Oxford Dictionary of Current English

I BOUGHT THIS
DICTIONARY TODAY
3/7/08 WHILE I WAS SPENDING
A QUALITY OF TIME WITH
MY DAUGHTER SARA.
MY RESOLUTION IS
TO USE IT AS MUCH
AS I NEED IT TO
BETTER MY SPELLING.

FOURTH EDITION

Edited by
Catherine Soanes
with Sara Hawker
and Julia Elliott

OXFORD
UNIVERSITY PRESS

OXFORD
UNIVERSITY PRESS

Great Clarendon Street, Oxford OX2 6DP

Oxford University Press is a department of the University of Oxford.
It furthers the University's objective of excellence in research, scholarship,
and education by publishing worldwide in

Oxford New York

Auckland Cape Town Dar es Salaam Hong Kong Karachi
Kuala Lumpur Madrid Melbourne Mexico City Nairobi
New Delhi Shanghai Taipei Toronto

With offices in

Argentina Austria Brazil Chile Czech Republic France Greece
Guatemala Hungary Italy Japan Poland Portugal Singapore
South Korea Switzerland Thailand Turkey Ukraine Vietnam

Oxford is a registered trade mark of Oxford University Press
in the UK and in certain other countries

Published in the United States
by Oxford University Press Inc., New York

© Oxford University Press 1993, 1996, 1998, 2001, 2006

Database right Oxford University Press (makers)
First edition 1993
Revised (second edition) 1996
Revised (second edition) 1998
Third edition 2001
Fourth edition 2006
First published in 2005 as the *Pocket Oxford English Dictionary* (tenth edition)

British Library Cataloguing in Publication Data
Data available

Library of Congress Cataloging in Publication Data
Data available

ISBN 978–0–19–861437–1
ISBN 978–0–19–929996–6 (USA edition)

2

Typeset in Frutiger and Parable
by Interactive Sciences Ltd, Gloucester
Printed in Great Britain by
Clays Ltd, Bungay, Suffolk

Contents

Preface

This new edition of the *Oxford Dictionary of Current English* has been fully revised, updated, and redesigned. It provides up-to-date and accessible information on the core vocabulary of today's English in a single pocket-sized volume, focusing on clear explanations of meaning and help with aspects of words which often cause difficulties, especially spelling, pronunciation, grammar, and usage. It will be particularly useful for secondary-school students in the 14–16 age range.

Part of the range based on the *Concise Oxford English Dictionary* (11th edition), the *Oxford Dictionary of Current English* is based on the evidence of how the language is actually used today, drawing on the analysis of hundreds of millions of words of real English contained in the Oxford English Corpus. Information in the dictionary is presented in a clear and concise way; definitions focus on the central meanings of words and are easier to understand than ever before, avoiding the use of difficult and technical terms. The new design and an open layout, with each new section of an entry (phrases, derivatives, usage notes, spelling notes, and etymologies) on a new line, ensure that finding individual sections and entries is easy to do.

In addition to giving clear information on the core language of current English, this new edition of the dictionary provides more help than ever before with tricky questions of grammar and usage (for example, on the difference between *pore* and *pour* and whether you should say *between you and me* or *between you and I*). The dictionary also includes a new feature: extra notes on words that people often find difficult to spell, such as *weird*, *skilful*, and *exaggerate*. Usage and spelling notes are based on evidence of real mistakes or problems that people have in their use of the language.

Pronunciations are given using a simple respelling system, making them very easy to understand: for the new edition, there is extra help with pronunciations of less straightforward or unfamiliar words, such as *anomalous*, *subtle*, and *unequivocal*. Etymologies (word origins) are written in a non-technical style to highlight the main words from which English words originate, with language names written out in full.

Guide to the use of the dictionary

1. STRUCTURE OF ENTRIES

The *Oxford Dictionary of Current English* is designed to be as easy to use as possible. Here is an explanation of the main types of information that you will find in the dictionary.

Headword

Verb forms (inflections)

bathe /bayth/ • v. (**bathes, bathing, bathed**) **1** wash by immersing the body in water. **2** Brit. take a swim. **3** soak or wipe gently with liquid to clean or soothe. • n. Brit. a swim.
– DERIVATIVES **bather** n.
– ORIGIN Old English.

Regional label (showing where word is used)

• Introduces new part of speech or word class

apogee /ap-uh-jee/ • n. **1** the highest point: *his creative activity reached its apogee in 1910.* **2** the point in the orbit of the moon or a satellite at which it is furthest from the earth.
– ORIGIN from Greek *apogaion diastēma*, 'distance away from earth'.

Sense number

Part of speech or word class

buck[1] • n. **1** the male of some animals, e.g. deer and rabbits. **2** a vertical jump performed by a horse. **3** old use: a fashionable young man. • v. **1** (of a horse) perform a buck. **2** go against: *the shares bucked the market trend.* **3** (**buck up** or **buck someone up**) informal become or make someone more cheerful.
– ORIGIN Old English.

Usage label (showing how word is used)

Typical pattern (in bold)

Example of use (taken from real evidence)

Homonym number (shows different word with the same spelling)

buck[2] • n. N. Amer. & Austral./NZ informal a dollar.

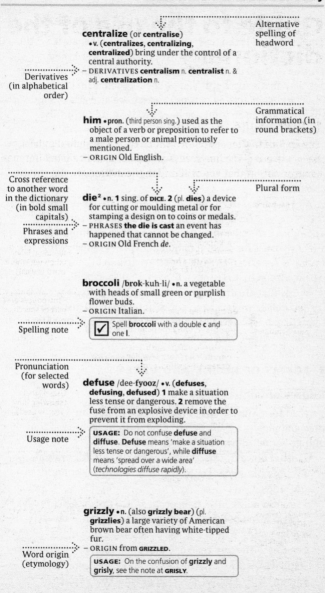

Alternative spelling of headword

centralize (or **centralise**)
• v. (**centralizes**, **centralizing**, **centralized**) bring under the control of a central authority.
– DERIVATIVES **centralism** n. **centralist** n. & adj. **centralization** n.

Derivatives (in alphabetical order)

Grammatical information (in round brackets)

him • pron. (third person sing.) used as the object of a verb or preposition to refer to a male person or animal previously mentioned.
– ORIGIN Old English.

Cross reference to another word in the dictionary (in bold small capitals)

Plural form

die² • n. **1** sing. of DICE. **2** (pl. **dies**) a device for cutting or moulding metal or for stamping a design on to coins or medals.
– PHRASES **the die is cast** an event has happened that cannot be changed.
– ORIGIN Old French *de*.

Phrases and expressions

broccoli /brok-kuh-li/ • n. a vegetable with heads of small green or purplish flower buds.
– ORIGIN Italian.

Spelling note

✓ Spell **broccoli** with a double **c** and one **l**.

Pronunciation (for selected words)

defuse /dee-fyooz/ • v. (**defuses**, **defusing**, **defused**) **1** make a situation less tense or dangerous. **2** remove the fuse from an explosive device in order to prevent it from exploding.

Usage note

USAGE: Do not confuse **defuse** and **diffuse**. Defuse means 'make a situation less tense or dangerous', while **diffuse** means 'spread over a wide area' (*technologies diffuse rapidly*).

grizzly • n. (also **grizzly bear**) (pl. **grizzlies**) a large variety of American brown bear often having white-tipped fur.
– ORIGIN from GRIZZLED.

Word origin (etymology)

USAGE: On the confusion of **grizzly** and **grisly**, see the note at GRISLY.

2. HEADWORD AND ALTERNATIVE SPELLINGS

The headword is the first word in each entry (separate section of the dictionary that deals with a particular word) and is printed in thick dark type (e.g. **score**). Although there is only one way that most words can be spelled, sometimes you can use other spellings (called *variants*) which are also acceptable. Such spellings are given after the headword, e.g. **adaptor** (also **adapter**), or before a particular sense if the alternative spelling only applies to that sense. In all such cases the spelling given as the headword is the one that most people use. The label *US* shows spellings that are used in American English, e.g. **colour** (*US* **color**).

Where verbs can be spelled with either an -**ize** or -**ise** ending, the two spellings are given in the following way: **apologize** (or **apologise**), to show that you can use either spelling. The spelling -**ise** is far more common in British English, while -**ize** is found in American writing and in English in other parts of the world, although it is used in British English as well.

Words that are different in meaning but spelled the same way (called *homographs*) are given small numbers to distinguish them (e.g. **buck¹**, meaning 'the male of an animal such as a deer' and **buck²**, meaning 'a dollar').

3. FORMS OF NOUNS AND VERBS

Plurals of nouns

You can form the plurals of most nouns by adding -*s*, or -*es* when they end in -*s*, -*x*, -*z*, -*sh*, or -*ch* (as in *church*). These kinds of plurals are not shown in the dictionary.

All other plural forms are spelled out in full, for example:

- nouns ending in -*i* or -*o*, e.g. **alibi** → **alibis**, **albino** → **albinos**
- nouns ending in -*a*, -*um*, or -*us* which are or appear to be Latin forms, e.g. **spectrum** → **spectra**, **larva** → **larvae**
- nouns ending in -*y*, e.g. **fly** → **flies**
- nouns with more than one plural, e.g. **storey** → **storeys** or **stories**
- nouns with a plural that changes markedly from the singular form, e.g. **foot** → **feet**

- nouns with a plural that has the same form as the singular, e.g. **sheep** → **sheep**

Verbs

Most verbs change their form (inflect) by adding *-s*, *-ing*, and *-ed* to the infinitive (e.g. **jump** → **jumps, jumping, jumped**). These kinds of verb forms are not shown in the dictionary.

Other verbs change their forms in the ways set out below and are shown in full:

- verbs whose infinitive (basic unchanged part) ends in *-e*, e.g. **change** → **changes, changing, changed**
- verbs which change by doubling a final consonant, e.g. **bat** → **bats, batting, batted**
- verbs ending in *-y* which change the *-y* to *-i*, e.g. **try** → **tries, trying, tried**
- verbs in which the past tense and/or the past participle do not follow the regular *-ed* pattern, e.g. **feel** → **feels, feeling, felt**; **wake** → **wakes, waking, woke**; past part. **woken**
- verbs ending in *-er*, showing whether the final *-r* is doubled or not, e.g. **confer** → **confers, conferring, conferred**; **shiver** → **shivers, shivering, shivered**

Adjectives

Adjectives have three different forms that express the level or intensity of a particular quality. The basic level is called the *positive*, e.g. **sweet**; the level expressing more of a quality is called the *comparative*, e.g. **sweeter**; and the level expressing most of a quality is called the *superlative*, e.g. **sweetest**. Most adjectives form their comparatives and superlatives in the following regular ways, and these are not shown in the dictionary:

- words of one syllable adding *-er* and *-est*, e.g. **great** → **greater, greatest**
- words of one syllable ending in silent (unspoken) *-e*, which drop the *-e* and add *-er* and *-est*, e.g. **brave** → **braver, bravest**
- words which form the comparative and superlative by adding 'more' and 'most'

In all other cases the forms are shown in the dictionary:

- adjectives which form the comparative and superlative by

doubling a final consonant, e.g. **hot → hotter**, **hottest**
- two-syllable adjectives which form the comparative and superlative with *-er* and *-est*, e.g. **happy → happier**, **happiest**

4. HYPHENATION

Although standard spelling in English is fixed, the use of hyphens is not. There are a few general rules that you should follow, and these are outlined below.

Noun compounds: there are no set rules as to whether you should write a compound (a word such as **airstream**) as one word, two words, or with a hyphen (unless the hyphen is used to show the word's grammatical function: see the next section): **airstream**, **air stream**, and **air-stream** are all acceptable. However, in modern English, people are tending to use hyphens less than before, and are writing compounds either as one word (**airstream**) or two words (**air raid**) rather than with a hyphen. While you will find one-word and two-word compounds in both British and American English, there is a general preference to write compounds as two words in British English and as one word in American English.

To save space and avoid confusion, we give only one of the three possible forms—the standard British one—in the dictionary. This does not, however, mean that other forms are incorrect or not used.

Grammatical information: hyphens are also used to show a word's grammatical function. When a noun compound which is made up of two separate words (e.g. **credit card**) is placed before another noun, the rule is that you should write the compound with a hyphen, so that you would write for example *I used my credit card* but *credit-card debt*. You will see this in example sentences in the dictionary but it is not otherwise mentioned in the dictionary entries.

There is a similar rule with compound adjectives such as **well known**. When you place them after the verb (in the *predicative* position) you should not write such adjectives with a hyphen, but when you put them before the noun (in the *attributive* position) you should use a hyphen: *he is well known* but *a well-known painter*.

The rule with verb compounds is that, where a noun compound is two words (e.g. **hero worship**) you should normally write any verb compound formed from it with a hyphen (to **hero-worship**). Compound verb forms of this type are always shown in the dictionary entries.

5. LABELS

The majority of the words and senses in this dictionary are all part of standard English, which means that they are the kinds of words we use in every type of situation, whether at home, with friends, or in a formal work situation. Some words, however, are suitable only for certain situations or are found only in certain types of writing, and where this is the case a label (or a combination of labels) is used.

Register labels

Register labels refer to the particular level of use in the language—indicating whether a term is informal, formal, historical, and so on.

> formal: normally used only in writing, such as in official documents (e.g. **abode**)

> informal: normally used only in speaking or writing to friends (e.g. **telly**)

> dated: no longer used by most English speakers, but still used by older people or to give a humorous or other effect (e.g. **charwoman**)

> old use: old-fashioned language, not in ordinary use today, though sometimes used to give an old-fashioned or humorous effect and also found in the literature of the past (e.g. **damsel**)

> hist.: historical—only used today to refer to something that is no longer part of modern life (e.g. **blunderbuss**)

> literary: found only or mainly in literature (e.g. **foe**)

> tech.: technical—normally used only in technical language, though not restricted to a particular subject field (e.g. **dorsal**)

> humorous: used to sound funny or playful (e.g. **tome**)

> euphem.: euphemistic—used instead of a more direct or rude term (e.g. **powder room** instead of 'women's toilet')

dialect: only used in certain local regions of the English-speaking world (e.g. **bide**)

derog.: derogatory—deliberately intended to express a low opinion or insult someone else (e.g. **bimbo**)

offens.: offensive—likely to cause offence, especially racial offence, whether the person using it means to or not

Geographical labels

English is spoken throughout the world, and, while most of the words used in British English will be the same as those used in American or Australian English, there are some words which are only found in one type of English. For example, the normal word in American English for a pavement is **sidewalk**, while the normal word in Australian English for a large sheep or cattle farm is **station**. These kinds of words are given a geographical label.

The main regional types of English are British, US and Canadian, Australian and New Zealand, South African, Indian, and West Indian. Most of the words and senses in the dictionary are found in all these types of English, but where important local differences exist these are shown. The geographical label Brit. means that the word is found typically in British English but is not found in American English, though it may be found in other varieties such as Australian English. The label US, on the other hand, means that the word is typically US and is not standard in British English, though it may be found elsewhere.

Subject labels

These are used to show that a word or sense is associated with a particular subject field or specialist activity, such as Music, Chemistry, or Football.

6. DEFINITIONS

Many words have only one meaning or definition, for example **bookcase** or **fearless**. Other words, such as **catch** or **fall**, have several meanings. In these types of entries the definitions are separated by numbers and listed with the most common and important senses first.

7. DERIVATIVES

Derivatives are words formed from another word with the addition of a suffix (ending): for example, **adjustable** is an adjective which is a derivative of the verb **adjust**, with the suffix **-able** added to it. Many derivatives do not need a definition because you can understand the meaning from the sense of the main word and the particular ending used; in such cases, you will find the derivatives listed alphabetically at the end of the entry for the main word (e.g. **eagerly** is at the end of the entry for **eager**). When a derivative has more than one meaning and needs to be explained in more detail, then it is given an entry in its own right (e.g. **agreeable**).

8. ETYMOLOGIES

Etymologies (word origins) are provided for many words: they explain the language that the word comes from and the meaning of that word if it is different from the meaning of the English word in the dictionary entry (e.g. **campaign** is from the French word *campagne*, which means 'open country'). You will find that some words in the dictionary do not have etymologies. These include the following: compounds, which are formed from two other words (e.g. **blue whale**, **half-hearted**, or **doorman**); words which are derivatives of other words or are clearly related in some other way (e.g. **fantastic** does not have an etymology but **fantasy** does); words whose origins are unknown or uncertain; words that derive from imitating a sound (e.g. **baa**, **hiss**).

9. SPELLING AND USAGE NOTES

The dictionary's usage notes give clear information about points of grammar (e.g. how to use **fewer** and **less** correctly), usage (e.g. whether it is best to say **fireman** or **firefighter**), and the differences between words which people often confuse with each other (e.g. **stationary** and **stationery**).

The spelling notes are shown by a tick enclosed in a box and give clear advice on words that are tricky to spell, such as **cemetery**, **February**, and **receive**.

10. PRONUNCIATIONS

The *Oxford Dictionary of Current English* uses a respelling system for pronunciations which is very easy to understand and to use. The dictionary gives a pronunciation for any word which native English speakers might find difficult; it does not provide pronunciations for everyday words that everyone knows how to say, such as *table* or *large*. Foreign pronunciations are always shown in the way an English speaker would say them, e.g. /kor-don **bler**/ (cordon bleu).

Pronunciations are divided into syllables by means of hyphens. The main stress is shown in thick dark type, e.g. /**ab**-duh-muhn/ (abdomen).

An apostrophe is used instead of the sound /uh/ in cases where there is a slight break between sounds, as in /**foh**-k'l/ (focal), or where the sound is a consonant that forms a whole syllable, as in /**har**-k'n/ (hearken).

The sound of the word 'eye' is shown in two ways: it is shown as /I/ in the first parts of words and in parts where it stands alone, as in /**I**-ther/ (either) or /kat-I-uhn/ (cation), but as /y/ in all other cases, as in /**a**-li-by/ (alibi).

A rhyming pronunciation is given where the alternative respelling would involve odd-looking word groups, as in aisle /*rhymes with* mile/.

List of respelling symbols

VOWELS	EXAMPLES		CONSONANTS	EXAMPLES
a	as in **cat**		b	as in **bat**
ah	as in **calm**		ch	as in **chin**
air	as in **hair**		d	as in **day**
ar	as in **bar**		f	as in **fat**
aw	as in **law**		g	as in **get**
ay	as in **say**		h	as in **hat**
e	as in **bed**		j	as in **jam**
ee	as in **meet**		k	as in **king**
eer	as in **beer**		kh	as in **loch**
er	as in **her**		l	as in **leg**
ew	as in **few**		m	as in **man**
i	as in **pin**		n	as in **not**
I	as in **eye**		ng	as in **sing, finger**
o	as in **top**		nk	as in **thank**
oh	as in **most**		p	as in **pen**
oi	as in **join**		r	as in **red**
oo	as in **soon**		s	as in **sit**
oor	as in **poor**		sh	as in **shop**
or	as in **corn**		t	as in **top**
ow	as in **cow**		th	as in **thin**
oy	as in **boy**		*th*	as in **this**
u	as in **cup**		v	as in **van**
uh	as in the 'a' in **along**		w	as in **will**
uu	as in **book**		y	as in **yes**
y	as in **cry**		z	as in **zebra**
yoo	as in **unit**		*zh*	as in **vision**
yoor	as in **Europe**			
yr	as in **fire**			

11. ABBREVIATIONS USED IN THE DICTIONARY

abbrev.	abbreviation	Med.	Medicine
adj.	adjective	Meteorol.	Meteorology
adv.	adverb	Mil.	Military
Anat.	Anatomy	n.	noun
Amer. Football	American Football	N. Amer.	North American
Archit.	Architecture	Naut.	Nautical
Astron.	Astronomy	N. English	Northern English
Austral.	Australian	NZ	New Zealand
Biochem.	Biochemistry	opp.	opposite of
Biol.	Biology	offens.	offensive
Bot.	Botany	part.	participle
Chem.	Chemistry	Philos.	Philosophy
comb. form	combining form	Phonet.	Phonetics
contr.	contraction	Physiol.	Physiology
derog.	derogatory	pl.	plural
det.	determiner	prep.	preposition
Electron.	Electronics	pres.	present
Engl. Law	English Law	pronunc.	pronunciation
esp.	especially	Rom. Myth.	Roman Mythology
euphem.	euphemistic	S. Afr.	South African
exclam.	exclamation	sing.	singular
fem.	feminine	Stat.	Statistics
Geol.	Geology	symb.	symbol
Geom.	Geometry	tech.	technical
Gk Myth.	Greek Mythology	usu.	usually
hist.	historical	v.	verb
Ind.	Indian	var.	variant
Math.	Mathematics	Zool.	Zoology

NOTE ON TRADEMARKS AND PROPRIETARY STATUS

This dictionary includes some words which have, or are asserted to have, proprietary status as trademarks or otherwise. Their inclusion does not imply that they have acquired for legal purposes a non-proprietary or general significance, nor any other judgement concerning their legal status. In cases where the editorial staff have some evidence that a word has proprietary status this is indicated in the entry for that word by the label trademark, but no judgement concerning the legal status of such words is made or implied thereby.

Aa

A¹ (also **a**) • n. (pl. **As** or **A's**) **1** the first letter of the alphabet. **2** referring to the first, best, or most important item in a group. **3** Music the sixth note of the scale of C major.
– PHRASES **from A to B** from one place to another.

A² • abbrev. **1** ampere(s). **2** answer. **3** (Å) angstrom(s).

a • det. **1** used when mentioning someone or something for the first time; the indefinite article. **2** one single: *a hundred*. **3** per: *typing 60 words a minute*.
– ORIGIN Old English.

a-¹ (often **an-** before a vowel) • prefix not; without: *atheistic*.
– ORIGIN Greek.

a-² • prefix **1** to; towards: *aside*. **2** in the process of: *a-hunting*. **3** in a specified state: *aflutter*.
– ORIGIN Old English.

a-³ • prefix **1** of: *anew*. **2** utterly: *abash*.
– ORIGIN Old French.

@ • symb. 'at', used: **1** to show cost or rate per unit. **2** in Internet addresses between the user's name and the domain name: *john.smith@oup.com*.

A1 • adj. informal excellent.

AA • abbrev. **1** Alcoholics Anonymous. **2** Automobile Association.

aardvark /ard-vark/ • n. an African mammal with a tubular snout and a long tongue.
– ORIGIN South African Dutch, 'earth pig'.

ab- (also **abs-**) • prefix away; from: *abdicate*.
– ORIGIN Latin.

aback • adv. (in phr. **take someone aback**) shock or surprise someone.
– ORIGIN Old English.

abacus /ab-uh-kuhss/ • n. (pl. **abacuses**) a frame with rows of wires along which beads are slid, used for counting.
– ORIGIN Greek *abax* 'slab'.

abaft /uh-bahft/ • adv. & prep. in or behind the stern of a ship.
– ORIGIN from the old word *baft* 'in the rear'.

abalone /a-buh-loh-ni/ • n. an edible sea creature which has a shell lined with mother-of-pearl.
– ORIGIN from an American Indian language.

abandon • v. **1** leave permanently. **2** give up an action or practice completely. **3** (**abandon yourself to**) give in to something completely. • n. complete lack of self-control: *dancers swung their bodies with wild abandon*.
– DERIVATIVES **abandonment** n.
– ORIGIN Old French *abandoner*.

abandoned • adj. wild; uncontrolled.

abase /uh-bayss/ • v. (**abases, abasing, abased**) (**abase yourself**) behave in a way that causes other people to lose their respect for you.
– DERIVATIVES **abasement** n.
– ORIGIN Old French *abaissier* 'to lower'.

abashed • adj. embarrassed or ashamed.
– ORIGIN Old French *esbair* 'utterly astound'.

abate /uh-bayt/ • v. (**abates, abating, abated**) (of something bad) become less severe or widespread.
– DERIVATIVES **abatement** n.
– ORIGIN Old French *abatre* 'to fell'.

abattoir /ab-uh-twar/ • n. Brit. a slaughterhouse.
– ORIGIN French.

abbess /ab-biss/ • n. a woman who is the head of an abbey of nuns.

abbey • n. (pl. **abbeys**) a building occupied by a community of monks or nuns.
– ORIGIN Old French *abbeie*.

abbot • n. a man who is the head of an abbey of monks.
– ORIGIN Greek *abbas* 'father'.

abbreviate /uh-bree-vi-ayt/ • v. (**abbreviates, abbreviating, abbreviated**) shorten a word, phrase, or piece of writing.
– ORIGIN Latin *abbreviare*.

abbreviation • n. a shortened form of a word or phrase.

a

USAGE: What is the difference between an **abbreviation**, an **acronym**, a **contraction**, and an **initialism**? An **abbreviation** is a shortened form of a word or phrase (for example, *miss* is an abbreviation of *mistress*). An **acronym** is a word formed from the first letters of other words (for example, *scuba* is an acronym made from the initials of the words *self-contained underwater breathing apparatus*). A **contraction** is a shortened form of a word or words, often joined by an apostrophe (*I'm* is a contraction of *I am*). Finally, an **initialism** is an abbreviation consisting of initial letters pronounced separately (for example, *BBC* is an initialism for *British Broadcasting Corporation*).

ABC • n. **1** the alphabet. **2** a guide to something arranged in alphabetical order. **3** the basic facts of a subject.

abdicate /ab-di-kayt/ • v. (**abdicates**, **abdicating**, **abdicated**) **1** give up the role of king or queen. **2** fail to carry out a duty.
– DERIVATIVES **abdication** n.
– ORIGIN Latin *abdicare* 'renounce'.

abdomen /ab-duh-muhn/ • n. **1** the part of the body containing the stomach, intestines, and reproductive organs; the belly. **2** the rear part of the body of an insect, spider, or crustacean.
– DERIVATIVES **abdominal** /ab-domm-in'l/ adj. **abdominally** adv.
– ORIGIN Latin.

abduct • v. take someone away, especially by force.
– DERIVATIVES **abductee** n. **abduction** n. **abductor** n.
– ORIGIN Latin *abducere*.

Aberdeen Angus • n. a Scottish breed of black beef cattle.

aberrant /uh-berr-uhnt/ • adj. not normal or acceptable.

aberration /a-buh-ray-sh'n/ • n. an action, event, or way of behaving that is not normal or acceptable.
– ORIGIN Latin *aberrare* 'to stray'.

abet /uh-bet/ • v. (**abets**, **abetting**, **abetted**) (usu. in phr. **aid and abet**) encourage or help someone to do something wrong.
– DERIVATIVES **abettor** (also **abetter**) n.
– ORIGIN Old French *abeter*.

abeyance /uh-bay-uhnss/ • n. (in phr. **in/into abeyance**) temporarily halted or not in use.
– ORIGIN Old French *abeer* 'aspire after'.

abhor /uhb-hor/ • v. (**abhors**, **abhorring**, **abhorred**) feel strong hatred for.
– ORIGIN Latin *abhorrere*.

abhorrent • adj. disgusting or hateful.
– DERIVATIVES **abhorrence** n.

abide • v. (**abides**, **abiding**, **abided**) **1** (**abide by**) accept or obey a rule or decision. **2** (**cannot abide**) dislike very much: *he could not abide lies.* **3** (of a feeling or memory) last for a long time. **4** old use live in a place.
– ORIGIN Old English, 'wait'.

abiding • adj. lasting; enduring.

ability • n. (pl. **abilities**) **1** the power or capacity to do something. **2** skill or talent.
– ORIGIN Latin *habilitas*.

abject /ab-jekt/ • adj. **1** very unpleasant and humiliating: *abject poverty.* **2** completely without pride or dignity: *an abject apology.*
– DERIVATIVES **abjectly** adv.
– ORIGIN Latin *abjectus* 'rejected'.

abjure /uhb-joor/ • v. (**abjures**, **abjuring**, **abjured**) formal swear to give up a belief or claim.
– ORIGIN Latin *abjurare*.

ablaze • adj. burning fiercely.

able • adj. (**abler**, **ablest**) **1** having the power, skill, or means to do something. **2** skilful and capable.
– DERIVATIVES **ably** adv.
– ORIGIN Latin *habilis* 'handy'.

-able • suffix forming adjectives meaning: **1** able to be: *calculable.* **2** having the quality of: *comfortable.*
– DERIVATIVES **-ability** suffix **-ably** suffix.

able-bodied • adj. physically fit and healthy.

ablutions /uh-bloo-shuhnz/ • pl. n. formal or humorous the act of washing yourself.
– ORIGIN Latin.

abnegation /ab-ni-gay-sh'n/ • n. formal the giving up of something wanted or valuable.
– DERIVATIVES **abnegate** v.
– ORIGIN Latin.

abnormal • adj. not normal or typical.
– DERIVATIVES **abnormally** adv.
– ORIGIN Greek *anōmalos* 'uneven'.

abnormality • n. (pl. **abnormalities**) **1** a feature or event which is not normal. **2** the state of being abnormal.

aboard • adv. & prep. on or into a ship, train, or other vehicle.

abode • n. formal or literary a house or home.
– ORIGIN from **ABIDE**.

abolish • v. officially put an end to a system, law, or custom.
– ORIGIN Latin *abolere* 'destroy'.

abolition • n. the official ending of a system, law, or custom.

abolitionist • n. a person who supports the abolition of something.

A-bomb • n. an atom bomb.

abominable • adj. **1** very unpleasant and causing disgust. **2** informal very bad.

– DERIVATIVES **abominably** adv.
– ORIGIN Latin *abominabilis*.

Abominable Snowman •n. the yeti.

abominate /uh-bom-i-nayt/
•v. (**abominates, abominating, abominated**) formal hate someone or something.

abomination •n. **1** a thing that causes disgust or hatred. **2** a feeling of hatred.

aboriginal •adj. **1** existing in a land from the earliest times or from before the arrival of colonists. **2** (**Aboriginal**) relating to the original peoples of Australia. •n. **1** an inhabitant of a land from the earliest times. **2** (**Aboriginal**) a member of one of the original peoples of Australia.

aborigine /ab-uh-ri-ji-nee/ (also **Aborigine**) •n. an original inhabitant of a land, especially an Australian Aboriginal.
– ORIGIN from Latin *ab origine* 'from the beginning'.

abort •v. **1** carry out the abortion of a fetus. **2** bring something to an early end because of a problem or fault.
– ORIGIN Latin *aboriri* 'miscarry'.

abortion •n. **1** the deliberate ending of a human pregnancy. **2** the natural ending of a pregnancy before the fetus is able to survive on its own.

abortionist •n. derog. a person who carries out abortions.

abortive •adj. failing to achieve the intended result; unsuccessful.

abound •v. **1** exist in large numbers or amounts. **2** (**abound in/with**) have something in large numbers or amounts.
– ORIGIN Latin *abundare* 'overflow'.

about •prep. & adv. **1** on the subject of; concerning. **2** used to indicate movement within an area or position in a place: *she looked about the room.* **3** approximately.
– PHRASES **be about to** be on the point of.
– ORIGIN Old English.

about-turn (also esp. N. Amer. **about-face**) •n. Brit. **1** a turn made by a soldier so as to face the opposite direction. **2** a complete change of opinion or policy.

above •prep. & adv. **1** at a higher level than. **2** rather or more than: *he valued safety above comfort.* **3** (in printed writing) mentioned earlier.
– PHRASES **above board** lawful and honest. **above yourself** having too high an opinion of yourself.
– ORIGIN Old English.

abracadabra •exclam. a word said by conjurors when performing a trick.
– ORIGIN Latin.

abrade /uh-brayd/ •v. (**abrades,**

abrading, abraded) scrape or wear away the surface of something.
– ORIGIN Latin *abradere*.

abrasion /uh-bray-zh'n/ •n. **1** the action of scraping or wearing away. **2** an area of skin that has been scraped or grazed.

abrasive /uh-bray-siv/ •adj. **1** able to polish or clean a hard surface by rubbing or grinding. **2** harsh or unkind.

abreast •adv. **1** side by side and facing the same way. **2** (**abreast of**) up to date with.

abridge •v. (**abridges, abridging, abridged**) shorten a written work or film.
– ORIGIN Old French *abregier*.

abridgement (also **abridgment**) •n. a shortened version of a larger work.

abroad •adv. **1** in or to a foreign country or countries. **2** felt or talked about by many people: *there is a new spirit abroad.* **3** over a wide area: *millions of seeds are scattered abroad.*

abrogate /ab-ruh-gayt/ •v. (**abrogates, abrogating, abrogated**) formal cancel or end a law or agreement.
– DERIVATIVES **abrogation** n.
– ORIGIN Latin *abrogare* 'repeal'.

abrupt •adj. **1** sudden and unexpected. **2** brief to the point of rudeness.
– DERIVATIVES **abruptly** adv. **abruptness** n.
– ORIGIN Latin *abruptus* 'broken off, steep'.

abscess •n. a swelling containing pus.
– ORIGIN Latin *abscessus*.

> ✓ **abscess** is spelled with **-sc-** in the middle and a double **s** at the end.

abscissa /ab-siss-uh/ •n. (pl. **abscissae** /ab-siss-ee/ or **abscissas**) Math. the distance from a point on a graph to the vertical or y-axis; the x-coordinate.
– ORIGIN from Latin *abscissa linea* 'cut-off line'.

abscond /uhb-skond/ •v. leave quickly and secretly to escape from custody or avoid arrest.
– DERIVATIVES **absconder** n.
– ORIGIN Latin *abscondere* 'hide'.

abseil /ab-sayl/ •v. Brit. climb down a rock face using a rope coiled round the body and fixed at a higher point.
– ORIGIN German *abseilen*.

absence •n. **1** the state of being away from a place or person. **2** (**absence of**) the non-existence or lack of: *the absence of reliable information.*

absent •adj. /ab-s'nt/ **1** not present. **2** not paying attention. •v. /uhb-**sent**/ (**absent yourself**) leave or stay away.
– DERIVATIVES **absently** adv.
– ORIGIN Latin *abesse* 'to be away'.

absentee •n. a person who is absent.

absenteeism • n. frequent absences from work or school without good reason.

absent-minded • adj. tending to forget things or not pay attention.
– DERIVATIVES **absent-mindedly** adv. **absent-mindedness** n.

absinthe /ab-sinth/ • n. a green aniseed-flavoured liqueur.
– ORIGIN French.

absolute • adj. **1** complete; total. **2** having unlimited power: *an absolute ruler*. **3** not related or compared to anything else: *absolute moral principles*.
– ORIGIN Latin *absolutus* 'freed'.

absolutely • adv. **1** completely; entirely. **2** used for emphasis or to express agreement.

absolute majority • n. a majority over all rivals considered as a group; more than half.

absolute pitch • n. = PERFECT PITCH.

absolute temperature • n. a temperature measured from absolute zero in kelvins.

absolute zero • n. the lowest temperature theoretically possible (zero kelvins, −273.15°C).

absolution • n. formal forgiveness of a person's sins.
– ORIGIN Latin.

absolutism • n. the principle that a ruler or government should have unlimited power.
– DERIVATIVES **absolutist** n. & adj.

absolve /uhb-zolv/ • v. (**absolves, absolving, absolved**) declare someone to be free from guilt, blame, or sin.
– ORIGIN Latin *absolvere* 'set free, acquit'.

absorb /uhb-zorb/ • v. **1** soak up liquid or another substance. **2** understand information. **3** take over something less powerful. **4** use up time or resources. **5** reduce the effect or strength of sound or an impact. **6** hold the attention of: *she was absorbed in her work*.
– DERIVATIVES **absorbable** adj. **absorber** n.
– ORIGIN Latin *absorbere* 'suck in'.

absorbent • adj. able to soak up liquid easily.
– DERIVATIVES **absorbency** n.

absorption • n. the process of absorbing or the state of being absorbed.
– DERIVATIVES **absorptive** adj.

abstain • v. **1** (**abstain from**) stop yourself from doing something enjoyable. **2** formally choose not to vote.
– DERIVATIVES **abstainer** n.
– ORIGIN Latin *abstinere* 'hold from'.

abstemious /uhb-stee-mi-uhss/ • adj. taking care to limit your intake of food or alcohol.
– ORIGIN Latin *abstemius*.

abstention /uhb-sten-sh'n/ • n. **1** a deliberate decision not to vote. **2** the avoidance of something enjoyable; abstinence.

abstinence /ab-sti-nuhnss/ • n. the avoidance of something enjoyable, such as food or alcohol.
– DERIVATIVES **abstinent** adj.
– ORIGIN Latin *abstinentia*.

abstract • adj. /ab-strakt/ **1** relating to ideas or qualities rather than physical things. **2** (of art) using colour and shapes to create an effect rather than attempting to represent real life accurately. • v. /uhb-strakt/ take out or remove something. • n. /ab-strakt/ a summary of a book or article.
– DERIVATIVES **abstractly** adv.
– ORIGIN Latin *abstrahere* 'draw away'.

abstracted • adj. not paying attention to what is happening; preoccupied.
– DERIVATIVES **abstractedly** adv.

abstraction • n. **1** the quality of being abstract. **2** something which exists only as an idea. **3** a preoccupied state of mind. **4** the action of removing something.

abstruse /uhb-strooss/ • adj. difficult to understand.
– ORIGIN Latin *abstrusus* 'concealed'.

absurd • adj. completely illogical or ridiculous.
– DERIVATIVES **absurdity** n. **absurdly** adv.
– ORIGIN Latin *absurdus* 'out of tune'.

abundance /uh-bun-duhnss/ • n. **1** a very large quantity. **2** the state of having a very large quantity: *vines grew in abundance*.
– ORIGIN Latin *abundare* 'to overflow'.

abundant • adj. **1** existing in large quantities; plentiful. **2** (**abundant in**) having plenty of.
– DERIVATIVES **abundantly** adv.

abuse • v. /uh-byooz/ (**abuses, abusing, abused**) **1** use badly or wrongly. **2** treat cruelly or violently. **3** speak to someone in an insulting and offensive way. • n. /uh-byooss/ **1** the wrong use of something. **2** cruel and violent treatment. **3** insulting and offensive language.
– DERIVATIVES **abuser** n.
– ORIGIN Latin *abuti* 'misuse'.

abusive • adj. **1** very offensive and insulting. **2** involving cruelty and violence.
– DERIVATIVES **abusively** adv.

abut /uh-but/ • v. (**abuts, abutting, abutted**) be next to or touching something.
– ORIGIN Old French *abouter*.

abysmal /uh-biz-m'l/ • adj. informal very bad.

– DERIVATIVES **abysmally** adv.
– ORIGIN Old French *abisme* 'abyss'.

abyss /uh-biss/ • n. a very deep hole.
– ORIGIN Greek *abussos* 'bottomless'.

AC • abbrev. alternating current.

Ac • symb. the chemical element actinium.

a/c • abbrev. account.

acacia /uh-kay-shuh/ • n. a tree or shrub with yellow or white flowers, found in warm climates.
– ORIGIN Greek *akakia*.

academia /a-kuh-dee-mi-uh/ • n. the world of higher education or the people involved in it.

academic • adj. **1** relating to education or study. **2** not related to a real situation; theoretical. • n. a teacher or scholar in a university or college.
– DERIVATIVES **academically** adv.

academician /uh-ka-duh-mish-uhn/ • n. a member of an academy.

academy • n. (pl. **academies**) **1** a place of study or training in a special field. **2** a society or institution of scholars, artists, or scientists. **3** US & Scottish a secondary school.
– ORIGIN Greek *akadēmeia*.

Academy award • n. an award given by the Academy of Motion Picture Arts and Sciences for achievement in the film industry; an Oscar.

acanthus /uh-kan-thuhss/ • n. a plant or shrub with spiny leaves.
– ORIGIN Greek *akanthos*.

a cappella /a kuh-pel-luh/ • adj. & adv. (of music) sung without being accompanied by instruments.
– ORIGIN Italian, 'in chapel style'.

accede /uhk-seed/ • v. (**accedes, acceding, acceded**) (usu. **accede to**) formal **1** agree to a demand or request. **2** take up an office or position.
– ORIGIN Latin *accedere* 'come to'.

accelerant • n. a substance used to help fire spread quickly.

accelerate /uhk-sel-uh-rayt/ • v. (**accelerates, accelerating, accelerated**) **1** begin to move more quickly. **2** increase in amount or scale.
– DERIVATIVES **acceleration** n.
– ORIGIN Latin *accelerare*.

accelerator • n. **1** a foot pedal which controls the speed of a vehicle. **2** Physics a device for making charged particles move at high speeds.

accent • n. /ak-s'nt, ak-sent/ **1** a way of pronouncing a language, related to a place or social background. **2** an emphasis given to a syllable, word, or note. **3** a mark on a letter or word showing how a sound is pronounced or stressed. **4** a particular emphasis: *the accent is on participation.* • v. /ak-sent/ **1** emphasize something. **2** (as adj. **accented**) spoken with a foreign accent.
– ORIGIN Latin *accentus* 'tone, signal, or intensity'.

accentuate /uhk-sen-tyuu-ayt/ • v. (**accentuates, accentuating, accentuated**) make more noticeable.
– DERIVATIVES **accentuation** n.

accept • v. **1** agree to receive or do something offered. **2** believe to be valid or correct. **3** admit responsibility for something. **4** make someone welcome. **5** put up with something unwelcome.
– DERIVATIVES **acceptance** n. **acceptor** n.
– ORIGIN Latin *acceptare*.

> **USAGE:** Do not confuse **accept** with **except**. **Accept** means 'agree to receive or do something' (*she accepted the job*), whereas **except** means 'not including' (*I work every day except Sunday*).

acceptable • adj. **1** able to be accepted. **2** good enough; adequate.
– DERIVATIVES **acceptability** n. **acceptably** adv.

access • n. **1** the means or opportunity to approach or enter a place. **2** the right or opportunity to use something or see someone. • v. **1** enter a place. **2** obtain data from a computer.
– ORIGIN Latin *accessus*.

accessible • adj. **1** able to be reached or used. **2** friendly and easy to talk to. **3** easily understood or enjoyed.
– DERIVATIVES **accessibility** n. **accessibly** adv.

accession • n. **1** the gaining of an important position or rank. **2** a new item added to a library or museum collection.

accessorize (or **accessorise**) • v. (**accessorizes, accessorizing, accessorized**) add a fashion accessory to an item of clothing.

accessory • n. (pl. **accessories**) **1** a thing which can be added to or worn with something else to make it more useful or attractive. **2** Law a person who helps someone commit a crime without taking part in it.
– ORIGIN Latin *accessorius* 'additional thing'.

accident • n. **1** an unpleasant and unexpected event. **2** an event that happens by chance.
– ORIGIN Latin *accidere* 'fall or happen'.

accidental • adj. happening by accident. • n. a sign attached to a musical note to show a momentary departure from the key signature.
– DERIVATIVES **accidentally** adv.

acclaim • v. praise enthusiastically and publicly. • n. enthusiastic public praise.

- ORIGIN Latin *acclamare*.

acclamation • n. loud and enthusiastic approval or praise.

acclimatize (or **acclimatise**)
• v. (**acclimatizes, acclimatizing, acclimatized**) adapt to a new climate or new conditions.
- DERIVATIVES **acclimatization** n.
- ORIGIN French *acclimater*.

accolade /ak-kuh-layd/ • n. something given as a special honour or as a reward for excellence.
- ORIGIN first meaning 'a touch on a person's shoulders with a sword when knighting them': from Provençal *acolada* 'embrace around the neck'.

accommodate • v. (**accommodates, accommodating, accommodated**)
1 provide lodging or space for. 2 adapt to or fit in with: *they tried to accommodate the children's needs.*
- ORIGIN Latin *accommodare*.

> ✓ Remember that **accommodate** and the related word **accommodation** are spelled with a double **c** and a double **m**.

accommodating • adj. willing to help or fit in with someone's wishes.

accommodation • n. 1 a place where someone may live or stay. 2 a settlement or compromise.

accompaniment • n. 1 a musical part which accompanies an instrument, voice, or group. 2 something that adds to or improves something else.

accompanist • n. a person who plays a musical accompaniment.

accompany • v. (**accompanies, accompanying, accompanied**) 1 go somewhere with someone. 2 be present or occur at the same time as something else. 3 play musical support or backing for an instrument, voice, or group.
- ORIGIN Old French *accompagner*.

accomplice /uh-kum-pliss/ • n. a person who helps another to commit a crime.
- ORIGIN Old French *complice*.

accomplish • v. achieve or complete something successfully.
- ORIGIN Old French *acomplir*.

accomplished • adj. highly skilled.

accomplishment • n. 1 something that has been achieved successfully. 2 a skill or special ability. 3 the successful achievement of a task.

accord • v. 1 give power or recognition to someone. 2 (**accord with**) be in agreement or consistent with something.
• n. 1 agreement in opinion. 2 an official agreement or treaty.
- PHRASES **of your own accord** willingly.
- ORIGIN Old French *acorder* 'reconcile, be of one mind'.

accordance • n. (in phr. **in accordance with**) in a way that agrees or conforms with.

according • adv. (**according to**) 1 as stated by. 2 following or agreeing with: *cook the rice according to the instructions.*

accordingly • adv. 1 in a way that is appropriate. 2 therefore.

accordion /uh-kor-di-uhn/ • n. a musical instrument played by stretching and squeezing with the hands to work a bellows, the notes being sounded by buttons or keys.
- DERIVATIVES **accordionist** n.
- ORIGIN German *Akkordion*.

accost • v. approach and speak to someone boldly or aggressively.
- ORIGIN French *accoster*.

account • n. 1 a description of an event. 2 a record of money spent and received. 3 a service through a bank or company by which funds are held on behalf of a customer or goods or services are supplied on credit. 4 importance: *money was of no account to her.* • v. regard in a particular way.
- PHRASES **account for 1** supply or make up an amount. 2 give a satisfactory explanation of. **call someone to account** ask someone to explain poor performance. **on someone's account** for someone's benefit. **on account of** because of. **on no account** under no circumstances. **take account of** take into consideration.
- ORIGIN Old French *acont*.

accountable • adj. responsible for your actions and expected to explain them.
- DERIVATIVES **accountability** n.

accountant • n. a person who keeps or inspects financial accounts.
- DERIVATIVES **accountancy** n.

accounting • n. the keeping of financial accounts.

accoutrement /uh-koo-truh-muhnt, uh-koo-ter-muhnt/ (US **accouterment**) • n. an extra item of clothing or equipment.
- ORIGIN French *accoutrer* 'clothe, equip'.

accredit • v. (**accredits, accrediting, accredited**) 1 (**accredit something to**) give someone the credit for something. 2 give official authorization to.
- DERIVATIVES **accreditation** n.
- ORIGIN French *accréditer*.

accretion /uh-kree-sh'n/ • n. 1 growth or increase by a gradual build-up of layers. 2 a thing formed or added in this way.
- ORIGIN Latin *accrescere* 'grow'.

accrue /uh-kroo/ • v. (**accrues, accruing, accrued**) 1 (of money) be received in regular or increasing amounts. 2 collect or receive payments or benefits.
- DERIVATIVES **accrual** n.

– ORIGIN Old French *acreistre* 'increase'.

accumulate /uh-kyoo-myuu-layt/
• v. (**accumulates, accumulating, accumulated**) **1** gather together a number or quantity of something. **2** increase: *large debts accumulated.*
– DERIVATIVES **accumulation** n. **accumulative** adj.
– ORIGIN Latin *accumulare* 'heap up'.

accumulator • n. Brit. **1** a large rechargeable electric cell. **2** a bet placed on a series of events, the winnings and stake from each being placed on the next.

accurate /ak-kyuu-ruht/ • adj. **1** correct in all details. **2** reaching an intended target.
– DERIVATIVES **accuracy** n. **accurately** adv.
– ORIGIN Latin *accurare* 'do with care'.

accursed /uh-ker-sid, uh-kerst/
• adj. literary under a curse.

accusation • n. a claim that someone has done something illegal or wrong.

accusative /uh-kyoo-zuh-tiv/
• n. Grammar the case used for the object of a verb.
– ORIGIN from Latin *casus accusativus* 'the case showing cause'.

accusatory /uh-kyoo-zuh-tuh-ri/
• adj. suggesting that you think that a person has done something wrong.

accuse • v. (**accuses, accusing, accused**) say that someone has done something wrong or illegal: *he was accused of murder.*
– DERIVATIVES **accuser** n.
– ORIGIN Latin *accusare* 'call to account'.

accustom • v. **1** (**accustom someone/ thing to**) make someone or something used to. **2** (**be accustomed to**) be used to. **3** (as adj. **accustomed**) usual; customary.
– ORIGIN Old French *acostumer.*

ace • n. **1** a playing card with a single spot on it, usually the highest card in its suit. **2** informal a person who is very good at a particular activity. **3** Tennis a service that an opponent is unable to return.
• adj. informal very good.
– PHRASES **ace up one's sleeve** a piece of information kept secret until needed.
– ORIGIN Latin *as* 'unity, a unit'.

acellular /ay-sel-yuu-ler/ • adj. Biol. **1** not divided into or containing cells. **2** consisting of one cell only.

acerbic /uh-ser-bik/ • adj. sharp and direct: *acerbic comments.*
– DERIVATIVES **acerbically** adv. **acerbity** n.
– ORIGIN Latin *acerbus* 'sour-tasting'.

acetate /a-si-tayt/ • n. **1** Chem. a salt or ester of acetic acid. **2** fibre or plastic made from a substance produced from cellulose.

acetic acid /uh-see-tik/ • n. the acid that gives vinegar its characteristic taste.
– ORIGIN Latin *acetum* 'vinegar'.

acetone /a-si-tohn/ • n. a colourless liquid used as a solvent.
– ORIGIN from ACETIC ACID.

acetylene /uh-set-i-leen/ • n. a gas which burns with a bright flame, used in welding.
– ORIGIN from ACETIC ACID.

ache • n. a continuous or long-lasting dull pain. • v. (**aches, aching, ached**) **1** suffer from an ache. **2** (**ache for/to do**) feel great desire for or to do.
– ORIGIN Old English.

achieve • v. (**achieves, achieving, achieved**) succeed in doing something by effort, skill, or courage.
– DERIVATIVES **achievable** adj. **achiever** n.
– ORIGIN Old French *achever* 'come or bring to a head'.

 achieve follows the usual rule of *i* before *e* except after *c*.

achievement • n. **1** a thing that is done successfully. **2** the action of achieving something.

Achilles heel /uh-kil-leez/ • n. a weak point.
– ORIGIN from *Achilles*, a hero in Greek myth whose mother plunged him into the River Styx when he was a baby, protecting his body from injury except for the heel by which she held him.

Achilles tendon • n. the tendon connecting calf muscles to the heel.

achromatic /a-kroh-mat-ik/
• adj. **1** transmitting light without separating it into colours. **2** without colour.

achy (also **achey**) • adj. suffering from an ache or aches.

acid • n. **1** a substance with chemical properties which include turning litmus red, neutralizing alkalis, and dissolving some metals. **2** informal the drug LSD.
• adj. **1** having the properties of an acid; having a pH of less than 7. **2** sharp-tasting or sour. **3** (of a remark) bitter or cutting.
– DERIVATIVES **acidic** adj. **acidly** adv. **acidy** adj.
– ORIGIN Latin *acidus.*

acidify • v. (**acidifies, acidifying, acidified**) make or become acid.
– DERIVATIVES **acidification** n.

acidity • n. **1** the level of acid in something. **2** sharpness in a person's remarks or tone.

acid rain • n. rainfall made acidic by pollution.

acid test • n. a decisive test of success or value.

a

– ORIGIN from the use of an acid to test whether or not a metal is gold.

acknowledge •v. (**acknowledges, acknowledging, acknowledged**)
1 accept that something exists or is true. **2** confirm that you have received or are grateful for something. **3** show that you have noticed someone by making a gesture.
– ORIGIN from the former verb *knowledge* (in the same sense).

acknowledgement (also **acknowledgment**) •n. **1** the action of acknowledging. **2** something done or given to show gratitude.

acme /ak-mi/ •n. the highest stage of development or the most excellent example of something.
– ORIGIN Greek *akmē*.

acne •n. a skin condition causing red pimples.
– ORIGIN Greek *aknas*.

acolyte /ak-uh-lyt/ •n. an assistant or follower.
– ORIGIN Greek *akolouthos*.

acorn •n. the fruit of the oak tree, an oval nut in a cup-shaped base.
– ORIGIN Old English.

acoustic /uh-koo-stik/ •adj. **1** relating to sound or hearing. **2** not electrically amplified: *an acoustic guitar.*
•n. (**acoustics**) **1** the aspects of a room or building that affect how well it trans-mits sound. **2** the branch of physics con-cerned with sound.
– DERIVATIVES **acoustical** adj. **acoustically** adv.
– ORIGIN Greek *akoustikos*.

acquaint •v. **1** (**acquaint someone with**) make someone aware of or familiar with. **2** (**be acquainted**) know someone personally.
– ORIGIN Latin *accognitare*.

acquaintance •n. **1** a person you know slightly. **2** knowledge of someone or something.

acquiesce /ak-wi-ess/ •v. (**acquiesces, acquiescing, acquiesced**) accept something without protest.
– ORIGIN Latin *acquiescere*.

acquiescent •adj. ready to accept or do something without protest.
– DERIVATIVES **acquiescence** n.

acquire •v. (**acquires, acquiring, acquired**) **1** come to have. **2** learn or develop a skill or quality.
– DERIVATIVES **acquirement** n. **acquirer** n.
– ORIGIN Latin *acquirere* 'get in addition'.

acquisition /ak-wi-zi-sh'n/
•n. **1** something that has recently been obtained. **2** the action of obtaining or learning something.

acquisitive •adj. too interested in gaining money or possessions.
– DERIVATIVES **acquisitiveness** n.

acquit •v. (**acquits, acquitting, acquitted**) **1** formally state that someone is not guilty of a criminal charge. **2** (**acquit yourself**) behave or perform in a particular way.
– ORIGIN Latin *acquitare* 'pay a debt'.

acquittal •n. a judgement that a person is not guilty of the crime with which they have been charged.

acre /ay-ker/ •n. a unit of land area equal to 4,840 square yards (0.405 hectare).
– DERIVATIVES **acreage** n.
– ORIGIN Old English.

acrid /ak-rid/ •adj. unpleasantly bitter or sharp.
– ORIGIN Latin *acer*.

acrimonious /ak-ri-moh-ni-uhss/
•adj. angry and bitter.

acrimony /ak-ri-muh-ni/ •n. feelings of bitterness or anger.
– ORIGIN Latin *acrimonia*.

acrobat •n. an entertainer who performs spectacular gymnastic feats.
– ORIGIN Greek *akrobatos* 'walking on tiptoe'.

acrobatic •adj. involving or skilled at spectacular gymnastic feats.
•n. (**acrobatics**) spectacular gymnastic feats.
– DERIVATIVES **acrobatically** adv.

acronym /ak-ruh-nim/ •n. a word formed from the first letters of other words (e.g. *laser*).
– ORIGIN from Greek *akron* 'end' + *onoma* 'name'.

acropolis /uh-krop-uh-liss/ •n. the citadel of an ancient Greek city, built on high ground.
– ORIGIN Greek.

across •prep. & adv. from one side to the other of something.
– PHRASES **across the board** applying to all.
– ORIGIN from Old French *a croix, en croix* 'in or on a cross'.

acrostic /uh-kross-tik/ •n. a poem or puzzle in which certain letters in each line form a word or words.
– ORIGIN Greek *akrostikhis*.

acrylic •adj. (of a synthetic fabric, plastic, or paint) made from acrylic acid (an organic acid).
– ORIGIN from Latin *acer* 'pungent' + *oleum* 'oil'.

act •v. **1** do something. **2** take effect or have a particular effect. **3** behave in a particular way. **4** (**act as**) perform the function of: *she often acted as an interpreter.* **5** (**act for/on behalf of**

someone) represent the interests of someone. **6** (as adj. **acting**) temporarily doing the duties of another person. **7** perform a role in a play or film. • n. **1** a thing done. **2** a law passed formally by a parliament. **3** a pretence: *putting on an act.* **4** a main division of a play, ballet, or opera. **5** a set performance or performing group.
– PHRASES **act of God** an event caused by natural forces beyond human control. **act up** informal behave badly. **get in on the act** informal become involved in something to share its benefits.
– ORIGIN Latin *actus* 'event, thing done'.

actinium /ak-tin-i-uhm/ • n. a rare radioactive metallic chemical element found in uranium ores.
– ORIGIN Greek *aktis* 'ray'.

action • n. **1** the process of doing something to achieve an aim. **2** a thing done. **3** the effect of something such as a chemical. **4** a lawsuit. **5** armed conflict. **6** the way in which something works or moves. • v. deal with something.
– PHRASES **in action** performing an activity. **out of action** not working.

actionable • adj. giving someone grounds to take legal action.

action replay • n. Brit. a playback of part of a television broadcast.

action stations • pl. n. esp. Brit. the positions taken up by soldiers in preparation for action.

activate • v. (**activates, activating, activated**) make something act or start working.
– DERIVATIVES **activation** n. **activator** n.

active • adj. **1** moving about often or energetically. **2** (of a person's mind) alert and lively. **3** doing something regularly: *an active member of the society.* **4** functioning; in operation. **5** Grammar (of verbs) in which the subject is the person or thing performing the action and which can take a direct object (e.g. *she loved him*).
– DERIVATIVES **actively** adv.
– ORIGIN Latin *activus.*

active service • n. direct involvement in military operations as a member of the armed forces.

activist • n. a person who campaigns for political or social change.
– DERIVATIVES **activism** n.

activity • n. (pl. **activities**) **1** a situation in which things are happening or being done. **2** busy or energetic action or movement. **3** an action or pursuit: *sporting activities.*

actor • n. a person whose profession is acting.

actress • n. a female actor.

actual • adj. existing in fact.
– ORIGIN Latin *actualis.*

actuality • n. (pl. **actualities**) the state of existing in fact; reality.

actualize (or **actualise**) • v. (**actualizes, actualizing. actualized**) make something real.
– DERIVATIVES **actualization** n.

actually • adv. in reality.

actuary /ak-choo-uh-ri/ • n. (pl. **actuaries**) a person who compiles and analyses statistics in order to calculate insurance risks and premiums.
– ORIGIN Latin *actuarius* 'bookkeeper'.

actuate /ak-choo-ayt/ • v. (**actuates, actuating, actuated**) **1** cause a machine to operate. **2** be the motive for someone to do something.

acuity /uh-kyoo-i-ti/ • n. sharpness of thought, vision, or hearing.
– ORIGIN Latin *acuitas.*

acumen /ak-yoo-muhn/ • n. the ability to make good judgements and take quick decisions.
– ORIGIN Latin, 'sharpness, point'.

acupuncture /ak-yoo-pungk-cher/ • n. a medical treatment in which very thin needles are inserted into the skin at specific points.
– DERIVATIVES **acupuncturist** n.
– ORIGIN from Latin *acu* 'with a needle' + PUNCTURE.

acute • adj. **1** (of something bad) serious. **2** (of an illness) coming rapidly to a crisis. **3** sharp-witted; shrewd. **4** (of a sense) highly developed. **5** (of an angle) less than 90°.
– DERIVATIVES **acutely** adv. **acuteness** n.
– ORIGIN Latin *acutus* 'sharpened'.

acute accent • n. a mark (´) placed over a letter to indicate pronunciation (e.g. in *fiancée*).

AD • abbrev. Anno Domini (used to indicate that a date comes the specified number of years after the traditional date of Jesus's birth).
– ORIGIN Latin, 'in the year of the Lord'.

> **USAGE:** With a date that is written in figures, **AD** should be placed **before** the numerals (*AD 375*), but when the date is spelled out, **AD** is placed after it (*the third century AD*).

ad • n. informal an advertisement.

adage /ad-ij/ • n. a popular saying expressing something that most people accept as true.
– ORIGIN Latin *adagium.*

adagio /uh-dah-ji-oh/ Music • adv. & adj. in slow time. • n. (pl. **adagios**) a passage in slow time.
– ORIGIN Italian.

adamant • adj. refusing to change your mind about something.
– DERIVATIVES **adamantly** adv.
– ORIGIN Greek *adamas* 'invincible'.

Adam's apple • n. the projection of cartilage at the front of the neck.
– ORIGIN from the belief that a piece of the forbidden fruit became lodged in Adam's throat.

adapt • v. 1 make suitable for a new use or purpose. 2 become adjusted to new conditions.
– DERIVATIVES **adaptive** adj.
– ORIGIN Latin *adaptare*.

adaptable • adj. able to adjust to or be altered for new conditions or uses.
– DERIVATIVES **adaptability** n.

adaptation (also **adaption**) • n. 1 the action of adapting something. 2 a film or play adapted from a written work.

adaptor (also **adapter**) • n. 1 a device for connecting pieces of equipment. 2 Brit. a device for connecting several electric plugs to one socket.

add • v. 1 join to or put with something else. 2 put together two or more numbers or amounts to find their total value. 3 (**add up**) increase in amount, number, or degree. 4 say as a further remark. 5 (**add up**) informal make sense.
– ORIGIN Latin *addere*.

addendum /uh-den-duhm/ • n. (pl. **addenda** /uh-den-duh/) an extra item added at the end of a book or other publication.
– ORIGIN Latin, 'that which is to be added'.

adder • n. a poisonous snake with a dark zigzag pattern on its back.
– ORIGIN Old English, 'serpent, adder'.

addict • n. a person who is addicted to something.

addicted • adj. 1 physically dependent on a particular substance. 2 devoted to a particular interest or activity.
– ORIGIN Latin *addicere* 'assign'.

addiction • n. the fact or condition of being addicted.
– DERIVATIVES **addictive** adj.

addition • n. 1 the action of adding. 2 a person or thing added.

additional • adj. extra to what is already present or available.
– DERIVATIVES **additionally** adv.

additive • n. a substance added to improve or preserve something.

addle • v. (**addles**, **addling**, **addled**) 1 confuse someone. 2 (as adj. **addled**) (of an egg) rotten.
– ORIGIN Old English, 'liquid filth'.

address • n. 1 the details of where someone lives or a building is situated. 2 a formal speech given to an audience.

3 a number indicating where to find a piece of information in a data storage system or computer memory. 4 a string of characters which identifies a destination for email messages.
• v. 1 write a name and address on an envelope or parcel. 2 formal speak to someone. 3 think about and begin to deal with.
– DERIVATIVES **addressee** n.
– ORIGIN from Latin *ad-* 'towards' + *directus* 'direct'.

adduce /uh-dyooss/ • v. (**adduces**, **adducing**, **adduced**) refer to something as evidence.
– ORIGIN Latin *adducere*.

adenoids /ad-uh-noydz/ • pl. n. a mass of tissue between the back of the nose and the throat.
– DERIVATIVES **adenoidal** adj.
– ORIGIN Greek *adēn* 'gland'.

adept • adj. /ad-ept, uh-dept/ skilled at doing something. • n. /ad-ept/ a person skilled at doing something.
– DERIVATIVES **adeptly** adv. **adeptness** n.
– ORIGIN Latin *adipisci* 'obtain, attain'.

adequate • adj. satisfactory or acceptable.
– DERIVATIVES **adequacy** n. **adequately** adv.
– ORIGIN Latin *adaequare* 'make equal to'.

adhere /uhd-heer/ • v. (**adheres**, **adhering**, **adhered**) (**adhere to**) 1 stick firmly to. 2 follow or observe: *members must adhere to a code of practice.*
– DERIVATIVES **adherence** n.
– ORIGIN Latin *adhaerere*.

adherent • n. a supporter of a party, person, or set of ideas. • adj. sticking firmly to something.

adhesion /uhd-hee-zh'n/ • n. the action of adhering to something.

adhesive /uhd-hee-siv/ • n. a substance used to stick things together; glue.
• adj. sticky.
– DERIVATIVES **adhesiveness** n.

ad hoc /ad hok/ • adj. & adv. formed or done for a particular purpose only.
– ORIGIN Latin, 'to this'.

adieu /uh-dyoo/ • exclam. literary goodbye.
– ORIGIN Old French.

Adi Granth /ah-di grunt/ • n. the main sacred scripture of Sikhism.
– ORIGIN Sanskrit, 'first book'.

ad infinitum /ad in-fi-ny-tuhm/
• adv. endlessly; forever.
– ORIGIN Latin, 'to infinity'.

adipose /ad-i-pohss/ • adj. tech. (of body tissue) used for storing fat.
– ORIGIN Latin *adiposus*.

adjacent /uh-jay-s'nt/ • adj. near or next to something else.

– ORIGIN Latin *adjacere* 'lie near to'.

adjective • n. a word used to describe a noun, such as *sweet*, *red*, or *technical*.
– DERIVATIVES **adjectival** /ad-jik-ty-vuhl/ adj.
– ORIGIN Old French *adjectif*.

adjoin • v. be next to and joined with.
– ORIGIN Latin *adjungere* 'join to'.

adjourn /uh-jern/ • v. **1** stop a meeting or legal case with the intention of continuing it later. **2** postpone a decision.
– DERIVATIVES **adjournment** n.
– ORIGIN Old French *ajorner*.

adjudge • v. (**adjudges**, **adjudging**, **adjudged**) decide to be the case formally or officially: *he was adjudged guilty*.
– ORIGIN Latin *adjudicare*.

adjudicate /uh-joo-di-kayt/ • v. (**adjudicates**, **adjudicating**, **adjudicated**) **1** make a formal judgement on an undecided matter. **2** judge a competition.
– DERIVATIVES **adjudication** n. **adjudicator** n.
– ORIGIN Latin *adjudicare* 'adjudge'.

adjunct /a-jungkt/ • n. an additional and supplementary part.
– ORIGIN Latin *adjungere* 'adjoin'.

adjure /uh-joor/ • v. (**adjures**, **adjuring**, **adjured**) formal solemnly urge someone to do something.
– ORIGIN Latin *adjurare*.

adjust • v. **1** alter slightly. **2** become used to a new situation. **3** decide the amount to be paid for loss or damages when settling an insurance claim.
– DERIVATIVES **adjustability** n. **adjustable** adj. **adjuster** n.
– ORIGIN Old French *ajoster* 'to estimate approximately'.

adjustment • n. **1** a minor change. **2** the action of adjusting.

adjutant /a-juu-tuhnt/ • n. a military officer acting as an administrative assistant to a senior officer.
– ORIGIN Latin *adjutare*.

ad-lib • v. (**ad-libs**, **ad-libbing**, **ad-libbed**) speak or perform in public without preparing beforehand. • adv. & adj. spoken or done without preparing beforehand. • n. an unprepared remark or speech.
– ORIGIN from Latin *ad libitum* 'according to pleasure'.

administer • v. (**administers**, **administering**, **administered**) **1** organize or put into effect. **2** give out a drug or remedy.
– ORIGIN Latin *administrare*.

administrate • v. (**administrates**,

administrating, **administrated**) manage an organization.
– DERIVATIVES **administrative** adj. **administrator** n.

administration • n. **1** the organization and running of a business or system. **2** the action of giving out or applying something. **3** the government in power.

admirable /ad-mi-ruh-b'l/ • adj. deserving respect and approval.
– DERIVATIVES **admirably** adv.

admiral • n. **1** the highest-ranking commander of a fleet or navy. **2** (**Admiral**) a naval officer of the second most senior rank.
– ORIGIN Old French *amiral*.

Admiralty • n. (in the UK) the government department formerly in charge of the Royal Navy.

admire • v. (**admires**, **admiring**, **admired**) **1** regard someone or something with respect or approval. **2** look at with pleasure.
– DERIVATIVES **admiration** n. **admirer** n.
– ORIGIN Latin *admirari* 'wonder at'.

admissible • adj. acceptable or valid.
– DERIVATIVES **admissibility** n.

admission • n. **1** entry to or permission to enter a place. **2** a confession. **3** a person who is admitted to hospital for treatment.

admit • v. (**admits**, **admitting**, **admitted**) **1** confess to be true or to be the case. **2** allow to enter. **3** accept someone into a hospital for treatment. **4** accept as valid.
– ORIGIN Latin *admittere* 'let into'.

admittance • n. the process of entering or the fact of being allowed to enter.

admixture • n. tech. a mixture.

admonish • v. reprimand firmly.
– DERIVATIVES **admonishment** n. **admonition** n. **admonitory** adj.
– ORIGIN Latin *admonere*.

ad nauseam /ad naw-zi-am/ • adv. to an annoyingly excessive extent.
– ORIGIN Latin, 'to sickness'.

ado • n. trouble; fuss.
– ORIGIN from dialect *at do* 'to do'.

adobe /uh-doh-bi/ • n. a kind of clay used to make sun-dried bricks.
– ORIGIN Spanish *adobar* 'to plaster'.

adolescent • adj. in the process of developing from a child into an adult. • n. an adolescent boy or girl.
– DERIVATIVES **adolescence** n.
– ORIGIN Latin *adolescere* 'to mature'.

Adonis /uh-doh-niss/ • n. a very handsome young man.
– ORIGIN the name of a beautiful youth in Greek myth.

adopt • v. **1** legally take another person's child and bring it up as your own.

2 choose an option or course of action. **3** take on an attitude or position: *he adopted a patronizing tone.*
– DERIVATIVES **adoptee** n. **adopter** n. **adoption** n.
– ORIGIN Latin *adoptare.*

adoptive • adj. (of a child or parent) in that relationship by adoption.

adorable • adj. very lovable or charming.
– DERIVATIVES **adorably** adv.

adore • v. (**adores, adoring, adored**) **1** love and respect deeply. **2** informal like very much.
– DERIVATIVES **adoration** n. **adorer** n.
– ORIGIN Latin *adorare* 'to worship'.

adorn • v. make more attractive or beautiful; decorate.
– DERIVATIVES **adornment** n.
– ORIGIN Latin *adornare.*

adrenal /uh-**dree**-n'l/ • adj. relating to a pair of glands found above the kidneys which produce adrenalin and other hormones.

adrenalin /uh-**dre**-nuh-lin/ (also **adrenaline**) • n. a hormone produced in response to stress, that increases rates of blood circulation, breathing, and metabolism.

adrift • adj. & adv. **1** (of a boat) drifting without control. **2** no longer fixed in position.

adroit /uh-**droyt**/ • adj. clever or skilful.
– ORIGIN from French *à droit* 'according to right, properly'.

adsorb /uhd-**zorb**/ • v. (of a solid) hold molecules of a gas or liquid in a layer on its surface.
– DERIVATIVES **adsorption** n.

adsorbent • n. a substance which adsorbs another.

adulation /ad-yuu-**lay**-sh'n/ • n. excessive admiration.
– DERIVATIVES **adulatory** adj.
– ORIGIN Latin.

adult /**ad**-ult, uh-**dult**/ • n. a person who is fully grown and developed. • adj. **1** fully grown and developed. **2** suitable for or typical of adults.
– DERIVATIVES **adulthood** n.
– ORIGIN Latin *adultus.*

adulterate /uh-**dul**-tuh-rayt/ • v. (**adulterates, adulterating, adulterated**) make something poorer in quality by adding another substance.
– DERIVATIVES **adulterant** adj. **adulteration** n.
– ORIGIN Latin *adulterare* 'to corrupt'.

adulterer • n. (fem. **adulteress**) a person who has committed adultery.
– ORIGIN Latin *adulterare* 'to corrupt'.

adultery • n. sexual intercourse between a married person and a person who is not their husband or wife.
– DERIVATIVES **adulterous** adj.

adumbrate /ad-um-**brayt**/ • v. (**adumbrates, adumbrating, adumbrated**) formal **1** give a general idea of; outline. **2** be a warning of something to come.
– DERIVATIVES **adumbration** n.
– ORIGIN Latin *adumbrare* 'shade, overshadow'.

advance • v. (**advances, advancing, advanced**) **1** move forwards. **2** make progress. **3** put forward a theory or suggestion. **4** hand over payment to someone as a loan or before it is due. • n. **1** a forward movement. **2** a development or improvement. **3** an amount of money advanced to someone. **4** (**advances**) approaches made to someone with the aim of beginning a sexual or romantic relationship. • adj. done or supplied beforehand.
– ORIGIN Old French *avancer.*

advanced • adj. **1** far on in development or progress. **2** complex; not basic.

advanced level • n. = A LEVEL.

advanced subsidiary level • n. (in the UK except Scotland) a GCE exam at a level between GCSE and advanced level.

advancement • n. **1** the process of helping something to progress. **2** the promotion of a person in rank or status. **3** a development or improvement.

advantage • n. **1** something that puts you in a favourable position. **2** Tennis a score marking a point between deuce and winning the game.
– PHRASES **take advantage of 1** make unfair use of someone or something for your own benefit. **2** make good use of the opportunities available.
– DERIVATIVES **advantageous** /ad-vuhn-**tay**-juhss/ adj.
– ORIGIN Old French *avantage.*

advent /**ad**-vent/ • n. **1** the arrival of an important person or thing. **2** (**Advent**) (in Christian belief) the coming or second coming of Jesus. **3** (**Advent**) (in the Christian Church) the period of time leading up to Christmas.
– ORIGIN Latin *adventus.*

Adventist • n. a member of a Christian sect which believes that the second coming of Jesus is about to happen.

adventitious /ad-vuhn-ti-**shuhss**/ • adj. happening by chance.
– ORIGIN Latin *adventicius* 'coming from abroad'.

adventure • n. **1** an unusual, exciting, and daring experience. **2** excitement arising from danger or risk.
– DERIVATIVES **adventuresome** adj.

– ORIGIN Latin *adventurus* 'about to happen'.

adventurer • n. (fem. **adventuress**) **1** a person willing to take risks or use dishonest methods to gain wealth or power: *a political adventurer*. **2** a person who looks for adventure.

adventurism • n. willingness to take risks in business or politics.

adventurous • adj. open to or involving new, interesting, or exciting experiences: *more adventurous meals*.

adverb • n. a word or phrase that gives more information about an adjective, verb, other adverb, or a sentence (e.g. *gently, very, fortunately*).
– DERIVATIVES **adverbial** adj.
– ORIGIN Latin *adverbium*.

adversarial /ad-ver-**sair**-i-uhl/ • adj. involving conflict or opposition.

adversary /**ad**-ver-suh-ri/ • n. (pl. **adversaries**) an opponent or enemy.
– ORIGIN Latin *adversarius* 'opposed, opponent'.

adverse /ad-**verss**/ • adj. harmful; unfavourable.
– DERIVATIVES **adversely** adv.
– ORIGIN Latin *adversus* 'against, opposite'.

> **USAGE:** Do not confuse **adverse** with **averse**. **Adverse** means 'harmful' or 'unfavourable' (*adverse publicity*), whereas **averse** means 'strongly disliking' or 'opposed' (*I am not averse to helping out*).

adversity • n. (pl. **adversities**) a difficult or unpleasant situation.

advert • n. Brit. informal an advertisement.

advertise • v. (**advertises, advertising, advertised**) **1** present or describe a product, service, or event in the media in order to increase sales. **2** publicize information about a vacancy for a job. **3** make a fact known.
– DERIVATIVES **advertiser** n. **advertising** n.
– ORIGIN Latin *advertere* 'turn to'.

advertisement • n. a notice or display advertising something.

advice • n. recommendations offered to someone about what they should do.
– ORIGIN Old French *avis*.

> **USAGE:** Do not confuse **advice** and **advise**. **Advice** is a noun meaning 'recommendations about what someone should do' (*your doctor can give you advice on diet*), whereas **advise** is a verb that means 'recommend that someone should do something' (*I advised him to go home*).

advisable • adj. to be recommended; sensible.
– DERIVATIVES **advisability** n.

advise • v. (**advises, advising, advised**) **1** suggest that someone should do something. **2** inform someone about a fact or situation.
– DERIVATIVES **adviser** (also **advisor**) n.
– ORIGIN Old French *aviser*.

> **USAGE:** On the confusion of **advise** with **advice**, see the note at **ADVICE**.

advised • adj. behaving as someone would recommend; sensible.
– DERIVATIVES **advisedly** adv.

advisory • adj. having the power to make recommendations but not to make sure that they are carried out.

advocaat /ad-vuh-**kah**/ • n. a liqueur made with eggs, sugar, and brandy.
– ORIGIN Dutch, 'advocate'.

advocate • n. /**ad**-vuh-kuht/ **1** a person who publicly supports or recommends a particular cause or policy. **2** a person who pleads a case on someone else's behalf. **3** Scottish = **BARRISTER**. • v. /**ad**-vuh-kayt/ (**advocates, advocating, advocated**) publicly recommend or support something.
– DERIVATIVES **advocacy** n.
– ORIGIN Latin *advocare* 'call to your aid'.

adze (US **adz**) • n. a tool similar to an axe, with an arched blade.
– ORIGIN Old English.

aegis /**ee**-jiss/ • n. the protection, backing, or support of someone: *talks conducted under the aegis of the UN*.
– ORIGIN Greek *aigis* 'shield of Zeus'.

aeon /**ee**-on/ (US or tech. also **eon**) • n. **1** a very long period of time. **2** a major division of time in geology, subdivided into eras.
– ORIGIN Greek *aiōn* 'age'.

aerate /**air**-ayt/ • v. (**aerates, aerating, aerated**) introduce air into something.
– DERIVATIVES **aeration** n. **aerator** n.
– ORIGIN Latin *aer* 'air'.

aerial • n. a structure that sends out or receives radio or television signals. • adj. **1** existing or taking place in the air. **2** involving the use of aircraft.
– ORIGIN Greek *aēr* 'air'.

aerie • n. US = **EYRIE**.

aero- /**air**-oh/ • comb. form **1** relating to air: *aerobic*. **2** relating to aircraft: *aerodrome*.
– ORIGIN Greek *aēr* 'air'.

aerobatics • n. exciting and skilful movements performed in an aircraft for entertainment.
– DERIVATIVES **aerobatic** adj.

aerobic /air-**oh**-bik/ • adj. **1** relating to physical exercise intended to improve the intake of oxygen and its movement

around the body. **2** using oxygen from the air: *aerobic bacteria.* •n. (**aerobics**) aerobic exercises.
– DERIVATIVES **aerobically** adv.
– ORIGIN from AERO- + Greek *bios* 'life'.

aerodrome •n. Brit. a small airport or airfield.

aerodynamic •adj. **1** relating to aerodynamics. **2** (of an object) having a shape which enables it to move through the air quickly. •n. (**aerodynamics**) the science concerned with the movement of objects through the air.
– DERIVATIVES **aerodynamically** adv.

aerofoil •n. Brit. a curved structure, such as a wing, designed to give an aircraft lift in flight.

aeronautics •n. the study or practice of travel through the air.
– DERIVATIVES **aeronautical** adj.
– ORIGIN from Greek *aēr* 'air' + *nautēs* 'sailor'.

aeroplane •n. Brit. a powered flying vehicle with fixed wings that is heavier than the air.
– ORIGIN from French *aéro-* 'air' + Greek *-planos* 'wandering'.

aerosol •n. a substance sealed in a container under pressure and released as a fine spray.
– ORIGIN from AERO- + SOLUTION.

aerospace •n. the technology and industry concerned with flight.

aesthete /eess-theet/ (US also **esthete**) •n. a person who appreciates art and beauty.

aesthetic /eess-thet-ik/ (US also **esthetic**) •adj. **1** concerned with beauty or the appreciation of beauty. **2** having a pleasant appearance. •n. **1** a set of principles behind the work of a particular artist or artistic movement. **2** (**aesthetics**) the branch of philosophy that deals with questions of beauty and artistic taste.
– DERIVATIVES **aesthetically** adv. **aestheticism** n.
– ORIGIN Greek *aisthētikos*.

aether •n. var. of ETHER (in sense 2).

afar •adv. literary at or to a distance.

affable •adj. good-natured and friendly.
– DERIVATIVES **affability** n. **affably** adv.
– ORIGIN Latin *affabilis*.

affair •n. **1** an event of a particular kind or that has previously been referred to. **2** a matter that a person is responsible for. **3** a love affair. **4** (**affairs**) matters of public interest. **5** (**affairs**) business dealings.
– ORIGIN from Old French *à faire* 'to do'.

affect[1] •v. **1** make a difference to: *the damp has affected my health.* **2** move someone emotionally.
– ORIGIN Latin *afficere* 'affect'.

USAGE: For an explanation of the difference between **affect** and **effect**, see the note at EFFECT.

affect[2] •v. **1** pretend to have or feel something. **2** use or wear in a false way or so as to impress: *he'd affected a French accent.*
– ORIGIN Latin *affectare* 'aim at'.

affectation /af-fek-tay-sh'n/ •n. behaviour, speech, or writing that is false and designed to impress.

affected •adj. false and designed to impress.
– DERIVATIVES **affectedly** adv.

affection •n. a feeling of fondness or liking.

affectionate •adj. showing fondness or liking for someone.
– DERIVATIVES **affectionately** adv.

affidavit /af-fi-day-vit/ •n. a written statement that is sworn on oath to be true, for use as evidence in a law court.
– ORIGIN Latin, 'he has stated on oath'.

affiliate •v. /uh-fil-i-ayt/ (**affiliates, affiliating, affiliated**) officially link a person or group to a larger organization. •n. /uh-fil-i-uht/ a person or group linked to a larger organization.
– DERIVATIVES **affiliation** n.
– ORIGIN Latin *affiliare* 'adopt as son'.

affinity •n. (pl. **affinities**) **1** a natural liking or understanding. **2** a close relationship between people or things with similar qualities. **3** the tendency of a chemical substance to combine with another.
– ORIGIN Latin *affinitas*.

affirm •v. state firmly or publicly.
– DERIVATIVES **affirmation** n.
– ORIGIN Latin *affirmare*.

affirmative •adj. agreeing with a statement or consenting to a request. •n. a statement or word that shows agreement.

affix •v. /uh-fiks/ attach or fasten something to something else. •n. /af-fiks/ a letter or letters added to a word in order to alter its meaning or create a new word; a prefix or suffix.
– ORIGIN Latin *affixare*.

afflict •v. cause pain or trouble to.
– DERIVATIVES **affliction** n.
– ORIGIN Latin *affligere* 'knock down'.

affluent •adj. having plenty of money; wealthy.
– DERIVATIVES **affluence** n.
– ORIGIN Latin *affluere* 'flow towards, flow freely'.

afford •v. **1** (**can/could afford**) have enough money or time for something.

2 provide or give: *the upper terrace affords beautiful views.*
– DERIVATIVES **affordable** adj.
– ORIGIN Old English, 'promote, perform'.

afforestation /uh-for-ris-**tay**-sh'n/ • n. the process of planting trees on an area of land in order to form a forest.

affray • n. Law, dated a breach of the peace by fighting in a public place.
– ORIGIN Old French *afrayer* 'disturb'.

affront • n. an action or remark that offends someone. • v. offend someone.
– ORIGIN Old French *afronter* 'slap in the face, insult'.

Afghan /af-gan/ • n. a person from Afghanistan. • adj. relating to Afghanistan.

Afghan hound • n. a silky-haired breed of dog used for hunting.

aficionado /uh-fi-shuh-**nah**-doh/ • n. (pl. **aficionados**) a person who knows a great deal about an activity or subject and is very interested in it.
– ORIGIN Spanish.

afield • adv. to or at a distance.

aflame • adj. in flames.

afloat • adj. & adv. **1** floating in water. **2** out of debt or difficulty.

aflutter • adj. in a state of agitated excitement.

afoot • adv. & adj. in preparation or progress.

afore • prep. old use or dialect before.

aforementioned • adj. referring to a thing or person previously mentioned.

afraid • adj. feeling fear or anxiety.
– PHRASES **I'm afraid** expressing polite regret.
– ORIGIN Old French *afrayer* 'disturb'.

afresh • adv. in a new or different way.

African • n. **1** a person from Africa, especially a black person. **2** a person descended from black African people. • adj. relating to Africa or Africans.

African American esp. US • n. an American of African origin. • adj. relating to African Americans.

Afrikaans /af-ri-**kahnz**/ • n. a language of southern Africa that developed from Dutch.
– ORIGIN Dutch, 'African'.

Afrikaner /af-ri-**kah**-ner/ • n. a white South African person whose native language is Afrikaans.

Afro • n. (pl. **Afros**) a hairstyle consisting of a mass of very tight curls all round the head.

Afro- • comb. form African: *Afro-American.*

Afro-American • adj. & n. = **AFRICAN AMERICAN**.

Afro-Caribbean • n. a person of African descent living in or coming from the Caribbean. • adj. relating to Afro-Caribbeans.

aft /ahft/ • adv. & adj. at or towards the rear of a ship or an aircraft.
– ORIGIN prob. related to **ABAFT**.

after • prep. **1** in the time following an event or another period of time. **2** next to and following in order or importance. **3** behind. **4** trying to find or get. **5** in reference to: *he was named after his grandfather.* • conj. & adv. in the time following an event.
– PHRASES **after all** in spite of what has been said or expected.
– ORIGIN Old English.

afterbirth • n. the placenta and other material that comes out of the mother's womb after a birth.

aftercare • n. care of a person after a stay in hospital or on release from prison.

after-effect • n. an effect that occurs some time after its cause has gone.

afterglow • n. **1** light remaining in the sky after the sun has set. **2** good feelings remaining after a pleasant experience.

afterlife • n. (in some religions) life after death.

aftermath • n. the effects or results of an unpleasant event.
– ORIGIN from dialect *math* 'mowing'.

afternoon • n. the time from noon to evening.

afters • pl. n. Brit. informal the dessert course of a meal.

aftershave • n. a scented liquid for men to apply to their skin after shaving.

aftershock • n. a smaller earthquake following a large earthquake.

aftertaste • n. a strong or unpleasant taste lingering in the mouth after eating or drinking.

afterthought • n. something thought of or added later.

afterwards (US also **afterward**) • adv. at a later or future time.

afterword • n. a section at the end of a book, usually by a person other than the author.

Ag • symb. the chemical element silver.
– ORIGIN Latin *argentum*.

again /uh-**gen**, uh-**gayn**/ • adv. **1** once more. **2** returning to a previous position or condition. **3** in addition to what has already been mentioned.
– ORIGIN Old English.

against • prep. **1** opposing or disagreeing with. **2** close to or touching. **3** so as to anticipate and prepare for a difficulty. **4** as protection from: *he turned up his collar against the wind.* **5** in contrast to. **6** so as to reduce, cancel, or secure money owed, due, or lent. **7** (in betting) in anticipation of the failure of.

agape /uh-**gayp**/ • adj. (of a person's mouth) wide open.

agate /ag-uht/ • n. a semi-precious variety of quartz that has a striped appearance.
– ORIGIN Greek *akhatēs*.

agave /uh-**gay**-vi, uh-**gah**-vi/ • n. an American plant with narrow spiny leaves.
– ORIGIN from *Agauē*, one of the daughters of Cadmus in Greek mythology.

age • n. **1** the length of time that a person or thing has existed. **2** a particular stage in someone's life: *children of primary school age.* **3** old age. **4** a distinct period of history: *the Elizabethan age.* • v. (**ages, ageing** or **aging, aged**) **1** grow older. **2** make someone or something appear older.
– PHRASES **come of age** be legally recognized as an adult (in UK law at 18).
– ORIGIN Old French.

-age • suffix forming nouns referring to: **1** an action or its result: *leverage.* **2** a number of: *mileage.* **3** a place or house: *vicarage.* **4** fees payable for: *postage.*
– ORIGIN Latin *-aticum*.

aged • adj. **1** /ayjd/ of a particular age. **2** /ay-jid/ old.

ageism • n. prejudice or discrimination against people on the grounds of their age.
– DERIVATIVES **ageist** adj.

ageless • adj. not ageing or appearing to age.

agency • n. **1** an organization or government department providing a particular service. **2** the action or intervention of someone or something: *channels carved by the agency of running water.*

agenda • n. **1** a list of items to be discussed at a meeting. **2** a list of matters to be dealt with.
– ORIGIN Latin, 'things to be done'.

agent • n. **1** a person who provides a particular service: *a travel agent.* **2** a spy. **3** a person or thing that takes an active role or produces a particular effect.
– ORIGIN Latin *agere* 'to do'.

agent noun • n. a noun which refers to a person or thing that carries out the action of a verb, usually ending in *-er* or *-or*, e.g. *worker, accelerator.*

agent provocateur /a-zhon pruh-vo-kuh-**ter**/ • n. (pl. **agents provocateurs** /a-zhon pruh-vo-kuh-**ter**/) a person employed to tempt suspected criminals to break the law so that they can then be convicted.

– ORIGIN French, 'provocative agent'.

age of consent • n. the age at which a person can legally agree to have sex.

age-old • adj. very old.

agglomerate • v. /uh-**glom**-uh-rayt/ (**agglomerates, agglomerating, agglomerated**) collect or form into a mass. • n. /uh-**glom**-uh-ruht/ a mass or collection of things.
– DERIVATIVES **agglomeration** n.
– ORIGIN Latin *agglomerare* 'add to'.

agglutinate /uh-**gloo**-ti-nayt/ • v. (**agglutinates, agglutinating, agglutinated**) firmly stick together to form a mass.
– DERIVATIVES **agglutination** n.
– ORIGIN Latin *agglutinare.*

aggrandize /uh-**gran**-dyz/ (or **aggrandise**) • v. (**aggrandizes, aggrandizing, aggrandized**) increase the power or importance of.
– DERIVATIVES **aggrandizement** n.
– ORIGIN French *agrandir.*

aggravate • v. (**aggravates, aggravating, aggravated**) **1** make a situation worse. **2** informal annoy someone.
– DERIVATIVES **aggravation** n.
– ORIGIN Latin *aggravare* 'make heavy'.

aggregate • n. /**ag**-gri-guht/ a whole formed by combining several different elements. • v. /**ag**-gri-gayt/ (**aggregates, aggregating, aggregated**) combine different elements into a whole. • adj. /**ag**-gri-guht/ formed or calculated by combining many separate items.
– ORIGIN Latin *aggregare* 'herd together'.

aggression • n. hostile or violent behaviour or attitudes.
– ORIGIN Latin.

aggressive • adj. **1** very angry or hostile. **2** too forceful or determined.
– DERIVATIVES **aggressively** adv. **aggressiveness** n.

aggressor • n. a person or country that attacks another without being provoked.

aggrieved • adj. resentful because you believe you have been treated unfairly.
– ORIGIN Old French *agrever* 'make heavier'.

> ✓ **aggrieved** follows the usual rule of *i* before *e* except after *c*; it has a double **g**.

aghast /uh-**gahst**/ • adj. filled with horror or shock.
– ORIGIN from former *gast* 'frighten'.

agile • adj. **1** able to move quickly and easily. **2** quick-witted or shrewd.
– DERIVATIVES **agility** n.
– ORIGIN Latin *agilis.*

agitate • v. (**agitates, agitating,**

agitated) 1 make someone troubled or nervous. **2** campaign to arouse public concern about something. **3** stir or shake a liquid briskly.
– DERIVATIVES **agitation** n.
– ORIGIN Latin *agitare* 'agitate, drive'.

agitator •n. a person who urges other people to protest or rebel.

AGM •abbrev. Brit. annual general meeting.

agnostic /ag-noss-tik/ •n. a person who believes that it is not possible to know whether or not God exists.
– DERIVATIVES **agnosticism** n.

ago •adv. before the present (used with a measurement of time).
– ORIGIN from former *ago* 'to pass'.

agog •adj. very eager to hear or see something.
– ORIGIN from Old French *en* 'in' + *gogue* 'fun'.

agonize (or **agonise**) •v. (**agonizes, agonizing, agonized**) **1** worry greatly. **2** (as adj. **agonizing**) very painful or worrying.

agony •n. (pl. **agonies**) great pain or distress.
– ORIGIN Greek *agōnia*.

agony aunt •n. Brit. informal a person who answers letters in an agony column.

agony column •n. Brit. informal a column in a newspaper or magazine offering advice on readers' personal problems.

agoraphobia /ag-uh-ruh-foh-bi-uh/ •n. abnormal fear of open or public places.
– DERIVATIVES **agoraphobic** adj. & n.
– ORIGIN Greek *agora* 'marketplace'.

agrarian /uh-grair-i-uhn/ •adj. relating to agriculture.
– ORIGIN Latin *agrarius*.

agree •v. (**agrees, agreeing, agreed**) **1** have the same opinion about something. **2** (**agree to**) be willing to do something which has been suggested by another person. **3** (of two or more people) decide on something. **4** (**agree with**) be consistent with: *your body language does not agree with what you are saying.* **5** (**agree with**) be good for.
– ORIGIN Old French *agreer*.

agreeable •adj. **1** pleasant. **2** willing to agree to something. **3** acceptable.
– DERIVATIVES **agreeably** adv.

agreement •n. **1** the sharing of opinion or feeling. **2** an arrangement or contract agreed between people.

agriculture •n. the science or practice of farming.
– DERIVATIVES **agricultural** adj.
agriculturally adv.
– ORIGIN Latin *ager* 'field'.

agronomy /uh-gron-uh-mi/ •n. the

science of soil management and crop production.
– DERIVATIVES **agronomic** adj.
agronomist n.
– ORIGIN French.

aground •adj. & adv. (with reference to a ship) on or on to the bottom in shallow water.

ague /ay-gyoo/ •n. old use malaria or another illness involving fever and shivering.
– ORIGIN from Latin *acuta febris* 'acute fever'.

ahead •adv. **1** further forward in space or time. **2** in the lead.
– PHRASES **ahead of 1** before. **2** earlier than planned or expected.

ahoy •exclam. a call made by people in ships to attract attention.

AI •abbrev. artificial intelligence.

aid •n. **1** help or support. **2** food or money given to a country in need. •v. help or support someone or something.
– ORIGIN Old French *aide*.

aide /ayd/ •n. an assistant to a political leader.

aide-de-camp /ayd-duh-kom/ •n. (pl. **aides-de-camp** /ayd-duh-kom/) a military officer acting as a personal assistant to a senior officer.
– ORIGIN French.

Aids •n. a disease, caused by the HIV virus and transmitted in body fluids, which breaks down the sufferer's natural defences against infection.
– ORIGIN from *acquired immune deficiency syndrome*.

aikido /I-kee-doh/ •n. a Japanese martial art.
– ORIGIN Japanese, 'way of adapting the spirit'.

ail •v. old use cause trouble or suffering to someone.
– ORIGIN Old English.

aileron /ayl-uh-ron/ •n. a hinged part of an aircraft's wing, used to control the balance of the aircraft.
– ORIGIN French, 'small wing'.

ailing •adj. in bad health or condition.

ailment •n. a minor illness.

aim •v. **1** point a weapon or camera at a target. **2** direct something at: *the programme is aimed at a wide audience.* **3** try to achieve something. •n. **1** a purpose or intention. **2** the aiming of a weapon or missile.
– PHRASES **take aim** point a weapon or camera at a target.
– ORIGIN Old French *amer*.

aimless •adj. without purpose or direction.

ain't •contr. informal **1** am not; are not; is

not. **2** has not; have not.

USAGE: Ain't is not good English and should not be used when writing or speaking in a formal situation.

air •n. **1** the invisible mixture of gases surrounding the earth. **2** the open space above the surface of the earth. **3** (before another noun) using aircraft: *air travel.* **4** (**an air of**) an impression of: *she answered with a faint air of boredom.* **5** (**airs**) a pretentious or condescending way of behaving, intended to impress other people. **6** a short, tuneful piece of music. •v. **1** express an opinion or complaint publicly. **2** broadcast a programme on radio or television. **3** expose a room or washed laundry to fresh or warm air.
– PHRASES **airs and graces** Brit. pretentious or condescending behaviour intended to impress other people. **on** (or **off**) **the air** being (or not being) broadcast on radio or television. **up in the air** (of an issue) not yet settled or resolved. **walk on air** feel very pleased or happy.
– DERIVATIVES **airless** adj.
– ORIGIN Greek *aēr.*

airbag •n. a safety device in a vehicle that fills rapidly with air when there is a sudden impact, so protecting the driver or passenger in a collision.

airbase •n. a base for military aircraft.

airborne •adj. **1** carried or spread through the air. **2** (of an aircraft) flying.

airbrick •n. Brit. a brick pierced with small holes in order to let air pass into a building.

airbrush •n. an artist's device for spraying paint by means of compressed air. •v. paint a picture or alter a photograph with an airbrush.

air conditioning •n. a system for controlling the temperature and circulation of the air in a building or vehicle.
– DERIVATIVES **air-conditioned** adj.

air corridor •n. a route over a foreign country which aircraft must take.

aircraft •n. (pl. **aircraft**) an aeroplane, helicopter, or other machine capable of flight.

aircraft carrier •n. a large warship from which aircraft can take off and land.

aircrew •n. (pl. **aircrews**) the crew of an aircraft.

Airedale •n. a large rough-coated black-and-tan breed of terrier.
– ORIGIN from *Airedale*, a district in Yorkshire.

airfield •n. an area of land where aircraft can take off and land.

air force •n. a branch of the armed forces concerned with fighting or defence in the air.

air gun •n. a gun which uses compressed air to fire pellets.

airhead •n. informal a stupid person.

air hostess •n. Brit. a stewardess in a passenger aircraft.

airing •n. **1** an act of exposing a room or washed laundry to warm or fresh air. **2** a public statement of an opinion or discussion of a subject.

airlift •n. an act of transporting supplies by aircraft.

airline •n. an organization which provides regular flights for public use.

airliner •n. a large passenger aircraft.

airlock •n. **1** a stoppage of the flow in a pump or pipe, caused by an air bubble. **2** a compartment with controlled air pressure and airtight doors at each end, to allow people to move between areas that are at different pressures.

airmail •n. a system of transporting mail overseas by air.

airman (or **airwoman**) •n. (pl. **airmen** or **airwomen**) a pilot or member of the crew of an aircraft in an air force.

air mile •n. **1** a nautical mile used as a measure of distance flown by aircraft. **2** (**Air Miles**) trademark points (equivalent to miles of free air travel) collected by buyers of airline tickets and other products.

air pistol (or **air rifle**) •n. a gun which uses compressed air to fire pellets.

airplane •n. N. Amer. an aeroplane.

airplay •n. broadcasting time devoted to a particular record, performer, or type of music.

air pocket •n. **1** a hollow space that contains air. **2** an area of low pressure that causes an aircraft to lose height suddenly.

airport •n. an area consisting of a set of runways and buildings where commercial aircraft can take off and land, together with facilities for passengers.

air raid •n. an attack in which bombs are dropped from aircraft on to a target on the ground.

air-sea rescue •n. a rescue from the sea using aircraft.

airship •n. a large power-driven aircraft filled with a gas which is lighter than air.

airspace •n. the part of the air above and subject to the laws of a particular country.

airspeed •n. the speed of an aircraft in

relation to the air through which it is moving.

airstream • n. a current of air.

airstrip • n. a strip of ground for the take-off and landing of aircraft.

airtight • adj. **1** not allowing air to escape or pass through. **2** having no weaknesses: *an airtight alibi.*

airtime • n. **1** the amount of time allocated to a particular subject or type of material on radio or television. **2** the time during which a mobile phone is in use.

air traffic control • n. the ground-based staff and equipment concerned with controlling and observing aircraft flying in a particular area.

airwaves • pl. n. the radio frequencies used for broadcasting.

airway • n. **1** the passage by which air reaches the lungs. **2** a recognized route followed by aircraft.

airworthy • adj. (of an aircraft) safe to fly.
– DERIVATIVES **airworthiness** n.

airy • adj. (**airier, airiest**) **1** spacious and well ventilated. **2** casual; dismissive: *an airy wave of the hand.*
– DERIVATIVES **airily** adv. **airiness** n.

airy-fairy • adj. informal, esp. Brit. vague and unrealistic or impractical.

aisle /rhymes with mile/ • n. a passage between rows of seats in a public building, aircraft, or train or between shelves in a shop.
– ORIGIN Latin *ala* 'wing'.

aitch • n. the letter H.
– PHRASES **drop your aitches** fail to pronounce the letter *h* at the beginning of words.
– ORIGIN Old French *ache.*

ajar • adv. & adj. (of a door or window) slightly open.
– ORIGIN Old English, 'a turn'.

aka • abbrev. also known as.

akimbo /uh-kim-boh/ • adv. with the hands on the hips and the elbows turned outwards.
– ORIGIN prob. from Old Norse.

akin • adj. similar in nature or type.
– ORIGIN from *of kin.*

Al • symb. the chemical element aluminium.

-al • suffix **1** (forming adjectives) relating to; of the kind of: *tidal.* **2** forming nouns chiefly referring to the action of a verb: *arrival.*
– ORIGIN Latin *-alis.*

alabaster /al-uh-bah-ster, al-uh-bass-ter/ • n. a white, semi-transparent form of the mineral gypsum, often carved into ornaments. • adj. literary smooth and

white: *pale, alabaster skin.*
– ORIGIN Greek *alabastos, alabastros.*

à la carte /ah lah kart/ • adj. (of a menu) listing dishes that can be ordered as separate items, rather than part of a set meal.
– ORIGIN French, 'according to the card'.

alacrity • n. brisk eagerness or enthusiasm.
– ORIGIN Latin *alacritas.*

Aladdin's cave • n. a place filled with a great number of interesting or precious items.
– ORIGIN from the story of *Aladdin* in the *Arabian Nights' Entertainments.*

à la mode /ah lah mohd/ • adv. & adj. up to date; fashionable.
– ORIGIN French.

alarm • n. **1** anxiety or fear caused by an awareness of danger. **2** a warning of danger. **3** a warning sound or device.
• v. **1** frighten or disturb. **2** (**be alarmed**) (of a building, car, etc.) be fitted with an alarm.
– ORIGIN from Italian *all' arme!* 'to arms!'

alarm clock • n. a clock that can be set to sound an alarm at a particular time to wake someone up.

alarmist • n. a person who exaggerates a danger, so causing unnecessary alarm.
• adj. causing unnecessary alarm.

alas • exclam. literary or humorous an expression of grief, pity, or concern.
– ORIGIN from Old French *a las, a lasse.*

Albanian • n. **1** a person from Albania. **2** the language of Albania. • adj. relating to Albania.

albatross /al-buh-tross/ • n. (pl. **albatrosses**) a very large seabird with long narrow wings, found chiefly in the southern oceans.
– ORIGIN Arabic, 'the diver'.

albeit /awl-bee-it/ • conj. though.
– ORIGIN from *all be it.*

albino /al-bee-noh/ • n. (pl. **albinos**) a person or animal born without pigment in the skin and hair (which are white) and the eyes (which are usually pink).
– ORIGIN Latin *albus* 'white'.

Albion • n. literary Britain or England.
– ORIGIN Latin.

album • n. **1** a blank book in which photographs, stamps, or other items can be kept and displayed. **2** a collection of musical recordings issued as a single item.
– ORIGIN Latin, 'blank tablet'.

albumen /al-byuu-muhn/ • n. egg white, or the protein contained in it.
– ORIGIN Latin.

albumin /al-byuu-min/ • n. a form of protein that is soluble in water and is

a

found especially in blood and egg white.

alchemy /al-kuh-mi/ •n. the medieval forerunner of chemistry, concerned particularly with attempts to convert common metals into gold.
– DERIVATIVES **alchemical** adj. **alchemist** n.
– ORIGIN Greek *khēmia, khēmeia* 'art of transforming metals'.

alcohol •n. **1** a colourless flammable liquid which is the ingredient that gives drinks such as wine, beer, and spirits their intoxicating effect. **2** drinks containing alcohol, such as wine, beer, and spirits. **3** Chem. any organic compound containing a group –OH.
– ORIGIN Arabic, 'the kohl'.

alcoholic •adj. relating to alcohol. •n. a person suffering from alcoholism.

alcoholism •n. addiction to alcoholic drink.

alcopop •n. Brit. informal a ready-mixed fizzy drink containing alcohol.

alcove •n. a recess in the wall of a room.
– ORIGIN French.

aldehyde /al-di-hyd/ •n. a chemical compound made by the oxidation of an alcohol.
– ORIGIN from Latin *alcohol dehydrogenatum* 'alcohol deprived of hydrogen'.

al dente /al den-tay/ •adj. & adv. (of food) cooked so as to be still firm when bitten.
– ORIGIN Italian, 'to the tooth'.

alder •n. a tree of the birch family, which bears catkins.
– ORIGIN Old English.

alderman •n. (pl. **aldermen**) **1** hist. a member of an English county or borough council, next in status to the Mayor. **2** (or **alderwoman**) N. Amer. & Austral. an elected member of a city council.
– ORIGIN Old English, 'chief, patriarch'.

ale •n. esp. Brit. beer other than lager, stout, or porter.
– ORIGIN Old English.

aleatory /ay-lee-uh-tri/ (also **aleatoric**) •adj. depending on the throw of a dice or on chance.
– ORIGIN Latin *aleator* 'dice player'.

alert •adj. **1** quick to notice and respond to danger or possible problems. **2** quick-thinking. •n. **1** the state of being alert. **2** a warning of danger. •v. warn someone of a danger or problem.
– DERIVATIVES **alertly** adv. **alertness** n.
– ORIGIN from Italian *all' erta* 'to the watchtower'.

A level •n. (in the UK except Scotland) the higher of the two main levels of the GCE exam.

– ORIGIN from **ADVANCED LEVEL**.

Alexander technique •n. a system designed to promote well-being through the control of posture.
– ORIGIN named after its originator, the Australian-born actor Frederick Matthias *Alexander*.

alexandrine /a-lig-**zahn**-dryn/ •adj. (of a line of verse) having six iambic feet.
– ORIGIN French.

alfalfa /al-**fal**-fuh/ •n. a plant with clover-like leaves and bluish flowers, used as fodder.
– ORIGIN Spanish.

alfresco /al-**fress**-koh/ •adv. & adj. in the open air.
– ORIGIN from Italian *al fresco*.

algae /al-jee, al-gee/ •pl. n. (sing. **alga** /al-guh/) simple plants that do not have true stems, roots, and leaves, e.g. seaweed.
– DERIVATIVES **algal** adj.
– ORIGIN Latin *alga* 'seaweed'.

algebra /al-ji-bruh/ •n. the branch of mathematics in which letters and other symbols are used to represent numbers and quantities.
– DERIVATIVES **algebraic** /al-ji-**bray**-ik/ adj.
– ORIGIN Latin.

Algerian •n. a person from Algeria. •adj. relating to Algeria.

algorithm /al-guh-ri-*th*'m/ •n. a process or set of rules used in calculations or other problem-solving operations.
– ORIGIN Latin *algorismus*.

alias /ay-li-uhss/ •adv. also known as. •n. **1** a false identity. **2** Computing an identifying label that can be used to access a file, command, or address.
– ORIGIN Latin, 'at another time, otherwise'.

alibi /a-li-by/ •n. (pl. **alibis**) a piece of evidence that someone was elsewhere when a crime was committed.
– ORIGIN Latin, 'elsewhere'.

alien •adj. **1** belonging to a foreign country. **2** unfamiliar or unacceptable: *a lifestyle that was now completely alien to me.* **3** relating to beings from other worlds. •n. **1** a foreigner. **2** a being from another world.
– DERIVATIVES **alienness** n.
– ORIGIN Latin *alienus*.

alienate •v. (**alienates, alienating, alienated**) **1** make someone feel isolated. **2** lose the support or sympathy of someone.
– DERIVATIVES **alienation** n.

alight[1] •v. **1** (of a bird) land on something. **2** formal get off a train or bus.

3 (**alight on**) happen to notice.
– ORIGIN Old English.

alight² • adv. & adj. **1** on fire. **2** shining brightly.

align • v. **1** place something in a straight line or in the correct position in relation to other things. **2** (**align yourself with**) be on the side of.
– DERIVATIVES **alignment** n.
– ORIGIN French *aligner*.

alike • adj. similar. • adv. in a similar way.
– ORIGIN Old English.

alimentary canal • n. the passage along which food passes during digestion.
– ORIGIN Latin *alimentum* 'nourishment'.

alimony /a-li-muh-ni/ • n. esp. N. Amer. financial support for a husband or wife after separation or divorce.
– ORIGIN Latin *alimonia* 'nutriment'.

A-line • adj. (of an item of clothing) slightly flared.

aliquot /a-li-kwot/ • n. tech. a portion or sample taken for analysis or treatment.
– ORIGIN Latin, 'some, so many'.

A-list (or **B-list**) • n. a list of the most (or second most) important or famous people, especially in show business.

alive • adj. **1** living; not dead. **2** continuing in existence or use: *keeping hope alive.* **3** alert and active. **4** (**alive with**) teeming with. **5** (**alive to**) aware of and willing to respond to.

alkali /al-kuh-ly/ • n. (pl. **alkalis**) a substance whose chemical properties include turning litmus blue and neutralizing acids.
– ORIGIN Arabic, 'fry, roast'.

alkaline /al-kuh-lyn/ • adj. having the properties of an alkali; having a pH greater than 7.
– DERIVATIVES **alkalinity** /al-kuh-lin-it-i/ n.

alkane /al-kayn/ • n. Chem. any of the series of saturated hydrocarbons whose simplest members are methane and ethane.
– ORIGIN German *Alkohol* 'alcohol'.

alkene /al-keen/ • n. Chem. any of the series of unsaturated hydrocarbons containing a double bond, of which the simplest member is ethylene.
– ORIGIN German *Alkohol* 'alcohol'.

all • det. & predet. **1** the whole quantity or extent of. **2** any whatever: *he denied all knowledge.* **3** the greatest possible: *with all speed.* • pron. everything or everyone. • adv. **1** completely. **2** indicating an equal score: *one-all.*
– PHRASES **all along** from the beginning. **all and sundry** everyone. **all but** very nearly. **all for** informal strongly in favour

of. **all in** informal exhausted. **all in all** on the whole. **all out** using all your effort. **all round 1** in all respects. **2** for or by each person: *drinks all round.* **all told** in total. **at all** in any way. **in all** in total. **on all fours** on hands and knees. **your all** your greatest effort.
– ORIGIN Old English.

Allah /al-luh/ • n. the name of God among Muslims (and Arab Christians).
– ORIGIN Arabic.

allay /uh-lay/ • v. reduce or end fear, concern, or difficulty.
– ORIGIN Old English, 'lay down or aside'.

all-clear • n. a signal that danger or difficulty is over.

allegation • n. a claim that someone has done something illegal or wrong.

allege /uh-lej/ • v. (**alleges, alleging, alleged**) claim that someone has done something illegal or wrong.
– DERIVATIVES **alleged** adj. **allegedly** adv.
– ORIGIN Old French *esligier.*

allegiance /uh-lee-juhnss/ • n. loyalty to a person of higher status or to a group or cause.
– ORIGIN Old French *ligeance.*

allegory /al-li-guh-ri/ • n. (pl. **allegories**) a story, poem, or picture which contains a hidden meaning.
– DERIVATIVES **allegorical** adj.
– ORIGIN Greek *allēgoria.*

allegretto /al-li-gret-toh/ • adv. & adj. Music at a fairly brisk speed.
– ORIGIN Italian.

allegro /uh-lay-groh/ Music • adv. & adj. at a brisk speed. • n. (pl. **allegros**) a piece of music to be played at a brisk speed.
– ORIGIN Italian, 'lively'.

alleluia /al-li-loo-yuh/ • exclam. & n. var. of HALLELUJAH.

Allen key • n. trademark a spanner designed to fit into and turn an **Allen screw** (one with a hexagonal socket in the head).
– ORIGIN from the *Allen* Manufacturing Company, Connecticut.

allergen /al-ler-juhn/ • n. a substance that causes an allergic reaction.

allergenic /al-ler-jen-ik/ • adj. likely to cause an allergic reaction.

allergic • adj. **1** caused by an allergy. **2** having an allergy.

allergy • n. (pl. **allergies**) a medical condition in which the body reacts badly when it comes into contact with a particular substance.
– ORIGIN Greek *allos* 'other'.

alleviate /uh-lee-vi-ayt/ • v. (**alleviates, alleviating, alleviated**) make pain or a problem less severe.
– DERIVATIVES **alleviation** n.

a

– ORIGIN Latin *alleviare* 'lighten'.

alley • n. (pl. **alleys**) **1** a narrow passageway between or behind buildings. **2** a path in a park or garden. **3** a long, narrow area in which skittles and bowling are played.
– ORIGIN Old French *alee* 'walking, passage'.

alleyway • n. an alley between or behind buildings.

alliance • n. **1** a relationship formed between countries or organizations for a joint purpose. **2** the state of being joined or associated.

allied • adj. **1** joined by an alliance. **2** (**Allied**) relating to Britain and its allies in the First and Second World Wars. **3** (**allied to/with**) combined with: *skilled craftsmanship allied to advanced technology.*

alligator • n. a large reptile similar to a crocodile but with a broader and shorter head.
– ORIGIN from Spanish *el lagarto* 'the lizard'.

all-in • adj. Brit. (especially of a price) including everything.

all-in wrestling • n. Brit. wrestling with few or no restrictions.

alliteration /uh-lit-uh-ray-sh'n/ • n. the occurrence of the same letter or sound at the beginning of words next to or close to each other.
– DERIVATIVES **alliterative** adj.
– ORIGIN Latin.

allocate • v. (**allocates**, **allocating**, **allocated**) give or distribute something.
– DERIVATIVES **allocation** n.
– ORIGIN Latin *allocare*.

allot • v. (**allots**, **allotting**, **allotted**) give or share out something.
– ORIGIN Old French *aloter*.

allotment • n. **1** Brit. a small plot of land rented for growing vegetables or flowers. **2** the action of allotting something. **3** an amount allotted to someone.

allotrope /al-luh-trohp/ • n. Chem. each of two or more different physical forms in which a particular element exists.
– DERIVATIVES **allotropic** adj.
– ORIGIN Greek *allotropos* 'of another form'.

allow • v. **1** let someone have or do something. **2** decide that something is legal or acceptable. **3** (**allow for**) take into consideration. **4** provide or set aside: *allow an hour or so for driving.* **5** admit that something is true.
– DERIVATIVES **allowable** adj.
– ORIGIN Old French *alouer*.

USAGE: On the confusion of **allowed** and **aloud**, see the note at **ALOUD**.

allowance • n. **1** the amount of something allowed. **2** a sum of money paid regularly to a person. **3** Brit. an amount of money that can be earned free of tax.
– PHRASES **make allowances for 1** take into consideration. **2** treat someone less harshly because of their difficult circumstances.

alloy • n. /al-loy/ **1** a mixture of two or more metals. **2** an inferior metal mixed with a precious one. • v. /uh-loy/ mix metals to make an alloy.
– ORIGIN Old French *aloier*, *aleier* 'combine'.

all right • adj. **1** satisfactory; acceptable. **2** allowed; permitted. • adv. fairly well. • exclam. expressing or asking for agreement or acceptance.

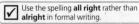

Use the spelling **all right** rather than **alright** in formal writing.

all-round (US **all-around**) • adj. **1** having a wide range of abilities or uses. **2** in many or all respects.

all-rounder • n. Brit. a person with a wide range of skills.

All Saints' Day • n. a Christian festival in honour of all the saints, held on 1 November.

All Souls' Day • n. a Roman Catholic festival with prayers for the souls of the dead in purgatory, held on 2 November.

allspice • n. the dried fruit of a Caribbean tree, used as a spice in cookery.

all-time • adj. not having been bettered or beaten: *the all-time record.*

allude /uh-lood/ • v. (**alludes**, **alluding**, **alluded**) (**allude to**) **1** mention briefly. **2** refer to indirectly.
– ORIGIN Latin *alludere*.

allure • n. powerful attractiveness or charm.
– ORIGIN Old French *aleurier*.

alluring • adj. very attractive or tempting.

allusion • n. an indirect reference to something.

allusive • adj. using or containing indirect references to something.

alluvium /uh-loo-vi-uhm/ • n. a fertile deposit of clay, silt, and sand left by flood water.
– DERIVATIVES **alluvial** adj.
– ORIGIN Latin.

ally • n. /al-ly/ (pl. **allies**) **1** a person, organization, or country that cooperates with another. **2** (**the Allies**) the

countries that fought with Britain in the First and Second World Wars. • v. /uh-**ly**/ (**allies, allying, allied**) 1 (**ally something to/with**) combine a resource or quality with another in a way that benefits both: *he allied his racing experience with his father's business skills.* 2 (**ally yourself with**) side with or support.
– ORIGIN Old French *alier*.

alma mater /al-muh **mah**-ter, al-muh **may**-ter/ • n. the school, college, or university that a person once attended.
– ORIGIN Latin, 'bountiful mother'.

almanac /al-muh-nak/ (also **almanack**) • n. 1 a calendar giving important dates and also information about the sun, moon, tides, etc. 2 a book published yearly which contains information relating to that year, usually about a particular subject or activity.
– ORIGIN Greek *almenikhiaka*.

almighty • adj. 1 having unlimited or very great power. 2 informal enormous. • n. (**the Almighty**) a name or title for God.

almond • n. an oval nut with a woody shell, growing on a tree found in warm climates.
– ORIGIN Old French *alemande*.

almost • adv. very nearly.
– ORIGIN Old English.

alms /ahmz/ • pl. n. (in the past) money or food given to poor people as charitable donations.
– ORIGIN Greek *eleēmosunē* 'compassion'.

almshouse • n. (in the past) a house built and funded through charitable donations which offered free accommodation for poor people.

aloe /a-loh/ • n. a tropical plant with thick tapering leaves.
– ORIGIN Greek *aloē*.

aloe vera /a-loh **veer**-uh/ • n. a jelly-like substance obtained from a kind of aloe, used to soothe the skin.
– ORIGIN Latin, 'true aloe'.

aloft • adj. & adv. up in or into the air.
– ORIGIN Old Norse.

alone • adj. & adv. 1 on your own. 2 isolated and lonely. 3 only; exclusively.
– PHRASES **leave someone/thing alone** stop interfering with someone or something.
– ORIGIN from ALL + ONE.

along • prep. & adv. 1 moving forward on a surface. 2 extending in a horizontal line on. 3 in or into company with other people: *he had brought along a friend.*
– PHRASES **along with** together with or at the same time as.
– ORIGIN Old English.

alongside (N. Amer. also **alongside of**)

• prep. 1 close to the side of; next to. 2 at the same time as.

aloof • adj. cool and distant.
– DERIVATIVES **aloofness** n.
– ORIGIN from LUFF.

alopecia /a-luh-**pee**-shuh/ • n. abnormal loss of hair.
– ORIGIN Greek *alōpekia* 'fox mange'.

aloud • adv. so as to be heard; out loud.

> USAGE: Do not confuse **aloud** with **allowed**. **Aloud** means 'out loud' (*I read the letter aloud*), whereas **allowed** means 'permitted' (*smoking is not allowed*).

alp • n. 1 a high mountain. 2 (**the Alps**) a high range of mountains in Switzerland and adjoining countries.
– ORIGIN Greek *Alpeis*.

alpaca /al-**pak**-uh/ • n. (pl. **alpaca** or **alpacas**) a long-haired South American mammal related to the llama.
– ORIGIN Spanish.

alpha /al-fuh/ • n. 1 the first letter of the Greek alphabet (A, α). 2 Brit. a first-class mark given for a piece of work.
• adj. referring to the dominant animal or person in a group: *the alpha male.*
– PHRASES **alpha and omega** the beginning and the end.

alphabet • n. an ordered set of letters or symbols used to represent the basic speech sounds of a language.
– ORIGIN from Greek *alpha* and *bēta*, the first two letters of the Greek alphabet.

alphabetical • adj. in the order of the letters of the alphabet.
– DERIVATIVES **alphabetically** adv.

alphanumeric /al-fuh-nyoo-**me**-rik/ • adj. using both letters and numerals.

alpha particle (also **alpha ray**) • n. Physics a helium nucleus, especially as given out by some radioactive substances.

alpine • adj. 1 relating to or found on high mountains. 2 (**Alpine**) relating to the Alps. • n. a plant which grows on high mountains.

already • adv. 1 before the time in question. 2 expressing surprise that something has happened so soon or early.

alright • adj., adv., & exclam. var. of ALL RIGHT.

> ✓ The spelling **alright** is best avoided in formal writing; use **all right** instead.

Alsatian • n. Brit. a German shepherd dog.
– ORIGIN Latin, 'Alsace', a region of NE France.

also • adv. in addition.
– ORIGIN Old English.

also-ran • n. a person who does not win a race or contest.

altar • n. **1** the table in a Christian church at which the bread and wine are consecrated in communion services. **2** a table on which religious offerings are made.
– ORIGIN Latin.

altar boy • n. a boy who assists a priest during a service.

altarpiece • n. a work of art set above and behind an altar.

alter • v. make or become different; change.
– DERIVATIVES **alteration** n.
– ORIGIN Latin *alterare*.

altercation /awl-ter-kay-sh'n/ • n. a noisy disagreement.
– ORIGIN Latin.

alter ego /awl-ter ee-goh/ • n. **1** another side to a person's normal personality. **2** a close friend who is very like yourself.
– ORIGIN Latin, 'other self'.

alternate • v. /awl-ter-nayt/ (**alternates, alternating, alternated**) **1** (of two people or things) repeatedly follow one another in turn. **2** continue to change between two contrasting states.
• adj. /awl-ter-nuht/ **1** every other. **2** (of two things) each following and succeeded by the other in a regular pattern.
– DERIVATIVES **alternately** adv. **alternation** n.
– ORIGIN Latin *alternare* 'do by turns'.

alternate angles • pl. n. two equal angles on opposite sides of a line crossing two parallel lines.

alternating current • n. an electric current that reverses its direction many times a second. Compare with DIRECT CURRENT.

alternative • adj. **1** (of one or more things) available as another possibility: *an alternative approach to the problem.* **2** differing from the usual or traditional form of something. • n. one of two or more available possibilities.
– DERIVATIVES **alternatively** adv.

alternative energy • n. energy produced in ways that do not use up natural resources or harm the environment.

alternative medicine • n. medical treatment that does not follow the usual practices of Western medicine, e.g. herbalism.

alternator • n. a dynamo that generates an alternating current.

although • conj. **1** in spite of the fact that. **2** but.

altimeter /al-ti-mee-ter/ • n. an instrument which shows the altitude reached by an aircraft.

altitude • n. the height of an object or point above sea level or ground level.
– ORIGIN Latin *altitudo*.

alto /al-toh/ • n. (pl. **altos**) **1** the highest adult male or lowest female singing voice. **2** (before another noun) referring to the second or third highest instrument in a family: *an alto sax.*
– ORIGIN from Italian *alto canto* 'high song'.

altogether • adv. **1** in total. **2** completely. **3** on the whole.

> **USAGE:** Altogether and all together do not mean the same thing. **Altogether** means 'in total' (*there are six bedrooms altogether*) or 'completely' (*I stopped seeing her altogether*), while **all together** means 'all in one place' (*it was good to have a group of friends all together*) or 'all at once' (*they came in all together*).

altruism /al-troo-i-z'm/ • n. unselfish concern for other people.
– DERIVATIVES **altruist** n. **altruistic** adj. **altruistically** adv.
– ORIGIN Italian *altrui* 'somebody else'.

alum /al-uhm/ • n. a compound of aluminium and potassium, used in dyeing and tanning animal skin.
– ORIGIN Latin *alumen*.

aluminium /al-yoo-min-i-uhm/ (US **aluminum** /uh-loo-mi-nuhm/) • n. a lightweight silvery-grey metallic element that resists rust or corrosion.

alumnus /uh-lum-nuhss/ • n. (pl. **alumni** /uh-lum-ny/; fem. **alumna** /uh-lum-nuh/, pl. **alumnae** /uh-lum-ni/) a former student of a particular school, college, or university.
– ORIGIN Latin, 'pupil'.

alveolus /al-vee-oh-luhss/ • n. (pl. **alveoli** /al-vee-oh-lee/) **1** any of the many tiny air sacs in the lungs. **2** the bony socket for the root of a tooth.
– DERIVATIVES **alveolar** adj.
– ORIGIN Latin, 'small cavity'.

always • adv. **1** at all times. **2** forever. **3** repeatedly. **4** if all else fails.

Alzheimer's disease /alts-hy-merz/ • n. a disorder affecting older people, which damages the functioning of the brain.
– ORIGIN named after the German neurologist Alois *Alzheimer.*

AM • abbrev. amplitude modulation.

Am • symb. the chemical element americium.

am 1st person sing. present of BE.

a.m. • abbrev. before noon.
– ORIGIN from Latin *ante meridiem.*

amalgam /uh-mal-guhm/ • n. **1** a mixture or blend. **2** an alloy of mercury with another metal.

amalgamate /uh-mal-guh-mayt/
• v. (**amalgamates, amalgamating, amalgamated**) **1** combine to form one organization or structure. **2** mix a metal with mercury to make an alloy.
– DERIVATIVES **amalgamation** n.

amanuensis /uh-man-yoo-en-siss/
• n. (pl. **amanuenses** /uh-man-yoo-en-seez/) a person who helps a writer with their work.
– ORIGIN Latin.

amaryllis /am-uh-**ril**-liss/ • n. a plant with large trumpet-shaped flowers.
– ORIGIN Greek *Amarullis*, a girl's name in poetry.

amass • v. build up over time.
– ORIGIN Latin *amassare*.

amateur • n. **1** a person who takes part in a sport or other activity without being paid. **2** a person who is not skilled at a particular activity. • adj. **1** non-professional. **2** unskilful or clumsy.
– DERIVATIVES **amateurism** n.
– ORIGIN French, 'lover'.

amateurish • adj. not done or made skilfully.

amatory /am-uh-tuh-ri/ • adj. relating to sexual love or desire.
– ORIGIN Latin *amatorius*.

amaze • v. (**amazes, amazing, amazed**) surprise greatly; astonish.
– DERIVATIVES **amazement** n.
– ORIGIN Old English.

Amazon /am-uh-zuhn/ • n. **1** a member of a legendary race of female warriors. **2** a very tall, strong woman.
– ORIGIN Greek.

Amazonian /am-uh-zoh-ni-uhn/
• adj. **1** relating to the River Amazon. **2** (of a woman) very tall and strong.

ambassador • n. **1** a diplomat sent by a state as its permanent representative in a foreign country. **2** a person who represents or promotes something: *he is a good ambassador for the industry.*
– ORIGIN Italian *ambasciator*.

amber • n. **1** a hard clear yellowish substance formed from the fossilized resin of certain ancient trees, used in jewellery. **2** a honey-yellow colour.
– ORIGIN Old French *ambre*.

ambergris /am-ber-greess/ • n. a waxy substance produced by sperm whales, used in making perfume.
– ORIGIN from Old French *ambre gris* 'grey amber'.

ambidextrous /am-bi-**dek**-struhss/
• adj. able to use the right and left hands equally well.
– ORIGIN from Latin *ambi*- 'on both sides' + *dexter* 'right-handed'.

ambience /am-bi-uhnss/ (also **ambiance**) • n. the character and atmosphere of a place.

ambient /am-bi-uhnt/ • adj. **1** relating to the surroundings of something: *there was no ambient light.* **2** (of music) quiet and relaxing.
– ORIGIN Latin.

ambiguity /am-bi-gyoo-i-ti/ • n. (pl. **ambiguities**) the quality of having more than one possible meaning.

ambiguous /am-big-yoo-uhss/
• adj. **1** (of language) having more than one possible meaning. **2** not clear or decided.
– DERIVATIVES **ambiguously** adv.
– ORIGIN Latin *ambiguus* 'doubtful'.

ambit • n. the scope or extent of something.
– ORIGIN Latin *ambitus* 'circuit'.

ambition • n. **1** a strong desire to do or achieve something. **2** desire for success, wealth, or fame.
– ORIGIN Latin.

ambitious • adj. **1** having or showing determination to succeed. **2** needing a great deal of effort, time, or money to succeed: *an ambitious enterprise.*
– DERIVATIVES **ambitiously** adv.

ambivalent /am-biv-uh-luhnt/
• adj. having mixed feelings about something or someone.
– DERIVATIVES **ambivalence** n.
– ORIGIN from Latin *ambi*- 'on both sides' + *valere* 'be worth'.

amble • v. (**ambles, ambling, ambled**) walk at a leisurely pace. • n. a leisurely walk.
– ORIGIN Latin *ambulare* 'to walk'.

ambrosia • n. **1** Gk & Rom. Myth. the food of the gods. **2** something very pleasing to taste or smell.
– DERIVATIVES **ambrosial** adj.
– ORIGIN Greek, 'elixir of life'.

ambulance • n. a vehicle for taking sick or injured people to and from hospital.
– ORIGIN French.

ambulatory /am-byoo-luh-tri/
• adj. **1** relating to walking or able to walk. **2** movable; mobile.

ambush • n. a surprise attack by people lying in wait in a hidden position. • v. attack a person or group of people from a hidden position.
– ORIGIN Old French *embusche*.

ameba • n. (pl. **amebae** or **amebas**) US = AMOEBA.

ameliorate /uh-mee-li-uh-rayt/
• v. (**ameliorates, ameliorating, ameliorated**) formal make something bad or unsatisfactory better.
– DERIVATIVES **amelioration** n.

a

– ORIGIN Latin *meliorare*.

amen /ah-men, ay-men/ • exclam. said at the end of a prayer or hymn, meaning 'so be it'.
– ORIGIN Greek.

amenable /uh-meen-uh-b'l/
• adj. **1** willing to cooperate or be persuaded. **2** (**amenable to**) able to be affected by.
– DERIVATIVES **amenability** n.
– ORIGIN Old French *amener* 'bring to'.

amend • v. make minor changes or improvements to.
– ORIGIN Latin *emendare* 'to correct'.

amendment • n. a minor improvement.

amends • pl. n. (in phr. **make amends**) make up for a wrongdoing.

amenity /uh-meen-i-ti/ • n. (pl. **amenities**) a useful or desirable feature of a place.
– ORIGIN Latin *amoenitas*.

American • adj. relating to the United States or to the continents of America. • n. a person from the United States or any of the countries of North, South, or Central America.
– DERIVATIVES **Americanize** (or **Americanise**) v.

American dream • n. the ideal of equality of opportunity associated with the US.

American football • n. a kind of football played in the US with an oval ball on a field marked out as a gridiron.

American Indian • n. a member of the native peoples of America.

Americanism • n. a word or phrase used or originating in the US.

americium /am-uh-riss-i-uhm/ • n. a radioactive metallic chemical element made by high-energy atomic collisions.
– ORIGIN from *America*.

Amerindian /am-uh-rin-di-uhn/ • n. & adj. = **AMERICAN INDIAN**.

amethyst /am-uh-thist/ • n. a precious stone consisting of a violet or purple variety of quartz.
– ORIGIN Greek *amethustos* 'not drunken' (because the stone was believed to prevent drunkenness).

amiable • adj. friendly and pleasant.
– DERIVATIVES **amiability** n. **amiably** adv.
– ORIGIN Old French.

amicable /am-i-kuh-b'l/ • adj. friendly and without disagreement.
– DERIVATIVES **amicably** adv.
– ORIGIN Latin *amicabilis*.

amid (or **amidst**) • prep. in the middle of.

amidships • adv. & adj. in the middle of a ship.

amino acid /uh-mee-noh/ • n. any of about twenty organic compounds which form the basic constituents of proteins.
– ORIGIN from **AMMONIA**.

amir /uh-meer/ • n. var. of **EMIR**.

amiss • adj. not quite right. • adv. wrongly or badly.
– PHRASES **take something amiss** be offended by something.
– ORIGIN prob. from Old Norse, 'so as to miss'.

amity /am-i-ti/ • n. formal friendly relations between people or countries.
– ORIGIN Old French *amitie*.

ammeter /am-mi-ter/ • n. an instrument for measuring electric current in amperes.

ammo • n. informal ammunition.

ammonia /uh-moh-ni-uh/ • n. a colourless, strong-smelling gas that forms a very alkaline solution in water, which is used as a cleaning fluid.
– ORIGIN first referring to a substance obtained near the temple of Jupiter *Ammon* in Egypt.

ammonite /am-uh-nyt/ • n. an extinct sea creature with a spiral shell, found as a fossil.
– ORIGIN from Latin *cornu Ammonis* 'horn of Ammon'.

ammunition /am-yuu-ni-sh'n/ • n. **1** a supply of bullets and shells. **2** points used to support a person's case in argument.
– ORIGIN from French *la munition* 'the fortification'.

amnesia /am-nee-zi-uh/ • n. loss of memory.
– ORIGIN Greek, 'forgetfulness'.

amnesiac /am-nee-zi-ak/ • n. a person who has lost their memory.

amnesty • n. (pl. **amnesties**) **1** an official pardon given to people convicted of political offences. **2** a period during which people admitting to particular offences are not punished.
– ORIGIN Greek *amnēstia* 'forgetfulness'.

amniocentesis /am-ni-oh-sen-tee-siss/ • n. (pl. **amnioceteses** /am-ni-oh-sen-tee-seez/) a medical procedure in which a sample of amniotic fluid is taken from a pregnant woman's womb to check for abnormalities in the fetus.
– ORIGIN from Greek *amnion* 'membrane surrounding an embryo' + *kentēsis* 'pricking'.

amniotic fluid • n. the fluid surrounding a fetus before birth.
– ORIGIN from Greek *amnion* 'membrane surrounding an embryo'.

amoeba /uh-mee-buh/ (US also **ameba**) • n. (pl. **amoebas** or **amoebae** /uh-mee-bee/) a microscopic animal that is made

up of a single cell and can change its shape.
– DERIVATIVES **amoebic** adj.
– ORIGIN Greek *amoibē* 'change'.

amok /uh-mok/ (also **amuck**) •adv. (in phr. **run amok**) behave in an uncontrolled and disorderly way.
– ORIGIN Malay.

among (also **amongst**) •prep. **1** surrounded by. **2** included or occurring in. **3** shared by; between.
– ORIGIN Old English.

amoral /ay-mo-ruhl/ • adj. without morals; not concerned about right or wrong.
– DERIVATIVES **amorality** n.

amorous •adj. showing or feeling sexual desire.
– DERIVATIVES **amorously** adv.
– ORIGIN Latin *amor* 'love'.

amorphous /uh-mor-fuhss/ •adj. without a definite shape or form.
– ORIGIN Greek *amorphos*.

amortize /uh-mor-tyz/ (or **amortise**) •v. (**amortizes, amortizing, amortized**) Finance gradually pay off a debt.
– ORIGIN Old French *amortir*.

amount •n. **1** the total number, size, or value of something. **2** a quantity. •v. (**amount to**) **1** add up to a total. **2** be the equivalent of something.
– ORIGIN Old French *amont* 'upward'.

amp •n. = AMPERE.

amperage /am-puh-rij/ •n. the strength of an electric current, measured in amperes.

ampere /am-pair/ •n. the base unit of electric current in the SI system.
– ORIGIN named after the French physicist André-Marie *Ampère*.

ampersand /am-per-sand/ •n. the sign &, standing for *and*.
– ORIGIN from *and per se and*, '& by itself is *and*'.

amphetamine /am-fet-uh-meen/ •n. a drug used illegally as a stimulant.
– ORIGIN from its chemical name.

amphibian /am-fib-i-uhn/ •n. a cold-blooded animal such as a frog or toad, which lives in the water when young and on the land as an adult.
– ORIGIN from Greek *amphi* 'both' + *bios* 'life'.

amphibious /am-fib-i-uhss/ •adj. **1** living in or suited for both land and water. **2** (of a military operation) involving forces landed from the sea.

amphitheatre (US **amphitheater**) •n. a round building consisting of tiers of seats surrounding a central space for dramatic or sporting events.
– ORIGIN from Greek *amphi* 'on both

sides' + *theatron* 'theatre'.

amphora /am-for-uh/ •n. (pl. **amphorae** /am-for-ee/ or **amphoras**) a tall ancient Greek or Roman jar with two handles and a narrow neck.
– ORIGIN Latin.

ample •adj. **1** enough or more than enough; plentiful. **2** large in size.
– DERIVATIVES **amply** adv.
– ORIGIN Latin *amplus*.

amplifier •n. an electronic device for increasing the strength of electrical signals.

amplify •v. (**amplifies, amplifying, amplified**) **1** increase the strength of sound or electrical signals. **2** add details to a story.
– DERIVATIVES **amplification** n.
– ORIGIN Latin *amplificare*.

amplitude •n. **1** Physics the maximum amount by which an alternating current or electromagnetic wave can vary from its average level. **2** great size or extent.

amplitude modulation •n. the modification of a radio wave by varying its amplitude, used as a means of broadcasting an audio signal.

ampoule /am-pool/ (US also **ampule** /am-pyool/) •n. a small sealed glass capsule containing a measured quantity of liquid ready for an injection.
– ORIGIN Latin *ampulla* 'flask'.

amputate /am-pyoo-tayt/ •v. (**amputates, amputating, amputated**) cut off an arm, leg, or similar part in a surgical operation.
– DERIVATIVES **amputation** n.
– ORIGIN Latin *amputare*.

amputee •n. a person who has had an arm or leg amputated.

amuck /uh-muk/ •adv. var. of AMOK.

amulet /am-yoo-lit/ •n. an ornament or small piece of jewellery worn as protection against evil.
– ORIGIN Latin *amuletum*.

amuse •v. (**amuses, amusing, amused**) **1** make someone laugh or smile. **2** give someone something enjoyable or interesting to do.
– ORIGIN Old French *amuser* 'entertain, deceive'.

amusement •n. **1** the state of finding something funny. **2** a game or activity that provides entertainment and pleasure.

an •det. the form of the indefinite article 'a' used before words beginning with a vowel sound.

an- •prefix var. of A-¹ before a vowel.

Anabaptist /an-uh-bap-tist/ •n. a member of a Protestant religious group

a

believing that only adults should be baptized.
– ORIGIN from Greek *ana-* 'again' + *baptismos* 'baptism'.

anabolic steroid /an-uh-bol-ik/ •n. a synthetic hormone taken illegally to improve a competitor's performance in a sport.

anabolism /uh-nab-uh-li-z'm/ •n. a metabolic process in which complex molecules are formed from simpler ones and energy is stored. Opp. CATABOLISM.
– DERIVATIVES **anabolic** adj.
– ORIGIN Greek *anabolē* 'ascent'.

anachronism /uh-nak-ruh-ni-z'm/ •n. a thing belonging to a period other than the one in which it exists.
– DERIVATIVES **anachronistic** adj. **anachronistically** adv.
– ORIGIN from Greek *ana-* 'backwards' + *khronos* 'time'.

anaconda /an-uh-kon-duh/ •n. a very large snake of the boa family, found in tropical South America.
– ORIGIN Sinhalese, 'whip snake'.

anaemia /uh-nee-mi-uh/ (US **anemia**) •n. a shortage of red cells or haemoglobin in the blood, causing tiredness.
– ORIGIN from Greek *an-* 'without' + *haima* 'blood'.

anaemic (US **anemic**) •adj. **1** suffering from anaemia. **2** not lively or exciting.

anaerobic /an-air-oh-bik/ •adj. (of an organism) not using oxygen from the air.
– DERIVATIVES **anaerobically** adv.

anaesthetic /an-iss-thet-ik/ (US **anesthetic**) •n. a drug or gas that makes you unable to feel pain.
– ORIGIN Greek *anaisthētos* 'unconscious'

anaesthetist /uh-neess-thuh-tist/ (US **anesthetist**) •n. a medical specialist who gives anaesthetics.

anaesthetize /uh-neess-thuh-tyz/ (or **anaesthetise**, US **anesthetize**) •v. (**anaesthetizes**, **anaesthetizing**, **anaesthetized**) give an anaesthetic to a patient.

anagram /an-uh-gram/ •n. a word or phrase formed by rearranging the letters of another.
– ORIGIN from Greek *ana-* 'back, anew' + *gramma* 'letter'.

anal /ay-n'l/ •adj. relating to the anus.
– DERIVATIVES **anally** adv.

analgesic /an-uhl-jee-zik/ •n. a painrelieving drug.
– ORIGIN from Greek *an-* 'not' + *algeein* 'feel pain'.

analogous /uh-nal-uh-guhss/ •adj. alike or comparable in some ways.

– ORIGIN Greek *analogos* 'proportionate'.

analogue /an-uh-log/ (US also **analog**) •adj. (also **analog**) relating to electronic information or signals represented by a varying physical effect (e.g. voltage, the position of a pointer, etc.) rather than by a digital display. •n. a person or thing that is like or comparable to another.

analogy /uh-nal-uh-ji/ •n. (pl. **analogies**) **1** a way of explaining something by comparing it to something else. **2** a partial similarity.
– DERIVATIVES **analogical** adj.

analyse (US **analyze**) •v. (**analyses**, **analysing**, **analysed**; US **analyzes**, **analyzing**, **analyzed**) **1** examine something in detail so as to explain it or to find out its structure or composition. **2** psychoanalyse someone.

analysis /uh-nal-i-siss/ •n. (pl. **analyses** /uh-nal-i-seez/) **1** a detailed examination of the elements or structure of something. **2** the separation of something into its component parts. **3** psychoanalysis.
– ORIGIN Greek *analuein* 'unloose'.

analyst •n. **1** a person who carries out an analysis. **2** a psychoanalyst.

analytical (also **analytic**) •adj. relating to analysis.
– DERIVATIVES **analytically** adv.

analyze •v. US = ANALYSE.

anarchic /uh-nar-kik/ •adj. with no controlling rules or principles.

anarchist /a-nuh-kist/ •n. a person who believes that government should be abolished and that society should be organized on a cooperative basis.
– DERIVATIVES **anarchism** n. **anarchistic** adj.

anarchy •n. a state of disorder due to lack of government or control.
– ORIGIN from Greek *an-* 'without' + *arkhos* 'ruler'.

anathema /uh-na-thuh-muh/ •n. something that you hate: *racism was anathema to her.*
– ORIGIN Greek, 'thing devoted to evil'.

anathematize /uh-na-thuh-muh-tyz/ (or **anathematise**) •v. (**anathematizes**, **anathematizing**, **anathematized**) curse or condemn.

anatomy •n. (pl. **anatomies**) **1** the scientific study of bodily structure. **2** the bodily structure of a person, animal, or plant. **3** a detailed examination or analysis.
– DERIVATIVES **anatomical** /an-uh-tom-i-k'l/ adj. **anatomically** adv. **anatomist** n.
– ORIGIN from Greek *ana-* 'up' + *tomia* 'cutting'.

ANC • abbrev. African National Congress.

-ance • suffix forming nouns referring to a quality, state, or action: *perseverance*.
– ORIGIN French.

ancestor • n. **1** a person from whom you are descended. **2** something from which a later species or version has developed.
– DERIVATIVES **ancestress** n.
– ORIGIN Latin *antecessor*.

ancestral /an-sess-truhl/ • adj. relating to or inherited from an ancestor or ancestors: *her ancestral home.*

ancestry • n. (pl. **ancestries**) a person's ancestors or the people that they are descended from.

anchor • n. a heavy metal object used to moor a ship to the bottom of the sea. • v. **1** moor a ship with an anchor. **2** fix firmly in position.
– ORIGIN Greek *ankura*.

anchorage • n. a place where ships may anchor safely.

anchorite /ang-kuh-ryt/ • n. hist. a person who lived apart from other people for religious reasons.
– ORIGIN Greek *anakhōrein* 'retire'.

anchorman (or **anchorwoman**) • n. (pl. **anchormen** or **anchorwomen**) a person who presents a live television or radio programme and coordinates the contributions of those taking part.

anchovy /an-chuh-vi/ • n. (pl. **anchovies**) a small fish of the herring family, with a strong flavour.
– ORIGIN Spanish and Portuguese *anchova*.

ancien régime /on-si-an ray-zheem/ • n. a political or social system that has been replaced by a more modern one.
– ORIGIN French, 'old rule'.

ancient • adj. **1** belonging to the very distant past. **2** very old. • pl. n. (**the ancients**) the people of ancient times.
– DERIVATIVES **anciently** adv.
– ORIGIN Old French *ancien*.

ancillary /an-sil-luh-ri/ • adj. **1** providing support to the main activities of an organization: *ancillary staff,* **2** additional; extra.
– ORIGIN Latin *ancilla* 'female servant'.

-ancy • suffix forming nouns referring to a quality or state: *expectancy.*
– ORIGIN Latin *-antia*.

and • conj. **1** used to connect words, clauses, or sentences. **2** used to connect two identical words to show gradual change, continuing action, or great extent: *getting better and better.* **3** (connecting two numbers) plus. **4** informal (after a verb) to: *try and do it.*
– ORIGIN Old English.

USAGE: Many people believe that it is incorrect to begin a sentence with **and** or other conjunctions such as **but** and **because**. It has, however, long been used in this way in both written and spoken English and is quite acceptable.

andante /an-dan-tay/ • adv. & adj. Music in a moderately slow tempo.
– ORIGIN Italian, 'going'.

androgynous /an-dro-ji-nuhss/ • adj. partly male and partly female.
– DERIVATIVES **androgyny** n.
– ORIGIN from Greek *anēr* 'man' + *gunē* 'woman'.

android /an-droyd/ • n. (in science fiction) a robot with a human appearance.
– ORIGIN from Greek *anēr* 'man'.

anecdotal /an-ik-doh-t'l/ • adj. (of a story) not necessarily true because not backed up by facts.
– DERIVATIVES **anecdotally** adv.

anecdote /an-ik-doht/ • n. a short entertaining story about a real incident or person.
– ORIGIN Greek *anekdota* 'things unpublished'.

anemia • n. US = ANAEMIA.

anemic • adj. US = ANAEMIC.

anemometer /an-i-mom-i-ter/ • n. an instrument for measuring the speed of the wind.
– ORIGIN Greek *anemos* 'wind'.

anemone /uh-nem-uh-ni/ • n. a plant having brightly coloured flowers with dark centres.
– ORIGIN Greek, 'windflower'.

aneroid barometer /an-uh-royd/ • n. a barometer that measures air pressure by the action of air on the flexible lid of a box containing a vacuum.
– ORIGIN from Greek *a-* 'without' + *nēros* 'water'.

anesthetic etc. • n. US = ANAESTHETIC etc.

aneurysm /an-yuu-ri-z'm/ (also **aneurism**) • n. an excessive swelling of the wall of an artery.
– ORIGIN Greek *aneurusma* 'widening'.

anew • adv. **1** in a new or different way. **2** once more; again.

angel • n. **1** a spiritual being acting as an attendant or messenger of God, pictured as a human being with wings. **2** a very beautiful, kind, or good person. **3** informal a person who gives financial backing to a theatrical production.
– ORIGIN Greek *angelos* 'messenger'.

angelfish • n. (pl. **angelfish** or **angelfishes**) a tropical fish with large fins, often vividly coloured or patterned.

angelic • adj. **1** relating to angels. **2** very beautiful, innocent, or kind.

a

– DERIVATIVES **angelically** adv.

angelica /an-jel-li-kuh/ • n. the stalks of
a plant of the parsley family, preserved
in sugar and used in cake decoration.
– ORIGIN from Latin *herba angelica*
'angelic herb'.

angelus /an-juh-luhss/ • n. a Roman
Catholic prayer commemorating the
Incarnation of Jesus, said at morning,
noon, and sunset.
– ORIGIN from Latin *Angelus domini* 'the
angel of the Lord'.

anger • n. a strong feeling of extreme
displeasure. • v. (**angers**, **angering**,
angered) make someone angry.
– ORIGIN Old Norse, 'grief'.

angina /an-jy-nuh/ (also **angina
pectoris** /pek-tuh-riss/) • n. severe pain
in the chest caused by an inadequate
supply of blood to the heart.
– ORIGIN from Greek *ankhonē* 'strangling'
+ Latin *pectoris* 'of the chest'.

angiosperm /an-ji-oh-sperm/ • n. a
plant of a large group that have flowers
and produce seeds enclosed in a carpel,
including herbaceous plants, shrubs,
grasses, and most trees.
– ORIGIN from Greek *angeion* 'container.'

Angle • n. a member of an ancient
Germanic people who founded king-
doms in the north and east of England in
the 5th century AD.
– ORIGIN Latin *Anglus* 'inhabitant of
Angul' (in northern Germany).

angle[1] • n. 1 the space between two lines
or surfaces that meet. 2 a position from
which something is viewed: *he was
filmed from a variety of camera angles.* 3 a
way of considering something: *a fresh
angle on life.* • v. (**angles**, **angling**,
angled) 1 move or place in a slanting
position. 2 present information from a
particular point of view.
– ORIGIN Latin *angulus* 'corner'.

angle[2] • v. (**angles**, **angling**, **angled**)
1 fish with a rod and line. 2 try to get
something by indirectly prompting
someone to offer it: *she was angling for
sympathy.*
– DERIVATIVES **angler** n.
– ORIGIN Old English.

Anglican • adj. relating to the Church of
England or any Church associated with
it. • n. a member of the Anglican Church.
– DERIVATIVES **Anglicanism** n.
– ORIGIN Latin *Anglicanus*.

Anglicism • n. a word or phrase that is
only found in British English.

anglicize (or **anglicise**) • v. (**anglicizes**,
anglicizing, **anglicized**) make English in
form or character.
– DERIVATIVES **anglicization** n.

Anglo- • comb. form 1 English: *Anglophile.*

2 English or British and ...: *Anglo-Indian.*
– ORIGIN Latin *Anglus* 'English'.

Anglo-Catholic • n. a member of a
section of the Church of England which
is close to Catholicism in its beliefs and
worship.

Anglo-Indian • adj. 1 relating to both
Britain and India. 2 of mixed British and
Indian parentage. 3 hist. British but
having lived for a long time in India.
• n. an Anglo-Indian person.

Anglo-Irish • adj. 1 relating to both
Britain and Ireland. 2 of mixed English
and Irish parentage. 3 having English
parents but born or living in Ireland.

Anglophile • n. a person who greatly
admires England or Britain.
– DERIVATIVES **Anglophilia** n.

Anglo-Saxon • n. 1 a Germanic inhabitant of England between the 5th century and the Norman Conquest. 2 an
English person. 3 the Old English
language.

Angolan /an-goh-luhn/ • n. a person
from Angola, a country in SW Africa.
• adj. relating to Angola.

angora /ang-gor-uh/ • n. 1 a cat, goat, or
rabbit of a long-haired breed. 2 fabric
made from the hair of the angora goat or
rabbit.
– ORIGIN from *Angora* (now Ankara) in
Turkey.

angostura /ang-guh-styoor-uh/ • n. the
bitter bark of a South American tree,
used as a flavouring.
– ORIGIN from *Angostura* (now Ciudad
Bolívar) in Venezuela.

angry • adj. (**angrier**, **angriest**) 1 feeling
or showing anger. 2 (of a wound or sore)
red and inflamed.
– DERIVATIVES **angrily** adv.

angst /angst/ • n. a strong feeling of
anxiety about life in general.
– DERIVATIVES **angsty** adj.
– ORIGIN German, 'fear'.

angstrom /ang-struhm/ • n. Physics a
unit of length equal to one hundred-
millionth of a centimetre.
– ORIGIN named after the Swedish
physicist A. J. *Ångström.*

anguish • n. severe pain or distress.
– DERIVATIVES **anguished** adj.
– ORIGIN Latin *angustia* 'tightness'.

angular /ang-gyuu-ler/ • adj. 1 having
angles or sharp corners. 2 lean and bony.
3 placed or directed at an angle. 4 Physics
measured by means of an angle.
– DERIVATIVES **angularity** n.

anhydrous /an-hy-druhss/ • adj. Chem.
containing no water.
– ORIGIN from Greek *an-* 'without' +
hudōr 'water'.

aniline /an-i-leen/ •n. an oily liquid used in making dyes, drugs, and plastics.
– ORIGIN Arabic, 'indigo'.

animadversion /an-im-uhd-**ver**-shu'n/ •n. formal a critical remark.
– ORIGIN from Latin *animus* 'mind' + *advertere* 'to turn'.

animal •n. **1** a living organism that can move about of its own accord and has specialized sense organs and nervous system. **2** a mammal, as opposed to a bird, reptile, fish, or insect. **3** a brutal or uncivilized person. **4** a particular type of person or thing: *she's a political animal.* •adj. **1** relating to animals. **2** physical rather than spiritual or intellectual: *animal lust.*
– ORIGIN Latin *animalis* 'having breath'.

animalcule /ani-**mal**-kyool/ •n. esp. literary a microscopic animal.

animality •n. physical and instinctive human behaviour, like that of animals.

animate •v. /an-i-mayt/ (**animates, animating, animated**) **1** bring life or vigour to. **2** give a film or character the appearance of movement using animation. •adj. /an-i-muht/ alive; having life.
– DERIVATIVES **animator** n.
– ORIGIN Latin *anima* 'life, soul'.

animated •adj. **1** lively. **2** (of a film) made using animation.
– DERIVATIVES **animatedly** adv.

animation •n. **1** liveliness or vigour. **2** the technique of filming a sequence of drawings or positions of models to give the appearance of movement. **3** (also **computer animation**) the creation of moving images by means of a computer.

animism /an-i-mi-z'm/ •n. the belief that all things in nature, such as plants and hills, have a soul.
– DERIVATIVES **animist** n. **animistic** adj.
– ORIGIN Latin *anima* 'life, soul'.

animosity /an-i-**moss**-i-ti/ •n. (pl. **animosities**) hatred or strong dislike.
– ORIGIN Latin *animositas*.

animus /an-i-**muhss**/ •n. hatred or strong dislike.
– ORIGIN Latin, 'spirit, mind'.

anion /an-I-uhn/ •n. Chem. an ion with a negative charge. Opp. **CATION**.
– ORIGIN from **ANODE** + **ION**.

anise /an-iss/ •n. a plant grown for its seeds (aniseed).
– ORIGIN Greek *anison* 'anise, dill'.

aniseed •n. the seed of the plant anise, used as a flavouring.

ankh /angk/ •n. an ancient Egyptian symbol of life in the shape of a cross with a loop instead of the top arm.
– ORIGIN Egyptian, 'life, soul'.

ankle •n. **1** the joint connecting the foot with the leg. **2** the narrow part of the leg between this joint and the calf.
– ORIGIN Old English.

anklet •n. a chain or band worn round the ankle.

annals /an-nuhlz/ •pl. n. a historical record of events year by year.
– DERIVATIVES **annalist** n.
– ORIGIN from Latin *annales libri* 'yearly books'.

anneal /uh-**neel**/ •v. heat metal or glass and allow it to cool slowly, to remove internal stresses.
– ORIGIN Old English, 'set on fire'.

annelid /an-ni-lid/ •n. a worm with a body made up of segments, such as an earthworm.
– ORIGIN Latin *annelus* 'small ring'.

annex •v. /an-**neks**/ **1** seize territory and add it to your own. **2** add or attach something. •n. /an-neks/ (esp. Brit. also **annexe**) (pl. **annexes**) **1** a building attached or near to a main building, used for additional space. **2** an addition to a document.
– DERIVATIVES **annexation** n.
– ORIGIN Latin *annectere* 'connect'.

annihilate /uh-**ny**-i-layt/ •v. (**annihilates, annihilating, annihilated**) **1** destroy completely. **2** defeat completely.
– DERIVATIVES **annihilation** n. **annihilator** n.
– ORIGIN Latin *annihilare* 'reduce to nothing'.

anniversary •n. (pl. **anniversaries**) the date on which an event took place in a previous year.
– ORIGIN Latin *anniversarius* 'returning yearly'.

Anno Domini /an-noh dom-i-ny/ •adv. full form of **AD**.

annotate /an-nuh-tayt/ •v. (**annotates, annotating, annotated**) add explanatory notes to a piece of writing.
– DERIVATIVES **annotation** n. **annotator** n.
– ORIGIN Latin *annotare* 'to mark'.

announce •v. (**announces, announcing, announced**) **1** make a public statement about something. **2** be a sign of: *lilies announce the arrival of summer.*
– DERIVATIVES **announcer** n.
– ORIGIN Latin *annuntiare*.

announcement •n. **1** a public statement. **2** the action of announcing.

annoy •v. make someone slightly angry.
– DERIVATIVES **annoyance** n.
– ORIGIN from Latin *mihi in odio est* 'it is hateful to me'.

annual •adj. **1** happening once a year. **2** calculated over or covering a year: *his annual income.* **3** (of a plant) living for a

year or less. •n. a book published once a year under the same title but with different contents.
– DERIVATIVES **annually** adv.
– ORIGIN Latin *annus* 'year'.

annuity /uh-nyoo-i-ti/ •n. (pl. **annuities**) a fixed sum of money paid to someone each year.
– ORIGIN Latin *annuitas*.

annul /uh-nul/ •v. (**annuls, annulling, annulled**) declare a law, marriage, or other legal contract to be invalid.
– DERIVATIVES **annulment** n.
– ORIGIN Latin *annullare*.

annular /an-yuu-ler/ •adj. tech. ring-shaped.
– ORIGIN Latin *anulus* 'small ring'.

Annunciation •n. (**the Annunciation**) the announcement by the angel Gabriel to the Virgin Mary that she was to be the mother of Jesus.

anode /an-ohd/ •n. an electrode with a positive charge. Opp. **CATHODE**.
– ORIGIN Greek *anodos* 'way up'.

anodized /an-uh-dyzd/ (or **anodised**) •adj. (of metal) coated with a protective oxide layer by electrolysis.

anodyne /an-uh-dyn/ •adj. unlikely to cause offence; bland. •n. a painkilling drug.
– ORIGIN Greek *anōdunos* 'painless'.

anoint •v. smear or rub with oil, especially as part of a religious ceremony.
– ORIGIN Old French *enoindre*.

anomalous /uh-nom-uh-luhs/ •adj. differing from what is standard or normal.
– ORIGIN from Greek *an-* 'not' + *homalos* 'even'.

anomaly /uh-nom-uh-li/ •n. (pl. **anomalies**) something that differs from what is standard or normal.

anomie /an-uh-mi/ •n. lack of the usual standards of good behaviour.
– ORIGIN Greek *anomos* 'lawless'.

anon •adv. old use or informal soon; shortly.
– ORIGIN Old English, 'in or into one'.

anonymous /uh-non-i-muhs/ •adj. **1** with a name that is not known or not made known. **2** having no outstanding or individual features: *her anonymous flat.*
– DERIVATIVES **anonymity** /an-uh-nim-iti/ n. **anonymously** adv.
– ORIGIN Greek *anōnumos* 'nameless'.

anorak •n. **1** a waterproof jacket with a hood. **2** Brit. informal a person with an obsessive interest in something.
– ORIGIN Eskimo.

anorexia /an-uh-rek-si-uh/ (also **anorexia nervosa** /ner-voh-suh/) •n.

a psychological disorder in which a person refuses to eat because they are afraid of becoming fat.
– ORIGIN from Greek *an-* 'without' + *orexis* 'appetite'.

anorexic (also **anorectic**) •adj. relating to anorexia. •n. a person with anorexia.

another •det. & pron. **1** one more; a further. **2** different from the one already mentioned: *she left him for another man.*

answer •n. **1** something said or written in reaction to a question or statement. **2** the solution to a problem.
•v. (**answers, answering, answered**) **1** give an answer. **2** (**answer back**) give a cheeky reply. **3** (**answer to/for**) be responsible to someone or for something. **4** meet a need.
– ORIGIN Old English.

answerable •adj. (**answerable to/for**) responsible to someone or for something.

answering machine •n. a machine which gives a recorded answer to a telephone call and can record a message from the caller.

ant •n. a small insect, usually wingless, living with many others in a highly organized group.
– ORIGIN Old English.

-ant •suffix **1** (forming adjectives) having a quality: *arrogant.* **2** (forming nouns) performing a function: *deodorant.*
– ORIGIN Latin.

antacid /an-tass-id/ •adj. (of a medicine) reducing excess acid in the stomach.

antagonism /an-tag-uh-ni-z'm/ •n. open hostility or opposition.

antagonist •n. an opponent or enemy.
– DERIVATIVES **antagonistic** adj.
– ORIGIN Greek *antagōnizesthai* 'struggle against'.

antagonize (or **antagonise**) •v. (**antagonizes, antagonizing, antagonized**) make someone hostile.

Antarctic •adj. relating to the region surrounding the South Pole.
– ORIGIN Greek *antarktikos* 'opposite to the north'.

> ✓ **Antarctic** has two **c**'s: there is one after the **r** as well as one at the end.

ante /an-ti/ •n. a stake put up by a player in poker or brag before receiving cards.
– PHRASES **up** (or **raise**) **the ante** increase what is at stake.
– ORIGIN Latin, 'before'.

ante- •prefix before; preceding: *antecedent.*

anteater •n. a mammal with a long snout, feeding on ants and termites.

antecedent /an-ti-see-duhnt/ •n.

1 a thing that occurs or exists before another. **2** (**antecedents**) a person's ancestors and background. **3** an earlier word, phrase, or clause to which a following pronoun refers back. ● adj. coming before in time or order.
– ORIGIN Latin *antecedere* 'go before'.

antechamber ● n. an anteroom.

antedate ● v. (**antedates, antedating, antedated**) **1** come before something in time. **2** indicate that a document or event belongs to an earlier date.

antediluvian /an-ti-di-**loo**-vi-uhn/ ● adj. **1** belonging to the time before the biblical Flood. **2** ridiculously old-fashioned.
– ORIGIN from ANTE- + Latin *diluvium* 'deluge'.

antelope ● n. a swift deer-like animal with long horns, found in Africa and Asia.
– ORIGIN Greek *antholops*.

antenatal ● adj. Brit. during pregnancy; before birth.

antenna /an-ten-nuh/ ● n. (pl. **antennae** /an-ten-nee/) **1** each of a pair of long, thin parts on the heads of some insects, shellfish, etc., used for feeling. **2** (pl. also **antennas**) an aerial.
– ORIGIN Latin *antemna* 'yard' (of a ship's mast).

antepenultimate ● adj. last but two in a series.

anterior ● adj. tech. at or nearer the front. Opp. POSTERIOR.
– ORIGIN Latin.

anteroom ● n. a small room leading to a larger one.

anthem ● n. **1** an uplifting song chosen by a country to express patriotic feelings. **2** a musical setting of a religious work to be sung by a choir during a church service.
– DERIVATIVES **anthemic** /an-thee-mik/ adj.
– ORIGIN Latin *antiphona* 'antiphon'.

anther ● n. the part of a flower's stamen that contains the pollen.
– ORIGIN Greek *anthos* 'flower'.

anthill ● n. a mound-shaped nest built by ants or termites.

anthology ● n. (pl. **anthologies**) a collection of poems or other pieces of writing or music.
– DERIVATIVES **anthologist** n. **anthologize** (or **anthologise**) v.
– ORIGIN Greek *anthos* 'flower'.

anthracite /an-thruh-syt/ ● n. hard coal that burns with little flame and smoke.
– ORIGIN Greek *anthrax* 'coal'.

anthrax /an-thraks/ ● n. a serious disease

of sheep and cattle, able to be transmitted to humans.
– ORIGIN Greek, 'coal, boil'.

anthropoid ● adj. relating to apes that are like humans in form, such as gorillas or chimpanzees.
– ORIGIN Greek *anthrōpos* 'human being'.

anthropology /an-thruh-pol-uh-ji/ ● n. the study of human origins, societies, and cultures.
– DERIVATIVES **anthropological** adj. **anthropologist** n.
– ORIGIN Greek *anthrōpos* 'human being'.

anthropomorphic /an-thruh-puh-mor-fik/ ● adj. (of a god, animal or object) treated as if having human feelings.

anti- ● prefix **1** opposed to; against: *antisocial*. **2** preventing or relieving: *antibiotic*. **3** the opposite of: *anticlimax*.
– ORIGIN Greek.

antibacterial ● adj. active against bacteria.

antibiotic ● n. a medicine that destroys bacteria or slows their growth.
– ORIGIN from Greek *biōtikos* 'fit for life'.

antibody ● n. (pl. **antibodies**) a protein produced in the blood to destroy an antigen (harmful substance).

Antichrist ● n. an enemy of Jesus believed by the early Church to appear before the end of the world.

anticipate ● v. (**anticipates, anticipating, anticipated**) **1** be aware of a future event and prepare for it. **2** expect something. **3** look forward to something. **4** do something earlier than someone else.
– DERIVATIVES **anticipatory** adj.
– ORIGIN Latin *anticipare*.

anticipation ● n. the action of anticipating; expectation.

anticlimax ● n. a disappointing end to an exciting series of events.
– DERIVATIVES **anticlimactic** adj.

anticline /an-ti-klyn/ ● n. a ridge or fold of rock in which the strata slope downwards from the crest.
– ORIGIN from Greek *klinein* 'lean'.

anticlockwise ● adv. & adj. Brit. in the opposite direction to the way in which the hands of a clock move round.

antics ● pl. n. foolish, outrageous, or amusing behaviour.
– ORIGIN Italian *antico* 'antique'.

anticyclone ● n. an area of high atmospheric pressure around which air slowly circulates, usually resulting in calm, fine weather.

antidote ● n. **1** a medicine taken to counteract a poison. **2** a thing that counteracts something unpleasant: *laughter is a good antidote to stress.*

– ORIGIN from Greek *didonai* 'give'.

antifreeze • n. a liquid added to water to prevent it from freezing, used in the radiator of a motor vehicle.

antigen /an-ti-jen/ • n. a harmful substance which causes the body to produce antibodies.

anti-hero (or **anti-heroine**) • n. a central character in a story, film, or play who lacks typical heroic qualities.

antihistamine • n. a drug that counteracts the effects of histamine, used in treating allergies.

antilogarithm • n. Math. the number of which a given number is the logarithm.

antimacassar /an-ti-muh-kass-er/ • n. a cloth put over the back of a chair to protect it from grease and dirt.
– ORIGIN from **ANTI-** + *Macassar*, a kind of hair oil formerly used by men.

antimatter • n. Physics matter consisting of the antiparticles of the particles that make up normal matter.

antimicrobial /an-ti-mi-kroh-bi-uhl/ • adj. active against microbes. • n. a substance which acts against microbes.

antimony /an-ti-muh-ni/ • n. a brittle silvery-white metallic element.
– ORIGIN Latin *antimonium*.

antioxidant • n. a substance that counteracts oxidation.

antiparticle • n. Physics a subatomic particle with the same mass as a corresponding particle but an opposite electric charge or magnetic effect.

antipathy /an-ti-puh-thi/ • n. (pl. **antipathies**) a strong feeling of dislike.
– DERIVATIVES **antipathetic** adj.
– ORIGIN from Greek *anti-* 'against' + *pathos* 'feeling'.

antiperspirant • n. a substance that is applied to the skin to prevent or reduce sweating.

antiphon /an-ti-fuhn/ • n. a short chant sung before or after a psalm or canticle.
– ORIGIN Greek *antiphōna* 'harmonies'.

antiphonal /an-tif-fuh-n'l/ • adj. sung or recited alternately between two groups.

Antipodes /an-ti-puh-deez/ • pl. n. (**the Antipodes**) Australia and New Zealand (because situated on the opposite side of the earth from Europe).
– DERIVATIVES **Antipodean** adj. & n.
– ORIGIN Greek, 'having the feet opposite'.

antiquarian /an-ti-kwair-i-uhn/ • adj. relating to the collection or study of antiques, rare books, or antiquities. • n. (also **antiquary**) a person who studies or collects antiquarian items.

antiquated • adj. old-fashioned or outdated.

antique • n. a decorative object or piece of furniture that is valuable because of its age. • adj. **1** valuable because of its age. **2** old-fashioned or outdated.
– ORIGIN Latin *antiquus* 'former, ancient'.

antiquity • n. (pl. **antiquities**) **1** the distant past, especially before the Middle Ages. **2** an object from the distant past. **3** great age.

antirrhinum /an-ti-ry-nuhm/ • n. (pl. **antirrhinums**) a snapdragon.
– ORIGIN from Greek *anti-* 'imitating' + *rhis* 'nose'.

anti-Semitism • n. hostility to or prejudice against Jews.
– DERIVATIVES **anti-Semite** n. **anti-Semitic** adj.

antiseptic • adj. preventing the growth of microorganisms that cause disease or infection. • n. an antiseptic substance.

antisocial • adj. **1** acting in a way that conflicts with accepted behaviour and causes annoyance. **2** not wanting to mix with other people.

antithesis /an-ti-thuh-siss/ • n. (pl. **antitheses** /an-ti-thuh-seez/) **1** a person or thing that is the direct opposite of another. **2** the putting together of contrasting ideas or words to produce an effect in writing or speaking.
– ORIGIN Greek *antitithenai* 'set against'.

antithetical /an-ti-thet-i-k'l/ • adj. opposed to or incompatible with each other.

antitoxin • n. an antibody that counteracts a toxin.

antivivisectionist • n. a person who is opposed to the use of live animals for scientific research.

antler • n. each of a pair of branched horns on the head of an adult male deer.
– ORIGIN Old French *antoillier*.

antonym /an-tuh-nim/ • n. a word opposite in meaning to another.
– ORIGIN from Greek *anti-* 'against' + *onoma* 'a name'.

anus /ay-nuhss/ • n. the opening at the end of the digestive system through which solid waste leaves the body.
– ORIGIN Latin.

anvil • n. an iron block on which metal can be hammered and shaped.
– ORIGIN Old English.

anxiety • n. (pl. **anxieties**) a feeling or state of unease or concern.

anxious • adj. **1** experiencing worry or unease. **2** very eager or concerned: *she was anxious to leave.*
– DERIVATIVES **anxiously** adv. **anxiousness** n.
– ORIGIN Latin *anxius*.

any • det. & pron. **1** one or some, no matter

how much or how many. **2** whichever or whatever you choose. •**adv.** at all.
– ORIGIN Old English.

> **USAGE:** As a pronoun **any** can be used with either a singular or a plural verb, depending on the rest of the sentence: *we needed more sugar but there wasn't any left* (singular verb) or *are any of the new videos available?* (plural verb).

anybody •**pron.** anyone.

anyhow •**adv. 1** anyway. **2** in a careless or disorderly way.

anyone •**pron.** any person or people.

anything •**pron.** a thing of any kind, no matter what.
– PHRASES **anything but** not at all.

anyway •**adv. 1** used to emphasize something just said or to change the subject. **2** nevertheless.

anywhere •**adv.** in or to any place. •**pron.** any place.

aorta /ay-**or**-tuh/ •**n.** the main artery supplying blood from the heart to the rest of the body.
– ORIGIN Greek *aortē*.

apace •**adv.** literary quickly.

Apache /uh-**pa**-chi/ •**n.** (pl. **Apache** or **Apaches**) a member of an American Indian people living chiefly in New Mexico and Arizona.

apart •**adv. 1** separated by a distance. **2** into pieces.
– PHRASES **apart from 1** except for. **2** as well as.
– ORIGIN from Latin *a parte* 'at the side'.

apartheid /uh-**par**-tayt/ •**n.** the former official system of segregation or discrimination on the grounds of a person's race in South Africa.
– ORIGIN Afrikaans, 'separateness'.

apartment •**n. 1** esp. N. Amer. a flat. **2** (**apartments**) a private set of rooms in a large house.
– ORIGIN French *appartement*.

apathetic /a-puh-**the**-tik/ •**adj.** not interested or enthusiastic.
– DERIVATIVES **apathetically** adv.

apathy /**ap**-uh-thi/ •**n.** lack of interest or enthusiasm.
– ORIGIN Greek *apathēs* 'without feeling'.

apatosaurus /uh-pa-tuh-**sor**-uhss/ •**n.** a huge plant-eating dinosaur with a long neck and tail; a brontosaurus.
– ORIGIN from Greek *apatē* 'deceit' + *sauros* 'lizard'.

ape •**n.** an animal like a monkey but without a tail, such as a chimpanzee or gorilla. •**v.** (**apes**, **aping**, **aped**) imitate someone or something.
– ORIGIN Old English.

aperitif /uh-pe-ri-**teef**/ •**n.** an alcoholic drink taken before a meal.
– ORIGIN French.

aperture /a-per-cher/ •**n. 1** an opening, hole, or gap. **2** the variable opening by which light enters a camera.
– ORIGIN Latin *apertura*.

apex /**ay**-peks/ •**n.** (pl. **apexes** or **apices** /**ay**-pi-seez/) the top or highest point.
– ORIGIN Latin, 'peak, tip'.

aphelion /ap-**hee**-li-uhn/ •**n.** (pl. **aphelia** /ap-**hee**-li-uh/) the point in a planet's orbit at which it is furthest from the sun. Opp. **PERIHELION**.
– ORIGIN from Greek *aph' hēlion* 'from the sun'.

aphid /**ay**-fid/ •**n.** a greenfly or similar insect that feeds on the sap of plants.
– ORIGIN Greek *aphis*.

aphorism /**af**-uh-ri-z'm/ •**n.** a short clever phrase which makes a true point.
– DERIVATIVES **aphoristic** adj.
– ORIGIN Greek *aphorismos* 'definition'.

aphrodisiac /af-ruh-**diz**-i-ak/ •**n.** a food, drink, or other thing that arouses sexual desire.
– ORIGIN from *Aphrodite*, the Greek goddess of love.

apiary /**ay**-pee-uh-ri/ •**n.** (pl. **apiaries**) a place where bees are kept.
– DERIVATIVES **apiarist** n.
– ORIGIN Latin *apis* 'bee'.

apical /**ay**-pi-k'l/ •**adj.** tech. relating to or forming an apex.

apices pl. of **APEX**.

apiece •**adv.** to, for, or by each one.

aplenty •**adj.** in abundance: *he has work aplenty*.

aplomb /uh-**plom**/ •**n.** calm self-confidence.
– ORIGIN from French *à plomb* 'straight as a plumb line'.

apocalypse /uh-**pok**-uh-lips/ •**n. 1** an event involving great destruction. **2** (**the Apocalypse**) the final destruction of the world, as described in the biblical book of Revelation.
– ORIGIN Greek *apokaluptein* 'reveal'.

apocalyptic /uh-po-kuh-**lip**-tik/ •**adj.** relating to or resembling the destruction of the world: *an apocalyptic war*.
– DERIVATIVES **apocalyptically** adv.

Apocrypha /uh-**pok**-ri-fuh/ •**n.** those books of the Old Testament not accepted as part of Hebrew scripture and excluded from the Protestant Bible at the Reformation.
– ORIGIN from Latin *apocrypha scripta* 'hidden writings'.

apocryphal •**adj. 1** widely known but unlikely to be true: *an apocryphal story.*

2 relating to the Apocrypha.

apogee /ap-uh-jee/ • n. **1** the highest point: *his creative activity reached its apogee in 1910.* **2** the point in the orbit of the moon or a satellite at which it is furthest from the earth.
– ORIGIN from Greek *apogaion diastēma*, 'distance away from earth'.

apolitical • adj. not interested or involved in politics.

apologetic • adj. admitting and showing regret for a wrongdoing.
• n. (**apologetics**) reasoned arguments defending a theory or belief.
– DERIVATIVES **apologetically** adv.

apologia /ap-uh-loh-ji-uh/ • n. a formal written statement defending your opinions or behaviour.
– ORIGIN Latin.

apologist • n. a person who offers an argument in defence of something controversial.

apologize (or **apologise**) • v. (**apologizes, apologizing, apologized**) say sorry for a wrongdoing.

apology • n. (pl. **apologies**) **1** an expression of regret for a wrong-doing. **2** (**an apology for**) a very poor example of something.
– ORIGIN Greek *apologia* 'a speech in your own defence'.

apophthegm /ap-uh-them/ • n. a short phrase stating a general truth.
– ORIGIN Greek *apophthengesthai* 'speak out'.

apoplectic /a-puh-plek-tik/
• adj. **1** overcome with anger. **2** dated relating to apoplexy (stroke).

apoplexy /a-puh-plek-si/ • n. (pl. **apoplexies**) **1** extreme anger. **2** Med., dated a stroke.
– ORIGIN Greek *apoplēssein* 'disable by a stroke'.

apostasy /uh-poss-tuh-si/ • n. the abandonment of a belief or principle.
– ORIGIN Greek *apostasis* 'desertion'.

apostate /ap-uh-stayt/ • n. a person who abandons a belief or principle.

apostle • n. **1** (**Apostle**) each of the twelve chief disciples of Jesus. **2** an enthusiastic supporter of an idea or cause.
– ORIGIN Greek *apostolos* 'messenger'.

apostolic /a-puh-stol-ik/ • adj. **1** relating to the Apostles. **2** relating to the Pope, regarded as the successor to St Peter.

apostrophe /uh-poss-truh-fi/ • n. a punctuation mark (') used to show either possession or the omission of letters or numbers.
– ORIGIN Greek *apostrephein* 'turn away'.

apothecary /uh-poth-uh-kuh-ri/ • n. (pl. **apothecaries**) old use a person who prepared and sold medicines.
– ORIGIN Greek *apothēkē* 'storehouse'.

apotheosis /uh-po-thi-oh-siss/ • n. (pl. **apotheoses** /uh-po-thi-oh-seez/) **1** the highest point: *science is the apotheosis of the intellect.* **2** the raising of someone to the rank of a god.
– ORIGIN Greek *apotheoun* 'make a god of'.

appal (US **appall**) • v. (**appals, appalling, appalled**) **1** shock or greatly dismay someone. **2** (as adj. **appalling**) informal very bad.
– ORIGIN Old French *apalir* 'grow pale'.

apparatchik /ap-puh-raht-chik/
• n. esp. derog. an official in a large political organization. **2** esp. hist. a member of the administrative system of a communist party.
– ORIGIN Russian.

apparatus /ap-puh-ray-tuhss/ • n. (pl. **apparatuses**) **1** the equipment needed for a particular activity or purpose. **2** the complex structure of an organization: *the apparatus of government.*
– ORIGIN Latin.

apparel /uh-pa-ruhl/ • n. formal clothing.
– ORIGIN Old French *apareillier*.

apparent • adj. **1** clearly seen or understood; obvious. **2** seeming real, but not necessarily so.
– DERIVATIVES **apparently** adv.
– ORIGIN Latin *apparere* 'appear'.

apparition • n. a remarkable thing that suddenly appears, especially a ghost.

appeal • v. **1** make a serious or earnest request. **2** be attractive or interesting: *activities that appeal to all.* **3** ask a higher court of law to reverse the decision of a lower court. **4** Cricket (of the bowler or fielders) call on the umpire to declare a batsman out. • n. **1** an act of appealing. **2** attractiveness or interest.
– ORIGIN Latin *appellare* 'to address'.

appealing • adj. attractive or interesting.

appear • v. **1** come into view or

existence. **2** seem: *she appeared calm and confident.* **3** present yourself publicly or formally, especially as a performer or in a law court.
– ORIGIN Latin *apparere*.

appearance • n. **1** the way that someone or something looks or seems. **2** an act of appearing.
– PHRASES **keep up appearances** keep up an impression of wealth or well-being.

appease • v. (**appeases, appeasing, appeased**) make someone calm or less hostile by agreeing to their demands.
– DERIVATIVES **appeasement** n. **appeaser** n.
– ORIGIN Old French *apaiser*.

appellation /ap-puh-**lay**-sh'n/ • n. formal a name or title.
– ORIGIN Latin *appellare* 'to address'.

append • v. add to the end of a document or piece of writing.
– ORIGIN Latin *appendere* 'hang on'.

appendage • n. a thing attached to or projecting from something larger or more important.

appendicitis /uh-pen-di-**sy**-tiss/ • n. inflammation of the appendix.

appendix • n. (pl. **appendices** or **appendixes**) **1** a small tube of tissue attached to the lower end of the large intestine. **2** a section of additional information at the end of a book.
– ORIGIN Latin.

appertain /ap-per-**tayn**/ • v. (**appertain to**) formal relate to.
– ORIGIN Latin *appertinere*.

appetite • n. **1** a natural desire to satisfy a bodily need, especially for food. **2** a liking or inclination: *my appetite for study had gone.*
– ORIGIN Latin *appetitus*.

appetizer (or **appetiser**) • n. a snack or a drink taken before a meal to stimulate the appetite.

appetizing (or **appetising**) • adj. causing a pleasant feeling of hunger.

applaud • v. **1** show approval by clapping. **2** express approval of: *teachers applauded the decision.*
– ORIGIN Latin *applaudere*.

☑ Spell **applaud** and the related word **applause** with a double **p**.

applause • n. approval shown by clapping.

apple • n. a round fruit that grows on a tree, with green or red skin and crisp flesh.
– PHRASES **the apple of your eye** a person who you are very fond of and proud of. [ORIGIN first referring to the pupil of

the eye.] **upset the apple cart** spoil a plan.
– DERIVATIVES **appley** adj.
– ORIGIN Old English.

apple-pie order • n. perfect order.

applet /ap-lit/ • n. Computing a small application running within a larger program.

appliance • n. a device designed to perform a specific task.

applicable • adj. able to be applied; appropriate.
– DERIVATIVES **applicability** n.

applicant • n. a person who applies for something.

application • n. **1** a formal request. **2** the action of applying something. **3** practical use or relevance. **4** continued effort. **5** a computer program designed to fulfil a particular purpose.

applicator • n. a device for putting something into or on to something.

applied • adj. practical rather than theoretical: *applied chemistry.*

appliqué /uh-**plee**-kay/ • n. decorative needlework in which fabric shapes are sewn or fixed on to a fabric background.
– DERIVATIVES **appliquéd** adj.
– ORIGIN French, 'applied'.

apply • v. (**applies, applying, applied**) **1** make a formal request: *he applied for a job as a carpenter.* **2** bring into operation or use. **3** be relevant. **4** put a substance on a surface. **5** (**apply yourself**) put all your efforts into a task.
– ORIGIN Latin *applicare* 'fold, fasten to'.

appoint • v. **1** give a job or role to someone. **2** decide on a time or place. **3** (as adj. **appointed**) equipped or furnished: *a luxuriously appointed lounge.*
– DERIVATIVES **appointee** n.
– ORIGIN Old French *apointer*.

appointment • n. **1** an arrangement to meet. **2** a job or position. **3** the action of appointing someone to a job. **4** (**appointments**) furniture or fittings.

apportion • v. share something out.
– DERIVATIVES **apportionment** n.
– ORIGIN Latin *apportionare*.

apposite /ap-puh-zit/ • adj. very appropriate.
– ORIGIN Latin *appositus* 'applied'.

apposition • n. Grammar a relationship in which a word or phrase is placed next to another so as to qualify or explain it (e.g. *my friend Sue*).

appraisal • n. **1** the action of assessing. **2** a formal assessment of an employee's performance.

appraise • v. (**appraises, appraising, appraised**) assess the quality, value, or nature of.

a

– DERIVATIVES **appraisee** n. **appraiser** n.
– ORIGIN from **APPRISE**.

> USAGE: **Appraise** is often confused with **apprise**. **Appraise** means 'assess', while **apprise** means 'inform' (*he was apprised of the problem*).

appreciable •adj. large or important enough to be noticed.
– DERIVATIVES **appreciably** adv.

appreciate /uh-pree-shi-ayt/
•v. (**appreciates, appreciating, appreciated**) **1** recognize the worth of: *he appreciates his time in the army.* **2** understand a situation fully. **3** be grateful for something. **4** rise in value or price.
– DERIVATIVES **appreciator** n.
– ORIGIN Latin *appretiare* 'appraise'.

appreciation •n. **1** recognition of the worth of something. **2** gratitude. **3** a favourable written assessment of a person or their work. **4** increase in value.

appreciative •adj. feeling or showing gratitude or pleasure.
– DERIVATIVES **appreciatively** adv.

apprehend •v. **1** seize or arrest someone for a crime. **2** understand something.
– ORIGIN Latin *prehendere* 'lay hold of'.

apprehension •n. **1** worry or fear about what might happen. **2** understanding of something. **3** the action of arresting someone.

apprehensive •adj. worried or afraid about what might happen.
– DERIVATIVES **apprehensively** adv.

apprentice •n. a person learning a skilled practical trade from an employer.
•v. (**apprentices, apprenticing, apprenticed**) employ as an apprentice.
– DERIVATIVES **apprenticeship** n.
– ORIGIN Old French *apprendre* 'to learn'.

apprise •v. (**apprises, apprising, apprised**) inform: *I apprised him of what had happened.*
– ORIGIN French *apprendre* 'learn, teach'.

> USAGE: On the confusion of **apprise** and **appraise**, see the note at **APPRAISE**.

approach •v. **1** come near to someone or something in distance, time, or quality. **2** go to someone with a proposal or request. **3** start to deal with something in a particular way. •n. **1** a way of dealing with something. **2** an initial proposal or request. **3** the action of approaching. **4** a way leading to a place.
– ORIGIN Old French *aprochier*.

approachable •adj. **1** friendly and easy to talk to. **2** able to be reached from a particular direction or by a particular means.
– DERIVATIVES **approachability** n.

approbation •n. approval; praise.
– ORIGIN Latin *approbare* 'approve'.

appropriate •adj. /uh-proh-pri-uht/ suitable or right in the circumstances.
•v. /uh-proh-pri-ayt/ (**appropriates, appropriating, appropriated**) **1** take something for your own use without permission. **2** set aside money for a special purpose.
– DERIVATIVES **appropriately** adv. **appropriateness** n. **appropriation** n.
– ORIGIN Latin *appropriare*.

approval •n. **1** a good opinion of someone or something. **2** official permission or agreement.
– PHRASES **on approval** (of goods) able to be returned to a supplier if not satisfactory.

approve •v. (**approves, approving, approved**) **1** believe to be good or acceptable: *he approved of stiff punishments for criminals.* **2** officially agree to or allow something.
– ORIGIN Latin *approbare*.

approximate •adj. /uh-prok-si-muht/ almost but not completely accurate.
•v. /uh-prok-si-mayt/ (**approximates, approximating, approximated**) be similar to something.
– DERIVATIVES **approximately** adv.
– ORIGIN Latin *approximatus*.

approximation /uh-prok-si-may-sh'n/
•n. **1** an approximate figure or result. **2** the estimation of something in a fairly accurate way.

appurtenances /uh-per-ti-nuhn-siz/
•pl. n. formal accessories associated with a particular activity.
– ORIGIN Old French *apertenance*.

APR •abbrev. annual percentage rate.

après-ski •n. social activities following a day's skiing.
– ORIGIN French.

apricot •n. an orange-yellow fruit like a small peach.
– ORIGIN Portuguese *albricoque* or Spanish *albaricoque*.

April •n. the fourth month of the year.
– ORIGIN Latin *Aprilis*.

April Fool's Day •n. 1 April, traditionally an occasion for playing tricks.

a priori /ay pry-or-I/ •adj. & adv. based on theoretical reasoning rather than actual observation.
– ORIGIN Latin, 'from what is before'.

apron •n. **1** a protective garment covering the front of your clothes.

2 an area on an airfield used for manoeuvring or parking aircraft. **3** (also **apron stage**) a strip of stage in a theatre extending in front of the curtain.
– PHRASES **tied to someone's apron strings** dominated or excessively influenced by someone.
– ORIGIN Old French *naperon* 'small tablecloth'.

apropos /a-pruh-poh/ • prep. (**apropos of**) with reference to.
– ORIGIN from French *à propos*.

apse /apss/ • n. a large recess with a domed or arched roof at the eastern end of a church.
– ORIGIN Greek *apsis* 'arch, vault'.

apt • adj. **1** appropriate; suitable. **2** (**apt to**) having a tendency to. **3** quick to learn.
– DERIVATIVES **aptly** adv. **aptness** n.
– ORIGIN Latin *aptus* 'fitted'.

aptitude • n. a natural ability or tendency.

aqualung • n. a portable breathing apparatus for divers, consisting of cylinders of compressed air attached to a mouthpiece or mask.
– ORIGIN Latin *aqua* 'water'.

aquamarine • n. **1** a light bluish-green precious stone. **2** a light bluish-green colour.
– ORIGIN from Latin *aqua marina* 'seawater'.

aquaplane • v. (**aquaplanes, aquaplaning, aquaplaned**) (of a vehicle) slide uncontrollably on a wet surface.
– ORIGIN from Latin *aqua* 'water' + PLANE¹.

aquarium • n. (pl. **aquaria** or **aquariums**) a water-filled glass tank for keeping fish and other water creatures and plants.
– ORIGIN Latin.

Aquarius /uh-kwair-i-uhss/ • n. a constellation (the Water Carrier) and sign of the zodiac, which the sun enters about 21 January.
– DERIVATIVES **Aquarian** n. & adj.

aquatic /uh-kwat-ik/ • adj. **1** relating to water. **2** living in or near water.

aqueduct /ak-wuh-dukt/ • n. a long channel or raised bridge-like structure, used for carrying water across country.
– ORIGIN from Latin *aquae ductus* 'conduit'.

aqueous /ay-kwee-uhss/ • adj. relating to or containing water.
– ORIGIN Latin *aqua* 'water'.

aqueous humour • n. the clear fluid in the eyeball in front of the lens.

aquifer /ak-wi-fer/ • n. a body of rock that holds water or through which water flows.

– ORIGIN Latin, 'water-bearing'.

aquiline /ak-wi-lyn/ • adj. **1** (of a nose) curved like an eagle's beak. **2** like an eagle.
– ORIGIN Latin *aquila* 'eagle'.

Ar • symb. the chemical element argon.

Arab • n. **1** a member of a Semitic people inhabiting much of the Middle East and North Africa. **2** a breed of horse that originated in Arabia.

arabesque /a-ruh-besk/ • n. **1** a ballet position in which one leg is extended horizontally backwards and the arms are outstretched. **2** an ornamental design of intertwined flowing lines.
– ORIGIN Italian *arabesco* 'in the Arabic style'.

Arabian • adj. relating to Arabia or its people.

Arabic • n. the Semitic language of the Arabs, written from right to left.
• adj. relating to the Arabs or Arabic.

Arabic numeral • n. any of the numerals 0, 1, 2, 3, 4, 5, 6, 7, 8, and 9.

arable /a-ruh-b'l/ • adj. (of land) able to be ploughed and used for growing crops.
– ORIGIN Latin *arare* 'to plough'.

arachnid /uh-rak-nid/ • n. an animal of a class of including spiders, scorpions, mites, and ticks.
– ORIGIN Greek *arakhnē* 'spider'.

arachnophobia /uh-rak-nuh-foh-bi-uh/ • n. extreme fear of spiders.
– ORIGIN from Greek *arakhnē* 'spider'.

Aramaic /a-ruh-may-ik/ • n. an ancient Semitic language still spoken in parts of the Middle East.
– ORIGIN Greek *Aramaios* 'of Aram' (the biblical name of Syria).

Aran • adj. (of knitwear) having a pattern involving cable stitch and large diamond designs, as made traditionally in the Aran Islands off the west coast of Ireland.

arbiter /ar-bi-ter/ • n. **1** a person who settles a dispute. **2** a person who has influence in a particular area: *an arbiter of taste.*
– ORIGIN Latin, 'judge, supreme ruler'.

arbitrary /ar-bi-truh-ri, ar-bi-tri/ • adj. **1** not seeming to be based on any reason, plan, or system. **2** (of power or authority) used without restraint.
– DERIVATIVES **arbitrarily** adv. **arbitrariness** n.
– ORIGIN Latin *arbitrarius*.

arbitrate • v. (**arbitrates, arbitrating, arbitrated**) (of an independent person or body) officially settle a dispute.
– DERIVATIVES **arbitration** n.
– ORIGIN Latin *arbitrari* 'give judgement'.

arbitrator • n. an independent person or

body officially appointed to settle a dispute.

arboreal /ar-bor-i-uhl/ • adj. **1** living in trees. **2** relating to trees.
– ORIGIN Latin *arbor* 'tree'.

arboretum /ar-buh-ree-tuhm/ • n. (pl. **arboretums** or **arboreta**) a garden where trees are grown for study and display to the public.
– ORIGIN Latin.

arbour (US **arbor**) • n. a shady place in a garden, formed by trees or climbing plants growing over a framework.
– ORIGIN Latin *herba* 'grass, herb', influenced by *arbor* 'tree'.

arc • n. **1** a curve forming part of the circumference of a circle. **2** a curving movement through the air. **3** a glowing electrical discharge between two points. • v. (**arcs**, **arcing**, **arced**) move in or form an arc.
– ORIGIN Latin *arcus* 'bow, curve'.

arcade • n. **1** a covered passage with arches along one or both sides. **2** a covered walk with shops along one or both sides.
– ORIGIN French.

Arcadian • adj. literary relating to an idyllic country scene or way of life.
– ORIGIN from *Arcadia*, a region of southern Greece.

arcana /ar-kay-nuh, ar-kah-nuh/ • pl. n. mysteries or secrets.
– ORIGIN Latin.

arcane /ar-kayn/ • adj. understood by only a few people; mysterious.
– ORIGIN Latin *arcere* 'shut up'.

arch[1] • n. **1** a curved structure that spans an opening or supports the weight of a bridge, roof, or wall. **2** the inner side of the foot. • v. form or make an arched shape.
– ORIGIN Latin *arcus* 'bow'.

arch[2] • adj. self-consciously playful or teasing.
– ORIGIN from the use of **ARCH-**, by association with the sense 'rogue' in words such as *arch-scoundrel*.

arch- • comb. form **1** chief: *archbishop*. **2** most extreme: *an arch-enemy*.
– ORIGIN Greek *arkhos* 'chief'.

archaeology (US also **archeology**) • n. the study of ancient history by examining objects dug up from the ground.
– DERIVATIVES **archaeological** adj. **archaeologist** n.
– ORIGIN Greek *arkhaios* 'ancient'.

archaeopteryx /ar-ki-op-tuh-riks/ • n. the oldest known fossil bird, which had feathers and wings like a bird, but teeth and a bony tail like a dinosaur.

– ORIGIN from Greek *arkhaios* 'ancient' + *pterux* 'wing'.

archaic /ar-kay-ik/ • adj. **1** very old or old-fashioned. **2** belonging to former or ancient times.
– ORIGIN Greek *arkhaios* 'ancient'.

archaism /ar-kay-is'm/ • n. an old or old-fashioned word or style of art or language.

archangel /ark-ayn-j'l/ • n. an angel of high rank.

archbishop • n. a bishop of the highest rank.

archdeacon • n. a senior Christian priest ranking immediately below a bishop.

archduke • n. a chief duke, especially (hist.) a son of the Emperor of Austria.

arch-enemy • n. a chief enemy.

archeology • n. US = ARCHAEOLOGY.

archer • n. a person who shoots with a bow and arrows.
– DERIVATIVES **archery** n.
– ORIGIN Latin *arcus* 'bow'.

archetype /ar-ki-typ/ • n. **1** a very typical example: *he was the archetype of the old-style football club chairman*. **2** an original model from which other forms are developed.
– DERIVATIVES **archetypal** adj.
– ORIGIN from Greek *arkhe-* 'primitive' + *tupos* 'a model'.

archipelago /ar-ki-pel-uh-goh/ • n. (pl. **archipelagos** or **archipelagoes**) a group of many islands.
– ORIGIN from Greek *arkhi-* 'chief' + *pelagos* 'sea'.

architect • n. **1** a person who designs buildings and supervises their construction. **2** a person who creates or is responsible for something: *the architect of the economic reforms*.
– ORIGIN Greek *arkhitektōn* 'chief builder'.

architectonic /ar-ki-tek-ton-ik/ • adj. relating to architecture or architects. • n. (**architectonics**) the scientific study of architecture.

architecture • n. **1** the design and construction of buildings. **2** the style in which a building is designed and constructed: *Gothic architecture*. **3** the complex structure of something.
– DERIVATIVES **architectural** adj.

architrave /ar-ki-trayv/ • n. **1** (in classical architecture) a main beam resting across the tops of columns. **2** the frame around a doorway or window.
– ORIGIN French.

archive /ar-kyv/ • n. **1** a collection of historical documents or records. **2** a complete record of the data in a

computer system, stored on a medium that is less frequently used.
• v. (**archives**, **archiving**, **archived**) place or store in an archive.
– DERIVATIVES **archival** adj.
– ORIGIN Greek *arkheia* 'public records'.

archivist /ar-ki-vist/ • n. a person who is in charge of archives of historical material.

archway • n. a curved structure forming a passage or entrance.

arc lamp (also **arc light**) • n. a light source using an electric arc.

Arctic • adj. **1** relating to the regions around the North Pole. **2** (**arctic**) informal (of weather) very cold.
– ORIGIN Greek *arktos* 'constellation of the Great Bear'.

☑ Arctic has two **c**'s: there is one after the **r** as well as one at the end.

ardent • adj. **1** very enthusiastic or passionate. **2** old use burning or glowing.
– DERIVATIVES **ardently** adv.
– ORIGIN Latin *ardere* 'to burn'.

ardour (US **ardor**) • n. great enthusiasm or passion.
– ORIGIN Latin *ardor*.

arduous • adj. difficult and tiring.
– ORIGIN Latin *arduus* 'steep, difficult'.

are 2nd person sing. present and 1st, 2nd, 3rd person pl. present of **BE**.

area • n. **1** a part of a place, object, or surface. **2** the extent or measurement of a surface. **3** a subject or range of activity. **4** a sunken enclosure that leads to a basement.
– ORIGIN Latin, 'piece of level ground'.

arena • n. **1** a level area surrounded by seating, in which sports and other public events are held. **2** an area of activity: *conflicts within the political arena.*
– ORIGIN Latin *harena*, *arena* 'sand, sand-covered place of combat'.

aren't • contr. **1** are not. **2** am not (only in questions): *I'm right, aren't I?*

areola /uh-ree-uh-luh/ • n. (pl. **areolae** /uh-ree-uh-lee/) the circular area of darker skin surrounding a human nipple.
– ORIGIN Latin, 'small open space'.

arête /uh-ret/ • n. a sharp mountain ridge.
– ORIGIN French.

Argentine • n. & adj. = **ARGENTINIAN**.

Argentinian • n. a person from Argentina. • adj. relating to Argentina.

argon /ar-gon/ • n. an inert element of the noble gas group, present in small amounts in the air.
– ORIGIN Greek *argos* 'idle'.

argot /ar-goh/ • n. the jargon or slang of a particular group or area of activity.
– ORIGIN French.

arguable • adj. **1** able to be supported by reasons. **2** open to disagreement.
– DERIVATIVES **arguably** adv.

argue • v. (**argues**, **arguing**, **argued**) **1** exchange conflicting views heatedly. **2** give reasons or evidence in support of something.
– ORIGIN Latin *arguere* 'accuse'.

argument • n. **1** a heated exchange of conflicting views. **2** a set of reasons given in support of something.

☑ Remember that there is no **e** after the **u** in **argument**.

argumentation • n. systematic reasoning in support of something.

argumentative • adj. tending to argue.

aria /ah-ri-uh/ • n. an accompanied song for a solo voice in an opera.
– ORIGIN Italian.

arid • adj. **1** very dry because having little or no rain. **2** dull and boring.
– DERIVATIVES **aridity** n.
– ORIGIN Latin *aridus*.

Aries /air-eez/ • n. a constellation (the Ram) and sign of the zodiac, which the sun enters about 20 March.
– ORIGIN Latin.

arise • v. (**arises**, **arising**, **arose**; past part. **arisen**) **1** come into being or come to notice. **2** (**arise from/out of**) occur as a result of. **3** formal get or stand up.

aristocracy /a-ris-tok-ruh-si/ • n. (pl. **aristocracies**) the highest social class, consisting of people with hereditary titles.
– ORIGIN Greek *aristokratia* 'rule by the best'.

aristocrat /ar-is-tuh-krat, uh-ris-tuh-krat/ • n. a member of the aristocracy.
– DERIVATIVES **aristocratic** adj.

arithmetic • n. /uh-rith-muh-tik/ **1** the branch of mathematics concerned with numbers. **2** the use of numbers in counting and calculation. • adj. /a-rith-met-ik/ relating to arithmetic.
– DERIVATIVES **arithmetical** adj. **arithmetically** adv.
– ORIGIN from Greek *arithmētikē tekhnē* 'art of counting'.

arithmetic progression • n. a sequence of numbers in which each differs from the next by a constant quantity (e.g. 9, 7, 5, 3, etc.).

ark • n. **1** (in the Bible) the ship built by Noah to save his family and two of every kind of animal from the Flood. **2** (also **Holy Ark**) a chest or cupboard containing the Torah scrolls in a synagogue. **3** (**Ark of the Covenant**) the

chest which contained the laws of the ancient Israelites.
– ORIGIN Latin *arca* 'chest'.

arm¹ • n. **1** each of the two upper limbs of the human body from the shoulder to the hand. **2** a side part of a chair that supports a sitter's arm. **3** a strip of water or land extending from a larger body. **4** a branch or division of an organization.
– PHRASES **cost an arm and a leg** informal be very expensive. **keep someone/thing at arm's length** avoid close or friendly contact with someone or something. **with open arms** with great warmth or enthusiasm.
– DERIVATIVES **armful** n.
– ORIGIN Old English.

arm² • v. **1** supply someone or something with weapons. **2** provide with essential equipment or information. **3** make a bomb ready to explode.
– ORIGIN Latin *arma* 'armour, arms'.

armada /ar-mar-duh/ • n. a fleet of warships.
– ORIGIN Spanish.

armadillo /ar-muh-dil-loh/ • n. (pl. **armadillos**) an insect-eating mammal of Central and South America, with a body covered in bony plates.
– ORIGIN Spanish, 'little armed man'.

Armageddon /ar-muh-ged-duhn/ • n. **1** (in the New Testament) the last battle between good and evil before the Day of Judgement. **2** a huge and very destructive conflict.
– ORIGIN Hebrew, 'hill of Megiddo' (Book of Revelation, chapter 16).

armament /ar-muh-muhnt/ • n. **1** (also **armaments**) military weapons and equipment. **2** the equipping of military forces for war.

armature /ar-muh-cher/ • n. **1** the rotating coil of a dynamo or electric motor. **2** a piece of iron placed across the poles of a magnet to preserve its power.
– ORIGIN Latin *armatura* 'armour'.

armchair • n. an upholstered chair with side supports for the sitter's arms.
• adj. experiencing something by reading about it, watching it on television, etc. rather than doing it: *an armchair traveller*.

armed • adj. equipped with or involving a firearm.

armed forces • pl. n. a country's army, navy, and air force.

Armenian /ah-meen-i-uhn/ • n. **1** a person from Armenia. **2** the language of Armenia. • adj. relating to Armenia.

armistice /ar-miss-tiss/ • n. a truce.
– ORIGIN from Latin *arma* 'arms' + *-stitium* 'stoppage'.

armorial • adj. relating to heraldry or coats of arms.

armour (US **armor**) • n. **1** the metal coverings worn in the past to protect the body in battle. **2** (also **armour plate**) the tough metal layer covering a military vehicle or ship. **3** the protective layer or shell of some animals and plants.
– DERIVATIVES **armoured** adj.
– ORIGIN Old French *armure*.

armourer (US **armorer**) • n. **1** a maker or supplier of weapons or armour. **2** an official in charge of the arms of a warship or regiment.

armoury (US **armory**) • n. (pl. **armouries**) a store or supply of arms.

armpit • n. a hollow under the arm at the shoulder.

arms • pl. n. **1** guns and other weapons. **2** the heraldic emblems on a coat of arms.
– PHRASES **up in arms** protesting about something vigorously.
– ORIGIN Latin *arma*.

arms race • n. a situation in which nations compete for superiority in developing and stockpiling weapons.

arm-wrestling • n. a contest in which two seated people engage hands and try to force each other's arm down.

army • n. (pl. **armies**) **1** an organized military force equipped for fighting on land. **2** a large number of people or things: *an army of researchers*.
– ORIGIN Old French *armee*.

aroma • n. a pleasant smell.
– ORIGIN Greek, 'spice'.

aromatherapy • n. the use of aromatic oils obtained from plants for healing or to promote well-being.
– DERIVATIVES **aromatherapist** n.

aromatic • adj. **1** having a pleasant smell. **2** (of an organic compound such as benzene) containing a flat ring of atoms in its molecule.

arose past of ARISE.

around • adv. & prep. **1** on every side. **2** in or to many places throughout an area.
• adv. **1** so as to face in the opposite direction. **2** approximately. **3** available or present. **4** without purpose.

arouse • v. (**arouses**, **arousing**, **aroused**) **1** bring about a feeling or response in someone. **2** excite someone sexually. **3** wake someone from sleep.
– DERIVATIVES **arousal** n.

arpeggio /ar-pej-ji-oh/ • n. (pl. **arpeggios**) the notes of a musical chord played in rapid succession.
– ORIGIN Italian.

arraign /uh-rayn/ • v. call someone

before a court to answer a criminal charge.
– DERIVATIVES **arraignment** n.
– ORIGIN Old French *araisnier*.

arrange • v. (**arranges, arranging, arranged**) **1** put tidily or in a particular order. **2** organize or plan. **3** adapt a piece of music for performance with different instruments or voices.
– DERIVATIVES **arranger** n.
– ORIGIN Old French *arangier*.

arrangement • n. **1** a plan for a future event. **2** something made up of things placed in an attractive or ordered way. **3** an arranged piece of music.

arrant /a-ruhnt/ • adj. utter; complete: *what arrant nonsense!*
– ORIGIN from ERRANT.

array • n. **1** an impressive display or range: *a bewildering array of choices.* **2** an ordered arrangement of troops. **3** literary elaborate or beautiful clothing.
• v. **1** display or arrange in a neat or impressive way. **2** (**be arrayed in**) be clothed in.
– ORIGIN Old French *arei*.

arrears • pl. n. money owed that should already have been paid.
– PHRASES **in arrears 1** behind with paying money that is owed. **2** (of wages or rent) paid at the end of each period of work or occupation.
– ORIGIN Old French *arere*.

arrest • v. **1** seize someone by legal authority and take them into custody. **2** stop the progress of something. **3** (as adj. **arresting**) attracting attention.
• n. **1** the action of arresting someone. **2** a sudden stop.
– ORIGIN Latin *restare* 'remain, stop'.

arrival • n. **1** the action of arriving. **2** a person or thing that has just arrived.

arrive • v. (**arrives, arriving, arrived**) **1** reach a destination. **2** (of a particular moment or event) happen. **3** (**arrive at**) reach a conclusion or decision. **4** informal become successful and well known.
– ORIGIN Old French *ariver*.

arriviste /a-ri-veest/ • n. usu. derog. a person who has recently become wealthy or risen in social status.
– ORIGIN French.

arrogant • adj. having too great a sense of your own importance or abilities.
– DERIVATIVES **arrogance** n. **arrogantly** adv.
– ORIGIN Latin *arrogare* 'claim for yourself'.

arrogate /a-ruh-gayt/ • v. (**arrogates, arrogating, arrogated**) take or claim something that you have no right to.
– ORIGIN Latin *arrogare*.

arrow • n. **1** a stick with a sharp pointed head, designed to be shot from a bow. **2** a symbol resembling an arrow, used to show direction or position.
– ORIGIN Old Norse.

arrowroot • n. a powdery starch obtained from a Caribbean plant, used as a thickener in cookery.
– ORIGIN from a word in a South American language meaning 'meal of meals'.

arsenal • n. a store of weapons and ammunition.
– ORIGIN Arabic, 'house of industry'.

arsenic • n. a brittle grey element with many highly poisonous compounds.
– ORIGIN Greek *arsenikon*.

arson • n. the criminal act of deliberately setting fire to property.
– DERIVATIVES **arsonist** n.
– ORIGIN Old French.

art[1] • n. **1** the expression of creative skill in a visual form such as painting or sculpture. **2** paintings, drawings, and sculpture as a whole. **3** (**the arts**) creative activities such as painting, music, and drama. **4** (**arts**) subjects of study concerned with human culture. **5** a skill: *the art of conversation.*
– ORIGIN Latin *ars*.

art[2] old-fashioned or dialect 2nd person sing. present of BE.

art deco /art dek-oh/ • n. a decorative art style of the 1920s and 1930s, characterized by geometric shapes.
– ORIGIN French *art décoratif* 'decorative art'.

artefact /ar-ti-fakt/ (US **artifact**) • n. a useful or decorative man-made object.
– ORIGIN from Latin *arte* 'using art' + *factum* 'something made'.

arterial /ar-teer-i-uhl/ • adj. **1** relating to an artery or arteries. **2** relating to an important transport route.

arteriosclerosis /ar-teer-i-oh-skluh-roh-siss/ • n. thickening and hardening of the walls of the arteries.

artery • n. (pl. **arteries**) **1** any of the tubes through which blood flows from the heart around the body. **2** an important transport route.
– ORIGIN Greek *artēria*.

artesian well /ar-tee-zh'n/ • n. a well that is bored vertically into a layer of water-bearing rock, the water coming to the surface through natural pressure.
– ORIGIN from *Artois*, a region in France.

artful • adj. clever in a cunning way.
– DERIVATIVES **artfully** adv.

arthritis /ar-thry-tiss/ • n. painful inflammation and stiffness of the joints.
– DERIVATIVES **arthritic** /ar-thri-tik/ adj. & n.
– ORIGIN Greek *arthron* 'joint'.

arthropod /ar-thruh-pod/ • n. an animal with a body divided into segments and an external skeleton, such as an insect, spider, crab, or lobster.
– ORIGIN from Greek *arthron* 'joint' + *pous* 'foot'.

artichoke • n. (also **globe artichoke**) a vegetable consisting of the unopened flower head of a thistle-like plant.
– ORIGIN Italian *articiocco*.

article • n. **1** a particular object. **2** a piece of writing in a newspaper or magazine. **3** a clause or paragraph of a legal document. **4** (**articles**) a period of professional training as a solicitor, architect, etc. • v. (**be articled**) (of a solicitor, architect, etc.) be employed under contract as a trainee.
– PHRASES **article of faith** a firmly held belief.
– ORIGIN Latin *articulus* 'small connecting part'.

articled clerk • n. a law student employed as a trainee.

articular • adj. Anat. relating to a joint.

articulate • adj. /ar-tik-yuu-luht/ **1** able to speak fluently and clearly. **2** having joints or jointed segments. • v. /ar-tik-yuu-layt/ (**articulates**, **articulating**, **articulated**) **1** pronounce words distinctly. **2** clearly express an idea or feeling. **3** (as adj. **articulated**) having sections connected by a flexible joint or joints.
– DERIVATIVES **articulacy** n. **articulately** adv. **articulation** n.
– ORIGIN Latin *articulare*.

artifact • n. US = ARTEFACT.

artifice /ar-ti-fiss/ • n. the use of cunning or skill in order to trick or deceive.
– ORIGIN from Latin *ars* 'art' + *facere* 'make'.

artificer /ar-ti-fi-ser/ • n. a person skilled in making or planning things.

artificial • adj. **1** made as a copy of something natural. **2** not sincere; affected: *an artificial smile*.
– DERIVATIVES **artificiality** n. **artificially** adv.

artificial insemination • n. the procedure of injecting semen into the vagina or womb of a woman or female animal.

artificial intelligence • n. the performance by computers of tasks that normally require human intelligence.

artificial respiration • n. the forcing of air into and out of a person's lungs to make them begin breathing again.

artillery /ar-til-luh-ri/ • n. **1** large guns used in warfare on land. **2** a branch of the armed forces that uses artillery.
– ORIGIN Old French *atillier* 'equip, arm'.

artisan • n. a skilled worker who makes things by hand.
– DERIVATIVES **artisanal** adj.
– ORIGIN French.

artist • n. **1** a person who paints or draws. **2** a person who practises or performs any of the creative arts.
– ORIGIN from Latin *ars* 'art'.

artiste /ar-teest/ • n. a professional singer or dancer.
– ORIGIN French.

artistic • adj. **1** having creative skill. **2** relating to art or artists.
– DERIVATIVES **artistically** adv.

artistry • n. creative skill or ability.

artless • adj. sincere and straightforward.

art nouveau /ar noo-voh, art noo-voh/ • n. a style of art and architecture of the late 19th and early 20th centuries, having intricate designs and flowing curves.
– ORIGIN French, 'new art'.

artwork • n. illustrations for inclusion in a publication.

arty (N. Amer. also **artsy**) • adj. (**artier**, **artiest**) informal interested or involved in the arts in an affected way.
– DERIVATIVES **artiness** n.

arum lily /air-uhm/ • n. a tall lily-like African plant.
– ORIGIN Greek *aron*.

-ary • suffix **1** forming adjectives: *budgetary*. **2** forming nouns: *dictionary*.

Aryan /air-i-uhn/ • n. **1** a member of an ancient people speaking an Indo-European language. **2** (in Nazi thought) a white person not of Jewish descent. • adj. relating to Aryans.
– ORIGIN Sanskrit, 'noble'.

As • symb. the chemical element arsenic.

as • adv. used in comparisons to refer to extent or amount. • conj. **1** while. **2** in the way that. **3** because. **4** even though. • prep. **1** in the role of; being: *a job as a cook*. **2** while; when.
– PHRASES **as for** with regard to. **as yet** until now or that time.
– ORIGIN Old English, 'similarly'.

asap • abbrev. as soon as possible.

asbestos • n. a fibrous mineral used in fire-resistant and insulating materials.
– ORIGIN Greek, 'unquenchable'.

asbestosis /az-bes-toh-sis/ • n. a serious lung disease, often accompanied by cancer, resulting from breathing asbestos dust.

ASBO (also **Asbo**) • abbrev. Brit. antisocial behaviour order.

ascend • v. go up; climb or rise.
– ORIGIN Latin *ascendere*.

ascendant • adj. **1** rising in power or status. **2** (of a planet or sign of the

zodiac) just above the eastern horizon.
– DERIVATIVES **ascendancy** n.

ascension • n. **1** the action of rising in status. **2 (the Ascension)** the ascent of Jesus into heaven after the Resurrection.

ascent • n. **1** an act of ascending something. **2** an upward slope.

ascertain /ass-er-tayn/ • v. find out for certain.
– ORIGIN Old French *acertener*.

ascetic /uh-set-ik/ • adj. strictly self-disciplined and avoiding any pleasures or luxuries. • n. an ascetic person.
– DERIVATIVES **asceticism** n.
– ORIGIN Greek *askētēs* 'monk'.

ASCII /ass-ki/ • abbrev. Computing American Standard Code for Information Interchange.

ascorbic acid /uh-skor-bik/ • n. vitamin C.
– ORIGIN Latin *scorbutus* 'scurvy'.

ascribe • v. (**ascribes, ascribing, ascribed**) (**ascribe something to**) consider something to be caused by: *he ascribed his breakdown to exhaustion.*
– DERIVATIVES **ascription** n.
– ORIGIN Latin *ascribere*.

aseptic /ay-sep-tik/ • adj. free from harmful bacteria, viruses, and other microorganisms.

asexual • adj. **1** not having sexual feelings or associations. **2** (of reproduction) not involving sexual activity. **3** not having sexual organs.
– DERIVATIVES **asexually** adv.

ash¹ • n. **1** the powder remaining after something has been burned. **2** (**ashes**) the remains of a human body after it has been cremated. **3** (**the Ashes**) a cricket trophy awarded for winning a test match series between England and Australia.
– ORIGIN Old English.

ash² • n. a tree with winged fruits and hard pale wood.
– ORIGIN Old English.

ashamed • adj. feeling embarrassed or guilty.

ashen • adj. very pale from shock, fear, or illness.

Ashkenazi /ash-kuh-nah-zi/ • n. (pl. **Ashkenazim** /ash-kuh-nah-zim/) a Jew of central or eastern European descent.
– ORIGIN from *Ashkenaz*, a grandson of Noah.

ashlar /ash-ler/ • n. large square-cut stones used as the surface layer of a wall.
– ORIGIN Old French *aisselier*.

ashore • adv. to or on the shore or land.

ashram /ash-ruhm/ • n. a Hindu religious retreat or community.
– ORIGIN Sanskrit, 'hermitage'.

ashtray • n. a small container for tobacco ash and cigarette ends.

Ash Wednesday • n. the first day of Lent in the Christian Church.

Asian /ay-zhh'n/ • n. a person from Asia or a person of Asian descent. • adj. relating to Asia.

Asiatic /ay-zi-at-ik/ • adj. relating to Asia.

aside • adv. **1** to one side; out of the way. **2** in reserve. • n. **1** an actor's remark spoken to the audience rather than the other characters. **2** a remark that is not directly related to the main subject of discussion.
– PHRASES **aside from** apart from.

asinine /ass-i-nyn/ • adj. very stupid or foolish.
– ORIGIN Latin *asinus* 'ass'.

ask • v. **1** say something so as to get an answer or some information. **2** say that you wants someone to do, give, or allow something. **3** (**ask for**) request to speak to. **4** expect something of someone. **5** invite someone to a social occasion. **6** (**ask someone out**) invite someone out on a date. **7** (**ask after**) Brit. make polite enquiries about someone's health or well-being.
– PHRASES **for the asking** for little or no effort or cost.
– ORIGIN Old English.

askance /uh-skanss, uh-skahnss/ • adv. with a suspicious or disapproving look.

askew /uh-skyoo/ • adv. & adj. not straight or level.

asking price • n. the price at which something is offered for sale.

aslant • adv. & prep. at or across at a slant.

asleep • adj. & adv. in or into a state of sleep.

asp • n. a small viper with an upturned snout.
– ORIGIN Greek *aspis*.

asparagus /uh-spa-ruh-guhss/ • n. a vegetable consisting of the tender young shoots of a tall plant.
– ORIGIN Greek *asparagos*.

aspartame /uh-spah-taym/ • n. a low-calorie artificial sweetener.
– ORIGIN from *aspartic acid*, a related chemical named after *asparagus*.

aspect • n. **1** a particular part or feature of something. **2** a particular appearance or quality: *the air of desertion lent the place a sinister aspect.* **3** the side of a building facing a particular direction.
– ORIGIN Latin *aspectus*.

aspen • n. a poplar tree with small rounded leaves.
– ORIGIN dialect.

asperity /uh-spe-ri-ti/ • n. harshness of tone or manner.
– ORIGIN Latin *asperitas*.

aspersions /uh-sper-sh'nz/ • pl. n. (in phr. **cast aspersions on**) make critical remarks about someone's character or reputation.
– ORIGIN Latin *aspergere* 'sprinkle'.

asphalt /ass-falt/ • n. a dark tar-like substance used in surfacing roads or waterproofing buildings.
– ORIGIN Greek *asphalton*.

asphodel /ass-fuh-del/ • n. a plant with clusters of yellow or white flowers on a long stem.
– ORIGIN Greek *asphodelos*.

asphyxia /uh-sfik-si-uh/ • n. a condition caused by the body being deprived of oxygen, leading to unconsciousness or death.
– ORIGIN from Greek *a-* 'without' + *sphuxis* 'pulse'.

asphyxiate • v. (**asphyxiates, asphyxiating, asphyxiated**) **1** kill someone by depriving them of oxygen. **2** die as a result of a lack of oxygen.
– DERIVATIVES **asphyxiation** n.

aspic • n. a savoury jelly made with meat stock.
– ORIGIN French, 'asp', the colours of the jelly being compared to those of the snake.

aspidistra /ass-pi-diss-truh/ • n. a plant of the lily family with broad tapering leaves.
– ORIGIN Greek *aspis* 'shield'.

aspirant /ass-pi-ruhnt/ • n. a person with ambitions to do or be something.

aspirate • v. /ass-pi-rayt/ (**aspirates, aspirating, aspirated**) pronounce a word with the sound of the letter *h* at the start. • n. /ass-pi-ruht/ the sound of the letter *h*.
– ORIGIN Latin *aspirare*.

aspiration • n. a hope or ambition.
– DERIVATIVES **aspirational** adj.

aspire • v. (**aspires, aspiring, aspired**) have ambitions to do or be something: *she aspired to be an actress.*
– ORIGIN Latin *aspirare*.

aspirin • n. (pl. **aspirin** or **aspirins**) a medicine used to relieve pain and reduce fever and inflammation.
– ORIGIN from its chemical name.

ass • n. **1** a donkey or related small wild horse. **2** informal a stupid person.
– ORIGIN Latin *asinus*.

assail • v. **1** attack violently. **2** (of an unpleasant feeling) disturb or upset someone severely.
– ORIGIN Latin *assalire*.

assailant • n. an attacker.

assassin • n. a person who assassinates someone.
– ORIGIN Arabic, 'hashish eater' (referring to a fanatical Muslim sect at the time of the Crusades who were said to use hashish before murdering people).

assassinate • v. (**assassinates, assassinating, assassinated**) murder an important person for political or religious reasons.
– DERIVATIVES **assassination** n.

assault • n. **1** a violent attack. **2** a determined attempt to achieve something dangerous or difficult: *an assault on Everest.* • v. attack someone violently.
– ORIGIN Old French *assauter*.

assault course • n. Brit. a series of demanding physical challenges, used for training soldiers.

assay /uh-say, ass-ay/ • n. the process of testing of a metal or ore to establish its quality. • v. test a metal or ore to establish its quality.
– ORIGIN Old French *assai*, *essai* 'trial'.

assegai /ass-uh-gy/ • n. (pl. **assegais**) an iron-tipped spear used by southern African peoples.
– ORIGIN Arabic, 'the spear'.

assemblage • n. **1** a collection or gathering of people or things. **2** something made of pieces fitted together.

assemble • v. (**assembles, assembling, assembled**) **1** come or bring together. **2** construct something by fitting parts together.
– DERIVATIVES **assembler** n.
– ORIGIN Old French *asembler*.

assembly • n. (pl. **assemblies**) **1** a group of people gathered together. **2** a body of people with powers to make decisions and laws. **3** the action of fitting the parts of something together.

assembly line • n. a series of workers and machines in a factory which assemble the parts of identical products in successive stages.

assent /uh-sent/ • n. approval or agreement. • v. agree to a request or suggestion.
– ORIGIN Latin *assentire*.

assert • v. **1** state a fact or belief confidently. **2** make other people recognize something: *cyclists asserted their rights to use the road.* **3** (**assert yourself**) behave in a confident and forceful way.
– ORIGIN Latin *asserere* 'claim, affirm'.

assertion • n. **1** a confident and forceful statement. **2** the action of asserting something.

assertive • adj. confident and forceful.
– DERIVATIVES **assertively** adv. **assertiveness** n.

assess • v. calculate or estimate the value, importance, or quality of someone or something.
– DERIVATIVES **assessment** n. **assessor** n.
– ORIGIN Latin *assidere* 'sit by, levy tax'.

> ✓ Spell **assess** with a double **s**, then another double **s**.

asset • n. **1** a useful or valuable thing or person. **2** (**assets**) property owned by a person or company.
– ORIGIN Old French *asez* 'enough'.

asset-stripping • n. the practice of buying a company that is in financial difficulties at a low price and selling its assets separately at a profit.

asseveration /uh-sev-uh-**ray**-sh'n/ • n. formal a solemn or emphatic declaration or statement.
– ORIGIN Latin *asseverare*.

assiduous /uh-**sid**-yoo-uhss/ • adj. showing great care and thoroughness: *an assiduous study of the classics.*
– DERIVATIVES **assiduity** /ass-i-**dyoo**-i-ti/ n. **assiduously** adv.
– ORIGIN Latin *assiduus*.

assign • v. **1** give a task or duty to someone. **2** regard something as being caused by or belonging to: *she assigned the text to the sixteenth century.*
– ORIGIN Latin *assignare*.

assignation • n. a secret meeting, especially one between lovers.

assignment • n. **1** a task or duty given to someone. **2** the giving of a task or duty to someone.

assimilate • v. (**assimilates, assimilating, assimilated**) **1** take in and understand information. **2** absorb people or ideas into a wider society or culture. **3** absorb and digest food or nutrients.
– DERIVATIVES **assimilation** n.
– ORIGIN Latin *assimilare*.

assist • v. give help or support to someone.
– ORIGIN Latin *assistere* 'stand by'.

assistance • n. help or support.

assistant • n. **1** a person who ranks below a senior person. **2** a person who provides help in a particular role or type of work.

assize /uh-**syz**/ (also **assizes**) • n. hist. a court which sat at intervals in each county of England and Wales.
– ORIGIN Old French *assise*.

associate • v. /uh-**soh**-shi-ayt/ (**associates, associating, associated**) **1** connect in the mind: *I associated wealth with freedom.* **2** frequently meet or have dealings with someone. **3** (**be associated with** or **associate yourself with**) be involved with. • n. /uh-**soh**-shi-uht/ a work partner or colleague. • adj. /uh-**soh**-shi-uht/ **1** connected with an organization: *an associate company.* **2** belonging to an association but not having full membership.
– DERIVATIVES **associative** adj.
– ORIGIN Latin *associare*.

association • n. **1** a group of people organized for a joint purpose. **2** a connection or link.

Association Football • n. formal = SOCCER.

assonance /ass-uh-nuhnss/ • n. rhyming of vowel sounds only (e.g. *hide, time*) or of consonants but not vowels (e.g. *cold, killed*).
– ORIGIN Latin *assonare* 'respond to'.

assorted • adj. of various sorts put together.
– ORIGIN Old French *assorter*.

assortment • n. a collection of different things.

assuage /uh-**swayj**/ • v. (**assuages, assuaging, assuaged**) **1** make an unpleasant feeling less intense. **2** satisfy an appetite or desire.
– ORIGIN Old French *assouagier*.

assume • v. (**assumes, assuming, assumed**) **1** accept that something is true without having proof. **2** take responsibility or control. **3** begin to have: *the island has recently assumed increased importance.* **4** pretend to have or feel.
– ORIGIN Latin *assumere*.

assuming • conj. based on the acceptance that something is true without having proof.

assumption • n. **1** a thing assumed to be true. **2** the assuming of responsibility or control. **3** (**Assumption**) the taking up of the Virgin Mary into heaven, according to Roman Catholic doctrine.

assurance • n. **1** a statement or promise intended to give confidence. **2** self-confidence. **3** Brit. life insurance.

assure • v. (**assures, assuring, assured**) **1** tell someone that something is definitely true. **2** make something certain to happen. **3** Brit. insure a person's life.
– ORIGIN Old French *assurer*.

assured • adj. **1** confident. **2** protected against change or ending: *an assured tenancy.*
– DERIVATIVES **assuredly** adv.

astatine /ass-tuh-teen/ • n. a very unstable radioactive chemical element

belonging to the halogen group.
– ORIGIN Greek *astatos* 'unstable'.

aster • n. a garden plant of the daisy family, typically having pink or purple flowers.
– ORIGIN Greek, 'star'.

asterisk • n. a symbol (*) used in printed or written material as a pointer to a note elsewhere.
– ORIGIN Greek *asteriskos* 'small star'.

astern • adv. behind or towards the rear of a ship or aircraft.

asteroid /ass-tuh-royd/ • n. a small rocky planet orbiting the sun.
– ORIGIN Greek *asteroeidēs* 'starlike'.

asthma /ass-muh/ • n. a medical condition in which a person has difficulty in breathing.
– DERIVATIVES **asthmatic** adj. & n.
– ORIGIN Greek.

astigmatism /uh-stig-muh-ti-z'm/ • n. a defect in an eye or lens, preventing proper focusing.
– ORIGIN from A-¹ + Greek *stigma* 'point'.

astir • adj. 1 in a state of excited movement. 2 awake and out of bed.

astonish • v. surprise or impress greatly.
– DERIVATIVES **astonishment** n.
– ORIGIN Old French *estoner* 'stun'.

astound • v. shock or greatly surprise.
– ORIGIN related to ASTONISH.

astrakhan /ass-truh-kan/ • n. the dark curly fleece of a type of young lamb from central Asia.
– ORIGIN named after the Russian city of *Astrakhan*.

astral /ass-truhl/ • adj. relating to the stars.
– ORIGIN Latin *astrum* 'star'.

astray • adv. away from the right path or direction.
– ORIGIN Old French *estraie*.

astride • prep. & adv. 1 with a leg on each side of. 2 (as adv.) (of a person's legs) wide apart.

astringent /uh-strin-juhnt/
• adj. 1 making body tissue contract.
2 harsh or severe in manner or style.
• n. an astringent lotion used medically or as a cosmetic.
– DERIVATIVES **astringency** n.
– ORIGIN Latin *astringere* 'pull tight'.

astrolabe /ass-truh-layb/ • n. an instrument formerly used for measuring the altitudes of stars and calculating latitude in navigation.
– ORIGIN Greek *astrolabos* 'star-taking'.

astrology • n. the study of the supposed influence of stars and planets on human affairs.
– DERIVATIVES **astrologer** n. **astrological** adj.

– ORIGIN Greek *astron* 'star'.

astronaut • n. a person trained to travel in a spacecraft.
– ORIGIN from Greek *astron* 'star' + *nautēs* 'sailor'.

astronomical • adj. 1 relating to astronomy. 2 informal very large: *he wanted an astronomical fee.*
– DERIVATIVES **astronomic** adj. **astronomically** adv.

astronomy • n. the scientific study of stars, planets, and the universe.
– DERIVATIVES **astronomer** n.
– ORIGIN Greek *astron* 'star'.

astrophysics • n. the branch of astronomy concerned with the physical nature of stars and planets.
– DERIVATIVES **astrophysicist** n.

astute /uh-styoot/ • adj. good at making accurate judgements; shrewd.
– DERIVATIVES **astutely** adv.
– ORIGIN Latin *astutus*.

asunder • adv. literary apart.
– ORIGIN Old English.

asylum • n. 1 protection from danger, especially for those who leave their own country because of persecution for their political beliefs. 2 dated an institution for people who are mentally ill.
– ORIGIN Greek *asulon* 'refuge'.

asymmetrical • adj. lacking symmetry.
– DERIVATIVES **asymmetric** adj.

asymmetry /ay-sim-mi-tri/ • n. (pl. **asymmetries**) lack of symmetry between the sides or parts of something.

asynchronous • adj. not existing or occurring at the same time.

At • symb. the chemical element astatine.

at • prep. used to express: 1 location, arrival, or time. 2 a value, rate, or point on a scale. 3 a state or condition. 4 direction towards. 5 the means by which something is done.
– ORIGIN Old English.

atavistic /at-uh-viss-tik/ • adj. relating or reverting to the feelings or behaviour of the earliest humans: *atavistic fears.*
– DERIVATIVES **atavism** n.
– ORIGIN Latin *atavus* 'forefather'.

ate past of EAT.

-ate¹ • suffix forming nouns referring to:
1 status, office, or function: *doctorate.*
2 a group: *electorate.* 3 Chem. a salt or ester: *chlorate.* 4 a product of a chemical process: *filtrate.*
– ORIGIN Old French *-at* or Latin *-atus.*

-ate² • suffix forming adjectives, nouns, and verbs: *associate.*
– ORIGIN Latin *-atus.*

atelier /uh-tel-i-ay/ • n. a workshop or studio used by an artist or designer.

– ORIGIN French.

atheism /ay-thi-i-z'm/ • n. disbelief in the existence of a god or gods.
– DERIVATIVES **atheist** n. **atheistic** adj.
– ORIGIN from Greek *a-* 'without' + *theos* 'god'.

atherosclerosis /ath-uh-roh-skluh-**roh**-siss/ • n. a disease of the arteries in which fatty material is deposited on their inner walls.
– ORIGIN from Greek *athērē* 'groats' + *sklērōsis* 'hardening'.

athlete • n. **1** a person who is good at sports. **2** a person who competes in track and field events.
– ORIGIN Greek *athlētēs*.

athlete's foot • n. a contagious fungal infection affecting the skin between the toes.

athletic • adj. **1** fit and good at sport. **2** relating to athletics. • n. (**athletics**) Brit. the sport of competing in track and field events.
– DERIVATIVES **athletically** adv. **athleticism** n.

athwart /uh-**thwort**/ • prep. & adv. across from side to side.

-ation • suffix (forming nouns) referring to an action or its result: *exploration*.
– ORIGIN French or Latin.

Atlantic • adj. relating to the Atlantic Ocean.
– ORIGIN first referring to Mount Atlas in Libya; named after the god *Atlas* (see ATLAS).

atlas • n. a book of maps or charts.
– ORIGIN named after the Greek god *Atlas*, shown on early atlases as supporting the heavens.

ATM • abbrev. automated teller machine.

atmosphere • n. **1** the gases that surround the earth or another planet. **2** the quality of the air in a place. **3** an overall tone or mood: *the hotel has a friendly atmosphere*. **4** a unit of pressure equal to the pressure of the atmosphere at sea level, 101,325 pascals.
– ORIGIN from Greek *atmos* 'vapour' + *sphaira* 'globe'.

atmospheric • adj. **1** relating to the atmosphere of a planet. **2** creating a distinctive mood: *atmospheric lighting*. • n. (**atmospherics**) electrical disturbances in the atmosphere, especially as causing interference with telecommunications.

atoll /a-**tol**/ • n. a ring-shaped coral reef or chain of islands.
– ORIGIN Maldivian.

atom • n. **1** the smallest particle of a chemical element that can exist. **2** a very small amount: *she did not have an atom of strength left*.

– ORIGIN Greek *atomos* 'indivisible'.

atom bomb (also **atomic bomb**) • n. a bomb whose explosive power comes from the fission (splitting) of the nuclei of atoms.

atomic • adj. **1** relating to an atom or atoms. **2** relating to nuclear energy or weapons.

atomic mass unit • n. a unit of mass used for atomic and molecular weights, equal to one twelfth of the mass of an atom of carbon-12.

atomic number • n. the number of protons in the nucleus of the atom of a chemical element.

atomic weight • n. = RELATIVE ATOMIC MASS.

atomize (or **atomise**) • v. (**atomizes, atomizing, atomized**) convert a substance into very fine particles or droplets.
– DERIVATIVES **atomizer** n.

atonal /ay-**toh**-n'l/ • adj. not written in any musical key.

atone • v. (**atones, atoning, atoned**) (**atone for**) make amends for a sin or other wrongdoing.
– ORIGIN from *at one*.

atonement • n. **1** the action of making amends for a sin or other wrongdoing. **2** (**the Atonement**) the reconciliation of God and humankind through the death of Jesus.

atop • prep. literary on the top of.

atrium /ay-tri-uhm/ • n. (pl. **atria** /ay-tri-uh/ or **atriums**) **1** a central hall rising through several storeys of a building and having a glazed roof. **2** an open central court in an ancient Roman house. **3** each of the two upper cavities of the heart.
– ORIGIN Latin.

atrocious /uh-**troh**-shuhss/ • adj. **1** horrifyingly wicked. **2** very bad or unpleasant.
– ORIGIN Latin *atrox* 'cruel'.

atrocity /uh-**tross**-i-ti/ • n. (pl. **atrocities**) a very wicked or cruel act.

atrophy /a-truh-fi/ • v. (**atrophies, atrophying, atrophied**) **1** (of body tissue or an organ) waste away. **2** gradually become weaker. • n. the condition or process of wasting away or becoming weaker.
– ORIGIN Greek *atrophia* 'lack of food'.

attach • v. **1** fasten; join. **2** regard as important or valuable. **3** appoint someone for special or temporary duties. **4** (**attached to**) very fond of.
– ORIGIN Old French *atachier*.

 The ending of **attach** is spelled **-ach**.

attaché /uh-tash-ay/ •n. a person on an ambassador's staff with a specific responsibility or field of activity: *a military attaché*.
– ORIGIN French, 'attached'.

attaché case •n. a small, flat briefcase for carrying documents.

attachment •n. 1 an extra part attached to something to perform a particular function. 2 a computer file sent with an email. 3 the action of attaching one thing to another.

attack •v. 1 take violent action against. 2 have a harmful effect on. 3 criticize fiercely. 4 tackle something with determination. 5 (in sport) try to score goals or points. •n. 1 an act of attacking. 2 a sudden short period of an illness.
– DERIVATIVES **attacker** n.
– ORIGIN Italian *attaccare*.

attain •v. 1 succeed in doing or achieving something. 2 reach: *the cheetah can attain speeds of 97 kph.*
– DERIVATIVES **attainable** adj.
– ORIGIN Latin *attingere*.

attainment •n. 1 the achieving of something. 2 an achievement.

attar /at-tar/ •n. a sweet-smelling oil made from rose petals.
– ORIGIN Arabic, 'perfume, essence'.

attempt •v. make an effort to do something; try. •n. an effort to do something.
– ORIGIN Latin *attemptare*.

attend •v. 1 be present at or go regularly to something. 2 (**attend to**) deal with or pay attention to. 3 occur at the same time or as a result of: *the work was attended by many difficulties.* 4 escort and assist an important person.
– DERIVATIVES **attendee** n. **attender** n.
– ORIGIN Latin *attendere*.

attendance •n. 1 the action of attending something. 2 the number of people present at a gathering or event.

attendant •n. 1 a person employed to provide a service. 2 an assistant to an important person. •adj. occurring with or as a result of: *obesity and its attendant health problems.*

attention •n. 1 the faculty of considering or taking notice. 2 special care or consideration. 3 (**attentions**) things done to express an interest in or please someone. 4 an erect position taken up by a soldier, with the feet together and the arms straight down the sides of the body.

attentive •adj. 1 paying close attention. 2 considerate and helpful.
– DERIVATIVES **attentively** adv. **attentiveness** n.

attenuate /uh-ten-yoo-ayt/

•v. (**attenuates, attenuating, attenuated**) 1 make weaker. 2 make thin or thinner.
– DERIVATIVES **attenuation** n.
– ORIGIN Latin *attenuare*.

attest /uh-test/ •v. 1 provide or act as clear evidence of. 2 declare that something is true or the case.
– DERIVATIVES **attestation** n.
– ORIGIN Latin *attestari*.

attic •n. a space or room inside the roof of a building.
– ORIGIN Latin *Atticus* 'relating to Athens or Attica' (a region of Greece).

attire •n. formal or literary clothes of a particular kind: *business attire.* •v. (**be attired**) be dressed in clothes of a particular kind.
– ORIGIN Old French *atirer* 'equip'.

attitude •n. 1 a way of thinking or feeling about someone or something. 2 a position of the body. 3 informal self-confident or uncooperative behaviour.
– ORIGIN Latin *aptitudo* 'suitability'.

attitudinize /at-ti-tyoo-di-nyz/ (or **attitudinise**) •v. (**attitudinizes, attitudinizing, attitudinized**) adopt an attitude just for effect.

attorney /uh-ter-ni/ •n. (pl. **attorneys**) 1 a person appointed to act for another in legal matters. 2 esp. US a lawyer.
– ORIGIN Old French *atorner* 'assign'.

Attorney General •n. (pl. **Attorneys General**) the most senior legal officer in some countries.

attract •v. 1 cause someone to come to a place or event or take part in something. 2 cause a reaction. 3 cause someone to have a liking for or interest in: *many men were attracted to her.* 4 draw something closer by exerting a force on it.
– DERIVATIVES **attractor** n.
– ORIGIN Latin *attrahere* 'draw near'.

attraction •n. 1 the action or power of attracting. 2 an interesting or appealing feature or quality.

attractive •adj. 1 pleasing in appearance. 2 arousing interest: *an attractive proposition.*
– DERIVATIVES **attractively** adv. **attractiveness** n.

attribute •v. /uh-trib-yoot/ (**attributes, attributing, attributed**) (**attribute something to**) regard something as belonging to, made, or caused by: *the moth's scarcity is attributed to pollution.* •n. /at-tri-byoot/ 1 a characteristic quality. 2 an object traditionally associated with a person or thing: *the hourglass is an attribute of Father Time.*
– DERIVATIVES **attributable** /uh-trib-yoo-tuh-b'l/ adj. **attribution** n.
– ORIGIN Latin *attribuere* 'assign to'.

attributive /uh-trib-yuu-tiv/
• adj. Grammar (of an adjective) coming before the word that it describes, for example *old* in *the old dog*.

attrition /uh-tri-sh'n/ • n. **1** gradual wearing down through prolonged attack or pressure. **2** wearing away by friction.
– ORIGIN Latin *atterere* 'to rub'.

attune • v. (**be attuned**) be receptive to and able to understand someone or something.

atypical • adj. not characteristic of a group, type, or class.
– DERIVATIVES **atypically** adv.

Au • symb. the chemical element gold.
– ORIGIN Latin *aurum*.

aubergine /oh-ber-zheen/ • n. esp. Brit. a purple egg-shaped vegetable.
– ORIGIN French.

aubretia /aw-bree-shuh/ (also **aubrietia**) • n. a trailing plant with purple, pink, or white flowers.
– ORIGIN named after the French botanist Claude *Aubriet*.

auburn /aw-bern/ • n. a reddish-brown colour.
– ORIGIN Old French *auborne*.

auction /awk-sh'n/ • n. a public sale in which goods or property are sold to the highest bidder. • v. sell an item or items at an auction.
– ORIGIN Latin, 'increase, auction'.

auctioneer • n. a person who conducts auctions.

audacious /aw-day-shuhss/ • adj. bold and daring.
– DERIVATIVES **audaciously** adv.
– ORIGIN Latin *audax* 'bold'.

audacity /aw-das-i-ti/ • n. **1** bold and daring actions or behaviour. **2** rude or disrespectful behaviour.

audible • adj. able to be heard.
– DERIVATIVES **audibility** n. **audibly** adv.
– ORIGIN Latin *audire* 'hear'.

audience • n. **1** the people gathered to see or listen to a play, concert, film, etc. **2** a formal interview with a person in authority.
– ORIGIN Latin *audire* 'hear'.

audio- • comb. form relating to hearing or sound: *audio-visual*.
– ORIGIN Latin *audire* 'hear'.

audio frequency • n. a frequency capable of being perceived by the human ear.

audio tape • n. magnetic tape on which sound can be recorded.

audio typist • n. a typist who types documents from recorded dictation.

audio-visual • adj. using both sight and sound.

audit /aw-dit/ • n. an official inspection of an organization's accounts.
• v. (**audits, auditing, audited**) inspect an organization's accounts.
– ORIGIN Latin *audire* 'hear'.

audition • n. an interview for a performer in which they give a practical demonstration of their skill. • v. take part in or assess someone by an audition.

auditor • n. **1** a person who inspects an organization's accounts. **2** a listener.

auditorium • n. (pl. **auditoriums** or **auditoria**) the part of a theatre or hall in which the audience sits.
– ORIGIN Latin.

auditory • adj. relating to hearing.

au fait /oh fay/ • adj. (**au fait with**) having a thorough knowledge of.
– ORIGIN French, 'to the point'.

auger /aw-ger/ • n. a tool resembling a large corkscrew, for boring holes.
– ORIGIN Old English.

aught /awt/ (also **ought**) • pron. old use anything at all.
– ORIGIN Old English.

augment /awg-ment/ • v. increase the amount, size, or value of something.
– DERIVATIVES **augmentation** n.
– ORIGIN Latin *augmentare*.

au gratin /oh gra-tan/ • adj. sprinkled with breadcrumbs or grated cheese and browned: *crab au gratin*.
– ORIGIN French, 'by grating'.

augur /aw-ger/ • v. (**augur well/badly**) be a sign of a good or bad outcome.
– ORIGIN Latin, 'person who interprets omens'.

augury /aw-gyuu-ri/ • n. (pl. **auguries**) a sign that shows what will happen in the future.

August • n. the eighth month of the year.
– ORIGIN named after the Roman emperor *Augustus*.

august /aw-gust/ • adj. inspiring respect and admiration.
– ORIGIN Latin *augustus* 'venerable'.

auk /awk/ • n. a black and white seabird with short wings.
– ORIGIN Old Norse.

auld lang syne /awld lang syn/
• n. times long past.
– ORIGIN Scots, 'old long since'.

aunt • n. the sister of a person's father or mother or the wife of a person's uncle.
– ORIGIN Old French *ante*.

au pair /oh pair/ • n. a foreign girl employed to look after children and help with housework in exchange for board and lodging.
– ORIGIN French, 'on equal terms'.

aura /aw-ruh/ • n. (pl. **auras**) **1** the distinctive atmosphere or quality associated with something or someone.

2 a supposed invisible force that surrounds a creature.
– ORIGIN Greek, 'breeze, breath'.

aural /aw-ruhl/ • adj. relating to the ear or hearing.
– DERIVATIVES **aurally** adv.
– ORIGIN Latin *auris* 'ear'.

> **USAGE:** Do not confuse **aural** with **oral**. See the note at **ORAL**.

aureole /aw-ri-ohl/ • n. **1** (in paintings) a bright circle surrounding a person to show that they are holy. **2** a circle of light around the sun or moon.
– ORIGIN from Latin *aureola corona* 'golden crown'.

au revoir /aw ruh-vwar/ • exclam. goodbye.
– ORIGIN French, 'to the seeing again'.

auricle /o-ri-k'l/ • n. **1** the external part of the ear. **2** an upper cavity of the heart.
– ORIGIN Latin *auricula* 'little ear'.

aurora australis /uh-raw-ruh oss-tray-liss/ • n. the Southern Lights, streamers of coloured light seen in the sky near the South Pole.
– ORIGIN Latin.

aurora borealis /uh-raw-ruh bo-ri-ay-liss/ • n. the Northern Lights, streamers of coloured light seen in the sky near the North Pole.
– ORIGIN Latin.

auspice /awss-piss/ • n. (in phr. **under the auspices of**) with the support or protection of.
– ORIGIN first meaning 'an omen', from Latin *auspicium*.

auspicious /aw-spi-shuhss/ • adj. suggesting that there is a good chance of success.

Aussie (also **Ozzie**) • n. (pl. **Aussies**) & adj. informal Australia or Australian.

austere /oss-teer/ • adj. **1** severe or strict in appearance or manner. **2** without comforts, luxuries, or decoration.
– ORIGIN Greek *austēros* 'severe'.

austerity /oss-te-ri-ti/ • n. (pl. **austerities**) **1** strictness or severity. **2** difficult economic conditions resulting from a cut in public spending.

Australasian /oss-truh-lay-*zh*'n, oss-struh-**lay**-sh'n/ • adj. relating to Australasia, a region made up of Australia, New Zealand, and islands of the SW Pacific.

Australian • n. a person from Australia.
• adj. relating to Australia.
– ORIGIN from Latin *Terra Australis* 'the southern land'.

Australian Rules • n. a form of football played on an oval field with an oval ball by teams of eighteen players.

Austrian • n. a person from Austria.

• adj. relating to Austria.

autarky (also **autarchy**) • n. (pl. **autarkies**) **1** economic independence or self-sufficiency. **2** an economically independent state or society.
– ORIGIN Greek *autarkēs*.

authentic • adj. **1** known to be real and genuine. **2** based on facts; accurate.
– DERIVATIVES **authentically** adv. **authenticity** n.
– ORIGIN Greek *authentikos*.

authenticate • v. (**authenticates, authenticating, authenticated**) prove or show to be genuine.
– DERIVATIVES **authentication** n.

author /aw-ther/ • n. **1** a writer of a book or article. **2** a person who thinks of a plan or idea.
– DERIVATIVES **authoress** n. **authorial** /aw-**thor**-i-uhl/ adj. **authorship** n.
– ORIGIN Latin *auctor*.

authoritarian /aw-tho-ri-**tair**-i-uhn/ • adj. in favour of or demanding strict obedience to authority. • n. an authoritarian person.

authoritative /aw-**tho**-ri-tuh-tiv/ • adj. **1** true or accurate and so able to be trusted. **2** expecting or likely to be respected and obeyed: *his authoritative manner.* **3** coming from an official source.
– DERIVATIVES **authoritatively** adv.

authority • n. (pl. **authorities**) **1** the power to give orders and enforce obedience. **2** a person or organization with official power. **3** official permission to do something. **4** recognized knowledge or expertise. **5** a person with expert knowledge of a particular subject.
– ORIGIN Old French *autorite*.

authorize (or **authorise**)
• v. (**authorizes, authorizing, authorized**) give official permission for.
– DERIVATIVES **authorization** n.

Authorized Version • n. an English translation of the Bible published in 1611.

autism /aw-ti-z'm/ • n. a mental condition in which a person has great difficulty in communicating with other people.
– DERIVATIVES **autistic** adj.
– ORIGIN Greek *autos* 'self'.

auto • adj. & n. = **AUTOMATIC**.

auto- • comb. form **1** self: *autocrat.* **2** a person's own: *autograph.*
– ORIGIN Greek *autos* 'self'.

autobiography • n. (pl. **autobiographies**) an account of a person's life written by that person.
– DERIVATIVES **autobiographer** n. **autobiographical** adj.

autoclave /or-toh-klayv/ • n. a strong heated container used for processes using high pressures and temperatures, e.g. steam sterilization.
– ORIGIN from AUTO- + Latin *clavis* 'key'.

autocracy /aw-tok-ruh-si/ • n. (pl. **autocracies**) 1 a system of government in which one person has total power. 2 a state governed by one person who has total power.
– ORIGIN from Greek *autos* 'self' + *kratos* 'power'.

autocrat • n. 1 a ruler who has total power. 2 a domineering person.
– DERIVATIVES **autocratic** adj.

autodidact /aw-toh-dy-dakt/ • n. a self-taught person.
– ORIGIN Greek *autodidaktos* 'self-taught'.

autogiro (also **autogyro**) • n. (pl. **autogiros**) a form of aircraft with unpowered rotating horizontal blades and a propeller.
– ORIGIN Spanish.

autograph • n. 1 a celebrity's signature written for an admirer. 2 a manuscript or musical score in an author's or composer's own handwriting. • v. write your signature on.
– ORIGIN Greek *autographos* 'written with a person's own hand'.

autoimmune • adj. (of disease) caused by antibodies or lymphocytes produced by the body to act against substances naturally present in it.

automate • v. (**automates, automating, automated**) convert a process or facility so that it can be operated by automatic equipment.

automated teller machine • n. a machine that provides banking services when a special card is inserted.

automatic • adj. 1 operating by itself without human control. 2 (of a firearm) self-loading and able to fire continuously until the bullets run out. 3 done or happening without conscious thought. 4 (of a punishment) applied without question because of a fixed rule.
– DERIVATIVES **automatically** adv.
– ORIGIN Greek *automatos*.

automatic pilot • n. a device for keeping an aircraft on a set course.
– PHRASES **on automatic pilot** doing something out of habit and without concentration.

automation /aw-tuh-may-sh'n/ • n. the use of automatic equipment instead of manual labour.

automaton /aw-tom-uh-tuhn/ • n. (pl. **automata** /aw-tom-uh-tuh/ or **automatons**) 1 a moving mechanical device resembling a human being. 2 a machine which operates automatically

according to a set of coded instructions.

automobile • n. N. Amer. a car.

automotive /aw-tuh-moh-tiv/ • adj. relating to motor vehicles.

autonomous • adj. self-governing or independent.
– DERIVATIVES **autonomously** adv.

autonomy /aw-ton-uh-mi/ • n. 1 self-government. 2 freedom of action.
– ORIGIN Greek *autonomia*.

autopilot • n. = AUTOMATIC PILOT.

autopsy /aw-top-si/ • n. (pl. **autopsies**) an examination of a dead body to discover the cause of death.
– ORIGIN Greek *autopsia*.

autumn • n. esp. Brit. the season after summer and before winter.
– DERIVATIVES **autumnal** adj.
– ORIGIN Latin *autumnus*.

auxiliary /awg-zil-yuh-ri/ • adj. providing extra help and support. • n. (pl. **auxiliaries**) a person or thing that provides extra help or support.
– ORIGIN Latin *auxilium* 'help'.

auxiliary verb • n. a verb used in forming the tenses, moods, and voices of other verbs (e.g. *be, do,* and *have*).

avail • v. (**avail yourself of**) formal use or take advantage of. • n. use or benefit: *his protests were to little avail.*
– ORIGIN Latin *valere* 'be strong'.

available • adj. 1 able to be used or obtained. 2 free to do something.
– DERIVATIVES **availability** n.

avalanche /av-uh-lahnsh/ • n. 1 a mass of snow and ice falling rapidly down the side of a mountain. 2 an overwhelming amount: *an avalanche of telephone calls.*
– ORIGIN French.

avant-garde /a-von gard/ • adj. (in the arts) new and experimental.
– ORIGIN French, 'vanguard'.

avarice /av-uh-riss/ • n. extreme greed for wealth or material things.
– ORIGIN Latin *avarus* 'greedy'.

avaricious /av-uh-ri-shuhss/ • adj. very greedy for wealth or material things.

avatar /av-uh-tar/ • n. Hinduism a god or goddess appearing in bodily form on earth.
– ORIGIN Sanskrit, 'descent'.

Ave Maria /ah-vay muh-ree-uh/ • n. a prayer to the Virgin Mary used in Roman Catholic worship.
– ORIGIN the opening words in Latin, 'hail, Mary!'

avenge • v. (**avenges, avenging, avenged**) punish or harm someone in return for a wrong.
– DERIVATIVES **avenger** n.
– ORIGIN Old French *avengier*.

avenue • n. 1 a broad road or path. 2 a

means of achieving something.
– ORIGIN French.

aver /uh-ver/ • v. (**avers, averring, averred**) formal declare to be the case.
– ORIGIN Old French *averer*.

average • n. **1** the result obtained by adding several amounts together and then dividing the total by the number of amounts. **2** a usual amount or level. • adj. **1** being an average: *the average temperature was 4°C below normal.* **2** usual or ordinary. • v. (**averages, averaging, averaged**) **1** amount to or achieve as an average. **2** calculate the average of.
– ORIGIN French *avarie* 'damage to ship or cargo'; the modern meaning comes from the sharing of the costs of things lost at sea.

averse • adj. (**averse to**) strongly disliking or opposed to.
– ORIGIN Latin *avertere* 'turn away from'.

> **USAGE:** On the confusion of averse and adverse, see the note at **ADVERSE**.

aversion • n. a strong dislike.

avert • v. **1** turn away the eyes. **2** prevent an unpleasant event.
– ORIGIN Latin *vertere* 'to turn'.

avian /ay-vi-uhn/ • adj. relating to birds.
– ORIGIN Latin *avis* 'bird'.

aviary /ay-vi-uh-ri/ • n. (pl. **aviaries**) a large enclosure for keeping birds in.

aviation • n. the activity of operating and flying aircraft.
– ORIGIN Latin *avis* 'bird'.

aviator • n. dated a pilot.

avid • adj. keenly interested or enthusiastic: *an avid reader.*
– DERIVATIVES **avidly** adv.
– ORIGIN Latin *avere* 'crave'.

avionics /ay-vi-on-iks/ • n. electronics used in aviation.

avocado • n. (pl. **avocados**) a pear-shaped fruit with pale green flesh and a large stone.
– ORIGIN Spanish.

avocet /av-uh-set/ • n. a wading bird with long legs and an upturned bill.
– ORIGIN Italian *avosetta*.

avoid • v. **1** keep away from, or stop yourself from doing something. **2** prevent something from happening.
– DERIVATIVES **avoidable** adj. **avoidance** n.
– ORIGIN Old French *evuider* 'clear out'.

avoirdupois /av-war-dyoo-pwah/ • n. a system of weights based on a pound of 16 ounces or 7,000 grains. Compare with TROY.
– ORIGIN from Old French *aveir de peis* 'goods of weight'.

avow • v. declare or confess openly.
– DERIVATIVES **avowal** n.

– ORIGIN Old French *avouer* 'acknowledge'.

avuncular /uh-vung-kyuu-ler/ • adj. friendly and kind towards a younger person.
– ORIGIN Latin *avunculus* 'maternal uncle'.

await • v. wait for someone or something.

awake • v. (**awakes, awaking, awoke**; past part. **awoken**) **1** stop sleeping. **2** make or become active again. • adj. not asleep.

awaken • v. **1** awake. **2** stir up a feeling.

awakening • n. **1** an act of becoming suddenly aware of something. **2** the beginning of a feeling or belief.

award • v. give something officially as a prize or reward. • n. **1** something awarded. **2** the giving of an award.
– ORIGIN Old French *esguarder* 'consider'.

aware • adj. having knowledge of a situation or fact.
– DERIVATIVES **awareness** n.
– ORIGIN Old English.

awash • adj. covered or flooded with water.

away • adv. **1** to or at a distance. **2** into a place for storage. **3** until disappearing: *the sound died away.* **4** constantly or continuously. • adj. (of a sports fixture) played at the opponents' ground.
– ORIGIN Old English.

awe • n. a feeling of great respect mixed with fear. • v. (**awes, awing, awed**) fill someone with awe.
– ORIGIN Old English.

awesome • adj. **1** very impressive or daunting. **2** informal excellent.

awful • adj. **1** very bad or unpleasant. **2** used for emphasis: *an awful lot.*
– DERIVATIVES **awfulness** n.

awfully • adv. **1** informal very or very much: *I'm awfully sorry.* **2** very badly or unpleasantly.

awhile • adv. for a short time.

awkward • adj. **1** hard to do or deal with. **2** causing or feeling embarrassment. **3** causing inconvenience. **4** not graceful; clumsy.
– DERIVATIVES **awkwardly** adv. **awkwardness** n.
– ORIGIN Old Norse.

awl /awl/ • n. a small pointed tool used for making holes.
– ORIGIN Old English.

awn /awn/ • n. a stiff bristle growing from the ear or flower of barley, rye, and grasses.
– ORIGIN Old Norse.

awning • n. a sheet of canvas on a frame, used for shelter.

awoke past of **AWAKE**.

awoken past part. of **AWAKE**.

AWOL /ay-wol/ • adj. Mil. absent but without intending to desert.
- ORIGIN from *absent without (official) leave*.

awry /uh-**ry**/ • adv. & adj. away from the expected course or position.
- ORIGIN from **wry**.

axe (US also **ax**) • n. a tool with a heavy blade, used for chopping wood. • v. (**axes, axing, axed**) **1** reduce something by a large amount. **2** dismiss someone ruthlessly.
- PHRASES **have an axe to grind** have a private reason for doing something.
- ORIGIN Old English.

axes pl. of **AXIS**.

axial /ak-si-uhl/ • adj. forming or relating to an axis.

axil /ak-sil/ • n. the upper angle where a leaf joins a stem.
- ORIGIN Latin *axilla*.

axiom /ak-si-uhm/ • n. a statement regarded as obviously true.
- DERIVATIVES **axiomatic** adj.
- ORIGIN Greek *axiōma* 'what is thought fitting'.

axis /ak-siss/ • n. (pl. **axes** /ak-seez/) **1** an imaginary line through a body, about which it rotates. **2** an imaginary line about which a regular figure is symmetrically arranged. **3** Math. a fixed reference line for the measurement of coordinates.

- ORIGIN Latin, 'axle, pivot'.

axle /ak-s'l/ • n. a rod passing through the centre of a wheel or group of wheels.
- ORIGIN Old Norse.

ayatollah /I-uh-**tol**-luh/ • n. a religious leader in Iran.
- ORIGIN Arabic, 'token of God'.

aye /*rhymes with* my/ (also **ay**) • exclam. old use or dialect yes. • n. a vote in favour of something.
- ORIGIN prob. from *I*, first person personal pronoun.

azalea /uh-**zay**-li-uh/ • n. a shrub with brightly coloured flowers.
- ORIGIN Greek *azaleos* 'dry' (because the shrubs flourish in dry soil).

Azerbaijani /a-zuh-by-**jah**-ni/ • n. (pl. **Azerbaijanis**) a person from Azerbaijan. • adj. relating to Azerbaijan or Azerbaijanis.

azimuth /az-i-muhth/ • n. Astron. the horizontal direction of a celestial object, measured from the north or south point of the horizon.
- ORIGIN Arabic, 'the way, direction'.

Aztec /az-tek/ • n. a member of the American Indian people dominant in Mexico before the Spanish conquest.
- ORIGIN from a Central American language.

azure /az-yuur/ • n. a bright blue colour.
- ORIGIN Old French *azur*.

Bb

B¹ (also **b**) • n. (pl. **Bs** or **B's**) **1** the second letter of the alphabet. **2** Music the seventh note of the scale of C major.

B² • abbrev. **1** (in chess) bishop. **2** black (used in describing grades of pencil lead). • symb. the chemical element boron.

b. • abbrev. born.

BA • abbrev. Bachelor of Arts.

Ba • symb. the chemical element barium.

baa • v. (**baas, baaing, baaed**) (of a sheep or lamb) bleat. • n. the cry of a sheep or lamb.

babble • v. (**babbles, babbling, babbled**) talk rapidly in a foolish or confused way. • n. foolish or confused talk.
– ORIGIN prob. from German *babbelen*.

babe • n. **1** literary a baby. **2** informal an attractive young woman.

babel /bay-b'l/ • n. a confused noise made by a number of people speaking together.
– ORIGIN from the Tower of *Babel* in the Bible, where God made the different peoples building the tower unable to understand each others' languages.

baboon • n. a large monkey with a long snout, large teeth, and a pink rump.
– ORIGIN Latin *babewynus*.

baby • n. (pl. **babies**) **1** a child or animal that is newly or recently born. **2** a timid or childish person. **3** informal a person's lover. • adj. small or very young: *baby carrots*. • v. (**babies, babying, babied**) treat someone too protectively.
– PHRASES **be left holding the baby** informal be given a responsibility that you do not want
– DERIVATIVES **babyhood** n. **babyish** adj.

baby boom • n. informal a temporary sharp rise in the birth rate, especially the one following the Second World War.

Babylonian /ba-bi-loh-ni-uhn/ • n. a person from Babylon or Babylonia, an ancient city and kingdom in Meso-potamia (part of what is now Iraq). • adj. relating to Babylon or Babylonia.

babysit • v. (**babysits, babysitting, babysat**) look after a child or children while the parents are out.
– DERIVATIVES **babysitter** n.

baccalaureate /ba-kuh-lor-i-uht/ • n. **1** an exam taken to qualify for higher education. **2** a university degree of bachelor.
– ORIGIN Latin *baccalaureus* 'bachelor'.

baccarat /bak-kuh-rah/ • n. a gambling card game in which players bet against a banker.
– ORIGIN French *baccara*.

bacchanalian /bak-kuh-nay-li-uhn/ • adj. (of a party or celebration) drunken and wild.
– ORIGIN from *Bacchus*, the Greek or Roman god of wine.

bachelor • n. **1** a man who has never been married. **2** a person who holds a first degree from a university.
– DERIVATIVES **bachelorhood** n.
– ORIGIN Old French *bacheler* 'a young man wishing to become a knight'.

bacillus /buh-sil-luhss/ • n. (pl. **bacilli** /buh-sil-lee/) a rod-shaped bacterium.
– ORIGIN Latin, 'little stick'.

back • n. **1** the rear surface of a person's body from the shoulders to the hips. **2** the upper part of an animal's body, equivalent to a person's back. **3** the side or part of something that is furthest from the front or that is not normally seen or used. **4** a player in a team game who plays in a defensive position behind the forwards. • adv. **1** in the opposite direction from that in which a person is facing or travelling. **2** so as to return to an earlier or normal position or state. **3** into the past. **4** in return. • v. **1** give support to. **2** walk or drive backwards. **3** bet money on a person or animal to win a race or contest. **4** (**back on/on to**) (of a building) have its back facing or next to. **5** cover the back of an object. **6** provide musical backing to a singer or musician. **7** (of the wind) change direction anticlockwise. • adj. **1** at or towards the back. **2** in a remote or less important position. **3** relating to the past.

– PHRASES **back and forth** to and fro. **the back of beyond** a very remote place. **back down** admit defeat. **back off** draw back from opposing someone. **back out** withdraw from something you have promised to do. **back to front** Brit. with the back at the front and the front at the back. **back something up** Computing make a spare copy of data or a disk. **behind someone's back** without a person knowing. **get** (or **put**) **someone's back up** annoy someone. **turn your back on** ignore; reject. **with your back to** (or **up against**) **the wall** in a very difficult situation.

– DERIVATIVES **backer** n.

– ORIGIN Old English.

backbencher • n. a member of parliament who does not hold a government or opposition post and who sits behind the front benches in the House of Commons.

– DERIVATIVES **backbench** adj.

backbiting • n. spiteful talk about a person who is not present.

backbone • n. **1** the spine. **2** the chief support of a system or organization. **3** strength of character.

back-breaking • adj. (of manual work) physically demanding.

back burner • n. (in phr. **on the back burner**) set aside because not very important.

backchat • n. Brit. informal rude or cheeky remarks.

backcomb • v. esp. Brit. comb the hair towards the scalp to make it look thicker.

backdate • v. (**backdates, backdating, backdated**) Brit. make something valid from an earlier date.

back door • n. (in phr. **by/through the back door**) in an underhand or secret way.

backdrop • n. **1** a painted cloth hung at the back of a theatre stage as part of the scenery. **2** the setting or background for a scene or event.

backfire • v. (**backfires, backfiring, backfired**) **1** (of a vehicle or its engine) make a bang as a result of fuel igniting wrongly. **2** (of a plan or action) produce the opposite effect to what was meant.

backgammon • n. a board game in which two players move their pieces around triangular points according to the throw of dice.

– ORIGIN from BACK + an Old English word meaning 'game'.

background • n. **1** part of a scene or description that forms a setting for the main figures or events. **2** information or circumstances that influence or explain something. **3** a person's education, experience, and social circumstances.

backhand • n. (in tennis and similar games) a stroke played with the back of the hand facing in the direction of the stroke.

backhanded • adj. **1** made with the back of the hand facing in the direction of movement. **2** expressed in a way that is indirect or has more than one meaning: *a backhanded compliment.*

backhander • n. **1** a backhand stroke or blow. **2** Brit. informal a bribe.

backing • n. **1** support. **2** a layer of material that forms or strengthens the back of something. **3** music or singing that accompanies a pop singer.

backlash • n. **1** a strong and angry reaction by a large number of people. **2** recoil or freedom of movement between parts of a machine.

backlog • n. a build-up of things needing to be dealt with.

backpack • n. a rucksack. • v. travel carrying your belongings in a rucksack.

– DERIVATIVES **backpacker** n.

back-pedal • v. **1** go back on something said or done. **2** move the pedals of a bicycle backwards.

back-seat driver • n. informal a passenger in a car who gives the driver unwanted advice.

backside • n. informal a person's bottom.

backslapping • n. hearty congratulations or praise.

backslide • v. (**backslides, backsliding, backslid**) return to former bad ways.

backspin • n. a backward spin given to a moving ball, making it stop more quickly or bounce back at a steeper angle.

back-stabbing • n. the action of criticizing someone while pretending to be friendly.

backstage • adv. & adj. behind the stage in a theatre.

backstreet • n. a less important street. • adj. secret, especially because illegal: *backstreet abortions.*

backstroke • n. a swimming stroke in which the swimmer lies on their back and lifts their arms alternately out of the water in a backward circular movement.

back-to-back • adj. **1** Brit. (of houses) built in a terrace backing on to another terrace, with a wall or an alley between. **2** following one after the other.

backtrack • v. **1** retrace your steps.

2 reverse your opinion or policy.

backup • n. 1 support. 2 a person or thing kept ready to be used when needed.

backward • adj. 1 directed towards the back. 2 having made less progress than is normal or expected. • adv. (also **backwards**) 1 towards your back. 2 back towards the starting point. 3 opposite to the usual direction or order.
– PHRASES **bend over backwards** informal try your hardest to be fair or helpful.
– DERIVATIVES **backwardly** adv. **backwardness** n.

backwash • n. waves flowing outwards behind a ship.

backwater • n. 1 a stretch of stagnant water on a river. 2 a place or state which always stays the same.

backwoods • pl. n. esp. N. Amer. 1 un-cleared forested land in a remote region. 2 a region that is remote or has few inhabitants.
– DERIVATIVES **backwoodsman** n. (pl. **backwoodsmen**).

backyard • n. 1 Brit. a yard at the back of a house. 2 N. Amer. a back garden.
– PHRASES **in your (own) backyard** informal in the area where you live.

bacon • n. salted or smoked meat from the back or sides of a pig.
– PHRASES **bring home the bacon** informal make money or achieve success.
– ORIGIN Old French.

bacteria • pl. n. (sing. **bacterium**) a group of microscopic organisms, each made up of a single cell, many kinds of which can cause disease.
– DERIVATIVES **bacterial** adj.
– ORIGIN Greek *baktērion* 'little rod'.

> **USAGE:** The word **bacteria** is the plural form of **bacterium** and it should always be used with a plural verb: *the bacteria were multiplying.*

bacteriology /bak-teer-i-**ol**-uh-ji/ • n. the study of bacteria.
– DERIVATIVES **bacteriological** adj. **bacteriologist** n.

Bactrian camel /bak-tri-uhn/ • n. a camel with two humps, found in central Asia.
– ORIGIN from the ancient empire of *Bactria* in central Asia.

bad • adj. (**worse**, **worst**) 1 poor in quality; well below standard. 2 un-pleasant. 3 severe; serious. 4 wicked or evil. 5 (**bad for**) harmful to. 6 injured, ill, or diseased. 7 (of food) decayed. 8 N. Amer. informal good; excellent.
– DERIVATIVES **badness** n.
– ORIGIN perh. from an Old English word meaning 'womanish man'.

bad blood • n. hostility or hatred between people.

bad debt • n. a debt that will not be repaid.

bade /bayd/ past of BID².

badge • n. a small flat object that a person wears to show who they are or what they do.

badger • n. a heavily built mammal with a black and white-striped head which lives underground and is active at night. • v. (**badgers**, **badgering**, **badgered**) pester someone to do something.
– ORIGIN perh. from BADGE, because of the animal's head markings.

badinage /bad-i-nahzh/ • n. witty conversation.
– ORIGIN French.

badlands • pl. n. poor land with very little soil.

badly • adv. (**worse**, **worst**) 1 in a way that is not acceptable or satisfactory. 2 severely; seriously. 3 very much.
– PHRASES **badly off** poor.

badminton • n. a game with rackets in which a shuttlecock is hit across a high net.
– ORIGIN named after *Badminton* in SW England.

bad-mouth • v. informal say unpleasant things about someone.

bad-tempered • adj. easily angered or annoyed.

baffle • v. (**baffles**, **baffling**, **baffled**) make someone feel puzzled. • n. a device for controlling or stopping the flow of sound, light, gas, or a fluid.
– DERIVATIVES **bafflement** n.
– ORIGIN perh. from French *bafouer* 'ridicule'.

bag • n. 1 a flexible container with an opening at the top. 2 (**bags**) loose folds of skin under a person's eyes. 3 (**bags of**) Brit. informal plenty of. 4 informal an unpleasant or unattractive woman. • v. (**bags**, **bagging**, **bagged**) 1 put in a bag. 2 manage to kill or catch an animal. 3 informal manage to get.
– PHRASES **in the bag** informal sure to be gained.
– ORIGIN perh. from Old Norse.

bagatelle /ba-guh-**tel**/ • n. 1 a game in which small balls are hit into numbered holes on a board. 2 something petty or unimportant.
– ORIGIN Italian *bagatella*.

bagel /**bay**-g'l/ • n. a ring-shaped bread roll with a heavy texture.
– ORIGIN Yiddish.

baggage • n. 1 luggage packed with belongings for travelling. 2 a person's past experiences or opinions seen as

weighing them down or holding them back: *emotional baggage.*
– ORIGIN Old French *bagage.*

baggy • adj. (**baggier**, **baggiest**) loose and hanging in bulges or folds.

bag lady • n. informal a homeless woman who carries her possessions in shopping bags.

bagpipe (also **bagpipes**) • n. a musical instrument with pipes that are sounded by wind squeezed from a bag.
– DERIVATIVES **bagpiper** n.

baguette /ba-get/ • n. a long, narrow French loaf of bread.
– ORIGIN French.

baht /baht/ • n. (pl. **baht**) the basic unit of money of Thailand.
– ORIGIN Thai.

bail¹ • n. **1** the temporary release of an accused person before they are tried, often on condition that a sum of money is promised to the court to make sure they attend the trial. **2** money paid to a court for this reason. • v. release an accused person on payment of bail.
– ORIGIN Old French, 'custody'.

bail² • n. **1** Cricket either of the two crosspieces resting on the stumps. **2** a bar on a typewriter or computer printer which holds the paper steady. **3** a bar separating horses in an open stable.
– ORIGIN Old French *baile* 'enclosure'.

bail³ (Brit. also **bale**) • v. **1** scoop water out of a ship or boat. **2** (**bail out**) make an emergency jump out of an aircraft, using a parachute. **3** (**bail someone/ thing out**) rescue someone or something from a difficulty.
– ORIGIN Old French *baille* 'bucket'.

bailey • n. (pl. **baileys**) the outer wall of a castle.
– ORIGIN prob. from Old French *baile* 'enclosure'.

bailiff • n. **1** esp. Brit. a sheriff's officer who delivers writs, seizes property to clear rent that is owed, and carries out arrests. **2** Brit. the agent of a landlord.
– ORIGIN Old French *baillif.*

bailiwick /bay-li-wik/ • n. **1** Law a district over which a bailiff has authority. **2** (**someone's bailiwick**) someone's area or activity or interest.
– ORIGIN from **BAILIFF.**

bairn • n. Scottish & N. English a child.
– ORIGIN Old English.

bait • n. food put on a hook or in a trap to attract fish or other animals. • v. **1** taunt or tease. **2** (as noun **baiting**) setting dogs on an animal (such as a badger or bear) that is trapped or tied up. **3** put bait on or in a trap or hook.
– PHRASES **rise to the bait** react to

taunting or temptation exactly as someone planned.
– ORIGIN Old Norse, 'pasture, food'.

baize • n. a thick green material, used for covering billiard and card tables.
– ORIGIN French *bai* 'chestnut-coloured'.

bake • v. (**bakes**, **baking**, **baked**) **1** cook food by dry heat in an oven. **2** heat something so as to dry or harden it. **3** informal be or become very hot in hot weather. • n. a dish in which a number of ingredients are mixed together and baked.
– ORIGIN Old English.

baked beans • pl. n. baked haricot beans, cooked in tomato sauce and tinned.

Bakelite • n. trademark an early form of plastic.
– ORIGIN named after Leo H. *Baekeland,* the Belgian-born American chemist who invented it.

baker • n. a person whose trade is making bread and cakes.
– PHRASES **baker's dozen** a group of thirteen.
– DERIVATIVES **bakery** n. (pl. **bakeries**).

baking powder • n. a mixture of sodium bicarbonate and cream of tartar, used to make cakes rise.

baking soda • n. sodium bicarbonate.

baksheesh /bak-sheesh/ • n. (in India and some other eastern countries) money given as charity, a tip, or a bribe.
– ORIGIN Persian.

balaclava /ba-luh-klah-vuh/ • n. a close-fitting woollen hat covering the head and neck except for the face.
– ORIGIN named after *Balaclava,* site of a battle in the Crimean War.

balalaika /ba-luh-ly-kuh/ • n. a Russian musical instrument like a guitar with a triangular body and three strings.
– ORIGIN Russian.

balance • n. **1** a state in which weight is evenly distributed, enabling a person or thing to remain steady and upright. **2** a situation in which different parts are in the correct proportions: *political balance in broadcasting.* **3** a device for weighing. **4** an amount that is the difference between money received and money spent in an account: *a healthy bank balance.* **5** an amount that is still owed when part of a debt has been paid.
• v. (**balances**, **balancing**, **balanced**) **1** be or put in a steady position. **2** compare the value of one thing with another. **3** give equal importance to two or more things. **4** compare sums of money owed and paid to an account to ensure that they are equal.
– PHRASES **be** (or **hang**) **in the balance** be

in an uncertain state. **on balance** when everything is taken into account.
– DERIVATIVES **balancer** n.
– ORIGIN from Latin *libra bilanx* 'balance having two scale pans'.

balance of payments • n. the difference in total value between payments into and out of a country over a period.

balance of power • n. **1** a situation in which states of the world have roughly equal power. **2** the power held by a small group when larger groups are of equal strength.

balance of trade • n. the difference in value between a country's imports and its exports.

balance sheet • n. a written statement setting out what a business owns and what it owes.

balcony • n. (pl. **balconies**) **1** an enclosed platform projecting from the outside of a building. **2** the highest level of seats in a theatre or cinema.
– ORIGIN Italian *balcone*.

bald • adj. **1** having no hair on the head. **2** (of an animal) not covered by the usual fur, hair, or feathers. **3** (of a tyre) having the tread worn away. **4** plain or blunt: *the bald facts*.
– DERIVATIVES **baldness** n.
– ORIGIN prob. from a former word meaning 'white patch'.

balderdash • n. nonsense.

balding • adj. going bald.

bale[1] • n. a large quantity of paper, hay, or cotton, tied or wrapped in a bundle. • v. (**bales, baling, baled**) make up paper, hay, or cotton into bales.
– DERIVATIVES **baler** n.
– ORIGIN prob. from Dutch.

bale[2] • n. & v. Brit. = BAIL[3].

baleen /buh-leen/ • n. whalebone.
– ORIGIN Latin *balaena* 'whale'.

baleen whale • n. any of the kinds of whale that have plates of whalebone in the mouth for straining plankton from the water.

baleful • adj. causing or threatening to cause harm.
– DERIVATIVES **balefully** adv.
– ORIGIN Old English.

balk • v. & n. esp. US = BAULK.

Balkan /bawl-k'n/ • adj. relating to the countries on the peninsula in SE Europe surrounded by the Adriatic, Ionian, Aegean, and the Black Seas.

ball[1] • n. **1** a rounded object that is kicked, thrown, or hit in a game. **2** a single throw or kick of the ball in a game. **3** a rounded part or thing: *the*

ball of the foot. • v. squeeze or form into a ball.
– PHRASES **on the ball** alert. **play ball** informal cooperate. **start** (or **set**) **the ball rolling** make a start.
– ORIGIN Old Norse.

ball[2] • n. a formal party for dancing.
– PHRASES **have a ball** informal have a very enjoyable time.
– ORIGIN French *bal* 'a dance'.

ballad • n. **1** a poem or song telling a popular story. **2** a slow sentimental or romantic song.
– ORIGIN Provençal *balada* 'dance, song to dance to'.

ball-and-socket joint • n. a joint in which a rounded end lies in a socket, allowing movement in all directions.

ballast • n. **1** a heavy substance carried by a ship or hot-air balloon to keep it stable. **2** gravel or coarse stone used to form the base of a railway track or road.
– ORIGIN prob. German or Scandinavian.

ball bearing • n. **1** a bearing in which the parts are separated by a ring of small metal balls which reduce rubbing. **2** a ball used in such a bearing.

ballboy (or **ballgirl**) • n. a boy (or girl) who fetches balls that go out of play during a tennis match or baseball game.

ballcock • n. a valve which automatically tops up a cistern when liquid is drawn from it.

ballerina • n. a female ballet dancer.

ballet • n. **1** an artistic form of dancing performed to music, using set steps and gestures. **2** a creative work in this form.
– DERIVATIVES **balletic** adj.
– ORIGIN Italian *balletto* 'a little dance'.

ballistic /buh-liss-tik/ • adj. relating to the flight through the air of missiles, bullets, or similar objects. • n. (**ballistics**) the science of missiles and firearms.
– PHRASES **go ballistic** informal fly into a rage.
– ORIGIN Greek *ballein* 'to throw'.

ballistic missile • n. a missile which is powered and guided when first launched, but falls under gravity on to its target.

balloon • n. **1** a small rubber bag which is inflated and used as a toy or a decoration. **2** (also **hot-air balloon**) a large bag filled with hot air or gas to make it rise in the air, with a basket attached to it for carrying passengers. **3** a rounded outline in which the words or thoughts of characters in a comic strip are written. • v. **1** swell outwards. **2** increase rapidly. **3** (as noun **ballooning**) travelling by hot-air balloon.
– DERIVATIVES **balloonist** n.
– ORIGIN French *ballon* 'large ball'.

ballot • n. **1** a way of voting on something secretly, usually by placing paper slips in a box. **2** (**the ballot**) the total number of votes cast in this way. • v. (**ballots, balloting, balloted**) obtain a secret vote from the members of an organization.
– ORIGIN Italian *ballotta* 'little ball' (from the former practice of voting by placing a ball in a container).

ballpark • n. **1** N. Amer. a baseball ground. **2** informal an area or range within which an estimate is likely to be correct. • adj. informal approximate: *a ballpark figure*.

ballpoint pen • n. a pen with a tiny ball as its writing point.

ballroom • n. a large room for formal dancing.

ballroom dancing • n. formal dancing in couples.

ballyhoo • n. informal excessive publicity or fuss.

balm • n. **1** a sweet-smelling ointment used to heal or soothe the skin. **2** something that soothes or heals.
– ORIGIN Latin *balsamum* 'balsam'.

balmy • adj. (of the weather) pleasantly warm.

baloney /buh-loh-ni/ • n. informal nonsense.
– ORIGIN perh. from *bologna*, a type of smoked sausage.

balsa /bawl-suh/ (also **balsa wood**) • n. very lightweight wood from a tropical American tree, used for making models.
– ORIGIN Spanish, 'raft'.

balsam /bawl-suhm/ • n. a scented resin obtained from some trees and shrubs, used in perfumes and medicines.
– DERIVATIVES **balsamic** /bawl-sam-ik/ adj.
– ORIGIN Greek *balsamon*.

balsamic vinegar • n. dark, sweet Italian vinegar.

balti /bawl-ti, bal-ti/ • n. (pl. **baltis**) a spicy Pakistani dish that is cooked in a small two-handled pan.
– ORIGIN Urdu, 'pail'.

Baltic /bawl-tik/ • adj. relating to the Baltic Sea or those states on its eastern shores.

baluster /ba-luh-ster/ • n. a short pillar forming part of a series supporting a rail.
– ORIGIN French *balustre*.

balustrade /ba-luh-strayd/ • n. a railing supported by balusters.

bamboo • n. a giant tropical grass with hollow woody stems.
– ORIGIN Malay.

bamboozle • v. (**bamboozles,**

bamboozling, bamboozled) informal cheat or deceive someone.

ban • v. (**bans, banning, banned**) forbid officially. • n. an official order forbidding something.
– ORIGIN Old English, 'call for by a public proclamation'.

banal /buh-nahl/ • adj. boring because not new or original.
– DERIVATIVES **banality** n. (pl. **banalities**).
– ORIGIN first meaning 'compulsory': from French *ban* 'proclamation'.

banana • n. a long curved fruit of a tropical tree, with yellow skin and soft flesh.
– PHRASES **go bananas** informal become mad or angry.
– ORIGIN from an African language.

band[1] • n. **1** a flat, thin strip or loop of material used as a fastener, for strengthening, or as decoration. **2** a stripe or strip of a different colour or nature from its surroundings: *a band of cloud.* **3** a range of values or frequencies within a series: *the lower-rate tax band.* • v. **1** put a band on or round. **2** mark with a stripe or stripes. **3** put in a range or category.
– ORIGIN Old English.

band[2] • n. **1** a small group of musicians and singers who play pop, jazz, or rock music. **2** a group of musicians who play brass, wind, or percussion instruments. **3** a group of people with the same aim or a shared feature. • v. form a group to achieve the same aim.
– ORIGIN Old French *bande*.

bandage • n. a strip of material used to tie around a wound or to protect an injury. • v. (**bandages, bandaging, bandaged**) tie a bandage around.
– ORIGIN French.

bandanna /ban-dan-nuh/ (also **bandana**) • n. a square of brightly coloured fabric worn on the head or around the neck.
– ORIGIN Hindi.

B. & B. • abbrev. bed and breakfast.

bandeau /ban-doh/ • n. (pl. **bandeaux** /ban-dohz/) **1** a narrow band worn round the head. **2** a woman's strapless top.
– ORIGIN Old French *bandel* 'small band'.

bandicoot /ban-di-koot/ • n. an insect-eating marsupial (mammal) found in Australia and New Guinea.
– ORIGIN from a word in an Indian language, meaning 'pig-rat'.

bandit /ban-dit/ • n. a member of a gang of armed robbers.
– DERIVATIVES **banditry** n.
– ORIGIN Italian *bandito* 'banned'.

bandolier /ban-duh-leer/ (also **bandoleer**) • n. a shoulder belt with

loops or pockets for cartridges.
– ORIGIN French *bandoulière*.

bandsaw • n. a power saw consisting of an endless moving steel belt with a serrated edge.

bandstand • n. a covered outdoor platform for a band to play on.

bandwagon • n. an activity or cause that has suddenly become fashionable or popular: *the company is jumping on the Green bandwagon.*

bandwidth • n. 1 a range of frequencies used in telecommunications. 2 the ability of a computer network or other telecommunications system to transmit signals.

bandy¹ • adj. (of a person's legs) curved outwards so that the knees are wide apart.
– ORIGIN perh. from a former word meaning 'curved hockey stick'.

bandy² • v. (**bandies, bandying, bandied**) mention an idea, term, or name frequently or in a casual way.
– PHRASES **bandy words** exchange angry remarks.
– ORIGIN perh. from French *bander* 'take sides at tennis'.

bane • n. a cause of great distress or annoyance.
– ORIGIN Old English.

bang • n. 1 a sudden loud sharp noise. 2 a sudden painful blow. • v. 1 hit or put down forcefully and noisily. 2 make or cause to make a bang. • adv. informal, esp. Brit. exactly: *bang on time.*
– PHRASES **bang on** Brit. informal exactly right.

banger • n. Brit. informal 1 a sausage. 2 an old car. 3 a loud explosive firework.

Bangladeshi /bang-gluh-**desh**-i/ • n. (pl. **Bangladeshis**) a person from Bangladesh. • adj. relating to Bangladesh.

bangle • n. a rigid band worn around the arm as jewellery.
– ORIGIN Hindi.

banish • v. 1 make someone leave a place, especially as an official punishment. 2 get rid of; drive away.
– DERIVATIVES **banishment** n.
– ORIGIN Old French *banir*.

banister (also **bannister**) • n. 1 the upright posts and handrail at the side of a staircase. 2 a single upright post at the side of a staircase.
– ORIGIN from **BALUSTER**.

banjo • n. (pl. **banjos** or **banjoes**) a musical instrument like a guitar, with five strings, a circular body, and a long neck.
– DERIVATIVES **banjoist** n.

– ORIGIN from *bandore*, a kind of lute.

bank¹ • n. 1 the land alongside a river or lake. 2 a long, high slope, mound, or mass: *mud banks.* 3 a set of similar things grouped together in rows. • v. 1 make or form into a bank. 2 (of an aircraft or vehicle) tilt sideways in making a turn.
– ORIGIN Old Norse.

bank² • n. 1 an organization offering financial services, especially loans and the safekeeping of customers' money. 2 a stock or supply available for use: *a blood bank.* 3 a site or container where something may be left for recycling: *a paper bank.* • v. 1 place in a bank. 2 have an account at a bank. 3 (**bank on**) rely on.
– PHRASES **break the bank** informal cost more than someone can afford.
– ORIGIN Latin *banca* 'bench' (first meaning a money dealer's table).

bankable • adj. certain to bring profit and success.
– DERIVATIVES **bankability** n.

bank card • n. a cheque card.

banker • n. a person who manages or owns a bank.

bank holiday • n. Brit. a public holiday, when banks are officially closed.

banking • n. the business activity of a bank.

banknote • n. a piece of paper money issued by a central bank.

bank rate • n. = BASE RATE.

bankroll • v. informal support financially. • n. N. Amer. available funds.

bankrupt • adj. 1 officially declared not to have enough money to pay your debts. 2 completely lacking in a particular good quality or value: *morally bankrupt.* • n. a bankrupt person. • v. make a person or organization bankrupt.
– DERIVATIVES **bankruptcy** n. (pl. **bankruptcies**).
– ORIGIN from Italian *banca rotta* 'broken bench' or 'broken bank'.

banner • n. a long strip of cloth with a slogan or design, hung up or carried on poles.
– ORIGIN Old French *baniere*.

bannister • n. = BANISTER.

banns • pl. n. a public announcement of an intended marriage read out in a parish church.
– ORIGIN plural of BAN.

banquet /**bang**-kwit/ • n. an elaborate, formal meal for many people. • v. (**banquets, banqueting, banqueted**) give or take part in a banquet.
– ORIGIN French, 'little bench'.

b

banquette /bang-ket/ • n. a padded bench along a wall.
– ORIGIN Italian *banchetta* 'little bench'.

banshee • n. (in Irish legend) a female spirit whose wailing warns that someone is going to die.
– ORIGIN from Old Irish *ben síde* 'woman of the fairies'.

bantam • n. a chicken of a small breed.
– ORIGIN prob. named after the province of *Bantam* in Java.

bantamweight • n. a weight in boxing and other sports, coming between flyweight and featherweight.

banter • n. friendly teasing between people. • v. (**banters, bantering, bantered**) make friendly teasing remarks.

Bantu /ban-too/ • n. (pl. **Bantu** or **Bantus**)
1 a member of a large group of peoples living in central and southern Africa.
2 the group of languages spoken by the Bantu.
– ORIGIN Bantu, 'people'.

> **USAGE: Bantu** is a very offensive word in South African English, especially when used to refer to individual black people.

banyan /ban-yan/ • n. an Indian fig tree with spreading branches from which roots grow downwards to the ground and form new trunks.
– ORIGIN Gujarati, 'trader' (because first used by Europeans to refer to a tree under which traders had built a pagoda).

baobab /bay-oh-bab/ • n. a short African tree with a very thick trunk and large fruit.
– ORIGIN prob. from an African language.

bap • n. Brit. a soft, round, flattish bread roll.

baptism • n. the Christian ceremony of sprinkling a person with water or dipping them in it, as a sign that they have been cleansed of sin and have entered the Church.
– PHRASES **baptism of fire** a difficult new experience.
– DERIVATIVES **baptismal** adj.
– ORIGIN Greek *baptizein*.

Baptist • n. a member of a Protestant group believing that only adults should be baptized and that this should be done by submerging them completely in water.

baptistery (also **baptistry**) • n. (pl. **baptisteries**) a building or part of a church used for baptism.

baptize (or **baptise**) • v. (**baptizes, baptizing, baptized**) **1** perform the ceremony of baptism on someone. **2** give someone a name or nickname.

bar¹ • n. **1** a long rigid piece of wood, metal, etc. **2** a counter, room, or place where alcohol or food and drink is served. **3** a small shop or counter serving food and drink or providing a service: *a snack bar.* **4** something that stops or delays progress. **5** any of the short units into which a piece of music is divided, shown on a sheet of music by vertical lines. **6** (**the bar**) the place in a court room where an accused person stands during a trial. **7** (**the Bar**) the profession of barrister, or barristers or (in America) lawyers as a group. **8** Brit. a metal strip added to a medal as an additional honour. • v. (**bars, barring, barred**) **1** fasten with a bar or bars. **2** forbid or prevent. • prep. esp. Brit. except for.
– PHRASES **be called** (or **go**) **to the Bar** Brit. be allowed to practise as a barrister.
behind bars in prison.
– ORIGIN Old French *barre*.

bar² • n. a unit of pressure equivalent to 100,000 newtons per square metre.
– ORIGIN Greek *baros* 'weight'.

barb • n. **1** a backward-pointing part of an arrowhead, fish hook, or similar object, that makes it difficult to take out from something it has pierced. **2** a spiteful remark.
– ORIGIN Latin *barba* 'beard'.

barbarian /bar-bair-i-uhn/ • n. **1** (in ancient times) a member of a people not belonging to the Greek, Roman, or Christian civilizations. **2** an uncivilized or cruel person. • adj. uncivilized or cruel.
– ORIGIN Greek *barbaros* 'foreign'.

barbaric /bar-ba-rik/ • adj. **1** savagely cruel. **2** lacking culture; coarse.

barbarism /bar-buh-ri-z'm/ • n. **1** great cruelty. **2** an uncivilized or primitive state.
– DERIVATIVES **barbarity** n. (pl. **barbarities**).

barbarous /bar-buh-ruhss/ • adj. **1** very cruel. **2** primitive; uncivilized.

barbecue • n. **1** an outdoor meal or party at which food is grilled over a charcoal fire. **2** a grill used at a barbecue. • v. (**barbecues, barbecuing, barbecued**) cook food on a barbecue.
– ORIGIN Spanish *barbacoa* 'wooden frame'.

barbed • adj. **1** having a barb or barbs. **2** (of a remark) spiteful.

barbed wire • n. wire with clusters of short, sharp spikes along it.

barbel /bar-b'l/ • n. **1** a long, thin growth hanging from the mouth or snout of some fish. **2** a large freshwater fish with barbels.
– ORIGIN Latin *barbellus* 'small barbel'.

b

barbell /bar-bel/ •n. a long metal bar to which discs of different weights are attached at each end, used for weightlifting.

barber •n. a person whose job is cutting men's hair and shaving or trimming their beards.
– ORIGIN Old French *barbe* 'beard'.

barbican /bar-bi-kuhn/ •n. a double tower above a gate or drawbridge of a castle or fortified city.
– ORIGIN Old French *barbacane*.

barbiturate /bar-bit-yuu-ruht/ •n. a kind of sedative drug.
– ORIGIN German *Barbitursäure*.

bar chart (also esp. N. Amer. **bar graph**) •n. a diagram in which different quantities are shown by rectangles of varying height.

bar code •n. a set of stripes printed on a product, able to be read by a computer to provide information on prices and quantities in stock.

bard •n. **1** old use or literary a poet. **2** (**the Bard**) Shakespeare. **3** (**Bard**) the winner of a prize for Welsh verse at an Eisteddfod.
– DERIVATIVES **bardic** adj.
– ORIGIN Celtic.

bare •adj. **1** not wearing clothes. **2** without the proper or usual covering or contents: *a big, bare room.* **3** without detail; basic. **4** only just enough: *the bare minimum.* •v. (**bares, baring, bared**) uncover or reveal.
– PHRASES **with your bare hands** without using tools or weapons.
– DERIVATIVES **barely** adv. **bareness** n.
– ORIGIN Old English.

bareback •adv. & adj. on a horse without a saddle.

barefaced •adj. done openly and without shame: *a barefaced lie.*

barefoot (also **barefooted**)
•adj. wearing nothing on the feet.

bargain •n. **1** an agreement made between people saying what each will do for the other. **2** a thing bought or put on sale at a low price. •v. **1** discuss the terms of an agreement. **2** (**bargain for/on**) expect.
– PHRASES **drive a hard bargain** press hard for a deal in your favour. **into the bargain** as well.
– ORIGIN Old French *bargaine*.

barge •n. a long flat-bottomed boat for carrying goods on canals and rivers. •v. (**barges, barging, barged**) **1** move forcefully or roughly. **2** (**barge in**) burst in on someone rudely or awkwardly.
– ORIGIN Old French.

bargee /bar-jee/ •n. esp. Brit. a person in charge of or working on a barge.

bargepole •n. a long pole used to push a barge along.
– PHRASES **would not touch someone/ thing with a bargepole** informal would not want to have anything to do with someone or something.

bar graph •n. esp. N. Amer. a bar chart.

barista /bar-is-tuh/ •n. a person who serves in a coffee bar.
– ORIGIN Italian, 'barman'.

baritone •n. a man's singing voice between tenor and bass. •adj. referring to a musical instrument that is second lowest in pitch in its family: *a baritone sax.*
– ORIGIN from Greek *barus* 'heavy' + *tonos* 'tone'.

barium /bair-i-uhm/ •n. a soft white metallic chemical element.
– ORIGIN Greek *barus* 'heavy'.

barium meal •n. a substance containing barium, which is swallowed so that the stomach or intestines can be seen on an X-ray.

bark[1] •n. the sharp sudden cry of a dog, fox, or seal. •v. **1** give a bark. **2** shout something in a fierce or sudden way.
– PHRASES **someone's bark is worse than their bite** someone is not as fierce as they seem. **be barking up the wrong tree** informal be doing or thinking something that is incorrect.
– ORIGIN Old English.

bark[2] •n. the tough outer covering of the trunk and branches of a tree. •v. scrape the skin off the knee or shin by accidentally knocking against something.
– ORIGIN Old Norse.

barker •n. informal a person at a fair who calls out to passers-by to persuade them to visit a sideshow.

barking •adj. Brit. informal completely mad.

barley •n. a type of cereal plant with bristly heads, the grains of which are used in brewing and animal feed.
– ORIGIN Old English.

barley sugar •n. an orange sweet made of boiled sugar.

barmaid •n. a woman who serves drinks in a bar or pub.

barman •n. (pl. **barmen**) esp. Brit. a man who serves drinks in a bar or pub.

bar mitzvah /bar mits-vuh/ •n. a religious ceremony in which a Jewish boy aged 13 takes on the responsibilities of an adult under Jewish law.
– ORIGIN Hebrew, 'son of the commandment'.

barmy •adj. (**barmier, barmiest**) Brit. informal mad.
– ORIGIN Old English, from a word

meaning 'froth on fermenting malt liquor'.

barn • n. a large farm building used for storing hay or grain or housing livestock.
– ORIGIN Old English, 'barley house'.

barnacle /bar-nuh-k'l/ • n. a small shellfish which fixes itself to rocks and other underwater surfaces.
– ORIGIN Latin *bernaca*.

barnacle goose • n. a goose with a white face and black neck.
– ORIGIN because the bird was once thought to hatch from barnacles.

barn dance • n. 1 a party with country dancing. 2 a dance for a number of couples moving round a circle.

barnet /bar-nit/ • n. Brit. informal a person's hair.
– ORIGIN from rhyming slang *barnet fair* (a horse fair held at *Barnet*, Herts.).

barney • n. (pl. **barneys**) Brit. informal a noisy quarrel.

barn owl • n. a pale-coloured owl with a heart-shaped face.

barnstorm • v. esp. N. Amer. 1 tour country districts putting on shows or giving flying displays. 2 make a rapid tour as part of a political campaign.

barnstorming • adj. done in a very showy, forceful, and successful way.

barnyard • n. esp. N. Amer. a farmyard.

barograph /ba-ruh-grahf/ • n. a barometer that records its readings on a moving chart.

barometer /buh-rom-i-ter/ • n. 1 an instrument that measures the pressure of the atmosphere, used to forecast the weather. 2 something that indicates change: *furniture is a barometer of changing tastes*.
– DERIVATIVES **barometric** adj.
– ORIGIN Greek *baros* 'weight'.

baron • n. 1 a man belonging to the lowest rank of the British nobility. 2 (in the Middle Ages) a man who held lands or property from the sovereign or an overlord. 3 a powerful person in business or industry: *a press baron*.
– DERIVATIVES **baronial** /buh-roh-ni-uhl/ adj.
– ORIGIN Latin *baro* 'man, warrior'.

baroness • n. 1 the wife or widow of a baron. 2 a woman holding the rank of baron.

baronet • n. a man who holds a title below that of baron.

baronetcy • n. (pl. **baronetcies**) the rank of a baronet.

barony • n. (pl. **baronies**) the rank and lands of a baron.

baroque /buh-rok/ • n. a highly decor-ated style of European architecture, art, and music of the 17th and 18th centuries. • adj. 1 relating to the baroque. 2 very elaborate or showy.
– ORIGIN French.

barque /bark/ • n. 1 a sailing ship with three masts. 2 literary a boat.
– ORIGIN Latin *barca* 'ship's boat'.

barrack[1] • v. provide soldiers with some-where to stay. • n. (**barracks**) a large building or group of buildings for housing soldiers.
– ORIGIN Spanish *barraca* 'soldier's tent'.

barrack[2] • v. Brit. shout loud insulting comments at a performer or speaker.
– ORIGIN prob. from Northern Irish dialect.

barracuda /ba-ruh-koo-duh/ • n. (pl. **barracuda** or **barracudas**) a large fish of tropical seas that preys on other fish.

barrage /ba-rahzh/ • n. 1 a continuous attack by heavy guns over a wide area. 2 an overwhelming number of questions or complaints coming one after the other. 3 a barrier placed across a river to control the water level.
– ORIGIN French.

barre /bar/ • n. a horizontal bar at waist level used by ballet dancers during exercises.
– ORIGIN French.

barrel • n. 1 a large cylindrical container bulging out in the middle and with flat ends. 2 a measure of capacity for oil and beer (36 imperial gallons for beer and 35 for oil). 3 a tube forming part of an object such as a gun.
– PHRASES **over a barrel** informal at a great disadvantage.
– ORIGIN Latin *barriclus* 'small cask'.

barrel organ • n. a small pipe organ that plays a set tune when a handle is turned.

barren • adj. 1 (of land) too poor to produce vegetation. 2 (of a female animal) not able to produce offspring. 3 bleak and lifeless. 4 unproductive or meaningless: *a barren spell*.
– DERIVATIVES **barrenness** n.
– ORIGIN Old French *barhaine*.

barrette /ba-ret/ • n. a hairslide.
– ORIGIN French, 'small bar'.

barricade /ba-ri-kayd/ • n. a make-shift barrier set up to block a road or entrance. • v. (**barricades**, **barricading**, **barricaded**) block or defend with a barricade.
– ORIGIN French.

barrier • n. 1 an obstacle that prevents movement or access. 2 an obstacle to communication or progress: *a language barrier*.
– ORIGIN Old French *barriere*.

barrier cream • n. Brit. a cream used to

protect the skin from damage or infection.

barrier reef •n. a coral reef close to the shore but separated from it by a channel of deep water.

barring •prep. except for; if not for.

barrister /ba-riss-ter/ •n. esp. Brit. a lawyer who is qualified to argue a case in court. Compare with SOLICITOR.
– ORIGIN from BAR¹.

barrow¹ •n. Brit. a two-wheeled cart pushed by hand and used by street traders.
– ORIGIN Old English.

barrow² •n. an ancient burial mound.
– ORIGIN Old English.

bartender •n. a person serving drinks at a bar.
– DERIVATIVES **bartending** n.

barter •v. (**barters, bartering, bartered**) exchange goods or services for other goods or services. •n. trading by bartering.
– ORIGIN prob. from Old French *barater* 'deceive'.

basal /bay-s'l/ •adj. forming or belonging to a base.

basalt /ba-sawlt/ •n. a dark fine-grained volcanic rock.
– DERIVATIVES **basaltic** /buh-sawl-tik/ adj.
– ORIGIN Latin *basaltes*.

base¹ •n. 1 the lowest or supporting part of something. 2 a foundation, support, or starting point: *the town's economic base collapsed.* 3 the main place where a person works or stays. 4 a centre of operations: *a military base.* 5 a main element to which others are added. 6 Chem. a substance able to react with an acid to form a salt and water. 7 Math. the number on which a system of counting is based, for example 10 in conventional notation. 8 Baseball each of the four stations that must be reached in turn to score a run. •v. (**bases, basing, based**) 1 use something as the foundation for something else. 2 put at a centre of operations.
– ORIGIN Greek *basis* 'base, pedestal'.

base² •adj. 1 bad or immoral. 2 old use of low social class.
– ORIGIN Latin *bassus* 'short'.

baseball •n. a game played with a bat and ball on a diamond-shaped circuit of four bases, around all of which a batsman must run to score.

baseball cap •n. a cotton cap with a large peak.

baseless •adj. not based on fact; untrue.

baseline •n. 1 a starting point for comparisons. 2 (in tennis, volleyball, etc.) the line marking each end of a court.

basement •n. a room or floor below ground level.

base metal •n. a common non-precious metal such as copper or tin.

base rate •n. the interest rate set by the Bank of England for lending to other banks, used as the basis for interest rates generally.

bases pl. of BASE¹ and BASIS.

bash informal •v. hit hard. •n. 1 a heavy blow. 2 a party. 3 Brit. an attempt: *she'll have a bash at anything.*
– ORIGIN perh. from BANG and SMASH.

bashful •adj. shy and easily embarrassed.
– DERIVATIVES **bashfully** adv. **bashfulness** n.
– ORIGIN from ABASHED.

BASIC •n. a high-level computer programming language.
– ORIGIN from *Beginners' All-purpose Symbolic Instruction Code.*

basic •adj. 1 forming an essential foundation; fundamental. 2 consisting of the minimum needed or offered: *a basic wage.* 3 containing or having the properties of a chemical base; alkaline. •n. (**basics**) essential facts or principles.

basically •adv. 1 in the most funda-mental respects. 2 used to sum up a situation: *I basically did the same thing every day.*

basil •n. a herb with leaves that are used in cookery.
– ORIGIN Greek *basilikos* 'royal'.

basilica /buh-zil-i-kuh/ •n. 1 (in ancient Rome) a large oblong building with two rows of columns and a curved end. 2 a Christian church of a similar design.
– ORIGIN Latin, 'royal palace'.

basilisk /baz-i-lisk/ •n. a mythical reptile whose look or breath could kill.
– ORIGIN Greek *basiliskos* 'little king, serpent'.

basin •n. 1 a large bowl or open con-tainer for preparing food or holding liquid. 2 a circular valley or natural depression. 3 an area drained by a river and its tributaries. 4 an enclosed area of water for mooring boats.
– ORIGIN Latin *bacinus*.

basis /bay-siss/ •n. (pl. **bases** /bay-seez/) 1 the underlying support for an idea or process. 2 the principles according to which an activity is carried on: *she needs coaching on a regular basis.*
– ORIGIN Greek, 'step, pedestal'.

bask •v. (usu. **bask in**) 1 lie in warmth and sunlight for pleasure. 2 take great pleasure in something.
– ORIGIN perh. from Old Norse, 'bathe'.

basket •n. 1 a container for carrying

things, made from woven cane or wire. **2** a net fixed on a hoop, used as the goal in basketball.
– ORIGIN Old French.

basketball • n. a team game in which goals are scored by throwing a ball through a hoop.

basket case • n. informal a useless person or thing.
– ORIGIN first referring to a soldier who had lost all four limbs.

basketry • n. **1** the craft of basket-making. **2** baskets as a whole.

basketwork • n. material woven in the style of a basket.

basking shark • n. a large shark which feeds on plankton and swims slowly close to the surface.

basmati rice /baz-mah-ti/ • n. a kind of long-grain Indian rice with a delicate fragrance.
– ORIGIN Hindi, 'fragrant'.

Basque /bask, bahsk/ • n. **1** a member of a people living in the western Pyrenees in France and Spain. **2** the language of the Basques.
– ORIGIN Latin *Vasco* 'inhabitant of Vasconia' (the Latin name also of Gascony in France).

basque /bask/ • n. a woman's close-fitting bodice.
– ORIGIN from **Basque**, referring to traditional Basque dress.

bas-relief /bass-ri-leef/ • n. Art low relief.
– ORIGIN Italian *basso-rilievo*.

bass¹ /bayss/ • n. **1** the lowest adult male singing voice. **2** informal a bass guitar or double bass. **3** the low-frequency output of transmitted or reproduced sound. • adj. referring to a musical instrument that is the lowest in pitch in its family: *a bass clarinet*.
– DERIVATIVES **bassist** n.
– ORIGIN from **BASE²**.

bass² /bass/ • n. (pl. **bass** or **basses**) the common freshwater perch (fish).
– ORIGIN Germanic.

bass clef • n. Music a clef placing F below middle C on the second-highest line of the stave.

basset hound • n. a breed of hunting dog with a long body, short legs, and long ears.
– ORIGIN from French *bas* 'low'.

bassoon /buh-**soon**/ • n. a large bass woodwind instrument with a double reed.
– DERIVATIVES **bassoonist** n.
– ORIGIN Italian *bassone*.

bastard • n. **1** old use or derog. a person born of unmarried parents. **2** informal an unpleasant person. • adj. no longer in a pure or original form.
– ORIGIN Latin *bastardus*.

bastardize (or **bastardise**)
• v. (**bastardizes, bastardizing, bastardized**) make impure by adding new elements.
– DERIVATIVES **bastardization** n.

baste¹ • v. (**bastes, basting, basted**) pour fat or juices over meat during cooking.

baste² • v. (**bastes, basting, basted**) sew with long, loose stitches in preparation for permanent sewing.
– ORIGIN Old French *bastir* 'sew lightly'.

bastion /bass-ti-uhn/ • n. **1** a projecting part of a fortification allowing an increased angle of fire. **2** something that protects or preserves particular principles or activities: *the town was a bastion of Conservatism*.
– ORIGIN Italian *bastione*.

bat¹ • n. an implement with a handle and a solid surface, used in sports for hitting the ball. • v. (**bats, batting, batted**) **1** (in sport) take the role of hitting the ball rather than throwing it. **2** hit with the flat of the hand.
– PHRASES **off your own bat** Brit. informal of your own accord.
– ORIGIN Old English, 'club, stick, staff'.

bat² • n. **1** a flying mammal that is active at night. **2** (**old bat**) informal a disliked woman.
– ORIGIN Scandinavian; sense 2 is from an old slang term for 'prostitute', or from **BATTLEAXE**.

bat³ • v. (**bats, batting, batted**) flutter the eyelashes.
– PHRASES **not bat an eyelid** informal show no surprise or concern.
– ORIGIN Old French *batre* 'to beat'.

batch • n. **1** a quantity of goods produced or dispatched at one time. **2** a group of people or things.
– ORIGIN Old English.

bated • adj. (in phr. **with bated breath**) in great suspense.
– ORIGIN from **ABATE**.

> ✓ The correct spelling is **with bated breath** (not *baited*).

bath • n. **1** a large tub that is filled with water for washing the body. **2** an act of washing in a bath. **3** (also **baths**) Brit. a building containing a public swimming pool or washing facilities. • v. Brit. wash in a bath.
– ORIGIN Old English.

bathe /bayth/ • v. (**bathes, bathing, bathed**) **1** wash by immersing the body in water. **2** Brit. take a swim. **3** soak or wipe gently with liquid to clean or soothe. • n. Brit. a swim.
– DERIVATIVES **bather** n.
– ORIGIN Old English.

bathos /bay-thoss/ • n. (in literature) a change in mood from the important and serious to the trivial or ridiculous.
– DERIVATIVES **bathetic** /buh-thet-ik/ adj.
– ORIGIN Greek, 'depth'.

bathrobe • n. a towelling dressing gown.

bathroom • n. **1** a room containing a bath, washbasin, and toilet. **2** N. Amer. a room containing a toilet.

bathysphere /bath-i-sfeer/ • n. a spherical vessel used for deep-sea observation.
– ORIGIN from Greek *bathus* 'deep'.

batik /ba-teek/ • n. a method of producing coloured designs on cloth by waxing the parts not to be dyed.
– ORIGIN Javanese, 'painted'.

batman • n. (pl. **batmen**) dated (in the British armed forces) an officer's personal attendant.
– ORIGIN Old French *bat* 'saddle for carrying loads'.

baton • n. **1** a thin stick used to conduct an orchestra or choir. **2** a short stick passed from runner to runner in a relay race.
– ORIGIN Latin *bastum* 'stick'.

batsman • n. (pl. **batsmen**) a player who bats in cricket.

battalion /buh-tal-i-uhn/ • n. a large body of troops, forming part of a brigade.
– ORIGIN French *bataillon*.

batten • n. a long wooden or metal strip that is used to strengthen or secure something.
– PHRASES **batten down the hatches** prepare for a difficult situation.
– ORIGIN Old French *batre* 'to beat'.

batter¹ • v. (**batters, battering, battered**) **1** hit hard and repeatedly. **2** damage or harm something.
– DERIVATIVES **batterer** n.
– ORIGIN Old French *batre* 'to beat'.

batter² • n. a mixture of flour, egg, and milk or water, used for making pancakes or coating food before frying.
– DERIVATIVES **battered** adj.
– ORIGIN Old French *batre* 'to beat'.

battering ram • n. a heavy object swung or rammed against a door to break it down.

battery • n. (pl. **batteries**) **1** a device containing one or more electrical cells, for use as a source of power. **2** an extensive series: *a battery of tests.* **3** Brit. a set of small cages for keeping poultry in a relatively small space. **4** Law the crime of physically attacking another person. **5** a group of heavy guns.
– ORIGIN Latin *battuere* 'to beat'.

battle • n. **1** a prolonged fight between organized armed forces. **2** a long and

difficult struggle: *a battle of wits.*
• v. (**battles, battling, battled**) fight or struggle with determination.
– DERIVATIVES **battler** n.
– ORIGIN Old French *bataille*.

battleaxe • n. **1** a large axe used in ancient warfare. **2** informal an aggressive older woman.

battledress • n. combat dress worn by soldiers.

battlefield (also **battleground**) • n. the piece of ground on which a battle is fought.

battlement • n. a parapet at the top of a wall with gaps for firing from.
– ORIGIN Old French *bataillier* 'fortify'.

battleship • n. a heavily armoured warship with large guns.

batty • adj. (**battier, battiest**) informal mad.
– DERIVATIVES **battiness** n.
– ORIGIN from **BAT**².

batwing • adj. (of a sleeve) having a deep armhole and a tight cuff.

bauble /baw-b'l/ • n. a small, showy trinket or decoration.
– ORIGIN Old French *baubel* 'child's toy'.

baud /rhymes with code/ • n. (pl. **baud** or **bauds**) Computing a unit of transmission speed for electronic signals, corresponding to one information unit or event per second.
– ORIGIN named after the French engineer Jean *Baudot*.

baulk /bawlk/ (esp. US also **balk**)
• v. **1** (**baulk at**) hesitate to accept an idea. **2** thwart or hinder a plan or person.
– ORIGIN Old Norse, 'partition'.

bauxite /bawk-syt/ • n. a clay-like rock from which aluminium is obtained.
– ORIGIN from the French village of *Les Baux*, where it was first found.

bawdy • adj. (**bawdier, bawdiest**) dealing with sex in an amusing way.
– DERIVATIVES **bawdiness** n.
– ORIGIN Old French *baude* 'shameless'.

bawl • v. **1** shout out noisily. **2** (**bawl someone out**) reprimand someone angrily. **3** weep noisily. • n. a loud shout.

bay¹ • n. a broad curved inlet of the sea.
– ORIGIN Old French *baie*.

bay² (also **bay laurel**) • n. an evergreen Mediterranean shrub, with leaves that are used in cookery.
– ORIGIN Old French *baie*.

bay³ • n. **1** a window area that projects outwards from a wall. **2** an area allocated for a purpose: *a loading bay.*
– ORIGIN Old French *baie*.

bay⁴ • adj. (of a horse) reddish-brown with black points. • n. a bay horse.
– ORIGIN Old French *bai*.

bay⁵ • v. (of a dog) howl loudly.
– PHRASES **at bay** trapped or cornered.
hold (or **keep**) **someone/thing at bay**
prevent someone or something from
approaching or having an effect.
– ORIGIN Old French *abaiier* 'to bark'.

bayonet • n. a long blade that is fixed to
a rifle for hand-to-hand fighting.
• v. (**bayonets, bayoneting, bayoneted**)
stab with a bayonet.
– ORIGIN French *baïonnette* 'dagger',
named after the French town of
Bayonne, where they were first made.

bay window • n. a window built to
project outwards from a wall.

bazaar /buh-**zar**/ • n. **1** a market in a
Middle Eastern country. **2** a sale of
goods to raise money for charity.
– ORIGIN Persian, 'market'.

bazooka • n. a short-range rocket
launcher used against tanks.
– ORIGIN prob. from US slang *bazoo*
'kazoo'.

BBC • abbrev. British Broadcasting
Corporation.

BC • abbrev. before Christ (used to show
that a date comes the specified number
of years before the traditional date of
Jesus's birth).

> **USAGE: BC** is normally written in small
> capitals and placed **after** the numerals, as
> in *72 BC.*

Be • symb. the chemical element
beryllium.

be • v. (sing. present **am; are; is**; pl. present **are**;
1st and 3rd sing. past **was**; 2nd sing. past and pl.
past **were**; present subjunctive **be**; past subjunctive
were; present part. **being**; past part. **been**)
1 exist; be present. **2** happen. **3** have the
specified state, nature, or role: *I want to
be a teacher.* **4** come; go; visit. • auxiliary
verb **1** used with a present participle to
form continuous tenses: *they are coming.*
2 used with a past participle to form the
passive voice: *it is said.* **3** used to show
something that is due to, may, or should
happen.
– PHRASES **the be-all and end-all** informal
the most important aspect.
– ORIGIN Old English.

be- • prefix forming verbs: **1** all over; all
round: *bespatter.* **2** thoroughly;
excessively: *bewilder.* **3** expressing
action: *bemoan.* **4** affect with or cause to
be: *befriend.* **5** (forming adjectives
ending in -*ed*) having; covered with:
bejewelled.
– ORIGIN Old English.

beach • n. a shore of sand or pebbles at
the edge of the sea or a lake. • v. bring on
to a beach from the water.
– ORIGIN perh. from Old English, 'brook'.

beachcomber • n. a person who

searches beaches for valuable things.

beachhead • n. a defended position on a
beach taken from the enemy by landing
forces.

beacon • n. **1** a fire lit on the top of a hill
as a signal. **2** a signal light for ships or
aircraft. **3** a radio transmitter signalling
the position of a ship or aircraft.
– ORIGIN Old English, 'sign'.

bead • n. **1** a small piece of glass, stone,
etc., threaded in a string with others to
make a necklace or rosary. **2** a drop of a
liquid on a surface. • v. decorate or cover
with beads.
– ORIGIN Old English, 'prayer' (each bead
on a rosary representing a prayer).

beadle • n. Brit. **1** a ceremonial officer of a
church, college, etc. **2** hist. a parish officer
who dealt with petty offenders.
– ORIGIN Old English, 'a person who
makes a proclamation'.

beady • adj. (of a person's eyes) small,
round, and observant.
– DERIVATIVES **beadily** adv.

beagle • n. a small short-legged breed of
hound.
– ORIGIN perh. from Old French *beegueule*
'open-mouthed'.

beak • n. **1** a bird's horny projecting jaws;
a bill. **2** Brit. informal a magistrate or
schoolmaster.
– DERIVATIVES **beaky** adj.
– ORIGIN Latin *beccus.*

beaker • n. Brit. **1** a tall plastic cup. **2** a
cylindrical glass container used in
laboratories.
– ORIGIN Old Norse.

beam • n. **1** a long piece of timber or
metal used as a support in building. **2** a
narrow horizontal length of timber for
balancing on in gymnastics. **3** a ray or
shaft of light or particles. **4** a glowing
smile. **5** a ship's breadth at its widest
point. • v. **1** transmit a radio signal.
2 shine brightly. **3** smile radiantly.
– PHRASES **off beam** informal on the wrong
track; mistaken.
– ORIGIN Old English.

bean • n. **1** an edible seed growing in long
pods on certain plants. **2** the hard seed
of a coffee or cocoa plant. **3** informal
nothing at all: *there is not a bean of truth
in the report.*
– PHRASES **full of beans** informal lively; in
high spirits.
– ORIGIN Old English.

beanbag • n. **1** a small bag filled with
dried beans and used in children's
games. **2** a large cushion filled with
polystyrene beads, used as a seat.

bean curd • n. = TOFU.

beanfeast • n. Brit. informal a party.
– ORIGIN first referring to an annual

dinner given to employees, which always featured beans and bacon.

beano • n. (pl. **beanos**) Brit. informal a party.
– ORIGIN from BEANFEAST.

beanpole • n. informal a tall, thin person.

bear¹ • v. (**bears, bearing, bore**; past part. **borne**) **1** carry someone or something. **2** have something as a quality or visible mark. **3** support a weight. **4** (**bear yourself**) behave in a specified way: *she bore herself with dignity.* **5** tolerate: *I can't bear it.* **6** give birth to a child. **7** (of a tree or plant) produce fruit or flowers. **8** turn and go in a specified direction: *bear left.*
– PHRASES **bear down on** approach in a purposeful or threatening way. **bear fruit** have good results. **bear someone a grudge** feel resentment against someone. **bear something in mind** take something into account. **bear on** relate to. **bear something out** support or confirm something. **bear up** remain cheerful in difficult circumstances. **bear with** be patient with. **bear witness to** provide evidence of. **bring something to bear** prepare something and use it effectively.
– ORIGIN Old English.

bear² • n. a large mammal with thick fur and a very short tail.
– DERIVATIVES **bearish** n.
– ORIGIN Old English.

bearable • adj. able to be accepted.
– DERIVATIVES **bearably** adv.

beard • n. a growth of hair on the chin and lower cheeks of a man's face. • v. boldly confront someone who is very powerful or important.
– DERIVATIVES **bearded** adj.
– ORIGIN Old English.

bearer • n. **1** a person or thing that carries something. **2** a person who presents a cheque or other order to pay money.

bear hug • n. a rough, tight embrace.

bearing • n. **1** a person's way of standing, moving, or behaving. **2** the way in which something is related to or influences something: *the case has no bearing on the issues.* **3** (**bearings**) a part of a machine that allows one part to rotate or move in contact with another. **4** direction or position relative to a fixed point. **5** (**your bearings**) awareness of your position relative to your surroundings.

bearskin • n. a tall cap of black fur worn ceremonially by certain troops.

beast • n. **1** an animal, especially a large or dangerous mammal. **2** a very cruel or wicked person.
– ORIGIN Latin *bestia.*

beastly • adj. Brit. informal very unpleasant.
– DERIVATIVES **beastliness** n.

beast of burden • n. an animal used for carrying loads.

beat • v. (**beats, beating, beat**; past part. **beaten**) **1** hit someone repeatedly and violently. **2** hit something repeatedly. **3** defeat or be better than: *he beat his own world record.* **4** informal baffle someone. **5** (of the heart) throb. **6** (of a bird) move the wings up and down. **7** stir cooking ingredients vigorously. • n. **1** an act of beating. **2** a main accent in music or poetry. **3** a brief pause. **4** an area patrolled by a police officer. • adj. informal completely exhausted.
– PHRASES **beat about the bush** discuss a matter without coming to the point. **beat down** shine very brightly. **beat it** informal leave. **beat someone up** attack someone and hit them repeatedly. **off the beaten track** isolated.
– DERIVATIVES **beater** n.
– ORIGIN Old English.

beatbox • n. informal a drum machine.

beatific /bee-uh-tif-ik/ • adj. intensely happy.
– DERIVATIVES **beatifically** adv.

beatify /bi-at-i-fy/ • v. (**beatifies, beatifying, beatified**) (in the Roman Catholic Church) announce that a dead person is in a state of bliss, the first step towards making them a saint.
– DERIVATIVES **beatification** n.
– ORIGIN Latin *beatus* 'blessed'.

beatitude /bi-at-i-tyood/ • n. very great happiness or blessedness.

beatnik • n. a young person in the 1950s and early 1960s who rejected the values and attitudes of conventional society.

beat-up • adj. informal worn out by overuse.

beau /boh/ • n. (pl. **beaux** or **beaus** /bohz, boh/) dated a boyfriend.
– ORIGIN French, 'handsome'.

Beaufort scale /boh-fert/ • n. a scale of wind speed ranging from force 0 to force 12.
– ORIGIN named after the English admiral Sir Francis *Beaufort.*

Beaujolais /boh-zhuh-lay/ • n. a light red wine produced in the Beaujolais district of SE France.

beauteous • adj. literary beautiful.

beautician • n. a person whose job is to give beauty treatments.

beautiful • adj. **1** very pleasing to the senses. **2** of a very high standard.
– DERIVATIVES **beautifully** adv.

> ☑ Spell **beautiful** and the related words **beauty** and **beautify** with **beau-** at the beginning.

beautify • v. (**beautifies, beautifying, beautified**) make beautiful.

– DERIVATIVES **beautification** n.

beauty •n. (pl. **beauties**) **1** a combination of qualities that delights the senses. **2** a beautiful woman. **3** an excellent example. **4** an attractive feature or advantage.
– ORIGIN Old French *beaute*.

beauty queen •n. the winner of a contest to choose the most beautiful woman.

beauty salon (also **beauty parlour**)
•n. a place in which hairdressing and cosmetic treatments are carried out.

beaux pl. of BEAU.

beaver •n. (pl. **beaver** or **beavers**) a large rodent that lives partly in water.
•v. (**beavers, beavering, beavered**) (**beaver away**) informal work hard.
– ORIGIN Old English.

bebop /bee-bop/ •n. a type of jazz characterized by complex harmony and rhythms.

becalm •v. (**be becalmed**) (of a sailing ship) be unable to move through lack of wind.

became past part. of BECOME.

because •conj. for the reason that.
– PHRASES **because of** by reason of.
– ORIGIN from *by cause*.

> **USAGE:** On starting a sentence with **because**, see the note at AND.

béchamel /bay-shuh-mel/ •n. a rich white sauce flavoured with herbs and other seasonings.
– ORIGIN named after the Marquis Louis de *Béchamel*.

beck •n. (in phr. **at someone's beck and call**) always having to be ready to obey someone's orders.
– ORIGIN from BECKON.

beckon •v. **1** gesture to someone to encourage them or to tell them to approach or follow. **2** seem appealing: *the Welsh hills beckoned.*
– ORIGIN Old English.

become •v. (**becomes, becoming, became**; past part. **become**) **1** begin to be. **2** develop into. **3** (**become of**) happen to. **4** suit or be appropriate to: *celebrity status did not become him.*
– ORIGIN from BE- + COME.

becoming •adj. **1** appropriate or suitable. **2** (of clothing) that suits someone.

becquerel /bek-kuh-rel/ •n. Physics a unit of radioactivity in the SI system.
– ORIGIN named after the French physicist A-H. *Becquerel*.

BEd •abbrev. Bachelor of Education.

bed •n. **1** a piece of furniture with a surface for sleeping on. **2** an area of ground where flowers and plants are grown. **3** a flat base or underlying layer. **4** informal a bed as a place for sexual activity. •v. (**beds, bedding, bedded**) **1** provide with or settle in sleeping accommodation. **2** (**bed something in/down**) fix something firmly. **3** informal have sex with someone.
– PHRASES **a bed of roses** a comfortable or easy situation.
– ORIGIN Old English.

bed and breakfast •n. sleeping accommodation and breakfast in a guest house or hotel.

bedbug •n. a bug which sucks the blood of sleeping humans.

bedclothes •pl. n. coverings for a bed, such as sheets and blankets.

bedding •n. **1** bedclothes. **2** straw or other material for animals to sleep on.

bedeck •v. decorate something lavishly.

bedevil •v. (**bedevils, bedevilling, bedevilled**; US **bedevils, bedeviling, bedeviled**) cause continual trouble to.

bedfellow •n. **1** a person or thing closely associated with another. **2** a person sharing a bed with another.

bedlam /bed-luhm/ •n. a scene of great confusion and noise.
– ORIGIN from the name of the mental hospital of St Mary of *Bethlehem* in London.

bedlinen •n. sheets, pillowcases, and duvet covers.

Bedouin /bed-oo-in/ •n. (pl. **Bedouin**) an Arab living as a nomad in the desert.
– ORIGIN Old French.

bedpan •n. a container used as a toilet by a bedridden patient.

bedraggled •adj. dishevelled or untidy.

bedridden •adj. having to stay in bed because of sickness or old age.

bedrock •n. **1** solid rock underlying soil. **2** the central principles on which something is based.

bedroom •n. a room for sleeping in.

Beds. •abbrev. Bedfordshire.

bedside manner •n. the way in which a doctor attends a patient.

bedsit •n. Brit. informal a rented room used for both living and sleeping.

bedsore •n. a sore caused by lying in bed in one position for a long time.

bedspread •n. a decorative cloth used to cover a bed.

bedstead •n. the framework of a bed.

bed-wetting •n. urinating while asleep.

bee •n. a winged insect with a sting, which collects nectar and pollen and makes wax and honey.
– PHRASES **have a bee in your bonnet**

b

informal be obsessed with something.
– ORIGIN Old English.

beech • n. a large tree with grey bark and pale wood.
– ORIGIN Old English.

beef • n. **1** the flesh of a cow, bull, or ox, used as food. **2** informal a complaint. • v. (**beef something up**) informal make something more powerful.
– ORIGIN Old French *boef*.

beefburger • n. a fried or grilled cake of minced beef eaten in a bun.

beefcake • n. informal men with well-developed muscles.

beefeater • n. a Yeoman Warder or Yeoman of the Guard in the Tower of London.

beefsteak • n. a thick slice of steak.

beefy • adj. informal muscular or strong.

beehive • n. a structure in which bees are kept.

beekeeping • n. the owning and breeding of bees for their honey.
– DERIVATIVES **beekeeper** n.

beeline • n. (in phr. **make a beeline for**) hurry straight to.

Beelzebub /bi-el-zi-bub/ • n. the Devil.
– ORIGIN Hebrew, 'lord of flies'.

been past part. of BE.

beep • n. a short, high-pitched sound made by electronic equipment or a vehicle horn. • v. produce a beep.
– DERIVATIVES **beeper** n.

beer • n. an alcoholic drink made from fermented malt flavoured with hops.
– ORIGIN Latin *biber* 'a drink'.

beer mat • n. Brit. a small cardboard mat for resting glasses on in a pub.

beery • adj. informal smelling or tasting of beer.

beeswax • n. wax produced by bees to make honeycombs, used for wood polishes and candles.

beet • n. a plant with a fleshy root, grown as food and for making into sugar.
– ORIGIN Latin *beta*.

beetle • n. an insect with a hard case on its back, covering its wings. • v. informal make your way hurriedly.
– ORIGIN Old English, 'biter'.

beetle-browed • adj. having large or bushy eyebrows.

beetroot • n. Brit. the edible dark-red root of a kind of beet.

befall • v. (**befalls, befalling, befell**; past part. **befallen**) literary (of something bad) happen to someone.

befit • v. (**befits, befitting, befitted**) be appropriate for: *as befits a Quaker, he was humane.*

before • prep., conj., & adv. **1** during the time preceding. **2** in front of. **3** rather than.
– ORIGIN Old English.

beforehand • adv. in advance.

befriend • v. become a friend to.

befuddle • v. (**befuddles, befuddling, befuddled**) confuse someone.
– DERIVATIVES **befuddlement** n.

beg • v. (**begs, begging, begged**) **1** ask humbly or solemnly for something. **2** ask for food or money as charity.
– PHRASES **beg the question 1** invite an obvious question. **2** assume the truth of something without arguing it. **go begging** be available because unwanted by other people.
– ORIGIN prob. Old English.

began past of BEGIN.

begat old-fashioned past of BEGET.

beget /bi-get/ • v. (**begets, begetting, begot**; past part. **begotten**) literary **1** cause something. **2** produce a child.
– DERIVATIVES **begetter** n.
– ORIGIN Old English.

beggar • n. **1** a person who lives by begging for food or money. **2** informal a particular type of person: *lucky beggar!* • v. make someone very poor.
– PHRASES **beggar belief** (or **description**) be too extraordinary to be believed or described.

beggarly • adj. very small in amount.

begin • v. (**begins, beginning, began**; past part. **begun**) **1** carry out or experience the first part of an action or activity. **2** come into being. **3** have as its starting point. **4** (**begin on**) set to work on. **5** informal have any chance of doing: *circuitry that Karen could not begin to comprehend.*
– DERIVATIVES **beginner** n. **beginning** n.
– ORIGIN Old English.

begone • exclam. old use go away at once!

begonia /bi-goh-ni-uh/ • n. a plant with brightly coloured flowers.
– ORIGIN named after the French botanist Michel *Bégon*.

begot past of BEGET.

begotten past part. of BEGET.

begrudge • v. (**begrudges, begrudging, begrudged**) **1** feel envious that some-one possesses or enjoys something. **2** give reluctantly or resentfully.

beguile • v. (**beguiles, beguiling, beguiled**) charm or trick someone.

begun past part. of BEGIN.

behalf • n. (in phr. **on behalf of** or **on someone's behalf**) **1** in the interests of a person, group, or principle. **2** as a representative of someone.
– ORIGIN from former *on his halve* and *bihalve him*, both meaning 'on his side'.

behave • v. (**behaves, behaving,**

behaved) **1** act in a certain way. **2** (also **behave yourself**) act in a polite or proper way.

behaved • adj. acting in a specified way: *a well-behaved child.*

behaviour (US **behavior**) • n. the way in which someone or something behaves.
– DERIVATIVES **behavioural** adj.

behaviourism (US **behaviorism**)
• n. the theory that behaviour can be explained in terms of conditioning, and that psychological disorders are best treated by altering behaviour patterns.
– DERIVATIVES **behaviourist** n. & adj.

behead • v. execute someone by cutting off their head.

beheld past and past part. of BEHOLD.

behemoth /bi-hee-moth/ • n. something very large, especially an organization.
– ORIGIN Hebrew, 'monstrous beast'.

behest /bi-hest/ • n. (in phr. **at the behest of**) literary at the request or order of.
– ORIGIN Old English.

behind • prep. & adv. **1** at or to the back or far side of. **2** further back than other members of a group. **3** in support of. **4** responsible for an event or plan. **5** less advanced than. **6** late in doing something. • n. informal a person's bottom.
– ORIGIN Old English.

behindhand • adj. late or slow in doing something.

behold • v. (**behold, beholding, beheld**) old use or literary see or observe.
– DERIVATIVES **beholder** n.
– ORIGIN Old English.

beholden • adj. (**beholden to**) having a duty to someone in return for a favour.

behove /bi-hohv/ • v. (**it behoves someone to do**) formal it is right or necessary for someone to do.
– ORIGIN Old English.

beige • n. a pale sandy colour.
– ORIGIN French.

being • n. **1** existence. **2** the nature of a person. **3** a living creature: *alien beings.*

bejewelled (US **bejeweled**)
• adj. decorated with jewels.

belabour (US **belabor**) • v. attack someone.

Belarusian /bel-ar-ru-sh'n, bel-ar-roo-si-uhn/ (also **Belarussian**) • n. a person from Belarus in eastern Europe.
• adj. relating to Belarus.

belated • adj. coming late or too late.
– DERIVATIVES **belatedly** adv.

belay /bi-lay/ • v. fix a rope round a rock, pin, or other object to secure it. **1** an act of fixing a rope round an object to secure it. **2** something used for belaying.

belch • v. **1** noisily discharge wind from

the stomach through the mouth. **2** give out smoke or flames with great force.
• n. an act of belching.
– ORIGIN Old English.

beleaguered • adj. **1** in difficulties. **2** (of a place) under siege.
– ORIGIN Dutch *belegeren* 'camp round'.

belfry • n. (pl. **belfries**) the place in a bell tower or steeple in which bells are housed.
– ORIGIN Old French *belfrei*.

Belgian • n. a person from Belgium.
• adj. relating to Belgium.

belie • v. (**belies, belying, belied**) **1** fail to give a true idea of. **2** show to be untrue or unjustified.
– ORIGIN Old English, 'deceive by lying'.

belief • n. **1** a feeling that something exists or is true, especially one without proof. **2** a firmly held opinion. **3** (**belief in**) trust or confidence in. **4** religious faith.
– ORIGIN Old English.

believe • v. (**believes, believing, believed**) **1** accept that something is true or someone is telling the truth. **2** (**believe in**) have faith in the truth or existence of. **3** think or suppose. **4** have religious faith.
– DERIVATIVES **believable** adj. **believer** n.

☑ **believe** and the related word **belief** follow the usual rule of *i* before *e* except after *c*.

belittle • v. (**belittles, belittling, belittled**) dismiss as unimportant.

Belizean /be-leez-i-uhn/ (also **Belizian**) • n. a person from Belize, a country in Central America. • adj. relating to Belize.

bell • n. **1** a deep metal cup held upside down, that sounds a clear musical note when struck. **2** a device that buzzes or rings to give a signal.
– PHRASES **give someone a bell** Brit. informal telephone someone. **ring a bell** informal sound vaguely familiar.
– ORIGIN Old English.

belladonna /bel-luh-don-nuh/ • n. a drug made from deadly nightshade.
– ORIGIN from Italian *bella donna* 'fair lady'.

bell-bottoms • pl. n. trousers with a wide flare below the knee.

belle /bel/ • n. a beautiful woman.
– ORIGIN French.

bellicose /bel-li-kohss/ • adj. aggressive and ready to fight.
– DERIVATIVES **bellicosity** /bel-li-koss-iti/ n.
– ORIGIN Latin *bellicosus*.

belligerence /buh-li-juh-ruhnss/
• n. aggressive or warlike behaviour.

belligerent • adj. **1** hostile and

aggressive. **2** engaged in a war or conflict.
– DERIVATIVES **belligerently** adv.
– ORIGIN Latin *belligerare* 'wage war'.

bellow • v. **1** give a deep roar of pain or anger. **2** shout or sing very loudly. • n. a deep shout or noise.
– ORIGIN perh. from Old English.

bellows • pl. n. a device consisting of a bag with two handles, used for blowing air into a fire.
– ORIGIN prob. from Old English, 'belly'.

bell-ringing • n. the activity of ringing church bells or handbells.

belly • n. (pl. **bellies**) **1** the front part of the body below the ribs, containing the stomach and bowels. **2** a person's stomach. **3** the rounded underside of a ship or aircraft.
– ORIGIN Old English, 'bag'.

bellyache • v. (**bellyaches, bellyaching, bellyached**) informal complain a great deal.

belly button • n. informal a person's navel.

bellyflop • n. informal a dive into water, landing flat on your front.

bellyful • n. (in phr. **have a bellyful of**) informal have more than enough of.

belly laugh • n. a loud unrestrained laugh.

belong • v. **1** (**belong to**) be the property of. **2** (**belong to**) be a member of. **3** be rightly put into a particular position or category. **4** feel at ease in a particular place or situation.

belongings • pl. n. a person's movable possessions.

beloved • adj. dearly loved.

below • prep. & adv. **1** at a lower level than. **2** mentioned further on in a piece of writing.

belt • n. **1** a strip of material worn round the waist to support or hold in clothes or to carry weapons. **2** a continuous band in machinery that transfers motion from one wheel to another. **3** a strip or encircling area: *the asteroid belt.*
• v. **1** fasten or secure with a belt. **2** hit very hard. **3** (**belt something out**) informal sing or play something loudly. **4** informal rush or dash. **5** (**belt up**) Brit. informal be quiet.
– PHRASES **below the belt** against the rules; unfair. **tighten your belt** cut your spending. **under your belt** achieved or acquired.
– ORIGIN Latin *balteus*.

beluga /buh-loo-guh/ • n. (pl. **beluga** or **belugas**) **1** a small whale of Arctic waters. **2** a very large sturgeon from which caviar is obtained.

– ORIGIN Russian, 'white'.

belying pres. part. of BELIE.

bemoan • v. express regret or sadness about something.

bemuse • v. (**bemuses, bemusing, bemused**) confuse or bewilder someone.
– DERIVATIVES **bemusement** n.

bench • n. **1** a long seat for more than one person. **2** a long work table in a workshop or laboratory. **3** (**the bench**) the office of judge or magistrate. **4** (**the bench**) a seat at the side of a sports field for coaches and players not taking part in a game.
– ORIGIN Old English.

benchmark • n. a standard against which things may be compared.

bend • v. (**bends, bending, bent**) **1** give or have a curved or angled shape, form, or course. **2** lean or curve the body downwards. **3** force or be forced to give in. **4** change a rule to suit yourself.
• n. **1** a curved or angled part or course. **2** a kind of knot used to join two ropes together, or one rope to another object. **3** (**the bends**) decompression sickness.
– PHRASES **round the bend** informal mad.
– DERIVATIVES **bendy** adj.
– ORIGIN Old English.

bender • n. informal a drinking bout.

beneath • prep. & adv. extending or directly underneath. • prep. of lower status or worth than.
– ORIGIN Old English.

Benedictine /ben-i-dik-teen/ • n. a monk or nun of a Christian religious order following the rule of St Benedict.

benediction • n. **1** the speaking of a blessing. **2** the state of being blessed.
– ORIGIN Latin *benedicere* 'bless'.

benefaction /ben-i-fak-sh'n/ • n. formal a donation.
– ORIGIN Latin.

benefactor • n. a person who gives money or other help.
– DERIVATIVES **benefactress** n.

benefice /ben-i-fiss/ • n. a Church office or position in which a member of the clergy receives accommodation and income in return for their duties.
– ORIGIN Latin *beneficium* 'favour'.

beneficent /bi-nef-i-suhnt/ • adj. doing or resulting in good.
– DERIVATIVES **beneficence** n.

beneficial • adj. having a good effect; favourable.
– DERIVATIVES **beneficially** adv.

beneficiary • n. (pl. **beneficiaries**) a person who benefits from something.

benefit • n. **1** advantage or profit. **2** a payment made by the state or an

insurance scheme to someone entitled to receive it. **3** a public performance to raise money for a charity. •v. (**benefits**, **benefiting**, **benefited**; also **benefits**, **benefitting**, **benefitted**) **1** receive an advantage; profit. **2** bring advantage to.
– PHRASES **the benefit of the doubt** an acceptance that a person is correct or innocent if the opposite cannot be proved.
– ORIGIN Latin *benefactum* 'good deed'.

benevolent /bi-nev-uh-luhnt/
•adj. **1** well meaning and kindly. **2** (of an organization) charitable rather than profit-making.
– DERIVATIVES **benevolence** n.
– ORIGIN Old French *benivolent*.

Bengali /ben-gaw-li/ •n. (pl. **Bengalis**) **1** a person from Bengal in the north-east of the Indian subcontinent. **2** the language of Bangladesh and West Bengal. •adj. relating to Bengal.

benighted •adj. lacking understanding of cultural, intellectual, or moral matters.

> ✓ **benighted** is spelled **ben-** at the beginning (it is related to *night*, not *knight*).

benign /bi-nyn/ •adj. **1** cheerful and kindly. **2** not harmful or harsh. **3** (of a tumour) not malignant.
– DERIVATIVES **benignity** /bi-**nig**-ni-ti/ n.
– ORIGIN Latin *benignus*.

Beninese /ben-i-neez/ •n. a person from Benin, a country in West Africa. •adj. relating to Benin.

bent past and past part. of **BEND**.
•adj. **1** having an angle or sharp curve. **2** Brit. informal dishonest; corrupt. **3** Brit. informal, derog. homosexual. **4** (**bent on**) determined to do or have. •n. a natural talent or inclination.

benumb •v. deprive someone of feeling.

benzene /ben-zeen/ •n. a liquid hydrocarbon present in coal tar and petroleum.
– ORIGIN French *benjoin*, referring to a resin obtained from a tree.

benzine /ben-zeen/ •n. a mixture of liquid hydrocarbons obtained from petroleum.

bequeath /bi-kweeth/ •v. **1** leave property to someone by a will. **2** hand down or pass on.
– ORIGIN Old English.

bequest •n. **1** a legacy that is left to someone by a will. **2** the action of bequeathing something.

berate •v. (**berates**, **berating**, **berated**) scold or criticize angrily.

Berber /ber-ber/ •n. a member of a people native to North Africa.

bereave •v. (**be bereaved**) be deprived of a close relation or friend through their death.
– DERIVATIVES **bereavement** n.
– ORIGIN Old English.

bereft •adj. **1** (**bereft of**) deprived of; without. **2** lonely and abandoned.
– ORIGIN from **BEREAVE**.

beret /be-ray/ •n. a flat round cap of felt or cloth.
– ORIGIN French.

bergamot /ber-guh-mot/ •n. **1** an oily substance extracted from Seville oranges, used as flavouring in Earl Grey tea. **2** a herb of the mint family.
– ORIGIN from *Bergamo* in Italy.

beriberi /be-ri-be-ri/ •n. a disease causing inflammation of the nerves and heart failure, due to a lack of vitamin B_1.
– ORIGIN Sinhalese.

berk /berk/ •n. Brit. informal a stupid person.

berkelium /ber-kee-li-uhm/ •n. a radioactive metallic chemical element.
– ORIGIN from the University of *Berkeley* (California).

Berks. •abbrev. Berkshire.

Bermuda shorts •pl. n. casual knee-length shorts.

berry •n. (pl. **berries**) **1** a small round juicy fruit without a stone. **2** Bot. a fruit that has its seeds enclosed in a fleshy pulp, e.g. a banana.
– ORIGIN Old English.

berserk /buh-zerk/ •adj. out of control with anger or excitement.
– ORIGIN Old Norse.

berth •n. **1** a place for a ship to moor at a wharf. **2** a bunk on a ship or train. •v. moor in a berth.
– PHRASES **give someone/thing a wide berth** stay well away from someone or something.
– ORIGIN prob. from **BEAR¹**.

beryl •n. a transparent pale green, blue, or yellow gemstone.
– ORIGIN Greek *bērullos*.

beryllium /buh-ril-li-uhm/ •n. a hard, grey, lightweight metallic element.

beseech •v. (**beseeches**, **beseeching**, **besought** or **beseeched**) literary ask in a pleading way.
– ORIGIN Old English.

beset •v. (**besets**, **besetting**, **beset**) (of something unwelcome) trouble or affect continuously.
– ORIGIN Old English.

beside •prep. **1** at the side of; next to. **2** compared with. **3** (also **besides**) as well as. •adv. (**besides**) as well.
– PHRASES **beside yourself** frantic with worry.

besiege • v. (**besieges, besieging, besieged**) 1 surround a place with armed forces so as to force it to surrender. 2 worry or overwhelm someone with requests or complaints.

besmirch /bi-smerch/ • v. damage someone's reputation.

besom /bee-zuhm/ • n. a broom made of twigs tied round a stick.
– ORIGIN Old English.

besotted /bi-sot-tid/ • adj. in love in an irrational and intense way.
– ORIGIN from **sot**.

besought past and past part. of **BESEECH**.

bespatter • v. (**bespatters, bespattering, bespattered**) spatter with liquid.

bespeak • v. (**bespeaks, bespeaking, bespoke**; past part. **bespoken**) 1 be evidence of. 2 formal order in advance.

bespoke • adj. Brit. made to a customer's requirements.

best • adj. 1 of the highest quality. 2 most suitable or sensible. • adv. 1 to the highest degree or standard; most. 2 most suitably or sensibly: *jokes are best avoided in essays.* • n. 1 (**the best**) that which is of the highest quality or most suitable. 2 (**your best**) the highest standard you can reach.
– PHRASES **at best** taking the most optimistic view. **get the best of** overcome someone. **had best** find it most sensible to. **make the best of** get what limited advantage you can from. **six of the best** Brit. six strokes of the cane as a punishment.
– ORIGIN Old English.

bestial /bess-ti-uhl/ • adj. 1 savagely cruel. 2 relating to or like an animal.
– ORIGIN Latin *bestia* 'beast'.

bestiality • n. 1 savagely cruel behaviour. 2 sexual intercourse between a person and an animal.

bestir • v. (**bestirs, bestirring, bestirred**) (**bestir yourself**) rouse yourself to action.

best man • n. a man chosen by a bridegroom to assist him at his wedding.

bestow • v. award an honour, right, or gift.
– DERIVATIVES **bestowal** n.
– ORIGIN Old English.

bestride • v. (**bestrides, bestriding, bestrode**; past part. **bestridden**) stand astride over something.

best-seller • n. a book or other product that sells in very large numbers.
– DERIVATIVES **best-selling** adj.

besuited /bi-soo-tid/ • adj. (of a man) wearing a suit.

bet • v. (**bets, betting, bet** or **betted**) 1 risk money or property against someone else's on the outcome of an unpredictable event such as a race. 2 informal feel sure. • n. 1 an act of betting or the money betted. 2 informal an option: *Austria is your best bet for summer skiing.* 3 (**your bet**) informal your opinion.
– PHRASES **you bet** informal certainly.
– DERIVATIVES **bettor** (also **better**) n.
– ORIGIN perh. from a former word meaning 'abetting'.

beta /bee-tuh/ • n. 1 the second letter of the Greek alphabet (B, β). 2 Brit. a second-class grade or mark.

beta blocker • n. a drug used to treat angina and reduce high blood pressure.

betake • v. (**betakes, betaking, betook**; past part. **betaken**) (**betake yourself to**) literary go to a place.

beta particle • n. Physics a fast-moving electron given off by some radioactive substances.

betel /bee-t'l/ • n. the leaf of an Asian plant, chewed as a mild stimulant.
– ORIGIN Portuguese.

bête noire /bet nwar/ • n. (pl. **bêtes noires** /bet nwar/) a person or thing that you particularly dislike.
– ORIGIN French, 'black beast'.

betide • v. (**betide, betiding, betided**) literary happen, or happen to someone.

betimes • adv. literary in good time.

betoken • v. literary be a sign of something.

betook past of **BETAKE**.

betray • v. 1 act treacherously towards your country by helping an enemy. 2 be disloyal to someone. 3 reveal something without meaning to: *she drew a deep breath that betrayed her indignation.*
– DERIVATIVES **betrayal** n. **betrayer** n.
– ORIGIN Latin *tradere* 'hand over'.

betrothed /bi-trohthd/ formal • adj. engaged to be married. • n. (**your betrothed**) the person to whom you are engaged.
– DERIVATIVES **betrothal** n.
– ORIGIN from **TROTH**.

better • adj. 1 more satisfactory or suitable. 2 partly or fully recovered from an illness or injury. • adv. 1 in a better way. 2 to a greater degree; more. • n. 1 something that is better. 2 (**your betters**) dated or humorous people who are more important than you. • v. 1 improve on something. 2 (**better yourself**) improve your social position.
– PHRASES **better off** in a more favourable position. **the better part of** most of. **get**

the better of defeat. **had better** ought to.
– ORIGIN Old English.

better half • n. informal a person's husband or wife.

betterment • n. the improvement of someone or something.

between • prep. & adv. **1** at, into, or across the space separating two things. **2** in the period separating two points in time. **3** (as prep.) indicating a connection or relationship. **4** (as prep.) shared by; together with.
– PHRASES **between ourselves** (or **you and me**) in confidence.
– ORIGIN Old English.

USAGE: A preposition such as **between** takes the object case and so should be followed by object pronouns such as **me** rather than subject pronouns such as **I**. You should therefore say **between you and me**, not **between you and I**.

betwixt • prep. & adv. old use between.
– ORIGIN Old English.

bevel • n. **1** (in carpentry) a sloping surface or edge. **2** (also **bevel square**) a tool for marking angles in carpentry and stonework. • v. (**bevels, bevelling, bevelled**; US **bevels, beveling, beveled**) cut a sloping surface or edge.
– ORIGIN Old French.

beverage • n. a drink other than water.
– ORIGIN Old French *bevrage*.

bevy /rhymes with heavy/ • n. (pl. **bevies**) a large group.

bewail • v. express great regret or sorrow over something.

beware • v. be cautious and alert to risks.
– ORIGIN from *be ware* 'be aware'.

bewilder • v. (**bewilders, bewildering, bewildered**) puzzle or confuse someone.
– DERIVATIVES **bewilderment** n.
– ORIGIN from a former word meaning 'lead or go astray'.

bewitch • v. **1** cast a spell over someone. **2** attract and delight someone.

beyond • prep. & adv. **1** at or to the further side of. **2** outside the range or limits of. **3** to or in a state where something is impossible: *the radio was beyond repair*. **4** happening or continuing after. **5** except.
– ORIGIN Old English.

bezel /bez-uhl/ • n. a groove holding a gemstone or the glass cover of a watch in position.
– ORIGIN Old French.

bezique /bi-zeek/ • n. a card game for two players.
– ORIGIN French *bésigue*.

Bh • symb. the chemical element bohrium.

bhaji /bah-ji/ (also **bhajia** /bah-juh/) • n. (pl. **bhajis, bhajia**) an Indian dish of vegetables fried in batter.
– ORIGIN Hindi.

bhang /bang/ (also **bang**) • n. the leaves and flower-tops of cannabis, used as a narcotic in India.
– ORIGIN Hindi.

bhangra /bahng-gruh/ • n. a type of popular music combining Punjabi folk music with Western pop.
– ORIGIN Punjabi.

b.h.p. • abbrev. brake horsepower.

Bi • symb. the chemical element bismuth.

bi- • comb. form **1** two; having two: *biathlon*. **2** occurring twice in every one or once in every two: *bicentennial*. **3** lasting for two: *biennial*.
– ORIGIN Latin.

biannual • adj. occurring twice a year.
– DERIVATIVES **biannually** adv.

bias /by-uhss/ • n. **1** an opinion or tendency to be strongly for or against a person or thing. **2** a slanting direction across the grain of a fabric. **3** a steady voltage, applied to an electronic device, that can be adjusted to change the way the device operates. • v. (**biases, biasing, biased**) be prejudiced for or against: *the courts were biased towards the police*.
– ORIGIN French *biais*.

bias binding • n. a narrow strip of fabric cut across the grain, used to bind edges.

biathlon /by-ath-lon/ • n. a sporting event combining cross-country skiing and rifle shooting.
– ORIGIN from Greek *athlon* 'contest'.

bib • n. **1** a piece of cloth or plastic fastened under a child's chin to protect their clothes. **2** the part of an apron or pair of dungarees that covers the chest.
– ORIGIN prob. from Latin *bibere* 'to drink'.

Bible • n. **1** the Christian scriptures, consisting of the Old and New Testaments. **2** the Jewish scriptures. **3** (**bible**) informal a book regarded as thorough and reliable.
– DERIVATIVES **biblical** adj. **biblically** adv.
– ORIGIN Greek *biblion* 'book'.

bibliography /bib-li-og-ruh-fi/ • n. (pl. **bibliographies**) **1** a list of the books referred to in a scholarly work. **2** a list of books on a particular subject or by a particular author. **3** the study of books and their production.
– DERIVATIVES **bibliographer** n. **bibliographic** adj.
– ORIGIN from Greek *biblion* 'book'.

bibliophile /bib-li-oh-fyl/ • n. a person who collects or loves books.

bibulous /bib-yuu-luhss/ •adj. formal very fond of drinking alcohol.
– ORIGIN Latin *bibulus* 'freely drinking'.

bicameral /by-kam-uh-ruhl/ •adj. (of a law-making body) having two chambers.
– ORIGIN from Latin *camera* 'chamber'.

bicarbonate •n. Chem. a compound containing HCO₃ negative ions together with a metallic element.

bicarbonate of soda •n. sodium bicarbonate.

bicentenary •n. (pl. **bicentenaries**) a two-hundredth anniversary.
– DERIVATIVES **bicentennial** n. & adj.

biceps /by-seps/ •n. (pl. **biceps**) a large muscle in the upper arm which flexes the arm and forearm.
– ORIGIN Latin, 'two-headed'.

bicker •v. (**bickers**, **bickering**, **bickered**) argue about unimportant things.

bicuspid /by-kuss-pid/ •adj. having two cusps or points. •n. a tooth with two cusps.

bicycle •n. a two-wheeled vehicle propelled by pedals. •v. (**bicycles**, **bicycling**, **bicycled**) ride a bicycle.
– DERIVATIVES **bicyclist** n.
– ORIGIN from Greek *kuklos* 'wheel'.

bid¹ •v. (**bids**, **bidding**, **bid**) **1** offer a price for something. **2** (**bid for**) try to get or achieve. •n. an act of bidding.
– DERIVATIVES **bidder** n. **bidding** n.
– ORIGIN Old English.

bid² •v. (**bids**, **bidding**, **bid** or **bade**; past part. **bid**) **1** say a greeting or farewell to someone. **2** old use command someone.
– ORIGIN Old English.

biddable •adj. willing to obey; obedient.

biddy •n. (pl. **biddies**) informal an old woman.

bide •v. (**bides**, **biding**, **bided**) old use or dialect stay in a place.
– PHRASES **bide your time** wait patiently for a good opportunity.
– ORIGIN Old English.

bidet /bee-day/ •n. a low basin used for washing the genitals and bottom.
– ORIGIN French, 'pony'.

biennial /by-en-ni-uhl/ •adj. **1** taking place every other year. **2** (of a plant) living for two years.
– DERIVATIVES **biennially** adv.
– ORIGIN from Latin *annus* 'year'.

bier /beer/ •n. a movable platform on which a coffin or corpse is placed before burial.
– ORIGIN Old English.

biff •v. informal hit hard with the fist.

bifocal •adj. (of a lens) made in two sections, one with a focus for seeing distant things and one for seeing things that are close. •n. (**bifocals**) a pair of glasses with bifocal lenses.

big •adj. (**bigger**, **biggest**) **1** large in size, amount, or extent. **2** very important or serious. **3** older or grown-up: *my big sister.* **4** informal very popular.
– PHRASES **the big screen** informal the cinema. **think big** informal be ambitious. **too big for your boots** informal too proud of yourself.
– DERIVATIVES **biggish** adj. **bigness** n.

bigamy /bi-guh-mi/ •n. the crime of marrying someone while already married to another person.
– DERIVATIVES **bigamist** n. **bigamous** adj.
– ORIGIN from **BI-** + Greek *-gamos* 'married'.

Big Bang •n. the rapid expansion of extremely dense matter which (according to current theories) marked the origin of the universe.

Big Brother •n. a person or organization exercising total control over people's lives.
– ORIGIN the head of state in George Orwell's novel *Nineteen Eighty-four.*

big end •n. the larger end of the connecting rod in a piston engine.

big-head •n. informal a conceited person.
– DERIVATIVES **big-headed** adj.

bight /rhymes with light/ •n. a long inward curve in a coastline.
– ORIGIN Old English.

big mouth •n. informal a person who boasts or cannot keep secrets.

bigot /bi-guht/ •n. a person with prejudiced views who does not tolerate the opinions of other people.
– DERIVATIVES **bigoted** adj. **bigotry** n.
– ORIGIN French.

> ✓ Remember that **bigoted** is spelled with a single **t**.

big top •n. the main tent in a circus.

big wheel •n. a Ferris wheel.

bigwig •n. informal an important person.

bijou /bee-zhoo/ •adj. small and elegant.
– ORIGIN French, 'jewel'.

bike informal •n. a bicycle or motorcycle. •v. (**bikes**, **biking**, **biked**) ride a bicycle or motorcycle.
– DERIVATIVES **biker** n.

bikini •n. (pl. **bikinis**) a women's two-piece swimsuit.
– ORIGIN named after *Bikini* atoll in the Pacific, where an atom bomb was exploded (because of the swimsuit's devastating effect).

bilateral •adj. **1** having two sides. **2** involving two parties.
– DERIVATIVES **bilaterally** adv.

bilberry •n. (pl. **bilberries**) the blue edible berry of a shrub.

– ORIGIN prob. Scandinavian.

bile • n. **1** a bitter fluid which is produced by the liver and aids digestion. **2** anger or irritability.
– ORIGIN Latin *bilis*.

bile duct • n. the tube which conveys bile from the liver and the gall bladder to the duodenum.

bilge • n. **1** the bottom of a ship's hull. **2** (also **bilge water**) dirty water that collects in the bilge. **3** informal nonsense.
– ORIGIN prob. from BULGE.

bilingual • adj. **1** speaking two languages fluently. **2** expressed in two languages.

bilious • adj. **1** affected by sickness; nauseous. **2** relating to bile. **3** bad-tempered.

bilk • v. informal cheat or defraud someone.
– ORIGIN perh. from BAULK.

Bill • n. (**the Bill** or **the Old Bill**) Brit. informal the police.
– ORIGIN familiar form of the man's name *William*.

bill¹ • n. **1** a written statement of charges for goods or services. **2** a draft of a proposed law presented to parliament for discussion. **3** a programme of entertainment at a theatre or cinema. **4** an advertising poster. **5** N. Amer. a banknote. • v. **1** list a person or event in a programme. **2** (**bill as**) describe as: *the show is billed as international.* **3** send a statement of charges to.
– PHRASES **a clean bill of health** a statement confirming good health or condition. **fit the bill** be suitable.
– DERIVATIVES **billing** n.
– ORIGIN Old French *bille*.

bill² • n. **1** the beak of a bird. **2** a narrow piece of land projecting into the sea: *Portland Bill.*
– PHRASES **bill and coo** informal behave in a loving and sentimental way.
– ORIGIN Old English.

billabong • n. Austral. a branch of a river forming a backwater or stagnant pool.
– ORIGIN from an Aboriginal word.

billboard • n. an advertisement hoarding.

billet • n. a civilian house where soldiers are lodged temporarily. • v. (**billets, billeting, billeted**) provide soldiers with accommodation in a billet.
– ORIGIN Old French *billette* 'small document'.

billet-doux /bil-li-doo/ • n. (pl. **billets-doux** /bil-li-dooz/) esp. humorous a love letter.
– ORIGIN French, 'sweet note'.

billhook • n. a tool with a curved blade, used for pruning.

billiards • n. a game played on a table with pockets at the sides and corners, into which balls are struck with a cue.
– ORIGIN French *billard.*

billion • cardinal number (pl. **billions** or (with numeral or quantifying word) **billion**) **1** a thousand million; 1,000,000,000 or 10⁹. **2** Brit. dated a million million (1,000,000,000,000 or 10¹²). **3** (**billions**) informal a very large number or amount.
– DERIVATIVES **billionth** ordinal number.
– ORIGIN French.

billionaire • n. a person owning money and property worth at least a billion pounds or dollars.

bill of rights • n. a statement of the rights of a country's citizens.

billow • v. **1** (of smoke, cloud, or steam) roll outward. **2** fill with air and swell out: *her dress billowed out behind her.* • n. a large rolling mass of cloud, smoke, or steam.
– DERIVATIVES **billowy** adj.
– ORIGIN Old Norse.

billy (also **billycan**) • n. (pl. **billies**) Brit. a metal cooking pot with a lid and handle, used in camping.
– ORIGIN perh. from an Aboriginal word meaning 'water'.

billy goat • n. a male goat.
– ORIGIN *Billy*, familiar form of the man's name *William*.

bimbo • n. (pl. **bimbos**) informal, derog. an attractive but unintelligent woman.
– ORIGIN Italian, 'little child'.

bin Brit. • n. **1** a container for rubbish. **2** a large storage container. • v. (**bins, binning, binned**) throw something away.
– ORIGIN Old English.

binary /by-nuh-ri/ • adj. **1** composed of or involving two things. **2** relating to a system of numbers with two as its base, using the digits 0 and 1.
– ORIGIN Latin *binarius.*

bind • v. (**binds, binding, bound**) **1** tie or fasten; tie up. **2** wrap or encircle tightly: *her hair was bound up in a towel.* **3** stick together in a mass. **4** hold together as a united group. **5** (**be bound by**) be hampered or restricted by. **6** require someone to do something by law or because of a contract. **7** (**bind someone over**) (of a court of law) require someone to do something: *he was bound over to keep the peace.* **8** fix together and enclose the pages of a book in a cover. **9** trim the edge of a piece of material with a fabric strip. • n. an informal annoying or difficult situation.
– ORIGIN Old English.

binder • n. **1** a cover for holding magazines or loose papers together. **2** a

reaping machine that binds grain into sheaves. **3** a person who binds books.
– DERIVATIVES **bindery** n. (pl. **binderies**)

binding • n. **1** a strong covering holding the pages of a book together. **2** fabric in a strip, used for binding the edges of material. • adj. (of an agreement) putting someone under a legal obligation.

bindweed • n. a plant that twines itself round things.

binge informal • n. a short period of uncontrolled eating or drinking.
• v. (**binges**, **bingeing**, **binged**) do something, especially eat, uncontrollably.
– DERIVATIVES **binger** n.

bingo • n. a game in which players mark off randomly called numbers on cards, the winner being the first to mark off all their numbers. • exclam. a call by someone who wins a game of bingo.

binnacle • n. a casing to hold a ship's compass.
– ORIGIN Spanish *bitácula*, *bitácora* or Portuguese *bitacola*.

binocular /bi-nok-yuu-ler/ • adj. for or using both eyes. • n. (**binoculars**) an instrument with a separate lens for each eye, used for viewing distant objects.
– ORIGIN from Latin *bini* 'two together' + *oculus* 'eye'.

binomial /by-noh-mi-uhl/ • n. Math. an algebraic expression consisting of two terms linked by a plus or minus sign.
– ORIGIN from Latin *bi-* 'having two' + Greek *nomos* 'part'.

bio- • comb. form **1** relating to life or living beings: *biosynthesis*. **2** biological; relating to biology: *biohazard*.
– ORIGIN Greek *bios* 'human life'.

biochemistry • n. the branch of science concerned with the chemical processes which occur within living organisms.
– DERIVATIVES **biochemical** adj. **biochemist** n.

biodegradable • adj. capable of being decomposed by bacteria or other living organisms.
– DERIVATIVES **biodegradability** n. **biodegrade** v.

biodiversity • n. the variety of plant and animal life in the world or in a habitat.

bioengineering • n. **1** genetic engineering. **2** the use of artificial tissues or organs in the body. **3** the use of organisms or biological processes in industry.

biography • n. (pl. **biographies**) an account of a person's life written by someone else.
– DERIVATIVES **biographer** n. **biographical** adj.

biohazard • n. a risk to human health or the environment arising from biological research.

biological • adj. **1** relating to biology or living organisms. **2** (of a parent or child) related by blood. **3** (of warfare) using harmful microorganisms. **4** (of a detergent) containing enzymes.
– DERIVATIVES **biologically** adv.

biological clock • n. a natural mechanism that controls certain regularly recurring physical processes in an animal or plant.

biology • n. the scientific study of living organisms.
– DERIVATIVES **biologist** n.

bionic • adj. relating to the use of electronically powered artificial body parts.

biopsy /by-op-si/ • n. (pl. **biopsies**) an examination of tissue taken from the body, to discover the presence or cause of a disease.
– ORIGIN from Greek *bios* 'life' + *opsis* 'sight'.

biorhythm • n. a recurring cycle in the functioning of an animal or plant.

biosphere • n. the parts of the earth that are inhabited by living things.

biosynthesis • n. the production of complex molecules within living organisms or cells.
– DERIVATIVES **biosynthetic** adj.

biotechnology • n. the use of microorganisms in industry and medicine for the production of antibiotics, hormones, etc.

bioterrorism • n. the use of harmful biological or biochemical substances as weapons of terrorism.
– DERIVATIVES **bioterrorist** n.

biotin /by-uh-tin/ • n. a vitamin of the B complex, found in egg yolk, liver, and yeast.
– ORIGIN from Greek *bios* 'life'.

bioweapon • n. a harmful organism or biological substance used as a weapon of war.

bipartisan • adj. involving the cooperation of two political parties.

bipartite • adj. **1** involving two separate parties. **2** tech. consisting of two parts.

biped /by-ped/ • n. an animal that walks on two feet.
– DERIVATIVES **bipedal** /by-pee-d'l/ adj.
– ORIGIN from Latin *bi-* 'having two' + *pes* 'foot'.

biplane • n. an early type of aircraft with two pairs of wings, one above the other.

bipolar • adj. (especially of an electronic device) having two poles.

birch • n. **1** a slender tree with thin,

peeling bark. **2** (**the birch**) a former punishment in which a person was beaten with a bundle of birch twigs.
– ORIGIN Old English.

bird • n. **1** a warm-blooded animal with feathers and wings, that lays eggs and is usually able to fly. **2** informal a person of a particular kind: *she's a sharp old bird.* **3** Brit. informal a young woman or a person's girlfriend.
– PHRASES **the birds and the bees** informal basic facts about sex.
– ORIGIN Old English.

birdie • n. (pl. **birdies**) **1** informal a little bird. **2** Golf a score of one stroke under par at a hole.

birdlime • n. a sticky substance spread on to twigs to trap small birds.

bird of paradise • n. (pl. **birds of paradise**) a tropical bird, the male of which has brightly coloured plumage.

bird of prey • n. (pl. **birds of prey**) a bird that feeds on animal flesh, such as an eagle, hawk, or owl.

bird's-eye view • n. a view of something from a height.

birdwatching • n. the hobby of observing birds in their natural environment.
– DERIVATIVES **birdwatcher** n.

biretta /bi-ret-tuh/ • n. a square cap worn by Roman Catholic clergymen.
– ORIGIN Italian *berretta* or Spanish *birreta.*

biriani /bi-ri-ah-ni/ (also **biryani**) • n. an Indian dish made with spiced rice and meat, fish, or vegetables.
– ORIGIN Persian, 'fried, grilled'.

biro • n. (pl. **biros**) Brit. trademark a ballpoint pen.
– ORIGIN named after the Hungarian inventor László József *Biró.*

birth • n. **1** the emergence of a baby or young animal from the body of its mother. **2** the beginning of something. **3** origin or ancestry: *he is of noble birth.*
– PHRASES **give birth** produce a child or young animal.
– ORIGIN Old Norse.

birth certificate • n. an official document recording a person's name, their place and date of birth, and the names of their parents.

birth control • n. the use of contra-ception to prevent unwanted pregnancies.

birthday • n. the annual anniversary of the day on which a person was born.

birthmark • n. an unusual mark on the body which is there from birth.

birthplace • n. the place where a person was born or where something began.

birth rate • n. the number of live births per thousand of population per year.

birthright • n. **1** a right or privilege that a person has through being born into a particular family, class, or place. **2** a natural right possessed by everyone.

biryani • n. var. of **BIRIANI.**

biscuit • n. **1** Brit. a small, flat, crisp cake. **2** a light brown colour.
– PHRASES **take the biscuit** (or **cake**) informal be the most surprising or annoying thing that has happened.
– ORIGIN from Latin *bis* 'twice' + *coquere* 'to cook'.

bisect • v. divide into two parts.
– DERIVATIVES **bisection** n. **bisector** n.
– ORIGIN from BI- + Latin *secare* 'to cut'.

bisexual • adj. **1** sexually attracted to both men and women. **2** Biol. having characteristics of both sexes. • n. a bisexual person.
– DERIVATIVES **bisexuality** n.

bishop • n. **1** a senior member of the Christian clergy who is in charge of a diocese. **2** a chess piece that can move diagonally in any direction.
– ORIGIN Greek *episkopos* 'overseer'.

bishopric • n. the position or diocese of a bishop.

bismuth /biz-muhth/ • n. a brittle reddish-grey metallic element resembling lead.
– ORIGIN German *Wismut.*

bison • n. (pl. **bison**) a shaggy-haired wild ox with a humped back.
– ORIGIN Latin.

bisque[1] /bisk/ • n. a rich soup made from lobster or other shellfish.
– ORIGIN French.

bisque[2] • n. = BISCUIT (in sense 2).

bistro /bee-stroh/ • n. (pl. **bistros**) a small, inexpensive restaurant.
– ORIGIN French.

bit[1] • n. **1** a small piece or quantity. **2** (**a bit**) a short time or distance.
– PHRASES **a bit** rather; slightly. **bit by bit** gradually. **do your bit** informal make a useful contribution. **to bits 1** into pieces. **2** informal very much.
– ORIGIN Old English, 'bite, mouthful'.

bit[2] past of BITE.

bit[3] • n. **1** a metal mouthpiece attached to a bridle, used to control a horse. **2** a tool or piece for boring or drilling.
– ORIGIN Old English, 'biting, a bite'.

bit[4] • n. Computing a unit of information expressed as either a 0 or 1 in binary notation.
– ORIGIN from BINARY and DIGIT.

bitch • n. **1** a female dog, wolf, fox, or

otter. **2** informal a spiteful or unpleasant woman. **3** (**a bitch**) informal something difficult or unpleasant: *life's a bitch.*
• v. informal make spiteful comments.
– ORIGIN Old English.

bitchy • adj. (**bitchier, bitchiest**) informal spiteful.
– DERIVATIVES **bitchily** adv. **bitchiness** n.

bite • v. (**bites, biting, bit**; past part. **bitten**) **1** cut into with the teeth. **2** (of a snake, insect, or spider) wound with a sting or fangs. **3** (of a fish) take a bait or lure into the mouth. **4** (of a tool, tyre, etc.) grip a surface. **5** take effect, with unpleasant consequences: *the cuts in education were starting to bite.* • n. **1** an act of biting or a piece bitten off. **2** informal a quick snack. **3** a feeling of cold in the air.
– PHRASES **bite the bullet** make yourself do something difficult. **bite the hand that feeds you** deliberately offend someone who is trying to help. **bite off more than you can chew** take on more than you can deal with. **bite your tongue** stop yourself saying something.
– DERIVATIVES **biter** n.
– ORIGIN Old English.

biting • adj. **1** (of a wind) very cold. **2** (of wit or criticism) harsh or sharp.

bitmap • n. the information used to control an image or display on a computer screen, in which each item corresponds to one or more bits of information.

bit part • n. a small acting role in a play or a film.

bitten past part. of BITE.

bitter • adj. **1** having a sharp taste or smell; not sweet. **2** painful or distressing. **3** feeling deep resentment. **4** (of a conflict) intense and full of hatred: *a bitter row broke out.* **5** intensely cold.
• n. **1** Brit. bitter-tasting beer that is strongly flavoured with hops. **2** (**bitters**) bitter alcoholic spirits used in cocktails.
– PHRASES **to the bitter end** to the very end, in spite of harsh difficulties.
– DERIVATIVES **bitterly** adv. **bitterness** n.
– ORIGIN Old English.

bittern • n. a bird found in marshland, noted for the male's booming call.
– ORIGIN Old French *butor.*

bittersweet • adj. **1** sweet with a bitter aftertaste. **2** pleasant but with a touch of sadness.

bitty • adj. Brit. informal made up of small unrelated parts.

bitumen /bit-yuu-muhn/ • n. a black sticky substance obtained naturally or from petroleum, used for road surfacing.
– DERIVATIVES **bituminous** /bi-tyoo-mi-nuhss/ adj.

– ORIGIN Latin.

bivalve • n. a mollusc that lives in water and has a shell divided into two parts, such as an oyster or mussel.

bivouac /bi-voo-ak/ • n. a temporary camp without tents. • v. (**bivouacs, bivouacking, bivouacked**) camp in a bivouac.
– ORIGIN French.

bizarre /bi-zar/ • adj. very strange or unusual.
– DERIVATIVES **bizarrely** adv.
– ORIGIN Italian *bizzarro* 'angry'.

Bk • symb. the chemical element berkelium.

blab • v. (**blabs, blabbing, blabbed**) informal reveal information that should have been kept secret.

blabber • v. (**blabbers, blabbering, blabbered**) informal talk excessively or carelessly.

black • adj. **1** of the very darkest colour. **2** relating to the human group having dark-coloured skin. **3** (of coffee or tea) served without milk. **4** marked by disaster or despair: *the future looks black.* **5** (of humour) presenting distressing situations in comic terms. **6** full of anger or hatred. • n. **1** black colour. **2** a black person. • v. **1** make something black. **2** Brit. dated refuse to deal with someone or something as a form of industrial action.
– PHRASES **black out** faint. **black something out** make a room or building dark by switching off lights and covering windows. **in the black** not owing any money.
– DERIVATIVES **blackish** adj. **blackly** adv. **blackness** n.
– ORIGIN Old English.

black and white • adj. involving clear-cut opposing opinions or issues.

black art (also **black arts**) • n. black magic.

blackball • v. reject a candidate for membership of a private club.
– ORIGIN from the practice of voting against something by placing a black ball in a box.

black belt • n. a black belt worn by an expert in judo, karate, and other martial arts.

blackberry • n. (pl. **blackberries**) the purple-black edible fruit of a prickly climbing shrub.

blackbird • n. a type of thrush, the male of which has black plumage and a yellow bill.

blackboard • n. a board with a dark surface for writing on with chalk.

black box • n. a flight recorder in an aircraft.

blackcurrant • n. the small round edible black berry of a shrub.

black economy • n. the part of a country's economy which is not recorded or taxed by its government.

blacken • v. 1 become or make black or dark. 2 damage or destroy someone's reputation.

black eye • n. an area of bruised skin around the eye.

blackfly • n. (pl. **blackflies**) a black or dark green flying insect which attacks crops.

blackguard /blag-gerd/ • n. dated a man who behaves in a dishonourable or contemptible way.
– ORIGIN first referring to a group of kitchen servants.

blackhead • n. a lump of oily matter blocking a pore in the skin.

black hole • n. a region of space having a gravitational field so intense that no matter or radiation can escape.

black ice • n. transparent ice on a road surface.

blackleg • n. Brit. derog. a person who continues to work when their fellow workers are on strike.

blacklist • n. a list of people or groups seen as unacceptable or untrustworthy. • v. put on a blacklist.

black magic • n. magic involving the summoning of evil spirits.

blackmail • n. 1 the demanding of money from someone in return for not revealing information that could disgrace them. 2 the use of threats or other pressure to influence someone: emotional blackmail. • v. use blackmail on someone.
– DERIVATIVES **blackmailer** n.
– ORIGIN Old Norse, 'speech, agreement'.

Black Maria /muh-ry-uh/ • n. informal a police vehicle for transporting prisoners.

black mark • n. informal a record of disapproval for something that someone has done.

black market • n. the illegal trade in goods that are officially controlled or hard to obtain.
– DERIVATIVES **black marketeer** n.

black mass • n. a blasphemous imitation of the Roman Catholic Mass, performed in worship of the Devil.

blackout • n. 1 a period when all lights must be switched off or covered during an enemy air raid. 2 a sudden failure of electric lights. 3 a short loss of consciousness. 4 an official restriction on publishing information: a total news blackout.

black pudding • n. Brit. a black sausage containing pork, dried pig's blood, and suet.

Black Rod (in full **Gentleman Usher of the Black Rod**) • n. the chief usher of the House of Lords and the Lord Chamberlain's department.

black sheep • n. informal a person who is regarded as a source of shame or embarrassment by their family or another group.

blackshirt • n. a member of a Fascist organization, especially in Italy before and during the Second World War.

blacksmith • n. a person who makes and repairs things made of iron.

black spot • n. Brit. a place marked by a particular problem: an accident black spot.

blackthorn • n. a thorny shrub with white flowers and blue-black fruits (sloes).

black tie • n. men's formal evening wear.

black widow • n. a highly poisonous American spider having a black body with red markings.

bladder • n. 1 a sac (bag-like structure) in the abdomen which stores urine before it is discharged from the body. 2 an inflated or hollow flexible bag.
– ORIGIN Old English.

blade • n. 1 the flat cutting edge of a knife or other tool or weapon. 2 the broad flat part of an oar, leaf, or other object. 3 a long narrow leaf of grass. 4 a shoulder bone in a joint of meat.
– ORIGIN Old English.

blag • v. (**blags, blagging, blagged**) Brit. informal get by clever persuasion or lying.
– DERIVATIVES **blagger** n.
– ORIGIN perh. from French blaguer 'tell lies'.

blame • v. (**blames, blaming, blamed**) think or say that someone or something is responsible for something bad or wrong: the terrorists were blamed for the bombings. • n. responsibility for something bad or wrong.
– DERIVATIVES **blameworthy** adj.
– ORIGIN Old French blasmer.

blameless • adj. having done nothing wrong; innocent.

blanch /blahnch/ • v. 1 make or become white or pale. 2 prepare vegetables by putting them briefly into water.
– ORIGIN Old French blanchir.

blancmange /bluh-monzh/ • n. Brit. a sweet jelly-like dessert made with cornflour and milk.

– ORIGIN from Old French *blanc* 'white' + *mangier* 'eat'.

bland • adj. **1** lacking strong qualities and therefore uninteresting: *a bland diet.* **2** showing little emotion: *his bland expression.*
– DERIVATIVES **blandly** adv. **blandness** n.
– ORIGIN Latin *blandus* 'soft, smooth'.

blandishments • pl. n. flattery intended to persuade someone to do something.

blank • adj. **1** not marked or decorated; bare or plain. **2** not understanding or reacting: *a blank look.* **3** complete; absolute: *a blank refusal.* • n. **1** a space left to be filled in a document. **2** an empty space or period of time. **3** a cartridge containing gunpowder but no bullet. • v. **1** hide or block out: *she blanked out her memories of him.* **2** Brit. informal deliberately ignore.
– PHRASES **draw a blank** fail to get a response or result.
– DERIVATIVES **blankly** adv. **blankness** n.
– ORIGIN Old French *blanc* 'white'.

blank cheque • n. **1** a cheque with the amount left for the person cashing it to fill in. **2** unlimited freedom of action.

blanket • n. **1** a large piece of woollen material used as a warm covering. **2** a thick mass or layer: *a blanket of cloud.* • adj. covering all cases; total: *a blanket ban.* • v. (**blankets, blanketing, blanketed**) cover with a thick layer.
– ORIGIN Old French *blanc* 'white'.

blanket stitch • n. a looped stitch used on the edges of material too thick to be hemmed.

blank verse • n. poetry which has a regular rhythm but does not rhyme.

blare • v. (**blares, blaring, blared**) sound loudly and harshly. • n. a loud, harsh sound.
– ORIGIN Dutch or German *blaren.*

blarney • n. charming or persuasive talk.
– ORIGIN from the *Blarney* Stone in Ireland, said to give persuasive speech to anyone who kisses it.

blasé /blah-zay/ • adj. not impressed with something because you have experienced it many times before.
– ORIGIN French.

blaspheme /blass-feem/ • v. (**blasphemes, blaspheming, blasphemed**) speak disrespectfully about God or sacred things.
– DERIVATIVES **blasphemer** n.
– ORIGIN Greek *blasphēmein.*

blasphemy /blass-fuh-mi/ • n. (pl. **blasphemies**) disrespectful talk about God or sacred things.
– DERIVATIVES **blasphemous** adj.

blast • n. **1** an explosion, or the destructive wave of air spreading outwards from it. **2** a strong gust of wind or air. **3** a single loud note of a horn or whistle. • v. **1** blow up with explosives. **2** (**blast off**) (of a rocket or spacecraft) take off. **3** produce loud music or noise. **4** hit a ball hard. **5** informal criticize fiercely. **6** (as adj. **blasted**) informal expressing annoyance. • exclam. Brit. informal expressing annoyance.
– PHRASES **(at) full blast** at maximum power or intensity.
– DERIVATIVES **blaster** n.
– ORIGIN Old English.

blast furnace • n. a smelting furnace using blasts of hot compressed air.

blatant • adj. open and unashamed: *a blatant act of racism.*
– DERIVATIVES **blatancy** n. **blatantly** adv.
– ORIGIN perh. from Scots *blatand* 'bleating'.

> ☑ The ending of **blatant** is spelled **-ant**.

blather • v. (**blathers, blathering, blathered**) talk at length without making much sense. • n. rambling talk.
– ORIGIN Old Norse.

blaze • n. **1** a very large or fierce fire. **2** a very bright light or display of colour. **3** an outburst: *he left in a blaze of glory.* **4** a white stripe down the face of a horse or other animal. • v. (**blazes, blazing, blazed**) **1** burn or shine fiercely or brightly. **2** (of guns) be fired repeatedly or wildly. **3** present news in a prominent way.
– PHRASES **blaze a trail 1** mark out a path. **2** be the first to do something.
– ORIGIN Old English; sense 3 of the verb is from German or Dutch *blāzen* 'to blow'.

blazer • n. **1** a jacket worn by schoolchildren or sports players as part of a uniform. **2** a man's smart jacket not forming part of a suit.

blazon /blay-zuhn/ • v. **1** display or describe prominently: *their names were blazoned all over the media.* **2** Heraldry depict a coat of arms. • n. a coat of arms.
– ORIGIN Old French *blason* 'shield'.

bleach • v. lighten by chemicals or sunlight. • n. a chemical used to lighten things and also to sterilize drains, sinks, etc.
– ORIGIN Old English.

bleak • adj. **1** bare and exposed to the weather. **2** dreary and unwelcoming: *a bleak little room.* **3** (of a situation) not hopeful.
– DERIVATIVES **bleakly** adv. **bleakness** n.
– ORIGIN Old English, 'white, shining'.

bleary • adj. (**blearier, bleariest**) (of the

eyes) dull and not focusing properly.
– DERIVATIVES **blearily** adv.
– ORIGIN prob. from German *blerre* 'blurred vision'.

bleat • v. **1** (of a sheep or goat) make a weak, wavering cry. **2** speak or complain in a weak or foolish way. • n. a bleating sound.
– ORIGIN Old English.

bleed • v. (**bleeds**, **bleeding**, **bled**) **1** lose blood from the body. **2** take blood from someone as a former medical treatment. **3** informal drain someone of money or resources. **4** (of dye or colour) seep into an adjoining colour or area. **5** allow fluid or gas to escape from a closed system through a valve. • n. an instance of bleeding.
– ORIGIN Old English.

bleeding • adj. Brit. informal used for emphasis or to express annoyance.

bleeding heart • n. informal, derog. a person who is thought to be too liberal or soft-hearted.

bleep • n. a short high-pitched sound made by an electronic device. • v. **1** make a bleep. **2** call with a device that makes a bleep.
– DERIVATIVES **bleeper** n.

blemish • n. a small mark or flaw. • v. spoil the appearance of something.
– ORIGIN Old French *blesmir* 'make pale'.

blench • v. flinch suddenly through fear or pain.
– ORIGIN Old English, 'deceive'.

blend • v. **1** mix and combine with something else. **2** become an unnoticeable part of a greater whole: *a bodyguard has to blend in.* • n. a mixture.
– ORIGIN prob. Scandinavian.

blender • n. an electric device for liquidizing or chopping food.

bless • v. **1** make holy by a religious ceremony. **2** ask God to protect. **3** (**be blessed with**) have or be given something desired.
– PHRASES **bless you!** said to a person who has just sneezed.
– ORIGIN Old English.

blessed /bless-id, blest/ • adj. **1** holy or protected by God. **2** bringing welcome pleasure or relief: *blessed sleep.* **3** informal expressing mild annoyance.
– DERIVATIVES **blessedly** adv.

blessing • n. **1** God's favour and protection, or a prayer asking for this. **2** something which you are very grateful for: *it's a blessing we're alive.* **3** a person's approval or support.

blew past of BLOW¹.

blight • n. **1** a plant disease, especially one caused by fungi. **2** a cause of harm or damage: *divorce is a great blight on your life.* • v. **1** infect with blight. **2** spoil or damage.

blighter • n. Brit. informal a person regarded with scorn or pity.

Blighty • n. Brit. informal (used by soldiers serving abroad) Britain or England.
– ORIGIN Urdu, 'foreign, European'.

blimey • exclam. Brit. informal expressing surprise or alarm.
– ORIGIN from *God blind* (or *blame*) *me!*

blind • adj. **1** not able to see. **2** lacking awareness, judgement, or reason: *blind hatred.* **3** done without being able to see or without certain information. **4** concealed, closed, or blocked: *a blind alley.* **5** informal the slightest: *it didn't do a blind bit of good.* • v. **1** make blind. **2** stop from thinking reasonably or clearly: *he was blinded by rage.* **3** (**blind someone with**) confuse or overawe someone with something hard to understand. • n. **1** a screen for a window. **2** something meant to hide your plans. • adv. without being able to see clearly.
– PHRASES **blind drunk** informal very drunk. **turn a blind eye** pretend not to notice.
– DERIVATIVES **blindly** adv. **blindness** n.
– ORIGIN Old English.

blind date • n. a meeting with a person you have not met before, with the aim of starting a romantic relationship.

blindfold • n. a piece of cloth tied around the head to cover someone's eyes. • v. cover someone's eyes with a blindfold. • adv. Brit. with a blindfold covering the eyes.
– ORIGIN Old English.

blinding • adj. **1** (of light) very bright. **2** (of pain) very severe. **3** informal very skilful and exciting.

blind man's buff • n. a game in which a blindfold player tries to catch other people while being pushed about by them.
– ORIGIN from the former word *buff* 'a blow'.

blind spot • n. **1** a small area of the retina in the eye that is insensitive to light. **2** an area where a person's view is obstructed. **3** a matter where a person lacks understanding: *he had a blind spot where ethics were concerned.*

bling-bling (also **bling**) • n. informal used to refer to showy, expensive clothing or jewellery, or the attitudes associated with them.
– ORIGIN perh. from the sound of jewellery clashing together.

blink • v. **1** shut and open the eyes quickly. **2** (of a light) flash on and off. • n. an act of blinking.

b

– PHRASES **on the blink** informal out of order.
– ORIGIN from **BLENCH**.

blinker • n. (**blinkers**) esp. Brit. **1** a pair of small screens attached to a horse's bridle to prevent it from seeing sideways. **2** a thing that prevents complete understanding. • v. (**blinkers, blinkering, blinkered**) **1** put blinkers on a horse. **2** (as adj. **blinkered**) having a limited point of view.

blinking • adj. Brit. informal used to express annoyance.

blip • n. **1** a very short high-pitched sound made by an electronic device. **2** a small flashing point of light on a radar screen. **3** an unexpected and temporary change in a steady situation or process: *a minor blip in the firm's growth rate.* • v. (**blips, blipped, blipping**) make a blip.

bliss • n. **1** perfect happiness. **2** a state of spiritual blessedness.
– ORIGIN Old English.

blissful • adj. very happy.
– DERIVATIVES **blissfully** adv.

blister • n. **1** a small bubble on the skin filled with watery liquid. **2** a similar swelling, filled with air or fluid, on a surface. • v. form or cause to form blisters.
– ORIGIN perh. from Old French *blestre*.

blistering • adj. **1** (of heat) intense. **2** very fierce or forceful.

blithe /blyth/ • adj. **1** without thought or care: *a blithe ignorance of the facts.* **2** literary happy.
– DERIVATIVES **blithely** adv.
– ORIGIN Old English.

blithering • adj. informal complete: *a blithering idiot.*
– ORIGIN from **BLATHER**.

BLitt • abbrev. Bachelor of Letters.
– ORIGIN from Latin *Baccalaureus Litterarum*.

blitz • n. **1** an intensive or sudden military attack. **2** (**the Blitz**) the German air raids on Britain in the Second World War. **3** informal a sudden and concentrated effort. • v. attack or damage in a blitz.
– ORIGIN German *Blitzkrieg* 'lightning war'.

blizzard • n. a severe snowstorm with high winds.

bloat • v. cause to swell with fluid or gas.
– ORIGIN perh. from Old Norse, 'soft'.

bloater • n. a salted and smoked herring.

blob • n. **1** a drop of a thick liquid or sticky substance. **2** a roundish mass or shape.
– DERIVATIVES **blobby** adj.

bloc • n. a group of countries or political parties who have formed an alliance.
– ORIGIN French, 'block'.

block • n. **1** a large solid piece of material with flat surfaces on each side. **2** Brit. a large single building divided into flats or offices. **3** a group of buildings with streets on all four sides. **4** a large quantity of things regarded as a unit: *a block of shares.* **5** an obstacle. **6** (also **cylinder block** or **engine block**) a large metal moulding containing the cylinders of an internal-combustion engine. **7** a pulley or system of pulleys mounted in a case. • v. **1** prevent movement or flow in something. **2** hinder or prevent: *the government tried to block the agreement.*
– PHRASES **knock someone's block off** informal hit someone on the head.
– DERIVATIVES **blocker** n.
– ORIGIN Dutch.

blockade • n. an act of sealing off a place to prevent goods or people from entering or leaving. • v. (**blockades, blockading, blockaded**) block the way in or out of a place.

blockage • n. an obstruction.

block and tackle • n. a lifting mechanism consisting of ropes, a pulley block, and a hook.

blockbuster • n. informal a film or book that is a great commercial success.

block capitals • pl. n. plain capital letters.

blockhead • n. informal a very stupid person.

blockhouse • n. a reinforced concrete shelter used as an observation point.

blog • n. a weblog. • v. (**blogs, blogging, blogged**) (usu. as noun **blogging**) regularly update a weblog.
– DERIVATIVES **blogger** n.

bloke • n. Brit. informal a man.
– DERIVATIVES **blokeish** (also **blokish**) adj.
– ORIGIN Shelta (a language used by Irish and Welsh Gypsies).

blonde • adj. (also **blond**) **1** (of hair) fair or pale yellow. **2** having fair hair and a light complexion. • n. a woman with blonde hair.
– ORIGIN French.

blood • n. **1** the red liquid that circulates in the arteries and veins, carrying oxygen and carbon dioxide. **2** family background: *she must have Irish blood.* • v. initiate someone in an activity.
– PHRASES **be** (or **run**) **in your blood** be a fundamental or inherited part of your character. **first blood** the first advantage gained in a contest. **have blood on your hands** be responsible for someone's death. **make someone's blood boil** informal make someone very angry. **new** (or **fresh**) **blood** new people who

join a group and often give it fresh ideas.
– ORIGIN Old English.

bloodbath • n. an event in which many people are killed violently.

blood brother • n. a man who has sworn to treat another man as a brother.

blood count • n. a calculation of the number of corpuscles (red and white blood cells) in a particular quantity of blood.

blood-curdling • adj. very frightening; horrifying.

blood group • n. any of the various types into which human blood is classified.

bloodhound • n. a large hound with a very keen sense of smell, used in tracking.

bloodless • adj. **1** without violence or killing: a bloodless coup. **2** (of the skin) drained of colour. **3** lacking emotion or vitality.

bloodletting • n. **1** hist. the surgical removal of some of a patient's blood. **2** violence during a war or conflict.

bloodline • n. a pedigree or set of ancestors.

blood money • n. **1** money paid to compensate the family of a murdered person. **2** money paid to a hired killer.

blood poisoning • n. a serious illness that results when harmful microorganisms have infected the blood.

blood pressure • n. the pressure of the blood in the circulatory system.

blood relation (also **blood relative**) • n. a person who is related to another by birth.

bloodshed • n. the killing or wounding of people.

bloodshot • adj. (of the eyes) inflamed or tinged with blood.

blood sport • n. a sport involving the hunting, wounding, or killing of animals.

bloodstock • n. thoroughbred horses.

bloodstream • n. the blood circulating through the body.

blood sugar • n. the concentration of glucose in the blood.

bloodthirsty • adj. taking pleasure in killing and violence.

blood vessel • n. a vein, artery, or capillary carrying blood through the body.

bloody • adj. (**bloodier**, **bloodiest**) **1** covered with or containing blood. **2** involving much violence or cruelty. **3** Brit. informal used to express anger or shock, or for emphasis. • v. (**bloodies**,

bloodying, **bloodied**) cover or stain with blood.
– DERIVATIVES **bloodily** adv. **bloodiness** n.

bloody-minded • adj. Brit. informal deliberately unhelpful.

bloom • v. **1** produce flowers; be in flower. **2** be or become very healthy. • n. **1** a flower. **2** the state or period of blooming: the apple trees were in bloom. **3** a healthy glow in a person's complexion. **4** a fine powdery coating on the surface of some fruit.
– DERIVATIVES **bloomer** n.
– ORIGIN Old Norse.

bloomers • pl. n. **1** women's loose-fitting knee-length knickers. **2** hist. women's loose-fitting trousers, gathered at the knee or ankle.
– ORIGIN named after the American social reformer Mrs Amelia J. Bloomer.

blooming • adj. Brit. informal used to express annoyance or for emphasis.

blossom • n. **1** a flower or a mass of flowers on a tree or bush. **2** the state or period of flowering. • v. **1** produce blossom. **2** develop in a promising or healthy way: our friendship blossomed into love.
– ORIGIN Old English.

blot • n. **1** a spot or stain made by ink. **2** a thing that spoils something good: the hotel is a blot on the coastline. • v. (**blots**, **blotting**, **blotted**) **1** dry with an absorbent material. **2** mark or spoil. **3** (**blot something out**) hide or cover something. **4** (**blot something out**) keep something from your mind: they wanted to blot out the bad news.
– PHRASES **blot your copybook** Brit. spoil your good reputation.
– ORIGIN prob. Scandinavian.

blotch • n. a large irregular mark.
– DERIVATIVES **blotched** adj. **blotchy** adj.
– ORIGIN from BLOT + BOTCH.

blotter • n. a pad of blotting paper.

blotting paper • n. absorbent paper used for soaking up excess ink when writing.

blotto • adj. informal very drunk.

blouse • n. a woman's top that is similar to a shirt.
– ORIGIN French.

blouson /bloo-zon/ • n. a short loose-fitting jacket.
– ORIGIN French.

blow¹ • v. (**blows**, **blowing**, **blew**; past part. **blown**) **1** (of wind) move or be moving. **2** send out air through pursed lips. **3** force air through the mouth into a musical instrument. **4** sound a horn. **5** (of an explosion) force out of place: the blast blew the windows out. **6** burst or burn out through pressure or over-

heating. **7** informal spend money in a reckless way. **8** informal reveal something secret: *his cover was blown.* **9** informal waste an opportunity. •n. **1** an act of blowing. **2** a strong wind.
– PHRASES **blow hot and cold** keep changing your mind. **blow someone's mind** informal impress or affect someone very strongly. **blow over** (of trouble) fade away without serious effects. **blow your top** informal lose your temper. **blow up 1** explode. **2** begin to develop or become public.
– ORIGIN Old English.

blow² •n. **1** a powerful stroke with a hand or weapon. **2** a sudden shock or disappointment.
– PHRASES **come to blows** start fighting after a disagreement.

blow-by-blow •adj. (of a description of an event) giving all the details in order.

blow-dry •v. arrange the hair while drying it with a hand-held dryer.

blower •n. **1** a device that creates a current of air to dry or heat something. **2** Brit. informal a telephone.

blowfly •n. (pl. **blowflies**) a bluebottle or similar large fly which lays its eggs on meat and carcasses.

blowhole •n. **1** the nostril of a whale or dolphin on the top of its head. **2** a hole in ice for breathing or fishing through.

blowlamp •n. Brit. a blowtorch.

blown past part. of BLOW¹.

blowout •n. **1** an occasion when a vehicle tyre bursts or an electric fuse melts. **2** informal a large meal.

blowpipe •n. a weapon consisting of a long tube through which an arrow or dart is blown.

blowsy /rhymes with drowsy/ (also **blowzy**) •adj. (of a woman) untidy and red-faced.
– ORIGIN from a former word meaning 'beggar's female companion'.

blowtorch •n. a portable device producing a hot flame, used to burn off paint.

blowy •adj. windy or windswept.

blub •v. (**blubs, blubbing, blubbed**) informal sob noisily.
– ORIGIN from BLUBBER².

blubber¹ •n. the fat of sea mammals, especially whales and seals.
– DERIVATIVES **blubbery** adj.

blubber² •v. (**blubbers, blubbering, blubbered**) informal sob noisily.

bludgeon •n. a thick stick with a heavy end, used as a weapon. •v. **1** hit with a bludgeon. **2** bully someone into doing something.

blue •adj. (**bluer, bluest**) **1** of the colour of the sky on a sunny day. **2** informal sad or depressed. **3** informal having sexual or pornographic content: *a blue movie.* **4** Brit. informal politically conservative. •n. **1** blue colour or material. **2** Brit. a person who has represented Cambridge University or Oxford University at a particular sport in a match between the two universities.
– PHRASES **once in a blue moon** informal very rarely. **out of the blue** informal unexpectedly.
– DERIVATIVES **blueness** n.
– ORIGIN Old French *bleu*.

bluebell •n. a woodland plant with clusters of blue bell-shaped flowers.

blueberry •n. (pl. **blueberries**) the small blue-black berry of a North American shrub.

bluebird •n. an American songbird, the male of which has a blue head, back, and wings.

blue-blooded •adj. of noble birth.

bluebottle •n. a blowfly with a metallic-blue body.

blue cheese •n. cheese containing veins of blue mould, such as Stilton.

blue-chip •adj. (of a company or shares) considered to be a reliable investment.
– ORIGIN from the *blue chip* used in gambling, which has a high value.

blue-collar •adj. esp. N. Amer. relating to manual work or workers.

blue-eyed boy •n. Brit. informal, derog. a person treated with special favour by someone.

blueish •adj. var. of BLUISH.

blueprint •n. **1** a design plan or other technical drawing. **2** something which acts as a plan or model.

blue ribbon •n. (also **blue riband**) a blue silk ribbon given to the winner of a competition.

blues •n. **1** slow, sad music of black American origin. **2** (**the blues**) informal feelings of sadness or depression.
– DERIVATIVES **bluesy** adj.
– ORIGIN from *blue devils* 'depression'.

bluestocking •n. usu. derog. an intellectual or literary woman.
– ORIGIN from the literary parties held in 18th-century London by society ladies, where some of the men wore blue worsted stockings.

blue tit •n. a small songbird with a blue cap and yellow underparts.

blue whale •n. a bluish-grey whale which is the largest living animal.

bluff¹ •n. an attempt to deceive someone into believing that you know or will do something. •v. try to make someone

believe that you know or will do something.
- PHRASES **call someone's bluff** challenge someone to do something, in the belief that they will not be able to.
- DERIVATIVES **bluffer** n.
- ORIGIN Dutch *bluffen* 'brag'.

bluff² • adj. frank and direct in a good-natured way.
- ORIGIN from BLUFF³.

bluff³ • n. a steep cliff or slope.

bluish (also **blueish**) • adj. tinged with blue.

blunder • n. a stupid or careless mistake. • v. (**blunders, blundering, blundered**) **1** make a blunder. **2** move clumsily or as if unable to see.
- ORIGIN prob. Scandinavian.

blunderbuss • n. hist. a gun with a short, wide barrel, firing balls or lead bullets.
- ORIGIN Dutch *donderbus* 'thunder gun'.

blunt • adj. **1** lacking a sharp edge or point. **2** very frank and direct: *a blunt statement of fact.* • v. **1** make or become blunt. **2** make weaker or less effective.
- DERIVATIVES **bluntly** adv. **bluntness** n.
- ORIGIN perh. Scandinavian.

blur • v. (**blurs, blurring, blurred**) make or become unclear or less distinct. • n. something that cannot be seen, heard, or recalled clearly.
- DERIVATIVES **blurry** adj.
- ORIGIN perh. from BLEARY.

blurb • n. informal a short description written to promote a book, film, or other product.
- ORIGIN coined by the American humorist Gelett Burgess.

blurt • v. say suddenly and without thinking.

blush • v. become red in the face through shyness or embarrassment. • n. **1** an instance of blushing. **2** literary a pink tinge.
- ORIGIN Old English.

blusher • n. esp. Brit. a cosmetic used to give a reddish tinge to the cheeks.

bluster • v. (**blusters, blustering, blustered**) **1** talk in a loud or aggressive way with little effect. **2** (of wind or rain) blow or beat fiercely and noisily. • n. loud and empty talk.
- DERIVATIVES **blustery** adj.

BM • abbrev. Bachelor of Medicine.

BMA • abbrev. British Medical Association.

B-movie • n. a low-budget film supporting a main film in a cinema programme.

BMX • abbrev. bicycle motocross (referring to bicycles designed for cross-country racing).

boa • n. **1** a large snake which winds itself round its prey and crushes it to death. **2** a long, thin stole of feathers or fur worn around a woman's neck.
- ORIGIN Latin.

boar • n. (pl. **boar** or **boars**) **1** (also **wild boar**) a wild pig with tusks. **2** an uncastrated male pig.
- ORIGIN Old English.

board • n. **1** a long, thin, flat piece of wood used in building. **2** a thin, flat, rectangular piece of stiff material used for various purposes. **3** a group of people who control an organization. **4** the provision of regular meals in return for payment. • v. **1** get on or into a ship, aircraft, or other vehicle. **2** receive meals and accommodation in return for payment. **3** (of a pupil) live in school during term time. **4** (**board something up/over**) cover or seal something with pieces of wood.
- PHRASES **go by the board** (of a plan or principle) be abandoned or rejected. [ORIGIN from nautical use meaning 'fall overboard'.] **on board** on or in a ship, aircraft, or other vehicle. **take something on board** informal fully consider or accept a new idea. **tread the boards** informal appear on stage as an actor.
- ORIGIN Old English.

boarder • n. **1** a pupil who lives in school during term time. **2** a person who forces their way on to a ship in an attack.

board game • n. a game that involves the movement of counters or other objects around a board.

boarding house • n. a private house providing food and lodging for paying guests.

boarding school • n. a school in which the pupils live during term time.

boardroom • n. a room in which a board of directors meets regularly.

boast • v. **1** talk about yourself with excessive pride. **2** possess an impressive or attractive feature: *the hotel boasts high standards of comfort.* • n. an act of boasting.
- DERIVATIVES **boaster** n.

boastful • adj. showing excessive pride in yourself.
- DERIVATIVES **boastfully** adv. **boastfulness** n.

boat • n. a vehicle for travelling on water.
- PHRASES **be in the same boat** informal be in the same difficult situation as other people. **miss the boat** informal be too slow to take advantage of something. **push the boat out** Brit. informal be extravagant. **rock the boat** informal disturb an existing situation.
- ORIGIN Old English.

boater •n. a flat-topped straw hat with a brim.

boathook •n. a long pole with a hook and a spike at one end, used for moving boats.

boathouse •n. a shed at the edge of a river or lake used for housing boats.

boating •n. the activity of using a small boat for pleasure.

boatman •n. (pl. **boatmen**) a person who provides transport by boat.

boat people •pl. n. refugees who have left a country by sea.

boatswain /boh-s'n/ (also **bo'sun** or **bosun**) •n. a ship's officer in charge of equipment and the crew.

Bob •n. (in phr. **Bob's your uncle**) Brit. informal said when a person thinks a task will be easy to complete.

bob[1] •v. (**bobs, bobbing, bobbed**) move quickly up and down. •n. a quick, short movement up and down.

bob[2] •n. 1 a short hairstyle hanging evenly all round. 2 a weight on a pendulum, plumb line, or kite-tail. 3 a bobsleigh. •v. (**bobs, bobbing, bobbed**) cut evenly all round.

bob[3] •n. (pl. **bob**) Brit. informal a shilling.

bobbin •n. a cylinder, cone, or reel holding thread.
– ORIGIN French *bobine*.

bobble •n. a small ball made of strands of wool.
– DERIVATIVES **bobbly** adj.
– ORIGIN from BOB[2].

bobby •n. (pl. **bobbies**) Brit. informal, dated a police officer.
– ORIGIN after Sir *Robert* Peel, the British Prime Minister who founded the Metropolitan Police.

bobsleigh (N. Amer. **bobsled**) •n. a sledge with brakes and a steering mechanism, used for racing down an ice-covered run.

Boche /bosh/ •n. (**the Boche**) informal, dated German soldiers.
– ORIGIN French, 'rascal'.

bod •n. informal 1 a body. 2 esp. Brit. a person.

bode •v. (**bodes, boding, boded**) (**bode well/ill**) be a sign of a good or bad outcome: *the film's success bodes well for similar projects.*
– ORIGIN Old English, 'proclaim, foretell'.

bodge •v. (**bodges, bodging, bodged**) Brit. informal make or repair badly or clumsily.
– DERIVATIVES **bodger** n.
– ORIGIN from BOTCH.

bodice •n. 1 the part of a dress above the waist. 2 a woman's sleeveless undergarment.
– ORIGIN formerly *bodies*, plural of BODY.

bodily •adj. relating to the body. •adv. by taking hold of a person's body with force.

bodkin •n. a thick, blunt needle with a large eye, used for drawing tape or cord through a hem.
– ORIGIN perh. Celtic.

body •n. (pl. **bodies**) 1 the whole physical structure of a person or an animal. 2 the main part of the body, apart from the head and limbs. 3 the main or central part: *the body of the aircraft was filled with smoke.* 4 a mass or collection. 5 an organized group set up for a particular purpose: *a regulatory body.* 6 tech. an object: *the path taken by the falling body.* 7 fullness of flavour or texture. 8 Brit. a woman's stretch garment for the upper body.
– PHRASES **keep body and soul together** stay alive in difficult circumstances.
– DERIVATIVES **bodied** adj. **bodiless** adj.
– ORIGIN Old English.

body blow •n. 1 a heavy punch to the body. 2 a severe setback.

bodybuilder •n. a person who strengthens and enlarges their muscles through exercise.

body clock •n. a person's biological clock.

bodyguard •n. a person employed to protect an important or famous person.

body language •n. the conveying of your feelings by the movement or position of your body.

body politic •n. the people of a nation or society considered as an organized group of citizens.

body stocking •n. a woman's one-piece undergarment covering the torso and legs.

bodysuit •n. = BODY (in sense 8).

bodywork •n. the metal outer shell of a vehicle.

Boer /*rhymes with* more *or* mower/ •n. an early Dutch or Huguenot settler of southern Africa. •adj. relating to the Boers.
– ORIGIN Dutch, 'farmer'.

boffin •n. Brit. informal a scientist.

bog •n. 1 an area of soft, wet, muddy ground. 2 Brit. informal a toilet. •v. (**be/get bogged down**) be prevented from progressing.
– DERIVATIVES **boggy** adj.
– ORIGIN Irish or Scottish Gaelic, 'soft'.

bogey[1] •n. (pl. **bogeys**) Golf a score of one stroke over par at a hole.
– ORIGIN perh. from BOGEY[2], referring to the Devil as an imaginary player.

bogey[2] (also **bogy**) •n. (pl. **bogeys**) 1 an evil or mischievous spirit. 2 a cause of

fear or alarm: *the bogey of recession.* **3** Brit. informal a piece of mucus in the nose.
– ORIGIN a former name for the Devil.

bogeyman (also **bogyman**) • n. (pl. **bogeymen**) an evil spirit.

boggle • v. (**boggles, boggling, boggled**) informal **1** be astonished or baffled: *the mind boggles at the complexity of the system.* **2** (**boggle at**) hesitate to do.
– ORIGIN prob. related to BOGEY².

bogie /boh-gi/ • n. (pl. **bogies**) esp. Brit. a supporting frame with wheels, fitted on a pivot beneath the end of a railway vehicle.

bog-standard • adj. Brit. informal, derog. ordinary; basic.

bogus • adj. not genuine or true.

bogy • n. (pl. **bogies**) var. of BOGEY².

Bohemian /boh-hee-mi-uhn/ • n. a person who does not follow accepted standards of behaviour. • adj. unconventional: *a Bohemian life.*
– DERIVATIVES **Bohemianism** n.
– ORIGIN from *Bohemia*, a region of the Czech Republic.

bohrium /bor-iuhm/ • n. a very unstable chemical element made by high-energy atomic collisions.
– ORIGIN named after the Danish physicist Niels *Bohr.*

boil¹ • v. **1** (with reference to a liquid) reach or cause to reach the temperature at which it bubbles and turns to vapour. **2** cook or be cooked in boiling water. **3** (**boil down to**) have as a main or basic part: *everything boils down to politics.* • n. **1** the action of boiling; boiling point. **2** a state of great activity or excitement: *the team have gone off the boil this season.*
– ORIGIN Latin *bullire* 'to bubble'.

boil² • n. an inflamed pus-filled swelling on the skin.
– ORIGIN Old English.

boiler • n. a fuel-burning device for heating water.

boiler suit • n. Brit. a one-piece suit worn as overalls for manual work.

boiling • adj. **1** at or near boiling point. **2** informal very hot.

boiling point • n. the temperature at which a liquid boils.

boisterous • adj. noisy, lively, and high-spirited.

bold • adj. **1** confident and brave. **2** (of a colour or design) strong or vivid. **3** dated lacking respect; impudent. **4** (of type) having thick strokes.
– PHRASES **as bold as brass** so confident as to be disrespectful.
– DERIVATIVES **boldly** adv. **boldness** n.
– ORIGIN Old English.

bole • n. a tree trunk.

– ORIGIN Old Norse.

bolero • n. (pl. **boleros**) **1** /buh-**lair**-oh/ a Spanish dance. **2** /**bol**-uh-roh/ a woman's short open jacket.
– ORIGIN Spanish.

Bolivian • n. a person from Bolivia. • adj. relating to Bolivia.

boll /rhymes with hole/ • n. the rounded seed capsule of plants such as cotton.
– ORIGIN Dutch *bolle* 'rounded object'.

bollard • n. **1** Brit. a short post used to prevent traffic from entering an area. **2** a short post on a ship or quayside for securing a rope.
– ORIGIN perh. from Old Norse, 'bole'.

Bollywood • n. the Indian popular film industry, based in Bombay.
– ORIGIN from *Bombay* and *Hollywood.*

Bolshevik /bol-shi-vik/ • n. hist. **1** a member of the majority group within the Russian Social Democratic Party, which seized power in the Revolution of 1917. **2** a person with revolutionary or radical political views.
– DERIVATIVES **Bolshevism** n.
– ORIGIN Russian *bol'she* 'greater'.

bolshie (also **bolshy**) • adj. Brit. informal hostile and uncooperative.
– ORIGIN from BOLSHEVIK.

bolster • n. a long, firm pillow.
• v. (**bolsters, bolstering, bolstered**) support or strengthen: *campaigns to bolster the president's image.*
– ORIGIN Old English.

bolt • n. **1** a long metal pin with a head that screws into a nut, used to fasten things together. **2** a bar that slides into a socket to fasten a door or window. **3** a short, heavy arrow shot from a crossbow. **4** a flash of lightning. **5** a roll of fabric. • v. **1** fasten with a bolt. **2** run away suddenly. **3** eat food quickly. **4** (of a plant) grow quickly upwards and stop flowering as seeds develop.
– PHRASES **a bolt from** (or **out of**) **the blue** a sudden and unexpected event. **bolt upright** with the back very straight. **have shot your bolt** informal have done everything possible but still not succeeded. **make a bolt for** try to escape by running suddenly towards.
– ORIGIN Old English.

bolt-hole • n. esp. Brit. a place where a person can escape to and hide.

bomb • n. **1** a container of material capable of exploding or causing a fire. **2** (**the bomb**) nuclear weapons. **3** (**a bomb**) Brit. informal a large sum of money. • v. **1** attack with a bomb or bombs. **2** Brit. informal move very quickly. **3** informal fail badly.
– PHRASES **go like a bomb** Brit. informal **1** be very successful. **2** move very fast.

– ORIGIN French *bombe*.

bombard /bom-bard/ • v. 1 attack continuously with bombs or other missiles. 2 direct a continuous flow of questions or information at someone. 3 Physics direct a stream of high-speed particles at a substance.
– DERIVATIVES **bombardment** n.
– ORIGIN French *bombarder*.

bombardier /bom-buh-deer/ • n. 1 a rank of non-commissioned officer in some artillery regiments, equivalent to corporal. 2 a member of a bomber crew in the US air force responsible for releasing bombs.
– ORIGIN French.

bombast /bom-bast/ • n. language that sounds impressive but has little meaning.
– DERIVATIVES **bombastic** adj. **bombastically** adv.
– ORIGIN Old French *bombace* 'cotton used as padding'.

bombazine /bom-buh-zeen/ • n. a twill dress fabric of worsted and silk or cotton.
– ORIGIN Latin *bombycinus* 'silken'.

bomber • n. 1 an aircraft that drops bombs. 2 a person who plants bombs.

bomber jacket • n. a short jacket gathered at the waist and cuffs by elasticated bands and having a full front.

bombshell • n. 1 something that comes as a great surprise and shock. 2 informal a very attractive woman.

bona fide /boh-nuh fy-di/ • adj. genuine; real.
– ORIGIN Latin, 'with good faith'.

bona fides /boh-nuh fy-deez/ • n. evidence proving that a person is what they claim to be; credentials.
– ORIGIN Latin, 'good faith'.

bonanza • n. 1 a situation creating wealth or success. 2 a large amount of something desirable.
– ORIGIN Spanish, 'fair weather'.

bonbon • n. a sweet.
– ORIGIN French *bon* 'good'.

bonce • n. Brit. informal a person's head.

bond • n. 1 a thing used to tie or fasten things together. 2 (**bonds**) ropes or chains used to hold someone prisoner. 3 a force or feeling that links people: *the bond between mother and son.* 4 an agreement with legal force. 5 a certificate issued by a government or a public company promising to repay money lent to it at a fixed rate of interest and at a specified time. 6 (also **chemical bond**) a strong force of attraction holding atoms together in a molecule. • v. 1 join or be joined securely to something else. 2 form a relationship based on shared feelings or experiences.
– ORIGIN from **BAND**[1].

bondage • n. 1 the state of being a slave. 2 sexual practice that involves the tying up of one partner.
– ORIGIN from Old Norse, 'tiller of the soil'.

bond paper • n. high-quality writing paper.

bone • n. 1 any of the pieces of hard, whitish tissue making up the skeleton in vertebrates. 2 the hard material of which bones consist. 3 a thing made or formerly made of bone, such as a strip of stiffening for a corset. • v. (**bones, boning, boned**) 1 remove the bones from meat or fish before cooking. 2 (**bone up on**) informal study a subject intensively.
– PHRASES **bone of contention** a source of continuing disagreement. **close to the bone** 1 (of a remark) accurate to the point of causing discomfort. 2 (of a joke or story) near the limit of decency. **have a bone to pick with** informal have reason to quarrel with. **in your bones** felt or believed deeply or instinctively. **make no bones about** be direct in stating or dealing with. **work your fingers to the bone** work very hard.
– DERIVATIVES **boneless** adj.
– ORIGIN Old English.

bone china • n. white porcelain containing the mineral residue of burnt bones.

bone dry • adj. very dry.

bonehead • n. informal a stupid person.

bone idle • adj. very idle.

bonemeal • n. ground bones used as a fertilizer.

boneshaker • n. Brit. informal an old vehicle with poor suspension.

bonfire • n. a large open-air fire lit to burn rubbish or as a celebration.
– ORIGIN first referring to a fire on which bones were burnt.

bongo • n. (pl. **bongos**) each of a pair of small drums, held between the knees and played with the fingers.
– ORIGIN Latin American Spanish.

bonhomie /bon-uh-mee/ • n. good-natured friendliness.
– ORIGIN French.

bonito /buh-nee-toh/ • n. (pl. **bonitos**) a small tuna with dark stripes.
– ORIGIN Spanish.

bonk informal • v. 1 hit someone or something. 2 have sex. • n. 1 a hit or knock. 2 an act of having sex.

bonkers • adj. informal mad.

bon mot /bon moh/ • n. (pl. **bons mots**

/bon **moh**, bon **mohz**/) a clever or witty remark.

– ORIGIN French, 'good word'.

bonnet • n. **1** a woman's or child's hat tied under the chin and with a brim framing the face. **2** a soft hat like a beret, worn by men and boys in Scotland. **3** Brit. the hinged metal cover over the engine of a motor vehicle.

– DERIVATIVES **bonneted** adj.

– ORIGIN Old French *bonet*.

bonny (also **bonnie**) • adj. (**bonnier**, **bonniest**) esp. Scottish & N. English **1** attractive; healthy-looking. **2** considerable: *it's worth a bonny sum.*

– ORIGIN perh. from Old French *bon* 'good'.

bonsai /bon-sy/ • n. the art of growing ornamental trees or shrubs in small pots so as to restrict their growth.

– ORIGIN Japanese, 'tray planting'.

bonus • n. **1** a sum of money added to a person's wages for good performance. **2** an unexpected and extra benefit.

– ORIGIN Latin, 'good'.

bon vivant /bon vee-von/ • n. (pl. **bon vivants** or **bons vivants** /bon vee-von/) a person who enjoys a sociable and luxurious lifestyle.

– ORIGIN French.

bon viveur /bon vee-ver/ • n. (pl. **bon viveurs** or **bons viveurs** /bon vee-ver/) = **BON VIVANT**.

– ORIGIN French.

bon voyage /bon voy-yah*z*h/ • exclam. have a good journey.

– ORIGIN French.

bony • adj. (**bonier**, **boniest**) **1** relating to or containing bones. **2** so thin that the bones can be seen.

– DERIVATIVES **boniness** n.

bonzer • adj. Austral./NZ informal excellent.

– ORIGIN perh. from **BONANZA**.

boo • exclam. **1** said suddenly to surprise someone. **2** said to show disapproval or contempt. • v. (**boos, booing, booed**) say 'boo' to show disapproval or contempt.

boob[1] Brit. informal • n. an embarrassing mistake. • v. make an embarrassing mistake.

– ORIGIN from **BOOBY**[1].

boob[2] • n. informal a woman's breast.

– ORIGIN from **BOOBY**[2].

boo-boo • n. informal a mistake.

– ORIGIN from **BOOB**[1].

boob tube • n. Brit. informal a woman's tight-fitting strapless top.

booby[1] • n. (pl. **boobies**) **1** informal a stupid person. **2** a large tropical seabird of the gannet family.

– ORIGIN prob. from Spanish *bobo*.

booby[2] • n. (pl. **boobies**) informal a woman's breast.

– ORIGIN dialect *bubby*.

booby prize • n. a prize given to the person who comes last in a contest.

booby trap • n. an object containing a hidden explosive device designed to explode when someone touches it. • v. (**booby-trap**) place a booby trap in or on an object or area.

boodle • n. informal money.

– ORIGIN Dutch *boedel, boel* 'possessions'.

boogie • n. (also **boogie-woogie**) (pl. **boogies**) **1** a style of blues played on the piano with a strong, fast beat. **2** informal a dance to pop or rock music. • v. (**boogies, boogieing, boogied**) informal dance to pop or rock music.

book • n. **1** a written or printed work consisting of pages fastened together along one side and bound in covers. **2** a main division of a literary work or of the Bible. **3** a set of blank sheets bound together for writing in: *an exercise book.* **4** (**books**) a set of records or accounts. **5** a set of tickets, stamps, etc., bound together. • v. **1** reserve accommodation, a ticket, etc. **2** (**book in**) register your arrival at a hotel. **3** engage a performer or guest for an event. **4** (**be booked up**) have all places or dates reserved. **5** make an official note of someone who has broken a law or rule.

– PHRASES **bring someone to book** officially ask someone to explain their behaviour. **by the book** strictly according to the rules. **in someone's bad** (or **good**) **books** in disfavour (or favour) with someone. **take a leaf out of someone's book** imitate someone in a particular way. **throw the book at** informal reprimand or punish severely.

– DERIVATIVES **bookable** adj. **booker** n. **booking** n.

– ORIGIN Old English, 'grant by charter'.

bookcase • n. an open cabinet containing shelves on which to keep books.

book club • n. an organization which sells its members selected books at reduced prices.

bookend • n. a support placed at the end of a row of books to keep them upright.

bookie • n. (pl. **bookies**) informal a bookmaker.

bookish • adj. devoted to reading and study.

bookkeeping • n. the activity of keeping records of financial dealings.

– DERIVATIVES **bookkeeper** n.

booklet • n. a small, thin book with paper covers.

bookmaker • n. a person whose job is to

take bets, calculate odds, and pay out winnings.

bookmark • n. **1** a strip of leather or card used to mark a place in a book. **2** a record of the address of a computer file, Internet page, etc., enabling quick access by a user. • v. record the address of a computer file, Internet page, etc.

bookworm • n. informal a person who greatly enjoys reading.

Boolean /boo-li-uhn/ • adj. Computing (of a system of notation) used to represent logical operations by means of the binary digits 0 (false) and 1 (true).
– ORIGIN named after the English mathematician George *Boole*.

boom[1] • n. **1** a loud, deep sound. **2** a period of rapid economic growth. • v. **1** make a loud, deep sound. **2** experience a period of rapid economic growth.
– ORIGIN perh. from Dutch *bommen* 'to hum, buzz'.

boom[2] • n. **1** a pivoted spar to which the foot of a ship's sail is attached. **2** a movable arm carrying a microphone or film camera. **3** a floating beam used to contain oil spills or to form a barrier across the mouth of a harbour.
– ORIGIN Dutch, 'beam, tree, pole'.

boomerang • n. a curved flat piece of wood that can be thrown so as to return to the person throwing it, used by Australian Aboriginals for hunting.
– ORIGIN from an Aboriginal language.

boon • n. a thing that is helpful or beneficial.
– ORIGIN Old Norse, 'a request'.

boon companion • n. a close friend.
– ORIGIN *boon* from Old French *bon* 'good'.

boor /bor, boor/ • n. a rough and bad-mannered person.
– DERIVATIVES **boorish** adj.
– ORIGIN German *bur* or Dutch *boer* 'farmer'.

boost • v. help or encourage to improve: *a range of measures to boost tourism.* • n. **1** a source of help or encouragement. **2** an increase.

booster • n. **1** a thing that helps or increases something. **2** a dose of a vaccine that increases or renews the effect of an earlier one. **3** the part of a rocket or spacecraft used to give acceleration after lift-off.

boot[1] • n. **1** an item of footwear covering the foot and ankle, and sometimes the lower leg. **2** Brit. a space at the back of a car for luggage. **3** informal a hard kick. • v. **1** kick hard. **2** (**boot someone out**) informal force someone to leave. **3** start a computer and make it ready to operate.
[ORIGIN from **pull yourself up by your bootstraps** (see **BOOTSTRAP**).]
– PHRASES **the boot is on the other foot** the situation is now reversed. **give** (or **get**) **the boot** informal dismiss (or be dismissed) from a job. **old boot** informal an ugly or disliked old woman. **put the boot in** Brit. informal attack someone when they are already in a vulnerable position.
– ORIGIN Old French *bote*.

boot[2] • n. (in phr. **to boot**) as well.
– ORIGIN Old English, 'advantage'.

bootee (also **bootie**) • n. **1** a baby's woollen shoe. **2** a woman's short boot.

booth • n. **1** an enclosed compartment allowing privacy when telephoning, voting, etc. **2** a small temporary structure used for selling goods or staging shows at a market or fair.
– ORIGIN Old Norse, 'dwell'.

bootleg • adj. (of alcoholic drink or a recording) made or distributed illegally. • v. (**bootlegs**, **bootlegging**, **bootlegged**) make or distribute alcoholic drink or a recording illegally. • n. an illegal musical recording.
– DERIVATIVES **bootlegger** n.
– ORIGIN from the smugglers' practice of hiding bottles in their boots.

bootstrap • n. a loop at the back of a boot, used to pull it on.
– PHRASES **pull yourself up by your bootstraps** improve your position by your own efforts.

booty • n. valuable stolen goods.
– ORIGIN German *büte, buite* 'exchange'.

booze informal • n. alcoholic drink. • v. (**boozes**, **boozing**, **boozed**) drink large quantities of alcohol.
– DERIVATIVES **boozy** adj.
– ORIGIN Dutch *busen*.

boozer • n. informal **1** a person who drinks large quantities of alcohol. **2** Brit. a pub.

booze-up • n. Brit. informal a heavy drinking session.

bop[1] informal • n. a dance to pop music. • v. (**bops**, **bopping**, **bopped**) dance to pop music.
– DERIVATIVES **bopper** n.
– ORIGIN from **BEBOP**.

bop[2] informal • v. (**bops**, **bopping**, **bopped**) hit or punch quickly. • n. a quick blow or punch.

boracic /buh-rass-ik/ • adj. relating to boric acid.

borax /bor-aks/ • n. a white mineral that is a compound of boron, used in making glass and ceramics.
– ORIGIN Latin.

Bordeaux /bor-doh/ • n. (pl. **Bordeaux** /bor-dohs/) a wine from the Bordeaux region of SW France.

border • n. **1** a boundary between two countries or other areas. **2** a decorative band around the edge of something. **3** a strip of ground along the edge of a lawn for planting flowers or shrubs.
• v. (**borders, bordering, bordered**) **1** form a border around or along. **2** (of a country or area) be next to another. **3** (**border on**) come close to: *his demands bordered on the impossible.*
– ORIGIN Old French *bordeure.*

borderline • n. a boundary. • adj. on the boundary between two states or categories: *references may be requested in borderline cases.*

bore¹ • v. (**bores, boring, bored**) make a hole in something with a drill or other tool. • n. **1** the hollow part inside a gun barrel or other tube. **2** the diameter of a bore: *a small-bore rifle.*
– DERIVATIVES **borer** n.
– ORIGIN Old English.

bore² • n. a dull and uninteresting person or activity: *it's a bore cooking when you're alone.* • v. (**bores, boring, bored**) make someone feel tired and unenthusiastic by being dull and uninteresting.
– DERIVATIVES **boring** adj.

bore³ • n. a high wave caused by the meeting of two tides or by a tide rushing up a narrow estuary.
– ORIGIN perh. from Old Norse, 'a wave'.

bore⁴ past of BEAR¹.

bored • adj. feeling tired and impatient because you are doing something dull or you have nothing to do.

> USAGE: Use **bored by** or **bored with** rather than **bored of**. Although **bored of** is often used in speech, you should not use it in writing.

boredom • n. the state of being bored.

borehole • n. a deep, narrow hole in the ground made to find water or oil.

boric acid • n. a compound derived from boron, used as a mild antiseptic.

born • adj. **1** existing as a result of birth. **2** (**-born**) having a particular nationality: *a Spanish-born footballer.* **3** having a particular natural ability: *he was a born engineer.* **4** (**born of**) existing as a result of a situation or feeling.
– PHRASES **born and bred** by birth and upbringing. **I** (or **she**, etc.) **wasn't born yesterday** I am (or she, etc. is) not easily deceived.
– ORIGIN Old English, from BEAR¹.

> USAGE: Do not confuse **born**, which means 'existing as a result of birth' (*I was born in Hull*) with **borne**, which is the past

participle of **bear** and means 'carried' (*the coffin was borne by eight soldiers*).

born-again • adj. **1** (of a person) newly converted to a personal faith in Jesus. **2** newly converted to and very enthusiastic about a cause: *born-again environmentalists.*

borne past part. of BEAR¹. • adj. (**-borne**) carried by the thing specified: *water-borne bacteria.*

Bornean /bor-ni-uhn/ • n. a person from Borneo. • adj. relating to Borneo.

boron /bor-on/ • n. a crystalline chemical element used in making alloy steel and in nuclear reactors.
– ORIGIN from BORAX.

borough /rhymes with thorough/ • n. **1** Brit. a town with a corporation and privileges granted by a royal charter. **2** an administrative division of London or of New York City.
– ORIGIN Old English, 'fortress, citadel'.

borrow • v. **1** take and use something belonging to someone else with the intention of returning it. **2** have money on a loan from a person or bank.
– DERIVATIVES **borrower** n.
– ORIGIN Old English.

borscht /borsht/ (also **borsch** /borsh/) • n. a Russian or Polish soup made with beetroot.
– ORIGIN Russian *borshch.*

borstal /bor-st'l/ • n. Brit. hist. a prison for young offenders.
– ORIGIN named after the English village of *Borstal.*

borzoi /bor-zoy/ • n. (pl. **borzois**) a breed of large Russian dog with a narrow head and silky coat.
– ORIGIN Russian *borzyĭ* 'swift'.

bosh • n. informal nonsense.
– ORIGIN Turkish *boş* 'empty, worthless'.

bosky /boss-ki/ • adj. literary covered by trees or bushes.
– ORIGIN from BUSH¹.

Bosnian /boz-ni-uhn/ • n. a person from Bosnia. • adj. relating to Bosnia.

bosom • n. **1** a woman's breasts or chest. **2** loving care or protection: *he went home to the bosom of his family.* • adj. (of a friend) very close.
– DERIVATIVES **bosomy** adj.
– ORIGIN Old English.

boss¹ informal • n. a person who is in charge of an employee or organization. • v. give orders in a domineering way.
– ORIGIN Dutch *baas* 'master'.

boss² • n. a projecting knob or stud, such as on the centre of a shield.
– ORIGIN Old French *boce.*

bossa nova /bos-suh noh-vuh/ • n. a Brazilian dance like the samba.

– ORIGIN Portuguese, 'new tendency'.

boss-eyed • adj. Brit. informal cross-eyed.

bossy • adj. (**bossier, bossiest**) informal fond of giving orders; domineering.
– DERIVATIVES **bossily** adv. **bossiness** n.

bosun /boh-s'n/ (also **bo'sun**) • n. var. of **BOATSWAIN**.

botanical • adj. relating to botany.
– DERIVATIVES **botanic** adj. **botanically** adv.

botanical garden (also **botanic garden**) • n. a place where plants are grown for scientific study and display to the public.

botany /bot-uh-ni/ • n. the scientific study of plants.
– DERIVATIVES **botanist** n.
– ORIGIN Greek *botanē* 'plant'.

botch informal • v. do badly or carelessly. • n. a badly performed action or task.

both • det., predet. & pron. two people or things, regarded together. • adv. applying equally to each of two alternatives.
– ORIGIN Old Norse.

bother • v. (**bothers, bothering, bothered**) 1 take the trouble: *the driver didn't bother to ask why.* 2 worry, disturb, or upset. 3 (**bother with/about**) be concerned about or interested in. • n. 1 trouble and fuss. 2 (**a bother**) a cause of trouble or fuss. • exclam. Brit. used to express irritation.
– ORIGIN Anglo-Irish.

bothersome • adj. annoying; troublesome.

Botswanan /bot-swah-nuhn/ • n. a person from Botswana, a country of southern Africa. • adj. relating to Botswana.

bottle • n. 1 a container with a narrow neck, used for storing liquids. 2 Brit. informal courage or confidence.
• v. (**bottles, bottling, bottled**) 1 put liquid in bottles. 2 (**bottle something up**) control and hide your feelings.
– PHRASES **hit the bottle** informal start to drink alcohol heavily.
– ORIGIN Latin *butticula* 'small cask'.

bottle bank • n. Brit. a place where used glass bottles may be left for recycling.

bottle green • adj. dark green.

bottleneck • n. a narrow section of road where traffic flow is restricted.

bottom • n. 1 the lowest or furthest point or part. 2 the lowest position in a competition or ranking: *life at the bottom of society.* 3 esp. Brit. a person's buttocks. 4 (also **bottoms**) the lower half of a two-piece garment. • adj. in the lowest or furthest position. • v. (**bottom out**) (of a situation) reach the lowest point before stabilizing or improving.
– PHRASES **at bottom** basically. **bottoms**

up! informal said as a toast before drinking. **get to the bottom of** find an explanation for.
– DERIVATIVES **bottomless** adj. **bottommost** adj.
– ORIGIN Old English.

bottom drawer • n. Brit. dated household linen stored by a woman in preparation for her marriage.

bottom line • n. informal 1 the final total of an account or balance sheet. 2 the basic and most important factor.

botulism /bot-yuu-li-z'm/ • n. food poisoning caused by a bacterium that grows on preserved foods that have not been properly sterilized.
– ORIGIN German *Botulismus* 'sausage poisoning'.

bouclé /boo-klay/ • n. yarn with a looped or curled strand.
– ORIGIN French, 'buckled, curled'.

boudoir /boo-dwar/ • n. a woman's bedroom or small private room.
– ORIGIN French, 'sulking-place'.

bouffant /boo-fon/ • adj. (of hair) styled so as to stand out from the head in a rounded shape.
– ORIGIN French, 'swelling'.

bougainvillea /boo-guhn-vil-li-uh/ (also **bougainvillaea**) • n. a tropical climbing plant with brightly coloured modified leaves (bracts) surrounding the flowers.
– ORIGIN named after the French explorer L. A. de *Bougainville*.

bough • n. a main branch of a tree.
– ORIGIN Old English, 'bough, shoulder'.

bought past and past part. of **BUY**.

> **USAGE:** Do not confuse **bought** and **brought**. **Bought** is the past tense and past participle of **buy** (*she bought a magazine*), whereas **brought** is the past tense and past participle of **bring** (*the article brought a massive response*).

bouillon /boo-yon/ • n. thin soup or stock.
– ORIGIN French.

boulder • n. a large rock.
– ORIGIN Scandinavian.

boule /bool/ (also **boules** /bool/) • n. a French game similar to bowls, played with metal balls.
– ORIGIN French, 'bowl'.

boulevard /boo-luh-vard/ • n. a wide street, typically one lined with trees.
– ORIGIN French, 'rampart'.

bounce • v. (**bounces, bouncing, bounced**) 1 move quickly up or away from a surface after hitting it. 2 move or jump up and down repeatedly. 3 (**bounce back**) recover well after a setback. 4 informal (of a cheque) be

returned by a bank when there is not enough money in an account for it to be paid. •n. **1** an act of bouncing. **2** high-spirited self-confidence: *the bounce was back in Jenny's step.*
– ORIGIN perh. from German *bunsen* 'beat' or Dutch *bons* 'a thump'.

bouncer •n. a person employed by a nightclub to prevent troublemakers entering or to remove them from the building.

bouncing •adj. (of a baby) lively and healthy.

bouncy •adj. (**bouncier**, **bounciest**) **1** able to bounce or making something bounce. **2** confident and lively.
– DERIVATIVES **bouncily** adv. **bounciness** n.

bound¹ •v. walk or run with leaping strides. •n. a leaping movement towards or over something.
– ORIGIN French *bondir* 'resound'.

bound² •n. a boundary or limit: *her grief knew no bounds.* •v. **1** form the boundary of; enclose. **2** restrict something.
– PHRASES **out of bounds 1** (in sport) beyond the field of play. **2** beyond permitted limits.
– ORIGIN Latin *bodina*.

bound³ •adj. going towards somewhere: *a train bound for Paris.*
– ORIGIN Old Norse, 'get ready'.

bound⁴ past and past part. of **BIND**. •adj. (**-bound**) restricted to or by a place or situation: *his job kept him city-bound.* **2** certain to be, do, or have: *there is bound to be a change of plan.* **3** obliged to do something.
– PHRASES **I'll be bound** Brit. I am sure.

boundary •n. (pl. **boundaries**) **1** a line marking the limits of an area. **2** Cricket a hit crossing the limits of the field, scoring four or six runs.
– ORIGIN from **BOUND²**.

bounden /bown-d'n/ •adj. (in phr. **your bounden duty**) a duty that you feel is morally right.
– ORIGIN from **BIND**.

bounder •n. Brit. informal, dated a dishonourable man.

boundless •adj. unlimited: *boundless energy.*

bounteous /bown-ti-uhs/ •adj. old use abundant or generous; bountiful.
– ORIGIN Old French *bontif* 'benevolent'.

bountiful •adj. **1** abundant: *bountiful crops.* **2** giving generously.
– DERIVATIVES **bountifully** adv.

bounty •n. (pl. **bounties**) **1** literary something provided in generous amounts. **2** literary generosity: *people along the Nile depend on its bounty.* **3** a reward for killing or capturing someone.

– ORIGIN Old French *bonte* 'goodness'.

bouquet /boo-kay, boh-kay/ •n. **1** a bunch of flowers. **2** the characteristic scent of a wine or perfume.
– ORIGIN French.

bourbon /ber-buhn/ •n. an American whisky made from maize and rye.
– ORIGIN named after *Bourbon* County, Kentucky.

bourgeois /boor-zhwah/ (also **bourgeoise** /boor-zhwahz/)
•adj. relating to the middle class, especially in being conventional and concerned with wealth.
– ORIGIN French.

bourgeoisie /boor-zhwah-zee/ •n. the middle class.
– ORIGIN French.

bout /bowt/ •n. **1** a short period of illness or intense activity. **2** a wrestling or boxing match.
– ORIGIN dialect *bought* 'bend, loop'.

boutique /boo-teek/ •n. a small shop selling fashionable clothes.
– ORIGIN French.

bouzouki /bu-zoo-ki/ •n. (pl. **bouzoukis**) a long-necked Greek form of mandolin.
– ORIGIN modern Greek *mpouzouki*.

bovine /boh-vyn/ •adj. **1** relating to cattle. **2** slow-witted or stupid.
– ORIGIN Latin *bovinus*.

bovine spongiform encephalopathy •n. see **BSE**.

bow¹ /rhymes with toe/ •n. **1** a knot tied with two loops and two loose ends. **2** a weapon for shooting arrows, made of curved wood joined at both ends by a taut string. **3** a rod with horsehair stretched along its length, used for playing some stringed instruments.
– ORIGIN Old English.

bow² /rhymes with cow/ •v. **1** bend the head or upper body as a sign of respect, greeting, or shame. **2** bend with age or under a heavy weight. **3** give in to pressure. **4** (**bow out**) withdraw or retire from an activity. •n. an act of bowing.
– PHRASES **bow and scrape** behave in a servile way. **take a bow** acknowledge applause by bowing.
– ORIGIN Old English, 'bend'.

bow³ /rhymes with cow/ (also **bows**) •n. the front end of a ship.
– ORIGIN German *boog* or Dutch *boeg*.

bowdlerize /bowd-luh-ryz/ (or **bowdlerise**) •v. (**bowdlerizes**, **bowdlerizing**, **bowdlerized**) remove indecent or offensive material from a written work.
– ORIGIN from Dr Thomas *Bowdler*, who published a censored edition of Shakespeare.

bowel /rhymes with towel/ •n. **1** the intestine. **2** (**bowels**) the deepest inner parts of something.
– ORIGIN Latin *botellus* 'little sausage'.

bowel movement •n. an act of defecation.

bower /rhymes with tower/ •n. **1** a pleasant shady place under climbing plants or trees. **2** literary a woman's private room.
– ORIGIN Old English.

bowerbird •n. an Australasian bird noted for the male's habit of building an elaborate structure to attract the female.

bowie knife /rhymes with snowy/ •n. a long knife with a blade double-edged at the point.
– ORIGIN named after the American pioneer Jim *Bowie*.

bowl¹ •n. **1** a round, deep dish or basin. **2** a rounded, hollow part of an object.
– ORIGIN Old English.

bowl² •v. **1** roll a round object along the ground. **2** Brit. move along rapidly and smoothly. **3** (**bowl someone over**) knock someone down. **4** (**bowl someone over**) informal greatly impress or overwhelm someone. **5** Cricket (of a bowler) throw the ball towards the wicket, or dismiss a batsman by hitting the wicket with a ball. •n. a heavy ball used in bowls or tenpin bowling.
– ORIGIN Old French *boule*.

bow-legged •adj. having legs that curve outwards at the knee.

bowler¹ •n. **1** Cricket a member of the fielding side who bowls. **2** a player of bowls or tenpin bowling.

bowler² •n. a man's hard felt hat with a dome-shaped crown.
– ORIGIN named after the English hatter William *Bowler*.

bowline /boh-lin/ •n. a simple knot for forming a non-slipping loop at the end of a rope.

bowling •n. the game of bowls, tenpin bowling, or skittles.

bowling alley •n. a long narrow track along which balls are rolled in skittles or tenpin bowling.

bowling green •n. an area of very short grass on which the game of bowls is played.

bowls /bohlz/ •n. a game played with wooden bowls, the object of which is to roll your bowl as close as possible to a small white ball (the jack).

bowsprit /boh-sprit/ •n. a pole that projects from a ship's bow, to which the ropes supporting the front mast are fastened.

bow tie •n. a necktie in the form of a bow.

bow window •n. a curved bay window.

box¹ •n. **1** a container with a flat base and sides and a lid. **2** an area within straight lines on a page or computer screen. **3** an enclosed area reserved for a group of people in a theatre, sports ground, or law court. **4** a small booth or building used for a particular purpose: *a tele-phone box*. **5** (**the box**) informal, esp. Brit. television. **6** a service at a newspaper office for receiving replies to an advertisement, or at a post office for keeping letters until collected. **7** Brit. a shield for protecting a man's genitals in sport. •v. **1** put in a box. **2** (**box someone in**) restrict or confine someone.
– ORIGIN Old English.

box² •v. fight an opponent with the fists in padded gloves as a sport. •n. a slap on the side of a person's head.
– PHRASES **box someone's ears** slap someone on the side of the head.
– DERIVATIVES **boxing** n.

box³ •n. an evergreen shrub with small glossy leaves.
– ORIGIN Greek *puxos*.

boxer •n. **1** a person who boxes as a sport. **2** a medium-sized breed of dog with a brown coat and pug-like face.

boxer shorts •pl. n. men's underpants resembling shorts.

Boxing Day •n. Brit. a public holiday on the first day after Christmas Day.
– ORIGIN from the former custom of giving tradesmen a Christmas gift on this day.

box junction •n. Brit. a road area at a junction marked with a yellow grid, which a vehicle should enter only if its exit is clear.

box number •n. a number identifying an advertisement in a newspaper, used as an address for replies.

box office •n. a place at a theatre, cinema, etc. where tickets are sold.

box pleat •n. a pleat consisting of two parallel creases forming a raised band.

box room •n. Brit. a very small room.

boxy •adj. (**boxier, boxiest**) **1** squarish in shape. **2** (of a room) cramped.

boy •n. **1** a male child or youth. **2** a man, especially one who comes from a particular place or who does a particular job: *the inspector was a local boy*.
– DERIVATIVES **boyhood** n. **boyish** adj.

boycott •v. refuse to deal with a person, organization, or country as a punish-ment or protest. •n. an act of boy-cotting someone or something.
– ORIGIN from Captain Charles *Boycott*, an Irish land agent so treated in 1880 in an attempt to get rents reduced.

boyfriend • n. a person's regular male companion in a romantic or sexual relationship.

Boyle's law • n. Chem. a law stating that the pressure of a given mass of an ideal gas is inversely proportional to its volume at a constant temperature.
– ORIGIN named after the English scientist Robert *Boyle*.

Boy Scout • n. dated or N. Amer. = **SCOUT** (in sense 2).

Br • symb. the chemical element bromine.

bra • n. a woman's undergarment worn to support the breasts.
– ORIGIN short for **BRASSIERE**.

brace • n. 1 a part that strengthens or supports something. 2 (**braces**) Brit. a pair of straps passing over the shoulders and fastening to the top of trousers to hold them up. 3 a wire device used to straighten the teeth. 4 (pl. **brace**) a pair: *a brace of grouse.* 5 either of two connecting marks { and }, used in printing and music. 6 (also **brace and bit**) a drilling tool with a crank handle and a socket to hold a bit. • v. (**braces, bracing, braced**) 1 make stronger or firmer with a brace. 2 press the body firmly against something to stay balanced. 3 (usu. **brace yourself**) prepare for something demanding or unpleasant.
– ORIGIN Old French *bracier* 'embrace'.

bracelet • n. an ornamental band or chain worn on the wrist or arm.
– ORIGIN Old French.

bracing • adj. refreshing; invigorating.

bracken • n. a tall fern with coarse fronds.
– ORIGIN Scandinavian.

bracket • n. 1 each of a pair of marks ( ) [ ] { } < > used to enclose words or figures. 2 a category of similar people or things: *a high income bracket.* 3 a right-angled support projecting from a wall. • v. (**brackets, bracketing, bracketed**) 1 enclose words or figures in brackets. 2 place in the same category. 3 hold or attach by means of a bracket.
– ORIGIN Spanish *bragueta* 'codpiece, bracket'.

brackish • adj. (of water) slightly salty.
– ORIGIN German or Dutch *brac*.

bract • n. a modified leaf with a flower in the angle where it meets the stem.
– ORIGIN Latin *bractea* 'thin metal plate'.

brad • n. a nail with a rectangular cross section and a small head.
– ORIGIN Old Norse.

brae /bray/ • n. Scottish a steep bank or hillside.
– ORIGIN Old Norse, 'eyelash'.

brag • v. (**brags, bragging, bragged**) say something boastfully. • n. 1 an act of bragging. 2 a simplified form of poker.

braggart /brag-gert/ • n. a person who boasts about something.
– ORIGIN French *bragard*.

Brahman /brah-muhn/ (also **Brahmin** /brah-min/) • n. (pl. **Brahmans**) a member of the highest Hindu caste, that of the priesthood.
– ORIGIN Sanskrit.

braid • n. 1 threads woven into a decorative band. 2 esp. N. Amer. a plaited length of hair. • v. 1 plait hair. 2 trim with braid.
– ORIGIN Old English, 'interweave'.

Braille /brayl/ • n. a written language for the blind using raised dots.
– ORIGIN named after the French educationist Louis *Braille*.

brain • n. 1 an organ of soft tissue inside the skull, functioning as the centre of the nervous system. 2 the ability to use your intelligence: *you're a girl with brains.* 3 (**the brains**) informal the main organizer within a group. • v. informal hit hard on the head.
– PHRASES **have something on the brain** informal be obsessed with something.
– ORIGIN Old English.

brainchild • n. (pl. **brainchildren**) informal a particular person's idea or invention.

brain death • n. irreversible brain damage causing the end of independent breathing.
– DERIVATIVES **brain-dead** adj.

brain drain • n. informal the emigration of highly skilled or qualified people from a country.

brainless • adj. stupid; very foolish.

brainstorm • n. 1 Brit. informal a moment in which you are suddenly unable to think clearly. 2 a group discussion to produce ideas. • v. have a group discussion to produce ideas.

brain-teaser • n. informal a problem or puzzle.

brainwash • v. force someone to accept an idea or belief by using repetition or mental pressure.

brainwave • n. 1 an electrical impulse in the brain. 2 informal a sudden clever idea.

brainy • adj. (**brainier, brainiest**) informal clever or intelligent.
– DERIVATIVES **braininess** n.

braise • v. (**braises, braising, braised**) fry food lightly and then stew it slowly in a closed container.
– ORIGIN French *braiser*.

brake • n. a device for slowing or stopping a moving vehicle. • v. (**brakes,**

b

braking, **braked**) slow or stop a vehicle with a brake.

> **USAGE:** Do not confuse **brake** with **break**. **Brake** means 'a device for slowing or stopping a vehicle' or 'slow or stop a vehicle' (*I had to brake hard*), whereas **break** mainly means 'separate into pieces' or 'a pause or short rest' (*a tea break*).

brake drum • n. a broad, short cylinder attached to a wheel, against which the brake shoes press to cause braking.

brake horsepower • n. an imperial unit equal to one horsepower, used in expressing the power available at the shaft of an engine.

brake shoe • n. a long curved block which presses on to a brake drum.

bramble • n. **1** a prickly shrub of the rose family, especially a blackberry. **2** Brit. the fruit of the blackberry.
– ORIGIN Old English.

bran • n. pieces of grain husk separated from flour after milling.
– ORIGIN Old French.

branch • n. **1** a part of a tree which grows out from the trunk or a bough. **2** a river, road, or railway extending out from a main one. **3** a division of a large organization, subject, etc. • v. **1** divide into one or more branches. **2** (**branch out**) start to undertake new activities.
– ORIGIN Old French *branche*.

brand • n. **1** a type of product made by a company under a particular name. **2** a brand name. **3** a mark burned on livestock with a hot iron. **4** a piece of burning wood. • v. **1** mark out as having a particular shameful quality: *she was branded a liar.* **2** give a brand name to a product. **3** mark with a branding iron.
– ORIGIN Old English, 'burning'.

brandish • v. wave something as a threat or in anger or excitement.
– ORIGIN Old French *brandir*.

brand name • n. a name given by the maker to a product.

brand new • adj. completely new.
– ORIGIN from the idea of a brand being 'straight from the fire'.

brandy • n. (pl. **brandies**) a strong alcoholic spirit distilled from wine or fermented fruit juice.
– ORIGIN from Dutch *branden* 'burn, distil' + *wijn* 'wine'.

brash • adj. **1** self-confident in a rude, noisy, or overbearing way. **2** showy or tasteless: *a brash new building.*
– DERIVATIVES **brashly** adv. **brashness** n.
– ORIGIN perh. from RASH[1].

brass • n. **1** a yellow alloy of copper and zinc. **2** (also **horse brass**) Brit. a flat brass ornament for the harness of a draught

horse. **3** Brit. a brass memorial plaque in the wall or floor of a church. **4** brass wind instruments forming a section of an orchestra. **5** (also **top brass**) informal people in authority. **6** Brit. informal money.
– PHRASES **brassed off** Brit. informal irritated or annoyed. **get down to brass tacks** informal start to consider the basic facts.
– ORIGIN Old English.

brass band • n. a group of musicians playing brass instruments.

brasserie /brass-uh-ri/ • n. (pl. **brasseries**) an inexpensive French or French-style restaurant.
– ORIGIN French, 'brewery'.

brassica /brass-ik-uh/ • n. a plant of a family that includes cabbage, swede, and rape.
– ORIGIN Latin, 'cabbage'.

brassiere /braz-i-er/ • n. formal a bra.
– ORIGIN French, 'bodice, child's vest'.

brass rubbing • n. the copying of the design on an engraved brass by rubbing chalk or wax over paper laid on it.

brassy • adj. (**brassier**, **brassiest**) **1** bright or harsh yellow. **2** tastelessly showy. **3** (of a sound) harsh or blaring like a brass instrument.

brat • n. derogatory or humorous a badly behaved child.
– DERIVATIVES **brattish** adj.
– ORIGIN perh. from Old French *brachet* 'hound, bitch'.

bravado • n. confidence or a show of confidence that is intended to impress.
– ORIGIN Spanish *bravada*.

brave • adj. having or showing courage. • n. dated an American Indian warrior. • v. (**braves**, **braving**, **braved**) face unpleasant conditions with courage.
– DERIVATIVES **bravely** adv. **bravery** n.
– ORIGIN Italian or Spanish *bravo* 'bold'.

bravo /brah-voh/ • exclam. shouted to express approval for a performer.
– ORIGIN Italian, 'bold'.

bravura /bruh-vyoor-uh/ • n. great skill and enthusiasm, typically shown in a performance.
– ORIGIN Italian.

brawl • n. a rough or noisy fight. • v. take part in a brawl.
– DERIVATIVES **brawler** n.

brawn • n. physical strength as opposed to intelligence.
– DERIVATIVES **brawny** adj.
– ORIGIN Old French *braon* 'fleshy part of the leg'.

bray • v. **1** (of a donkey) make a loud, harsh cry. **2** (of a person) speak or laugh loudly and harshly. • n. the loud, harsh cry of a donkey.

– ORIGIN Old French *braire* 'to cry'.

braze • v. (**brazes**, **brazing**, **brazed**) solder something with an alloy of copper and zinc.
– ORIGIN French *braser* 'solder'.

brazen • adj. bold and shameless.
• v. (**brazen it out**) endure a difficult situation with an apparent lack of shame.
– DERIVATIVES **brazenly** adv.
– ORIGIN Old English, 'made of brass'.

brazier /bray-zi-er/ • n. a portable heater holding lighted coals.
– ORIGIN French *brasier*.

Brazilian • n. a person from Brazil.
• adj. relating to Brazil.

Brazil nut • n. the large three-sided nut of a South American tree.

breach • v. 1 make a hole in; break through. 2 break a rule or agreement.
• n. 1 a gap made in a wall or barrier. 2 an act of breaking a rule or agreement. 3 a break in relations between people or groups.
– PHRASES **breach of the peace** the criminal offence of behaving in a violent or noisy way in public. **step into the breach** replace someone who is suddenly unable to do a job.
– ORIGIN Old French *breche*.

> **USAGE:** Do not confuse **breach** and **breech**. Breach means 'break through something' (*the river breached its bank*), 'break a law or agreement', or 'a gap'; **breech** means 'the back part of a gun barrel'.

bread • n. 1 food made of flour, water, and yeast mixed together and baked. 2 informal money.
– PHRASES **bread and butter** a person's main source of income. **break bread** celebrate Holy Communion.
– ORIGIN Old English.

breadcrumb • n. a small fragment of bread.

breaded • adj. (of food) coated with breadcrumbs and fried.

breadfruit • n. a large round starchy fruit of a tropical tree, used as a vegetable.

breadline • n. (usu. in phr. **on the breadline**) Brit. the level of income of people who are very poor.

breadth • n. 1 the distance from side to side of something. 2 wide range: *her breadth of experience*.
– ORIGIN related to **BROAD**.

breadwinner • n. a person who supports their family with the money they earn.

break • v. (**breaks**, **breaking**, **broke**; past part. **broken**) 1 separate into pieces as a result of a blow or strain. 2 stop working. 3 interrupt a sequence or course. 4 fail to observe a rule or agreement. 5 crush the spirit of. 6 beat a record. 7 work out a code. 8 make a rush or dash. 9 soften a fall. 10 suddenly make or become public. 11 (of a person's voice) falter and change tone. 12 (of a boy's voice) become deeper at puberty. 13 (of the weather) change suddenly. 14 (of a storm, the dawn, or a day) begin. • n. 1 a pause, gap, or short rest. 2 an instance of breaking, or the point where something is broken. 3 a sudden rush or dash. 4 informal a chance: *his big break had finally come.* 5 (also **break of serve** or **service break**) Tennis the winning of a game against an opponent's serve. 6 Snooker & Billiards an uninterrupted series of successful shots.
– PHRASES **break away** escape. **break the back of** accomplish the main part of. **break down** 1 suddenly stop functioning. 2 lose control of your emotions when upset. **break in** 1 force entry to a building. 2 interrupt with a remark. **break something in** 1 make a horse used to being ridden. 2 make new shoes comfortable by wearing them. **break into** burst into laughter, song, a run, etc. **break off** stop suddenly. **break out** 1 (of something unwelcome) start suddenly. 2 escape. **break out in** suddenly be affected by: *she broke out in spots.* **break up** 1 (of a gathering) end. 2 (of a couple) end a relationship. 3 esp. Brit. end the school term. **break wind** release gas from the anus. **give someone a break** informal stop putting pressure on someone.
– DERIVATIVES **breakable** adj.
– ORIGIN Old English.

> **USAGE:** On the confusion of **break** with **brake**, see the note at **BRAKE**.

breakage • n. the action of breaking something or the fact of being broken.

breakaway • n. 1 a departure or change from something long-standing. 2 (in sport) a sudden attack or forward movement.

break-dancing • n. an energetic and acrobatic style of street dancing.

breakdown • n. 1 a failure or collapse. 2 an analysis of costs or figures.

breaker • n. 1 a heavy sea wave that breaks on the shore. 2 a person who breaks up old machinery.

breakfast • n. the first meal of the day.
• v. eat breakfast.
– ORIGIN from **BREAK** + **FAST**².

break-in • n. an illegal forced entry in order to steal something.

b

breakneck • adj. dangerously fast.

breakthrough • n. a sudden important development or success.

breakwater • n. a barrier built out into the sea to protect a coast or harbour from the force of waves.

bream • n. (pl. **bream**) a greenish-bronze freshwater fish.
– ORIGIN Old French *bresme*.

breast • n. **1** either of the two organs on a woman's chest which produce milk after childbirth. **2** a person's or animal's chest region. • v. **1** face and move forwards against or through: *I watched him breast the wave.* **2** reach the top of a hill.
– ORIGIN Old English.

breastbone • n. a thin flat bone that runs down the centre of the chest and connects the ribs.

breastfeed • v. (**breastfeeds, breastfeeding, breastfed**) feed a baby with milk from the breast.

breastplate • n. a piece of armour covering the chest.

breaststroke • n. a style of swimming in which the arms are pushed forwards and then swept back while the legs are tucked in and kicked out.

breath • n. **1** air taken into or sent out of the lungs. **2** an instance of breathing in or out. **3** a slight movement of air. **4** a sign or hint: *he avoided the slightest breath of scandal.*
– PHRASES **take someone's breath away** astonish or inspire someone. **under your breath** in a very quiet voice.
– DERIVATIVES **breathable** adj.
– ORIGIN Old English, 'smell, scent'.

breathalyser (US trademark **Breathalyzer**) • n. a device for measuring the amount of alcohol in a driver's breath.
– DERIVATIVES **breathalyse** (US **breathalyze**) v.
– ORIGIN from **BREATH** and **ANALYSE**.

breathe • v. (**breathes, breathing, breathed**) **1** take air into the lungs and send it out again. **2** say quietly. **3** let air or moisture in or out. **breathe your last** die.

breather • n. informal a brief pause for rest.

breathing space • n. an opportunity to relax or decide what to do next.

breathless • adj. **1** gasping for breath. **2** feeling or causing great excitement, fear, etc.
– DERIVATIVES **breathlessly** adv. **breathlessness** n.

breathtaking • adj. astonishing or impressive.

breath test • n. a test in which a driver is made to blow into a breathalyser.

breathy • adj. (of a voice) having an audible sound of breathing.
– DERIVATIVES **breathily** adv.

bred past and past part. of **BREED**.

breech • n. the back part of a rifle or gun barrel.
– ORIGIN Old English, 'garment covering the loins and thighs'.

USAGE: On the confusion of **breech** and **breach**, see the note at **BREACH**.

breech birth • n. a birth in which the baby's buttocks or feet are delivered first.

breeches • pl. n. short trousers fastened just below the knee.

breed • v. (**breeds, breeding, bred**) **1** (of animals) mate and produce offspring. **2** keep animals for the purpose of producing young. **3** bring up in a particular way: *she'd had rebellion bred into her.* **4** produce: *familiarity breeds contempt.* • n. **1** a particular type within a species of animals or plants. **2** a type: *a new breed of businessman.*
– DERIVATIVES **breeder** n.
– ORIGIN Old English.

breeding • n. upper-class good manners seen as being passed on from one generation to another.

breeze • n. **1** a gentle wind. **2** informal something easy to do. • v. (**breezes, breezing, breezed**) informal come or go in a casual way.
– ORIGIN prob. from Spanish and Portuguese *briza*.

breeze block • n. Brit. a lightweight building brick made from cinders, sand, and cement.
– ORIGIN French *braise* 'live coals'.

breezy • adj. (**breezier, breeziest**) **1** pleasantly windy. **2** relaxed and cheerily brisk: *his breezy manner.*

brethren old-fashioned pl. of **BROTHER**. • pl. n. fellow Christians or members of a group.

Breton /bre-tuhn/ • n. **1** a person from Brittany. **2** the language of Brittany.
– ORIGIN Old French, 'Briton'.

breve /rhymes with sleeve/ • n. Music a note twice as long as a semibreve.
– ORIGIN from **BRIEF**.

breviary /bree-vi-uh-ri/ • n. (pl. **breviaries**) a book containing the service for each day, used in the Roman Catholic Church.
– ORIGIN Latin *breviarium* 'summary'.

brevity /brev-i-ti/ • n. **1** concise and exact use of words. **2** shortness of time.
– ORIGIN Latin *brevitas*.

brew • v. **1** make beer by soaking, boiling, and fermentation. **2** make tea or coffee by mixing it with hot water. **3** begin to

develop: *trouble is brewing.* •n. a drink that has been brewed.
– DERIVATIVES **brewer** n.
– ORIGIN Old English.

brewery •n. (pl. **breweries**) a place where beer is made.

briar (also **brier**) •n. a prickly shrub, especially a wild rose.
– ORIGIN Old English.

bribe •v. (**bribes, bribing, bribed**) dishonestly persuade someone to help you, especially by paying them. •n. something offered in an attempt to bribe someone.
– DERIVATIVES **bribery** n.
– ORIGIN Old French *briber* 'beg'.

bric-a-brac •n. various objects of little value.
– ORIGIN French.

brick •n. **1** a small rectangular block of fired clay, used in building. **2** Brit. informal, dated a helpful and reliable person. •v. block or enclose with a wall of bricks.
– PHRASES **bricks and mortar** buildings.
– ORIGIN German or Dutch *bricke, brike*.

brickbat •n. a critical remark.

bricklayer •n. a person whose job is to build structures with bricks.

bridal •adj. relating to a bride or a newly married couple.

bride •n. a woman on her wedding day or just before and after the event.
– ORIGIN Old English.

bridegroom •n. a man on his wedding day or just before and after the event.
– ORIGIN Old English, 'bride man'.

bridesmaid •n. a girl or woman who accompanies a bride on her wedding day.

bridge¹ •n. **1** a structure carrying a road, path, or railway across a river, road, etc. **2** the platform on a ship from which the captain and officers direct its course. **3** the upper bony part of a person's nose. **4** a false tooth or teeth held in place by natural teeth on either side. **5** the part on a stringed instrument over which the strings are stretched. •v. (**bridges, bridging, bridges**) **1** be or make a bridge over or between. **2** reduce a difference or gap between two groups or things.
– ORIGIN Old English.

bridge² •n. a card game played by two teams of two players.

bridgehead •n. a strong position gained by an army inside enemy territory.

bridging loan (N. Amer. **bridge loan**) •n. a sum of money lent by a bank to cover the period of time between the buying of one thing and the selling of another.

bridle •n. the headgear used to control a horse. •v. (**bridles, bridling, bridled**) **1** put a bridle on. **2** bring under control. **3** show resentment or anger.
– ORIGIN Old English.

bridleway (also **bridle path**) •n. Brit. a path along which horse riders have right of way.

Brie /bree/ •n. a kind of soft, mild, creamy cheese.
– ORIGIN named after *Brie* in northern France.

brief •adj. **1** lasting a short time. **2** using few words. **3** (of clothing) not covering much of the body. •n. **1** Brit. a set of instructions about a task. **2** a summary of the facts in a case given to a barrister to argue in court. **3** informal a solicitor or barrister. •v. give someone information so as to prepare them for a task. **hold no brief for** not support.
– DERIVATIVES **briefly** adv.
– ORIGIN Old French.

> ✓ **brief** follows the usual rule of *i* before *e* except after c.

briefcase •n. a flat rectangular case for carrying books and documents.

briefing •n. a meeting for giving information or instructions.

briefs •pl. n. short underpants.

brier •n. var. of BRIAR.

brig •n. a square-rigged sailing ship with two masts.
– ORIGIN from BRIGANTINE.

brigade •n. **1** a subdivision of an army, made up of battalions and forming part of a division. **2** informal, usu. derog. a particular group of people: *the anti-smoking brigade.*
– ORIGIN French.

brigadier /bri-guh-**deer**/ •n. a rank of officer in the British army, above colonel.

brigand /**brig**-uhnd/ •n. a member of a gang of bandits.
– ORIGIN Italian *brigante* '(person) contending'.

brigantine /**brig**-uhn-teen/ •n. a sailing ship with two masts.
– ORIGIN Italian *brigantino*.

bright •adj. **1** giving out or filled with light. **2** (of colour) vivid and bold. **3** intelligent and quick-witted. **4** cheerfully lively. **5** (of prospects) good.
– DERIVATIVES **brightly** adv. **brightness** n.
– ORIGIN Old English.

brighten •v. **1** make or become brighter. **2** make or become more cheerful.

bright spark •n. informal, often ironic a clever or witty person.

brill •n. a flatfish similar to the turbot.

b

brilliant •adj. **1** (of light or colour) very bright or vivid. **2** very clever or talented. **3** Brit. informal excellent.
– DERIVATIVES **brilliance** (also **brilliancy**) n. **brilliantly** adv.
– ORIGIN French *brillant*.

brilliantine •n. dated scented oil used on men's hair to make it look glossy.

brim •n. **1** the projecting edge around the bottom of a hat. **2** the lip of a cup, bowl, etc. •v. (**brims**, **brimming**, **brimmed**) fill or be full to the point of overflowing.
– DERIVATIVES **brimful** adj.
– ORIGIN perh. from German *Bräme* 'trimming'.

brimstone /brim-stohn/ •n. old use sulphur.
– ORIGIN Old English.

brindle (also **brindled**) •adj. (of an animal) brownish with streaks of another colour.
– ORIGIN prob. Scandinavian.

brine •n. water containing dissolved salt.
– ORIGIN Old English.

bring •v. (**brings**, **bringing**, **brought**) **1** carry or accompany to a place. **2** cause to be in a particular position or state. **3** cause someone to receive: *his first novel brought him a great deal of money.* **4** (**bring yourself to do**) force yourself to do something unpleasant. **5** begin legal action.
– PHRASES **bring something about** cause something to happen. **bring something forward** move a planned event to an earlier time. **bring the house down** make an audience laugh or applaud very enthusiastically. **bring something off** achieve something successfully. **bring something on** cause something unpleasant to occur. **bring something out 1** produce and launch a new product or publication. **2** emphasize a feature. **bring someone round 1** make someone conscious again. **2** persuade someone to agree to something. **bring something to bear** apply influence or pressure. **bring someone/thing up 1** look after a child until it is an adult. **2** raise a matter for discussion.
– DERIVATIVES **bringer** n.
– ORIGIN Old English.

brink •n. **1** the edge of land before a steep slope or an area of water. **2** the point where a new or unpleasant situation is about to begin: *a country on the brink of civil war.*
– ORIGIN Scandinavian.

brinkmanship (US also **brinksmanship**) •n. the pursuing of a dangerous course of action to the limits of safety before stopping.

briny /rhymes with tiny/ •adj. salty. •n. (**the briny**) Brit. informal the sea.

brio /bree-oh/ •n. energy or liveliness.
– ORIGIN Italian.

brioche /bree-osh/ •n. a small, round, sweet French roll.
– ORIGIN French.

briquette /bri-ket/ (also **briquet**) •n. a block of compressed coal dust or peat used as fuel.
– ORIGIN French, 'small brick'.

brisk •adj. **1** active and energetic. **2** practical and efficient: *a brisk, businesslike tone.*
– DERIVATIVES **briskly** adv.
– ORIGIN prob. from French *brusque* 'lively, fierce'.

brisket •n. meat from the breast of a cow.
– ORIGIN perh. from Old Norse, 'cartilage, gristle'.

bristle •n. a short, stiff hair. •v. (**bristles**, **bristling**, **bristled**) **1** (of hair or fur) stand upright away from the skin. **2** react angrily or defensively. **3** (**bristle with**) be covered with.
– DERIVATIVES **bristly** adj.
– ORIGIN Old English.

Brit •n. informal a British person.

Britannia /bri-tan-yuh/ •n. a woman wearing a helmet and carrying a shield and trident, used to represent Britain.
– ORIGIN Latin, 'Britain'.

British •adj. relating to Great Britain.
– DERIVATIVES **Britishness** n.
– ORIGIN Old English.

Briton •n. **1** a British person. **2** a Celtic inhabitant of southern Britain before and during Roman times.

brittle •adj. **1** hard but likely to break easily. **2** sharp or artificial: *a brittle laugh.*
– ORIGIN from Old English, 'break up'.

broach •v. **1** raise a difficult subject for discussion. **2** pierce or open a container to draw out liquid.
– ORIGIN Old French *brochier*.

broad •adj. **1** larger than usual from side to side; wide. **2** of a particular distance wide. **3** large in area or range: *a broad expanse of water.* **4** without detail: *a broad outline.* **5** (of a hint) clear and unmistakable. **6** (of a regional accent) very strong. •n. N. Amer. informal a woman.
– PHRASES **broad daylight** full daylight.
– DERIVATIVES **broadly** adv.
– ORIGIN Old English.

broadband •n. a telecommunications technique which uses a wide range of frequencies, enabling messages to be sent at the same time.

broad bean •n. a large flat green bean.

broadcast •v. (**broadcasts**,

broadcasting, broadcast; past part. **broadcast** or **broadcasted**) **1** transmit a programme by radio or television. **2** tell something to many people. **3** scatter seeds. •n. a radio or television programme.
– DERIVATIVES **broadcaster** n.

broadcloth •n. a fine cloth of wool or cotton.

broaden •v. make or become broader.

broadleaved (also **broadleaf**) •adj. having fairly wide flat leaves.

broadloom •n. carpet woven in wide widths.

broad-minded •adj. tolerant or open-minded.

broadsheet •n. a newspaper printed on large sheets of paper.

broadside •n. **1** a strongly worded critical attack. **2** hist. a firing of all the guns from one side of a warship.

broadsword •n. a sword with a wide blade.

brocade •n. a rich fabric woven with a raised pattern.
– ORIGIN Spanish and Portuguese *brocado*.

broccoli /brok-kuh-li/ •n. a vegetable with heads of small green or purplish flower buds.
– ORIGIN Italian.

> ✓ Spell **broccoli** with a double **c** and one **l**.

brochure /broh-sher/ •n. a magazine containing information about a product or service.
– ORIGIN French, 'something stitched'.

broderie anglaise /broh-duh-ri ong-glayz/ •n. open embroidery on fine white cotton or linen.
– ORIGIN French, 'English embroidery'.

brogue •n. **1** a strong outdoor shoe with perforated patterns in the leather. **2** a noticeable Irish or Scottish accent when speaking English.
– ORIGIN Scottish Gaelic and Irish *bróg*.

broil •v. N. Amer. grill meat or fish.
– ORIGIN Old French *bruler* 'to burn'.

broiler •n. a young chicken suitable for roasting, grilling, or barbecuing.

broke past of BREAK. •adj. informal having no money.
– PHRASES **go for broke** informal risk everything in one determined effort.

broken past part. of BREAK. •adj. (of a language) spoken hesitantly and with many mistakes.

broken-down •adj. in a bad condition or not working.

broken-hearted •adj. overwhelmed by grief or disappointment.

broken home •n. a family in which the parents are divorced or separated.

broker •n. a person who buys and sells goods or shares for other people.
•v. (**brokers, brokering, brokered**) arrange a deal or plan.
– DERIVATIVES **brokerage** n.
– ORIGIN Old French *brocour*.

brolly •n. (pl. **brollies**) Brit. informal an umbrella.

bromide /broh-myd/ •n. a compound of bromine with another chemical element or group.

bromine /broh-meen/ •n. a dark red liquid chemical element.
– ORIGIN Greek *brōmos* 'a stink'.

bronchi pl. of BRONCHUS.

bronchial /brong-ki-uhl/ •adj. relating to the bronchi or to the smaller tubes into which they divide.

bronchitis /brong-ky-tiss/ •n. inflammation of the bronchial tubes.

bronchus /brong-kuhss/ •n. (pl. **bronchi** /brong-kee/) any of the major air passages of the lungs which spread out from the windpipe.
– ORIGIN Greek *bronkhos* 'windpipe'.

bronco •n. (pl. **broncos**) a wild or half-tamed horse of the western US.
– ORIGIN Spanish, 'rough, rude'.

brontosaurus /bron-tuh-sor-uhss/ •n. former term for APATOSAURUS.
– ORIGIN from Greek *brontē* 'thunder' + *sauros* 'lizard'.

bronze •n. **1** a yellowish-brown alloy of copper and tin. **2** a yellowish-brown colour. **3** an object made of bronze.
•v. (**bronzes, bronzing, bronzed**) make suntanned.
– ORIGIN Italian *bronzo*.

Bronze Age •n. a period that came after the Stone Age and before the Iron Age, when weapons and tools were made of bronze.

bronze medal •n. a medal made of or coloured bronze, awarded for third place in a competition.

brooch •n. an ornament fastened to clothing with a hinged pin and catch.
– ORIGIN Old French *broche* 'spit for roasting'.

brood •n. **1** a family of young animals produced at one hatching or birth. **2** informal all the children in a family.
•v. **1** think deeply about an unpleasant subject. **2** (as adj. **brooding**) darkly menacing: *the brooding ruins of a castle.* **3** (of a bird) sit on eggs to hatch them.
– ORIGIN Old English.

broody •adj. **1** (of a hen) wanting to lay or sit on eggs. **2** informal (of a woman) wanting very much to have a baby. **3** thoughtful and unhappy.

brook[1] • n. a small stream.
– ORIGIN Old English.

brook[2] • v. formal tolerate: *she would brook no criticism.*
– ORIGIN Old English 'use, possess'.

broom • n. 1 a long-handled brush used for sweeping. 2 a shrub with yellow flowers and small or few leaves.
– ORIGIN Old English.

broomstick • n. a brush with twigs at one end and a long handle, on which witches are said to fly.

Bros • pl. n. brothers.

broth • n. soup made of meat or vegetable chunks cooked in stock.
– ORIGIN Old English.

brothel • n. a house where men visit prostitutes.
– ORIGIN related to an Old English word meaning 'degenerate, deteriorate'.

brother • n. 1 a man or boy in relation to other children of his parents. 2 a male colleague or friend. 3 (pl. also **brethren**) a (male) fellow Christian. 4 a member of a religious order of men: *a Benedictine brother.*
– DERIVATIVES **brotherly** adj.
– ORIGIN Old English.

brotherhood • n. 1 the relationship between brothers. 2 a feeling of fellowship and understanding. 3 a group of people linked by a shared interest or belief: *a religious brotherhood.*

brother-in-law • n. (pl. **brothers-in-law**) 1 the brother of a person's wife or husband. 2 the husband of a person's sister or sister-in-law.

brougham /broo-uhm/ • n. hist. a horse-drawn carriage with a roof and an open driver's seat in front.
– ORIGIN named after Lord *Brougham.*

brought past and past part. of **BRING**.

> **USAGE:** For an explanation of the difference between **brought** and **bought**, see the note at **BOUGHT**.

brouhaha /broo-hah-hah/ • n. a noisy and overexcited reaction.
– ORIGIN French.

brow • n. 1 a person's forehead. 2 an eyebrow. 3 the highest point of a hill or pass.
– ORIGIN Old English.

browbeat • v. (**browbeats, browbeating, browbeat;** past part. **browbeaten**) bully or frighten someone with stern or threatening words.

brown • adj. 1 of a colour produced by mixing red, yellow, and blue, as of rich soil. 2 dark-skinned or suntanned. • n. brown colour or material. • v. 1 make or become brown. 2 (**be browned off**)

Brit. informal be irritated or depressed.
– DERIVATIVES **brownish** adj.
– ORIGIN Old English.

brown bear • n. a large bear with a coat colour ranging from cream to black.

brownfield • adj. Brit. (of an urban site for development) having been built on before. Compare with **GREENFIELD**.

Brownian motion • n. Physics the irregular movement of tiny particles in a fluid, caused by the surrounding molecules striking against them.
– ORIGIN named after the Scottish botanist Robert *Brown.*

Brownie • n. (pl. **Brownies**) 1 (Brit. also **Brownie Guide**) a member of the junior branch of the Guides Association. 2 (**brownie**) a small square of rich chocolate cake.
– PHRASES **brownie point** informal an imaginary good mark given for an attempt to please.

brown owl • n. = **TAWNY OWL**.

brown rice • n. unpolished rice with only the husk of the grain removed.

brownstone • n. N. Amer. a building faced with a reddish-brown sandstone.

brown sugar • n. unrefined or partially refined sugar.

brown trout • n. the common trout of European lakes and rivers.

browse • v. (**browses, browsing, browsed**) 1 look at goods or written material in a leisurely way. 2 look at computer files via a network. 3 (of an animal) feed on leaves, twigs, etc. • n. an act of browsing.
– DERIVATIVES **browsable** adj.
– ORIGIN Old French *brost* 'young shoot'.

browser • n. 1 a person or animal that browses. 2 a computer program used to navigate the World Wide Web.

bruise • n. 1 an area of discoloured skin on the body, caused by a blow bursting underlying blood vessels. 2 a similar area of damage on a fruit, vegetable, or plant. • v. (**bruises, bruising, bruised**) cause or develop a bruise.
– ORIGIN Old English.

bruiser • n. informal, derog. a tough, aggressive person.

bruit /rhymes with fruit/ • v. spread a report or rumour widely.
– ORIGIN Old French *bruire* 'to roar'.

brunch • n. a late morning meal eaten instead of breakfast and lunch.

brunette (US also **brunet**) • n. a woman or girl with dark brown hair.
– ORIGIN French *brun* 'brown'.

brunt • n. the chief impact of something

bad: *education will bear the brunt of the cuts.*

brush[1] •n. **1** an implement with a handle and a block of bristles, hair, or wire. **2** an act of brushing. **3** a brief encounter with something bad. **4** the bushy tail of a fox. •v. **1** clean, smooth, or apply something with a brush. **2** touch lightly. **3** (**brush someone/thing off**) dismiss someone or something in an abrupt way. **4** (**brush up on something** or **brush something up**) work to improve a skill that has not been used for some time.
– ORIGIN Old French *broisse*.

brush[2] •n. N. Amer. & Austral./NZ small trees, undergrowth, and shrubs.
– ORIGIN Old French *broce*.

brushed •adj. (of fabric) having soft raised fibres.

brush-off •n. informal a rejection or dismissal.

brushwood •n. undergrowth, twigs, and small branches.

brusque /bruusk/ •adj. abrupt or offhand.
– DERIVATIVES **brusquely** adv.
– ORIGIN French, 'lively, fierce'.

Brussels sprout (also **Brussel sprout**) •n. the bud of a variety of cabbage, eaten as a vegetable.

brut /rhymes with *loot*/ •adj. (of sparkling wine) very dry.
– ORIGIN French, 'raw, rough'.

brutal •adj. **1** savagely violent. **2** not attempting to hide unpleasantness: *brutal honesty.*
– DERIVATIVES **brutality** n. **brutally** adv.

brutalize (or **brutalise**) •v. (**brutalizes, brutalizing, brutalized**) **1** make someone cruel, violent, or callous by repeatedly exposing them to violence. **2** treat someone in a violent way.

brute •n. **1** a violent person or animal. **2** informal a cruel person. •adj. involving physical strength rather than reasoning: *brute force.*
– DERIVATIVES **brutish** adj.
– ORIGIN Latin *brutus* 'dull, stupid'.

bryony /bry-uh-ni/ •n. (pl. **bryonies**) a climbing hedgerow plant with red berries.
– ORIGIN Greek *bruōnia*.

BS •abbrev. **1** Bachelor of Surgery. **2** British Standard(s).

BSc •abbrev. Bachelor of Science.

BSE •abbrev. bovine spongiform encephalopathy, a fatal disease of cattle which is believed to be related to Creutzfeldt–Jakob disease in humans.

BSI •abbrev. British Standards Institution.

BST •abbrev. British Summer Time (time as advanced one hour ahead of Greenwich Mean Time in the UK between March and October).

BT •abbrev. British Telecom.

bubble •n. **1** a thin sphere of liquid enclosing a gas. **2** an air- or gas-filled sphere in a liquid or a solidified liquid e.g. glass. **3** a transparent dome. •v. (**bubbles, bubbling, bubbled**) **1** (of a liquid) contain rising bubbles of gas. **2** (**bubble with**) be filled with: *she was bubbling with enthusiasm.*

bubble and squeak •n. Brit. a dish of cooked cabbage fried with cooked potatoes.

bubble bath •n. sweet-smelling liquid added to bathwater to make it foam.

bubblegum •n. chewing gum that can be blown into bubbles.

bubbly •adj. **1** containing bubbles. **2** cheerful and high-spirited. •n. informal champagne.

bubonic plague •n. a form of plague passed on by rat fleas, causing swellings in the groin or armpits.
– ORIGIN Greek *boubōn* 'groin or swelling in the groin'.

buccaneer /buk-kuh-neer/ •n. **1** hist. a pirate. **2** a recklessly adventurous person.
– ORIGIN French *boucanier*.

buck[1] •n. **1** the male of some animals, e.g. deer and rabbits. **2** a vertical jump performed by a horse. **3** old use a fashionable young man. •v. **1** (of a horse) perform a buck. **2** go against: *the shares bucked the market trend.* **3** (**buck up** or **buck someone up**) informal become or make someone more cheerful.
– ORIGIN Old English.

buck[2] •n. N. Amer. & Austral./NZ informal a dollar.

buck[3] •n. an object placed in front of a poker player whose turn it is to deal.
– PHRASES **the buck stops here** informal the responsibility for something cannot be avoided. **pass the buck** informal shift responsibility to someone else.

bucket •n. **1** an open container with a handle, used to carry liquids. **2** (**buckets**) informal large quantities of liquid. •v. (**buckets, bucketing, bucketed**) (**bucket down**) Brit. informal rain heavily.
– DERIVATIVES **bucketful** n.
– ORIGIN Old French *buquet.*

bucket shop •n. Brit. a travel agency that sells cheap air tickets.

buckle •n. a flat frame with a hinged pin, used as a fastener. •v. (**buckles, buckling, buckled**) **1** fasten with a buckle. **2** bend and give way under

b

pressure. **3** (**buckle down**) tackle a task with determination.
– ORIGIN Latin *buccula* 'cheek strap of a helmet'; sense 2 is from French *boucler* 'to bulge'.

buckram • n. coarse cloth stiffened with paste, used in binding books.
– ORIGIN Old French *boquerant*.

Bucks. • abbrev. Buckinghamshire.

buckshot • n. coarse lead shot used in shotgun shells.

buckskin • n. soft leather made from the skin of deer or sheep.

buck teeth • pl. n. upper teeth that project over the lower lip.
– DERIVATIVES **buck-toothed** adj.

buckthorn • n. a thorny shrub which bears black berries.

buckwheat • n. the starchy seeds of a plant, used for animal fodder or making flour.
– ORIGIN Dutch *boecweite* 'beech wheat'.

bucolic /byoo-kol-ik/ • adj. relating to country life.
– ORIGIN Greek *boukolikos*.

bud • n. a growth on a plant which develops into a leaf, flower, or shoot.
• v. (**buds, budding, budded**) form a bud or buds.

Buddhism /buud-di-z'm/ • n. a religion based on the teachings of Siddartha Gautama (Buddha; *c.*563–*c.*460 BC).
– DERIVATIVES **Buddhist** n. & adj.

budding • adj. beginning and showing signs of promise: *their budding relationship*.

buddleia /bud-dli-uh/ • n. a shrub with clusters of lilac, white, or yellow flowers.
– ORIGIN named after the English botanist Adam *Buddle*.

buddy • n. (pl. **buddies**) N. Amer. informal a close friend.
– ORIGIN perh. from **BROTHER**.

budge • v. (**budges, budging, budged**) **1** make or cause to make the slightest movement. **2** change or cause to change an opinion.
– ORIGIN French *bouger* 'to stir'.

budgerigar • n. a small Australian parakeet.
– ORIGIN Aboriginal.

budget • n. **1** an estimate of income and spending for a set period of time. **2** the amount of money needed or available for a purpose. **3** (**Budget**) a regular estimate of national income and spending put forward by a finance minister. • v. (**budgets, budgeting, budgeted**) allow for in a budget.
• adj. inexpensive.
– DERIVATIVES **budgetary** adj.

– ORIGIN Old French *bougette* 'little leather bag'.

budgie • n. (pl. **budgies**) informal a budgerigar.

buff¹ • n. a yellowish-beige colour.
• v. polish something.
– PHRASES **in the buff** informal naked.
– ORIGIN prob. from French *buffle* 'buffalo'.

buff² • n. informal a person who knows a lot about a particular subject: *a film buff.*
– ORIGIN from **BUFF¹**, first referring to spectators of fires in New York, because of the firemen's buff uniforms.

buffalo • n. (pl. **buffalo** or **buffaloes**) **1** a heavily built wild ox with backward-curving horns. **2** the North American bison.
– ORIGIN Latin *bufalus*.

buffer¹ • n. **1** (**buffers**) Brit. shock-absorbing devices at the end of a railway track or on a railway vehicle. **2** a person or thing that lessens the impact of something harmful: *friends can provide a buffer against stress.* **3** (also **buffer solution**) Chem. a solution which resists changes in pH when acid or alkali is added to it.
– ORIGIN prob. from former *buff* 'deaden the force of something'.

buffer² • n. Brit. informal a foolish or incompetent elderly man.
– ORIGIN prob. from former *buff* (see **BUFFER¹**).

buffet¹ /boo-fay, buf-fay/ • n. **1** a meal made up of several dishes from which guests serve themselves. **2** a room or counter selling light meals or snacks.
– ORIGIN Old French *bufet* 'stool'.

buffet² /buf-fit/ • v. (**buffets, buffeting, buffeted**) (especially of wind or waves) strike someone or something repeatedly and violently.
– ORIGIN Old French *buffeter*.

buffoon /buh-foon/ • n. a ridiculous but amusing person.
– DERIVATIVES **buffoonery** n.
– ORIGIN French *bouffon*.

bug • n. **1** informal a harmful micro-organism, or an illness caused by one. **2** esp. N. Amer. a small insect. **3** informal an enthusiasm for something: *the sailing bug.* **4** a microphone used for secret recording. **5** an error in a computer program or system. • v. (**bugs, bugging, bugged**) **1** hide a microphone in a room or telephone. **2** informal annoy someone.

bugbear • n. a cause of anxiety or irritation.
– ORIGIN prob. from former *bug* 'evil spirit' + **BEAR²**.

bug-eyed • adj. with bulging eyes.

buggery • n. anal intercourse.

buggy • n. (pl. **buggies**) **1** a small motor vehicle with an open top. **2** hist. a light horse-drawn vehicle for one or two people.

bugle • n. a brass instrument like a small trumpet.
– DERIVATIVES **bugler** n.
– ORIGIN Latin *buculus* 'little ox'.

build • v. (**builds, building, built**) **1** construct by putting parts together. **2** (often **build up**) increase over time. **3** (**build on**) use as a basis for further development. **4** (**build something in/into**) make something a permanent part of a larger structure. • n. the size or shape of a person's or animal's body: *she was of slim build.*
– DERIVATIVES **builder** n.
– ORIGIN Old English.

building • n. **1** a structure with a roof and walls. **2** the process or trade of building houses and other structures.

building society • n. Brit. a financial organization which pays interest on members' investments and lends money for mortgages.

build-up • n. **1** a gradual increase. **2** a period of excitement and preparation before an event.

built past and past part. of **BUILD**. • adj. of a particular physical build: *a slightly built woman.*

built-in • adj. included as part of a larger structure: *a worktop with a built-in cooker.*

built-up • adj. (of an area) covered by many buildings.

bulb • n. **1** the rounded base of the stem of some plants, from which the roots grow. **2** a light bulb.
– ORIGIN Greek *bolbos* 'onion'.

bulbous • adj. **1** round or bulging. **2** (of a plant) growing from a bulb.

Bulgarian • n. **1** a person from Bulgaria. **2** the language of Bulgaria. • adj. relating to Bulgaria.

bulge • n. **1** a rounded swelling on a flat surface. **2** informal a temporary increase: *a bulge in the birth rate.* • v. (**bulges, bulging, bulged**) **1** swell or stick out. **2** be full of: *a briefcase bulging with documents.*
– DERIVATIVES **bulgy** adj.
– ORIGIN Latin *bulga* 'leather bag'.

bulimia /buu-lim-i-uh/ (also **bulimia nervosa** /ner-voh-suh/) • n. a disorder in which a person repeatedly overeats and then fasts or makes themself vomit.
– DERIVATIVES **bulimic** adj. & n.
– ORIGIN Greek *boulimia* 'ravenous hunger'.

bulk • n. **1** the mass or size of something large. **2** the greater part. **3** a large mass or shape. • adj. large in quantity: *bulk orders.* • v. (**bulk something up/out**) make something bigger, thicker, or heavier.
– PHRASES **bulk large** be or seem to be very important. **in bulk** (of goods) in large quantities.
– ORIGIN prob. from Old Norse, meaning 'cargo'.

bulkhead • n. a barrier between separate areas inside a ship, aircraft, etc.

bulky • adj. (**bulkier, bulkiest**) large and awkward to handle.

bull¹ • n. **1** an uncastrated male animal of the cattle family. **2** a large male animal, e.g. a whale or elephant. **3** Brit. a bullseye.
– PHRASES **like a bull in a china shop** behaving clumsily in a delicate situation. **take the bull by the horns** deal decisively with a difficult situation.
– ORIGIN Old Norse.

bull² • n. an order or announcement issued by the Pope.
– ORIGIN Latin *bulla* 'bubble, seal'.

bulldog • n. a short breed of dog with a powerful lower jaw and a flat, wrinkled face.

bulldog clip • n. Brit. trademark a device with two flat pieces of metal held together by a spring, used to hold papers together.

bulldoze • v. (**bulldozes, bulldozing, bulldozed**) **1** clear ground or destroy buildings with a bulldozer. **2** informal use force to do something or deal with someone.
– ORIGIN from **BULL¹** + **-doze**, from **DOSE**.

bulldozer • n. a tractor with a broad curved blade at the front for clearing ground.

bullet • n. **1** a small missile fired from a gun. **2** a solid circle printed before each item in a list.
– ORIGIN French *boulet* 'small ball'.

bulletin • n. **1** a short official statement or summary of news. **2** a regular newsletter or report.
– ORIGIN Italian *bullettino* 'little passport'.

bulletin board • n. **1** N. Amer. a notice-board. **2** a site on a computer system where any user can read or write messages.

bullfighting • n. the sport of baiting and killing a bull for public entertainment.
– DERIVATIVES **bullfight** n. **bullfighter** n.

bullfinch • n. a finch with grey and black plumage and a pink breast.

bullfrog •n. a very large frog with a deep croak.

bullion /buul-li-uhn/ •n. gold or silver in bulk before being made into coins.
– ORIGIN Old French *bouillon*.

bullish •adj. aggressively confident.

bull-necked •adj. (of a man) having a thick, strong neck.

bullock •n. a castrated male animal of the cattle family, raised for beef.
– ORIGIN Old English.

bullring •n. an arena where bullfights are held.

bullrush •n. var. of BULRUSH.

bullseye •n. the centre of the target in sports such as archery and darts.

bull terrier •n. a dog that is a cross-breed of bulldog and terrier.

bully •n. (pl. **bullies**) a person who intimidates or frightens weaker people. •v. (**bullies, bullying, bullied**) intimidate or frighten someone.
– PHRASES **bully for you!** an ironic expression of admiration or approval.
– ORIGIN prob. from Dutch *boele* 'lover'.

bulrush (also **bullrush**) •n. a tall waterside plant with a long brown head.
– ORIGIN prob. from BULL¹ in the sense 'large, coarse'.

bulwark /buul-werk/ •n. 1 a defensive wall. 2 a person or thing that acts as a defence. 3 an extension of a ship's sides above deck level.
– ORIGIN German and Dutch *bolwerk*.

bum¹ •n. Brit. informal a person's bottom.

bum² informal •n. N. Amer. 1 a homeless person or beggar. 2 a lazy or worthless person. •v. (**bums, bumming, bummed**) get something by asking or begging for it. •adj. bad: *not one bum note was played.*
– ORIGIN prob. from BUMMER.

bumbag •n. Brit. informal a small pouch on a belt, worn round the hips.

bumble •v. (**bumbles, bumbling, bumbled**) move or speak in an awkward or confused way.
– ORIGIN from BOOM¹.

bumblebee •n. a large hairy bee with a loud hum.

bumf (also **bumph**) •n. Brit. informal useless or dull printed information.
– ORIGIN from slang *bum-fodder*.

bummer •n. informal an annoying or disappointing thing.
– ORIGIN perh. from German *Bummler* 'loafer'.

bump •n. 1 a light blow or collision. 2 a hump or swelling on a level surface. •v. 1 knock or run into with a jolt. 2 travel with a jolting movement. 3 (**bump into**) meet by chance. 4 (**bump someone off**) informal murder someone.

5 (**bump something up**) informal increase or raise something.
– DERIVATIVES **bumpy** adj. (**bumpier, bumpiest**).
– ORIGIN perh. Scandinavian.

bumper •n. a bar fixed across the front or back of a motor vehicle to reduce damage in a collision. •adj. exceptionally large or successful: *a bumper crop.*

bumph •n. var. of BUMF.

bumpkin •n. an unsophisticated person from the countryside.
– ORIGIN perh. from Dutch *boomken* 'little tree' or *bommekijn* 'little barrel'.

bumptious •adj. irritatingly confident or self-important.
– ORIGIN from BUMP.

bun •n. 1 a small cake or bread roll. 2 a tight coil of hair at the back of the head.

bunch •n. 1 a number of things grouped or held together. 2 informal a group of people. •v. collect or form into a bunch.

bundle •n. 1 a group of things or a quantity of material tied or wrapped up together. 2 informal a large amount of money. •v. (**bundles, bundling, bundled**) 1 tie or roll something up in a bundle. 2 (**be bundled up**) be dressed in many warm clothes. 3 informal push or carry forcibly.
– ORIGIN perh. from Old English.

bunfight •n. Brit. humorous a grand party or other social function.

bung¹ •n. a stopper for a hole in a container. •v. 1 close with a bung. 2 (**bung something up**) block something up.
– ORIGIN Dutch *bonghe*.

bung² Brit. informal •v. put or throw something somewhere carelessly or casually. •n. a bribe.

bungalow •n. a house with only one storey.
– ORIGIN Hindi, 'belonging to Bengal'.

bungee /bun-ji/ (also **bungee cord** or **rope**) •n. a long rubber band encased in nylon, used for securing luggage and in bungee jumping.

bungee jumping •n. the sport of leaping from a high place, held by a bungee around the ankles.

bungle •v. (**bungles, bungling, bungled**) perform a task in a clumsy or unskilful way. •n. a mistake or failure.
– DERIVATIVES **bungler** n.

bunion •n. a painful swelling on the big toe.
– ORIGIN Old French *buignon*.

bunk¹ •n. a narrow shelf-like bed.

bunk² •v. (**bunk off**) Brit. informal stay away from school or work without permission.

– PHRASES **do a bunk** leave hurriedly.

bunk bed • n. a structure made up of two beds, one above the other.

bunker • n. 1 a large container for storing fuel. 2 an underground shelter for use in wartime. 3 a hollow filled with sand, forming an obstacle on a golf course.
– ORIGIN Scots 'seat or bench'.

bunkum • n. informal, dated nonsense.
– ORIGIN named after *Buncombe* County in North Carolina.

bunny • n. (pl. **bunnies**) informal 1 a child's term for a rabbit. 2 (also **bunny girl**) a nightclub hostess wearing a skimpy costume with ears and a tail.
– ORIGIN dialect *bun* 'squirrel, rabbit'.

Bunsen burner /bun-s'n/ • n. a small gas burner used in laboratories.
– ORIGIN named after the German chemist Robert *Bunsen*.

bunting[1] • n. a songbird with brown streaked plumage and a boldly marked head.

bunting[2] • n. flags and streamers used as decorations.

buoy /boy/ • n. a floating object that marks safe navigation channels for boats. • v. 1 keep afloat. 2 make or remain cheerful and confident: *he was buoyed up by his success.*
– ORIGIN prob. from Dutch *boye, boeie*; the verb is from Spanish *boyar* 'to float'.

☑ Spell **buoy** and the related word **buoyant** with a **u** before the **o**.

buoyant • adj. 1 able to keep afloat. 2 cheerful and optimistic.
– DERIVATIVES **buoyancy** n.

BUPA /boo-puh/ • abbrev. British United Provident Association, a private health insurance organization.

bur • n. see BURR.

burble • v. (**burbles, burbling, burbled**) 1 make a continuous murmuring noise. 2 speak at length in a way that is hard to understand. • n. continuous murmuring noise.

burden • n. 1 a heavy load. 2 a cause of hardship, worry, or grief. 3 the main responsibility for a task. • v. 1 load heavily. 2 cause worry, hardship, or grief to.
– ORIGIN Old English.

burdensome • adj. causing worry or difficulty.

burdock • n. a plant with large leaves and prickly flowers.
– ORIGIN from BUR + DOCK[3].

bureau /byoor-oh/ • n. (pl. **bureaux** or **bureaus**) 1 Brit. a writing desk with a sloping top that opens downwards to form a writing surface. 2 N. Amer. a chest of drawers. 3 an office for carrying out particular business: *a news bureau.* 4 a government department.
– ORIGIN French.

bureaucracy /byuu-rok-ruh-si/ • n. (pl. **bureaucracies**) 1 a system of government in which most decisions are taken by state officials rather than by elected representatives. 2 administrative procedure that is too complicated.

bureaucrat • n. an official who is seen as being too concerned with following administrative guidelines.
– DERIVATIVES **bureaucratic** adj.

bureau de change /byoo-roh duh shonzh/ • n. (pl. **bureaux de change** /byoo-roh duh shonzh/) a place where foreign money can be exchanged.
– ORIGIN French, 'office of exchange'.

burette /byuu-ret/ (US also **buret**) • n. a glass tube with measurements on it and a tap at one end, for delivering known amounts of a liquid.
– ORIGIN French.

burgeon /ber-juhn/ • v. grow or increase rapidly.
– ORIGIN Old French *bourgeonner* 'put out buds'.

burger • n. a hamburger.

burgher /ber-guh/ • n. old use a citizen of a town or city.
– ORIGIN from BOROUGH.

burglar • n. a person who commits burglary.
– ORIGIN Old French *burgier* 'pillage'.

burglary • n. (pl. **burglaries**) the crime of entering a building illegally and stealing its contents.

burgle • v. (**burgles, burgling, burgled**) esp. Brit. enter a building illegally and steal its contents.

burgundy /ber-guhn-di/ • n. (pl. **burgundies**) 1 a red wine from Burgundy, a region of east central France. 2 a deep red colour.

burial • n. the burying of a dead body.

burlesque /ber-lesk/ • n. 1 a performance or piece of writing which makes fun of something by representing it in a comically exaggerated way. 2 N. Amer. a variety show.
– ORIGIN French.

burly • adj. (**burlier, burliest**) (of a person) large and strong.
– DERIVATIVES **burliness** n.
– ORIGIN prob. from Old English 'stately'.

Burmese • n. (pl. **Burmese**) 1 a member of the largest ethnic group of Burma (now Myanmar) in SE Asia. 2 a person from Burma. •adj. relating to Burma or the Burmese.

burn¹ •v. (**burns, burning, burned** or esp. Brit. **burnt**) **1** (of a fire) flame or glow while using up a fuel. **2** be or cause to be harmed by fire. **3** use a fuel as a source of heat or energy. **4** (of the skin) become red and painful through exposure to the sun. **5** (**be burning with**) experience a very strong desire or emotion. **6** (**burn out**) become exhausted through overwork. **7** produce a CD by copying from an original or master copy. •n. an injury caused by burning.
– PHRASES **burn your boats** (or **bridges**) do something which makes it impossible to return to the previous situation. **burn the candle at both ends** go to bed late and get up early. **burn the midnight oil** work late into the night.
– ORIGIN Old English.

burn² •n. Scottish & N. English a small stream.
– ORIGIN Old English.

burner •n. **1** a part of a cooker, lamp, etc. that gives out a flame. **2** a device for burning something.

burning •adj. **1** very deeply felt. **2** of great interest or importance: *the burning issues of the day.*

burnish •v. polish something by rubbing it.
– ORIGIN Old French *brunir* 'make brown'.

burnous /ber-nooss/ (US also **burnoose**) •n. a long hooded cloak worn by Arabs.
– ORIGIN Arabic.

burnout •n. physical or mental collapse.

burnt (also **burned**) past and past part. of **BURN¹**.

burp informal •v. **1** belch. **2** make a baby belch after feeding. •n. a belch.

burr •n. **1** a whirring sound. **2** a strong pronunciation of the letter *r*. **3** (also **bur**) a prickly seed case or flower head that clings to clothing and animal fur. •v. make a whirring sound.
– ORIGIN prob. Scandinavian.

burrow •n. a hole or tunnel dug by a small animal as a home. •v. **1** make a burrow. **2** hide underneath something. **3** search for something.
– DERIVATIVES **burrower** n.
– ORIGIN from **BOROUGH**.

bursar •n. esp. Brit. a person who manages the finances of a college or school.
– ORIGIN Latin *bursarius*.

bursary •n. (pl. **bursaries**) Brit. a grant for study.

burst •v. (**bursts, bursting, burst**) **1** break suddenly and violently apart. **2** be very full. **3** move or be opened suddenly and forcibly. **4** (**be bursting with**) feel a very strong emotion. **5** suddenly do something: *she burst out crying.* •n. **1** an instance of bursting. **2** a sudden brief outbreak: *a burst of activity.* **3** a period of continuous effort.
– ORIGIN Old English.

burton •n. (in phr. **go for a burton**) Brit. informal be ruined, destroyed, or killed.
– ORIGIN perh. referring to *Burton* ale, from Burton-upon-Trent.

bury •v. (**buries, burying, buried**) **1** put something underground. **2** place a dead body in the earth or a tomb. **3** cover completely. **4** (**bury yourself**) involve yourself deeply in something.
– ORIGIN Old English.

bus •n. (pl. **buses**; US also **busses**) **1** a large motor vehicle that carries customers along a fixed route. **2** a distinct set of conductors within a computer system, to which pieces of equipment may be connected in parallel. •v. (**buses, busing, bused**; also **busses, bussing, bussed**) transport or travel in a bus.
– ORIGIN from **OMNIBUS**.

busby •n. (pl. **busbies**) a tall fur hat worn by certain military regiments.

bush¹ •n. **1** a shrub or clump of shrubs. **2** (**the bush**) (in Australia and Africa) wild or uncultivated country.
– ORIGIN Old French *bois* 'wood'.

bush² •n. Brit. **1** a metal lining for a hole in which something fits or revolves. **2** a sleeve that protects an electric cable.
– ORIGIN Dutch *busse*.

bushbaby •n. (pl. **bushbabies**) a small African mammal with very large eyes.

bushed •adj. informal exhausted.

bushel •n. **1** Brit. a measure of capacity equal to 8 gallons (equivalent to 36.4 litres). **2** US a measure of capacity equal to 64 US pints (equivalent to 35.2 litres).
– ORIGIN Old French *boissel*.

Bushman •n. (pl. **Bushmen**) **1** a member of any of several peoples native to southern Africa. **2** (**bushman**) a person who lives or travels in the Australian bush.

bush telegraph •n. an informal network by which information is spread quickly.

bushy •adj. (**bushier, bushiest**) **1** growing thickly. **2** covered with bush or bushes.

business •n. **1** a person's regular occupation. **2** commercial activity. **3** a commercial organization. **4** work to be done or things to be attended to. **5** a person's concern: *it's none of your business.* **6** informal a difficult matter. **7** (**the business**) Brit. informal an excellent person or thing.
– PHRASES **mind your own business** avoid

interfering in other people's affairs.
– ORIGIN Old English, 'anxiety'.

✓ Remember that **business** begins with busi-.

businesslike •adj. efficient and practical.

businessman (or **businesswoman**) •n. (pl. **businessmen** or **businesswomen**) a person who works in commerce.

busk •v. play music in the street in the hope of being given money by people passing by.
– DERIVATIVES **busker** n.
– ORIGIN from former French *busquer* 'seek'.

busman's holiday •n. leisure time spent doing the same thing that you do at work.

bust[1] •n. 1 a woman's breasts. 2 a sculpture of a person's head, shoulders, and chest.
– ORIGIN French *buste*.

bust[2] informal •v. (**busts**, **busting**, **busted** or **bust**) 1 break, split, or burst. 2 esp. N. Amer. raid or search a building, or arrest someone. •n. 1 a period of economic difficulty. 2 a police raid. •adj. 1 Brit. damaged; broken. 2 bankrupt.
– ORIGIN from **burst**.

bustard /buss-terd/ •n. a large swift-running bird of open country.
– ORIGIN perh. from Old French *bistarde* and *oustarde*.

buster •n. informal, esp. N. Amer. a form of address to a man or boy.

bustier /buss-ti-ay/ •n. a woman's close-fitting strapless top.
– ORIGIN French.

bustle[1] •v. (**bustles**, **bustling**, **bustled**) 1 move energetically or noisily. 2 (often as adj. **bustling**) (of a place) be full of activity. •n. excited activity and movement.
– ORIGIN perh. from former *busk* 'prepare'.

bustle[2] •n. hist. a pad or frame worn under a skirt to puff it out behind.

bust-up •n. informal a serious quarrel or fight.

busty •adj. informal having large breasts.

busy •adj. (**busier**, **busiest**) 1 having a great deal to do. 2 occupied with an activity. 3 crowded or full of activity. 4 too detailed or decorated. •v. (**busies**, **busying**, **busied**) (**busy yourself**) keep yourself occupied.
– DERIVATIVES **busily** adv. **busyness** n.
– ORIGIN Old English.

busybody •n. (pl. **busybodies**) an interfering or nosy person.

busy Lizzie •n. Brit. a plant with many red, pink, or white flowers.

but •conj. 1 in spite of that; however. 2 on the contrary. 3 other than; otherwise than. 4 old use without it being the case that: *it never rains but it pours*. •prep. except; apart from: *the last but one*. •adv. only. •n. an objection.
– PHRASES **but for** 1 except for. 2 if it were not for.
– ORIGIN Old English, 'outside, except'.

butane /byoo-tayn/ •n. a flammable gas present in petroleum and natural gas, used as a fuel.
– ORIGIN Latin *butyrum* 'butter'.

butch •adj. informal aggressively masculine.
– ORIGIN perh. from **BUTCHER**.

butcher •n. 1 a person who cuts up and sells meat as a trade. 2 a person who slaughters animals for food. 3 a person who kills brutally. •v. (**butchers**, **butchering**, **butchered**) 1 slaughter or cut up an animal for food. 2 kill someone brutally. 3 spoil something by doing it badly: *the film was butchered by the studio*.
– DERIVATIVES **butchery** n.
– ORIGIN Old French *bochier*.

butler •n. the chief manservant of a house.
– ORIGIN Old French *bouteillier* 'cup-bearer'.

butt[1] •v. 1 hit with the head or horns. 2 (**butt in**) interrupt a conversation or activity. •n. a rough push with the head.
– ORIGIN Old French *boter*.

butt[2] •n. 1 an object of criticism or ridicule. 2 a target or range in archery or shooting.
– ORIGIN Old French *but*.

butt[3] •n. 1 the thicker end of a tool or a weapon. 2 the stub of a cigar or a cigarette. 3 N. Amer. informal a person's bottom. •v. be next to or against.
– ORIGIN Dutch *bot* 'stumpy'.

butt[4] •n. a cask used for wine, beer, or water.
– ORIGIN Latin *buttis*.

butter •n. a pale yellow fatty substance made by churning cream. •v. (**butters**, **buttering**, **buttered**) 1 spread something with butter. 2 (**butter someone up**) informal flatter someone.
– PHRASES **look as if butter wouldn't melt in your mouth** informal appear innocent while being the opposite.
– ORIGIN Latin *butyrum*.

butter bean •n. Brit. a large flat edible bean.

buttercream •n. a mixture of butter and icing sugar used in cake making.

buttercup •n. a plant with bright yellow cup-shaped flowers.

b

butterfingers • n. informal a person who often drops things.

butterfly • n. **1** an insect with two pairs of large wings, which feeds on nectar. **2** a showy or frivolous person: *a social butterfly.* **3** (**butterflies**) informal a fluttering sensation felt in the stomach as a result of nervousness. **4** a stroke in swimming in which both arms are raised out of the water and lifted forwards together.
– ORIGIN Old English.

buttermilk • n. the slightly sour liquid left after cream has been churned to produce butter.

butterscotch • n. a sweet made with butter and brown sugar.

buttery[1] • adj. containing, tasting like, or covered with butter.

buttery[2] • n. (pl. **butteries**) Brit. a room in a college where food is kept and sold to students.
– ORIGIN Old French *boterie* 'cask store'.

buttie • n. (pl. **butties**) var. of BUTTY.

buttock • n. either of the two round fleshy parts of the human body that form the bottom.
– ORIGIN Old English.

button • n. **1** a small disc sewn on to a garment to fasten it by being pushed through a buttonhole. **2** a knob on a piece of equipment which is pressed to operate it. • v. fasten or be fastened with buttons.
– ORIGIN Old French *bouton*.

buttonhole • n. **1** a slit made in a garment through which a button is pushed to fasten it. **2** Brit. a flower worn in a buttonhole on the lapel of a jacket or coat. • v. (**buttonholes, buttonholing, buttonholed**) informal stop and hold someone in conversation.

button mushroom • n. a young unopened mushroom.

buttress /but-triss/ • n. **1** a projecting support built against a wall. **2** a projecting part of a hill or mountain. • v. support or strengthen.
– ORIGIN from Old French *ars bouterez* 'thrusting arch'.

butty (also **buttie**) • n. (pl. **butties**) Brit. informal a sandwich.
– ORIGIN from BUTTER.

buxom /buk-suhm/ • adj. (of a woman) attractively plump and large-breasted.
– ORIGIN Old English, 'to bend'.

buy • v. (**buys, buying, bought**) **1** get something in return for payment. **2** get something by sacrifice or great effort. **3** informal accept the truth of. • n. informal a purchase.
– PHRASES **buy someone out** pay some-

one to give up a share in something.
– ORIGIN Old English.

buyer • n. **1** a person who buys. **2** a person employed to buy stock for a business.

buyer's market • n. a situation in which goods or shares are plentiful and buyers can keep prices down.

buyout • n. the purchase of a controlling share in a company.

buzz • n. **1** a low, continuous humming sound. **2** the sound of a buzzer or telephone. **3** an atmosphere of excitement and activity. **4** informal a thrill. • v. **1** make a humming sound. **2** call someone with a buzzer. **3** move quickly. **4** (**buzz off**) informal go away. **5** have an air of excitement or activity. **6** informal (of an aircraft) fly very close to something at high speed.

buzzard /buz-zerd/ • n. **1** a large bird of prey which soars in wide circles. **2** N. Amer. a vulture.
– ORIGIN Old French *busard*.

buzzer • n. an electrical device that makes a buzzing noise to attract attention.

buzzword • n. informal a technical word or phrase that has become fashionable.

by • prep. **1** through the action or means of. **2** indicating an amount or the size of a margin: *the shot missed her by miles.* **3** showing multiplication. **4** indicating the end of a time period. **5** beside. **6** past and beyond. **7** during. **8** according to. • adv. so as to go past. • n. (pl. **byes**) var. of BYE[1].
– PHRASES **by and by** before long. **by the by** in passing. **by and large** on the whole.
– ORIGIN Old English.

by- (also **bye-**) • prefix less important; secondary: *by-election.*

bye[1] • n. **1** the moving of a competitor straight to the next round of a competition because they have no opponent. **2** Cricket a run scored from a ball that passes the batsman without being hit.
– ORIGIN from BY.

bye[2] • exclam. informal goodbye.

by-election • n. Brit. an election held during a government's term of office to fill a vacant seat.

bygone • adj. belonging to an earlier time.
– PHRASES **let bygones be bygones** forget past disagreements.

by-law (also **bye-law**) • n. **1** Brit. a rule made by a local authority. **2** a rule made by a company or society.

– ORIGIN prob. from former *byrlaw* 'local law or custom'.

byline •n. **1** a line in a newspaper naming the writer of an article. **2** (also **byeline**) (in football) the part of the goal line to either side of the goal.

bypass •n. **1** a road passing round a town. **2** an operation to help the circulation of blood by directing it through a new passage. •v. go past or round.

by-product •n. a product produced in the making of something else.

byre /*rhymes with* fire/ •n. Brit. a cow-shed.
– ORIGIN Old English.

Byronic /by-**ron**-ik/ •adj. **1** referring to the poet Lord Byron. **2** (of a man) interestingly mysterious and moody.

bystander •n. a person who is present at an event but does not take part in it.

byte /*rhymes with* white/ •n. a unit of information stored in a computer, equal to eight bits.
– ORIGIN from BIT⁴ and BITE.

byway •n. a minor road or path.

byword •n. **1** a notable example of something: *his name became a byword for luxury.* **2** a saying.

Byzantine /bi-**zan**-tyn/ •adj. **1** relating to Byzantium (now Istanbul), the Byzantine Empire, or the Eastern Orthodox Church. **2** very complicated.

Cc

C¹ (also **c**) • n. (pl. **Cs** or **C's**) **1** the third letter of the alphabet. **2** referring to the third item in a set. **3** Music the first note of the scale of C major. **4** the Roman numeral for 100. [ORIGIN from Latin *centum* 'hundred'.]

C² • abbrev. **1** Celsius or centigrade. **2** (©) copyright. **3** Physics coulomb(s). • symb. the chemical element carbon.

c • abbrev. **1** cent(s). **2** (before a date or amount) circa. **3** (**c.**) century or centuries.

Ca • symb. the chemical element calcium.

ca. • abbrev. (before a date or amount) circa.

CAB • abbrev. Citizens' Advice Bureau.

cab • n. **1** (also **taxi cab**) a taxi. **2** the driver's compartment in a lorry, bus, or train.
– ORIGIN from CABRIOLET.

cabal /kuh-bal/ • n. a secret political group.
– ORIGIN Latin *cabala* 'Kabbalah'.

cabaret /kab-uh-ray/ • n. entertainment held in a nightclub or restaurant while the audience sit at tables.
– ORIGIN Old French, 'inn'.

cabbage • n. a vegetable with thick green or purple leaves around a core of young leaves.
– ORIGIN Old French *caboche* 'head'.

cabbage white • n. a white butterfly whose caterpillars are pests of cabbages and related plants.

cabby (also **cabbie**) • n. (pl. **cabbies**) informal a taxi driver.

caber /kay-ber/ • n. a roughly trimmed tree trunk that is thrown in the Scottish Highland sport of tossing the caber.
– ORIGIN Scottish Gaelic *cabar* 'pole'.

cabin • n. **1** a private room on a ship. **2** the passenger compartment in an aircraft. **3** a small wooden shelter or house.
– ORIGIN Old French *cabane*.

cabin cruiser • n. a motor boat with a living area.

cabinet • n. **1** a cupboard with drawers or shelves for storing articles. **2** a piece of furniture housing a radio, television, or speaker. **3** (also **Cabinet**) a committee of senior government ministers.
– ORIGIN from CABIN.

cabinetmaker • n. a person who makes fine wooden furniture as a job.

cable • n. **1** a thick rope of wire or fibre. **2** a wire or wires for transmitting electricity or telecommunications signals.
– ORIGIN Old French *chable*.

cable car • n. a small carriage hung from a moving cable and travelling up and down a mountainside.

cable television • n. a system in which television programmes are transmitted by cable.

caboodle • n. (in phr. **the whole caboodle** or **the whole kit and caboodle**) informal all the people or things in question.

cabriolet /kab-ri-oh-lay/ • n. **1** a car with a roof that folds down. **2** a light two-wheeled carriage with a hood, drawn by one horse.
– ORIGIN French.

cacao /kuh-kah-oh/ • n. the bean-like seeds of a tropical American tree, from which cocoa and chocolate are made.
– ORIGIN Nahuatl (a language of Central America).

cache /kash/ • n. a hidden store of things.
– ORIGIN French.

cachet /ka-shay/ • n. the state of being respected or admired; prestige: *the brand has lost some of its cachet.*
– ORIGIN French.

cack-handed • adj. Brit. informal clumsy.

cackle • v. (**cackles, cackling, cackled**) **1** laugh in a loud, raucous way. **2** (of a hen or goose) make a loud clucking cry • n. a loud cry or laugh.
– ORIGIN prob. from German *kākelen*.

cacophony /kuh-koff-uh-ni/ • n. (pl. **cacophonies**) a mixture of loud and unpleasant sounds.
– DERIVATIVES **cacophonous** adj.
– ORIGIN Greek *kakophōnia*.

cactus /kak-tuhss/ • n. (pl. **cacti** /kak-ty/ or **cactuses**) a plant with a thick fleshy

stem bearing spines but no leaves.
– ORIGIN Greek *kaktos* 'cardoon'.

cad •n. dated or humorous a man who behaves dishonourably.
– DERIVATIVES **caddish** adj.
– ORIGIN from **CADDIE** OR **CADET**.

cadaver /kuh-da-ver/ •n. Med. or literary a dead body.
– ORIGIN Latin.

cadaverous /kuh-dav-uh-ruhss/ •adj. very pale and thin.

caddie (also **caddy**) •n. (pl. **caddies**) a person who carries a golfer's clubs during a match. •v. (**caddies, caddying, caddied**) work as a caddie.
– ORIGIN French *cadet*.

caddis /kad-iss/ (also **caddis fly**) •n. a small winged insect having larvae that live in water and build cases of sticks, stones, etc.

caddy •n. (pl. **caddies**) a small storage container.
– ORIGIN Malay, referring to a unit of weight of 1⅓ lb (0.61 kg).

cadence /kay-duhnss/ •n. **1** the rise and fall in pitch of a person's voice. **2** a sequence of notes or chords making up the close of a musical phrase.
– ORIGIN Italian *cadenza*.

cadenza /kuh-den-zuh/ •n. a difficult solo passage in a musical work.
– ORIGIN Italian.

cadet •n. a young trainee in the armed services or police.
– ORIGIN French.

cadge •v. (**cadges, cadging, cadged**) informal, esp. Brit. ask for or get something without paying or working for it.
– ORIGIN northern English and Scottish *cadger*, 'travelling dealer'.

cadmium /kad-mi-uhm/ •n. a silvery-white metallic chemical element resembling zinc.
– ORIGIN Latin *cadmia* 'calamine'.

cadre /kah-der/ •n. a small group of people chosen and trained for a particular purpose or at the centre of a political organization.
– ORIGIN French.

caecum /see-kuhm/ (US **cecum**) •n. (pl. **caeca** /see-kuh/) a pouch at the place where the small and large intestines join.
– ORIGIN from Latin *intestinum caecum* 'blind gut'.

Caesar /see-zer/ •n. a title of Roman emperors.
– ORIGIN family name of the Roman statesman Gaius Julius *Caesar*.

Caesarean /si-zair-i-uhn/ (also **Caesarean section**) •n. an operation for delivering a child by cutting through the wall of the mother's abdomen.
– ORIGIN from the story that Julius Caesar was delivered by this method.

caesium /see-zi-uhm/ (US **cesium**) •n. a soft, silvery, extremely reactive metallic chemical element.
– ORIGIN Latin *caesius* 'greyish-blue'.

caesura /si-zyoor-uh/ •n. a pause near the middle of a line of verse.
– ORIGIN Latin.

cafe /ka-fay/ •n. a small restaurant selling light meals and drinks.
– ORIGIN French, 'coffee or coffee house'.

cafeteria /ka-fuh-teer-i-uh/ •n. a self-service restaurant.
– ORIGIN Latin American Spanish, 'coffee shop'.

cafetière /ka-fuh-tyair/ •n. a coffee pot containing a plunger with which the grounds are pushed to the bottom.
– ORIGIN French.

caffeine /kaf-feen/ •n. a substance found in tea and coffee plants which stimulates the central nervous system.
– DERIVATIVES **caffeinated** adj.
– ORIGIN French *caféine*.

caftan •n. var. of **KAFTAN**.

cage •n. **1** a structure of bars or wires in which animals are confined. **2** any similar structure. •v. (**cages, caging, caged**) confine a person or animal in a cage.
– ORIGIN Old French.

cagey (also **cagy**) •adj. informal cautiously reluctant to speak.
– DERIVATIVES **cagily** adv.

cagoule /kuh-gool/ •n. Brit. a light waterproof jacket with a hood.
– ORIGIN French, 'cowl'.

cahoots /kuh-hoots/ •pl. n. (in phr. **in cahoots**) informal making secret plans together in order to achieve something dishonest or underhand.

caiman /kay-muhn/ (also **cayman**) •n. a tropical American reptile similar to an alligator.
– ORIGIN Carib.

cairn •n. a mound of rough stones built as a memorial or landmark.
– ORIGIN Scottish Gaelic *carn*.

caisson /kay-suhn/ •n. a large watertight box or chamber in which underwater construction work may be carried out.
– ORIGIN French, 'large chest'.

cajole /kuh-johl/ •v. (**cajoles, cajoling, cajoled**) persuade someone to do something by coaxing or flattery.
– ORIGIN French *cajoler*.

Cajun /kay-juhn/ •n. a member of a French-speaking community in areas of southern Louisiana.

- ORIGIN from *Acadian* 'relating to Acadia', a former French colony in Canada.

cake •n. **1** an item of soft, sweet food made from baking a mixture of flour, fat, eggs, and sugar. **2** a flat, round item of savoury food that is baked or fried. •v. (**cakes, caking, caked**) (of a thick or sticky substance) cover and form a hard layer on something.
- PHRASES **a piece of cake** informal something easily achieved. **sell like hot cakes** informal be sold quickly and in large amounts.
- ORIGIN Scandinavian.

Cal •abbrev. large calorie(s).

cal •abbrev. small calorie(s).

calabash /kal-uh-bash/ •n. a water container made from the dried shell of a gourd.
- ORIGIN Spanish *calabaza*.

calabrese /kal-uh-breez/ •n. a bright green variety of broccoli.
- ORIGIN Italian.

calamine /kal-uh-myn/ •n. a pink powder used to make a soothing lotion.
- ORIGIN Latin *calamina*.

calamity •n. (pl. **calamities**) a sudden event causing great damage or distress.
- DERIVATIVES **calamitous** adj.
- ORIGIN Latin *calamitas*.

calcareous /kal-kair-i-uhss/ •adj. containing calcium carbonate; chalky.
- ORIGIN Latin *calcarius*.

calciferol /kal-si-fuh-rol/ •n. vitamin D₂, essential for the storing of calcium in bones.

calcify /kal-si-fy/ •v. (**calcifies, calcifying, calcified**) harden by a deposit of calcium salts.

calcine /kal-syn/ •v. (**calcines, calcining, calcined**) reduce, oxidize, or dry a substance by exposing it to strong heat.
- ORIGIN Latin *calcinare*.

calcite /kal-syt/ •n. a mineral consisting of calcium carbonate.
- ORIGIN German *Calcit*.

calcium •n. a soft grey metallic chemical element.
- ORIGIN Latin *calx* 'lime'.

calcium carbonate •n. a white compound found as chalk, limestone, and marble.

calculate •v. (**calculates, calculating, calculated**) **1** work out a number or amount by using mathematics. **2** intend an action to have a particular effect.
- DERIVATIVES **calculable** adj.
- ORIGIN Latin *calculare* 'count'.

calculated •adj. done with awareness of the likely effect.

calculating •adj. craftily planning things so as to benefit yourself.

calculation •n. **1** an act of working out a number or amount by using mathematics. **2** an assessment of the results of a course of action.

calculator •n. a small electronic device used for making mathematical calculations.

calculus /kal-kyuu-luhss/ •n. the branch of mathematics concerned with problems involving rates of variation.
- ORIGIN Latin, 'small pebble' (as used on an abacus).

caldron •n. US = CAULDRON.

Caledonian /ka-li-doh-ni-uhn/ •adj. relating to Scotland or the Scottish Highlands.
- ORIGIN from *Caledonia*, the Latin name for northern Britain.

calendar /ka-lin-der/ •n. **1** a chart or series of pages showing the days, weeks, and months of a particular year. **2** a system by which the beginning, length, and subdivisions of the year are fixed. **3** a list of special days or events.
- ORIGIN Latin *kalendarium* 'account book'.

calf¹ •n. (pl. **calves**) **1** a young cow or bull. **2** the young of some other large mammals, e.g. elephants.
- ORIGIN Old English.

calf² •n. (pl. **calves**) the back of a person's leg below the knee.
- ORIGIN Old Norse.

calibrate /ka-li-brayt/ •v. (**calibrates, calibrating, calibrated**) **1** mark a gauge or instrument with a standard scale of readings. **2** compare the readings of an instrument with those of a standard.
- DERIVATIVES **calibration** n.
- ORIGIN from CALIBRE.

calibre /ka-li-ber/ (US **caliber**) •n. **1** the quality of a person's ability: *musicians of the highest calibre*. **2** the diameter of the inside of a gun barrel, or of a bullet or shell.
- ORIGIN French.

calico /ka-li-koh/ •n. (pl. **calicoes** or US also **calicos**) **1** Brit. a type of plain white or unbleached cotton cloth. **2** N. Amer. printed cotton fabric.
- ORIGIN from *Calicut*, a port in SW India where the fabric was first made.

californium /ka-li-for-ni-uhm/ •n. a radioactive metallic chemical element made by high-energy atomic collisions.
- ORIGIN from *California* University.

caliper /ka-li-per/ (also **calliper**) •n. **1** (also **calipers**) a measuring instrument with two hinged legs. **2** a metal support for a person's leg.
- ORIGIN prob. from CALIBRE.

caliph /kay-lif/ • n. hist. the chief Muslim ruler.
– ORIGIN Arabic, 'deputy of God'.

calisthenics • pl. n. US = CALLISTHENICS.

calk • n. & v. US = CAULK.

call • v. **1** shout to someone so as to summon them or attract their attention. **2** order or ask someone to go or come somewhere. **3** telephone someone. **4** pay a brief visit. **5** give a particular name or description to. **6** fix a date or time for: *he called an election.* **7** predict the outcome of a future event. **8** (of a bird or animal) make its typical cry. • n. **1** an act or instance of calling. **2** the typical cry of a bird or animal. **3** (**call for**) demand or need for: *there is little call for antique furniture.*
– PHRASES **call for** require. **call something in** demand payment of a loan. **call something off** cancel an event or agreement. **call on** turn to for help. **call of nature** euphem. a need to go to the toilet. **call the shots** (or **tune**) control a situation. **call someone up** summon someone to serve in the army or to play in a team. **on call** available to provide a service if necessary.
– DERIVATIVES **caller** n.
– ORIGIN Old Norse.

call centre • n. an office in which large numbers of telephone calls are handled for an organization.

call girl • n. a female prostitute who accepts appointments by telephone.

calligraphy /kuh-lig-ruh-fi/ • n. decorative handwriting.
– DERIVATIVES **calligrapher** n. **calligraphic** adj.
– ORIGIN Greek *kalligraphia.*

calling • n. **1** a profession or occupation. **2** a vocation.

calliper • n. var. of CALIPER.

callisthenics /kal-liss-then-iks/ (US **calisthenics**) • pl. n. gymnastic exercises to achieve fitness and grace of movement.
– ORIGIN from Greek *kallos* 'beauty' + *sthenos* 'strength'.

callous /kal-luhss/ • adj. insensitive and cruel.
– DERIVATIVES **callously** adv. **callousness** n.
– ORIGIN Latin *callosus* 'hard-skinned'.

calloused (also **callused**) • adj. having hardened skin.

callow • adj. (of a young person) inexperienced and immature.
– ORIGIN Old English, 'bald'.

callus /kal-luhss/ • n. an area of skin which has become thick and hard.
– ORIGIN Latin, 'hardened skin'.

calm • adj. **1** not nervous, angry, or excited. **2** peaceful and undisturbed. • n. a calm state or period. • v. (often **calm down**) make or become calm.
– DERIVATIVES **calmly** adv. **calmness** n.
– ORIGIN Greek *kauma* 'heat of the day'.

Calor gas /ka-ler/ • n. Brit. trademark liquefied butane stored under pressure in containers, for domestic use.
– ORIGIN Latin *calor* 'heat'.

caloric /kuh-lo-rik/ • adj. N. Amer. or tech. relating to heat.

calorie • n. (pl. **calories**) **1** (also **large calorie**) a unit of energy equal to the energy needed to raise the temperature of 1 kilogram of water through 1 °C (4.1868 kilojoules). **2** (also **small calorie**) a unit of energy equal to one-thousandth of a large calorie.
– ORIGIN Latin *calor* 'heat'.

calorific • adj. relating to the amount of energy contained in food or fuel.

calorimeter /ka-luh-rim-i-ter/ • n. a device for measuring the amount of heat involved in a chemical reaction or other process.

calumny /ka-luhm-ni/ • n. (pl. **calumnies**) the making of false and damaging statements about someone.
– ORIGIN Latin *calumnia.*

calve • v. (**calves, calving, calved**) give birth to a calf.
– ORIGIN Old English.

calves pl. of CALF¹, CALF².

Calvinism • n. the form of Protestantism of John Calvin (1509–64), centring on the belief that God has decided everything that happens in advance.
– DERIVATIVES **Calvinist** n. **Calvinistic** adj.

calypso /kuh-lip-soh/ • n. (pl. **calypsos**) a kind of West Indian song with improvised words on a subject of current interest.

calyx /kay-liks/ • n. (pl. **calyces** /kay-li-seez/ or **calyxes**) the sepals of a flower, forming a protective layer around a bud.
– ORIGIN Greek *kalux* 'husk'.

cam • n. **1** a projecting part on a wheel or shaft, designed to come into contact with another part while rotating and cause it to move. **2** a camshaft.
– ORIGIN Dutch *kam* 'comb'.

camaraderie /kam-uh-rah-duh-ri/ • n. trust and friendship between people.
– ORIGIN French.

camber /kam-ber/ • n. a slight upward curve on a horizontal surface e.g. a road.
– ORIGIN Old French *chambre* 'arched'.

cambium /kam-bi-uhm/ • n. (pl. **cambia** /kam-bi-uh/ or **cambiums**) a layer of cells in a plant stem from which new

tissue grows by the division of cells.
– ORIGIN Latin, 'change, exchange'.

Cambodian /kam-boh-di-uhn/ •n. a person from Cambodia. •adj. relating to Cambodia.

Cambrian /kam-bri-uhn/ •adj. **1** Welsh. **2** Geol. relating to the first period in the Palaeozoic era (about 570 to 510 million years ago).
– ORIGIN Latin *Cambria*.

cambric /kam-brik/ •n. a light, closely woven white linen or cotton fabric.
– ORIGIN named after the town of *Cambrai* in northern France.

Cambs. •abbrev. Cambridgeshire.

camcorder •n. a portable combined video camera and video recorder.

came past tense of COME.

camel •n. a large mammal of desert countries, with a long neck and either one or two humps on the back.
– ORIGIN Greek *kamēlos*.

camellia /kuh-mee-li-uh/ •n. a shrub with showy flowers and shiny leaves.
– ORIGIN named after the botanist Joseph *Kamel*.

Camembert /kam-uhm-bair/ •n. a rich, soft cheese originally made near Camembert in Normandy.

cameo /kam-i-oh/ •n. (pl. **cameos**) **1** a piece of jewellery consisting of a carving of a head shown in outline against a differently coloured background. **2** a short piece of writing giving a good description of a person or thing. **3** a small part in a play or film for a well-known actor.
– ORIGIN Latin *cammaeus*.

camera •n. a device for taking photographs or recording moving images.
– PHRASES **in camera** Law in the private rooms of a judge, without the press and public being present.
– ORIGIN Latin, 'vault, arched chamber'.

camera obscura /ob-skyoor-uh/ •n. a darkened box or building with a lens or opening for casting the image of an outside object on to a screen inside.
– ORIGIN Latin, 'dark chamber'.

Cameroonian /ka-muh-roo-ni-uhn/ •n. a person from Cameroon, a country on the west coast of Africa. •adj. relating to Cameroon.

camiknickers •pl. n. Brit. a woman's one-piece undergarment which combines a camisole and a pair of French knickers.

camisole /kam-i-sohl/ •n. a woman's loose-fitting undergarment for the upper body.
– ORIGIN French.

camomile •n. var. of CHAMOMILE.

camouflage /kam-uh-flahzh/ •n. **1** the painting or covering of soldiers and military equipment to make them blend in with their surroundings. **2** clothing or materials used for this purpose. **3** the natural colouring or form of an animal which allows it to blend in with its surroundings. •v. (**camouflages, camouflaging, camouflaged**) hide by means of camouflage.
– ORIGIN French.

camp¹ •n. **1** a place with temporary accommodation of tents, huts, etc. for soldiers, refugees, or travelling people. **2** a complex of buildings for holiday accommodation. **3** the supporters of a particular party or set of beliefs. •v. stay in a tent while on holiday.
– ORIGIN Latin *campus* 'level ground'.

camp² informal •adj. **1** (of a man) effeminate in an exaggerated way. **2** deliberately exaggerated and theatrical in style. •n. camp behaviour or style. •v. (**camp it up**) behave in a camp way.

campaign •n. **1** a series of military operations intended to achieve a particular aim. **2** an organized course of action to achieve a goal. •v. work in an organized way towards a goal.
– DERIVATIVES **campaigner** n.
– ORIGIN French *campagne* 'open country'.

campanile /kam-puh-nee-lay/ •n. a bell tower.
– ORIGIN Italian.

campanology /kam-puh-nol-uh-ji/ •n. the art of bell-ringing.
– ORIGIN Latin *campana* 'bell'.

campanula /kam-pan-yu-luh/ •n. a plant with blue, purple, or white bell-shaped flowers.
– ORIGIN from Latin *campana* 'bell'.

camp bed •n. Brit. a folding portable bed.

camper •n. **1** a person who spends a holiday in a tent or holiday camp. **2** (also **camper van**) a large motor vehicle with a living area.

campfire •n. an open-air fire in a camp.

camp follower •n. **1** a civilian attached to a military camp. **2** a person who associates with a group without being a full member of it.

camphor /kam-fer/ •n. a white substance with an aromatic smell and bitter taste, used in insect repellents.
– ORIGIN Latin *camphora*.

campion •n. a plant of the pink family, typically having pink or white flowers.
– ORIGIN perh. related to CHAMPION.

campsite •n. a place used for camping.

campus •n. (pl. **campuses**) the grounds and buildings of a university or college.
– ORIGIN Latin, 'level ground'.

camshaft /kam-shahft/ • n. a shaft with one or more cams attached to it.

can[1] • modal verb (3rd sing. present **can**; past **could**) **1** be able to. **2** used to express doubt or surprise: *he can't have finished.* **3** used to indicate that something is often the case: *he could be very moody.* **4** be allowed to.
– ORIGIN Old English, 'know'.

> USAGE: The verb **can** is mainly used to mean 'be able to', as in the sentence *can he move?* = is he physically able to move? Although it is not incorrect to use **can** when asking to be allowed to do something, it is more polite to say **may** (*may we leave now?* rather than *can we leave now?*).

can[2] • n. a cylindrical metal container. • v. (**cans, canning, canned**) preserve food in a can.
– PHRASES **a can of worms** a complex matter that is full of possible problems.
– ORIGIN Old English.

Canada goose • n. a common brownish-grey North American goose, introduced in Britain and elsewhere.

Canadian • n. a person from Canada. • adj. relating to Canada.

canal • n. **1** a waterway cut through land for the passage of boats or for conveying water for irrigation. **2** a tubular passage in a plant or animal carrying food, liquid, or air.
– ORIGIN Latin *canalis* 'pipe, channel'.

canalize /kan-uh-lyz/ (or **canalise**) • v. (**canalizes, canalizing, canalized**) **1** convert a river into a canal. **2** convey something through a duct or channel.

canapé /kan-uh-pay/ • n. a small piece of bread or pastry with a savoury topping.
– ORIGIN French, 'sofa, couch'.

canard /ka-nard/ • n. an unfounded rumour or story.
– ORIGIN French, 'duck, hoax'.

canary • n. (pl. **canaries**) a bright yellow finch with a tuneful song.
– ORIGIN from the *Canary* Islands, to which one species of the bird is native.

cancan • n. a lively, high-kicking stage dance originating in 19th-century Parisian music halls.
– ORIGIN French.

cancel • v. (**cancels, cancelling, cancelled**; US also **cancels, canceling, canceled**) **1** decide that a planned event will not take place. **2** withdraw from or end an agreement. **3** (**cancel something out**) have an equal but opposite effect on something. **4** mark a stamp, ticket, etc. to show that it has been used.
– DERIVATIVES **cancellation** n.
– ORIGIN Latin *cancellare*.

Cancer • n. a constellation (the Crab) and sign of the zodiac, which the sun enters about 21 June.
– DERIVATIVES **Cancerian** /kan-seer-ri-uhn/ n. & adj.
– ORIGIN Latin, 'crab'.

cancer • n. **1** a disease caused by an uncontrolled division of abnormal cells in a part of the body. **2** a harmful growth or tumour resulting from an uncontrolled division of abnormal cells. **3** something evil or destructive that spreads quickly and is hard to destroy.
– DERIVATIVES **cancerous** adj.
– ORIGIN Latin, 'crab, ulcer'.

candela /kan-dee-luh/ • n. Physics the SI unit of luminous intensity.
– ORIGIN Latin, 'candle'.

candelabrum /kan-di-lah-bruhm/ • n. (pl. **candelabra** /kan-di-lah-bruh/) a large candlestick or other object for holding several candles or lights.
– ORIGIN Latin.

candid • adj. truthful and straight-forward; frank.
– DERIVATIVES **candidly** adv.
– ORIGIN Latin *candidus* 'white'.

candidate /kan-di-duht/ • n. **1** a person who applies for a job or is nominated for election. **2** Brit. a person taking an exam. **3** a person or thing seen as suitable for a particular fate, treatment, or position: *she was the perfect candidate for a biography.*
– DERIVATIVES **candidacy** n.
– ORIGIN Latin *candidatus* 'white-robed'.

candied • adj. (of fruit) preserved in a sugar syrup.

candle • n. a stick of wax with a central wick which is lit to produce light as it burns.
– ORIGIN Latin *candela*.

Candlemas /kan-d'l-mass/ • n. a Christian festival held on 2 February to commemorate the purification of the Virgin Mary and the presentation of Jesus in the Temple.

candlestick • n. a support or holder for a candle.

candlewick • n. a thick, soft cotton fabric with a raised, tufted pattern.

candour (US **candor**) • n. the quality of being open and honest.
– ORIGIN Latin *candor* 'whiteness, purity'.

candy • n. (pl. **candies**) N. Amer. sweets.
– ORIGIN from French *sucre candi* 'crystallized sugar'.

candyfloss • n. Brit. a mass of pink or white fluffy spun sugar wrapped round a stick.

candy-striped • adj. patterned with alternating stripes of white and another colour.

cane • n. **1** the hollow jointed stem of tall reeds, grasses, etc. **2** the slender, flexible stem of plants such as rattan. **3** a woody stem of a raspberry or related plant. **4** a length of cane used as a support for plants, a walking stick, or for hitting someone as a punishment. • v. (**canes, caning, caned**) hit someone with a cane as a punishment.
– ORIGIN Greek *kanna, kannē*.

canine /kay-nyn/ • adj. relating to a dog or dogs. • n. **1** a dog or other animal of the dog family. **2** (also **canine tooth**) a pointed tooth next to the incisors.
– ORIGIN Latin *caninus*.

canister • n. a round or cylindrical container.
– ORIGIN Greek *kanastron* 'wicker basket'.

canker • n. **1** a destructive disease of trees and plants, caused by a fungus. **2** a condition in animals that causes open sores.
– ORIGIN Latin *cancer* 'crab, ulcer'.

cannabis • n. a drug obtained from the hemp plant.
– ORIGIN Greek *kannabis*.

canned • adj. **1** preserved in a can. **2** informal, esp. derog. (of music, applause, etc.) pre-recorded.

cannelloni /kan-nuh-**loh**-ni/ • pl. n. rolls of pasta stuffed with a meat or vegetable mixture, cooked in a cheese sauce.
– ORIGIN Italian, 'large tubes'.

cannery • n. (pl. **canneries**) a factory where food is canned.

cannibal • n. a person who eats the flesh of other human beings.
– DERIVATIVES **cannibalism** n. **cannibalistic** adj.
– ORIGIN Spanish *Caribes*, a West Indian people said to eat humans.

cannibalize (or **cannibalise**) • v. (**cannibalizes, cannibalizing, cannibalized**) use a machine as a source of spare parts for others.

cannon • n. (pl. **cannon** or **cannons**) **1** a large, heavy gun formerly used in warfare. **2** an automatic heavy gun that fires shells from an aircraft or tank. • v. (**cannons, cannoning, cannoned**) (**cannon into/off**) esp. Brit. collide with.
– ORIGIN Italian *cannone* 'large tube'.

cannonade /kan-nuh-**nayd**/ • n. a period of continuous heavy gunfire.

cannonball • n. a metal or stone ball fired from a cannon.

cannon fodder • n. soldiers seen only as a resource to be used up in war.

cannot • contr. can not.

canny • adj. (**cannier, canniest**) shrewd, especially in financial matters.

– DERIVATIVES **cannily** adv.
– ORIGIN from CAN¹.

canoe • n. a narrow shallow boat with pointed ends, propelled with a paddle. • v. (**canoes, canoeing, canoed**) travel in a canoe.
– DERIVATIVES **canoeist** n.
– ORIGIN Spanish *canoa*.

canon • n. **1** a general rule or principle by which something is judged: *his designs break the canons of fashion.* **2** a Church decree or law. **3** the works of a particular author or artist that are recognized as genuine. **4** a list of literary works which are considered to be permanently established as being of the highest quality. **5** a member of the clergy on the staff of a cathedral. **6** a piece of music in which a theme is taken up by two or more parts that overlap.
– ORIGIN Greek *kanōn* 'rule'.

canonical /kuh-**non**-i-k'l/ • adj. **1** accepted as being authentic or established as a standard: *the canonical works of science fiction.* **2** according to the laws of the Christian Church.

canonize (or **canonise**) • v. (**canonizes, canonizing, canonized**) (in the Roman Catholic Church) officially declare a dead person to be a saint.
– DERIVATIVES **canonization** n.

canon law • n. the laws of the Christian Church.

canoodle • v. (**canoodles, canoodling, canoodled**) informal kiss and cuddle lovingly.

canopy • n. (pl. **canopies**) **1** a cloth covering hung or held up over a throne or bed. **2** a roof-like covering or shelter. **3** the part of a parachute that opens.
– DERIVATIVES **canopied** adj.
– ORIGIN Latin *conopeum* 'mosquito net over a bed'.

cant¹ /rhymes with rant/ • n. **1** insincere talk about moral or religious matters. **2** derog. the language typical of a particular group: *thieves' cant.*
– ORIGIN prob. from Latin *cantare* 'to sing'.

cant² /rhymes with rant/ • v. be or cause to be in a slanting position; tilt. • n. a slope or tilt.
– ORIGIN German *kant, kante* or Dutch *cant* 'point, side, edge'.

can't • contr. cannot.

Cantab. /kan-**tab**/ • abbrev. relating to Cambridge University.
– ORIGIN Latin *Cantabrigia* 'Cambridge'.

cantabile /kan-**tah**-bi-lay/ • adv. & adj. Music in a smooth singing style.
– ORIGIN Italian, 'singable'.

cantaloupe /kan-tuh-**loop**/ • n. a small round melon with orange flesh.

– ORIGIN from *Cantaluppi* near Rome.

cantankerous /kan-**tang**-kuh-ruhss/
• adj. bad-tempered and uncooperative.
– ORIGIN perh. from Anglo-Irish *cant* 'auction' and *rancorous*.

cantata /kan-**tah**-tuh/ • n. a sung musical composition based on a narrative work and usually accompanied by a chorus and orchestra.
– ORIGIN from Italian *cantata aria* 'sung air'.

canteen • n. 1 a restaurant in a workplace, school, or college. 2 Brit. a case containing a set of cutlery. 3 a small water bottle, as used by soldiers or campers.
– ORIGIN Italian *cantina* 'cellar'.

canter • n. a pace of a horse between a trot and a gallop. • v. (**canters, cantering, cantered**) move at a canter.
– ORIGIN from *Canterbury pace*, the easy pace at which medieval pilgrims travelled to Canterbury.

canticle /kan-ti-k'l/ • n. a hymn or chant forming a regular part of a church service.
– ORIGIN Latin *canticulum* 'little song'.

cantilever /kan-ti-lee-ver/ • n. a long projecting beam or girder fixed at only one end, used in bridge construction.

canto /kan-toh/ • n. (pl. **cantos**) one of the sections into which some long poems are divided.
– ORIGIN Italian, 'song'.

canton /kan-ton/ • n. a political or administrative subdivision of a country, especially in Switzerland.
– ORIGIN Old French, 'corner'.

cantonment /kan-ton-muhnt/
• n. (especially in the Indian subcontinent) a military garrison or camp.
– ORIGIN French *cantonnement*.

cantor /kan-tor/ • n. 1 an official who leads the prayers in a Jewish synagogue. 2 a person who sings solo verses to which the choir or congregation respond in a Christian service.
– ORIGIN Latin, 'singer'.

canvas • n. (pl. **canvases** or **canvasses**) 1 a strong, coarse cloth used to make sails, tents, etc. 2 an oil painting on canvas.
– ORIGIN Old French *canevas*.

canvass • v. 1 visit someone to ask for their vote in an election. 2 question someone to find out their opinion. 3 Brit. suggest an idea for discussion.
– DERIVATIVES **canvasser** n.
– ORIGIN first meaning 'toss someone in a canvas sheet' (as a game or form of punishment).

canyon • n. a deep gorge.
– ORIGIN Spanish *cañón* 'tube'.

CAP • abbrev. Common Agricultural Policy.

cap • n. 1 a soft, flat hat with a peak. 2 a soft, close-fitting head covering worn for a particular purpose: *a shower cap.* 3 Brit. a cap awarded to members of a national sports team. 4 a lid or cover. 5 an upper limit set on spending or borrowing. 6 Brit. informal a contraceptive diaphragm. 7 a small amount of explosive powder in a metal or paper case that explodes when struck.
• v. (**caps, capping, capped**) 1 put or form a cap, lid, or cover on. 2 provide a fitting end to: *he capped a memorable season by becoming champion.* 3 place a limit on prices, spending, etc. 4 (**be capped**) Brit. be chosen as a member of a national sports team.
– PHRASES **cap in hand** humbly asking for a favour.
– ORIGIN Latin *cappa*.

capability • n. (pl. **capabilities**) the power or ability to do something.

capable • adj. 1 (**capable of**) having the necessary ability or quality to do something. 2 able to achieve what needs to be done; competent.
– DERIVATIVES **capably** adv.
– ORIGIN Latin *capere* 'take or hold'.

capacious • adj. having a lot of space inside; roomy.
– ORIGIN Latin *capax* 'capable'.

capacitance /kuh-**pass**-i-tuhnss/ • n. the ability to store electric charge.

capacitor • n. a device used to store electric charge.

capacity • n. (pl. **capacities**) 1 the maximum amount that something can contain or produce: *the room was filled to capacity.* 2 (before another noun) fully occupying the available space: *a capacity crowd.* 3 the ability or power to do something. 4 a particular role or position: *I was engaged in a voluntary capacity.*
– ORIGIN Latin *capere* 'take or hold'.

caparison /kuh-pa-ri-s'n/ • v. (**be caparisoned**) be dressed in rich decorative coverings or clothes.
– ORIGIN Spanish *caparazón* 'saddlecloth'.

cape[1] • n. a short cloak.
– DERIVATIVES **caped** adj.
– ORIGIN Latin *cappa* 'head covering'.

cape[2] • n. a piece of land that projects into the sea.
– ORIGIN Latin *caput* 'head'.

caper[1] • v. (**capers, capering, capered**) skip or dance about in a lively or playful way. • n. 1 a playful skipping movement. 2 informal a light-hearted or dishonest activity, or a film or novel portraying one: *I'm too old for this kind of caper.*

– ORIGIN Latin *capreolus* 'little goat'.

caper² • n. a flower bud of a southern European shrub, pickled for use in cooking.
– ORIGIN Greek *kapparis*.

capercaillie /kap-er-**kay**-li/ • n. (pl. **capercaillies**) a large turkey-like grouse of forests in northern Europe.
– ORIGIN from Scottish Gaelic *capull coille*, 'horse of the wood'.

capillarity /ka-pi-**la**-ri-ti/ • n. the tendency of a liquid in a narrow tube or pore to rise or fall as a result of surface tension.

capillary /kuh-**pil**-luh-ri/ • n. (pl. **capillaries**) **1** any of the fine branching blood vessels that form a network between the arteries and veins. **2** (also **capillary tube**) a tube with an internal diameter of hair-like thinness.
– ORIGIN Latin *capillus* 'hair'.

capillary action • n. = CAPILLARITY.

capital¹ • n. **1** the most important city or town of a country or region. **2** wealth owned by a person or organization or invested, lent, or borrowed. **3** a capital letter. • adj. **1** (of an offence) punishable by death. **2** (of a letter of the alphabet) large in size and of the form used to begin sentences and names. **3** informal, dated excellent.
– PHRASES **make capital out of** use something to your advantage.
– ORIGIN Latin *caput* 'head'.

capital² • n. the top part of a pillar.
– ORIGIN Latin *capitellum* 'little head'.

capital gain • n. a profit from the sale of property or an investment.

capital goods • pl. n. goods that are used in producing other goods.

capitalism • n. an economic and political system in which a country's trade and industry are controlled by private owners for profit.
– DERIVATIVES **capitalist** n. & adj.

capitalize (or **capitalise**)
• v. (**capitalizes**, **capitalizing**, **capitalized**) **1** (**capitalize on**) take advantage of a situation. **2** convert income into financial capital. **3** provide a company with financial capital. **4** write or print a word or letter in capital letters or with a capital initial letter.
– DERIVATIVES **capitalization** n.

capital punishment • n. the punishment of a crime by death.

capital sum • n. a lump sum of money payable to an insured person or paid as an initial fee or investment.

capitation • n. the payment of a fee or grant to a doctor, school, etc., the amount being determined by the number of people involved.
– ORIGIN Latin.

capitulate /kuh-**pit**-yuu-layt/
• v. (**capitulates**, **capitulating**, **capitulated**) give in to an opponent or an unwelcome demand.
– DERIVATIVES **capitulation** n.
– ORIGIN Latin *capitulare* 'draw up under headings'.

capon /**kay**-pon/ • n. a domestic cock that has been castrated and fattened for eating.
– ORIGIN Latin *capo*.

cappuccino /kap-puh-**chee**-noh/ • n. (pl. **cappuccinos**) coffee made with milk that has been frothed up with pressurized steam.
– ORIGIN Italian, 'Capuchin' (because the colour of the coffee resembles that of a Capuchin monk's habit).

caprice /kuh-**preess**/ • n. a sudden change of mood or behaviour.
– ORIGIN Italian *capriccio* 'sudden start'.

capricious /kuh-**pri**-shuhss/ • adj. prone to sudden, unpredictable changes of mood or behaviour.

Capricorn /**kap**-ri-korn/ • n. a constellation and sign of the zodiac (the Goat), which the sun enters about 21 December.
– ORIGIN Latin *capricornus*.

capri pants /kuh-**pree**/ • pl. n. close-fitting tapered trousers for women.
– ORIGIN from the Italian island of *Capri*.

capsicum /**kap**-si-kuhm/ • n. (pl. **capsicums**) a sweet pepper or chilli pepper.
– ORIGIN Latin.

capsize • v. (**capsizes**, **capsizing**, **capsized**) (of a boat) be overturned in the water.
– ORIGIN perh. from Spanish *capuzar* 'sink a ship by the head'.

cap sleeve • n. a short sleeve which tapers to nothing under the arm.

capstan /**kap**-stuhn/ • n. a broad revolving upright cylinder, used for winding a rope or cable.
– ORIGIN Provençal *cabestan*.

capsule • n. **1** a small case of gelatin containing a dose of medicine, that dissolves after it is swallowed. **2** a small case or container. **3** a dry fruit that releases its seeds by bursting open when ripe.
– ORIGIN Latin *capsula*.

captain • n. **1** the person in command of a ship or civil aircraft. **2** a rank of naval officer above commander. **3** a rank of officer in the army above lieutenant. **4** a leader of a team. • v. be the captain of.
– DERIVATIVES **captaincy** n.
– ORIGIN Old French *capitain* 'chief'.

caption • n. **1** a title or brief explanation printed with an illustration or cartoon. **2** a piece of writing appearing on screen as part of a film or television broadcast. • v. provide with a caption.
– ORIGIN Latin, 'taking'.

captious /kap-shuhss/ • adj. formal tending to find fault or raise trivial objections.
– ORIGIN Latin captiosus.

captivate • v. (**captivates**, **captivating**, **captivated**) attract and hold the interest of; charm.

captive • n. a person who has been captured or held in confinement. • adj. **1** confined. **2** not free to choose an alternative: advertisements at the cinema reach a captive audience.
– DERIVATIVES **captivity** n.
– ORIGIN Latin captivus.

captor • n. a person who captures another.

capture • v. (**captures**, **capturing**, **captured**) **1** take or get by force. **2** take prisoner. **3** record accurately in words or pictures: photographers tried to capture her soulful blue eyes. **4** cause data to be stored in a computer. • n. the action of capturing or the state of being captured.
– ORIGIN Latin capere 'seize, take'.

Capuchin /kap-uh-chin/ • n. **1** a friar belonging to a strict branch of the Franciscan order. **2** (**capuchin**) a South American monkey with a hood-like cap of hair on the head.
– ORIGIN Italian cappuccino 'small hood'.

capybara /ka-pi-bah-ruh/ • n. (pl. **capybara** or **capybaras**) a large South American rodent resembling a long-legged guinea pig.
– ORIGIN from an American Indian word meaning 'grass eater'.

car • n. **1** a powered road vehicle designed to carry a small number of people. **2** a railway carriage or (N. Amer.) wagon.
– ORIGIN Latin carrus 'two-wheeled vehicle'.

carafe /kuh-raf/ • n. an open-topped glass flask used for serving wine or water in a restaurant.
– ORIGIN French.

carambola /ka-ruhm-boh-luh/ • n. a golden-yellow fruit which is shaped like a star when cut through.
– ORIGIN Portuguese.

caramel • n. **1** a soft toffee made with sugar and butter. **2** sugar or syrup heated until it turns brown, used as a flavouring or colouring for food.
– ORIGIN Spanish caramelo.

caramelize /ka-ruh-muh-lyz/ (or **caramelise**) • v. (**caramelizes**, **caramelizing**, **caramelized**) turn or be turned into caramel.

carapace /ka-ruh-payss/ • n. the hard upper shell of a tortoise, lobster, or related animal.
– ORIGIN Spanish carapacho.

carat /ka-ruht/ • n. **1** a unit of weight for precious stones and pearls, equivalent to 200 milligrams. **2** (US also **karat**) a measure of the purity of gold, pure gold being 24 carats.
– ORIGIN Greek keration 'fruit of the carob'.

caravan • n. **1** Brit. a vehicle equipped for living in, designed to be towed by a vehicle or a horse. **2** a group of people with vehicles or animals who are travelling together.
– DERIVATIVES **caravanner** n. **caravanning** n.
– ORIGIN Persian.

caravanserai /ka-ruh-van-suh-ry/ • n. (pl. **caravanserais**) **1** a group of people travelling together. **2** hist. an inn with a central courtyard in the deserts of Asia or North Africa.
– ORIGIN Persian, 'caravan palace'.

caravel /ka-ruh-vel/ • n. hist. a small, fast Spanish or Portuguese ship of the 15th–17th centuries.
– ORIGIN Portuguese caravela.

caraway /ka-ruh-way/ • n. the seeds of a plant of the parsley family, used for flavouring.
– ORIGIN Latin carui.

carbide • n. a compound of carbon with a metal or other element.

carbine • n. a light automatic rifle.
– ORIGIN French carabine.

carbohydrate • n. any of a large group of compounds (including sugars and starch) which contain carbon, hydrogen, and oxygen, found in food and used to give energy.

carbolic acid (also **carbolic**) • n. phenol, used as a disinfectant.

carbon • n. a non-metallic chemical element which has two main pure forms (diamond and graphite), and is present in all organic compounds.
– ORIGIN Latin carbo 'coal, charcoal'.

carbonaceous /kar-buh-nay-shuhss/ • adj. consisting of or containing carbon or its compounds.

carbonate /kar-buh-nayt/ • n. a compound containing CO_3 negative ions together with a metallic element.

carbonated • adj. (of a drink) containing dissolved carbon dioxide and therefore fizzy.

carbon copy • n. **1** a copy made with carbon paper. **2** a person or thing identical to another.

carbon dating •n. a method of finding out the age of an organic object by measuring the amount of radioactive carbon-14 that it contains.

carbon dioxide •n. a gas produced by burning carbon and by breathing, and absorbed by plants in photosynthesis.

carbonic acid •n. a very weak acid formed when carbon dioxide dissolves in water.

Carboniferous /kar-buh-**nif**-uh-ruhss/ •adj. Geol. relating to the fifth period in the Palaeozoic era (about 363 to 290 million years ago), when extensive coal-bearing strata were formed.

carbonize (or **carbonise**)
•v. (**carbonizes, carbonizing, carbonized**) convert into carbon, by heating or burning.
– DERIVATIVES **carbonization** n.

carbon monoxide •n. a poisonous flammable gas formed by incomplete burning of carbon.

carbon paper •n. thin paper coated with carbon, used for making a copy as a document is being written or typed.

car boot sale •n. Brit. a sale at which people sell things from the boots of their cars.

carborundum /kar-buh-**run**-duhm/ •n. a very hard black solid consisting of silicon and carbon, used for grinding, smoothing, and polishing.
– ORIGIN from CARBON and CORUNDUM.

carboy •n. a large rounded glass bottle with a narrow neck, used for holding acids.
– ORIGIN Persian.

carbuncle /kar-**bung**-k'l/ •n. **1** a severe abscess or multiple boil in the skin. **2** a polished garnet (gem).
– ORIGIN Latin *carbunculus* 'small coal'.

carburettor /kar-buh-**ret**-ter/ (US also **carburetor**) •n. a device in an internal-combustion engine for mixing air with a fine spray of liquid fuel.
– ORIGIN from former *carburet* 'combine or fill with carbon'.

carcass (Brit. also **carcase**) •n. **1** the dead body of an animal. **2** the remains of a cooked bird after all the edible parts have been removed. **3** the structural framework or remains of something.
– ORIGIN Old French *carcois*.

carcinogen /kar-**sin**-uh-juhn/ •n. a substance that can cause cancer.
– DERIVATIVES **carcinogenic** /kar-sin-uh-**jen**-ik/ adj.

carcinoma /kar-si-**noh**-muh/ •n. (pl. **carcinomas** or **carcinomata** /kar-si-**noh**-muh-tuh/) a cancer arising in the tissues

of the skin or the lining of the internal organs.
– ORIGIN from Greek *karkinos* 'crab'.

card[1] •n. **1** thick, stiff paper or thin cardboard. **2** a piece of card for writing on or printed with information: *a business card.* **3** a small rectangular piece of plastic containing personal details in a form that can be read by a computer: *a credit card.* **4** a playing card. **5** (**cards**) a game played with playing cards. **6** informal, dated an odd or amusing person.
– PHRASES **give someone their cards** (or **get your cards**) Brit. informal dismiss someone (or be dismissed) from employment. **on the cards** informal likely. **play your cards right** make the best use of your assets and opportunities. **put your cards on the table** state your plans openly.
– ORIGIN Greek *khartēs* 'papyrus leaf'.

card[2] •v. comb and clean raw wool or similar material with a sharp-toothed instrument to disentangle the fibres.
•n. a toothed implement or machine for combing and cleaning wool.
– ORIGIN Latin *carduus* 'thistle'.

cardamom /**kar**-duh-muhm/ •n. the seeds of a SE Asian plant, used as a spice.
– ORIGIN from Greek *kardamon* 'cress' + *amōmon*, a kind of spice plant.

cardboard •n. thin board made from layers of paper pasted together or from paper pulp. •adj. not realistic: *the novel's cardboard characters.*

card-carrying •adj. registered as a member of a political party or trade union.

cardiac /**kar**-di-ak/ •adj. relating to the heart.
– ORIGIN Greek *kardia* 'heart'.

cardigan •n. a knitted jumper fastening with buttons down the front.
– ORIGIN named after the 7th Earl of *Cardigan*, whose troops first wore such garments.

cardinal •n. a leading Roman Catholic clergyman, nominated by and having the power to elect the Pope. •adj. most important; chief.
– ORIGIN Latin *cardinalis*.

cardinal number •n. a number expressing quantity (one, two, three, etc.), rather than order (first, second, third, etc.).

cardinal point •n. each of the four main points of the compass (north, south, east, and west).

cardinal sin •n. **1** any of the seven deadly sins. **2** esp. humorous a serious error of judgement.

cardiograph /**kar**-di-uh-grahf/ •n. an

instrument for recording heart movements.

cardiology /kar-di-ol-uh-ji/ •n. the branch of medicine concerned with diseases and abnormalities of the heart.
– DERIVATIVES **cardiological** adj. **cardiologist** n.
– ORIGIN Greek *kardia* 'heart'.

cardiovascular /kar-di-oh-**vass**-kyuu-ler/ •adj. relating to the heart and blood vessels.

cardoon /kar-**doon**/ •n. a tall thistle-like plant with edible leaves and roots.
– ORIGIN Latin *carduus* 'thistle'.

card sharp (also **card sharper**) •n. a person who cheats at cards.

care •n. 1 the provision of welfare and protection: *the care of the elderly*. 2 Brit. the responsibility of a local authority to look after children: *he was taken into care*. 3 serious attention to avoid damage, risk, or error: *handle with care*. 4 a feeling of or cause for anxiety.
•v. (**cares**, **caring**, **cared**) 1 feel concern or interest: *he doesn't really care about anybody*. 2 feel affection or liking. 3 (**care for/to do**) like to have or be willing to do. 4 (**care for**) look after and provide for the needs of.
– PHRASES **care of** at the address of. **take care 1** be careful. **2** make sure to do. **take care of** look after or deal with.
– ORIGIN Old English.

careen /kuh-**reen**/ •v. tilt a ship on its side.
– ORIGIN Latin *carina* 'a keel'.

career •n. an occupation that a person undertakes for a substantial period of their life. •adj. (of a woman) choosing to pursue a profession rather than devoting herself to childcare or housekeeping. •v. (**careers**, **careering**, **careered**) move along swiftly and in an uncontrolled way.
– ORIGIN French *carrière* 'racecourse'.

careerist •n. a person whose main concern is to progress in their career.
– DERIVATIVES **careerism** n.

carefree •adj. free from anxiety or responsibility.

careful •adj. 1 taking care to avoid harm or trouble; cautious. 2 (**careful with**) sensible in the use of something. 3 done with or showing thought and attention.
– DERIVATIVES **carefully** adv. **carefulness** n.

careless •adj. 1 not giving enough attention or thought to avoiding harm or mistakes. 2 (**careless of/about**) not concerned about.
– DERIVATIVES **carelessly** adv. **carelessness** n.

carer •n. Brit. a family member or paid

helper who cares for a sick, elderly, or disabled person.

caress •v. touch or stroke gently or lovingly. •n. a gentle or loving touch.
– ORIGIN French *caresser*.

caretaker •n. a person employed to look after a public building. •adj. holding power temporarily: *a caretaker government*.

careworn •adj. tired and unhappy because of prolonged worry.

cargo •n. (pl. **cargoes** or **cargos**) goods carried on a ship, aircraft, or lorry.
– ORIGIN Spanish.

Carib /ka-rib/ •n. 1 a member of a people living mainly in coastal regions of north-east South America. 2 the language of the Carib.
– ORIGIN Spanish *caribe*.

Caribbean /ka-rib-bee-uhn/ •adj. relating to the region consisting of the Caribbean Sea, its islands, and the surrounding coasts.

> ✓ Remember that **Caribbean** is spelled with one **r** and a double **b**.

caribou /ka-ri-boo/ •n. (pl. **caribou**) N. Amer. a reindeer.
– ORIGIN Canadian French.

caricature /ka-ri-kuh-tewr, ka-ri-kuh-cher/ •n. a picture in which a person's distinctive features are exaggerated for comic effect.
•v. (**caricatures**, **caricaturing**, **caricatured**) make a caricature of.
– DERIVATIVES **caricaturist** n.
– ORIGIN Italian *caricare* 'exaggerate'.

caries /kair-eez/ •n. decay of a tooth or bone.
– ORIGIN Latin.

carillon /ka-ril-lyuhn/ •n. a set of bells sounded from a keyboard or by an automatic mechanism.
– ORIGIN Old French *quarregnon* 'peal of four bells'.

carjacking •n. the action of stealing a car after violently removing its driver.

Carmelite /kar-muh-lyt/ •n. a friar or nun of an order founded at Mount Carmel in Israel during the Crusades.

carmine /kar-myn/ •n. a vivid crimson colour.
– ORIGIN French *carmin*.

carnage /kar-nij/ •n. the killing of a large number of people.
– ORIGIN Latin *caro* 'flesh'.

carnal •adj. relating to sexual urges and activities.
– DERIVATIVES **carnality** n. **carnally** adv.
– ORIGIN Latin *caro* 'flesh'.

carnation •n. a cultivated variety of

pink, with double pink, white, or red flowers.
– ORIGIN perh. from a misreading of an Arabic word.

carnelian /kar-nee-li-uhn/ (also **cornelian**) • n. a dull red or pink semi-precious variety of chalcedony (a form of quartz).
– ORIGIN Old French *corneline*.

carnival • n. **1** an annual public festival involving processions, music, and dancing. **2** N. Amer. a travelling funfair or circus.
– ORIGIN Italian *carnevale*.

carnivore /kar-ni-vor/ • n. an animal that eats meat.

carnivorous /kar-niv-uh-ruhss/ • adj. (of an animal) eating meat.
– ORIGIN from Latin *caro* 'flesh'.

carob /ka-ruhb/ • n. the edible pod of an Arabian tree, from which a substitute for chocolate is made.
– ORIGIN Old French *carobe*.

carol • n. a religious song or popular hymn sung at Christmas. • v. (**carols, carolling, carolled**; US **carols, caroling, caroled**) **1** (**go carolling**) sing carols in the streets. **2** sing or say happily.
– DERIVATIVES **caroller** (US **caroler**) n.
– ORIGIN Old French *carole*.

carotene /ka-ruh-teen/ • n. an orange or red substance found in carrots and many other plants, important in the formation of vitamin A.
– ORIGIN from Latin *carota* 'carrot'.

carotid /kuh-rot-id/ • adj. relating to the two main arteries carrying blood to the head and neck.
– ORIGIN Latin *carotides*.

carouse /kuh-rowz/ • v. (**carouses, carousing, caroused**) drink alcohol and enjoy yourself with other people in a noisy, lively way.
– DERIVATIVES **carousal** n. **carouser** n.
– ORIGIN from German *gar aus trinken* 'drink heavily'.

carousel /ka-ruh-sel/ • n. **1** a merry-go-round at a fair. **2** a conveyor system for baggage collection at an airport.
– ORIGIN Italian *carosello* 'tournament for knights on horseback'.

carp[1] • n. (pl. **carp**) an edible freshwater fish.
– ORIGIN Latin *carpa*.

carp[2] • v. complain continually.
– DERIVATIVES **carper** n.
– ORIGIN Old Norse, 'brag'.

carpal /kar-p'l/ • adj. relating to the bones in the wrist. • n. a bone in the wrist.
– ORIGIN Greek *karpos* 'wrist'.

car park • n. Brit. an area or building where cars may be left temporarily.

carpel /kar-p'l/ • n. the female reproductive organ of a flower, consisting of an ovary, a stigma, and usually a style.
– ORIGIN Greek *karpos* 'fruit'.

carpenter • n. a person who makes wooden objects and structures.
– DERIVATIVES **carpentry** n.
– ORIGIN from Latin *carpentarius artifex* 'carriage-maker'.

carpet • n. **1** a floor covering made from thick woven fabric. **2** a thick or soft layer: *a carpet of bluebells*. • v. (**carpets, carpeting, carpeted**) **1** cover with a carpet. **2** Brit. informal reprimand severely.
– PHRASES **sweep something under the carpet** conceal or ignore a problem in the hope that it will be forgotten.
– ORIGIN Old French *carpite* 'woollen covering for a table or bed'.

carpet bag • n. a travelling bag originally made of carpet-like fabric.

carpetbagger • n. informal, derog. a politician who tries to get elected in an area where they have no local connections.

carpet-bomb • v. bomb an area intensively.

carpeting • n. material for carpets or carpets in general.

carpet slipper • n. a soft slipper with an upper of wool or thick cloth.

carport • n. an open-sided shelter for a car, projecting from the side of a house.

carpus /kar-puhss/ • n. (pl. **carpi** /kar-py/) the group of small bones in the wrist.
– ORIGIN Greek *karpos* 'wrist'.

carrel /ka-ruhl/ • n. a small cubicle with a desk for a reader in a library.
– ORIGIN prob. from **CAROL** in the former sense 'a ring or enclosure'.

carriage • n. **1** a four-wheeled horse-drawn vehicle for passengers. **2** Brit. a passenger vehicle in a train. **3** Brit. the carrying of goods from one place to another. **4** a person's way of standing or moving. **5** a moving part of a machine that carries other parts into the required position: *a typewriter carriage*. **6** a wheeled support for moving a gun.
– ORIGIN Old French *cariage*.

carriage clock • n. Brit. a portable clock in a rectangular case with a handle on top.

carriageway • n. Brit. **1** each of the two sides of a dual carriageway or motorway. **2** the part of a road intended for vehicles.

carrier • n. **1** a person or thing that carries or holds something. **2** a company that transports goods or people for payment. **3** a person or animal that

transmits a disease to other people without suffering from it themselves.
carrier bag • n. Brit. a plastic or paper shopping bag.
carrier pigeon • n. a homing pigeon trained to carry messages.
carrion • n. the decaying flesh of dead animals.
– ORIGIN Old French *caroine, charoigne*.
carrot • n. **1** a tapering orange root vegetable. **2** something offered to someone to persuade them to do something: *they're throwing a carrot to investors in the form of a lower price.*
– ORIGIN Greek *karōton*.
carroty • adj. (of a person's hair) orange-red.
carry • v. (**carries, carrying, carried**) **1** move or take from one place to another. **2** have with you wherever you go: *I never carry money.* **3** support the weight of. **4** assume or accept responsibility or blame. **5** have as a feature or result: *the bike carries a ten-year guarantee.* **6** take or develop an idea or activity to a particular point: *he carried the criticism much further.* **7** publish or broadcast. **8** (of a sound or voice) travel. **9** approve a proposal by a majority of votes. **10** (**carry yourself**) stand and move in a specified way. **11** be pregnant with a baby. • n. (pl. **carries**) an act of carrying.
– PHRASES **be/get carried away** lose self-control. **carry the can** Brit. informal take responsibility for a mistake. **carry forward** transfer figures to a new page or account. **carry someone/thing off 1** take someone or something away by force. **2** succeed in doing something. **carry on 1** continue with something. **2** informal have a love affair. **carry something out** perform a task. **carry something over 1** keep something to use or deal with in a new situation. **2** postpone an event. **carry something through** bring something to completion.
– ORIGIN Old French *carier*.
carrycot • n. Brit. a small portable baby's cot.
carry-on • n. Brit. informal **1** a fuss. **2** (also **carryings-on**) improper behaviour.
cart • n. **1** an open horse-drawn vehicle with two or four wheels, for carrying loads or passengers. **2** a shallow open container on wheels, pulled or pushed by hand. • v. **1** carry in a cart or similar vehicle. **2** informal carry a heavy object with difficulty. **3** convey or remove roughly: *the demonstrators were carted off by the police.*
– PHRASES **put the cart before the horse** do things in the wrong order.
– ORIGIN Old Norse.

carte blanche /kart blahnsh/
• n. complete freedom to do what you want.
– ORIGIN French, 'blank paper'.
cartel /kar-tel/ • n. an association of manufacturers or suppliers formed to keep prices high and restrict competition.
– ORIGIN German *Kartell*.
Cartesian /kar-tee-zi-uhn/ • adj. relating to the French philosopher René Descartes (1596–1650) and his ideas.
– ORIGIN from *Cartesius*, Latin form of *Descartes*.
Cartesian coordinates • pl. n. a system for locating a point by reference to its distance from axes intersecting at right angles.
carthorse • n. Brit. a large, strong horse suitable for heavy work.
Carthusian /kar-thyoo-zi-uhn/ • n. a monk or nun of a strict order founded at Chartreuse in France in 1084.
– ORIGIN Latin *Carthusia* 'Chartreuse'.
cartilage /kar-ti-lij/ • n. firm, flexible tissue which covers the ends of joints and forms structures such as the external ear.
– DERIVATIVES **cartilaginous** /kar-ti-laj-in-uhs/ adj.
– ORIGIN Latin *cartilago*.
cartography /kar-tog-ruh-fi/ • n. the science or practice of drawing maps.
– DERIVATIVES **cartographer** n. **cartographic** adj.
– ORIGIN French *carte* 'card, map'.
carton • n. a light cardboard box or container.
– ORIGIN Italian *cartone* 'cartoon'.
cartoon • n. **1** a humorous drawing in a newspaper or magazine. **2** (also **cartoon strip**) a sequence of cartoons that tell a story. **3** an animated film made from a sequence of drawings. **4** a full-size drawing made as a preliminary design for a painting or other work of art.
– DERIVATIVES **cartoonist** n.
– ORIGIN Italian *cartone*.
cartouche /kar-toosh/ • n. **1** a carved decoration or drawing in the form of a scroll with rolled-up ends. **2** an oval or oblong containing Egyptian hieroglyphs representing the name and title of a monarch.
– ORIGIN French.
cartridge • n. **1** a container holding film, a quantity of ink, or other item or substance, to be inserted into a mechanism. **2** a casing containing a charge and a bullet or shot for a gun.
– ORIGIN from CARTOUCHE.
cartridge paper • n. thick, rough-textured drawing paper.

cartwheel • n. a circular sideways handspring with the arms and legs extended. • v. perform cartwheels.

carve • v. (**carves**, **carving**, **carved**) 1 cut into or shape a hard material to produce an object or design. 2 produce by carving. 3 cut cooked meat into slices for eating. 4 (**carve something out**) develop a career, reputation, etc. through great effort. 5 (**carve something up**) divide something up ruthlessly.
– ORIGIN Old English.

carver • n. 1 a person or tool that carves. 2 Brit. the principal chair, with arms, in a set of dining chairs.

carvery • n. (pl. **carveries**) a buffet or restaurant where cooked joints are carved as required.

carving • n. an object or design carved from wood or stone as a work of art.

Casanova /ka-suh-noh-vuh/ • n. a man who is known for seducing many women.
– ORIGIN named after the Italian Giovanni Jacopo *Casanova*.

casbah • n. var. of KASBAH.

cascade • n. 1 a small waterfall, especially one in a series. 2 a mass of something that falls, hangs, or occurs in large quantities: *a cascade of blossoms*. • v. (**cascades**, **cascading**, **cascaded**) pour downwards rapidly and in large quantities.
– ORIGIN Italian *cascata*.

case[1] • n. 1 an instance of something occurring: *a case of mistaken identity*. 2 an incident being investigated by the police. 3 a legal action that is to be or has been decided in a court of law. 4 a set of facts or arguments supporting one side of a debate or lawsuit. 5 a person or problem requiring or receiving the attention of a doctor, social worker, etc. 6 Grammar a form of a noun, adjective, or pronoun expressing the relationship of the word to others in the sentence: *the possessive case*.
– PHRASES **be the case** be so. **in case** so as to allow for the possibility of something happening.
– ORIGIN Latin *casus* 'fall, chance'.

case[2] • n. 1 a container or protective covering. 2 Brit. a suitcase. 3 a box containing twelve bottles of wine or other drink, sold as a unit. • v. (**cases**, **casing**, **cased**) 1 enclose within a case. 2 informal look around a place before carrying out a robbery.
– ORIGIN Latin *capsa*.

case history • n. a record of a person's background or medical history kept by a doctor or social worker.

casein /kay-seen/ • n. the main protein present in milk and cheese.
– ORIGIN from Latin *caseus* 'cheese'.

case law • n. the law as established by the outcome of former cases rather than by legislation.

caseload • n. the number of cases being dealt with by a doctor, lawyer, or social worker at one time.

casement • n. a window set on a hinge at the side, so that it opens like a door.
– ORIGIN Latin *cassimentum*.

case study • n. 1 a detailed study of the development of a person, group, or situation over a period of time. 2 a particular instance used to illustrate a general principle.

casework • n. social work concerned with a person's family history and their personal circumstances.

cash • n. 1 money in coins or notes. 2 money: *he was always short of cash*. • v. 1 give or receive notes or coins for a cheque or money order. 2 (**cash something in**) convert an insurance policy, savings account, etc. into money. 3 (**cash in on**) informal take advantage of.
– PHRASES **cash in hand** Brit. payment in cash rather than by cheque or other means.
– DERIVATIVES **cashless** adj.
– ORIGIN Old French *casse* 'box for money'.

cash and carry • n. a system of wholesale trading in which the buyer pays for goods in full and takes them away.

cashback • n. 1 a cash refund offered as an incentive to buyers. 2 a service offered by a shop whereby a customer may withdraw cash when buying goods with a debit card.

cash book • n. a book in which amounts of money paid and received are recorded.

cash card • n. Brit. a plastic card issued by a bank or building society which enables the holder to withdraw money from a cash dispenser.

cash crop • n. a crop produced for sale rather than for use by the grower.

cash dispenser • n. Brit. an automated teller machine.

cashew /ka-shoo/ • n. (also **cashew nut**) the edible kidney-shaped nut of a tropical American tree.
– ORIGIN from an American Indian language.

cash flow • n. the total amount of money passing into and out of a business.

cashier¹ • n. a person whose job is to pay out and receive money in a shop, bank, or business.
– ORIGIN French *caissier*.

cashier² • v. (**cashiers, cashiering, cashiered**) dismiss from the armed forces because of serious wrongdoing.
– ORIGIN French *casser* 'revoke, dismiss'.

cashmere • n. fine soft wool, originally that from a breed of Himalayan goat.
– ORIGIN from *Kashmir*, a region on the border of India and NE Pakistan.

cashpoint • n. Brit. trademark an automated teller machine.

cash register • n. a machine used in shops for totalling and recording the amount of each sale and storing the money received.

cash-strapped • adj. informal very short of money.

casing • n. a cover or shell that protects or encloses something.

casino • n. (pl. **casinos**) a public building or room for gambling.
– ORIGIN Italian, 'little house'.

cask • n. a large barrel for storing alcoholic drinks.
– ORIGIN French *casque* or Spanish *casco* 'helmet'.

casket • n. 1 a small ornamental box or chest for holding valuable objects. 2 esp. N. Amer. a coffin.
– ORIGIN perh. from Old French *cassette* 'little box'.

Cassandra /kuh-san-druh/ • n. a person who makes gloomy predictions.
– ORIGIN from *Cassandra* in Greek mythology, whose prophecies were not believed.

cassava /kuh-sah-vuh/ • n. the starchy root of a tropical American tree, used as food.
– ORIGIN from an extinct Caribbean language.

casserole • n. 1 a large dish with a lid, used for cooking food slowly in an oven. 2 a kind of stew cooked slowly in an oven. • v. (**casseroles, casseroling, casseroled**) cook food in a casserole.
– ORIGIN French.

cassette • n. a sealed plastic case containing audio tape, videotape, film, etc., to be inserted into a recorder, camera, or other device.
– ORIGIN French, 'little box'.

cassock • n. a long item of clothing worn by some Christian clergy and members of church choirs.
– ORIGIN Italian *casacca* 'riding coat'.

cassowary /kass-uh-wuh-ri/ • n. (pl. **cassowaries**) a very large flightless bird, native mainly to New Guinea.
– ORIGIN Malay.

cast • v. (**casts, casting, cast**) 1 throw forcefully. 2 cause light or shadow to appear on a surface. 3 direct your eyes or thoughts towards something. 4 express: *journalists cast doubt on this account.* 5 register a vote. 6 give a part to an actor or allocate parts in a play or film. 7 leave aside: *Sam jumped in, casting caution to the wind.* 8 throw the end of a fishing line out into the water. 9 shape metal or other material by pouring it into a mould while molten. 10 produce by casting metal: *a figure cast in bronze.* 11 cause a magic spell to take effect.
• n. 1 the actors taking part in a play or film. 2 an object made by casting metal or other material. 3 (also **plaster cast**) a bandage stiffened with plaster of Paris, moulded to support and protect a broken limb. 4 appearance or character: *minds of a philosophical cast.*
– PHRASES **be cast away** be stranded after a shipwreck. **be cast down** feel discouraged or depressed. **cast about** (or **around** or **round**) search far and wide. **cast off** Knitting take the stitches off the needle by looping each over the next. **cast something off** release a boat or ship from its moorings. **cast on** Knitting make the first row of loops on the needle.
– ORIGIN Old Norse.

castanets • pl. n. a pair of small curved pieces of wood, clicked together by the fingers to accompany Spanish dancing.
– ORIGIN Spanish *castañeta* 'little chestnut'.

castaway • n. a person who has been shipwrecked in an isolated place.

caste • n. each of the hereditary classes of Hindu society.
– ORIGIN Spanish and Portuguese *casta* 'lineage, breed'.

castellated /kass-tuh-lay-tid/ • adj. having battlements.
– ORIGIN Latin *castellum* 'little fort'.

caster • n. var. of CASTOR.

caster sugar (also **castor sugar**) • n. Brit. white sugar in fine granules.

castigate /kass-ti-gayt/ • v. (**castigates, castigating, castigated**) reprimand severely.
– DERIVATIVES **castigation** n.
– ORIGIN Latin *castigare*.

Castilian /ka-stil-i-uhn/ • n. 1 a person from the Spanish region of Castile. 2 the language of Castile, the standard form of both spoken and literary Spanish.
• adj. relating to Castile or Castilian.

casting • n. an object made by casting molten metal or other material.

casting vote • n. an extra vote used by a chairperson to decide an issue when votes on each side are equal.

cast iron •n. a hard alloy of iron and carbon which can be cast in a mould.
•adj. firm and unchangeable: *a cast-iron guarantee*.

castle •n. **1** a large fortified building or group of buildings of the medieval period. **2** Chess, informal, dated = ROOK².
– PHRASES **castles in the air** (or **in Spain**) dreams or plans that will never be achieved.
– ORIGIN Latin *castellum* 'little fort'.

cast-off •adj. abandoned or discarded.
•n. an item of clothing that is no longer wanted.

castor /kah-ster/ (also **caster**) •n. **1** each of a set of small swivelling wheels fixed to the legs or base of a piece of furniture. **2** a small container with holes in the top, used for sprinkling salt, sugar, etc.
– ORIGIN from CASTER.

castor oil •n. an oil obtained from the seeds of an African shrub, used as a laxative.
– ORIGIN Greek *kastōr* 'beaver'; perh. because a substance produced by beavers was used as a laxative.

castor sugar •n. var. of CASTER SUGAR.

castrate •v. (**castrates, castrating, castrated**) **1** remove the testicles of a man or male animal. **2** deprive of power or vigour.
– DERIVATIVES **castration** n. **castrator** n.
– ORIGIN Latin *castrare*.

casual •adj. **1** relaxed and unconcerned. **2** lacking care or thought: *a casual remark*. **3** not regular or firmly established; occasional or temporary: *casual jobs*. **4** happening by chance. **5** (of clothes) informal. •n. **1** Brit. a temporary or occasional worker. **2** (**casuals**) informal clothes or shoes.
– DERIVATIVES **casually** adv. **casualness** n.
– ORIGIN Latin *casualis*.

casualty •n. (pl. **casualties**) **1** a person killed or injured in a war or accident. **2** a person or thing badly affected by an event or situation: *the firm was one of the casualties of the recession*.

casuistry /kazh-oo-iss-tri/ •n. the use of clever but false reasoning.
– DERIVATIVES **casuist** n.
– ORIGIN Latin *casus* 'fall, chance'.

cat •n. **1** a small furry mammal that is kept as a pet. **2** a wild animal related to or resembling this, e.g. a lion.
– PHRASES **the cat's whiskers** informal an excellent person or thing. **let the cat out of the bag** informal reveal a secret by mistake. **put** (or **set**) **the cat among the pigeons** Brit. do something likely to cause trouble.
– DERIVATIVES **catlike** adj.

– ORIGIN Old English.

catabolism /kuh-tab-uh-li-z'm/ •n. a metabolic process in which complex molecules are broken down to form simpler ones and energy is released. Opp. ANABOLISM.
– DERIVATIVES **catabolic** adj.
– ORIGIN Greek *katabolē* 'throwing down'.

cataclysm /kat-uh-kli-z'm/ •n. a violent upheaval or disaster.
– DERIVATIVES **cataclysmic** adj. **cataclysmically** adv.
– ORIGIN Greek *kataklusmos* 'deluge'.

catacomb /kat-uh-koom/ •n. an underground cemetery consisting of tunnels with recesses for tombs.
– ORIGIN Latin *catacumbas*, the name of an underground cemetery near Rome.

catafalque /kat-uh-falk/ •n. a decorated wooden framework used to support a coffin.
– ORIGIN Italian *catafalco*.

Catalan /kat-uh-lan/ •n. **1** a person from Catalonia in NE Spain. **2** the language of Catalonia. •adj. relating to Catalonia.

catalepsy /kat-uh-lep-si/ •n. a medical condition in which a person suffers a loss of consciousness and their body becomes rigid.
– DERIVATIVES **cataleptic** adj. & n.
– ORIGIN Greek *katalambanein* 'seize on'.

catalogue (US also **catalog**) •n. **1** a list of items arranged in alphabetical or other systematic order. **2** a publication containing details of items for sale. **3** a series of bad things: *a catalogue of failures*. •v. (**catalogues, cataloguing, catalogued**; US also **catalogs, cataloging, cataloged**) list in a catalogue.
– DERIVATIVES **cataloguer** n.
– ORIGIN Greek *katalogos*.

Catalonian /kat-uh-loh-ni-uhn/ •adj. & n. = CATALAN.

catalyse /kat-uh-lyz/ (US **catalyze**)
•v. (**catalyses, catalysing, catalysed**; US **catalyzes, catalyzing, catalyzed**) cause or speed up a reaction by acting as a catalyst.
– DERIVATIVES **catalyser** n.

catalysis /kuh-tal-i-siss/ •n. the speeding up of a chemical reaction by a catalyst.
– DERIVATIVES **catalytic** /kat-uh-**lit**-ik/ adj.
– ORIGIN Greek *katalusis* 'dissolving'.

catalyst /kat-uh-list/ •n. **1** a substance that increases the rate of a chemical reaction while remaining unchanged itself. **2** a person or thing that causes something to happen.

catalytic converter •n. a device in the exhaust system of a motor vehicle, containing a catalyst for converting pollutant gases into less harmful ones.

catamaran /kat-uh-muh-ran/ •n. a boat with twin parallel hulls.
– ORIGIN Tamil, 'tied wood'.

catamite /kat-uh-myt/ •n. literary a boy kept by an older man as a homosexual partner.
– ORIGIN Latin *catamitus*.

catapult •n. **1** esp. Brit. a forked stick with an elastic band fastened to the two prongs, used for shooting small stones. **2** a mechanical device for launching a glider or aircraft. •v. **1** throw forcefully: *the explosion catapulted the car along the road.* **2** move suddenly or very fast.
– ORIGIN Latin *catapulta*.

cataract /kat-uh-rakt/ •n. **1** a large waterfall. **2** a medical condition in which the lens of the eye becomes cloudy, resulting in blurred vision.
– ORIGIN Greek *kataraktēs* 'down-rushing'.

catarrh /kuh-tar/ •n. excessive mucus in the nose or throat.
– ORIGIN Greek *katarrhein* 'flow down'.

catastrophe /kuh-tass-truh-fi/ •n. a sudden event causing great damage or suffering.
– DERIVATIVES **catastrophic** /kat-uh-strof-ik/ adj. **catastrophically** adv.
– ORIGIN Greek *katastrophē* 'overturning'.

catatonia /kat-uh-toh-ni-uh/ •n. a form of schizophrenia in which a person experiences periods of unconsciousness or overactivity.
– DERIVATIVES **catatonic** adj.
– ORIGIN from Greek *tonos* 'tone'.

cat burglar •n. a thief who enters a building by climbing to an upper storey.

catcall •n. a shrill whistle or shout of mockery or disapproval. •v. make a catcall.

catch •v. (**catches, catching, caught**) **1** seize and hold something moving. **2** capture a person or animal. **3** reach in time and board a vehicle or be in time to see a person or event. **4** entangle or become entangled: *she caught her foot in the bedspread.* **5** surprise someone in the act of doing something wrong or embarrassing. **6** (**be caught in**) unexpectedly find yourself in an unwelcome situation. **7** gain a person's interest. **8** see, hear, or understand: *he said something Jess couldn't catch.* **9** hit someone or something. **10** become infected with an illness. **11** start burning. **12** Cricket dismiss a batsman by catching the ball before it touches the ground. •n. **1** an act of catching. **2** a device for fastening a door, window, etc. **3** a hidden problem. **4** a break in a person's voice caused by emotion. **5** an

amount of fish caught.
– PHRASES **catch your breath 1** breathe in sharply from emotion. **2** recover your breath after exercise. **catch someone's eye 1** be noticed by someone. **2** attract someone's attention. **catch on** informal **1** become popular. **2** understand. **catch someone out** Brit. **1** discover that someone has done something wrong. **2** take unawares: *you might get caught out by the weather.* **catch the sun 1** be in a sunny position. **2** Brit. become tanned or sunburnt. **catch up** do tasks which you should have done earlier. **catch someone up** succeed in reaching a person ahead of you.
– DERIVATIVES **catcher** n.
– ORIGIN Latin *captare* 'try to catch'.

catch-all •n. a term or category intended to cover all possibilities.

catching •adj. (of a disease) infectious.

catchment area (also **catchment**) •n. **1** the area from which a hospital's patients or a school's pupils are drawn. **2** the area from which rainfall flows into a river, lake, or reservoir.

catchpenny •adj. outwardly attractive so as to sell quickly.

catchphrase •n. a well-known sentence or phrase.

catch-22 •n. a difficult situation from which there is no escape because it involves conditions which conflict with each other.
– ORIGIN a novel by Joseph Heller.

catchword •n. a frequently used word or phrase that is associated with or sums up something.

catchy •adj. (**catchier, catchiest**) (of a tune or phrase) appealing and easy to remember.
– DERIVATIVES **catchiness** n.

catechism /kat-i-ki-z'm/ •n. a summary of the principles of Christian religion in the form of questions and answers, used for teaching.

catechist •n. a Christian teacher.

catechize (or **catechise**) •v. (**catechizes, catechizing, catechized**) teach someone about Christianity by using a catechism.
– ORIGIN Greek *katēkhein* 'instruct orally'.

categorical (also **categoric**) •adj. completely clear and direct.
– DERIVATIVES **categorically** adv.

categorize (or **categorise**) •v. (**categorizes, categorizing, categorized**) place in a category.
– DERIVATIVES **categorization** n.

category •n. (pl. **categories**) a class or group of people or things with shared characteristics.

– ORIGIN Greek *katēgoria* 'statement'.

cater • v. (**caters, catering, catered**)
1 (**cater for**) Brit. provide food and drink at a social event. **2** (**cater for/to**) provide with what is needed or required: *the school caters for children from 5 to 11.*
3 (**cater for**) take into account. **4** (**cater to**) satisfy a need or demand.
– DERIVATIVES **caterer** n.
– ORIGIN Old French *acater* 'buy'.

caterpillar • n. **1** the larva of a butterfly or moth. **2** (also **caterpillar track** or **tread**) trademark a steel band passing round the wheels of a vehicle for travel on rough ground.
– ORIGIN perh. from Old French *chatepelose* 'hairy cat'.

caterwaul /kat-er-wawl/ • v. make a shrill howling or wailing noise.

catfight • n. informal a fight between women.
– DERIVATIVES **catfighting** n.

catfish • n. (pl. **catfish** or **catfishes**) a freshwater or sea fish with whisker-like growths round the mouth.

catgut • n. material used for the strings of musical instruments and formerly for sewing up wounds, made of the dried intestines of sheep or horses.

catharsis /kuh-thar-siss/ • n. the release of pent-up emotions.
– DERIVATIVES **cathartic** adj.
– ORIGIN Greek *kathairein* 'cleanse'.

cathedral • n. the principal church of a diocese.
– ORIGIN Greek *kathedra* 'seat'.

Catherine wheel • n. Brit. a firework in the form of a spinning coil.
– ORIGIN named after St *Catherine*, who was martyred on a spiked wheel.

catheter /kath-i-ter/ • n. a flexible tube inserted into the bladder or another body cavity to remove fluid.
– ORIGIN Greek *kathienai* 'send down'.

cathode /kath-ohd/ • n. an electrode with a negative charge. Opp. **ANODE**.
– ORIGIN Greek *kathodos* 'way down'.

cathode ray tube • n. a vacuum tube in which beams of electrons produce a luminous image on a fluorescent screen, used in televisions and visual display units.

catholic • adj. **1** including a wide variety of things: *catholic tastes.* **2** (**Catholic**) Roman Catholic. • n. (**Catholic**) a Roman Catholic.
– DERIVATIVES **Catholicism** /kuh-thol-i-siz'm/ n.
– ORIGIN Greek *katholikos* 'universal'.

cation /kat-I-uhn/ • n. Chem. an ion with a positive charge. Opp. **ANION**.
– ORIGIN from **CATHODE** + **ION**.

catkin • n. a spike of small soft flowers hanging from trees such as the willow.
– ORIGIN former Dutch *katteken* 'kitten'.

catnap • n. a short sleep during the day. • v. (**catnaps, catnapping, catnapped**) have a catnap.

cat-o'-nine-tails • n. hist. a rope whip with nine knotted cords.

cat's cradle • n. a game in which patterns are formed in a loop of string held between the fingers of each hand.

catseye • n. Brit. trademark each of a series of reflective studs marking the lanes or edges of a road.

cat's paw • n. a person used by someone else to carry out an unpleasant task.

catsuit • n. esp. Brit. a woman's close-fitting one-piece garment with trouser legs.

cattery • n. (pl. **catteries**) a place where cats are bred, or looked after while their owners are away.

cattle • pl. n. cows, bulls, and oxen.
– ORIGIN Old French *chatel* 'chattel'.

cattle grid • n. Brit. a metal grid covering a trench across a road, allowing vehicles to pass over but not animals.

catty • adj. (**cattier, cattiest**) spiteful.
– DERIVATIVES **cattily** adv.

catwalk • n. **1** a narrow platform along which models walk to display clothes. **2** a raised narrow walkway.

Caucasian /kaw-kay-zh'n/ • adj. **1** relating to a division of humankind which covers peoples from Europe, western Asia, and parts of India and North Africa. **2** white-skinned; of European origin. • n. a Caucasian person.

caucus /kaw-kuhss/ • n. (pl. **caucuses**) **1** a meeting of a policy-making committee of a political party. **2** a group of people with shared concerns within a larger organization.
– ORIGIN perh. from an American Indian word meaning 'adviser'.

caudal /kaw-duhl/ • adj. relating to the tail or the rear part of the body.
– DERIVATIVES **caudally** adv.
– ORIGIN Latin *cauda* 'tail'.

caught past and past part. of **CATCH**.

caul /rhymes with ball/ • n. a membrane enclosing a fetus, part of which is sometimes found on a baby's head at birth.
– ORIGIN perh. from Old French *cale* 'head covering'.

cauldron (US **caldron**) • n. a large metal cooking pot.
– ORIGIN Old French *caudron*.

cauliflower • n. a variety of cabbage with a large white flower head.
– ORIGIN from former French *chou fleuri* 'flowered cabbage'.

caulk /kawk/ (US also **calk**) • n. a water-

proof substance used to fill cracks and seal joins. •v. seal with caulk.
– ORIGIN Latin *calcare* 'to tread'.

causal •adj. relating to or being a cause: *a causal connection between smoking and lung cancer.*
– DERIVATIVES **causally** adv.

causality •n. the relationship between something that happens and the effect it produces.

causation •n. **1** the action of causing something. **2** = CAUSALITY.

causative •adj. causing an effect: *HIV is the causative agent of Aids.*

cause •n. **1** a person or thing that produces an effect. **2** good reason for thinking or doing something: *cause for concern.* **3** a principle or movement which you are prepared to support. **4** a lawsuit. •v. (**causes, causing, caused**) make something, especially something bad, happen. **make common cause** come together to achieve a shared aim.
– ORIGIN Latin *causa*.

cause célèbre /kawz se-**leb**-ruh/ •n. (pl. **causes célèbres** /kawz se-**leb**-ruh/) an issue arousing great public interest.
– ORIGIN French, 'famous case'.

causeway •n. a raised road or track across low or wet ground.
– ORIGIN Old French *causee*.

caustic /**kaw**-stik/ •adj. **1** able to burn through or wear away living tissue by chemical action. **2** sarcastic in a hurtful way.
– DERIVATIVES **caustically** adv.
– ORIGIN Greek *kaustikos*.

caustic soda •n. sodium hydroxide.

cauterize /**kaw**-tuh-ryz/ (or **cauterise**) •v. (**cauterizes, cauterizing, cauterized**) burn the skin or flesh of a wound to stop bleeding or prevent infection.
– DERIVATIVES **cauterization** n.
– ORIGIN Greek *kautēriazein*.

caution •n. **1** care taken to avoid danger or mistakes. **2** warning: *advisers sounded a note of caution.* **3** Brit. an official or legal warning given to someone who has committed a minor offence. •v. **1** warn or advise. **2** Brit. give a caution to someone.
– PHRASES **throw caution to the wind** act in a reckless way.
– ORIGIN Latin *cavere* 'take heed'.

cautionary •adj. acting as a warning.

cautious •adj. careful to avoid possible problems or dangers.
– DERIVATIVES **cautiously** adv.

cavalcade /ka-vuhl-**kayd**/ •n. a procession of vehicles or riders.
– ORIGIN Italian *cavalcare* 'to ride'.

cavalier •n. (**Cavalier**) a supporter of King Charles I in the English Civil War.
•adj. showing a lack of proper concern: *the cavalier treatment of mental illness.*
– ORIGIN Italian *cavaliere* 'knight, gentleman'.

cavalry •n. (pl. **cavalries**) soldiers who used to fight on horseback, but who now use armoured vehicles.
– DERIVATIVES **cavalryman** n. (pl. **cavalrymen**).
– ORIGIN from Italian *cavallo* 'horse'.

cave •n. a large natural hollow in the side of a hill or cliff, or underground.
•v. (**caves, caving, caved**) **1** (**cave in**) give way or collapse. **2** (**cave in**) finally give in to someone's demands.
– ORIGIN Latin *cavus* 'hollow'.

caveat /**ka**-vi-at/ •n. a warning.
– ORIGIN Latin, 'let a person beware'.

caveman (or **cavewoman**) •n. (pl. **cavemen** or **cavewomen**) a prehistoric person who lived in caves.

cavern •n. a large cave.
– ORIGIN Latin *caverna*.

cavernous /**kav**-er-nuhss/ •adj. like a cavern in being huge or gloomy.

caviar /**ka**-vi-ar/ (also **caviare**) •n. the pickled roe of the sturgeon (a large fish).
– ORIGIN French.

cavil /**ka**-vuhl/ •v. (**cavils, cavilling, cavilled**; US **cavils, caviling, caviled**) make petty objections. •n. a petty objection.
– ORIGIN Latin *cavillari*.

caving •n. the activity of exploring caves as a sport.
– DERIVATIVES **caver** n.

cavity •n. (pl. **cavities**) **1** a hollow space within a solid object. **2** a decayed part of a tooth.
– ORIGIN Latin *cavitas*.

cavity wall •n. a wall formed from two layers of bricks with a space between them.

cavort •v. jump or dance around excitedly.
– ORIGIN perh. from CURVET.

cavy /**kay**-vi/ •n. (pl. **cavies**) a guinea pig or related South American rodent.
– ORIGIN Latin *cavia*.

caw •v. (of a rook, crow, etc.) make a harsh cry.

cayenne /kay-**en**/ (also **cayenne pepper**) •n. a hot-tasting red powder made from dried chillies.
– ORIGIN from a South American language.

cayman •n. var. of CAIMAN.

CB •abbrev. **1** Citizens' Band. **2** (in the UK) Companion of the Order of the Bath.

CBE •abbrev. (in the UK) Commander of the Order of the British Empire.

CBI • abbrev. Confederation of British Industry.

cc (also **c.c.**) • abbrev. **1** carbon copy (showing that a copy has been or should be sent to another person). **2** cubic centimetre(s).

CCTV • abbrev. closed-circuit television.

CD • abbrev. compact disc.

Cd • symb. the chemical element cadmium.

cd • abbrev. candela.

CD-R • abbrev. compact disc recordable, a CD which can be recorded on once only.

CD-ROM • n. a compact disc used in a computer as a read-only device for displaying data.

CD-RW • abbrev. compact disc rewritable, a CD on which recordings can be made and erased a number of times.

CE • abbrev. Church of England.

Ce • symb. the chemical element cerium.

cease • v. (**ceases**, **ceasing**, **ceased**) come or bring to an end; stop.
– ORIGIN Latin *cessare*.

ceasefire • n. a temporary period when fighting in a war stops.

ceaseless • adj. never stopping.
– DERIVATIVES **ceaselessly** adv.

cecum • n. (pl. **ceca**) US = CAECUM.

cedar • n. a tall coniferous tree with hard, sweet-smelling wood.
– ORIGIN Greek *kedros*.

cede /seed/ • v. (**cedes**, **ceding**, **ceded**) give up power or territory.
– ORIGIN Latin *cedere*.

cedilla /si-dil-luh/ • n. a mark ( ) written under the letter *c* to show that it is pronounced like an *s* (e.g. *soupçon*).
– ORIGIN Spanish *zedilla* 'little z'.

ceilidh /kay-li/ • n. a social event with Scottish or Irish folk music and dancing.
– ORIGIN Old Irish *céilide* 'visit, visiting'.

ceiling • n. **1** the upper inside surface of a room. **2** an upper limit set on prices, wages, or spending.
– ORIGIN from former *ceil* 'line or plaster the roof of a building'.

> ✓ **ceiling** follows the usual rule of *i* before *e* except after *c*.

celandine /sel-uhn-dyn/ • n. a yellow-flowered plant of the buttercup family.
– ORIGIN Greek *khelidōn* 'swallow' (because the plant flowers at the time swallows arrive).

celebrant /sel-i-bruhnt/ • n. a person who performs a religious ceremony, especially a priest who leads Holy Communion.

celebrate • v. (**celebrates**, **celebrating**, **celebrated**) **1** mark an important occasion by doing something special and enjoyable. **2** honour or praise someone publicly. **3** perform a religious ceremony.
– DERIVATIVES **celebration** n. **celebrator** n. **celebratory** adj.
– ORIGIN Latin *celebrare*.

celebrity • n. (pl. **celebrities**) **1** a famous person. **2** the state of being famous.

celeriac /suh-lair-i-ak/ • n. a variety of celery which forms a large edible root.

celerity /si-le-ri-ti/ • n. old use or literary speed of movement.
– ORIGIN Latin *celeritas*.

celery • n. a vegetable with crisp juicy stalks.
– ORIGIN Greek *selinon* 'parsley'.

celesta /si-les-tuh/ (also **celeste** /si-lest/) • n. a small keyboard instrument in which felt-covered hammers strike a row of steel plates.
– ORIGIN from French *céleste* 'heavenly'.

celestial /si-less-ti-uhl/ • adj. **1** relating to heaven. **2** relating to the sky or outer space.
– DERIVATIVES **celestially** adv.
– ORIGIN Latin *caelum* 'heaven'.

celibate /sel-i-buht/ • adj. not marrying or having sex, often for religious reasons. • n. a person who is celibate.
– DERIVATIVES **celibacy** n.
– ORIGIN Latin *caelibatus* 'unmarried state'.

cell • n. **1** a small room for a prisoner, monk, or nun. **2** the smallest unit of a living organism that is able to reproduce and perform other functions. **3** a small compartment in a larger structure. **4** a small group that is part of a larger political organization. **5** a device for producing electricity by chemical action or light.
– ORIGIN Latin *cella* 'storeroom'.

cellar • n. **1** a storage space or room below ground level in a building. **2** a stock of wine.
– ORIGIN Latin *cellarium* 'storehouse'.

cello /chel-loh/ • n. (pl. **cellos**) an instrument like a large violin, held upright on the floor between the legs of the seated player.
– DERIVATIVES **cellist** n.
– ORIGIN from VIOLONCELLO.

cellophane /sel-luh-fayn/ • n. trademark a thin transparent wrapping material.
– ORIGIN from CELLULOSE.

cellphone • n. a mobile phone.

cellular /sel-yuu-ler/ • adj. **1** relating to or made up of cells. **2** relating to a mobile telephone system that uses a number of short-range radio stations to cover the area it serves.

cellulite /sel-yuu-lyt/ • n. fat that builds

up under the skin, causing a dimpled effect.
– ORIGIN French.

celluloid • n. a kind of transparent plastic formerly used for cinema film.

cellulose /sel-yuu-lohz/ • n. a substance found in all plant tissues, used in making paint, plastics, and man-made fibres.
– ORIGIN French.

Celsius /sel-si-uhss/ • adj. relating to a scale of temperature on which water freezes at 0° and boils at 100°.
– ORIGIN named after the Swedish astronomer Anders *Celsius*.

Celt /kelt/ • n. **1** a member of a people inhabiting much of Europe and Asia Minor in pre-Roman times. **2** a person from a modern region in which a Celtic language is (or was) spoken.
– ORIGIN Greek *Keltoi* 'Celts'.

Celtic /kel-tik/ • n. a group of languages including Irish, Scottish Gaelic, Welsh, Breton, Manx, and Cornish.
• adj. relating to Celtic or to the Celts.

cement • n. **1** a powdery substance made by heating lime and clay, used in making mortar and concrete. **2** a soft glue that hardens on setting. • v. **1** fix with cement. **2** strengthen: *the occasion cemented our friendship.*
– ORIGIN Latin *caementum* 'quarry stone'.

cemetery • n. (pl. **cemeteries**) a large burial ground.
– ORIGIN Greek *koimētērion* 'dormitory'.

> ✓ Remember that all the vowels in **cemetery** are e's.

cenotaph /sen-uh-tahf/ • n. a memorial to members of the armed forces killed in a war.
– ORIGIN from Greek *kenos* 'empty' + *taphos* 'tomb'.

Cenozoic /see-nuh-zoh-ik/ • adj. Geol. relating to the era following the Mesozoic era (from about 65 million years ago to the present).
– ORIGIN from Greek *kainos* 'new' + *zōion* 'animal'.

censer • n. a container in which incense is burnt.
– ORIGIN Old French *censier*.

censor • n. an official who examines material that is to be published and bans anything considered to be offensive or a threat to security. • v. ban unacceptable parts of a book, film, etc.
– DERIVATIVES **censorship** n.
– ORIGIN Latin.

censorious /sen-sor-i-uhss/ • adj. very critical.

censure /sen-sher/ • v. (**censures, censuring, censured**) criticize strongly.

• n. strong disapproval or criticism.
– ORIGIN Latin *censura* 'judgement'.

census • n. (pl. **censuses**) an official count or survey of a population.
– ORIGIN Latin.

cent • n. a unit of money equal to one hundredth of a dollar, euro, or other decimal currency unit.
– ORIGIN Latin *centum* 'hundred'.

centaur /sen-tor/ • n. Gk Myth. a creature with a man's head, arms, and upper body and a horse's lower body and legs.
– ORIGIN Greek *kentauros*.

centenarian /sen-ti-nair-i-uhn/ • n. a person who is a hundred or more years old.

centenary /sen-tee-nuh-ri/ • n. (pl. **centenaries**) Brit. the hundredth anniversary of an event.
– ORIGIN Latin *centenarius* 'containing a hundred'.

centennial • adj. relating to a hundredth anniversary. • n. a hundredth anniversary.

center etc. • n. US = CENTRE etc.

centi- • comb. form **1** one hundredth: *centilitre*. **2** hundred: *centipede*.
– ORIGIN Latin *centum* 'hundred'.

centigrade • adj. relating to the Celsius scale of temperature.
– ORIGIN from Latin *centum* 'a hundred' + *gradus* 'step'.

centilitre (US **centiliter**) • n. a metric unit equal to one hundredth of a litre.

centime /son-teem/ • n. a unit of money equal to one hundredth of a franc or some other decimal currency units (used in France, Belgium, and Luxembourg until the introduction of the euro in 2002).
– ORIGIN French.

centimetre (US **centimeter**) • n. a metric unit equal to one hundredth of a metre.

centipede • n. an insect-like creature with a long thin body made up of many segments, most of which have a pair of legs.
– ORIGIN from Latin *centum* 'a hundred' + *pes* 'foot'.

central • adj. **1** in or near the centre. **2** very important.
– DERIVATIVES **centrality** n. **centrally** adv.

central bank • n. a national bank that provides services for its country's government and commercial banking system, and issues currency.

central heating • n. a system for warming a building by heating water or air in one place and circulating it through pipes and radiators or vents.

centralize (or **centralise**)
• v. (**centralizes, centralizing,**

centralized) bring under the control of a central authority.
– DERIVATIVES **centralism** n. **centralist** n. & adj. **centralization** n.

central nervous system •n. the complex of nerve tissues that controls the activities of the body, consisting of the brain and spinal cord in vertebrates.

central processing unit •n. the part of a computer in which operations are controlled and carried out.

central reservation •n. Brit. the strip of land between the carriageways of a motorway or dual carriageway.

centre (US **center**) •n. **1** a point or part in the middle of something. **2** a place which is devoted to a particular activity: *a conference centre.* **3** a point from which something spreads or to which something is directed: *the city was a centre of discontent.* **4** a moderate political group. •v. (**centres, centring, centred**; US **centers, centering, centered**) **1** place in the centre. **2** (**centre on/around**) have as a major concern or theme: *the case centres around their adopted children.*
– PHRASES **centre of gravity** the central point in an object, about which its mass is evenly balanced.
– ORIGIN Latin *centrum.*

centre back •n. Football a defender who plays in the middle of the field.

centreboard (US **centerboard**) •n. a board lowered through the keel of a sailing boat to reduce sideways movement.

centrefold (US **centerfold**) •n. the two middle pages of a magazine, containing illustrations or a special feature.

centre forward •n. Sport an attacker who plays in the middle of the field.

centre half •n. Football a centre back.

centrepiece (US **centerpiece**) •n. an object or item that is meant to attract attention.

-centric •comb. form **1** having a specified centre: *concentric.* **2** coming from a specified viewpoint: *Eurocentric.*
– DERIVATIVES **-centricity** comb. form.

centrifugal /sen-tri-fyoo-g'l/ •adj. Physics moving away from a centre.
– DERIVATIVES **centrifugally** adv.
– ORIGIN from Latin *centrum* 'centre' + *-fugus* 'fleeing'.

centrifugal force •n. Physics a force which tends to cause a body to move directly away from a central point.

centrifuge /sen-tri-fyooj/ •n. a machine with a rapidly rotating container, used to separate liquids from solids.

centripetal /sen-tri-pee-t'l/ •adj. Physics moving towards a centre.
– DERIVATIVES **centripetally** adv.
– ORIGIN from Latin *centrum* 'centre' + *-petus* 'seeking'.

centripetal force •n. Physics a force which tends to cause a body to move directly towards a central point.

centrist •n. a person having moderate political views or policies.
– DERIVATIVES **centrism** n.

centurion •n. the commander of a hundred men in the ancient Roman army.
– ORIGIN Latin.

century •n. (pl. **centuries**) **1** a period of one hundred years. **2** a batsman's score of a hundred runs in cricket.
– ORIGIN Latin *centuria.*

CEO •abbrev. chief executive officer.

cephalic /si-fal-ik/ •adj. tech. relating to the head.
– ORIGIN Greek *kephalē* 'head'.

cephalopod /sef-uh-luh-pod/ •n. a mollusc of a class including octopuses and squids.
– ORIGIN from Greek *kephalē* 'head' + *pous* 'foot'.

ceramic •adj. made of clay that is permanently hardened by heat.
•n. (**ceramics**) the art of making ceramic articles.
– DERIVATIVES **ceramicist** n.
– ORIGIN Greek *keramos* 'pottery'.

cereal •n. **1** a grass producing an edible grain, such as wheat, maize, or rye. **2** a breakfast food made from a cereal grain or grains.
– ORIGIN from *Ceres*, the Roman goddess of agriculture.

cerebellum /se-ri-bel-luhm/ •n. (pl. **cerebellums** or **cerebella** /se-ri-bel-uh/) the part of the brain at the back of the skull, which coordinates muscular activity.
– DERIVATIVES **cerebellar** adj.
– ORIGIN Latin, 'little brain'.

cerebral /suh-ree-bruhl/ •adj. **1** relating to the cerebrum of the brain. **2** intellectual rather than emotional or physical: *cerebral pursuits such as chess.*
– DERIVATIVES **cerebrally** adv.

cerebral palsy •n. a condition in which a person has difficulty in controlling or moving their muscles, caused by brain damage before or at birth.

cerebration /se-ri-bray-sh'n/ •n. formal the working of the brain; thinking.

cerebrospinal /suh-ree-broh-spy-n'l/ •adj. relating to the brain and spine.

cerebrum /se-ri-bruhm/ •n. (pl. **cerebra** /se-ri-bruh/) the main part of the brain,

located in the front of the skull.
– ORIGIN Latin, 'brain'.

ceremonial • adj. relating to or used in ceremonies. • n. = CEREMONY.
– DERIVATIVES **ceremonially** adv.

ceremonious • adj. done in a way appropriate to a grand and formal occasion.
– DERIVATIVES **ceremoniously** adv.

ceremony • n. (pl. **ceremonies**) 1 a formal religious or public occasion celebrating an event. 2 the set procedures performed at grand and formal occasions.
– PHRASES **stand on ceremony** insist on formal behaviour.
– ORIGIN Latin *caerimonia* 'religious worship'.

cerise /suh-reess/ • n. a light, clear red colour.
– ORIGIN French, 'cherry'.

cerium /seer-i-uhm/ • n. a silvery-white metallic chemical element.
– ORIGIN named after the asteroid *Ceres*.

cert • n. Brit. informal 1 an event that is certain to happen. 2 a competitor that is certain to win.

certain • adj. 1 able to be relied on to happen or be the case: *it seems certain that he will be recalled to the England team.* 2 completely sure about something. 3 specific but not directly named or stated: *he raised certain problems.* • pron. (**certain of**) some but not all.
– ORIGIN Latin *certus* 'settled, sure'.

certainly • adv. 1 without doubt; definitely. 2 yes.

certainty • n. (pl. **certainties**) 1 the state of being certain. 2 a fact that is true or an event that is definitely going to take place.

certifiable • adj. 1 able or needing to be officially recorded. 2 officially recognized as needing treatment for mental disorder.
– DERIVATIVES **certifiably** adv.

certificate • n. 1 an official document recording a particular fact, event, or achievement. 2 an official classification given to a cinema film, indicating its suitability for a particular age group.
– DERIVATIVES **certification** n.

certify • v. (**certifies, certifying, certified**) 1 declare or confirm in a certificate or other official document. 2 officially declare insane.
– DERIVATIVES **certifier** n.
– ORIGIN Latin *certificare*.

certitude • n. a feeling of complete certainty.

cerulean /si-roo-li-uhn/ • adj. deep blue in colour.
– ORIGIN from Latin *caelum* 'sky'.

cervical /ser-vi-k'l, ser-vy-k'l/ • adj. relating to the cervix.

cervical smear • n. Brit. a specimen of cells from the neck of the womb, spread on a microscope slide for examination for signs of cancer.

cervix /ser-viks/ • n. (pl. **cervices** /ser-vi-seez/) the narrow neck-like passage forming the lower end of the womb.
– ORIGIN Latin.

cesium • n. US = CAESIUM.

cessation • n. the ending of something.
– ORIGIN Latin.

cession • n. the formal giving up of rights or territory by a state.
– ORIGIN Latin.

cesspool (also **cesspit**) • n. an underground tank or covered pit where liquid waste and sewage is stored before disposal.
– ORIGIN prob. from Old French *souspirail* 'air hole'.

cetacean /si-tay-sh'n/ Zool. • n. a sea mammal of a group including whales and dolphins.
– ORIGIN Greek *kētos* 'whale'.

Cf • symb. the chemical element californium.

cf. • abbrev. compare with.
– ORIGIN Latin *confer* 'compare'.

CFC • abbrev. chlorofluorocarbon, a gas that is a compound of carbon, hydrogen, chlorine, and fluorine, used in refrigerators and aerosols and harmful to the ozone layer.

CFE • abbrev. (in the UK) College of Further Education.

CH • abbrev. (in the UK) Companion of Honour.

ch. • abbrev. chapter.

Chablis /shab-lee/ • n. a dry white wine from Chablis in France.

cha-cha • n. a modern ballroom dance performed to a Latin American rhythm.
– ORIGIN Latin American Spanish.

Chadian /chad-i-uhn/ • n. a person from Chad in central Africa. • adj. relating to Chad or Chadians.

chador /chah-dor/ (also **chaddar**) • n. a piece of dark cloth worn by Muslim women around the head and upper body, so that only part of the face can be seen.
– ORIGIN Persian.

chafe • v. (**chafes, chafing, chafed**) 1 make or become sore or worn by rubbing against something. 2 rub a part of the body to warm it. 3 become

impatient, especially because you are restricted by something.
– ORIGIN Old French *chaufer* 'make hot'.

chafer • n. a large flying beetle.
– ORIGIN Old English.

chaff[1] /chahf/ • n. **1** husks of grain separated from the seed by winnowing or threshing. **2** chopped hay and straw as food for cattle.
– PHRASES **separate** (or **sort**) **the wheat from the chaff** pick out what is valuable from what is worthless.
– ORIGIN Old English.

chaff[2] /chahf/ • v. tease someone.
– ORIGIN perh. from **CHAFE**.

chaffinch • n. a finch, the male of which has a bluish head, pink underparts, and dark wings.
– ORIGIN Old English.

chagrin /sha-grin/ • n. annoyance or shame at having failed. • v. (**be chagrined**) feel annoyed or ashamed.
– ORIGIN French, 'rough skin'.

chain • n. **1** a series of connected metal links. **2** a connected series, set, or sequence: *a chain of superstores.* **3** a part of a molecule consisting of a number of atoms bonded together in a series. **4** a measure of length equal to 66 ft. • v. fasten or restrain with a chain.
– ORIGIN Old French *chaine*.

chain gang • n. a group of convicts chained together while working outside the prison.

chain letter • n. a letter which is sent to a number of people, all of whom are asked to send copies to other people, who then do the same.

chain mail • n. hist. armour made of small metal rings linked together.

chain reaction • n. **1** a series of events, each caused by the previous one. **2** a chemical reaction in which the products of the reaction cause other changes.

chainsaw • n. a power-driven saw with teeth set on a moving chain.

chain-smoke • v. smoke cigarettes one after the other.

chain store • n. one of a group of shops owned by one firm and selling the same goods.

chair • n. **1** a separate seat for one person, with a back and four legs. **2** the person in charge of a meeting or an organization. **3** a post as professor. • v. be in charge of a meeting.
– ORIGIN Old French *chaiere*.

chairlift • n. a series of chairs hung from a moving cable, used for carrying passengers up and down a mountain.

chairman (or **chairwoman**) • n. (pl. **chairmen** or **chairwomen**) a person in charge of a meeting or organization.

chairperson • n. a chairman or chairwoman.

chaise /shayz/ • n. esp. hist. a two-wheeled horse-drawn carriage for one or two people.
– ORIGIN French.

chaise longue /shayz long/ • n. (pl. **chaises longues** /shayz long/) a sofa with a backrest at only one end.
– ORIGIN French, 'long chair'.

chakra /chuk-ruh/ • n. (in Indian thought) each of seven centres of spiritual power in the human body.
– ORIGIN Sanskrit, 'wheel or circle'.

chalcedony /kal-sed-uh-ni/ • n. (pl. **chalcedonies**) a type of quartz with very small crystals, such as onyx.
– ORIGIN Greek *khalkēdōn*.

chalet /sha-lay/ • n. **1** a wooden house with overhanging eaves, found in the Swiss Alps. **2** a small cabin used by holidaymakers.
– ORIGIN Old French *chasel* 'farmstead'.

chalice /cha-liss/ • n. **1** hist. a goblet. **2** the wine cup used in Holy Communion.
– ORIGIN Latin *calix* 'cup'.

chalk • n. **1** a white soft limestone formed from the skeletons of sea creatures. **2** a similar substance made into sticks and used for drawing or writing. • v. **1** draw or write with chalk. **2** (**chalk something up**) achieve something noteworthy.
– PHRASES **as different as chalk and cheese** Brit. completely different. **not by a long chalk** Brit. by no means; not at all.
– DERIVATIVES **chalky** adj.
– ORIGIN Latin *calx* 'lime'.

challenge • n. **1** a demanding task or situation. **2** a call to someone to take part in a contest. **3** an act or statement that calls something into question. • v. (**challenges**, **challenging**, **challenged**) **1** raise doubt as to whether something is true or genuine. **2** invite someone to do something difficult or take part in a fight. **3** (of a sentry) call on someone to prove their identity.
– DERIVATIVES **challenger** n.
– ORIGIN Old French *chalenge*.

challenging • adj. presenting a test of your abilities; demanding: *a challenging job.*

chalybeate /kuh-lib-i-uht/ • adj. (of a natural mineral spring) containing iron salts.
– ORIGIN Latin *chalybeatus*.

chamaeleon • n. var. of **CHAMELEON**.

chamber • n. **1** a large room used for formal or public events. **2** one of the parts of a parliament. **3** (**chambers**) Law,

Brit. rooms used by a barrister or barristers. **4** old use a bedroom. **5** a space or cavity within something. **6** the part of a gun bore that contains the charge.
– ORIGIN Old French *chambre*.

chamberlain /chaym-ber-lin/ •n. hist. an officer who managed the household of a monarch or noble.
– ORIGIN Old French.

chambermaid •n. a woman who cleans rooms in a hotel.

chamber music •n. instrumental music played by a small group of musicians, such as a string quartet.

Chamber of Commerce •n. a local association to promote the interests of the business community.

chamber pot •n. a bowl kept in a bedroom and used as a toilet.

chambray /sham-bray/ •n. a fabric with a white weft and a coloured warp.
– ORIGIN from the French town of *Cambrai*.

chameleon /kuh-mee-li-uhn/ (also **chamaeleon**) •n. a small lizard that is able change colour according to its surroundings.
– ORIGIN from Greek *khamai* 'on the ground' + *leōn* 'lion'.

chamfer /sham-fer/ •v. (**chamfers, chamfering, chamfered**) Carpentry cut away a right-angled edge or corner to make a symmetrical sloping edge.
– ORIGIN from French *chant* 'point, edge' + *fraint* 'broken'.

chamois •n. **1** /sham-wah/ (pl. **chamois** /sham-wahz/) an agile wild antelope found in mountainous areas of southern Europe. **2** /sham-mi/ (pl. **chamois** /sham-miz/) (also **chamois leather**) soft leather made from the skin of sheep, goats, or deer.
– ORIGIN French.

chamomile /kam-uh-myl/ (also **camomile**) •n. a plant with white and yellow flowers, used in herbal medicine.
– ORIGIN Greek *khamaimēlon* 'earth-apple'.

champ[1] •v. munch noisily.
– PHRASES **champ at the bit** be very impatient.

champ[2] •n. informal a champion.

champagne /sham-payn/ •n. a white sparkling wine from the Champagne region of France.

champion •n. **1** the winner of a sporting contest or other competition. **2** a person who argues or fights for a cause or another person. •v. strongly support the cause of: *priests who championed human rights*. •adj. Brit. informal or dialect excellent.
– ORIGIN Latin *campion* 'fighter'.

championship •n. **1** a sporting contest for the position of champion. **2** the strong support of a person or cause.

chance •n. **1** a possibility of something happening. **2** (**chances**) the probability of something happening. **3** an opportunity. **4** the way in which things happen without any obvious plan or cause: *they met by chance in a bookshop*. •v. (**chances, chancing, chanced**) **1** happen or do something by chance. **2** informal do something even though it is risky.
– PHRASES **on the off chance** just in case. **stand a chance** have a likelihood of success. **take a chance** (or **chances**) take a risk.
– ORIGIN Old French *cheance*.

chancel /chahn-s'l/ •n. the part of a church near the altar, reserved for the clergy and choir.
– ORIGIN Latin *cancelli* 'crossbars'.

chancellery /chahn-suh-luh-ri/ •n. (pl. **chancelleries**) the post or department of a chancellor.

chancellor •n. **1** a senior state or legal official of various kinds. **2** (**Chancellor**) the head of the government in some European countries. **3** Brit. the honorary head of a university.
– DERIVATIVES **chancellorship** n.
– ORIGIN Latin *cancellarius* 'porter'.

Chancellor of the Exchequer •n. the chief finance minister of the United Kingdom.

chancer •n. Brit. informal a person who makes the most of any opportunity.

Chancery (also **Chancery Division**) •n. (pl. **Chanceries**) (in the UK) the Lord Chancellor's court, a division of the High Court of Justice.
– ORIGIN from **CHANCELLERY**.

chancre /shang-ker/ •n. a painless ulcer that develops on the genitals as a symptom of syphilis.
– ORIGIN French.

chancy •adj. (**chancier, chanciest**) informal risky; uncertain.

chandelier /shan-duh-leer/ •n. a large hanging light with branches for several light bulbs or candles.
– ORIGIN French.

chandler /chahnd-ler/ (also **ship chandler**) •n. a dealer in supplies and equipment for ships.
– DERIVATIVES **chandlery** n. (pl. **chandleries**).
– ORIGIN Old French *chandelier* 'candle maker or candle seller'.

change •v. (**changes, changing, changed**) **1** make or become different. **2** exchange one thing for another. **3** move from one to another: *he changed* jobs frequently. **4** (**change over**) move from one system or situation to another. **5** exchange a sum of money for the same sum in a different currency or denomination. **6** (**change down** or **up**) Brit. engage a lower (or higher) gear in a vehicle or on a bicycle. • n. **1** the action of changing. **2** a different experience. **3** money returned to someone as the balance of the sum paid. **4** money given in exchange for the same sum in larger units. **5** coins as opposed to banknotes. **6** a clean set of clothes.

– PHRASES **change hands** pass to a different owner. **change your tune** express a very different attitude. **ring the changes** vary the ways of doing something.

– DERIVATIVES **changeless** adj. **changer** n.

– ORIGIN Old French *changer*.

changeable • adj. **1** likely to change in an unpredictable way. **2** able to be changed.

– DERIVATIVES **changeability** n.

changeling • n. a child believed to have been secretly exchanged by fairies for the parents' real child.

changeover • n. a change from one system or situation to another.

channel • n. **1** a band of frequencies used in radio and television transmission, or a station using such a band. **2** a means of communication: *apply through the proper channels.* **3** a passage along which liquid or a watercourse may flow. **4** a wide stretch of water joining two seas: *the English Channel.* **5** a passage that boats can pass through in a stretch of water. **6** an electric circuit which acts as a path for a signal. • v. (**channels, channelling, channelled**; US **channels, channeling, channeled**) **1** direct towards a purpose. **2** pass along or through a channel.

– ORIGIN Latin *canalis* 'pipe, channel'.

chant • n. **1** a repeated rhythmic phrase, shouted or sung together by a group. **2** a tune to which the words of psalms or other works with irregular rhythm are fitted by singing several syllables or words to the same note. • v. say, shout, or sing in a chant.

– DERIVATIVES **chanter** n.

– ORIGIN Old French *chanter* 'sing'.

Chanukkah • n. var. of **HANUKKAH**.

chaos /kay-oss/ • n. complete disorder and confusion.

– ORIGIN Greek *khaos* 'vast chasm, void'.

chaotic /kay-ot-ik/ • adj. in a state of complete confusion and disorder.

– DERIVATIVES **chaotically** adv.

chap • n. Brit. informal a man.

– ORIGIN from former *chapman*, 'pedlar'.

chapatti /chuh-pah-ti/ • n. (pl. **chapattis**) (in Indian cookery) a flat round piece of

unleavened wholemeal bread.

– ORIGIN Hindi.

chapel • n. **1** a small building or room for Christian worship. **2** a part of a large church with its own altar.

– ORIGIN Old French *chapele*.

chaperone /shap-uh-rohn/ • n. **1** a person who looks after and accompanies another person or people. **2** dated an older woman who ensures that an unmarried girl behaves correctly at social occasions. • v. (**chaperones, chaperoning, chaperoned**) accompany and look after someone.

– ORIGIN French.

chaplain • n. a member of the clergy attached to a chapel in a private house or an institution, or to a military unit.

– DERIVATIVES **chaplaincy** n.

– ORIGIN Old French *chapelain*.

chaplet • n. a decorative circular band worn on the head.

– ORIGIN Old French *chapelet* 'little hat'.

chapped • adj. (of the skin) cracked and sore through exposure to cold weather.

chapter • n. **1** a main division of a book. **2** a particular period in history or in a person's life. **3** the governing body of a cathedral or other religious community. **4** esp. N. Amer. a local branch of a society.

– PHRASES **chapter and verse** an exact reference or authority.

– ORIGIN Old French *chapitre*.

char[1] • v. (**chars, charring, charred**) partially burn something so as to blacken the surface.

– ORIGIN prob. from **CHARCOAL**.

char[2] Brit. informal • n. a charwoman. • v. (**chars, charring, charred**) work as a charwoman.

char[3] • n. Brit. informal tea.

– ORIGIN Chinese.

charabanc /sha-ruh-bang/ • n. Brit. an early form of bus.

– ORIGIN French *char-à-bancs* 'carriage with benches'.

character • n. **1** the qualities that make a person different from other people. **2** the particular nature of something: *the industrial character of the Midlands.* **3** strength and originality in a person's nature. **4** a person's good reputation. **5** a person in a novel, play, or film. **6** informal an eccentric or amusing person. **7** a printed or written letter or symbol.

– DERIVATIVES **characterful** adj. **characterless** adj.

– ORIGIN Greek *kharaktēr* 'a stamping tool'.

characteristic • n. a quality typical of a person or thing. • adj. typical of a particular person or thing: *he began with a characteristic attack on extremism.*

– DERIVATIVES **characteristically** adv.

characterize (or **characterise**)
• v. (**characterizes, characterizing, characterized**) **1** describe the character or nature of. **2** be typical of: *the dance is characterized by a quick pace.*
– DERIVATIVES **characterization** n.

charade /shuh-rahd/ • n. **1** an absurd pretence. **2** (**charades**) a game of guessing a word or phrase from written or acted clues.
– ORIGIN Provençal *charrado* 'conversation'.

charcoal • n. **1** a black form of carbon obtained when wood is heated in the absence of air. **2** a dark grey colour.
– ORIGIN prob. related to **COAL**.

chard /chard/ (also **Swiss chard**) • n. a variety of beet with edible broad white leaf stalks and green blades.
– ORIGIN French *carde*.

Chardonnay /shah-duh-nay/ • n. a white wine made from a variety of grape used for making champagne and other wines.
– ORIGIN French.

charge • v. (**charges, charging, charged**)
1 ask an amount of money as a price.
2 formally accuse someone of something. **3** rush forward in attack.
4 rush in a particular direction.
5 entrust with a task. **6** store electrical energy in a battery. **7** load or fill a container, gun, etc. **8** fill with a quality or emotion: *the air was charged with menace.* • n. **1** a price asked. **2** a formal accusation made against a prisoner brought to trial. **3** responsibility for care or control. **4** a person or thing entrusted to someone's care. **5** a headlong rush forward. **6** a property of matter that is responsible for electrical phenomena, existing in a positive or negative form.
7 energy stored chemically in a battery for conversion into electricity. **8** a quantity of explosive needed to fire a gun or similar weapon.
– PHRASES **press charges** accuse someone formally of a crime so that they can be brought to trial.
– DERIVATIVES **chargeable** adj.
– ORIGIN Old French *charger*.

charge card • n. a credit card issued by a chain store or bank.

chargé d'affaires /shar-zhay da-fair/
• n. (pl. **chargés d'affaires** /shar-zhay da-fair/) **1** an ambassador's deputy.
2 the diplomatic representative in a country to which an ambassador has not been sent.
– ORIGIN French.

charge nurse • n. Brit. a nurse in charge of a ward in a hospital.

charger • n. **1** a device for charging a

battery. **2** hist. a horse ridden by a knight or cavalryman.

chargrill • v. grill food quickly at a very high heat.

chariot • n. a two-wheeled horse-drawn vehicle, used in ancient warfare and racing.
– DERIVATIVES **charioteer** n.
– ORIGIN Old French.

charisma /kuh-riz-muh/ • n. attractiveness or charm that can inspire admiration or enthusiasm in other people.
– ORIGIN Greek *kharisma*.

charismatic • adj. **1** having a charm that can inspire admiration in other people.
2 (of a Christian movement) that believes in special gifts from God, such as healing the sick.
– DERIVATIVES **charismatically** adv.

charitable • adj. **1** relating to the assistance of those in need. **2** tolerant in judging other people.
– DERIVATIVES **charitably** adv.

charity • n. (pl. **charities**) **1** an organization set up to help those in need.
2 the voluntary giving of money or other help to those in need. **3** help or money given to those in need.
4 tolerance in judging other people.
– ORIGIN Latin *caritas* 'affection'.

charlatan /shar-luh-tuhn/ • n. a person who falsely claims to have a particular skill.
– DERIVATIVES **charlatanism** n.
– ORIGIN Italian *ciarlatano* 'babbler'.

charleston • n. a lively dance of the 1920s which involved turning the knees inwards and kicking out the lower legs.
– ORIGIN named after the US city of *Charleston.*

charlie • n. (pl. **charlies**) informal **1** Brit. a fool. **2** cocaine.
– ORIGIN from the man's name *Charles.*

charm • n. **1** the power or quality of delighting or fascinating other people.
2 a small ornament worn on a necklace or bracelet. **3** an object, act, or saying believed to have magic power.
• v. **1** delight someone greatly. **2** use your charm in order to influence someone: *he charmed her into going out.* **3** (as adj. **charmed**) unusually lucky, as if protected by magic.
– DERIVATIVES **charmer** n. **charmless** adj.
– ORIGIN Old French *charme.*

charming • adj. **1** delightful; attractive.
2 very polite, friendly, and likeable.
– DERIVATIVES **charmingly** adv.

charnel house • n. hist. a building in which corpses or bones were kept.
– ORIGIN Latin *carnalis* 'relating to flesh'.

Charolais /sha-roh-lay/ • n. (pl.

Charolais) an animal of a breed of large white beef cattle.
– ORIGIN named after the *Monts du Charollais*, hills in eastern France.

chart •n. **1** a sheet of information in the form of a table, graph, or diagram. **2** a geographical map used for navigation by sea or air. **3** (**the charts**) a weekly listing of the current best-selling pop records.
•v. **1** make a map of an area. **2** plot or record on a chart.
– ORIGIN Greek *khartēs* 'papyrus leaf'.

charter •n. **1** a document granted by a ruler or government, by which an institution such as a university is created or its rights are defined. **2** a written constitution or description of an organization's functions. **3** the hiring of an aircraft, ship, or motor vehicle.
•v. (**charters, chartering, chartered**) **1** hire an aircraft, ship, or motor vehicle. **2** grant a charter to an institution.
– DERIVATIVES **charterer** n.
– ORIGIN Latin *chartula* 'little paper'.

chartered •adj. Brit. (of an accountant, engineer, etc.) qualified as a member of a professional body that has a royal charter.

charter flight •n. a flight by an aircraft chartered for a specific journey.

Chartism •n. a UK movement (1837–48) for social and parliamentary reform, the principles of which were set out in *The People's Charter*.
– DERIVATIVES **Chartist** n. & adj.

chartreuse /sha-trerz/ •n. a pale green or yellow liqueur.
– ORIGIN named after *La Grande Chartreuse*, a monastery near Grenoble where the liqueur was first made.

charwoman •n. (pl. **charwomen**) Brit. dated a woman employed as a cleaner in a house or office.
– ORIGIN from former *char* or *chare* 'a chore'.

chary /chair-i/ •adj. cautiously reluctant: *leaders are chary of reform.*
– ORIGIN Old English, 'sorrowful'.

chase[1] •v. (**chases, chasing, chased**) **1** follow or run after someone or something so as to catch them. **2** hurry or cause to hurry. **3** try to get: *the company employs people to chase up debts.*
•n. **1** an act of chasing. **2** (**the chase**) hunting as a sport.
– PHRASES **give chase** pursue so as to catch.
– ORIGIN Old French *chacier*.

chase[2] •v. (**chases, chasing, chased**) engrave metal, or a design on metal.
– ORIGIN prob. from Old French *enchasser* 'enclose'.

chaser •n. **1** a person or thing that chases. **2** informal a strong alcoholic drink taken after a weaker one.

chasm •n. **1** a deep crack or opening in the earth. **2** a marked difference between people, opinions, etc.
– ORIGIN Greek *khasma*.

chassis /shas-si/ •n. (pl. **chassis** /shas-siz/) the base frame of a wheeled vehicle such as a car.
– ORIGIN French.

chaste •adj. **1** not having sex at all or not having sex outside marriage. **2** without unnecessary decoration.
– ORIGIN Latin *castus* 'morally pure'.

chasten /chay-s'n/ •v. (often as adj. **chastened**) make someone feel subdued or ashamed.
– ORIGIN Old French *chastier*.

chastise •v. (**chastises, chastising, chastised**) reprimand severely.
– DERIVATIVES **chastisement** n.

chastity •n. the practice of not having sex at all, or of not having sex outside marriage.

chasuble /chaz-yuu-b'l/ •n. a sleeveless outer garment worn by a Christian priest when celebrating Mass.
– ORIGIN Latin *casula* 'hooded cloak, little cottage'.

chat •v. (**chats, chatting, chatted**) **1** talk in an informal way. **2** (**chat someone up**) informal talk flirtatiously to someone.
•n. an informal conversation.
– ORIGIN from **CHATTER**.

chateau /sha-toh/ •n. (pl. **chateaux** or **chateaus** /sha-toh, sha-tohz/) a large French country house or castle.
– ORIGIN French.

chatelaine /sha-tuh-layn/ •n. dated a woman in charge of a large house.
– ORIGIN French.

chatline •n. a telephone service which allows a number of separate callers to talk to each other.

chat room •n. an area on the Internet where users can communicate.

chat show •n. Brit. a television or radio programme in which celebrities talk informally to a presenter.

chattel /chat-t'l/ •n. a personal possession.
– ORIGIN Old French *chatel*.

chatter •v. (**chatters, chattering, chattered**) **1** talk informally about minor matters. **2** (of a bird or monkey) make a series of short high-pitched sounds. **3** (of a person's teeth) click together from cold or fear.
•n. **1** informal talk. **2** a series of short high-pitched sounds.

chatterbox •n. informal a person who chatters.

chatty • adj. (**chattier, chattiest**) **1** fond of chatting. **2** (of a letter) informal and lively.
– DERIVATIVES **chattily** adv. **chattiness** n.

chauffeur • n. a person employed to drive a car. • v. drive a car or a passenger in a car.
– ORIGIN French, 'stoker'.

chauvinism /shoh-vin-i-z'm/
• n. **1** extreme or unreasonable support for your own country or group. **2** the belief held by some men that men are superior to women.
– ORIGIN named after Nicolas *Chauvin*, a French soldier noted for his extreme patriotism.

chauvinist • n. a person who has an extreme or unreasonable belief in the superiority of their country, group, or sex. • adj. relating to chauvinists or chauvinism.
– DERIVATIVES **chauvinistic** adj.

cheap • adj. **1** low in price. **2** charging low prices. **3** low in price and quality. **4** worthless because achieved in a regrettable way: *her moment of cheap triumph.* • adv. at or for a low price.
– DERIVATIVES **cheaply** adv. **cheapness** n.
– ORIGIN Old English 'bargaining, trade'.

cheapen • v. lower the price or worth of.

cheapskate • n. informal a miserly person.

cheat • v. **1** act dishonestly or unfairly to gain an advantage. **2** deprive someone of something by dishonest or unfair means. **3** avoid by luck or skill: *she cheated death in a spectacular crash.* • n. **1** a person who cheats. **2** an act of cheating.
– ORIGIN from former *escheat* 'return of property to the state on the owner's dying without heirs'.

Chechen /che-chen/ • n. (pl. **Chechen** or **Chechens**) a person from Chechnya, an self-governing republic in SW Russia.

check¹ • v. **1** examine the accuracy, quality, or condition of something. **2** make sure that something is the case: *I checked that my passport was still valid.* **3** stop or slow the progress of something. **4** Chess move a piece or pawn to a square where it directly attacks the opposing king. • n. **1** an act of checking accuracy, quality, or condition. **2** a control or restraint. **3** Chess a position in which a king is directly threatened. **4** N. Amer. the bill in a restaurant.
– PHRASES **check in** register at a hotel or airport. **check out** settle your hotel bill before leaving. **check something out** (or **check up on**) investigate something. **in check** under control.
– DERIVATIVES **checker** n.
– ORIGIN Persian, 'king'.

check² • n. a pattern of small squares.

• adj. (also **checked**) having a pattern of small squares.
– ORIGIN prob. from CHEQUER.

check³ • n. US = CHEQUE.

checker • n. & v. US = CHEQUER.

checklist • n. a list of items to be done or considered.

checkmate Chess • n. a position of check from which a king cannot escape.
• v. (**checkmates, checkmating, checkmated**) put a king into checkmate.
– ORIGIN Persian, 'the king is dead'.

checkout • n. a place where goods are paid for in a supermarket or similar shop.

checkpoint • n. a barrier where security checks are carried out on travellers.

check-up • n. a thorough medical or dental examination to detect any problems.

Cheddar • n. a kind of firm smooth cheese originally made in Cheddar in SW England.

cheek • n. **1** either side of the face below the eye. **2** either of the buttocks. **3** rude or disrespectful remarks or behaviour: *he had the cheek to complain.* • v. informal speak rudely or disrespectfully to someone.
– PHRASES **cheek by jowl** close together. **turn the other cheek** choose not to retaliate to an attack. [ORIGIN Gospel of Matthew, chapter 5.]
– ORIGIN Old English.

cheekbone • n. the bone below the eye.

cheeky • adj. (**cheekier, cheekiest**) showing a lack of respect.
– DERIVATIVES **cheekily** adv. **cheekiness** n.

cheep • n. a shrill squeaky cry made by a young bird. • v. make a cheep.

cheer • v. **1** shout for joy or in praise or encouragement. **2** praise or encourage with shouts. **3** (**cheer up** or **cheer someone up**) become or make someone less miserable. **4** give comfort to someone. • n. **1** a shout of encouragement, joy, or praise. **2** (also **good cheer**) cheerfulness; optimism.
– ORIGIN first meaning 'face, expression, mood': from Old French *chiere* 'face'.

cheerful • adj. **1** noticeably happy and optimistic. **2** bright and pleasant: *cheerful colours.*
– DERIVATIVES **cheerfully** adv. **cheerfulness** n.

cheerio • exclam. Brit. informal goodbye.

cheerleader • n. (in North America) a girl belonging to a group that performs organized chanting and dancing at sporting events.

cheerless • adj. gloomy; depressing.

cheers • exclam. informal **1** expressing good

wishes before drinking. **2** Brit. said to express thanks or on parting.

cheery • adj. (**cheerier, cheeriest**) happy and optimistic.
– DERIVATIVES **cheerily** adv. **cheeriness** n.

cheese¹ • n. a firm or soft food made from the pressed curds of milk.
– ORIGIN Latin *caseus*.

cheese² • v. (**be cheesed off**) Brit. informal be irritated or bored.

cheeseburger • n. a beefburger with a slice of cheese on it, served in a bread roll.

cheesecake • n. a rich sweet tart made with cream and soft cheese on a biscuit base.

cheesecloth • n. thin, loosely woven cotton cloth.

cheese-paring • adj. very careful about spending money; mean.

cheesy • adj. (**cheesier, cheesiest**) **1** like cheese in taste or smell. **2** informal cheap, tasteless, or unoriginal: *a cheesy plastic purse.*
– DERIVATIVES **cheesiness** n.

cheetah /chee-tuh/ • n. a large swift-running spotted cat found in Africa and parts of Asia.
– ORIGIN Hindi.

chef • n. a professional cook in a restaurant or hotel.
– ORIGIN French, 'head'.

chef-d'œuvre /shay derv-ruh/ • n. (pl. **chefs-d'œuvre** /shay derv-ruh/) a masterpiece.
– ORIGIN French, 'chief work'.

chemical • adj. relating to chemistry or chemicals. • n. a compound or substance which has been artificially prepared or purified.
– DERIVATIVES **chemically** adv.
– ORIGIN French *chimique*.

chemical engineering • n. the branch of engineering concerned with the design and operation of industrial chemical plants.

chemise /shuh-meez/ • n. a woman's loose-fitting dress, nightdress, or petticoat.
– ORIGIN Latin *camisia* 'shirt, nightgown'.

chemist • n. **1** Brit. a person who is authorized to dispense medicines prescribed by a doctor. **2** Brit. a shop where medicines, toiletries, and cosmetics are sold. **3** a scientist who studies chemistry.
– ORIGIN Latin *alchimista* 'alchemist'.

chemistry • n. **1** the branch of science concerned with the nature and properties of substances and how they react with each other. **2** attraction or interaction between two people: *sexual chemistry.*

chemotherapy /kee-moh-the-ruh-pi/ • n. the treatment of disease, especially cancer, by the use of chemicals.

chenille /shuh-neel/ • n. fabric with a long velvety pile.
– ORIGIN French, 'hairy caterpillar'.

cheque (US **check**) • n. a written order to a bank to pay a stated sum from an account to a specified person.
– ORIGIN from **CHECK**¹, in the former sense 'means of checking an amount'.

chequebook • n. a book of forms for writing cheques.

cheque card • n. Brit. a card issued by a bank to guarantee that a customer's cheques will be paid.

chequer (US **checker**) • n. **1** (**chequers**) a pattern of alternately coloured squares. **2** (**checkers**) N. Amer. the game of draughts. • v. **1** (**be chequered**) be divided into or marked with chequers. **2** (as adj. **chequered**) having successful and unsuccessful periods: *a chequered career.*
– ORIGIN from **EXCHEQUER**.

cherish • v. **1** protect and care for lovingly. **2** keep in your mind: *I will always cherish memories of those days.*
– ORIGIN Old French *cherir*.

Cherokee /che-ruh-kee/ • n. (pl. **Cherokee** or **Cherokees**) a member of an American Indian people formerly living in much of the southern US.

cheroot /shuh-root/ • n. a cigar with both ends open.
– ORIGIN Tamil, 'roll of tobacco'.

cherry • n. (pl. **cherries**) **1** a small, round bright or dark red fruit with a stone. **2** a bright deep red colour.
– PHRASES **a bite at the cherry** Brit. an attempt or opportunity.
– ORIGIN Greek *kerasos*.

cherry-pick • v. choose the best things or people from those available.

cherry tomato • n. a small sweet tomato.

cherub • n. **1** (pl. **cherubim** or **cherubs**) a type of angel, shown in art as a chubby child with wings. **2** (pl. **cherubs**) a beautiful or innocent-looking child.
– DERIVATIVES **cherubic** /chuh-roo-bik/ adj.
– ORIGIN Hebrew.

chervil /cher-vil/ • n. a herb with an aniseed flavour, used in cooking.
– ORIGIN Greek *khairephullon*.

Ches. • abbrev. Cheshire.

Cheshire /che-sher/ • n. a kind of firm crumbly cheese, originally made in Cheshire.

chess • n. a board game for two players,

the object of which is to put the opponent's king under a direct attack, leading to checkmate.
– ORIGIN named after the *Chianti* Mountains, Italy.

chiaroscuro /ki-ah-ruh-**skoor**-oh/
• n. the treatment of light and shade in drawing and painting.
– ORIGIN Italian.

chessboard • n. a square board divided into sixty-four chequered squares, used for playing chess or draughts.

chic /sheek/ • adj. (**chicer, chicest**) elegant and fashionable. • n. stylishness and elegance.
– DERIVATIVES **chicly** adv.
– ORIGIN French.

chest • n. **1** the front surface of a person's body between the neck and the stomach. **2** a large strong box in which things may be stored or transported.
– PHRASES **get something off your chest** informal say something that you have wanted to say for a long time. **keep** (or **play**) **your cards close to your chest** informal be very secretive about your plans.
– ORIGIN Greek *kistē* 'box'.

chicane /shi-**kayn**/ • n. a sharp double bend created to form an obstacle on a motor-racing track.
– ORIGIN French *chicaner* 'quibble'.

chicanery • n. the use of trickery to achieve your aims.

chick • n. **1** a young bird that is newly hatched. **2** informal a young woman.
– ORIGIN from **CHICKEN**.

chesterfield • n. a sofa whose padded back and outward-curving arms are of the same height.
– ORIGIN named after an Earl of *Chesterfield*.

chicken • n. **1** a domestic fowl kept for its eggs or meat. **2** informal a coward. • adj. informal cowardly. • v. (**chicken out**) informal be too scared to do something.
– PHRASES **chicken-and-egg** (of a situation) in which each of two things appears to be necessary to the other.
– ORIGIN Old English.

chestnut • n. **1** a shiny brown edible nut. **2** (also **sweet chestnut** or **Spanish chestnut**) the large tree that produces chestnuts. **3** a deep reddish-brown colour. **4** a reddish-brown horse. **5** (**old chestnut**) a joke or story that has become uninteresting because it has been repeated too often.
– ORIGIN from Greek *kastanea* + **NUT**.

chicken feed • n. informal a very small sum of money.

chickenpox • n. a disease causing a mild fever and itchy inflamed pimples.

chest of drawers • n. a piece of furniture consisting of an upright frame fitted with a set of drawers.

chickpea • n. a yellowish seed eaten as a vegetable.
– ORIGIN Latin *cicer*.

chesty • adj. Brit. informal having a lot of catarrh in the lungs.
– DERIVATIVES **chestiness** n.

chickweed • n. a small white-flowered plant, often growing as a garden weed.

Cheviot /**chev**-i-uht/ • n. a large sheep of a breed with short thick wool.
– ORIGIN from the *Cheviot* Hills between England and Scotland.

chicory /**chi**-kuh-ri/ • n. (pl. **chicories**) **1** a plant with a root which is added to or used instead of coffee. **2** N. Amer. = **ENDIVE**.
– ORIGIN Greek *kikhorion*.

chevron • n. a V-shaped line or stripe, especially one on the sleeve of a soldier's or police officer's uniform to show their rank.
– ORIGIN Old French.

chide /chyd/ • v. (**chides, chiding, chided** or **chid**) scold or rebuke someone.
– ORIGIN Old English.

chew • v. **1** bite and work food in the mouth to make it easier to swallow. **2** (**chew something over**) discuss or consider something at length. • n. **1** an act of chewing. **2** a thing meant for chewing.
– DERIVATIVES **chewable** adj. **chewer** n.
– ORIGIN Old English.

chief • n. **1** a leader or ruler of a people. **2** the head of an organization. • adj. **1** having the highest rank or authority. **2** most important: *the chief reason.*
– ORIGIN Old French.

chief constable • n. Brit. the head of the police force of a county or other region.

chiefly • adv. mainly; mostly.

chewing gum • n. flavoured gum for chewing.

chief of staff • n. the senior staff officer of an armed service or command.

chewy • adj. (**chewier, chewiest**) (of food) needing to be chewed a lot.
– DERIVATIVES **chewiness** n.

chieftain • n. the leader of a people or clan.
– DERIVATIVES **chieftaincy** n. (pl. **chieftaincies**).
– ORIGIN Old French.

Chianti /ki-**an**-ti/ • n. (pl. **Chiantis**) a dry red Italian wine produced in Tuscany.

chiffchaff • n. a warbler (songbird) with brownish plumage.

chiffon • n. a light, see-through silk or nylon fabric.
– ORIGIN French.

chignon /sheen-yon/ • n. a knot or coil of hair arranged on the back of a woman's head.
– ORIGIN French, 'nape of the neck'.

chihuahua /chi-wah-wuh/ • n. a very small breed of dog with smooth hair and large eyes.
– ORIGIN named after *Chihuahua* in northern Mexico.

chilblain • n. a painful, itching swelling on a hand or foot caused by poor circulation in the skin when exposed to cold.
– ORIGIN from CHILL + an Old English word meaning 'inflamed swelling'.

child • n. (pl. **children**) 1 a young human being below the age of full physical development. 2 a son or daughter of any age.
– PHRASES **child's play** an easy task. **with child** old use pregnant.
– DERIVATIVES **childless** adj.
– ORIGIN Old English.

childbirth • n. the process of giving birth to a child.

childhood • n. the state or period of being a child.

childish • adj. 1 silly and immature. 2 like or appropriate to a child.
– DERIVATIVES **childishly** adv. **childishness** n.

childlike • adj. (of an adult) having the good qualities associated with a child, such as innocence.

childminder • n. Brit. a person who is paid to look after children in his or her own house.

children pl. of CHILD.

Chilean /chil-i-uhn/ • n. a person from Chile. • adj. relating to Chile.

chill • n. 1 an unpleasant feeling of coldness. 2 a feverish cold. • v. 1 make cold. 2 frighten or horrify. 3 informal relax: *switch on the TV and chill out.* • adj. chilly.
– ORIGIN Old English.

chiller • n. a cold cabinet or refrigerator for keeping stored food a few degrees above freezing point.

chilli (US **chili**) • n. (pl. **chillies**) 1 (also **chilli pepper**) a small hot-tasting kind of pepper, used in cooking and as a spice. 2 chilli con carne.
– ORIGIN from a Central American Indian language.

chilli con carne /chil-li kon kar-ni/ • n. a stew of minced beef and beans flavoured with chilli.
– ORIGIN Spanish *chile con carne*.

chilly • adj. (chillier, chilliest) 1 too cold to be comfortable. 2 unfriendly.
– DERIVATIVES **chilliness** n.

chime • n. 1 a tuneful ringing sound. 2 a bell or a metal bar used in a set to produce chimes when struck.
• v. (**chimes**, **chiming**, **chimed**) 1 (of a bell or clock) make a tuneful ringing sound. 2 (**chime in**) interrupt a conversation with a remark.
– ORIGIN prob. from CYMBAL.

chimera /ky-meer-uh/ (also **chimaera**) • n. 1 an unrealistic idea or hope. 2 Gk Myth. a female monster with a lion's head, a goat's body, and a serpent's tail.
– ORIGIN Greek *khimaira*.

chimerical /ky-me-ri-k'l/ • adj. impossible to achieve; unrealistic: *chimerical projects.*

chimney • n. (pl. **chimneys**) a vertical pipe which takes smoke and gases up from a fire or furnace.
– ORIGIN Old French *cheminee*.

chimney breast • n. a part of an inside wall that comes out to surround a chimney.

chimney pot • n. a pipe at the top of a chimney.

chimney stack • n. the part of a chimney that sticks up above a roof.

chimp • n. informal a chimpanzee.

chimpanzee • n. an ape native to west and central Africa.
– ORIGIN from a language of the Congo.

chin • n. the part of the face below the mouth.
– PHRASES **keep your chin up** informal remain cheerful in difficult circumstances. **take it on the chin** informal accept a difficult situation bravely or without complaining.
– DERIVATIVES **chinned** adj.
– ORIGIN Old English.

china • n. 1 a fine white ceramic material. 2 household objects made from china.
– ORIGIN Persian, 'relating to China'.

china clay • n. = KAOLIN.

chinchilla /chin-chil-luh/ • n. a small South American rodent with soft grey fur and a long bushy tail.
– ORIGIN from South American Indian languages.

chine /chyn/ • n. the backbone of an animal, or a joint of meat containing part of it.
– ORIGIN Old French *eschine*.

Chinese • n. (pl. **Chinese**) 1 the language of China. 2 a person from China.
• adj. relating to China.

Chinese leaves • pl. n. a kind of cabbage which does not form a firm heart.

chink¹ • n. 1 a narrow opening or crack.

2 a beam of light entering through a chink.
– ORIGIN Old English.

chink² • v. make a light, high-pitched ringing sound. • n. a high-pitched ringing sound.

Chinky (also **Chink**) • n. (pl. **Chinkies**) informal, offens. a Chinese person.

chinless • adj. **1** having a very small chin. **2** informal having a weak character.

chino /chee-noh/ • n. **1** a woven cotton fabric. **2** (**chinos**) casual cotton trousers.
– ORIGIN Latin American Spanish, 'toasted' (referring to the typical colour of the fabric).

chinoiserie /shin-wah-zuh-ri/ • n. **1** the use of Chinese styles in Western art, furniture, and architecture. **2** objects or decorations in this style.
– ORIGIN French.

chintz • n. multicoloured shiny cotton fabric, used for curtains and upholstery.
– ORIGIN Hindi, 'spattering, stain'.

chintzy • adj. **1** decorated or covered with chintz. **2** colourful but fussy or tasteless.

chinwag • n. Brit. informal a chat.

chip • n. **1** a small, thin piece cut or broken off from a hard material. **2** a mark left by the removal of such a piece. **3** Brit. a long rectangular piece of deep-fried potato. **4** (also **potato chip**) N. Amer. a potato crisp. **5** a microchip. **6** a counter used in certain gambling games to represent money. **7** (in football or golf) a short, high kick or shot. • v. (**chips, chipping, chipped**) **1** cut or break a small piece from a hard material. **2** (**chip away**) gradually make something smaller or weaker. **3** (in football or golf) strike the ball to produce a short, high shot or pass.
– PHRASES **chip in 1** contribute to a joint fund. **2** informal interrupt with a remark. **a chip off the old block** informal someone who resembles their mother or father in character. **a chip on your shoulder** informal a long-held grievance. **when the chips are down** informal when a very serious situation arises.
– ORIGIN Old English.

chipboard • n. material made from compressed wood chips and resin.

chipmunk • n. a burrowing squirrel with light and dark stripes running down the body.
– ORIGIN from an American Indian language.

chipolata • n. Brit. a small thin sausage.
– ORIGIN Italian *cipollata* 'dish of onions'.

Chippendale • adj. (of furniture) designed by or in the style of the English furniture-maker Thomas Chippendale.

chipper • adj. informal cheerful and lively.
– ORIGIN perh. from northern English dialect *kipper* 'lively'.

chipping • n. Brit. a small fragment of stone, wood, or similar material.

chippy (also **chippie**) • n. Brit. informal (pl. **chippies**) **1** a fish-and-chip shop. **2** a carpenter.

chiropody /ki-rop-uh-di/ • n. the medical treatment of the feet.
– DERIVATIVES **chiropodist** n.
– ORIGIN from Greek *kheir* 'hand' + *pous* 'foot'.

chiropractic /ky-roh-prak-tik/ • n. a system of complementary medicine based on the manipulation of the joints, especially those of the spinal column.
– DERIVATIVES **chiropractor** n.
– ORIGIN from Greek *kheir* 'hand' + *praktikos* 'practical'.

chirp • v. (of a small bird) make a short, high-pitched sound. • n. a chirping sound.

chirpy • adj. informal cheerful and lively.
– DERIVATIVES **chirpily** adv. **chirpiness** n.

chirrup • v. (**chirrups, chirruping, chirruped**) (of a small bird) make repeated short high-pitched sounds. • n. a chirruping sound.

chisel • n. a hand tool with a long blade, used to cut or shape wood, stone, or metal. • v. (**chisels, chiselling, chiselled**; US **chisels, chiseling, chiseled**) **1** cut or shape with a chisel. **2** (as adj. **chiselled**) (of a man's facial features) strongly defined.
– ORIGIN Old French.

chit¹ • n. Brit. derog. a rude or disrespectful young woman.
– ORIGIN perh. from dialect, 'sprout'.

chit² • n. a short official note recording money owed.
– ORIGIN Hindi, 'note, pass'.

chit-chat informal • n. conversation about unimportant things. • v. talk about unimportant things.

chitin /ky-tin/ • n. a tough substance which forms the external skeletons of some insects, spiders, and crustaceans.
– ORIGIN Greek *khitōn* 'tunic'.

chivalrous • adj. (of a man) polite and gallant, especially towards women.

chivalry • n. **1** the religious, moral, and social code of behaviour which a medieval knight was expected to follow. **2** polite behaviour, especially that of a man towards women.
– DERIVATIVES **chivalric** adj.
– ORIGIN Old French *chevalerie*.

chives • pl. n. a herb with long tubular

leaves and an onion taste, used in cooking.
– ORIGIN Old French.

chivvy •v. (**chivvies, chivvying, chivvied**) esp. Brit. repeatedly tell someone to do something.
– ORIGIN first meaning 'a hunting cry'.

chlamydia /kluh-mid-i-uh/ •n. (pl. **chlamydia**) a very small parasitic bacterium which can cause various diseases.
– ORIGIN Greek *khlamus* 'cloak'.

chloral /klor-uhl/ •n. Chem. a liquid used as a sedative.
– ORIGIN French.

chlorate •n. Chem. a salt containing ClO_3 negative ions together with a metallic element: *sodium chlorate.*

chloride /klor-yd/ •n. a compound of chlorine with another element or group.

chlorinate /klor-in-ayt/ •v. (**chlorinates, chlorinating, chlorinated**) fill or treat with chlorine.
– DERIVATIVES **chlorination** n.

chlorine /klor-een/ •n. a poisonous green gaseous chemical element, used as a disinfectant.
– ORIGIN Greek *khlōros* 'green'.

chlorofluorocarbon /klor-oh-floor-oh-kar-b'n/ •n. see **CFC.**

chloroform •n. a liquid used as a solvent and formerly as an anaesthetic.
– ORIGIN from **CHLORINE + FORMIC ACID.**

chlorophyll /klo-ruh-fil/ •n. a green pigment in plants which enables them to absorb light to provide energy for photosynthesis.
– ORIGIN from Greek *khlōros* 'green' + *phullon* 'leaf'.

chloroplast /klo-ruh-plahst/ •n. a structure in green plant cells which contains chlorophyll and in which photosynthesis takes place.
– ORIGIN from Greek *khlōros* 'green' + *plastos* 'formed'.

choc ice •n. Brit. a bar of ice cream with a coating of chocolate.

chock •n. a wedge or block placed against a wheel to prevent it from moving.
– ORIGIN Old French *çoche.*

chock-a-block •adj. informal, esp. Brit. crammed full with people or things.
– ORIGIN first referring to blocks (pulleys) in tackle running close together.

chock-full •adj. informal filled to overflowing.

chocoholic •n. informal a person who is very fond of chocolate.

chocolate •n. 1 a food made from roasted cacao seeds, eaten as a sweet or mixed with milk or water to make a drink. 2 a sweet covered with chocolate. 3 a deep brown colour.
– DERIVATIVES **chocolatey** (also **chocolaty**) adj.
– ORIGIN from a language of Central America.

choice •n. 1 an act of choosing. 2 the right or ability to choose. 3 a range from which to choose: *a choice of over forty fabrics.* 4 a person or thing chosen. •adj. of very good quality.
– ORIGIN Old French *chois.*

choir •n. an organized group of singers.
– ORIGIN Old French *quer.*

choirboy (or **choirgirl**) •n. a boy (or girl) who sings in a church choir.

choke •v. (**chokes, choking, choked**) 1 prevent someone from breathing by squeezing or blocking the throat or depriving them of air. 2 have trouble breathing. 3 (**be choked with**) (of a space) be filled or blocked with people or things. •n. a valve in the carburettor of a petrol engine used to reduce the amount of air in the fuel mixture.
– ORIGIN Old English.

choker •n. a close-fitting necklace.

cholecalciferol /ko-li-kal-sif-uh-rol/ •n. vitamin D_3, produced naturally in the skin by the action of sunlight.
– ORIGIN from Greek *kholē* 'gall, bile'.

choler /kol-uh/ •n. 1 (in medieval science and medicine) one of the four bodily humours, believed to be associated with an irritable temperament. 2 old use anger or bad temper.
– ORIGIN Greek *kholē* 'bile'.

cholera /kol-uh-ruh/ •n. an infectious disease of the small intestine, causing severe vomiting and diarrhoea.
– ORIGIN Latin, 'diarrhoea, bile'.

choleric /kol-uh-rik/ •adj. bad-tempered or irritable.

cholesterol /kuh-less-tuh-rol/ •n. a compound which occurs normally in most body tissues and is believed to cause disease of the arteries if present in high concentrations in the blood.
– ORIGIN from Greek *kholē* 'bile' + *stereos* 'stiff'.

chomp •v. munch or chew noisily or vigorously.

choose •v. (**chooses, choosing, chose**; past part. **chosen**) 1 pick out as being the best of the available alternatives. 2 decide on a course of action.
– ORIGIN Old English.

choosy •adj. (**choosier, choosiest**) informal very careful in making a choice.
– DERIVATIVES **choosiness** n.

chop¹ • v. (**chops, chopping, chopped**) **1** cut with repeated heavy blows of an axe or knife. **2** strike with a short, heavy blow. **3** get rid of something or reduce it by a large amount. • n. **1** a thick slice of pork, lamb, or veal next to and usually including a rib. **2** a downward cutting blow or movement. **3** (**the chop**) Brit. informal the dismissal of someone or cancellation of something.
– ORIGIN from CHAPPED.

chop² • v. (**chops, chopping, chopped**) (in phr. **chop and change**) Brit. informal repeatedly change your opinions or behaviour.
– ORIGIN perh. related to CHEAP.

chop-chop • adv. & exclam. quickly.
– ORIGIN pidgin English.

chopper • n. **1** a short axe with a large blade. **2** informal a helicopter. **3** (**choppers**) informal teeth.

choppy • adj. (of the sea) rough, with many small waves.
– DERIVATIVES **choppiness** n.

chops • pl. n. informal a person's or animal's mouth, jaws, or cheeks.

chopstick • n. each of a pair of thin, tapered sticks held in one hand and used as eating utensils by the Chinese and Japanese.
– ORIGIN pidgin English.

chop suey /chop soo-i/ • n. a Chinese-style dish of meat with bean sprouts, bamboo shoots, and onions.
– ORIGIN Chinese, 'mixed bits'.

choral • adj. relating to or sung by a choir or chorus.

chorale • n. a simple, stately hymn tune for a choir or chorus.
– ORIGIN from Latin *cantus choralis*.

chord¹ • n. a group of three or more musical notes sounded together in harmony.
– ORIGIN from ACCORD.

> **USAGE:** Do not confuse **chord** with **cord**. **Chord** means 'a group of musical notes' (*an E major chord*), whereas **cord** means 'thin string or rope' or 'a part of the body resembling string or rope' (*the spinal cord*).

chord² • n. a straight line joining the ends of an arc.
– PHRASES **strike a chord** affect or stir someone's emotions.
– ORIGIN from CORD.

chore • n. a routine or boring task, especially a household one.
– ORIGIN from former *char* or *chare* 'an odd job'.

choreograph /ko-ri-uh-grahf/ • v. compose the sequence of steps and moves for a ballet or other dance.

choreographer /ko-ri-og-ruh-fer/ • n. a person who designs the steps and moves for a dance.

choreography /ko-ri-og-ruh-fi/ • n. **1** the sequence of steps and movements in dance. **2** the practice of designing dance steps and movements.
– DERIVATIVES **choreographic** adj.
– ORIGIN Greek *khoreia* 'dancing together'.

chorister • n. a member of a church choir.
– ORIGIN Old French *cueriste*.

chortle • v. (**chortles, chortling, chortled**) laugh loudly.
– ORIGIN coined by Lewis Carroll in *Through the Looking-Glass*.

chorus • n. (pl. **choruses**) **1** part of a song which is repeated after each verse. **2** a group of singers performing with an orchestra. **3** a group of singers or dancers in a musical or an opera. **4** something said at the same time by many people. **5** (in ancient Greek tragedy) a group of performers who comment on the action of the play. • v. (**choruses, chorusing, chorused**) (of a group) say the same thing all together.
– ORIGIN Greek *khoros*.

chorus girl • n. a young woman who sings or dances in the chorus of a musical.

chose past of CHOOSE.

chosen past part. of CHOOSE.

chough /chuff/ • n. a black bird of the crow family with a red or yellow bill.

choux pastry /shoo/ • n. very light pastry made with egg.
– ORIGIN French *chou* 'cabbage'.

chow /chow/ • n. **1** informal food. **2** a Chinese breed of dog with a tail curled over its back.
– ORIGIN from pidgin English *chow chow* 'mixed pickle'.

chowder • n. a rich soup containing fish, clams, or corn.
– ORIGIN perh. from French *chaudière* 'stew pot'.

chow mein /chow mayn/ • n. a Chinese-style dish of fried noodles served with shredded meat or seafood and vegetables.
– ORIGIN Chinese, 'stir-fried noodles'.

Christ • n. the title given to Jesus.
– ORIGIN Greek *Khristos* 'anointed one'.

christen • v. **1** name a baby at baptism to mark their entry to a Christian Church. **2** informal use for the first time.
– DERIVATIVES **christening** n.
– ORIGIN Old English, 'make Christian'.

Christendom • n. literary the worldwide body of Christians.

Christian • adj. relating to or believing

in Christianity or its teachings. •n. a person who has received Christian baptism or is a believer in Christianity.
– DERIVATIVES **Christianize** (or **Christianise**) v.

Christianity •n. the religion based on the teaching and works of Jesus Christ.

Christian name •n. a forename, especially one given at baptism.

Christian Science •n. the beliefs and practices of the Church of Christ Scientist, a Christian sect.
– DERIVATIVES **Christian Scientist** n.

Christmas •n. (pl. **Christmases**) 1 (also **Christmas Day**) the annual Christian festival celebrating the birth of Jesus, held on 25 December. 2 the period immediately before and after 25 December.
– ORIGIN Old English, 'Mass of Christ'.

Christmas pudding •n. Brit. a rich pudding eaten at Christmas, made with flour, suet, and dried fruit.

Christmas tree •n. an evergreen or artificial tree decorated with ornaments at Christmas.

chromatic •adj. 1 (of a musical scale) rising or falling by semitones. 2 relating to or produced by colour.
– ORIGIN Greek *khrōmatikos*.

chromatography /kroh-muh-tog-ruh-fi/ •n. Chem. a technique for separating a mixture by passing it through a medium in which the components move at different rates.
– DERIVATIVES **chromatograph** n. **chromatographic** adj.
– ORIGIN from Greek *khrōma* 'colour'.

chrome •n. a hard shiny metal coating made from chromium.
– ORIGIN Greek *khrōma* 'colour'.

chromium •n. a hard white metallic chemical element used in stainless steel and other alloys.

chromosome •n. a thread-like structure in a cell nucleus, carrying the genes.
– DERIVATIVES **chromosomal** adj.
– ORIGIN from Greek *khrōma* 'colour' + *sōma* 'body'.

chronic •adj. 1 (of an illness or problem) lasting for a long time. 2 having a bad habit: *a chronic liar.* 3 Brit. informal very bad.
– DERIVATIVES **chronically** adv.
– ORIGIN Greek *khronikos* 'of time'.

chronic fatigue syndrome •n. a medical condition of unknown cause, with aching and prolonged tiredness.

chronicle •n. a written account of historical events in the order in which they occurred. •v. (**chronicles**,

chronicling, **chronicled**) record events in a factual way.
– DERIVATIVES **chronicler** n.
– ORIGIN Greek *khronika* 'annals'.

chronograph •n. an instrument for recording time very accurately.

chronological •adj. 1 (of a record of events) following the order in which they occurred. 2 relating to the establishment of dates of past events.
– DERIVATIVES **chronologically** adv.

chronology /kruh-nol-uh-ji/ •n. (pl. **chronologies**) 1 the arrangement of events in the order in which they occurred. 2 the study of records to establish the dates of past events. 3 a list of events in chronological order.
– ORIGIN Greek *khronos* 'time'.

chronometer /kruh-nom-i-ter/ •n. an instrument for measuring time accurately in spite of motion or varying conditions.

chrysalis /kriss-uh-liss/ •n. (pl. **chrysalises**) 1 an insect pupa, especially of a butterfly or moth. 2 the hard case enclosing an insect pupa.
– ORIGIN Greek *khrusallis*.

chrysanthemum /kri-san-thi-muhm/ •n. (pl. **chrysanthemums**) a garden plant with brightly coloured flowers.
– ORIGIN from Greek *khrusos* 'gold' + *anthemon* 'flower'.

chub •n. a thick-bodied river fish.

Chubb •n. trademark a lock with a device for fixing the bolt to prevent it from being picked.
– ORIGIN named after the London locksmith Charles *Chubb*.

chubby •adj. (**chubbier**, **chubbiest**) plump and rounded.
– ORIGIN from **CHUB**.

chuck¹ •v. informal 1 throw something carelessly or casually. 2 (**chuck something away/out**) throw something away.
– ORIGIN from **CHUCK²**.

chuck² •v. touch someone playfully under the chin.
– ORIGIN prob. from Old French *chuquer* 'to knock, bump'.

chuck³ •n. 1 a device for holding an object being worked on in a lathe or a tool in a drill. 2 (also **chuck steak**) a cut of beef extending from the neck to the ribs.
– ORIGIN from **CHOCK**.

chuckle •v. (**chuckles**, **chuckling**, **chuckled**) laugh quietly or inwardly. •n. a quiet laugh.
– ORIGIN from a former word meaning 'to cluck'.

chuff •v. (of a steam engine) move with a

regular puffing sound.

chuffed • adj. Brit. informal delighted.
– ORIGIN dialect *chuff* 'plump, pleased'.

chug • v. (**chugs**, **chugging**, **chugged**) move with the regular puffing sound of an engine running slowly.

chukka • n. each of six periods into which play in a game of polo is divided.
– ORIGIN Sanskrit, 'circle or wheel'.

chum • n. informal a close friend.
– DERIVATIVES **chummy** adj.
– ORIGIN Oxford University slang for a room-mate: prob. from *chamber-fellow*.

chump • n. **1** informal a foolish person. **2** Brit. the thick end of a loin of lamb or mutton.
– ORIGIN prob. from **CHUNK** and **LUMP**[1].

chunder informal, esp. Austral./NZ • v. (**chunders**, **chundering**, **chundered**) vomit.
– ORIGIN prob. from rhyming slang *Chunder Loo* 'spew'.

chunk • n. **1** a thick, solid piece. **2** a large amount.
– ORIGIN prob. from **CHUCK**[3].

chunky • adj. (**chunkier**, **chunkiest**) **1** bulky and thick. **2** containing chunks.

church • n. **1** a building used for public Christian worship. **2** (**Church**) a particular Christian organization. **3** the Christian religion as an institution with political or social influence.
– ORIGIN from Greek *kuriakon dōma* 'Lord's house'.

churchman (or **churchwoman**) • n. (pl. **churchmen** or **churchwomen**) a member of the Christian clergy or of a Church.

Church of England • n. the English branch of the Western Christian Church, which has the reigning king or queen as its head.

Church of Scotland • n. the national (Presbyterian) Christian Church in Scotland.

churchwarden • n. either of two people who are elected by an Anglican congregation to take care of church property.

churchyard • n. an enclosed area surrounding a church.

churl • n. a rude or bad-tempered person.
– ORIGIN Old English.

churlish • adj. rude or bad-tempered.
– DERIVATIVES **churlishly** adv.

churn • n. **1** a machine for making butter by shaking milk or cream. **2** Brit. a large metal milk can. • v. **1** (of liquid) move about vigorously. **2** (**churn something out**) produce something in large quantities and without much thought. **3** shake milk or cream in a churn to produce butter.

– ORIGIN Old English.

chute (also **shoot**) • n. **1** a sloping channel for moving things to a lower level. **2** a water slide into a swimming pool.
– ORIGIN French, 'fall'.

chutney • n. (pl. **chutneys**) a spicy pickle made of fruits or vegetables with vinegar and sugar.
– ORIGIN Hindi.

chutzpah /khuuts-puh/ • n. informal extreme self-confidence.
– ORIGIN Yiddish.

chyle /kyl/ • n. a milky fluid which drains from the small intestine into the lymphatic system during digestion.
– ORIGIN Greek *khūlos*.

chyme /kym/ • n. the fluid which passes from the stomach to the small intestine, consisting of gastric juices and partly digested food.
– ORIGIN Greek *khūmos*.

Ci • abbrev. curie.

CIA • abbrev. Central Intelligence Agency.

ciabatta /chuh-bah-tuh/ • n. a flattish Italian bread made with olive oil.
– ORIGIN Italian, 'slipper' (from its shape).

ciao /chow/ • exclam. informal hello or goodbye.
– ORIGIN Italian.

cicada /si-kah-duh/ • n. a large insect with long wings, which makes a continuous high sound after dark.
– ORIGIN Latin.

cicatrix /sik-uh-triks/ (also **cicatrice** /sik-uh-triss/) • n. (pl. **cicatrices** /sik-uh-try-seez/) a scar.
– ORIGIN Latin.

CID • abbrev. (in the UK) Criminal Investigation Department.

-cide • comb. form **1** referring to a person or thing that kills: *insecticide*. **2** referring to an act of killing: *suicide*.
– ORIGIN Latin *-cida*, *-cidium*.

cider • n. Brit. an alcoholic drink made from apple juice.
– ORIGIN Old French *sidre*.

cigar • n. a cylinder of tobacco rolled in tobacco leaves for smoking.
– ORIGIN French.

cigarette • n. a cylinder of finely cut tobacco rolled in paper for smoking.
– ORIGIN French, 'little cigar'.

cigarillo /sig-uh-ril-loh/ • n. (pl. **cigarillos**) a small cigar.
– ORIGIN Spanish.

cilium /si-li-uhm/ • n. (pl. **cilia** /si-li-uh/) Biol. a microscopic hair-like structure, occurring on the surface of certain cells.
– ORIGIN Latin.

C.-in-C. • abbrev. Commander-in-Chief.

cinch • n. informal **1** a very easy task. **2** esp. N. Amer. a certainty.
– ORIGIN Spanish *cincha* 'girth'.

cinchona /sing-koh-nuh/ • n. a medicinal drug obtained from the bark of a South American tree, containing quinine.
– ORIGIN named after the Countess of *Chinchón*.

cinder • n. a piece of partly burnt coal or wood.
– ORIGIN Old English.

cine • adj. relating to film-making: *a cine camera*.

cinema • n. esp. Brit. **1** a place where films are shown. **2** the production of films as an art or industry.
– ORIGIN Greek *kinēma* 'movement'.

cinematic • adj. relating to films and film-making.

cinematography • n. the art of photography and camerawork in film-making.
– DERIVATIVES **cinematographer** n.

cinnabar /sin-nuh-bar/ • n. a bright red mineral consisting of mercury sulphide.
– ORIGIN Greek *kinnabari*.

cinnamon /sin-uh-muhn/ • n. a spice made from the dried bark of an Asian tree.
– ORIGIN Greek *kinnamōmon*.

cinquefoil /singk-foyl/ • n. a plant with leaves made up of five small leaves.
– ORIGIN from Latin *quinque* 'five' + *folium* 'leaf'.

cipher (also **cypher**) • n. **1** a code. **2** a key to a code. **3** an unimportant person.
– ORIGIN Old French *cifre*.

circa /ser-kuh/ • prep. approximately.
– ORIGIN Latin.

circadian /ser-kay-di-uhn/ • adj. relating or referring to biological processes that happen regularly once every twenty-four hours.
– ORIGIN from Latin *circa* 'about' + *dies* 'day'.

circle • n. **1** a round plane figure whose boundary is made up of points at an equal distance from the centre. **2** a thing or group of people forming or shaped like a circle. **3** Brit. a curved upper tier of seats in a theatre. **4** a group of people with a shared job, interests, or friends. • v. (**circles, circling, circled**) **1** move or be placed all the way around. **2** draw a line around.
– PHRASES **come full circle** return to a previous position.
– ORIGIN Latin *circulus* 'small ring'.

circlet • n. a circular band worn on the head as an ornament.

circuit • n. **1** a roughly circular line, route, or movement. **2** Brit. a track used

for motor racing. **3** a system of components forming a complete path for an electric current. **4** a series of sporting events or entertainments. **5** a regular journey by a judge around a district to hear court cases.
– ORIGIN Latin *circuitus*.

circuit-breaker • n. an automatic safety device for stopping the flow of current in an electric circuit.

circuitous /ser-kyoo-i-tuhss/ • adj. (of a route or journey) long and not direct.

circuitry • n. (pl. **circuitries**) a system of electric circuits.

circular • adj. **1** having the form of a circle. **2** (of an argument) false because it uses as evidence the point which is to be proved. **3** (of a letter or advertisement) for distribution to a large number of people. • n. a circular letter or advertisement.

circular saw • n. a power saw with a toothed metal disc that rotates at high speed.

circulate • v. (**circulates, circulating, circulated**) **1** move continuously through a closed system or area. **2** pass from place to place or person to person. **3** move around at a social function, talking to many people.

circulation • n. **1** movement around something. **2** the continuous movement of blood round the body. **3** the public availability of something. **4** the number of copies sold of a newspaper or magazine.
– DERIVATIVES **circulatory** adj.

circum- • prefix about; around: *circumnavigate*.
– ORIGIN Latin *circum* 'round'.

circumcise • v. (**circumcises, circumcising, circumcised**) **1** cut off a young boy's or man's foreskin. **2** cut off a girl's or young woman's clitoris.
– DERIVATIVES **circumcision** n.
– ORIGIN Latin *circumcidere* 'cut around'.

circumference • n. **1** the boundary which encloses a circle. **2** the distance around something.
– ORIGIN Latin *circumferentia*.

> ✓ The second part of **circumference** has three e's in it: -**ference**.

circumflex • n. a mark (ˆ) placed over a vowel in some languages to show that it is pronounced differently.
– ORIGIN Latin *circumflexus*.

circumlocution /ser-kuhm-luh-kyoo-sh'n/ • n. a way of saying something which uses more words than are necessary.
– DERIVATIVES **circumlocutory** adj.
– ORIGIN Latin.

circumnavigate • v. (**circumnavigates, circumnavigating, circumnavigated**) sail all the way around.
– DERIVATIVES **circumnavigation** n.

circumscribe • v. (**circumscribes, circumscribing, circumscribed**)
1 restrict; limit. **2** Geom. draw a figure round another, touching it at points but not cutting it.
– DERIVATIVES **circumscription** n.
– ORIGIN Latin *circumscribere*.

circumspect • adj. unwilling to take risks; cautious.
– DERIVATIVES **circumspection** n. **circumspectly** adv.
– ORIGIN Latin *circumspectus*.

circumstance • n. **1** a fact or condition connected with an event or action. **2** unforeseen events outside a person's control: *he was a victim of circumstance.* **3** (**circumstances**) a person's situation in life, especially the money they have. **4** old use ceremony and public display: *pomp and circumstance.*
– ORIGIN Latin *circumstantia*.

circumstantial • adj. (of evidence) consisting of facts that strongly suggest something but do not prove it.

circumvent /ser-kuhm-**vent**/ • v. find a way of avoiding a problem, obstacle, etc.
– ORIGIN Latin *circumvenire*.

circus • n. (pl. **circuses**) **1** a travelling group of acrobats, trained animals, and clowns. **2** informal a scene of frantic or hectic activity: *a media circus.*
– ORIGIN Latin.

cirque /serk/ • n. a steep-sided hollow at the head of a valley or on a mountain-side.
– ORIGIN French.

cirrhosis /si-**roh**-siss/ • n. a chronic liver disease typically caused by alcoholism or hepatitis.
– ORIGIN Greek *kirrhos* 'tawny' (the colour of the liver in many cases).

cirrus /**sir**-ruhss/ • n. (pl. **cirri** /**sir**-ry/) cloud in the form of wispy streaks high in the sky.
– ORIGIN Latin, 'a curl'.

CIS • abbrev. Commonwealth of Independent States.

Cistercian /si-**ster**-sh'n/ • n. a monk or nun of an order that is a stricter branch of the Benedictines.
– ORIGIN from *Cîteaux* in France, where the order was founded.

cistern • n. a water storage tank, especially as part of a flushing toilet.
– ORIGIN Latin *cisterna*.

citadel • n. a fortress protecting or overlooking a city.
– ORIGIN French *citadelle* or Italian *cittadella*.

citation /sy-**tay**-sh'n/ • n. **1** a quotation from or reference to a book or author. **2** a mention of a praiseworthy act in an official report. **3** a note accompanying an award, giving reasons for it.

cite • v. (**cites, citing, cited**) quote a book or author as evidence for an argument.
– ORIGIN Latin *citare*.

citizen • n. **1** a person who is legally recognized as a member of a country. **2** an inhabitant of a town or city.
– DERIVATIVES **citizenship** n.
– ORIGIN Old French *citezein*.

citizenry • n. the citizens of a particular place seen as a group.

Citizens' Band • n. a range of radio frequencies which are able to be used for local communication by private individuals.

citric acid • n. a sharp-tasting acid present in the juice of lemons and other sour fruits.

citron • n. the lemon-like fruit of an Asian tree.
– ORIGIN Latin *citrus* 'citron tree'.

citronella • n. a fragrant natural oil used as an insect repellent and in perfume.

citrus (also **citrus fruit**) • n. (pl. **citruses**) a fruit of a group that includes lemons, limes, oranges, and grapefruit.
– ORIGIN Latin.

city • n. (pl. **cities**) **1** a large town, in particular (Brit.) a town created a city by charter and usually containing a cathedral. **2** (**the City**) the part of London governed by the Lord Mayor and the Corporation, especially with regard to its financial and commercial institutions.
– ORIGIN Latin *civitas*.

cityscape • n. a city landscape.

city slicker • n. informal, derog. a person with the sophisticated tastes or values associated with people who live in a city.

city state • n. esp. hist. a city that with its surrounding territory forms an independent state.

City Technology College • n. (in the UK) a type of secondary school set up to teach technology and science in inner-city areas.

civet /**siv**-it/ • n. **1** a cat native to Africa and Asia. **2** a strong perfume obtained from the scent glands of the civet.
– ORIGIN Arabic.

civic • adj. relating to a city or town or to the duties or activities of its citizens.
– ORIGIN Latin *civicus*.

civic centre • n. Brit. a building which contains municipal offices.

civics • n. the study of the rights and duties of citizenship.

civil •adj. **1** relating to ordinary citizens, rather than to church or church matters. **2** Law non-criminal: *a civil court*. **3** polite.
– ORIGIN Latin *civilis*.

civil disobedience •n. the refusal to obey certain laws as a political protest.

civil engineer •n. an engineer who designs roads, bridges, dams, etc.

civilian •n. a person not in the armed services or the police force. •adj. relating to a civilian.
– ORIGIN Old French *civilien*.

> ✓ There is only one **l** in **civilian**.

civility •n. (pl. **civilities**) politeness.

civilization (or **civilisation**) •n. **1** an advanced stage or system of human social development. **2** the process of achieving this. **3** a civilized nation or area.

civilize (or **civilise**) •v. (**civilizes, civilizing, civilized**) **1** bring a person or people to an advanced stage of social development. **2** (as adj. **civilized**) polite and good-mannered.

civil law •n. law concerned with ordinary citizens.

civil liberty •n. **1** freedom of action and speech subject to laws established for the good of the community. **2** (**civil liberties**) a person's rights to be subject only to laws established for the good of the community.

Civil List •n. (in the UK) an annual allowance voted by Parliament to fund the official expenses of the Queen in her role as head of state.

civil rights •pl. n. the rights of citizens to political and social freedom.

civil servant •n. a member of the civil service.

civil service •n. the branches of state administration, excluding the military and legal branches and elected politicians.

civil war •n. a war between people of the same country.

CJD •abbrev. Creutzfeldt–Jakob disease.

Cl •symb. the chemical element chlorine.

cl •abbrev. centilitre.

clack •v. make a sharp sound as of a hard object striking another. •n. a clacking sound.

clad old-fashioned or literary past part. of CLOTHE. •adj. clothed.

cladding •n. a covering or coating on a structure or material.

claim •v. **1** state that something is the case, without being able to give proof. **2** ask for something which you believe you have a right to. **3** cause the loss of someone's life. **4** ask for money under the terms of an insurance policy. **5** call for someone's attention. •n. **1** a statement that something is the case. **2** a request for something which you believe you have a right to. **3** a request for compensation under the terms of an insurance policy.
– ORIGIN Latin *clamare* 'call out'.

claimant •n. a person who makes a claim.

clairvoyance /klair-voy-uhnss/ •n. the supposed ability to see events in the future or communicate with people who are dead.
– ORIGIN from French *clair* 'clear' + *voir* 'to see'.

clairvoyant •n. a person claiming to be able to see into the future or communicate with the dead. •adj. able to predict the future.

clam •n. a large shellfish with two shells of equal size. •v. (**clams, clamming, clammed**) (**clam up**) informal stop talking suddenly.
– ORIGIN Old English 'bond, bondage'.

clamber •v. (**clambers, clambering, clambered**) climb or move in an awkward way, using the hands and feet.
– ORIGIN prob. from CLIMB.

clammy •adj. (**clammier, clammiest**) **1** unpleasantly damp and sticky. **2** (of air) cold and damp.
– DERIVATIVES **clamminess** n.
– ORIGIN dialect *clam* 'to be sticky'.

clamour (US **clamor**) •n. **1** a loud and confused noise. **2** a strong protest or demand. •v. (of a group) shout or demand something loudly.
– DERIVATIVES **clamorous** adj.
– ORIGIN Latin *clamor*.

clamp •n. a brace, band, or clasp for strengthening or holding things together. •v. **1** fasten in place or together with a clamp. **2** (**clamp down**) take strict action to prevent something. **3** fit a wheel clamp to an illegally parked car.
– ORIGIN prob. from Dutch.

clampdown •n. informal a determined attempt to prevent something.

clan •n. a group of related families, especially in the Scottish Highlands.
– DERIVATIVES **clansman** n. (pl. **clansmen**).
– ORIGIN Scottish Gaelic, 'offspring'.

clandestine /klan-dess-tin/ •adj. done secretly or kept secret.
– DERIVATIVES **clandestinely** adv.
– ORIGIN Latin *clandestinus*.

clang •n. a loud metallic sound. •v. make a clang.

clanger •n. Brit. informal an embarrassing mistake.

clangour /klang-ger/ (US **clangor**) •n. a continuous clanging sound.
– ORIGIN Latin *clangor*.

clank •n. a sharp sound as of pieces of metal being struck together. •v. make a clank.

clannish •adj. (of a group) excluding other people outside the group.

clap[1] •v. (**claps**, **clapping**, **clapped**) **1** strike the palms of the hands together repeatedly, especially to applaud. **2** slap someone encouragingly on the back. **3** put or place somewhere quickly or suddenly: *he clapped a hand to his forehead.* •n. **1** an act of clapping. **2** an explosive sound, especially of thunder.
– ORIGIN Old English.

clap[2] •n. informal gonorrhoea.
– ORIGIN Old French *clapoir*.

clapped-out •adj. Brit. informal worn out.

clapper •n. the striker of a bell.
– PHRASES **like the clappers** Brit. informal very fast or hard.

clapperboard •n. hinged boards that are struck together at the beginning of filming to ensure that the picture and sound machinery start at the same time.

claptrap •n. nonsense.
– ORIGIN first referring to something designed to make people applaud.

claque /klak/ •n. **1** a group of people who admire or support someone in an excessively obedient or respectful way. **2** a group of people hired to applaud or heckle a performer.
– ORIGIN French.

claret /kla-ruht/ •n. **1** a red wine, especially from Bordeaux in France. **2** a purplish red colour.
– ORIGIN from Latin *claratum vinum* 'clarified wine'.

clarify •v. (**clarifies**, **clarifying**, **clarified**) **1** make something easier to understand. **2** melt butter in order to separate out the impurities.
– DERIVATIVES **clarification** n.
– ORIGIN Old French *clarifier*.

clarinet •n. a woodwind instrument with holes stopped by keys and a mouthpiece with a single reed.
– DERIVATIVES **clarinettist** (US **clarinetist**) n.
– ORIGIN French *clarinette*.

clarion /kla-ri-uhn/ •adj. literary loud and clear.
– PHRASES **clarion call** a clear, strongly expressed demand for action.
– ORIGIN Latin, 'war trumpet'.

clarity •n. **1** the state or quality of being clear and easily understood. **2** transparency or purity.
– ORIGIN Latin *claritas*.

clash •n. **1** a conflict or disagreement. **2** an inconvenient occurrence of dates or events at the same time. **3** a loud discordant sound. •v. **1** (of opposing groups) come into violent conflict. **2** disagree or be at odds. **3** (of colours) look unpleasant when put together. **4** (of dates or events) occur inconveniently at the same time. **5** strike cymbals together, producing a loud harsh sound.

clasp •v. **1** grasp something tightly with your hand. **2** place your arms tightly around something. **3** fasten something with a clasp. •n. **1** a device with interlocking parts used for fastening. **2** an act of clasping.

clasp knife •n. a knife with a blade that folds into the handle.

class •n. **1** a set or category of things having a common characteristic. **2** a system that divides members of a society into sets based on social or economic status. **3** a set in a society based on social or economic status. **4** a group of students or pupils who are taught together. **5** a lesson. **6** Biol. a category into which animals and plants with similar characteristics are divided, ranking above order and below phylum. **7** informal impressive stylishness. •v. put in a particular category.
– ORIGIN Latin *classis*.

classic •adj. **1** judged over a period of time to be of the highest quality. **2** typical. •n. **1** a work of art which is generally agreed to be of high quality. **2** (**Classics**) the study of ancient Greek and Latin literature, philosophy, and history. **3** (**the classics**) the works of ancient Greek and Latin writers.
– ORIGIN Latin *classicus*.

classical •adj. **1** relating to ancient Greek or Latin literature, art, or culture. **2** (of a form of art or a language) representing the highest standard within a long-established form. **3** (of music) written in the European tradition between approximately 1750 and 1830.
– DERIVATIVES **classically** adv.

classicism •n. the use of a simple and elegant style characteristic of the art, architecture, or literature of ancient Greece and Rome.

classicist •n. a person who studies Classics.

classification •n. **1** the action of classifying something. **2** a category into which something is put.
– DERIVATIVES **classificatory** adj.

classified •adj. **1** (of newspaper or magazine advertisements) organized in categories. **2** (of information or documents) officially classed as secret. ● n. (**classifieds**) classified advertisements.

classify ● v. (**classifies, classifying, classified**) **1** arrange a group in classes. **2** put in a class or category. **3** make documents or information officially secret.
– DERIVATIVES **classifiable** adj. **classifier** n.

classless ● adj. **1** not divided into social classes. **2** not showing characteristics of a particular social class.

classroom ● n. a room in which a class of pupils or students is taught.

classy ● adj. (**classier, classiest**) informal stylish and sophisticated.

clatter ● n. a loud rattling sound as of hard objects striking each other. ● v. (**clatters, clattering, clattered**) make a clatter.
– ORIGIN Old English.

clause ● n. **1** a group of words that includes a subject and a verb, forming a sentence or part of a sentence. **2** a particular and separate item of a treaty, bill, or contract.
– ORIGIN Old French.

claustrophobia /kloss-truh-foh-bi-uh/ ● n. extreme fear of being in an enclosed place.
– DERIVATIVES **claustrophobic** adj.
– ORIGIN Latin *claustrum* 'lock'.

clavichord /klav-i-kord/ ● n. a small early keyboard instrument with a soft tone.
– ORIGIN Latin *clavichordium*.

clavicle ● n. the collarbone.
– ORIGIN Latin *clavicula* 'small key'.

claw ● n. **1** a curved horny nail on each digit of the foot in birds, lizards, and some mammals. **2** the pincer of a shellfish. ● v. **1** scratch or tear at with the claws or fingernails. **2** (**claw something back**) manage to get back something that has been lost.
– ORIGIN Old English.

claw hammer ● n. a hammer with one side of the head split and curved.

clay ● n. a heavy, sticky earth that can be moulded when wet and baked to make bricks and pottery.
– ORIGIN Old English.

claymore ● n. hist. a type of large sword used in Scotland.
– ORIGIN Scottish Gaelic, 'great sword'.

clay pigeon ● n. a saucer-shaped piece of baked clay thrown up in the air as a target for shooting.

clean ● adj. **1** free from dirt or harmful substances. **2** not obscene or immoral. **3** showing or having no record of offences or crimes: *a clean driving licence.*

4 done according to the rules: *a good clean fight.* **5** having a smooth and regular surface: *a clean fracture.* **6** (of an action) smoothly and skilfully done. ● v. **1** make clean. **2** (**clean someone out**) informal use up or take all someone's money. **3** (**clean up**) informal make a large gain or profit. ● adv. **1** so as to be free from dirt. **2** informal completely: *I clean forgot.* ● n. an act of cleaning.
– PHRASES **come clean** (or **make a clean breast of it**) informal fully confess something.
– DERIVATIVES **cleaner** n.
– ORIGIN Old English.

clean-cut ● adj. (of a person) looking neat and respectable.

cleanliness /klen-li-nuhss/ ● n. the state of being clean or the habit of keeping clean.

cleanly /kleen-li/ ● adv. in a clean way.

cleanse /klenz/ ● v. (**cleanses, cleansing, cleansed**) **1** make thoroughly clean. **2** rid of something unpleasant or unwanted.
– ORIGIN Old English.

clean-shaven ● adj. (of a man) not having a beard or moustache.

clear ● adj. **1** easy to see, hear, or understand. **2** leaving or feeling no doubt. **3** transparent. **4** free of obstructions or unwanted objects. **5** (of a period of time) free of commitments. **6** free from disease or guilt. **7** (**clear of**) not touching. **8** complete: *seven clear days' notice.* ● adv. **1** so as to be out of the way of or not obstructed by. **2** so as to be easily heard or seen. ● v. **1** make or become clear. **2** get past or over something safely or without touching it. **3** show or declare someone to be innocent. **4** give official approval to. **5** make people leave a building or place. **6** (of a cheque) be paid into a person's account.
– PHRASES **clear the air 1** make the air less humid. **2** improve a tense situation by frank discussion. **clear off** (or **out**) informal go away. **clear something out** informal empty something. **clear up 1** (of an illness or other medical condition) become cured. **2** (of the weather) become fine. **clear something up 1** tidy something. **2** solve or explain something. **in the clear** no longer in danger or under suspicion.
– DERIVATIVES **clearness** n.
– ORIGIN Old French *cler.*

clearance ● n. **1** the action of clearing. **2** official authorization for something to take place. **3** clear space allowed for a thing to move past or under another.

clear-cut ● adj. easy to see or understand.

clearing[1] • n. an open space in a forest.

clearing[2] • n. Brit. a system used by universities to fill the remaining available undergraduate places before the start of the academic year.

clearing house • n. a bankers' establishment where cheques and bills from member banks (**clearing banks**) are exchanged.

clearly • adv. 1 in a clear way. 2 without doubt.

clear-sighted • adj. thinking clearly.

clearway • n. Brit. a main road other than a motorway on which vehicles are not allowed to stop.

cleat • n. 1 a T-shaped projection to which a rope may be attached. 2 a projecting piece of rubber or metal on the sole of a shoe, to prevent a person from slipping.
– ORIGIN Germanic.

cleavage • n. 1 the space between a woman's breasts. 2 a marked difference or division between people.

cleave[1] • v. (**cleaves**, **cleaving**, **clove** or **cleft** or **cleaved**; past part. **cloven** or **cleft** or **cleaved**) 1 split along a natural grain or line. 2 divide; split.
– ORIGIN Old English.

cleave[2] • v. (**cleaves**, **cleaving**, **cleaved**) (**cleave to**) literary 1 stick fast to. 2 become emotionally attached to.
– ORIGIN Old English.

cleaver • n. a tool with a heavy broad blade, used for chopping meat.

clef • n. Music any of several symbols placed on a stave to show the pitch of the notes written on the stave.
– ORIGIN French.

cleft past part. of **CLEAVE**[1]. • adj. split, divided, or partly divided into two. • n. a split, crack, or partial division in the ground or part of a person's body.
– PHRASES **in a cleft stick** in a situation in which any action that is taken will have undesirable results.

cleft lip • n. a split in the upper lip on one or both sides of the centre, present from birth.

cleft palate • n. a split in the roof of the mouth which is present from birth.

clematis /klem-uh-tiss/ • n. a climbing plant with white, pink, or purple flowers.
– ORIGIN Greek klēmatis.

clement • adj. 1 (of weather) mild. 2 merciful.
– DERIVATIVES **clemency** n.
– ORIGIN Latin clemens.

clementine /klem-uhn-tyn/ • n. an orange-red variety of tangerine.
– ORIGIN French, from the man's name Clément.

clench • v. 1 close or press your teeth or fists together tightly, as a reaction to stress or anger. 2 contract a set of muscles sharply. 3 hold something tightly.
– ORIGIN Old English.

clerestory /kleer-stor-i/ • n. (pl. **clerestories**) the upper part of the nave, choir, and transepts of a large church, with windows which allow light into the building.
– ORIGIN from **CLEAR** + **STOREY**.

clergy /kler-ji/ • n. all the people ordained for religious duties, especially those in the Christian Church.
– ORIGIN Latin clericus 'clergyman'.

clergyman (or **clergywoman**) • n. (pl. **clergymen** or **clergywomen**) a Christian priest or minister.

cleric /kle-rik/ • n. a priest or religious leader.
– ORIGIN Latin clericus.

clerical • adj. 1 relating to the work of an office clerk. 2 relating to the clergy.

clerical collar • n. a stiff white collar worn by the clergy in some churches.

clerk /klark/ • n. 1 a person employed in an office or bank to keep records or accounts and to carry out other administrative tasks. 2 a person in charge of the records of a local council or court.
– ORIGIN Latin clericus 'clergyman'.

clever • adj. (**cleverer**, **cleverest**) 1 quick to understand and learn things. 2 skilled at doing something.
– DERIVATIVES **cleverly** adv. **cleverness** n.
– ORIGIN perh. Dutch or German.

cliché /klee-shay/ (also **cliche**) • n. a phrase or idea that has been used so often that it is no longer interesting or effective.
– DERIVATIVES **clichéd** (also **cliched**) adj.
– ORIGIN French.

click • n. 1 a short, sharp sound as of two hard objects coming into contact. 2 Computing an act of pressing one of the buttons on a mouse. • v. 1 make or cause to make a click. 2 move with a click. 3 Computing press a mouse button. 4 informal become suddenly clear. 5 informal become friendly.

client • n. a person using the services of a professional person or organization.
– ORIGIN Latin cliens.

clientele /klee-on-tel/ • n. clients or customers seen as a group.
– ORIGIN French.

cliff • n. a steep rock face at the edge of the sea.
– ORIGIN Old English.

cliffhanger • n. a story or situation that

is exciting because its outcome is uncertain.

climacteric /kly-mak-tuh-rik/ •n. the period of life when fertility is in decline; (in women) the menopause.
– ORIGIN Greek *klimaktēr*.

climactic /kly-mak-tik/ •adj. forming an exciting climax.
– DERIVATIVES **climactically** adv.

climate •n. 1 the general weather conditions in an area over a long period. 2 a widespread trend or public attitude: *the current economic climate.*
– ORIGIN Greek *klima* 'zone'.

climatic /kly-mat-ik/ •adj. relating to climate.

climax •n. 1 the most intense, exciting, or important point of something. 2 an orgasm. •v. reach a climax.
– ORIGIN Greek *klimax* 'ladder, climax'.

climb •v. 1 go or come up to a higher position. 2 go up a hill, rock face, etc. 3 move somewhere, especially with effort or difficulty. 4 increase in scale, amount, or power. 5 (**climb down**) withdraw from a position taken up in an argument or negotiation. •n. 1 an act of climbing. 2 a route up a mountain or cliff.
– ORIGIN Old English.

climber •n. a person who climbs rocks or mountains as a sport.

climbing frame •n. Brit. a structure of joined bars for children to climb on.

clime •n. literary a region with a particular climate: *tropical climes.*
– ORIGIN Greek *klima.*

clinch •v. 1 succeed in securing or winning a contract, contest, etc. 2 settle an argument or debate. •n. 1 an act of grappling at close quarters in a fight. 2 informal an embrace.
– ORIGIN from CLENCH.

clincher •n. informal a fact, argument, or event that decisively settles something.

cling •v. (**clings, clinging, clung**) (**cling to/on to**) 1 hold on tightly to. 2 stick to. 3 be unwilling to give up a belief or hope. 4 be emotionally dependent on.
– ORIGIN Old English.

cling film •n. Brit. a thin transparent plastic film used to wrap or cover food.

clingy •adj. (**clingier, clingiest**) 1 (of a garment) clinging to the body. 2 (of a person) too emotionally dependent.

clinic •n. a place where specialized medical treatment or advice is given.
– ORIGIN from Greek *klinikē tekhnē* 'bedside art'.

clinical •adj. 1 relating to the observation and treatment of patients (rather than theoretical studies). 2 calm and

without feeling or sympathy. 3 (of a place) very clean and plain.
– DERIVATIVES **clinically** adv.

clinician •n. a doctor having direct contact with and responsibility for treating patients.

clink •n. a sharp ringing sound, like that made when metal or glass are struck. •v. make or cause to make a clink.
– ORIGIN Dutch *klinken.*

clinker •n. the stony remains from burnt coal or from a furnace.

clip[1] •n. 1 a flexible or spring-loaded device for holding an object or objects together or in place. 2 a piece of jewellery that can be fastened on to a garment with a clip. •v. (**clips, clipping, clipped**) fasten with a clip.
– ORIGIN Old English.

clip[2] •v. (**clips, clipping, clipped**) 1 cut or cut out with shears or scissors. 2 trim an animal's hair or wool. 3 strike sharply or with a glancing blow. •n. 1 an act of clipping. 2 a short sequence taken from a film or broadcast. 3 informal a sharp blow.
– ORIGIN Old Norse.

clipboard •n. a small board with a clip at the top, used for holding papers and providing support for writing.

clipped •adj. (of speech) having short, sharp vowel sounds and clear pronunciation.

clipper •n. 1 (**clippers**) a tool for clipping. 2 a fast sailing ship of the 19th century.

clipping •n. 1 a small piece trimmed from something: *hedge clippings.* 2 an article cut from a newspaper or magazine.

clique /*rhymes with* seek/ •n. a small group of people who spend time together and do not allow other people to join them.
– DERIVATIVES **cliquey** adj. **cliquish** adj.
– ORIGIN French.

clitoris /kli-tuh-riss/ •n. a small sensitive organ at the front end of the external female genitals.
– DERIVATIVES **clitoral** adj.
– ORIGIN Greek *kleitoris.*

cloak •n. 1 an outer garment that hangs loosely from the shoulders over the arms to the knees or ankles. 2 something that hides or covers: *a cloak of secrecy.* •v. cover or hide.
– DERIVATIVES **cloaked** adj.
– ORIGIN Old French *cloke.*

cloak-and-dagger •adj. involving secret activities.

cloakroom •n. 1 a room in a public

building where outdoor clothes and bags may be left. **2** Brit. a room that contains a toilet or toilets.

clobber informal •n. Brit. clothing and personal belongings. •v. (**clobbers, clobbering, clobbered**) **1** hit hard. **2** defeat heavily.

cloche /klosh/ •n. **1** a glass or plastic cover for protecting outdoor plants. **2** (also **cloche hat**) a woman's close-fitting bell-shaped hat.
– ORIGIN French, 'bell'.

clock •n. **1** an instrument that measures and indicates the time. **2** informal a measuring device such as a milometer or speedometer. •v. **1** reach or show a particular time, distance, or speed. **2** (**clock in/out** or Brit. **on/off**) record your arrival at or departure from work, especially by inserting a card in a special clock. **3** Brit. informal see or watch.
– PHRASES **round the clock** all day and all night.
– ORIGIN Latin *clocca* 'bell'.

clockwise •adv. & adj. in the direction of the movement of the hands of a clock.

clockwork •n. a mechanism with a spring and toothed gearwheels, used to drive a mechanical clock or other device.
– PHRASES **like clockwork** very smoothly and easily.

clod •n. **1** a lump of earth. **2** informal a stupid person.
– ORIGIN from CLOT.

clodhopper •n. informal **1** a large, heavy shoe. **2** a stupid or clumsy person.

clog •n. a shoe with a thick wooden sole. •v. (**clogs, clogging, clogged**) block or become blocked.

cloister /kloy-ster/ •n. a covered passage round an open courtyard in a convent, monastery, college, or cathedral.
– ORIGIN Old French *cloistre*.

cloistered •adj. **1** having or enclosed by a cloister. **2** protected from the problems of ordinary life.

clomp •v. walk heavily.

clone •n. **1** an animal or plant produced from the cells of another, to which it is genetically identical. **2** a person or thing regarded as identical to another. •v. (**clones, cloning, cloned**) **1** create as a clone. **2** make an identical copy of.
– ORIGIN Greek *klōn* 'twig'.

clop •n. a sound made by a horse's hooves on a hard surface. •v. (**clops, clopping, clopped**) move with such a sound.

close¹ /rhymes with dose/ •adj. **1** only a short distance away or apart in space or time. **2** (of a connection or likeness) strong. **3** (of a person) part of someone's immediate family. **4** (of a relationship or the people in it) very affectionate or intimate. **5** (of observation or examination) done in a careful and thorough way. **6** uncomfortably humid or airless. •adv. so as to be very near.
•n. Brit. **1** a residential street from which there is no access to other streets. **2** the grounds surrounding a cathedral.
– PHRASES **at** (or **from**) **close quarters** (or **range**) very near. **close-knit** (of a group of people) united by strong relationships and common interests. **close-run** (of a contest) won or lost by a very small margin. **close shave** (also **close call**) informal a narrow escape from danger or disaster.
– DERIVATIVES **closely** adv. **closeness** n.
– ORIGIN Old French *clos*.

close² /rhymes with nose/ •v. (**closes, closing, closed**) **1** move something so as to cover an opening. **2** bring two parts of something together. **3** (**close on/in on**) gradually get nearer to or surround. **4** (**close in**) (of bad weather or darkness) gradually surround one. **5** (**close around/over**) encircle and hold. **6** bring or come to an end. **7** finish speaking or writing. **8** (often **close down/up**) (with reference to a business or other organization) stop or cause to stop trading or operating. **9** bring a deal or transaction to a conclusion. •n. the end of a period of time or an activity.
– ORIGIN Old French *clore*.

closed •adj. **1** not open or allowing access. **2** not communicating with or influenced by other people.
– PHRASES **behind closed doors** in private.

closed-circuit television •n. a television system in which the signals are sent by cable to a restricted set of monitors.

closed shop •n. a place of work where all employees must belong to a particular trade union.

close season (also **closed season**) •n. **1** a period when fishing or the killing of particular animals or game birds is officially forbidden. **2** Brit. a part of the year when a particular sport is not played.

closet •n. esp. N. Amer. a cupboard or wardrobe. •adj. secret. •v. (**closets, closeting, closeted**) shut yourself away in private to talk to someone or to be alone.
– PHRASES **in** (or **out of**) **the closet** not open (or open) about being homosexual.
– ORIGIN Old French.

close-up •n. a photograph or film sequence taken at close range.

closure • n. **1** an act or the process of closing. **2** a device that closes or seals. **3** a feeling that an emotional or upsetting experience has been resolved.

clot • n. **1** a thick semi-solid mass formed from a liquid substance, especially blood. **2** Brit. informal a foolish or clumsy person. • v. (**clots**, **clotting**, **clotted**) form into clots.
– ORIGIN Old English.

cloth • n. (pl. **cloths**) **1** fabric made by weaving or knitting a soft fibre such as wool or cotton. **2** a piece of cloth used for a particular purpose. **3** (**the cloth**) Christian priests as a group.
– ORIGIN Old English.

clothe • v. (**clothes**, **clothing**, **clothed**) **1** provide with clothes. **2** (**be clothed in**) be dressed in.
– ORIGIN Old English.

clothes • pl. n. things worn to cover the body.

clothes horse • n. a frame on which washed clothes are hung to dry.

clothes peg • n. Brit. a wooden or plastic clip for fastening washed clothes to a rope or wire for drying.

clothier /kloh-*thi*-er/ • n. a person who makes or sells clothes or cloth.

clothing • n. clothes.

clotted cream • n. esp. Brit. thick cream made by heating milk slowly and then allowing it to cool while the cream rises to the top in lumps.

cloud • n. **1** a white or grey mass of condensed watery vapour floating in the atmosphere. **2** a mass of smoke, dust, etc. **3** a large number of insects or birds moving together. **4** a state or cause of gloom or anxiety: *inflation is a cloud on the horizon.* • v. **1** (**cloud over**) (of the sky) become full of clouds. **2** make or become less clear. **3** (of someone's face or eyes) show sadness, anxiety, or anger.
– PHRASES **have your head in the clouds** be full of unrealistic thoughts. **on cloud nine** very happy. **under a cloud** under suspicion of having done wrong.
– DERIVATIVES **cloudless** adj.
– ORIGIN Old English, 'mass of rock'.

cloudburst • n. a sudden violent storm with heavy rain.

cloud cuckoo land • n. a state of unrealistic fantasy.
– ORIGIN Greek *Nephelokokkugia*, a city built by the birds in Aristophanes' comedy *Birds*.

cloudy • adj. (**cloudier**, **cloudiest**) **1** having many clouds. **2** (of a liquid) not clear or transparent.
– DERIVATIVES **cloudiness** n.

clout informal • n. **1** a heavy blow.

2 influence or power. • v. hit hard.
– ORIGIN Old English, 'a patch or metal plate'.

clove[1] • n. the dried flower bud of a tropical tree, used as a spice.
– ORIGIN Old French.

clove[2] • n. any of the small bulbs making up a compound bulb of garlic.
– ORIGIN Old English.

clove[3] past of CLEAVE[1].

clove hitch • n. a knot used to fasten a rope to a spar or another rope.
– ORIGIN *clove*, past tense of CLEAVE[1].

cloven past part. of CLEAVE[1].

cloven hoof • n. the divided hoof of animals such as cattle, sheep, goats, and deer.

clover • n. a plant with round white or pink flowers and leaves with three rounded parts.
– PHRASES **in clover** living a comfortable life with plenty of money.
– ORIGIN Old English.

clown • n. **1** a comic entertainer in a circus, wearing a traditional costume and exaggerated make-up. **2** a playful and amusing person. • v. behave in a silly or playful way.
– DERIVATIVES **clownish** adj.
– ORIGIN perh. German.

cloying • adj. unpleasant as a result of being too sweet or sentimental.
– ORIGIN Old French *encloyer* 'drive a nail into'.

club[1] • n. **1** an association dedicated to a particular activity. **2** an organization where members can meet, eat meals, or stay overnight. **3** a nightclub with dance music. • v. (**clubs**, **clubbing**, **clubbed**) **1** (**club together**) combine with other people to do something. **2** informal go out to nightclubs.
– DERIVATIVES **clubber** n.
– ORIGIN from CLUB[2].

club[2] • n. **1** a heavy stick with a thick end, used as a weapon. **2** (also **golf club**) a club used to hit the ball in golf. **3** (**clubs**) one of the four suits in a conventional pack of playing cards, represented by a design of three black leaves on a short stem. • v. (**clubs**, **clubbing**, **clubbed**) beat with a club or similar object.
– ORIGIN Old Norse.

clubbable • adj. sociable and popular.

club class • n. Brit. the class of seating on an aircraft designed for business travellers.

club foot • n. a deformed foot which is twisted so that the sole cannot be placed flat on the ground.

clubhouse • n. a building having a bar

and other facilities for club members.

club sandwich • n. a sandwich consisting typically of chicken and bacon, tomato, and lettuce, layered between three slices of bread.

cluck • v. **1** (of a hen) make a short, low sound. **2** (**cluck over/around**) express fussy concern about. • n. the short, low sound made by a hen.

clue • n. a fact or piece of evidence that helps to clear up a mystery or solve a problem.
– PHRASES **not have a clue** informal be confused or incompetent.
– ORIGIN first meaning a ball of thread, as used to guide a person out of a maze.

clued-up • adj. informal well informed.

clueless • adj. informal having no knowledge, understanding, or ability.

clump • n. **1** a small group of trees or plants growing closely together. **2** a mass or lump of something. • v. **1** form into a clump or mass. **2** walk heavily.
– ORIGIN from CLUB².

clumpy • adj. Brit. (of shoes or boots) heavy and clumsy-looking.

clumsy • adj. (**clumsier, clumsiest**) **1** not smooth or graceful in movement or action. **2** difficult to use. **3** tactless.
– DERIVATIVES **clumsily** adv. **clumsiness** n.
– ORIGIN prob. Scandinavian.

clung past and past part. of CLING.

clunk • n. a dull, heavy sound like that made by thick pieces of metal striking together. • v. move with or make a clunk.

cluster • n. a group of similar things placed or occurring closely together. • v. (**cluster, clustering, clustered**) form a cluster.
– ORIGIN Old English.

clutch¹ • v. grasp tightly. • n. **1** a tight grasp. **2** (**clutches**) power or control. **3** a mechanism for connecting and disconnecting the engine and the transmission system in a vehicle.
– ORIGIN Old English.

clutch² • n. **1** a group of eggs fertilized at the same time and laid in a single session. **2** a brood of chicks.
– ORIGIN Old Norse.

clutch bag • n. a slim, flat handbag without handles or a strap.

clutter • v. (**clutters, cluttering, cluttered**) cover or fill with an untidy collection of things. • n. **1** things lying about untidily. **2** an untidy state.
– ORIGIN dialect *clotter* 'to clot'.

Cm • symb. the chemical element curium.

cm • abbrev. centimetre or centimetres.

CMG • abbrev. (in the UK) Companion of St Michael and St George (or Companion of the Order of St Michael and St George).

CND • abbrev. Campaign for Nuclear Disarmament.

CO • abbrev. Commanding Officer.

Co • symb. the chemical element cobalt.

Co. • abbrev. **1** company. **2** county.

c/o • abbrev. care of.

co- • prefix **1** (forming nouns) joint; mutual; common: *co-pilot*. **2** (forming adjectives) jointly; mutually: *coaxial*. **3** (forming verbs) together with another or others: *co-star*.
– ORIGIN Latin.

coach¹ • n. **1** Brit. a single-decker bus with comfortable seats, used for longer journeys. **2** a railway carriage. **3** a closed horse-drawn carriage.
– ORIGIN French *coche*.

coach² • n. **1** an instructor or trainer in sport. **2** a tutor who gives private or specialized teaching. • v. train or teach as a coach.
– ORIGIN from COACH¹.

coachman • n. (pl. **coachmen**) a driver of a horse-drawn carriage.

coachwork • n. the bodywork of a road or railway vehicle.

coagulant /koh-ag-yoo-luhnt/ • n. a substance that causes a fluid to change to a solid or semi-solid state.

coagulate /koh-ag-yoo-layt/
• v. (**coagulates, coagulating, coagulated**) (of a fluid, especially blood) change to a solid or semi-solid state.
– DERIVATIVES **coagulation** n.
– ORIGIN Latin *coagulare* 'curdle'.

coal • n. **1** a black rock consisting mainly of carbon formed from the remains of ancient trees and other vegetation and used as fuel. **2** Brit. a piece of coal.
– PHRASES **haul someone over the coals** reprimand someone severely.
– ORIGIN Old English.

coalesce /koh-uh-less/ • v. (**coalesces, coalescing, coalesced**) come or bring together to form a mass or whole.
– ORIGIN Latin *coalescere*.

coalface • n. an exposed area of coal in a mine.

coalfield • n. a large area which is rich in underground coal.

coalition /koh-uh-li-sh'n/ • n. a temporary alliance, especially one enabling political parties to form a government.
– ORIGIN Latin.

coal tar • n. a thick black liquid distilled from coal, containing organic chemicals.

coal tit • n. a small songbird with a grey back and a black cap and throat.

coaming • n. a raised border round the cockpit or hatch of a boat to keep out water.

coarse • adj. **1** having a rough texture. **2** consisting of large grains or particles. **3** rude or vulgar in behaviour or speech.
– DERIVATIVES **coarsely** adv. **coarseness** n.
– ORIGIN perh. from **COURSE**.

USAGE: Do not confuse **coarse** with **course**. **Coarse** means 'rough' (*my hair is coarse and wavy*), whereas **course** means 'a direction' (*the plane changed course*).

coarse fish • n. (pl. **coarse fish**) Brit. any freshwater fish other than salmon and trout.

coarsen • v. make or become coarse.

coast • n. land next to or near the sea. • v. **1** move easily without using power. **2** achieve something without making much effort: *United coasted to victory.*
– PHRASES **the coast is clear** there is no danger of being seen or caught.
– DERIVATIVES **coastal** adj.
– ORIGIN Latin *costa* 'rib, side'.

coaster • n. **1** a small mat for a glass. **2** a ship carrying cargo along the coast from port to port.

coastguard • n. an organization or person that keeps watch over coastal waters.

coastline • n. a stretch of coast: *a rugged coastline.*

coat • n. **1** a full-length outer garment with sleeves. **2** an animal's covering of fur or hair. **3** an enclosing or covering layer or structure. **4** a single application of paint or similar substance. • v. provide with or form a layer or covering.
– ORIGIN Old French *cote*.

coating • n. a thin layer or covering.

coat of arms • n. a heraldic design or shield that is the symbol of a person, family, corporation, or country.

coat of mail • n. hist. a jacket made of metal rings or plates, used as armour.

coat-tail • n. each of the flaps formed by the back of a tailcoat.
– PHRASES **on someone's coat-tails** benefiting from another person's success.

coax /kohks/ • v. **1** gradually or gently persuade someone to do something. **2** move something carefully into a particular situation or position.

coaxial /koh-ak-si-uhl/ • adj. **1** having a common axis. **2** (of a cable or line) transmitting by means of two concentric conductors separated by an insulator.

cob • n. **1** Brit. a loaf of bread. **2** a corncob. **3** (also **cobnut**) a hazelnut or filbert. **4** a sturdily built horse.

cobalt /koh-bolt/ • n. a silvery-white metallic chemical element.
– ORIGIN German *Kobalt* 'goblin, demon' (from the belief that cobalt had been placed in silver mines by goblins to cause the miners problems).

cobber • n. Austral./NZ informal a companion or friend.
– ORIGIN perh. from English dialect *cob* 'take a liking to'.

cobble¹ • n. (also **cobblestone**) a small round stone used to cover road surfaces.
– DERIVATIVES **cobbled** adj.
– ORIGIN from **COB**.

cobble² • v. (**cobbles, cobbling, cobbled**) (**cobble something together**) put something together quickly and without great care.
– ORIGIN from **COBBLER**.

cobbler • n. **1** a person whose job is mending shoes. **2** (**cobblers**) Brit. informal nonsense. [ORIGIN rhyming slang *cobbler's awls* 'balls'.]

cobra /koh-bruh/ • n. a poisonous snake native to Africa and Asia.
– ORIGIN from Portuguese *cobra de capello* 'snake with hood'.

cobweb • n. a spider's web, especially an old or dusty one.
– DERIVATIVES **cobwebbed** adj.
– ORIGIN from former *coppe* 'spider'.

coca /koh-kuh/ • n. a tropical American shrub grown for its leaves, which are the source of cocaine.
– ORIGIN Spanish.

cocaine /koh-kayn/ • n. an addictive drug made from coca, used as an illegal stimulant and sometimes in medicine as a local anaesthetic.

coccus /kok-kuhss/ • n. (pl. **cocci** /kok-ky/) Biol. any rounded bacterium.
– ORIGIN Greek *kokkos* 'berry'.

coccyx /kok-siks/ • n. (pl. **coccyges** /kok-si-jeez/ or **coccyxes**) a small triangular bone at the base of the spinal column in humans.
– ORIGIN Greek *kokkux* 'cuckoo' (because the bone resembles a cuckoo's bill).

cochineal /koch-i-neel/ • n. a scarlet dye used for colouring food, made from the crushed bodies of an insect.
– ORIGIN French *cochenille* or Spanish *cochinilla.*

cochlea /kok-li-uh/ • n. (pl. **cochleae** /kok-li-ee/) the spiral cavity of the inner ear.
– ORIGIN Latin, 'snail shell or screw'.

cock • n. **1** a male bird, especially of a domestic fowl. **2** a firing lever in a gun which can be raised to be released by the trigger. • v. **1** tilt or bend something in a particular direction. **2** raise the cock of a gun to make it ready for firing. **3** (**cock**

something up) Brit. informal spoil or ruin something.
– ORIGIN Latin *coccus*.

cockade /kok-**ayd**/ • n. a rosette or knot of ribbons worn in a hat to show rank or as part of a uniform.
– ORIGIN French *cocarde*.

cock-a-hoop • adj. very pleased.
– ORIGIN from *set cock a hoop*, prob. referring to the action of turning on a tap and allowing alcohol to flow.

cock and bull story • n. informal an unbelievable story or excuse.

cockatiel /kok-uh-**teel**/ • n. a small crested Australian parrot.
– ORIGIN Dutch *kaketielje*.

cockatoo • n. a crested parrot.
– ORIGIN Dutch *kaketoe*.

cockcrow • n. literary dawn.

cockerel • n. a young domestic cock.

cocker spaniel • n. a small breed of spaniel with a silky coat.
– ORIGIN from **cock**, because the dog was bred to drive game birds such as wood-cock out into the open.

cockeyed • adj. informal 1 crooked or askew; not level. 2 absurd; impractical.

cockfighting • n. the sport (illegal in the UK) of setting two cocks to fight each other.

cockle • n. an edible shellfish with a ribbed shell.
– PHRASES **warm the cockles of someone's heart** give someone a feeling of contentment.
– ORIGIN Old French *coquille* 'shell'.

cockney /kok-ni/ • n. (pl. **cockneys**) 1 a person from of the East End of London. 2 the dialect or accent used in this area.

cockpit • n. 1 a compartment for the pilot and crew in an aircraft or space-craft. 2 the driver's compartment in a racing car. 3 an enclosure where cockfighting takes place.

cockroach • n. a beetle-like insect with long antennae and legs.
– ORIGIN Spanish *cucaracha*.

cockscomb • n. the crest or comb of a domestic cock.

cocksure • adj. arrogantly confident.
– ORIGIN from former *cock* (a euphemism for *God*) + **SURE**.

cocktail • n. 1 an alcoholic drink consisting of a spirit mixed with other ingredients. 2 a dish consisting of a mixture of small pieces of food. 3 a mixture of different substances or factors: *a cocktail of chemicals*.
– ORIGIN first meaning a horse with a docked tail.

cock-up • n. Brit. informal something done badly.

cocky • adj. (**cockier**, **cockiest**) conceited

in a bold or cheeky way.
– DERIVATIVES **cockily** adv. **cockiness** n.
– ORIGIN from **cock**.

cocoa • n. 1 a powder made from roasted and ground cacao seeds. 2 a hot drink made from cocoa powder.
– ORIGIN from **CACAO**.

cocoa butter • n. a fatty substance obtained from cocoa beans.

coconut • n. 1 the large brown seed of a tropical palm, consisting of a woody husk lined with edible white flesh and containing a clear liquid. 2 the white flesh of a coconut.
– ORIGIN Spanish and Portuguese *coco* 'grinning face'.

> The middle of **coconut** is spelled **-co-** (no **a**).

coconut shy • n. Brit. a fairground sideshow where balls are thrown at coconuts in an attempt to knock them off stands.

cocoon /kuh-**koon**/ • n. 1 a protective silky case spun by the larvae of many insects, in which the pupa develops. 2 something that envelops in a protective or comforting way. • v. envelop in a protective or comforting way.
– ORIGIN French *cocon*.

cod¹ • n. (pl. **cod**) a large sea fish which is important as a food fish.
– ORIGIN perh. from Old English 'bag'.

cod² • adj. Brit. informal fake.

coda /koh-duh/ • n. Music the concluding passage of a piece or movement.
– ORIGIN Italian.

coddle • v. (**coddles**, **coddling**, **coddled**) treat in an overprotective way.

code • n. 1 a system of words, figures, or symbols used to represent others, especially for the purposes of secrecy. 2 a series of numbers or letters used to classify or identify something. 3 (also **dialling code**) a sequence of numbers dialled to connect a telephone line with another exchange. 4 Computing program instructions. 5 a set of principles or rules of behaviour. 6 a systematic collection of laws or statutes: *the penal code*. • v. (**codes**, **coding**, **coded**) 1 convert into a code. 2 (as adj. **coded**) expressed in an indirect way.
– ORIGIN Latin *codex* 'block of wood'.

codeine /koh-**deen**/ • n. a painkilling drug obtained from morphine.
– ORIGIN Greek *kōdeia* 'poppy head'.

codex /koh-deks/ • n. (pl. **codices** /koh-di-seez/ or **codexes**) an ancient manuscript in book form.
– ORIGIN Latin, 'block of wood'.

codger • n. informal, derog. an elderly man.
– ORIGIN perh. from **CADGE**.

codicil /koh-di-sil/ • n. an addition or supplement that explains, alters, or cancels a will or part of one.
– ORIGIN Latin *codicillus* 'little book'.

codify /koh-di-fy/ • v. (**codifies, codifying, codified**) organize procedures or rules into a system.
– DERIVATIVES **codification** n.

cod liver oil • n. oil obtained from the fresh liver of cod, which is rich in vitamins D and A.

codpiece • n. (in the 15th and 16th centuries) a pouch covering a man's genitals, attached to a pair of breeches.
– ORIGIN from former *cod* 'scrotum'.

codswallop • n. Brit. informal nonsense.

co-education • n. the education of pupils of both sexes together.
– DERIVATIVES **co-educational** adj.

coefficient /koh-i-fi-sh'nt/ • n. 1 Math. a quantity multiplying the variable in an algebraic expression (e.g. 4 in $4x^2$).
2 Physics a multiplier or factor that measures a particular property.

coelacanth /seel-uh-kanth/ • n. a large sea fish with a tail fin in three rounded parts.
– ORIGIN from Greek *koilos* 'hollow' + *akantha* 'spine'.

coelenterate /see-len-tuh-ruht/ • n. Zool. a member of a group of invertebrate sea animals, including jellyfish, corals, and sea anemones.
– ORIGIN from Greek *koilos* 'hollow' + *enteron* 'intestine'.

coeliac disease /seel-i-ak/ (US **celiac**) • n. a disease in which the small intestine fails to digest and absorb food, caused by a reaction to gluten.
– ORIGIN from Greek *koilia* 'belly'.

coerce /koh-erss/ • v. (**coerces, coercing, coerced**) persuade an unwilling person to do something by force or threats.
– DERIVATIVES **coercion** n. **coercive** adj.
– ORIGIN Latin *coercere* 'restrain'.

coeval /koh-ee-vuhl/ • adj. having the same age or date of origin; contemporary. • n. a person of roughly the same age as yourself; a contemporary.
– ORIGIN Latin *coaevus*.

coexist • v. 1 exist at the same time or in the same place. 2 exist together in harmony.
– DERIVATIVES **coexistence** n.

C. of E. • abbrev. Church of England.

coffee • n. 1 a hot drink made from the roasted and ground seeds of a tropical shrub. 2 the seeds used to make coffee.
– ORIGIN Arabic.

coffee table • n. a small, low table.

coffee-table book • n. a large book with many illustrations.

coffer • n. 1 a small chest for holding valuables. 2 (**coffers**) the money that a government or organization has available.
– ORIGIN Old French *coffre*.

coffin • n. a long box in which a dead body is buried or cremated.
– ORIGIN Old French *cofin* 'little basket'.

cog • n. 1 (also **cogwheel**) a wheel or bar with projections on its edge, which transfers motion by engaging with projections on another wheel or bar. 2 any one of these projections.
– ORIGIN prob. Scandinavian.

cogent /koh-juhnt/ • adj. (of an argument) clear, logical, and convincing.
– DERIVATIVES **cogency** n. **cogently** adv.
– ORIGIN Latin *cogere* 'compel'.

cogitate /koj-i-tayt/ • v. (**cogitates, cogitating, cogitated**) formal think deeply.
– DERIVATIVES **cogitation** n.
– ORIGIN Latin *cogitare* 'to consider'.

cognac /kon-yak/ • n. a high-quality brandy made in Cognac in France.

cognate /kog-nayt/ • adj. 1 (of a word) having the same origin as another word in a different language (e.g. English *father*, German *Vater*, and Latin *pater*). 2 formal related; connected. • n. a word that has the same origin as another in a different language.
– ORIGIN Latin *cognatus* 'born together'.

cognition /kog-ni-sh'n/ • n. the process of obtaining knowledge through thought, experience, and the senses.
– DERIVATIVES **cognitive** adj.
– ORIGIN Latin.

cognizance /kog-ni-zuhnss/ (or **cognisance**) • n. formal knowledge or awareness.
– DERIVATIVES **cognizant** adj.
– ORIGIN Old French *conoisance*.

cognoscenti /kog-nuh-shen-ti/ • pl. n. people who are well informed about a particular subject.
– ORIGIN Italian.

cohabit • v. (**cohabits, cohabiting, cohabited**) live together and have a sexual relationship without being married.
– DERIVATIVES **cohabitation** n. **cohabitee** n.
– ORIGIN Latin *cohabitare*.

cohere /koh-heer/ • v. (**coheres, cohering, cohered**) hold firmly together; form a whole.
– ORIGIN Latin *cohaerere*.

coherent /coh-heer-uhnt/ • adj. 1 (of an argument or theory) logical and consistent. 2 able to speak clearly and logically.

– DERIVATIVES **coherence** n.

cohesion /koh-hee-zh'n/ • n. the fact of forming a united whole.

cohesive • adj. **1** forming a whole. **2** causing people or things to form a whole.

cohort /koh-hort/ • n. **1** an ancient Roman military unit equal to one tenth of a legion. **2** a group of people with a shared feature.
– ORIGIN Latin *cohors* 'yard, retinue'.

coif /koyf/ • n. a close-fitting cap worn by nuns under a veil. • v. /kwuhf/ (**coifs, coiffed, coiffing**) style or arrange someone's hair.
– ORIGIN Old French *coife*.

coiffure /kwah-fyoor/ • n. a person's hairstyle.

coil • n. **1** a length of something wound in a joined sequence of loops. **2** a contraceptive device in the form of a coil, placed in the womb. **3** an electrical device consisting of a coiled wire, for converting the level of a voltage, producing a magnetic field, or adding inductance to a circuit. • v. arrange or form into a coil.
– ORIGIN Old French *coillir*.

coin • n. a flat disc or piece of metal used as money. • v. **1** invent a new word or phrase. **2** make coins by stamping metal.
– ORIGIN Old French 'wedge, die'.

coinage • n. **1** coins as a whole. **2** the process of producing coins. **3** a system of coins; a currency. **4** a newly invented word.

coincide /koh-in-syd/ • v. (**coincides, coinciding, coincided**) **1** happen at the same time or place. **2** be the same or similar.
– ORIGIN Latin *coincidere*.

coincidence /koh-in-si-duhnss/ • n. **1** a remarkable instance of things happening at the same time by chance. **2** the fact of things existing together or being the same: *the firms' coincidence of interest.*
– DERIVATIVES **coincidental** adj. **coincidentally** adv.

coir /koy-uh/ • n. fibre from the outer husk of the coconut, used in potting compost and for making ropes and matting.
– ORIGIN from a language of southern India.

coitus /koh-i-tuhss/ • n. tech. sexual intercourse.
– DERIVATIVES **coital** adj.
– ORIGIN Latin.

coke[1] • n. a solid fuel made by heating coal in the absence of air.

coke[2] • n. informal cocaine.

Col. • abbrev. Colonel.

col • n. the lowest point between two peaks of a mountain ridge.
– ORIGIN French, 'neck'.

colander /kol-uhn-der/ • n. a bowl with holes in it, used for draining food.
– ORIGIN Latin *colare* 'to strain'.

cold • adj. **1** relating to or at a low or relatively low temperature. **2** not feeling, showing, or affected by emotion: *the cold facts.* **3** (of a colour) containing pale blue or grey and giving no impression of warmth. **4** (of a scent or trail) no longer fresh and easy to follow. **5** without preparation; unawares: *he went into the test cold.* • n. **1** cold weather or surroundings. **2** an infection causing a streaming nose and sneezing.
– PHRASES **get cold feet** lose your nerve. **the cold shoulder** deliberate unfriendliness or rejection. **in cold blood** without mercy; deliberately cruel.
– DERIVATIVES **coldly** adv. **coldness** n.
– ORIGIN Old English.

cold-blooded • adj. **1** (of reptiles and fish) having a body whose temperature varies with that of the environment. **2** without emotion or pity.

cold-call • v. visit or telephone someone without their agreement in an attempt to sell them something.

cold cream • n. a cream for cleansing and softening the skin.

cold frame • n. a frame with a glass top in which small plants are grown and protected.

cold-hearted • adj. lacking affection or warmth; unfeeling.

cold snap • n. a brief spell of cold weather.

cold sore • n. an inflamed blister in or near the mouth, caused by a virus.

cold sweat • n. a state of sweating caused by nervousness or illness.

cold turkey • n. informal the unpleasant state caused by abrupt withdrawal from a drug to which you are addicted.

cold war • n. a state of hostility between the countries allied to the former Soviet Union and the Western powers after the Second World War.

coleslaw • n. a salad dish of shredded raw cabbage and carrots mixed with mayonnaise.
– ORIGIN Dutch *koolsla*.

colic • n. severe pain in the abdomen caused by wind or obstruction in the intestines.
– DERIVATIVES **colicky** adj.
– ORIGIN Latin *colicus*.

collaborate /kuh-lab-uh-rayt/

• v. (**collaborates**, **collaborating**, **collaborated**) **1** work jointly on an activity or project. **2** betray your country by cooperating with an enemy.
– DERIVATIVES **collaboration** n. **collaborative** adj. **collaborator** n.
– ORIGIN Latin *collaborare*.

collage /kol-lahzh/ • n. a form of art in which various materials are arranged and stuck to a backing.
– ORIGIN French, 'gluing'.

collagen /kol-luh-juhn/ • n. a protein forming the main structural component of animal connective tissue.
– ORIGIN French *collagène*.

collapse • v. (**collapses**, **collapsing**, **collapsed**) **1** suddenly fall down or give way. **2** fall down as a result of illness. **3** fail suddenly and completely. • n. **1** an instance of a structure collapsing. **2** a sudden failure or breakdown.
– ORIGIN Latin *collabi*.

collapsible • adj. able to be folded down.

collar • n. **1** a band of material around the neck of a shirt or other garment. **2** a band put around the neck of a domestic animal. • v. informal seize or arrest someone.
– ORIGIN Latin *collare*.

collarbone • n. either of the pair of bones joining the breastbone to the shoulder blades.

collate /kuh-layt/ • v. (**collates**, **collating**, **collated**) **1** collect and combine documents or information. **2** compare sources of information.
– DERIVATIVES **collation** n. **collator** n.
– ORIGIN Latin *collatus* 'brought together'.

collateral /kuh-lat-uh-ruhl/ • n. something promised to someone if you are unable to repay a loan. • adj. additional but less important.
– ORIGIN Latin *collateralis*.

colleague • n. a person with whom you work.
– ORIGIN Latin *collega*.

collect¹ /kuh-lekt/ • v. **1** bring or come together. **2** call for and take away; fetch. **3** ask for money or receive a prize or award. **4** buy or find items of a particular kind as a hobby. **5** (**collect yourself**) regain your self-control.
– ORIGIN Latin *colligere*.

collect² /kol-lekt/ • n. (in the Christian Church) a short prayer, especially one used on a particular day.
– ORIGIN Latin *collecta* 'a gathering'.

collectable (also **collectible**) • adj. worth collecting as a hobby. • n. an item valued by collectors.
– DERIVATIVES **collectability** n.

collected • adj. **1** calm and self-controlled. **2** (of works) brought together in one volume or edition.

collection • n. **1** the action of collecting. **2** a group of things that have been collected. **3** a regular removal of mail or rubbish.

collective • adj. **1** done by or belonging to all the members of a group. **2** taken as a whole. • n. a business owned or run as a cooperative venture.
– DERIVATIVES **collectively** adv. **collectivity** n.

collective bargaining • n. negotiation of wages and other conditions of employment by an organized group of employees.

collective farm • n. a farm or group of farms owned by the state and run by a group of people.

collective noun • n. a noun that refers to a group of people or things (e.g. *staff*, *herd*).

> **USAGE:** A **collective noun** refers to a group of people or things and can be used with either a singular verb (*my family was always hard-working*) or a plural verb (*his family were disappointed in him*). You should remember that, if the verb is singular, any following pronouns (words such as 'he', 'it', or 'they') must be too: *the government is prepared to act, but not until it knows the outcome of the talks* (not … *until they know the outcome…*).

collectivism • n. the ownership of land, business, and industry by the people or the state.
– DERIVATIVES **collectivize** (or **collectivise**) v.

collector • n. a person who collects things of a particular type.

colleen /kol-leen/ • n. Irish a girl or young woman.
– ORIGIN Irish *cailín*.

college • n. **1** an educational establishment providing higher education or specialized training. **2** (in Britain) any of the independent institutions into which some universities are separated.
– ORIGIN Latin *collegium* 'partnership'.

collegiate /kuh-lee-ji-uht/ • adj. **1** (also **collegial**) relating to a college or its students. **2** (of a university) composed of different colleges.

collide • v. (**collides**, **colliding**, **collided**) **1** hit by accident when moving. **2** come into conflict.
– ORIGIN Latin *collidere*.

collie • n. (pl. **collies**) a breed of sheepdog with a pointed nose and long hair.
– ORIGIN perh. from COAL (the breed

originally being black).

collier /kol-li-er/ • n. esp. Brit. **1** a coal miner. **2** a ship carrying coal.

colliery • n. (pl. **collieries**) a coal mine.

collision • n. an instance of colliding with someone or something.

collocation • n. **1** the frequent occurrence of a word with another word or words. **2** a word or group of words that occur together frequently (e.g. *heavy drinker*).
– DERIVATIVES **collocate** v.
– ORIGIN Latin.

colloid /kol-loyd/ • n. a homogeneous substance consisting of submicroscopic particles of one substance dispersed in another, as in an emulsion or gel.
– DERIVATIVES **colloidal** adj.
– ORIGIN Greek *kolla* 'glue'.

colloquial /kuh-loh-kwi-uhl/ • adj. (of language) used in ordinary conversation; not formal or literary.
– DERIVATIVES **colloquially** adv.
– ORIGIN Latin *colloquium* 'conversation'.

colloquialism • n. an informal word or phrase.

colloquium /kuh-loh-kwi-uhm/ • n. (pl. **colloquiums** or **colloquia** /kuh-loh-kwi-uh/) an academic conference or seminar.
– ORIGIN Latin.

colloquy /kol-luh-kwi/ • n. (pl. **colloquies**) formal a conference or conversation.
– ORIGIN Latin *colloquium*.

collude /kuh-lood/ • v. (**colludes**, **colluding**, **colluded**) cooperate secretly for a dishonest or underhand purpose.
– ORIGIN Latin *colludere*.

collusion • n. secret cooperation in order to deceive.

colobus /kol-uh-buhss/ • n. (pl. **colobus**) an African monkey with silky fur.
– ORIGIN Greek *kolobos* 'curtailed' (referring to its shortened thumbs).

cologne /kuh-lohn/ • n. eau de cologne or similarly scented toilet water.

Colombian • n. a person from Colombia. • adj. relating to Colombia.

colon[1] /koh-luhn, koh-lon/ • n. a punctuation mark (:) used before a list, a quotation, or an explanation.
– ORIGIN Greek *kōlon* 'limb, clause'.

colon[2] /koh-luhn, koh-lon/ • n. the main part of the large intestine, which passes from the caecum to the rectum.
– DERIVATIVES **colonic** adj.
– ORIGIN Greek *kolon* 'food, meat'.

colonel /ker-nuhl/ • n. a rank of officer in the army and in the US air force, above a lieutenant colonel.
– DERIVATIVES **colonelcy** n. (pl. **colonelcies**).

– ORIGIN Italian *colonnello* 'column of soldiers'.

colonial • adj. relating to a colony or colonialism. • n. a person who lives in a colony.
– DERIVATIVES **colonially** adv.

colonialism • n. the practice by which one country acquires control over another, occupying it with settlers, and exploiting it economically.
– DERIVATIVES **colonialist** n. & adj.

colonist • n. an inhabitant of a colony.

colonize (or **colonise**) • v. (**colonizes**, **colonizing**, **colonized**) **1** make a colony in a place. **2** take over a place for your own use.
– DERIVATIVES **colonization** n. **colonizer** n.

colonnade /kol-uh-nayd/ • n. a row of evenly spaced columns supporting a roof.
– ORIGIN French.

colony • n. (pl. **colonies**) **1** a country or area under the control of another country and occupied by settlers from that country. **2** a group of people of one nationality or race living in a foreign place. **3** a place where a group of people with a common interest live together: *a nudist colony.* **4** a community of animals or plants of one kind living close together.
– ORIGIN Latin *colonia*.

Colorado beetle • n. an American beetle whose larvae are very destructive to potato plants.
– ORIGIN from the US state of *Colorado*.

coloration (also **colouration**) • n. the natural colouring of something.

coloratura /kol-uh-ruh-tyoor-uh/ • n. elaborate ornamentation of a vocal melody, e.g. in opera.
– ORIGIN Italian, 'colouring'.

colossal • adj. very large.
– DERIVATIVES **colossally** adv.

colossus /kuh-loss-uhss/ • n. (pl. **colossi** /kuh-loss-I/) a person or thing of great size or importance.
– ORIGIN Latin.

colostomy /kuh-loss-tuh-mi/ • n. (pl. **colostomies**) a surgical operation in which the colon is shortened and the cut end diverted to an opening in the wall of the abdomen.
– ORIGIN from **colon**[2] + Greek *stoma* 'mouth'.

colour (US **color**) • n. **1** the property of an object of producing different sensations on the eye as a result of the way it reflects or gives out light. **2** one of the parts into which light can be separated. **3** the use of all colours in photography

or television. **4** the shade of the skin as an indication of someone's race. **5** redness of the complexion. **6** interest and excitement: *a town full of colour and character.* • v. **1** change the colour of something. **2** blush. **3** influence, especially in a bad way: *the experiences had coloured her whole life.*
– ORIGIN Latin *color.*

colourant (US **colorant**) • n. a dye or pigment used to colour something.

colouration • n. var. of COLORATION.

colour-blind • adj. unable to tell the difference between certain colours.
– DERIVATIVES **colour blindness** n.

coloured (US **colored**) • adj. **1** having a colour or colours. **2** offens. wholly or partly of non-white descent. • n. offens. a person who is wholly or partly of non-white descent.

colour-fast • adj. dyed in colours that will not fade or be washed out.

colourful (US **colorful**) • adj. **1** having many or varied colours. **2** lively and exciting; vivid.
– DERIVATIVES **colourfully** adv.

colouring (US **coloring**) • n. **1** the process or art of applying colour. **2** the appearance of something with regard to its colour. **3** the natural colours of a person's skin, hair, and eyes. **4** a substance used to colour something.

colourist (US **colorist**) • n. an artist or designer who uses colour in a special or skilful way.

colourless (US **colorless**) • adj. **1** without colour. **2** lacking character or interest; dull.

colt /kohlt/ • n. **1** a young uncastrated male horse. **2** Brit. a member of a junior sports team.
– ORIGIN Old English.

coltish • adj. (of a person) lively and long-limbed but rather ungainly.

columbine /kol-uhm-byn/ • n. a plant with purplish-blue flowers.
– ORIGIN from Latin *columba* 'dove'.

column • n. **1** an upright pillar that supports a structure or stands alone as a monument. **2** a line of people or vehicles moving in the same direction. **3** a vertical division of a page. **4** a regular section of a newspaper or magazine on a particular subject or by a particular person.
– ORIGIN Latin *columna.*

columnist /kol-uhm-ist/ • n. a journalist who writes a column in a newspaper or magazine.

com- (also **co-**, **col-**, **con-**, or **cor-**) • prefix with; together; altogether: *combine.*
– ORIGIN Latin *cum.*

coma /koh-muh/ • n. a state of deep and prolonged unconsciousness.
– ORIGIN Greek *kōma* 'deep sleep'.

Comanche /kuh-man-chi/ • n. (pl. **Comanche** or **Comanches**) a member of an American Indian people of the southwestern US.

comatose /koh-muh-tohss/ • adj. in a coma.

comb • n. **1** an object with a row of narrow teeth, used for arranging the hair. **2** a device for separating and dressing textile fibres. **3** the red fleshy crest on the head of a domestic fowl. • v. **1** arrange the hair with a comb. **2** search in an organized way. **3** prepare wool, flax, or cotton for manufacture with a comb.
– ORIGIN Old English.

combat • n. fighting, especially between armed forces. • v. (**combats**, **combating**, **combated**; also **combats**, **combatting**, **combatted**) take action to reduce or prevent something undesirable: *new measures to combat crime.*
– ORIGIN Latin *combattere.*

combatant /kom-buh-tuhnt/ • n. a person or nation engaged in fighting during a war.

combative /kom-buh-tiv/ • adj. ready or eager to fight or argue.

combat trousers • pl. n. loose trousers with large pockets halfway down each leg.

combe /koom/ • n. Brit. a short valley or hollow on a hillside or coastline.
– ORIGIN Old English.

combination • n. **1** something made up of distinct elements. **2** the action of combining different things. **3** a sequence of numbers or letters used to open a combination lock.

combination lock • n. a lock that is opened using a specific sequence of letters or numbers.

combine • v. /kuhm-byn/ (**combines**, **combining**, **combined**) **1** join or mix together. **2** do at the same time: *combine shopping and sightseeing.* • n. /kom-byn/ a group acting together for a commercial purpose.
– DERIVATIVES **combiner** n.
– ORIGIN Latin *combinare.*

combine harvester • n. a farming machine that reaps, threshes, and cleans a cereal crop in one operation.

combining form • n. a form of a word used in combination with another element to form a word (e.g. *bio-* 'life' in *biology*).

combo • n. (pl. **combos**) informal a small

jazz, rock, or pop band.

combust /kuhm-bust/ • v. burn or be burnt by fire.
– ORIGIN Latin *comburere* 'burn up'.

combustible • adj. able to catch fire and burn easily.

combustion • n. **1** the process of burning. **2** rapid chemical combination with oxygen, involving the production of heat.

come • v. (**comes, coming, came**; past part. **come**) **1** move or reach towards or into a place: *Jess came into the kitchen.* **2** arrive at a place. **3** happen. **4** have or achieve a certain position: *she came second.* **5** pass into a specified condition or state of mind: *his shirt came undone.* **6** be sold or available in a particular form: *they come in three sizes.* **7** (as adj. **coming**) likely to be successful in the future: *a coming man.* **8** informal have an orgasm. • prep. informal when a specified time is reached.
– PHRASES **come about** happen. **come across 1** give a particular impression. **2** meet or find by chance. **come by** manage to get. **come down to** be dependent on a factor. **come from** originate in. **come in** prove to be: *it came in handy.* **come into** inherit money or property. **come of** result from. **come off 1** succeed. **2** end up in a specified situation. **come on 1** (of a state or condition) begin. **2** (also **come upon**) meet or find by chance. **come out 1** (of a fact) become known. **2** declare yourself as being for or against something. **come out with** say in a sudden or incautious way. **come round** esp. Brit. **1** recover consciousness. **2** be converted to another person's opinion. **come to 1** recover consciousness. **2** (of an expense) amount to. **come up** (of a situation or problem) arise. **come what may** no matter what happens.
– ORIGIN Old English.

comeback • n. **1** a return to fame or popularity. **2** informal a quick reply.

comedian • n. (fem. **comedienne**) **1** an entertainer whose act is intended to make people laugh. **2** a comic actor.

comedown • n. informal **1** a loss of status or importance. **2** a feeling of disappointment or depression.

comedy • n. (pl. **comedies**) **1** entertainment consisting of jokes and sketches intended to make people laugh. **2** an amusing film, play, or programme. **3** a humorous play in which the characters find happiness after experiencing difficulty.
– DERIVATIVES **comedic** /kuh-mee-dik/ adj.

– ORIGIN Greek *kōmōidia*.

come-hither • adj. informal flirtatious.

comely /kum-li/ • adj. (**comelier, comeliest**) old use pleasant to look at.
– DERIVATIVES **comeliness** n.
– ORIGIN prob. from former *becomely* 'becoming'.

come-on • n. informal a gesture or remark intended to attract someone sexually.

comestible /kuh-mess-ti-b'l/ • n. formal an item of food.
– ORIGIN Latin *comestibilis*.

comet /kom-it/ • n. a mass of ice and dust with a long tail, moving around the solar system.
– ORIGIN Greek *komētēs* 'long-haired star'.

comeuppance • n. informal a punishment or fate that someone deserves.

comfort • n. **1** a pleasant state of relaxation and well-being. **2** (**comforts**) things that contribute to comfort. **3** relief for unhappiness or worry: *a few words of comfort.* • v. make someone less unhappy.
– ORIGIN Old French *confort*.

comfortable • adj. **1** giving or enjoying physical comfort. **2** free from financial worry. **3** (of a victory) easily achieved.
– DERIVATIVES **comfortably** adv.

comforter • n. a person or thing that comforts.

comfrey /kum-fri/ • n. (pl. **comfreys**) a plant with clusters of purplish or white flowers.
– ORIGIN Old French *cumfirie*.

comfy • adj. (**comfier, comfiest**) informal comfortable.

comic • adj. **1** causing or meant to cause laughter. **2** relating to comedy: *a comic actor.* • n. **1** a comedian. **2** a children's magazine containing comic strips.
– ORIGIN Greek *kōmikos*.

comical • adj. causing laughter, especially through being ridiculous.
– DERIVATIVES **comically** adv.

comic strip • n. a sequence of drawings in boxes that tell an amusing story.

comity /kom-i-ti/ • n. (pl. **comities**) formal considerate behaviour towards other people.
– ORIGIN Latin *comitas*.

comma • n. a punctuation mark (,) showing a pause between parts of a sentence or separating items in a list.
– ORIGIN Greek *komma*.

command • v. **1** give an order. **2** be in charge of a military unit. **3** be in a position to receive: *emeralds command a high price.* • n. **1** an order. **2** authority: *the officer in command.* **3** a group of officers in control of a particular group or operation. **4** the ability to use or control something: *her poor command of English.*

5 an instruction causing a computer to perform a basic function.
– ORIGIN Latin *commandare*.

commandant /kom-muhn-dant/ •n. an officer in charge of a particular force or institution.

commandeer /kom-muhn-**deer**/ •v. (**commandeers, commandeering, commandeered**) officially take possession of something for military purposes.
– ORIGIN Afrikaans *kommandeer*.

commander •n. **1** a person in command. **2** a rank of naval officer next below captain.

commander-in-chief •n. (pl. **commanders-in-chief**) an officer in charge of all of the armed forces of a country.

commanding •adj. **1** indicating or expressing authority; imposing. **2** having or giving superior strength: *a commanding lead*.

commandment •n. a rule given by God, especially one of the Ten Commandments.

commando •n. (pl. **commandos**) **1** a soldier trained for carrying out raids. **2** a unit of commandos.
– ORIGIN Portuguese.

command performance •n. a presentation of a play, concert, or film at the request of royalty.

commedia dell'arte /ko-med-i-uh del-**ah**-tay/ •n. an Italian kind of comedy popular in the 16th–18th centuries, with stock characters.
– ORIGIN Italian, 'comedy of art'.

commemorate •v. (**commemorates, commemorating, commemorated**) honour the memory of someone or something.
– DERIVATIVES **commemoration** n.
– ORIGIN Latin *commemorare*.

commemorative /kuh-mem-muh-ruh-tiv/ •adj. acting to honour the memory of an event or person.

commence •v. (**commences, commencing, commenced**) start or be started; begin.
– ORIGIN Old French *commencier*.

commencement •n. the beginning of something.

commend •v. **1** praise formally or publicly. **2** present as suitable or good; recommend.
– DERIVATIVES **commendation** n.
– ORIGIN Latin *commendare*.

commendable •adj. deserving praise.
– DERIVATIVES **commendably** adv.

commensal /kuh-men-s'l/ •adj. Biol. (of two organisms) having an association in

which one benefits and the other is not harmed but does not benefit.
– ORIGIN Latin *commensalis*.

commensurable /kuh-men-shuh-ruh-b'l/ •adj. formal (of things) able to be measured by the same standard.
– ORIGIN Latin *commensurabilis*.

commensurate /kuh-men-shuh-ruht/ •adj. corresponding in size or degree; in proportion: *salary will be commensurate with age and experience*.

comment •n. **1** a remark expressing an opinion or reaction. **2** discussion of an issue or event. •v. express an opinion or reaction.
– ORIGIN Latin *commentum* 'contrivance'.

commentary •n. (pl. **commentaries**) **1** a broadcast spoken account of a sports match or other event as it happens. **2** the expression of opinions about an event or situation. **3** a set of explanatory notes on a written work.

commentate •v. (**commentates, commentating, commentated**) provide a commentary on a sports match or other event.

commentator •n. a person who broadcasts or writes a commentary.

commerce •n. the activity of buying and selling, especially on a large scale.
– ORIGIN Latin *commercium*.

commercial •adj. **1** relating to or involved in commerce. **2** making or intended to make a profit. **3** (of radio or television) funded by broadcast advertisements. •n. a television or radio advertisement.
– DERIVATIVES **commercially** adv.

commercialism •n. emphasis on making as much profit as possible.

commercialize (or **commercialise**) •v. (**commercializes, commercializing, commercialized**) manage something in a way designed to make a profit.
– DERIVATIVES **commercialization** n.

Commie •n. (pl. **Commies**) informal, derog. a communist.

commingle /kom-ming-g'l/ •v. (**commingles, commingling, commingled**) literary mix or blend.

commiserate /kuh-miz-uh-rayt/ •v. (**commiserates, commiserating, commiserated**) express sympathy or pity; sympathize.
– DERIVATIVES **commiseration** n.
– ORIGIN Latin *commiserari*.

commissar /kom-mi-sar/ •n. an official of the Communist Party responsible for political education.
– ORIGIN Russian *komissar*.

commissariat /kom-mi-**sair**-i-uht/ •n. a military department for the supply of food and equipment.

commission • n. **1** an instruction, command, or duty. **2** a formal request for something to be designed or made. **3** a group of people given official authority to do something. **4** payment to an agent for selling something. **5** the position of officer in the armed forces. • v. **1** order the production of something. **2** bring into working order.
– PHRASES **in** (or **out of**) **commission** in (or not in) working order.
– ORIGIN Latin.

commissionaire /kuh-mi-shuh-**nair**/ • n. Brit. a uniformed door attendant at a hotel, theatre, or other building.
– ORIGIN French.

commissioner • n. **1** a member of an official commission. **2** a representative of the highest authority in an area.

commit • v. (**commits, committing, committed**) **1** do something wrong or illegal. **2** dedicate or allocate to a use or course of action: *we believe in committing our resources to education.* **3** (**commit oneself**) promise to do something. **4** (**commit something to**) put something in a safe place. **5** send to prison or a psychiatric hospital.
– ORIGIN Latin *committere*.

commitment • n. **1** dedication to a cause or policy. **2** a promise. **3** an engagement or duty that restricts freedom of action: *business commitments.*

> ✓ Spell **commitment** with a double **m** and a single **t** in the middle.

committal • n. the sending of someone to prison or a psychiatric hospital, or for trial.

committed • adj. dedicated to a cause, activity, job, etc.

committee • n. a group of people appointed for a particular function by a larger group.

commode • n. a piece of furniture containing a concealed chamber pot.
– ORIGIN French, 'convenient, suitable'.

commodify /kuh-**mod**-i-fy/ • v. (**commodifies, commodifying, commodified**) turn into or treat purely as a commodity: *art has become commodified.*
– DERIVATIVES **commodification** n.

commodious /kuh-**moh**-di-uhss/ • adj. formal roomy and comfortable.
– ORIGIN Latin *commodus* 'convenient'.

commodity /kuh-**mod**-i-ti/ • n. (pl. **commodities**) **1** a raw material or agricultural product that can be bought and sold. **2** something that is useful or valuable.
– ORIGIN Latin *commoditas.*

commodore /**kom**-muh-dor/ • n. **1** a naval rank above captain and below rear admiral. **2** the president of a yacht club.
– ORIGIN prob. from Dutch *komandeur.*

common • adj. (**commoner, commonest**) **1** occurring, found, or done often; not rare. **2** without special qualities or position; ordinary. **3** shared by two or more people or things. **4** belonging to or affecting the whole of a community: *common land.* **5** Brit. not well-mannered, in a way supposedly typical of lower-class people. • n. a piece of open land for public use.
– PHRASES **common or garden** Brit. informal of the usual or ordinary type; with no special features. **in common** shared.
– DERIVATIVES **commonly** adv. **commonness** n.
– ORIGIN Latin *communis.*

commonality • n. (pl. **commonalities**) the sharing of features.

common denominator • n. **1** Math. a common multiple of the denominators of several fractions. **2** a feature shared by all members of a group.

commoner • n. an ordinary person as opposed to an aristocrat.

common ground • n. views shared by each of two or more parties.

common law • n. English law that has been developed from custom and judges' decisions rather than created by Parliament.

common-law husband (or **wife**) • n. a man or woman who has lived with a person long enough to be recognized as a husband or wife, but has not been married in a civil or religious ceremony.

common market • n. **1** a group of countries imposing few duties on trade with one another. **2** (**the Common Market**) the European Union.

common noun • n. a noun referring to a thing (e.g. *tree*) as opposed to a particular person or thing. Opp. PROPER NOUN.

commonplace • adj. not unusual or original; ordinary. • n. **1** a usual or ordinary thing. **2** a cliché.

common room • n. esp. Brit. a room in a school or college for use of students or staff outside teaching hours.

Commons • pl. n. (**the Commons**) the House of Commons.

common sense • n. good sense and sound judgement in practical matters.

commonsensical • adj. having or showing common sense.

common time • n. a rhythmic musical pattern in which there are two or four beats in a bar.

commonwealth •n. 1 (**the Commonwealth** or **the Commonwealth of Nations**) an association consisting of the UK together with states that were previously part of the British Empire, and dependencies. 2 an independent state or community.

commotion •n. noisy confusion or disturbance.
– ORIGIN Latin.

communal /kuh-myoo-n'l/ •adj. shared or done by all members of a community.
– DERIVATIVES **communally** adv.
– ORIGIN Latin *communalis*.

commune¹ /kom-myoon/ •n. a group of people living together and sharing possessions and responsibilities.
– ORIGIN Latin *communia*.

commune² /kuh-myoon/ •v. (**communes**, **communing**, **communed**) (**commune with**) share your thoughts or feelings with: *she lives in Wales and communes with nature.*
– ORIGIN Old French *comuner*.

communicable •adj. (of a disease) able to be passed on to other people.

communicant •n. a person who receives Holy Communion.

communicate •v. (**communicates**, **communicating**, **communicated**) 1 share or exchange information. 2 pass on or convey an emotion, disease, heat, etc. 3 (as adj. **communicating**) (of two rooms) having a common connecting door.
– DERIVATIVES **communicator** n.
– ORIGIN Latin *communicare*.

communication •n. 1 the action of communicating. 2 a letter or message. 3 (**communications**) means of sending information or travelling, such as telephone lines or roads.

communication cord •n. Brit. a cord which a train passenger may pull in an emergency, causing the train to brake.

communicative •adj. willing or eager to talk or give information.

communion •n. 1 the sharing of intimate thoughts and feelings. 2 (also **Holy Communion**) the service of Christian worship at which bread and wine are made sacred and shared; the Eucharist.

communiqué /kuh-myoo-ni-kay/ •n. an official announcement or statement.
– ORIGIN French, 'communicated'.

communism •n. 1 a political system whereby all property is owned by the community and each person contributes and receives according to their ability and needs. 2 a system of this kind based on Marxism.

– DERIVATIVES **communist** n. & adj.
– ORIGIN French *communisme*.

community •n. (pl. **communities**) 1 a group of people living together in one place. 2 (**the community**) the people of an area as a group; society. 3 a group of people sharing a religion, race, or profession: *the scientific community.* 4 a group of animals or plants living or growing in the same place.
– ORIGIN Old French *comunete*.

community care •n. long-term care for mentally ill, elderly, and disabled people within the community rather than in hospitals or institutions.

community centre •n. a place which provides educational or recreational activities for a neighbourhood.

community service •n. socially useful work that an offender is required to do instead of going to prison.

commutate /kom-yuu-tayt/ •v. (**commutates**, **commutating**, **commutated**) regulate the direction of an alternating electric current, especially to make it a direct current.
– DERIVATIVES **commutation** n. **commutator** n.

commutative /kuh-myoo-tuh-tiv/ •adj. Math. unchanged in result by altering the order of quantities, such that for example $a \times b = b \times a$.

commute •v. (**commutes**, **commuting**, **commuted**) 1 regularly travel some distance between your home and place of work. 2 reduce a judicial sentence to a less severe one.
– DERIVATIVES **commuter** n.
– ORIGIN Latin *commutare*; sense 1 is from *commutation ticket*, the US term for a season ticket.

compact¹ •adj. /kuhm-pakt/ 1 closely and neatly packed together; dense. 2 having all the necessary parts fitted into a small space. •v. /kuhm-**pakt**/ press firmly together. •n. /kom-pakt/ a small case containing face powder, a mirror, and a powder puff.
– DERIVATIVES **compactor** n.
– ORIGIN Latin *compingere* 'fasten together'.

compact² /kom-pakt/ •n. a formal agreement.
– ORIGIN Latin *compactum*.

compact disc •n. a small disc on which music or other digital information is stored.

companion •n. 1 a person that you spend time or travel with. 2 each of a pair of things intended to complement or match each other.
– DERIVATIVES **companionship** n.
– ORIGIN Old French *compaignon* 'a

person who breaks bread with another'.

companionable • adj. friendly and sociable.
– DERIVATIVES **companionably** adv.

companionway • n. a set of steps leading from a ship's deck down to a cabin or lower deck.
– ORIGIN from former Dutch *kompanje* 'quarterdeck'.

company • n. (pl. **companies**) **1** a commercial business. **2** the fact of being with another person or other people: *she is excellent company.* **3** a guest or guests: *we're expecting company.* **4** a gathering of people. **5** a division of an infantry battalion. **6** a group of actors, singers, or dancers who perform together.
– PHRASES **keep someone company** spend time with someone to prevent them feeling lonely or bored.
– ORIGIN Old French *compainie*.

comparable /kom-puh-ruh-b'l/ • adj. able to be compared with someone or something; similar.
– DERIVATIVES **comparability** n. **comparably** adv.

comparative /kuhm-pa-ruh-tiv/ • adj. **1** measured by comparing one thing with another; relative. **2** involving comparison between subjects. **3** (of an adjective or adverb) expressing a higher degree of a quality (e.g. *braver*), but not the highest possible. Contrasted with POSITIVE, SUPERLATIVE.
– DERIVATIVES **comparatively** adv.

> ✓ Remember that **comparative** is spelled with **-ara-** in the middle.

comparator /kuhm-pa-ruh-ter/ • n. a device that is used for comparing something measurable with a reference or standard.

compare • v. (**compares, comparing, compared**) **1** estimate, measure, or note the similarity or difference between: *there was a drop in sales compared to last year.* **2** (**compare something to**) describe the resemblances of something with something else. **3** (usu. **compare with**) be similar to or have a specified relationship with another thing or person.
– ORIGIN Latin *comparare*.

comparison • n. **1** an instance of comparing things or people. **2** the quality of being similar or equivalent.

compartment • n. **1** a separate section of a structure or container. **2** a division of a railway carriage marked by partitions.
– ORIGIN French *compartiment*.

compartmentalize (or **compartmentalise**)

• v. (**compartmentalizes, compartmentalizing, compartmentalized**) divide into categories or sections.

compass • n. **1** an instrument containing a magnetized pointer which shows the direction of magnetic north. **2** (also **compasses**) an instrument for drawing circles, consisting of two arms linked by a movable joint. **3** the range or scope of something.
– ORIGIN Old French *compas*.

compassion • n. sympathetic pity and concern for the sufferings of other people.
– ORIGIN Latin.

compassionate • adj. feeling or showing compassion.

compatible • adj. **1** able to exist or be used together without conflict. **2** (of two people) able to have a good relationship; well suited. **3** (usu. **compatible with**) consistent or in keeping.
– DERIVATIVES **compatibility** n. **compatibly** adv.
– ORIGIN Latin *compatibilis*.

compatriot /kuhm-pat-ri-uht/ • n. a fellow citizen of a country.
– ORIGIN French *compatriote*.

compel • v. (**compels, compelling, compelled**) **1** force to do something. **2** bring about by force or pressure.
– ORIGIN Latin *compellere*.

compelling • adj. strongly arousing attention or admiration.

compendious • adj. formal presenting facts in a detailed but concise way.
– ORIGIN Latin *compendiosus*.

compendium /kuhm-pen-di-uhm/ • n. (pl. **compendiums** or **compendia** /kuhm-pen-di-uh/) **1** a collection of concise but detailed information about a subject. **2** a collection of similar items.
– ORIGIN Latin, 'profit, saving'.

compensate • v. (**compensates, compensating, compensated**) **1** give something to someone in recognition of loss, distress, or injury suffered. **2** (**compensate for**) reduce or balance something undesirable by having an opposite force or effect.
– DERIVATIVES **compensator** n. **compensatory** adj.
– ORIGIN Latin *compensare* 'weigh against'.

compensation • n. **1** something given to compensate for loss, suffering, or injury. **2** something that makes up for an undesirable situation.

compère /kom-pair/ Brit. • n. a person who introduces the acts in a variety

show. •v. (**compères, compèring, compèred**) act as a compère for a variety show.
– ORIGIN French, 'godfather'.

compete •v. (**competes, competing, competed**) try to gain or win something by defeating or being better than other people.
– ORIGIN Latin *competere*.

competence (also **competency**) •n. **1** the ability to do something well. **2** the authority of a court or other body to deal with something.

competent •adj. **1** having the necessary skill or knowledge to do something successfully. **2** acceptable and satisfactory: *she spoke quite competent French.* **3** having legal authority to deal with something.
– DERIVATIVES **competently** adv.
– ORIGIN Latin *competere*.

✓ Spell **competent** with **-ent** at the end.

competition •n. **1** the activity of competing against other people. **2** an event or contest in which people compete. **3** the person or people that you are competing with.

competitive •adj. **1** relating to competition. **2** strongly wanting to be more successful than other people. **3** as good as or better than others of a similar nature.
– DERIVATIVES **competitively** adv. **competitiveness** n.

competitor •n. **1** a person who takes part in a sporting contest. **2** an organization competing with others in business.

compilation •n. **1** the action of compiling. **2** a thing, especially a book or record, compiled from different sources.

compile •v. (**compiles, compiling, compiled**) **1** produce a book, report, etc. by assembling material from other sources. **2** gather material to produce a book, report, etc.
– DERIVATIVES **compiler** n.
– ORIGIN Latin *compilare* 'plunder'.

complacent /kuhm-**play**-s'nt/ •adj. satisfied with yourself in a smug or uncritical way.
– DERIVATIVES **complacency** n. **complacently** adv.
– ORIGIN Latin *complacere* 'to please'.

complain •v. **1** express dissatisfaction or annoyance. **2** (**complain of**) state that you are suffering from a symptom of illness.
– DERIVATIVES **complainer** n.
– ORIGIN Old French *complaindre*.

complainant •n. Law a person who

brings a case against another in certain lawsuits.

complaint •n. **1** an act of complaining. **2** a reason for being dissatisfied. **3** the expression of dissatisfaction: *a letter of complaint.* **4** a minor illness or medical condition.

complaisant /kuhm-**play**-z'nt/ •adj. willing to please other people or to accept their behaviour without protest.
– ORIGIN French.

complement •n. /**kom**-pli-muhnt/ **1** a thing that contributes extra features to something else so as to improve it. **2** the number or quantity that makes something complete: *we have a full complement of staff.* **3** a word or words used with a verb to complete the meaning of the subject (e.g. *happy* in the sentence *we are happy*). •v. /**kom**-pli-ment/ add to something in a way that improves it.
– ORIGIN Latin *complementum*.

USAGE: Do not confuse **complement** and **compliment**. As a verb, **complement** means 'add to in a way that improves' (*her accessories complement her outfit*), while **compliment** means 'politely congratulate or praise' (*I complimented her on her appearance*).

complementary •adj. combining so as to form a complete whole or to improve each other.

complementary angle •n. either of two angles whose sum is 90°.

complementary medicine •n. medical therapy that is not part of scientific medicine but may be used alongside it, e.g. acupuncture.

complete •adj. **1** having all the necessary parts; entire. **2** having run its course; finished. **3** to the greatest extent or degree; total. **4** skilled at every aspect of an activity. •v. (**completes, completing, completed**) **1** finish making or doing something. **2** provide with the items necessary to make something complete. **3** write the required information on a form.
– DERIVATIVES **completely** adv.
– ORIGIN Latin *complere*.

completion •n. the action of completing something or the state of being completed.

complex •adj. **1** consisting of many different and connected parts. **2** hard to understand; complicated. •n. **1** a group of similar buildings or facilities on the same site. **2** an interlinked system; a network. **3** a group of repressed feelings which lead to abnormal mental states or behaviour.

– DERIVATIVES **complexity** n. (pl. **complexities**).
– ORIGIN Latin *complexus*.

complexion • n. **1** the colour and texture of the skin of a person's face. **2** the general character of something.
– ORIGIN Latin, 'combination'.

complex number • n. Math. a number containing both a real and an imaginary part.

compliance /kuhm-**ply**-uhnss/ • n. the action of obeying an order, rule, or request.

compliant • adj. **1** too obedient or ready to accept something. **2** in accordance with rules.

complicate • v. (**complicates**, **complicating**, **complicated**) make more intricate or confusing.
– ORIGIN Latin *complicare* 'fold together'.

complicated • adj. **1** consisting of many connected parts or elements; intricate. **2** involving many confusing aspects.

complication • n. **1** a thing that complicates something; a difficulty. **2** an involved or confused state. **3** a secondary disease or condition which makes an existing one worse.

complicity • n. involvement with other people in an unlawful activity.
– DERIVATIVES **complicit** adj.
– ORIGIN Old French *complice* 'an associate'.

compliment • n. /kom-pli-muhnt/ **1** an expression of praise or admiration. **2** (**compliments**) formal greetings. • v. /kom-pli-ment/ politely congratulate or praise.
– PHRASES **with the compliments of someone** provided free of charge.
– ORIGIN Italian *complimento*.

USAGE: On the difference between **compliment** and **complement**, see the note at **COMPLEMENT**.

complimentary • adj. **1** praising or approving. **2** given free of charge.

comply /kuhm-**ply**/ • v. (**complies**, **complying**, **complied**) (often **comply with**) **1** do what is requested or ordered. **2** meet specified standards.
– ORIGIN Latin *complere*.

component /kuhm-**poh**-nuhnt/ • n. a part of a larger whole. • adj. being part of a larger whole.
– ORIGIN Latin *componere* 'put together'.

comport /kuhm-**port**/ • v. (**comport yourself**) formal behave in a particular way.
– ORIGIN Latin *comportare*.

compose • v. (**composes**, **composing**, **composed**) **1** make up a whole: *the National Congress is composed of ten senators.* **2** create a work of art, especially music or poetry. **3** arrange parts in an orderly or artistic way to form a whole. **4** (as adj. **composed**) calm and in control of your feelings.
– ORIGIN Old French *composer*.

composer • n. a person who writes music.

composite /**kom**-puh-zit/ • adj. **1** made up of various parts. **2** /**kom**-puh-zyt/ (of a plant) having flower heads consisting of numerous small flowers. • n. a thing made up of several parts.
– ORIGIN Latin *componere* 'put together'.

composition • n. **1** the way in which something is made up from different elements: *the molecular composition of cells.* **2** a work of music, literature, or art. **3** a thing composed of various elements. **4** the action of composing. **5** the arrangement of the parts of a picture.

compositor /kuhm-**poz**-i-ter/ • n. a person who arranges type or keys material for printing.

compos mentis /kom-poss **men**-tiss/ • adj. having full control of your mind.
– ORIGIN Latin.

compost • n. decayed organic material used as a fertilizer.
– ORIGIN Latin *composita* 'something put together'.

composure • n. the state of being calm and self-controlled.

compound[1] • n. /**kom**-pownd/ **1** a thing composed of two or more separate elements. **2** a substance formed from two or more elements chemically united in fixed proportions. **3** a word that is made up of two or more existing words. • adj. /**kom**-pownd/ **1** made up or consisting of several parts. **2** (of interest) payable on both capital and the accumulated interest. Compare with **SIMPLE**. • v. /kuhm-**pownd**/ **1** make up a whole. **2** make something bad worse.
– ORIGIN Latin *componere* 'put together'.

compound[2] /**kom**-pownd/ • n. a large open area enclosed by a fence.
– ORIGIN Malay.

compound fracture • n. an injury in which a broken bone pierces the skin.

comprehend /kom-pri-**hend**/ • v. fully understand something.
– ORIGIN Latin *comprehendere*.

comprehensible • adj. able to be understood.
– DERIVATIVES **comprehensibility** n.

comprehension • n. **1** the ability to understand: *mysteries beyond human comprehension.* **2** Brit. the school exercise of answering questions on a set passage to test understanding.

comprehensive • adj. **1** including or

dealing with all or nearly all aspects of something. **2** Brit. (of secondary education) in which children of all abilities are educated in one school. **3** (of motor-vehicle insurance) providing cover for most risks. **4** (of a victory or defeat) by a large margin. • n. Brit. a comprehensive school.
– DERIVATIVES **comprehensively** adv.

compress • v. /kuhm-**press**/ **1** press or squeeze so as to occupy less space. **2** squeeze or press two things together. **3** alter the form of computer data so that it occupies less space on a disk or magnetic tape. • n. /**kom**-press/ an absorbent pad pressed on to part of the body to relieve inflammation or stop bleeding.
– DERIVATIVES **compressibility** n. **compressible** adj.
– ORIGIN Old French *compresser*.

compressed air • n. air that is at more than atmospheric pressure.

compression • n. **1** the action of compressing something. **2** the reduction in volume (causing an increase in pressure) of the fuel mixture in an internal-combustion engine before ignition.

compressor • n. a device used for compressing something, especially a machine used to supply air at increased pressure.

comprise • v. (**comprises, comprising, comprised**) **1** be made up of; consist of: *the country comprises twenty states.* **2** (also **be comprised of**) make up a whole.
– ORIGIN French, 'comprised'.

compromise • n. **1** an agreement reached by each side giving way on some points. **2** something that is halfway between different elements: *a compromise between greed and caution.* • v. (**compromises, compromising, compromised**) **1** settle a dispute by giving way on some points. **2** accept standards that are lower than is desirable for practical reasons. **3** cause embarrassment or danger to someone by reckless or indiscreet behaviour.
– DERIVATIVES **compromiser** n.
– ORIGIN Old French *compromis*.

compromising • adj. revealing an embarrassing or incriminating secret.

comptroller /kuhn-**troh**-ler, komp-**troh**-ler/ • n. a controller of financial affairs.
– ORIGIN from **controller** (see **CONTROL**).

compulsion • n. **1** pressure forcing someone to do something. **2** an irresistible urge to do something.

compulsive • adj. **1** resulting from or acting on an irresistible urge.

2 powerfully exciting.
– DERIVATIVES **compulsively** adv.

compulsory • adj. required by law or a rule; obligatory.
– DERIVATIVES **compulsorily** adv.

compunction • n. a feeling of guilt that prevents or follows wrongdoing: *he felt no compunction in letting her worry.*
– ORIGIN Latin.

computation • n. **1** mathematical calculation. **2** the use of computers.
– DERIVATIVES **computational** adj.

compute • v. (**computes, computing, computed**) calculate a figure or amount.
– ORIGIN Latin *computare*.

computer • n. an electronic device capable of storing and processing information in accordance with a set of instructions.

computerize (or **computerise**) • v. (**computerizes, computerizing, computerized**) convert something to a system which is controlled, stored, or processed by computer.

computing • n. the use or operation of computers.

comrade • n. **1** (among men) a companion who shares your activities or is a fellow member of an organization. **2** (also **comrade-in-arms**) a fellow soldier.
– DERIVATIVES **comradeship** n.
– ORIGIN Spanish *camarada* 'room-mate'.

con[1] informal • v. (**cons, conning, conned**) deceive someone into doing or believing something. • n. an act of deceiving someone.
– ORIGIN from *confidence trick*.

con[2] • n. (usu. in phr. **pros and cons**) a disadvantage of or argument against something.
– ORIGIN Latin *contra* 'against'.

concatenation /kon-ka-ti-**nay**-sh'n/ • n. a series of interconnected things.
– ORIGIN Latin *concatenare* 'link together'.

concave /kon-**kayv**/ • adj. having an outline or surface that curves inwards. Compare with **CONVEX**.
– DERIVATIVES **concavity** n.
– ORIGIN Latin *concavus*.

conceal • v. **1** prevent from being seen. **2** keep something secret.
– DERIVATIVES **concealer** n. **concealment** n.
– ORIGIN Latin *concelare*.

concede • v. (**concedes, conceding, conceded**) **1** finally admit that something is true. **2** give up a possession, advantage, or right. **3** admit defeat in a match or contest. **4** fail to

prevent an opponent scoring a goal or point.
– ORIGIN Latin *concedere*.

conceit • n. **1** excessive pride in yourself. **2** an artistic effect. **3** a complicated metaphor.
– ORIGIN from **CONCEIVE**.

conceited • adj. excessively proud of yourself.

conceivable • adj. capable of being imagined or understood.
– DERIVATIVES **conceivably** adv.

conceive • v. (**conceives, conceiving, conceived**) **1** become pregnant with a child. **2** create in the mind.
– ORIGIN Latin *concipere*.

> ✓ **conceive** follows the usual rule of *i* before *e* except after *c*.

concentrate • v. (**concentrates, concentrating, concentrated**) **1** focus all your attention on something. **2** gather together in numbers or a mass at one point. **3** increase the strength of a solution. • n. a concentrated substance or solution.
– DERIVATIVES **concentrator** n.
– ORIGIN from Latin *con-* 'together' + *centrum* 'centre'.

concentration • n. **1** the action or power of concentrating. **2** a close gathering of people or things. **3** the amount of a particular substance within a solution or mixture.

concentration camp • n. a camp for holding political prisoners.

concentric • adj. (of circles or arcs) sharing the same centre.
– ORIGIN Latin *concentricus*.

concept • n. an abstract idea.
– ORIGIN Latin *conceptum*.

conception • n. **1** the creation of a child in the womb. **2** the forming of a plan or idea. **3** a concept or idea. **4** ability to imagine or understand.

conceptual • adj. relating to concepts or ideas.
– DERIVATIVES **conceptually** adv.

conceptualize (or **conceptualise**) • v. (**conceptualizes, conceptualizing, conceptualized**) form an idea of something in the mind.

concern • v. **1** relate to; be about. **2** affect or involve: *stop interfering in matters that don't concern you.* **3** make anxious or worried. • n. **1** worry; anxiety. **2** a matter of interest or importance. **3** a business.
– ORIGIN Latin *concernere*.

concerned • adj. worried or anxious.

concerning • prep. about.

concert • n. a musical performance given in public.

– PHRASES **in concert** acting together.
– ORIGIN Italian *concerto*.

concerted /kuhn-ser-tid/ • adj. **1** jointly arranged or carried out: *a concerted campaign.* **2** determined: *a concerted effort.*

concertina /kon-ser-tee-nuh/ • n. a small musical instrument with bellows, the notes being sounded by buttons.
• v. (**concertinas, concertinaing, concertinaed**) compress in folds like those of a concertina.

concerto /kuhn-cher-toh/ • n. (pl. **concertos** or **concerti** /kuhn-cher-ti/) a musical composition for an orchestra and one or more solo instruments.
– ORIGIN Italian.

concession • n. **1** a thing given up or allowed to settle a dispute. **2** a reduction in price for a certain kind of person. **3** the right to use land or other property for a particular purpose, granted by a government. **4** a commercial operation set up within a larger business.
– DERIVATIVES **concessionary** adj.
– ORIGIN Latin.

conch /konch/ • n. (pl. **conchs** or **conches** /kon-chiz/) a mollusc of tropical seas, with a spiral shell.
– ORIGIN Greek *konkhē*.

concierge /kon-si-airzh/ • n. **1** (especially in France) a resident caretaker of a block of flats or small hotel. **2** a hotel employee who makes entertainment bookings for guests.
– ORIGIN French.

conciliate /kuhn-sil-i-ayt/
• v. (**conciliates, conciliating, conciliated**) **1** make calm and content. **2** try to bring the sides in a dispute together.
– DERIVATIVES **conciliation** n. **conciliator** n. **conciliatory** adj.
– ORIGIN Latin *conciliare* 'combine'.

concise • adj. giving information clearly and in few words.
– DERIVATIVES **concisely** adv. **concision** n.
– ORIGIN Latin *concisus* 'cut up'.

conclave /kong-klayv/ • n. **1** a private meeting. **2** (in the Roman Catholic Church) a meeting of cardinals for the election of a pope.
– ORIGIN Latin, 'lockable room'.

conclude • v. (**concludes, concluding, concluded**) **1** bring or come to an end. **2** arrive at an opinion by reasoning. **3** formally settle or arrange an agreement.
– ORIGIN Latin *concludere*.

conclusion • n. **1** an end or finish. **2** the summing-up of an argument or written work. **3** a decision reached by reasoning.

conclusive • adj. decisive or convincing.

– DERIVATIVES **conclusively** adv.

concoct /kuhn-kokt/ • v. **1** make a dish or meal by combining ingredients. **2** invent a story or plan.
– DERIVATIVES **concoction** n.
– ORIGIN Latin *concoquere*.

concomitant /kuhn-kom-i-tuhnt/ formal • adj. occurring or naturally connected with something else. • n. something that occurs or is connected with something else.
– ORIGIN Latin *concomitari*.

concord • n. literary agreement; harmony.
– ORIGIN Latin *concordia*.

concordance /kuhn-kor-duhnss/ • n. an alphabetical list of the important words in a written work.

concordat /kuhn-kor-dat/ • n. an agreement, especially one between the Vatican and a government.

concourse • n. a large open area inside or in front of a public building.
– ORIGIN Latin *concursus*.

concrete • n. a building material made from gravel, sand, cement, and water, forming a stone-like mass when dry. • adj. **1** existing in a physical form; not abstract. **2** definite: *concrete proof*. • v. (**concretes, concreting, concreted**) cover with concrete.
– ORIGIN Latin *concretus* 'grown together'.

concretion • n. a hard solid mass.

concubine /kong-kyuu-byn/ • n. esp. hist. (in societies in which a man may have more than one wife) a woman who lives with a man but has lower status than his wife or wives.
– ORIGIN Latin *concubina*.

concupiscence /kuhn-kyoo-pi-suhns/ • n. formal lust.
– DERIVATIVES **concupiscent** adj.
– ORIGIN Latin *concupiscentia*.

concur /kuhn-ker/ • v. (**concurs, concurring, concurred**) **1** (often **concur with**) agree. **2** happen at the same time.
– ORIGIN Latin *concurrere* 'run together'.

concurrent • adj. existing or happening at the same time.
– DERIVATIVES **concurrence** n. **concurrently** adv.

concussion • n. **1** temporary unconsciousness or confusion caused by a blow on the head. **2** a violent shock as from a heavy blow.
– DERIVATIVES **concussed** adj.
– ORIGIN Latin.

condemn • v. **1** express complete disapproval of. **2** (usu. **condemn someone to**) sentence someone to a punishment. **3** (**condemn someone to**) force someone to endure something unpleasant. **4** officially declare to be unfit for use.
– DERIVATIVES **condemnation** n. **condemnatory** adj.
– ORIGIN Latin *condemnare*.

condensation • n. **1** water from humid air collecting as droplets on a cold surface. **2** the conversion of a vapour or gas to a liquid.

condense • v. (**condenses, condensing, condensed**) **1** make more concentrated. **2** change from a gas or vapour to a liquid. **3** express a piece of writing or speech in fewer words.
– DERIVATIVES **condenser** n.
– ORIGIN Latin *condensare*.

condensed milk • n. a kind of milk that has been thickened by evaporation and sweetened.

condescend • v. **1** behave as if you are better than other people. **2** do something that you regard as being below your dignity: *he condescended to see me at my hotel*.
– DERIVATIVES **condescension** n.
– ORIGIN Latin *condescendere*.

condescending • adj. behaving as if you are better than other people.

condiment • n. a substance such as salt or mustard, used to flavour food.
– ORIGIN Latin *condimentum*.

condition • n. **1** the state of something or someone, with regard to appearance, fitness, or working order. **2** (**conditions**) the circumstances affecting something. **3** a situation that must exist before something else is possible: *for a country to borrow money, three conditions must be met.* **4** an illness or medical problem. • v. **1** influence something. **2** bring into a good or desirable state or condition. **3** train to become used to something or to behave in a certain way: *the child is conditioned to dislike the food.*
– PHRASES **in** (or **out of**) **condition** in a fit (or unfit) physical state.
– ORIGIN Latin *condicion* 'agreement'.

conditional • adj. **1** depending on one or more conditions being fulfilled. **2** (of a clause, phrase, conjunction, or verb form) expressing a condition. • n. the conditional form of a verb (e.g. *should* in *if I should die*).
– DERIVATIVES **conditionally** adv.

conditioner • n. a thing used to improve the condition of something.

condo • n. (pl. **condos**) N. Amer. informal = CONDOMINIUM (in sense 1).

condole /kuhn-dohl/ • v. (**condoles, condoling, condoled**) (**condole with**) express sympathy for someone.

– ORIGIN Latin *condolere*.

condolence • n. an expression of sympathy.

condom • n. a rubber sheath worn on the penis during sex as a contraceptive or to protect against infection.

condominium /kon-duh-**min**-i-uhm/ • n. (pl. **condominiums**) **1** N. Amer. a building which contains a number of individually owned flats. **2** the joint control of a state's affairs by other states.
– ORIGIN Latin.

condone /kuhn-**dohn**/ • v. (**condones**, **condoning**, **condoned**) accept or forgive an offence or wrongdoing.
– ORIGIN Latin *condonare* 'refrain from punishing'.

condor • n. a very large South American vulture with a bare head and black plumage.
– ORIGIN Spanish.

conducive • adj. (**conducive to**) contributing to or helping to bring something about.

conduct • n. /**kon**-dukt/ **1** the way in which a person behaves. **2** management or direction: *the conduct of foreign affairs*. • v. /kuhn-**dukt**/ **1** organize and carry out. **2** direct the performance of an orchestra or choir. **3** guide someone to or around a place. **4** (**conduct yourself**) behave in a particular way. **5** transmit heat, electricity, etc. by conduction.
– ORIGIN Latin *conducere* 'bring together'.

conductance • n. the degree to which a material conducts electricity.

conduction • n. the transmission of heat or electricity directly through a substance.
– DERIVATIVES **conductive** adj.

conductivity • n. the degree to which a particular material conducts electricity or heat.

conductor • n. **1** a person who conducts an orchestra or choir. **2** a material or device that conducts heat or electricity. **3** a person who collects fares on a bus.

conduit /**kon**-dwit, **kon**-dyuu-it/ • n. **1** a channel for carrying fluid from one place to another. **2** a tube or trough protecting electric wiring.
– ORIGIN Old French.

cone • n. **1** an object which tapers from a circular base to a point. **2** (also **traffic cone**) a plastic cone used to separate off sections of a road. **3** the dry fruit of a conifer. **4** a type of light-sensitive cell in the eye, responsible for sharpness of vision and colour perception. Compare with ROD.

– ORIGIN Greek *kōnos*.

coney /**koh**-ni/ • n. (pl. **coneys**) Brit. a rabbit.
– ORIGIN Old French *conin*.

confab • n. informal an informal conversation.

confabulation /kuhn-**fab**-yuu-lay-sh'n/ • n. formal a conversation.
– ORIGIN Latin *confabulari*.

confection • n. **1** an elaborate sweet dish. **2** an elaborately constructed thing.
– ORIGIN Latin, 'making'.

confectionery • n. sweets and chocolates.
– DERIVATIVES **confectioner** n.

confederacy • n. (pl. **confederacies**) an alliance, especially of confederate states.

confederate • adj. /kuhn-**fed**-uh-ruht/ **1** joined by an agreement or treaty. **2** (**Confederate**) relating to the southern states which separated from the US in 1860–1. • n. /kuhn-**fed**-uh-ruht/ an accomplice. • v. /kuhn-**fed**-uh-rayt/ (**confederates**, **confederating**, **confederated**) bring into an alliance.
– ORIGIN Latin *confoederatus*.

confederation • n. **1** an alliance of a number of groups. **2** a union of states with some political power belonging to a central authority.

confer /kuhn-**fer**/ • v. (**confers**, **conferring**, **conferred**) **1** grant a title, degree, or right to someone. **2** have discussions.
– DERIVATIVES **conferment** n. **conferral** n.
– ORIGIN Latin *conferre* 'bring together'.

conference • n. a formal meeting for discussion or debate.

confess • v. **1** admit to a crime or wrongdoing. **2** acknowledge reluctantly. **3** formally declare your sins to a priest.
– ORIGIN Old French *confesser*.

confession • n. **1** an act of confessing, especially a statement admitting to a crime. **2** an account of your sins given privately to a priest.

confessional • n. **1** an enclosed stall in a church, in which a priest sits to hear confessions. **2** a confession.

confessor • n. a priest who hears confessions.

confetti • n. small pieces of coloured paper traditionally thrown over a bride and groom after a marriage ceremony.
– ORIGIN Italian, 'sweets'.

confidant /**kon**-fi-dant/ • n. (fem. **confidante** /kon-fi-dant/) a person that you confide in.

confide /kuhn-**fyd**/ • v. (**confides**, **confiding**, **confided**) tell someone about

a secret or private matter in confidence.
– ORIGIN Latin *confidere*.

confidence • n. **1** faith in someone or something. **2** self-assurance arising from a belief in your ability to achieve things. **3** a feeling of trust that someone will keep secret information private.
– PHRASES **in someone's confidence** in a position of trust with someone.

confidence trick • n. an act of cheating someone by gaining their trust.

confident • adj. **1** feeling confidence in yourself. **2** feeling certain about something.
– DERIVATIVES **confidently** adv.

confidential • adj. intended to be kept secret.
– DERIVATIVES **confidentiality** n. **confidentially** adv.

configuration /kuhn-fi-guh-**ray**-sh'n/ • n. an arrangement of parts in a particular way.

configure • v. (**configures, configuring, configured**) **1** arrange in a particular way. **2** arrange a computer system so that it is able to do a particular task.
– DERIVATIVES **configurable** adj.
– ORIGIN Latin *configurare*.

confine • v. /kuhn-**fyn**/ (**confines, confining, confined**) **1** (**confine someone/thing to**) keep someone or something within certain limits of space, scope, or time. **2** (**be confined to**) be unable to leave your bed, home, etc. due to illness or disability. **3** (**be confined**) dated (of a woman) remain in bed for a period before, during, and after giving birth. • n. /**kon**-fynz/ (**confines**) boundaries or limits.
– ORIGIN Latin *confinis*.

confined • adj. (of a space) small and enclosed.

confinement • n. **1** the state of being confined. **2** dated the time around which a woman gives birth to a baby.

confirm • v. **1** state or show that something is true or correct. **2** make definite or valid. **3** (**confirm someone in**) make someone believe or feel something more strongly. **4** (**be confirmed**) go through the religious ceremony of confirmation.
– ORIGIN Latin *confirmare*.

confirmation • n. **1** the action of confirming. **2** the ceremony at which a baptized person is admitted as a full member of the Christian Church.

confirmed • adj. firmly established in a habit or way of life: *a confirmed bachelor*.

confiscate /**kon**-fi-skayt/ • v. (**confiscates, confiscating,** confiscated) officially take or seize property.
– DERIVATIVES **confiscation** n.
– ORIGIN Latin *confiscare* 'put in a chest'.

conflagration /kon-fluh-**gray**-sh'n/ • n. a large and destructive fire.
– ORIGIN Latin.

conflate • v. (**conflates, conflating, conflated**) combine into one.
– DERIVATIVES **conflation** n.
– ORIGIN Latin *conflare* 'kindle, fuse'.

conflict • n. /**kon**-flikt/ **1** a serious disagreement. **2** a long-lasting armed struggle. **3** a lack of agreement between opinions, principles, etc.: *a conflict of interests*. • v. /kuhn-**flikt**/ be different or in opposition: *he condemned views that conflicted with his own*.
– ORIGIN Latin *conflictus*.

confluence /**kon**-floo-uhnss/ • n. the junction of two rivers.
– ORIGIN Latin *confluere*.

conform • v. (usu. **conform to**) **1** obey or follow rules or standards. **2** be similar in form or type.
– ORIGIN Latin *conformare*.

conformation • n. the structure or shape of something.

conformist • n. a person who behaves or thinks in an expected or conventional way. • adj. following accepted standards; conventional.

conformity • n. **1** the fact of following conventions, rules, or laws. **2** similarity in form or type.

confound • v. **1** surprise or bewilder someone. **2** prove a theory or expectation wrong. **3** defeat a plan or hope.
– ORIGIN Latin *confundere* 'mix up'.

confounded • adj. informal, dated used to express annoyance.

confraternity • n. (pl. **confraternities**) an association with a religious or charitable purpose.
– ORIGIN Latin *confraternitas*.

confront • v. **1** meet face to face in a hostile or defiant way. **2** (of a problem) present itself to someone. **3** face up to and deal with a problem. **4** force someone to face something.
– ORIGIN Latin *confrontare*.

confrontation • n. a situation of angry disagreement or opposition.
– DERIVATIVES **confrontational** adj.

Confucian /kuhn-**fyoo**-sh'n/ • adj. relating to the Chinese philosopher Confucius.
– DERIVATIVES **Confucianism** n.

confuse • v. (**confuses, confusing, confused**) **1** make someone unable to understand or think clearly. **2** make less

easy to understand. **3** mistake one person or thing for another.
– DERIVATIVES **confusable** adj.
– ORIGIN Latin *confusus*.

confused • adj. **1** bewildered. **2** lacking order and so difficult to understand.

confusion • n. **1** the state of being confused. **2** a situation of panic or disorder. **3** the mistaking of one person or thing for another.

confute • v. (**confutes, confuting, confuted**) formal prove to be wrong.
– ORIGIN Latin *confutare*.

conga /kong-guh/ • n. a dance performed by people in single file.
– ORIGIN Spanish.

congeal /kuhn-jeel/ • v. (of a liquid) become semi-solid, especially on cooling.
– ORIGIN Latin *congelare*.

congenial /kuhn-jee-ni-uhl/ • adj. **1** pleasant because of qualities or interests similar to your own: *congenial company.* **2** suited to your taste.
– DERIVATIVES **congeniality** n. **congenially** adv.

congenital /kuhn-jen-i-t'l/ • adj. **1** (of a disease or abnormality) present from birth. **2** having a trait as part of your character: *a congenital liar.*
– DERIVATIVES **congenitally** adv.
– ORIGIN Latin *congenitus*.

conger eel /kong-ger/ • n. a large eel of coastal waters.
– ORIGIN Greek *gongros*.

congested • adj. **1** so crowded that it is difficult or impossible to move freely. **2** abnormally full of blood. **3** blocked with mucus.
– DERIVATIVES **congestion** n.
– ORIGIN Latin *congerere* 'heap up'.

conglomerate • n. /kuhn-glom-muh-ruht/ **1** something consisting of a number of different and distinct things. **2** a large corporation formed by the merging of separate firms.
– DERIVATIVES **conglomeration** n.
– ORIGIN Latin *conglomerare*.

Congolese /kong-guh-leez/ • n. (pl. **Congolese**) **1** a person from the Congo or the Democratic Republic of Congo (formerly Zaire). **2** any of the languages that are spoken in the Congo region. • adj. relating to the Congo or the Democratic Republic of Congo.

congratulate • v. (**congratulates, congratulating, congratulated**) **1** express good wishes at the happiness or success of someone. **2** (**congratulate yourself**) think yourself lucky or clever.
– DERIVATIVES **congratulatory** adj.
– ORIGIN Latin *congratulari*.

congratulation • n. **1** (**congratulations**) praise or good wishes on a special occasion. **2** the action of congratulating.

congregate • v. (**congregates, congregating, congregated**) gather into a crowd or mass.
– ORIGIN Latin *congregare*.

congregation • n. **1** a group of people gathered for religious worship. **2** a gathering of people or things.
– DERIVATIVES **congregational** adj.

congress • n. **1** a formal meeting or series of meetings between delegates. **2** (**Congress**) a national law-making body, especially that of the US.
– DERIVATIVES **congressional** adj.
– ORIGIN Latin *congressus*.

congressman (or **congresswoman**) • n. (pl. **congressmen** or **congresswomen**) a male (or female) member of the US Congress.

congruent /kong-groo-uhnt/ • adj. **1** in agreement or harmony. **2** Geom. (of figures) identical in form.
– DERIVATIVES **congruence** n.
– ORIGIN Latin *congruere* 'agree'.

conical • adj. shaped like a cone.

conic section • n. the figure of a circle, ellipse, parabola, or hyperbola formed by the intersection of a plane and a circular cone.

conifer /kon-i-fer/ • n. a tree bearing cones and evergreen needle-like or scale-like leaves.
– DERIVATIVES **coniferous** adj.
– ORIGIN Latin, 'cone-bearing'.

conjecture /kuhn-jek-cher/ • n. an opinion based on incomplete information; a guess. • v. (**conjectures, conjecturing, conjectured**) make a guess.
– DERIVATIVES **conjectural** adj.
– ORIGIN Latin *conjectura*.

conjoin • v. formal join; combine.

conjoined twins • pl. n. tech. = SIAMESE TWINS.

conjugal /kon-juu-g'l/ • adj. relating to marriage or the relationship between husband and wife.
– ORIGIN Latin *conjugalis*.

conjugate /kon-juu-gayt/ • v. (**conjugates, conjugating, conjugated**) give the different forms of a verb.
– DERIVATIVES **conjugation** n.
– ORIGIN Latin *conjugare* 'yoke together'.

conjunction • n. **1** a word used to connect words or clauses (e.g. *and, if*). **2** an instance of two or more events occurring together.

USAGE: A **conjunction** is used to connect words or clauses, as in the sentence *it was Monday morning and I was in bed*. Some people believe that it is wrong to start a sentence with a conjunction such as **and**, **because**, or **but**, but it is acceptable to do this as a way of creating a particular effect, for example: *What are the government's chances of winning in court? And what are the consequences?*

conjunctiva /kon-jungk-ty-vuh/ • n. (pl. **conjunctivae** /kon-jungk-ty-vi/) the mucous membrane that covers the front of the eye and lines the inside of the eyelids.
– ORIGIN from Latin *membrana conjunctiva* 'linking membrane'.

conjunctivitis /kuhn-jungk-ti-vy-tiss/ • n. inflammation of the conjunctiva of the eye.

conjuncture • n. a combination of events.

conjure /kun-jer/ • v. (**conjures**, **conjuring**, **conjured**) (usu. **conjure something up**) 1 cause something to appear as if by magic. 2 make something appear in the mind. 3 call on a spirit to appear by magic.
– ORIGIN Latin *conjurare* 'conspire'.

conjuror (also **conjurer**) • n. a person who performs seemingly magical tricks for entertainment.
– DERIVATIVES **conjuring** n.

conk¹ • v. (**conk out**) informal (of a machine) break down.

conk² • n. Brit. informal a person's nose.
– ORIGIN perh. from CONCH.

conker • n. Brit. 1 the dark brown nut of a horse chestnut tree. 2 (**conkers**) a children's game in which each has a conker on a string and tries to break another's with it.
– ORIGIN dialect, 'snail shell' (with which the game was originally played).

con man • n. informal a man who cheats people using confidence tricks.

connect • v. 1 bring together so as to establish a link. 2 join together so as to provide access and communication. 3 (**be connected**) be related in some way. 4 (of a train, bus, etc.) arrive at its destination just before another leaves so that passengers can transfer.
– DERIVATIVES **connector** n.
– ORIGIN Latin *connectere*.

connection (Brit. also **connexion**) • n. 1 a link or relationship. 2 (**connections**) influential people that you know or are related to. 3 a train, bus, or ferry that connects with another.
– PHRASES **in connection with** with reference to; concerning.

connective • adj. connecting one thing to another.

connective tissue • n. body tissue that connects, supports, binds, or separates other tissues or organs.

conning tower • n. a raised structure on a submarine, containing the periscope.

connive /kuh-nyv/ • v. (**connives**, **conniving**, **connived**) 1 (**connive at/in**) secretly allow a wrongdoing. 2 (often **connive with**) conspire to do something.
– DERIVATIVES **connivance** n.
– ORIGIN Latin *connivere* 'shut the eyes (to)'.

connoisseur /kon-nuh-ser/ • n. an expert in matters involving the judgement of beauty, quality, or skill.
– ORIGIN French.

connotation /kon-nuh-tay-sh'n/ • n. an idea or feeling suggested by a word in addition to its main meaning.

connote /kuh-noht/ • v. (**connotes**, **connoting**, **connoted**) (of a word) suggest something in addition to its main meaning.
– ORIGIN Latin *connotare*.

connubial /kuh-nyoo-bi-uhl/ • adj. literary relating to marriage; conjugal.
– ORIGIN Latin *connubialis*.

conquer • v. (**conquers**, **conquering**, **conquered**) 1 overcome and take control of a place or its people by military force. 2 successfully overcome a problem or climb a mountain.
– DERIVATIVES **conqueror** n.
– ORIGIN Latin *conquirere*.

conquest • n. 1 the action of conquering. 2 a conquered territory. 3 a person whose affection you have won.

conquistador /kon-kwiss-tuh-dor/ • n. (pl. **conquistadores** /kon-kwiss-tuh-dor-ayz/ or **conquistadors**) a Spanish conqueror of Mexico or Peru in the 16th century.
– ORIGIN Spanish.

consanguinity /kon-sang-gwin-it-i/ • n. formal descent from the same ancestor.
– DERIVATIVES **consanguineous** adj.
– ORIGIN Latin *consanguineus* 'of the same blood'.

conscience • n. a person's moral sense of right and wrong.
– ORIGIN Latin *conscientia*.

conscientious /kon-shi-en-shuhss/ • adj. 1 careful and thorough in carrying out your work or duty. 2 relating to a person's conscience.
– DERIVATIVES **conscientiously** adv.

conscientious objector • n. a person who refuses to serve in the armed forces for moral reasons.

conscious • adj. **1** aware of and responding to your surroundings. **2** (usu. **conscious of**) aware of something. **3** deliberate; intentional.
– DERIVATIVES **consciously** adv.
– ORIGIN Latin *conscius*.

consciousness • n. **1** the state of being conscious. **2** awareness of something.

conscript • v. /kuhn-skript/ call someone up for compulsory military service. • n. /kon-skript/ a person called up for compulsory military service.
– DERIVATIVES **conscription** n.
– ORIGIN Latin *conscriptus*.

consecrate /kon-si-krayt/
• v. (**consecrates**, **consecrating**, **consecrated**) **1** make or declare something to be holy or sacred. **2** (in Christian belief) declare that bread or wine represents or is the body and blood of Jesus. **3** officially make someone a bishop.
– DERIVATIVES **consecration** n.
– ORIGIN Latin *consecrare*.

consecutive /kuhn-sek-yuu-tiv/
• adj. following in unbroken sequence.
– DERIVATIVES **consecutively** adv.
– ORIGIN Latin *consecutivus*.

consensual /kuhn-sen-syoo-uhl/
• adj. relating to or involving general agreement.

consensus /kuhn-sen-suhss/ • n. general agreement.
– ORIGIN Latin, 'agreement'.

> ✓ Remember that **consensus** and the related word **consensual** are spelled with **-sen-** in the middle.

consent • n. permission or agreement.
• v. **1** give permission. **2** agree to do something.
– ORIGIN Latin *consentire*.

consequence • n. **1** a result or effect. **2** importance or relevance: *the past is of no consequence*.
– ORIGIN Latin *consequentia*.

consequent • adj. following as a result or effect.
– DERIVATIVES **consequential** adj. **consequently** adv.

conservancy /kuhn-ser-vuhn-si/ • n. (pl. **conservancies**) an organization which is concerned with the preservation of natural resources.

conservation • n. **1** preservation or restoration of the natural environment. **2** preservation and repair of archaeological and historical sites and objects. **3** careful use of a resource: *energy conservation*.

– DERIVATIVES **conservationist** n.

conservative • adj. **1** opposed to change and holding traditional values. **2** (in politics) favouring free enterprise and private ownership. **3** (**Conservative**) relating to the Conservative Party. **4** (of an estimate) deliberately low for the sake of caution. • n. **1** a conservative person. **2** (**Conservative**) a supporter or member of the Conservative Party.
– DERIVATIVES **conservatism** n. **conservatively** adv.

Conservative Party • n. a British right-wing political party which favours free enterprise and private ownership.

conservatoire /kuhn-ser-vuh-twar/
• n. a college for the study of classical music.
– ORIGIN French.

conservatory • n. (pl. **conservatories**) Brit. a room with a glass roof and walls, attached to a house.

conserve /kuhn-serv/ • v. (**conserves**, **conserving**, **conserved**) protect from harm or overuse. • n. /also kon-serv/ jam or marmalade.
– ORIGIN Latin *conservare*.

consider • v. (**considers**, **considering**, **considers**) **1** think carefully about something. **2** believe or think. **3** take into account when making a judgement.
– ORIGIN Latin *considerare*.

considerable • adj. great in size, amount, or importance.
– DERIVATIVES **considerably** adv.

considerate • adj. careful not to harm or inconvenience other people.

consideration • n. **1** careful thought. **2** a fact taken into account when making a decision. **3** thoughtfulness towards other people. **4** a payment or reward.

considering • prep. & conj. taking something into consideration.
• adv. informal taking everything into account.

consign /kuhn-syn/ • v. **1** deliver something to someone. **2** (**consign someone/thing to**) put someone or something in a place so as to be rid of them.
– ORIGIN Latin *consignare* 'mark with a seal'.

consignment • n. a batch of goods sent or delivered.

consist • v. **1** (**consist of**) be composed of. **2** (**consist in**) have something as an essential feature.
– ORIGIN Latin *consistere* 'stand firm'.

consistency • n. (pl. **consistencies**) **1** the state of being consistent. **2** the thickness of a liquid or semi-liquid substance.

consistent • adj. **1** following a regular

pattern; unchanging. **2** (usu. **consistent with**) in agreement.
– DERIVATIVES **consistently** adv.

consolation /kon-suh-lay-sh'n/
• n. **1** comfort received after a loss or disappointment. **2** a source of such comfort.

consolation prize • n. a prize given to a competitor who just fails to win.

console¹ /kuhn-sohl/ • v. (**consoles, consoling, consoled**) comfort someone who is unhappy or disappointed about something.
– ORIGIN Latin *consolari*.

console² /kon-sohl/ • n. **1** a panel or unit containing a set of controls. **2** (also **games console**) a small machine for playing computerized video games.
– ORIGIN French.

consolidate /kuhn-sol-i-dayt/
• v. (**consolidates, consolidating, consolidated**) **1** make stronger or more stable. **2** combine things into a single unit.
– DERIVATIVES **consolidation** n. **consolidator** n.
– ORIGIN Latin *consolidare*.

consommé /kuhn-som-may/ • n. a clear soup made with concentrated stock.
– ORIGIN French.

consonance /kon-suh-nuhnss/
• n. agreement or compatibility.

consonant /kon-suh-nuhnt/ • n. **1** a speech sound in which the breath is partly or completely obstructed. **2** a letter that represents such a sound (e.g. *c*, *t*). • adj. (**consonant with**) in agreement or harmony with.
– ORIGIN Latin *consonare* 'sound together'.

consort • n. /kon-sort/ a wife, husband, or companion. • v. /kuhn-sort/ (**consort with**) regularly associate with.
– ORIGIN Latin *consors* 'sharing'.

consortium /kuhn-sor-ti-uhm/ • n. (pl. **consortia** /kuhn-sor-ti-uh, kuhn-sor-shuh/ or **consortiums**) an association of several companies.
– ORIGIN Latin, 'partnership'.

conspicuous /kuhn-spik-yoo-uhss/
• adj. **1** clearly visible. **2** notable: *conspicuous bravery*.
– DERIVATIVES **conspicuously** adv.
– ORIGIN Latin *conspicuus*.

conspiracy • n. (pl. **conspiracies**) **1** a secret plan by a group to do something unlawful or harmful. **2** the action of conspiring.

conspire • v. (**conspires, conspiring, conspired**) **1** jointly make secret plans to commit a wrongful act. **2** (of circumstances) seem to be acting together to bring about an unfortunate result.

– DERIVATIVES **conspirator** n. **conspiratorial** adj. **conspiratorially** adv.
– ORIGIN Latin *conspirare*.

constable • n. Brit. a police officer of the lowest rank.
– ORIGIN Old French *conestable* 'chief court officer'.

constabulary /kuhn-stab-yuu-luh-ri/
• n. (pl. **constabularies**) Brit. a police force.

constant • adj. **1** occurring continuously. **2** remaining the same. **3** faithful and dependable. • n. **1** an unchanging situation. **2** Math. & Physics a number or quantity that does not change its value.
– DERIVATIVES **constancy** n. **constantly** adv.
– ORIGIN Old French.

constellation • n. a group of stars forming a recognized pattern.
– ORIGIN Latin.

consternation • n. anxiety or dismay.
– ORIGIN Latin.

constipated • adj. affected with constipation.
– ORIGIN Latin *constipare* 'to crowd'.

constipation • n. difficulty in emptying the bowels.

constituency /kuhn-stit-yoo-uhn-si/
• n. (pl. **constituencies**) **1** the group of voters in a particular area who elect a representative to a law-making body. **2** esp. Brit. an area that elects a representative to a law-making body.

constituent • adj. being a part of a whole. • n. **1** a voter in a constituency. **2** a part of a whole.

constitute /kon-sti-tyoot/
• v. (**constitutes, constituting, constituted**) **1** be a part of a whole. **2** be or be equivalent to something. **3** (**be constituted**) be established by law.
– ORIGIN Latin *constituere*.

constitution • n. **1** a body of principles according to which a state or organization is governed. **2** the composition or formation of something. **3** a person's physical or mental state.

constitutional • adj. **1** relating to or in accordance with a constitution. **2** relating to a person's physical or mental state. • n. dated a regular walk taken to stay in good health.
– DERIVATIVES **constitutionally** adv.

constitutive • adj. **1** forming a constituent of something. **2** having the power to establish something.

constrain • v. **1** force someone to do something. **2** (as adj. **constrained**) appearing forced or unnatural. **3** severely restrict the scope or activity of.

– ORIGIN Old French *constraindre*.

constraint • n. **1** a limitation or restriction. **2** strict control of your behaviour or feelings.

constrict • v. **1** make or become narrower or tighter. **2** prevent someone from moving or acting freely.
– DERIVATIVES **constriction** n.
– ORIGIN Latin *constringere*.

constrictor • n. a snake that kills by squeezing and choking its prey.

construct • v. /kuhn-**strukt**/ **1** build something. **2** form from different elements. • n. /**kon**-strukt/ **1** an idea or theory containing various elements. **2** a thing that has been built.
– DERIVATIVES **constructor** n.
– ORIGIN Latin *construere*.

construction • n. **1** the action of constructing. **2** a building or other structure. **3** the industry of erecting buildings. **4** an interpretation.

constructive • adj. useful and helpful.
– DERIVATIVES **constructively** adv.

construe • v. (**construes, construing, construed**) interpret in a particular way: *her silence could be construed as an admission of guilt.*
– ORIGIN Latin *construere* 'build'.

consul /**kon**-s'l/ • n. **1** a state official living in a foreign city and protecting the state's citizens and interests there. **2** (in ancient Rome) each of two elected magistrates who ruled jointly for a year.
– DERIVATIVES **consular** /**kon**-syuu-ler/ adj.
– ORIGIN Latin.

consulate • n. the place where a consul works.

consult • v. **1** ask someone for advice or information. **2** ask someone for permission or approval.
– DERIVATIVES **consultation** n. **consultative** adj.
– ORIGIN Latin *consultare*.

consultancy • n. (pl. **consultancies**) a company giving expert advice in a particular field.

consultant • n. **1** a person who provides expert advice professionally. **2** Brit. a senior hospital doctor.

consume • v. (**consumes, consuming, consumed**) **1** eat or drink. **2** use up a resource. **3** (especially of a fire) completely destroy. **4** (of a feeling) completely fill the mind of: *she was consumed with guilt.*
– DERIVATIVES **consumable** adj.
– ORIGIN Latin *consumere*.

consumer • n. a person who buys a product or service for personal use.

consumerism • n. **1** the preoccupation

of society with buying goods. **2** the protection of the interests of consumers.
– DERIVATIVES **consumerist** adj. & n.

consummate • v. /**kon**-syuu-mayt/ (**consummates, consummating, consummated**) **1** make a marriage or relationship complete by having sex. **2** complete a transaction. • adj. /kuhn-**sum**-muht/ showing great skill and flair.
– DERIVATIVES **consummation** n.
– ORIGIN Latin *consummare*.

consumption • n. **1** the action of consuming. **2** an amount consumed. **3** dated tuberculosis.
– DERIVATIVES **consumptive** adj. & n. (dated).

contact • n. /**kon**-takt/ **1** the state of touching something. **2** the state of communicating or meeting: *I've lost contact with him.* **3** a relationship established with someone. **4** a person who may be asked for information or help. **5** a connection for the passage of an electric current from one thing to another. • v. /**kon**-takt, kuhn-**takt**/ get in touch with someone.
– ORIGIN Latin *contactus*.

contact lens • n. a plastic lens placed on the surface of the eye to correct visual defects.

contagion /kuhn-**tay**-juhn/ • n. the passing of disease from one person to another by close contact.
– ORIGIN Latin.

contagious • adj. **1** (of a disease) spread by contact between people. **2** having a contagious disease. **3** (of an emotion) likely to spread to and affect other people.

contain • v. **1** have or hold something inside. **2** control or restrain yourself or a feeling. **3** prevent a problem from becoming worse.
– ORIGIN Latin *continere*.

container • n. **1** a box or similar object for holding something. **2** a large metal box for transporting goods.

containment • n. the limitation of something harmful.

contaminate • v. (**contaminates, contaminating, contaminated**) make something impure by exposing it to a poisonous or polluting substance.
– DERIVATIVES **contaminant** n. **contamination** n.
– ORIGIN Latin *contaminare*.

contemplate /**kon**-tuhm-playt/ • v. (**contemplates, contemplating, contemplated**) **1** look at thoughtfully. **2** think about. **3** think deeply and at length.

– ORIGIN Latin *contemplari*.

contemplation • n. **1** the action of contemplating. **2** religious meditation.

contemplative /kuhn-tem-pluh-tiv/ • adj. showing or involving deep thought or meditation.

contemporaneous /kuhn-tem-puh-**ray**-ni-uhss/ • adj. existing at or occurring in the same period of time.

– DERIVATIVES **contemporaneity** /kuhn-tem-puh-ruh-**nay**-i-ti/ n.

– ORIGIN Latin.

contemporary /kuhn-**tem**-puh-ruh-ri, kuhn-**tem**-puh-ri/ • adj. **1** living or occurring at the same time. **2** belonging to or occurring in the present. **3** modern in style. • n. (pl. **contemporaries**) **1** a person or thing existing at the same time as another. **2** a person of roughly the same age as another.

– ORIGIN Latin *contemporarius*.

contempt • n. **1** the feeling that a person or thing is worthless or unworthy of respect. **2** (also **contempt of court**) the offence of being disobedient to or disrespectful of a court of law.

– PHRASES **beneath contempt** utterly worthless.

– ORIGIN Latin *contemptus*.

contemptible • adj. deserving hatred or lack of respect.

– DERIVATIVES **contemptibly** adv.

contemptuous • adj. showing or feeling a lack of respect.

– DERIVATIVES **contemptuously** adv.

contend • v. **1** (**contend with/against**) struggle to deal with a difficulty. **2** (**contend for**) struggle to achieve. **3** state as a view in an argument.

– DERIVATIVES **contender** n.

– ORIGIN Latin *contendere*.

content¹ /kuhn-**tent**/ • adj. happy and satisfied. • v. satisfy or please someone. • n. happiness or satisfaction.

– DERIVATIVES **contentment** n.

– ORIGIN Latin *contentus*.

content² /**kon**-tent/ • n. **1** (**contents**) the things that are contained in something. **2** the amount of a particular thing occurring in a substance: *soya milk has a low fat content.* **3** (**contents**) a list of chapters at the front of a book or magazine. **4** the material dealt with in a piece of writing, as distinct from its form or style.

– ORIGIN Latin *contentum*.

contented • adj. happy and satisfied.

– DERIVATIVES **contentedly** adv.

contention • n. **1** strong disagreement. **2** a point of view that is put forward.

– PHRASES **in** (or **out of**) **contention** having (or not having) a good chance of success in a contest.

– ORIGIN Latin.

contentious • adj. **1** causing disagreement or controversy. **2** tending to cause arguments.

contest • n. /**kon**-test/ **1** an event in which people compete to see who is the best. **2** a struggle for power or control. • v. /kuhn-**test**/ **1** take part in a competition, election, or struggle for power. **2** challenge or dispute something.

– ORIGIN Latin *contestari* 'call to witness'.

contestant • n. a person who takes part in a contest.

context • n. **1** the circumstances that form the setting for an event, statement, or idea. **2** the parts that come immediately before and after a word or passage and make its meaning clear.

– DERIVATIVES **contextual** adj. **contextually** adv.

– ORIGIN Latin *contextus*.

contiguous /kuhn-**tig**-yoo-uhss/ • adj. **1** sharing a border. **2** next or together in sequence.

– DERIVATIVES **contiguity** n.

– ORIGIN Latin *contiguus* 'touching'.

continent¹ • n. **1** any of the world's main continuous expanses of land (Europe, Asia, Africa, North and South America, Australia, Antarctica). **2** (also **the Continent**) the mainland of Europe as distinct from the British Isles.

– ORIGIN from Latin *terra continens* 'continuous land'.

continent² • adj. **1** able to control the bowels and bladder. **2** self-restrained, especially sexually.

– DERIVATIVES **continence** n.

– ORIGIN Latin *continere*.

continental • adj. **1** forming or belonging to a continent. **2** (also **Continental**) coming from or typical of mainland Europe. • n. (also **Continental**) a person from mainland Europe.

continental breakfast • n. a light breakfast of coffee and bread rolls.

continental drift • n. the gradual movement of the continents across the earth's surface through geological time.

continental shelf • n. an area of seabed around a large land mass where the sea is relatively shallow.

contingency /kuhn-**tin**-juhn-si/ • n. (pl. **contingencies**) a future event which is possible but cannot be predicted with certainty.

contingent /kuhn-**tin**-juhnt/ • n. a group of people with a common feature, forming part of a larger group. • adj. **1** (**contingent on**) dependent on: *the merger is contingent on government approval.* **2** depending on chance.

– ORIGIN Latin *contingere* 'befall'.

continual • adj. **1** constantly or often occurring. **2** having no interruptions.
– DERIVATIVES **continually** adv.

continuance • n. formal **1** the state of continuing. **2** the time for which something lasts.

continuation • n. **1** the action or state of continuing. **2** a part that is attached to and is an extension of something else.

continue • v. (**continues, continuing, continued**) **1** keep happening or existing without stopping. **2** carry on doing something. **3** carry on travelling in the same direction. **4** start again after a break.
– ORIGIN Latin *continuare*.

continuity /kon-ti-**nyoo**-i-ti/ • n. (pl. **continuities**) **1** the uninterrupted and unchanged existence or operation of something. **2** an unbroken connection or line of development. **3** the maintaining of continuous action and consistent details in the scenes of a film or broadcast.

continuous • adj. forming an unbroken whole or sequence without interruptions or exceptions.
– DERIVATIVES **continuously** adv.

> USAGE: **Continuous** and **continual** can both mean 'without interruption' (*years of continuous/continual warfare*), but only **continual** can be used to mean 'happening frequently' (*the continual arguments*).

continuous assessment • n. Brit. the evaluation of a pupil's progress throughout a course of study, rather than by exams.

continuum /kuhn-**tin**-yoo-uhm/ • n. (pl. **continua**/ kuhn-**tin**-yoo-uh/) a continuous sequence in which the elements next to each other are very similar, but the last and the first are very different.
– ORIGIN Latin.

contort • v. twist or bend something out of its normal shape.
– DERIVATIVES **contortion** n.
– ORIGIN Latin *contorquere*.

contortionist • n. an entertainer who twists and bends their body into unnatural positions.

contour • n. **1** an outline of the shape or form of something. **2** (also **contour line**) a line on a map joining points of equal height. • v. mould into a shape.
– ORIGIN French.

contra- • prefix against; opposite: *contraception*.
– ORIGIN Latin *contra*.

contraband /kon-truh-band/
• n. **1** goods that have been imported or

exported illegally. **2** trade in smuggled goods.
– ORIGIN Italian *contrabando*.

contraception • n. the use of devices or drugs to prevent pregnancy.

contraceptive • n. a device or drug used to prevent a woman becoming pregnant. • adj. preventing pregnancy.

contract • n. /kon-trakt/ **1** a written or spoken agreement intended to be legally binding. **2** informal an arrangement for someone to be killed by a hired assassin. • v. /kuhn-**trakt**/ **1** decrease in size, number, or range. **2** (of a muscle) become shorter and tighter in order to move part of the body. **3** enter into a legally binding agreement. **4** catch a disease.
– DERIVATIVES **contractual** adj. **contractually** adv.
– ORIGIN Latin *contractus*.

contract bridge • n. the standard form of the card game bridge.

contractible • adj. able to be shrunk or capable of contracting.

contractile /kuhn-**trak**-tyl/ • adj. tech. able to contract or produce contraction.

contraction • n. **1** the process of contracting. **2** a shortening of the muscles of the womb occurring at intervals during childbirth. **3** a shortened form of a word or words.

contractor • n. a person who undertakes a contract to provide materials or labour for a job.

contradict • v. deny the truth of a statement made by someone by saying the opposite.
– ORIGIN Latin *contradicere*.

contradiction • n. **1** a combination of statements, ideas, or features which are opposed to one another. **2** the action of contradicting something already said.

contradictory • adj. **1** opposed or inconsistent. **2** containing opposing elements.

contradistinction • n. distinction made by contrasting the different qualities of two things.

contraflow • n. Brit. an arrangement by which the lanes of a dual carriageway or motorway normally carrying traffic in one direction become two-directional.

contralto /kuhn-**tral**-toh/ • n. (pl. **contraltos**) the lowest female singing voice.
– ORIGIN Italian.

contraption • n. a machine or device that appears strange or unnecessarily complicated.
– ORIGIN perh. from **contrive**.

contrapuntal /kon-truh-**pun**-t'l/
• adj. Music relating to or in counterpoint.
– DERIVATIVES **contrapuntally** adv.
– ORIGIN Italian *contrapunto*.

contrariwise /kuhn-**trair**-i-wyz/
• adv. in the opposite way.

contrary /kon-truh-ri/ • adj. 1 opposite
in nature, direction, or meaning. 2 (of
two or more statements, beliefs, etc.)
opposed to one another. 3 /kuhn-**trair**-i/
deliberately inclined to do the opposite
of what is expected or desired. • n. (**the
contrary**) the opposite.
– DERIVATIVES **contrarily** adv.
contrariness n.
– ORIGIN Latin *contrarius*.

contrast • n. /kon-trahst/ 1 the state of
being noticeably different from
something else when put or considered
together. 2 a thing or person noticeably
different from another. 3 the amount of
difference between tones in a television
picture, photograph, etc. • v. /kuhn-
trahst/ 1 differ noticeably. 2 compare
people or things so as to emphasize
differences.
– DERIVATIVES **contrastive** adj.
– ORIGIN Latin *contrastare*.

contravene /kon-truh-**veen**/
• v. (**contravenes, contravening,
contravened**) 1 commit an act that is
not allowed by a law, treaty, etc.
2 conflict with a right or principle.
– DERIVATIVES **contravention** n.
– ORIGIN Latin *contravenire*.

contretemps /kon-truh-ton/ • n. (pl.
contretemps /kon-truh-ton/ or /kon-
truh-tonz/) a minor disagreement.
– ORIGIN French.

contribute /kuhn-**trib**-yoot/
• v. (**contributes, contributing,
contributed**) 1 give in order to help
achieve or provide something.
2 (**contribute to**) help to cause.
– DERIVATIVES **contribution** n.
contributor n.
– ORIGIN Latin *contribuere* 'bring
together'.

contributory /kuhn-**trib**-yuu-tuh-ri/
• adj. 1 playing a part in bringing
something about. 2 (of a pension or
insurance scheme) operated by means
of a fund into which people pay.

con trick • n. informal a confidence trick.

contrite /kuhn-**tryt**, kon-tryt/ • adj. very
sorry for having done wrong.
– DERIVATIVES **contrition** n.
– ORIGIN Latin *contritus*.

contrivance • n. 1 a clever device or
scheme. 2 the use of skill to create or
achieve something.

contrive /kuhn-**tryv**/ • v. (**contrives,
contriving, contrived**) 1 plan or achieve

in a clever or skilful way. 2 manage to do
something foolish.
– ORIGIN Old French *controver*.

contrived • adj. deliberately created
rather than arising naturally, and often
seeming artificial.

control • n. 1 the power to influence
people's behaviour or the course of
events. 2 the restriction of something:
crime control. 3 a means of limiting or
regulating something: *exchange controls*.
4 a person or thing used as a standard of
comparison for checking the results of a
survey or experiment. • v. (**controls,
controlling, controlled**) 1 have control
of; direct. 2 limit or regulate.
– DERIVATIVES **controllability** n,
controllable adj. **controller** n.
– ORIGIN Old French *contreroller* 'keep a
copy of a roll of accounts'.

control tower • n. a tall building from
which the movements of air traffic are
controlled.

controversial • adj. causing or likely to
cause controversy.
– DERIVATIVES **controversially** adv.

controversy /kon-truh-ver-si,
kuhn-**trov**-er-si/ • n. (pl. **controversies**)
public debate about a matter which
arouses conflicting opinions.
– ORIGIN Latin *controversia*.

contumely /kon-**tyoom**-li/ • n. old use
insulting language or treatment.
– ORIGIN Latin *contumelia*.

contusion /kuhn-**tyoo**-zh'n/ • n. Med.
a bruise.
– ORIGIN Latin.

conundrum /kuh-**nun**-druhm/ • n. (pl.
conundrums) 1 a confusing and difficult
problem or question. 2 a riddle.

conurbation /kon-er-**bay**-sh'n/ • n. a
large urban area consisting of several
towns merging with the suburbs of a
city.
– ORIGIN Latin *urbs* 'city'.

convalesce /kon-vuh-**less**/
• v. (**convalesces, convalescing,
convalesced**) gradually get better after
an illness or medical treatment.
– ORIGIN Latin *convalescere*.

convalescent • adj. recovering from an
illness or medical treatment. • n. a
convalescent person.
– DERIVATIVES **convalescence** n.

convection • n. transference of mass or
heat within a fluid caused by the
tendency of warmer material to rise.
– DERIVATIVES **convective** adj.
– ORIGIN Latin.

convector • n. a heater that circulates
warm air by convection.

convene /kuhn-**veen**/ • v. (**convenes,**

convening, **convened**) come or bring together for a meeting or activity.
– ORIGIN Latin *convenire* 'assemble, fit'.

convener (also **convenor**) • n. a person whose job is to arrange the meetings of a committee.

convenience • n. 1 freedom from effort or difficulty. 2 a useful or helpful thing. 3 Brit. a public toilet.
– PHRASES **at your convenience** when or where it suits you.
– ORIGIN Latin *convenientia*.

convenience food • n. a frozen, canned, or packaged food that needs little preparation by the consumer.

convenient • adj. 1 fitting in well with a person's needs, activities, and plans. 2 involving little trouble or effort.
– DERIVATIVES **conveniently** adv.

convenor • n. var. of **CONVENER**.

convent • n. a Christian community of nuns living under monastic vows.
– ORIGIN Old French.

convention • n. 1 a way in which something is usually done. 2 behaviour that is acceptable to most people in a society. 3 an agreement between states or countries. 4 a large meeting or conference.
– ORIGIN Latin.

conventional • adj. 1 based on or in accordance with what is generally done. 2 following social conventions; not individual or adventurous. 3 (of weapons or power) non-nuclear.
– DERIVATIVES **conventionally** adv.

converge /kuhn-verj/ • v. (**converges**, **converging**, **converged**) 1 come together from different directions so as eventually to meet. 2 (**converge on**) come from different directions and meet at.
– DERIVATIVES **convergent** adj.
– ORIGIN Latin *convergere*.

conversant • adj. (**conversant with**) familiar with or knowledgeable about.

conversation • n. an informal spoken exchange between people.
– DERIVATIVES **conversational** adj.

conversationalist • n. a person who is good at or fond of talking to people.

converse[1] /kuhn-verss/ • v. (**converses**, **conversing**, **conversed**) hold a conversation.
– ORIGIN Latin *conversari* 'keep company with'.

converse[2] /kon-verss/ • n. (**the converse**) the opposite of a fact or statement. • adj. opposite.
– DERIVATIVES **conversely** adv.
– ORIGIN Latin *conversus* 'turned about'.

conversion • n. 1 the action of con-

verting. 2 Brit. a building that has been converted to a new purpose. 3 Rugby a successful kick at goal after a try.

convert • v. /kuhn-vert/ 1 change in form, character, or function. 2 change money or units into others of a different kind. 3 adapt a building for a new purpose. 4 change your religious faith or other beliefs. • n. /kon-vert/ a person who has changed their religious faith or other beliefs.
– DERIVATIVES **converter** (also **convertor**) n.
– ORIGIN Latin *convertere* 'turn about'.

convertible • adj. 1 able to be converted. 2 (of a car) having a folding or detachable roof. • n. a convertible car.

convex /kon-veks/ • adj. having an outline or surface that curves outwards. Compare with **CONCAVE**.
– ORIGIN Latin *convexus* 'vaulted, arched'.

convey /kuhn-vay/ • v. 1 transport to a place. 2 communicate an idea or feeling.
– DERIVATIVES **conveyor** (also **conveyer**) n.
– ORIGIN Latin *conviare*.

conveyance • n. 1 the action of conveying. 2 formal a means of transport. 3 the legal process of transferring property from one owner to another.
– DERIVATIVES **conveyancer** n. **conveyancing** n.

conveyor belt • n. a continuous moving belt used for transporting objects within a building.

convict • v. /kuhn-vikt/ officially declare that someone is guilty of a criminal offence. • n. /kon-vikt/ a person convicted of a criminal offence and serving a prison sentence.
– ORIGIN Latin *convictus* 'demonstrated'.

conviction • n. 1 an instance of being convicted of a criminal offence. 2 a firmly held belief or opinion. 3 the quality of showing that you are convinced of what you believe or say.

convince • v. (**convinces**, **convincing**, **convinced**) 1 cause someone to believe firmly in the truth of something. 2 persuade someone to do something.
– ORIGIN Latin *convincere* 'overcome'.

convincing • adj. 1 able to convince. 2 (of a victory or a winner) leaving no margin of doubt.

convivial /kuhn-viv-i-uhl/ • adj. 1 (of an atmosphere or event) friendly and lively. 2 cheerfully sociable.
– DERIVATIVES **conviviality** n.
– ORIGIN Latin *convivium* 'a feast'.

convocation /kon-vuh-kay-sh'n/ • n. a large formal assembly of people.
– ORIGIN Latin.

convoke /kuhn-vohk/ • v. (**convokes**,

c

convoking, **convoked**) formal call together an assembly or meeting.
– ORIGIN Latin *convocare*.

convoluted /kon-vuh-**loo**-tid/
• adj. **1** (of an argument or story) very complex. **2** folded or twisted in a complex way.

convolution • n. **1** a coil or twist. **2** a complex argument, story, etc.
– ORIGIN Latin.

convolvulus /kuhn-**volv**-yuu-luhss/
• n. (pl. **convolvuluses**) a twining plant with trumpet-shaped flowers.
– ORIGIN Latin.

convoy /kon-voy/ • n. a group of ships or vehicles travelling together under armed protection.
– ORIGIN French *convoyer*.

convulse /kuhn-**vulss**/ • v. (**convulses**, **convulsing**, **convulsed**) **1** suffer convulsions. **2** (**be convulsed**) make sudden, uncontrollable movements because of laughter or emotion.
– DERIVATIVES **convulsive** adj.
– ORIGIN Latin *convellere* 'pull violently'.

convulsion • n. **1** a sudden, irregular movement of the body caused by the muscles contracting uncontrollably. **2** (**convulsions**) uncontrollable laughter. **3** a violent upheaval.

coo • v. (**coos**, **cooing**, **cooed**) **1** (of a pigeon or dove) make a soft murmuring sound. **2** speak in a soft, gentle voice. • n. a cooing sound.

cook • v. **1** prepare food or a meal by heating the ingredients. **2** (of food) be heated so as to become edible. **3** informal alter dishonestly. **4** (**cook something up**) informal invent a story or plan. • n. a person who cooks.
– ORIGIN Latin *coquus* 'a cook'.

cooker • n. Brit. an appliance for cooking food.

cookery • n. the practice or skill of preparing and cooking food.

cookie • n. (pl. **cookies**) **1** N. Amer. a sweet biscuit. **2** informal a person of a specified kind: *she's a tough cookie*.
– ORIGIN Dutch *koekje* 'little cake'.

cool • adj. **1** fairly cold. **2** preventing you from becoming too hot. **3** unfriendly or unenthusiastic. **4** not excited or emotional: *he kept a cool head*. **5** informal fashionably attractive or impressive. **6** informal excellent. • n. (**the cool**) a fairly low temperature: *the cool of the day*. • v. make or become cool.
– PHRASES **keep** (or **lose**) **your cool** informal stay (or fail to stay) calm and controlled.
– DERIVATIVES **cooler** n. **coolly** adv. **coolness** n.
– ORIGIN Old English.

coolant • n. a fluid used to cool an engine or other device.

coolie /koo-li/ • n. (pl. **coolies**) dated an unskilled labourer in some Asian countries.
– ORIGIN Hindi.

cooling tower • n. an open-topped cylindrical tower, used for cooling water or condensing steam from an industrial process.

coombe (also **coomb**) • n. var. of COMBE.

coon • n. **1** N. Amer. a raccoon. **2** informal, offens. a black person.

coop • n. a cage or pen for poultry. • v. (**coop someone/thing up**) confine a person or animal in a small space.
– ORIGIN Latin *cupa* 'cask, tub'.

co-op • n. informal a cooperative organization.

cooper • n. a person who makes or repairs casks and barrels.
– ORIGIN Latin *cupa* 'cask, tub'.

cooperate /koh-op-uh-rayt/ (also **co-operate**) • v. (**cooperates**, **cooperating**, **cooperated**) **1** work together to achieve something. **2** do what is requested.
– DERIVATIVES **cooperation** n.
– ORIGIN Latin *cooperari*.

cooperative (also **co-operative**)
• adj. **1** involving cooperation. **2** willing to help. **3** (of a farm or business) owned and run jointly by its members, with profits shared among them. • n. a cooperative organization.
– DERIVATIVES **cooperatively** adv.

co-opt • v. **1** make someone a member of a committee or other body by invitation of the existing members. **2** divert to a role different from the usual one. **3** adopt an idea or policy for your own use.
– DERIVATIVES **co-optation** n. **co-option** n.
– ORIGIN Latin *cooptare*.

coordinate (also **co-ordinate**)
• v. /koh-or-di-nayt/ (**coordinates**, **coordinating**, **coordinated**) **1** bring the different elements of a complex activity or organization into an efficient relationship. **2** (**coordinate with**) negotiate with other people to work together effectively. **3** match or harmonize attractively. • n. /koh-or-di-nuht/ **1** Math. each of a group of numbers used to indicate the position of a point, line, or plane. **2** (**coordinates**) matching items of clothing.
– DERIVATIVES **coordinator** n.
– ORIGIN Latin *ordinare* 'put in order'.

coordination (also **co-ordination**)
• n. **1** the action of coordinating. **2** the ability to move different parts of the body smoothly and at the same time.

coot • n. (pl. **coot** or **coots**) a black waterbird with a white bill.

– ORIGIN prob. Dutch or German.

cop informal • n. a police officer. • v. (**cops,
copping, copped**) **1** arrest an offender.
2 experience or receive something
unwelcome. **3** (**cop off**) Brit. have a
sexual encounter. **4** (**cop out**) avoid
doing something that you ought to do.
– PHRASES **cop hold of** Brit. take hold of.
cop it Brit. **1** get into trouble. **2** be killed.
not much cop Brit. not very good.
– ORIGIN perh. from Old French *caper*
'seize'.

cope[1] • v. (**copes, coping, coped**) deal
effectively with something difficult.
– ORIGIN Old French *coper* 'to strike'.

cope[2] • n. a long cloak worn by a priest on
ceremonial occasions.
– ORIGIN Latin *cappa* 'head covering'.

copeck • n. var. of KOPEK.

Copernican system /kuh-per-
ni-kuhn/ (also **Copernican theory**)
• n. the theory proposed by the
astronomer Nicolaus Copernicus that
the sun is the centre of the solar system,
with the planets orbiting round it.
Compare with PTOLEMAIC SYSTEM.

copier • n. a machine that makes exact
copies of something.

co-pilot • n. a second pilot in an aircraft.

coping • n. the top layer of a brick or
stone wall.
– ORIGIN from COPE[2].

copious • adj. abundant; plentiful.
– DERIVATIVES **copiously** adv.
– ORIGIN Latin *copia* 'plenty'.

copper[1] • n. **1** a red-brown metallic
chemical element which is used as a
component of brass and bronze.
2 (**coppers**) Brit. coins made of copper or
bronze. **3** a reddish-brown colour.
– ORIGIN from Latin *cyprium aes* 'Cyprus
metal'.

copper[2] • n. Brit. informal a police officer.
– ORIGIN from COP.

copper-bottomed • adj. Brit. totally
reliable.
– ORIGIN with reference to copper
covering applied to the bottom of a ship.

copperplate • n. a neat style of handwriting with slanted letters.
– ORIGIN the copybooks for this were
originally printed from copper plates.

copper sulphate • n. a blue solid used
in electroplating and as a fungicide.

coppice • n. an area of woodland in
which the trees or shrubs are
periodically cut back to ground level.
– ORIGIN Old French *copeiz*.

copra /kop-ruh/ • n. dried coconut
kernels, from which oil is obtained.
– ORIGIN Portuguese and Spanish.

copse • n. a small group of trees.

– ORIGIN from COPPICE.

Copt /kopt/ • n. **1** a member of the Coptic
Church, the native Christian Church in
Egypt. **2** a native Egyptian in the periods
of Greek and Roman rule.
– ORIGIN Latin *Coptus*.

copula /kop-yuu-luh/ • n. a verb,
especially the verb *be*, that links a
subject and complement (e.g. *was* in
I was happy).
– ORIGIN Latin, 'connection'.

copulate /kop-yuu-layt/ • v. (**copulates,
copulating, copulated**) have sexual
intercourse.
– DERIVATIVES **copulation** n.
– ORIGIN Latin *copulare* 'fasten together'.

copy • n. (pl. **copies**) **1** a thing made to be
similar or identical to another. **2** a single
example of a particular book, record,
etc. **3** matter to be printed in a book,
newspaper, or magazine. • v. (**copies,
copying, copied**) **1** make a copy of.
2 imitate the behaviour or style of.
– ORIGIN Latin *copia* 'abundance'.

copybook • n. a book containing models
of handwriting for learners to imitate.
• adj. exactly following established
standards: *a copybook landing*.

copycat • n. informal a person who copies
another.

copyist • n. a person who makes copies.

copyright • n. the exclusive legal right
to publish, perform, film, or record
literary, artistic, or musical material.

copywriter • n. a person who writes
advertisements or publicity material.

coquette /ko-ket/ • n. a woman who
flirts.
– DERIVATIVES **coquetry** n. **coquettish** adj.
– ORIGIN French.

coracle /ko-ruh-k'l/ • n. a small, round
boat made of wickerwork covered with a
watertight material, propelled with a
paddle.
– ORIGIN Welsh *corwgl*.

coral • n. **1** a hard substance produced by
certain sea creatures as an external
skeleton. **2** precious red coral, used in
jewellery. **3** a pinkish-red colour.
– ORIGIN Greek *korallion, kouralion*.

cor anglais /kor ong-glay/ • n. (pl. **cors
anglais** /kor ong-glay/) a woodwind
instrument of the oboe family, sounding
a fifth lower than the oboe.
– ORIGIN French, 'English horn'.

corbel /kor-b'l/ • n. a projection jutting
out from a wall to support a structure
above it.
– ORIGIN Old French 'little crow'.

cord • n. **1** thin string or rope made from
several twisted strands. **2** a length of
cord. **3** a structure in the body

resembling a cord. **4** an electric flex.
5 corduroy. **6** (**cords**) corduroy trousers.
– ORIGIN Greek *khordē*.

> **USAGE:** On the confusion of **chord** and
> **cord**, see the note at **CHORD**¹.

cordial • adj. **1** warm and friendly.
2 deeply felt: *a cordial loathing*. • n. Brit.
a sweet fruit-flavoured drink.
– DERIVATIVES **cordiality** n. **cordially** adv.
– ORIGIN Latin *cordialis*.

cordite • n. a smokeless explosive.
– ORIGIN from **CORD**.

cordless • adj. (of an electrical
appliance) working without connection
to a mains supply or central unit.

cordon /kor-d'n/ • n. a line or circle of
police, soldiers, or guards forming a
barrier. • v. (**cordon something off**)
close somewhere off by means of a
cordon.
– ORIGIN Italian *cordone* and French
cordon.

cordon bleu /kor-don bler/ • adj. (of a
cook or cooking) of the highest class.
– ORIGIN French, 'blue ribbon'.

corduroy /kor-duh-roy/ • n. a thick
cotton fabric with velvety ribs.
– ORIGIN prob. from **CORD** + *duroy*, a
former kind of lightweight fabric.

core • n. **1** the tough central part of
various fruits. **2** the central or most
important part of something. **3** the
dense central region of a planet. **4** the
central part of a nuclear reactor.
• v. (**cores, coring, cored**) remove the
core from a fruit.
– DERIVATIVES **corer** n.

co-respondent • n. a person named in a
divorce case as having committed
adultery with the husband or wife of
the person who wants a divorce.

corgi (also **Welsh corgi**) • n. (pl. **corgis**) a
breed of dog with short legs and a fox-
like head.
– ORIGIN Welsh.

coriander /ko-ri-an-der/ • n. a herb of
the parsley family, used in cookery.
– ORIGIN Old French *coriandre*.

cork • n. **1** the buoyant, brown substance
obtained from the bark of a kind of oak
tree. **2** a bottle stopper made of cork.
• v. **1** seal a bottle with a cork. **2** (as adj.
corked) (of wine) spoilt by a faulty cork.
– ORIGIN Dutch and German *kork*.

corkage • n. a charge made by a
restaurant for serving wine that has
been brought in by a customer.

corker • n. informal an excellent person or
thing.
– DERIVATIVES **corking** adj.

corkscrew • n. a device with a spiral
metal rod, used for pulling corks from

bottles. • v. move or twist in a spiral.

corm • n. an underground storage organ
of some plants.
– ORIGIN Greek *kormos* 'trunk stripped of
its boughs'.

cormorant /kor-muh-ruhnt/ • n. a
diving seabird with a long hooked bill
and black plumage.
– ORIGIN Old French *cormaran*.

corn¹ • n. **1** Brit. the chief cereal crop of a
district (in England, wheat). **2** N. Amer. &
Austral./NZ maize.
– ORIGIN Old English.

corn² • n. a painful area of thickened skin
on the foot, caused by pressure.
– ORIGIN Latin *cornu* 'horn'.

corncob • n. the central part of an ear of
maize, to which the grains are attached.

cornea /kor-ni-uh/ • n. the transparent
layer forming the front of the eye.
– ORIGIN from Latin *cornea tela* 'horny
tissue'.

corned beef • n. Brit. pressed beef
preserved in salt, typically sold in tins.

cornelian /kor-nee-li-uhn/ • n. var. of
CARNELIAN.

corner • n. **1** a place or angle where two
or more sides or edges meet. **2** a place
where two streets meet. **3** a remote area.
4 a difficult or awkward position. **5** (also
corner kick) Football a free kick taken by
the attacking side from a corner of the
field. • v. (**corners, cornering, cornered**)
1 force into a place or situation from
which it is hard to escape. **2** go round a
bend in a road. **3** control a market by
dominating the supply of particular
goods.
– ORIGIN Latin *cornu* 'horn, corner'.

corner shop • n. Brit. a small shop selling
groceries and general goods in a residential area.

cornerstone • n. **1** a vital part: *sugar was
the cornerstone of the economy*. **2** a stone
that forms the base of a corner of a
building.

cornet /kor-nit/ • n. **1** a brass instrument
resembling a trumpet but shorter and
wider. **2** Brit. a cone-shaped wafer for
holding ice cream.
– DERIVATIVES **cornetist** /kor-nett-ist/
(also **cornettist**) n.
– ORIGIN Old French, 'little horn'.

cornflakes • pl. n. a breakfast cereal
consisting of toasted flakes made from
maize flour.

cornflour • n. Brit. ground maize flour,
used for thickening sauces.

cornflower • n. a plant with deep blue
flowers.

cornice /kor-niss/ • n. **1** a decorative
moulding round the wall of a room just

below the ceiling. **2** a horizontal moulded projection crowning a building or structure.
– ORIGIN Italian.

Cornish •adj. relating to Cornwall.
•n. the ancient Celtic language of Cornwall.

Cornish pasty •n. Brit. a pasty containing meat and vegetables.

cornucopia /kor-nyuu-koh-pi-uh/ •n. **1** an abundant supply of good things. **2** a symbol of plenty consisting of a goat's horn overflowing with flowers, fruit, and corn.
– ORIGIN from Latin *cornu copiae* 'horn of plenty'.

corny •adj. (**cornier, corniest**) informal unoriginal or very sentimental.
– ORIGIN from **CORN**[1].

corolla /kuh-**rol**-luh/ •n. the petals of a flower.
– ORIGIN Latin, 'little crown'.

corollary /kuh-**rol**-luh-ri/ •n. (pl. **corollaries**) **1** a direct consequence or result. **2** a logical proposition that follows from one already proved.
– ORIGIN Latin *corollarium* 'gratuity'.

corona /kuh-**roh**-nuh/ •n. (pl. **coronae** /kuh-**roh**-nee/) **1** the envelope of gas around the sun or a star. **2** a small circle of light seen round the sun or moon.
– ORIGIN Latin, 'crown'.

coronary /ko-ruh-nuh-ri/ •adj. relating to the arteries which surround and supply the heart. •n. (pl. **coronaries**) (also **coronary thrombosis**) a blockage of the flow of blood to the heart, caused by a clot in a coronary artery.
– ORIGIN Latin *coronarius* 'resembling or forming a crown'.

coronation •n. the ceremony of crowning a king or queen.
– ORIGIN Latin.

coroner /ko-ruh-ner/ •n. an official who holds inquests into violent, sudden, or suspicious deaths.
– ORIGIN Old French *coruner*.

coronet /ko-ruh-net/ •n. **1** a small or simple crown. **2** a decorative band worn around the head.
– ORIGIN Old French *coronete*.

corpora pl. of **CORPUS**.

corporal[1] •n. a rank of non-commissioned officer in the army, below sergeant.
– ORIGIN Italian *caporale*.

corporal[2] •adj. relating to the human body.
– ORIGIN Latin *corporalis*.

corporal punishment •n. physical punishment, such as caning.

corporate •adj. **1** relating to a business

corporation. **2** relating to or shared by all members of a group: *corporate responsibility*.
– ORIGIN Latin *corporare* 'form into a body'.

corporation •n. **1** a large company or group of companies, recognized by law as a single unit. **2** Brit. a group of people elected to govern a city, town, or borough.

corporatism •n. the control of a state or organization by large interest groups.
– DERIVATIVES **corporatist** adj. & n.

corporeal /kor-**por**-i-uhl/ •adj. relating to a person's body; physical rather than spiritual.
– ORIGIN Latin *corporealis*.

corps /kor/ •n. (pl. **corps** /korz/) **1** a main subdivision of an army in the field. **2** a branch of an army given a particular kind of work. **3** a group of people engaged in a particular activity: *the press corps*.
– ORIGIN French.

corps de ballet /kor duh **bal**-lay/ •n. the members of a ballet company who dance together as a group.

corpse •n. a dead body, especially of a person.
– ORIGIN Latin *corpus*.

corpulent /kor-pyuu-luhnt/ •adj. (of a person) fat.
– DERIVATIVES **corpulence** n.
– ORIGIN Latin *corpulentus*.

corpus /kor-puhss/ •n. (pl. **corpora** /kor-puh-ruh/ or **corpuses**) a collection of written works.
– ORIGIN Latin, 'body'.

corpuscle /kor-pus-s'l/ •n. a red or white blood cell.
– ORIGIN Latin *corpusculum* 'small body'.

corral /kuh-**rahl**/ •n. N. Amer. a pen for livestock on a farm or ranch. •v. (**corrals, corralling, corralled**) **1** N. Amer. put or keep livestock in a corral. **2** gather a group together.
– ORIGIN Spanish and Portuguese.

correct •adj. **1** free from error; true; right. **2** following accepted social standards. •v. **1** put right an error or fault. **2** mark the errors in written work. **3** tell someone that they are mistaken.
– DERIVATIVES **correctly** adv. **correctness** n. **corrector** n.
– ORIGIN Latin *corrigere*.

correction •n. **1** the action of correcting. **2** a change that corrects something wrong.

corrective •adj. designed to correct something undesirable. •n. a corrective measure.

correlate /ko-ruh-layt/ •v. (**correlates,**

correlating, correlated) be in or bring into a relationship in which one thing depends on another and vice versa: *the Victorian attempt to correlate head size with brain power.*

correlation • n. **1** a relationship in which one thing depends on another and vice versa. **2** the process of correlating things.
– DERIVATIVES **correlative** adj.

correspond • v. **1** match or agree almost exactly. **2** be comparable or equivalent in character or form. **3** communicate by exchanging letters.
– ORIGIN Latin *correspondere.*

correspondence • n. **1** a close similarity, link, or equivalence. **2** letters sent or received.

correspondence course • n. a course of study in which student and tutors communicate by post.

correspondent • n. **1** a journalist who reports on a particular subject. **2** a person who writes letters.

corridor • n. **1** a passage in a building or train, with doors leading into rooms or compartments. **2** a strip of land linking two other areas.
– PHRASES **the corridors of power** the senior levels of government or administration.
– ORIGIN Italian *corridore.*

corroborate /kuh-rob-uh-rayt/
• v. (**corroborates, corroborating, corroborated**) confirm or give support to a statement or theory.
– DERIVATIVES **corroboration** n.
– ORIGIN Latin *corroborare* 'strengthen'.

corrode /kuh-rohd/ • v. (**corrodes, corroding, corroded**) **1** (of metal or other hard material) wear or be worn away slowly by chemical action. **2** gradually weaken or destroy: *the affair corroded her self-esteem.*
– ORIGIN Latin *corrodere.*

corrosion /kuh-roh-zh'n/ • n. **1** the process of wearing something away. **2** the damage caused by this.

corrosive • adj. causing corrosion.

corrugate /ko-ruh-gayt/
• v. (**corrugates, corrugating, corrugated**) **1** contract into wrinkles or folds. **2** (as adj. **corrugated**) shaped into alternate ridges and grooves.
– DERIVATIVES **corrugation** n.
– ORIGIN Latin *corrugare.*

corrupt • adj. **1** willing to act dishonestly in return for money or personal gain. **2** evil or immoral. **3** (of a written work or computer data) made unreliable by errors or alterations. • v. make corrupt.
– DERIVATIVES **corrupter** n. **corruptible** adj.

– ORIGIN Latin *corrumpere* 'bribe, destroy'.

corruption • n. **1** dishonest or illegal behaviour. **2** the action of corrupting.

corsage /kor-sahzh/ • n. a spray of flowers worn pinned to a woman's clothes.
– ORIGIN French.

corsair /kor-sair/ • n. old use a pirate.
– ORIGIN French *corsaire.*

corset • n. **1** a woman's tight-fitting undergarment worn to shape the figure. **2** a similar garment worn to support a weak or injured back.
– DERIVATIVES **corsetry** n.
– ORIGIN Old French, 'little body'.

Corsican • n. **1** a person from Corsica. **2** the language of Corsica. • adj. relating to Corsica.

cortège /kor-tezh/ • n. a solemn funeral procession.
– ORIGIN Italian *corteggio* 'entourage'.

cortex /kor-teks/ • n. (pl. **cortices** /kor-ti-seez/) the outer layer of a bodily organ or structure, especially the outer, folded layer of the brain (**cerebral cortex**).
– DERIVATIVES **cortical** adj.
– ORIGIN Latin, 'bark of a tree'.

cortisone /kor-ti-zohn/ • n. a steroid hormone used to treat inflammation and allergies.
– ORIGIN from its chemical name.

corundum /kuh-run-duhm/ • n. an extremely hard form of aluminium oxide, used for grinding, smoothing, and polishing.
– ORIGIN Tamil.

coruscating /ko-ruh-skay-ting/
• adj. literary flashing or sparkling.
– ORIGIN Latin *coruscare* 'glitter'.

corvette /kor-vet/ • n. a small warship used to escort convoys.
– ORIGIN French.

cos[1] /koss/ • n. Brit. a variety of lettuce with crisp narrow leaves.
– ORIGIN named after the Greek island of *Cos* (now *Kos*).

cos[2] /koz/ • abbrev. cosine.

cosec /koh-sek/ • abbrev. cosecant.

cosecant /koh-see-kuhnt, koh-sek-uhnt/ • n. (in a right-angled triangle) the ratio of the hypotenuse to the side opposite an acute angle.

cosh Brit. • n. a thick heavy stick or bar used as a weapon. • v. hit with a cosh.

cosine /koh-syn/ • n. (in a right-angled triangle) the ratio of the side adjacent to a particular acute angle to the hypotenuse.

cosmetic • adj. **1** relating to treatment intended to improve a person's

appearance. **2** improving something only outwardly: *the reforms were merely a cosmetic exercise*. • n. (**cosmetics**) cosmetic substances for the face and body.
– DERIVATIVES **cosmetically** adv.
– ORIGIN Greek *kosmein* 'arrange'.

cosmic • adj. relating to the universe.
– DERIVATIVES **cosmical** adj. **cosmically** adv.

cosmogony /koz-**mog**-uh-ni/ • n. (pl. **cosmogonies**) the branch of science concerned with the origin of the universe, especially the solar system.
– ORIGIN from Greek *kosmos* 'order or world' + *-gonia* '-creating'.

cosmology • n. (pl. **cosmologies**) the science of the origin and development of the universe.
– DERIVATIVES **cosmological** adj. **cosmologist** n.

cosmonaut • n. a Russian astronaut.
– ORIGIN from **cosmos** + Greek *nautēs* 'sailor'.

cosmopolitan /koz-muh-**pol**-i-tuhn/ • adj. **1** consisting of people from many different countries: *Barcelona is a cosmopolitan city*. **2** familiar with and at ease in many different countries.
– ORIGIN from Greek *kosmos* 'world' + *politēs* 'citizen'.

cosmos • n. the universe.
– ORIGIN Greek *kosmos* 'order or world'.

Cossack /**koss**-ak/ • n. a member of a people of southern Russia, Ukraine, and Siberia, noted for their horsemanship and military skill.
– ORIGIN Russian *kazak* 'nomad'.

cosset • v. (**cossets, cosseting, cosseted**) care for and protect someone in an excessively soft-hearted way.

cost • v. (**costs, costing, cost**) **1** be able to be bought or done for a specific price. **2** involve the loss of: *his heroism cost him his life*. **3** (**costs, costing, costed**) estimate the cost of something. • n. **1** an amount given or required as payment. **2** the effort or loss necessary to achieve something: *the cuts came at the cost of customer service*. **3** (**costs**) legal expenses.
– PHRASES **to someone's cost** with loss or disadvantage to someone.
– ORIGIN Latin *constare* 'stand firm'.

co-star • n. a film or stage star appearing with another or other stars of equal importance. • v. **1** appear in a film or play as a co-star. **2** (of a production) include someone as a co-star.

Costa Rican /kos-tuh **ree**-kuhn/ • n. a person from Costa Rica, a republic in Central America. • adj. relating to Costa Rica.

cost-effective (also **cost-efficient**)

• adj. effective or productive in relation to its cost.

costermonger /**koss**-ter-mung-ger/ • n. Brit. dated a person who sells fruit and vegetables from a barrow in the street.
– ORIGIN from *Costard* (a type of apple) + **-MONGER**.

costing • n. the estimated cost of doing or producing something.

costly • adj. (**costlier, costliest**) **1** expensive; not cheap. **2** causing suffering, loss, or disadvantage: *a costly mistake*.
– DERIVATIVES **costliness** n.

cost price • n. the price at which goods are bought by a retailer.

costume • n. **1** a set of clothes in a style typical of a particular country or historical period. **2** a set of clothes worn by an actor or performer for a role. • v. (**costumes, costuming, costumed**) dress in a costume.
– ORIGIN Italian, 'custom, fashion'.

costume jewellery • n. jewellery made with inexpensive materials or imitation gems.

costumier /koss-**tyoo**-mi-er/ • n. a maker or supplier of theatrical or fancy-dress costumes.

cosy (US **cozy**) • adj. (**cosier, cosiest**) **1** comfortable, warm, and secure. **2** not difficult or demanding: *the cosy belief that man is master*. • n. (pl. **cosies**) a cover to keep a teapot or a boiled egg hot.
– DERIVATIVES **cosily** adv. **cosiness** n.

cot[1] • n. Brit. a small bed with high barred sides for a baby or very young child.
– ORIGIN Hindi, 'bedstead, hammock'.

cot[2] • abbrev. cotangent.

cotangent /koh-**tan**-juhnt/ • n. (in a right-angled triangle) the ratio of the side (other than the hypotenuse) adjacent to a particular acute angle to the side opposite the angle.

cot death • n. Brit. the unexplained death of a baby in its sleep.

coterie /**koh**-tuh-ri/ • n. (pl. **coteries**) a small exclusive group of people with shared interests.
– ORIGIN French.

cottage • n. a small house in the country.
– DERIVATIVES **cottager** n. **cottagey** adj.
– ORIGIN Latin *cotagium*.

cottage cheese • n. soft, lumpy white cheese made from the curds of skimmed milk.

cottage industry • n. a business or manufacturing activity carried on in people's homes.

cottage pie • n. Brit. a dish of minced meat topped with mashed potato.

cotter pin • n. **1** a metal pin used to

c

fasten two parts of a mechanism together. **2** a split pin that is opened out after being passed through a hole.

cotton • n. the soft white fibres which surround the seeds of a tropical and subtropical plant, used to make cloth or thread for sewing. • v. (**cotton on**) informal begin to understand.
– DERIVATIVES **cottony** adj.
– ORIGIN Arabic.

cotton wool • n. Brit. fluffy soft material, used for applying or removing cosmetics or bathing wounds.

cotyledon /ko-ti-lee-duhn/ • n. the first leaf to grow from a germinating seed.
– ORIGIN Greek *kotulēdōn* 'cup-shaped cavity'.

couch /kowch/ • n. **1** a long padded piece of furniture for several people to sit on. **2** a long seat with a headrest at one end on which a person lies during medical treatment or psychoanalysis. • v. express in language of a particular style: *some warnings are couched in general terms.*
– ORIGIN Old French *couche*.

couchette /koo-shet/ • n. **1** a railway carriage with seats convertible into sleeping berths. **2** a berth in a couchette.
– ORIGIN French, 'small couch'.

couch potato • n. informal a person who spends a great deal of time watching television.

cougar /koo-ger/ • n. N. Amer. a puma.
– ORIGIN French *couguar*.

cough • v. **1** send out air from the lungs with a sudden sharp sound. **2** (**cough something up**) informal give money or information reluctantly. • n. **1** an act of coughing. **2** an illness of the throat or lungs causing coughing.

could • modal verb past of CAN¹.

couldn't • contr. could not.

coulomb /koo-lom/ • n. the unit of electric charge in the SI system.
– ORIGIN named after the French military engineer Charles-Augustin de *Coulomb*.

council • n. **1** an assembly of people meeting regularly to advise on, discuss, or organize something. **2** a group of people elected to manage a city, county, or district. • adj. Brit. (of housing) provided by a local council.
– ORIGIN Latin *concilium* 'assembly'.

> **USAGE:** Do not confuse **council** with **counsel**. **Council** means 'a group that manages an area or advises on something' (*the city council*), whereas **counsel** means 'advice' (*wise counsel*) or 'advise someone'.

councillor (US also **councilor**) • n. a member of a council.

council tax • n. (in Britain) a tax charged on households by local

authorities, based on the estimated value of a property.

counsel • n. **1** advice given to someone. **2** (pl. **counsel**) a barrister or other legal adviser conducting a case. • v. (**counsels, counselling, counselled**; US **counsels, counseling, counseled**) **1** advise or recommend. **2** give professional help and advice to someone with psychological or personal problems.
– PHRASES **keep your own counsel** keep your plans or opinions to yourself.
– ORIGIN Latin *consilium* 'advice'.

counsellor (US **counselor**) • n. a person trained to give advice on personal or psychological problems.

count¹ • v. **1** find the total number of a collection of people or things. **2** say numbers in ascending order. **3** include when calculating a total. **4** regard as being: *people she had counted as her friends.* **5** be important. **6** (**count on**) rely on. **7** (**count someone in** or **out**) include (or not include) someone in an activity. • n. **1** an act of counting. **2** a total found by counting: *a low pollen count.* **3** a point to be discussed or considered. **4** Law each of the charges against an accused person.
– PHRASES **out for the count 1** Boxing defeated by being knocked to the ground and unable to get up within ten seconds. **2** unconscious or asleep.
– DERIVATIVES **countable** adj.
– ORIGIN Latin *computare*.

count² • n. a foreign nobleman whose rank corresponds to that of an earl.
– ORIGIN Old French *conte*.

countdown • n. **1** an act of counting backwards to zero to launch a rocket. **2** the final moments before a significant event.

countenance /kown-tuh-nuhnss/ • n. a person's face or facial expression. • v. (**countenances, countenancing, countenanced**) tolerate or allow.
– ORIGIN Old French *contenance* 'bearing'.

counter¹ • n. **1** a long flat surface over which goods are sold or served or across which business is conducted with customers. **2** a small disc used in board games for keeping the score or as a place marker. **3** a person or thing that counts something.
– PHRASES **over the counter** by ordinary sale in a shop. **under the counter** bought or sold secretly and illegally.
– ORIGIN Old French *conteor*.

counter² • v. (**counters, countering, countered**) speak or act in opposition or response to: *he helped to counter an invasion.* • adv. (**counter to**) in the opposite direction or in opposition to.

• **adj.** opposing. • **n.** an act which opposes something else.
− ORIGIN Latin *contra* 'against'.

counter- • **prefix 1** opposing or done in return: *counter-attack.* **2** corresponding: *counterpart.*

counteract • **v.** act against something so as to reduce its force or cancel it out.

counter-attack • **n.** an attack made in response to an attack. • **v.** attack in response.

counterbalance • **n.** /kown-ter-bal-uhnss/ **1** a weight that balances another. **2** a factor that has the opposite effect to that of another and balances it out. • **v.** /kown-ter-**bal**-uhnss/ (**counterbalances, counterbalancing, counterbalanced**) have an opposing and balancing effect on.

counter-espionage • **n.** activities designed to prevent spying by an enemy.

counterfeit /kown-ter-fit/ • **adj.** made to imitate something valuable exactly so as to deceive or cheat people. • **n.** a forgery. • **v. 1** imitate fraudulently. **2** pretend to feel or possess: *no pretence could have counterfeited such terror.*
− DERIVATIVES **counterfeiter** n.
− ORIGIN Old French *contrefait* 'made in opposition'.

> ☑ Spell **counterfeit** with **-eit** at the end.

counterfoil • **n.** Brit. the part of a cheque, ticket, or receipt that is kept as a record by the person issuing it.

countermand /kown-ter-**mahnd**/ • **v.** cancel an order.
− ORIGIN Latin *contramandare.*

countermeasure • **n.** an action taken to counteract a danger or threat.

counterpane • **n.** a bedspread.
− ORIGIN Old French *contrepointe.*

counterpart • **n.** a person or thing that corresponds to another.

counterpoint • **n. 1** the technique of writing or playing a melody or melodies together with another. **2** a melody played together with another. **3** a pleasing or notable contrast: *the sauce made a piquant counterpoint to the ham.*

counterpoise • **n. & v.** (**counterpoises, counterpoising, counterpoised**) = COUNTERBALANCE.

counterproductive • **adj.** having the opposite of the desired effect.

countersign • **v.** sign a document already signed by another person.

countersink • **v.** (**countersinks, countersinking, countersunk**) insert a screw or bolt so that the head lies flat with the surface.

countertenor • **n.** the highest male adult singing voice.

counterterrorism • **n.** political or military activities designed to prevent terrorism.
− DERIVATIVES **counterterrorist** n. & adj.

countervail /kown-ter-**vayl**/ • **v.** (usu. as adj. **countervailing**) counteract something with something else of equal force: *countervailing pressure.*
− ORIGIN from Latin *contra valere* 'be of worth against'.

countess • **n. 1** the wife or widow of a count or earl. **2** a woman holding the rank of count or earl.

counting • **prep.** taking account of; including.

countless • **adj.** too many to be counted; very many.

count noun • **n.** a noun that can form a plural and, in the singular, can be used with *a*, e.g. *books, a book.* Contrasted with MASS NOUN.

countrified • **adj.** characteristic of the country or country life.

country • **n.** (pl. **countries**) **1** a nation with its own government. **2** districts outside large city areas. **3** an area with particular physical features: *hill country.*
− PHRASES **across country** not keeping to roads.
− ORIGIN Old French *cuntree.*

country and western • **n.** country music.

country club • **n.** a club in a country area with sporting and social facilities.

country dance • **n.** a traditional type of English dance, performed by couples facing each other in long lines.

countryman (or **countrywoman**) • **n.** (pl. **countrymen** or **countrywomen**) **1** a person living or born in the country. **2** a person from the same country as someone else.

country music • **n.** a form of popular music originating in the rural southern US, featuring ballads and dance tunes.

countryside • **n.** the land and scenery of a rural area.

county • **n.** (pl. **counties**) **1** each of the main areas into which some countries are divided for the purposes of local government. **2** US a political and administrative division of a state.
− ORIGIN Old French *conte* 'land of a count'.

county council • **n.** (in the UK) the elected governing body of a county.

county court • **n.** (in England and Wales) a local court for civil cases.

county town • **n.** the town that is the administrative capital of a county.

coup /koo/ •n. (pl. **coups** /kooz/) **1** (also **coup d'état** /koo day-tah/) a sudden violent seizure of power from a government. [ORIGIN French, 'blow of state'.] **2** a successful move: *the deal is a major coup for the company.*
– ORIGIN French.

coup de grâce /koo duh grahss/ •n. (pl. **coups de grâce** /koo duh grahss/) a final blow or shot given to kill a wounded person or animal.
– ORIGIN French, 'stroke of grace'.

coupé /koo-pay/ (also **coupe** /koop/) •n. a car with a fixed roof, two doors, and a sloping back.
– ORIGIN from French *carrosse coupé* 'cut carriage'.

couple •n. **1** two people or things of the same sort considered together. **2** two people who are married or in a romantic or sexual relationship. **3** informal an indefinite small number. •v. (**couples, coupling, coupled**) **1** connect or combine: *my routine, coupled with a good diet, will build up your biceps.* **2** have sex.
– DERIVATIVES **coupler** n.
– ORIGIN Latin *copula* 'connection'.

couplet •n. a pair of rhyming lines of poetry one after another.

coupling •n. a device for connecting railway vehicles or parts of machinery together.

coupon •n. **1** a voucher which entitles the holder to a discount or to buy something. **2** a detachable form used to send for information or to enter a competition.
– ORIGIN French, 'piece cut off'.

courage •n. **1** the ability to do something frightening. **2** strength in the face of pain or grief.
– PHRASES **have the courage of your convictions** act on your beliefs despite danger or disapproval.
– ORIGIN Old French *corage.*

courageous •adj. having courage; brave.
– DERIVATIVES **courageously** adv.

courgette /koor-zhet/ •n. Brit. a variety of small vegetable marrow.
– ORIGIN French, 'little gourd'.

courier /kuu-ri-er/ •n. **1** a person employed to deliver goods or documents quickly. **2** esp. Brit. a person employed to guide and help a group of tourists.
– ORIGIN Old French *coreor.*

course •n. **1** a direction taken or intended: *the aircraft changed course.* **2** the way in which something progresses or develops: *the course of history.* **3** (also **course of action**) a way of dealing with a situation. **4** a dish forming one of the stages of a meal. **5** a

series of lectures or lessons in a particular subject. **6** a series of repeated treatments or doses of medication. **7** an area of land or water prepared for golf, racing, or another sport. •v. (**courses, coursing, coursed**) **1** (of liquid) flow. **2** (as noun **coursing**) hunting game, especially hares, with greyhounds using sight rather than scent.
– PHRASES **in (the) course of 1** in the process of. **2** during. **of course 1** as expected. **2** certainly; yes.
– ORIGIN Latin *cursus* 'running'.

> **USAGE:** On the difference between **course** and **coarse**, see the note at **COARSE**.

coursework •n. work done during a course of study, counting towards a final mark.

court •n. **1** (also **court of law**) the judge, jury, and law officers before whom legal cases are heard. **2** the place where a court of law meets. **3** a quadrangular area marked out for ball games such as tennis. **4** a quadrangle surrounded by a building or group of buildings. **5** the home, councillors, and household staff of a sovereign. •v. **1** try to win the support of someone. **2** behave in a way that makes you vulnerable to: *he often courted controversy.* **3** dated try to win the love of someone you want to marry.
– PHRASES **hold court** be the centre of attention. **out of court** before a legal hearing can take place. **pay court to** pay flattering attention to.
– ORIGIN Old French *cort.*

court card •n. Brit. a playing card that is a king, queen, or jack of a suit.

courteous /ker-ti-uhss/ •adj. polite and considerate.
– DERIVATIVES **courteously** adv.
– ORIGIN Old French *corteis* 'having manners fit for a royal court'.

courtesan /kor-ti-zan/ •n. a prostitute with wealthy or upper-class clients.
– ORIGIN French *courtisane.*

courtesy /ker-tuh-si/ •n. (pl. **courtesies**) **1** polite and considerate behaviour. **2** a polite speech or action.
– PHRASES **(by) courtesy of** given or allowed by.

courthouse •n. a building in which a court of law is held.

courtier /kor-ti-er/ •n. a sovereign's companion or adviser.

courtly •adj. (**courtlier, courtliest**) very dignified and polite.
– DERIVATIVES **courtliness** n.

court martial •n. (pl. **courts martial**) a court for trying members of the armed services accused of breaking military law. •v. (**court-martial**) (**court-martials,**

court-martialling, court-martialled; US **court-martials, court-martialing, court-martialed**) try someone by court martial.

court order • n. a direction issued by a court or a judge requiring a person to do or not do something.

courtroom • n. the room or building in which a court of law meets.

courtship • n. 1 a period during which a couple develop a romantic relationship. 2 the process of trying to win a person's love or support.

court shoe • n. Brit. a woman's plain shoe with a low-cut upper and no fastening.

courtyard • n. an open area enclosed by walls or buildings.

couscous /**kuuss**-kuuss, **kooss**-kooss/ • n. a North African dish of steamed or soaked semolina, served with spicy meat or vegetables.
– ORIGIN Arabic.

cousin • n. 1 (also **first cousin**) a child of your uncle or aunt. 2 a person of a similar people or nation.
– PHRASES **second cousin** a child of your parent's first cousin.
– ORIGIN Old French *cosin*.

couture /koo-**tyoor**/ • n. the design and manufacture of fashionable clothes to a client's specific requirements.
– ORIGIN French, 'dressmaking'.

couturier /koo-**tyoo**-ri-ay/ • n. (fem. **couturière** /koo-**tyoo**-ri-**air**/) a person who designs and sells couture clothes.

cove • n. a small sheltered bay.
– ORIGIN Old English, 'chamber, cave'.

coven /**kuv**-uhn/ • n. a group of witches who meet regularly.
– ORIGIN Latin *convenire* 'come together'.

covenant /**kuv**-uh-nuhnt/ • n. 1 a formal agreement, especially a written contract by which you agree to make regular payments to a charity. 2 (in Judaism and Christianity) an agreement which brings about a commitment between God and his people. • v. agree or pay by covenant.
– ORIGIN Old French, 'agreeing'.

cover • v. (**covers, covering, covered**) 1 put something over or in front of someone or something so as to protect or hide them. 2 spread or extend over: *the grounds covered eight acres.* 3 deal with or report on: *the course covers a range of subjects.* 4 travel a specified distance. 5 (of money) be enough to pay for something. 6 (of insurance) protect against a loss or accident. 7 (**cover something up**) try to hide or deny a mistake or crime. 8 (**cover for**) temporarily take over the job of a colleague. • n. 1 something that covers or

protects. 2 a thick protective outer part or page of a book or magazine. 3 shelter: *they ran for cover.* 4 a means of concealing an illegal or secret activity: *his neat office was a cover for his real work.* 5 Brit. protection by insurance. 6 (also **cover version**) a recording or performance of a song previously recorded by a different artist.
– PHRASES **break cover** suddenly leave shelter when being chased. **under cover of** concealed by.
– DERIVATIVES **covering** n.
– ORIGIN Old French *covrir*.

coverage • n. 1 the treatment of a subject by the media. 2 the extent to which something is covered.

cover charge • n. a service charge per person added to the bill in a restaurant.

covering letter • n. an explanatory letter sent with another document or a parcel.

coverlet • n. a bedspread.
– ORIGIN from Old French *covrir* 'to cover' + *lit* 'bed'.

cover note • n. Brit. a temporary certificate showing that a person has a current insurance policy.

covert • adj. /**kuv**-ert, koh-**vert**/ not done openly; secret. • n. /**kuv**-ert/ an area of bushes or trees where game can hide.
– DERIVATIVES **covertly** adv.
– ORIGIN Old French, 'covered'.

cover-up • n. an attempt to conceal a mistake or crime.

covet /**kuv**-it/ • v. (**covets, coveting, coveted**) long to possess something belonging to someone else.
– ORIGIN Old French *cuveitier*.

covetous • adj. longing to possess something.

covey /**kuv**-i/ • n. (pl. **coveys**) a small flock of game birds.
– ORIGIN Old French *cover* 'sit on, hatch'.

coving • n. a concave arched moulding, especially one at the junction of a wall with a ceiling.
– ORIGIN related to **cove**.

cow[1] • n. 1 a mature female animal of a domesticated breed of ox. 2 the female of certain other large animals, such as the elephant. 3 informal, derog. a disliked woman.
– ORIGIN Old English.

cow[2] • v. frighten someone into giving in to your wishes.
– ORIGIN prob. from Old Norse, 'oppress'.

coward • n. a person who is afraid to do dangerous or unpleasant things.
– DERIVATIVES **cowardliness** n. **cowardly** adj.
– ORIGIN Old French *couard*.

cowardice /kow-er-diss/ • n. lack of courage.

cowboy • n. **1** a man on horseback who herds cattle in the western US. **2** Brit. informal a dishonest or unqualified tradesman.

cower • v. (**cowers, cowering, cowered**) crouch down or shrink back in fear.
– ORIGIN German *küren* 'lie in wait'.

cowl • n. **1** a large loose hood forming part of a monk's robe. **2** a covering for a chimney or ventilation shaft.
– ORIGIN Latin *cucullus* 'hood of a cloak'.

cowlick • n. a lock of hair hanging over the forehead.

cowling • n. a removable cover for a vehicle or aircraft engine.

cowpat • n. Brit. a flat, round piece of cow dung.

cowrie /kow-ri/ • n. (pl. **cowries**) a sea mollusc having a glossy shell with a long, narrow opening.
– ORIGIN Hindi.

cowslip • n. a wild plant with clusters of yellow flowers.
– ORIGIN Old English, 'cow slime'.

cox • n. a coxswain. • v. act as a coxswain for.

coxcomb /koks-kohm/ • n. old use a vain and conceited man; a dandy.
– ORIGIN from **cockscomb**.

coxswain /kok-suhn/ • n. a person who steers a boat.
– ORIGIN from former *cock* 'small boat' + **swain**.

coy • adj. (**coyer, coyest**) **1** pretending to be shy or modest. **2** reluctant to give details about something sensitive: *he's coy about his age.*
– DERIVATIVES **coyly** adv. **coyness** n.
– ORIGIN Old French *coi*.

coyote /koy-oh-ti/ • n. (pl. **coyote** or **coyotes**) a wolf-like wild dog found in North America.
– ORIGIN from a North American Indian language.

coypu /koy-pyoo/ • n. (pl. **coypus**) a large beaver-like South American rodent, farmed for its fur.
– ORIGIN from a Chilean language.

cozen /kuz-uhn/ • v. literary deceive someone.
– ORIGIN perh. from former Italian *cozzonare* 'to cheat'.

cozy • adj. US = **cosy**.

CPS • abbrev. (in the UK) Crown Prosecution Service.

CPU • abbrev. Computing central processing unit.

Cr • symb. the chemical element chromium.

crab • n. a marine shellfish with a broad shell and five pairs of legs.
– PHRASES **catch a crab** make a faulty stroke in rowing in which the oar is jammed under the water or misses the water completely.
– ORIGIN Old English.

crab apple • n. a small, sour kind of apple.
– ORIGIN prob. Scandinavian.

crabbed • adj. **1** (of writing) hard to read. **2** bad-tempered.

crabby • adj. (**crabbier, crabbiest**) bad-tempered.
– DERIVATIVES **crabbily** adv. **crabbiness** n.

crabwise • adv. & adj. (of movement) sideways.

crack • n. **1** a narrow opening between two parts of something which has split or been broken. **2** a sudden sharp noise. **3** a sharp blow. **4** informal a joke. **5** informal an attempt to do something. **6** (also **crack cocaine**) a very strong form of cocaine. • v. **1** break apart or without complete separation of the parts: *take care not to crack the glass.* **2** give way under pressure or strain. **3** make a sudden sharp sound. **4** hit hard. **5** (of a person's voice) suddenly change in pitch. **6** informal solve or decipher: *he took a day to crack the code.* **7** tell a joke.
• adj. very good or skilful: *a crack shot.*
– PHRASES **crack down on** informal take strong action against. **crack of dawn** daybreak. **crack of the whip** Brit. informal a chance to try or take part in something. **crack on** informal proceed or progress quickly. **crack up** informal **1** suffer an emotional breakdown. **2** (**be cracked up to be**) be said to be. **get cracking** informal begin immediately and work quickly.
– ORIGIN Old English.

crackbrained • adj. informal very foolish.

crackdown • n. a series of severe measures against undesirable or illegal behaviour.

cracked • adj. informal mad; crazy.

cracker • n. **1** a paper cylinder which, when pulled apart, makes a sharp noise and releases a small toy. **2** a firework that explodes with a crack. **3** a thin, dry biscuit. **4** Brit. informal a very good example of something.

crackers • adj. Brit. informal mad; crazy.

cracking • adj. Brit. informal **1** excellent. **2** fast: *a cracking pace.*

crackle • v. (**crackles, crackling, crackled**) make a series of slight cracking noises. • n. a crackling sound.
– DERIVATIVES **crackly** adj.

crackling • n. the crisp fatty skin of roast pork.

crackpot informal • n. an eccentric or

foolish person. • adj. eccentric; impractical.

-cracy • comb. form referring to a particular form of government or rule: *democracy*.
– ORIGIN Greek *-kratia* 'power, rule'.

cradle • n. 1 a baby's bed on rockers. 2 a place in which something originates or flourishes: *the Middle East is believed to be the cradle of agriculture*. 3 a supporting framework. • v. (**cradles, cradling, cradled**) hold gently and protectively.
– ORIGIN Old English.

craft • n. 1 an activity involving skill in making things by hand. 2 skill in carrying out work. 3 (**crafts**) things made by hand. 4 skill in deceiving people; cunning. 5 (pl. **craft**) a boat, ship, or aircraft. • v. make something skilfully.
– DERIVATIVES **crafter** n.
– ORIGIN Old English.

craftsman (or **craftswoman**) • n. (pl. **craftsmen** or **craftswomen**) a worker skilled in a particular craft.
– DERIVATIVES **craftsmanship** n.

craftwork • n. 1 the making of things by hand. 2 items produced by hand.
– DERIVATIVES **craftworker** n.

crafty • adj. (**craftier, craftiest**) clever at deceiving people; cunning.
– DERIVATIVES **craftily** adv. **craftiness** n.

crag • n. a steep or rugged rock face.
– DERIVATIVES **craggy** adj.
– ORIGIN Celtic.

cram • v. (**crams, cramming, crammed**) 1 force too many people or things into a space. 2 fill something to overflowing. 3 study hard just before an exam.
– ORIGIN Old English.

crammer • n. Brit. a college that gives students concentrated preparation for exams.

cramp • n. painful and uncontrollable tightening of a muscle or muscles. • v. restrict the development of: *tighter rules will cramp economic growth*.
– ORIGIN German and Dutch *krampe*.

cramped • adj. 1 uncomfortably small or crowded. 2 (of handwriting) small and difficult to read.

crampon /kram-pon/ • n. a plate with spikes, fixed to a boot for climbing on ice or rock.
– ORIGIN Old French.

cranberry • n. (pl. **cranberries**) a small sour-tasting red berry used in cooking.
– ORIGIN German *Kranbeere* 'crane-berry'.

crane • n. 1 a tall machine used for moving heavy objects by suspending them from a projecting arm. 2 a grey or white wading bird with long legs and a long neck. • v. (**cranes, craning, craned**) stretch out your neck to see something.
– ORIGIN Old English.

crane fly • n. a fly with very long legs; a daddy-long-legs.

cranesbill • n. a plant with purple, violet, or pink flowers.

cranium /kray-ni-uhm/ • n. (pl. **craniums** or **crania** /kray-ni-uh/) the part of the skull enclosing the brain.
– DERIVATIVES **cranial** adj.
– ORIGIN Latin.

crank¹ • v. 1 turn a crankshaft or handle. 2 (**crank something up**) informal make something more intense. 3 (**crank something out**) informal produce regularly and routinely: *researchers cranked out worthy studies*. • n. a right-angled part of an axle or shaft, for converting linear to circular motion or vice versa.
– ORIGIN Old English.

crank² • n. an eccentric person.
– ORIGIN from CRANKY.

crankshaft • n. a shaft driven by a crank.

cranky • adj. (**crankier, crankiest**) informal 1 Brit. eccentric or strange. 2 esp. N. Amer. bad-tempered.
– DERIVATIVES **crankily** adv. **crankiness** n.
– ORIGIN perh. from Dutch or German *krank* 'sick'.

cranny • n. (pl. **crannies**) a small, narrow space or opening.
– ORIGIN Latin *crena* 'notch'.

crape • n. black silk, formerly used for mourning clothes.
– ORIGIN from CRÊPE.

craps • n. a North American gambling game played with two dice.
– ORIGIN perh. from CRAB or *crab's eyes*, referring to a throw of two ones.

crapulous /krap-yuu-luhss/ (also **crapulent**) • adj. literary relating to the drinking of alcohol or to drunkenness.
– ORIGIN Latin *crapulentus* 'very drunk'.

crash • v. 1 (of a vehicle) collide violently with an obstacle or another vehicle. 2 (of an aircraft) fall from the sky and hit the land or sea. 3 move with force and sudden loud noise: *huge waves crashed down on us*. 4 (of shares) fall suddenly in value. 5 (of a computer, software, or system) fail suddenly. 6 (also **crash out**) informal fall deeply asleep. • n. an instance or sound of crashing. • adj. rapid and concentrated: *a crash course in Italian*.

crash helmet • n. a helmet worn by a motorcyclist to protect the head.

crashing • adj. informal complete; total: *a crashing bore*.

crash-land • v. (of an aircraft) land roughly in an emergency.

crass • adj. very thoughtless and stupid.
– DERIVATIVES **crassly** adv. **crassness** n.
– ORIGIN Latin *crassus* 'solid, thick'.

-crat • comb. form referring to a member or supporter of a particular form of government or rule: *democrat*.
– ORIGIN Greek *-kratia* 'power, rule'.

crate • n. 1 a wooden case used for transporting goods. 2 a square container divided into sections for holding bottles. 3 informal an old and ramshackle vehicle. • v. (**crates, crating, crated**) pack in a crate.
– ORIGIN perh. from Dutch *krat* 'flap at the back of a wagon'.

crater • n. a large hollow caused by an explosion or impact or forming the mouth of a volcano.
– ORIGIN Greek *kratēr* 'mixing bowl'.

-cratic • comb. form referring to a particular form of government or rule: *democratic*.

cravat /kruh-vat/ • n. a strip of fabric worn by men round the neck and tucked inside a shirt.
– ORIGIN French *cravate*.

crave • v. (**craves, craving, craved**) 1 feel a powerful desire for something. 2 old use ask for something.
– ORIGIN Old English.

craven • adj. not brave; cowardly.
– ORIGIN perh. from Old French *cravanter* 'crush'.

craving • n. a powerful desire for something.

craw • n. dated the crop (part of the throat) of a bird.
– ORIGIN Dutch *crāghe* or German *krage* 'neck'.

crawl • v. 1 move forward on the hands and knees or with the body close to the ground. 2 move along very slowly. 3 (**be crawling with**) be unpleasantly covered or crowded with: *the place was crawling with journalists.* 4 informal behave in an excessively friendly or submissive way to win someone's favour. • n. 1 an act of crawling. 2 a very slow rate of movement. 3 a swimming stroke involving alternate overarm movements and rapid kicks of the legs.
– DERIVATIVES **crawler** n.
– ORIGIN perh. from Swedish *kravla* and Danish *kravle*.

crayfish • n. (pl. **crayfish** or **crayfishes**) a shellfish resembling a small lobster.
– ORIGIN Old French *crevice*.

crayon • n. a stick of coloured chalk or wax, used for drawing. • v. draw with a crayon or crayons.
– ORIGIN French.

craze • n. a widespread but short-lived enthusiasm for something.
– ORIGIN perh. Scandinavian.

crazed • adj. 1 behaving in a wild or mad way. 2 covered with fine cracks.

crazy • adj. (**crazier, craziest**) 1 insane; mad. 2 informal very enthusiastic: *I'm crazy about Cindy.* 3 foolish or ridiculous.
– PHRASES **like crazy** to a great degree.
– DERIVATIVES **crazily** adv. **craziness** n.

crazy paving • n. Brit. paving made of irregular pieces of flat stone.

creak • v. make or move with a scraping or squeaking sound. • n. a creaking sound.
– DERIVATIVES **creaky** adj.

cream • n. 1 the thick fatty liquid which rises to the top when milk is left to stand. 2 a food containing cream or having a creamy texture. 3 a thick liquid cosmetic or medical substance. 4 the very best of a group: *the cream of Paris society.* 5 a very pale yellow or off-white colour. • v. 1 mash a cooked vegetable with milk or cream. 2 work butter to form a smooth soft paste. 3 (**cream someone/thing off**) take away the best of a group.
– ORIGIN Old French *cresme*.

cream cheese • n. soft cheese made from unskimmed milk and cream.

creamer • n. a cream or milk substitute for adding to coffee or tea.

creamery • n. (pl. **creameries**) a factory that produces butter and cheese.

cream of tartar • n. see TARTAR.

creamy • adj. (**creamier, creamiest**) resembling or containing a lot of cream.
– DERIVATIVES **creamily** adv. **creaminess** n.

crease • n. 1 a line or ridge produced on paper or cloth by folding or pressing. 2 Cricket any of a number of lines marked on the pitch at specified places. • v. (**creases, creasing, creased**) 1 make or become crumpled. 2 (**crease up**) Brit. informal burst out laughing.
– ORIGIN prob. from CREST.

create • v. (**creates, creating, created**) 1 bring into existence. 2 cause to happen: *I want to create a good impression.* 3 Brit. informal make a fuss; complain.
– ORIGIN Latin *creare*.

creation • n. 1 the action of bringing something into existence. 2 a thing which has been made or invented. 3 (**the Creation**) the making of the universe regarded as an act of God. 4 (**Creation**) literary the universe.

creative • adj. involving the use of the imagination in order to create something.
– DERIVATIVES **creatively** adv. **creativity** n.

creator • n. 1 a person or thing that creates. 2 (**the Creator**) God.

creature • n. **1** a living being, in particular an animal rather than a person. **2** a person viewed in a particular way: *the poor creature!*
– ORIGIN Latin *creatura* 'thing created'.

creature comforts • pl. n. things that make life comfortable, such as good food.

crèche /kresh/ • n. Brit. a day nursery for babies and young children.
– ORIGIN French.

credence /kree-duhnss/ • n. belief that something is true: *he gave no credence to the witness's statement.*
– ORIGIN Latin *credentia*.

credential /kri-den-sh'l/ • n. **1** a qualification, achievement, or quality, used to indicate a person's suitability for something: *his academic credentials cannot be doubted.* **2** (**credentials**) documents proving a person's identity or qualifications.

credible • adj. able to be believed; convincing.
– DERIVATIVES **credibility** n. **credibly** adv.
– ORIGIN Latin *credere* 'believe'.

credit • n. **1** an arrangement in which a shop or other business enables a customer to pay at a later date for goods or services supplied. **2** public recognition or praise. **3** a source of pride: *the fans are a great credit to the club.* **4** a written acknowledgement of a contributor's role displayed at the beginning or end of a film or television programme. **5** a unit of study counting towards a degree or diploma. **6** an entry in an account recording a sum received. • v. (**credits, crediting, credited**) **1** (usu. **credit someone with**) believe that someone has done something or has a particular quality: *he was credited with changing politics.* **2** Brit. believe something surprising. **3** add an amount of money to an account.
– PHRASES **be in credit** (of an account) have money in it. **do someone credit** make someone worthy of praise or respect.
– ORIGIN Latin *creditum*.

creditable • adj. deserving recognition and praise.
– DERIVATIVES **creditably** adv.

credit card • n. a plastic card allowing the holder to buy things and pay for them later.

creditor • n. a person or company to whom money is owed.

creditworthy • adj. considered suitable to receive financial credit.
– DERIVATIVES **creditworthiness** n.

credo /kree-doh/ • n. (pl. **credos**) a statement of a person's beliefs or aims.

– ORIGIN Latin, 'I believe'.

credulous /kred-yuu-luhss/ • adj. too ready to believe things.
– DERIVATIVES **credulity** /kri-dyoo-li-ti/ n.
– ORIGIN Latin *credulus*.

creed • n. **1** a system of religious belief; a faith. **2** a statement of beliefs or principles.
– ORIGIN Latin *credo* 'I believe'.

creek • n. **1** esp. Brit. an inlet in a shoreline. **2** N. Amer. & Austral./NZ a stream or small river.
– PHRASES **up the creek** informal in severe difficulty.
– ORIGIN Old French *crique*.

creel • n. a large basket for carrying fish.

creep • v. (**creeps, creeping, crept**) **1** move slowly and cautiously. **2** progress or develop gradually: *interest rates are creeping up.* **3** (as adj. **creeping**) (of a plant) growing along the ground or another surface. • n. **1** informal a person who behaves in an excessively friendly or submissive way to win favour. **2** slow and gradual movement.
– PHRASES **give you the creeps** informal make you feel disgust or fear.
– ORIGIN Old English.

creeper • n. a plant that grows along the ground or another surface.

creepy • adj. (**creepier, creepiest**) informal causing fear or unease.
– DERIVATIVES **creepily** adv. **creepiness** n.

creepy-crawly • n. (pl. **creepy-crawlies**) informal a spider or small insect.

cremate • v. (**cremates, cremating, cremated**) dispose of a dead body by burning it to ashes.
– DERIVATIVES **cremation** n.
– ORIGIN Latin *cremare* 'burn'.

crematorium /kre-muh-tor-i-uhm/ • n. (pl. **crematoria** /kre-muh-tor-i-uh/ or **crematoriums**) a building where dead bodies are cremated.

crème de la crème /krem duh la krem/ • n. the best person or thing of a particular kind.
– ORIGIN French, 'cream of the cream'.

crème fraiche /krem fresh/ • n. a type of thick cream with buttermilk, sour cream, or yogurt.
– ORIGIN French, 'fresh cream'.

crenellations /kren-uh-lay-shunz/ • pl. n. battlements.
– DERIVATIVES **crenellated** adj.

Creole /kree-ohl/ • n. **1** a person of mixed European and black descent. **2** a descendant of French settlers in the southern US. **3** a language formed from a combination of a European language and an African language.
– ORIGIN French.

creosote /kree-uh-soht/ • n. a dark

brown oil used as a wood preservative.
– ORIGIN from Greek *kreas* 'flesh' + *sōtēr* 'preserver'.

crêpe /krayp/ (also **crepe**, **crape**) • n. **1** a light, thin fabric with a wrinkled surface. **2** hard-wearing wrinkled rubber used for the soles of shoes. **3** /also krep/ a thin pancake.
– ORIGIN Old French *crespe* 'curled'.

crêpe paper • n. thin, crinkled paper used for making decorations.

crept past and past part. of **CREEP**.

crepuscular /kri-pus-kyuu-ler/ • adj. esp. literary resembling or relating to twilight.
– ORIGIN Latin *crepusculum* 'twilight'.

crescendo /kri-shen-doh/ • n. (pl. **crescendos** or **crescendi** /kri-shen-di/) a gradual increase in loudness in a piece of music. **2** a climax: *the hysteria reached a crescendo before the festival.* • adv. & adj. Music gradually becoming louder.
– ORIGIN Italian.

crescent /krez-uhnt/ • n. a narrow curved shape tapering to a point at each end, as seen in the waxing or waning moon: *a crescent of golden sand.*
– ORIGIN Old French *creissant*.

cress • n. a plant with hot-tasting leaves, some kinds of which are eaten in salads.
– ORIGIN Old English.

crest • n. **1** a tuft or growth of feathers, fur, or skin on the head of a bird or animal. **2** a plume of feathers on a helmet. **3** the top of a ridge, wave, etc. **4** a distinctive heraldic design which represents a family or organization. • v. **1** reach the top of: *he finally crested the hill.* **2** (as adj. **crested**) having a crest.
– ORIGIN Latin *crista*.

crestfallen • adj. sad and disappointed.

Cretaceous /kri-tay-shuhss/ • adj. Geol. relating to the last period of the Mesozoic era (about 146 to 65 million years ago), at the end of which dinosaurs and many other organisms died out.
– ORIGIN from Latin *creta* 'chalk'.

cretin /kret-in/ • n. **1** a stupid person. **2** Med., dated a person who is deformed and has learning difficulties because of a lack of thyroid hormone.
– ORIGIN Swiss French *crestin* 'Christian', prob. as a reminder that disabled people are human.

cretinous • adj. very stupid.

cretonne /kri-ton/ • n. a heavy cotton fabric with a floral pattern, used for upholstery.
– ORIGIN French.

Creutzfeldt–Jakob disease /kroyts-felt-yak-ob/ • n. a fatal disease affecting nerve cells in the brain, a form of which

is possibly linked to BSE.
– ORIGIN named after the German neurologists H. G. *Creutzfeldt* and A. *Jakob*.

crevasse /kri-vass/ • n. a deep open crack in a glacier or ice field.
– ORIGIN Old French *crevace* 'crevice'.

crevice /kre-viss/ • n. a narrow opening or crack in a rock or wall.
– ORIGIN Old French *crevace*.

crew[1] • n. **1** a group of people who work on a ship, aircraft, or train. **2** a group of such people excluding the officers. **3** a group of people who work together: *a film crew.* **4** informal, usu. derog. a group of people. • v. act as a member of a crew.
– ORIGIN Old French *creue* 'increase'.

crew[2] past of **CROW**[2].

crew cut • n. a very short haircut for men and boys.

crew neck • n. a close-fitting round neckline.

crib • n. **1** esp. N. Amer. a child's cot. **2** informal a list of answers or other information, often used by students to cheat in a test. **3** a rack for animal fodder. **4** informal, esp. N. Amer. a house or flat. **5** the game cribbage. • v. (**cribs**, **cribbing**, **cribbed**) informal copy someone's work dishonestly or without acknowledgement.
– ORIGIN Old English.

cribbage • n. a card game for two players, in which the objective is to reach a certain number of points.
– ORIGIN from **CRIB**.

crick • n. a painful stiff feeling in the neck or back. • v. twist or strain the neck or back.

cricket[1] • n. an outdoor game played with a bat, ball, and wickets, between two teams of eleven players.
– PHRASES **not cricket** Brit. informal not fair or honourable.
– DERIVATIVES **cricketer** n.

cricket[2] • n. an insect like a grasshopper, the male of which produces a shrill chirping sound.
– ORIGIN Old French *criquet*.

cried past and past part. of **CRY**.

crikey • exclam. Brit. informal an expression of surprise.
– ORIGIN euphemism for **CHRIST**.

crime • n. **1** an act that is illegal and can be punished by law. **2** illegal actions as a whole: *the fight against organized crime.* **3** something disgraceful or immoral.
– ORIGIN Latin *crimen* 'judgement'.

criminal • n. a person who has committed a crime. • adj. **1** relating to crime or a crime. **2** informal disgraceful and shocking.

– DERIVATIVES **criminality** n. **criminally** adv.

criminalize (or **criminalise**)
• v. (**criminalizes**, **criminalizing**, **criminalized**) make an activity illegal.
– DERIVATIVES **criminalization** n.

criminology /kri-mi-**nol**-uh-ji/ • n. the scientific study of crime and criminals.
– DERIVATIVES **criminologist** n.

crimp • v. press into small folds or ridges.
– DERIVATIVES **crimper** n.
– ORIGIN Old English.

crimplene /**krimp**-leen/ • n. trademark a synthetic crease-resistant fabric.
– ORIGIN prob. from CRIMP + TERYLENE.

crimson /**krim**-z'n/ • n. a deep red colour.
– ORIGIN Arabic.

cringe /krinj/ • v. (**cringes**, **cringing**, **cringed**) **1** shrink back or cower in fear or in a submissive way. **2** have a sudden feeling of embarrassment or disgust.
– ORIGIN Old English, 'bend'.

crinkle • v. (**crinkle**, **crinkling**, **crinkled**) form small creases or wrinkles. • n. a small crease or wrinkle.
– DERIVATIVES **crinkly** adj.
– ORIGIN from CRINGE.

crinoline /**krin**-uh-lin/ • n. a petticoat stiffened with hoops, formerly worn to make a long skirt stand out.
– ORIGIN French.

cripple • n. old use or offens. a person who is unable to walk or move properly because they are disabled or injured. • v. (**cripples**, **crippling**, **crippled**) **1** make someone unable to move or walk properly. **2** damage or weaken some-thing severely.
– ORIGIN Old English.

crisis • n. (pl. **crises**) **1** a time of severe difficulty or danger. **2** a time when a difficult or important decision must be made: *she's having a midlife crisis.*
– ORIGIN Greek *krisis* 'decision'.

crisp • adj. **1** firm, dry, and brittle. **2** (of the weather) cool and fresh. **3** brisk and decisive: *her answer was crisp.* • n. (also **potato crisp**) Brit. a thin slice of fried potato eaten as a snack. • v. give food a crisp surface by grilling or baking.
– DERIVATIVES **crisply** adv. **crispness** n.
– ORIGIN Latin *crispus* 'curled'.

crispbread • n. a thin, crisp biscuit made from rye or wheat.

crispy • adj. (**crispier**, **crispiest**) firm and brittle; crisp.

criss-cross • adj. with a pattern of crossing lines. • v. make or move in a criss-cross pattern on or across: *the governor will criss-cross the state next month.*

criterion /kry-**teer**-i-uhn/ • n. (pl. **criteria** /kry-**teer**-i-uh/) a standard by which something may be judged or decided.
– ORIGIN Greek *kritērion.*

USAGE: The singular form is **criterion** and the plural form is **criteria**. Do not use **criteria** as if it were a singular: say a *further criterion needs to be considered,* not a *further criteria needs to be considered.*

critic • n. **1** a person who expresses disapproval of someone or something. **2** a person who assesses the quality of literary or artistic works.
– ORIGIN Greek *kritēs* 'a judge'.

critical • adj. **1** expressing disapproving comments. **2** assessing a literary or artistic work. **3** having a decisive importance. **4** at a point of danger or crisis: *the floods were rising and the situation was critical.* **5** (of a nuclear reactor or fuel) maintaining a chain reaction that can sustain itself.
– DERIVATIVES **critically** adv.

criticism • n. **1** the expression of disapproval. **2** the assessment of literary or artistic works.

criticize (or **criticise**) • v. (**criticizes**, **criticizing**, **criticized**) **1** express disapproval of. **2** assess a literary or artistic work.

critique /kri-**teek**/ • n. a critical assessment.
– ORIGIN French.

croak • n. a deep hoarse sound, like that made by a frog. • v. **1** utter a croak. **2** informal die.
– DERIVATIVES **croaky** adj.

Croatian /kroh-**ay**-sh'n/ • n. (also **Croat** /kroh-at/) **1** a person from Croatia. **2** the language of the Croatians. • adj. relating to Croatia or Croatian.

crochet /**kroh**-shay/ • n. a handicraft in which yarn is looped into a fabric of connected stitches by means of a hooked needle. • v. (**crochets** /**kroh**-shayz/, **crocheting** /**kroh**-shay-ing/, **crocheted** /**kroh**-shayd/) make an article in this way.
– ORIGIN French, 'little hook'.

croci pl. of CROCUS.

crock[1] • n. Brit. informal **1** a feeble and useless old person. **2** an old worn-out vehicle.
– ORIGIN prob. from CRACK.

crock[2] • n. an earthenware pot or jar.
– ORIGIN Old English.

crockery • n. plates, dishes, cups, etc., made of earthenware or china.

crocodile • n. **1** a large tropical reptile living partly in water, with long jaws and a long tail. **2** Brit. informal a line of schoolchildren walking in pairs.

c

– ORIGIN Greek *krokodilos* 'worm of the stones'.

crocodile tears • pl. n. insincere tears or sorrow.
– ORIGIN from a belief that crocodiles wept while eating or luring their prey.

crocus /kroh-kuhss/ • n. (pl. **crocuses** or **croci** /kroh-kee/) a small plant with bright yellow, purple, or white flowers.
– ORIGIN Greek *krokos*.

Croesus /kree-suhss/ • n. a person of great wealth.
– ORIGIN the name of a wealthy king of ancient Lydia in Asia.

croft • n. a small rented farm in Scotland or northern England.
– DERIVATIVES **crofter** n.
– ORIGIN Old English.

croissant /krwass-on/ • n. a crescent-shaped flaky bread roll.
– ORIGIN French, 'crescent'.

cromlech /krom-lek/ • n. **1** (in Wales) an ancient tomb consisting of a large flat stone laid on upright ones. **2** (in Brittany) a circle of standing stones.
– ORIGIN Welsh, 'arched flat stone'.

crone • n. an ugly old woman.
– ORIGIN Old French *caroigne* 'carrion'.

crony /kroh-ni/ • n. (pl. **cronies**) informal, usu. derog. a close friend or companion.
– ORIGIN Greek *khronios* 'long-lasting'.

cronyism • n. the improper appointment of friends and associates to positions of authority.

crook • n. **1** a shepherd's or bishop's hooked staff. **2** a bend at a person's elbow. **3** informal a criminal or dishonest person. • v. bend a finger or leg.
• adj. Austral./NZ informal bad or unwell.
– ORIGIN Old Norse, 'hook'.

crooked /kruu-kid/ • adj. **1** bent or twisted out of shape or position. **2** informal dishonest or illegal.
– DERIVATIVES **crookedly** adv. **crookedness** n.

croon • v. hum, sing, or speak in a soft, low voice.
– DERIVATIVES **crooner** n.
– ORIGIN German and Dutch *krōnen* 'groan'.

crop • n. **1** a plant grown for food or other use. **2** an amount of a crop harvested at one time. **3** an amount of people or things appearing at one time: *the current crop of politicians*. **4** a very short hair-style. **5** a riding crop. **6** a pouch in a bird's throat where food is stored or prepared for digestion. • v. (**crops**, **cropping**, **cropped**) **1** cut something very short. **2** (of an animal) bite off and eat the tops of plants. **3** (**crop up**) occur unexpectedly. **4** produce a food crop.
– ORIGIN Old English.

crop circle • n. an area of crops which has been flattened in the shape of a circle or other pattern by unexplained means.

cropper • n. (in phr. **come a cropper**) informal fall or fail heavily.

croquet /kroh-kay/ • n. a game played on a lawn, in which wooden balls are hit through hoops with a mallet.
– ORIGIN perh. from French *crochet* 'hook'.

croquette /kruh-ket/ • n. a small cake or roll of vegetables, meat, or fish, fried in breadcrumbs.
– ORIGIN French.

crosier /kroh-zi-er/ • n. var. of CROZIER.

cross • n. **1** a mark, object, or shape formed by two short intersecting lines or pieces (+ or ×). **2** a cross-shaped medal or monument. **3** (**the Cross**) the wooden cross on which Jesus was crucified. **4** a thing that has to be endured: *she's just a cross we have to bear.* **5** an animal or plant resulting from cross-breeding. **6** a mixture of two things: *a cross between a bar and a restaurant.* **7** Football a pass of the ball across the field towards the centre.
• v. **1** go or extend across or to the other side of: *he started to cross the road.* **2** pass in an opposite or different direction. **3** place crosswise: *Michele crossed her legs.* **4** oppose or thwart someone. **5** draw a line or lines across. **6** Brit. mark a cheque with a pair of parallel lines to indicate that it must be paid into a named bank account. **7** Football pass the ball across the field towards the centre. **8** cause an animal of one species or breed to interbreed with one of another.
• adj. annoyed.
– PHRASES **at cross purposes** (of two people) misunderstanding one another. **cross something off** delete an item from a list. **cross yourself** make the sign of the Cross in front of your chest as a sign of Christian reverence or to call on God for protection. **cross something out/through** delete a word or phrase by drawing a line through it. **cross swords** have an argument or dispute. **crossed line** a telephone connection that has been wrongly made with the result that another call can be heard.
– DERIVATIVES **crossly** adv. **crossness** n.
– ORIGIN Latin *crux*.

crossbar • n. **1** a horizontal bar between the two upright posts of a football goal. **2** a bar between the handlebars and saddle on a bicycle.

cross-bencher • n. a member of the House of Lords who is independent of any political party.

crossbow •n. a bow fixed across a wooden support, with a mechanism for drawing and releasing the string.

cross-breed •n. an animal or plant produced by crossing two different species, breeds, or varieties. •v. produce an animal or plant in this way.

cross-check •v. check figures or information by using an alternative source or method.

cross-country •adj. 1 across fields or countryside, rather than keeping to roads or tracks. 2 across a region or country.

cross-dressing •n. the wearing of clothing usually worn by the opposite sex.

cross-examine •v. question a witness called by the other party in a court of law to challenge or extend the testimony that they have already given.
– DERIVATIVES **cross-examination** n.

cross-eyed •adj. having one or both eyes turned inwards towards the nose.

cross-fertilize (or **cross-fertilise**) •v. fertilize a plant using pollen from another plant of the same species.
– DERIVATIVES **cross-fertilization** n.

crossfire •n. gunfire from two or more directions passing through the same area.

cross-hatch •v. shade an area with many intersecting parallel lines.

crossing •n. 1 a place where roads or railway lines cross. 2 a place at which a street or railway line may be crossed safely. 3 a journey across water in a ship.

cross-legged •adj. & adv. (of a seated person) with the legs crossed at the ankles and the knees bent outwards.

crossover •n. 1 a point or place of crossing. 2 the production of work in a new style or in a combination of styles, especially in popular music: *a perfect dance/soul crossover.*

crosspiece •n. a beam or bar fixed or placed across something else.

cross-question •v. question in great detail.

cross reference •n. a reference to another written work or part of a written work, given to provide further information.

crossroads •n. a place where two or more roads cross each other.

cross section •n. 1 a surface exposed by making a straight cut through a solid object at right angles to its length. 2 a typical sample of a larger group.

crosswind •n. a wind blowing across the direction of travel.

crosswise (also **crossways**) •adv. 1 in the form of a cross. 2 diagonally.

crossword •n. a puzzle consisting of a grid of squares and blanks into which words crossing vertically and horizontally are written according to clues.

crotch •n. the part of the human body between the legs where they join the torso.
– ORIGIN partly from **CRUTCH**.

crotchet /kro-chit/ •n. Brit. a musical note having the time value of half a minim, shown by a large solid dot with a plain stem.
– ORIGIN Old French *crochet* 'little hook'.

crotchety •adj. irritable.

crouch •v. bend the knees and bring the upper body forward and down. •n. a crouching position.
– ORIGIN perh. from Old French *crochir* 'be bent'.

croup[1] /kroop/ •n. inflammation of the throat in children, causing coughing and breathing difficulties.
– ORIGIN dialect, 'to croak'.

croup[2] /kroop/ •n. the rump of a horse.
– ORIGIN Old French.

croupier /kroo-pi-ay/ •n. the person in charge of a gambling table, gathering in and paying out money or tokens.
– ORIGIN French.

crouton /kroo-ton/ •n. a small piece of fried or toasted bread served with soup or used as a garnish.
– ORIGIN French.

crow[1] •n. a large black bird with a harsh call.
– PHRASES **as the crow flies** in a straight line across country.
– ORIGIN Old English.

crow[2] •v. (**crows, crowing, crowed** or **crew**) 1 (of a cock) make its loud shrill cry. 2 express pride or triumph in a gloating way. •n. the cry of a cock.
– ORIGIN Old English.

crowbar •n. an iron bar with a flattened end, used as a lever.

crowd •n. 1 a large number of people gathered together. 2 informal, often derog. a group of people with a shared quality: *he hangs around with a fancy writing crowd.* •v. 1 fill an area or space almost completely. 2 move or come together as a crowd. 3 move or stand too close to. 4 (**crowd someone/thing out**) keep someone or something out by taking their place.
– DERIVATIVES **crowded** adj.
– ORIGIN Old English, 'press, hasten'.

crown •n. 1 a circular ornamental headdress worn by a king or queen as a symbol of authority. 2 (**the Crown**) the

monarchy or the reigning king or queen. **3** a wreath of leaves or flowers worn as an emblem of victory. **4** an award gained by a victory: *the world heavyweight crown.* **5** the top or highest part of something, such as a person's head or a hat. **6** an artificial replacement or covering for the upper part of a tooth. **7** a former British coin worth five shillings (25 pence). •v. **1** place a crown on someone's head to formally declare them to be king or queen. **2** rest on or form the top of. **3** be the triumphant conclusion of: *his ride crowned an amazing sporting comeback.*
– ORIGIN Latin *corona.*

Crown Colony •n. a British colony controlled by the Crown.

Crown court •n. (in England and Wales) a court which deals with serious cases referred from the magistrates' courts.

Crown jewels •pl. n. the crown and other jewellery worn or carried by the king or queen on state occasions.

Crown prince •n. (in some countries) a male heir to a throne.

Crown princess •n. **1** the wife of a Crown prince. **2** (in some countries) a female heir to a throne.

crow's feet •pl. n. wrinkles at the outer corner of a person's eye.

crow's-nest •n. a platform for a lookout at the masthead of a ship.

crozier /kroh-zi-er/ (also **crosier**) •n. a hooked staff carried by a bishop.
– ORIGIN Old French *croisier* 'cross-bearer'.

crucial /kroo-sh'l/ •adj. of great importance, especially in the success or failure of something: *negotiations were at a crucial stage.*
– DERIVATIVES **crucially** adv.
– ORIGIN Latin *crux* 'cross'.

crucible /kroo-si-b'l/ •n. a container in which metals or other substances may be melted or subjected to very high temperatures.
– ORIGIN Latin *crucibulum.*

cruciferous /kroo-sif-uh-ruhss/ •adj. (of a plant) belonging to the cabbage family, with four equal petals arranged in a cross.
– ORIGIN from Latin *crux* 'cross' + *-fer* 'bearing'.

crucifix /kroo-si-fiks/ •n. a model of a cross with a figure of Jesus on it.
– ORIGIN from Latin *cruci fixus* 'fixed to a cross'.

crucifixion •n. **1** the execution of a person by crucifying them. **2** (**the Crucifixion**) the killing of Jesus in this way.

cruciform /kroo-si-form/ •adj. having the shape of a cross.

crucify /kroo-si-fy/ •v. (**crucifies, crucifying, crucified**) **1** put someone to death by nailing or binding them to a cross. **2** informal criticize someone very severely.
– ORIGIN from Latin *crux* 'cross' + *figere* 'fix'.

crud •n. informal **1** an unpleasantly dirty or messy substance. **2** nonsense.
– DERIVATIVES **cruddy** adj.
– ORIGIN from **CURD.**

crude •adj. **1** in a natural state; not yet processed: *crude oil.* **2** rough or simple: *a pair of crude huts.* **3** coarse or vulgar. •n. natural mineral oil.
– DERIVATIVES **crudely** adv. **crudity** n.
– ORIGIN Latin *crudus* 'raw, rough'.

crudités /kroo-di-tay/ •pl. n. mixed raw vegetables served with a sauce in which they may be dipped.
– ORIGIN French *crudité* 'rawness'.

cruel •adj. (**crueller, cruellest** or **crueler, cruelest**) **1** taking pleasure in the suffering of other people. **2** causing pain or suffering.
– DERIVATIVES **cruelly** adv.
– ORIGIN Latin *crudelis.*

cruelty •n. (pl. **cruelties**) cruel behaviour or attitudes.

cruet /kroo-it/ •n. a small container or set of containers for salt, pepper, oil, or vinegar, for use at a dining table.
– ORIGIN Old French, 'small pot'.

cruise •v. (**cruises, cruising, cruised**) **1** sail, travel, or move slowly around without a precise destination. **2** travel smoothly at a moderate speed that is economical on fuel. **3** easily achieve an objective: *United cruised to a 2-0 win.* •n. a voyage on a ship taken as a holiday, calling in at several places.
– ORIGIN prob. from Dutch *kruisen* 'to cross'.

cruise missile •n. a low-flying missile which is guided to its target by an on-board computer.

cruiser •n. **1** a large fast warship. **2** a yacht or motor boat with passenger accommodation.

cruiserweight •n. esp. Brit. = **LIGHT HEAVYWEIGHT.**

crumb •n. **1** a small fragment of bread, cake, or biscuit. **2** a very small amount: *the Budget provided few crumbs of comfort.*
– ORIGIN Old English.

crumble •v. (**crumbles, crumbling, crumbled**) **1** break or fall apart into small fragments. **2** gradually decline or disintegrate. •n. Brit. a baked pudding made with fruit and a crumbly topping.

– ORIGIN Old English.

crumbly • adj. easily crumbling into small fragments.

crummy • adj. informal bad or unpleasant.

crumpet • n. 1 a soft, flat cake with an open texture, eaten toasted and buttered. 2 Brit. informal sexually attractive women.

crumple • v. (**crumples, crumpling, crumpled**) 1 crush something so as to make it creased. 2 collapse.
– ORIGIN Old English, 'bent, crooked'.

crunch • v. 1 crush something hard or brittle with the teeth. 2 make or move with a grinding sound. • n. 1 a crunching sound. 2 (**the crunch**) informal the crucial point of a situation.
– DERIVATIVES **crunchy** adj. (**crunchier, crunchiest**).

crupper /krup-per/ • n. a strap at the back of a saddle which is looped under a horse's tail to prevent the saddle or harness from slipping.
– ORIGIN Old French *cropiere*.

crusade • n. 1 any of a series of medieval military expeditions made by Europeans to recover the Holy Land from the Muslims. 2 an energetic organized campaign: *a crusade against crime*. • v. (**crusades, crusading, crusaded**) lead or take part in a crusade.
– DERIVATIVES **crusader** n.
– ORIGIN French *croisée* 'the state of being marked with the cross'.

crush • v. 1 press something so as to squash, crease, or break it. 2 defeat or subdue completely: *he sent in the army to crush the militants*. • n. 1 a crowd of people pressed closely together. 2 informal a strong, usually short-lived feeling of love for someone: *she had a crush on Dr Jones*. 3 a drink made from the juice of pressed fruit.
– DERIVATIVES **crusher** n.
– ORIGIN Old French *cruissir* 'crack'.

crust • n. 1 the tough outer part of a loaf of bread. 2 Brit. informal a living or livelihood: *I've been earning a crust where I can.* 3 a hardened layer, coating, or deposit. 4 the outermost rocky layer of the earth. 5 a layer of pastry covering a pie. • v. form into or cover with a crust.
– ORIGIN Latin *crusta*.

crustacean /kruss-tay-sh'n/ • n. an animal with a hard shell, usually living in water, such as a crab or lobster.
– ORIGIN Latin *crusta* 'shell, crust'.

crusty • adj. (**crustier, crustiest**) 1 having or consisting of a crust. 2 (of an old person) easily irritated.

crutch • n. 1 a long stick with a crosspiece at the top, used as a support by a person who is lame. 2 a person's crotch.

– ORIGIN Old English.

crux /kruks/ • n. (**the crux**) the most important point under discussion.
– ORIGIN Latin, 'cross'.

cry • v. (**cries, crying, cried**) 1 shed tears. 2 shout or scream loudly. 3 (of a bird or other animal) make a distinctive call. 4 (**cry out for**) demand: *the scheme cries out for reform.* 5 (**cry off**) informal fail to keep to an arrangement. • n. (pl. **cries**) 1 a period of shedding tears. 2 a loud shout or scream. 3 a distinctive call of a bird or other animal.
– ORIGIN Old French *crier*.

crying • adj. very great: *a crying shame.*

cryogenics /kry-uh-jen-iks/ • n. the branch of physics concerned with the production and effects of very low temperatures.
– DERIVATIVES **cryogenic** adj.
– ORIGIN from Greek *kruos* 'frost'.

crypt • n. an underground room or vault beneath a church, used as a chapel or burial place.
– ORIGIN Greek *kruptē*.

cryptic • adj. mysterious or obscure in meaning: *he gave us a cryptic message to pass on.*
– DERIVATIVES **cryptically** adv.
– ORIGIN Greek *kruptos* 'hidden'.

cryptogram /krip-tuh-gram/ • n. a document written in code.

cryptography • n. the art of writing or solving codes.
– DERIVATIVES **cryptographer** n. **cryptographic** adj.

crystal • n. 1 a transparent mineral, especially quartz. 2 a piece of a solid substance with a regular internal structure and plane faces arranged symmetrically. 3 very clear glass. • adj. completely clear: *the crystal waters of the lake.*
– ORIGIN Greek *krustallos* 'ice, crystal'.

crystal ball • n. a solid globe of glass or crystal, used for predicting the future.

crystalline /kriss-tuh-lyn/ • adj. 1 having the structure and form of a crystal. 2 literary very clear.

crystallize (or **crystallise**) • v. (**crystallizes, crystallizing, crystallized**) 1 form crystals. 2 make or become definite and clear: *his book helped me to crystallize my thoughts.* 3 (as adj. **crystallized**) (of fruit) coated with and preserved in sugar.
– DERIVATIVES **crystallization** n.

crystallography /kriss-tuh-log-ruh-fi/ • n. the branch of science concerned with the structure and properties of crystals.
– DERIVATIVES **crystallographer** n. **crystallographic** adj.

Cs • symb. the chemical element caesium.

c/s • abbrev. cycles per second.

CS gas • n. a powerful form of tear gas used in the control of riots.
– ORIGIN from the initials of the American chemists Ben B. *Corson* and Roger W. *Stoughton*.

ct • abbrev. **1** carat. **2** cent.

CTC • abbrev. City Technology College.

Cu • symb. the chemical element copper.
– ORIGIN Latin *cuprum*.

cu. • abbrev. cubic.

cub • n. the young of a fox, bear, lion, or other meat-eating mammal. **2** (also **Cub Scout**) a member of the junior branch of the Scout Association, for boys aged about 8 to 11.

Cuban /kyoo-buhn/ • n. a person from Cuba. • adj. relating to Cuba.

cubbyhole • n. a small enclosed space or room.
– ORIGIN from dialect *cub* 'pen, hutch'.

cube • n. **1** a three-dimensional shape with six equal square faces. **2** the product of a number multiplied by itself twice. • v. **1** cut food into small cube-shaped pieces. **2** find the cube of a number.
– ORIGIN Greek *kubos*.

cube root • n. the number which, when multiplied by itself twice, produces a particular number.

cubic /kyoo-bik/ • adj. **1** having the shape of a cube. **2** referring to a volume equal to that of a cube whose edge is a given unit of length: *a cubic metre*.

cubicle • n. a small area of a room that is partitioned off for privacy.
– ORIGIN Latin *cubiculum* 'bedroom'.

cubism • n. an early 20th-century style of painting in which objects are represented as being made up of geometric shapes.
– DERIVATIVES **cubist** n. & adj.

cubit /kyoo-bit/ • n. an ancient measure of length, approximately equal to the length of a forearm.
– ORIGIN Latin *cubitum* 'elbow, cubit'.

cuboid /kyoo-boyd/ • adj. having the shape of a cube. • n. a solid which has six rectangular faces at right angles to each other.

cuckold /kuk-ohld/ • n. a man whose wife has committed adultery. • v. make a married man a cuckold.
– ORIGIN Old French *cucu* 'cuckoo' (from the cuckoo's habit of laying its egg in another bird's nest).

cuckoo • n. a grey or brown bird with a two-note call, known for laying its eggs in the nests of other birds. • adj. informal crazy.
– ORIGIN Old French *cucu*.

cucumber • n. a long, green fruit with watery flesh, eaten in salads.
– ORIGIN Latin *cucumis*.

cud • n. partly digested food returned from the first stomach of cattle and similar animals to the mouth for further chewing.
– ORIGIN Old English.

cuddle • v. (**cuddles, cuddling, cuddled**) **1** hold someone closely and lovingly in your arms. **2** (often **cuddle up to**) lie or sit close to someone. • n. an affectionate hug.

cuddly • adj. (**cuddlier, cuddliest**) pleasantly soft or plump.

cudgel /ku-juhl/ • n. a short thick stick used as a weapon. • v. (**cudgels, cudgelling, cudgelled**; US **cudgels, cudgeling, cudgeled**) beat with a cudgel.
– PHRASES **take up the cudgels** start to defend someone or something strongly.
– ORIGIN Old English.

cue¹ • n. **1** a signal to an actor to enter or to begin their speech or performance. **2** a signal or reminder for someone to do something. • v. (**cues, cueing** or **cuing, cued**) **1** give someone a cue. **2** set a piece of audio or video equipment in readiness to play a particular part of a recording.
– PHRASES **on cue** at the correct moment.

cue² • n. a long tapering wooden rod for striking the ball in snooker, billiards, or pool. • v. (**cues, cueing** or **cuing, cued**) use a cue to strike the ball.
– ORIGIN from QUEUE.

cuff¹ • n. the end part of a sleeve, where the material is turned back or a separate band is sewn on.
– PHRASES **off the cuff** informal without preparation.

cuff² • v. hit someone with an open hand. • n. a blow given with an open hand.

cufflink • n. a device for fastening the sides of a shirt cuff together.

cuirass /kwi-rass/ • n. hist. a piece of armour covering the chest and the back.
– ORIGIN Old French *cuirace*.

cuisine /kwi-zeen/ • n. a style of cooking, especially as typical of a country or region: *classic French cuisine*.
– ORIGIN French, 'kitchen'.

cul-de-sac /kul-duh-sak/ • n. (pl. **cul-de-sacs** /kul-duh-saks/) a street or passage closed at one end.
– ORIGIN French, 'bottom of a sack'.

culinary /cul-i-nuh-ri/ • adj. relating to cooking.
– ORIGIN Latin *culina* 'kitchen'.

cull • v. **1** slaughter a selected number of a

certain kind of animal to reduce its population. **2** select from a wide range or large quantity: *anecdotes culled from Roman history.* •n. a selective slaughter of a certain kind of animal.
– ORIGIN Latin *colligere* 'gather together'.

culminate /kul-mi-nayt/
•v. (**culminates, culminating, culminated**) reach a climax or point of highest development: *the disorders which culminated in World War II.*
– DERIVATIVES **culmination** n.
– ORIGIN Latin *culminare*.

culottes /kyuu-lots/ •pl. n. women's knee-length trousers, cut with full legs to resemble a skirt.
– ORIGIN French.

culpable /kul-puh-b'l/ •adj. deserving blame.
– DERIVATIVES **culpability** n.
– ORIGIN Latin *culpabilis*.

culprit •n. a person who is responsible for a crime or offence.
– ORIGIN perh. from *cul. prist*, the abbreviation for Old French *Culpable: prest d'averrer notre bille* '(You are) guilty: (We are) ready to prove our charge'.

cult •n. **1** a system of religious worship directed towards a particular person or object. **2** a small religious group regarded by other people as strange or as having too great a control over its members. **3** something popular or fashionable among a particular group of people: *the series has become a cult in the UK.*
– DERIVATIVES **cultish** adj. **cultist** n.
– ORIGIN Latin *cultus* 'worship'.

cultivar /kul-ti-var/ •n. a plant variety that has been produced by selective breeding.

cultivate •v. (**cultivates, cultivating, cultivated**) **1** prepare and use land for crops or gardening. **2** grow plants or crops. **3** try to develop or gain: *he cultivated an air of detachment.* **4** try to win the friendship or support of. **5** (as adj. **cultivated**) refined and well educated.
– DERIVATIVES **cultivable** adj. **cultivation** n.
– ORIGIN Latin *cultivare*.

cultivator •n. a mechanical implement for breaking up the ground.

cultural •adj. **1** relating to the culture of a society. **2** relating to the arts and to intellectual achievements.
– DERIVATIVES **culturally** adv.

culture •n. **1** the arts and other instances of human intellectual achievement regarded as a whole. **2** an understanding or appreciation of this. **3** the arts, customs, ideas, etc. of a nation, people,

or group. **4** a preparation of cells or bacteria grown for medical or scientific study. **5** the growing of plants.
•v. (**cultures, culturing, cultured**) grow cells or bacteria for medical or scientific study.
– ORIGIN Latin *cultura* 'growing'.

cultured •adj. **1** well educated and able to appreciate art, literature, music, etc. **2** (of a pearl) formed round a foreign body inserted into an oyster.

culvert /kul-vert/ •n. a tunnel carrying a stream or open drain under a road or railway.

cum /kum/ •prep. combined with: *a study-cum-bedroom.*
– ORIGIN Latin.

cumbersome •adj. **1** difficult to carry or use through size or weight. **2** complicated and inefficient or time-consuming: *cumbersome business procedures.*
– ORIGIN from **ENCUMBER**.

cumbrous /kum-bruhss/ •adj. literary cumbersome.

cumin /kyoo-min/ (also **cummin**) •n. the seeds of a plant of the parsley family, used as a spice.
– ORIGIN Greek *kuminon*.

cummerbund /kum-mer-bund/ •n. a sash worn around the waist, especially as part of a man's formal evening suit.
– ORIGIN Urdu and Persian.

cumulative /kyoo-myuu-luh-tiv/ •adj. increasing in amount, strength, or effect by successive additions: *the cumulative effect of years of drought.*
– ORIGIN Latin *cumulus* 'a heap'.

cumulonimbus /kyoo-myuu-loh-nim-buhss/ •n. (pl. **cumulonimbi** /kyoo-myuu-loh-**nim**-by/) cloud forming a towering mass with a flat base, as in thunderstorms.

cumulus /kyoo-myuu-luhss/ •n. (pl. **cumuli** /kyoo-myuu-lee/) cloud forming rounded masses heaped on a flat base.
– ORIGIN Latin, 'heap'.

cuneiform /kyoo-ni-form, kyoo-**nay**-i-form/ •adj. relating to the wedge-shaped characters used in the ancient writing systems of Mesopotamia, Persia, and Ugarit in Syria. •n. cuneiform writing.
– ORIGIN from Latin *cuneus* 'wedge'.

cunning •adj. **1** skilled at deceiving people. **2** ingenious or clever. •n. craftiness.
– DERIVATIVES **cunningly** adv.
– ORIGIN perh. from Old Norse, 'knowledge'.

cup •n. **1** a small bowl-shaped container with a handle for drinking from. **2** a cup-shaped trophy with a stem and two

handles, awarded as a prize in a sports contest. **3** either of the two parts of a bra shaped to contain or support one breast. • v. (**cups, cupping, cupped**) **1** form your hand or hands into the curved shape of a cup. **2** hold something with your hand or hands in a curved shape.
– PHRASES **not someone's cup of tea** informal not what someone likes or enjoys.
– ORIGIN Latin *cuppa*.

cupboard • n. a piece of furniture or small recess with a door, used for storage.

cupboard love • n. Brit. a show of affection put on in order to obtain something.

Cupid • n. **1** Rom. Myth. the god of love. **2** (also **cupid**) a picture or statue of a naked winged child carrying a bow.

cupidity /kyoo-**pid**-i-ti/ • n. greed for money or possessions.
– ORIGIN Latin *cupiditas*.

cupola /**kyoo**-puh-luh/ • n. a rounded dome forming or decorating a roof or ceiling.
– ORIGIN Latin *cupula* 'small cask'.

cupro-nickel • n. an alloy of copper and nickel, especially as used in 'silver' coins.

cur /ker/ • n. an aggressive mongrel dog.
– ORIGIN perh. from Old Norse, 'grumbling'.

curacy • n. (pl. **curacies**) the role or position of a curate.

curare /kyuu-**rah**-ri/ • n. a type of poison obtained from some South American plants.
– ORIGIN Carib.

curate /**kyoor**-uht/ • n. a member of the clergy who assists a parish priest.
– ORIGIN Latin *curatus*.

curative • adj. able to cure disease.

curator • n. a keeper of a museum or other collection.
– DERIVATIVES **curatorial** adj.
– ORIGIN Latin.

curb • v. control or put a limit on. • n. **1** a control or limit on something. **2** a type of bit with a strap or chain attached which passes under a horse's lower jaw. **3** US = KERB.
– ORIGIN Old French *courber* 'to bend'.

curd (also **curds**) • n. a soft, white substance formed when milk coagulates, used for making cheese.

curd cheese • n. a soft cheese made from skimmed milk curd.

curdle • v. (**curdles, curdling, curdled**) (of a liquid) form lumps.

cure • v. (**cures, curing, cured**) **1** make a person who is ill well again. **2** end a disease, condition, or problem by treatment or appropriate action. **3** preserve meat, fish, etc. by salting, drying, or smoking. • n. **1** a remedy. **2** the healing of a person who is ill.
– DERIVATIVES **curable** adj.
– ORIGIN Latin *cura* 'care'.

curfew /**ker**-fyoo/ • n. **1** a regulation requiring people to remain indoors between specific hours of the night. **2** the time at which a curfew begins.
– ORIGIN first meaning a regulation requiring that fires be put out at a particular time: from Old French *cuevrefeu*.

Curia /**kyoor**-i-uh/ • n. the papal court at the Vatican, by which the Roman Catholic Church is governed.
– ORIGIN Latin.

curie /**kyoor**-i/ • n. (pl. **curies**) a unit of radioactivity.
– ORIGIN named after the French physicists Pierre and Marie *Curie*.

curio /**kyoor**-i-oh/ • n. (pl. **curios**) an object that is interesting because it is rare or unusual.

curiosity • n. (pl. **curiosities**) **1** a strong desire to know or learn something. **2** an unusual or interesting object.

curious • adj. **1** eager to know or learn something. **2** strange; unusual.
– DERIVATIVES **curiously** adv.
– ORIGIN Latin *curiosus* 'careful'.

curium /**kyoo**-ri-uhm/ • n. a radioactive metallic chemical element made by high-energy atomic collisions.
– ORIGIN named after Marie and Pierre *Curie*.

curl • v. **1** form or cause to form a curved or spiral shape. **2** move in a spiral or curved course: *smoke curled into the air.* • n. something in the shape of a spiral or coil.
– DERIVATIVES **curly** adj.
– ORIGIN Dutch *krul*.

curler • n. a roller around which a lock of hair is wrapped to curl it.

curlew /**ker**-lyoo/ • n. (pl. **curlew** or **curlews**) a large wading bird with a long bill that curves downwards and brown streaked plumage.
– ORIGIN Old French *courlieu*.

curlicue /**ker**-li-kyoo/ • n. a decorative curl or twist.
– ORIGIN from curly + CUE².

curling • n. a game played on ice, in which large flat circular stones are slid across the surface towards a mark.

curmudgeon /ker-**muj**-uhn/ • n. a bad-tempered person.
– DERIVATIVES **curmudgeonly** adj.

currant • n. **1** a dried fruit made from a small seedless variety of grape. **2** a

shrub producing small edible black, red, or white berries.
– ORIGIN from Old French *raisins de Coarantz* 'grapes of Corinth'.

currency • n. (pl. **currencies**) **1** a system of money in general use in a country. **2** the state or period of being current: *the term has gained new currency.*

current • adj. **1** happening or being used or done now: *current events.* **2** in common or general use. • n. **1** a body of water or air moving in a particular direction. **2** a flow of electrically charged particles.
– ORIGIN Latin *currere* 'run'.

> **USAGE:** Do not confuse **current** with **currant**. **Current** means 'happening now' or 'a flow of water, air, or electricity', whereas **currant** means 'a dried grape'.

current account • n. Brit. an account with a bank or building society from which money may be withdrawn without notice.

currently • adv. at the present time.

curriculum /kuh-rik-yuu-luhm/ • n. (pl. **curricula** or **curriculums**) the subjects included in a course of study in a school or college.
– DERIVATIVES **curricular** adj.
– ORIGIN Latin, 'course, racing chariot'.

curriculum vitae /kuh-rik-yuu-luhm vee-ty/ • n. (pl. **curricula vitae**) a brief account of a person's qualifications and previous occupations, sent with a job application.
– ORIGIN Latin, 'course of life'.

curried • adj. made as a curry with a hot, spicy sauce.

curry[1] • n. (pl. **curries**) a dish of meat, vegetables, or fish, cooked in a hot, spicy sauce of Indian origin.
– ORIGIN Tamil.

curry[2] • v. (**curries, currying, curried**) esp. N. Amer. groom a horse with a curry comb.
– PHRASES **curry favour** try to win someone's favour by flattering and trying to please them.
– ORIGIN Old French *correier.*

curry comb • n. a hand-held device with serrated ridges, used for grooming horses.

curse • n. **1** an appeal to a supernatural power to harm someone or something. **2** a cause of harm or misery: *the curse of drug addiction.* **3** an offensive word or phrase used to express anger or annoyance. • v. (**curses, cursing, cursed**) **1** use a curse against. **2** (**be cursed with**) continuously suffer from or be affected by. **3** say offensive words; swear.
– ORIGIN Old English.

cursive /ker-siv/ • adj. (of handwriting)

written with the characters joined.
– ORIGIN Latin *cursivus* 'running'.

cursor • n. **1** a movable indicator on a computer screen identifying the point where input from the user will take effect. **2** the sliding part, bearing a hairline, used to locate points on a slide rule.
– ORIGIN Latin, 'runner'.

> ✓ Remember that **cursor** ends with **-or**.

cursory /ker-suh-ri/ • adj. hasty and therefore not thorough.
– DERIVATIVES **cursorily** adv.

curt • adj. so brief or abrupt as to be rude.
– DERIVATIVES **curtly** adv.
– ORIGIN Latin *curtus* 'cut short'.

curtail /ker-tayl/ • v. limit or cut short.
– DERIVATIVES **curtailment** n.
– ORIGIN French *courtault* 'horse with a docked tail'.

curtain • n. **1** a piece of material suspended at the top to form a screen, hung at a window or between the stage and auditorium of a theatre. **2** (**the curtain**) the rise or fall of a stage curtain between acts or scenes. **3** (**curtains**) informal a disastrous end: *it's curtains for the bank.* • v. provide or screen something with a curtain or curtains.
– ORIGIN Latin *cortina.*

curtain call • n. the appearance of one or more performers on stage after a performance to acknowledge the audience's applause.

curtain-raiser • n. an event happening just before a longer or more important one.

curtsy (also **curtsey**) • n. (pl. **curtsies** or **curtseys**) a woman's or girl's respectful greeting, made by bending the knees with one foot in front of the other. • v. (**curtsies, curtsying, curtsied**; also **curtseys, curtseying, curtseyed**) perform a curtsy.
– ORIGIN from **COURTESY**.

curvaceous /ker-vay-shuhss/ • adj. having an attractively curved shape.

curvature /ker-vuh-cher/ • n. the fact of being curved or the degree to which something is curved: *curvature of the spine.*

curve • n. **1** a line or outline which gradually bends. **2** a line on a graph showing how one quantity varies with respect to another. • v. (**curves, curving, curved**) form or move in a curve.
– ORIGIN Latin *curvus* 'bent'.

curvet /ker-vet/ • v. (**curvets, curvetting, curvetted**; also **curvets, curveting,**

curveted) (of a horse) make a short energetic leap.
– ORIGIN Italian *corvetta* 'little curve'.

curvilinear /ker-vi-lin-i-er/
• adj. contained by or consisting of a curved line or lines: *a curvilinear building*.

curvy • adj. (**curvier, curviest**) 1 having many curves. 2 informal curvaceous.

cushion • n. 1 a bag of cloth stuffed with soft material, used to provide comfort when sitting. 2 a means of protection against impact or something unpleasant. 3 the inner sides of a billiard table, from which the balls rebound. • v. 1 soften the effect of an impact on. 2 lessen the unpleasant effects of: *he relied on his savings to cushion the blow of losing his job*.
– ORIGIN Old French *cuissin*.

cushy • adj. (**cushier, cushiest**) informal easy and undemanding: *a cushy job*.
– ORIGIN Urdu, 'pleasure'.

cusp /kusp/ • n. 1 a pointed end where two curves meet, such as each of the ends of a crescent moon. 2 a cone-shaped projection on the surface of a tooth. 3 the initial point of an astrological sign or house. 4 a point of changing from one state to another: *those on the cusp of adulthood*.
– ORIGIN Latin *cuspis* 'point or apex'.

cuss informal • n. an annoying or stubborn person or animal. • v. swear or curse.

cussed /kuss-id/ • adj. informal stubborn and awkward.
– DERIVATIVES **cussedness** n.

custard • n. 1 a sweet sauce made with milk and eggs, or milk and flavoured cornflour. 2 a baked dessert made from eggs and milk.
– ORIGIN first meaning a pie containing meat or fruit in a sauce: from Old French *crouste* 'crust'.

custodian /kuss-toh-di-uhn/ • n. a person who has responsibility for or looks after something.

custody /kuss-tuh-di/ • n. 1 protective care. 2 Law parental responsibility as allocated to one of two parents who are getting divorced. 3 imprisonment, especially while waiting for trial: *he was taken into custody*.
– DERIVATIVES **custodial** /kuss-toh-di-uhl/ adj.
– ORIGIN Latin *custos* 'guardian'.

custom • n. 1 a traditional way of behaving or doing something in a particular society or place, or at a particular time: *the English custom of dancing round the maypole*. 2 a thing that a person often does; a habit: *it was my custom to nap for an hour every day*. 3 Brit. regular dealings with a shop or business by customers.

– ORIGIN Old French *coustume*.

customary • adj. in accordance with custom; usual.
– DERIVATIVES **customarily** adv.

custom-built (also **custom-made**)
• adj. made to a particular customer's order.

customer • n. 1 a person who buys goods or services from a shop or business. 2 a person or thing of a particular kind that has to be dealt with: *he's a tough customer*.

customize (or **customise**)
• v. (**customizes, customizing, customized**) modify something to suit a particular person or task.

customs • pl. n. 1 the duties charged by a government on imported goods. 2 the official department that administers and collects such duties.

cut • v. (**cuts, cutting, cut**) 1 make an opening or wound in something with a sharp implement. 2 make, shorten, divide, or remove with a sharp implement: *she cut his photo out of the paper*. 3 (usu. as adj. **cut**) make or design a garment in a particular way: *an impeccably cut suit*. 4 reduce the amount or quantity of: *I should cut down my salt intake*. 5 end or interrupt the supply of something. 6 go across or through: *is it illegal to cut across a mini-roundabout?* 7 move to another shot in a film. 8 divide a pack of playing cards by lifting a portion from the top. • n. 1 an act of cutting. 2 a result of cutting: *a cut on his jaw*. 3 a reduction. 4 the style in which a garment or the hair is cut. 5 a piece of meat cut from a carcass. 6 informal a share of profits. 7 a version of a film after editing.
– PHRASES **be cut out for** (or **to be**) informal have exactly the right qualities for a role. **a cut above** informal better than. **cut and dried** decided or planned in advance. **cut and run** informal make a rapid departure from a difficult situation. **cut and thrust** a difficult or competitive situation. **cut both ways 1** (of a point) serve both sides of an argument. **2** have both good and bad effects. **cut corners** do something with a lack of thoroughness in order to save time or money. **cut a dash** Brit. be stylish or impressive. **cut someone dead** completely ignore someone. **cut in 1** interrupt someone. **2** pull in too closely in front of another vehicle. **3** (of a machine) begin operating automatically. **cut it out** informal stop it. **cut the mustard** informal reach the required standard. **cut no ice** informal have no influence or effect. **cut someone/thing off 1** block the usual means of

access to a place. **2** deprive someone of a supply of power, water, etc. **3** break a telephone connection with someone. **cut out** (of an engine) suddenly stop operating. **cut someone out** exclude someone. **cut your teeth** get initial experience of an activity. **cut a tooth** (of a baby) have a tooth appear through the gum. **cut up** informal very upset. **cut up rough** Brit. informal behave in an aggressive or awkward way.
– ORIGIN prob. Germanic.

cutaneous /kyoo-**tay**-ni-uhss/ • adj. relating to or affecting the skin.
– ORIGIN Latin *cutis* 'skin'.

cutback • n. a reduction.

cute • adj. **1** charmingly pretty; sweet. **2** N. Amer. informal clever; shrewd.
– DERIVATIVES **cutely** adv. **cuteness** n.
– ORIGIN from ACUTE.

cut glass • n. glass with decorative patterns cut into it.

cuticle /**kyoo**-ti-k'l/ • n. **1** the dead skin at the base of a fingernail or toenail. **2** the epidermis of the body.
– ORIGIN Latin *cuticula* 'little skin'.

cutlass /kut-luhss/ • n. a short sword with a slightly curved blade, formerly used by sailors.
– ORIGIN Latin *cultellus* 'small knife'.

cutler • n. a maker or seller of cutlery.
– ORIGIN Latin *cultellus* 'small knife'.

cutlery • n. knives, forks, and spoons used for eating or serving food.

cutlet • n. **1** a lamb or veal chop from just behind the neck. **2** a flat cake of minced meat, nuts, etc., covered in breadcrumbs and fried.
– ORIGIN French *côtelette*.

cut-off • n. **1** a point or level marking a set limit. **2** a device for interrupting a power or fuel supply. **3** (**cut-offs**) shorts made by cutting off the legs of a pair of jeans.

cut-out • n. **1** a shape cut out of board or paper. **2** a device that automatically breaks an electric circuit for safety.

cut-price • adj. for sale at a reduced price; cheap.

cutter • n. **1** a person or thing that cuts. **2** a light, fast patrol boat or sailing boat.

cut-throat • adj. ruthless and fierce: *cut-throat competition*. • n. dated a murderer or other violent criminal.

cut-throat razor • n. Brit. a razor with a long blade which folds like a penknife.

cutting • n. **1** a piece cut off, especially a piece cut from a plant to grow a new one. **2** Brit. an article cut from a newspaper or magazine. **3** Brit. an open passage dug through higher ground for a railway, road, or canal. • adj. **1** capable

of cutting. **2** (of a remark) hurtful.

cutting edge • n. the most advanced stage; the forefront. • adj. (**cutting-edge**) innovative; pioneering.

cuttlefish • n. (pl. **cuttlefish** or **cuttlefishes**) a sea creature resembling a squid, that squirts out a black liquid when attacked.
– ORIGIN Old English.

CV • abbrev. curriculum vitae.

cwt • abbrev. hundredweight.
– ORIGIN from Latin *centum* 'a hundred'.

cyan /sy-uhn/ • n. a greenish-blue colour.
– ORIGIN Greek *kuaneos* 'dark blue'.

cyanide /sy-uh-nyd/ • n. a highly poisonous compound containing a metal combined with carbon and nitrogen atoms.

cyanocobalamin /sy-uh-noh-kuh-**bal**-uh-min/ • n. vitamin B_{12}, found in liver, fish, and eggs.
– ORIGIN from Greek *kuanos* 'dark blue' + COBALT and VITAMIN.

cyanosis /sy-uh-**noh**-siss/ • n. a bluish discoloration of the skin due to poor circulation or a lack of oxygen in the blood.
– ORIGIN Greek *kuanōsis* 'blueness'.

cyber- /sy-ber/ • comb. form relating to information technology, the Internet, and virtual reality: *cyberspace*.
– ORIGIN from CYBERNETICS.

cybercafe • n. a cafe where customers can also use computer terminals and access the Internet.

cybernetics • n. the science of communications and automatic control systems in both machines and living things.
– DERIVATIVES **cybernetic** adj.
– ORIGIN Greek *kubernētēs* 'steersman'.

cyberspace • n. the hypothetical environment in which communication over computer networks occurs.

cyborg /sy-borg/ • n. (in science fiction) a person having mechanical elements built into the body to extend their normal physical abilities.
– ORIGIN from CYBER- and ORGANISM.

cyclamen /sik-luh-muhn/ • n. (pl. **cyclamen** or **cyclamens**) a plant having pink, red, or white flowers with petals that curve backwards.
– ORIGIN Greek *kuklaminos*.

cycle • n. **1** a series of events that are regularly repeated in the same order: *the cycle of birth and death*. **2** a complete sequence of changes associated with a recurring phenomenon such as an alternating electric current. **3** a series of musical or literary works composed

around a particular theme. **4** a bicycle.
• v. (**cycles**, **cycling**, **cycled**) ride a
bicycle.
– ORIGIN Greek *kuklos* 'circle'.

cyclic /syk-lik, sik-lik/ • adj. **1** occurring
in cycles. **2** Chem. having a molecular
structure containing one or more closed
rings of atoms.
– DERIVATIVES **cyclical** adj. **cyclically** adv.

cyclist • n. a person who rides a bicycle.

cyclone /sy-klohn/ • n. **1** a system of
winds rotating inwards to an area of low
atmospheric pressure. **2** a violent
tropical storm.
– DERIVATIVES **cyclonic** adj.
– ORIGIN prob. from Greek *kuklōma*
'wheel, coil of a snake'.

cyclopean /sy-kluh-pee-uhn, sy-kloh-
pi-uhn/ • adj. relating to a Cyclops.

Cyclops /sy-klops/ • n. (pl. **Cyclops**) Gk
Myth. a member of a race of one-eyed
giants.
– ORIGIN Greek *Kuklōps* 'round-eyed'.

cyclotron /sy-kluh-tron/ • n. an
apparatus for accelerating charged
atomic and subatomic particles by
making them move spirally in a
magnetic field.

cygnet /sig-nit/ • n. a young swan.
– ORIGIN Old French.

cylinder /si-lin-der/ • n. **1** a three-
dimensional shape with straight parallel
sides and circular or oval ends. **2** a
piston chamber in a steam or internal-
combustion engine. **3** a cylindrical
container for liquefied gas under
pressure.
– ORIGIN Greek *kulindros* 'roller'.

cylindrical /si-lin-dri-k'l/ • adj. having
the shape of a cylinder.

cymbal /sim-buhl/ • n. a musical
instrument consisting of a round brass
plate which is either struck against
another one or hit with a stick.
– ORIGIN Greek *kumbalon*.

cyme /sym/ • n. a flower cluster with a
central stem bearing a single flower on
the end that develops first. Compare
with RACEME.
– ORIGIN Latin *cyma* 'summit'.

cynic /si-nik/ • n. **1** a person who believes
that people always act from selfish
motives. **2** a person who raises doubts
about something. **3** (**Cynic**) a member of
an ancient Greek school of philosophers
who despised wealth and pleasure.
– DERIVATIVES **cynicism** n.
– ORIGIN Greek *kunikos*.

cynical • adj. **1** believing that people
always act from selfish motives. **2** (of an
action) done to benefit yourself,
without any concern for accepted
standards of behaviour: *a cynical
professional foul.* **3** doubtful; sceptical.
– DERIVATIVES **cynically** adv.

cynosure /sin-uh-zyoor/ • n. a person or
thing that is the centre of attention or
admiration.
– ORIGIN Greek *kunosoura* 'dog's tail',
also 'Ursa Minor' (the constellation
contains the pole star, which was used as
a guide by sailors).

cypher • n. var. of CIPHER.

cypress • n. an evergreen coniferous tree
with small dark leaves.
– ORIGIN Greek *kuparissos*.

Cypriot • n. a person from Cyprus.
• adj. relating to Cyprus.

Cyrillic /si-ril-lik/ • adj. relating to the
alphabet used for Russian, Ukrainian,
Bulgarian, and related languages.
– ORIGIN named after the 9th-century
missionary St *Cyril*.

cyst /sist/ • n. a thin-walled abnormal sac
or cavity in the body, containing fluid.
– ORIGIN Greek *kustis* 'bladder'.

cystic • adj. **1** relating to cysts. **2** relating
to the urinary bladder or the gall
bladder.

cystic fibrosis • n. an inherited disease
in which the production of abnormally
thick mucus leads to the blockage of the
pancreatic ducts, intestines, and
bronchi.

cystitis /si-sty-tiss/ • n. inflammation of
the bladder.

cytology /sy-tol-uh-ji/ • n. the branch of
biology concerned with the structure
and function of cells.
– DERIVATIVES **cytological** adj.
cytologist n.

cytoplasm /sy-toh-pla-z'm/ • n. the
material of a living cell, excluding the
nucleus.
– DERIVATIVES **cytoplasmic** adj.

czar etc. • n. var. of TSAR etc.

Czech /chek/ • n. **1** a person from the
Czech Republic or (formerly)
Czechoslovakia. **2** the Slavic language
spoken in the Czech Republic.
• adj. relating to the Czech Republic.

Czechoslovak /chek-uh-sloh-vak/ (also
Czechoslovakian) • n. a person from the
former country of Czechoslovakia, now
divided between the Czech Republic
and Slovakia. • adj. relating to the former
country of Czechoslovakia.

Dd

D¹ (also **d**) • n. (pl. **Ds** or **D's**) **1** the fourth letter of the alphabet. **2** Music the second note of the scale of C major. **3** the Roman numeral for 500.

D² • abbrev. **1** depth (in the sense of the dimension of an object from front to back). **2** (with a numeral) dimension(s) or dimensional.

d • abbrev. **1** deci-. **2** (in travel timetables) departs. **3** (**d.**) died (used to indicate a date of death). **4** Brit. penny or pence (of pre-decimal currency). [ORIGIN Latin *denarius* 'penny'.]

'd • contr. **1** had. **2** would.

DA • abbrev. US district attorney.

dab¹ • v. (**dabs**, **dabbing**, **dabbed**) **1** press lightly with a cloth, sponge, etc. **2** apply with light quick strokes. • n. a small amount lightly applied.

dab² • n. a small North Atlantic flatfish.

dabble • v. (**dabbles**, **dabbling**, **dabbled**) **1** move the hands or feet around gently in water. **2** take part in an activity in a casual way.
– DERIVATIVES **dabbler** n.
– ORIGIN from former Dutch *dabbelen* or from **DAB¹**.

dab hand • n. Brit. informal a person who is very skilled in a particular activity.

dace /dayss/ • n. (pl. **dace**) a small freshwater fish related to the carp.
– ORIGIN Old French *dars*.

dacha /da-chuh/ • n. (in Russia) a house or cottage in the country, used as a holiday home.
– ORIGIN Russian.

dachshund /dak-suhnd/ • n. a breed of dog with a long body and very short legs.
– ORIGIN German, 'badger dog'.

dactyl /dak-til/ • n. Poetry a metrical foot consisting of one stressed syllable followed by two unstressed syllables.
– ORIGIN Greek *daktulos* 'finger'.

dad • n. informal a person's father.

Dada /dah-dah/ • n. an early 20th-century movement in the arts which mocked conventions and emphasized the illogical and absurd.
– ORIGIN French, 'hobby horse'.

daddy • n. (pl. **daddies**) informal a person's father.

daddy-long-legs • n. (pl. **daddy-long-legs**) Brit. informal a crane fly.

dado /day-doh/ • n. (pl. **dados**) the lower part of the wall of a room, when decorated differently from the upper part.
– ORIGIN Italian, 'dice or cube'.

dado rail • n. a waist-high moulding round the wall of a room.

daemon /dee-muhn/ • n. old-fashioned var. of **DEMON**.
– DERIVATIVES **daemonic** adj.
– ORIGIN Greek *daimon*.

daffodil • n. a plant bearing bright yellow flowers with a long trumpet-shaped centre.
– ORIGIN Latin *asphodilus* 'asphodel'.

daffy • adj. informal silly.
– ORIGIN northern English dialect *daff* 'simpleton'.

daft • adj. Brit. informal silly; foolish.
– ORIGIN Old English, 'mild, meek'.

dagger • n. a short pointed knife, used as a weapon.
– PHRASES **be at daggers drawn** Brit. be bitterly hostile.
– ORIGIN perh. from former *dag* 'pierce'.

dago /day-goh/ • n. (pl. **dagos** or **dagoes**) informal, offens. a Spanish, Portuguese, or Italian-speaking person.
– ORIGIN from the Spanish man's name *Diego* 'James'.

daguerreotype /duh-ger-ruh-typ/ (also **daguerrotype**) • n. an early kind of photograph produced using silver-coated copper plate and mercury vapour.
– ORIGIN named after L.-J.-M. *Daguerre*, its French inventor.

dahlia /day-li-uh/ • n. a garden plant with brightly coloured flowers.
– ORIGIN named after the Swedish botanist Andreas *Dahl*.

Dáil /doyl/ (in full **Dáil Éireann** /doyl air-uhn/) • n. the lower house of Parliament in the Republic of Ireland.

d

– ORIGIN Irish, 'assembly' (in full 'assembly of Ireland').

daily • adj. done, happening, or produced every day or every weekday. • adv. every day. • n. (pl. **dailies**) informal a newspaper published every day except Sunday.

dainty • adj. (**daintier, daintiest**) delicately small and pretty. • n. (pl. **dainties**) a small appetizing item of food.
– DERIVATIVES **daintily** adv. **daintiness** n.
– ORIGIN Old French *daintie* 'choice morsel, pleasure'.

daiquiri /da-ki-ri/ • n. (pl. **daiquiris**) a cocktail containing rum and lime juice.
– ORIGIN *Daiquiri*, a district in Cuba.

dairy • n. (pl. **dairies**) a building for treating and distributing milk and milk products. • adj. **1** made from milk. **2** involved in milk production: *a dairy farmer*.
– ORIGIN Old English, 'female servant'.

dairymaid • n. old use a woman employed in a dairy.

dais /day-iss/ • n. a low platform for a lectern or throne.
– ORIGIN Old French *deis*.

daisy • n. (pl. **daisies**) a small plant having flowers with a yellow centre and white petals.
– ORIGIN Old English, 'day's eye'.

daisy wheel • n. a disc bearing spokes with printing characters on the ends, used in word processors and typewriters.

Dalai Lama /da-ly lah-muh/ • n. the spiritual head of Tibetan Buddhism.
– ORIGIN Tibetan, 'ocean monk'.

dale • n. (in northern England) a valley.
– ORIGIN Old English.

dalliance • n. a casual romantic or sexual relationship.

dally • v. (**dallies, dallying, dallied**) **1** act or move slowly **2** (**dally with**) have a casual romantic or sexual relationship with.
– ORIGIN Old French *dalier* 'to chat'.

Dalmatian /dal-**may**-sh'n/ • n. a breed of large dog with short white hair and dark spots.
– ORIGIN named after *Dalmatia*, a region of Croatia.

dam[1] • n. a barrier built across a river to hold back water. • v. (**dams, damming, dammed**) build a dam across.
– ORIGIN German or Dutch.

dam[2] • n. the female parent of an animal.
– ORIGIN from **DAME**.

damage • n. **1** physical harm reducing the value or usefulness of something. **2** harmful effects. **3** (**damages**) financial compensation for a loss or injury.
• v. (**damages, damaging, damaged**) cause harm to.
– ORIGIN Old French.

damaging • adj. harmful or undesirable: *the damaging effects of the sun*.

damask /dam-uhsk/ • n. a rich heavy fabric with a pattern woven into it.
– ORIGIN from *Damascus*, where the fabric was first produced.

dame • n. **1** (**Dame**) (in the UK) the title of a woman awarded a knighthood, equivalent to *Sir*. **2** N. Amer. informal a woman. **3** (also **pantomime dame**) Brit. a comic female character in pantomime, played by a man.
– ORIGIN Old French.

damn /dam/ • v. **1** (**be damned**) (in Christian belief) be condemned by God to eternal punishment in hell. **2** criticize strongly. • exclam. informal expressing anger. • adj. informal used to emphasize anger.
– PHRASES **damn someone/thing with faint praise** praise someone or something so unenthusiastically that it seems as though you are actually criticizing them.
– ORIGIN Latin *dampnare* 'inflict loss on'.

damnable /dam-nuh-b'l/ • adj. very bad or unpleasant.
– DERIVATIVES **damnably** adv.

damnation /dam-nay-sh'n/ • n. condemnation to eternal punishment in hell. • exclam. expressing anger.

damned /damd/ • adj. used to emphasize anger.
– PHRASES **do your damnedest** do your utmost.

damning /dam-ing/ • adj. strongly suggesting guilt.

damp • adj. slightly wet. • n. moisture in the air, on a surface, or in a solid substance. • v. **1** make something damp. **2** (**damp something down**) control a feeling or situation.
– DERIVATIVES **dampness** n.
– ORIGIN Germanic.

damp course (also **damp-proof course**) • n. a layer of waterproof material in a wall near the ground, to prevent rising damp.

dampen • v. **1** make damp. **2** make less strong or intense.
– DERIVATIVES **dampener** n.

damper • n. **1** a pad for silencing a piano string. **2** a movable metal plate used to regulate the air flow in a chimney.
– PHRASES **put a damper on** informal make something less enjoyable.

damp squib • n. Brit. something that

turns out to be much less impressive than expected.

damsel /dam-z'l/ • n. old use or humorous a young unmarried woman.
– ORIGIN Old French *dameisele*.

damselfly • n. (pl. **damselflies**) a slender insect related to the dragonflies.

damson /dam-zuhn/ • n. a small purple-black plum-like fruit.
– ORIGIN from Latin *damascenum prunum* 'plum of Damascus'.

dan • n. 1 any of ten degrees of advanced skill in judo or karate. 2 a person who has achieved a dan.
– ORIGIN Japanese.

dance • v. (**dances, dancing, danced**) 1 move rhythmically to music. 2 move in a quick and lively way. • n. 1 a series of steps and movements that match the rhythm of a piece of music. 2 an act of dancing. 3 a social gathering at which people dance. 4 (also **dance music**) pop music for dancing to in clubs.
– PHRASES **dance attendance on** esp. Brit. try hard to please someone. **lead someone a merry dance** Brit. cause someone a great deal of trouble.
– DERIVATIVES **dancer** n. **dancing** n.
– ORIGIN Old French *dancer*.

dandelion • n. a weed with large bright yellow flowers followed by rounded heads of seeds with downy tufts.
– ORIGIN French *dent-de-lion* 'lion's tooth'.

dander • n. (in phr. **get your dander up**) informal lose your temper.

dandified • adj. (of a man) too concerned about his clothes and appearance.

dandle • v. (**dandles, dandling, dandled**) gently bounce a young child on your knees or in your arms.

dandruff • n. flakes of dead skin on a person's scalp and in the hair.

dandy • n. (pl. **dandies**) a man who is too concerned with having a stylish and fashionable appearance. • adj. N. Amer. informal excellent.
– DERIVATIVES **dandyish** adj.
– ORIGIN an informal form of the man's name *Andrew*.

Dane • n. a person from Denmark.

danger • n. 1 the possibility of suffering harm or of something unpleasant happening: *he was in danger of being killed.* 2 a cause of harm.
– ORIGIN Old French *dangier*.

dangerous • adj. likely to cause harm or problems.
– DERIVATIVES **dangerously** adv. **dangerousness** n.

dangle • v. (**dangles, dangling, dangled**) 1 hang so as to swing freely. 2 offer something to someone to persuade them to do something.
– DERIVATIVES **dangler** n. **dangly** adj.

Danish /day-nish/ • adj. relating to Denmark or the Danes. • n. the language of Denmark.

Danish blue • n. a strong-flavoured blue-veined white cheese.

Danish pastry • n. a cake of sweetened yeast pastry topped with icing, fruit, or nuts.

dank • adj. damp and cold.
– ORIGIN prob. Scandinavian.

dapper • adj. (of a man) neat in dress and appearance.
– ORIGIN prob. from German or Dutch, 'strong, stout'.

dapple • v. (**dapples, dappling, dappled**) mark with spots or small patches.
– ORIGIN perh. from Old Norse, 'spot'.

dapple grey • adj. (of a horse) grey or white with darker ring-like markings.

dare • v. (**dares, daring, dared**) 1 have the courage to do something. 2 challenge someone to do something. • n. a challenge to do something brave or risky.
– PHRASES **I dare say** it is probable.
– ORIGIN Old English.

daredevil • n. a person who enjoys doing dangerous things.

daring • adj. 1 willing to do dangerous or risky things. 2 involving risk or danger. • n. adventurous courage.
– DERIVATIVES **daringly** adv.

dark • adj. 1 with little or no light. 2 of a deep colour. 3 (of skin, hair, or eyes) brown or black. 4 unpleasant or gloomy: *the dark days of the war.* 5 evil. 6 mysterious: *a dark secret.* 7 (**darkest**) humorous most remote or uncivilized. • n. 1 (**the dark**) the absence of light. 2 nightfall.
– PHRASES **in the dark** in a state of ignorance. **a shot** (or **stab**) **in the dark** a wild guess.
– DERIVATIVES **darkish** adj. **darkly** adv. **darkness** n.
– ORIGIN Old English.

Dark Ages • pl. n. the period in Europe between the fall of the Roman Empire and the Middle Ages, *c.*500–1100, seen as lacking culture and learning.

darken • v. 1 make or become darker. 2 become unhappy or angry.
– PHRASES **never darken someone's door** keep away from someone's home.

dark horse • n. a person about whom little is known, often one with unexpected talents.

darkroom •n. a room for developing photographs, from which normal light is excluded.

darling •n. **1** used as an affectionate form of address. **2** a lovable person. **3** a person popular with a particular group: *she's the darling of the media.* •adj. **1** beloved. **2** charming.
– ORIGIN Old English.

darn¹ •v. mend knitted material by interweaving yarn across it.
– DERIVATIVES **darning** n.
– ORIGIN perh. from Old English, 'to hide'.

darn² •v., adj., & exclam. informal euphemism for **DAMN**.

darned •adj. informal euphemism for **DAMNED**.

dart •n. **1** a small pointed missile thrown or fired as a weapon. **2** a small pointed missile used in the game of darts. **3** (**darts**) an indoor game in which darts are thrown at a dartboard. **4** a sudden rapid movement. **5** a tapered tuck in a garment. •v. move suddenly or rapidly.
– ORIGIN Old French.

dartboard •n. a circular board used as a target in the game of darts.

Darwinism •n. the theory of the evolution of species by natural selection, proposed by the English natural historian Charles Darwin.
– DERIVATIVES **Darwinian** n. & adj. **Darwinist** n. & adj.

dash •v. **1** run or travel in a great hurry. **2** hit or throw with great force. **3** destroy: *his hopes were dashed.* **4** (**dash something off**) write something hurriedly. •n. **1** an act of dashing. **2** a small amount added: *a dash of soda.* **3** a horizontal stroke in writing, marking a pause or omission. **4** the longer of the signals used in Morse code. **5** style and confidence.

dashboard •n. the panel of instruments and controls facing the driver of a vehicle.
– ORIGIN first meaning a board in front of a carriage, to keep out mud.

dashing •adj. (of a man) attractive and confident.

dastardly /dass-terd-li/ •adj. dated or humorous wicked and cruel.
– ORIGIN from the old word *dastard* 'despicable person'.

DAT •abbrev. digital audiotape.

data /day-tuh/ •n. **1** facts or statistics used for reference or analysis. **2** the quantities, characters, or symbols operated on by a computer.
– ORIGIN Latin, plural of **DATUM**.

databank •n. a large store of computer data on a particular topic.

database •n. a structured set of data held in a computer.

datable (also **dateable**) •adj. able to be dated to a particular time.

data capture •n. the process of gathering data and putting it into a form accessible by computer.

data protection •n. legal control over access to data stored in computers.

date¹ •n. **1** the day of the month or year as specified by a number. **2** a day or year when a particular event occurred or will occur. **3** a social or romantic appointment. **4** a musical or theatrical performance. •v. (**dates, dating, dated**) **1** establish the date of something. **2** mark with a date. **3** (**date from** or **back to**) start at a particular time in the past. **4** (as adj. **dated**) old-fashioned. **5** informal go on a date or regular dates with someone.
– PHRASES **to date** until now.
– ORIGIN Latin *data* 'given'.

date² •n. the sweet, dark brown fruit of a palm tree of North Africa and western Asia.
– ORIGIN Greek *daktulos* 'finger'.

dateable •adj. var. of **DATABLE**.

date rape •n. rape by a person with whom the victim has gone on a date.

dating agency •n. a service which arranges introductions for people seeking romantic partners or friends.

dative /day-tiv/ •adj. (in Latin, Greek, German, etc.) referring to the case of nouns and pronouns indicating an indirect object or the person or thing affected by a verb.
– ORIGIN from Latin *casus dativus* 'case of giving'.

datum /day-tuhm/ •n. (pl. **data**) a piece of information.
– ORIGIN Latin, 'something given'.

daub /dawb/ •v. **1** smear carelessly or heavily with a thick substance. **2** spread a thick substance on a surface. •n. **1** plaster, clay, or a similar substance, used in building. **2** a smear of a thick substance. **3** an unskilful painting.
– DERIVATIVES **dauber** n.
– ORIGIN Old French *dauber*.

daughter •n. **1** a girl or woman in

relation to her parents. **2** a female descendant.
– DERIVATIVES **daughterly** adj.
– ORIGIN Old English.

daughterboard (also **daughtercard**) • n. a small printed circuit board that attaches to a larger one.

daughter-in-law • n. (pl. **daughters-in-law**) the wife of a person's son.

daunt /dawnt/ • v. make someone feel nervous or discouraged.
– DERIVATIVES **daunting** adj.
– ORIGIN Old French *danter*.

dauntless • adj. fearless and determined.

dauphin /doh-fan/ • n. hist. the eldest son of the King of France.
– ORIGIN French.

davenport • n. Brit. an ornamental writing desk with drawers and a sloping surface for writing.
– ORIGIN named after a Captain *Davenport*, for whom a desk of this type was first made.

davit /da-vit/ • n. a small crane on a ship.
– ORIGIN Old French *daviot*.

dawdle • v. (**dawdles**, **dawdling**, **dawdled**) move slowly; take your time.
– DERIVATIVES **dawdler** n.
– ORIGIN from dialect *daddle* 'dally'.

dawn • n. **1** the first appearance of light in the sky in the morning. **2** the beginning of something: *the dawn of civilization.* • v. **1** (of a day) begin. **2** come into existence. **3** (**dawn on**) become obvious to someone.
– ORIGIN Old English.

dawn chorus • n. the early-morning singing of birds.

day • n. **1** a period of twenty-four hours, reckoned from midnight to midnight. **2** the time between sunrise and sunset. **3** a particular period of the past: *laws were strict in those days.* **4** (**the day**) the present time or the time in question. **5** (**your day**) the youthful or successful period of your life.
– PHRASES **call it a day** decide to stop doing something. **day by day** gradually. **day in, day out** continuously or repeatedly over a long period. **day-to-day 1** happening every day. **2** routine. **that will be the day** informal that is very unlikely. **these days** at present.
– ORIGIN Old English.

day boy (or **day girl**) • n. Brit. a boy (or girl) who lives at home and attends a school that also takes boarders.

daybreak • n. dawn.

day centre (also **day-care centre**) • n. a place providing daytime care and social facilities for elderly or disabled people.

daydream • n. a series of pleasant thoughts that distract your attention from the present. • v. have a daydream.
– DERIVATIVES **daydreamer** n.

daylight • n. **1** the natural light of the day. **2** dawn. **3** visible distance between one person or thing and another.
– PHRASES —— **the living daylights out of someone** do something to someone very severely: *you scared the living daylights out of me.*

daylight robbery • n. Brit. informal blatant and unfair overcharging.

day release • n. Brit. a system in which employees are granted days off work to go on educational courses.

day return • n. Brit. a ticket at a reduced rate for a return journey on public transport within one day.

day school • n. **1** a school for pupils who live at home. **2** a short educational course.

daytime • n. **1** the time between sunrise and sunset. **2** the period of time corresponding to normal working hours.

day trip • n. a journey or outing that is completed in one day.
– DERIVATIVES **day tripper** n.

daze • v. (**dazes**, **dazing**, **dazed**) stun or bewilder someone. • n. a state of stunned confusion or bewilderment.
– ORIGIN Old Norse, 'weary'.

dazzle • v. (**dazzles**, **dazzling**, **dazzled**) **1** (of a bright light) blind someone temporarily. **2** impress greatly: *I was dazzled by her beauty.* • n. blinding brightness.
– DERIVATIVES **dazzler** n.
– ORIGIN from DAZE.

Db • symb. the chemical element dubnium.

dB • abbrev. decibel(s).

DC • abbrev. **1** direct current. **2** District of Columbia.

DD • abbrev. Doctor of Divinity.

D-Day • n. the day (6 June 1944) in the Second World War on which Allied forces invaded northern France.
– ORIGIN from *D* for *day* + DAY.

DDR • abbrev. hist. German Democratic Republic.
– ORIGIN short for German *Deutsche Demokratische Republik*.

DDT • abbrev. dichlorodiphenyltrichloroethane, a compound used as an insecticide but now banned in many countries.

de- • prefix forming or added to verbs or their derivatives: **1** down; away: *deduct.* **2** completely: *denude.* **3** indicating removal or reversal: *de-ice.*
– ORIGIN Latin *de* 'off, from' or *dis-*.

deacon /dee-kuhn/ •n. **1** (in the Roman Catholic, Anglican, and Orthodox Churches) a minister ranking below a priest. **2** (in some Protestant Churches) a person who assists a minister but is not a member of the clergy.
– ORIGIN Greek *diakonos* 'servant'.

deaconess •n. a woman with duties similar to those of a deacon.

deactivate •v. (**deactivates, deactivating, deactivated**) make equipment or a virus inactive by disconnecting or destroying it.

dead •adj. **1** no longer alive. **2** (of a part of the body) numb. **3** showing no emotion: *a cold, dead voice.* **4** no longer current or important. **5** lacking activity or excitement. **6** (of equipment) not working. **7** complete: *dead silence.* •adv. **1** completely; exactly: *dead on time.* **2** directly: *dead ahead.* **3** Brit. informal very.
– PHRASES **the dead of night** the quietest, darkest part of the night. **the dead of winter** the coldest part of the year. **from the dead** from being dead.
– DERIVATIVES **deadness** n.
– ORIGIN Old English.

deadbeat •adj. (**dead beat**) informal completely exhausted. •n. informal a lazy or unreliable person.

dead duck •n. informal an unsuccessful or useless person or thing.

deaden •v. **1** make a noise or feeling less intense. **2** make something numb.

dead end •n. a road or passage that is closed at one end.

dead hand •n. an undesirable and long-lasting influence.

dead heat •n. a result in a race in which two or more competitors finish at exactly the same time.

dead letter •n. a law or treaty which is no longer applied in practice.

deadline •n. the latest time or date by which something should be completed.

deadlock •n. **1** a situation in which no progress can be made. **2** a lock operated by a key. •v. (**be deadlocked**) be unable to make progress.

dead loss •n. an unproductive or useless person or thing.

deadly •adj. (**deadlier, deadliest**) **1** causing or able to cause death. **2** (of a voice, glance, etc.) filled with hate. **3** very accurate or effective. **4** informal very boring. •adv. **1** in a way that resembles death. **2** very: *she was deadly serious.*
– DERIVATIVES **deadliness** n.

deadly nightshade •n. a poisonous plant with purple flowers and round black fruit.

deadly sin •n. (in Christian tradition) a sin seen as leading to damnation.

deadpan •adj. not showing any emotion; expressionless.

dead reckoning •n. a way of finding out your position by estimating the direction and distance travelled.

dead ringer •n. a person or thing that looks very like another.

deadweight •n. **1** a person or thing that is very heavy and difficult to lift. **2** the total weight which a ship can carry.

dead wood •n. useless or unproductive people or things.

deaf •adj. **1** wholly or partially unable to hear. **2** (**deaf to**) unwilling to listen to.
– PHRASES **fall on deaf ears** be ignored. **turn a deaf ear** refuse to listen or respond.
– DERIVATIVES **deafness** n.
– ORIGIN Old English.

deafen •v. **1** make someone deaf. **2** (as adj. **deafening**) very loud.

deaf mute •n. offens. a person who is deaf and unable to speak.

deal[1] •v. (**deals, dealing, dealt**) **1** (**deal something out**) distribute something. **2** (usu. **deal in**) buy and sell a product commercially. **3** buy and sell illegal drugs. **4** give out cards to players for a game or round. •n. **1** an agreement between two or more parties. **2** a particular form of treatment given or received: *working mothers get a bad deal.*
– PHRASES **a big deal** informal an important thing. **deal someone/thing a blow** hit or be harmful to someone or something. **a deal of** a large amount of. **deal with 1** do business with. **2** take action to put right. **3** cope with. **4** have something as a subject. **a good** (or **great**) **deal 1** a large amount. **2** much; a lot. **a square deal** a fair bargain or treatment.
– ORIGIN Old English.

deal[2] •n. fir or pine wood (as a building material).
– ORIGIN German and Dutch *dele* 'plank'.

dealer •n. **1** a person who buys and sells goods. **2** a person who sells illegal drugs. **3** a player who deals cards in a card game.
– DERIVATIVES **dealership** n.

dealt past part. of DEAL[1].

dean •n. **1** the head of the governing body of a cathedral. **2** the head of a university department or of a medical school. **3** a college officer who deals with discipline and welfare.
– ORIGIN Old French *deien*.

deanery •n. (pl. **deaneries**) the official house of a dean.

dear • adj. **1** much loved. **2** used in the polite introduction to a letter. **3** esp. Brit. expensive. • n. **1** a lovable person. **2** used as an affectionate form of address. • adv. esp. Brit. at a high cost. • exclam. used in expressions of surprise or dismay.
– ORIGIN Old English.

dearly • adv. **1** very much. **2** at great cost.

dearth /derth/ • n. a lack or inadequate amount of something: *a dearth of evidence.*
– ORIGIN from **DEAR**.

death • n. **1** the action of dying. **2** an instance of a person or an animal dying. **3** the state of being dead. **4** the end of something.
– PHRASES **at death's door** so ill that you may die. **catch your death (of cold)** informal catch a severe cold. **die a death** fail or come to an end. **put someone to death** execute someone. **to death** used for emphasis: *I'm sick to death of him.*
– DERIVATIVES **deathless** adj.
– ORIGIN Old English.

deathbed • n. the bed where someone is dying or has died.

death certificate • n. an official statement of a person's death.

death duty • n. dated = INHERITANCE TAX.

death knell • n. an event that signals the end of something.
– ORIGIN from the ringing of a bell to mark a person's death.

deathly • adj. suggesting death: *a deathly hush.*

death penalty • n. punishment by execution.

death rate • n. the number of deaths per one thousand people per year.

death row • n. a prison block for those sentenced to death.

death toll • n. the number of deaths resulting from a particular cause.

deathtrap • n. a dangerous building, vehicle, etc.

death-watch beetle • n. a beetle whose larvae bore into dead wood and timbers.
– ORIGIN so called because it makes a ticking sound, formerly believed to be an omen of death.

deb • n. informal a debutante.

debacle /day-bah-k'l/ • n. a complete failure or disaster.
– ORIGIN French.

debar • v. (**debars, debarring, debarred**) officially ban someone from doing something.
– ORIGIN Old French *desbarrer* 'unbar'.

debark • v. leave a ship or aircraft.
– ORIGIN French *débarquer.*

debase /di-bayss/ • v. (**debases,**
debasing, debased**) lower the quality, value, or character of: *killing debases and demeans us all.*
– DERIVATIVES **debasement** n.

debatable • adj. open to discussion or argument.

debate • n. **1** a formal discussion in which opposing arguments are presented. **2** an argument. • v. (**debates, debating, debated**) **1** discuss or argue about something. **2** consider a course of action.
– DERIVATIVES **debater** n.
– ORIGIN Old French.

debauched /di-bawchd/ • adj. over-indulging in sex, alcohol, and drugs.
– DERIVATIVES **debauchery** n.
– ORIGIN Old French *desbaucher* 'turn away from your duty'.

debenture /di-ben-cher/ • n. Brit. a certificate issued by a company acknowledging that it has borrowed money on which interest is being paid.
– ORIGIN Latin *debentur* 'are owing'.

debilitate /di-bil-i-tayt/ • v. (**debilitates, debilitating, debilitated**) severely weaken someone or something.
– DERIVATIVES **debilitation** n.
– ORIGIN Latin *debilitare.*

debility • n. (pl. **debilities**) physical weakness.

debit • n. **1** an entry in an account recording a sum owed. **2** a payment made or owed. • v. (**debits, debiting, debited**) (of a bank) take money from a customer's account.
– ORIGIN French.

debit card • n. a card allowing the holder to take money from a bank account electronically when buying something.

debonair /deb-uh-nair/ • adj. (of a man) confident, stylish, and charming.
– ORIGIN from Old French *de bon aire* 'of good disposition'.

debouch /di-bowch/ • v. emerge from a confined space into a wide, open area.
– ORIGIN French.

debrief • v. question someone in detail about a completed mission.

debris /deb-ree/ • n. scattered pieces of rubbish or the remains of something that has been destroyed.
– ORIGIN French.

debt • n. **1** a sum of money owed. **2** the state of owing money. **3** a feeling of gratitude for a favour or service.
– ORIGIN Latin *debitum.*

debtor • n. a person who owes money.

debug • v. (**debugs, debugging, debugged**) remove errors from computer hardware or software.

- DERIVATIVES **debugger** n.

debunk •v. show that a widely held belief is false or exaggerated.
- DERIVATIVES **debunker** n.

debut /day-byoo/ •n. a person's first appearance in a role. •v. perform in public for the first time.
- ORIGIN French.

debutant /deb-yoo-ton(t)/ •n. a person making a first public appearance in a role.

debutante /deb-yuh-tahnt/ •n. a young upper-class woman making her first appearance in society.

Dec. •abbrev. December.

deca- (also **dec-** before a vowel) •comb. form ten; having ten: decahedron.
- ORIGIN Greek deka 'ten'.

decade /dek-ayd/ •n. a period of ten years.
- ORIGIN Old French.

decadent •adj. having low moral standards and interested only in pleasure.
- DERIVATIVES **decadence** n. **decadently** adv.
- ORIGIN French.

decaffeinated /dee-kaf-fi-nay-tid/ •adj. (of tea or coffee) having had most or all of its caffeine removed.

decagon /dek-uh-guhn/ •n. a plane figure with ten straight sides and angles.

decahedron /dek-uh-hee-druhn/ •n. (pl. **decahedra** or **decahedrons**) a solid figure with ten plane faces.

decalitre (US **decaliter**) •n. a metric unit of volume, equal to 10 litres.

Decalogue /dek-uh-log/ •n. the Ten Commandments.
- ORIGIN from Greek dekalogos biblos 'book of the Ten Commandments'.

decametre (US **decameter**) •n. a metric unit of length, equal to 10 metres.

decamp •v. leave suddenly or secretly.

decant /di-kant/ •v. pour liquid from one container into another to remove any sediment.
- ORIGIN Latin decanthare.

decanter •n. a glass container with a stopper, into which wine or spirits are decanted.

decapitate /di-kap-i-tayt/
•v. (**decapitates**, **decapitating**, **decapitated**) kill someone by cutting off their head.
- DERIVATIVES **decapitation** n.
- ORIGIN Latin decapitare.

decapod /dek-uh-pod/ •n. a crustacean with five pairs of walking legs, such as a crab.
- ORIGIN from Greek deka 'ten' + pous 'foot'.

decarbonize (or **decarbonise**)
•v. (**decarbonizes**, **decarbonizing**, **decarbonized**) remove carbon deposits from an engine.

decathlon /di-kath-lon/ •n. an athletic event in which each competitor takes part in the same ten events.
- DERIVATIVES **decathlete** n.
- ORIGIN from Greek deka 'ten' + athlon 'contest'.

decay •v. **1** (of plant or animal material) rot. **2** gradually become worse or weaker: the authority of the party is decaying. **3** Physics (of a radioactive substance, particle, etc.) undergo change to a different form by giving out radiation. •n. **1** the state or process of decaying. **2** rotten matter or tissue.
- ORIGIN Old French decair.

decease •n. formal or Law death.
- ORIGIN Latin decessus.

deceased formal or Law •n. (**the deceased**) the recently dead person in question.
•adj. recently dead.

deceit •n. behaviour intended to make someone believe something that is not true.

deceitful •adj. deliberately causing other people to believe things that are not true.
- DERIVATIVES **deceitfully** adv.

deceive •v. (**deceives**, **deceiving**, **deceived**) **1** deliberately cause someone to believe something that is not true. **2** (of a thing) give a mistaken impression.
- DERIVATIVES **deceiver** n.
- ORIGIN Old French deceivre.

☑ **deceive** follows the usual rule of i before e except after c.

decelerate /dee-sel-uh-rayt/
•v. (**decelerates**, **decelerating**, **decelerated**) begin to move more slowly.
- DERIVATIVES **deceleration** n.

December •n. the twelfth month of the year.
- ORIGIN Latin.

decency •n. (pl. **decencies**) **1** behaviour that follows generally accepted standards of morality or respectability. **2** (**decencies**) standards of acceptable behaviour.

decennial /di-sen-ni-uhl/ •adj. lasting for or happening every ten years.
- ORIGIN from Latin decem 'ten' + annus 'year'.

decent •adj. **1** following generally accepted standards of morality or respectability. **2** of an acceptable quality. **3** Brit. informal kind or generous.
- DERIVATIVES **decently** adv.

– ORIGIN Latin *decere* 'to be fit'.

decentralize (or **decentralise**)
• v. (**decentralizes, decentralizing, decentralized**) transfer authority from central to local government.
– DERIVATIVES **decentralization** n.

deception • n. **1** the action of deceiving someone. **2** a thing that deceives someone into believing something that is not true.

deceptive • adj. giving a misleading impression.

deceptively • adv. **1** to a lesser extent than appears to be the case: *a deceptively smooth surface.* **2** to a greater extent than appears to be the case: *a deceptively spacious room.*

deci- • comb. form one tenth: *decilitre.*
– ORIGIN Latin *decimus* 'tenth'.

decibel /dess-i-bel/ • n. a unit of measurement expressing the intensity of a sound or the power of an electrical signal.
– ORIGIN from **DECI-** + *bel*, a unit (= 10 decibels) named after Alexander Graham *Bell*, inventor of the telephone.

decide • v. (**decides, deciding, decided**) **1** think about something carefully and make a judgement or choice. **2** settle a matter or contest. **3** give a judgement concerning a legal case.
– DERIVATIVES **decidable** adj.
– ORIGIN Latin *decidere* 'determine'.

decided • adj. definite; clear: *a decided improvement.*
– DERIVATIVES **decidedly** adv.

decider • n. a contest that settles the winner of a series of contests.

deciduous /di-sid-yoo-uhss/ • adj. **1** (of a tree or shrub) shedding its leaves annually. Contrasted with **EVERGREEN**. **2** (of teeth or horns) shed after a time.
– ORIGIN Latin *deciduus.*

decilitre (US **deciliter**) • n. a metric unit of volume, equal to one tenth of a litre.

decimal • adj. relating to a system of numbers based on the number ten. • n. a fraction whose denominator is a power of ten, expressed by numbers placed to the right of a decimal point.
– DERIVATIVES **decimalize** (or **decimalise**) v. **decimally** adv.
– ORIGIN Latin *decimus* 'tenth'.

decimal place • n. the position of a digit to the right of a decimal point.

decimal point • n. a full point placed after the figure representing units in a decimal fraction.

decimate /dess-i-mayt/ • v. (**decimates, decimating, decimated**) **1** kill or destroy a large proportion of a group. **2** severely reduce the strength of something.

– DERIVATIVES **decimation** n.
– ORIGIN Latin *decimare* 'take as a tenth'.

decimetre (US **decimeter**) • n. a metric unit of length, equal to one tenth of a metre.

decipher /di-sy-fer/ • v. (**deciphers, deciphering, deciphered**) **1** convert something from code into normal language. **2** succeed in understanding something hard to interpret.
– DERIVATIVES **decipherable** adj. **decipherment** n.

decision • n. **1** a choice or judgement made after considering something. **2** the action of deciding something. **3** the ability to decide things quickly.

decisive • adj. **1** having great importance for the outcome of a situation: *a decisive battle.* **2** able to make decisions quickly.
– DERIVATIVES **decisively** adv. **decisiveness** n.

deck • n. **1** a floor of a ship. **2** a floor or platform. **3** esp. N. Amer. a pack of cards. **4** a piece of sound-reproduction equipment, made up of a player or recorder for discs or tapes. • v. decorate or dress festively or attractively.
– PHRASES **hit the deck** informal fall to the ground.
– ORIGIN Dutch *dec* 'covering, roof'.

deckchair • n. a folding chair with a wooden frame and a canvas seat.

decking • n. material used in making a deck.

declaim • v. speak or recite in a dramatic or passionate way.
– ORIGIN Latin *declamare.*

declamation • n. the action of declaiming something.
– DERIVATIVES **declamatory** adj.

declaration • n. **1** a formal statement or announcement. **2** the action of declaring something.

declarative /di-kla-ruh-tiv/
• adj. **1** making a declaration: *declarative statements.* **2** (of a sentence or phrase) taking the form of a simple statement.

declare • v. (**declares, declaring, declared**) **1** announce solemnly or officially. **2** (**declare yourself**) reveal your intentions or identity. **3** (as adj. **declared**) having stated something openly: *a declared atheist.* **4** state that you have income or goods on which tax or duty should be paid. **5** Cricket close an innings voluntarily with wickets remaining.
– ORIGIN Latin *declarare.*

declassify • v. (**declassifies, declassifying, declassified**) officially declare information or documents to be no longer secret.

declension /di-klen-sh'n/ • n. the changes in the form of a noun, pronoun, or adjective that identify its grammatical case, number, and gender.
– ORIGIN Old French *decliner* 'to decline'.

declination /dek-li-nay-sh'n/
• n. **1** Astron. the position of a point in the sky equivalent to latitude on the earth. **2** the angular deviation of a compass needle from true north.

decline • v. (**declines, declining, declined**) **1** become smaller, weaker, or worse: *the birth rate continued to decline.* **2** politely refuse to accept or do something. **3** form a noun, pronoun, or adjective according to case, number, and gender. • n. a gradual and continuous loss of strength, numbers, or value.
– ORIGIN Latin *declinare* 'bend down'.

declivity /di-kliv-i-ti/ • n. (pl. **declivities**) a downward slope.
– ORIGIN Latin *declivitas*.

decoction • n. a concentrated liquid produced produced by heating or boiling a substance.
– ORIGIN Latin.

decode • v. (**decodes, decoding, decoded**) **1** convert a coded message into understandable language. **2** convert audio or video signals from analogue to digital.
– DERIVATIVES **decoder** n.

décolletage /day-kol-i-tahzh/ • n. a low neckline on a woman's dress or top.
– ORIGIN French.

décolleté /day-kol-tay/ • adj. having a low neckline.
– ORIGIN French.

decommission • v. **1** take a ship out of service. **2** dismantle a nuclear reactor or weapon and make it safe.

decompose • v. (**decomposes, decomposing, decomposed**) **1** (of plant or animal matter) decay. **2** (of a substance) break down into its component elements.
– DERIVATIVES **decomposition** n.

decompress /dee-kuhm-press/
• v. **1** reduce the air pressure on a deep-sea diver. **2** expand compressed computer data to its normal size.
– DERIVATIVES **decompressor** n.

decompression • n. **1** reduction in air pressure. **2** a gradual reduction of air pressure on a person who has been experiencing high pressure while deep-sea diving. **3** the process of decompressing computer data.

decompression sickness • n. a serious condition that results when too rapid decompression by a diver causes nitrogen bubbles to form in the tissues of the body.

decongestant /dee-kuhn-jess-tuhnt/
• n. a medicine used to relieve a blocked nose.

deconstruct /dee-kuhn-strukt/
• v. reduce something to its constituent parts in order to reinterpret it.
– DERIVATIVES **deconstructive** adj.

decontaminate • v. (**decontaminates, decontaminating, decontaminated**) remove dangerous substances from something.
– DERIVATIVES **decontamination** n.

decor /day-kor, dek-or/ • n. the furnishing and decoration of a room.
– ORIGIN French.

decorate • v. (**decorates, decorating, decorated**) **1** make more attractive by adding extra items. **2** esp. Brit. apply paint or wallpaper to walls. **3** give an award or medal to someone.
– ORIGIN Latin *decorare* 'embellish'.

decoration • n. **1** the process or art of decorating. **2** a decorative object or pattern. **3** the way in which something is decorated. **4** a medal or award given as an honour.

decorative /dek-uh-ruh-tiv/
• adj. **1** making something look more attractive: *decorative patterns.* **2** relating to decoration.
– DERIVATIVES **decoratively** adv.

decorator • n. Brit. a person whose job is to paint interior walls or hang wallpaper.

decorous /dek-uh-ruhss/ • adj. in good taste; polite and restrained.
– DERIVATIVES **decorously** adv.
– ORIGIN Latin *decorus* 'seemly'.

decorum /di-kor-uhm/ • n. polite and socially acceptable behaviour.
– ORIGIN Latin, 'seemly thing'.

decoy • n. /dee-koy/ **1** a real or imitation bird or mammal, used by hunters to lure game. **2** a person or thing used to mislead or lure someone into a trap.
• v. /di-koy/ lure by means of a decoy.
– ORIGIN Dutch *de kooi*.

decrease • v. /di-kreess/ (**decreases, decreasing, decreased**) make or become smaller or fewer in size, amount, or strength. • n. /dee-kreess/ **1** the amount by which something decreases: *an 88 per cent decrease in demand.* **2** the process of decreasing.
– ORIGIN Latin *decrescere*.

decree • n. **1** an official order that has the force of law. **2** a judgement of certain law courts. • v. (**decrees, decreeing, decreed**) order by decree.
– ORIGIN Latin *decretum* 'something decided'.

decree absolute • n. (pl. **decrees absolute**) Engl. Law a final order by a court of law which officially ends a marriage.

decree nisi /di-kree **ny**-sy/ • n. (pl.
decrees nisi) Engl. Law an order by a court
of law that states the date on which a
marriage will end, unless a good reason
to prevent a divorce is produced.
– ORIGIN Latin *nisi* 'unless'.

decrepit /di-**krep**-it/ • adj. worn out or
ruined because of age or neglect.
– DERIVATIVES **decrepitude** n.
– ORIGIN Latin *decrepitus*.

decriminalize (or **decriminalise**)
• v. (**decriminalizes, decriminalizing,
decriminalized**) change the law so that
something is no longer illegal.
– DERIVATIVES **decriminalization** n.

decry /di-**kry**/ • v. (**decries, decrying,
decried**) criticize something publicly.
– ORIGIN French *décrier* 'cry down'.

decrypt /dee-**kript**/ • v. convert a coded
or unclear message into understandable
language.
– DERIVATIVES **decryption** n.

dedicate • v. (**dedicates, dedicating,
dedicated**) 1 devote to a particular
subject, task, or purpose: *twenty hours
will be dedicated to lectures.* 2 address a
book to a person as a sign of respect or
affection. 3 hold a ceremony to devote a
building to a god, goddess, or saint.
– DERIVATIVES **dedicatee** n. **dedicator** n.
dedicatory adj.
– ORIGIN Latin *dedicare*.

dedicated • adj. 1 devoted to a task or
purpose. 2 used or designed for one
particular purpose only: *dedicated bike
lanes.*

dedication • n. 1 devotion to a purpose
or task. 2 the action of dedicating
something. 3 the words with which a
book is dedicated.

deduce • v. (**deduces, deducing,
deduced**) form an opinion or conclusion
on the basis of available information.
– DERIVATIVES **deducible** adj.
– ORIGIN Latin *deducere* 'lead away'.

deduct • v. take an amount away from a
total.
– ORIGIN Latin *deducere*.

deductible • adj. able to be taken away
from a total.
– DERIVATIVES **deductibility** n.

deduction • n. 1 the action of taking an
amount away from a total. 2 an amount
that is or may be deducted. 3 a method
of reasoning in which a general rule or
principle is used to draw a particular
conclusion.
– DERIVATIVES **deductive** adj.

deed • n. 1 an action that is performed
deliberately. 2 (usu. **deeds**) a legal
document that is signed and delivered,
especially one relating to property
ownership.
– ORIGIN Old English.

deed of covenant • n. Brit. an
agreement to pay a regular amount of
money.

deed poll • n. Engl. Law a legal deed made
and carried out by one party only,
especially to change a person's name.

deejay • n. informal a disc jockey.

deem • v. formal consider something in a
particular way.
– ORIGIN Old English.

deep • adj. 1 extending far down or in
from the top or surface. 2 extending a
specified distance from the top, surface,
or outer edge. 3 (of sound) low in pitch.
4 (of colour) dark. 5 very intense or
extreme: *a deep sleep.* 6 difficult to
understand. 7 (in ball games) far down
or across the field. • n. (**the deep**) literary
the sea. • adv. far down or in; deeply.
– PHRASES **go off the deep end** informal
give way suddenly to an outburst of
emotion. **in deep water** informal in
trouble. **be thrown in at the deep end**
informal have to face a difficult situation
with little experience.
– DERIVATIVES **deepness** n.
– ORIGIN Old English.

deepen • v. make or become deep or
deeper.

deep freeze • n. (also **deep freezer**) a
freezer.

deep-frozen • adj. stored at a very low
temperature.

deep-fry • v. fry food in enough fat or oil
to cover it completely.

deeply • adv. 1 far down or in.
2 intensely.

deep-seated (also **deep-rooted**)
• adj. firmly established.

deer • n. (pl. **deer**) a hoofed animal, the
male of which usually has antlers.
– ORIGIN Old English.

deerstalker • n. a soft cloth cap, with
peaks in front and behind and ear flaps
which can be tied together over the top.

de-escalate • v. (**de-escalates,
de-escalating, de-escalated**) reduce
the intensity of a conflict or crisis.
– DERIVATIVES **de-escalation** n.

deface • v. (**defaces, defacing, defaced**)
spoil the appearance of something.
– DERIVATIVES **defacement** n.

de facto /day **fak**-toh/ • adj. existing in
fact, whether legally accepted or not.
– ORIGIN Latin, 'of fact'.

defame • v. (**defames, defaming,
defamed**) write or say something that
damages someone's reputation.

- DERIVATIVES **defamation** n. **defamatory** adj.
- ORIGIN Latin *diffamare* 'spread evil rumour'.

default • n. **1** failure to do something required by law, especially to repay a loan. **2** a previously selected option adopted by a computer program or other mechanism when no alternative is specified. • v. **1** fail to do something required by law. **2** (**default to**) go back automatically to a previously selected option.
- PHRASES **by default** because of a lack of opposition or positive action.
- DERIVATIVES **defaulter** n.
- ORIGIN Old French *defaillir* 'to fail'.

defeat • v. **1** win a victory over. **2** prevent from achieving an aim. **3** reject or block a proposal or motion. • n. an instance of defeating or of being defeated.
- ORIGIN Old French *desfaire*.

defeatist • n. a person who gives in to failure too readily. • adj. accepting failure too readily.
- DERIVATIVES **defeatism** n.

defecate /def-uh-kayt/ • v. (**defecates**, **defecating**, **defecated**) discharge waste matter from the bowels.
- DERIVATIVES **defecation** n.
- ORIGIN Latin *defaecare*.

defect[1] /dee-fekt/ • n. an imperfection or fault.
- ORIGIN Latin *defectus*.

defect[2] /di-fekt/ • v. abandon your country or cause in favour of an opposing one.
- DERIVATIVES **defection** n. **defector** n.
- ORIGIN Latin *deficere*.

defective • adj. imperfect or faulty.

defence (US **defense**) • n. **1** the action of defending something against attack. **2** military measures or resources for protecting a country. **3** (**defences**) fortifications against attack. **4** attempted justification: *he spoke in defence of his actions.* **5** the case presented by the party being accused or sued in a lawsuit. **6** (**the defence**) the lawyer acting for the defendant in a lawsuit. **7** (in sport) the players who prevent the other team from scoring.

defenceless (US **defenseless**) • adj. without protection; completely vulnerable.

defend • v. **1** protect from attack or danger. **2** attempt to justify. **3** act as a lawyer for the party being accused or sued in a lawsuit. **4** compete to hold on to a title or seat in a contest or election. **5** (in sport) prevent the other team from scoring.

- DERIVATIVES **defendable** adj. **defender** n.
- ORIGIN Latin *defendere*.

defendant • n. a person sued or accused in a court of law. Compare with PLAINTIFF.

defensible • adj. **1** able to be justified by argument. **2** able to be protected.

defensive • adj. **1** used or intended to defend or protect. **2** very anxious to challenge or avoid criticism.
- PHRASES **on the defensive** expecting or resisting criticism or attack.
- DERIVATIVES **defensively** adv. **defensiveness** n.

defer[1] /di-fer/ • v. (**defers**, **deferring**, **deferred**) put off to a later time.
- DERIVATIVES **deferment** n. **deferral** n.
- ORIGIN Latin *differre*.

defer[2] /di-fer/ • v. (**defers**, **deferring**, **deferred**) (**defer to**) give in to or agree to accept.
- ORIGIN Latin *deferre* 'carry away, refer'.

deference /def-uh-ruhnss/ • n. polite respect.

deferential • adj. showing polite respect.
- DERIVATIVES **deferentially** adv.

defiance • n. open refusal to obey.
- DERIVATIVES **defiant** adj. **defiantly** adv.
- ORIGIN Old French.

deficiency • n. (pl. **deficiencies**) **1** a lack or shortage. **2** a failing or shortcoming.

deficient /di-fi-sh'nt/ • adj. **1** not having enough of a specified quality or ingredient. **2** inadequate in amount or quantity.
- ORIGIN Latin.

deficit /def-i-sit/ • n. **1** the amount by which something falls short of a target or total. **2** an excess of money spent over money earned.
- ORIGIN Latin, 'it is lacking'.

defile[1] /di-fyl/ • v. (**defiles**, **defiling**, **defiled**) **1** make dirty. **2** treat something holy with disrespect.
- DERIVATIVES **defilement** n. **defiler** n.
- ORIGIN Old French *defouler* 'trample down'.

defile[2] /dee-fyl/ • n. a steep-sided narrow gorge or mountain pass.
- ORIGIN French.

define • v. (**defines**, **defining**, **defined**) **1** describe the exact nature of something. **2** give the meaning of a word or phrase. **3** mark out the limits or outline of something.
- DERIVATIVES **definable** adj.
- ORIGIN Latin *definire*.

definite • adj. **1** clearly stated or decided. **2** (of a person) certain about something. **3** known to be true or real. **4** having exact and measurable physical limits.
- DERIVATIVES **definiteness** n.

☑ Remember that **definite** ends with -ite.

definite article • n. Grammar the word *the*.

definitely • adv. without doubt; certainly.

definition • n. 1 a statement of the exact meaning of a word or the nature of something. 2 the action of defining something. 3 the degree of sharpness in outline of an object or image.

definitive • adj. 1 (of a conclusion or agreement) final and not able to be changed. 2 (of a written work) the most accurate and trusted of its kind.
– DERIVATIVES **definitively** adv.

deflate • v. (**deflates, deflating, deflated**) 1 let air or gas out of a tyre, balloon, etc. 2 make someone feel suddenly discouraged or gloomy. 3 reduce price levels in an economy.
– DERIVATIVES **deflator** n.

deflation • n. 1 the action of deflating something. 2 reduction of the general level of prices in an economy.
– DERIVATIVES **deflationary** adj.

deflect • v. 1 turn aside from a straight course or intended purpose. 2 prevent something undesirable from being aimed at you.
– DERIVATIVES **deflection** n. **deflector** n.
– ORIGIN Latin *deflectere*.

deflower • v. (**deflowers, deflowering, deflowered**) literary have sex with a woman who is a virgin.

defoliant • n. a chemical used to remove the leaves from trees and plants.

defoliate /dee-foh-li-ayt/
• v. (**defoliates, defoliating, defoliated**) remove leaves from trees and plants.
– DERIVATIVES **defoliation** n.
– ORIGIN Latin *defoliare*.

deforest • v. clear an area of trees.
– DERIVATIVES **deforestation** n.

deform • v. change or spoil the usual shape of.
– DERIVATIVES **deformable** adj. **deformation** n. **deformed** adj.

deformity • n. (pl. **deformities**) 1 a deformed part. 2 the state of being deformed.

DEFRA • abbrev. (in the UK) Department for Environment, Food, and Rural Affairs.

defraud • v. illegally obtain money from someone by deception.
– ORIGIN Latin *defraudare*.

defray • v. provide money to pay a cost.
– ORIGIN French *défrayer*.

defrock • v. officially remove a Christian priest from their job because of wrongdoing.

defrost • v. 1 remove ice from a freezer or refrigerator. 2 thaw frozen food.

deft • adj. quick and neatly skilful.
– DERIVATIVES **deftly** adv. **deftness** n.
– ORIGIN from DAFT.

defunct /di-fungkt/ • adj. no longer existing or functioning.
– ORIGIN Latin *defunctus* 'dead'.

defuse /dee-fyooz/ • v. (**defuses, defusing, defused**) 1 make a situation less tense or dangerous. 2 remove the fuse from an explosive device in order to prevent it from exploding.

USAGE: Do not confuse **defuse** and **diffuse**. **Defuse** means 'make a situation less tense or dangerous', while **diffuse** means 'spread over a wide area' (*technologies diffuse rapidly*).

defy • v. (**defies, defying, defied**) 1 openly resist or refuse to obey. 2 challenge someone to do or prove something.
– ORIGIN Old French *desfier*.

degenerate • v. /di-jen-uh-rayt/ (**degenerates, degenerating, degenerated**) become worse or weaker. • adj. /di-jen-uh-ruht/ having very low moral standards. • n. /di-jen-uh-ruht/ a person with very low moral standards.
– DERIVATIVES **degeneracy** n. **degeneration** n.
– ORIGIN Latin *degeneratus* 'no longer of its kind'.

degenerative • adj. (of a disease) becoming progressively worse.

degradation /deg-ruh-day-sh'n/
• n. 1 the state of being humiliated. 2 the process of being broken down or made worse.

degrade • v. (**degrades, degrading, degraded**) 1 cause someone to suffer a loss of dignity. 2 make worse in quality. 3 cause something to break down or deteriorate chemically.
– DERIVATIVES **degradable** adj. **degradative** adj.

degrading • adj. causing a loss of self-respect; humiliating.

degree • n. 1 the amount, level, or extent to which something happens or is present: *a degree of caution is wise.* 2 a unit of measurement of angles, equivalent to one ninetieth of a right angle. 3 a stage in a scale, e.g. of temperature. 4 an academic rank awarded by a college or university after examination or completion of a course.
– PHRASES **by degrees** gradually.
– ORIGIN Old French.

dehisce /di-hiss/ • v. (**dehisces, dehiscing, dehisced**) tech. (especially of a seed case) gape or burst open.

- DERIVATIVES **dehiscence** n. **dehiscent** adj.
- ORIGIN Latin *dehiscere*.

dehumanize (or **dehumanise**)
• v. (**dehumanizes, dehumanizing, dehumanized**) deprive someone of good qualities such as kindness.
- DERIVATIVES **dehumanization** n.

dehumidify • v. (**dehumidifies, dehumidifying, dehumidified**) remove moisture from the air or a gas.
- DERIVATIVES **dehumidifier** n.

dehydrate /dee-hy-drayt/
• v. (**dehydrates, dehydrating, dehydrated**) 1 cause someone to lose a large amount of water from their body. 2 remove water from food in order to preserve it.
- DERIVATIVES **dehydration** n.
- ORIGIN Greek *hudros* 'water'.

de-ice • v. (**de-ices, de-icing, de-iced**) remove ice from something.
- DERIVATIVES **de-icer** n.

deify /day-i-fy/ • v. (**deifies, deifying, deified**) worship or treat someone as a god.
- DERIVATIVES **deification** n.
- ORIGIN Latin *deificare*.

deign /dayn/ • v. do something that you consider to be beneath your dignity: *I didn't deign to respond.*
- ORIGIN Latin *dignare* 'consider worthy'.

deindustrialization (or **deindustrialisation**) • n. the reduction of industrial activity in a region or economy.

deism /day-i-z'm, dee-i-z'm/ • n. belief in the existence of an all-powerful creator who does not intervene in the universe. Compare with THEISM.
- DERIVATIVES **deist** n.

deity /day-i-ti, dee-i-ti/ • n. (pl. **deities**) 1 a god or goddess. 2 the state or quality of being a god or goddess.
- ORIGIN Latin *deitas*.

déjà vu /day-zhah voo/ • n. a feeling of having already experienced the present situation.
- ORIGIN French, 'already seen'.

dejected • adj. sad and in low spirits.
- DERIVATIVES **dejectedly** adv.

dejection • n. sadness or low spirits.
- ORIGIN Latin.

de jure /day joo-ray/ • adv. rightfully; by right. • adj. rightful.
- ORIGIN Latin, 'of law'.

dekko • n. Brit. informal a quick look.
- ORIGIN Hindi, 'look!'

delay • v. 1 make or be late or slow. 2 put off to a later time. • n. 1 a period of time by which someone or something is delayed. 2 the action of delaying.
- ORIGIN Old French *delayer*.

delectable • adj. delightful or delicious.
- DERIVATIVES **delectably** adv.

delectation /dee-lek-tay-sh'n/ • n. formal, humorous pleasure and delight.
- ORIGIN Latin.

delegate • n. /del-i-guht/ 1 a person sent to represent other people. 2 a member of a committee. • v. /del-i-gayt/ (**delegates, delegating, delegated**) 1 give a task or responsibility to a less important person. 2 authorize someone to act as a representative.
- DERIVATIVES **delegator** n.
- ORIGIN Latin *delegare* 'send away'.

delegation • n. 1 a group of delegates. 2 the action of delegating work or a responsibility.

delete • v. (**deletes, deleting, deleted**) 1 remove or cross out written or printed matter. 2 remove data from a computer's memory.
- DERIVATIVES **deletion** n.
- ORIGIN Latin *delere*.

deleterious /del-i-teer-i-uhss/
• adj. formal causing harm or damage.
- ORIGIN Greek *dēlētērios* 'harmful'.

delft /delft/ • n. glazed earthenware, decorated in blue on a white background.
- ORIGIN named after the town of *Delft* in the Netherlands.

deli • n. (pl. **delis**) informal a delicatessen.

deliberate • adj. /di-lib-uh-ruht/ 1 done on purpose. 2 careful and unhurried: *a deliberate worker.* • v. /di-lib-uh-rayt/ (**deliberates, deliberating, deliberated**) consider carefully and for a long time.
- DERIVATIVES **deliberately** adv. **deliberateness** n.
- ORIGIN Latin *deliberare*.

deliberation • n. 1 long and careful consideration. 2 carefulness and lack of haste.

deliberative • adj. relating to consideration or discussion.

delicacy • n. (pl. **delicacies**) 1 fine, intricate, or fragile texture or structure. 2 discretion and tact. 3 a delicious or expensive food.

delicate • adj. 1 very fine in quality or structure. 2 easily broken or damaged. 3 tending to become ill easily. 4 requiring tact, sensitivity, or skill: *a delicate issue.* 5 (of colour or flavour) light and pleasant.
- DERIVATIVES **delicately** adv.
- ORIGIN Latin *delicatus*.

delicatessen /de-li-kuh-tess-uhn/ • n. a shop selling cooked meats, cheeses, and unusual or foreign prepared foods.
- ORIGIN German or Dutch.

delicious • adj. 1 very pleasant to eat or

drink. **2** delightful: *a delicious irony.*
– DERIVATIVES **deliciously** adv.
deliciousness n.
– ORIGIN Latin *deliciosus*.

delight • v. **1** please someone greatly.
2 (**delight in**) take great pleasure in.
• n. **1** great pleasure. **2** a source of great
pleasure.
– DERIVATIVES **delighted** adj.
– ORIGIN Latin *delectare* 'to charm'.

delightful • adj. very pleasing.
– DERIVATIVES **delightfully** adv.

delimit /di-lim-it/ • v. (**delimits,**
delimiting, delimited) determine the
limits or boundaries of something.
– DERIVATIVES **delimitation** n.
delimiter n.

delineate /di-lin-i-ayt/ • v. (**delineates,**
delineating, delineated) describe or
indicate something precisely.
– DERIVATIVES **delineation** n.
– ORIGIN Latin *delineare*.

delinquency • n. (pl. **delinquencies**)
1 minor crime. **2** formal neglect of your
duty.

delinquent /di-ling-kwuhnt/
• adj. **1** tending to commit crime. **2** formal
failing in your duty. • n. a person who
tends to commit crime.
– ORIGIN Latin *delinquere* 'to offend'.

deliquescent /del-i-kwess-uhnt/
• adj. tech. or literary becoming or tending to
become liquid.
– DERIVATIVES **deliquescence** n.
deliquesce v.
– ORIGIN Latin *deliquescere* 'dissolve'.

delirious • adj. **1** in a very disturbed
mental state. **2** very excited or happy.
– DERIVATIVES **deliriously** adv.

delirium /di-li-ri-uhm/ • n. a disturbed
state of mind marked by restlessness,
illusions, and incoherent thought and
speech.
– ORIGIN Latin.

delirium tremens /di-li-ri-uhm tree-
menz/ • n. a condition in which
alcoholics who are trying to give up
alcohol experience tremors and
hallucinations.
– ORIGIN Latin, 'trembling delirium'.

deliver • v. (**delivers, delivering,**
delivered) **1** bring and hand over
something to the person who is to
receive it. **2** provide something
promised or expected. **3** present in a
formal way. **4** launch or aim a blow.
5 save or set someone free. **6** assist in
the birth of a baby. **7** (also **be delivered**
of) give birth to a baby.
– DERIVATIVES **deliverable** adj. **deliverer** n.
– ORIGIN Old French *delivrer*.

deliverance • n. the process of being
rescued or set free.

delivery • n. (pl. **deliveries**) **1** the action
of delivering something. **2** the process
of giving birth. **3** an act of throwing or
bowling a ball. **4** the manner or style of
giving a speech.

dell • n. literary a small valley.
– ORIGIN Old English.

Delphic /del-fik/ • adj. deliberately
difficult to understand: *Delphic*
utterances.
– ORIGIN from the ancient Greek oracle at
Delphi.

delphinium /del-fin-i-uhm/ • n. (pl.
delphiniums) a garden plant having tall
spikes of blue flowers.
– ORIGIN Greek *delphinion* 'larkspur' (a
flowering plant).

delta • n. **1** a triangular area of land
where a river has split into several
channels just before entering the sea.
2 the fourth letter of the Greek alphabet
(Δ, δ).

delude /di-lood/ • v. (**deludes, deluding,**
deluded) persuade someone to believe
something that is not true.
– DERIVATIVES **deluded** adj.
– ORIGIN Latin *deludere* 'to mock'.

deluge /del-yooj/ • n. **1** a severe flood or
very heavy fall of rain. **2** a large number
of things arriving at the same time: *a*
deluge of complaints. • v. (**deluges,**
deluging, deluged) **1** overwhelm with a
large number of things. **2** flood a place.
– ORIGIN Old French.

delusion • n. a false belief or impression
about yourself.
– DERIVATIVES **delusional** adj. **delusive** adj.
delusory adj.

de luxe /di luks/ • adj. of a higher quality
than usual.
– ORIGIN French, 'of luxury'.

delve • v. (**delves, delving, delved**)
1 reach inside a container and search for
something. **2** research something very
thoroughly.
– ORIGIN Old English.

demagnetize (or **demagnetise**)
• v. (**demagnetizes, demagnetizing,**
demagnetized) remove magnetic
properties from something.
– DERIVATIVES **demagnetization** n.

demagogue /dem-uh-gog/ • n. a
political leader who appeals to the
desires and prejudices of the public.
– DERIVATIVES **demagogic** /dem-uh-gog-
ik/ adj. **demagoguery** /dem-uh-gog-
uh-ri/ n.
– ORIGIN Greek *dēmagōgos*.

demand • n. **1** a very firm and forceful
request. **2** (**demands**) things that are
urgent, necessary, or difficult. **3** the
desire of consumers for a particular
product or service. • v. **1** ask or ask for

firmly or forcefully. **2** need a quality, skill, etc.
– PHRASES **in demand** sought after. **on demand** as soon as or whenever required.
– ORIGIN Latin *demandare* 'hand over'.

demanding •adj. requiring much skill or effort.

demarcate /dee-mar-kayt/ •v. (**demarcates, demarcating, demarcated**) set the boundaries of something.

demarcation •n. **1** the action of fixing boundaries. **2** a dividing line.
– ORIGIN Spanish *demarcación*.

dematerialize (or **dematerialise**) •v. (**dematerializes, dematerializing, dematerialized**) become no longer physically present; disappear.
– DERIVATIVES **dematerialization** n.

demean /di-meen/ •v. **1** make someone lose dignity or respect. **2** (**demean yourself**) do something that is beneath your dignity.
– DERIVATIVES **demeaning** adj.
– ORIGIN from DE- + MEAN².

demeanour (US **demeanor**) •n. outward behaviour or bearing.
– ORIGIN Old French *demener* 'to lead'.

demented •adj. **1** suffering from dementia. **2** informal wild and irrational.
– DERIVATIVES **dementedly** adv.
– ORIGIN Latin *demens* 'insane'.

dementia /di-men-shuh/ •n. a mental disorder marked by memory failures and an inability to think clearly.
– ORIGIN Latin.

demerara sugar /dem-uh-rair-uh/ •n. Brit. light brown cane sugar coming originally from Demerara in Guyana.

demerit •n. a fault or disadvantage.

demesne /di-mayn/ •n. **1** hist. land attached to a manor. **2** old use a domain.
– ORIGIN Old French *demeine* 'belonging to a lord'.

demi- •prefix **1** half: *demisemiquaver.* **2** partially: *demigod.*
– ORIGIN Latin *dimidius* 'half'.

demigod (or **demigoddess**) •n. a partly divine or less important god (or goddess).

demijohn •n. a narrow-necked bottle holding from 3 to 10 gallons of liquid.
– ORIGIN prob. from French *dame-jeanne* 'Lady Jane'.

demilitarize (or **demilitarise**) •v. (**demilitarizes, demilitarizing, demilitarized**) remove all military forces from an area.
– DERIVATIVES **demilitarization** n.

demi-monde /dem-i-mond/ •n. a group on the fringes of respectable society.

– ORIGIN French, 'half-world'.

demise /di-myz/ •n. **1** a person's death. **2** the end or failure of something.
– ORIGIN Old French.

demi-sec /de-mi-sek/ •adj. (of wine) medium dry.
– ORIGIN French, 'half-dry'.

demisemiquaver /dem-i-sem-i-kway-ver/ •n. Music, esp. Brit. a note having the time value of half a semiquaver.

demist /dee-mist/ •v. Brit. clear condensation from a windscreen
– DERIVATIVES **demister** n.

demo informal •n. (pl. **demos**) **1** esp. Brit. a public demonstration. **2** a tape or disc containing a demonstration of a performer's music or a piece of software. •v. (**demos, demoing, demoed**) demonstrate software or equipment.

demob /dee-mob/ •v. (**demobs, demobbing, demobbed**) Brit. informal demobilize troops.

demobilize /dee-moh-bi-lyz/ (or **demobilise**) •v. (**demobilizes, demobilizing, demobilized**) take troops out of active service.
– DERIVATIVES **demobilization** n.

democracy /di-mok-ruh-si/ •n. (pl. **democracies**) **1** a form of government in which the people can vote for representatives to govern the state on their behalf. **2** a state governed by elected representatives. **3** control of a group by the majority of its members.
– ORIGIN Greek *dēmokratia.*

democrat •n. **1** a supporter of democracy. **2** (**Democrat**) (in the US) a member of the Democratic Party.

democratic •adj. **1** relating to or supporting democracy. **2** based on the principle that everyone in society is equal. **3** (**Democratic**) (in the US) relating to the Democratic Party.
– DERIVATIVES **democratically** adv.

democratize (or **democratise**) •v. (**democratizes, democratizing, democratized**) introduce a democratic system or ideas to something.
– DERIVATIVES **democratization** n.

demodulate •v. (**demodulates, demodulating, demodulated**) Electron. extract a modulating signal from its carrier.
– DERIVATIVES **demodulation** n. **demodulator** n.

demographic /de-muh-graf-ik/ •adj. relating to the structure of populations. •n. **1** (**demographics**) statistics relating to the population and groups within it. **2** a particular section of a population: *a young demographic.*
– DERIVATIVES **demographically** adv.

demography /di-**mog**-ruh-fi/ • n. the study of the structure of human populations using records of the numbers of births, deaths, etc.
– DERIVATIVES **demographer** n.

demolish /di-**mol**-ish/ • v. **1** pull or knock down a building. **2** informal thoroughly defeat someone. **3** humorous eat food quickly.
– ORIGIN Latin *demoliri*.

demolition /de-muh-**li**-shuhn/ • n. the action of demolishing something.

demon • n. **1** an evil spirit or devil. **2** usu. humorous an evil or destructive person or thing. • adj. forceful or skilful: *a demon cook*.
– ORIGIN Greek *daimōn* 'deity, spirit'.

demonetize /dee-**mun**-i-tyz/ (or **demonetise**) • v. (**demonetizes, demonetizing, demonetized**) make a coin or currency no longer valid as money.
– DERIVATIVES **demonetization** n.
– ORIGIN French *démonétiser*.

demoniac /di-**moh**-ni-ak/ • adj. relating to or like a demon; demonic.
– DERIVATIVES **demoniacal** adj.

demonic /di-**mon**-ik/ • adj. relating to or like demons or evil spirits.
– DERIVATIVES **demonically** adv.

demonize (or **demonise**) • v. (**demonizes, demonizing, demonized**) portray someone as wicked or threatening.
– DERIVATIVES **demonization** n.

demonology • n. the study of demons or belief in demons.

demonstrable /di-**mon**-struh-b'l, de-**muhn**-struh-b'l/ • adj. clearly apparent or able to be proved.
– DERIVATIVES **demonstrably** adv.

demonstrate • v. (**demonstrates, demonstrating, demonstrated**) **1** clearly show something by giving proof or evidence. **2** show and explain how something works or is done. **3** express a feeling or quality by your actions. **4** take part in a public demonstration.
– DERIVATIVES **demonstrator** n.
– ORIGIN Latin *demonstrare* 'point out'.

demonstration • n. **1** the action of demonstrating. **2** a public meeting or march expressing an opinion on an issue.

demonstrative /di-**mon**-struh-tiv/ • adj. **1** tending to show your feelings openly. **2** showing or proving something. **3** Grammar (of a determiner or pronoun) indicating the person or thing referred to (e.g. *this, that, those*).
– DERIVATIVES **demonstratively** adv.

demoralize (or **demoralise**)

• v. (**demoralizes, demoralizing, demoralized**) cause someone to lose confidence or hope.
– DERIVATIVES **demoralization** n.
– ORIGIN French *démoraliser* 'to corrupt'.

demote • v. (**demotes, demoting, demoted**) move someone to a less senior position.
– DERIVATIVES **demotion** n.
– ORIGIN from DE- + PROMOTE.

demotic /di-**mot**-ik/ • adj. (of language) used by ordinary people.
– ORIGIN Greek *dēmotikos*.

demotivate • v. (**demotivates, demotivating, demotivated**) make someone less eager to work or make an effort.
– DERIVATIVES **demotivation** n.

demur /di-**mer**/ • v. (**demurs, demurring, demurred**) raise objections or show reluctance.
– PHRASES **without demur** without objecting or hesitating.
– DERIVATIVES **demurral** n.
– ORIGIN Old French *demourer*.

demure /di-**myoor**/ • adj. (of a woman) reserved, modest, and shy.
– DERIVATIVES **demurely** adv.
– ORIGIN perh. from Old French *demourer* 'remain'.

demutualize (or **demutualise**)
• v. (**demutualizes, demutualizing, demutualized**) change an organization (such as a building society) that is owned by its members to one owned by shareholders.

demystify • v. (**demystifies, demystifying, demystified**) make a subject easier to understand.
– DERIVATIVES **demystification** n.

den • n. **1** a wild animal's lair or home. **2** informal a person's private room. **3** a place where people meet to do something wrong or forbidden: *a den of vice*.
– ORIGIN Old English.

denarius /di-**nair**-i-uhss/ • n. (pl. **denarii** /di-**nair**-i-I/) an ancient Roman silver coin.
– ORIGIN Latin, 'containing ten'.

denationalize (or **denationalise**)
• v. (**denationalizes, denationalizing, denationalized**) transfer a nationalized industry to private ownership.
– DERIVATIVES **denationalization** n.

denature /dee-**nay**-cher/ • v. (**denatures, denaturing, denatured**) **1** alter the natural qualities of something. **2** make alcohol unfit for drinking by adding poisonous or unpleasant-tasting substances.

dendrite /**den**-dryt/ • n. a short extension of a nerve cell that carries

impulses to the cell body.
- DERIVATIVES **dendritic** /den-**dri**-tik/ adj.
- ORIGIN Greek *dendritēs* 'tree-like'.

dene /deen/ •n. Brit. a deep, narrow, wooded valley.
- ORIGIN Old English.

dengue /deng-gi/ (also **dengue fever**)
•n. a tropical disease transmitted by mosquitoes, causing sudden fever and pains in the joints.
- ORIGIN Swahili.

deniable •adj. able to be denied.
- DERIVATIVES **deniability** n.

denial •n. **1** a statement that something is not true. **2** the action of denying. **3** refusal to accept that something unpleasant is true: *Tim was in denial of his illness.*

denier /den-yer/ •n. a unit by which the fineness of yarn is measured.
- ORIGIN Latin *denarius* (see **DENARIUS**).

denigrate /den-i-grayt/ •v. (**denigrates, denigrating, denigrated**) criticize someone or something unfairly.
- DERIVATIVES **denigration** n.
- ORIGIN Latin *denigrare* 'make dark'.

denim •n. **1** a hard-wearing cotton twill fabric. **2** (**denims**) jeans or other clothes made of denim.
- ORIGIN from French *serge de Nîmes*, referring to serge from the town of Nîmes.

denizen /den-i-zuhn/ •n. formal or humorous an inhabitant or occupant of a place.
- ORIGIN Old French *deinz* 'within'.

denominate /di-nom-i-nayt/
•v. (**denominates, denominating, denominated**) formal give a name to.
- ORIGIN Latin *denominare*.

denomination •n. **1** a recognized branch of a church or religion. **2** the face value of a banknote, coin, postage stamp, etc.
- DERIVATIVES **denominational** adj.

denominator •n. Math. the number below the line in a fraction.

denote /di-noht/ •v. (**denotes, denoting, denoted**) **1** be a sign of. **2** (of a word) have something as a main meaning.
- DERIVATIVES **denotation** n.
- ORIGIN Latin *denotare*.

denouement /day-noo-mon/ (also **dénouement**) •n. the final part of a play, film, or story, in which matters are explained or settled.
- ORIGIN French.

denounce •v. (**denounces, denouncing, denounced**) publicly declare to be wrong or evil.
- DERIVATIVES **denouncement** n.

- ORIGIN Latin *denuntiare* 'give official information'.

dense •adj. **1** containing many people or things crowded closely together: *dense jungle.* **2** having a thick texture: *dense rye bread.* **3** informal stupid.
- DERIVATIVES **densely** adv.
- ORIGIN Latin *densus*.

density •n. (pl. **densities**) **1** the degree to which a substance is dense; mass per unit volume. **2** the quantity of people or things in a particular area.

dent •n. a slight hollow in a surface made by a blow or pressure. •v. **1** mark with a dent. **2** have a bad effect on: *the experience dented his enthusiasm.*
- ORIGIN from **DINT**.

dental •adj. relating to the teeth or to dentistry.
- DERIVATIVES **dentally** adv.
- ORIGIN Latin *dentalis*.

dentine /den-teen/ •n. hard dense bony tissue forming the main part of a tooth.

dentist •n. a person who is qualified to treat the diseases and conditions that affect the teeth and gums.
- DERIVATIVES **dentistry** n.

dentition /den-ti-sh'n/ •n. the arrangement or condition of the teeth in a particular species.

denture /den-cher/ •n. a removable plate or frame holding one or more false teeth.

denude •v. (**denudes, denuding, denuded**) make bare: *the land was denuded of trees.*
- DERIVATIVES **denudation** n.
- ORIGIN Latin *denudare*.

denunciation /di-nun-si-ay-sh'n/
•n. public criticism or condemnation.
- DERIVATIVES **denunciatory** adj.

deny •v. (**denies, denying, denied**) **1** state that something is not true. **2** refuse to admit or accept something. **3** refuse to give something requested or desired to someone. **4** (**deny yourself**) go without something wanted.
- ORIGIN Old French *deneier*.

deodorant /di-oh-duh-ruhnt/ •n. a substance which removes or conceals bodily smells.
- ORIGIN Latin *odor* 'smell'.

deodorize (or **deodorise**)
•v. (**deodorizes, deodorizing, deodorized**) remove or conceal an unpleasant smell in a place.
- DERIVATIVES **deodorizer** n.

deoxygenated /dee-ok-si-juh-nay-tid/
•adj. having had the oxygen removed.

deoxyribonucleic acid /di-ok-si-ry-boh-nyoo-klay-ik/ •n. see **DNA**.

depart •v. **1** leave somewhere. **2** (**depart**

from) do something different from a usual course of action.
– ORIGIN Old French *departir*.

departed • adj. (of a person) dead.

department • n. **1** a division of a business, government, or other large organization, dealing with a specific area of activity. **2** an administrative district, especially in France. **3** (**your department**) informal an area of special skill or responsibility.
– DERIVATIVES **departmental** adj. **departmentally** adv.

department store • n. a large shop stocking many types of goods in different departments.

departure • n. **1** the action of leaving. **2** a change from a usual course of action.

depend • v. (**depend on**) **1** be determined or influenced by. **2** rely on.
– ORIGIN Latin *dependere* 'hang down'.

dependable • adj. trustworthy and reliable.
– DERIVATIVES **dependability** n. **dependably** adv.

dependant (also **dependent**) • n. a person who relies on another for financial support.

> ☑ As a noun, **dependant** can also be spelled **dependent** (*elderly dependants* or *dependents*). The adjective is always spelled **dependent** (*we were dependent on his good will*).

dependency • n. (pl. **dependencies**) **1** a country or province controlled by another. **2** the state of being dependent.

dependent • adj. **1** (**dependent on**) determined or influenced by. **2** relying on someone or something for support. **3** (**dependent on**) unable to do without. • n. var. of DEPENDANT.
– DERIVATIVES **dependence** n. **dependently** adv.

depersonalize (or **depersonalise**) • v. take away human qualities from someone or something.
– DERIVATIVES **depersonalization** n.

depict /di-pikt/ • v. **1** represent by a drawing, painting, or other art form. **2** describe in words.
– DERIVATIVES **depiction** n.
– ORIGIN Latin *depingere*.

depilate /dep-i-layt/ • v. (**depilates, depilating, depilated**) remove the hair from.
– ORIGIN Latin *depilare*.

depilatory /di-pil-uh-tri/ • adj. used to remove hair. • n. (pl. **depilatories**) a cream or lotion used to remove hair.

deplete /di-pleet/ • v. (**depletes, depleting, depleted**) reduce the number

or quantity of: *fish stocks are severely depleted.*
– DERIVATIVES **depletion** n.
– ORIGIN Latin *deplere* 'empty out'.

deplorable /di-plor-uh-b'l/ • adj. shockingly bad.
– DERIVATIVES **deplorably** adv.

deplore • v. (**deplores, deploring, deplored**) feel or express strong disapproval of.
– ORIGIN Latin *deplorare*.

deploy /di-ploy/ • v. **1** bring or move troops into position for military action. **2** use something effectively.
– DERIVATIVES **deployable** adj. **deployment** n.
– ORIGIN French *déployer*.

depoliticize (or **depoliticise**) • v. (**depoliticizes, depoliticizing, depoliticized**) remove something from political influence.
– DERIVATIVES **depoliticization** n.

depopulate • v. (**depopulates, depopulating, depopulated**) greatly reduce the population of a place.
– DERIVATIVES **depopulation** n.

deport • v. force a foreigner or immigrant to leave a country.
– DERIVATIVES **deportation** n. **deportee** n.
– ORIGIN Latin *deportare*.

deportment • n. **1** Brit. the way a person stands and walks. **2** N. Amer. a person's behaviour or manners.

depose • v. (**deposes, deposing, deposed**) remove someone from power suddenly and forcefully.
– ORIGIN Old French *deposer*.

deposit • n. **1** a sum of money paid into a bank or building society account. **2** a payment made as a first instalment in buying something. **3** a returnable sum paid when renting something, to cover possible loss or damage. **4** a layer of a substance that has accumulated or been laid down. • v. (**deposits, depositing, deposited**) **1** put down in a specific place. **2** put in a place for safekeeping. **3** pay as a deposit. **4** lay down matter as a layer or covering.
– DERIVATIVES **depositor** n.
– ORIGIN Latin *depositum*.

deposit account • n. Brit. a bank account that pays interest on money placed in it.

deposition /dep-uh-zi-shuhn/ • n. **1** the action of removing someone from power. **2** a sworn statement to be used as evidence in a court of law. **3** the action of depositing.

depository • n. (pl. **depositories**) a place where things are stored.

depot /dep-oh/ • n. **1** a place where large quantities of goods are stored. **2** a place

where vehicles are housed and repaired.
– ORIGIN French.

deprave /di-prayv/ • v. (**depraves, depraving, depraved**) make someone immoral or wicked.
– DERIVATIVES **depraved** adj.
– ORIGIN Latin *depravare*.

depravity /di-prav-i-ti/ • n. the state of being morally corrupt.

deprecate /dep-ri-kayt/ • v. (**deprecates, deprecating, deprecated**) express disapproval of.
– DERIVATIVES **deprecation** n. **deprecatory** adj.
– ORIGIN Latin *deprecari* 'pray to ward off evil'.

depreciate /di-pree-shi-ayt/ • v. (**depreciates, depreciating, depreciated**) 1 reduce in value over time. 2 dismiss as unimportant.
– DERIVATIVES **depreciation** n.
– ORIGIN Latin *depreciare*.

depredation /dep-ri-day-sh'n/ • n. an act that causes harm or damage.
– ORIGIN Latin.

depress • v. 1 make someone feel very unhappy. 2 reduce the level of activity in: *alcohol depresses the nervous system.* 3 push or pull down.
– DERIVATIVES **depressing** adj. **depressingly** adv.
– ORIGIN Latin *depressare*.

depressant • n. a drug or other substance that slows down bodily processes.

depressed • adj. 1 very unhappy and dispirited. 2 suffering the effects of an economic slump: *depressed rural areas.*

depression • n. 1 a mental state in which a person has feelings of great unhappiness and hopelessness. 2 a long and severe slump in an economy or market. 3 a sunken place or hollow. 4 an area of low pressure which may bring rain.

depressive • adj. tending to cause depression. • n. a person who tends to suffer from depression.

deprivation /dep-ri-vay-sh'n/ • n. 1 hardship resulting from the lack of basic necessities. 2 the lack or denial of something necessary.

deprive • v. (**deprives, depriving, deprived**) prevent from having or using something: *the city was deprived of its water supply.*
– ORIGIN Latin *deprivare*.

deprived • adj. suffering a damaging lack of the basic necessities of life.

Dept • abbrev. Department.

depth • n. 1 the distance from the top or surface down, or from front to back.

2 complex or meaningful thought: *the book has unexpected depth.* 3 extensive and detailed study. 4 strength of emotion. 5 (**the depths**) the deepest, lowest, or inmost part.
– PHRASES **out of your depth** 1 in water too deep to stand in. 2 in a situation that you cannot cope with.
– DERIVATIVES **depthless** adj.
– ORIGIN from **DEEP**.

depth charge • n. a charge designed to explode under water, used for attacking submarines.

deputation • n. a group of people who are appointed to act on behalf of a larger group.

depute /di-pyoot/ • v. (**deputes, deputing, deputed**) instruct someone to perform a task for which you are responsible.
– ORIGIN Latin *deputare* 'assign'.

deputize /dep-yuu-tyz/ (or **deputise**) • v. (**deputizes, deputizing, deputized**) temporarily act on behalf of someone else.

deputy • n. (pl. **deputies**) a person appointed to perform the duties of a more senior person in that person's absence.

derail • v. 1 cause a train to leave the tracks. 2 obstruct a process by diverting it from its intended course: *an attempt to derail the negotiations.*
– DERIVATIVES **derailment** n.

derange • v. (**deranges, deranging, deranged**) 1 (usu. as adj. **deranged**) make someone insane. 2 throw something into disorder.
– DERIVATIVES **derangement** n.
– ORIGIN French *déranger*.

Derby /dar-bi/ • n. (pl. **Derbies**) 1 an annual flat race at Epsom in Surrey for three-year-old horses, founded by the 12th Earl of Derby. 2 (**derby**; also **local derby**) a sports match between two rival teams from the same area.

deregulate • v. (**deregulates, deregulating, deregulated**) remove regulations from something.
– DERIVATIVES **deregulation** n.

derelict /de-ri-likt/ • adj. in a very poor condition as a result of disuse and neglect. • n. a person without a home, job, or possessions.
– ORIGIN Latin *derelinquere* 'to abandon'.

dereliction • n. 1 the state of having been abandoned and become run down. 2 (**dereliction of duty**) shameful failure to fulfil your duty.

deride /di-ryd/ • v. (**derides, deriding, derided**) express contempt for; ridicule.
– ORIGIN Latin *deridere* 'scoff at'.

de rigueur /duh ri-ger/ • adj. necessary

for acceptance in fashionable society: *large bathroom suites are de rigueur.*
– ORIGIN French, 'in strictness'.

derision /di-ri-zh'n/ • n. scornful ridicule or mockery.
– ORIGIN Latin.

derisive /di-ry-siv/ • adj. expressing contempt or ridicule.
– DERIVATIVES **derisively** adv.

derisory /di-ry-suh-ri/ • adj. 1 ridiculously small or inadequate. 2 derisive.

derivation • n. 1 the deriving of something from a source. 2 the formation of a word from another word.

derivative /di-riv-uh-tiv/
• adj. imitating the work of another artist, writer, etc.; not original.
• n. 1 something which is based on or comes from something else. 2 Math. an expression representing the rate of change of one quantity in relation to another.

derive /di-ryv/ • v. (**derives, deriving, derived**) 1 (**derive something from**) obtain something from something else. 2 (**derive from**) originate or develop from.
– DERIVATIVES **derivable** adj.
– ORIGIN Latin *derivare* 'draw off water'.

dermatitis /der-muh-ty-tiss/
• n. inflammation of the skin as a result of irritation or an allergic reaction.
– ORIGIN Greek *derma* 'skin'.

dermatology • n. the branch of medicine concerned with skin disorders.
– DERIVATIVES **dermatological** adj. **dermatologically** adv. **dermatologist** n.

dermis /der-miss/ • n. the thick layer of the skin below the epidermis.
– ORIGIN Latin.

derogate /der-uh-gayt/ • v. (**derogates, derogating, derogated**) formal 1 (**derogate from**) deviate from an agreement or rule. 2 be critical of.
– DERIVATIVES **derogation** n.
– ORIGIN Latin *derogare* 'abrogate'.

derogatory /di-rog-uh-tri/ • adj. critical or disrespectful.
– DERIVATIVES **derogatorily** adv.

derrick /derr-ik/ • n. 1 a kind of crane with a movable pivoted arm. 2 the framework over an oil well, holding the drilling machinery.
– ORIGIN from *Derrick*, the surname of a 17th-century hangman.

derring-do /derr-ing-doo/ • n. dated or humorous heroic or courageous action.
– ORIGIN from former *dorryng do* 'daring to do'.

dervish /der-vish/ • n. a member of a Muslim religious group vowed to poverty, some orders of which are

known for their wild rituals.
– ORIGIN Persian, 'religious beggar'.

desalinate /dee-sal-i-nayt/
• v. (**desalinates, desalinating, desalinated**) remove salt from seawater.
– DERIVATIVES **desalination** n.

descant /dess-kant/ • n. an independent melody sung or played above a basic melody.
– ORIGIN Latin *discantus* 'part song'.

descend • v. 1 move downwards or down. 2 slope or lead downwards. 3 (**descend to**) act in a shameful way that is below your usual standards. 4 (**descend on**) make a sudden attack on or unwelcome visit to. 5 (**be descended from**) be a blood relative of a particular ancestor.
– DERIVATIVES **descendent** adj. **descender** n.
– ORIGIN Latin *descendere* 'climb down'.

descendant • n. a person, animal, etc. that is descended from a particular ancestor.

descent • n. 1 an act of descending. 2 a downward slope. 3 a person's origin or nationality.

describe • v. (**describes, describing, described**) 1 give a detailed account of someone or something in words. 2 draw or form a shape.
– DERIVATIVES **describable** adj. **describer** n.
– ORIGIN Latin *describere* 'write down'.

description • n. 1 a spoken or written account. 2 the action of describing. 3 a sort, kind, or class: *people of any description.*

descriptive • adj. describing someone or something.
– DERIVATIVES **descriptively** adv.

descry /di-skry/ • v. (**descries, descrying, descried**) literary catch sight of.
– ORIGIN Old French *descrier* 'publish, proclaim'.

desecrate /dess-i-krayt/ • v. (**desecrates, desecrating, desecrated**) treat something sacred with violent disrespect.
– DERIVATIVES **desecration** n. **desecrator** n.
– ORIGIN from DE- + CONSECRATE.

desegregate • v. (**desegregates, desegregating, desegregated**) end racial segregation in a school or similar institution.
– DERIVATIVES **desegregation** n.

deselect • v. Brit. reject an existing MP as a candidate in a forthcoming election.
– DERIVATIVES **deselection** n.

desensitize (or **desensitise**)
• v. (**desensitizes, desensitizing, desensitized**) 1 make something less

sensitive. **2** make someone less likely to be distressed by cruelty or suffering.
– DERIVATIVES **desensitization** n.

desert[1] /di-zert/ • v. **1** leave someone without help or support. **2** (usu. as adj. **deserted**) leave a place, making it seem empty. **3** illegally leave the armed forces.
– DERIVATIVES **deserter** n. **desertion** n.
– ORIGIN Latin *desertare*.

desert[2] /dez-ert/ • n. a waterless, empty area of land with little or no vegetation.
– ORIGIN Latin *desertum* 'something left waste'.

desert island • n. a remote uninhabited tropical island.

deserts /di-zerts/ • pl. n. (usu. in phr. **get** or **receive your just deserts**) the reward or punishment that a person deserves.
– ORIGIN Old French *desert*.

deserve • v. (**deserves, deserving, deserved**) do something or show qualities worthy of a reward or punishment.
– DERIVATIVES **deservedly** adv.
– ORIGIN Latin *deservire* 'serve well'.

deserving • adj. worthy of favourable treatment or help.

déshabillé /day-za-bee-**yay**/ (also **dishabille**) /diss-uh-**beel**/ • n. the state of being only partly clothed.
– ORIGIN French, 'undressed'.

desiccate /dess-i-kayt/ • v. (**desiccates, desiccating, desiccated**) remove the moisture from.
– DERIVATIVES **desiccation** n.
– ORIGIN Latin *desiccare*.

desideratum /di-zi-duh-**rah**-tuhm/ • n. (pl. **desiderata** /di-zi-duh-**rah**-tuh/) something that is needed or wanted.
– ORIGIN Latin.

design • n. **1** a plan or drawing produced to show the appearance and workings of something before it is made. **2** the action of producing a design. **3** a decorative pattern. **4** underlying purpose or planning. • v. **1** produce a design for. **2** intend for a purpose: *the video is designed to help someone train their dog.*
– PHRASES **by design** on purpose. **have designs on** aim to obtain.
– ORIGIN Latin *designare* 'mark out'.

designate • v. /dez-ig-nayt/ (**designates, designating, designated**) **1** officially give a particular status or name to: *certain schools are designated 'science schools'.* **2** appoint someone to a particular job. • adj. /dez-ig-nuht/ (after a noun) appointed to a post but not yet having taken it up: *the Director designate.*
– DERIVATIVES **designator** n.
– ORIGIN Latin *designare*.

designation • n. **1** the action of designating or choosing. **2** an official title or description.

designer • n. a person who designs things. • adj. made by a famous fashion designer.

designer baby • n. a baby whose genetic make-up has been selected in order to remove a particular defect, or to ensure that a particular gene is present.

designing • adj. cunning and deceitful.

desirable • adj. **1** wished for as being attractive, useful, or necessary. **2** sexually attractive.
– DERIVATIVES **desirability** n. **desirably** adv.

desire • n. **1** a strong feeling of wanting to have something or wishing for something to happen. **2** strong sexual appetite. • v. (**desires, desiring, desired**) **1** strongly wish for or want. **2** want someone sexually.
– ORIGIN Latin *desiderare*.

desirous /di-zy-ruhss/ • adj. strongly wishing to have: *the pope was desirous of peace.*

desist /di-sisst/ • v. stop doing something.
– ORIGIN Latin *desistere*.

desk • n. **1** a piece of furniture with a flat or sloping surface for writing on. **2** a counter in a hotel, bank, or airport. **3** a particular section of a news organization: *the sports desk.*
– ORIGIN Latin *discus* 'plate'.

deskill • v. reduce the level of skill needed to carry out a job.

desktop • n. **1** the working area of a computer screen. **2** a microcomputer suitable for use at a desk.

desktop publishing • n. the production of high-quality printed matter by means of a printer linked to a computer, with special software.

desolate • adj. /dess-uh-luht/ **1** (of a place) bleak and empty. **2** very unhappy. • v. /dess-uh-layt/ (**desolates, desolating, desolated**) make very unhappy.
– DERIVATIVES **desolation** n.
– ORIGIN Latin *desolare* 'abandon'.

despair • n. the complete loss or absence of hope. • v. lose or be without hope.
– ORIGIN Latin *desperare*.

despatch • v. & n. var. of DISPATCH.

desperado /dess-puh-**rah**-doh/ • n. (pl. **desperadoes** or **desperados**) a desperate or reckless criminal.
– ORIGIN pseudo-Spanish.

desperate • adj. **1** completely without hope. **2** done when everything else has

failed: *the firm shut the factory in a desperate bid to cut costs.* **3** very serious. **4** having a great need for something.
– DERIVATIVES **desperately** adv. **desperation** n.
– ORIGIN Latin *desperatus*.

> ✓ Spell **desperate** with **-per-** in the middle.

despicable /di-spik-uh-b'l/
• adj. deserving hatred and contempt.
– DERIVATIVES **despicably** adv.
– ORIGIN Latin *despicabilis*.

despise /di-spyz/ • v. (**despise, despising, despised**) feel hatred or disgust for.
– ORIGIN Latin *despicere* 'look down'.

despite /di-spyt/ • prep. in spite of.
– ORIGIN Latin *despectus* 'looking down on'.

despoil /di-spoyl/ • v. literary steal valuable possessions from a place.
– DERIVATIVES **despoiler** n. **despoliation** /di-spoh-li-ay-sh'n/ n.
– ORIGIN Latin *despoliare* 'rob, plunder'.

despondent • adj. in low spirits from loss of hope or courage.
– DERIVATIVES **despondency** n. **despondently** adv.
– ORIGIN Latin *despondere* 'give up'.

despot /dess-pot/ • n. a ruler with total power, especially one who uses it in a cruel way.
– DERIVATIVES **despotic** adj. **despotism** n.
– ORIGIN Greek *despotēs*.

dessert /di-zert/ • n. the sweet course eaten at the end of a meal.
– ORIGIN French.

dessertspoon • n. a spoon used for dessert, smaller than a tablespoon and larger than a teaspoon.

destabilize (or **destabilise**)
• v. (**destabilizes, destabilizing, destabilized**) upset the stability of something.
– DERIVATIVES **destabilization** n.

destination • n. the place to which someone or something is going or being sent.

destine • v. (**be destined**) **1** be intended for or certain to do something: *he was destined to be an engineer.* **2** be intended for a particular destination.
– ORIGIN Latin *destinare* 'make firm'.

destiny • n. (pl. **destinies**) **1** the events that will happen to a person in the future. **2** the power believed to control future events; fate.
– ORIGIN Latin *destinata*.

destitute /dess-ti-tyoot/ • adj. very poor and without a home or other basic necessities.
– DERIVATIVES **destitution** n.

– ORIGIN Latin *destituere* 'forsake'.

destroy • v. **1** end the existence of something by badly damaging it. **2** kill an animal in a painless way.
– ORIGIN Latin *destruere*.

destroyer • n. **1** a person or thing that destroys. **2** a small fast warship.

destructible • adj. able to be destroyed.

destruction • n. **1** the action of destroying or the state of being destroyed. **2** a cause of someone's ruin: *gambling was his destruction.*
– ORIGIN Latin.

destructive • adj. causing severe damage or destruction.
– DERIVATIVES **destructively** adv. **destructiveness** n.

desuetude /dess-wi-tyood/ • n. formal a state of disuse.
– ORIGIN Latin *desuetudo*.

desultory /dess-uhl-tuh-ri/
• adj. **1** lacking purpose or enthusiasm. **2** aimlessly going from one subject to another: *a desultory conversation.*
– DERIVATIVES **desultorily** adv.
– ORIGIN Latin *desultorius* 'superficial'.

detach • v. **1** disconnect something and remove it. **2** (**detach yourself from**) distance yourself from a group or situation. **3** (**be detached**) (of a group of soldiers) be sent on a separate mission.
– DERIVATIVES **detachable** adj.
– ORIGIN French *détacher*.

> ✓ **detach** only has one **t**; the ending is spelled **-ach**.

detached • adj. **1** separate or disconnected. **2** not involved; objective.

detachment • n. **1** the state of being uninvolved: *a sense of detachment from what was going on.* **2** a group of troops, ships, etc. sent on a separate mission. **3** the action of detaching.

detail • n. **1** a small individual item or fact. **2** small items or facts as a whole: *attention to detail.* **3** a small detachment of troops or police officers given a special duty. • v. **1** describe something fully. **2** order to undertake a task.
– ORIGIN French *détail*.

detailed • adj. having many details.

detailing • n. small decorative features on a building, garment, or work of art.

detain • v. **1** prevent someone from going somewhere. **2** keep someone in official custody.
– DERIVATIVES **detainment** n.
– ORIGIN Latin *detinere*.

detainee /dee-tay-nee/ • n. a person kept in custody, especially for political reasons.

detect • v. **1** discover the presence of:

cancer may soon be detected in its earliest stages. **2** notice something very slight. **3** discover or investigate a crime.
– DERIVATIVES **detectable** adj. **detectably** adv. **detection** n.
– ORIGIN Latin *detegere* 'uncover'.

detective • n. a person whose occupation is to investigate crimes.

detector • n. a device that discovers the presence of something and sends out a signal.

détente /day-**tahnt**/ • n. the easing of hostility or unfriendly relations between countries.
– ORIGIN French, 'loosening, relaxation'.

detention • n. **1** the state of being detained in official custody. **2** the punishment of being kept in school after hours.

detention centre • n. an institution where people, especially refugees or those awaiting trial, are kept in custody.

deter /di-**ter**/ • v. (**deters**, **deterring**, **deterred**) **1** discourage someone from doing something, especially by making them afraid of the consequences. **2** prevent something from happening.
– ORIGIN Latin *deterrere*.

detergent • n. a liquid or powder used for removing dirt and grease.
– ORIGIN Latin *detergere* 'wipe away'.

deteriorate /di-**teer**-i-uh-rayt/ • v. (**deteriorates**, **deteriorating**, **deteriorated**) become gradually worse.
– DERIVATIVES **deterioration** n.
– ORIGIN Latin *deteriorare*.

determinant /di-**ter**-mi-nuhnt/ • n. **1** a factor which decisively affects the nature or outcome of something: *force of will was the main determinant of his success.* **2** Math. a quantity obtained by adding products of the elements of a square matrix according to a given rule.

determinate /di-**ter**-mi-nuht/ • adj. having fixed and definite limits.

determination • n. **1** firmness of purpose. **2** the action of establishing or deciding something.

determine • v. (**determines**, **determining**, **determined**) **1** cause to happen in a particular way or to have a particular nature: *it is biological age that determines our looks.* **2** firmly decide something. **3** establish by research or calculation.
– DERIVATIVES **determinable** adj.
– ORIGIN Latin *determinare* 'limit, fix'.

determined • adj. having firmness of purpose; resolute.
– DERIVATIVES **determinedly** adv.

determiner • n. **1** a person or thing that determines. **2** Grammar a word that comes

before a noun to show how the noun is being used, for example *a*, *the*, *every*.

determinism • n. the belief that people are not free to do as they wish because their lives are determined by factors outside their control.
– DERIVATIVES **determinist** n. & adj.

deterrent /di-**terr**-uhnt/ • n. a thing that deters or is intended to deter.
– DERIVATIVES **deterrence** n.

detest • v. dislike intensely.
– ORIGIN Latin *detestari* 'denounce, hate'.

detestable • adj. deserving intense dislike.

detestation /dee-tess-**tay**-sh'n/ • n. intense dislike.

dethrone • v. (**dethrones**, **dethroning**, **dethroned**) remove a monarch from power.

detonate /**det**-uh-nayt/ • v. (**detonates**, **detonating**, **detonated**) explode or cause to explode.
– DERIVATIVES **detonation** n.
– ORIGIN Latin *detonare*.

detonator • n. a device used to detonate an explosive.

detour /**dee**-toor/ • n. a long or roundabout route taken to avoid something or to visit something along the way.
– ORIGIN French, 'change of direction'.

detox informal • n. /**dee**-toks/ detoxification. • v. /**dee**-toks/ detoxify.

detoxify • v. (**detoxifies**, **detoxifying**, **detoxified**) **1** remove harmful or poisonous substances from. **2** stop taking or help to stop taking drink or drugs.
– DERIVATIVES **detoxification** n. **detoxifier** n.

detract • v. (**detract from**) cause something to seem less valuable or impressive.
– ORIGIN Latin *detrahere* 'draw away'.

detractor • n. a person who criticizes someone or something.

detriment /**det**-ri-muhnt/ • n. harm or damage: *she fasted to the detriment of her health.*
– DERIVATIVES **detrimental** adj. **detrimentally** adv.
– ORIGIN Latin *detrimentum*.

detritus /di-**try**-tuhss/ • n. debris or waste material.
– ORIGIN Latin.

de trop /duh **troh**/ • adj. not wanted; unwelcome.
– ORIGIN French, 'excessive'.

deuce[1] /dyooss/ • n. Tennis the score of 40 all in a game, at which two consecutive points are needed to win the game.
– ORIGIN Old French *deus*.

deuce[2] /dyooss/ • exclam. (**the deuce**) informal used as a euphemism for 'devil'.
– ORIGIN German *duus*.

deus ex machina /day-uuss eks mak-i-nuh/ • n. an unexpected event that saves a seemingly hopeless situation.
– ORIGIN Latin, 'god from the machinery'.

deuterium /dyoo-teer-i-uhm/ • n. Chem. a stable isotope of hydrogen with a mass approximately twice that of the usual isotope.
– ORIGIN Latin.

Deutschmark /doych-mark/ • n. (until the introduction of the euro in 2002) the basic unit of money of Germany.
– ORIGIN from German *deutsche Mark* 'German mark'.

devalue • v. (**devalues, devaluing, devalued**) **1** reduce the worth of: *people seem to devalue my achievement.* **2** reduce the official value of a currency in relation to other currencies.
– DERIVATIVES **devaluation** n.

devastate /dev-uh-stayt/
• v. (**devastates, devastating, devastated**) **1** destroy or ruin. **2** (**be devastated**) be overwhelmed with shock or grief.
– DERIVATIVES **devastation** n. **devastator** n.
– ORIGIN Latin *devastare*.

devastating • adj. **1** highly destructive. **2** very distressing. **3** informal very impressive or attractive.
– DERIVATIVES **devastatingly** adv.

develop • v. (**develops, developing, developed**) **1** become or make larger or more advanced. **2** start to exist, experience, or possess. **3** convert land to a new purpose. **4** treat a photographic film with chemicals to make a visible image.
– DERIVATIVES **developable** adj. **developer** n.
– ORIGIN French *développer* 'unfold'.

developing country • n. a poor agricultural country that is seeking to become more advanced.

development • n. **1** the action of developing or the state of being developed. **2** a new product or idea. **3** a new stage in a changing situation. **4** an area of land with new buildings on it.
– DERIVATIVES **developmental** adj. **developmentally** adv.

deviant • adj. departing from normal standards. • n. a person who departs from normal standards.
– DERIVATIVES **deviance** n. **deviancy** n.

deviate /dee-vi-ayt/ • v. (**deviates, deviating, deviated**) depart from an established course or from normal standards.

– DERIVATIVES **deviation** n.
– ORIGIN Latin *deviare* 'turn out of the way'.

device • n. **1** a piece of equipment made for a particular purpose. **2** a plan or method with a particular aim: *a clever marketing device.* **3** a drawing or design.
– PHRASES **leave someone to their own devices** leave someone to do as they wish.
– ORIGIN Old French *devis*.

devil • n. **1** (**the Devil**) (in Christian and Jewish belief) the most powerful evil spirit. **2** an evil spirit. **3** a very wicked or cruel person. **4** a mischievous person. **5** informal a person with specified characteristics: *the poor devil.* **6** (**the devil**) expressing surprise or annoyance.
– PHRASES **between the devil and the deep blue sea** caught in a dilemma. **devil-may-care** cheerful and reckless. **speak** (or **talk**) **of the devil** said when a person appears just after being mentioned.
– ORIGIN Greek *diabolos* 'accuser'.

devilish • adj. **1** evil and cruel. **2** mischievous: *a devilish grin.*
– DERIVATIVES **devilishly** adv.

devilment • n. reckless mischief.

devilry • n. **1** wicked activity. **2** reckless mischief.

devil's advocate • n. a person who expresses an unpopular opinion in order to provoke debate.

devious /dee-vi-uhss/ • adj. **1** skilful in using underhand tactics. **2** (of a route or journey) indirect.
– DERIVATIVES **deviously** adv. **deviousness** n.
– ORIGIN Latin *devius* 'out of the way'.

devise /di-vyz/ • v. (**devises, devising, devised**) plan or invent a complex procedure or device.
– DERIVATIVES **deviser** n.
– ORIGIN Old French *deviser*.

devoid /di-voyd/ • adj. (**devoid of**) completely lacking in: *her voice was devoid of emotion.*
– ORIGIN Old French *devoidier* 'cast out'.

devolution /dee-vuh-loo-sh'n/ • n. the transfer of power by central government to local or regional governments.
– DERIVATIVES **devolutionist** n.

devolve /di-volv/ • v. (**devolves, devolving, devolved**) **1** transfer power to a lower level. **2** (**devolve on/to**) (of responsibility) pass to a deputy or successor.
– ORIGIN Latin *devolvere* 'roll down'.

Devonian /di-voh-ni-uhn/ • adj. Geol. relating to the fourth period of the Palaeozoic era (about 409 to 363 million years ago), when the first amphibians appeared.

devote • v. (**devotes, devoting, devoted**) (**devote something to**) give time or resources to.
– ORIGIN Latin *devovere* 'consecrate'.

devoted • adj. very loving or loyal.
– DERIVATIVES **devotedly** adv.

devotee /dev-oh-tee/ • n. **1** a person who is very enthusiastic about someone or something. **2** a person with a strong belief in a particular religion or god.

devotion • n. **1** great love or loyalty. **2** religious worship. **3** (**devotions**) prayers or religious observances.
– DERIVATIVES **devotional** adj.

devour /di-vow-er/ • v. **1** eat greedily. **2** (of a force) destroy completely: *fire devoured the old house.* **3** read quickly and eagerly.
– DERIVATIVES **devourer** n.
– ORIGIN Latin *devorare*.

devout /di-vowt/ • adj. **1** deeply religious. **2** earnestly sincere: *my devout hope.*
– DERIVATIVES **devoutly** adv.
– ORIGIN Latin *devotus* 'devoted'.

dew • n. tiny drops of moisture that form on cool surfaces at night, when water vapour in the air condenses.
– ORIGIN Old English.

dewlap • n. a fold of loose skin hanging from the neck or throat of an animal or bird.

dewy • adj. wet with dew.

dewy-eyed • adj. sentimental or naive.

dexterity /dek-ste-ri-ti/ • n. **1** skill in using the hands. **2** the ability to do something skilfully: *mental dexterity.*
– ORIGIN Latin *dexteritas.*

dexterous /dek-stuh-ruhss/ (also **dextrous** /dek-struhss/) • adj. showing skill with the hands.
– DERIVATIVES **dexterously** adv.

dextrose • n. a naturally occurring form of glucose.
– ORIGIN from Latin *dexter* 'on the right'.

DfES • abbrev. (in the UK) Department for Education and Skills.

DG • abbrev. director general.

dhal /dahl/ (also **dal**) • n. (in Indian cookery) split pulses.
– ORIGIN Hindi.

dharma /dar-muh/ • n. (in Indian religion) the eternal law of the universe.
– ORIGIN Sanskrit, 'decree or custom'.

dhoti /doh-ti/ • n. (pl. **dhotis**) a long piece of cloth tied around the waist, worn by some Indian men.
– ORIGIN Hindi.

dhow /dow/ • n. a sailing ship with one or two masts, used in the Arabian region.
– ORIGIN Arabic.

di- • comb. form two-; double: *dioxide.*
– ORIGIN Greek *dis* 'twice'.

dia- (also **di-** before a vowel) • prefix **1** through; across: *diameter.* **2** apart: *diaeresis.*
– ORIGIN Greek *dia* 'through'.

diabetes /dy-uh-bee-teez/ • n. a disorder of the metabolism in which a lack of the hormone insulin results in a failure to absorb sugar and starch properly.
– ORIGIN Greek, 'siphon.'

diabetic • adj. relating to diabetes. • n. a person with diabetes.

diabolical • adj. **1** (also **diabolic**) relating to or like the Devil; evil. **2** Brit. informal very bad.
– DERIVATIVES **diabolically** adv.
– ORIGIN Greek *diabolos* 'accuser'.

diaconal /dy-ak-uh-nuhl/ • adj. (in the Christian Church) relating to a deacon or deacons.
– ORIGIN Latin *diaconus* 'deacon'.

diaconate /dy-ak-uh-nayt/ • n. the office or post of deacon.

diacritic /dy-uh-krit-ik/ • n. a mark that is put above or below a letter of a foreign word to show how a sound is pronounced or stressed.
– ORIGIN Greek *diakritikos.*

diadem /dy-uh-dem/ • n. a jewelled crown or headband worn as a symbol of royalty.
– ORIGIN Greek *diadēma.*

diaeresis /dy-eer-i-siss/ (US **dieresis**) • n. (pl. **diaereses** /dy-eer-i-seez/) a mark (¨) placed over a vowel to indicate that it is sounded separately, as in *Brontë.*
– ORIGIN Greek *diairesis* 'separation'.

diagnose /dy-uhg-nohz/ • v. (**diagnoses, diagnosing, diagnosed**) identify the nature of an illness or problem by examining the symptoms.

diagnosis • n. (pl. **diagnoses**) the identification of the nature of an illness or problem by examination of the symptoms.
– DERIVATIVES **diagnostic** /dy-uhg-noss-tik/ adj. **diagnostically** adv.
– ORIGIN Greek.

diagonal /dy-ag-uh-n'l/ • adj. **1** (of a straight line) joining two opposite corners of a rectangle, square, or other shape. **2** (of a line) straight and at an angle; slanting. • n. a diagonal line.
– DERIVATIVES **diagonally** adv.
– ORIGIN Greek *diagōnios* 'from angle to angle'.

diagram • n. a simplified drawing

showing the appearance or structure of something.
- DERIVATIVES **diagrammatic** adj. **diagrammatically** adv.
- ORIGIN Greek *diagramma*.

dial • n. **1** a disc marked to show the time on a clock or to indicate a measurement by means of a pointer. **2** a disc with numbered holes on a telephone, turned to make a call. **3** a disc turned to select a setting on a radio, cooker, etc. • v. (**dials, dialling, dialled;** US **dials, dialing, dialed**) call a telephone number.
- DERIVATIVES **dialler** (also **dialer**) n.
- ORIGIN Latin *diale*.

dialect /dy-uh-lekt/ • n. a form of a language used in a particular region: *Yorkshire dialect.*
- DERIVATIVES **dialectal** adj.
- ORIGIN Greek *dialektos* 'discourse'.

dialectic /dy-uh-lek-tik/ (also **dialectics**) • n. Philos. the investigation of the truth of opposing opinions by logical discussion.
- DERIVATIVES **dialectical** adj.
- ORIGIN from Greek *dialektikē tekhnē* 'art of debate'.

dialling code • n. Brit. a sequence of numbers dialled to connect a telephone to an exchange in another area or country.

dialling tone • n. a sound produced by a telephone which indicates that a caller may start to dial.

dialog box (Brit. also **dialogue box**) • n. a small area on a computer screen in which the user is prompted to provide information or select commands.

dialogue (US also **dialog**) • n. **1** conversation between two or more people as a feature of a book, play, or film. **2** a discussion intended to explore a subject or to solve a problem.
- ORIGIN Greek *dialogos*.

dialysis /dy-al-i-siss/ • n. (pl. **dialyses** /dy-al-i-seez/) **1** Chem. the separation of particles in a liquid on the basis of differences in their ability to pass through a membrane. **2** the purifying of blood by dialysis, as a substitute for the normal function of the kidney.
- ORIGIN Greek *dialusis*.

diamanté /dy-uh-mon-tay/ • adj. decorated with glass cut to resemble diamonds.
- ORIGIN French, 'set with diamonds'.

diameter /dy-am-i-ter/ • n. a straight line passing from side to side through the centre of a circle or sphere.
- ORIGIN from Greek *diametros grammē* 'line measuring across'.

diametrical /dy-uh-met-ri-k'l/ • adj. **1** (of opposites) completely

different. **2** relating to a diameter.
- DERIVATIVES **diametrically** adv.

diamond • n. **1** a precious stone consisting of a clear, colourless form of pure carbon, the hardest naturally occurring substance. **2** a figure with four straight sides of equal length forming two opposite acute angles and two opposite obtuse angles. **3** (**diamonds**) one of the four suits in a pack of playing cards.
- ORIGIN Old French *diamant*.

diamond jubilee • n. the sixtieth anniversary of a notable event.

diamond wedding • n. Brit. the sixtieth anniversary of a wedding.

diapason /dy-uh-pay-suhn, dy-uh-pay-zuhn/ • n. a stop controlling the tone of a pipe organ.
- ORIGIN from Greek *dia pasōn khordōn* 'through all notes'.

diaper /dy-uh-per/ • n. N. Amer. a baby's nappy.
- ORIGIN Greek *diaspros*.

diaphanous /dy-af-fuh-nuhss/ • adj. light, delicate, and transparent.
- ORIGIN Greek *diaphanēs*.

diaphragm /dy-uh-fram/ • n. **1** a muscular partition which separates the thorax from the abdomen in mammals. **2** a taut flexible membrane in mechanical or sound systems. **3** a thin contraceptive cap fitting over the neck of the womb.
- ORIGIN Latin *diaphragma*.

diarist • n. a person who writes a diary.

diarrhoea /dy-uh-ree-uh/ (US **diarrhea**) • n. a condition in which a person frequently discharges liquid faeces from the bowels.
- ORIGIN Greek *diarrhoia*.

> ✓ Spell **diarrhoea** with a double **r**; the ending is **-hoea** in British English.

diary • n. (pl. **diaries**) **1** a book in which someone keeps a daily record of their experiences. **2** a book with each day's date, in which to note appointments or important information.
- ORIGIN Latin *diarium*.

diaspora /dy-ass-puh-ruh/ • n. **1** (**the diaspora**) the dispersion of the Jews beyond Israel. **2** the dispersion of any people from their traditional homeland.
- ORIGIN Greek.

diastole /dy-ass-tuh-li/ • n. the phase of the heartbeat when the heart muscle relaxes and the chambers fill with blood.
- DERIVATIVES **diastolic** adj.
- ORIGIN Greek, 'separation, expansion'.

diatom /dy-uh-tuhm/ • n. a single-celled alga which has a cell wall of silica.
- ORIGIN Greek *diatomos* 'cut in two'.

diatomic /dy-uh-tom-ik/ •adj. Chem. consisting of two atoms.

diatonic /dy-uh-ton-ik/ •adj. Music involving only the notes of the major or minor scale, without additional sharps, flats, etc.
– ORIGIN Greek *diatonikos* 'at intervals of a tone'.

diatribe /dy-uh-tryb/ •n. a harsh and forceful verbal attack.
– ORIGIN Greek, 'discourse'.

dice •n. (pl. **dice**; sing. also **die**) a small cube with faces bearing from one to six spots, used in games of chance.
•v. (**dices, dicing, diced**) **1** cut food into small cubes. **2** (**dice with**) take great risks with: *he enjoyed dicing with death.*
– ORIGIN Old French *des.*

dicey •adj. (**dicier, diciest**) informal risky or difficult.

dichotomy /dy-kot-uh-mi/ •n. (pl. **dichotomies**) a separation between two things that are opposed or different: *the dichotomy between good and evil.*
– DERIVATIVES **dichotomous** adj.
– ORIGIN Greek *dikhotomia* 'a cutting in two'.

dickens •n. informal used to express annoyance or surprise.
– ORIGIN a euphemism for 'devil'.

Dickensian /di-ken-zi-uhn/ •adj. like the novels of Charles Dickens, especially in terms of the poverty that they portray.

dicky •adj. Brit. informal not strong, healthy, or functioning reliably.
– ORIGIN perh. from the man's name *Dick,* in the old saying *as queer as Dick's hatband.*

dicky bow •n. informal a bow tie.

dicotyledon /dy-kot-i-lee-duhn/ •n. a plant with an embryo bearing two cotyledons (seed leaves).

dicta pl. of DICTUM.

dictate •v. /dik-tayt/ (**dictates, dictating, dictated**) **1** state or order something with authority. **2** control or influence: *choice is often dictated by availability.* **3** say or read aloud words to be typed or written down. •n. /dik-tayt/ an order or principle that must be obeyed: *the dictates of fashion.*
– DERIVATIVES **dictation** n.
– ORIGIN Latin *dictare.*

dictator /dik-tay-ter/ •n. a ruler with total power over a country.

dictatorial /dik-tuh-tor-i-uhl/ •adj. **1** relating to or controlled by a dictator. **2** insisting on total obedience; domineering.

dictatorship •n. **1** government by a

dictator. **2** a country governed by a dictator.

diction •n. **1** the choice and use of words in speech or writing: *poetic diction.* **2** a person's way of pronouncing words.
– ORIGIN Latin.

dictionary •n. (pl. **dictionaries**) a book that lists the words of a language and gives their meaning, or their equivalent in a different language.
– ORIGIN from Latin *dictionarium manuale* or *dictionarius liber* 'manual or book of words'.

dictum /dik-tuhm/ •n. (pl. **dicta** /dik-tuh/ or **dictums**) **1** a formal or authoritative statement. **2** a short statement that expresses a general truth.
– ORIGIN Latin, 'something said'.

did past of DO¹.

didactic /dy-dak-tik/ •adj. intended to teach or give moral guidance.
– DERIVATIVES **didactically** adv. **didacticism** n.
– ORIGIN Greek *didaskein* 'teach'.

diddle •v. (**diddles, diddling, diddled**) informal cheat or swindle someone.
– ORIGIN prob. from Jeremy *Diddler,* a character in a farce.

didgeridoo /di-juh-ri-doo/ •n. an Australian Aboriginal wind instrument in the form of a long wooden tube, blown to produce a deep booming sound.
– ORIGIN from an Aboriginal language.

didn't •contr. did not.

die¹ •v. (**dies, dying, died**) **1** stop living. **2** (**die out**) become extinct. **3** become less loud or strong: *the noise died down.* **4** (**be dying for/to do**) informal be very eager to have or do.
– PHRASES **die hard** change very slowly. **never say die** do not give up hope. **to die for** informal very good or desirable.
– ORIGIN Old Norse.

die² •n. **1** sing. of DICE. **2** (pl. **dies**) a device for cutting or moulding metal or for stamping a design on to coins or medals.
– PHRASES **the die is cast** an event has happened that cannot be changed.
– ORIGIN Old French *de.*

die-cast •adj. formed by pouring molten metal into a mould.

diehard •n. a person who strongly supports something in spite of opposition or changing circumstances: *diehard Marxists.*

dielectric /dy-i-lek-trik/ Physics •adj. that does not conduct electricity; insulating. •n. an insulator.

dieresis •n. US = DIAERESIS.

diesel /dee-z'l/ •n. **1** an internal-

combustion engine in which the heat of compressed air is used to ignite the fuel. **2** (also **diesel oil**) a form of petroleum used to fuel diesel engines.
– ORIGIN named after the German engineer Rudolf *Diesel*.

diet¹ • n. **1** the kinds of food that a person or animal usually eats. **2** a limited range or amount of food, eaten in order to lose weight or for medical reasons. • adj. with reduced fat or sugar content: *diet drinks.* • v. (**diets**, **dieting**, **dieted**) eat a limited range or amount of food to lose weight.
– DERIVATIVES **dieter** n.
– ORIGIN Greek *diaita* 'a way of life'.

diet² • n. a law-making assembly in certain countries.
– ORIGIN Latin *dieta* 'day's work'.

dietary /dy-uh-tri/ • adj. **1** relating to diets or dieting. **2** provided by the diet: *dietary fibre.*

dietetics /dy-uh-tet-iks/ • n. the branch of knowledge concerned with diet and its effects on health.
– DERIVATIVES **dietetic** adj.

dietitian /dy-uh-ti-sh'n/ (also **dietician**) • n. an expert on diet and nutrition.

differ • v. (**differs**, **differing**, **differed**) **1** be unlike: *the second set of data differed from the first.* **2** disagree with someone.
– ORIGIN Latin *differre* 'differ, defer'.

difference • n. **1** a way in which people or things are not the same. **2** the state of being unlike: *there's little difference between his public and private self.* **3** a disagreement or dispute: *they patched up their differences.* **4** the remainder left after one value is subtracted from another.
– PHRASES **make a** (or **no**) **difference** have an effect (or no effect).

different • adj. **1** not the same as another or each other. **2** separate. **3** informal new and unusual.
– DERIVATIVES **differently** adv.

> USAGE: **Different** can be followed by **from**, **to**, or **than**. In British English **different from** is the most common use, while **different than** is mainly found in North America.

differential /dif-fuh-ren-sh'l/ • adj. relating to or depending on a difference: *the differential achievements of boys and girls.* • n. **1** Brit. a difference in wages between industries or between categories of employees in the same industry. **2** Math. a minute difference between successive values of a variable. **3** a gear allowing a vehicle's driven wheels to revolve at different speeds in cornering.
– DERIVATIVES **differentially** adv.

differential calculus • n. Math. the part of calculus concerned with the derivatives of functions.

differential equation • n. an equation involving derivatives of a function or functions.

differentiate /dif-fuh-ren-shi-ayt/ • v. (**differentiates**, **differentiating**, **differentiated**) **1** recognize as different; distinguish. **2** cause to appear different: *little differentiates the firm's products from its rivals.* **3** Math. transform a function into its derivative.
– DERIVATIVES **differentiation** n. **differentiator** n.

difficult • adj. **1** needing much effort or skill to do or understand. **2** causing or full of problems: *a difficult economic climate.* **3** not easy to please or satisfy.

difficulty • n. (pl. **difficulties**) **1** the state of being difficult. **2** a problem. **3** a difficult or dangerous situation.
– ORIGIN Latin *difficultas.*

diffident • adj. modest or shy because of a lack of self-confidence.
– DERIVATIVES **diffidence** n. **diffidently** adv.
– ORIGIN Latin *diffidere* 'fail to trust'.

diffraction • n. Physics the process by which a beam of light or other system of waves is spread out as a result of passing through a narrow opening or across an edge.
– DERIVATIVES **diffract** v.
– ORIGIN Latin *diffringere* 'break into pieces'.

diffuse • v. /dif-fyooz/ (**diffuses**, **diffusing**, **diffused**) **1** spread over a wide area: *technologies diffuse rapidly.* **2** Physics (of a gas or liquid) intermingle with another substance by movement. • adj. /dif-fyooss/ **1** spread out over a large area; not concentrated: *a diffuse cloud of gas.* **2** not clear or concise.
– DERIVATIVES **diffusely** adv. **diffuser** n.
– ORIGIN Latin *diffundere* 'pour out'.

> USAGE: On the confusion of **diffuse** and **defuse**, see the note at **DEFUSE**.

diffusion • n. **1** the action of spreading over a wide area. **2** Physics the intermingling of substances by the natural movement of their particles.
– DERIVATIVES **diffusive** adj.

dig • v. (**digs**, **digging**, **dug**) **1** break up and turn over or move earth. **2** remove or do by digging. **3** push or poke sharply: *he dug his hands into his pockets.* **4** (**dig into/through**) search or rummage in. **5** (**dig something out/up**) discover facts. **6** (**dig in**) begin eating heartily. **7** informal, dated like: *I really dig heavy rock.* • n. **1** an act of digging. **2** an archaeological excavation. **3** a sharp push or poke.

4 informal a critical remark. **5** (**digs**) informal lodgings.
– PHRASES **dig in your heels** stubbornly refuse to do something.
– DERIVATIVES **digger** n.
– ORIGIN perh. from Old English, 'ditch'.

digest • v. /dy-**jest**/ **1** break down food in the stomach and intestines into substances that can be absorbed by the body. **2** think about and absorb information. • n. /**dy**-jest/ a summary or collection of material or information.
– DERIVATIVES **digestible** adj.
– ORIGIN Latin *digerere* 'distribute'.

digestion • n. **1** the process of digesting food. **2** a person's capacity to digest food: *he suffered with his digestion.*

digestive • adj. relating to the digestion of food. • n. Brit. a semi-sweet wholemeal biscuit.

digit /di-jit/ • n. **1** any of the numerals from 0 to 9. **2** a finger or thumb.
– ORIGIN Latin *digitus* 'finger, toe'.

digital • adj. **1** relating to information represented as a series of binary digits, as in a computer. **2** relating to computer technology: *the digital revolution.* **3** (of a clock or watch) showing the time by displaying numbers electronically. **4** relating to a finger or fingers.
– DERIVATIVES **digitally** adv.

digital audiotape • n. audio tape on which sound is recorded digitally.

digital camera • n. a camera which produces digital images that can be stored in a computer and displayed on screen.

digitalis /di-ji-**tay**-liss/ • n. a drug prepared from foxglove leaves, used to stimulate the heart muscle.
– ORIGIN Latin genus name of the foxglove.

digitalize (or **digitalise**) • v. (**digitalizes, digitalizing, digitalized**) = DIGITIZE.
– DERIVATIVES **digitalization** n.

digitize (or **digitise**) • v. (**digitizes, digitizing, digitized**) convert pictures or sound into a digital form that can be processed by a computer.
– DERIVATIVES **digitization** n. **digitizer** n.

dignified • adj. having a serious manner that is worthy of respect.

dignify • v. (**dignifies, dignifying, dignified**) make impressive or worthy of respect: *they dignified their departure with a ceremony.*
– ORIGIN Latin *dignificare.*

dignitary /**dig**-ni-tuh-ri/ • n. (pl. **dignitaries**) a high-ranking person.

dignity • n. (pl. **dignities**) **1** the state of being worthy of respect. **2** a calm or serious manner. **3** a sense of pride in

yourself: *it was beneath his dignity to shout.*
– ORIGIN Latin *dignitas.*

digraph /**dy**-grahf/ • n. a combination of two letters representing one sound, as in *ph.*

digress /dy-**gress**/ • v. leave the main subject temporarily in speech or writing.
– DERIVATIVES **digression** n. **digressive** adj.
– ORIGIN Latin *digredi* 'step away'.

dihedral /dy-**hee**-druhl/ • adj. having or contained by two plane faces.

dike[1] • n. var. of DYKE[1].

dike[2] • n. var. of DYKE[2].

diktat /**dik**-tat/ • n. a decree imposed by someone in power without popular consent.
– ORIGIN German.

dilapidated /di-**lap**-i-day-tid/ • adj. in a state of disrepair or ruin.
– DERIVATIVES **dilapidation** n.
– ORIGIN Latin *dilapidare* 'demolish'.

dilate /dy-**layt**/ • v. (**dilates, dilating, dilated**) make or become wider, larger, or more open.
– DERIVATIVES **dilation** n. **dilator** n.
– ORIGIN Latin *dilatare* 'spread out'.

dilatory /**di**-luh-tri/ • adj. **1** slow to act. **2** intended to cause delay.
– DERIVATIVES **dilatoriness** n.
– ORIGIN Latin *dilatorius.*

dildo • n. (pl. **dildos** or **dildoes**) an object shaped like an erect penis, used for sexual stimulation.

dilemma /di-**lem**-muh/ • n. **1** a situation in which a difficult choice has to be made between alternatives that are equally undesirable. **2** informal a difficult situation or problem.
– ORIGIN Greek.

dilettante /di-li-**tan**-tay/ • n. (pl. **dilettanti** /di-li-**tan**-ti/ or **dilettantes**) a person who dabbles in a subject for enjoyment but without serious study.
– DERIVATIVES **dilettantish** adj. **dilettantism** n.
– ORIGIN Italian, 'person loving the arts'.

diligent • adj. careful and conscientious in carrying out a task or duties.
– DERIVATIVES **diligence** n. **diligently** adv.
– ORIGIN Latin *diligens.*

dill • n. a herb used in cookery or for medicinal purposes.
– ORIGIN Old English.

dilly-dally • v. (**dilly-dallies, dilly-dallying, dilly-dallied**) informal dawdle or be indecisive.
– ORIGIN from DALLY.

dilute /dy-**lyoot**/ • v. (**dilutes, diluting, diluted**) **1** make a liquid thinner or

weaker by adding water or another solvent. **2** weaken something by changing it or adding other things. •adj. /also dy-lyoot/ (of a liquid) containing little dissolved matter; weak.
– DERIVATIVES **dilution** n. **dilutive** adj.
– ORIGIN Latin *diluere* 'wash away'.

dim •adj. (**dimmer, dimmest**) **1** not bright or well lit. **2** made difficult to see by darkness or distance: *dim shapes of men passed to and fro.* **3** (of the eyes) not able to see clearly. **4** not clearly remembered. **5** informal stupid. •v. (**dims, dimming, dimmed**) make or become dim.
– PHRASES **take a dim view of** regard with disapproval.
– DERIVATIVES **dimly** adv. **dimmable** adj. **dimness** n.
– ORIGIN Old English.

dime /dym/ •n. N. Amer. a ten-cent coin.
– ORIGIN Old French *disme* 'tenth part'.

dimension /di-men-sh'n/ •n. **1** a measurable extent, such as length, breadth, or height. **2** an aspect or feature: *we modern types lack a spiritual dimension.*
– DERIVATIVES **dimensional** adj. **dimensionally** adv.
– ORIGIN Latin.

diminish •v. make or become smaller, weaker, or less.
– ORIGIN Latin *deminuere.*

diminuendo /di-min-yoo-en-doh/ •adv. & adj. Music with a decrease in loudness.
– ORIGIN Italian, 'diminishing'.

diminution /di-mi-nyoo-sh'n/ •n. a reduction in size, extent, or importance.

diminutive /di-min-yuh-tiv/ •adj. **1** extremely or unusually small. **2** (of a word, name, or suffix) used to convey smallness (e.g. *-let* in *booklet*). •n. a shortened form of a name, used informally.
– ORIGIN Latin *diminutivus.*

dimmer (also **dimmer switch**) •n. a device for varying the brightness of an electric light.

dimple •n. **1** a small depression formed in the fleshy part of the cheeks when someone smiles. **2** any small depression in a surface. •v. (**dimples, dimpling, dimpled**) produce a dimple or dimples in the surface of.
– ORIGIN Germanic.

dimwit •n. informal a stupid person.
– DERIVATIVES **dim-witted** adj.

din •n. a prolonged loud and unpleasant noise. •v. (**dins, dinning, dinned**) (**din something into someone**) repeat information constantly in order to make someone remember it.

– ORIGIN Old English.

dinar /dee-nar/ •n. the basic unit of money of Bosnia, the Union of Serbia and Montenegro, and some Middle Eastern and North African countries.
– ORIGIN Arabic and Persian.

dine •v. (**dines, dining, dined**) **1** eat dinner. **2** (**dine out on**) regularly entertain friends with an amusing story.
– ORIGIN Old French *disner.*

diner •n. **1** a person eating a meal in a restaurant. **2** a dining car on a train. **3** N. Amer. a small roadside restaurant.

dinette /dy-net/ •n. a small room or part of a room used for eating meals.

ding-dong •n. Brit. informal a fierce argument or fight.
– ORIGIN from the sound of a bell.

dinghy /ding-gi, ding-i/ •n. (pl. **dinghies**) **1** a small open sailing boat. **2** a small inflatable rubber boat.
– ORIGIN Hindi, 'rowing boat'.

dingle •n. literary a deep wooded valley.

dingo /ding-goh/ •n. (pl. **dingoes** or **dingos**) a wild Australian dog.
– ORIGIN from an Aboriginal language.

dingy /din-ji/ •adj. (**dingier, dingiest**) gloomy and drab.
– DERIVATIVES **dinginess** n.
– ORIGIN perh. from Old English, 'dung'.

dining car •n. a railway carriage equipped as a restaurant.

dining room •n. a room in which meals are eaten.

dinkum /ding-kuhm/ •adj. Austral./NZ informal genuine.
– PHRASES **fair dinkum** used for emphasis or to query whether something is true.

dinky •adj. (**dinkier, dinkiest**) Brit. informal attractively small and neat.
– ORIGIN Scots and northern English *dink* 'neat, trim'.

dinner •n. **1** the main meal of the day, eaten either around midday or in the evening. **2** a formal evening meal.
– ORIGIN Old French *disner* 'to dine'.

dinner jacket •n. a man's short jacket, worn with a bow tie for formal evening occasions.

dinosaur /dy-nuh-sor/ •n. **1** an extinct reptile of the Mesozoic era, often reaching an enormous size. **2** a person or thing that is outdated.
– ORIGIN from Greek *deinos* 'terrible' + *sauros* 'lizard'.

dint •n. (in phr. **by dint of**) by means of.
– ORIGIN Old English, 'a blow'.

diocese /dy-uh-siss/ •n. (pl. **dioceses** /dy-uh-seez, dy-uh-seez-iz/) (in the Christian church) a district for which a bishop is responsible.
– DERIVATIVES **diocesan** /dy-oss-i-z'n/ adj.

– ORIGIN Latin *diocesis*.

diode /dy-ohd/ •n. a semiconductor device with two terminals, allowing the flow of current in one direction only.
– ORIGIN from **DI-** + **ELECTRODE**.

Dionysian /dy-uh-**niss**-i-uhn/ (also **Dionysiac** /dy-uh-**niss**-i-ak/)
•adj. 1 relating to Dionysus, the Greek god of fertility and wine. 2 wild and uninhibited.

dioptric •adj. relating to the refraction of light.

diorama /dy-uh-**rah**-muh/ •n. a model representing a scene with three-dimensional figures against a painted background.
– ORIGIN French.

diorite /dy-uh-ryt/ •n. a speckled, coarse-grained igneous rock.
– ORIGIN French.

dioxide /dy-**ok**-syd/ •n. Chem. an oxide with two atoms of oxygen to one of a metal or other element.

dioxin /dy-**ok**-sin/ •n. a highly poisonous organic compound produced as a by-product in some manufacturing processes.

dip •v. (**dips, dipping, dipped**) 1 (**dip something in/into**) put or lower something briefly in or into. 2 sink, drop, or slope downwards. 3 (of a level or amount) temporarily become lower or smaller. 4 lower briefly: *the plane dipped its wings.* 5 (**dip into**) reach into a bag or container to take something out. 6 (**dip into**) spend some of your financial resources. •n. 1 an act of dipping. 2 a thick sauce in which pieces of food are dipped before eating. 3 a brief swim. 4 a brief downward slope followed by an upward one.
– ORIGIN Old English.

diphtheria /dip-**theer**-i-uh/ •n. a serious infectious disease causing inflammation of the mucous membranes, especially in the throat.
– ORIGIN Greek *diphthera* 'skin, hide'.

diphthong /dif-thong, dip-thong/ •n. a sound formed by the combination of two vowels in a single syllable (as in *coin*).
– ORIGIN from Greek *di-* 'twice' + *phthongos* 'sound'.

diploid /dip-loyd/ •adj. (of a cell or nucleus) containing two complete sets of chromosomes, one from each parent. Compare with **HAPLOID**.
– ORIGIN Greek *diplous* 'double'.

diploma •n. a certificate awarded by a school or college for successfully completing a course of study.
– ORIGIN Greek, 'folded paper'.

diplomacy •n. 1 the profession or skill

of managing international relations. 2 skill and tact in dealing with people.
– ORIGIN French *diplomatie*.

diplomat •n. an official representing a country abroad.

diplomatic •adj. 1 relating to diplomacy. 2 tactful.
– DERIVATIVES **diplomatically** adv.

dipole /dy-pohl/ •n. 1 Physics a pair of equal and oppositely charged or magnetized poles separated by a distance. 2 an aerial consisting of a horizontal metal rod with a connecting wire at its centre.
– DERIVATIVES **dipolar** adj.

dipper •n. 1 a songbird able to dive into fast-flowing streams to feed. 2 a ladle.

dippy •adj. informal foolish or eccentric.

dipsomania /dip-suh-**may**-ni-uh/
•n. alcoholism.
– DERIVATIVES **dipsomaniac** n.
– ORIGIN Greek *dipsa* 'thirst'.

dipstick •n. a rod for measuring the depth of a liquid.

diptych /**dip**-tik/ •n. a painting on two hinged wooden panels, forming an altarpiece.
– ORIGIN Greek *diptukha* 'pair of writing tablets'.

dire •adj. 1 very serious or urgent. 2 Brit. informal of a very poor quality.
– ORIGIN Latin *dirus* 'fearful'.

direct /di-rekt, dy-rekt/ •adj. 1 going from one place to another without changing direction or stopping. 2 with nothing or no one in between: *he relied on direct contact with the leaders.* 3 frank. 4 clear and explicit. •adv. in a direct way or by a direct route. •v. 1 aim towards: *he should have directed his criticism at the press.* 2 control the operations of. 3 supervise and control a film, play, or other production. 4 tell or show someone the way. 5 give an order to.
– DERIVATIVES **directness** n.
– ORIGIN Latin *directus*.

direct action •n. the use of public forms of protest rather than negotiation to achieve your aims.

direct current •n. an electric current flowing in one direction only. Compare with **ALTERNATING CURRENT**.

direct debit •n. Brit. an arrangement with a bank that allows money to be taken from a person's account to pay a particular person or organization.

direction /di-rek-sh'n, dy-**rek**-sh'n/
•n. 1 a course along which someone or something moves, or which leads to a destination. 2 a point to or from which a person or thing moves or faces: *a house with views in all directions.* 3 the

management or guidance of someone or something. **4** (**directions**) instructions on how to reach a destination or how to do something.

directional • adj. **1** relating to or indicating direction. **2** operating or sending radio signals in one direction only: *a directional microphone.*

directive • n. an official instruction.

directly • adv. **1** in a direct way. **2** exactly in a particular position: *the house directly opposite.* **3** immediately. • conj. Brit. as soon as.

direct mail • n. advertising material sent to possible customers without them having asked for it.

direct object • n. a person or thing that is directly affected by the action of a transitive verb (e.g. *the dog* in *I fed the dog*).

director • n. **1** a person who is in charge of a department, organization, or activity. **2** a member of the managing board of a business. **3** a person who directs a film, play, etc.
– DERIVATIVES **directorial** adj. **directorship** n.

directorate • n. **1** the board of directors of a company. **2** a section of a government department which is in charge of a particular activity.

director general • n. (pl. **directors general**) esp. Brit. the chief executive of a large organization.

directory • n. (pl. **directories**) a book listing people or organizations with details such as addresses and telephone numbers.

direct speech • n. the reporting of speech by repeating the actual words of a speaker, for example *'I'm going', she said.* Contrasted with REPORTED SPEECH.

direct tax • n. a tax, such as income tax, which is charged on the income or profits of the person who pays it.

dirge /derj/ • n. **1** a lament for the dead. **2** a mournful song or piece of music.
– ORIGIN Latin *dirige!* 'direct!', the first word of a psalm used in a religious service for the dead.

dirham /dee-ruhm/ • n. the basic unit of money of Morocco and the United Arab Emirates.
– ORIGIN Arabic.

dirigible /di-rij-i-b'l/ • n. an airship.
– ORIGIN Latin *dirigere* 'to direct'.

dirk /derk/ • n. a short dagger formerly carried by Scottish Highlanders.

dirndl /dern-d'l/ (also **dirndl skirt**) • n. a full, wide skirt gathered into a tight waistband.
– ORIGIN German dialect, 'little girl'.

dirt • n. **1** a substance that makes something unclean. **2** soil or earth. **3** informal excrement. **4** informal scandalous or damaging information: *what's the dirt on Jack?*
– ORIGIN Old Norse.

dirt cheap • adj. & adv. very cheap.

dirt track • n. a racing track made of earth or rolled cinders.

dirty • adj. (**dirtier**, **dirtiest**) **1** covered or marked with dirt; not clean. **2** obscene. **3** dishonest or dishonourable. **4** (of weather) rough and unpleasant.
• adv. Brit. informal used for emphasis: *a dirty great stone.* • v. (**dirties**, **dirtying**, **dirtied**) make dirty.
– PHRASES **do the dirty on** Brit. informal cheat or betray. **play dirty** informal act in a dishonest or unfair way.

dirty look • n. informal a look expressing disapproval, disgust, or anger.

dirty weekend • n. Brit. informal a weekend spent away with a lover.

dirty word • n. a thing regarded with dislike: *VAT is a dirty word among small businesses.*

dirty work • n. unpleasant or dishonest activities that are passed to someone else.

dis- • prefix expressing **1** not; the reverse of: *disadvantage.* **2** separation or removal: *disperse.*
– ORIGIN Latin.

disability • n. (pl. **disabilities**) **1** a physical or mental condition that limits a person's movements, senses, or activities. **2** a disadvantage.

disable • v. (**disables**, **disabling**, **disabled**) **1** (of a disease, injury, or accident) limit someone in their movements, senses, or activities. **2** put out of action.
– DERIVATIVES **disablement** n.

disabled • adj. having a physical or mental disability.

disabuse /diss-uh-byooz/
• v. (**disabuses**, **disabusing**, **disabused**) persuade someone that an idea or belief is mistaken: *he disabused her of this idea.*

disadvantage • n. something that makes success or progress less likely or causes a problem. • v. (**disadvantages**, **disadvantaging**, **disadvantaged**) **1** put in an unfavourable position. **2** (as adj. **disadvantaged**) having less money and fewer opportunities than most people.
– DERIVATIVES **disadvantageous** adj.

disaffected • adj. dissatisfied with an organization, group, etc. and no longer loyal to it: *disaffected Labour voters.*
– DERIVATIVES **disaffection** n.

disagree • v. (**disagrees**, **disagreeing**,

disagreed) 1 have a different opinion. **2** be inconsistent: *results which disagree with the findings reported so far.* **3** (**disagree with**) make slightly ill.
– DERIVATIVES **disagreement** n.

disagreeable • adj. **1** unpleasant. **2** bad-tempered.

disallow • v. declare to be invalid.

disappear • v. **1** cease to be visible. **2** cease to exist.
– DERIVATIVES **disappearance** n.

disappoint • v. **1** fail to fulfil someone's hopes. **2** prevent hopes from becoming a reality.
– DERIVATIVES **disappointing** adj.
– ORIGIN Old French *desappointer*.

disappointed • adj. sad or displeased because your hopes have not been fulfilled.

disappointment • n. **1** sadness or displeasure felt when your hopes are not fulfilled. **2** a person or thing that causes disappointment.

disapprobation /diss-ap-ruh-**bay**-sh'n/ • n. strong disapproval.

disapprove • v. (**disapproves, disapproving, disapproved**) think that someone or something is wrong or bad: *he disapproved of gambling.*
– DERIVATIVES **disapproval** n.

disarm • v. **1** take a weapon or weapons away from. **2** win over a hostile or suspicious person. **3** remove the fuse from a bomb.

disarmament /diss-**arm**-uh-muhnt/ • n. the reduction or withdrawal of military forces and weapons.

disarming • adj. making people feel less hostile or suspicious.
– DERIVATIVES **disarmingly** adv.

disarrange • v. (**disarranges, disarranging, disarranged**) make untidy or disordered.

disarray • n. a state of disorder or confusion.

disassemble • v. (**disassembles, disassembling, disassembled**) take to pieces.

disassociate • v. = DISSOCIATE.

disaster • n. **1** a sudden accident or a natural catastrophe that causes great damage or loss of life. **2** a sudden misfortune: *a string of personal disasters.*
– ORIGIN Italian *disastro* 'unlucky event'.

disastrous • adj. **1** causing great damage. **2** informal very unsuccessful.
– DERIVATIVES **disastrously** adv.

> ✓ Although **disastrous** is related to *disaster*, it is spelled **-str-** in the middle.

disavow • v. deny any responsibility or support for.

– DERIVATIVES **disavowal** n.

disband • v. (with reference to an organized group) break up or cause to break up: *the team was disbanded.*

disbar • v. (**disbars, disbarring, disbarred**) expel a barrister from the Bar.

disbelief • n. inability or refusal to accept that something is true or real.

disbelieve • v. (**disbelieves, disbelieving, disbelieved**) be unable to believe someone or something.

disburse /diss-**berss**/ • v. (**disburses, disbursing, disbursed**) pay out money from a fund.
– DERIVATIVES **disbursement** n.
– ORIGIN Old French *desbourser*.

disc (US also **disk**) • n. **1** a flat, thin, round object. **2** (**disk**) an information storage device for a computer, on which data is stored either magnetically or optically. **3** a layer of cartilage which separates vertebrae in the spine. **4** dated a gramophone record.
– ORIGIN Greek *diskos* 'discus'.

> ✓ Generally speaking, **disc** is spelled with a **c** at the end (the spelling **disk** is American). However, the spelling for computer-related senses is usually **disk**: *floppy disk.*

discard • v. /diss-**kard**/ get rid of a useless or unwanted item. • n. /**diss**-kard/ a discarded item.
– ORIGIN from DIS- + CARD¹.

discern /di-**sern**/ • v. **1** recognize or become aware of. **2** see or hear with difficulty.
– DERIVATIVES **discernible** adj.
– ORIGIN Latin *discernere*.

discerning • adj. having or showing good judgement.
– DERIVATIVES **discernment** n.

discharge • v. /diss-**charj**/ (**discharges, discharging, discharged**) **1** officially tell someone that they can or must leave: *he was discharged from the RAF.* **2** send out a liquid, gas, or other substance. **3** fire a gun or missile. **4** fulfil a responsibility. **5** Physics release or neutralize the electric charge of a battery or electric field. • n. /**diss**-charj, diss-**charj**/ **1** the action of discharging. **2** a substance that has been discharged. **3** a flow of electricity through the air or other gas.
– ORIGIN Old French *descharger* 'unload'.

disciple /di-**sy**-p'l/ • n. **1** a follower of Jesus during his life, especially one of the twelve Apostles. **2** a follower of a teacher, leader, or philosopher.
– ORIGIN Latin *discipulus* 'learner'.

disciplinarian /diss-i-pli-**nair**-i-uhn/

• **n.** a person who enforces firm discipline.

disciplinary /diss-i-plin-uh-ri/ • **adj.** relating to or enforcing discipline.

discipline /diss-i-plin/ • **n. 1** the training of people to obey rules or a code of behaviour. **2** controlled behaviour resulting from such training: *he was able to maintain discipline among his men.* **3** a branch of academic study.
• **v. (disciplines, disciplining, disciplined) 1** train to be obedient or self-controlled. **2** punish formally for an offence. **3** (as adj. **disciplined**) behaving in a controlled way.
– ORIGIN Latin *disciplina* 'instruction'.

disc jockey • **n.** a DJ.

disclaim • **v.** deny responsibility for or knowledge of something.

disclaimer • **n.** a statement denying responsibility for something.

disclose • **v. (discloses, disclosing, disclosed) 1** make secret or new information known. **2** allow to be seen.

disclosure • **n. 1** the disclosing of new or secret information. **2** a fact that is made known.

disco • **n.** (pl. **discos**) a club or party at which people dance to pop music.
– ORIGIN short for **DISCOTHEQUE**.

discolour (US **discolor**) • **v.** change to a different and unattractive colour.
– DERIVATIVES **discoloration** (also **discolouration**) n.

discomfit /diss-kum-fit/ • **v. (discomfits, discomfiting, discomfited)** make uneasy or embarrassed.
– DERIVATIVES **discomfiture** n.
– ORIGIN Old French *desconfire* 'defeat'.

discomfort • **n. 1** slight pain. **2** slight anxiety or embarrassment. • **v.** cause discomfort to.

discompose • **v. (discomposes, discomposing, discomposed)** disturb or agitate.
– DERIVATIVES **discomposure** n.

disconcert /diss-kuhn-sert/ • **v.** make someone feel anxious, uneasy, or confused.
– ORIGIN former French *desconcerter*.

disconnect • **v. 1** break the connection between. **2** detach an electrical device from a power supply.
– DERIVATIVES **disconnection** n.

disconnected • **adj.** (of speech, thoughts, etc.) not having a logical sequence.

disconsolate /diss-kon-suh-luht/ • **adj.** very unhappy and unable to be comforted.

discontent • **n.** lack of contentment or satisfaction.

– DERIVATIVES **discontented** adj. **discontentment** n.

discontinue • **v. (discontinues, discontinuing, discontinued)** stop doing, providing, or making: *he discontinued his visits.*
– DERIVATIVES **discontinuation** n.

discontinuous /diss-kuhn-tin-yoo-uhss/ • **adj.** having intervals or gaps; not continuous.
– DERIVATIVES **discontinuity** n. (pl. **discontinuities**).

discord • **n. 1** lack of agreement or harmony: *those who promote racial discord.* **2** lack of harmony between musical notes sounding together.
– ORIGIN Latin *discors* 'discordant'.

discordant • **adj. 1** not in harmony or agreement. **2** (of a sound) harsh and unpleasant.
– DERIVATIVES **discordance** n.

discotheque /diss-kuh-tek/ • **n.** a disco.
– ORIGIN French.

discount • **n.** /diss-kownt/ a deduction from the usual cost of something.
• **v.** /diss-kownt/ **1** deduct a discount from the usual price of something. **2** choose not to believe something because it seems unlikely: *she'd heard rumours, but discounted them.*

discourage • **v. (discourages, discouraging, discouraged) 1** cause someone to lose confidence or enthusiasm. **2** try to persuade someone not to do something: *we want to discourage children from smoking.*
– DERIVATIVES **discouragement** n.
– ORIGIN Old French *descouragier*.

discourse • **n.** /diss-korss/ **1** written or spoken communication or debate. **2** a formal discussion of a topic.
• **v.** /diss-korss/ **(discourses, discoursing, discoursed)** speak or write about a topic authoritatively.
– ORIGIN Latin *discursus* 'running to and fro'.

discourteous • **adj.** rude and without consideration for other people.

discourtesy • **n.** (pl. **discourtesies**) **1** rude and inconsiderate behaviour. **2** a rude or inconsiderate act or remark.

discover • **v. (discovers, discovering, discovered) 1** find unexpectedly or during a search. **2** become aware of a fact or situation. **3** be the first to find or observe a place, substance, or scientific phenomenon.
– DERIVATIVES **discoverer** n.

discovery • **n.** (pl. **discoveries**) **1** the action of discovering something. **2** a person or thing discovered.

discredit • **v. (discredits, discrediting, discredited) 1** harm a person's good reputation. **2** make something seem false or unreliable. • n. loss or lack of reputation or respect.

discreditable • adj. bringing discredit; shameful.

discreet • adj. careful to keep something secret or to avoid causing someone embarrassment.
– DERIVATIVES **discreetly** adv.
– ORIGIN Old French *discret*.

> **USAGE:** The words **discrete** and **discreet** are often confused. **Discreet** means 'careful to keep something secret or avoid causing embarrassment' (*we made some discreet inquiries*), while **discrete** means 'separate' (*a number of discrete categories*).

discrepancy /diss-krep-uhn-si/ • n. (pl. **discrepancies**) a difference between facts or figures that should be the same.
– ORIGIN Latin *discrepantia*.

discrete • adj. individually separate and distinct.
– DERIVATIVES **discretely** adv.
– ORIGIN Latin *discretus* 'separate'.

discretion • n. **1** the quality of being discreet. **2** the freedom to decide what should be done in a particular situation: *booksellers may offer discounts at their own discretion.*

discretionary • adj. done or used according to a person's judgement.

discriminate /diss-krim-i-nayt/ • v. (**discriminates, discriminating, discriminated**) **1** recognize a difference between one thing and another. **2** treat different categories of people unfairly on the grounds of race, sex, or age.
– ORIGIN Latin *discriminare*.

discriminating • adj. having or showing good taste or judgement.

discrimination • n. **1** unfair treatment of different categories of people on the grounds of race, sex, or age. **2** recognition of the difference between one thing and another. **3** good judgement or taste.

discriminatory • adj. showing discrimination or prejudice.

discursive /diss-ker-siv/ • adj. moving from subject to subject.
– ORIGIN Latin *discursivus* 'running to and fro'.

discus • n. (pl. **discuses**) a heavy disc thrown in athletic contests.
– ORIGIN Greek *diskos*.

discuss • v. **1** talk about something so as to reach a decision. **2** talk or write about a topic in detail.
– ORIGIN Latin *discutere* 'dash to pieces'.

discussion • n. **1** the action of discussing something. **2** a detailed written treatment of a topic .

disdain • n. the feeling that someone or something does not deserve consideration or respect. • v. consider to be unworthy of consideration or respect.
– DERIVATIVES **disdainful** adj. **disdainfully** adv.
– ORIGIN Old French *desdeign*.

disease • n. a disorder in a human, animal, or plant, caused by infection, diet, or by faulty functioning of a process.
– DERIVATIVES **diseased** adj.
– ORIGIN Old French *desaise* 'lack of ease'.

disembark • v. leave a ship, aircraft, or train.
– DERIVATIVES **disembarkation** n.

disembodied • adj. **1** separated from the body, or existing without a body. **2** (of a sound) coming from a person who cannot be seen.

disembowel • v. (**disembowels, disembowelling, disembowelled**; US **disembowels, disemboweling, disemboweled**) cut open and remove the internal organs of.
– DERIVATIVES **disembowelment** n.

disempower • v. (**disempowers, disempowering, disempowered**) make someone less powerful or confident.

disenchant • v. make disillusioned: *those who are disenchanted with science.*
– DERIVATIVES **disenchantment** n.

disenfranchise • v. (**disenfranchises, disenfranchising, disenfranchised**) deprive of a right, especially the right to vote.

disengage • v. (**disengages, disengaging, disengaged**) **1** release or detach: *I disengaged his hand from mine.* **2** remove troops from an area of conflict.
– DERIVATIVES **disengagement** n.

disentangle • v. (**disentangles, disentangling, disentangled**) free someone or something from something they are entangled with.

disestablish • v. put an end to the official status of a national Church.
– DERIVATIVES **disestablishment** n.

disfavour (US **disfavor**) • n. **1** disapproval or dislike. **2** the state of being disliked.

disfigure • v. (**disfigures, disfiguring, disfigured**) spoil the appearance of.
– DERIVATIVES **disfigurement** n.

disgorge • v. (**disgorges, disgorging, disgorged**) **1** cause to pour out: *a bus disgorged a group of youths.* **2** bring up food.
– ORIGIN Old French *desgorger*.

disgrace • n. **1** the loss of other people's respect as the result of behaving badly.

2 a shameful person or thing: *he's a disgrace to the legal profession.* • v. (**disgraces, disgracing, disgraced**) bring disgrace on.

disgraceful • adj. shockingly unacceptable.
– DERIVATIVES **disgracefully** adv.

disgruntled • adj. angry or dissatisfied.
– DERIVATIVES **disgruntlement** n.
– ORIGIN from dialect *gruntle* 'grumble'.

disguise • v. (**disguises, disguising, disguised**) **1** change the appearance or nature of someone or something to prevent recognition: *he was disguised as a priest.* **2** hide a feeling or situation. • n. **1** a means of disguising your identity. **2** the state of being disguised.
– ORIGIN Old French *desguisier.*

disgust • n. revulsion or strong disapproval. • v. cause disgust in.
– ORIGIN from **DIS-** + Latin *gustus* 'taste'.

disgusting • adj. causing revulsion or strong disapproval.

dish • n. **1** a shallow container for cooking or serving food. **2** (**the dishes**) all the crockery and utensils used for a meal. **3** a particular kind of food: *a classic Italian dish.* **4** a shallow concave object. **5** informal an attractive person. • v. **1** (**dish something out/up**) put food on to a plate or plates before a meal. **2** (**dish something out**) distribute something in a casual or random way.
– ORIGIN Greek *diskos* 'discus'.

disharmony • n. lack of harmony.

dishearten • v. make someone lose determination or confidence.
– DERIVATIVES **disheartening** adj.

dishevelled /di-shev-v'ld/ (US **disheveled**) • adj. very untidy: *his dirty and dishevelled appearance.*
– ORIGIN Old French *deschevele.*

dishonest • adj. not honest, trustworthy, or sincere.
– DERIVATIVES **dishonestly** adv. **dishonesty** n.

dishonour (US **dishonor**) • n. a state of shame or disgrace. • v. **1** bring shame or disgrace to. **2** fail to keep an agreement.

dishonourable (US **dishonorable**) • adj. bringing shame or disgrace.

dishwasher • n. a machine for washing dishes automatically.

dishy • adj. (**dishier, dishiest**) informal, esp. Brit. sexually attractive.

disillusion • n. disappointment from discovering that your beliefs are mistaken or unrealistic. • v. make someone realize that a belief they hold is mistaken or unrealistic.
– DERIVATIVES **disillusioned** adj. **disillusionment** n.

disincentive • n. a factor that discourages a particular action: *rising house prices are a disincentive to development.*

disinclination • n. a reluctance to do something.

disinclined • adj. reluctant; unwilling.

disinfect • v. clean with disinfectant in order to destroy bacteria.
– DERIVATIVES **disinfection** n.

disinfectant • n. a chemical liquid that destroys bacteria.

disinformation • n. information which is intended to mislead.

disingenuous /diss-in-jen-yoo-uhss/ • adj. not sincere, especially in pretending ignorance about something.
– DERIVATIVES **disingenuously** adv.

disinherit • v. (**disinherits, disinheriting, disinherited**) prevent a person who was your heir from inheriting your property.

disintegrate • v. (**disintegrates, disintegrating, disintegrated**) break up into small parts as a result of impact or decay.
– DERIVATIVES **disintegration** n.

disinter /diss-in-ter/ • v. (**disinters, disinterring, disinterred**) dig up something buried.

disinterest • n. **1** impartiality. **2** lack of interest.

disinterested • adj. **1** not influenced by personal feelings; impartial. **2** not interested.

> **USAGE:** Strictly speaking, **disinterested** should only be used to mean 'impartial' (as in *a banker is under an obligation to give disinterested advice*), and should not be used to mean 'not interested'. This second meaning is very common, but it should be avoided in careful writing as it is not accepted by everyone.

disjointed • adj. lacking a logical sequence or connection; disconnected.

disjunction • n. a difference between things expected to be similar.

disk • n. US & Computing = **DISC**.

disk drive • n. a device which allows a computer to read from and write on to computer disks.

diskette • n. = **FLOPPY**.

dislike • v. (**dislike, disliking, disliked**) feel distaste for or hostility towards. • n. **1** a feeling of distaste or hostility. **2** a thing that is disliked.
– DERIVATIVES **dislikable** (also **dislikeable**) adj.

dislocate /diss-luh-kayt/ • v. (**dislocates, dislocating, dislocated**) **1** displace a

bone from its proper position in a joint.
2 disrupt.
– DERIVATIVES **dislocation** n.

dislodge • v. (**dislodges, dislodging, dislodged**) remove from a fixed position.

disloyal • adj. not loyal or faithful.
– DERIVATIVES **disloyalty** n.

dismal • adj. **1** causing or showing gloom or depression. **2** informal shockingly bad.
– DERIVATIVES **dismally** adv.
– ORIGIN from Latin *dies mali* 'evil days'.

dismantle • v. (**dismantles, dismantling, dismantled**) take to pieces.
– DERIVATIVES **dismantlement** n.
– ORIGIN Old French *desmanteler*.

dismay • n. discouragement and distress resulting from an unpleasant surprise.
• v. cause someone to feel dismay.
– ORIGIN Old French.

dismember • v. (**dismembers, dismembering, dismembered**) **1** tear or cut the limbs from a person or animal.
2 divide up a territory or organization.
– DERIVATIVES **dismemberment** n.
– ORIGIN Old French *desmembrer*.

dismiss • v. **1** order or allow to leave.
2 order an employee to leave a job.
3 treat as unworthy of consideration.
4 refuse to allow a legal case to continue. **5** Cricket end the innings of a batsman or side.
– DERIVATIVES **dismissal** n.
– ORIGIN Latin *dimittere* 'send away'.

dismissive • adj. showing that you feel something is not worth consideration.
– DERIVATIVES **dismissively** adv.

dismount • v. get off or down from a horse or bicycle.

disobedient • adj. failing or refusing to be obedient.
– DERIVATIVES **disobedience** n.

disobey • v. fail or refuse to obey.

disorder • n. **1** a lack of order; confusion.
2 the breakdown of peaceful and law-abiding behaviour. **3** an illness.
• v. (**disorders, disordering, disordered**) (usu. as adj. **disordered**) bring disorder to.

disorderly • adj. **1** disorganized or untidy. **2** involving a breakdown of peaceful and law-abiding behaviour.

disorganized (or **disorganised**)
• adj. **1** not properly planned and controlled. **2** not able to plan your activities efficiently.
– DERIVATIVES **disorganization** n.

disorient • v. = DISORIENTATE.

disorientate • v. (**disorientates, disorientating, disorientated**) Brit. cause someone to lose their bearings or feel confused.

– DERIVATIVES **disorientation** n.

disown • v. refuse to have anything further to do with someone.

disparage /di-spa-rij/ • v. (**disparages, disparaging, disparaged**) talk about someone or something in a critical or negative way.
– DERIVATIVES **disparagement** n.
– ORIGIN Old French *desparagier* 'marry someone of unequal rank'.

disparate /diss-puh-ruht/ • adj. **1** very different from one another. **2** containing elements very different from one another: *a culturally disparate country*.
– ORIGIN Latin *disparatus* 'separated'.

disparity • n. (pl. **disparities**) a great difference.

dispassionate • adj. not influenced by strong emotion; rational and impartial.
– DERIVATIVES **dispassionately** adv.

dispatch (Brit. also **despatch**) • v. **1** send off to a destination, especially for a particular purpose. **2** send a letter, parcel, etc. somewhere. **3** deal with a task or opponent quickly and efficiently.
4 kill. • n. **1** the action of dispatching.
2 an official report on the latest situation in state or military affairs. **3** a report sent in from abroad by a journalist. **4** promptness and efficiency: *proceed with dispatch.*
– DERIVATIVES **dispatcher** n.
– ORIGIN Italian *dispacciare* or Spanish *despachar* 'expedite'.

dispel • v. (**dispels, dispelling, dispelled**) make a doubt, feeling, or belief disappear.
– ORIGIN Latin *dispellere* 'drive apart'.

dispensable • adj. able to be replaced or done without.

dispensary • n. (pl. **dispensaries**) a room where medicines are prepared and provided.

dispensation • n. **1** permission to be exempt from a rule or usual require-ment. **2** the religious or political system existing at a particular time: *the capitalist dispensation*. **3** the action of dispensing something.

dispense • v. (**dispenses, dispensing, dispensed**) **1** distribute or supply to a number of people. **2** (of a chemist) prepare and supply medicine according to a doctor's prescription. **3** (**dispense with**) get rid of or manage without.
– DERIVATIVES **dispenser** n.
– ORIGIN Latin *dispensare* 'continue to weigh out'.

dispensing optician • n. see OPTICIAN.

disperse • v. (**disperses, dispersing, dispersed**) **1** go in different directions: *the crowd dispersed*. **2** spread over a wide area. **3** (of gas, smoke, etc.) thin out and

eventually disappear. **4** Physics separate light into constituents with different wavelengths.
– DERIVATIVES **dispersal** n. **dispersion** n.
– ORIGIN Latin *dispergere*.

dispirited • adj. discouraged or depressed.
– DERIVATIVES **dispiriting** adj.

displace • v. (**displaces, displacing, displaced**) **1** move from the proper or usual position. **2** take over the position or role of. **3** (especially of a war or natural disaster) force someone to leave their home.

displacement • n. **1** the action of displacing someone or something. **2** the amount by which something is displaced from its position. **3** the volume or weight of water displaced by a floating ship, used as a measure of the ship's size.

display • v. **1** put on show in a noticeable and attractive way. **2** show a quality or feeling. **3** show data or an image on a screen. • n. **1** a show or other event for public entertainment. **2** the action of showing something: *a display of emotion.* **3** objects, data, or images that are displayed. **4** an electronic device for displaying data.
– ORIGIN Old French *despleier* 'unfold'.

displease • v. (**displeases, displeasing, displeased**) annoy or upset.

displeasure • n. annoyance or dissatisfaction.

disport • v. (**disport yourself**) old use enjoy yourself in an unrestrained way.
– ORIGIN Old French *desporter* 'carry away'.

disposable • adj. **1** (of an article) intended to be used once and then thrown away. **2** (of income or financial assets) available for use as required.

disposal • n. the action of disposing of something.
– PHRASES **at someone's disposal** available for someone to use whenever or however they wish.

dispose • v. (**disposes, disposing, disposed**) **1** (**dispose of**) get rid of. **2** make someone likely to do or think something: *I was disposed to quarrel with this.* **3** (as adj. **disposed**) having a specified attitude: *they were favourably disposed towards him.* **4** arrange in a particular position.
– DERIVATIVES **disposer** n.
– ORIGIN Old French *disposer*.

disposition • n. **1** the natural qualities of a person's character: *a lady of a kindly disposition.* **2** an inclination or tendency. **3** the arrangement of something.

dispossess • v. deprive someone of land or property.
– DERIVATIVES **dispossession** n.

disproportion • n. a lack of proportion or equality.
– DERIVATIVES **disproportional** adj. **disproportionally** adv.

disproportionate • adj. too large or too small in comparison with something else.
– DERIVATIVES **disproportionately** adv.

disprove • v. (**disproves, disproving, disproved**) prove to be false.

disputable • adj. open to question.

disputation • n. debate or argument.

disputatious • adj. fond of arguing.

dispute • v. /diss-pyoot/ (**disputes, disputing, disputed**) **1** argue about. **2** question the truth or validity of. **3** compete for. • n. /diss-pyoot, diss-pyoot/ **1** an argument or disagreement. **2** a disagreement between management and employees.
– ORIGIN Latin *disputare* 'to estimate'.

disqualify • v. (**disqualifies, disqualifying, disqualified**) **1** ban someone from a job or activity because of a breach of the law or rules. **2** make someone unsuitable for a job or activity: *a heart complaint disqualified him from military service.*
– DERIVATIVES **disqualification** n.

disquiet • n. a feeling of worry or unease. • v. make someone worried or uneasy.

disquisition /diss-kwi-zi-sh'n/ • n. a long or complex discussion of a subject in speech or writing.
– ORIGIN Latin, 'investigation'.

disregard • v. fail to consider or pay attention to. • n. lack of attention or consideration: *his disregard for truth.*

disrepair • n. a poor condition resulting from neglect.

disreputable • adj. not respectable in appearance or character.

disrepute • n. the state of having a bad reputation.

disrespect • n. lack of respect or courtesy.
– DERIVATIVES **disrespectful** adj. **disrespectfully** adv.

disrobe • v. (**disrobes, disrobing, disrobed**) undress.

disrupt • v. interrupt the normal operation of an activity or process.
– DERIVATIVES **disruption** n.
– ORIGIN Latin *disrumpere* 'break apart'.

disruptive • adj. causing disruption.

dissatisfied • adj. not content or happy.
– DERIVATIVES **dissatisfaction** n.

dissect /di-sekt, dy-sekt/

•v. **1** methodically cut up a body, part, or plant in order to study its internal parts. **2** analyse something in great detail.
– DERIVATIVES **dissection** n.
– ORIGIN Latin *dissecare*.

dissemble •v. (**dissembles, dissembling, dissembled**) hide or disguise your true motives or feelings.
– ORIGIN Latin *dissimulare*.

disseminate •v. (**disseminates, disseminating, disseminated**) spread information widely.
– DERIVATIVES **dissemination** n. **disseminator** n.
– ORIGIN Latin *disseminare* 'scatter'.

dissension •n. disagreement causing trouble within a group.
– ORIGIN Latin.

dissent •v. **1** express disagreement with an official or widely held view. **2** disagree with the doctrine of an established Church. •n. disagreement with an official or widely held view.
– DERIVATIVES **dissenter** n.
– ORIGIN Latin *dissentire*.

dissertation •n. a long essay, especially one written for a university degree or diploma.
– ORIGIN Latin *dissertare* 'continue to discuss'.

disservice •n. a harmful action.

dissident •n. a person who opposes official policy. •adj. opposing official policy.
– DERIVATIVES **dissidence** n.
– ORIGIN Latin *dissidere* 'sit apart'.

dissimilar •adj. not similar; different.
– DERIVATIVES **dissimilarity** n.

dissimulate •v. (**dissimulates, dissimulating, dissimulated**) hide or disguise your thoughts or feelings.
– DERIVATIVES **dissimulation** n.
– ORIGIN Latin *dissimulare*.

dissipate •v. (**dissipates, dissipating, dissipated**) **1** disperse or disappear: *the cloud of smoke dissipated in the air.* **2** waste money, energy, or resources. **3** (as adj. **dissipated**) overindulging in sex and alcohol.
– ORIGIN Latin *dissipare*.

dissipation •n. **1** a lifestyle which is characterized by overindulgence in sex and alcohol. **2** the action of dissipating something.

dissociate •v. (**dissociates, dissociating, dissociated**) **1** disconnect or separate. **2** (**dissociate yourself from**) declare that you are not connected with.
– DERIVATIVES **dissociation** n.
– ORIGIN Latin *dissociare*.

dissolute /diss-uh-loot/ •adj. indulging in immoral activities.
– ORIGIN Latin *dissolutus* 'loose'.

dissolution •n. **1** the formal closing down or ending of an assembly or agreement. **2** the action of dissolving or decomposing. **3** immoral living.

dissolve •v. (**dissolves, dissolving, dissolved**) **1** (of a solid) disperse in a liquid so as to form a solution. **2** close down or end an assembly or agreement. **3** (**dissolve into/in**) give way to strong emotion.
– ORIGIN Latin *dissolvere*.

dissonant •adj. lacking harmony; discordant.
– DERIVATIVES **dissonance** n.
– ORIGIN Latin *dissonare* 'be discordant'.

dissuade /dis-swayd/ •v. (**dissuades, dissuading, dissuaded**) persuade or advise not to do something: *they tried to dissuade him from going.*
– DERIVATIVES **dissuasion** n.
– ORIGIN Latin *dissuadere*.

distaff /diss-tahf/ •n. a stick or spindle on to which wool or flax is wound for spinning.
– PHRASES **distaff side** the female side of a family.
– ORIGIN Old English.

distance •n. **1** the length of the space between two points: *I cycled the short distance home.* **2** the state of being distant. **3** a far-off point or place. **4** an interval of time. **5** the full length or time of a race or other contest.
•v. (**distances, distancing, distanced**) (**distance yourself from**) become less involved with or supportive of.
– ORIGIN Latin *distantia*.

distant •adj. **1** far away in space or time. **2** at a specified distance: *the star is 15 light years distant from Earth.* **3** far apart in resemblance or relationship: *a distant acquaintance.* **4** aloof or reserved.
– DERIVATIVES **distantly** adv.

distaste •n. the feeling that something is unpleasant or offensive.

distasteful •adj. unpleasant or offensive.

distemper •n. **1** a kind of paint made of powdered pigment mixed with glue or size, used on walls. **2** a disease affecting dogs, causing fever and coughing.
– ORIGIN Latin *distemperare* 'soak'.

distend •v. swell because of internal pressure.
– DERIVATIVES **distension** n.
– ORIGIN Latin *distendere*.

distil (US **distill**) •v. (**distils, distilling, distilled**; US **distills, distilling, distilled**) **1** purify a liquid by heating it so that it vaporizes, then condensing the vapour and collecting the resulting liquid. **2** make spirits such as whisky in this way. **3** extract the most important

aspects of: *my notes were distilled into a book.*
- DERIVATIVES **distillation** n.
- ORIGIN Latin *distillare*.

distiller • n. a person or company that manufactures spirits.
- DERIVATIVES **distillery** n. (pl. **distilleries**).

distinct • adj. **1** noticeably different: *there are two distinct types of the disease.* **2** able to be perceived clearly by the senses.
- DERIVATIVES **distinctly** adv. **distinctness** n.
- ORIGIN Latin *distinctus*.

distinction • n. **1** a noticeable difference or contrast. **2** the action of distinguishing. **3** outstanding excellence. **4** a special honour or recognition.

distinctive • adj. characteristic of a person or thing, so making it different from others: *the car's distinctive design.*
- DERIVATIVES **distinctively** adv. **distinctiveness** n.

distinguish • v. **1** recognize or treat as different: *she can distinguish reality from fantasy.* **2** manage to see or hear. **3** be a distinctive characteristic of: *what distinguishes the Americans from the British?* **4** (**distinguish yourself**) do something very well.
- DERIVATIVES **distinguishable** adj.
- ORIGIN Latin *distinguere*.

distinguished • adj. **1** successful and greatly respected. **2** dignified in appearance.

distort • v. **1** pull or twist out of shape. **2** give a false or misleading account of. **3** change the form of an electrical signal or sound wave during transmission or amplification.
- DERIVATIVES **distortion** n.
- ORIGIN Latin *distorquere* 'twist apart'.

distract • v. **1** prevent someone from concentrating on something. **2** divert attention from something.
- DERIVATIVES **distracting** adj.
- ORIGIN Latin *distrahere* 'draw apart'.

distraction • n. **1** a thing that distracts someone's attention. **2** an activity providing entertainment. **3** mental turmoil.

distraught • adj. very worried and upset.
- ORIGIN Latin *distractus* 'pulled apart'.

distress • n. **1** extreme anxiety, sorrow, or difficulty. **2** the state of a ship or aircraft when in danger or difficulty. • v. cause distress to.
- DERIVATIVES **distressing** adj.
- ORIGIN Old French *destresce*.

distribute • v. (**distributes, distributing, distributed**) **1** hand or share out to a

number of people. **2** (**be distributed**) be spread over an area. **3** supply goods to retailers.
- DERIVATIVES **distributable** adj.
- ORIGIN Latin *distribuere* 'divide up'.

distribution • n. **1** the action of distributing something. **2** the way in which something is distributed: *the uneven distribution of wealth.*

distributive • adj. relating to distribution.

distributor • n. **1** an agent who supplies goods to retailers. **2** a device in a petrol engine for passing electric current to each spark plug in turn.

district • n. an area of a town or region, regarded as a unit for administrative purposes or because of a particular feature.
- ORIGIN Latin *districtus* 'territory of jurisdiction'.

district attorney • n. (in the US) a public official who acts as prosecutor for the state in a particular district.

district nurse • n. (in the UK) a nurse who treats patients in their homes, operating within a particular district.

distrust • n. lack of trust. • v. have little trust in.
- DERIVATIVES **distrustful** adj.

disturb • v. **1** interrupt someone's sleep, relaxation, or privacy. **2** interfere with the normal arrangement or functioning of something. **3** make someone anxious. **4** (as adj. **disturbed**) having emotional or mental problems.
- DERIVATIVES **disturbing** adj.
- ORIGIN Latin *disturbare*.

disturbance • n. **1** the interruption or disruption of a settled or normal condition. **2** a breakdown of peaceful behaviour.

disunited • adj. lacking unity or agreement.
- DERIVATIVES **disunity** n.

disuse • n. the state of not being used; neglect.
- DERIVATIVES **disused** adj.

ditch • n. a narrow channel dug to hold or carry water. • v. **1** informal abandon or get rid of. **2** (with reference to an aircraft) bring or come down in a forced landing on the sea.
- ORIGIN Old English.

dither • v. (**dithers, dithering, dithered**) be indecisive. • n. informal a state of agitation or indecision.
- DERIVATIVES **dithery** adj.
- ORIGIN from dialect *didder* 'tremble'.

ditto • n. **1** the same thing again (used in lists). **2** (also **ditto mark**) a symbol

consisting of two apostrophes („) placed
under the item to be repeated.
– ORIGIN Italian *detto* 'said'.

ditty • n. (pl. **ditties**) a short simple song.
– ORIGIN Old French *dite* 'composition'.

diuretic /dy-uh-**ret**-ik/ • adj. causing an
increase in the flow of urine.
– ORIGIN Greek *diourein* 'urinate'.

diurnal /dy-**er**-nuhl/ • adj. 1 relating to
or during the daytime. 2 daily.
– ORIGIN Latin *diurnalis*.

diva /**dee**-vuh/ • n. a famous female opera
singer.
– ORIGIN Latin, 'goddess'.

Divali • n. var. of DIWALI.

divan /di-**van**/ • n. 1 Brit. a bed consisting
of a base and mattress but no footboard
or headboard. 2 a long, low sofa without
a back or arms.
– ORIGIN Persian, 'bench, court'.

dive • v. (**dives, diving, dived**; US past and
past part. also **dove** /*rhymes with* rove/)
1 plunge head first into water. 2 (of a
submarine or diver) go under water.
3 plunge steeply downwards through
the air. 4 move quickly or suddenly: *he
dived into an office building.* • n. 1 an act of
diving. 2 informal a disreputable nightclub
or bar.
– ORIGIN Old English.

dive-bomb • v. bomb a target while
diving steeply in an aircraft.

diver • n. 1 a person who dives under
water as a sport or for their work. 2 a
large diving waterbird.

diverge • v. (**diverges, diverging,
diverged**) 1 (of a route or line) separate
from another route and go in a different
direction. 2 be different.
– DERIVATIVES **divergence** n.
– ORIGIN Latin *divergere*.

divergent • adj. different.

divers /**dy**-verz/ • adj. old use of many
different kinds.

diverse /dy-**verss**/ • adj. widely varied.
– ORIGIN Latin *diversus*.

diversify • v. (**diversifies, diversifying,
diversified**) 1 make or become more
varied. 2 (of a company) expand its
range of products or field of operation.
– DERIVATIVES **diversification** n.

diversion • n. 1 an instance of diverting
something. 2 Brit. an alternative route for
use when the usual road is closed.
3 something intended to distract
attention. 4 a pastime or pleasant
activity.
– DERIVATIVES **diversionary** adj.

diversity • n. (pl. **diversities**) 1 the state
of being varied. 2 a range of different
things.

divert /dy-**vert**/ • v. 1 change the

direction or course of. 2 distract
someone or their attention. 3 amuse or
entertain.
– ORIGIN Latin *divertere* 'turn in separate
ways'.

divest /dy-**vest**/ • v. 1 (**divest someone/
thing of**) deprive someone or something of. 2 (**divest yourself of**) remove
or get rid of.
– ORIGIN Old French *desvestir*.

divide • v. (**divides, dividing, divided**)
1 separate into parts. 2 share out.
3 cause disagreement between people or
groups: *the question had divided the
French for years.* 4 form a boundary
between. 5 find how many times a
number contains another. • n. a wide
difference between two groups: *the
North–South divide.*
– ORIGIN Latin *dividere* 'force apart'.

dividend • n. 1 a sum of money that is
divided among a number of people, such
as the part of a company's profits paid to
its shareholders. 2 (**dividends**) benefits:
persistence pays dividends. 3 Math. a
number to be divided by another
number.
– ORIGIN Latin *dividendum* 'something to
be divided'.

divider • n. 1 a screen or piece of
furniture that divides a room into
separate parts. 2 (**dividers**) a measuring
compass.

divination • n. the use of supernatural
means to find out about the future or
the unknown.

divine[1] • adj. 1 relating to God or a god:
divine forces. 2 informal excellent. • n. dated
a priest, religious leader, or theologian.
– DERIVATIVES **divinely** adv.
– ORIGIN Latin *divinus*.

divine[2] • v. (**divines, divining, divined**)
1 discover by guesswork or intuition.
2 have supernatural insight into the
future.
– DERIVATIVES **diviner** n.
– ORIGIN Latin *divinare* 'predict'.

diving board • n. a board projecting
over a swimming pool, from which
people dive in.

diving suit • n. a watertight suit with a
helmet and an air supply, worn for
working or exploring deep under water.

divining rod • n. a forked stick or rod
supposed to move when held over
ground in which water or minerals can
be found.

divinity • n. (pl. **divinities**) 1 the state of
being divine. 2 a god or goddess. 3 the
study of religion; theology.

divisible • adj. 1 capable of being
divided. 2 (of a number) containing
another number a number of times

without a remainder.
– DERIVATIVES **divisibility** n.

division •n. **1** the action of dividing something or the state of being divided. **2** each of the parts into which something is divided. **3** a major section of an organization. **4** a number of sports teams grouped together for competitive purposes. **5** a partition.
– DERIVATIVES **divisional** adj.

division sign •n. the sign ÷, placed between two numbers to show that the first is to be divided by the second.

divisive /di-vy-siv/ •adj. causing disagreement or hostility between people.
– DERIVATIVES **divisiveness** n.

divisor •n. Math. a number by which another number is to be divided.

divorce •n. the legal ending of a marriage. •v. (**divorces, divorcing, divorced**) **1** legally end your marriage with your husband or wife. **2** (**divorce someone/thing from**) separate someone or something from: *jazz has become divorced from its origins.*
– ORIGIN Old French.

divorcee /di-vor-see/ •n. a divorced person.

divot /di-vuht/ •n. a piece of turf cut out of the ground.

divulge /dy-vulj/ •v. (**divulges, divulging, divulged**) reveal information that is meant to be private or secret.
– ORIGIN Latin *divulgare* 'publish widely'.

Diwali /di-wah-li/ (also **Divali**) •n. a Hindu festival with lights, held in October and November to celebrate the end of the monsoon.
– ORIGIN Sanskrit, 'row of lights'.

Dixie •n. informal the Southern states of the US.

DIY •n. esp. Brit. the activity of decorating and making repairs in the home yourself rather than employing a professional.
– ORIGIN from *do-it-yourself*.

dizzy •adj. (**dizzier, dizziest**) **1** having a sensation of spinning around and losing your balance. **2** informal (of a woman) silly but attractive. •v. (**dizzies, dizzying, dizzied**) make someone feel unsteady or confused.
– DERIVATIVES **dizzily** adv. **dizziness** n.
– ORIGIN Old English, 'foolish'.

DJ¹ •n. **1** a person who introduces and plays recorded pop music on radio or at a club. **2** a person who uses samples of recorded music to make techno or rap music. •v. (**DJ's, DJ'ing, DJ'd**) perform as a DJ.
– ORIGIN from **DISC JOCKEY**.

DJ² •n. Brit. a dinner jacket.

djellaba /jel-luh-buh/ •n. a loose woollen hooded cloak traditionally worn by Arabs.
– ORIGIN Arabic.

dl •abbrev. decilitre(s).

DLitt •abbrev. Doctor of Letters.
– ORIGIN Latin *Doctor Litterarum*.

DM (also **D-mark**) •abbrev. Deutschmark.

dm •abbrev. decimetre(s).

DMA •abbrev. Computing direct memory access.

DMus •abbrev. Doctor of Music.

DNA •n. deoxyribonucleic acid, a substance carrying genetic information that is found in the cell nuclei of nearly all organisms.

DNA fingerprinting •n. = GENETIC FINGERPRINTING.

do¹ •v. (**does, doing, did**; past part. **done**) **1** carry out or complete an action, duty, or task. **2** act or progress in a particular way: *the team were doing badly.* **3** work on something to bring it to a required state. **4** have a particular effect on: *the walk will do me good.* **5** work at for a living or take as your subject of study. **6** make or provide. **7** be suitable or acceptable: *if he's like you, he'll do.* **8** (**be/have done with**) stop being concerned about. **9** Brit. informal swindle. •auxiliary verb **1** used before a verb in questions and negative statements. **2** used to refer back to a verb already mentioned: *he looks better than he did before.* **3** used in commands, or to give emphasis to a verb: *do sit down.* •n. (pl. **dos** or **do's**) Brit. informal a party or other social event.
– PHRASES **can** (or **could**) **do with** informal would find useful or would like. **do away with** informal put an end to; kill. **do for** informal defeat or kill. **2** be good enough for. **do someone in** informal **1** kill someone. **2** (**be done in**) be tired out. **dos and don'ts** rules of behaviour. **do something up 1** fasten or wrap something. **2** informal renovate or redecorate a building or room.
– DERIVATIVES **doable** adj. (informal) **doer** n.
– ORIGIN Old English.

do² •n. var. of DOH.

Dobermann /doh-ber-muhn/ (also **Doberman** or **Dobermann pinscher** /pin-sher/) •n. a large breed of dog with powerful jaws.
– ORIGIN named after the German dog breeder Ludwig *Dobermann* + German *Pinscher* 'terrier'.

docile •adj. willing to accept control or instruction; submissive.
– DERIVATIVES **docilely** adv. **docility** n.
– ORIGIN Latin *docilis* 'easily taught'.

dock¹ •n. an enclosed area of water in a port for the loading, unloading, and

repair of ships. •v. **1** (with reference to a ship) come or bring into a dock. **2** (of a spacecraft) join with a space station or another spacecraft in space.
– ORIGIN Dutch or German *docke*.

dock² •n. the enclosure in a criminal court for a person on trial.
– ORIGIN prob. from Flemish *dok* 'chicken coop'.

dock³ •n. a weed with broad leaves.
– ORIGIN Old English.

dock⁴ •v. **1** deduct money from a person's wages. **2** cut an animal's tail short.

docker •n. a person employed in a port to load and unload ships.

docket •n. Brit. a document sent with a batch of goods that lists its contents, confirms that duty has been paid, or entitles the holder to delivery.
– ORIGIN perh. from **DOCK⁴**.

dockland •n. (also **docklands**) Brit. the area containing a city's docks.

dockyard •n. an area with docks and equipment for repairing and building ships.

doctor •n. **1** a person who is qualified to practise medicine. **2** (**Doctor**) a person who holds the highest university degree. •v. **1** change information, figures, etc. in order to deceive other people. **2** add a harmful or strong ingredient to a food or drink. **3** Brit. remove an animal's sexual organs.
– ORIGIN Latin, 'teacher'.

doctoral •adj. relating to a doctorate.

doctorate •n. the highest degree awarded by a university.

doctrinaire /dok-tri-**nair**/ •adj. very strict in applying beliefs or principles.
– ORIGIN French.

doctrine /dok-trin/ •n. a set of beliefs or principles held and taught by a religious, political, or other group.
– DERIVATIVES **doctrinal** /dok-**try**-n'l/ adj.
– ORIGIN Latin *doctrina* 'teaching'.

docudrama •n. a television film based on a dramatized version of real events.

document •n. /dok-yoo-muhnt/ a piece of written, printed, or electronic matter that provides information or evidence. •v. /dok-yoo-ment/ record something in written, photographic, or other form.
– ORIGIN Latin *documentum* 'lesson'.

documentary •n. (pl. **documentaries**) a film or television or radio programme giving a factual account of something, using film, photographs, and sound recordings of real events. •adj. consisting of documents and other material which provide a factual account of something: *documentary evidence*.

documentation •n. **1** documents providing official information or evidence. **2** written specifications or instructions for a computer.

dodder •v. (**dodders, doddering, doddered**) be slow and unsteady in movement.
– DERIVATIVES **doddery** adj.
– ORIGIN from **DITHER**.

doddle •n. Brit. informal a very easy task.

dodecagon /doh-**dek**-uh-guhn/ •n. a plane figure with twelve straight sides and angles.
– ORIGIN Greek *dōdekagōnos* 'twelve-angled'.

dodecahedron /doh-de-kuh-**hee**-druhn/ •n. (pl. **dodecahedra** /doh-de-kuh-**hee**-druh/ or **dodecahedrons**) a three-dimensional shape with twelve plane faces.
– ORIGIN Greek *dōdekagōnos* 'twelve-faced'.

dodge •v. (**dodges, dodging, dodged**) **1** avoid something by a making sudden quick movement. **2** cunningly avoid doing or paying something. •n. an act of avoiding something.

dodgem •n. a small electric car with rubber bumpers, driven at a funfair with the aim of bumping other such cars.
– ORIGIN US trademark, from *dodge them*.

dodger •n. informal a person who avoids doing or paying something: *a tax dodger*.

dodgy •adj. (**dodgier, dodgiest**) Brit. informal **1** dishonest. **2** risky. **3** not working well or in good condition.

dodo /doh-doh/ •n. (pl. **dodos** or **dodoes**) a large extinct flightless bird formerly found on Mauritius.
– ORIGIN Portuguese *doudo* 'simpleton'.

doe •n. **1** a female deer or reindeer. **2** the female of some other animals, such as a rabbit or hare.
– ORIGIN Old English.

does 3rd person sing. present of **DO¹**.

doesn't •contr. does not.

doff •v. remove your hat when greeting someone.
– ORIGIN from *do off*.

dog •n. **1** a four-legged meat-eating mammal, kept as a pet or used for work or hunting. **2** any member of the dog family, such as the wolf. **3** the male of an animal of the dog family. •v. (**dogs, dogging, dogged**) **1** follow closely and persistently. **2** cause continual trouble for: *he was dogged by ankle problems*.
– PHRASES **dog eat dog** (of a situation) very competitive. **a dog in the manger** a person who prevents other people from having things that they do not need themselves. [ORIGIN from the fable of the dog that lay in a manger to prevent

the ox and horse from eating the hay.]
go to the dogs informal get much worse.
– ORIGIN Old English.

dog collar • n. informal a white upright collar worn by Christian priests.

dog days • pl. n. the hottest period of the year (formerly calculated from the first time Sirius, the Dog Star, rose at the same time as the sun).

doge /dohj/ • n. hist. the chief magistrate of Venice or Genoa.
– ORIGIN Italian *doze*.

dog-eared • adj. (of a book, magazine, etc.) having worn or battered corners.

dog-end • n. Brit. informal a cigarette end.

dogfight • n. a close combat between military aircraft.

dogfish • n. (pl. **dogfish** or **dogfishes**) a small shark with a long tail, living close to the seabed.

dogged /dog-gid/ • adj. very persistent.
– DERIVATIVES **doggedly** adv.
doggedness n.

doggerel /dog-guh-ruhl/ • n. badly written poetry.
– ORIGIN prob. from **DOG**.

doggo • adv. (in phr. **lie doggo**) informal remain still and quiet to avoid being discovered.

doggy • adj. **1** relating to dogs. **2** fond of dogs.

doggy bag • n. a bag used to take home leftover food from a restaurant.

doggy-paddle • n. a simple swimming stroke like that of a dog.

doghouse • n. N. Amer. a dog's kennel.
– PHRASES **in the doghouse** informal having displeased someone.

dog-leg • n. a sharp bend.

dogma • n. a principle or principles laid down by an authority and intended to be accepted without question.
– ORIGIN Greek, 'opinion'.

dogmatic • adj. forcefully putting forward your own opinions and unwilling to accept those of other people.
– DERIVATIVES **dogmatically** adv.
dogmatism n. **dogmatist** n.

do-gooder • n. a well-meaning but unrealistic or interfering person.

dog rose • n. a wild rose with pink or white flowers.

dogsbody • n. (pl. **dogsbodies**) Brit. informal a person who is given boring, menial tasks.

dog-tired • adj. very tired.

dog-tooth • n. a small check pattern with notched corners.

dogwood • n. a shrub or small tree with red stems and hard wood.
– ORIGIN from the use of the wood to

make skewers known as 'dogs'.

DoH • abbrev. (in the UK) Department of Health.

doh /doh/ (also **do**) • n. Music the first note of a major scale, coming before 'ray'.
– ORIGIN Italian *do*.

doily • n. (pl. **doilies**) a small ornamental mat made of lace or paper.
– ORIGIN from *Doiley* or *Doyley*, a London draper.

doings • pl. n. a person's actions or activities.

Dolby /dol-bi/ • n. trademark **1** a noise-reduction system used in tape recording. **2** an electronic system providing stereo sound for cinemas and televisions.
– ORIGIN named after the American engineer Ray M. *Dolby*.

doldrums /dol-druhmz/ • pl. n. (**the doldrums**) **1** a state of inactivity or depression. **2** a region of the Atlantic Ocean where the wind is erratic or scarce.
– ORIGIN perh. from **DULL**.

dole • n. Brit. informal benefit paid by the state to unemployed people. • v. (**doles, doling, doled**) (**dole something out**) distribute something.
– ORIGIN Old English, 'division or share'.

doleful • adj. sad or depressing.
– DERIVATIVES **dolefully** adv.
– ORIGIN Old French *doel* 'mourning'.

dolerite /dol-luh-ryt/ • n. a dark igneous rock.
– ORIGIN Greek *doleros* 'deceptive' (because it resembles diorite).

doll • n. a small model of a human figure, used as a child's toy. • v. (**be dolled up**) informal be dressed in smart, attractive clothes.
– ORIGIN from the woman's name *Dorothy*.

dollar • n. the basic unit of money of the US, Canada, Australia, and some other countries.
– ORIGIN German *Thaler*, referring to a silver coin.

dollar sign (also **dollar mark**) • n. the sign $, representing a dollar.

dollop informal • n. a shapeless mass or lump, especially of soft food.
• v. (**dollops, dolloping, dolloped**) serve out soft food casually.
– ORIGIN perh. Scandinavian.

dolly bird • n. Brit. informal an attractive and fashionable young woman.

dolman sleeve /dol-muhn/ • n. a loose sleeve cut in one piece with the body of a garment.
– ORIGIN Turkish *dolama* 'open robe'.

dolmen /dol-men/ • n. a prehistoric

tomb with a large flat stone laid on upright ones.
– ORIGIN Cornish, 'hole of a stone'.

dolomite /dol-uh-myt/ •n. a mineral or rock consisting chiefly of a carbonate of calcium and magnesium.
– DERIVATIVES **dolomitic** adj.
– ORIGIN named after the French geologist M. *Dolomieu*.

dolour /dol-er/ (US **dolor**) •n. literary great sorrow or distress.
– DERIVATIVES **dolorous** adj.
– ORIGIN Latin *dolor* 'pain, grief'.

dolphin •n. a small whale with a beak-like snout and a curved fin on the back.
– ORIGIN Greek *delphin*.

dolphinarium /dol-fi-nair-i-uhm/ •n. (pl. **dolphinariums** or **dolphinaria**) an aquarium in which dolphins are kept and trained for public entertainment.

dolt •n. a stupid person.
– DERIVATIVES **doltish** adj.
– ORIGIN perh. from **DULL**.

-dom •suffix forming nouns referring to: **1** a state or condition: *freedom*. **2** status: *earldom*. **3** a place or area: *kingdom*. **4** a class of people: *officialdom*.
– ORIGIN Old English, 'decree'.

domain /doh-mayn/ •n. **1** an area controlled by a ruler or government. **2** an area of activity or knowledge. **3** a part of the Internet with addresses sharing a common element.
– ORIGIN Old French *demeine* 'belonging to a lord'.

domain name •n. the part of a computer network address which identifies it as belonging to a particular domain.

dome •n. **1** a rounded roof of a building, with a circular base. **2** a stadium or other building with a rounded roof.
– ORIGIN Italian *duomo* 'cathedral, dome'.

domestic •adj. **1** relating to a home or family: *domestic chores*. **2** for use in the home. **3** (of an animal) tame and kept by humans. **4** existing or occurring within a country; not foreign. •n. a person who is employed to do household tasks.
– DERIVATIVES **domestically** adv.
– ORIGIN Latin *domesticus*.

domesticate •v. (**domesticates, domesticating, domesticated**) **1** tame an animal and keep it as a pet or for farm produce. **2** grow a plant for food.
– DERIVATIVES **domestication** n.

domesticity /dom-e-sti-si-ti/ •n. home or family life.

domicile /dom-i-syl/ formal or Law •n. the country in which a person lives permanently. •v. (**be domiciled**) be living in a particular country or place.
– ORIGIN Latin *domicilium* 'dwelling'.

domiciliary /dom-i-sil-i-uh-ri/ •adj. in someone's home: *a domiciliary visit*.

dominant •adj. **1** most important, powerful, or influential: *a dominant position in the market*. **2** (of a gene) appearing in offspring even if a contrary gene is also inherited. Compare with **RECESSIVE**.
– DERIVATIVES **dominance** n. **dominantly** adv.

dominate •v. (**dominates, dominating, dominated**) **1** have a very strong influence over. **2** be the most important or noticeable person or thing in: *she dominated the race from start to finish*.
– DERIVATIVES **domination** n. **dominator** n.
– ORIGIN Latin *dominari* 'rule'.

domineering •adj. arrogant and overbearing.
– ORIGIN Latin *dominari* 'rule'.

Dominican /duh-min-i-kuhn/ •n. a member of an order of friars founded by St Dominic, or of a corresponding order of nuns.

dominion •n. **1** supreme power or control. **2** the territory of a sovereign or government.
– ORIGIN Latin *dominium*.

domino •n. (pl. **dominoes**) any of 28 small oblong pieces marked with 0–6 pips in each half, used in the game of **dominoes**.
– ORIGIN prob. from Latin *dominus* 'lord'.

domino effect •n. a situation in which one event appears to cause a series of similar events to happen elsewhere.

don¹ •n. a university teacher, especially at Oxford or Cambridge.
– ORIGIN Spanish.

don² •v. (**dons, donning, donned**) put on an item of clothing.
– ORIGIN from *do on*.

donate •v. (**donates, donating, donated**) **1** give something to a good cause. **2** allow blood or an organ to be removed from your body and given to another person.
– ORIGIN Latin *donare*.

donation •n. something that is given to a charity.

done past part. of **DO¹**. •adj. **1** cooked thoroughly. **2** no longer happening or existing. **3** informal socially acceptable: *the done thing*. •exclam. (in response to an offer) I accept.

doner kebab /don-er/ •n. a Turkish dish of spiced lamb cooked on a spit and served in slices.
– ORIGIN from Turkish *döner* 'rotating' and *kebap* 'roast meat'.

donjon /don-juhn/ •n. the strongest or central tower of a castle.
– ORIGIN from DUNGEON.

Don Juan /don hwahn, don joo-uhn/ •n. a man who seduces many women.
– ORIGIN the name of a legendary Spanish nobleman.

donkey •n. (pl. **donkeys**) **1** a domesticated mammal of the horse family with long ears and a braying call. **2** informal a foolish person.
– PHRASES **donkey's years** Brit. informal a very long time.
– ORIGIN perh. from DUN, or from the man's name *Duncan*.

donkey jacket •n. Brit. a heavy jacket with a patch of waterproof material across the shoulders.

donkey work •n. Brit. informal the part of a job that is demanding and boring.

donnish •adj. like a university don; concerned with scholarly rather than practical matters.

donor •n. a person who donates something.

don't •contr. do not.

donut •n. US = DOUGHNUT.

doodle •v. (**doodles, doodling, doodled**) draw or scribble absent-mindedly. •n. a drawing made absent-mindedly.
– ORIGIN German *dudeldopp* 'simpleton'.

doolally /doo-lal-li/ •adj. Brit. informal temporarily insane.
– ORIGIN from *Deolali* (a town near Mumbai) + Urdu *tap* 'fever'.

doom •n. death, destruction, or another terrible fate. •v. (**be doomed**) be fated to fail or be destroyed.
– ORIGIN Old English, 'decree'.

doomsday •n. **1** the last day of the world's existence. **2** (in religious belief) the day of the Last Judgement.

door •n. **1** a movable barrier at the entrance to a building, room, or vehicle, or as part of a cupboard. **2** the distance from one building in a row to another: *he lived two doors away.*
– PHRASES **out of doors** in or into the open air.
– ORIGIN Old English.

doorbell •n. a bell in a building which can be rung by visitors outside.

do-or-die •adj. showing or requiring great determination to succeed.

doorkeeper •n. a person on duty at the entrance to a building.

doorknob •n. a rounded door handle.

doorman •n. (pl. **doormen**) a man who is on duty at the entrance to a large building.

doormat •n. **1** a mat placed in a doorway for wiping the shoes. **2** informal a person

who allows other people to control them.

doorstep •n. a step leading up to the outer door of a house. •v. (**doorsteps, doorstepping, doorstepped**) Brit. informal (of a journalist) try to get an interview with or photograph of someone by waiting outside their home.

doorstop •n. an object that keeps a door open or in place.

doorway •n. an entrance with a door.

dope •n. **1** informal an illegal drug, especially cannabis. **2** a drug used to improve the performance of an athlete, racehorse, or greyhound. **3** informal a stupid person. •v. (**dopes, doping, doped**) give a drug to.
– ORIGIN Dutch *doop* 'sauce'.

dopey (also **dopy**) •adj. (**dopier, dopiest**) informal **1** in a semi-conscious state from sleep or a drug. **2** stupid.
– DERIVATIVES **dopily** adv. **dopiness** n.

doppelgänger /dop-puhl-gang-er/ •n. a ghost or double of a living person.
– ORIGIN German, 'double-goer'.

Doppler effect /dop-pler/ •n. Physics an increase (or decrease) in the apparent frequency of sound, light, or other waves as the source and the observer move towards (or away from) each other.
– ORIGIN named after the Austrian physicist Johann Christian *Doppler*.

dork •n. informal a stupid person.
– ORIGIN perh. from DIRK.

dormant •adj. **1** (of an animal) in or as if in a deep sleep. **2** (of a plant or bud) alive but not growing. **3** (of a volcano) temporarily inactive.
– DERIVATIVES **dormancy** n.
– ORIGIN Old French, 'sleeping'.

dormer (also **dormer window**) •n. a window set vertically into a sloping roof.
– ORIGIN Old French *dormir* 'to sleep'.

dormitory •n. (pl. **dormitories**) a bedroom for a number of people in a school or similar institution. •adj. referring to a place from which people travel to work in a nearby city.
– ORIGIN Latin *dormitorium*.

dormouse •n. (pl. **dormice**) a small mouse-like rodent with a bushy tail.

dorsal •adj. tech. relating to the upper side or back. Compare with VENTRAL.
– DERIVATIVES **dorsally** adv.
– ORIGIN Latin *dorsum* 'back'.

dory /*rhymes with* story/ •n. (pl. **dories**) a narrow sea fish with a large mouth.
– ORIGIN French *dorée* 'gilded'.

DOS •abbrev. Computing disk operating system.

dosage • n. the size of a dose of medicine or radiation.

dose • n. **1** a quantity of a medicine or drug taken at one time. **2** an amount of radiation received or absorbed at one time. • v. (**doses, dosing, dosed**) give someone a drug or medicine.
– ORIGIN Greek *dosis* 'gift'.

dosh • n. Brit. informal money.

doss • v. Brit. informal **1** sleep in rough or makeshift conditions. **2** spend time in a lazy or aimless way.
– DERIVATIVES **dosser** n.
– ORIGIN perh. from Latin *dorsum* 'back'.

dossier /doss-i-er, doss-i-ay/ • n. a collection of documents about a person or subject.
– ORIGIN French.

dot • n. **1** a small round mark or spot. **2** the shorter signal of the two used in Morse code. • v. (**dots, dotting, dotted**) **1** mark with a dot or dots. **2** scatter something over an area.
– PHRASES **on the dot** informal exactly on time. **the year dot** Brit. informal a very long time ago.
– ORIGIN Old English, 'head of a boil'.

dotage /doh-tij/ • n. the period of life in which a person is old and weak.
– ORIGIN from DOTE.

dotard /doh-terd/ • n. an old person who is weak or senile.

dot-com (also **dot.com**) • n. a company that conducts its business on the Internet.
– ORIGIN from '.com' in an Internet address, indicating a commercial site.

dote • v. (**dotes, doting, doted**) (**dote on**) be very fond of someone, ignoring their faults.
– ORIGIN Dutch *doten* 'be silly'.

dotty • adj. (**dottier, dottiest**) informal slightly mad or eccentric.
– DERIVATIVES **dottily** adv. **dottiness** n.
– ORIGIN perh. from former *dote* 'fool'.

double • adj. **1** consisting of two equal, identical, or similar parts or things. **2** having twice the usual size, quantity, or strength: *a double brandy.* **3** designed to be used by two people. **4** having two different roles or interpretations: *she began a double life.* **5** (of a flower) having more than one circle of petals. • adv. twice the amount or quantity. • n. **1** a thing which is twice as large as usual or is made up of two parts. **2** a person who looks exactly like another. **3** (**doubles**) a game involving sides made up of two players. • pron. an amount twice as large as usual. • v. (**doubles, doubling, doubled**) **1** make or become double. **2** fold or bend over on itself. **3** (**double up**) bend over or

curl up with pain or laughter. **4** (**double (up) as**) be used in or play a different role: *the van doubled as a mobile kitchen.* **5** (**double back**) go back in the direction you have come from.
– PHRASES **at the double** very fast.
– DERIVATIVES **doubleness** n. **doubler** n. **doubly** adv.
– ORIGIN Latin *duplus*.

double agent • n. an agent who pretends to act as a spy for one country while in fact acting for its enemy.

double-barrelled • adj. Brit. (of a surname) having two parts joined by a hyphen.

double bass • n. the largest and lowest-pitched instrument of the violin family.

double-book • v. mistakenly reserve something for two different customers at the same time.

double-breasted • adj. (of a jacket or coat) having a large overlap at the front and two rows of buttons.

double-check • v. check again to make certain.

double chin • n. a roll of flesh below a person's chin.

double cream • n. Brit. thick cream with a high fat content.

double-cross • v. betray a person that you are supposed to be helping.

double-dealing • n. deceitful behaviour.

double-decker • n. a bus with two floors.

double Dutch • n. Brit. informal language that is hard to understand.

double-edged • adj. having two opposing aspects or possible outcomes.

double entendre /doo-b'l on-ton-druh/ • n. (pl. **double entendres** /doo-b'l on-ton-druh/) a word or phrase with two meanings, one of which is usually slightly indecent or rude.
– ORIGIN from former French, 'double understanding'.

double figures • pl. n. esp. Brit. a number from 10 to 99 inclusive.

double glazing • n. esp. Brit. windows having two layers of glass with a space between them.
– DERIVATIVES **double-glazed** adj.

double helix • n. a pair of parallel helices with a common axis, especially that in the structure of DNA.

double-jointed • adj. (of a person) having unusually flexible joints.

double negative • n. a negative statement containing two negative elements (e.g. *he didn't say nothing*).

USAGE: If you say *I don't know nothing*, this is not good English. The structure is called a **double negative** because it uses two negative words in the same clause to convey a single negative. This is bad English because the two negative elements cancel each other out to give a positive statement, so that *I don't know nothing* could be taken to mean *I know something*; you should say *I don't know anything* to avoid confusion.

double pneumonia • n. pneumonia affecting both lungs.

doublespeak • n. language that is deliberately unclear or has more than one meaning.
– ORIGIN coined by George Orwell (see **DOUBLETHINK**).

double standard • n. a rule or principle applied unfairly in different ways to different people.

doublet • n. hist. a man's short close-fitting padded jacket.
– ORIGIN Old French, 'something folded'.

double take • n. a second reaction to something unexpected, immediately after your first reaction.

doublethink • n. the acceptance of conflicting opinions or beliefs at the same time.
– ORIGIN coined by George Orwell in his novel *Nineteen Eighty-Four*.

double time • n. a rate of pay equal to double the standard rate.

doubloon /dub-loon/ • n. hist. a Spanish gold coin.
– ORIGIN Spanish *doblón*.

doubt • n. a feeling of uncertainty. • v. 1 feel uncertain about something. 2 disbelieve or mistrust someone.
– PHRASES **no doubt** certainly; probably.
– DERIVATIVES **doubter** n.
– ORIGIN Latin *dubius* 'doubtful'.

doubtful • adj. 1 feeling uncertain. 2 causing uncertainty. 3 not likely or probable.
– DERIVATIVES **doubtfully** adv.

doubting Thomas • n. a person who refuses to believe something without proof.
– ORIGIN referring to the apostle Thomas (Gospel of John, Chapter 20).

doubtless • adv. very probably.
– DERIVATIVES **doubtlessly** adv.

douche /doosh/ • n. 1 a shower of water. 2 a jet of liquid applied to part of the body for cleansing or medicinal purposes. • v. (**douches, douching, douched**) spray or clean with a jet of water.
– ORIGIN French.

dough • n. 1 a thick mixture of flour and liquid, for baking into bread or pastry. 2 informal money.

– DERIVATIVES **doughy** adj.
– ORIGIN Old English.

doughnut (also US **donut**) • n. a small fried cake or ring of sweetened dough.

doughty /dow-ti/ • adj. (**doughtier, doughtiest**) brave and determined.
– ORIGIN Old English.

dour /doo-er, dow-er/ • adj. very severe, stern, or gloomy.
– ORIGIN prob. from Scottish Gaelic *dúr* 'dull, obstinate'.

douse /dowss/ (also **dowse**) • v. (**douses, dousing, doused**; also **dowses, dowsing, dowsed**) 1 drench with liquid. 2 extinguish a fire or light.
– ORIGIN perh. from Dutch and German *dossen* 'strike, beat'.

dove[1] /duv/ • n. 1 a bird with a small head and a cooing voice, very similar to a pigeon. 2 a person who favours a policy of peace and negotiation.
– DERIVATIVES **dovish** (also **doveish**) adj.
– ORIGIN Old Norse.

dove[2] /dohv/ N. Amer. past of **DIVE**.

dovecote /duv-kot/ • n. a shelter with nest holes for domesticated pigeons.
– ORIGIN Old English.

dovetail • v. 1 fit together easily or conveniently: *flights that dovetail with the working day*. 2 join by means of a dovetail joint. • n. a wedge-shaped joint formed by interlocking two pieces of wood.

dowager /dow-uh-jer/ • n. 1 a widow who holds a title or property that belonged to her late husband. 2 a dignified elderly woman.
– ORIGIN Old French *douagiere*.

dowdy • adj. (**dowdier, dowdiest**) (especially of a woman) unfashionable and dull in appearance.
– DERIVATIVES **dowdily** adv. **dowdiness** n.

dowel /rhymes with towel/ • n. a headless peg used for holding together components.
– ORIGIN perh. from German *dovel*.

dower /rhymes with tower/ • n. a widow's share for life of her late husband's estate.
– ORIGIN Old French *douaire*.

down[1] • adv. 1 towards, in, or at a lower place, position, or level. 2 to a smaller amount or size, or a more basic state. 3 in or into a weaker or worse position or condition. 4 away from a central place or the north. 5 from an earlier to a later point in time or order: *farms were passed down within the family*. 6 in or into writing. 7 (of a computer system) out of action. • prep. 1 from a higher to a lower point of. 2 at a point further along the course of: *he lived down the street*. 3 along. 4 informal at or to a place.

•adj. **1** directed or moving downwards. **2** unhappy. •v. informal **1** knock or bring to the ground. **2** consume a drink.
– PHRASES **be down to 1** be caused by. **2** be left with the specified amount. **down with —** expressing strong dislike.
– ORIGIN Old English.

down² •n. soft fine feathers or hairs.
– ORIGIN Old Norse.

down³ •n. **1** a gently rolling hill. **2** (**the Downs**) an area of hills in southern England.
– ORIGIN Old English.

down and out •adj. homeless and without money; destitute. •n. (**down-and-out**) a destitute person.

down at heel •adj. esp. Brit. shabby because of lack of money.

downbeat •adj. **1** gloomy or pessimistic. **2** relaxed and low-key. •n. Music an accented beat, usually the first of the bar.

downcast •adj. **1** (of the eyes) looking downwards. **2** sad or depressed.

downer •n. informal **1** a tranquillizing or depressant drug. **2** a depressing experience or situation.

downfall •n. a loss of power, wealth, or status.

downgrade •v. (**downgrades, downgrading, downgraded**) reduce to a lower rank or level of importance.

downhearted •adj. feeling sad or discouraged.

downhill •adv. & adj. **1** towards the bottom of a slope. **2** into a steadily worsening situation: *the business is going downhill*.

download •v. copy data from one computer system to another or to a disk.

downmarket •adj. esp. Brit. cheap and of poor quality.

down payment •n. an initial payment made when buying on credit.

downplay •v. make something appear less important than it really is.

downpour •n. a heavy fall of rain.

downright •adj. utter; complete. •adv. extremely.

downriver •adv. & adj. towards or at a point nearer the mouth of a river.

downshift •v. adopt a simpler and less stressful lifestyle.

downside •n. the negative aspect of something.

downsize •v. (**downsizes, downsizing, downsized**) reduce the number of staff employed by a company in order to cut costs.

Down's syndrome •n. a disorder caused by a genetic defect, causing physical abnormalities and a lower than average intellectual ability.
– ORIGIN named after the English physician John L. H. *Down*.

downstairs •adv. & adj. down a flight of stairs; to a lower floor. •n. the ground floor or lower floors of a building.

downstream •adv. & adj. in the direction in which a stream or river flows.

downtime •n. time during which a computer or other machine is out of action.

down-to-earth •adj. practical and realistic.

downtown •adj. & adv. esp. N. Amer. in, to, or towards the central or main business area of a city.

downtrodden •adj. treated badly by people in power.

downturn •n. a decline in economic or other activity.

down under •n. informal Australia and New Zealand.

downward •adv. (also **downwards**) towards a lower point or level. •adj. moving towards a lower point or level.
– DERIVATIVES **downwardly** adv.

downwind •adv. & adj. in the direction in which the wind is blowing.

downy •adj. covered with fine soft hair or feathers.

dowry /dow-ri/ •n. (pl. **dowries**) property or money brought by a bride to her husband on their marriage.
– ORIGIN Old French *dowarie*.

dowse¹ /dowz/ •v. (**dowses, dowsing, dowsed**) search for underground water or minerals with a pointer which is supposedly moved by unseen influences.
– DERIVATIVES **dowser** n.

dowse² •v. var. of DOUSE.

doxology /dok-sol-uh-ji/ •n. (pl. **doxologies**) a set form of prayer praising God.
– ORIGIN Greek *doxologia*.

doyen /doy-yen/ •n. (fem. **doyenne** /doy-yen/) the most respected or prominent person in a particular field: *he was the doyen of British physicists*.
– ORIGIN French.

doze •v. (**dozes, dozing, dozed**) sleep lightly. •n. a short light sleep.
– ORIGIN perh. from Danish *døse* 'make drowsy'.

dozen •n. **1** (pl. **dozen**) a group or set of twelve. **2** (**dozens**) a lot.
– PHRASES **talk nineteen to the dozen** Brit. talk fast and continuously.
– DERIVATIVES **dozenth** adj.

– ORIGIN Old French *dozeine*.

dozy • adj. **1** feeling drowsy and lazy. **2** Brit. informal stupid.
– DERIVATIVES **dozily** adv. **doziness** n.

DP • abbrev. data processing.

DPhil • abbrev. (in the UK) Doctor of Philosophy.

DPP • abbrev. (in the UK) Director of Public Prosecutions.

Dr • abbrev. (as a title) Doctor.

drab • adj. (**drabber**, **drabbest**) dull and uninteresting. • n. a dull light brown colour.
– DERIVATIVES **drably** adv. **drabness** n.
– ORIGIN prob. from Old French *drap* 'cloth'.

drachm /dram/ • n. hist. a unit of measure equivalent to one eighth of an ounce or one eighth of a fluid ounce.
– ORIGIN see DRACHMA.

drachma /drak-muh/ • n. (pl. **drachmas** or **drachmae** /drak-mee/) (until the introduction of the euro in 2002) the basic unit of money in Greece.
– ORIGIN Greek *drakhmē*, an ancient weight and coin.

draconian /druh-koh-ni-uhn, dray-koh-ni-uhn/ • adj. (of laws) excessively harsh.
– ORIGIN named after the ancient Athenian legislator *Draco*.

draft • n. **1** a preliminary version of a piece of writing. **2** a written order requesting a bank to pay a specified sum. **3** (**the draft**) US compulsory recruitment for military service. **4** US = DRAUGHT. • v. **1** prepare a preliminary version of a piece of writing. **2** select for a particular purpose: *he was drafted in to oversee security.* **3** US recruit someone for compulsory military service.
– DERIVATIVES **drafter** n.
– ORIGIN from DRAUGHT.

drafty • adj. US = DRAUGHTY.

drag • v. (**drags**, **dragging**, **dragged**) **1** pull along forcefully, roughly, or with difficulty. **2** trail along the ground. **3** (of time) pass slowly. **4** (**drag something out**) make something last longer than necessary. **5** (**drag something up**) informal deliberately mention something unwelcome. **6** move an image across a computer screen using a mouse. **7** search the bottom of an area of water with grapnels or nets. **8** (**drag on**) informal inhale the smoke from a cigarette. • n. **1** informal a boring or tiresome person or thing. **2** a person or thing that hinders progress. **3** informal an act of inhaling smoke from a cigarette. **4** the force exerted by air or water to slow down a moving object.
– PHRASES **drag your feet** be slow or

reluctant. **in drag** (of a man) wearing women's clothes.
– ORIGIN Old English.

dragnet • n. **1** a net drawn through water or across ground to trap fish or game. **2** a systematic search for criminals.

dragon • n. **1** a mythical monster like a giant reptile, able to breathe out fire. **2** derog. a fierce and frightening woman.
– ORIGIN Greek *drakōn* 'serpent'.

dragonfly • n. (pl. **dragonflies**) a long-bodied insect with two pairs of large transparent wings.

dragoon /druh-goon/ • n. a member of any of several British cavalry regiments. • v. make someone do something that they do not want to do.
– ORIGIN French *dragon* 'dragon'.

drag queen • n. informal a man who dresses up in showy clothes usually worn by women.

drag race • n. a short race between two cars to see which can accelerate fastest from a standstill.

drain • v. **1** make the liquid in something run out. **2** (of liquid) run off or out. **3** become dry as liquid runs off. **4** make someone feel weak or tired. **5** cause a resource to be used up: *my mother's hospital bills are draining my income.* **6** drink the entire contents of a glass or cup. • n. **1** a channel or pipe carrying off surplus liquid. **2** a thing that uses up a resource or your strength.
– PHRASES **go down the drain** informal be totally wasted.
– DERIVATIVES **drainer** n.
– ORIGIN Old English.

drainage • n. **1** the action of draining. **2** a system of drains.

draining board • n. Brit. a surface next to a sink, on which crockery is left to drain.

drainpipe • n. **1** a pipe for carrying off rainwater from a building. **2** (**drainpipes** or **drainpipe trousers**) trousers with very narrow legs.

drake • n. a male duck.
– ORIGIN Germanic.

dram • n. **1** a small drink of spirits. **2** a drachm.
– ORIGIN Greek *drakhmē* 'drachma'.

drama • n. **1** a play. **2** plays as a literary form. **3** an exciting series of events.
– ORIGIN Greek.

dramatic • adj. **1** relating to drama. **2** sudden and striking: *a dramatic increase.* **3** exciting or impressive. • n. (**dramatics**) **1** the practice of acting in and producing plays. **2** exaggerated or overemotional behaviour.
– DERIVATIVES **dramatically** adv.

d

dramatis personae /dra-muh-tiss per-**soh**-ny/ • **pl. n.** the characters of a play or novel.
– ORIGIN Latin.

dramatist • n. a person who writes plays.

dramatize (or **dramatise**)
• v. (**dramatizes, dramatizing, dramatized**) **1** present a novel, event, etc. as a play or film. **2** make something seem more exciting or serious than it actually is.
– DERIVATIVES **dramatization** n.

drank past of **DRINK**.

drape • v. (**drapes, draping, draped**) **1** arrange cloth or clothing loosely on or round something. **2** rest a part of the body on something in a relaxed way. • n. (**drapes**) esp. N. Amer. long curtains.
– ORIGIN from **DRAPERY**.

draper • n. Brit. dated a person who sells fabrics.

drapery • n. (pl. **draperies**) cloth or clothing hanging in loose folds.
– ORIGIN Old French *drap* 'cloth'.

drastic • adj. having a strong or far-reaching effect.
– DERIVATIVES **drastically** adv.
– ORIGIN Greek *drastikos*.

drat • exclam. used to express mild annoyance.
– ORIGIN from *od rat*, a euphemism for *God rot*.

draught (US **draft**) • n. **1** a current of cool air indoors. **2** an act of drinking or breathing in. **3** old use a quantity of a medicinal liquid. **4** the depth of water needed to float a particular ship. **5** (**draughts**) Brit. a game for two players using 24 pieces, played on a draught-board. • v. var. of **DRAFT**. • adj. **1** (of beer) served from a cask. **2** (of an animal) used for pulling heavy loads.
– ORIGIN Old Norse.

draughtboard • n. Brit. a square chequered board of sixty-four squares, used for playing draughts.

draughtsman (or **draughtswoman**) • n. (pl. **draughtsmen** or **draughts-women**) **1** a person who makes detailed technical plans or drawings. **2** an artist skilled in drawing.
– DERIVATIVES **draughtsmanship** n.

draughty (US **drafty**) • adj. (of an enclosed space) uncomfortable because of draughts of cold air.

draw • v. (**draws, drawing, drew**; past part. **drawn**) **1** produce a picture or diagram by making lines and marks on paper. **2** pull or drag a vehicle so as to make it follow behind. **3** pull or move in a particular direction: *the train drew into the station.* **4** open or shut curtains.

5 arrive at a point in time: *the campaign drew to a close.* **6** take from a container: *he drew his gun.* **7** (**draw something from/out**) get or take something from a source. **8** take in a breath. **9** be the cause of a particular response. **10** attract to a place or an event. **11** persuade to reveal something: *he refused to be drawn on what would happen.* **12** reach a conclusion. **13** finish a contest or game with an even score. • n. **1** an even score at the end of a game or match. **2** an act of selecting names at random for prizes, sporting fixtures, etc. **3** a person or thing that is very attractive or interesting. **4** an act of inhaling smoke from a cigarette.
– PHRASES **draw in** (of successive days) become shorter. **draw the line at** refuse to do or tolerate. **draw on 1** (of a period of time) pass by and approach its end. **2** suck smoke from a cigarette or pipe. **draw something out** make something last longer. **draw someone out** persuade someone to be more talkative. **draw up** come to a halt. **draw something up** prepare a plan or document.
– ORIGIN Old English.

> USAGE: Do not confuse **draw** with **drawer**. As a noun, **draw** chiefly means 'an even score at the end of a game or match' (*he scored twice to force a 4–4 draw*), whereas **drawer** means 'a sliding storage compartment'.

drawback • n. a disadvantage.

drawbridge • n. a bridge which is hinged at one end so that it can be raised.

drawer • n. **1** /draw/ a storage compartment made to slide horizontally in and out of a desk or chest. **2** (**drawers**) /drawz/ dated knickers or underpants. **3** /draw-er/ a person who draws something.

drawing • n. a picture or diagram made with a pencil, pen, or crayon.

drawing board • n. a board on which paper can be spread for artists or designers to work on.
– PHRASES **back to the drawing board** a plan has failed and a new one is needed.

drawing pin • n. Brit. a short flat-headed pin for fastening paper to a surface.

drawing room • n. a room in a large house in which guests can be received.
– ORIGIN from *withdrawing-room* 'a room to withdraw to'.

drawl • v. speak in a slow, lazy way with prolonged vowel sounds. • n. a drawling accent.
– ORIGIN German or Dutch *dralen* 'delay'.

drawn past part. of **DRAW**. • adj. looking

strained from illness or exhaustion.

drawn-out • adj. lasting longer than is necessary.

drawstring • n. a string in the seam of a garment or bag, which can be pulled to tighten or close it.

dray • n. a low lorry or cart without sides, for delivering barrels or other heavy loads.
– ORIGIN perh. from Old English, 'dragnet'.

dread • v. think about with great fear or anxiety. • n. great fear or anxiety.
– ORIGIN Old English.

dreadful • adj. 1 very bad or serious. 2 used for emphasis: *he's a dreadful flirt.*
– DERIVATIVES **dreadfully** adv.

dreadlocks • pl. n. a Rastafarian hairstyle in which the hair is twisted into tight braids or ringlets.
– DERIVATIVES **dreadlocked** adj.

dream • n. 1 a series of images and feelings occurring in a person's mind during sleep. 2 a long-held ambition or wish. 3 informal a wonderful or perfect person or thing. • v. (**dreams, dreaming, dreamed** or **dreamt** /dremt/) 1 experience dreams during sleep. 2 have daydreams. 3 think of as possible: *I never dreamed she'd take offence.* 4 (**dream something up**) invent something.
– PHRASES **like a dream** informal very easily or successfully.
– DERIVATIVES **dreamer** n. **dreamless** adj.
– ORIGIN Germanic.

dreamy • adj. (**dreamier, dreamiest**) 1 tending to daydream. 2 having a pleasantly unreal quality.
– DERIVATIVES **dreamily** adv. **dreaminess** n.

dreary • adj. (**drearier, dreariest**) dull, bleak, and depressing.
– DERIVATIVES **drearily** adv. **dreariness** n.
– ORIGIN Old English, 'gory, melancholy'.

dredge • v. (**dredges, dredging, dredged**) 1 scoop out mud or objects from the bed of a harbour or river. 2 (**dredge something up**) mention something unpleasant that has been forgotten. • n. a machine for scooping up mud or objects from a river or seabed.
– DERIVATIVES **dredger** n.
– ORIGIN perh. from Dutch *dregghe* 'grappling hook'.

dregs • n. 1 the last drops of a liquid left in a container, together with any sediment. 2 the most worthless parts: *the dregs of society.*
– ORIGIN prob. from Scandinavian.

drench • v. 1 wet thoroughly. 2 (often as adj. **drenched**) cover with large amounts of something: *a sun-drenched clearing.*
– ORIGIN Old English.

dress • v. 1 (also **get dressed**) put on your clothes. 2 put clothes on someone. 3 wear clothes in a particular way or of a particular type: *she dresses well.* 4 decorate or arrange in an attractive way. 5 clean and cover a wound. 6 clean and prepare food for cooking or eating. 7 treat or smooth the surface of leather, fabric, or stone. • n. 1 a woman's garment that covers the body and extends down over the legs. 2 clothing of a particular kind: *evening dress.*
– PHRASES **dress up** dress in smart clothes or in a special costume.
– ORIGIN Old French *dresser* 'arrange'.

dressage /dress-ahzh/ • n. the training of a horse to perform a set of controlled movements at the rider's command.
– ORIGIN French.

dress circle • n. Brit. the first level of seats above the ground floor in a theatre.

dresser • n. 1 a sideboard with shelves above for storing and displaying crockery. 2 a person who dresses in a particular way.

dressing • n. 1 a sauce for salads, usually consisting of oil and vinegar with flavourings. 2 a piece of material placed on a wound to protect it. 3 a layer of fertilizer spread over land.

dressing-down • n. informal a severe reprimand.

dressing gown • n. a long robe worn after getting out of bed or having a bath or shower.

dressing room • n. 1 a room in which actors or other performers change clothes. 2 a room attached to a bedroom for storing clothes.

dressing table • n. a table with a mirror and drawers, used while dressing or applying make-up.

dressmaker • n. a person who makes women's clothes.
– DERIVATIVES **dressmaking** n.

dress rehearsal • n. a final rehearsal in which everything is done as it would be in a real performance.

dress shirt • n. a man's white shirt worn with a bow tie on formal occasions.

dressy • adj. (**dressier, dressiest**) (of clothes) smart or formal.

drew past of DRAW.

dribble • v. (**dribbles, dribbling, dribbled**) 1 (of a liquid) fall slowly in drops or a thin stream. 2 allow saliva to run from the mouth. 3 (in sport) take the ball forward with slight touches or (in basketball) by continuous bouncing. • n. a thin stream of liquid.
– DERIVATIVES **dribbler** n.

d

– ORIGIN from **DRIP**.

dribs and drabs • pl. n. (in phr. **in dribs and drabs**) informal in small amounts over a period of time.

dried past and past part. of **DRY**.

drier[1] • n. var. of **DRYER**.

drier[2] • adj. comparative of **DRY**.

drift • v. **1** be carried slowly by a current of air or water. **2** walk or move slowly or casually. **3** (of snow, leaves, etc.) be blown into heaps by the wind. • n. **1** a continuous slow movement from one place to another. **2** the general meaning of someone's remarks: *he got her drift.* **3** a large mass of snow, leaves, etc. piled up by the wind.

– ORIGIN Old Norse.

drifter • n. **1** a person who continually moves from place to place, without any fixed home or job. **2** a fishing boat with a drift net.

drift net • n. a large fishing net allowed to drift in the sea.

driftwood • n. pieces of wood floating on the sea or washed ashore.

drill[1] • n. **1** a tool or machine for boring holes. **2** training in military exercises. **3** instruction by means of repeated exercises. **4** (**the drill**) informal the correct procedure. • v. **1** bore a hole with a drill. **2** give military training or other thorough instruction to someone.

– DERIVATIVES **driller** n.

– ORIGIN Dutch *drillen*.

drill[2] • n. a machine which makes small furrows, sows seed in them, and then covers the sown seed.

– ORIGIN perh. from **DRILL**[1].

drill[3] • n. a strong cotton fabric woven with parallel diagonal lines.

– ORIGIN Latin *trilix* 'triple-twilled'.

drily /dry-li/ (also **dryly**) • adv. in a matter-of-fact or ironically humorous way.

drink • v. (**drinks, drinking, drank**; past part. **drunk**) **1** take a liquid into the mouth and swallow it. **2** consume alcohol, especially regularly. **3** (**drink something in**) watch or listen eagerly to something. • n. **1** a liquid for drinking. **2** a quantity of liquid swallowed at one time. **3** alcohol or an alcoholic drink.

– DERIVATIVES **drinkable** adj. **drinker** n.

– ORIGIN Old English.

drink-driving • n. Brit. the crime of driving a vehicle after drinking too much alcohol.

drip • v. (**drips, dripping, dripped**) fall or let fall in small drops of liquid. • n. **1** a small drop of a liquid. **2** a device which slowly passes a substance into a patient's body through a vein. **3** informal

a weak or foolish person.

– ORIGIN Old English.

drip-dry • adj. (of an item of clothing) able to dry without creases if hung up when wet.

drip-feed • v. supply a patient with fluid through a drip.

dripping • n. Brit. fat that has melted and dripped from roasting meat. • adj. very wet.

drippy • adj. informal weak, silly, or very sentimental.

drive • v. (**drives, driving, drove**; past part. **driven**) **1** operate and control a motor vehicle. **2** carry in a motor vehicle. **3** carry or urge along. **4** make someone act in a particular way. **5** provide the energy to keep an engine or machine in motion. • n. **1** a journey in a car. **2** (also **driveway**) a short private road leading to a house. **3** an inborn desire or urge. **4** an organized effort to achieve a particular purpose. **5** determination and ambition.

– PHRASES **what someone is driving at** the point that someone is trying to make.

– DERIVATIVES **drivable** (also **driveable**) adj. **driver** n.

– ORIGIN Old English.

drive-by shooting • n. esp. N. Amer. a shooting carried out from a passing vehicle.

drive-in • adj. (of a cinema, restaurant, etc.) that you can visit without leaving your car.

drivel /driv-uhl/ • n. nonsense.

– ORIGIN Old English.

driven past part. of **DRIVE**.

driving • adj. **1** having a controlling influence: *the driving force behind the plan.* **2** (of rain or snow) being blown by the wind with great force.

– PHRASES **in the driving seat** in control.

driving licence • n. a document permitting a person to drive a motor vehicle.

drizzle • n. light rain falling in fine drops. • v. (**drizzles, drizzling, drizzled**) **1** (**it drizzles, it is drizzling**, etc.) rain lightly. **2** pour a thin stream of a liquid ingredient over a dish.

– DERIVATIVES **drizzly** adj.

– ORIGIN prob. from Old English, 'to fall'.

droll /drohl/ • adj. amusing in a strange or unexpected way.

– DERIVATIVES **drollery** n. **drolly** /drohl-li/ adv.

– ORIGIN French.

dromedary /drom-i-duh-ri/ • n. (pl. **dromedaries**) an Arabian camel, with one hump.

– ORIGIN from Latin *dromedarius camelus* 'swift camel'.

drone • v. (**drones, droning, droned**) **1** make a low continuous humming sound. **2** (**drone on**) talk for a long time in a boring way. • n. **1** a low continuous humming sound. **2** a male bee which does no work but can fertilize a queen.
– ORIGIN Old English, 'male bee'.

drool • v. (**drools, drooling, drooled**) **1** drop saliva uncontrollably from the mouth. **2** (**drool over**) informal show great pleasure or desire for.
– ORIGIN from **DRIVEL**, in the earlier sense 'spittle'.

droop • v. **1** bend or hang downwards limply. **2** sag down from tiredness or low spirits. • n. an act of drooping.
– ORIGIN Old Norse, 'hang the head'.

droopy • adj. **1** hanging down limply. **2** lacking strength or spirit.

drop • v. (**drops, dropping, dropped**) **1** fall or cause to fall. **2** sink to the ground. **3** make or become lower or less: *he dropped his voice*. **4** abandon a course of action. **5** (often **drop someone/thing off**) set down or unload a passenger or goods. **6** mention something casually. **7** lose a point, match, etc. • n. **1** a small round or pear-shaped amount of liquid. **2** an instance of dropping. **3** a small drink: *a drop of water*. **4** an abrupt fall or slope. **5** a sweet.
– PHRASES **drop by/in** visit informally and briefly. **drop someone a line** informal send someone a short letter. **drop off** fall asleep. **drop out 1** stop participating. **2** live an alternative lifestyle.
– ORIGIN Old English.

drop goal • n. Rugby a goal scored by a drop kick over the crossbar.

drop kick • n. a kick made by dropping the ball and kicking it as it bounces.

droplet • n. a very small drop of a liquid.

dropout • n. a person who has dropped out of society or a course of study.

dropper • n. a short glass tube with a rubber bulb at one end, for measuring out drops of liquid.

droppings • pl. n. the excrement of animals.

dropsy /drop-si/ • n. dated = **OEDEMA**.
– ORIGIN from former *hydropsy*.

dross • n. rubbish.
– ORIGIN Old English.

drought /drowt/ • n. a very long period of abnormally low rainfall.
– ORIGIN Old English, 'dryness'.

drove[1] past of **DRIVE**.

drove[2] • n. **1** a flock of animals being moved along as a group. **2** a large number of people doing the same thing: *tourists arrived in droves.*
– DERIVATIVES **drover** n.
– ORIGIN Old English.

drown • v. **1** die or kill through submersion in water. **2** flood an area. **3** (usu. **drown someone/thing out**) make someone or something impossible to hear by making a very loud noise.
– ORIGIN Old Norse, 'be drowned'.

drowse /drowz/ • v. (**drowses, drowsing, drowsed**) be half asleep; doze.
– ORIGIN prob. from Old English, 'be slow'.

drowsy • adj. sleepy.
– DERIVATIVES **drowsily** adv. **drowsiness** n.

drubbing • n. informal a thorough defeat in a match or contest.
– ORIGIN prob. from Arabic.

drudge • n. a person made to do hard, menial, or dull work.

drudgery • n. hard, menial, or dull work.

drug • n. **1** a substance used to treat or prevent disease or infection. **2** an illegal substance taken for the effects it has on the body. • v. (**drugs, drugging, drugged**) give someone a drug in order to make them unconscious.
– ORIGIN Old French *drogue*.

drugstore • n. N. Amer. a pharmacy which also sells toiletries and other articles.

Druid /droo-id/ • n. a priest in the ancient Celtic religion.
– DERIVATIVES **Druidic** adj.
– ORIGIN Gaulish (the language of the ancient Gauls).

drum • n. **1** a percussion instrument with a skin stretched across a frame, sounded by being hit with sticks or the hands. **2** a cylindrical container or part. • v. (**drums, drumming, drummed**) **1** play on a drum. **2** make a continuous rhythmic noise. **3** (**drum something into**) teach something to someone by constantly repeating it. **4** (**drum something up**) try hard to get support or business.
– ORIGIN Dutch or German *tromme*.

drum and bass • n. a type of dance music consisting largely of electronic drums and bass.

drumbeat • n. a stroke or pattern of strokes on a drum.

drum kit • n. a set of drums, cymbals, and other percussion instruments.

drum majorette • n. the female leader of a marching band.

drummer • n. a person who plays a drum or drums.

drum roll • n. a rapid succession of drumbeats.

drumstick • n. **1** a stick used for beating a drum. **2** the lower joint of the leg of a cooked chicken or similar bird.

d

drunk past part. of DRINK. • adj. affected by alcohol to such an extent that you are not in control of yourself. • n. a person who is drunk or who often drinks too much.

drunkard • n. a person who is often drunk.

drunken • adj. **1** drunk. **2** caused by or showing the effects of drink.
– DERIVATIVES **drunkenly** adv. **drunkenness** n.

☑ **drunkenness** is spelled with a double n (*drunken* + *-ness*).

drupe /droop/ • n. a fleshy fruit with a central stone, e.g. a plum or olive.
– ORIGIN Latin *drupa* 'overripe olive'.

dry • adj. (**drier, driest**) **1** free from moisture or liquid. **2** without grease or other lubrication: *his throat was dry and sore.* **3** serious and boring. **4** (of humour) subtle and expressed in a matter-of-fact way. **5** (of wine) not sweet. • v. (**dries, drying, dried**) **1** make or become dry. **2** preserve something by evaporating the moisture from it. **3** (**dry up**) (of a supply) decrease and stop.
– DERIVATIVES **dryness** n.
– ORIGIN Old English.

dry cell (also **dry battery**) • n. an electric cell (or battery) in which the electrolyte is in the form of a paste.

dry-clean • v. clean clothes with a chemical, without using water.

dryer (also **drier**) • n. a machine or device for drying something.

dry ice • n. **1** solid carbon dioxide. **2** white mist produced with this as a theatrical effect.

dryly • adv. var. of DRILY.

dry rot • n. a fungus causing wood to decay.

dry run • n. informal a rehearsal.

drystone • adj. Brit. (of a stone wall) built without using mortar.

DSC • abbrev. (in the UK) Distinguished Service Cross.

DSO • abbrev. (in the UK) Distinguished Service Order.

DTI • abbrev. (in the UK) Department of Trade and Industry.

DTP • abbrev. desktop publishing.

DTs • pl. n. informal delirium tremens.

dual • adj. consisting of two parts or aspects.
– DERIVATIVES **dually** adv.
– ORIGIN Latin *dualis*.

dual carriageway • n. Brit. a road consisting of two or more lanes in each direction.

dualism • n. **1** division into two opposed aspects, such as good and evil. **2** duality.
– DERIVATIVES **dualist** n. & adj. **dualistic** adj.

duality • n. the state of having two parts or aspects.

dub¹ • v. (**dubs, dubbing, dubbed**) **1** give someone an unofficial name. **2** knight someone by touching their shoulder with a sword.
– ORIGIN Old French *adober* 'equip with armour'.

dub² • v. (**dubs, dubbing, dubbed**) **1** provide a film with a soundtrack in a different language from the original. **2** add sound effects or music to a film or a recording. • n. an act of dubbing sound effects or music.
– ORIGIN from DOUBLE.

dubbin /dub-bin/ • n. Brit. prepared grease used for softening and water-proofing leather.
– ORIGIN from DUB¹ (in the sense 'smear leather with grease').

dubiety /dyoo-by-i-ti/ • n. formal uncertainty.

dubious /dyoo-bi-uhss/ • adj. **1** hesitating or doubting. **2** probably not honest. **3** of questionable value.
– DERIVATIVES **dubiously** adv.
– ORIGIN Latin *dubiosus*.

dubnium /dub-ni-uhm/ • n. a very unstable chemical element made by high-energy atomic collisions.
– ORIGIN from *Dubna* in Russia.

ducal /dyoo-k'l/ • adj. relating to a duke or dukedom.

ducat /duk-uht/ • n. a former European gold coin.
– ORIGIN Italian *ducato*.

duchess • n. **1** the wife or widow of a duke. **2** a woman holding a rank equivalent to duke.
– ORIGIN Old French.

duchy /duch-i/ • n. (pl. **duchies**) the territory of a duke or duchess.
– ORIGIN Old French *duche*.

duck¹ • n. (pl. **duck** or **ducks**) **1** a waterbird with a broad bill, short legs, and webbed feet. **2** a female duck. Contrasted with DRAKE.
– PHRASES **like water off a duck's back** (of a critical remark) having no effect.
– ORIGIN Old English.

duck² • v. **1** lower the head or body quickly to avoid being hit or seen. **2** push someone under water. **3** informal avoid an unwelcome duty.
– DERIVATIVES **ducker** n.
– ORIGIN Germanic.

duck³ • n. Cricket a batsman's score of nought.
– ORIGIN short for *duck's egg*, used for the figure o.

duck-billed platypus •n. see PLATYPUS.

duckboards • pl. n. wooden slats joined together to form a path over muddy ground.

ducking stool •n. hist. a chair on the end of a pole, in which offenders were plunged into a pond or river as a punishment.

duckling •n. a young duck.

duct •n. 1 a tube or passageway for air, cables, etc. 2 a tube in the body through which fluid passes. •v. convey through a duct.
– ORIGIN Latin *ductus* 'leading'.

ductile /duk-tyl/ •adj. (of a metal) able to be drawn out into a thin wire.
– DERIVATIVES **ductility** n.

dud informal •n. a thing that fails to work properly. •adj. failing to work or meet a standard.

dude /dyood/ •n. N. Amer. informal a man.
– ORIGIN prob. from German dialect *Dude* 'fool'.

dudgeon /duj-uhn/ •n. (in phr. **in high dudgeon**) angry or resentful.

due •adj. 1 expected at a certain time. 2 owed or deserving something: *he was due for a rise.* 3 needing to be paid; owing. 4 required as a legal or moral duty: *driving without due care and attention.* •n. 1 (**someone's due/dues**) what a person deserves or is owed. 2 (**dues**) fees. •adv. (with reference to a point of the compass) directly: *head due south.*
– PHRASES **due to 1** caused by. 2 because of. **in due course** at the appropriate time.
– ORIGIN Old French *deu* 'owed'.

duel •n. 1 hist. a prearranged contest with deadly weapons between two people to settle a point of honour. 2 a contest between two parties. •v. (**duels, duelling, duelled;** US **duels, dueling, dueled**) fight a duel.
– DERIVATIVES **duellist** (US **duelist**) n.
– ORIGIN Latin *duellum* 'war'.

duet •n. 1 a performance by two singers, musicians, or dancers. 2 a musical composition for two performers. •v. (**duets, duetting, duetted**) perform a duet.
– ORIGIN Italian *duetto*.

duff[1] •adj. Brit. informal worthless or false.

duff[2] •v. (**duff someone up**) Brit. informal beat someone up.

duffel bag (also **duffle bag**) •n. a cylindrical canvas bag closed by a draw-string.

duffel coat (also **duffle coat**) •n. a hooded coat made of a coarse woollen material.

– ORIGIN named after the Belgian town of *Duffel*.

duffer •n. informal an incompetent or stupid person.
– ORIGIN Scots *dowfart*.

dug[1] past and past part. of DIG.

dug[2] •n. the udder, teat, or nipple of a female animal.
– ORIGIN perh. from Old Norse.

dugong /dyoo-gong/ •n. (pl. **dugong** or **dugongs**) a sea cow (mammal) found in the Indian Ocean.
– ORIGIN Malay.

dugout •n. 1 a trench that is roofed over as a shelter for troops. 2 a low shelter at the side of a sports field for a team's coaches and substitutes. 3 (also **dugout canoe**) a canoe made from a hollowed tree trunk.

duiker /dy-ker/ •n. (pl. **duiker** or **duikers**) a small African antelope.
– ORIGIN Dutch, 'diver'.

duke •n. 1 a man holding the highest hereditary title in Britain and certain other countries. 2 hist. (in parts of Europe) a male ruler of a small independent state.
– DERIVATIVES **dukedom** n.
– ORIGIN Old French *duc*.

dulcet /dul-sit/ •adj. usu. ironic (of a sound) sweet and soothing.
– ORIGIN Old French *doucet*.

dulcimer /dul-si-mer/ •n. a musical instrument with strings which are struck with hand-held hammers.
– ORIGIN Old French *doulcemer*.

dull •adj. 1 not interesting. 2 not bright or shiny. 3 (of the weather) overcast. 4 slow to understand. •v. make or become dull.
– DERIVATIVES **dullness** n. **dully** adv.
– ORIGIN Old English.

dullard /dul-lerd/ •n. a slow or stupid person.

duly •adv. in accordance with what is required or expected.

dumb •adj. 1 offens. unable to speak; lacking the power of speech. 2 temporarily unable or unwilling to speak. 3 N. Amer. informal stupid. •v. (**dumb something down**) informal make something less intellectually challenging.
– DERIVATIVES **dumbly** adv. **dumbness** n.
– ORIGIN Old English.

dumb-bell •n. a short bar with a weight at each end, used for exercise.

dumbfound •v. greatly astonish someone.
– ORIGIN from DUMB and CONFOUND.

dumbo •n. (pl. **dumbos**) informal a stupid person.

dumbshow • n. gestures used to communicate something without speech.

dumbstruck • adj. so shocked or surprised as to be unable to speak.

dumb waiter • n. a small lift for carrying food and crockery between floors.

dumdum (also **dumdum bullet**) • n. a kind of soft-nosed bullet that expands on impact.
– ORIGIN from *Dum Dum*, a town in India.

dummy • n. (pl. **dummies**) 1 a model of a human being. 2 an object designed to resemble and take the place of the real one. 3 Brit. a rubber or plastic teat for a baby to suck on. 4 (in sport) a pretended pass or kick. • v. (**dummies, dummying, dummied**) pretend to pass or kick the ball.
– ORIGIN from **DUMB**.

dummy run • n. Brit. a practice or trial.

dump • n. 1 a site where rubbish or waste is left. 2 a heap of rubbish left at a dump. 3 informal an unpleasant or dull place. 4 Mil. a temporary store of weapons or provisions. • v. 1 get rid of rubbish. 2 put something down carelessly. 3 informal abandon someone.
– ORIGIN perh. from Old Norse.

dumper • n. 1 a person or thing that dumps something. 2 (also **dumper truck**) Brit. a lorry with a body that tilts or opens at the back for unloading.

dumpling • n. a small savoury ball of dough boiled in water or in a stew.
– ORIGIN perh. from former *dump* 'of the consistency of dough'.

dumps • pl. n. (in phr. (**down) in the dumps**) informal depressed or unhappy.
– ORIGIN prob. from Dutch *domp* 'haze'.

dumpy • adj. (**dumpier, dumpiest**) short and stout.

dun • n. a dull greyish-brown colour.
– ORIGIN Old English.

dunce • n. a person who is slow at learning.
– ORIGIN from the name of the Scottish theologian John *Duns* Scotus, whose followers were ridiculed.

dunce's cap • n. a paper cone formerly put on the head of a dunce at school as a mark of disgrace.

dunderhead • n. informal a stupid person.
– ORIGIN perh. from former Scots *dunder, dunner* 'resounding noise'.

dune • n. a mound or ridge of sand formed by the wind.
– ORIGIN Dutch.

dung • n. manure.
– ORIGIN Old English.

dungarees /dung-guh-reez/ • pl. n. esp. Brit. a garment consisting of trousers held up by straps over the shoulders.
– ORIGIN Hindi.

dungeon • n. a strong underground prison cell.
– ORIGIN Old French.

dunghill • n. a heap of dung or refuse.

dunk • v. 1 dip food into a drink or soup before eating it. 2 immerse in water.
– ORIGIN German *tunken*.

dunlin • n. (pl. **dunlin** or **dunlins**) a sandpiper with a bill that curves downwards and (in winter) greyish-brown upper parts.
– ORIGIN prob. from **DUN** + **-LING**.

dunnock /dun-nuhk/ • n. a songbird with a grey head and a reddish-brown back.
– ORIGIN prob. from **DUN**.

dunny • n. (pl. **dunnies**) Austral./NZ informal a toilet.
– ORIGIN prob. from **DUNG** + former slang *ken* 'house'.

duo • n. (pl. **duos**) 1 a pair of people or things, especially in music or entertainment. 2 Music a duet.
– ORIGIN Latin, 'two'.

duodecimal /dyoo-oh-**dess**-i-m'l/ • adj. relating to a system of counting that has twelve as a base.
– ORIGIN Latin *duodecimus* 'twelfth'.

duodenum /dyoo-oh-**dee**-nuhm/ • n. (pl. **duodenums**) the first part of the small intestine immediately beyond the stomach.
– DERIVATIVES **duodenal** adj.
– ORIGIN Latin.

duologue /dyoo-uh-log/ • n. a play or part of a play with speaking roles for only two actors.

duopoly /dyoo-op-uh-li/ • n. (pl. **duopolies**) a situation in which two suppliers dominate a commercial market.
– ORIGIN Latin *duplus*.

dupe • v. (**dupes, duping, duped**) deceive or trick someone. • n. a person who has been deceived or tricked.
– ORIGIN French dialect, 'hoopoe'.

duple /dyoo-p'l/ • adj. Music (of rhythm) based on two main beats to the bar.
– ORIGIN Latin *duplus*.

duplex /dyoo-pleks/ • n. N. Amer. 1 a residential building divided into two apartments. 2 a flat on two floors. 3 N. Amer. & Austral. a semi-detached house.
– ORIGIN Latin.

duplicate • adj. /dyoo-pli-kuht/ 1 exactly like something else. 2 having two corresponding parts. • n. /dyoo-pli-kuht/ one of two or more identical things. • v. /dyoo-pli-kayt/ (**duplicates, duplicating, duplicated**) 1 make or be an exact copy of something. 2 multiply

something by two. **3** do something again unnecessarily.
– DERIVATIVES **duplication** n.
– ORIGIN Latin *duplicare*.

duplicator •n. a machine for copying something.

duplicity /dyoo-pli-si-ti/ •n. dishonest behaviour that is intended to deceive.
– DERIVATIVES **duplicitous** adj.

durable •adj. **1** hard-wearing. **2** (of goods) not for immediate consumption and so able to be kept.
– DERIVATIVES **durability** n. **durably** adv.
– ORIGIN Latin *durabilis*.

dura mater /dyoo-ruh may-ter/ •n. the tough outermost membrane enclosing the brain and spinal cord.
– ORIGIN Latin, 'hard mother'.

duration •n. the time during which something continues.
– ORIGIN Latin.

duress /dyuu-ress/ •n. threats or violence used to force a person to do something: *confessions extracted under duress*.
– ORIGIN Latin *durus* 'hard'.

during •prep. **1** throughout the course of a period of time. **2** at a particular point in the course of a period of time.
– ORIGIN Latin *durare* 'endure'.

durum wheat /dyoo-ruhm/ •n. a kind of hard wheat, yielding flour that is used to make pasta.
– ORIGIN Latin.

dusk •n. the darker stage of twilight.
– ORIGIN Old English, 'dark, swarthy'.

dusky •adj. (**duskier**, **duskiest**) darkish in colour.
– DERIVATIVES **duskily** adv. **duskiness** n.

dust •n. **1** fine, dry powder made up of tiny particles of earth or waste matter. **2** any material in the form of tiny particles: *coal dust*. •v. **1** remove dust from something. **2** cover lightly with a powdered substance.
– ORIGIN Old English.

dustbin •n. Brit. a large container for household rubbish.

dust bowl •n. an area where vegetation has been lost and the soil eroded and reduced to dust.

dustcart •n. Brit. a vehicle used for collecting household rubbish.

dust cover •n. a dust jacket or dust sheet.

duster •n. a cloth for dusting furniture.

dust jacket •n. a removable paper cover on a book.

dustman •n. (pl. **dustmen**) Brit. a man employed to collect household rubbish.

dustpan •n. a hand-held container into which dust and waste can be swept.

dust sheet •n. Brit. a sheet for covering furniture to protect it from dust or while decorating.

dust-up •n. informal a fight or quarrel.

dusty •adj. (**dustier**, **dustiest**) **1** covered with or resembling dust. **2** solemn and uninteresting.
– DERIVATIVES **dustily** adv. **dustiness** n.

Dutch •adj. relating to the Netherlands or its language. •n. the language of the Netherlands.
– PHRASES **go Dutch** share the cost of a meal equally.
– DERIVATIVES **Dutchman** n. (pl. **Dutchmen**). **Dutchwoman** n. (pl. **Dutchwomen**).

Dutch courage •n. confidence gained from drinking alcohol.

Dutch elm disease •n. a disease of elm trees, caused by a fungus.

Dutch oven •n. a covered earthenware container for cooking casseroles.

dutiable /dyoo-ti-uh-b'l/ •adj. (of goods) on which customs or other duties have to be paid.

dutiful •adj. doing your duty in a conscientious way.
– DERIVATIVES **dutifully** adv.

duty •n. (pl. **duties**) **1** something you have to do because it is morally or legally necessary. **2** a task required as part of your job. **3** a payment charged on the import, export, manufacture, or sale of goods.
– PHRASES **on** (or **off**) **duty** doing (or not doing) your regular work.
– ORIGIN Old French *duete*.

duty-bound •adj. morally or legally obliged to do something.

duty-free •adj. & adv. (of goods) not requiring payment of duty.

duvet /doo-vay/ •n. esp. Brit. a thick quilt used instead of an upper sheet and blankets.
– ORIGIN French, 'down'.

DVD •abbrev. digital versatile disc.

DVD-R •abbrev. DVD recordable, a DVD which can be recorded on once only.

DVD-ROM •abbrev. DVD read-only memory, a DVD used in a computer for displaying data.

DVD-RW (also **DVD-RAM**) •abbrev. DVD rewritable (or random-access memory), a DVD on which recordings can be made and erased a number of times.

DVLA •abbrev. Driver and Vehicle Licensing Agency.

dwarf •n. (pl. **dwarfs** or **dwarves**) **1** a member of a mythical race of short human-like creatures. **2** a person who is unusually small. •v. make something seem small in comparison with

something larger. •adj. (of an animal or plant) much smaller than is usual for its type or species.
– DERIVATIVES **dwarfish** adj.
– ORIGIN Old English.

dwarfism •n. unusually low stature or small size.

dwell •v. (**dwells**, **dwelling**, **dwelt** or **dwelled**) 1 formal live in or at a place. 2 (**dwell on**) think about something at length.
– DERIVATIVES **dweller** n.
– ORIGIN Old English.

dwelling •n. formal a house or other place where someone lives.

dwindle •v. (**dwindles**, **dwindling**, **dwindled**) gradually become smaller or weaker.
– ORIGIN Scots and dialect *dwine*.

DWP •abbrev. (in the UK) Department for Work and Pensions.

Dy •symb. the chemical element dysprosium.

dye •n. a natural or synthetic substance used to colour something. •v. (**dyes**, **dyeing**, **dyed**) colour something with dye.
– PHRASES **dyed in the wool** having firm beliefs that never change.
– DERIVATIVES **dyer** n.
– ORIGIN Old English.

dyestuff •n. a substance used as or yielding a dye.

dying pres. part. of DIE¹.

dyke¹ (also **dike**) •n. 1 a barrier built to prevent flooding from the sea. 2 a ditch or watercourse. 3 Geol. an intrusion of igneous rock cutting across existing strata.
– ORIGIN Old Norse.

dyke² (also **dike**) •n. informal a lesbian.

dynamic •adj. 1 (of a process) constantly changing or active. 2 full of energy and new ideas. 3 Physics relating to forces producing motion. Often contrasted with STATIC. •n. a force that stimulates change.
– DERIVATIVES **dynamical** adj. **dynamically** adv.
– ORIGIN Greek *dunamikos*.

dynamics •n. 1 the branch of mechanics concerned with the motion of bodies under the action of forces. 2 the forces which stimulate change within a process. 3 the varying levels of volume of sound in a musical performance.

dynamism •n. the quality of being full of energy, vigour, or enthusiasm.

dynamite •n. 1 a high explosive made of nitroglycerine. 2 informal an extremely impressive or dangerous person or thing. •v. (**dynamites**, **dynamiting**, **dynamited**) blow up with dynamite.
– ORIGIN Greek *dunamis* 'power'.

dynamo •n. (pl. **dynamos**) esp. Brit. a machine for converting mechanical energy into electrical energy.
– ORIGIN from *dynamo-electric machine*.

dynamometer /dy-nuh-**mom**-iter/ •n. an instrument which measures the power output of an engine.

dynast /**dy**-nuhst, **dy**-nast/ •n. a member of a dynasty, especially a hereditary ruler.

dynasty /di-nuh-sti/ •n. (pl. **dynasties**) 1 a series of rulers who belong to the same family. 2 a succession of powerful people from the same family.
– DERIVATIVES **dynastic** adj.
– ORIGIN Greek *dunasteia* 'lordship'.

dyne /dyn/ •n. Physics a unit of force.
– ORIGIN Greek *dunamis* 'force, power'.

dys- •comb. form bad; difficult: *dyspepsia*.
– ORIGIN Greek *dus-*.

dysentery /**diss**-uhn-tri/ •n. a disease in which the intestines are infected, resulting in severe diarrhoea.
– ORIGIN Greek *dusenteria*.

dysfunctional •adj. 1 not operating normally. 2 unable to deal with normal relationships between people.
– DERIVATIVES **dysfunction** n. **dysfunctionally** adv.

dyslexia /diss-**lek**-si-uh/ •n. a disorder involving difficulty in learning to read words, letters, and other symbols.
– DERIVATIVES **dyslexic** adj. & n.
– ORIGIN Greek *lexis* 'speech'.

dysmenorrhoea /diss-men-uh-**ree**-uh/ (US **dysmenorrhea**) •n. Med. painful menstruation.

dyspepsia /diss-**pep**-si-uh/ •n. indigestion.
– ORIGIN Greek *duspepsia*.

dyspeptic •adj. 1 relating to or suffering from indigestion. 2 irritable; bad-tempered.

dysprosium /diss-**proh**-zi-uhm/ •n. a soft silvery-white metallic chemical element.
– ORIGIN Greek *dusprositos* 'hard to get at'.

dystopia /diss-**toh**-pi-uh/ •n. an imaginary place or society in which everything is bad.
– DERIVATIVES **dystopian** adj. & n.
– ORIGIN from DYS- + UTOPIA.

dystrophy /**diss**-truh-fi/ •n. a disorder in which an organ or tissue of the body wastes away. See also MUSCULAR DYSTROPHY.
– ORIGIN from Greek *-trophia* 'nourishment'.

Ee

E¹ (also **e**) •n. (pl. **Es** or **E's**) **1** the fifth letter of the alphabet. **2** Music the third note of the scale of C major.

E² •abbrev. **1** East or Eastern. **2** informal the drug Ecstasy or a tablet of Ecstasy. **3** Physics energy.

e •symb. **1** (€) euro or euros. **2** (*e*) Mathematics the transcendental number that is the base of natural logarithms, approximately equal to 2.71828.

e- •prefix referring to the use of electronic data transfer or commerce, especially through the Internet: *e-ticket*.
– ORIGIN from **ELECTRONIC**.

each •det. & pron. every one of two or more people or things, regarded separately. •adv. to, for, or by every one of a group.
– ORIGIN Old English.

each other •pron. the other one or ones.

eager •adj. **1** strongly wanting to do or have something. **2** keenly expectant or interested.
– DERIVATIVES **eagerly** adv. **eagerness** n.
– ORIGIN Old French *aigre* 'keen'.

eagle •n. a large keen-sighted bird of prey with long broad wings.
– ORIGIN Old French *aigle*.

eagle-eyed •adj. sharp-sighted and very observant.

ear¹ •n. **1** the organ of hearing and balance in humans and other vertebrates. **2** an ability to recognize and appreciate music or language. **3** willingness to listen: *a sympathetic ear*.
– PHRASES **be all ears** informal be listening attentively. **keep your ear to the ground** be well informed about recent events or developments. **be out on your ear** informal be abruptly dismissed from a job. **be up to your ears in** informal be very busy with.
– ORIGIN Old English.

ear² •n. the seed-bearing head of a cereal plant.
– ORIGIN Old English.

earache •n. pain inside the ear.

eardrum •n. the membrane of the middle ear, which vibrates in response to sound waves.

earful •n. informal a lengthy reprimand.

earhole •n. the outer opening of the ear.

earl •n. a British nobleman ranking above a viscount and below a marquess.
– DERIVATIVES **earldom** n.
– ORIGIN Old English.

ear lobe •n. see LOBE (sense 2).

early •adj. (**earlier, earliest**) & adv. **1** before the usual or expected time. **2** near the beginning of a particular period or sequence.
– PHRASES **at the earliest** not before the time or date specified. **early** (or **earlier**) **on** at an early (or earlier) stage.
– DERIVATIVES **earliness** n.
– ORIGIN Old English.

earmark •v. set aside for a particular purpose. •n. **1** an identifying feature. **2** an identifying mark on the ear of a domesticated animal.

earmuffs •pl. n. a pair of fabric coverings worn over the ears to protect them from cold or noise.

earn •v. **1** receive money in return for work or services. **2** receive something as a reward for achievements or behaviour. **3** (of money invested) gain money as interest or profit.
– DERIVATIVES **earner** n.
– ORIGIN Old English.

earnest •adj. very serious.
– PHRASES **in earnest 1** with greater intensity than before. **2** sincere and serious about your intentions.
– DERIVATIVES **earnestly** adv. **earnestness** n.
– ORIGIN Old English.

earnings •pl. n. money or income earned.

earphone •n. an electrical device worn on the ear to listen to radio or recorded sound.

earpiece •n. the part of a telephone, radio receiver, or other device for listening that is applied to the ear during use.

ear-piercing •adj. loud and shrill.

earplug •n. a piece of wax, cotton wool, etc., placed in the ear as protection against noise or water.

earring • n. a piece of jewellery worn on the lobe or edge of the ear.

earshot • n. the distance over which you can hear or be heard.

ear-splitting • adj. very loud.

earth • n. 1 (also **Earth**) the planet on which we live. 2 the substance of the land surface; soil. 3 Brit. electrical connection to the ground, regarded as having zero electrical potential. 4 the underground lair of a badger or fox. • v. Brit. connect an electrical device to earth.
– PHRASES **come back** (or **down**) **to earth** return to reality. **the earth** Brit. a very large amount: *her hat cost the earth.* **on earth** used for emphasis: *what on earth are you doing?*
– ORIGIN Old English.

earthbound • adj. 1 confined to the earth or earthly things. 2 moving towards the earth.

earthen • adj. 1 made of compressed earth. 2 (of a pot) made of baked clay.

earthenware • n. pottery made of baked clay.

earthling • n. (in science fiction) a person from the earth.

earthly • adj. 1 relating to the earth or human life. 2 material; worldly. 3 informal used for emphasis: *there's no earthly reason to rush.*

earthquake • n. a sudden violent shaking of the ground, caused by movements within the earth's crust.

earth sciences • pl. n. the branches of science concerned with the physical composition of the earth and its atmosphere.

earth-shattering • adj. informal very important or shocking.

earthwork • n. a large man-made bank of soil.

earthworm • n. a burrowing worm that lives in the soil.

earthy • adj. (**earthier**, **earthiest**) 1 resembling soil. 2 treating sex or bodily functions in a direct and unembarrassed way.
– DERIVATIVES **earthily** adv. **earthiness** n.

earwig • n. a small insect with a pair of pincers at its rear end.
– ORIGIN Old English.

ease • n. 1 lack of difficulty or effort. 2 freedom from problems. • v. (**eases**, **easing**, **eased**) 1 make something less serious. 2 (**ease off/up**) become less intense or unpleasant. 3 move carefully or gradually.
– ORIGIN Old French *aise*.

easel /ee-z'l/ • n. a wooden frame on legs for holding an artist's work in progress.

– ORIGIN Dutch *ezel* 'ass'.

easily • adv. 1 without difficulty or effort. 2 without doubt.

east • n. 1 the direction in which the sun rises at the equinoxes, on the right of a person facing north. 2 the eastern part of a place. 3 (**the East**) the regions or countries lying to the east of Europe. 4 (**the East**) hist. the former communist states of eastern Europe. • adj. 1 lying towards or facing the east. 2 (of a wind) blowing from the east. • adv. to or towards the east.
– DERIVATIVES **eastbound** adj. & adv.
– ORIGIN Old English.

Easter (also **Easter Day** or **Easter Sunday**) • n. the Christian festival celebrating the resurrection of Jesus.
– ORIGIN Old English.

Easter egg • n. a chocolate egg given as a gift at Easter.

easterly • adj. & adv. 1 towards or facing the east. 2 (of a wind) blowing from the east.

eastern • adj. 1 situated in or facing the east. 2 (usu. **Eastern**) coming from or typical of the regions to the east of Europe.

easterner • n. a person from the east of a region.

east-north-east • n. the direction halfway between east and north-east.

east-south-east • n. the direction halfway between east and south-east.

eastward • adj. in an easterly direction. • adv. (also **eastwards**) towards the east.

easy • adj. (**easier**, **easiest**) 1 achieved without great effort; not difficult. 2 free from worry or problems. 3 not anxious or awkward: *his easy and agreeable manner.*
– PHRASES **take it easy** relax.
– DERIVATIVES **easiness** n.

easy chair • n. a large, comfortable armchair.

easy-going • adj. relaxed and open-minded.

easy listening • n. popular music that is tuneful and undemanding.

eat • v. (**eats**, **eating**, **ate** /et, ayt/; past part. **eaten**) 1 put food into the mouth and chew and swallow it. 2 (**eat something away**) gradually wear away or destroy something. 3 (**eat something up**) use resources in very large quantities.
– PHRASES **eat your words** admit that what you said before was wrong.
– DERIVATIVES **eater** n.
– ORIGIN Old English.

eatable • adj. fit to be eaten as food. • pl. n. (**eatables**) items of food.

eatery • n. (pl. **eateries**) informal a cafe or restaurant.

eau de cologne /oh duh kuh-**lohn**/ • n. (pl. **eaux de cologne** /oh duh kuh-**lohn**/) = COLOGNE.
– ORIGIN French, 'water of Cologne'.

eau de toilette /oh duh twah-**let**/ • n. (pl. **eaux de toilette** /oh duh twah-**let**/) a dilute form of perfume; toilet water.
– ORIGIN French.

eaves • pl. n. the part of a roof that meets or overhangs the walls of a building.
– ORIGIN Old English.

eavesdrop • v. (**eavesdrops, eavesdropping, eavesdropped**) secretly listen to a conversation.
– DERIVATIVES **eavesdropper** n.
– ORIGIN from former *eavesdrop* 'the ground on to which water drips from the eaves'.

ebb • n. the movement of the tide out to sea. • v. 1 (of tidewater) move away from the land. 2 gradually become less or weaker: *my enthusiasm was ebbing away.*
– PHRASES **at a low ebb** in a weakened or depressed state.
– ORIGIN Old English.

ebony /eb-uh-ni/ • n. 1 heavy blackish or dark brown wood from a tree of tropical and warm regions. 2 a very dark brown or black colour.
– ORIGIN Greek *ebenos* 'ebony tree'.

ebullient /i-**bul**-yuhnt/ • adj. cheerful and full of energy.
– DERIVATIVES **ebullience** n.
– ORIGIN Latin *ebullire* 'boil up'.

EC • abbrev. European Community.

eccentric /ik-**sen**-trik/ • adj. 1 unconventional and rather strange. 2 tech. not placed centrally or not having its axis placed centrally. • n. an unconventional and rather strange person.
– DERIVATIVES **eccentrically** adv.
– ORIGIN Greek *ekkentros*.

eccentricity /ek-sen-**triss**-i-ti/ • n. (pl. **eccentricities**) 1 the quality of being eccentric. 2 an eccentric act or habit.

ecclesiastic /i-klee-zi-**ass**-tik/ • n. formal a Christian priest.

ecclesiastical /i-klee-zi-**ass**-ti-k'l/ • adj. relating to the Christian Church or its clergy.
– ORIGIN Greek *ekklēsiastikos*.

echelon /**esh**-uh-lon/ • n. a level or rank in an organization, profession, or society.
– ORIGIN French *échelon*.

echinoderm /i-**ky**-nuh-derm/ • n. an invertebrate sea creature of a large group including starfishes and sea urchins.

– ORIGIN from Greek *ekhinos* 'hedgehog, sea urchin' + *derma* 'skin'.

echo • n. (pl. **echoes**) 1 a sound caused by the reflection of sound waves from a surface back to the listener. 2 a reflected radio or radar beam. 3 something suggestive of or similar to something else. • v. (**echoes, echoing, echoed**) 1 (of a sound) reverberate or be repeated after the original sound has stopped. 2 be suggestive of or similar to something else. 3 repeat someone's words or opinions.
– DERIVATIVES **echoey** adj.
– ORIGIN Greek *ēkhō*.

echo chamber • n. an enclosed space for producing echoes.

echolocation /e-koh-loh-**kay**-sh'n/ • n. the location of objects by reflected sound, especially as used by animals such as bats.

echo sounder • n. a device used for determining the depth of the seabed or detecting objects in water by measuring the time taken for echoes to return to the listener.

eclair /i-**klair**/ • n. a long cake of choux pastry filled with cream and topped with chocolate icing.
– ORIGIN French *éclair* 'lightning'.

eclampsia /i-**klamp**-si-uh/ • n. a condition in which a pregnant woman with high blood pressure experiences convulsions.
– ORIGIN Greek *eklampsis* 'sudden development'.

éclat /ay-**klah**/ • n. a notably brilliant or successful effect.
– ORIGIN French.

eclectic /i-**klek**-tik/ • adj. using ideas from a wide variety of sources.
– DERIVATIVES **eclectically** adv. **eclecticism** n.
– ORIGIN Greek *eklektikos*.

eclipse /i-**klips**/ • n. 1 an occasion when one planet, the moon, etc. passes between another and the observer, or in front of a planet's source of light. 2 a sudden loss of significance or power. • v. (**eclipses, eclipsing, eclipsed**) 1 (of a planet, the moon, etc.) obscure the light coming from or shining on another. 2 make less significant or powerful.
– ORIGIN Greek *ekleipsis*.

ecliptic /i-**klip**-tik/ • n. Astron. the sun's apparent circular path among the stars during the year.

eco- /ee-koh/ • comb. form = ECOLOGY.

eco-friendly • adj. not harmful to the environment.

E. coli /ee koh-ly/ • n. the bacterium

Escherichia coli, some strains of which can cause severe food poisoning.

ecology /i-kol-uh-ji/ •n. the branch of biology concerned with the relations of organisms to one another and to their surroundings.
– DERIVATIVES **ecological** adj. **ecologically** adv. **ecologist** n.
– ORIGIN Greek *oikos* 'house'.

e-commerce (also **e-business**)
•n. commercial dealings conducted on the Internet.

economic /ee-kuh-nom-ik, ek-uh-nom-ik/ •adj. **1** relating to economics or the economy of a country or region.
2 profitable, or relating to profitability.

economical •adj. **1** giving good value in relation to the resources used or money spent. **2** careful in the use of resources or money.
– DERIVATIVES **economically** adv.

economics •n. the branch of knowledge concerned with the production, consumption, and transfer of wealth.

economist •n. an expert in economics.

economize (or **economise**)
•v. (**economizes**, **economizing**, **economized**) spend or use less.

economy •n. (pl. **economies**) **1** the state of a country or region in terms of the production and consumption of goods and services and the supply of money.
2 careful management of resources. **3** a financial saving. **4** (also **economy class**) the cheapest class of air or rail travel.
•adj. offering good value for money: *an economy pack.*
– ORIGIN Greek *oikonomia* 'household management'.

ecosystem •n. a biological community of interacting animals and plants and their environment.

ecotourism •n. tourism intended to support conservation efforts in unspoilt natural environments.
– DERIVATIVES **ecotourist** n.

ecru /ek-roo/ •n. a light cream or beige colour.
– ORIGIN French, 'unbleached'.

ecstasy /ek-stuh-si/ •n. (pl. **ecstasies**)
1 an overwhelming feeling of great happiness or joyful excitement.
2 (**Ecstasy**) an illegal amphetamine-based drug.
– ORIGIN Greek *ekstasis* 'standing outside yourself'.

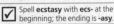
Spell **ecstasy** with **ecs-** at the beginning; the ending is **-asy**.

ecstatic /ik-stat-ik/ •adj. very happy, excited, or enthusiastic.
– DERIVATIVES **ecstatically** adv.

ectopic pregnancy /ek-top-ik/ •n. a pregnancy in which the fetus develops outside the womb.
– ORIGIN Greek *ektopos* 'out of place'.

ectoplasm /ek-toh-pla-z'm/ •n. a substance that supposedly comes out of the body of a medium during a trance.
– ORIGIN from Greek *ektos* 'outside' + *plasma* 'formation'.

Ecuadorean /ek-wuh-dor-i-uhn/ (also **Ecuadorian**) •n. a person from Ecuador.
•adj. relating to Ecuador.

ecumenical /ee-kyoo-men-i-k'l, ek-yoo-men-i-k'l/ •adj. **1** representing a number of different Christian Churches. **2** promoting unity among the world's Christian Churches.
– DERIVATIVES **ecumenically** adv.
– ORIGIN Greek *oikoumenikos*.

ecumenism /i-kyoo-muh-ni-z'm/
•n. the aim of promoting unity among the world's Christian Churches.

eczema /eks-(i)-muh/ •n. a condition in which patches of skin become rough and inflamed, causing itching and bleeding.
– ORIGIN Greek *ekzema*.

Edam /ee-dam/ •n. a round yellow cheese with a red wax coating.
– ORIGIN from *Edam* in the Netherlands.

eddy •n. (pl. **eddies**) a circular movement of water causing a small whirlpool.
•v. (**eddies**, **eddying**, **eddied**) (of water, air, etc.) move in a circular way.
– ORIGIN prob. from Old English, 'again, back'.

edelweiss /ay-duhl-vyss/ •n. a mountain plant with small flowers.
– ORIGIN German.

edema •n. US = OEDEMA.

Eden /ee-duhn/ •n. **1** (also **Garden of Eden**) the place where Adam and Eve lived in the story of the Creation in the Bible. **2** a place or state of happiness or unspoilt beauty.
– DERIVATIVES **Edenic** /i-den-ik/ adj.
– ORIGIN Hebrew.

edge •n. **1** the outside limit of an object, area, or surface. **2** the sharpened side of a blade. **3** the line along which two surfaces of a solid meet. **4** a slight advantage over close rivals. **5** an intense or striking quality: *there was an edge to Khan's voice.* •v. (**edges**, **edging**, **edged**)
1 provide with an edge or border.
2 move carefully or furtively.
– PHRASES **on edge** tense or irritable.
– DERIVATIVES **edger** n.
– ORIGIN Old English.

edgeways (US **edgewise**) •adv. with the edge uppermost or towards the viewer.
– PHRASES **get a word in edgeways** manage to break into a conversation.

edging • n. something forming an edge or border.

edgy • adj. (**edgier**, **edgiest**) tense, nervous, or irritable.
– DERIVATIVES **edgily** adv. **edginess** n.

edible • adj. fit to be eaten. • pl. n. (**edibles**) items of food.
– ORIGIN Latin *edibilis*.

edict /ee-dikt/ • n. an official order or proclamation.
– ORIGIN Latin *edictum*.

edifice /ed-i-fiss/ • n. formal a large and impressive building.
– ORIGIN Latin *aedificium*.

edify /ed-i-fy/ • v. (**edifies**, **edifying**, **edified**) teach someone something that is educational or morally improving.
– DERIVATIVES **edification** n.
– ORIGIN Latin *aedificare* 'build'.

edit • v. (**edits**, **editing**, **edited**) 1 prepare written material for publication by correcting, shortening, or improving it. 2 prepare material for a recording, film, or broadcast. 3 be editor of a newspaper or magazine. • n. a change made as a result of editing.
– DERIVATIVES **editable** adj.
– ORIGIN from EDITOR.

edition • n. 1 a particular form of a published written work. 2 the total number of copies of a book, newspaper, etc. issued at one time. 3 a particular instance of a regular television or radio programme.
– ORIGIN Latin.

editor • n. 1 a person who is in charge of a newspaper or magazine. 2 a person who prepares or selects written or recorded material for publication or broadcasting.
– DERIVATIVES **editorship** n.
– ORIGIN Latin.

editorial • adj. relating to the selection or preparation of material for publication. • n. a newspaper article giving an opinion on a topical issue.
– DERIVATIVES **editorialist** n. **editorially** adv.

editorialize (or **editorialise**) • v. (**editorializes**, **editorializing**, **editorialized**) (of a newspaper or editor) express opinions rather than just report news.

educate /ed-yuu-kayt/ • v. (**educates**, **educating**, **educated**) 1 give intellectual or moral instruction to someone. 2 give someone information about a particular subject. 3 (as adj. **educated**) showing or having had a good education.
– DERIVATIVES **educative** adj. **educator** n.
– ORIGIN Latin *educare* 'lead out'.

educated guess • n. a guess based on knowledge and experience.

education • n. 1 the process of teaching or learning. 2 the theory and practice of teaching. 3 information about or training in a particular subject.
– DERIVATIVES **educational** adj. **educationalist** n. **educationally** adv. **educationist** n.

Edwardian /ed-wor-di-uhn/ • adj. relating to the reign of King Edward VII (1901–10).

-ee • suffix forming nouns: 1 referring to the person affected by the action of a verb: *employee*. 2 referring to a person described as or concerned with: *absentee*.
– ORIGIN Old French *-é*.

EEC • abbrev. European Economic Community.

eel • n. a snake-like fish with a very long thin body and small fins.
– ORIGIN Old English.

e'er /air/ • adv. literary = EVER.

eerie /eer-i/ • adj. (**eerier**, **eeriest**) strange and frightening.
– DERIVATIVES **eerily** adv. **eeriness** n.
– ORIGIN prob. from Old English, 'cowardly'.

efface /i-fayss/ • v. (**effaces**, **effacing**, **effaced**) 1 cause something to disappear. 2 (**efface yourself**) make yourself appear unimportant. 3 erase a mark from a surface.
– DERIVATIVES **effacement** n.
– ORIGIN French *effacer*.

effect • n. 1 a change which is a result of an action or other cause. 2 the state of being or becoming operative: *the ban took effect in 2004*. 3 the extent to which something succeeds: *wind power can be used to great effect*. 4 (**effects**) personal belongings. 5 (**effects**) the lighting, sound, or scenery used in a play or film. 6 Physics a physical phenomenon, named after its discoverer: *the Doppler effect*. • v. bring about a result.
– PHRASES **in effect** in practice, even if not formally acknowledged.
– ORIGIN Latin *effectus*.

USAGE: Do not confuse **affect** and **effect**. **Affect** is a verb meaning 'make a difference to' (*the changes will affect everyone*). **Effect** is used both as a noun meaning 'a result' (*the substance has a painkilling effect*) and as a verb meaning 'bring about a result' (*she effected a cost-cutting exercise*).

effective • adj. 1 producing an intended result. 2 (of a law or policy) operative. 3 existing in fact, though not formally acknowledged as such: *he is in effective control of the military*.
– DERIVATIVES **effectively** adv. **effectiveness** n.

effectual /i-fek-choo-uhl/ • adj. producing an intended result; effective.
– DERIVATIVES **effectually** adv.

effeminate /i-fem-i-nuht/ • adj. (of a man) having characteristics regarded as typical of a woman.
– DERIVATIVES **effeminacy** n.
– ORIGIN Latin *effeminare* 'make feminine'.

effervescent /e-fuh-ve-suhnt/ • adj. **1** (of a liquid) giving off bubbles; fizzy. **2** lively and enthusiastic.
– DERIVATIVES **effervesce** v. **effervescence** n.
– ORIGIN Latin *effervescere* 'boil up'.

effete /i-feet/ • adj. **1** no longer effective; weak. **2** (of a man) effeminate or affected.
– ORIGIN Latin *effetus* 'worn out by bearing young'.

efficacious /ef-fi-kay-shuhss/ • adj. formal producing an intended effect; effective.
– ORIGIN Latin *efficere* 'accomplish'.

efficacy /ef-fi-kuh-si/ • n. formal the ability to produce an intended result.

efficiency • n. (pl. **efficiencies**) the quality of being efficient.

efficient • adj. working well with minimum waste of money or effort.
– DERIVATIVES **efficiently** adv.
– ORIGIN Latin *efficere* 'accomplish'.

effigy /ef-fi-ji/ • n. (pl. **effigies**) a sculpture or model of a person.
– ORIGIN Latin *effigies*.

efflorescence /ef-fluh-ress-uhnss/ • n. literary a very high stage of development.
– ORIGIN Latin *efflorescere* 'begin to bloom'.

effluent • n. liquid waste or sewage discharged into a river or the sea.
– ORIGIN Latin *effluere* 'flow out'.

effluvium /i-floo-vi-uhm/ • n. (pl. **effluvia** /i-floo-vi-uh/) an unpleasant or harmful smell or discharge.
– ORIGIN Latin.

effort • n. **1** a vigorous or determined attempt. **2** the physical or mental vigour needed to do something.
– DERIVATIVES **effortful** adj.
– ORIGIN French.

effortless • adj. done or achieved without effort; natural and easy.
– DERIVATIVES **effortlessly** adv.

effrontery /i-frun-tuh-ri/ • n. insolent or disrespectful behaviour.
– ORIGIN French *effronterie*.

effusion • n. **1** a discharge of something, especially a liquid. **2** an unrestrained expression of feelings in speech or writing.
– ORIGIN Latin.

effusive • adj. expressing pleasure or approval in an unrestrained way.

EFL • abbrev. English as a foreign language.

e.g. • abbrev. for example.
– ORIGIN from Latin *exempli gratia* 'for the sake of example'.

egalitarian /i-gal-i-tair-i-uhn/ • adj. believing that all people are equal and deserve equal rights and opportunities. • n. a person who believes in equal rights for all.
– DERIVATIVES **egalitarianism** n.
– ORIGIN French *égalitaire*.

egg¹ • n. **1** an oval or round object laid by a female bird, reptile, fish, or invertebrate and containing an ovum which can develop into a new organism. **2** the cell in female animals that is capable of producing young; an ovum. **3** informal, dated a person of a specified kind: *you're a good egg.*
– PHRASES **with egg on your face** informal appearing foolish.
– DERIVATIVES **eggy** adj.
– ORIGIN Old English.

egg² • v. (**egg someone on**) urge someone to do something foolish or risky.
– ORIGIN Old Norse.

egghead • n. informal a very intelligent or studious person.

eggplant • n. N. Amer. = AUBERGINE.

eggshell • n. the fragile outer layer of an egg. • adj. **1** (of china) very thin and delicate. **2** (of a paint) that dries with a slight sheen.

ego /ee-goh/ • n. (pl. **egos**) **1** a person's sense of their own worth and importance. **2** the part of the mind that is responsible for the interpretation of reality and a sense of personal identity. Compare with ID and SUPEREGO.
– ORIGIN Latin, 'I'.

egocentric • adj. thinking only of yourself; self-centred.
– DERIVATIVES **egocentrically** adv. **egocentricity** n. **egocentrism** n.

egoism • n. = EGOTISM.
– DERIVATIVES **egoist** n. **egoistic** adj.

egomania • n. an obsessive concern with yourself.
– DERIVATIVES **egomaniac** n. **egomaniacal** adj.

egotism • n. the quality of being excessively conceited or self-centred.
– DERIVATIVES **egotist** n. **egotistic** adj. **egotistical** adj.

ego trip • n. informal something that a person does to feel important.

egregious /i-gree-juhss/

• **adj.** outstandingly bad.
– ORIGIN Latin *egregius* 'illustrious'.

egress /ee-gress/ • **n.** formal **1** the action of going out of a place. **2** a way out.
– ORIGIN Latin *egressus*.

egret /ee-grit/ • **n.** a heron with mainly white plumage.
– ORIGIN Old French *aigrette*.

Egyptian • **n. 1** a person from Egypt. **2** the language used in ancient Egypt. • **adj.** relating to Egypt.

Egyptology /ee-jip-tol-uh-ji/ • **n.** the study of the language, history, and culture of ancient Egypt.
– DERIVATIVES **Egyptological** adj. **Egyptologist** n.

Eid /eed/ (also **Id**) • **n. 1** (in full **Eid ul-Fitr** /eed uul **fee**-truh/) the Muslim festival marking the end of the fast of Ramadan. **2** (in full **Eid ul-Adha** /eed uul **aa**-duh/) the festival marking the culmination of the annual pilgrimage to Mecca.
– ORIGIN Arabic, 'feast'.

eider /I-der/ (also **eider duck**) • **n.** (pl. **eider** or **eiders**) a northern sea duck with black-and-white plumage.
– ORIGIN Old Norse.

eiderdown • **n.** Brit. a quilt filled with down (originally from the female eider duck) or another soft material.

eight • **cardinal number 1** one more than seven; 8. (Roman numeral: **viii** or **VIII**.) **2** an eight-oared rowing boat or its crew.
– ORIGIN Old English.

eighteen • **cardinal number** one more than seventeen; 18. (Roman numeral: **xviii** or **XVIII**.)
– DERIVATIVES **eighteenth** ordinal number.

eighth • **ordinal number 1** that is number eight in a sequence; 8th. **2** (**an eighth/ one eighth**) each of eight equal parts of something.

☑ Remember that **eighth** has two **h**'s; it ends with **-hth**.

eighty • **cardinal number** (pl. **eighties**) ten less than ninety; 80. (Roman numeral: **lxxx** or **LXXX**.)
– DERIVATIVES **eightieth** ordinal number.

einsteinium /yn-sty-ni-uhm/ • **n.** an unstable radioactive chemical element made by high-energy atomic collisions.
– ORIGIN named after the German-born physicist Albert *Einstein*.

eisteddfod /I-steth-vod/ • **n.** (pl. **eisteddfods** or **eisteddfodau** /I-steth- vod-I/) a competitive festival of music and poetry in Wales.
– ORIGIN Welsh, 'session'.

either /I-ther, ee-ther/ • **conj. & adv. 1** used before the first of two alternatives specified. **2** (adv.) used to indicate a similarity or link with a

statement just made: *You don't like him, do you? I don't either.* **3** for that matter; moreover. • **det. & pron. 1** one or the other of two people or things. **2** each of two.
– ORIGIN Old English.

> **USAGE:** In good English, it is important that **either** and **or** are correctly placed so that the structures following each word balance each other. For example, it is better to say *I'm going to buy either a new camera or a new video* rather than *I'm either going to buy a new camera or a video.*

ejaculate /i-jak-yuu-layt/
• **v.** (**ejaculates, ejaculating, ejaculated**) **1** (of a man or male animal) eject semen from the penis at the moment of orgasm. **2** dated say something suddenly.
– DERIVATIVES **ejaculation** n. **ejaculator** n. **ejaculatory** /i-jak-yoo-luh-tri/ adj.
– ORIGIN Latin *ejaculari* 'dart out'.

eject • **v. 1** force or throw out violently or suddenly. **2** force someone to leave a place or post. **3** (of a pilot) escape from an aircraft by means of an ejection seat.
– DERIVATIVES **ejection** n. **ejector** n.
– ORIGIN Latin *eicere*.

ejection seat (also **ejector seat**) • **n.** an aircraft seat that can throw its occupant from the craft in an emergency.

eke /eek/ • **v.** (**ekes, eking, eked**) (**eke something out**) **1** use something sparingly: *young mothers hunting for bargains to eke out their social security money.* **2** make a living with difficulty.
– ORIGIN Old English, 'increase'.

elaborate • **adj.** /i-lab-uh-ruht/ involving many carefully arranged parts; complicated. • **v.** /i-lab-uh-rayt/ (**elaborates, elaborating, elaborated**) **1** develop or present an idea or policy in detail. **2** (**elaborate on**) add more detail to something already said.
– DERIVATIVES **elaborately** adv. **elaboration** n.
– ORIGIN Latin *elaborare* 'work out'.

élan /ay-lan/ (also **elan**) • **n.** energy and stylishness.
– ORIGIN French.

eland /ee-luhnd/ • **n.** an African antelope with spiral horns.
– ORIGIN Dutch, 'elk'.

elapse • **v.** (**elapses, elapsing, elapsed**) (of time) pass.
– ORIGIN Latin *elabi* 'slip away'.

elastane /i-las-tayn/ • **n.** a synthetic elastic material, used for clothing.

elastic /i-lass-tik/ • **adj. 1** able to return to normal size or shape after being stretched or squeezed. **2** flexible and adaptable. • **n.** cord or fabric which

returns to its original size or shape after being stretched.
– DERIVATIVES **elastically** adv. **elasticity** /i-lass-**tiss**-i-ti/ n.
– ORIGIN Greek *elastikos* 'propulsive'.

elasticated • adj. Brit. (of clothing or material) made elastic with rubber thread or tape.

elastic band • n. Brit. a rubber band.

elated /i-lay-tid/ • adj. very happy and excited.
– ORIGIN Latin *elatus* 'raised'.

elation /i-lay-sh'n/ • n. great happiness and excitement.

elbow • n. the joint between the forearm and the upper arm. • v. hit or push with the elbow.
– ORIGIN Old English.

elbow grease • n. informal hard physical work, especially vigorous cleaning.

elbow room • n. informal enough space to move or work in.

elder[1] • adj. (of one or more out of a group of people) of a greater age. • n. 1 (**your elder**) a person who is older than you are. 2 a leader or senior figure in a community.
– ORIGIN Old English.

elder[2] • n. a small tree or shrub with white flowers and bluish-black or red berries.
– ORIGIN Old English.

elderberry • n. (pl. **elderberries**) the berry of the elder, used for making jelly or wine.

elderflower • n. the flower of the elder, used to make wines and cordials.

elderly • adj. old or ageing.

eldest • adj. (of one out of a group of people) oldest.

El Dorado /el duh-**rah**-doh/ • n. (pl. **El Dorados**) a place of great wealth.
– ORIGIN Spanish, 'the golden one'.

eldritch /**el**-drich/ • adj. literary weird and sinister or ghostly.
– ORIGIN perh. related to ELF.

elect • v. 1 choose someone to hold a public position by voting. 2 choose to do something. • adj. 1 chosen or singled out. 2 elected to a position but not yet in office: *the President Elect*.
– ORIGIN Latin *eligere*.

election • n. 1 a procedure by which a person is elected. 2 the action of electing someone.

electioneering • n. the action of campaigning to be elected to a political position.

elective • adj. 1 relating to or chosen by election. 2 (of a course of study, treatment, etc.) chosen by the person concerned; not compulsory.

elector • n. a person who has the right to vote in an election.

electoral • adj. relating to elections or electors.
– DERIVATIVES **electorally** adv.

electoral college • n. a group of people chosen to represent the members of a political party in the election of a leader.

electoral roll (also **electoral register**) • n. (in the UK) an official list of the people in a district who are entitled to vote in an election.

electorate /i-lek-tuh-ruht/ • n. the group of people in a country or area who are entitled to vote in an election.

electric • adj. 1 relating to, using, or producing electricity. 2 very exciting. • n. (**electrics**) Brit. the system of electric wiring in a house or vehicle.
– ORIGIN Greek *ēlektron* 'amber'.

electrical • adj. relating to, using, or producing electricity.
– DERIVATIVES **electrically** adv.

electric blanket • n. an electrically wired blanket used for heating a bed.

electric blue • n. a bright blue colour.

electric chair • n. a chair in which convicted criminals are executed by electrocution.

electric eel • n. a large eel-like South American fish which uses pulses of electricity to kill its prey.

electric guitar • n. a guitar with a built-in pickup which converts sound vibrations into electrical signals.

electrician • n. a person who installs and repairs electrical equipment.

electricity • n. 1 a form of energy resulting from the existence of charged particles, either statically as a build-up of charge or dynamically as a current. 2 the supply of electric current to a building for heating, lighting, etc. 3 great excitement.

electric shock • n. a sudden discharge of electricity through a part of the body.

electrify • v. (**electrifies, electrifying, electrified**) 1 pass an electric current through something. 2 convert a system or device to the use of electrical power. 3 (as adj. **electrifying**) very exciting.
– DERIVATIVES **electrification** n.

electroconvulsive • adj. (of therapy for mental illness) using electric shocks applied to the brain.

electrocute • v. (**electrocutes, electrocuting, electrocuted**) injure or kill by electric shock.
– DERIVATIVES **electrocution** n.

electrode /i-lek-trohd/ • n. a conductor through which electricity enters or leaves something.

– ORIGIN from **ELECTRIC** + Greek *hodos* 'way'.

electrolysis /i-lek-**trol**-i-siss/
• n. **1** chemical decomposition produced by passing an electric current through a conducting liquid. **2** the breaking up and removal of hair roots or small blemishes on the skin by means of an electric current.
– DERIVATIVES **electrolytic** /i-lek-truh-**lit**-ik/ adj.

electrolyte /i-lek-truh-lyt/ • n. a liquid or gel which contains ions and can be decomposed by electrolysis, e.g. that present in a battery.
– ORIGIN Greek *lutos* 'released'.

electromagnet • n. a metal core made into a magnet by the passage of electric current through a surrounding coil.

electromagnetic • adj. relating to the interrelation of electric currents or fields and magnetic fields.
– DERIVATIVES **electromagnetism** n.

electromagnetic radiation
• n. radiation in which electric and magnetic fields vary at the same time.

electromotive /i-lek-truh-**moh**-tiv/
• adj. tending to produce an electric current.

electromotive force • n. a difference in potential that tends to give rise to an electric current.

electron • n. Physics a negatively charged subatomic particle found in all atoms and acting as the primary carrier of electricity in solids.

electronic • adj. **1** having components such as microchips and transistors that control and direct electric currents. **2** relating to electrons or electronics. **3** relating to or carried out by means of a computer: *electronic shopping.*
– DERIVATIVES **electronically** adv.

electronics • n. **1** the branch of physics and technology concerned with the design of circuits using transistors and microchips, and with the behaviour and movement of electrons. **2** circuits or devices using transistors, microchips, etc.

electron microscope • n. a microscope with high magnification and resolution, using electron beams in place of light.

electroplate /i-lek-troh-**playt**/
• v. (**electroplates, electroplating, electroplated**) coat a metal object with another metal using electrolysis.

electroscope • n. an instrument for detecting and measuring electric charge.

electrostatic • adj. relating to stationary electric charges or fields as opposed to electric currents.

elegant • adj. **1** graceful and stylish. **2** pleasingly clever but simple.
– DERIVATIVES **elegance** n. **elegantly** adv.
– ORIGIN Latin *elegans* 'discriminating'.

elegiac /el-i-jy-uhk/ • adj. **1** relating to or like an elegy. **2** sad.

elegy /**el**-i-ji/ • n. (pl. **elegies**) a sad poem, especially for someone who has died.
– ORIGIN Greek *elegos.*

element • n. **1** a basic part of something. **2** (also **chemical element**) each of more than one hundred substances that cannot be chemically changed or broken down. **3** any of the four substances (earth, water, air, and fire) formerly believed to be the basic constituents of all matter. **4** a trace: *an element of danger.* **5** a distinct group within a larger group. **6** (**the elements**) rain or other bad weather. **7** a part in an electric device through which an electric current is passed to provide heat.
– PHRASES **in your element** in a situation in which you feel happy or relaxed.
– ORIGIN Latin *elementum* 'principle'.

elemental /el-i-**men**-t'l/ • adj. **1** basic and fundamental. **2** relating to or like the forces of nature; wild and powerful: *elemental passions.*

elementary • adj. **1** relating to the most basic aspects of a subject. **2** straightforward and uncomplicated.

elephant • n. (pl. **elephant** or **elephants**) a very large mammal with a trunk, curved tusks, and large ears, found in Africa and southern Asia.
– ORIGIN Greek *elephas.*

elephantine /el-i-**fan**-tyn/ • adj. like an elephant, especially in being large or clumsy.

elevate /**el**-i-vayt/ • v. (**elevates, elevating, elevated**) **1** lift to a higher position. **2** raise to a higher level or status.
– ORIGIN Latin *elevare.*

elevated • adj. having a high intellectual or moral level.

elevation • n. **1** the action of elevating. **2** the height of a place above sea level. **3** the angle of something with the horizontal.

elevator • n. N. Amer. a lift in a building.

eleven • cardinal number **1** one more than ten; 11. (Roman numeral: **xi** or **XI**.) **2** a sports team of eleven players.
– ORIGIN Old English.

eleven-plus • n. (in the UK, especially formerly) an exam taken at the age of 11–12 to decide the type of secondary school a child should enter.

elevenses • pl. n. Brit. informal a mid-morning break for light refreshments.

eleventh • ordinal number **1** that is number eleven in a sequence; 11th. **2** (**an eleventh/one eleventh**) each of eleven equal parts into which something is divided.
– PHRASES **the eleventh hour** the latest possible moment.

elf • n. (pl. **elves**) a supernatural creature of folk tales, shown as a small human figure with pointed ears.
– ORIGIN Old English.

elfin • adj. like an elf, especially in being small and delicate.

elicit /i-liss-it/ • v. (**elicits, eliciting, elicited**) produce or draw out a response or reaction.
– ORIGIN Latin *elicere* 'draw out by trickery'.

elide /i-lyd/ • v. (**elides, eliding, elided**) **1** omit a sound or syllable when speaking. **2** join things together.
– ORIGIN Latin *elidere* 'crush out'.

eligible /el-i-ji-b'l/ • adj. **1** meeting the conditions to do or receive something: *you may be eligible for a refund.* **2** desirable or suitable as a wife or husband.
– DERIVATIVES **eligibility** n.
– ORIGIN Latin *eligibilis.*

eliminate /i-lim-i-nayt/ • v. (**eliminates, eliminating, eliminated**) **1** completely remove or get rid of. **2** remove a competitor from a sporting competition by beating them.
– DERIVATIVES **elimination** n.
– ORIGIN Latin *eliminare* 'turn out of doors'.

elision /i-li-zh'n/ • n. the omission of a sound or syllable in speech.
– ORIGIN Latin.

elite /i-leet/ • n. a group of people regarded as the best in a particular society or organization.
– ORIGIN French, 'selection'.

elitism • n. **1** the belief that a society should be run by an elite. **2** the feeling of being superior to other people that is associated with belonging to an elite.
– DERIVATIVES **elitist** adj. & n.

elixir /i-lik-seer/ • n. a magical potion, especially one supposedly able to make people live forever.
– ORIGIN Arabic.

Elizabethan /i-liz-uh-bee-thuhn/ • adj. relating to the reign of Queen Elizabeth I (1558–1603).

elk • n. (pl. **elk** or **elks**) a large northern deer with a growth of skin hanging from the neck.
– ORIGIN prob. from Old English.

ellipse /i-lips/ • n. a regular oval shape created when a cone is cut by an oblique plane which does not intersect the base.

ellipsis /i-lip-siss/ • n. (pl. **ellipses** /i-lip-seez/) **1** the omission of words from speech or writing. **2** a set of dots indicating such an omission.
– ORIGIN Greek *elleipsis.*

elliptic • adj. relating to or having the form of an ellipse.

elliptical • adj. **1** (of speech or writing) having a word or words deliberately omitted. **2** = ELLIPTIC.

elm • n. a tall deciduous tree with rough leaves.
– ORIGIN Old English.

El Niño /el neen-yoh/ • n. (pl. **El Niños**) a complex cycle of climatic changes affecting the Pacific region.
– ORIGIN Spanish, 'the Christ child', so called because the signs of an El Niño appear around Christmas time.

elocution /el-uh-kyoo-sh'n/ • n. the skill of speaking clearly and pronouncing words distinctly.
– ORIGIN Latin.

elongate /ee-long-gayt/ • v. (**elongates, elongating, elongated**) (usu. as adj. **elongated**) make or become longer.
– DERIVATIVES **elongation** n.
– ORIGIN Latin *elongare* 'place at a distance'.

elope • v. (**elopes, eloping, eloped**) run away secretly in order to get married.
– DERIVATIVES **elopement** n.
– ORIGIN Old French *aloper.*

eloquence /el-uh-kwuhnss/ • n. fluent or persuasive speaking or writing.
– ORIGIN Latin *eloquentia.*

eloquent • adj. **1** fluent or persuasive in speech or writing. **2** clearly expressive.
– DERIVATIVES **eloquently** adv.

else • adv. **1** in addition. **2** different.
– PHRASES **or else** used to introduce the second of two alternatives.
– ORIGIN Old English.

elsewhere • adv. in, at, or to another place or other places. • pron. another place.

elucidate /i-loo-si-dayt/ • v. (**elucidates, elucidating, elucidated**) make something easier to understand.
– DERIVATIVES **elucidation** n.
– ORIGIN Latin *elucidare.*

elude /i-lood/ • v. (**eludes, eluding, eluded**) **1** cleverly escape from or avoid. **2** fail to be understood or achieved by: *the racing championship which has so far eluded him.*
– ORIGIN Latin *eludere.*

elusive • adj. difficult to find, catch, or achieve.
– ORIGIN Latin *eludere* 'elude'.

elver • n. a young eel.
– ORIGIN from dialect *eel-fare* 'the

passage of young eels up a river'.

elves pl. of **ELF**.

Elysian /i-liz-i-uhn/ • adj. relating to or like paradise.
– ORIGIN from *Elysium* or the *Elysian Fields* in Greek mythology, where heroes were taken when they died.

em- • prefix var. of **EN-**.

emaciated /i-may-si-ay-tid/ • adj. abnormally thin and weak.
– DERIVATIVES **emaciation** n.
– ORIGIN Latin *emaciare* 'make thin'.

email (also **e-mail**) • n. **1** a message sent electronically from one computer user to another or others via a network. **2** the system of sending of emails. • v. contact someone or send a message using email.
– ORIGIN from *electronic mail*.

emanate /em-uh-nayt/ • v. (**emanates, emanating, emanated**) **1** (**emanate from**) come or spread out from a source. **2** give out: *he emanated a brooding air.*
– ORIGIN Latin *emanare* 'flow out'.

emanation • n. **1** something which comes or spreads out from a source. **2** the action of emanating.

emancipate /i-man-si-payt/ • v. (**emancipates, emancipating, emancipated**) **1** free from legal, social, or political restrictions. **2** free from slavery.
– DERIVATIVES **emancipation** n.
– ORIGIN Latin *emancipare* 'transfer as property'.

emasculate /i-mass-kyuu-layt/ • v. (**emasculates, emasculating, emasculated**) **1** make weaker or less effective. **2** deprive a man of his male role or identity.
– DERIVATIVES **emasculation** n.
– ORIGIN Latin *emasculare* 'castrate'.

embalm /im-bahm/ • v. treat a dead body to preserve it from decay.
– DERIVATIVES **embalmer** n.
– ORIGIN Old French *embaumer*.

embankment • n. **1** a wall or bank built to prevent flooding by a river. **2** a bank of earth or stone built to carry a road or railway over low ground.

embargo /em-bar-goh, im-bar-goh/ • n. (pl. **embargoes**) an official ban, especially on trade with a particular country. • v. (**embargoes, embargoing, embargoed**) put an embargo on; ban officially.
– ORIGIN Spanish.

embark • v. **1** go on board a ship or aircraft. **2** (**embark on**) begin a new project or course of action.
– DERIVATIVES **embarkation** n.
– ORIGIN French *embarquer*.

embarrass /im-ba-ruhss, em-ba-ruhss/ • v. **1** make someone feel awkward or ashamed. **2** (**be embarrassed**) be in financial difficulties.
– DERIVATIVES **embarrassing** adj. **embarrassment** n.
– ORIGIN French *embarrasser*.

> ☑ Remember that **embarrass** and related words have a double **r** and a double **s**.

embassy • n. (pl. **embassies**) the official home or offices of an ambassador.
– ORIGIN Old French *ambasse*.

embattled • adj. **1** facing many problems and difficulties: *the embattled Chancellor.* **2** surrounded by enemy forces.

embed (also **imbed**) • v. (**embeds, embedding, embedded**; also **imbeds, imbedding, imbedded**) **1** fix firmly in a surrounding mass. **2** fix an idea or feeling firmly in a society or a person's mind. **3** attach a journalist to a military unit during a conflict.

embellish • v. **1** make more attractive by adding decorations. **2** make a story more interesting by adding extra details.
– DERIVATIVES **embellishment** n.
– ORIGIN Old French *embellir*.

ember /em-ber/ • n. a piece of burning wood or coal in a dying fire.
– ORIGIN Old English.

embezzle • v. (**embezzles, embezzling, embezzled**) steal money placed in your trust or under your control.
– DERIVATIVES **embezzlement** n. **embezzler** n.
– ORIGIN Old French *embesiler*.

embitter • v. (**embitters, embittering, embittered**) (usu. as adj. **embittered**) make bitter or resentful.

emblazon /im-blay-zuhn/ • v. display a design on something in a noticeable way.

emblem /em-bluhm/ • n. **1** a heraldic design or symbol as a badge of a nation, organization, or family. **2** something which represents a quality or an idea.
– ORIGIN Greek *emblēma* 'insertion'.

emblematic • adj. representing a particular quality or idea.

embody • v. (**embodies, embodying, embodied**) **1** give a physical or visible form to an idea or quality. **2** include or contain as a part of a whole.
– DERIVATIVES **embodiment** n.

embolden • v. give courage or confidence to.

embolism /em-buh-li-z'm/ • n. the obstruction of an artery by a clot of blood or an air bubble.
– ORIGIN Greek *embolismos*.

emboss • v. carve or mould a raised design on.
– ORIGIN from former French *embosser*.

embrace • v. (**embraces, embracing, embraced**) **1** hold someone closely in your arms as a sign of affection. **2** include or contain. **3** accept or support a belief or change willingly. • n. an act of embracing someone.
– ORIGIN Old French *embracer*.

embrocation /em-bruh-**kay**-sh'n/ • n. a liquid rubbed on the body to relieve pain in the muscles.
– ORIGIN Latin.

embroider • v. (**embroiders, embroidering, embroidered**) **1** sew decorative needlework patterns on. **2** add false or exaggerated details to.
– ORIGIN Old French *enbrouder*.

embroidery • n. (pl. **embroideries**) **1** the art of embroidering. **2** embroidered cloth.

embroil • v. involve deeply in a conflict or difficult situation.
– ORIGIN French *embrouiller* 'to muddle'.

embryo /em-bri-oh/ • n. (pl. **embryos**) **1** an unborn animal in the process of development, especially an unborn human being in the first eight weeks from conception. Compare with FETUS. **2** the part of a seed which develops into a new plant. **3** something at an early stage of development.
– ORIGIN Greek *embruon*.

embryonic /em-bri-on-ik/ • adj. **1** relating to an embryo. **2** in an early stage of development.

emend /i-**mend**/ • v. correct and revise written material.
– DERIVATIVES **emendation** n.
– ORIGIN Latin *emendare*.

emerald • n. **1** a bright green precious stone consisting of a variety of beryl. **2** a bright green colour.
– ORIGIN Old French *esmeraud*.

emerge • v. (**emerges, emerging, emerged**) **1** become gradually visible. **2** (of facts) become known. **3** survive a difficult period.
– DERIVATIVES **emergence** n.
– ORIGIN Latin *emergere*.

emergency • n. (pl. **emergencies**) a serious and unexpected situation requiring immediate action. • adj. arising from or used in an emergency: *an emergency exit.*
– ORIGIN Latin *emergentia*.

emergent • adj. in the process of coming into being.

emeritus /i-me-ri-tuhss/ • adj. having retired but allowed to keep a title as an honour: *an emeritus professor.*
– ORIGIN Latin.

emery • n. a form of corundum (aluminium oxide), used in powdered form for smoothing and polishing.
– ORIGIN Old French *esmeri*.

emery board • n. a strip of thin wood or card coated with emery and used as a nail file.

emetic /i-met-ik/ • adj. (of a substance) causing vomiting.
– ORIGIN Greek *emetikos*.

emf • abbrev. electromotive force.

emigrant • n. a person who emigrates to another country.

emigrate /em-i-grayt/ • v. (**emigrates, emigrating, emigrated**) leave your own country in order to settle permanently in another.
– DERIVATIVES **emigration** n.
– ORIGIN Latin *emigrare*.

émigré /em-i-gray/ • n. a person who has emigrated.
– ORIGIN French.

eminence /em-i-nuhnss/ • n. **1** the quality of being very accomplished and respected in a particular area of activity. **2** an important person.
– ORIGIN Latin *eminentia*.

eminent • adj. **1** distinguished. **2** out-standing or obvious.
– DERIVATIVES **eminently** adv.

emir /e-meer/ (also **amir**) • n. a title of various Muslim (mainly Arab) rulers.
– ORIGIN Arabic, 'commander'.

emirate /em-i-ruht/ • n. the lands or rank of an emir.

emissary /em-i-suh-ri/ • n. (pl. **emissaries**) a person sent as a diplomatic representative on a special mission.
– ORIGIN Latin *emissarius* 'scout, spy'.

emission /i-mi-sh'n/ • n. **1** the action of emitting something. **2** a substance which is emitted.

emit • v. (**emits, emitting, emitted**) **1** discharge or give out gas, radiation, etc. **2** make a sound.
– DERIVATIVES **emitter** n.
– ORIGIN Latin *emittere*.

emollient /i-mol-li-uhnt/ • adj. **1** having a softening or soothing effect on the skin. **2** attempting to avoid confrontation; calming.
– DERIVATIVES **emollience** n.
– ORIGIN Latin *emollire* 'make soft'.

emolument /i-mol-yuu-muhnt/ • n. formal a salary or fee.
– ORIGIN Latin *emolumentum*.

emote /i-moht/ • v. (**emotes, emoting, emoted**) show emotion in an exaggerated way.

emotion • n. **1** a strong feeling, such as joy or anger. **2** instinctive feeling as

distinguished from logic or reasoning.
– ORIGIN Latin *emovare* 'disturb'.

emotional •adj. **1** relating to the emotions. **2** showing intense feeling. **3** readily showing emotion.
– DERIVATIVES **emotionalism** n. **emotionally** adv.

emotive •adj. arousing intense feeling.

> USAGE: **Emotive** and **emotional** are similar in meaning but they are not exactly the same. **Emotive** means 'arousing intense feeling' (*hunting is a highly emotive issue*), while **emotional** tends to mean 'showing intense feeling' (*an emotional speech*).

empathize (or **empathise**) •v. (**empathizes, empathizing, empathized**) understand and share the feelings of another person.

empathy /em-puh-thi/ •n. the ability to understand and share the feelings of other people.
– DERIVATIVES **empathetic** adj. **empathic** /em-**path**-ik/ adj.
– ORIGIN Greek *empatheia*.

emperor •n. the ruler of an empire.
– ORIGIN Latin *imperator* 'military commander'.

emperor penguin •n. the largest kind of penguin, found in the Antarctic and having a yellow patch on each side of the head.

emphasis /em-fuh-siss/ •n. (pl. **emphases** /em-fuh-seez/) **1** special importance or value given to something. **2** stress given to a word or words in speaking.
– ORIGIN Greek.

emphasize (or **emphasise**) •v. (**emphasizes, emphasizing, emphasized**) give special importance or prominence to.

emphatic •adj. **1** showing or giving emphasis. **2** definite and clear.
– DERIVATIVES **emphatically** adv.

emphysema /em-fi-see-muh/ (also **pulmonary emphysema**) •n. a condition in which the air sacs of the lungs are damaged and enlarged, causing breathlessness.
– ORIGIN Greek *emphusēma*.

empire •n. **1** a large group of states ruled over by a single monarch or ruling authority. **2** a large commercial organization under the control of one person or group.
– ORIGIN Latin *imperium*.

empirical •adj. based on observation or experience rather than theory or logic.
– DERIVATIVES **empirically** adv.
– ORIGIN Greek *empeirikos*.

empiricism /em-pi-ri-si-z'm/ •n. the theory that all knowledge comes from

experience and observation.
– DERIVATIVES **empiricist** n. & adj.

emplacement •n. a structure or platform where a gun is placed for firing.

employ •v. **1** give work to someone and pay them for it. **2** make use of. **3** keep someone occupied.
– DERIVATIVES **employability** n. **employable** adj.
– ORIGIN Old French *employer*.

employee •n. a person employed for wages or a salary.

employer •n. a person or organization that employs people.

employment •n. **1** the action of employing someone or something. **2** the state of having paid work. **3** a person's work or profession.

emporium /em-por-i-uhm/ •n. (pl. **emporia** /em-por-i-uh/ or **emporiums**) a large store selling a wide variety of goods.
– ORIGIN Greek *emporion*.

empower •v. (**empowers, empowering, empowered**) **1** give authority or power to. **2** give strength and confidence to.
– DERIVATIVES **empowerment** n.

empress /em-priss/ •n. **1** a female emperor. **2** the wife or widow of an emperor.

empty •adj. (**emptier, emptiest**) **1** containing nothing; not filled or occupied. **2** not likely to be fulfilled: *an empty threat.* **3** having no meaning or purpose. •v. (**empties, emptying, emptied**) **1** make or become empty. **2** (of a river) flow into the sea or a lake. •n. (**empties**) informal a bottle or glass whose contents have been drunk.
– DERIVATIVES **emptily** adv. **emptiness** n.
– ORIGIN Old English, 'at leisure'.

empty-handed •adj. having failed to get or achieve what you wanted.

empty-headed •adj. foolish.

empyrean /em-py-ree-uhn/ •n. (**the empyrean**) literary heaven or the sky.
– ORIGIN Greek *empurios*.

EMS •abbrev. European Monetary System.

EMU •abbrev. Economic and Monetary Union.

emu •n. a flightless Australian bird similar to an ostrich.
– ORIGIN Portuguese *ema*.

emulate /em-yuu-layt/ •v. (**emulates, emulating, emulated**) try to do as well as or be better than.
– DERIVATIVES **emulation** n. **emulator** n.
– ORIGIN Latin *aemulari*.

emulsifier •n. a substance that stabilizes an emulsion, especially one used to stabilize processed foods.

emulsify /i-mul-si-fy/ • v. (**emulsifies, emulsifying, emulsified**) make into or become an emulsion.

emulsion • n. 1 a mixture of two liquids in which particles of one are evenly distributed in the other. 2 a type of matt paint for walls. 3 a light-sensitive coating for photographic film.
– ORIGIN Latin.

en- (also **em-**) • prefix forming verbs: 1 put into or on: *engulf.* 2 bring into the condition of: *enliven.* 3 in, into, or on: *ensnare.*
– ORIGIN French.

enable • v. (**enables, enabling, enabled**) 1 provide with the ability or means to do something. 2 make possible. 3 (as adj. **-enabled**) adapted for use with a particular application or system: *WAP-enabled mobile phones.*

enact • v. 1 make a bill or other proposal law. 2 act out a role or play.
– DERIVATIVES **enactment** n. **enactor** n.

enamel • n. 1 a coloured shiny substance applied to metal, glass, or pottery for decoration or protection. 2 the hard substance that covers the crown of a tooth. 3 a paint that dries to give a smooth, hard coat. • v. (**enamels, enamelling, enamelled;** US **enamels, enameling, enameled**) coat or decorate with enamel.
– ORIGIN Old French *enamailler.*

enamour /i-nam-er/ (US **enamor**) • v. (**be enamoured of/with**) be filled with love or admiration for.
– ORIGIN Old French *enamourer.*

en bloc /on blok/ • adv. all together or all at once.
– ORIGIN French.

encamp • v. settle in or establish a camp.

encampment • n. a place where a camp is set up.

encapsulate /in-kap-syuu-layt/ • v. (**encapsulates, encapsulating, encapsulated**) 1 express clearly and in few words. 2 enclose something in a capsule or other container.
– DERIVATIVES **encapsulation** n.

encase • v. (**encases, encasing, encased**) enclose or cover in a case.

-ence • suffix forming nouns referring to a quality or action: *impertinence.*
– ORIGIN Latin *-entia, -antia.*

encephalitis /en-sef-uh-ly-tiss/ • n. inflammation of the brain.
– ORIGIN Greek *enkephalos* 'brain'.

enchant • v. 1 fill with delight. 2 put under a spell.
– DERIVATIVES **enchanter** n. **enchantress** n.
– ORIGIN French *enchanter.*

enchanting • adj. delightfully charming or attractive.

enchantment • n. 1 the state of being under a magic spell. 2 delight or fascination.

enchilada /en-chi-lah-duh/ • n. a tortilla filled with meat or cheese and served with chilli sauce.
– ORIGIN Latin American Spanish.

encircle • v. (**encircles, encircling, encircled**) form a circle around.

enclave /en-klayv/ • n. 1 a small territory surrounded by a larger territory whose inhabitants are of a different culture or nationality. 2 a group that is different from those surrounding it: *a male enclave.*
– ORIGIN Old French *enclaver* 'enclose'.

enclose • v. (**encloses, enclosing, enclosed**) 1 surround or close off on all sides. 2 place in an envelope together with a letter.
– ORIGIN Old French *enclore.*

enclosure • n. 1 an enclosed area. 2 a document or object placed in an envelope together with a letter.

encode • v. (**encodes, encoding, encoded**) convert into a coded form.
– DERIVATIVES **encoder** n.

encomium /en-koh-mi-uhm/ • n. (pl. **encomiums** or **encomia** /en-koh-mi-uh/) formal a speech or piece of writing which expresses praise.
– ORIGIN Greek *enkōmion.*

encompass /in-kum-puhss/ • v. 1 include a wide range of things. 2 surround or cover.

encore /ong-kor/ • n. a repeated or additional performance at the end of a concert, as called for by an audience. • exclam. again!
– ORIGIN French.

encounter • v. (**encounters, encountering, encountered**) unexpectedly meet or be faced with. • n. 1 an unexpected or casual meeting. 2 a confrontation or difficult struggle.
– ORIGIN Old French *encontrer.*

encourage • v. (**encourages, encouraging, encouraged**) 1 give support, confidence, or hope to. 2 help the development of.
– DERIVATIVES **encouragement** n. **encouraging** adj.
– ORIGIN French *encourager.*

encroach • v. 1 (**encroach on**) gradually intrude on a person's territory, rights, etc. 2 gradually advance beyond expected or acceptable limits: *the sea has encroached all round the coast.*
– ORIGIN Old French *encrochier* 'seize'.

encrust • v. cover with a hard crust.

– DERIVATIVES **encrustation** n.

encrypt /en-kript/ • v. convert into code.
– DERIVATIVES **encryption** n.
– ORIGIN Greek *kruptos* 'hidden'.

encumber /in-kum-ber/
• v. (**encumbers, encumbering, encumbered**) prevent from moving or acting freely.
– ORIGIN Old French *encombrer* 'block up'.

encumbrance • n. something that prevents freedom of movement or activity.

-ency • suffix forming nouns referring to a quality or state: *efficiency*.
– ORIGIN Latin *-entia*.

encyclical /en-sik-li-k'l/ • n. a letter sent by the pope to all bishops of the Roman Catholic Church.
– ORIGIN Greek *enkuklios* 'circular'.

encyclopedia /en-sy-kluh-pee-di-uh/ (also **encyclopaedia**) • n. a book or set of books giving information on many subjects.
– ORIGIN from Greek *enkuklios paideia* 'all-round education'.

encyclopedic /en-sy-kluh-pee-dik/ (also **encyclopaedic**) • adj. **1** having detailed information on a wide variety of subjects: *an encyclopedic knowledge of politics*. **2** relating to encyclopedias.

end • n. **1** the final part of something. **2** the furthest part. **3** the stopping of a state or situation: *they called for an end to violence*. **4** a person's death or downfall. **5** a goal or desired result. **6** a part or share of an activity: *your end of the deal*.
• v. **1** come or bring to an end. **2** (**end in**) have as its result. **3** (**end up**) eventually reach or come to a particular state or place.
– PHRASES **in the end** eventually. **make ends meet** earn just enough money to live on. **on end** continuously.
– ORIGIN Old English.

endanger • v. (**endangers, endangering, endangered**) **1** put in danger. **2** (as adj. **endangered**) in danger of becoming extinct.

endear /in-deer/ • v. make someone popular or well liked.

endearing • adj. inspiring love or affection.
– DERIVATIVES **endearingly** adv.

endearment • n. **1** a word or phrase expressing affection. **2** love or affection.

endeavour /in-dev-er/ (US **endeavor**)
• v. try hard to do or achieve something.
• n. **1** a serious effort to achieve something. **2** hard work; effort.
– ORIGIN from former *put yourself in devoir* 'do your utmost'.

endemic /en-dem-ik/ • adj. **1** (of a disease or condition) regularly found among particular people or in a certain area. **2** (of a plant or animal) native or restricted to a certain area.
– ORIGIN Greek *endēmios*.

ending • n. an end or final part.

endive /en-dyv/ • n. a plant with bitter curly or smooth leaves, eaten in salads.
– ORIGIN Old French.

endless • adj. **1** seeming to have no limits in size or amount. **2** continuing indefinitely. **3** (of a belt, chain, or tape) having the ends joined to allow for continuous action.
– DERIVATIVES **endlessly** adv.

endo- • comb. form internal; within: *endoskeleton*.
– ORIGIN Greek *endon*.

endocrine /en-duh-krin/ • adj. (of a gland) producing and discharging hormones or other products directly into the blood.
– ORIGIN Greek *krinein* 'sift'.

endometriosis /en-doh-mee-tri-oh-sis/
• n. a condition in which tissue from the mucous membrane lining the womb appears in other parts of the body, causing pain in the pelvic area.
– ORIGIN Greek *mētra* 'womb'.

endorphin /en-dor-fin/ • n. any of a group of chemical compounds produced in the brain that have a painkilling effect.
– ORIGIN from *endogenous* 'having an internal cause' and **MORPHINE**.

endorse /in-dorss/ • v. (**endorses, endorsing, endorsed**) **1** publicly state that you support someone or something. **2** sign a cheque on the back so that it can be paid into another person's account. **3** Brit. enter a note on a driving licence recording the penalty for a driving offence.
– ORIGIN Latin *indorsare*.

endorsement • n. **1** a declaration of approval. **2** (in the UK) a note on a driving licence recording the penalty for a driving offence.

endoskeleton • n. an internal skeleton, such as that of vertebrates.

endosperm • n. the part of a seed which acts as a food store for the developing plant embryo.

endothermic • adj. (of a chemical reaction) absorbing heat.

endow /in-dow/ • v. **1** give or leave an income or property to a person or institution. **2** establish a university post, annual prize, etc., by donating the funds needed to maintain it. **3** (**be endowed**) have something as a natural quality or characteristic: *he was endowed with*

tremendous physical strength.
– ORIGIN Old French *endouer.*

endowment •n. **1** property or a regular income that has been given or left to a person or an institution. **2** a natural quality or ability.

endowment mortgage •n. Brit. a mortgage linked to an insurance policy, in which the sum received when the policy matures is used to pay back the money borrowed.

endpaper •n. a leaf of paper at the beginning or end of a book, fixed to the inside of the cover.

endurance •n. the ability to endure something unpleasant and prolonged.

endure /in-dyoor/ •v. (**endures, enduring, endured**) **1** suffer something unpleasant and prolonged and patiently. **2** remain in existence: *these cities have endured through time.*
– DERIVATIVES **endurable** adj.
– ORIGIN Latin *indurare* 'harden'.

ENE •abbrev. east-north-east.

enema /en-i-muh/ •n. (pl. **enemas**) a medical procedure in which fluid is injected into the rectum to empty it.
– ORIGIN Greek.

enemy •n. (pl. **enemies**) **1** a person who is actively opposed or hostile to someone or something. **2** (**the enemy**) a hostile nation or its armed forces in time of war. **3** a thing that harms or weakens something.
– ORIGIN Old French *enemi.*

energetic •adj. showing or involving great energy.
– DERIVATIVES **energetically** adv.
– ORIGIN Greek *energein* 'operate'.

energize (or **energise**) •v. (**energizes, energizing, energized**) give energy and enthusiasm to: *people were energized by his ideas.*

energy •n. (pl. **energies**) **1** the strength and vitality required to keep active. **2** (**energies**) a person's physical and mental powers. **3** power derived from physical or chemical resources to provide light and heat or to work machines. **4** Physics the capacity of matter or radiation to perform work.
– ORIGIN Greek *energeia.*

enervate /en-er-vayt/ •v. (**enervates, enervating, enervated**) make someone feel drained of energy.
– DERIVATIVES **enervation** n.
– ORIGIN Latin *enervare* 'weaken'.

enfant terrible /on-fon te-ree-bluh/ •n. (pl. **enfants terribles** /on-fon te-ree-bluh/) a person who behaves in a controversial or unconventional way.
– ORIGIN French, 'terrible child'.

enfeeble •v. (**enfeebles, enfeebling, enfeebled**) weaken.

enfilade /en-fi-layd/ •n. a volley of gunfire directed along a line of soldiers from end to end.
– ORIGIN French.

enfold •v. surround or envelop.

enforce •v. (**enforces, enforcing, enforced**) **1** make sure a law, rule, or duty is obeyed or fulfilled. **2** (often as adj. **enforced**) force something to happen: *months of enforced idleness.*
– DERIVATIVES **enforceable** adj. **enforcement** n. **enforcer** n.

enfranchise /in-fran-chyz/ •v. (**enfranchises, enfranchising, enfranchised**) **1** give the right to vote to. **2** hist. free a slave.
– DERIVATIVES **enfranchisement** n.

engage •v. (**engages, engaging, engaged**) **1** attract or involve someone's interest or attention. **2** (**engage in/with**) become involved in. **3** employ. **4** enter into a contract to do something. **5** enter into combat with. **6** (of a part of a machine or engine) move into position so as to begin to operate: *the clutch will not engage.*
– ORIGIN French *engager.*

engaged •adj. **1** occupied: *I was otherwise engaged.* **2** Brit. (of a telephone line) unavailable because already in use. **3** having formally agreed to marry.

engagement •n. **1** a formal agreement to get married. **2** an appointment. **3** the state of being involved in something. **4** a battle between armed forces.

engaging •adj. charming and attractive.
– DERIVATIVES **engagingly** adv.

engender /in-jen-der/ •v. (**engenders, engendering, engendered**) give rise to a feeling, situation, or condition.
– ORIGIN Old French *engendrer.*

engine •n. **1** a machine with moving parts that converts power into motion. **2** (also **railway engine**) a locomotive.
– ORIGIN Latin *ingenium* 'talent, device'.

engineer •n. **1** a person who designs, builds, or maintains engines, machines, or structures. **2** a person who controls an engine on an aircraft or ship.
•v. (**engineers, engineering, engineered**) **1** design and build. **2** skilfully arrange for something to happen: *she engineered a meeting with him.*

engineering •n. the branch of science and technology concerned with the design, building, and use of engines, machines, and structures.

English •n. the language of England, now used in many varieties throughout the world. •adj. relating to England.

– DERIVATIVES **Englishness** n.

Englishman (or **Englishwoman**) •n. (pl. **Englishmen** or **Englishwomen**) a person from England.

engorge /in-gorj/ •v. (**engorges, engorging, engorged**) (often as adj. **engorged**) swell or cause to swell with blood, water, etc.
– DERIVATIVES **engorgement** n.
– ORIGIN Old French *engorgier* 'feed to excess'.

engrained •adj. var. of **INGRAINED**.

engrave •v. (**engraves, engraving, engraved**) **1** carve words or a design on a hard surface. **2** cut a design as lines on a metal plate for printing. **3** (**be engraved on** or **in**) be permanently fixed in the mind.
– DERIVATIVES **engraver** n.
– ORIGIN from **EN-** + former *grave* 'engrave'.

engraving •n. **1** a print made from an engraved plate or block. **2** the process or art of cutting or carving a design on a hard surface.

engross /in-grohss/ •v. (**be engrossed in**) be completely involved in.
– DERIVATIVES **engrossing** adj.
– ORIGIN from Latin *in grosso* 'wholesale'.

engulf •v. **1** (of a natural force) sweep over something so as to completely surround or cover it. **2** (of a feeling) overwhelm someone.

enhance /in-hahnss/ •v. (**enhances, enhancing, enhanced**) increase the quality, value, or extent of.
– DERIVATIVES **enhancement** n. **enhancer** n.
– ORIGIN Old French *enhaucer*.

enigma /i-nig-muh/ •n. a mysterious or puzzling person or thing.
– ORIGIN Greek *ainigma* 'riddle'.

enigmatic •adj. difficult to understand; mysterious.
– DERIVATIVES **enigmatically** adv.

enjoin •v. instruct or urge to do.
– ORIGIN Old French *enjoindre*.

enjoy •v. **1** take pleasure in. **2** (**enjoy yourself**) have a pleasant time. **3** possess and benefit from: *these professions enjoy high status*.
– DERIVATIVES **enjoyment** n.
– ORIGIN Old French *enjoier* 'give joy to' or *enjoïr* 'enjoy'.

enjoyable •adj. giving pleasure.
– DERIVATIVES **enjoyably** adv.

enlarge •v. (**enlarges, enlarging, enlarged**) **1** make or become bigger. **2** (**enlarge on**) speak or write about in greater detail.
– DERIVATIVES **enlarger** n.

enlargement •n. **1** the action of enlarging something or the state of being enlarged. **2** a photograph that is larger than the original negative or than an earlier print.

enlighten •v. **1** give someone greater knowledge and understanding. **2** (as adj. **enlightened**) reasonable, tolerant, and well-informed.

enlightenment •n. **1** knowledge and understanding. **2** (**the Enlightenment**) a European intellectual movement of the late 17th and 18th centuries which emphasized reason and individualism rather than tradition.

enlist •v. **1** enrol or be enrolled in the armed services. **2** ask for someone's help in doing something.
– DERIVATIVES **enlistment** n.

enliven •v. **1** make something more interesting. **2** make someone more cheerful or lively.

en masse /on mass/ •adv. all together.
– ORIGIN French, 'in a mass'.

enmesh •v. (usu. **be enmeshed in**) involve in complicated circumstances.

enmity •n. (pl. **enmities**) hostility.
– ORIGIN Old French *enemistie*.

ennoble •v. (**ennobles, ennobling, ennobled**) **1** give a noble rank or title to. **2** give greater dignity to: *a man ennobled by tragedy*.

ennui /on-wee/ •n. listlessness and dissatisfaction caused by boredom.
– ORIGIN French.

enormity •n. (pl. **enormities**) **1** (**the enormity of**) the extreme seriousness of something bad. **2** great size or scale: *the enormity of the task*. **3** a serious crime or sin.
– ORIGIN Latin *enormitas*.

enormous •adj. very large.
– DERIVATIVES **enormously** adv.

enough •det. & pron. as much or as many as is necessary or desirable. •adv. **1** to the required degree. **2** to a moderate degree.
– ORIGIN Old English.

enquire •v. (**enquires, enquiring, enquired**) esp. Brit. **1** ask someone for information. **2** (**enquire after**) ask about someone's health or well-being. **3** (**enquire into**) investigate.
– DERIVATIVES **enquirer** n.
– ORIGIN Latin *inquirere*.

enquiry •n. (pl. **enquiries**) esp. Brit. **1** an act of asking for information. **2** an official investigation.

enrage •v. (**enrages, enraging, enraged**) make someone very angry.

enrapture •v. (**enraptures, enrapturing,**

enraptured) give someone great pleasure.

enrich • v. **1** improve the quality or value of. **2** make wealthier.
– DERIVATIVES **enrichment** n.

enrol /in-rohl/ (US **enroll**) • v. (**enrols, enrolling, enrolled**; US **enrolls, enrolling, enrolled**) officially register or recruit as a member or student.
– DERIVATIVES **enrolment** n.
– ORIGIN Old French *enroller*.

en route /on root/ • adv. on the way.
– ORIGIN French.

ensconce /in-skonss/ • v. (**ensconces, ensconcing, ensconced**) settle yourself in a comfortable, safe, or secret place.
– ORIGIN from former *sconce*, referring to a small fort.

ensemble /on-som-b'l/ • n. **1** a group of musicians, actors, or dancers who perform together. **2** a group of items viewed as a whole: *her ensemble of tweed and cashmere.* **3** a passage for a whole choir or group of instruments.
– ORIGIN French.

enshrine • v. (**enshrines, enshrining, enshrined**) **1** preserve a right, tradition, or idea in a form that ensures it will be respected: *rights enshrined in the constitution.* **2** place a precious or holy object in an appropriate receptacle.

enshroud /in-shrowd/ • v. literary cover completely and hide from view.

ensign /en-syn/ • n. **1** a flag showing a ship's nationality. **2** the lowest rank of commissioned officer in the US and some other navies.
– ORIGIN Old French *enseigne*.

enslave • v. (**enslaves, enslaving, enslaved**) **1** make someone a slave. **2** make someone completely dominated by someone or something: *they were enslaved by their need to take drugs.*
– DERIVATIVES **enslavement** n.

ensnare • v. (**ensnares, ensnaring, ensnared**) trap someone in a difficult situation or gain control over them.

ensue • v. (**ensues, ensuing, ensued**) happen afterwards or as a result.
– ORIGIN Old French *ensivre*.

en suite /on sweet/ • adj. & adv. Brit. (of a bathroom) leading directly off a bedroom.
– ORIGIN French, 'in sequence'.

ensure /in-shoor/ • v. (**ensures, ensuring, ensured**) **1** make certain that something will happen or be so. **2** (**ensure against**) make sure that a problem does not occur.
– ORIGIN Old French *enseurer*.

USAGE: On the difference between **ensure** and **insure**, see the note at **INSURE**.

-ent • suffix **1** (forming adjectives) referring to a state or an occurrence of action: *convenient.* **2** (forming nouns) performing a function: *coefficient.*
– ORIGIN Latin.

entail • v. involve something that is unavoidable.
– ORIGIN Old French *taille* 'notch, tax'.

entangle • v. (**entangles, entangling, entangled**) (usu. **be entangled in/with**) **1** make tangled. **2** involve someone in a complicated situation.
– DERIVATIVES **entanglement** n.

entente /on-tont/ (also **entente cordiale** /on-tont kor-di-ahl/) • n. a friendly understanding between countries.
– ORIGIN from French *entente cordiale* 'friendly understanding'.

enter • v. (**enters, entering, entered**) **1** come or go into. **2** (often **enter into**) begin to be involved in or do. **3** join an institution or profession. **4** register as a participant in a competition, exam, etc. **5** (**enter into**) undertake to be bound by an agreement. **6** write or key information in a book, computer, etc.
– ORIGIN Old French *entrer*.

enteric /en-terr-ik/ • adj. relating to the intestines.
– ORIGIN Greek *enterikos*.

enteritis /en-tuh-ry-tis/ • n. inflammation of the intestine, especially the small intestine.

enterprise • n. **1** a large project or undertaking. **2** a business or company. **3** initiative and resourcefulness: *success was the result of talent and enterprise.*
– ORIGIN Old French.

enterprising • adj. showing initiative and resourcefulness.

entertain • v. **1** provide with amusement or enjoyment. **2** receive someone as a guest and give them food and drink. **3** give consideration to: *he entertained little hope of success.*
– ORIGIN French *entretenir*.

entertainer • n. a person whose job is to entertain other people.

entertaining • adj. providing amusement or enjoyment.
– DERIVATIVES **entertainingly** adv.

entertainment • n. **1** the action of entertaining someone. **2** an event, performance, or activity designed to entertain other people.

enthral /in-thrawl/ (US **enthrall**) • v. (**enthrals, enthralling, enthralled**; US **enthralls, enthralling, enthralled**) fascinate someone and hold their attention.

enthrone • v. (**enthrones, enthroning, enthroned**) mark the new reign or

period of office of a king, queen, or bishop by a ceremony in which they sit on a throne.
– DERIVATIVES **enthronement** n.

enthuse /in-thyooz/ • v. (**enthuses, enthusing, enthused**) **1** (often **enthuse over**) express great enthusiasm for something. **2** make someone enthusiastic.

enthusiasm • n. great enjoyment, interest, or approval.
– ORIGIN Greek *enthous* 'possessed by a god'.

enthusiast • n. a person who is full of enthusiasm for something.

enthusiastic • adj. having or showing great enjoyment, interest, or approval.
– DERIVATIVES **enthusiastically** adv.

entice /in-tyss/ • v. (**entices, enticing, enticed**) attract by offering something pleasant or desirable.
– DERIVATIVES **enticement** n.
– ORIGIN Old French *enticier*.

entire /in-tyr/ • adj. including everything, everyone, or every part; whole.
– ORIGIN Old French *entier*.

entirely • adv. wholly; completely.

entirety • n. (**the entirety**) the whole of something.
– PHRASES **in its entirety** as a whole.

entitle • v. (**entitles, entitling, entitled**) **1** give someone a right to do or have something. **2** give a title to a book, play, etc.
– DERIVATIVES **entitlement** n.

entity /en-ti-ti/ • n. (pl. **entities**) a thing which exists separately from other things.
– ORIGIN French *entité*.

entomb • v. **1** place in a tomb. **2** bury in or under something.

entomology /en-tuh-mol-uh-ji/ • n. the scientific study of insects.
– DERIVATIVES **entomological** adj. **entomologist** n.
– ORIGIN Greek *entomon* 'insect'.

entourage /on-toor-ahzh/ • n. a group of people accompanying an important person.
– ORIGIN French.

entrails • pl. n. a person's or animal's intestines or internal organs.
– ORIGIN Latin *intralia* 'internal things'.

entrance[1] /en-truhnss/ • n. **1** a door or passageway into a place. **2** an act of entering a place. **3** the right, means, or opportunity to enter a place: *fifty people attempted to gain entrance.*

entrance[2] /in-trahnss/ • v. (**entrances, entrancing, entranced**) **1** fill with wonder and delight. **2** cast a spell on.

entrant • n. a person who enters, joins,

or takes part in something.

entrap • v. (**entraps, entrapping, entrapped**) **1** catch in a trap. **2** (of a police officer) deceive someone into committing a crime in order to have them prosecuted.
– DERIVATIVES **entrapment** n.

entreat • v. ask someone to do something in an earnest or emotional way.
– ORIGIN Old French *entraitier*.

entreaty • n. (pl. **entreaties**) an earnest or emotional request.

entrecôte /on-truh-koht/ • n. a steak cut off the sirloin.
– ORIGIN French.

entrée /on-tray/ • n. **1** the main course of a meal. **2** the right to enter a place or social group: *an entrée into fashionable society.*
– ORIGIN French.

entrench • v. **1** establish something so firmly that change is difficult: *prejudice is entrenched in our society.* **2** establish a military force in fortified positions.
– DERIVATIVES **entrenchment** n.

entrepreneur /on-truh-pruh-ner/ • n. a person who sets up a business or businesses, taking financial risks in the hope of profit.
– DERIVATIVES **entrepreneurial** adj.
– ORIGIN French.

entropy /en-truh-pi/ • n. Physics a quantity expressing how much of a system's thermal energy is unavailable for conversion into mechanical work.
– DERIVATIVES **entropic** /en-trop-ik/ adj.
– ORIGIN Greek *tropē* 'transformation'.

entrust • v. **1** (**entrust someone with**) make someone responsible for doing something. **2** (**entrust something to**) put something into someone's care.

entry • n. (pl. **entries**) **1** an act of entering a place. **2** an entrance. **3** the right, means, or opportunity to enter a place. **4** an item entered in a list, reference book, etc.

entry-level • adj. suitable for a beginner or first-time user.

entwine • v. (**entwines, entwining, entwined**) wind or twist together.

E-number • n. Brit. a code number beginning with the letter E, given to food additives.

enumerate /i-nyoo-muh-rayt/ • v. (**enumerates, enumerating, enumerated**) mention a number of things one by one.
– DERIVATIVES **enumeration** n.
– ORIGIN Latin *enumerare* 'count out'.

enunciate /i-nun-si-ayt/
• v. (**enunciates, enunciating,**

enunciated) **1** pronounce clearly. **2** set out a policy or theory precisely.
– DERIVATIVES **enunciation** n.
– ORIGIN Latin *enuntiare* 'announce'.

envelop /in-vel-uhp/ • v. (**envelops, enveloping, enveloped**) wrap up, cover, or surround completely.
– ORIGIN Old French *envoluper*.

envelope /en-vuh-lohp/ • n. **1** a flat paper container with a sealable flap, used to enclose a letter or document. **2** a structure or layer that covers or encloses something.
– ORIGIN French *enveloppe* 'envelop'.

enviable /en-vi-uh-b'l/ • adj. desirable and so likely to cause envy in other people.
– DERIVATIVES **enviably** adv.

envious • adj. feeling or showing envy.
– DERIVATIVES **enviously** adv.

environment • n. **1** the surroundings or conditions in which a person, animal, or plant lives or operates. **2** (**the environment**) the natural world.
– DERIVATIVES **environmental** adj. **environmentally** adv.

> ☑ Remember that **environment** has an n before the **m**.

environmentalist • n. a person who is concerned with the protection of the environment.
– DERIVATIVES **environmentalism** n.

environs • pl. n. the area surrounding a place.
– ORIGIN French.

envisage /in-viz-ij/ • v. (**envisages, envisaging, envisaged**) **1** think of as a possible future event. **2** form a mental picture of.
– ORIGIN French *envisager*.

envision • v. imagine as a possible future event.

envoy /en-voy/ • n. a messenger or representative.
– ORIGIN French *envoyé* 'sent'.

envy • n. (pl. **envies**) **1** discontented longing aroused by someone else's possessions, qualities, etc. **2** (**the envy of**) a person or thing that arouses this feeling. • v. (**envies, envying, envied**) long to have something that belongs to another person.
– ORIGIN Old French *envie*.

enzyme /en-zym/ • n. a substance produced by a living organism that acts as a catalyst to bring about a particular biochemical reaction.
– ORIGIN modern Greek *enzumos* 'leavened'.

Eocene /ee-oh-seen/ • adj. Geol. relating to the second epoch of the Tertiary period (56.5 to 35.4 million years ago).

– ORIGIN from Greek *ēōs* 'dawn' + *kainos* 'new'.

eon • n. US and tech. var. of AEON.

EP • abbrev. **1** (of a record or compact disc) extended-play. **2** European Parliament.

ep- • prefix var. of EPI-.

epaulette /ep-puh-let/ (US also **epaulet**) • n. an ornamental shoulder piece on a military uniform.
– ORIGIN French, 'little shoulder'.

ephemera /i-fem-uh-ruh/ • pl. n. items of short-lived interest or usefulness.
– ORIGIN Greek, 'things lasting only a day'.

ephemeral /i-fem-uh-ruhl/ • adj. lasting or living for a very short time.

epi- (also **ep-** before a vowel or *h*) • prefix **1** upon: *epigraph*. **2** above: *epidermis*.
– ORIGIN Greek *epi*.

epic • n. **1** a long poem describing the actions of heroic or legendary figures or the history of a nation. **2** a long film or book portraying heroic actions or covering a long period of time. • adj. **1** relating to an epic. **2** grand or heroic in scale: *an epic journey around the world*.
– ORIGIN Greek *epikos*.

epicene /e-pi-seen/ • adj. having both male and female characteristics or no characteristics of either sex.
– ORIGIN Greek *epikoinos*.

epicentre (US **epicenter**) • n. the point on the earth's surface directly above the origin of an earthquake.

epicure /e-pi-kyoor/ • n. a person who takes particular pleasure in good food and drink.
– DERIVATIVES **epicurean** n. & adj.
– ORIGIN from the ancient Greek philosopher *Epicurus*.

epidemic • n. **1** a widespread occurrence of an infectious disease in a community at a particular time. **2** a sudden and widespread occurrence of something undesirable: *an epidemic of crime*.
– ORIGIN Greek *epidēmia*.

epidemiology /e-pi-dee-mi-ol-uh-ji/ • n. the study of the spread and control of diseases.
– DERIVATIVES **epidemiological** adj. **epidemiologist** n.

epidermis /e-pi-der-miss/ • n. **1** the surface layer of an animal's skin, overlying the dermis. **2** the outer layer of tissue in a plant.
– DERIVATIVES **epidermal** adj.
– ORIGIN Greek.

epidural /e-pi-dyoor-uhl/ • n. an anaesthetic put into the space around the outermost membrane of the spinal cord, used especially in childbirth.

epiglottis /e-pi-**glot**-tiss/ • n. a flap of cartilage at the root of the tongue, that descends during swallowing to cover the opening of the windpipe.
– ORIGIN Greek.

epigram /**e**-pi-gram/ • n. **1** a concise and witty saying. **2** a short witty poem.
– DERIVATIVES **epigrammatic** adj.
– ORIGIN Greek *epigramma*.

epigraph /**e**-pi-grahf/ • n. **1** an inscription on a building, statue, or coin. **2** a short quotation introducing a book or chapter.
– ORIGIN Greek *epigraphein* 'write on'.

epilepsy /**e**-pi-lep-si/ • n. a disorder of the nervous system causing periodic loss of consciousness or convulsions.
– DERIVATIVES **epileptic** adj. & n.
– ORIGIN Greek *epilēpsia*.

epilogue /**e**-pi-log/ (US also **epilog**) • n. a section at the end of a book or play which comments on what has happened.
– ORIGIN Greek *epilogos*.

epiphany /i-**pif**-uh-ni/ • n. (pl. **epiphanies**) **1** (**Epiphany**) the occasion when Jesus appeared to the Magi (Gospel of Matthew, chapter 2). **2** (**Epiphany**) the festival which commemorates this, on 6 January.
– ORIGIN Greek *epiphainein* 'reveal'.

episcopacy /i-**piss**-kuh-puh-si/ • n. (pl. **episcopacies**) **1** government of a Church by bishops. **2** (**the episcopacy**) the bishops of a region or church as a group.

episcopal /i-**piss**-kuh-puhl/ • adj. relating to a bishop or bishops.
– DERIVATIVES **episcopally** adv.
– ORIGIN Latin *episcopus* 'bishop'.

episcopalian /i-piss-kuh-**pay**-li-uhn/ • adj. relating to the government of a Church by bishops. • n. a supporter of government of a Church by bishops.
– DERIVATIVES **episcopalianism** n.

episcopate /i-**piss**-kuh-puht/ • n. **1** the position or period of office of a bishop. **2** (**the episcopate**) the bishops of a church or region as a group.

episode • n. **1** an event or a sequence of events. **2** each of the parts into which a serialized story or programme is divided.
– ORIGIN Greek *epeisodion*.

episodic /e-pi-**sod**-ik/ • adj. **1** made up of a series of separate events. **2** occurring at irregular intervals.
– DERIVATIVES **episodically** adv.

epistemology /i-piss-ti-**mol**-uh-ji/ • n. the branch of philosophy that deals with knowledge.
– DERIVATIVES **epistemic** adj.
epistemological adj. **epistemologist** n.
– ORIGIN Greek *epistēmē* 'knowledge'.

epistle /i-**piss**-uhl/ • n. **1** formal or humorous a letter. **2** (**Epistle**) a book of the New Testament in the form of a letter from an Apostle.
– ORIGIN Greek *epistolē*.

epistolary /i-**piss**-tuh-luh-ri/ • adj. **1** relating to the writing of letters. **2** (of a literary work) in the form of letters.

epitaph /**e**-pi-tahf/ • n. words written in memory of a person who has died.
– ORIGIN Greek *epitaphion* 'funeral oration'.

epithelium /ep-i-**thee**-li-uhm/ • n. (pl. **epithelia** /ep-i-**thee**-li-uh/) the thin tissue forming the outer layer of the body's surface and lining the alimentary canal and other hollow structures.
– ORIGIN Latin.

epithet /**e**-pi-thet/ • n. a word or phrase used to describe the most important quality of a person or thing.
– ORIGIN Greek *epitheton*.

epitome /i-**pit**-uh-mi/ • n. (**the epitome of**) a perfect example of a quality or type: *she was the epitome of elegance.*
– ORIGIN Greek.

epitomize (or **epitomise**) • v. (**epitomizes**, **epitomizing**, **epitomized**) be a perfect example of a quality or type.

epoch /**ee**-pok/ • n. **1** a period of time in history marked by particular events or features: *the Victorian epoch.* **2** the beginning of a period of history. **3** Geol. a division of time that is a subdivision of a period and is itself subdivided into ages.
– ORIGIN Greek *epokhē* 'fixed point of time'.

epoch-making • adj. likely to have a very important effect on a period of history.

eponym /**e**-puh-nim/ • n. **1** a word or name that comes from the name of a person. **2** a person after whom something is named.

eponymous /i-**pon**-i-muhss/ • adj. **1** (of a person) giving their name to something. **2** (of a thing) named after a particular person.
– ORIGIN Greek *epōnumos*.

epoxy /i-**pok**-si/ (also **epoxy resin**) • n. (pl. **epoxies**) a type of strong glue made from synthetic polymers.
– ORIGIN from EPI- + OXYGEN.

Epsom salts • pl. n. crystals of magnesium sulphate used as a laxative.
– ORIGIN named after the town of *Epsom* in Surrey.

equable /**ek**-wuh-b'l/ • adj. **1** calm and even-tempered. **2** not varying greatly: *an equable climate.*
– DERIVATIVES **equably** adv.

e

– ORIGIN Latin *aequabilis*.

equal • adj. **1** being the same in quantity, size, degree, value, or status. **2** evenly balanced. **3** (**equal to**) having the ability to meet a challenge. • n. a person or thing that is equal to another.
• v. (**equals, equalling, equalled**; US **equals, equaling, equaled**) **1** be equal or equivalent to something. **2** reach the same standard as; match.
– ORIGIN Latin *aequalis*.

equality • n. the state of being equal.

equalize (or **equalise**) • v. (**equalizes, equalizing, equalized**) **1** make or become equal. **2** Brit. level the score in a match by scoring a goal.
– DERIVATIVES **equalization** n.

equalizer (or **equaliser**) • n. **1** a thing that has an equalizing effect. **2** Brit. a goal that levels the score in a match.

equally • adv. **1** in an equal way or to an equal extent. **2** in amounts that are equal.

> **USAGE:** You should not use the words **equally** as together, as in the sentence *follow-up discussion is equally as important*: just say **equally** or **as** on its own.

equals sign (also **equal sign**) • n. the symbol =.

equanimity /ek-wuh-**nim**-i-ti/ • n. calmness of temper.
– ORIGIN Latin *aequanimitas*.

equate /i-**kwayt**/ • v. (**equates, equating, equated**) **1** consider one thing as equal to another: *customers equate the brand with reliability.* **2** make two or more things the same.

equation /i-**kway**-zh'n/ • n. **1** Math. a statement that the values of two mathematical expressions are equal (indicated by the sign =). **2** Chem. a formula representing the changes which occur in a chemical reaction. **3** the process of equating one thing with another.

equator /i-**kway**-ter/ • n. an imaginary line around the earth at equal distances from the poles, dividing the earth into northern and southern hemispheres.
– ORIGIN Latin *aequator*.

equatorial /ek-wuh-**tor**-i-uhl/ • adj. relating to the equator.
– DERIVATIVES **equatorially** adv.

equerry /ek-wuh-**ri**/ • n. (pl. **equerries**) a male officer of the British royal household acting as an attendant to a member of the royal family.
– ORIGIN Old French *esquierie* 'company of squires'.

equestrian /i-**kwess**-tri-uhn/ • adj. relating to horse riding. • n. (fem.

equestrienne /i-kwess-tri-**en**/) a person on horseback.
– ORIGIN Latin *equus* 'horse'.

equestrianism • n. the skill or sport of horse riding.

equi- /ee-kwi, ek-wi/ • comb. form equal; equally: *equidistant.*
– ORIGIN Latin *aequus* 'equal'.

equidistant • adj. at equal distances.
– DERIVATIVES **equidistance** n.

equilateral • adj. (of a triangle) having all its sides of the same length.

equilibrium /ee-kwi-**lib**-ri-uhm, ek-wi-**lib**-ri-uhm/ • n. (pl. **equilibria** /ee-kwi-**lib**-ri-uh, ek-wi-**lib**-ri-uh/) **1** a state in which opposing forces are balanced. **2** the state of being physically balanced. **3** a calm state of mind.
– ORIGIN Latin *aequilibrium*.

equine /ek-wyn/ • adj. **1** relating to horses or other members of the horse family. **2** resembling a horse.
– ORIGIN Latin *equus* 'horse'.

equinoctial /ee-kwi-**nok**-sh'l, ek-wi-**nok**-sh'l/ • adj. **1** relating to the equinox. **2** at or near the equator.

equinox /ee-kwi-noks/ • n. the time or date (twice each year, about 22 September and 20 March) when day and night are of equal length.
– ORIGIN Latin *aequinoctium*.

equip • v. (**equips, equipping, equipped**) **1** supply with the items needed for a purpose. **2** prepare someone for a situation or task: *people seeking jobs need to be better equipped to make decisions.*
– ORIGIN French *équiper*.

equipment • n. **1** the items needed for a particular purpose. **2** the supply of these items.

equipoise /ek-wi-poyz/ • n. a state of balance between different forces or interests.

equitable /ek-wi-tuh-b'l/ • adj. treating everyone equally; fair.
– DERIVATIVES **equitably** adv.

equitation /ek-wi-**tay**-sh'n/ • n. formal the art and practice of horse riding.
– ORIGIN Latin.

equity /ek-wi-ti/ • n. (pl. **equities**) **1** the quality of being fair and impartial. **2** a branch of law that developed alongside common law and is concerned with fairness and justice. **3** the value of a mortgaged property after all the charges and debts secured against it have been paid. **4** the value of the shares issued by a company. **5** (**equities**) stocks and shares that do not pay a fixed amount of interest.
– ORIGIN Latin *aequitas*.

equivalent /i-**kwiv**-uh-luhnt/

• **adj.** equal in value, amount, meaning, etc.: *a brightness equivalent to a billion suns.* • **n.** a person or thing that is equivalent to another.
– DERIVATIVES **equivalence** n. **equivalency** n. **equivalently** adv.
– ORIGIN Latin *aequivalere* 'be of equal worth'.

equivocal /i-kwiv-uh-k'l/ • **adj.** unclear because able to be understood in more than one way.
– DERIVATIVES **equivocally** adv.
– ORIGIN from Latin *aequus* 'equal' + *vocare* 'to call'.

equivocate /i-kwiv-uh-kayt/ • **v.** (**equivocates, equivocating, equivocated**) use language that can be understood in more than one way in order to avoid the truth.
– DERIVATIVES **equivocation** n.

ER • **abbrev. 1** Queen Elizabeth. [ORIGIN from Latin *Elizabetha Regina*.] **2** N. Amer. emergency room.

Er • **symb.** the chemical element erbium.

-er[1] • **suffix** referring to: **1** a person or thing that performs a specified action or that has a specified quality: *farmer*. **2** a person concerned with a specified thing: *milliner*. **3** a person belonging to a specified place or group: *city-dweller*.
– ORIGIN Old English.

-er[2] • **suffix** forming the comparative of adjectives (as in *bigger*) and adverbs (as in *faster*).
– ORIGIN Old English.

era /eer-uh/ • **n. 1** a long and distinct period of history. **2** Geol. a major division of time that is a subdivision of an aeon and is itself subdivided into periods.
– ORIGIN Latin *aera* 'counters'.

eradicate /i-rad-i-kayt/ • **v.** (**eradicates, eradicating, eradicated**) remove or destroy completely.
– DERIVATIVES **eradication** n. **eradicator** n.
– ORIGIN Latin *eradicare* 'tear up by the roots'.

erase /i-rayz/ • **v.** (**erases, erasing, erased**) **1** rub something out. **2** remove all traces of.
– DERIVATIVES **erasable** adj. **erasure** n.
– ORIGIN Latin *eradere* 'scrape away'.

eraser • **n.** a piece of rubber or plastic used to rub out something written.

erbium /er-bi-uhm/ • **n.** a soft silvery-white metallic chemical element.
– ORIGIN from *Ytterby* in Sweden.

ere /air/ • **prep. & conj.** old use before (in time).
– ORIGIN Old English.

erect • **adj. 1** rigidly upright. **2** (of a body part) enlarged and rigid. • **v. 1** build something. **2** create or establish: *the*

party that erected the welfare state.
– DERIVATIVES **erector** n.
– ORIGIN Latin *erigere* 'set up'.

erectile /i-rek-tyl/ • **adj.** able to become erect.

erection • **n. 1** the action of erecting a structure or object. **2** a building or other upright structure. **3** an erect state of the penis.

erg • **n.** Physics a unit of work or energy.
– ORIGIN Greek *ergon* 'work'.

ergo /er-goh/ • **adv.** therefore.
– ORIGIN Latin.

ergonomics /er-guh-nom-iks/ • **n.** the study of people's efficiency in their working environment.
– DERIVATIVES **ergonomic** adj. **ergonomically** adv.
– ORIGIN Greek *ergon* 'work'.

ergot /er-got/ • **n.** a disease of rye and other cereals, caused by a fungus.
– ORIGIN French.

Erin /e-rin/ • **n.** old use or literary Ireland.
– ORIGIN Irish.

Eritrean /e-ri-tray-uhn/ • **n.** a person from the independent state of Eritrea in NE Africa. • **adj.** relating to Eritrea.

ERM • **abbrev.** Exchange Rate Mechanism.

ermine /er-min/ • **n.** (pl. **ermine** or **ermines**) **1** a stoat. **2** the white winter fur of the stoat, used to trim the ceremonial robes of judges or nobles.
– ORIGIN Old French *hermine*.

erode /i-rohd/ • **v.** (**erodes, eroding, eroded**) **1** gradually wear or be worn away. **2** gradually destroy: *this humiliation has eroded Jean's confidence.*
– ORIGIN Latin *erodere*.

erogenous /i-roj-i-nuhss/ • **adj.** (of a part of the body) sensitive to sexual stimulation.
– ORIGIN from Greek *erōs* 'sexual love'.

erosion /i-roh-zh'n/ • **n.** the process of eroding or the result of being eroded.

erotic /i-rot-ik/ • **adj.** relating to or causing sexual desire or excitement.
– DERIVATIVES **erotically** adv.
– ORIGIN Greek *erōtikos*.

erotica • **n.** erotic literature or art.

eroticism • **n. 1** the quality of being erotic. **2** sexual desire or excitement.

eroticize (or **eroticise**) • **v.** (**eroticizes, eroticizing, eroticized**) make something able to arouse sexual desire or excitement.
– DERIVATIVES **eroticization** n.

err • **v. 1** make a mistake. **2** (usu. as adj. **erring**) do wrong: *her erring husband.*
– PHRASES **err on the side of** display more rather than less of a quality: *it is best to err on the side of caution.*
– ORIGIN Latin *errare* 'to stray'.

errand •n. a short journey made to deliver or collect something.
– ORIGIN Old English, 'message, mission'.

errant /e-ruhnt/ •adj. **1** formal or humorous straying from the accepted course or standards. **2** old use travelling in search of adventure: *a knight errant*.
– ORIGIN sense 1 from Latin *errare* 'err'; sense 2 from Old French, 'travelling'.

erratic /i-rat-ik/ •adj. not happening at regular times or following a regular pattern.
– DERIVATIVES **erratically** adv.

erratum /e-rah-tuhm/ •n. (pl. **errata** /e-rah-tuh/) an error in printing or writing.
– ORIGIN Latin.

erroneous /i-roh-ni-uhss/ •adj. incorrect; wrong.
– DERIVATIVES **erroneously** adv.
– ORIGIN Latin *erroneus*.

error •n. **1** a mistake. **2** the state of being wrong in behaviour or judgement: *the money was paid in error*.
– ORIGIN Latin.

ersatz /er-sats/ •adj. **1** (of a product) made or used as a poor-quality substitute for something else. **2** not genuine: *ersatz emotion*.
– ORIGIN German, 'replacement'.

Erse /erss/ •n. the Scottish or Irish Gaelic language.
– ORIGIN early Scots form of **IRISH**.

erstwhile •adj. former.
– ORIGIN Old English.

erudite /e-roo-dyt/ •adj. having or showing knowledge or learning.
– DERIVATIVES **erudition** n.
– ORIGIN Latin *eruditus*.

erupt •v. **1** (of a volcano) forcefully throw out lava, ash, and gases. **2** break out suddenly: *noise erupted from the next room*. **3** express feelings in a sudden and noisy way. **4** (of a spot or rash) suddenly appear on the skin.
– DERIVATIVES **eruptive** adj.
– ORIGIN Latin *erumpere* 'break out'.

eruption •n. an act or the action of erupting.

-ery (also **-ry**) •suffix forming nouns referring to: **1** a class or kind: *greenery*. **2** an occupation, a state, or behaviour: *archery*. **3** a place set aside for an activity or a group of things or animals: *rookery*.
– ORIGIN Latin *-arius* and *-ator*.

erysipelas /e-ri-sip-i-luhs/ •n. a skin disease causing large raised red patches on the face and legs.
– ORIGIN Greek *erusipelas*.

erythrocyte /i-rith-ruh-syt/ •n. a blood cell which contains haemoglobin and

transports oxygen to the tissues; a red blood cell.
– ORIGIN Greek *eruthros* 'red'.

Es •symb. the chemical element einsteinium.

escalate /ess-kuh-layt/ •v. (**escalates**, **escalating**, **escalated**) **1** increase rapidly. **2** become more serious or intense: *the crisis escalated*.
– DERIVATIVES **escalation** n.
– ORIGIN from **ESCALATOR**.

escalator •n. a moving staircase consisting of a circulating belt of steps driven by a motor.
– ORIGIN French *escalade*, referring to a former method of military attack using ladders.

escalope /i-ska-luhp/ •n. a thin slice of meat, coated in breadcrumbs and fried.
– ORIGIN Old French, 'shell'.

escapade /ess-kuh-payd/ •n. an incident involving daring and adventure.

escape •v. (**escapes**, **escaping**, **escaped**) **1** break free from imprisonment or control. **2** get free from someone. **3** succeed in avoiding something unpleasant. **4** fail to be noticed or remembered by: *his name escapes me*. **5** (of gas, liquid, or heat) leak from a container. •n. **1** an act of escaping. **2** a means of escaping.
– DERIVATIVES **escapee** n. **escaper** n.
– ORIGIN Old French *eschaper*.

escapement /i-skayp-muhnt/ •n. a mechanism that connects and regulates the moving parts of a clock or watch.

escapism •n. the habit of trying to distract yourself from unpleasant realities through fantasy or entertainment.
– DERIVATIVES **escapist** n. & adj.

escapologist /ess-kuh-pol-uh-jist/ •n. an entertainer who specializes in breaking free from ropes, handcuffs, and chains.

escarpment /i-skarp-muhnt/ •n. a long, steep slope that separates an area of high ground from an area of lower ground.
– ORIGIN French *escarpement*.

eschatology /ess-kuh-tol-uh-ji/ •n. the part of theology concerned with death, judgement, and destiny.
– DERIVATIVES **eschatological** adj.
– ORIGIN Greek *eskhatos* 'last'.

eschew /iss-choo/ •v. deliberately avoid doing something.
– ORIGIN Old French *eschiver*.

escort •n. /ess-kort/ **1** a person, vehicle, or group accompanying another to provide protection or as a mark of rank. **2** a person who accompanies a member of the opposite sex to a social event.

• v. /i-**skort**/ accompany a person, vehicle, or group to a place.
– ORIGIN French *escorte*.

escritoire /ess-kri-**twar**/ • n. a small writing desk with drawers and compartments.
– ORIGIN French.

escudo /ess-**kyoo**-doh/ • n. (pl. **escudos**) the former basic unit of money of Portugal (replaced by the euro in 2002).
– ORIGIN Portuguese.

escutcheon /i-sku-**chuhn**/ • n. a shield or emblem bearing a coat of arms.
– ORIGIN Old French *escuchon*.

ESE • abbrev. east-south-east.

-ese • suffix forming adjectives and nouns: **1** referring to an inhabitant or language of a country or city: *Chinese*. **2** usu. derog. referring to character or style of language: *journalese*.
– ORIGIN Latin *-ensis*.

Eskimo • n. (pl. **Eskimo** or **Eskimos**) **1** a member of a people inhabiting northern Canada, Alaska, Greenland, and eastern Siberia. **2** the language of the Eskimo.
• adj. relating to Eskimos.
– ORIGIN a North American Indian word.

> **USAGE:** The word **Eskimo** is regarded by some people as offensive and the peoples inhabiting the regions of northern Canada and parts of Greenland and Alaska prefer to call themselves **Inuit**. The term **Eskimo**, however, is the only one that covers both the Inuit and the Yupik (peoples of Siberia, the Aleutian islands, and Alaska), and is still widely used.

ESL • abbrev. English as a second language.

esophagus • n. US = OESOPHAGUS.

esoteric /e-suh-**te**-rik, ee-suh-**te**-rik/ • adj. intended for or understood by only a small number of people with a specialized knowledge.
– DERIVATIVES **esoterically** adv.
– ORIGIN Greek *esōterikos*.

ESP • abbrev. extrasensory perception.

espadrille /ess-puh-**dril**/ • n. a light canvas shoe with a plaited fibre sole.
– ORIGIN French.

espalier /i-**spal**-yuh, e-**spal**-yuh/ • n. a fruit tree or ornamental shrub whose branches are trained to grow flat against a wall.
– ORIGIN French.

especial • adj. **1** special: *the interior carvings are of especial interest*. **2** for or belonging chiefly to one person or thing.
– ORIGIN Latin *specialis*.

especially • adv. **1** used to single out one person or thing; particularly: *a song written especially for Jonathan*. **2** to a great extent: *he didn't especially like dancing*.

Esperanto /ess-puh-**ran**-toh/ • n. an

artificial language invented as a means of international communication.
– ORIGIN from *Dr Esperanto*, a pen name of the inventor.

espionage /ess-pi-uh-**nahzh**/ • n. the practice of spying or of using spies.
– ORIGIN French.

esplanade /ess-pluh-**nayd**/ • n. a long, level area along which people may walk for pleasure.
– ORIGIN French.

espousal /i-**spow**-z'l/ • n. an act of adopting or supporting a cause, belief, or way of life.

espouse /i-**spowz**/ • v. (**espouses**, **espousing**, **espoused**) adopt or support a cause, belief, or way of life.
– ORIGIN Old French *espouser*.

espresso /ess-**press**-oh/ (also **expresso** /ex-**press**-oh/) • n. (pl. **espressos**) strong black coffee made by forcing steam through ground coffee beans.
– ORIGIN from Italian *caffè espresso* 'pressed out coffee'.

esprit de corps /e-spree duh **kor**/ • n. a feeling of pride and loyalty uniting the members of a group.
– ORIGIN French, 'spirit of the body'.

espy /i-**spy**/ • v. (**espies**, **espying**, **espied**) literary catch sight of.
– ORIGIN Old French *espier*.

Esq. • abbrev. Esquire.

-esque • suffix (forming adjectives) in the style of: *Kafkaesque*.
– ORIGIN French.

esquire /i-**skwyr**/ • n. **1** (**Esquire**) Brit. a polite title placed after a man's name when no other title is used. **2** hist. a young nobleman who acted as an attendant to a knight.
– ORIGIN Old French *esquier*.

-ess • suffix forming nouns referring to females: *abbess*.
– ORIGIN French *-esse*.

essay • n. /**ess**-ay/ **1** a piece of writing on a particular subject. **2** formal an attempt or effort. • v. /e-**say**/ formal attempt: *Donald essayed a smile*.
– DERIVATIVES **essayist** n.
– ORIGIN Old French *essai* 'trial'; the verb is from ASSAY.

essence • n. **1** the basic or most important feature of something, which determines its character: *conflict is the essence of drama*. **2** an extract obtained from a plant or other substance and used for flavouring or perfume.
– PHRASES **in essence** basically. **of the essence** very important.
– ORIGIN Latin *essentia*.

essential • adj. **1** absolutely necessary. **2** central to the nature of: *the essential*

weakness of the case. • n. (**essentials**)
1 things that are absolutely necessary.
2 the basic elements of something.
– DERIVATIVES **essentially** adv.

essential oil • n. a natural oil extracted
from a plant.

-est • suffix forming the superlative of
adjectives (such as *shortest*) and of
adverbs (such as *soonest*).
– ORIGIN Old English.

establish • v. **1** set up on a firm or
permanent basis. **2** start or bring about:
*the countries established diplomatic
relations.* **3** make something accepted or
recognized by other people: *she had
established her reputation as a journalist.*
4 find out the facts of a situation. **5** (as
adj. **established**) recognized by the state
as the national Church or religion.
– ORIGIN Old French *establir*.

establishment • n. **1** the action of
establishing something or the state of
being established. **2** an organization,
institution, or hotel. **3** (**the Establishment**) a group in a society who have
power and influence in matters of policy
or opinion, and who oppose change.

estate • n. **1** a property consisting of a
large house and extensive grounds. **2** Brit.
an area of land and modern buildings
used for housing, industrial, or business
purposes. **3** a property where crops such
as coffee are grown or where wine is
produced. **4** all the money and property
owned by a person at the time of their
death.
– ORIGIN Old French *estat*.

estate agency • n. Brit. a business that
sells and rents out buildings and land
for clients.
– DERIVATIVES **estate agent** n.

estate car • n. Brit. a car which has a large
carrying area behind the seats and an
extra door at the rear.

esteem • n. respect and admiration.
• v. **1** respect and admire someone or
something. **2** formal think or consider.
– ORIGIN Latin *aestimare* 'to estimate'.

ester /ess-ter/ • n. an organic compound
formed by a reaction between an acid
and an alcohol.

esthete • n. US = AESTHETE.

esthetic • adj. US = AESTHETIC.

estimable • adj. worthy of great respect.
– DERIVATIVES **estimably** adv.

estimate • v. /ess-ti-mayt/ (**estimates,
estimating, estimated**) roughly
calculate the value, number, or amount
of something. • n. /ess-ti-muht/ **1** an
approximate calculation. **2** a written
statement giving the likely price that
will be charged for specified work. **3** a
judgement or opinion.

– DERIVATIVES **estimation** n. **estimator** n.
– ORIGIN Latin *aestimare* 'determine'.

Estonian • n. a person from Estonia.
• adj. relating to Estonia.

estranged • adj. **1** no longer friendly or
close to someone. **2** no longer living
with your husband or wife.
– DERIVATIVES **estrangement** n.
– ORIGIN Old French *estranger*.

estrogen • n. US = OESTROGEN.

estrus • n. US = OESTRUS.

estuary /ess-tyuh-ri/ • n. (pl. **estuaries**)
the mouth of a large river, where it
becomes affected by the tide.
– DERIVATIVES **estuarine** /es-tyuh-ryn/
adj.
– ORIGIN Latin *aestuarium* 'tidal part of a
shore'.

 Spell **estuary** with **-tua-** in the
middle.

ETA /ee-tee-ay/ • abbrev. estimated time of
arrival.

e-tailer • n. a retailer who sells goods
over the Internet.

et al. /et al/ • abbrev. and others.
– ORIGIN Latin *et alii*.

etc. • abbrev. et cetera.

et cetera /et set-uh-ruh/ (also **etcetera**)
• adv. and other similar things; and so on.
– ORIGIN Latin.

etch • v. **1** engrave metal, glass, or stone
by drawing on a protective coating with
a needle, and then covering it with acid
to attack the exposed parts. **2** cut
writing or a design on a surface. **3** (**be
etched**) be clearly visible. **4** (**be etched
on/in**) be fixed permanently in someone's mind: *the setting will be forever etched in my brain.*
– DERIVATIVES **etcher** n.
– ORIGIN Dutch *etsen*.

etching • n. **1** the art or process of
etching. **2** a print produced by etching.

eternal • adj. **1** lasting or existing
forever. **2** valid for all time: *eternal
truths.*
– PHRASES **eternal triangle** a relationship
between three people involving sexual
rivalry.
– DERIVATIVES **eternally** adv.
– ORIGIN Latin *aeternalis*.

eternity • n. (pl. **eternities**) **1** unending
time: *Shakespeare wrote plays that will last
for eternity.* **2** (**an eternity**) informal an
undesirably long period of time.

ethane /ee-thayn/ • n. a flammable
hydrocarbon gas present in petroleum
and natural gas.
– ORIGIN from ETHER.

ethanol /eth-uh-nol/ • n. = ALCOHOL (in sense 1).

ether /ee-ther/ • n. **1** a highly flammable liquid used as an anaesthetic and as a solvent. **2** (also **aether**) esp. literary the sky or the upper regions of air.
– ORIGIN Greek *aithēr* 'upper air'.

ethereal /i-theer-i-uhl/ (also **etherial**) • adj. **1** very delicate and light: *she has a weirdly ethereal voice.* **2** heavenly or spiritual.
– DERIVATIVES **ethereality** n. **ethereally** adv.

Ethernet • n. a system for connecting a number of computer systems to form a local area network.
– ORIGIN from ETHER and NETWORK.

ethic • n. a set of moral principles: *the puritan ethic.*
– ORIGIN Latin *ethice.*

ethical • adj. **1** relating to moral principles. **2** morally correct.
– DERIVATIVES **ethically** adv.

ethics • n. **1** the moral principles that govern a person's behaviour or how an activity is conducted: *medical ethics.* **2** the branch of knowledge concerned with moral principles.
– DERIVATIVES **ethicist** n.

Ethiopian • n. a person from Ethiopia. • adj. relating to Ethiopia.

ethnic • adj. **1** relating to a group of people who have a common national or cultural tradition. **2** referring to origin by birth rather than by present nationality: *ethnic Albanians.* **3** belonging to a non-Western cultural tradition.
– DERIVATIVES **ethnically** adv. **ethnicity** n.
– ORIGIN Greek *ethnikos* 'heathen'.

ethnic cleansing • n. the forcible removal or killing of members of one ethnic or religious group in an area by those of another.

ethnic minority • n. a group within a community which has a different ethnic origin from the main population.

ethnocentric • adj. assessing other cultures according to the particular values or characteristics of your own.

ethnography • n. the scientific description of peoples and cultures.
– DERIVATIVES **ethnographer** n. **ethnographic** adj.

ethnology /eth-nol-uh-ji/ • n. the study of the characteristics of different peoples and the differences and relationships between them.
– DERIVATIVES **ethnological** adj. **ethnologist** n.

ethos /ee-thoss/ • n. the characteristic spirit of a culture, era, or community.
– ORIGIN Greek *ēthos* 'nature'.

ethyl /eth-yl/ • n. Chem. a radical ($-C_2H_5$) derived from ethane, present in alcohol and ether.
– ORIGIN German.

ethyl alcohol • n. = ALCOHOL (in sense 1).

ethylene /eth-i-leen/ • n. a flammable hydrocarbon gas, present in natural gas and coal gas.

etiolated /ee-ti-uh-lay-tid/ • adj. (of a plant) pale and weak due to a lack of light.
– ORIGIN French *étioler.*

etiquette /et-i-ket/ • n. the rules of polite or correct behaviour in a society or among members of a profession.
– ORIGIN French, 'list of ceremonial observances of a court'.

et seq. • adv. and what follows (used in page references).
– ORIGIN from Latin *et sequens.*

-ette • suffix forming nouns referring to: **1** small size: *kitchenette.* **2** an imitation or substitute: *flannelette.* **3** female gender: *suffragette.*
– ORIGIN Old French.

étude /ay-tyood/ • n. a short musical composition or exercise.
– ORIGIN French, 'study'.

etymology /et-i-mol-uh-ji/ • n. (pl. **etymologies**) an account of the origins and the developments in meaning of a word.
– DERIVATIVES **etymological** adj. **etymologically** adv. **etymologist** n.
– ORIGIN Greek *etumologia.*

EU • abbrev. European Union.

Eu • symb. the chemical element europium.

eucalyptus /yoo-kuh-lip-tuhss/ (also **eucalypt**) • n. (pl. **eucalyptuses**) an evergreen Australasian tree important for its wood, oil, gum, and resin.
– ORIGIN Latin.

Eucharist /yoo-kuh-rist/ • n. **1** the Christian ceremony commemorating the Last Supper, in which consecrated bread and wine are consumed. **2** the consecrated bread and wine used in this ceremony.
– DERIVATIVES **Eucharistic** adj.
– ORIGIN Greek *eukharistia* 'thanksgiving'.

Euclidean /yoo-klid-i-uhn/ • adj. (of systems of geometry) based on the principles of the ancient Greek mathematician Euclid.

eugenics /yoo-jen-iks/ • n. the science of improving a population by controlled breeding, so as to increase the occurrence of desirable characteristics which are able to be inherited.

- DERIVATIVES **eugenic** adj. **eugenicist** n. & adj.
- ORIGIN from Greek *eu* 'well' + *genēs* 'born'.

eulogize /yoo-luh-jyz/ (or **eulogise**)
• v. (**eulogizes, eulogizing, eulogized**) praise highly.
- DERIVATIVES **eulogist** n. **eulogistic** adj.

eulogy /yoo-luh-ji/ • n. (pl. **eulogies**) a speech or piece of writing that praises someone or something highly.
- ORIGIN Greek *eulogia* 'praise'.

eunuch /yoo-nuhk/ • n. a man who has been castrated.
- ORIGIN Greek *eunoukhos* 'bedroom guard'.

euphemism /yoo-fuh-mi-z'm/ • n. a less direct word used to refer to something unpleasant or embarrassing, often so as to avoid offence.
- DERIVATIVES **euphemistic** adj. **euphemistically** adv.
- ORIGIN Greek *euphēmismos*.

euphonious /yoo-foh-ni-uhss/
• adj. sounding pleasant.
- DERIVATIVES **euphoniously** adv.

euphonium /yoo-foh-ni-uhm/ • n. a brass musical instrument resembling a small tuba.
- ORIGIN Greek *euphōnos* 'having a pleasing sound'.

euphony /yoo-fuh-ni/ • n. the quality of having a pleasant sound.
- DERIVATIVES **euphonic** adj.
- ORIGIN Greek *euphōnia*.

euphoria /yoo-for-i-uh/ • n. a feeling of great happiness.
- DERIVATIVES **euphoric** adj. **euphorically** adv.
- ORIGIN Greek.

Eurasian • adj. **1** of mixed European (or European-American) and Asian parentage. **2** relating to Eurasia (the land mass of Europe and Asia together).

eureka /yoo-ree-kuh/ • exclam. a cry of joy or satisfaction when you find or discover something.
- ORIGIN Greek *heurēka* 'I have found it'.

euro • n. (pl. **euros**) the basic unit of money of twelve member states of the European Union.

Eurocentric • adj. seeing European culture as the most important.
- DERIVATIVES **Eurocentrism** n.

European • n. **1** a person from Europe. **2** a person who is white or of European parentage. • adj. relating to Europe or the European Union.
- DERIVATIVES **Europeanism** n. **Europeanize** (or **Europeanise**) v.

European Union • n. an economic and political association of certain European countries, with free trade between member countries.

europium /yoo-roh-pi-uhm/ • n. a soft silvery-white metallic element.
- ORIGIN from *Europe*.

Eurosceptic • n. a person who is opposed to increasing the powers of the European Union.

Eustachian tube /yoo-stay-sh'n/ • n. a narrow passage leading from the pharynx to the cavity of the middle ear, which equalizes the pressure on each side of the eardrum.
- ORIGIN named after the Italian anatomist Bartolomeo *Eustachio*.

euthanasia /yoo-thuh-nay-zi-uh/
• n. the painless killing of a person who has an incurable disease or who is in an irreversible coma.
- ORIGIN from Greek *eu* 'well' + *thanatos* 'death'.

evacuate • v. (**evacuates, evacuating, evacuated**) **1** remove someone from a place of danger to a safer place. **2** leave a dangerous place. **3** tech. remove the contents from a container. **4** empty the bowels.
- DERIVATIVES **evacuation** n.
- ORIGIN Latin *evacuare*.

evacuee • n. a person evacuated from a place of danger.

evade • v. (**evades, evading, evaded**) **1** escape or avoid, especially by cunning. **2** avoid dealing with or discussing something. **3** avoid paying tax or duty.
- DERIVATIVES **evader** n.
- ORIGIN Latin *evadere*.

evaluate • v. (**evaluates, evaluating, evaluated**) form an idea of the amount or value of.
- DERIVATIVES **evaluation** n. **evaluative** adj. **evaluator** n.

evanescent /ev-uh-ness-uhnt/
• adj. literary soon passing out of sight, memory, or existence.
- DERIVATIVES **evanescence** n.
- ORIGIN Latin *evanescere* 'disappear'.

evangelical • adj. **1** relating to a tradition within Protestant Christianity that emphasizes the authority of the Bible and salvation through personal faith in Jesus. **2** relating to the teaching of the gospel or Christianity. **3** showing passionate support for something: *evangelical feminists*. • n. a member of the evangelical tradition in the Christian Church.
- DERIVATIVES **evangelicalism** n. **evangelically** adv.
- ORIGIN Greek *euangelos* 'bringing good news'.

evangelist • n. **1** a person who tries to convert other people to Christianity.

2 the writer of one of the four Gospels. **3** a passionate supporter of something.
– DERIVATIVES **evangelism** n. **evangelistic** adj.

evangelize (or **evangelise**)
• v. (**evangelizes, evangelizing, evangelized**) **1** convert or try to convert someone to Christianity. **2** preach the gospel.

evaporate • v. (**evaporates, evaporating, evaorated**) **1** turn from liquid into vapour. **2** cease to exist: *my patience evaporated.*
– DERIVATIVES **evaporation** n. **evaporative** adj. **evaporator** n.
– ORIGIN Latin *evaporare.*

evaporated milk • n. thick sweetened milk that has had some of the liquid removed by evaporation.

evasion • n. **1** the action of avoiding or evading. **2** a statement that avoids dealing with something.

evasive • adj. **1** avoiding a direct answer to a question. **2** intended to avoid or escape something: *evasive action.*
– DERIVATIVES **evasively** adv. **evasiveness** n.

eve • n. **1** the day or period of time immediately before an event. **2** literary evening.
– ORIGIN from EVEN².

even¹ • adj. **1** flat and smooth; level. **2** equal in number, amount, or value. **3** regular: *an even pace.* **4** equally balanced. **5** placid; calm: *an even temper.* **6** (of a number) able to be divided by two without a remainder. • v. make or become even. • adv. used for emphasis: *he knows even less than I do.*
– PHRASES **even as** at the very same time as. **even if** despite the possibility that. **even so** nevertheless. **even though** despite the fact that.
– DERIVATIVES **evenly** adv. **evenness** n.
– ORIGIN Old English.

even² • n. old use evening.
– ORIGIN Old English.

even-handed • adj. fair and impartial.

evening • n. the period of time at the end of the day.
– ORIGIN Old English.

evening primrose • n. a plant with pale yellow flowers that open in the evening, used for a medicinal oil.

evening star • n. (**the evening star**) the planet Venus, seen shining in the western sky after sunset.

even money • n. (in betting) odds offering an equal chance of winning or losing.

evens • pl. n. Brit. even money.

evensong • n. (in the Anglican Church) a service of evening prayers, psalms, and canticles.

event • n. **1** a thing that happens. **2** a public or social occasion. **3** each of several contests making up a sports competition.
– PHRASES **in any event** (or **at all events**) whatever happens or may have happened. **in the event** **1** as it turned out. **2** (**in the event of/that**) if the specified thing happens.
– ORIGIN Latin *eventus.*

eventful • adj. marked by interesting or exciting events.

eventide • n. old use evening.

eventing • n. a riding competition in which competitors must take part in each of several contests.
– DERIVATIVES **eventer** n.

eventual • adj. occurring at the end of a process or period of time.
– DERIVATIVES **eventually** adv.

eventuality • n. (pl. **eventualities**) a possible event or outcome.

ever • adv. **1** at any time. **2** used in comparisons for emphasis: *better than ever.* **3** always. **4** increasingly: *ever larger sums.*
– ORIGIN Old English.

evergreen • adj. **1** (of a plant) having green leaves throughout the year. Contrasted with DECIDUOUS. **2** having a lasting freshness or appeal: *this symphony is an evergreen favourite.* • n. an evergreen plant.

everlasting • adj. lasting forever or a very long time.
– DERIVATIVES **everlastingly** adv.

evermore • adv. literary forever.

every • det. **1** used to refer to all the members of a set without exception. **2** indicating how often something happens: *every thirty minutes.* **3** all possible: *every effort was made.*
– PHRASES **every other** each alternate one in a series.

everybody • pron. every person.

everyday • adj. **1** daily. **2** ordinary: *everyday activities.*

Everyman • n. an ordinary or typical person.

everyone • pron. every person.

every one • pron. each one.

everything • pron. **1** all things, or all the things of a group. **2** the most important thing: *money isn't everything.*

everywhere • adv. **1** in or to all places. **2** in many places: *sandwich bars are everywhere.*

evict • v. legally force someone to leave a building or piece of land.
– DERIVATIVES **eviction** n.

– ORIGIN Latin *evincere* 'overcome'.

evidence • n. **1** information indicating whether something is true or valid. **2** information used to establish facts in a legal investigation or acceptable as testimony in a law court. • v. (**evidences, evidencing, evidenced**) be or show evidence of: *his popularity was evidenced by a large turnout.*
– PHRASES **in evidence** noticeable.
– ORIGIN Latin *evidentia*.

evident • adj. clear or obvious.
– DERIVATIVES **evidently** adv.

evidential • adj. formal relating to evidence.

evil • adj. **1** very immoral and wicked. **2** very unpleasant: *an evil smell.* • n. **1** extreme wickedness. **2** something harmful or undesirable: *unpleasant social evils.*
– PHRASES **the evil eye** a gaze superstitiously believed to cause harm.
– DERIVATIVES **evilly** adv. **evilness** n.
– ORIGIN Old English.

evince • v. (**evinces, evincing, evinced**) formal reveal the presence of: *his letters evince the excitement he felt.*
– ORIGIN Latin *evincere* 'overcome'.

eviscerate /i-viss-uh-rayt/ • v. (**eviscerates, eviscerating, eviscerated**) formal remove the intestines of.
– DERIVATIVES **evisceration** n.
– ORIGIN Latin *eviscerare*.

evocative /i-vok-uh-tiv/ • adj. bringing strong images or feelings to mind.

evoke /i-vohk/ • v. (**evokes, evoking, evoked**) **1** bring to the mind. **2** obtain a response.
– DERIVATIVES **evocation** n.
– ORIGIN Latin *evocare* 'call on a spirit'.

evolution • n. **1** the process by which different kinds of living organism develop from earlier forms. **2** gradual development.
– DERIVATIVES **evolutionarily** adv. **evolutionary** adj.
– ORIGIN Latin, 'unrolling'.

evolutionist • n. a person who believes in the theories of evolution and natural selection.
– DERIVATIVES **evolutionism** n.

evolve • v. (**evolves, evolving, evolved**) **1** develop gradually. **2** (of an organism) develop from earlier forms by evolution.
– ORIGIN Latin *evolvere*.

ewe • n. a female sheep.
– ORIGIN Old English.

ewer /yoo-er/ • n. a large jug with a wide mouth.
– ORIGIN Old French *aiguiere*.

ex¹ • prep. Brit. not including.

ex² • n. informal a former husband, wife, or partner in a relationship.

ex- (also **e-**; **ef-** before *f*) • prefix **1** out: *exclude.* **2** upward: *extol.* **3** thoroughly: *excruciating.* **4** former: *ex-husband.*
– ORIGIN Latin or Greek.

exacerbate /ig-zass-er-bayt/ • v. (**exacerbates, exacerbating, exacerbated**) make something bad worse.
– DERIVATIVES **exacerbation** n.
– ORIGIN Latin *exacerbare* 'make harsh'.

exact • adj. **1** correct in every detail: *an exact copy.* **2** precise; not approximate. • v. **1** demand and obtain something from someone. **2** take revenge on someone.
– DERIVATIVES **exactness** n.
– ORIGIN Latin *exigere* 'enforce'.

exacting • adj. demanding much effort or skill.

exaction • n. formal **1** the action of demanding payment. **2** a sum of money demanded.

exactitude • n. the quality of being exact.

exactly • adv. **1** in an exact way; precisely. **2** used to confirm or agree with what has just been said.

exaggerate • v. (**exaggerates, exaggerating, exaggerated**) **1** make something seem larger, better, or worse than it really is. **2** (as adj. **exaggerated**) larger or more noticeable than normal.
– DERIVATIVES **exaggeration** n.
– ORIGIN Latin *exaggerare* 'heap up'.

> ✓ Spell **exaggerate** and the related word **exaggeration** with a double **g** and one **r**.

exalt /ig-zawlt/ • v. **1** praise highly. **2** raise to a higher rank or position.
– ORIGIN Latin *exaltare*.

exaltation • n. **1** extreme happiness. **2** the action of exalting.

exalted • adj. **1** at a high level: *her exalted position.* **2** (of an idea) noble.

exam • n. = EXAMINATION (in sense 2).

examination • n. **1** a detailed inspection. **2** a formal test of knowledge or ability in a subject or skill. **3** the action of examining.

examine • v. (**examines, examining, examined**) **1** inspect someone or something closely to find out their nature or condition. **2** test someone's knowledge or ability. **3** Law formally question a person on trial or a witness in court.
– DERIVATIVES **examinee** n. **examiner** n.
– ORIGIN Latin *examinare* 'weigh, test'.

example • n. **1** a thing that is typical of its kind or that illustrates a general rule.

2 a person or thing seen in terms of their suitability to be imitated.
– PHRASES **for example** used to introduce something chosen as a typical case. **make an example of** punish someone as a warning to other people.
– ORIGIN Latin *exemplum*.

exasperate /ig-zass-puh-rayt/
• v. (**exasperates, exasperating, exasperated**) greatly irritate someone.
– DERIVATIVES **exasperated** adj. **exasperating** adj. **exasperation** n.
– ORIGIN Latin *exasperare*.

excavate • v. (**excavates, excavating, excavated**) **1** make a hole or channel by digging. **2** carefully remove earth from an area in order to find buried remains. **3** dig out material or objects from the ground.
– DERIVATIVES **excavation** n. **excavator** n.
– ORIGIN Latin *excavare* 'hollow out'.

exceed • v. **1** be greater in number or size than. **2** go beyond what is set down by a limit. **3** be better than: *they exceeded expectations.*
– ORIGIN Latin *excedere*.

exceedingly • adv. extremely.

excel • v. (**excels, excelling, excelled**) **1** be very good at something. **2** (**excel yourself**) perform exceptionally well.
– ORIGIN Latin *excellere*.

Excellency • n. (pl. **Excellencies**) (**His, Your,** etc. **Excellency**) a title or form of address for certain high officials of state or of the Roman Catholic Church.

excellent • adj. very good; outstanding.
– DERIVATIVES **excellence** n.

except • prep. not including. • conj. used before a statement that is not included in one just made. • v. exclude: *present company excepted.*
– ORIGIN Latin *excipere* 'take out'.

USAGE: On the confusion of **except** and **accept**, see the note at **ACCEPT**.

excepting • prep. except for.

exception • n. a person or thing that is not included in a general statement or that does not follow a rule.
– PHRASES **take exception to** object strongly to.

exceptionable • adj. formal causing disapproval or offence.

exceptional • adj. **1** unusually good. **2** unusual; not typical.
– DERIVATIVES **exceptionally** adv.

excerpt • n. /ek-serpt/ a short extract from a film or piece of music or writing. • v. /ik-serpt/ take a short extract from a piece of writing.
– ORIGIN Latin *excerpere* 'pluck out'.

excess • n. /ik-sess/ **1** an amount that is more than necessary, allowed, or

desirable. **2** extreme behaviour, especially in eating or drinking too much: *bouts of alcoholic excess.* **3** (**excesses**) unacceptable or illegal behaviour. **4** Brit. a part of an insurance claim to be paid by the person insured. • adj. /usu. ek-sess/ exceeding an allowed or desirable amount: *excess fat.*
– ORIGIN Latin *excessus.*

excess baggage • n. luggage weighing more than the limit allowed on an aircraft, liable to an extra charge.

excessive • adj. more than is necessary, normal, or desirable.
– DERIVATIVES **excessively** adv.

exchange • n. **1** an act of giving something and receiving something else in return. **2** a short conversation or argument. **3** the changing of money to its equivalent in another currency. **4** a building that is used for financial trading. **5** a set of equipment that connects telephone lines during a call. • v. (**exchanges, exchanging, exchanged**) give something and receive something else in return.
– DERIVATIVES **exchangeable** adj. **exchanger** n.
– ORIGIN Old French *eschangier.*

exchange rate • n. the value at which one currency may be exchanged for another.

exchequer /iks-chek-er/ • n. **1** a royal or national treasury. **2** (**Exchequer**) the account at the Bank of England into which public money is paid.
– ORIGIN Old French *eschequier* 'chessboard' (accounts were kept on a chequered tablecloth by means of counters).

excise¹ /ek-syz/ • n. a tax charged on certain goods, such as alcohol.
– ORIGIN Dutch *excijs.*

excise² /ik-syz/ • v. (**excises, excising, excised**) **1** cut something out surgically. **2** remove a section from a piece of writing or music.
– DERIVATIVES **excision** n.
– ORIGIN Latin *excidere.*

excitable • adj. easily excited.
– DERIVATIVES **excitability** n. **excitably** adv.

excite • v. (**excites, exciting, excited**) **1** make someone feel very enthusiastic and eager. **2** arouse someone sexually. **3** give rise to: *the report excited great controversy.* **4** increase the energy or activity in a physical or biological system.
– DERIVATIVES **excitation** n. **excited** adj.
– ORIGIN Latin *excitare.*

excitement • n. **1** great enthusiasm and eagerness. **2** something that arouses

great enthusiasm and eagerness.
3 sexual arousal.

exciting • adj. causing great enthusiasm and eagerness.
– DERIVATIVES **excitingly** adv.

exclaim • v. cry out suddenly.
– ORIGIN Latin *exclamare*.

exclamation • n. a sudden cry or remark.
– DERIVATIVES **exclamatory** adj.

exclamation mark • n. a punctuation mark (!) indicating an exclamation.

exclude • v. (**excludes, excluding, excluded**) **1** prevent from entering or taking part in something. **2** deliberately leave out when considering or doing something: *this information was excluded from the investigation.* **3** expel a pupil from a school.
– DERIVATIVES **excludable** adj. **excluder** n.
– ORIGIN Latin *excludere*.

excluding • prep. not including; except.

exclusion • n. the action of excluding.
– DERIVATIVES **exclusionary** adj.

exclusive • adj. **1** restricted to the person, group, or area concerned: *a problem exclusive to London.* **2** high-class and expensive. **3** not including other things. **4** unable to exist or be true if something else exists or is true. **5** (of a story) not published or broadcast elsewhere. • n. an exclusive story or broadcast.
– DERIVATIVES **exclusively** adv. **exclusiveness** n. **exclusivity** n.
– ORIGIN Latin *exclusivus*.

excommunicate /eks-kuh-myoo-ni-kayt/ • v. (**excommunicates, excommunicating, excommunicated**) officially ban someone from the sacraments and services of the Christian Church.
– DERIVATIVES **excommunication** n.
– ORIGIN Latin *excommunicare*.

excoriate /ik-skor-i-ayt/ • v. (**excoriates, excoriating, excoriated**) **1** formal criticize severely. **2** Med. damage or remove part of the surface of the skin.
– DERIVATIVES **excoriation** n.
– ORIGIN Latin *excoriare* 'to skin'.

excrement /eks-kri-muhnt/ • n. waste matter emptied from the bowels.
– ORIGIN Latin *excrementum*.

excrescence /iks-kress-uhnss/ • n. an abnormal growth protruding from a body or plant.
– ORIGIN Latin *excrescentia*.

excreta /ik-skree-tuh/ • n. waste discharged from the body.
– ORIGIN Latin.

excrete • v. (**excretes, excreting, excreted**) discharge a waste substance from the body.
– DERIVATIVES **excretion** n. **excretory** adj.
– ORIGIN Latin *excernere* 'sift out'.

excruciating • adj. **1** very painful. **2** very embarrassing, awkward, or boring.
– ORIGIN Latin *excruciare* 'torment'.

exculpate /eks-kul-payt/ • v. (**exculpates, exculpating, exculpated**) formal show or declare that someone is not guilty of wrongdoing.
– DERIVATIVES **exculpation** n. **exculpatory** adj.
– ORIGIN Latin *exculpare*.

excursion • n. a short journey or trip taken for pleasure.
– ORIGIN Latin.

excuse • v. /ik-skyooz/ (**excuses, excusing, excused**) **1** try to find reasons for a fault or offence. **2** forgive a minor fault or a person committing one. **3** allow someone to not do something that is usually required. **4** allow someone to leave. • n. /ik-skyooss/ **1** a reason given to justify a fault or offence. **2** something said to conceal the real reason for an action. **3** informal a poor example of: *that pathetic excuse for a man.*
– PHRASES **excuse me** a polite apology.
– DERIVATIVES **excusable** adj.
– ORIGIN Latin *excusare* 'free from blame'.

ex-directory • adj. Brit. not listed in a telephone directory at your own request.

execrable /ek-si-kruh-b'l/ • adj. very bad or unpleasant.
– DERIVATIVES **execrably** adv.
– ORIGIN Latin *execrabilis*.

execrate /ek-si-krayt/ • v. (**execrates, execrating, execrated**) feel or express great hatred for.
– DERIVATIVES **execration** n.
– ORIGIN Latin *exsecrari* 'curse'.

execute • v. (**executes, executing, executed**) **1** carry out a plan, order, etc. **2** perform a skilful action or manoeuvre. **3** carry out a sentence of death on a condemned person.
– ORIGIN Latin *executare*.

execution • n. **1** the carrying out or performance of something. **2** the killing of a person who has been condemned to death. **3** the way in which something is produced or carried out.

executioner • n. an official who executes condemned criminals.

executive /ig-zek-yuu-tiv/ • n. **1** a senior manager in a business. **2** a decision-making committee in an organization. **3** (**the executive**) the branch of a government responsible for putting plans or laws into effect. • adj. having the power to put plans, actions, or laws into effect.

executor /ig-zek-yuu-ter/ • n. a person appointed by someone to carry out the terms of their will.

executrix /ig-zek-yoo-triks/ • n. (pl. **executrices** /ig-zek-yoo-tri-seez/ or **executrixes**) a female executor of a will.

exegesis /ek-si-jee-siss/ • n. (pl. **exegeses** /ek-si-jee-seez/) critical explanation of a written work.
– DERIVATIVES **exegetical** adj.
– ORIGIN Greek.

exemplar /ig-zem-pler/ • n. a person or thing serving as a typical example or appropriate model.
– ORIGIN Latin *exemplarium*.

exemplary • adj. **1** providing a good example to other people: *exemplary behaviour.* **2** (of a punishment) serving as a warning.

exemplify /ig-zem-pli-fy/
• v. (**exemplifies, exemplifying, exemplified**) be or give a typical example of.
– DERIVATIVES **exemplification** n.

exempt /ig-zempt/ • adj. free from a duty or requirement imposed on other people: *these patients are exempt from all charges.* • v. free someone from a duty or requirement.
– DERIVATIVES **exemption** n.
– ORIGIN Latin *exemptus* 'taken out'.

exercise • n. **1** physical activity carried out for the sake of health and fitness. **2** an activity carried out for a purpose: *a public relations exercise.* **3** a task set to practise or test a skill. **4** (**exercises**) military drills or training manoeuvres. **5** the use of a power, right, or quality: *the exercise of authority.* • v. (**exercises, exercising, exercised**) **1** use a power, right, or quality. **2** do physical exercise. **3** worry or puzzle someone.
– DERIVATIVES **exercisable** adj. **exerciser** n.
– ORIGIN Latin *exercitium*.

exercise book • n. Brit. a booklet with blank pages for students to write in.

exert /ig-zert/ • v. **1** apply or bring to bear a force, influence, or quality. **2** (**exert yourself**) make a physical or mental effort.
– DERIVATIVES **exertion** n.
– ORIGIN Latin *exserere* 'put forth'.

exeunt /ek-si-uhnt/ • v. (as a stage direction) (actors) leave the stage.
– ORIGIN Latin, 'they go out'.

exfoliate /iks-foh-li-ayt/ • v. (**exfoliates, exfoliating, exfoliated**) **1** shed or be shed from a surface in scales or layers. **2** wash or rub part of the body with a rough substance to remove dead skin cells.

– DERIVATIVES **exfoliation** n. **exfoliator** n.
– ORIGIN Latin *exfoliare* 'strip of leaves'.

ex gratia /eks gray-shuh/ • adv. & adj. (of payment) given as a gift or favour rather than because of any legal requirement.
– ORIGIN Latin, 'from favour'.

exhale • v. (**exhales, exhaling, exhaled**) **1** breathe out. **2** give off vapour or fumes.
– DERIVATIVES **exhalation** n.
– ORIGIN Latin *exhalare*.

exhaust • v. **1** make someone very tired. **2** use up resources completely. **3** explore a subject so fully that there is nothing left to be said. • n. **1** waste gases that are discharged from an engine. **2** the system through which waste gases are discharged.
– DERIVATIVES **exhauster** n. **exhaustible** adj. **exhausting** adj.
– ORIGIN Latin *exhaurire* 'drain out'.

exhaustion • n. **1** extreme tiredness. **2** the action of using something up.

exhaustive • adj. covering all aspects fully.
– DERIVATIVES **exhaustively** adv.

exhibit • v. **1** publicly display an item in an art gallery or museum. **2** show: *they exhibited great humility.* • n. **1** an object or collection on display in an art gallery or museum. **2** Law an object produced in a court as evidence.
– DERIVATIVES **exhibitor** n.
– ORIGIN Latin *exhibere* 'hold out'.

exhibition • n. **1** a public display of items in an art gallery or museum. **2** a display or demonstration of a skill or quality.
– PHRASES **make an exhibition of yourself** behave very foolishly in public.

exhibitionism • n. behaviour that is intended to attract attention to yourself.
– DERIVATIVES **exhibitionist** n. **exhibitionistic** adj.

exhilarate /ig-zil-uh-rayt/
• v. (**exhilarates, exhilarating, exhilarated**) make someone feel very happy or lively.
– DERIVATIVES **exhilarating** adj. **exhilaration** n.
– ORIGIN Latin *exhilarare*.

exhort /ig-zort/ • v. strongly urge someone to do something.
– DERIVATIVES **exhortation** n.
– ORIGIN Latin *exhortari*.

exhume /eks-syoom/ • v. (**exhumes, exhuming, exhumed**) dig out something buried from the ground.
– DERIVATIVES **exhumation** n.
– ORIGIN Latin *exhumare*.

exigency /ek-si-juhn-si/ • n. (pl. **exigencies**) formal an urgent need or demand.

– ORIGIN Latin *exigentia*.

exigent /ek-si-juhnt/ •adj. formal urgent; pressing: *exigent demands*.

exiguous /ig-zig-yoo-uhss/ •adj. formal very small.
– ORIGIN Latin *exiguus* 'scanty'.

exile •n. **1** the state of being banned from your native country. **2** a person who lives in exile. •v. (**exiles, exiling, exiled**) expel and ban someone from their native country.
– ORIGIN Latin *exilium* 'banishment'.

exist •v. **1** be real or present: *they say the deal never existed.* **2** be alive.
– ORIGIN Latin *exsistere* 'come into being'.

existence •n. **1** the fact or state of existing. **2** a way of living: *a rural existence.*
– DERIVATIVES **existent** adj.

existential /eg-zi-sten-sh'l/ •adj. **1** relating to existence. **2** relating to existentialism.
– DERIVATIVES **existentially** adv.

existentialism •n. a philosophical theory which emphasizes that people are free agents, responsible for their own actions.
– DERIVATIVES **existentialist** n. & adj.

exit •n. **1** a way out of a place or passenger vehicle. **2** an act of leaving. **3** a place for traffic to leave a major road or roundabout. •v. (**exits, exiting, exited**) **1** go out of or leave somewhere. **2** end a computer process or program.
– ORIGIN Latin, 'he or she goes out'.

exit poll •n. a poll of people leaving a polling station, asking how they voted.

exo- •prefix external: *exoskeleton.*
– ORIGIN Greek *exō* 'outside'.

exocrine /ek-soh-kryn/ •adj. (of a gland) producing hormones or other products through ducts rather than directly into the blood.
– ORIGIN Greek *krinein* 'sift'.

exodus •n. a mass departure of people.
– ORIGIN Greek *exodos*.

ex officio /eks uh-fish-i-oh/ •adv. & adj. as a result of a person's position or status.
– ORIGIN from Latin *ex* 'out of' + *officium* 'duty'.

exonerate /ig-zon-uh-rayt/ •v. (**exonerates, exonerating, exonerated**) officially state that someone has not done something wrong or illegal.
– DERIVATIVES **exoneration** n.
– ORIGIN Latin *exonerare* 'free from a burden'.

exorbitant /ig-zor-bi-tuhnt/ •adj. (of an amount charged) unreasonably high.
– DERIVATIVES **exorbitantly** adv.

– ORIGIN Latin *exorbitare* 'go off the track'.

exorcize /ek-sor-syz/ (or **exorcise**) •v. (**exorcizes, exorcizing, exorcizes**) drive out a supposed evil spirit from a person or place.
– DERIVATIVES **exorcism** n. **exorcist** n.
– ORIGIN Greek *exorkizein*.

exoskeleton •n. the rigid outer covering of the body in some invertebrate animals.

exothermic /ek-soh-ther-mik/ •adj. (of a chemical reaction) releasing heat.

exotic •adj. **1** coming from or typical of a distant foreign country. **2** strikingly colourful or unusual: *an exotic outfit.*
– DERIVATIVES **exotically** adv. **exoticism** n.
– ORIGIN Greek *exōtikos* 'foreign'.

expand •v. **1** make or become larger or more extensive. **2** (**expand on**) give more details about.
– DERIVATIVES **expandable** adj. **expander** n.
– ORIGIN Latin *expandere* 'spread out'.

expanse •n. a wide continuous area: *the green expanse of forest.*

expansion •n. **1** the action of becoming larger or expanding. **2** the political strategy of extending a state's territory by advancing gradually into that of other nations.
– DERIVATIVES **expansionary** adj. **expansionism** n. **expansionist** adj.

expansive •adj. **1** covering a wide area. **2** relaxed, friendly, and communicative.
– DERIVATIVES **expansively** adv.

expat •n. informal = EXPATRIATE.

expatiate /ik-spay-shi-ayt/ •v. (**expatiates, expatiating, expatiated**) (**expatiate on**) speak or write at length or in detail about.
– ORIGIN Latin *exspatiari* 'move beyond your usual bounds'.

expatriate /eks-pat-ri-uht/ •n. a person who lives outside their native country.
– DERIVATIVES **expatriation** n.
– ORIGIN Latin *expatriare*.

expect •v. **1** think that something is likely to happen. **2** regard someone as likely to do or be something. **3** believe that someone will arrive soon. **4** require or demand something because it is appropriate or a person's duty: *we expect great things of you.* **5** (**be expecting**) informal be pregnant.
– DERIVATIVES **expectable** adj.
– ORIGIN Latin *exspectare* 'look out for'.

expectancy •n. (pl. **expectancies**) hope or anticipation that something will happen.

expectant •adj. **1** hoping or anticipating

that something is about to happen. **2** (of a woman) pregnant.
– DERIVATIVES **expectantly** adv.

expectation • n. **1** belief that something will happen or be the case. **2** a thing that is expected to happen.

expectorant • n. a medicine which helps to bring up phlegm from the air passages, used to treat coughs.

expectorate /ik-spek-tuh-rayt/ • v. (**expectorates**, **expectorating**, **expectorated**) cough or spit out phlegm from the throat or lungs.
– DERIVATIVES **expectoration** n.
– ORIGIN Latin *expectorare* 'expel from the chest'.

expedient /ik-spee-di-uhnt/ • adj. necessary to achieve something, though not always right or fair. • n. a means of achieving something.
– DERIVATIVES **expediency** (also **expedience**) n.
– ORIGIN Latin.

expedite /eks-pi-dyt/ • v. (**expedites**, **expediting**, **expedited**) cause to happen sooner or be achieved more quickly: *he promised to expedite economic reforms*.
– DERIVATIVES **expediter** (also **expeditor**) n.
– ORIGIN Latin *expedire* 'extricate'.

expedition • n. a journey undertaken by a group of people for a particular purpose.
– DERIVATIVES **expeditionary** adj.

expeditious /eks-pi-di-shuhss/ • adj. quick and efficient.
– DERIVATIVES **expeditiously** adv.

expel • v. (**expels**, **expelling**, **expelled**) **1** force someone to leave a school, organization, or place. **2** force something out, especially from the body.
– ORIGIN Latin *expellere*.

expend • v. spend or use up a resource.
– ORIGIN Latin *expendere*.

expendable • adj. able to be sacrificed because of little importance when compared to an overall purpose.

expenditure /ik-spen-di-cher/ • n. **1** the action of spending funds. **2** the amount of money spent. **3** the use of energy or other resources.

expense • n. **1** the cost of something. **2** (**expenses**) money spent in carrying out a job or task. **3** something on which money must be spent.
– PHRASES **at the expense of 1** paid for by. **2** so as to harm.
– ORIGIN Old French.

expense account • n. an arrangement under which money spent in the course of business is later repaid by a person's employer.

expensive • adj. costing a lot of money.
– DERIVATIVES **expensively** adv.

experience • n. **1** practical contact with and observation of facts or events. **2** knowledge or skill gained over time. **3** an event which affects you: *a frightening experience.* • v. (**experiences**, **experiencing**, **experienced**) **1** undergo or be affected by a situation: *some areas experienced heavy showers.* **2** feel an emotion.
– ORIGIN Latin *experientia*.

experienced • adj. having knowledge or skill in a particular job or field gained over time.

experiential /ik-speer-i-en-sh'l/ • adj. relating to experience and observation.
– DERIVATIVES **experientially** adv.

experiment • n. **1** a scientific test undertaken to make a discovery, investigate a theory, or demonstrate a known fact. **2** a new course of action adopted without being sure of the outcome. • v. **1** perform a scientific experiment. **2** try out new ideas or methods.
– DERIVATIVES **experimentation** n. **experimenter** n.
– ORIGIN Latin *experimentum*.

experimental • adj. **1** based on new ideas and not yet fully tested or finalized. **2** relating to scientific experiments. **3** (of art, music, etc.) not following tradition; innovative.
– DERIVATIVES **experimentally** adv.

expert • n. a person who has great knowledge or skill in a particular area. • adj. having or involving great knowledge or skill: *an expert witness.*
– DERIVATIVES **expertly** adv.
– ORIGIN Latin *expertus*.

expertise /ek-sper-teez/ • n. great skill or knowledge in a particular area.

expiate /ek-spi-ayt/ • v. (**expiates**, **expiating**, **expiated**) make amends for having done something wrong.
– DERIVATIVES **expiation** n.
– ORIGIN Latin *expiare* 'appease by sacrifice'.

expire /ik-spyr/ • v. (**expires**, **expiring**, **expired**) **1** (of a document or agreement) cease to be valid. **2** (of a period of time) come to an end. **3** (of a person) die. **4** tech. breathe out air from the lungs.
– DERIVATIVES **expiration** n. **expiratory** adj.
– ORIGIN Latin *exspirare*.

expiry • n. Brit. the time when something ends or ceases to be valid.

explain • v. **1** make clear by giving a detailed description. **2** give a reason for.

3 (explain yourself) justify your motives or behaviour. **4 (explain something away)** make something seem less embarrassing by giving an excuse for it.
– DERIVATIVES **explainable** adj. **explainer** n. **explanation** n.
– ORIGIN Latin *explanare*.

explanatory /ik-splan-uh-tuh-ri/ •adj. intended to explain something.

expletive /ik-splee-tiv/ •n. a swear word.
– ORIGIN Latin *expletivus* 'acting to fill out'.

explicable /ik-splik-uh-b'l/ •adj. able to be explained.
– ORIGIN Latin *explicare* 'unfold'.

explicate /eks-pli-kayt/ •v. (**explicates, explicating, explicated**) analyse and explain something in detail.
– DERIVATIVES **explication** n. **explicator** n.
– ORIGIN Latin *explicare* 'unfold'.

explicit /ik-spli-sit/ •adj. **1** clear and detailed, with no room for confusion. **2** describing or showing sexual activity in a direct and detailed way.
– DERIVATIVES **explicitly** adv. **explicitness** n.
– ORIGIN Latin *explicare* 'unfold'.

explode •v. (**explodes, exploding, exploded**) **1** burst or shatter violently as a result of the release of internal energy. **2** sudden express an emotion. **3** increase suddenly in number or extent: *the use of this drug exploded in the nineties.* **4** show a belief to be false.
– DERIVATIVES **exploder** n.
– ORIGIN Latin *explodere* 'drive out by clapping'.

exploit •v. /ik-sployt/ **1** make use of a person or situation in an unfair way, so as to benefit yourself. **2** make good use of a resource. •n. /ek-sployt/ a daring act.
– DERIVATIVES **exploitable** adj. **exploitation** n. **exploiter** n.
– ORIGIN Old French *esploit* 'success'.

exploitative (also **exploitive**) •adj. treating someone unfairly so as to make money or gain an advantage.

explore •v. (**explores, exploring, explored**) **1** travel through an unfamiliar area in order to learn about it. **2** inquire into or discuss in detail. **3** examine by touch.
– DERIVATIVES **exploration** n. **exploratory** adj. **explorer** n.
– ORIGIN Latin *explorare* 'search out'.

explosion •n. **1** an act of exploding. **2** a sudden increase in amount or extent.

explosive •adj. **1** able or likely to explode. **2** likely to cause an outburst of anger or controversy. **3** (of an increase)

sudden and dramatic. •n. a substance which can be made to explode.
– DERIVATIVES **explosively** adv. **explosiveness** n.

exponent /ik-spoh-nuhnt/ •n. **1** a person who promotes an idea or theory. **2** a person who does a particular thing skilfully. **3** Math. a raised figure beside a number indicating how many times that number is to be multiplied by itself (e.g. 3 in $2^3 = 2 \times 2 \times 2$).
– ORIGIN Latin.

exponential /eks-puh-nen-sh'l/ •adj. **1** (of an increase) becoming more and more rapid. **2** relating to a mathematical exponent.
– DERIVATIVES **exponentially** adv.

export •v. /ik-sport/ **1** send goods or services to another country for sale. **2** introduce ideas or customs to another country. •n. /ek-sport/ **1** an exported article or service. **2** the exporting of goods or services.
– DERIVATIVES **exportable** adj. **exportation** n. **exporter** n.
– ORIGIN Latin *exportare*.

expose •v. (**exposes, exposing, exposed**) **1** make something visible by uncovering it. **3** reveal the true nature of. **3 (expose someone to)** make someone vulnerable to possible harm. **4** (as adj. **exposed**) unprotected from the weather. **5** subject photographic film to light. **6 (expose yourself)** publicly display your genitals.
– DERIVATIVES **exposer** n.
– ORIGIN Latin *exponere* 'to present'.

exposé /ik-spoh-zay/ •n. a report in the media that reveals something shocking.
– ORIGIN French, 'shown'.

exposition •n. **1** a full description and explanation of a theory. **2** a large public exhibition of art or trade goods. **3** Music the part of a movement in which the principal themes are first presented.
– ORIGIN Latin.

expositor /ik-spoz-i-ter/ •n. a person who explains complicated ideas or theories.
– DERIVATIVES **expository** adj.

expostulate /ik-sposs-tyoo-layt/ •v. (**expostulates, expostulating, expostulated**) express strong disapproval or disagreement.
– DERIVATIVES **expostulation** n.
– ORIGIN Latin *expostulare* 'demand'.

exposure •n. **1** the state of being exposed to something harmful. **2** a physical condition resulting from being exposed to severe weather conditions. **3** the revealing of something secret. **4** the publicizing of information or an event: *the meetings received regular* *exposure in the media.* **5** the quantity of light reaching a photographic film.

expound • v. present and explain a theory or idea systematically.
– DERIVATIVES **expounder** n.
– ORIGIN Latin *exponere* 'to present'.

express¹ /ik-spress/ • v. **1** convey a thought or feeling in words or by gestures and behaviour. **2** squeeze out liquid or air.
– DERIVATIVES **expressible** adj.
– ORIGIN Old French *expresser*.

express² /ik-spress/ • adj. **1** operating at high speed. **2** (of a delivery service) using a special messenger. • adv. by express train or delivery service. • n. (also **express train**) a train that stops at few stations and so travels quickly. • v. send by express messenger or delivery.
– ORIGIN Latin *expressus* 'distinctly presented'.

express³ /ik-spress/ • adj. **1** stated clearly. **2** specific: *the firm was founded with the express purpose of building aircraft.*
– DERIVATIVES **expressly** adv.

expression • n. **1** the action of expressing something. **2** a look on someone's face: *a happy expression.* **3** a word or phrase expressing an idea. **4** Math. a collection of symbols expressing a quantity.
– DERIVATIVES **expressionless** adj.

expressionism • n. a style in art, music, or drama in which the artist or writer tries to express inner emotion rather than external reality.
– DERIVATIVES **expressionist** n. & adj.

expressive • adj. **1** effectively conveying thought or feeling. **2** (**expressive of**) conveying a quality or idea.
– DERIVATIVES **expressively** adv. **expressiveness** n. **expressivity** n.

expresso • n. var. of **ESPRESSO**.

expressway • n. N. Amer. an urban motorway.

expropriate /iks-proh-pri-ayt/ • v. (**expropriates**, **expropriating**, **expropriated**) (of the state) take property from its owner for public use or benefit.
– DERIVATIVES **expropriation** n. **expropriator** n.
– ORIGIN Latin *expropriare*.

expulsion • n. the action of expelling.
– ORIGIN Latin.

expunge /ik-spunj/ • v. (**expunges**, **expunging**, **expunged**) completely remove something undesirable.
– ORIGIN Latin *expungere* 'mark for deletion by means of points'.

expurgate /eks-per-gayt/ • v. (**expurgates**, **expurgating**, **expurgated**) remove matter regarded as obscene or unsuitable from a piece of writing.
– DERIVATIVES **expurgation** n.
– ORIGIN Latin *expurgare* 'cleanse thoroughly'.

exquisite /ik-skwi-zit, ek-skwi-zit/ • adj. **1** very beautiful and delicate. **2** highly refined: *exquisite taste.* **3** intensely felt.
– DERIVATIVES **exquisitely** adv.
– ORIGIN Latin *exquirere* 'seek out'.

extant /ik-stant, ek-stuhnt/ • adj. still in existence.
– ORIGIN Latin *exstare* 'be visible'.

extempore /ik-stem-puh-ri/ • adj. & adv. spoken or done without preparation: *extempore public speaking.*
– ORIGIN from Latin *ex tempore* 'on the spur of the moment'.

extemporize /ik-stem-puh-ryz/ (or **extemporise**) • v. (**extemporizes**, **extemporizing**, **extemporized**) improvise: *he extemporized at the piano.*
– DERIVATIVES **extemporization** n.

extend • v. **1** make larger or longer in space or time. **2** occupy a specified area or continue for a specified distance. **3** offer: *she extended an invitation to her to stay.* **4** stretch out the body or a limb.
– DERIVATIVES **extendable** (also **extendible**) adj. **extender** n. **extensible** adj.
– ORIGIN Latin *extendere* 'stretch out'.

extended family • n. a family which extends beyond the parents and children to include grandparents and other relatives.

extension • n. **1** the action of extending something. **2** a part added to a building to enlarge it. **3** an additional period of time allowed for something. **4** an extra telephone on the same line as the main one. **5** (**extensions**) lengths of long artificial hair woven into a person's own hair. **6** (Brit. also **extension lead** or **cable**) an extra length of electric cable which can be plugged into a fixed socket and has another socket on the end.
– ORIGIN Latin.

extensive • adj. **1** covering a large area. **2** large in amount or scale. **3** (of agriculture) obtaining a relatively small crop from a large area.
– DERIVATIVES **extensively** adv.

extensor /ik-sten-ser/ • n. a muscle which causes a part of the body to extend.

extent • n. **1** the area covered by something. **2** size or scale: *the extent of global warming.* **3** the degree to which something is the case: *everyone*

compromises to some extent.
– ORIGIN Old French *extente*.

extenuating /ik-sten-yoo-ay-ting/
• adj. showing reasons why an offence should be treated less seriously.
– DERIVATIVES **extenuation** n.
– ORIGIN Latin *extenuare* 'make thin'.

exterior • adj. relating to or on the outside of something. • n. the outer surface or structure of something.
– ORIGIN Latin.

exterminate /ik-ster-mi-nayt/
• v. (**exterminates, exterminating, exterminated**) destroy completely.
– DERIVATIVES **extermination** n. **exterminator** n.
– ORIGIN Latin *exterminare* 'drive out'.

external • adj. **1** relating to the outside of something. **2** coming from a source outside the person or thing affected: *external factors can influence cancer.* **3** relating to another country.
• n. (**externals**) the outward features of something.
– DERIVATIVES **externally** adv.
– ORIGIN Latin.

externalize (or **externalise**)
• v. (**externalizes, externalizing, externalized**) express a thought or feeling in words or actions.
– DERIVATIVES **externalization** n.

extinct • adj. **1** (of a species or other large group) having no living members. **2** no longer in existence. **3** (of a volcano) not having erupted in recorded history.
– ORIGIN Latin *exstinguere* 'extinguish'.

extinction • n. the state of being or process of becoming extinct.

extinguish • v. **1** put out a fire or light. **2** put an end to.
– DERIVATIVES **extinguisher** n.
– ORIGIN Latin *exstinguere*.

extirpate /ek-ster-payt/ • v. (**extirpates, extirpating, extirpated**) destroy something completely.
– DERIVATIVES **extirpation** n.
– ORIGIN Latin *exstirpare*.

extol /ik-stohl/ • v. (**extols, extolling, extolled**) praise enthusiastically.
– ORIGIN Latin *extollere*.

extort /ik-stort/ • v. obtain by force, threats, or other unfair means.
– DERIVATIVES **extortion** n. **extortionist** n.
– ORIGIN Latin *extorquere*.

extortionate /ik-stor-shuh-nuht/
• adj. (of a price) much too high.
– DERIVATIVES **extortionately** adv.

extra • adj. added to an existing or usual amount or number. • adv. **1** more than usual. **2** in addition. • n. **1** an additional item, for which an extra charge is made. **2** a person taking part in a crowd scene in a film or play.

– ORIGIN prob. from **EXTRAORDINARY**.

extra- • prefix **1** outside: *extramarital.* **2** beyond the scope of: *extra-curricular.*
– ORIGIN Latin *extra*.

extract • v. /ik-strakt/ **1** remove with care or effort. **2** obtain something from someone unwilling to give it: *I tried to extract a promise from him.* **3** obtain a substance or resource from something by a special method. **4** select a passage from a written work, film, or piece of music for quotation, performance, or reproduction. • n. /ek-strakt/ **1** a short passage taken from a written work, film, or piece of music. **2** the concentrated form of the active ingredient of a substance.
– DERIVATIVES **extractable** adj. **extractive** adj.
– ORIGIN Latin *extrahere* 'draw out'.

extraction • n. **1** the action of extracting. **2** the ethnic origin of someone's family.

extractor • n. a machine or device used to extract something.

extra-curricular • adj. (of an activity at a school or college) done in addition to the normal curriculum.

extradite /ek-struh-dyt/ • v. (**extradites, extraditing, extradited**) hand over a person accused or convicted of a crime in a foreign state to the legal authority of that state.
– DERIVATIVES **extradition** n.
– ORIGIN French *extradition*.

extramarital /eks-truh-ma-ri-t'l/
• adj. occurring outside marriage.

extramural /eks-truh-myoor-uhl/
• adj. Brit. (of a course of study) arranged for people who are not full-time members of a college or other educational establishment.
– ORIGIN from Latin *extra muros* 'outside the walls'.

extraneous /ik-stray-ni-uhss/
• adj. unrelated to the subject being dealt with.
– ORIGIN Latin *extraneus*.

extraordinaire /ek-struh-or-di-nair/
• adj. outstanding in a particular area: *a singer extraordinaire.*
– ORIGIN French.

extraordinary • adj. **1** very unusual or remarkable. **2** (of a meeting) held for a particular reason rather than being one of a regular series.
– DERIVATIVES **extraordinarily** adv. **extraordinariness** n.
– ORIGIN Latin *extraordinarius*.

> ✓ Spell **extraordinary** with **extra-** at the beginning (it is made up of the words *extra* and *ordinary*).

extrapolate /ik-**strap**-uh-layt/
• v. (**extrapolates, extrapolating, extrapolated**) use a fact or conclusion that is valid for one situation and apply it to a different or wider one.
– DERIVATIVES **extrapolation** n.
– ORIGIN from EXTRA- + INTERPOLATE.

extrasensory perception /eks-truh-**sen**-suh-ri/ • n. the supposed ability to perceive things by means other than the known senses, e.g. by telepathy.

extraterrestrial /eks-truh-tuh-**ress**-tri-uhl/ • adj. relating to things outside the earth or its atmosphere. • n. a fictional being from outer space.

extravagant /ik-**strav**-uh-guhnt/ • adj. **1** spending or using more than is necessary or more than you can afford. **2** costing a great deal. **3** exceeding what is reasonable: *extravagant claims.*
– DERIVATIVES **extravagance** n. **extravagantly** adv.
– ORIGIN Latin *extravagari* 'diverge greatly'.

extravaganza /ik-stra-vuh-**gan**-zuh/ • n. an elaborate and spectacular entertainment.
– ORIGIN Italian *estravaganza* 'extravagance'.

extra virgin • adj. (of olive oil) of a very high grade, made from the first pressing of the olives.

extreme • adj. **1** to the highest degree; very great. **2** highly unusual: *extreme cases.* **3** very severe or serious. **4** not moderate: *extreme socialists.* **5** furthest from the centre or a given point. **6** (of a sport) performed in a dangerous environment. • n. **1** either of two things that are as different from each other as possible. **2** the most extreme degree: *extremes of temperature.*
– DERIVATIVES **extremely** adv.
– ORIGIN Latin *extremus* 'outermost'.

extremist • n. a person who holds extreme political or religious views.
– DERIVATIVES **extremism** n.

extremity /ik-**strem**-i-ti/ • n. (pl. **extremities**) **1** the furthest point or limit. **2** (**extremities**) the hands and feet. **3** severity: *the extremity of the violence.* **4** extreme hardship.

extricate /**eks**-tri-kayt/ • v. (**extricates, extricating, extricated**) free from a difficult or restrictive situation or place.
– DERIVATIVES **extrication** n.
– ORIGIN Latin *extricare* 'unravel'.

extrinsic /eks-**trin**-sik/ • adj. coming from outside; not part of the basic nature of something.
– DERIVATIVES **extrinsically** adv.
– ORIGIN Latin *extrinsecus* 'outward'.

extrovert /**ek**-struh-vert/ • n. an outgoing, socially confident person. • adj. relating to an extrovert.
– DERIVATIVES **extroversion** n. **extroverted** adj.
– ORIGIN from EXTRA- + Latin *vertere* 'to turn'.

extrude /ik-**strood**/ • v. (**extrudes, extruding, extruded**) thrust or force something out.
– DERIVATIVES **extrusion** n.
– ORIGIN Latin *extrudere*.

extrusive • adj. (of rock) that has been forced out at the earth's surface as lava or other volcanic deposits.

exuberant /ig-**zyoo**-buh-ruhnt/ • adj. lively and cheerful.
– DERIVATIVES **exuberance** n. **exuberantly** adv.
– ORIGIN Latin *exuberare* 'be abundantly fruitful'.

exude /ig-**zyood**/ • v. (**exudes, exuding, exuded**) **1** (of a liquid or smell) discharge or be discharged slowly and steadily. **2** clearly display an emotion or quality.
– DERIVATIVES **exudation** n.
– ORIGIN Latin *exsudare*.

exult • v. show or feel triumphant joy.
– DERIVATIVES **exultant** adj. **exultantly** adv. **exultation** n.
– ORIGIN Latin *exsultare*.

eye • n. **1** the organ of sight in humans and animals. **2** the small hole in a needle through which the thread is passed. **3** a small metal loop into which a hook is fitted as a fastener on a garment. **4** a person's opinion or feelings: *to European eyes, the city seems overcrowded.* **5** a round, dark spot on a potato from which a new shoot grows. **6** the calm region at the centre of a storm. • v. (**eyes, eyeing** or **eying, eyed**) **1** look at closely or with interest. **2** (**eye someone up**) informal look at someone with sexual interest.
– PHRASES **be all eyes** be watching eagerly. **an eye for an eye and a tooth for a tooth** doing the same thing in return is the appropriate way to deal with an offence or crime. **have an eye for** be able to recognize and judge something wisely. **have your eye on** aim to acquire. **have** (or **with**) **an eye to** have (or having) as your objective. **make eyes at** look at someone with sexual interest. **one in the eye for** a setback for. **see eye to eye** be in full agreement. **a twinkle** (or **gleam**) **in someone's eye** something that is as yet no more than an idea or dream. **up to your eyes** informal very busy.
– ORIGIN Old English.

eyeball • n. the round part of the eye of a vertebrate, within the eyelids and

socket. • v. informal stare at closely.
– PHRASES **eyeball to eyeball** face to face
with someone.

eyebrow • n. the strip of hair growing
on the ridge above a person's eye socket.
– PHRASES **raise your eyebrows** show
surprise or mild disapproval.

eye-catching • adj. immediately
appealing or noticeable.

eyeful • n. informal **1** a long steady look.
2 an eye-catching person or thing.

eyeglass • n. a single lens for correcting
poor eyesight.

eyelash • n. each of the short hairs
growing on the edges of the eyelids.

eyelet • n. **1** a small round hole made in
leather or cloth, used for threading a
lace, string, or rope through. **2** a metal
ring strengthening an eyelet.
– ORIGIN Old French *oillet*.

eyelid • n. each of the upper and lower
folds of skin which cover the eye when
closed.

eyeliner • n. a cosmetic applied as a line
round the eyes.

eye-opener • n. informal an unexpectedly
revealing event or situation.

eyepiece • n. the lens that is closest to
the eye in a microscope or other optical
instrument.

eyeshade • n. a translucent visor used to
protect the eyes from strong light.

eyeshadow • n. a coloured cosmetic
applied to the eyelids or to the skin
around the eyes.

eyesight • n. a person's ability to see.

eye socket • n. the cavity in the skull
which encloses an eyeball with its
surrounding muscles.

eyesore • n. a very ugly thing.

eye tooth • n. a canine tooth.
– PHRASES **give your eye teeth for** (or **to
do**) do anything in order to have or to be
or do.

eyewitness • n. a person who has seen
something happen and so can give a
first-hand description of it.

eyrie /eer-i, I-ri/ (US also **aerie**) • n. a
large nest of a bird of prey.
– ORIGIN prob. from Old French *aire*.

Ff

F¹ (also **f**) • n. (pl. **Fs** or **F's**) **1** the sixth letter of the alphabet. **2** the fourth note of the musical scale of C major.

F² • abbrev. **1** Fahrenheit. **2** farad(s). **3** female. **4** Brit. fine (used in describing grades of pencil lead). **5** franc(s). • symb. **1** the chemical element fluorine. **2** Physics force.

f • abbrev. **1** Grammar feminine. **2** (in references in documents) folio. **3** Music forte. • symb. Electron. frequency.

FA • abbrev. (in the UK) Football Association.

fa • n. var. of **FAH**.

fab • adj. informal fabulous.

Fabian /fay-bi-uhn/ • n. a supporter of the Fabian Society, an organization aiming to achieve socialism in a gradual way rather than by revolution. • adj. relating to the Fabians.
– ORIGIN from Roman general Quintus *Fabius* Maximus Verrucosus, known for his delaying tactics.

fable • n. **1** a short story with a message about right and wrong. **2** a story about mythical characters or events.
– ORIGIN Old French.

fabled • adj. famous for being impressive: *a fabled art collection.* **2** mentioned in myths or legends.

fabric • n. **1** cloth. **2** the walls, floor, and roof of a building. **3** the underlying structure of a system or organization: *the fabric of society.*
– ORIGIN Latin *fabrica* 'something skilfully produced'.

fabricate • v. (**fabricates, fabricating, fabricated**) **1** invent false information. **2** construct or make an industrial product.
– DERIVATIVES **fabrication** n. **fabricator** n.
– ORIGIN Latin *fabricare*.

fabulous • adj. **1** great; extraordinary. **2** informal excellent. **3** existing in myths or legends.
– DERIVATIVES **fabulously** adv.
– ORIGIN Latin *fabulosus* 'celebrated in fable'.

facade /fuh-**sahd**/ • n. **1** any of the sides of a building. **2** a false or misleading appearance.
– ORIGIN French.

face • n. **1** the front part of the head from the forehead to the chin. **2** an expression on someone's face. **3** the main surface of something. **4** a vertical or sloping side of a mountain or cliff. **5** an aspect: *the hidden face of American politics.* • v. (**faces, facing, faced**) **1** be positioned with the face or front towards someone or something or in a specified direction. **2** confront and deal with. **3** have a difficulty ahead of you. **4** cover the surface of something with a layer of a different material.
– PHRASES **face the music** experience the unpleasant consequences of your actions. **face to face** close together and looking directly at one another. **in the face of** when confronted with. **lose** (or **save**) **face** lose (or keep) your credibility or good reputation. **on the face of it** according to appearances. **to your face** openly in your presence.
– ORIGIN Latin *facies* 'form, face'.

facecloth • n. a small towelling cloth for washing the face.

faceless • adj. remote and impersonal: *faceless accountants.*

facelift • n. an operation to tighten the skin of the face to make someone look younger.

face mask • n. **1** a protective mask covering the mouth and nose or the whole face. **2** a face pack.

face pack • n. Brit. a cream or gel which is spread over the face and then removed, to improve the skin.

face-saving • adj. preserving your reputation or dignity.

facet /fa-set/ • n. **1** one of the sides of a cut gemstone. **2** an aspect: *different facets of the truth.*
– DERIVATIVES **faceted** adj.
– ORIGIN French *facette* 'little face'.

facetious /fuh-**see**-shuhss/ • adj. treating serious issues with inappropriate humour.

- DERIVATIVES **facetiously** adv. **facetiousness** n.
- ORIGIN French *facétieux*.

face value • n. the value printed or shown on a coin, postage stamp, etc.
- PHRASES **take something at face value** accept that something is what it appears to be.

facia • n. esp. Brit. var. of FASCIA.

facial /fay-sh'l/ • adj. relating to the face. • n. a beauty treatment for the face.
- DERIVATIVES **facially** adv.

facile /fa-syl/ • adj. **1** lacking careful thought. **2** too easily achieved.
- ORIGIN Latin *facilis* 'easy'.

facilitate /fuh-sil-i-tayt/ • v. (**facilitates, facilitating, facilitated**) make something easy or easier.
- DERIVATIVES **facilitation** n. **facilitator** n.
- ORIGIN French *faciliter*.

facility • n. (pl. **facilities**) **1** a building, service, or piece of equipment provided for a particular purpose. **2** a natural ability to do something well and easily.

facing • n. **1** a piece of material sewn to the inside edge of a garment at the neck, armhole, etc., to strengthen it. **2** a layer covering the surface of a wall. • adj. positioned so as to face.

facsimile /fak-sim-i-li/ • n. an exact copy of written or printed material.
- ORIGIN from Latin *fac!* 'make!' and *simile* 'like'.

fact • n. **1** a thing that is known to be true. **2** (**facts**) information used as evidence or as part of a report.
- PHRASES **before** (or **after**) **the fact** Law before (or after) the committing of a crime. **a fact of life** something that must be accepted, even if unpleasant. **the facts of life** information explaining things relating to sex. **in fact** in reality.
- ORIGIN Latin *factum* 'an act'.

faction • n. a small group within a larger one that disagrees with some of its beliefs.
- DERIVATIVES **factional** adj.
- ORIGIN Latin *facere* 'do, make'.

factious /fak-shuhss/ • adj. relating to opposition or disagreement.
- ORIGIN Latin *factiosus*.

factitious /fak-ti-shuhss/ • adj. not genuine; made up.
- ORIGIN Latin *facticius* 'made by art'.

factor • n. **1** a circumstance, fact, or influence that contributes to a result. **2** Math. a number or quantity that when multiplied with another produces a given number or expression. **3** a level on a scale of measurement: *a high sun protection factor*. **4** any of a number of substances in the blood which are involved in clotting. **5** an agent who buys and sells goods on commission. • v. (**factor something in/out**) include (or exclude) something as relevant when making a decision.
- ORIGIN Latin *facere* 'do, make'.

factorial • n. Math. the product of a whole number and all the whole numbers below it, e.g. $4 \times 3 \times 2 \times 1$ (*factorial 4*, written as 4! and equal to 24).

factorize (or **factorise**) • v. (**factorizes, factorizing, factorized**) Math. break down or be able to be broken down into factors.
- DERIVATIVES **factorization** n.

factory • n. (pl. **factories**) a building where goods are manufactured or assembled chiefly by machine.
- ORIGIN Latin *factorium* 'oil press'.

factory farming • n. a system of rearing poultry, pigs, or cattle indoors under strictly controlled conditions.

factory floor • n. the workers in a company or industry, rather than the management.

factotum /fak-toh-tuhm/ • n. (pl. **factotums**) an employee who does all kinds of work.
- ORIGIN from Latin *fac!* 'do!' + *totum* 'the whole thing'.

factual • adj. based on or concerned with fact or facts.
- DERIVATIVES **factually** adv.

faculty • n. (pl. **faculties**) **1** a basic mental or physical power. **2** an ability to do a particular thing well. **3** a group of university departments concerned with a particular area of knowledge. **4** N. Amer. the teaching or research staff of a university or college.
- ORIGIN Latin *facultas*.

fad • n. **1** a craze. **2** a fussy like or dislike.
- DERIVATIVES **faddish** adj.

faddy • adj. Brit. having many fussy likes and dislikes about food.

fade • v. (**fades, fading, faded**) **1** gradually grow faint and disappear. **2** gradually lose colour. **3** (of a film or video image or recorded sound) become more or less clear or loud.
- ORIGIN Old French *fader*.

faeces /fee-seez/ (US **feces**) • pl. n. waste material that is left after food has been digested and is expelled from the bowels.
- DERIVATIVES **faecal** /fee-k'l/ adj.
- ORIGIN Latin, 'dregs'.

faff • v. (**faff about/around**) Brit. informal bustle about without achieving much.
- ORIGIN dialect, 'blow in gusts'.

fag¹ • n. Brit. informal a cigarette.
- ORIGIN from FAG END.

fag² Brit. • n. **1** a tiring or unwelcome task.

2 informal a junior pupil at a public school who does minor chores for a senior pupil. •v. (**fags, fagging, fagged**) **1** (of a junior public-school pupil) do minor chores for a senior pupil. **2** (**fagged out**) exhausted.

fag³ •n. N. Amer. informal, derog. a male homosexual.
– ORIGIN from **FAGGOT** (in sense 3).

fag end •n. informal, esp. Brit. **1** a cigarette end. **2** an unimportant remaining part.
– ORIGIN from former *fag* 'a flap'.

faggot /fag-guht/ •n. **1** Brit. a ball of seasoned chopped liver, baked or fried. **2** (US **fagot**) a number of sticks for fuel, tied together in a bundle. **3** N. Amer. informal, derog. a male homosexual.
– ORIGIN Greek *phakelos* 'bundle'.

fah (also **fa**) •n. Music the fourth note of a major scale, coming between 'me' and 'soh'.
– ORIGIN the first syllable of *famuli*, taken from a Latin hymn.

Fahrenheit /fa-ruhn-hyt/ •adj. relating to a scale of temperature in which water freezes at 32° and boils at 212°.
– ORIGIN named after the German physicist Gabriel Daniel *Fahrenheit*.

fail •v. **1** be unsuccessful in achieving something. **2** be unable to meet the standards set by a test. **3** neglect to do: *the firm failed to give adequate warnings.* **4** stop working properly. **5** become weaker or less good. **6** let someone down: *her nerve failed her.* •n. a mark which is not high enough to pass an exam or test.
– PHRASES **without fail** whatever happens.
– ORIGIN Latin *fallere* 'deceive'.

failing •n. a weakness in a person's character. •prep. if not.

fail-safe •adj. **1** causing machinery to return to a safe condition in the event of a breakdown. **2** unlikely to fail.

failure •n. **1** lack of success. **2** an unsuccessful person or thing. **3** a situation in which something stops functioning. **4** an instance of not doing something that is expected: *her failure to comply with the rules.*

fain old use •adv. gladly. •adj. willing or obliged to do something.
– ORIGIN Old English, 'happy'.

faint •adj. **1** not clearly seen, heard, or smelt. **2** slight: *a faint chance.* **3** close to losing consciousness. •v. briefly lose consciousness. •n. a sudden loss of consciousness.
– DERIVATIVES **faintly** adv. **faintness** n.
– ORIGIN Old French *faindre* 'feign'.

faint-hearted •adj. not brave; timid.

fair¹ •adj. **1** treating people equally. **2** just

and reasonable in the circumstances. **3** considerable in size or amount: *he did a fair bit of coaching.* **4** moderately good. **5** (of hair or complexion) light; blonde. **6** (of weather) fine and dry. **7** old use beautiful. •adv. in a just and reasonable way.
– PHRASES **fair and square 1** with absolute accuracy. **2** honestly and straightforwardly. **the fair sex** (also **the fairer sex**) dated or humorous women.
– DERIVATIVES **fairish** adj. **fairness** n.
– ORIGIN Old English.

fair² •n. **1** an event at which sideshows and rides are set up for public entertainment. **2** an event held to promote or sell goods: *a fine art fair.*
– ORIGIN Latin *feriae* 'holy days'.

fair copy •n. a corrected copy of written or printed material.

fair game •n. a person or thing regarded as an acceptable target for criticism or ridicule.

fairground •n. an outdoor area where a fair is held.

fairing •n. a structure added to a vehicle, boat, or aircraft to make it more streamlined.

Fair Isle •n. a traditional multicoloured geometric design used in knitwear.
– ORIGIN from *Fair Isle* in the Shetlands.

fairly •adv. **1** with justice. **2** moderately.

fair play •n. action that conforms to accepted and reasonable rules or standards.

fairway •n. **1** the part of a golf course between a tee and a green. **2** a channel in a river or harbour which can be used by shipping.

fair-weather friend •n. a person who stops being a friend when things become difficult.

fairy •n. (pl. **fairies**) **1** a small imaginary being of human form that has magical powers. **2** informal, derog. a male homosexual.
– ORIGIN Old French *fae.*

fairy godmother •n. a female character in fairy stories who regularly helps a young hero or heroine.

fairyland •n. the imaginary home of fairies.

fairy lights •pl. n. Brit. small electric lights used to decorate a Christmas tree.

fairy ring •n. a ring of dark grass caused by fungi, once believed to have been made by fairies dancing.

fairy story •n. **1** a children's tale about magical and imaginary beings and lands. **2** an untrue account.

fairy tale •n. a fairy story. •adj. (**fairy-**

tale) magical or wonderful: *a fairy-tale romance*.

fait accompli /fayt uh-kom-pli/ • n. a thing that has been done or decided and cannot now be altered.
– ORIGIN French, 'accomplished fact'.

faith • n. **1** complete trust or confidence. **2** strong belief in a religion. **3** a system of religious belief.
– ORIGIN Latin *fides*.

faithful • adj. **1** remaining loyal. **2** remaining sexually loyal to a lover, husband, or wife. **3** true to the facts or the original: *a faithful copy of a painting.* • n. (**the faithful**) people who are faithful to a particular religion or political party.
– DERIVATIVES **faithfully** adv. **faithfulness** n.

faith healing • n. healing achieved by religious faith and prayer.

faithless • adj. disloyal, especially to a lover, husband, or wife.

fajitas /fuh-hee-tuhz/ • pl. n. a Mexican dish consisting of strips of spiced meat with vegetables and cheese, wrapped in a soft tortilla.
– ORIGIN Mexican Spanish, 'little strips'.

fake • adj. not genuine: *fake designer clothing.* • n. a person or thing that is not genuine. • v. (**fakes, faking, faked**) **1** make or do something that is not genuine in order to deceive. **2** pretend to feel or have an emotion or illness.
– DERIVATIVES **faker** n. **fakery** n.

fakir /fay-keer/ • n. a Muslim (or Hindu) holy man who lives by asking people for money or food.
– ORIGIN Arabic, 'needy man'.

falcon /fawl-k'n/ • n. a fast-flying bird of prey with long pointed wings.
– ORIGIN Latin *falco* 'hawk'.

falconry • n. the skill of keeping birds of prey and training them to hunt.
– DERIVATIVES **falconer** n.

fall • v. (**falls, falling, fell;** past part. **fallen**) **1** move downwards quickly and without control. **2** collapse to the ground. **3** hang or slope down: *the land fell away in a steep bank.* **4** become less or lower. **5** become: *he fell silent.* **6** happen; come about. **7** (of someone's face) show dismay. **8** be captured or defeated in a battle or contest. • n. **1** an act of falling. **2** a thing which falls or has fallen. **3** a waterfall. **4** a drop in size or number. **5** a defeat or downfall. **6** N. Amer. autumn.
– PHRASES **fall back** retreat. **fall back on** turn to something already tried or known when things are difficult. **fall for** informal **1** fall in love with. **2** be tricked by. **fall foul of** come into conflict with. **fall in line** do what you are told or what

other people do. **fall in with 1** meet and become involved with. **2** agree to. **fall on 1** attack fiercely or unexpectedly. **2** be the duty of someone to do something. **fall out** have an argument. **fall short** (**of**) fail to reach a required standard or target. **fall through** (of a plan) fail to happen or be completed. **fall to** become the duty of someone to do something.
– ORIGIN Old English.

fallacious /fuh-lay-shuhss/ • adj. based on a mistaken belief: *a fallacious explanation.*

fallacy /fal-luh-si/ • n. (pl. **fallacies**) **1** a mistaken belief. **2** a mistake in reasoning which makes an argument invalid.
– ORIGIN Latin *fallere* 'deceive'.

fallback • n. an alternative plan for use in an emergency.

fallen past part. of **FALL**.

fall guy • n. informal a person who is blamed for something that is not their fault; a scapegoat.

fallible /fal-li-b'l/ • adj. capable of making mistakes or being wrong.
– DERIVATIVES **fallibility** n.
– ORIGIN Latin *fallibilis*.

falling star • n. a meteor or shooting star.

Fallopian tube /fuh-loh-pi-uhn/ • n. either of a pair of tubes along which eggs travel from the ovaries to the womb of a female mammal.
– ORIGIN named after the Italian anatomist Gabriello *Fallopio*.

fallout • n. **1** radioactive particles that are spread over a wide area after a nuclear explosion. **2** the unfavourable side effects of a situation.

fallow • adj. **1** (of farmland) ploughed but left for a period without being planted with crops. **2** (of a period of time) when very little is done or achieved.
– ORIGIN Old English.

fallow deer • n. a small deer that has a white-spotted reddish-brown coat in summer.
– ORIGIN Old English, 'pale brown'.

false • adj. **1** not correct or true; wrong. **2** fake; artificial: *false eyelashes.* **3** based on something that is not true or correct: *a false sense of security.* **4** literary not faithful; disloyal.
– DERIVATIVES **falsely** adv. **falsity** n.
– ORIGIN Latin *falsum* 'fraud'.

false alarm • n. a warning given about something that then fails to take place.

falsehood • n. **1** the state of being untrue. **2** a lie.

false move • n. an unwise action that

could have dangerous consequences.

false pretences • pl. n. behaviour intended to deceive.

false step • n. **1** a slip or stumble. **2** a mistake.

falsetto /fawl-set-toh/ • n. (pl. **falsettos**) a high-pitched voice above someone's natural range, used by male singers.
– ORIGIN Italian.

falsify /fawl-si-fy/ • v. (**falsifies, falsifying, falsified**) alter information or evidence so as to mislead.
– DERIVATIVES **falsifiable** adj. **falsification** n.

falter /fawl-ter/ • v. (**falters, faltering, faltered**) **1** lose strength or momentum. **2** move or speak hesitantly.
– ORIGIN perh. from **FOLD**[1].

fame • n. the state of being famous.

famed • adj. famous; well known.

familial /fuh-mil-i-uhl/ • adj. relating to a family.

familiar • adj. **1** well known. **2** often encountered; common. **3** (**familiar with**) having a good knowledge of. **4** (of a relationship) friendly. **5** more friendly or informal than is proper. • n. (also **familiar spirit**) a spirit which supposedly accompanies and obeys a witch.
– DERIVATIVES **familiarly** adv.
– ORIGIN Latin *familiaris*.

> ✓ Remember that **familiar** is spelled with a single **l**.

familiarity • n. **1** the state of knowing or recognizing something. **2** the state of being friendly and close.

familiarize (or **familiarise**) • v. (**familiarizes, familiarizing, familiarized**) (**familiarize someone with**) give someone knowledge or understanding of something.
– DERIVATIVES **familiarization** n.

family • n. (pl. **families**) **1** a group consisting of parents and their children. **2** a group of people related by blood or marriage. **3** the children of a person or couple. **4** all the descendants of a common ancestor: *the house has been in the family for years.* **5** a group of things that are alike in some way. **6** a group of related plants or animals. • adj. suitable for children as well as adults.
– PHRASES **in the family way** informal pregnant.
– ORIGIN Latin *familia* 'household servants, family'.

family credit • n. (in the UK) a regular payment by the state to a family with an income below a certain level.

family name • n. a surname.

family planning • n. the use of contraception to control the number of children born in a family.

family tree • n. a diagram showing the relationship between people in several generations of a family.

famine • n. extreme scarcity of food.
– ORIGIN Latin *fames* 'hunger'.

famished • adj. informal very hungry.
– ORIGIN Latin *fames* 'hunger'.

famous • adj. **1** known about by many people. **2** informal excellent.
– DERIVATIVES **famously** adv.
– ORIGIN Latin *fama* 'fame'.

fan[1] • n. **1** a device with rotating blades that creates a current of air. **2** a hand-held folding device that is waved so as to cool the user. • v. (**fans, fanning, fanned**) **1** drive a current of air towards: *he fanned himself with his hat.* **2** strengthen an emotion. **3** (**fan out**) spread out from a central point to cover a wide area.
– ORIGIN Latin *vannus*.

fan[2] • n. a person who supports or has great enthusiasm for a sport, celebrity, etc.
– ORIGIN from **FANATIC**.

fanatic • n. **1** a person who holds extreme or dangerous political or religious opinions. **2** informal a person with an extreme enthusiasm for a pastime or hobby.
– DERIVATIVES **fanatical** adj. **fanatically** adv. **fanaticism** n.
– ORIGIN Latin *fanaticus* 'of a temple'.

fan belt • n. a belt driving the fan that cools the radiator of a motor vehicle.

fanciable • adj. informal sexually attractive.

fancier • n. a person who has a special interest in or breeds a particular animal: *a pigeon fancier.*

fanciful • adj. **1** existing only in the imagination. **2** highly ornamental or imaginative: *lavish and fanciful costumes.*
– DERIVATIVES **fancifully** adv.

fancy • v. (**fancies, fancying, fancied**) **1** Brit. informal want or want to do. **2** Brit. informal find someone sexually attractive. **3** think: *he fancied he could smell roses.* **4** Brit. regard as a likely winner in a competition. • adj. (**fancier, fanciest**) elaborate or highly decorated. • n. (pl. **fancies**) **1** a brief feeling of attraction. **2** the power of imagining things. **3** something that is imagined.
– PHRASES **take someone's fancy** appeal to someone. **take a fancy to** become fond of.
– DERIVATIVES **fancily** adv. **fanciness** n.
– ORIGIN from **FANTASY**.

fancy dress • n. a costume worn to make someone look like a famous person, a fictional character, or an animal.

fancy-free •adj. not in a relationship or in love.

fancy man (or **woman**) •n. informal, usu. derog. a lover.

fandango /fan-dang-goh/ •n. (pl. **fandangoes** or **fandangos**) a lively Spanish dance for two people.
– ORIGIN Spanish.

fanfare •n. a short tune played on brass instruments to announce someone or something.
– ORIGIN French.

fang •n. **1** a canine tooth of a dog or wolf. **2** a tooth with which a snake injects poison.
– ORIGIN Old Norse, 'capture, grasp'.

fanlight •n. a small semicircular window over a door or another window.

fantasia /fan-tay-zi-uh/ •n. **1** a piece of music that does not follow a conventional form. **2** a piece of music based on several familiar tunes.
– ORIGIN Italian, 'fantasy'.

fantasize (or **fantasise**) •v. (**fantasizes, fantasizing, fantasized**) imagine something desired: *he fantasized about emigrating.*
– DERIVATIVES **fantasist** n.

fantastic •adj. **1** hard to believe; fanciful. **2** strange or exotic. **3** informal very good or large.
– DERIVATIVES **fantastical** adj. **fantastically** adv.

fantasy •n. (pl. **fantasies**) **1** the imagining of improbable or impossible things. **2** an imagined situation or event that is desirable but unlikely to happen: *fantasies about the lives we'd live.* **3** a type of fiction involving magic and adventure.
– ORIGIN Greek *phantasia* 'imagination'.

fanzine /fan-zeen/ •n. a magazine for fans.
– ORIGIN from **FAN**² and **MAGAZINE**.

FAQ •abbrev. Computing frequently asked questions.

far •adv. (**further, furthest** or **farther, farthest**) **1** at, to, or by a great distance. **2** over a long time. **3** by a great deal: *he's functioning far better than usual.* •adj. **1** situated at a great distance. **2** distant from the centre. **3** more distant than another object of the same kind.
– PHRASES **as far as** to the extent that. **be a far cry from** be very different to. **far and away** by a very large amount. **far and wide** over a large area. **far gone** in a bad or worsening state. **go far 1** achieve a great deal. **2** be worth much. **go too far** go beyond what is acceptable.
– ORIGIN Old English.

farad /fa-rad/ •n. the SI unit of electrical capacitance.
– ORIGIN named after the English physicist Michael *Faraday*.

faraway •adj. **1** distant in space or time. **2** remote from your present situation: *a faraway look.*

farce •n. **1** a comic play involving ridiculously improbable situations. **2** an absurd event.
– ORIGIN French, 'stuffing' (from the former practice of 'stuffing' comic passages into religious plays).

farcical •adj. absurd or ridiculous.
– DERIVATIVES **farcically** adv.

fare •n. **1** the money a passenger on public transport has to pay. **2** a passenger in a taxi. **3** a range of food: *English fare.* •v. (**fares, faring, fared**) perform in a specified way: *the party fared badly in the elections.*
– ORIGIN Old English.

Far East •n. China, Japan, and other countries of east Asia.

farewell •exclam. old use goodbye. •n. an act of leaving or of marking someone's departure.

far-fetched •adj. far from reality and therefore unlikely: *a far-fetched plot.*

far-flung •adj. distant or remote.

farinaceous /fa-ri-nay-shuhss/ •adj. containing or resembling starch.
– ORIGIN Latin *farina* 'flour'.

farm •n. **1** an area of land and its buildings used for growing crops and rearing animals. **2** a farmhouse. **3** a place for breeding or growing something: *a fish farm.* •v. **1** make a living by growing crops or keeping livestock. **2** breed or grow a type of livestock or crop commercially. **3** (**farm something out**) send out or subcontract work to other people.
– DERIVATIVES **farming** n.
– ORIGIN Old French *ferme* 'fixed payment'.

farmer •n. a person who owns or manages a farm.

farmhouse •n. the main house on a farm.

farmland •n. (also **farmlands**) land used for farming.

farmstead •n. a farm and its buildings.

farmyard •n. a yard or enclosure attached to a farmhouse.

far-off •adj. distant in time or space.

farrago /fuh-rah-goh/ •n. (pl. **farragos** or US **farragoes**) a confused mixture.
– ORIGIN Latin, 'mixed fodder'.

far-reaching •adj. having a widespread and important effect.

farrier /fa-ri-er/ • n. a blacksmith who shoes horses.
– ORIGIN Old French *ferrier*.

farrow • n. a litter of pigs. • v. (of a sow) give birth to piglets.
– ORIGIN Old English, 'young pig'.

far-seeing • adj. able to predict and prepare for the future.

Farsi /far-see/ • n. the modern form of the Persian language.
– ORIGIN Persian, 'Persia'.

far-sighted • adj. able to think about and prepare for the future.

fart informal • v. 1 let out wind from the anus. 2 (**fart about/around**) waste time on unimportant things. • n. 1 an act of letting out wind from the anus. 2 a boring or unpleasant person.
– ORIGIN Old English.

farther • adv. & adj. var. of **FURTHER**.

> **USAGE:** For an explanation of the difference between **farther** and **further**, see the note at **FURTHER**.

farthest • adj. & adv. var. of **FURTHEST**.

farthing • n. a former coin of the UK, worth a quarter of an old penny.
– ORIGIN Old English.

farthingale /far-thing-gayl/ • n. a hooped petticoat or circular pad of fabric around the hips, formerly worn under women's skirts to give a pronounced shape.
– ORIGIN French *verdugale*.

fascia /fay-shuh/ (also esp. Brit. **facia**) • n. 1 a board covering the ends of rafters or other fittings. 2 Brit. a signboard on a shopfront. 3 Brit. the dashboard of a motor vehicle. 4 a detachable cover for the front of a mobile phone.
– ORIGIN Latin, 'band, door frame'.

fascinate • v. (**fascinates, fascinating, fascinated**) interest or charm someone greatly.
– ORIGIN Latin *fascinare* 'bewitch'.

> ✓ Spell **fascinate** and the related word **fascination** with an **s** before the **c**.

fascinating • adj. very interesting or attractive.

fascination • n. 1 the quality of being very interesting or attractive: *the fascination of science*. 2 a strong feeling of interest.

fascism /fash-i-z'm/ • n. 1 a right-wing system of government characterized by extreme nationalistic beliefs and strict obedience to a leader or the state. 2 extreme right-wing or intolerant views or behaviour.
– DERIVATIVES **fascist** n. & adj. **fascistic** adj.
– ORIGIN Italian *fascismo*.

fashion • n. 1 a popular trend, especially in clothes. 2 the production and marketing of new styles of clothing and cosmetics. 3 a way of doing something: *the work was done in a casual fashion*. • v. make or shape.
– PHRASES **after a fashion** to a certain extent but not entirely or perfectly.
– ORIGIN Old French *façon*.

fashionable • adj. in or adopting a style that is currently popular.
– DERIVATIVES **fashionability** n. **fashionably** adv.

fast¹ • adj. 1 moving or capable of moving at high speed. 2 taking place or acting rapidly. 3 (of a clock or watch) ahead of the correct time. 4 firmly fixed or attached: *he made a rope fast to each corner*. 5 (of a dye) not fading in light or when washed. 6 devoting yourself to pleasurable or immoral activities.
• adv. 1 quickly. 2 firmly or securely.
– PHRASES **fast asleep** in a deep sleep. **pull a fast one** informal try to gain an unfair advantage.
– ORIGIN Old English.

fast² • v. go without food or drink, especially for religious reasons. • n. a period of fasting.
– ORIGIN Old English.

fast breeder • n. a nuclear reactor using high-speed neutrons.

fasten • v. 1 close or do up securely. 2 fix or hold in place. 3 (**fasten on**) pick out and concentrate on.
– ORIGIN Old English, 'make sure'.

fastener (also **fastening**) • n. a device for fastening something.

fast food • n. cooked food sold in snack bars and restaurants as a quick meal.

fastidious /fa-stid-i-uhss/ • adj. 1 very careful about accuracy and detail. 2 very concerned about cleanliness.
– DERIVATIVES **fastidiously** adv. **fastidiousness** n.
– ORIGIN Latin *fastidium* 'loathing'.

fastness • n. 1 a secure place well protected by natural features. 2 the ability of a dye to maintain its colour.

fast track • n. the quickest way to become effective or successful.
• v. (**fast-track**) speed up the progress of.

fat • n. 1 a natural oily substance found in animal bodies. 2 such a substance, or a similar one made from plants, used in cooking. • adj. (**fatter, fattest**) 1 (of a person or animal) having much excess fat. 2 (of food) containing much fat. 3 informal large: *fat profits*. 4 informal very little: *fat chance*.
– PHRASES **live off the fat of the land** have the best of everything.
– DERIVATIVES **fatness** n. **fattish** adj.

– ORIGIN Old English.

fatal • adj. **1** causing death. **2** leading to failure or disaster: *the strategy contained three fatal flaws.*
– DERIVATIVES **fatally** adv.
– ORIGIN Latin *fatalis*.

fatalism • n. the belief that events are decided in advance by a supernatural power and that humans have no control over them.
– DERIVATIVES **fatalist** n. **fatalistic** adj.

fatality • n. (pl. **fatalities**) an occurrence of death by accident, in war, or from disease.

fat cat • n. derog. a wealthy and powerful businessman or businesswoman.

fate • n. **1** the development of events outside a person's control, regarded as decided in advance by a supernatural power. **2** the outcome of a situation: *the pink pigeon narrowly escaped the same fate as the dodo.* **3** (**the Fates**) Gk & Rom. Myth. the three goddesses who control people's lives. • v. (**be fated**) be destined to happen in a particular way: *they were fated to meet again.*
– ORIGIN Latin *fatum* 'that which has been spoken'.

fateful • adj. having far-reaching, often unpleasant, consequences.
– DERIVATIVES **fatefully** adv.

fathead • n. informal a stupid person.

father • n. **1** a male parent. **2** an important figure in the origin and early history of something: *Pasteur, the father of microbiology.* **3** literary a male ancestor. **4** (often as a title or form of address) a priest. **5** (**the Father**) (in Christian belief) God. • v. (**fathers, fathering, fathered**) be the father of.
– DERIVATIVES **fatherhood** n.
– ORIGIN Old English.

Father Christmas • n. Brit. an imaginary man said to bring presents for children on Christmas Eve.

father-in-law • n. (pl. **fathers-in-law**) the father of a person's husband or wife.

fatherland • n. a person's native country.

fatherly • adj. protective and affectionate.
– DERIVATIVES **fatherliness** n.

fathom • n. a unit of length equal to six feet (1.8 metres), used in measuring the depth of water. • v. understand something after much thought: *I can't fathom him out.*
– ORIGIN Old English, 'something which embraces' (the original measurement was based on the span of a person's outstretched arms).

fatigue • n. **1** extreme tiredness.

2 brittleness in metal or other materials caused by repeated stress. **3** (**fatigues**) loose-fitting clothing of a sort worn by soldiers. • v. (**fatigues, fatiguing, fatigued**) make someone very tired.
– ORIGIN Latin *fatigare*.

fatten • v. make or become fat or fatter.

fatty • adj. (**fattier, fattiest**) containing a large amount of fat. • n. (pl. **fatties**) informal a fat person.
– DERIVATIVES **fattiness** n.

fatty acid • n. an organic acid whose molecule contains a hydrocarbon chain.

fatuity /fuh-tyoo-i-ti/ • n. (pl. **fatuities**) **1** a silly remark. **2** foolishness.

fatuous • adj. silly and pointless.
– DERIVATIVES **fatuously** adv.
– ORIGIN Latin *fatuus*.

fatwa /fat-wah/ • n. an authoritative ruling on a point of Islamic law.
– ORIGIN Arabic.

faucet /faw-sit/ • n. N. Amer. a tap.
– ORIGIN Old French *fausset*.

fault • n. **1** a defect or mistake. **2** responsibility for something that happens: *it's not my fault that she left.* **3** (in tennis) a service that breaks the rules. **4** an extended break in the continuity of layers of rock, caused by movement of the earth's crust. • v. criticize for being unsatisfactory.
– PHRASES **find fault** make a criticism or objection. —— **to a fault** to an excessive extent: *you're generous to a fault.*
– DERIVATIVES **faultless** adj.
– ORIGIN Latin *fallere* 'deceive'.

faulty • adj. (**faultier, faultiest**) **1** not working or made correctly. **2** (of reasoning) containing mistakes.

faun /fawn/ • n. Rom. Myth. a god in the form of a man with a goat's horns, ears, legs, and tail.
– ORIGIN Latin *Faunus*.

fauna /faw-nuh/ • n. (pl. **faunas**) the animals of a particular region, habitat, or geological period. Compare with **FLORA**.
– ORIGIN Latin *Fauna*, a rural goddess.

faux pas /foh pah/ • n. (pl. **faux pas**) an embarrassing mistake made in a social situation.
– ORIGIN French, 'false step'.

favour (US **favor**) • n. **1** approval or liking. **2** an act of kindness: *I've come to ask you a favour.* **3** special treatment given to one person at the expense of another. • v. **1** regard or treat with favour. **2** work to the advantage of: *natural selection has favoured bats.* **3** (**favour someone with**) give someone something they wish for.

– PHRASES **in favour of 1** to be replaced by. **2** in support or to the advantage of.
– ORIGIN Latin *favor*.

favourable (US **favorable**) • adj. **1** expressing approval or agreement. **2** advantageous or helpful.
– DERIVATIVES **favourably** adv.

favourite (US **favorite**) • adj. preferred to all others of the same kind. • n. **1** a favourite person or thing. **2** the competitor thought most likely to win.

favouritism (US **favoritism**) • n. the unfair favouring of one person or group at the expense of another.

fawn[1] • n. **1** a young deer in its first year. **2** a light brown colour.
– ORIGIN Old French *faon*.

fawn[2] • v. try to please someone by flattering them and being too attentive.
– DERIVATIVES **fawning** adj.
– ORIGIN Old English, 'make or be glad'.

fax • n. **1** an exact copy of a document made by electronic scanning and sent by telecommunications links. **2** the making and sending of documents in such a way. **3** (also **fax machine**) a machine for sending and receiving such documents. • v. **1** send a document by fax. **2** contact someone by fax.
– ORIGIN from FACSIMILE.

faze • v. (**fazes, fazing, fazed**) informal disturb or unsettle.
– ORIGIN Old English, 'drive off'.

FBI • abbrev. (in the US) Federal Bureau of Investigation.

FC • abbrev. Football Club.

FCO • abbrev. (in the UK) Foreign and Commonwealth Office.

FE • abbrev. (in the UK) further education.

Fe • symb. the chemical element iron.
– ORIGIN Latin *ferrum*.

fealty /fee-uhl-ti/ • n. hist. the loyalty sworn to a feudal lord by his tenant.
– ORIGIN Old French *feaulte*.

fear • n. **1** an unpleasant emotion caused by the threat of danger, pain, or harm. **2** the likelihood of something unwelcome happening. • v. **1** be afraid of. **2** (**fear for**) be anxious about.
– ORIGIN Old English, 'danger'.

fearful • adj. **1** showing or causing fear. **2** informal very great.
– DERIVATIVES **fearfully** adv.

fearless • adj. lacking fear; brave.
– DERIVATIVES **fearlessly** adv.

fearsome • adj. frightening.

feasible • adj. **1** able to be done easily. **2** likely; probable.
– DERIVATIVES **feasibility** n. **feasibly** adv.
– ORIGIN Old French *faisible*.

USAGE: Although some people say that you should not use **feasible** to mean 'likely' or 'probable' (*the most feasible explanation*), this sense has been in the language for centuries and is generally considered to be acceptable.

feast • n. **1** a large meal marking a special occasion. **2** an annual religious celebration. • v. **1** have a large or lavish meal. **2** (**feast on**) eat large quantities of.
– PHRASES **feast your eyes on** gaze at something with pleasure.
– ORIGIN Latin *festa*.

feat • n. an achievement requiring great courage, skill, or strength.
– ORIGIN Old French *fait*.

feather • n. any of the flat structures growing from a bird's skin, consisting of a partly hollow shaft fringed with fine strands. • v. (**feathers, feathering, feathered**) **1** (as adj. **feathered**) covered or decorated with feathers. **2** turn an oar so that the blade passes through the air edgeways.
– PHRASES **a feather in your cap** an achievement to be proud of. **feather your nest** make money dishonestly.
– DERIVATIVES **feathery** adj.
– ORIGIN Old English.

feather bed • n. a bed with a mattress stuffed with feathers. • v. (**feather-bed**) provide with very comfortable or profitable conditions.

feather-brained • adj. silly or absent-minded.

featherweight • n. **1** a weight in boxing between bantamweight and lightweight. **2** a person or thing of little or no importance.

feature • n. **1** a distinctive element or aspect: *the software has some welcome new features.* **2** a distinctive part of the face, such as the mouth. **3** a newspaper or magazine article or a broadcast programme on a particular topic. **4** (also **feature film**) a full-length film forming the main item in a cinema programme. • v. (**features, featuring, featured**) **1** have as a distinctive element: *the hotel features a restaurant and a sauna.* **2** take an important part in. **3** have as an important actor or participant.
– DERIVATIVES **featureless** adj.
– ORIGIN Old French *faiture* 'form'.

Feb. • abbrev. February.

febrile /fee-bryl/ • adj. **1** having or showing the symptoms of a fever. **2** overactive and excitable: *her febrile imagination.*
– ORIGIN Latin *febris* 'fever'.

February /feb-yuu-ri, feb-ruu-uh-ri/

•n. (pl. **Februaries**) the second month of the year.
– ORIGIN Latin *februarius*.

 February has two **r**'s; one after the **b** and one near the end.

feces •pl. n. US = FAECES.

feckless •adj. irresponsible and lacking strength of character.
– ORIGIN from EFFECT.

fecund /fek-uhnd/ •adj. very fertile.
– DERIVATIVES **fecundity** n.
– ORIGIN Latin *fecundus*.

fed past and past part. of FEED.

federal •adj. **1** relating to a system of government in which several states unite under a central authority but remain independent in internal affairs. **2** relating to the central government of a federation: *federal laws*. **3** (**Federal**) US hist. relating to the Northern States in the Civil War.
– DERIVATIVES **federally** adv.
– ORIGIN Latin *foedus* 'league, covenant'.

federalism •n. the federal principle or system of government.
– DERIVATIVES **federalist** n. & adj.

federate /fed-uh-rayt/ •v. (**federates, federating, federated**) (of states) unite under a central authority while remaining independent in internal affairs.

federation •n. **1** a group of states with a central government but independence in internal affairs. **2** an organization within which smaller divisions have some internal independence.

fedora /fi-dor-uh/ •n. a soft felt hat with a curled brim and the crown creased lengthways.
– ORIGIN *Fédora*, a drama written by the French dramatist Victorien Sardou.

fed up •adj. informal annoyed or bored.

fee •n. **1** a payment given for professional advice or services. **2** a sum payable to be allowed to do something: *an admission fee*.
– ORIGIN Old French *feu* 'a piece of land held in return for feudal service'.

feeble •adj. (**feebler, feeblest**) **1** lacking strength. **2** failing to convince or impress: *a feeble excuse*.
– DERIVATIVES **feebleness** n. **feebly** adv.
– ORIGIN Latin *flebilis* 'lamentable'.

feeble-minded •adj. foolish; stupid.

feed •v. (**feeds, feeding, fed**) **1** give food to. **2** provide enough food for. **3** eat. **4** supply with material, power, or information. **5** pass something gradually through a confined space. •n. **1** an act of feeding. **2** food for domestic animals. **3** a device for supplying material to a

machine. **4** the supply of raw material to a machine.
– ORIGIN Old English.

feedback •n. **1** comments about a product or a person's performance, used as a basis for improvement. **2** the return of a fraction of the output of an amplifier, microphone, or other device to the input of the same device, causing distortion or a whistling sound.

feeder •n. **1** a person or animal that eats a particular food or in a particular way. **2** a device that feeds or supplies something. **3** a road or rail route linking outlying districts with a main system.

feel •v. (**feels, feeling, felt**) **1** be aware of, examine, or search by touch. **2** be aware of through physical sensation. **3** give a sensation when touched: *the wool feels soft*. **4** experience an emotion or sensation. **5** be affected by. **6** have a belief or opinion. **7** (**feel up to**) have the strength or energy to. •n. **1** an act of feeling. **2** the sense of touch. **3** an impression: *the restaurant has a bistro feel*.
– PHRASES **get a feel for** become used to. **have a feel for** have a sensitive appreciation of.
– ORIGIN Old English.

feeler •n. **1** an organ such as an antenna, used by some animals for testing things by touch. **2** a cautious proposal intended to find out someone's attitude or opinion.

feeling •n. **1** an emotional state or reaction: *a feeling of joy*. **2** (**feelings**) the emotional side of a person's character. **3** strong emotion. **4** the capacity to feel. **5** the sensation of touching or being touched: *the feeling of water against your skin*. **6** a belief or opinion. **7** (**feeling for**) an understanding of.
– DERIVATIVES **feelingly** adv.

feet pl. of FOOT.

feign •v. pretend to feel or have: *she feigned nervousness*.
– ORIGIN Old French *feindre*.

feint¹ /faynt/ •n. a pretended attacking movement in boxing or fencing, designed to distract your opponent. •v. make a pretended attacking movement in boxing or fencing.
– ORIGIN French *feindre* 'pretend'.

feint² /faynt/ •adj. (of paper) printed with faint lines as a guide for handwriting.
– ORIGIN from FAINT.

feisty /fy-sti/ •adj. (**feistier, feistiest**) lively and spirited.
– DERIVATIVES **feistily** adv. **feistiness** n.
– ORIGIN from former *feist* 'small dog'.

feldspar /feld-spar/ (also **felspar**) •n. a

mineral forming igneous rocks, consisting chiefly of aluminium silicates.
– ORIGIN German *Feldspat* 'field spar'.

felicitations • pl. n. formal congratulations.

felicitous /fuh-liss-i-tuhss/ • adj. well chosen or appropriate.
– DERIVATIVES **felicitously** adv.

felicity • n. (pl. **felicities**) 1 great happiness. 2 an apt and pleasing feature of a work of literature.
– ORIGIN Latin *felicitas*.

feline /fee-lyn/ • adj. relating to or like a cat or cats. • n. a cat or other animal of the cat family.
– ORIGIN Latin *feles* 'cat'.

fell¹ past of FALL.

fell² • v. 1 cut down a tree. 2 knock down.
– ORIGIN Old English.

fell³ • n. a hill or stretch of high moorland in northern England.
– ORIGIN Old Norse.

fell⁴ • adj. literary very evil or fierce.
– PHRASES **in** (or **at**) **one fell swoop** all in one go.
– ORIGIN Old French *fel*.

fellatio /fe-lay-shi-oh/ • n. stimulation of a man's penis using the tongue or lips.
– ORIGIN Latin *fellare* 'to suck'.

fellow • n. 1 a man or boy. 2 a person involved in the same activity or belonging to the same group as another person: *the rebel was murdered by his fellows*. 3 a thing of the same kind as another. 4 a member of a learned society. 5 Brit. a member of the governing body of certain colleges. • adj. sharing a particular situation or condition: *a fellow sufferer*.
– ORIGIN Old English, 'partner'.

fellow feeling • n. sympathy based on shared experiences.

fellowship • n. 1 friendliness and companionship based on shared interests. 2 a group of people meeting to pursue a shared interest or aim. 3 the position of a fellow of a college or society.

fellow-traveller • n. esp. hist. a person who sympathizes with the Communist Party but is not a member of it.

felon /fe-luhn/ • n. a person who has committed a serious crime.
– DERIVATIVES **felonious** /fi-loh-ni-uhss/ adj.
– ORIGIN Old French, 'wicked person'.

felony /fe-luh-ni/ • n. (pl. **felonies**) (in the US and many other judicial systems) a crime regarded as more serious than a misdemeanour.

felspar /fel-spar/ • n. var. of FELDSPAR.

felt¹ • n. cloth made by rolling and pressing wool in a damp or heated atmosphere, which causes the fibres to become matted.
– ORIGIN Old English.

felt² past and past part. of FEEL.

female • adj. 1 referring to the sex that can bear offspring or produce eggs. 2 relating to women or girls: *a female name*. 3 (of a plant or flower) having a pistil but no stamens. 4 (of a fitting) having a hollow opening so that a corresponding male part can be inserted. • n. a female person, animal, or plant.
– ORIGIN Latin *femina* 'woman'.

feminine • adj. 1 having qualities associated with women, especially delicacy and prettiness. 2 female. 3 Grammar (of a gender of nouns and adjectives in certain languages) treated as female.
– DERIVATIVES **femininity** n.
– ORIGIN Latin *femina* 'woman'.

feminism • n. a movement supporting women's rights on the grounds of equality of the sexes.
– DERIVATIVES **feminist** n. & adj.

feminize (or **feminise**) • v. (**feminizes**, **feminizing**, **feminized**) make more feminine or female.
– DERIVATIVES **feminization** n.

femme fatale /fam fuh-tahl/ • n. (pl. **femmes fatales** /fam fuh-tahl/) an attractive woman whose sexuality gives her power over men.
– ORIGIN French, 'disastrous woman'.

femur /fee-mer/ • n. (pl. **femurs** or **femora** /fem-uh-ruh/) the bone of the thigh.
– DERIVATIVES **femoral** /fem-uh-ruhl/ adj.
– ORIGIN Latin, 'thigh'.

fen • n. a low and marshy or frequently flooded area of land.
– ORIGIN Old English.

fence • n. 1 a barrier enclosing an area of land, consisting of posts connected by wire mesh or wooden boards or panels. 2 a large upright obstacle in steeplechasing, showjumping, or cross-country. 3 informal a dealer in stolen goods. • v. (**fences**, **fencing**, **fenced**) 1 surround or protect with a fence. 2 informal deal in stolen goods. 3 practise the sport of fencing.
– PHRASES **sit on the fence** avoid making a decision.
– DERIVATIVES **fencer** n.
– ORIGIN from DEFENCE.

fencing • n. 1 the sport of fighting with blunted swords in order to score points. 2 fences or material for making fences.

fend •v. 1 (**fend for yourself**) look after and provide for yourself. 2 (**fend off**) defend yourself from.
– ORIGIN from **DEFEND**.

fender •n. 1 a low frame around a fireplace to keep in falling coals. 2 a cushioning device hung over a ship's side to protect it against impact. 3 N. Amer. the mudguard or area around the wheel well of a vehicle.

feng shui /feng shoo-i, fung shway/ •n. an ancient Chinese system of designing buildings and positioning objects inside buildings to ensure a favourable flow of energy.
– ORIGIN Chinese, 'wind' and 'water'.

fennel /fen-n'l/ •n. a plant whose leaves and seeds are used as a herb and whose bulb is eaten as a vegetable.
– ORIGIN Latin *faeniculum*.

fenugreek /fen-yuu-greek/ •n. a plant with seeds that are used as a spice.
– ORIGIN from Latin *faenum graecum* 'Greek hay'.

feral /fe-ruhl/ •adj. 1 (of an animal or plant) wild, especially after having been domesticated. 2 fierce.
– ORIGIN Latin *ferus* 'wild'.

ferment •v. /fer-ment/ 1 (of a substance) undergo a chemical breakdown by the action of bacteria, yeasts, or other microorganisms. 2 stir up disorder. •n. /fer-ment/ a state of widespread unrest or excitement.
– DERIVATIVES **fermenter** n.
– ORIGIN Latin *fermentum* 'yeast'.

fermentation •n. the chemical breakdown of a substance by bacteria, yeasts, or other microorganisms, such as when sugar is converted into alcohol.

fermium /fer-mi-uhm/ •n. an unstable radioactive chemical element made by high-energy atomic collisions.

fern •n. (pl. **fern** or **ferns**) a flowerless plant which has feathery or leafy fronds and reproduces by means of spores.
– DERIVATIVES **ferny** adj.
– ORIGIN Old English.

ferocious /fuh-roh-shuss/ •adj. savagely fierce, cruel, or violent.
– DERIVATIVES **ferociously** adv.
– ORIGIN Latin *ferox* 'fierce'.

ferocity /fuh-ross-i-ti/ •n. the state of being savagely fierce, cruel, or violent.

-ferous (usu. **-iferous**) •comb. form having or containing: *Carboniferous*.
– ORIGIN Latin *-fer* 'producing'.

ferret /ferr-it/ •n. a domesticated albino or brown polecat, used for catching rabbits. •v. (**ferrets, ferreting, ferreted**) 1 search for something in a container or confined space. 2 (**ferret something out**) discover something by determined searching. 3 (as noun **ferreting**) hunting with ferrets.
– DERIVATIVES **ferrety** adj.
– ORIGIN Old French *fuiret*.

ferric /ferr-ik/ •adj. Chem. relating to iron with a valency of three.
– ORIGIN Latin *ferrum* 'iron'.

Ferris wheel •n. a fairground ride consisting of a giant vertical revolving wheel with passenger cars hanging from its outer edge.
– ORIGIN named after the American engineer George W. G. Ferris.

ferroconcrete •n. concrete reinforced with steel.

ferrous /ferr-uhss/ •adj. 1 (of metals) containing iron. 2 Chem. relating to iron with a valency of two.

ferrule /ferr-ool/ •n. a metal ring or cap which strengthens the end of a handle, stick, or tube.
– ORIGIN Old French *virelle*.

ferry •n. (pl. **ferries**) a boat that transports passengers and goods as a regular service. •v. (**ferries, ferrying, ferried**) carry by ferry or other transport.
– DERIVATIVES **ferryman** n. (pl. **ferrymen**).
– ORIGIN Old Norse.

fertile •adj. 1 (of soil or land) producing abundant vegetation or crops. 2 (of a person, animal, or plant) able to conceive young or produce seed. 3 productive in generating ideas: *a fertile debate*.
– DERIVATIVES **fertility** n.
– ORIGIN Latin *fertilis*.

fertilize (or **fertilise**) •v. (**fertilizes, fertilizing, fertilized**) 1 introduce sperm or pollen into an egg, female animal, or plant to develop a new individual. 2 add fertilizer to land.
– DERIVATIVES **fertilization** n.

fertilizer (also **fertiliser**) •n. a chemical or natural substance added to soil to increase its fertility.

fervent /fer-vuhnt/ •adj. very passionate.
– DERIVATIVES **fervently** adv.
– ORIGIN Latin *fervere* 'to boil'.

fervid •adj. fervent.
– ORIGIN Latin *fervidus*.

fervour (US **fervor**) •n. passionate feeling.

festal •adj. relating to a festival.
– ORIGIN Latin *festa* 'feast'.

fester •v. (**festers, festering, festered**) 1 (of a wound or sore) become septic. 2 become rotten. 3 become worse: *tensions began to fester between Rose and Nick*.
– ORIGIN Old French *festrir*.

festival • n. **1** a day or period of celebration. **2** an organized series of concerts, films, or talks.
– ORIGIN Latin *festa* 'feast'.

festive • adj. relating to a period of celebration: *the festive season*.

festivity • n. (pl. **festivities**) **1** joyful celebration. **2** (**festivities**) activities or events celebrating a special occasion.

festoon /fess-toon/ • v. decorate with chains of flowers or other decorations. • n. a decorative chain of flowers, leaves, or ribbons, hung in a curve.
– ORIGIN Italian *festone* 'festive ornament'.

feta /fet-uh/ • n. a salty Greek cheese made from the milk of ewes or goats.
– ORIGIN modern Greek *pheta*.

fetal /fee-t'l/ • adj. relating to a fetus.

fetch • v. **1** go for something and bring it back. **2** sell for a particular price. **3** (**fetch up**) informal arrive or come to rest somewhere. **4** (as adj. **fetching**) attractive.
– DERIVATIVES **fetcher** n.
– ORIGIN Old English.

fete /fayt/ (also **fête**) • n. Brit. an outdoor event to raise funds for charity, involving the sale of goods and stalls with games. • v. (**fetes**, **feting**, **feted**) honour or entertain someone lavishly.
– ORIGIN French.

fetid /fet-id/ (also **foetid**) • adj. smelling very unpleasant.
– ORIGIN Latin *fetidus*.

fetish • n. **1** an object worshipped for its supposed magical powers. **2** a form of sexual desire in which sexual pleasure is gained from an object or a part of the body. **3** something to which a person is obsessively devoted: *he had a fetish about purity*.
– DERIVATIVES **fetishism** n. **fetishist** n. **fetishize** (or **fetishise**) v.
– ORIGIN French *fétiche*.

fetlock • n. a joint of a horse's leg between the knee and the hoof.
– ORIGIN Germanic.

fetor /fee-ter/ • n. a very unpleasant smell.
– ORIGIN Latin.

fetter • v. (**fetters**, **fettering**, **fettered**) **1** restrict the freedom of. **2** restrain with chains or shackles. • n. **1** (**fetters**) restraints or controls. **2** a chain placed around a prisoner's ankle to restrict their movement.
– ORIGIN Old English.

fettle • n. condition: *the aircraft is in fine fettle*.
– ORIGIN Old English, 'strip of material'.

fettuccine /fet-tuh-chee-ni/ • pl. n. pasta made in ribbons.
– ORIGIN Italian, 'little ribbons'.

fetus /fee-tuhss/ (Brit. (in non-technical use) also **foetus**) • n. (pl. **fetuses**) an unborn mammal, in particular an unborn human more than eight weeks after conception.
– ORIGIN Latin, 'pregnancy, birth'.

feud • n. a long-lasting and bitter dispute. • v. take part in a feud.
– ORIGIN Old French *feide* 'hostility'.

feudal • adj. relating to feudalism.
– ORIGIN Latin *feodum* 'fee'.

feudalism • n. the main social system in medieval Europe, in which a person worked for a lord in exchange for land, and in which a lord was given land by the monarch in exchange for military service.

fever • n. **1** an abnormally high body temperature. **2** a state of nervous excitement or agitation.
– DERIVATIVES **feverish** adj.
– ORIGIN Latin *febris*.

fevered • adj. **1** having an abnormally high body temperature. **2** nervously excited or agitated.

feverfew • n. a plant with daisy-like flowers, used as a herbal remedy for headaches.
– ORIGIN from Latin *febris* 'fever' + *fugare* 'drive away'.

few • det., pron., & adj. **1** (**a few**) a small number of; some. **2** not many: *he had few friends*.
– PHRASES **few and far between** scarce. **a good few** Brit. a fairly large number. **quite a few** a fairly large number.
– ORIGIN Old English.

> **USAGE:** Many people use the words **fewer** and **less** incorrectly. The rule is that **fewer** should be used with plural nouns, as in *eat fewer cakes* or *there are fewer people here today*. Use **less** with nouns referring to things that cannot be counted, as in *there is less blossom on this tree*. It is wrong to use **less** with a plural noun (*less people, less cakes*).

fey /fay/ • adj. **1** unworldly and vague. **2** able to see into the future.
– ORIGIN Old English, 'fated to die soon'.

fez • n. (pl. **fezzes**) a flat-topped conical red hat, worn by men in some Muslim countries.
– ORIGIN named after the city of *Fez* in Morocco.

ff. • abbrev. following pages.

fiancé /fi-on-say/ • n. (fem. **fiancée** /fi-on-say/) a person to whom you are engaged to be married.
– ORIGIN French.

fiasco /fi-ass-koh/ • n. (pl. **fiascos**) a ridiculous or humiliating failure.
– ORIGIN from Italian *far fiasco* 'fail in a performance' (literally 'make a bottle').

fiat /fee-at/ • n. an official order or authorization.
– ORIGIN Latin, 'let it be done'.

fib • n. a trivial lie. • v. (**fibs, fibbing, fibbed**) tell a trivial lie.
– DERIVATIVES **fibber** n.
– ORIGIN perh. from FABLE.

fiber • n. US = FIBRE.

fiberboard • n. US = FIBREBOARD.

fiberglass • n. US = FIBREGLASS.

Fibonacci series /fi-buh-nah-chi/ • n. Math. a series of numbers in which each number (**Fibonacci number**) is the sum of the two preceding numbers (e.g. the series 1, 1, 2, 3, 5, 8, etc.).
– ORIGIN named after the Italian mathematician Leonardo *Fibonacci*.

fibre (US **fiber**) • n. **1** a thread or strand from which a plant or animal tissue, mineral substance, or textile is formed. **2** a substance formed of fibres. **3** substances in vegetables, fruit, and some other foods, that are difficult to digest and therefore help food to pass through the body. **4** strength of character: *he's lacking in moral fibre*.
– ORIGIN Latin *fibra* 'fibre, entrails'.

fibreboard (US **fiberboard**) • n. a building material made of compressed wood fibres.

fibreglass (US **fiberglass**) • n. **1** a rigid plastic material containing glass fibres. **2** a material made from woven glass fibres, used for heat insulation.

fibre optics • n. the use of thin flexible transparent fibres to transmit light signals, used for telecommunications or for internal inspection of the body.
– DERIVATIVES **fibre-optic** adj.

fibril /fy-bril/ • n. tech. a small or slender fibre.
– ORIGIN Latin *fibrilla*.

fibrillate /fy-bri-layt, fib-ri-layt/ • v. (of a muscle, especially in the heart) twitch irregularly, owing to uncoordinated contraction of the individual fibres.
– DERIVATIVES **fibrillation** n.

fibrin /fy-brin/ • n. an insoluble protein formed as a fibrous mesh during the clotting of blood.

fibroid • adj. relating to fibres or fibrous tissue. • n. a non-cancerous tumour of fibrous tissues, developing in the womb.

fibrosis /fy-broh-siss/ • n. Med. the thickening and scarring of connective tissue, as a result of injury.

fibrous • adj. relating to or made of fibres.

fibula /fib-yuu-luh/ • n. (pl. **fibulae** /fib-yuu-lee/ or **fibulas**) the outer of the two bones between the knee and the ankle, parallel with the tibia.
– ORIGIN Latin, 'brooch'.

fickle • adj. changeable with regard to your loyalty to someone or something.
– ORIGIN Old English, 'deceitful'.

fiction • n. **1** writing in prose that describes imaginary events and people. **2** a false belief or statement.
– ORIGIN Latin.

fictional • adj. relating to writing that describes imaginary events and people.
– DERIVATIVES **fictionally** adv.

fictionalize (or **fictionalise**) • v. (**fictionalizes, fictionalizing, fictionalized**) make into a fictional story.

fictitious /fik-tish-uhss/ • adj. **1** imaginary or invented; not real. **2** referring to fiction.

fiddle • n. informal **1** a violin. **2** esp. Brit. an act of fraud or cheating. • v. (**fiddles, fiddling, fiddled**) **1** touch or handle something restlessly or nervously. **2** informal, esp. Brit. falsify: *everyone is fiddling their expenses.* **3** informal play the violin.
– PHRASES **fit as a fiddle** very healthy. **play second fiddle** take a less important role than someone else.
– DERIVATIVES **fiddler** n.
– ORIGIN Old English.

fiddlesticks • exclam. informal, dated nonsense.

fiddly • adj. Brit. informal complicated and awkward to do or use.

fidelity /fi-del-i-ti/ • n. **1** continuing faithfulness to a person, cause, or belief. **2** the degree of exactness with which something is copied or reproduced.
– ORIGIN Latin *fidelis* 'faithful'.

fidget /fi-jit/ • v. (**fidgets, fidgeting, fidgeted**) make small movements through nervousness or impatience. • n. a person who fidgets.
– DERIVATIVES **fidgety** adj.
– ORIGIN from former *fidge* 'to twitch'.

fief /feef/ • n. **1** a person's area of operation or control. **2** hist. a piece of land held in return for feudal service.
– DERIVATIVES **fiefdom** n.
– ORIGIN Old French.

field • n. **1** an area of open land, planted with crops or used for grazing animals. **2** a piece of land used for a sport or game. **3** a subject of study or area of activity. **4** a space within which a particular property has an effect: *a magnetic field.* **5** a range within which objects are visible. **6** (**the field**) all the participants in a contest or sport. **7** a

scene of a battle or a military campaign. • v. **1** Cricket & Baseball attempt to catch or stop the ball and return it after it has been hit. **2** select someone to play in a game or to stand in an election. **3** try to deal with: *we frantically fielded phone calls.* • adj. **1** carried out or working in the natural environment, rather than in a laboratory or office. **2** (of military equipment) light and mobile for use on campaign.
– PHRASES **in the field 1** (of troops) engaged in combat or manoeuvres. **2** engaged in practical work in the natural environment. **play the field** informal have a series of casual sexual relationships.
– DERIVATIVES **fielder** n.
– ORIGIN Old English.

field day • n. an opportunity to do something in a free and unrestricted way.

field events • pl. n. athletic sports other than races, such as throwing and jumping events.

fieldfare • n. a large thrush with a grey head.
– ORIGIN Old English.

field glasses • pl. n. binoculars.

field marshal • n. the highest rank of officer in the British army.

field mouse • n. a common dark brown mouse with a long tail and large eyes.

field officer • n. a major, lieutenant colonel, or colonel.

field sports • pl. n. the sports of hunting, shooting, and fishing.

field test (also **field trial**) • n. a test carried out in the place in which a product is to be used.

field trip • n. an expedition made by students or research workers to study something at first hand.

fieldwork • n. practical work carried out by a researcher in the field.

fiend /feend/ • n. **1** an evil spirit. **2** a very wicked or cruel person. **3** informal an enthusiast: *an exercise fiend.*
– ORIGIN Old English, 'an enemy'.

fiendish • adj. **1** very cruel or unpleasant. **2** informal very difficult.
– DERIVATIVES **fiendishly** adv.

fierce • adj. **1** violent or aggressive. **2** intense or powerful: *fierce opposition.*
– DERIVATIVES **fiercely** adv. **fierceness** n.
– ORIGIN Latin *ferus* 'untamed'.

☑ **fierce** follows the usual rule of *i* before *e* except after *c*.

fiery • adj. (**fierier, fieriest**) **1** consisting of or resembling fire. **2** quick-tempered or passionate.

fiesta /fi-ess-tuh/ • n. (in Spanish-speaking countries) a religious festival.
– ORIGIN Spanish.

FIFA /fee-fuh/ • abbrev. Fédération Internationale de Football Association, the international governing body of football.

fife • n. a small high-pitched flute played in military bands.
– ORIGIN German *Pfeife* 'pipe'.

fifteen • cardinal number **1** one more than fourteen; 15. (Roman numeral: **xv** or **XV**.) **2** a Rugby Union team of fifteen players.
– DERIVATIVES **fifteenth** ordinal number.
– ORIGIN Old English.

fifth • ordinal number **1** that is number five in a sequence; 5th. **2** (**a fifth/one fifth**) each of five equal parts into which something is divided. **3** a musical interval spanning five consecutive notes in a scale.

fifth column • n. a group within a country at war who are working for its enemies.
– DERIVATIVES **fifth columnist** n.
– ORIGIN from a general in the Spanish Civil War, who while leading four columns of troops towards Madrid, said that he had a fifth column inside the city.

fifty • cardinal number (pl. **fifties**) ten less than sixty; 50. (Roman numeral: **l** or **L**.)
– DERIVATIVES **fiftieth** ordinal number.
– ORIGIN Old English.

fifty-fifty • adj. & adv. with equal shares or chances.

fig • n. a soft sweet pear-shaped fruit with many small seeds.
– ORIGIN Latin *ficus*.

fight • v. (**fights, fighting, fought**) **1** take part in a violent struggle involving physical force or weapons. **2** take part in a war or contest. **3** (**fight someone off**) defend yourself against an attack. **4** struggle to overcome or prevent. **5** try very hard to obtain or do: *doctors fought to save his life.* • n. an act of fighting.
– PHRASES **fight shy of** avoid something you are worried or unhappy about. **fight your way** move forward with difficulty.
– ORIGIN Old English.

fighter • n. **1** a person or animal that fights. **2** a fast military aircraft designed for attacking other aircraft.

fighting chance • n. a possibility of success if great effort is made.

fighting fit • adj. in excellent health.

fig leaf • n. a leaf of a fig tree, often in art depicted as covering the genitals of naked figures.

figment /fig-muhnt/ • n. a thing that

exists only in the imagination.
– ORIGIN Latin *figmentum*.

figurative • adj. **1** not using words in their literal sense; metaphorical. **2** (of art) representing people or things as they appear in real life.
– DERIVATIVES **figuratively** adv.

figure • n. **1** a number or numerical symbol. **2** a person's bodily shape, especially that of a woman. **3** an important or distinctive person: *senior figures in politics.* **4** a geometric or decorative shape defined by one or more lines. **5** a diagram or illustrative drawing. **6** a short succession of musical notes from which longer passages are developed. • v. (**figures, figuring, figured**) **1** play an important part: *nuclear policy figured prominently in the talks.* **2** calculate arithmetically. **3** (**figure someone/thing out**) informal understand someone or something. **4** N. Amer. informal think; consider.
– ORIGIN Latin *figura*.

figurehead • n. **1** a leader without real power. **2** a carved bust or full-length figure at the prow of an old-fashioned sailing ship.

figure of speech • n. a word or phrase used in a non-literal sense to add interest to speech or writing.

figure skating • n. ice skating in which the skater combines a number of movements including steps, jumps, and turns.

figurine /fi-guh-reen/ • n. a small statue of a human form.
– ORIGIN Italian *figurina* 'small figure'.

Fijian /fee-jee-uhn/ • n. a person from Fiji, a country in the South Pacific consisting of some 840 islands. • adj. relating to Fiji.

filament /fil-uh-muhnt/ • n. **1** a slender thread-like object. **2** a metal wire in an electric light bulb, which glows white-hot when an electric current is passed through it.
– ORIGIN Latin *filamentum*.

filbert • n. a cultivated hazelnut.
– ORIGIN from French *noix de filbert* (because it ripens around 20 August, the feast day of St *Philibert*).

filch • v. informal steal something.

file¹ • n. **1** a folder or box for keeping loose papers together and in order. **2** a collection of computer data or programs stored under a single identifying name. **3** a line of people or things one behind another. • v. (**files, filing, filed**) **1** place in a file. **2** place a legal document, application, or charge on record. **3** walk one behind the other.
– ORIGIN Latin *filum* 'a thread'.

file² • n. a tool with a roughened surface, used for smoothing or shaping. • v. (**files, filing, filed**) smooth or shape with a file.
– ORIGIN Old English.

filename • n. an identifying name given to a computer file.

filial /fil-i-uhl/ • adj. relating to a son or daughter.
– ORIGIN Latin *filialis*.

filibuster /fil-i-buss-ter/ • n. (in parliament) the prolonging of speeches in order to obstruct the passing of a new law. • v. (**filibusters, filibustering, filibustered**) obstruct legislation with prolonged speeches.
– ORIGIN French *flibustier*, first referring to pirates in the West Indies.

filigree /fil-i-gree/ • n. delicate ornamental work of fine interlaced gold, silver, or copper wire.
– DERIVATIVES **filigreed** adj.
– ORIGIN from Latin *filum* 'thread' + *granum* 'seed'.

filings • pl. n. small particles rubbed off by a file.

Filipino /fi-li-pee-noh/ • n. (pl. **Filipinos**; fem. **Filipina**, pl. **Filipinas**) **1** a person from the Philippines. **2** the national language of the Philippines. • adj. relating to the Philippines or to Filipinos.

fill • v. **1** make or become full. **2** block up a hole or gap. **3** be an overwhelming presence in: *the smell of garlic filled the air.* **4** make someone experience a feeling. **5** satisfy a need. **6** occupy time. **7** hold and perform the duties of a position or role. • n. (**your fill**) as much as you want or can bear.
– PHRASES **fill in** act as a substitute. **fill someone in** give someone information. **fill something in** Brit. complete a form. **fill out** put on weight.
– ORIGIN Old English.

filler • n. something used to fill a gap or cavity, or to increase bulk.

fillet • n. **1** a boneless cut of meat or piece of fish. **2** a band or ribbon used for tying back the hair. • v. (**fillets, filleting, filleted**) remove the bones from a fish.
– ORIGIN Old French *filet* 'thread'.

filling • n. a quantity or piece of material used to fill something. • adj. (of food) leaving you with a pleasantly full feeling.

filling station • n. a petrol station.

fillip /fil-lip/ • n. a stimulus or boost.

filly • n. (pl. **fillies**) **1** a young female horse. **2** humorous a lively girl or young woman.
– ORIGIN Old Norse.

film • n. **1** a thin flexible strip of plastic or other material coated with light-

sensitive material, used in a camera to make photos or motion pictures. **2** a story or event recorded by a camera and shown in a cinema or on television. **3** motion pictures considered as an art or industry: *feminist writings on film.* **4** material in the form of a very thin flexible sheet. **5** a thin layer covering a surface. • v. make a film of.
– ORIGIN Old English, 'membrane'.

filmy • adj. **1** thin and almost transparent: *a filmy black dress.* **2** covered with a thin film.

filo /fee-loh/ (also **phyllo**) • n. a kind of flaky pastry in the form of very thin sheets, made in Greece.
– ORIGIN modern Greek *phullo* 'leaf'.

Filofax /fy-loh-faks/ • n. trademark a loose-leaf notebook for recording appointments, addresses, and notes.

filter • n. **1** a device or substance that allows liquid or gas to pass through it, but holds back any solid particles. **2** a screen, plate, or layer which absorbs some of the light passing through it. **3** Brit. an arrangement at a junction whereby vehicles may turn while traffic waiting to go straight ahead is stopped by a red light. • v. (**filters**, **filtering**, **filtered**) **1** pass through a filter. **2** move gradually in or out of somewhere. **3** (of information) gradually become known.
– ORIGIN Latin *filtrum* 'felt used as a filter'.

filter tip • n. a filter attached to a cigarette that traps impurities from the smoke.

filth • n. **1** disgusting dirt. **2** obscene and offensive language or printed material.
– ORIGIN Old English.

filthy • adj. (**filthier**, **filthiest**) **1** disgustingly dirty. **2** obscene and offensive. **3** informal very unpleasant. • adv. informal extremely: *filthy rich.*
– DERIVATIVES **filthily** adv. **filthiness** n.

filtrate /fil-trayt/ • n. a liquid that has passed through a filter.

filtration /fil-tray-sh'n/ • n. the action of passing something through a filter.

fin • n. **1** a flattened part that projects from the body of a fish, dolphin, or whale, used for swimming and balancing. **2** a part that projects from an aircraft, rocket, or car, for providing stability.
– ORIGIN Old English.

final • adj. **1** coming at the end; last. **2** allowing no further doubt or discussion: *the decision of the judges is final.* • n. **1** the last game in a tournament, which will decide the overall winner. **2** (**finals**) Brit. a series of exams at the end of a degree course.
– ORIGIN Latin *finalis.*

finale /fi-nah-li/ • n. the last part of a piece of music, an entertainment, or a public event.
– ORIGIN Italian.

finalist • n. a person or team competing in a final.

finality • n. the fact or quality of being final.

finalize (or **finalise**) • v. (**finalizes**, **finalizing**, **finalized**) decide on or complete a plan or agreement.
– DERIVATIVES **finalization** n.

finally • adv. **1** after a long time and much difficulty. **2** as a final point.

finance /fy-nanss/ • n. **1** the management of large amounts of money by governments or large organizations. **2** funds to support an enterprise. **3** (**finances**) the money available to a state, organization, or person. • v. (**finances**, **financing**, **financed**) provide funding for.
– ORIGIN Old French.

financial • adj. relating to finance.
– DERIVATIVES **financially** adv.

financial year • n. a year as reckoned for taxing or accounting purposes, especially the British tax year reckoned from 6 April.

financier /fy-nan-si-er/ • n. a person who manages the finances of large organizations.
– ORIGIN French.

finch • n. a songbird of a large group including the chaffinch and goldfinch, most of which have short stubby bills.
– ORIGIN Old English.

find • v. (**finds**, **finding**, **found**) **1** discover by chance or by searching. **2** recognize or discover to be present or to be the case. **3** work out or confirm by research or calculation. **4** (of a law court) officially declare to be the case: *he was found guilty of speeding.* **5** reach or arrive at a state or point by a natural or normal process: *water finds its own level.* • n. a valuable or interesting discovery.
– PHRASES **find your feet** become confident in a new situation. **find someone out** discover that someone has lied or been dishonest. **find something out** discover information.
– ORIGIN Old English.

finder • n. **1** a person who finds someone or something. **2** a viewfinder in a camera.

finding • n. a conclusion reached as a result of an inquiry, investigation, or trial.

fine¹ • adj. **1** of very high quality. **2** satisfactory. **3** healthy and feeling

well. **4** (of the weather) bright and clear. **5** (of a thread, strand, or hair) thin. **6** consisting of small particles: *fine sand.* **7** of delicate or complex workmanship. **8** difficult to distinguish because precise or subtle: *the ear makes fine distinctions between different noises.* • **adv.** informal in a satisfactory or pleasing way.
– PHRASES **cut it fine** allow only just enough time for something.
– DERIVATIVES **finely** adv. **fineness** n.
– ORIGIN Old French *fin.*

fine² • n. a sum of money imposed as a punishment by a court of law or other authority. • v. (**fines, fining, fined**) punish someone by ordering them to pay a sum of money.
– ORIGIN Old French *fin* 'end, payment'.

fine art • n. art intended to appeal to the sense of beauty, such as painting or sculpture.

fine print • n. = SMALL PRINT.

finery /fy-nuh-ri/ • n. showy clothes or decoration.

finesse /fi-ness/ • n. **1** elegant or delicate skill: *his acting showed dignity and finesse.* **2** subtle skill in handling people or situations. • v. (**finesses, finessing, finessed**) do something in a skilful and delicate way.
– ORIGIN French.

fine-tooth comb (also **fine-toothed comb**) • n. (in phr. **with a fine-tooth comb**) with a very thorough search or examination.

fine-tune • v. (**fine-tunes, fine-tuning, fine-tuned**) make small adjustments to something so as to improve its performance.

finger • n. **1** each of the four jointed parts attached along with the thumb to either side of the hand. **2** a measure of a drink in a glass, based on the breadth of a finger. **3** a long, narrow object or area: *a finger of white sand.* • v. (**fingers, fingering, fingered**) touch or feel with the fingers.
– PHRASES **be all fingers and thumbs** Brit. informal be clumsy. **lay a finger on** touch someone with the intention of harming them. **pull your finger out** Brit. informal stop hesitating and start to act. **put your finger on** identify something exactly.
– ORIGIN Old English.

fingerboard • n. a flat strip on the neck of a stringed instrument, against which the strings are pressed in order to vary the pitch.

finger food • n. food that can conveniently be eaten with the fingers.

fingering • n. a technique of using the fingers to play a musical instrument.

fingernail • n. the nail on the upper surface of the tip of each finger.

fingerprint • n. a mark made on a surface by a person's fingertip, used for identification. • v. record the fingerprints of.

fingertip • n. the tip of a finger.
– PHRASES **at your fingertips** (of information) readily available to you.

finial /fin-i-uhl/ • n. an ornament at the top of an architectural structure such as a gable or spire.
– ORIGIN Latin *finis* 'end'.

finicky • adj. **1** fussy. **2** excessively detailed or elaborate.
– ORIGIN prob. from FINE¹.

finish • v. **1** bring or come to an end. **2** consume what is left of a meal or drink. **3** (**finish with**) Brit. have nothing more to do with. **4** reach the end of a race or other sporting competition. **5** (**finish someone off**) kill or completely defeat someone. **6** complete the manufacture or decoration of something by giving it an attractive surface appearance. • n. **1** an end or final stage. **2** the place at which a race or competition ends. **3** the way in which a manufactured article is finished.
– DERIVATIVES **finisher** n.
– ORIGIN Latin *finire.*

finishing school • n. a private college where girls are taught how to behave correctly in fashionable society.

finishing touch • n. a detail that completes and improves a piece of work.

finite /fy-nyt/ • adj. limited in size or extent: *every computer has a finite amount of memory.*
– DERIVATIVES **finitely** adv.
– ORIGIN Latin *finitus* 'finished'.

Finn • n. a person from Finland.

Finnish • n. the language of the Finns. • adj. relating to the Finns.

fiord • n. var. of FJORD.

fir • n. an evergreen coniferous tree with upright cones and needle-shaped leaves.
– ORIGIN prob. Old Norse.

fire • n. **1** the state of burning, in which substances combine with oxygen from the air and give out light, heat, and smoke. **2** an instance of burning in which something is destroyed. **3** wood or coal that is burning in a hearth or stove for heating or cooking. **4** (also **electric fire** or **gas fire**) esp. Brit. a heater for a room that uses electricity or gas as fuel. **5** passionate emotion or enthusiasm. **6** the firing of guns.
• v. (**fires, firing, fired**) **1** shoot a bullet, shell, or missile from a gun or other weapon. **2** informal dismiss an employee from a job. **3** direct a rapid series of questions or statements towards someone. **4** stimulate: *the idea fired his*

imagination. **5** supply a furnace, power station, etc. with fuel. **6** bake pottery or bricks at high temperatures in a kiln. **7** old use set fire to.
– PHRASES **catch fire** begin to burn. **fire away** informal go ahead. **set fire to** (or **set something on fire**) cause something to burn. **set the world on fire** do something remarkable or sensational. **under fire** being shot at or strongly criticized.
– ORIGIN Old English.

fire alarm • n. a device that rings loudly to give warning of a fire.

firearm • n. a rifle, pistol, or other portable gun.

firebomb • n. a bomb intended to cause a fire.

firebrand • n. a person who passionately supports a particular cause.

firebreak • n. a strip of open space in a forest, created to stop a fire from spreading.

fire brigade • n. Brit. an organized body of firefighters employed to put out fires.

firecracker • n. a firework that makes a loud bang.

fire door • n. a door made of fire-resistant material to prevent the spread of fire.

fire drill • n. a practice of the emergency procedures to be used in case of fire.

fire engine • n. a vehicle carrying firefighters and their equipment.

fire escape • n. a staircase or ladder used for escaping from a building if there is a fire.

fire extinguisher • n. a portable device that discharges a jet of liquid, foam, or gas to put out a fire.

firefighter • n. a person whose job is to put out fires.

firefly • n. (pl. **fireflies**) a kind of beetle which glows in the dark.

fireguard • n. a protective screen placed in front of an open fire.

firelighter • n. Brit. a piece of flammable material used to help start a fire.

fireman • n. (pl. **firemen**) a male firefighter.

fireplace • n. a partially enclosed space at the base of a chimney for a domestic fire.

firepower • n. the destructive capacity of guns, missiles, or a military force.

fireproof • adj. able to withstand fire or great heat.

fireside • n. the part of a room round a fireplace.

fire station • n. the headquarters of a fire brigade.

firestorm • n. a very fierce fire, fanned by strong currents of air drawn in from the surrounding area.

firetrap • n. a building without enough fire exits for use in the case of a fire.

firewall • n. a part of a computer system or network that blocks unauthorized access while allowing outward communication.

firewater • n. informal strong alcoholic drink.

firewood • n. wood that is burnt as fuel.

firework • n. **1** a device containing chemicals that is ignited to produce spectacular effects and explosions. **2** (**fireworks**) an outburst of anger or a display of skill.

firing line • n. **1** the front line of troops in a battle. **2** a position in which someone is likely to be criticized: *the prime minister is in the firing line again.*

firing squad • n. a group of soldiers ordered to shoot a condemned person.

firm¹ • adj. **1** having a surface or structure that does not give way or sink under pressure. **2** solidly in place and stable. **3** having steady power or strength: *a firm grip.* **4** showing determination and strength of character. **5** fixed or definite: *she had no firm plans.* • v. make firm. • adv. in a determined way: *she stood firm against the proposal.*
– DERIVATIVES **firmly** adv. **firmness** n.
– ORIGIN Latin *firmus.*

firm² • n. a business organization.
– ORIGIN Latin *firmare* 'settle'.

firmament /fer-muh-muhnt/ • n. literary the heavens; the sky.
– ORIGIN Latin *firmamentum.*

firmware • n. permanent computer software programmed into a read-only memory.

first • ordinal number **1** coming before all others in time, order, or importance; 1st. **2** before doing something else. **3** informal something never previously done or occurring: *travelling by air was a first for us.* **4** Brit. a place in the top grade in an exam for a degree.
– PHRASES **at first** at the beginning. **of the first order** of the highest quality.
– ORIGIN Old English.

first aid • n. emergency medical help given to a sick or injured person before full treatment is available.

firstborn • n. the first child to be born to someone.

first class • n. **1** a set of people or things grouped together as the best. **2** the best accommodation in an aircraft, train, or ship. **3** Brit. the highest division in the results of the exams for a university degree. •adj. & adv. relating to the best class or grade.

first-day cover •n. an envelope with one or more stamps postmarked on their day of issue.

first-degree •adj. (of burns) affecting only the surface of the skin and causing reddening.

first-foot •v. be the first person to cross someone's threshold in the New Year. •n. (also **first-footer**) the first person to cross someone's threshold in the New Year.

first-hand •adj. & adv. from the original source or personal experience; direct.
– PHRASES **at first hand** directly.

first lady •n. the wife of the President of the United States.

firstly •adv. first (used to introduce a first point).

first mate •n. the officer second in command to the master of a merchant ship.

first name •n. a personal name given to someone at birth or baptism and used before a surname.
– PHRASES **be on first-name terms** have a friendly relationship.

first night •n. the first public performance of a play or show.

first officer •n. **1** the first mate on a merchant ship. **2** the second in command to the captain on an aircraft.

first person •n. see PERSON (sense 3).

first-rate •adj. excellent.

firth •n. a narrow inlet of the sea, especially in Scotland.
– ORIGIN Old Norse.

fiscal /fiss-k'l/ •adj. relating to the income received by a government, especially as raised through taxes.
– DERIVATIVES **fiscally** adv.
– ORIGIN Latin *fiscalis*.

fish¹ •n. (pl. **fish** or **fishes**) **1** a cold-blooded animal with a backbone, gills, and fins, living in water. **2** the flesh of fish as food. •v. **1** catch or try to catch fish. **2** (**fish something out**) pull or take something out of water or a container. **3** (**fish for**) search or feel for something hidden. **4** (**fish for**) try to obtain a response by indirect means: *I was not fishing for compliments.*
– PHRASES **a big fish** an important person. **a fish out of water** a person who feels out of place in their surroundings. **have other** (or **bigger**) **fish to fry** have more important matters to attend to.
– DERIVATIVES **fishing** n.
– ORIGIN Old English.

USAGE: When referring to more than one fish, the normal plural is **fish** (*he caught two fish*). When talking about different kinds of fish, however, you can use **fishes**: *freshwater fishes of the British Isles.*

fish² (also **fishplate**) •n. a flat piece fixed across a joint to strengthen or connect it.
– ORIGIN prob. from French *ficher* 'to fix'.

fish cake •n. a flattened round cake of shredded fish mixed with mashed potato.

fisherman •n. (pl. **fishermen**) a person who catches fish for a living or for sport.

fishery •n. (pl. **fisheries**) **1** a place where fish are reared for food, or caught in numbers. **2** the industry of catching or rearing fish.

fisheye •n. a highly curved lens for a camera, covering a very wide angle of view.

fish finger •n. Brit. a small oblong piece of flaked or minced fish coated in batter or breadcrumbs.

fishing line •n. a long thread of silk or nylon attached to a baited hook and used for catching fish.

fishing rod •n. a long, tapering rod to which a fishing line is attached.

fishmonger •n. a person who sells fish for food.

fishnet •n. an open mesh fabric resembling a fishing net.

fishtail •n. an object which is forked like a fish's tail.

fishwife •n. a coarse-mannered woman with a loud voice.

fishy •adj. (**fishier**, **fishiest**) **1** relating to or like fish. **2** informal causing feelings of doubt or suspicion.

fissile /fiss-yl/ •adj. **1** (of an atom or element) able to undergo nuclear fission. **2** (of rock) easily split.
– ORIGIN Latin *fissilis*.

fission /fi-sh'n/ •n. **1** the action of splitting into two or more parts. **2** a reaction in which an atomic nucleus splits in two, releasing much energy. **3** Biol. reproduction by means of a cell dividing into two or more new cells.

fissure /fish-er/ •n. a long, narrow crack.
– ORIGIN Latin *fissura*.

fist •n. a person's hand when the fingers are bent in towards the palm and held there tightly.
– DERIVATIVES **fistful** n.
– ORIGIN Old English.

fisticuffs •pl. n. fighting involving punches with the fists.

fit¹ •adj. (**fitter**, **fittest**) **1** of a suitable quality or type to meet the required

purpose: *food fit for human consumption.*
2 having the necessary qualities or skills to do something well. **3** in good health. •v. (**fits, fitting, fitted**) **1** be the right shape and size for. **2** be able to occupy a particular position or space. **3** fix into place. **4** provide with a part or article. **5** be in harmony with; match: *the punishment should fit the crime.* **6** make someone ready for a role or task: *an MSc fits the student for a professional career.* **7** try clothing on someone in order to alter it to the correct size. •n. the way in which something fits.
– PHRASES **fit in** be well suited or in harmony. **fit someone/thing out** (or **up**) provide someone or something with necessary items. **fit to bust** informal with great energy. **see** (or **think**) **fit to** consider it correct or acceptable.
– DERIVATIVES **fitness** n.

fit² •n. **1** a sudden attack of an illness, in which a person makes violent, uncontrolled movements and often loses consciousness. **2** a sudden short period of coughing, laughing, etc. **3** a sudden burst of strong feeling. •v. (**fits, fitting, fitted**) have an epileptic fit.
– PHRASES **in** (or **by**) **fits and starts** with irregular bursts of activity.
– ORIGIN Old English, 'conflict'.

fitful •adj. disturbed and erratic or restless: *a few hours' fitful sleep.*
– DERIVATIVES **fitfully** adv.

fitment •n. Brit. a fixed item of furniture or piece of equipment.

fitted •adj. **1** made to fill a space or to cover something closely. **2** esp. Brit. (of a room) equipped with matching units of furniture.

fitter •n. **1** a person who fits together or installs machinery. **2** a person who fits clothes.

fitting •n. **1** a small part attached to furniture or equipment. **2** (**fittings**) esp. Brit. items which are fixed in a building but can be removed when the owner moves. **3** an occasion when someone tries on a garment that is being made or altered. •adj. appropriate.
– DERIVATIVES **fittingly** adv.

five •cardinal number one more than four; 5. (Roman numeral: **v** or **V**.)
– DERIVATIVES **fivefold** adj. & adv.
– ORIGIN Old English.

fiver •n. Brit. informal a five-pound note.

fix •v. **1** attach or position securely. **2** repair something. **3** decide or settle on. **4** make arrangements for. **5** make unchanging or permanent: *the rate of interest is fixed for five years.* **6** (**fix on**) direct a look or the eyes steadily towards. **7** informal influence the outcome

of something in an underhand way: *the club attempted to fix the match.* •n. informal **1** a difficult or awkward situation. **2** a dose of a narcotic drug to which you are addicted. **3** an act of fixing.
– PHRASES **be fixed for** informal be provided with: *how are you fixed for money?* **fix something up** arrange or organize something. **fix someone up** informal provide someone with something. **get a fix on** find out the position, nature, or facts of.
– DERIVATIVES **fixer** n.
– ORIGIN Latin *fixus* 'fixed'.

fixate /fik-sayt/ •v. (**fixates, fixating, fixated**) (**fixate on** or **be fixated on**) be interested in someone or something to an excessive extent.

fixation •n. **1** an excessive interest in someone or something. **2** the process by which some plants and microorganisms combine chemically with nitrogen or carbon dioxide in the air to form solid compounds.

fixative /fiks-uh-tiv/ •n. a substance used to fix, protect, or stabilize something.

fixings •pl. n. Brit. screws, bolts, or other items used to fix or assemble building components, furniture, or equipment.

fixity •n. the state of being permanent.

fixture •n. **1** a piece of equipment or furniture which is fixed in position. **2** (**fixtures**) articles attached to a house or land and considered legally part of it so that they normally remain in place when an owner moves. **3** Brit. a sporting event which takes place on a particular date. **4** informal a person or thing that has become firmly established.

fizz •v. make a hissing sound, as when gas escapes in bubbles from a liquid. •n. **1** the quality of being fizzy. **2** informal a fizzy drink. **3** liveliness.

fizzle •v. (**fizzles, fizzling, fizzled**) **1** make a weak hissing sound. **2** (**fizzle out**) end or fail in a weak or disappointing way.

fizzy •adj. (**fizzier, fizziest**) (of a drink) containing bubbles of gas.
– DERIVATIVES **fizziness** n.

fjord /fyord, fee-ord/ (also **fiord**) •n. a long, narrow, deep inlet of the sea between high cliffs, especially in Norway.
– ORIGIN Norwegian.

fl. •abbrev. **1** floruit. **2** fluid.

flab •n. informal excess fat on a person's body.

flabbergast /flab-ber-gahst/ •v. (usu. as adj. **flabbergasted**) informal surprise someone greatly.

flabby • adj. (**flabbier**, **flabbiest**) **1** (of a part of a person's body) fat and floppy. **2** weak or unsuccessful because not tightly controlled: *a flabby documentary epic.*
– DERIVATIVES **flabbiness** n.
– ORIGIN from **FLAP**.

flaccid /ˈflass-id, ˈflak-sid/ • adj. soft and limp.
– DERIVATIVES **flaccidity** n.
– ORIGIN Latin *flaccus* 'flabby'.

flag[1] • n. a piece of cloth that is attached to a pole or rope and used as a symbol of a country or organization or as a signal. • v. (**flags**, **flagging**, **flagged**) **1** mark something for attention. **2** (**flag someone down**) signal to a driver to stop.

flag[2] (also **flagstone**) • n. a flat rectangular or square stone slab, used for paving.
– DERIVATIVES **flagged** adj.
– ORIGIN prob. Scandinavian.

flag[3] • n. a plant of the iris family.

flag[4] • v. (**flags**, **flagging**, **flagged**) **1** become tired or less enthusiastic. **2** (as adj. **flagging**) losing vigour or strength: *a flagging computer business.*
– ORIGIN related to **FLAG**[1].

flag day • n. Brit. a day on which street collections are made for a charity and contributors are given paper badges to wear.

flagellate[1] /ˈfla-juh-layt/ • v. (**flagellates**, **flagellating**, **flagellated**) whip someone, either as a form of religious punishment or for sexual pleasure.
– DERIVATIVES **flagellation** n.
– ORIGIN Latin *flagellare.*

flagellate[2] /ˈfla-juh-luht/ • adj. (of a single-celled organism) having a flagellum or flagella for swimming.

flagellum /fluh-ˈjel-luhm/ • n. (pl. **flagella** /fluh-ˈjel-luh/) Biol. a long, thin projection which enables many single-celled organisms to swim.
– ORIGIN Latin, 'little whip'.

flageolet /ˈfla-juh-lay/ • n. a very small flute-like instrument resembling a recorder.
– ORIGIN French.

flagon /ˈfla-guhn/ • n. a large bottle or other container in which wine, cider, or beer is sold or served.
– ORIGIN Latin *flasco.*

flagpole (also **flagstaff**) • n. a pole used for flying a flag.

flagrant /ˈflay-gruhnt/ • adj. very obvious and unashamed: *a flagrant violation of the law.*
– DERIVATIVES **flagrantly** adv.
– ORIGIN Latin *flagrare* 'blaze'.

flagship • n. **1** the ship in a fleet which carries the commanding admiral. **2** the best or most important thing owned or produced by an organization.

flail /flayl/ • v. **1** swing the arms or legs wildly. **2** (**flail around/about**) struggle to make your way. • n. a tool or machine with a swinging action, used for threshing grain.
– ORIGIN Latin *flagellum* 'little whip'.

flair • n. **1** a natural ability or talent. **2** stylishness.
– ORIGIN French.

> USAGE: On the confusion of **flair** with **flare**, see the note at **FLARE**.

flak • n. **1** anti-aircraft fire. **2** strong criticism.
– ORIGIN from German *Fliegerabwehrkanone* 'aviator-defence gun'.

flake[1] • n. a small, flat, very thin piece of something. • v. (**flakes**, **flaking**, **flaked**) **1** come away from a surface in flakes: *the paint was flaking off.* **2** separate into flakes.
– ORIGIN prob. Germanic.

flake[2] • v. (**flakes**, **flaking**, **flaked**) (**flake out**) informal fall asleep or drop from exhaustion.
– ORIGIN from **FLAG**[4].

flak jacket • n. a sleeveless jacket reinforced with metal, worn as protection against bullets and shrapnel.

flaky • adj. (**flakier**, **flakiest**) breaking or separating easily into flakes.
– DERIVATIVES **flakiness** n.

flambé /ˈflom-bay/ • v. (**flambés**, **flambéing**, **flambéed**) cover food with spirits and set it alight briefly.
– ORIGIN French, 'singed'.

flamboyant /flam-ˈboy-uhnt/ • adj. **1** confident and lively in a noticeable way. **2** brightly coloured or highly decorated.
– DERIVATIVES **flamboyance** n. **flamboyantly** adv.
– ORIGIN French, 'flaming, blazing'.

flame • n. **1** a hot glowing body of ignited gas produced by something on fire. **2** a brilliant orange-red colour. • v. (**flames**, **flaming**, **flamed**) **1** give off flames. **2** (of a strong emotion) appear suddenly. **3** informal send insulting or hostile email messages to.
– PHRASES **old flame** informal a former lover.
– ORIGIN Latin *flamma.*

flamenco /fluh-ˈmeng-koh/ • n. a style of Spanish guitar music accompanied by singing and dancing.
– ORIGIN Spanish, 'like a Gypsy, Flemish'.

flame-thrower • n. a weapon that

sprays out burning fuel.

flaming •adj. **1** sending out flames. **2** very hot. **3** (of an argument) passionate. **4** informal expressing annoyance.

flamingo /fluh-**ming**-goh/ •n. (pl. **flamingos** or **flamingoes**) a wading bird with mainly pink or scarlet plumage and a long neck and legs.
– ORIGIN Spanish *flamengo*.

flammable /**flam**-muh-b'l/ •adj. easily set on fire.

flan •n. a baked dish consisting of an open pastry case with a savoury or sweet filling.
– ORIGIN Old French *flaon*.

flange /flanj/ •n. a projecting flat rim on an object, for strengthening it or attaching it to something.
– DERIVATIVES **flanged** adj.
– ORIGIN perh. from Old French *flanchir* 'to bend'.

flank •n. **1** the side of the body between the ribs and the hip. **2** the side of something such as a building or mountain. **3** the left or right side of a group of people. •v. be on each or one side of: *the hall was flanked by two towers.*
– ORIGIN Old French *flanc*.

flanker •n. Rugby a wing forward.

flannel •n. **1** a kind of softly woven woollen fabric. **2** (**flannels**) men's trousers made of a soft woollen fabric. **3** Brit. a small piece of towelling for washing yourself. **4** Brit. informal empty or flattering talk used to avoid a difficult subject. •v. (**flannels, flannelling, flannelled**) Brit. informal use empty or flattering talk to avoid a difficult subject.
– ORIGIN prob. from Welsh *gwlanen* 'woollen article'.

flannelette /flan-nuh-**let**/ •n. a soft brushed cotton fabric resembling flannel.

flap •v. (**flaps, flapping, flapped**) **1** move up and down or from side to side. **2** Brit. informal be agitated. •n. **1** a piece attached to something on one side only, to cover an opening. **2** a movable section of an aircraft wing, used to control upward movement. **3** a single flapping movement. **4** informal a minor panic.
– DERIVATIVES **flappy** adj.

flapjack •n. Brit. a soft thick biscuit made from oats and butter.
– ORIGIN from FLAP (in the dialect sense 'toss a pancake') + JACK.

flapper •n. informal a fashionable and unconventional young woman of the 1920s.

flare •n. **1** a sudden brief burst of flame or light. **2** a device producing a very bright flame as a signal or marker. **3** a gradual widening towards the hem of a garment. **4** (**flares**) trousers whose legs widen from the knees down. •v. (**flares, flaring, flared**) **1** burn or shine with a sudden intensity. **2** suddenly become angry or more intense: *in 1943 the Middle East crisis flared up again.* **3** gradually become wider at one end.

> **USAGE:** Do not confuse **flare** with **flair**: **flare** means 'burn' or 'gradually become wider', whereas **flair** means 'a natural ability or talent'. Trousers whose legs widen from the knees down are **flared** not **flaired**.

flash •v. **1** shine with a bright but brief or irregular light. **2** move, pass, or send swiftly in a particular direction: *the scenery flashed by.* **3** display briefly or repeatedly. **4** informal display in an obvious way so as to impress: *they flash their money about.* **5** informal (of a man) show the genitals in public. •n. **1** a sudden brief burst of bright light. **2** a camera attachment that produces a flash of light, for taking photographs in poor light. **3** a sudden or brief occurrence: *a flash of inspiration.* **4** Brit. a coloured patch on a uniform, used to identify a regiment, country, etc. •adj. informal, esp. Brit. stylish or expensive in a showy way.
– PHRASES **flash in the pan** a sudden but brief success. **in a flash** very quickly.
– DERIVATIVES **flasher** n.

flashback •n. **1** a scene in a film or story set in a time earlier than the main story. **2** a sudden vivid memory of a past event.

flashbulb •n. a bulb for a flashgun.

flash flood •n. a sudden local flood resulting from very heavy rainfall.

flashgun •n. a device which gives a brief flash of light, used for taking photographs in poor light.

flashing •n. a strip of metal used to seal the junction of a roof with another surface.

flashlight •n. **1** an electric torch with a strong beam. **2** a flashgun.

flashpoint •n. **1** a point or place at which anger or violence flares up. **2** the temperature at which a flammable compound gives off enough vapour to ignite in air.

flashy •adj. (**flashier, flashiest**) attractive in a showy or cheap way.
– DERIVATIVES **flashily** adv. **flashiness** n.

flask •n. **1** a conical or round bottle with a narrow neck. **2** Brit. a vacuum flask.
– ORIGIN Latin *flasca* 'cask or bottle'.

flat¹ •adj. (**flatter, flattest**) **1** having a level and even surface. **2** not sloping; horizontal. **3** with a level surface and

little height: *a flat cap*. **4** lacking liveliness or interest: *a flat voice*. **5** (of a sparkling drink) no longer fizzy. **6** (of something kept inflated) having lost some or all of its air. **7** Brit. (of a battery) having used up its charge. **8** (of a charge or price) fixed. **9** definite and firm: *his statement was a flat denial*. **10** (of musical sound) below true or normal pitch. **11** (of a note or key) lower by a semitone than a specified note or key: *E flat*. • adv. **1** in or into a flat position or state. **2** informal completely; absolutely: *she turned him down flat*. **3** emphasizing speed: *in ten minutes flat*. • n. **1** the flat part of something. **2** (**flats**) an area of low level ground near water. **3** (**the Flat**) Brit. flat racing. **4** a musical note that is a semitone lower than the corresponding one of natural pitch, shown by the sign ♭.
– PHRASES **fall flat** fail to produce the intended effect. **flat out** as fast or as hard as possible.
– DERIVATIVES **flatly** adv. **flatness** n. **flattish** adj.
– ORIGIN Old Norse.

flat² • n. esp. Brit. a set of rooms forming an individual home within a larger building.
– DERIVATIVES **flatlet** n.
– ORIGIN Germanic.

flatbed • n. **1** a vehicle with a flat load-carrying area. **2** a scanner, plotter, or other device which keeps paper flat during use.

flat feet • pl. n. feet with arches that are lower than usual.

flatfish • n. (pl. **flatfish** or **flatfishes**) a sea fish, such as a plaice, that swims on its side and has both eyes on the upper side of its flattened body.

flat-footed • adj. **1** having flat feet. **2** informal clumsy.

flat iron • n. hist. an iron heated on a hotplate or fire.

flatmate • n. Brit. a person with whom you share a flat.

flat race • n. a horse race over a course with no jumps.
– DERIVATIVES **flat racing** n.

flatten • v. **1** make flat or flatter. **2** informal knock down.

flatter • v. (**flatters, flattering, flattered**) **1** compliment someone excessively or without meaning what you say. **2** (**be flattered**) feel honoured and pleased. **3** make someone appear attractive: *a green dress that flattered her skin*. **4** paint or draw someone so that they appear more attractive than in reality.
– DERIVATIVES **flatterer** n.
– ORIGIN Old French *flater*.

flattery • n. (pl. **flatteries**) excessive or insincere praise.

flatulent /flat-yuu-luhnt/
• adj. suffering from a build-up of gas in the intestines or stomach.
– DERIVATIVES **flatulence** n.
– ORIGIN Latin *flatus* 'blowing'.

flatworm • n. a type of worm, such as a tapeworm, with a simple flattened body.

flaunt • v. display proudly or obviously: *she flaunted her wealth*.

flautist /flaw-tist/ • n. a flute player.
– ORIGIN Italian *flautista*.

flavour (US **flavor**) • n. **1** the distinctive taste of a food or drink. **2** a particular quality: *balconies gave the building a Spanish flavour*. • v. give flavour to food or drink by adding an ingredient.
– PHRASES **flavour of the month** a person or thing that has recently become very popular.
– ORIGIN Old French *flaor* 'a smell'.

flavouring (US **flavoring**) • n. a substance used to give more flavour to food or drink.

flaw • n. **1** a mark or fault that spoils something. **2** a weakness or mistake. • v. (usu. as adj. **flawed**) spoil or weaken.
– DERIVATIVES **flawless** adj. **flawlessly** adv.
– ORIGIN perh. from Old Norse, 'stone slab'.

flax • n. **1** a blue-flowered plant that is grown for its seed (linseed) and for thread made from its stalks. **2** thread made from flax, used to make linen.
– ORIGIN Old English.

flaxen • adj. literary (of hair) pale yellow.

flay • v. **1** strip the skin from a body or carcass. **2** whip or beat very harshly. **3** criticize harshly.
– ORIGIN Old English.

flea • n. a small wingless jumping insect which feeds on the blood of mammals and birds.
– PHRASES **a flea in your ear** a sharp reprimand.
– ORIGIN Old English.

flea market • n. a street market selling second-hand goods.

fleapit • n. Brit. informal a run-down, dirty cinema.

fleck • n. **1** a very small patch of colour or light. **2** a small particle. • v. mark or dot with flecks.
– ORIGIN perh. from Old Norse.

fled past and past part. of FLEE.

fledge /flej/ • v. (**fledges, fledging, fledged**) **1** (of a young bird) develop wing feathers that are large enough for flight. **2** (as adj. **fledged**) having just taken on a particular role: *a newly fledged Detective Inspector*.

– ORIGIN Old English, 'ready to fly'.

fledgling (also **fledgeling**) •n. a young bird that has just acquired the ability to fly. •adj. new and inexperienced: *fledgling democracies.*

flee •v. (**flees, fleeing, fled**) run away.
– ORIGIN Old English.

fleece •n. **1** the wool coat of a sheep. **2** a soft, warm fabric with a pile, or a garment made from this. •v. (**fleeces, fleecing, fleeced**) informal swindle someone by charging them too much money.
– DERIVATIVES **fleecy** adj.
– ORIGIN Old English.

fleet¹ •n. **1** a group of ships, vehicles, or aircraft travelling together or having the same owner. **2** (**the fleet**) a country's navy.
– ORIGIN Old English.

fleet² •adj. fast and nimble.
– PHRASES **fleet of foot** able to walk or move swiftly.
– ORIGIN prob. from Old Norse.

fleeting •adj. lasting for a very short time.
– DERIVATIVES **fleetingly** adv.

Fleming /flem-ing/ •n. **1** a Flemish person. **2** a member of the Flemish-speaking people living in northern and western Belgium.

Flemish /flem-ish/ •n. **1** (**the Flemish**) the people of Flanders, a region divided between Belgium, France, and the Netherlands. **2** the Dutch language as spoken in Flanders. •adj. relating to Flanders or the Flemish.
– ORIGIN Dutch *Vlämisch.*

flesh •n. **1** the soft substance in the body consisting of muscle and fat. **2** the edible soft part of a fruit or vegetable. **3** (**the flesh**) the physical aspects and needs of the body: *pleasures of the flesh.* •v. (**flesh something out**) make something more detailed.
– PHRASES **your flesh and blood** a close relative; your family. **in the flesh** in person or (of a thing) in its actual state.
– ORIGIN Old English.

fleshly •adj. relating to the body and its needs.

fleshpots •pl. n. places where people can satisfy their sexual desires.
– ORIGIN from the *fleshpots of Egypt* mentioned in the Bible (Book of Exodus).

flesh wound •n. a wound that breaks the skin but does not damage bones or organs.

fleshy •adj. (**fleshier, fleshiest**) **1** having much flesh; plump. **2** (of leaves or fruit) soft and thick.
– DERIVATIVES **fleshiness** n.

fleur-de-lis /fler-duh-lee/ (also **fleur-de-lys**) •n. (pl. **fleurs-de-lis** /fler-duh-lee/) a representation of a lily made up of three petals tied together near their bases.
– ORIGIN Old French *flour de lys* 'flower of the lily'.

flew past of FLY¹.

flex¹ •v. **1** bend a limb or joint. **2** tighten a muscle. **3** warp or bend and then return to shape.
– ORIGIN Latin *flectere.*

flex² •n. Brit. a flexible insulated cable used for carrying electric current to an appliance.
– ORIGIN from FLEXIBLE.

flexible •adj. **1** able to bend easily without breaking. **2** able to change or be changed to adapt to different circumstances.
– DERIVATIVES **flexibility** n. **flexibly** adv.

flexion /flek-sh'n/ •n. the action of bending or the state of being bent.

flexitime •n. a system allowing some flexibility as to when employees start and finish work, as long as they work a set number of hours.

flibbertigibbet /flib-ber-ti-jib-bit/ •n. a person who is not interested in serious things.

flick •v. **1** make a sudden sharp movement. **2** hit or remove with a quick light movement. **3** (**flick through**) look quickly through a book, magazine, etc. •n. **1** a sudden sharp movement up and down or from side to side. **2** (**the flicks**) Brit. informal the cinema.

flicker •v. (**flickers, flickering, flickered**) **1** shine or burn unsteadily. **2** appear briefly: *amusement flickered in his eyes.* **3** make small, quick movements. •n. **1** a flickering movement or light. **2** a brief stirring of a feeling.
– ORIGIN Old English, 'to flutter'.

flick knife •n. Brit. a knife with a blade that springs out from the handle when a button is pressed.

flier •n. var. of FLYER.

flight •n. **1** the action of flying. **2** a journey made in an aircraft or in space. **3** the path of something through the air. **4** the action of running away: *the enemy were in flight.* **5** a highly imaginative idea or story: *a flight of fancy.* **6** a group of birds or aircraft flying together. **7** a series of steps between floors or levels. **8** the tail of an arrow or dart.
– PHRASES **take flight 1** (of a bird) take off and fly. **2** run away.
– ORIGIN Old English.

flight attendant •n. a steward or stewardess on an aircraft.

flight deck • n. **1** the cockpit of a large aircraft. **2** the deck of an aircraft carrier, used as a runway.

flightless • adj. (of a bird or insect) naturally unable to fly.

flight recorder • n. an electronic device in an aircraft that records technical details during a flight.

flighty • adj. (**flightier, flightiest**) unreliable and uninterested in serious things.

flimsy • adj. (**flimsier, flimsiest**) **1** weak and fragile. **2** (of clothing) light and thin. **3** not convincing: *a flimsy excuse*.
– DERIVATIVES **flimsily** adv. **flimsiness** n.

flinch • v. **1** make a quick, nervous movement as a reaction to fear or pain. **2** (**flinch from**) avoid something through fear or anxiety.
– ORIGIN Old French *flenchir* 'turn aside'.

fling • v. (**flings, flinging, flung**) **1** throw or move forcefully: *she flung the tray against the wall*. **2** (**fling something on/off**) put on or take off clothes carelessly and rapidly. • n. **1** a short period of unrestrained enjoyment. **2** a short sexual relationship.
– ORIGIN perh. from Old Norse, 'flog'.

flint • n. **1** a hard grey rock consisting of nearly pure silica. **2** a piece of flint or a metal alloy, used to produce a spark in a cigarette lighter.
– ORIGIN Old English.

flintlock • n. an old-fashioned type of gun fired by a spark from a flint.

flinty • adj. **1** relating to or like flint. **2** stern and showing no emotion: *a flinty stare*.
– DERIVATIVES **flintiness** n.

flip • v. (**flips, flipping, flipped**) **1** turn over with a quick, smooth movement. **2** move or throw with a sudden sharp movement: *he flipped a switch*. **3** (also **flip your lid**) informal suddenly become very angry or lose your self-control. • n. a flipping action or movement. • adj. not serious or respectful.
– ORIGIN prob. from FILLIP.

flip chart • n. a very large pad of paper bound so that pages can be turned over at the top, used on a stand at presentations.

flip-flop • n. a light sandal with a thong that passes between the big and second toes.

flippant • adj. not showing proper seriousness or respect.
– DERIVATIVES **flippancy** n. **flippantly** adv.
– ORIGIN from FLIP.

flipper • n. **1** a broad, flat limb used for swimming by sea animals such as turtles. **2** each of a pair of flat rubber

attachments worn on the feet for underwater swimming.

flip side • n. informal **1** the less important side of a pop single. **2** the reverse or unwelcome aspect of a situation.

flirt • v. **1** behave as if trying to attract someone sexually but without serious intentions. **2** (**flirt with**) show a casual interest in. **3** (**flirt with**) deliberately risk danger or death. • n. a person who likes to flirt.
– DERIVATIVES **flirtation** n. **flirty** adj.

flirtatious /fler-tay-shuhss/ • adj. liking to flirt.

flit • v. (**flits, flitting, flitted**) move quickly and lightly.
– PHRASES **do a (moonlight) flit** Brit. informal leave home secretly at night, especially to avoid paying debts.
– ORIGIN Old Norse.

flitter • v. (**flitters, flittering, flittered**) move quickly here and there.
– ORIGIN from FLIT.

float • v. **1** rest on the surface of a liquid without sinking. **2** move or be held in a liquid or the air: *clouds floated across the sky*. **3** put forward an idea as a suggestion. **4** (as adj. **floating**) unsettled in your life or your opinions. **5** offer the shares of a company for sale on the stock market for the first time. **6** allow a currency to have a variable rate of exchange against other currencies. • n. **1** a lightweight object or device designed to float on water. **2** a small vehicle powered by electricity: *a milk float*. **3** a platform mounted on a lorry and carrying a display in a procession. **4** Brit. a sum of money available for minor expenses or to provide change.
– DERIVATIVES **floater** n.
– ORIGIN Old English.

floatation • n. var. of FLOTATION.

floating voter • n. Brit. a person who votes for different parties in different elections.

floaty • adj. (of a woman's garment or a fabric) light and flimsy.

flocculent /flok-kyuu-luhnt/ • adj. resembling tufts of wool.
– ORIGIN Latin *flocculus* 'tuft of wool'.

flock¹ • n. **1** a number of birds, sheep, or goats moving or kept together. **2** (a **flock/flocks**) a large number or crowd. **3** a Christian congregation under the charge of a particular minister. • v. gather or move in a flock.
– ORIGIN Old English.

flock² • n. a soft material for stuffing cushions and quilts, made of torn-up cloth or waste wool.
– ORIGIN Latin *floccus* 'tuft of wool'.

flock wallpaper • n. wallpaper with a

raised pattern made from powdered cloth.

floe /floh/ • n. a sheet of floating ice.
– ORIGIN prob. from Norwegian *flo* 'layer'.

flog • v. (**flogs, flogging, flogged**) **1** beat with a whip or stick as a punishment. **2** Brit. informal sell something.
– PHRASES **flog a dead horse** Brit. waste energy on something that can never be successful.
– DERIVATIVES **flogger** n.
– ORIGIN perh. from Latin *flagellare* 'to whip'.

flood • n. **1** an overflow of a large amount of water over dry land. **2** (**the Flood**) the flood described in the Bible, brought by God because of the wickedness of the human race. **3** an overwhelming quantity or outpouring: *a flood of complaints.* **4** the rising of the tide. • v. **1** cover or become covered with water in a flood. **2** (of a river) fill up and overflow its banks. **3** arrive in very large numbers. **4** fill completely.
– ORIGIN Old English.

floodgate • n. **1** a gate that can be opened or closed to control a flow of water. **2** (**floodgates**) controls holding back something powerful: *success could open the floodgates for similar mergers.*

floodlight • n. a large, powerful lamp used to light up a stage, a building, or an area such as a sports ground.
• v. (**floodlights, floodlighting, floodlit**) light up with floodlights.

flood plain • n. an area of low ground next to a river that regularly becomes flooded.

flood tide • n. an incoming tide.

floor • n. **1** the lower surface of a room, on which you stand. **2** a storey of a building. **3** the bottom of the sea, a cave, etc. **4** (**the floor**) the part of a law-making body in which members sit and from which they speak. **5** (**the floor**) the right to speak in a debate: *other speakers have the floor.* • v. **1** provide a room with a floor. **2** informal knock someone to the ground. **3** informal baffle someone completely.
– ORIGIN Old English.

floorboard • n. a long plank used with others to make a wooden floor.

flooring • n. the boards or other material of which a floor is made.

floor show • n. an entertainment presented on the floor of a nightclub or restaurant.

floozy (also **floozie**) • n. (pl. **floozies**) informal, esp. humorous a girl or woman who has many sexual partners.

flop • v. (**flops, flopping, flopped**) **1** hang or swing loosely. **2** sit or lie down

heavily. **3** informal fail totally. • n. **1** a heavy and clumsy fall. **2** informal a total failure.
– ORIGIN from **FLAP**.

floppy • adj. not firm or rigid. • n. (pl. **floppies**) (also **floppy disk**) a flexible removable magnetic disk used in a computer for storing data.

flora • n. (pl. **floras**) **1** the plants of a particular area or period of time. Compare with **FAUNA**. **2** the bacteria found naturally in the intestines.
– ORIGIN Latin *flos* 'flower'.

floral • adj. relating to or decorated with flowers.

floret /flo-rit/ • n. **1** one of the small flowers making up a composite flower head. **2** one of the flowering stems making up a head of cauliflower or broccoli.
– ORIGIN Latin *flos* 'flower'.

florid /flo-rid/ • adj. **1** having a red or flushed complexion. **2** over-elaborate: *florid prose.*
– ORIGIN Latin *floridus.*

florin /flo-rin/ • n. a former British coin worth two shillings.
– ORIGIN Italian *fiorino* 'little flower'.

florist • n. a person who sells and arranges cut flowers.
– DERIVATIVES **floristry** n.

floruit /flo-ruu-it/ • v. used to indicate when a historical figure lived, worked, or was most active.
– ORIGIN Latin, 'he or she flourished'.

floss • n. **1** (also **dental floss**) a soft thread used to clean between the teeth. **2** untwisted silk thread used in embroidery. • v. clean between the teeth with dental floss.
– DERIVATIVES **flossy** adj.
– ORIGIN Old French *flosche* 'down'.

flotation /floh-tay-sh'n/ (also **floatation**) • n. **1** the action of floating. **2** the process of offering a company's shares for sale on the stock market for the first time.

flotilla /fluh-til-luh/ • n. a small fleet of ships or boats.
– ORIGIN Spanish.

flotsam /flot-suhm/ • n. wreckage found floating on the sea.
– PHRASES **flotsam and jetsam** useless or discarded objects.
– ORIGIN Old French *floteson.*

flounce¹ • v. (**flounces, flouncing, flounced**) move in a way that emphasizes your anger or impatience. • n. an exaggerated action expressing annoyance or impatience.
– ORIGIN perh. from Norwegian *flunsa* 'hurry'.

flounce² • n. a wide strip of material gathered and sewn to a skirt or dress.

– DERIVATIVES **flouncy** adj.
– ORIGIN Old French *fronce* 'a fold'.

flounder¹ • v. (**flounders, floundering, floundered**) **1** have trouble doing or understanding something. **2** stagger clumsily in mud or water.
– ORIGIN perh. from **FOUNDER³** and **BLUNDER**.

USAGE: On the confusion of **flounder** and **founder**, see the note at **FOUNDER³**.

flounder² • n. a small flatfish of shallow coastal waters.
– ORIGIN Old French *flondre*.

flour • n. a powder produced by grinding grain, used to make bread, cakes, and pastry. • v. sprinkle with flour.
– ORIGIN from **FLOWER** in the sense 'the best part' (of ground wheat).

flourish • v. **1** grow or develop in a healthy or vigorous way. **2** be successful during a specified period. **3** wave something about in a noticeable way. • n. **1** a bold or exaggerated gesture. **2** an ornamental flowing curve in hand-writing. **3** a fanfare played by brass instruments.
– ORIGIN Old French *florir*.

floury • adj. **1** covered with flour. **2** (of a potato) soft and fluffy when cooked.

flout /flowt/ • v. openly fail to follow a rule, law, or custom.
– ORIGIN perh. from Dutch *fluiten* 'play the flute, hiss derisively'.

flow • v. **1** move steadily and continuously in a current or stream. **2** move steadily and freely: *people flowed into the courtyard.* **3** (often as adj. **flowing**) hang loosely and elegantly. **4** (of the sea) move towards the land. • n. **1** the action of flowing. **2** a steady, continuous stream. **3** the rise of a tide.
– PHRASES **in full flow** fully engaged in saying or doing something.
– ORIGIN Old English.

flow chart (also **flow diagram**) • n. a diagram showing a sequence of stages making up a complex process or computer program.

flower • n. **1** the part of a plant from which the seed or fruit develops, usually having brightly coloured petals. **2** the state or period in which a plant is flowering. **3** (**the flower of**) the best of a group. • v. (**flowers, flowering, flowered**) **1** produce flowers. **2** develop fully and richly: *she flowered into a striking beauty.*
– DERIVATIVES **flowered** adj.
– ORIGIN Old French *flour, flor.*

flower head • n. a compact mass of flowers at the top of a stem.

flowerpot • n. an earthenware or plastic container in which to grow a plant.

flowery • adj. **1** full of, decorated with, or like flowers. **2** (of speech or writing) elaborate.

flown past part. of **FLY¹**.

flu • n. influenza.

fluctuate /fluk-chuu-ayt/ • v. (**fluctuates, fluctuating, fluctuated**) rise and fall irregularly in number or amount.
– DERIVATIVES **fluctuation** n.
– ORIGIN Latin *fluctuare* 'undulate'.

flue /floo/ • n. **1** a passage in a chimney for smoke and waste gases. **2** a pipe or passage for conveying heat.

fluent /floo-uhnt/ • adj. **1** speaking or writing clearly and naturally. **2** (of a language) used easily and accurately. **3** smoothly graceful and easy: *a runner in fluent motion.*
– DERIVATIVES **fluency** n. **fluently** adv.
– ORIGIN Latin *fluere* 'to flow'.

fluff • n. **1** soft fibres gathered in small light clumps. **2** the soft fur or feathers of a young mammal or bird. **3** informal a mistake. • v. **1** (**fluff something up/out**) make something fuller and softer by shaking or patting. **2** informal fail to do something properly: *he fluffed his only line.*
– ORIGIN prob. from Flemish *vluwe*.

fluffy • adj. (**fluffier, fluffiest**) **1** like or covered with fluff. **2** (of food) light in texture.
– DERIVATIVES **fluffiness** n.

flugelhorn /floo-g'l-horn/ • n. a brass musical instrument like a cornet but with a broader tone.
– ORIGIN German.

fluid • n. a substance, such as a liquid or gas, that has no fixed shape and gives way to outside pressure. • adj. **1** able to flow easily. **2** not stable: *a fluid political situation.* **3** graceful.
– DERIVATIVES **fluidity** n. **fluidly** adv.
– ORIGIN Latin *fluidus*.

fluid ounce • n. Brit. one twentieth of a pint (approximately 0.028 litre).

fluke¹ • n. a lucky chance occurrence.
– DERIVATIVES **fluky** (also **flukey**) adj.
– ORIGIN perh. dialect.

fluke² • n. a parasitic flatworm.
– ORIGIN Old English.

flume /floom/ • n. **1** an artificial channel carrying water. **2** a water slide at a swimming pool or amusement park.
– ORIGIN Latin *flumen* 'river'.

flummery /flum-muh-ri/ • n. empty talk or compliments.
– ORIGIN Welsh *llymru*.

flummox /flum-muhks/ • v. informal baffle someone completely.

– ORIGIN prob. dialect.

flung past and past part. of **FLING**.

flunk • v. informal, esp. N. Amer. fail an exam.
– ORIGIN perh. from **FUNK**[1].

flunkey (also **flunky**) • n. (pl. **flunkeys** or **flunkies**) esp. derog. **1** a uniformed male servant or porter. **2** a person who performs menial tasks.
– ORIGIN perh. from **FLANK**.

fluoresce /fluu-uh-ress/ • v. (**fluoresces, fluorescing, fluoresced**) shine or glow brightly due to fluorescence.

fluorescence /fluu-uh-ress-uhnss/ • n. **1** light given out by a substance when it is exposed to radiation such as ultraviolet light or X-rays. **2** the property of giving out light in this way.
– ORIGIN from **FLUORSPAR**.

fluorescent • adj. **1** having or showing fluorescence. **2** (of lighting) based on fluorescence from a substance lit by ultraviolet light. **3** vividly colourful.

> ✓ Remember that **fluorescent** and the related word **fluorescence** begin with fluor-.

fluoridate /fluu-uh-ri-dayt/ • v. (**fluoridates, fluoridating, fluoridated**) add traces of fluorides to.
– DERIVATIVES **fluoridation** n.

fluoride /fluu-uh-ryd/ • n. **1** a compound of fluorine with another element or group. **2** a fluorine-containing salt added to water supplies or toothpaste to reduce tooth decay.

fluorine /fluu-uh-reen/ • n. an extremely reactive pale yellow poisonous gas.
– ORIGIN from Latin *fluor* 'a flow'.

fluorite • n. a mineral form of calcium fluoride.

fluorspar /fluu-uh-spar/ • n. = **FLUORITE**.
– ORIGIN from Latin *fluor* 'a flow' + **SPAR**[3].

flurried • adj. agitated or nervous.

flurry • n. (pl. **flurries**) **1** a small swirling mass of snow, leaves, or dust moved by a gust of wind. **2** a sudden short spell of activity or excitement. **3** a number of things arriving suddenly and at the same time.
– ORIGIN from former *flurr* 'fly up'.

flush[1] • v. **1** (of a person's skin or face) become red and hot. **2** (**be flushed with**) be very pleased by: *he was flushed with success.* **3** clean or remove something by passing large quantities of water through it. **4** force a person or animal into the open: *their task was to flush out the rebels.* • n. **1** a reddening of the face or skin. **2** a sudden rush of strong emotion. **3** a period of freshness and vigour: *the first flush of youth.* **4** an act of flushing with water.

– ORIGIN perh. influenced by **FLASH** and **BLUSH**.

flush[2] • adj. (usu. **flush with**) **1** completely level with another surface. **2** informal having plenty of money.
– ORIGIN prob. from **FLUSH**[1].

flush[3] • n. (in poker or brag) a hand of cards all of the same suit.
– ORIGIN French *flux*.

fluster • v. (**fluster, flustering, flustered**) make someone agitated or confused. • n. a flustered state.
– ORIGIN perh. Scandinavian.

flute • n. **1** a high-pitched wind instrument consisting of a tube with holes along it. **2** a tall, narrow wine glass. • v. (**flutes, fluting, fluted**) speak in a tuneful way.
– ORIGIN Old French *flahute*.

fluted • adj. decorated with a series of gently rounded grooves.

flutter • v. (**flutters, fluttering, fluttered**) **1** fly unsteadily by flapping the wings quickly and lightly. **2** move or fall with a light trembling motion. **3** (of a pulse or heartbeat) beat irregularly. • n. **1** a trembling or unsteady flight or fall. **2** an irregular beating of the heart or pulse. **3** a state of nervous excitement. **4** Brit. informal a small bet.
– DERIVATIVES **fluttery** adj.
– ORIGIN Old English.

fluvial /floo-vi-uhl/ • adj. Geol. relating to a river.
– ORIGIN Latin *fluvialis*.

flux /fluks/ • n. **1** continuous change. **2** an abnormal discharge from or within the body. **3** Physics the total amount of radiation, or of electric or magnetic field lines, passing through an area. **4** a substance mixed with a solid to lower the melting point, used in soldering or smelting.
– ORIGIN Latin *fluxus*.

fly[1] • v. (**flies, flying, flew**; past part. **flown**) **1** (of a winged creature or aircraft) move through the air. **2** control the flight of an aircraft. **3** travel or transport in an aircraft. **4** go or move quickly. **5** move quickly through the air. **6** flutter in the wind. **7** (of a flag) be displayed on a flagpole. **8** (**fly at**) attack verbally or physically. **9** old use run away. • n. (pl. **flies**) **1** (Brit. also **flies**) an opening at the crotch of a pair of trousers, closed with a zip or buttons. **2** a flap of material covering the opening of a tent.
– PHRASES **fly in the face of** be the opposite of what is usual or expected. **fly into a rage** (or **temper**) become suddenly angry. **fly off the handle** informal lose your temper suddenly.
– ORIGIN Old English.

fly² •n. (pl. **flies**) **1** a flying insect with a single pair of transparent wings and sucking or piercing mouthparts. **2** used in names of other flying insects, e.g. **dragonfly**. **3** a fishing bait consisting of a natural or artificial flying insect.
– PHRASES **a fly in the ointment** a minor irritation that spoils something. **a fly on the wall** an unnoticed observer. **there are no flies on ——** the person specified can quickly judge a person or situation.
– ORIGIN Old English.

fly³ •adj. Brit. informal knowing and clever.

flyaway •adj. (of hair) fine and difficult to control.

flyblown •adj. contaminated by contact with flies.

fly-by-night •adj. unreliable or untrustworthy.

flycatcher •n. a perching bird that catches flying insects.

flyer (also **flier**) •n. **1** a person or thing that flies. **2** informal a fast-moving person or thing. **3** a small leaflet advertising something. **4** a flying start.

fly-fishing •n. the sport of fishing using a rod and an artificial fly as bait.

fly half •n. Rugby = STAND-OFF HALF.

flying •adj. **1** able to fly. **2** brief: *a flying visit.*
– PHRASES **with flying colours** particularly well.

flying fish •n. a fish of warm seas which leaps out of the water and uses its wing-like fins to glide.

flying fox •n. a large fruit bat with a foxlike face, found in Madagascar, SE Asia, and northern Australia.

flying saucer •n. a disc-shaped flying craft supposedly piloted by aliens.

flying squad n. •n. Brit. a division of a police force which is capable of reaching an incident quickly.

flying start •n. **1** a start of a race in which the competitors are already moving at speed as they pass the starting point. **2** a good beginning giving an advantage over competitors.

flyleaf •n. (pl. **flyleaves**) a blank page at the beginning or end of a book.

flyover •n. esp. Brit. a bridge carrying one road or railway line over another.

flypaper •n. sticky, poison-treated strips of paper that are hung indoors to catch and kill flies.

fly-past •n. Brit. a ceremonial flight of aircraft past a person or place.

fly-post •v. Brit. put up advertising posters in places where they are not permitted.

flysheet •n. Brit. a fabric cover pitched over a tent to keep the rain out.

fly-tipping •n. Brit. illegal dumping of waste.

flyweight •n. a weight in boxing and other sports coming between light flyweight and bantamweight.

flywheel •n. a heavy revolving wheel in a machine used to increase the machine's momentum and make it more stable or provide it with a reserve of available power.

FM •abbrev. frequency modulation.

Fm •symb. the chemical element fermium.

FO •abbrev. Foreign Office.

foal •n. a young horse or related animal.
•v. (of a mare) give birth to a foal.
– ORIGIN Old English.

foam •n. **1** a mass of small bubbles formed on or in liquid. **2** a liquid substance containing many small bubbles: *shaving foam.* **3** a lightweight form of rubber or plastic made by solidifying foam. •v. form or produce foam.
– DERIVATIVES **foamy** adj.
– ORIGIN Old English.

fob¹ •n. **1** a chain attached to a watch for carrying in the pocket of a waistcoat. **2** a tab on a key ring.
– ORIGIN prob. from German dialect *Fuppe* 'pocket'.

fob² •v. (**fobs, fobbing, fobbed**) **1** (**fob someone off**) try to deceive someone into accepting excuses or something inferior. **2** (**fob something off on**) give something inferior to.
– ORIGIN perh. from German *foppen* 'deceive, banter'.

fob watch •n. a pocket watch.

focaccia /fuh-kach-uh/ •n. a type of flat Italian bread made with olive oil and flavoured with herbs.
– ORIGIN Italian.

focal /foh-k'l/ •adj. relating to a focus.

focal length •n. the distance between the centre of a lens or curved mirror and its focus.

focal point •n. **1** the point at which rays or waves from a lens or mirror meet, or the point from which rays or waves going in different directions appear to proceed. **2** the centre of interest or activity.

fo'c's'le /fohk-s'l/ •n. var. of FORECASTLE.

focus /foh-kuhss/ •n. (pl. **focuses** or **foci** /foh-sy/) **1** the centre of interest or activity. **2** the state of having or producing a clear and defined image: *his face is out of focus.* **3** the point at which an object must be situated in order for a lens or mirror to produce a clear image of it. **4** a focal point. **5** the point of origin

of an earthquake. Compare with
EPICENTRE. **6** Geom. a fixed point with
reference to which an ellipse, parabola,
or other curve is drawn. •v. (**focuses,
focusing, focused** or **focusses,
focussing, focussed**) **1** adapt to the
available level of light and become able
to see clearly. **2** (**focus on**) pay particular
attention to. **3** adjust the focus of a
telescope, camera, etc. **4** (of rays or
waves) meet at a single point.
– DERIVATIVES **focuser** n.
– ORIGIN Latin, 'domestic hearth'.

focus group •n. a group of people
assembled to assess a new product,
political campaign, etc.

fodder •n. **1** food for cattle and other
livestock. **2** people or things regarded
only as material to satisfy a need: *young
people ending up as factory fodder.*
– ORIGIN Old English.

foe •n. literary an enemy or opponent.
– ORIGIN Old English, 'hostile'.

foetid •adj. var. of **FETID**.

foetus •n. Brit. var. of **FETUS**.
– DERIVATIVES **foetal** adj.

fog •n. **1** a thick cloud of tiny water
droplets suspended in the atmosphere
at or near the earth's surface which
reduces visibility. **2** a state or cause of
confusion: *a fog of detail.* •v. (**fogs,
fogging, fogged**) **1** cover or become
covered with steam. **2** confuse someone.
– ORIGIN perh. from **FOGGY**.

fogey /foh-gi/ (also **fogy**) •n. (pl. **fogeys**
or **fogies**) a very old-fashioned or
conservative person.

foggy •adj. (**foggier, foggiest**) full of
fog.
– PHRASES **not have the foggiest (idea)**
informal, esp. Brit. have no idea at all.
– ORIGIN perh. from Norwegian *fogg*
'grass which grows in a field after a crop
of hay has been cut'.

foghorn •n. a device making a loud,
deep sound as a warning to ships in fog.

foible /foy-b'l/ •n. a minor weakness or
eccentricity.
– ORIGIN from former French form of Old
French *fieble* 'feeble'.

foie gras /fwah grah/ (also **pâté de foie
gras**) •n. a pâté made from the liver of a
fattened goose.

foil[1] •v. **1** prevent something undesirable
from succeeding. **2** stop someone from
doing something.
– ORIGIN perh. from Old French *fouler* 'to
trample'.

foil[2] •n. **1** metal hammered or rolled into
a thin flexible sheet. **2** a person or thing
that contrasts with and so emphasizes
the qualities of another.
– ORIGIN Latin *folium* 'leaf'.

foil[3] •n. a light, blunt-edged fencing
sword with a button on its point.

foist /foysst/ •v. (**foist something on**)
impose an unwelcome person or thing
on someone.
– ORIGIN Dutch dialect *vuisten* 'take in
the hand'.

fold[1] •v. **1** bend something over on itself
so that one part of it covers another.
2 be able to be folded into a flatter
shape. **3** use a flexible material to wrap
something. **4** informal (of a company) go
out of business. **5** (**fold something
in/into**) mix an ingredient gently with
another. •n. **1** a folded part or thing. **2** a
line produced by folding.
– PHRASES **fold someone in your arms**
affectionately hug someone. **fold your
arms** cross your arms over your chest.
– DERIVATIVES **foldable** adj.
– ORIGIN Old English.

fold[2] •n. **1** a pen or enclosure for sheep.
2 (**the fold**) a group with shared aims
and values.
– ORIGIN Old English.

-fold •suffix forming adjectives and
adverbs from cardinal numbers: **1** in an
amount multiplied by: *threefold.*
2 consisting of so many parts: *twofold.*
– ORIGIN Old English.

folder •n. **1** a folding cover or wallet for
storing loose papers. **2** Computing a directory containing related files.

foliage /foh-li-ij/ •n. the leaves of
plants.
– ORIGIN Old French *feuillage*.

folic acid /foh-lik/ •n. a vitamin of the B
complex found especially in leafy green
vegetables, liver, and kidney.
– ORIGIN Latin *folium* 'leaf'.

folio /foh-li-oh/ •n. (pl. **folios**) **1** a sheet
of paper folded once to form two leaves
(four pages) of a book. **2** a book made up
of such sheets.
– ORIGIN Latin *folium* 'leaf'.

folk /fohk/ •pl. n. **1** (also **folks**) informal
people in general. **2** (**your folks**) esp. N.
Amer. your family. **3** (also **folk music**)
traditional music whose composer is
unknown and which is passed on
through performance. •adj. originating
from the beliefs, culture, and customs of
ordinary people: *folk wisdom.*
– ORIGIN Old English.

folk dance •n. a traditional dance of a
particular people or area.

folklore •n. the traditional beliefs,
stories, and customs of a community,
passed on by word of mouth.

folksy •adj. traditional and homely: *the
shop's folksy, small-town image.*
– DERIVATIVES **folksiness** n.

folk tale •n. a traditional story

originally passed on by word of mouth.

follicle /fol-li-k'l/ • n. a small cavity in the body, especially one in which the root of a hair develops.
– DERIVATIVES **follicular** /fol-lik-yuu-ler/ adj.
– ORIGIN Latin *folliculus* 'little bag'.

follow • v. 1 move behind someone or something. 2 go after someone so as to observe them. 3 go along a route. 4 come after in time or order. 5 (also **follow on from**) occur as a result of. 6 be a logical consequence. 7 act according to an instruction or example. 8 accept someone as a guide, example, or leader of a movement. 9 be interested in or pay close attention to. 10 understand: *I still don't follow you.* 11 undertake a career or course of action. 12 (**follow something through**) continue an action or task to its end. 13 (**follow something up**) further pursue or investigate something.
– PHRASES **follow your nose 1** trust to your instincts. **2** go straight ahead. **follow suit 1** do the same as someone else. **2** (in card games) play a card of the suit led.
– ORIGIN Old English.

follower • n. 1 a supporter, fan, or disciple. 2 a person who follows.
– DERIVATIVES **followership** n.

following • prep. coming after or as a result of. • n. a group of supporters or admirers. • adj. next in time or order.

follow-through • n. the continuing of an action or task to its end.

follow-up • n. 1 an activity carried out to check or further develop earlier work. 2 a work that follows or builds on an earlier work.

folly • n. (pl. **follies**) 1 foolishness. 2 a foolish act or idea. 3 an ornamental building with no practical purpose.
– ORIGIN Old French *folie* 'madness'.

foment /foh-ment/ • v. stir up trouble or conflict.
– ORIGIN Latin *fomentare*.

fond • adj. 1 (**fond of**) having an affection or liking for. 2 affectionate: *fond memories.* 3 (of a hope or belief) unlikely to be fulfilled.
– DERIVATIVES **fondly** adv. **fondness** n.

fondant /fon-duhnt/ • n. a thick paste made of sugar and water, used in making sweets and icing cakes.
– ORIGIN French, 'melting'.

fondle • v. (**fondles, fondling, fondled**) stroke or caress lovingly or sexually.
– ORIGIN from **FOND**.

fondue /fon-doo/ • n. a dish in which small pieces of food are dipped into melted cheese or a hot sauce.

– ORIGIN French, 'melted'.

font[1] • n. a large stone bowl in a church for the water used in baptism.
– ORIGIN Latin *fons* 'fountain'.

font[2] (Brit. also **fount**) • n. Printing a set of type of a particular size and design.
– ORIGIN French *fonte* 'casting'.

fontanelle /fon-tuh-nel/ (US **fontanel**) • n. a soft area between the bones of the skull in a baby or fetus.
– ORIGIN Old French, 'little fountain'.

food • n. any substance that people or animals eat or drink or that plants absorb to maintain life and growth.
– PHRASES **food for thought** something that makes you think carefully about an issue.
– ORIGIN Old English.

food chain • n. a series of organisms, each of which depends on the next as a source of food.

foodie • n. (pl. **foodies**) informal a person with a strong interest in food and cooking.

food poisoning • n. illness caused by food contaminated by bacteria or other organisms.

foodstuff • n. a substance suitable to be eaten as food.

fool[1] • n. 1 a person who acts unwisely. 2 hist. a jester or clown. • v. 1 trick or deceive someone. 2 (**fool about/around**) act in a joking or silly way.
– DERIVATIVES **foolery** n.
– ORIGIN Old French *fol*.

fool[2] • n. esp. Brit. a cold dessert made of puréed fruit mixed with cream or custard.
– ORIGIN perh. from **FOOL**[1].

foolhardy • adj. bold in a reckless way.
– DERIVATIVES **foolhardiness** n.
– ORIGIN Old French *folhardi*.

foolish • adj. silly or unwise.
– DERIVATIVES **foolishly** adv. **foolishness** n.

foolproof • adj. incapable of going wrong or being wrongly used.

foolscap /foolz-kap/ • n. Brit. a size of paper, about 330 × 200 (or 400) mm.
– ORIGIN perh. from a former watermark of a fool's cap.

fool's gold • n. pyrites, a brassy yellow mineral that can be mistaken for gold.

fool's paradise • n. a state of happiness based on not knowing about or ignoring possible trouble.

foot • n. (pl. **feet**) 1 the part of the leg below the ankle, on which a person walks. 2 the bottom of something vertical. 3 the end of a bed. 4 a unit of length equal to 12 inches (30.48 cm). 5 Poetry a group of syllables making up a

basic unit of metre. •v. informal pay a bill.
– PHRASES **have** (or **keep**) **your feet on the ground** be (or remain) practical and sensible. **have** (or **get**) **a foot in the door** have (or gain) a first introduction to a profession or organization. **land** (or **fall**) **on your feet** have good luck or easy success. **on** (or **by**) **foot** walking. **put your best foot forward** begin with as much effort and determination as possible. **put your foot down** informal be firm when faced with opposition or disobedience. **put your foot in it** informal say or do something tactless. **put a foot wrong** make a mistake. **under your feet** in your way.
– DERIVATIVES **footless** adj.
– ORIGIN Old English.

footage •n. **1** part of a film made for cinema or television. **2** size or length measured in feet.

foot-and-mouth disease •n. a disease caused by a virus in cattle and sheep, causing ulcers on the hoofs and around the mouth.

football •n. **1** a team game involving kicking a ball, in particular (in the UK) soccer or (in the US) American football. **2** a large inflated ball used in football.
– DERIVATIVES **footballer** n.

footboard •n. **1** an upright panel forming the foot of a bed. **2** a board acting as a step up to a vehicle such as a train.

footbridge •n. a bridge for pedestrians.

footer /fuut-er/ •n. **1** a person or thing of a specified number of feet in length or height: *a six-footer.* **2** a line of writing appearing at the foot of each page of a book or document.

footfall •n. the sound of a footstep or footsteps.

foot fault •n. (in tennis or squash) an act of overstepping the baseline when serving, not allowed by the rules.

foothill •n. a low hill at the base of a mountain or mountain range.

foothold •n. **1** a secure position from which further progress may be made. **2** a place where you can lodge a foot to give secure support while climbing.

footing •n. **1** (**your footing**) a secure grip with your feet. **2** the basis on which something is established or operates.

footlights •pl. n. a row of spotlights along the front of a stage at the level of the actors' feet.

footling /foot-ling/ •adj. unimportant and irritating.

footloose •adj. free to do as you please.

footman •n. a uniformed servant whose duties include admitting visitors and waiting at table.

footmark •n. a footprint.

footnote •n. an additional piece of information printed at the bottom of a page.

footpad •n. hist. a highwayman who operated on foot.

footpath •n. a path for people to walk along.

footprint •n. the mark left by a foot or shoe on the ground.

footsie /fuut-si/ •n. (in phr. **play footsie**) informal touch someone's feet lightly and playfully with your own to express romantic interest.

footsore •adj. having sore feet from much walking.

footstep •n. a step taken in walking.
– PHRASES **follow in someone's footsteps** do as another person did before.

footstool •n. a low stool for resting the feet on when sitting.

footwear •n. shoes, boots, and other coverings for the feet.

footwork •n. the way in which a person moves their feet in dancing and sport.

fop •n. a man who is too concerned about his clothes and appearance.
– DERIVATIVES **foppish** adj.

for •prep. **1** affecting or relating to: *tickets for the show.* **2** in favour or on behalf of. **3** because of: *I could dance for joy.* **4** so as to get, have, or do: *shall we go for a walk?* **5** in place of or in exchange for. **6** in the direction of. **7** over a distance or during a period. **8** so as to happen at. •conj. literary because.
– ORIGIN Old English.

fora pl. of FORUM (in sense 2).

forage /fo-rij/ •v. (**forages, foraging, foraged**) **1** search for food. **2** search for something. •n. food for horses and cattle.
– DERIVATIVES **forager** n.
– ORIGIN Old French *fourrager.*

forage cap •n. a soldier's peaked cap.

foray /fo-ray/ •n. **1** a sudden attack or move into enemy territory. **2** a brief but spirited attempt to become involved in a new activity.
– ORIGIN Old French *forrier* 'forager'.

forbade (also **forbad**) past of FORBID.

forbear[1] /for-bair/ •v. (**forbears, forbearing, forbore**; past part. **forborne**) stop yourself from doing something.
– ORIGIN Old English.

forbear[2] /for-bair/ •n. var. of FOREBEAR.

forbearance •n. the quality of being patient and tolerant towards other people.

forbearing •adj. patient and self-controlled.

forbid /for-bid/ •v. (**forbids, forbidding, forbade** /for-bad, for-bayd/ or **forbad**; past part. **forbidden**) **1** refuse to allow. **2** order not to do something.
– PHRASES **forbidden fruit** a thing that is desired all the more because it is not allowed. [ORIGIN referring to the Book of Genesis, chapter 2.]
– ORIGIN Old English.

forbidding •adj. appearing unfriendly or threatening.
– DERIVATIVES **forbiddingly** adv.

forbore past of FORBEAR¹.

forborne past part. of FORBEAR¹.

force •n. **1** physical strength or energy accompanying action or movement. **2** pressure to do something backed by the use or threat of violence. **3** influence or power. **4** a person or thing having influence: *a force for peace.* **5** an organized group of soldiers, police, or workers. **6** (**the forces**) Brit. the army, navy, and air force. **7** Physics a measurable influence that causes something to move. •v. (**forces, forcing, forced**) **1** make a way through or into by force. **2** push into position using force. **3** achieve by effort: *force a smile.* **4** make someone do something against their will. **5** (**force something on**) impose something on. **6** make a plant develop or mature more quickly than normal.
– PHRASES **force someone's hand** make someone do something. **in force 1** in great strength or numbers. **2** (**in/into force**) in or in effect.
– ORIGIN Old French.

force-feed •v. force someone to eat food.

forceful •adj. powerful and confident.
– DERIVATIVES **forcefully** adv. **forcefulness** n.

forcemeat •n. a mixture of chopped and seasoned meat or vegetables used as a stuffing or garnish.

forceps /for-seps/ •pl. n. **1** a pair of pincers used in surgery or in a laboratory. **2** a large surgical instrument with broad blades, used to help to deliver a baby.
– ORIGIN Latin.

forcible •adj. done by force.
– DERIVATIVES **forcibly** adv.

ford •n. a shallow place in a river or stream where it can be crossed. •v. cross a river or stream at a ford.
– ORIGIN Old English.

fore •adj. found or placed in front.
– PHRASES **to the fore** in or to a noticeable or leading position.
– ORIGIN Old English.

fore- •comb. form **1** before; in advance: *forebode.* **2** in front of: *forecourt.*

forearm¹ /for-arm/ •n. the part of a person's arm from the elbow to the wrist.

forearm² /for-arm/ •v. (**be forearmed**) be prepared in advance for danger or attack.

forebear (also **forbear**) •n. an ancestor.
– ORIGIN from FORE + former *bear* 'someone who exists'.

forebode •v. (**forebodes, foreboding, foreboded**) old use act as an advance warning of something bad.

foreboding •n. a feeling that something bad is going to happen.

forecast •v. (**forecasts, forecasting, forecast** or **forecasted**) predict or estimate a future event or trend. •n. a prediction or estimate.
– DERIVATIVES **forecaster** n.

forecastle /fohk-s'l/ (also **fo'c's'le**) •n. the front part of a ship below the deck.

foreclose •v. (**forecloses, foreclosing, foreclosed**) **1** take possession of a mortgaged property when someone fails to keep up their mortgage payments. **2** rule out or prevent a course of action.
– DERIVATIVES **foreclosure** n.
– ORIGIN Old French *forclore* 'shut out'.

forecourt •n. an open area in front of a large building or petrol station.

forefather (or **foremother**) •n. an ancestor.

forefinger •n. the finger next to the thumb.

forefoot •n. (pl. **forefeet**) each of the two front feet of a four-footed animal.

forefront •n. the leading position.

foregather (also **forgather**) •v. formal assemble or gather together.

forego¹ •v. var. of FORGO.

forego² •v. (**foregoes, foregoing, forewent**; past part. **foregone**) old use come before in place or time.

foregoing •adj. previously mentioned.

foregone past part. of FOREGO².
– PHRASES **a foregone conclusion** a result that can be easily predicted.

foreground •n. **1** the part of a view or picture nearest to the observer. **2** the most important position. •v. make something the most important feature.

forehand •n. (in racket sports) a stroke played with the palm of the hand facing in the direction of the stroke.

forehead /for-hed/ •n. the part of the face above the eyebrows.

f

foreign /fo-rin, fo-ruhn/ • adj. **1** relating to a country or language other than your own. **2** dealing with other countries: *foreign policy*. **3** coming from outside: *a foreign influence*. **4** (**foreign to**) not known to or typical of: *cruelty is foreign to him*.
– DERIVATIVES **foreignness** n.
– ORIGIN Old French *forein, forain*.

> 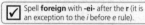 Spell **foreign** with **-ei-** after the **r** (it is an exception to the *i* before *e* rule).

Foreign and Commonwealth Office (also **Foreign Office**) • n. the British government department dealing with foreign affairs.

foreign body • n. a very small object or piece of material that has entered the body from outside.

foreigner • n. **1** a person from a foreign country. **2** informal a stranger or outsider.

foreign exchange • n. the currency of other countries.

Foreign Legion • n. a military formation of the French army made up chiefly of non-Frenchmen.

Foreign Secretary • n. (in the UK) the government minister who heads the Foreign and Commonwealth Office.

foreknowledge • n. awareness of something before it happens or exists.

foreland • n. **1** an area of land in front of a particular feature. **2** a piece of land that projects into the sea.

foreleg • n. either of the front legs of a four-footed animal.

forelimb • n. either of the front limbs of an animal.

forelock • n. a lock of hair growing just above the forehead.

foreman (or **forewoman**) • n. **1** a worker who supervises other workers. **2** (in a law court) a person who is head of a jury and speaks on its behalf.

foremast • n. the mast of a ship nearest the bow.

foremost • adj. highest in importance or position. • adv. in the first place.

forename • n. = FIRST NAME.

forensic /fuh-ren-sik/ • adj. **1** relating to the use of scientific methods in the investigation of crime. **2** relating to a court of law.
– ORIGIN Latin *forensis* 'in open court'.

forensic medicine • n. medical knowledge used in the investigation of crime.

foreplay • n. sexual activity that occurs before intercourse.

forerunner • n. a person or thing that comes before and influences someone or something else.

foresail /for-sayl, for-s'l/ • n. the main sail on a foremast.

foresee • v. (**foresees, foreseeing, foresaw**; past part. **foreseen**) be aware of something in advance of it happening.
– DERIVATIVES **foreseeable** adj.

foreshadow • v. be a warning or indication of a future event.

foreshore • n. the part of a shore between high- and low-water marks, or between the water and land that has been cultivated or built on.

foreshorten • v. **1** portray an object or view as closer or shallower than it really is as an effect of perspective. **2** reduce in time or scale.

foresight • n. the ability to predict and prepare for future events and needs.

foreskin • n. the roll of skin covering the end of the penis.

forest • n. **1** a large area covered thickly with trees and plants. **2** a large number of tangled or upright objects: *a forest of flags*. • v. (usu. as adj. **forested**) plant an area with trees.
– DERIVATIVES **forestation** n.
– ORIGIN from Latin *forestis silva* 'outside wood'.

forestall /for-stawl/ • v. prevent or delay something by taking action before it happens.
– ORIGIN Old English, 'an ambush'.

forester • n. a person in charge of a forest or skilled in forestry.

forestry • n. the science or practice of planting, managing, and caring for forests.

foretaste • n. a sample of something that lies ahead.

foretell • v. (**foretells, foretelling, foretold**) predict the future.

forethought • n. careful consideration of what will be necessary or may happen in the future.

foretold past and past part. of FORETELL.

forever • adv. **1** (also **for ever**) for all future time. **2** for a very long time. **3** continually: *she is forever complaining*.

forewarn • v. warn someone about a possible future problem.

forewent past of FOREGO[1], FOREGO[2].

forewing • n. either of the two front wings of a four-winged insect.

foreword • n. a short introduction to a book.

forfeit /for-fit/ • v. (**forfeits, forfeiting, forfeited**) **1** lose property or a right as a punishment for a fault or mistake. **2** lose or give up as a necessary result of choosing something else: *forfeit a night's sleep for a night on the town*. • n. a punishment for a fault or mistake.

– ORIGIN Old French *forfet* 'crime'.

forgave past of **FORGIVE**.

forge¹ • v. (**forges, forging, forged**)
1 make or shape a metal object by heating and hammering the metal.
2 create: *forge a close relationship.*
3 produce a copy of a banknote, work of art, or signature for the purpose of deception. • n. **1** a blacksmith's workshop. **2** a furnace for melting or refining metal.
– DERIVATIVES **forger** n.
– ORIGIN Old French *forger.*

forge² • v. (**forges, forging, forged**)
1 move forward gradually or steadily.
2 (**forge ahead**) make good progress.
– ORIGIN perh. from **FORCE**.

forgery • n. (pl. **forgeries**) **1** the action of forging a banknote, work of art, or signature. **2** a forged item.

forget • v. (**forgets, forgetting, forgot**; past part. **forgotten** or US **forgot**) **1** fail to remember. **2** fail to remember to do something. **3** no longer think of.
4 (**forget yourself**) behave in an inappropriate way.
– DERIVATIVES **forgettable** adj.
– ORIGIN Old English.

forgetful • adj. tending not to remember things.
– DERIVATIVES **forgetfully** adv.
forgetfulness n.

forget-me-not • n. a low-growing plant with bright blue flowers.

forgive • v. (**forgives, forgiving, forgave**; past part. **forgiven**) **1** stop feeling angry or resentful towards someone for an offence or mistake. **2** no longer feel angry about or wish to punish an offence or mistake.
– DERIVATIVES **forgivable** adj.
– ORIGIN Old English.

forgiveness • n. the action of forgiving or the state of being forgiven.

forgo (also **forego**) • v. (**forgoes, forgoing, forwent**; past part. **forgone**) go without something you want.
– ORIGIN Old English.

forgot past of **FORGET**.

forgotten past part. of **FORGET**.

fork • n. **1** a small tool with two or more prongs used for lifting or holding food.
2 a larger pronged tool used in gardening for digging or lifting. **3** the point where a road, path, or river divides into two parts. **4** either of two such parts. • v. **1** divide into two parts.
2 take one route or the other at a fork.
3 dig or lift with a fork. **4** (**fork something out/up**) informal pay money for something.
– ORIGIN Latin *furca* 'pitchfork'.

forked • adj. having a divided or fork-shaped end.

forked lightning • n. lightning seen as a zigzag or branching line across the sky.

forklift truck • n. a vehicle with a forked device in front for lifting and carrying heavy loads.

forlorn /fer-lorn/ • adj. **1** very sad and lonely. **2** unlikely to succeed or be achieved: *a forlorn attempt to escape.*
– DERIVATIVES **forlornly** adv.
– ORIGIN Old English, 'depraved, lost'.

form • n. **1** the visible shape or arrangement of something. **2** a particular way in which a thing exists: *passages in the form of poems.* **3** a type.
4 what is usually done: *the Englishman knew the form.* **5** a printed document with blank spaces for information to be filled in. **6** the current standard of play of a sports player. **7** details of previous performances by a racehorse or greyhound. **8** a person's mood and state of health: *she was on good form.* **9** esp. Brit. a class or year in a school. • v. **1** bring together parts to create something. **2** to make up: *this information should form the basis of a report.* **3** establish or develop. **4** make or be made into a certain form.
– PHRASES **in** (or Brit. **on**) **form** playing or performing well. **off** (or Brit. **out of**) **form** not playing or performing well.
– DERIVATIVES **formless** adj.
– ORIGIN Latin *forma* 'a mould or form'.

formal • adj. **1** suitable for or referring to an official or important occasion.
2 officially recognized: *a formal complaint.* **3** having a recognized form, structure, or set of rules: *he had little formal education.* **4** (of language) very correct and used in official situations.
– DERIVATIVES **formally** adv.

formaldehyde /for-mal-di-hyd/
• n. a colourless strong-smelling gas, used in solution as a preservative and disinfectant.
– ORIGIN from **FORMIC ACID** and **ALDEHYDE**.

formalin /for-muh-lin/ • n. a solution of formaldehyde in water.

formalism • n. (in art, music, or literature) concern with rules and outward form rather than the content of something.
– DERIVATIVES **formalist** n.

formality • n. (pl. **formalities**) **1** a thing done to follow rules or usual practices: *all the formalities have been complied with.*
2 correct and formal behaviour. **3** (**a formality**) a thing done or occurring as a matter of course.

formalize (or **formalise**)
• v. (**formalizes, formalizing,**

formalized) **1** give something formal or legal status. **2** give a definite shape to.
– DERIVATIVES **formalization** n.

format • n. **1** the way in which something is arranged or presented. **2** the shape, size, and presentation of a book or other publication or a document. **3** the medium in which a sound recording is made available: *LP and CD formats.* **4** a structure for the processing, storage, or display of computer data. • v. (**formats, formatting, formatted**) put into a particular format or arrangement.
– ORIGIN from Latin *formatus liber* 'shaped book'.

formation • n. **1** the action of coming together or taking shape. **2** a structure or arrangement: *a cloud formation.* **3** a formal arrangement of aircraft in flight or troops.

formative • adj. having a strong influence in the development of someone or something.

former[1] • adj. **1** having been previously. **2** in the past: *in former times.* **3** (**the former**) referring to the first of two things mentioned.
– ORIGIN Old English.

former[2] • n. **1** a person or thing that forms something. **2** Brit. a person in a particular school year: *a fifth-former.*

formerly • adv. in the past.

Formica /for-**my**-kuh/ • n. trademark a hard, strong plastic material used for worktops, cupboard doors, etc.

formic acid /for-mik/ • n. an acid present in the fluid produced by some ants.
– ORIGIN Latin *formica* 'ant'.

formidable /for-mi-duh-b'l, for-**mid**-uh-b'l/ • adj. causing fear or respect through being very large, powerful, or capable.
– DERIVATIVES **formidably** adv.
– ORIGIN Latin *formidabilis.*

formula /for-myuu-luh/ • n. (pl. **formulae** /for-myuu-lee/ (in senses 1 and 2) or **formulas**) **1** a mathematical relationship or rule expressed in symbols. **2** (also **chemical formula**) a set of chemical symbols showing the elements present in a compound and the amounts in which they are present. **3** a method for achieving something. **4** a fixed form of words used in a particular situation. **5** a list of ingredients with which something is made. **6** a classification of racing car: *formula one.*
– ORIGIN Latin, 'small shape or mould'.

formulaic /for-myuu-**lay**-ik/ • adj. **1** containing a set form of words. **2** following a rule or style too closely:

much romantic fiction is formulaic.

formulate /for-myuu-layt/ • v. (**formulates, formulating, formulated**) **1** create or prepare methodically. **2** express an idea in a brief or orderly way.

formulation • n. **1** the action of creating or preparing something. **2** a mixture prepared according to a formula.

fornicate • v. (**fornicates, fornicating, fornicated**) formal or humorous have sex with someone you are not married to.
– DERIVATIVES **fornication** n. **fornicator** n.
– ORIGIN Latin.

forsake • v. (**forsakes, forsaking, forsook**; past part. **forsaken**) literary **1** abandon someone. **2** give up something valued or pleasant.
– ORIGIN Old English.

forsooth /fer-**sooth**/ • adv. old use or humorous indeed.

forswear • v. (**forswears, forswearing, forswore**; past part. **forsworn**) formal agree to give up or do without something.

forsythia /for-sy-thi-uh/ • n. a shrub whose bright yellow flowers appear before its leaves.
– ORIGIN named after the Scottish botanist William *Forsyth.*

fort • n. a building constructed to defend a place against attack.
– PHRASES **hold the fort** be responsible for something while someone is away.
– ORIGIN Latin *fortis* 'strong'.

forte[1] /for-tay/ • n. a thing for which someone has a particular talent.
– ORIGIN French, 'strong'.

forte[2] /for-tay/ • adv. & adj. Music loud or loudly.
– ORIGIN Italian.

forth • adv. formal or literary **1** out and away from a starting point. **2** so as to be seen. **3** onwards in time.
– PHRASES **and so forth** and so on.
– ORIGIN Old English.

forthcoming • adj. **1** about to happen or appear. **2** made available when required: *help was not forthcoming.* **3** willing to reveal information.

forthright • adj. direct and outspoken.
– DERIVATIVES **forthrightly** adv. **forthrightness** n.
– ORIGIN Old English.

forthwith • adv. without delay.

fortification • n. **1** a defensive structure built to strengthen a place against attack. **2** the action of strengthening a place with defensive structures.

fortify /for-ti-fy/ • v. (**fortifies, fortifying, fortified**) **1** strengthen a place with defensive structures as

protection against attack. **2** invigorate or encourage someone. **3** strengthen an alcoholic drink with extra alcohol: *fortified wine.* **4** make food more nutritious by adding vitamins.
– DERIVATIVES **fortifier** n.
– ORIGIN Latin *fortificare*.

fortissimo /for-tiss-i-moh/ • adv. & adj. Music very loud or loudly.
– ORIGIN Italian.

fortitude /for-ti-tyood/ • n. courage and strength when facing pain or trouble.
– ORIGIN Latin *fortitudo*.

fortnight • n. Brit. a period of two weeks.
– ORIGIN Old English, 'fourteen nights'.

fortnightly Brit. • adj. happening or produced every two weeks. • adv. every two weeks.

fortress • n. a fort or a strongly fortified town.
– ORIGIN Old French *forteresse* 'strong place'.

fortuitous /for-tyoo-i-tuhss/ • adj. **1** happening by chance. **2** lucky.
– DERIVATIVES **fortuitously** adv.
– ORIGIN Latin *fortuitus*.

fortunate • adj. **1** involving or having good luck. **2** advantageous or favourable: *I'm in the fortunate position of having a purpose-made workshop.*

fortunately • adv. it is fortunate that.

fortune • n. **1** chance as an external force affecting people's lives. **2** luck: *a piece of good fortune.* **3** (**fortunes**) the success or failure of a person or undertaking. **4** a large amount of money or property.
– PHRASES **a small fortune** informal a large amount of money.
– ORIGIN Latin *Fortuna*, a goddess of luck or chance.

fortune-teller • n. a person who predicts what will happen in people's lives.
– DERIVATIVES **fortune-telling** n.

forty • cardinal number (pl. **forties**) ten less than fifty; 40. (Roman numeral: **xl** or **XL**.)
– PHRASES **forty winks** informal a short daytime sleep.
– DERIVATIVES **fortieth** ordinal number.
– ORIGIN Old English.

> ✓ Remember that **forty** begins with **for-** (no **u**).

forum /for-uhm/ • n. (pl. **forums**) **1** a meeting or opportunity for an exchange of views. **2** (pl. **fora** /for-uh/) (in the cities of ancient Rome) a square or marketplace used for public business.
– ORIGIN Latin, 'what is out of doors'.

forward • adv. (also **forwards**) **1** in the direction that you are facing or travelling. **2** onward so as to make

progress. **3** ahead in time. **4** in or near the front of a ship or aircraft. • adj. **1** towards the direction that you are facing or travelling. **2** relating to the future. **3** bold or overfamiliar in manner. **4** situated in or near the front of a ship or aircraft. • n. an attacking player in a sport. • v. **1** send a letter or email on to a further address. **2** send something.
– DERIVATIVES **forwarder** n. **forwardly** adv. **forwardness** n.
– ORIGIN Old English.

forward-looking (also **forward-thinking**) • adj. open to new ideas and developments.

forwent past of FORGO.

fossil /foss-uhl/ • n. the remains or impression of a prehistoric plant or animal that have become hardened into rock.
– ORIGIN French *fossile*.

fossil fuel • n. a natural fuel such as coal or gas, formed from the remains of animals and plants.

fossilize (or **fossilise**) • v. (**fossilizes, fossilizing, fossilized**) preserve an animal or plant so that it becomes a fossil.
– DERIVATIVES **fossilization** n.

foster • v. (**fosters, fostering, fostered**) **1** encourage the development of. **2** bring up a child that is not your own by birth.
– ORIGIN Old English, 'feed, nourish'.

fought past and past part. of FIGHT.

foul • adj. **1** having a disgusting smell or taste. **2** very unpleasant. **3** wicked or obscene. **4** not allowed by the rules of a sport. **5** polluted. • n. (in sport) a piece of play that is not allowed by the rules. • v. **1** make foul or dirty. **2** (in sport) commit a foul against. **3** (**foul something up**) make a mistake with or spoil something. **4** cause a cable or anchor to become entangled or jammed.
– DERIVATIVES **foully** adv. **foulness** n.
– ORIGIN Old English.

foul-mouthed • adj. regularly using bad language.

foul play • n. **1** unfair play in a game or sport. **2** criminal or violent activity.

found¹ past and past part. of FIND.

found² • v. **1** establish an institution. **2** (**be founded on**) be based on a particular idea.
– ORIGIN Old French *fonder*.

found³ • v. **1** melt and mould metal. **2** make an object by melting and moulding metal.
– ORIGIN French *fondre*.

foundation • n. **1** the lowest weight-bearing part of a building, set below the

ground. **2** an underlying basis for something. **3** reason: *there was no foundation for the claim.* **4** the action of establishing an institution. **5** an institution established for a purpose. **6** a cream or powder applied to the face as a base for other make-up.
– DERIVATIVES **foundational** adj.

foundation stone •n. a stone laid at a ceremony to celebrate the building of a new institution.

founder[1] •n. a person who establishes a new institution or settlement.

founder[2] •n. the owner or operator of a foundry.

founder[3] •v. (**founders, foundering, foundered**) **1** (of a plan or undertaking) fail or break down. **2** (of a ship) fill with water and sink.
– ORIGIN Old French *fondrer* 'to collapse'.

> USAGE: The words **founder** and **flounder** are often confused. **Founder** chiefly means 'fail', while **flounder** means 'have trouble doing or understanding something' or 'stagger in mud or water'.

foundling •n. a young child that has been abandoned by its parents and is discovered and cared for by other people.

foundry •n. (pl. **foundries**) a workshop or factory for casting metal.

fount[1] •n. **1** a source of a desirable quality. **2** literary a spring or fountain.

fount[2] •n. Brit. var. of FONT[2].

fountain •n. **1** a decorative structure in a pool or lake from which a jet of water is pumped into the air. **2** a source of something desirable. **3** literary a natural spring of water.
– ORIGIN Old French *fontaine*.

fountainhead •n. an original source of something.

fountain pen •n. a pen with a container from which ink flows continuously to the nib.

four •cardinal number **1** one more than three; 4. (Roman numeral: **iv** or **IV**.) **2** Cricket a hit that reaches the boundary after first striking the ground, scoring four runs. **3** a four-oared rowing boat or its crew.
– DERIVATIVES **fourfold** adj. & adv.
– ORIGIN Old English.

four-by-four (also **4 × 4**) •n. a vehicle with four-wheel drive.

four-letter word •n. any of several short words referring to sex or excretion, regarded as rude.

four-poster (also **four-poster bed**) •n. a bed with a post at each corner supporting a canopy.

foursome •n. a group of four people.

four-square •adj. **1** (of a building) having a square shape and solid appearance. **2** firm and determined. •adv. with firmness and determination.

fourteen •cardinal number one more than thirteen; 14. (Roman numeral: **xiv** or **XIV**.)
– DERIVATIVES **fourteenth** ordinal number.

fourth •ordinal number **1** that is number four in a sequence; 4th. **2** (**a fourth/one fourth**) esp. N. Amer. a quarter. **3** an interval spanning four consecutive notes in a musical scale.
– PHRASES **the fourth estate** the press.
– DERIVATIVES **fourthly** adv.

four-wheel drive •n. a system which provides power directly to all four wheels of a vehicle.

fowl •n. (pl. **fowl** or **fowls**) **1** (also **domestic fowl**) a domesticated bird kept for its eggs or meat, such as a chicken. **2** birds as a group.
– ORIGIN Old English.

fox •n. **1** an animal with a pointed muzzle, bushy tail, and a reddish coat. **2** a sly or crafty person. •v. informal baffle or deceive someone.
– ORIGIN Old English.

foxglove •n. a tall plant with flowers shaped like the fingers of gloves growing up the stem.

foxhole •n. a hole in the ground used by troops as a shelter against enemy fire or as a firing point.

foxhound •n. a breed of dog trained to hunt in packs for foxes.

fox-hunting •n. the sport of hunting a fox across country with a pack of hounds.

foxtrot •n. a ballroom dance which involves switching between slow and quick steps.

foxy •adj. (**foxier, foxiest**) **1** like a fox. **2** crafty or sly.

foyer /foy-ay/ •n. a large entrance hall in a hotel or theatre.
– ORIGIN French, 'hearth, home'.

Fr •abbrev. Father (as a title of priests). [ORIGIN French *frère* 'brother'.] •symb. the chemical element francium.

fr. •abbrev. franc(s).

fracas /fra-kah/ •n. (pl. **fracas** /fra-kahz/) a noisy disturbance or quarrel.
– ORIGIN French.

fraction •n. **1** a number that is not a whole number (e.g. ½, 0.5). **2** a very small part or amount. **3** Chem. each of the parts into which a mixture may be separated by fractionation.
– ORIGIN Latin.

fractional •adj. **1** relating to fractions.

2 very small in amount.
– DERIVATIVES **fractionally** adv.

fractionation • n. Chem. separation of a mixture into its constituent parts by using the fact that they condense or vaporize at different temperatures.

fractious /frak-shuhss/ • adj. **1** bad-tempered. **2** difficult to control.
– ORIGIN from **FRACTION**.

fracture • n. **1** a crack or break. **2** the cracking or breaking of a hard object or hard material. • v. (**fractures, fracturing, fractured**) **1** break or crack. **2** (of a group) break up.
– ORIGIN Latin *fractura*.

fragile • adj. **1** easily broken or damaged. **2** (of a person) delicate and vulnerable.
– DERIVATIVES **fragility** n.
– ORIGIN Latin *fragilis*.

fragment • n. /frag-muhnt/ **1** a small part broken or separated off. **2** an incomplete part: *a fragment of conversation.* • v. /frag-ment/ break into fragments.
– DERIVATIVES **fragmentary** adj. **fragmentation** n.
– ORIGIN Latin *fragmentum*.

fragrance /fray-gruhnss/ • n. **1** a pleasant, sweet smell. **2** a perfume or aftershave.

fragrant • adj. having a pleasant, sweet smell.
– ORIGIN Latin.

frail • adj. **1** (of a person) weak and delicate. **2** easily damaged or broken.
– ORIGIN Old French *fraile*.

frailty • n. (pl. **frailties**) **1** the condition of being weak and delicate. **2** weakness in character or morals: *human frailty.*

frame • n. **1** a rigid structure surrounding a picture, door, etc. **2** (**frames**) a metal or plastic structure holding the lenses of a pair of glasses. **3** the rigid supporting structure of something such as a building or car. **4** the structure of a person's body: *her slim frame.* **5** the underlying structure that supports a system or idea. **6** a single complete picture in a series forming a cinema or video film. **7** a single game of snooker. • v. (**frames, framing, framed**) **1** place a picture in a frame. **2** surround something so as to create an attractive image: *hair cut to frame the face.* **3** create or develop a plan or system. **4** informal produce false evidence against an innocent person to make them appear guilty of a crime.
– PHRASES **frame of mind** a particular mood. **frame of reference** a set of values according to which judgements can be made.
– DERIVATIVES **framer** n.

– ORIGIN Old English, 'be useful'.

frame-up • n. informal a plot to make an innocent person appear guilty of a crime.

framework • n. a supporting or underlying structure.

franc /frangk/ • n. the basic unit of money of France, Belgium, Switzerland, Luxembourg, and several other countries (replaced in France, Belgium, and Luxembourg by the euro in 2002).
– ORIGIN Old French.

franchise /fran-chyz/ • n. **1** formal permission granted by a government or company to a person or group allowing them to sell certain products or services. **2** a business or service run under a franchise. **3** the right to vote in public elections. • v. (**franchises, franchising, franchised**) give someone official permission to sell products or a service.
– DERIVATIVES **franchisee** n. **franchiser** (also **franchisor**) n.
– ORIGIN Old French.

Franciscan /fran-siss-kuhn/ • n. a monk or nun of a Christian religious order following the rule of St Francis of Assisi. • adj. relating to St Francis or the Franciscans.

francium /fran-si-uhm/ • n. an unstable radioactive chemical element.
– ORIGIN from *France*.

Franco- (also **franco-**) • comb. form **1** French; French and ...: *francophone.* **2** relating to France: *Francophile.*
– ORIGIN from Latin *Francus* 'Frank'.

frangible /fran-ji-b'l/ • adj. literary or tech. fragile; brittle.
– ORIGIN Latin *frangibilis*.

frangipani /fran-zhi-pah-ni/ • n. (pl. **frangipanis**) **1** a tropical American tree or shrub with sweet-smelling white, pink, or yellow flowers. **2** perfume obtained from the frangipani plant.
– ORIGIN named after the Italian Marquis Muzio *Frangipani*, who invented a perfume for gloves.

Frank • n. a member of a Germanic people that conquered Gaul in the 6th century.
– DERIVATIVES **Frankish** adj. & n.
– ORIGIN Old English *Franca*.

frank¹ • adj. **1** honest and direct. **2** open or undisguised: *frank admiration.*
– DERIVATIVES **frankness** n.
– ORIGIN Latin *francus* 'free'.

frank² • v. stamp an official mark on a letter or parcel to indicate that postage has been paid or does not need to be paid. • n. a franking mark on a letter or parcel.

Frankenstein | freebie

– ORIGIN from **FRANK**[1], in the former sense 'free of obligation'.

Frankenstein /frang-kuhn-styn/ (also **Frankenstein's monster**) • n. a thing that becomes out of control and terrifying or destructive to its maker.
– ORIGIN from Victor *Frankenstein*, a character in a novel by Mary Shelley.

frankfurter • n. a seasoned smoked sausage made of beef and pork.
– ORIGIN from German *Frankfurter Wurst* 'Frankfurt sausage'.

frankincense /frang-kin-senss/ • n. a kind of sweet-smelling gum obtained from an African tree and burnt as incense.
– ORIGIN from Old French *franc encens* 'high-quality incense'.

frankly • adv. 1 in a frank way. 2 to be frank.

frantic • adj. 1 very agitated as a result of fear or anxiety. 2 done in a very hurried and confused way.
– DERIVATIVES **frantically** adv.
– ORIGIN Old French *frenetique* 'violently mad'.

fraternal /fruh-ter-n'l/ • adj. 1 like a brother. 2 relating to a group of people sharing a common profession or interest. 3 (of twins) developed from separate ova (female reproductive cells) and therefore not identical.
– DERIVATIVES **fraternally** adv.
– ORIGIN Latin *fraternalis*.

fraternity /fruh-ter-ni-ti/ • n. (pl. **fraternities**) 1 a group of people sharing a common profession or interest. 2 friendship and shared support within a group.

fraternize /frat-er-nyz/ (or **fraternise**) • v. (**fraternizes, fraternizing, fraternized**) (usu. **fraternize with**) be on friendly terms.
– DERIVATIVES **fraternization** n.

fratricide /frat-ri-syd/ • n. 1 the killing of your brother or sister. 2 the accidental killing of your own forces in war.
– DERIVATIVES **fratricidal** adj.
– ORIGIN from Latin *frater* 'brother'.

Frau /frow/ • n. (pl. **Frauen** /frow-uhn/) a form of address for a married or widowed German woman.
– ORIGIN German.

fraud /frawd/ • n. 1 the crime of deceiving someone to gain money or personal advantage. 2 a person who deceives people into believing that they have certain qualities or abilities.
– DERIVATIVES **fraudster** n.
– ORIGIN Old French *fraude*.

fraudulent /fraw-dyuu-luhnt/ • adj. 1 involving the use of deception to gain money or personal advantage.

2 deceitful or dishonest.
– DERIVATIVES **fraudulently** adv.

fraught /frawt/ • adj. 1 (**fraught with**) involving something difficult or unwelcome: *the next three weeks were fraught with dangers.* 2 causing or feeling anxiety or stress.
– ORIGIN from Dutch *uracht* 'ship's cargo'.

Fräulein /froy-lyn/ • n. a form of address for an unmarried German woman.
– ORIGIN German.

fray[1] • v. 1 (of a fabric, rope, or cord) unravel or become worn at the edge. 2 (of a person's nerves or temper) show the effects of strain.
– ORIGIN Old French *freiier*.

fray[2] • n. (**the fray**) 1 a very competitive situation. 2 a battle or fight.
– ORIGIN Old French *afrayer* 'disturb'.

frazzle • n. (**a frazzle**) informal 1 an exhausted state. 2 a burnt state.
– ORIGIN perh. from **FRAY**[1] and former *fazle* 'ravel out'.

frazzled • adj. informal highly stressed or exhausted.

freak • n. 1 informal a person who is obsessed with a particular interest: *a fitness freak.* 2 a very unusual and unexpected event. 3 (also **freak of nature**) a person, animal, or plant with a physical abnormality. • adj. very unusual and unexpected: *a freak accident.* • v. (usu. **freak out**) informal react or cause to react in a wild, shocked, or excited way.
– DERIVATIVES **freakish** adj.
– ORIGIN prob. from a dialect word.

freaky • adj. (**freakier, freakiest**) informal very strange.

freckle • n. a small light brown mark on the skin. • v. (**freckles, freckling, freckled**) become marked with freckles.
– DERIVATIVES **freckly** adj.
– ORIGIN Old Norse.

free • adj. (**freer, freest**) 1 not under the control of anyone else; able to do what you want. 2 not confined, obstructed, or fixed. 3 not having or filled with things to do: *free time.* 4 not in use. 5 (**free of/from**) not containing or affected by something undesirable. 6 available without charge. 7 (usu. **free with**) giving things or behaving without restraint. • adv. without cost or payment. • v. (**frees, freeing, freed**) 1 make free. 2 make available for a purpose.
– PHRASES **free and easy** informal and relaxed. **a free hand** freedom to do what you want.
– ORIGIN Old English.

freebie • n. informal a thing given free of charge.

freebooter • n. a person who behaves in an illegal way for their own advantage.
– DERIVATIVES **freebooting** n.
– ORIGIN Dutch *vrijbuiter*.

freeborn • adj. not born in slavery.

Free Church • n. a Christian Church which has separated from an established Church.

freedom • n. 1 the power or right to act, speak, or think freely. 2 the state of being free. 3 (**freedom from**) the state of not being affected by something undesirable. 4 Brit. a special privilege or right of access: *freedom of the City of Glasgow.*

freedom fighter • n. a person who takes part in a struggle to achieve political freedom.

free enterprise • n. an economic system in which private businesses compete with each other with little state control.

free fall • n. 1 downward movement under the force of gravity. 2 a sudden decline that cannot be stopped: *her career was in free fall.*

free-for-all • n. a situation or event in which everyone can take part without restraints or controls.

free-form • adj. not in a regular or formal structure.

freehand • adj. & adv. done by hand without the aid of instruments such as rulers.

freehold • n. esp. Brit. permanent and absolute ownership of land or property with the freedom to sell it when you wish.
– DERIVATIVES **freeholder** n.

free house • n. Brit. a pub that is not controlled by a brewery and therefore not restricted to selling only that brewery's beers.

free kick • n. (in football and rugby) an unopposed kick of the ball awarded when the opposing team breaks the rules.

freelance /free-lahnss/ • adj. self-employed and hired to work for different companies on particular jobs. • n. (also **freelancer**) a freelance worker. • v. (**freelances, freelancing, freelanced**) earn your living as a freelance.

freeloader • n. informal a person who takes advantage of other people's generosity without giving anything in return.
– DERIVATIVES **freeload** v.

free love • n. dated the practice of having sexual relationships freely, without being faithful to one partner.

freely • adv. 1 not under the control of another person. 2 without restriction or restraint. 3 in abundant amounts. 4 willingly and readily.

freeman • n. (pl. **freemen**) 1 Brit. a person who has been given a special privilege or right of access in a city or borough. 2 hist. a person who is not a slave or serf.

free market • n. an economic system in which prices are determined by supply and demand rather than controlled by a government.

Freemason • n. a member of an international order whose members help each other and hold secret ceremonies.
– DERIVATIVES **Freemasonry** n.

free port • n. 1 a port open to all traders. 2 a port area where goods being transported are not subject to customs duty.

free radical • n. Chem. a highly reactive molecule with one odd electron not paired up in a chemical bond.

free-range • adj. (of livestock or eggs) kept or produced in natural conditions, where the animals may move around freely.

freesia /free-zi-uh/ • n. a plant with sweet-smelling, colourful flowers, native to southern Africa.
– ORIGIN named after the German physician Friedrich H. T. *Freese*.

free-standing • adj. not attached to or supported by another structure.

freestyle • adj. (of a contest, race, or type of sport) having few restrictions on the style or technique that competitors use. • v. perform or compete in an unrestricted or improvised fashion.
– DERIVATIVES **freestyler** n.

freethinker • n. a person who has independent ideas and challenges accepted opinions.

free trade • n. international trade left to its natural course without the controls of tariffs or quotas.

free verse • n. poetry that does not rhyme or have a regular rhythm.

free vote • n. esp. Brit. a vote in which members of parliament do not have to conform to the policy of their party.

freeway • n. N. Amer. a dual-carriageway main road.

freewheel • v. 1 ride a bicycle without using the pedals. 2 (as adj. **freewheeling**) not concerned with rules or the results of your actions. • n. a bicycle wheel which is able to turn freely when no power is being applied to the pedals.

free will • n. the power to act according to your own wishes.

freeze • v. (**freezes, freezing, froze**; past part. **frozen**) 1 (with reference to a

liquid) turn or be turned into a solid as a result of extreme cold. **2** become blocked or rigid with ice. **3** be very cold. **4** preserve something by storing it at a very low temperature. **5** become suddenly motionless with fear or shock. **6** keep or stop at a fixed level or in a fixed state. **7** (of a computer screen) suddenly become locked. **8** (**freeze someone out**) informal make someone feel left out by treating them in a cold or hostile way. •n. **1** an act of freezing. **2** a period of very cold weather.
– ORIGIN Old English.

freeze-dry •v. preserve something by rapidly freezing it and then removing the ice in a vacuum.

freeze-frame •n. the facility or process of stopping a film or videotape to obtain a single still image.

freezer •n. a refrigerated cabinet for preserving food at very low temperatures.

freezing •adj. **1** having a temperature below 0°C. **2** very cold. **3** (of fog or rain) consisting of droplets which freeze rapidly on contact with a surface. •n. the freezing point of water (0°C).

freezing point •n. the temperature at which a liquid turns into a solid when cooled.

freight /frayt/ •n. **1** transport of goods in bulk by lorry, train, ship, or aircraft. **2** goods transported by freight. •v. transport by freight.
– ORIGIN Dutch and German *vrecht*.

freighter •n. a large ship or aircraft designed to carry freight.

French •adj. relating to France or its people or language. •n. the language of France, also used in parts of Belgium, Switzerland, Canada, and elsewhere.
– ORIGIN Old English.

French bean •n. Brit. an edible green bean.

French bread •n. white bread in a long, crisp loaf.

French Canadian •n. a Canadian whose native language is French.

French dressing •n. a salad dressing of vinegar, oil, and seasonings.

French fries •pl. n. esp. N. Amer. chips.

French horn •n. a brass instrument with a coiled tube, valves, and a wide bell.

French kiss •n. a kiss with contact between tongues.

Frenchman (or **Frenchwoman**) •n. (pl. **Frenchmen** or **Frenchwomen**) a person who is French by birth or descent.

French polish •n. a kind of polish that produces a high gloss on wood.

•v. (**French-polish**) treat wood with French polish.

French window •n. each of a pair of glazed doors in an outside wall.

frenetic /fruh-net-ik/ •adj. fast and energetic in a disorganized way.
– DERIVATIVES **frenetically** adv.
– ORIGIN Old French *frenetique* 'violently mad'.

frenzy •n. (pl. **frenzies**) a state or period of uncontrolled excitement or wild behaviour.
– DERIVATIVES **frenzied** adj. **frenziedly** adv.
– ORIGIN Latin *phrenesia*.

frequency •n. (pl. **frequencies**) **1** the rate at which something occurs in a given period or sample. **2** the state of being frequent. **3** the number of cycles per second of a sound, light, or radio wave. **4** the particular waveband at which radio signals are transmitted.

frequency modulation •n. the varying of the frequency of a wave, used as a means of broadcasting an audio signal by radio.

frequent •adj. /free-kwuhnt/ **1** occurring or done many times at short intervals. **2** doing something often: *a frequent visitor.* •v. /fri-kwent/ visit a place often.
– DERIVATIVES **frequenter** n. **frequently** adv.
– ORIGIN Latin *frequens* 'crowded'.

fresco /fress-koh/ •n. (pl. **frescoes** or **frescos**) a painting done on wet plaster on a wall or ceiling, in which the colours become fixed as the plaster dries.
– ORIGIN Italian, 'cool, fresh'.

fresh •adj. **1** new or different. **2** (of food) recently made or obtained. **3** recently created and not faded: *the memory was fresh in their minds.* **4** (of water) not salty. **5** (of the wind) cool and fairly strong. **6** pleasantly clean and cool: *fresh air.* **7** full of energy and vigour. **8** informal overfamiliar in a sexual way. •adv. newly; recently.
– DERIVATIVES **freshly** adv. **freshness** n.
– ORIGIN Old English.

freshen •v. make or become fresh or fresher.
– DERIVATIVES **freshener** n.

fresher •n. Brit. informal a first-year student at college or university.

freshman •n. a first-year student at university or (N. Amer.) at high school.

freshwater •adj. relating to or found in fresh water.

fret[1] •v. (**frets, fretting, fretted**) be constantly or visibly anxious.
– ORIGIN Old English, 'devour, consume'.

fret[2] •n. each of a sequence of ridges on

the fingerboard of some stringed instruments, used for fixing the positions of the fingers.

fretful • adj. anxious or irritated.
– DERIVATIVES **fretfully** adv.

fretsaw • n. a saw with a narrow blade for cutting designs in thin wood or metal.

fretwork • n. decorative designs cut into wood.
– ORIGIN Old French *frete* 'trelliswork'.

Freudian /froy-di-uhn/ • adj. relating to the Austrian psychotherapist Sigmund Freud and his methods of psycho-analysis.

Fri. • abbrev. Friday.

friable /fry-uh-b'l/ • adj. easily crumbled.
– DERIVATIVES **friability** n.
– ORIGIN Latin *friabilis*.

friar • n. a member of certain religious orders of men.
– ORIGIN Old French *frere*.

friary • n. (pl. **friaries**) a building occupied by friars.

fricassée /fri-kuh-say/ • n. a dish of stewed or fried pieces of meat served in a thick white sauce.
– ORIGIN French.

friction • n. 1 the resistance that one surface or object encounters when moving over another. 2 the action of one surface or object rubbing against another. 3 conflict or disagreement.
– DERIVATIVES **frictional** adj. **frictionless** adj.
– ORIGIN Latin.

Friday • n. the day of the week before Saturday and following Thursday.
– ORIGIN Old English, named after the Germanic goddess *Frigga*.

fridge • n. a refrigerator.

fridge-freezer • n. an upright unit made up of a separate refrigerator and freezer.

fried past and past part. of FRY¹.

friend • n. 1 a person you like and know well. 2 a person who supports a particular cause or organization. 3 (**Friend**) a Quaker.
– DERIVATIVES **friendless** adj. **friendship** n.
– ORIGIN Old English.

☑ Spell **friend** with **-ie-** in the middle.

friendly • adj. (**friendlier**, **friendliest**) 1 warm and pleasant to other people. 2 (in combination) not harmful to a specified thing: *environment-friendly*. 3 Mil. relating to your own forces: *friendly fire*. • n. (pl. **friendlies**) Brit. a game not forming part of a serious competition.

– DERIVATIVES **friendlily** adv. **friendliness** n.

friendly society • n. (in the UK) an association owned by its members and providing sickness benefits, life assurance, and pensions.

Friesian /free-zh'n/ • n. Brit. an animal of a black-and-white breed of dairy cattle.

frieze /freez/ • n. a broad horizontal band of sculpted or painted decoration.
– ORIGIN Latin *frisium*.

frigate /fri-guht/ • n. a warship with mixed weapons.
– ORIGIN Italian *fregata*.

fright • n. 1 a sudden strong feeling of fear. 2 a shock.
– ORIGIN Old English.

frighten • v. 1 make a person or animal afraid. 2 (**frighten someone/thing off**) make someone or something too afraid to do something.
– DERIVATIVES **frightened** adj. **frightening** adj.

frightener • n. (in phr. **put the frighteners on**) Brit. informal threaten or intimidate.

frightful • adj. 1 very unpleasant, serious, or shocking. 2 informal very bad; awful.
– DERIVATIVES **frightfully** adv.

frigid /fri-jid/ • adj. 1 very cold. 2 (of a woman) unable to be sexually aroused.
– DERIVATIVES **frigidity** n. **frigidly** adv.
– ORIGIN Latin *frigidus*.

frill • n. 1 a strip of gathered or pleated material used as a decorative edging. 2 a frill-like growth of feathers, hair, skin, or scales on an animal. 3 (**frills**) unnecessary extra features.
– DERIVATIVES **frilled** adj. **frilly** adj.
– ORIGIN Flemish *frul*.

fringe • n. 1 a border of threads, tassels, or twists, used to edge clothing or soft furnishings. 2 esp. Brit. the front part of someone's hair, cut so as to hang over the forehead. 3 a natural border of hair or fibres in an animal or plant. 4 the outer part of something. • adj. not part of the mainstream: *fringe theatre*.
• v. (**fringes**, **fringing**, **fringed**) provide with or form a fringe.
– ORIGIN Old French *frenge*.

fringe benefit • n. a benefit received in addition to your regular pay.

frippery • n. (pl. **fripperies**) 1 showy or unnecessary ornament. 2 a frivolous thing.
– ORIGIN Old French *freperie* 'second-hand clothes'.

frisbee • n. trademark a plastic disc

designed for skimming through the air as an outdoor game.
- ORIGIN said to be named after the pie tins of the *Frisbie* bakery in Connecticut.

Frisian /free-zi-uhn, free-zhuhn/ •n. **1** a person from Frisia or Friesland in the Netherlands. **2** the Germanic language spoken in northern parts of the Netherlands and adjacent islands.
•adj. relating to Frisia or Friesland.

frisk •v. **1** pass the hands over someone in a search for hidden weapons or drugs. **2** skip or move playfully.
- ORIGIN Old French *frisque* 'alert'.

frisky •adj. (**friskier, friskiest**) playful and full of energy.

frisson /free-son/ •n. a sudden shiver of excitement.
- ORIGIN French.

fritillary /fri-til-luh-ri/ •n. (pl. **fritillaries**) **1** a plant with hanging bell-like flowers. **2** a butterfly with orange-brown wings chequered with black.
- ORIGIN Latin *fritillaria*.

fritter¹ •v. (**fritters, frittering, frittered**) (**fritter away**) waste time, money, or energy on unimportant matters.
- ORIGIN from former *fitter* 'break into fragments'.

fritter² •n. a piece of food that is coated in batter and deep-fried.
- ORIGIN Old French *friture*.

frivolous •adj. **1** not having any serious purpose or value. **2** (of a person) failing to give serious consideration to something.
- DERIVATIVES **frivolity** n. **frivolously** adv.
- ORIGIN Latin *frivolus* 'silly, trifling'.

frizz •v. (of hair) form into a mass of tight curls. •n. a mass of tightly curled hair.
- ORIGIN French *friser*.

frizzy •adj. (**frizzier, frizziest**) made up of a mass of small, tight curls.
- DERIVATIVES **frizziness** n.

fro •adv. see **to and fro** (at **TO**).
- ORIGIN Old Norse.

frock •n. **1** esp. Brit. a dress. **2** a loose outer garment, worn by priests.
- ORIGIN Old French *froc*.

frock coat •n. a man's double-breasted, long-skirted coat.

frog¹ •n. an amphibian with a short body and no tail and very long hind legs for leaping.
- PHRASES **have a frog in your throat** informal be slightly hoarse
- DERIVATIVES **froggy** adj.
- ORIGIN Old English

frog² •n. **1** a thing used to hold or fasten something. **2** an ornamental coat

fastener consisting of a spindle-shaped button and a loop.
- ORIGIN perh. from **FROG**¹.

frog³ •n. a horny pad in the sole of a horse's hoof.
- ORIGIN perh. from **FROG**¹.

frogman •n. (pl. **frogmen**) a diver equipped with a rubber suit, flippers, and breathing equipment.

frogmarch •v. force someone to walk forward by pinning their arms back and pushing them from behind.

frogspawn •n. a mass of frogs' eggs surrounded by transparent jelly.

frolic •v. (**frolics, frolicking, frolicked**) play or move about in a cheerful and lively way. •n. a playful action or activity.
- ORIGIN Dutch *vrolijk* 'merry, cheerful'.

frolicsome •adj. lively and playful.

from •prep. **1** indicating the point at which a journey, process, or action starts. **2** indicating the source of something. **3** indicating the starting point of a range. **4** indicating separation, removal, or prevention. **5** indicating a cause. **6** indicating a difference.
- ORIGIN Old English.

fromage frais /from-ahzh fray/ •n. a type of smooth soft fresh cheese.
- ORIGIN French, 'fresh cheese'.

frond •n. the leaf or leaf-like part of a palm, fern, or similar plant.
- ORIGIN Latin *frons*.

front •n. **1** the part of an object that faces forwards and is normally seen first. **2** the position directly ahead. **3** the forward-facing part of a person's body. **4** a face of a building: *the west front of the Cathedral.* **5** the furthest position that an army has reached. **6** Meteorol. the forward edge of an advancing mass of air. **7** a particular situation or sphere: *good news on the jobs front.* **8** an organized political group. **9** a false appearance or way of behaving. **10** a person or organization serving as a cover for secret or illegal activities. **11** a bold and confident manner.
•adj. relating to the front. •v. **1** have the front facing towards. **2** place or be at the front of. **3** provide with a part at the front: *fronted with iron bars.* **4** be at the forefront of. **5** present a television or radio programme. **6** act as a cover for someone who is doing something illegal.
- PHRASES **front of house** Brit. the parts of a theatre in front of the stage. **in front of** in the presence of.
- ORIGIN Latin *frons* 'forehead, front'.

frontage •n. **1** the front of a building. **2** a strip of land next to a street or waterway.

frontal • adj. relating to the front.
– DERIVATIVES **frontally** adv.

frontbencher • n. a member of the cabinet or shadow cabinet, who sits in the front benches in the House of Commons.
– DERIVATIVES **front-bench** adj.

frontier • n. **1** a border separating two countries. **2** the extreme limit of settled land beyond which lies wilderness. **3** the extreme limit of understanding or achievement in a particular area.
– ORIGIN Old French *frontiere*.

frontispiece /frun-tiss-peess/ • n. an illustration facing the title page of a book.
– ORIGIN Latin *frontispicium* 'facade'.

front line • n. the part of an army that is closest to the enemy.

frontman • n. (pl. **frontmen**) **1** the leader of a band. **2** a person who represents an illegal organization to make it seem respectable.

front runner • n. the contestant who is leading in a competition.

front-wheel drive • n. a system that provides power to the front wheels of a motor vehicle.

frost • n. **1** a deposit of white ice crystals formed on surfaces when the temperature falls below freezing. **2** a period of cold weather when frost forms. • v. cover with frost.
– ORIGIN Old English.

frostbite • n. injury to body tissues caused by exposure to extreme cold.
– DERIVATIVES **frostbitten** adj.

frosted • adj. **1** covered with frost. **2** (of glass) having a textured surface.

frosting • n. N. Amer. icing.

frosty • adj. (**frostier, frostiest**) **1** (of the weather) very cold with frost forming on surfaces. **2** cold and unfriendly.
– DERIVATIVES **frostily** adv. **frostiness** n.

froth • n. **1** a mass of small bubbles in liquid. **2** unimportant talk, ideas, or activities. • v. form or contain froth.
– DERIVATIVES **frothy** adj.
– ORIGIN Old Norse.

frown • v. **1** crease your forehead to show displeasure or concentration. **2** (**frown on**) disapprove of. • n. a creasing of the forehead to show displeasure or concentration.
– ORIGIN Old French *froignier*.

frowsty /frow-sti/ • adj. Brit. having a stale and stuffy atmosphere.
– ORIGIN from **FROWZY**.

frowzy /frow-zi/ (also **frowsy**) • adj. scruffy, dingy, and neglected in appearance.

froze past of **FREEZE**.

frozen past part. of **FREEZE**.

fructify /fruk-ti-fy/ • v. (**fructifies, fructifying, fructified**) formal **1** make or become fruitful. **2** bear fruit.
– ORIGIN Latin *fructificare*.

fructose /fruk-tohz/ • n. a simple sugar found chiefly in honey and fruit.
– ORIGIN Latin *fructus* 'fruit'.

frugal /froo-g'l/ • adj. **1** using only as much money or food as is necessary. **2** (of a meal) plain and cheap.
– DERIVATIVES **frugality** n. **frugally** adv.
– ORIGIN Latin *frugalis*.

fruit • n. **1** the sweet and fleshy product of a plant that contains seed and can be eaten as food. **2** Bot. the seed-bearing part of a plant, e.g. an acorn. **3** the positive result of work or activity. • v. produce fruit.
– PHRASES **bear fruit** have good results.
– ORIGIN Latin *fructus* 'enjoyment of produce'.

fruit bat • n. a large bat which feeds chiefly on fruit or nectar.

fruitcake • n. informal an eccentric or mad person.

fruiterer • n. esp. Brit. a person who sells fruit.

fruit fly • n. a small fly which feeds on fruit.

fruitful • adj. **1** producing much fruit. **2** producing good results.
– DERIVATIVES **fruitfully** adv. **fruitfulness** n.

fruiting body • n. the spore-producing organ of a fungus, often seen as a toadstool.

fruition /fruu-i-sh'n/ • n. the fulfilment of a plan or project.
– ORIGIN Latin.

fruitless • adj. failing to achieve the desired results.
– DERIVATIVES **fruitlessly** adv.

fruit machine • n. Brit. a coin-operated gambling machine that generates combinations of symbols, certain combinations winning money for the player.

fruit salad • n. a mixture of different types of chopped fruit served in syrup or juice.

fruity • adj. (**fruitier, fruitiest**) **1** relating to fruit. **2** (of a voice) deep and rich. **3** Brit. informal sexually suggestive.
– DERIVATIVES **fruitiness** n.

frump • n. an unattractive woman who wears old-fashioned clothes.
– DERIVATIVES **frumpy** adj.
– ORIGIN prob. from Dutch *verrompelen* 'wrinkle'.

frustrate • v. (**frustrates, frustrating, frustrated**) **1** prevent a plan or action

from progressing or succeeding.
2 prevent someone from doing or achieving something. **3** make someone feel dissatisfied as a result of being unable to do something.
– DERIVATIVES **frustrated** adj. **frustrating** adj. **frustration** n.
– ORIGIN Latin *frustrare* 'disappoint'.

fry[1] • v. (**fries, frying, fried**) cook in hot fat or oil. • n. (**fries**) French fries.
– ORIGIN Old French *frire*.

fry[2] • pl. n. young fish.
– ORIGIN Old Norse.

fryer • n. a large, deep container for frying food.

frying pan • n. a shallow pan with a long handle, used for frying food.
– PHRASES **out of the frying pan into the fire** from a bad situation to one that is worse.

fry-up • n. Brit. informal a dish of fried food.

ft • abbrev. foot or feet.

FTSE index (also **FT index**) • n. a figure (published by the *Financial Times*) indicating the relative prices of shares on the London Stock Exchange.
– ORIGIN short for *Financial Times Stock Exchange*.

fuchsia /fyoo-shuh/ • n. **1** an ornamental shrub with drooping tubular flowers. **2** a vivid purplish-red colour.
– ORIGIN named after the German botanist Leonhard *Fuchs*.

fuddled • adj. not able to think clearly, especially as a result of drinking alcohol.

fuddy-duddy • n. (pl. **fuddy-duddies**) informal a person who is old-fashioned and disapproving.

fudge • n. **1** a soft sweet made from sugar, butter, and milk or cream. **2** an attempt to present an issue in a vague way in order to avoid the truth. • v. (**fudges, fudging, fudged**) **1** present in a vague way. **2** manipulate facts or figures so as to present a more desirable picture.
– ORIGIN prob. from former *fadge* 'to fit'.

fuehrer • n. var. of FÜHRER.

fuel • n. **1** material such as coal, gas, or oil that is burned to produce heat or power. **2** food, drink, or drugs as a source of energy. **3** something that stirs up argument or strong emotion. • v. (**fuels, fuelling, fuelled**; US **fuels, fueling, fueled**) **1** supply or power with fuel. **2** stir up feeling or activity.
– ORIGIN Old French *fouaille*.

fuel injection • n. the direct introduction of fuel into the cylinders of an internal-combustion engine.

fug • n. Brit. informal a warm, stuffy atmosphere.

– DERIVATIVES **fuggy** adj.

fugitive /fyoo-ji-tiv/ • n. a person who has escaped from captivity or is in hiding. • adj. quick to disappear: *a fugitive memory*.
– ORIGIN Latin *fugitivus*.

fugue /fyoog/ • n. Music a composition in which a short melody or phrase is introduced by one part and successively taken up by others.
– ORIGIN Latin *fuga* 'flight'.

führer /fyoo-uh-ruh/ (also **fuehrer**) • n. the title used by Hitler as leader of Germany.
– ORIGIN German, 'leader'.

-ful • suffix **1** (forming adjectives) full of: *sorrowful*. **2** (forming adjectives from verbs) accustomed to: *forgetful*. **3** forming nouns referring to the amount needed to fill the specified container: *bucketful*.

fulcrum /fuul-kruhm/ • n. (pl. **fulcra** /fuul-kruh/ or **fulcrums**) the point on which a lever turns or is supported.
– ORIGIN Latin, 'post of a couch'.

fulfil (US **fulfill**) • v. (**fulfils, fulfilling, fulfilled**; US **fulfills, fulfilling, fulfilled**) **1** achieve or realize something desired, promised, or predicted. **2** meet a requirement. **3** (**fulfil yourself**) gain satisfaction by fully developing your abilities.
– ORIGIN Old English, 'fill up, make full'.

fulfilment (US **fulfillment**) • n. **1** a feeling of satisfaction resulting from fully developing your abilities. **2** the action of fulfilling something.

> ☑ There is only one **l** in the middle of **fulfilment** (the spelling **fulfillment** is American).

full[1] • adj. **1** holding as much as or as many as possible. **2** (**full of**) having a large number or quantity of. **3** complete: *full details on request*. **4** (**full of**) unable to stop talking or thinking about. **5** plump or rounded. **6** (of flavour, sound, or colour) strong or rich. • adv. **1** straight. **2** very.
– PHRASES **full of yourself** too proud of yourself. **full on 1** running at or providing maximum power or capacity. **2** so as to make a direct impact. **full steam** (or **speed**) **ahead** proceeding with as much speed or energy as possible. **full up** filled to capacity. **to the full** to the greatest possible extent.
– ORIGIN Old English.

full[2] • v. clean, shrink, and thicken cloth using heat, pressure, and moisture.
– ORIGIN prob. from FULLER.

full back • n. a player in a defensive

position near the goal in a game such as football.

full-blooded • adj. wholehearted and enthusiastic.

full-blown • adj. fully developed.

full board • n. Brit. a type of accommodation at a hotel or guest house which includes all meals.

full-bodied • adj. rich and satisfying in flavour or sound.

fuller • n. a person whose occupation is preparing cloth by cleaning, shrinking, and thickening it.
– ORIGIN Old English *fullere*.

fuller's earth • n. a type of clay used in preparing and thickening cloth.

full-frontal • adj. fully exposing the genitals.

full house • n. 1 a theatre or meeting that is filled to capacity. 2 a winning card at bingo.

full moon • n. the phase of the moon in which its whole disc is lit up.

fullness (also **fulness**) • n. the state of being full.
– PHRASES **in the fullness of time** after a due length of time has gone by.

full-scale • adj. 1 (of a model or plan) of the same size as the thing represented. 2 complete and thorough: *a full-scale invasion.*

full stop • n. a punctuation mark (.) used at the end of a sentence or an abbreviation.

full-time • adj. using the whole of a person's available working time. • adv. on a full-time basis. • n. (**full time**) the end of a sports match.
– DERIVATIVES **full-timer** n.

fully • adv. 1 completely. 2 no less or fewer than: *fully 65 per cent.*

-fully • suffix forming adverbs corresponding to adjectives ending in -*ful*: *sorrowfully.*

fully fledged • adj. Brit. completely developed or established: *a fully fledged pilot.*

fulmar /fuul-mer/ • n. a grey and white northern seabird.
– ORIGIN Old Norse, 'stinking gull'.

fulminate /fuul-mi-nayt/
• v. (**fulminates, fulminating, fulminated**) express strong protest.
– DERIVATIVES **fulmination** n.
– ORIGIN Latin *fulminare* 'strike with lightning'.

fulness • n. var. of fullness (see **FULL¹**).

fulsome • adj. 1 excessively flattering. 2 of large size or quantity: *fulsome details.*
– DERIVATIVES **fulsomely** adv.

fumble • v. (**fumbles, fumbling,**

fumbled) 1 use the hands clumsily while doing something. 2 (of the hands) do something clumsily. 3 (**fumble about/around**) move about clumsily using your hands to find your way. 4 express yourself or deal with something clumsily or nervously. • n. an act of fumbling.
– ORIGIN German *fommeln* or Dutch *fommelen*.

fume • n. a gas or vapour that smells strongly or is dangerous to breathe in.
• v. (**fumes, fuming, fumed**) 1 send out fumes. 2 feel very angry.
– ORIGIN Latin *fumus* 'smoke'.

fumigate /fyoo-mi-gayt/
• v. (**fumigates, fumigating, fumigated**) use the fumes of certain chemicals to disinfect a contaminated area.
– DERIVATIVES **fumigation** n. **fumigator** n.
– ORIGIN Latin *fumigare*.

fun • n. 1 light-hearted enjoyment. 2 a source of light-hearted enjoyment. 3 playfulness: *she's full of fun.* • adj. informal enjoyable.
– PHRASES **make fun of** laugh at in a mocking way.

function • n. 1 an activity that is natural to or the purpose of a person or thing. 2 a large or formal social event. 3 a basic task of a computer. 4 Math. a relationship between one element and another, or between several elements and one another. • v. 1 operate in a proper or particular way. 2 (**function as**) fulfil the purpose of.
– ORIGIN French *fonction*.

functional • adj. 1 relating to a function. 2 designed to be practical and useful. 3 working or operating.
– DERIVATIVES **functionality** n. **functionally** adv.

functionalism • n. the theory that the design of an object should be governed by its use rather than a pleasant appearance.
– DERIVATIVES **functionalist** n. & adj.

functionary • n. (pl. **functionaries**) an official.

fund • n. 1 a sum of money saved or made available for a purpose. 2 (**funds**) financial resources. 3 a large stock.
• v. provide with a sum of money.
– DERIVATIVES **funding** n.
– ORIGIN Latin *fundus* 'bottom'.

fundamental • adj. of basic importance. • n. a basic rule or principle: *the fundamentals of navigation.*
– DERIVATIVES **fundamentally** adv.
– ORIGIN Latin *fundamentum* 'foundation'.

fundamentalism • n. 1 a form of Protestant Christianity which promotes

the belief that the Bible is literally true. **2** the strict following of the basic underlying doctrines of any religion or system of thought.
– DERIVATIVES **fundamentalist** n. & adj.

fundamental note • n. Music the lowest note of a chord.

fund-raiser • n. **1** a person who raises money for an organization or cause. **2** an event held to raise money for an organization or cause.
– DERIVATIVES **fund-raising** n.

funeral • n. a ceremony in which a dead person is buried or cremated.
– ORIGIN Latin *funeralia*.

funeral director • n. an undertaker.

funeral parlour (also **funeral home**) • n. a place where someone who has died is prepared for burial or cremation.

funerary /fyoo-nuh-ruh-ri/ • adj. relating to a funeral or other rites in which people who have died are remembered.

funereal /fyoo-neer-i-uhl/ • adj. having the solemn character appropriate to a funeral.

funfair • n. esp. Brit. a fair consisting of rides, sideshows, and other amusements.

fungi pl. of FUNGUS.

fungicide /fun-ji-syd, fung-gi-syd/ • n. a chemical that destroys fungi.
– DERIVATIVES **fungicidal** adj.

fungus /fung-guhss/ • n. (pl. **fungi** /fung-gy/) a spore-producing organism, such as a mushroom, that has no leaves or flowers and grows on other plants or on decaying matter.
– DERIVATIVES **fungal** adj.
– ORIGIN Latin.

funicular /fuh-nik-yuu-ler/ • adj. (of a railway on a steep slope) operated by cables attached to cars which balance each other while one goes up and the other goes down.
– ORIGIN Latin *funiculus* 'little rope'.

funk[1] informal • n. (also **blue funk**) a state of panic or depression. • v. avoid something out of fear.
– ORIGIN perh. from FUNK[2] in the informal sense 'tobacco smoke'.

funk[2] • n. a style of popular dance music of US black origin, having a strong rhythm.
– ORIGIN perh. from French dialect *funkier* 'blow smoke on'.

funky • adj. (**funkier**, **funkiest**) informal **1** (of music) having a strong dance rhythm. **2** strikingly stylish and unusual.
– DERIVATIVES **funkily** adv. **funkiness** n.

funnel • n. **1** a utensil that is wide at the top and narrow at the bottom, used for guiding liquid or powder into a small opening. **2** a metal chimney on a ship or steam engine. • v. (**funnels, funnelling, funnelled**; US **funnels, funneling, funneled**) guide or move through a funnel or narrow space.
– ORIGIN Provençal *fonilh*.

funny • adj. (**funnier, funniest**) **1** causing laughter or amusement. **2** strange. **3** suspicious: *something funny is going on.* **4** informal slightly unwell.
– DERIVATIVES **funnily** adv.

funny bone • n. informal the part of the elbow over which a very sensitive nerve passes.

fun run • n. informal an uncompetitive run held to raise money for charity.

fur • n. **1** the short, soft hair of some animals. **2** the skin of an animal with fur on it, used in making garments. **3** a coat made from fur. **4** a coating formed on the tongue as a sign of illness. • v. (**furs, furring, furred**) Brit. coat or clog with a deposit of a substance.
– ORIGIN Old French *forrer* 'to line'.

furbelow • n. **1** a strip of gathered or pleated material attached to a skirt or petticoat. **2** (**furbelows**) showy trimmings.
– ORIGIN French *falbala* 'trimming'.

furious • adj. **1** very angry. **2** full of anger or energy: *he drove at a furious speed.*
– DERIVATIVES **furiously** adv.
– ORIGIN Latin *furiosus*.

furl • v. roll or fold up neatly and securely.
– ORIGIN French *ferler*.

furlong • n. an eighth of a mile, 220 yards.
– ORIGIN from the Old English words for 'furrow' + 'long'.

furlough /fer-loh/ • n. permission to leave your duties or job for a period of time.
– ORIGIN Dutch *verlof*.

furnace • n. **1** an enclosed chamber in which material can be heated to very high temperatures. **2** a very hot place.
– ORIGIN Latin *fornax*.

furnish • v. **1** provide a room or building with furniture and fittings. **2** (**furnish someone/thing with**) supply someone or something with equipment or information. **3** provide something.
– ORIGIN Old French *furnir*.

furnishings • pl. n. furniture and fittings in a room or building.

furniture • n. the movable objects that are used to make a room or building suitable for living or working in.
– ORIGIN French *fourniture*.

furore /fyoo-ror-i/ (US **furor** /fyoo-ror/)
• n. an outbreak of public anger or excitement.
– ORIGIN Italian.

furrier /furr-i-er/ • n. a person who prepares or deals in furs.

furrow • n. **1** a long, narrow trench made in the ground by a plough. **2** a rut or groove. **3** a deep wrinkle on a person's face. • v. make a furrow in.
– ORIGIN Old English.

furry • adj. (**furrier, furriest**) covered with or like fur.

further • adv. (also **farther**) **1** at or to a greater distance. **2** for a longer way: *he had walked further than intended.*
3 beyond the point already reached. **4** at or to a more advanced stage. **5** in addition. • adj. **1** (also **farther**) more distant in space. **2** additional.
• v. (**furthers, furthering, furthered**) help the progress of.
– PHRASES **further to** formal following on from.
– ORIGIN comparative of FAR.

> USAGE: When should you use **further** and when is it better to say **farther**? When talking about distance, either form can be used: *she moved further down the train* and *she moved farther down the train* are both correct. However, you should use **further** when you mean 'beyond or in addition to what has already been done' (*I won't trouble you any further*) or when you mean 'additional' (*phone for further information*).

furtherance • n. the action of helping a plan to progress.

further education • n. Brit. education below degree level for people above school age.

furthermore • adv. in addition.

furthest (also **farthest**) • adj. **1** situated at the greatest distance. **2** covering the greatest area or distance. • adv. **1** at or by the greatest distance. **2** over the greatest distance or area. **3** to the most extreme or advanced point.

furtive • adj. trying to avoid being noticed in a secretive or guilty way.
– DERIVATIVES **furtively** adv.
– ORIGIN Latin *furtivus*.

fury • n. (pl. **furies**) **1** extreme anger.
2 extreme strength or violence: *the fury of a gathering storm.* **3** (**Furies**) Gk Myth. three goddesses who punished people for doing wrong.
– ORIGIN Latin *furia*.

furze • n. = GORSE.
– ORIGIN Old English.

fuse¹ • v. (**fuses, fusing, fused**) **1** join or become combined to form a whole.
2 melt a material or object with intense

heat, so as to join it with something else. **3** Brit. (of an electrical appliance) stop working when a fuse melts. **4** provide a circuit or electrical appliance with a fuse. • n. a safety device consisting of a strip of wire that melts and breaks an electric circuit if the current goes beyond a safe level.
– ORIGIN Latin *fundere* 'pour, melt'.

fuse² (US also **fuze**) • n. **1** a length of material along which a small flame moves to explode a bomb or firework.
2 a device in a bomb that controls the timing of the explosion. • v. (**fuses, fusing, fused**; US **fuzes, fuzing, fuzed**) fit a fuse to a bomb.
– ORIGIN Latin *fusus* 'spindle'.

fuse box • n. a box containing the fuses for electrical circuits in a building.

fuselage /fyoo-zuh-lahzh/ • n. the main body of an aircraft.
– ORIGIN French.

fusible • adj. able to be melted easily.

Fusilier /fyoo-zi-leer/ • n. a member of any of several British regiments formerly armed with fusils (light muskets).
– ORIGIN French.

fusillade /fyoo-zi-layd/ • n. a series of shots fired at the same time or quickly one after the other.
– ORIGIN French.

fusion • n. **1** the process or result of fusing things to form a whole. **2** a reaction in which light atomic nuclei fuse to form a heavier nucleus, releasing much energy. **3** popular music that is a mixture of different styles, especially jazz and rock. • adj. referring to food or cooking which combines elements of both eastern and western cuisine.
– ORIGIN Latin.

fuss • n. **1** a display of unnecessary excitement or anxiety. **2** a protest or complaint. • v. **1** show unnecessary concern about something. **2** treat with excessive attention or affection.
– PHRASES **not be fussed** Brit. informal not have strong feelings about something.
– ORIGIN perh. Anglo-Irish.

fusspot • n. informal a fussy person.

fussy • adj. (**fussier, fussiest**) **1** hard to please. **2** full of unnecessary detail.
– DERIVATIVES **fussily** adv. **fussiness** n.

fustian /fuss-ti-uhn/ • n. a thick, hard-wearing cloth woven with parallel diagonal lines.
– ORIGIN from Latin *pannus fustaneus* 'cloth from *Fostat*', a suburb of Cairo.

fusty • adj. **1** smelling stale and damp or stuffy. **2** old-fashioned.
– DERIVATIVES **fustiness** n.

– ORIGIN Old French *fuste* 'smelling of the cask'.

futile • adj. producing no useful results; pointless.
– DERIVATIVES **futilely** adv. **futility** n.
– ORIGIN Latin *futilis*.

futon /foo-ton/ • n. a Japanese padded mattress that can be rolled up.
– ORIGIN Japanese.

future • n. 1 (**the future**) time that is still to come. 2 events or conditions occurring or existing in time still to come. 3 a prospect of success or happiness: *I might have a future as an artist.* 4 Grammar a tense of verbs expressing events that have not yet happened. • adj. 1 existing or occurring in the future. 2 destined to hold a specified position: *his future wife.* 3 Grammar (of a tense) expressing an event yet to happen.
– PHRASES **in future** from now onward.
– ORIGIN Latin *futurus* 'going to be'.

future perfect • n. Grammar a tense of verbs expressing an action that will be completed in the future, as in English *will have done.*

Futurism • n. an early 20th-century artistic movement which strongly rejected traditional forms and embraced modern technology.
– DERIVATIVES **Futurist** n. & adj.

futuristic • adj. 1 having or involving very modern technology or design. 2 (of a film or book) set in the future.

futurity /fyoo-tyoor-i-ti/ • n. (pl. **futurities**) 1 the future time. 2 a future event.

fuze • n. US = FUSE².

fuzz¹ • n. a frizzy mass of hair or fibre.
– ORIGIN prob. German or Dutch.

fuzz² • n. (**the fuzz**) informal the police.

fuzzy • adj. (**fuzzier**, **fuzziest**) 1 having a frizzy texture or appearance. 2 not clear: *the picture is very fuzzy.*
– DERIVATIVES **fuzzily** adv. **fuzziness** n.

FX • abbrev. visual or sound effects.
– ORIGIN from the pronunciation of *effects.*

FYI • abbrev. for your information.

Gg

G¹ (also **g**) • n. (pl. **Gs** or **G's**) **1** the seventh letter of the alphabet. **2** Music the fifth note in the scale of C major.

G² • abbrev. **1** giga- (10⁹). **2** N. Amer. informal grand (a thousand dollars). **3** the force exerted by the earth's gravitational field.

g • abbrev. **1** Chem. gas. **2** gram(s). • symb. Physics the acceleration due to gravity (9.81 m s⁻²).

Ga • symb. the chemical element gallium.

gab • v. (**gabs, gabbing, gabbed**) informal talk at length.
– PHRASES **the gift of the gab** the ability to speak fluently and persuasively.
– ORIGIN from GOB¹.

gabardine • n. var. of GABERDINE.

gabble • v. (**gabbles, gabbling, gabbled**) talk quickly and in a way that is difficult to understand. • n. talk that is fast and difficult to understand.
– ORIGIN Dutch *gabbelen*.

gaberdine /ga-ber-**deen**/ • n. a smooth, hard-wearing worsted or cotton cloth used especially for making raincoats.
– ORIGIN Old French *gauvardine*.

gable • n. the triangular upper part of a wall at the end of a ridged roof.
– DERIVATIVES **gabled** adj.
– ORIGIN Old Norse.

Gabonese /ga-buh-**neez**/ • n. (pl. **Gabonese**) a person from Gabon, a country in West Africa. • adj. relating to Gabon.

gad • v. (**gads, gadding, gadded**) (**gad about/around**) informal enjoy yourself by visiting many different places or travelling from one place to another.
– ORIGIN Germanic.

gadabout • n. informal a person who is always travelling from one place to another enjoying themselves.

gadfly • n. (pl. **gadflies**) **1** a fly that bites livestock. **2** an annoying person.
– ORIGIN from GAD, or an old word meaning 'a goad'.

gadget • n. a small mechanical device.
– DERIVATIVES **gadgetry** n.

– ORIGIN prob. from French *gâchette* 'lock mechanism'.

gadolinium /gad-uh-**lin**-i-uhm/ • n. a soft silvery-white metallic chemical element.
– ORIGIN named after the Finnish mineralogist Johan *Gadolin*.

Gael /gayl/ • n. a Gaelic-speaking person.
– ORIGIN Scottish Gaelic.

Gaelic /**gay**-lik, ga-lik/ • n. **1** (also **Scottish Gaelic**) a Celtic language spoken in western Scotland. **2** (also **Irish Gaelic**) the Celtic language of Ireland.

gaff¹ • n. a stick with a hook for landing large fish.
– ORIGIN Provençal *gaf* 'hook'.

gaff² • n. (in phr. **blow the gaff**) Brit. informal reveal a plot or secret.

gaff³ • n. Brit. informal a person's home.

gaffe /gaf/ (also **gaff**) • n. an embarrassing blunder or mistake.
– ORIGIN French.

gaffer • n. **1** Brit. informal a person's supervisor or boss. **2** informal an old man. **3** the chief electrician on a film or television set.
– ORIGIN prob. from GODFATHER.

gag¹ • n. **1** a piece of cloth put in or over a person's mouth to prevent them from speaking. **2** a restriction on free speech. • v. (**gags, gagging, gagged**) **1** put a gag on. **2** choke or retch.

gag² • n. a joke or funny story.

gaga /**gah**-gah/ • adj. informal rambling in speech or thought, especially as a result of old age.
– ORIGIN French.

gage¹ /gayj/ • n. old use **1** a valued object given as a guarantee of someone's good faith. **2** a glove or other object thrown down as a challenge to fight.
– ORIGIN Old French.

gage² • n. & v. var. of GAUGE.

gaggle • n. **1** a flock of geese. **2** informal a noisy group of people.

gaiety (US also **gayety**) • n. (pl. **gaieties**) **1** the state or quality of being light-hearted and cheerful. **2** lively celebrations or festivities.

– ORIGIN French *gaieté*.

gaily • adv. **1** in a light-hearted and cheerful way. **2** without thinking of the consequences of your actions. **3** with a bright appearance.

gain • v. **1** obtain or secure: *they fought to gain control of the island*. **2** reach a place: *we gained the summit*. **3** (**gain on**) come closer to a person or thing being chased. **4** increase the amount or rate of weight or speed. **5** increase in value. **6** (**gain in**) improve or progress in some way: *she has gained in confidence*. **7** (of a clock or watch) become fast. • n. **1** a thing that is gained. **2** an increase in wealth or resources.

– ORIGIN Old French *gagnier*.

gainful • adj. (of employment) paid; profitable.

– DERIVATIVES **gainfully** adv.

gainsay /gayn-say/ • v. (**gainsays, gainsaying; gainsaid**) formal deny or contradict.

– ORIGIN from former *gain-* 'against' + SAY.

gait /gayt/ • n. **1** a person's way of walking. **2** a way in which a horse moves along, such as a trot.

– ORIGIN Old Norse, 'street'.

gaiter • n. a covering of cloth or leather for the ankle and lower leg.

– ORIGIN French *guêtre*.

gal • n. informal, esp. N. Amer. a girl or young woman.

gal. • abbrev. gallon(s).

gala /gah-luh/ • n. **1** a social occasion with special entertainments. **2** Brit. a special sports event, especially a swimming competition.

– ORIGIN Old French *gale* 'rejoicing'.

galactic /guh-lak-tik/ • adj. relating to a galaxy or galaxies.

galaxy • n. (pl. **galaxies**) **1** a system of millions or billions of stars. **2** (**the Galaxy**) the galaxy of which the solar system is a part; the Milky Way.

– ORIGIN from Greek *galaxias kuklos* 'milky vault' (referring to the Milky Way).

gale • n. **1** a very strong wind. **2** an outburst of laughter.

– ORIGIN perh. from Old Norse, 'mad, frantic'.

gall[1] /gawl/ • n. bold and disrespectful or rude behaviour.

– ORIGIN Old English.

gall[2] /gawl/ • n. **1** annoyance or resentment. **2** a sore on the skin made by rubbing. • v. make someone feel annoyed or resentful.

– ORIGIN Old English.

gall[3] /gawl/ • n. an abnormal growth on plants or trees, caused by the presence

of insect larvae, mites, or fungi.

– ORIGIN Latin *galla*.

gall. • abbrev. gallon(s).

gallant • adj. **1** /gal-luhnt/ brave or heroic. **2** /guh-lant/ (of a man) polite and charming towards women. • n. /guh-lant/ a man who is charmingly attentive to women.

– DERIVATIVES **gallantly** adv.

– ORIGIN Old French *galant*.

gallantry • n. (pl. **gallantries**) **1** bravery. **2** polite attention given by men to women.

gall bladder • n. a small sac-shaped organ beneath the liver, in which bile is stored.

galleon • n. hist. a large square-rigged sailing ship with three or more decks and masts.

– ORIGIN French *galion* or Spanish *galeón*.

gallery • n. (pl. **galleries**) **1** a room or building in which works of art are displayed or sold. **2** a balcony or upper floor projecting from a back or side wall inside a hall or church. **3** the highest balcony in a theatre, having the cheapest seats. **4** a horizontal underground passage in a mine.

– PHRASES **play to the gallery** do something intended to win people's approval or make yourself popular.

– DERIVATIVES **galleried** adj.

– ORIGIN Italian *galleria*.

galley • n. (pl. **galleys**) **1** hist. a low, flat ship with one or more sails and up to three banks of oars. **2** a narrow kitchen in a ship or aircraft.

– ORIGIN Greek *galaia*.

Gallic /gal-lik/ • adj. relating to France or the French.

– ORIGIN Latin *Gallicus*.

gallimaufry /gal-li-maw-fri/ • n. a jumble or mixture.

– ORIGIN a former French word *galimafrée* 'unappetizing dish'.

gallium /gal-li-uhm/ • n. a soft, silvery-white metallic chemical element.

– ORIGIN Latin *Gallia* 'France' or *gallus* 'cock'.

gallivant /gal-li-vant/ • v. informal go from place to place enjoying yourself.

– ORIGIN perh. from GALLANT.

gallon /gal-luhn/ • n. **1** Brit. a unit of volume for measuring liquids, equal to eight pints (4.55 litres). **2** (**gallons**) informal large quantities.

– ORIGIN Old French *galon*.

gallop • n. **1** the fastest pace of a horse, with all the feet off the ground together in each stride. **2** a ride on a horse at a gallop. • v. (**gallops, galloping, galloped**) **1** go at the pace of a gallop. **2** go very fast.

– ORIGIN Old French *galoper*.

gallows • pl. n. **1** a structure consisting of two uprights and a crosspiece, used for hanging a person. **2** (**the gallows**) execution by hanging.
– ORIGIN Old English.

gallows humour • n. grim humour in a desperate or hopeless situation.

gallstone /gawl-stohn/ • n. a hard mass formed abnormally in the gall bladder or bile ducts, causing pain and obstruction.

Gallup poll /gal-luhp/ • n. trademark an assessment of public opinion by the questioning of a representative cross-section of the population.
– ORIGIN from the name of the American statistician George H. *Gallup*.

galore • adj. in abundance: *there were prizes galore.*
– ORIGIN from Irish *go leor* 'to sufficiency'.

galosh /guh-losh/ • n. a waterproof rubber overshoe.
– ORIGIN from Latin *gallica solea* 'Gallic shoe'.

galumph /guh-lumf/ • v. informal move in a clumsy or noisy way.
– ORIGIN coined by Lewis Carroll in *Through the Looking-Glass.*

galvanic /gal-van-ik/ • adj. relating to electric currents produced by chemical action.
– ORIGIN French *galvanique.*

galvanize /gal-vuh-nyz/ (or **galvanise**) • v. (**galvanizes, galvanizing, galvanized**) **1** shock or excite someone into doing something. **2** (as adj. **galvanized**) (of iron or steel) coated with a protective layer of zinc.
– ORIGIN from the name of the Italian physiologist Luigi *Galvani.*

galvanometer /gal-vuh-nom-i-ter/ • n. an instrument for detecting and measuring small electric currents.

Gambian /gam-bi-uhn/ • n. a person from Gambia, a country in West Africa. • adj. relating to Gambia.

gambit • n. an action or remark intended to gain someone an advantage.
– ORIGIN Italian *gambetto* 'tripping up'.

gamble • v. (**gambles, gambling, gambled**) **1** play games of chance for money. **2** bet a sum of money. **3** take risky action in the hope of a successful result. • n. a risky action or undertaking.
– DERIVATIVES **gambler** n.
– ORIGIN from former *gamel* 'play games', or from GAME¹.

gambol • v. (**gambols, gambolling, gambolled**; US **gambols, gamboling, gamboled**) run or jump about playfully.

– ORIGIN Italian *gambata* 'trip up'.

game¹ • n. **1** an activity taken part in for amusement. **2** a form of competitive activity or sport played according to rules. **3** a complete period of play, ending in a final result. **4** a part of a tennis match, forming a unit of scoring. **5** (**games**) a meeting for sporting contests. **6** the equipment used in playing a board game, computer game, etc. **7** informal a type of activity or business regarded as a game. **8** wild mammals or birds hunted for sport or food. • adj. eager and willing to do something new or challenging: *they were game for anything.* • v. (**games, gaming, gamed**) play at games of chance for money.
– PHRASES **the game is up** the deception or crime is revealed and so cannot succeed. **on the game** Brit. informal working as a prostitute.
– DERIVATIVES **gamely** adv.
– ORIGIN Old English.

game² • adj. dated (of a person's leg) lame.

game bird • n. a bird shot for sport or food.

gamekeeper • n. a person employed to breed and protect game for a large estate.

game plan • n. a plan for success in sport, politics, or business.

gamer • n. a participant in a computer or role-playing game.

game show • n. a programme on television in which people compete to win prizes.

gamesmanship • n. the art of winning games by using tactics to make your opponent less confident.

gamete /gam-eet/ • n. a cell which is able to unite with another of the opposite sex in sexual reproduction to form a zygote.
– ORIGIN Greek, 'wife'.

gamey • adj. var. of GAMY.

gamine /ga-meen/ • adj. (of a girl) having a mischievous, boyish charm.
– ORIGIN French.

gamma /gam-muh/ • n. the third letter of the Greek alphabet (Γ, γ).

gamma rays (also **gamma radiation**) • pl. n. electromagnetic radiation of shorter wavelength than X-rays.

gammon • n. Brit. **1** ham which has been cured like bacon. **2** the part of a side of bacon that includes the hind leg.
– ORIGIN Old French *gambon.*

gammy • adj. Brit. informal (of a person's leg or knee) injured or painful.
– ORIGIN dialect form of GAME².

gamut /gam-uht/ • n. **1** the complete

range or scope of something. **2** a complete scale of musical notes.
– PHRASES **run the gamut** experience or perform the complete range of something.
– ORIGIN from Latin *gamma ut*, the lowest musical note in the medieval scale.

gamy (also **gamey**) • adj. (of meat) having the strong flavour or smell of game when it is slightly decomposed and so ready to cook.

gander • n. **1** a male goose. **2** informal a look.
– ORIGIN Old English.

gang • n. **1** an organized group of criminals or rowdy young people. **2** informal a group of people who regularly meet and do things together. **3** an organized group of people doing manual work. • v. **1** (**gang together**) form a group or gang. **2** (**gang up**) join together to oppose or intimidate someone.
– ORIGIN Old Norse, 'course, going'.

gangland • n. the world of criminal gangs.

gangling (also **gangly**) • adj. (of a person) tall, thin, and awkward in their movements.
– ORIGIN Old English, 'go'.

ganglion /gang-gli-uhn/ • n. (pl. **ganglia** /gang-gli-uh/ or **ganglions**) **1** a structure containing a number of nerve cells, often forming a swelling on a nerve fibre. **2** a harmless swelling on a tendon.
– ORIGIN Greek.

gangmaster • n. Brit. a person who organizes and oversees the work of casual manual workers.

gangplank • n. a movable plank used to board or leave a ship or boat.

gang rape • n. the rape of one person by a group of other people.

gangrene /gang-green/ • n. the death of body tissue, caused by an obstructed blood supply or by infection.
– DERIVATIVES **gangrenous** /gang-gri-nuhss/ adj.
– ORIGIN Greek *gangraina*.

gangster • n. a member of an organized gang of violent criminals.

gangway • n. **1** Brit. a passage between rows of seats in an aircraft, theatre, etc. **2** a movable bridge placed between a ship and the shore. **3** a raised platform or walkway providing a passage.

ganja /gan-juh/ • n. cannabis.
– ORIGIN Hindi.

gannet /gan-nit/ • n. **1** a large seabird with mainly white plumage. **2** Brit. informal a greedy person.
– ORIGIN Old English.

gantry • n. (pl. **gantries**) a bridge-like

overhead structure supporting equipment such as a crane or railway signals.
– ORIGIN prob. from GALLON + TREE.

gaol • n. Brit. var. of JAIL.

gap • n. **1** a break or hole in an object or between two objects. **2** a space, interval, or break.
– DERIVATIVES **gappy** adj.
– ORIGIN Old Norse, 'chasm'.

gape • v. (**gapes, gaping, gaped**) **1** be or become wide open. **2** stare with the mouth open wide in amazement. • n. **1** a wide opening. **2** an open-mouthed stare.
– ORIGIN Old Norse.

gap year • n. a period taken by a student as a break between school and university or college education.

garage /ga-rahj, ga-rij/ • n. **1** a building in which a car or other motor vehicle is kept. **2** a place which sells fuel or which repairs and sells motor vehicles. **3** a type of music with elements of drum and bass, house, and soul. • v. (**garages, garaging, garaged**) put or keep a motor vehicle in a garage.
– ORIGIN French.

garb • n. distinctive or special clothes. • v. (usu. **be garbed in**) dress in distinctive clothes.
– ORIGIN Italian *garbo* 'elegance'.

garbage • n. esp. N. Amer. **1** domestic rubbish or waste. **2** something worthless or meaningless.
– ORIGIN Old French.

garble • v. (**garbles, garbling, garbled**) reproduce a message or transmission in a confused and distorted way.
– ORIGIN Arabic, 'sift'.

garden • n. **1** esp. Brit. a piece of ground next to a house, with a lawn or flowers. **2** (**gardens**) an ornamental area of ground laid out for public use and enjoyment. • v. work in a garden.
– DERIVATIVES **gardener** n.
– ORIGIN Old French *jardin*.

garden centre • n. a place that sells plants and gardening equipment.

garden city • n. Brit. a new town designed as a whole and incorporating much open space and greenery.

gardenia /gar-dee-ni-uh/ • n. a tree or shrub with large white or yellow flowers.
– ORIGIN named after the Scottish naturalist Dr Alexander *Garden*.

garden party • n. a social event held on a lawn in a garden.

gargantuan /gar-gan-tyuu-uhn/ • adj. enormous.
– ORIGIN from *Gargantua*, a giant in a book by the French writer Rabelais.

gargle • v. (**gargles, gargling, gargled**) wash the mouth and throat with a liquid that is kept in motion by breathing through it.
– ORIGIN French *gargouiller* 'to gurgle'.

gargoyle /gar-goyl/ • n. a spout in the form of a grotesque face or figure, carved on the roof of a building to carry the rain away.
– ORIGIN Old French *gargouille*.

garish /gair-ish/ • adj. unpleasantly bright and showy; lurid.
– DERIVATIVES **garishly** adv.

garland • n. a wreath of flowers and leaves, worn on the head or hung as a decoration. • v. decorate with a garland.
– ORIGIN Old French *garlande*.

garlic • n. the bulb of a plant of the onion family, having a strong taste and smell.
– DERIVATIVES **garlicky** adj.
– ORIGIN Old English.

garment • n. an item of clothing.
– ORIGIN Old French *garnement* 'equipment'.

garner • v. (**garners, garnering, garnered**) gather or collect.
– ORIGIN Old French *gernier*.

garnet /gar-nit/ • n. a red semi-precious stone.
– ORIGIN Old French *grenat*.

garnish • v. decorate food. • n. a decoration for food.
– ORIGIN Old French *garnir* 'equip'.

garret • n. a top-floor or attic room.
– ORIGIN Old French *garite* 'watchtower'.

garrison • n. a body of troops stationed in a fortress or town to defend it. • v. provide a place with a garrison.
– ORIGIN Old French *garison*.

garrotte /guh-rot/ (US **garrote**) • v. (**garrottes, garrotting, garrotted**; US **garrotes, garroting, garroted**) strangle someone with a wire or cord. • n. a wire or cord used for garrotting someone.
– ORIGIN Spanish *garrote*.

garrulous /ga-rjuh-luhss/ • adj. very talkative.
– DERIVATIVES **garrulity** /guh-**roo**-li-ti/ n.
– ORIGIN Latin *garrulus*.

garter • n. 1 a band worn around the leg to keep up a stocking or sock. 2 N. Amer. a suspender for a sock or stocking.
– ORIGIN Old French *gartier*.

gas • n. (pl. **gases** or esp. US **gasses**) 1 an air-like substance which expands to fill any space available. 2 a flammable substance of this type used as a fuel. 3 a gas used as an anaesthetic. 4 N. Amer. informal petrol. • v. (**gases, gassing, gassed**) 1 harm or kill with gas. 2 informal chatter.
– ORIGIN invented by the Belgian chemist J. B. van Helmont.

gasbag • n. informal a person who talks too much.

gas chamber • n. an airtight room that can be filled with poisonous gas to kill people or animals.

gaseous /gass-i-uhss/ • adj. relating to or like a gas.

gash • n. a long slash, cut, or wound. • v. make a gash in something.
– ORIGIN Old French *garcer* 'to crack'.

gasify • v. (**gasifies, gasifying, gasified**) convert a solid or liquid into a gas.
– DERIVATIVES **gasification** n.

gasket /gass-kit/ • n. a sheet or ring of rubber sealing the junction between two surfaces in an engine or other device.
– ORIGIN perh. from French *garcette* 'thin rope'.

gaslight • n. light from a gas lamp.
– DERIVATIVES **gaslit** adj.

gas mask • n. a protective mask used to cover the face as a defence against poisonous gas.

gasoline • n. N. Amer. petrol.

gasometer /gass-om-i-ter/ • n. a large tank in which gas is stored before being distributed to consumers.

gasp • v. 1 take a quick breath with the mouth open, from pain, breathlessness, or astonishment. 2 (**gasp for**) struggle for air by gasping. 3 (**be gasping for**) Brit. informal be desperate to have. • n. a sudden quick breath.
– ORIGIN Old Norse, 'to yawn'.

gassy • adj. (**gassier, gassiest**) resembling or full of gas.

gastric • adj. relating to the stomach.
– ORIGIN Greek *gastēr* 'stomach'.

gastric flu • n. a short-lived stomach upset of unknown cause.

gastric juice • n. an acidic substance produced by the stomach glands which helps digestion.

gastritis /gas-try-tiss/ • n. inflammation of the lining of the stomach.

gastro-enteritis • n. inflammation of the stomach and intestines, causing vomiting and diarrhoea.

gastronomy /gass-tron-uh-mi/ • n. the practice or art of cooking and eating good food.
– DERIVATIVES **gastronomic** adj.
– ORIGIN Greek *gastronomia*.

gastropod /gass-truh-pod/ • n. Zool. any of a large class of molluscs including snails and slugs.
– ORIGIN from Greek *gastēr* 'stomach' + *pous* 'foot'.

gasworks • pl. n. a place where gas is manufactured and processed.

gate • n. 1 a hinged barrier used to close an opening in a wall, fence, or hedge.

2 an exit from an airport building to an aircraft. **3** a hinged or sliding barrier that controls the flow of water on a river or canal. **4** the number of people who pay to attend a sports event. **5** an electric circuit with an output which depends on the combination of several inputs.
– ORIGIN Old English.

gateau /gat-oh/ •n. (pl. **gateaus** or **gateaux** /gat-ohz/) Brit. a rich cake with layers of cream or fruit.
– ORIGIN French.

gatecrash •v. go to a party without an invitation or ticket.
– DERIVATIVES **gatecrasher** n.

gatefold •n. an oversized page in a book or magazine, intended to be opened out for reading.

gatehouse •n. a house standing by the gateway to a country estate.

gatekeeper •n. an attendant at a gate.

gateleg table •n. a table with hinged legs that may be swung out from the centre to support folding leaves.

gatepost •n. a post on which a gate is hinged or against which it shuts.

gateway •n. **1** an opening that can be closed by a gate. **2** (**gateway to**) a means of entering somewhere or achieving something: *the gateway to success.*

gather •v. (**gathers, gathering, gathered**) **1** come or bring together; assemble. **2** increase in speed, force, etc. **3** understand something to be the case as a result of information or evidence: *I gather he's resigned.* **4** collect plants or fruits for food. **5** harvest a crop. **6** draw together or towards yourself: *she gathered the child in her arms.* **7** pull fabric together in a series of folds by drawing thread through it. •n. (**gathers**) a part of a garment that is gathered.
– DERIVATIVES **gatherer** n.
– ORIGIN Old English.

gathering •n. a group of people assembled for a purpose.

gauche /gohsh/ •adj. unsophisticated and awkward when dealing with other people.
– ORIGIN French, 'left'.

gaucho /gow-choh/ •n. (pl. **gauchos**) a cowboy from the South American plains.
– ORIGIN Latin American Spanish.

gaudy /gaw-di/ •adj. (**gaudier, gaudiest**) tastelessly bright or showy.
– DERIVATIVES **gaudily** adv. **gaudiness** n.
– ORIGIN prob. from Old French *gaudir* 'rejoice'.

gauge /gayj/ (US also **gage**) •n. **1** an instrument that measures and gives a visual display of the amount, level, or contents of something. **2** the thickness, size, or capacity of a wire, tube, bullet, etc. **3** the distance between the rails of a railway track. •v. (**gauges, gauging, gauged**; US **gages, gaging, gaged**) **1** judge a situation or mood. **2** estimate or measure the amount or level of.
– ORIGIN Old French.

☑ Spell **gauge** with **-au-** in the middle (the spelling **gage** is American).

Gaul /gorl/ •n. a person from the ancient European region of Gaul.

gaunt •adj. **1** (of a person) looking thin and exhausted. **2** (of a place) grim or desolate.

gauntlet¹ •n. **1** a strong glove with a long loose wrist. **2** a glove worn as part of medieval armour.
– PHRASES **take up** (or **throw down**) **the gauntlet** accept (or give) a challenge.
– ORIGIN Old French *gantelet*.

gauntlet² •n. (in phr. **run the gauntlet**) go through an intimidating crowd or experience in order to reach a goal.
– ORIGIN from Swedish *gata* 'lane' + *lopp* 'course'.

gauze /gawz/ •n. **1** a thin transparent fabric. **2** thin cloth used for covering and protecting wounds. **3** (also **wire gauze**) a fine wire mesh.
– DERIVATIVES **gauzy** adj.
– ORIGIN French *gaze*.

gave past of GIVE.

gavel /gav-uhl/ •n. a small hammer with which an auctioneer or judge hits a surface to call for attention or order.

gavotte /guh-vot/ •n. a medium-paced French dance, popular in the 18th century.
– ORIGIN Provençal *gavoto* 'dance of the mountain people'.

gawk •v. stare in a rude or stupid way.
– ORIGIN perh. from Old Norse 'to heed'.

gawky •adj. awkward and clumsy in behaviour or movement.
– DERIVATIVES **gawkily** adv. **gawkiness** n.

gawp •v. Brit. informal stare in a rude or stupid way.
– DERIVATIVES **gawper** n.
– ORIGIN perh. from GAPE.

gay •adj. (**gayer, gayest**) **1** (especially of a man) homosexual. **2** relating to homosexuals. **3** dated light-hearted and carefree. **4** dated brightly coloured. •n. a homosexual person, especially a man.
– ORIGIN Old French *gai*.

gayety •n. US = GAIETY.

gaze •v. (**gazes, gazing, gazed**) look steadily and intently. •n. a steady, intent look.
– DERIVATIVES **gazer** n.

– ORIGIN perh. from **GAWK**.

gazebo /guh-zee-boh/ • n. (pl. **gazebos**) a summer house with a pleasant view of the surrounding area.
– ORIGIN perh. from **GAZE**.

gazelle • n. a small antelope with curved horns and white underparts.
– ORIGIN French.

gazette • n. a journal or newspaper.
– ORIGIN from Venetian *gazeta de la novità* 'a halfpennyworth of news'.

gazetteer /ga-zuht-**teer**/ • n. a dictionary or list of places or place names.

gazump /guh-**zump**/ • v. Brit. informal offer or accept a higher price for a house after a lower offer has already been accepted from a prospective buyer.
– ORIGIN Yiddish, 'overcharge'.

GB • abbrev. **1** Great Britain. **2** (also **Gb**) Computing gigabyte(s).

GBH • abbrev. Brit. grievous bodily harm.

GC • abbrev. George Cross.

GCE • abbrev. General Certificate of Education.

GCSE • abbrev. (in the UK except Scotland) General Certificate of Secondary Education (the lower of the two main levels of the GCE exam).

Gd • symb. the chemical element gadolinium.

GDP • abbrev. gross domestic product.

Ge • symb. the chemical element germanium.

gear • n. **1** (**gears**) a set of toothed wheels that connect the engine to the wheels of a vehicle and work together to alter its speed. **2** a particular setting of gears in a vehicle. **3** informal equipment or clothing. • v. **1** design or adjust gears to give a particular speed or power output. **2** adapt for a particular purpose: *an activity programme geared towards senior citizens.* **3** (**gear something up**) make something ready or prepared.
– PHRASES **in** (or **out of**) **gear** with a gear (or no gear) engaged.
– ORIGIN Scandinavian.

gearbox • n. a set of gears with its casing, especially in a motor vehicle.

gear lever (also **gearstick**) • n. Brit. a lever used to engage or change gear in a motor vehicle.

gearwheel • n. **1** a toothed wheel in a set of gears. **2** (on a bicycle) a cogwheel driven directly by the chain.

gecko /gek-koh/ • n. (pl. **geckos** or **geckoes**) a lizard of warm regions, with adhesive pads on the feet.
– ORIGIN Malay.

gee • exclam. **1** (**gee up**) a command to a horse to go faster. **2** (also **gee whiz**) N.

Amer. informal a mild expression of surprise, enthusiasm, or sympathy.

geek /geek/ • n. informal **1** a person who is unfashionable or awkward in the company of other people. **2** a person who is obsessed with something: *a computer geek.*
– DERIVATIVES **geeky** adj.
– ORIGIN from dialect *geck* 'fool'.

geese pl. of **GOOSE**.

geezer /gee-zer/ • n. informal a man.
– ORIGIN from former *guiser* 'mummer'.

Geiger counter • n. a device for measuring radioactivity.
– ORIGIN named after the German physicist Hans *Geiger*.

geisha /gay-shuh/ • n. (pl. **geisha** or **geishas**) a Japanese hostess trained to entertain men with conversation, dance, and song.
– ORIGIN Japanese.

gel¹ /jel/ • n. **1** a jelly-like substance, especially one used cosmetically on the hair or skin. **2** Chem. a semi-solid suspension of a solid dispersed in a liquid. • v. (**gels, gelling, gelled**) **1** Chem. form into a gel. **2** smooth or style the hair with gel.
– ORIGIN from **GELATIN**.

gel² /jel/ • v. (**gels, gelling, gelled**) **1** (of jelly or a similar substance) set or become firmer. **2** take definite form or begin to work well.

gelatin /jel-uh-tin/ (also **gelatine** /jel-uh-teen/) • n. a clear water-soluble substance obtained from animal bones, used in food preparation, in photographic processing, and for making glue.
– DERIVATIVES **gelatinous** /je-lat-i-nuhss/ adj.
– ORIGIN French *gélatine*.

geld • v. castrate a male animal.
– ORIGIN Old Norse, 'barren'.

gelding • n. a castrated male horse.

gelid /jel-id/ • adj. esp. literary very cold; icy.
– ORIGIN Latin *gelidus*.

gelignite /jel-ig-nyt/ • n. a high explosive made from nitroglycerine in a base of wood pulp and sodium.
– ORIGIN prob. from **GELATIN** + Latin *lignis* 'wood'.

gem • n. **1** a precious or semi-precious stone. **2** an outstanding person or thing.
– ORIGIN Latin *gemma* 'bud, jewel'.

Gemini • n. a constellation (the Twins) and sign of the zodiac, which the sun enters about 21 May.
– ORIGIN Latin, 'twins'.

gemstone • n. a gem used in a piece of jewellery.

gen /jen/ Brit. informal • n. information.

• v. (**gens, genning, genned**) (**gen up on**) obtain information about something.
– ORIGIN perh. from *general information*.

gendarme /zhon-darm/ • n. a police officer in French-speaking countries.
– ORIGIN French.

gender • n. **1** Grammar a class (usually masculine, feminine, common, or neuter) into which nouns and pronouns are placed in some languages. **2** the state of being male or female (with reference to social or cultural differences rather than biological ones). **3** the members of one or other sex.
– ORIGIN Old French *gendre*.

gene /jeen/ • n. a distinct sequence of DNA forming part of a chromosome, by which offspring inherit characteristics from a parent.
– ORIGIN German *Gen*.

genealogy /jee-ni-al-uh-ji/ • n. (pl. **genealogies**) **1** a line of descent traced from an ancestor. **2** the study of lines of descent.
– DERIVATIVES **genealogical** adj. **genealogist** n.
– ORIGIN Greek *genealogia*.

gene pool • n. the stock of different genes in a particular species of animal or plant.

genera pl. of GENUS.

general • adj. **1** affecting or concerning all or most people or things. **2** involving only the main features or elements of something; not detailed. **3** chief: *the general manager*. • n. a commander of an army, or an army officer ranking above lieutenant general.
– PHRASES **in general 1** usually; mainly. **2** as a whole.
– ORIGIN Latin *generalis*.

general anaesthetic • n. an anaesthetic that affects the whole body and causes a loss of consciousness.

general election • n. the election of representatives to a parliament from constituencies throughout the country.

generalist • n. a person who is competent in several different fields or activities.

generality • n. (pl. **generalities**) **1** a statement that is general rather than specific. **2** the quality or state of being general. **3** (**the generality**) the majority.

generalize (or **generalise**)
• v. (**generalizes, generalizing, generalized**) **1** make a general or broad statement based on specific cases. **2** make something more common or more widely applicable.
– DERIVATIVES **generalization** n.

generally • adv. **1** in most cases or by most people. **2** without discussing the

details of something. **3** widely.

general meeting • n. a meeting open to all members of an organization.

general practitioner • n. a doctor based in a local community rather than a hospital, who treats patients with minor or long-lasting illnesses.
– DERIVATIVES **general practice** n.

general staff • n. the staff assisting a military commander.

general strike • n. a strike of workers in all or most industries.

generate • v. (**generates, generating, generated**) create or produce something.
– ORIGIN Latin *generare*.

generation • n. **1** all of the people born and living at about the same time. **2** the average period in which children grow up and have children of their own (usually considered to be about thirty years). **3** a set of members of a family regarded as a single stage in descent. **4** a group of people of similar age involved in an activity: *a new generation of actors*. **5** a stage in the development of a product: *the next generation of mobile phones*. **6** the production or creation of something.
– DERIVATIVES **generational** adj.

generation gap • n. a difference in attitudes between people of different generations.

generative • adj. capable of producing something.

generator • n. a dynamo or similar machine for converting mechanical energy into electricity.

generic /ji-ne-rik/ • adj. **1** referring to a class or group of things; not specific. **2** (of goods) having no brand name.
– DERIVATIVES **generically** adv.
– ORIGIN Latin *genus* 'stock, race'.

generous • adj. **1** freely giving more than is necessary or expected. **2** kind towards other people. **3** larger or more plentiful than is usual: *a generous sprinkle of pepper*.
– DERIVATIVES **generosity** n. **generously** adv.
– ORIGIN Latin *generosus* 'noble'.

genesis /jen-i-siss/ • n. the origin of something.
– ORIGIN Greek.

gene therapy • n. the introduction of normal genes into cells in order to correct genetic disorders.

genetic • adj. **1** relating to genes and heredity. **2** relating to genetics.
– DERIVATIVES **genetical** adj. **genetically** adv.

genetically modified • adj. (of a plant

g

or animal) containing genetic material that has been artificially altered so as to produce a desired characteristic.

genetic code • n. the means by which DNA and RNA molecules carry genetic information.

genetic engineering • n. the deliberate alteration of the characteristics of an animal or plant by altering its genetic material.

genetic fingerprinting • n. the analysis of DNA from samples of body tissues or fluids in order to identify individual people.

genetics • n. the study of the way inherited characteristics are passed from one generation to another.
– DERIVATIVES **geneticist** n.

genial /jee-ni-uhl/ • adj. friendly and cheerful.
– DERIVATIVES **geniality** n. **genially** adv.
– ORIGIN Latin *genialis* 'productive'.

-genic • comb. form **1** producing or produced by: *carcinogenic*. **2** well suited to: *photogenic*.

genie /jee-ni/ • n. (pl. **genies** or **genii** /jee-ni-I/) (in Arabian folklore) a spirit.
– ORIGIN Latin *genius* (see GENIUS).

genital • adj. referring to the human or animal reproductive organs.
• n. (**genitals**) a person's or animal's external reproductive organs.
– DERIVATIVES **genitally** adv.
– ORIGIN Latin *genitalis*.

genitalia /jen-i-tay-li-uh/ • pl. n. formal or tech. the genitals.
– ORIGIN Latin.

genitive /jen-i-tiv/ • n. Grammar the form of a noun, pronoun, or adjective used to show possession.
– ORIGIN from Latin *genitivus casus* 'case of production or origin'.

genius /jee-ni-uhss/ • n. (pl. **geniuses**) **1** exceptional natural ability. **2** an exceptionally intelligent or able person.
– ORIGIN Latin.

genocide /jen-uh-syd/ • n. the deliberate killing of a very large number of people from a particular ethnic group or nation.
– DERIVATIVES **genocidal** adj.
– ORIGIN from Greek *genos* 'race' + -CIDE.

genome /jee-nohm/ • n. Biol. **1** the full set of the chromosomes of an animal, plant, or other life form. **2** the complete set of genetic material present in an animal, plant, or other life form.
– ORIGIN from GENE and CHROMOSOME.

genotype /jen-uh-typ/ • n. Biol. the genetic make-up of an individual animal, plant, or other life form.

genre /zhon-ruh/ • n. a style or category of art or literature.
– ORIGIN French.

gent • n. informal **1** a gentleman. **2** (**the Gents**) Brit. a men's public toilet.

genteel • adj. polite and refined in an affected or exaggerated way.
– DERIVATIVES **genteelly** adv.
– ORIGIN French *gentil* 'well-born'.

gentian /jen-sh'n/ • n. a plant with violet or blue trumpet-shaped flowers.
– ORIGIN Latin *gentiana*.

Gentile /jen-tyl/ • adj. not Jewish. • n. a person who is not Jewish.
– ORIGIN Latin *gentilis* 'of a family or nation'.

gentility • n. polite and refined behaviour.
– ORIGIN Old French *gentil* 'high-born'.

gentle • adj. (**gentler, gentlest**) **1** (of a person) mild and kind. **2** not harsh or severe: *a gentle breeze*.
– DERIVATIVES **gentleness** n. **gently** adv.
– ORIGIN Old French *gentil* 'high-born'.

gentlefolk • pl. n. old use people of noble birth or good social position.

gentleman • n. (pl. **gentlemen**) **1** a courteous or honourable man. **2** a man of good social position. **3** (in polite or formal use) a man.
– DERIVATIVES **gentlemanly** adj.

gentleman's agreement • n. an arrangement which is based on trust rather than a legal contract.

gentrify • v. (**gentrifies, gentrifying, gentrified**) renovate a house or district so that it is in keeping with middle-class tastes.
– DERIVATIVES **gentrification** n.

gentry • n. (**the gentry**) people of good social position, specifically the class next below the nobility.
– ORIGIN Old French *genterie*.

genuflect /jen-yuu-flekt/ • v. lower the body briefly by bending one knee to the ground in worship or as a sign of respect.
– DERIVATIVES **genuflection** n.
– ORIGIN Latin *genuflectere*.

genuine • adj. **1** truly what it is said to be; authentic. **2** able to be trusted; honest and sincere.
– DERIVATIVES **genuinely** adv.
– ORIGIN Latin *genuinus*.

genus /jee-nuhss/ • n. (pl. **genera** /jen-uh-ruh/) **1** a category in the classification of animals and plants that ranks above species and below family. **2** a class of things which have common characteristics.
– ORIGIN Latin, 'race, stock'.

geo- /jee-oh/ • comb. form relating to the earth: geology.
– ORIGIN Greek gē 'earth'.

geode /jee-ohd/ • n. 1 a small cavity in rock lined with crystals. 2 a rock containing such a cavity.
– ORIGIN Greek geōdēs 'earthy'.

geodesic /jee-oh-dess-ik/ • adj. 1 referring to the shortest possible line between two points on a curved surface. 2 (of a dome) constructed from struts which follow geodesic lines.

geodesy /ji-od-i-si/ • n. the branch of mathematics concerned with the shape and area of the earth.
– ORIGIN Greek geōdaisia.

geographical • adj. relating to geography.
– DERIVATIVES **geographic** adj. **geographically** adv.

geography • n. 1 the study of the physical features of the earth and of human activity as it relates to these. 2 the way in which the physical features of a place are arranged: the geography of post-war London.
– DERIVATIVES **geographer** n.

geology • n. 1 the science which deals with the physical structure and substance of the earth. 2 the geological features of a particular area.
– DERIVATIVES **geological** adj. **geologically** adv. **geologist** n.

geometric /ji-uh-met-rik/ • adj. 1 relating to geometry. 2 (of a design) consisting of regular lines and shapes.
– DERIVATIVES **geometrical** adj. **geometrically** adv.

geometric mean • n. the central number in a geometric progression (e.g. 9 in 3, 9, 27).

geometric progression (also **geometric series**) • n. a sequence of numbers with a constant ratio between each number and the one before (e.g. 1, 3, 9, 27, 81).

geometry /ji-om-uh-tri/ • n. (pl. **geometries**) 1 the branch of mathematics concerned with the properties and relations of points, lines, surfaces, and solids. 2 the shape and relative arrangement of the parts of something.
– ORIGIN Greek geometria.

geophysics • n. the physics of the earth.
– DERIVATIVES **geophysical** adj. **geophysicist** n.

geopolitical • adj. relating to political relations between the countries of the world.

Geordie • n. Brit. informal a person from Tyneside.
– ORIGIN from the man's name George.

georgette /jor-jet/ • n. a thin silk or crêpe dress material.
– ORIGIN named after the French dressmaker Georgette de la Plante.

Georgian • adj. 1 relating to the reigns of the British Kings George I–IV (1714–1830). 2 relating to British architecture of this period.

geostationary • adj. (of a satellite) orbiting in such a way that it appears to be stationary above a fixed point on the earth's surface.

geothermal • adj. relating to or produced by the internal heat of the earth.

geranium • n. a garden plant with red, white, or pink flowers.
– ORIGIN Greek geranion.

gerbil • n. a mouse-like rodent, often kept as a pet.
– ORIGIN Latin gerbillus 'little jerboa'.

geriatric /je-ri-at-rik/ • adj. relating to old people. • n. an old person, especially one receiving special care.
– ORIGIN from Greek gēras 'old age' + iatros 'doctor'.

geriatrics • n. the branch of medicine or social science concerned with the health and care of old people.

germ • n. 1 a microorganism, especially one which causes disease. 2 a part of a plant or animal capable of developing into a new one or part of one. 3 an initial stage from which something may develop: the germ of an idea.
– ORIGIN Latin germen 'seed, sprout'.

German • n. 1 a person from Germany. 2 the language of Germany, Austria, and parts of Switzerland. • adj. relating to Germany or German.

germane /jer-mayn/ • adj. relevant to the subject which is being considered.
– ORIGIN Latin germanus 'genuine'.

Germanic • adj. 1 referring to the language family that includes English, German, Dutch, and the Scandinavian languages. 2 referring to the peoples of ancient northern and western Europe speaking such languages. 3 relating to Germans or Germany. • n. 1 the Germanic languages collectively. 2 the ancient language from which these developed.

germanium /jer-may-ni-uhm/ • n. a shiny grey chemical element with semiconducting properties.
– ORIGIN Latin Germanus 'German'.

German measles • pl. n. = RUBELLA.

German shepherd • n. a large breed of dog often used as guard dogs; an Alsatian.

g

germicide •n. a substance which destroys germs.
– DERIVATIVES **germicidal** adj.

germinal •adj. **1** relating to a gamete or embryo. **2** in the earliest stage of development.
– ORIGIN Latin *germen* 'sprout, seed'.

germinate •v. (**germinates, germinating, germinated**) (of a seed or spore) begin to grow and put out shoots after a period of being dormant.
– DERIVATIVES **germination** n.
– ORIGIN Latin *germinare*.

germ warfare •n. the use of microorganisms which spread disease as a military weapon.

gerontology /je-ruhn-**tol**-uh-ji/ •n. the scientific study of old age and old people.

gerrymander •v. (**gerrymanders, gerrymandering, gerrymandered**) alter the boundaries of a constituency so as to favour one political party in an election.
– ORIGIN from Governor Elbridge *Gerry* of Massachusetts + SALAMANDER, from the similarity between a salamander and the shape of a voting district created when he was in office.

gerund /je-ruhnd/ •n. Grammar a verb form which functions as a noun, in English ending in -*ing* (e.g. *asking* in *do you mind my asking you?*).
– ORIGIN Latin *gerundum*.

gesso /jess-oh/ •n. a hard compound of plaster of Paris, used in sculpture.
– ORIGIN Italian.

Gestapo /ge-stah-poh/ •n. the German secret police under Nazi rule.
– ORIGIN German.

gestation /jess-tay-sh'n/ •n. **1** the process of developing in the womb between conception and birth. **2** the development of a plan or idea over a period of time.
– ORIGIN Latin.

gesticulate /jess-tik-yuu-layt/ •v. (**gesticulates, gesticulating, gesticulated**) gesture dramatically instead of speaking or to emphasize speech.
– DERIVATIVES **gesticulation** n.
– ORIGIN Latin *gesticulari*.

gesture •n. **1** a movement of part of the body to express an idea or meaning. **2** an action performed as an indication of feelings or intentions: *sharing food is a gesture of hospitality.* •v. (**gestures, gesturing, gestured**) make a gesture.
– ORIGIN Latin *gestura*.

get •v. (**gets, getting, got**; past part. **got**, N. Amer. **gotten**) **1** come to have or hold; receive. **2** succeed in achieving or experiencing. **3** experience or suffer: *I*

got a sudden pain in my eye. **4** fetch something. **5** reach a particular state or condition: *it's getting late.* **6** catch or thwart. **7** move to or from a particular place. **8** travel by or catch a form of transport. **10** begin to be or do something: *we got talking.*
– PHRASES **get something across** (or **over**) manage to communicate an idea clearly. **get at 1** reach somewhere. **2** informal mean something. **get away with** escape blame or punishment for something. **get back at** take revenge on. **get by** manage with difficulty to live or do something. **get down to** begin to do or give serious attention to. **get off** informal escape a punishment. **get on 1** make progress with a task. **2** esp. Brit. have a friendly relationship. **3** (**be getting on**) informal be old. **get over** recover from an illness or an unpleasant experience. **get your own back** informal have your revenge. **get round** persuade someone to do or allow something. **get round to** find the time to deal with a task.
– ORIGIN Old Norse.

getaway •n. an escape or quick departure.

get-together •n. an informal social gathering.

get-up •n. informal an outfit, especially an unusual one.

gewgaw /gyoo-gor/ •n. a showy trinket, especially one that is of little or no value.

geyser /gee-zer, gy-zer/ •n. a hot spring in which water intermittently boils, sending a column of water and steam into the air.
– ORIGIN named after a spring in Iceland.

Ghanaian /gah-nay-uhn/ •n. a person from Ghana. •adj. relating to Ghana.

ghastly •adj. (**ghastlier, ghastliest**) **1** causing great horror or fear. **2** informal very unpleasant. **3** deathly pale.
– DERIVATIVES **ghastliness** n.
– ORIGIN Old English, 'terrify'.

ghee /gee/ •n. clarified butter used in Indian cooking.
– ORIGIN Sanskrit, 'sprinkled'.

gherkin /ger-kin/ •n. a small pickled cucumber.
– ORIGIN Dutch *gurkje*.

ghetto /get-toh/ •n. (pl. **ghettos** or **ghettoes**) **1** a part of a city occupied by people of a particular race, nationality, or ethnic group. **2** hist. the Jewish quarter in a city.
– ORIGIN perh. from Italian *getto* 'foundry' (because the first ghetto was established on the site of a foundry in Venice).

ghetto blaster •n. informal a large

portable radio and cassette or CD player.

ghost • n. **1** an apparition of a dead person which is believed to appear to the living. **2** a faint trace: *the ghost of a smile.*
– ORIGIN Old English, 'spirit, soul'.

ghosting • n. the appearance of a secondary image on a television or other display screen.

ghostly • adj. (**ghostlier, ghostliest**) like a ghost; eerie.

ghost town • n. a town with few or no remaining inhabitants.

ghost writer • n. a person employed to write material for another person who is the named author.

ghoul /gool/ • n. **1** an evil spirit believed to rob graves and eat dead bodies. **2** a person with an unhealthy interest in death or disaster.
– DERIVATIVES **ghoulish** adj.
– ORIGIN Arabic.

GHQ • abbrev. General Headquarters.

GHz (also **gHz**) • abbrev. gigahertz.

GI • n. (pl. **GIs**) a private soldier in the US army.
– ORIGIN from *government* (or *general*) *issue* (referring to military equipment).

giant • n. **1** an imaginary being of human form but superhuman size and strength. **2** an unusually tall or large person, animal, or plant. • adj. unusually large.
– ORIGIN Old French *geant.*

gibber /jib-ber/ • v. (**gibbers, gibbering, gibbered**) speak rapidly in a way that is difficult to understand.

gibberish /jib-buh-rish/ • n. speech or writing that is meaningless or difficult to understand.

gibbet /jib-bit/ • n. hist. **1** a gallows. **2** an upright post with an arm on which the bodies of executed criminals were left hanging.
– ORIGIN Old French *gibet* 'little cudgel, or gallows'.

gibbon • n. a small ape with long, powerful arms, native to the forests of SE Asia.
– ORIGIN French.

gibbous /gib-buhss/ • adj. (of the moon) having the illuminated part greater than a semicircle and less than a circle.
– ORIGIN Latin *gibbosus.*

gibe /jib/ • n. & v. var. of JIBE[1].

giblets /jib-lits/ • pl. n. the liver, heart, gizzard, and neck of a chicken, turkey, or other bird.
– ORIGIN Old French *gibelet* 'game bird stew'.

giddy • adj. (**giddier, giddiest**) **1** having a sensation of spinning around and losing your balance. **2** excitable and not

interested in serious things.
– DERIVATIVES **giddily** adv. **giddiness** n.
– ORIGIN Old English, 'insane'.

GIF • n. Computing **1** a format for image files. **2** (also **gif**) a file in this format.
– ORIGIN from *graphic interchange format.*

gift • n. **1** a thing given willingly to someone; a present. **2** a natural ability or talent. **3** informal a very easy task.
• v. **1** give something as a gift. **2** (as adj. **gifted**) having exceptional talent or ability.
– ORIGIN Old Norse.

gift token (also **gift voucher**) • n. Brit. a voucher which can be exchanged for goods in a particular shop, given as a present.

gift-wrap • v. wrap a present in decorative paper.

gig[1] /gig/ • n. esp. hist. a light two-wheeled carriage pulled by one horse.
– ORIGIN perh. from former *gig*, 'a flighty girl'.

gig[2] /gig/ • n. informal a live performance by a musician or other performer.

giga- (also **gHz**, **jig-uh**/ • comb. form **1** referring to a factor of one thousand million (10^9). **2** Computing referring to a factor of 2^{30}.
– ORIGIN Greek *gigas* 'giant'.

gigabit /gig-uh-bit, jig-uh-bit/ • n. a unit of information stored in a computer equal to one thousand million (10^9) or (strictly) 2^{30} bits.

gigabyte /gig-uh-byt, jig-uh-byt/ • n. a unit of information stored in a computer, equal to one thousand million (10^9) or (strictly) 2^{30} bytes.

gigahertz • n. a unit of frequency equivalent to one thousand million hertz.

gigantic • adj. very large.
– DERIVATIVES **gigantically** adv.
– ORIGIN Latin *gigas* 'giant'.

gigawatt • n. a unit of power equal to one thousand million watts.

giggle • v. (**giggles, giggling, giggled**) laugh lightly in a nervous or silly way.
• n. **1** a nervous or silly laugh. **2** Brit. informal an amusing person or thing.
– DERIVATIVES **giggly** adj.

gigolo /jig-uh-loh/ • n. (pl. **gigolos**) a young man paid by an older woman to be her companion or lover.
– ORIGIN French.

gild • v. **1** cover thinly with gold. **2** (as adj. **gilded**) wealthy and privileged: *gilded youth.*
– DERIVATIVES **gilding** n.
– ORIGIN Old English.

gilet /zhi-lay/ • n. (pl. **gilets** /zhi-lay/) a

g

light sleeveless padded jacket.
– ORIGIN French, 'waistcoat'.

gill[1] /gil/ •n. **1** the breathing organ in fish and some amphibians. **2** the plates on the underside of mushrooms and many toadstools.
– ORIGIN Old Norse.

gill[2] /jil/ •n. a unit of measure for liquids, equal to a quarter of a pint.
– ORIGIN Old French *gille* 'measure or container for wine'.

gillie /ˈgil-li/ •n. (in Scotland) a man or boy who assists someone who is shooting or fishing for sport.
– ORIGIN Scottish Gaelic *gille* 'lad'.

gilt •adj. covered thinly with gold leaf or gold paint. •n. **1** gold leaf or gold paint applied in a thin layer to a surface. **2** (**gilts**) fixed-interest loan securities issued by the UK government.
– ORIGIN from GILD.

gilt-edged •adj. referring to stocks or securities (such as gilts) that are regarded as very reliable investments.

gimcrack /ˈjim-krak/ •adj. showy but cheap or badly made.

gimlet /ˈgim-lit/ •n. a T-shaped tool with a screw-tip for boring holes.
– ORIGIN Old French *guimbelet* 'little drill'.

gimmick •n. something intended to attract attention rather than fulfil a useful purpose.
– DERIVATIVES **gimmickry** n. **gimmicky** adj.

gin[1] •n. a clear alcoholic spirit flavoured with juniper berries.
– ORIGIN from *genever*, a kind of Dutch gin.

gin[2] •n. **1** a machine for separating cotton from its seeds. **2** a trap for catching small game.
– ORIGIN Old French *engin* 'engine'.

ginger •n. **1** a hot spice made from the root of a SE Asian plant. **2** a light reddish-yellow colour. •v. (**gingers, gingering, gingered**) (**ginger someone/thing up**) make someone or something more lively or exciting.
– DERIVATIVES **gingery** adj.
– ORIGIN Latin *gingiber*.

ginger ale •n. a fizzy soft drink flavoured with ginger.

ginger beer •n. a fizzy drink made by fermenting a mixture of ginger and syrup.

gingerbread •n. cake made with treacle or syrup and flavoured with ginger.

gingerly •adv. in a careful or cautious way.

– ORIGIN perh. from Old French *gensor* 'delicate'.

gingham /ˈging-uhm/ •n. lightweight cotton cloth with a checked pattern.
– ORIGIN Malay, 'striped'.

gingivitis /jin-ji-vy-tiss/ •n. inflammation of the gums.
– ORIGIN Latin *gingiva* 'gum'.

ginormous •adj. Brit. informal very large.
– ORIGIN from GIANT and ENORMOUS.

ginseng /ˈjin-seng/ •n. the tuber of an east Asian and North American plant, supposed to have medicinal properties.
– ORIGIN from Chinese 'man' + the name of a kind of herb.

gip •n. var. of GYP.

Gipsy •n. var. of GYPSY.

giraffe •n. (pl. **giraffe** or **giraffes**) a large African mammal with a very long neck and legs, the tallest living animal.
– ORIGIN French *girafe*.

gird •v. (**girds, girding, girded**; past part. **girded** or **girt**) literary encircle or secure with a belt or band.
– PHRASES **gird (up) your loins** prepare and strengthen yourself for something difficult.
– ORIGIN Old English.

girder •n. a large metal beam used in building bridges and large buildings.
– ORIGIN from GIRD.

girdle •n. **1** a belt or cord worn round the waist. **2** a woman's elasticated corset extending from waist to thigh.
•v. (**girdles, girdling, girdled**) encircle with a girdle or belt.
– ORIGIN Old English.

girl •n. **1** a female child. **2** a young woman. **3** a person's girlfriend.
– DERIVATIVES **girlhood** n. **girlish** adj.
– ORIGIN perh. from German *gör* 'child'.

girlfriend •n. **1** a person's regular female companion in a romantic or sexual relationship. **2** a woman's female friend.

Girl Guide •n. Brit. a member of the Guides Association.

girlie (also **girly**) •adj. **1** usu. derog. typical of or resembling a girl. **2** showing nude young women in erotic poses: *girlie magazines.* •n. (pl. **girlies**) informal a girl or young woman.

giro •n. (pl. **giros**) **1** a system of electronic credit transfer involving banks, post offices, and public utilities. **2** a cheque or payment by giro.
– ORIGIN Italian, 'circulation (of money)'.

girt past part. of GIRD.

girth •n. **1** the measurement around the middle of something. **2** a band attached to a saddle and fastened around a horse's belly.

– ORIGIN Old Norse.

gist /jist/ •n. the main or general meaning of a speech or piece of writing.
– ORIGIN from Old French *cest action gist* 'this action lies', meaning that there were enough grounds to proceed in a legal case.

git •n. Brit. informal an unpleasant or disliked person.
– ORIGIN from dialect *get* 'a stupid or unpleasant person'.

give •v. (**gives, giving, gave**; past part. **given**) 1 cause someone to have, get, or experience something. 2 carry out an action or make a sound. 3 show: *he gave no sign of life*. 4 put forward information. 5 have something as a result. 6 admit that someone deserves recognition for something: *to give him his due, he tried*. 7 bend under pressure. •n. the ability of something to bend under pressure.
– PHRASES **give and take** willingness on both sides of a relationship to make allowances. **give something away** reveal something secret. **give in** stop opposing something. **give something off/out** send out a smell, heat, etc. **give out** stop operating. **give rise to** make something happen. **give up** stop making an effort and accept that you have failed. **give someone up** hand over a wanted person. **give something up** stop doing, eating, or drinking something regularly.
– DERIVATIVES **giver** n.
– ORIGIN Old English.

giveaway •n. informal 1 something that reveals the truth about something. 2 something given free, especially for promotional purposes.

given past part. of GIVE. •adj. 1 specified or stated. 2 (**given to**) inclined to. •prep. taking into account. •n. an established fact.

given name •n. = FIRST NAME.

gizmo •n. (pl. **gizmos**) informal a clever device; a gadget.

gizzard •n. a muscular part of a bird's stomach for grinding food.
– ORIGIN Old French.

GLA •abbrev. Greater London Authority.

glacé /gla-say/ •adj. (of fruit) preserved in sugar.
– ORIGIN French, 'iced'.

glacé icing •n. icing made with icing sugar and water.

glacial /glay-si-uhl/ •adj. 1 relating to ice, especially in the form of glaciers. 2 very cold or unfriendly.
– DERIVATIVES **glacially** adv.
– ORIGIN Latin *glacialis* 'icy'.

glacial period •n. an ice age.

glaciated /glay-si-ay-tid/ •adj. covered or having been covered by glaciers or ice sheets.

glaciation •n. the state or result of being covered by glaciers.

glacier /gla-si-er, glay-si-er/ •n. a slowly moving mass of ice formed by the accumulation of snow on mountains or near the poles.
– ORIGIN French.

glad •adj. (**gladder, gladdest**) 1 pleased; delighted. 2 grateful: *he was glad of my company*. 3 causing happiness.
– DERIVATIVES **gladly** adv. **gladness** n.
– ORIGIN Old English, 'bright, shining'.

gladden •v. make someone glad.

glade •n. an open space in a wood or forest.

gladiator •n. (in ancient Rome) a man trained to fight against other men or wild animals in an arena.
– DERIVATIVES **gladiatorial** adj.
– ORIGIN Latin.

gladiolus /glad-i-oh-luhss/ •n. (pl. **gladioli** /glad-i-oh-ly/) a plant with tall stems carrying brightly coloured flowers.
– ORIGIN Latin.

glad rags •pl. n. informal clothes for a party or special occasion.

Glam. •abbrev. Glamorgan.

glamorize (or **glamorise**) •v. (**glamorizes, glamorizing, glamorized**) make something, especially something bad, seem attractive or desirable.
– DERIVATIVES **glamorization** n.

glamorous •adj. attractive and appealing.
– DERIVATIVES **glamorously** adv.

> ☑ **glamorous** and **glamorize** drop the *u* of **glamour**.

glamour (US also **glamor**) •n. an attractive and exciting quality.
– ORIGIN first meaning 'magic': from GRAMMAR, with reference to the magical practices associated with learning in medieval times.

glance •v. (**glances, glancing, glanced**) 1 take a brief or hurried look. 2 strike and bounce off at an angle. •n. a brief or hurried look.
– ORIGIN Old French *glacier* 'to slip'.

gland •n. 1 an organ of the body which produces particular chemical substances. 2 a lymph node.
– ORIGIN Latin *glandulae* 'throat glands'.

glandular •adj. relating to or affecting a gland or glands.

glandular fever •n. Brit. an infectious disease that causes swelling of the lymph glands and persistent lack of energy.

glare • v. (**glares, glaring, glared**) **1** stare in an angry way. **2** shine with a dazzling light. **3** (as adj. **glaring**) very obvious: *a glaring omission*. • n. **1** an angry stare. **2** dazzling light.
– ORIGIN Dutch and German *glaren*.

glasnost /ˈglaz-nosst/ • n. (in the former Soviet Union) the policy or practice of more open government.
– ORIGIN Russian.

glass • n. **1** a hard transparent substance made by fusing sand with soda and lime. **2** a drinking container made of glass. **3** esp. Brit. a mirror. • v. cover or enclose with glass.
– DERIVATIVES **glassful** n. **glassware** n.
– ORIGIN Old English.

glass-blowing • n. the craft of making glassware by blowing semi-liquid glass through a long tube.

glass ceiling • n. a situation in which certain groups, especially women and minorities, find that progress in a profession is blocked although there are no official barriers to advancement.

glasses • pl. n. a pair of lenses set in a frame that rests on the nose and ears, used to correct eyesight.

glass fibre • n. esp. Brit. a strong material containing embedded glass filaments for reinforcement.

glasshouse • n. Brit. a greenhouse.

glasspaper • n. paper covered with powdered glass, used for smoothing and polishing.

glassy • adj. (**glassier, glassiest**) **1** resembling glass. **2** (of a person's eyes or expression) showing no interest.
– DERIVATIVES **glassily** adv.

Glaswegian /glaz-ˈwee-jən/ • n. a person from Glasgow. • adj. relating to Glasgow.

glaucoma /glaw-ˈkoh-muh/ • n. Med. a condition of increased pressure within the eyeball, causing gradual loss of sight.
– ORIGIN Greek *glaukōma*.

glaze • v. (**glazes, glazing, glazed**) **1** fit panes of glass into a window frame or similar structure. **2** enclose or cover with glass. **3** cover with a glaze. **4** lose brightness and liveliness: *her eyes glazed over*. • n. **1** a glass-like substance fused on to the surface of pottery to form a hard coating. **2** a liquid such as milk or beaten egg, used to form a shiny coating on food.
– ORIGIN from GLASS.

glazier /ˈglay-zi-er/ • n. a person whose trade is fitting glass into windows and doors.

gleam • v. shine brightly with reflected light. • n. **1** a faint or brief light. **2** a brief or faint sign of a quality or emotion: *a gleam of humour*.
– ORIGIN Old English.

glean • v. **1** collect things gradually from various sources. **2** hist. gather grain that is left over from a harvest.
– DERIVATIVES **gleaner** n.
– ORIGIN Latin *glennare*.

gleanings • pl. n. things gathered from various sources.

glebe /gleeb/ • n. hist. a piece of land serving as part of a clergyman's benefice and providing income.
– ORIGIN Latin *gleba* 'land, soil'.

glee • n. **1** great delight. **2** a song for men's voices in three or more parts.
– ORIGIN Old English, 'entertainment, music'.

gleeful • adj. very happy, often in a gloating way.
– DERIVATIVES **gleefully** adv.

glen • n. a narrow valley, especially in Scotland or Ireland.
– ORIGIN Scottish Gaelic and Irish *gleann*.

glib • adj. (**glibber, glibbest**) using words easily, but without much thought or sincerity.
– DERIVATIVES **glibly** adv. **glibness** n.
– ORIGIN Germanic.

glide • v. (**glides, gliding, glided**) **1** move with a smooth, quiet motion. **2** fly without power or in a glider. • n. an instance of gliding.
– ORIGIN Old English.

glider • n. a light aircraft designed to fly without using an engine.

glimmer • v. (**glimmers, glimmering, glimmered**) shine faintly with a wavering light. • n. **1** a faint or wavering light. **2** a faint sign of a feeling or quality: *a glimmer of hope*.
– ORIGIN prob. from Scandinavian.

glimpse • n. a brief or partial view. • v. (**glimpses, glimpsing, glimpsed**) see briefly or partially.
– ORIGIN prob. Germanic.

glint • v. give out or reflect small flashes of light. • n. a small flash of reflected light.
– ORIGIN prob. from Scandinavian.

glissando /glis-ˈsan-doh/ • n. (pl. **glissandi** /glis-ˈsan-di/ or **glissandos**) Music a slide upwards or downwards between two notes.
– ORIGIN Italian.

glisten • v. (of something wet or greasy) shine or sparkle. • n. a sparkling light reflected from something wet.
– ORIGIN Old English.

glitch • n. informal **1** a sudden fault or

failure of equipment. **2** an unexpected setback.

glitter • v. (**glitters, glittering, glittered**) **1** shine with a shimmering reflected light. **2** (as adj. **glittering**) impressively successful or glamorous: *a glittering career.* • n. **1** a shimmering reflected light. **2** tiny pieces of sparkling material used for decoration. **3** an attractive but superficial quality.
– DERIVATIVES **glittery** adj.
– ORIGIN Old Norse.

glitterati /glit-tuh-**rah**-ti/ • pl. n. informal fashionable people involved in show business or another glamorous activity.
– ORIGIN from **GLITTER** and **LITERATI**.

glitz • n. informal showy but superficial display.
– DERIVATIVES **glitzy** adj.
– ORIGIN from **GLITTER**.

gloaming • n. (**the gloaming**) literary twilight; dusk.
– ORIGIN Old English.

gloat • v. be smug or pleased about your own success or another person's misfortune.

glob • n. informal a lump of a semi-liquid substance.
– ORIGIN perh. from **BLOB** and **GOB**².

global • adj. **1** relating to the whole world; worldwide. **2** relating to or including the whole of something, or of a group of things. **3** Computing operating or applying through the whole of a file or program.
– DERIVATIVES **globalist** n. **globally** adv.

globalization (or **globalisation**) • n. the process by which businesses start operating on a global scale.
– DERIVATIVES **globalize** v.

global warming • n. the gradual increase in the overall temperature of the earth's atmosphere due to increased levels of carbon dioxide and other pollutants.

globe • n. **1** a spherical or rounded object. **2** (**the globe**) the earth. **3** a spherical model of the earth with a map on the surface.
– ORIGIN Latin *globus*.

globetrotter • n. informal a person who travels widely.
– DERIVATIVES **globetrotting** n. & adj.

globular • adj. **1** spherical. **2** composed of globules.

globule • n. a small round particle of a substance; a drop.
– ORIGIN Latin *globulus* 'little globe'.

globulin /glob-yuu-lin/ • n. any of a group of simple proteins found in blood serum.

glockenspiel /glok-uhn-shpeel/ • n. a

musical instrument containing metal pieces which are struck with small hammers.
– ORIGIN German, 'bell play'.

gloom • n. **1** partial or total darkness. **2** a state of depression or despair.

gloomy • adj. (**gloomier, gloomiest**) **1** dark or poorly lit. **2** causing or feeling depression or despair.
– DERIVATIVES **gloomily** adv. **gloominess** n.

gloop • n. informal sloppy or sticky semi-fluid matter.
– DERIVATIVES **gloopy** adj.

glorify • v. (**glorifies, glorifying, glorified**) **1** represent something as admirable. **2** (as adj. **glorified**) made to appear more important than is the case: *he was nothing more than a glorified janitor.* **3** praise and worship God.
– DERIVATIVES **glorification** n.

glorious • adj. **1** having or bringing glory. **2** very beautiful or impressive: *a glorious autumn day.* **3** very enjoyable.
– DERIVATIVES **gloriously** adv.

glory • n. (pl. **glories**) **1** fame or honour won by notable achievements. **2** magnificence; great beauty. **3** a very beautiful or impressive thing: *the glories of Paris.* **4** worship and thanksgiving offered to God. • v. (**glories, glorying, gloried**) (**glory in**) take great pride or pleasure in.
– ORIGIN Latin *gloria*.

Glos. • abbrev. Gloucestershire.

gloss¹ • n. **1** the shine on a smooth surface. **2** a type of paint which dries to a shiny surface. **3** an attractive appearance that conceals something ordinary or less pleasant. • v. **1** give a shiny appearance to. **2** (**gloss over**) try to conceal or pass over something by mentioning it briefly or misleadingly.

gloss² • n. a translation or explanation of a word, phrase, or passage. • v. provide a gloss for.
– ORIGIN Old French *glose*.

glossary • n. (pl. **glossaries**) an alphabetical list of words relating to a specific subject or written work, with explanations.
– ORIGIN Latin *glossarium*.

glossy • adj. (**glossier, glossiest**) **1** shiny and smooth. **2** appearing attractive and stylish. • n. (pl. **glossies**) informal a magazine printed on shiny paper with many colour photographs.
– DERIVATIVES **glossily** adv. **glossiness** n.

glottal • adj. relating to the glottis (part of the larynx).

glottal stop • n. a speech sound made

by opening and closing the glottis, sometimes used instead of a properly sounded *t*.

glottis /glot-tiss/ •n. the part of the larynx made up of the vocal cords and the slit-like opening between them.
– ORIGIN Greek.

glove •n. **1** a covering for the hand with separate parts for each finger. **2** a padded covering for the hand used in boxing and other sports.
– DERIVATIVES **gloved** adj.
– ORIGIN Old English.

glove compartment (also **glovebox**) •n. a small storage compartment in the dashboard of a motor vehicle.

glove puppet •n. Brit. a cloth puppet fitted on the hand and worked by the fingers.

glow •v. **1** give out steady light without flame. **2** look or feel warm or pink: *I was glowing with excitement.* **3** look very pleased or happy. •n. **1** a steady light. **2** a feeling or appearance of warmth. **3** a strong feeling of pleasure or well-being.
– ORIGIN Old English.

glower /glow-er/ •v. (**glowers**, **glowering**, **glowered**) have an angry or sullen expression. •n. an angry or sullen look.
– ORIGIN perh. from Scandinavian.

glowing •adj. expressing great praise: *a glowing report.*

glow-worm •n. a type of beetle, the female of which glows to attract males.

gloxinia /glok-sin-i-uh/ •n. a tropical plant with large, bell-shaped flowers.
– ORIGIN named after the German botanist Benjamin P. *Gloxin*.

glucose /gloo-kohz/ •n. a simple sugar which is an important energy source in living organisms.
– ORIGIN Greek *gleukos* 'sweet wine'.

glue •n. an adhesive substance used for sticking things together. •v. (**glues**, **gluing** or **glueing**, **glued**) **1** fasten or join with glue. **2** (**be glued to**) informal be paying very close attention to.
– DERIVATIVES **gluey** adj.
– ORIGIN Latin *gluten*.

glue-sniffing •n. the habit of breathing in intoxicating fumes from some types of glue.

glug •v. informal (**glugs**, **glugging**, **glugged**) pour or drink liquid with a gurgling sound.

glum •adj. (**glummer**, **glummest**) sad and unhappy.
– DERIVATIVES **glumly** adv.
– ORIGIN from **GLOOM**.

glut •n. an excessively large supply.

•v. (**gluts**, **glutting**, **glutted**) supply or fill to excess.
– ORIGIN prob. from Latin *gluttire* 'to swallow'.

gluten /gloo-tuhn/ •n. a substance containing a number of proteins that is found in wheat and other cereal grains.
– ORIGIN Latin, 'glue'.

glutinous /gloo-ti-nuhss/ •adj. like glue in texture; sticky.
– ORIGIN Latin *glutinosus*.

glutton •n. **1** a very greedy eater. **2** a person who is very eager for something difficult or challenging: *a glutton for punishment.*
– DERIVATIVES **gluttonous** adj.
– ORIGIN Latin *glutto*.

gluttony •n. the habit of eating too much.

glycerine /gli-suh-reen/ (US **glycerin** /gli-suh-rin/) •n. = GLYCEROL.
– ORIGIN French *glycérin*.

glycerol /gli-suh-rol/ •n. a liquid formed as a by-product in soap manufacture, used in making cosmetics, explosives, and antifreeze.

glycogen /gly-kuh-juhn/ •n. a substance deposited in bodily tissues as a store of glucose.

GM •abbrev. **1** genetically modified. **2** George Medal. **3** (of a school) grant-maintained.

gm •abbrev. gram(s).

GMO •abbrev. genetically modified organism.

GMT •abbrev. Greenwich Mean Time.

gnarled (also **gnarly**) •adj. knobbly, rough, and twisted.
– ORIGIN from former *knarre* 'rugged rock'.

gnash /nash/ •v. grind your teeth together in anger.
– ORIGIN perh. from Old Norse.

gnashers •pl. n. Brit. informal teeth.

gnat /nat/ •n. a small two-winged fly resembling a mosquito.
– ORIGIN Old English.

gnaw /naw/ •v. **1** bite at or nibble persistently. **2** cause persistent anxiety or pain: *doubts continued to gnaw at me.*
– ORIGIN Old English.

gneiss /nyss/ •n. a metamorphic rock with a banded or layered structure, typically consisting of feldspar, quartz, and mica.
– ORIGIN German.

gnome •n. an imaginary creature like a tiny man, who guards the earth's treasures underground.
– DERIVATIVES **gnomish** adj.

– ORIGIN Latin *gnomus*.

gnomic /noh-mik/ • adj. clever but often difficult to understand: *a gnomic explanation.*
– DERIVATIVES **gnomically** adv.
– ORIGIN Greek *gnōmē* 'thought, opinion'

Gnosticism /noss-ti-si-z'm/ • n. a former heretical movement of the Christian Church, teaching that mystical knowledge (gnosis) of the supreme divine being enabled the human spirit to be redeemed.
– DERIVATIVES **Gnostic** adj.
– ORIGIN Greek *gnosis* 'knowledge'.

GNP • abbrev. gross national product.

gnu /noo/ • n. a large African antelope with a long head and a beard and mane.
– ORIGIN from a southern African language.

GNVQ • abbrev. General National Vocational Qualification.

go • v. (**goes, going, went;** past part. **gone**) **1** move to or from a place. **2** pass into or be in a particular state: *her mind went blank.* **3** lie or extend in a certain direction. **4** come to an end. **5** disappear or be used up. **6** (of time) pass. **7** pass time in a particular way: *they went for months without talking.* **8** engage in a specified activity. **9** have a particular outcome: *it all went off smoothly.* **10** (**be going to be/do**) used to express a future tense. **11** function or operate. **12** match something. **13** be acceptable or allowed. **14** fit into or be regularly kept in a particular place. **15** make a specified sound. • n. (pl. **goes**) informal, esp. Brit. **1** an attempt. **2** a turn to do or use something. **3** spirit or energy.
– PHRASES **go about** begin or carry on work at. **go along with** agree to. **go back on** fail to keep a promise. **go down 1** be defeated in a contest. **2** obtain a specified reaction: *the show went down well.* **go for 1** decide on. **2** attempt to gain. **3** attack. **go in for 1** Brit. enter a contest. **2** like something. **going!, gone!** an auctioneer's announcement that bidding is closing or closed. **go into 1** investigate or enquire into. **2** (of a whole number) be capable of dividing another. **go off 1** (of a gun or bomb) explode or fire. **2** Brit. (of food) begin to decompose. **3** Brit. informal begin to dislike. **go on 1** continue. **2** take place. **go out 1** stop shining or burning. **2** carry on a regular romantic relationship with someone. **go over** examine or check the details of. **go round** be enough to supply everybody present. **go through 1** undergo a difficult experience. **2** examine carefully. **3** informal use up or spend. **go without** suffer lack or

hardship. **have a go at** esp. Brit. attack or criticize. **make a go of** informal be successful in. **on the go** informal very active or busy.
– ORIGIN Old English.

goad /gohd/ • v. keep annoying or criticizing someone until they react. • n. **1** a thing that stimulates someone into action. **2** a spiked stick used for driving cattle.
– ORIGIN Old English.

go-ahead informal • n. (**the go-ahead**) permission to proceed. • adj. enterprising and ambitious: *a go-ahead director.*

goal • n. **1** (in football, rugby, etc.) a pair of posts linked by a crossbar and forming a space into or over which the ball has to be sent to score. **2** an instance of sending the ball into or over a goal. **3** an aim or desired result.
– DERIVATIVES **goalless** adj.

goalie • n. informal a goalkeeper.

goalkeeper • n. a player in football or field hockey whose role is to stop the ball from entering the goal.

goal kick • n. **1** Football a free kick taken by the defending side after attackers send the ball over the byline. **2** Rugby an attempt to kick a goal.

goal line • n. a line across a football or hockey field on which the goal is placed or which acts as the boundary beyond which a try or touchdown is scored.

goalpost • n. either of the two upright posts of a goal.
– PHRASES **move the goalposts** unfairly alter the conditions or rules of something while it is still happening.

goat • n. **1** a domesticated mammal that has backward-curving horns and (in the male) a beard. **2** a wild mammal related to the goat.
– PHRASES **get someone's goat** informal irritate someone.
– ORIGIN Old English.

goatee /goh-tee/ • n. a small pointed beard like that of a goat.

goatherd • n. a person who looks after goats.

gob[1] • n. Brit. informal a person's mouth.
– ORIGIN perh. from Scottish Gaelic.

gob[2] informal • n. a lump or clot of a slimy substance. • v. (**gobs, gobbing, gobbed**) Brit. spit.
– ORIGIN Old French *gobe* 'mouthful'.

gobbet /gob-bit/ • n. a piece of flesh, food, or other matter.
– ORIGIN Old French *gobet*.

gobble • v. (**gobbles, gobbling, gobbled**) **1** eat hurriedly and noisily. **2** (often **gobble something up**) use a large amount of something very quickly. **3** (of

g

a turkey) make a swallowing sound in the throat.
– DERIVATIVES **gobbler** n.
– ORIGIN prob. from GOB².

gobbledegook /gob-b'l-di-gook/ (also **gobbledygook**) • n. informal complicated language that is difficult to understand.

go-between • n. an intermediary or negotiator.

goblet • n. 1 a drinking glass with a foot and a stem. 2 Brit. a container forming part of a liquidizer.
– ORIGIN Old French *gobelet* 'little cup'.

goblin • n. (in fairy stories) a small, ugly, mischievous creature.
– ORIGIN Old French *gobelin*.

gobsmacked • adj. Brit. informal completely astonished.

gobstopper • n. esp. Brit. a hard round sweet.

goby /goh-bi/ • n. (pl. **gobies**) a small sea fish, typically with a sucker on the underside.
– ORIGIN Greek *kōbios*.

go-cart • n. = GO-KART.

God • n. 1 (in Christianity and other religions which believe in only one God) the creator and supreme ruler of the universe. 2 (**god**) a superhuman being or spirit: *a moon god*. 3 (**god**) a greatly admired or influential person.
• exclam. used to express surprise, anger, etc. or for emphasis. (in Christian doctrine) the persons of the Trinity.
– PHRASES **God Save the Queen** (or **King**) the British national anthem.
– DERIVATIVES **godlike** adj.
– ORIGIN Old English.

godchild • n. (pl. **godchildren**) a person in relation to a godparent.

god-daughter • n. a female godchild.

goddess • n. a female god.

godfather • n. 1 a male godparent. 2 the male head of the Mafia.

God-fearing • adj. earnestly religious.

godforsaken • adj. (of a place) unattractive, remote, or depressing.

godhead • n. 1 (**the Godhead**) God. 2 divine nature.

godless • adj. 1 not believing in a god or God. 2 wicked; bad.

godly • adj. very religious.
– DERIVATIVES **godliness** n.

godmother • n. a female godparent.

godparent • n. a person who presents a child at baptism and promises to be responsible for their religious education.

godsend • n. something very helpful or welcome at a particular time.

godson • n. a male godchild.

goer • n. a person who regularly attends a particular place or event: *a theatregoer*.

goes 3rd person sing. present of GO.

go-getter • n. informal an energetic and very enterprising person.
– DERIVATIVES **go-getting** adj.

goggle • v. (**goggles**, **goggling**, **goggled**) 1 look with wide open eyes. 2 (of the eyes) stick out or open wide.
• n. (**goggles**) close-fitting protective glasses.

go-go • adj. referring to an erotic style of dancing to pop music.

going • n. 1 the condition of the ground in terms of its suitability for horse racing or walking. 2 conditions for an activity: *the going gets tough*. • adj. 1 esp. Brit. existing or available: *any jobs going?* 2 (of a price) usual or current.

going concern • n. a thriving business.

going-over • n. informal 1 a thorough cleaning or inspection. 2 an attack or heavy defeat.

goings-on • pl. n. informal strange or dishonest activities.

goitre /goy-ter/ • n. a swelling of the neck resulting from enlargement of the thyroid gland.
– ORIGIN French.

go-kart (also **go-cart**) • n. a small racing car with a lightweight body.

gold • n. 1 a yellow precious metal, used as an ornament and as money. 2 a deep yellow or yellow-brown colour. 3 articles made of gold.
– ORIGIN Old English.

goldcrest • n. a very small warbler with a yellow or orange crest.

gold-digger • n. informal a woman who forms relationships with men purely for financial gain.

gold disc • n. a golden disc awarded to a recording artist or group for sales above a specified figure.

gold dust • n. fine particles of gold.
– PHRASES **be like gold dust** Brit. be very rare and valuable.

golden • adj. 1 made of or resembling gold. 2 (of a period) very happy and prosperous. 3 excellent.

golden age • n. the period when something is most successful: *the golden age of cinema*.

golden boy (or **golden girl**) • n. informal a very popular or successful young person.

golden eagle • n. a large eagle with yellow-tipped head feathers.

golden handshake • n. informal a payment given to someone who is made redundant or retires early.

golden jubilee • n. the fiftieth anniversary of an important event.

golden mean • n. the ideal middle position between two extremes.

golden retriever • n. a breed of retriever with a thick golden-coloured coat.

goldenrod • n. a plant with tall stems carrying spikes of bright yellow flowers.

golden rule • n. a principle which should always be followed.

golden syrup • n. Brit. a pale treacle.

golden wedding • n. Brit. the fiftieth anniversary of a wedding.

goldfield • n. a district in which gold is found as a mineral.

goldfinch • n. a brightly coloured finch with a yellow patch on each wing.

goldfish • n. (pl. **goldfish** or **goldfishes**) a small reddish-golden carp popular in ponds and aquaria.

gold leaf • n. gold beaten into a very thin sheet, used in gilding.

gold medal • n. a medal made of or coloured gold, awarded for first place in a competition.

gold mine • n. **1** a place where gold is mined. **2** a source of great wealth or resources.

gold plate • n. **1** a thin layer of gold applied as a coating to another metal. **2** plates, dishes, etc. made of or plated with gold.

gold rush • n. a rapid movement of people to a newly discovered goldfield.

goldsmith • n. a person who makes gold articles.

gold standard • n. hist. the system by which the value of a currency was defined in terms of gold.

golf • n. a game played on an outdoor course, the aim of which is to strike a small ball with a club into a series of small holes.
– DERIVATIVES **golfer** n.
– ORIGIN perh. from Dutch *kolf* 'club'.

golf club • n. see CLUB² (sense 2).

Goliath /guh-ly-uth/ • n. a very large or strong person or thing.
– ORIGIN a Philistine giant in the Bible, killed by David.

golliwog • n. a soft doll with a black face and fuzzy hair.
– ORIGIN from *Golliwogg*, a doll character in books by the US writer Bertha Upton.

golly • exclam. informal used to express surprise or delight.
– ORIGIN from GOD.

gonad /goh-nad/ • n. a bodily organ that produces gametes; a testis or ovary.
– ORIGIN Latin *gonades*.

gondola /gon-duh-luh/ • n. **1** a flat-bottomed boat used on Venetian canals, worked by one oar at the stern. **2** a cabin

on a ski lift, or hanging from an airship or balloon.
– ORIGIN Venetian Italian.

gondolier /gon-duh-leer/ • n. a person who propels and steers a gondola.

gone past part. of GO. • adj. no longer present, available, or in existence. • prep. Brit. (of time) past.

goner /gon-er/ • n. informal a person or thing that cannot be saved.

gong • n. **1** a metal disc with a turned rim, giving a resonant note when struck. **2** Brit. informal a medal or decoration.
– ORIGIN Malay.

gonorrhoea /gon-uh-ree-uh/ (US **gonorrhea**) • n. a sexually transmitted disease causing discharge from the urethra or vagina.
– ORIGIN Greek *gonorrhoia*.

goo • n. informal a sticky or slimy substance.
– ORIGIN perh. from *burgoo*, a nautical slang term for porridge.

good • adj. (**better, best**) **1** having the right qualities; of a high standard. **2** behaving in a way that is right, polite, or obedient. **3** enjoyable or satisfying. **4** appropriate or suitable. **5** (**good for**) of benefit to. **6** thorough: *a really good clear-up.* **7** at least. • n. **1** behaviour that is right or acceptable. **2** something beneficial: *he resigned for the good of the country.* **3** (**goods**) products or possessions. **4** (**goods**) Brit. freight.
– PHRASES **as good as** very nearly. **for good** forever. **the Good Book** the Bible. **a good word** words in favour of or defending a person. **in good time 1** with no risk of being late. **2** (also **all in good time**) in due course but without haste. **make something good 1** compensate for loss, damage, or expense. **2** fulfil a promise or claim.
– ORIGIN Old English.

goodbye (US also **goodby**) • exclam. used to express good wishes when parting or ending a conversation.
– ORIGIN from *God be with you!*

good faith • n. honesty or sincerity of intention.

good-for-nothing • adj. worthless and lazy.

Good Friday • n. the Friday before Easter Sunday, on which the Crucifixion of Jesus is commemorated in the Christian Church.

good-hearted • adj. kind and well meaning.

good-humoured • adj. friendly or cheerful.

goodie • n. var. of GOODY.

g

goodish • adj. **1** fairly good. **2** fairly large.

good-looking • adj. attractive.

goodly • adj. dated considerable in size or quantity.

good-natured • adj. kind and unselfish.

goodness • n. **1** the quality of being good. **2** the nutritious element of food. • exclam. expressing surprise or anger.

goodnight • exclam. expressing good wishes on parting at night or before going to bed.

goods and chattels • pl. n. all kinds of personal possessions.

good-tempered • adj. not easily angered.

goodwill • n. friendly or helpful feelings or attitude.

goody • n. (also **goodie**) (pl. **goodies**) informal **1** Brit. a good person, especially a hero in a story or film. **2** (**goodies**) tasty things to eat. • exclam. expressing childish delight.

goody-goody informal • n. a person who behaves well so as to impress other people.

gooey • adj. (**gooier, gooiest**) informal soft and sticky.

goof informal, esp. N. Amer. • n. a mistake. • v. **1** fool around. **2** make a mistake.

goofy • adj. (**goofier, goofiest**) informal **1** esp. N. Amer. foolish. **2** having front teeth that stick out.
– DERIVATIVES **goofily** adv. **goofiness** n.

goon • n. informal **1** a foolish person. **2** N. Amer. a thug.
– ORIGIN perh. from dialect *gooney* 'stupid person'.

goose • n. (pl. **geese**) **1** a large waterbird with a long neck and webbed feet. **2** a female goose. **3** informal a foolish person. • v. (**gooses, goosing, goosed**) informal poke someone in the bottom.
– ORIGIN Old English.

gooseberry • n. (pl. **gooseberries**) **1** an edible yellowish-green berry with a hairy skin. **2** Brit. informal a third person in the company of two lovers.
– ORIGIN perh. from **goose**, or perh. from Old French *groseille*.

gooseflesh (also **goose pimples**) • n. a pimply state of the skin with the hairs erect, produced by cold or fright.

goose step • n. a military marching step in which the legs are kept straight. • v. (**goose-step**) march with the legs kept straight.

gopher /goh-fer/ • n. (also **pocket gopher**) a burrowing American rodent with pouches on its cheeks.
– ORIGIN perh. from Canadian French *gaufre* 'honeycomb' (because the gopher 'honeycombs' the ground with its burrows).

Gordian knot /gor-di-uhn/ • n. (in phr. **cut the Gordian knot**) solve a difficult problem in a forceful or direct way.
– ORIGIN from the legendary knot tied by King *Gordius* and cut through by Alexander the Great in response to the prophecy that whoever untied it would rule Asia.

gore¹ • n. blood that has been shed.
– ORIGIN Old English, 'dung, dirt'.

gore² • v. (**gores, goring, gored**) (of an animal such as a bull) pierce or stab with a horn or tusk.

gore³ • n. a triangular piece of material used in making a garment, sail, or umbrella.
– DERIVATIVES **gored** adj.
– ORIGIN Old English, 'triangular piece of land'.

gorge • n. a narrow valley or ravine. • v. (**gorges, gorging, gorged**) eat a large amount greedily.
– PHRASES **your gorge rises** you feel sick or disgusted.
– ORIGIN Old French, 'throat'.

gorgeous • adj. **1** beautiful. **2** informal very pleasant.
– DERIVATIVES **gorgeously** adv. **gorgeousness** n.
– ORIGIN Old French *gorgias* 'fine'.

gorgon /gor-guhn/ • n. **1** Gk Myth. each of three sisters with snakes for hair, who had the power to turn anyone who looked at them to stone. **2** a fierce or repulsive woman.
– ORIGIN Greek *Gorgō*.

Gorgonzola /gor-guhn-zoh-luh/ • n. a strong-flavoured Italian cheese with bluish-green veins.
– ORIGIN named after the Italian village of *Gorgonzola*.

gorilla • n. a powerfully built great ape of central Africa, the largest living primate.
– ORIGIN Greek.

gormless • adj. Brit. informal stupid or foolish.
– ORIGIN from dialect *gaum* 'understanding'.

gorse • n. a yellow-flowered shrub with thin prickly leaves.
– ORIGIN Old English.

gory • adj. (**gorier, goriest**) **1** involving violence and bloodshed. **2** covered in blood.

gosh • exclam. informal used to express surprise or for emphasis.
– ORIGIN euphemism for **God**.

goshawk /goss-hawk/ • n. a short-

winged hawk resembling a large sparrowhawk.
– ORIGIN Old English, 'goose-hawk'.

gosling • n. a young goose.
– ORIGIN Old Norse.

go-slow • n. Brit. a form of industrial action in which work is done more slowly than usual.

gospel • n. **1** the teachings of Jesus. **2** (**Gospel**) the record of Jesus's life and teaching in the first four books of the New Testament. **3** (**Gospel**) each of the first four books of the New Testament. **4** (also **gospel truth**) something absolutely true. **5** (also **gospel music**) a style of black American religious singing.
– ORIGIN Old English, 'good news'.

gossamer • n. a fine substance consisting of cobwebs spun by small spiders. • adj. very fine and insubstantial.
– ORIGIN prob. from GOOSE + SUMMER, perh. from the time around St Martin's day (11 November) when geese were eaten and gossamer is seen.

gossip • n. **1** casual conversation or unproven reports about other people. **2** derog. a person who likes talking about other people's private lives. • v. (**gossips, gossiping, gossiped**) engage in gossip.
– DERIVATIVES **gossiper** n. **gossipy** adj.
– ORIGIN Old English, 'godfather or godmother'.

got past and past part. of GET.

Goth /goth/ • n. a member of a Germanic people that invaded the Roman Empire between the 3rd and 5th centuries.
– ORIGIN Greek Gothoi.

Gothic • adj. **1** relating to the style of architecture common in western Europe in the 12th–16th centuries. **2** very gloomy or horrifying. **3** relating to the ancient Goths. • n. **1** Gothic architecture. **2** the extinct language of the Goths.

gotten N. Amer. past part. of GET.

gouache /goo-ash/ • n. **1** a method of painting using watercolours thickened with a type of glue. **2** paint used in this method.
– ORIGIN French.

Gouda /gow-duh/ • n. a flat round Dutch cheese with a yellow rind.
– ORIGIN first made in Gouda in the Netherlands.

gouge /gowj/ • v. (**gouges, gouging, gouged**) **1** make a rough hole in a surface. **2** (**gouge something out**) cut or force something out roughly. • n. **1** a chisel with a concave blade. **2** a hole or groove made by gouging.
– ORIGIN Old French.

goulash /goo-lash/ • n. a spicy Hungarian stew of meat and vegetables.

– ORIGIN from Hungarian gulyás 'herdsman' + hús 'meat'.

gourd /gord/ • n. **1** the large hard-skinned fruit of a climbing or trailing plant. **2** a container made from the hollowed skin of a gourd.
– ORIGIN Old French gourde.

gourmand /gor-muhnd/ • n. **1** a person who enjoys eating, sometimes to excess. **2** a person who is knowledgeable about good food.
– ORIGIN Old French.

gourmet /gor-may/ • n. a person who is knowledgeable about good food. • adj. (of food or a meal) high quality.
– ORIGIN French.

gout /gowt/ • n. **1** a disease causing the joints to swell and become painful. **2** literary a drop or spot.
– DERIVATIVES **gouty** adj.
– ORIGIN Latin gutta.

govern • v. **1** control the policy and affairs of a state, organization, or people. **2** control or influence: your actions are governed by your desires.
– ORIGIN Old French governer.

governance • n. the action or style of governing something.

governess • n. a woman employed to teach children in a private household.

government • n. **1** the group of people who govern a state. **2** the system by which a state or community is governed. **3** the action or way of governing a state: she believed in strong government.
– DERIVATIVES **governmental** adj.

> ✓ Remember that **government** is spelled with an **n** before the **m**.

governor • n. **1** an official appointed to govern a town or region. **2** the elected executive head of a US state. **3** the representative of the British Crown in a colony or in a Commonwealth state that regards the monarch as head of state. **4** the head of a public institution. **5** a member of a group of people who govern a school or other institution.
– DERIVATIVES **governorship** n.

Governor General • n. (pl. **Governors General**) the chief representative of the Crown in a Commonwealth country of which the British monarch is head of state.

gown • n. **1** a long dress worn on formal occasions. **2** a protective garment worn in hospital by surgical staff or patients. **3** a loose cloak showing a person's profession or status, worn by a lawyer, academic, or university student. • v. (**be gowned**) be dressed in a gown.
– ORIGIN Old French goune.

GP • abbrev. general practitioner.

gr. •abbrev. **1** grain(s). **2** gram(s). **3** gross.

grab •v. (**grabs, grabbed, grabbing**)
1 seize suddenly and roughly. **2** informal obtain quickly or when an opportunity arises. **3** informal impress: *how does that grab you?* •n. a sudden attempt to seize something or someone.
– PHRASES **up for grabs** informal available.
– DERIVATIVES **grabber** n.
– ORIGIN German and Dutch *grabben*.

grace •n. **1** elegance of movement. **2** polite good will: *she had the grace to look sheepish.* **3** (**graces**) attractive qualities or behaviour. **4** (in Christian belief) the unearned favour of God. **5** a person's favour. **6** a period officially allowed for an obligation to be met: *three days' grace.* **7** a short prayer of thanks said before or after a meal. **8** (**His, Her,** or **Your Grace**) used as a form of address to a duke, duchess, or archbishop. •v. (**graces, gracing, graced**) **1** bring honour to something by your presence. **2** make more attractive: *the room is graced with Scandinavian-style furniture.*
– PHRASES **with good** (or **bad**) **grace** in a willing (or reluctant) way.
– ORIGIN Latin *gratia*.

graceful •adj. having or showing grace or elegance.
– DERIVATIVES **gracefully** adv. **gracefulness** n.

graceless •adj. lacking grace or charm.

grace note •n. Music an extra note added to ornament a melody.

gracious •adj. **1** polite, kind, and pleasant. **2** elegant in a way that is associated with upper-class status or wealth. •exclam. expressing polite surprise.
– DERIVATIVES **graciously** adv. **graciousness** n.

gradation /gruh-day-sh'n/ •n. **1** a scale of successive changes, stages, or degrees. **2** a stage in a such a scale.

grade •n. **1** a specified level of rank, quality, ability, or value. **2** a mark indicating the quality of a student's work. **3** N. Amer. a class in school comprising children grouped according to age or ability: *I was in fourth grade.* •v. (**grades, grading, graded**) arrange people or things in groups according to quality, size, ability, etc.
– PHRASES **make the grade** informal succeed.
– ORIGIN Latin *gradus* 'step'.

gradient /gray-di-uhnt/ •n. **1** a sloping part of a road or railway. **2** the degree to which the ground slopes.
– ORIGIN from GRADE.

gradual •adj. **1** taking place in stages over an extended period. **2** (of a slope) not steep.
– DERIVATIVES **gradually** adv.
– ORIGIN Latin *gradualis*.

graduate •n. /grad-yuu-uht/ a person who has been awarded a first academic degree. •v. /grad-yoo-ayt/ (**graduates, graduating, graduated**) **1** successfully complete a degree or course. **2** (**graduate to**) move up to something more advanced. **3** arrange or mark out in a scale of gradations. **4** change gradually.
– DERIVATIVES **graduation** n.
– ORIGIN Latin *graduare* 'take a degree'.

Graeco- /gree-koh/ (also **Greco-**) •comb. form Greek; Greek and ...: *Graeco-Roman.*
– ORIGIN Latin *Graecus.*

graffiti /gruh-fee-ti/ •n. writing or drawings on a surface in a public place.
– ORIGIN Italian.

graft[1] •n. **1** a shoot from one plant inserted into another to form a new growth. **2** a piece of living body tissue that is transplanted surgically to replace diseased or damaged tissue. •v. **1** insert or transplant as a graft. **2** add something to something else, especially in a way that seems inappropriate.
– ORIGIN Old French *grafe.*

graft[2] Brit. informal •n. hard work. •v. work hard.
– DERIVATIVES **grafter** n.
– ORIGIN perh. from *spade's graft* 'the amount of earth that one stroke of a spade will move'.

graft[3] informal •n. bribery and other corrupt measures adopted to gain power or money in politics or business.

Grail (also **Holy Grail**) •n. (in medieval legend) the cup or platter used by Jesus at the Last Supper, especially as the object of quests by knights.
– ORIGIN Old French *graal.*

grain •n. **1** wheat or other cultivated cereal used as food. **2** a single seed or fruit of a cereal. **3** a small, hard particle of a substance such as sand. **4** the smallest unit of weight in the troy and avoirdupois systems. **5** the smallest possible amount: *there wasn't a grain of truth in the rumours.* **6** the lengthwise arrangement of fibres, particles, or layers in wood, paper, rock, etc.
– PHRASES **against the grain** conflicting with your nature or instinct.
– ORIGIN Latin *granum.*

grainy •adj. (**grainier, grainiest**) **1** (of a photograph) showing visible grains of emulsion; granular. **2** consisting of grains; granular.
– DERIVATIVES **graininess** n.

gram (Brit. also **gramme**) •n. a metric

unit of mass equal to one thousandth of a kilogram.
– ORIGIN French *gramme*.

-gram • comb. form forming nouns referring to something written or recorded: *anagram*.
– ORIGIN Greek *gramma* 'thing written'.

grammar • n. **1** the whole structure of a language, including the rules for the way words are formed and their relationship to each other in a sentence. **2** knowledge and use of the rules of grammar: *bad grammar*. **3** a book on grammar.
– ORIGIN from Greek *grammatikē tekhnē* 'art of letters'.

☑️ **grammar** is spelled with a double **m**; the ending is **-ar**.

grammarian /gruh-mair-i-uhn/ • n. a person who studies and writes about grammar.

grammar school • n. (in the UK, especially formerly) a state secondary school which admits pupils on the basis of their ability.

grammatical /gruh-mat-i-k'l/ • adj. relating to or following the rules of grammar.
– DERIVATIVES **grammaticality** n. **grammatically** adv.

gramme • n. var. of GRAM.

gramophone • n. dated a record player.
– ORIGIN formed by reversing the elements of *phonogram* 'sound recording'.

gramophone record • n. = RECORD (in sense 3).

grampus /gram-puhss/ • n. (pl. **grampuses**) a killer whale or other dolphin-like sea animal.
– ORIGIN Old French *grapois*.

gran • n. Brit. informal a person's grandmother.

granary • n. (pl. **granaries**) a storehouse for grain.
– ORIGIN Latin *granarium*.

granary bread • n. Brit. trademark a type of brown bread containing whole grains of wheat.

grand • adj. **1** magnificent and impressive. **2** large or ambitious in scale: *his grand design for peace*. **3** of the highest importance or rank. **4** dignified, noble, or proud. **5** informal excellent. • n. **1** (pl. **grand**) informal a thousand dollars or pounds. **2** a grand piano.
– DERIVATIVES **grandly** adv.
– ORIGIN Latin *grandis* 'great'.

grandad (also **granddad**) • n. informal a person's grandfather. • adj. (of a shirt) having a collar in the form of a narrow upright band.

grandchild • n. (pl. **grandchildren**) a child of a person's son or daughter.

granddaughter • n. a daughter of a person's son or daughter.

grand duke • n. (in Europe, especially formerly) a prince or nobleman ruling over a small independent state.

grande dame /grond dam/ • n. a woman who is influential within a particular area of activity.
– ORIGIN French, 'grand lady'.

grandee /gran-dee/ • n. **1** a Spanish or Portuguese nobleman of the highest rank. **2** a high-ranking or important man.
– ORIGIN Spanish and Portuguese *grande* 'grand'.

grandeur /gran-dyer/ • n. **1** the quality of being grand and impressive. **2** high rank or social importance.

grandfather • n. **1** the father of a person's father or mother. **2** a founder or originator: *the grandfather of liberalism*.

grandfather clock • n. a clock in a tall wooden case.

grandiloquent /gran-dil-uh-kwuhnt/ • adj. using long or difficult words in order to impress.
– DERIVATIVES **grandiloquence** n. **grandiloquently** adv.
– ORIGIN Latin *grandiloquus* 'grand-speaking'.

grandiose /gran-di-ohss/ • adj. very large or ambitious, especially in a way which is intended to impress.
– DERIVATIVES **grandiosely** adv. **grandiosity** /gran-di-os-it-i/ n.
– ORIGIN Italian *grandioso*.

grand jury • n. US Law a jury selected to examine the validity of an accusation prior to trial.

grandma • n. informal a person's grandmother.

grand mal /gron mal/ • n. a serious form of epilepsy with prolonged loss of consciousness. Compare with PETIT MAL.
– ORIGIN French, 'great sickness'.

grand master (also **grandmaster**) • n. a chess player of the highest class.

grandmother • n. the mother of a person's father or mother.

Grand National • n. an annual steeplechase held at Aintree, Liverpool.

grandpa • n. informal a person's grandfather.

grandparent • n. a grandmother or grandfather.

grand piano • n. a large piano which has the strings arranged horizontally.

Grand Prix /gron pree/ • n. (pl. **Grands**

Prix /gron pree/) a race forming part of a motor-racing or motorcycling world championship.
– ORIGIN French, 'great or chief prize'.

grandsire •n. old use = GRANDFATHER.

grand slam •n. the winning of each of a group of major championships or matches in a particular sport in the same year.

grandson •n. the son of a person's son or daughter.

grandstand •n. the main stand at a racecourse or sports ground.

grand total •n. the final amount after everything is added up.

grand tour •n. a cultural tour of Europe formerly undertaken by upper-class young men.

grange •n. Brit. 1 a country house with farm buildings attached. 2 old use a barn.
– ORIGIN Old French.

granite /gran-it/ •n. a very hard rock made up of quartz, mica, and feldspar.
– DERIVATIVES **granitic** adj.
– ORIGIN Italian *granito* 'grained'.

granny (also **grannie**) •n. (pl. **grannies**) informal a person's grandmother.

granny flat •n. informal, esp. Brit. a part of a house made into self-contained accommodation suitable for an elderly relative.

granny knot •n. a reef knot with the ends crossed the wrong way and therefore liable to slip.

grant •v. 1 agree to give something to someone or allow them to do something. 2 give something formally or legally to. 3 admit to someone that something is true. •n. a sum of money given by a government or public body for a particular purpose.
– PHRASES **take someone/thing for granted** 1 fail to appreciate someone or something as a result of being over-familiar with them. 2 assume that something is true.
– DERIVATIVES **grantor** n.
– ORIGIN Old French *granter* 'consent to support'.

granted •adv. it is true. •conj. (**granted that**) even assuming that.

grant-maintained •adj. Brit. (of a school) funded by central rather than local government.

granular •adj. 1 resembling or consisting of granules. 2 having a roughened surface.

granulated •adj. in the form of granules.
– DERIVATIVES **granulation** n.

granule /gran-yool/ •n. a small hard particle of a substance.

– ORIGIN Latin *granulum* 'little grain'.

grape •n. a green, purple, or black berry growing in clusters on a vine, eaten as fruit and used in making wine.
– ORIGIN Old French, 'bunch of grapes'.

grapefruit •n. (pl. **grapefruit**) a large yellow citrus fruit with a slightly bitter taste.

grapeshot •n. hist. ammunition consisting of a number of small iron balls fired together from a cannon.

grapevine •n. 1 a vine bearing grapes. 2 (**the grapevine**) informal the spreading of information through rumour and informal conversation.

graph •n. a diagram showing the relation between two or more sets of numbers or quantities.
– ORIGIN from *graphic formula*.

-graph •comb. form 1 referring to something written or drawn in a particular way: *autograph*. 2 referring to an instrument that records something: *seismograph*.
– ORIGIN Greek *graphos* 'written'.

graphic •adj. 1 relating to visual art, especially involving drawing, engraving, or the design of printed material. 2 giving vividly explicit detail: *a graphic description*. 3 in the form of a graph. •n. 1 a visual image displayed on a computer screen or stored as data. 2 (**graphics**) the use of drawings, designs, or pictures to illustrate books, magazines, etc.
– DERIVATIVES **graphically** adv.
– ORIGIN Greek *graphikos*.

graphical •adj. 1 relating to or in the form of a graph. 2 relating to visual art or computer graphics.

graphic design •n. the art of combining words and pictures in advertisements, magazines, or books.

graphic equalizer •n. a device for controlling the strength and quality of selected frequency bands.

graphic novel •n. a novel in comic-strip format.

graphite •n. a grey form of carbon used as pencil lead and as a lubricant in machinery.
– ORIGIN Greek *graphein* 'write'.

graphology •n. the study of handwriting to analyse a person's character.
– DERIVATIVES **graphologist** n.
– ORIGIN Greek *graphē* 'writing'.

graph paper •n. paper printed with a network of small squares, used for drawing graphs or other diagrams.

-graphy •comb. form forming nouns

meaning: **1** a descriptive science: *geography.* **2** a technique of producing images: *radiography.* **3** a style of writing or drawing: *calligraphy.* **4** writing about a particular subject: *hagiography.* **5** a list: *bibliography.*
– DERIVATIVES **-graphic** comb. form.
– ORIGIN Greek *-graphia* 'writing'.

grapnel /grap-nuhl/ •n. a device with iron claws, attached to a rope and used for dragging or grasping.
– ORIGIN Old French *grapon.*

grapple •v. (**grapples, grappling, grappled**) **1** struggle or fight physically, without using weapons. **2** (**grapple with**) struggle to deal with or understand.
– ORIGIN Old French *grapil* 'small hook'.

grappling hook •n. a grapnel.

grasp •v. **1** seize and hold firmly. **2** understand fully. •n. **1** a firm grip. **2** a person's capacity to achieve or understand something: *meanings that are beyond my grasp.*
– ORIGIN perh. from **GROPE**.

grasping •adj. greedy.

grass •n. **1** vegetation consisting of short plants with long narrow leaves. **2** ground covered with grass. **3** informal cannabis. **4** Brit. informal a police informer. •v. **1** cover with grass. **2** Brit. informal inform the police of someone's criminal activity.
– DERIVATIVES **grassy** adj.
– ORIGIN Old English.

grasshopper •n. an insect with long hind legs which are used for jumping and for producing a chirping sound.

grass roots •pl. n. the most basic level of an activity or organization.

grass snake •n. a harmless grey-green snake with a yellowish band around the neck.

grass widow •n. a woman whose husband is away often or for a long time.
– ORIGIN first referring to an unmarried woman with a child: perh. from the idea of a couple having lain on the grass rather than a bed.

grate¹ •v. (**grates, grating, grated**) **1** shred food by rubbing it on a grater. **2** make an unpleasant scraping sound. **3** have an irritating effect: *he grated on her nerves.*
– ORIGIN Old French *grater.*

grate² •n. a metal frame preventing coal or wood from falling out of a fireplace.
– ORIGIN Old French.

grateful •adj. feeling or showing that you value or appreciate something that has been done for you.
– DERIVATIVES **gratefully** adv.

– ORIGIN Latin *gratus* 'thankful'.

 The beginning of **grateful** is spelled **grate-** (it is not related to *great*).

grater •n. a device having a surface covered with sharp-edged holes, used for grating food.

gratify •v. (**gratifies, gratifying, gratified**) **1** give someone pleasure or satisfaction: *it gratified him to be seen in her company.* **2** indulge or satisfy a desire.
– DERIVATIVES **gratification** n.
– ORIGIN Latin *gratificari* 'give or do as a favour'.

gratin /gra-tan/ •n. a dish with a browned crust of breadcrumbs or melted cheese.
– ORIGIN French.

grating¹ •adj. **1** sounding harsh and unpleasant. **2** irritating.

grating² •n. a framework of parallel or crossed bars that covers an opening.

gratis /grah-tiss/ •adv. & adj. free of charge.
– ORIGIN Latin.

gratitude •n. the feeling of being grateful.
– ORIGIN Latin *gratitudo.*

gratuitous /gruh-tyoo-i-tuhss/ •adj. having no justifiable reason or purpose: *gratuitous violence.*
– DERIVATIVES **gratuitously** adv.
– ORIGIN Latin *gratuitus* 'given freely'.

gratuity /gruh-tyoo-i-ti/ •n. (pl. **gratuities**) formal a sum of money given to someone who has provided a service; a tip.
– ORIGIN Latin *gratuitas* 'gift'.

grave¹ •n. **1** a hole dug in the ground for a coffin or a dead body. **2** (**the grave**) death.
– PHRASES **turn in his** (or **her**) **grave** (of a dead person) be likely to have been angry or distressed about something had they been alive.
– ORIGIN Old English.

grave² •adj. **1** giving cause for alarm or concern. **2** solemn or serious.
– DERIVATIVES **gravely** adv.
– ORIGIN Old French.

grave accent /grahv/ •n. a mark (`) placed over a vowel to indicate a change in its sound quality.
– ORIGIN French *grave* 'serious'.

gravel •n. a loose mixture of small stones and coarse sand, used for paths and roads.
– ORIGIN Old French.

gravelly •adj. **1** containing or made of gravel. **2** (of a voice) deep and rough-sounding.

gravestone •n. an inscribed headstone marking a grave.

graveyard •n. a burial ground beside a church.

gravid /gra-vid/ •adj. tech. pregnant.
– ORIGIN Latin *gravidus*.

gravitas /gra-vi-tass/ •n. a serious and dignified manner.
– ORIGIN Latin.

gravitate /gra-vi-tayt/ •v. (**gravitates, gravitating, gravitated**) (**gravitate to/towards**) be drawn towards a place, person, or thing.

gravitation •n. **1** movement, or a tendency to move, towards a centre of gravity. **2** Physics gravity.
– DERIVATIVES **gravitational** adj.

gravity •n. **1** the force that attracts a body towards the centre of the earth, or towards any other physical body having mass. **2** great importance or seriousness: *crimes of the utmost gravity*. **3** a solemn or serious manner.
– ORIGIN Latin *gravitas*.

gravy •n. (pl. **gravies**) a sauce made by adding stock, flour, etc. to the fat and juices that come out of meat during cooking.
– ORIGIN perh. from Old French *grané*.

gravy boat •n. a narrow jug used for serving gravy.

gravy train •n. informal a situation in which someone can easily make a lot of money.

gray •adj. US = GREY.

graze¹ •v. (**grazes, grazing, grazed**) (of cattle, sheep, etc.) eat grass in a field.
– ORIGIN Old English.

graze² •v. (**grazes, grazing, grazed**) **1** scrape and break the skin on part of the body. **2** touch something lightly in passing. •n. an injury caused by grazing the skin.
– ORIGIN perh. from GRAZE¹.

grazing •n. grassland suitable for use as pasture.

grease •n. **1** a thick oily substance, especially one used to lubricate machinery. **2** animal fat used or produced in cooking. •v. (**greases, greasing, greased**) smear or lubricate with grease.
– ORIGIN Old French *graisse*.

greasepaint •n. a waxy substance used as make-up by actors.

greaseproof paper •n. Brit. paper that does not allow grease to pass through it, used in cooking.

greasy •adj. (**greasier, greasiest**) **1** covered with or resembling grease. **2** polite or friendly in a way that seems excessive and insincere.
– DERIVATIVES **greasiness** n.

greasy spoon •n. informal a shabby cafe serving cheap fried meals.

great •adj. **1** considerably above average in amount, extent, or strength. **2** considerably above average in ability, quality, or importance. **3** informal excellent. **4** used to emphasize something: *he's a great cricket fan*. **5** (**Greater**) referring to an area that includes the centre of a city and a large urban area round it: *Greater London*. •n. a famous and successful person.
– DERIVATIVES **greatness** n.
– ORIGIN Old English.

great ape •n. a large ape of a family closely related to humans, including the gorilla and chimpanzees.

great-aunt •n. an aunt of a person's father or mother.

great circle •n. a circle on the surface of a sphere which lies in a plane passing through the sphere's centre.

greatcoat •n. a long, heavy overcoat.

Great Dane •n. a very large breed of dog with short hair.

greatly •adv. very much.

great-uncle •n. an uncle of a person's mother or father.

Great War •n. the First World War.

greave •n. hist. a piece of armour for the shin.
– ORIGIN Old French *greve* 'shin, greave'.

grebe /greeb/ •n. a diving waterbird with a long neck.
– ORIGIN French.

Grecian /gree-sh'n/ •adj. relating to ancient Greece.

greed •n. **1** a strong and selfish desire for possessions, wealth, or power. **2** a desire to eat more food than is necessary.

greedy •adj. (**greedier, greediest**) having or showing greed.
– DERIVATIVES **greedily** adv. **greediness** n.
– ORIGIN Old English.

Greek •n. **1** a person from Greece. **2** the ancient or modern language of Greece. •adj. relating to Greece.

Greek cross •n. a cross of which all four arms are of equal length.

Greek Orthodox Church •n. the national church of Greece.

green •adj. **1** of the colour between blue and yellow in the spectrum; coloured like grass. **2** covered with grass or other vegetation. **3** (**Green**) concerned with or supporting protection of the environment. **4** (of a plant or fruit) young or unripe. **5** inexperienced or naive: *a green recruit*. •n. **1** green colour or material. **2** a piece of grassy land for public use. **3** an area of very short grass

surrounding a hole on a golf course.
4 (**greens**) green vegetables. **5** (**Green**) a
member or supporter of a Green
political party.
– DERIVATIVES **greenish** adj. **greenness** n.
– ORIGIN Old English.

green belt • n. an area of open land
around a city, on which building is
restricted.

green card • n. (in the US) a permit
allowing a foreigner to live and work
permanently in the US.

greenery • n. green leaves or plants.

greenfield • adj. (of an area of land)
previously undeveloped or built on.

greenfinch • n. a large finch with green
and yellow plumage.

green fingers • pl. n. Brit. informal natural
ability in growing plants.

greenfly • n. (pl. **greenflies**) a green
aphid.

greengage • n. a sweet greenish fruit
resembling a small plum.
– ORIGIN named after the English
botanist Sir William *Gage*.

greengrocer • n. Brit. a person who sells
fruit and vegetables.

greenhouse • n. a glass building in
which plants are kept to protect them
from cold weather.

greenhouse effect • n. the trapping of
the sun's warmth in the earth's lower
atmosphere, because visible radiation
from the sun passes through the
atmosphere more readily than infrared
radiation coming from the earth's
surface.

greenhouse gas • n. a gas, such as
carbon dioxide, that contributes to the
greenhouse effect by absorbing infrared
radiation.

green light • n. **1** a green traffic light
giving permission to proceed. **2** permission to go ahead with a project.

green pepper • n. an unripe sweet
pepper, green in colour and eaten as a
vegetable.

green room • n. a room in a theatre or
studio in which performers can relax
when they are not performing.

greensward /green-sword/ • n. literary
grass-covered ground.

green tea • n. tea made from unfer-
mented leaves, produced mainly in
China and Japan.

Greenwich Mean Time /gren-ich/
• n. the time measured at the Greenwich
meridian, used as the standard time in a
zone that includes the British Isles.
– ORIGIN from *Greenwich* in London,
former site of the Royal Observatory.

Greenwich meridian • n. the

meridian of zero longitude, passing
through Greenwich.

greenwood • n. old use a wood or forest
in leaf.

greet • v. **1** give a word or sign of
welcome when meeting someone.
2 react to or acknowledge in a particular
way: *everyone greeted the idea warmly.*
3 (of a sight or sound) become apparent
to a person arriving somewhere.
– ORIGIN Old English.

greeting • n. **1** a word or sign of
welcome when meeting someone.
2 (**greetings**) a formal expression of
good wishes.

greetings card (N. Amer. **greeting card**)
• n. a decorative card sent to express
good wishes on a particular occasion.

gregarious /gri-gair-i-uhss/ • adj. **1** fond
of company; sociable. **2** (of animals)
living in flocks or colonies.
– ORIGIN Latin *gregarius*.

Gregorian chant /gri-gor-i-uhn/
• n. medieval church music for voices.
– ORIGIN named after St *Gregory* the
Great.

gremlin • n. an imaginary mischievous
creature regarded as responsible for
unexplained mechanical or electrical
faults.
– ORIGIN perh. from GOBLIN.

grenade /gruh-nayd/ • n. a small bomb
that is thrown by hand or launched
mechanically.
– ORIGIN from Old French *pome grenate*
'pomegranate'.

grenadier /gren-uh-deer/ • n. **1** hist. a
soldier armed with grenades.
2 (**Grenadiers** or **Grenadier Guards**) the
first regiment of the royal household
infantry.

grew past of GROW.

grey (US **gray**) • adj. **1** of a colour between
black and white, as of ashes. **2** (of hair)
turning grey or white with age. **3** (of the
weather) cloudy and dull. **4** lacking
interest or distinctive characteristics:
grey, faceless men. **5** not accounted for in
official statistics: *the grey economy.*
• n. grey colour. • v. (of hair) become grey
with age.
– DERIVATIVES **greyish** adj. **greyness** n.
– ORIGIN Old English.

grey area • n. an area of activity that
does not easily fit into an existing
category and is difficult to deal with.

greyhound • n. a swift, slender breed of
dog used in racing.
– ORIGIN Old English.

greylag • n. a large goose with mainly
grey plumage.
– ORIGIN prob. from dialect *lag* 'goose'.

grey matter •n. informal intelligence.

grey seal •n. a large North Atlantic seal with a spotted greyish coat.

grey squirrel •n. a tree squirrel with mainly grey fur.

grid •n. **1** a framework of bars that are parallel to or cross each other. **2** a network of lines that cross each other to form a series of squares or rectangles. **3** a network of cables or pipes for distributing electricity or gas.
– ORIGIN from GRIDIRON.

griddle •n. a circular iron plate that is heated and used for cooking food.
•v. (**griddles, griddling, griddled**) cook on a griddle.
– ORIGIN Old French *gredil*.

gridiron /grid-I-uhn/ •n. **1** a frame of parallel metal bars used for grilling meat or fish over an open fire. **2** a field for American football, marked with regularly spaced parallel lines.
– ORIGIN from former *gredile* 'griddle'.

gridlock •n. a traffic jam affecting a whole network of linked streets.
– DERIVATIVES **gridlocked** adj.

grief •n. **1** intense sorrow, especially caused by someone's death. **2** informal trouble or annoyance.
– ORIGIN Old French.

grievance •n. a cause for complaint.

grieve •v. (**grieves, grieving, grieved**) **1** feel intense sorrow, especially as a result of someone's death. **2** cause great distress to.
– ORIGIN Old French *grever* 'burden'.

☑ **grieve** and the related word **grief** follow the usual rule of *i* before *e* except after c.

grievous •adj. formal (of something bad) very severe or serious: *his death was a grievous blow.*
– DERIVATIVES **grievously** adv.

grievous bodily harm •n. Law, Brit. serious physical injury inflicted on a person by the deliberate action of another.

griffin (also **gryphon** or **griffon**) •n. a mythical creature with the head and wings of an eagle and the body of a lion.
– ORIGIN Old French *grifoun*.

griffon /grif-fuhn/ •n. a small dog resembling a terrier.
– ORIGIN from GRIFFIN.

grill •n. Brit. **1** a device on a cooker that directs heat downwards for cooking food. **2** a gridiron used for cooking food on an open fire. **3** a dish of food cooked using a grill. **4** a restaurant serving grilled food. **5** var. of GRILLE. •v. **1** cook with a grill. **2** informal question in a

relentless or aggressive way; interrogate.
– ORIGIN Old French *graille* 'grille'.

grille (also **grill**) •n. a grating or screen of metal bars or wires.
– ORIGIN French.

grilse /grilss/ •n. a salmon that has returned to fresh water after a single winter at sea.

grim •adj. (**grimmer, grimmest**) **1** very serious and forbidding. **2** horrifying, depressing, or worrying: *the grim reality of unemployment.*
– DERIVATIVES **grimly** adv. **grimness** n.
– ORIGIN Old English.

grimace /gri-mayss, gri-muhss/ •n. a twisted expression on a person's face, showing disgust, pain, or wry amusement. •v. (**grimaces, grimacing, grimaced**) make a grimace.
– ORIGIN French.

grime •n. dirt ingrained on a surface.
•v. (**grimes, griming, grimed**) blacken or make dirty with grime.
– DERIVATIVES **grimy** adj.
– ORIGIN German and Dutch.

grin •v. (**grins, grinning, grinned**) smile broadly. •n. a broad smile.
– PHRASES **grin and bear it** suffer pain or misfortune without complaining.
– ORIGIN Old English.

grind •v. (**grinds, grinding, ground**) **1** reduce to small particles or powder by crushing. **2** make something sharp or smooth by rubbing it against a hard or abrasive surface or tool. **3** rub together or move gratingly. **4** (**grind someone down**) wear someone down by continuous harsh treatment. **5** (**grind something out**) produce something slowly and with effort. **6** (as adj. **grinding**) (of a difficult situation) seemingly endless: *grinding poverty.*
•n. hard dull work: *the daily grind.*
– DERIVATIVES **grinder** n.
– ORIGIN Old English.

grindstone •n. a revolving disc of abrasive material used for sharpening or polishing metal objects.
– PHRASES **keep your nose to the grindstone** keep working hard.

gringo /gring-goh/ •n. (pl. **gringos**) informal, derogatory (in Latin America) a white English-speaking person.
– ORIGIN Spanish, 'foreign'.

grip •v. (**grips, gripping, gripped**) **1** take and keep a firm hold of: *she was gripped by a feeling of excitement.* **2** deeply affect: **3** hold the attention or interest of.
•n. **1** a firm hold. **2** understanding. **3** a part or attachment by which something is held in the hand. **4** a travelling bag.
– PHRASES **come** (or **get**) **to grips with**

begin to deal with or understand.
– ORIGIN Old English.

gripe • v. (**gripes, griping, griped**)
1 informal complain or grumble. **2** (as adj.
griping) (of pain in the stomach or
intestines) sudden and acute.
• n. **1** informal a minor complaint. **2** pain in
the stomach or intestines.
– ORIGIN Old English, 'grasp, clutch'.

gripping • adj. very interesting or
exciting.

grisly /griz-li/ • adj. (**grislier, grisliest**)
causing horror or disgust.
– ORIGIN Old English.

USAGE: Do not confuse **grisly** with
grizzly. **Grisly** means 'causing horror or
disgust' (*a grisly murder case*), while a
grizzly is a kind of large American bear.

grist • n. corn that is ground to make
flour.
– PHRASES **grist to the mill** useful
experience or knowledge.
– ORIGIN Old English, 'grinding'.

gristle /griss-uhl/ • n. tough inedible
cartilage in meat.
– DERIVATIVES **gristly** adj.
– ORIGIN Old English.

grit • n. **1** small loose particles of stone or
sand. **2** (also **gritstone**) a coarse sandstone. **3** courage and determination.
• v. (**grits, gritting, gritted**) spread
grit on an icy road.
– PHRASES **grit your teeth 1** clench your
teeth. **2** resolve to do something
difficult.
– ORIGIN Old English.

grits • pl. n. US coarsely ground maize
kernels, served boiled with water or
milk.
– ORIGIN Old English, 'bran, mill dust'.

gritty • adj. (**grittier, grittiest**)
1 containing or covered with grit.
2 brave and determined **3** showing
something unpleasant as it really is: *a
gritty prison drama*.
– DERIVATIVES **grittily** adv. **grittiness** n.

grizzle • v. (**grizzles, grizzling, grizzled**)
Brit. informal (of a child) cry or whimper
fretfully.

grizzled • adj. having grey or grey-
streaked hair.
– ORIGIN Old French *gris* 'grey'.

grizzly • n. (also **grizzly bear**) (pl.
grizzlies) a large variety of American
brown bear often having white-tipped
fur.
– ORIGIN from **GRIZZLED**.

USAGE: On the confusion of **grizzly** and
grisly, see the note at **GRISLY**.

groan • v. **1** make a deep sound of pain or
despair. **2** make a low creaking sound

when pressure or weight is applied. • n. a
groaning sound.
– ORIGIN Old English.

groat • n. hist. an English silver coin worth
four old pence.
– ORIGIN Dutch *groot* or German *grōte*
'great, thick'.

grocer • n. a person who sells food and
small household goods.
– ORIGIN Old French *grossier*.

grocery • n. (pl. **groceries**) **1** a grocer's
shop or business. **2** (**groceries**) items of
food sold in a grocer's shop or supermarket.

grog • n. **1** spirits (originally rum) mixed
with water. **2** informal or Austral./NZ alcoholic
drink.
– ORIGIN said to be from the nickname of
Admiral Vernon, who ordered diluted
rum to be served out to sailors.

groggy • adj. feeling dazed, weak, or
unsteady.
– DERIVATIVES **groggily** adv.

groin[1] • n. **1** the area between the
abdomen and the thigh. **2** informal the
region of the genitals. **3** Archit. a curved
edge formed by two intersecting roof
arches.
– ORIGIN perh. from Old English,
'depression, abyss'.

groin[2] • n. US = **GROYNE**.

grommet /grom-mit/ • n. **1** a protective
eyelet in a hole that a rope or cable
passes through. **2** Brit. a tube implanted
in the eardrum to drain fluid from the
middle ear.
– ORIGIN from former French *gourmer* 'to
curb'.

groom • v. **1** brush and clean the coat of a
horse or dog. **2** (often as adj. **groomed**)
keep yourself neat and tidy in
appearance. **3** prepare or train for a
particular purpose or activity: *pupils who
are groomed for higher things.* • n. **1** a
person employed to take care of horses.
2 a bridegroom.

groove • n. **1** a long, narrow cut in a hard
material. **2** a spiral track cut in a
gramophone record. **3** an established
routine or habit. • v. (**grooves, grooving,
grooved**) **1** make a groove or grooves in.
2 informal dance to or play pop or jazz
music.
– ORIGIN Dutch *groeve* 'furrow, pit'.

groovy • adj. (**groovier, grooviest**)
informal, dated fashionable and exciting.

grope • v. (**gropes, groping, groped**)
1 feel about uncertainly with your
hands. **2** informal fondle someone for
sexual pleasure. • n. informal an act of
groping someone.
– ORIGIN Old English.

grosgrain /groh-grayn/ • n. a heavy

ribbed fabric of silk or rayon.
– ORIGIN French, 'coarse grain'.

gross •adj. **1** unattractively large. **2** very obvious and unacceptable: *gross misconduct*. **3** informal very unpleasant. **4** rude or vulgar. **5** (of income, profit, or interest) before tax has been deducted. **6** (of weight) including contents or other variable items. •adv. without tax having been deducted. •v. produce or earn an amount of money as gross profit or income. •n. **1** (pl. **gross**) an amount equal to twelve dozen; 144. **2** (pl. **grosses**) a gross profit or income.
– DERIVATIVES **grossly** adv. **grossness** n.
– ORIGIN Old French *gros*.

gross domestic product •n. the total value of goods produced and services provided within a country during one year.

gross national product •n. the total value of goods produced and services provided by a country during one year, equal to the gross domestic product plus the net income from foreign investments.

grotesque /groh-tesk/ •adj. **1** comically or repulsively ugly or distorted. **2** shocking. •n. a grotesque figure or image.
– DERIVATIVES **grotesquely** adv.
– ORIGIN Italian *grottesca*.

grotesquerie /groh-tesk-uh-ri/ •n. (pl. **grotesqueries**) the quality of being grotesque, or things that are grotesque.

grotto •n. (pl. **grottoes** or **grottos**) a small cave, especially an artificial one in a park or garden.
– ORIGIN Italian *grotta*.

grotty •adj. (**grottier**, **grottiest**) Brit. informal **1** unpleasant and of poor quality. **2** unwell.
– ORIGIN from **GROTESQUE**.

grouch /growch/ •n. informal **1** a person who is often grumpy. **2** a complaint or grumble.
– ORIGIN Old French *grouchier* 'to grumble, murmur'.

grouchy •adj. irritable and bad-tempered; grumpy.

ground[1] •n. **1** the solid surface of the earth. **2** land or soil of a particular kind: *marshy ground*. **3** an area of land or sea with a particular use: *fishing grounds*. **4** (**grounds**) an area of enclosed land surrounding a large house. **5** (**grounds**) reasons for doing or thinking something: *there are some grounds for optimism*. **6** (**grounds**) small pieces of solid matter in a liquid, especially coffee, which settle at the bottom.
•v. **1** ban or prevent a pilot or aircraft from flying. **2** run a ship aground. **3** (**be**

grounded in/on) have as a basis. **4** informal (of a parent) refuse to allow a child to go out socially, as a punishment.
– PHRASES **be thick** (or **thin**) **on the ground** exist in large (or small) numbers or amounts. **break new ground** achieve or create something new. **get off the ground** start happening or functioning successfully. **give** (or **lose**) **ground** retreat or lose your advantage. **hold** (or **stand**) **your ground** not retreat or lose your advantage.
– ORIGIN Old English.

ground[2] past and past part. of **GRIND**.

groundbreaking •adj. involving completely new methods or discoveries.

ground control •n. the personnel and equipment that monitor and direct the flight and landing of aircraft or spacecraft.

ground floor •n. the floor of a building at ground level.

ground frost •n. Brit. frost formed on the surface of the ground or in the top layer of soil.

groundhog •n. N. Amer. = **WOODCHUCK**.

grounding •n. basic training or instruction in a subject.

groundless •adj. not based on any good reason.

groundnut •n. = **PEANUT**.

ground rent •n. Brit. rent paid by the owner of a building to the owner of the land on which it is built.

ground rules •pl. n. basic rules controlling the way in which something is done.

groundsel /grownd-s'l/ •n. a plant of the daisy family with small yellow flowers.
– ORIGIN Old English.

groundsheet •n. a waterproof sheet spread on the ground inside a tent.

groundsman (N. Amer. **groundskeeper**) •n. (pl. **groundsmen**) Brit. a person who maintains a sports ground or the grounds of a large building.

ground squirrel •n. a burrowing squirrel of a large group including the chipmunks.

groundswell /grownd-swel/ •n. a build-up of opinion in a large section of the population.

groundwater •n. water held underground in the soil or in rock.

groundwork •n. preliminary or basic work.

group •n. **1** a number of people or things gathered or classed together. **2** a number of musicians who play popular music together. **3** Chem. a set of elements occupying a column in the periodic

table. • v. place in or form a group or groups.
– ORIGIN Italian *gruppo*.

groupie • n. informal a young woman who follows a pop group or celebrity around.

grouping • n. a group of people with a shared interest or aim, especially within a larger organization.

group therapy • n. a form of psychiatric therapy in which patients meet to discuss their problems.

grouse[1] • n. (pl. **grouse**) a game bird with a plump body and feathered legs.
– ORIGIN perh. from Latin *gruta* or Old French *grue* 'crane'.

grouse[2] • v. (**grouses**, **grousing**, **groused**) complain or grumble. • n. a grumble or complaint.

grout /growt/ • n. (also **grouting**) a mortar or paste for filling crevices, especially the gaps between tiles. • v. fill in crevices with grout.
– ORIGIN perh. from French dialect *grouter* 'grout a wall'.

grove • n. a small orchard or group of trees.
– ORIGIN Old English.

grovel • v. (**grovels**, **grovelling**, **grovelled**; US **grovels**, **groveling**, **groveled**) 1 crouch or crawl on the ground. 2 act very humbly to make someone forgive you or treat you favourably.
– ORIGIN Old Norse, 'face downwards'.

grow • v. (**grows**, **growing**, **grew**; past part. **grown**) 1 (of a living thing) develop by increasing in size and changing physically. 2 (**grow up**) become an adult. 3 (of a plant) germinate and develop. 4 become larger or greater over time. 5 become gradually or increasingly: *we grew braver*. 6 (**grow on**) become gradually more appealing to.
– DERIVATIVES **grower** n.
– ORIGIN Old English.

growing pains • pl. n. 1 pains which can occur in the limbs of young children. 2 difficulties experienced in the early stages of an enterprise.

growl • v. 1 (especially of a dog) make a low sound of hostility in the throat. 2 say something in a low, angry voice. 3 make a rumbling sound. • n. a growling sound.

grown past part. of GROW.

grown-up • adj. adult. • n. informal an adult.

growth • n. 1 the process of growing. 2 something that has grown or is growing. 3 a tumour or other formation which is not normal.

growth industry • n. an industry that

is developing particularly quickly.

groyne (US **groin**) • n. a low wall built out into the sea from a beach to prevent the beach from shifting or being eroded.
– ORIGIN Latin *gronium* 'pig's snout'.

grub • n. 1 the larva of an insect. 2 informal food. • v. (**grubs**, **grubbing**, **grubbed**) 1 dig shallowly in soil. 2 (**grub something up**) dig something up. 3 search clumsily and unmethodically: *I began grubbing about in the waste-paper basket.*
– ORIGIN perh. from Dutch *grobbelen*.

grubby • adj. (**grubbier**, **grubbiest**) 1 dirty. 2 not respectable; sordid.
– DERIVATIVES **grubbiness** n.

grudge • n. a long-lasting feeling of resentment or dislike. • v. (**grudges**, **grudging**, **grudged**) 1 be unwilling to give or allow something. 2 feel resentful that someone has achieved something.
– ORIGIN from GROUCH.

grudging • adj. given or allowed only reluctantly or resentfully: *a grudging apology.*

gruel • n. a thin liquid food of oatmeal boiled in milk or water.
– ORIGIN Old French.

gruelling (US **grueling**) • adj. very tiring and demanding.
– ORIGIN from former *gruel* 'exhaust'.

gruesome • adj. causing disgust or horror.
– ORIGIN Scottish *grue* 'feel horror'.

gruff • adj. 1 (of a voice) rough and low in pitch. 2 abrupt or unfriendly in manner.
– DERIVATIVES **gruffly** adv.
– ORIGIN Flemish and Dutch *grof* 'rude'.

grumble • v. (**grumbles**, **grumbling**, **grumbled**) 1 complain in a bad-tempered way. 2 make a low rumbling sound. • n. a complaint.
– ORIGIN prob. from Germanic.

grump • n. informal a grumpy person.

grumpy • adj. (**grumpier**, **grumpiest**) bad-tempered and sulky.
– DERIVATIVES **grumpily** adv.

grunge • n. 1 a style of rock music with a loud, harsh guitar sound. 2 a casual, deliberately untidy style of fashion.
– DERIVATIVES **grungy** adj.
– ORIGIN perh. from GRUBBY and DINGY.

grunt • v. 1 (of an animal) make a low, short sound. 2 make a low sound as a result of physical effort or to show agreement. • n. a grunting sound.
– ORIGIN Old English.

Gruyère /groo-yair/ • n. a Swiss cheese with a firm texture.
– ORIGIN named after *Gruyère*, a district in Switzerland.

gryphon • n. var. of GRIFFIN.

g

G-string • n. a skimpy undergarment covering the genitals, consisting of a narrow strip of cloth attached to a waistband.

GT • n. a high-performance car.
– ORIGIN short for Italian *gran turismo* 'great touring'.

guacamole /gwa-kuh-**moh**-lay/ • n. a dish of mashed avocado mixed with chilli peppers and other ingredients.
– ORIGIN from a Central American Indian language.

guano /**gwah**-noh/ • n. the excrement of seabirds, used as a fertilizer.
– ORIGIN from a language of Peru.

guarantee • n. 1 an assurance that certain things will be done. 2 an assurance that a product will remain in working order for a particular length of time. 3 something that makes a particular outcome certain. 4 money or a valuable item given or promised as an assurance that something will be done.
• v. (**guarantees, guaranteeing, guaranteed**) 1 provide a guarantee for something. 2 promise with certainty. 3 provide financial security for.
– ORIGIN perh. from Spanish *garante*.

guarantor /ga-ruhn-**tor**/ • n. a person or organization that gives or acts as a guarantee.

guard • v. 1 watch over in order to protect or control. 2 (**guard against**) take precautions against. • n. 1 a person who guards or keeps watch. 2 a group of soldiers guarding a place or person. 3 (**Guards**) the troops of the British army whose original duty was to protect the king or queen. 4 a defensive position taken up in a fight. 5 a state of looking out for possible danger or difficulties: *she was on guard*. 6 a device worn or fitted on something to prevent injury or damage: *a blade guard*. 7 Brit. an official who rides on and is in general charge of a train.
– ORIGIN Old French *garder*.

> ✓ Spell **guard** and the related word **guardian** with **gua-** at the beginning.

guarded • adj. cautious and having possible reservations: *a guarded welcome*.

guardhouse (also **guardroom**) • n. a building for soldiers guarding the entrance to a military camp or for the detention of military prisoners.

guardian • n. 1 a person who defends or protects something. 2 a person legally responsible for someone who cannot manage their own affairs.
– DERIVATIVES **guardianship** n.
– ORIGIN Old French *garden*.

guardian angel • n. a spirit believed to watch over and protect a person.

guardsman • n. (pl. **guardsmen**) 1 (in the UK) a soldier of a regiment of Guards. 2 (in the US) a member of the National Guard.

Guatemalan /gwah-tuh-**mah**-luhn/ • n. a person from Guatemala in Central America. • adj. relating to Guatemala.

guava /**gwah**-vuh/ • n. a tropical fruit with pink juicy flesh.
– ORIGIN prob. from a Caribbean language.

gubbins • pl. n. Brit. informal 1 an assortment of various items. 2 a gadget.
– ORIGIN Old French.

gubernatorial /goo-ber-nuh-**tor**-i-uhl/ • adj. relating to a governor of a US state.
– ORIGIN Latin *gubernator* 'governor'.

gudgeon¹ /**guj**-uhn/ • n. a small freshwater fish often used as bait by anglers.
– ORIGIN Old French *goujon*.

gudgeon² /**guj**-uhn/ • n. 1 a pivot or spindle on which something swings or rotates. 2 the tubular part of a hinge into which the pin fits.
– ORIGIN Old French *goujon*.

guelder rose /**gel**-der/ • n. a shrub with creamy-white flowers followed by semi-transparent red berries.
– ORIGIN from Dutch *geldersche roos* 'rose of *Gelderland*' (a province of the Netherlands).

Guernsey /**gern**-zi/ • n. (pl. **Guernseys**) an animal of a breed of dairy cattle from Guernsey in the Channel Islands.

guerrilla /guh-**ril**-luh/ (also **guerilla**) • n. a member of a small independent group fighting against the government or regular forces.
– ORIGIN Spanish, 'little war'.

guess • v. 1 estimate or suppose something without enough information to be sure of being correct. 2 correctly estimate. • n. an attempt to guess something.
– ORIGIN perh. from Dutch *gissen*.

guesstimate /**gess**-ti-muht/ • n. informal an estimate based on a mixture of guesswork and calculation.

guesswork • n. the process or results of guessing.

guest • n. 1 a person invited to visit someone's home or to a social occasion. 2 a person invited to take part in a broadcast or entertainment. 3 a person staying at a hotel or guest house.
• v. appear as a guest in a broadcast or entertainment.
– ORIGIN Old Norse.

guest house • n. a private house offering accommodation to paying guests.

guest worker • n. a person with temporary permission to work in another country.

guff • n. informal ridiculous talk or ideas; nonsense.

guffaw /guhf-faw/ • n. a loud, deep laugh. • v. give a loud, deep laugh.

guidance • n. advice or information aimed at solving a problem.

guide • n. 1 a person who advises or shows the way to other people. 2 something which helps a person make a decision or form an opinion. 3 a book providing information on a subject. 4 a structure or marking which directs the movement or positioning of something. 5 (**Guide**) a member of the Guides Association, a girls' organization corresponding to the Scouts. • v. (**guides**, **guiding**, **guided**) 1 show someone the way. 2 direct the positioning or movement of. 3 (as adj. **guided**) directed by remote control or internal equipment: *a guided missile.*
– ORIGIN Old French.

guidebook • n. a book containing information about a place for visitors or tourists.

guide dog • n. a dog that has been trained to lead a blind person.

guideline • n. a general rule, principle, or piece of advice.

guild • n. 1 a medieval association of craftsmen or merchants. 2 an association of people who do the same work or have the same interests or aims.
– ORIGIN Old English.

guilder /gil-der/ • n. (pl. **guilder** or **guilders**) (until the introduction of the euro in 2002) the basic unit of money of the Netherlands.
– ORIGIN Dutch.

guildhall • n. 1 the meeting place of a guild or corporation. 2 Brit. a town hall.

guile /gyl/ • n. clever but dishonest or devious behaviour.
– DERIVATIVES **guileful** adj.
– ORIGIN Old French.

guileless • adj. very honest and sincere.

guillemot /gil-li-mot/ • n. an auk (seabird) with a narrow pointed bill.
– ORIGIN French.

guillotine /gil-luh-teen/ • n. 1 a machine with a heavy blade that slides down a frame, used for beheading people. 2 a device with a descending or sliding blade, used for cutting paper or sheet metal. • v. (**guillotines**, **guillotining**, **guillotined**) execute with a guillotine.

– ORIGIN named after the French physician Joseph-Ignace *Guillotin*, who recommended its use for executions.

guilt • n. 1 the fact of having committed an offence or crime. 2 a feeling of having done something wrong.
– ORIGIN Old English.

guiltless • adj. having no guilt; innocent.

guilty • adj. (**guiltier**, **guiltiest**) 1 (often **guilty of**) responsible for a particular wrongdoing, fault, or mistake. 2 having or showing a feeling of guilt.
– DERIVATIVES **guiltily** adv.

guinea /gi-ni/ • n. Brit. 1 a former British gold coin with a value of 21 shillings (now £1.05). 2 the sum of £1.05, used mainly for professional fees and auction prices.
– ORIGIN named after *Guinea* in West Africa (the source of the gold for the first guineas).

guineafowl • n. (pl. **guineafowl**) a large African game bird with grey, white-spotted plumage.

Guinean /gin-i-uhn/ • n. a person from Guinea, a country on the west coast of Africa. • adj. relating to Guinea.

guinea pig • n. 1 a domesticated South American rodent. 2 a person or thing used as a subject for experiment.

guise /gyz/ • n. an outward form, appearance, or way of presenting someone or something: *he visited in the guise of an inspector.*
– ORIGIN Old French.

guitar • n. a stringed musical instrument with six strings, played by plucking or strumming.
– DERIVATIVES **guitarist** n.
– ORIGIN Spanish *guitarra*.

Gujarati /goo-juh-rah-ti/ (also **Gujerati**) • n. (pl. **Gujaratis**) 1 a person from the Indian state of Gujarat. 2 the language of the Gujaratis. • adj. relating to the Gujaratis or their language.

Gulag /goo-lag/ • n. (**the Gulag**) a system of harsh labour camps in the former Soviet Union.
– ORIGIN Russian.

gulch /gulch/ • n. N. Amer. a narrow, steep-sided ravine.
– ORIGIN perh. from dialect *gulch* 'to swallow'.

gulf • n. 1 a deep inlet of the sea almost surrounded by land, with a narrow mouth. 2 a deep ravine. 3 a large difference between two people, opinions, or situations: *the gulf between rich and poor.*
– ORIGIN Italian *golfo*.

gull[1] • n. a long-winged seabird having

white plumage with a grey or black back.
– ORIGIN Celtic.

gull² • v. fool or deceive someone.

gullet • n. the passage by which food passes from the mouth to the stomach.
– ORIGIN Old French *goulet* 'little throat'.

gullible • adj. easily persuaded to believe something.
– DERIVATIVES **gullibility** n.
– ORIGIN from **GULL²**.

> ✓ **gullible** has a double **l** in the middle; the ending is **-ible**.

gully (also **gulley**) • n. (pl. **gullies** or **gulleys**) a ravine or deep channel caused by the action of running water.
– ORIGIN French *goulet*.

gulp • v. 1 swallow drink or food quickly or in large mouthfuls. 2 swallow with difficulty as a result of strong emotion: *she gulped back the tears*. • n. 1 an act of gulping. 2 a large mouthful of liquid hastily drunk.
– ORIGIN prob. from Dutch *gulpen*.

gum¹ • n. 1 a sticky substance produced by some trees and shrubs. 2 glue used for sticking paper or other light materials together. 3 chewing gum or bubble gum. • v. (**gums, gumming, gummed**) 1 cover or fasten with gum or glue. 2 (**gum something up**) clog up a mechanism.
– ORIGIN Old French *gomme*.

gum² • n. the firm area of flesh around the roots of the teeth.
– ORIGIN Old English.

gum arabic • n. a gum produced by some kinds of acacia tree, used as glue and in incense.

gumboil • n. a small swelling formed on the gum at the root of a tooth.

gumboot • n. Brit. dated a wellington boot.

gumdrop • n. a firm, jelly-like sweet.

gummy¹ • adj. sticky.

gummy² • adj. toothless: *a gummy grin*.

gumption /gump-sh'n/ • n. informal initiative and resourcefulness.

gumshield • n. a pad or plate used by a sports player to protect the teeth and gums.

gun • n. 1 a weapon with a metal tube from which bullets or shells are propelled by means of a small explosion. 2 a device using pressure to send out a substance or object: *a glue gun*. • v. (**guns, gunning, gunned**) 1 (**gun someone down**) shoot someone with a gun. 2 (**be gunning for**) be actively looking for an opportunity to blame or attack someone.
– PHRASES **jump the gun** informal act before

the proper or right time. **stick to your guns** informal refuse to compromise or change.
– ORIGIN perh. from the Scandinavian name *Gunnhildr*, meaning 'war'.

gunboat • n. a small ship armed with guns.

gunboat diplomacy • n. foreign policy supported by the use or threat of military force.

gun carriage • n. a framework with wheels used to support a piece of artillery.

gun dog • n. a dog trained to collect game that has been shot.

gunfight • n. a fight involving an exchange of gunfire.
– DERIVATIVES **gunfighter** n.

gunfire • n. the repeated firing of a gun or guns.

gunge • n. Brit. informal an unpleasantly sticky or messy substance.
– ORIGIN perh. from **GOO** and **GUNK**.

gung-ho /gung-hoh/ • adj. too eager to take part in fighting or warfare.
– ORIGIN Chinese, 'work together'.

gunk • n. informal an unpleasantly sticky or messy substance.
– ORIGIN the trademark of a US detergent.

gunman • n. (pl. **gunmen**) a man who uses a gun to commit a crime.

gunmetal • n. 1 a grey corrosion-resistant form of bronze containing zinc. 2 a dull bluish-grey colour.

gunnel • n. var. of **GUNWALE**.

gunner • n. 1 a person who operates a gun. 2 a British artillery soldier.

gunnery • n. the design, manufacture, and firing of heavy guns.

gunpoint • n. (in phr. **at gunpoint**) while threatening or being threatened with a gun.

gunpowder • n. an explosive consisting of a powdered mixture of saltpetre, sulphur, and charcoal.

gunrunner • n. a person involved in the illegal sale or importing of firearms.
– DERIVATIVES **gunrunning** n.

gunship • n. a heavily armed helicopter.

gunshot • n. a shot fired from a gun.

gunsight • n. a device on a gun enabling it to be aimed accurately.

gunslinger • n. informal a man who carries a gun.

gunsmith • n. a person who makes and sells small firearms.

gunwale /gun-n'l/ (also **gunnel**) • n. the upper edge or planking of the side of a boat.
– ORIGIN from **GUN** + *wale* 'strip of wood

on a boat's side' (formerly used to support guns).

guppy /gup-pi/ •n. (pl. **guppies**) a small freshwater fish native to tropical America.
– ORIGIN named after the Trinidadian clergyman R. J. Lechmere *Guppy*.

gurdwara /goor-dwah-ruh/ •n. a Sikh place of worship.
– ORIGIN from Sanskrit words meaning 'teacher' and 'door'.

gurgle •v. (**gurgles, gurgling, gurgled**) make a hollow bubbling sound. •n. a gurgling sound.
– ORIGIN perh. from Latin *gurgulio* 'gullet'.

Gurkha /ger-kuh/ •n. 1 a member of a people of Nepal noted for their ability as soldiers. 2 a member of a Nepalese regiment in the British army.
– ORIGIN a Nepalese place name.

gurn /gern/ (also **girn**) •v. Brit. pull a grotesque face.
– ORIGIN from GRIN.

gurnard /ger-nerd/ •n. a small sea fish with three finger-like bony parts to its fins.
– ORIGIN Old French *gornart* 'grunter'.

guru /guu-roo/ •n. 1 a Hindu spiritual teacher. 2 each of the ten first leaders of the Sikh religion. 3 an influential teacher or expert on a particular subject: *a management guru.*
– ORIGIN Sanskrit, 'weighty, grave'.

gush •v. 1 flow in a strong, fast stream. 2 express approval in a very enthusiastic way. •n. a strong, fast stream.

gushing (also **gushy**) •adj. expressing approval in a very enthusiastic way.

gusset /guss-it/ •n. a piece of material sewn into a garment to strengthen or enlarge a part of it.
– ORIGIN Old French *gousset.*

gust •n. 1 a brief, strong rush of wind. 2 a sudden burst of rain, sound, etc. •v. blow in gusts.
– DERIVATIVES **gusty** adj.
– ORIGIN Old Norse.

gusto •n. enthusiasm and energy.
– ORIGIN Italian.

gut •n. 1 the stomach or intestine. 2 (**guts**) the internal parts or essence of something. 3 (**guts**) informal courage and determination. •v. (**guts, gutting, gutted**) 1 take out the internal organs of a fish or other animal before cooking. 2 remove or destroy the internal parts of: *the fire gutted most of the factory.* •adj. informal instinctive: *a gut feeling.*
– ORIGIN Old English.

gutless •adj. informal lacking courage or determination.

gutsy •adj. (**gutsier, gutsiest**) informal brave and determined.

gutted •adj. Brit. informal bitterly disappointed or upset.

gutter •n. 1 a shallow trough beneath the edge of a roof, or a channel at the side of a street, for carrying off rainwater. 2 (**the gutter**) a very poor or squalid environment. •v. (**gutters, guttering, guttered**) (of a flame) flicker and burn unsteadily.
– ORIGIN Old French *gotiere.*

guttering •n. esp. Brit. the gutters of a building.

gutter press •n. newspapers that focus on scandalous or sensational stories rather than serious news.

guttersnipe •n. a scruffy, badly behaved child.

guttural /gut-tuh-ruhl/ •adj. 1 (of a speech sound) produced in the throat; harsh-sounding. 2 (of a way of speaking) characterized by guttural sounds.
– ORIGIN Latin *gutturalis.*

guv (also **guv'nor**) •n. Brit. informal (as a form of address) sir.

guy[1] •n. 1 informal a man. 2 (**guys**) informal, esp. N. Amer. people of either sex. 3 Brit. a figure representing Guy Fawkes, burnt on a bonfire on 5 November. •v. make fun of.

guy[2] •n. a rope or line fixed to the ground to secure a tent.
– ORIGIN prob. from German.

Guyanese /gy-uh-neez/ •n. (pl. **Guyanese**) a person from Guyana, a country on the NE coast of South America. •adj. relating to Guyana.

guzzle •v. (**guzzles, guzzling, guzzled**) eat or drink greedily.
– ORIGIN perh. from Old French *gosillier* 'chatter, vomit'.

gybe /jyb/ (US **jibe**) Sailing •v. (**gybes, gybing, gybed**) change course by swinging the sail across a following wind. •n. an act of gybing.
– ORIGIN from former Dutch *gijben.*

gym •n. 1 a gymnasium. 2 a private club with facilities for improving physical fitness. 3 gymnastics.

gymkhana /jim-kah-nuh/ •n. an event consisting of a series of competitions on horseback.
– ORIGIN Urdu, 'racket court'.

gymnasium /jim-nay-zi-uhm/ •n. (pl. **gymnasiums** or **gymnasia** /jim-nay-zi-uh/) a hall or building equipped for gymnastics and other physical exercise.
– ORIGIN Latin.

gymnast •n. a person trained in gymnastics.

g

gymnastics •n. exercises involving physical agility, flexibility, and coordination.
– DERIVATIVES **gymnastic** adj.

gymnosperm /jim-noh-sperm/ •n. a plant of a large group that have seeds unprotected by an ovary or fruit, including conifers.
– ORIGIN Greek *gumnos* 'naked'.

gymslip •n. Brit. a belted pinafore dress reaching from the shoulder to the knee, formerly worn by schoolgirls.

gynaecology /gy-ni-kol-uh-ji/ (US **gynecology**) •n. the branch of medicine concerned with conditions and diseases specific to women and girls.
– DERIVATIVES **gynaecological** adj. **gynaecologist** n.
– ORIGIN Greek *gunē* 'woman, female'.

gyp /jip/ (also **gip**) •n. Brit. informal pain or discomfort.

gypsophila /jip-sof-fi-luh/ •n. a garden plant with small pink or white flowers.
– ORIGIN Latin.

gypsum /jip-suhm/ •n. a soft white or grey mineral used to make plaster of Paris and in the building industry.

– ORIGIN Latin.

Gypsy (also **Gipsy**) •n. (pl. **Gypsies** or **Gipsies**) a member of a travelling people speaking the Romany language.
– ORIGIN from **EGYPTIAN** (because Gypsies were believed to have come from Egypt).

gyrate /jy-rayt/ •v. (**gyrates, gyrating, gyrated**) move in a circle or spiral.
– DERIVATIVES **gyration** n.
– ORIGIN Latin *gyrare* 'revolve'.

gyrfalcon /jer-fawl-kuhn/ •n. a large arctic falcon, with mainly grey or white plumage.
– ORIGIN prob. from German *gēr* 'spear'.

gyro /jy-roh/ •n. (pl. **gyros**) a gyroscope or gyrocompass.

gyrocompass •n. a compass in which the direction of true north is maintained by a gyroscope rather than magnetism.
– ORIGIN Greek *guros* 'a ring'.

gyroscope •n. a device, used to provide stability or maintain a fixed direction, consisting of a wheel or disc spinning rapidly about an axis which is itself free to alter in direction.

Hh

H¹ (also **h**) •n. (pl. **Hs** or **H's**) the eighth letter of the alphabet.

H² •abbrev. **1** (of a pencil lead) hard. **2** height. **3** Physics henry(s). •symb. the chemical element hydrogen.

h •abbrev. hour(s).

ha •abbrev. hectare(s).

habeas corpus /hay-bi-uhss kor-puhss/ •n. Law a written order that an arrested person be brought before a judge or into court, to decide whether their detention is lawful.
– ORIGIN Latin, 'you shall have the body (in court)'.

haberdasher /hab-er-dash-er/ •n. **1** Brit. a person who sells dressmaking and sewing goods. **2** N. Amer. a person who sells men's clothing.
– DERIVATIVES **haberdashery** n.
– ORIGIN prob. from Old French *hapertas*.

habiliment /huh-bil-i-muhnt/ •n. old use clothing.
– ORIGIN Old French *habillement*.

habit •n. **1** something that a person does often. **2** informal an addiction to a drug. **3** a long, loose garment worn by a monk or nun.
– ORIGIN Latin *habitus* 'condition'.

habitable •adj. of a good enough condition to live in.
– ORIGIN Latin *habitabilis*.

habitat •n. the natural home or environment of an animal or plant.
– ORIGIN Latin, 'it inhabits'.

habitation •n. **1** the fact of living somewhere. **2** formal a house or home.

habit-forming •adj. (of a drug) addictive.

habitual /huh-bit-yuu-uhl/ •adj. **1** done often or as a habit. **2** regular; usual: *his habitual dress.*
– DERIVATIVES **habitually** adv.

habituate •v. (**habituates, habituating, habituated**) make or become used to something.
– DERIVATIVES **habituation** n.

habitué /huh-bit-yuu-ay/ •n. a person who goes regularly to a particular place.
– ORIGIN French, 'accustomed'.

hachures /ha-shyoorz/ •pl. n. parallel lines used on maps to shade in hills.
– ORIGIN French.

hacienda /ha-si-en-duh/ •n. (in Spanish-speaking countries) a large estate with a house.
– ORIGIN Spanish.

hack¹ •v. **1** cut with rough or heavy blows. **2** kick wildly or roughly. **3** use a computer to gain unauthorized access to another computer system. •n. a rough cut or blow.
– DERIVATIVES **hacker** n.
– ORIGIN Old English.

hack² •n. **1** a writer, especially a journalist, who produces mediocre or unoriginal work. **2** a horse for ordinary riding, or one that can be hired. •v. ride a horse.
– ORIGIN short for **HACKNEY**.

hacking cough •n. a dry, frequent cough.

hackles •pl. n. hairs along an animal's back which rise when it is angry or alarmed.
– PHRASES **make someone's hackles rise** make someone angry.
– ORIGIN Germanic.

hackney •n. (pl. **hackneys**) hist. a horse-drawn vehicle which could be hired.
– ORIGIN prob. from *Hackney* in East London, where horses were formerly kept.

hackney carriage •n. Brit. the official term for a taxi.

hackneyed •adj. (of a phrase or idea) unoriginal and used too often.
– ORIGIN from former *hackney* 'use a horse for general purposes'.

hacksaw •n. a saw with a narrow blade set in a frame.

had past and past part. of **HAVE**.

haddock •n. (pl. **haddock**) a silvery-grey edible fish of North Atlantic coastal waters.
– ORIGIN Old French *hadoc*.

Hades /hay-deez/ •n. **1** Gk Myth. the underworld. **2** informal hell.

– ORIGIN Greek *Haidēs*, a name of Pluto, the god of the dead.

hadn't • contr. had not.

haematite /hee-muh-tyt/ (US **hematite**)
• n. a reddish-black mineral consisting of iron oxide.
– ORIGIN from Greek *haimatitēs lithos* 'blood-like stone'.

haematology /hee-muh-tol-uh-ji/ (US **hematology**) • n. the branch of medicine concerned with the blood.
– DERIVATIVES **haematologist** n.
– ORIGIN Greek *haima* 'blood'.

haemoglobin /hee-muh-gloh-bin/ (US **hemoglobin**) • n. a red protein which transports oxygen in the blood.
– ORIGIN from Greek *haima* 'blood' + GLOBULE.

haemophilia /hee-muh-fi-li-uh/ (US **hemophilia**) • n. a medical condition in which the ability of the blood to clot is greatly reduced, causing serious bleeding from even a slight injury.
– ORIGIN from Greek *haima* 'blood' + -PHILIA.

haemophiliac (US **hemophiliac**) • n. a person with haemophilia.

haemorrhage /hem-uh-rij/ (US **hemorrhage**) • n. 1 a severe loss of blood from a burst blood vessel. 2 a damaging loss of valuable people or resources.
• v. (**haemorrhages, haemorrhaging, haemorrhaged**; US **hemorrhages, hemorrhaging, hemorrhaged**) 1 bleed heavily from a burst blood vessel. 2 use or spend something valuable in large amounts: *the business was haemorrhaging cash*.
– ORIGIN Greek *haimorrhagia*.

haemorrhoid /hem-uh-royd/ (US **hemorrhoid**) • n. a swollen vein in the region of the anus.
– ORIGIN from Greek *haimorrhoides phlebes* 'bleeding veins'.

hafnium /haf-ni-uhm/ • n. a hard silver-grey metal resembling zirconium.
– ORIGIN from *Hafnia*, the Latin form of *Havn*, a former name of Copenhagen.

haft /hahft/ • n. the handle of a knife, axe, or spear.
– ORIGIN Old English.

hag • n. 1 an ugly old woman. 2 a witch.
– ORIGIN perh. from Old English.

haggard • adj. looking exhausted and ill.
– ORIGIN French *hagard*.

haggis • n. (pl. **haggis**) a Scottish dish consisting of seasoned sheep's or calf's offal mixed with suet and oatmeal.
– ORIGIN prob. from Old Norse, 'hack'.

haggle • v. (**haggles, haggling, haggled**) argue or negotiate with someone about the price of something.

– ORIGIN Old Norse.

hagiography /ha-gi-og-ruh-fi/
• n. 1 literature which deals with the lives of saints. 2 a biography which idealizes its subject.
– DERIVATIVES **hagiographer** n.

hag-ridden • adj. suffering from nightmares or anxieties.

ha-ha • n. a ditch with a wall below ground level, forming a boundary to a garden without interrupting the view.
– ORIGIN perh. from the cry of surprise made on coming across such an obstacle.

haiku /hy-koo/ • n. (pl. **haiku** or **haikus**) a Japanese poem with seventeen syllables.
– ORIGIN Japanese.

hail[1] • n. 1 pellets of frozen rain falling in showers. 2 a large number of things hurled forcefully through the air: *a hail of bullets*. • v. (**it hails, it is hailing, it hailed**) hail falls.
– ORIGIN Old English.

hail[2] • v. 1 call out to someone to attract their attention. 2 describe enthusiastically: *he has been hailed as the new James Dean*. 3 (**hail from**) have your home or origins in a particular place.
– ORIGIN from former *hail* 'healthy'.

hail-fellow-well-met • adj. showing too much friendliness or familiarity.

Hail Mary • n. (pl. **Hail Marys**) a prayer to the Virgin Mary used chiefly by Roman Catholics.

hailstone • n. a pellet of hail.

hair • n. 1 any of the fine thread-like strands growing from the skin of mammals and other animals, or from a plant. 2 strands of hair.
– PHRASES **hair of the dog** informal an alcoholic drink taken to cure a hangover. [ORIGIN from *hair of the dog that bit you*, formerly thought to be a remedy for the bite of a mad dog.] **a hair's breadth** a very small margin. **let your hair down** informal behave wildly or in a very relaxed way. **split hairs** make trivial and unnecessary distinctions.
– DERIVATIVES **hairless** adj.
– ORIGIN Old English.

hairband • n. a band worn over the top of the head and behind the ears to keep the hair off the face.

hairbrush • n. a brush for smoothing the hair.

haircut • n. 1 the style in which someone's hair is cut. 2 an act of cutting someone's hair.

hairdo • n. (pl. **hairdos**) informal the style of someone's hair.

hairdresser • n. a person who cuts and styles hair.
– DERIVATIVES **hairdressing** n.

hairdryer (also **hairdrier**) • n. an electrical device for drying the hair with warm air.

hairgrip • n. Brit. a flat hairpin with the ends close together.

hairline • n. the edge of a person's hair. • adj. very thin or fine: *a hairline fracture.*

hairnet • n. a fine net for holding the hair in place.

hairpiece • n. a piece of false hair used to add to a person's natural hair.

hairpin • n. a U-shaped pin for fastening the hair.

hairpin bend • n. a sharp U-shaped bend in a road.

hair-raising • adj. very frightening.

hair shirt • n. a shirt made of stiff prickly cloth woven from horsehair, worn in the past by people who wished to punish themselves for doing wrong.

hairslide • n. Brit. a clip for keeping a woman's hair in position.

hairspray • n. a solution sprayed on to hair to keep it in place.

hairspring • n. a flat coiled spring which regulates the timekeeping in some clocks and watches.

hairstyle • n. a way in which someone's hair is cut or arranged.
– DERIVATIVES **hairstylist** n.

hair trigger • n. a firearm trigger set for release at the slightest pressure.

hairy • adj. (**hairier, hairiest**) 1 covered with or like hair. 2 informal dangerous or frightening: *a hairy mountain road.*
– DERIVATIVES **hairiness** n.

Haitian /hay-shi-uhn, hay-shuhn/ • n. a person from Haiti. • adj. relating to Haiti.

hajj /haj/ (also **haj**) • n. the pilgrimage to Mecca which all Muslims are expected to make at least once if they can afford to do so.
– ORIGIN Arabic.

haka /hah-kuh/ • n. a ceremonial Maori war dance.
– ORIGIN Maori.

hake • n. a long-bodied edible fish with strong teeth.
– ORIGIN perh. from Old English, 'hook'.

halal /huh-lahl/ • adj. (of meat) prepared according to Muslim law.
– ORIGIN Arabic.

halberd /hal-berd/ • n. hist. a combined spear and battleaxe.
– ORIGIN German *helmbarde.*

halcyon /hal-si-uhn/ • adj. (of a past time) very happy and peaceful: *halcyon days.*
– ORIGIN Greek *alkuōn* 'kingfisher' (first referring to a mythical bird said to calm the sea).

hale • adj. (of an old person) strong and healthy.
– ORIGIN Old English, 'whole'.

half • n. (pl. **halves**) 1 either of two equal or matching parts into which something is or can be divided. 2 either of two equal periods into which a match or performance is divided. 3 Brit. informal half a pint of beer. • predet. & pron. an amount equal to a half: *half an hour.* • adj. forming a half. • adv. 1 to the extent of half. 2 partly: *half-cooked.*
– PHRASES **at half mast** (of a flag) flown halfway down its mast, as a mark of respect for a person who has died. **not do things by halves** do things thoroughly. **not half 1** not nearly. **2** Brit. informal to an extreme degree: *she didn't half flare up.* **too —— by half** excessively ——: *too superstitious by half.*
– ORIGIN Old English.

half-and-half • adv. & adj. in equal parts.

halfback • n. a player in a ball game whose position is between the forwards and full backs.

half-baked • adj. informal not well planned or considered.

half board • n. Brit. a type of accommodation at a hotel or guest house which includes breakfast and one main meal.

half-breed • n. offens. a person whose parents are of different races.

half-brother (or **half-sister**) • n. a brother (or sister) with whom you have only one parent in common.

half-caste • n. offens. a person whose parents are of different races.

half-crown (also **half a crown**) • n. a former British coin equal to two shillings and sixpence (12½p).

half-cut • adj. Brit. informal drunk.

half-dozen (also **half a dozen**) • n. a group of six.

half-hearted • adj. without enthusiasm or energy.
– DERIVATIVES **half-heartedly** adv.

half hitch • n. a knot formed by passing the end of a rope round itself and then through the loop created.

half-hour • n. (also **half an hour**) a period of thirty minutes.
– DERIVATIVES **half-hourly** adj. & adv.

half-life • n. the time taken for the radioactivity of a substance to fall to half its original value.

half-light • n. dim light, such as that at dusk.

half measures • pl. n. actions or policies that are not forceful or decisive enough.

half-moon • n. 1 the moon when only half its surface is visible from the earth.

2 a semicircular or crescent-shaped object.

halfpenny /hayp-ni/ (also **ha'penny**) •n. (pl. **halfpennies** (for separate coins); **halfpence** /hay-p'nss/ (for a sum of money)) a former British coin equal to half an old or new penny.

half-term •n. Brit. a short holiday halfway through a school term.

half-timbered •adj. (of a building) having walls with a timber frame and a brick or plaster filling.

half-time •n. (in sport) a short gap between two halves of a match.

half-truth •n. a statement which is only partly true.

half-volley •n. (in sport) a strike or kick of the ball immediately after it bounces.

halfway •adv. & adj. 1 at or to a point equal in distance between two others. 2 to some extent: *halfway decent*.

halfway house •n. 1 the halfway point in a process. 2 Brit. a compromise.

halfwit •n. informal a stupid person.
– DERIVATIVES **half-witted** adj.

halibut /ha-li-buht/ •n. (pl. **halibut**) a large edible sea fish.
– ORIGIN from former *haly* 'holy' + *butt* 'flatfish' (because it was often eaten on holy days).

halide /hay-lyd/ •n. a chemical compound formed from a halogen and another element or group: *silver halide*.

halitosis /ha-li-toh-siss/ •n. unpleasant-smelling breath.
– ORIGIN Latin *halitus* 'breath'.

hall •n. 1 the room or space just inside the front entrance of a house. 2 a large room in which meetings, concerts, etc. are held. 3 (also **hall of residence**) Brit. a university building in which students live. 4 the dining room of a college, university, or school. 5 Brit. a large country house.
– ORIGIN Old English.

hallelujah /hal-li-loo-yuh/ (also **alleluia**) •exclam. God be praised.
– ORIGIN Hebrew, 'praise ye the Lord'.

hallmark •n. 1 an official mark stamped on objects made of gold, silver, or platinum as a guarantee of their purity. 2 a distinctive feature: *tiny bubbles are the hallmark of fine champagnes.* •v. stamp an object with a hallmark.
– ORIGIN from *Goldsmiths' Hall* in London, where objects were tested and stamped.

hallo •exclam. var. of **HELLO**.

hallowed /hal-lohd/ •adj. 1 made holy. 2 greatly respected: *the hallowed turf of Wimbledon.*
– ORIGIN Old English.

Halloween (also **Hallowe'en**) •n. the night of 31 October, the eve of All Saints' Day.
– ORIGIN from *All Hallow Even*.

hallucinate /huh-loo-si-nayt/ •v. (**hallucinates, hallucinating, hallucinated**) see something which is not actually present.
– DERIVATIVES **hallucination** n.
– ORIGIN Latin *hallucinari* 'go astray in thought'.

hallucinatory /huh-loo-si-nuh-tuh-ri/ •adj. resembling or causing hallucinations.

hallucinogen /huh-loo-si-nuh-juhn/ •n. a drug causing hallucinations.
– DERIVATIVES **hallucinogenic** adj.

hallway •n. = **HALL** (in sense 1).

halo /hay-loh/ •n. (pl. **haloes** or **halos**) 1 (in a painting) a circle of light surrounding the head of a holy person. 2 a circle of light round the sun or moon, refracted through ice crystals in the atmosphere.
– ORIGIN Greek *halōs* 'disc of the sun or moon'.

halogen /hal-uh-juhn/ •n. any of the chemical elements fluorine, chlorine, bromine, iodine, and astatine.
•adj. using a filament surrounded by iodine vapour or that of another halogen: *a halogen bulb*.
– ORIGIN Greek *hals* 'salt'.

halt¹ •v. bring or come to a sudden stop.
•n. 1 a stopping of movement or activity. 2 Brit. a minor stopping place on a railway line.
– ORIGIN German *halten* 'to hold'.

halt² •adj. old use lame.
– ORIGIN Old English.

halter •n. a rope or strap placed around the head of an animal and used to lead it or tie it to something.
– ORIGIN Old English.

halter neck •n. a style of woman's top that is fastened behind the neck, leaving the shoulders, upper back, and arms bare.

halting •adj. slow and hesitant.
– DERIVATIVES **haltingly** adv.

halve •v. (**halves, halving, halved**) 1 divide into two parts of equal size. 2 reduce or be reduced by half.

halves pl. of **HALF**.

halyard /hal-yerd/ •n. a rope used for raising and lowering a sail, yard, or flag on a ship.
– ORIGIN Old French *haler* 'haul'.

ham¹ •n. 1 meat from the upper part of a pig's leg which has been salted and dried or smoked. 2 (**hams**) the back of the thigh or the thighs and buttocks.

– ORIGIN Germanic, 'be crooked'.

ham² • n. 1 a bad actor, especially one who overacts. 2 (also **radio ham**) informal an amateur radio operator. • v. (**hams, hamming, hammed**) informal overact.
– DERIVATIVES **hammy** adj.
– ORIGIN perh. from AMATEUR.

hamburger • n. a small cake of minced beef, fried or grilled and typically served in a bread roll.
– ORIGIN German.

ham-fisted (also **ham-handed**) • adj. informal clumsy; awkward.

hamlet • n. a small village.
– ORIGIN Old French *hamelet*.

hammer • n. 1 a tool consisting of a heavy metal head mounted at the end of a handle, used for breaking things and driving in nails. 2 an auctioneer's mallet. 3 a part of a mechanism that hits another, e.g. one exploding the charge in a gun. 4 a heavy metal ball attached to a wire for throwing in an athletic contest. • v. (**hammers, hammering, hammered**) 1 hit repeatedly. 2 (**hammer away**) work hard and persistently. 3 (**hammer something in/into**) make something stick in someone's mind by constantly repeating it. 4 (**hammer something out**) work out the details of a plan or agreement.
– PHRASES **hammer and tongs** informal with great energy or enthusiasm.
– ORIGIN Old English.

hammer and sickle • n. the symbols of the industrial worker and the peasant used as the emblem of the former Soviet Union.

hammerhead • n. a shark with flattened extensions on either side of the head.

hammer toe • n. a toe that is bent permanently downwards.

hammock • n. a wide strip of canvas or rope mesh suspended at both ends, used as a bed.
– ORIGIN from an extinct Caribbean language.

hamper¹ • n. 1 a basket used for food, cutlery, etc. on a picnic. 2 Brit. a box containing a selection of food and drink, given as a gift.
– ORIGIN Old French *hanaper* 'case for a goblet'.

hamper² • v. (**hampers, hampering, hampered**) slow down or prevent the movement or progress of.
– ORIGIN perh. from German *hemmen* 'restrain'.

hamster • n. a burrowing rodent with a short tail and large cheek pouches.
– ORIGIN German *hamustro* 'corn weevil'.

hamstring • n. any of five tendons at the

back of a person's knee. • v. (**hamstrings, hamstringing, hamstrung**) 1 cripple someone by cutting their hamstrings. 2 severely restrict.

hand • n. 1 the end part of the arm beyond the wrist. 2 a pointer on a clock or watch indicating the passing of time. 3 (**hands**) a person's power or control: *taking the law into their own hands*. 4 an active role. 5 help in doing something. 6 a person who does physical work. 7 informal a round of applause. 8 the set of cards dealt to a player in a card game. 9 a unit of measurement of a horse's height, equal to 4 inches (10.16 cm). • v. give or pass something to someone. • adj. 1 operated by or held in the hand: *hand luggage*. 2 done or made by hand.
– PHRASES **at hand** easy to reach; near. **get** (or **keep**) **your hand in** become (or remain) practised in something. **hand in glove** in close association. (**from**) **hand to mouth** meeting only your immediate needs; with no money in reserve. **hands-on** involving direct participation in something. **in hand 1** in progress. 2 ready for use if needed. **on hand** present and available. **out of hand 1** not under control. 2 without taking time to think: *the proposal was rejected out of hand*. **to hand** within easy reach.
– ORIGIN Old English.

handbag • n. Brit. a small bag used by a woman to carry everyday personal items.

handball • n. 1 a game in which the ball is hit with the hand in a walled court. 2 Football unlawful touching of the ball with the hand or arm.

handbill • n. a small printed advertisement handed out in the street.

handbook • n. a book giving basic information or instructions.

handbrake • n. a brake operated by hand, used to hold an already stationary vehicle.

handcrafted • adj. made skilfully by hand.

handcuff • n. (**handcuffs**) a pair of lockable linked metal rings for securing a prisoner's wrists. • v. put handcuffs on.

handful • n. 1 a quantity that fills the hand. 2 a small number or amount. 3 informal a person who is difficult to deal with or control.

hand grenade • n. a hand-thrown grenade.

handgun • n. a gun designed for use with one hand.

handhold • n. something for a hand to grip on.

handicap • n. 1 a condition that restricts a person's ability to function physically,

mentally, or socially. **2** something that makes progress or success difficult. **3** a disadvantage given to a superior competitor in a sport in order to make the chances more equal, such as the extra weight given to a racehorse. **4** the number of strokes by which a golfer normally exceeds par for a course.
• v. (**handicaps, handicapping, handicapped**) make it difficult for someone to do something.
– ORIGIN from *hand in cap*, an old gambling game involving players putting their hands into a cap in which money had been deposited.

handicapped • adj. having a handicap.

> USAGE: When used to refer to people with physical and mental disabilities, the word **handicapped** sounds old-fashioned and may cause offence; it is better to say **disabled**, or, when referring to mental disability, **having learning difficulties**.

handicraft • n. **1** an activity involving the making of decorative objects by hand. **2** decorative objects made by hand.

handiwork • n. **1** (**your handiwork**) something that you have made or done. **2** the making of things by hand.

handkerchief /hang-ker-cheef/ • n. (pl. **handkerchiefs** or **handkerchieves**) a square of material for wiping the nose.

> ☑ Remember that there is a **d** in **handkerchief**.

handle • v. (**handles, handling, handled**) **1** feel or move something with the hands. **2** control a vehicle or animal. **3** deal or cope with. **4** control or manage something commercially. **5** (**handle yourself**) behave in a particular way.
• n. **1** the part by which a thing is held, carried, or controlled. **2** a means of understanding or controlling a person or situation. **3** informal the name of a person or place.
– ORIGIN Old English.

handlebar (also **handlebars**) • n. the steering bar of a bicycle or motorbike.

handler • n. **1** a person who handles a particular type of article: *a baggage handler*. **2** a person who trains or controls an animal.

handmade • adj. made by hand rather than machine.

handmaid (also **handmaiden**) • n. old use a female servant.

hand-me-down • n. a piece of clothing or other item that has been passed on from another person.

handout • n. **1** an amount of money or other aid given to a needy person. **2** a

piece of printed information provided free of charge.

handover • n. an act of handing something over.

hand-pick • v. select carefully.

handset • n. **1** the part of a telephone that is held up to speak into and listen to. **2** a hand-held control device for a piece of electronic equipment.

handshake • n. an act of shaking a person's hand.

handsome • adj. (**handsomer, handsomest**) **1** (of a man) good-looking. **2** (of a woman) striking and impressive rather than pretty. **3** (of a thing) well made and of obvious quality. **4** (of an amount) large: *a handsome majority*.
– DERIVATIVES **handsomely** adv.
– ORIGIN from HAND + -SOME, first meaning 'easy to handle or use'.

handspring • n. a jump through the air on to the hands followed by another on to the feet.

handstand • n. an act of balancing upside down on the hands.

hand-to-hand • adj. (of fighting) at close quarters and involving physical contact between the opponents.

handwriting • n. **1** writing with a pen or pencil rather than by typing or printing. **2** a person's particular style of writing.

handwritten • adj. written with a pen or pencil.

handy • adj. (**handier, handiest**) **1** convenient to handle or use; useful. **2** in a convenient place or position.
– DERIVATIVES **handily** adv.

handyman • n. (pl. **handymen**) a person employed to do general decorating or domestic repairs.

hang • v. (**hangs, hanging,** past and past part. **hung** except in sense 2) **1** suspend or be suspended from above with the lower part not attached. **2** (past and past part. **hanged**) kill someone by suspending them from a rope tied around the neck. **3** attach something so as to allow free movement about the point of attachment (e.g. a hinge): *hanging a door*. **4** (of fabric or a garment) fall or drape in a particular way. **5** attach meat or game to a hook and leave it until dry, tender, and ready to cook.
– PHRASES **get the hang of** informal learn how to do something. **hang around** wait around. **hang on 1** hold tightly. **2** informal wait for a short time. **hang out** informal spend time relaxing or enjoying yourself. **hang up** end a telephone conversation by cutting the connection.
– ORIGIN Old English.

USAGE: **Hang** has two past tense and past participle forms: **hanged** and **hung**. You should use **hung** in general situations, as in *they hung out the washing*, while **hanged** should only be used when talking about executing someone by hanging, as in *the prisoner was hanged*.

hangar /hang-er/ • n. a large building in which aircraft are kept.
– ORIGIN French.

hangdog • adj. having a sad or guilty appearance; shamefaced.

hanger • n. **1** a person who hangs something. **2** (also **coat hanger**) a curved frame with a hook at the top, for hanging clothes from a rail.

hanger-on • n. (pl. **hangers-on**) a person who tries to be friends with a rich or powerful person in order to benefit from the relationship.

hang-glider • n. an unpowered flying apparatus consisting of a frame with fabric stretched over it from which the operator is suspended.
– DERIVATIVES **hang-gliding** n.

hanging • n. **1** the practice of hanging criminals as a form of capital punishment. **2** a decorative piece of fabric hung on the wall of a room or around a bed.

hanging valley • n. a valley that ends in a very steep descent to a main valley, the main valley having been deepened through erosion by a glacier.

hangman • n. (p. **hangmen**) an executioner who hangs condemned people.

hangnail • n. a piece of torn skin at the root of a fingernail.
– ORIGIN Old English.

hang-out • n. informal a place where someone spends a great deal of time.

hangover • n. **1** a severe headache or other after-effects caused by drinking too much alcohol. **2** a thing that has survived from the past.

hang-up • n. informal an emotional problem.

hank • n. a coil or length of wool, hair, or other material.
– ORIGIN Old Norse.

hanker • v. (**hankers, hankering, hankered**) (**hanker after/for/to do**) feel a desire for or to do.
– ORIGIN prob. from **HANG**.

hanky (also **hankie**) • n. (pl. **hankies**) informal a handkerchief.

hanky-panky • n. informal **1** sexual activity that is seen as slightly improper. **2** slightly dishonest behaviour.

Hanoverian /han-uh-veer-i-uhn/ • adj. relating to the royal house of Hanover, who ruled as monarchs in Britain from 1714 to 1901.

Hansard /han-sard/ • n. the official record of debates in the British, Canadian, Australian, New Zealand, or South African parliament.
– ORIGIN named after the English printer Thomas C. *Hansard*.

hansom /han-suhm/ (also **hansom cab**) • n. hist. a two-wheeled horse-drawn cab for two passengers, with the driver seated behind.
– ORIGIN named after the English architect Joseph A. *Hansom*.

Hants • abbrev. Hampshire.

Hanukkah /han-uu-kuh/ (also **Chanukkah**) • n. a Jewish festival of lights held in December, commemorating the occasion when the Jewish Temple in Jerusalem was dedicated to God again.
– ORIGIN Hebrew, 'consecration'.

ha'penny • n. var. of **HALFPENNY**.

haphazard • adj. having no particular order or plan; disorganized.
– DERIVATIVES **haphazardly** adv.

hapless • adj. unlucky.

haploid /hap-loyd/ • adj. (of a cell or nucleus) containing a single set of unpaired chromosomes. Compare with **DIPLOID**.

happen • v. **1** take place by chance or as a result of something. **2** (**happen on**) come across by chance. **3** (**happen to**) be experienced by. **4** (**happen to**) become of: *I don't care what happens to the money.*
– ORIGIN Old Norse, 'chance'.

happening • n. an event or occurrence. • adj. informal fashionable.

happy • adj. (**happier, happiest**) **1** feeling or showing pleasure. **2** willing to do something. **3** fortunate and convenient: *a happy coincidence.*
– DERIVATIVES **happily** adv. **happiness** n.
– ORIGIN Old Norse, 'luck'.

happy-go-lucky • adj. cheerfully unconcerned about the future.

happy hour • n. a period of the day when drinks are sold at reduced prices in a bar.

hara-kiri /ha-ruh-ki-ri/ • n. (formerly, in Japan) a method of ritual suicide involving cutting open the stomach with a sword.
– ORIGIN Japanese, 'belly-cutting'.

harangue /huh-rang/ • v. (**harangues, haranguing, harangued**) address a person or group in a loud and aggressive or critical way. • n. a forceful and aggressive or critical speech.
– ORIGIN Latin *harenga*.

harass /ha-ruhss, huh-rass/ • v. **1** torment someone by subjecting

them to constant interference or bullying. **2** (as adj. **harassed**) feeling tired or tense as a result of having too many demands made on you: *harassed parents.*
– DERIVATIVES **harassment** n.
– ORIGIN French *harasser.*

> Spell **harass** with a single **r** and a double **s**.

harbinger /har-bin-jer/ • n. a person or thing that announces or signals the approach of something: *the harbingers of spring.*
– ORIGIN Old French *herbergier* 'provide lodging for.'

harbour (US **harbor**) • n. a place on the coast where ships can be moored.
• v. **1** keep a thought or feeling secretly in your mind. **2** give a refuge or shelter to. **3** carry the germs of a disease.
– ORIGIN Old English, 'shelter'.

hard • adj. **1** solid, firm, and rigid. **2** requiring a great deal of endurance or effort; difficult. **3** (of a person) not showing any signs of weakness; tough. **4** done with a great deal of force or strength: *a hard whack.* **5** harsh or unpleasant to the senses. **6** (of information or a subject of study) concerned with precise facts that can be proved: *hard science.* **7** (of drink) strongly alcoholic. **8** (of a drug) very addictive. **9** (of water) containing mineral salts. • adv. **1** with a great deal of effort or force. **2** so as to be solid or firm.
– PHRASES **hard and fast** (of a rule) fixed and definitive. **hard done by** Brit. harshly or unfairly treated. **hard feelings** feelings of resentment. **hard up** informal short of money.
– DERIVATIVES **hardness** n.
– ORIGIN Old English.

hardback • n. a book bound in stiff covers.

hardbitten • adj. tough and cynical.

hardboard • n. stiff board made of compressed wood pulp.

hard-boiled • adj. **1** (of an egg) boiled until the yolk is firm. **2** (of a person) tough and cynical.

hard cash • n. coins and banknotes as opposed to other forms of payment.

hard copy • n. a printed version on paper of data held in a computer.

hard core • n. **1** the most committed or uncompromising members of a group. **2** very explicit pornography. **3** (usu. **hardcore**) a type of rock or dance music that is experimental, loud, and played aggressively.

hard disk (also **hard drive**) • n. Computing a rigid magnetic disk on which a large amount of data can be stored.

harden • v. **1** make or become hard or harder. **2** (as adj. **hardened**) fixed in a bad habit or way of life: *hardened criminals.*

hard-headed • adj. tough and realistic.

hard-hearted • adj. unsympathetic, harsh, or uncaring.

hard labour • n. a type of punishment that takes the form of heavy physical work.

hard line • n. a strict and uncompromising policy or attitude.
– DERIVATIVES **hardliner** n.

hardly • adv. **1** scarcely; barely. **2** only with great difficulty. **3** no or not: *I hardly think so.*

hard-nosed • adj. informal realistic and tough-minded.

hard palate • n. the bony front part of the roof of the mouth.

hard-pressed • adj. in difficulties or under pressure.

hard sell • n. a policy or technique of aggressive selling or advertising.

hardship • n. severe suffering.

hard shoulder • n. Brit. a strip of road alongside a motorway for use in an emergency.

hardware • n. **1** tools and other items used in the home and in activities such as gardening. **2** the machines, wiring, and other physical parts of a computer. **3** heavy military equipment such as tanks and missiles.

hardwood • n. the wood from a broadleaved tree as distinguished from that of conifers.

hardy • adj. (**hardier**, **hardiest**) **1** capable of surviving difficult conditions. **2** (of a plant) able to survive outside during winter.
– DERIVATIVES **hardiness** n.
– ORIGIN Old French *hardi.*

hare • n. a fast-running mammal like a large rabbit, with very long hind legs.
• v. (**hares**, **haring**, **hared**) esp. Brit. run very fast.
– ORIGIN Old English.

harebell • n. a plant with pale blue bell-shaped flowers.

hare-brained • adj. foolish and unlikely to succeed.

Hare Krishna /ha-ri krish-nuh/ • n. a member of a religious sect based on the worship of the Hindu god Krishna.
– ORIGIN Sanskrit.

harelip • n. offens. = CLEFT LIP.

harem /hah-reem/ • n. **1** the separate part of a Muslim household reserved for women. **2** the women living in a harem.
– ORIGIN Arabic, 'prohibited place'.

haricot /ha-ri-koh/ • n. esp. Brit. a round white edible bean.
– ORIGIN French.

hark • v. 1 literary listen. 2 (**hark back to**) recall or remind you of something in the past.
– ORIGIN Germanic.

harken • v. var. of HEARKEN.

harlequin /har-li-kwin/ • n. (**Harlequin**) a character in traditional pantomime, wearing a mask and a diamond-patterned costume. • adj. in varied colours.
– ORIGIN former French.

harlot • n. old use a prostitute.
– ORIGIN Old French, 'young man'.

harm • n. 1 physical injury to a person. 2 damage done to a thing. 3 a bad effect: *there's no harm in telling him.* • v. 1 physically injure. 2 damage or have a bad effect on.
– ORIGIN Old English.

harmful • adj. causing or likely to cause harm.
– DERIVATIVES **harmfully** adv.

harmless • adj. not able or likely to cause harm.
– DERIVATIVES **harmlessly** adv.

harmonic /har-mon-ik/ • adj. relating to harmony. • n. Music a tone produced by vibration of a string in any of certain fractions (half, third, etc.) of its length.
– DERIVATIVES **harmonically** adv.

harmonica • n. a small rectangular wind instrument with a row of metal reeds that produce different notes.

harmonious • adj. 1 tuneful. 2 arranged in a pleasing way so that each part goes well with the others. 3 free from con-flict: *harmonious relationships.*
– DERIVATIVES **harmoniously** adv.

harmonium • n. a keyboard instrument in which the notes are produced by air driven through metal reeds by foot-operated bellows.
– ORIGIN Greek *harmonios* 'harmonious'.

harmonize (or **harmonise**)
• v. (**harmonizes, harmonizing, harmonized**) 1 add notes to a melody to produce harmony. 2 sing or play in harmony. 3 make or be harmonious.
– DERIVATIVES **harmonization** n.

harmony • n. (pl. **harmonies**) 1 the combination of musical notes sounded at the same time to produce chords with a pleasing effect. 2 a pleasing quality when things are arranged together well. 3 agreement.
– ORIGIN Latin *harmonia* 'joining'.

harness • n. 1 a set of straps by which a horse or other animal is fastened to a cart, plough, etc. and is controlled by its driver. 2 a similar arrangement of straps, such as those for fastening a parachute to a person's body. • v. 1 fit with a harness. 2 control and make use of: *attempts to harness solar energy.*
– ORIGIN Old French *harneis* 'military equipment'.

harp • n. a musical instrument consisting of a frame supporting a series of strings of different lengths, played by plucking with the fingers. • v. (**harp on**) keep talking about something in a boring way.
– DERIVATIVES **harpist** n.
– ORIGIN Old English.

harpoon • n. a barbed spear-like missile used for catching whales and other large sea creatures. • v. spear with a harpoon.
– ORIGIN French *harpon*.

harpsichord • n. a keyboard instrument with horizontal strings plucked by points operated by pressing the keys.
– DERIVATIVES **harpsichordist** n.
– ORIGIN from Latin *harpa* 'harp' + *chorda* 'string'.

harpy • n. (pl. **harpies**) 1 Gk & Rom. Myth. a monster with a woman's head and body and a bird's wings and claws. 2 an unpleasant woman.
– ORIGIN Greek *harpuiai* 'snatchers'.

harridan • n. a bossy or aggressive old woman.
– ORIGIN perh. from French *haridelle* 'old horse'.

harrier[1] • n. a breed of hound used for hunting hares.
– ORIGIN from HARE.

harrier[2] • n. a long-winged bird of prey.
– ORIGIN from HARRY.

harrow • n. an implement consisting of a heavy frame set with teeth which is drawn over ploughed land to break up or spread the soil. • v. 1 draw a harrow over. 2 (as adj. **harrowing**) very distressing.
– ORIGIN Old Norse.

harry • v. (**harries, harrying, harried**) 1 carry out repeated attacks on an enemy. 2 pester someone continuously.
– ORIGIN Old English.

harsh • adj. 1 unpleasantly rough or jarring to the senses. 2 cruel or severe. 3 (of climate or conditions) difficult to survive in.
– DERIVATIVES **harshly** adv. **harshness** n.
– ORIGIN German *harsch*.

hart • n. an adult male deer.
– ORIGIN Old English.

hartebeest /har-ti-beest/ • n. a large African antelope with a long head and sloping back.
– ORIGIN from Dutch *hert* 'hart' + *beest* 'beast'.

h

harum-scarum •adj. reckless.
– ORIGIN from HARE and SCARE.

harvest •n. 1 the process or period of gathering in crops. 2 the season's yield or crop. •v. gather a crop as a harvest.
– DERIVATIVES **harvester** n.
– ORIGIN Old English, 'autumn'.

harvest mouse •n. a small mouse which nests among the stalks of growing cereal crops.

has 3rd person sing. present of HAVE.

has-been •n. informal a person or thing that is old-fashioned or no longer important.

hash[1] •n. a dish of diced cooked meat reheated with potatoes.
– PHRASES **make a hash of** informal make a mess of.
– ORIGIN French *hacher*.

hash[2] •n. informal hashish.

hash[3] •n. Brit. the symbol #.
– ORIGIN prob. from HATCH[3].

hashish /ha-sheesh/ •n. cannabis.
– ORIGIN Arabic, 'dry herb'.

hasn't •contr. has not.

hasp •n. a hinged metal plate that forms part of a fastening and is fitted over a metal loop and secured by a pin or padlock.
– ORIGIN Old English.

hassium /hass-i-uhm/ •n. a very unstable chemical element made by high-energy atomic collisions.
– ORIGIN from *Hassias*, the Latin name for the German state of *Hesse*.

hassle informal •n. 1 annoying inconvenience. 2 a situation involving argument or conflict. •v. (**hassles, hassling, hassled**) harass or pester.

hassock •n. a cushion for kneeling on in church.
– ORIGIN Old English, 'clump of grass'.

haste •n. speed or urgency when doing something.
– ORIGIN Old French.

hasten •v. 1 be quick to do something. 2 cause something to happen sooner than expected.

hasty •adj. (**hastier, hastiest**) done or acting with speed or urgency.
– DERIVATIVES **hastily** adv.

hat •n. a shaped covering for the head, typically with a brim and a crown.
– PHRASES **pass the hat round** collect contributions of money. **take your hat off to** used to express admiration or praise for someone.
– ORIGIN Old English.

hatband •n. a decorative ribbon around a hat.

hatch[1] •n. 1 a small opening in a floor, wall, or roof allowing access from one area to another. 2 a door in an aircraft, spacecraft, or submarine.
– ORIGIN Old English.

hatch[2] •v. 1 (of a young bird, fish, or reptile) come out of its egg. 2 (of an egg) open and produce a young animal. 3 form a plot or plan.

hatch[3] •v. (in drawing) shade an area with closely drawn parallel lines.
– ORIGIN Old French *hacher*.

hatchback •n. a car with a door across the full width at the back end that opens upwards.

hatchet •n. a small axe with a short handle.
– PHRASES **bury the hatchet** end a quarrel.
– ORIGIN Old French *hachette* 'little axe'.

hatchet job •n. informal a fierce spoken or written attack.

hatchet man •n. informal a person who carries out unpleasant tasks on behalf of an employer.

hatchling •n. a newly hatched young animal.

hatchway •n. an opening or hatch, especially in a ship's deck.

hate •v. (**hates, hating, hated**) feel very strong dislike for. •n. 1 very strong dislike. 2 informal a disliked thing.
– DERIVATIVES **hater** n.
– ORIGIN Old English.

hateful •adj. very unkind or unpleasant.

hatred •n. very strong hate.

hatter •n. a person who makes and sells hats.
– PHRASES (**as**) **mad as a hatter** informal completely insane.

hat-trick •n. three successes of the same kind, especially (in football) three goals scored by the same player in a game or (in cricket) three wickets taken by a bowler with successive balls.
– ORIGIN first referring to the presentation of a new hat to a bowler taking a hat-trick.

haughty •adj. (**haughtier, haughtiest**) behaving in an arrogant and superior way towards other people.
– DERIVATIVES **haughtily** adv. **haughtiness** n.
– ORIGIN Old French *hault* 'high'.

haul •v. 1 pull or drag with effort. 2 transport in a lorry or cart. •n. 1 a quantity of something obtained, especially illegally. 2 a number of fish caught at one time.
– ORIGIN Old French *haler*.

haulage •n. Brit. the commercial transport of goods.

haulier •n. Brit. a person or company

employed in the commercial transport of goods by road.

haulm /hawm/ • n. a plant stalk or stem.
– ORIGIN Old English.

haunch • n. **1** the buttock and thigh of a human or animal. **2** the leg and loin of an animal, as food.
– ORIGIN Old French *hanche*.

haunt • v. **1** (of a ghost) appear regularly in a place. **2** (of a person) visit a place frequently. **3** be persistently and disturbingly present in a person's mind. • n. a place that a particular person often visits: *a favourite haunt of pickpockets.*
– ORIGIN Old French *hanter*.

haunted • adj. **1** (of a place) visited by a ghost. **2** having or showing signs of mental suffering: *haunted eyes.*

haunting • adj. beautiful or sad in a way that is hard to forget.
– DERIVATIVES **hauntingly** adv.

haute couture /oht kuu-tyoor/ • n. the designing and making of high-quality clothes by leading fashion houses.
– ORIGIN French 'high dressmaking'.

haute cuisine /oht kwi-zeen/ • n. high-quality cooking in the traditional French style.
– ORIGIN French, 'high cookery'.

hauteur /oh-ter/ • n. the quality of behaving in an arrogant and superior way towards other people.
– ORIGIN French.

have • v. (**has, having, had**) **1** possess or own. **2** experience: *have difficulty.* **3** be able to make use of: *how much time have I got?* **4** (**have to**) be obliged to; must. **5** perform an action: *he had a look round.* **6** show a personal characteristic. **7** suffer from an illness or disability. **8** cause to be or be done: *I want to have everything ready.* **9** place, hold, or keep in a particular position. **10** eat or drink. • auxiliary verb used with a past participle to form the perfect, pluperfect, and future perfect tenses, and the conditional mood.
– PHRASES **have had it** informal be beyond repair. **have someone on** informal try to make someone believe something untrue.
– ORIGIN Old English.

> USAGE: Be careful not to write **of** when you mean **have** or **'ve**: *I could've told you that* not *I could of told you that.* The mistake occurs because the pronunciation of **have** can be the same as that of **of** in certain contexts, so that the two words are confused when they are written down.

haven • n. **1** a place of safety. **2** a harbour or small port.
– ORIGIN Old English.

haven't • contr. have not.

haver /hay-ver/ • v. (**havers, havering, havered**) **1** Scottish talk foolishly. **2** Brit. be indecisive.

haversack • n. a small, sturdy bag carried on the back or over the shoulder.
– ORIGIN from former German *Habersack* 'bag used to carry oats'.

havoc • n. **1** widespread destruction. **2** great confusion or disorder.
– PHRASES **play havoc with** completely disrupt.
– ORIGIN Old French *havot.*

haw • n. the red fruit of the hawthorn.
– ORIGIN Old English.

Hawaiian /huh-wy-uhn/ • n. **1** a person from Hawaii. **2** the language of Hawaii. • adj. relating to Hawaii.

hawk[1] • n. **1** a fast-flying bird of prey with broad wings and a long tail. **2** a person in favour of aggressive policies in foreign affairs. • v. hunt game with a trained hawk.
– DERIVATIVES **hawkish** adj.
– ORIGIN Old English.

hawk[2] • v. offer goods for sale in the street.
– ORIGIN prob. from **HAWKER**.

hawk[3] • v. **1** clear the throat noisily. **2** (**hawk something up**) bring phlegm up from the throat.

hawker • n. a person who travels about selling goods.
– ORIGIN prob. from German or Dutch.

hawser /haw-zer/ • n. a thick rope or cable for mooring or towing a ship.
– ORIGIN Old French *haucier* 'to hoist'.

hawthorn • n. a thorny shrub or tree with white, pink, or red blossom and small dark red fruits.
– ORIGIN Old English.

hay • n. grass that has been mown and dried for use as fodder.
– PHRASES **make hay (while the sun shines)** make good use of an opportunity while it lasts.
– ORIGIN Old English.

haycock • n. a cone-shaped heap of hay left in a field to dry.

hay fever • n. an allergy to pollen or dust, causing sneezing and watery eyes.

haystack (also **hayrick**) • n. a large packed pile of hay.

haywire • adj. informal out of control.
– ORIGIN from the fact that wire used to tie up bales of hay was often also used in makeshift repairs.

hazard • n. **1** a danger. **2** an obstacle, such as a bunker, on a golf course. • v. **1** say tentatively. **2** put something at risk.
– ORIGIN Old French *hasard.*

hazard lights • pl. n. flashing lights on a

vehicle, used as a warning that the vehicle is stationary or moving unexpectedly slowly.

hazardous • adj. dangerous.

haze • n. 1 a thin mist caused by fine particles of dust, water vapour, etc. 2 a state of mental confusion: *he went to bed in an alcoholic haze.* • v. cover or conceal with a haze.

hazel • n. 1 a shrub or small tree bearing catkins in spring and nuts in autumn. 2 a rich reddish-brown colour.
– ORIGIN Old English.

hazelnut • n. the round brown edible nut of the hazel.

hazy • adj. (**hazier**, **haziest**) 1 covered by a haze. 2 vague or unclear: *hazy memories.*
– DERIVATIVES **hazily** adv. **haziness** n.

HB • abbrev. 1 half board. 2 hard black (as a grade of pencil lead).

H-bomb • n. = HYDROGEN BOMB.

He • symb. the chemical element helium.

he • pron. (third person sing.) 1 used to refer to a man, boy, or male animal previously mentioned or easily identified. 2 used to refer to a person or animal of unspecified sex.
– ORIGIN Old English.

> USAGE: Until quite recently, **he** was used to talk about both males and females when a person's sex was not specified: *every child needs to know that he is loved.* Many people now think of this as outdated and sexist. One solution is to use **he or she**, but this can be awkward if used frequently. An alternative solution is to use **they**, especially where it occurs after an indefinite pronoun such as **everyone** or **someone** (as in *everyone needs to feel that they matter*).

head • n. 1 the upper part of the body, containing the brain, mouth, and sense organs. 2 a person in charge. 3 the front, forward, or upper part of something. 4 a person considered as a unit: *fifty pounds per head.* 5 (treated as pl.) a number of cattle or sheep: *seventy head of cattle.* 6 a compact mass of leaves or flowers at the top of a stem. 7 a part of a computer or a tape or video recorder which transfers information to and from a tape or disk. 8 the source of a river or stream. 9 (**heads**) the side of a coin which has the image of a head. 10 pressure of water or steam in an enclosed space: *a good head of steam.* • adj. chief. • v. 1 be or act as the head of: *the mayor headed the procession.* 2 give a heading to. 3 move in a specified direction: *we headed north.* 4 (**head someone/thing off**) intercept someone or something and force them to change direction. 5 Football hit the ball with the head.

– PHRASES **come to a head** reach a crisis. **go to someone's head** 1 (of alcohol) make someone slightly drunk. 2 (of success) make someone feel too proud. **head first** 1 with the head in front of the rest of the body. 2 without thinking beforehand. **a head for** a talent for or ability to cope with: *a head for heights.* **head over heels** madly in love. **a head start** an advantage gained at the beginning. **make head or tail of** understand at all. **off the top of your head** without careful thought.
– DERIVATIVES **headless** adj.
– ORIGIN Old English.

headache • n. 1 a continuous pain in the head. 2 informal something that causes worry.

headband • n. a band of fabric worn around the head, especially to keep the hair off the face.

headboard • n. an upright panel at the head of a bed.

headbutt • v. attack someone by hitting them hard with the head. • n. an act of headbutting someone.

headcase • n. informal a mentally unstable person.

headcount • n. a count of the number of people present.

headdress • n. an ornamental covering for the head.

header • n. 1 Football a shot or pass made with the head. 2 informal a headlong fall or dive. 3 a line of writing at the top of each page of a book or document.

headgear • n. items worn on the head.

headhunt • v. 1 approach someone already employed elsewhere to fill a vacant post. 2 (as noun **headhunting**) the practice among some peoples of collecting the heads of dead enemies as trophies.
– DERIVATIVES **headhunter** n.

heading • n. 1 a title at the top of a page or section of a book. 2 a direction or bearing.

headland • n. a narrow piece of land that juts out into the sea.

headlight (also **headlamp**) • n. a powerful light at the front of a motor vehicle.

headline • n. 1 a heading at the top of a newspaper or magazine article. 2 (**the headlines**) a summary of the most important items of news. • v. (**headlines**, **headlining**, **headlined**) 1 provide an article with a headline. 2 appear as the star performer at a concert.

headlock • n. a method of restraining someone by holding an arm firmly around their head.

headlong •adv. & adj. **1** with the head first. **2** in a rush.

headman •n. (pl. **headmen**) the leader of a tribe.

headmaster (or **headmistress**) •n. esp. Brit. a head teacher.

head of state •n. the official leader of a country, who may also be the head of government.

head-on •adj. & adv. **1** with or involving the front of a vehicle. **2** with or involving direct confrontation.

headphones •pl. n. a pair of earphones joined by a band placed over the head.

headpiece •n. a device worn on the head.

headquarter •v. (**be headquartered**) have headquarters at a specified place.

headquarters •n. **1** the centre of an organization from which operations are directed. **2** the premises occupied by a military commander and the commander's staff.

headrest •n. a padded support for the head on the back of a seat.

headroom •n. the space between the top of a vehicle or a person's head and the ceiling or other structure above.

headscarf •n. (pl. **headscarves**) a square of fabric worn as a covering for the head.

headset •n. a set of headphones with a microphone attached.

headship •n. **1** the position of leader. **2** esp. Brit. the position of head teacher in a school.

headstone •n. a stone slab placed at the head of a grave.

headstrong •adj. determined to do things your own way, regardless of other people's advice.

head teacher •n. esp. Brit. the teacher in charge of a school.

head-to-head •adj. & adv. involving two parties confronting each other in a dispute or contest.

headwaters •pl. n. streams forming the source of a river.

headway •n. (in phr. **make headway**) make progress.

headwind •n. a wind blowing from directly in front.

headword •n. a word which begins a separate entry in a reference book such as a dictionary or encyclopedia.

heady •adj. (**headier, headiest**) **1** exhilarating or exciting: *the heady days of the 1960s.* **2** (of alcohol) strong.

heal •v. **1** make or become healthy again. **2** put right: *the rift between them was never healed.*
– DERIVATIVES **healer** n.

– ORIGIN Old English.

health •n. **1** the state of being free from illness or injury. **2** a person's mental or physical condition.
– ORIGIN Old English.

health centre •n. a building in which a group of doctors see their patients and where local medical services have their offices.

health club •n. a private club with exercise facilities and health and beauty treatments.

health farm •n. esp. Brit. a place where people stay to try to improve their health by dieting, taking exercise, and having various treatments.

health food •n. natural food that is believed to be good for your health.

healthful •adj. good for the health.

health service •n. a public service providing medical care.

health visitor •n. Brit. a nurse who visits the homes of patients who are ill for a long time or parents with very young children.

healthy •adj. (**healthier, healthiest**) **1** having or helping towards good health. **2** normal, sensible, or desirable: *a healthy balance between work and home.* **3** of a very satisfactory size or amount: *a healthy profit.*
– DERIVATIVES **healthily** adv. **healthiness** n.

heap •n. **1** a pile of a substance or of a number of objects. **2** informal a large amount or number: *heaps of room.* **3** informal an old vehicle in bad condition. •adv. (**heaps**) Brit. informal much: *I feel heaps better.* •v. **1** put in or form a heap. **2** (**heap something with**) load something heavily with. **3** (**heap something on**) give much praise, criticism, etc. to: *the press heaped abuse on him.*
– ORIGIN Old English.

hear •v. (**hears, hearing, heard**) **1** be aware of a sound with the ears. **2** be told about. **3** (**have heard of**) be aware of the existence of. **4** (**hear from**) receive a letter or phone call from. **5** listen to. **6** listen to and judge a case or person bringing a case in a law court.
– PHRASES **hear! hear!** used to show agreement with something said in a speech.
– DERIVATIVES **hearer** n.
– ORIGIN Old English.

hearing •n. **1** the ability to hear sounds. **2** the range within which sounds can be heard. **3** an opportunity to state your case: *a fair hearing.* **4** an act of listening to evidence before an official or in a law court.

hearing aid • n. a small device worn on the ear by a partially deaf person, which increases the strength of sounds.

hearken /har-k'n/ (also **harken**) • v. (usu. **hearken to**) old use listen.
– ORIGIN Old English.

hearsay • n. information received from other people which may not be true.

hearse /herss/ • n. a vehicle for carrying the coffin at a funeral.
– ORIGIN Old French *herce* 'harrow'.

heart • n. **1** the hollow muscular organ in the chest that pumps the blood around the body. **2** the central or innermost part of something: *the heart of the city.* **3** a person's capacity for feeling love or compassion. **4** mood or feeling: *a change of heart.* **5** courage or enthusiasm. **6** a shape representing a heart with two equal curves meeting at a point at the bottom and a cusp at the top. **7** (**hearts**) one of the four suits in a pack of playing cards.
– PHRASES **after your own heart** sharing your tastes. **at heart** in your real nature. **break someone's heart** make someone deeply sad. **by heart** from memory. **from the** (or **the bottom of your**) **heart** in a very sincere way. **have a heart of gold** have a very kind nature. **have your heart in your mouth** be very alarmed or anxious. **tug** (or **pull**) **at your heartstrings** arouse deep feelings of love or compassion. **take something to heart** be very upset by criticism. **wear your heart on your sleeve** show your feelings openly.
– ORIGIN Old English.

heartache • n. worry or grief.

heart attack • n. a sudden failure of the heart to function normally.

heartbeat • n. a pulsation of the heart.
– PHRASES **a heartbeat away** very close.

heartbreak • n. extreme distress.
– DERIVATIVES **heartbreaking** adj. **heartbroken** adj.

heartburn • n. a form of indigestion felt as a burning sensation in the chest.

hearten • v. make more cheerful or confident.
– DERIVATIVES **heartening** adj.

heart failure • n. severe failure of the heart to function properly.

heartfelt • adj. deeply and strongly felt.

hearth /harth/ • n. the floor or surround of a fireplace.
– ORIGIN Old English.

hearthrug • n. a rug laid in front of a fireplace.

heartily • adv. **1** in a hearty way. **2** very: *I'm heartily sick of them.*

heartland • n. the central or most important part of a country or area.

heartless • adj. feeling no pity for other people; very unkind.
– DERIVATIVES **heartlessly** adv.

heart-rending • adj. very sad or distressing.

heart-searching • n. thorough examination of your feelings and motives.

heart-throb • n. informal a well-known man who is very good-looking.

heart-to-heart • adj. (of a conversation) intimate and personal.

heart-warming • adj. emotionally rewarding or uplifting.

heartwood • n. the dense inner part of a tree trunk, where the hardest wood is to be found.

hearty • adj. (**heartier**, **heartiest**) **1** enthusiastic and friendly. **2** strong and healthy. **3** heartfelt. **4** (of a meal) nourishing and filling.
– DERIVATIVES **heartiness** n.

heat • n. **1** the quality of being hot; high temperature. **2** heat as a form of energy produced by the movement of molecules. **3** a source of heat for cooking. **4** strength of feeling. **5** (**the heat**) informal great pressure to do or achieve something: *the heat is on.* **6** a preliminary round in a race or contest.
• v. **1** make or become hot or warm. **2** (**heat up**) become more intense and exciting. **3** (as adj. **heated**) passionate: *a heated argument.*
– PHRASES **on heat** (of a female mammal) ready for mating.
– DERIVATIVES **heatedly** adv.
– ORIGIN Old English.

heater • n. a device for heating something.

heath • n. **1** esp. Brit. an area of open uncultivated land, usually covered with heather, gorse, and coarse grasses. **2** a shrub with small pink or purple bell-shaped flowers, found on heaths and moors.
– ORIGIN Old English.

heathen /hee-*th*uhn/ • n. derog. a person who does not belong to a widely held religion.
– ORIGIN Old English.

heather • n. a shrub with small purple flowers, found on moors and heaths.
– ORIGIN Old English.

heating • n. equipment used to provide heat.

heat-seeking • adj. (of a missile) able to detect and home in on heat sent out by a target.

heatstroke • n. a feverish condition

caused by being exposed to very high temperatures.

heatwave • n. a period of unusually hot weather.

heave • v. (**heaves, heaving, heaved** or Naut. **hove**) **1** lift or drag with great effort. **2** produce a sigh noisily. **3** informal throw something heavy. **4** rise and fall: *his shoulders heaved.* **5** try to vomit. **6** (**heave to**) Naut. come to a stop. • n. an act of heaving.
– PHRASES **heave in sight** (or **into view**) come into view.
– ORIGIN Old English.

heave-ho • n. (**the heave-ho**) informal dismissal from a position or contest.

heaven • n. **1** (in various religions) the place where God or the gods live and where good people go after death. **2** (**the heavens**) literary the sky. **3** a place or state of extreme happiness: *lying in the sun is my idea of heaven.*
– PHRASES **in seventh heaven** very happy.
– ORIGIN Old English.

heavenly • adj. **1** relating to heaven. **2** relating to the sky. **3** informal wonderful.

heavenly body • n. a planet, star, etc.

heaven-sent • adj. happening unexpectedly and at a very good time.

heaving • adj. Brit. informal very crowded.

heavy • adj. (**heavier, heaviest**) **1** of great weight. **2** thick or dense. **3** of more than the usual size, amount, or force. **4** doing something to excess: *a heavy smoker.* **5** forceful: *a heavy blow.* **6** not delicate or graceful. **7** needing much physical effort. **8** informal serious or difficult to understand. **9** informal involving strong feelings and difficult to deal with: *things were getting heavy.* **10** (of ground) muddy or full of clay. • n. (pl. **heavies**) informal a large, strong man.
– DERIVATIVES **heavily** adv. **heaviness** n.
– ORIGIN Old English.

heavy-duty • adj. designed to withstand a lot of use or wear.

heavy-handed • adj. clumsy, insensitive, or too forceful.

heavy industry • n. the large-scale production of heavy articles and materials such as vehicles or metal.

heavy metal • n. a type of very loud harsh-sounding rock music with a strong beat.

heavy petting • n. sexual activity between two people that stops short of intercourse.

heavyset • adj. (of a person) broad and strongly built.

heavyweight • n. **1** the heaviest weight in boxing and other sports. **2** informal an influential person. • adj. **1** of above-average weight. **2** informal serious or influential: *heavyweight news coverage.*

Hebraic /hi-bray-ik/ • adj. relating to the Hebrew language or people.

Hebrew /hee-broo/ • n. **1** a member of an ancient people living in what is now Israel and Palestine, who established the kingdoms of Israel and Judah. **2** the language of the Hebrews.
– ORIGIN Greek *Hebraios.*

Hebridean /heb-ri-dee-uhn/ • n. a person from the Hebrides off the NW coast of Scotland. • adj. relating to the Hebrides.

heck • exclam. used for emphasis, or to express surprise, annoyance, etc.
– ORIGIN from HELL.

heckle • v. (**heckles, heckling, heckled**) interrupt a public speaker with comments or abuse.
– DERIVATIVES **heckler** n.
– ORIGIN from *hackle* 'flax comb' (from HACKLES).

hectare /hek-tair/ • n. a unit of area, equal to 10,000 square metres (2.471 acres).
– ORIGIN Greek *hekaton* 'hundred'.

hectic • adj. full of frantic activity.
– DERIVATIVES **hectically** adv.
– ORIGIN Greek *hektikos* 'habitual'.

hector /hek-ter/ • v. talk to someone in a bullying way.
– ORIGIN from the Trojan warrior *Hector* in Homer's *Iliad.*

he'd • contr. **1** he had. **2** he would.

hedge • n. a fence formed by bushes growing closely together. • v. (**hedges, hedging, hedged**) **1** surround with a hedge. **2** avoid making a definite statement or decision.
– PHRASES **hedge your bets** avoid committing yourself when faced with a difficult choice.
– ORIGIN Old English.

hedgehog • n. a small mammal with a spiny coat, able to roll itself into a ball for defence.

hedgerow • n. a hedge of wild bushes and trees bordering a field.

hedging • n. **1** the planting or trimming of hedges. **2** bushes planted to form hedges.

hedonism /hee-duh-ni-z'm/ • n. behaviour based on the belief that pleasure is the most important thing in life.
– DERIVATIVES **hedonist** n. **hedonistic** adj.
– ORIGIN Greek *hēdonē* 'pleasure'.

heebie-jeebies • pl. n. (**the heebie-jeebies**) informal a state of nervous fear or anxiety.

heed • v. pay attention to.

– PHRASES **pay** (or **take**) **heed** pay careful attention.
– ORIGIN Old English.

heedless •adj. showing a reckless lack of care or attention.
– DERIVATIVES **heedlessly** adv.

hee-haw •n. the loud, harsh cry of a donkey or mule.

heel[1] •n. **1** the back part of the foot below the ankle. **2** the part of a shoe or boot supporting the heel. **3** the part of the palm of the hand next to the wrist.
•v. renew a heel on a shoe or boot.
– PHRASES **bring someone to heel** bring someone under control. **cool** (or Brit. **kick**) **your heels** be kept waiting. **take to your heels** run away.
– ORIGIN Old English.

heel[2] •v. (of a ship) lean over to one side.
– ORIGIN Germanic.

heft •v. lift or carry something heavy.
– ORIGIN prob. from HEAVE.

hefty •adj. (**heftier, heftiest**) **1** large, heavy, and powerful. **2** (of a number or amount) large or larger than expected.

hegemony /hi-jem-uh-ni, hi-gem-uh-ni/ •n. dominance of one group or state over another.
– ORIGIN Greek *hēgemonia*.

Hegira /hej-i-ruh/ (also **Hejira** or **Hijra** /hij-ruh/) •n. **1** Muhammad's departure from Mecca to Medina in AD 622, marking the consolidation of the first Muslim community. **2** the Muslim era reckoned from this date.
– ORIGIN Arabic, 'departure'.

heifer /hef-fer/ •n. a young cow, especially one that has not had a calf.
– ORIGIN Old English.

height •n. **1** the measurement of someone or something from head to foot or from base to top. **2** the distance of something above ground or sea level. **3** the quality of being tall or high. **4** a high place. **5** the most intense part: *the height of the attack.* **6** an extreme example of something: *the height of folly.*
– ORIGIN Old English.

> ✓ Spell **height** with the e before the i; the ending is **-ght**.

heighten •v. **1** make or become more intense. **2** make higher.

heinous /hay-nuhss, hee-nuhss/ •adj. very wicked: *a heinous crime.*
– ORIGIN Old French *haineus*.

heir /air/ •n. **1** a person who has the legal right to inherit the property or rank of someone else on that person's death. **2** a person who continues someone else's work.
– ORIGIN Old French.

heir apparent •n. (pl. **heirs apparent**)

1 an heir whose rights cannot be taken away by the birth of another heir. **2** a person who is most likely to take the job or role of another.

heiress •n. a female heir.

heirloom •n. a valuable object that has belonged to a family for several generations.
– ORIGIN from HEIR + LOOM[1].

heir presumptive •n. (pl. **heirs presumptive**) an heir whose right may be taken away by the birth of another heir.

heist /hysst/ •n. informal a robbery.
– ORIGIN from HOIST.

held past and past part. of HOLD[1].

helical /hel-i-k'l/ •adj. in the shape of a helix.

helices pl. of HELIX.

helicopter •n. a type of aircraft with one or two sets of horizontally revolving blades.
– ORIGIN French *hélicoptère*.

heliograph /hee-li-uh-grahf/ •n. a device which reflects sunlight in flashes from a movable mirror, used to send signals.
– ORIGIN Greek *hēlios* 'sun'.

heliotrope /heel-i-uh-trohp/ •n. a plant with fragrant purple or blue flowers.
– ORIGIN from Greek *hēlios* 'sun' + *trepein* 'to turn'.

helipad •n. a landing and take-off area for helicopters.

heliport •n. an airport or landing place for helicopters.

helium /hee-li-uhm/ •n. a light colourless gas that does not burn.
– ORIGIN Greek *hēlios* 'sun'.

helix /hee-liks/ •n. (pl. **helices** /hee-li-seez/) an object in the shape of a spiral.
– ORIGIN Greek.

hell •n. **1** (in various religions) a place of evil and suffering where wicked people are sent after death. **2** a state or place of great suffering.
– PHRASES **come hell or high water** whatever difficulties may occur. **hell for leather** as fast as possible. **like hell** informal very fast, much, hard, etc.
– ORIGIN Old English.

he'll •contr. he shall or he will.

hell-bent •adj. determined to achieve something at all costs.

Hellenic /hel-len-ik/ •adj. Greek.
– ORIGIN named after *Hellen*, the mythical ancestor of all the Greeks.

Hellenism •n. **1** the national character or culture of Greece. **2** the study or imitation of ancient Greek culture.

Hellenistic •adj. relating to Greek

culture from 323 BC to 31 BC.

hellfire • n. the fire said to exist in hell.

hellhole • n. a very unpleasant place.

hellish • adj. **1** relating to or like hell.
2 informal very difficult or unpleasant.
– DERIVATIVES **hellishly** adv.

hello (also **hallo** or **hullo**) • exclam. **1** used
as a greeting. **2** Brit. used to express surprise or to attract someone's attention.
– ORIGIN from French *ho* 'ho!' + *là* 'there'.

hellraiser • n. a person who causes
trouble by violent, drunken, or outrageous behaviour.

Hell's Angel • n. a member of a gang of
male motorcycle enthusiasts, originally
known for their lawless behaviour.

helm • n. **1** a tiller or wheel for steering a
ship or boat. **2** (**the helm**) a position of
leadership.
– ORIGIN Old English.

helmet • n. a hard or padded protective
hat.
– ORIGIN Old French, 'little helmet'.

helmsman • n. (pl. **helmsmen**) a person
who steers a boat.

helot /hel-uht/ • n. (in part of ancient
Greece) a member of a class of people
having a status in between slaves and
citizens.
– ORIGIN Greek *Heilōtes*.

help • v. **1** make it easier for someone to
do something. **2** improve a situation or
problem. **3** (**help someone to**) serve
someone with food or drink. **4** (**help
yourself**) take something without
asking for it first. **5** (**can/could not help**)
cannot or could not stop yourself doing.
• n. **1** the action of helping someone. **2** a
person or thing that helps someone.
– DERIVATIVES **helper** n.
– ORIGIN Old English.

helpful • adj. **1** giving or ready to give
help. **2** useful.
– DERIVATIVES **helpfully** adv.
helpfulness n.

helping • n. a portion of food served to
one person at one time.

helpless • adj. **1** unable to defend
yourself or to act without help.
2 uncontrollable: *helpless laughter*.
– DERIVATIVES **helplessly** adv.
helplessness n.

helpline • n. a telephone service
providing help with problems.

helpmate (also **helpmeet**) • n. a helpful
companion.

helter-skelter • adj. & adv. in a hasty and
confused or disorganized way. • n. Brit. a
tall slide winding around a tower at a
fair.

hem • n. the edge of a piece of cloth or
clothing which has been turned under

and sewn. • v. (**hems, hemming,
hemmed**) **1** turn under and sew the
edge of. **2** (**hem someone/thing in**)
surround someone or something and
restrict their space or movement.
– ORIGIN Old English.

he-man • n. informal a very well-built,
masculine man.

hematite etc. • n. US = **HAEMATITE** etc.

hemi- • prefix half: *hemisphere*.
– ORIGIN Greek *hēmi-*.

hemisphere • n. **1** a half of a sphere. **2** a
half of the earth.
– DERIVATIVES **hemispherical** adj.

hemline • n. the level of the lower edge
of a garment such as a skirt or coat.

hemlock • n. **1** a very poisonous plant
with fern-like leaves and small white
flowers. **2** a poison obtained from
hemlock.
– ORIGIN Old English.

hemp • n. **1** the cannabis plant. **2** the
fibre of this plant, used to make rope,
strong fabrics, paper, etc. **3** the drug
cannabis.
– ORIGIN Old English.

hen • n. **1** a female bird, especially of a
domestic fowl. **2** (**hens**) domestic fowls
of either sex.
– ORIGIN Old English.

hence • adv. **1** for this reason. **2** from
now.
– ORIGIN Old English.

henceforth (also **henceforward**)
• adv. from this or that time on.

henchman • n. (pl. **henchmen**) esp. derog. a
faithful follower or assistant.
– ORIGIN from Old English, 'male horse' +
MAN.

henge /henj/ • n. a prehistoric monument consisting of a circle of stone or
wooden uprights.
– ORIGIN from *Stonehenge*, a monument
of this type in Wiltshire.

henna • n. a reddish-brown dye made
from the powdered leaves of a tropical
shrub, used especially to colour the hair.
• v. (**hennas, hennaing, hennaed**) dye
the hair with henna.
– ORIGIN Arabic.

hen night • n. Brit. informal a celebration
held for a woman who is about to get
married, attended only by women.

hen party • n. informal a social gathering
for women only.

henpecked • adj. (of a man) continually
nagged or criticized by his wife.

henry • n. (pl. **henries** or **henrys**) Physics
the SI unit of inductance.
– ORIGIN named after the American
physicist Joseph *Henry* .

h

hepatic /hi-**pat**-ik/ • adj. relating to the liver.
– ORIGIN Greek *hēpatikos*.

hepatitis /hep-uh-**ty**-tiss/ • n. a disease in which the liver becomes inflamed, mainly transmitted by viruses in blood or food.

hepta- • comb. form seven: *heptathlon*.
– ORIGIN Greek.

heptagon /**hep**-tuh-guhn/ • n. a plane figure with seven straight sides and angles.

heptathlon /hep-**tath**-lon/ • n. an athletic contest for women that consists of seven separate events.
– DERIVATIVES **heptathlete** n.
– ORIGIN from **HEPTA-** + Greek *athlon* 'contest'.

her • pron. (third person sing.) **1** used as the object of a verb or preposition to refer to a female person or animal previously mentioned. **2** referring to a ship, country, or other thing regarded as female. • possess. det. **1** belonging to or associated with a female person or animal previously mentioned. **2** (**Her**) used in titles.
– ORIGIN Old English.

herald • n. **1** (in the UK) an official who oversees matters concerning state ceremonies and coats of arms. **2** hist. a person who carried official messages, made announcements, and oversaw tournaments. **3** a sign that something is about to happen. • v. **1** signal the future arrival of. **2** describe in enthusiastic terms.
– ORIGIN Old French *herault*.

heraldic /hi-**ral**-dik/ • adj. relating to heraldry.

heraldry • n. the system by which coats of arms are drawn up and controlled.

herb • n. **1** a plant whose leaves, seeds, or flowers are used for flavouring food or in medicine. **2** Bot. a seed-bearing plant which does not have a woody stem and dies down to the ground after flowering.
– ORIGIN Latin *herba*.

herbaceous /her-**bay**-shuhss/ • adj. relating to herbs (in the botanical sense).

herbaceous border • n. a garden border containing mainly flowering plants which live for several years.

herbage • n. herbaceous plants.

herbal • adj. relating to or made from herbs. • n. a book that describes herbs and their uses.

herbalism • n. the study or practice of using plants in medicine and cookery.
– DERIVATIVES **herbalist** n.

herbarium /her-**bair**-i-uhm/ • n. (pl. **herbaria** /her-**bair**-i-uh/) a collection of dried plants organized in a systematic way.

herbicide /**her**-bi-syd/ • n. a substance used to destroy unwanted plants.

herbivore /**her**-bi-vor/ • n. an animal that feeds on plants.
– DERIVATIVES **herbivorous** /her-**biv**-uh-ruhss/ adj.

Herculean /her-kyuu-**lee**-uhn/ • adj. requiring great strength or effort.
– ORIGIN named after *Hercules*, a hero of Roman and Greek myth.

herd • n. **1** a large group of animals that live or are kept together. **2** derog. a large group of people. • v. **1** move in a large group. **2** look after livestock.
– ORIGIN Old English.

herdsman • n. (pl. **herdsmen**) the owner or keeper of a herd of animals.

here • adv. **1** in, at, or to this place, position, or point. **2** (usu. **here is/are**) used when introducing or handing over something or someone.
– PHRASES **here and there** in various places. **neither here nor there** of no importance.
– ORIGIN Old English.

hereabouts (also **hereabout**) • adv. near this place.

hereafter • adv. formal **1** from now on or at some time in the future. **2** after death. • n. (**the hereafter**) life after death.

hereby • adv. formal as a result of this.

hereditary /hi-**red**-i-tuh-ri/ • adj. **1** relating to the inheriting of something. **2** (of a characteristic or disease) able to be passed on from parents to their offspring.

heredity /hi-**red**-i-ti/ • n. **1** the passing on of physical or mental characteristics from one generation to another. **2** the inheriting of a title, office, or right.
– ORIGIN Latin *hereditas* 'status of an heir'.

herein • adv. formal in this document, book, or matter.

heresy /**he**-ri-si/ • n. (pl. **heresies**) **1** belief or opinion which goes against traditional religious doctrine. **2** opinion which differs greatly from what is generally accepted.
– ORIGIN Greek *hairesis* 'choice, sect'.

heretic /**he**-ri-tik/ • n. a person who is guilty of heresy.
– DERIVATIVES **heretical** /hi-**ret**-i-k'l/ adj.

hereto • adv. formal to this matter or document.

heretofore • adv. formal before now.

hereupon • adv. old use after or as a result of this.

herewith • adv. formal with this letter or document.

heritable • adj. able to be inherited.

heritage • n. **1** property that is or may be inherited. **2** valued things such as historic buildings that have been passed down from previous generations.
– ORIGIN Old French.

hermaphrodite /her-maf-ruh-dyt/ • n. **1** a person or animal with both male and female sex organs or characteristics. **2** Bot. a plant having stamens and pistils in the same flower.
– DERIVATIVES **hermaphroditic** adj.
– ORIGIN Greek *hermaphroditos*.

hermetic /her-met-ik/ • adj. (of a seal or closure) complete and airtight.
– DERIVATIVES **hermetically** adv.
– ORIGIN from Latin *Hermes Trismegistus*, the mythical founder of alchemy and astrology.

hermit • n. **1** a person who lives alone for religious reasons. **2** a person who prefers to live alone.
– ORIGIN Greek *erēmitēs*.

hermitage • n. the home of a hermit.

hermit crab • n. a crab with a soft abdomen which lives in shells cast off by other shellfish.

hernia /her-ni-uh/ • n. (pl. **hernias**) a condition in which part of an organ protrudes through the wall of the cavity containing it.
– ORIGIN Latin.

hero • n. (pl. **heroes**) **1** a person who is admired for their courage or outstanding achievements. **2** the chief male character in a book, play, or film.
– ORIGIN Greek *hērōs*.

heroic • adj. **1** very brave. **2** grand or ambitious in scale or planning.
• n. (**heroics**) brave or dramatic behaviour or talk.
– DERIVATIVES **heroically** adv.

heroin • n. a highly addictive painkilling drug obtained from morphine.
– ORIGIN German.

heroine • n. **1** a woman admired for her courage or outstanding achievements. **2** the chief female character in a book, play, or film.

heroism • n. great bravery.

heron • n. a large fish-eating bird with long legs, a long neck, and a long pointed bill.
– ORIGIN Old French.

hero worship • n. extreme admiration for someone. • v. (**hero-worship**) greatly admire.

herpes /her-peez/ • n. a disease caused by a virus, affecting the skin or the nervous system.

– ORIGIN Greek *herpēs* 'shingles'.

Herr /hair/ • n. a form of address for a German-speaking man.
– ORIGIN German *hërro* 'more exalted'.

herring • n. a silvery edible fish which is found in shoals in coastal waters.
– ORIGIN Old English.

herringbone • n. a zigzag pattern consisting of columns of short parallel lines, with all the lines in one column sloping one way and all the lines in the next column sloping the other way.

herring gull • n. a common northern gull with grey black-tipped wings.

hers • possess. pron. used to refer to a thing or things belonging to or associated with a female person or animal previously mentioned.

 No apostrophe: **hers** not *her's*.

herself • pron. (third person sing.) **1** used as the object of a verb or preposition to refer to a female person or animal previously mentioned as the subject of the clause. **2** she or her personally.

Herts. /harts/ • abbrev. Hertfordshire.

hertz /herts/ • n. (pl. **hertz**) the SI unit of frequency, equal to one cycle per second.
– ORIGIN named after the German physicist H. R. *Hertz*.

he's • contr. **1** he is. **2** he has.

hesitant • adj. slow to act or speak as a result of indecision or reluctance.
– DERIVATIVES **hesitancy** n. **hesitantly** adv.

hesitate • v. (**hesitates, hesitating, hesitated**) **1** pause indecisively. **2** be reluctant to do something.
– DERIVATIVES **hesitation** n.
– ORIGIN Latin *haesitare* 'stick fast'.

hessian • n. esp. Brit. a strong, coarse fabric made from hemp or jute.
– ORIGIN from the German state of *Hesse*.

hetero- • comb. form different: *heterosexual*.
– ORIGIN Greek *heteros* 'other'.

heterodox /het-uh-ruh-doks/ • adj. not following traditional standards or beliefs.
– DERIVATIVES **heterodoxy** n.
– ORIGIN Greek *doxa* 'opinion'.

heterogeneous /het-uh-ruh-jee-ni-uhss/ • adj. varied: *a heterogeneous collection*.
– DERIVATIVES **heterogeneity** /het-uh-ruh-juh-nee-i-ti/ n.
– ORIGIN Greek *genos* 'a kind'.

heterosexual • adj. **1** sexually attracted to the opposite sex. **2** (of a sexual relationship) between a man and a

woman. •n. a heterosexual person.
– DERIVATIVES **heterosexuality** n.
heterosexually adv.

het up •adj. informal angry and agitated.
– ORIGIN from dialect *het* 'heated, hot'.

heuristic /hyuu-uh-**riss**-tik/
•adj. allowing a person to discover or
learn something for themselves.
– ORIGIN Greek *heuriskein* 'to find'.

hew /hyoo/ •v. (**hews, hewing, hewed**,
past part. **hewn** or **hewed**) **1** chop or cut
wood, coal, etc. with an axe or other
tool. **2** (**be hewn**) be cut or formed from
a hard material: *a seat hewn out of a fallen
tree trunk.*
– ORIGIN Old English.

hex N. Amer. •v. cast a spell on. •n. a magic
spell.
– ORIGIN German *hexen*.

hexa- (also **hex-** before a vowel) •comb.
form six: *hexagon*.
– ORIGIN Greek *hex*.

hexagon /hek-suh-guhn/ •n. a plane
figure with six straight sides and angles.
– DERIVATIVES **hexagonal** adj.

hexagram •n. a six-pointed star formed
by two intersecting equilateral
triangles.

hexameter /hek-**sam**-i-ter/ •n. a line of
verse made up of six metrical feet.

hey •exclam. used to attract attention or
to express surprise, interest, etc.

heyday •n. (**someone's heyday**) the
period of someone's greatest success,
activity, or energy.

HF •abbrev. Physics high frequency.

Hf •symb. the chemical element hafnium.

Hg •symb. the chemical element mercury.
– ORIGIN from Latin *hydrargyrum*.

HGV •abbrev. Brit. heavy goods vehicle.

hi •exclam. informal used as a friendly
greeting.

hiatus /hy-**ay**-tuhss/ •n. (pl. **hiatuses**) a
pause or gap in a series or sequence.
– ORIGIN Latin, 'gaping'.

hibernate •v. (**hibernates, hibernating**,
hibernated) (of an animal) spend the
winter in a state like deep sleep.
– DERIVATIVES **hibernation** n.
– ORIGIN Latin *hibernare*.

Hibernian /hy-**ber**-ni-uhn/ •adj. Irish.
•n. an Irish person.
– ORIGIN Latin *Hibernia*.

hibiscus /hi-**biss**-kuhss/ •n. a plant with
large brightly coloured flowers.
– ORIGIN Greek *hibiskos* 'marsh mallow'.

hiccup (also **hiccough** /hik-kup/) •n. **1** a
gulping sound in the throat caused by an
involuntary spasm of the diaphragm. **2** a
minor setback. •v. (**hiccups, hiccuping**,
hiccuped; also **hiccoughs, hiccoughing**,

hiccoughed) make the sound of a hiccup
or hiccups.

hick •n. informal, esp. N. Amer. an unsophisticated person from the country.
– ORIGIN informal form of the man's
name *Richard*.

hickory •n. a tree found chiefly in North
America, having tough, heavy wood and
edible nuts.
– ORIGIN from an American Indian
language.

hid past of HIDE¹.

hidden past part. of HIDE¹.

hidden agenda •n. a secret motive or
plan.

hide¹ •v. (**hides, hiding, hid**; past part.
hidden) **1** put or keep out of sight.
2 conceal yourself. **3** keep secret. •n. Brit.
a concealed shelter used to watch wild
animals or birds at close quarters.
– PHRASES **hide your light under a bushel**
keep quiet about your talents. [ORIGIN
with biblical reference to the Gospel of
Matthew, chapter 15.]
– ORIGIN Old English.

hide² •n. the skin of an animal.
– ORIGIN Old English.

hideaway •n. a hiding place.

hidebound •adj. unwilling or unable to
abandon old-fashioned ideas or customs
in favour of new ways of thinking.

hideous •adj. **1** very ugly. **2** very
unpleasant.
– DERIVATIVES **hideously** adv.
hideousness n.
– ORIGIN Old French *hidos, hideus*.

hideout •n. a hiding place.

hiding¹ •n. **1** a physical beating. **2** informal
a severe defeat.
– PHRASES **be on a hiding to nothing** Brit.
be unlikely to succeed.
– ORIGIN from HIDE².

hiding² •n. the action of hiding or the
state of being hidden: *he had gone into
hiding.*

hie /hi/ •v. (**hies, hieing** or **hying, hied**)
old use go quickly.
– ORIGIN Old English, 'strive, pant'.

hierarchical /hy-uh-**rar**-ki-k'l/
•adj. arranged in order of rank.
– DERIVATIVES **hierarchically** adv.

hierarchy /hy-uh-**rar**-ki/ •n. (pl.
hierarchies) **1** a system in which people
are ranked one above the other
according to status or authority. **2** a
classification of things according to
their relative importance.
– ORIGIN Greek *hierarkhia*.

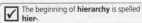 The beginning of **hierarchy** is spelled
hier-.

hieroglyph /hy-ruh-glif/ • n. a picture of an object representing a word, syllable, or sound, especially as used in the ancient Egyptian writing system.

hieroglyphic • n. (**hieroglyphics**) writing consisting of hieroglyphs. • adj. relating to hieroglyphs.
– ORIGIN Greek *hierogluphikos*.

hi-fi informal • adj. relating to high fidelity sound. • n. (pl. **hi-fis**) a set of equipment for reproducing high-fidelity sound.

higgledy-piggledy • adv. & adj. in confusion or disorder.
– ORIGIN prob. with reference to the irregular herding together of pigs.

high • adj. **1** extending far upwards: *a high mountain.* **2** of a specified height. **3** far above ground or sea level. **4** large in amount, value, size, or intensity: *a high temperature.* **5** (of a period or movement) at its peak: *high summer.* **6** great in status; important. **7** culturally or morally superior. **8** (of a sound or note) not deep or low. **9** informal under the influence of drugs or alcohol. **10** (of food) strong-smelling because beginning to go bad. • n. **1** a high point, level, or figure. **2** an area of high atmospheric pressure. **3** informal a state of high spirits. • adv. **1** at or to a high or specified level or position: *the sculpture stood about five feet high.* **2** (of a sound) at or to a high pitch.
– PHRASES **high and dry 1** stranded by the sea as it retreats. **2** in a difficult position. **high and low** in many different places. **high and mighty** informal arrogant. **on your high horse** informal behaving arrogantly or pompously.
– ORIGIN Old English.

highball • n. N. Amer. a long drink consisting of a spirit and a mixer such as soda, served with ice.

highbrow • adj. usu. derog. intellectual or refined in taste.

high chair • n. a small long-legged chair for an infant, fitted with a tray and used at mealtimes.

High Church • n. a tradition within the Anglican Church which gives an important place to ritual and the authority of bishops and priests.

high command • n. the commander-in-chief and senior staff of an army, navy, or air force.

high commission • n. an embassy of one Commonwealth country in another.
– DERIVATIVES **high commissioner** n.

high court • n. a supreme court of justice.

Higher • n. (in Scotland) the more advanced of the two main levels of the Scottish Certificate of Education.

higher education • n. education to degree level or equivalent, provided at universities or colleges.

highest common factor • n. Math. the highest number that can be divided exactly into each of two or more numbers.

high explosive • n. a powerful chemical explosive of the kind used in shells and bombs.

highfalutin /hy-fuh-loo-tin/
• adj. informal grand or self-important in a pompous or pretentious way.
– ORIGIN perh. from HIGH + *fluting*.

high fidelity • n. the reproduction of sound with little distortion.

high five • n. informal, esp. N. Amer. a gesture of celebration or greeting in which two people slap each other's palms with their arms raised.

high-flown • adj. grand-sounding: *high-flown prose.*

high-flyer (also **high-flier**) • n. a very successful person.

high frequency • n. (in radio) a frequency of 3–30 megahertz.

high-handed • adj. using authority without considering the feelings of other people.

high jinks • pl. n. high-spirited fun.

high jump • n. (**the high jump**) an athletic event in which competitors jump as high as possible over a bar which is raised after each round.

highland • n. (also **highlands**) **1** an area of high or mountainous land. **2** (**the Highlands**) the mountainous northern part of Scotland.
– DERIVATIVES **highlander** n.

Highland fling • n. a lively solo Scottish dance consisting of a series of complex steps.

high-level • adj. **1** involving senior people. **2** (of a computer programming language) resembling an existing language such as English, making it relatively easy to use.

high life • n. an extravagant social life as enjoyed by wealthy people.

highlight • n. **1** an outstanding part of an event or period of time. **2** a bright area in a painting, picture, or design. **3** (**highlights**) bright tints in the hair, produced by bleaching or dyeing. • v. **1** draw attention to. **2** mark with a highlighter. **3** create highlights in hair.

highlighter • n. **1** a broad marker pen used to mark transparent fluorescent colour on a part of a document or plan. **2** a powder or cream used to emphasize facial features.

h

highly • adv. **1** to a high degree or level. **2** favourably.

highly strung • adj. Brit. very nervous and easily upset.

high-minded • adj. having strong moral principles.

Highness • n. (**His, Her, Your Highness**) a title given to a person of royal rank.

high-octane • adj. **1** (of petrol) having a high octane number and therefore allowing an engine to run smoothly. **2** powerful or dynamic: *a high-octane career.*

high-powered • adj. informal (of a person) dynamic and forceful.

high priest • n. **1** a chief priest of a non-Christian religion. **2** (also **high priestess**) the leader of a cult or movement.

high-rise • adj. (of a building) having many storeys.

high road • n. a main road.

high school • n. **1** N. Amer. a secondary school. **2** (in the UK except Scotland) a grammar school or independent secondary school.

high seas • pl. n. (**the high seas**) the areas of the sea that are not under the control of any one country.

high season • n. esp. Brit. the most popular time of year for a holiday, when prices are highest.

high sheriff • n. see SHERIFF.

high spirits • pl. n. lively and cheerful behaviour or mood.
– DERIVATIVES **high-spirited** adj.

high spot • n. the most enjoyable part of an experience or period of time.

high street • n. Brit. the main street of a town. • adj. (**high-street**) catering to the needs of the ordinary public: *high-street fashion.*

hightail • v. informal, esp. N. Amer. move or travel fast.

high tea • n. Brit. a meal eaten in the late afternoon or early evening.

high-tech (also **hi-tech**) • adj. using high technology.

high technology • n. advanced technology.

high-tensile • adj. (of metal) very strong under tension.

high tide (also **high water**) • n. the time when the sea is closest to the land.

high treason • n. see TREASON.

high-water mark • n. the level reached by the sea at high tide, or by a lake or river during a flood.

highway • n. **1** esp. N. Amer. a main road. **2** a public road.

highwayman • n. (pl. **highwaymen**) hist. a man who held up and robbed travellers.

high wire • n. a high tightrope.

hijack • v. **1** illegally seize control of an aircraft, ship, etc. while it is travelling somewhere. **2** take over something and use it for a different purpose. • n. an instance of hijacking.
– DERIVATIVES **hijacker** n.

Hijra • n. var. of HEGIRA.

hike • n. **1** a long walk or walking tour. **2** a sharp increase. • v. (**hikes, hiking, hiked**) **1** go on a hike. **2** pull or lift clothing. **3** increase a price sharply.
– DERIVATIVES **hiker** n.

hilarious /hi-lair-i-uhss/ • adj. very funny.
– DERIVATIVES **hilariously** adv.
– ORIGIN Greek *hilaros* 'cheerful'.

hilarity /hi-la-ri-ti/ • n. a state of great amusement causing loud laughter.

hill • n. a naturally raised area of land, not as high as a mountain.
– PHRASES **over the hill** informal old and past your best.
– ORIGIN Old English.

hillbilly • n. (pl. **hillbillies**) N. Amer. informal, esp. derog. an unsophisticated country person.
– ORIGIN from HILL + *Billy* (informal form of the man's name *William*).

hillock • n. a small hill or mound.

hillwalking • n. the pastime of walking in hilly country.

hilly • adj. (**hillier, hilliest**) having many hills.

hilt • n. the handle of a sword, dagger, or knife.
– PHRASES **to the hilt** completely.
– ORIGIN Old English.

him • pron. (third person sing.) used as the object of a verb or preposition to refer to a male person or animal previously mentioned.
– ORIGIN Old English.

himself • pron. (third person sing.) **1** used as the object of a verb or preposition to refer to a male person or animal previously mentioned as the subject of the clause. **2** he or him personally.

hind[1] • adj. situated at the back.
– ORIGIN perh. from Old English.

hind[2] • n. a female deer.
– ORIGIN Old English.

hinder /hin-der/ • v. (**hinders, hindering, hindered**) delay or obstruct.
– ORIGIN Old English, 'damage'.

Hindi /hin-di/ • n. a language of northern India derived from Sanskrit.
– ORIGIN Urdu.

hindmost • adj. furthest back.

hindquarters • pl. n. the hind legs and

adjoining parts of a four-legged animal.

hindrance /hin-druhnss/ •n. a thing that delays or obstructs someone or something.

> ☑ Although **hindrance** is related to *hinder* there is no **e** in the middle.

hindsight •n. understanding of a situation or event after it has happened.

Hindu /hin-doo/ •n. (pl. **Hindus**) a follower of Hinduism. •adj. relating to Hinduism.
– ORIGIN Urdu.

Hinduism •n. a major religious and cultural tradition of the Indian subcontinent, including belief in reincarnation and the worship of a large number of gods and goddesses.

Hindustani /hin-duu-stah-ni/ •n. a group of languages and dialects spoken in northern India which includes Hindi and Urdu.

hinge •n. a movable joint or mechanism by which a door, gate, or lid opens and closes or which connects linked objects. •v. (**hinges**, **hingeing** or **hinging**, **hinged**) 1 attach or join with a hinge. 2 (**hinge on**) depend entirely on.
– ORIGIN from HANG.

hint •n. 1 a slight or indirect suggestion. 2 a very small trace. 3 a small item of practical information. •v. 1 suggest indirectly. 2 (**hint at**) be a slight suggestion of.
– ORIGIN prob. from Old English, 'grasp'.

hinterland /hin-ter-land/ •n. 1 the remote areas of a country, away from the coast and major rivers. 2 the area around a major town or port.
– ORIGIN German.

hip¹ •n. a projection formed by the pelvis and upper thigh bone on each side of the body.
– ORIGIN Old English.

hip² •n. the fruit of a rose.
– ORIGIN Old English.

hip³ •adj. (**hipper**, **hippest**) informal fashionable.
– DERIVATIVES **hipness** n.

hip bath •n. a bath shaped to sit rather than lie down in.

hip bone •n. a large bone forming the main part of the pelvis on each side of the body.

hip flask •n. a small flask for spirits, carried in a hip pocket.

hip hop •n. a style of pop music of US black and Hispanic origin, featuring rap with an electronic backing.
– ORIGIN prob. from HIP³.

hippie •n. var. of HIPPY.

hippo •n. (pl. **hippo** or **hippos**) informal a hippopotamus.

Hippocratic oath /hip-puh-krat-ik/ •n. an oath (formerly taken by medical doctors) to observe a code of professional behaviour.
– ORIGIN from the ancient Greek physician *Hippocrates*.

hippodrome /hip-puh-drohm/ •n. 1 a theatre or concert hall. 2 (in ancient Greece or Rome) a course for chariot or horse races.
– ORIGIN Greek *hippodromos*.

hippopotamus /hip-puh-pot-uh-muhss/ •n. (pl. **hippopotamuses** or **hippopotami** /hip-puh-pot-uh-my/) a large African mammal with a thick skin and massive jaws, living partly on land and partly in water.
– ORIGIN from Greek *hippos ho potamios* 'river horse'.

hippy (also **hippie**) •n. (pl. **hippies**) (especially in the 1960s) a young person who rejects traditional social values and dresses unconventionally.
– ORIGIN from HIP³.

hipsters •pl. n. Brit. trousers cut to fit and fasten at the hips rather than the waist.
– ORIGIN from HIP¹.

hire •v. (**hires**, **hiring**, **hired**) 1 esp. Brit. pay to be allowed to use something temporarily. 2 (**hire something out**) allow something to be used temporarily in return for payment. 3 take someone on as an employee. 4 temporarily employ someone to do a particular job. •n. the action of hiring.
– PHRASES **for hire** available to be hired.
– ORIGIN Old English.

hireling •n. esp. derog. a person who is willing to do any kind of work provided they are paid.

hire purchase •n. Brit. a system by which someone pays for a thing in regular instalments while having the use of it.

hirsute /her-syoot/ •adj. hairy.
– ORIGIN Latin *hirsutus*.

his •possess. det. 1 belonging to or associated with a male person or animal previously mentioned. 2 (**His**) used in titles. •possess. pron. used to refer to a thing belonging to or associated with a male person or animal previously mentioned.
– ORIGIN Old English.

Hispanic /hi-span-ik/ •adj. relating to Spain or the Spanish-speaking countries of Central and South America. •n. a Spanish-speaking person living in the US.
– ORIGIN Latin *Hispanicus*.

hiss •v. 1 make a sharp sound like that

made when pronouncing the letter *s*, often as a sign of disapproval or mockery. **2** whisper something in an urgent or angry way. •n. a hissing sound.

histamine /hiss-tuh-meen/ •n. a substance which is released by cells in response to injury and in allergic reactions.
– ORIGIN from Greek *histos* 'web' and *amine* (a compound containing an amino group).

histology /hi-stol-uh-ji/ •n. the branch of biology concerned with the microscopic structure of tissues.
– DERIVATIVES **histological** adj. **histologist** n.
– ORIGIN Greek *histos* 'web'.

historian •n. an expert in history.

historic •adj. **1** famous or important in history, or likely to be so in the future: *a historic occasion*. **2** Grammar (of a tense) used in describing past events.

> USAGE: **Historic** and **historical** do not have the same meaning. **Historic** means 'famous or important in history' (*a historic occasion*), whereas **historical** chiefly means 'relating to history' (*historical evidence*).

historical •adj. **1** relating to history. **2** belonging to or set in the past. **3** (of the study of a subject) looking at its development over a period.
– DERIVATIVES **historically** adv.

historicism •n. **1** the theory that social and cultural developments are determined by history. **2** excessive regard for former styles of art and architecture.
– DERIVATIVES **historicist** n.

historiography /hi-sto-ri-og-ruh-fi/ •n. the study of the writing of history and of written histories.
– DERIVATIVES **historiographer** n. **historiographical** adj.

history •n. (pl. **histories**) **1** the study of past events. **2** the past considered as a whole. **3** the past events connected with someone or something. **4** a continuous record of past events or trends.
– ORIGIN Greek *historia*.

histrionic /hiss-tri-on-ik/ •adj. excessively dramatic. •n. (**histrionics**) exaggerated behaviour intended to attract attention.
– DERIVATIVES **histrionically** adv.
– ORIGIN Latin *histrionicus*.

hit •v. (**hits, hitting, hit**) **1** strike with the hand or a tool, bat, etc. **2** (of something moving) come into contact with someone or something quickly and forcefully. **3** strike a target. **4** cause harm or distress to. **5** (**hit out**) criticize or attack strongly. **6** be suddenly

realized by: *it hit me that I was successful.* **7** (**hit on**) suddenly discover or think of.
•n. **1** an instance of hitting or being hit. **2** a successful film, pop record, etc. **3** Computing an instance of picking out an item of data which matches the requirements of a search. **4** an instance of a particular website being accessed by a user. **5** informal, esp. N. Amer. a murder carried out by a criminal organization. **6** informal a dose of an addictive drug.
– PHRASES **hit-and-miss** done or occurring at random. **hit-and-run** (of a road accident) from which the driver responsible leaves rapidly without helping the other people involved. **hit someone below the belt** Boxing give an opponent an illegal low blow. **2** behave unfairly towards someone. **hit it off** informal be naturally well suited. **hit the nail on the head** be exactly right.
– DERIVATIVES **hitter** n.
– ORIGIN Old Norse, 'come upon'.

hitch •v. **1** move something into a different position with a jerk. **2** fasten with a rope. **3** informal travel or obtain a lift by hitchhiking. •n. **1** a temporary difficulty. **2** a temporary knot used to fasten one thing to another.
– PHRASES **get hitched** informal get married.

hitchhike •v. travel by getting free lifts in passing vehicles.
– DERIVATIVES **hitchhiker** n.

hither •adv. old use to or towards this place.
– PHRASES **hither and thither** (also **hither and yon**) to and fro.
– ORIGIN Old English.

hitherto •adv. until this point in time.

hit list •n. a list of people to be killed for criminal or political reasons.

hit man •n. informal a person paid to kill someone.

HIV •abbrev. human immunodeficiency virus (the virus causing Aids).

hive •n. **1** a beehive. **2** a place full of people working hard.
– PHRASES **hive something off** esp. Brit. transfer part of a business to new ownership.
– ORIGIN Old English.

hives •pl. n. a rash of round, red, itchy weals on the skin, caused by an allergy.

HK •abbrev. Hong Kong.

HM •abbrev. (in the UK) Her or His Majesty or Majesty's.

HMS •abbrev. Her or His Majesty's Ship.

HMSO •abbrev. (in the UK) Her or His Majesty's Stationery Office, which publishes government documents.

HNC •abbrev. (in the UK) Higher National Certificate.

HND • abbrev. (in the UK) Higher National Diploma.

Ho • symb. the chemical element holmium.

hoard • n. a secret store of something valuable. • v. collect something over time and store it away.
– DERIVATIVES **hoarder** n.
– ORIGIN Old English.

> USAGE: **Hoard** and **horde** are sometimes confused. A **hoard** is 'a secret store' (*a hoard of treasure*), while **horde** is a word showing disapproval when talking about 'a large group of people' (*hordes of greedy shareholders*).

hoarding • n. Brit. a large board used to display advertisements.
– ORIGIN prob. from Old French *hourd*.

hoar frost • n. a greyish-white feathery deposit of frost.
– ORIGIN from HOARY.

hoarse • adj. (of a voice) rough and harsh.
– DERIVATIVES **hoarsely** adv. **hoarseness** n.
– ORIGIN Old English.

hoary • adj. (**hoarier, hoariest**) **1** having grey hair. **2** old and unoriginal: *a hoary old adage*.
– ORIGIN Old English.

hoax • n. a humorous or cruel trick. • v. deceive with a hoax.
– DERIVATIVES **hoaxer** n.
– ORIGIN prob. from HOCUS-POCUS.

hob • n. Brit. the flat top part of a cooker, with hotplates or burners.
– ORIGIN from HUB.

hobble • v. (**hobbles, hobbling, hobbled**) **1** walk with difficulty or painfully. **2** strap together the legs of a horse to stop it wandering away.
– ORIGIN prob. from Dutch *hobbelen* 'rock from side to side'.

hobby • n. (pl. **hobbies**) a leisure activity that a person does regularly for pleasure.
– ORIGIN from an informal form of the man's name *Robin*.

hobby horse • n. **1** a child's toy consisting of a stick with a model of a horse's head at one end. **2** a rocking horse. **3** a person's favourite topic of conversation.

hobbyist • n. a person with a particular hobby.

hobgoblin • n. a mischievous imp.
– ORIGIN from *hob*, informal form of *Robin* and *Robert*, used in the sense 'country fellow'.

hobnail • n. a short heavy-headed nail used to strengthen the soles of boots.
– DERIVATIVES **hobnailed** adj.

hobnob • v. (**hobnobs, hobnobbing, hobnobbed**) informal spend time socially

with rich or important people.
– ORIGIN from former *hob or nob*, or *hob and nob*, prob. meaning 'give and take'.

hobo • n. (pl. **hoboes** or **hobos**) N. Amer. a homeless person.

Hobson's choice • n. a choice of taking what is offered or nothing at all.
– ORIGIN named after Thomas *Hobson*, who hired out horses, making the customer take the one nearest the door or none at all.

hock[1] • n. the joint in the back leg of a four-legged animal, between the knee and the fetlock.
– ORIGIN Old English, 'heel'.

hock[2] • n. Brit. a dry white wine from the German Rhineland.
– ORIGIN from German *Hochheimer Wein* 'wine from Hochheim'.

hock[3] • v. informal pawn an object.
– PHRASES **in hock 1** having been pawned. **2** in debt.
– ORIGIN Dutch *hok* 'prison, debt'.

hockey /hok-ki/ • n. a game played between two teams of eleven players each, using hooked sticks to drive a small hard ball towards a goal.

hocus-pocus • n. meaningless talk used to deceive people.
– ORIGIN from *hax pax max Deus adimax*, a mock Latin phrase used by magicians.

hod • n. **1** a builder's V-shaped open trough attached to a short pole, used for carrying bricks. **2** a metal container for storing coal.
– ORIGIN Old French *hotte* 'pannier'.

hodgepodge • n. N. Amer. = HOTCHPOTCH.

Hodgkin's disease • n. a cancerous disease causing enlargement of the lymph nodes, liver, and spleen.
– ORIGIN named after the English physician Thomas *Hodgkin*.

hoe • n. a long-handled gardening tool with a thin metal blade. • v. (**hoes, hoeing, hoed**) use a hoe to turn earth or cut through weeds.
– ORIGIN Old French *houe*.

hog • n. a castrated male pig reared for slaughter. • v. (**hogs, hogging, hogged**) informal take or hoard selfishly.
– PHRASES **go the whole hog** informal do something fully.
– DERIVATIVES **hogger** n. **hoggish** adj.
– ORIGIN Old English.

Hogmanay /hog-muh-nay/ • n. (in Scotland) New Year's Eve.
– ORIGIN perh. from Old French *aguillanneuf* 'last day of the year'.

hogshead • n. **1** a large cask. **2** a measure of liquid volume for wine or beer.

hogwash • n. informal nonsense.

– ORIGIN first meaning 'kitchen scraps for pigs'.

hoick • v. Brit. informal lift or pull with a jerk.
– ORIGIN perh. from HIKE.

hoi polloi /hoy puh-loy/ • pl. n. derog. the ordinary people.
– ORIGIN Greek, 'the many'.

hoist • v. 1 raise by means of ropes and pulleys. 2 haul or lift up. • n. 1 an act of hoisting. 2 a device for hoisting.
– ORIGIN prob. from Dutch *hijsen* or German *hiesen*.

hoity-toity • adj. snobbish; haughty.
– ORIGIN from former *hoit* 'romp'.

hokum /hoh-kuhm/ • n. informal 1 nonsense. 2 unoriginal or sentimental material in a film, book, etc.

hold¹ • v. (**holds, holding, held**) 1 grasp, carry, or support. 2 contain or be able to contain. 3 have, own, or occupy. 4 keep or detain someone. 5 stay or keep at a certain level. 6 (**hold someone to**) cause someone to keep to a promise. 7 continue to follow a course. 8 arrange and take part in a meeting or conversation. 9 (**hold someone/thing in**) regard someone or something in a particular way. • n. 1 a grip. 2 a place to grip while climbing. 3 a degree of control.
– PHRASES **get hold of** 1 grasp. 2 informal find or contact. **hold something against** continue to feel resentful about something that someone has done. **hold back** hesitate. **hold something down** informal succeed in keeping a job. **hold fast** 1 remain tightly secured. 2 stick to a principle. **hold forth** talk at length. **hold it** informal wait or stop doing something. **hold off** (of bad weather) fail to occur. **hold someone/thing off** 1 resist an attacker or challenge. 2 postpone something. **hold on** 1 wait. 2 keep going in difficult circumstances. **hold out** 1 resist difficult circumstances. 2 continue to be enough. **hold out for** continue to demand. **hold something over** postpone something. **hold someone/thing up** 1 delay someone or something. 2 rob someone using the threat of violence. 3 present someone or something as an example. **no holds barred** without restrictions. **on hold** waiting to be dealt with or connected by telephone. **take hold** start to have an effect.
– DERIVATIVES **holder** n.
– ORIGIN Old English.

hold² • n. a storage space in the lower part of a ship or aircraft.
– ORIGIN from HOLE.

holdall • n. Brit. a large bag with handles and a shoulder strap.

holding • n. 1 an area of land held by lease. 2 (**holdings**) stocks and property owned by a person or organization.

hold-up • n. 1 a cause of delay. 2 a robbery carried out with the threat of violence.

hole • n. 1 a hollow space in a solid object or surface. 2 an opening in or passing through something. 3 (in golf) a hollow in the ground into which the ball must be hit. 4 informal an awkward or unpleasant place or situation. • v. (**holes, holing, holed**) 1 make a hole or holes in. 2 Golf hit the ball into a hole. 3 (**hole up**) informal hide yourself.
– PHRASES **make a hole in** use a large amount of.
– DERIVATIVES **holey** adj.
– ORIGIN Old English.

hole in the heart • n. an abnormal opening present from birth in the wall between the chambers of the heart.

Holi /hoh-li/ • n. a Hindu spring festival celebrated in honour of Krishna.
– ORIGIN Sanskrit.

holiday esp. Brit. • n. 1 an extended period of leisure. 2 a day of national or religious celebration when no work is done. 3 a short period during which the payment of instalments, tax, etc. may be suspended. • v. spend a holiday.
– ORIGIN Old English, 'holy day'.

holidaymaker • n. Brit. a tourist.

holier-than-thou • adj. offensively certain that you are morally superior to other people.

holiness • n. 1 the state of being holy. 2 (**His/Your Holiness**) the title of the Pope and some other religious leaders.

holistic /hoh-liss-tik/ • n. Med. treating the whole person rather than just the symptoms of a disease.
– DERIVATIVES **holism** n.
– ORIGIN Greek *holos* 'whole'.

hollandaise sauce /hol-uhn-dayz/ • n. a creamy sauce made of butter, egg yolks, and vinegar.
– ORIGIN French *hollandais* 'Dutch'.

holler informal • v. (**hollers, hollering, hollered**) give a loud shout. • n. a loud shout.
– ORIGIN from *halloo*, a call used to urge on dogs during a hunt.

hollow • adj. 1 having empty space inside. 2 curving inwards: *hollow cheeks*. 3 (of a sound) echoing. 4 worthless or not sincere: *a hollow promise*. • n. 1 a hole. 2 a small valley. • v. 1 form by making a hole: *the pond was hollowed out by hand*. 2 make something hollow.
– DERIVATIVES **hollowly** adv. **hollowness** n.

– ORIGIN Old English, 'cave'.

holly • n. an evergreen shrub with prickly dark green leaves and red berries.
– ORIGIN Old English.

hollyhock • n. a tall plant with large showy flowers.
– ORIGIN from **HOLY** + former *hock* 'mallow'.

holmium /hohl-mi-uhm/ • n. a soft silvery-white metallic element.
– ORIGIN from *Holmia*, Latin form of *Stockholm*, the capital of Sweden.

holocaust /hol-uh-kawst/
• n. **1** destruction or killing on a mass scale. **2** (**the Holocaust**) the mass murder of Jews under the German Nazi regime in World War II.
– ORIGIN from Greek *holos* 'whole' + *kaustos* 'burnt'.

Holocene /hol-uh-seen/ • adj. Geol. relating to the present epoch (from about 10,000 years ago).
– ORIGIN French.

hologram /hol-uh-gram/ • n. a photographic image formed in such a way that it looks three-dimensional when it is lit up.
– DERIVATIVES **holographic** adj. **holography** n.
– ORIGIN from Greek *holos* 'whole'.

holster /hohl-ster/ • n. a holder for carrying a handgun.

holy • adj. (**holier, holiest**) **1** dedicated to God or a religious purpose. **2** very good in a moral and spiritual way.
– ORIGIN Old English.

holy day • n. a religious festival.

Holy Father • n. the Pope.

holy of holies • n. **1** hist. the inner chamber of the sanctuary in the Jewish Temple in Jerusalem. **2** a place regarded as sacred.

holy orders • pl. n. see **ORDER** (in sense 10 of the noun).

Holy Roman Empire • n. the western part of the Roman Empire, as revived by Charlemagne in 800.

Holy See • n. the office of or the court surrounding the Pope.

Holy Spirit (or **Holy Ghost**) • n. (in Christianity) God as spiritually active in the world.

Holy Week • n. the week before Easter.

homage /hom-ij/ • n. honour shown publicly to someone.
– ORIGIN Old French.

homburg /hom-berg/ • n. a man's felt hat with a narrow curled brim and a dented crown.
– ORIGIN named after the German town of *Homburg*.

home • n. **1** the place where someone lives. **2** an institution for people needing special care. **3** a place where something flourishes or from which it originated.
• adj. **1** relating to the home. **2** made, done, or intended for use in the home. **3** relating to a person's own country. **4** (in sport) referring to a team's own ground. • adv. **1** to or at a person's home. **2** to the end of something. **3** to the intended position: *slide the bolt home*.
• v. (**homes, homing, homed**) **1** (of an animal) return by instinct to its territory. **2** (**home in on**) move or be aimed towards.
– PHRASES **at home 1** comfortable and at ease. **2** ready to receive visitors. **bring something home to** make someone realize the significance of something. **close to home** (of a remark) uncomfortably accurate. **home and dry** Brit. having achieved your objective.
– ORIGIN Old English.

homeboy (or **homegirl**) • n. informal, esp. US a person from your own town or neighbourhood.

homebuyer • n. a person who buys a house or flat.

homecoming • n. an instance of returning home.

home economics • n. the study of cookery and household management.

home-grown • adj. grown or produced in a person's own garden or country.

Home Guard • n. the British volunteer force organized in 1940 to defend the UK against invasion.

home help • n. Brit. a person employed to help with household work.

homeland • n. **1** a person's native land. **2** hist. any of ten partially self-governing areas in South Africa assigned to particular black African peoples.

homeless • adj. not having anywhere to live.
– DERIVATIVES **homelessness** n.

homely • adj. (**homelier, homeliest**) **1** Brit. simple but comfortable. **2** Brit. ordinary or unsophisticated. **3** N. Amer. unattractive.
– DERIVATIVES **homeliness** n.

home-made • adj. made at home.

Home Office • n. the British government department dealing with law and order, immigration, etc. in England and Wales.

homeopathy /hoh-mi-op-uh-thi/ (also **homoeopathy**) • n. a system of complementary medicine in which disease is treated by minute doses of natural substances that would normally cause symptoms of the disease.
– DERIVATIVES **homeopath** n. **homeopathic** adj.

h

– ORIGIN from Greek *homoios* 'like' + *patheia* 'feeling'.

homeostasis /hoh-mi-uh-**stay**-siss/ (also **homeoestasis**) • n. the tendency of the body to keep its own temperature, blood pressure, etc. at a constant level.
– DERIVATIVES **homeostatic** adj.
– ORIGIN from Greek *homoios* 'like' + *stasis* 'stoppage'.

home page • n. a person's or organization's introductory document on the Internet.

Homeric /hoh-**merr**-ik/ • adj. relating to the ancient Greek poet Homer or to the poems he is believed to have written.

home rule • n. the government of a place by its own citizens.

Home Secretary • n. (in the UK) the Secretary of State in charge of the Home Office.

homesick • adj. missing your home during a time away from it.

homespun • adj. 1 simple and unsophisticated. 2 (of cloth or yarn) made at home.

homestead • n. a farmhouse with surrounding land and outbuildings.
– DERIVATIVES **homesteader** n.

home straight (also **home stretch**) • n. the final stretch of a racecourse.

home truth • n. an unpleasant fact about yourself that someone else tells you.

homeward • adv. (also **homewards**) towards home. • adj. going or leading towards home.

homework • n. 1 school work that a pupil is required to do at home. 2 preparation for something. 3 paid work done in your own home.
– DERIVATIVES **homeworker** n.

homicide /hom-i-syd/ • n. esp. N. Amer. the killing of another person.
– DERIVATIVES **homicidal** adj.
– ORIGIN from Latin *homo* 'man' + -CIDE.

homiletic /hom-i-let-ik/ • adj. relating to or like a homily; morally uplifting.

homily /hom-i-li/ • n. (pl. **homilies**) 1 a talk on a religious subject. 2 a dull talk on a moral issue.
– ORIGIN Greek *homilia* 'discourse'.

homing • adj. 1 (of an animal) able to return home from a great distance. 2 (of a weapon) able to find and hit a target electronically.

hominid /hom-i-nid/ • n. a member of a family of primates which includes humans and their prehistoric ancestors.
– ORIGIN Latin *homo* 'man'.

homo- • comb. form 1 same: *homogeneous*. 2 relating to homosexual love: *homoerotic*.

– ORIGIN Greek *homos* 'same'.

homoeopathy • n. var. of HOMEOPATHY.

homoeostasis • n. var. of HOMEOSTASIS.

homoerotic /hoh-moh-i-**rot**-ik, hom-oh-i-rot-ik/ • adj. concerning sexual desire centred on a person of the same sex.

homogeneous /hom-uh-jee-ni-uhss/ • adj. 1 of the same kind; alike. 2 made up of parts of the same kind.
– DERIVATIVES **homogeneity** /hom-uh-ji-**nee**-i-ti/ n.
– ORIGIN Greek *homogenēs*.

✓ The ending is **-eous**, with an **e**.

homogenize (or **homogenise**) • v. (**homogenizes**, **homogenizing**, **homogenized**) 1 treat milk so that the particles of fat are broken down and cream does not separate. 2 make different things more alike.
– DERIVATIVES **homogenization** n.

homograph • n. each of two or more words having the same spelling but different meanings and origins and often different pronunciations (e.g. BOW¹ and BOW² in this dictionary).

homologous /huh-**mol**-uh-guhss/ • adj. having a related or similar position or structure; corresponding.
– DERIVATIVES **homology** n.
– ORIGIN Greek *homologos* 'agreeing'.

homonym /hom-uh-nim/ • n. each of two or more words having the same spelling and pronunciation but different meanings and origins (e.g. CAN¹ and CAN² in this dictionary).
– ORIGIN Greek *homōnumos* 'having the same name'.

homophobia • n. extreme hatred or fear of homosexuality and homosexuals.
– DERIVATIVES **homophobe** n. **homophobic** adj.

homophone • n. each of two or more words having the same pronunciation but different meanings, origins, or spelling (e.g. *new* and *knew*).
– ORIGIN Greek *phōnē* 'sound, voice'.

Homo sapiens /hoh-moh sap-i-enz/ • n. the species to which modern humans belong.
– ORIGIN Latin, 'wise man'.

homosexual • adj. feeling or involving sexual attraction to people of your own sex. • n. a homosexual person.
– DERIVATIVES **homosexuality** n.

Hon. • abbrev. 1 (in official job titles) Honorary. 2 (in titles of the British nobility and members of parliament) Honourable.

honcho /hon-choh/ • n. (pl. **honchos**) informal a leader.

– ORIGIN Japanese, 'group leader'.

Honduran /hon-**dyoo**-ruhn/ •n. a person from Honduras, a country in Central America. •adj. relating to Honduras.

hone /hohn/ •v. (**hones, honing, honed**) **1** make better or more efficient: *she honed her singing skills.* **2** sharpen a tool with a stone.
– ORIGIN Old English, 'stone'.

honest •adj. **1** truthful and sincere. **2** fairly earned through hard work: *an honest living.* **3** simple and straightforward: *good, honest food.* •adv. informal really.
– ORIGIN Latin *honestus*.

honestly •adv. **1** in an honest way. **2** really (used for emphasis).

honesty •n. the quality of being honest.

honey •n. (pl. **honeys**) **1** a sweet, sticky yellowish-brown fluid made by bees from flower nectar. **2** darling. **4** informal an attractive girl.
– ORIGIN Old English.

honeybee •n. the common bee.

honeycomb •n. **1** a structure of six-sided cells of wax, made by bees to store honey and eggs. **2** a structure like a bee's honeycomb.

honeydew •n. a sweet, sticky substance produced by small insects feeding on the sap of plants.

honeydew melon •n. a variety of melon with sweet green flesh.

honeyed •adj. **1** containing or coated with honey. **2** soothing and soft: *honeyed words.* **3** having a warm yellow colour.

honeymoon •n. **1** a holiday taken by a newly married couple. **2** an initial period of enthusiasm or goodwill. •v. go on honeymoon.
– DERIVATIVES **honeymooner** n.
– ORIGIN first referring to affection waning like the moon.

honeypot •n. a place to which many people are attracted.

honeysuckle •n. a climbing shrub with sweet-smelling yellow and pink flowers.

honk •n. **1** the cry of a goose. **2** the sound of a car horn. •v. make a honk.

honky-tonk •n. informal **1** N. Amer. a cheap bar or club, or one with a bad reputation. **2** ragtime piano music.

honor •n. & v. US = **HONOUR**.

honorable •adj. US = **HONOURABLE**.

honorarium /on-uh-**rair**-i-uhm/ •n. (pl. **honorariums** or **honoraria** /on-uh-**rair**-i-uh/) a voluntary payment for professional services which are offered without charge.
– ORIGIN Latin.

honorary •adj. **1** (of a title or position) given as an honour. **2** Brit. (of a position

or its holder) unpaid.

 Spell **honorary** with **-nor-** in the middle (no **u**).

honorific •adj. given as a mark of respect.

honour (US **honor**) •n. **1** great respect. **2** something that is a privilege or pleasure. **3** a clear sense of what is morally right. **4** a person or thing that brings credit. **5** an award or title given as a reward for achievement. **6** (**honours**) a course of degree studies more specialized than for an ordinary pass. **7** (**His, Your,** etc. **Honour**) a title of respect for a judge. •v. **1** regard with great respect. **2** pay public respect to. **3** fulfil a duty or keep an agreement.
– ORIGIN Latin *honor*.

honourable (US **honorable**) •adj. **1** bringing or worthy of honour. **2** (**Honourable**) a title given to certain high officials, members of the nobility, and MPs.
– DERIVATIVES **honourably** adv.

hooch /hooch/ (also **hootch**) •n. informal strong alcoholic drink.
– ORIGIN from *Hoochinoo*, an Alaskan Indian people who made alcoholic spirits.

hood¹ •n. **1** a covering for the head and neck with an opening for the face. **2** Brit. a folding waterproof cover of a vehicle or pram. **3** N. Amer. the bonnet of a vehicle. **4** a protective cover. •v. put a hood on or over.
– DERIVATIVES **hooded** adj.
– ORIGIN Old English.

hood² •n. informal, esp. N. Amer. a gangster or violent criminal.
– ORIGIN from **HOODLUM**.

-hood •suffix forming nouns referring to: **1** a condition or quality: *womanhood.* **2** a collection or group: *brotherhood.*
– ORIGIN Old English.

hoodlum /**hood**-luhm/ •n. a gangster or violent criminal.

hoodoo •n. **1** a run or cause of bad luck. **2** voodoo.
– ORIGIN from **VOODOO**.

hoodwink •v. deceive or trick someone.
– ORIGIN from **HOOD¹** + **WINK** in the former sense 'close the eyes'.

hoody (also **hoodie**) •n. (pl. **hoodies**) a hooded sweatshirt or other top.

hooey •n. informal, esp. N. Amer. nonsense.

hoof •n. (pl. **hoofs** or **hooves**) the horny part of the foot of a horse, cow, etc. •v. (**hoof it**) informal go on foot.
– PHRASES **on the hoof** Brit. informal without great thought or preparation.
– DERIVATIVES **hoofed** adj.
– ORIGIN Old English.

hoo-ha • n. informal a fuss or commotion.

hook • n. **1** a piece of curved metal or other hard material for catching hold of things or hanging things on. **2** a short punch made with the elbow bent and rigid. **3** something designed to catch people's attention. • v. **1** attach or fasten with a hook. **2** bend into a curved shape: *he hooked his arm under Mum's.* **3** catch a fish with a hook. **4** (**be hooked**) informal be very interested or addicted. **5** (in sport) hit the ball in a curving path.
– PHRASES **by hook or by crook** by any possible means. **hook, line, and sinker** completely. **hook up 1** link to electronic equipment. **2** meet or join another person or people. **off the hook 1** informal no longer in trouble. **2** (of a telephone receiver) not on its rest.
– DERIVATIVES **hooked** adj.
– ORIGIN Old English.

hookah /huuk-uh/ • n. an oriental tobacco pipe with a long tube which draws the smoke through water in a bowl.
– ORIGIN Urdu.

hook and eye • n. a small metal hook and loop used to fasten a garment.

hooker • n. **1** informal a prostitute. **2** Rugby the player in the middle of the front row of the scrum.

hook-up • n. a connection to mains electricity, a communications system, etc.

hookworm • n. a worm with hook-like mouthparts which can infest the intestines.

hooligan • n. a violent young trouble-maker.
– DERIVATIVES **hooliganism** n.
– ORIGIN perh. from *Hooligan*, the surname of a fictional rowdy Irish family.

hoop • n. **1** a rigid circular band. **2** a large ring used as a toy or for circus perform-ers to jump through. **3** a metal arch through which the balls are hit in croquet. • v. surround with a hoop or hoops.
– PHRASES **jump through hoops** undergo a difficult test.
– ORIGIN Old English.

hoopla /hoop-lah/ • n. Brit. a game in which rings are thrown in an attempt to encircle a prize.

hoopoe /hoo-poo/ • n. a salmon-pink bird with a long bill, a large crest, and black-and-white wings and tail.
– ORIGIN Latin *upupa*.

hooray • exclam. hurrah.

hoot • n. **1** a low sound made by owls or a similar sound made by a horn, siren, etc. **2** a short laugh or mocking shout. **3** (a hoot) informal an amusing person or thing. • v. make or cause to make a hoot.
– PHRASES **not give a hoot** (or **two hoots**) informal not care at all.

hootch • n. var. of HOOCH.

hooter • n. **1** Brit. a siren, steam whistle, or horn. **2** informal a person's nose.

Hoover Brit. • n. trademark a vacuum cleaner. • v. (**hoover**) (**hoovers, hoovering, hoovered**) **1** clean with a vacuum cleaner. **2** (usu. **hoover something up**) eat, drink, or use all of something very quickly and eagerly.
– ORIGIN named after the American industrialist William H. *Hoover*.

hooves pl. of HOOF.

hop[1] • v. (**hops, hopping, hopped**) **1** jump along on one foot. **2** (of a bird or animal) jump along with two or all feet at once. **3** informal move or go quickly. **4** (**hop it**) Brit. informal go away. • n. **1** a hopping movement. **2** a short journey or distance. **3** an informal dance.
– PHRASES **hopping mad** informal very angry. **on the hop** Brit. informal unprepared.
– ORIGIN Old English.

hop[2] • n. a climbing plant whose dried flowers (**hops**) are used in brewing to give beer a bitter flavour.
– ORIGIN German or Dutch.

hope • n. **1** a feeling of expectation and desire for something to happen. **2** a cause or source of hope. • v. (**hopes, hoping, hoped**) **1** expect and want something to happen. **2** intend if possible to do something.
– ORIGIN Old English.

hopeful • adj. feeling or inspiring hope. • n. a person likely or hoping to succeed.
– DERIVATIVES **hopefulness** n.

hopefully • adv. **1** in a hopeful way. **2** it is to be hoped that.

> **USAGE:** The traditional sense of **hopefully** is 'in a hopeful way'. The newer use, meaning 'it is to be hoped that' (as in *hopefully, we'll see you tomorrow*), is now the most common, although some people still think that it is incorrect.

hopeless • adj. **1** feeling or causing despair. **2** esp. Brit. very bad or unskilful.
– DERIVATIVES **hopelessly** adv. **hopelessness** n.

hopper • n. a container that tapers downwards and empties its contents at the bottom.

hopscotch • n. a children's game of hopping into and over squares marked on the ground to retrieve a marker.
– ORIGIN from HOP[1] + SCOTCH in the sense 'put an end to'.

horde • n. esp. derog. a large group of people.

– ORIGIN Polish *horda*.

> **USAGE:** On the confusion of **horde** with **hoard**, see the note at **HOARD**.

horizon • n. **1** the line at which the earth's surface and the sky appear to meet. **2** the limit of a person's understanding, experience, or interest.
– PHRASES **on the horizon** about to happen.
– ORIGIN Greek *horizōn* 'limiting'.

horizontal • adj. parallel to the ground; at right angles to the vertical. • n. a horizontal line or surface.
– DERIVATIVES **horizontally** adv.

hormone • n. a substance produced by a living thing and carried by blood or sap to regulate the action of specific cells or tissues.
– DERIVATIVES **hormonal** adj.
– ORIGIN Greek *hormōn* 'setting in motion'.

horn • n. **1** a hard bony outgrowth found in pairs on the heads of cattle, sheep, and other animals. **2** the substance of which horns are made. **3** a brass wind instrument, shaped like a cone or wound into a spiral. **4** an instrument sounding a signal.
– PHRASES **on the horns of a dilemma** faced with a decision involving equally unfavourable alternatives.
– DERIVATIVES **horned** adj.
– ORIGIN Old English.

hornbeam • n. a tree with hard pale wood.

hornbill • n. a tropical bird with a horn-like structure on its large curved bill.

hornblende /horn-blend/ • n. a dark brown, black, or green mineral present in many rocks.
– ORIGIN German.

hornet • n. a kind of large wasp.
– PHRASES **stir up a hornets' nest** cause difficulties or angry feelings to arise.
– ORIGIN Old English.

hornpipe • n. **1** a lively solo dance traditionally performed by sailors. **2** a piece of music for a hornpipe.

horny • adj. (**hornier**, **horniest**) **1** made of or resembling horn. **2** hard and rough. **3** informal sexually aroused or arousing.
– DERIVATIVES **horniness** n.

horology /ho-rol-uh-ji/ • n. **1** the study and measurement of time. **2** the art of making clocks and watches.
– ORIGIN Greek *hōra* 'time'.

horoscope • n. a forecast of a person's future based on the positions of the stars and planets at the time of their birth.
– ORIGIN Greek *hōroskopos*.

horrendous /huh-ren-duhss/ • adj. very

unpleasant or horrifying.
– DERIVATIVES **horrendously** adv.
– ORIGIN Latin *horrendus*.

horrible • adj. **1** causing or likely to cause horror. **2** very unpleasant.
– DERIVATIVES **horribly** adv.

horrid • adj. **1** causing horror. **2** very unpleasant.

horrific • adj. causing horror.
– DERIVATIVES **horrifically** adv.

horrify • v. (**horrifies**, **horrifying**, **horrified**) fill someone with horror.
– ORIGIN Latin *horrificare*.

horror • n. **1** a strong feeling of fear, shock, or disgust. **2** a cause of horror. **3** informal a badly behaved child.
– ORIGIN Latin.

hors de combat /or duh kom-bah/ • adj. out of action due to injury or damage.
– ORIGIN French, 'out of the fight'.

hors d'oeuvre /or derv/ • n. (pl. **hors d'oeuvre** or **hors d'oeuvres** /or derv/, or **dervz**/) a small item of savoury food eaten before a meal.
– ORIGIN French, 'outside the work'.

horse • n. **1** a large four-legged mammal with a flowing mane and tail, used for riding and for pulling heavy loads. **2** an adult male horse. **3** cavalry. **4** a structure on which something is mounted or supported: *a clothes horse.* • v. (**horses**, **horsing**, **horsed**) (**horse around/about**) informal fool about.
– PHRASES **from the horse's mouth** from a person directly concerned. **hold your horses** informal wait a moment.
– ORIGIN Old English.

horseback • n. (in phr. **on horseback**) mounted on a horse.

horsebox • n. Brit. a vehicle or trailer for transporting one or more horses.

horse chestnut • n. **1** a large tree producing nuts (conkers) enclosed in a spiny case. **2** a conker.

horseflesh • n. horses as a group.

horsefly • n. (pl. **horseflies**) a large fly that bites horses and other large mammals.

horsehair • n. hair from the mane or tail of a horse, used in furniture for padding.

horseman (or **horsewoman**) • n. (pl. **horsemen** or **horsewomen**) a rider on horseback.
– DERIVATIVES **horsemanship** n.

horseplay • n. rough, high-spirited play.

horsepower • n. (pl. **horsepower**) an imperial unit of power equal to 550 foot-pounds per second (about 750 watts).

horseradish • n. a plant grown for its

h

strong-tasting root which is often made into a sauce.

horse sense • n. informal common sense.

horseshoe • n. a U-shaped iron band attached to the base of a horse's hoof.

horsetail • n. a flowerless plant with a jointed stem and narrow leaves.

horsewhip • n. a long whip used for controlling horses. • v. (**horsewhips, horsewhipping, horsewhipped**) beat with a horsewhip.

horsey (also **horsy**) • adj. 1 relating to or like a horse. 2 very interested in horses or horse racing.

horst • n. Geol. a raised elongated block of the earth's crust lying between two faults.
– ORIGIN German, 'heap'.

hortatory /hor-tuh-tuh-ri/ • adj. formal strongly urging someone to do something.
– ORIGIN Latin *hortatorius*.

horticulture /hor-ti-kul-cher/ • n. the art or practice of cultivating and managing gardens.
– DERIVATIVES **horticultural** adj. **horticulturist** (also **horticulturalist**) n.
– ORIGIN Latin *hortus* 'garden'.

hosanna (also **hosannah**) • n. & exclam. a biblical cry of praise or joy.
– ORIGIN Greek.

hose • n. 1 (Brit. also **hosepipe**) a flexible tube conveying water. 2 stockings, socks, and tights. • v. (**hoses, hosing, hosed**) wash or spray with a hose.
– ORIGIN Old English.

hosiery /hoh-zi-uh-ri/ • n. stockings, socks, and tights.

hospice • n. 1 a home providing care for people who are sick or terminally ill. 2 old use a lodging for travellers.
– ORIGIN French.

hospitable /hoss-pit-uh-b'l/ • adj. 1 friendly and welcoming to strangers or guests. 2 (of an environment) pleasant and favourable for living in.
– DERIVATIVES **hospitably** adv.

hospital • n. an institution providing medical treatment and nursing care for sick or injured people.
– ORIGIN Latin *hospitale*.

hospitality • n. the friendly and generous treatment of guests or strangers.

hospitalize (or **hospitalise**) • v. (**hospitalizes, hospitalizing, hospitalized**) admit someone to hospital for treatment.
– DERIVATIVES **hospitalization** n.

host¹ • n. 1 a person who receives or entertains guests. 2 the presenter of a television or radio programme. 3 a place or organization that holds an event to

which other people are invited. 4 an animal or plant on or in which a parasite lives. • v. act as host at an event or for a television or radio programme.
– ORIGIN Old French *hoste*.

host² • n. (**a host/hosts of**) a large number of.
– ORIGIN Latin *hostis* 'stranger, enemy'.

Host³ • n. (**the Host**) the consecrated bread used in the service of Holy Communion.
– ORIGIN Latin *hostia* 'victim'.

hostage • n. a person held prisoner in an attempt to make other people give in to a demand.
– PHRASES **a hostage to fortune** an act or remark regarded as unwise because it invites trouble in the future.
– ORIGIN Old French.

hostel • n. a place which provides cheap food and lodging for a particular group of people.
– ORIGIN Old French.

hostelry • n. (pl. **hostelries**) old use or humorous an inn or pub.
– ORIGIN Old French *hostelerie*.

hostess • n. 1 a female host. 2 a woman employed to welcome and entertain customers at a nightclub or bar.

hostile • adj. 1 showing or feeling dislike or opposition. 2 relating to a military enemy. 3 (of a takeover bid) opposed by the company to be bought.
– ORIGIN Latin *hostilis*.

hostility /hoss-til-i-ti/ • n. (pl. **hostilities**) 1 hostile behaviour. 2 (**hostilities**) acts of warfare.

hot • adj. (**hotter, hottest**) 1 having a high temperature. 2 feeling or producing an uncomfortable sensation of heat. 3 feeling or showing anger, lust, or other strong emotion. 4 informal currently popular or interesting. 5 informal (of goods) stolen. 6 (**hot on**) informal very knowledgeable about. 7 (**hot on**) informal strict about. • v. (**hots, hotting, hotted**) (**hot up**) Brit. informal become more exciting or intense.
– PHRASES **have the hots for** informal be sexually attracted to. **hot under the collar** informal angry or annoyed. **in hot water** informal in trouble.
– DERIVATIVES **hotly** adv. **hotness** n.
– ORIGIN Old English.

hot air • n. informal empty or boastful talk.

hot-air balloon • n. = BALLOON (in sense 2).

hotbed • n. a place where a particular activity happens or flourishes: *a hotbed of crime.*

hot-blooded • adj. passionate.

hotchpotch (N. Amer. **hodgepodge**) • n. a confused mixture.

– ORIGIN Old French *hochepot*.

hot cross bun • n. a bun marked with a cross, traditionally eaten on Good Friday.

hot dog • n. a hot sausage served in a long, soft roll.

hotel • n. a place providing accommodation and meals for travellers and tourists.
– ORIGIN French.

hotelier /hoh-tel-i-er/ • n. a person who owns or manages a hotel.

hotfoot • adv. in eager haste.
• v. (**hotfoot it**) hurry eagerly.

hothead • n. a rash or quick-tempered person.
– DERIVATIVES **hot-headed** adj.

hothouse • n. **1** a heated greenhouse. **2** an environment that encourages rapid development.

hot key • n. Computing a key or combination of keys providing quick access to a function within a program.

hotline • n. a direct telephone line set up for a specific purpose.

hot pants • pl. n. women's tight, brief shorts.

hotplate • n. a flat heated metal or ceramic surface on an electric cooker.

hotpot (also **Lancashire hotpot**) • n. Brit. a casserole of meat and vegetables with a covering layer of sliced potato.

hot potato • n. informal a controversial and difficult issue.

hot rod • n. a motor vehicle that has been specially adapted to give it extra power and speed.

hot seat • n. (**the hot seat**) informal the position of a person who carries full responsibility for something.

hotshot • n. informal an important or very able person.

hot spot • n. **1** a small area with a high temperature in comparison to its surroundings. **2** a place where there is a lot of activity or danger.

hot stuff • n. informal **1** a person or thing of outstanding talent or interest. **2** a sexually exciting person, book, etc.

hot-tempered • adj. easily angered.

Hottentot /hot-tuhn-tot/ • n. & adj. offens. formerly used to refer to the Khoikhoi peoples of South Africa and Namibia.
– ORIGIN Dutch.

hot ticket • n. informal a person or thing that is in great demand.

hot tub • n. a large tub filled with hot bubbling water.

hot-water bottle • n. a rubber container that is filled with hot water and used for warming a bed or part of the body.

hot-wire • v. informal start the engine of a vehicle without using the ignition switch.

houmous • n. var. of HUMMUS.

hound • n. a hunting dog. • v. harass someone.
– ORIGIN Old English.

houndstooth • n. a large check pattern with notched corners.

hour • n. **1** a period of 60 minutes, one of the twenty-four parts that a day is divided into. **2** a point in time: *you can't turn him away at this hour.* **3** a period set aside for a particular purpose or activity: *leisure hours.*
– ORIGIN Greek *hōra.*

hourglass • n. a device with two connected glass bulbs containing sand that takes an hour to fall from the upper to the lower bulb. • adj. shaped like an hourglass.

houri /hoo-ri/ • n. (pl. **houris**) one of the virgin companions of the faithful in the Muslim Paradise.
– ORIGIN Arabic, 'having eyes with a contrast of black and white'.

hourly • adj. **1** done or occurring every hour. **2** calculated hour by hour: *hourly rates.* • adv. **1** every hour. **2** by the hour.

house • n. /howss/ **1** a building for people to live in. **2** a building devoted to a particular activity: *a house of prayer.* **3** a firm or institution: *a fashion house.* **4** a religious community that occupies a particular building. **5** esp. Brit. a group of pupils living in the same building at a boarding school. **6** a law-making assembly. **7** a dynasty: *the House of Stewart.* **8** (also **house music**) a style of fast electronic dance music. • adj. **1** (of an animal or plant) kept in or infesting buildings. **2** relating to medical staff who have living quarters at a hospital. **3** relating to a firm or institution.
• v. /howz/ (**houses**, **housing**, **housed**) **1** provide with accommodation. **2** provide space for. **3** enclose something.
– PHRASES **get on like a house on fire** informal have a very good relationship. **on the house** at the management's expense. **put your house in order** make necessary reforms.
– DERIVATIVES **houseful** n.
– ORIGIN Old English.

house arrest • n. the state of being kept as a prisoner in your own house.

houseboat • n. a boat that people can live in.

housebound • adj. unable to leave your house because of illness or old age.

housebreaking •n. the action of breaking into a building to commit a crime.
– DERIVATIVES **housebreaker** n.

housecoat •n. a woman's long, loose robe worn casually around the house.

housefly •n. (pl. **houseflies**) a common small fly often found in houses.

household •n. a house and its occupants.
– DERIVATIVES **householder** n.

household name (also **household word**) •n. a famous person or thing.

house-hunting •n. the process of looking for a house to buy or rent.
– DERIVATIVES **house-hunter** n.

housekeeper •n. a person employed to manage a household.
– DERIVATIVES **housekeeping** n.

house lights •pl. n. the lights in the part of a theatre where the audience sits.

housemaid •n. a female employee who carries out household tasks.

housemaid's knee •n. swelling of the fluid-filled cavity covering the kneecap.

house martin •n. a black-and-white bird which nests on buildings.

housemaster (or **housemistress**) •n. esp. Brit. a teacher in charge of a house at a boarding school.

housemate •n. a person with whom you share a house.

House of Commons •n. the part of Parliament in the UK whose members have been elected by voters.

House of Keys •n. the part of Tynwald, the parliament of the Isle of Man, whose members have been elected by voters.

House of Lords •n. the part of Parliament in the UK whose members are peers and bishops and have not been elected by voters.

House of Representatives •n. the lower house of the US Congress.

house-proud •adj. very concerned with the cleanliness and appearance of your home.

Houses of Parliament •pl. n. the Houses of Lords and Commons in the UK regarded together.

house-train •v. train a pet to urinate and defecate outside the house.

house-warming •n. a party celebrating a move to a new home.

housewife •n. (pl. **housewives**) a woman whose main occupation is caring for her family and running the household.
– DERIVATIVES **housewifery** /howss-wif-uh-ri/ n.

housework •n. cleaning and other work done in running a home.

housing •n. **1** houses and flats as a whole. **2** a casing for a piece of equipment.

housing estate •n. Brit. a number of houses in an area planned and built as a unit.

hove Naut. past tense of **HEAVE**.

hovel •n. a small dirty or run-down dwelling.

hover •v. (**hovers**, **hovering**, **hovered**) **1** remain in one place in the air. **2** wait about uncertainly. **3** remain near a particular level or between two states: *the temperature hovered around ten degrees.*

hovercraft •n. (pl. **hovercraft**) a vehicle that travels over land or water on a cushion of air.

how •adv. **1** in what way or by what means. **2** in what condition. **3** to what extent or degree. **4** the way in which.
– PHRASES **how about?** would you like? **how do you do?** said when meeting someone for the first time in a formal situation. **how many** what number. **how much** what amount or price.
– ORIGIN Old English.

howdah /how-duh/ •n. a seat for riding on the back of an elephant.
– ORIGIN Urdu.

however •adv. **1** used to introduce a statement that contrasts with a previous one. **2** in whatever way or to whatever extent.

howitzer /how-it-ser/ •n. a short gun for firing shells at a high angle.
– ORIGIN Dutch *houwitser*.

howl •n. **1** a long wailing cry made by an animal. **2** a loud cry of pain, amusement, etc. •v. make a howling sound.

howler •n. informal a stupid mistake.

howling •adj. informal great: *the meal was a howling success.*

hoyden /hoy-duhn/ •n. dated a girl who behaves in a high-spirited or wild way.
– ORIGIN prob. from Dutch *heiden* 'heathen'.

h.p. (also **HP**) •abbrev. **1** Brit. hire purchase. **2** horsepower.

HQ •abbrev. headquarters.

hr •abbrev. hour.

HRH •abbrev. Brit. Her (or His) Royal Highness.

HRT •abbrev. hormone replacement therapy, in which a patient is treated with certain hormones to ease symptoms of the menopause or osteoporosis.

Hs •symb. the chemical element hassium.

HTML •n. Computing Hypertext Markup Language.

HTTP • abbrev. Computing Hypertext Transport (or Transfer) Protocol.

hub • n. **1** the central part of a wheel, rotating on or with the axle. **2** the centre of an activity or region.

hubbub • n. **1** a loud confused noise caused by a crowd. **2** a busy, noisy situation.
– ORIGIN perh. Irish.

hubby • n. (pl. **hubbies**) informal a husband.

hubcap • n. a cover for the hub of a motor vehicle's wheel.

hubris /hyoo-briss/ • n. excessive pride or self-confidence.
– DERIVATIVES **hubristic** adj.
– ORIGIN Greek.

huckster • n. a person who sells small items, either door-to-door or from a stall.
– ORIGIN prob. German.

huddle • v. (**huddles, huddling, huddled**) **1** crowd together. **2** curl the body into a small space. • n. a number of people or things crowded together.
– ORIGIN perh. German.

hue • n. **1** a colour or shade. **2** an aspect: *men of all political hues.*
– ORIGIN Old English.

hue and cry • n. a strong public outcry.
– ORIGIN from Old French *hu e cri* 'outcry and cry'.

huff • v. (usu. in phr. **huff and puff**) **1** breathe out noisily. **2** show annoyance in an obvious way. • n. a fit of annoyance.

huffy • adj. easily offended.
– DERIVATIVES **huffily** adv.

hug • v. (**hugs, hugging, hugged**) **1** hold tightly in your arms or against your body. **2** keep close to: *a few craft hugged the shore.* • n. an act of hugging.
– DERIVATIVES **huggable** adj. **hugger** n.
– ORIGIN prob. Scandinavian.

huge • adj. (**huger, hugest**) very large.
– DERIVATIVES **hugeness** n.
– ORIGIN Old French *ahuge.*

hugely • adv. **1** very much. **2** very.

hugger-mugger • n. **1** confusion or disorder. **2** secrecy.
– ORIGIN prob. from **HUDDLE** and dialect *mucker* 'hoard money'.

Huguenot /hyoo-guh-noh/ • n. a French Protestant of the 16th–17th centuries.
– ORIGIN French.

hula /hoo-luh/ • n. a dance performed by Hawaiian women, in which the dancers sway their hips.
– ORIGIN Hawaiian.

hula hoop (also US trademark **Hula-Hoop**) • n. a large hoop spun round the body by moving the hips in a circular way.

hulk • n. **1** an old ship stripped of fittings and permanently moored. **2** a large or clumsy person or thing.
– ORIGIN Old English, 'fast ship'.

hulking • adj. informal very large or clumsy.

hull[1] • n. the main body of a ship.
– ORIGIN perh. the same as **HULL**[2], or from **HOLD**[2].

hull[2] • n. **1** the outer covering of a fruit or seed. **2** the stalk and cluster of leaves on a strawberry or raspberry. • v. remove the hulls from strawberries or raspberries.
– ORIGIN Old English.

hullabaloo • n. informal an uproar.
– ORIGIN from *hullo.*

hullo • exclam. var. of **HELLO.**

hum • v. (**hums, humming, hummed**) **1** make a low continuous sound like that of a bee. **2** sing with closed lips. **3** informal be in a state of great activity. **4** Brit. informal smell unpleasant. • n. a low, steady continuous sound.
– DERIVATIVES **hummable** adj.

human • adj. **1** relating to human beings. **2** showing the better qualities of human beings, such as kindness. • n. (also **human being**) a person.
– DERIVATIVES **humanly** adv. **humanness** n.
– ORIGIN Latin *humanus.*

humane /hyuu-mayn/ • adj. showing concern and kindness towards other people.
– DERIVATIVES **humanely** adv.

humanism • n. **1** a system of thought that regards people as capable of using their intelligence to live their lives, rather than relying on religious belief. **2** a Renaissance cultural movement which revived interest in ancient Greek and Roman thought.
– DERIVATIVES **humanist** n. & adj. **humanistic** adj.

humanitarian /hyuu-man-i-tair-i-uhn/ • adj. concerned with human welfare. • n. a humanitarian person.
– DERIVATIVES **humanitarianism** n.

humanity • n. (pl. **humanities**) **1** human beings as a whole. **2** the condition of being human. **3** sympathy and kindness towards other people. **4** (**humanities**) studies concerned with human culture, such as literature or history.

humanize (or **humanise**) • v. (**humanizes, humanizing, humanized**) make more pleasant or suitable for people.
– DERIVATIVES **humanization** n.

humankind • n. human beings as a whole.

human nature • n. the general

characteristics and feelings shared by all people.

humanoid /hyoo-muh-noyd/
• adj. having an appearance or character like that of a human. • n. a humanoid being.

human rights • pl. n. basic rights to which every person is entitled, such as freedom.

humble • adj. (**humbler, humblest**)
1 having or showing a modest or low opinion of your own importance. **2** of low rank. **3** not large or special: *humble brick bungalows.* • v. (**humbles, humbling, humbled**) make someone seem less dignified or important.
– PHRASES **eat humble pie** make a humble apology. [ORIGIN from former *umbles* meaning 'offal'.]
– DERIVATIVES **humbly** adv.
– ORIGIN Latin *humilis* 'low, lowly'.

humbug • n. **1** false or misleading talk or behaviour. **2** a person who is not sincere or honest. **3** Brit. a boiled peppermint sweet.

humdinger /hum-ding-er/ • n. informal an outstanding person or thing.

humdrum • adj. lacking excitement or variety; dull.
– ORIGIN prob. from **HUM**.

humerus /hyoo-muh-ruhss/ • n. (pl. **humeri** /hyoo-muh-ry/) the bone of the upper arm, between the shoulder and the elbow.
– DERIVATIVES **humeral** adj.
– ORIGIN Latin, 'shoulder'.

humid /hyoo-mid/ • adj. (of the air or weather) damp and warm.
– ORIGIN Latin *humidus*.

humidify • v. (**humidifies, humidifying, humidified**) increase the level of moisture in air.
– DERIVATIVES **humidification** n. **humidifier** n.

humidity • n. **1** the state of being humid. **2** the amount of moisture in the air.

humiliate • v. (**humiliates, humiliating, humiliated**) make someone feel ashamed or stupid in front of another.
– DERIVATIVES **humiliation** n.
– ORIGIN Latin *humiliare* 'make humble'.

humility • n. the quality of being humble.

hummingbird • n. a small, chiefly tropical American bird able to hover by beating its wings very fast.

hummock • n. a small hill or mound.

hummus /huu-muhss/ (also **houmous**)
• n. a thick Middle Eastern dip made from chickpeas puréed with olive oil and garlic.
– ORIGIN Arabic.

humor • n. US = **HUMOUR**.

humorist • n. a writer or speaker who is known for being amusing.

humorous • adj. **1** causing amusement. **2** showing a sense of humour.
– DERIVATIVES **humorously** adv.

> ✓ **humorous** and **humorist** drop the *u* before the *r* of **humour**.

humour (US **humor**) • n. **1** the quality of being amusing. **2** a state of mind: *her good humour vanished.* **3** (also **cardinal humour**) each of four fluids of the body, formerly believed to determine a person's physical and mental qualities.
• v. agree with the wishes of someone so as to keep them happy.
– PHRASES **out of humour** in a bad mood.
– DERIVATIVES **humourless** adj.
– ORIGIN Latin *humor* 'moisture'.

hump • n. **1** a rounded raised mass of earth or land. **2** a rounded part projecting from the back of a camel or other animal or as an abnormality on a person's back. • v. **1** informal, esp. Brit. carry a heavy object with difficulty. **2** (as adj. **humped**) having a hump.
– PHRASES **get the hump** Brit. informal become annoyed or sulky.
– DERIVATIVES **humpy** adj.
– ORIGIN prob. from German *humpe*.

humpback • n. = **HUNCHBACK**.
– DERIVATIVES **humpbacked** adj.

humpback bridge • n. Brit. a small road bridge that slopes steeply on both sides.

humus /hyoo-muhss/ • n. a substance found in soil, formed from dead or dying leaves and other plant material.
– ORIGIN Latin, 'soil'.

Hun • n. **1** a member of a people from Asia who invaded Europe in the 4th–5th centuries. **2** informal, derog. a German (especially during the First and Second World Wars).
– ORIGIN Greek *Hounnoi.*

hunch • v. raise the shoulders and bend the top of the body forward. • n. a belief that something is true, based on a feeling rather than evidence.

hunchback • n. offens. a person with a hump on their back.

hundred • cardinal number **1** ten more than ninety; 100. (Roman numeral: **c** or **C**.) **2** (**hundreds**) informal a large number.
– PHRASES **a** (or **one**) **hundred per cent** completely.
– DERIVATIVES **hundredfold** adj. & adv. **hundredth** ordinal number.
– ORIGIN Old English.

hundreds and thousands • pl. n. Brit. tiny coloured sugar strands used for decorating cakes and desserts.

hundredweight • n. (pl.

hundredweight or **hundredweights)**
1 Brit. a unit of weight equal to 112 lb (about 50.8 kg). **2** US a unit of weight equal to 100 lb (about 45.4 kg).

hung past and past part. of **HANG**.
• adj. **1** (of an elected body in the UK and Canada) having no political party with an overall majority. **2** (of a jury) unable to agree on a verdict. **3** (**hung up**) informal emotionally confused or disturbed.

Hungarian /hung-**gair**-i-uhn/ • n. **1** a person from Hungary. **2** the language of Hungary. • adj. relating to Hungary.

hunger • n. **1** a feeling of discomfort and a need to eat, caused by lack of food. **2** a strong desire: *her hunger for knowledge.*
• v. (**hungers, hungering, hungered**) (**hunger after/for**) have a strong desire for.
– ORIGIN Old English.

hunger strike • n. a refusal to eat for a long period, carried out as a protest by a prisoner.

hungover • adj. suffering from a hangover.

hungry • adj. (**hungrier, hungriest**)
1 feeling hunger. **2** having a strong desire: *a party hungry for power.*
– DERIVATIVES **hungrily** adv.

hunk • n. **1** a large piece cut or broken from something larger. **2** informal a strong, sexually attractive man.
– DERIVATIVES **hunky** adj.
– ORIGIN prob. Dutch or German.

hunker • v. (**hunkers, hunkering, hunkered**) squat or crouch down low.
– ORIGIN prob. from German *hocken*.

hunkers • pl. n. informal a person's haunches.

hunky-dory • adj. informal excellent.
– ORIGIN *hunky* from Dutch *honk* 'home'; the origin of *dory* is unknown.

hunt • v. **1** chase and kill a wild animal for sport or food. **2** try to find by thorough searching: *scientists are hunting for alternatives to many overused drugs.*
3 (**hunt someone down**) chase and capture someone. **4** (as adj. **hunted**) appearing alarmed or harassed. • n. **1** an act of hunting. **2** a group of people who meet regularly to hunt animals as a sport.
– DERIVATIVES **hunting** n.
– ORIGIN Old English.

hunter • n. **1** a person or animal that hunts. **2** a watch with a hinged cover protecting the glass.
– DERIVATIVES **huntress** n.

hunting ground • n. a place where people can easily find what they are looking for.

huntsman • n. (pl. **huntsmen**) **1** a person

who hunts. **2** an official in charge of hounds during a fox hunt.

hurdle • n. **1** one of a series of upright frames which athletes in a race must jump over. **2** an obstacle or difficulty. **3** a portable rectangular frame used as a temporary fence. • v. (**hurdles, hurdling, hurdled**) jump over a hurdle or other obstacle while running.
– DERIVATIVES **hurdler** n.
– ORIGIN Old English.

hurdy-gurdy /her-di-**ger**-di/ • n. (pl. **hurdy-gurdies**) a musical instrument with a droning sound played by turning a handle, with keys worked by the other hand.

hurl • v. **1** throw with great force. **2** shout abuse or insults.

hurling (also **hurley**) • n. an Irish game resembling hockey.

hurly-burly • n. busy and noisy activity.
– ORIGIN from **HURL**.

hurrah (also **hooray, hurray**)
• exclam. used to express joy or approval.

hurricane • n. a severe storm with a violent wind, especially in the Caribbean.
– ORIGIN Spanish *huracán*.

hurricane lamp • n. an oil lamp in which the flame is protected from the wind by a glass tube.

hurry • v. (**hurries, hurrying, hurried**)
1 move or act quickly. **2** do quickly or too quickly: *guided tours tend to be hurried.* • n. great haste or urgency.
– DERIVATIVES **hurriedly** adv.

hurt • v. (**hurts, hurting, hurt**) **1** cause pain or injury to. **2** feel pain. **3** upset someone. • n. **1** injury or pain.
2 unhappiness.
– ORIGIN Old French *hurter* 'to strike'.

hurtful • adj. causing mental pain or distress.

hurtle • v. (**hurtles, hurtling, hurtled**) move at great speed.
– ORIGIN from **HURT**.

husband • n. a married man in relation to his wife. • v. use resources carefully and without waste.
– ORIGIN Old Norse, 'master of a house'.

husbandry • n. **1** farming. **2** careful use of resources.

hush • v. **1** make or become quiet. **2** (**hush something up**) prevent something from becoming public. • n. a silence.

hush-hush • adj. informal highly secret.

hush money • n. informal money paid to someone to prevent them from revealing information.

husk • n. the dry outer covering of some fruits or seeds.

– ORIGIN prob. from German *hüske* 'sheath'.

husky[1] •adj. (**huskier**, **huskiest**) **1** sounding low-pitched and slightly hoarse. **2** big and strong.
– DERIVATIVES **huskily** adv.

husky[2] •n. (pl. **huskies**) a powerful dog of a breed used in the Arctic for pulling sledges.
– ORIGIN North American dialect, 'Eskimo'.

hussar /huu-zar/ •n. (now only in titles) a soldier in a light cavalry regiment.
– ORIGIN Hungarian *huszár*.

hussy •n. (pl. **hussies**) an immoral or cheeky girl or woman.
– ORIGIN from **HOUSEWIFE**.

hustings •n. (**the hustings**) the political meetings and other campaigning that take place before an election.
– ORIGIN Old Norse, 'household assembly'.

hustle •v. (**hustles**, **hustling**, **hustled**) **1** push or move roughly. **2** (**hustle someone into**) make someone act quickly and without time for consideration. •n. busy movement and activity.
– ORIGIN Dutch *hutselen* 'shake, toss'.

hustler •n. informal, esp. N. Amer. **1** a person who is good at aggressive selling or dishonest dealing. **2** a prostitute.

hut •n. a small simple house or shelter.
– ORIGIN German *hütte*.

hutch •n. a box with a wire mesh front, used for keeping small animals such as rabbits.
– ORIGIN Latin *hutica* 'storage chest'.

hyacinth /hy-uh-sinth/ •n. a plant with sweet-smelling bell-shaped flowers.
– ORIGIN named after *Hyacinthus*, a youth loved by the god Apollo in Greek mythology.

hyaena •n. var. of **HYENA**.

hybrid /hy-brid/ •n. **1** the offspring of two plants or animals of different species or varieties, such as a mule. **2** a thing made by combining two different elements.
– DERIVATIVES **hybridity** n.
– ORIGIN Latin *hybrida*.

hybridize (or **hybridise**) •v. (**hybridizes**, **hybridizing**, **hybridized**) breed individuals of two different species or varieties to produce hybrids.
– DERIVATIVES **hybridization** n.

hydra •n. a minute freshwater invertebrate animal with a tubular body and tentacles around the mouth.
– ORIGIN named after the *Hydra* of Greek mythology, a snake with many heads that grew again if cut off.

hydrangea /hy-drayn-juh/ •n. a shrub with white, blue, or pink flowers growing in clusters.
– ORIGIN from Greek *hudro-* 'water' + *angeion* 'container'.

hydrant /hy-druhnt/ •n. a water pipe with a nozzle to which a fire hose can be attached.

hydrate •n. /hy-drayt/ a compound in which water molecules are chemically bound to another compound or an element. •v. /hy-drayt/ (**hydrates**, **hydrating**, **hydrated**) make something absorb or combine with water.
– DERIVATIVES **hydration** n.

hydraulic /hy-dro-lik/ •adj. relating to or operated by a liquid moving in a confined space under pressure. •n. (**hydraulics**) the branch of science concerned with the use of liquids moving under pressure to provide mechanical force.
– DERIVATIVES **hydraulically** adv.
– ORIGIN from Greek *hudro-* 'water' + *aulos* 'pipe'.

hydro •n. (pl. **hydros**) Brit. a hotel or health farm providing hydropathic and other treatment.

hydro- (also **hydr-**) •comb. form **1** water; relating to water: *hydroelectric*. **2** combined with hydrogen: *hydrocarbon*.
– ORIGIN Greek *hudōr* 'water'.

hydrocarbon •n. any of the many compounds of hydrogen and carbon.

hydrocephalus /hy-druh-sef-uh-luhss/ •n. a condition in which fluid collects in the brain.
– ORIGIN from Greek *hudro-* 'water' + *kephalē* 'head'.

hydrochloric acid •n. a corrosive acid containing hydrogen and chlorine.

hydrodynamics •n. the branch of science concerned with the forces acting on or generated by liquids.
– DERIVATIVES **hydrodynamic** adj.

hydroelectric •adj. relating to the use of flowing water to generate electricity.
– DERIVATIVES **hydroelectricity** n.

hydrofoil •n. **1** a boat fitted with structures (known as foils) which lift the hull clear of the water at speed. **2** each of the foils of such a craft.

hydrogen /hy-druh-juhn/ •n. a highly flammable gas which is the lightest of the chemical elements.

hydrogenated /hy-droj-uh-nay-tid/ •adj. combined with hydrogen.
– DERIVATIVES **hydrogenation** n.

hydrogen bomb •n. a nuclear bomb whose destructive power comes from the fusion of hydrogen nuclei.

hydrogen peroxide •n. a liquid used

in some disinfectants and bleaches.

hydrogen sulphide •n. a poisonous gas with a smell of bad eggs.

hydrography /hy-drog-ruh-fi/ •n. the science of charting seas, lakes, and rivers.
– DERIVATIVES **hydrographer** n. **hydrographic** adj.

hydrology /hy-drol-uh-ji/ •n. the branch of science concerned with the properties and distribution of water on the earth's surface.
– DERIVATIVES **hydrological** adj. **hydrologist** n.

hydrolyse /hy-druh-lyz/ (or US **hydrolyze**) •v. (**hydrolyses, hydrolysing, hydrolysed**) break down a compound by chemical reaction with water.

hydrolysis /hy-drol-i-siss/ •n. the chemical breakdown of a compound due to reaction with water.
– DERIVATIVES **hydrolytic** adj.

hydrometer /hy-drom-i-ter/ •n. an instrument for measuring the density of liquids.

hydropathy /hy-drop-uh-thi/ •n. the treatment of illness through the use of water, either internally or by external means such as steam baths.
– DERIVATIVES **hydropathic** adj.

hydrophilic /hy-druh-fil-ik/ •adj. having a tendency to mix with or dissolve in water.

hydrophobia •n. **1** extreme fear of water, especially as a symptom of rabies. **2** rabies.

hydrophobic •adj. **1** repelling or failing to mix with water. **2** relating to hydrophobia.

hydroplane •n. a light, fast motor boat designed to skim over the surface of water.

hydroponics /hy-druh-pon-iks/ •n. the growing of plants in sand, gravel, or liquid, with added nutrients but without soil.
– DERIVATIVES **hydroponic** adj.
– ORIGIN from Greek *hudōr* 'water' + *ponos* 'labour'.

hydrosphere •n. the seas, lakes, and other waters of the earth's surface.

hydrostatic /hy-druh-stat-ik/ •adj. relating to the pressure and other characteristics of liquid at rest.

hydrotherapy •n. the use of exercises in a pool to treat conditions such as arthritis.

hydrothermal •adj. relating to the action of heated water in the earth's crust.
– DERIVATIVES **hydrothermally** adv.

hydrous •adj. containing water.

hydroxide •n. a compound containing OH negative ions together with a metallic element.

hyena (also **hyaena**) •n. a doglike African mammal.
– ORIGIN Greek *huaina* 'female pig'.

hygiene •n. the practice of keeping yourself and your surroundings clean in order to prevent illness or disease.
– ORIGIN Greek *hugieinē* 'of health'.

> ✓ **hygiene** follows the usual rule of *i* before e except after c.

hygienic •adj. clean and free of the organisms which spread disease.
– DERIVATIVES **hygienically** adv.

hygienist •n. an expert in hygiene.

hygrometer /hy-grom-i-ter/ •n. an instrument for measuring humidity.
– ORIGIN Greek *hugros* 'wet'.

hygroscopic •adj. (of a substance) tending to absorb moisture from the air.

hymen /hy-muhn/ •n. a membrane which partially closes the opening of the vagina and is usually broken when a woman or girl first has sex.
– ORIGIN Greek *humēn* 'membrane'.

hymenopterous /hy-muh-nop-tuh-ruhss/ •adj. (of an insect) belonging to a large group that includes the bees, wasps, and ants, having four transparent wings.
– ORIGIN Greek *humenopteros* 'membrane-winged'.

hymn •n. a religious song of praise, especially a Christian one. •v. praise or celebrate.
– ORIGIN Greek *humnos*.

hymnal /him-nuhl/ •n. a book of hymns.

hymnody /him-nuh-di/ •n. the singing or composition of hymns.
– ORIGIN Greek *humnōidia*.

hype informal •n. excessive or exaggerated publicity. •v. (**hypes, hyping, hyped**) **1** publicize in an excessive way. **2** (**be hyped up**) be very excited or tense. [ORIGIN from **HYPODERMIC**.]

hyper •adj. informal full of nervous energy.

hyper- •prefix **1** over; above: *hypersonic*. **2** excessively: *hyperactive*.
– ORIGIN Greek *huper*.

hyperactive •adj. abnormally or extremely active.
– DERIVATIVES **hyperactivity** n.

hyperbola /hy-per-buh-luh/ •n. (pl. **hyperbolas**) a symmetrical curve formed when a cone is cut by a plane nearly parallel to the cone's axis.
– ORIGIN Greek *huperbolē* 'excess'.

hyperbole /hy-per-buh-li/ •n. a way of speaking or writing that deliberately exaggerates things to create an effect.

– ORIGIN Greek *huperbolē*.

hyperbolic /hy-per-bol-ik/ • adj. **1** (of language) deliberately exaggerated. **2** relating to a hyperbola.
– DERIVATIVES **hyperbolically** adv.

hypercritical • adj. excessively critical.

hyperglycaemia /hy-per-gly-see-mi-uh/ (US **hyperglycemia**) • n. an excess of glucose in the bloodstream, often associated with the most common form of diabetes.
– DERIVATIVES **hyperglycaemic** adj.

hyperinflation • n. inflation of prices or wages occurring at a very high rate.

hyperlink • n. Computing a link from a hypertext document to another location.

hypermarket • n. Brit. a very large supermarket.

hypermedia • n. Computing an extension to hypertext providing multimedia facilities, such as sound and video.

hypersensitive • adj. excessively sensitive.

hypersonic • adj. **1** relating to speeds of more than five times the speed of sound. **2** relating to sound frequencies above about a thousand million hertz.

hypertension • n. abnormally high blood pressure.
– DERIVATIVES **hypertensive** adj.

hypertext • n. Computing a software system allowing users to move quickly between related documents or sections of data.

hypertrophy /hy-per-truh-fi/ • n. abnormal enlargement of an organ or tissue resulting from an increase in size of its cells.
– DERIVATIVES **hypertrophied** adj.
– ORIGIN Greek *-trophia* 'nourishment'.

hyperventilate • v. (**hyperventilates, hyperventilating, hyperventilated**) breathe at an abnormally rapid rate.
– DERIVATIVES **hyperventilation** n.

hyphen /hy-fuhn/ • n. the sign (-) used to join words together or to divide a word into parts between one line and the next.
– ORIGIN Greek *huphen* 'together'.

> **USAGE:** When a phrasal verb such as **build up** is made into a noun it is usually hyphenated (*a build-up of pressure*). However, a normal phrasal verb should not be hyphenated: *continue to build up your pension*.

hyphenate • v. write or separate with a hyphen.
– DERIVATIVES **hyphenation** n.

hypnosis • n. the practice of causing a person to enter a state of consciousness in which they respond very readily to suggestions or commands.
– ORIGIN Greek *hupnos* 'sleep'.

hypnotherapy • n. the use of hypnosis to treat physical or mental problems.
– DERIVATIVES **hypnotherapist** n.

hypnotic • adj. **1** relating to hypnosis. **2** causing a very relaxed or drowsy state: *her voice had a hypnotic quality.* **3** (of a drug) producing sleep.
– DERIVATIVES **hypnotically** adv.

hypnotism • n. the study or practice of hypnosis.
– DERIVATIVES **hypnotist** n.

hypnotize (or **hypnotise**) • v. (**hypnotizes, hypnotizing, hypnotized**) put someone in a state of hypnosis.

hypo- (also **hyp-**) • prefix **1** under: *hypodermic.* **2** below normal: *hypothermia.*
– ORIGIN Greek *hupo.*

hypoallergenic • adj. unlikely to cause an allergic reaction.

hypochondria /hy-per-kon-dri-uh/ • n. constant and excessive anxiety about your health.
– ORIGIN Greek *hupokhondria* 'abdomen below the ribs' (once thought to be the source of melancholy).

hypochondriac • n. a person who is excessively anxious about their health.

hypocrisy /hi-pok-ruh-si/ • n. behaviour in which a person pretends to have higher standards than is the case.
– ORIGIN Greek *hupokrisis* 'acting of a theatrical part'.

hypocrite • n. a person who pretends to have higher standards than is the case.
– DERIVATIVES **hypocritical** adj. **hypocritically** adv.

hypodermic • adj. (of a needle or syringe) used to inject a drug or other substance beneath the skin. • n. a hypodermic syringe or injection.
– ORIGIN Greek *derma* 'skin'.

hypoglycaemia /hy-poh-gly-see-mi-uh/ (US **hypoglycemia**) • n. lack of glucose in the bloodstream.
– DERIVATIVES **hypoglycaemic** adj.

hypotension • n. abnormally low blood pressure.
– DERIVATIVES **hypotensive** adj.

hypotenuse /hy-pot-uh-nyooz/ • n. the longest side of a right-angled triangle, opposite the right angle.
– ORIGIN from Greek *hupoteinousa grammē* 'subtending line'.

hypothermia /hy-puh-ther-mi-uh/ • n. the condition of having an abnormally low body temperature.
– ORIGIN Greek *thermē* 'heat'.

hypothesis /hy-poth-i-siss/ •n. (pl.
hypotheses /hy-poth-i-seez/) a proposed
explanation based on limited evidence,
used as a starting point for further
investigation.
– ORIGIN Greek *hupothesis* 'foundation'.

hypothesize (or **hypothesise**)
•v. (**hypothesizes, hypothesizing,
hypothesized**) put forward an
explanation as a hypothesis.

hypothetical /hy-puh-thet-i-k'l/
•adj. based on an imagined situation
rather than fact.
– DERIVATIVES **hypothetically** adv.

hyrax /hy-raks/ •n. a small mammal with
a short tail, found in Africa and Arabia.
– ORIGIN Greek *hurax* 'shrew-mouse'.

hyssop /hiss-uhp/ •n. a bushy plant
whose bitter minty leaves are used in
cookery and herbal medicine.
– ORIGIN Greek *hyssōpos*.

hysterectomy /hiss-tuh-rek-tuh-mi/
•n. (pl. **hysterectomies**) a surgical
operation to remove all or part of the
womb.
– ORIGIN from Greek *hustera* 'womb'.

hysteria •n. 1 extreme or uncontrollable
emotion or excitement: *election hysteria*.
2 dated a mental disorder in which a
person converts psychological stress
into physical symptoms.
– ORIGIN from Greek *hustera* 'womb'
(hysteria once being thought to be
caused by a disorder of the womb).

hysterical •adj. 1 affected by wildly
uncontrolled emotion. 2 informal very
funny.
– DERIVATIVES **hysterically** adv.

hysterics •pl. n. 1 wildly emotional
behaviour. 2 informal uncontrollable
laughter.

Hz •abbrev. hertz.

h

Ii

I¹ (also **i**) • n. (pl. **Is** or **I's**) **1** the ninth letter of the alphabet. **2** the Roman numeral for one.

I² • pron. (first person sing.) used by a speaker to refer to himself or herself.
– ORIGIN Old English.

> USAGE: On whether to say *you have more than me* or *you have more than I*, see the note at **THAN**.

I³ • symb. the chemical element iodine.

I.³ • abbrev. Island(s) or Isle(s).

iambic /I-am-bik/ • adj. Poetry having one short or unstressed syllable followed by one long or stressed syllable.
– ORIGIN Greek *iambos*.

IBA • abbrev. (in the UK) Independent Broadcasting Authority.

Iberian /I-beer-i-uhn/ • adj. relating to Iberia (the peninsula that consists of modern Spain and Portugal). • n. a person from Iberia.

ibex /I-beks/ • n. (pl. **ibexes**) a wild mountain goat with long, curved horns.
– ORIGIN Latin.

ibid. /ib-id/ • adv. in the same source (referring to a work previously mentioned).
– ORIGIN Latin *ibidem* 'in the same place'.

ibis /I-biss/ • n. (pl. **ibis** or **ibises**) a large wading bird with a long curved bill.
– ORIGIN Greek.

-ible • suffix forming adjectives: **1** able to be: *defensible.* **2** suitable for being: *edible.* **3** causing: *horrible.*
– DERIVATIVES **-ibility** suffix. **-ibly** suffix.
– ORIGIN Latin *-ibilis.*

ibuprofen /I-byoo-proh-fen/ • n. a synthetic compound used as a painkiller and to reduce inflammation.
– ORIGIN from the chemical name.

IC • abbrev. integrated circuit.

-ic • suffix **1** forming adjectives: *Islamic.* **2** forming nouns: *mechanic.*
– ORIGIN Latin *-icus* or Greek *-ikos.*

-ical • suffix forming adjectives: **1** from nouns or adjectives ending in *-ic* (such as *comical* from *comic*). **2** from nouns ending in *-y* (such as *pathological* from *pathology*).

– DERIVATIVES **-ically** suffix.

ICBM • abbrev. intercontinental ballistic missile.

ice • n. **1** frozen water, a brittle transparent solid. **2** esp. Brit. an ice cream or water ice. • v. (**ices, icing, iced**) **1** decorate with icing. **2** (**ice up/over**) become covered or blocked with ice.
– PHRASES **break the ice** help people who do not know each other well to feel more relaxed. **on ice** (of a plan) waiting to be dealt with at a later time. **on thin ice** in a risky situation.
– ORIGIN Old English.

ice age • n. a period when ice sheets covered much of the earth's surface, especially during the Pleistocene period.

iceberg • n. a large mass of ice floating in the sea.
– PHRASES **the tip of the iceberg** the small visible part of a much larger problem that remains hidden.
– ORIGIN Dutch *ijsberg.*

iceberg lettuce • n. a kind of lettuce having a closely packed round head of crisp leaves.

icebox • n. **1** a chilled container for keeping food cold. **2** Brit. a compartment in a refrigerator for making and storing ice.

icebreaker • n. a ship designed for breaking a channel through ice.

ice cap • n. a permanent covering of ice over a large area, especially at the North and South Poles.

ice cream • n. a frozen dessert made with sweetened and flavoured milk fat.

iced • adj. **1** cooled or mixed with ice: *iced water.* **2** decorated with icing.

ice field • n. a large permanent expanse of ice at the North and South Poles.

ice hockey • n. a form of hockey played on an ice rink.

Icelander • n. a person from Iceland.

Icelandic /Is-lan-dik/ • n. the language of Iceland. • adj. relating to Iceland.

ice lolly • n. Brit. a piece of flavoured

water ice or ice cream on a stick.

ice pack • n. a bag filled with ice and held against part of the body to reduce swelling or lower temperature.

ice skate • n. a boot with a blade attached to the sole, used for skating on ice. • v. (**ice-skate**) skate on ice as a sport or pastime.
– DERIVATIVES **ice skater** n. **ice skating** n.

ichneumon /ik-nyoo-muhn/ • n. a small wasp which lays its eggs in or on the larvae of other insects.
– ORIGIN Greek *ikhneumōn* 'tracker'.

ichthyology /ik-thi-ol-uh-ji/ • n. the branch of zoology concerned with fish.
– DERIVATIVES **ichthyologist** n.
– ORIGIN Greek *ikhthus* 'fish'.

ichthyosaur /ik-thi-uh-sor/ (also **ichthyosaurus** /ik-thi-uh-sor-uhss/) • n. a fossil reptile that lived in the sea, having a long pointed head, four flippers, and a vertical tail.

icicle • n. a hanging, tapering piece of ice formed when dripping water freezes.
– ORIGIN Old English.

icing • n. a mixture of sugar with liquid or fat, used to coat or fill cakes or biscuits.
– PHRASES **the icing on the cake** an additional thing which makes something good even better.

icing sugar • n. Brit. finely powdered sugar used to make icing.

icon /I-kon/ • n. 1 (also **ikon**) (in the Orthodox Church) a painting of Jesus or another holy figure which itself is treated as holy and used as an aid to prayer. 2 a person or thing seen as a symbol of something: *he's an iron-jawed icon of American manhood.* 3 a symbol on a computer screen of a program or option.
– DERIVATIVES **iconic** adj.
– ORIGIN Greek *eikōn* 'image'.

iconify /I-kon-i-fy/ • v. (**iconifies, iconifying, iconified**) reduce a window on a computer screen to an icon.

iconoclast /I-kon-uh-klast/ • n. 1 a person who attacks popular beliefs or established values and practices. 2 hist. a person who destroyed images used in religious worship.
– DERIVATIVES **iconoclasm** n. **iconoclastic** adj.
– ORIGIN from Greek *eikōn* 'image' + *klan* 'to break'.

iconography /I-kuh-nog-ruh-fi/ • n. 1 the use or study of pictures or symbols in visual arts. 2 the pictures or symbols associated with a person or movement.
– DERIVATIVES **iconographer** n. **iconographic** adj.

icosahedron /I-koss-uh-hee-druhn/ • n. (pl. **icosahedra** /I-koss-uh-hee-druh/ or **icosahedrons**) a three-dimensional shape with twenty plane faces.
– ORIGIN Greek *eikosaedros* 'twenty-faced'.

ICT • abbrev. information and computing technology.

icy • adj. (**icier, iciest**) 1 covered with ice. 2 very cold. 3 very unfriendly.
– DERIVATIVES **icily** adv. **iciness** n.

ID • abbrev. identification or identity.

Id • n. var. of EID.

I'd • contr. 1 I had. 2 I should; I would.

id /id/ • n. the part of the unconscious mind consisting of a person's basic inherited instincts, needs, and feelings. Compare with EGO and SUPEREGO.
– ORIGIN Latin, 'that'.

idea • n. 1 a thought or suggestion about a possible course of action. 2 a mental impression. 3 a belief. 4 (**the idea**) the aim or purpose.
– ORIGIN Greek, 'form, pattern'.

ideal • adj. 1 most suitable; perfect. 2 desirable or perfect but existing only in the imagination: *in an ideal world, we might have made a different decision.* • n. 1 a person or thing regarded as perfect. 2 a principle or standard that is worth trying to achieve: *tolerance and freedom, the liberal ideals.*
– DERIVATIVES **ideally** adv.

idealism • n. 1 the belief that ideals can be achieved, even when this is unrealistic. 2 (in art or literature) the presenting of things as perfect or better than in reality.
– DERIVATIVES **idealist** n. **idealistic** adj.

idealize (or **idealise**) • v. (**idealizes, idealizing, idealized**) (often as adj. **idealized**) regard or present as perfect or better than in reality: *a porcelain figure of idealized beauty.*
– DERIVATIVES **idealization** n.

idée fixe /ee-day feeks/ • n. (pl. **idées fixes** /ee-day feeks/) an idea that dominates the mind; an obsession.
– ORIGIN French, 'fixed idea'.

identical • adj. 1 exactly alike. 2 the same. 3 (of twins) developed from a single fertilized ovum, and therefore of the same sex and very similar in appearance.
– DERIVATIVES **identically** adv.
– ORIGIN Latin *identicus*.

identification • n. 1 the action of identifying or the fact of being identified. 2 an official document or other proof of your identity.

identify • v. (**identifies, identifying, identified**) 1 prove or recognize as being

a specified person or thing: *he couldn't identify his attackers.* **2** recognize something as being worthy of attention. **3** (**identify with**) feel that you understand or feel the same as someone else. **4** (**identify someone/thing with**) associate someone or something closely with.
– DERIVATIVES **identifiable** adj. **identifier** n.

identikit • n. trademark a picture of a person wanted by the police, put together according to witnesses' descriptions from a set of typical facial features.

identity • n. (pl. **identities**) **1** the fact of being who or what a person or thing is: *she knew the identity of the bomber.* **2** a close similarity or feeling of understanding.
– ORIGIN Latin *identitas.*

identity parade • n. Brit. a group of people assembled so that an eyewitness may identify a suspect for a crime from among them.

ideogram /id-i-uh-gram/ (also **ideograph**) • n. a symbol used in a writing system to represent the idea of a thing rather than the sounds used to say it (e.g. a number).

ideologue /I-di-uh-log/ • n. a person who follows a system of ideas and principles in a strict and inflexible way.

ideology /I-di-ol-uh-ji/ • n. (pl. **ideologies**) **1** a system of ideas and principles forming the basis of an economic or political theory. **2** the set of beliefs held by a particular group: *bourgeois ideology.*
– DERIVATIVES **ideological** adj. **ideologically** adv. **ideologist** n.
– ORIGIN Greek *idea* 'form'.

ides /*rhymes with* hides/ • pl. n. (in the ancient Roman calendar) a day falling roughly in the middle of each month, from which other dates were calculated.
– ORIGIN Latin *idus.*

idiocy /id-i-uh-si/ • n. (pl. **idiocies**) very stupid behaviour.

idiom /id-i-uhm/ • n. **1** a group of words whose meaning is different from the meanings of the individual words (e.g. *over the moon*). **2** a form of language and grammar used by particular people at a particular time or place. **3** a style of expression in music or art that is characteristic of a particular group or place: *an Impressionist idiom.*
– ORIGIN Greek *idiōma* 'private property'.

idiomatic • adj. using or relating to expressions that are natural to a native speaker.

idiosyncrasy /id-i-oh-sing-kruh-si/

• n. (pl. **idiosyncrasies**) **1** a person's particular way of behaving or thinking. **2** a distinctive or peculiar feature of a thing.
– ORIGIN Greek *idiosunkrasia.*

> ☑ The ending of **idiosyncrasy** is spelled **-asy**.

idiosyncratic /id-i-oh-sing-krat-ik/ • adj. individual or peculiar.

idiot • n. informal a stupid person.
– ORIGIN Greek *idiōtēs* 'layman, ignorant person'.

idiotic • adj. very stupid.
– DERIVATIVES **idiotically** adv.

idle • adj. (**idler, idlest**) **1** tending to avoid work; lazy. **2** not working or in use. **3** having no purpose or effect: *she did not make idle threats.* • v. (**idles, idling, idled**) **1** spend time doing nothing. **2** (of an engine) run slowly while out of gear.
– DERIVATIVES **idleness** n. **idler** n. **idly** adv.
– ORIGIN Old English, 'empty, useless'.

idol • n. **1** a statue or picture of a god which itself is worshipped. **2** a person who is greatly admired: *a soccer idol.*
– ORIGIN Greek *eidōlon.*

idolatry /I-dol-uh-tri/ • n. **1** the worship of a statue or picture representing a god. **2** extreme admiration or devotion.
– DERIVATIVES **idolater** n. **idolatrous** adj.
– ORIGIN from Greek *eidōlon* 'idol' + *-latreia* 'worship'.

idolize (or **idolise**) • v. (**idolizes, idolizing, idolized**) admire or love someone greatly or excessively.
– DERIVATIVES **idolization** n.

idyll /i-dil/ • n. **1** a very happy or peaceful period or situation. **2** a short poem or piece of writing describing a picturesque scene or incident in country life.
– ORIGIN Greek *eidullion* 'little form'.

idyllic • adj. very happy, peaceful, or beautiful.
– DERIVATIVES **idyllically** adv.

i.e. • abbrev. that is to say.
– ORIGIN from Latin *id est* 'that is'.

if • conj. **1** on the condition or in the event that: *if you have a complaint, write to the manager.* **2** despite the possibility that. **3** whether. **4** whenever. **5** expressing surprise, regret, or an opinion: *if you ask me, he's in love.*
– ORIGIN Old English.

> **USAGE:** Although **if** can mean 'whether', it is better to use the word **whether** rather than **if** in writing (*I'll see whether he left an address* rather than *I'll see if he left an address*).

iffy • adj. informal **1** uncertain. **2** of doubtful quality or legality.

igloo • n. a dome-shaped Eskimo house

built from blocks of solid snow.
– ORIGIN Inuit, 'house'.

igneous /ig-ni-uhss/ • adj. (of rock)
formed when molten rock has solidified.
– ORIGIN Latin *ignis* 'fire'.

ignite /ig-nyt/ • v. (**ignites, igniting,
ignited**) **1** catch fire or set on fire.
2 provoke or stir up: *the words ignited
new fury in him.*
– DERIVATIVES **igniter** n.
– ORIGIN Latin *ignire.*

ignition • n. **1** the action of catching fire
or setting on fire. **2** the mechanism
providing the spark that ignites the fuel
in an internal-combustion engine.

ignoble • adj. not good or honest;
dishonourable.
– ORIGIN from Latin *in-* 'not' + *gnobilis*
'noble'.

ignominious /ig-nuh-**min**-i-uhss/
• adj. deserving or causing public
disgrace: *they risked ignominious defeat.*
– DERIVATIVES **ignominiously** adv.
– ORIGIN Latin *ignominiosus.*

ignominy /ig-nuh-mi-ni/ • n. public
disgrace.

ignoramus /ig-nuh-**ray**-muhss/ • n. (pl.
ignoramuses) an ignorant or stupid
person.
– ORIGIN Latin, 'we do not know'.

ignorance • n. lack of knowledge or
information.

ignorant • adj. **1** lacking knowledge or
awareness. **2** informal not polite; rude.
– ORIGIN Latin *ignorare* 'not know'.

ignore • v. (**ignores, ignoring, ignored**)
1 deliberately take no notice of
someone. **2** fail to consider something
important.
– ORIGIN Latin *ignorare* 'not know'.

iguana /i-**gwah**-nuh/ • n. a large tropical
American lizard with a spiny crest along
the back.
– ORIGIN Spanish.

ikon • n. var. of **ICON**.

ileum /il-i-uhm/ • n. (pl. **ilea** /il-i-uh/) the
third and lowest part of the small
intestine.
– ORIGIN Latin.

iliac /il-i-ak/ • adj. relating to the ilium or
the nearby regions of the lower body.

ilium /il-i-uhm/ • n. (pl. **ilia** /il-i-uh/) the
large broad bone forming the upper part
of each half of the pelvis.
– ORIGIN Latin.

ilk • n. a type: *fascists, racists, and others of
that ilk.*
– ORIGIN Old English, 'same'.

I'll • contr. I shall; I will.

ill • adj. **1** not in good health; unwell.
2 harmful, hostile, or unfavourable.
• adv. **1** badly or wrongly: *ill-chosen.*

2 only with difficulty: *she could ill afford
the cost.* • n. **1** a problem or misfortune.
2 evil or harm.
– PHRASES **ill at ease** uncomfortable or
embarrassed.
– ORIGIN Old Norse, 'evil, difficult'.

ill-advised • adj. unwise or badly
thought out.

ill-bred • adj. badly brought up or rude.

ill-disposed • adj. unfriendly or
unsympathetic.

illegal • adj. against the law.
– DERIVATIVES **illegality** n. **illegally** adv.

illegible /il-**lej**-i-b'l/ • adj. not clear
enough to be read.
– DERIVATIVES **illegibility** n. **illegibly** adv.

illegitimate /il-li-**jit**-i-muht/ • adj. **1** not
allowed by law or rules. **2** (of a child)
born to parents who are not married to
each other.
– DERIVATIVES **illegitimacy** n.

ill-fated • adj. destined to fail or be
unlucky.

ill-favoured (US **ill-favored**) • adj. unattractive.

ill-gotten • adj. obtained by illegal or
unfair means.

illiberal • adj. restricting freedom of
thought or behaviour.

illicit /il-**li**-sit/ • adj. forbidden by law,
rules, or accepted standards.
– DERIVATIVES **illicitly** adv.
– ORIGIN Latin *illicitus.*

illiterate /il-**lit**-uh-ruht/ • adj. **1** unable
to read or write. **2** not knowledgeable
about a particular subject: *politically
illiterate.*
– DERIVATIVES **illiteracy** n.

illness • n. a disease or period of
sickness.

illogical • adj. not sensible or based on
sound reasoning: *an illogical fear of the
dark.*
– DERIVATIVES **illogicality** n. (pl.
illogicalities). **illogically** adv.

ill-starred • adj. unlucky.

ill-tempered • adj. irritable or surly.

ill-treat • v. treat cruelly.

illuminate /il-**lyoo**-mi-nayt/
• v. (**illuminates, illuminating,
illuminated**) **1** light up. **2** (usu. as adj.
illuminating) help to explain or make
clear: *an illuminating discussion.*
3 decorate a manuscript with gold,
silver, or coloured designs.
– DERIVATIVES **illuminator** n.
– ORIGIN Latin *illuminare.*

illumination • n. **1** lighting or light.
2 (**illuminations**) lights used in
decorating a building or other structure.
3 understanding of something.

illumine • v. (**illumines, illumining,**

illumined) literary illuminate.

illusion /il-lyoo-zh'n/ • n. **1** a false idea or belief: *he had no illusions about his playing.* **2** a thing that seems to be something that it is not or seems to exist but does not.
– ORIGIN Latin *illudere* 'to mock'.

illusionist • n. a magician or conjuror.

illusory /il-lyoo-suh-ri/ (also **illusive**) • adj. not real, although seeming to be.

illustrate • v. (**illustrates, illustrating, illustrated**) **1** provide a book or magazine with pictures. **2** make something clear by using examples, charts, etc. **3** act as an example of.
– DERIVATIVES **illustrator** n.
– ORIGIN Latin *illustrare* 'light up'.

illustration • n. **1** a picture in a book or magazine. **2** the action of illustrating. **3** an example that proves something or helps to explain it.

illustrative • adj. **1** acting as an example or explanation. **2** relating to pictures in a book or magazine.

illustrious /il-luss-tri-uhss/ • adj. famous and admired for past achievements.
– ORIGIN Latin *illustris* 'clear, bright'.

ill will • n. hostility towards someone.

I'm • contr. I am.

image • n. **1** a likeness of someone or something in the form of a picture or statue. **2** a picture seen on a television or computer screen, through a lens, or reflected in something. **3** a picture in the mind. **4** the impression that a person or thing presents to the public: *she tries to project an image of youth.* **5** a person or thing that looks very similar to another: *Gwen was the image of Judy, down to her red hair.* **6** a word or phrase describing something in an imaginative way; a simile or metaphor. • v. (**images, imaging, imaged**) make or form an image of.
– ORIGIN Latin *imago.*

imager • n. an electronic or other device which records images.

imagery • n. **1** language using similes and metaphors that produces images in the mind. **2** images as a whole.

imaginable • adj. possible to be thought of or believed.

imaginary • adj. **1** existing only in the imagination. **2** Math. (of a number or quantity) expressed in terms of the square root of −1 (represented by *i* or *j*).

> ✓ Remember that **imaginary** ends in -ary.

imagination • n. **1** the ability to form ideas or images in the mind. **2** the ability of the mind to be creative or solve problems.

imaginative • adj. using the imagination in a creative or inventive way.
– DERIVATIVES **imaginatively** adv.

imagine • v. (**imagines, imagining, imagined**) **1** form a mental picture of. **2** think that something is probable; assume. **3** believe something unreal to exist.
– ORIGIN from Latin *imaginare* 'form an image of' and *imaginari* 'imagine'.

imaginings • pl. n. thoughts or fantasies.

imago /i-may-goh/ • n. (pl. **imagos** or **imagines** /i-may-ji-neez/) the final and fully developed adult stage of an insect.
– ORIGIN Latin, 'image'.

imam /i-mahm/ • n. **1** the person who leads prayers in a mosque. **2** (**Imam**) a title of various Muslim religious leaders.
– ORIGIN Arabic, 'leader'.

imbalance • n. a lack of proportion or balance.

imbecile /im-bi-seel/ • n. informal a stupid person.
– DERIVATIVES **imbecilic** adj. **imbecility** n. (pl. **imbecilities**).
– ORIGIN Latin *imbecillus* 'weak'.

imbed • v. var. of EMBED.

imbibe /im-byb/ • v. (**imbibes, imbibing, imbibed**) **1** formal drink alcohol. **2** literary absorb ideas or knowledge.
– ORIGIN Latin *imbibere.*

imbroglio /im-broh-li-oh/ • n. (pl. **imbroglios**) a very confused or complicated situation.
– ORIGIN Italian.

imbue /im-byoo/ • v. (**imbues, imbuing, imbued**) fill with a feeling or quality: *we were imbued with a sense of purpose.*
– ORIGIN Latin *imbuere* 'moisten'.

IMF • abbrev. International Monetary Fund.

imitate • v. (**imitates, imitating, imitated**) **1** take someone or something as a model to follow. **2** copy a person's speech or behaviour to amuse people. **3** make a copy of; simulate.
– DERIVATIVES **imitator** n.
– ORIGIN Latin *imitari.*

imitation • n. **1** a copy. **2** the action of copying someone or of following something as a model.

imitative /im-i-tuh-tiv/ • adj. following a model or example.

immaculate • adj. **1** completely clean or tidy. **2** free from flaws or mistakes; perfect.
– DERIVATIVES **immaculately** adv.
– ORIGIN Latin *immaculatus.*

i

Immaculate Conception •n. (in the Roman Catholic Church) the doctrine that the Virgin Mary was free of the sin common to all human beings from the moment she was conceived by her mother .

immanent /im-muh-nuhnt/ •adj. present within or throughout: *love is a force immanent in the world.*
– DERIVATIVES **immanence** n.
– ORIGIN Latin *immanere* 'remain within'.

immaterial •adj. **1** unimportant under the circumstances; irrelevant. **2** spiritual rather than physical.

immature •adj. **1** not fully developed. **2** behaving in a way that is typical of someone younger; childish.
– DERIVATIVES **immaturity** n.

immeasurable •adj. too large or extreme to measure.
– DERIVATIVES **immeasurably** adv.

immediacy •n. **1** the quality of providing direct and instant involvement with something. **2** lack of delay; speed.

immediate •adj. **1** occurring or done at once. **2** nearest in time, space, or relationship. **3** most urgent; current. **4** direct: *a coronary was the immediate cause of death.*
– ORIGIN Latin *immediatus.*

immediately •adv. **1** at once. **2** very close in time, space, or relationship. •conj. esp. Brit. as soon as.

> ☑ Spell **immediately** with an **e** after the **t**.

immemorial •adj. existing from before what can be remembered or found in records: *they had lived there from time immemorial.*

immense •adj. very large or great.
– DERIVATIVES **immensity** n.
– ORIGIN Latin *immensus* 'immeasurable'.

immensely •adv. to a great extent; extremely.

immerse •v. (**immerses, immersing, immersed**) **1** dip or cover completely in a liquid. **2** (**immerse yourself** or **be immersed**) involve yourself deeply in an activity or interest.
– ORIGIN Latin *immergere.*

immersion •n. **1** the action of dipping or covering someone or something in a liquid. **2** deep involvement.

immersion heater •n. an electric device that is positioned in a domestic water tank to heat the water.

immigrant •n. a person who comes to live permanently in a foreign country.

immigration •n. the action of coming to live permanently in a foreign country.
– ORIGIN Latin *immigrare.*

imminent •adj. about to happen.
– DERIVATIVES **imminence** n.
– ORIGIN Latin *imminere* 'overhang'.

immiscible /im-miss-i-b'l/ •adj. (of liquids) not able to be mixed together.

immobile •adj. **1** not moving. **2** not able to move.
– DERIVATIVES **immobility** n.

immobilize (or **immobilise**) •v. (**immobilizes, immobilizing, immobilized**) prevent from moving or operating as normal.
– DERIVATIVES **immobilization** n.

immoderate •adj. not sensible or controlled; excessive.

immodest •adj. **1** tending to be boastful. **2** tending to show off your body.

immolate /im-muh-layt/ •v. (**immolates, immolating, immolated**) kill or sacrifice a person or animal by burning.
– DERIVATIVES **immolation** n.
– ORIGIN Latin *immolare* 'sprinkle with sacrificial meal'.

immoral •adj. not following accepted standards of morality.
– DERIVATIVES **immorality** n.

immortal •adj. **1** living forever. **2** deserving to be remembered forever. •n. **1** an immortal god or other being. **2** a person who will be famous for a very long time.
– DERIVATIVES **immortality** n.

immortalize (or **immortalise**) •v. (**immortalizes, immortalizing, immortalized**) cause to be remembered for a very long time.

immovable •adj. **1** not able to be moved. **2** unable to be changed or persuaded: *an immovable truth.*
– DERIVATIVES **immovably** adv.

immune •adj. **1** having a natural resistance to a particular infection. **2** not affected by something: *no one is immune to his charm.* **3** protected from being punished or having to do a duty.
– ORIGIN Latin *immunis.*

immune system •n. the organs and processes of the body that provide resistance to infection and toxins.

immunity •n. (pl. **immunities**) **1** the ability of a person or animal to resist a particular infection. **2** protection from having to do a duty or be punished.

immunize (or **immunise**) •v. (**immunizes, immunizing, immunized**) make a person or animal resistant to infection.
– DERIVATIVES **immunization** n.

immunodeficiency •n. failure of the body's ability to resist infection.

immunology • n. the branch of medicine and biology concerned with resistance to infection.
– DERIVATIVES **immunological** adj. **immunologist** n.

immunotherapy • n. the prevention or treatment of disease with substances that stimulate the body's resistance to infection.

immure /im-myoor/ • v. (**immures, immuring, immured**) literary confine or imprison someone.
– ORIGIN Latin *immurare*.

immutable /im-myoo-tuh-b'l/ • adj. unchanging or unchangeable.

imp • n. 1 a small, mischievous devil or sprite. 2 a mischievous child.
– ORIGIN Old English, 'young shoot'.

impact • n. /im-pakt/ 1 an act of one object hitting another. 2 a noticeable effect or influence: *man's impact on the environment.* • v. /im-**pakt**/ 1 hit another object. 2 have a strong effect: *the cuts impacted on the service the company provided.* 3 press firmly into something. 4 (as adj. **impacted**) (of a tooth) wedged between another tooth and the jaw.
– ORIGIN Latin *impingere* 'drive something in'.

impair • v. weaken or damage.
– DERIVATIVES **impairment** n.
– ORIGIN Old French *empeirier*.

impala /im-pah-luh/ • n. (pl. **impala**) an antelope of southern and East Africa, with lyre-shaped horns.
– ORIGIN Zulu.

impale • v. (**impales, impaling, impaled**) pierce with a sharp object.
– DERIVATIVES **impalement** n.
– ORIGIN Latin *impalare*.

impalpable • adj. 1 unable to be felt by touch. 2 not easily perceived or understood.

impart • v. 1 provide information. 2 give a particular quality to.
– ORIGIN Latin *impartire* 'give a share of'.

impartial • adj. treating everyone or everything equally; not biased.
– DERIVATIVES **impartiality** n. **impartially** adv.

impassable • adj. impossible to travel along or over.

impasse /am-pahss/ • n. a situation in which no progress is possible; a deadlock.
– ORIGIN French.

impassioned • adj. filled with or showing great emotion.

impassive • adj. not feeling or showing emotion.
– DERIVATIVES **impassively** adv. **impassivity** n.

impasto /im-pass-toh/ • n. the technique of laying on paint thickly so that it stands out from the surface of a painting.
– ORIGIN Italian.

impatient • adj. 1 lacking patience or tolerance. 2 restlessly eager: *they are impatient for change.*
– DERIVATIVES **impatience** n. **impatiently** adv.

impeach • v. 1 question the worth of. 2 esp. US charge someone who holds a responsible public position with bad behaviour.
– DERIVATIVES **impeachment** n.
– ORIGIN Old French *empecher* 'impede'.

impeccable /im-pek-kuh-b'l/ • adj. without faults or mistakes; perfect.
– DERIVATIVES **impeccably** adv.
– ORIGIN Latin *impeccabilis* 'not liable to sin'.

impecunious /im-pi-kyoo-ni-uhss/ • adj. having little or no money.
– ORIGIN from IN-¹ + Latin *pecuniosus* 'wealthy'.

impedance /im-pee-duhnss/ • n. the total resistance of an electric circuit to the flow of alternating current.

impede /im-peed/ • v. (**impedes, impeding, impeded**) delay or block the progress or action of: *matters which would impede progress.*
– ORIGIN Latin *impedire* 'shackle the feet of'.

impediment /im-ped-i-muhnt/ • n. 1 a hindrance or obstruction. 2 (also **speech impediment**) a defect in a person's speech, such as a stammer.

impedimenta /im-ped-i-men-tuh/ • pl. n. equipment for an activity or expedition, seen as slowing you down.
– ORIGIN Latin.

impel /im-pel/ • v. (**impels, impelling, impelled**) drive or urge someone to do something.
– ORIGIN Latin *impellere*.

impending • adj. be about to happen.
– ORIGIN Latin *impendere* 'overhang'.

impenetrable /im-pen-i-truh-b'l/ • adj. 1 impossible to get through or into. 2 impossible to understand.

impenitent • adj. not feeling shame or regret.

imperative /im-pe-ruh-tiv/ • adj. 1 of vital importance. 2 giving a command. 3 Grammar (of a mood of a verb) expressing a command, as in *come here!* • n. an essential or urgent thing.
– ORIGIN Latin *imperativus* 'specially ordered'.

imperceptible • adj. too slight or gradual to be seen or felt.

– DERIVATIVES **imperceptibly** adv.

imperfect • adj. **1** faulty or incomplete. **2** Grammar (of a tense) referring to a past action in progress but not completed.
– DERIVATIVES **imperfection** n. **imperfectly** adv.

imperial • adj. **1** relating to an empire or an emperor. **2** (of weights and measures) conforming to a non-metric system formerly used in the UK.
– ORIGIN Latin *imperialis*.

imperialism • n. a policy of extending a country's power and influence through means such as establishing colonies or by military force.
– DERIVATIVES **imperialist** n. & adj.

imperil • v. (**imperils**, **imperilling**, **imperilled**; US **imperils**, **imperiling**, **imperiled**) put in danger.

imperious /im-peer-i-uhss/ • adj. expecting to be obeyed without question; domineering.
– ORIGIN Latin *imperiosus*.

impermanent • adj. not permanent.
– DERIVATIVES **impermanence** n.

impermeable /im-per-mi-uh-b'l/ • adj. not allowing fluid to pass through.
– DERIVATIVES **impermeability** n.

impermissible • adj. not permitted or allowed.

impersonal • adj. **1** not influenced by personal feelings. **2** lacking human feelings or atmosphere: *an impersonal tower block*. **3** Grammar (of a verb) used only with *it* as a subject (as in *it is snowing*).
– DERIVATIVES **impersonality** n. **impersonally** adv.

impersonal pronoun • n. the pronoun *it* when not referring to a thing, as in *it was snowing*.

impersonate • v. (**impersonates**, **impersonating**, **impersonated**) pretend to be another person to entertain or trick people.
– DERIVATIVES **impersonation** n. **impersonator** n.

impertinent • adj. not showing proper respect; cheeky.
– DERIVATIVES **impertinence** n.

imperturbable /im-per-ter-buh-b'l/ • adj. not easily upset or worried.

impervious /im-per-vi-uhss/ • adj. **1** not allowing fluid to pass through. **2** (**impervious to**) unaffected by.

impetigo /im-pi-ty-goh/ • n. a skin infection forming spots and yellow crusty sores.
– ORIGIN Latin.

impetuous • adj. acting or done quickly and without thought or care.
– DERIVATIVES **impetuosity** n.

– ORIGIN Latin *impetuosus*.

impetus • n. **1** the force or energy with which a body moves. **2** a driving force: *the impetus for change*.
– ORIGIN Latin, 'assault, force'.

impiety /im-py-i-ti/ • n. lack of religious respect or reverence.

impinge • v. (**impinges**, **impinging**, **impinged**) have an effect: *parents impinge on our lives*.
– DERIVATIVES **impingement** n.
– ORIGIN Latin *impingere* 'drive something in or at'.

impious /im-pi-uhss/ • adj. not showing respect or reverence.

implacable • adj. **1** unwilling to stop being hostile towards someone or something: *an implacable enemy*. **2** unstoppable.
– DERIVATIVES **implacably** adv.
– ORIGIN from IN-¹ + Latin *placabilis* 'easily calmed'.

implant • v. /im-plahnt/ **1** insert tissue or an artificial object into the body. **2** establish an idea in the mind. • n. /im-plahnt/ a thing that has been inserted.
– DERIVATIVES **implantation** n.

implausible • adj. not seeming reasonable or probable.
– DERIVATIVES **implausibility** n. **implausibly** adv.

implement • n. /im-pli-muhnt/ a tool, utensil, or instrument that is used for a particular purpose. • v. /im-pli-ment/ put a decision or planned change into effect.
– DERIVATIVES **implementation** n.
– ORIGIN Latin *implere* 'fill up, employ'.

implicate /im-pli-kayt/ • v. (**implicates**, **implicating**, **implicated**) **1** show someone to be involved in a crime. **2** (**be implicated in**) bear some of the responsibility for. **3** imply something.
– ORIGIN Latin *implicare* 'involve, imply'.

implication • n. **1** the conclusion that can be drawn from something although it is not directly stated. **2** a likely consequence. **3** the state of being involved in something.

implicit /im-pliss-it/ • adj. **1** suggested though not directly expressed. **2** (**implicit in**) always to be found in. **3** with no doubt or question: *an implicit faith in God*.
– DERIVATIVES **implicitly** adv.
– ORIGIN Latin *implicare* 'involve, imply'.

implode /im-plohd/ • v. (**implodes**, **imploding**, **imploded**) collapse violently inwards.
– DERIVATIVES **implosion** n.
– ORIGIN from IN-² + Latin *plodere*, *plaudere* 'to clap'.

implore • v. (**implores**, **imploring**,

implored) beg earnestly or desperately.
– ORIGIN Latin *implorare* 'invoke with tears'.

imply • v. (**implies, implying, implied**)
1 suggest something rather than state it directly. **2** suggest as a likely result: *the forecast traffic increase implied more pollution*.
– ORIGIN Latin *implicare* 'involve, imply'.

> **USAGE:** Do not confuse **imply** and **infer**. These words can describe the same situation, but from different points of view. If a person **implies** something, as in *he implied that the General was a traitor*, it means that they are suggesting something but not saying it directly. If you **infer** something from what has been said, as in *we inferred from his words that the General was a traitor*, this means that you come to the conclusion that this is what they really mean.

impolite • adj. not having or showing good manners.

impolitic • adj. unwise.

imponderable • adj. difficult or impossible to assess.
– ORIGIN from **PONDER**.

import • v. /im-port/ **1** bring goods or services into a country from abroad. **2** transfer data into a computer file or document. • n. /im-port/ **1** an imported article or service. **2** the action of importing. **3** the implied meaning of something. **4** importance.
– DERIVATIVES **importation** n. **importer** n.
– ORIGIN Latin *importare*.

important • adj. **1** of great significance or value. **2** (of a person) having great authority or influence.
– DERIVATIVES **importance** n. **importantly** adv.

importunate /im-por-tyuu-nuht/
• adj. very persistent.
– ORIGIN Latin *importunus* 'inconvenient'.

importune /im-por-tyoon/
• v. (**importunes, importuning, importuned**) bother someone with persistent requests.

impose • v. (**imposes, imposing, imposed**) **1** introduce something that must be obeyed or done: *they plan to impose a tax on fuel*. **2** force something to be accepted. **3** (**impose on**) take unreasonable advantage of someone.
– ORIGIN French *imposer*.

imposing • adj. grand and impressive.

imposition • n. **1** the action of introducing something that must be done. **2** something that has been forced on you that seems unreasonable.

impossible • adj. **1** not able to occur, exist, or be done. **2** very difficult to deal with.
– DERIVATIVES **impossibility** n. (pl. **impossibilities**). **impossibly** adv.

impostor (also **imposter**) • n. a person who pretends to be someone else in order to deceive or cheat other people.
– ORIGIN Latin.

imposture • n. an act of pretending to be someone else so as to deceive.

impotent /im-puh-tuhnt/
• adj. **1** helpless or powerless. **2** (of a man) unable to achieve an erection.
– DERIVATIVES **impotence** n.

impound • v. **1** seize and take legal possession of something. **2** shut up domestic animals in an enclosure.

impoverish • v. **1** make someone poor. **2** make something worse in quality.
– DERIVATIVES **impoverishment** n.
– ORIGIN Old French *empoverir*.

impracticable • adj. not able to be done in practice: *it was impracticable to widen the road here*.

impractical • adj. not adapted for use or action: *impractical high heels*.

imprecation • n. formal a spoken curse.
– ORIGIN Latin.

imprecise • adj. not exact.
– DERIVATIVES **imprecision** n.

impregnable • adj. **1** unable to be captured or broken into. **2** unable to be overcome: *an impregnable half-time lead*.
– ORIGIN Old French *imprenable*.

impregnate /im-preg-nayt/
• v. (**impregnates, impregnating, impregnated**) **1** saturate with a substance. **2** fill with a feeling or quality. **3** make pregnant.
– DERIVATIVES **impregnation** n.
– ORIGIN Latin *impregnare*.

impresario /im-pri-sah-ri-oh/ • n. (pl. **impresarios**) a person who organizes theatrical or musical productions.
– ORIGIN Italian.

impress • v. /im-press/ **1** make someone feel admiration and respect. **2** make a mark or design on something using a stamp or seal. **3** (**impress something on**) cause someone to understand the significance of something. • n. /im-press/ a mark or impression.
– ORIGIN Old French *empresser* 'press in'.

impression • n. **1** an idea, feeling, or opinion. **2** an effect produced on someone: *her courtesy made a good impression*. **3** an imitation of a person or thing, done to entertain. **4** a mark made by pressing on a surface.

impressionable • adj. easily influenced by someone or something.

Impressionism • n. a style of painting

concerned with showing the visual impression of a particular moment, especially the shifting effects of light.
- DERIVATIVES **Impressionist** n. & adj.

impressionist • n. an entertainer who impersonates famous people.

impressionistic • adj. based on personal feelings and responses.

impressive • adj. arousing admiration through size, quality, or skill.
- DERIVATIVES **impressively** adv. **impressiveness** n.

imprimatur /im-pri-mah-ter/ • n. **1** authority or approval. **2** an official licence issued by the Roman Catholic Church to print a religious book.
- ORIGIN Latin, 'let it be printed'.

imprint • v. /im-**print**/ **1** make a mark on an object by pressure. **2** have an effect on someone's mind or memory. • n. /**im**-print/ **1** a mark made by pressure. **2** a printer's or publisher's name and other details in a publication.
- ORIGIN Latin *imprimere*.

imprison • v. put or keep in prison.
- DERIVATIVES **imprisonment** n.

improbable • adj. not likely to be true or to happen.
- DERIVATIVES **improbability** n. (pl. **improbabilities**). **improbably** adv.

impromptu /im-promp-tyoo/ • adj. & adv. done without being planned or rehearsed.
- ORIGIN from Latin *in promptu* 'in readiness'.

improper • adj. **1** not in accordance with accepted standards of behaviour. **2** not modest or decent.

improper fraction • n. a fraction in which the numerator is greater than the denominator, such as ⁵⁄₄.

impropriety /im-pruh-**pry**-uh-ti/ • n. (pl. **improprieties**) behaviour that does not conform to accepted standards or principles.

improve • v. (**improves, improving, improved**) **1** make or become better. **2** (**improve on**) produce something better than.
- DERIVATIVES **improver** n.
- ORIGIN Old French *empower*.

improvement • n. **1** the action of making or becoming better: *there's still room for improvement.* **2** a thing that makes something better or is better than something else.

improvident • adj. not providing for future needs.

improvise • v. (**improvises, improvising, improvised**) **1** invent and perform music, drama, or a speech without any preparation. **2** make something from

whatever is available.
- DERIVATIVES **improvisation** n.
- ORIGIN Latin *improvisus* 'unforeseen'.

imprudent • adj. not showing care for the results of an action; rash.

impudent /im-pyoo-duhnt/ • adj. not showing proper respect to someone; cheeky.
- DERIVATIVES **impudence** n. **impudently** adv.
- ORIGIN Latin *impudens* 'shameless'.

impugn /im-**pyoon**/ • v. express doubts about the honesty or validity of a fact or statement.
- ORIGIN Latin *impugnare* 'attack'.

impulse • n. **1** a sudden urge to act, without thought for the results. **2** a driving force: *the impulse for the book came from personal experience.* **3** a pulse of electrical energy.
- ORIGIN Latin *impulsus* 'a push'.

impulsion • n. **1** an urge to do something. **2** a driving force.

impulsive • adj. acting or done without thinking ahead.
- DERIVATIVES **impulsively** adv.

impunity /im-pyoo-ni-ti/ • n. freedom from punishment or harm: *rebels crossed the border with impunity.*
- ORIGIN Latin *impunitas*.

impure • adj. **1** mixed with unwanted substances: *impure coal.* **2** morally wrong.

impurity • n. (pl. **impurities**) **1** the state of being impure. **2** a thing which spoils the purity of something.

impute /im-**pyoot**/ • v. (**imputes, imputing, imputed**) believe that something has been done or caused by someone or something: *madness among the troops was imputed to shell shock.*
- DERIVATIVES **imputation** n.
- ORIGIN Latin *imputare* 'enter in the account'.

In • symb. the chemical element indium.

in • prep. **1** so as to be enclosed, surrounded, or inside. **2** expressing a period of time during which an event takes place. **3** expressing the length of time before an event is to take place. **4** expressing a state or quality: *he's in love.* **5** so as to be included or involved. **6** indicating the means of expression used: *put it in writing.* **7** expressing a value as a proportion of a whole. • adv. **1** expressing the state of being enclosed, surrounded, or inside: *we were locked in.* **2** present at your home or office. **3** expressing arrival. **4** (of the tide) rising or at its highest level. • adj. informal fashionable.
- PHRASES **in that** for the reason that. **the ins and outs** informal all the details.

– ORIGIN Old English.

in. •abbrev. inch(es).

in-¹ •prefix **1** not: *infertile*. **2** without; a lack of: *inaction*.
– ORIGIN Latin.

in-² •prefix in; into; towards: *influx*.
– ORIGIN from **in** or Latin *in*.

inability •n. the state of being unable to do something.

in absentia /in ab-sen-ti-uh/ •adv. while not present.
– ORIGIN Latin, 'in absence'.

inaccessible •adj. **1** unable to be reached or used. **2** difficult to understand or appreciate.
– DERIVATIVES **inaccessibility** n.

inaccurate •adj. not accurate.
– DERIVATIVES **inaccuracy** n. (pl. **inaccuracies**). **inaccurately** adv.

inaction •n. lack of action where some is expected or appropriate.

inactive •adj. not active or working.
– DERIVATIVES **inactivity** n.

inadequate •adj. **1** not enough or not good enough. **2** unable to deal with a situation or with life.
– DERIVATIVES **inadequacy** n. (pl. **inadequacies**). **inadequately** adv.

inadmissible •adj. (of evidence in court) not accepted as valid.

inadvertent •adj. not deliberate; unintentional.
– DERIVATIVES **inadvertently** adv.
– ORIGIN from **in-¹** + Latin *advertere* 'turn the mind to'.

> ☑ **inadvertent** ends with **-ent**.

inadvisable •adj. likely to have unwelcome results; unwise.

inalienable •adj. unable to be taken away or given away: *inalienable rights*.

inamorato /i-nam-uh-rah-toh/ •n. (pl. **inamoratos**; fem. **inamorata**, pl. **inamoratas**) a person's lover.
– ORIGIN Italian.

inane •adj. lacking sense; silly.
– DERIVATIVES **inanity** n. (pl **inanities**).
– ORIGIN Latin *inanis* 'empty, vain'.

inanimate •adj. not alive.

inapplicable •adj. not relevant or appropriate.

inappropriate •adj. not suitable or appropriate.
– DERIVATIVES **inappropriately** adv.

inarticulate /in-ar-tik-yuu-luht/ •adj. **1** unable to express your ideas clearly. **2** not expressed in words: *inarticulate cries*.

inasmuch •adv. (**inasmuch as**) **1** to the extent that. **2** considering that; since.

inattentive •adj. not paying attention.

– DERIVATIVES **inattention** n.

inaudible •adj. unable to be heard.

inaugural /in-aw-gyuu-ruhl/ •adj. marking the beginning of an organization or period of office.

inaugurate /in-aw-gyuu-rayt/ •v. (**inaugurates, inaugurating, inaugurated**) **1** begin or introduce a system, project, or period of activity. **2** admit someone formally to a new position or office. **3** mark the opening of an institution with a ceremony.
– DERIVATIVES **inauguration** n.
– ORIGIN Latin *inauguratus* 'consecrated after interpreting omens'.

inauspicious •adj. not likely to lead to success.

inauthentic •n. not genuine or sincere.

inboard •adv. & adj. within or towards the centre of a ship, aircraft, or vehicle.

inborn •adj. existing from birth.

inbound •adj. & adv. travelling back to an original point of departure.

in-box •n. the window on a computer screen in which received emails are displayed.

inbred •adj. **1** produced by breeding from closely related people or animals. **2** existing from birth; inborn.

inbreeding •n. breeding from closely related people or animals.

inbuilt •adj. present as an original or vital part.

Inc. •abbrev. N. Amer. Incorporated.

Inca •n. a member of a South American Indian people living in the central Andes before the Spanish conquest in the early 1530s.
– ORIGIN from an American Indian word meaning 'lord, royal person'.

incalculable •adj. **1** too great to be calculated or estimated: *an archive of incalculable value*. **2** not able to be calculated or estimated.

in camera •adv. see **CAMERA**.

incandescent /in-kan-dess-uhnt/ •adj. **1** glowing as a result of being heated. **2** (of an electric light) containing a filament which glows white-hot when heated by an electric current. **3** informal very angry.
– DERIVATIVES **incandescence** n.
– ORIGIN Latin *incandescere* 'glow'.

incantation •n. words said as a magic spell or charm.
– DERIVATIVES **incantatory** adj.
– ORIGIN Latin *incantare* 'chant'.

incapable •adj. **1** (**incapable of**) lacking the ability or required quality to do. **2** not able to look after yourself.

incapacitate /in-kuh-pa-si-tayt/ •v. (**incapacitates, incapacitating,**

incapacitated) prevent someone from functioning in a normal way.
– DERIVATIVES **incapacitation** n.

incapacity • n. (pl. **incapacities**) inability to do something.

incarcerate /in-kar-suh-rayt/
• v. (**incarcerates, incarcerating, incarcerated**) imprison someone.
– DERIVATIVES **incarceration** n.
– ORIGIN Latin *incarcerare*.

incarnate • adj. /in-kar-nuht/ **1** (of a god or spirit) in human form. **2** in physical form: *she was beauty incarnate.* • v. /in-kar-nayt/ be the living embodiment of a quality.
– ORIGIN Latin *incarnare* 'make flesh'.

incarnation • n. **1** a living embodiment of a god, spirit, or quality. **2** (**the Incarnation**) (in Christian belief) the embodiment of God the Son in human flesh as Jesus.

incautious • adj. not concerned about possible problems.

incendiary /in-sen-di-uh-ri/ • adj. **1** (of a bomb) designed to cause fires. **2** tending to stir up conflict. • n. (pl. **incendiaries**) an incendiary bomb.
– ORIGIN Latin *incendiarius*.

incense¹ /in-senss/ • n. a gum or other substance that is burned for the sweet smell it produces.
– ORIGIN Latin *incensum*.

incense² /in-senss/ • v. (**incenses, incensing, incensed**) make someone very angry.
– ORIGIN Latin *incendere* 'set fire to'.

incentive • n. a thing that influences or encourages someone to do something.
– ORIGIN Latin *incentivum* 'something that incites'.

inception • n. the establishment or starting point of an organization or activity.
– ORIGIN Latin.

incessant • adj. never stopping.
– DERIVATIVES **incessantly** adv.
– ORIGIN Latin.

incest • n. sex between people who are too closely related to marry each other.
– ORIGIN Latin *incestus*.

incestuous /in-sess-tyoo-uhss/
• adj. **1** involving sex between two closely related people. **2** excessively close and wishing to keep out outside influences: *a small, incestuous legal community.*

inch • n. **1** a unit of length equal to one twelfth of a foot (2.54 cm). **2** a quantity of rainfall that would cover a surface to a depth of one inch. **3** a very small amount or distance: *don't move an inch.* • v. move along slowly and carefully.

– ORIGIN Latin *uncia* 'twelfth part'.

inchoate /in-koh-uht/ • adj. just begun and so not fully formed or developed.
– ORIGIN Latin *inchoatus*.

incidence • n. **1** the occurrence, rate, or frequency of something: *an increased incidence of cancer.* **2** Physics the meeting of a line or ray with a surface.

incident • n. **1** an event. **2** a violent event, such as an attack. **3** the occurrence of dangerous or exciting events: *the plane landed without incident.* • adj. **1** (**incident to**) resulting from. **2** (of light or other radiation) falling on a surface.
– ORIGIN Latin *incidere* 'happen to'.

incidental • adj. **1** occurring in connection with or as a result of something else. **2** occurring as a minor result: *incidental expenses.*

incidentally • adv. **1** by the way. **2** in an incidental way.

incidental music • n. music used in a film or play as a background.

incinerate /in-sin-uh-rayt/
• v. (**incinerates, incinerating, incinerated**) destroy by burning.
– DERIVATIVES **incineration** n.
– ORIGIN Latin *incinerare* 'burn to ashes'.

incinerator • n. a device for burning rubbish.

incipient /in-sip-i-uhnt/ • adj. beginning to happen or develop.
– ORIGIN Latin *incipere* 'begin'.

incise • v. (**incises, incising, incised**) **1** make a cut or cuts in a surface. **2** cut a mark into a surface.
– ORIGIN Latin *incidere*.

incision • n. **1** a cut made as part of a surgical operation. **2** the action of cutting into something.

incisive • adj. **1** showing clear thought and sharp insight: *incisive criticism.* **2** quick and direct.

incisor • n. a narrow-edged tooth at the front of the mouth.

incite • v. (**incites, inciting, incited**) **1** stir up violent or unlawful behaviour. **2** urge someone to act in a violent or unlawful way.
– DERIVATIVES **incitement** n.
– ORIGIN Latin *incitare*.

incivility • n. (pl. **incivilities**) rude speech or behaviour.

inclement /in-klem-uhnt/ • adj. (of the weather) unpleasantly cold or wet.
– DERIVATIVES **inclemency** n.

inclination • n. **1** a natural tendency to act or feel in a particular way: *John was a scientist by inclination.* **2** (**inclination for/to/towards**) an interest in or liking for. **3** a slope or slant. **4** the angle at which a straight line or plane slopes away from another.

incline • v. /in-klyn/ (**inclines, inclining, inclined**) **1** (**be inclined to/to do something**) tend or be willing to think or do something. **2** (**be inclined**) have a particular tendency or talent: *Sam was mathematically inclined.* **3** lean or slope. **4** bend your head forwards and downwards. • n. /in-klyn/ a slope.
– ORIGIN Latin *inclinare*.

inclined plane • n. a plane inclined at an angle to the horizontal, used to make it easier to raise a load.

include • v. (**includes, including, included**) **1** have or contain something as part of a whole: *the price includes bed and breakfast.* **2** make or treat as part of a whole.
– ORIGIN Latin *includere* 'shut in'.

including • prep. containing as part of the whole in question.

inclusion • n. **1** the action of including or the state of being included. **2** a person or thing that is included.
– DERIVATIVES **inclusionary** adj.

inclusive • adj. **1** including everything expected or required. **2** (after a noun) including the limits specified: *the ages of 55 to 59 inclusive.*
– DERIVATIVES **inclusiveness** n. **inclusivity** n.

incognito /in-kog-nee-toh/ • adj. & adv. having your true identity concealed.
– ORIGIN Italian, 'unknown'.

incoherent • adj. **1** hard to understand; unclear. **2** not logical or well organized.
– DERIVATIVES **incoherence** n. **incoherently** adv.

income • n. money received during a certain period for work or from investments.

incomer • n. Brit. a person who has come to live in an area in which they have not grown up.

income support • n. (in the UK and Canada) payment made by the state to people on a low income.

income tax • n. tax that must be paid on personal income.

incoming • adj. **1** coming in. **2** coming into office to replace another person.

incommensurable /in-kuh-men-shuh-ruh-b'l/ • adj. not able to be judged or measured by the same standards.

incommensurate /in-kuh-men-shuh-ruht/ • adj. (**incommensurate with**) not in keeping or in proportion with.

incommode • v. (**incommodes, incommoding, incommoded**) formal cause inconvenience to.
– ORIGIN Latin *incommodare*.

incommunicado /in-kuh-myoo-ni-kah-doh/ • adj. & adv. not able to communicate with other people.
– ORIGIN Spanish *incomunicado*.

incomparable /in-kom-puh-ruh-b'l/ • adj. so good that nothing can be compared to it: *the incomparable beauty of Venice.*
– DERIVATIVES **incomparably** adv.

incompatible • adj. **1** (of two things) not able to exist or be used together. **2** (of two people) unable to live or work together without disagreeing.
– DERIVATIVES **incompatibility** n.

incompetent • adj. not skilful enough to do something successfully.
– DERIVATIVES **incompetence** n.

incomplete • adj. not finished or having all the necessary parts.

incomprehensible • adj. not able to be understood.
– DERIVATIVES **incomprehension** n.

inconceivable • adj. not able to be imagined or grasped mentally.
– DERIVATIVES **inconceivably** adv.

inconclusive • adj. not leading to a firm conclusion.

incongruous /in-kong-groo-uhss/ • adj. out of place.
– DERIVATIVES **incongruity** n. (pl. **incongruities**). **incongruously** adv.
– ORIGIN from IN-¹ + Latin *congruus* 'in agreement'.

inconsequential • adj. not important.

inconsiderable • adj. small in size, amount, etc.: *a not inconsiderable number.*

inconsiderate • adj. thoughtlessly causing hurt or trouble to other people.

inconsistent • adj. **1** having parts or elements that differ from or contradict each other. **2** (**inconsistent with**) not in keeping with.
– DERIVATIVES **inconsistency** n. (pl. **inconsistencies**).

inconsolable • adj. not able to be comforted.

inconspicuous • adj. not noticeable.

inconstant • adj. frequently changing.

incontestable • adj. not able to be disputed.

incontinent • adj. **1** unable to control when you pass urine or faeces. **2** lacking self-control.
– DERIVATIVES **incontinence** n.

incontrovertible • adj. not able to be denied or disputed.
– DERIVATIVES **incontrovertibly** adv.

inconvenience • n. slight trouble or difficulty. • v. (**inconveniences, inconveniencing, inconvenienced**)

cause someone slight trouble or difficulty.
– DERIVATIVES **inconvenient** adj. **inconveniently** adv.

incorporate • v. (**incorporates, incorporating, incorporated**) include something as part of a whole.
– DERIVATIVES **incorporation** n.
– ORIGIN Latin *incorporare* 'embody'.

incorporated • adj. (of a company) formed into a legal corporation.

incorporeal /in-kor-por-i-uhl/ • adj. without a physical body or form.

incorrect • adj. not true, accurate, or following accepted standards; wrong.
– DERIVATIVES **incorrectly** adv. **incorrectness** n.

incorrigible /in-kor-i-jib'l/ • adj. having bad habits that cannot be changed: *an incorrigible liar.*
– DERIVATIVES **incorrigibility** n. **incorrigibly** adv.
– ORIGIN Latin *incorrigibilis.*

incorruptible • adj. **1** too honest to be corrupted by taking bribes. **2** not prone to death or decay.
– DERIVATIVES **incorruptibility** n.

increase • v. /in-kreess/ (**increases, increasing, increased**) make or become greater in size, amount, or intensity. • n. /in-kreess/ a rise in amount, size, or intensity.
– ORIGIN Latin *increscere.*

increasingly • adv. more and more.

incredible • adj. **1** impossible or hard to believe. **2** informal very good.
– DERIVATIVES **incredibility** n. **incredibly** adv.

incredulity /in-kri-dyoo-li-ti/ • n. the state of being unwilling or unable to believe something.

incredulous • adj. unwilling or unable to believe something.

increment /ing-kri-muhnt/ • n. an increase in a number or an amount: *salary increments.*
– DERIVATIVES **incremental** adj. **incrementally** adv.
– ORIGIN Latin *incrementum.*

incriminate /in-krim-i-nayt/ • v. (**incriminates, incriminating, incriminated**) make someone appear guilty of a crime or wrongdoing.
– DERIVATIVES **incrimination** n.
– ORIGIN Latin *incriminare* 'accuse'.

incubate /ing-kyuu-bayt/ • v. (**incubates, incubating, incubated**) **1** (of a bird) sit on eggs to keep them warm and hatch them. **2** keep bacteria, cells, etc. at a suitable temperature so that they develop. **3** (of an infectious disease) develop slowly without obvious signs.
– DERIVATIVES **incubation** n.
– ORIGIN Latin *incubare* 'lie on'.

incubator • n. **1** an apparatus used to hatch eggs or grow microorganisms. **2** a heated enclosed apparatus like a cot in which a premature baby can be cared for.

incubus /ing-kyuu-buhss/ • n. (pl. **incubi** /ing-kyuu-by/) a male demon believed to have sex with sleeping women.
– ORIGIN Latin *incubo* 'nightmare'.

inculcate /in-kul-kayt/ • v. (**inculcates, inculcating, inculcated**) fix an idea in someone's mind by constantly repeating it.
– DERIVATIVES **inculcation** n.
– ORIGIN Latin *inculcare* 'press in'.

incumbency • n. (pl. **incumbencies**) the period during which a person holds an office or post.

incumbent /in-kum-buhnt/ • adj. **1** (**incumbent on**) necessary for someone as a duty. **2** currently holding an office or post: *the incumbent President.* • n. the holder of an office or post.
– ORIGIN Latin *incumbere* 'lie or lean on'

incur /in-ker/ • v. (**incurs, incurring, incurred**) bring something unwelcome on yourself: *he incurred the crowd's anger.*
– ORIGIN Latin *incurrere* 'run into'.

incurable • adj. **1** not able to be cured. **2** not able to be changed: *he's an incurable romantic.*
– DERIVATIVES **incurably** adv.

incurious • adj. not eager to know about things.

incursion • n. a sudden or brief invasion or attack.
– ORIGIN Latin.

indebted • adj. **1** grateful to someone. **2** owing money.

indecent • adj. **1** not following accepted standards of behaviour in relation to sexual matters. **2** not appropriate.
– DERIVATIVES **indecency** n. **indecently** adv.

indecent assault • n. sexual assault that does not involve rape.

indecent exposure • n. the crime of deliberately showing your genitals in public.

indecipherable /in-di-sy-fuh-ruh-b'l/ • adj. not able to be read or understood.

indecisive • adj. **1** not able to make decisions quickly. **2** not settling an issue: *an indecisive battle.*
– DERIVATIVES **indecision** n. **indecisively** adv. **indecisiveness** n.

indeed • adv. **1** used to emphasize a statement or answer: *this is praise indeed.*

2 used to introduce a further and stronger point.

indefatigable /in-di-fat-i-guh-b'l/ • adj. never tiring or stopping.
– DERIVATIVES **indefatigably** adv.
– ORIGIN Latin *indefatigabilis*.

indefensible • adj. not able to be justified or defended.

indefinable • adj. not able to be defined or described exactly.
– DERIVATIVES **indefinably** adv.

indefinite • adj. **1** not clearly expressed or defined; vague. **2** lasting for an unknown or unstated length of time.
– DERIVATIVES **indefinitely** adv.

indefinite article • n. Grammar the words *a* or *an*.

indelible /in-del-i-b'l/ • adj. **1** (of ink or a mark) unable to be removed. **2** unable to be forgotten.
– DERIVATIVES **indelibly** adv.
– ORIGIN Latin *indelebilis*.

indelicate • adj. **1** lacking sensitive understanding. **2** slightly indecent.
– DERIVATIVES **indelicacy** n.

indemnify /in-dem-ni-fy/ • v. (**indemnifies**, **indemnifying**, **indemnified**) **1** pay money to someone to compensate them for harm or loss. **2** protect or insure someone against legal responsibility for their actions.
– DERIVATIVES **indemnification** n.

indemnity /in-dem-ni-ti/ • n. (pl. **indemnities**) **1** insurance against or protection from legal responsibility for your actions. **2** a sum of money paid to compensate for damage or loss.
– ORIGIN Latin *indemnitas*.

indent • v. /in-dent/ **1** form hollows, dents, or notches in. **2** begin a line of writing further from the margin than the other lines. **3** Brit. make a written order for something. • n. /in-dent/ Brit. an official order for goods.
– ORIGIN Latin *indentare*.

indentation • n. **1** a hollow or notch. **2** the action of indenting something.

indenture /in-den-cher/ • n. a formal agreement or contract, such as one formerly binding an apprentice to work for his employer.

independence • n. the state of being independent.

independent • adj. **1** free from outside control or influence: *you should take independent advice.* **2** (of a country) self-governing. **3** having or earning enough money to support yourself. **4** not connected with someone or something else; separate. **5** (of broadcasting, a school, etc.) not supported by public funds. • n. an independent person or organization.
– DERIVATIVES **independently** adv.

☑ Remember that **independent** ends with **-ent**.

in-depth • adj. thorough and detailed.

indescribable • adj. too extreme or vague to be described.
– DERIVATIVES **indescribably** adv.

indestructible • adj. not able to be destroyed.

indeterminate /in-di-ter-mi-nuht/ • adj. not exactly known or defined: *a woman of indeterminate age.*
– DERIVATIVES **indeterminacy** n.

index /in-deks/ • n. (pl. **indexes** or in technical use **indices** /in-di-seez/) **1** an alphabetical list of names or subjects with references to the places in a book where they occur. **2** an alphabetical list or catalogue of books or documents. **3** a sign or measure of something. **4** a number indicating the relative level of prices or wages compared with a standard: *a price index.* **5** Math. an exponent. • v. record in or provide with an index.
– DERIVATIVES **indexation** n. **indexer** n.
– ORIGIN Latin, 'forefinger, sign'.

index finger • n. the forefinger.

index-linked • adj. Brit. (of wages, pensions, etc.) adjusted according to rises or falls in the retail price index.

Indian • n. **1** a person from India. **2** an American Indian. • adj. **1** relating to India. **2** relating to American Indians.

USAGE: Do not use **Indian** or **Red Indian** to talk about American native peoples, as these terms are now outdated; use **American Indian** instead.

Indian file • n. single file.

Indian ink • n. deep black ink used in drawing.

Indian summer • n. a period of dry, warm weather in late autumn.

India rubber • n. natural rubber.

indicate • v. (**indicates**, **indicating**, **indicated**) **1** point out; show. **2** be a sign of. **3** give a reading of a measurement. **4** state briefly. **5** (**be indicated**) be necessary or recommended: *in certain cases, surgery may be indicated.*
– DERIVATIVES **indication** n.
– ORIGIN Latin *indicare*.

indicative /in-dik-uh-tiv/ • adj. **1** acting as a sign: *the film's poor showing is indicative of a wider problem in Hollywood.* **2** Grammar (of a form of a verb) expressing a simple statement of fact (e.g. *she left*).

indicator • n. **1** a thing that shows a state

or level. **2** a device that gives particular information: *a speed indicator*. **3** Brit. a flashing light on a vehicle to show that it is about to change lanes or turn. **4** a chemical compound which changes colour at a specific pH value or in the presence of a particular substance.

indices pl. of INDEX.

indict /in-dyt/ • v. esp. N. Amer. formally accuse someone of or charge them with a crime.
– DERIVATIVES **indictable** adj.
– ORIGIN Latin *indicere* 'proclaim'.

indictment /in-dyt-muhnt/ • n. **1** esp. N. Amer. a formal charge or accusation of a crime. **2** an indication that something is bad and deserves to be condemned: *rising crime is an indictment of our society*.

indifferent • adj. **1** having no interest in or feelings about something. **2** not very good.
– DERIVATIVES **indifference** n. **indifferently** adv.

indigenous /in-dij-i-nuhss/ • adj. originating or occurring naturally in a place; native.
– ORIGIN Latin *indigena* 'a native'.

indigent /in-di-juhnt/ • adj. very poor.
– ORIGIN Latin, 'lacking'.

indigestible • adj. difficult or impossible to digest.

indigestion • n. pain or discomfort in the stomach caused by difficulty in digesting food.

indignant • adj. feeling or showing offence and annoyance.
– DERIVATIVES **indignantly** adv.
– ORIGIN Latin, 'regarding as unworthy'.

indignation • n. annoyance caused by what is seen as unfair treatment.

indignity • n. (pl. **indignities**) treatment or circumstances that make you feel ashamed or embarrassed.

indigo /in-di-goh/ • n. a dark blue colour or dye.
– ORIGIN Greek *indikos* 'Indian'.

indirect • adj. **1** not direct. **2** (of taxation) charged on goods and services rather than income or profits.
– DERIVATIVES **indirectly** adv.

indirect object • n. a person or thing that is affected by the action of a transitive verb but is not the main object (e.g. *him* in *give him the book*).

indirect question • n. Grammar a question in reported speech (e.g. *they asked who I was*).

indirect speech • n. = REPORTED SPEECH.

indiscernible /in-di-ser-ni-b'l/ • adj. impossible to see or clearly distinguish.

indiscipline • n. disorderly or uncontrolled behaviour.

indiscreet • adj. too ready to reveal things that should remain private.

indiscretion • n. **1** indiscreet behaviour. **2** an indiscreet act or remark.

indiscriminate /in-diss-krim-i-nuht/ • adj. done or acting without careful judgement.
– DERIVATIVES **indiscriminately** adv.

indispensable • adj. absolutely necessary.
– DERIVATIVES **indispensability** n.

indisposed • adj. **1** slightly unwell. **2** unwilling.

indisposition • n. a slight illness.

indisputable • adj. unable to be challenged or denied.
– DERIVATIVES **indisputably** adv.

indissoluble /in-dis-sol-yuu-b'l/ • adj. unable to be destroyed; lasting.

indistinct • adj. not clear or sharply defined.
– DERIVATIVES **indistinctly** adv.

indistinguishable • adj. not able to be identified as different or distinct.

indium /in-di-uhm/ • n. a soft silvery-white metallic chemical element, used in some alloys and semiconductor devices.
– ORIGIN from INDIGO.

individual • adj. **1** single; separate. **2** relating to one particular person: *the individual needs of the children*. **3** striking or unusual; original. • n. **1** a single person or item as distinct from a group. **2** a person of a particular kind: *a selfish individual*. **3** an independent or unusual person.
– DERIVATIVES **individually** adv.
– ORIGIN from Latin *in-* 'not' + *dividere* 'to divide'.

individualism • n. **1** the quality of being independent and original. **2** the belief that individual people should have freedom of action rather than be controlled by society or the state.
– DERIVATIVES **individualist** n. & adj. **individualistic** adj.

individuality • n. the quality or character of a person or thing that makes them different from other people or things.

individualize (or **individualise**) • v. (**individualizes**, **individualizing**, **individualized**) make something different to suit the needs of an individual person.

indivisible • adj. **1** unable to be divided or separated. **2** (of a number) unable to be divided by another number exactly without leaving a remainder.

indoctrinate /in-dok-tri-nayt/

- v. (**indoctrinates, indoctrinating, indoctrinated**) make someone accept a set of beliefs without considering any alternatives.
- DERIVATIVES **indoctrination** n.
- ORIGIN from **DOCTRINE**.

Indo-European • adj. relating to the family of languages spoken over most of Europe and Asia as far as northern India.

indolent /in-duh-luhnt/ • adj. lazy.
- DERIVATIVES **indolence** n.
- ORIGIN Latin, 'not giving pain'.

indomitable /in-dom-i-tuh-b'l/
• adj. impossible to defeat or subdue.
- DERIVATIVES **indomitably** adv.
- ORIGIN Latin *indomitabilis* 'unable to be tamed'.

Indonesian • n. 1 a person from Indonesia. 2 the group of languages spoken in Indonesia. • adj. relating to Indonesia.

indoor • adj. situated, done, or used inside a building or under cover.
• adv. (**indoors**) into or inside a building.

indrawn • adj. (of breath) taken in.

indubitable /in-dyoo-bi-tuh-b'l/
• adj. formal impossible to doubt; unquestionable.
- DERIVATIVES **indubitably** adv.
- ORIGIN Latin *indubitabilis*.

induce /in-dyooss/ • v. (**induces, inducing, induced**) 1 persuade someone to do something. 2 bring about or cause: *herbs to induce sleep*. 3 bring on the start of childbirth by drugs or other artificial means.
- DERIVATIVES **inducer** n. **inducible** adj.
- ORIGIN Latin *inducere* 'lead in'.

inducement • n. 1 a thing that persuades someone to do something. 2 a bribe.

induct • v. formally admit someone to an organization or establish them in a post.
- ORIGIN Latin *inducere* 'lead in'.

inductance • n. Physics the property of an electric conductor or circuit that causes an electromotive force to be generated by a change in the current flowing.

induction • n. 1 the action of introducing someone to a post or organization. 2 the action of bringing something about. 3 a method of reasoning in which a general rule or conclusion is drawn from particular facts or examples. 4 the production of an electric or magnetic state in an object by bringing an electrified or magnetized object close to but not touching it.

inductive • adj. 1 using a method of reasoning that draws general conclusions from particular facts or examples. 2 relating to electric or magnetic induction.

inductor • n. a component of an electrical circuit which possesses inductance.

indulge • v. (**indulges, indulging, indulged**) 1 (**indulge in**) allow yourself to enjoy the pleasure of something. 2 satisfy a desire or interest. 3 allow someone to do or have whatever they wish.
- ORIGIN Latin *indulgere*.

indulgence • n. 1 the action of indulging in something. 2 a thing that is indulged in; a luxury. 3 willingness to tolerate someone's faults. 4 esp. hist. (in the Roman Catholic Church) the setting aside or cancellation by the Pope of the punishment still due for sins after formal forgiveness.

indulgent • adj. readily allowing someone to do or have whatever they want or overlooking their faults.
- DERIVATIVES **indulgently** adv.

industrial • adj. relating to industry.
- DERIVATIVES **industrially** adv.

industrial action • n. Brit. a strike or other action taken by employees as a protest.

industrial estate • n. esp. Brit. an area of land developed as a site for factories and other industrial use.

industrialism • n. a social system in which industry forms the basis of the economy.

industrialist • n. a person who owns or controls a manufacturing business.

industrialize (or **industrialise**)
• v. (**industrializes, industrializing, industrialized**) develop industries in a country or region on a wide scale.
- DERIVATIVES **industrialization** n.

industrial relations • pl. n. the relations between management and workers.

industrious • adj. hard-working.
- DERIVATIVES **industriously** adv.

industry • n. (pl. **industries**) 1 the manufacture of goods in factories. 2 a branch of economic or commercial activity: *the tourist industry*. 3 hard work.
- ORIGIN Latin *industria*.

-ine • suffix 1 (forming adjectives) relating to; resembling: *canine*. 2 forming feminine or abstract nouns: *heroine*. 3 Chem. forming names of amino acids and certain other substances: *cocaine*.

inebriate /i-nee-bri-ayt/ • v. (**inebriates, inebriating, inebriated**) (usu. as adj. **inebriated**) make someone drunk.

– DERIVATIVES **inebriation** n.
– ORIGIN Latin *inebriare*.

inedible • adj. not fit for eating.

ineducable /in-ed-yuu-kuh-b'l/
• adj. considered incapable of being
educated.

ineffable /in-ef-fuh-b'l/ • adj. too great
or extreme to be expressed in words: *the
ineffable beauty of the Everglades.*
– ORIGIN Latin *ineffabilis*.

ineffective • adj. not producing any or
the desired effect.

ineffectual • adj. **1** not producing any or
the desired effect. **2** lacking the
required forcefulness to achieve something.
– DERIVATIVES **ineffectually** adv.

inefficient • adj. failing to make the best
use of time or resources.
– DERIVATIVES **inefficiency** n.

inelegant • adj. not elegant or graceful.
– DERIVATIVES **inelegance** n.

ineligible • adj. not satisfying the
conditions required for a post or benefit.
– DERIVATIVES **ineligibility** n.

ineluctable /in-i-luk-tuh-b'l/
• adj. unable to be resisted or avoided.
– ORIGIN Latin *ineluctabilis*.

inept • adj. lacking skill.
– DERIVATIVES **ineptitude** n.
– ORIGIN Latin *ineptus* 'unsuitable'.

inequality • n. (pl. **inequalities**) lack of
equality.

inequitable • adj. unfair; unjust.

inequity • n. (pl. **inequities**) lack of
fairness or justice.

ineradicable /in-i-rad-i-kuh-b'l/
• adj. unable to be destroyed or removed.

inert • adj. **1** lacking the ability or
strength to move or act. **2** without active
chemical properties.
– ORIGIN Latin *iners* 'unskilled, inactive'.

inertia /i-ner-shuh/ • n. **1** a tendency to
do nothing or to remain unchanged.
2 Physics a property by which matter
remains in a state of rest or continues
moving in a straight line, unless
changed by an external force.

inescapable • adj. unable to be avoided
or denied.

inessential • adj. not absolutely
necessary.

inestimable • adj. too great to be
measured.

inevitable • adj. certain to happen;
unavoidable.
– DERIVATIVES **inevitability** n. **inevitably**
adv.
– ORIGIN Latin *inevitabilis*.

inexact • adj. not quite accurate.

inexcusable • adj. too bad to be justified
or tolerated.

inexhaustible • adj. (of a supply)
available in unlimited quantities.

inexorable /in-ek-suh-ruh-b'l/
• adj. impossible to stop or prevent.
– DERIVATIVES **inexorably** adv.
– ORIGIN Latin *inexorabilis*.

inexpensive • adj. not costing a great
deal; cheap.

inexperience • n. lack of experience.
– DERIVATIVES **inexperienced** adj.

inexpert • adj. lacking skill or
knowledge in a particular field.

inexplicable /in-ik-splik-uh-b'l/
• adj. unable to be explained.
– DERIVATIVES **inexplicably** adv.

inexpressible • adj. not able to be
defined or described.
– DERIVATIVES **inexpressibly** adv.

inexpressive • adj. showing no
emotion.

in extremis /in ek-stree-miss/ • adv. **1** in
a very difficult situation. **2** at the point
of death.
– ORIGIN Latin.

inextricable /in-ik-strik-uh-b'l/
• adj. impossible to untangle or separate:
the past and the present are inextricable.
– DERIVATIVES **inextricably** adv.

infallible /in-fal-li-b'l/ • adj. **1** incapable
of making mistakes or being wrong.
2 never failing.
– DERIVATIVES **infallibility** n. **infallibly**
adv.

infamous /in-fuh-muhss/ • adj. **1** well
known for a bad quality or act. **2** wicked.

infamy /in-fuh-mi/ • n. (pl. **infamies**)
1 the state of being known for something bad. **2** a wicked act.

infancy • n. **1** the state or period of being
a baby or young child. **2** the early stage
in the development of something.

infant • n. **1** a baby or very young child.
2 Brit. a schoolchild between the ages of
five and seven.
– ORIGIN Old French *enfant*.

infanta /in-fan-tuh/ • n. hist. a daughter
of the king or queen of Spain or
Portugal.
– ORIGIN Spanish and Portuguese.

infanticide /in-fan-ti-syd/ • n. the
killing of an infant.

infantile /in-fuhn-tyl/ • adj. **1** relating to
babies or young children. **2** derog.
childish.

infantry • n. soldiers who fight on foot.
– DERIVATIVES **infantryman** n. (pl.
infantrymen).
– ORIGIN Italian *infanteria*.

infatuate • v. (**be infatuated with**) have
an intense passion for.
– DERIVATIVES **infatuation** n.
– ORIGIN Latin *infatuare* 'make foolish'.

infect • v. **1** affect a body or part of the body with an organism that causes disease. **2** contaminate; affect badly.
– ORIGIN Latin *inficere* 'to taint'.

infection • n. **1** the process of infecting or the state of being infected. **2** an infectious disease.

infectious • adj. **1** (of a disease or disease-causing organism) able to be transmitted through the environment. **2** likely to spread infection. **3** likely to spread to or influence other people.

infelicity • n. (pl. **infelicities**) an inappropriate remark or action.

infer • v. (**infers, inferring, inferred**) work something out from evidence or suggestions rather than from direct statements.
– ORIGIN Latin *inferre* 'bring in'.

USAGE: For an explanation of the difference between **imply** and **infer**, see the note at **IMPLY**.

inference /in-fuh-ruhnss/ • n. **1** a conclusion reached on the basis of evidence or something suggested. **2** the process of reaching a conclusion in this way.

inferior • adj. **1** lower in rank, status, or quality. • n. a person who is lower than other people in rank, status, or ability.
– DERIVATIVES **inferiority** n.
– ORIGIN Latin.

inferiority complex • n. a feeling that you are of lower status or have less ability than other people, resulting in aggressive or withdrawn behaviour.

infernal • adj. **1** relating to hell or the underworld. **2** informal very annoying: *an infernal nuisance.*
– ORIGIN Latin *infernus* 'below'.

inferno • n. (pl. **infernos**) a large uncontrollable fire.
– ORIGIN Italian.

infertile • adj. **1** unable to have children or (of an animal) bear young. **2** (of land) unable to produce crops or vegetation.
– DERIVATIVES **infertility** n.

infest • v. (of insects) be present in large numbers, so as to cause damage or disease.
– DERIVATIVES **infestation** n.
– ORIGIN Latin *infestare* 'to attack'.

infidel /in-fi-duhl/ • n. old use a person who has no religion or whose religion is not that of the majority.
– ORIGIN Latin *infidelis*.

infidelity • n. (pl. **infidelities**) the action of being unfaithful to your sexual partner.

infighting • n. conflict within a group or organization.

infiltrate /in-fil-trayt/ • v. (**infiltrates,**

infiltrating, infiltrated) **1** secretly and gradually gain access to an organization or place. **2** pass slowly into or through something.
– DERIVATIVES **infiltration** n. **infiltrator** n.

infinite /in-fi-nit/ • adj. **1** limitless in space or size. **2** very great in amount or degree: *with infinite care.*
– DERIVATIVES **infinitely** adv.
– ORIGIN Latin *infinitus*.

infinitesimal /in-fi-ni-tess-i-m'l/ • adj. very small.
– DERIVATIVES **infinitesimally** adv.
– ORIGIN Latin *infinitesimus*.

infinitive /in-fin-i-tiv/ • n. the basic form of a verb, normally occurring in English with the word *to*, as in *to see, to ask.*
– ORIGIN Latin *infinitus*.

infinity • n. (pl. **infinities**) **1** the state of being limitless in space or size. **2** a very great number or amount. **3** Math. a number greater than any quantity or countable number (symbol ∞).

infirm • adj. physically weak.
– ORIGIN Latin *infirmus*.

infirmary • n. (pl. **infirmaries**) a hospital or place set aside for the care of sick or injured people.

infirmity • n. (pl. **infirmities**) physical or mental weakness.

in flagrante delicto /in fluh-gran-tay di-lik-toh/ • adv. in the middle of an act of doing wrong.
– ORIGIN Latin, 'in the heat of the crime'.

inflame • v. (**inflames, inflaming, inflamed**) **1** make something worse. **2** make someone very angry. **3** cause inflammation in a part of the body.

inflammable • adj. easily set on fire.
– DERIVATIVES **inflammability** n.

USAGE: The words **inflammable** and **flammable** both mean 'easily set on fire'. To avoid confusion it is better to say **flammable**, as the *in-* part of **inflammable** can give the impression that the word means 'not flammable'.

inflammation • n. a condition in which a part of the body becomes reddened, swollen, hot, and often painful.

inflammatory • adj. **1** causing inflammation. **2** arousing angry feelings.

inflatable • adj. capable of being inflated. • n. a plastic or rubber object that is inflated before use.

inflate • v. (**inflates, inflating, inflated**) **1** expand by filling with air or gas. **2** (as adj. **inflated**) exaggerated: *an inflated view of her own importance.* **3** bring about inflation of a currency or in an economy.
– ORIGIN Latin *inflare* 'blow into'.

inflation •n. **1** the action of expanding something by filling it with air or gas. **2** a general increase in prices.
– DERIVATIVES **inflationary** adj.

inflect •v. **1** Grammar (of a word) change by inflection. **2** vary the tone or pitch of the voice.
– ORIGIN Latin *inflectere*.

inflection •n. **1** Grammar a change in the form of a word to show a grammatical function or a quality such as tense, person, or number. **2** a variation in tone or pitch of the voice. **3** esp. Math. a change of curvature from convex to concave.

inflexible •adj. **1** not able to be altered or adapted. **2** unwilling to change or compromise. **3** not able to be bent.
– DERIVATIVES **inflexibility** n.

inflict •v. (**inflict something on**) **1** cause someone to experience something unpleasant. **2** impose something unwelcome on someone.
– DERIVATIVES **infliction** n.
– ORIGIN Latin *infligere* 'strike against'.

inflorescence /in-fluh-ress-uhnss/ •n. Bot. the complete flower head of a plant.
– ORIGIN Latin *inflorescere* 'come into flower'.

influence •n. **1** the capacity to have an effect on someone's beliefs or actions. **2** a person or thing with the capacity to affect someone's beliefs or actions. **3** the power arising out of status or wealth.
•v. (**influences, influencing, influenced**) have an effect on.
– ORIGIN Latin *influere* 'flow in'.

influential •adj. having great influence.

influenza •n. an infection of the nose, throat, and lungs, spread by a virus and causing fever, aching, and catarrh.
– ORIGIN Italian, 'influence'.

influx •n. the arrival or entry of large numbers of people or things.
– ORIGIN Latin *influxus*.

inform •v. **1** give facts or information to. **2** (**inform on someone**) give information about someone's involvement in a crime to the police.
– ORIGIN Latin *informare* 'describe'.

informal •adj. **1** relaxed, friendly, or unofficial. **2** (of clothes) suitable for everyday wear; casual. **3** referring to the language of everyday speech and writing, rather than that used in official situations.
– DERIVATIVES **informality** n. **informally** adv.

informant •n. a person who gives information to someone else.

information •n. **1** facts or knowledge that are provided or learned. **2** computer data.

information superhighway •n. an extensive electronic network such as the Internet, used for the rapid transfer of information.

information technology •n. the study or use of systems such as computers and telecommunications for storing, retrieving, and sending information.

informative •adj. providing useful information.

informed •adj. **1** having or showing knowledge. **2** (of a judgement) based on a sound understanding of the facts.

informer •n. a person who informs on another person to the police.

infra- •prefix below: *infrared*.
– ORIGIN Latin *infra*.

infraction •n. a breaking of a law or agreement.
– ORIGIN Latin.

infra dig /in-fruh **dig**/ •adj. informal, esp. Brit. beneath your dignity.
– ORIGIN from Latin *infra dignitatem*.

infrared •n. electromagnetic radiation having a wavelength just greater than that of red light but less than that of microwaves. •adj. relating to such radiation.

infrastructure •n. the basic structures (e.g. buildings, roads, power supplies) needed for a society or organization to function.

infrequent •adj. not occurring often; rare.
– DERIVATIVES **infrequency** n. **infrequently** adv.

infringe •v. (**infringes, infringing, infringed**) **1** break a law or agreement. **2** curb or limit a right or privilege.
– DERIVATIVES **infringement** n.
– ORIGIN Latin *infringere*.

infuriate /in-fyoor-i-ayt/ •v. (**infuriates, infuriating, infuriated**) make someone very angry.
– ORIGIN Latin *infuriare*.

infuse •v. (**infuses, infusing, infused**) **1** fill with a quality. **2** soak tea or herbs to extract the flavour or healing properties.
– DERIVATIVES **infuser** n.
– ORIGIN Latin *infundere* 'pour in'.

infusion •n. **1** a drink prepared by soaking tea or herbs. **2** the action of infusing.

-ing¹ •suffix **1** referring to a verbal action, activity, or result: *building*. **2** referring to material used for a process: *piping*. **3** forming the gerund of verbs (such as *painting* as in *I love painting*).
– ORIGIN Old English.

-ing² •suffix **1** forming the present

participle of verbs: *calling*. **2** forming adjectives from nouns: *hulking*.
– ORIGIN Latin -*ent*.

ingenious /in-jee-ni-uhss/ • adj. clever and inventive.
– DERIVATIVES **ingeniously** adv.
– ORIGIN Latin *ingeniosus*.

ingénue /an-zhuh-nyoo/ • n. an innocent or inexperienced young woman.
– ORIGIN French.

ingenuity /in-ji-nyoo-i-ti/ • n. the quality of being clever and inventive.
– ORIGIN Latin *ingenuitas* 'the quality of being ingenuous'.

ingenuous /in-jen-yoo-uhss/ • adj. innocent and unsuspecting.
– ORIGIN Latin *ingenuus* 'native, inborn'.

ingest • v. take a substance into the body by swallowing or absorbing it.
– DERIVATIVES **ingestion** n.
– ORIGIN Latin *ingerere* 'bring in'.

inglenook • n. a space on either side of a large fireplace.
– ORIGIN from dialect *ingle* 'fire, fireplace' + NOOK.

inglorious • adj. causing shame; dishonourable.

ingoing • adj. going towards or into.

ingot /ing-guht/ • n. a rectangular block of steel, gold, or other metal.
– ORIGIN perh. from Old English, 'pour, cast'.

ingrained (also **engrained**) • adj. **1** (of a habit or attitude) firmly established and hard to change. **2** (of dirt) deeply embedded.
– ORIGIN from the old use of *grain* meaning 'cochineal' (the first meaning was 'dyed with cochineal').

ingrate /in-grayt/ • n. literary an ungrateful person.
– ORIGIN Latin *ingratus*.

ingratiate /in-gray-shi-ayt/ • v. (**ingratiates, ingratiating, ingratiated**) (**ingratiate yourself**) gain favour with someone by flattering or trying to please them.
– DERIVATIVES **ingratiating** adj.
– ORIGIN from Latin *in gratiam* 'into favour'.

ingratitude • n. a lack of thankfulness and appreciation.

ingredient • n. **1** any of the substances that are combined to make a dish. **2** a part or element.
– ORIGIN Latin *ingredi* 'enter'.

ingress /in-gress/ • n. **1** the action of entering. **2** a place or means of access.
– ORIGIN Latin *ingressus*.

ingrown • adj. (of a toenail) having grown into the flesh.
– DERIVATIVES **ingrowing** adj.

inhabit • v. (**inhabits, inhabiting, inhabited**) live in or occupy a place.
– DERIVATIVES **inhabitable** adj.
– ORIGIN Latin *inhabitare*.

inhabitant • n. a person or animal that lives in or occupies a place.

inhalant • n. a medicine that is breathed in.

inhale /in-hayl/ • v. (**inhales, inhaling, inhaled**) breathe in air, smoke, or a gas.
– DERIVATIVES **inhalation** n.
– ORIGIN Latin *inhalare*.

inhaler • n. a portable device used for inhaling a drug.

inharmonious • adj. not forming a pleasing whole; discordant.

inhere /in-heer/ • v. (**inhere, inhering, inhered**) (**inhere in/within**) formal be an essential or permanent part of something.
– ORIGIN Latin *inhaerere* 'stick to'.

inherent /in-herr-uhnt/ • adj. existing in something as a permanent or essential part or quality.
– DERIVATIVES **inherently** adv.

inherit • v. (**inherits, inheriting, inherited**) **1** receive money, property, or a title as an heir at the death of the previous holder. **2** derive a quality or characteristic from your parents or ancestors. **3** receive or be left with an object or a situation from a former owner.
– DERIVATIVES **inheritor** n.
– ORIGIN Latin *inhereditare* 'appoint as heir'.

inheritance • n. **1** money, property, or a title received on someone's death. **2** the action of inheriting.

inheritance tax • n. (in the UK) tax on property and money that has been inherited.

inhibit • v. (**inhibits, inhibiting, inhibited**) **1** hinder or prevent an action or process. **2** make someone unable to act in a relaxed and natural way.
– DERIVATIVES **inhibited** adj.
– ORIGIN Latin *inhibere*.

inhibition • n. **1** a feeling that makes you unable to act in a relaxed and natural way. **2** the action of inhibiting.

inhospitable • adj. **1** (of an environment) harsh and difficult to live in. **2** unwelcoming.

in-house • adj. & adv. within an organization.

inhuman • adj. **1** lacking good human qualities; cruel or brutal. **2** not human.

inhumane • adj. without pity for misery or suffering; cruel.

inhumanity • n. (pl. **inhumanities**) cruel or brutal behaviour.

inimical /i-nim-i-k'l/ • adj. tending to obstruct or harm; hostile.
– ORIGIN Latin *inimicalis*.

inimitable /in-im-i-tuh-b'l/
• adj. impossible to imitate; unique.
– DERIVATIVES **inimitably** adv.

iniquity /i-ni-kwi-ti/ • n. (pl. **iniquities**) a highly unfair or immoral action.
– DERIVATIVES **iniquitous** adj.
– ORIGIN Latin *iniquitas*.

initial • adj. existing or occurring at the beginning. • n. the first letter of a name or word. • v. (**initials, initialling, initialled**; US **initials, initialing, initialed**) mark with your initials as a sign of approval or agreement.
– DERIVATIVES **initially** adv.
– ORIGIN Latin *initialis*.

initialism • n. an abbreviation consisting of initial letters pronounced separately (e.g. *BBC*).

initiate /i-ni-shi-ayt/ • v. (**initiates, initiating, initiated**) **1** cause a process or action to begin. **2** admit someone to a society or group with a formal ceremony. **3** (**initiate someone into**) introduce someone to a new activity.
– DERIVATIVES **initiation** n. **initiator** n.
– ORIGIN Latin *initiare* 'begin'.

initiative • n. **1** the ability to act independently and with a fresh approach. **2** the power or opportunity to act before other people do: *we have lost the initiative*. **3** a fresh approach to a problem.

inject • v. **1** introduce a drug or other substance into the body with a syringe. **2** give a drug to a person or animal using a syringe. **3** introduce a different quality: *she tried to inject scorn into her tone*.
– ORIGIN Latin *inicere* 'throw in'.

injection • n. **1** an act of injecting a person or animal. **2** a large sum of additional money used to help an organization.

in-joke • n. a joke that is shared only by a small group.

injudicious • adj. showing poor judgement; unwise.

injunction • n. **1** an order by a court of law stating that someone must or must not do something. **2** a strong warning.
– ORIGIN Latin.

injure • v. (**injures, injuring, injured**) **1** do physical harm to. **2** damage: *their reputation could be injured by a libel*.

injured • adj. **1** harmed. **2** offended.

injurious /in-joor-i-uhss/ • adj. causing or likely to cause harm or damage.

injury • n. (pl. **injuries**) **1** an instance of being harmed. **2** harm or damage.

– ORIGIN Latin *injuria* 'a wrong'.

injury time • n. Brit. (in football and other sports) extra playing time to make up for time lost as a result of injuries.

injustice • n. **1** lack of fairness or right judgement. **2** an unjust act or occurrence.

ink • n. **1** a coloured fluid used for writing, drawing, or printing. **2** a black liquid produced by a cuttlefish, octopus, or squid. • v. **1** write or mark words or a design with ink. **2** cover metal type or a stamp with ink before printing.
– ORIGIN Old French *enque*.

inkling • n. a slight suspicion; a hint.
– ORIGIN from former *inkle* 'say in an undertone'.

inkstand • n. a stand for ink bottles, pens, and other stationery items.

inkwell • n. a container for ink that fits into a hole in a desk.

inky • adj. **1** as dark as ink. **2** stained with ink.

inlaid past and past part. of INLAY.

inland • adj. & adv. in or into the interior of a country.

Inland Revenue • n. (in the UK) the government department responsible for collecting income tax and some other taxes.

in-law • n. a relative by marriage. • comb. form related by marriage: *father-in-law*.

inlay • v. (**inlays, inlaying, inlaid**) decorate an object by embedding pieces of a different material in its surface. • n. **1** inlaid decoration. **2** a material used for inlaying.

inlet • n. **1** a small arm of the sea, a lake, or a river. **2** a place or means of entry.

in-line skate • n. a type of roller skate in which the wheels are fixed in a single line along the sole.

in loco parentis /in loh-koh puh-ren-tiss/ • adv. (of an adult responsible for children) in the place of a parent.
– ORIGIN Latin.

inmate • n. a person living in an institution such as a prison or hospital.
– ORIGIN prob. from INN + MATE¹.

in memoriam /in mi-mor-i-am/
• prep. in memory of a dead person.
– ORIGIN Latin.

inmost • adj. furthest in; closest to the centre.

inn • n. a pub.
– ORIGIN Old English.

innards • pl. n. informal **1** internal organs. **2** the internal workings of a device or machine.
– ORIGIN from INWARDS.

innate /in-nayt/ • adj. inborn; natural.
– DERIVATIVES **innately** adv.

– ORIGIN Latin *innatus*.

inner • adj. **1** situated inside; close to the centre. **2** mental or spiritual: *inner strength.* **3** private; not expressed.

inner city • n. an area in or near the centre of a city.

innermost • adj. **1** furthest in; closest to the centre. **2** (of thoughts) most private.

inner tube • n. a separate inflatable tube inside a tyre casing.

innings • n. (pl. **innings**) (treated as *sing.*) Cricket each of the divisions of a game during which one side has a turn at batting.

innkeeper • n. old use a person who runs an inn.

innocent • adj. **1** not guilty of a crime or offence. **2** having little experience of life, especially of sex. **3** not intended to cause offence: *an innocent mistake.* • n. an innocent person.
– DERIVATIVES **innocence** n. **innocently** adv.
– ORIGIN Latin, 'not harming'.

innocuous /in-nok-yoo-uhss/ • adj. not harmful or offensive.
– ORIGIN Latin *innocuus*.

innovate /in-nuh-vayt/ • v. (**innovates, innovating, innovated**) introduce new methods, ideas, or products.
– DERIVATIVES **innovator** n. **innovatory** adj.
– ORIGIN Latin *innovare* 'renew, alter'.

innovation • n. **1** the introduction of new methods, ideas, or products. **2** a new method, idea, or product.

innovative /in-nuh-vuh-tiv/ • adj. **1** featuring new ideas or methods: *innovative designs.* **2** original and creative in thinking.

innuendo /in-yuu-en-doh/ • n. (pl. **innuendoes** or **innuendos**) a remark which makes an indirect reference to something.
– ORIGIN Latin, 'by pointing to'.

innumerable • adj. too many to be counted.
– ORIGIN Latin *innumerabilis*.

innumerate • adj. without a basic knowledge of mathematics and arithmetic.

inoculate /i-nok-yuu-layt/ • v. = VACCINATE.
– DERIVATIVES **inoculation** n.
– ORIGIN Latin *inoculare* 'graft a shoot of a plant'.

inoffensive • adj. not objectionable or harmful.

inoperable • adj. **1** (of an illness) not able to be cured by a medical operation. **2** not able to be used or operated.

inoperative • adj. not working or taking effect.

inopportune • adj. occurring at an inconvenient time.

inordinate /in-or-di-nuht/ • adj. unusually large; excessive.
– DERIVATIVES **inordinately** adv.
– ORIGIN Latin *inordinatus* 'not arranged'.

inorganic • adj. **1** not consisting of or coming from living matter. **2** referring to chemical compounds that do not contain carbon.

inpatient • n. a patient who is staying day and night in a hospital while receiving treatment.

input • n. **1** what is put or taken in by a system or process. **2** a person's contribution. **3** the action of putting data into a computer. **4** a place or device from which electricity or information enters a computer or other machine. • v. (**inputs, inputting, input**) put data into a computer.

inquest • n. **1** an official inquiry to gather the facts relating to an incident. **2** Brit. an inquiry by a coroner's court into the cause of a death.
– ORIGIN Old French *enqueste*.

inquire • v. = ENQUIRE.

inquiry • n. (pl. **inquiries**) an enquiry.

inquisition • n. **1** a long period of intensive questioning or investigation. **2** the verdict of a coroner's jury.
– ORIGIN Latin.

inquisitive • adj. **1** eagerly seeking to find out about things. **2** prying.

inquisitor /in-kwiz-i-ter/ • n. a person conducting an inquisition.

inroad • n. (usu. in phr. **make inroads in/into**) a gradual entry into or effect on a situation.

inrush • n. a sudden inward flow.

insalubrious /in-suh-loo-bri-uhss/ • adj. seedy; unwholesome.

insane • adj. **1** seriously mentally ill. **2** very foolish; irrational.
– DERIVATIVES **insanely** adv. **insanity** n. (pl. **insanities**).
– ORIGIN Latin *insanus*.

insanitary • adj. so dirty as to be a danger to health.

insatiable /in-say-shuh-b'l/ • adj. impossible to satisfy.
– DERIVATIVES **insatiability** n. **insatiably** adv.

inscribe • v. (**inscribes, inscribing, inscribed**) **1** write or carve words or symbols on a surface. **2** write a dedication to someone in a book. **3** Geom. draw a figure within another so that their boundaries touch but do not intersect.

– ORIGIN Latin *inscribere*.

inscription • n. words or symbols inscribed on a surface or in a book.

inscrutable /in-skroo-tuh-b'l/
• adj. impossible to understand or interpret.
– DERIVATIVES **inscrutability** n. **inscrutably** adv.
– ORIGIN Latin *inscrutabilis*.

insect • n. a small invertebrate animal with six legs and a body divided into three segments (head, thorax, and abdomen).
– ORIGIN from Latin *animal insectum* 'segmented animal'.

insecticide • n. a substance used for killing insects.

insectivore /in-sek-ti-vor/ • n. an animal that feeds on insects.
– DERIVATIVES **insectivorous** /in-sek-tiv-uh-ruhss/ adj.

insecure • adj. 1 not confident or assured. 2 not firm or firmly fixed. 3 (of a place) easily broken into.
– DERIVATIVES **insecurely** adv. **insecurity** n. (pl. **insecurities**).

inseminate /in-sem-i-nayt/
• v. (**inseminates, inseminating, inseminated**) introduce semen into the vagina of a woman or a female animal.
– DERIVATIVES **insemination** n.
– ORIGIN Latin *inseminare* 'sow'.

insensate • adj. 1 lacking physical sensation. 2 lacking sensitivity towards other people; unfeeling.

insensible • adj. 1 unconscious. 2 numb; without feeling.
– DERIVATIVES **insensibility** n.

insensitive • adj. 1 having no concern for the feelings of other people. 2 not able to feel physical sensation. 3 not aware of or able to respond to something.
– DERIVATIVES **insensitivity** n.

inseparable • adj. 1 unable to be separated or treated separately. 2 very friendly and close.
– DERIVATIVES **inseparably** adv.

insert • v. /in-sert/ place, fit, or add something into something else. • n. /in-sert/ a loose page or section in a magazine.
– ORIGIN Latin *inserere*.

insertion • n. 1 the action of inserting something into something else. 2 a change or new item inserted into a piece of writing.

in-service • adj. (of training) intended to take place during the course of employment.

inset • n. /in-set/ 1 a thing inserted. 2 a small picture or map inserted within the

border of a larger one. • v. /in-set/ (**insets, insetting, inset**) put something in as an inset.

inshore • adj. at sea but close to the shore. • adv. towards or closer to the shore.

inside • n. 1 the inner side, part, or surface of something. 2 (**insides**) informal the stomach and bowels. 3 the side of a bend where the edge is shorter.
• adj. situated on or in, or coming from, the inside. • prep. & adv. 1 situated or moving within. 2 informal in prison. 3 in less than the period of time specified.

inside job • n. informal a crime committed by or with the help of a person associated with the place where it occurred.

inside leg • n. the length of a person's leg or trouser leg from crotch to ankle.

inside out • adv. with the inner surface turned outwards.

insider • n. a person within an organization who has information not known to those outside it.

insidious /in-sid-i-uhss/ • adj. proceeding in a gradual and harmful way.
– DERIVATIVES **insidiously** adv.
– ORIGIN Latin *insidiosus* 'cunning'.

insight • n. 1 the ability to understand the truth about someone or something. 2 an understanding of the truth about someone or something.
– DERIVATIVES **insightful** adj.

insignia /in-sig-ni-uh/ • n. (pl. **insignia** or **insignias**) a badge or symbol showing a person's rank, position, or membership of an organization.
– ORIGIN Latin.

insignificant • adj. having little or no importance or value.
– DERIVATIVES **insignificance** n.

insincere • adj. saying things that you do not mean.
– DERIVATIVES **insincerely** adv. **insincerity** n.

insinuate /in-sin-yuu-ayt/
• v. (**insinuates, insinuating, insinuated**) 1 suggest something bad in an indirect and unpleasant way. 2 (**insinuate yourself into**) move yourself gradually into a favourable position.
– ORIGIN Latin *insinuare*.

insinuation • n. an unpleasant hint or suggestion.

insipid /in-si-pid/ • adj. 1 lacking flavour. 2 lacking liveliness or interest.
– ORIGIN Latin *insipidus*.

insist • v. 1 demand or state something forcefully, without accepting refusal. 2 (**insist on**) persist in: *when everyone*

sat, he'd insist on standing.
– ORIGIN Latin *insistere* 'persist'.

insistent • adj. **1** demanding that something must be done. **2** sustained and demanding attention: *the traffic's insistent roar.*
– DERIVATIVES **insistence** n. **insistently** adv.

in situ /in sit-yoo/ • adv. & adj. in the original or appropriate position.
– ORIGIN Latin.

insole • n. **1** a removable sole worn inside a shoe. **2** the fixed inner sole of a boot or shoe.

insolent • adj. rude and disrespectful.
– DERIVATIVES **insolence** n. **insolently** adv.
– ORIGIN Latin, 'arrogant'.

insoluble • adj. **1** impossible to solve. **2** (of a substance) unable to be dissolved.
– DERIVATIVES **insolubility** n.

insolvent • adj. not having enough money to pay your debts.
– DERIVATIVES **insolvency** n.

insomnia • n. the condition of being unable to sleep.
– DERIVATIVES **insomniac** n. & adj.
– ORIGIN Latin.

insomuch • adv. (**insomuch that/as**) to the extent that.

insouciant /in-soo-si-uhnt/ • adj. casually unconcerned.
– DERIVATIVES **insouciance** n.
– ORIGIN French.

inspect • v. **1** look at closely. **2** make an official visit to an organization to check on standards.
– DERIVATIVES **inspection** n.
– ORIGIN Latin *inspicere*.

inspector • n. **1** an official who makes sure that regulations are obeyed. **2** a police officer ranking below a chief inspector.
– DERIVATIVES **inspectorate** n.

inspiration • n. **1** the process of being filled with a feeling or with the urge to do something. **2** a person or thing that inspires. **3** a sudden clever idea.
– DERIVATIVES **inspirational** adj.

inspire • v. (**inspires, inspiring, inspired**) **1** fill someone with the urge to do something. **2** create a feeling in a person. **3** give rise to: *the film was successful enough to inspire a sequel.*
– DERIVATIVES **inspiring** adj.
– ORIGIN Latin *inspirare* 'breathe into'.

inspired • adj. showing creativity or feeling.

instability • n. (pl. **instabilities**) lack of steadiness.

install • v. (**installs, installing, installed**) **1** place or fix equipment in position

ready for use. **2** establish someone in a new place or role.
– DERIVATIVES **installer** n.
– ORIGIN Latin *installare*.

installation • n. **1** the action of installing. **2** a large piece of equipment installed for use. **3** a military or industrial establishment. **4** an art exhibit constructed within a gallery.

instalment (US also **installment**) • n. **1** a sum of money due as one of several payments made over a period of time. **2** one of several parts of something published or broadcast at intervals.

> ✓ **instalment** is spelled with one l (the spelling **installment** is American).

instance • n. **1** an example or single occurrence of something. **2** a particular case. • v. (**instances, instancing, instanced**) give something as an example.
– ORIGIN Latin *instantia* 'presence, urgency'.

instant • adj. **1** happening immediately. **2** (of food) processed to allow quick preparation. • n. **1** a precise moment of time. **2** a very short time.
– DERIVATIVES **instantly** adv.
– ORIGIN Latin.

instantaneous /in-stuhn-tay-ni-uhss/ • adj. happening or done immediately.
– DERIVATIVES **instantaneously** adv.

instead • adv. **1** as an alternative. **2** (**instead of**) in place of.

instep • n. the part of a person's foot between the ball and the ankle.

instigate /in-sti-gayt/ • v. (**instigates, instigating, instigated**) **1** make something happen or begin. **2** (**instigate someone to/to do**) encourage someone to do.
– DERIVATIVES **instigation** n. **instigator** n.
– ORIGIN Latin *instigare* 'urge'.

instil /in-stil/ (US **instill**) • v. (**instils, instilling, instilled**; US **instills, instilling, instilled**) gradually establish an idea in someone's mind.
– DERIVATIVES **instillation** n.
– ORIGIN Latin *instillare* 'put in by drops'.

instinct • n. **1** an inborn tendency to behave in a certain way. **2** a natural ability or skill.
– DERIVATIVES **instinctual** adj.
– ORIGIN Latin *instinctus* 'impulse'.

instinctive • adj. based on instinct rather than thought or training.
– DERIVATIVES **instinctively** adv.

institute • n. an organization for the promotion of educational, cultural, or professional activities. • v. (**institutes, instituting, instituted**) set something

up; establish something.
– ORIGIN Latin *instituere* 'establish'.

institution • n. **1** an important organization such as a university, bank, or Church. **2** an organization providing residential care for people with special needs. **3** an established law or custom.

institutional • adj. relating to or typical of a large organization.
– DERIVATIVES **institutionally** adv.

institutionalize (or **institutionalise**) • v. (**institutionalizes, institutionalizing, institutionalized**) **1** establish something as an accepted part of an organization or culture. **2** place someone in a residential institution. **3** (**be/become institutionalized**) be or become apathetic and dependent after a long period of residence in an institution.

instruct • v. **1** direct or command. **2** teach someone. **3** inform someone of a fact or situation.
– ORIGIN Latin *instruere* 'equip, teach'.

instruction • n. **1** a direction or order. **2** teaching or education.
– DERIVATIVES **instructional** adj.

instructive • adj. useful and informative.

instructor (or **instructress**) • n. a teacher.

instrument • n. **1** a tool or implement for precise work. **2** a measuring device. **3** (also **musical instrument**) a device for producing musical sounds.
– ORIGIN Latin *instrumentum*.

instrumental • adj. **1** acting as a means of achieving something. **2** (of music) performed on instruments. • n. a piece of music performed by instruments only.
– DERIVATIVES **instrumentally** adv.

instrumentalist • n. a player of a musical instrument.

instrumentation • n. **1** the instruments used in measuring. **2** the arrangement of a piece of music for particular instruments.

insubordinate • adj. disobedient.
– DERIVATIVES **insubordination** n.

insubstantial • adj. lacking strength and solidity.

insufferable • adj. **1** too extreme to bear; intolerable. **2** unbearably arrogant or conceited.
– DERIVATIVES **insufferably** adv.
– ORIGIN Latin *sufferre* 'suffer'.

insufficient • adj. not enough.
– DERIVATIVES **insufficiency** n. **insufficiently** adv.

insular • adj. **1** not open to outside influences; narrow-minded. **2** relating to an island.
– DERIVATIVES **insularity** n.
– ORIGIN Latin *insula* 'island'.

insulate • v. (**insulates, insulating, insulated**) **1** place material between one thing and another to prevent loss of heat or intrusion of sound. **2** cover something with non-conducting material to prevent the passage of electricity. **3** protect someone from something unpleasant.
– DERIVATIVES **insulator** n.
– ORIGIN Latin *insula* 'island'.

insulation • n. **1** material used to prevent the escape of heat or sound or the passage of electricity. **2** the action of insulating or state of being insulated.

insulin /in-syuu-lin/ • n. a hormone produced in the pancreas, which regulates glucose levels in the blood, and the lack of which causes diabetes.
– ORIGIN Latin *insula* 'island' (with reference to the islets of Langerhans in the pancreas).

insult • v. /in-sult/ speak to or treat someone with disrespect or abuse. • n. /in-sult/ **1** a disrespectful or abusive remark or action. **2** something that is worth so little that it causes offence: *the pay offer is an absolute insult.*
– ORIGIN Latin *insultare* 'jump on'.

insuperable /in-soo-puh-ruh-b'l/ • adj. impossible to overcome.
– ORIGIN Latin *insuperabilis*.

insupportable • adj. **1** unable to be supported or justified. **2** unable to be endured; intolerable.

insurance • n. **1** an arrangement by which a company or the state guarantees to provide compensation for loss, damage, illness, or death in return for payment of a regular amount of money. **2** money paid to an insured person in the event of damage, loss, injury, or death. **3** a thing providing protection against a possible event.

insure • v. (**insures, insuring, insured**) **1** arrange for compensation in the event of damage, loss, illness, or death, in exchange for regular payments to a company. **2** (**insure someone against**) protect someone against a possible event. **3** = ENSURE.
– DERIVATIVES **insurable** adj. **insurer** n.
– ORIGIN from ENSURE.

insurgent /in-ser-juhnt/ • n. a rebel or revolutionary.
– DERIVATIVES **insurgency** n. (pl. **insurgencies**).
– ORIGIN Latin *insurgere* 'rise up'.

insurmountable /in-ser-mown-tuh-b'l/ • adj. too great to be overcome.

insurrection /in-suh-rek-sh'n/ • n. a violent uprising against authority.
– DERIVATIVES **insurrectionary** adj.
– ORIGIN Latin.

intact • adj. not damaged.
– ORIGIN Latin *intactus* 'untouched'.

intaglio /in-ta-li-oh/ • n. (pl. **intaglios**) an incised or engraved design.
– ORIGIN Italian.

intake • n. **1** an amount or quantity taken in. **2** an act of taking in.

intangible • adj. **1** unable to be touched; not solid or real. **2** vague and abstract. • n. an intangible thing.
– DERIVATIVES **intangibly** adv.

integer /in-ti-jer/ • n. a whole number.
– ORIGIN Latin, 'whole'.

integral • adj. /in-ti-gruhl, in-teg-ruhl/ **1** necessary to make a whole complete; fundamental. **2** included as part of a whole. • n. /in-ti-gruhl/ Math. a function of which a given function is the derivative, and which may express the area under the curve of a graph of the function.
– DERIVATIVES **integrally** adv.

integral calculus • n. Math. the part of calculus concerned with the integrals of functions.

integrate • v. /in-ti-grayt/ (**integrates, integrating, integrated**) **1** combine or be combined to form a whole. **2** make someone accepted as part of a group.
– ORIGIN Latin *integrare* 'make whole'.

integrated circuit • n. an electronic circuit on a small piece of semiconducting material, performing the same function as a larger circuit of separate components.

integration • n. **1** the action of combining things to form a whole. **2** the mixing of peoples or groups previously kept apart.

integrity /in-teg-ri-ti/ • n. **1** the quality of being honest and morally upright. **2** the state of being whole or unified.
– ORIGIN Latin *integritas*.

integument /in-teg-yuu-muhnt/ • n. a tough outer protective layer, especially of an animal or plant.
– ORIGIN Latin *integumentum*.

intellect • n. the ability to use the mind to think logically and understand things.
– ORIGIN Latin *intellectus*.

intellectual /in-tuh-lek-chyuu-uhl/ • adj. **1** having a highly developed ability to think logically and understand things. **2** relating to a person's mental powers. • n. a person with a highly developed intellect.
– DERIVATIVES **intellectually** adv.

intellectualize (or **intellectualise**) • v. (**intellectualizes, intellectualizing, intellectualized**) talk or write in an intellectual way.

intelligence • n. **1** the ability to gain and apply knowledge and skills. **2** secret information collected about an enemy or competitor.
– ORIGIN Latin *intelligentia*.

intelligence quotient • n. a number representing a person's reasoning ability, 100 being the average.

intelligent • adj. **1** having intelligence, especially of a high level. **2** (of a device) able to vary its state or action in response to varying situations and past experience.
– DERIVATIVES **intelligently** adv.

intelligentsia /in-tel-li-jent-si-uh/ • n. intellectuals or highly educated people.

intelligible /in-tel-li-ji-b'l/ • adj. able to be understood.
– DERIVATIVES **intelligibility** n. **intelligibly** adv.
– ORIGIN Latin *intelligibilis*.

intemperate • adj. lacking self-control.

intend • v. **1** have something as your aim or plan. **2** plan that something should be, do, or mean something: *the book was intended as a satire.* **3** (**intend something for/to do**) design or plan something for a particular purpose.
– ORIGIN Latin *intendere* 'intend, extend'.

intended • adj. planned or meant. • n. (**your intended**) informal your fiancé(e).

intense • adj. (**intenser, intensest**) **1** very great in force, degree, or strength. **2** very earnest or serious.
– DERIVATIVES **intensely** adv.
– ORIGIN Latin *intensus* 'stretched tightly'.

intensify • v. (**intensifies, intensifying, intensified**) increase in degree, force, or strength.
– DERIVATIVES **intensification** n.

intensity • n. (pl. **intensities**) the quality of being great in force, degree, or strength.

intensive • adj. **1** very thorough or vigorous. **2** (of agriculture) aiming to achieve maximum production within a limited area. **3** (in combination) making much use of something: *labour-intensive methods.*
– DERIVATIVES **intensively** adv.

intensive care • n. special medical treatment given to a dangerously ill patient.

intent • n. an aim, plan, or purpose. • adj. **1** (**intent on**) determined to do. **2** (**intent on**) concentrating hard on an

activity. **3** showing earnest and eager attention.
– DERIVATIVES **intently** adv.
– ORIGIN Old French *entente*.

intention • n. **1** an aim or plan. **2** (**your intentions**) your plans in respect to marriage.

intentional • adj. deliberate.
– DERIVATIVES **intentionally** adv.

inter /in-ter/ • v. (**inters**, **interring**, **interred**) place a dead body in a grave or tomb.
– ORIGIN Old French *enterrer*.

inter- • prefix **1** between: *interbreed*. **2** so as to affect both: *interact*.
– ORIGIN Latin *inter*.

interact • v. (of two people or things) act so as to affect each other.
– DERIVATIVES **interaction** n.

interactive • adj. **1** influencing each other. **2** (of a computer or other electronic device) allowing a two-way flow of information between it and a user.

inter alia /in-ter ay-li-uh/ • adv. among other things.
– ORIGIN Latin.

interbreed • v. (**interbreeds**, **interbreeding**, **interbred**) breed with an animal of a different race or species.

intercede /in-ter-seed/ • v. (**intercedes**, **interceding**, **interceded**) intervene on behalf of someone.
– ORIGIN Latin *intercedere*.

intercept • v. /in-ter-**sept**/ stop a person, vehicle, or communication and prevent them from continuing to a destination. • n. /**in**-ter-sept/ Math. the point at which a line cuts the axis of a graph.
– DERIVATIVES **interception** n. **interceptor** n.
– ORIGIN Latin *intercipere* 'catch between'.

intercession /in-ter-sesh-uhn/ • n. the action of intervening on behalf of someone.
– ORIGIN Latin.

interchange • v. /in-ter-**chaynj**/ (**interchanges**, **interchanging**, **interchanged**) **1** (of people) exchange things with each other. **2** put each of two things in the other's place. • n. /**in**-ter-chaynj/ **1** the action of exchanging things. **2** an exchange of words. **3** a road junction on several levels so that traffic streams do not intersect.
– DERIVATIVES **interchangeability** n. **interchangeable** adj. **interchangeably** adv.

intercity • adj. existing or travelling between cities.

intercom • n. an electrical device allowing one-way or two-way communication.
– ORIGIN short for *intercommunication*.

intercommunication • n. the process of communicating between people or groups.

interconnect • v. connect with each other.

intercontinental • adj. relating to or travelling between continents.

intercourse • n. **1** communication or dealings between people. **2** the act of having sex.
– ORIGIN Latin *intercursus*.

intercut • v. (**intercuts**, **intercutting**, **intercut**) alternate scenes with contrasting scenes in a film.

interdenominational • adj. relating to more than one religious denomination.

interdepartmental • adj. relating to more than one department.

interdependent • adj. dependent on each other.

interdict • n. /**in**-ter-dikt/ an order forbidding something. • v. /in-ter-**dikt**/ esp. N. Amer. prohibit or forbid.
– DERIVATIVES **interdiction** n.
– ORIGIN Latin *interdictum*.

interdisciplinary • adj. relating to more than one branch of knowledge.

interest • n. **1** the state of wanting to know about something or someone. **2** the quality of arousing someone's curiosity or holding their attention. **3** a subject about which you are concerned or enthusiastic. **4** money paid for the use of money that is being lent. **5** a person's advantage or benefit: *it is in his own interest*. **6** a share, right, or stake in property or a business. • v. **1** arouse someone's curiosity or attention. **2** (**interest someone in**) persuade someone to do or obtain. **3** (as adj. **interested**) not impartial: *interested parties*.
– ORIGIN Latin *interesse* 'be important'.

interesting • adj. arousing curiosity or attention.

interface • n. **1** a point where two things meet and interact. **2** a device or program enabling a user to communicate with a computer, or for connecting two items of hardware or software. • v. (**interfaces**, **interfacing**, **interfaced**) (**interface with**) Computing connect with something by an interface.

interfacing • n. an extra layer of material or an adhesive stiffener, applied to the facing of a garment to add support.

interfere • v. (**interferes**, **interfering**,

interfered) **1** (**interfere with**) prevent
something from continuing or being
carried out properly. **2** (**interfere with**)
handle or adjust something without
permission. **3** become involved in
something without being asked.
4 (**interfere with**) Brit. euphem. fondle or
assault someone sexually.
– DERIVATIVES **interfering** adj.
– ORIGIN Old French *s'entreferir* 'strike
each other'.

interference • n. **1** the action of
interfering. **2** disturbance to radio
signals caused by unwanted signals
from other sources. **3** Physics the
combination of waves of the same
wavelength from two or more sources,
producing a new wave pattern.

interferon /in-ter-feer-on/ • n. a protein
released by animal cells which prevents
a virus from reproducing itself.

intergalactic • adj. relating to or
situated between galaxies.

interim /in-tuh-rim/ • n. (**the interim**)
the time between two events. • adj. lasting for a short time; provisional.
– ORIGIN Latin, 'meanwhile'.

interior • adj. **1** situated within or inside;
inner. **2** remote from the coast or
frontier; inland. • n. **1** the interior part.
2 the internal affairs of a country.
– ORIGIN Latin 'inner'.

interior angle • n. the angle between
adjacent sides of a straight-sided figure.

interior design • n. the design,
decoration, and furnishings of the
interior of a room or building.

interject /in-ter-jekt/ • v. say something
suddenly as an interruption.
– ORIGIN Latin *interjicere* 'interpose'.

interjection • n. an exclamation (e.g.
ah!).

interlace • v. (**interlaces, interlacing,
interlaced**) weave together.

interleave • v. (**interleaves,
interleaving, interleaved**) place
something between the layers of.

interlining • n. material used in a
garment or curtain as an additional
layer between the lining and surface
fabric.

interlink • v. join or connect together.

interlock • v. (of two parts) engage with
each other by overlapping or fitting
together. • n. (also **interlock fabric**) a
fabric with closely interlocking stitches
allowing it to stretch.

interlocutor /in-ter-lok-yuu-ter/
• n. formal a person who takes part in a
conversation or dialogue.
– ORIGIN Latin *interloqui* 'interrupt'.

interlocutory /in-ter-lok-yuu-tuh-ri/

• adj. relating to conversation or
dialogue.

interloper /in-ter-loh-per/ • n. a person
who interferes in someone else's affairs.
– ORIGIN from INTER- + former *landloper*
'vagabond'.

interlude • n. **1** a period of time or
activity that contrasts with what goes
before or after: *a romantic interlude.* **2** a
pause between the acts of a play. **3** a
piece of music played between other
pieces.
– ORIGIN Latin *interludium.*

intermarry • v. (**intermarries,
intermarrying, intermarried**) (of people
of different races, castes, or religions)
marry each other.
– DERIVATIVES **intermarriage** n.

intermediary /in-ter-mee-di-uh-ri/
• n. (pl. **intermediaries**) a person who
tries to settle a dispute.

intermediate /in-ter-mee-di-uht/
• adj. **1** coming between two things in
time, place, or character. **2** having more
than basic knowledge or skills but not
yet advanced. • n. an intermediate
person or thing.
– ORIGIN from Latin *inter-* 'between' +
medius 'middle'.

interment /in-ter-muhnt/ • n. the burial
of a dead body.

intermezzo /in-ter-met-zoh/ • n. (pl.
intermezzi /in-ter-met-zi/ or
intermezzos) a short connecting
instrumental movement between parts
of an opera or other musical work, or
between the acts of a play.
– ORIGIN Italian.

interminable • adj. endless or seem-
ingly endless: *interminable discussions.*
– DERIVATIVES **interminably** adv.
– ORIGIN Latin *interminabilis.*

intermingle • v. (**intermingles,
intermingling, intermingled**) mix
together.

intermission • n. **1** a pause or break.
2 an interval between parts of a play or
film.
– ORIGIN Latin.

intermittent • adj. happening at
irregular intervals.
– DERIVATIVES **intermittently** adv.
– ORIGIN Latin.

intermix • v. mix together.

intern • v. /in-tern/ confine someone as a
prisoner. • n. /in-tern/ N. Amer. **1** a recent
medical graduate receiving supervised
training in a hospital. **2** a student or
trainee who does a job to gain work
experience.
– DERIVATIVES **internment** n.
– ORIGIN Latin *internus* 'internal'.

internal • adj. **1** relating to the inside. **2** inside the body. **3** relating to affairs and activities within a country. **4** existing or used within an organization. **5** in the mind or soul.
– DERIVATIVES **internally** adv.
– ORIGIN Latin *internalis*.

internal-combustion engine • n. an engine in which power is generated by the expansion of hot gases from the burning of fuel with air inside the engine.

internalize (or **internalise**) • v. (**internalizes, internalizing, internalized**) unconsciously make a belief or attitude part of your behaviour or thinking.

international • adj. **1** existing or occurring between nations. **2** agreed on or used by all or many nations. • n. Brit. **1** a game or contest between teams from different countries. **2** a player who has taken part in a contest between teams from different countries.
– DERIVATIVES **internationally** adv.

International Date Line • n. an imaginary North–South line through the Pacific Ocean, to the east of which the date is a day earlier than it is to the west.

internationalism • n. belief in cooperation and understanding between nations.

internationalize (or **internationalise**) • v. (**internationalizes, internationalizing, internationalized**) make something international in scope.
– DERIVATIVES **internationalization** n.

international law • n. a body of rules recognized by nations as binding in their relations with one another.

internecine /in-ter-nee-syn/ • adj. (of conflict) happening between members of a group: *internecine rivalries*.
– ORIGIN Latin *internecinus*.

internee • n. a prisoner.

Internet • n. a global computer network providing a variety of information and communication facilities.

interpersonal • adj. relating to relationships between people.

interplanetary • adj. situated or travelling between planets.

interplay • n. the way in which things interact.

Interpol /in-ter-pol/ • n. an international organization that coordinates investigations made by the police forces of member countries into international crimes.
– ORIGIN from *Inter*(*national*) *pol*(*ice*).

interpolate /in-ter-puh-layt/ • v. (**interpolates, interpolating, interpolated**) **1** insert something different or additional. **2** add a remark to a conversation. **3** Math. insert an intermediate term into a series by estimating it from surrounding known values.
– DERIVATIVES **interpolation** n.
– ORIGIN Latin *interpolare* 'refurbish'.

interpose • v. (**interposes, interposing, interposed**) **1** place something between one thing and another. **2** intervene between parties.
– ORIGIN French *interposer*.

interpret • v. (**interprets, interpreting, interpreted**) **1** explain the meaning of something. **2** translate aloud the words of a person speaking a different language. **3** understand something as having a particular meaning.
– DERIVATIVES **interpretable** adj. **interpretative** adj. **interpretive** adj.
– ORIGIN Latin *interpretari* 'explain'.

interpretation • n. **1** the action of explaining the meaning of something. **2** an explanation. **3** the way in which a performer expresses a creative work.

interpreter • n. a person who translates foreign speech aloud while it is being spoken.

interracial • adj. existing between or involving different races.

interregnum /in-ter-reg-nuhm/ • n. (pl. **interregnums**) a period between reigns or political regimes when normal government is suspended.
– ORIGIN Latin.

interrelate • v. (**interrelates, interrelating, interrelated**) relate or connect to one other.
– DERIVATIVES **interrelation** n.

interrogate • v. (**interrogates, interrogating, interrogated**) ask someone questions thoroughly or aggressively.
– DERIVATIVES **interrogation** n. **interrogator** n.
– ORIGIN Latin *interrogare*.

interrogative /in-ter-rog-uh-tiv/ • adj. in the form of a question or used in questions. • n. a word used in questions, e.g. *how* or *what*.

interrogatory /in-ter-rog-uh-tuh-ri/ • adj. questioning.

interrupt • v. **1** stop the continuous progress of something. **2** stop a person who is speaking by saying or doing something. **3** break the continuity of a line, surface, or view.
– DERIVATIVES **interrupter** (also **interruptor**) n. **interruption** n.
– ORIGIN Latin *interrumpere*.

> ✓ Spell **interrupt** and the related word **interruption** with a double **r**.

intersect • v. **1** divide something by passing or lying across it. **2** (of lines, roads, etc.) cross or cut each other.
– ORIGIN Latin *intersecare*.

intersection • n. a place at which two roads, lines, etc. intersect.

intersperse • v. (**intersperses, interspersing, interspersed**) scatter or place among or between other things: *the debate was interspersed with angry exchanges.*
– ORIGIN Latin *interspergere*.

interstate • adj. existing or carried on between states. • n. one of a system of motorways running between US states.

interstellar /in-ter-stel-ler/ • adj. occurring or situated between stars.

interstice /in-ter-stiss/ • n. a small space in something.
– ORIGIN Latin *interstitium*.

interstitial /in-ter-sti-sh'l/ • adj. found in or relating to small spaces within something.

intertwine • v. (**intertwines, intertwining, intertwined**) twist or twine together.

interval • n. **1** a period of time between two events. **2** a pause. **3** Brit. a pause between parts of a performance or a sports match. **4** the difference in pitch between two sounds.
– ORIGIN Latin *intervallum* 'space between ramparts'.

intervene • v. (**intervenes, intervening, intervened**) **1** come between two people or things so as to prevent or alter a situation. **2** (as adj. **intervening**) occurring between or among.
– ORIGIN Latin *intervenire*.

intervention • n. the action of coming between people or things to improve or control a situation.

interventionist • adj. favouring intervention as a way of influencing an outcome.

interview • n. **1** an occasion when a journalist or broadcaster puts questions to a person. **2** a spoken examination of an applicant for a job or college place. **3** a session of formal questioning of a person by the police. • v. hold an interview with.
– DERIVATIVES **interviewee** n. **interviewer** n.
– ORIGIN French *entrevue*.

interwar • adj. existing in the period between the two world wars.

interweave • v. (**interweaves, interweaving, interwove**; past part. **interwoven**) weave or become woven together.

intestate /in-tess-tayt/ • adj. not having made a will before you die.
– DERIVATIVES **intestacy** /in-tes-tuh-si/ n.
– ORIGIN Latin *intestatus*.

intestine (also **intestines**) • n. the long tubular organ leading from the end of the stomach to the anus.
– DERIVATIVES **intestinal** /in-tes-ty-n'l/ adj.
– ORIGIN Latin *intestinum*.

intimacy • n. (pl. **intimacies**) **1** close familiarity or friendship. **2** a familiar or private act or remark.

intimate¹ /in-ti-muht/ • adj. **1** close and friendly. **2** private and personal: *intimate details.* **3** euphem. having a sexual relationship. **4** involving very close connection. **5** (of knowledge) detailed. **6** having a cosy and relaxed atmosphere. • n. a very close friend.
– DERIVATIVES **intimately** adv.
– ORIGIN Latin *intimare* 'impress'.

intimate² /in-ti-mayt/ • v. (**intimates, intimating, intimated**) state something indirectly; hint.
– DERIVATIVES **intimation** n.
– ORIGIN Latin *intimare* (see **INTIMATE¹**).

intimidate • v. (**intimidates, intimidating, intimidated**) frighten someone into doing something.
– DERIVATIVES **intimidation** n.
– ORIGIN Latin *intimidare* 'make timid'.

into • prep. **1** expressing movement or direction to a point on or within. **2** expressing a change of state or the result of an action. **3** in the direction of. **4** about or concerning. **5** expressing division: *three into twelve.*

intolerable • adj. unable to be endured.
– DERIVATIVES **intolerably** adv.

intolerant • adj. unwilling to tolerate ideas or behaviour that are different from your own.
– DERIVATIVES **intolerance** n.

intonation • n. **1** the rise and fall of the voice in speaking. **2** the action of reciting something with little rise and fall in the voice.

intone /in-tohn/ • v. (**intones, intoning, intoned**) say or recite something with little rise and fall of the voice.
– ORIGIN Latin *intonare*.

in toto /in toh-toh/ • adv. as a whole.
– ORIGIN Latin.

intoxicate • v. (**intoxicates, intoxicating, intoxicated**) **1** (of alcoholic drink or a drug) make someone lose control of themselves. **2** excite or exhilarate someone.
– DERIVATIVES **intoxication** n.
– ORIGIN Latin *intoxicare*.

intra- /in-truh/ • prefix (added to

adjectives) on the inside; within:
intramural.
– ORIGIN Latin.

intractable /in-trak-tuh-b'l/
• adj. **1** hard to deal with. **2** stubborn.
– DERIVATIVES **intractability** n.

intramural /in-truh-**myoor**-uhl/
• adj. esp. N. Amer. forming part of normal
university or college studies.
– ORIGIN from **INTRA-** + Latin *murus* 'wall'.

intranet /in-truh-net/ • n. a private
communications network created with
Internet software.

intransigent /in-**tran**-zi-juhnt/
• adj. refusing to change your views or
behaviour.
– DERIVATIVES **intransigence** n.
– ORIGIN from Spanish *los intransigentes*
(a name adopted by extreme repub-
licans).

intransitive /in-**tran**-zi-tiv/ • adj. (of a
verb) not taking a direct object, e.g. *look*
in *look at the sky*. Opp. **TRANSITIVE**.

intrauterine /in-truh-**yoo**-tuh-ryn/
• adj. within the womb.

intrauterine device • n. a contraceptive device in the form of a coil,
inserted into the womb.

intravenous /in-truh-**vee**-nuhss/
• adj. within or into a vein or veins.
– DERIVATIVES **intravenously** adv.

intrepid • adj. fearless; adventurous.
– DERIVATIVES **intrepidity** n.
– ORIGIN Latin *intrepidus* 'not alarmed'.

intricacy /in-tri-kuh-si/ • n. (pl.
intricacies) **1** the quality of being very
complicated or detailed. **2** (**intricacies**)
details.

intricate • adj. very complicated or
detailed.
– DERIVATIVES **intricately** adv.
– ORIGIN Latin *intricare* 'entangle'.

intrigue • v. /in-**treeg**/ (**intrigues,
intriguing, intrigued**) **1** arouse
someone's curiosity or interest. **2** plot
something illegal or harmful. • n. /**in**-
treeg/ **1** the plotting of something
illegal or harmful. **2** a secret love affair.
– DERIVATIVES **intriguing** adj.
– ORIGIN French *intriguer* 'tangle, plot'.

intrinsic /in-**trin**-sik/ • adj. belonging to
the basic nature of someone or some-
thing; essential.
– DERIVATIVES **intrinsically** adv.
– ORIGIN Latin *intrinsecus* 'inwardly'.

intro- • prefix into; inwards: *introvert*.
– ORIGIN Latin *intro* 'to the inside'.

introduce • v. (**introduces, introducing,
introduced**) **1** bring something into use
or operation for the first time. **2** present
someone by name to another person.
3 (**introduce something to**) bring a

subject to someone's attention for the
first time. **4** insert or bring into something: *a device which introduces chlorine
into the pool*. **5** occur at the start of.
6 provide an opening announcement for.
– ORIGIN Latin *introducere*.

introduction • n. **1** the action of
introducing. **2** an act of introducing one
person to another. **3** a thing which
introduces another, such as a section at
the beginning of a book. **4** a thing newly
brought in. **5** a book or course of study
intended to introduce a subject. **6** a
person's first experience of a subject or
activity.

introductory • adj. serving as an
introduction; basic.

introspection • n. the examination of
your own thoughts or feelings.
– DERIVATIVES **introspective** adj.
– ORIGIN Latin *introspicere* 'look into'.

introvert • n. a shy, quiet person who is
mainly concerned with their own
thoughts and feelings. • adj. relating to
an introvert.
– DERIVATIVES **introversion** n.
introverted adj.
– ORIGIN from Latin *intro-* 'to the inside'
+ *vertere* 'to turn'.

intrude • v. (**intrudes, intruding,
intruded**) come into a place or situation
where you are unwelcome or uninvited.
– ORIGIN Latin *intrudere*.

intruder • n. **1** a person who enters a
place illegally. **2** a person who goes
somewhere where they are not
welcome.

intrusion • n. **1** the action of coming into
a place or situation where you are
unwelcome or uninvited. **2** a thing that
intrudes.

intrusive • adj. **1** having an unwelcome
effect. **2** (of igneous rock) that has been
forced when molten into cracks in
neighbouring rocks.

intuit /in-tyoo-it/ • v. understand or work
out by intuition.
– ORIGIN Latin *intueri* 'contemplate'.

intuition • n. the ability to understand
or know something immediately,
without conscious reasoning.

intuitive • adj. based on what you feel to
be true; instinctive.
– DERIVATIVES **intuitively** adv.

Inuit /in-yuu-it/ • n. **1** (pl. **Inuit** or **Inuits**) a
member of a people of northern Canada
and parts of Greenland and Alaska. **2** the
language of the Inuit.
– ORIGIN Inuit, 'people'.

USAGE: For an explanation of the terms
Inuit and **Eskimo**, see the note at **ESKIMO**.

inundate /in-uhn-dayt/ • v. (**inundates,**

inundating, inundated) 1 overwhelm someone with things to be dealt with. **2** flood something.
– DERIVATIVES **inundation** n.
– ORIGIN Latin *inundare* 'flood'.

inure /i-nyoor/ • v. (**be inured to**) become used to something unpleasant.
– ORIGIN Old French, 'in practice'.

invade • v. (**invades, invading, invaded**) **1** enter a country so as to conquer or occupy it. **2** enter a place in large numbers. **3** (of a parasite or disease) spread into the body. **4** intrude on: *his privacy was being invaded.*
– DERIVATIVES **invader** n.
– ORIGIN Latin *invadere*.

invalid[1] /in-vuh-lid/ • n. a person made weak or disabled by illness or injury.
• v. (**be invalided**) be removed from service in the armed forces because of injury or illness.
– ORIGIN from **INVALID**[2].

invalid[2] /in-val-id/ • adj. **1** not valid or officially recognized. **2** not true because based on incorrect information or faulty reasoning.
– ORIGIN Latin *invalidus* 'not strong'.

invalidate • v. (**invalidates, invalidating, invalidated**) make something invalid.
– DERIVATIVES **invalidation** n.

invalidity • n. **1** Brit. the condition of being an invalid. **2** the fact of being invalid.

invaluable • adj. very useful.

invariable • adj. **1** never changing. **2** Math. (of a quantity) constant.

invariably • adv. always.

invasion • n. **1** an act of invading a country. **2** the arrival of a large number of people or things. **3** an intrusion.

invasive • adj. **1** tending to invade or intrude: *invasive grasses.* **2** (of medical procedures) involving the introduction of instruments or other objects into the body.

invective • n. strongly abusive or critical language.
– ORIGIN Latin *invectivus* 'attacking'.

inveigh /in-vay/ • v. (**inveigh against**) speak or write about someone with great hostility.
– ORIGIN Latin *invehere* 'carry in'.

inveigle /in-vay-g'l/ • v. (**inveigles, inveigling, inveigled**) (**inveigle someone into**) persuade someone to do something by trickery or flattery.
– ORIGIN Old French *aveugler* 'to blind'.

invent • v. **1** create or design a new device or process. **2** make up a false story, identity, etc.
– DERIVATIVES **inventor** n.

– ORIGIN Latin *invenire* 'contrive'.

invention • n. **1** the action of creating a new device or process. **2** a newly created device or process. **3** a false story. **4** creative ability.

inventive • adj. having or showing creativity or original thought.
– DERIVATIVES **inventiveness** n.

inventory /in-vuhn-tuh-ri/ • n. (pl. **inventories**) **1** a complete list of items. **2** a quantity of goods in stock.
– ORIGIN Latin *inventarium* 'a list of what is found'.

inverse /in-verss/ • adj. opposite in position, direction, order, or effect.
• n. **1** a thing that is the opposite or reverse of another. **2** Math. a reciprocal quantity.
– ORIGIN Latin *inversus*.

inverse proportion (also **inverse ratio**) • n. a relation between two quantities such that one increases in proportion as the other decreases.

inversion • n. the action of inverting or the state of being inverted.

invert /in-vert/ • v. put something upside down or in the opposite position or order.
– ORIGIN Latin *invertere* 'turn inside out'.

invertebrate /in-ver-ti-bruht/ • n. an animal having no backbone.
• adj. relating to invertebrates.

inverted comma • n. esp. Brit. a quotation mark.

invest • v. **1** put money into financial schemes, shares, or property with the expectation of making a profit. **2** devote time or energy to an undertaking with the expectation of a worthwhile result. **3** (**invest in**) informal buy something whose usefulness will repay the cost. **4** (**invest something with**) provide something with an added quality. **5** give a rank or office to.
– DERIVATIVES **investor** n.
– ORIGIN Latin *investire* 'clothe'.

investigate • v. **1** carry out a systematic inquiry into something so as to establish the truth. **2** carry out research into a subject.
– DERIVATIVES **investigation** n. **investigator** n.
– ORIGIN Latin *investigare* 'trace out'.

investigative /in-vess-ti-guh-tiv/ • adj. **1** relating to the process of investigating something. **2** (of journalism or a journalist) investigating and seeking to expose dishonesty or injustice.

investiture /in-vess-ti-cher/ • n. **1** the action of formally investing a person with honours or rank. **2** a ceremony at which this takes place.

investment •n. **1** the action of investing. **2** a thing worth buying because it may be profitable or useful in the future.

inveterate /in-vet-uh-ruht/ •adj. **1** having a long-standing and firmly established habit: *an inveterate gambler*. **2** (of a feeling or habit) firmly established.
– ORIGIN Latin *inveteratus* 'made old'.

invidious /in-vid-i-uhss/ •adj. unacceptable, unfair, and likely to arouse resentment or anger in other people.
– ORIGIN Latin *invidiosus*.

invigilate /in-vij-i-layt/ •v. (**invigilates, invigilating, invigilated**) Brit. supervise candidates during an exam.
– DERIVATIVES **invigilation** n. **invigilator** n.
– ORIGIN Latin *invigilare* 'watch over'.

invigorate /in-vig-uh-rayt/ •v. (**invigorates, invigorating, invigorated**) give strength or energy to.
– DERIVATIVES **invigorating** adj.
– ORIGIN Latin *invigorare* 'make strong'.

invincible /in-vin-si-b'l/ •adj. too powerful to be defeated or overcome.
– DERIVATIVES **invincibility** n.
– ORIGIN Latin *invincibilis*.

inviolable /in-vy-uh-luh-b'l/ •adj. never to be attacked or dishonoured.
– DERIVATIVES **inviolability** n.

inviolate /in-vy-uh-luht/ •adj. free from injury or harm.
– ORIGIN Latin *inviolatus*.

invisible •adj. **1** unable to be seen, either by nature or because concealed. **2** relating to earnings which a country makes from the sale of services rather than commodities.
– DERIVATIVES **invisibility** n. **invisibly** adv.

invitation •n. **1** a request inviting someone to go somewhere or to do something. **2** the action of inviting. **3** a situation or action likely to provoke a particular outcome: *his tactics were an invitation to disaster*.

invite •v. (**invites, inviting, invited**) **1** ask someone in a friendly or formal way to go somewhere or do something. **2** ask for something formally or politely. **3** tend to provoke a particular outcome or response. •n. informal an invitation.
– ORIGIN Latin *invitare*.

inviting •adj. tempting or attractive.

in vitro /in vee-troh/ •adj. & adv. (of biological processes) taking place in a test tube or other environment outside the body.
– ORIGIN Latin, 'in glass'.

invocation /in-vuh-kay-sh'n/ •n. **1** the action of appealing to someone or something as an authority or in support of an argument. **2** an appeal to a god or spirit.

invoice •n. a list of goods or services provided, with a statement of the sum due. •v. (**invoices, invoicing, invoiced**) send an invoice to.
– ORIGIN French *envoyer* 'send'.

invoke /in-vohk/ •v. (**invokes, invoking, invoked**) **1** appeal to someone or something as an authority or to support an argument. **2** call on a god or spirit in prayer or as a witness. **3** call earnestly for.
– ORIGIN Latin *invocare*.

involuntary •adj. **1** done without conscious control. **2** (especially of muscles or nerves) unable to be consciously controlled. **3** done against someone's will.
– DERIVATIVES **involuntarily** adv.

involve •v. (**involves, involving, involved**) **1** (of a situation or event) include something as a necessary part or result. **2** cause to experience or participate in an activity or situation: *what organizations will be involved in these projects?* **3** (**be/get involved**) be or become occupied or engrossed in something. **4** (**be involved**) be in a romantic relationship with someone.
– DERIVATIVES **involvement** n.
– ORIGIN Latin *involvere* 'entangle'.

involved •adj. difficult to understand; complicated.

invulnerable •adj. impossible to harm or damage.
– DERIVATIVES **invulnerability** n.

-in-waiting •comb. form referring to a position as attendant to a royal person: *lady-in-waiting*.

inward •adj. **1** directed or proceeding towards the inside. **2** mental or spiritual. •adv. var. of **INWARDS**.
– DERIVATIVES **inwardly** adv. **inwardness** n.

inwards (also **inward**) •adv. **1** towards the inside. **2** towards the mind or spirit.

iodide /I-uh-dyd/ •n. a compound of iodine with another element or group.

iodine /I-uh-deen/ •n. **1** a black non-metallic chemical element of the halogen group. **2** an antiseptic solution of iodine in alcohol.
– ORIGIN Greek *iōdēs* 'violet-coloured'.

ion /I-uhn/ •n. an atom or molecule with a net electric charge through loss or gain of electrons.
– DERIVATIVES **ionic** adj.
– ORIGIN Greek, 'going'.

ionize /I-uh-nyz/ (or **ionise**) •v. (**ionizes, ionizing, ionized**) convert an atom,

molecule, or substance into an ion or ions.
– DERIVATIVES **ionization** n.

ionizer (or **ioniser**) • n. a device which produces ions, used to improve the quality of the air in a room.

ionosphere /I-on-uh-sfeer/ • n. the layer of the atmosphere above the mesosphere.

iota /I-oh-tuh/ • n. a very small amount: *it won't make an iota of difference.*
– ORIGIN Greek; the letter *iota* is the smallest in the Greek alphabet.

IOU • n. a signed document acknowledging a debt.
– ORIGIN from *I owe you.*

ipso facto /ip-soh fak-toh/ • adv. by that very fact or act.
– ORIGIN Latin.

IQ • abbrev. intelligence quotient.

Ir • symb. the chemical element iridium.

IRA • abbrev. Irish Republican Army.

Iranian • n. a person from Iran. • adj. relating to Iran.

Iraqi • n. (pl. **Iraqis**) a person from Iraq. • adj. relating to Iraq.

irascible /i-rass-i-b'l/ • adj. hot-tempered; irritable.
– DERIVATIVES **irascibility** n.
– ORIGIN Latin *irascibilis.*

irate /I-rayt/ • adj. very angry.
– DERIVATIVES **irately** adv.
– ORIGIN Latin *iratus.*

ire /rhymes with fire/ • n. literary anger.
– ORIGIN Latin *ira.*

iridescent /i-ri-dess-uhnt/ • adj. showing bright colours that seem to change when seen from different angles.
– DERIVATIVES **iridescence** n.
– ORIGIN Latin *iris* 'rainbow'.

iridium /i-rid-i-uhm/ • n. a hard, dense silvery-white metallic element.
– ORIGIN Latin *iris* 'rainbow'.

iris • n. 1 a coloured ring-shaped membrane behind the cornea of the eye, with the pupil in the centre. 2 a plant with sword-shaped leaves and purple or yellow flowers.
– ORIGIN Greek, 'rainbow, iris'.

Irish • n. (also **Irish Gaelic**) the Celtic language of Ireland. • adj. relating to Ireland or Irish.
– DERIVATIVES **Irishman** n. (pl. **Irishmen**). **Irishness** n. **Irishwoman** n. (pl. **Irishwomen**).

Irish coffee • n. coffee mixed with a dash of Irish whisky.

irk /erk/ • v. irritate; annoy.
– DERIVATIVES **irksome** adj.
– ORIGIN perh. from Old Norse, 'to work'.

iron • n. 1 a strong magnetic silvery-grey metal. 2 a hand-held implement with a heated steel base, used to smooth clothes and linen. 3 a golf club used for hitting the ball at a high angle. 4 (**irons**) chains or handcuffs used as a restraint. • v. 1 smooth clothes with an iron. 2 (**iron something out**) settle a difficulty or problem.
– ORIGIN Old English.

Iron Age • n. the period that followed the Bronze Age, when weapons and tools came to be made of iron.

Iron Curtain • n. (**the Iron Curtain**) an imaginary barrier separating the former Soviet bloc and the West before the decline of communism in eastern Europe.

ironic /I-ron-ik/ • adj. 1 expressing an idea with words that normally mean the opposite in order to be humorous or to emphasize a point. 2 happening in the opposite way to what is expected.
– DERIVATIVES **ironical** adj. **ironically** adv.

ironing • n. clothes and linen that need to be or have just been ironed.

ironmonger • n. Brit. a person who sells tools and other hardware.
– DERIVATIVES **ironmongery** n.

ironstone • n. 1 sedimentary rock containing iron compounds. 2 a kind of dense, opaque stoneware.

ironworks • n. a place where iron is smelted or iron goods are made.

irony /I-ruh-ni/ • n. (pl. **ironies**) 1 the expression of meaning through the use of words which normally mean the opposite in order to be humorous or to emphasize a point 2 a situation that appears to be opposite to what is expected.
– ORIGIN Greek *eirōneia* 'simulated ignorance'.

irradiate • v. (**irradiates, irradiating, irradiated**) 1 expose to radiation. 2 shine light on.
– DERIVATIVES **irradiation** n.
– ORIGIN Latin *irradiare.*

irrational • adj. not logical or reasonable.
– DERIVATIVES **irrationality** n. **irrationally** adv.

irreconcilable • adj. 1 incompatible. 2 not able to be settled: *irreconcilable differences.*

irrecoverable • adj. not able to be recovered.

irredeemable • adj. not able to be saved, improved, or corrected.
– DERIVATIVES **irredeemably** adv.

irredentist /ir-ri-den-tist/ • n. a person who believes that territory formerly

belonging to their country should be given back to it.
– ORIGIN Italian *irredentista*.

irreducible • adj. not able to be reduced or simplified.

irrefutable /ir-ri-fyoo-tuh-b'l/ • adj. impossible to deny or disprove.

irregular • adj. **1** not regular in shape, arrangement, or occurrence. **2** not according to a rule or standard. **3** not belonging to regular army units. **4** Grammar (of a word) having inflections that are not formed in the usual way.
– DERIVATIVES **irregularity** n. (pl. **irregularities**). **irregularly** adv.

irrelevant • adj. not relating to the subject or matter in question.
– DERIVATIVES **irrelevance** n. **irrelevancy** n. (pl. **irrelevancies**). **irrelevantly** adv.

> ☑ **irrelevant** has a double **r** at the beginning; the ending is **-ant**.

irreligious • adj. indifferent or hostile to religion.

irremediable /ir-ri-mee-di-uh-b'l/ • adj. impossible to remedy.

irremovable • adj. impossible to remove.

irreparable /ir-rep-uh-ruh-b'l/ • adj. impossible to put right or repair.
– DERIVATIVES **irreparably** adv.

irreplaceable • adj. impossible to replace if lost or damaged.

irrepressible • adj. not able to be restrained.

irreproachable • adj. very good and unable to be criticized.

irresistible • adj. too tempting or powerful to be resisted.
– DERIVATIVES **irresistibly** adv.

irresolute • adj. uncertain.

irrespective • adj. (**irrespective of**) regardless of.

irresponsible • adj. not showing a proper sense of responsibility.
– DERIVATIVES **irresponsibility** n. **irresponsibly** adv.

irretrievable • adj. not able to be improved or set right.
– DERIVATIVES **irretrievably** adv.

irreverent • adj. disrespectful.
– DERIVATIVES **irreverence** n. **irreverently** adv.

irreversible • adj. impossible to be reversed or altered.
– DERIVATIVES **irreversibility** n. **irreversibly** adv.

irrevocable /ir-rev-uh-kuh-b'l/ • adj. not able to be changed, reversed, or recovered.
– DERIVATIVES **irrevocability** n. **irrevocably** adv.

– ORIGIN Latin *irrevocabilis*.

irrigate /ir-ri-gayt/ • v. (**irrigates, irrigating, irrigated**) supply water to land or crops by means of channels.
– DERIVATIVES **irrigation** n.
– ORIGIN Latin *irrigare* 'moisten'.

irritable • adj. easily annoyed or angered.
– DERIVATIVES **irritability** n. **irritably** adv.

irritant • n. **1** a substance that irritates part of the body. **2** a source of continual annoyance.

irritate • v. (**irritates, irritating, irritated**) **1** make someone annoyed. **2** cause inflammation in a part of the body.
– DERIVATIVES **irritation** n.
– ORIGIN Latin *irritare*.

irruption /ir-rup-sh'n/ • n. formal a sudden forcible entry.
– ORIGIN Latin *irrumpere* 'break into'.

is 3rd person sing. present of BE.

ISA • abbrev. individual savings account.

-ise • suffix var. of -IZE.

> **USAGE:** Most verbs ending in **-ise**, e.g. *realise*, *authorise*, can also be spelled **-ize**. However, there are some verbs which must always be spelled **-ise** and are not variants of the **-ize** spelling. The most common ones are: *advertise*, *compromise*, *devise*, *televise*, *surprise*, *exercise*, *improvise*, *surmise*, *chastise*, *despise*, *supervise*, and *enfranchise*.

-ish • suffix forming adjectives: **1** having the qualities of: *girlish*. **2** of the nationality of: *Swedish*. **3** rather: *yellowish*.
– ORIGIN Old English.

Islam /iz-lahm/ • n. **1** the religion of the Muslims, based on belief in one God and revealed through Muhammad as the Prophet of Allah. **2** the Muslim world.
– ORIGIN Arabic, 'submission'.

Islamic /iz-lam-ik/ • adj. relating to Islam.

island • n. a piece of land surrounded by water.
– DERIVATIVES **islander** n.
– ORIGIN Old English.

isle • n. literary (except in place names) an island.
– ORIGIN Old French *ile*.

islet /I-lit/ • n. a small island.

islets of Langerhans /lang-er-hanz/ • pl. n. groups of cells in the pancreas that produce insulin.
– ORIGIN named after the German anatomist Paul *Langerhans*.

-ism • suffix forming nouns referring to: **1** an action or its result: *baptism*. **2** a state or quality: *barbarism*. **3** a system, principle, or movement: *Anglicanism*. **4** a

basis for prejudice: *racism.* **5** a medical condition: *alcoholism.*
– ORIGIN Greek *-ismos.*

isn't • contr. is not.

isobar /I-soh-bar/ • n. Meteorol. a line on a map connecting points having the same atmospheric pressure.
– ORIGIN Greek *isobaros* 'of equal weight'.

isohyet /I-soh-hy-it/ • n. Meteorol. a line on a map connecting points having the same amount of rainfall.
– ORIGIN from Greek *isos* 'equal' + *huetos* 'rain'.

isolate • v. (**isolates, isolating, isolated**) **1** place apart or alone; cut off. **2** Chem. & Biol. obtain or extract a compound, microorganism, etc. in a pure form.
– ORIGIN from ISOLATED.

isolated • adj. **1** remote; lonely. **2** single; exceptional: *isolated incidents.*
– ORIGIN French *isolé.*

isolation • n. the action of isolating or the fact of being isolated.

isolationism • n. a policy of remaining apart from the political affairs of other countries.
– DERIVATIVES **isolationist** n.

isomer /I-suh-mer/ • n. Chem. each of two or more compounds with the same formula but a different arrangement of atoms and different properties.
– DERIVATIVES **isomeric** adj.
– ORIGIN Greek *isomerēs* 'sharing equally'.

isometric • adj. having equal dimensions.
– ORIGIN Greek *isometria.*

isosceles /I-soss-i-leez/ • adj. (of a triangle) having two sides of equal length.
– ORIGIN Greek *isoskelēs.*

isotherm /I-soh-therm/ • n. a line on a map or diagram connecting points having the same temperature.
– DERIVATIVES **isothermal** adj. & n.
– ORIGIN from Greek *isos* 'equal' + *thermē* 'heat'.

isotope /I-suh-tohp/ • n. Chem. each of two or more forms of the same element that contain equal numbers of protons but different numbers of neutrons in their nuclei.
– ORIGIN from Greek *isos* 'equal' + *topos* 'place'.

ISP • abbrev. Internet service provider.

Israeli /iz-ray-li/ • n. (pl. **Israelis**) a person from Israel. • adj. relating to the modern country of Israel.

Israelite /iz-ruh-lyt/ • n. a member of the ancient Hebrew nation.

issue • n. **1** an important topic to be debated or settled. **2** the action of supplying or giving out. **3** each of a

regular series of publications. **4** (**issues**) personal problems or difficulties.
• v. (**issues, issuing, issued**) **1** supply or give out. **2** formally send out or make known: *issue a statement.* **3** (**issue from**) come, go, or flow out from.
– PHRASES **at issue** under discussion. **take issue with** challenge someone or something.
– ORIGIN Old French.

-ist • suffix forming nouns and related adjectives referring to: **1** a person who believes something or is prejudiced: *sexist.* **2** a member of a profession: *dentist.* **3** a person who uses something: *guitarist.*
– ORIGIN Greek *-istēs.*

isthmus /iss-muhss/ • n. (pl. **isthmuses**) a narrow strip of land with sea on either side, linking two larger areas of land.
– ORIGIN Greek *isthmos.*

> ✓ Remember that **isthmus** begins with isth-.

IT • abbrev. information technology.

it • pron. (third person sing.) **1** used to refer to a thing previously mentioned or easily identified. **2** referring to an animal or child of unspecified sex. **3** used to identify a person: *it's me.* **4** used as a subject in statements about time, distance, or weather: *it is raining.* **5** used to refer to something specified later in the sentence: *it is impossible to get there today.* **6** used to refer to the situation or circumstances: *if it's convenient.*
– ORIGIN Old English.

Italian • n. **1** a person from Italy. **2** the language of Italy. • adj. relating to Italy or Italian.

italic /i-tal-ik/ • adj. referring to the sloping typeface used especially for emphasis and in foreign words. • n. (also **italics**) an italic typeface or letter.
– ORIGIN Greek *Italikos* 'Italian'.

italicize (or **italicise**) • v. (**italicizes, italicizing, italicized**) print words in italics.

itch • n. **1** an uncomfortable sensation that causes a desire to scratch the skin. **2** informal an impatient desire. • v. **1** have an itch. **2** informal feel an impatient desire to do something: *we itch to explore.*
– ORIGIN Old English.

itchy • adj. (**itchier, itchiest**) having or causing an itch.
– PHRASES **have itchy feet** informal have a strong urge to travel.
– DERIVATIVES **itchiness** n.

it'd • contr. **1** it had. **2** it would.

-ite • suffix **1** forming names of people from a certain country: *Israelite.* **2** usu. derog. referring to followers of a

movement: *Luddite*. **3** forming names of minerals, rocks, fossils, or structures of anatomy: *ammonite*. **4** Chem. forming names of salts or esters of acids ending in -*ous*: *nitrite*.
– ORIGIN Greek *ites*.

item • n. an individual article or unit.
– ORIGIN Latin, 'in like manner, also'.

itemize (or **itemise**) • v. (**itemizes, itemizing, itemized**) present as a list of individual items or parts.

iterate /it-uh-rayt/ • v. (**iterates, iterating, iterated**) do or say something repeatedly.
– DERIVATIVES **iteration** n.
– ORIGIN Latin *iterare*.

itinerant /I-tin-uh-ruhnt/ • adj. travelling from place to place. • n. an itinerant person.
– ORIGIN Latin *itinerari* 'travel'.

itinerary /I-tin-uh-ruh-ri/ • n. (pl. **itineraries**) a planned route or journey.

-itis • suffix forming names of diseases which cause inflammation: *cystitis*.
– ORIGIN Greek -*itēs*.

it'll • contr. **1** it shall. **2** it will.

its • possess. det. **1** belonging to or associated with a thing previously mentioned or easily identified. **2** belonging to or associated with a child or animal of unspecified sex.

> **USAGE:** Do not confuse the possessive **its** meaning 'belonging to it' (as in *turn the camera on its side*) with the form **it's** (short for either **it is** or **it has**), as in *it's my fault*.

it's • contr. **1** it is. **2** it has.

itself • pron. (third person sing.) **1** used to refer to something previously mentioned as the subject of the clause: *his horse hurt itself*. **2** used to emphasize a particular thing or animal mentioned: *she wanted him more than life itself*.

ITV • abbrev. Independent Television.

-ity • suffix forming nouns referring to a quality or condition: *humility*.
– ORIGIN Latin -*itas*.

IUD • abbrev. intrauterine device.

I've • contr. I have.

IVF • abbrev. in vitro fertilization.

Ivorian /I-vor-i-uhn/ • n. a person from the Ivory Coast, a country in West Africa. • adj. relating to the Ivory Coast.

ivory • n. (pl. **ivories**) **1** a hard creamy-white substance which forms the tusks of an elephant or walrus. **2** the creamy-white colour of ivory.
– ORIGIN Old French *ivurie*.

ivory tower • n. a situation in which someone leads a privileged life and does not have to face normal difficulties.

ivy • n. an evergreen climbing plant, typically with five-pointed leaves.
– ORIGIN Old English.

Ivy League • n. a group of long-established universities in the eastern US.
– ORIGIN with reference to the ivy traditionally growing over their walls.

-ize (or **-ise**) • suffix forming verbs meaning: **1** make or become: *privatize*. **2** cause to resemble: *Americanize*. **3** treat in a specified way: *pasteurize*. **4** treat or cause to combine with a specified substance: *carbonize*.
– ORIGIN Greek -*izein*.

Jj

J[1] (also **j**) • n. (pl. **Js** or **J's**) the tenth letter of the alphabet.

J[2] • abbrev. Physics joule(s).

jab • v. (**jabs, jabbing, jabbed**) poke roughly or quickly with a sharp or pointed object. • n. **1** a quick, sharp poke or blow. **2** Brit. informal an injection, especially a vaccination.

jabber • v. (**jabbers, jabbering, jabbered**) talk quickly and excitedly but with little sense.

jabot /zha-boh/ • n. a ruffle on the front of a shirt or blouse.
– ORIGIN French.

jacaranda /ja-kuh-ran-duh/ • n. a tropical American tree with blue flowers and sweet-smelling wood.
– ORIGIN from a South American Indian language.

jack • n. **1** a device for lifting a motor vehicle off the ground. **2** a playing card ranking next below a queen. **3** (also **jack socket**) a socket designed to receive a jack plug. **4** (in bowls) a small white ball at which players aim the bowls. **5** a small metal piece used in games of tossing and catching. • v. (**jack something up**) **1** raise something with a jack. **2** informal increase a quantity by a large amount.
– ORIGIN from *Jack*, familiar form of the man's name *John*.

jackal /ja-k'l/ • n. a wild dog that feeds on dead animals, found in Africa and Asia.
– ORIGIN Turkish *çakal*.

jackass • n. **1** a stupid person. **2** a male ass or donkey.

jackboot • n. a leather military boot reaching to the knee.

jackdaw • n. a small grey-headed crow.
– ORIGIN from JACK + earlier *daw* (of Germanic origin).

jacket • n. **1** an outer garment extending to the waist or hips, with sleeves. **2** a covering placed around something for protection or insulation. **3** Brit. the skin of a potato.
– ORIGIN Old French *jaquet*.

jacket potato • n. Brit. a baked potato served with the skin on.

jack-in-the-box • n. a toy consisting of a box containing a figure on a spring which pops up when the lid is opened.

jackknife • n. (pl. **jackknives**) a large knife with a folding blade.
• v. (**jackknifes, jackknifing, jackknifed**) (of a lorry or other articulated vehicle) bend into a V-shape in an uncontrolled skidding movement.

jack-o'-lantern • n. a lantern made from a hollowed-out pumpkin or turnip in which holes are cut to resemble a face.

jack plug • n. a plug consisting of a single shaft used to make a connection which transmits a signal.

jackpot • n. a large cash prize in a game or lottery.
– PHRASES **hit the jackpot** informal have great or unexpected success.
– ORIGIN term first used in poker.

jackrabbit • n. a North American prairie hare.
– ORIGIN short for *jackass-rabbit*, because of its long ears.

Jack Russell (also **Jack Russell terrier**) • n. a small breed of terrier with short legs.
– ORIGIN named after the English clergyman Revd John (*Jack*) *Russell*.

Jack the Lad • n. Brit. informal a cocky young man.
– ORIGIN nickname of *Jack* Sheppard, a thief.

Jacobean /jak-uh-bee-uhn/ • adj. relating to the reign of James I of England (1603–1625).
– ORIGIN Latin *Jacobus* 'James'.

Jacobite /jak-uh-byt/ • n. a supporter of the deposed James II and his descendants in their claim to the British throne.

jacquard /ja-kard/ • n. a fabric with a woven pattern.
– ORIGIN named after the French weaver Joseph M. *Jacquard*.

jacuzzi /juh-koo-zi/ • n. (pl. **jacuzzis**) trademark a large bath with jets of water to massage the body.

– ORIGIN named after the Italian-born American inventor Candido *Jacuzzi*.

jade • n. **1** a hard bluish green precious stone. **2** a light bluish green.
– ORIGIN from French *le jade*.

jaded • adj. tired out or lacking enthusiasm after having had too much of something.
– ORIGIN from former *jade* 'a worn-out horse'.

jag • v. (**jags**, **jagging**, **jagged**) stab, pierce, or prick.

jagged /jag-gid/ • adj. with rough, sharp points sticking out.

jaguar /jag-yuu-er/ • n. a large, heavily built cat that has a yellowish-brown coat with black spots, found in Central and South America.
– ORIGIN from a South American Indian language.

jail (Brit. also **gaol**) • n. a place for holding people accused or convicted of a crime. • v. put someone in jail.
– DERIVATIVES **jailer** (Brit. also **gaoler**) n.
– ORIGIN Old French *jaiole* and *gayole*.

jailbait • n. informal a sexually attractive young woman who is too young to have sex legally.

jailbird • n. informal a person who is or has repeatedly been in prison.

jailbreak • n. an escape from jail.

jalapeño /ha-luh-**pay**-nyoh, ha-luh-**pee**-noh/ • n. (pl. **jalapeños**) a very hot green chilli pepper.
– ORIGIN Spanish.

jalopy /juh-**lop**-i/ • n. (pl. **jalopies**) informal an old car.

jalousie /zha-loo-zee/ • n. a blind or shutter made of a row of angled slats.
– ORIGIN French, 'jealousy'.

jam¹ • v. (**jams**, **jamming**, **jammed**) **1** squeeze or pack tightly into a space. **2** push something roughly and forcibly into position. **3** block a road through crowding. **4** become or make something unable to operate due to a part becoming stuck. **5** (**jam something on**) apply forcibly: *he jammed on the brakes.* **6** block a radio transmission by causing interference. **7** informal improvise with other musicians. • n. **1** an instance of being blocked. **2** informal a difficult situation. **3** informal an improvised performance by a group of musicians.

jam² • n. esp. Brit. a thick spread made from fruit and sugar.
– ORIGIN perh. from **jam¹**.

Jamaican • n. a person from Jamaica. • adj. relating to Jamaica.

jamb /jam/ • n. a side post of a doorway or window.
– ORIGIN Old French *jambe* 'leg'.

jamboree /jam-buh-**ree**/ • n. a lavish or noisy celebration or party.

jammy • adj. **1** covered or filled with jam. **2** Brit. informal lucky.

jam-packed • adj. informal very crowded or full to capacity.

Jan. • abbrev. January.

jangle • v. (**jangles**, **jangling**, **jangled**) **1** make a ringing metallic sound. **2** (of your nerves) be set on edge. • n. an instance of jangling.
– DERIVATIVES **jangly** adj.
– ORIGIN Old French *jangler*.

janitor /jan-i-ter/ • n. esp. N. Amer. a caretaker of a building.
– ORIGIN Latin.

January • n. (pl. **Januaries**) the first month of the year.
– ORIGIN from Latin *Januarius mensis* 'month of *Janus*'.

japan • n. a black glossy varnish originating in Japan. • v. (**japans**, **japanning**, **japanned**) cover something with japan.

Japanese • n. (pl. **Japanese**) **1** a person from Japan. **2** the language of Japan. • adj. relating to Japan.

jape • n. a practical joke.
– ORIGIN prob. from Old French *japer* 'to yelp, yap' and *gaber* 'to mock'.

japonica /juh-**pon**-i-kuh/ • n. an Asian shrub with bright red flowers and edible fruits.
– ORIGIN Latin, 'Japanese'.

jar¹ • n. a cylindrical container made of glass or pottery.
– ORIGIN French *jarre*.

jar² • v. (**jars**, **jarring**, **jarred**) **1** send a painful shock through a part of the body. **2** strike against something with a jolt. **3** have an unpleasant effect. • n. an instance of jarring.

jardinière /zhar-din-**yair**/ • n. an ornamental pot or stand for displaying plants.
– ORIGIN French, 'female gardener'.

jargon • n. words or expressions used by a particular group that are difficult for other people to understand.
– ORIGIN Old French *jargoun*.

jasmine • n. a shrub or climbing plant with sweet-smelling flowers.
– ORIGIN French *jasmin*.

jasper • n. a reddish-brown variety of quartz.
– ORIGIN Old French *jaspre*.

jaundice /**jawn**-diss/ • n. **1** yellowing of the skin due to a disorder of the liver. **2** bitterness or resentment.
– DERIVATIVES **jaundiced** adj.
– ORIGIN Old French *jaunice* 'yellowness'.

jaunt • n. a short trip for pleasure.

j

jaunty • adj. lively and self-confident.
– DERIVATIVES **jauntily** adv. **jauntiness** n.
– ORIGIN French *gentil* 'well-born'.

javelin /jav-lin/ • n. a long spear thrown in a competitive sport or as a weapon.
– ORIGIN Old French *javeline*.

jaw • n. **1** each of the upper and lower bony structures forming the framework of the mouth and containing the teeth. **2** (**jaws**) the grasping, biting, or crushing mouthparts of an invertebrate animal. **3** (**jaws**) the gripping parts of a tool such as a wrench or vice. • v. informal talk or gossip at length.
– ORIGIN Old French *joe*.

jawbone • n. a bone forming the lower jaw.

jaw-dropping • adj. informal amazing.

jay • n. a noisy bird of the crow family with boldly patterned plumage.
– ORIGIN Latin *gaius, gaia*.

jaywalk • v. esp. N. Amer. walk along or across a road without regard for the traffic.
– DERIVATIVES **jaywalker** n.
– ORIGIN from **JAY** in the former sense 'silly person'.

jazz • n. a type of music of black American origin in which the players often improvise. • v. (**jazz something up**) make something more lively or attractive.

jazzy • adj. (**jazzier, jazziest**) **1** in the style of jazz. **2** bright, colourful, and showy.

jealous • adj. **1** envious of someone else's achievements or advantages. **2** resentful of someone who you think is a sexual rival. **3** very protective of your rights or possessions: *they kept a jealous eye over their interests.*
– DERIVATIVES **jealously** adv. **jealousy** n. (pl. **jealousies**).
– ORIGIN Old French *gelos*.

jeans • pl. n. casual trousers made of denim.
– ORIGIN Latin *Janua* 'Genoa', where *jean*, a type of hard-wearing cloth, was originally made.

jeep • n. trademark a sturdy motor vehicle with four-wheel drive.
– ORIGIN prob. from the vehicle's model code *GP*.

jeer • v. (**jeers, jeering, jeered**) make rude and mocking remarks at someone. • n. a rude and mocking remark.

Jehovah /ji-hoh-vuh/ • n. a form of the Hebrew name of God used in some translations of the Bible.
– ORIGIN Hebrew.

Jehovah's Witness • n. a member of a Christian sect that denies many traditional Christian doctrines and believes that Jesus will return to earth at the Last Judgement.

jejune /ji-joon/ • adj. **1** unsophisticated; simplistic. **2** (of ideas or writings) dull.
– ORIGIN Latin *jejunus* 'fasting, barren'.

jejunum /ji-joo-nuhm/ • n. the part of the small intestine between the duodenum and ileum.
– ORIGIN Latin, 'fasting'.

Jekyll /je-k'l/ • n. (in phr. **a Jekyll and Hyde**) a person displaying alternately good and evil personalities.
– ORIGIN after the central character in Robert Louis Stevenson's story *The Strange Case of Dr Jekyll and Mr Hyde*.

jell • v. var. of **GEL²**.

jellied • adj. (of food) set in a jelly.

jelly • n. (pl. **jellies**) **1** Brit. a dessert consisting of a sweet, fruit-flavoured liquid set with gelatin to form a semi-solid mass. **2** a small sweet made with gelatin.
– ORIGIN Old French *gelee* 'frost, jelly'.

jellyfish • n. (pl. **jellyfish** or **jellyfishes**) a sea animal with a soft body that has stinging tentacles around the edge.

jemmy (also **jimmy**) • n. (pl. **jemmies**) a short crowbar.
– ORIGIN familiar form of the man's name *James*.

je ne sais quoi /zhuh nuh say kwah/ • n. a quality that is hard to describe.
– ORIGIN French, 'I do not know what'.

jenny • n. (pl. **jennies**) a female donkey or ass.
– ORIGIN familiar form of the woman's name *Janet*.

jeopardize /jep-er-dyz/ (or **jeopardise**) • v. (**jeopardizes, jeopardizing, jeopardized**) put at risk of being harmed or lost.

jeopardy /jep-er-di/ • n. danger of loss or harm.
– ORIGIN from Old French *ieu parti* '(evenly) divided game'.

jerboa /jer-boh-uh/ • n. a rodent with very long hind legs that lives in the desert.
– ORIGIN Arabic.

jeremiad /je-ri-my-ad/ • n. a long complaint.
– ORIGIN with reference to the Lamentations of Jeremiah in the Old Testament.

jerk • n. **1** a quick, sharp, sudden movement. **2** informal a stupid person. • v. move or raise with a jerk.

jerkin • n. a sleeveless jacket.

jerky • adj. moving in abrupt stops and starts.
– DERIVATIVES **jerkily** adv. **jerkiness** n.

Jerry • n. (pl. **Jerries**) Brit. informal, derog. a German or Germans.

– ORIGIN prob. from **German**.

jerry-built •adj. badly or hastily built.

jerrycan •n. a large flat-sided metal container for storing or carrying liquids.
– ORIGIN from **Jerry** + **can²**, because first used in Germany.

jersey •n. (pl. **jerseys**) **1** a knitted garment with long sleeves. **2** a distinctive shirt worn by a player of certain sports. **3** a soft knitted fabric. **4** (**Jersey**) an animal of a breed of light brown dairy cattle.
– ORIGIN from *Jersey* in the Channel Islands.

Jerusalem artichoke •n. a knobbly root vegetable with white flesh.
– ORIGIN Italian *girasole* 'sunflower'.

jest •n. a joke. •v. speak or act in a joking way.
– ORIGIN Old French *geste* 'an exploit'.

jester •n. hist. a professional joker or 'fool' at a medieval court.

Jesuit /jez-yuu-it/ •n. a member of the Society of Jesus, a Roman Catholic order of priests founded by St Ignatius Loyola.
– DERIVATIVES **Jesuitical** adj.

Jesus (also **Jesus Christ**) •n. the central figure of the Christian religion, believed by Christians to be the Messiah and the Son of God.

jet¹ •n. **1** a rapid stream of liquid or gas forced out of a small opening. **2** an aircraft powered by jet engines. •v. (**jets, jetting, jetted**) **1** spurt out in a jet. **2** travel by jet aircraft.
– ORIGIN French *jeter* 'to throw'.

jet² •n. **1** a hard black semi-precious mineral. **2** (also **jet black**) a glossy black colour.
– ORIGIN Old French *jaiet*.

jeté /zhe-tay/ •n. Ballet a spring from one foot to the other, with the following leg extended backwards while in the air.
– ORIGIN French.

jet engine •n. an aircraft engine which provides force for forward movement by ejecting a high-speed jet of gas obtained by burning fuel in air.

jet lag •n. extreme tiredness and other effects felt by a person after a long flight across different time zones.
– DERIVATIVES **jet-lagged** adj.

jetsam /jet-suhm/ •n. unwanted material thrown overboard from a ship and washed ashore.
– ORIGIN from **jettison**.

jet set •n. (**the jet set**) informal fashionable and wealthy people who regularly travel abroad for pleasure.
– DERIVATIVES **jet-setter** n.

jet ski •n. trademark a small jet-propelled vehicle which skims across the surface of water and is ridden in a similar way to a motorcycle.
– DERIVATIVES **jet-skiing** n.

jettison /jet-ti-suhn/ •v. throw or drop something from an aircraft or ship.
– ORIGIN Old French *getaison*.

jetty •n. (pl. **jetties**) a landing stage or small pier.
– ORIGIN Old French *jetee*.

Jew •n. a member of the people whose traditional religion is Judaism and who trace their origins to the ancient Hebrew people of Israel.
– ORIGIN Hebrew, 'Judah'.

jewel •n. **1** a precious stone. **2** (**jewels**) pieces of jewellery. **3** a highly valued person or thing: *she was a jewel of a housekeeper.*
– DERIVATIVES **jewelled** (US **jeweled**) adj.
– ORIGIN Old French *joel*.

jeweller (US **jeweler**) •n. a person who makes or sells jewellery.

jewellery (US **jewelry**) •n. personal ornaments such as necklaces, rings, or bracelets.

Jewess •n. usu. offens. a Jewish woman or girl.

Jewish •adj. relating to Jews or Judaism.
– DERIVATIVES **Jewishness** n.

Jewry /joo-ri/ •n. Jews as a group.

Jew's harp •n. a small musical instrument like a U-shaped harp, held between the teeth and struck with a finger.

Jezebel /jez-uh-bel/ •n. an immoral woman.
– ORIGIN the name of the wife of King Ahab in the Bible.

jib¹ •n. **1** Sailing a triangular sail in front of the mast. **2** the projecting arm of a crane.

jib² •v. (**jibs, jibbing, jibbed**) (**jib at**) **1** be unwilling to do or accept something. **2** (of a horse) refuse to go on.
– ORIGIN perh. from French *regimber* 'to buck'.

jibe¹ (also **gibe**) •n. an insulting remark. •v. (**jibes, jibing, jibed**) make insulting remarks.
– ORIGIN perh. from Old French *giber* 'handle roughly'.

jibe² •v. & n. US = **gybe**.

jiffy (also **jiff**) •n. informal a moment.

jig •n. **1** a lively leaping dance. **2** a device that holds a piece of work and guides the tools working on it. •v. (**jigs, jigging, jigged**) **1** move up and down jerkily. **2** dance a jig.

jigger •n. **1** a machine or vehicle with a part that rocks or moves to and fro. **2** a measure of spirits or wine. •v. (**jiggers, jiggering, jiggered**) Brit. informal **1** tamper with. **2** (as adj. **jiggered**) broken or exhausted.

jiggery-pokery • n. informal, esp. Brit. suspicious behaviour.
– ORIGIN prob. from Scots *jouk* 'dodge, skulk'.

jiggle • v. (**jiggles, jiggling, jiggled**) move lightly and quickly from side to side or up and down.
– DERIVATIVES **jiggly** adj.
– ORIGIN partly from **JOGGLE**.

jigsaw • n. **1** a puzzle in the form of a picture printed on cardboard or wood and cut into many interlocking shapes that have to be fitted together. **2** a machine saw with a fine blade allowing it to cut curved lines in a sheet of wood or metal.

jihad /ji-hahd/ • n. (in Islam) a war or struggle against unbelievers.
– ORIGIN Arabic, 'effort'.

jihadi /ji-hah-di/ (also **jihadist**) • n. (pl. **jihadis**) (in Islam) a person involved in a war or struggle against unbelievers.
– ORIGIN Arabic.

jilt • v. abruptly break off a relationship with a lover.

jimmy • n. US = **JEMMY**.

jingle • n. **1** a light ringing sound such as that made by metal objects being shaken together. **2** a short easily remembered slogan, verse, or tune. • v. (**jingles, jingling, jingled**) make a light ringing sound.
– DERIVATIVES **jingly** adj.

jingoism • n. esp. derog. excessive pride in your country.
– DERIVATIVES **jingoistic** adj.
– ORIGIN from *by jingo!* in a song adopted by those who supported the sending of a British fleet into Turkish waters to resist Russia in 1878.

jink • v. change direction suddenly and nimbly.
– ORIGIN from **HIGH JINKS**, referring to antics at drinking parties.

jinx • n. a person or thing that brings bad luck. • v. bring bad luck to.
– ORIGIN prob. from Latin *jynx* 'wryneck' (a bird).

jitterbug • n. a fast dance performed to swing music, popular in the 1940s.

jitters • pl. n. (**the jitters**) informal a feeling of extreme nervousness.
– DERIVATIVES **jitteriness** n. **jittery** adj.

jiu-jitsu • n. var. of **JU-JITSU**.

jive • n. a lively dance popular in the 1940s and 1950s, performed to swing music or rock and roll. • v. (**jives, jiving, jived**) dance the jive.

job • n. **1** a paid position of regular employment. **2** a task. **3** informal a crime.

4 informal a procedure to improve the appearance of something: *a nose job.* • v. (**jobs, jobbing, jobbed**) do casual or occasional work.
– PHRASES **a good job** informal, esp. Brit. a fortunate fact or circumstance. **on the job** at work.

jobcentre • n. (in the UK) a government office in a local area, which gives out benefits and information about available jobs to unemployed people.

jobless • adj. without a paid job.
– DERIVATIVES **joblessness** n.

job lot • n. a batch of articles sold or bought at one time.

job-share • v. (of two part-time employees) share a single full-time job.

Jock • n. informal, usu. offens. a Scotsman.
– ORIGIN Scottish form of the man's name *Jack*.

jockey • n. (pl. **jockeys**) a professional rider in horse races. • v. (**jockeys, jockeying, jockeyed**) struggle to gain or achieve something: *two men will be jockeying for the top job.*
– ORIGIN from **JOCK**.

jockstrap • n. a pouch worn to support or protect a man's genitals.
– ORIGIN from slang *jock* 'genitals'.

jocose /juh-**kohss**/ • adj. formal playful or humorous.
– ORIGIN Latin *jocosus*.

jocular /jok-**yuu**-ler/ • adj. humorous or amusing.
– DERIVATIVES **jocularity** n. **jocularly** adv.
– ORIGIN Latin *jocularis*.

☑ The ending of **jocular** is spelled **-ar**.

jocund /jok-**uhnd**/ • adj. formal cheerful and light-hearted.
– ORIGIN Latin *jocundus*.

jodhpurs /jod-perz/ • pl. n. trousers worn for horse riding that are close-fitting below the knee.
– ORIGIN named after the Indian city of *Jodhpur*.

joey • n. (pl. **joeys**) Austral. a young kangaroo, wallaby, or possum.
– ORIGIN Aboriginal.

jog • v. (**jogs, jogging, jogged**) **1** run at a steady, gentle pace. **2** (**jog along/on**) continue in a steady, uneventful way. **3** knock something slightly. • n. **1** a spell of jogging. **2** a slight knock or nudge.
– PHRASES **jog someone's memory** make someone remember something.
– ORIGIN from **JAG**.

jogger • n. **1** a person who jogs as a form of exercise. **2** (**joggers**) tracksuit trousers worn for jogging.

joggle • v. (**joggles, joggling, joggled**) move with repeated small jerks.

– ORIGIN from **JOG**.

john • n. informal, esp. N. Amer. a toilet.
– ORIGIN from the man's name *John*.

John Bull • n. a character representing England or the typical Englishman.
– ORIGIN from a character in John Arbuthnot's satire *Law is a Bottomless Pit; or, the History of John Bull*.

joie de vivre /zhwah duh vee-vruh/ • n. lively and cheerful enjoyment of life.
– ORIGIN French.

join • v. **1** link or become linked to. **2** come together to form a whole. **3** become a member or employee of an organization. **4** (**join up**) become a member of the armed forces. **5** take part in an activity. **6** meet or go somewhere with someone. • n. a place where things are joined.
– ORIGIN Old French *joindre*.

joiner • n. esp. Brit. a person who makes the wooden parts of a building.

joinery • n. **1** the wooden parts of a building. **2** the work of a joiner.

joint • n. **1** a point at which parts are joined. **2** a structure in the body which joins two bones. **3** the part of a plant stem from which a leaf or branch grows. **4** Brit. a large piece of meat. **5** informal a place of a specified kind: *a burger joint*. **6** informal a cannabis cigarette.
• adj. **1** shared, held, or made by two or more people. **2** sharing in an achievement or activity: *a joint winner*.
• v. **1** (as adj. **jointed**) having joints. **2** cut the body of an animal into joints.
– PHRASES **out of joint 1** (of a joint of the body) out of position. **2** in a state of disorder.
– DERIVATIVES **jointly** adv.
– ORIGIN Old French *joindre* 'to join'.

joist /joysst/ • n. a length of timber or steel supporting the floor or ceiling of a building.
– ORIGIN Old French *giste*.

jojoba /hoh-hoh-buh/ • n. an oil extracted from the seeds of a North American shrub, used in cosmetics.
– ORIGIN Mexican Spanish.

joke • n. **1** a thing that someone says to cause amusement or laughter. **2** a trick played for fun. **3** informal a person or thing that is ridiculously inadequate: *public transport is a joke*. • v. (**jokes, joking, joked**) make jokes.
– DERIVATIVES **jokey** adj.
– ORIGIN perh. from Latin *jocus*.

joker • n. **1** a person who is fond of joking. **2** a playing card with the figure of a jester, used as a wild card.

jollification • n. time spent having fun.

jollity • n. (pl. **jollities**) **1** lively and cheerful activity. **2** the quality of being cheerful and lively.

jolly • adj. (**jollier, jolliest**) **1** happy and cheerful. **2** lively and entertaining.
• v. (**jollies, jollying, jollied**) informal encourage in a friendly way: *he jollied her along*. • adv. Brit. informal very.
– DERIVATIVES **jollily** adv. **jolliness** n.
– ORIGIN Old French *jolif* 'pretty'.

Jolly Roger • n. a pirate's flag with a white skull and crossbones on a black background.

jolt • v. **1** push or shake abruptly and roughly. **2** shock someone into taking action. • n. **1** a rough and abrupt push or shake. **2** a shock.

Jordanian • n. a person from Jordan.
• adj. relating to Jordan.

josh • v. informal tease someone playfully.

joss stick • n. a thin stick of a sweet-smelling substance, burnt as incense.
– ORIGIN from *joss*, referring to a Chinese religious statue.

jostle • v. (**jostles, jostling, jostled**) **1** roughly push or bump against. **2** (**jostle for**) struggle forcefully for: *they jostled for control of the bathroom*.
– ORIGIN from **JOUST**.

jot • v. (**jots, jotting, jotted**) write something quickly. • n. a very small amount: *it made not a jot of difference*.
– ORIGIN Greek *iōta*, the smallest letter of the Greek alphabet.

jotter • n. Brit. a small notebook.

jotting • n. a brief note.

joule /jool/ • n. the SI unit of work or energy.
– ORIGIN named after the English physicist James P. *Joule*.

journal • n. **1** a newspaper or magazine dealing with a particular subject. **2** a diary or daily record.
– ORIGIN Old French *jurnal*.

journalese • n. informal a poor writing style supposedly used by journalists, containing many clichés.

journalism • n. the activity or profession of being a journalist.

journalist • n. a person who writes for newspapers or magazines or prepares news or features to be broadcast on radio or television.
– DERIVATIVES **journalistic** adj.

journey • n. (pl. **journeys**) an act of travelling from one place to another.
• v. (**journeys, journeying, journeyed**) travel somewhere.
– ORIGIN Old French *jornee* 'day'.

journeyman • n. (pl. **journeymen**) **1** a skilled worker who is employed by another. **2** a worker who is reliable but not outstanding.

– ORIGIN from **JOURNEY** in the former sense 'day's work'.

joust /jowst/ • v. (of medieval knights) fight on horseback with lances. • n. a jousting contest.
– DERIVATIVES **jouster** n.
– ORIGIN Old French *jouster* 'bring together'.

Jove /johv/ • n. (in phr. **by Jove**) dated used for emphasis or to indicate surprise.
– ORIGIN another name for the Roman god Jupiter.

jovial /joh-vi-uhl/ • adj. cheerful and friendly.
– DERIVATIVES **joviality** n. **jovially** adv.
– ORIGIN Latin *jovialis* 'of Jupiter'.

jowl • n. **1** the lower part of a cheek when it is fleshy. **2** the loose skin at the throat of cattle.
– DERIVATIVES **jowly** adj.
– ORIGIN Old English.

joy • n. **1** great pleasure and happiness. **2** a cause of great pleasure and happiness. **3** Brit. informal success or satisfaction: *you'll get no joy out of her.*
– DERIVATIVES **joyless** adj.
– ORIGIN Old French *joie*.

joyful • adj. feeling or causing great pleasure and happiness.
– DERIVATIVES **joyfully** adv.

joyous • adj. esp. literary full of happiness and joy.
– DERIVATIVES **joyously** adv.

joypad • n. a device for a computer games console which uses buttons to control an image on the screen.

joyride • n. informal **1** a fast ride in a stolen vehicle. **2** a ride for enjoyment.
– DERIVATIVES **joyrider** n. **joyriding** n.

joystick • n. informal **1** the control column of an aircraft. **2** a lever for controlling the movement of an image on a computer screen.

JP • abbrev. Justice of the Peace.

jubilant • adj. happy and triumphant.
– DERIVATIVES **jubilantly** adv.

jubilation /joo-bi-lay-sh'n/ • n. a feeling of great happiness and triumph.
– ORIGIN Latin *jubilare* 'shout for joy'.

jubilee • n. a special anniversary.
– ORIGIN from Latin *jubilaeus annus* 'year of jubilee'.

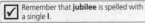 Remember that **jubilee** is spelled with a single **l**.

Judaic /joo-day-ik/ • adj. relating to Judaism or the ancient Jews.

Judaism /joo-day-i-z'm/ • n. the religion of the Jews, based on the Old Testament and the Talmud.
– ORIGIN Greek *Ioudaïsmos*.

Judas /joo-duhss/ • n. a person who betrays a friend.
– ORIGIN from *Judas* Iscariot, the disciple who betrayed Christ.

judder • v. (**judders, juddering, juddered**) shake rapidly and forcefully.
– DERIVATIVES **juddery** adj.

judge • n. **1** a public officer who decides cases in a law court. **2** a person who decides the results of a competition. **3** a person with the necessary knowledge or skill to give an opinion. • v. (**judges, judging, judged**) **1** form an opinion about something. **2** give a verdict on a case or person in a law court. **3** decide the results of a competition.
– ORIGIN Latin *judex*.

judgement (also **judgment**) • n. **1** the ability to make sound decisions or form sensible opinions. **2** an opinion or conclusion. **3** a decision of a law court or judge.

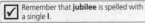 **judgement** is usually spelled with an e after the g. The spelling **judgment** is used in legal situations and in American English.

judgemental (also **judgmental**) • adj. **1** relating to the use of judgement. **2** excessively critical of other people.

Judgement Day • n. the time of the Last Judgement.

judicature /joo-dik-uh-cher/ • n. **1** the organization and administration of a country's system of justice. **2** (**the judicature**) judges as a group.
– ORIGIN Latin *judicare* 'to judge'.

judicial /joo-di-sh'l/ • adj. relating to a law court or judge.
– DERIVATIVES **judicially** adv.
– ORIGIN Latin *judicium* 'judgement'.

judiciary /joo-di-shuh-ri/ • n. (**the judiciary**) judges as a group.

judicious /joo-di-shuhss/ • adj. having or done with good judgement.
– DERIVATIVES **judiciously** adv.

judo • n. a sport of unarmed combat, using holds and leverage to unbalance your opponent.
– ORIGIN Japanese, 'gentle way'.

jug • n. **1** Brit. a container with a handle and a lip, for holding and pouring liquids. **2** N. Amer. a large container for liquids, with a narrow mouth.
– ORIGIN perh. from *Jug*, informal form of the woman's names *Joan, Joanna,* and *Jenny.*

jugged • adj. (of a hare) stewed in a covered container.

juggernaut /jug-ger-nawt/ • n. Brit. a large heavy vehicle.
– ORIGIN Sanskrit 'Lord of the world',

referring to an image of the Hindu god Krishna carried on a heavy chariot.

juggle •v. (**juggles, juggling, juggled**) **1** continuously toss and catch a number of objects so as to keep at least one in the air at any time. **2** manage to do several activities at the same time.
– DERIVATIVES **juggler** n.
– ORIGIN Old French *jogler*.

jugular /jug-yuu-ler/ •adj. relating to the neck or throat. •n. (also **jugular vein**) any of several large veins in the neck, carrying blood from the head.
– ORIGIN Latin *jugulum* 'throat'.

juice •n. **1** the liquid present in fruit or vegetables, often made into a drink. **2** (**juices**) fluid produced by the stomach. **3** (**juices**) liquid coming from food during cooking. **4** informal electrical energy. **5** informal petrol. **6** (**juices**) informal a person's creative abilities. •v. (**juices, juicing, juiced**) extract the juice from.
– DERIVATIVES **juicer** n.
– ORIGIN Latin *jus* 'broth, juice'.

juicy •adj. (**juicier, juiciest**) **1** full of juice. **2** informal interestingly scandalous: *juicy gossip*.
– DERIVATIVES **juiciness** n.

ju-jitsu /joo jit-soo/ (also **jiu-jitsu**) •n. a Japanese system of unarmed combat and physical training.
– ORIGIN Japanese, 'gentle skill'.

jukebox •n. a machine that plays a selected musical recording when a coin is inserted.
– ORIGIN *juke* is from a word in a Creole language meaning 'disorderly'.

Jul. •abbrev. July.

julep /joo-lep/ •n. a sweet drink made from sugar syrup.
– ORIGIN Latin *julapium*.

Julian calendar •n. a calendar introduced by the Roman general Julius Caesar, in which the year consisted of 365 days, every fourth year having 366 (replaced by the Gregorian calendar).

julienne /joo-li-en/ •n. a portion of food cut into short, thin strips.
– ORIGIN French.

July •n. (pl. **Julys**) the seventh month of the year.
– ORIGIN from Latin *Julius mensis* 'month of July', named after the Roman general Julius Caesar.

jumble •n. **1** an untidy collection of things. **2** Brit. articles collected for a jumble sale. •v. (**jumbles, jumbling, jumbled**) mix things up in a confused way.

jumble sale •n. Brit. a sale of various second-hand goods.

jumbo informal •n. (pl. **jumbos**) **1** a very large person or thing. **2** (also **jumbo jet**) a very large airliner. •adj. very large.
– ORIGIN prob. from MUMBO-JUMBO.

jump •v. **1** push yourself off the ground using the muscles in your legs and feet. **2** move over, on to, or down from a place by jumping. **3** move suddenly and quickly. **4** (**jump at/on**) accept eagerly. **5** (**jump on**) informal attack suddenly. **6** pass abruptly from one subject or state to another. •n. **1** an act of jumping. **2** a large or sudden increase. **3** an obstacle to be jumped by a horse.
– PHRASES **jump down someone's throat** informal respond to someone in a sudden and angry way. **jump the queue** move ahead of your proper place in a queue. **jump ship** (of a sailor) leave a ship without permission. **one jump ahead** one stage ahead of a rival.

jumped-up •adj. informal considering yourself to be more important than you really are.

jumper[1] •n. **1** Brit. a pullover or sweater. **2** N. Amer. a pinafore dress.
– ORIGIN perh. from Old French *jupe* 'loose tunic'.

jumper[2] •n. a person or animal that jumps.

jump jet •n. a jet aircraft that can take off and land vertically.

jump lead •n. Brit. each of a pair of cables for recharging a battery in a motor vehicle by connecting it to the battery in another.

jump-start •v. start a car with a flat battery with jump leads or by a sudden release of the clutch while it is being pushed.

jumpsuit •n. a one-piece garment incorporating trousers and a sleeved top.
– ORIGIN first referring to a garment worn when parachuting.

jumpy •adj. (**jumpier, jumpiest**) informal **1** anxious and uneasy. **2** stopping and starting abruptly.
– DERIVATIVES **jumpily** adv. **jumpiness** n.

Jun. •abbrev. June.

junction •n. **1** a point where two or more things meet or are joined. **2** a place where two or more roads or railway lines meet.
– ORIGIN Latin.

juncture /jungk-cher/ •n. **1** a particular point in time. **2** a place where things join.
– ORIGIN Latin *junctura* 'joint'.

June •n. the sixth month of the year.
– ORIGIN from Latin *Junius mensis* 'month

of June', named after the goddess Juno.

jungle •n. **1** an area of thick tropical forest and tangled vegetation. **2** a very bewildering or competitive situation: *a jungle of market forces.*
– ORIGIN Sanskrit, 'rough arid land'.

junior •adj. **1** relating to young or younger people. **2** Brit. relating to schoolchildren aged 7–11. **3** (after a name) referring to the younger of two people with the same name in a family. **4** low or lower in status. •n. **1** a person who is a specified number of years younger than someone else: *he's five years her junior.* **2** Brit. a child at a junior school. **3** (in sport) a young competitor. **4** a person with low status.
– ORIGIN Latin.

juniper /joo-ni-per/ •n. an evergreen shrub or small tree with berries that are used to flavour gin.
– ORIGIN Latin *juniperus.*

junk[1] informal •n. useless or worthless articles. •v. get rid of something abruptly.

junk[2] •n. a flat-bottomed sailing boat used in China and the East Indies.
– ORIGIN Malay.

junket /jung-kit/ •n. **1** a dish of sweetened curds of milk. **2** informal an extravagant trip or party. •v. (**junkets, junketing, junketed**) informal take part in an extravagant trip at public expense.
– ORIGIN first meaning a cream cheese made in a rush basket: from Old French *jonquette* 'rush basket'.

junk food •n. unhealthy food.

junkie (also **junky**) •n. informal a drug addict.
– ORIGIN from **junk**[1] in the sense 'heroin'.

junk mail •n. informal advertising material received in the post which has not been requested.

junta /jun-tuh/ •n. a military group that rules a country after taking power by force.
– ORIGIN Spanish and Portuguese, 'deliberative or administrative council'.

Jupiter •n. the largest planet in the solar system, fifth in order from the sun.

Jurassic /juu-rass-ik/ •adj. Geol. relating to the second period of the Mesozoic era (about 208 to 146 million years ago), a time when large reptiles flourished and the first birds appeared.
– ORIGIN French *jurassique.*

jurisdiction /joo-riz-dik-sh'n, joo-riss-dik-sh'n/ •n. **1** the official power to make legal decisions. **2** the area over which the legal authority of a court or other institution extends. **3** a system of law courts.

– DERIVATIVES **jurisdictional** adj.
– ORIGIN Latin.

jurisprudence /joo-riss-proo-duhnss/ •n. **1** the theory and philosophy of law. **2** a legal system.
– ORIGIN Latin *jurisprudentia.*

jurist /joor-ist/ •n. an expert in law.
– ORIGIN Latin *jurista.*

juror •n. a member of a jury.

jury •n. (pl. **juries**) **1** a group of people who have to attend a legal case and give a verdict on the basis of evidence given in court. **2** a group of people judging a competition.
– ORIGIN Old French *juree* 'oath'.

just •adj. **1** right and fair. **2** deserved. •adv. **1** exactly. **2** exactly or nearly at this or that moment. **3** very recently. **4** by a small amount. **5** only.
– PHRASES **just so** arranged or done very carefully.
– DERIVATIVES **justly** adv.
– ORIGIN Latin *justus.*

justice •n. **1** behaviour or treatment that is right and fair. **2** the quality of being right and fair. **3** the administration of law in a fair and reasonable way. **4** a judge or magistrate.
– PHRASES **do yourself justice** perform as well as you are able. **do someone/thing justice** treat someone or something with due fairness.
– ORIGIN Old French *justise.*

Justice of the Peace •n. (in the UK) a non-professional magistrate appointed to hear minor cases in a town or county.

justifiable •adj. able to be shown to be right or reasonable.
– DERIVATIVES **justifiably** adv.

justify •v. (**justifies, justifying, justified**) **1** prove something to be right or reasonable. **2** be a good reason for a decision or action. **3** adjust text so that the lines of type form straight edges at both sides.
– DERIVATIVES **justification** n.
– ORIGIN Latin *justificare* 'do justice to'.

jut •v. (**juts, jutting, jutted**) extend out, over, or beyond the main body or line of something.
– ORIGIN from **jet**[1].

jute /joot/ •n. rough fibre obtained from the stems of a tropical plant, made into rope or sacking.
– ORIGIN Bengali.

juvenile /joo-vuh-nyl/ •adj. **1** relating to young people or animals. **2** childish. •n. **1** a young person or animal. **2** Law a person below the age at which they have adult status in law (18 in most countries).
– ORIGIN Latin *juvenilis.*

juvenile delinquency • n. the regular committing of criminal acts by a young person.
– DERIVATIVES **juvenile deliquent** n.

juvenilia /joo-vuh-**nil**-i-uh/ • pl. n. works produced by an author or artist when young.

– ORIGIN Latin.

juxtapose /juk-stuh-**pohz**/
• v. (**juxtaposes, juxtaposing, juxtaposed**) place something closely alongside something else.
– DERIVATIVES **juxtaposition** n.
– ORIGIN French *juxtaposer*.

Kk

K¹ (also **k**) • n. (pl. **Ks** or **K's**) the eleventh letter of the alphabet.

K² • abbrev. **1** kelvin(s). **2** kilobyte(s). **3** kilometre(s). **4** informal thousand. [ORIGIN from KILO-.] • symb. the chemical element potassium. [ORIGIN Latin *kalium*.]

k • abbrev. kilo-.

Kabbalah /kuh-bah-luh/ (also **Kabbala**) • n. the ancient Jewish tradition of mystical interpretation of the Bible.
– DERIVATIVES **Kabbalist** n. **Kabbalistic** adj.
– ORIGIN Hebrew, 'tradition'.

Kafkaesque /kaf-kuh-esk/ • adj. relating to the Czech novelist Franz Kafka or his nightmarish fictional world.

kaftan /kaf-tan/ (also **caftan**) • n. **1** a woman's long, loose dress. **2** a man's long belted tunic, worn in parts of the Middle East and south-west Asia.
– ORIGIN Persian.

kaiser /ky-zer/ • n. hist. the German Emperor, the Emperor of Austria, or the head of the Holy Roman Empire.
– ORIGIN German.

Kalashnikov /kuh-lash-ni-kof/ • n. a type of rifle or sub-machine gun made in Russia.
– ORIGIN named after the Russian designer Mikhail T. *Kalashnikov*.

kale • n. a type of cabbage with large leaves and a loosely packed head.
– ORIGIN Latin *caulis*.

kaleidoscope /kuh-ly-duh-skohp/ • n. **1** a tube containing mirrors and pieces of coloured glass or paper, whose reflections produce changing patterns when the tube is turned. **2** a constantly changing pattern: *a kaleidoscope of colour*.
– DERIVATIVES **kaleidoscopic** adj.
– ORIGIN from Greek *kalos* 'beautiful' + *eidos* 'form' + -SCOPE.

☑ Spell **kaleidoscope** with **-ei-** in the middle.

Kama Sutra /kah-muh soo-truh/ • n. an ancient book on the art of love and sexual technique.
– ORIGIN Sanskrit, 'love thread'.

kameez /kuh-meez/ • n. (pl. **kameez** or **kameezes**) a long tunic worn by people from the Indian subcontinent.
– ORIGIN Arabic.

kamikaze /ka-mi-kah-zi/ • n. (in the Second World War) a Japanese aircraft loaded with explosives and making a deliberate suicidal crash on an enemy target. • adj. having the potential to kill or harm yourself.
– ORIGIN Japanese, 'holy wind'.

kangaroo • n. a large Australian marsupial with a long powerful tail and strong hind legs that enable it to travel by leaping.
– ORIGIN from an Aboriginal language.

kangaroo court • n. an unofficial court formed by a group of people to try someone seen as guilty of an offence.

kaolin /kay-uh-lin/ • n. a fine, soft white clay, used for making china and in medicine.
– ORIGIN Chinese word, 'high hill'.

kapok /kay-pok/ • n. a substance resembling cotton wool which grows around the seeds of a tropical tree, used as padding.
– ORIGIN Malay.

kaput /kuh-puut/ • adj. informal broken and useless.
– ORIGIN German *kaputt*.

karaoke /ka-ri-oh-ki/ • n. a form of entertainment in which people sing popular songs over pre-recorded backing tracks.
– ORIGIN Japanese, 'empty orchestra'.

karat • n. US = CARAT (in sense 2).

karate /kuh-rah-ti/ • n. an oriental system of unarmed combat using the hands and feet to deliver and block blows.
– ORIGIN Japanese, 'empty hand'.

karma /kar-muh/ • n. (in Hinduism and Buddhism) the sum of a person's actions in this and previous lives, seen as affecting their future fate.

– DERIVATIVES **karmic** adj.
– ORIGIN Sanskrit, 'action, effect, fate'.

karst /*rhymes with* cast/ • n. Geol. a limestone region with underground streams and many cavities in the rock.
– ORIGIN from German *der Karst*, a limestone region in Slovenia.

kart • n. a small racing car with no suspension and with the engine at the back.
– DERIVATIVES **karting** n.
– ORIGIN from GO-KART.

kasbah /kaz-bah/ (also **casbah**) • n. a fortress in the old part of a North African city, and the narrow streets that surround it.
– ORIGIN Arabic.

Kashmiri /kash-mee-ri/ • n. 1 a person from Kashmir. 2 the language of Kashmir. • adj. relating to Kashmir.

kayak /ky-ak/ • n. a canoe made of a light frame with a watertight covering.
– DERIVATIVES **kayaker** n.
– ORIGIN Inuit.

kazoo /kuh-zoo/ • n. a musical instrument consisting of a pipe with a hole in it, over which is a membrane that produces a buzzing sound when the player hums into it.

KB (also **Kb**) • abbrev. kilobyte(s).

KBE • abbrev. (in the UK) Knight Commander of the Order of the British Empire.

KC • abbrev. King's Counsel.

kcal • abbrev. kilocalorie(s).

KCB • abbrev. (in the UK) Knight Commander of the Order of the Bath.

kebab /ki-bab/ • n. a dish of pieces of meat, fish, or vegetables roasted or grilled on a skewer or spit.
– ORIGIN Arabic.

kecks • pl. n. Brit. informal trousers.
– ORIGIN from former *kicks*.

kedgeree /kej-uh-ree/ • n. a dish of smoked fish, rice, and hard-boiled eggs.
– ORIGIN Sanskrit.

keel • n. a structure running along the bottom of a ship, often extended downwards to increase stability. • v. (**keel over**) 1 (of a boat or ship) turn over on its side. 2 fall over.
– ORIGIN Old Norse.

keelhaul • v. humorous punish someone severely.
– ORIGIN from a former punishment in which a person was dragged through the water under a boat.

keen[1] • adj. 1 esp. Brit. eager and enthusiastic. 2 (**keen on**) interested in. 3 (of a blade) sharp. 4 quick to understand. 5 (of a sense) highly developed. 6 Brit. (of prices) very low.

– DERIVATIVES **keenly** adv. **keenness** n.
– ORIGIN Old English, 'wise, clever'.

keen[2] • v. 1 wail in grief for a dead person. 2 make an eerie wailing sound.
– ORIGIN Irish *caoinim* 'I wail'.

keep • v. (**keeps, keeping, kept**) 1 continue to have something. 2 continue in a specified condition, position, or activity: *she kept quiet about it.* 3 save or retain something for use in the future. 4 store something in a regular place. 5 do something promised, agreed, or necessary. 6 (of food) remain in good condition. 7 make a note about something or keep a diary. 8 make someone late. 9 provide accommodation and food for someone. 10 (as adj. **kept**) dated (of a woman) supported financially in return for sex. • n. 1 food, clothes, and other essentials for living. 2 the strongest or central tower of a castle.
– PHRASES **for keeps** informal permanently. **keep from** avoid doing something. **keep someone from** protect someone from. **keep something from** cause something to remain a secret from someone. **keep on** continue to do. **keep someone/thing on** continue to use or employ someone or something. **keep to 1** avoid leaving a path, road, or place. 2 stick to a schedule or to the point being discussed. 3 fulfil a promise. **keep up** move at the same rate as someone or something else. **keep something up** continue a course of action. **keep up with the Joneses** try hard not to be outdone by your neighbours or friends.
– ORIGIN Old English.

keeper • n. 1 a person who manages or looks after something or someone. 2 a goalkeeper or wicketkeeper.

keep-fit • n. esp. Brit. regular exercises to improve your fitness and health.

keeping • n. (in phr. **in** (or **out of**) **keeping with**) fitting (or not fitting) in with.

keepsake • n. a small item kept in memory of the person who gave it or originally owned it.

keg • n. a small barrel.
– ORIGIN Old Norse.

kelp • n. a very large brown seaweed.

kelvin • n. the SI base unit of temperature, equal to one degree Celsius.
– ORIGIN named after the British physicist William T. *Kelvin*.

Kelvin scale • n. the scale of temperature with absolute zero as zero and the freezing point of water as 273.15 kelvins.

ken • n. (**your ken**) your range of knowledge or experience. • v. (**kens,**

k

kenning, kenned or **kent**) Scottish & N. English **1** know someone or something. **2** recognize someone or something.
– ORIGIN Old English, 'tell, make known'.

kendo /ken-doh/ • n. a Japanese form of fencing with two-handed bamboo swords.
– ORIGIN Japanese, 'sword way'.

kennel • n. **1** a small shelter for a dog. **2** (**kennels**) a boarding or breeding establishment for dogs.
– ORIGIN Old French *chenil*.

kent past and past part. of **KEN**.

Kenyan /ken-yuhn/ • n. a person from Kenya. • adj. relating to Kenya.

kepi /kep-i/ • n. (pl. **kepis**) a French military cap with a horizontal peak.
– ORIGIN French.

kept past and past part. of **KEEP**.

keratin /ke-ruh-tin/ • n. a protein forming the basis of hair, feathers, hoofs, claws, and horns.
– ORIGIN Greek *keras* 'horn'.

kerb (US **curb**) • n. a stone edging to a pavement.
– ORIGIN variant of **CURB**.

kerb-crawling • n. Brit. driving slowly along beside a pavement in search of a prostitute.
– DERIVATIVES **kerb-crawler** n.

kerb drill • n. Brit. a set of rules followed in order to cross a road safely, as taught to children.

kerbside (US **curbside**) • n. the side of a road or pavement that is nearer to the kerb.

kerbstone • n. a long, narrow stone or concrete block, laid end to end with others to form a kerb.

kerchief /ker-chif/ • n. **1** a piece of fabric used to cover the head. **2** dated a handkerchief.
– ORIGIN Old French *cuevrechief*.

kerfuffle /ker-fuf-f'l/ • n. Brit. informal a commotion or fuss.
– ORIGIN perh. from Scots *curfuffle*.

kernel /ker-n'l/ • n. **1** the softer part of a nut, seed, or fruit stone contained within its hard shell. **2** the seed and hard husk of a cereal. **3** the central part of something.
– ORIGIN Old English, 'small corn'.

☑ The ending of **kernel** is spelled **-el**.

kerosene /ke-ruh-seen/ (also **kerosine**) • n. esp. N. Amer. paraffin oil.
– ORIGIN Greek *kēros* 'wax'.

kestrel • n. a small falcon that hunts by hovering with rapidly beating wings.
– ORIGIN perh. from Old French *crecerelle*.

ketch • n. a small sailing boat with two masts.
– ORIGIN prob. from **CATCH**.

ketchup (US also **catsup**) • n. a spicy sauce made from tomatoes and vinegar.
– ORIGIN perh. from Chinese, 'tomato juice'.

ketone /kee-tohn/ • n. any of a class of organic chemical compounds including acetone.
– ORIGIN German *Aketon* 'acetone'.

kettle • n. a metal or plastic container with a lid, spout, and handle, used for boiling water.
– PHRASES **a different kettle of fish** informal something completely different from something just mentioned.
– ORIGIN Latin *catillus* 'little pot'.

kettledrum • n. a large drum shaped like a bowl, with adjustable pitch.

key¹ • n. (pl. **keys**) **1** a small piece of shaped metal which is inserted into a lock and turned to open or close it. **2** an instrument for turning a screw, peg, or nut. **3** a lever pressed down by the finger in playing an instrument such as the piano or flute. **4** each of several buttons on a panel for operating a computer or typewriter. **5** a thing providing access or understanding: *a key to success.* **6** a list explaining the symbols used in a map or table. **7** a word or system for solving a code. **8** Music a group of notes based on a particular note and making up a scale. • adj. of central importance: *he was a key figure in the negotiations.* • v. (**keys, keying, keyed**) **1** enter data using a computer keyboard. **2** (**be keyed up**) be nervous, tense, or excited.
– ORIGIN Old English.

key² • n. a low-lying island or reef in the Caribbean or off the coast of Florida.
– ORIGIN Spanish *cayo* 'reef'.

keyboard • n. **1** a panel of keys for use with a computer or typewriter. **2** a set of keys on a musical instrument. **3** an electronic musical instrument with keys arranged as on a piano. • v. enter data by means of a keyboard.
– DERIVATIVES **keyboarder** n.

keyhole • n. a hole in a lock into which the key is inserted.

keyhole surgery • n. surgery carried out through a very small cut made in the affected area.

keynote • n. **1** a central theme. **2** Music the note on which a key is based. • adj. (of a speech) setting out the central theme of a conference.

keypad • n. a small keyboard or set of buttons for operating a portable electronic device or telephone.

key ring • n. a metal ring for holding

keys together in a bunch.

key signature •n. Music a combination of sharps or flats after the clef at the beginning of each stave, indicating the key of a composition.

keystone •n. **1** the central part of a policy or system. **2** a central stone at the top of an arch, locking the whole together.

keystroke •n. a single depression of a key on a keyboard.

keyword •n. **1** a word or idea of great importance. **2** a word used in a computer system to indicate the content of a document. **3** a significant word mentioned in an index.

KG •abbrev. (in the UK) Knight of the Order of the Garter.

kg •abbrev. kilogram(s).

khaki /kah-ki/ •n. (pl. **khakis**) **1** a cotton or wool fabric of a dull yellowish-brown colour. **2** a dull greenish- or yellowish-brown colour.
– ORIGIN Urdu, 'dust-coloured'.

Khalsa /kul-suh/ •n. the group of fully initiated Sikhs to which devout orthodox Sikhs are ritually admitted at puberty.
– ORIGIN from Arabic, 'pure, belonging to'.

khan /kahn/ •n. a title given to rulers and officials in central Asia, Afghanistan, and certain other Muslim countries.
– ORIGIN Turkic, 'lord, prince'.

khazi /kah-zi/ •n. (pl. **khazies**) Brit. informal a toilet.
– ORIGIN Italian *casa* 'house'.

kHz •abbrev. kilohertz.

kibbutz /kib-buuts/ •n. (pl. **kibbutzim** /kib-buuts-im/) a farming settlement in Israel in which work is shared between its members.
– ORIGIN modern Hebrew, 'gathering'.

kibosh /ky-bosh/ •n. (in phr. **put the kibosh on**) informal firmly put an end to.

kick •v. **1** strike or propel forcibly with the foot. **2** strike out with the foot. **3** informal succeed in giving up a habit. **4** (of a gun) spring back when fired. •n. **1** an instance of kicking. **2** informal a thrill of excitement. **3** informal the strong effect of alcohol or a drug.
– PHRASES **kick the bucket** informal die. **kick in** come into effect. **a kick in the teeth** informal a serious setback. **kick off** (of a football match) start or restart with a kick from the centre spot. **kick someone out** informal force someone to leave.
– DERIVATIVES **kicker** n.

kickback •n. **1** a sudden forceful springing back. **2** informal an underhand

payment made to someone who has helped to arrange a business or political deal.

kick-boxing •n. a form of martial art which combines boxing with kicking with bare feet.

kick-off •n. the start of a football match.

kick-pleat •n. an inverted pleat in a narrow skirt to allow freedom of movement.

kickstand •n. a rod attached to a bicycle or motorcycle that may be kicked upright to support the vehicle when it is not being ridden.

kick-start •v. **1** start an engine on a motorcycle with a downward thrust of a pedal. **2** stimulate: *the government should kick-start the economy.* •n. a device to kick-start an engine.

kid¹ •n. **1** informal a child or young person. **2** a young goat.
– PHRASES **kids' stuff** informal something that is easy or simple to do.
– ORIGIN Old Norse.

kid² •v. (**kids, kidding, kidded**) informal fool someone into believing something.
– ORIGIN perh. from **KID¹**, expressing the idea 'make a child or goat of'.

kid brother (or **kid sister**) •n. informal a younger brother or sister.

kiddie (also **kiddy**) •n. (pl. **kiddies**) informal a young child.

kidnap •v. (**kidnaps, kidnapping, kidnapped**; US also **kidnaps, kidnaping, kidnaped**) take someone by force and hold them captive in order to obtain money for their release. •n. an instance of kidnapping.
– DERIVATIVES **kidnapper** n.
– ORIGIN from **KID¹** + slang *nap* 'seize'.

kidney •n. (pl. **kidneys**) **1** each of a pair of organs that remove waste products from the blood and produce urine. **2** the kidney of a sheep, ox, or pig as food.

kidney bean •n. a dark red kidney-shaped bean, eaten as a vegetable.

kidney machine •n. a machine that performs the functions of a kidney, used when a person's kidneys are failing.

kidney stone •n. a hard mass formed in a kidney.

kilim /ki-leem/ •n. a carpet or rug woven without a pile, made in Turkey, Kurdistan, and neighbouring areas.
– ORIGIN Persian.

kill •v. **1** cause the death of. **2** put an end to. **3** informal overwhelm someone with an emotion: *the suspense is killing me.* **4** informal cause someone pain. **5** pass time. •n. **1** an act of killing. **2** an animal or animals killed by a hunter or another animal.

k

– ORIGIN prob. Germanic.

killer • n. **1** a person or thing that kills. **2** informal a very impressive or difficult thing.

killer instinct • n. a ruthless determination to succeed or win.

killer whale • n. a large toothed whale with black-and-white markings and a prominent fin on its back.

killing • n. an act of causing death. • adj. informal exhausting.
– PHRASES **make a killing** make a great deal of money out of something.

killjoy • n. a person who spoils the enjoyment of other people by behaving very seriously or disapprovingly.

kiln • n. a furnace for baking or burning pottery, bricks, or lime.
– ORIGIN Latin *culina* 'kitchen'.

kilo • n. (pl. **kilos**) a kilogram.

kilo- /ki-loh, kee-loh/ • comb. form referring to a factor of one thousand (10³): *kilolitre*.
– ORIGIN Greek *khilioi* 'thousand'.

kilobyte • n. a unit of information stored in a computer, equal to 1,024 bytes.

kilocalorie • n. a unit of energy of one thousand calories (equal to one large calorie).

kilogram (also **kilogramme**) • n. the SI unit of mass, equal to 1,000 grams (approximately 2.205 lb).

kilohertz • n. a measure of frequency equivalent to 1,000 cycles per second.

kilojoule • n. 1,000 joules.

kilolitre (US **kiloliter**) • n. 1,000 litres (equivalent to 220 imperial gallons).

kilometre /kil-uh-mee-ter, ki-lom-i-ter/ (US **kilometer**) • n. a metric unit of measurement equal to 1,000 metres (approximately 0.62 miles).
– DERIVATIVES **kilometric** adj.

kiloton (also **kilotonne**) • n. a unit of explosive power equivalent to 1,000 tons of TNT.

kilovolt • n. 1,000 volts.

kilowatt • n. 1,000 watts.

kilowatt-hour • n. a measure of electrical energy equivalent to one kilowatt operating for one hour.

kilt • n. a knee-length skirt of pleated tartan cloth, traditionally worn by men as part of Scottish Highland dress.
– DERIVATIVES **kilted** adj.
– ORIGIN Scandinavian.

kilter • n. (in phr. **out of kilter**) out of balance.

kimono /ki-moh-noh/ • n. (pl. **kimonos**) a long, loose Japanese robe having wide sleeves and tied with a sash.
– ORIGIN Japanese, 'wearing thing'.

kin • n. (treated as pl.) your family and relations.
– ORIGIN Old English.

-kin • suffix forming nouns referring to things of small size: *catkin*.
– ORIGIN Dutch *-kijn*, *-ken* or German *-kin*.

kind¹ • n. **1** a class or type of similar people or things. **2** character; nature: *the US is different in kind to other countries.* **3** each of the elements (bread and wine) of the Eucharist.
– PHRASES **in kind 1** in the same way. **2** (of payment) in goods or services instead of money. **kind of** informal rather. **one of a kind** unique. **two of a kind** the same or very similar.
– ORIGIN Old English.

> **USAGE:** When using **kind** to refer to a plural noun, it is wrong to say *these kind of questions are not relevant* (that is, to have *kind* in the singular): you should use *kinds* instead (*these kinds of questions are not relevant*).

kind² • adj. considerate and generous.
– ORIGIN Old English, 'natural, native'.

kindergarten /kin-der-gar-tuhn/ • n. a nursery school.
– ORIGIN German, 'children's garden'.

kindle /kin-d'l/ • v. (**kindles**, **kindling**, **kindled**) **1** light a flame. **2** arouse an emotion.
– ORIGIN Old Norse, 'candle, torch'.

kindling • n. small sticks used for lighting fires.

kindly • adv. **1** in a kind way. **2** please (used in a polite request). • adj. (**kindlier**, **kindliest**) kind; warm-hearted.
– PHRASES **not take kindly to** not be pleased by.
– DERIVATIVES **kindliness** n.

kindness • n. **1** the quality of being considerate and generous. **2** a kind act.

kindred /kin-drid/ • n. **1** (treated as pl.) your family and relations. **2** relationship by blood. • adj. having similar qualities.
– ORIGIN Old English.

kindred spirit • n. a person whose interests or attitudes are similar to your own.

kinematics /kin-i-mat-iks/ • n. the branch of mechanics concerned with the motion of objects without reference to the forces which cause the motion.
– DERIVATIVES **kinematic** adj.
– ORIGIN Greek *kinēma* 'motion'.

kinetic /ki-net-ik/ • adj. relating to or resulting from motion.
– DERIVATIVES **kinetically** adv.
– ORIGIN Greek *kinētikos*.

kinetic energy • n. Physics energy which a body possesses as a result of being in motion. Compare with POTENTIAL ENERGY.

kinetics /ki-net-iks/ • n. **1** the branch of chemistry concerned with the rates of chemical reactions. **2** Physics = DYNAMICS (in sense 1).

kinfolk • pl. n. = KINSFOLK.

king • n. **1** the male ruler of an independent state. **2** the best or most important person or thing in a field or group. **3** a playing card bearing a picture of a king, ranking next below an ace. **4** the most important chess piece, which the opponent has to checkmate in order to win.
– DERIVATIVES **kingly** adj. **kingship** n.
– ORIGIN Old English.

King Charles spaniel • n. a small breed of spaniel with a white, black, and tan coat.
– ORIGIN named after King Charles II of England, Scotland, and Ireland.

kingdom • n. **1** a country, state, or territory ruled by a king or queen. **2** an area in which a particular person or thing is dominant. **3** the spiritual authority of God. **4** each of the three divisions (animal, vegetable, and mineral) in which natural objects are classified.

kingfisher • n. a colourful bird with a long sharp beak, which dives to catch fish in streams and rivers.

kingmaker • n. a person who uses their political influence to bring a leader to power.
– ORIGIN first referring to the Earl of Warwick.

kingpin • n. **1** a large bolt in a central position. **2** a vertical bolt used as a pivot. **3** a person or thing that is essential to the success of an organization or operation.

king-sized (also **king-size**) • adj. of a larger than normal size.

kink • n. **1** a sharp twist in something long and narrow. **2** a flaw or difficulty in a plan or operation. **3** a peculiar habit or characteristic. • v. form a kink.
– ORIGIN German *kinke*.

kinky • adj. (**kinkier**, **kinkiest**) **1** informal relating to or liking unusual sexual activities. **2** having kinks or twists.
– DERIVATIVES **kinkily** adv. **kinkiness** n.

kinsfolk (also **kinfolk**) • pl. n. a person's family and relations.

kinship • n. **1** family relationship. **2** a sharing of characteristics or origins: *they felt a kinship with architects.*

kinsman (or **kinswoman**) • n. (pl. **kinsmen** or **kinswomen**) one of a person's family or relations.

kiosk /kee-ossk/ • n. **1** a small open-

fronted hut from which newspapers, refreshments, or tickets are sold. **2** Brit. a public telephone booth.
– ORIGIN Turkish *köşk* 'pavilion'.

kip Brit. informal • n. a sleep. • v. (**kips**, **kipping**, **kipped**) sleep.
– ORIGIN perh. from Danish *kippe* 'hovel'.

kipper • n. a herring that has been split open, salted, and dried or smoked.
– ORIGIN Old English, referring to a male salmon in the spawning season.

kipper tie • n. a very wide tie.

kirk • n. Scottish & N. English **1** a church. **2** (**the Kirk** or **the Kirk of Scotland**) the Church of Scotland.
– ORIGIN related to CHURCH.

Kirk session • n. the lowest court in the Church of Scotland.

kirsch /keersh/ • n. brandy distilled from the fermented juice of cherries.
– ORIGIN German.

kismet /kiz-met/ • n. fate or destiny.
– ORIGIN Arabic, 'division, lot'.

kiss • v. touch with the lips as a sign of love, affection, or greeting. • n. a touch with the lips.
– PHRASES **kiss of life 1** mouth-to-mouth resuscitation. **2** something that revives a failing enterprise.
– DERIVATIVES **kissable** adj.
– ORIGIN Old English.

kiss curl • n. a small curl of hair on the forehead, at the nape of the neck, or in front of the ear.

kisser • n. **1** a person who kisses someone. **2** informal a person's mouth.

kissogram • n. a novelty greeting delivered by a man or woman who accompanies it with a kiss.

kit[1] • n. **1** a set of articles or equipment for a specific purpose. **2** Brit. the clothes and items needed for an activity: *boys in football kit.* • v. (**kits**, **kitting**, **kitted**) (**kit someone out**) provide someone with appropriate clothing or equipment.
– ORIGIN Dutch *kitte* 'wooden container'.

kit[2] • n. the young of certain animals, such as the beaver, ferret, and mink.

kitbag • n. a long, cylindrical canvas bag for carrying a soldier's possessions.

kitchen • n. **1** a room where food is prepared and cooked. **2** a set of fittings and units installed in a kitchen.
– ORIGIN Old English.

kitchenette • n. a small kitchen or part of a room equipped as a kitchen.

kitchen garden • n. a garden where vegetables and fruit are grown for household use.

kitchen-sink • adj. (of drama) realistic in dealing with harsh everyday subjects.

k

kitchenware • n. kitchen utensils.

kite • n. **1** a toy consisting of a light frame with thin material stretched over it, flown in the wind at the end of a long string. **2** a long-winged bird of prey with a forked tail. **3** Geom. a four-sided figure having two pairs of equal sides next to each other.
– ORIGIN Old English.

Kitemark • n. trademark (in the UK) an official kite-shaped mark on goods approved by the British Standards Institution.

kith /kith/ • n. (in phr. **kith and kin**) your family and relations.
– ORIGIN Old English.

kitsch /rhymes with rich/ • n. art, objects, or design considered to be tastelessly showy or sentimental.
– DERIVATIVES **kitschy** adj.
– ORIGIN German.

kitten • n. **1** a young cat. **2** the young of certain other animals, such as the rabbit and beaver.
– PHRASES **have kittens** Brit. informal be very nervous or upset.
– ORIGIN Old French chitoun.

kitten heel • n. a type of low stiletto heel.

kittenish • adj. playful, lively, or flirtatious.

kittiwake /kit-ti-wayk/ • n. a small gull that nests on sea cliffs and has a loud call that resembles its name.

kitty • n. (pl. **kitties**) **1** a fund of money for use by a number of people. **2** a pool of money in some card games.

kiwi • n. (pl. **kiwis**) **1** a flightless, tailless New Zealand bird with hair-like feathers and a long downwardly curved bill. **2** (**Kiwi**) informal a New Zealander.
– ORIGIN Maori.

kiwi fruit • n. (pl. **kiwi fruit**) the fruit of an Asian climbing plant, with a thin hairy skin, green flesh, and black seeds.

kJ • abbrev. kilojoule(s).

kl • abbrev. kilolitre(s).

klaxon /klak-suhn/ • n. trademark a vehicle horn or warning hooter.
– ORIGIN the name of the manufacturers.

kleptomania /klep-tuh-**may**-ni-uh/ • n. a recurring urge to steal.
– DERIVATIVES **kleptomaniac** n. & adj.
– ORIGIN Greek kleptēs 'thief'.

km • abbrev. kilometre(s).

knack • n. **1** a skill at performing a task. **2** a habit of doing something.
– ORIGIN prob. from former knack 'sharp blow or sound'.

knacker Brit. • n. a person who disposes of dead or unwanted animals.
• v. (**knackers, knackering, knackered**) informal wear out.
– ORIGIN orig. referring to a harness-maker, perh. from former knack 'trinket'.

knacker's yard • n. Brit. a place where old or injured animals are slaughtered.

knapsack • n. a small rucksack.
– ORIGIN Dutch knapzack.

knave • n. **1** old use a dishonest man. **2** (in cards) a jack.
– DERIVATIVES **knavery** n. **knavish** adj.
– ORIGIN Old English, 'boy, servant'.

knead • v. **1** work dough or clay with the hands. **2** massage a part of the body by squeezing and pressing it.
– ORIGIN Old English.

knee • n. **1** the joint between the thigh and the lower leg. **2** the upper surface of the thigh if you are in a sitting position.
• v. (**knees, kneeing, kneed**) hit someone with the knee.
– ORIGIN Old English.

kneecap • n. the outward-curving bone in front of the knee joint. • v. (**kneecaps, kneecapping, kneecapped**) shoot someone in the knee.

knee-jerk • n. an involuntary kick caused by a blow on the tendon just below the knee. • adj. automatic and unthinking: a knee-jerk reaction.

kneel • v. (**kneels, kneeling, knelt** or N. Amer. also **kneeled**) rest on your knees.
– ORIGIN Old English.

kneeler • n. a cushion or bench for kneeling on.

knees-up • n. Brit. informal a lively party.

knell /nel/ • n. literary the sound of a bell rung solemnly.
– ORIGIN Old English.

knelt past and past part. of KNEEL.

knew past of KNOW.

knickerbockers • pl. n. loose-fitting trousers or long knickers gathered at the knee or calf.
– ORIGIN named after Diedrich Knickerbocker, the pretended author of Washington Irving's History of New York.

knickers • pl. n. Brit. an item of women's or girls' underclothes, covering the bottom and with two holes for the legs.
– ORIGIN from knickerbockers.

knick-knack • n. a cheap decorative object.
– ORIGIN from KNACK.

knife • n. (pl. **knives**) **1** a cutting instrument consisting of a blade fixed into a handle. **2** a cutting blade on a machine. • v. (**knifes, knifing, knifed**) stab someone with a knife.

– PHRASES **at knifepoint** under threat of injury from a knife.
– ORIGIN Old Norse.

knife-edge • n. a very tense or dangerous situation.

knight • n. 1 (in the Middle Ages) a man raised to military rank after serving his sovereign or lord as a page and squire. 2 (in the UK) a man awarded a title by the King or Queen and entitled to use 'Sir' in front of his name. 3 a chess piece that moves by jumping to the opposite corner of a rectangle two squares by three. • v. give a man the title of knight.
– DERIVATIVES **knighthood** n. **knightly** adj.
– ORIGIN Old English, 'boy, servant'.

knight errant • n. a medieval knight who wandered in search of adventure.

knit • v. (**knits, knitting, knitted** or **knit**) 1 make a garment by looping yarn together with knitting needles or on a machine. 2 make a plain stitch in knitting. 3 (of parts of a wound or broken bone) join together. 4 tighten your eyebrows in a frown. • n. (**knits**) knitted garments.
– DERIVATIVES **knitter** n. **knitting** n.
– ORIGIN Old English.

knitting needle • n. a long, thin, pointed rod used as part of a pair for hand knitting.

knitwear • n. knitted garments.

knives pl. of KNIFE.

knob • n. 1 a rounded lump at the end or on the surface of something. 2 a ball-shaped handle. 3 a round control switch on a machine. 4 a small lump of something.
– DERIVATIVES **knobbed** adj. **knobby** adj.
– ORIGIN German *knobbe*.

knobble • n. Brit. a small lump on something.
– DERIVATIVES **knobbly** adj.
– ORIGIN from KNOB.

knock • v. 1 strike a surface noisily to attract attention. 2 collide with. 3 strike someone or something so that they move or fall. 4 make a hole or dent in something by striking it. 5 informal criticize someone or something. 6 (of a motor) make a rattling noise. • n. 1 a sudden short sound caused by a blow. 2 a blow or collision. 3 a setback.
– PHRASES **knock about** (or **around**) informal travel or spend time aimlessly. **knock something back** informal consume a drink quickly. **knock something down** informal reduce the price of an article. **knock off** informal stop work. **knock something off** informal 1 produce a piece of work quickly and easily. 2 Brit. steal something. **knock someone out 1** make someone unconscious. 2 informal astonish

or greatly impress someone. 3 eliminate someone from a knockout competition.
– ORIGIN Old English.

knockabout • adj. (of comedy) rough and slapstick.

knock-back • n. informal a refusal or setback.

knock-down • adj. informal (of a price) very low.

knocker • n. 1 a hinged object fixed to a door and rapped by visitors to attract attention. 2 informal a person who continually finds fault. 3 (**knockers**) informal a woman's breasts. 2 Austral./NZ (of payment) immediately.

knock-kneed • adj. having legs that curve inwards at the knee.

knock-on effect • n. esp. Brit. an effect or result that creates a further effect.

knockout • n. 1 an act of making someone unconscious. 2 Brit. a tournament in which the loser in each round is eliminated. 3 informal a very impressive person or thing.

knock-up • n. Brit. (in racket sports) a period of practice play before a game.

knoll /nol/ • n. a small hill or mound.
– ORIGIN Old English.

knot[1] • n. 1 a fastening made by looping a piece of string or rope on itself and tightening it. 2 a tangled mass in hair, wool, or other fibres. 3 a hard mass in wood at the point where the trunk and a branch join. 4 a hard lump of tissue in the body. 5 a small group of people. 6 a unit used to measure the speed of ships, aircraft, or winds, equivalent to one nautical mile per hour. • v. (**knots, knotting, knotted**) 1 fasten something with a knot. 2 tangle something. 3 make a muscle tense and hard. 4 (of the stomach) tighten as a result of tension.
– PHRASES **at a rate of knots** Brit. informal very fast.
– ORIGIN Old English; sense 6 comes from the former practice of measuring a ship's speed by using a float attached to a long knotted line.

knot garden • n. a formal garden laid out in a complex design.

knothole • n. a hole in a piece of wood where a knot has fallen out.

knotty • adj. (**knottier, knottiest**) 1 full of knots. 2 very complex: *a knotty problem.*

know • v. (**knows, knowing, knew**; past part. **known**) 1 be aware of something as a result of observing, asking, or being informed. 2 be absolutely sure of something. 3 be familiar with. 4 have a good command of a subject or language. 5 have personal experience of. 6 (**be**

k

known as) be thought of as having a specified characteristic or title.
– PHRASES **be in the know** informal be aware of something known only to a few people. **know the ropes** have experience of the correct way of doing something.
– DERIVATIVES **knowable** adj.
– ORIGIN Old English, 'recognize'.

know-all • n. informal a person who behaves as if they know everything.

know-how • n. practical knowledge or skill.

knowing • adj. suggesting that you know something that is supposed to be secret: *a knowing smile*.
– PHRASES **there is no knowing** no one can tell whether something is the case.
– DERIVATIVES **knowingly** adv. **knowingness** n.

knowledge • n. **1** information and skills gained through experience or education. **2** the total of what is known. **3** awareness gained by experience of a fact or situation: *he denied all knowledge of the incident*.
– PHRASES **to (the best of) my knowledge 1** so far as I know. **2** as I know for certain.

 Remember that **knowledge** ends with **-edge**.

knowledgeable (also **knowledgable**) • adj. intelligent and well informed.
– DERIVATIVES **knowledgeably** adv.

known past part. of KNOW. • adj. **1** that is recognized, familiar, or can be known. **2** publicly acknowledged to be: *a known criminal*. **3** Math. (of a quantity or variable) having a value that can be stated.

knuckle • n. **1** each of the joints of a finger. **2** a knee-joint of a four-legged animal, or the part joining the leg to the foot, especially as a joint of meat.
• v. (**knuckles, knuckling, knuckled**) rub or press something with the knuckles.
– PHRASES **knuckle down 1** approach a task seriously. **2** (also **knuckle under**) submit to someone's authority. **a rap on (or over) the knuckles** a reprimand.
– ORIGIN German or Dutch *knökel* 'little bone'.

knuckleduster • n. a metal fitting worn over the knuckles in fighting to increase the effect of blows.

knucklehead • n. informal a stupid person.

knurl /rhymes with curl/ • n. a small projecting knob or ridge.
– DERIVATIVES **knurled** adj.
– ORIGIN prob. from German *knorre* 'knob'.

KO¹ • abbrev. kick-off.

KO² • n. a knockout in a boxing match.
• v. (**KO's, KO'ing, KO'd**) knock someone out in a boxing match.

koala /koh-ah-luh/ • n. a bear-like tree-dwelling Australian marsupial that has thick grey fur and feeds on eucalyptus leaves.
– ORIGIN from an Aboriginal language.

kohl /kohl/ • n. a black powder used as eye make-up.
– ORIGIN Arabic.

kohlrabi /kohl-rah-bi/ • n. (pl. **kohlrabies**) a variety of cabbage with an edible turnip-like stem.
– ORIGIN German.

koi /koy/ • n. (pl. **koi**) a large common Japanese carp.
– ORIGIN Japanese.

kook • n. N. Amer. informal a mad or unconventional person.
– DERIVATIVES **kooky** adj.
– ORIGIN prob. from CUCKOO.

kookaburra /kuu-kuh-bur-ruh/ • n. a very large, noisy Australasian kingfisher that feeds on reptiles and birds.
– ORIGIN from an Aboriginal language.

kopek /koh-pek/ (also **copeck** or **kopeck**) • n. a unit of money of Russia and some other countries of the former Soviet Union, equal to one hundredth of a rouble.
– ORIGIN Russian *kopeïka* 'small lance'.

Koran /ko-rahn/ (also **Quran** or **Qur'an** /kuu-rahn/) • n. the sacred book of Islam, believed to be the word of God as told to Muhammad and written down in Arabic.
– DERIVATIVES **Koranic** /ko-ran-ik/ adj.
– ORIGIN Arabic, 'recitation'.

Korean • n. **1** a person from Korea. **2** the language of Korea. • adj. relating to Korea.

korma /kor-muh/ • n. a mild Indian curry of meat or fish marinaded in yogurt or curds.
– ORIGIN Urdu.

koruna • n. the basic unit of money of the Czech Republic and Slovakia.
– ORIGIN Czech, 'crown'.

kosher /koh-sher/ • adj. **1** (of food) prepared according to the requirements of Jewish law. **2** informal genuine and legitimate.
– ORIGIN Hebrew, 'proper'.

Kosovar /koss-uh-var/ • n. a person from Kosovo, a province of Serbia whose population is largely of Albanian descent.
– DERIVATIVES **Kosovan** n. & adj.

kowtow /kow-tow/ • v. **1** be very meek and obedient towards someone. **2** hist.

kneel and touch the ground with the forehead in submission as part of Chinese custom.
– ORIGIN Chinese.

kph • abbrev. kilometres per hour.

Kr • symb. the chemical element krypton.

kraal /krahl/ • n. S. Afr. **1** a traditional African village of huts. **2** an enclosure for sheep and cattle.
– ORIGIN Dutch.

Kraut /krowt/ • n. informal, offens. a German.
– ORIGIN from SAUERKRAUT.

Kremlin /krem-lin/ • n. (**the Kremlin**) the building in Moscow that houses the Russian government.
– ORIGIN Russian *kreml'*.

krill • pl. n. small shrimp-like crustaceans which are the main food of baleen whales.
– ORIGIN Norwegian *kril* 'small fish fry'.

krona /kroh-nuh/ • n. **1** (pl. **kronor** /kroh-nuh/) the basic unit of money of Sweden. **2** (pl. **kronur** /kroh-nuh/) the basic unit of money of Iceland.
– ORIGIN Swedish and Icelandic, 'crown'.

krone /kroh-nuh/ • n. (pl. **kroner** /kroh-nuh/) the basic unit of money of Denmark and Norway.
– ORIGIN Danish and Norwegian, 'crown'.

krugerrand /kroo-ger-rand/ (also **Kruger**) • n. a South African gold coin with a portrait of President Kruger on it.
– ORIGIN named after Paul *Kruger*, a President of Transvaal.

krypton /krip-ton/ • n. an inert odourless gaseous chemical element, present in small amounts in the air and used in some kinds of electric light.
– ORIGIN Greek *krupton* 'hidden'.

KStJ • abbrev. Knight of the Order of St John.

KT • abbrev. (in the UK) Knight of the Order of the Thistle.

kt • abbrev. knot(s).

kudos /kyoo-doss/ • n. praise and honour.
– ORIGIN Greek.

> **USAGE:** Although it ends in *-s*, **kudos**, meaning 'praise' is not a plural word. This means that there is no singular form **kudo** and that use of it as if it were a plural, as in *he received many kudos for his work*, is wrong.

kudu /koo-doo/ • n. (pl. **kudu** or **kudus**) a striped African antelope, the male of which has long spirally curved horns.
– ORIGIN Afrikaans.

Ku Klux Klan /koo kluks klan/ • n. a secret organization of white people in the US who are violently opposed to black people.
– ORIGIN perh. from Greek *kuklos* 'circle' and CLAN.

kumquat /kum-kwot/ • n. a small orange-like fruit.
– ORIGIN Chinese, 'little orange'.

kuna /koo-nuh/ • n. (pl. **kune**) the basic unit of money of Croatia.
– ORIGIN Serbo-Croat, 'marten' (the fur of the marten was once used as a form of currency).

kung fu /kung foo/ • n. a Chinese martial art resembling karate.
– ORIGIN Chinese, from words meaning 'merit' and 'master'.

Kurd /kerd/ • n. a member of a mainly Islamic people living in Kurdistan.
– DERIVATIVES **Kurdish** n. & adj.

kurta /kertuh/ • n. a loose collarless shirt worn by people from the Indian subcontinent.
– ORIGIN Urdu and Persian.

Kuwaiti /kuu-way-ti/ • n. a person from Kuwait. • adj. relating to Kuwait.

kV • abbrev. kilovolt(s).

kW • abbrev. kilowatt(s).

kWh • abbrev. kilowatt-hour(s).

k

LI

L¹ (also **l**) •n. (pl. **Ls** or **L's**) **1** the twelfth letter of the alphabet. **2** the Roman numeral for 50.

L² •abbrev. **1** (**L.**) Lake, Loch, or Lough. **2** large (as a clothes size). **3** Brit. learner driver. **4** lire.

l •abbrev. **1** left. **2** (**l.**) line. **3** litre(s). •symb. (in mathematical formulae) length.

£ •abbrev. pound(s).
– ORIGIN from Latin *libra* 'pound, balance'.

LA •abbrev. Los Angeles.

La •symb. the chemical element lanthanum.

la •n. Music var. of LAH.

lab •n. informal a laboratory.

label •n. **1** a small piece of card, fabric, or other material attached to an object and giving information about it. **2** the name or trademark of a fashion company. **3** a company that produces recorded music. **4** a classifying name given to a person or thing. •v. (**labels, labelling, labelled**; US **labels, labeling, labeled**) **1** attach a label to. **2** put something in a category.
– ORIGIN Old French, 'ribbon'.

labia /lay-bi-uh/ •pl. n. (sing. **labium** /lay-bi-uhm/) the inner and outer folds of a woman's genitals.
– ORIGIN Latin, 'lips'.

labial •adj. esp. Anat. & Biol. relating to the lips or labia.

labiate /lay-bi-uht/ •adj. Bot. relating to plants of the mint family, having distinctive two-lobed flowers.
– ORIGIN Latin *labiatus*.

labor etc. •n. US & Austral. = LABOUR etc.

laboratory /luh-bo-ruh-tuh-ri/ •n. (pl. **laboratories**) a room or building for scientific experiments or teaching, or for the making of drugs or chemicals.
– ORIGIN Latin *laboratorium*.

laborious /luh-bor-i-uhss/ •adj. **1** requiring much time and effort. **2** showing obvious signs of effort: *a slow, laborious speech.*
– DERIVATIVES **laboriously** adv.

labour (US & Austral. **labor**) •n. **1** work.

2 workers as a group. **3** (**Labour**) the Labour Party. **4** the process of childbirth. •v. **1** do hard physical work. **2** have difficulty despite working hard. **3** move with difficulty. **4** (**labour under**) be misled by a mistaken belief.
– PHRASES **labour the point** talk about something at excessive length.
– ORIGIN Latin *labor* 'toil, trouble'.

labour camp •n. a prison camp where prisoners must do hard physical work.

Labour Day •n. a public holiday held in some countries in honour of working people.

laboured (US **labored**) •adj. **1** done with great difficulty. **2** not spontaneous or natural: *a laboured joke.*

labourer (US **laborer**) •n. a person doing unskilled manual work.

labour exchange •n. former term for JOBCENTRE.

labour force •n. the members of a population who are able to work.

labour-intensive •adj. needing a large workforce or a large amount of work in relation to what is produced.

Labour Party •n. a British political party formed to represent the interests of ordinary working people.

labour-saving •adj. designed to reduce the amount of work needed to do something.

Labrador /lab-ruh-dor/ (also **Labrador retriever**) •n. a breed of retriever with a black or yellow coat, also used as a guide dog.
– ORIGIN named after the *Labrador* Peninsula of eastern Canada.

laburnum /luh-ber-nuhm/ •n. (pl. **laburnums**) a small hardwood tree with hanging clusters of yellow flowers followed by pods of poisonous seeds.
– ORIGIN Latin.

labyrinth /lab-i-rinth/ •n. **1** a complicated irregular network of passages. **2** a complex and confusing arrangement: *a labyrinth of laws and regulations.* **3** a complex structure in the

inner ear which contains the organs of hearing and balance.
– DERIVATIVES **labyrinthine** /lab-i-**rin**-thyn/ adj.
– ORIGIN Greek *laburinthos*.

lac • n. a substance produced by an Asian insect (the **lac insect**), used to make varnish and shellac.
– ORIGIN Hindi or Persian.

lace • n. **1** a fine open fabric of cotton or silk made by looping, twisting, or knitting thread in patterns. **2** a cord used to fasten a shoe or garment. • v. (**laces, lacing, laced**) **1** fasten a shoe or garment with a lace or laces. **2** entwine. **3** add an ingredient to a drink or dish to improve the flavour or to make it stronger: *chefs laced their pastas with caviar.*
– ORIGIN Old French *laz*.

lacerate /**lass**-uh-rayt/ • v. (**lacerates, lacerating, lacerated**) tear or deeply cut the flesh or skin.
– DERIVATIVES **laceration** n.
– ORIGIN Latin *lacerare*.

lachrymal /**lak**-ri-muhl/ (also **lacrimal**) • adj. tech. or literary connected with weeping or tears.
– ORIGIN Latin *lachrymalis*.

lachrymose /**lak**-ri-mohss/ • adj. formal or literary **1** tearful. **2** sad: *a lachrymose children's classic.*

lacing • n. a laced fastening of a shoe or garment.

lack • n. the state of being without or not having enough of something. • v. (also **lack for**) be without or without enough of.
– ORIGIN perh. partly from German *lak*, Dutch *laken*.

lackadaisical /lak-uh-**day**-zi-k'l/ • adj. lacking enthusiasm and thoroughness.
– ORIGIN from former *lackaday*, expressing surprise or grief.

lackey • n. (pl. **lackeys**) **1** a servant. **2** a person who is too willing to serve or obey other people.
– ORIGIN French *laquais*.

lacking • adj. missing or deficient.

lacklustre (US **lackluster**) • adj. **1** lacking in energy or inspiration. **2** (of the hair or eyes) not shining.

laconic /luh-**kon**-ik/ • adj. using very few words.
– DERIVATIVES **laconically** adv.
– ORIGIN Greek *Lakōnikos*.

lacquer /**lak**-ker/ • n. **1** a varnish made of shellac, the sap of an Asian tree, or of synthetic substances. **2** decorative wooden goods coated with lacquer. **3** a chemical substance sprayed on hair to keep it in place. • v. (**lacquers,** **lacquering, lacquered**) coat with lacquer.
– ORIGIN Hindi or Persian.

lacrimal • adj. var. of LACHRYMAL.

lacrosse /luh-**kross**/ • n. a team game in which a ball is thrown, carried, and caught with a long-handled stick bearing a net at one end.
– ORIGIN from French *le jeu de la crosse* 'the game of the hooked stick'.

lactate /lak-**tayt**/ • v. (**lactates, lactating, lactated**) (of a female mammal) produce milk.
– ORIGIN Latin *lactare* 'suckle'.

lactation • n. **1** the production of milk by the mammary glands. **2** the suckling of a baby or young animal.

lacteal /**lak**-ti-uhl/ • adj. conveying milk or milky fluid. • n. (**lacteals**) Anat. vessels in the small intestine which absorb digested fats.
– ORIGIN Latin *lacteus*.

lactic /**lak**-tik/ • adj. relating to or obtained from milk.

lactic acid • n. an organic acid present in sour milk, and produced in the muscles during strenuous exercise.

lactose /**lak**-tohz/ • n. Chem. a sugar present in milk.

lacto-vegetarian • n. a person who eats only dairy products and vegetables.

lacuna /luh-**kyoo**-nuh/ • n. (pl. **lacunae** /luh-**kyoo**-nee/ or **lacunas**) **1** a gap or missing portion. **2** a cavity or depression in bone.
– ORIGIN Latin, 'pool'.

lacy • adj. (**lacier, laciest**) made of, resembling, or trimmed with lace.

lad • n. informal **1** a boy or young man. **2** (**the lads**) Brit. a group of male friends. **3** Brit. a very macho or high-spirited man.
– DERIVATIVES **laddish** adj.

ladder • n. **1** a structure consisting of a series of bars or steps between two uprights, used for climbing up or down. **2** a series of stages by which progress can be made: *the career ladder.* **3** Brit. a strip of unravelled fabric in tights or stockings, leading from a torn thread. • v. (**ladders, laddering, laddered**) Brit. make a ladder in tights or stockings.
– ORIGIN Old English.

laden • adj. heavily loaded or weighed down.
– ORIGIN Old English.

la-di-da • adj. informal affected or snobbish.
– ORIGIN imitating an affected way of speaking.

ladies pl. of LADY.

ladies' man • n. informal a man who

enjoys spending time and flirting with women.

ladle • n. a large long-handled spoon with a cup-shaped bowl, for serving soup, stew, or a sauce. • v. (**ladles, ladling, ladled**) **1** serve or transfer soup, stew, or a sauce with a ladle. **2** (**ladle something out**) give something out in large amounts.
– DERIVATIVES **ladleful** n.
– ORIGIN Old English.

lady • n. (pl. **ladies**) **1** (in polite or formal use) a woman. **2** a woman of a high social position. **3** (**Lady**) a title used by peeresses, female relatives of peers, and the wives and widows of knights. **4** a well-mannered and sophisticated woman. **5** (**the Ladies**) Brit. a women's public toilet.
– PHRASES **My Lady** a polite form of address to female judges and certain women of high rank.
– ORIGIN Old English.

ladybird • n. a small beetle with a red or yellow back with black spots.

Lady Day • n. the Christian feast of the Annunciation, 25 March.

lady-in-waiting • n. (pl. **ladies-in-waiting**) a woman who accompanies and looks after a queen or princess.

ladykiller • n. informal a man who is successful in seducing women.

ladylike • adj. appropriate for or typical of a well-mannered woman or girl.

Ladyship • n. (**Her/Your Ladyship**) a respectful way of referring to or addressing a Lady.

lady's maid • n. esp. hist. a maid who attended to the personal needs of her mistress.

lag¹ • v. (**lags, lagging, lagged**) fall behind. • n. (also **time lag**) a period of time between two events; a delay.
– ORIGIN perh. Scandinavian.

lag² • v. (**lags, lagging, lagged**) cover a water tank or pipes with material designed to prevent heat loss.
– ORIGIN from earlier *lag* 'piece of insulating cover'.

lag³ • n. Brit. informal a person who has repeatedly been sent to prison.

lager • n. a light fizzy beer.
– ORIGIN German *Lagerbier* 'beer brewed for keeping'.

laggard /lag-gerd/ • n. a person who falls behind other people.
– ORIGIN from **LAG¹**.

lagging • n. material providing protection against heat loss for a water tank or pipes.

lagoon • n. a stretch of salt water separated from the sea by a low sandbank or coral reef.
– ORIGIN Italian and Spanish *laguna*.

lah (also **la**) • n. Music the sixth note of a major scale, coming after 'soh' and before 'te'.
– ORIGIN from *labii*, taken from a Latin hymn.

laid past and past part. of **LAY¹**.

laid-back • adj. informal relaxed and easy-going.

lain past part. of **LIE¹**.

lair • n. **1** a wild animal's resting place. **2** a person's hiding place or den.
– ORIGIN Old English.

laird /rhymes with scared/ • n. (in Scotland) a person who owns a large estate.
– ORIGIN Scots form of **LORD**.

laissez-faire /less-ay-fair/ • n. a policy of leaving things to take their own course, without interfering.
– ORIGIN French, 'allow to do'.

laity /lay-i-ti/ • n. (**the laity**) people who do not belong to the clergy.
– ORIGIN from **LAY²**.

lake¹ • n. **1** a large area of water surrounded by land. **2** (**the Lakes**) = the **LAKE DISTRICT**.
– ORIGIN Latin *lacus* 'pool, lake'.

lake² • n. a purplish-red pigment originally made with a substance produced by an insect.
– ORIGIN from **LAC**.

Lake District • n. a region of lakes and mountains in Cumbria.

lam • v. (**lams, lamming, lammed**) informal hit hard or repeatedly.
– ORIGIN perh. Scandinavian.

lama /lah-muh/ • n. **1** a title given as a mark of respect to a spiritual leader in Tibetan Buddhism. **2** a Tibetan or Mongolian Buddhist monk.
– ORIGIN Tibetan, 'superior one'.

lamb • n. **1** a young sheep. **2** a good and gentle or innocent person. • v. (of a ewe) give birth to lambs.
– PHRASES **the Lamb of God** a title of Jesus.
– ORIGIN Old English.

lambada /lam-bah-duh/ • n. a fast Brazilian dance which couples perform in close physical contact.
– ORIGIN Portuguese, 'a beating'.

lambaste /lam-baysst/ (also **lambast** /lam-bast/) • v. (**lambastes** or **lambasts, lambasting, lambasted**) criticize harshly.
– ORIGIN from **LAM** + former *baste*, also meaning 'beat'.

lambent /lam-buhnt/ • adj. literary lit up or flickering with a soft glow.
– ORIGIN Latin *lambere* 'to lick'.

lame • adj. **1** walking with difficulty

because of an injury or illness affecting the leg or foot. **2** (of an explanation or excuse) unconvincing and feeble. **3** (of something meant to be entertaining) dull and uninspiring.
– DERIVATIVES **lamely** adv. **lameness** n.
– ORIGIN Old English.

lamé /lah-may/ • n. fabric with interwoven gold or silver threads.
– ORIGIN French.

lame duck • n. **1** an unsuccessful person or thing. **2** esp. N. Amer. an official in the final period of office, after the election of a successor.

lament /luh-ment/ • n. **1** a passionate expression of grief. **2** a song or poem expressing grief or regret. • v. **1** mourn a person's death. **2** (as adj. **lamented** or **late lamented**) a way of referring to a dead person. **3** express regret or disappointment about something.
– DERIVATIVES **lamentation** n.
– ORIGIN Latin *lamenta* 'weeping'.

lamentable /la-muhn-tuh-b'l/ • adj. very bad or regrettable.
– DERIVATIVES **lamentably** adv.

lamina /lam-i-nuh/ • n. (pl. **laminae** /lam-i-nee/) tech. a thin layer, plate, or scale of rock, tissue, or other material.
– DERIVATIVES **laminar** adj.
– ORIGIN Latin.

laminate • v. /lam-i-nayt/ (**laminates**, **laminating**, **laminated**) **1** cover a flat surface with a layer of protective material. **2** make something by sticking layers together. **3** split into layers or leaves. **4** beat or roll metal into thin plates. • n. /lam-i-nuht/ a laminated structure or material.
– DERIVATIVES **lamination** n.

Lammas /lam-muhss/ (also **Lammas Day**/) • n. the first day of August, formerly observed as harvest festival.
– ORIGIN Old English, 'loaf mass'.

lammergeier /lam-mer-gy-er/ (also **lammergeyer**) • n. a long-winged, long-tailed vulture, noted for dropping bones to break them and get at the marrow.
– ORIGIN German.

lamp • n. **1** an electric, oil, or gas device for giving light. **2** an electrical device producing radiation.
– ORIGIN Greek *lampas* 'torch'.

lampblack • n. a black pigment made from soot.

lampoon /lam-poon/ • v. publicly mock or ridicule someone. • n. a mocking attack.
– ORIGIN French *lampon*.

lamp post • n. a tall pole with a light at the top, used to light a street.

lamprey /lam-pri/ • n. (pl. **lampreys**) an eel-like jawless fish that has a sucker

mouth with horny teeth.
– ORIGIN Latin *lampreda*.

LAN • abbrev. local area network.

Lancastrian /lang-kass-tri-uhn/ • n. **1** a person from Lancashire or Lancaster. **2** a follower of the House of Lancaster in the Wars of the Roses. • adj. relating to Lancashire or Lancaster, or the House of Lancaster.

lance • n. **1** a long weapon with a wooden shaft and a pointed steel head, formerly used by people on horseback. **2** a metal pipe supplying a jet of oxygen to a furnace or to make a very hot flame for cutting. • v. (**lances**, **lancing**, **lanced**) **1** Med. prick or cut open a boil or wound with a sharp instrument. **2** pierce something.
– ORIGIN Latin *lancea*.

lance corporal • n. a rank of non-commissioned officer in the British army, above private and below corporal.

lanceolate /lahn-si-uh-luht/ • adj. tech. having a narrow oval shape tapering to a point at each end.
– ORIGIN Latin *lanceolatus*.

lancer • n. a cavalry soldier armed with a lance.

lancet /lahn-sit/ • n. a small, broad two-edged knife with a sharp point, used in surgery.
– ORIGIN Old French *lancette* 'small lance'.

lancet window • n. a narrow window with a pointed arch at the top.

Lancs. • abbrev. Lancashire.

land • n. **1** the part of the earth's surface that is not covered by water. **2** an area of ground in terms of its ownership or use: *waste land.* **3** (**the land**) ground or soil used for farming. **4** a country or state. • v. **1** arrive at the shore. **2** come down to the ground. **3** bring a fish out of the water with a net or rod. **4** informal succeed in obtaining or achieving something desirable. **5** (**land up**) reach a place or destination. **6** (**land up with**) end up with an unwelcome situation. **7** (**land someone in**) informal put someone in a difficult situation. **8** informal inflict a blow on someone.
– PHRASES **how the land lies** Brit. what the situation is.
– DERIVATIVES **landless** adj.
– ORIGIN Old English.

land agent • n. Brit. **1** a person employed to manage an estate on behalf of its owners. **2** a person who deals with the sale of land.

landau /lan-dor/ • n. a four-wheeled enclosed horse-drawn carriage.
– ORIGIN named after *Landau* in Germany, where it was first made.

landed •adj. owning much land.

landfall •n. an arrival at land on a sea or air journey.

landfill •n. **1** the disposal of waste material by burying it. **2** buried waste material.

landform •n. a natural feature of the earth's surface.

landing •n. **1** a place where people and goods can be landed from a boat. **2** a level area at the top of a staircase.

landing craft •n. a boat for putting troops and military equipment ashore on a beach.

landing gear •n. the undercarriage of an aircraft.

landing stage •n. a platform on to which passengers or cargo can be landed from a boat.

landlady •n. **1** a woman who rents out property or land. **2** Brit. a woman who runs a pub.

landline •n. a conventional telecommunications connection by cable laid across land.

landlocked •adj. almost or entirely surrounded by land.

landlord •n. **1** a man (in legal use also a woman) who rents out property or land. **2** Brit. a man who runs a pub.

landlubber •n. informal a person who is unfamiliar with the sea or sailing.
– ORIGIN from former *lubber* 'clumsy person'.

landmark •n. **1** an object or feature of a landscape or town that is easily seen from a distance. **2** an event, discovery, or change marking an important stage: *a landmark of research*.

land mass •n. a continent or other large body of land.

landmine •n. an explosive mine laid on or just under the surface of the ground.

landowner •n. a person who owns land.

landscape •n. **1** all the visible features of an area of land. **2** a picture of an area of countryside. •v. (**landscapes**, **landscaping**, **landscaped**) improve the appearance of a piece of land by changing its contours and planting trees and shrubs.
– ORIGIN Dutch *lantscap*.

landscape gardening •n. the art and practice of laying out grounds.

landslide •n. **1** (Brit. also **landslip**) a mass of earth or rock that slides down from a mountain or cliff. **2** an overwhelming majority of votes for one party in an election.

landward •adv. (also **landwards**) towards land. •adj. facing towards land rather than the sea.

lane •n. **1** a narrow road. **2** a division of a road for a single line of traffic. **3** each of a number of parallel strips of track or water for competitors in a race. **4** a course at sea or in the sky followed by ships or aircraft.
– ORIGIN Old English.

language •n. **1** the means of human communication, consisting of the use of spoken or written words in a structured way. **2** the system of communication used by a particular community or country. **3** a particular style of speaking or writing: *legal language*. **4** a system of symbols and rules for writing computer programs.
– ORIGIN Old French *langage*.

> ✓ Spell **language** with **-ua-** after the first **g**.

language laboratory •n. a room with audio and visual equipment for learning a foreign language.

languid /lang-gwid/ •adj. **1** relaxed and not inclined to be physically active. **2** weak or faint.
– DERIVATIVES **languidly** adv.

languish •v. **1** grow weak or feeble. **2** be kept in an unpleasant place or situation: *he was languishing in jail*.
– ORIGIN Old French *languir*.

languor /lang-ger/ •n. pleasurable inactivity.
– DERIVATIVES **languorous** adj.

lank •adj. (of hair) long, limp, and straight.
– ORIGIN Old English, 'thin'.

lanky •adj. awkwardly thin and tall.
– DERIVATIVES **lankiness** n.

lanolin •n. a fatty substance found naturally on sheep's wool and used to make ointments.
– ORIGIN from Latin *lana* 'wool' + *oleum* 'oil'.

lantern •n. **1** a lamp enclosed in a metal frame with glass panels. **2** the light chamber at the top of a lighthouse.
– ORIGIN Latin *lanterna*.

lantern-jawed •adj. having long, thin jaws.

lanthanum /lan-thuh-nuhm/ •n. a silvery-white metallic chemical element.
– ORIGIN Greek *lanthanein* 'escape notice'.

lanyard /lan-yerd/ •n. **1** a rope used to secure or raise and lower something such as a ship's sails. **2** a cord passed round the neck, shoulder, or wrist for holding a whistle or similar object.
– ORIGIN Old French *laniere*.

Laotian /lay-oh-shuhn/ •n. a person from the country of Laos in SE Asia.

•adj. relating to Laos.

lap¹ •n. the flat area between the waist and knees of a seated person.
– ORIGIN Old English, 'fold, flap'.

lap² •n. **1** one circuit of a track. **2** a part of a journey. **3** an overlapping or projecting part. •v. (**laps**, **lapping**, **lapped**) overtake a competitor in a race to become one or more laps ahead.
– ORIGIN from LAP¹.

lap³ •v. (**laps**, **lapping**, **lapped**) **1** (of an animal) take up liquid with the tongue. **2** (**lap something up**) accept something with obvious pleasure. **3** (of water) wash against something with a gentle rippling sound.
– ORIGIN Old English.

lap dance •n. an erotic dance or strip-tease performed near to or on the lap of a person watching.
– DERIVATIVES **lap dancer** n.

lapdog •n. **1** a small pampered pet dog. **2** a person who is completely under the influence of someone else.

lapel •n. the part which is folded back at the front opening of a jacket or coat.
– ORIGIN from LAP¹.

lapidary /la-pi-duh-ri/ •adj. **1** relating to the engraving, cutting, or polishing of stones and gems. **2** (of language) elegant and concise.
– ORIGIN Latin *lapidarius*.

lapis lazuli /la-piss laz-yuu-li/ (also **lapis**) •n. a bright blue rock used in jewellery.
– ORIGIN Latin, 'stone of lapis lazuli'.

lap of honour •n. a celebratory circuit of a sports field or track by the winning person or team.

Lapp •n. **1** a member of a people of the extreme north of Scandinavia. **2** the language of this people.
– ORIGIN Swedish.

> **USAGE:** Although the term **Lapp** is still very common, the people themselves prefer to be called **Sami**.

lappet /lap-pit/ •n. **1** a fold or hanging piece of flesh in some animals. **2** a loose or overlapping part of a garment.
– ORIGIN from LAP¹.

lapse •n. **1** a brief failure of concentration, memory, or judgement. **2** a decline from previously high standards. **3** a period of time between two events. •v. (**lapses**, **lapsing**, **lapsed**) **1** (of a right or agreement) become invalid because it is not used or renewed. **2** cease to follow the rules of a religion. **3** (**lapse into**) pass gradually into a quieter or weaker state.
– ORIGIN Latin *lapsus*.

laptop •n. a portable computer.

lapwing •n. a large crested plover with a dark green back and a black-and-white head.
– ORIGIN Old English.

larboard /lar-bord, lar-berd/ •n. Naut. old use = PORT³.
– ORIGIN from former *lade* 'load a ship', referring to the side on which cargo was loaded.

larceny /lar-suh-ni/ •n. (pl. **larcenies**) N. Amer. or dated theft of personal property.
– ORIGIN Old French *larcin*.

larch •n. a coniferous tree with bunches of bright green needles and hard wood.
– ORIGIN High German *larche*.

lard •n. fat from the abdomen of a pig, used in cooking. •v. **1** insert strips of fat or bacon in meat before cooking. **2** add technical or obscure expressions to talk or writing.
– DERIVATIVES **lardy** adj.
– ORIGIN Latin *lardum*.

larder •n. a room or large cupboard for storing food.
– ORIGIN Latin *lardarium*.

large •adj. **1** relatively great in size, extent, or capacity. **2** of wide range or scope. •v. (**larges**, **larging**, **larged**) (**large it**) Brit. informal go out and have a good time.
– PHRASES **at large 1** escaped or not yet captured. **2** as a whole.
– DERIVATIVES **largeness** n.
– ORIGIN Latin *larga* 'copious'.

large intestine •n. Anat. the caecum, colon, and rectum as a whole.

largely •adv. on the whole; mostly.

large-scale •adj. extensive.

largesse /lar-zhess/ (also **largess**) •n. **1** generosity. **2** money or gifts given generously.
– ORIGIN Old French.

largo /lar-goh/ •adv. & adj. Music in a slow tempo and dignified style.
– ORIGIN Italian.

lariat /la-ri-uht/ •n. a rope used as a lasso or for tethering animals.
– ORIGIN from Spanish *la reata*.

lark¹ •n. a brown songbird that sings in flight.
– ORIGIN Old English.

lark² informal •n. **1** an enjoyable adventure or escapade. **2** Brit. an activity regarded as foolish or a waste of time: *he's serious about this music lark.* •v. (**lark about/ around**) Brit. behave in a playful and mischievous way.
– ORIGIN perh. from dialect *lake* 'play'.

larva /lar-vuh/ •n. (pl. **larvae** /lar-vee/) an active immature form of an insect or other animal that undergoes metamorphosis, e.g. a caterpillar.

– DERIVATIVES **larval** adj.
– ORIGIN Latin, 'ghost, mask'.

laryngitis /la-rin-**jy**-tiss/ • n. inflammation of the larynx.

larynx /**la**-ringks/ • n. (pl. **larynxes** or **larynges** /luh-**rin**-jeez/) the hollow muscular organ forming an air passage to the lungs and containing the vocal cords.
– ORIGIN Greek *larunx*.

lasagne /luh-**zan**-yuh, luh-**zahn**-yuh/ • n. **1** pasta in the form of wide strips. **2** an Italian dish consisting of this baked with meat or vegetables and a cheese sauce.
– ORIGIN Italian.

lascivious /luh-**siv**-i-uhss/ • adj. feeling or showing an open or offensive sexual desire.
– DERIVATIVES **lasciviously** adv.
– ORIGIN Latin *lascivia* 'lustfulness'.

laser • n. a device that produces an intense narrow beam of light.
– ORIGIN from the initial letters of *light amplification (by) stimulated emission (of) radiation*.

laserdisc • n. a disc resembling a large compact disc, used for high-quality video and for interactive multimedia.

laser printer • n. a computer printer in which a laser is used to form a pattern on a light-sensitive drum, which attracts toner.

lash • v. **1** beat a person or animal with a whip or stick. **2** beat against: *waves lashed the coast.* **3** (**lash out**) launch an attack with words or punches. **4** (of an animal) move the tail quickly and violently. **5** fasten something securely with a cord or rope. • n. **1** a sharp blow or stroke with a whip or stick. **2** the flexible part of a whip. **3** an eyelash.

lashings • pl. n. Brit. informal a large amount of food or drink.

lass (also **lassie**) • n. Scottish & N. English a girl or young woman.
– ORIGIN Old Norse, 'unmarried'.

Lassa fever /**lass**-uh/ • n. an often fatal disease transmitted by a virus and occurring chiefly in West Africa.
– ORIGIN named after the village of *Lassa* in Nigeria.

lassitude /**lass**-i-tyood/ • n. physical or mental weariness; lack of energy.
– ORIGIN Latin *lassitudo*.

lasso /luh-**soo**/ • n. (pl. **lassos**) a rope with a noose at one end, used for catching cattle. • v. (**lassoes, lassoing, lassoed**) catch an animal with a lasso.
– ORIGIN Spanish *lazo*.

last¹ • adj. **1** coming after all other people or things in time or order. **2** most recent.

3 lowest in importance or rank. **4** (**the last**) the least likely or suitable. **5** only remaining. • adv. on the last occasion before the present: *a woman last heard of in Cornwall.* • n. (pl. **last**) **1** the last person or thing. **2** (**the last of**) the only remaining part of.
– PHRASES **at last** (or **at long last**) in the end; eventually. **the last minute** the latest possible time before an event. **the last word 1** a final statement on a subject. **2** the most modern or advanced example of something: *the new flat is the last word in luxury.* **to the last** up to the final moment.
– ORIGIN Old English.

last² • v. **1** continue for a specified period of time. **2** remain operating or usable for a considerable or specified length of time. **3** (of provisions or resources) be enough for someone for a specified length of time: *enough food to last him for three months.*
– ORIGIN Old English.

last³ • n. a shaped stand or block used by a shoemaker for shaping or repairing a shoe or boot.
– ORIGIN Old English.

last-ditch • adj. referring to a final desperate attempt to achieve something.

last-gasp • adj. informal done or happening at the last possible moment.

lasting • adj. enduring for a long time: *a lasting impression.*

Last Judgement • n. the judgement of humankind expected in some religions to take place at the end of the world.

lastly • adv. in the last place; last.

last name • n. a person's surname.

last post • n. (in the British armed forces) the second of two bugle calls signalling the end of the day, played also at military funerals and acts of remembrance.

last rites • pl. n. (in the Christian Church) rites administered to a person who is about to die.

lat. • abbrev. latitude.

latch • n. **1** a bar with a catch and lever used for fastening a door or gate. **2** a spring lock for an outer door, which can only be opened from the outside with a key. • v. **1** fasten a door or gate with a latch. **2** (**latch on to**) informal associate yourself enthusiastically with.
– PHRASES **on the latch** esp. Brit. (of a door or gate) closed but not locked.
– ORIGIN Old English, 'to grasp'.

late • adj. **1** acting, arriving, or happening after the proper or usual time. **2** belonging or taking place far on in a

particular time or period. **3** far on in the day or night. **4** (**the/a person's late**) (of a person) no longer alive: *her late husband.* **5** (**latest**) of most recent date or origin. • adv. **1** after the proper or usual time. **2** towards the end of a period. **3** far on in the day or night. **4** (**later**) at a time in the near future; afterwards. • n. (**the latest**) the most recent news or fashion.
– PHRASES **of late** recently.
– DERIVATIVES **lateness** n. **latish** (also **lateish**) adj.
– ORIGIN Old English.

latecomer • n. a person who arrives late.

lateen sail /la-teen/ • n. a triangular sail set at an angle of 45° to the mast.
– ORIGIN from French *voile Latine* 'Latin sail'.

lately • adv. recently; not long ago.

latent • adj. existing but not yet developed, apparent, or active: *her latent talent.*
– DERIVATIVES **latency** n.
– ORIGIN Latin *latere* 'be hidden'.

lateral /lat-uh-ruhl/ • adj. relating to, towards, or from the side or sides: *lateral roots.*
– DERIVATIVES **laterally** adv.
– ORIGIN Latin *lateralis.*

lateral thinking • n. esp. Brit. the solving of problems by an indirect and creative approach.

latex /lay-teks/ • n. **1** a milky fluid found in many plants, which thickens on exposure to the air. **2** a synthetic product resembling this, used to make paints, coatings, etc.
– ORIGIN Latin, 'liquid, fluid'.

lath /lath/ • n. (pl. **laths** /laths/) a thin, flat strip of wood.
– ORIGIN Old English.

lathe /rhymes with bathe/ • n. a machine for shaping wood or metal by means of a rotating drive which turns the piece being worked on against different cutting tools.
– ORIGIN prob. from Danish *lad* 'frame'.

lather /lah-*ther*, la-*ther*/ • n. **1** a frothy mass of bubbles produced by soap when mixed with water. **2** heavy sweat visible on a horse's coat as a white foam.
• v. (**lathers, lathering, lathered**) **1** form a lather. **2** rub something with soap until a lather is produced. **3** spread a sub-stance generously over an area.
– ORIGIN Old English.

Latin • n. the language of ancient Rome and its empire. • adj. relating to the Latin language.
– ORIGIN Latin *Latinus* 'of Latium' (an ancient region in central Italy).

Latin American • adj. relating to the parts of the American continent where Spanish or Portuguese is the national language. • n. a person from this region.

Latinate /lat-i-nayt/ • adj. (of language) having the character of Latin.

Latino /luh-tee-noh/ • n. (pl. **Latinos**; fem. **Latina**, pl. **Latinas**) N. Amer. a Latin American inhabitant of the United States.
– ORIGIN Latin American Spanish.

latitude /la-ti-tyood/ • n. **1** the distance of a place north or south of the equator. **2** (**latitudes**) regions with reference to their temperature and distance from the equator: *northern latitudes.* **3** scope for freedom of action or thought.
– DERIVATIVES **latitudinal** adj.
– ORIGIN Latin *latitudo* 'breadth'.

latrine /luh-treen/ • n. a communal toilet in a camp or barracks.
– ORIGIN Latin *latrina.*

latte /lat-tay/ • n. a drink of frothy steamed milk to which a shot of espresso coffee is added.
– ORIGIN Italian.

latter • adj. **1** nearer to the end than to the beginning. **2** recent: *in latter years.* **3** (**the latter**) referring to the second-mentioned of two people or things.
– ORIGIN Old English, 'slower'.

latter-day • adj. modern or contem-porary: *a latter-day Noah.*

Latter-Day Saints • pl. n. the Mormons' name for themselves.

latterly • adv. **1** recently. **2** in the later stages of a period of time.

lattice • n. a structure or pattern consisting of strips crossing each other with square or diamond-shaped spaces left between.
– DERIVATIVES **latticed** adj. **latticework** n.
– ORIGIN Old French *lattis.*

laud /lawd/ • v. formal praise someone highly.
– ORIGIN Latin *laudare.*

laudable • adj. deserving praise.

laudanum /law-duh-nuhm/ • n. a solution prepared from opium and formerly used as a painkiller.
– ORIGIN Latin.

laudatory /law-duh-tuh-ri/ • adj. expressing praise.

laugh • v. **1** make the sounds and movements that express great amusement. **2** (**laugh at**) make fun of. **3** (**laugh something off**) dismiss something by treating it light-heartedly. • n. **1** an act of laughing. **2** (**a laugh**) informal something that makes people laugh.
– PHRASES **have the last laugh** eventually be proved to be right or at an advantage.
– ORIGIN Old English.

laughable • adj. so ridiculous as to be amusing.
– DERIVATIVES **laughably** adv.

laughing gas • n. non-technical term for NITROUS OXIDE.

laughing stock • n. a person who is ridiculed by everyone.

laughter • n. the action or sound of laughing.

launch¹ • v. 1 move a boat or ship from land into the water. 2 send a rocket or other missile on its course. 3 hurl forcefully. 4 begin or introduce an enterprise or a new product. 5 (**launch into**) begin something energetically and enthusiastically. • n. an act of launching.
– ORIGIN Old French *launcher*.

launch² • n. a large motor boat.
– ORIGIN Spanish *lancha* 'pinnace'.

launcher • n. a structure that holds a rocket or missile during launching.

launder • v. (**launders, laundering, laundered**) 1 wash and iron clothes or linen. 2 informal pass illegally obtained money through legitimate businesses or foreign banks to conceal its origins.
– ORIGIN Latin *lavanda* 'things to be washed'.

launderette (also **laundrette**) • n. Brit. a place with coin-operated washing machines and dryers for public use.

laundress • n. a woman employed to launder clothes and linen.

laundry • n. (pl. **laundries**) 1 clothes and linen that need to be washed or that have been newly washed. 2 a room or building where clothes and linen are washed and ironed.

laureate /lo-ri-uht/ • n. a person given an award for outstanding creative or intellectual achievement.
– ORIGIN Latin *laurea* 'laurel wreath'.

laurel • n. 1 an evergreen shrub or small tree with dark green glossy leaves. 2 (**laurels**) a crown woven from bay leaves and awarded in classical times as a sign of victory or mark of honour. 3 (**laurels**) honour or praise.
– PHRASES **rest on your laurels** be so satisfied with what you have already achieved that you make no further effort.
– ORIGIN Latin *laurus*.

lava • n. hot molten rock that erupts from a volcano or fissure, or solid rock formed when this cools.
– ORIGIN Italian.

lava lamp • n. a transparent electric lamp containing a thick liquid in which a suspended waxy substance rises and falls in constantly changing shapes.

lavatorial • adj. esp. Brit. (of conversation or humour) referring to lavatories and excretion.

lavatory • n. (pl. **lavatories**) a toilet.
– ORIGIN Latin *lavatorium* 'place for washing'.

lavender • n. 1 a small strong-smelling shrub with narrow leaves and bluish-purple flowers. 2 a pale bluish-mauve colour.
– ORIGIN Latin *lavandula*.

lavender water • n. a perfume made from lavender.

lavish • adj. 1 very rich, elaborate, or luxurious. 2 giving or given in great amounts. • v. (**lavish something on**) give something in generous or extravagant quantities to: *he lavished praise on the band.*
– DERIVATIVES **lavishly** adv.
– ORIGIN Old French *lavasse* 'deluge of rain'.

law • n. 1 a rule or system of rules recognized by a country or community as governing the actions of its members. 2 such rules as a subject of study or as the basis of the legal profession. 3 a rule that controls correct behaviour in a sport. 4 a statement of the fact that a particular phenomenon always occurs if certain conditions are present: *the second law of thermodynamics.*
– PHRASES **lay down the law** issue instructions in an authoritative way.
– ORIGIN Old Norse, 'something fixed'.

law-abiding • adj. obeying the laws of a society.

lawbreaker • n. a person who breaks the law.

law court • n. a court of law.

lawful • adj. allowed by or obeying the law or a set of rules.
– DERIVATIVES **lawfully** adv.

lawless • adj. not governed by or obedient to the law or a set of rules.
– DERIVATIVES **lawlessness** n.

law lord • n. (in the UK) a member of the House of Lords qualified to perform its legal work.

lawmaker • n. a member of a government who makes laws.

lawn¹ • n. an area of mown grass in a garden or park.
– ORIGIN Old French *launde* 'wooded district, heath'.

lawn² • n. a fine linen or cotton fabric.
– ORIGIN prob. from *Laon*, a French city important for linen manufacture.

lawnmower • n. a machine for cutting the grass on a lawn.

lawn tennis • n. dated or formal tennis.

law of averages • n. the supposed principle that future events are likely to balance any past events.

lawrencium /lo-ren-si-uhm/ • n. a very unstable chemical element made by high-energy collisions.
– ORIGIN named after the American physicist Ernest O. *Lawrence*.

lawsuit • n. a claim brought to a law court to be decided.

lawyer • n. a person who practises law.

lax • adj. **1** not strict, severe, or careful enough. **2** (of limbs or muscles) relaxed.
– DERIVATIVES **laxity** n.
– ORIGIN Latin *laxus* 'loose, lax'.

laxative • n. a medicine that causes a person to empty their bowels.
– ORIGIN Latin *laxare* 'loosen'.

lay¹ • v. (**lays, laying, laid**) **1** put down gently or carefully. **2** put something down and set it in position for use: *have your carpet laid by a professional.* **3** assign or place: *lay the blame.* **4** (**lay something before**) present information or evidence to someone. **5** (of a female bird, reptile, etc.) produce an egg from inside the body. **6** stake an amount of money in a bet. • n. the general appearance of an area of land.
– PHRASES **lay something down 1** draw up and enforce a rule or principle. **2** build up a deposit of a substance. **3** store wine in a cellar. **4** pay or bet money. **lay something in/up** build up a stock in case of need. **lay someone off** discharge a worker because of a shortage of work. **lay something on** Brit. provide a service or amenity. **lay something out 1** construct or arrange buildings or gardens according to a plan. **2** arrange and present material for printing. **lay someone up** put someone out of action through illness or injury.
– ORIGIN Old English.

> **USAGE:** Make sure that you use the words **lay** and **lie** correctly. **Lay** generally means 'put something down', as in *they are going to lay the carpet,* whereas **lie** means 'be in a horizontal position to rest', as in *why don't you lie down?* The past tense and past participle of **lay** is **laid,** as in *they laid the carpet;* the past tense of **lie** is **lay** (*he lay on the floor*) and the past participle is **lain** (*she had lain awake for hours*).

lay² • adj. **1** not belonging to the clergy. **2** not having particular professional qualifications or expert knowledge.
– ORIGIN Latin *laicus.*

lay³ • n. a short lyric or narrative poem intended to be sung.
– ORIGIN Old French *lai.*

lay⁴ past of **LIE¹.**

layabout • n. derog., esp. Brit. a person who does little or no work.

lay-by • n. (pl. **lay-bys**) Brit. an area at the side of a road where vehicles may pull off the road and stop.

layer • n. **1** a sheet or thickness of material covering a surface. **2** (in combination) a person or thing that lays something: *a cable-layer.* • v. (**layers, layering, layered**) arrange or cut something in a layer or layers.
– ORIGIN from **LAY¹.**

layette • n. a set of clothing and bed-clothes for a newborn child.
– ORIGIN French.

layman (or **laywoman** or **layperson**) • n. (pl. **laymen, laywomen, laypersons,** or **laypeople**) **1** a member of a Church who is not a priest or minister. **2** a person without a particular professional or specialized knowledge.

lay-off • n. **1** a discharge of a worker or workers because of a shortage of work. **2** a temporary break from an activity.

layout • n. **1** the way in which some-thing, especially a page, is laid out. **2** a thing set out in a particular way.

lay reader • n. (in the Anglican Church) a layperson licensed to preach and to conduct some services.

laywoman • n. see **LAYMAN.**

laze • v. (**lazes, lazing, lazed**) spend time relaxing or doing very little.

lazy • adj. (**lazier, laziest**) **1** unwilling to work or use energy. **2** showing a lack of effort or care.
– DERIVATIVES **lazily** adv. **laziness** n.
– ORIGIN perh. from German *lasich* 'languid, idle'.

lazy eye • n. an eye with poor vision due to lack of use.

lb • abbrev. pound(s) (in weight).
– ORIGIN from Latin *libra.*

lbw • abbrev. Cricket leg before wicket.

LCD • abbrev. **1** Electron. & Computing liquid crystal display. **2** Math. lowest (or least) common denominator.

LCM • abbrev. Math. lowest (or least) common multiple.

LEA • abbrev. (in the UK) Local Education Authority.

lea • n. literary an open area of grassy land.
– ORIGIN Old English.

leach • v. (of a soluble substance) drain away from soil or other material by the action of water passing through it.
– ORIGIN Old English, 'to water'.

lead¹ /leed/ • v. (**leads, leading, led**) **1** cause a person or animal to go with you. **2** be a route or means of access: *the street led into the square.* **3** (**lead to**) result in. **4** influence someone to do or believe something. **5** be in charge of other people. **6** have the advantage in a

race or game. **7** be superior to a competitor. **8** have a particular way of life. **9** (**lead up to**) come before or result in. **10** (**lead someone on**) deceive someone into believing that you are attracted to them. •n. **1** an example for other people to follow: *others followed our lead.* **2** (**the lead**) a position of advantage in a contest. **3** the chief part in a play or film. **4** a clue to be followed in solving a problem. **5** Brit. a strap or cord for restraining and guiding a dog. **6** Brit. a wire taking electric current from a source to an appliance, or connecting two points of a circuit together. •adj. playing the chief part in a musical group: *the lead singer.*
– PHRASES **lead someone up the garden path** informal give misleading clues or signals to someone.
– ORIGIN Old English.

lead² /led/ •n. **1** a heavy bluish-grey metallic element. **2** graphite used as the part of a pencil that makes a mark.
– ORIGIN Old English.

leaded •adj. **1** framed, covered, or weighted with lead. **2** (of petrol) containing lead.

leaden •adj. **1** dull, heavy, or slow. **2** dull grey: *a leaden sky.*

leader •n. **1** a person or thing that leads. **2** a person or thing that is the most successful or advanced in a particular area. **3** the main player in a music group. **4** Brit. a leading article in a newspaper.
– DERIVATIVES **leadership** n.

leading /lee-ding/ •adj. most important or in first place: *leading politicians.*

leading article •n. Brit. a newspaper article giving the editor's opinion.

leading light •n. a person who is important or inspiring in a particular field or organization.

leading question •n. a question that prompts the answer wanted.

leaf •n. (pl. **leaves**) **1** a flat green structure that grows from the stem of a plant. **2** the state of having leaves: *the trees were in leaf.* **3** a single sheet of paper. **4** gold, silver, or other metal in the form of very thin foil. **5** a hinged or detachable part of a table. •v. **1** (of a plant) put out new leaves. **2** (**leaf through**) turn over the pages of something, reading them quickly or casually.
– PHRASES **turn over a new leaf** start to act or behave in a better way.
– ORIGIN Old English.

leaflet •n. **1** a printed sheet of paper containing information or advertising. **2** a small leaf. •v. (**leaflets, leafleted,**

leafleting) distribute leaflets to.

leafy •adj. (**leafier, leafiest**) **1** having many leaves. **2** full of trees and shrubs: *a leafy avenue.*

league¹ •n. **1** a collection of people, countries, or groups that combine to help or protect each other. **2** a group of sports clubs which play each other over a period for a championship. **3** a class of quality or excellence: *the two men were not in the same league.*
– PHRASES **in league** (of two or more people) plotting with each other.
– ORIGIN Italian *lega.*

league² •n. a former measure of distance, usually about three miles.
– ORIGIN Latin *leuga, leuca.*

league table •n. Brit. **1** a list of the competitors in a league ranked according to performance. **2** a list in order of merit or achievement.

leak •v. **1** (of a container or covering) accidentally allow contents to escape or enter through a hole or crack. **2** (of a liquid or gas) escape or enter accidentally through a hole or crack. **3** deliberately give out secret information. •n. **1** a hole or crack through which contents leak. **2** an instance of leaking.
– DERIVATIVES **leakage** n. **leaky** adj.
– ORIGIN prob. from German or Dutch.

lean¹ •v. (**leans, leaning, leaned** or Brit. **leant**) **1** be in or move into a sloping position. **2** (**lean against/on**) slope and rest against. **3** (**lean on**) rely on someone for support. **4** (**lean to/towards**) favour a point of view.
– ORIGIN Old English.

lean² •adj. **1** (of a person) having little fat; thin. **2** (of meat) containing little fat. **3** (of a period of time) difficult and unprofitable. **4** informal (of an industry or company) efficient. •n. the part of a cut of meat that has little fat.
– DERIVATIVES **leanness** n.
– ORIGIN Old English.

leaning •n. a tendency or preference: *communist leanings.*

lean-to •n. (pl. **lean-tos**) a small building sharing a wall with a larger building and having a roof that leans against it.

leap •v. (**leaps, leaping, leaped** or **leapt**) **1** jump high or a long way. **2** move quickly and suddenly: *Polly leapt to her feet.* **3** (**leap at**) accept something eagerly. **4** increase dramatically. •n. **1** an act of leaping. **2** a sudden change or increase.
– PHRASES **a leap in the dark** a daring step or enterprise with an unpredictable outcome. **by** (or **in**) **leaps and bounds** with very rapid progress.

– ORIGIN Old English.

leapfrog • n. a game in which people take it in turns to vault over other players who are bending down.
• v. (**leapfrogs, leapfrogging, leapfrogged**) 1 perform such a vault. 2 reach a leading position by overtaking other people.

leap year • n. a year, occurring once every four years, which has 366 days.

learn • v. (**learns, learning, learned** or **learnt**) 1 gain knowledge of or skill in something through study or experience or by being taught. 2 become aware of something through receiving information or through observation. 3 memorize something.
– DERIVATIVES **learner** n.
– ORIGIN Old English.

learned /ler-nid/ • adj. having gained much knowledge by study.

learning • n. knowledge or skills gained through study or by being taught.

learning curve • n. the rate of a person's progress in gaining experience or new skills.

learning difficulties • pl. n. Brit. difficulties in gaining knowledge and skills to the normal level expected of people of the same age.

> USAGE: The term **learning difficulties** covers general conditions such as Down's syndrome as well as more specific conditions such as dyslexia. In Britain, it has now replaced terms such as **mentally handicapped** in official situations.

lease • n. a contract by which one party lets land, property, or services to another for a specified time, in return for payment. • v. (**leases, leasing, leased**) let or rent something on lease.
– PHRASES **a new lease of life** a chance to live or last longer, or to have an improved quality of life.
– ORIGIN Old French *lesser*.

leasehold • n. the holding of property by a lease.

leash • n. a dog's lead.
– ORIGIN Old French *laissier* 'let an animal run on a slack lead'.

least • det. & pron. (usu. **the least**) smallest in amount, extent, or significance. • adv. to the smallest extent or degree.
– PHRASES **at least** 1 not less than. 2 if nothing else. 3 anyway. **at the least** (or **very least**) 1 not less than. 2 taking the most unfavourable view. **not least** notably; in particular.
– ORIGIN Old English.

leastways • adv. dialect or informal at least.

leather • n. 1 a material made from the skin of an animal by tanning or a similar process. 2 (**leathers**) leather clothes worn by a motorcyclist.
– ORIGIN Old English.

leatherjacket • n. Brit. the tough-skinned larva of a large crane fly.

leathery • adj. having a tough, hard texture like leather.

leave[1] • v. (**leaves, leaving, left**) 1 go away from. 2 stop living at: *he left home at 16.* 3 stop attending or working for. 4 go away without taking something; allow to remain. 5 (**be left**) remain to be used or dealt with. 6 cause to be in a particular state or position: *leave the door open.* 7 let someone do something without helping or interfering. 8 (**leave something to**) entrust a decision or action to someone. 9 deposit something to be collected or attended to.
– PHRASES **leave someone/thing be** informal avoid disturbing or interfering with someone or something. **leave off** stop doing something. **leave someone/thing out** fail to include someone or something.
– DERIVATIVES **leaver** n.
– ORIGIN Old English.

leave[2] • n. 1 (also **leave of absence**) time when you have permission to be absent from work or duty. 2 formal permission: *seeking leave to appeal.*
– PHRASES **take your leave** formal say goodbye.
– ORIGIN Old English.

leaven /lev-uhn/ • n. a substance added to dough to make it ferment and rise. • v. 1 (as adj. **leavened**) (of dough or bread) fermented by adding leaven. 2 make less serious or dull: *the debate was leavened by humour.*
– ORIGIN Latin *levamen* 'relief'.

leaves pl. of LEAF.

leave-taking • n. an act of saying goodbye.

leavings • pl. n. things that have been left as worthless.

Lebanese /le-buh-neez/ • n. (pl. **Lebanese**) a person from Lebanon. • adj. relating to Lebanon.

lecher • n. a lecherous man.
– DERIVATIVES • **lechery** n.

lecherous • adj. showing excessive or offensive sexual desire.
– ORIGIN Old French *lecheros.*

lectern /lek-tern/ • n. a tall stand with a sloping top from which a speaker can read while standing up.
– ORIGIN Latin *lectrum.*

lecture • n. 1 an educational talk to an audience. 2 a lengthy reprimand. • v. (**lectures, lecturing, lectured**) 1 give an educational talk or series of talks.

2 criticize or reprimand someone.
– DERIVATIVES **lecturer** n. **lectureship** n.
– ORIGIN Latin *lectura*.

LED • abbrev. light-emitting diode, a semiconductor diode which glows when a voltage is applied.

led past and past part. of LEAD[1].

ledge • n. **1** a narrow horizontal surface sticking out from a wall, cliff, or other vertical surface. **2** an underwater ridge.
– ORIGIN perh. from LAY[1].

ledger • n. a book in which financial accounts are kept.
– ORIGIN prob. from LAY[1] and LIE[1].

ledger line (also **leger line**) • n. Music a short line added for notes above or below the range of a stave.

lee • n. **1** (also **lee side**) the side sheltered from the wind. Contrasted with WEATHER. **2** shelter from wind or weather given by an object.
– ORIGIN Old English, 'shelter'.

leech • n. **1** a worm that sucks the blood of animals or people. **2** a person who makes a profit from or lives off other people.
– ORIGIN Old English.

leek • n. a vegetable related to the onion, with flat overlapping leaves forming a long cylindrical bulb.
– ORIGIN Old English.

leer • v. (**leers**, **leering**, **leered**) look or gaze in a lustful or unpleasant way. • n. a lustful or unpleasant look.
– ORIGIN perh. from Old English, 'cheek'.

leery • adj. (**leerier**, **leeriest**) cautious or wary.
– ORIGIN from LEER.

lees /leez/ • pl. n. the sediment found in the bottom of a bottle or barrel of wine.
– ORIGIN Latin *liae*.

leeward /lee-werd, loo-erd/ • adj. & adv. on or towards the side sheltered from the wind or towards which the wind is blowing. Contrasted with WINDWARD.

leeway • n. the amount of freedom available to you to move or act: *we have a lot of leeway in how we do our jobs.*

left[1] • adj. **1** on or towards the side of a person or of a thing which is to the west when the person or thing is facing north. **2** relating to a left-wing person or group. • adv. on or to the left side. • n. **1** (**the left**) the left-hand side or direction. **2** a left turn. **3** a person's left fist, or a blow given with it. **4** (**the Left**) a left-wing group or party.
– DERIVATIVES **leftward** adj. & adv.
– ORIGIN Old English, 'weak'.

left[2] past and past part. of LEAVE[1].

left-field • adj. informal unconventional or experimental.

left hand • n. the region or direction on the left side. • adj. (**left-hand**) **1** on or towards the left side. **2** done with or using the left hand.

left-hand drive • n. a motor-vehicle steering system with the steering wheel and other controls fitted on the left side.

left-handed • adj. **1** using or done with the left hand. **2** turning to the left.

left-hander • n. **1** a left-handed person. **2** a blow struck with a person's left hand.

leftie • n. var. of LEFTY.

leftism • n. the political views or policies of the Left.
– DERIVATIVES **leftist** n. & adj.

left luggage • n. Brit. travellers' luggage left in temporary storage at a railway station, bus station, or airport.

leftovers • pl. n. food remaining after the rest has been used.

left wing • n. **1** the radical, reforming, or socialist section of a political party. [ORIGIN with reference to the National Assembly in France (1789–91), where the nobles sat to the president's right and the commoners to the left.] **2** the left side of a sports team on the field.
– DERIVATIVES **left-winger** n.

lefty (also **leftie**) • n. (pl. **lefties**) informal, esp. Brit. a left-wing person.

leg • n. **1** each of the limbs on which a person or animal moves and stands. **2** a long, thin support or prop, especially of a chair or table. **3** a section of a journey, process, or race. **4** (in sport) each of two or more games or stages that make up a round or match.
– PHRASES **leg before wicket** Cricket (of a batsman) judged to be out through obstructing the ball with the leg when the ball would otherwise have hit the wicket. **leg it** Brit. informal **1** travel by foot. **2** run away. **not have a leg to stand on** not be able to give reasons for your arguments or actions. **on your** (or **its**) **last legs** exhausted or worn out.
– ORIGIN Old Norse.

legacy • n. (pl. **legacies**) **1** an amount of money or property left to someone in a will. **2** something handed down by a predecessor.
– ORIGIN Old French *legacie*.

legal • adj. **1** relating to or required by the law. **2** permitted by law.
– DERIVATIVES **legally** adv.
– ORIGIN Latin *legalis*.

legal aid • n. payment from public funds given to people who cannot afford to pay for legal advice.

legalese /lee-guh-**leez**/ • n. informal the formal and technical language of legal documents.

legality • n. (pl. **legalities**) **1** the state of being legal. **2** (**legalities**) rules and obligations imposed by law.

legalize (or **legalise**) • v. (**legalizes**, **legalizing**, **legalized**) make something legal.
– DERIVATIVES **legalization** n.

legal tender • n. coins or banknotes that must be accepted if offered in payment of a debt.

legate /**leg**-uht/ • n. a member of the clergy who represents the Pope.
– ORIGIN Latin *legatus*.

legation /li-**gay**-sh'n/ • n. **1** a diplomatic minister and staff. **2** the official residence of a diplomat.

legato /li-**gah**-toh/ • adv. & adj. Music in a smooth, flowing way.
– ORIGIN Italian, 'bound'.

legend • n. **1** a traditional story from the past which may or may not be true. **2** a very famous person: *a screen legend.* **3** an inscription, caption, or key.
– ORIGIN Latin *legenda* 'things to be read'.

legendary • adj. **1** relating to traditional stories from the past. **2** remarkable enough to be famous.

legerdemain /**lej**-er-di-**mayn**/ • n. **1** skilful use of your hands when performing conjuring tricks. **2** trickery.
– ORIGIN from French *léger de main* 'dexterous'

leggings • pl. n. **1** tight-fitting stretchy trousers worn by women. **2** strong protective coverings for the legs from knee to ankle.

leggy • adj. (**leggier**, **leggiest**) **1** long-legged. **2** (of a plant) having a long, straggly stem or stems.

legible • adj. (of handwriting or print) clear enough to read.
– DERIVATIVES **legibility** n. **legibly** adv.
– ORIGIN Latin *legibilis*.

legion • n. **1** a division of 3,000–6,000 men in the army of ancient Rome. **2** (a **legion**/**legions of**) a vast number of people or things. • adj. great in number: *her fans are legion.*
– ORIGIN Latin.

legionary • n. (pl. **legionaries**) a soldier in an ancient Roman legion.

legionnaire /lee-juh-**nair**/ • n. a member of the Foreign Legion, or of an association of former servicemen and servicewomen.

legionnaires' disease • n. a form of pneumonia spread chiefly in water droplets through air conditioning systems.

– ORIGIN because identified after an outbreak at an American Legion meeting.

leg iron • n. a metal band or chain placed around a prisoner's ankle as a restraint.

legislate /**lej**-iss-layt/ • v. (**legislates**, **legislating**, **legislated**) **1** make laws. **2** (**legislate for/against**) prepare for or try to prevent a situation.

legislation • n. laws as a whole.
– ORIGIN Latin.

legislative /**lej**-iss-luh-tiv/ • adj. **1** having the power to make laws. **2** relating to laws or a law-making body.

legislator • n. a person who makes laws.

legislature /**lej**-iss-luh-cher/ • n. the law-making body of a state.

legitimate • adj. /li-**jit**-i-muht/ **1** allowed by the law or rules. **2** able to be defended; reasonable: *a legitimate excuse.* **3** (of a child) born of parents who are lawfully married to each other.
• v. /li-**jit**-i-mayt/ (**legitimates**, **legitimating**, **legitimated**) make something obey the law or rules.
– DERIVATIVES **legitimacy** n. **legitimately** adv. **legitimation** n.
– ORIGIN Latin *legitimare*.

> ✓ **legitimate** begins with **leg-** and ends with **-ate**.

legitimize /li-**jit**-i-myz/ (or **legitimise**) • v. (**legitimizes**, **legitimizing**, **legitimized**) make something conform to the law or rules.
– DERIVATIVES **legitimization** n.

legless • adj. **1** having no legs. **2** Brit. informal very drunk.

legroom • n. space in which a seated person can put their legs.

legume /**leg**-yoom/ • n. a plant of the pea family grown as a crop.
– ORIGIN Latin *legumen*.

leguminous /li-**gyoo**-mi-nuhss/ • adj. relating to plants that bear their seeds in pods, such as peas.

leg warmers • pl. n. a pair of knitted garments covering the legs from ankle to knee or thigh.

legwork • n. work that involves tiring or boring movement from place to place.

lei /lay/ • n. a Polynesian garland of flowers.
– ORIGIN Hawaiian.

Leics. • abbrev. Leicestershire.

leisure • n. time free for relaxation or enjoyment.
– PHRASES **at leisure 1** not occupied; free. **2** in an unhurried way. **at your leisure** when it is convenient for you.
– ORIGIN Old French *leisir*.

leisure centre • n. Brit. a public building

offering facilities for sport and recreation.

leisurely • adj. relaxed and unhurried. • adv. without hurry.

leisurewear • n. casual clothes worn for leisure activities.

leitmotif /lyt-moh-teef/ (also **leitmotiv**) • n. a frequently repeated theme in a musical or literary work.
– ORIGIN German *Leitmotiv*.

lemming • n. a short-tailed Arctic rodent, which periodically migrates in large numbers.
– ORIGIN Norwegian and Danish.

lemon • n. 1 a pale yellow citrus fruit with thick skin and acidic juice. 2 a drink made from or flavoured with lemon juice. 3 a pale yellow colour.
– DERIVATIVES **lemony** adj.
– ORIGIN Old French *limon*.

lemonade • n. a sweetened drink made from lemon juice or flavouring and water.

lemon balm • n. a bushy lemon-scented herb of the mint family.

lemon curd • n. a sweet spread made from lemons, butter, eggs, and sugar.

lemon grass • n. a tropical grass which yields an oil that smells of lemon, used in Asian cooking.

lemon sole • n. a common flatfish of the plaice family.
– ORIGIN French *limande*.

lemur /lee-mer/ • n. a primate with a pointed snout, that lives in trees in Madagascar.
– ORIGIN Latin *lemures* 'spirits of the dead'.

lend • v. (**lends, lending, lent**) 1 allow someone to use something on the understanding that it will be returned. 2 allow someone the use of a sum of money under an agreement to pay it back later. 3 contribute or add a quality to. 4 (**lend itself to**) (of a thing) be suitable for.
– DERIVATIVES **lender** n.
– ORIGIN Old English.

lending library • n. a public library from which books may be borrowed for a limited time.

length • n. 1 the measurement or extent of something from end to end. 2 the amount of time occupied by something. 3 the quality of being long. 4 the full distance that a thing extends for. 5 the extent of a garment in a vertical direction when worn. 6 the length of a horse or boat as a measure of the lead in a race. 7 a stretch or piece of something. 8 a degree to which a course of action is taken: *they go to great lengths to avoid the press.*
– PHRASES **at length 1** in detail; fully. **2** after a long time.
– ORIGIN Old English.

lengthen • v. make or become longer.

lengthways (also **lengthwise**) • adv. in a direction parallel with a thing's length.

lengthy • adj. (**lengthier, lengthiest**) very long in time or extent: *lengthy delays.*
– DERIVATIVES **lengthily** adv.

lenient /lee-ni-uhnt/ • adj. not strict or severe; merciful.
– DERIVATIVES **leniency** n.
– ORIGIN Latin *lenire* 'soothe'.

lens /lenz/ • n. 1 a curved piece of glass or other transparent material for concentrating or spreading light rays. 2 the light-gathering device of a camera. 3 Anat. the transparent structure behind the iris in the eye, by which light is focused on to the retina.
– ORIGIN Latin, 'lentil'.

Lent • n. (in the Christian Church) the period immediately before Easter, during which fasting takes place.
– ORIGIN short for **LENTEN**.

lent past and past part. of **LEND**.

Lenten • adj. relating to Lent.
– ORIGIN Old English, 'spring, Lent'.

lentil • n. a pulse (edible seed) which is dried and then soaked and cooked before eating.
– ORIGIN Latin *lenticula*.

lento • adv. & adj. Music slow or slowly.
– ORIGIN Italian.

Leo • n. a constellation (the Lion) and sign of the zodiac, which the sun enters about 23 July.
– ORIGIN Latin.

leonine /lee-uh-nyn/ • adj. relating to or resembling a lion or lions.
– ORIGIN Latin *leoninus*.

leopard • n. (fem. **leopardess**) a large solitary cat that has a fawn or brown coat with black spots, found in the forests of Africa and southern Asia.
– ORIGIN Greek *leopardos*.

leotard /lee-uh-tard/ • n. a close-fitting, stretchy one-piece garment covering the body to the top of the thighs, worn for dance, gymnastics, and exercise.
– ORIGIN named after the French trapeze artist Jules *Léotard*.

leper • n. 1 a person suffering from leprosy. 2 a person who is rejected by other people: *a social leper.*
– ORIGIN Old French *lepre*.

Lepidoptera /lep-i-dop-tuh-ruh/ • pl. n. an order of insects comprising the butterflies and moths.

- DERIVATIVES **lepidopteran** adj. & n.
- ORIGIN from Greek *lepis* 'scale' + *pteron* 'wing'.

lepidopterist /lep-i-dop-tuh-rist/ • n. a person who studies or collects butterflies or moths.

leprechaun /lep-ruh-kawn/ • n. (in Irish folklore) a small, mischievous sprite.
- ORIGIN Old Irish *luchorpán*.

leprosy • n. a contagious disease that causes discoloration and lumps on the skin and, in severe cases, disfigurement and deformities.

leprous • adj. referring to or suffering from leprosy.

lesbian • n. a woman who is sexually attracted to other women.
• adj. referring to lesbians or lesbianism.
- DERIVATIVES **lesbianism** n.
- ORIGIN from *Lesbos*, Greek island and home of Sappho, who expressed affection for women in her poetry.

lesion /lee-zhuhn/ • n. an area of skin or part of an organ which has been damaged.
- ORIGIN Latin *laedere* 'injure'.

less • det. & pron. 1 a smaller amount of something. 2 fewer in number. • adv. to a smaller extent; not so much.
• prep. minus.
- ORIGIN Old English.

> USAGE: For an explanation of the difference between **less** and **fewer**, see the note at FEW.

-less • suffix forming adjectives and adverbs: 1 (from nouns) without: *flavourless*. 2 (from verbs) not affected by: *tireless*.
- ORIGIN Old English, 'devoid of'.

lessee • n. a person who holds the lease of a property.
- ORIGIN Old French *lesse*.

lessen • v. make or become less.

lesser • adj. not so great, large, or important as the other or the rest.

lesson • n. 1 a period of learning or teaching. 2 a thing learned. 3 a thing that acts as a warning or encouragement. 4 a passage from the Bible read aloud during a church service.
- ORIGIN Old French *leçon*.

lessor • n. a person who leases or lets a property to another person.
- ORIGIN Old French.

lest • conj. formal 1 to avoid the risk of. 2 because of the possibility of.
- ORIGIN Old English.

let¹ • v. (lets, letting, let) 1 allow someone to do something or something to happen. 2 used to express an intention, suggestion, or order: *let's have a drink*. 3 used to express an assumption

on which a theory or calculation is to be based: *let A stand for X.* 4 esp. Brit. allow someone to have the use of a room or property in return for payment. • n. Brit. a period during which a room or property is rented.
- PHRASES **let alone** not to mention. **let someone down** fail to support or help someone. **let someone go** allow someone to go free. **let yourself go** 1 act in a relaxed way. 2 become careless in your habits or appearance. **let someone off** 1 choose not to punish someone. 2 excuse someone from a task. **let something off** cause a gun, firework, or bomb to fire or explode. **let up** informal become less intense. **to let** available for rent.
- ORIGIN Old English, 'leave behind'.

let² • n. (in racket sports) a situation in which a point is not counted and is played for again.
- PHRASES **without let or hindrance** formal without obstruction; freely.
- ORIGIN Old English, 'hinder'.

-let • suffix 1 (forming nouns) referring to a smaller or lesser kind: *booklet.* 2 referring to articles worn as decoration: *anklet.*
- ORIGIN related to French *-ette.*

let-down • n. a disappointment.

lethal • adj. 1 able to cause death. 2 very harmful.
- DERIVATIVES **lethally** adv.
- ORIGIN Latin *lethalis.*

lethargic /li-thar-jik/ • adj. lacking energy or enthusiasm.
- DERIVATIVES **lethargically** adv.

lethargy /leth-er-ji/ • n. a lack of energy and enthusiasm.
- ORIGIN Greek *lēthargos* 'forgetful'.

let-off • n. informal an instance of avoiding or being excused from doing something.

let's • contr. let us.

letter • n. 1 a sign representing one or more of the sounds used in speech; any of the symbols of an alphabet. 2 a written communication, sent by post or messenger. 3 the precise terms of something: *the letter of the law.* 4 (**letters**) knowledge of literature.
• v. (**letters, lettering, lettered**) write something with letters.
- PHRASES **to the letter** precisely and accurately.
- DERIVATIVES **lettering** n.
- ORIGIN Latin *litera.*

letter bomb • n. an explosive device hidden in a small package, which explodes when the package is opened.

letter box • n. Brit. a slot in a door through which mail is delivered.

letterhead • n. a printed heading on stationery.

lettuce • n. a cultivated plant with leaves that are eaten in salads.
– ORIGIN Old French *letues*.

let-up • n. informal a brief time when something becomes less intense or difficult.

leucocyte /loo-koh-syt/ (also **leukocyte**) • n. a cell which circulates in the blood and bodily fluids and acts against foreign substances and disease; a white blood cell.
– ORIGIN from Greek *leukos* 'white' + *kutos* 'vessel'.

leukaemia /loo-kee-mi-uh/ (US **leukemia**) • n. a serious disease in which increased numbers of immature or abnormal white cells are produced, stopping the production of normal blood cells.
– ORIGIN from Greek *leukos* 'white' + *haima* 'blood'.

levee¹ /lev-ay/ • n. N. Amer. or old use a formal reception of visitors or guests.
– ORIGIN French.

levee² /lev-i/ • n. 1 an embankment built to prevent a river from overflowing. 2 a ridge of sediment deposited naturally alongside a river.
– ORIGIN French.

level • n. 1 a horizontal line or surface. 2 a position or stage on a scale of quantity, extent, rank, or quality: *a high level of unemployment*. 3 a height or distance from the ground or another base. 4 a floor within a multi-storey building. • adj. 1 having a flat, horizontal surface. 2 at the same height as someone or something else. 3 having the same position or value. • v. (**levels, levelling, levelled;** US **levels, leveling, leveled**) 1 make or become level. 2 aim or direct a weapon, criticism, or accusation. 3 (**level with**) informal be honest with.
– PHRASES **on the level** informal honest; truthful.
– DERIVATIVES **leveller** n. **levelly** adv.
– ORIGIN Old French *livel*.

level crossing • n. Brit. a place where a railway and a road cross at the same level.

level-headed • adj. calm and sensible.

lever • n. 1 a bar resting on a pivot, used to move a load with one end when pressure is applied to the other. 2 an arm or handle that is moved to operate a mechanism. • v. (**levers, levering, levered**) 1 lift or move with a lever. 2 move with effort: *she levered herself up*.
– ORIGIN Old French *levier*.

leverage • n. 1 the exertion of force by means of a lever. 2 the power to

influence: *political leverage*.

leveret /lev-uh-rit/ • n. a young hare in its first year.
– ORIGIN Old French.

leviathan /li-vy-uh-thuhn/ • n. 1 (in biblical use) a sea monster. 2 a very large or powerful thing.
– ORIGIN Hebrew.

levitate /lev-i-tayt/ • v. (**levitates, levitating, levitated**) rise and hover in the air.
– DERIVATIVES **levitation** n.
– ORIGIN Latin *levis* 'light'.

levity • n. the treatment of a serious matter with humour or lack of respect.
– ORIGIN Latin *levitas*.

levy • v. (**levies, levying, levied**) impose a tax, fee, or fine. • n. (pl. **levies**) 1 the imposing of a tax, fee, or fine. 2 a sum of money raised by a tax, fee, or fine.
– ORIGIN Old French *lever* 'raise'.

lewd • adj. crude and offensive in a sexual way.
– ORIGIN Old English.

lexical • adj. 1 relating to the words of a language. 2 relating to a dictionary.
– DERIVATIVES **lexically** adv.
– ORIGIN Greek *lexikos* 'of words'.

lexicography /leks-i-kog-ruh-fi/ • n. the practice of writing dictionaries.
– DERIVATIVES **lexicographer** n.

lexicon • n. 1 the vocabulary of a person, language, or branch of knowledge. 2 a dictionary.
– ORIGIN from Greek *lexikon biblion* 'book of words'.

ley¹ /rhymes with pay/ • n. a piece of land where grass is grown temporarily.
– ORIGIN Old English, 'fallow'.

ley² /rhymes with pay or pea/ (also **ley line**) • n. a supposed straight line connecting ancient sites, associated by some people with lines of energy.
– ORIGIN from LEA.

LF • abbrev. low frequency.

Li • symb. the chemical element lithium.

liability • n. (pl. **liabilities**) 1 the state of being legally responsible for something. 2 a sum of money that is owed. 3 a person or thing likely to cause embarrassment or trouble.

liable • adj. 1 responsible by law. 2 (**liable to**) legally required to do something. 3 (**liable to**) likely to do or to be affected by something.
– ORIGIN perh. from French *lier* 'to bind'.

liaise /li-ayz/ • v. (**liaises, liaising, liaised**) 1 cooperate on a matter of shared concern. 2 (**liaise between**) act as a link to assist communication between.
– ORIGIN from LIAISON.

☑ **liaise** and **liason** are spelled with two **i**'s, one before and one after the **a**.

liaison •n. **1** communication or cooperation between people or organizations. **2** a sexual relationship.
– ORIGIN French.

liana /li-ah-nuh/ (also **liane** /li-ahn/) •n. a woody climbing plant that hangs from trees in tropical forests.
– ORIGIN French *liane* 'clematis, liana'.

liar •n. a person who tells lies.

lias /ly-uhss/ •n. a blue-grey clayey limestone found chiefly in SW England.
– ORIGIN Old French *liais*.

libation /ly-**bay**-sh'n/ •n. **1** a drink poured out as an offering to a god. **2** humorous an alcoholic drink.
– ORIGIN Latin.

libel •n. the crime of publishing a false statement that harms a person's reputation. Compare with **SLANDER**. •v. (**libels, libelling, libelled**; US **libels, libeling, libeled**) publish a false statement about someone.
– DERIVATIVES **libellous** (US also **libelous**) adj.
– ORIGIN Latin *libellus* 'little book'.

liberal •adj. **1** willing to respect and accept behaviour or opinions that differ from your own. **2** (in politics) favouring individual liberty, free trade, and moderate reform. **3** (**Liberal**) relating to Liberals or a Liberal Party, especially (in the UK) relating to the Liberal Democrat party. **4** (of an interpretation) not strictly literal. **5** given, used, or giving in generous amounts. •n. **1** a person of liberal views. **2** (**Liberal**) a supporter or member of a Liberal Party, especially (in the UK) a Liberal Democrat.
– DERIVATIVES **liberalism** n. **liberality** n. **liberally** adv.
– ORIGIN Latin *liberalis*.

Liberal Democrat •n. (in the UK) a member of a party formed from the Liberal Party and members of the Social Democratic Party.

liberalize (or **liberalise**) •v. (**liberalizes, liberalizing, liberalized**) remove or loosen restrictions on something.
– DERIVATIVES **liberalization** n.

liberate •v. (**liberates, liberating, liberated**) **1** set someone free. **2** (as adj. **liberated**) free from conventional ideas about behaviour.
– DERIVATIVES **liberation** n. **liberator** n.
– ORIGIN Latin *liberare*.

Liberian /ly-**beer**-i-uhn/ •n. a person from Liberia, a country in West Africa. •adj. relating to Liberia.

libertarian •n. a person who believes in very limited state intervention in people's lives.
– DERIVATIVES **libertarianism** n.

libertine /li-ber-teen/ •n. a man who behaves in an unprincipled way, especially in sexual matters.
– DERIVATIVES **libertinism** n.
– ORIGIN Latin *libertinus* 'freed slave'.

liberty •n. (pl. **liberties**) **1** the state of being free. **2** a right or privilege. **3** the ability to act as you please. **4** informal a disrespectful remark or action.
– PHRASES **take liberties with 1** behave in an excessively familiar way towards a person. **2** deal with something without strict faithfulness to the facts or to an original.
– ORIGIN Latin *libertas*.

libidinous /li-**bid**-i-nuhss/ •adj. having a strong sexual drive.
– ORIGIN Latin *libidinosus*.

libido /li-**bee**-doh/ •n. (pl. **libidos**) sexual desire.
– ORIGIN Latin, 'desire, lust'.

Libra /**lee**-bruh/ •n. a constellation (the Scales) and sign of the zodiac, which the sun enters about 23 September.
– DERIVATIVES **Libran** n. & adj.
– ORIGIN Latin.

librarian •n. a person who works in a library.

library •n. (pl. **libraries**) **1** a building or room containing a collection of books and periodicals for use by the public or the members of an institution. **2** a private collection of books. **3** a collection of films or recorded music kept for research or borrowing.
– ORIGIN Latin *libraria* 'bookshop'.

☑ Remember that **library** is spelled with two **r**'s, one before and one after the **a**.

libretto /li-**bret**-toh/ •n. (pl. **libretti** /li-**bret**-ti/ or **librettos**) the words of an opera or other long vocal work.
– DERIVATIVES **librettist** n.
– ORIGIN Italian, 'small book'.

Libyan •n. a person from Libya. •adj. relating to Libya.

lice pl. of **LOUSE**.

licence (US **license**) •n. **1** a permit from an authority to own, use, or do something. **2** freedom to behave without restraint. **3** freedom to disregard accepted rules: *poetic licence.*
– ORIGIN Latin *licentia* 'freedom'.

license (also **licence**) •v. (**licenses, licensing, licensed**; also **licences, licencing, licenced**) **1** grant a permit to. **2** authorize something.
– ORIGIN from **LICENCE**.

licensee •n. the holder of a licence,

especially to sell alcoholic drinks.

licentiate /ly-sen-shi-uht/ •n. a person who holds a certificate allowing them to practise a particular profession.
– ORIGIN Latin *licentiatus* 'having freedom'.

licentious /ly-sen-shuhss/ •adj. unprincipled in sexual matters.
– ORIGIN Latin *licentiosus*.

lichen /ly-kuhn, li-chuhn/ •n. a simple plant consisting of a fungus living in close association with an alga, growing on rocks, walls, and trees.
– ORIGIN Greek *leikhēn*.

licit /lis-it/ •adj. formal not forbidden; lawful.
– ORIGIN Latin *licitus* 'allowed'.

lick •v. 1 pass the tongue over. 2 move lightly and quickly like a tongue: *the flames licked around the wood.* 3 informal totally defeat. •n. 1 an act of licking. 2 informal a small amount or quick application of something: *a lick of paint.*
– ORIGIN Old English.

lickspittle •n. a person who behaves with excessive obedience to those in power.

licorice •n. US = LIQUORICE.

lid •n. 1 a removable or hinged cover for the top of a container. 2 an eyelid.
– DERIVATIVES **lidded** adj.
– ORIGIN Old English.

lido /lee-doh/ •n. (pl. **lidos**) Brit. a public open-air swimming pool.
– ORIGIN Italian, 'shore'.

lie¹ •v. (**lies**, **lying**, **lay**; past part. **lain**) 1 be in or take up a horizontal position on a supporting surface. 2 be in a particular state: *the abbey lies in ruins.* 3 be found: *the solution lies in a return to traditional values.* 4 be situated in a specified position. •n. the way, direction, or position in which something lies.
– PHRASES **lie low** avoid attention. **the lie** (N. Amer. **lay**) **of the land** 1 the features of an area. 2 the current situation.
– ORIGIN Old English.

> USAGE: For the correct use of **lay** and **lie**, see the note at LAY¹.

lie² •n. 1 a deliberately false statement. 2 a situation involving deception. •v. (**lies**, **lying**, **lied**) 1 tell a lie or lies. 2 (of a thing) present a false impression.
– ORIGIN Old English.

lied /leed/ •n. (pl. **lieder** /lee-der/) a type of German song sung as a solo with piano accompaniment.
– ORIGIN German.

lie detector •n. an instrument for determining whether a person is telling the truth.

lie-down •n. Brit. a short rest on a bed or sofa.

liege /leej/ •n. hist. 1 (also **liege lord**) a lord under the feudal system. 2 a person who served a feudal lord.
– ORIGIN Old French.

lie-in •n. Brit. a prolonged stay in bed in the morning.

lieu /loo/ •n. (in phr. **in lieu** or **in lieu of**) instead (of).
– ORIGIN French.

lieutenant /lef-ten-uhnt/ •n. 1 a deputy or substitute acting for a person of higher rank. 2 a rank of officer in the British army or in the navy.
– ORIGIN Old French, 'place-holding'.

lieutenant colonel •n. a rank of officer in the army and the US air force, above major and below colonel.

life •n. (pl. **lives**) 1 the condition of being alive and able to grow, breathe, and reproduce. 2 the existence of an individual human being or animal. 3 a particular type or aspect of people's existence: *school life.* 4 living things and their activity. 5 the period during which something continues to exist, function, or be valid. 6 vitality or energy. 7 informal a sentence of imprisonment for life.
– ORIGIN Old English.

life assurance •n. Brit. = LIFE INSURANCE.

lifebelt •n. an inflatable ring used to help a person who has fallen into water to stay afloat.

lifeblood •n. a vital factor or force: *the cash is the lifeblood of our business.*

lifeboat •n. 1 a boat launched from land to rescue people at sea. 2 a small boat kept on a ship for use in an emergency.

life cycle •n. the series of changes in the life of an organism.

life expectancy •n. the period that a person may expect to live.

life form •n. any living thing.

lifeguard •n. a person employed to rescue bathers who get into difficulty at a beach or swimming pool.

life insurance •n. insurance that pays out a sum of money either on the death of the insured person or after a set period.

life jacket •n. an inflatable jacket for keeping a person afloat in water.

lifeless •adj. 1 dead or apparently dead. 2 not containing living things. 3 lacking energy or excitement.

lifelike •adj. exactly like a living person or thing.

lifeline •n. 1 a thing which on which someone or something depends. 2 a rope or line thrown to rescue someone in difficulties in water.

lifelong • adj. lasting throughout a person's life.

life peer • n. (in the UK) a peer whose title cannot be inherited.

life raft • n. an inflatable raft for use in an emergency at sea.

lifesaver • n. informal a thing that saves you from serious illness or difficulty.

life sciences • pl. n. the sciences concerned with the study of living organisms, including biology, botany, and zoology.

lifespan • n. the length of time for which a person or animal lives or a thing functions.

lifestyle • n. the way in which someone lives.

life-support • adj. (of medical equipment) that keeps the body functioning after serious illness or injury.

lifetime • n. the length of time that a person lives or a thing lasts.

lift • v. 1 raise or be raised to a higher position. 2 pick up and move to a different position. 3 formally end a legal restriction. 4 (**lift off**) (of an aircraft or spacecraft) become airborne; take off. • n. 1 Brit. a platform or compartment housed in a shaft for raising and lowering people or things. 2 an act of lifting. 3 a free ride in another person's vehicle. 4 a device for carrying people up or down a mountain. 5 a feeling of increased cheerfulness. 6 upward force exerted by the air on an aerofoil or similar structure.
– DERIVATIVES **lifter** n.
– ORIGIN Old Norse.

lift-off • n. the vertical take-off of a spacecraft or rocket.

ligament /lig-uh-muhnt/ • n. 1 a short band of tough, flexible tissue which connects two bones or cartilages or holds together a joint. 2 a structure that supports an organ and keeps it in position.
– ORIGIN Latin *ligamentum* 'bond'.

ligature /lig-uh-cher/ • n. 1 a cord used to tie up a bleeding artery. 2 Music a slur or tie.
– ORIGIN Latin *ligatura*.

light¹ • n. 1 the natural form of energy that makes things visible. 2 a source of illumination such as a lamp. 3 a window or section of a window. 4 a device producing a flame or spark. 5 an expression in someone's eyes. 6 understanding: *she saw light dawn on the woman's face.* • v. (**lights**, **lighting**, **lit**; past part. **lit** or **lighted**) 1 provide an area or object with light. 2 ignite or be ignited. • adj. 1 having a considerable amount of light. 2 (of a colour) pale.

– PHRASES **come to light** become widely known. **in (the) light of** taking something into consideration. **light up** become lively or happy: *his face lit up with delight.* **light something up** ignite a cigarette, pipe, or cigar before smoking it. **see the light** understand or realize something.
– ORIGIN Old English.

light² • adj. 1 not heavy or heavy enough. 2 not strongly or heavily built. 3 relatively low in density, amount, or intensity. 4 carrying or suitable for small loads: *light commercial vehicles.* 5 gentle or delicate. 6 not serious. 7 (of sleep or a sleeper) easily disturbed.
– PHRASES **make light of** treat something as unimportant.
– DERIVATIVES **lightly** adv. **lightness** n.
– ORIGIN Old English.

light³ • v. (**lights**, **lighting**, **lit** or **lighted**) (**light on**) discover by chance.
– ORIGIN Old English, 'descend, alight'.

light bulb • n. a glass bulb containing inert gas, which provides light when an electric current is passed through it.

lighten¹ • v. 1 make or become lighter in weight. 2 make or become less serious.

lighten² • v. make or become brighter.

lighter¹ • n. a device producing a small flame, used to light cigarettes.

lighter² • n. a flat-bottomed barge used to transfer goods to and from ships in harbour.
– ORIGIN German *luchter*.

light-fingered • adj. informal prone to steal.

light-footed • adj. fast and nimble on your feet.

light-headed • adj. dizzy and slightly faint.

light-hearted • adj. 1 amusing and entertaining. 2 cheerful or carefree.

light heavyweight • n. a weight in boxing and other sports between middleweight and heavyweight.

lighthouse • n. a tower or other structure containing a light to warn and guide ships at sea.

light industry • n. the manufacture of small or light articles.

lighting • n. 1 equipment for producing light. 2 the arrangement or effect of lights.

lighting-up time • n. Brit. the time at which motorists are required by law to switch their vehicles' lights on.

light meter • n. an instrument measuring the intensity of light, used when taking photographs.

lightning • n. the occurrence of a high-

voltage electrical discharge between a cloud and the ground or within a cloud, accompanied by a bright flash. • adj. very quick: *lightning speed*.
– ORIGIN from LIGHTEN².

> ☑ **lightning** is not spelled with an **e**; the different word **lightening** is part of the verb *lighten* and means 'getting lighter'.

lightning conductor (also N. Amer. **lightning rod**) • n. Brit. a metal rod or wire fixed in a high place to divert lightning into the ground.

light pen • n. a hand-held pen-like device used for passing information to a computer.

lights • pl. n. the lungs of sheep, pigs, or bullocks as food for pets.
– ORIGIN from LIGHT² (because of their lightness).

lightweight • n. 1 a weight in boxing and other sports between featherweight and welterweight. 2 informal a person of little importance: *a political lightweight*.

light year • n. Astron. a unit of distance equivalent to the distance that light travels in one year, nearly 6 million million miles.

ligneous /lig-ni-uhss/ • adj. consisting of or resembling wood.
– ORIGIN Latin *ligneus* 'relating to wood'.

lignin • n. an organic substance found in the cell walls of many plants, making them rigid and woody.
– ORIGIN Latin *lignum* 'wood'.

lignite • n. soft brownish coal.
– ORIGIN Latin *lignum* 'wood'.

likable • adj. var. of LIKEABLE.

like¹ • prep. 1 similar to. 2 in a similar way to. 3 in a way appropriate to. 4 such as. • conj. informal 1 in the same way that. 2 as if. • n. (**the like**) things of the same kind. • adj. having similar characteristics to someone or something else.
– PHRASES (**as**) **like as not** probably. **like so** informal in this way.
– ORIGIN Old Norse.

> **USAGE:** When writing, do not use **like** to mean 'as if', as in *he's behaving like he owns the place*; you should use **as if** or **as though** instead.

like² • v. (**likes, liking, liked**) 1 find pleasant or satisfactory. 2 wish for; want. • n. (**likes**) the things you like.
– ORIGIN Old English, 'be pleasing'.

-like • comb. form (added to nouns) similar to; characteristic of: *crust-like*.

likeable (also **likable**) • adj. pleasant; easy to like.

likelihood • n. the state of being likely.

likely • adj. (**likelier, likeliest**) 1 probable.

2 promising: *a likely-looking spot*. • adv. probably.

like-minded • adj. having similar tastes or opinions.

liken • v. (**liken someone/thing to**) point out the resemblance of someone or something to.

likeness • n. 1 resemblance. 2 outward appearance: *humans are made in God's likeness*. 3 a picture of a person.

likewise • adv. 1 also; moreover. 2 similarly.

liking • n. 1 a fondness for someone or something. 2 a person's taste: *the coffee was just to her liking*.

lilac • n. 1 a shrub or small tree with sweet-smelling violet, pink, or white blossom. 2 a pale pinkish-violet colour.
– ORIGIN Persian, 'bluish'.

Lilliputian /lil-li-pyoo-sh'n/ • adj. very small or unimportant.
– ORIGIN from the country of *Lilliput* in Jonathan Swift's *Gulliver's Travels*, inhabited by 6-inch high people.

lilo /ly-loh/ (also trademark **Li-lo**) • n. (pl. **lilos**) Brit. an inflatable mattress used for floating on water or as a bed.
– ORIGIN from *lie low*.

lilt • n. 1 a characteristic rising and falling of the voice when speaking. 2 a gentle rhythm in a tune. • v. speak, sing, or sound with a lilt.

lily • n. (pl. **lilies**) a plant with large trumpet-shaped flowers on a tall, slender stem.
– ORIGIN Greek *leirion*.

lily-livered • adj. cowardly.

lily of the valley • n. a plant of the lily family, with broad leaves and small white bell-shaped flowers.

lily pad • n. the flat leaf of a water lily.

lily-white • adj. 1 pure white. 2 totally innocent or pure.

limb • n. 1 an arm, leg, or wing. 2 a large branch of a tree. 3 a projecting part of a structure, object, or natural feature.
– PHRASES **out on a limb** in a position not supported by anyone else.
– DERIVATIVES **limbless** adj.
– ORIGIN Old English.

limber /rhymes with timber/ • v. (**limbers, limbering, limbered**) (**limber up**) warm up in preparation for exercise or activity. • adj. supple; flexible.
– ORIGIN perh. from *limber* in the dialect sense 'cart shaft'.

limbo¹ • n. 1 (in some Christian beliefs) the place between heaven and hell where the souls of people who have not been baptized go when they die. 2 an uncertain period of waiting.
– ORIGIN Latin *limbus* 'hem, limbo'.

limbo² •n. (pl. **limbos**) a West Indian dance in which the dancer bends backwards to pass under a horizontal bar which is gradually lowered towards the ground.
– ORIGIN from **LIMBER**.

lime¹ •n. **1** a product obtained from burning chalk or limestone, used in agriculture or in traditional building to make mortar and plaster. **2** any salt or alkali containing calcium.
– ORIGIN Old English.

lime² •n. **1** a rounded green citrus fruit similar to a lemon. **2** a bright light green colour.
– ORIGIN French.

lime³ (also **lime tree**) •n. a deciduous tree with heart-shaped leaves and yellowish blossom.
– ORIGIN Old English.

limekiln •n. a kiln for burning limestone to produce quicklime and lime.

limelight •n. **1** (**the limelight**) the focus of public attention. **2** a strong white light produced by heating lime, formerly used in theatres.

limerick •n. a humorous five-line poem with a rhyme scheme *aabba*.
– ORIGIN said to be from the chorus 'will you come up to Limerick?', sung between verses at a party.

limescale •n. Brit. a hard white substance consisting chiefly of calcium carbonate, deposited by water on the inside of pipes, kettles, etc.

limestone •n. a hard sedimentary rock composed mainly of calcium carbonate.

Limey •n. (pl. **Limeys**) N. Amer. & Austral. informal a British person.
– ORIGIN from the former practice in the British navy of giving lime juice to sailors.

limit •n. **1** a point beyond which something does not or may not pass. **2** a restriction on the size or amount of something. **3** the furthest extent of energy or endurance: *the horses were reaching their limit.* •v. (**limits, limiting, limited**) put a limit on.
– PHRASES **off limits** out of bounds.
– DERIVATIVES **limiter** n. **limitless** adj.
– ORIGIN Latin *limes* 'boundary'.

limitation •n. **1** a restriction. **2** a fault or failing. **3** the action of limiting.

limited •adj. restricted in size, amount, extent, or ability.

limited company •n. Brit. a private company whose owners have only a limited responsibility for its debts.

limn /lim/ •v. literary depict or describe in painting or words.
– ORIGIN Latin *luminare* 'make light'.

limousine •n. a large, luxurious car.
– ORIGIN French.

limp¹ •v. **1** walk with difficulty because of an injured leg or foot. **2** (of a damaged ship or aircraft) move with difficulty. •n. a limping walk.
– ORIGIN from former *limphalt* 'lame'.

limp² •adj. **1** not stiff or firm. **2** without energy or will.
– DERIVATIVES **limply** adv.
– ORIGIN perh. from **LIMP¹**.

limpet •n. a shellfish with a muscular foot for clinging tightly to rocks.
– ORIGIN Latin *lampreda*.

limpid •adj. **1** (of a liquid or the eyes) clear. **2** (of writing or music) clear or tuneful.
– ORIGIN Latin *limpidus*.

linchpin (also **lynchpin**) •n. **1** a very important person or thing. **2** a pin through the end of an axle keeping a wheel in position.
– ORIGIN Old English.

Lincs. •abbrev. Lincolnshire.

linctus •n. Brit. thick liquid cough medicine.
– ORIGIN Latin.

linden •n. a lime tree.
– ORIGIN Old English.

line¹ •n. **1** a long, narrow mark or band. **2** a length of cord, wire, etc. **3** a row or series of people or things. **4** a row of written or printed words. **5** a direction, course, or channel: *direct lines of communication.* **6** a telephone connection. **7** a railway track or route. **8** an imaginary limit. **9** a series of military defences facing an enemy force. **10** a wrinkle in the skin. **11** the shape or outline of something. **12** a range of commercial goods. **13** an area of activity: *their line of work.* **14** (**lines**) the words of an actor's part. **15** informal a remark intended to achieve a purpose: *a cheesy chat-up line.* **16** (**lines**) Brit. a number of repetitions of a sentence written out as a school punishment. •v. (**lines, lining, lined**) **1** stand or be positioned at intervals along a route. **2** (**line someone/thing up**) arrange people or things in a row. **3** (**line someone/thing up**) have someone or something prepared. **4** (as adj. **lined**) marked or covered with lines.
– PHRASES **in line** under control. **in line for** likely to receive something. **on the line** at serious risk. **out of line** informal behaving badly or wrongly.
– ORIGIN Old English.

line² •v. (**lines, lining, lined**) cover the inner surface of something with a layer of different material.
– PHRASES **line your pocket** make money by dishonest means.

– ORIGIN from former *line* 'flax'.

lineage /lin-i-ij/ • n. ancestry or pedigree.

lineal /lin-i-uhl/ • adj. **1** in a direct line of descent or ancestry. **2** linear.

lineaments /lin-i-uh-muhntz/ • pl. n. literary the features of the face.
– ORIGIN Latin *lineamentum*.

linear /lin-i-er/ • adj. **1** arranged in or extending along a straight line. **2** consisting of lines or outlines. **3** involving one dimension only. **4** progressing from one stage to another in a series of steps: *linear narrative*. **5** Math. able to be represented by a straight line on a graph.
– DERIVATIVES **linearity** n.

line dancing • n. a type of country and western dancing in which a line of dancers follow a set pattern of steps.

line drawing • n. a drawing based on the use of line rather than shading.

linen • n. **1** cloth woven from flax. **2** articles such as sheets and clothes that were traditionally made of linen.
– ORIGIN Old English.

linen basket • n. esp. Brit. a basket for dirty clothing.

liner[1] • n. **1** a large passenger ship. [ORIGIN because such a ship travelled on a regular line or route.] **2** a cosmetic for outlining or emphasizing the eyes or lips.

liner[2] • n. a lining of a garment, container, etc.

linesman • n. (pl. **linesmen**) **1** (in sport) an official who assists the referee or umpire in deciding whether the ball is out of play. **2** Brit. a person who repairs telephone or electricity power lines.

line-up • n. a group of people or things assembled for a particular purpose.

ling[1] • n. a long-bodied edible sea fish of the cod family.
– ORIGIN prob. from Dutch.

ling[2] • n. the common heather.
– ORIGIN Old Norse.

-ling • suffix **1** forming nouns: *sapling*. **2** forming nouns indicating smallness: *gosling*.
– ORIGIN Old English.

linger • v. (**lingers, lingering, lingered**) **1** be slow or reluctant to leave. **2** (**linger over**) spend a long time over. **3** (usu. **linger on**) be slow to disappear or die.
– ORIGIN Germanic.

lingerie /lan-zhuh-ri/ • n. women's underwear and nightclothes.
– ORIGIN French.

lingo • n. (pl. **lingos** or **lingoes**) informal **1** a foreign language. **2** the jargon of a particular subject or group.

– ORIGIN prob. from Latin *lingua* 'tongue'.

lingua franca /ling-gwuh frang-kuh/ • n. (pl. **lingua francas**) a language used as a common language between speakers whose native languages are different.
– ORIGIN Italian, 'Frankish tongue'.

linguine /ling-gwee-ni/ • pl. n. small ribbons of pasta.
– ORIGIN Italian, 'little tongues'.

linguist • n. **1** a person skilled in foreign languages. **2** a person who studies linguistics.
– ORIGIN Latin *lingua* 'language'.

linguistic • adj. relating to language or linguistics. • n. (**linguistics**) the scientific study of language.
– DERIVATIVES **linguistically** adv.

liniment • n. an ointment rubbed on the body to relieve pain or bruising.
– ORIGIN Latin *linimentum*.

lining • n. a layer of different material covering or attached to the inside of something.

link • n. **1** a relationship or connection between people or things. **2** something that enables people to communicate. **3** a means of contact or transport between two places: *a satellite link*. **4** a code or instruction connecting one part of a computer program, website, etc. to another. **5** a loop in a chain. • v. make or suggest a link with or between.
– ORIGIN Old Norse.

linkage • n. **1** the action of linking people or things. **2** a system of links.

links • pl. n. a golf course, especially on grassland near the sea.
– ORIGIN Old English, 'rising ground'.

link-up • n. **1** an instance of two or more people or things connecting. **2** a connection enabling people or machines to communicate with each other.

linnet • n. a mainly brown and grey finch with a reddish breast and forehead.
– ORIGIN Old French *linette*.

lino • n. (pl. **linos**) informal, esp. Brit. linoleum.

linocut • n. a design carved in a block of linoleum, used for printing.

linoleum /li-noh-li-uhm/ • n. a floor covering consisting of a canvas backing thickly coated with a preparation of linseed oil and powdered cork.
– ORIGIN from Latin *linum* 'flax' + *oleum* 'oil'.

linseed • n. the seeds of the flax plant.
– ORIGIN Old English.

linseed oil • n. oil extracted from linseed, used in paint and varnish.

lint • n. **1** short, fine fibres which separate from cloth or yarn during processing. **2** a fabric used for dressing wounds.

– ORIGIN perh. from Old French *linette* 'linseed'.

lintel • n. a horizontal support across the top of a door or window.
– ORIGIN Old French.

lion • n. (fem. **lioness**) **1** a large tawny-coloured cat of Africa and NW India, the male of which has a shaggy mane. **2** a brave, strong, or fierce person.
– PHRASES **the lion's share** Brit. the largest part of something.
– ORIGIN Old French *liun*.

lionize (or **lionise**) • v. (**lionizes**, **lionizing**, **lionized**) treat someone as a celebrity.

lip • n. **1** either of the two fleshy parts forming the edges of the mouth opening. **2** the edge of a hollow container or an opening. **3** informal cheeky talk.
– PHRASES **bite your lip** stop yourself from laughing or saying something. **pay lip service to** express only superficial respect or support for.
– ORIGIN Old English.

lipase /lip-ayz/ • n. an enzyme produced by the pancreas that promotes the breakdown of fats.
– ORIGIN Greek *lipos* 'fat'.

lipgloss • n. a glossy cosmetic applied to the lips.

lipid /lip-id/ • n. any of a class of fats that are insoluble in water.
– ORIGIN Greek *lipos* 'fat'.

liposuction /lip-oh-suk-sh'n/ • n. a technique in cosmetic surgery for removing excess fat from under the skin by suction.

lippy • adj. informal cheeky.

lip-read • v. understand speech from watching a speaker's lip movements.
– DERIVATIVES **lip-reader** n.

lip salve • n. Brit. a preparation to prevent or relieve sore or chapped lips.

lipstick • n. coloured cosmetic applied to the lips from a small solid stick.

lip-sync • v. (of a singer) move the lips in time to pre-recorded music or speech.

liquefy /lik-wi-fy/ • v. (**liquefies**, **liquefying**, **liquefied**) make or become liquid.
– DERIVATIVES **liquefaction** n.
– ORIGIN Latin *liquefacere*.

> ✓ Remember that **liquefy** ends with **-efy**.

liqueur /li-kyoor/ • n. a strong, sweet flavoured alcoholic spirit.
– ORIGIN French.

liquid • n. a substance that flows freely but remains at a constant volume, such as water or oil. • adj. **1** relating to or in the form of a liquid. **2** clear, like water: *liquid dark eyes.* **3** (of a sound) clear and flowing. **4** (of assets) held in or easily converted into cash.
– ORIGIN Latin *liquidus*.

liquidate • v. (**liquidates**, **liquidating**, **liquidated**) **1** close a business and sell what it owns in order to pay its debts. **2** sell something in order to get money. **3** pay off a debt. **4** informal kill someone.
– DERIVATIVES **liquidation** n. **liquidator** n.
– ORIGIN Latin *liquidare* 'make clear'.

liquid crystal display • n. an electronic visual display in which the application of an electric current to a liquid crystal layer makes it no longer transparent.

liquidity /li-kwid-i-ti/ • n. the availability of liquid assets to a market or company.

liquidize (or **liquidise**) • v. (**liquidizes**, **liquidizing**, **liquidized**) Brit. convert solid food into a liquid or purée.
– DERIVATIVES **liquidizer** n.

liquor /lik-er/ • n. **1** alcoholic drink, especially spirits. **2** liquid that has been produced in or used for cooking.
– ORIGIN Latin.

liquorice /lik-uh-riss, lik-uh-rish/ (US **licorice**) • n. a black substance made from the juice of a root and used as a sweet and in medicine.
– ORIGIN Old French *licoresse*.

lira /leer-uh/ • n. (pl. **lire** /leer-uh, leer-ay/) **1** (until the introduction of the euro in 2002) the basic unit of money of Italy. **2** the basic unit of money of Turkey.
– ORIGIN Italian.

lisp • n. a speech defect in which *s* is pronounced like *th* in *thick* and *z* is pronounced like *th* in *this*. • v. speak with a lisp.
– ORIGIN Old English.

lissom (also **lissome**) • adj. slim, supple, and graceful.
– ORIGIN from LITHE + -SOME.

list[1] • n. a number of connected items or names written as a series. • v. **1** make a list of. **2** include something in a list.
– ORIGIN Old French *liste*.

list[2] • v. (of a ship) lean over to one side. • n. an instance of listing.

listed • adj. (of a building in the UK) officially named as being of historical or architectural importance and so protected.

listen • v. **1** give your attention to a sound. **2** make an effort to hear something. **3** (**listen in**) listen to a private conversation. **4** respond to advice or a request. • n. an act of

attending to a sound or hearing something.
– DERIVATIVES **listener** n.
– ORIGIN Old English, 'pay attention to'.

listeria /li-steer-i-uh/ •n. a type of bacterium which infects humans and other animals through contaminated food.
– ORIGIN named after the English surgeon Joseph *Lister*.

listing •n. **1** a list or catalogue. **2** an entry in a list.

listless •adj. lacking energy or enthusiasm.
– DERIVATIVES **listlessly** adv. **listlessness** n.
– ORIGIN from former *list* 'desire'.

list price •n. the price of an article as listed by the manufacturer.

lit¹ past and past part. of LIGHT¹, LIGHT³.

lit² •n. = LITERATURE: *chick lit*.

litany /lit-uh-ni/ •n. (pl. **litanies**) **1** a series of prayers to God used in church services. **2** a long and boring list of complaints, reasons, etc.
– ORIGIN Greek *litaneia* 'prayer'.

liter •n. US = LITRE.

literacy •n. **1** the ability to read and write. **2** ability or knowledge in a specified area: *computer literacy*.

literal •adj. **1** being the usual or most basic sense of a word. **2** (of a translation) representing the exact words of the original piece of writing.
– ORIGIN Latin *litera* 'letter of the alphabet'.

literally •adv. **1** in a literal way or sense. **2** informal used for emphasis while not being actually true.

literary •adj. **1** relating to literature. **2** (of language) typical of or suitable for literary works or formal writing.
– ORIGIN Latin *litera* 'letter of the alphabet'.

literate •adj. **1** able to read and write. **2** knowledgeable in a particular field: *computer literate*.

literati /li-tuh-rah-ti/ •pl. n. educated people who are interested in literature.
– ORIGIN Latin.

literature •n. **1** written works that are regarded as having artistic merit. **2** books and writings on a particular subject. **3** leaflets used to give information.

lithe /lyth/ •adj. slim, supple, and graceful.
– ORIGIN Old English, 'gentle, meek'.

lithium /lith-i-uhm/ •n. a silver-white metallic chemical element.
– ORIGIN Greek *lithos* 'stone'.

lithograph /li-thuh-grahf/ •n. a print made by lithography.

– DERIVATIVES **lithographic** adj.

lithography /li-thog-ruh-fi/ •n. the process of printing from a flat metal surface treated so as to repel the ink except where it is required for printing.
– ORIGIN Greek *lithos* 'stone'.

Lithuanian •n. **1** a person from Lithuania. **2** the language of Lithuania. •adj. relating to Lithuania.

litigant •n. a person involved in a dispute or claim being heard in a law court.

litigate /lit-i-gayt/ •v. (**litigates**, **litigating**, **litigated**) take a dispute or claim to a law court.
– DERIVATIVES **litigation** n. **litigator** n.
– ORIGIN Latin *litigare*.

litigious /li-ti-juhss/ •adj. having a tendency to turn to the law to settle disputes.

litmus /lit-muhss/ •n. a dye that is red under acid conditions and blue under alkaline conditions.
– ORIGIN from Old Norse words meaning 'dye' and 'moss'.

litmus paper •n. paper stained with litmus, used to test for acids or alkalis.

litmus test •n. a reliable test of value or truth.

litotes /ly-toh-teez/ •n. understatement in which something is expressed by the negative of its opposite (e.g. *I shan't be sorry* for *I shall be glad*).
– ORIGIN Greek.

litre (US **liter**) •n. a metric unit of capacity equal to 1,000 cubic centimetres (about 1.75 pints).
– ORIGIN French.

litter •n. **1** rubbish left in a public place. **2** an untidy collection of things. **3** a number of young born to an animal at one time. **4** (also **cat litter**) absorbent material lining a tray for a cat to urinate and defecate in indoors. **5** straw used as animal bedding. **6** (also **leaf litter**) decomposing leaves forming a layer on top of soil. **7** hist. a vehicle containing a bed or seat enclosed by curtains and carried by men or animals. •v. (**litters**, **littering**, **littered**) make a place or area untidy with scattered articles.
– ORIGIN Old French *litiere*.

little •adj. **1** small in size, amount, or degree. **2** (of a person) young or younger: *her little sister*. **3** short in time or distance. •det. & pron. **1** (**a little**) a small amount of. **2** (**a little**) a short time or distance. **3** not much. •adv. (**less**, **least**) **1** (**a little**) to a small extent. **2** hardly or not at all.
– ORIGIN Old English.

little end •n. the smaller end of the connecting rod in a piston engine, attached to the piston.

Little Englander • n. informal a person opposed to an international role or policy for Britain.

little finger • n. (in phr. **twist someone around your little finger**) be able to make someone do whatever you want.

little people • pl. n. fairies or leprechauns.

littoral /lit-tuh-ruhl/ • adj. relating to the shore of the sea or a lake.
– ORIGIN Latin *littoralis*.

liturgy /lit-er-ji/ • n. (pl. **liturgies**) a set form of public worship used in the Christian Church.
– DERIVATIVES **liturgical** adj.
– ORIGIN Greek *leitourgia*.

live¹ /liv/ • v. (**lives**, **living**, **lived**) 1 remain alive. 2 be alive at a particular time. 3 spend your life in a particular way: *they are living in fear*. 4 make your home in a place or with a person. 5 (**live in/out**) reside at (or away from) the place where you work or study. 6 supply yourself with the means of staying alive: *they live by hunting and fishing*.
– PHRASES **live something down** succeed in making other people forget something embarrassing. **live it up** informal lead a life of extravagance and exciting social activity. **live rough** live outdoors as a result of being homeless.
– ORIGIN Old English.

live² /lyv/ • adj. 1 living. 2 (of a musical performance) played in front of an audience. 3 (of a broadcast) transmitted at the time of occurrence. 4 of interest and importance: *a live issue*. 5 (of a wire or device) connected to a source of electric current. 6 (of ammunition or explosive) able to explode. • adv. at the time of something's occurrence or performance: *the match will be televised live*.
– ORIGIN from **ALIVE**.

liveable (US also **livable**) • adj. 1 fit to live in. 2 worth living.

lived-in • adj. (of a room or building) showing comforting signs of wear and use.

live-in • adj. 1 (of a nanny, nurse, or home help) living in an employer's house. 2 living with someone in a sexual relationship: *his live-in girlfriend*.

livelihood • n. a means of earning enough money to live on.
– ORIGIN Old English, 'way of life'.

livelong /liv-long/ • adj. literary (of a period of time) entire.

lively • adj. (**livelier**, **liveliest**) 1 full of life and energy. 2 (of a place) full of activity. 3 mentally quick and active.
– DERIVATIVES **liveliness** n.

liven • v. (**liven someone/thing up** or **liven up**) make or become more lively or interesting.

liver • n. 1 a large organ in the abdomen that produces bile. 2 an animal's liver as food.
– ORIGIN Old English.

liverish • adj. 1 slightly unwell, as though having a liver disorder. 2 unhappy and bad-tempered.

Liverpudlian /li-ver-pud-li-uhn/ • n. a person from the city of Liverpool in NW England. • adj. relating to Liverpool.
– ORIGIN from *Liverpool* + **PUDDLE**.

liver sausage • n. a savoury meat paste in the form of a sausage containing cooked liver or a mixture of cooked liver and pork.

liver spot • n. a small brown spot on the skin.

livery • n. (pl. **liveries**) 1 a special uniform worn by an official or a servant such as a footman. 2 a distinctive design and colour scheme used on the vehicles or products of a company.
– PHRASES **at livery** (of a horse) kept for the owner and fed and cared for at a fixed charge.
– DERIVATIVES **liveried** adj.
– ORIGIN first meaning 'the giving of food or clothing to servants': from Old French *livree* 'delivered'.

lives pl. of **LIFE**.

livestock • n. farm animals.

live wire • n. informal an energetic and lively person.

livid • adj. 1 informal furiously angry. 2 dark bluish grey in colour.
– ORIGIN Latin *lividus*.

living • n. 1 a way or style of life. 2 an income which is enough to live on, or the means of earning it. • adj. 1 alive. 2 (of a language) still used. 3 for daily life: *living quarters*.

living room • n. a room in a house for general everyday use.

living wage • n. a wage which is high enough to maintain a normal standard of living.

living will • n. a written statement of a person's wishes regarding their medical treatment should they become too ill to give consent.

lizard • n. a four-legged reptile with a long body and tail and a rough or spiny skin.
– ORIGIN Old French *lesard*.

'll • contr. shall; will.

llama /lah-muh/ • n. a domesticated animal of the camel family found in the Andes.
– ORIGIN Spanish.

lo • exclam. old use used to draw attention to an interesting event.

loach /lohch/ • n. a small freshwater fish with several long, thin growths near the mouth.
– ORIGIN Old French *loche*.

load • n. **1** a heavy or bulky thing being or about to be carried. **2** a weight or source of pressure. **3** the total number or amount carried in a vehicle or container. **4** (**a load/loads of**) informal a large quantity of. **5** the amount of work to be done by a person or machine. • v. **1** place a load or large quantity of something on or in a vehicle or container. **2** insert something into a device so that it will operate. **3** put ammunition into a firearm.
– DERIVATIVES **loader** n.
– ORIGIN Old English.

loaded • adj. **1** carrying a load. **2** biased towards a particular outcome. **3** having an underlying meaning: *a loaded question.* **4** informal wealthy.

loaf[1] • n. (pl. **loaves**) a quantity of bread that is shaped and baked in one piece.
– ORIGIN Old English.

loaf[2] • v. spend time being idle.
– ORIGIN prob. from **LOAFER**.

loafer • n. **1** a person who spends time being idle. **2** trademark a flat casual leather shoe.
– ORIGIN perh. from German *Landläufer* 'tramp'.

loam • n. a fertile soil of clay and sand containing humus.
– DERIVATIVES **loamy** adj.
– ORIGIN Old English, 'clay'.

loan • n. **1** a sum of money that is lent to someone. **2** the action of lending something. • v. give something as a loan.
– ORIGIN Old Norse.

loan shark • n. informal a moneylender who charges very high rates of interest.

loath /lohth/ (also **loth**) • adj. reluctant; unwilling: *I was loath to leave.*
– ORIGIN Old English, 'hostile'.

loathe /lohth/ • v. (**loathes, loathing, loathed**) feel hatred or disgust for.
– ORIGIN Old English.

loathsome • adj. causing hatred or disgust.

loaves pl. of **LOAF**[1].

lob • v. (**lobs, lobbing, lobbed**) throw or hit something in a high arc. • n. (in football or tennis) a ball lobbed over an opponent.
– ORIGIN prob. from German or Dutch.

lobby • n. (pl. **lobbies**) **1** a room out of which one or more other rooms or corridors lead, usually one near the entrance of a public building. **2** (also **division lobby**) each of two corridors in the Houses of Parliament to which MPs go to vote. **3** a group of people who try to influence politicians on a particular issue. • v. (**lobbies, lobbying, lobbied**) try to influence a politician on an issue.
– DERIVATIVES **lobbyist** n.
– ORIGIN Latin *lobia* 'covered walk'.

lobe • n. **1** a roundish projecting part or division of something. **2** (also **ear lobe**) the rounded fleshy part at the lower edge of the outer ear. **3** a major division of an organ such as the brain.
– DERIVATIVES **lobed** adj.
– ORIGIN Greek *lobos*.

lobelia /luh-bee-li-uh/ • n. a garden plant with blue or scarlet flowers.
– ORIGIN named after the Flemish botanist Matthias de *Lobel*.

lobotomy /luh-bot-uh-mi/ • n. (pl. **lobotomies**) a surgical operation involving cutting into part of the brain, formerly used to treat mental illness.

lobster • n. a large edible shellfish with large pincers.
– ORIGIN Old English.

lobster pot • n. a basket-like trap in which lobsters are caught.

local • adj. **1** relating to a particular area or to the area in which you live: *the local post office.* **2** affecting a particular part of the body: *a local anaesthetic.* **3** Computing (of a device) that can be accessed without the use of a network. • n. **1** a person who lives in a particular area. **2** Brit. informal a pub near to a person's home.
– DERIVATIVES **locally** adv.
– ORIGIN Latin *locus* 'place'.

local area network • n. a computer network that links devices within a building or group of buildings.

local authority • n. Brit. an administrative body responsible for local government.

locale /loh-kahl/ • n. a place where something happens.
– ORIGIN French *local* 'locality'.

local government • n. the administration of a particular county or district, with representatives elected by those who live there.

locality • n. (pl. **localities**) **1** an area or neighbourhood. **2** the position or site of something.

localize (or **localise**) • v. (**localizes, localizing, localized**) restrict or assign something to a particular place.
– DERIVATIVES **localization** n. **localizer** n.

local time • n. time as reckoned in a particular region or time zone.

locate • v. (**locates, locating, located**)

1 discover the exact place or position of. **2** (**be located**) be situated in a particular place.
– DERIVATIVES **locator** n.
– ORIGIN Latin *locare* 'to place'.

location • n. **1** a place where something is situated. **2** the action of discovering where something is. **3** an actual place in which a film or broadcast is made, as distinct from in a studio.
– DERIVATIVES **locational** adj.

loc. cit. • abbrev. in the passage already mentioned.
– ORIGIN Latin *loco citato*.

loch /lokh/ • n. (in Scotland) a lake or a narrow strip of sea almost surrounded by land.
– ORIGIN Scottish Gaelic.

loci pl. of LOCUS.

lock¹ • n. **1** a mechanism for keeping a door or container fastened, operated by a key. **2** a similar device used to prevent a vehicle or other machine from operating. **3** a structure constructed within a canal or river, having gates at each end which can be opened or closed to change the water level and so raise and lower boats. **4** (in wrestling and martial arts) a hold that prevents an opponent from moving a limb.
• v. **1** fasten a door or container with a lock. **2** (**lock someone in/up/away**) shut someone in or imprison someone. **3** (**lock something in/up/away**) keep something safe by locking a door or lid. **4** make or become fixed or immovable. **5** (**be locked in**) be deeply involved in: *they were locked in a legal battle.*
– PHRASES **lock, stock, and barrel** including everything.
– DERIVATIVES **lockable** adj.
– ORIGIN Old English.

lock² • n. **1** a section of a person's hair that coils or hangs in a piece. **2** (**locks**) literary a person's hair.
– ORIGIN Old English.

locker • n. a small lockable cupboard or compartment where belongings may be left.

locket • n. a small ornamental case worn on a chain round a person's neck, used to hold an item such as a tiny photograph.
– ORIGIN Old French *locquet* 'small lock'.

lockjaw • n. a form or sign of tetanus in which the jaws become stiff and tightly closed.

lockout • n. a situation in which an employer refuses to allow employees to enter their place of work until they agree to certain conditions.

locksmith • n. a person who makes and repairs locks.

lock-up • n. **1** a makeshift jail. **2** Brit. a garage or small shop separate from living quarters, that can be locked up.

loco¹ • n. (pl. **locos**) informal a locomotive.

loco² • adj. informal crazy.
– ORIGIN Spanish.

locomotion • n. movement or the ability to move from one place to another.
– ORIGIN from Latin *loco* 'from a place' + *motio* 'motion'.

locomotive • n. a powered railway vehicle used for pulling trains.
• adj. relating to locomotion.

locum /loh-kuhm/ • n. Brit. a doctor or priest standing in for another who is temporarily away.
– ORIGIN from Latin *locum tenens* 'a person holding a place'.

locus /loh-kuhss/ • n. (pl. **loci** /loh-sy/) **1** tech. a particular position, point, or place. **2** Math. a curve or other figure formed by all the points satisfying a particular condition.
– ORIGIN Latin.

locust • n. a large tropical grasshopper which migrates in vast swarms, eating and destroying all the vegetation in an area.
– ORIGIN Latin *locusta*.

locution /luh-kyoo-sh'n/ • n. **1** a word or phrase. **2** a person's particular style of speech.
– ORIGIN Latin.

lode /rhymes with rode/ • n. a vein of metal ore in the earth.
– ORIGIN Old English, 'way, course'.

lodestar • n. the pole star.

lodestone • n. **1** a piece of magnetic iron ore used as a magnet. **2** a focus of attention or attraction.

lodge • n. **1** a small house at the gates of a large house with grounds, occupied by an employee. **2** a porter's quarters at the entrance of a college or other large building. **3** a small country house where people stay while hunting or shooting. **4** a branch of an organization such as the Freemasons. **5** a beaver's den.
• v. (**lodges, lodging, lodged**) **1** formally present a complaint or appeal. **2** fix or be fixed in a place. **3** rent accommodation in another person's house. **4** (**lodge something in/with**) leave something valuable for safekeeping in a place or with someone.
– ORIGIN Old French *loge* 'hut'.

lodger • n. esp. Brit. a person who pays rent to live in a property with the owner.

lodging • n. **1** temporary accommodation. **2** (**lodgings**) a rented room or rooms in the same house as the owner.

lodging house • n. a private house providing rented accommodation.

loess /loh-iss/ • n. a loose, fine soil originally deposited by the wind.
– ORIGIN Swiss German *lösch* 'loose'.

lo-fi (also **low-fi**) • adj. relating to sound reproduction of a lower quality than hi-fi.
– ORIGIN from **LOW¹** + *-fi* on the pattern of *hi-fi*.

loft • n. 1 a room or storage space directly under the roof of a house or other building. 2 a large, open living area in a converted warehouse or other large building. 3 a gallery in a church or hall. • v. kick, hit, or throw a ball high into the air.
– ORIGIN Old Norse, 'air, upper room'.

lofty • adj. (**loftier, loftiest**) 1 tall and impressive. 2 morally good; noble: *lofty ideals.* 3 proud and superior.
– DERIVATIVES **loftily** adv. **loftiness** n.

log¹ • n. 1 a sawn section of the trunk or a large branch of a tree. 2 (also **logbook**) an official record of events during the voyage of a ship or aircraft. • v. (**logs, logging, logged**) 1 enter facts in an official record. 2 achieve a certain distance, speed, or time. 3 (**log in/on** or **out/off**) begin (or finish) using a computer. 4 cut down an area of forest to use the wood commercially.
– DERIVATIVES **logger** n.

log² • n. a logarithm.

loganberry • n. (pl. **loganberries**) an edible red soft fruit, similar to a large raspberry.
– ORIGIN named after the American horticulturalist John H. *Logan*.

logarithm /log-uh-ri-thuhm/ • n. one of a series of numbers, representing the power to which a fixed number (the base) must be raised to produce a given number, used to simplify calculations.
– DERIVATIVES **logarithmic** adj.
– ORIGIN from Greek *logos* 'reckoning, ratio' + *arithmos* 'number'.

logbook • n. 1 a log of a ship or aircraft. 2 Brit. an official document recording details about a vehicle and its owner.

loggerheads • pl. n. (in phr. **at loggerheads**) in strong disagreement.
– ORIGIN from dialect *logger* 'block of wood for hobbling a horse' + **HEAD**.

loggia /loh-ji-uh/ • n. a long room with one or more open sides, especially one facing a garden.
– ORIGIN Italian, 'lodge'.

logic • n. 1 the science of reasoning. 2 good reasoning: *the strategy has a certain logic to it.* 3 an underlying system or set of principles used in preparing a

computer or electronic device to perform a specified task.
– DERIVATIVES **logician** n.
– ORIGIN from Greek *logikē tekhnē* 'art of reason'.

logical • adj. 1 following the rules of logic. 2 showing clear, sound reasoning. 3 expected or reasonable under the circumstances: *a bridge is the logical choice.*
– DERIVATIVES **logically** adv.

-logical • comb. form forming adjectives from nouns ending in *-logy* (such as *biological* from *biology*).
– DERIVATIVES **-logic** comb. form.

logistics /luh-jiss-tiks/ • n. 1 the detailed organization of a large and complex project or event. 2 the commercial activity of transporting goods to customers.
– DERIVATIVES **logistic** adj. **logistical** adj.
– ORIGIN French *logistique* 'movement and supply of troops and equipment'.

logjam • n. a situation that seems unable to be settled; a deadlock.

logo /loh-goh/ • n. (pl. **logos**) a design or symbol chosen by an organization to identify its products.
– ORIGIN Greek *logos* 'word'.

-logy • comb. form forming words referring to: 1 (also **-ology**) a subject of study or interest: *psychology.* 2 a type of writing or speech: *trilogy.*
– ORIGIN Greek *logos* 'word'.

loin • n. 1 the part of the body between the ribs and the hip bones. 2 a joint of meat from this part of an animal. 3 (**loins**) literary a person's sexual organs.
– ORIGIN Old French *loigne*.

loincloth • n. a piece of cloth wrapped round the hips, worn by men in some hot countries.

loiter • v. (**loiters, loitering, loitered**) stand around without any obvious purpose.
– DERIVATIVES **loiterer** n.
– ORIGIN perh. from Dutch *loteren* 'wag about'.

loll • v. 1 sit, lie, or stand in a lazy, relaxed way. 2 hang loosely: *he let his head loll back.*

lollipop • n. a large, flat, rounded boiled sweet on the end of a stick.
– ORIGIN perh. from dialect *lolly* 'tongue' + **POP¹**.

lollipop lady (or **lollipop man**) • n. Brit. informal a person employed to help children cross the road safely by holding up a circular sign on a pole to stop the traffic.

lollop • v. (**lollops, lolloping, lolloped**)

move in a series of clumsy bounding steps.
– ORIGIN prob. from **LOLL** and **TROLLOP**.

lolly • n. (pl. **lollies**) Brit. informal **1** a lollipop. **2** money.

Londoner • n. a person from London.

lone • adj. **1** having no companions; solitary. **2** lacking the support of other people: *I am certainly not a lone voice.*
– ORIGIN from **ALONE**.

lonely • adj. (**lonelier**, **loneliest**) **1** sad because of having no friends or company. **2** spent alone: *lonely days.* **3** (of a place) remote.
– DERIVATIVES **loneliness** n.

lonely hearts • pl. n. people looking for a lover or friend through the personal columns of a newspaper.

loner • n. a person who prefers to be alone.

lonesome • adj. esp. N. Amer. lonely.

long[1] • adj. (**longer**, **longest**) **1** having a great length in space or time. **2** having or lasting a particular length, distance, or time: *the ship will be 150 metres long.* **3** relatively great in extent: *a long list.* **4** (of odds in betting) reflecting a low level of probability. **5** (of a vowel) pronounced in a way that takes longer than a short vowel in the same position (e.g. in standard British English the vowel /oo/ in *food*). **6** (**long on**) informal well supplied with. **7** (of a drink) large and refreshing. • n. a long time. • adv. (**longer**, **longest**) **1** for a long time. **2** at a distant time: *long ago.* **3** throughout a specified period of time: *all day long.*
– PHRASES **as** (or **so**) **long as** provided that. **in the long run** (or **term**) eventually. **the long and the short of it** all that can or need be said. **long in the tooth** rather old.
– DERIVATIVES **longish** adj.
– ORIGIN Old English.

long[2] • v. (**long for/to do**) have a strong wish for or to do something.
– ORIGIN Old English, 'grow long, yearn'.

long. • abbrev. longitude.

longboat • n. **1** hist. the largest boat carried by a sailing ship. **2** = **LONGSHIP**.

longbow • n. hist. a large bow for shooting arrows.

long-distance • adj. travelling or operating between distant places. • adv. between distant places.

long division • n. the process of dividing one number by another with all calculations written down.

longe • n. var. of **LUNGE** (in sense 2).

longevity /lon-jev-i-ti/ • n. long life.
– ORIGIN Latin *longaevitas.*

long face • n. an unhappy or disappointed expression.

longhand • n. ordinary handwriting (as opposed to shorthand, typing, or printing).

long haul • n. **1** a long distance over which goods or passengers are transported. **2** a long and difficult task.

longing • n. a strong wish to do or have something.
– DERIVATIVES **longingly** adv.

longitude /long-i-tyood/ • n. the distance of a place east or west of the Greenwich meridian, measured in degrees.
– ORIGIN Latin *longitudo.*

longitudinal /long-i-tyoo-di-n'l/ • adj. **1** extending lengthwise. **2** relating to the distance of a place east or west of the Greenwich meridian.
– DERIVATIVES **longitudinally** adv.

long johns • pl. n. informal underpants with closely fitted legs reaching to the ankles.

long jump • n. an athletic event in which competitors jump as far as possible along the ground in one leap.

long-life • adj. (of perishable goods) treated so as to stay fresh for longer than usual.

long-lived • adj. living or lasting a long time.

long-playing • adj. (of a gramophone record) about 30 cm in diameter and rotating at 33⅓ revolutions per minute.

long-range • adj. **1** able to travel long distances. **2** relating to a period of time far into the future.

longship • n. a long, narrow warship with oars and a sail, used by the Vikings.

longshore • adj. relating to or moving along the seashore.
– ORIGIN from *along shore.*

long shot • n. a scheme or guess that has only the slightest chance of succeeding or being accurate.
– PHRASES (**not**) **by a long shot** informal (not) by any means or at all.

long-sighted • adj. Brit. unable to see things clearly if they are close to the eyes.

long-standing • adj. having existed for a long time.

long-suffering • adj. bearing problems or annoying behaviour with patience.

long wave • n. a radio wave of a wavelength above one kilometre (and a frequency below 300 kilohertz).

longways • adv. lengthways.

long-winded • adj. long and boring.

loo • n. Brit. informal a toilet.

loofah /loo-fuh/ • n. a long rough object

used like a bath sponge, consisting of the dried inner parts of a tropical fruit.
– ORIGIN Egyptian Arabic.

look • v. **1** direct your gaze in a particular direction. **2** give the impression of being: *her father looked unhappy.* **3** face in a particular direction: *the rooms look out over the harbour.* • n. **1** an act of looking. **2** a particular appearance. **3** (**looks**) a person's facial appearance. **4** a style or fashion.
– PHRASES **look after** take care of. **look down on** (also **look down your nose at**) think that you are better than. **look for** try to find. **look in** make a short visit. **look into** investigate. **look on** watch without getting involved. **look out** be alert for possible trouble. **look something out** Brit. search for and produce something. **look to** rely on someone to do something. **look up** improve. **look someone up** informal visit or contact a friend. **look something up** search for information in a reference book. **look up to** have a great deal of respect for.
– ORIGIN Old English.

lookalike • n. a person who looks very similar to someone else.

looker • n. informal a person with a specified appearance: *she's not a bad looker.*

look-in • n. Brit. informal a chance to take part in something.

looking glass • n. a mirror.

lookout • n. **1** a place from which to keep watch. **2** a person keeping watch for danger or trouble. **3** (**your lookout**) Brit. informal your own concern.
– PHRASES **be on the lookout** (or **keep a lookout**) **for 1** be alert to. **2** keep searching for.

lookup • n. the systematic retrieval of electronic information.

loom¹ • n. a machine for weaving cloth.
– ORIGIN Old English, 'tool'.

loom² • v. **1** appear as a vague and threatening shape: *vehicles loomed out of the darkness.* **2** (of an unfavourable event) seem about to happen.
– ORIGIN prob. from German or Dutch.

loony informal • n. (pl. **loonies**) a mad or silly person. • adj. (**loonier, looniest**) mad or silly.
– DERIVATIVES **looniness** n.
– ORIGIN from LUNATIC.

loop • n. **1** a shape produced by a curve that bends round and crosses itself. **2** an endless strip of tape or film allowing sounds or images to be continuously repeated. **3** a complete circuit for an electric current. **4** Computing a programmed sequence of instructions

that is repeated until or while a particular condition is satisfied. • v. **1** form into a loop or loops: *she looped her arms around his neck.* **2** follow a course that forms a loop or loops.
– PHRASES **loop the loop** (of an aircraft) fly in a vertical circle.

loophole • n. an inexact wording or omission in a law or contract that enables someone to avoid doing something.
– ORIGIN from former *loop* 'opening in a wall'.

loopy • adj. (**loopier, loopiest**) informal mad or silly.
– DERIVATIVES **loopiness** n.

loose /looss/ • adj. **1** not firmly or tightly fixed in place. **2** not fastened or packaged together. **3** not tied up or shut in: *the horses broke loose.* **4** (of a garment) not fitting tightly. **5** not dense or compact in structure. **6** not strict; inexact: *a loose interpretation.* **7** careless and indiscreet: *loose talk.* **8** dated immoral. • v. (**looses, loosing, loosed**) **1** unfasten or set free. **2** (**loose something off**) fire a shot, bullet, etc.
– PHRASES **on the loose** having escaped from prison.
– DERIVATIVES **loosely** adv. **looseness** n.
– ORIGIN Old Norse.

> **USAGE:** Do not confuse the words **loose** and **lose**; **loose** means 'not fixed in place or tied up' (*a loose tooth*), while **lose** means 'no longer have' or 'become unable to find' (*I need to lose about a stone*).

loose box • n. Brit. a stable or stall in which a horse is kept without a tether.

loose cannon • n. a person who behaves in a way that is unexpected and that may cause harm.

loose end • n. a detail that is not yet settled or explained.
– PHRASES **be at a loose end** have nothing definite to do.

loose forward • n. Rugby a forward who plays at the back of the scrum.

loose-leaf • adj. (of a folder) allowing sheets of paper to be added or removed.

loosen • v. **1** make or become loose. **2** (**loosen up**) warm up in preparation for exercise.

loot • n. **1** goods stolen from empty buildings during a war or riot. **2** goods stolen by a thief. **3** informal money. • v. steal goods from empty buildings during a war or riot.
– DERIVATIVES **looter** n.
– ORIGIN Sanskrit.

lop • v. (**lops, lopping, lopped**) **1** cut off a branch or limb from a tree or body.

2 informal make smaller or less by a particular amount.
– DERIVATIVES **lopper** n.

lope • v. (**lopes, loping, loped**) run with a long bounding stride. • n. a long bounding stride.
– ORIGIN Old Norse, 'leap'.

lop-eared • adj. (of an animal) having drooping ears.
– ORIGIN from former *lop* 'hang loosely'.

lopsided • adj. with one side lower or smaller than the other.

loquacious /luh-kway-shuhss/ • adj. tending to talk a great deal; talkative.
– DERIVATIVES **loquacity** /luh-kwass-i-ti/ n.
– ORIGIN Latin *loqui* 'to talk'.

lord • n. **1** a nobleman. **2** (**Lord**) a title given to certain British peers or high officials: *Lord Derby.* **3** (**the Lords**) the House of Lords. **4** a master or ruler. **5** (**Lord**) a name for God or Christ.
– PHRASES **lord it over** act in an arrogant and bullying way towards. **the Lord's Prayer** the prayer taught by Christ to his disciples, beginning 'Our Father'.
– ORIGIN Old English, 'bread-keeper'.

Lord Chamberlain • n. (in the UK) the official in charge of the royal household.

Lord Chancellor • n. the highest judge in the United Kingdom and Speaker of the House of Lords.

Lord Chief Justice • n. the second highest judge in the United Kingdom.

Lord Lieutenant • n. (in the UK) the representative of the Queen and head of magistrates in each county.

lordly • adj. (**lordlier, lordliest**) suitable for or like a lord.

Lord Mayor • n. the title of the mayor in London and some other large cities.

Lord Privy Seal • n. (in the UK) a senior cabinet minister without particular official duties.

Lordship • n. (**His/Your Lordship**) a form of address to a judge, bishop, or nobleman.

Lords spiritual • pl. n. the bishops in the House of Lords.

Lords temporal • pl. n. the members of the House of Lords other than the bishops.

lore • n. a body of traditions and knowledge in a particular subject: *farming lore.*
– ORIGIN Old English, 'instruction'.

lorgnette /lor-nyet/ (also **lorgnettes**) • n. a pair of glasses or opera glasses held by a long handle at one side.
– ORIGIN French.

lorry • n. (pl. **lorries**) Brit. a large, heavy

motor vehicle for transporting goods.

lose /looz/ • v. (**loses, losing, lost**) **1** have something or someone taken away from you; no longer have or keep: *she lost her job in a hotel.* **2** become unable to find. **3** fail to win a game or contest. **4** earn less money than you are spending. **5** waste time or an opportunity. **6** (**be lost**) be destroyed or killed. **7** escape from someone in pursuit. **8** (**lose yourself in/be lost in**) be or become deeply involved in. **9** (of a watch or clock) become slow by a specified amount of time.
– PHRASES **lose out** not get a full chance or advantage.
– ORIGIN Old English.

> USAGE: For an explanation of the difference between **lose** and **loose**, see the note at **LOOSE**.

loser • n. **1** a person or thing that loses or has lost a game or contest. **2** informal a person who is generally unsuccessful in life.

losing battle • n. a struggle in which failure seems certain.

loss • n. **1** the fact or action of losing something or someone. **2** a person, thing, or amount lost. **3** the feeling of sadness after losing a valued person or thing. **4** a person or thing that is badly missed when lost.
– PHRASES **at a loss** uncertain or puzzled.
– ORIGIN Old English, 'destruction'.

loss-leader • n. a product sold at a loss but justified because it attracts customers.

lost past and past part. of **LOSE**.
– PHRASES **be lost for words** be so surprised or upset that you cannot think what to say. **be lost on** fail to be understood by: *the irony is lost on him.*

lost cause • n. something that has no chance of success.

lot • pron. & adv. (**a lot** or **lots**) informal a large number or amount. • n. **1** an item or set of items for sale at an auction. **2** informal a group of people or things: *you lot think you're clever.* **3** a method of deciding something by chance, especially by choosing one from a number of pieces of paper. **4** a person's situation in life: *schemes to improve the lot of the poor.* **5** esp. N. Amer. a plot of land.
– PHRASES **draw** (or **cast**) **lots** decide by choosing one from a number of pieces of paper, or by a similar method of chance. **the lot** esp. Brit. the whole number or quantity. **throw in your lot with** decide to join a person or group and share their fate.
– ORIGIN Old English.

☑️ The correct spelling is **a lot**; do not spell it as one word (*alot*).

USAGE: Although **a lot of** and **lots of** are often used in speech, it is better not to use them when writing; use **many** or **a large number** instead.

---

loth • adj. var. of LOATH.

Lothario /luh-thair-i-oh/ • n. (pl. **Lotharios**) a man who has many casual sexual relationships with women.
– ORIGIN from a character in Nicholas Rowe's play *The Fair Penitent*.

lotion • n. a creamy liquid put on the skin as a medicine or cosmetic.
– ORIGIN Latin.

lottery • n. (pl. **lotteries**) 1 a means of raising money by selling numbered tickets and giving prizes to the holders of numbers drawn at random. 2 something whose success is controlled by luck.
– ORIGIN prob. from Dutch *loterij*.

lotus • n. 1 a kind of large water lily. 2 (in Greek mythology) a fruit that causes dreamy forgetfulness.
– ORIGIN Greek *lōtos*.

lotus position • n. a cross-legged position for meditation, with the feet resting on the thighs.

louche /loosh/ • adj. having a bad reputation but still attractive: *his louche, creepy charm.*
– ORIGIN French, 'squinting'.

loud • adj. 1 producing much noise. 2 expressed forcefully: *loud protests.* 3 very bright and lacking good taste: *a loud checked suit.* • adv. with much noise.
– PHRASES **out loud** aloud.
– DERIVATIVES **loudly** adv. **loudness** n.
– ORIGIN Old English.

loudhailer • n. Brit. an electronic device for making the voice louder.

loudmouth • n. informal a person who talks too much or who makes offensive remarks.

loudspeaker • n. a device that converts electrical impulses into sound.

lough /lokh/ • n. (in Ireland) a lake or narrow strip of sea; a loch.

lounge • v. (**lounges**, **lounging**, **lounged**) lie, sit, or stand in a relaxed way. • n. 1 Brit. a sitting room. 2 a room in a hotel, theatre, or airport in which to relax or wait.

lounge bar • n. Brit. a bar in a pub or hotel that is more comfortable or smarter than the public bar.

lounger • n. 1 an outdoor chair that allows a person to lie back. 2 a person spending their time lazily.

lounge suit • n. Brit. a man's suit for ordinary day wear.

lour /rhymes with flour/ (also **lower**) • v. (of the sky) appear dark and threatening.

louse • n. 1 (pl. **lice**) a small insect which lives as a parasite on animals or plants. 2 (pl. **louses**) informal an unpleasant person. • v. (**louses**, **lousing**, **loused**) (**louse something up**) informal spoil something.
– ORIGIN Old English.

lousy • adj. (**lousier**, **lousiest**) 1 informal very poor or bad. 2 infested with lice.

lout • n. a rude or aggressive man.
– DERIVATIVES **loutish** adj.
– ORIGIN perh. from Old English, 'bow down'.

louvre /loo-ver/ (US also **louver**) • n. each of a set of slanting slats fixed at intervals in a door or other opening to allow air or light through.
– DERIVATIVES **louvred** adj.
– ORIGIN Old French *lover* 'skylight'.

lovable (also **loveable**) • adj. easy to love or feel affection for.
– DERIVATIVES **lovably** adv.

lovage /luv-ij/ • n. a herb used in cookery.
– ORIGIN Old French *luvesche*.

love • n. 1 a strong feeling of affection. 2 a strong feeling of affection linked with sexual attraction. 3 a great interest and pleasure in something. 4 a person or thing that you love. 5 (in tennis, squash, etc.) a score of zero. • v. (**loves**, **loving**, **loved**) 1 feel love for. 2 like very much.
– PHRASES **make love** have sex.
– DERIVATIVES **loveless** adj.
– ORIGIN Old English.

love affair • n. a romantic or sexual relationship between two people who are not married to each other.

love bite • n. Brit. a temporary red mark on the skin caused by biting or sucking during sexual play.

love child • n. a child born to parents who are not married to each other.

lovelorn • adj. unhappy because you love someone who does not feel the same way about you.
– ORIGIN from LOVE + a former word meaning 'lost'.

lovely • adj. (**lovelier**, **loveliest**) 1 very beautiful. 2 very pleasant.
– DERIVATIVES **loveliness** n.

lovemaking • n. sex and other sexual activity.

love nest • n. informal a private place where two lovers spend time together.

lover • n. 1 a person having a sexual or romantic relationship with someone. 2 a person who enjoys a specified thing: *a music lover.*

lovesick • adj. pining or feeling weak due to being in love.

low[1] • adj. **1** not high or tall or far above the ground. **2** below average in amount, extent, or strength: *cook over a low heat.* **3** lacking importance or quality; inferior. **4** (of a sound) deep or quiet. **5** depressed or lacking in energy. **6** unfavourable: *she had a low opinion of him.* **7** lacking moral principles: *low cunning.* • n. **1** a low point, level, or figure. **2** an area of low atmospheric pressure. • adv. **1** at or into a low position or state. **2** (of a sound) at a low pitch.
– ORIGIN Old Norse.

low[2] • v. (of a cow) moo.
– ORIGIN Old English.

lowbrow • adj. usu. derog. not intellectual or interested in culture.

Low Church • n. the part of the Church of England that places comparatively little emphasis on ritual and the authority of bishops and priests.

low-down informal • adj. unfair or dishonest. • n. (**the low-down**) the important facts about something.

lower[1] • adj. **1** less high. **2** (of a geological period or formation) earlier: *the Lower Cretaceous.* **3** (in place names) situated to the south. • v. (**lowers, lowering, lowered**) **1** make or become lower. **2** move downwards. **3** (**lower yourself**) behave in a way that is humiliating.
– DERIVATIVES **lowermost** adj.

lower[2] • v. var. of LOUR.

lower case • n. small letters as opposed to capitals.

lower class • n. the working class.

lower house (also **lower chamber**) • n. the larger body of a parliament with two chambers, usually with elected members.

lowest common denominator • n. Math. the lowest common multiple of the denominators of several fractions.

lowest common multiple • n. Math. the lowest quantity that is a multiple of two or more given quantities.

low-fi • adj. var. of LO-FI.

low frequency • n. (in radio) 30–300 kilohertz.

low gear • n. a gear that causes a vehicle to move slowly.

low-key (also **low-keyed**) • adj. not elaborate or showy; modest.

lowland /loh-luhnd/ • n. **1** (also **lowlands**) low-lying country. **2** (**the Lowlands**) the part of Scotland lying south and east of the Highlands.
– DERIVATIVES **lowlander** n.

low-level • adj. (of a computer programming language) similar to machine code in form.

low life • n. dishonest or immoral people or activities.

lowly • adj. (**lowlier, lowliest**) low in status or importance: *I'm just a lowly engineer.*
– DERIVATIVES **lowliness** n.

low-lying • adj. (of land) not far above sea level.

low-rise • adj. **1** (of a building) having few storeys. **2** (of trousers) cut so as to fit low on the hips rather than on the waist.

low season • n. Brit. the least popular time of year for a holiday, when prices are lowest.

low-slung • adj. lower in height or closer to the ground than usual.

low tide (also **low water**) • n. the state of the tide when at its lowest level.

low-water mark • n. the level reached by the sea at low tide.

loyal • adj. committed and faithful in your support for a person, an organization, or your country.
– DERIVATIVES **loyally** adv.
– ORIGIN Old French *loial.*

loyalist • n. **1** a person who remains loyal to the established ruler or government. **2** (**Loyalist**) a supporter of union between Great Britain and Northern Ireland.
– DERIVATIVES **loyalism** n.

loyalty • n. (pl. **loyalties**) **1** the state of being loyal or faithful to a person, an organization, or your country. **2** a strong feeling of support and commitment.

lozenge /loz-inj/ • n. **1** a small tablet of medicine that is sucked to soothe a sore throat. **2** a diamond shape.
– ORIGIN Old French *losenge.*

LP • abbrev. long-playing (gramophone record).

L-plate • n. Brit. a sign with the letter L on it, attached to a vehicle to indicate that the driver is a learner.

Lr • symb. the chemical element lawrencium.

LSD • n. lysergic acid diethylamide, a powerful illegal drug that causes hallucinations.

Lt • abbrev. Lieutenant.

Ltd • abbrev. Brit. (after a company name) Limited.

Lu • symb. the chemical element lutetium.

lubricant • n. a substance for lubricating machinery or part of the body.

lubricate /loo-bri-kayt/ • v. (**lubricates, lubricating, lubricated**) apply a

substance such as oil or grease to machinery or part of the body to allow smooth movement.
– DERIVATIVES **lubrication** n.
– ORIGIN Latin *lubricare* 'make slippery'.

lubricious /loo-bri-shuhss/ • adj. referring to sexual matters in a rude or offensive way.
– ORIGIN Latin *lubricus* 'slippery'.

lucent /loo-suhnt/ • adj. literary shining.
– ORIGIN Latin *lucere* 'shine'.

lucerne /loo-sern/ • n. = ALFALFA.
– ORIGIN Provençal *luzerno* 'glow-worm'.

lucid /loo-sid/ • adj. **1** easy to understand; clear. **2** showing an ability to think clearly.
– DERIVATIVES **lucidity** n. **lucidly** adv.
– ORIGIN Latin *lucidus* 'bright'.

Lucifer /loo-si-fer/ • n. **1** the Devil. **2** (**lucifer**) old use a match.
– ORIGIN Latin, 'light-bringing'.

luck • n. **1** good or bad things that happen by chance. **2** good fortune.
– ORIGIN German *lucke*.

luckily • adv. it is fortunate that.

luckless • adj. unlucky; unfortunate.

lucky • adj. (**luckier, luckiest**) having, bringing, or resulting from good luck: *he had a lucky escape.*

lucky dip • n. Brit. a game in which small prizes are concealed in a container for people to pick out at random.

lucrative /loo-kruh-tiv/ • adj. making a large profit.
– ORIGIN Latin *lucrativus*.

lucre /loo-ker/ • n. literary money.
– ORIGIN Latin *lucrum*.

Luddite /lud-dyt/ • n. derog. a person opposed to new technology.
– ORIGIN perh. from Ned *Lud*, one of the workers who in 1811–16 destroyed machinery which they thought was threatening their jobs.

ludicrous /loo-di-kruhss/ • adj. absurd; ridiculous.
– DERIVATIVES **ludicrously** adv.
– ORIGIN Latin *ludicrus*.

ludo • n. Brit. a board game in which players move counters according to throws of a dice.
– ORIGIN Latin, 'I play'.

luff • v. steer a sailing ship nearer the wind.
– ORIGIN Old French *lof*.

lug[1] • v. (**lugs, lugging, lugged**) carry or drag something with great effort.
– ORIGIN prob. Scandinavian.

lug[2] • n. **1** Brit. informal an ear. **2** a projection on an object by which it may be carried or fixed in place.
– ORIGIN prob. Scandinavian.

luge /loozh/ • n. a light toboggan ridden in a sitting or lying position.
– ORIGIN Swiss French.

luggage • n. suitcases or other bags for a traveller's belongings.
– ORIGIN from LUG[1].

lugger • n. a small ship with two or three masts and a four-sided sail on each.

lugubrious /luu-goo-bri-uhss/ • adj. sad or gloomy.
– ORIGIN Latin *lugubris*.

lugworm • n. a worm living in muddy sand by the sea, used as fishing bait.

lukewarm • adj. **1** only slightly warm. **2** unenthusiastic.
– ORIGIN from dialect *luke* 'tepid'.

lull • v. **1** calm someone or send them to sleep with soothing sounds or movements. **2** make someone feel safe or confident, even if they are at risk. **3** (of noise or a storm) quieten or become calm. • n. a quiet period between times of activity.

lullaby • n. (pl. **lullabies**) a soothing song sung to send a child to sleep.

lumbago /lum-bay-goh/ • n. pain in the lower back.
– ORIGIN Latin.

lumbar /lum-ber/ • adj. relating to the lower back.
– ORIGIN Latin *lumbaris*.

lumber • n. **1** Brit. disused articles of furniture that take up space. **2** esp. N. Amer. timber sawn into rough planks. • v. (**lumbers, lumbering, lumbered**) **1** Brit. informal give someone an unwanted responsibility. **2** move in a slow, awkward way.

lumberjack (also **lumberman**) • n. a person who fells trees, cuts them into logs, or transports them.

lumen /loo-muhn/ • n. Physics the SI unit of flux of light.
– ORIGIN Latin, 'light'.

luminary /loo-mi-nuh-ri/ • n. (pl. **luminaries**) a person who inspires or influences people: *sporting luminaries.*

luminescence /loo-mi-ness-uhnss/ • n. the production of light by a substance that has not been heated, as occurs in fluorescence.
– DERIVATIVES **luminescent** adj.

luminosity • n. (pl. **luminosities**) the quality of being bright or shining.

luminous /loo-mi-nuhss/ • adj. **1** bright or shining, especially in the dark. **2** Physics relating to visible light.
– ORIGIN Latin *luminosus*.

lump[1] • n. **1** an irregular piece of something hard or solid. **2** a swelling under the skin. • v. treat people or things as being alike, without regard for

differences: *alternative therapies are often lumped together.*
– PHRASES **a lump in the throat** a feeling of tightness in the throat caused by strong emotion.
– ORIGIN perh. Germanic.

lump² •v. (**lump it**) informal put up with something whether you like it or not.

lumpectomy •n. (pl. **lumpectomies**) a surgical operation in which a tumour or other lump is removed from the breast.

lumpen •adj. **1** lumpy and misshapen. **2** unthinking or stupid.
– ORIGIN German *Lumpen* 'rag, rogue'.

lumpish •adj. stupid and slow.

lump sum •n. a single payment made at one time, as opposed to a number of smaller payments on several occasions.

lumpy •adj. (**lumpier**, **lumpiest**) full of or covered with lumps.
– DERIVATIVES **lumpiness** n.

lunacy •n. **1** insanity (not in technical use). **2** great stupidity.

lunar /loo-ner/ •adj. relating to or resembling the moon: *a lunar landscape.*
– ORIGIN Latin *luna* 'moon'.

lunar eclipse •n. an eclipse in which the moon passes into the earth's shadow.

lunar month •n. a month measured between one new moon and the next (roughly 29½ days).

lunatic •n. **1** a person who is mentally ill (not in technical use). **2** a very foolish person.
– ORIGIN Latin *luna* 'moon' (from the former belief that changes of the moon caused insanity).

lunatic fringe •n. a small section of people within a group with extreme or eccentric views.

lunch •n. a meal eaten in the middle of the day. •v. eat lunch.
– DERIVATIVES **luncher** n.
– ORIGIN from LUNCHEON.

luncheon •n. formal lunch.
– ORIGIN perh. from Spanish *lonja* 'slice'.

luncheon meat •n. minced cooked pork mixed with cereal, sold in a tin.

lung •n. each of the pair of organs within the ribcage of humans and most vertebrates, into which air is drawn in breathing.
– DERIVATIVES **lungful** n.
– ORIGIN Old English.

lunge •n. **1** a sudden forward movement of the body. **2** (also **longe**) a long rein on which a horse is made to move in a circle round its trainer. •v. (**lunges**, **lunging** or **lungeing**, **lunged**) make a sudden forward movement of the body.
– ORIGIN French *allonger* 'lengthen'.

lupin /loo-pin/ •n. a plant with a tall

stem bearing many small colourful flowers.
– ORIGIN Latin *lupinus*.

lupine /loo-pyn/ •adj. relating to wolves.
– ORIGIN Latin *lupus* 'wolf'.

lurch¹ •v. make a sudden unsteady movement. •n. a sudden unsteady movement.

lurch² •n. (in phr. **leave someone in the lurch**) leave someone in a difficult situation without help or support.
– ORIGIN French *lourche*, a game resembling backgammon.

lurcher •n. Brit. a dog that is a cross between a greyhound and a retriever, collie, or sheepdog.
– ORIGIN related to LURK.

lure /lyoor/ •v. (**lures**, **luring**, **lured**) tempt someone to do something. •n. **1** the attractive and tempting qualities of something: *the lure of the city.* **2** a type of bait used in fishing or hunting.
– ORIGIN Old French *luere*.

lurex /lyoo-reks/ •n. trademark yarn or fabric containing a glittering metallic thread.

lurid /lyoor-id/ •adj. **1** unpleasantly bright in colour. **2** (of a description) deliberately containing vivid and shocking material.
– DERIVATIVES **luridly** adv.
– ORIGIN Latin *luridus* 'pale yellow'.

lurk •v. wait in hiding so as to attack someone or something.
– DERIVATIVES **lurker** n.
– ORIGIN perh. from LOUR.

luscious •adj. **1** having a pleasingly rich, sweet taste. **2** pleasing to the senses: *luscious harmonies.* **3** (of a person) sexually attractive.
– ORIGIN perh. from DELICIOUS.

lush¹ •adj. **1** (of plants) growing thickly and strongly. **2** rich or luxurious: *a lush red fabric.*
– DERIVATIVES **lushly** adv. **lushness** n.
– ORIGIN perh. from Old French *lasche* 'lax'.

lush² •n. N. Amer. informal a drunkard.
– ORIGIN perh. from LUSH¹.

lust •n. **1** strong sexual desire. **2** a passionate desire for something. •v. (usu. **lust for/after**) feel a strong desire for someone or something.
– ORIGIN Old English.

lustful •adj. filled with strong sexual desire.
– DERIVATIVES **lustfully** adv.

lustre (US **luster**) •n. **1** a soft glow or shine. **2** prestige or honour: *a celebrity player added lustre to the line-up.*
– ORIGIN French.

lustrous • adj. having a soft glow or shine.

lusty • adj. (**lustier, lustiest**) healthy and strong; vigorous.
– DERIVATIVES **lustily** adv.

lute • n. a stringed instrument having a long neck and a rounded body with a flat front, played by plucking.
– ORIGIN Old French *lut*.

lutenist /loo-tuh-nist/ • n. a lute player.

lutetium /loo-tee-shi-uhm/ • n. a rare silvery-white metallic chemical element.
– ORIGIN Latin *Lutetia*, the ancient name of Paris.

Lutheran • n. a member of the Lutheran Church, a Protestant Church based on the beliefs of the German theologian Martin Luther. • adj. relating to the teachings of Martin Luther or to the Lutheran Church.

lux /luks/ • n. (pl. **lux**) the SI unit of illumination.
– ORIGIN Latin, 'light'.

Luxembourger /luk-suhm-ber-ger/ • n. a person from Luxembourg.

luxuriant /lug-zhoor-i-uhnt/ • adj. (of vegetation or hair) growing thickly and strongly.
– DERIVATIVES **luxuriance** n. **luxuriantly** adv.
– ORIGIN Latin *luxuriare* 'grow very thickly'.

luxuriate /lug-zhoor-i-ayt/ • v. (**luxuriates, luxuriating, luxuriated**) (**luxuriate in/over**) take pleasure in something enjoyable.

luxurious • adj. **1** very comfortable, elegant, and expensive. **2** giving pleasure to the senses: *a luxurious scented bath*.
– DERIVATIVES **luxuriously** adv.

luxury • n. (pl. **luxuries**) **1** comfortable and expensive living or surroundings: *a life of luxury*. **2** an item that is expensive and enjoyable but not essential.
– ORIGIN Latin *luxuria* 'lechery'.

LW • abbrev. long wave.

-ly • suffix **1** having the qualities of: *brotherly*. **2** recurring at intervals of: *hourly*. **3** forming adverbs from adjectives: *greatly*.
– ORIGIN Old English.

lychee /ly-chee/ • n. a small rounded fruit with sweet white flesh and thin rough skin.
– ORIGIN Chinese.

lychgate /lich-gayt/ • n. a roofed gateway to a churchyard.
– ORIGIN from Old English *līc* 'body' (referring to the former practice of using such a gateway to shelter a coffin before burial).

Lycra /ly-kruh/ • n. trademark a synthetic elastic fibre or fabric used for close-fitting clothes.

lye • n. a strongly alkaline solution used for washing or cleaning.
– ORIGIN Old English.

lying[1] pres. part. of LIE[1].

lying[2] pres. part. of LIE[2].

lymph /limf/ • n. a colourless fluid containing white blood cells, which bathes the tissues of the body.
– ORIGIN Latin *lympha, limpa* 'water'.

lymphatic /lim-fat-ik/ • adj. relating to lymph or its production.

lymphatic system • n. the network of vessels through which lymph drains from the tissues into the blood.

lymph node (also **lymph gland**) • n. each of a number of small swellings in the lymphatic system where lymph is filtered and lymphocytes are formed.

lymphocyte /lim-fuh-syt/ • n. a type of small white blood cell with a single round nucleus.

lymphoma /lim-foh-muh/ • n. (pl. **lymphomas** or **lymphomata** /lim-foh-muh-tuh/) cancer of the lymph nodes.

lynch • v. (of a group) kill someone for an alleged crime without a legal trial, especially by hanging.
– ORIGIN named after Captain William *Lynch* of Virginia, who set up his own court of justice.

lynchpin • n. var. of LINCHPIN.

lynx • n. a wild cat with a short tail and tufted ears.
– ORIGIN Greek *lunx*.

lyre • n. a stringed instrument like a small U-shaped harp with strings fixed to a crossbar, used in ancient Greece.
– ORIGIN Greek *lura*.

lyric • n. **1** (also **lyrics**) the words of a song. **2** a poem that expresses the writer's thoughts and emotions. • adj. (of poetry) expressing the writer's thoughts and emotions.
– ORIGIN Greek *lura* 'lyre'.

lyrical • adj. **1** (of literature or music) expressing the writer's emotions in an imaginative and pleasing way. **2** relating to the words of a popular song.
– PHRASES **wax lyrical** talk in a very enthusiastic and unrestrained way.
– DERIVATIVES **lyrically** adv.

lyricism • n. expression of emotion in writing or music in an imaginative and pleasing way.

lyricist • n. a person who writes the words to popular songs.

Mm

M¹ (also **m**) • n. (pl. **Ms** or **M's**) **1** the thirteenth letter of the alphabet. **2** the Roman numeral for 1,000. [ORIGIN from Latin *mille*.]

M² • abbrev. **1** medium. **2** mega-. **3** Monsieur. **4** motorway.

m • abbrev. **1** Physics mass. **2** metre(s). **3** mile(s). **4** milli-. **5** million(s).

m- • prefix referring to commercial activity carried out electronically by means of mobile phones: *m-commerce*.

MA • abbrev. Master of Arts.

ma'am • n. madam.

mac • n. Brit. informal a mackintosh.

macabre /muh-**kah**-bruh/ • adj. disturbing because concerned with death or injury.
– ORIGIN French.

macadam /muh-**kad**-uhm/ • n. broken stone used with tar or bitumen for surfacing roads and paths.
– ORIGIN named after the British surveyor John L. *McAdam*.

macadamia /ma-kuh-**day**-mi-uh/ • n. the edible nut of an Australian tree.
– ORIGIN named after the Australian chemist John *Macadam*.

macaque /muh-**kak**/ • n. a medium-sized monkey with a long face and cheek pouches for holding food.
– ORIGIN Bantu *makaku* 'some monkeys'.

macaroni /ma-kuh-**roh**-ni/ • n. pasta in the form of narrow tubes.
– ORIGIN Italian *maccaroni*.

macaroon • n. a light biscuit made with egg white and ground almonds or coconut.
– ORIGIN French *macaron*.

macaw /muh-**kaw**/ • n. a brightly coloured parrot with a long tail, native to Central and South America.
– ORIGIN from former Portuguese *macau*.

McCarthyism • n. a campaign against suspected communists in American public life carried out under Senator Joseph McCarthy from 1950–4.
– DERIVATIVES **McCarthyite** adj. & n.

McCoy • n. (in phr. **the real McCoy**) informal the real thing.

mace¹ • n. **1** hist. a heavy club with a spiked metal head. **2** a ceremonial staff carried by an official such as a mayor. **3** (**Mace**) trademark a stinging chemical sprayed from an aerosol to disable attackers.
– ORIGIN Old French *masse* 'large hammer'.

mace² • n. a spice made from the dried outer covering of the nutmeg.
– ORIGIN Latin *macir*.

Macedonian /mass-i-**doh**-ni-uhn/ • n. a person from the republic of Macedonia (formerly part of Yugoslavia), ancient Macedonia, or the modern Greek region of Macedonia. • adj. relating to Macedonia.

macerate /**mass**-uh-rayt/
• v. (**macerates**, **macerating**, **macerated**) soften food by soaking it in a liquid.
– DERIVATIVES **maceration** n.
– ORIGIN Latin *macerare*.

Mach /mak/ • n. used with a numeral (as **Mach 1**, **Mach 2**, etc.) to indicate the speed of sound, twice the speed of sound, etc.
– ORIGIN named after the Austrian physicist Ernst *Mach*.

machete /muh-**shet**-i/ • n. a broad, heavy knife used as a tool or weapon.
– ORIGIN Spanish.

Machiavellian /mak-i-uh-**vel**-li-uhn/ • adj. using cunning and underhand methods to get what you want.
– ORIGIN named after the Italian statesman Niccolò *Machiavelli*.

machinations /mash-i-**nay**-sh'nz/ • pl. n. plots and scheming.
– ORIGIN Latin *machinari* 'contrive'.

machine • n. **1** a device using mechanical power and having several parts, for performing a particular task. **2** an efficient group of influential people: *the council's publicity machine*. • v. (**machines**, **machining**, **machined**) make or work on something with a device using mechanical power.
– ORIGIN Greek *mēkhanē*.

machine code (also **machine**

language) •n. a computer programming language consisting of instructions which a computer can respond to directly.

machine gun •n. an automatic gun that fires bullets in rapid succession.

machine-readable •adj. in a form that a computer can process.

machinery •n. **1** machines as a whole, or the parts of a machine. **2** an organized system or structure: *the machinery of the state.*

machine tool •n. a fixed powered tool for cutting or shaping metal, wood, etc.

machinist •n. a person who operates a machine or who makes machinery.

machismo /muh-**kiz**-moh/ •n. strong or aggressive male pride.
– ORIGIN Mexican Spanish.

macho /**mach**-oh/ •adj. showing aggressive pride in being male.
– ORIGIN Mexican Spanish.

mackerel •n. an edible sea fish with a greenish-blue back.
– ORIGIN Old French *maquerel.*

mackintosh (also **macintosh**) •n. Brit. a full-length water-resistant coat.
– ORIGIN named after the Scottish inventor Charles *Macintosh.*

macramé /muh-**krah**-may/ •n. the craft of knotting cord or string in patterns to make decorative articles.
– ORIGIN French.

macro- •comb. form large or large-scale: *macroeconomics.*
– ORIGIN Greek *makros.*

macrobiotic /mak-roh-by-**ot**-ik/ •adj. (of diet) consisting of organic unprocessed foods.
– ORIGIN from MACRO- + Greek *bios* 'life'.

macrocosm /**mak**-roh-ko-z'm/ •n. the whole of a complex structure (such as the world) contrasted with a small or representative part of it (a microcosm).
– ORIGIN from Greek *makros kosmos* 'big world'.

macroeconomics •n. the branch of economics concerned with large-scale economic factors, such as interest rates.

macromolecule •n. Chem. a molecule containing a very large number of atoms, such as a protein.

macron •n. a written or printed mark (¯) used to indicate a long vowel in some languages, or a stressed vowel in verse.

macroscopic •adj. **1** large enough to be seen without a microscope. **2** relating to general analysis.

macula /**mak**-yuu-luh/ •n. (pl. **maculae** /**mak**-yuu-lee/) Med. an area of skin discoloration.
– ORIGIN Latin.

mad •adj. (**madder**, **maddest**) **1** insane. **2** very foolish; not sensible. **3** done without thought or control: *a mad dash to get ready.* **4** informal very enthusiastic about something. **5** informal very angry.
– DERIVATIVES **madly** adv. **madness** n.
– ORIGIN Old English.

Madagascan /mad-uh-**gas**-k'n/ •n. a person from Madagascar. •adj. relating to Madagascar.

madam •n. **1** a polite form of address for a woman. **2** Brit. informal an arrogant or cheeky girl. **3** a woman who runs a brothel.
– ORIGIN from French *ma dame* 'my lady'.

Madame /muh-**dam**/ •n. (pl. **Mesdames** /may-**dam**/) a title or form of address for a French-speaking woman.
– ORIGIN French.

madcap •adj. acting without thought; reckless.

mad cow disease •n. informal = BSE.

madden •v. make someone very annoyed.

madder •n. a red dye obtained from the roots of a plant.
– ORIGIN Old English.

made past and past part. of MAKE.

Madeira /muh-**deer**-uh/ •n. a strong sweet white wine from the island of Madeira.

Madeira cake •n. Brit. a rich kind of sponge cake.

Mademoiselle /ma-duh-mwah-**zel**/ •n. (pl. **Mesdemoiselles** /may-duh-mwa-**zel**/) a title or form of address for an unmarried French-speaking woman.
– ORIGIN French.

made-up •adj. **1** wearing make-up. **2** invented; untrue.

madhouse •n. informal a scene of great confusion or uproar.

madman (or **madwoman**) •n. (pl. **madmen** or **madwomen**) **1** a person who is mentally ill. **2** a foolish or reckless person.

Madonna •n. (**the Madonna**) the Virgin Mary.
– ORIGIN Italian.

madras /muh-**drass**, muh-**drahss**/ •n. **1** a hot spiced curry dish. **2** a colourful striped or checked cotton fabric.
– ORIGIN named after the Indian city of *Madras.*

madrigal •n. a 16th- or 17th-century song for several voices without instrumental accompaniment.
– ORIGIN Italian *madrigale.*

maelstrom /**mayl**-struhm/ •n. **1** a powerful whirlpool. **2** a situation of confusion or upheaval.
– ORIGIN Dutch.

maenad /mee-nad/ • n. (in ancient Greece) a female follower of the god Bacchus.
– ORIGIN Greek *Mainas*.

maestro /my-stroh/ • n. (pl. **maestri** /my-stri/ or **maestros**) **1** a distinguished male conductor or classical musician. **2** a distinguished man in any field of activity.
– ORIGIN Italian, 'master'.

Mafia • n. **1** (**the Mafia**) an international criminal organization originating in Sicily. **2** (**mafia**) a powerful group who secretly influence matters: *the top tennis mafia.*
– ORIGIN Italian.

Mafioso /ma-fi-oh-soh/ • n. (pl. **Mafiosi** /ma-fi-oh-si/) a member of the Mafia.

magazine • n. **1** a periodical publication containing articles and pictures. **2** a chamber holding cartridges to be fed automatically to the breech of a gun. **3** a store for arms, ammunition, and explosives.
– ORIGIN Arabic, 'storehouse'.

magenta /muh-jen-tuh/ • n. a light mauvish crimson.
– ORIGIN named after *Magenta* in Italy.

maggot • n. a soft-bodied larva of a fly or other insect, found in decaying matter.
– ORIGIN perh. from Old Norse.

magi pl. of **MAGUS**.

magic • n. **1** the apparent use of mysterious or supernatural forces to make something happen. **2** conjuring tricks. **3** a mysterious or wonderful quality: *the magic of the theatre.*
• adj. **1** having supernatural powers. **2** Brit. informal very good. • v. (**magics**, **magicking**, **magicked**) use magic to make something happen.
– ORIGIN from Greek *magikē tekhnē* 'art of a magus'.

magical • adj. **1** relating to or using magic. **2** very pleasant or enjoyable.
– DERIVATIVES **magically** adv.

magician • n. **1** a person with magic powers. **2** a conjuror.

magic lantern • n. an early form of projector for showing photographic slides.

magisterial /ma-ji-steer-i-uhl/ • adj. **1** having or showing great authority: *a magisterial pronouncement.* **2** relating to a magistrate.
– DERIVATIVES **magisterially** adv.
– ORIGIN Latin *magister* 'master'.

magistracy /ma-jiss-truh-si/ • n. (pl. **magistracies**) **1** the post of magistrate. **2** magistrates as a group.

magistrate • n. an official with authority to judge minor legal cases and hold preliminary hearings.
– ORIGIN Latin *magistratus* 'administrator'.

magma /mag-muh/ • n. very hot fluid or semi-fluid material under the earth's crust, from which igneous rock is formed by cooling.
– ORIGIN Greek.

magnanimous /mag-nan-i-muhss/ • adj. generous or forgiving towards a rival or enemy.
– DERIVATIVES **magnanimity** n.
– ORIGIN from Latin *magnus* 'great' + *animus* 'soul'.

magnate /mag-nayt/ • n. a wealthy and influential businessman or business-woman.
– ORIGIN Latin *magnas* 'great man'.

magnesium /mag-nee-zi-uhm/ • n. a silvery-white metallic element which burns with a brilliant white flame.
– ORIGIN Greek *Magnēsia*, relating to a mineral from Magnesia in Asia Minor.

magnet • n. **1** a piece of iron or other material that can attract iron-containing objects and that points north and south when suspended. **2** a person or thing that has a powerful attraction: *the beach is a magnet for sun-worshippers.*
– ORIGIN from Greek *magnēs lithos* 'lodestone'.

magnetic • adj. **1** having the property of magnetism. **2** very attractive.
– DERIVATIVES **magnetically** adv.

magnetic field • n. a region around a magnet within which the force of magnetism acts.

magnetic north • n. the direction in which the north end of a compass needle will point in response to the earth's magnetic field.

magnetic pole • n. each of the points near the geographical North and South Poles, indicated by the needle of a magnetic compass.

magnetic storm • n. a disturbance of the magnetic field of the earth.

magnetic tape • n. tape used in recording sound, pictures, or computer data.

magnetism • n. **1** the property displayed by magnets and produced by the movement of electric charges, which results in objects being attracted or pushed away. **2** the ability to attract and charm people.

magnetize (or **magnetise**)
• v. (**magnetizes**, **magnetizing**, **magnetized**) make something magnetic.

magneto /mag-nee-toh/ • n. (pl. **magnetos**) a small electric generator containing a permanent magnet and

m

used to provide high-voltage pulses.

Magnificat /mag-**nif**-i-kat/ • n. a hymn beginning 'my soul magnifies the Lord', sung as a regular part of a Christian service.
– ORIGIN Latin, 'magnifies'.

magnification • n. **1** the effect of a lens or microscope in making something appear larger than it is. **2** the degree to which something can be made to appear larger by means of a lens or microscope.

magnificent • adj. **1** very attractive and impressive; splendid. **2** very good.
– DERIVATIVES **magnificence** n. **magnificently** adv.
– ORIGIN Latin, 'making something great'.

magnify • v. (**magnifies**, **magnifying**, **magnified**) **1** make something appear larger than it is with a lens or microscope. **2** make larger or more intense: *the tin roof magnified the tropical heat.* **3** old use praise highly.
– DERIVATIVES **magnifier** n.
– ORIGIN Latin *magnificare*.

magnifying glass • n. a lens that produces an enlarged image, used to examine small or finely detailed things.

magnitude • n. **1** great size or importance: *they were discouraged at the magnitude of the task.* **2** size. **3** the degree of brightness of a star.
– ORIGIN Latin *magnitudo*.

magnolia • n. a tree or shrub with large white or pink flowers.
– ORIGIN named after the French botanist Pierre *Magnol*.

magnum • n. (pl. **magnums**) a wine bottle of twice the standard size, normally 1½ litres.
– ORIGIN Latin, 'great thing'.

magnum opus /mag-nuhm **oh**-puhss, mag-nuhm **op**-uhss/ • n. a work of art, music, or literature that is the most important that a person has produced.
– ORIGIN Latin, 'great work'.

magpie • n. **1** a black and white bird with a long tail and a noisy cry. **2** a person who collects trivial objects.
– ORIGIN prob. from *Magot*, a former form of the woman's name *Marguerite*, + Latin *pica* 'magpie'.

magus /**may**-guhss/ • n. (pl. **magi** /**may**-jy/) **1** a priest of ancient Persia. **2** a sorcerer.
– ORIGIN Latin.

Magyar /**mag**-yar/ • n. **1** a member of the predominant people in Hungary. **2** the Hungarian language.
– ORIGIN Hungarian.

maharaja /mah-huh-**rah**-juh/ (also **maharajah**) • n. hist. an Indian prince.
– ORIGIN Hindi.

maharani /mah-huh-**rah**-ni/ • n. hist. a maharaja's wife or widow.
– ORIGIN Hindi.

Maharishi /mah-huh-**ri**-shi/ • n. a great Hindu wise man or spiritual leader.
– ORIGIN Sanskrit.

mahatma /muh-**hat**-muh/ • n. a wise or holy Hindu leader.
– ORIGIN Sanskrit, 'great soul'.

mah-jong /mah-**jong**/ (also **mah-jongg**) • n. a Chinese game played with very small rectangular tiles.
– ORIGIN Chinese dialect, 'sparrows'.

mahogany • n. **1** hard reddish-brown wood from a tropical tree, used for furniture. **2** a rich reddish-brown colour.

maid • n. **1** a female servant. **2** old use a girl or young woman.

maiden • n. **1** old use a girl or young woman, especially a virgin. **2** (also **maiden over**) Cricket an over in which no runs are scored. • adj. **1** (of an older woman) unmarried. **2** first of its kind: *a maiden voyage.*
– ORIGIN Old English.

maidenhair fern • n. a fern with fine stems and delicate foliage.

maidenhead • n. old use **1** a girl's or woman's virginity. **2** the hymen.

maiden name • n. the surname of a married woman before her marriage.

maid of honour • n. an unmarried noblewoman who waits on a queen or princess.

maidservant • n. dated a female servant.

mail[1] • n. **1** letters and parcels sent by post. **2** the postal system. **3** email. • v. **1** send a letter or parcel by post. **2** send post or email to.
– ORIGIN Old French *male* 'wallet'.

mail[2] • n. hist. armour made of metal rings or plates.
– ORIGIN Old French *maille*.

mailbox • n. **1** N. Amer. a box for mail at the entrance to a person's house. **2** a computer file in which emails are stored.

mailing • n. a piece of advertising material posted to a large number of people.

mailing list • n. a list of people to whom advertising material or information may be mailed regularly.

mail order • n. the buying or selling of goods by post.

mailshot • n. Brit. a piece of advertising material posted to a large number of people; a mailing.

maim • v. injure someone so that part of the body is permanently damaged.
– ORIGIN Old French *mahaignier*.

main • adj. greatest or most important: *a*

main road. • n. **1** a chief water or gas pipe or electricity cable. **2 (the mains)** Brit. public water, gas, or electricity supply through pipes or cables. **3 (the main)** old use the open ocean.
– PHRASES **in the main** on the whole.
– ORIGIN Old English, 'physical force'.

mainboard • n. = MOTHERBOARD.

mainframe • n. a large high-speed computer, especially one supporting a network of workstations.

mainland • n. the main area of land of a country, not including islands and separate territories.

mainline • v. (**mainlines, mainlining, mainlined**) informal inject a drug into a vein.

mainly • adv. for the most part; chiefly.

mainmast • n. the principal mast of a ship.

mainspring • n. the most important or influential part: *faith was the mainspring of her life.*

mainstay • n. a thing on which something else is based or depends: *cotton is the mainstay of the economy.*

mainstream • n. the ideas, attitudes, or activities that are shared by most people.

maintain • v. **1** cause something to continue in the same state or at the same level: *he maintained close links with India.* **2** keep a building, vehicle, or machine in good condition by checking or repairing it regularly. **3** support someone financially. **4** strongly state that something is the case.
– ORIGIN Old French *maintenir*.

maintenance • n. **1** the action of keeping something in the same state or in good condition. **2** Brit. the provision of financial support for a former husband or wife after divorce.

> ✓ Spell **maintenance** with -ten- in the middle; the ending is -ance.

maisonette • n. a flat on two storeys of a larger building.
– ORIGIN French *maisonnette* 'small house'.

maître d'hôtel /may-truh doh-**tel**/ • n. (pl. **maîtres d'hôtel** /may-truh doh-**tel**/) the head waiter of a restaurant.
– ORIGIN French, 'master of the house'.

maize • n. Brit. a cereal plant with large grains set in rows on a cob.
– ORIGIN Spanish *maíz*.

majestic • adj. impressively beautiful or grand.
– DERIVATIVES **majestically** adv.

majesty • n. (pl. **majesties**) **1** impressive beauty or grandeur: *the awesome majesty of the sea.* **2** royal power. **3 (His, Your,** etc. **Majesty)** a title given to a king or queen or their wife or widow.
– ORIGIN Latin *majestas.*

major • adj. **1** important or serious. **2** greater or more important; main. **3** Music (of a scale) having intervals of a semitone between the third and fourth, and seventh and eighth notes. Contrasted with MINOR. • n. **1** a rank of army officer above captain. **2** Music a major key, interval, or scale. **3** N. Amer. a student specializing in a specified subject. • v. (**major in**) N. Amer. & Austral./NZ specialize in a particular subject at college or university.
– ORIGIN Latin, 'greater'.

major-domo • n. (pl. **major-domos**) the chief steward or butler of a large household.
– ORIGIN Spanish and Italian.

major general • n. a rank of army officer above brigadier.

majority • n. (pl. **majorities**) **1** the greater number. **2** Brit. the number of votes by which one party or candidate in an election defeats the opposition. **3** the age when a person is legally a full adult, usually 18 or 21.

> USAGE: The main meaning of **majority** is 'the greater number' and it should be used with plural nouns: *the majority of cases.* Do not use **majority** with nouns that do not take a plural to mean 'the greatest part', as in *she ate the majority of the meal.*

majority rule • n. the principle that the greater number of people should exercise greater power.

make • v. (**makes, making, made**) **1** form something by putting parts together or mixing substances. **2** bring something about; cause: *the drips had made a pool on the floor.* **3** force someone to do something. **4** add up to. **5** be suitable as. **6** estimate something as or decide on. **7** earn an amount of money or profit. **8** arrive at or achieve. **9** (**make it**) become successful. **10** prepare to go in a particular direction or to do something: *he made towards the car.* • n. the manufacturer or trade name of a product.
– PHRASES **make do** manage with something that is not satisfactory. **make for 1** move towards. **2** tend to result in: *the film makes for uncomfortable viewing.* **3** (**be made for**) be very suitable for. **make something of 1** give attention or importance to. **2** understand the meaning of. **make off** leave hurriedly. **make off with** steal. **make someone out**

represent someone as being of a specified nature. **make something out 1** manage with difficulty to see, hear, or understand something. **2** draw up a list or document. **make someone over** give a new image to someone. **make something over** transfer the ownership of something. **make sail** spread a sail or sails to begin a voyage. **make time** find time to do something. **make up** be friendly again after a quarrel. **make someone up** apply cosmetics to someone. **make something up 1** put something together from parts or ingredients. **2** invent a story. **3** (also **make up for**) do something to set right a bad situation. **make up your mind** make a decision. **make way** allow room for someone or something else. **on the make** informal trying to make money or gain an advantage.

– DERIVATIVES **maker** n.
– ORIGIN Old English.

make-believe •n. a state of fantasy or pretence. •adj. imitating something real.

makeover •n. a complete transformation of the appearance of someone or something.

makeshift •adj. acting as a temporary substitute: *chairs formed a makeshift bed.*

make-up •n. **1** cosmetics. **2** the way in which something is formed or put together: *the make-up of the rock.*

makeweight •n. **1** an unimportant person or thing that is only included to complete something. **2** something added to make up a required weight.

making •n. **1** (in phr. **be the making of**) bring about the success of. **2** (**makings**) the necessary qualities.

mal- •comb. form **1** bad: *malnourished.* **2** in a faulty or incorrect way: *malfunction.*

– ORIGIN Latin *male*.

malachite /ˈmal-uh-kyt/ •n. a bright green mineral that contains copper.

– ORIGIN Greek *molokhitis.*

maladjusted •adj. (of a person) failing to cope with normal social situations.

maladroit /ˈmal-uh-droyt/ •adj. clumsy.

malady •n. (pl. **maladies**) literary a disease or illness.

– ORIGIN Old French *malade* 'ill'.

Malagasy /ˈma-luh-gass-i/ •n. (pl. **Malagasy** or **Malagasies**) **1** a person from Madagascar. **2** the language of Madagascar.

malaise /ma-ˈlayz/ •n. a general feeling of unease, illness, or low spirits.

– ORIGIN French.

malapropism /ˈmal-uh-prop-i-z'm/ (US also **malaprop**) •n. the mistaken use of a word in place of a similar-sounding one

(e.g. 'dance a *flamingo*' instead of *flamenco*).

– ORIGIN named after Mrs *Malaprop* in Richard Sheridan's play *The Rivals.*

malaria •n. a disease that causes recurrent fever, caused by a parasite transmitted by mosquitoes.

– DERIVATIVES **malarial** adj.
– ORIGIN from Italian *mala aria* 'bad air' (once thought to cause the disease).

malarkey /muh-ˈlar-ki/ •n. informal nonsense.

Malawian /muh-ˈlah-wi-uhn/ •n. a person from Malawi in south central Africa. •adj. relating to Malawi.

Malay •n. **1** a member of a people inhabiting Malaysia and Indonesia. **2** the language of the Malays.

Malayan •n. = MALAY. •adj. relating to Malays or Malaya (now part of Malaysia).

Malaysian /muh-ˈlay-zi-uhn, muh-ˈlay-zh'n/ •n. a person from Malaysia. •adj. relating to Malaysia.

Maldivian /mawl-ˈdiv-i-uhn/ •n. **1** a person from the Maldives, a country consisting of a chain of islands in the Indian Ocean. **2** the language of the Maldives. •adj. relating to the Maldives.

male •adj. **1** relating to the sex that can fertilize or inseminate the female. **2** relating to men: *a deep male voice.* **3** (of a plant or flower) having stamens but not a pistil. **4** (of a fitting) manufactured to fit inside a corresponding female part. •n. a male person, animal, or plant.

– ORIGIN Old French *masle.*

malediction /mal-i-ˈdik-sh'n/ •n. a curse.

– ORIGIN Latin *maledicere* 'speak evil of'.

malefactor /ˈmal-i-fak-ter/ •n. formal a criminal or wrongdoer.

– ORIGIN Latin.

malevolent /muh-ˈlev-uh-luhnt/ •adj. wishing harm to other people.

– DERIVATIVES **malevolence** n.
– ORIGIN Latin.

malformation •n. the state of being abnormally shaped or formed.

– DERIVATIVES **malformed** adj.

malfunction •v. (of equipment or machinery) fail to function normally. •n. a failure to function normally.

Malian /ˈmah-li-uhn/ •n. a person from Mali, a country in West Africa. •adj. relating to Mali.

malice •n. the desire to harm someone.

– ORIGIN Old French.

malicious •adj. meaning or meant to do harm.

– DERIVATIVES **maliciously** adv.

malign /muh-lyn/ • adj. harmful or evil.
• v. say unpleasant things about.
– DERIVATIVES **malignity** /muh-lig-ni-ti/ n.
– ORIGIN Latin *malignus* 'tending to evil'.

malignancy • n. (pl. **malignancies**)
1 cancer. **2** a cancerous growth. **3** the quality of being harmful or evil.

malignant • adj. **1** harmful; malevolent. **2** (of a tumour) growing uncontrollably or likely to recur after removal; cancerous.
– ORIGIN Latin *malignare* 'plan maliciously'.

malinger • v. (**malingers, malingering, malingered**) pretend to be ill in order to avoid work.
– DERIVATIVES **malingerer** n.
– ORIGIN French *malingre* 'weak, sickly'.

mall /mal, mawl/ • n. **1** a large enclosed pedestrian shopping area. **2** a sheltered walk.
– ORIGIN from *The Mall*, a walk in St James's Park, London.

mallard • n. a wild duck, the male of which has a dark green head.
– ORIGIN Old French, 'wild drake'.

malleable /mal-li-uh-b'l/ • adj. **1** able to be hammered or pressed into shape without breaking or cracking. **2** easily influenced: *a malleable youth*.
– DERIVATIVES **malleability** n.
– ORIGIN Latin *malleus* 'a hammer'.

mallet • n. **1** a hammer with a large wooden head. **2** an implement with a long handle and a head like a hammer, for hitting a croquet or polo ball.
– ORIGIN Latin *malleus*.

mallow • n. a plant with pink or purple flowers.
– ORIGIN Latin *malva*.

malnourished • adj. suffering from lack of food or of the right foods.

malnutrition • n. the state of not having enough food or not eating enough of the right foods.

malodorous • adj. smelling bad.

malpractice • n. illegal, corrupt, or careless professional behaviour.

malt • n. barley or other grain that has been soaked in water, allowed to sprout, and dried, used for brewing or distilling.
• v. **1** make grain into malt. **2** (as adj. **malted**) mixed with malt or a malt extract.
– ORIGIN Old English.

Malthusian /mal-thyoo-zi-uhn/
• adj. relating to the theory of the English economist Thomas Malthus that, if unchecked, the population tends to increase at a greater rate than its food supplies.

maltose /mawl-tohz/ • n. a sugar produced by the breakdown of starch, for example by enzymes found in malt and saliva.

maltreat • v. treat a person or animal badly or cruelly.
– DERIVATIVES **maltreatment** n.

malt whisky • n. whisky made only from malted barley.

mama (also **mamma**) • n. dated or N. Amer. a person's mother.

mamba • n. a large, highly poisonous African snake.
– ORIGIN Zulu.

mambo • n. (pl. **mambos**) a Latin American dance similar to the rumba.
– ORIGIN American Spanish.

mammal • n. a warm-blooded animal that has hair or fur, produces milk, and bears live young.
– DERIVATIVES **mammalian** adj.
– ORIGIN Latin *mamma* 'breast'.

mammary • adj. relating to the breasts or the milk-producing organs of other mammals.
– ORIGIN Latin *mamma* 'breast'.

mammography /mam-mog-ruh-fi/
• n. a technique using X-rays to examine the breasts for tumours.
– DERIVATIVES **mammogram** n.

Mammon • n. wealth thought of as a false object of worship.
– ORIGIN Aramaic, 'riches'; see Gospel of Matthew, chapter 6 and Gospel of Luke, chapter 16.

mammoth • n. a large extinct elephant with a hairy coat and long curved tusks.
• adj. huge; enormous.
– ORIGIN Russian.

man • n. (pl. **men**) **1** an adult human male. **2** a husband or lover. **3** a person. **4** human beings in general: *places untouched by man*. **5** a piece used in a board game. • v. (**mans, manning, manned**) provide a place or machine with the people to run, operate, or defend it.
– PHRASES **the man in the street** the average person. **to a man** with no exceptions.
– DERIVATIVES **manned** adj.
– ORIGIN Old English.

> **USAGE:** Many people now think that the use of the word **man** to mean 'human beings in general' is outdated or sexist; you could use **the human race** or **humankind** instead.

-man • comb. form forming nouns referring to: **1** a man of a particular nationality or origin: *Frenchman*. **2** a person belonging to a particular group or having a particular role: *chairman*. **3** a ship of a particular kind: *merchantman*.

manacle • n. a metal band or chain fastened around a person's hands or ankles to restrict their movement. • v. (**manacles, manacling, manacled**) restrict someone with a manacle.
– ORIGIN Old French *manicle* 'handcuff'.

manage • v. (**manages, managing, managed**) 1 be in charge of people or an organization. 2 succeed in doing: *she finally managed to call a cab.* 3 be able to cope despite difficulties. 4 control the use of money or other resources. 5 be free to attend an appointment.
– ORIGIN Italian *maneggiare* 'train a horse'.

manageable • adj. able to be managed without difficulty.

management • n. 1 the action of managing. 2 the managers of an organization.

manager • n. 1 a person who manages staff, an organization, or a sports team. 2 a person in charge of the business affairs of a sports player, actor, etc.
– DERIVATIVES **managerial** adj.

manageress • n. Brit. a female manager.

mañana /man-yah-nuh/ • adv. tomorrow, or at some time in the future.
– ORIGIN Spanish.

man-at-arms • n. old use a soldier.

manatee /man-uh-tee/ • n. a large plant-eating mammal that lives in the sea near tropical Atlantic coasts.
– ORIGIN Carib.

Mancunian • n. a person from Manchester. • adj. relating to Manchester.
– ORIGIN Latin *Mancunium* 'Manchester'.

mandala /man-duh-luh/ • n. a circular design symbolizing the universe in Hinduism and Buddhism.
– ORIGIN Sanskrit, 'disc'.

mandarin • n. 1 (**Mandarin**) the official form of the Chinese language. 2 a high-ranking official in the former Chinese empire. 3 a powerful official. 4 a small citrus fruit with a loose yellow-orange skin.
– ORIGIN Hindi, 'counsellor'.

mandate • n. /man-dayt/ 1 an official order or permission to do something. 2 the authority to carry out a policy, seen as given by a country's voters to the winner of an election: *a government with a popular mandate.* • v. /man-dayt/ (**mandates, mandating, mandated**) give someone authority to do something.
– ORIGIN Latin *mandatum* 'something commanded'.

mandatory /man-duh-tuh-ri/ • adj. required by law or rules; compulsory.
– DERIVATIVES **mandatorily** adv.

mandible • n. 1 the lower jawbone in mammals or fish. 2 either of the upper and lower parts of a bird's beak. 3 either half of the crushing organ in an insect's mouthparts.
– ORIGIN Latin *mandibula*.

mandolin • n. a musical instrument like a lute, having metal strings that are plucked with a plectrum.
– ORIGIN Italian *mandolino* 'little lute'.

mandrake • n. a plant with a forked fleshy root that is used in herbal medicine and magic.
– ORIGIN Latin *mandragora*.

mandrel • n. 1 a shaft or spindle in a lathe to which work is fixed while being turned. 2 a cylindrical rod round which metal or other material is forged or shaped.

mandrill • n. a large West African baboon with a red and blue face.
– ORIGIN prob. from **man** + a local word.

mane • n. 1 a growth of long hair on the neck of a horse, lion, or other mammal. 2 a person's long hair.
– ORIGIN Old English.

maneuver • n. & v. US = MANOEUVRE.

manful • adj. brave and determined.
– DERIVATIVES **manfully** adv.

manga • n. Japanese comic books and cartoon films with a science-fiction or fantasy theme.
– ORIGIN Japanese.

manganese /mang-guh-neez/ • n. a hard grey metallic element used in special steels and magnetic alloys.
– ORIGIN Italian.

mange /maynj/ • n. a skin disease in some animals caused by mites, resulting in severe itching and hair loss.
– ORIGIN Old French *mangeue*.

mangel-wurzel /mang-g'l wer-z'l/ • n. = MANGOLD.

manger • n. a long trough from which horses or cattle feed.
– ORIGIN Old French *mangeure*.

mangetout /monzh-too/ • n. (pl. **mangetout** or **mangetouts** /monzh-too/) Brit. a variety of pea with an edible pod.

– ORIGIN French, 'eat all'.

mangle[1] • n. Brit. a machine with two or more cylinders turned by a handle, between which wet laundry is squeezed to remove water.
– ORIGIN Greek *manganon* 'axis, engine'.

mangle[2] • v. (**mangles, mangling, mangled**) destroy or severely damage by crushing and twisting.
– ORIGIN Old French *mahaignier* 'maim'.

mango • n. (pl. **mangoes** or **mangos**) an oval tropical fruit with yellow flesh.
– ORIGIN Portuguese *manga*.

mangold • n. a variety of beet grown as feed for farm animals.
– ORIGIN German *Mangoldwurzel*.

mangrove • n. a tropical tree or shrub found in coastal swamps, with tangled roots that grow above ground.
– ORIGIN prob. from an extinct Caribbean language.

mangy /mayn-ji/ • adj. **1** having mange. **2** in poor condition; shabby.

manhandle • v. (**manhandles, manhandling, manhandled**) **1** move a heavy object with effort. **2** push or drag someone roughly.

manhole • n. a covered opening through which a person can enter a sewer or other underground structure.

manhood • n. **1** the state or period of being a man. **2** the men of a country or society. **3** the qualities associated with men, such as strength or courage.

mania /may-ni-uh/ • n. **1** mental illness characterized by an overactive imagination and excited activity. **2** an extreme enthusiasm: *his mania for cars*.
– ORIGIN Greek, 'madness'.

-mania • comb. form referring to a particular type of mental abnormality or obsession: *kleptomania*.
– DERIVATIVES **-maniac** comb. form.

maniac /may-ni-ak/ • n. **1** a person who behaves in a very wild or violent way. **2** informal a person with an extreme enthusiasm for something.
– DERIVATIVES **maniacal** /muh-**ny**-uh-k'l/ adj. **maniacally** adv.

manic • adj. **1** relating to a mental illness characterized by an overactive imagination and excited activity. **2** showing wild excitement and energy.
– DERIVATIVES **manically** adv.

manic depression • n. a mental disorder with alternating periods of excited activity and depression.
– DERIVATIVES **manic-depressive** adj. & n.

manicure • n. a cosmetic treatment of the hands and nails. • v. (**manicures, manicuring, manicured**) give a manicure to.

– DERIVATIVES **manicurist** n.
– ORIGIN from Latin *manus* 'hand' + *cura* 'care'.

manifest[1] • adj. clear and obvious.
• v. **1** show or display: *Liz manifested signs of depression.* **2** (of an illness or disorder) become noticeable.
– DERIVATIVES **manifestly** adv.
– ORIGIN Latin *manifestus* 'flagrant'.

manifest[2] • n. a document listing the cargo, crew, or passengers of a ship or aircraft.
– ORIGIN Italian *manifesto* 'manifesto'.

manifestation • n. **1** a sign or evidence of something. **2** an appearance of a god or spirit in physical form.

manifesto • n. (pl. **manifestos**) a public declaration of the policy and aims of a group such as a political party.
– ORIGIN Italian.

manifold • adj. many and various. • n. a pipe with several openings that connect to other parts, especially one in an internal-combustion engine.
– ORIGIN Old English.

manikin (also **mannikin**) • n. a very small person.
– ORIGIN Dutch *manneken* 'little man'.

Manila (also **Manilla**) • n. strong brown paper made from a Philippine plant.
– ORIGIN from *Manila*, the capital of the Philippines.

manioc /man-i-ok/ • n. = CASSAVA.
– ORIGIN from a South American Indian language.

manipulate • v. (**manipulates, manipulating, manipulated**) **1** handle or control something skilfully. **2** control or influence someone in a clever or underhand way.
– DERIVATIVES **manipulation** n. **manipulator** n.
– ORIGIN Latin *manipulus* 'handful'.

manipulative • adj. manipulating other people in a clever or underhand way.

mankind • n. human beings as whole.

manky • adj. Brit. informal dirty.
– ORIGIN prob. from Latin *mancus* 'maimed'.

manly • adj. (**manlier, manliest**) **1** having qualities associated with men, such as courage and strength. **2** suitable for a man.
– DERIVATIVES **manliness** n.

man-made • adj. made or caused by human beings.

manna • n. **1** (in the Bible) the substance supplied by God as food to the Israelites in the wilderness (Book of Exodus, chapter 16). **2** something unexpected and beneficial.
– ORIGIN Hebrew.

m

mannequin /man-ni-kin/ • n. **1** a dummy used to display clothes in a shop. **2** dated a fashion model.
– ORIGIN French.

manner • n. **1** a way in which something is done or happens: *he was dancing in a peculiar manner*. **2** a person's outward behaviour or attitude towards other people: *her shy manner*. **3** (**manners**) polite behaviour. **4** literary a kind or sort.
– PHRASES **all manner of** many different kinds of.
– ORIGIN Latin *manuarius* 'of the hand'.

mannered • adj. **1** behaving in a specified way: *well-mannered*. **2** (of an artistic style) artificial or exaggerated.

mannerism • n. **1** a distinctive personal gesture, habit, or way of speaking. **2** (**Mannerism**) a style of 16th-century Italian art in which people or objects were shown in an exaggerated or distorted way.
– DERIVATIVES **mannerist** n. & adj.

mannerly • adj. well-mannered; polite.

mannikin • n. var. of MANIKIN.

mannish • adj. (of a woman) looking or behaving like a man.

manoeuvrable (US **maneuverable**) • adj. (of a boat or aircraft) able to be manoeuvred easily.

manoeuvre /muh-noo-ver/ (US **maneuver**) • n. **1** a movement or series of moves requiring skill and care. **2** a carefully planned scheme or action. **3** (**manoeuvres**) a large-scale military exercise. • v. (**manoeuvres, manoeuvring, manoeuvred**; US **maneuvers, maneuvering, maneuvered**) **1** make a movement or series of moves skilfully and carefully. **2** guide skilfully or craftily.
– ORIGIN French *manœuvrer*.

> ✓ The British spelling of **manoeuvre** has **-oeu-** in the middle and **-re** at the end.

man-of-war (also **man-o'-war**) • n. hist. an armed sailing ship.

manometer /muh-nom-i-ter/ • n. an instrument for measuring the pressure of fluids.
– ORIGIN Greek *manos* 'thin'.

manor • n. **1** a large country house with lands. **2** (in medieval times) an area of land controlled by a lord.
– DERIVATIVES **manorial** adj.
– ORIGIN Old French *maner* 'dwelling'.

manpower • n. the number of people working or available for work or service.

manqué /mong-kay/ • adj. having never become what you might have been: *an actor manqué*.
– ORIGIN French.

mansard /man-sard/ • n. a roof with four sides, in each of which the lower part of the slope is steeper than the upper part.
– ORIGIN named after the French architect François *Mansart*.

manse /manss/ • n. the house provided for a minister of certain Christian Churches, especially the Scottish Presbyterian Church.
– ORIGIN Latin *mansus*.

manservant • n. (pl. **menservants**) a male servant.

mansion • n. a large, impressive house.
– ORIGIN Latin, 'dwelling'.

manslaughter • n. the crime of killing a person without meaning to do so.

mantel • n. a mantelpiece or mantel-shelf.
– ORIGIN from MANTLE.

mantelpiece • n. **1** a structure surrounding a fireplace. **2** a mantelshelf.

mantelshelf • n. a shelf forming the top of a structure surrounding a fireplace.

mantilla /man-til-luh/ • n. (in Spain) a lace or silk scarf traditionally worn by women over the hair and shoulders.
– ORIGIN Spanish.

mantis (also **praying mantis**) • n. (pl. **mantis** or **mantises**) an insect with a long body, that waits motionless for its prey with its forelegs folded.
– ORIGIN Greek, 'prophet'.

mantle • n. **1** a woman's loose sleeveless cloak. **2** a close covering, such as that of snow. **3** a mesh cover fixed round a gas jet, producing a glowing light when heated. **4** a role or responsibility that passes from one person to another. **5** the region of very hot dense rock between the earth's crust and its core.
• v. (**mantles, mantling, mantled**) literary cover or envelop.
– ORIGIN Latin *mantellum*.

mantra /man-truh/ • n. (originally in Hinduism and Buddhism) a word or sound repeated to aid concentration when meditating.
– ORIGIN Sanskrit, 'instrument of thought'.

manual • adj. **1** relating to or operated by the hands. **2** working with the hands: *a manual worker*. • n. a book giving instructions.
– DERIVATIVES **manually** adv.
– ORIGIN Latin *manualis*.

manufacture • v. (**manufactures, manufacturing, manufactured**) **1** make something on a large scale using machinery. **2** invent evidence or a story. • n. the making of goods on a large scale using machinery.
– DERIVATIVES **manufacturer** n.
– ORIGIN French.

manure • n. animal dung used for fertilizing land. • v. (**manures, manuring, manured**) spread manure on.
– ORIGIN Old French *manouvrer* 'manoeuvre'.

manuscript • n. 1 a handwritten book, document, or piece of music. 2 an author's handwritten or typed work, before printing and publication.
– ORIGIN from Latin *manu* 'by hand' + *scriptus* 'written'.

Manx • adj. relating to the Isle of Man.
– ORIGIN Old Norse.

Manx cat • n. a breed of cat that has no tail.

many • det., pron., & adj. (**more, most**) a large number of. • n. (**the many**) the majority of people.
– ORIGIN Old English.

Maoism /mow-i-z'm/ • n. the communist policies and theories of the former Chinese head of state Mao Zedong.
– DERIVATIVES **Maoist** n. & adj.

Maori /mow-ri/ • n. (pl. **Maori** or **Maoris**) 1 a member of the aboriginal people of New Zealand. 2 the language of the Maori.

map • n. 1 a diagram of an area showing physical features, cities, roads, etc. 2 a diagram or collection of data showing the way in which something is arranged or spread over an area. • v. (**maps, mapping, mapped**) 1 show something on a map. 2 (**map something out**) plan something in detail.
– ORIGIN Latin *mappa* 'sheet, napkin'.

maple • n. a tree with five-pointed leaves and a syrupy sap.
– ORIGIN Old English.

Maquis /ma-kee/ • n. the French resistance movement during the German occupation of France in the Second World War.
– ORIGIN French, 'brushwood'.

Mar. • abbrev. March.

mar • v. (**mars, marring, marred**) spoil the appearance or quality of.
– ORIGIN Old English.

marabou /ma-ruh-boo/ • n. 1 an African stork with a large neck pouch. 2 down feathers from the marabou used as trimming for hats or clothes.
– ORIGIN Arabic, 'holy man'.

maraca /muh-rak-uh/ • n. a hollow club-shaped gourd or container filled with small beans, stones, etc., shaken as a musical instrument.
– ORIGIN Portuguese.

maraschino cherry • n. a cherry preserved in maraschino, a liqueur made from small black Dalmatian cherries.
– ORIGIN Italian.

marathon • n. 1 a long-distance running race, strictly one of 26 miles 385 yards (42.195 km). 2 a long and difficult task.
– ORIGIN from *Marathōn* in Greece, where the Greeks defeated the Persians in 490 BC; a messenger is said to have run from Marathon to Athens with the news.

maraud /muh-rawd/ • v. go about in search of things to steal or people to attack.
– DERIVATIVES **marauder** n.
– ORIGIN French, 'rogue'.

marble • n. 1 a hard form of limestone, typically with coloured lines running through it, which is polished and used in sculpture and building. 2 a small ball of coloured glass used as a toy. 3 (**your marbles**) informal your mental powers.
– ORIGIN Greek *marmaros* 'shining stone'.

marbled • adj. having coloured streaks like marble.

marbling • n. colouring or marking that resembles marble.

marcasite /mar-kuh-syt, mar-kuh-zeet/ • n. a semi-precious stone consisting of iron pyrites.
– ORIGIN Latin *marcasita*.

March • n. the third month of the year.
– ORIGIN from Latin *Martius mensis* 'month of Mars'.

march • v. 1 walk in time and with regular paces, like a soldier. 2 walk quickly and with determination. 3 force someone to walk quickly. 4 take part in an organized procession to make a protest. • n. 1 an act of marching. 2 a procession organized as a protest. 3 a piece of music written to accompany marching.
– DERIVATIVES **marcher** n.
– ORIGIN French *marcher* 'to walk'.

Marches • pl. n. land on the border between two countries or territories.
– ORIGIN Old French *marche*.

March hare • n. informal a brown hare in the breeding season, noted for its wild behaviour.

marching orders • n. 1 instructions for troops to depart. 2 informal a dismissal.

marchioness /mar-shuh-ness/ • n. 1 the wife or widow of a marquess. 2 a woman holding the rank of marquess in her own right.
– ORIGIN Latin *marchionissa*.

Mardi Gras /mar-di grah/ • n. a carnival held in some countries on Shrove Tuesday.
– ORIGIN French, 'fat Tuesday', the last day of feasting before the fast of Lent.

m

mare /mair/ •n. the female of a horse or related animal.
– ORIGIN Old English.

mare's nest •n. 1 a muddle. 2 a discovery that turns out to be worthless.

margarine •n. a butter substitute made from vegetable oils or animal fats.
– ORIGIN French.

margarita /mar-guh-**ree**-tuh/ •n. a cocktail made with tequila and citrus fruit juice.
– ORIGIN Spanish equivalent of the woman's name *Margaret*.

margin •n. 1 an edge or border. 2 the blank border on each side of the print on a page. 3 an amount by which something is won. 4 an amount included or allowed for so as to be sure of success or safety: *there was no margin for error.*
– ORIGIN Latin *margo*.

marginal •adj. 1 relating to an edge or border. 2 of minor importance. 3 Brit. (of a parliamentary seat) held by a small majority and so at risk in an election.
– DERIVATIVES **marginality** n.

marginalia /mar-ji-**nay**-li-uh/ •pl. n. notes written or printed in the margin of a book or manuscript.

marginalize (or **marginalise**)
•v. (**marginalizes, marginalizing, marginalized**) make a person or group feel less important or powerful.
– DERIVATIVES **marginalization** n.

marginally •adv. slightly.

marigold •n. a plant of the daisy family with yellow or orange flowers.
– ORIGIN from the woman's name *Mary* + dialect *gold* 'marigold'.

marijuana /ma-ri-**hwah**-nuh/
•n. cannabis.
– ORIGIN Latin American Spanish.

marimba •n. a deep-toned xylophone of African origin.
– ORIGIN from Kimbundu (a Bantu language of western Angola).

marina •n. a purpose-built harbour with moorings for yachts and small boats.
– ORIGIN Italian or Spanish.

marinade •n. /ma-ri-**nayd**/ a mixture of ingredients in which food is soaked before cooking in order to flavour or soften it. •v. /**ma**-ri-nayd/ (**marinades, marinading, marinaded**) = MARINATE.
– ORIGIN French.

marinate •v. (**marinates, marinating, marinated**) soak meat or fish in a marinade.

marine •adj. 1 relating to the sea. 2 relating to shipping or a navy. •n. a member of a body of troops trained to serve on land or sea.
– ORIGIN Latin *marinus*.

mariner •n. formal or literary a sailor.

marionette •n. a puppet worked by strings.
– ORIGIN French.

marital •adj. relating to marriage or the relations between husband and wife.
– ORIGIN Latin *maritus* 'husband'.

maritime •adj. 1 relating to shipping or other activity taking place at sea. 2 living or found in or near the sea. 3 (of a climate) moist and mild due to the influence of the sea.
– ORIGIN Latin *maritimus*.

marjoram •n. a plant of the mint family, used as a herb in cooking.
– ORIGIN Latin *majorana*.

mark¹ •n. 1 a small area on a surface having a different colour from its surroundings. 2 something that acts as a pointer. 3 a sign or symbol that identifies something. 4 a sign of a quality or feeling: *a mark of respect.* 5 a characteristic feature. 6 a stage: *the runner had passed the ten-mile mark.* 7 esp. Brit. a point awarded for a correct answer or for a good performance in an exam. 8 a particular model of a vehicle or machine. •v. 1 make a mark on. 2 write a word or symbol on an object to identify it. 3 indicate the position of. 4 (**mark someone/thing out**) show someone or something to be different or special. 5 acknowledge an important event. 6 (**mark something up** or **down**) increase or reduce the price of an item. 7 give a mark to written work. 8 pay careful attention to. 9 Brit. (in team games) stay close to an opponent to prevent them getting or passing the ball.
– PHRASES **be quick off the mark** be fast in responding. **make a mark** have a notable effect. **mark time** 1 (of troops) march on the spot. 2 pass time while waiting for something. **on your marks** be ready to start (used to instruct competitors in a race). **up to the mark** up to the required standard.
– ORIGIN Old English.

mark² •n. (until the introduction of the euro in 2002) the basic unit of money of Germany.
– ORIGIN Old Norse.

marked •adj. 1 having an identifying mark. 2 clearly noticeable. 3 singled out as a target for attack: *a marked man.*
– DERIVATIVES **markedly** adv.

marker •n. 1 an object used to indicate a position, place, or route. 2 a felt-tip pen with a broad tip.

market •n. 1 a regular gathering for the buying and selling of food, livestock, or other goods. 2 an outdoor space or large hall where people offer goods for sale. 3 a particular area of trade or business.

4 demand for a particular product or service. • v. (**markets**, **marketing**, **marketed**) advertise or promote something.
– PHRASES **on the market** available for sale.
– DERIVATIVES **marketable** adj.
– ORIGIN Latin *mercatus*.

marketeer • n. a person who is in favour of a particular system of trade: *a free marketeer*.

market garden • n. Brit. a place where vegetables and fruit are grown for sale.

marketing • n. the promoting and selling of products or services.

marketplace • n. a competitive or commercial arena: *the global marketplace*.

market research • n. the gathering of information about consumers' needs, likes, and dislikes.

market town • n. a town where a regular market is held.

market value • n. the amount for which something can be sold in a competitive market.

marking • n. **1** an identifying mark. **2** (also **markings**) a pattern of marks on an animal.

marksman • n. (pl. **marksmen**) a person skilled in shooting.
– DERIVATIVES **marksmanship** n.

markup • n. **1** an amount added to the cost of producing something, to cover the producer's costs and profit. **2** a set of codes given to elements of a body of computer data to indicate their relationship to the rest of the data.

marl[1] • n. rock or soil consisting of clay and lime.
– ORIGIN Old French *marle*.

marl[2] • n. a type of fabric with differently coloured threads.
– ORIGIN from **MARBLED**.

marlin • n. a large, edible fish of warm seas, with a pointed snout.
– ORIGIN from **MARLINSPIKE**.

marlinspike • n. a pointed metal tool used by sailors to separate strands of rope or wire.
– ORIGIN Dutch *marlen* 'keep binding'.

marmalade • n. a preserve made from oranges.
– ORIGIN Portuguese *marmelada* 'quince jam'.

marmoreal /mar-mor-i-uhl/ • adj. literary made of or resembling marble.
– ORIGIN Latin *marmoreus*.

marmoset /mar-muh-zet/ • n. a small tropical American monkey with a silky coat and a long tail.

– ORIGIN Old French *marmouset* 'grotesque image'.

marmot /mar-muht/ • n. a heavily built burrowing rodent.
– ORIGIN French *marmotte*.

maroon[1] • n. a dark brownish-red colour.
– ORIGIN French *marron* 'chestnut'.

maroon[2] • v. (**be marooned**) be abandoned alone in a remote place.
– ORIGIN Spanish *cimarrón* 'runaway slave'.

marque • n. a make of car, as distinct from a specific model.
– ORIGIN French.

marquee • n. esp. Brit. a large tent used for social or business events.
– ORIGIN from **MARQUISE**.

marquess • n. a British nobleman ranking above an earl and below a duke.
– ORIGIN from **MARQUIS**.

marquetry /mar-ki-tri/ • n. work in which small pieces of coloured wood are inlaid into a surface, used to decorate furniture.
– ORIGIN French *marqueter* 'become variegated'.

marquis /mar-kwiss/ • n. (in some European countries) a nobleman ranking above a count and below a duke.
– ORIGIN Old French *marchis*.

marquise /mar-keez/ • n. the wife or widow of a marquis, or a woman holding the rank of marquis in her own right.
– ORIGIN French, feminine of **MARQUIS**.

marram grass • n. a coarse grass that grows on sand dunes.
– ORIGIN Old Norse.

marriage • n. **1** the formal union of a man and a woman, by which they are or become husband and wife. **2** a combination of two or more elements.
– ORIGIN Old French *mariage*.

marriageable • adj. suitable for marriage.

married • adj. joined in marriage.

marrow • n. **1** Brit. a long vegetable with a thin green skin and white flesh. **2** (also **bone marrow**) a soft fatty substance in the cavities of bones, in which blood cells are produced.
– ORIGIN Old English.

marrowbone • n. a bone containing edible marrow.

marry • v. (**marries**, **marrying**, **married**) **1** become the husband or wife of. **2** join two people in marriage. **3** (**marry into**) become a member of a family by marriage. **4** join two things together.
– ORIGIN Old French *marier*.

Mars • n. a planet of the solar system, fourth in order from the sun and the nearest to the earth.

m

marsh •n. an area of low-lying land which remains waterlogged.
– DERIVATIVES **marshy** adj.
– ORIGIN Old English.

marshal •n. **1** an officer of the highest rank in the armed forces of some countries. **2** (in the US) a type of law enforcement officer. **3** an official responsible for supervising public events. •v. (**marshals, marshalling, marshalled;** US **marshals, marshaling, marshaled**) **1** assemble a group of people in an orderly way. **2** bring together facts or thoughts in an organized way.
– ORIGIN Old French *mareschal* 'farrier, commander'.

marshmallow •n. a spongy sweet made from sugar, egg white, and gelatin.
– ORIGIN formerly made from the root of a plant growing in marshes.

marsh marigold •n. a plant with large yellow flowers which grows in damp ground and shallow water.

marsupial /mar-soo-pi-uhl/ •n. a mammal, such as a kangaroo, whose young are born before they are fully developed and are carried and suckled in a pouch on the mother's belly.
– ORIGIN Greek *marsupion* 'little purse'.

mart •n. **1** N. Amer. a shop. **2** a market.
– ORIGIN Dutch.

marten •n. a weasel-like forest animal.
– ORIGIN from Old French *peau martrine* 'marten fur'.

martial •adj. relating to war.
– ORIGIN Latin *martialis*.

martial arts •pl. n. sports which originated as forms of self-defence or attack, such as judo and karate.

martial law •n. government by the military forces of a country, when ordinary laws do not apply.

Martian •n. a supposed inhabitant of the planet Mars.

martin •n. a small short-tailed swallow.
– ORIGIN prob. from St *Martin* of Tours.

martinet •n. a person who enforces strict discipline.
– ORIGIN named after Jean *Martinet*, a French drill master.

martingale •n. a strap or set of straps running from the noseband or reins to the girth of a horse, used to prevent the horse from raising its head too high.
– ORIGIN French.

martyr •n. **1** a person who is killed because of their religious or political beliefs. **2** a person who exaggerates their difficulties in order to gain sympathy. •v. make someone a martyr.
– DERIVATIVES **martyrdom** n.

– ORIGIN Greek *martur* 'witness'.

marvel •v. (**marvels, marvelling,** US **marvels, marveling, marveled**) be filled with wonder. •n. a person or thing that causes a feeling of wonder.
– ORIGIN Old French *merveille*.

marvellous (US **marvelous**) •adj. **1** causing great wonder. **2** very good.
– DERIVATIVES **marvellously** adv.

Marxism •n. the political and economic theories of Karl Marx and Friedrich Engels which formed the basis for communism.
– DERIVATIVES **Marxian** n. & adj. **Marxist** n. & adj.

marzipan •n. a sweet paste of ground almonds, sugar, and egg white.
– ORIGIN Italian *marzapane*.

mascara •n. a cosmetic for darkening and thickening the eyelashes.
– ORIGIN Italian, 'mask'.

mascarpone /mas-kuh-poh-nay/ •n. a soft, mild Italian cream cheese.
– ORIGIN Italian.

mascot •n. a person, animal, or object that is supposed to bring good luck.
– ORIGIN French *mascotte*.

masculine •adj. **1** relating to men. **2** having qualities associated with men. **3** Grammar (of a gender of nouns and adjectives in certain languages) treated as male.
– DERIVATIVES **masculinity** n.
– ORIGIN Latin *masculus* 'male'.

maser /may-zer/ •n. a form of laser generating a beam of microwaves.
– ORIGIN from *microwave amplification by the stimulated emission of radiation*.

mash •v. crush or beat something to a soft mass. •n. **1** a soft mass made by crushing a substance. **2** Brit. informal boiled and mashed potatoes. **3** bran mixed with hot water, given as food to horses.
– ORIGIN Old English.

mask •n. **1** a covering for all or part of the face, worn as a disguise or for protection. **2** a device used to filter air breathed in or to supply gas for breathing. **3** a likeness of a person's face moulded in clay or wax. **4** a face pack. •v. **1** cover someone's face or part of their face with a mask. **2** conceal or disguise. **3** cover an area so as to protect it during painting or similar work.
– ORIGIN French *masque*.

masking tape •n. sticky tape used to cover areas on which paint is not wanted.

masochism /mass-uh-ki-z'm/ •n. the enjoyment of your own pain or humiliation.

– DERIVATIVES **masochist** n. **masochistic** adj.

– ORIGIN named after the Austrian novelist Leopold von Sacher-*Masoch*.

mason • n. **1** a builder and worker in stone. **2** (**Mason**) a Freemason.

– ORIGIN Old French *masson*.

Masonic • adj. relating to Freemasons.

masonry • n. stonework.

masque /mahsk/ • n. a form of dramatic entertainment popular in the 16th and 17th centuries, consisting of dancing and acting performed by masked players.

– ORIGIN prob. from former *masker* 'person wearing a mask'.

masquerade /mahss-kuh-**rayd**/ • n. **1** a pretence. **2** esp. N. Amer. a ball at which people wear masks. • v. (**masquerades, masquerading, masqueraded**) pretend to be someone or something.

– ORIGIN French *mascarade*.

Mass • n. **1** the Christian service of the Eucharist or Holy Communion. **2** a musical setting of parts of this service.

– ORIGIN Latin *missa*.

mass • n. **1** a body of matter with no definite shape. **2** a large number of people or objects gathered together. **3** (**the masses**) the ordinary people. **4** (**the mass of**) the majority of. **5** (**a mass of**) a large amount of. **6** Physics the quantity of matter which a body contains. • adj done by or affecting large numbers: *a mass exodus.* • v. gather together in a mass.

– ORIGIN Latin *massa*.

massacre • n. **1** a brutal slaughter of a large number of people. **2** informal a very heavy defeat. • v. (**massacres, massacring, massacred**) **1** brutally kill a large number of people. **2** informal defeat heavily.

– ORIGIN French.

massage • n. the rubbing and kneading of parts of the body with the hands to relieve tension or pain. • v. (**massages, massaging, massaged**) **1** give a massage to. **2** manipulate figures to give a more acceptable result.

– ORIGIN French.

massage parlour • n. **1** an establishment in which massage is provided for payment. **2** euphem. a brothel.

masseur /ma-**ser**/ • n. (fem. **masseuse** /ma-**serz**/) a person who provides massage professionally.

– ORIGIN French.

massif /ma-**seef**/ • n. a compact group of mountains.

– ORIGIN French, 'massive'.

massive • adj. **1** large and heavy or solid. **2** very large or severe.

– DERIVATIVES **massively** adv.

– ORIGIN French *massif*.

mass-market • adj. (of goods) produced in large quantities and appealing to most people.

mass noun • n. a noun referring to something which cannot be counted, usually without a plural and not used with *a* or *an*, e.g. *luggage, happiness.* Contrasted with **COUNT NOUN**.

mass number • n. Physics the total number of protons and neutrons in a nucleus.

mass-produce • v. produce goods in large quantities, using machinery.

mast • n. **1** a tall upright post on a boat, carrying a sail or sails. **2** a tall upright post such as a radio transmitter.

– ORIGIN Old English.

mastectomy /ma-**stek**-tuh-mi/ • n. (pl. **mastectomies**) an operation to remove a breast.

– ORIGIN Greek *mastos* 'breast'.

master • n. **1** a man in a position of authority, control, or ownership. **2** a person skilled in a particular art or activity. **3** the head of a college or school. **4** esp. Brit. a male schoolteacher. **5** a person who holds a second or further degree. **6** an original film, recording, or document from which copies are made. **7** a title placed before the name of a boy. • adj. **1** skilled in a particular trade: *a master builder.* **2** main; principal: *the master bedroom.* • v. (**masters, mastering, mastered**) **1** gain complete knowledge or skill in. **2** gain control of.

– ORIGIN Latin *magister*.

masterclass • n. a class given to students by an expert musician.

masterful • adj. **1** powerful and able to control other people. **2** performed or performing very skilfully.

– DERIVATIVES **masterfully** adv.

master key • n. a key that opens several locks, each of which also has its own key.

masterly • adj. performed or performing very skilfully.

mastermind • n. **1** a person who is very intelligent. **2** a person who plans and directs a complex scheme. • v. plan and direct a complex scheme.

master of ceremonies • n. a person in charge of proceedings at a formal event, who introduces the speakers or performers.

masterpiece • n. a work of outstanding skill.

mastery • n. **1** complete knowledge or command of a subject or skill. **2** control or superiority: *man's mastery over nature.*

masthead •n. **1** the highest part of a ship's mast. **2** the name of a newspaper or magazine printed at the top of the first page.

mastic /mass-tik/ •n. **1** a gum from the bark of a Mediterranean tree, used in making varnish and chewing gum. **2** a putty-like waterproof substance used for filling and sealing in building work.
– ORIGIN Greek *mastikhē*.

masticate •v. (**masticates, masticating, masticated**) chew food.
– DERIVATIVES **mastication** n.
– ORIGIN Latin *masticare*.

mastiff •n. a dog of a large, strong breed with drooping ears and lips.
– ORIGIN Old French *mastin*.

mastitis /ma-sty-tiss/ •n. inflammation of the mammary gland in the breast or udder.
– ORIGIN from Greek *mastos* 'breast'.

mastodon /mass-tuh-don/ •n. a large extinct elephant-like mammal.
– ORIGIN from Greek *mastos* 'breast' + *odous* 'tooth'.

mastoid /mass-toyd/ (also **mastoid process**) •n. a part of the bone behind the ear, to which neck muscles are attached, and which has air spaces linked to the middle ear.

masturbate /mass-ter-bayt/ •v. (**masturbates, masturbating, masturbated**) stimulate your genitals with your hand for sexual pleasure.
– DERIVATIVES **masturbation** n. **masturbatory** adj.
– ORIGIN Latin *masturbari*.

mat •n. **1** a thick piece of decorative or protective material placed on the floor. **2** a piece of springy material for landing on in some sports. **3** a small piece of material placed on a surface to protect it. **4** a thick, untidy layer of hairy or woolly material.
– ORIGIN Old English.

matador /mat-uh-dor/ •n. a bullfighter whose task is to kill the bull.
– ORIGIN Spanish, 'killer'.

match¹ •n. **1** a contest in which people or teams compete against each other. **2** a person or thing that can compete with another as an equal in quality or strength. **3** an exact equivalent. **4** a pair of things which correspond or are very similar. **5** a marriage or possible marriage partner. •v. **1** correspond or fit with something. **2** be equal to. **3** place a person or team in competition with another.
– ORIGIN Old English, 'companion'.

match² •n. a short, thin stick tipped with a mixture that is set alight when rubbed against a rough surface.

– ORIGIN Old French *meche*.

matchbox •n. a small box in which matches are sold.

matchless •adj. so good that nothing is an equal.

matchmaker •n. a person who tries to arrange marriages or relationships between other people.

match point •n. (in tennis and some other sports) a point which if won by one of the players will also win them the match.

mate¹ •n. **1** Brit. informal a friend. **2** (in combination) a fellow member or occupant: *his teammates.* **3** the sexual partner of an animal. **4** esp. Brit. an assistant to a skilled worker. **5** an officer on a merchant ship below a master. •v. (**mates, mating, mated**) (of animals or birds) come together for breeding.
– ORIGIN German, 'comrade'.

mate² •n. & v. Chess = **CHECKMATE**.

mater /may-ter/ •n. Brit. informal, dated mother.
– ORIGIN Latin.

material •n. **1** the substance from which something is or can be made. **2** items needed for doing or creating something. **3** cloth. •adj. **1** relating to physical objects rather than the mind or spirit. **2** essential or relevant: *evidence material to the case.*
– DERIVATIVES **materially** adv.
– ORIGIN Latin *materia* 'matter'.

materialism •n. the belief that material possessions and physical comfort are more important than spiritual values.
– DERIVATIVES **materialist** n. & adj. **materialistic** adj.

materialize (or **materialise**) •v. (**materialize, materializing, materialized**) **1** become fact; happen. **2** appear suddenly.
– DERIVATIVES **materialization** n.

maternal •adj. **1** characteristic of or relating to a mother. **2** related through the mother's side of the family.
– DERIVATIVES **maternally** adv.
– ORIGIN French *maternel*.

maternity •n. the state of being or becoming a mother.

matey •adj. Brit. informal familiar and friendly.
– DERIVATIVES **mateyness** n. **matily** adv.

mathematics •n. the branch of science concerned with number, quantity, and space.
– DERIVATIVES **mathematical** adj. **mathematically** adv. **mathematician** n.
– ORIGIN Greek *mathēma* 'science'.

maths (N. Amer. **math**) •n. = **MATHEMATICS**.

matinee /ma-ti-nay/ •n. an afternoon

performance in a theatre or cinema.
– ORIGIN French, 'morning'.

matins /ma-tinz/ • n. a service of morning prayer.
– ORIGIN Old French *matines* 'mornings'.

matriarchy • n. (pl. **matriarchies**) **1** a form of social organization in which the mother or eldest female is the head of the family. **2** a society in which women hold most or all of the power.

matriarch /may-tri-ark/ • n. **1** a woman who is the head of a family or tribe. **2** a powerful older woman.
– DERIVATIVES **matriarchal** adj.
– ORIGIN Latin *mater* 'mother'.

matrices pl. of MATRIX.

matricide /ma-tri-syd/ • n. **1** the killing of a mother by her child. **2** a person who kills their mother.
– ORIGIN Latin *mater* 'mother'.

matriculate /muh-trik-yuu-layt/ • v. (**matriculates, matriculating, matriculated**) enrol at a college or university.
– DERIVATIVES **matriculation** n.
– ORIGIN Latin *matriculare*.

matrimony • n. marriage.
– DERIVATIVES **matrimonial** adj.
– ORIGIN Latin *matrimonium*.

matrix /may-triks/ • n. (pl. **matrices** /may-tri-seez/ or **matrixes**) **1** an environment or material in which something develops. **2** a mass of rock in which crystals or fossils are embedded. **3** a mould in which something is cast or shaped. **4** Math. a rectangular arrangement of quantities in rows and columns that is manipulated according to particular rules. **5** a grid-like arrangement of elements.
– ORIGIN Latin, 'womb'.

matron • n. **1** a woman in charge of medical and living arrangements at a boarding school. **2** a dignified or sedate married woman. **3** Brit. dated a woman in charge of nursing in a hospital.
– DERIVATIVES **matronly** adj.
– ORIGIN Latin *matrona*.

matron of honour • n. a married woman attending the bride at a wedding.

matt (also **matte**) • adj. not shiny.
– ORIGIN French *mat*.

matted • adj. (of hair or fur) tangled into a thick mass.

matter • n. **1** physical substance or material; (in physics) that which occupies space and has mass. **2** a subject to be dealt with. **3** (**the matter**) the reason for a problem. **4** written or printed material. • v. (**matters, mattering, mattered**) be important.
– PHRASES **a matter of** no more than a specified period. **a matter of course** the natural or expected thing. **no matter** it is of no importance.
– ORIGIN Latin *materia*.

matter-of-fact • adj. unemotional and practical.

matting • n. material used for mats.

mattock • n. a farming tool similar to a pickaxe.
– ORIGIN Old English.

mattress • n. a fabric case filled with soft, firm, or springy material used for sleeping on.
– ORIGIN Arabic, 'carpet or cushion'.

maturation /mat-yuu-ray-sh'n/ • n. the action of maturing.

mature • adj. (**maturer, maturest**) **1** fully grown. **2** like an adult in being reasonable and sensible. **3** (of certain foods or drinks) full-flavoured.
• v. (**matures, maturing, matured**) **1** become mature. **2** (of an insurance policy) reach the end of its term and so become payable.
– DERIVATIVES **maturely** adv.
– ORIGIN Latin *maturus* 'timely, ripe'.

maturity • n. **1** the state or period of being fully grown. **2** the time when an insurance policy reaches the end of its term and becomes payable.

matutinal /ma-tyuu-ty-n'l/ • adj. formal relating to the morning.
– ORIGIN Latin *matutinus* 'early'.

maudlin /mawd-lin/ • adj. sentimental and full of self-pity.
– ORIGIN from Mary *Magdalen* in the Bible.

maul • v. **1** (of an animal) wound by scratching and tearing. **2** treat someone savagely or roughly. • n. Rugby Union a loose scrum formed around a player with the ball off the ground.
– ORIGIN Latin *malleus* 'hammer'.

maunder • v. (**maunders, maundering, maundered**) talk in a rambling way.
– ORIGIN perh. from former *maunder* 'to beg'.

Maundy Thursday • n. the Thursday before Easter, when the British king or queen gives out specially minted coins (**Maundy money**) to a group of people at a public ceremony.
– ORIGIN from Latin *mandatum novum* 'new commandment'.

Mauritanian /mor-i-tay-ni-uhn/ • n. a person from Mauritania, a country in West Africa. • adj. relating to Mauritania.

mausoleum /maw-suh-lee-uhm/ • n. (pl. **mausolea** /maw-suh-lee-uh/ or

m

mausoleums) a building housing a tomb or tombs.
– ORIGIN Greek *Mausōleion*.

mauve •n. a pale purple colour.
– ORIGIN French, 'mallow'.

maverick •n. an unconventional or independent-minded person.
– ORIGIN first meaning an unbranded calf: from Samuel A. *Maverick*, a 19th-century Texas rancher who did not brand his cattle.

maw •n. the jaws or throat.
– ORIGIN Old English.

mawkish •adj. sentimental in a feeble way.
– ORIGIN from former *mawk* 'maggot'.

max •abbrev. maximum.

maxi •n. (pl. **maxis**) a skirt or coat reaching to the ankle.

maxilla /mak-sil-luh/ •n. (pl. **maxillae** /mak-sil-lee/) 1 the bone of the upper jaw. 2 (in an insect or other arthropod) each of a pair of mouthparts.
– DERIVATIVES **maxillary** adj..
– ORIGIN Latin, 'jaw'.

maxim •n. a short statement expressing a general truth or rule of behaviour.
– ORIGIN from Latin *propositio maxima* 'most important proposition'.

maximize (or **maximise**)
•v. (**maximizes, maximizing, maximized**) 1 make as large or great as possible. 2 make the best use of.
– DERIVATIVES **maximization** n.

maximum •n. (pl. **maxima** or **maximums**) the greatest amount, size, or strength possible or gained.
•adj. greatest in amount, size, or strength.
– DERIVATIVES **maximal** adj.
– ORIGIN Latin, 'greatest thing'.

May •n. 1 the fifth month of the year. 2 (**may**) the hawthorn or its blossom.
– ORIGIN from Latin *Maius mensis* 'month of the goddess *Maia*'.

may •modal verb (3rd sing. present **may**; past **might**) 1 expressing possibility. 2 asking for or giving permission. 3 expressing a wish.
– ORIGIN Old English.

> USAGE: For an explanation of when to use **may** and **can**, see the note at **CAN**.

Maya /my-uh/ •n. (pl. **Maya** or **Mayas**) a member of a Central American people whose civilization died out *c*.900 AD.
– DERIVATIVES **Mayan** adj. & n.

maybe •adv. perhaps.

May Day •n. 1 May, celebrated as a spring festival or as a holiday in honour of workers.

Mayday •n. an international radio distress signal used by ships and aircraft.
– ORIGIN French *m'aidez* 'help me'.

mayfly •n. (pl. **mayflies**) an insect with transparent wings which lives for only a very short time.

mayhem •n. violent disorder.
– ORIGIN Old French.

mayn't •contr. may not.

mayonnaise /may-uh-nayz/ •n. a thick creamy dressing made from egg yolks, oil, and vinegar.
– ORIGIN French.

mayor •n. the elected head of a city or borough council.
– DERIVATIVES **mayoral** adj.
– ORIGIN Latin *major* 'greater'.

mayoralty /mair-uhl-ti/ •n. (pl. **mayoralties**) the time during which a mayor is in office.

mayoress •n. 1 a woman elected as mayor. 2 the wife of a mayor.

maypole •n. a decorated pole with long ribbons attached to the top, traditionally used for dancing round on May Day.

maze •n. a complicated network of paths and walls or hedges designed as a challenge to find a way through.
– ORIGIN from AMAZE.

mazurka /muh-zer-kuh/ •n. a lively Polish dance.
– ORIGIN Polish, 'woman from the province of Mazovia'.

MB •abbrev. 1 Bachelor of Medicine. [ORIGIN Latin *Medicinae Baccalaureus*.] 2 (also **Mb**) megabyte(s).

MBA •abbrev. Master of Business Administration.

MBE •abbrev. Member of the Order of the British Empire.

MC •abbrev. 1 Master of Ceremonies. 2 Military Cross. •n. a person who provides entertainment at a club or party by instructing the DJ and performing rap music. •v. (**MC's, MC'ing, MC'd**) perform as an MC.

MCC •abbrev. Marylebone Cricket Club.

m-commerce •n. commercial dealings carried out electronically by mobile phone.

MD •abbrev. 1 Doctor of Medicine. [ORIGIN Latin *Medicinae Doctor*.] 2 Brit. Managing Director.

Md •symb. the chemical element mendelevium.

MDF •abbrev. medium density fibreboard.

MDMA
•abbrev. methylenedioxymethampheta-mine, the drug Ecstasy.

ME •abbrev. myalgic encephalomyelitis, a

medical condition with fever, aching, and severe tiredness.

me¹ • pron. (first person sing.) used as the object of a verb or preposition or after 'than', 'as', or the verb 'to be', to refer to the speaker himself or herself.
– ORIGIN Old English.

> **USAGE:** For an explanation of when to use **me** and when to use **I**, see the note at **PERSONAL PRONOUN**.

me² (also **mi**) • n. Music the third note of a major scale, coming after 'ray' and before 'fah'.
– ORIGIN from *mira* in a Latin hymn.

mea culpa /may-uh kuul-puh/ • exclam. used as an acknowledgement that something is your fault.
– ORIGIN Latin, 'by my fault'.

mead • n. an alcoholic drink made from honey and water.
– ORIGIN Old English.

meadow • n. an area of grassland.
– ORIGIN Old English.

meadowsweet • n. a tall plant with creamy-white sweet-smelling flowers.

meagre (US **meager**) • adj. small in quantity and poor in quality: *a meagre diet of bread and beans*.
– DERIVATIVES **meagreness** n.
– ORIGIN Old French *maigre*.

meal¹ • n. 1 any of the regular daily occasions when food is eaten. 2 the food eaten on such an occasion.
– PHRASES **make a meal of** Brit. informal do something with unnecessary care and effort.
– ORIGIN Old English.

meal² • n. any grain or pulse that has been ground to a powder, used to make flour or feed animals.
– ORIGIN Old English.

meal ticket • n. a person or thing that is treated just as a source of money.

mealy • adj. relating to ground grain or pulses: *a mealy flavour*.

mealy-mouthed • adj. afraid to speak frankly.
– ORIGIN perh. from German *Mehl im Maule behalten* 'carry meal in the mouth'.

mean¹ • v. (**means, meaning, meant**) 1 intend to say or refer to something. 2 (of a word) have as its explanation in the same language or its equivalent in another language. 3 intend to be or do: *it was meant to be a secret*. 4 have something as a result or purpose. 5 be of specified importance: *animals mean more to him than people*.
– PHRASES **mean business** be serious. **mean well** have good intentions, but not always carry them out.
– ORIGIN Old English.

mean² • adj. 1 esp. Brit. unwilling to give or share things. 2 unkind or unfair. 3 N. Amer. bad-tempered or aggressive. 4 poor in quality or appearance. 5 dated of a low social class. 6 informal excellent.
– DERIVATIVES **meanly** adv. **meanness** n.
– ORIGIN Old English.

mean³ • n. 1 the average value of a set of quantities. 2 something in the middle of two extremes. • adj. 1 calculated as an average. 2 equally far from two extremes.
– ORIGIN Latin *medianus* 'middle'.

meander /mi-an-der/ • v. (**meanders, meandering, meandered**) 1 follow a winding course. 2 wander in an aimless way. • n. a bend of a river that curves back on itself.
– ORIGIN from the river *Maeander* in Turkey.

meaning • n. 1 what is meant by a word, idea, or action. 2 a sense of purpose.

meaningful • adj. 1 having meaning. 2 worthwhile. 3 intended to express something: *meaningful glances*.
– DERIVATIVES **meaningfully** adv.

meaningless • adj. having no meaning or significance.
– DERIVATIVES **meaninglessly** adv. **meaninglessness** n.

means • n. 1 a thing or method for achieving a result. 2 money. 3 wealth: *a man of means*.
– PHRASES **by all means** of course. **by no means** certainly not. **a means to an end** a thing that is not valued in itself but is useful in achieving an aim.
– ORIGIN plural of **MEAN³**.

means test • n. an official investigation of a person's finances to find out whether they qualify for welfare benefits from the state.

meant past and past part. of **MEAN¹**.

meantime • adv. (also **in the meantime**) meanwhile.

meanwhile • adv. 1 (also **in the meanwhile**) in the period of time between two events. 2 at the same time.

measles • n. an infectious disease causing fever and a red rash.
– ORIGIN prob. from Dutch *masel* 'spot'.

measly • adj. informal ridiculously small or few.

measure • v. (**measures, measuring, measured**) 1 find out the size, amount, or degree of something by comparing it with a standard. 2 be of a specified size. 3 (**measure something out**) take an exact quantity of something. 4 (**measure up**) reach the required standard. • n. 1 a means of achieving a purpose. 2 a

m

proposal for a law. **3** a standard unit used to express size, amount, or degree. **4** a measuring device marked with standard units of size, amount, or degree. **5** (**a measure of**) a certain amount of. **6** (**a measure of**) an indication of the extent or quality of. **7** a unit of metre in poetry.
– PHRASES **for good measure** as an amount or item that is additional to what is strictly required. **have the measure of** understand the character or abilities of.
– DERIVATIVES **measurer** n. **measurable** adj. **measurably** adv.
– ORIGIN Latin *mensura*.

measured • adj. **1** slow and regular in rhythm. **2** carefully considered: *measured prose*.

measureless • adj. literary having no limits.

measurement • n. **1** the action of measuring. **2** an amount, size, or extent found by measuring. **3** a standard unit used in measuring.

meat • n. **1** the flesh of an animal as food. **2** the chief part: *let's get to the meat of the matter.*
– ORIGIN Old English, 'food'.

meatball • n. a ball of minced or chopped meat.

meaty • adj. (**meatier, meatiest**) **1** resembling or full of meat. **2** fleshy or muscular. **3** substantial or satisfying: *the play offered meaty roles for actors.*

Mecca • n. a place which attracts many people.
– ORIGIN from the city of *Mecca* in Saudi Arabia, the holiest city for Muslims.

mechanic • n. a skilled worker who repairs and maintains machinery.
– ORIGIN Greek *mēkhanē* 'machine'.

mechanical • adj. **1** relating to or operated by a machine or machinery. **2** done without thought. **3** relating to physical forces or motion.
– DERIVATIVES **mechanically** adv.

mechanical engineering • n. the branch of engineering concerned with the design, building, and use of machines.

mechanics • n. **1** the branch of study concerned with motion and forces producing motion. **2** machinery or working parts. **3** the practical aspects of something: *the mechanics of cello playing.*

mechanism • n. **1** a piece of machinery. **2** the way in which something works or is brought about.

mechanize (or **mechanise**)
• v. (**mechanizes, mechanizing, mechanized**) equip with machines or automatic devices.

– DERIVATIVES **mechanization** n.

medal • n. a metal disc with an inscription or design, awarded for an achievement or to mark an event.
– ORIGIN Latin *medalia* 'half a denarius'.

medallion • n. a piece of jewellery in the shape of a medal, worn as a pendant.

medallist (US **medalist**) • n. a person awarded a medal.

meddle • v. (**meddles, meddling, meddled**) interfere in something that is not your concern.
– DERIVATIVES **meddler** n.
– ORIGIN Old French.

meddlesome • adj. tending to interfere in other people's business.

media • n. **1** television, radio, and newspapers as the means of mass communication. **2** pl. of MEDIUM.

> **USAGE:** The word **media** comes from the plural of the Latin word **medium**. In the normal sense 'television, radio, and newspapers', it often behaves as a collective noun (one referring to a group of people or things, such as **staff**), and can correctly be used with either a singular or a plural verb: *the media was informed* or *the media were informed*.

mediaeval • adj. var. of MEDIEVAL.

medial /mee-di-uhl/ • adj. situated in the middle.
– DERIVATIVES **medially** adv.
– ORIGIN Latin *medialis*.

median /mee-di-uhn/ • adj. **1** tech. situated in the middle. **2** having a value in the middle of a series of values. • n. **1** a median value. **2** Geom. a straight line drawn from one of the angles of a triangle to the middle of the opposite side.
– ORIGIN Latin *medianus*.

mediate /mee-di-ate/ • v. (**mediates, mediating, mediated**) try to settle a dispute between other people.
– DERIVATIVES **mediation** n. **mediator** n.
– ORIGIN Latin *mediare* 'place in the middle'.

medic • n. informal, esp. Brit. a doctor or medical student.

medical • adj. relating to the science or practice of medicine. • n. an examination to assess a person's physical health.
– DERIVATIVES **medically** adv.
– ORIGIN Latin *medicus* 'physician'.

medicament /muh-dik-uh-muhnt/ • n. a medicine.

medicate • v. (**medicates, medicating, medicated**) **1** give medicine or a drug to. **2** (as adj. **medicated**) containing a medicinal substance.
– ORIGIN Latin *medicari*.

medication • n. **1** a medicine or drug.

2 treatment with medicines.

medicinal • adj. **1** having healing properties. **2** relating to medicines.
– DERIVATIVES **medicinally** adv.

medicine • n. **1** the science or practice of the treatment and prevention of disease. **2** a substance taken by mouth in order to treat or prevent disease.
– ORIGIN Latin *medicus* 'physician'.

> ☑ Spell **medicine** with an **i** after the **d**.

medicine man • n. a person believed to have magical powers of healing.

medieval /med-i-ee-v'l/ (also **mediaeval**) • adj. **1** relating to the Middle Ages. **2** informal very old-fashioned.
– ORIGIN from Latin *medium aevum* 'middle age'.

medievalist (also **mediaevalist**) • n. a person who studies medieval history or literature.

medina /me-dee-nuh/ • n. the old quarter of a North African town.
– ORIGIN Arabic, 'town'.

mediocre /mee-di-oh-ker/ • adj. of only average quality.
– ORIGIN Latin *mediocris* 'of middle height or degree'.

mediocrity /mee-di-ok-ri-ti/ • n. (pl. **mediocrities**) **1** the state of being average in quality. **2** a person of average ability and lacking flair or inspiration.

meditate • v. (**meditates, meditating, meditated**) **1** focus your mind as a spiritual exercise or for relaxation. **2** (**meditate on/about**) think carefully about.
– ORIGIN Latin *meditari* 'contemplate'.

meditation • n. **1** the action of meditating. **2** a speech or piece of writing expressing considered thoughts on a subject.

meditative • adj. involving or absorbed in focused thought or deep reflection.
– DERIVATIVES **meditatively** adv.

Mediterranean /med-i-tuh-ray-ni-uhn/ • adj. relating to the Mediterranean Sea or the countries around it.
– ORIGIN Latin *mediterraneus* 'inland'.

> ☑ **Mediterranean** is spelled with one **d**, one **t** and a double **r**.

medium • n. (pl. **media** or **mediums**) **1** a means by which something is communicated or achieved. **2** a substance through which a force or other influence is transmitted. **3** a liquid with which pigments are mixed to make paint. **4** (pl. **mediums**) a person claiming to be able to communicate between the dead and the living. **5** the middle state

between two extremes. • adj. between two extremes.
– ORIGIN Latin, 'middle'.

medium wave • n. esp. Brit. a radio wave of a frequency between 300 kilohertz and 3 megahertz.

medlar • n. a small brown apple-like fruit.
– ORIGIN Old French *medler*.

medley • n. (pl. **medleys**) **1** a varied mixture of people or things. **2** a collection of musical items performed as a continuous piece.
– ORIGIN Old French *medlee* 'melee'.

medulla /mi-dul-luh/ • n. **1** Anat. a separate inner region of an organ or tissue. **2** Bot. the soft internal tissue of a plant.
– ORIGIN Latin, 'pith or marrow'.

medulla oblongata /mi-dul-luh ob-long-gah-tuh/ • n. the part of the spinal cord extending into the brain.

meek • adj. quiet, gentle, and obedient.
– DERIVATIVES **meekly** adv. **meekness** n.
– ORIGIN Old Norse, 'soft, gentle'.

meerkat • n. a small southern African mongoose.
– ORIGIN Dutch, 'sea cat'.

meerschaum /meer-shuhm, meer-shawm/ • n. **1** a soft white clay-like material. **2** a tobacco pipe with a bowl made from meerschaum.
– ORIGIN German, 'sea foam'.

meet¹ • v. (**meets, meeting, met**) **1** come together with someone at the same place and time. **2** see or be introduced to someone for the first time. **3** touch or join. **4** experience a situation. **5** (**meet with**) receive a reaction. **6** satisfy a requirement. • n. a meeting for races or (Brit.) fox-hunting.
– ORIGIN Old English.

meet² • adj. old use suitable or proper.
– ORIGIN from **METE**.

meeting • n. **1** an organized gathering of people for a discussion or other purpose. **2** a situation in which people meet by chance or arrangement.

mega • adj. informal **1** very large. **2** excellent.

mega- • comb. form **1** large. **2** referring to a factor of one million (10^6).
– ORIGIN Greek *megas* 'great'.

megabyte • n. Computing a unit of information equal to one million or (strictly) 1,048,576 bytes.

megahertz • n. (pl. **megahertz**) a unit of frequency equal to one million hertz.

megalith • n. a large stone that forms a prehistoric monument or part of one.
– DERIVATIVES **megalithic** adj.

megalomania /meg-uh-luh-may-ni-uh/ • n. **1** the false belief that you are very powerful and important. **2** a strong desire for power.
– DERIVATIVES **megalomaniac** n. & adj.

megaphone • n. a large cone-shaped device for amplifying the voice.

megapixel • n. Computing a unit of graphic resolution equal to 2²⁰ or (strictly) 1,048,576 pixels.

megastar • n. informal a very famous entertainer or sports player.

megaton • n. a unit of explosive power equivalent to one million tons of TNT.

megawatt • n. a unit of power equal to one million watts.

meiosis /my-oh-siss/ • n. (pl. **meioses** /my-oh-seez/) Biol. the division of a cell that results in four cells, each with half the number of chromosomes of the original cell. Compare with **MITOSIS**.
– DERIVATIVES **meiotic** adj.
– ORIGIN Greek *meiōsis* 'lessening'.

meitnerium /myt-neer-i-uhm/ • n. a very unstable chemical element made by high-energy atomic collisions.
– ORIGIN named after the Swedish physicist Lise *Meitner*.

melamine /mel-uh-meen/ • n. a hard, heat-resistant plastic used to coat surfaces.
– ORIGIN German *Melamin*.

melancholia /me-luhn-koh-li-uh/ • n. dated severe depression.

melancholy • n. deep and long-lasting sadness. • adj. feeling or causing sadness.
– DERIVATIVES **melancholic** adj.
– ORIGIN Greek *melankholia*.

melange /may-lonzh/ • n. a varied mixture.
– ORIGIN French.

melanin /mel-uh-nin/ • n. a dark pigment in the hair and skin, responsible for the tanning of skin exposed to sunlight.
– ORIGIN Greek *melas* 'black'.

melanoma /mel-uh-noh-muh/ • n. a form of skin cancer which develops in melanin-forming cells.

meld • v. blend or mix together.
– ORIGIN perh. from **MELT** and **WELD**.

melee /mel-ay/ • n. **1** a confused fight. **2** a disorderly mass of people.
– ORIGIN French.

mellifluous /mel-lif-luu-uhsss/ • adj. pleasingly smooth and musical to hear.
– ORIGIN from Latin *mel* 'honey' + *fluere* 'to flow'.

mellow • adj. **1** pleasantly smooth or soft in sound, taste, or colour. **2** relaxed and good-humoured. • v. become mellow.

– ORIGIN perh. related to **MEAL²**.

melodeon /mel-oh-di-ihn/ • n. **1** a small accordion. **2** a small organ similar to the harmonium.

melodic /muh-lod-ik/ • adj. **1** relating to melody. **2** pleasant-sounding.
– DERIVATIVES **melodically** adv.

melodious • adj. tuneful.

melodrama • n. **1** a sensational play with exaggerated characters and exciting events. **2** exaggerated behaviour.
– ORIGIN from Greek *melos* 'music' + French *drame* 'drama'.

melodramatic • adj. too dramatic or exaggerated.
– DERIVATIVES **melodramatically** adv.

melody • n. (pl. **melodies**) **1** a tune. **2** the main part in harmonized music.
– ORIGIN Greek *melos* 'song'.

melon • n. a large round fruit with sweet pulpy flesh and many seeds.
– ORIGIN Greek *mēlopepōn*.

melt • v. **1** make or become liquid by heating. **2** gradually disappear.
– ORIGIN Old English.

meltdown • n. **1** an accident in a nuclear reactor in which the fuel overheats and melts the reactor core. **2** a disastrous collapse: *the 1987 stock market meltdown*.

melting point • n. the temperature at which a solid will melt.

melting pot • n. a place where different peoples, ideas, or styles are mixed together.

member • n. **1** a person or organization belonging to a group or society. **2** a part of a complex structure. **3** old use a part of the body.
– DERIVATIVES **membership** n.
– ORIGIN Latin *membrum* 'limb'.

membrane • n. **1** a skin-like structure that lines, connects, or covers a cell or part of the body. **2** a thin pliable sheet of material forming a barrier or lining.
– DERIVATIVES **membranous** adj.
– ORIGIN Latin.

memento • n. (pl. **mementos** or **mementoes**) an object kept as a reminder.
– ORIGIN Latin, 'remember!'

memento mori /mi-men-toh mor-i/ • n. (pl. **memento mori**) an object kept as a reminder that death is inevitable.
– ORIGIN Latin, 'remember (that you have) to die'.

memo • n. (pl. **memos**) a memorandum.

memoir /mem-war/ • n. **1** a historical account or biography written from personal knowledge. **2** (**memoirs**) an account written by a public figure of their life and experiences.

– ORIGIN French *mémoire* 'memory'.

memorabilia /mem-uh-ruh-**bil**-i-uh/
• pl. n. objects kept or collected because
of their associations with memorable
people or events.

memorable • adj. worth remembering
or easily remembered.
– DERIVATIVES **memorably** adv.

memorandum • n. (pl. **memoranda** or
memorandums) **1** a note sent from one
person to another in an organization. **2** a
note recording something for future
use.
– ORIGIN Latin, 'something to be brought
to mind'.

memorial • n. an object or structure
established in memory of a person or
event. • adj. in memory of someone.

memorize (or **memorise**)
• v. (**memorizes, memorizing,
memorized**) learn something by heart.

memory • n. (pl. **memories**) **1** the faculty
by which the mind stores and
remembers information. **2** a person or
thing remembered. **3** the length of time
over which you can remember things.
4 a computer's equipment or capacity
for storing information.
– PHRASES **in memory of** intended to
remind people of.
– ORIGIN Old French *memorie*.

memsahib /**mem**-sahb, mem-**suh**-
heeb/ • n. dated (in India) a respectful
form of address for a married white
woman.
– ORIGIN from an Indian pronunciation of
ma'am + SAHIB.

men pl. of MAN.

menace • n. **1** a dangerous or troublesome person or thing. **2** a threatening
quality. • v. (**menaces, menacing,
menaced**) threaten someone.
– ORIGIN Latin *minax* 'threatening'.

ménage à trois /may-nah*zh* ah **trwah**/
• n. an arrangement in which a married
couple and the lover of one of them live
together.
– ORIGIN French, 'household of three'.

menagerie /muh-**naj**-uh-ri/ • n. a
collection of wild animals kept in
captivity for showing to the public.
– ORIGIN French.

menaquinone /men-uh-**kwin**-ohn/
• n. a member of the vitamin K group, a
compound produced by bacteria in the
intestines, and essential for blood-
clotting.
– ORIGIN from its chemical name.

mend • v. **1** restore something to its
correct or working condition. **2** improve
an unpleasant situation.
– PHRASES **on the mend** improving in
health or condition.

– ORIGIN shortening of AMEND.

mendacious /men-**day**-shuss/
• adj. untruthful.
– DERIVATIVES **mendacity** n.
– ORIGIN Latin *mendax* 'lying'.

mendelevium /men-duh-**lee**-vi-uhm/
• n. a very unstable chemical element
made by high-energy collisions.
– ORIGIN named after the Russian
chemist Dimitri *Mendeleev*.

mendicant /**men**-di-kuhnt/
• adj. **1** living by begging. **2** (of a
religious order) originally dependent on
charitable donations. • n. **1** a beggar. **2** a
member of a mendicant order.
– ORIGIN Latin *mendicus* 'beggar'.

menfolk • pl. n. the men of a family or
community.

menhir /**men**-heer/ • n. a tall stone set
up as a monument in prehistoric times.
– ORIGIN Breton, 'long stone'.

menial /**mee**-ni-uhl/ • adj. (of work)
requiring little skill and lacking status.
• n. a person with a menial job.
– ORIGIN Old French.

meninges /mi-**nin**-jeez/ • pl. n. (sing.
meninx) the three membranes that
enclose the brain and spinal cord.
– ORIGIN Greek *mēninx* 'membrane'.

meningitis /men-in-**jy**-tiss/ • n. a
disease in which the meninges become
inflamed owing to infection.

meniscus /muh-**niss**-kuhss/ • n. (pl.
menisci /muh-**niss**-I/) **1** Physics the curved
upper surface of a liquid in a tube. **2** a
thin lens curving outwards on one side
and inwards on the other.
– ORIGIN Greek *mēniskos* 'crescent'.

menopause • n. the period in a
woman's life (between about 45 and 50)
when menstruation gradually stops.
– DERIVATIVES **menopausal** adj.
– ORIGIN from Greek *mēn* 'month' + PAUSE.

menorah /mi-**nor**-uh/ • n. a large
candlestick used in Jewish worship,
typically with eight branches.
– ORIGIN Hebrew.

menses /**men**-seez/ • pl. n. blood discharged from the lining of the womb
during menstruation.
– ORIGIN Latin, 'months'.

menstrual • adj. relating to the monthly
discharge of blood from the lining of the
womb.
– ORIGIN Latin *menstrualis*.

menstruate • v. (**menstruates,
menstruating, menstruated**) (of a non-
pregnant woman) discharge blood from
the lining of the womb each month.
– DERIVATIVES **menstruation** n.

mensuration /men-syuu-**ray**-sh'n/
• n. **1** measurement. **2** the part of

m

geometry concerned with finding lengths, areas, and volumes.
– ORIGIN Latin.

-ment • suffix **1** forming nouns expressing the means or result of an action: *treatment*. **2** forming nouns from adjectives: *merriment*.
– ORIGIN French or Latin.

mental • adj. **1** relating to the mind. **2** relating to disorders or illnesses of the mind. **3** informal mad.
– DERIVATIVES **mentally** adv.
– ORIGIN Latin *mens* 'mind'.

mental age • n. a person's mental ability expressed as the age at which an average person reaches the same ability.

mental handicap • n. a condition in which a person's intellectual ability is underdeveloped and prevents them from functioning normally in society.
– DERIVATIVES **mentally handicapped** adv.

USAGE: In Britain, the terms **mental handicap** and **mentally handicapped** have been largely replaced in official situations by the term **learning difficulties**.

mentality • n. (pl. **mentalities**) a typical way of thinking.

menthol • n. a substance found in peppermint oil, used as a flavouring and in decongestant medicines.
– DERIVATIVES **mentholated** adj.
– ORIGIN Latin *mentha* 'mint'.

mention • v. **1** refer to something briefly. **2** refer to someone by name. • n. **1** a reference to someone or something. **2** a formal acknowledgement of something noteworthy.
– PHRASES **mention someone in your will** leave a legacy to someone.
– ORIGIN Latin.

mentor • n. an experienced person in an organization or institution who trains and advises new employees or students.
– ORIGIN named after *Mentor*, the adviser of Telemachus in Homer's *Odyssey*.

menu • n. **1** a list of dishes available in a restaurant. **2** the food to be served at a meal. **3** a list of commands or facilities displayed on a computer screen.
– ORIGIN French, 'detailed list'.

meow • n. & v. var. of MIAOW.

MEP • abbrev. Member of the European Parliament.

mercantile /mer-kuhn-tyl/ • adj. relating to trade or commerce.
– ORIGIN Italian *mercante* 'merchant'.

mercenary • adj. motivated chiefly by the desire to make money. • n. (pl. **mercenaries**) a professional soldier hired to serve in a foreign army.
– ORIGIN Latin *mercenarius* 'hireling'.

merchandise • n. /mer-chuhn-dyss/ goods for sale. • v. /mer-chuhn-dyz/ (**merchandises**, **merchandising**, **merchandised**) promote the sale of goods.
– DERIVATIVES **merchandiser** n.
– ORIGIN Old French *marchand* 'merchant'.

merchant • n. **1** a trader who sells goods in large quantities. **2** informal, derog. a person fond of a particular activity: *a speed merchant*. • adj. (of sailors or shipping) involved with commerce.
– ORIGIN Old French *marchant*.

merchantable • adj. suitable for sale.

merchant bank • n. Brit. a bank dealing in commercial loans and investment.

merchantman • n. (pl. **merchantmen**) a ship carrying merchandise.

merchant navy (N. Amer. **merchant marine**) • n. a country's commercial shipping.

merciful • adj. **1** showing compassion and forgiveness. **2** giving relief from suffering: *a merciful release*.

mercifully • adv. **1** in a compassionate and forgiving way. **2** to your great relief.

merciless • adj. showing no compassion or forgiveness.
– DERIVATIVES **mercilessly** adv.

mercurial /mer-kyoor-i-uhl/ • adj. **1** tending to change mood suddenly. **2** relating to mercury.
– ORIGIN Latin *mercurialis* 'relating to the god Mercury'.

Mercury • n. a small planet that is the closest to the sun in the solar system.

mercury • n. a heavy silvery-white liquid metallic element used in some thermometers and barometers.
– ORIGIN from *Mercury*, the Roman messenger of the gods.

mercy • n. (pl. **mercies**) **1** compassion or forgiveness shown towards an enemy or offender in your power. **2** something to be grateful for. • adj. motivated by pity: *a mercy killing*.
– PHRASES **at the mercy of** in the power of.
– ORIGIN Latin *merces* 'reward, pity'.

mere¹ • adj. **1** that is nothing more than what is specified. **2** (**the merest**) the slightest.
– ORIGIN Latin *merus* 'pure, undiluted'.

mere² • n. literary (except in place names) a lake or pond.
– ORIGIN Old English.

merely • adv. only.

meretricious /me-ri-tri-shuhss/ • adj. appearing attractive but in reality having no value.
– ORIGIN Latin *meretrix* 'prostitute'.

merganser /mer-gan-zer/ • n. a fish-

eating diving duck with a long, thin jagged bill.
– ORIGIN from Latin *mergus* 'diver' + *anser* 'goose'.

merge •v. (**merges, merging, merged**) **1** combine or be combined into a whole. **2** blend gradually into something else.
– ORIGIN Latin *mergere* 'to dip'.

merger •n. a merging of two organizations into one.

meridian •n. a circle of constant longitude passing through a given place on the earth's surface and the poles.
– ORIGIN Latin *meridianum* 'noon' (because the sun crosses a meridian at noon).

meridional /muh-**rid**-i-uh-nuhl/ •adj. **1** relating to southern Europe. **2** relating to a meridian.

meringue /muh-**rang**/ •n. beaten egg whites and sugar baked until crisp.
– ORIGIN French.

merino /muh-**ree**-noh/ •n. (pl. **merinos**) **1** a breed of sheep with long, fine wool. **2** a soft woollen material.
– ORIGIN Spanish.

meristem /**me**-ri-stem/ •n. a region of plant tissue consisting of actively dividing cells.
– ORIGIN Greek *meristos* 'divisible'.

merit •n. **1** excellence. **2** a good point or quality. •v. (**merits, meriting, merited**) deserve something.
– ORIGIN Latin *meritum* 'due reward'.

meritocracy /mer-i-**tok**-ruh-si/ •n. (pl. **meritocracies**) a society in which power is held by the people with the greatest ability.
– DERIVATIVES **meritocrat** n. **meritocratic** adj.

meritorious •adj. deserving reward or praise.

merlin •n. a small dark falcon.
– ORIGIN Old French *merilun*.

mermaid •n. a mythical sea creature with a woman's head and trunk and a fish's tail.
– ORIGIN from MERE² (in the former sense 'sea') + MAID.

merriment •n. cheerfulness and fun.

merry •adj. (**merrier, merriest**) **1** cheerful and lively. **2** informal slightly drunk.
– DERIVATIVES **merrily** adv. **merriness** n.
– ORIGIN Old English, 'pleasing'.

merry-go-round •n. **1** a revolving machine with model horses or cars on which people ride for amusement. **2** a continuous cycle of activities or events.

merrymaking •n. cheerful celebration and fun.

mesa /**may**-suh/ •n. an isolated flat-topped hill with steep sides.
– ORIGIN Spanish, 'table'.

Mesdames pl. of MADAME.

Mesdemoiselles pl. of MADEMOISELLE.

mesh •n. **1** material made of a network of wire or thread. **2** the spacing of the strands of a net. **3** a complex or restricting situation. •v. **1** become entangled or entwined. **2** (**mesh with**) be in harmony with. **3** (of a gearwheel) lock together with another.
– ORIGIN prob. from Old English.

mesmeric /mez-**me**-rik/ •adj. causing a person to become transfixed; hypnotic: *his mesmeric gaze.*

mesmerism •n. dated hypnotism.
– ORIGIN named after the Austrian physician Franz A. *Mesmer*.

mesmerize (or **mesmerise**) •v. (**mesmerizes, mesmerizing, mesmerized**) capture someone's attention so that they are transfixed.

meso- /**me**-zoh, **mee**-zoh/ •comb. form middle: *mesosphere.*
– ORIGIN Greek *mesos*.

Mesolithic •adj. relating to the middle part of the Stone Age.
– ORIGIN from Greek *mesos* 'middle' + *lithos* 'stone'.

Mesopotamian /mess-uh-puh-**tay**-mi-uhn/ •adj. relating to Mesopotamia, an ancient region of what is now Iraq.

mesosphere •n. the region of the earth's atmosphere above the stratosphere and below the thermosphere.

Mesozoic •adj. Geol. relating to the era between the Palaeozoic and Cenozoic eras, about 245 to 65 million years ago, with evidence of the first mammals, birds, and flowering plants.
– ORIGIN from Greek *mesos* 'middle' + *zōion* 'animal'.

mess •n. **1** a dirty or untidy state. **2** a state of confusion or difficulty. **3** euphem. a dog's or cat's excrement. **4** a place where members of the armed forces have their meals and relax. •v. **1** make something untidy or dirty. **2** (**mess about/around**) behave in a silly or playful way. **3** (**mess someone about/around**) Brit. informal cause someone problems. **4** **mess something up** informal handle something badly. **5** (**mess with**) informal meddle with.
– ORIGIN Old French *mes* 'portion of food'.

message •n. **1** a spoken, written, or electronic communication. **2** an important point or central theme of a novel, speech, etc. •v. (**messages, messaging, messaged**) send a message to.

– PHRASES **on** (or **off**) **message** (of a politician) following (or not following) the official party line.
– ORIGIN Old French.

messenger •n. a person who carries a message.

messiah •n. **1** (**the Messiah**) the person sent by God to save the Jewish people, as prophesied in the Hebrew Bible (the Old Testament). **2** (**the Messiah**) Jesus regarded by Christians as the Messiah of the Hebrew prophecies. **3** a leader or saviour.
– ORIGIN Hebrew, 'anointed'.

messianic /mess-i-**an**-ik/ •adj. **1** relating to the Messiah or belief in a messiah. **2** intense or passionate: *messianic zeal*.

Messieurs pl. of **MONSIEUR**.

Messrs pl. of **MR**.
– ORIGIN short for **MESSIEURS**.

messy •adj. (**messier, messiest**) **1** untidy or dirty. **2** confused and difficult to deal with.
– DERIVATIVES **messily** adv. **messiness** n.

met past and past part. of **MEET**¹.

meta- (also **met-** before a vowel or h) •comb. form forming words referring to: **1** a change of position or condition: *metamorphosis*. **2** position behind, after, or beyond: *metacarpus*.
– ORIGIN Greek *meta* 'with, across, after'.

metabolism /mi-**tab**-uh-li-z'm/ •n. the chemical processes in a living thing by which food is used for tissue growth or energy production.
– DERIVATIVES **metabolic** adj.
– ORIGIN Greek *metabolē* 'change'.

metabolize (or **metabolise**) •v. (**metabolizes, metabolizing, metabolized**) process or be processed by metabolism.

metacarpus /met-uh-**kar**-puhss/ •n. (pl. **metacarpi** /met-uh-**kar**-pi/) the group of five bones in the hand between the wrist and the fingers.
– DERIVATIVES **metacarpal** adj. & n.
– ORIGIN Greek *metakarpion*.

metal •n. a hard, shiny, solid material which is able to be shaped and can conduct electricity and heat.
– ORIGIN Greek *metallon*.

metal detector •n. an electronic device that makes a noise when it is close to metal.

metallic •adj. **1** relating to or resembling metal. **2** (of sound) sharp and ringing.
– DERIVATIVES **metallically** adv.

metallography /met-uh-**log**-ruh-fi/ •n. the descriptive science of the structure and properties of metals.

metallurgy /mi-**tal**-ler-ji, met-uh-ler-ji/ •n. the scientific study of the properties, production, and purification of metals.

– DERIVATIVES **metallurgical** adj. **metallurgist** n.

metalwork •n. **1** the art of making things from metal. **2** metal objects as a group.

metamorphic •adj. (of rock) having been changed by heat or pressure.

metamorphose /met-uh-**mor**-fohz/ •v. (**metamorphoses, metamorphosing, metamorphosed**) **1** change completely in form or nature. **2** (of an insect or amphibian) undergo metamorphosis.

metamorphosis /met-uh-**mor**-fuh-siss/ •n. (pl. **metamorphoses** /met-uh-**mor**-fuh-seez/) **1** the transformation of an insect or amphibian from an immature form or larva to an adult form. **2** a change in form or nature.
– ORIGIN Greek.

metaphor /met-uh-fer/ •n. a word or phrase used in an imaginative way to represent or stand for something else (e.g. *the long arm of the law*).
– ORIGIN Greek.

metaphorical /met-uh-**fo**-ri-k'l/ (also **metaphoric**) •adj. relating to or making use of metaphor.
– DERIVATIVES **metaphorically** adv.

metaphysical •adj. **1** relating to metaphysics. **2** beyond physical matter: *the metaphysical battle of Good and Evil*.
– DERIVATIVES **metaphysically** adv.

metaphysics •n. philosophy concerned with abstract ideas such as the nature of existence, truth, and knowledge.
– ORIGIN from Greek *ta meta ta phusika* 'the things after the Physics', referring to the sequence of Aristotle's works.

metatarsus /met-uh-**tar**-suhss/ •n. (pl. **metatarsi** /met-uh-**tar**-si/) the bones of the foot, between the ankle and the toes.
– DERIVATIVES **metatarsal** adj. & n.

mete •v. (**metes, meting, meted**) (**mete something out**) deal out justice, punishment, etc.
– ORIGIN Old English, 'measure'.

meteor •n. a small body of matter from outer space that glows as a result of friction with the earth's atmosphere and appears as a shooting star.
– ORIGIN Greek.

meteoric •adj. **1** relating to meteors or meteorites. **2** (of progress or development) very rapid.

meteorite •n. a piece of rock or metal that has fallen to the earth from space.

meteoroid •n. a small body that would become a meteor if it entered the earth's atmosphere.

meteorology /mee-ti-uh-**rol**-uh-ji/ •n. the study of conditions in the

atmosphere, used for weather forecasting.
– DERIVATIVES **meteorological** adj. **meteorologist** n.

meter[1] • n. a device that measures and records the quantity, degree, or rate of something. • v. (**meters, metering, metered**) measure quantity, degree, or rate with a meter.
– ORIGIN from METE.

meter[2] • n. US = METRE[1], METRE[2].

-meter • comb. form **1** in names of measuring instruments: *thermometer.* **2** in nouns referring to lines of poetry with a specified number of measures: *hexameter.*
– ORIGIN Greek *metron* 'measure'.

methadone /meth-uh-dohn/ • n. a powerful painkiller, used as a substitute for morphine and heroin in the treatment of addiction.
– ORIGIN from its chemical name.

methane /mee-thayn/ • n. a flammable gas which is the main constituent of natural gas.
– ORIGIN from METHYL.

methanol • n. a poisonous flammable alcohol, used to make methylated spirit.

methinks • v. old use or humorous it seems to me.
– ORIGIN Old English.

method • n. **1** a way of doing something. **2** the quality of being well organized in your thinking and actions.
– ORIGIN Greek *methodos* 'pursuit of knowledge'.

method acting • n. an acting technique in which an actor tries to identify completely with a character's emotions.

methodical (also **methodic**) • adj. well organized and systematic.
– DERIVATIVES **methodically** adv.

Methodist • n. a member of a Christian Protestant group originating in the 18th century, based on the ideas of Charles and John Wesley. • adj. relating to Methodists or their beliefs.
– DERIVATIVES **Methodism** n.
– ORIGIN prob. from the idea of following a specified 'method' of Bible study.

methodology • n. (pl. **methodologies**) a system of methods used in a particular field.
– DERIVATIVES **methodological** adj.

meths • n. Brit. informal methylated spirit.

methyl /mee-thyl/ • n. Chem. the radical –CH₃, derived from methane.
– ORIGIN from Greek *methu* 'wine' + *hulē* 'wood'.

methyl alcohol • n. methanol.

methylated spirit (also **methylated spirits**) • n. alcohol for use as a solvent or fuel, made unfit for drinking by the addition of methanol and a violet dye.

meticulous /mi-tik-yuu-luhss/ • adj. very careful and precise.
– DERIVATIVES **meticulously** adv. **meticulousness** n.
– ORIGIN Latin *meticulosus* 'fearful'.

métier /may-ti-ay/ • n. **1** a profession or occupation. **2** an occupation or activity that someone is good at.
– ORIGIN French.

metonym /met-uh-nim/ • n. a word or phrase used as a substitute for something with which it is closely associated, e.g. *Washington* for the US government.
– DERIVATIVES **metonymic** adj. **metonymy** n.
– ORIGIN Greek *metōnumia* 'change of name'.

metre[1] (US **meter**) • n. the basic unit of length in the metric system, equal to 100 centimetres (approx. 39.37 inches).
– ORIGIN French.

metre[2] (US **meter**) • n. **1** the rhythm of a piece of poetry, determined by the number and length of feet in a line. **2** the basic rhythmic pattern of a piece of music.
– ORIGIN Greek *metron* 'measure'.

metric • adj. relating to or using the metric system.

metrical • adj. relating to poetic metre.
– DERIVATIVES **metrically** adv.

metricate • v. (**metricates, metricating, metricated**) convert to a metric system of measurement.
– DERIVATIVES **metrication** n.

metric system • n. the decimal measuring system based on the metre, litre, and gram.

metric ton (also **metric tonne**) • n. a unit of weight equal to 1,000 kilograms (2,205 lb).

metro • n. (pl. **metros**) an underground railway system in a city.
– ORIGIN French.

metronome /met-ruh-nohm/ • n. a musicians' device that marks time at a selected rate by giving a regular tick.
– DERIVATIVES **metronomic** adj.
– ORIGIN from Greek *metron* 'measure' + *nomos* 'law'.

metropolis /mi-trop-uh-liss/ • n. the main city of a country or region.
– ORIGIN Greek.

metropolitan /met-ruh-pol-i-t'n/ • adj. relating to a large or capital city.

mettle • n. spirit and strength in the face of difficulty.
– ORIGIN from METAL.

mew • v. (of a cat or gull) make a high-pitched crying noise. •n. a high-pitched crying noise.

mewl •v. **1** cry feebly. **2** make a high-pitched crying noise.

mews •n. (pl. **mews**) Brit. a row of houses or flats converted from stables in a small street or square.
– ORIGIN from *mew* 'place for keeping hawks' (first referring to stables on the site of hawk mews in London).

Mexican •n. a person from Mexico. •adj. relating to Mexico.

Mexican wave •n. an effect like a moving wave produced by sections of a stadium crowd standing and sitting down again one after the other while raising and lowering their arms.
– ORIGIN first seen at the soccer World Cup in Mexico City.

mezzanine /mez-zuh-neen, mets-uh-neen/ •n. a floor extending over part of the area of a building, built between two full floors.
– ORIGIN Italian *mezzano* 'middle'.

mezzo /met-zoh/ (also **mezzo-soprano**) •n. (pl. **mezzos**) a female singer with a voice pitched between soprano and contralto.
– ORIGIN Italian.

Mg •symb. the chemical element magnesium.

mg •abbrev. milligram(s).

MHz •abbrev. megahertz.

mi •n. var. of ME².

mi. •abbrev. mile(s).

MI5 •abbrev. Military Intelligence section 5, the former name for the UK government agency responsible for internal security and the gathering of political and military information on British territory.

MI6 •abbrev. Military Intelligence section 6, the former name for the UK government agency responsible for gathering political and military information overseas.

miaow (also **meow**) •n. the cry of a cat. •v. make a miaow.

miasma /mi-az-muh, my-az-muh/ •n. literary **1** an unpleasant or unhealthy vapour. **2** a heavy or unpleasant atmosphere.
– ORIGIN Greek, 'defilement'.

mica /my-kuh/ •n. a mineral found as tiny shiny scales in rocks.
– ORIGIN Latin, 'crumb'.

mice pl. of MOUSE.

Michaelmas /mi-k'l-muhss/ •n. the day of the Christian festival of St Michael, 29 September.
– ORIGIN Old English, 'Saint Michael's Mass'.

mickey •n. (in phr. **take the mickey**) Brit. informal tease someone.

micro •n. (pl. **micros**) a microcomputer or microprocessor. •adj. very small.

micro- •comb. form **1** very small: *microchip*. **2** referring to a factor of one millionth (10^{-6}): *microgram*.
– ORIGIN Greek *mikros*.

microbe /my-krohb/ •n. a microscopic organism.
– DERIVATIVES **microbial** adj.
– ORIGIN from Greek *mikros* 'small' + *bios* 'life'.

microbiology •n. the scientific study of microorganisms.

microchip •n. a tiny wafer of silicon or similar material used to make an integrated circuit. •v. (**microchips, microchipping, microchipped**) implant a microchip under the skin of a cat or dog so that they can be identified.

microclimate •n. the climate of a very small or restricted area.

microcomputer •n. a small computer with a microprocessor as its central processor.

microcosm /my-kroh-ko-z'm/ •n. a thing that represents something much larger.
– DERIVATIVES **microcosmic** adj.
– ORIGIN from Greek *mikros kosmos* 'little world'.

microdot •n. a photograph reduced to a very small size.

microeconomics •pl. n. (treated as sing.) the branch of economics concerned with single factors and the effects of individual decisions.

microelectronics •n. the design, manufacture, and use of microchips and minute electric circuits.

microfiche /my-kroh-feesh/ •n. a piece of film containing greatly reduced photographs of the pages of a news-paper, catalogue, or archive material.
– ORIGIN from Greek *mikros* 'small' + French *fiche* 'slip of paper'.

microfilm •n. a length of film contain-ing greatly reduced photographs of the pages of a newspaper, catalogue, or archive material.

microgram •n. one millionth of a gram.

microlight •n. esp. Brit. a very small, light aircraft for one or two people.

micrometer /my-krom-i-ter/ •n. an instrument which measures small distances or thicknesses.

micrometre (US **micrometer**) •n. one millionth of a metre.

micron •n. one millionth of a metre.

microorganism •n. an organism so

small that it can only be seen with a microscope.

microphone • n. an instrument for changing sound waves into electrical energy which may then be amplified, transmitted, or recorded.

microprocessor • n. an integrated circuit which can perform the role of a central processing unit of a computer.

microscope • n. an instrument for magnifying very small objects.
– ORIGIN from Greek *mikros* 'small' + *skopein* 'look at'.

microscopic • adj. **1** so small as to be visible only with a microscope. **2** relating to a microscope.
– DERIVATIVES **microscopically** adv.

microscopy /my-kross-kuh-pi/ • n. the use of a microscope.

microsecond • n. one millionth of a second.

microsurgery • n. complex surgery performed using very small instruments and a microscope.

microwave • n. **1** an electromagnetic wave with a wavelength in the range 0.001–0.3 m. **2** (also **microwave oven**) an oven that uses microwaves to cook or heat food. • v. (**microwaves, microwaving, microwaved**) cook or heat food in a microwave oven.

mid • adj. relating to the middle point of a range. • prep. literary in the middle of.

mid- • comb. form in the middle of: *midway*.
– ORIGIN Old English.

Midas touch • n. the ability to make money out of anything you do.
– ORIGIN from King *Midas*, who in Greek mythology had the power to turn everything he touched into gold.

midday • n. twelve o'clock in the day; noon.

midden • n. a dunghill or rubbish heap.
– ORIGIN Scandinavian.

middle • adj. **1** at an equal distance from the edges or ends of something. **2** medium in rank, quality, or ability. • n. **1** a middle point or position. **2** informal a person's waist and stomach.
– ORIGIN Old English.

middle age • n. the period after early adulthood and before old age, about 45 to 60.
– DERIVATIVES **middle-aged** adj.

Middle Ages • pl. n. the period of European history from about 1000 to the mid 15th century.

Middle America • n. the conservative middle classes of the United States.

middlebrow • adj. informal needing only moderate intellectual effort: *a middle-brow magazine*.

middle C • n. Music the C near the middle of the piano keyboard, written on the first ledger line below the treble stave or the first ledger line above the bass stave.

middle class • n. the social group made up of business and professional people, between the upper and working classes.

middle ear • n. the air-filled central cavity of the ear, behind the eardrum.

Middle East • n. an area of SW Asia and northern Africa, stretching from the Mediterranean to Pakistan.
– DERIVATIVES **Middle Eastern** adj.

Middle England • n. the conservative middle classes in England.

Middle English • n. the English language from *c*.1150 to *c*.1470.

middle ground • n. an area of possible agreement between two opposing positions.

middleman • n. (pl. **middlemen**) **1** a person who buys goods from producers and sells them to retailers or consumers. **2** a person who arranges business or political deals between other people.

middle-of-the-road • adj. **1** (of views) not extreme. **2** (of music) popular with a wide range of people but rather unadventurous.

middleweight • n. a weight in boxing and other sports coming between welterweight and light heavyweight.

middling • adj. average in size, amount, or rank.

Middx • abbrev. Middlesex.

midfield • n. **1** the central part of a sports field. **2** the players who play in a central position between attack and defence.
– DERIVATIVES **midfielder** n.

midge • n. a small two-winged fly that forms swarms near water, of which many kinds feed on blood.
– ORIGIN Old English.

midget • n. a very small person. • adj. very small: *a midget submarine*.

MIDI • n. a standard for interconnecting electronic musical instruments and computers.
– ORIGIN from *musical instrument digital interface*.

midi- • comb. form of medium size or length.

midi system • n. Brit. a set of compact pieces of stacking hi-fi equipment.

Midlands • n. (**the Midlands**) the inland counties of central England.

midlife • n. the central period of a person's life, between around 45 and 60.

midnight • n. twelve o'clock at night.

midnight blue • n. a very dark blue.

midnight sun • n. the sun when seen at

midnight during the summer within either the Arctic or Antarctic Circle.

midpoint • n. **1** a point halfway through a period or process. **2** the exact middle point.

midriff • n. the front of the body between the chest and the waist.
– ORIGIN Old English.

midshipman • n. (pl. **midshipmen**) a low-ranking officer in the Royal Navy.

midst old use or literary • prep. in the middle of. • n. the middle point or part.
– PHRASES **in our** (or **your** or **their**) **midst** among us (or you or them).

midsummer • n. **1** the middle part of summer. **2** the summer solstice.

Midsummer Day (Brit. also **Midsummer's Day**) • n. 24 June.

midterm • n. the middle of a period of office, an academic term, or a pregnancy.

midway • adv. & adj. in or towards the middle.

midweek • n. the middle of the week. • adj. & adv. in the middle of the week.

Midwest • n. the region of northern states of the US from Ohio west to the Rocky Mountains.
– DERIVATIVES **Midwestern** adj.

midwife /mid-wyf/ • n. (pl. **midwives**) a nurse who is trained to assist women in childbirth.
– DERIVATIVES **midwifery** /mid-wif-uh-ri/ n.
– ORIGIN prob. from former *mid* 'with' + WIFE.

midwinter • n. **1** the middle part of winter. **2** the winter solstice.

mien /meen/ • n. a person's look or manner.
– ORIGIN prob. from French *mine* 'expression'.

miffed • adj. informal offended or irritated.

might[1] • modal verb (3rd sing. present **might**) past of MAY. **1** used to express possibility or make a suggestion. **2** used politely in questions and requests.

might[2] • n. great power or strength.
– ORIGIN Old English.

mightn't • contr. might not.

mighty • adj. (**mightier**, **mightiest**) **1** powerful or strong. **2** informal very large. • adv. informal, esp. N. Amer. extremely.
– DERIVATIVES **mightily** adv.

migraine /mee-grayn, my-grayn/ • n. a severe headache, often accompanied by nausea and disturbed vision.
– ORIGIN French.

migrant • n. **1** a worker who moves from one place to another to find work. **2** an animal that moves from one habitat to another according to the seasons.

• adj. tending to migrate or having migrated.

migrate • v. (**migrates**, **migrating**, **migrated**) **1** (of an animal) move from one habitat to another according to the seasons. **2** move to settle in a new area in order to find work.
– DERIVATIVES **migration** n. **migratory** adj.
– ORIGIN Latin *migrare* 'move, shift'.

mike • n. informal a microphone.

mil • abbrev. **1** millilitres. **2** millimetres. **3** informal millions.

milady • n. hist. used to address or refer to an English noblewoman.

milch /milsh, milch/ • adj. (of an animal) giving or kept for milk.
– ORIGIN Old English.

milch cow • n. a source of easy profit.

mild • adj. **1** not severe, harsh, or extreme. **2** (of weather) fairly warm. **3** not sharp or strong in flavour. **4** gentle and calm. • n. Brit. a kind of dark beer not strongly flavoured with hops.
– DERIVATIVES **mildly** adv. **mildness** n.
– ORIGIN Old English.

mildew • n. a coating of tiny fungi on plants or damp material such as paper or leather. • v. affect with mildew.
– ORIGIN Old English.

mild steel • n. strong steel containing a small percentage of carbon.

mile • n. **1** (also **statute mile**) a unit of length equal to 1,760 yards (approximately 1.609 kilometres). **2** (**miles**) informal a very long way. • adv. (**miles**) informal by a great amount or a long way.
– PHRASES **be miles away** informal be lost in thought. **stand** (or **stick**) **out a mile** informal be very obvious.
– ORIGIN Latin *milia* 'thousands'; a Roman 'mile' consisted of 1,000 paces.

mileage (also **milage**) • n. **1** a number of miles covered. **2** informal benefit or advantage: *he got a lot of mileage out of the mix-up.*

mileometer • n. var. of MILOMETER.

milestone • n. **1** a stone set up beside a road to mark the distance in miles to a particular place. **2** an event marking a significant new development or stage.

milieu /mee-lyer/ • n. (pl. **milieux** or **milieus**) /mee-lyers/ a person's social environment.
– ORIGIN French.

militant • adj. prepared to take aggressive action in support of a political or social cause. • n. a militant person.
– DERIVATIVES **militancy** n. **militantly** adv.

militarism • n. the belief that a country should possess and readily use strong armed forces.

m

- DERIVATIVES **militarist** n. & adj.
militaristic adj.
militarize (or **militarise**)
• v. (**militarizes**, **militarizing**,
militarized) (often as adj. **militarized**)
1 supply with soldiers and military
equipment. **2** make military in nature: *a
militarized civilian police force.*

military • adj. relating to soldiers or
armed forces. • n. (**the military**) the
armed forces of a country.
- DERIVATIVES **militarily** adv.
- ORIGIN Latin *militaris.*

military honours • pl. n. ceremonies
performed by troops as a mark of
respect at the burial of a member of the
armed forces.

military police • n. a military body
responsible for policing and disciplinary
duties in the armed forces.

militate • v. (**militates**, **militating**,
militated) (**militate against**) be a
powerful or decisive factor in
preventing something.
- ORIGIN Latin *militare* 'wage war'.

> **USAGE:** For an explanation of the
> difference between **militate** and **mitigate**,
> see the note at **MITIGATE**.

militia /mi-li-shuh/ • n. **1** a military force
made up of civilians, used to
supplement a regular army in an
emergency. **2** a rebel force opposing a
regular army.
- DERIVATIVES **militiaman** n. (pl.
militiamen).
- ORIGIN Latin, 'military service'.

milk • n. **1** a white fluid produced by
female mammals to feed their young.
2 the milk of cows as a food and drink
for humans. • v. **1** draw milk from an
animal. **2** take money from someone
dishonestly over a period of time. **3** take
full personal advantage of a situation.
- ORIGIN Old English.

milk chocolate • n. solid chocolate
made with milk.

milk float • n. Brit. an electrically
powered van used for delivering milk to
houses.

milkmaid • n. old use a girl or woman who
works in a dairy.

milkman • n. (pl. **milkmen**) a man who
delivers milk to houses.

milk run • n. a routine, uneventful
journey.
- ORIGIN RAF slang for a sortie that was
as simple as a milkman's round.

milkshake • n. a cold drink made from
milk whisked with a flavouring such as
syrup or fruit.

milksop • n. a timid and indecisive
person.

milk tooth • n. a temporary tooth in a
child or young mammal.

milky • adj. **1** containing milk. **2** having
a soft white colour or clouded
appearance.
- DERIVATIVES **milkily** adv. **milkiness** n.

Milky Way • n. the galaxy of which our
solar system is a part.

mill • n. **1** a building equipped with
machinery for grinding grain into flour.
2 a device for grinding solid substances,
such as peppercorns. **3** a building fitted
with machinery for a manufacturing
process: *a steel mill.* • v. **1** grind
something in a mill. **2** cut or shape metal
with a rotating tool. **3** (as adj. **milled**)
(of a coin) having ribbed markings on
the edge. **4** (**mill about/around**) move
around in a confused mass.
- ORIGIN Latin *mola* 'grindstone, mill'.

millennial • adj. relating to a
millennium.

millennium /mil-len-i-uhm/ • n. (pl.
millennia or **millenniums**) **1** a period of
a thousand years. **2** (**the millennium**)
the point at which one period of a
thousand years ends and another
begins. **3** an anniversary of a thousand
years.
- ORIGIN from Latin *mille* 'thousand' +
annus 'year'.

> ✓ The correct spelling is **millennium**,
> with a double **l** and a double **n**.

millennium bug • n. an inability in
older computing software to deal with
dates of 1 January 2000 or later.

miller • n. a person who owns or works in
a grain mill.

millet • n. a cereal which bears a large
crop of small seeds, used to make flour
or alcoholic drinks.
- ORIGIN French.

milli- • comb. form a thousand: *milligram.*
- ORIGIN Latin *mille* 'thousand'.

millibar • n. a unit for measuring
atmospheric pressure.

milligram (also **milligramme**) • n. one
thousandth of a gram.

millilitre (US **milliliter**) • n. one
thousandth of a litre.

millimetre (US **millimeter**) • n. one
thousandth of a metre.

milliner • n. a person who makes or sells
women's hats.
- DERIVATIVES **millinery** n.
- ORIGIN from the Italian city *Milan.*

million • cardinal number (pl. **millions** or
(with numeral or quantifying word)
million) **1** the number equivalent to a

thousand multiplied by a thousand; 1,000,000 or 10⁶. **2** (also **millions**) informal a very large number or amount.
– DERIVATIVES **millionth** ordinal number.

millionaire • n. (fem. **millionairess**) a person whose money and property are worth one million pounds or dollars or more.

millipede • n. a small invertebrate animal with a long body composed of many segments, most of which bear two pairs of legs.
– ORIGIN from Latin *mille* 'thousand' + *pes* 'foot'.

millisecond • n. one thousandth of a second.

millpond • n. **1** a very still and calm stretch of water. **2** an artificial pool providing a head of water to power a watermill.

millstone • n. **1** each of a pair of circular stones used for grinding grain. **2** a burden of responsibility.

mill wheel • n. a wheel used to drive a watermill.

milometer /my-lom-i-ter/ (also **mileometer**) • n. Brit. an instrument on a vehicle for recording the number of miles travelled.

milord • n. hist. used to address or refer to an English nobleman.

mime • n. the use of silent gestures and facial expressions to tell a story or convey a feeling. • v. (**mimes, miming, mimed**) **1** use mime to act out a story or convey a feeling. **2** pretend to sing or play an instrument as a recording is being played.
– ORIGIN Greek *mimos*.

mimesis /mi-mee-siss/ • n. **1** the use of imitation to represent reality in art and literature. **2** Biol. mimicry of another animal or plant.
– ORIGIN Greek.

mimetic /mi-met-ik/ • adj. relating to mimicry in biology or to the imitation of reality in art and literature.

mimic • v. (**mimics, mimicking, mimicked**) **1** imitate someone's voice or behaviour. **2** (of an animal or plant) take on the appearance of another in order to hide or for protection. • n. **1** a person skilled in mimicking. **2** an animal or plant that mimics another.

mimicry • n. **1** imitation of someone or something. **2** the close external resemblance of an animal or plant to another.

mimosa /mi-moh-zuh/ • n. an acacia tree with delicate fern-like leaves and yellow flowers.
– ORIGIN prob. from Latin *mimus* 'mime'.

mimsy • adj. rather feeble and prim.
– ORIGIN coined by Lewis Carroll from MISERABLE and FLIMSY.

min. • abbrev. **1** minimum. **2** minute(s).

minaret /min-uh-ret/ • n. a slender tower of a mosque, with a balcony from which Muslims are called to prayer.
– ORIGIN Arabic.

minatory /min-uh-tuh-ri/ • adj. formal threatening.
– ORIGIN Latin *minari* 'threaten'.

mince • v. **1** cut up meat into very small pieces. **2** walk in an affected way with short, quick steps and swinging hips. • n. Brit. minced meat.
– PHRASES **not mince (your) words** speak plainly.
– ORIGIN Old French *mincier*.

mincemeat • n. a mixture of dried fruit, candied peel, sugar, spices, and suet.
– PHRASES **make mincemeat of** informal defeat someone decisively.

mince pie • n. esp. Brit. a small tart containing mincemeat, typically eaten at Christmas.

mind • n. **1** the faculty of consciousness and thought. **2** a person's intellect or memory. **3** a person's attention or will. • v. **1** be distressed or annoyed by. **2** remember or take care to do. **3** watch out for. **4** take care of someone or something temporarily. **5** (**be minded**) be inclined to do.
– PHRASES **be in two minds** be unable to decide between alternatives. **never mind 1** do not be concerned or upset. **2** let alone. **out of your mind** not thinking sensibly; mad.
– ORIGIN Old English.

mind-bending • adj. informal altering your state of mind.

mind-blowing • adj. informal very impressive.

mind-boggling • adj. informal overwhelming.

minded • adj. inclined to think in a particular way: *liberal-minded*.

minder • n. **1** a person employed to look after someone or something. **2** informal a bodyguard.

mindful • adj. **1** (**mindful of/that**) aware of or recognizing that. **2** formal inclined to do something.

mindless • adj. **1** acting or done without good reason and with no concern for the consequences. **2** (**mindless of**) not thinking of or concerned about. **3** (of an activity) simple and repetitive.
– DERIVATIVES **mindlessly** adv. **mindlessness** n.

mindset • n. a person's particular way of thinking.

mine[1] • possess. pron. referring to a thing or things belonging to or associated with the speaker.
– ORIGIN Old English.

mine[2] • n. **1** a hole or passage dug in the earth for extracting coal or other minerals. **2** an abundant source: *the book is a mine of information.* **3** a type of bomb placed on or in the ground or water, which explodes on contact. • v. (**mines, mining, mined**) **1** obtain something from a mine. **2** dig for coal or other minerals. **3** lay explosive mines on or in.
– ORIGIN Old French.

minefield • n. **1** an area planted with explosive mines. **2** a subject or situation presenting hidden dangers.

miner • n. a person who works in a mine.

mineral • n. **1** a solid inorganic substance occurring naturally, such as copper. **2** an inorganic substance needed by the human body for good health, such as calcium. **3** a substance obtained by mining.
– ORIGIN Latin *minera* 'ore'.

mineralogy • n. the scientific study of minerals.
– DERIVATIVES **mineralogical** adj. **mineralogist** n.

mineral water • n. water containing dissolved salts.

mineshaft • n. a deep, narrow shaft leading to a mine.

minestrone /mi-ni-stroh-ni/ • n. an Italian soup containing vegetables and pasta.
– ORIGIN Italian *minestrare* 'serve at table'.

minesweeper • n. a warship equipped for detecting and removing or destroying explosive mines.

Ming • adj. (of Chinese porcelain) made during the Ming dynasty (1368–1644), having elaborate designs and vivid colours.
– ORIGIN Chinese, 'clear or bright'.

mingle • v. (**mingles, mingling, mingled**) **1** mix together. **2** move around and chat at a social function.
– ORIGIN from former *meng* 'to mix'.

mingy /min-ji/ • adj. informal not generous.
– ORIGIN perh. from MEAN[2] and STINGY.

mini • adj. very small of its kind. • n. (pl. **minis**) a very short skirt or dress.

mini- • comb. form miniature: *minibus.*

miniature • adj. of a much smaller size than normal. • n. **1** a thing that is much smaller than normal. **2** a very small and minutely detailed portrait.
– ORIGIN Latin *minium* 'red lead' (formerly used to mark words in manuscripts).

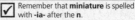
☑ Remember that **miniature** is spelled with **-ia-** after the **n**.

miniaturist • n. an artist who paints miniatures.

miniaturize (or **miniaturise**) • v. (**miniaturizes, miniaturizing, miniaturized**) make something on a smaller scale.

minibar • n. a refrigerator in a hotel room containing a selection of drinks.

minibus • n. a small bus for about ten to fifteen passengers.

minicab • n. Brit. an ordinary car that is available for hire as a taxi.

minicomputer • n. a computer of medium power.

minidisc • n. a disc similar to a small CD, used for recording and playing back sound or data.

minim • n. Music, Brit. a note having the time value of two crotchets or half a semibreve, represented by a ring with a stem.
– ORIGIN Latin *minimus* 'smallest'.

minima pl. of MINIMUM.

minimal • adj. **1** of a minimum amount, quantity, or degree. **2** Art using simple forms or structures. **3** Music characterized by the repetition and gradual alteration of short phrases.
– DERIVATIVES **minimally** adv.

minimalist • adj. **1** relating to minimal art or music. **2** deliberately simple or basic in design. • n. a person who produces minimal art or music.
– DERIVATIVES **minimalism** n.

minimize (or **minimise**) • v. (**minimizes, minimizing, minimized**) **1** reduce something to the smallest possible amount or degree. **2** represent something as less important than it really is.

minimum • n. (pl. **minima** or **minimums**) the smallest amount, extent, or strength possible. • adj. smallest in amount, extent, or strength.
– ORIGIN Latin.

minimum wage • n. the lowest wage permitted by law.

minion • n. a lowly worker or assistant.
– ORIGIN French *mignon* 'pretty'.

miniskirt • n. a very short skirt.

minister • n. **1** a head of a government department. **2** a diplomat representing a state, or a king or queen, in a foreign country. **3** a member of the clergy. • v. (**ministers, ministering, ministered**) (**minister to**) attend to the needs of.
– ORIGIN Latin, 'servant'.

ministerial /min-is-teer-i-uhl/ • adj. relating to a minister or ministers.

m

Minister of State •n. (in the UK) a government minister ranking below a Secretary of State.

Minister of the Crown •n. (in the UK and Canada) a member of the cabinet.

Minister without Portfolio •n. a government minister with cabinet status but not in charge of a specific department of state.

ministrations •pl. n. formal the provision of help or care.

ministry •n. (pl. **ministries**) **1** a government department headed by a minister. **2** a period of government under one Prime Minister. **3** the work or office of a minister of religion.

mink •n. a small stoat-like animal farmed for its fur.
– ORIGIN Swedish.

minke /ming-kuh/ •n. a small whale with a dark grey back and white underparts.

minnow •n. **1** a small freshwater fish. **2** a small or unimportant person.
– ORIGIN prob. from Old English.

Minoan /mi-noh-uhn/ •adj. relating to a Bronze Age civilization based on Crete (c.3000–1050 BC).
– ORIGIN named after the legendary Cretan king *Minos*.

minor •adj. **1** not important or serious. **2** Music (of a scale) having intervals of a semitone between the second and third, fifth and sixth, and seventh and eighth notes. Contrasted with **MAJOR**. •n. **1** a person under the age of full legal responsibility. **2** Music a minor key, interval, or scale.
– ORIGIN Latin, 'smaller, less'.

minority •n. (pl. **minorities**) **1** the smaller number or part. **2** a relatively small group of people differing from the majority in race or religion.

minster •n. Brit. a large or important church originally associated with a monastery.
– ORIGIN Greek *monastērion* 'monastery'.

minstrel •n. a medieval singer or musician.
– ORIGIN Old French *menestral* 'entertainer, servant'.

mint¹ •n. **1** a plant used as a herb in cookery. **2** the flavour of mint. **3** a peppermint sweet.
– DERIVATIVES **minty** adj.
– ORIGIN Old English *minthe*.

mint² •n. **1** a place where coins are made. **2** (**a mint**) informal a large sum of money. •adj. as new: *the car was in mint condition*. •v. **1** make a coin by stamping metal. **2** produce something for the first time.
– ORIGIN Latin *moneta* 'money'.

minuet •n. a slow ballroom dance popular in the 18th century.
– ORIGIN French *menuet* 'fine, delicate'.

minus •prep. **1** with the subtraction of. **2** (of temperature) falling below zero by a specific number of degrees: *minus 40° centigrade*. **3** informal lacking: *he was minus a finger*. •adj. **1** (before a number) below zero. **2** (after a grade) slightly below. **3** having a negative electric charge. •n. **1** (also **minus sign**) the symbol −, indicating subtraction or a negative value. **2** informal a disadvantage.
– ORIGIN Latin, 'less'.

minuscule /min-uhss-kyool/ •adj. very tiny.
– ORIGIN from Latin *minuscula littera* 'somewhat smaller letter'.

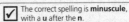 The correct spelling is **minuscule**, with a **u** after the **n**.

minute¹ /min-it/ •n. **1** a period of time equal to sixty seconds or a sixtieth of an hour. **2** (**a minute**) informal a very short time. **3** (also **arc minute** or **minute of arc**) a measurement of an angle equal to one sixtieth of a degree.
– PHRASES **up to the minute** up to date.
– ORIGIN from Latin *pars minuta prima* 'first very small part'.

minute² /my-nyoot/ •adj. **1** very small. **2** precise and careful: *a minute examination of the facts*.
– DERIVATIVES **minutely** adv.
– ORIGIN Latin *minutus* 'made small'.

minute³ /min-it/ •n. **1** (**minutes**) a written summary of the points discussed at a meeting. **2** an official written message. •v. (**minutes**, **minuting**, **minuted**) record the points discussed at a meeting.
– ORIGIN French.

minutiae /mi-nyoo-shi-ee/ •pl. n. small or precise details.
– ORIGIN Latin.

minx •n. a cheeky, cunning, or flirtatious girl or young woman.

Miocene /my-oh-seen/ •adj. Geol. relating to the fourth epoch of the Tertiary period (23.3 to 5.2 million years ago), a time when the first apes appeared.
– ORIGIN from Greek *meiōn* 'less' + *kainos* 'new'.

miracle •n. **1** an extraordinary and welcome event believed to be the work of God or a saint. **2** a remarkable and very welcome occurrence. **3** an outstanding example or achievement: *a miracle of modern design*.
– ORIGIN Latin *miraculum* 'object of wonder'.

miracle play •n. a medieval play based on biblical stories or the lives of saints.

miraculous •adj. like a miracle; very surprising and welcome: *a miraculous escape*.
– DERIVATIVES **miraculously** adv.

mirage /mi-rahzh/ •n. **1** an effect caused by hot air, in which a sheet of water seems to appear in a desert or on a hot road. **2** something that appears real or possible but is not in fact so.
– ORIGIN French.

mire •n. **1** a stretch of swampy or boggy ground. **2** a difficult situation from which it is hard to escape. •v. (**be mired**) **1** become stuck in mud. **2** become involved in a difficult situation.
– ORIGIN Old Norse.

mirror •n. **1** a surface which reflects a clear image. **2** something that accurately represents something else. •v. reflect something.
– ORIGIN Old French *mirour*.

mirror image •n. an image which is identical in form to another but has the structure reversed, as if seen in a mirror.

mirth •n. laughter.
– DERIVATIVES **mirthful** adj. **mirthless** adj.
– ORIGIN Old English.

miry •adj. very muddy or boggy.

mis- •prefix **1** (added to verbs and their derivatives) wrongly, badly, or unsuitably: *mismanage*. **2** (added to some nouns) expressing a negative sense: *misadventure*.
– ORIGIN Old English.

misadventure •n. **1** (also **death by misadventure**) Engl. Law death caused accidentally and not involving crime. **2** a mishap.

misalliance •n. an unsuitable or unhappy relationship or marriage.

misanthrope /miz-uhn-throhp/ •n. a person who dislikes and avoids other people.
– DERIVATIVES **misanthropic** adj. **misanthropy** n.
– ORIGIN from Greek *misein* 'to hate' + *anthrōpos* 'man'.

misapprehension •n. a mistaken belief.

misappropriate •v. (**misappropriates, misappropriating, misappropriated**) dishonestly take something for your own use.
– DERIVATIVES **misappropriation** n.

misbegotten •adj. not carefully thought about or planned.

misbehave •v. (**misbehaves, misbehaving, misbehaved**) behave badly.
– DERIVATIVES **misbehaviour** n.

miscalculate •v. (**miscalculates, miscalculating, miscalculated**) calculate or assess something wrongly.
– DERIVATIVES **miscalculation** n.

miscarriage •n. the early and unplanned birth of a fetus, before it is able to survive independently.

miscarriage of justice •n. a failure of a court of law to achieve justice.

miscarry •v. (**miscarries, miscarrying, miscarried**) **1** (of a pregnant woman) have a miscarriage. **2** (of a plan) fail.

miscast •v. (**be miscast**) (of an actor) be given an unsuitable role.

miscellaneous /mi-suh-lay-ni-uhss/ •adj. **1** (of items or people) of various types. **2** (of a collection or group) made up of things of different kinds.
– ORIGIN Latin *miscellus* 'mixed'.

miscellany /mi-sel-luh-ni/ •n. (pl. **miscellanies**) a collection of different things.

mischance •n. bad luck.

mischief •n. **1** playful misbehaviour. **2** harm or trouble caused by someone or something.
– ORIGIN Old French *meschief*.

mischievous /miss-chi-vuhss/ •adj. **1** (of a person) causing harm or trouble. **2** (of an act) intended to cause trouble.
– DERIVATIVES **mischievously** adv. **mischievousness** n.

> ✓ **mischievous** follows the rule of *i* before *e* except after *c*; the ending is **-vous**.

miscible /miss-i-b'l/ •adj. (of liquids) capable of being mixed together.
– ORIGIN Latin *miscere* 'to mix'.

misconceive •v. (**misconceives, misconceiving, misconceived**) **1** fail to understand something correctly. **2** (**be misconceived**) be badly judged or planned.

misconception •n. a false or mistaken idea or belief.

misconduct /miss-kon-dukt/ •n. unacceptable or improper behaviour.

misconstruction •n. the action of misunderstanding something.

misconstrue •v. (**misconstrues, misconstruing, misconstrued**) understand or interpret something wrongly.

miscreant /miss-kri-uhnt/ •n. a person who behaves badly or unlawfully.
– ORIGIN Old French *mescreant* 'disbelieving'.

misdeed •n. a wrongful act.

misdemeanour (US **misdemeanor**) •n. **1** a minor wrongdoing. **2** Law (in the

US) an offence regarded as less serious than a felony.

misdiagnose • v. (**misdiagnoses, misdiagnosing, misdiagnosed**) diagnose a symptom or illness incorrectly.
– DERIVATIVES **misdiagnosis** n.

misdial • v. (**misdials, misdialling, misdialled**; US **misdials, misdialing, misdialed**) dial a telephone number incorrectly.

misdirect • v. direct or instruct someone wrongly.
– DERIVATIVES **misdirection** n.

miser • n. a person who hoards wealth and spends as little as possible.
– ORIGIN Latin, 'wretched'.

miserabilism /miz-er-uh-buh-lis'm/ • n. the tendency to be gloomy or pessimistic.
– DERIVATIVES **miserabilist** n. & adj.

miserable • adj. **1** very unhappy or depressed. **2** causing unhappiness or discomfort. **3** (of a person) gloomy and humourless. **4** too small; inadequate.
– DERIVATIVES **miserably** adv.

misericord /mi-ze-ri-kord/ • n. a ledge projecting from the underside of a hinged seat in the choir stall of a church, giving support to someone standing when the seat is folded up.
– ORIGIN Latin *misericors* 'compassionate'.

miserly • adj. **1** unwilling to spend money; ungenerous. **2** (of a quantity) too small.
– DERIVATIVES **miserliness** n.

misery • n. (pl. **miseries**) **1** great unhappiness. **2** a cause of great unhappiness. **3** Brit. informal a person who is always miserable.

misfire • v. (**misfires, misfiring, misfired**) **1** (of a gun) fail to fire properly. **2** (of an internal-combustion engine) fail to ignite the fuel correctly. **3** fail to produce the intended result.

misfit • n. a person whose attitudes and actions set them apart from other people.

misfortune • n. **1** bad luck. **2** an unfortunate event.

misgivings • pl. n. feelings of doubt or worry.

misgovern • v. govern unfairly or poorly.

misguided • adj. showing faulty judgement or reasoning.

mishandle • v. (**mishandles, mishandling, mishandled**) handle a situation unwisely or wrongly.

mishap • n. an unlucky accident.

mishear • v. (**mishears, mishearing,** **misheard**) hear something incorrectly.

mishit • v. (**mishits, mishitting, mishit**) hit or kick a ball badly.

mishmash • n. a confused mixture.
– ORIGIN from MASH.

misinform • v. give false or inaccurate information to.
– DERIVATIVES **misinformation** n.

misinterpret • v. (**misinterprets, misinterpreting, misinterpreted**) interpret something wrongly.
– DERIVATIVES **misinterpretation** n.

misjudge • v. (**misjudges, misjudging, misjudged**) **1** form an incorrect opinion of. **2** estimate something wrongly: *the horse misjudged the fence.*
– DERIVATIVES **misjudgement** (also **misjudgment**) n.

mislay • v. (**mislays, mislaying, mislaid**) lose an object by temporarily forgetting where you have left it.

mislead • v. (**misleads, misleading, misled**) give someone inaccurate or false information.

mismanage • v. (**mismanages, mismanaging, mismanaged**) manage something badly or wrongly.
– DERIVATIVES **mismanagement** n.

mismatch • n. a combination of people or things that do not match or suit each other. • v. match people or things unsuitably or incorrectly.

misnomer /miss-noh-mer/ • n. **1** an inaccurate name. **2** the wrong use of a name or term.
– ORIGIN Old French *mesnommer* 'misname'.

misogynist /mi-soj-uh-nist/ • n. a man who hates women.
– DERIVATIVES **misogynistic** adj.

misogyny /mi-soj-uh-ni/ • n. hatred of women.
– ORIGIN from Greek *misos* 'hatred' + *gunē* 'woman'.

misplace • v. (**misplaces, misplacing, misplaced**) **1** put something in the wrong place. **2** (**misplaced**) unwise or inappropriate.

misprint • n. a mistake in a printed document or publication. • v. print something wrongly.

mispronounce • v. (**mispronounces, mispronouncing, mispronounced**) pronounce something wrongly.
– DERIVATIVES **mispronunciation** n.

misquote • v. (**misquotes, misquoting, misquoted**) quote inaccurately.
– DERIVATIVES **misquotation** n.

misread • v. (**misreads, misreading, misread**) read or interpret something wrongly.

misrepresent • v. give a false or

misleading account of.
– DERIVATIVES **misrepresentation** n.

misrule •n. **1** unfair or inefficient government. **2** public disorder.

miss[1] •v. **1** fail to hit, reach, or come into contact with. **2** be too late for. **3** fail to notice, hear, or understand. **4** fail to be present at: *he missed the game with a leg injury.* **5** avoid or escape. **6** (**miss someone/thing out**) Brit. omit someone or something. **7** notice or feel the loss or absence of. •n. a failure to hit, catch, or reach something.
– ORIGIN Old English.

miss[2] •n. **1** (**Miss**) a title coming before the name of an unmarried woman or girl. **2** (**Miss**) used as a form of address to a female teacher. **3** a girl or young woman, especially one regarded as headstrong.
– ORIGIN short for *mistress*.

missal •n. a book containing the prayers and responses used in the Roman Catholic Mass.
– ORIGIN Latin *missa* 'Mass'.

misshapen •adj. not having the normal or natural shape.

missile •n. **1** an object which is thrown at a target. **2** an explosive weapon that is self-propelled or directed by remote control.
– ORIGIN Latin.

missing •adj. **1** absent and unable to be found. **2** not present when supposed to be.

missing link •n. a supposed fossil form believed to form a link between humans and apes.

mission •n. **1** an important assignment involving travel abroad. **2** an organization or institution involved in a long-term assignment abroad. **3** a military or scientific expedition. **4** the requirement of a religious organization to spread its faith. **5** a strongly felt aim or calling.
– ORIGIN Latin.

missionary •n. (pl. **missionaries**) a person sent on a religious mission. •adj. relating to missionaries or a religious mission: *missionary zeal.*

mission statement •n. a summary of the aims and values of an organization.

missis •n. var. of MISSUS.

missive •n. formal a letter.
– ORIGIN Latin *missivus*.

misspell •v. (**misspells, misspelling, misspelt** or **misspelled**) spell wrongly.

misspend •v. (**misspends, misspending, misspent**) spend foolishly.

missus (also **missis**) •n. informal or humorous a person's wife.

missy •n. (pl. **missies**) an affectionate or scornful form of address to a young girl.

mist •n. **1** a cloud of tiny water droplets in the atmosphere, limiting the ability to see. **2** a condensed vapour settling on a surface. •v. cover or become covered with mist.
– ORIGIN Old English.

mistake •n. **1** a thing that is incorrect. **2** an error of judgement: *coming here was a mistake.* •v. (**mistakes, mistaking, mistook**; past part. **mistaken**) **1** be wrong about. **2** (**mistake someone/thing for**) confuse someone or something with.
– ORIGIN Old Norse, 'take in error'.

mistaken •adj. **1** wrong in your opinion or judgement. **2** based on a misunderstanding or faulty judgement.
– DERIVATIVES **mistakenly** adv.

mister •n. **1** var. of MR. **2** informal a form of address to a man.

mistime •v. (**mistimes, mistiming, mistimed**) choose an unsuitable moment to do or say something.

mistle thrush •n. a large thrush with a spotted breast.
– ORIGIN from the bird's fondness for mistletoe berries.

mistletoe •n. a plant which grows as a parasite on trees, and bears white berries in winter.
– ORIGIN Old English.

mistook past of MISTAKE.

mistral /miss-truhl/ •n. a strong north-westerly wind that blows through southern France.
– ORIGIN French.

mistreat •v. treat a person or animal badly.
– DERIVATIVES **mistreatment** n.

mistress •n. **1** a woman in a position of authority or control. **2** a woman skilled in a particular subject or activity. **3** a woman having a sexual relationship with a man who is married to someone else. **4** Brit. a female schoolteacher. **5** (**Mistress**) old use Mrs.
– ORIGIN Old French *maistresse*.

mistrial •n. a trial made invalid through a mistake in proceedings.

mistrust •v. have no trust in. •n. lack of trust.
– DERIVATIVES **mistrustful** adj.

misty •adj. (**mistier, mistiest**) **1** full of or covered with mist. **2** indistinct or unclear.
– DERIVATIVES **mistiness** n.

misunderstand •v. (**misunderstands, misunderstanding, misunderstood**) fail to understand correctly.

misunderstanding •n. **1** a failure to understand correctly. **2** a minor disagreement.

misuse • v. (**misuses, misusing, misused**) /mis-**yooz**/ 1 use wrongly. 2 treat someone badly. • n. /mis-**yooss**/ the action of using something wrongly.

mite[1] • n. a very tiny creature like a spider.
– ORIGIN Old English.

mite[2] • n. 1 a small child or animal. 2 a very small amount. • adv. (**a mite**) informal slightly.
– ORIGIN Dutch.

mitigate • v. (**mitigates, mitigating, mitigated**) 1 make something less severe, serious, or painful. 2 (as adj. **mitigating**) (of a fact or circumstance) lessening the seriousness of or blame attached to an action.
– DERIVATIVES **mitigation** n.
– ORIGIN Latin *mitigare* 'soften'.

> **USAGE:** Do not confuse **mitigate** and **militate**. **Mitigate** means 'make something less severe' (*drainage schemes helped to mitigate the problem*), while **militate** is used with **against** to mean 'be a powerful factor in preventing' (*laws that militate against personal freedom*).

mitochondrion /my-tuh-kon-dri-uhn/ • n. (pl. **mitochondria** /my-tuh-**kon**-dri-uh/) Biol. a structure found in large numbers in most cells, in which respiration and energy production occur.
– DERIVATIVES **mitochondrial** adj.
– ORIGIN from Greek *mitos* 'thread' + *khondrion* 'small granule'.

mitosis /my-**toh**-siss/ • n. (pl. **mitoses** /my-**toh**-seez/) Biol. the division of a cell that results in two daughter cells, each with the same number and kind of chromosomes as the original cell. Compare with MEIOSIS.
– ORIGIN Greek *mitos* 'thread'.

mitre (US **miter**) • n. 1 a tall headdress that tapers to a point at front and back, worn by bishops. 2 a joint made between two pieces of wood cut at an angle so as to form a corner of 90°.
– ORIGIN Greek *mitra* 'belt or turban'.

mitt • n. 1 a mitten. 2 a fingerless glove.

mitten • n. a glove having a single section for all four fingers, with a separate section for the thumb.
– ORIGIN Old French *mitaine*.

mix • v. 1 combine or be combined to form a whole. 2 make something by combining ingredients. 3 combine different recordings to produce a piece of music. 4 (**mix something up**) spoil the arrangement of something. 5 (**mix someone/thing up**) confuse someone or something with another person or thing. 6 meet people socially. • n. 1 a

mixture. 2 the proportion of different people or things making up a mixture. 3 a version of a piece of music mixed in a different way from the original.
– PHRASES **be mixed up in** be involved in underhand or dishonest activities.
– ORIGIN from MIXED.

mixed • adj. 1 consisting of different kinds, qualities, or elements. 2 relating to both males and females.
– ORIGIN Latin *mixtus*.

mixed economy • n. an economic system combining private and state enterprise.

mixed farming • n. farming of both crops and livestock.

mixed marriage • n. a marriage between people of different races or religions.

mixed metaphor • n. a combination of metaphors that produces a ridiculous effect (e.g. *this tower of strength will forge ahead*).

mixer • n. 1 a device for mixing things. 2 a person considered in terms of their ability to mix socially. 3 a soft drink that can be mixed with alcohol.

mixer tap • n. a single tap through which both hot and cold water can flow at the same time.

mixture • n. 1 a substance made by mixing other substances together. 2 (**a mixture of**) a combination of different things in which each thing is distinct.

mix-up • n. informal a confusion or misunderstanding.

mizzen • n. (also **mizzenmast**) the mast behind a ship's mainmast.
– ORIGIN Italian *mezzano* 'middle'.

ml • abbrev. 1 miles. 2 millilitres.

Mlle • abbrev. (pl. **Mlles**) Mademoiselle.

mm • abbrev. millimetres.

Mme • abbrev. (pl. **Mmes**) Madame.

MMR • abbrev. measles, mumps, and rubella (a vaccination given to children).

MMS • abbrev. Multimedia Messaging Service, a system that enables mobile phones to send and receive colour pictures and sound clips as well as text messages.

Mn • symb. the chemical element manganese.

mnemonic /ni-mon-ik/ • n. a pattern of letters or words used to help you remember something. • adj. aiding the memory.
– ORIGIN Greek *mnēmōn* 'mindful'.

MO • abbrev. Medical Officer.

Mo • symb. the chemical element molybdenum.

mo • n. informal, esp. Brit. a moment.

moa /moh-uh/ • n. a large extinct flightless bird resembling the emu, formerly found in New Zealand.
– ORIGIN Maori.

moan • n. 1 a low mournful sound, expressing suffering. 2 informal a trivial complaint. • v. 1 make a moan. 2 grumble.
– DERIVATIVES **moaner** n.

moat • n. a wide ditch filled with water, surrounding and protecting a castle or town.
– ORIGIN Old French *mote* 'mound'.

mob • n. 1 a disorderly crowd of people. 2 Brit. informal a group of people. 3 (**the Mob**) N. Amer. the Mafia. 4 (**the mob**) derog. ordinary people. • v. (**mobs, mobbing, mobbed**) crowd round someone or into a place in an unruly way.
– ORIGIN from Latin *mobile vulgus* 'excitable crowd'.

mobile • adj. 1 able to move or be moved freely or easily. 2 (of a shop or library) set up inside a vehicle so as to travel around. 3 able or willing to move between occupations, homes, or social classes. 4 (of the features of the face) readily changing expression. • n. 1 a decorative structure hung so as to turn freely in the air. 2 a mobile phone.
– PHRASES **upwardly mobile** moving to a higher social class.
– ORIGIN Latin *mobilis*.

mobile home • n. a large caravan used as permanent living accommodation.

mobile phone • n. a portable telephone.

mobility • n. the quality of being mobile.

mobilize (or **mobilise**) • v. (**mobilizes, mobilizing, mobilized**) 1 prepare and organize troops for war. 2 organize people or resources for a task.
– DERIVATIVES **mobilization** n.

Möbius strip /mer-bi-uhss/ • n. a surface with one continuous side formed by joining the ends of a rectangle after twisting one end through 180°.
– ORIGIN named after the German mathematician August F. *Möbius*.

mobster • n. informal a gangster.

moccasin • n. a soft leather shoe with the sole turned up and sewn to the upper, originally worn by North American Indians.
– ORIGIN from a North American Indian language.

mocha /mok-uh/ • n. 1 a fine-quality coffee. 2 a drink made with coffee and chocolate.
– ORIGIN named after *Mocha*, a port in Yemen on the Red Sea.

mock • v. 1 tease scornfully; ridicule.

2 imitate someone in an unkind way. 3 (**mock something up**) make a replica or imitation of something. • adj. 1 not genuine or real. 2 (of an exam, battle, etc.) arranged for training or practice. • n. (**mocks**) Brit. informal exams taken in school as training for public exams.
– ORIGIN Old French *mocquer* 'deride'.

mockery • n. (pl. **mockeries**) 1 scornful teasing; ridicule. 2 an action or situation that is an absurd or worthless version of something: *after a mockery of a trial, he was executed.*

mockingbird • n. a long-tailed American songbird, noted for copying the calls of other birds.

mock-up • n. a model of a machine or structure that is used for teaching or testing.

MOD • abbrev. (in the UK) Ministry of Defence.

mod • n. Brit. (especially in the 1960s) a young person of a group who wore smart fashionable clothes and rode motor scooters.

modal • adj. 1 relating to the way something is done. 2 Grammar relating to the mood of a verb.
– DERIVATIVES **modality** n.

modal verb • n. Grammar an auxiliary verb expressing necessity or possibility, e.g. *must, shall, will.*

mod cons • pl. n. Brit. informal modern conveniences, the equipment and features characteristic of a well-equipped modern house.

mode • n. 1 a way in which something occurs or is done. 2 a style in clothes or art; a fashion. 3 Music a set of notes forming a scale and from which melodies and harmonies are constructed.
– ORIGIN Latin *modus* 'measure, manner'.

model • n. 1 a three-dimensional copy of a person or thing, typically on a smaller scale. 2 something used as an example. 3 a simplified mathematical description of a system or process. 4 an excellent example of a quality. 5 a person employed to display clothes by wearing them. 6 a person employed to pose for an artist. 7 a particular version of a product. • v. (**models, modelling, modelled**; US **models, modeling, modeled**) 1 make or shape a figure in clay or wax. 2 (in drawing and painting) make something appear three-dimensional. 3 make a mathematical model of something. 4 (**model something on**) use something as an example for something else. 5 work as a model.

modem /moh-dem/ • n. a device for

converting digital and analogue signals, especially to allow a computer to be connected to a telephone line.
– ORIGIN from *modulator* and *demodulator*.

moderate • adj. /mod-uh-ruht/ **1** average in amount, intensity, or degree. **2** (of a political position) not extreme. • n. /mod-uh-ruht/ a person with moderate views. • v. /mod-uh-rayt/ (**moderates, moderating, moderated**) **1** make or become less extreme or intense. **2** Brit. review exam papers or results to ensure consistency of marking.
– DERIVATIVES **moderately** adv.
– ORIGIN Latin *moderare* 'reduce'.

moderation • n. **1** the avoidance of extremes in your actions or opinions. **2** the process of moderating.

moderator • n. **1** a person who helps people to solve a dispute. **2** a chairman of a debate. **3** Brit. a person who moderates exam papers.

modern • adj. **1** relating to the present or to recent times. **2** having or using the most up-to-date techniques or equipment. **3** (in art, architecture, etc.) marked by a significant break from traditional values.
– DERIVATIVES **modernity** n.
– ORIGIN Latin *modernus*.

modernism • n. **1** modern ideas, methods, or styles. **2** a movement in the arts that aims to break with traditional styles or ideas.
– DERIVATIVES **modernist** n. & adj.

modernize (or **modernise**) • v. (**modernizes, modernizing, modernized**) bring up to date with modern equipment, techniques, or ideas.
– DERIVATIVES **modernization** n. **modernizer** n.

modest • adj. **1** having an unassuming view of your abilities or achievements. **2** relatively moderate, limited, or small. **3** not showing off the body; decent.
– DERIVATIVES **modestly** adv.
– ORIGIN Latin *modestus* 'keeping due measure'.

modesty • n. the quality of being modest.

modicum /mod-i-kuhm/ • n. a small quantity of something.
– ORIGIN Latin *modicus* 'moderate'.

modification • n. **1** the action of partially changing something. **2** a change made.

modifier • n. Grammar a word that qualifies the sense of a noun (e.g. *good* and *family* in *a good family house*).

modify • v. (**modifies, modifying,** modified) make partial changes to.
– ORIGIN Latin *modificare*.

modish /moh-dish/ • adj. fashionable.

modular • adj. made up of separate units.

modulate • v. (**modulates, modulating, modulated**) **1** control or regulate. **2** vary the strength, tone, or pitch of your voice. **3** adjust the amplitude or frequency of an oscillation or signal. **4** Music change from one key to another.
– DERIVATIVES **modulation** n.
– ORIGIN Latin *modulari* 'measure'.

module • n. **1** each of a set of parts or units that can be used to create a more complex structure. **2** each of a set of independent units of study or training forming part of a course. **3** an independent unit of a spacecraft.
– ORIGIN Latin *modulus*.

modulus /mod-yuu-luhss/ • n. (pl. **moduli** /mod-yuu-li/) **1** Math. the magnitude of a number irrespective of whether it is positive or negative. **2** Physics a constant factor relating a physical effect to the force producing it.

modus operandi /moh-duhss op-uh-ran-di/ • n. (pl. **modi operandi** /moh-di op-uh-ran-di/) a way of operating or doing something.
– ORIGIN Latin.

modus vivendi /moh-duhss vi-ven-di/ • n. (pl. **modi vivendi** /moh-di vi-ven-di/) a way of existing together peacefully; a way of living.
– ORIGIN Latin.

moggie (also **moggy**) • n. (pl. **moggies**) Brit. informal a cat.
– ORIGIN from *Maggie*, familiar form of the woman's name *Margaret*.

Mogul /moh-guhl/ (also **Moghul** or **Mughal**) • n. **1** a member of the Muslim dynasty of Mongol origin which ruled much of India in the 16th–19th centuries. **2** (**mogul**) an important or powerful person.
– ORIGIN Persian, 'Mongol'.

mohair • n. a yarn or fabric made from the hair of the angora goat.
– ORIGIN Arabic.

Mohican /moh-hee-kuhn/ • n. a hair style in which the sides of the head are shaved and a central strip of hair is made to stand up.
– ORIGIN from the name of a North American Indian people.

moiety /moy-i-ti/ • n. (pl. **moieties**) formal a half.
– ORIGIN Old French *moite*.

moire /mwar/ (also **moiré** /mwah-ray/) • n. silk fabric treated to have an appearance like that of rippled water.

– ORIGIN French, 'mohair' (the treatment first being used on mohair).

moist • adj. slightly wet; damp.
– DERIVATIVES **moisten** v. **moistness** n.
– ORIGIN Old French *moiste*.

moisture • n. tiny drops of water or other liquid in the air, in a substance, or condensed on a surface.

moisturize (or **moisturise**)
• v. (**moisturizes, moisturizing, moisturized**) make something, especially skin, less dry.
– DERIVATIVES **moisturizer** n.

molar[1] /moh-ler/ • n. a grinding tooth at the back of a mammal's mouth.
– ORIGIN Latin *mola* 'millstone'.

molar[2] • adj. Chem. 1 relating to one mole of a substance. 2 (of a solution) containing one mole of solute per litre of solvent.

molasses /muh-lass-iz/ • n. 1 a thick, dark brown liquid obtained from raw sugar. 2 N. Amer. golden syrup.
– ORIGIN Latin *mellacium* 'must'.

mold • n. & v. US = MOULD[1], MOULD[2], and MOULD[3].

molder • v. US = MOULDER.

molding • n. US = MOULDING.

Moldovan /mol-doh-vuhn/ • n. a person from Moldova, a country in SE Europe.
• adj. relating to Moldova.

moldy • adj. US = MOULDY.

mole[1] • n. 1 a small burrowing mammal with dark fur, a long muzzle, and very small eyes. 2 a person within an organization who secretly passes confidential information to another organization or country.
– ORIGIN Germanic.

mole[2] • n. a dark blemish on the skin where there is a high concentration of melanin.
– ORIGIN Old English.

mole[3] • n. 1 a large solid structure serving as a pier, breakwater, or causeway. 2 a harbour formed by a mole.
– ORIGIN Latin *moles* 'mass'.

mole[4] • n. Chem. the SI unit of amount of a substance, equal to the quantity containing as many elementary units as there are atoms in 0.012 kg of carbon-12.
– ORIGIN German *Molekul* 'molecule'.

molecular /muh-lek-yuu-ler/ • adj. relating to or made up of molecules.

molecule /mol-i-kyool/ • n. a group of atoms chemically bonded together, representing the smallest fundamental unit of a compound that can take part in a chemical reaction.
– ORIGIN French.

molehill • n. a small mound of earth thrown up by a burrowing mole.

– PHRASES **make a mountain out of a molehill** exaggerate the importance of a small problem.

moleskin • n. a thick cotton fabric with a soft pile surface.

molest • v. 1 assault someone sexually. 2 dated pester or harass someone in a hostile way.
– DERIVATIVES **molestation** n. **molester** n.
– ORIGIN Latin *molestare* 'annoy'.

moll • n. informal a gangster's girlfriend.
– ORIGIN from the woman's name *Mary*.

mollify • v. (**mollifies, mollifying, mollified**) make someone feel less anxious or angry.
– ORIGIN Latin *mollis* 'soft'.

mollusc /mol-luhsk/ (US **mollusk**) • n. an invertebrate animal of a group with a soft body and often an external shell, such as a snail or slug.
– ORIGIN Latin *mollis* 'soft'.

mollycoddle • v. (**mollycoddles, mollycoddling, mollycoddled**) treat someone indulgently or too protectively.
– ORIGIN from *molly* 'girl' (see MOLL) + CODDLE.

Molotov cocktail /mol-uh-tof/ • n. a device that bursts into flames when thrown by hand, made up of a bottle of flammable liquid ignited by a wick.
– ORIGIN named after the Soviet statesman Vyacheslav *Molotov*.

molt • v. & n. US = MOULT.

molten • adj. (especially of metal and glass) made liquid by heat.
– ORIGIN former past participle of MELT.

molto /mol-toh/ • adv. Music very.
– ORIGIN Italian.

molybdenum /muh-lib-duh-nuhm/ • n. a brittle silver-grey metallic element used in some steels and other alloys.
– ORIGIN Greek *molubdos* 'lead'.

mom • n. N. Amer. = MUM[1].

moment • n. 1 a brief period of time. 2 an exact point in time. 3 formal importance: *the issues were of little moment.*
– ORIGIN Latin *momentum*.

momentarily • adv. 1 for a very short time. 2 N. Amer. very soon.

momentary • adj. very brief or short-lived.

momentous • adj. very important.

momentum • n. (pl. **momenta**) 1 the force gained by a moving object. 2 the force caused by the development of something. 3 Physics the quantity of motion of a moving body, equal to its mass multiplied by its velocity.
– ORIGIN Latin *movimentum*.

m

mommy • n. (pl. **mommies**) N. Amer. = **MUMMY**[1].

Mon. • abbrev. Monday.

monarch • n. a king or queen who rules a country.
– DERIVATIVES **monarchical** adj.
– ORIGIN from Greek *monos* 'alone' + *arkhein* 'to rule'.

monarchism • n. support for the principle that a king or queen should rule a country.
– DERIVATIVES **monarchist** n. & adj.

monarchy • n. (pl. **monarchies**) **1** rule by a monarch. **2** a state ruled by a monarch.

monastery • n. (pl. **monasteries**) a community of monks living under religious vows.
– ORIGIN Greek *monastērion*.

monastic • adj. **1** relating to monks or nuns or their communities.
2 resembling monks or their way of life.
– DERIVATIVES **monasticism** n.

Monday • n. the day of the week before Tuesday and following Sunday.
– ORIGIN Old English, 'day of the moon'.

monetarism • n. the theory that inflation is best controlled by limiting the supply of money circulating in an economy.
– DERIVATIVES **monetarist** n. & adj.

monetary • adj. relating to money or currency.

money • n. **1** a means of payment in the form of coins and banknotes. **2** wealth. **3** payment or profit. **4** (**moneys** or **monies**) formal sums of money.
– ORIGIN Latin *moneta* 'mint, money'.

moneyed (also **monied**) • adj. having much money; rich.

money-grubbing • adj. informal greedily concerned with making money.

money order • n. a printed order for payment of a specified sum, issued by a bank or post office.

money spider • n. a very small black spider.

money-spinner • n. esp. Brit. a thing that brings in a large profit.

money supply • n. the total amount of money in circulation or in existence in a country.

-monger • comb. form **1** referring to someone who trades in something specified: *fishmonger*. **2** esp. derog. referring to a person who engages in a particular activity: *rumour-monger*.
– ORIGIN Latin *mango* 'dealer'.

Mongol • n. **1** a person from Mongolia. **2** (**mongol**) offens. a person with Down's syndrome.
– DERIVATIVES **mongolism** n. (offens.).

Mongolian • n. **1** a person from Mongolia. **2** the language of Mongolia.
• adj. relating to Mongolia.

mongoose • n. (pl. **mongooses**) a small meat-eating mammal with a long body and tail, native to Africa and Asia.
– ORIGIN from a central Indian language.

mongrel • n. a dog of a mixed breed.
– ORIGIN prob. from **MINGLE** and **AMONG**.

monied • adj. var. of **MONEYED**.

monies pl. of **MONEY**.

moniker /mon-i-ker/ • n. informal a name.

monitor • n. **1** a person or device that monitors something. **2** a display screen used to view a picture from a particular camera or a computer. **3** a school pupil with special duties. **4** (also **monitor lizard**) a large tropical lizard. • v. observe someone or something in order to record or regulate their activity or progress.
– ORIGIN Latin *monere* 'warn'.

monk • n. a man belonging to a religious community and living under vows of poverty, chastity, and obedience.
– ORIGIN Greek *monakhos* 'solitary'.

monkey • n. (pl. **monkeys**) **1** a primate typically having a long tail and living in trees in tropical countries. **2** a mischievous child. • v. (**monkeys**, **monkeying**, **monkeyed**) **1** (**monkey about/around**) behave in a silly or playful way. **2** (**monkey with**) tamper with.

monkey business • n. informal mischievous or underhand activity.

monkey nut • n. Brit. a peanut.

monkey puzzle • n. a coniferous tree with branches covered in spirals of tough spiny leaves.

monkey wrench • n. a spanner with large adjustable jaws.

monkfish • n. (pl. **monkfish** or **monkfishes**) an edible sea fish with a long fleshy growth on the snout.

mono • adj. monophonic. • n. monophonic sound reproduction.

mono- (also **mon-** before a vowel) • comb. form one; single: *monochrome*.
– ORIGIN Greek *monos*.

monochrome • adj. consisting of or displaying images in black and white or in varying tones of one colour.
– DERIVATIVES **monochromatic** adj.
– ORIGIN Greek *monokhrōmatos* 'of a single colour'.

monocle • n. a single lens worn to improve the sight in one eye.
– ORIGIN Latin *monoculus* 'one-eyed'.

monocotyledon /mon-oh-kot-i-lee-duhn/ • n. a flowering plant whose seeds have a single cotyledon (seed leaf).

monocular • adj. relating to the use of just one eye.

– ORIGIN Latin *monoculus* 'having one eye'.

monogamy /muh-**nog**-uh-mi/ • n. the state of having only one husband, wife, or sexual partner at any one time.
– DERIVATIVES **monogamist** n. **monogamous** adj.
– ORIGIN from Greek *monos* 'single' + *gamos* 'marriage'.

monogram • n. a design of interwoven letters, typically a person's initials.
– DERIVATIVES **monogrammed** adj.

monograph /**mon**-uh-grahf/ • n. a scholarly written study of a single subject.

monolingual • adj. speaking or expressed in only one language.

monolith • n. a large single upright block of stone.
– ORIGIN from Greek *monos* 'single' + *lithos* 'stone'.

monolithic • adj. **1** formed of a single large block of stone. **2** massive and uniform: *a monolithic European superstate.*

monologue • n. **1** a long speech by one actor in a play or film. **2** a long, boring speech by one person during a conversation.
– ORIGIN Greek *monologos* 'speaking alone'.

monomania /mon-oh-**may**-ni-uh/ • n. an obsession with one thing.
– DERIVATIVES **monomaniac** n.

monomer /**mon**-uh-mer/ • n. Chem. a molecule that can be linked to other identical molecules to form a polymer.

monophonic • adj. (of sound reproduction) using only one transmission channel.

monoplane • n. an aircraft with one pair of wings.

monopolistic • adj. relating to control of the supply of a product or service by one person or organization.

monopolize (or **monopolise**) • v. (**monopolizes, monopolizing, monopolized**) dominate or take control of.

monopoly • n. (pl. **monopolies**) **1** the control of the supply of a product or service by one person or organization. **2** an organization having a monopoly, or a product or service controlled by one.
– ORIGIN Greek *monopōlion*.

monorail • n. a railway in which the track consists of a single rail.

monosaccharide • n. a sugar that cannot be broken down to give a simpler sugar.

monosodium glutamate • n. a compound used to add flavour to food.

monosyllabic • adj. **1** consisting of one syllable. **2** saying little more than 'yes' or 'no'; saying very little.

monosyllable • n. a word of one syllable.

monotheism /mon-oh-**thee**-i-z'm/ • n. the belief that there is a single god.
– DERIVATIVES **monotheist** n. **monotheistic** adj.

monotone • n. a continuing sound that is unchanging in pitch.

monotonous /muh-**not**-uh-nuhss/ • adj. (of a sound, activity, or process) not interesting because of lack of change or variety.
– DERIVATIVES **monotonously** adv. **monotony** n.

monoxide • n. Chem. an oxide containing one atom of oxygen.

Monseigneur /mon-sen-**yer**/ • n. a title or form of address for a French-speaking prince, cardinal, archbishop, or bishop.
– ORIGIN French, 'my lord'.

Monsieur /muh-**syer**/ • n. (pl. **Messieurs** /mess-**yer**/) a title or form of address for a French-speaking man, corresponding to *Mr* or *sir*.
– ORIGIN French, 'my lord'.

Monsignor /mon-**seen**-yer/ • n. (pl. **Monsignori** /mon-seen-**yor**-i/) the title of various senior Roman Catholic priests and officials.
– ORIGIN Italian.

monsoon • n. **1** a seasonal wind in the Indian subcontinent and SE Asia, bringing rain when blowing from the south-west. **2** the rainy season accompanying the monsoon.
– ORIGIN Arabic, 'season'.

monster • n. **1** a large and frightening imaginary creature. **2** a very cruel or wicked person. • adj. informal very large.
– ORIGIN Latin *monstrum.*

monstrosity • n. (pl. **monstrosities**) **1** a very large and ugly object. **2** a thing that is evil.

monstrous • adj. **1** very large and ugly or frightening. **2** very evil or wrong.

montage /mon-**tahzh**/ • n. **1** the technique of making a picture or film by putting together pieces from other pictures or films. **2** a picture or film resulting from this.
– ORIGIN French.

Montenegrin /mon-ti-**nee**-grin/ • n. a person from Montenegro, a republic that is part of the Union of Serbia and Montenegro. • adj. relating to Montenegro.

month • n. **1** each of the twelve named periods into which a year is divided. **2** a period of time between the same dates

m

in successive calendar months, usually about 28 days.
– ORIGIN Old English.

monthly •adj. done or occurring once a month. •adv. once a month.

monty •n. (in phr. **the full monty**) Brit. informal the full amount expected, desired, or possible.

monument •n. **1** a statue or structure built to commemorate a person or event. **2** a structure or site of historical importance. **3** a notable or lasting example: *a monument to good taste.*
– ORIGIN Latin *monumentum.*

monumental •adj. **1** very large or impressive. **2** acting as a monument.
– DERIVATIVES **monumentally** adv.

moo •v. (**moos, mooing, mooed**) (of a cow) make a long deep sound. •n. (pl. **moos**) the long deep sound made by a cow.

mooch •v. Brit. informal stand or walk around in a bored or listless way.
– ORIGIN prob. from Old French *muscher* 'hide, skulk'.

mood •n. **1** a temporary state of mind. **2** a fit of bad temper or depression. **3** the atmosphere of a work of art. **4** Grammar a form of a verb expressing a fact, command, question, wish, or condition.
– ORIGIN Old English.

moody •adj. (**moodier, moodiest**) **1** having moods that change quickly, especially tending to become bad-tempered or sulky. **2** giving a sad or mysterious impression.
– DERIVATIVES **moodily** adv. **moodiness** n.

moon •n. **1** (also **Moon**) the natural satellite of the earth. **2** a natural satellite of any planet. **3** literary a month. •v. **1** (**moon about/around**) behave in a listless or dreamy way. **2** informal expose your buttocks to someone as an insult or joke.
– PHRASES **over the moon** informal delighted.
– ORIGIN Old English.

moonlight •n. the light of the moon. •v. (**moonlights, moonlighting, moonlighted**) informal do a second job without declaring it for tax purposes.
– DERIVATIVES **moonlit** adj.

moonscape •n. a rocky and barren landscape like the moon's surface.

moonshine •n. informal **1** foolish talk or ideas. **2** N. Amer. secretly made or smuggled alcoholic drink.

moonstone •n. a white semi-precious form of feldspar.

moony •adj. dreamy because in love.

Moor •n. a member of a Muslim people of NW Africa.

– DERIVATIVES **Moorish** adj.
– ORIGIN Greek *Mauros* 'inhabitant of Mauretania' (an ancient region of N. Africa).

moor¹ •n. esp. Brit. a stretch of open uncultivated upland.
– ORIGIN Old English.

moor² •v. fasten a boat to the shore or to an anchor.
– ORIGIN prob. from Germanic.

moorhen •n. a black water bird with a red and yellow bill.

mooring (also **moorings**) •n. **1** a place where a boat is moored. **2** the ropes or cables by which a boat is moored.

moorland (also **moorlands**) •n. esp. Brit. a large area of moor.

moose •n. (pl. **moose**) N. Amer. = **ELK**.
– ORIGIN from an American Indian language.

moot •adj. debatable; uncertain: *a moot point.* •v. put forward for discussion.
– ORIGIN Old English, 'assembly'.

mop •n. **1** a bundle of thick strings or a sponge attached to a handle, used for wiping floors. **2** a thick mass of untidy hair. •v. (**mops, mopping, mopped**) **1** clean or soak up by wiping. **2** (**mop something up**) complete something by dealing with the things that remain.
– ORIGIN perh. from Latin *mappa* 'napkin'.

mope •v. (**mopes, moping, moped**) be listless and in low spirits.
– ORIGIN perh. Scandinavian.

moped /moh-ped/ •n. a light motorcycle with an engine capacity below 50 cc.
– ORIGIN from a Swedish term.

moppet •n. informal an endearing small child.
– ORIGIN from former *moppe* 'baby, rag doll'.

moraine /muh-rayn/ •n. a mass of rocks and sediment carried down and deposited by a glacier.
– ORIGIN French dialect *morre* 'snout'.

moral •adj. **1** concerned with the principles of right and wrong behaviour. **2** following accepted standards of behaviour. **3** psychological rather than practical: *moral support.* •n. **1** a lesson about right or wrong that can be learned from a story or experience. **2** (**morals**) standards of good behaviour, or principles of right and wrong.
– DERIVATIVES **morally** adv.
– ORIGIN Latin *moralis.*

morale •n. a feeling of confidence and satisfaction.
– ORIGIN French *moral.*

moralist •n. a person who teaches or promotes a sense of right and wrong.

– DERIVATIVES **moralistic** adj.

morality • n. (pl. **moralities**) **1** principles concerning the difference between right and wrong. **2** the extent to which an action is right or wrong. **3** good behaviour.

morality play • n. a play about right and wrong in which characters represent qualities such as goodness or evil, popular in the 15th and 16th centuries.

moralize (or **moralise**) • v. (**moralizes, moralizing, moralized**) comment on matters of right and wrong in a disapproving way.

moral victory • n. a defeat that can be interpreted as a victory because you have done the right thing.

morass /muh-**rass**/ • n. **1** an area of muddy or boggy ground. **2** a complicated situation: *a morass of lies.*
– ORIGIN Dutch *moeras*.

moratorium /mo-ruh-**tor**-i-uhm/ • n. (pl. **moratoriums** or **moratoria** /mo-ruh-**tor**-i-uh/) a temporary ban on an activity.
– ORIGIN Latin.

moray /mo-ray/ (also **moray eel**) • n. an eel-like fish of warm seas.
– ORIGIN Portuguese *moréia*.

morbid • adj. **1** having an unhealthy interest in death and disease. **2** Med. relating to or indicating disease.
– DERIVATIVES **morbidity** n. **morbidly** adv.
– ORIGIN Latin *morbus* 'disease'.

mordant • adj. (of humour) sharply sarcastic. • n. a substance that combines with a dye and is used to fix it in a material.
– ORIGIN Latin *mordere* 'to bite'.

more • det. & pron. a greater or additional amount or degree. • adv. **1** forming the comparative of adjectives and adverbs. **2** to a greater extent. **3** again. **4** (**more than**) very.
– PHRASES **more or less 1** to a certain extent. **2** approximately. **no more 1** nothing or no further. **2** (**be no more**) no longer exist.
– ORIGIN Old English.

USAGE: Do not use **more** with an adjective that is already in a comparative (the **-er**) form (as in *more better, more hungrier*); the correct use is *better* or *hungrier* (or *more hungry*).

moreish • adj. Brit. informal so pleasant to eat that you want more.

morel /muh-**rel**/ • n. an edible fungus with a brown oval or pointed cap.
– ORIGIN French *morille*.

morello /muh-**rel**-loh/ • n. (pl. **morellos**) a kind of sour dark cherry used in cooking.

– ORIGIN Italian, 'blackish'.

moreover • adv. as a further matter; besides.

✓ Remember that **moreover** has an **e** before the **o**.

mores /mor-ayz/ • pl. n. the customs and conventions of a community.
– ORIGIN Latin.

morgue • n. a place in which dead bodies are kept; a mortuary.
– ORIGIN French.

moribund /mo-ri-bund/ • adj. **1** at the point of death. **2** losing effectiveness and about to end.
– ORIGIN Latin *moribundus*.

Mormon • n. a member of the Church of Jesus Christ of Latter-Day Saints.
– DERIVATIVES **Mormonism** n.
– ORIGIN *Mormon*, a prophet on whose book of supposed revelations the religion is based.

morn • n. literary morning.
– ORIGIN Old English.

morning • n. **1** the period of time between midnight and noon, especially from sunrise to noon. **2** sunrise.
• adv. (**mornings**) informal every morning.
– ORIGIN from **MORN**.

morning-after pill • n. a contraceptive pill that is effective within about seventy-two hours after sex.

morning dress • n. a man's formal outfit consisting of a tailcoat and striped trousers.

morning glory • n. a climbing plant with trumpet-shaped flowers.

morning sickness • n. nausea occurring in the mornings during early pregnancy.

morning star • n. the planet Venus, when visible in the east before sunrise.

Moroccan • n. a person from Morocco in North Africa. • adj. relating to Morocco.

moron • n. informal a stupid person.
– DERIVATIVES **moronic** adj.
– ORIGIN Greek *mōros* 'foolish'.

morose • adj. sullen and bad-tempered.
– DERIVATIVES **morosely** adv.
– ORIGIN Latin *morosus* 'peevish'.

morph • v. (in computer animation) change smoothly and gradually from one image to another.
– ORIGIN from **METAMORPHOSIS**.

morpheme /mor-feem/ • n. the smallest unit of meaning that a word can be divided into (e.g. the units *like* and *-ly*, forming *likely*).

morphia • n. dated morphine.

morphine /mor-feen/ • n. a drug obtained from opium and used in medicine to relieve pain.

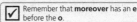

– ORIGIN named after the Roman god of sleep, *Morpheus*.

morphology •n. (pl. **morphologies**) **1** the scientific study of forms, especially of living organisms or words. **2** a shape or structure.
– DERIVATIVES **morphological** adj.

morris dancing •n. traditional English folk dancing performed by dancers wearing costumes with small bells attached and carrying handkerchiefs or sticks.
– ORIGIN from *Moorish* (see **Moor**).

morrow •n. (**the morrow**) old use the following day.
– ORIGIN Old English.

Morse (also **Morse code**) •n. a code in which letters are represented by combinations of long and short light or sound signals.
– ORIGIN named after its American inventor Samuel F. B. *Morse*.

morsel •n. a small piece of food.
– ORIGIN Old French, 'little bite'.

mortal •adj. **1** having to die at some time. **2** causing death. **3** (of fear or pain) very strong. **4** (of conflict or an enemy) lasting until death. **5** (in Christian belief) referring to a sin that will deprive the soul of divine grace. Often contrasted with **VENIAL**. •n. a human being.
– DERIVATIVES **mortally** adv.
– ORIGIN Latin *mors* 'death'.

mortality •n. **1** the state of having to die at some time. **2** death. **3** (also **mortality rate**) the number of deaths in a particular area or period.

mortar •n. **1** a mixture of lime, cement, sand, and water, used to hold bricks or stones together. **2** a cup-shaped container in which substances are crushed with a pestle. **3** a short cannon for firing shells at high angles.
– ORIGIN Latin *mortarium*.

mortar board •n. a hat with a flat square top and a tassel, worn as part of formal academic dress.

mortgage •n. **1** a legal agreement by which a person takes out a loan using their house or other property as a security. **2** an amount of money borrowed in a mortgage. •v. (**mortgages, mortgaging, mortgaged**) give a bank or building society the right to hold a person's house as security for the loan borrowed from them.
– ORIGIN Old French, 'dead pledge'.

mortgagee •n. the lender in a mortgage agreement.

mortgagor •n. the borrower in a mortgage agreement.

mortician •n. N. Amer. an undertaker.

mortify •v. (**mortifies, mortifying, mortified**) **1** make someone feel embarrassed or humiliated. **2** use self-discipline to control your physical needs.
– DERIVATIVES **mortification** n.
– ORIGIN Old French *mortifier*.

mortise /mor-tiss/ (also **mortice**) •n. a hole or recess designed to receive a projection (a tenon) so that the two are held together.
– ORIGIN Old French *mortaise*.

mortise lock •n. a lock set into the framework of a door in a recess or mortise.

mortuary •n. (pl. **mortuaries**) a room or building in which dead bodies are kept until burial or cremation. •adj. relating to burial or tombs.
– ORIGIN Latin *mortuus* 'dead'.

Mosaic •adj. relating to the biblical prophet Moses.

mosaic •n. a picture or pattern produced by fitting together small coloured pieces of stone, tile, or glass.
– ORIGIN French *mosaïque*.

mosey •v. (**moseys, moseying, moseyed**) informal walk or move in a leisurely way.

Moslem •n. & adj. var. of **Muslim**.

mosque •n. a Muslim place of worship.
– ORIGIN French.

mosquito •n. (pl. **mosquitoes**) a small fly, some kinds of which transmit diseases through the bite of the female.
– ORIGIN Spanish and Portuguese, 'little fly'.

mosquito net •n. a fine net hung across a door or window or around a bed to keep mosquitoes away.

moss •n. a small green spreading plant which grows in damp conditions.
– DERIVATIVES **mossy** adj.
– ORIGIN Old English.

most •det. & pron. **1** greatest in amount or degree. **2** the majority of. •adv. **1** to the greatest extent. **2** forming the superlative of adjectives and adverbs. **3** very.
– PHRASES **make the most of** use something to the best advantage.
– ORIGIN Old English.

-most •suffix forming superlative adjectives and adverbs: *innermost*.
– ORIGIN Old English.

mostly •adv. **1** on the whole; mainly. **2** usually.

Most Reverend •n. the title of an Anglican archbishop or an Irish Roman Catholic bishop.

MOT •n. (in the UK) a compulsory annual test of motor vehicles of more than a specified age.

m

– ORIGIN from *Ministry of Transport*.

mote • n. a speck of a substance.
– ORIGIN Old English.

motel • n. a roadside hotel for motorists.
– ORIGIN from **MOTOR** and **HOTEL**.

motet /moh-tet/ • n. a short piece of sacred choral music.
– ORIGIN Old French, 'little word'.

moth • n. an insect like a butterfly which is mainly active at night.
– ORIGIN Old English.

mothball • n. a small ball made from a strong-smelling chemical, placed among stored clothes to prevent the larvae of moths from eating the fabric. • v. put a plan or piece of equipment into storage or on hold.

moth-eaten • adj. shabby or very worn.

mother • n. 1 a female parent. 2 (**Mother**) (especially as a title or form of address) the head of a convent. 3 informal an extreme or very large example of something: *the mother of all traffic jams.* • v. (**mothers, mothering, mothered**) 1 bring up a child as its mother. 2 look after someone kindly and protectively.
– DERIVATIVES **motherhood** n.
– ORIGIN Old English.

motherboard (also **mainboard**) • n. a printed circuit board containing the main components of a microcomputer.

mother country • n. a country in relation to its colonies.

Mothering Sunday (also **Mother's Day**) • n. Brit. the fourth Sunday in Lent, traditionally a day in which people give gifts to their mother.

mother-in-law • n. (pl. **mothers-in-law**) the mother of a person's husband or wife.

motherland • n. a person's native country.

motherly • adj. kind and protective.

mother-of-pearl • n. a smooth pearly substance lining the shells of oysters and some other molluscs.

Mother's Day (Brit. also **Mothering Sunday**) • n. a day of the year on which people give gifts to their mother (in Britain the fourth Sunday in Lent and in North America and South Africa the second Sunday in May).

Mother Superior • n. the head of a convent.

mother tongue • n. a person's native language.

motif /moh-teef/ • n. 1 a single or repeated image forming a design. 2 a theme that is repeated in a work of art or literature or piece of music.
– ORIGIN French.

motion • n. 1 the action of moving. 2 a movement or gesture. 3 a formal proposal put to a meeting. 4 Brit. an emptying of the bowels. • v. direct someone with a gesture.
– DERIVATIVES **motionless** adj.
– ORIGIN Latin *movere* 'to move'.

motion picture • n. esp. N. Amer. a cinema film.

motivate • v. (**motivates, motivating, motivated**) 1 provide someone with a motive for doing something. 2 stimulate someone's interest in something.
– DERIVATIVES **motivator** n.

motivation • n. 1 the reason for a person's actions or behaviour. 2 enthusiasm.
– DERIVATIVES **motivational** adj.

motive • n. a factor influencing a person to act in a particular way. • adj. producing motion.
– ORIGIN Latin *motivus*.

motive power • n. the energy used to drive machinery.

mot juste /moh zhoost/ • n. (pl. **mots justes** /moh zhoost/) (**the mot juste**) the most appropriate word or expression.
– ORIGIN French.

motley • adj. made up of a variety of very different people or things.

motocross • n. cross-country racing on motorcycles.

motor • n. 1 a machine that supplies the power to drive a vehicle or other device. 2 Brit. informal a car. • adj. 1 giving or producing motion. 2 relating to muscular movement or the nerves activating it. • v. travel in a car.
– DERIVATIVES **motorize** (or **motorise**) v.
– ORIGIN Latin, 'mover'.

motorbike • n. Brit. a motorcycle.

motorboat • n. a boat powered by a motor.

motorcade • n. a procession of motor vehicles.

motor car • n. Brit. a car.

motorcycle • n. a two-wheeled vehicle that is powered by a motor and has no pedals.
– DERIVATIVES **motorcycling** n. **motorcyclist** n.

motorist • n. the driver of a car.

motor racing • n. the sport of racing in specially developed fast cars.

motor vehicle • n. a road vehicle powered by an internal-combustion engine.

motorway • n. Brit. a road designed for fast traffic, with three lanes in each direction.

motte /mot/ • n. hist. a mound forming the site of a castle or camp.
– ORIGIN French, 'mound'.

mottled • adj. marked with patches of a different colour.
– ORIGIN prob. from **MOTLEY**.

motto • n. (pl. **mottoes** or **mottos**) a short sentence or phrase expressing the aims or beliefs of a person or group.
– ORIGIN Italian, 'word'.

moue /moo/ • n. a pout.
– ORIGIN French.

mould[1] (US **mold**) • n. 1 a hollow container used to give shape to hot liquid material when it cools and hardens. 2 a jelly or mousse. 3 a distinctive type, style, or character: *he's a leader in the mould of Winston Churchill.* • v. 1 form a soft substance into something. 2 influence the formation or development of something.
– ORIGIN prob. from Old French *modle*.

mould[2] (US **mold**) • n. a furry growth of tiny fungi occurring in moist warm conditions.
– ORIGIN prob. from former *moul* 'grow mouldy'.

mould[3] (US **mold**) • n. esp. Brit. soft loose earth.
– ORIGIN Old English.

moulder (US **molder**) • v. (**moulders, mouldering, mouldered**; US **molders, moldering, moldered**) slowly decay.
– ORIGIN perh. from **MOULD**[3].

moulding (US **molding**) • n. a shaped strip of wood, stone, or plaster fitted as a decorative architectural feature.

mouldy (US **moldy**) • adj. 1 covered with or smelling of mould. 2 informal, esp. Brit. boring or dull.

moult (US **molt**) • v. shed old feathers, hair, or skin, to make way for a new growth. • n. a period of moulting.
– ORIGIN Latin *mutare* 'to change'.

mound • n. 1 a raised mass of earth or other material. 2 a small hill. 3 a heap or pile. • v. heap something up into a mound.

mount[1] • v. 1 climb up or on to something. 2 get up on an animal or bicycle to ride it. 3 (**be mounted**) be on horseback. 4 grow larger, more numerous, or more intense. 5 organize: *the company had successfully mounted takeover bids.* 6 put or fix something in place or on a support. • n. 1 (also **mounting**) something on which an object is mounted for support or display. 2 a horse used for riding.
– ORIGIN Old French *munter*.

mount[2] • n. old use or in place names a mountain or hill.
– ORIGIN Old English.

mountain • n. 1 a very high, steep hill. 2 a large pile or quantity.
– ORIGIN Old French *montaigne*.

mountain ash • n. a rowan tree.

mountain bike • n. a sturdy bicycle with broad deep-treaded tyres.

mountaineering • n. the sport or activity of climbing mountains.
– DERIVATIVES **mountaineer** n.

mountain lion • n. N. Amer. a puma.

mountainous • adj. 1 having many mountains. 2 huge: *mountainous debts.*

mountebank /mown-ti-bangk/ • n. a person who deceives other people.
– ORIGIN from Italian *monta in banco!* 'climb on the bench!', referring to the raised platform used by people who sold patent medicines in public.

Mountie • n. informal a member of the Royal Canadian Mounted Police.

mourn • v. feel deep sorrow following the death or loss of someone.
– ORIGIN Old English.

mourner • n. a person who attends a funeral as a relative or friend of the dead person.

mournful • adj. feeling, showing, or causing sadness or grief.
– DERIVATIVES **mournfully** adv.

mourning • n. 1 the expression of deep sorrow for someone who has died. 2 black clothes worn in a period of mourning.

mouse • n. (pl. **mice**) 1 a small rodent with a pointed snout and a long thin tail. 2 a timid and quiet person. 3 (pl. also **mouses**) a small hand-held device which controls cursor movements on a computer screen.
– ORIGIN Old English.

moussaka /moo-sah-kuh/ • n. a Greek dish of minced lamb layered with aubergines and tomatoes and topped with a cheese sauce.
– ORIGIN Turkish, 'that which is fed liquid'.

mousse • n. 1 a light sweet or savoury dish made with cream or egg white and flavoured with fruit, fish, etc. 2 a light substance used to style the hair.
– ORIGIN French, 'moss or froth'.

moustache (US also **mustache**) • n. a strip of hair left to grow above a man's upper lip.
– DERIVATIVES **moustached** adj.
– ORIGIN French.

mousy (also **mousey**) • adj. 1 (of hair) light brown. 2 shy and timid.

mouth • n. 1 the opening in the body through which food is taken and sounds are made. 2 an opening or entrance. 3 the place where a river enters the sea. • v. 1 move the lips as if to form words. 2 say something in an insincere way.
– ORIGIN Old English.

m

mouthful •n. **1** a quantity of food or drink that fills or can be put in the mouth. **2** a long or complicated word or phrase.

mouth organ •n. a harmonica.

mouthpart •n. any of the projections surrounding the mouth of an insect and adapted for feeding.

mouthpiece •n. a part of a musical instrument, telephone, or breathing apparatus that is designed to be put in or against the mouth.

mouth-to-mouth •adj. (of artificial respiration) in which a person breathes into someone's lungs through their mouth.

mouthwash •n. an antiseptic liquid for rinsing the mouth or gargling.

mouth-watering •adj. **1** smelling or looking delicious. **2** very attractive or tempting.

mouthy •adj. (**mouthier**, **mouthiest**) informal inclined to talk a lot, especially in a disrespectful way.

movable (also **moveable**) •adj. **1** able to be moved. **2** (of a religious festival) occurring on a different date each year.

move •v. (**moves**, **moving**, **moved**) **1** go or cause to go in a specified direction or way. **2** change position. **3** change the place where you live. **4** change from one state or activity to another. **5** take or cause to take action. **6** make progress. **7** provoke sympathy, affection, or other feelings in someone. •n. **1** an instance of moving. **2** an action taken towards achieving a purpose. **3** a player's turn during a board game.
– PHRASES **make a move 1** take action. **2** Brit. set off.
– ORIGIN Latin *movere*.

movement •n. **1** an act or the process of moving. **2** a group of people with a shared cause. **3** a trend or development. **4** (**movements**) a person's activities during a particular period of time. **5** a main division of a musical work.

movie •n. N. Amer. a cinema film.

moving •adj. **1** in motion. **2** arousing sadness or sympathy.

mow •v. (**mows**, **mowing**, **mowed**; past part. **mowed** or **mown**) **1** cut down or trim grass or a cereal crop. **2** (**mow someone down**) kill someone by gunfire or by knocking them down with a car.
– DERIVATIVES **mower** n.
– ORIGIN Old English.

Mozambican /moh-zam-beek-uhn/ •n. a person from Mozambique. •adj. relating to Mozambique.

mozzarella /mot-suh-rel-luh/ •n. a firm white Italian cheese made from buffalo's or cow's milk.
– ORIGIN Italian.

MP •abbrev. Member of Parliament.

mpg •abbrev. miles per gallon.

mph •abbrev. miles per hour.

MPhil •abbrev. Master of Philosophy.

Mr •n. a title used before a man's surname or full name.
– ORIGIN from MASTER.

Mrs •n. a title used before a married woman's surname or full name.
– ORIGIN from MISTRESS.

MS •abbrev. **1** manuscript. **2** multiple sclerosis.

Ms •n. a title used before the surname or full name of a married or unmarried woman.

MSc •abbrev. Master of Science.

MS-DOS •abbrev. Computing, trademark Microsoft disk operating system.

MSP •abbrev. Member of the Scottish Parliament.

Mt •abbrev. (in place names) Mount. •symb. the chemical element meitnerium.

much •det. & pron. (**more**, **most**) a large amount. •adv. **1** to a great extent. **2** often.
– PHRASES **not much of a** not a good example of: *I'm not much of a gardener.*
– ORIGIN Old English.

muchness •n. (in phr. (**much**) of a **muchness**) very similar.

mucilage /myoo-si-lij/ •n. **1** a thick bodily fluid. **2** a thick or sticky solution extracted from plants, used in medicines and adhesives.
– DERIVATIVES **mucilaginous** /myoo-si-**laj**-i-nuhss/ adj.
– ORIGIN Latin *mucilago* 'musty juice'.

muck •n. **1** dirt, mud, or manure. **2** informal something unpleasant or worthless. •v. **1** (**muck something up**) informal spoil something. **2** (**muck about/around**) Brit. informal behave in a silly way. **3** (**muck about/around with**) Brit. informal interfere with. **4** (**muck in**) Brit. informal share tasks or accommodation. **5** (**muck something out**) esp. Brit. remove manure from a stable.
– ORIGIN prob. Scandinavian.

muckraking •n. the action of searching out and publicizing scandal about famous people.
– ORIGIN coined by President Theodore Roosevelt in a speech referring to the man with the *muck rake* in Bunyan's *Pilgrim's Progress*.

mucky •adj. (**muckier**, **muckiest**) **1** dirty. **2** sordid or indecent.

mucous /myoo-kuhss/ •adj. relating to or covered with mucus.

mucous membrane • n. a tissue that produces many body cavities and organs.

mucus /myoo-kuhss/ • n. a slimy substance produced by the mucous membranes and glands of animals for lubrication, protection, etc.
– ORIGIN Latin.

mud • n. soft, sticky matter consisting of mixed earth and water.
– ORIGIN prob. from German *mudde*.

muddle • v. (**muddles, muddling, muddled**) **1** bring into a disordered or confusing state. **2** confuse someone. **3** (**muddle something up**) confuse two or more things with each other. **4** (**muddle through** (or Brit. **along**)) cope more or less satisfactorily. • n. a disordered or confusing state.
– DERIVATIVES **muddly** adj.
– ORIGIN perh. from Dutch *modden* 'dabble in mud'.

muddy • adj. (**muddier, muddiest**) **1** covered in or full of mud. **2** not bright or clear. • v. (**muddies, muddying, muddied**) make something muddy or unclear.

mudflap • n. a flap hung behind the wheel of a vehicle to protect against mud and stones thrown up from the road.

mudflat • n. a stretch of muddy land left uncovered at low tide.

mudguard • n. a curved strip fitted over a wheel of a bicycle or motorcycle to protect against water and dirt thrown up from the road.

mud pack • n. a paste applied to the face to improve the skin.

mud-slinging • n. informal the casting of insults and accusations.

muesli /myooz-li/ • n. (pl. **mueslis**) a mixture of oats, dried fruit, and nuts, eaten with milk at breakfast.
– ORIGIN Swiss German.

muezzin /moo-ez-zin/ • n. a man who calls Muslims to prayer.
– ORIGIN Arabic, 'proclaim'.

muff[1] • n. a short tube made of fur or other warm material into which the hands are placed for warmth.
– ORIGIN Dutch *mof*.

muff[2] • v. informal handle something clumsily; bungle.
– ORIGIN unknown.

muffin • n. **1** (N. Amer. **English muffin**) a flattened bread roll eaten toasted with butter. **2** a small cake with a rounded top.

muffle • v. (**muffles, muffling, muffled**) **1** wrap or cover yourself or a part of the body for warmth. **2** make a sound quieter or less distinct by covering its source.
– ORIGIN Old French *moufle* 'thick glove'.

muffler • n. a scarf worn around the neck and face.

mufti[1] /muf-ti/ • n. (pl. **muftis**) a Muslim legal expert who gives rulings on religious matters.
– ORIGIN Arabic, 'decide a point of law'.

mufti[2] /muf-ti/ • n. non-uniform clothes when worn by military or police staff.
– ORIGIN perh. from **MUFTI**[1].

mug[1] • n. **1** a large cylindrical cup with a handle. **2** informal a person's face. **3** Brit. informal a stupid or gullible person. • v. (**mugs, mugging, mugged**) **1** attack and rob someone in a public place. **2** informal make faces in front of an audience or a camera.
– ORIGIN prob. Scandinavian.

mug[2] • v. (**mugs, mugging, mugged**) (**mug something up**) Brit. informal learn or study a subject quickly and intensively.

mugger • n. a person who attacks and robs someone in a public place.

muggins • n. Brit. informal a foolish person.
– ORIGIN perh. a use of the surname *Muggins*, with reference to **MUG**[1].

muggy • adj. (**muggier, muggiest**) (of the weather) unpleasantly warm and humid.
– ORIGIN from dialect *mug* 'mist, drizzle'.

Mughal • n. var. of **MOGUL**.

mugshot • n. informal a photograph of a person's face made for an official purpose.

mujahedin /muu-jah-hi-deen/ (also **mujaheddin, mujahideen**) • pl. n. Islamic guerrilla fighters.
– ORIGIN Persian and Arabic, 'people who fight a holy war'.

mulatto /muu-lat-toh/ • n. (pl. **mulattoes** or **mulattos**) offens. a person with one white and one black parent.
– ORIGIN Spanish *mulato*.

mulberry • n. (pl. **mulberries**) **1** a dark red or white fruit resembling the loganberry. **2** a dark red or purple colour.
– ORIGIN Latin *morum* 'mulberry'.

mulch /mulch/ • n. a mass of leaves, bark, or compost spread around a plant for protection or to enrich the soil. • v. cover soil or the base of a plant with mulch.
– ORIGIN prob. from dialect *mulch* 'soft'.

mule[1] • n. the offspring of a male donkey and a female horse.
– ORIGIN Latin *mulus, mula*.

mule[2] • n. a slipper or light shoe without a back.
– ORIGIN French, 'slipper'.

muleteer /myoo-li-**teer**/ • n. a person who drives mules.

mulish • adj. stubborn.

mull[1] • v. (**mull something over**) think about something at length.

mull[2] • v. warm wine or beer and add sugar and spices to it.

mull[3] • n. (in Scottish place names) a point of high land jutting out into the sea or a lake.
– ORIGIN perh. from Scottish Gaelic or Icelandic.

mullah /**muul**-luh/ • n. a Muslim who is an expert in Islamic theology and sacred law.
– ORIGIN Arabic.

mullet • n. a sea fish that is caught for food.
– ORIGIN Greek *mullos*.

mulligatawny /mul-li-guh-**taw**-ni/ • n. a spicy meat soup originally made in India.
– ORIGIN Tamil, 'pepper water'.

mullion • n. a vertical bar between the panes of glass in a window.
– DERIVATIVES **mullioned** adj.
– ORIGIN prob. from Old French *moinel* 'middle'.

multi- • comb. form more than one; many: *multicultural*.
– ORIGIN Latin *multus*.

multicoloured (also **multicolour**; US **multicolored**, **multicolor**) • adj. having many colours.

multicultural • adj. relating to or made up of several cultural or ethnic groups.
– DERIVATIVES **multiculturalism** n.

multifaceted • adj. having many sides or aspects.

multifarious /mul-ti-**fair**-i-uhss/ • adj. having great variety.
– ORIGIN Latin *multifarius*.

multilateral • adj. involving three or more participants.

multilingual • adj. in or using several languages.

multimedia • adj. using more than one means of providing information. • n. Computing a system providing video and audio material as well as documents.

multimillion • adj. consisting of several million.

multimillionaire • n. a person with assets worth several million pounds or dollars.

multinational • adj. involving several countries or nationalities. • n. a company operating in several countries.

multiparty • adj. involving several political parties.

multiple • adj. **1** having or involving several different people or things. **2** (of a disease or injury) affecting several parts of the body. • n. a number that may be divided by another a certain number of times without a remainder.
– ORIGIN Latin *multiplus*.

multiple-choice • adj. (of a question in an exam) giving several possible answers, from which the candidate must choose the correct one.

multiple sclerosis • n. see SCLEROSIS.

multiplex • adj. made up of many elements in a complex relationship. • n. a cinema with several separate screens.
– ORIGIN Latin.

multiplicand /mul-ti-pli-**kand**, mul-ti-pli-**kand**/ • n. a quantity which is to be multiplied by another (the multiplier).

multiplication • n. the process of multiplying.

multiplication sign • n. the sign ×, used to indicate that one quantity is to be multiplied by another.

multiplication table • n. a list of multiples of a particular number.

multiplicity • n. (pl. **multiplicities**) a large number or variety.

multiplier • n. **1** a quantity by which a given number (the multiplicand) is to be multiplied. **2** a device for increasing the intensity of an electric current, force, etc.

multiply[1] /**mul**-ti-ply/ • v. (**multiplies**, **multiplying**, **multiplied**) **1** add a number to itself a specified number of times. **2** increase in number or quantity. **3** reproduce in large numbers.
– ORIGIN Latin *multiplicare*.

multiply[2] /**mul**-ti-pli/ • adv. in different ways or respects.

multi-purpose • adj. having several purposes.

multiracial • adj. relating to a situation involving people of many races.

multi-storey • adj. (of a building) having several storeys.

multitask • v. (usu. as noun **multitasking**) **1** Computing carry out more than one program or task at the same time. **2** (of a person) do more than one task at the same time.

multitude • n. **1** a large number of people or things. **2** (**the multitude**) the mass of ordinary people.
– ORIGIN Latin *multitudo*.

multitudinous /mul-ti-**tyoo**-di-nuhss/ • adj. very numerous.

mum[1] • n. Brit. informal a person's mother.

mum[2] • adj. (in phr. **keep mum**) informal say nothing so as not to reveal a secret.
– PHRASES **mum's the word** do not (or I will not) reveal a secret.

mumble • v. (**mumbles, mumbling,**

mumbled) say something indistinctly and quietly. •n. a quiet and indistinct way of speaking.
– ORIGIN from MUM².

mumbo-jumbo •n. informal language that is complicated but has no real meaning.
– ORIGIN from *Mumbo Jumbo*, the supposed name of an African idol.

mummer •n. an actor in a traditional English folk play.
– ORIGIN Old French *momeur*.

mummify •v. (**mummifies, mummifying, mummified**) (especially in ancient Egypt) preserve a body by embalming and wrapping it in cloth.
– DERIVATIVES **mummification** n.

mummy¹ •n. (pl. **mummies**) Brit. informal a person's mother.

mummy² •n. (pl. **mummies**) (especially in ancient Egypt) a body that has been preserved for burial by embalming and wrapping in cloth.
– ORIGIN Arabic, 'embalmed body'.

mumps •pl. n. an infectious disease causing swelling of the glands at the sides of the face.
– ORIGIN from former *mump* 'grimace'.

munch •v. eat steadily and in a way that can be heard by other people.

mundane /mun-**dayn**/ •adj. **1** lacking interest or excitement. **2** relating to the physical world rather than a heavenly or spiritual one.
– DERIVATIVES **mundanity** n.
– ORIGIN Latin *mundus* 'world'.

mung bean •n. a small round green bean grown in the tropics as a source of bean sprouts.
– ORIGIN Hindi.

municipal •adj. relating to a town or city or its governing council.
– ORIGIN Latin *municipalis*.

municipality /myoo-ni-si-**pal**-i-ti/ •n. (pl. **municipalities**) a town or district that has local government.

munificent /myoo-**nif**-i-suhnt/ •adj. very generous.
– DERIVATIVES **munificence** n.
– ORIGIN Latin *munificus*.

munitions •pl. n. military weapons, ammunition, equipment, and stores.
– ORIGIN Latin, 'fortification'.

mural •n. a painting done directly on a wall.
– ORIGIN Latin *murus* 'wall'.

murder •n. **1** the deliberate killing of one person by another. **2** informal a very difficult or unpleasant situation.
•v. (**murders, murdering, murdered**) **1** kill someone deliberately. **2** informal spoil something by poor performance.

– DERIVATIVES **murderer** n. **murderess** n.
– ORIGIN Old English.

murderous •adj. **1** capable of or involving murder or extreme violence. **2** informal very difficult or unpleasant.

murk •n. darkness or fog causing poor visibility.
– ORIGIN Old English.

murky •adj. (**murkier, murkiest**) **1** dark and gloomy. **2** (of water) dirty or cloudy. **3** suspicious because secret.
– DERIVATIVES **murkiness** n.

murmur •n. **1** something that is said quietly. **2** a low continuous background noise. **3** a quiet complaint. **4** Med. a recurring sound heard in the heart through a stethoscope and usually indicating disease or damage. •v. **1** say something in a murmur. **2** make a low continuous sound. **3** complain quietly.
– ORIGIN Latin.

Murphy's Law •n. a supposed law of nature, to the effect that anything that can go wrong will go wrong.

muscle •n. **1** a band of tissue in the body that can contract so as to move or hold the position of a part of the body. **2** power or strength. •v. (**muscles, muscling, muscled**) (**muscle in**) informal involve yourself in something that does not concern you.
– DERIVATIVES **muscly** adj.
– ORIGIN Latin *musculus*.

USAGE: Do not confuse **muscle** with **mussel**. **Muscle** means 'the tissue that moves a body part' (*tone up your thigh muscles*), whereas **mussel** means 'a shellfish'.

muscle-bound •adj. (of a person) having overdeveloped muscles.

Muscovite •n. a person from Moscow.

muscular •adj. **1** relating to muscles. **2** having well-developed muscles.
– DERIVATIVES **muscularity** n.

muscular dystrophy •n. an inherited condition in which the muscles gradually get weaker and waste away.

musculature •n. the muscular system or arrangement of a body or an organ.

muse¹ •n. **1** (**Muse**) (in Greek and Roman mythology) each of nine goddesses who encouraged the arts and sciences. **2** a woman who is the inspiration for a creative artist.
– ORIGIN Greek *mousa*.

muse² •v. (**muses, musing, mused**) **1** be absorbed in thought. **2** say something to yourself in a thoughtful way.
– ORIGIN Old French *muser*.

museum •n. a building in which objects of interest or importance are stored and displayed.

– ORIGIN Greek *mouseion* 'seat of the Muses'.

museum piece •n. something that is very old or no longer working.

mush •n. **1** a soft, wet mass. **2** excessive sentimentality.
– ORIGIN prob. from MASH.

mushroom •n. a spore-producing body of a fungus, having a rounded head on a stalk and often edible. •v. increase or develop rapidly.
– ORIGIN Old French *mousseron*.

mushroom cloud •n. a mushroom-shaped cloud of dust and debris formed after a nuclear explosion.

mushy •adj. (**mushier, mushiest**) **1** soft and pulpy. **2** excessively sentimental.

music •n. **1** the art of combining the sounds of a voice or instrument in a pleasing way. **2** the sound so produced. **3** the signs in which music is written or printed.
– ORIGIN Old French *musique*.

musical •adj. **1** relating to or accompanied by music. **2** fond of or skilled in music. **3** pleasant-sounding. •n. a play or film in which the story is regularly interrupted with singing and dancing.
– DERIVATIVES **musicality** n. **musically** adv.

musical box •n. Brit. a small box which plays a tune when the lid is opened.

musical chairs •pl. n. **1** a party game in which players compete for a decreasing number of chairs when the accompanying music is stopped. **2** a situation in which people frequently exchange positions.

music centre •n. Brit. a combined radio, cassette player, and record or compact disc player.

music hall •n. **1** a form of entertainment involving singing, dancing, and comedy, popular in Britain in the 19th and early 20th centuries. **2** a theatre where such entertainment took place.

musician •n. a person who plays a musical instrument or writes music.
– DERIVATIVES **musicianship** n.

musicology •n. the study of music as an academic subject.
– DERIVATIVES **musicological** adj. **musicologist** n.

musk •n. a strong-smelling substance produced by a type of male deer, used in making perfume.
– DERIVATIVES **musky** adj.
– ORIGIN Persian.

musket •n. hist. a light gun with a long barrel.
– ORIGIN French *mousquet*.

musketeer •n. hist. **1** a soldier armed with a musket. **2** a member of the household troops of the French king in the 17th and 18th centuries.

muskrat •n. a large North American rodent with a musky smell, valued for its fur.

Muslim (also **Moslem**) •n. a follower of Islam. •adj. relating to Muslims or Islam.
– ORIGIN Arabic.

muslin •n. lightweight cotton cloth in a plain weave.
– ORIGIN Italian *mussolina*.

musquash /muss-kwosh/ •n. Brit. the fur of the muskrat.
– ORIGIN from an American Indian language.

muss •v. informal, esp. N. Amer. make untidy or messy.
– ORIGIN prob. from MESS.

mussel •n. an edible shellfish with a dark brown or purplish-black shell, found in the sea or in fresh water.
– ORIGIN Latin *musculus* 'muscle'.

> **USAGE:** On the confusion of **mussel** with **muscle**, see the note at **MUSCLE**.

must[1] •modal verb (past **had to** or in reported speech **must**) **1** be obliged to; should. **2** used to insist on something. **3** expressing an opinion about something that is very likely: *you must be tired.* •n. informal something that should not be missed.
– ORIGIN Old English.

must[2] •n. grape juice before or during fermentation.
– ORIGIN Latin *mustus* 'new'.

mustache •n. US = MOUSTACHE.

mustachios /muh-stah-shi-ohz/ •pl. n. a long or elaborate moustache.
– ORIGIN Italian *mostaccio*.

mustang •n. a small wild horse of the south-western US.
– ORIGIN from Spanish *mestengo* and *mostrenco*, both meaning 'wild cattle'.

mustard •n. **1** a hot-tasting yellow or brown paste made from the crushed seeds of a plant. **2** a brownish yellow colour.
– ORIGIN Old French *moustarde*.

mustard gas •n. a liquid whose vapour causes severe irritation and blistering, used in chemical weapons.

muster •v. (**musters, mustering, mustered**) **1** bring troops together. **2** (of people) gather together. **3** summon up a feeling or attitude. •n. an instance of mustering troops.
– PHRASES **pass muster** be accepted as satisfactory.

– ORIGIN Old French *moustrer*.

mustn't • contr. must not.

musty • adj. having a stale or mouldy smell or taste.
– DERIVATIVES **mustiness** n.
– ORIGIN perh. from *moisty* 'moist'.

mutable /myoo-tuh-b'l/ • adj. liable to change.
– DERIVATIVES **mutability** n.
– ORIGIN Latin *mutabilis*.

mutant • adj. resulting from or showing the effect of a change in genetic structure. • n. a mutant form.

mutate • v. (**mutates, mutating, mutated**) change in form or nature; undergo mutation.

mutation • n. **1** a change in genetic structure which results in a variant form and may be passed on to subsequent generations. **2** a form resulting from such a change. **3** the process or an instance of changing.
– ORIGIN Latin.

mute • adj. **1** not speaking or temporarily speechless. **2** lacking the power of speech. **3** (of a letter) not pronounced. • n. **1** dated a person who is unable to speak. **2** a device used to dampen the sound of a musical instrument.
• v. (**mutes, muting, muted**) **1** deaden or muffle the sound of a musical instrument. **2** reduce the strength or intensity of something. **3** (as adj. **muted**) (of colour or lighting) not bright; subdued.
– ORIGIN Latin *mutus*.

mute swan • n. the commonest Eurasian swan, having an orange-red bill with a black knob at the base.

mutilate • v. (**mutilates, mutilating, mutilated**) **1** cause a severe injury to someone. **2** cause serious damage to something.
– DERIVATIVES **mutilation** n.
– ORIGIN Latin *mutilare* 'maim'.

mutineer • n. a rebel soldier or sailor.

mutinous • adj. rebellious.

mutiny • n. (pl. **mutinies**) an open rebellion against authority, especially by soldiers or sailors against their officers.
• v. (**mutinies, mutinying, mutinied**) engage in mutiny; rebel.
– ORIGIN French *mutin* 'mutineer'.

mutt • n. informal a dog, especially a mongrel.
– ORIGIN from *muttonhead* 'stupid person'.

mutter • v. (**mutters, muttering, muttered**) **1** say something in a voice which can barely be heard. **2** talk or grumble in secret or in private.
• n. something said which can barely be heard.

mutton • n. the flesh of mature sheep used as food.
– ORIGIN Old French *moton*.

mutual • adj. **1** experienced or done by two or more people equally. **2** (of two or more people) having the same specified relationship to each other. **3** shared by two or more people: *a mutual friend*. **4** (of a building society or insurance company) owned by its members and dividing its profits between them.
– DERIVATIVES **mutuality** n. **mutually** adv.
– ORIGIN Old French *mutuel*.

muzak • n. trademark recorded light background music played in public places.
– ORIGIN from **MUSIC**.

muzzle • n. **1** the nose and mouth of an animal. **2** a guard fitted over an animal's nose and mouth to stop it biting or feeding. **3** the open end of the barrel of a firearm. • v. (**muzzles, muzzling, muzzled**) **1** fit a guard over an animal's nose and mouth. **2** prevent someone expressing their opinions freely.
– ORIGIN Latin *musum*.

muzzy • adj. (**muzzier, muzziest**) **1** dazed or confused. **2** blurred or indistinct.
– DERIVATIVES **muzziness** n.

MW • abbrev. **1** medium wave. **2** megawatt(s).

my • possess. det. belonging to or associated with me (that is, the speaker).
– ORIGIN Old English.

myalgia /my-al-juh/ • n. pain in a muscle or group of muscles.
– ORIGIN from Greek *mus* 'muscle' + *algos* 'pain'.

mycelium /my-see-li-uhm/ • n. (pl. **mycelia**) Bot. a network of fine white threads making up the vegetative part of a fungus.
– ORIGIN Greek *mukēs* 'fungus'.

Mycenaean /my-si-nee-uhn/ • adj. relating to a late Bronze Age civilization in Greece represented by archaeological discoveries at Mycenae and other ancient cities.

mycology /my-kol-uh-ji/ • n. the scientific study of fungi.
– DERIVATIVES **mycologist** n.
– ORIGIN Greek *mukēs* 'fungus'.

myelin /my-uh-lin/ • n. a whitish fatty substance forming a sheath around nerve fibres.
– ORIGIN Greek *muelos* 'marrow'.

mynah (also **mynah bird**) • n. a southern Asian or Australasian starling with a loud call, some kinds of which can mimic human speech.
– ORIGIN Hindi.

m

myopia /my-oh-pi-uh/ • n. short-sightedness.
– ORIGIN from Greek *muein* 'shut' + *ōps* 'eye'.

myopic /my-op-ik/ • adj. (of a person) short-sighted.

myriad /mi-ri-uhd/ • n. (also **myriads**) a countless or very great number. • adj. countless.
– ORIGIN Greek *murias*.

myriapod /mi-ri-uh-pod/ • n. a centipede, millipede, or other insect having a long body with numerous leg-bearing segments.
– ORIGIN from Greek *murioi* 'ten thousand' + *pous* 'foot'.

myrrh /mer/ • n. a sweet-smelling resin obtained from certain trees and used in perfumes, medicines, and incense.
– ORIGIN Greek *murra*.

myrtle • n. an evergreen shrub with white flowers followed by purple-black berries.
– ORIGIN Greek *murtos*.

myself • pron. (first person sing.) **1** used by a speaker to refer to himself or herself as the object of a verb or preposition when he or she is the subject of the clause: *I hurt myself.* **2** I or me personally: *I wrote it myself.*
– ORIGIN Old English.

mysterious • adj. difficult or impossible to understand or explain.
– DERIVATIVES **mysteriously** adv.

mystery • n. (pl. **mysteries**) **1** something that is difficult or impossible to understand or explain. **2** secrecy. **3** a novel, play, or film dealing with a puzzling crime. **4** (**mysteries**) secret religious ceremonies.
– ORIGIN Greek *mustērion*.

mystery play • n. a type of popular medieval play based on biblical stories or the lives of saints.

mystery tour • n. Brit. a trip to an unspecified destination.

mystic • n. a person who devotes their time to profound thought in order to become closer to God and to reach truths beyond human understanding. • adj. mystical.
– ORIGIN Greek *mustēs* 'initiated person'.

mystical • adj. **1** relating to mystics or mysticism. **2** having a spiritual significance that goes beyond human understanding. **3** inspiring a sense of spiritual mystery and awe.
– DERIVATIVES **mystically** adv.

mysticism • n. **1** the belief that knowledge of God can be gained by profound thought. **2** vague or ill-defined religious or spiritual belief.

mystify • v. (**mystifies, mystifying, mystified**) **1** utterly bewilder someone. **2** make something seem obscure or mysterious.
– DERIVATIVES **mystification** n.
– ORIGIN French *mystifier*.

mystique • n. **1** a quality of mystery, glamour, or power surrounding someone or something. **2** an air of secrecy surrounding a subject, making it impressive or baffling to those not involved in it.
– ORIGIN French.

myth • n. **1** a traditional story concerning the early history of a people or explaining a natural or social fact. **2** a widely held but false belief. **3** an imaginary person or thing.
– ORIGIN Greek *muthos*.

mythical • adj. **1** occurring in or relating to myths or folk tales. **2** imaginary or not real.
– DERIVATIVES **mythic** adj.

mythological • adj. relating to or occurring in myths or folk tales.

mythology • n. (pl. **mythologies**) **1** a collection of myths. **2** a set of widely held but exaggerated or false stories or beliefs.
– DERIVATIVES **mythologist** n.

myxomatosis /mik-suh-muh-toh-siss/ • n. a highly infectious and usually fatal disease of rabbits, causing inflammation and discharge around the eyes.
– ORIGIN Greek *muxa* 'slime, mucus'.

m

Nn

N¹ (also **n**) • n. (pl. **Ns** or **N's**) the fourteenth letter of the alphabet.

N² • abbrev. North or Northern. • symb. the chemical element nitrogen.

n • symb. an unspecified or variable number.

'n' (also **'n**) • contr. informal and: *rock 'n roll.*

Na • symb. the chemical element sodium.
– ORIGIN Latin *natrium.*

n/a • abbrev. not applicable.

NAAFI /na-fi/ • abbrev. Brit. Navy, Army, and Air Force Institutes, an organization running shops or canteens for those in the armed forces.

naan • n. var. of NAN².

nab • v. (**nabs, nabbing, nabbed**) informal **1** catch a wrongdoer. **2** take or grab suddenly.

nacho /na-choh/ • n. (pl. **nachos**) a small piece of tortilla topped with melted cheese, peppers, etc.
– ORIGIN perh. from Mexican Spanish *Nacho*, familiar form of *Ignacio*, first name of the chef credited with creating the dish.

nacre /nay-ker/ • n. mother-of-pearl.
– ORIGIN French.

nadir /nay-deer/ • n. **1** the lowest or worst point. **2** Astron. the point in the sky directly opposite the zenith and below an observer.
– ORIGIN Arabic, 'opposite to the zenith'.

naevus /nee-vuhss/ (US **nevus**) • n. (pl. **naevi** /nee-vy/) a birthmark or a mole on the skin.
– ORIGIN Latin.

naff Brit. informal • v. (**naff off**) go away.
• adj. lacking taste or style.

nag¹ • v. (**nags, nagging, nagged**) **1** constantly tell someone to do something they dislike. **2** be constantly worrying or painful to: *I was nagged by the feeling that something was wrong.* • n. a persistent feeling of anxiety.
– ORIGIN perh. Scandinavian or German.

nag² • n. informal a horse, especially one that is old or in poor condition.

naiad /ny-ad/ • n. (in classical mythology) a water nymph.
– ORIGIN Greek *Naias.*

naif /ny-eef/ • adj. naive. • n. a naive person.
– ORIGIN French.

nail • n. **1** a small metal spike with a flat head, used to join things together or as a hook. **2** a thin hard layer on the upper surface of the tip of the finger and toe.
• v. **1** fasten with a nail or nails. **2** informal catch a suspected criminal.
– PHRASES **a nail in the coffin** an action or event likely to cause something to fail or come to an end.
– ORIGIN Old English.

nail-biting • adj. causing great anxiety or tension.

nail file • n. a small file for shaping the fingernails and toenails.

nail polish (also **nail varnish**) • n. a glossy substance put on the fingernails or toenails.

naive /ny-eev/ (also **naïve**)
• adj. **1** lacking experience, wisdom, or judgement. **2** (of art) in a style which rejects sophisticated techniques.
– DERIVATIVES **naively** adv.
– ORIGIN French.

naivety /ny-eev-ti/ (also **naiveté** /ny-eev-tay/) • n. lack of experience, wisdom, or judgement.

naked • adj. **1** without clothes. **2** (of an object) without the usual covering. **3** not hidden; open: *naked aggression.* **4** exposed to harm.
– PHRASES **the naked eye** the normal power of the eyes, without using a microscope, telescope, etc.
– DERIVATIVES **nakedly** adv. **nakedness** n.
– ORIGIN Old English.

namby-pamby • adj. lacking courage or vigour; feeble.
– ORIGIN from the name of *Ambrose* Philips, an English poet ridiculed for his poor verse.

name • n. **1** a word or words by which someone or something is known. **2** a famous person. **3** a reputation: *he made a name for himself in the theatre.*
• v. (**names, naming, named**) **1** give a

name to. **2** identify or mention by name. **3** specify a sum of money, time, or place.
– PHRASES **call someone names** insult someone verbally. **in someone's name 1** registered as belonging to or reserved for someone. **2** on behalf of someone. **in the name of** for the sake of.
– ORIGIN Old English.

namecheck • v. publicly mention the name of.

name-dropping • n. the mentioning of famous people's names as if you know them, so as to impress other people.

nameless • adj. **1** having no name. **2** having a name that is not made known; anonymous.

namely • adv. that is to say.

namesake • n. a person or thing with the same name as another.
– ORIGIN from *for the name's sake*.

Namibian /nuh-mib-i-uhn/ • n. a person from Namibia, a country in southern Africa. • adj. relating to Namibia.

nan[1] /nan/ • n. Brit. informal your grandmother.
– ORIGIN from **NANNY**.

nan[2] /nahn/ (also **naan**) • n. a type of soft flat Indian bread.
– ORIGIN Urdu and Persian.

nancy boy (also **nancy**) • n. informal, derog. an effeminate or homosexual man.
– ORIGIN familiar form of the name *Ann*.

nanny • n. (pl. **nannies**) **1** a woman employed to look after a child in its own home. **2** (also **nanny goat**) a female goat. • adj. interfering and overprotective: *the nanny state*.
– ORIGIN familiar form of the name *Ann*.

nano- /na-noh/ • comb. form **1** referring to a factor of one thousand millionth (10^{-9}): *nanosecond*. **2** very small; submicroscopic: *nanotechnology*.
– ORIGIN Greek *nanos* 'dwarf'.

nanosecond • n. one thousand millionth of a second.

nanotechnology • n. technology on an atomic or molecular scale.

nap[1] • n. a short sleep during the day. • v. (**naps, napping, napped**) have a nap.
– ORIGIN Old English.

nap[2] • n. short raised fibres on the surface of fabrics such as velvet.
– ORIGIN Dutch or German *noppe*.

napalm /nay-pahm/ • n. a highly flammable jelly-like form of petrol, used in firebombs and flame-throwers.
– ORIGIN from *naphthenic* and *palmitic acids* (compounds used in its manufacture).

nape • n. the back of a person's neck.

naphtha /naf-thuh/ • n. a flammable oil obtained from coal, shale, or petroleum.

– ORIGIN Greek.

naphthalene /naf-thuh-leen/ • n. a crystalline compound used in mothballs and for chemical manufacture.

napkin • n. a square piece of cloth or paper used at a meal to wipe the fingers or lips and to protect clothes.
– ORIGIN Old French *nappe* 'tablecloth'.

nappy • n. (pl. **nappies**) Brit. a piece of material wrapped round a baby's bottom and between its legs to absorb urine and faeces.
– ORIGIN short for **NAPKIN**.

narcissism /nar-siss-i-z'm/ • n. excessive or sexual interest in yourself and your appearance.
– DERIVATIVES **narcissist** n. **narcissistic** adj.
– ORIGIN from *Narcissus*, a beautiful youth in Greek mythology who fell in love with his reflection.

narcissus /nar-siss-uhss/ • n. (pl. **narcissi** or **narcissuses**) a daffodil with a flower that has white or pale outer petals and an orange or yellow centre.
– ORIGIN Greek *narkissos*.

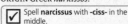
Spell **narcissus** with **-ciss-** in the middle.

narcotic • n. **1** an addictive drug which affects mood or behaviour. **2** a drug which causes drowsiness or unconsciousness, or relieves pain. • adj. relating to narcotics.
– ORIGIN Greek *narkōtikos*.

nark Brit. informal • n. a police informer. • v. annoy someone.
– ORIGIN Romany *nāk* 'nose'.

narrate • v. (**narrates, narrating, narrated**) **1** give an account of something. **2** provide a commentary for a film, television programme, etc.
– DERIVATIVES **narration** n. **narrator** n.
– ORIGIN Latin *narrare*.

narrative • n. **1** a story. **2** the part of a fictional work that tells the story, as distinct from dialogue. • adj. relating to stories or the telling of stories.

narrow • adj. (**narrower, narrowest**) **1** of small width in comparison to length. **2** limited in extent, amount, or scope. **3** only just achieved: *a narrow escape*. • v. **1** become or make narrower. **2** (**narrow something down**) reduce the number of possibilities of something. • n. (**narrows**) a narrow channel connecting two larger areas of water.
– DERIVATIVES **narrowly** adv. **narrowness** n.
– ORIGIN Old English.

narrowboat • n. Brit. a canal boat less than 7 ft (2.1 metres) wide.

narrow-minded • adj. unwilling to

listen to or accept the views of other people.

narwhal /nar-wuhl/ • n. a small Arctic whale, the male of which has a long spiral tusk.
– ORIGIN Danish *narhval*.

NASA /na-suh/ • abbrev. (in the US) National Aeronautics and Space Administration.

nasal • adj. relating to the nose.
– DERIVATIVES **nasally** adv.
– ORIGIN Latin *nasus* 'nose'.

nascent /nay-suhnt/ • adj. just coming into existence and beginning to develop.
– ORIGIN Latin *nasci* 'be born'.

nasturtium /nuh-ster-shuhm/ • n. a garden plant with round leaves and orange, yellow, or red flowers.
– ORIGIN Latin.

nasty • adj. (**nastier, nastiest**)
1 unpleasant or disgusting. **2** spiteful, violent, or bad-tempered. **3** dangerous or serious: *a nasty bang on the head*.
– DERIVATIVES **nastily** adv. **nastiness** n.

natal /nay-t'l/ • adj. relating to the place or time of your birth.
– ORIGIN Latin *natalis*.

nation • n. a large group of people sharing the same culture, language, or history, and inhabiting a particular state or area.
– ORIGIN Latin.

national • adj. **1** relating to a nation. **2** owned, controlled, or financially supported by the state. • n. a citizen of a particular country.
– DERIVATIVES **nationally** adv.

national curriculum • n. a curriculum of study laid down to be taught in state schools.

national debt • n. the total amount of money which a country's government has borrowed.

national grid • n. Brit. the network of high-voltage power lines between major power stations.

National Insurance • n. (in the UK) a system of payments by employees and employers to provide health care or financial help for people who are sick, unemployed, or retired.

nationalism • n. **1** patriotic feeling, often to an excessive degree. **2** belief in political independence for a particular country.
– DERIVATIVES **nationalist** n. & adj. **nationalistic** adj.

nationality • n. (pl. **nationalities**) **1** the status of belonging to a particular nation. **2** an ethnic group forming a part of one or more political nations.

nationalize (or **nationalise**)

• v. (**nationalizes, nationalizing, nationalized**) transfer a private industry or business to state ownership or control.
– DERIVATIVES **nationalization** n.

national park • n. an area of countryside protected by the state for the preservation of wildlife and for public enjoyment.

national service • n. a period of compulsory service in the armed forces during peacetime.

nationwide • adj. & adv. throughout the whole nation.

native • n. **1** a person born in a specified place. **2** a local inhabitant. **3** an animal or plant that lives or grows naturally in a place. **4** dated, offens. a non-white original inhabitant of a country as regarded by Europeans. • adj. **1** associated with a person's place of birth. **2** (of a plant or animal) occurring naturally in a place. **3** relating to the original inhabitants of a place. **4** in a person's character: *native wit*.
– ORIGIN Latin *nativus*.

Native American • n. a member of any of the original inhabitants of North and South America and the Caribbean Islands. • adj. relating to Native Americans.

native speaker • n. a person who has spoken a particular language from earliest childhood.

nativity • n. (pl. **nativities**) **1** (**the Nativity**) the birth of Jesus. **2** formal a person's birth.

NATO (also **Nato**) • abbrev. North Atlantic Treaty Organization.

natter informal • v. (**natters, nattering, nattered**) chat for a long time. • n. a long chat.

natterjack toad • n. a small toad with a bright yellow stripe down its back.
– ORIGIN perh. from **NATTER** + **JACK**.

natty • adj. (**nattier, nattiest**) informal smart and fashionable.
– DERIVATIVES **nattily** adv.
– ORIGIN perh. from **NEAT**.

natural • adj. **1** existing in or obtained from nature; not made or caused by humans. **2** in accordance with nature; normal: *a natural death*. **3** born with a particular skill or quality: *a natural leader*. **4** relaxed and unaffected. **5** (of a parent or child) related by blood. **6** Music (of a note) not sharp or flat. • n. **1** a person with an inborn gift or talent. **2** an off-white colour. **3** Music a natural note or a sign (♮) indicating one.
– DERIVATIVES **naturalness** n.

natural gas • n. gas consisting largely of

methane, occurring underground and used as fuel.

natural history • n. the scientific study of animals or plants.

naturalism • n. an artistic or literary style based on the highly detailed and realistic description of daily life.

naturalist • n. an expert in or student of natural history.

naturalistic • adj. **1** imitating real life or nature. **2** based on the theory of naturalism in art or literature.
– DERIVATIVES **naturalistically** adv.

naturalize (or **naturalise**)
• v. (**naturalizes, naturalizing, naturalized**) **1** make a foreigner a citizen of a country. **2** establish a plant or animal in a region where it is not native.
– DERIVATIVES **naturalization** (or **naturalisation**) n.

natural law • n. **1** a group of unchanging moral principles regarded as a basis for all human behaviour. **2** an observable law relating to natural phenomena.

naturally • adv. **1** in a natural way. **2** of course.

natural selection • n. the evolutionary process by which organisms that are better adapted to their environment tend to survive and produce more offspring.

nature • n. **1** the physical world, including plants, animals, the landscape, natural phenomena such as the weather, and all other things not made by people. **2** the inborn qualities or characteristics of a person or thing. **3** a kind, sort, or class: *topics of a religious nature*.
– ORIGIN Latin *natura* 'birth, nature'.

nature reserve • n. an area of land managed so as to preserve its plants, animals, and physical features.

nature trail • n. a signposted path through the countryside designed to draw attention to natural features.

naturism • n. esp. Brit. nudism.
– DERIVATIVES **naturist** n. & adj.

naturopathy /nay-chuh-**rop**-uh-thi/ • n. a system of alternative medicine involving the treatment or prevention of diseases by diet, exercise, and massage rather than by using drugs.
– DERIVATIVES **naturopath** n. **naturopathic** adj.

naught • pron. old use nothing.
– ORIGIN Old English.

naughty • adj. (**naughtier, naughtiest**) **1** (of a child) disobedient; badly behaved. **2** informal mildly indecent.

– DERIVATIVES **naughtily** adv. **naughtiness** n.
– ORIGIN from NAUGHT.

nausea /naw-zi-uh/ • n. **1** a feeling of sickness with the need to vomit. **2** disgust.
– ORIGIN Greek *nausia* 'seasickness'.

nauseate • v. (**nauseates, nauseating, nauseated**) make someone feel sick or disgusted.

nauseous • adj. **1** feeling sick. **2** causing a feeling of sickness.

nautical • adj. relating to sailors or navigation; maritime.
– DERIVATIVES **nautically** adv.
– ORIGIN Greek *nautikos*.

nautical mile • n. a unit used in measuring distances at sea, equal to 1,852 metres (approximately 2,025 yards).

nautilus /naw-ti-luhss/ • n. (pl. **nautiluses**) a swimming mollusc with a spiral shell and short tentacles around the mouth.
– ORIGIN Greek *nautilos* 'sailor'.

naval • adj. relating to a navy or navies.
– ORIGIN Latin *navalis*.

nave • n. the central part of a church.
– ORIGIN Latin *navis* 'ship'.

navel • n. the small hollow in the centre of a person's belly where the umbilical cord was cut at birth.
– ORIGIN Old English.

navel-gazing • n. narrow concern with yourself or a single issue.

navigable • adj. wide and deep enough to be used by boats and ships.

navigate • v. (**navigates, navigating, navigated**) **1** plan and direct the route of a ship, aircraft, or other form of transport. **2** guide a boat or vehicle over a route. **3** sail or travel over water or land.
– DERIVATIVES **navigator** n.
– ORIGIN Latin *navigare* 'to sail'.

navigation • n. **1** the activity of navigating. **2** the movement of ships.
– DERIVATIVES **navigational** adj.

navvy • n. (pl. **navvies**) Brit. dated a labourer employed in building a road, canal, or railway.
– ORIGIN from navigator (see NAVIGATE) in the former sense 'builder of a *navigation*' (a dialect word for a canal).

navy • n. (pl. **navies**) **1** the branch of a country's armed services which fights at sea. **2** (also **navy blue**) a dark blue colour.
– ORIGIN Latin *navis* 'ship'.

nay • adv. **1** or rather: *it will take months, nay years*. **2** old use or dialect no.
– ORIGIN Old Norse.

n

Nazi /naht-si/ • n. (pl. **Nazis**) hist. a member of the far-right National Socialist German Workers' Party.
– DERIVATIVES **Nazism** n.
– ORIGIN German, from the pronunciation of *Nati-* in *Nationalsozialist*.

NB • abbrev. note well.
– ORIGIN from Latin *nota bene*.

Nb • symb. the chemical element niobium.

NCO • abbrev. non-commissioned officer.

Nd • symb. the chemical element neodymium.

NE • abbrev. north-east or north-eastern.

Ne • symb. the chemical element neon.

Neanderthal /ni-an-der-tahl/
• n. **1** (also **Neanderthal man**) an extinct human living in Europe between about 120,000–35,000 years ago. **2** informal a man who is uncivilized or who holds very old-fashioned views.
– ORIGIN named after a region in Germany where remains of Neanderthal man were found.

neap /neep/ (also **neap tide**) • n. a tide just after the first or third quarters of the moon when there is least difference between high and low water.
– ORIGIN Old English.

Neapolitan /ni-uh-pol-i-tuhn/ • n. a person from the Italian city of Naples.
• adj. relating to Naples.

near • adv. **1** at or to a short distance in space or time. **2** almost: *a near perfect fit*.
• prep. (also **near to**) **1** at or to a short distance in space or time from. **2** close to: *she was near to death*. • adj. **1** at a short distance away in space or time. **2** close to being: *a near disaster*. **3** closely related.
• v. come near to; approach.
– DERIVATIVES **nearness** n.
– ORIGIN Old Norse.

nearby • adj. & adv. not far away.

Near East • n. the countries of SW Asia between the Mediterranean and India (including the Middle East).

nearly • adv. very close to; almost.
– PHRASES **not nearly** far from.

near miss • n. **1** a narrowly avoided collision or accident. **2** a bomb or shot that just misses its target.

nearside • n. Brit. the side of a vehicle nearest the kerb.

nearsighted • adj. esp. N. Amer. short-sighted.

neat • adj. **1** tidy or carefully arranged. **2** clever but simple: *a neat solution to the labour shortage*. **3** (of a drink of spirits) not diluted. **4** N. Amer. informal excellent.
– DERIVATIVES **neatly** adv. **neatness** n.
– ORIGIN French *net* 'clean'.

neaten • v. make something neat.

neath • prep. literary beneath.

nebula /neb-yuu-luh/ • n. (pl. **nebulae**
/neb-yuu-lee/ or **nebulas**) a cloud of gas or dust in outer space.
– DERIVATIVES **nebular** adj.
– ORIGIN Latin, 'mist'.

nebulizer /neb-yuu-ly-zer/ (or **nebuliser**) • n. a device for producing a fine spray of liquid, used for inhaling a medicinal drug.

nebulous • adj. not clearly defined; vague: *nebulous concepts*.

necessarily • adv. as a necessary result; unavoidably.

necessary • adj. **1** needing to be done or present; essential: *major changes are necessary*. **2** that must be; unavoidable: *a necessary result*. • n. (**necessaries**) the basic requirements of life, such as food.
– ORIGIN Latin *necessarius*.

> ☑ Remember that **necessary** and related words are spelled with one **c** and a double **s**.

necessitate • v. (**necessitates, necessitating, necessitated**) **1** make necessary: *the cut necessitated eighteen stitches*. **2** cause someone to have to do something.

necessity • n. (pl. **necessities**) **1** the state of being needed or unavoidable. **2** a thing that is essential. **3** a situation that requires a particular course of action: *political necessity forced him to consider it*.

neck • n. **1** the part of the body connecting the head to the rest of the body. **2** a narrow connecting or end part, such as the part of a bottle near the mouth. **3** the length of a horse's head and neck as a measure of its lead in a race. • v. informal kiss and caress passionately.
– PHRASES **neck and neck** level in a race or other competition. **neck of the woods** informal a particular place.
– ORIGIN Old English, 'nape of the neck'.

neckerchief • n. a square of cloth worn round the neck.

necklace • n. an ornamental chain or string of beads, jewels, or links worn round the neck.

necklet • n. a close-fitting rigid ornament worn around the neck.

neckline • n. the edge of a dress or top at or below the neck.

necktie • n. N. Amer. or dated a tie worn around the neck.

necromancy /nek-ruh-man-si/
• n. **1** prediction of the future by supposedly communicating with dead people. **2** witchcraft or black magic.
– DERIVATIVES **necromancer** n. **necromantic** adj.
– ORIGIN from Greek *nekros* 'corpse' + *manteia* 'divination'.

necrophilia /nek-ruh-fil-i-uh/
• n. sexual intercourse with or attraction towards corpses.
– DERIVATIVES **necrophiliac** n.

necropolis /ne-krop-uh-liss/ • n. a cemetery.
– ORIGIN from Greek *nekros* 'corpse' + *polis* 'city'.

necrosis /ne-kroh-siss/ • n. Med. the death of cells in the body due to disease, injury, or failure of the blood supply.
– DERIVATIVES **necrotic** adj.

nectar • n. **1** a sugary fluid produced by flowers and made into honey by bees. **2** (in Greek and Roman mythology) the drink of the gods.
– ORIGIN Greek *nektar*.

nectarine /nek-tuh-reen/ • n. a variety of peach with smooth skin and rich firm flesh.
– ORIGIN from NECTAR.

née /nay/ • adj. born (used in giving a married woman's maiden name): *Mrs. Hargreaves, née Liddell.*
– ORIGIN French.

need • v. **1** want something because it is essential or very important. **2** used to express what should or must be done: *need I say more?* • n. **1** a situation in which something is necessary or must be done: *I was in need of a haircut.* **2** a thing that is needed. **3** a state of being poor or in great difficulty.
– ORIGIN Old English.

needful • adj. formal necessary.

needle • n. **1** a very thin pointed piece of metal with a hole or eye for thread at the blunter end, used in sewing. **2** a long thin metal or plastic rod with a pointed end, used in knitting. **3** the pointed hollow end of a hypodermic syringe. **4** a stylus used to play records. **5** a thin pointer on a dial, compass, etc. **6** the thin, stiff leaf of a fir or pine tree.
• v. (**needles, needling, needled**) informal deliberately annoy someone.
– ORIGIN Old English.

needlecord • n. Brit. corduroy fabric with narrow ridges.

needlepoint • n. closely stitched embroidery worked over canvas.

needless • adj. unnecessary; avoidable.
– DERIVATIVES **needlessly** adv.

needlewoman • n. (pl. **needlewomen**) a woman who has particular sewing skills.

needlework • n. sewing or embroidery.

needn't • contr. need not.

needy • adj. (**needier, neediest**) very poor.
– DERIVATIVES **neediness** n.

ne'er /nair/ • contr. literary or dialect never.

ne'er-do-well • n. a person who is lazy or useless.

nefarious /ni-fair-i-uhss/ • adj. wicked or criminal.
– ORIGIN Latin *nefas* 'wrong'.

negate /ni-gayt/ • v. (**negates, negating, negated**) **1** prevent from having an effect: *alcohol negates the effects of the drug.* **2** deny that something exists.
– ORIGIN Latin *negare*.

negation • n. **1** the denial of something. **2** the lack or opposite of something: *evil is not merely the negation of goodness.*

negative • adj. **1** showing the absence rather than the presence of particular features: *a negative test result.* **2** expressing denial, disagreement, or refusal. **3** not hopeful or favourable. **4** (of a quantity) less than zero. **5** relating to the kind of electric charge carried by electrons. **6** (of a photograph) showing light and shade or colours reversed from those of the original. **7** Grammar containing a word such as *not, no,* or *never.* • n. **1** a negative word or statement. **2** a negative photograph, from which positive prints may be made.
– DERIVATIVES **negatively** adv. **negativity** n.

neglect • v. **1** fail to give proper care or attention to. **2** fail to do something. • n. the action of neglecting or the state of being neglected: *animals dying through neglect.*
– ORIGIN Latin *neglegere* 'disregard'.

neglectful • adj. failing to give proper care or attention.

negligee /neg-li-zhay/ • n. a woman's light, flimsy dressing gown.
– ORIGIN French, 'given little thought'.

negligence • n. failure to give proper care and attention.
– DERIVATIVES **negligent** adj.

negligible /neg-li-juh-b'l/ • adj. so small or unimportant as to be not worth considering.
– DERIVATIVES **negligibly** adv.
– ORIGIN French *négliger* 'to neglect'.

negotiable • adj. able to be changed after discussion: *the price was not negotiable.*

negotiate • v. (**negotiates, negotiating, negotiated**) **1** try to reach an agreement by discussion. **2** bring about by discussion. **3** find a way over or through an obstacle or difficult route.
– DERIVATIVES **negotiator** n.
– ORIGIN Latin *negotiari* 'do in the course of business'.

negotiation (also **negotiations**) • n. discussion aimed at reaching an agreement.

Negress /nee-gress/ •n. dated, offens. a woman or girl of black African origin.

Negro •n. (pl. **Negroes**) a member of a group of black peoples that originated in Africa.
– ORIGIN Latin *niger* 'black'.

> USAGE: The terms **Negro** and **Negress** are now thought to be old-fashioned and offensive; you should use **black** instead.

neigh •n. a high-pitched cry made by a horse. •v. make a neigh.

neighbour (US **neighbor**) •n. 1 a person living next door to or very near to another. 2 a person or place next to or near another. •v. (usu. as adj. **neighbouring**) be next to or very near something.
– DERIVATIVES **neighbourly** adj.
– ORIGIN Old English.

neighbourhood (US **neighborhood**) •n. 1 a district within a town or city. 2 the area surrounding a place, person, or object.
– PHRASES **in the neighbourhood of** about; approximately.

neighbourhood watch •n. a scheme in which local groups of householders watch each other's homes to discourage burglary and other crimes.

neither /ny-ther, nee-ther/ •det. & pron. not either. •adv. 1 used to show that a negative statement is true of two things: *I am neither a liberal nor a conservative.* 2 used to show that a negative statement is also true of something else: *he didn't remember, and neither did I.*
– ORIGIN Old English.

> ☑ **neither** is spelled with the e before the *i*.

nematode /nem-uh-tohd/ •n. a worm of a group with slender, cylindrical bodies.
– ORIGIN Greek *nēma* 'thread'.

nemesis /nem-i-siss/ •n. (pl. **nemeses** /nem-i-seez/) a means of punishment or downfall that is deserved or unavoidable.
– ORIGIN Greek, 'retribution'.

neo- /nee-oh/ •comb. form 1 new: *neologism.* 2 a new or revived form of: *neoclassicism.*
– ORIGIN Greek *neos.*

neoclassical (also **neoclassic**) •adj. relating to the revival of a classical style in the arts.
– DERIVATIVES **neoclassicism** n.

neodymium /nee-oh-dim-i-uhm/ •n. a silvery-white metallic element.
– ORIGIN from **NEO-** + Greek *didumos* 'twin'.

Neolithic /nee-uh-lith-ik/ •adj. relating

to the later part of the Stone Age.
– ORIGIN from **NEO-** + Greek *lithos* 'stone'.

neologism /ni-ol-uh-ji-z'm/ •n. a new word or expression.
– ORIGIN from **NEO-** + Greek *logos* 'word'.

neon •n. an inert gas that glows when electricity is passed through it, used in fluorescent lighting.
– ORIGIN Greek, 'something new'.

neonatal •adj. relating to newborn children.

neophyte /nee-uh-fyt/ •n. 1 a person who is new to a subject, skill, or belief. 2 a novice in a religious order, or a newly ordained priest.
– ORIGIN Greek *neophutos* 'newly planted'.

neoprene /nee-oh-preen/ •n. a synthetic substance resembling rubber.

Nepalese /ne-puh-leez/ •n. a person from Nepal. •adj. relating to Nepal.

Nepali /ni-paw-li/ •n. (pl. **Nepali** or **Nepalis**) 1 a person from Nepal. 2 the language of Nepal.

nephew •n. a son of a person's brother or sister.
– ORIGIN Latin *nepos* 'grandson, nephew'.

nephritis /ni-fry-tiss/ •n. inflammation of the kidneys.
– ORIGIN Greek *nephros* 'kidney'.

nepotism /nep-uh-ti-z'm/ •n. favouritism shown to relatives or friends, especially by giving them jobs.
– ORIGIN Italian *nipote* 'nephew'.

Neptune •n. a planet of the solar system, eighth in order from the sun.

neptunium /nep-tyoo-ni-uhm/ •n. a rare radioactive metallic element.
– ORIGIN from **NEPTUNE**.

nerd •n. informal a person who is excessively interested in something and finds it difficult to get on with people.

nerve •n. 1 a fibre or bundle of fibres in the body that transmits impulses of sensation between the brain or spinal cord and other parts of the body. 2 (**nerves** or **your nerve**) steadiness and courage in a demanding situation: *the journey tested her nerves to the full.* 3 (**nerves**) nervousness. 4 informal cheeky boldness. •v. (**nerves, nerving, nerved**) (**nerve yourself**) brace yourself for a demanding situation.
– PHRASES **get on someone's nerves** informal irritate someone.
– ORIGIN Latin *nervus.*

nerve cell •n. a neuron.

nerve centre •n. 1 the control centre of an organization or operation. 2 a group of connected nerve cells performing a particular function.

nerve gas • n. a poisonous gas which affects the nervous system.

nerveless • adj. **1** lacking strength or feeling. **2** confident.

nerve-racking (also **nerve-wracking**) • adj. stressful or frightening.

nervous • adj. **1** easily frightened or worried. **2** anxious. **3** relating to the nerves.
– DERIVATIVES **nervously** adv. **nervousness** n.

nervous breakdown • n. a period of mental illness resulting from severe depression or stress.

nervous system • n. the network of nerves which transmits nerve impulses between parts of the body.

nervy • adj. (**nervier**, **nerviest**) Brit. nervous or tense.

ness • n. a headland.
– ORIGIN Old English.

-ness • suffix forming nouns referring to: **1** a state or condition: *liveliness*. **2** something in a certain state: *wilderness*.
– ORIGIN Old English.

nest • n. **1** a structure made by a bird for laying eggs and sheltering its young. **2** a place where an animal or insect breeds or shelters. **3** a set of similar objects that are designed to fit inside each other. • v. use or build a nest.
– ORIGIN Old English.

nest egg • n. a sum of money saved for the future.

nestle • v. (**nestles**, **nestling**, **nestled**) **1** settle comfortably within or against something: *the baby deer nestled in her arms*. **2** (of a place) lie in a sheltered position.
– ORIGIN Old English.

nestling • n. a bird that is too young to leave the nest.

net¹ • n. **1** a material made of strands of twine or cord that are woven or knotted together to form small open squares. **2** a piece or structure of net for catching fish, surrounding a goal, etc. **3** a light fabric with a very open weave. **4** a way of catching someone: *unregistered boats slipped through the net*. **5** (**the Net**) the Internet. • v. (**nets**, **netting**, **netted**) **1** catch something in a net. **2** catch or get something: *customs officials netted large hauls of drugs*.
– ORIGIN Old English.

net² (Brit. also **nett**) • adj. **1** (of a sum of money) remaining after tax, discounts, or expenses have been deducted. **2** (of a weight) not including that of the packaging. **3** (of an effect or result)

overall. • v. (**nets**, **netting**, **netted**) gain a sum of money as clear profit.
– ORIGIN French *net* 'neat'.

netball • n. a team game in which goals are scored by throwing a ball through a net hanging from a hoop.

nether /neth-er/ • adj. lower in position.
– ORIGIN Old English.

nether regions (also **netherworld**) • pl. n. hell.

net profit • n. the actual profit after working expenses have been paid.

nett • adj. & v. Brit. = NET².

netting • n. material made of net.

nettle • n. a plant with leaves that are covered with stinging hairs. • v. (**nettles**, **nettling**, **nettled**) annoy someone.
– PHRASES **grasp the nettle** Brit. tackle a difficulty boldly.
– ORIGIN Old English.

network • n. **1** an arrangement of horizontal and vertical lines that cross each other. **2** a system of railways, roads, etc., that cross or connect with each other. **3** a group of radio or television stations that connect to broadcast a programme at the same time. **4** a number of interconnected computers, operations, etc. **5** a group of people who keep in contact with each other to exchange information. • v. keep in contact with other people to exchange information.
– DERIVATIVES **networker** n.

neural /nyoor-uhl/ • adj. relating to a nerve or the nervous system.

neuralgia /nyoo-ral-juh/ • n. intense pain along a nerve in the head or face.
– DERIVATIVES **neuralgic** adj.

neuro- • comb. form relating to nerves or the nervous system: *neurosurgery*.
– ORIGIN Greek *neuron* 'nerve, sinew'.

neurology • n. the branch of medicine and biology concerned with the nervous system.
– DERIVATIVES **neurological** adj. **neurologist** n.

neuron (also **neurone**) • n. a specialized cell that transmits nerve impulses.
– ORIGIN Greek, 'nerve, sinew'.

neurosis /nyoo-roh-siss/ • n. (pl. **neuroses** /nyoo-roh-seez/) a mild mental illness involving symptoms such as depression, anxiety, or obsessive behaviour.

neurosurgery • n. surgery performed on the nervous system.

neurotic • adj. **1** relating to neurosis. **2** informal excessively sensitive, anxious, or obsessive.
– DERIVATIVES **neurotically** adv.

neurotransmitter • n. a chemical substance released from a nerve fibre and bringing about the transfer of an impulse to another nerve, muscle, etc.

neuter • adj. **1** Grammar (of a noun) not masculine or feminine. **2** having no sexual or reproductive organs.
• v. (**neuters, neutering, neutered**) **1** operate on an animal so that it cannot produce young. **2** take away the power of: *their only purpose is to neuter local democracy.*
– ORIGIN Latin, 'neither'.

neutral • adj. **1** not supporting either side in a dispute or war. **2** lacking noticeable or strong qualities: *his tone was neutral, without sentiment.* **3** Chem. neither acid nor alkaline; having a pH of about 7. **4** electrically neither positive nor negative. • n. **1** a state or person that does not take sides during a dispute or war. **2** a position of a gear mechanism in which the engine is disconnected from the driven parts.
– DERIVATIVES **neutrality** n. **neutrally** adv.
– ORIGIN Latin *neutralis* 'of neuter gender'.

neutralize (or **neutralise**)
• v. (**neutralizes, neutralizing, neutralized**) **1** stop something from having an effect. **2** make something chemically neutral.
– DERIVATIVES **neutralization** (or **neutralisation**) n.

neutrino /nyoo-tree-noh/ • n. (pl. **neutrinos**) a subatomic particle with a mass close to zero and no electric charge.
– ORIGIN Italian.

neutron • n. a subatomic particle of about the same mass as a proton but without an electric charge.
– ORIGIN from **NEUTRAL**.

neutron bomb • n. a nuclear weapon that produces large numbers of neutrons, killing people but doing little harm to property.

never • adv. **1** not ever. **2** not at all.
– PHRASES **the never-never** Brit. informal hire purchase.
– ORIGIN Old English.

nevermore • adv. literary never again.

nevertheless • adv. in spite of that.

nevus • n. (pl. **nevi**) US = **NAEVUS**.

new • adj. **1** made, introduced, discovered, or experienced recently: *his new book.* **2** not used or owned by anyone before. **3** (**new to/at**) not familiar with or experienced at: *I'm new to Canberra.* **4** different from a recent previous one. **5** better than before; renewed or reformed. • adv. newly.
– DERIVATIVES **newness** n.

– ORIGIN Old English.

New Age • n. a movement concerned with alternative approaches to traditional Western religion, culture, medicine, etc.

newborn • adj. recently born.

newcomer • n. **1** a person who has recently arrived. **2** a person who is new to an activity or situation.

newel /nyoo-uhl/ • n. **1** (also **newel post**) the post at the top or bottom of a stair rail. **2** the central supporting pillar of a winding staircase.
– ORIGIN Old French *nouel* 'knob'.

newfangled • adj. derog. newly developed and unfamiliar.
– ORIGIN from dialect *newfangle* 'liking what is new'.

Newfoundland /nyoo-fuhnd-luhnd/ • n. a very large breed of dog with a thick coarse coat.
– ORIGIN named after *Newfoundland* in Canada.

newly • adv. **1** recently. **2** again; afresh: *confidence for the newly single.*

newly-wed • n. a recently married person.

new man • n. a man who rejects traditional male attitudes, often taking on childcare and housework.

new maths • n. a system of teaching mathematics to children, with emphasis on investigation by them and on set theory.

new moon • n. the phase of the moon when it first appears as a thin crescent.

news • n. **1** new information about recent events. **2** (**the news**) a broadcast or published news report. **3** (**news to**) informal information not previously known to someone.

news agency • n. an organization that collects and distributes news items to newspapers or broadcasters.

newsagent • n. Brit. a shopkeeper who sells newspapers, magazines, etc.

newscast • n. N. Amer. a broadcast news report.
– DERIVATIVES **newscaster** n.

news conference • n. N. Amer. a press conference.

newsflash • n. a brief item of important news, interrupting other radio or television programmes.

newsgroup • n. a group of Internet users who exchange email on a subject of shared interest.

newsletter • n. a bulletin issued periodically to the members of a society or organization.

newspaper • n. a daily or weekly publication containing news, articles, and advertisements.

newspeak • n. deliberately misleading and indirect language, used by politicians.
– ORIGIN from George Orwell's novel *Nineteen Eighty-Four*.

newsprint • n. cheap, low-quality printing paper used for newspapers.

newsreader • n. Brit. a person who reads the news on radio or television.

newsreel • n. a short cinema film of news and current affairs.

newsroom • n. the area in a newspaper or broadcasting office where news is processed.

newsworthy • adj. important enough to be mentioned as news.

newsy • adj. informal full of news.

newt • n. a small animal with a thin body and a long tail, that can live in water or on land.
– ORIGIN Old English.

New Testament • n. the second part of the Christian Bible, recording the life and teachings of Jesus and his earliest followers.

newton • n. Physics the SI unit of force.
– ORIGIN named after the English scientist Sir Isaac *Newton*.

new town • n. a town planned and built in an undeveloped or rural area.

New World • n. North and South America.

new year • n. the calendar year that has just begun or is about to begin, following 31 December.

New Year's Day • n. 1 January.

New Year's Eve • n. 31 December.

New Zealander • n. a person from New Zealand.

next • adj. 1 coming immediately after the present one in time, space, or order. 2 (of a day of the week) nearest (or the nearest but one) after the present. • adv. 1 immediately afterwards. 2 following in the specified order: *Joe was the next oldest after Martin*. • n. the next person or thing.
– PHRASES **next of kin** a person's closest living relative or relatives. **next to** 1 beside. 2 following in order or importance. 3 almost. **the next world** (in some religious beliefs) the place where you go after death.
– ORIGIN Old English.

next door • adv. & adj. in or to the next house or room.

nexus /nek-suhss/ • n. (pl. **nexus** or **nexuses**) a connection or series of connections: *the nexus between industry and political power*.
– ORIGIN Latin, 'a binding together'.

NGO • abbrev. non-governmental organization.

NHS • abbrev. (in the UK) National Health Service.

NI • abbrev. 1 (in the UK) National Insurance. 2 Northern Ireland.

Ni • symb. the chemical element nickel.

niacin /ny-uh-sin/ • n. = NICOTINIC ACID.

nib • n. the pointed end part of a pen.
– ORIGIN prob. from Dutch *nib* or German *nibbe* 'beak, nose'.

nibble • v. (**nibbles, nibbling, nibbled**) 1 take small bites out of something. 2 bite something gently. • n. 1 a small bite of food. 2 (**nibbles**) informal small savoury snacks.
– ORIGIN prob. German or Dutch.

nibs • n. (**his nibs**) informal a mock title used to refer to a man who thinks he is important.

Nicam /ny-kam/ • n. a digital system used in British television to provide video signals with high-quality stereo sound.
– ORIGIN from *near instantaneously companded* (i.e. compressed and expanded) *audio multiplex*.

Nicaraguan /ni-kuh-**rag**-yuu-uhn, ni-kuh-**rag**-wuhn/ • n. a person from Nicaragua in Central America. • adj. relating to Nicaragua.

nice • adj. 1 pleasant, enjoyable, or attractive. 2 good-natured; kind. 3 involving a very fine detail or difference: *a nice distinction*.
– DERIVATIVES **nicely** adv. **niceness** n.
– ORIGIN Latin *nescius* 'ignorant'.

nicety • n. (pl. **niceties**) 1 a fine detail or difference. 2 accuracy or preciseness.

niche /neesh, nich/ • n. 1 a shallow recess in a wall, in which an ornament may be displayed. 2 (**your niche**) a position or role that suits you: *he found his niche as a writer*. 3 a group of people seen as a potential market for a product: *targeting the urban-youth niche*.
– ORIGIN French.

nick • n. 1 a small cut. 2 (**the nick**) Brit. informal prison or a police station. 3 Brit. informal condition: *the car's in good nick*. • v. 1 make a nick or nicks in something. 2 Brit. informal steal something. 3 Brit. informal arrest someone.
– PHRASES **in the nick of time** only just in time.

nickel • n. 1 a silvery-white metallic element used in alloys. 2 N. Amer. informal a five-cent coin.
– ORIGIN German *Kupfernickel*, the ore from which nickel was first obtained.

nicker • n. (pl. **nicker**) Brit. informal a pound sterling.

nickname •n. an informal, often amusing, name for a person or thing. •v. (**nicknames, nicknaming, nicknamed**) give a nickname to.
– ORIGIN from former *eke-name* 'additional name'.

nicotine •n. a poisonous oily liquid found in tobacco.
– ORIGIN named after Jaques *Nicot*, who introduced tobacco to France.

nicotinic acid •n. a vitamin of the B group, found in foods such as milk and meat.

nictitating membrane •n. a whitish membrane forming an inner eyelid in birds, reptiles, and some mammals.
– ORIGIN Latin *nictare* 'to blink'.

niece •n. a daughter of a person's brother or sister.
– ORIGIN Old French.

niff Brit. informal •n. an unpleasant smell. •v. smell unpleasant.
– ORIGIN perh. from SNIFF.

nifty •adj. (**niftier, niftiest**) informal particularly good, fast, or useful.

Nigerian /ny-jeer-i-uhn/ •n. a person from Nigeria. •adj. relating to Nigeria.

niggardly •adj. not generous; mean.
– ORIGIN Scandinavian.

nigger •n. offens. a black person.
– ORIGIN Spanish *negro* 'black'.

niggle •v. (**niggles, niggling, niggled**) worry or annoy someone slightly. •n. a minor worry or criticism.
– DERIVATIVES **niggly** adj.
– ORIGIN prob. Scandinavian.

nigh •adv., prep., & adj. literary or old use near.
– ORIGIN Old English.

night •n. **1** the time from sunset to sunrise. **2** an evening until bedtime.
– ORIGIN Old English.

nightcap •n. **1** a hot or alcoholic drink taken at bedtime. **2** hist. a cap worn in bed.

nightclub •n. a club that is open at night, with a bar and music.

nightdress (also **nightgown**) •n. a light, loose garment worn by a woman or girl in bed.

nightfall •n. dusk.

nightie •n. informal a nightdress.

nightingale •n. a small brownish thrush with a tuneful song, often heard at night.
– ORIGIN Old English.

nightjar •n. a bird with grey-brown plumage and a distinctive call, active at night.

nightlife •n. social activities or entertainment available at night.

night light •n. a lamp or candle providing a dim light during the night.

nightly •adj. & adv. happening every night.

nightmare •n. **1** a frightening or unpleasant dream. **2** a very unpleasant experience.
– DERIVATIVES **nightmarish** adj.
– ORIGIN Old English, 'male demon believed to have sex with sleeping women'.

night owl •n. informal a person who enjoys staying up late at night.

night school •n. classes provided in the evening for people who work during the day.

nightshirt •n. a long, loose shirt worn in bed.

nightspot •n. informal a nightclub.

nightwatchman •n. (pl. **nightwatchmen**) a person who guards a building at night.

nihilism /ny-hi-li-z'm/ •n. the belief that nothing has any value, especially religious and moral principles.
– DERIVATIVES •n. **nihilist** n. **nihilistic** adj.
– ORIGIN Latin *nihil* 'nothing'.

nil •n. nothing; zero.
– ORIGIN Latin *nihil*.

nimble •adj. (**nimbler, nimblest**) quick and agile in movement or thought.
– DERIVATIVES **nimbly** adv.
– ORIGIN Old English.

nimbus /nim-buhss/ •n. (pl. **nimbi** /nim-by/ or **nimbuses**) a large grey rain cloud.
– ORIGIN Latin.

Nimby /nim-bi/ •n. (pl. **Nimbys**) informal a person who objects to the siting of unpleasant developments in their neighbourhood.
– ORIGIN from *not in my back yard*.

nincompoop /ning-kuhm-poop/ •n. a stupid person.

nine •cardinal number one less than ten; 9. (Roman numeral: **ix** or **IX**.)
– PHRASES **to** (or Brit. **up to**) **the nines** to a great or elaborate extent: *the women were dressed to the nines.*
– ORIGIN Old English.

ninepins •n. the traditional form of the game of skittles, using nine pins.

nineteen •cardinal number one more than eighteen; 19. (Roman numeral: **xix** or **XIX**.)
– DERIVATIVES **nineteenth** ordinal number.

ninety •cardinal number (pl. **nineties**) ten less than one hundred; 90. (Roman numeral: **xc** or **XC**.)
– DERIVATIVES **ninetieth** ordinal number.

ninny •n. (pl. **ninnies**) informal a foolish and weak person.
– ORIGIN perh. from INNOCENT.

ninth •ordinal number **1** that is number nine in a sequence; 9th. **2** (**a ninth/one ninth**) each of nine equal parts into which something is divided. **3** a musical interval spanning nine consecutive notes in a scale.

niobium /ny-oh-bi-uhm/ •n. a silver-grey metallic element.
– ORIGIN from *Niobe*, daughter of Tantalus in Greek mythology.

nip¹ •v. (**nips, nipping, nipped**) **1** pinch or bite sharply. **2** Brit. informal go quickly. •n. **1** a sharp bite or pinch. **2** a feeling of sharp coldness.
– PHRASES **nip something in the bud** stop something at an early stage.
– ORIGIN prob. German or Dutch.

nip² •n. a small quantity or sip of spirits.
– ORIGIN prob. from former *nipperkin*.

nipper •n. informal a child.

nipple •n. **1** a small projection in the centre of each breast, containing (in females) the outlets of the organs that produce milk. **2** a small projection on a machine from which oil or other fluid is dispensed.
– ORIGIN perh. from Scots and northern English *neb* 'nose, beak'.

nippy •adj. (**nippier, nippiest**) informal **1** quick; nimble. **2** chilly.

nirvana /neer-vah-nuh/ •n. (in Buddhism) a state of perfect happiness in which there is no suffering or desire, and no sense of self.
– ORIGIN Sanskrit.

Nissen hut /niss-uhn/ •n. Brit. a tunnel-shaped hut of corrugated iron.
– ORIGIN named after the British engineer Peter N. *Nissen*.

nit •n. informal **1** the egg of a human head louse. **2** Brit. a stupid person.
– ORIGIN Old English.

nit-picking •n. informal petty criticism.

nitrate /ny-trayt/ •n. a salt or ester of nitric acid.

nitric acid •n. a very corrosive acid.

nitrify /ny-tri-fy/ •v. (**nitrifies, nitrifying, nitrified**) convert ammonia or another nitrogen compound into nitrites or nitrates.
– DERIVATIVES **nitrification** n.

nitrite /ny-tryt/ •n. a salt or ester of nitrous acid.

nitrogen /ny-truh-juhn/ •n. a gas forming about 78 per cent of the earth's atmosphere.
– ORIGIN Greek *nitron* 'nitre' (saltpetre).

nitrogenous /ny-troj-i-nuhss/ •adj. containing nitrogen in chemical combination.

nitroglycerine (US also **nitroglycerin**) •n. an explosive liquid used in dynamite.

nitrous /ny-truhss/ •adj. relating to or containing nitrogen.

nitrous acid •n. a weak acid made by the action of acids on nitrites.

nitrous oxide •n. a gas used as an anaesthetic.

nitty-gritty •n. informal the most important details.

nitwit •n. informal a foolish person.

No¹ •symb the chemical element nobelium.

No² •n. var. of **Noh**.

no •det. **1** not any. **2** the opposite of: *she's no fool*. •exclam. used to refuse, deny, or disagree with something. •adv. not at all. •n. (pl. **noes**) a decision or vote against something.
– PHRASES **no way** informal certainly not.
– ORIGIN Old English.

no. •abbrev. number.
– ORIGIN Latin *numero* 'by number'.

nob •n. Brit. informal an upper-class person.

no-ball •n. a ball in cricket that is unlawfully bowled, counting as an extra run to the batting side.

nobble •v. (**nobbles, nobbling, nobbled**) Brit. informal **1** try to influence or thwart by underhand methods: *an attempt to nobble the jury*. **2** tamper with a race-horse to prevent it from winning a race. **3** stop someone so as to talk to them.
– ORIGIN prob. from dialect *knobble*, *knubble* 'to knock'.

nobelium /noh-bee-li-uhm/ •n. a very unstable chemical element made by high-energy collisions.
– ORIGIN named after Alfred *Nobel* (see **Nobel Prize**).

Nobel Prize •n. any of six international prizes awarded annually for outstanding work in various fields.
– ORIGIN named after the Swedish chemist and engineer Alfred *Nobel*.

nobility •n. **1** the quality of being noble. **2** the aristocracy.

noble •adj. (**nobler, noblest**) **1** belonging to the aristocracy. **2** having admirable personal qualities or high moral principles. **3** magnificent; impressive. •n. a nobleman or noblewoman.
– DERIVATIVES **nobly** adv.
– ORIGIN Latin *nobilis* 'noted, high-born'.

noble gas •n. any of the gases helium, neon, argon, krypton, xenon, and radon, which seldom or never combine with other elements to form compounds.

nobleman (or **noblewoman**) •n. (pl. **noblemen** or **noblewomen**) a member of the aristocracy.

noblesse oblige /noh-bless oh-bleezh/ •n. the idea that noble or wealthy people should help those who are less fortunate.
– ORIGIN French.

nobody •pron. no person. •n. (pl. **nobodies**) an unimportant person.

no-claims bonus •n. Brit. a reduction in

an insurance premium when no claim has been made during an agreed period.

nocturnal • adj. done or active at night.
– DERIVATIVES **nocturnally** adv.
– ORIGIN Latin *nocturnus* 'of the night'.

nocturne /nok-tern/ • n. a short piece of music of a dreamy, romantic nature.
– ORIGIN French.

nod • v. (**nods, nodding, nodded**) **1** lower and raise your head briefly to show agreement or as a greeting or signal. **2** let your head fall forward when drowsy or asleep. **3** (**nod off**) informal fall asleep. • n. an act of nodding.
– PHRASES **give someone/thing the nod** approve someone or something. **a nodding acquaintance** a slight acquaintance.
– ORIGIN perh. German.

noddle • n. informal a person's head.

node • n. tech. **1** a point in a network at which lines cross or branch. **2** the part of a plant stem from which one or more leaves grows. **3** a small mass of distinct tissue in the body.
– DERIVATIVES **nodal** adj.
– ORIGIN Latin *nodus* 'knot'.

nodule /nod-yool/ • n. a small swelling or lump.
– DERIVATIVES **nodular** adj.
– ORIGIN Latin *nodulus* 'little knot'.

Noel • n. Christmas.
– ORIGIN French.

noggin • n. informal **1** a person's head. **2** a small quantity of alcoholic drink.

no-go area • n. Brit. an area which is dangerous or impossible to enter.

Noh /noh/ (also **No**) • n. traditional Japanese drama with dance and song.
– ORIGIN Japanese.

noise • n. **1** a sound or series of sounds that is loud or unpleasant. **2** disturbances that accompany and interfere with an electrical signal. • v. (**noises, noising, noised**) dated make something public.
– DERIVATIVES **noiseless** adj.
– ORIGIN Old French.

noisette /nwah-zet/ • n. a small round piece of meat.
– ORIGIN French, 'little nut'.

noisome /noy-suhm/ • adj. literary **1** having a very unpleasant smell. **2** very unpleasant.
– ORIGIN from **ANNOY**.

noisy • adj. (**noisier, noisiest**) full of or making a lot of noise.
– DERIVATIVES **noisily** adv. **noisiness** n.

nomad • n. a member of a people that travels from place to place to find fresh pasture for its animals.
– ORIGIN Greek *nomas*.

nomadic • adj. having the life of a nomad; wandering.

no-man's-land • n. an area between two opposing armies that is not controlled by either.

nom de plume /nom duh ploom/ • n. (pl. **noms de plume** /nom duh ploom/) a name used by a writer instead of their real name; a pen name.
– ORIGIN French.

nomenclature /noh-men-kluh-cher/ • n. a system of names used in a particular subject.
– ORIGIN Latin *nomenclatura*.

nominal • adj. **1** in name but not in reality: *a purely nominal Arsenal fan.* **2** (of a sum of money) very small, but charged or paid as a sign that payment is necessary. **3** Grammar relating to or acting as a noun.
– DERIVATIVES **nominally** adv.
– ORIGIN Latin *nominalis*.

nominal value • n. the value that is stated on a coin, note, etc.

nominate • v. (**nominates, nominating, nominated**) **1** put someone forward as a candidate for a job, award, etc. **2** formally specify something.
– DERIVATIVES **nomination** n.
– ORIGIN Latin *nominare* 'to name'.

nominative /nom-i-nuh-tiv/ • n. Grammar the case used for the subject of a verb.

nominee • n. a person who is nominated for a job, award, etc.

non- • prefix not: *non-specific.*
– ORIGIN Latin.

> **USAGE:** The prefixes (word beginnings) **non-** and **un-** both mean 'not', but they tend to be used in slightly different ways. **Non-** is more neutral, while **un-** often suggests a particular bias or standpoint. For example, **unnatural** means that something is not natural in a bad way, whereas **nonnatural** simply means 'not natural'.

nonagenarian /non-uh-juh-**nair**-i-uhn, noh-nuh-juh-**nair**-i-uhn/ • n. a person between 90 and 99 years old.
– ORIGIN Latin *nonagenarius*.

nonagon /non-uh-guhn/ • n. a plane figure with nine straight sides and angles.
– ORIGIN Latin *nonus* 'ninth'.

non-aligned • adj. (of a country during the cold war) not allied to any of the major world powers.

nonce /nonss/ • adj. (of a word or expression) coined for one occasion.
– PHRASES **for the nonce** for the present; temporarily.
– ORIGIN wrong division of former *then anes* 'the one (purpose)'.

nonchalant /non-shuh-luhnt/

• adj. calm and relaxed.
– DERIVATIVES **nonchalance** n. **nonchalantly** adv.
– ORIGIN French, 'not being concerned'.

non-combatant • n. a person who is not engaged in fighting during a war, especially a civilian, army chaplain, or army doctor.

non-commissioned • adj. (of a military officer) appointed from the lower ranks rather than holding a commission.

non-committal • adj. not showing what you think or which side you support.

non compos mentis /non kom-poss men-tiss/ • adj. mentally unbalanced or insane.
– ORIGIN Latin, 'not having control of your mind'.

non-conductor • n. a substance that does not conduct heat or electricity.

nonconformist • n. **1** a person who does not follow accepted ideas or behaviour. **2** (**Nonconformist**) a member of a Protestant Church which does not follow the beliefs of the established Church of England.
– DERIVATIVES **nonconformity** n.

non-contributory • adj. (of a pension) funded by regular payments by the employer, not the employee.

nondescript /non-di-skript/ • adj. lacking special or interesting features: *a nondescript apartment building.*
– ORIGIN from NON- + former *descript* 'described'.

none • pron. **1** not any. **2** no one.
• adv. (**none the**) not at all: *none the wiser.*
– ORIGIN Old English.

> **USAGE:** When you use **none of** with a plural noun or pronoun (such as *them*), or a singular noun that refers to a group of people or things, you can correctly use either a singular or plural verb: *none of them is coming* or *none of them are coming; none of the family was present* or *none of the family were present.*

nonentity /non-en-ti-ti/ • n. (pl. **nonentities**) an unimportant person or thing.
– ORIGIN Latin *nonentitas* 'non-existence'.

nonetheless (also **none the less**) • adv. in spite of that; nevertheless.

non-event • n. an event which is not as interesting as it was expected to be.

non-existent • adj. not real or present.

non-ferrous • adj. (of metal) not iron or steel.

non-fiction • n. prose writing that deals with real people, facts, or events.

non-flammable • adj. not catching fire easily.

non-functional • adj. **1** not having a particular function. **2** not in working order.

non-intervention • n. the policy of not becoming involved in the affairs of other countries.

non-invasive • adj. (of medical procedures) not involving the introduction of instruments into the body.

non-member • n. a person who is not a member of a particular organization.

non-natural • adj. not produced by or involving natural processes.

no-no • n. (pl. **no-nos**) informal a thing that is not possible or acceptable.

no-nonsense • adj. simple and straightforward; sensible.

nonpareil /non-puh-rayl/ • n. a person or thing that has no match or equal.
– ORIGIN French.

nonplussed /non-plusst/ • adj. surprised and confused as to how to react.
– ORIGIN from Latin *non plus* 'not more'.

non-profit • adj. not intended to make a profit.

non-proliferation • n. the prevention of an increase in the number of nuclear weapons that are produced.

non-resident • adj. not living in a particular country or a place of work.
• n. a person not living in a particular place.

nonsense • n. **1** words that make no sense. **2** silly ideas or behaviour.

nonsensical • adj. making no sense; ridiculous.

non sequitur /non sek-wi-ter/ • n. a conclusion that does not logically follow from the previous statement.
– ORIGIN Latin, 'it does not follow'.

non-standard • adj. **1** not average or usual. **2** (of language) not of the form accepted as standard.

non-starter • n. informal something that has no chance of succeeding.

non-stick • adj. (of a pan or surface) covered with a substance that prevents food sticking to it during cooking.

non-stop • adj. **1** continuing without stopping. **2** having no stops on the way to a destination. • adv. without stopping.

non-verbal • adj. not using words or speech: *non-verbal communication.*

non-white • adj. (of a person) not white or not of European origin.

noodle • n. informal a silly person.

noodles • pl. n. long, thin strips of pasta.
– ORIGIN German *Nudel.*

nook • n. a corner or place that is sheltered or hidden.

nooky (also **nookie**) • n. informal sexual activity or intercourse.
– ORIGIN perh. from NOOK.

noon • n. twelve o'clock in the day; midday.
– ORIGIN from Latin *nona hora* 'ninth hour' (from sunrise).

noonday • adj. happening or appearing in the middle of the day.

no one • pron. no person.

noose • n. a loop with a knot which tightens as the rope or wire is pulled, used to hang people or trap animals.
– ORIGIN prob. from Old French *nous*.

nor • conj. & adv. and not; and not either.
– ORIGIN Old English.

Nordic • adj. 1 relating to Scandinavia, Finland, and Iceland. 2 referring to a tall, blonde type of person typical of northern Europe.
– ORIGIN French *nordique*.

norm • n. 1 (**the norm**) the usual or standard thing: *strikes were the norm*. 2 a standard that is required or acceptable.
– ORIGIN Latin *norma* 'rule'.

normal • adj. 1 usual, typical, or expected. 2 tech. (of a line) intersecting a line or surface at right angles.
• n. the normal state or condition: *her temperature was above normal*.
– DERIVATIVES **normality** (N. Amer. also **normalcy**) n. **normally** adv.

normalize (or **normalise**)
• v. (**normalizes, normalizing, normalized**) make or become normal.
– DERIVATIVES **normalization** (or **normalisation**) n.

Norman • n. a member of a people of Normandy in northern France who conquered England in 1066.
• adj. 1 relating to the Normans. 2 relating to the style of Romanesque architecture used in Britain under the Normans.

normative • adj. formal relating to or setting a standard or norm.

Norse • n. an ancient or medieval form of Norwegian or a related Scandinavian language. • adj. relating to ancient or medieval Norway or Scandinavia.
– ORIGIN Dutch *noordsch*.

north • n. 1 the direction in which a compass needle normally points, on the left-hand side of a person facing east. 2 the northern part of a place.
• adj. 1 lying towards or facing the north. 2 (of a wind) blowing from the north.
• adv. to or towards the north.
– DERIVATIVES **northbound** adj. & adv.
– ORIGIN Old English.

North American • n. a person from

North America. • adj. relating to North America.

Northants • abbrev. Northamptonshire.

north-east • n. the direction or region halfway between north and east.
• adj. 1 lying towards or facing the north-east. 2 (of a wind) blowing from the north-east. • adv. to or towards the north-east.
– DERIVATIVES **north-eastern** adj.

north-easterly • adj. & adv. in a north-eastward position or direction.

north-eastward • adv. (also **north-eastwards**) towards the north-east.
• adj. in, towards, or facing the north-east.

northerly • adj. & adv. 1 towards or facing the north. 2 (of a wind) blowing from the north.

northern • adj. 1 situated in or facing the north. 2 (usu. **Northern**) coming from or characteristic of the north.
– DERIVATIVES **northernmost** adj.

northerner • n. a person from the north of a region.

Northern Lights • pl. n. the aurora borealis.

north-north-east • n. the direction halfway between north and north-east.

north-north-west • n. the direction halfway between north and north-west.

North Star • n. the Pole Star.

Northumb. • abbrev. Northumberland.

northward • adj. in a northerly direction. • adv. (also **northwards**) towards the north.

north-west • n. the direction or region halfway between north and west.
• adj. 1 lying towards or facing the north-west. 2 (of a wind) blowing from the north-west. • adv. to or towards the north-west.
– DERIVATIVES **north-western** adj.

north-westerly • adj. & adv. in a north-westward position or direction.

north-westward • adv. (also **north-westwards**) towards the north-west.
• adj. in, towards, or facing the north-west.

Norwegian /nor-wee-juhn/ • n. 1 a person from Norway. 2 the language spoken in Norway. • adj. relating to Norway.
– ORIGIN Latin *Norvegia* 'Norway'.

nose • n. 1 the part of the face containing the nostrils and used in breathing and smelling. 2 the front end of an aircraft, car, or other vehicle. 3 the sense of smell. 4 a talent for finding something: *he had a nose for an opportunity*. 5 the characteristic smell of a wine. • v. (**noses, nosing, nosed**) 1 (of an animal) thrust

its nose against or into something.
2 look around or pry into something.
3 make your way slowly forward.
– PHRASES **cut off your nose to spite your face** do something which is supposed to harm someone else but which also harms yourself. **put someone's nose out of joint** informal offend someone. **turn your nose up at** informal show distaste or contempt for.
– ORIGIN Old English.

nosebag • n. Brit. a bag containing fodder, hung from a horse's head.

nosebleed • n. an instance of bleeding from the nose.

nosedive • n. **1** a steep downward plunge by an aircraft. **2** a sudden marked decline: *his fortunes took a nosedive*. • v. (**nosedives, nosediving, nosedived**) make a nosedive.

nosegay • n. a small bunch of flowers.
– ORIGIN from GAY in the former sense 'ornament'.

nosey • adj. var. of NOSY.

nosh informal • n. Brit. food. • v. eat enthusiastically or greedily.
– ORIGIN Yiddish.

nosh-up • n. Brit. informal a large meal.

nostalgia • n. /no-**stal**-juh/ wistful longing for a happier or better time in the past.
– DERIVATIVES **nostalgic** adj. **nostalgically** adv.
– ORIGIN from Greek *nostos* 'return home' + *algos* 'pain'.

nostril • n. either of the two external openings of the nose through which air passes to the lungs.
– ORIGIN Old English, 'nose hole'.

nostrum • n. **1** a favourite method for improving something: *right-wing nostrums such as cutting public spending.* **2** a medicine that is prepared by an unqualified person and is not effective.
– ORIGIN Latin, 'something of our own making'.

nosy (also **nosey**) • adj. (**nosier, nosiest**) informal too inquisitive about other people's business.

nosy parker • n. Brit. informal a very inquisitive person.

not • adv. **1** used to form or express a negative: *she would not leave.* **2** less than: *not ten feet away.*
– ORIGIN from NOUGHT.

notable • adj. deserving to be noticed or given attention. • n. a famous or important person.

notably • adv. **1** in particular. **2** in a way that is noticeable or remarkable.

notary (in full **notary public**) • n. (pl. **notaries**) a lawyer who is officially authorized to draw up and witness the signing of contracts and other documents.
– ORIGIN Latin *notarius* 'secretary'.

notation • n. a system of written symbols used to represent numbers, amounts, or elements in a subject such as music or mathematics.

notch • n. **1** a V-shaped cut or indentation on an edge or surface. **2** a point or level on a scale: *her opinion of him dropped a few notches.* • v. **1** make notches in. **2** (**notch something up**) score or achieve something.
– ORIGIN Old French *osche*.

note • n. **1** a brief written record of something, used as an aid to memory. **2** a short written message. **3** Brit. a banknote. **4** a single sound of a particular pitch and length made by a musical instrument or voice, or a symbol representing this. **5** a particular quality: *there was a note of scorn in his voice.* • v. (**notes, noting, noted**) **1** pay attention to. **2** record in writing.
– PHRASES **of note** important. **take note** pay attention.
– ORIGIN Latin *nota* 'a mark'.

notebook • n. **1** a small book for writing notes in. **2** a portable computer smaller than a laptop.

noted • adj. well known.

notepad • n. a pad of paper for writing notes on.

notepaper • n. paper for writing letters on.

noteworthy • adj. interesting or important.

nothing • pron. **1** not anything. **2** something that is not important or interesting. **3** nought. • adv. not at all.
– PHRASES **for nothing 1** without payment or charge. **2** with no result. **nothing but** only. **sweet nothings** words of affection between lovers.
– ORIGIN Old English.

nothingness • n. the state of not existing or a state where nothing exists.

notice • n. **1** the fact of being aware of or paying attention to something: *his silence did not escape my notice.* **2** information or warning that something is going to happen: *interest rates may change without notice.* **3** a formal statement that someone is going to leave a job or end an agreement. **4** a sheet or placard put on display to give information. **5** a small announcement or advertisement published in a newspaper. **6** a short published review of a new film, play, or book. • v. (**notices, noticing, noticed**) become aware of.
– PHRASES **take notice (of)** pay attention (to).

– ORIGIN Latin *notitia*.

noticeable • adj. easily seen or noticed.
– DERIVATIVES **noticeably** adv.

> ✓ Remember that **noticeable** has an **e** in the middle.

noticeboard • n. Brit. a board for displaying notices.

notifiable • adj. (of an infectious disease) so dangerous or serious that it must be reported to the health authorities.

notify • v. (**notifies, notifying, notified**) formally tell someone about something.
– DERIVATIVES **notification** n.
– ORIGIN Latin *notificare*.

notion • n. **1** an idea or belief. **2** an understanding: *I had no notion of what she meant.*
– ORIGIN Latin.

notional • adj. based on a guess or theory; hypothetical.
– DERIVATIVES **notionally** adv.

notoriety /noh-tuh-ry-i-ti/ • n. the state of being famous for a bad quality or action.

notorious • adj. famous for a bad quality or action: *the prison housed the most notorious criminals in the US.*
– DERIVATIVES **notoriously** adv.
– ORIGIN Latin *notorius* 'generally known'.

Notts. • abbrev. Nottinghamshire.

notwithstanding • prep. in spite of.
• adv. nevertheless.

nougat /noo-gah, nug-uht/ • n. a sweet made from sugar or honey, nuts, and egg white.
– ORIGIN French.

nought • n. Brit. the figure 0.
• pron. nothing.
– DERIVATIVES **noughth** adj.

noun • n. a word (other than a pronoun) that refers to a person, place, or thing.
– ORIGIN Latin *nomen* 'name'.

nourish • v. **1** provide with the food or other substances necessary for growth and health. **2** keep a feeling or belief in your mind for a long time.
– ORIGIN Latin *nutrire*.

nourishment • n. the food or other substances necessary for growth and health.

nous /nowss/ • n. Brit. informal common sense.
– ORIGIN Greek, 'mind'.

nouveau riche /noo-voh reesh/
• n. people who have recently become rich and who like to display their wealth in an obvious or tasteless way.
– ORIGIN French, 'new rich'.

Nov. • abbrev. November.

nova /noh-vuh/ • n. (pl. **novae** /noh-vee/ or **novas**) a star that suddenly becomes very bright for a short period.
– ORIGIN Latin, 'new'.

novel[1] • n. a story about imaginary people and events, long enough to fill a complete book.
– ORIGIN from Italian *novella storia* 'new story'.

novel[2] • adj. new in an interesting or unusual way: *a novel approach to architecture.*
– ORIGIN Latin *novus* 'new'.

novelette • n. a short novel, especially a romantic novel regarded as not very well written.

novelist • n. a person who writes novels.

novella /nuh-vel-luh/ • n. a short novel or long short story.
– ORIGIN Italian.

novelty • n. (pl. **novelties**) **1** the quality of being new and unusual. **2** a new or unfamiliar thing: *in 1914 air travel was still a novelty.* **3** a small toy or ornament.

November • n. the eleventh month of the year.
– ORIGIN from Latin *novem* 'nine' (November being originally the ninth month of the Roman year).

novena /noh-vee-nuh/ • n. (in the Roman Catholic Church) a set of special prayers or services on nine successive days.
– ORIGIN Latin.

novice • n. **1** a person who is new to a job or situation and lacks experience. **2** a person who has entered a religious order but has not yet taken their vows.
– ORIGIN Latin *novicius*.

novitiate /noh-vi-shi-uht/ • n. the period or state of being a novice in a religious order.

now • adv. **1** at the present time. **2** at or from this precise moment; immediately.
• conj. as a result of the fact.
– PHRASES **now and again** (or **then**) from time to time.
– ORIGIN Old English.

nowadays • adv. at the present time, in contrast with the past.

nowhere • adv. not anywhere. • pron. no place.

nowt • pron. & adv. N. English nothing.

noxious /nok-shuhss/ • adj. harmful or very unpleasant.
– ORIGIN Latin *noxius*.

nozzle • n. a spout used to control a stream of liquid or gas.
– ORIGIN from **NOSE**.

Np • symb. the chemical element neptunium.

NSPCC • abbrev. (in the UK) National Society for the Prevention of Cruelty to Children.

NSW • abbrev. New South Wales.

NT • abbrev. **1** National Trust. **2** New Testament.

-n't • contr. not, used with auxiliary verbs (e.g. *can't*).

nth /enth/ • adj. referring to the last or latest item in a long series.
– PHRASES **to the nth degree** to an extreme degree.

nuance /nyoo-ahnss/ • n. a very slight difference in meaning, expression, sound, etc.
– ORIGIN French.

nub • n. **1** (**the nub**) the central point of a matter. **2** a small lump.
– DERIVATIVES **nubby** adj.
– ORIGIN prob. from German *knubbe* 'knob'.

nubile /nyoo-byl/ • adj. (of a girl or young woman) sexually attractive.
– ORIGIN Latin *nubilis* 'fit for marriage'.

nubuck /nyoo-buk/ • n. leather which has been rubbed on the flesh side of the skin to give a suede-like effect.

nuclear • adj. **1** relating to the nucleus of an atom or cell. **2** using energy released in the fission (splitting) or fusion of atomic nuclei. **3** referring to, possessing, or involving nuclear weapons: *a nuclear bomb.*

nuclear family • n. a couple and their children, as a basic unit of society.

nuclear fuel • n. a substance that will undergo nuclear fission and can be used as a source of nuclear energy.

nuclear physics • n. the science of atomic nuclei and the way they interact.

nuclear power • n. power generated by a nuclear reactor.

nuclear waste • n. radioactive waste material from the use or reprocessing of nuclear fuel.

nucleate /nyoo-kli-ayt/ • v. (**nucleates, nucleating, nucleated**) form a nucleus.

nuclei pl. of **NUCLEUS**.

nucleic acid /nyoo-klee-ik, nyoo-klay-ik/ • n. either of two organic substances, DNA and RNA, that are present in all living cells.

nucleus /nyoo-kli-uhss/ • n. (pl. **nuclei** /nyoo-kli-I/) **1** the central and most important part of an object or group. **2** Physics the positively charged central core of an atom. **3** Biol. a structure present in most cells, containing the genetic material.
– ORIGIN Latin, 'kernel'.

nude • adj. wearing no clothes. • n. a painting or sculpture of a naked human figure.
– DERIVATIVES **nudity** n.
– ORIGIN Latin *nudus* 'plain, explicit'.

nudge • v. (**nudges, nudging, nudged**) **1** prod someone with your elbow to attract their attention. **2** touch or push gently. • n. a light prod or push.

nudist • n. a person who prefers to wear no clothes wherever possible.
– DERIVATIVES **nudism** n.

nugatory /nyoo-guh-tuh-ri/ • adj. formal having no purpose or value.
– ORIGIN Latin *nugatorius*.

nugget • n. **1** a small lump of gold or other precious metal found in the earth. **2** a small but valuable fact.

nuisance • n. a person or thing causing annoyance or difficulty.
– ORIGIN Old French, 'hurt'.

nuke informal • n. a nuclear weapon. • v. (**nukes, nuking, nuked**) attack with nuclear weapons.

null • adj. tech. having the value zero.
– PHRASES **null and void** having no legal force; invalid.
– ORIGIN Latin *nullus* 'none'.

nullify • v. (**nullifies, nullifying, nullified**) **1** make legally invalid. **2** cancel out the effect of.
– DERIVATIVES **nullification** n.

nullity • n. (pl. **nullities**) **1** the state of being legally invalid. **2** a thing of no value or importance.

numb • adj. **1** (of a part of the body) having no sensation. **2** lacking the power to feel, think, or react. • v. make numb.
– DERIVATIVES **numbly** adv. **numbness** n.
– ORIGIN Germanic, 'taken'.

number • n. **1** a quantity or value expressed by a word or symbol. **2** a quantity or amount. **3** (**a number of**) several. **4** esp. Brit. a single issue of a magazine. **5** a song, dance, or piece of music. **6** a grammatical classification of words depending on whether one or more people or things are being referred to. • v. (**numbers, numbering, numbered**) **1** amount to. **2** give a number to each thing in a series. **3** count people or things. **4** include as a member of a group: *he numbered Grieg among his friends.*
– PHRASES **someone's days are numbered** someone will not survive for much longer. **someone's number is up** informal someone is finished or about to die.
– ORIGIN Latin *numerus*.

number cruncher • n. informal **1** a computer for performing complicated calculations. **2** usu. derog. an accountant, statistician, or other person whose job

n

involves dealing with large amounts of numerical data.

numberless •adj. too many to be counted; innumerable.

number one •n. informal yourself.
•adj. most important; top.

number plate •n. Brit. a sign on the front and rear of a vehicle showing its registration number.

numbskull (also **numskull**) •n. informal a stupid person.

numeral /nyoo-muh-ruhl/ •n. a symbol or word representing a number.

numerate /nyoo-muh-ruht/
•adj. having a good basic knowledge of arithmetic.
– DERIVATIVES **numeracy** n.
– ORIGIN Latin *numerus* 'a number'.

numeration •n. the action of calculating or giving a number to something.

numerator •n. Math. the number above the line in a fraction.

numerical •adj. relating to or expressed as a number or numbers.
– DERIVATIVES **numeric** adj. **numerically** adv.

numerology •n. the study of the supposed magical power of numbers.
– DERIVATIVES **numerologist** n.

numerous •adj. **1** many. **2** consisting of many members.

numinous /nyoo-mi-nuhss/ •adj. having a strong religious or spiritual quality.
– ORIGIN Latin *numen* 'divine will'.

numismatic /nyoo-miz-mat-ik/
•adj. relating to coins or medals.
•n. (**numismatics**) the study or collection of coins, banknotes, and medals.
– DERIVATIVES **numismatist** n.
– ORIGIN Greek *nomisma* 'current coin'.

numskull •n. var. of NUMBSKULL.

nun •n. a woman belonging to a female religious community who has taken vows of poverty, chastity, and obedience.
– ORIGIN Latin *nonna*.

nuncio /nun-si-oh/ •n. (pl. **nuncios**) (in the Roman Catholic Church) a person who represents the pope in a foreign country.
– ORIGIN Latin *nuntius* 'messenger'.

nunnery •n. (pl. **nunneries**) a convent.

nuptial /nup-sh'l/ •adj. relating to marriage or weddings. •n. (**nuptials**) a wedding.
– ORIGIN Latin *nuptiae* 'wedding'.

nurse •n. **1** a person trained to care for sick or injured people. **2** dated a person employed to look after young children.
•v. (**nurses**, **nursing**, **nursed**) **1** give medical and other care to a sick person.

2 treat or hold carefully or protectively. **3** cling to a belief or feeling for a long time. **4** feed a baby at the breast.
– ORIGIN Old French *nourice*.

nursemaid •n. dated a woman or girl employed to look after a young child or children.

nursery •n. (pl. **nurseries**) **1** a room in a house where young children sleep or play. **2** (also **day nursery**) a nursery school. **3** a place where young plants and trees are grown for sale or for planting elsewhere.

nurseryman •n. (pl. **nurserymen**) a person who works in or owns a plant or tree nursery.

nursery nurse •n. Brit. a person trained to look after young children and babies in a nursery or crèche.

nursery rhyme •n. a simple traditional song or poem for children.

nursery school •n. a school for young children between three and five.

nursery slopes •pl. n. gentle ski slopes suitable for beginners.

nursing home •n. a private home providing accommodation and health care for elderly people.

nurture •v. (**nurtures**, **nurturing**, **nurtured**) **1** care for and protect a child or young plant while they are growing and developing. **2** have a hope, belief, or ambition for a long time. •n. the action of nurturing or the state of being nurtured.
– ORIGIN Old French *noureture* 'nourishment'.

nut •n. **1** a fruit consisting of a hard shell around an edible kernel. **2** the kernel of such a fruit. **3** a small flat piece of metal or other material with a hole through the centre for screwing on to a bolt. **4** informal a crazy person. **5** informal a person's head.
– PHRASES **do your nut** Brit. informal be extremely angry. **nuts and bolts** informal the basic practical details.
– ORIGIN Old English.

nutcase •n. informal a mad or foolish person.

nutcrackers •pl. n. a device for cracking nuts.

nuthatch •n. a small songbird which climbs up and down tree trunks.
– ORIGIN from a former word related to HACK¹, from the bird's habit of hacking at nuts with its beak.

nutmeg •n. a spice obtained from the seed of a tropical tree.
– ORIGIN from Old French *nois muguede* 'musky nut'.

nutrient /nyoo-tri-uhnt/ •n. a substance that is essential for life and growth.
– ORIGIN Latin, 'nourishing'.

 The ending of **nutrient** is spelled -ient.

nutriment •n. nourishment.

nutrition •n. **1** the process of taking in and absorbing nutrients. **2** the branch of science concerned with this process.
– DERIVATIVES **nutritional** adj. **nutritionist** n.
– ORIGIN Latin.

nutritious •adj. full of nutrients; nourishing.

nutritive •adj. **1** relating to nutrition. **2** nutritious.

nuts •adj. informal mad.

nutshell •n. (in phr. **in a nutshell**) in the fewest possible words.

nutter •n. Brit. informal a mad person.

nutty •adj. (**nuttier, nutties**) **1** containing or tasting like nuts. **2** informal mad.
– DERIVATIVES **nuttiness** n.

nuzzle •v. (**nuzzles, nuzzling, nuzzled**) rub or push against gently with the nose.
– ORIGIN from **NOSE**.

NVQ •abbrev. (in the UK) National Vocational Qualification.

NW •abbrev. north-west or north-western.

NY •abbrev. New York.

NYC •abbrev. New York City.

nylon •n. **1** a strong, lightweight, synthetic material which can be made into fabric, yarn, and many other products. **2** (**nylons**) nylon stockings or tights.
– ORIGIN an invented word.

nymph •n. **1** (in Greek and Roman mythology) a spirit of nature in the form of a beautiful young woman. **2** an immature form of an insect such as a dragonfly.
– ORIGIN Greek *numphē* 'nymph, bride'.

nymphet •n. an attractive and sexually mature young girl.

nymphomania •n. uncontrollable or abnormally strong sexual desire in a woman.
– DERIVATIVES **nymphomaniac** n.

NZ •abbrev. New Zealand.

Oo

O¹ (also **o**) • n. (pl. **Os** or **O's**) **1** the fifteenth letter of the alphabet. **2** (also **oh**) zero.

O² • symb. the chemical element oxygen.

O³ • exclam. used when addressing someone: *give us peace, O Lord.*

oaf • n. a stupid, rude, or clumsy man.
– DERIVATIVES **oafish** adj.
– ORIGIN Old Norse, 'elf'.

oak • n. a large tree which produces acorns and a hard wood used for building and furniture.
– ORIGIN Old English.

oak apple • n. a growth which forms on oak trees, caused by wasp larvae.

oaken • adj. literary made of oak.

oakum • n. hist. loose fibre obtained by untwisting old rope, used to fill cracks in wooden ships.
– ORIGIN Old English, 'off-combings'.

OAP • abbrev. Brit. old-age pensioner.

oar • n. a pole with a flat blade, used for rowing a boat.
– PHRASES **put** (or **stick**) **your oar in** informal, esp. Brit. give an opinion without being asked.
– ORIGIN Old English.

oarsman (or **oarswoman**) • n. (pl. **oarsmen** or **oarswomen**) a rower.

oasis • n. (pl. **oases**) **1** a fertile place in a desert where water rises to ground level. **2** a pleasant or peaceful area or period in the midst of a difficult or hectic place or situation.
– ORIGIN Greek.

oast house • n. a building containing a kiln for drying hops.
– ORIGIN Old English.

oat • n. **1** a cereal plant grown in cool climates. **2** (**oats**) the edible grain of this plant.
– PHRASES **sow your wild oats** have many casual sexual relationships while young.
– ORIGIN Old English.

oatcake • n. a savoury oatmeal biscuit.

oath • n. (pl. **oaths**) **1** a solemn promise to do something or that something is true. **2** a swear word.
– PHRASES **under** (or **on**) **oath** having

sworn to tell the truth in a court of law.
– ORIGIN Old English.

oatmeal • n. meal made from ground oats, used in making porridge and oatcakes.

obdurate /ob-dyuu-ruht/
• adj. stubbornly refusing to change your mind.
– DERIVATIVES **obduracy** n.
– ORIGIN Latin *obduratus* 'hardened'.

OBE • abbrev. Officer of the Order of the British Empire.

obedient • adj. willingly doing what you are told.
– DERIVATIVES **obedience** n. **obediently** adv.
– ORIGIN Latin *oboedire* 'obey'.

obeisance /oh-bay-suhnss/ • n. **1** respect for someone and willingness to obey them. **2** a gesture expressing this, such as a bow.
– ORIGIN Old French *obeissance.*

obelisk • n. a four-sided stone pillar that tapers to a point, set up as a monument.
– ORIGIN Greek *obeliskos.*

obese • adj. very fat.
– DERIVATIVES **obesity** n.
– ORIGIN Latin *obesus.*

obey • v. **1** do what a person or a rule or law requires you to do. **2** behave in accordance with a general principle or natural law.
– ORIGIN Latin *oboedire.*

obfuscate /ob-fuss-kayt/
• v. (**obfuscates, obfuscating, obfuscated**) make unclear or hard to understand.
– DERIVATIVES **obfuscation** n.
– ORIGIN Latin *obfuscare* 'darken'.

obituary /oh-bi-chuu-ri, oh-bi-tyuu-ri/
• n. (pl. **obituaries**) a short biography of a person, published in a newspaper after their death.
– ORIGIN Latin *obitus* 'death'.

object • n. /ob-jikt/ **1** a physical thing that can be seen and touched. **2** a person or thing to which an action or feeling is directed: *he was an object of ridicule among his staff.* **3** a purpose. **4** Grammar a

noun acted on by a transitive verb or by a preposition. • v. /uhb-**jekt**/ express disapproval or opposition: *residents objected to the noise.*
– PHRASES **no object** not influencing or restricting choices: *money is no object.*
– DERIVATIVES **objector** n.
– ORIGIN Latin *objectum* 'thing presented to the mind'.

objectify • v. (**objectifies, objectifying, objectified**) **1** refer to something abstract as if it has a physical form. **2** treat someone as an object rather than a person.
– DERIVATIVES **objectification** n.

objection • n. a statement expressing disapproval or opposition.

objectionable • adj. unpleasant or offensive.

objective • adj. **1** not influenced by personal feelings or opinions: *historians try to be objective.* **2** having actual existence outside the mind: *a matter of objective fact.* **3** Grammar relating to a case of nouns and pronouns used for the object of a transitive verb or a preposition. • n. a goal or aim.
– DERIVATIVES **objectively** adv. **objectivity** n.

object lesson • n. a clear practical example of what should or should not be done in a particular situation.

objet d'art /ob-zhay **dar**/ • n. (pl. **objets d'art** /ob-zhay **dar**/) a small decorative or artistic object.
– ORIGIN French, 'object of art'.

oblate /ob-layt/ • adj. Geom. (of a sphere) flattened at each pole.
– ORIGIN Latin *oblatus* 'carried inversely'.

oblation • n. a thing presented or offered to a god.
– ORIGIN Latin.

obligate • v. (**be obligated**) be obliged to do something.
– ORIGIN Latin *obligare.*

obligation • n. **1** something a person must do because of a law, agreement, promise, etc. **2** the state of having to do something of this kind.
– PHRASES **under an obligation** owing gratitude to someone for something.

obligatory • adj. required by a law, rule, or custom; compulsory.

oblige • v. (**obliges, obliging, obliged**) **1** make someone do something because it is a law, a necessity, or their duty: *he was obliged to do military service.* **2** perform a service or favour for. **3** (**be obliged**) be grateful.
– ORIGIN Latin *obligare.*

obliging • adj. willing to help.
– DERIVATIVES **obligingly** adv.

oblique /uh-**bleek**/ • adj. **1** at an angle;

slanting. **2** not done in a direct way: *an oblique reference to the US.* **3** Geom. (of a line, plane figure, or surface) inclined at other than a right angle.
– DERIVATIVES **obliquely** adv.
– ORIGIN Latin *obliquus.*

obliterate /uh-**blit**-uh-rayt/
• v. (**obliterates, obliterating, obliterated**) **1** destroy completely. **2** cover completely: *the clouds obliterated the moon.*
– DERIVATIVES **obliteration** n.
– ORIGIN Latin *obliterare* 'erase'.

oblivion • n. **1** the state of being unaware of what is happening around you. **2** the state of being forgotten. **3** the state of being completely destroyed.
– ORIGIN Latin.

oblivious • adj. not aware of what is happening around you.
– DERIVATIVES **obliviousness** n.

oblong • adj. rectangular in shape. • n. an oblong shape.
– ORIGIN Latin *oblongus* 'longish'.

obloquy /**ob**-luh-kwi/ • n. **1** strong public criticism. **2** disgrace brought about by strong public criticism.
– ORIGIN Latin *obloqui* 'speak against'.

obnoxious /uhb-**nok**-shuhss/ • adj. very unpleasant.
– ORIGIN Latin *obnoxius* 'exposed to harm'.

oboe /**oh**-boh/ • n. a woodwind instrument of treble pitch, played with a double reed.
– DERIVATIVES **oboist** n.
– ORIGIN Italian, or from French *hautbois.*

obscene • adj. **1** dealing with sexual matters in an offensive or disgusting way. **2** (especially of an amount of money) unacceptably large: *obscene pay rises.*
– DERIVATIVES **obscenely** adv.
– ORIGIN Latin *obscaenus* 'hateful'.

obscenity • n. (pl. **obscenities**) **1** obscene language or behaviour. **2** an obscene act or word.

obscurantism /ob-skyuu-**rant**-i-z'm/ • n. the practice of deliberately preventing something from becoming known or understood.
– DERIVATIVES **obscurantist** n. & adj.

obscure • adj. **1** not discovered or known about. **2** not well known. **3** hard to understand or see: *obscure references to Proust.* • v. (**obscures, obscuring, obscured**) make something difficult to see, hear, or understand.
– DERIVATIVES **obscurely** adv.
– ORIGIN Latin *obscurus* 'dark'.

obscurity • n. (pl. **obscurities**) **1** the state of being unknown or forgotten. **2** the quality of being hard to understand.

obsequies /ob-si-kwiz/ •pl. n. funeral rites.
– ORIGIN Latin *obsequiae*.

obsequious /uhb-see-kwi-uhss/ •adj. too obedient or respectful; trying too hard to please someone.
– DERIVATIVES **obsequiously** adv. **obsequiousness** n.
– ORIGIN Latin *obsequium* 'compliance'.

observance •n. 1 the obeying of a rule or following of a custom. 2 (**observances**) acts performed for religious or ceremonial reasons.

observant •adj. quick to notice things.

observation •n. 1 the action of watching someone or something closely. 2 the ability to notice important details. 3 a comment based on something you have heard or noticed.
– DERIVATIVES **observational** adj.

observatory •n. (pl. **observatories**) a building equipped with a telescope or other scientific equipment for the study of natural phenomena.

observe •v. (**observes, observing, observed**) 1 notice. 2 watch carefully. 3 make a remark. 4 obey a law or rule. 5 celebrate or take part in a festival or ritual.
– DERIVATIVES **observable** adj. **observer** n.
– ORIGIN Latin *observare*.

obsess •v. preoccupy someone to a disturbing extent: *she's obsessed with her appearance.*
– ORIGIN Latin *obsidere* 'besiege'.

obsession •n. 1 the state of being obsessed. 2 a thing that someone is unable to stop thinking about.
– DERIVATIVES **obsessional** adj.

obsessive •adj. thinking continually about someone or something.
– DERIVATIVES **obsessively** adv.

obsidian /uhb-sid-i-uhn/ •n. a dark glass-like rock, formed when lava solidifies rapidly.
– ORIGIN Latin *obsidianus*.

obsolescent /ob-suh-less-uhnt/ •adj. becoming obsolete.
– DERIVATIVES **obsolescence** n.
– ORIGIN Latin *obsolescere* 'fall into disuse'.

obsolete •adj. no longer produced or used; out of date.
– ORIGIN Latin *obsoletus* 'grown old'.

obstacle •n. a thing that blocks the way or makes it difficult to do something.
– ORIGIN Latin *obstaculum*.

obstetrician /ob-stuh-tri-sh'n/ •n. a doctor who is trained in obstetrics.

obstetrics •n. the branch of medicine and surgery concerned with childbirth.
– DERIVATIVES **obstetric** adj.

– ORIGIN Latin *obstetrix* 'midwife'.

obstinate •adj. 1 stubbornly refusing to change your mind. 2 hard to deal with.
– DERIVATIVES **obstinacy** n. **obstinately** adv.
– ORIGIN Latin *obstinatus*.

obstreperous /uhb-strep-uh-ruhss/ •adj. noisy and difficult to control.
– ORIGIN Latin *obstrepere* 'shout at'.

obstruct •v. 1 be in the way of; block. 2 prevent or hinder.
– ORIGIN Latin *obstruere*.

obstruction •n. 1 an obstacle or blockage. 2 the action of obstructing.

obstructive •adj. deliberately causing difficulties or delays.

obtain •v. 1 come into possession of; get. 2 formal be established or usual: *the standards which obtain in this school.*
– DERIVATIVES **obtainable** adj.
– ORIGIN Latin *obtinere*.

obtrude •v. (**obtrudes, obtruding, obtruded**) become noticeable in an unwelcome way.
– ORIGIN Latin *obtrudere*.

obtrusive •adj. noticeable in an unwelcome way.

obtuse /uhb-tyooss/ •adj. 1 annoyingly slow to understand. 2 (of an angle) more than 90° and less than 180°. 3 not sharp or pointed; blunt.
– DERIVATIVES **obtuseness** n.
– ORIGIN Latin *obtusus*.

obverse •n. 1 the side of a coin or medal bearing the head or main design. 2 the opposite of something.
– ORIGIN Latin *obversus* 'turned towards'.

obviate /ob-vi-ayt/ •v. (**obviates, obviating, obviated**) remove or prevent a need or difficulty.
– ORIGIN Latin *obviare*.

obvious •adj. easily seen or understood; clear.
– DERIVATIVES **obviously** adv. **obviousness** n.
– ORIGIN from Latin *ob viam* 'in the way'.

ocarina /ok-uh-ree-nuh/ •n. a small egg-shaped wind instrument with holes for the fingers.
– ORIGIN Italian.

occasion •n. 1 a particular event, or the time at which it happens. 2 a special event or celebration. 3 a suitable time for something. 4 formal reason or cause: *we have occasion to rejoice.* •v. formal cause something.
– PHRASES **on occasion** from time to time.
– ORIGIN Latin.

> ✓ Spell **occasion** with a double **c** and a single **s**.

occasional •adj. happening or done from time to time.
– DERIVATIVES **occasionally** adv.

occidental •adj. literary relating to the countries of the West.
– ORIGIN Latin *occidentalis*.

occiput /ok-si-put/ •n. Anat. the back of the head.
– DERIVATIVES **occipital** /ok-si-pi-t'l/ adj.
– ORIGIN Latin.

occlude /uh-klood/ •v. (**occludes, occluding, occluded**) tech. close up or block an opening or passage.
– ORIGIN Latin *occludere*.

occluded front •n. a weather front produced when a cold front catches up with a warm front, so that the warm air in between them is forced upwards.

occult /ok-kult, ok-kult/ •n. (**the occult**) magical or supernatural powers, practices, or phenomena. •adj. relating to the occult.
– DERIVATIVES **occultism** n. **occultist** n.
– ORIGIN Latin *occulere* 'conceal'.

occupancy •n. **1** the action of occupying a place. **2** the proportion of accommodation that is occupied.

occupant •n. a person who occupies a place or job.

occupation •n. **1** a job or profession. **2** a way of spending time. **3** the action of occupying a place: *the Roman occupation of Britain.*

occupational •adj. relating to a job or profession.

occupational therapy •n. the use of particular activities to help someone recover from an illness.

occupy •v. (**occupies, occupying, occupied**) **1** live or work in. **2** enter and take control of a place. **3** fill or take up a space, time, or position. **4** keep busy: *he has occupied himself with research.*
– DERIVATIVES **occupier** n.
– ORIGIN Latin *occupare* 'seize'.

occur •v. (**occurs, occurring, occurred**) **1** happen. **2** be found or present: *radon occurs in rocks such as granite.* **3** (**occur to**) come into someone's mind.
– ORIGIN Latin *occurrere* 'go to meet'.

occurrence /uh-ku-ruhnss/ •n. **1** an incident or event. **2** the fact of something happening or existing: *the occurrence of cancer increases with age.*

> **occurrence** is spelled with a double **c** and a double **r**.

ocean •n. a very large expanse of sea, especially each of the Atlantic, Pacific, Indian, Arctic, and Antarctic Oceans.
– ORIGIN Greek *ōkeanos* 'great stream encircling the earth'.

oceanic /oh-si-an-ik, oh-shi-an-ik/ •adj. relating to the ocean.

oceanography •n. the branch of science concerned with the study of the sea.
– DERIVATIVES **oceanographer** n.

ocelot /oss-i-lot/ •n. a striped and spotted wild cat, found in South and Central America.
– ORIGIN French.

ochre /oh-ker/ (US also **ocher**) •n. a type of earth varying from light yellow to brown or red, used as a pigment.
– ORIGIN Greek *ōkhra*.

o'clock •adv. used to specify the hour when telling the time.
– ORIGIN from *of the clock*.

Oct. •abbrev. October.

octagon •n. a plane figure with eight straight sides and eight angles.
– DERIVATIVES **octagonal** adj..
– ORIGIN Greek *octagōnos* 'eight-angled'.

octahedron /ok-tuh-hee-druhn/ •n. (pl. **octahedra** /ok-tuh-hee-druh/ or **octahedrons**) a three-dimensional shape with eight plane faces.
– ORIGIN Greek *oktaedron* 'eight-faced thing'.

octane •n. a liquid hydrocarbon present in petroleum spirit.
– ORIGIN from Greek *octō* 'eight' (referring to eight carbon atoms).

octave /ok-tiv/ •n. **1** a series of eight musical notes occupying the interval between (and including) two notes. **2** the interval between two such notes.
– ORIGIN Latin *octavus* 'eighth'.

octavo /ok-tah-voh/ •n. (pl. **octavos**) a size of book page that results from folding each printed sheet into eight leaves (sixteen pages).
– ORIGIN from Latin *in octavo* 'in an eighth'.

octet •n. **1** a group of eight musicians. **2** a musical composition for eight voices or instruments.
– ORIGIN from Latin *octo* 'eight'.

October •n. the tenth month of the year.
– ORIGIN from Latin *octo* 'eight' (October being originally the eighth month of the Roman year).

octogenarian /ok-tuh-ji-nair-i-uhn/ •n. a person who is between 80 and 89 years old.
– ORIGIN Latin *octoginta* 'eighty'.

octopus •n. (pl. **octopuses**) a sea animal with a soft body and eight long tentacles.
– ORIGIN from Greek *oktō* 'eight' + *pous* 'foot'.

ocular /ok-yuu-ler/ • adj. relating to the eyes or vision.
– ORIGIN Latin *oculus* 'eye'.

oculist /ok-yuu-list/ • n. dated a doctor who treats diseases or defects of the eye.
– ORIGIN Latin *oculus* 'eye'.

OD • v. (**OD's, OD'ing, OD'd**) informal take an overdose of a drug.

odalisque /oh-duh-lisk/ • n. hist. a female slave or concubine in a harem.
– ORIGIN French.

odd • adj. **1** unusual or unexpected; strange. **2** (of whole numbers such as 3 and 5) having one left over as a remainder when divided by two. **3** occasional: *we have the odd drink together.* **4** spare; available: *an odd five minutes.* **5** separated from a pair or set. **6** in the region of: *fifty-odd years.*
– PHRASES **odd one out** a person or thing that differs from the other members of a group. **odds and ends** various small items that are not part of a larger set.
– DERIVATIVES **oddly** adv. **oddness** n.
– ORIGIN Old Norse.

oddball • n. informal a strange or eccentric person.

oddity • n. (pl. **oddities**) **1** the quality of being strange. **2** a strange person or thing.

oddment • n. an item or piece left over from a larger piece or set.

odds • pl. n. **1** the ratio between the amount placed as a bet and the money which would be received if the bet was won: *odds of 8-1.* **2** (**the odds**) the chances of something happening. **3** (**the odds**) the advantage thought to be possessed by one person compared to another: *she won against all the odds.*
– PHRASES **at odds** in conflict or disagreement. **over the odds** Brit. (of a price) above what is thought acceptable.

odds-on • adj. very likely to win, succeed, or happen.

ode • n. a poem addressed to a person or thing or celebrating an event.
– ORIGIN Greek *ōidē* 'song'.

odious • adj. very unpleasant.
– ORIGIN Latin *odium* 'hatred'.

odium • n. widespread hatred or disgust.
– ORIGIN Latin.

odoriferous /oh-duh-rif-uh-ruhss/ • adj. giving off a smell, especially an unpleasant one.

odour (US **odor**) • n. a smell.
– DERIVATIVES **odorous** adj. **odourless** adj.
– ORIGIN Latin *odor*.

odyssey /od-i-si/ • n. (pl. **odysseys**) a long, eventful journey.
– ORIGIN the title of a Greek poem describing the adventures of Odysseus.

OECD • abbrev. Organization for Economic Cooperation and Development.

oedema /i-dee-muh/ (US **edema**) • n. an excess of watery fluid in the cavities or tissues of the body.
– ORIGIN Greek *oidēma*.

Oedipus complex /ee-di-puhss/ • n. (in the theory of Sigmund Freud) the emotions aroused in a young child by an unconscious sexual desire for the parent of the opposite sex.
– DERIVATIVES **Oedipal** adj.
– ORIGIN from *Oedipus* in Greek mythology, who unknowingly killed his father and married his mother.

o'er • adv. & prep. old use or literary = **OVER**.

oesophagus /i-sof-fuh-guhss/ (US **esophagus**) • n. (pl. **oesophagi** /i-sof-fuh-jy/) the muscular tube which connects the throat to the stomach.
– ORIGIN Greek *oisophagos*.

oestrogen /ee-struh-juhn, ess-truh-juhn/ (US **estrogen**) • n. any of a group of hormones which produce and maintain female physical and sexual characteristics.
– ORIGIN from **OESTRUS**.

oestrus /ee-struhss, ess-truhss/ (US **estrus**) • n. a regularly occurring period of time during which female mammals are fertile and sexually receptive to males.
– ORIGIN Greek *oistros* 'gadfly, frenzy'.

oeuvre /er-vruh/ • n. all the works of a particular artist, composer, author, etc.
– ORIGIN French.

of • prep. **1** expressing the relationship between a part and a whole. **2** belonging to; coming from. **3** used in expressions of measurement, value, or age. **4** made from. **5** used to show position: *north of Watford.* **6** used to show that something belongs to a category: *the city of Prague.*
– ORIGIN Old English.

> **USAGE:** It is wrong to write the word **of** instead of **have** or **'ve** in sentences such as *I could have told you that* (not *I could of told you that*).

off • adv. **1** away from a place. **2** so as to be removed or separated: *he took off his coat.* **3** starting a journey or race. **4** so as to finish or be discontinued. **5** (of an electrical appliance or power supply) not working or connected. **6** having a particular level of wealth: *badly off.*
• prep. **1** away from. **2** situated or leading in a direction away from. **3** so as to be removed or separated from. **4** having a temporary dislike of. • adj. **1** (of food) no longer fresh. **2** Brit. informal annoying or

unfair. •n. Brit. informal the start of a race or journey.
– PHRASES **off and on** now and then.
– ORIGIN Old English.

> USAGE: Say **off**, not **off of**, in a sentence such as *the cup fell off the table*; **off of** is not good English and should not be used in writing.

offal •n. the internal organs of an animal used as food.
– ORIGIN prob. from Dutch *afval*.

offbeat •adj. unconventional; unusual.

off-colour •adj. Brit. slightly unwell.

offcut •n. Brit. a piece of wood, fabric, etc. that is left behind after a larger piece has been cut off.

off day •n. a day when a person is not at their best.

offence (US **offense**) •n. **1** an act that breaks a law or rule. **2** a feeling of hurt or annoyance: *I didn't mean to give offence.*

offend •v. **1** make someone feel upset, insulted, or annoyed. **2** be displeasing to. **3** do something illegal.
– DERIVATIVES **offender** n.
– ORIGIN Latin *offendere* 'strike against'.

offensive •adj. **1** causing someone to feel upset, insulted, or annoyed. **2** used in attack: *an offensive weapon.* •n. a campaign to attack or achieve something: *an offensive against crime.*
– PHRASES **be on the offensive** be ready to act aggressively.
– DERIVATIVES **offensively** adv.

offer •v. (**offers, offering, offered**) **1** present something for someone to accept or reject as they wish. **2** express willingness to do something for someone. **3** provide: *the mall offers a variety of shops.* •n. **1** an expression of readiness to do or give something. **2** an amount of money that someone is willing to pay for something. **3** a specially reduced price.
– PHRASES **on offer 1** available. **2** for sale at a reduced price.
– ORIGIN Latin *offerre.*

offering •n. something that is offered; a gift or contribution.

offertory /of-fer-tuh-ri/ •n. (pl. **offertories**) **1** (in the Christian Church) the offering of the bread and wine at Holy Communion. **2** a collection of money made at a Christian church service.
– ORIGIN Latin *offertorium.*

offhand •adj. rudely casual or abrupt in manner. •adv. without previous thought.

office •n. **1** a room, set of rooms, or building in which business or clerical work is carried out. **2** a position of authority. **3** the holding of an official position. **4** (**offices**) things done for other people: *the good offices of the rector.* **5** (also **Divine Office**) daily Christian services of prayers and psalms.
– ORIGIN Latin *officium* 'performance of a task'.

officer •n. **1** a person holding a position of authority in the armed services. **2** a person holding a position of authority in an organization or the government. **3** a policeman or policewoman.

official •adj. **1** relating to an authority or public organization. **2** permitted or done by a person or group in a position of authority. •n. a person holding public office or having official duties.
– DERIVATIVES **officialdom** n. **officially** adv.

official secret •n. Brit. a piece of information that is important for national security and is officially classified as confidential.

officiate /uh-fi-shi-ayt/ •v. (**officiates, officiating, officiated**) **1** act as an official in charge of a sporting event or other occasion. **2** perform a religious service or ceremony.
– ORIGIN Latin *officiare.*

officious •adj. too ready to assert your authority or tell people what to do.

offing •n. (in phr. **in the offing**) likely to happen soon.

off-key •adj. & adv. **1** Music not in the correct key or of the correct pitch. **2** inappropriate.

off-licence •n. Brit. a shop selling alcoholic drink to be drunk elsewhere.

off-limits •adj. out of bounds.

offline •adj. not connected to a computer.

offload •v. **1** unload a cargo. **2** get rid of something by passing it on to someone else.

off-peak •adj. & adv. at a time when demand is less.

off-putting •adj. unpleasant or unsettling.

off season •n. a time of year when people do not take part in a particular activity or a business is quiet.

offset •v. (**offsets, offsetting, offset**) counteract something by having an equal and opposite force or effect.

offshoot •n. **1** a side shoot on a plant. **2** a thing that develops from something else.

offshore •adj. & adv. **1** situated at sea some distance from the shore. **2** (of the wind) blowing towards the sea from the land. **3** made, situated, or registered abroad.

offside • adj. & adv. (in games such as football) occupying a position on the field where playing the ball is not allowed. • n. Brit. the side of a vehicle furthest from the kerb.

offspring • n. (pl. **offspring**) a person's child or children, or the young of an animal.

offstage • adj. & adv. (in a theatre) not on the stage and so not visible to the audience.

off-white • n. a white colour with a grey or yellowish tinge.

oft • adv. old use or literary often.
– ORIGIN Old English.

often (also old use or N. Amer. **oftentimes**) • adv. **1** frequently. **2** in many cases.

ogle • v. (**ogles, ogling, ogled**) stare at someone in a lecherous way.
– ORIGIN prob. from German or Dutch.

ogre /oh-guh/ • n. (fem. **ogress**) **1** (in folklore) a man-eating giant. **2** a cruel or terrifying person.
– ORIGIN French.

oh • exclam. expressing surprise, disappointment, joy, acknowledgement, etc.

ohm /ohm/ • n. the SI unit of electrical resistance. (Symbol: Ω)
– ORIGIN named after the German physicist G. S. *Ohm*.

OHMS • abbrev. on Her (or His) Majesty's Service.

-oid • suffix (forming adjectives and nouns) similar to: *asteroid*.
– ORIGIN Greek *-oeidēs*.

oik (also **oick**) • n. Brit. informal a rude or unpleasant person.

oil • n. **1** a thick, sticky liquid obtained from petroleum. **2** any of various thick liquids which cannot be dissolved in water and are obtained from animals or plants. **3** (also **oils**) oil paint. • v. treat or coat with oil.
– ORIGIN Latin *oleum*.

oilcloth • n. cotton fabric treated with oil to make it waterproof.

oilfield • n. an area where oil is found beneath the ground or the seabed.

oil paint • n. artist's paint made from ground pigment mixed with linseed or other oil.

oil rig (also **oil platform**) • n. a structure that stands on the seabed to provide a stable base above water for drilling oil wells.

oilskin • n. **1** heavy cotton cloth waterproofed with oil. **2** (**oilskins**) a set of garments made of oilskin.

oil slick • n. a layer of oil floating on an area of water.

oil well • n. a shaft dug in the ground so as to extract oil.

oily • adj. (**oilier, oiliest**) **1** containing or covered with oil. **2** resembling oil. **3** (of a person) insincerely polite and flattering.
– DERIVATIVES **oiliness** n.

oink • n. the grunting sound made by a pig. • v. make such a sound.

ointment • n. a smooth substance that is rubbed on the skin for medicinal purposes.
– ORIGIN Old French *oignement*.

OK (also **okay**) informal • exclam. expressing agreement or acceptance.
• adj. **1** satisfactory, but not especially good. **2** allowed. • adv. in a satisfactory way. • n. an act of allowing or agreeing to something. • v. (**OK's, OK'ing, OK'd**) agree to or authorize.
– ORIGIN prob. from *orl korrect*, humorous form of *all correct*.

okapi /oh-kah-pi/ • n. (pl. **okapi** or **okapis**) a large African mammal having a dark chestnut coat with stripes on the hindquarters and upper legs.
– ORIGIN a local word.

okra /ok-ruh, oh-kruh/ • n. a vegetable consisting of the long seed pods of a tropical plant.
– ORIGIN a West African word.

old • adj. (**older, oldest**) **1** having lived for a long time. **2** made or built long ago. **3** possessed or used for a long time. **4** long established or known. **5** former: *they moved back to their old house.* **6** of a specified age: *he was four years old.* **7** informal expressing affection or contempt.
– PHRASES **of old 1** in or belonging to the past. **2** for a long time. **the old days** a period in the past. **the old school** the traditional form or type: *a gentleman of the old school.*
– ORIGIN Old English.

old age • n. the later part of normal life.

old-age pensioner • n. Brit. an old person receiving a retirement pension.

old boy (or **old girl**) • n. Brit. a former student of a school or college.

olden • adj. relating to a long time ago.

Old English • n. the language spoken in England up to about 1150.

Old English sheepdog • n. a large breed of sheepdog with a shaggy grey and white coat.

old-fashioned • adj. no longer current or modern; dated.

Old French • n. the French language up to about 1400.

old gold • n. a dull brownish-gold colour.

old guard • n. the long-standing members of a group, who are often unwilling to accept change.

old hand • n. a very experienced person.

old hat • n. informal something that is boringly familiar or outdated.

old lady • n. informal a person's mother, wife, or girlfriend.

old maid • n. **1** derog. a single woman regarded as too old for marriage. **2** a prim and fussy person.

old man • n. informal a person's father, husband, or boyfriend.

old master • n. a great artist of the past.

Old Nick • n. informal the Devil.

Old Norse • n. the language of medieval Norway, Iceland, Denmark, and Sweden.

Old Testament • n. the first part of the Christian Bible, comprising the sacred writings of Judaism in thirty-nine books.

old-time • adj. relating to or typical of the past.

old-timer • n. informal a person who has worked for an organization for a long time.

old wives' tale • n. a widely held traditional belief that is now thought to be unscientific or incorrect.

old woman • n. **1** informal a person's mother, wife, or girlfriend. **2** derog. a fussy or timid person.

Old World • n. Europe, Asia, and Africa, regarded as the part of the world known before the discovery of the Americas.

old-world • adj. belonging to or associated with the past; quaint.

oleaginous /oh-li-aj-i-nuhss/ • adj. **1** oily or greasy. **2** excessively flattering: *oleaginous speeches.*
– ORIGIN Latin *oleaginus* 'of the olive tree'.

oleander /oh-li-an-der/ • n. an evergreen shrub of warm countries with clusters of white, pink, or red flowers.
– ORIGIN Latin.

O level • n. hist. (in the UK except Scotland) the lower of the two main levels of the GCE exam.
– ORIGIN short for ORDINARY LEVEL.

olfactory /ol-fak-tuh-ri/ • adj. relating to the sense of smell.
– ORIGIN Latin *olfacere* 'to smell'.

oligarch /ol-i-gark/ • n. a ruler in an oligarchy.

oligarchy • n. (pl. **oligarchies**) **1** a small group of people having control of a state. **2** a state governed by a small group of people.
– DERIVATIVES **oligarchic** adj.
– ORIGIN from Greek *oligoi* 'few' + *arkhein* 'to rule'.

Oligocene /ol-i-goh-seen/ • adj. Geol. relating to the third epoch of the Tertiary period (35.4 to 23.3 million years ago), a time when the first primates appeared.
– ORIGIN from Greek *oligos* 'few' + *kainos* 'new'.

oligopoly /oli-gop-uh-li/ • n. (pl. **oligopolies**) a state of limited competition, in which a market is shared by a small number of producers or sellers.
– DERIVATIVES **oligopolistic** adj.

olive • n. **1** a small oval fruit with a hard stone and bitter green or black flesh. **2** the small evergreen tree which produces olives. **3** (also **olive green**) a greyish-green colour. • adj. (of a person's complexion) yellowish brown.
– ORIGIN Latin *oliva.*

olive branch • n. an offer to restore friendly relations.
– ORIGIN with reference to Noah in the Book of Genesis, to whom a dove returned with an olive branch after the Flood.

olive oil • n. an oil obtained from olives, used in cookery and salad dressings.

Olympiad /uh-lim-pi-ad/ • n. a staging of the Olympic Games.

Olympian • adj. **1** relating to the Olympic Games. **2** like a god, especially in being powerful or aloof: *Olympian detachment.* **2** relating to Mount Olympus in Greece, traditional home of the Greek gods. • n. **1** a competitor in the Olympic Games. **2** a person who is greatly admired. **3** any of the twelve main Greek gods.

Olympic • adj. relating to the Olympic Games. • n. (**the Olympics**) the Olympic Games.

Olympic Games • pl. n. **1** a sports festival held every four years in different countries. **2** an ancient Greek festival with athletic and arts competitions, held every four years.

OM • abbrev. (in the UK) Order of Merit.

ombudsman /om-buudz-muhn/ • n. (pl. **ombudsmen**) an official appointed to investigate people's complaints against an organization.
– ORIGIN Swedish, 'legal representative'.

omega /oh-mi-guh/ • n. the last letter of the Greek alphabet (Ω, ω).

omelette (US also **omelet**) • n. a dish of beaten eggs cooked in a frying pan, usually with a savoury filling.
– ORIGIN French.

 Spell **omelette** with an **e** after the **m**; the ending is **-ette**.

omen • n. **1** an event seen as a sign of

future good or bad luck. **2** future significance: *a bird of evil omen.*
– ORIGIN Latin.

ominous • adj. suggesting that something bad is going to happen.
– DERIVATIVES **ominously** adv.
– ORIGIN Latin *ominosus*.

omission • n. **1** the action of leaving something out. **2** a failure to do something. **3** something that has been left out or not done.

> ✓ **omission** and the related word **omit** are spelled with one **m**.

omit • v. (**omits, omitting, omitted**) **1** leave out or exclude. **2** fail to do.
– ORIGIN Latin *omittere* 'let go'.

omni- • comb. form **1** of all things: *omniscient.* **2** in all ways or places: *omnipresent.*
– ORIGIN Latin *omnis* 'all'.

omnibus • n. **1** a book containing several works previously published separately. **2** Brit. a television or radio programme consisting of two or more programmes previously broadcast separately. **3** dated a bus.
– ORIGIN Latin, 'for all'.

omnipotent /om-ni-puh-tuhnt/ • adj. having total power.
– DERIVATIVES **omnipotence** n.
– ORIGIN Latin *omnipotens.*

omnipresent • adj. widespread: *the omnipresent threat of natural disasters.*
– DERIVATIVES **omnipresence** n.

omniscient /om-niss-i-uhnt/ • adj. knowing everything.
– DERIVATIVES **omniscience** n.
– ORIGIN Latin *omnisciens.*

omnivore /om-ni-vor/ • n. an animal that eats both plants and meat.

omnivorous /om-niv-uh-ruhss/ • adj. (of an animal) eating both plants and meat.

on • prep. **1** in contact with and supported by a surface. **2** on to. **3** in the possession of. **4** forming part of the surface of: *a scratch on her arm.* **5** about: *a book on careers.* **6** as a member of a committee, jury, etc. **7** stored in or broadcast by. **8** in the course of a journey or while travelling in a vehicle. **9** indicating the day or time of an event. **10** engaged in: *she's out on errands.* **11** regularly taking a drug or medicine. **12** paid for by someone. **13** added to something. • adv. **1** in contact with and supported by a surface. **2** (of clothing) being worn. **3** with continued movement or action. **4** taking place or being presented: *there's a good film on today.* **5** (of an electrical appliance or power supply) functioning.
– PHRASES **be on about** Brit. informal talk

about. **be on at** Brit. informal nag at. **be on to** informal **1** be close to discovering that someone has done something wrong. **2** have an idea that is likely to lead to an important discovery. **on to** moving to a place on the surface of or aboard.
– ORIGIN Old English.

onanism /oh-nuh-ni-z'm/ • n. formal **1** masturbation. **2** sexual intercourse in which the penis is withdrawn before ejaculation.
– ORIGIN from *Onan* in the Bible (Book of Genesis, chapter 38).

once • adv. **1** on one occasion only. **2** on even one occasion: *he never once complained.* **3** formerly. **4** multiplied by one. • conj. as soon as.
– PHRASES **all at once** suddenly. **at once 1** immediately. **2** at the same time. **once upon a time** at some time in the past.

once-over • n. informal a rapid inspection, search, or piece of work.

oncology /ong-kol-uh-ji/ • n. the study and treatment of tumours.
– DERIVATIVES **oncological** adj. **oncologist** n.

oncoming • adj. moving towards you.

one • cardinal number **1** the lowest cardinal number; 1. (Roman numeral: **i** or **I**.) **2** single, or a single person or thing. **3** (before a person's name) a certain. **4** the same. • pron. **1** used to refer to a person or thing previously mentioned or easily identified. **2** a person of a specified kind: *her loved ones.* **3** (third person sing.) used to refer to the speaker or to represent people in general.
– PHRASES **at one** in agreement. **be one up on** informal have an advantage over. **one and all** everyone. **one and only** unique. **one another** each other. **one day** at some time in the past or future. **one or two** informal a few.
– ORIGIN Old English.

one-armed bandit • n. informal a fruit machine operated by pulling a long handle at the side.

one-dimensional • adj. not complex or deep; superficial.

one-liner • n. informal a short joke or witty remark.

one-man band • n. **1** a street entertainer who plays many instruments at the same time. **2** a person who runs a business alone.

oneness • n. the state of being unified, whole, or in agreement.

one-night stand • n. informal a sexual relationship lasting only one night.

one-off Brit. informal • adj. made or happening only once. • n. something made or happening only once.

onerous /oh-nuh-ruhss/ • adj. involving

great effort and difficulty.
– ORIGIN Latin *onerosus*.

oneself • pron. (third person sing.) **1** used as the object of a verb or preposition when this is the same as the subject of the clause and the subject is 'one'. **2** used to emphasize that one does something individually or without help. **3** in one's normal state of body or mind.

one-sided • adj. **1** unfairly biased. **2** (of a contest or conflict) very unequal.

one-time • adj. former.

one-track mind • n. informal a mind preoccupied with one subject.

one-upmanship • n. informal the technique of gaining an advantage over someone else.

one-way • adj. moving or allowing movement in one direction only.

ongoing • adj. still in progress.

onion • n. a vegetable consisting of a bulb with a strong taste and smell.
– PHRASES **know your onions** informal be very knowledgeable.
– ORIGIN Old French *oignon*.

online • adj. & adv. **1** controlled by or connected to a computer. **2** available on or carried out via the Internet: *online banking*.

onlooker • n. a spectator.

only • adv. **1** and no one or nothing more besides. **2** no longer ago than. **3** not until. **4** with the negative result that: *he turned, only to find his way blocked.* • adj. **1** single or solitary. **2** alone deserving consideration. • conj. informal except that.
– PHRASES **only just 1** by a very small margin. **2** very recently.
– ORIGIN Old English.

o.n.o. • abbrev. Brit. or nearest offer.

onomatopoeia /on-uh-mat-uh-pee-uh/ • n. the use of a word that sounds similar to the noise described (e.g. *sizzle*).
– DERIVATIVES **onomatopoeic** adj.
– ORIGIN Greek *onomatopoiia* 'word-making'.

onrush • n. a surging rush forward.
– DERIVATIVES **onrushing** adj.

onset • n. the beginning of something.

onshore • adj. & adv. **1** situated on land. **2** (of the wind) blowing from the sea towards the land.

onside • adj. & adv. (in sport) not offside.

onslaught • n. **1** a fierce or destructive attack. **2** an overwhelmingly large quantity of people or things.
– ORIGIN Dutch *aenslag*.

onstage • adj. & adv. (in a theatre) on the stage and so visible to the audience.

onto • prep. var. of on to (see **ON**).

USAGE: There is a difference between the preposition **onto** or **on to** and the use of the adverb **on** followed by the preposition **to**: *she climbed on to* (or *onto*) *the roof* (in other words, so as to be on the surface of it) but *let's go on to* (continue to) *the next point.*

ontology /on-tol-uh-ji/ • n. philosophy concerned with the nature of being.
– DERIVATIVES **ontological** adj.

onus /oh-nuhss/ • n. a responsibility: *the onus is on you to spot mistakes.*
– ORIGIN Latin.

onward • adv. (also **onwards**) **1** in a continuing forward direction. **2** so as to make progress. • adj. moving forward.

onyx /on-iks/ • n. a semi-precious variety of agate with different colours in layers.
– ORIGIN Greek *onux* 'fingernail, onyx'.

oodles • pl. n. informal a very great number or amount.

oolite /oh-uh-lyt/ • n. limestone consisting of a mass of rounded grains.
– ORIGIN Latin *oolites* 'egg stone'.

oomph • n. informal excitement or energy.

oops • exclam. informal used to show a person's awareness of a mistake or minor accident.

ooze • v. (**oozes**, **oozing**, **oozed**) **1** (of a fluid) slowly seep out. **2** give a powerful impression of: *she oozes sex appeal.* • n. wet mud or slime.
– DERIVATIVES **oozy** adj.
– ORIGIN Old English, 'juice or sap'.

Op. (also **op.**) • abbrev. Music opus.

op • n. informal a surgical operation.

opacity /oh-pa-si-ti/ • n. **1** the state of being opaque or difficult to see through. **2** the quality of being difficult to understand.

opal • n. a semi-transparent gemstone in which many small points of shifting colour can be seen.
– ORIGIN Latin *opalus*.

opalescent • adj. showing many small points of shifting colour.

opaque /oh-payk/ • adj. (**opaquer**, **opaquest**) **1** not able to be seen through. **2** difficult or impossible to understand.
– ORIGIN Latin *opacus* 'darkened'.

op. cit. • adv. in the work already mentioned.
– ORIGIN from Latin *opere citato*.

OPEC • abbrev. Organization of the Petroleum Exporting Countries.

open • adj. **1** not closed, fastened, or restricted. **2** not covered or protected. **3** (**open to**) likely to suffer from or be affected by. **4** spread out, expanded, or unfolded. **5** accessible or available. **6** frank and communicative. **7** not

disguised or hidden: *open hostility.* **8** not finally settled. **9** (**open to**) making possible: *a message open to different interpretations.* • v. **1** make or become open. **2** formally begin or establish. **3** (**open on to/into**) give access to. **4** (**open out/up**) begin to talk frankly. • n. **1** (**the open**) fresh air or open countryside. **2** (**Open**) a competition with no restrictions on who may compete.
– PHRASES **the open air** an unenclosed space outdoors. **in** (or **into**) **the open** not secret. **open-and-shut** not disputed; straightforward. **open up** (or **open fire**) begin shooting.
– DERIVATIVES **openness** n.
– ORIGIN Old English.

opencast • adj. Brit. (of mining) in which coal or ore is extracted from a level near the earth's surface, rather than from shafts.

open day • n. Brit. a day when the public may visit a place to which they do not usually have access.

open-ended • adj. having no limit decided in advance.

opener • n. **1** a device for opening something. **2** a person or thing that opens or begins something.

open-handed • adj. giving willingly; generous.

open-hearted • adj. kind and friendly.

open-heart surgery • n. surgery in which the heart is exposed and the blood made to bypass it.

open house • n. a place or situation in which all visitors are welcome.

opening • n. **1** a gap. **2** a beginning. **3** a ceremony at which a building, show, etc. is declared to be open. **4** an opportunity or available job. • adj. coming at the beginning.

open letter • n. a letter addressed to a particular person but intended to be published in a newspaper or journal.

openly • adv. frankly or honestly.

open market • n. a situation in which companies can trade without restrictions.

open marriage • n. a marriage in which both people agree that each may have other sexual partners.

open-minded • adj. willing to consider new ideas.

open-plan • adj. having large rooms with few or no dividing walls.

open prison • n. Brit. a prison with the minimum of restrictions on prisoners' movements and activities.

open season • n. the period of the year when restrictions on the killing of certain types of wildlife are lifted.

open secret • n. a supposed secret that is in fact known to many people.

open verdict • n. Law a verdict of a coroner's jury which states that a suspicious death has occurred but the cause is not known.

opera¹ • n. a dramatic work set to music for singers and musicians.
– ORIGIN Italian.

opera² pl. of OPUS.

operable • adj. **1** able to be used. **2** able to be treated by a surgical operation.

opera glasses • pl. n. small binoculars for use at the opera or theatre.

opera house • n. a theatre for the performance of opera.

operand /op-uh-rand/ • n. Math. the quantity on which an operation is to be done.
– ORIGIN Latin *operandum* 'thing to be operated on'.

operate • v. (**operates**, **operating**, **operated**) **1** work or function. **2** control or use a machine. **3** (of an organization or armed force) carry out activities. **4** be in effect: *a powerful law operates in politics.* **5** perform a surgical operation.
– ORIGIN Latin *operari*.

operatic • adj. relating to opera.
– DERIVATIVES **operatically** adv.

operating system • n. the low-level software that supports a computer's basic functions.

operating theatre (N. Amer. **operating room**) • n. a room in which surgical operations are performed.

operation • n. **1** the action of operating. **2** an act of surgery performed on a patient to remove or repair a damaged part. **3** an organized action involving a number of people. **4** a business organization. **5** Math. a process in which a number, quantity, etc. is altered according to particular rules.

operational • adj. **1** being used or ready for use. **2** relating to the functioning of an organization.
– DERIVATIVES **operationally** adv.

operative • adj. **1** working or functioning. **2** (of a word) having the most importance in a phrase. **3** relating to surgery. • n. **1** a worker. **2** esp. N. Amer. a secret agent.

operator • n. **1** a person who operates equipment or a machine. **2** a person who works at the switchboard of a telephone exchange. **3** a person or company that runs a business. **4** informal a person who acts in a specified way: *a smooth operator.* **5** a mathematical symbol referring to an operation (e.g. ×, +).

operculum /oh-per-kyuu-luhm/ • n. (pl. **opercula** /oh-per-kyuu-luh/) **1** a flap of skin protecting a fish's gills. **2** a plate that closes the opening of a mollusc's shell.
– ORIGIN Latin, 'lid, covering'.

operetta • n. a short opera on a light or humorous theme.
– ORIGIN Italian, 'little opera'.

ophthalmia /off-thal-mi-uh/ • n. inflammation of the eye.
– ORIGIN Greek.

ophthalmic • adj. relating to the eye and its diseases.

ophthalmic optician • n. see OPTICIAN.

ophthalmology /off-thal-mol-uh-ji/ • n. the study and treatment of disorders and diseases of the eye.
– DERIVATIVES **ophthalmologist** n.

opiate /oh-pi-uht/ • n. **1** a drug containing opium. **2** something that causes a false sense of contentment: *movies are the new opiate of the people.* • adj. relating to opium.

opine • v. (**opines, opining, opined**) formal state something as your opinion.
– ORIGIN Latin *opinari* 'think, believe'.

opinion • n. **1** a personal view not necessarily based on fact or knowledge. **2** the views of people in general: *public opinion.* **3** a formal statement of advice by an expert.
– PHRASES **a matter of opinion** something not able to be proven either way.
– ORIGIN Latin.

opinionated • adj. tending to put forward your views forcefully.

opinion poll • n. the questioning of a small sample of people in order to assess wider public opinion.

opium • n. an addictive drug made from the juice of a poppy.
– ORIGIN Latin.

opossum /uh-poss-uhm/ • n. **1** an American marsupial mammal with a tail which it can use for grasping. **2** Austral./NZ a possum.
– ORIGIN Algonquian (an American Indian language), 'white dog'.

opponent • n. **1** a person who opposes or competes with another in a contest, argument, or fight. **2** a person who disagrees with a proposal or practice.
– ORIGIN Latin *opponere* 'set against'.

opportune /op-per-tyoon, op-per-tyoon/ • adj. done or happening at an especially convenient or appropriate time.
– ORIGIN Latin *opportunus.*

opportunist • n. a person who takes advantage of opportunities when they arise, regardless of whether or not they

are right to do so. • adj. opportunistic.
– DERIVATIVES **opportunism** n.

opportunistic • adj. taking advantage of opportunities when they arise.
– DERIVATIVES **opportunistically** adv.

opportunity • n. (pl. **opportunities**) **1** a favourable time or situation for doing something. **2** a career opening: *job opportunities.*

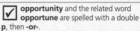

opportunity and the related word **opportune** are spelled with a double p, then -or-.

opposable • adj. (of the thumb of a primate mammal) capable of facing and touching the other digits on the same hand.

oppose • v. (**opposes, opposing, opposed**) **1** (also **be opposed to**) disagree with and try to prevent or resist. **2** compete with or fight. **3** (as adj. **opposed**) (of two or more things) conflicting. **4** (as adj. **opposing**) opposite.
– ORIGIN Old French *opposer.*

opposite • adj. **1** on the other or further side; facing. **2** completely different. **3** being the other of a contrasted pair: *the opposite ends of the price range.* **4** (of angles) between opposite sides of the intersection of two lines. • n. an opposite person or thing. • adv. in an opposite position. • prep. in a position opposite to.
– DERIVATIVES **oppositely** adv.
– ORIGIN Latin *oppositus.*

opposite number • n. a person's counterpart in another organization.

opposite sex • n. (**the opposite sex**) women in relation to men or vice versa.

opposition • n. **1** resistance or disagreement. **2** a group of opponents. **3** (**the Opposition**) Brit. the main party in parliament that is opposed to the one in the government. **4** a contrast or direct opposite.
– DERIVATIVES **oppositional** adj.

oppress • v. **1** treat in a very harsh and unfair way. **2** make someone feel distressed or anxious.
– DERIVATIVES **oppression** n. **oppressor** n.
– ORIGIN Old French *oppresser.*

oppressive • adj. **1** harsh and demanding strict obedience. **2** causing distress or anxiety. **3** (of weather) hot and close.
– DERIVATIVES **oppressively** adv.

opprobrious /uh-proh-bri-uhss/ • adj. formal critical or scornful.

opprobrium /uh-proh-bri-uhm/ • n. formal **1** criticism or scorn. **2** public disgrace as a result of bad behaviour.
– ORIGIN Latin, 'infamy'.

opt • v. make a choice.
– PHRASES **opt out 1** choose not to

participate. **2** Brit. (of a school or hospital) withdraw from local authority control.
– ORIGIN Latin *optare*.

optic • adj. relating to the eye or vision. • n. Brit. trademark a device fastened to the neck of an upside-down bottle for measuring out spirits.
– ORIGIN Greek *optikos*.

optical • adj. relating to vision, light, or optics.
– DERIVATIVES **optically** adv.

optical fibre • n. a thin glass fibre through which light can be transmitted.

optical illusion • n. a thing that deceives the eye by appearing to be something that it is not.

optician • n. Brit. a person qualified to prescribe and dispense glasses and contact lenses, and to detect eye diseases (**ophthalmic optician**), or to make and supply glasses and contact lenses (**dispensing optician**).

optic nerves • pl. n. the pair of nerves transmitting impulses from the eyes to the brain.

optics • n. the branch of science concerned with vision and the behaviour of light.

optimal • adj. best or most favourable.
– DERIVATIVES **optimally** adv.

optimism • n. hopefulness and confidence about the future or success of something.
– DERIVATIVES **optimist** n.
– ORIGIN French *optimisme*.

optimistic • adj. hopeful and confident about the future.
– DERIVATIVES **optimistically** adv.

optimize (or **optimise**) • v. (**optimizes**, **optimizing**, **optimized**) make the best use of a situation or resource.
– DERIVATIVES **optimization** n.

optimum • adj. most likely to lead to a favourable outcome: *the optimum level of security.* • n. (pl. **optima** or **optimums**) the most favourable conditions for growth or success.
– ORIGIN Latin, 'best thing'.

option • n. **1** a thing that is or may be chosen. **2** the freedom or right to choose. **3** a right to buy or sell something in the future.
– PHRASES **keep** (or **leave**) **your options open** not commit yourself.

optional • adj. available to be chosen but not compulsory.
– DERIVATIVES **optionally** adv.

optometry • n. the occupation of measuring eyesight, prescribing lenses, and detecting eye disease.
– DERIVATIVES **optometrist** n.

opulent /op-yuu-luhnt/ • adj. expensive and luxurious.
– DERIVATIVES **opulence** n. **opulently** adv.
– ORIGIN Latin *opulens* 'wealthy'.

opus /oh-puhss/ • n. (pl. **opuses** or **opera** /op-uh-ruh/) **1** a musical composition or set of compositions. **2** an artistic work.
– ORIGIN Latin, 'work'.

or • conj. **1** used to link alternatives. **2** introducing a word that means the same as a preceding word or phrase, or that explains it. **3** otherwise.
– ORIGIN Old English.

-or • suffix **1** forming nouns referring to a person or thing that performs the action of a verb: *escalator.* **2** forming nouns referring to a state: *terror.*
– ORIGIN Latin.

oracle • n. **1** (in ancient Greece or Rome) a priest or priestess who acted as a channel for advice or prophecy from the gods. **2** an authority which is always correct.
– ORIGIN Latin *oraculum*.

oracular /o-rak-yuu-ler/ • adj. **1** relating to an oracle. **2** hard to interpret.

oral • adj. **1** spoken rather than written. **2** relating to or done by the mouth. • n. a spoken exam.
– DERIVATIVES **orally** adv.
– ORIGIN Latin *oralis*.

> **USAGE:** Do not confuse **oral** with **aural**. **Oral** means 'spoken' or 'relating to the mouth' (*oral communication skills*), whereas **aural** means 'relating to the ears or hearing' (*the album provides pure aural pleasure*).

orange • n. **1** a large round citrus fruit with a tough reddish-yellow rind. **2** esp. Brit. a drink made from or flavoured with orange juice. **3** a bright reddish-yellow colour. • adj. reddish yellow.
– DERIVATIVES **orangey** (also **orangy**) adj.
– ORIGIN Old French *orenge*.

orangeade • n. Brit. a fizzy soft drink flavoured with orange.

Orange Order • n. a Protestant political society in Northern Ireland.
– DERIVATIVES **Orangeman** n. (pl. **Orangemen**).
– ORIGIN named after the Protestant king William of *Orange* (William III of Great Britain and Ireland).

orangery • n. (pl. **orangeries**) a type of large conservatory where orange trees are grown.

orang-utan /uh-rang-oo-tan/ (also **orang-utang** /uh-rang-oo-tang/) • n. a large ape with long red hair, found in forests in Borneo and Sumatra.
– ORIGIN Malay, 'forest person'.

oration /o-ray-sh'n/ • n. a formal speech.
– ORIGIN Latin.

orator /o-ruh-ter/ • n. a skilful public speaker.

oratorio /o-ruh-tor-i-oh/ • n. (pl. **oratorios**) a large-scale musical work on a religious theme for orchestra and voices.
– ORIGIN Italian.

oratory¹ /o-ruh-tri/ • n. (pl. **oratories**) a small chapel for private worship.

oratory² /o-ruh-tri/ • n. powerful and persuasive public speaking.
– DERIVATIVES **oratorical** /o-ruh-to-ri-k'l/ adj.

orb • n. 1 a spherical object or shape. 2 a golden globe with a cross on top, carried by a king or queen.
– ORIGIN Latin *orbis* 'ring'.

orbit • n. 1 the regularly repeated elliptical course of a planet, moon, spacecraft, etc. around a star or planet. 2 an area of activity or influence. • v. (**orbits**, **orbiting**, **orbited**) move in orbit round a star or planet.
– DERIVATIVES **orbiter** n.
– ORIGIN Latin *orbita* 'course'.

orbital • adj. 1 relating to an orbit or orbits. 2 Brit. (of a road) passing round the outside of a town.

orca /or-kuh/ • n. a killer whale.
– ORIGIN French *orque* or Latin *orca*.

Orcadian /or-kay-di-uhn/ • adj. relating to the Orkney Islands. • n. a person from the Orkney Islands.
– ORIGIN Latin *Orcades* 'Orkney Islands'.

orchard • n. a piece of enclosed land planted with fruit trees.
– ORIGIN Old English.

orchestra • n. 1 a large group of musicians with string, woodwind, brass, and percussion sections. 2 (also **orchestra pit**) the part of a theatre where the orchestra plays.
– DERIVATIVES **orchestral** adj. **orchestrally** adv.
– ORIGIN Greek *orkhēstra*.

orchestrate • v. (**orchestrates**, **orchestrating**, **orchestrated**) 1 arrange music to be performed by an orchestra. 2 direct a situation to produce a desired effect.
– DERIVATIVES **orchestration** n. **orchestrator** n.

orchid • n. a plant of a large family with complex showy flowers.
– ORIGIN Greek *orkhis* 'testicle'.

ordain • v. 1 make someone a priest or minister. 2 order something officially. 3 (of God or fate) decide in advance.
– ORIGIN Latin *ordinare*.

ordeal • n. a prolonged painful or horrific experience.
– ORIGIN Old English.

order • n. 1 the arrangement of people or things according to a particular sequence or method. 2 a state in which everything is in its correct place. 3 a state in which the laws regulating public behaviour are followed. 4 a command. 5 a request for something to be made, supplied, or served. 6 the set procedure followed in a meeting, law court, or religious service. 7 quality: *poetry of the highest order.* 8 a social class or system. 9 (**orders** or **holy orders**) the rank of an ordained minister in the Christian Church. 10 a society of monks, nuns, or friars living under the same rule. 11 an institution founded by a king or queen to honour good behaviour: *the Order of the Garter.* 12 a main classifying category of plants and animals that ranks below class and above family. • v. (**orders**, **ordering**, **ordered**) 1 give a command. 2 request that something be made, supplied, or served. 3 arrange methodically.
– PHRASES **in order 1** in the correct condition for use. 2 suitable in the circumstances. **in order for** (or **that**) so that. **in order to** so as to. **of** (or **in**) **the order of** approximately. **on order** (of goods) requested but not yet received. **out of order 1** not working properly or at all. 2 Brit. informal unacceptable.
– ORIGIN Latin *ordo* 'row, series'.

orderly • adj. 1 neatly and methodically arranged. 2 well behaved. • n. (pl. **orderlies**) 1 a hospital attendant responsible for various non-medical tasks. 2 a soldier who carries orders or performs minor tasks for an officer.
– DERIVATIVES **orderliness** n.

order of magnitude • n. size or quantity.

ordinal • adj. relating to order in a series.
– ORIGIN Latin *ordinalis*.

ordinal number • n. a number defining a thing's position in a series, such as 'first' or 'second'.

ordinance • n. formal 1 an official order. 2 a religious rite.
– ORIGIN Old French *ordenance*.

ordinand /or-di-nand/ • n. a person who is training to be ordained as a priest or minister.
– ORIGIN Latin *ordinandus*.

ordinary • adj. 1 normal or usual. 2 not interesting or exceptional.
– DERIVATIVES **ordinarily** adv. **ordinariness** n.
– ORIGIN Latin *ordinarius* 'orderly'.

ordinary grade • n. (in Scotland) the lower of the two main levels of the Scottish Certificate of Education exam.

ordinary level • n. = O LEVEL.

ordinate /or-di-nuht/ •n. Math. a straight line from a point on a graph drawn parallel to the vertical axis and meeting the other; the y-coordinate.
– ORIGIN from Latin *linea ordinata applicata* 'line applied parallel'.

ordination •n. the action of ordaining someone as a priest or minister.

ordnance /ord-nuhnss/ •n. 1 large guns mounted on wheels. 2 US military equipment and stores.
– ORIGIN variant of ORDINANCE.

Ordnance Survey •n. (in the UK) an official survey organization preparing detailed maps of the country.

Ordovician /or-duh-vish-i-uhn/ •adj. Geol. relating to the second period of the Palaeozoic era, about 510 to 439 million years ago, when the first vertebrates appeared.
– ORIGIN Latin *Ordovices*, an ancient British tribe in North Wales.

ordure /or-dyuur/ •n. dung.
– ORIGIN Old French.

ore •n. a naturally occurring material from which a metal or valuable mineral can be extracted.
– ORIGIN Old English, 'unwrought metal'.

oregano /o-ri-gah-noh/ •n. a plant whose leaves are used as a herb in cookery.
– ORIGIN Spanish.

organ •n. 1 a part of an animal or plant that has a particular function, for example the heart. 2 a large musical keyboard instrument with rows of pipes supplied with air from bellows. 3 a smaller keyboard instrument producing sounds electronically. 4 a newspaper or journal which puts forward the views of a political party or movement.
– DERIVATIVES **organist** n.
– ORIGIN Greek *organon* 'tool, organ'.

organdie /or-guhn-di/ (US also **organdy**) •n. a fine, semi-transparent, stiff cotton muslin.
– ORIGIN French *organdi*.

organelle /or-guh-nel/ •n. a specialized structure within a cell.
– ORIGIN Latin *organella* 'little tool'.

organic •adj. 1 relating to living matter. 2 produced without artificial chemicals such as fertilizers. 3 (of a chemical compound) containing carbon and chiefly or ultimately of biological origin. 4 relating to a bodily organ or organs. 5 (of the parts of a whole) fitting together harmoniously. 6 (of development or change) continuous or natural.
– DERIVATIVES **organically** adv.

organism •n. 1 an individual animal, plant, or other life form. 2 a whole made up of parts which are dependent on each other.

organization (or **organisation**) •n. 1 the action of organizing. 2 a systematic arrangement or approach. 3 an organized group of people with a particular purpose, e.g. a business.
– DERIVATIVES **organizational** adj. **organizationally** adv.

organize (or **organise**) •v. (**organizes, organizing, organized**) 1 arrange in an orderly way: *the book is organized into nine thematic chapters.* 2 make arrangements for an event or activity.
– DERIVATIVES **organizer** n.
– ORIGIN Latin *organizare*.

organza /or-gan-zuh/ •n. a thin, stiff, transparent fabric.

orgasm •n. the climax of sexual excitement, when feelings of sexual pleasure are most intense. •v. have an orgasm.
– DERIVATIVES **orgasmic** adj.
– ORIGIN Greek *orgasmos*.

orgiastic /or-ji-ass-tik/ •adj. relating to or like an orgy.

orgy •n. (pl. **orgies**) 1 a wild party with much drinking and sexual activity. 2 an excessive amount of a specified activity: *an orgy of killing.*
– ORIGIN Greek *orgia* 'secret rites'.

oriel window /or-i-uhl/ •n. a window in a large bay built in the upper storey of a building.
– ORIGIN Old French *oriol* 'gallery'.

orient •n. /or-i-uhnt/ (**the Orient**) literary the countries of the East. •v. /or-i-ent/ 1 position something in relation to the points of a compass or other specified positions. 2 (**orient yourself**) find your position in relation to unfamiliar surroundings. 3 tailor to meet particular needs: *magazines oriented to students.*
– ORIGIN Latin *oriens* 'rising or east'.

oriental •adj. relating to the Far East. •n. dated or offens. a person of Far Eastern descent.

orientate •v. (**orientates, orientating, orientated**) = ORIENT.

orientation •n. 1 the action of orienting or positioning someone or something. 2 a position in relation to something else. 3 a person's attitude or natural tendency: *her sexual orientation.*

orienteering •n. a competitive sport in which runners have to find their way across rough country with the aid of a map and compass.

orifice /o-ri-fiss/ •n. an opening in the body.
– ORIGIN French.

origami /o-ri-gah-mi/ • n. the Japanese art of folding paper into decorative shapes.
– ORIGIN Japanese.

origin • n. 1 the point where something begins. 2 a person's social background or ancestry. 3 Math. a fixed point from which coordinates are measured.
– ORIGIN Latin *origo*.

original • adj. 1 existing from the beginning. 2 produced by an artist, author, etc. rather than copied. 3 new and different from what has been done before; inventive. • n. the earliest form of something, from which copies can be made.
– DERIVATIVES **originally** adv.

originality • n. 1 the ability to think independently or creatively. 2 the quality of being new or inventive.

original sin • n. (in Christian belief) the tendency to be sinful that is thought to be present in all people.

originate • v. (**originates, originating, originated**) 1 begin in a particular place or situation. 2 create or initiate something.
– DERIVATIVES **origination** n. **originator** n.

oriole /or-i-ohl/ • n. a brightly coloured bird with a musical call.
– ORIGIN Latin *oriolus*.

ormolu /or-muh-loo/ • n. a gold-coloured alloy of copper, zinc, and tin used in decoration.
– ORIGIN from French *or moulu* 'powdered gold'.

ornament • n. 1 an object designed to add beauty to something. 2 decorative items as a whole. 3 (**ornaments**) Music embellishments made to a melody.
– DERIVATIVES **ornamentation** n. **ornamented** adj.
– ORIGIN Latin *ornamentum*.

ornamental • adj. used as an ornament; decorative.
– DERIVATIVES **ornamentally** adv.

ornate • adj. highly decorated.
– DERIVATIVES **ornately** adv.
– ORIGIN Latin *ornare* 'adorn'.

ornithology /or-ni-thol-uh-ji/ • n. the scientific study of birds.
– DERIVATIVES **ornithological** adj. **ornithologist** n.
– ORIGIN Greek *ornis* 'bird'.

orotund /o-roh-tund/ • adj. 1 (of a person's voice) deep and impressive. 2 (of writing or style) pompous.
– ORIGIN from Latin *ore rotundo* 'with rounded mouth'.

orphan • n. a child whose parents are dead. • v. (**be orphaned**) (of a child) be made an orphan.
– ORIGIN Greek *orphanos* 'bereaved'.

orphanage • n. a home which cares for orphans.

ortho- • comb. form 1 straight; rectangular; upright: *orthodontics*. 2 correct: *orthography*.
– ORIGIN Greek *orthos*.

orthodontics /or-thuh-**don**-tiks/ • n. the treatment of irregularities in the teeth and jaws.
– DERIVATIVES **orthodontic** adj. **orthodontist** n.
– ORIGIN Greek *odous* 'tooth'.

orthodox • adj. 1 following traditional or generally accepted beliefs. 2 conventional or normal. 3 (**Orthodox**) relating to Orthodox Judaism or the Orthodox Church.
– ORIGIN Greek *orthodoxos*.

Orthodox Church • n. any of the ancient branches of the Christian Church which originated in eastern Europe and do not accept the authority of the Pope.

Orthodox Judaism • n. a branch of Judaism which teaches that the requirements of Jewish law and traditional custom must be strictly followed.

orthodoxy • n. (pl. **orthodoxies**) 1 traditional beliefs, theories, or practices. 2 an idea which is generally accepted. 3 the whole community of Orthodox Jews or Orthodox Christians.

orthography /or-**thog**-ruh-fi/ • n. the conventional spelling system of a language.
– DERIVATIVES **orthographic** adj.

orthopaedics /or-thuh-**pee**-diks/ (US **orthopedics**) • n. the branch of medicine concerned with the correction of deformities of bones or muscles.
– DERIVATIVES **orthopaedic** adj.
– ORIGIN Greek *paideia* 'rearing of children'.

ortolan /or-tuh-luhn/ • n. a small songbird with an olive-green head and yellow throat.
– ORIGIN Provençal, 'gardener'.

Orwellian • adj. relating to the work of the British novelist George Orwell, especially the oppressive state depicted in *Nineteen Eighty-four*.

-ory[1] • suffix forming nouns referring to a place for a particular function: *dormitory*.
– ORIGIN Latin *-oria, -orium*.

-ory[2] • suffix forming adjectives relating to a verbal action: *compulsory*.
– ORIGIN Latin *-orius*.

oryx /o-riks/ • n. a large antelope with long horns, found in arid regions of Africa and Arabia.
– ORIGIN Latin.

Os • symb. the chemical element osmium.

Oscar • n. (trademark in the US) the nickname for a gold statuette given as an Academy award.

oscillate /oss-i-layt/ • v. (**oscillates, oscillating, oscillated**) **1** move or swing back and forth in a regular rhythm. **2** waver between extremes of opinion or emotion. **3** Physics move or vary with periodic regularity.
– DERIVATIVES **oscillation** n. **oscillator** n.
– ORIGIN Latin *oscillare* 'to swing'.

oscilloscope • n. a device for showing changes in electrical current as a display on the screen of a cathode ray tube.

osier /oh-zi-er/ • n. a type of willow tree with long flexible shoots used in making baskets.
– ORIGIN Old French.

osmium /oz-mi-uhm/ • n. a hard, dense silvery-white metallic element.
– ORIGIN Greek *osmē* 'smell'.

osmoregulation • n. Biol. the control of water content and salt concentration in the body of an organism.

osmosis /oz-moh-siss/ • n. **1** a process by which molecules of a solvent pass through a membrane from a less concentrated solution into a more concentrated one. **2** the gradual absorbing of ideas.
– DERIVATIVES **osmotic** adj.
– ORIGIN Greek *ōsmos* 'a push'.

osprey • n. (pl. **ospreys**) a large fish-eating bird of prey with a white under-side and crown.
– ORIGIN Old French *ospres*.

osseous /oss-i-uhss/ • adj. tech. consisting of or turned into bone.
– ORIGIN Latin *osseus* 'bony'.

ossify /oss-i-fy/ • v. (**ossifies, ossifying, ossified**) **1** turn into bone or bony tissue. **2** (usu. as adj. **ossified**) stop developing: *an ossified tradition*.
– DERIVATIVES **ossification** n.
– ORIGIN Latin *os* 'bone'.

ostensible • adj. apparently true, but not necessarily so.
– DERIVATIVES **ostensibly** adv.
– ORIGIN Latin *ostensibilis*.

ostentation • n. showy display which is intended to impress.
– ORIGIN Latin *ostendere* 'stretch out to view'.

ostentatious /oss-ten-tay-shuhss/ • adj. showy in a way which is intended to impress.
– DERIVATIVES **ostentatiously** adv.

osteo- /oss-ti-oh/ • comb. form relating to the bones: *osteoporosis*.
– ORIGIN Greek *osteon* 'bone'.

osteoarthritis /oss-ti-oh-ar-thry-tiss/ • n. a condition in which cartilage in the joints decays, causing pain and stiffness.

osteopathy /oss-ti-op-uh-thi/ • n. a system of complementary medicine involving the manipulation of the bones and muscles.
– DERIVATIVES **osteopath** n. **osteopathic** adj.

osteoporosis /oss-ti-oh-puh-roh-siss/ • n. a medical condition in which the bones become brittle and fragile.
– ORIGIN Greek *poros* 'passage, pore'.

ostinato /oss-ti-nah-toh/ • n. (pl. **ostinatos** or **ostinati** /oss-ti-nah-ti/) a continually repeated musical phrase or rhythm.
– ORIGIN Italian, 'obstinate'.

ostler /oss-ler/ • n. hist. a man employed at an inn to look after customers' horses.
– ORIGIN Old French *hostelier* 'innkeeper'.

ostracize /oss-truh-syz/ (or **ostracise**) • v. (**ostracizes, ostracizing, ostracized**) exclude someone from a society or group.
– DERIVATIVES **ostracism** n.
– ORIGIN Greek *ostrakizein*.

ostrich • n. a large African bird with a long neck and long legs, that runs fast but cannot fly.
– ORIGIN Old French *ostriche*.

OT • abbrev. Old Testament.

other • adj. & pron. **1** used to refer to a person or thing that is different from one already mentioned or known. **2** additional. **3** the alternative of two. **4** those people or things not already mentioned.
– PHRASES **the other woman** the mistress of a married man.
– ORIGIN Old English.

other half • n. Brit. informal a person's wife, husband, or partner.

otherness • n. the quality or fact of being different.

otherwise • adv. **1** in different circum-stances. **2** in other respects. **3** in a different way. **4** alternatively.

other-worldly • adj. **1** relating to an imaginary or spiritual world. **2** not aware of the realities of life.

otiose /oh-ti-ohss, oh-shi-ohss/ • adj. serving no practical purpose.
– ORIGIN Latin *otiosus*.

OTT • abbrev. Brit. informal over the top.

otter • n. a fish-eating mammal with a long body and webbed feet, living partly in water and partly on land.
– ORIGIN Old English.

Ottoman • adj. hist. relating to the Turkish dynasty of Osman I (Othman I), founded in about 1300, or to the Ottoman Empire ruled by his successors. • n. (pl. **Ottomans**) a Turk of the Ottoman period.

– ORIGIN Arabic.

ottoman • n. (pl. **ottomans**) a low padded seat without a back or arms.

OU • abbrev. (in the UK) Open University.

oubliette /oo-bli-et/ • n. a secret dungeon with access only through a trapdoor in its ceiling.
– ORIGIN French.

ought • modal verb (3rd sing. present and past **ought**) **1** used to indicate duty or correctness. **2** used to indicate something that is probable. **3** used to indicate a desirable or expected state. **4** used to give or ask advice.
– ORIGIN Old English.

> USAGE: The correct way of forming negative sentences with **ought** is *he ought not to have gone*. The sentences *he didn't ought to have gone* and *he hadn't ought to have gone* are found in dialect but should not be used in writing.

oughtn't • contr. ought not.

Ouija board /wee-juh/ • n. trademark a board with letters and other signs around its edge, to which a pointer moves, supposedly in answer to questions at a seance.
– ORIGIN from French *oui* 'yes' + German *ja* 'yes'.

ounce • n. **1** a unit of weight of one sixteenth of a pound (approximately 28 grams). **2** a very small amount.
– ORIGIN Latin *uncia* 'twelfth part of a pound or foot'.

our • possess. det. **1** belonging to or connected with the speaker and one or more other people. **2** belonging to or associated with people in general.
– ORIGIN Old English.

> USAGE: Do not confuse **our** and **are**. **Our** mainly means 'belonging to or connected with us', as in *Jo and I had our hair cut*, whereas **are** is one of the forms of the present tense of the verb **to be**, as in *you are a bully*.

Our Father • n. God.

Our Lady • n. the Virgin Mary.

Our Lord • n. God or Jesus.

ours • possess. pron. used to refer to something belonging to or connected with the speaker and one or more other people.

> ☑ No apostrophe: **ours** not *our's*.

ourselves • pron. (first person pl.) **1** used as the object of a verb or preposition when this is the same as the subject of the clause and the subject is the speaker and one or more other people. **2** we or us personally.

-ous • suffix forming adjectives: **1** characterized by: *mountainous*. **2** Chem. referring to an element in a lower valency: *sulphurous*.
– ORIGIN Latin *-osus*.

oust /owsst/ • v. force out of a job or position of power.
– ORIGIN Old French *ouster* 'take away'.

out • adv. **1** moving away from a place. **2** away from your home or place of work. **3** outdoors. **4** so as to be revealed, heard, or known. **5** at or to an end: *the romance fizzled out*. **6** at a specified distance away from the target. **7** to sea, away from the land. **8** (of the tide) falling or at its lowest level. • adj. **1** not at home or your place of work. **2** made public or available. **3** not possible or worth considering: *under-age drinking is out*. **4** no longer existing or current. **5** unconscious. **6** (of the ball in tennis, squash, etc.) not in the playing area. **7** Cricket & Baseball no longer batting. • v. informal reveal that someone is homosexual.
– PHRASES **out for** intent on having. **out of 1** from. **2** not having a supply of. **out to do** trying hard to do.
– ORIGIN Old English.

> USAGE: You should write **out of** rather than just **out** in sentences such as *he threw it out of the window*.

out- • prefix **1** to the point of exceeding or going beyond: *outperform*. **2** external; separate: *outbuildings*. **3** away from: *outpost*.

outage • n. a period when a power supply or other service is not available.

out-and-out • adj. in every way; complete: *an out-and-out lie*.

outback • n. (**the outback**) the part of Australia that is remote and has few inhabitants.

outbid • v. (**outbids**, **outbidding**, **outbid**) bid more for something than someone else.

outboard • adj. & adv. on, towards, or near the outside of a ship or aircraft.

outboard motor • n. a portable motor which can be attached to the outside of a boat.

outbound • adj. & adv. travelling from a place rather than arriving in it.

outbreak • n. a sudden or violent occurrence of war, disease, etc.

outbuilding • n. a smaller building in the grounds of a main building.

outburst • n. **1** a sudden release of strong emotion. **2** a sudden or violent occurrence of something.

outcast • n. a person rejected by their society or social group.

outclass • v. be far better than.

outcome • n. the result or consequence of something.

outcrop • n. a part of a rock formation that is visible on the surface.

outcry • n. (pl. **outcries**) a strong expression of public disapproval.

outdated • adj. no longer used or fashionable.

outdistance • v. (**outdistances**, **outdistancing**, **outdistanced**) leave a competitor or pursuer far behind.

outdo • v. (**outdoes**, **outdoing**, **outdid**; past part. **outdone**) do better than someone else.

outdoor • adj. 1 done, situated, or used outdoors. 2 fond of being outdoors.

outdoors • adv. in or into the open air. • n. any area outside buildings.

outer • adj. 1 outside. 2 further from the centre or the inside.
– DERIVATIVES **outermost** adj.

outer space • n. the universe beyond the earth's atmosphere.

outface • v. (**outfaces**, **outfacing**, **outfaced**) unsettle or defeat someone by confronting them boldly.

outfall • n. the place where a river, drain, or sewer empties into the sea, a river, or a lake.

outfit • n. 1 a set of clothes worn together. 2 informal a group of people working together as a business, team, etc. • v. (**outfits**, **outfitting**, **outfitted**) provide with a set of clothes.

outfitter (also **outfitters**) • n. Brit. dated a shop selling men's clothing.

outflank • v. 1 move round the side of an enemy so as to attack them. 2 gain an advantage over; outwit.

outflow • n. a large amount of something that moves or is transferred out of a place.

outfox • v. informal defeat someone by being more cunning than they are.

outgoing • adj. 1 friendly and confident. 2 leaving a job or position. 3 going out or away from a place. • n. (**outgoings**) Brit. money that has to be spent regularly.

outgrow • v. (**outgrows**, **outgrowing**, **outgrew**; past part. **outgrown**) 1 grow too big for. 2 stop doing or having an interest in something as you grow older. 3 grow faster or taller than.

outgrowth • n. 1 something that grows out of something else. 2 a natural development or result.

outgun • v. (**outguns**, **outgunning**, **outgunned**) have more or better weapons than.

outhouse • n. a smaller building built on to or in the grounds of a house.

outing • n. 1 a short trip taken for pleasure. 2 informal an occasion when a competitor takes part in a sporting event, or an actor appears in a film, play, etc.: *an actress in her first screen outing*.

outlandish • adj. bizarre or unfamiliar.
– ORIGIN Old English, 'not native'.

outlast • v. last longer than.

outlaw • n. a person who has broken the law and remains at large. • v. make illegal.

outlay • n. an amount of money spent.

outlet • n. 1 a pipe or hole through which water or gas may escape. 2 a point from which goods are sold or distributed. 3 a way of expressing your talents, energy, or emotions.

outlier /owt-ly-er/ • n. a thing which is separate or detached from a main body or system.

outline • n. 1 a drawing or diagram showing the shape of an object. 2 the outer edges of an object. 3 a description of the main points of something.
• v. (**outlines**, **outlining**, **outlined**) 1 draw the outer edge or shape of. 2 give a summary of.

outlive • v. (**outlives**, **outliving**, **outlived**) live or last longer than.

outlook • n. 1 a person's attitude to life. 2 a view. 3 what is likely to happen in the future.

outlying • adj. situated far from a centre.

outmanoeuvre • v. (**outmanoeuvres**, **outmanoeuvring**, **outmanoeuvred**) gain an advantage over an opponent by using skill and cunning.

outmoded • adj. old-fashioned.

outnumber • v. (**outnumbers**, **outnumbering**, **outnumbered**) be more numerous than.

out of date • adj. 1 old-fashioned. 2 no longer valid.

outpace • v. (**outpaces**, **outpacing**, **outpaced**) go faster than.

outpatient • n. a patient attending a hospital for treatment without staying overnight.

outperform • v. perform better than.

outplay • v. play better than.

outpost • n. 1 a small military camp at a distance from the main army. 2 a remote part of a country or empire.

outpouring • n. 1 something that streams out rapidly. 2 an outburst of strong emotion.

output • n. 1 the amount of something produced. 2 the process of producing something. 3 the power, energy, etc. supplied by a device or system. 4 Electron. a place where power or information leaves a system. • v. (**outputs**,

outputting, **output** or **outputted**) (of a computer) produce data.

outrage • n. **1** a very strong reaction of anger and shock. **2** a very cruel, wicked, or shocking act. • v. (**outrages**, **outraging**, **outraged**) make someone feel very angry and shocked.
– ORIGIN Old French.

outrageous • adj. **1** shockingly bad or unacceptable. **2** very unusual and slightly shocking: *an outrageous dress.*
– DERIVATIVES **outrageously** adv.

☑ Spell **outrageous** with an **e** after the **g**.

outran past of OUTRUN.

outrank • v. be of a higher rank or quality than.

outré /oo-tray/ • adj. unusual and rather shocking.
– ORIGIN French, 'exceeded'.

outreach • n. an organization's involvement with the community, especially in providing a service or advice outside its usual centres of operation.

outrider • n. a person in a vehicle or on horseback who escorts another vehicle.

outrigger • n. a structure fixed to the side of a boat in order to help keep it stable.

outright • adv. **1** altogether. **2** openly. **3** immediately. • adj. **1** open and direct. **2** complete.

outrun • v. (**outruns**, **outrunning**, **outran**; past part. **outrun**) run or travel faster or further than.

outsell • v. (**outsells**, **outselling**, **outsold**) be sold in greater quantities than.

outset • n. the beginning.

outshine • v. (**outshines**, **outshining**, **outshone**) **1** shine more brightly than. **2** be much better than.

outside • n. **1** the external side, part, or surface of something. **2** the side of a bend or curve where the edge is longer. **3** the external appearance of someone or something. • adj. **1** situated on or near the outside. **2** not belonging to a particular group. • prep. & adv. **1** situated or moving beyond the boundaries of. **2** not being a member of.
– PHRASES **at the outside** at the most. **an outside chance** a remote possibility.

outsider • n. **1** a person who does not belong to a particular group. **2** a competitor thought to have little chance of success.

outsize (also **outsized**) • adj. very large.

outskirts • pl. n. the outer parts of a town or city.

outsmart • v. defeat someone by being cleverer than they are.

outsold past and past part. of OUTSELL.

outsource • v. arrange for work to be done outside a company.

outspoken • adj. stating your opinions in an open and direct way.
– DERIVATIVES **outspokenness** n.

outspread • adj. extended or stretched out as far as possible.

outstanding • adj. **1** exceptionally good. **2** clearly noticeable. **3** not yet dealt with or paid.
– DERIVATIVES **outstandingly** adv.

outstay • v. stay for longer than the expected or permitted time.

outstretched • adj. extended or stretched out.

outstrip • v. (**outstrips**, **outstripping**, **outstripped**) **1** move faster than and overtake. **2** go beyond or be better than.

out-take • n. a scene or sequence filmed or recorded for a film or television programme but not included in the final version.

outvote • v. (**outvotes**, **outvoting**, **outvoted**) defeat by gaining more votes.

outward • adj. **1** on or from the outside. **2** going out or away from a place. • adv. (also esp. Brit. **outwards**) towards the outside.
– DERIVATIVES **outwardly** adv.

outweigh • v. be greater or more important than.

outwit • v. (**outwits**, **outwitting**, **outwitted**) defeat or gain an advantage over someone by being cleverer than they are.

ouzo /oo-zoh/ • n. an aniseed-flavoured Greek alcoholic drink.
– ORIGIN modern Greek.

ova pl. of OVUM.

oval • adj. having a rounded and slightly elongated outline. • n. an oval object or design.
– ORIGIN Latin *ovalis.*

ovary /oh-vuh-ri/ • n. (pl. **ovaries**) **1** a female reproductive organ in which eggs are produced. **2** the base of the reproductive organ of a flower.
– DERIVATIVES **ovarian** /oh-vair-i-uhn/ adj.
– ORIGIN Latin *ovarium.*

ovate /oh-vayt/ • adj. tech. egg-shaped; oval.
– ORIGIN Latin *ovatus.*

ovation • n. a long, enthusiastic round of applause.
– ORIGIN Latin.

oven • n. **1** an enclosed compartment in which food is cooked or heated. **2** a small furnace or kiln.

– ORIGIN Old English.

ovenproof • adj. suitable for use in an oven.

over • prep. **1** extending upwards from or above. **2** above so as to cover or protect. **3** expressing movement or a route across. **4** beyond and falling or hanging from: *the car toppled over the cliff.* **5** expressing length of time. **6** higher or more than. **7** expressing authority or control. **8** on the subject of; concerning. • adv. **1** expressing movement or a route across an area. **2** beyond and falling or hanging from a point. **3** in or to the place indicated. **4** expressing action and result: *the car flipped over.* **5** finished. **6** expressing repetition of a process. • n. Cricket a sequence of six balls bowled by a bowler from one end of the pitch.
– PHRASES **be over** be no longer affected by. **over and above** in addition to.
– ORIGIN Old English.

over- • prefix **1** excessively: *overambitious.* **2** completely: *overjoyed.* **3** upper; outer: *overcoat.* **4** over; above: *overcast.*

overachieve • v. (**overachieves, overachieving, overachieved**) do better than expected.
– DERIVATIVES **overachiever** n.

overact • v. act a role in a play or film in an exaggerated way.

overactive • adj. more active than is normal or desirable.

overall • adj. including everything. • adv. taken as a whole. • n. (also **overalls**) Brit. a loose-fitting garment worn over ordinary clothes to protect them.

overambitious • adj. too ambitious.

overarching • adj. covering or dealing with everything: *a single overarching principle.*

overarm • adj. & adv. esp. Brit. (of a throw, stroke with a racket, etc.) made with the hand brought forward and down from above shoulder level.

overate past of OVEREAT.

overawe • v. (**overawes, overawing, overawed**) impress someone so much that they are silent or nervous.

overbalance • v. (**overbalances, overbalancing, overbalanced**) fall due to loss of balance.

overbearing • adj. trying to control people in an unpleasant way.

overblown • adj. made to seem more important or impressive than is really the case.

overboard • adv. from a ship into the water.
– PHRASES **go overboard** be very or too enthusiastic.

overbook • v. accept more bookings for a flight or hotel than there is room for.

overburden • v. give too much work to.

overcame past of OVERCOME.

overcast • adj. (of the sky or weather) cloudy.

overcharge • v. (**overcharges, overcharging, overcharged**) charge too high a price.

overcoat • n. **1** a long, warm coat. **2** a top layer of paint or varnish.

overcome • v. (**overcomes, overcoming, overcame;** past part. **overcome**) **1** succeed in dealing with a problem. **2** defeat someone. **3** (**be overcome**) be overwhelmed by a strong emotion.

overcompensate • v. (**overcompensates, overcompensating, overcompensated**) do something which is too extreme in an attempt to correct a problem.

overconfident • adj. too confident.
– DERIVATIVES **overconfidence** n.

overcook • v. cook food for too long.

overcrowded • adj. filled with more people or things than is usual or comfortable.
– DERIVATIVES **overcrowding** n.

overdevelop • v. (**overdevelops, overdeveloping, overdeveloped**) develop too much.

overdo • v. (**overdoes, overdoing, overdid;** past part. **overdone**) **1** do something excessively or in an exaggerated way. **2** use too much of: *don't overdo the garlic.* **3** (as adj. **overdone**) overcooked.

overdose • n. an excessive and dangerous dose of a drug. • v. (**overdoses, overdosing, overdosed**) take an overdose.

overdraft • n. an arrangement with a bank that allows someone to take out more money than there is in their account.

overdrawn • adj. (of a bank account) in a state in which more money has been taken out than the account holds.

overdressed • adj. wearing clothes that are too elaborate or formal for a particular occasion.

overdrive • n. **1** a mechanism in a motor vehicle providing an extra gear above the usual top gear. **2** a state of great activity.

overdue • adj. not having arrived, happened, or been done at the expected or required time.

overeager • adj. too eager.

overeat • v. (**overeats, overeating, overate;** past part. **overeaten**) eat too much.

overemphasize (or **overemphasise**) • v. (**overemphasizes, overemphasizing,**

overemphasized) place too much emphasis or importance on.
– DERIVATIVES **overemphasis** n.

overenthusiastic •adj. too enthusiastic.

overestimate •v. (**overestimates**, **overestimating**, **overestimated**) estimate someone or something to be larger or better than in reality. •n. an estimate of size, cost, etc. which is too high.

overexcited •adj. too excited to behave in a sensible way.

overexert •v. (**overexert yourself**) exhaust yourself by making too much physical effort.
– DERIVATIVES **overexertion** n.

overexpose •v. (**overexposes**, **overexposing**, **overexposed**) 1 subject photographic film to too much light. 2 (as adj. **overexposed**) seen too much on television, in the newspapers, etc.
– DERIVATIVES **overexposure** n.

overfamiliar •adj. 1 too well known. 2 behaving or speaking in an inappropriately informal way.
– DERIVATIVES **overfamiliarity** n.

overfeed •v. (**overfeeds**, **overfeeding**, **overfed**) give too much food to.

overfill •v. put more into a container than there is room for.

overflow •v. 1 flow over the brim of a container. 2 be too full or crowded. 3 (**overflow with**) be very full of an emotion. •n. 1 the overflowing of a liquid. 2 the number of people or things that do not fit into a particular space. 3 (also **overflow pipe**) an outlet for excess water.

overground •adv. & adj. on or above the ground.

overgrown •adj. 1 covered with plants that have been allowed to grow wild. 2 having grown too large.

overgrowth •n. too much growth of something.

overhang •v. (**overhangs**, **overhanging**, **overhung**) hang outwards over. •n. an overhanging part.

overhaul •v. 1 examine and repair equipment or machinery. 2 analyse and improve a system or process. 3 Brit. overtake. •n. an act of overhauling something.

overhead •adv. above the head. •adj. situated above the head. •n. (**overheads**) the regular expenses involved in running a business or organization, such as rent, electricity, wages, etc.

overhead projector •n. a device that projects an enlarged image of a transparent photograph printed on

plastic, by means of an overhead mirror.

overhear •v. (**overhears**, **overhearing**, **overheard**) hear accidentally.

overheat •v. make or become too hot.

overindulge •v. (**overindulges**, **overindulging**, **overindulged**) 1 have too much of something enjoyable. 2 give in to someone's wishes too readily.
– DERIVATIVES **overindulgence** n.

overjoyed •adj. very happy.

overkill •n. too much of something.

overlaid past and past part. of OVERLAY.

overlain past part. of OVERLIE.

overland •adj. & adv. by land.

overlap •v. (**overlaps**, **overlapping**, **overlapped**) 1 extend over so as to partly cover. 2 (of two events) occur at the same time for part of their duration. •n. an overlapping part or amount.

overlay •v. /oh-ver-lay/ (**overlays**, **overlaying**, **overlaid**) 1 coat the surface of. 2 (of a quality or feeling) become more noticeable than a previous one. •n. /oh-ver-lay/ 1 a covering. 2 a transparent sheet over artwork or a map, giving additional detail.

overleaf •adv. on the other side of the page.

overlie •v. (**overlies**, **overlying**, **overlay**; past part. **overlain**) lie on top of.

overload •v. /oh-ver-lohd/ 1 load too heavily. 2 put too great a demand on. •n. /oh-ver-lohd/ an excessive amount.

overlook /oh-ver-luuk/ •v. 1 fail to notice. 2 choose to ignore a fault, wrongdoing, etc. 3 have a view of from above.

overlord •n. a ruler.

overly •adv. excessively.

overlying pres. part. of OVERLIE.

overmuch •adv., det., & pron. too much.

overnight •adv. 1 for the duration of a night. 2 during a night. 3 very quickly. •adj. 1 done, happening, or for use overnight. 2 very sudden or quick: an overnight success.

overpass •n. a bridge by which a road or railway line passes over another.

overpay •v. (**overpays**, **overpaying**, **overpaid**) pay too much.
– DERIVATIVES **overpayment** n.

overplay •v. give too much importance to.
– PHRASES **overplay your hand** spoil your chance of success by being too confident.

overpopulated •adj. (of a country, city, or area) having too many people living in it.
– DERIVATIVES **overpopulation** n.

overpower •v. (**overpowers**,

overpowering, overpowered) **1** defeat with greater strength. **2** overwhelm: *they were overpowered by the fumes.*

overpriced • adj. too expensive.

overprotective • adj. too protective.

overqualified • adj. too highly qualified.

overran past of OVERRUN.

overrate • v. (**overrates, overrating, overrated**) have too high an opinion of.

overreach • v. (**overreach yourself**) fail as a result of being too ambitious or trying too hard.

overreact • v. react more strongly than is justified.
– DERIVATIVES **overreaction** n.

override • v. (**overrides, overriding, overrode**; past part. **overridden**) **1** use your authority to reject or cancel someone else's decision or order. **2** interrupt the action of an automatic device. **3** be more important than. • n. a device on a machine for overriding an automatic process.

overrule • v. (**overrules, overruling, overruled**) use your authority to reverse or disallow someone else's decision or order.

overrun • v. (**overruns, overrunning, overran**; past part. **overrun**) **1** spread over or occupy in large numbers. **2** use more time or money than intended.

overseas • adv. in or to a foreign country. • adj. relating to a foreign country.

oversee • v. (**oversees, overseeing, oversaw**; past part. **overseen**) supervise someone or something.
– DERIVATIVES **overseer** n.

oversensitive • adj. too sensitive.
– DERIVATIVES **oversensitivity** n.

oversexed • adj. having unusually strong sexual desires.

overshadow • v. **1** appear more important or successful than. **2** cast a feeling of sadness over. **3** tower above and cast a shadow over.

overshirt • n. a loose shirt worn over other clothes.

overshoe • n. a protective shoe worn over a normal shoe.

overshoot • v. (**overshoots, overshooting, overshot**) accidentally go further than an intended place.

oversight • n. an unintentional failure to notice or do something.

oversimplify • v. (**oversimplifies, oversimplifying, oversimplified**) simplify something so much that an inaccurate impression is given.
– DERIVATIVES **oversimplification** n.

oversized (also **oversize**) • adj. bigger than the usual size.

oversleep • v. (**oversleeps, oversleeping, overslept**) sleep longer or later than you intended.

overspend • v. (**overspends, overspending, overspent**) spend too much.

overspill • n. Brit. part of the population of a city or town moving from an overcrowded area to live elsewhere.

overstaffed • adj. having more members of staff than are necessary.

overstate • v. (**overstates, overstating, overstated**) express or state too strongly; exaggerate.
– DERIVATIVES **overstatement** n.

overstay • v. stay longer than an allowed time.

overstep • v. (**oversteps, overstepping, overstepped**) go beyond a limit.
– PHRASES **overstep the mark** behave in an unacceptable way.

overstretch • v. make excessive demands on.

oversubscribed • adj. **1** (of something for sale) applied for in greater quantities than are available. **2** (of a course, school, etc.) having more applications than available places.

oversupply • n. an excessive supply of something.

overt /oh-vert, oh-vert/ • adj. done or shown openly.
– DERIVATIVES **overtly** adv.
– ORIGIN Old French, 'opened'.

overtake • v. (**overtakes, overtaking, overtook**; past part. **overtaken**) **1** catch up with and pass while travelling in the same direction. **2** become greater or more successful than. **3** suddenly affect: *weariness overtook him.*

overthrow • v. (**overthrows, overthrowing, overthrew**; past part. **overthrown**) remove from power by force. • n. a forcible removal from power.

overtime • n. time worked in addition to normal working hours.

overtone • n. **1** a subtle additional quality or implication: *the decision had political overtones.* **2** a musical tone which is a part of the harmonic series above a fundamental note, and may be heard with it.

overture • n. **1** an orchestral piece at the beginning of a musical work. **2** an independent orchestral composition in one movement. **3** (**overtures**) approaches made with the aim of opening negotiations or establishing a relationship.
– ORIGIN Old French.

overturn • v. **1** turn over and come to rest upside down. **2** abolish or reverse a decision, system, etc.

overuse • v. (/oh-ver-**yooz**/) (**overuses, overusing, overused**) use too much. • n. /oh-ver-**yooss**/ excessive use.

overview • n. a general survey or summary.

overweening • adj. (especially of a quality) excessive: *overweening ambition*.
– ORIGIN Old English, 'think'.

overweight • adj. above a normal, desirable, or permitted weight.

overwhelm • v. **1** have a strong emotional effect on. **2** give someone too much of something. **3** cover with a huge mass of water.
– ORIGIN Old English, 'engulf or submerge'.

overwinter • v. (**overwinters, overwintering, overwintered**) **1** spend the winter in a particular place. **2** (of an insect, plant, etc.) survive through the winter.

overwork • v. **1** work too hard. **2** use a word or idea too much and so make it less effective. • n. too much work.

overwrite • v. (**overwrites, overwriting, overwrote**; past part. **overwritten**) destroy computer data or the data in a file by entering new data in its place.

overwrought • adj. **1** in a state of nervous excitement or anxiety. **2** (of writing or a work of art) too elaborate.

overzealous • adj. showing too much enthusiasm.

oviduct /oh-vi-dukt/ • n. the tube through which an ovum or egg passes from an ovary.
– ORIGIN from Latin *ovum* 'egg'.

ovine /oh-vyn/ • adj. relating to sheep.
– ORIGIN Latin *ovinus*.

oviparous /oh-vip-uh-ruhss/ • adj. (of an animal such as a bird) producing young by means of eggs which are hatched after they have been laid by the parent. Compare with VIVIPAROUS.

ovoid /oh-voyd/ • adj. **1** egg-shaped. **2** oval. • n. an ovoid shape.
– ORIGIN Latin *ovoides*.

ovulate /ov-yuu-layt/ • v. (**ovulates, ovulating, ovulated**) (of a woman or female animal) discharge ova (reproductive cells) from the ovary.
– DERIVATIVES **ovulation** n.

ovule /ov-yool/ • n. the part of the ovary of plants that after fertilization becomes the seed.
– ORIGIN Latin *ovulum* 'little egg'.

ovum /oh-vuhm/ • n. (pl. **ova**) a mature female reproductive cell, which can divide to develop into an embryo if fertilized by a male cell.
– ORIGIN Latin, 'egg'.

owe • v. (**owes, owing, owed**) **1** be required to give money or goods to someone in return for something received. **2** be obliged to do or give something to someone: *I owe you an apology*. **3** (**owe something to**) have something because of: *I owe my life to you*.
– ORIGIN Old English.

owing • adj. esp. Brit. yet to be paid or supplied.
– PHRASES **owing to** because of.

owl • n. a bird of prey with large eyes and a hooked beak, active at night.
– ORIGIN Old English.

owlish • adj. **1** like an owl, especially in appearing to be serious or wise. **2** (of glasses) resembling the large round eyes of an owl.

own • adj. & pron. **1** belonging or relating to the person specified. **2** done by the person specified. • v. **1** possess something. **2** formal admit that something is the case. **3** (**own up**) admit that you have done something wrong.
– PHRASES **come into its** (or **your**) **own** become fully effective. **hold your own** remain in a strong position despite difficulties.
– ORIGIN Old English.

owner • n. a person who owns something.
– DERIVATIVES **ownership** n.

owner-occupier • n. Brit. a person who owns the house or flat in which they live.

own goal • n. **1** (in football) a goal scored when a player accidentally hits the ball into their own team's goal. **2** Brit. informal an act that unintentionally harms your own interests.

ox • n. (pl. **oxen**) **1** a cow or bull. **2** a castrated bull, used for pulling heavy loads.
– ORIGIN Old English.

oxbow • n. a loop formed by a horseshoe bend in a river.

Oxbridge • n. Oxford and Cambridge universities considered together.

oxidation • n. Chem. the process of oxidizing or the result of being oxidized.

oxide /ok-syd/ • n. a compound of oxygen with another element or group.

oxidize (or **oxidise**) • v. (**oxidizes, oxidizing, oxidized**) **1** cause to combine with oxygen. **2** Chem. cause to undergo a reaction in which electrons are lost to another substance or molecule. Opp. REDUCE.
– DERIVATIVES **oxidization** n.

Oxon • abbrev. **1** Oxfordshire. **2** (in degree titles) of Oxford University.

– ORIGIN from *Oxonia*, Latin form of Oxford.

oxtail •n. the tail of an ox (used in making soup or stews).

oxyacetylene /ok-si-uh-set-i-leen/ •adj. (of welding or cutting techniques) using a very hot flame produced by mixing acetylene and oxygen.

oxygen •n. a colourless, odourless gas forming about 20 per cent of the earth's atmosphere and essential to life.
– ORIGIN from French *principe oxygène* 'acidifying constituent'.

oxygenate /ok-si-juh-nayt/ •v. (**oxygenates**, **oxygenating**, **oxygenated**) supply with oxygen.

oxygen mask •n. a mask placed over the nose and mouth and connected to a supply of oxygen, used when a person cannot gain enough oxygen by breathing air.

oxymoron /ok-si-mor-on/ •n. a figure of speech in which apparently contradictory terms appear together (e.g. *a deafening silence*).
– ORIGIN Greek *oxumōros* 'pointedly foolish'.

oyster •n. **1** a shellfish with two hinged shells, several kinds of which are farmed for food or pearls. **2** a shade of greyish white.
– PHRASES **the world is your oyster** you have a wide range of opportunities available to you.
– ORIGIN Old French *oistre*.

oystercatcher •n. a wading bird with black or black-and-white plumage and a strong orange-red bill.

Oz •n. & adj. informal Australia or Australian.
– ORIGIN short for *Australia*.

oz •abbrev. ounce(s).
– ORIGIN Italian *onza* 'ounce'.

ozone •n. **1** a strong-smelling poisonous form of oxygen, formed in electrical discharges or by ultraviolet light. **2** Brit. informal fresh invigorating air.
– ORIGIN German *Ozon*.

ozone hole •n. an area of the ozone layer where the ozone is greatly reduced, due to CFCs and other pollutants.

ozone layer •n. a layer in the earth's stratosphere containing a high concentration of ozone, which absorbs most of the ultraviolet radiation reaching the earth from the sun.

Ozzie •n. & adj. var. of **Aussie**.

o

Pp

P¹ (also **p**) • n. (pl. **Ps** or **P's**) the sixteenth letter of the alphabet.

P² • symb. the chemical element phosphorus.

p • abbrev. **1** page. **2** Brit. penny or pence.

PA • abbrev. **1** Brit. personal assistant. **2** public address.

Pa • abbrev. pascal(s). • symb. the chemical element protactinium.

pa • n. informal father.
– ORIGIN from PAPA.

p.a. • abbrev. per annum.

pace¹ /payss/ • n. **1** a single step taken when walking or running. **2** speed in moving. **3** the rate at which something happens or develops. **4** a way in which a horse is trained to run or walk. • v. (**paces, pacing, paced**) **1** walk up and down in a small area. **2** measure a distance by walking it and counting the number of steps taken. **3** set the speed at which something happens or develops. **4** (**pace yourself**) do something in a controlled and steady rate.
– PHRASES **keep pace with** progress at the same speed as. **put someone through their paces** make someone demonstrate their abilities.
– ORIGIN Latin *passus* 'stretch (of the leg)'.

pace² /pah-chay, pay-si/ • prep. with due respect to someone.
– ORIGIN Latin, 'in peace'.

pacemaker • n. an artificial device for stimulating and regulating the heart muscle.

pacey • adj. var. of PACY.

pachyderm /pak-i-derm/ • n. a very large mammal with thick skin, e.g. an elephant.
– ORIGIN Greek *pakhudermos*.

pacific • adj. **1** peaceful. **2** (**Pacific**) relating to the Pacific Ocean.
– ORIGIN Latin *pacificus* 'peacemaking'.

pacifism • n. the belief that disputes should be settled peacefully and that war and violence are always wrong.
– DERIVATIVES **pacifist** n. & adj.

pacify • v. (**pacifies, pacifying, pacified**) **1** make someone less angry or upset. **2** bring peace to a country or groups in conflict.
– DERIVATIVES **pacification** n. **pacifier** n.
– ORIGIN Latin *pacificare*.

pack¹ • n. **1** a cardboard or paper container and the items inside it. **2** Brit. a set of playing cards. **3** a collection of related documents. **4** a group of animals that live and hunt together. **5** esp. derog. a group of similar things or people. **6** (**the pack**) the main body of competitors following the leader in a race. **7** Rugby a team's forwards. **8** (**Pack**) an organized group of Cub Scouts or Brownies. **9** a rucksack. **10** a pad of absorbent material, used for treating an injury. • v. **1** fill a bag with items needed for travel. **2** place something in a container for transport or storage. **3** cram a large number of things into something. **4** (as adj. **packed**) crowded. **5** cover, surround, or fill. **6** informal carry a gun.
– PHRASES **pack something in** informal give up an activity or job. **pack someone off** informal send someone somewhere without much notice. **pack up** Brit. informal (of a machine) break down. **send someone packing** informal dismiss someone abruptly.
– ORIGIN German *pak*.

pack² • v. fill a jury or committee with people likely to support a particular verdict or decision.
– ORIGIN prob. from former *pact* 'enter into an agreement with'.

package • n. **1** an object or group of objects wrapped in paper or packed in a box. **2** N. Amer. a packet. **3** (also **package deal**) a set of proposals or terms offered or agreed as a whole. **4** Computing a collection of related programs or sets of instructions. • v. (**packages, packaging, packaged**) **1** put something into a box or wrapping. **2** present something in a favourable way.

package holiday (also **package tour**) • n. a holiday organized by a travel agent, the price of which includes arrangements for transport and accommodation.

p

packaging •n. materials used to wrap or protect goods.

packet •n. **1** a paper or cardboard container. **2 (a packet)** informal a large sum of money.
– ORIGIN from **PACK**[1].

packhorse •n. a horse used to carry loads.

pack ice •n. a large mass of ice floating in the sea.

packing •n. material used to protect fragile goods while they are being transported.

packing case •n. a large, strong box used for transporting or storing things.

pact •n. a formal agreement between people or groups.
– ORIGIN Latin *pactum* 'something agreed'.

pacy (also **pacey**) •adj. (**pacier, paciest**) fast-moving.

pad[1] •n. **1** a thick piece of soft or absorbent material. **2** the fleshy underpart of an animal's foot or of a human finger. **3** a protective guard worn over a part of the body by a sports player. **4** a number of sheets of blank paper fastened together at one edge. **5** a flat-topped structure or area used for helicopter take-off and landing or for launching rockets. **6** informal a person's home. •v. (**pads, padding, padded**) **1** fill or cover something with a pad or padding. **2 (pad something out)** lengthen a speech or piece of writing with unnecessary material.

pad[2] •v. (**pads, padding, padded**) walk with soft, steady steps.
– ORIGIN German *padden*.

padding •n. **1** soft material used to pad or stuff something. **2** unnecessary material added to lengthen a speech or piece of writing.

paddle[1] •n. **1** a short pole with a broad blade at one or both ends, used to propel a small boat. **2** a tool or part of a machine shaped like a paddle, used for stirring or mixing. •v. (**paddles, paddling, paddled**) **1** propel a boat with a paddle or paddles. **2** (of a bird or other animal) swim with short fast strokes.

paddle[2] •v. (**paddles, paddling, paddled**) walk with bare feet in shallow water. •n. an act of paddling.

paddle steamer (also **paddle boat**) •n. a boat powered by steam and propelled by large wheels at the side or stern.

paddling pool •n. Brit. a shallow artificial pool for children to paddle in.

paddock •n. **1** a small field or enclosure for horses. **2** an enclosure next to a racecourse or track where horses or cars are displayed before a race.

Paddy •n. (pl. **Paddies**) informal, offens. an Irishman.
– ORIGIN informal form of the Irish man's name *Padraig*.

paddy[1] •n. (pl. **paddies**) a field where rice is grown.
– ORIGIN Malay.

paddy[2] •n. Brit. informal a fit of temper.
– ORIGIN from **PADDY**.

padlock •n. a detachable lock hanging by a hinged hook through a ring on the object fastened. •v. secure with a padlock.

paean /pee-uhn/ •n. a song of praise or triumph.
– ORIGIN Greek *paian* 'hymn of thanksgiving to Apollo'.

paediatrics /pee-di-at-riks/ (US **pediatrics**) •n. the branch of medicine concerned with children and their diseases.
– DERIVATIVES **paediatric** adj. **paediatrician** n.
– ORIGIN from Greek *pais* 'child' + *iatros* 'physician'.

paedophile /pee-duh-fyl/ (US **pedophile**) •n. a person who is sexually attracted to children.
– DERIVATIVES **paedophilia** n.
– ORIGIN Greek *pais* 'child' + *philos* 'loving'.

paella /py-el-luh/ •n. a Spanish dish of rice, saffron, chicken, seafood, and vegetables, cooked in a large shallow pan.
– ORIGIN Catalan.

pagan •n. a person who holds religious beliefs other than those of the main world religions. •adj. relating to pagans or their beliefs.
– DERIVATIVES **paganism** n.
– ORIGIN Latin *paganus* 'rustic'.

page[1] •n. **1** one side of a leaf of a book, magazine, or newspaper. **2** both sides of such a leaf considered as a single unit. **3** a section of data displayed on a computer screen at one time. •v. (**pages, paging, paged**) (**page through**) turn the pages of a book or display information on a computer screen one page at a time.
– ORIGIN Latin *pagina*.

page[2] •n. **1** a boy or young man employed in a hotel or club to run errands, open doors, etc. **2** a young boy attending a bride at a wedding. **3** hist. a boy training to be a knight. •v. (**pages, paging, paged**) summon someone over a public address system or by means of a pager.
– ORIGIN Old French.

pageant /paj-uhnt/ •n. an

entertainment performed by people in elaborate or historical costumes.

pageantry • n. elaborate display or ceremony.

pageboy • n. a page in a hotel or attending a bride at a wedding.

pager • n. a small radio device which bleeps or vibrates to inform the wearer that someone wishes to contact them or that it has received a message.

paginate /paj-i-nayt/ • v. (**paginates, paginating, paginated**) give numbers to the pages of a book or other publication or a document.
– DERIVATIVES **pagination** n.

pagoda /puh-goh-duh/ • n. a Hindu or Buddhist temple or other sacred building.
– ORIGIN Portuguese *pagode*.

paid past and past part. of PAY.
– PHRASES **put paid to** informal stop abruptly.

paid-up • adj. **1** with all money due paid in full. **2** committed to a cause or group: *a fully paid-up socialist*.

pail • n. a bucket.

pain • n. **1** a strongly unpleasant sensation caused by illness or injury. **2** mental suffering. **3** (also **pain in the neck**) informal an annoying or boring person or thing. **4** (**pains**) great care or trouble. • v. **1** cause pain to. **2** (as adj. **pained**) showing that you are annoyed or upset.
– PHRASES **on** (or **under**) **pain of** with the threat of the punishment of.
– ORIGIN Old French *peine*.

painful • adj. **1** affected with or causing pain. **2** informal very bad: *their attempts at reggae are painful*.
– DERIVATIVES **painfully** adv.

painkiller • n. a medicine for relieving pain.
– DERIVATIVES **painkilling** adj.

painless • adj. **1** not causing pain. **2** involving little effort or stress.
– DERIVATIVES **painlessly** adv.

painstaking • adj. very careful and thorough.
– DERIVATIVES **painstakingly** adv.

paint • n. **1** a coloured substance which is spread over a surface to give a thin decorative or protective coating. **2** dated cosmetic make-up. • v. **1** apply paint to. **2** apply a liquid to a surface with a brush. **3** produce a picture with paint. **4** give a description of.
– ORIGIN Old French *peindre*.

paintball • n. a combat game in which participants shoot capsules of paint at each other with air guns.

paintbox • n. a box holding a palette of dry paints for painting pictures.

paintbrush • n. a brush for applying paint.

painter[1] • n. **1** an artist who paints pictures. **2** a person who paints buildings.

painter[2] • n. a rope attached to the bow of a boat for tying it to a quay.

painterly • adj. like a painter; artistic: *she has a painterly eye*.

painting • n. a painted picture.

paintwork • n. esp. Brit. painted surfaces in a building or on a vehicle.

pair • n. **1** a set of two things used together or seen as a unit. **2** an article consisting of two joined or corresponding parts. **3** two people or animals that are related or considered together. • v. **1** join or connect to form a pair. **2** (**pair off/up**) form a couple.
– ORIGIN Old French *paire*.

paisley /payz-li/ • n. an intricate pattern of curved shapes like feathers.
– ORIGIN named after the town of *Paisley* in Scotland.

pajamas • pl. n. US = PYJAMAS.

Pakistani /pak-i-stah-ni, pak-i-sta-ni/ • n. a person from Pakistan. • adj. relating to Pakistan.

pal informal • n. a friend. • v. (**pals, palling, palled**) (**pal up**) form a friendship.
– ORIGIN Romany, 'brother, mate'.

palace • n. a large, impressive building forming the official residence of a king or queen, president, archbishop, etc.
– ORIGIN Old French *paleis*.

palace coup • n. the non-violent overthrow of a king or queen or a government by senior officials within the ruling group.

palaeo- /pa-li-oh, pay-li-oh/ (US **paleo-**) • comb. form older or ancient: *Palaeolithic*.
– ORIGIN Greek *palaios*.

Palaeocene /pa-li-oh-seen, pay-li-oh-seen/ (US **Paleocene**) • adj. Geol. relating to the earliest epoch of the Tertiary period (about 65 to 56.5 million years ago), a time of rapid development of mammals.
– ORIGIN from Greek *palaios* 'ancient' + *kainos* 'new'.

palaeography /pa-li-og-ruh-fi, pay-li-og-ruh-fi/ (US **paleography**) • n. the study of ancient writing systems and manuscripts.

Palaeolithic /pa-li-uh-li-thik, pay-li-uh-li-thik/ (US **Paleolithic**) • adj. Archaeol. relating to the early phase of the Stone Age.
– ORIGIN from Greek *palaios* 'ancient' + *lithos* 'stone'.

palaeontology /pa-li-on-tol-uh-ji, pay-li-on-tol-uh-ji/ (US **paleontology**) • n. the

branch of science concerned with fossil animals and plants.
– DERIVATIVES **palaeontologist** n.
– ORIGIN from Greek *palaios* 'ancient' + *onta* 'beings'.

Palaeozoic /pa-li-uh-**zoh**-ik, pay-li-uh-**zoh**-ik/ (US **Paleozoic**) •adj. Geol. relating to the era between the Precambrian aeon and the Mesozoic era (about 570 to 245 million years ago), which ended with the dominance of the reptiles.
– ORIGIN from Greek *palaios* 'ancient' + *zōē* 'life'.

palanquin /pa-luhn-**keen**/ •n. (in India and the East) a seat having a canopy and carried on poles, serving as a form of transport for one person.
– ORIGIN Portuguese *palanquim*.

palatable /pa-luh-tuh-b'l/ •adj. 1 pleasant to taste. 2 acceptable.

palate •n. 1 the roof of the mouth. 2 a person's ability to distinguish between different flavours.
– ORIGIN Latin *palatum*.

palatial /puh-**lay**-sh'l/ •adj. spacious or impressive, like a palace.

palatinate /puh-**lat**-i-nuht/ •n. hist. a territory ruled by a palatine official or feudal lord.

palatine /pa-luh-**tyn**/ •adj. hist. 1 (of an official or feudal lord) having local authority that elsewhere belongs only to a sovereign. 2 (of a territory) subject to such authority.
– ORIGIN French.

palaver /puh-**lah**-ver/ •n. informal lengthy or boring fuss about something.
– ORIGIN Portuguese *palavra* 'word'.

palazzo /puh-**lat**-soh/ •n. (pl. **palazzos** or **palazzi** /puh-**lat**-see/) a large, grand building in Italy.
– ORIGIN Italian, 'palace'.

pale[1] •adj. 1 of a light shade or colour. 2 (of a person's face) having little colour, through shock, illness, or tiredness. 3 not very good or impressive: *a pale imitation.* •v. (**pales, paling, paled**) 1 become pale in your face. 2 seem less important: *his version of the song pales in comparison to the original.*
– DERIVATIVES **paleness** n.
– ORIGIN Old French.

pale[2] •n. 1 a wooden stake used with others to form a fence. 2 a boundary.
– PHRASES **beyond the pale** outside the boundaries of acceptable behaviour.
– ORIGIN Old French *pal*.

paleo- •comb. form US = PALAEO-.

Palestinian /pa-li-**stin**-i-uhn/ •adj. relating to Palestine. •n. a member of the native Arab population of Palestine.

palette /pa-lit/ •n. 1 a thin board on which an artist lays and mixes paints. 2 the range of colours used by an artist.
– ORIGIN French, 'little shovel'.

palette knife •n. 1 a thin blade with a handle, for mixing, applying, or removing paint. 2 Brit. a kitchen knife with a long, blunt, round-ended blade.

palimpsest /pa-**limp**-sesst/ •n. 1 a parchment on which writing has been applied over earlier writing which has been erased. 2 something used again or altered but still bearing traces of its earlier form: *the house is a palimpsest of the taste of successive owners.*
– ORIGIN from Greek *palin* 'again' + *psēstos* 'rubbed smooth'.

palindrome /**pal**-in-drohm/ •n. a word or phrase that reads the same backwards as forwards, e.g. *madam*.
– ORIGIN Greek *palindromos* 'running back again'.

paling /**pay**-ling/ •n. 1 a fence made from stakes. 2 a stake used in such a fence.

palisade /pa-li-**sayd**/ •n. a fence of stakes or iron railings.
– ORIGIN French *palissade*.

pall[1] /pawl/ •n. 1 a cloth spread over a coffin, hearse, or tomb. 2 a dark cloud of smoke or dust. 3 a general atmosphere of gloom or fear: *the murder has cast a pall of terror over the village.*
– ORIGIN Latin *pallium* 'covering, cloak'.

pall[2] /pawl/ •v. become less appealing through being too familiar.
– ORIGIN from APPAL.

palladium /puh-**lay**-di-uhm/ •n. a rare silvery-white metallic element resembling platinum.
– ORIGIN from *Pallas*, an asteroid discovered just before the element.

pall-bearer •n. a person helping to carry or escorting a coffin at a funeral.

pallet[1] •n. a straw mattress or makeshift bed.
– ORIGIN Old French *paillete*.

pallet[2] •n. a portable platform on which goods can be moved, stacked, and stored.
– ORIGIN French, 'little blade'.

palliasse /pal-li-**ass**/ •n. a straw mattress.
– ORIGIN French *paillasse*.

palliate /**pal**-li-ayt/ •v. (**palliates, palliating, palliated**) 1 make the symptoms of a disease less severe without curing it. 2 make something bad less severe.
– DERIVATIVES **palliation** n.
– ORIGIN Latin *palliare* 'to cloak'.

palliative /**pal**-li-uh-tiv/ •adj. 1 (of

medicine) relieving pain without curing the cause of it. **2** intended to make a problem less severe without dealing with the cause of it. • n. a palliative medicine or remedy.

pallid • adj. **1** pale, especially because of poor health. **2** feeble.
– ORIGIN Latin *pallidus*.

pallor • n. an unhealthy pale appearance.
– ORIGIN Latin.

pally • adj. informal having a close, friendly relationship.

palm¹ • n. **1** (also **palm tree**) an evergreen tree of warm regions, with a crown of long feathered or fan-shaped leaves. **2** a prize or symbol of victory.
– ORIGIN Latin *palma* 'palm (of a hand)'.

palm² • n. the inner surface of the hand between the wrist and fingers. • v. **1** palm a small object in the hand. **2** (**palm something off**) sell or dispose of something in a way that is dishonest or unfair. **3** (**palm someone off**) informal persuade someone to accept something that has little value.
– ORIGIN Latin *palma*.

palmate /pal-mayt/ • adj. esp. Bot. & Zool. shaped like a hand with the fingers spread out.

palmistry • n. the supposed interpretation of a person's character or prediction of their future by examining the hand.
– DERIVATIVES **palmist** n.

Palm Sunday • n. the Sunday before Easter.

palmtop • n. a computer small and light enough to be held in one hand.

palmy • adj. (**palmier, palmiest**) comfortable and prosperous: *the palmy days of the 1970s*.

palomino /pa-luh-mee-noh/ • n. (pl. **palominos**) a pale golden or tan-coloured horse with a white mane and tail.
– ORIGIN Latin American Spanish.

palp /rhymes with scalp/ • n. each of a pair of long segmented feelers near the mouth of some insects and crustaceans.
– ORIGIN Latin *palpus*.

palpable /pal-puh-b'l/ • adj. **1** able to be touched or felt. **2** so strong that you seem able to touch it or feel it as a physical sensation: *a palpable sense of loss*.
– DERIVATIVES **palpably** adv.
– ORIGIN Latin *palpabilis*.

palpate /pal-payt/ • v. (**palpates, palpating, palpated**) medically examine a part of the body by touch.

palpitate /pal-pi-tayt/ • v. (**palpitates, palpitating, palpitated**) **1** (of the heart) beat rapidly or irregularly. **2** shake; tremble.
– ORIGIN Latin *palpitare* 'tremble, throb'.

palpitation • n. **1** throbbing or trembling. **2** (**palpitations**) a noticeably rapid, strong, or irregular heartbeat.

palsy /pawl-zi/ • n. (pl. **palsies**) dated paralysis. • v. (**be palsied**) be paralysed or partially paralysed.
– ORIGIN Old French *paralisie*.

paltry • adj. (**paltrier, paltriest**) **1** (of an amount) very small. **2** petty; trivial.
– ORIGIN prob. from dialect *pelt* 'rubbish'.

pampas /pam-puhss/ • n. large treeless plains in South America.
– ORIGIN from an American Indian language.

pampas grass • n. a tall South American grass with silky flowering plumes.

pamper • v. (**pampers, pampering, pampered**) give someone a great deal of care and attention.
– ORIGIN first meaning 'cram with food': prob. from German or Dutch.

pamphlet /pam-flit/ • n. a small leaflet containing information about something. • v. (**pamphlets, pamphleting, pamphleted**) distribute pamphlets to.
– ORIGIN from the name of a 12th-century Latin love poem *Pamphilus, seu de Amore*.

pamphleteer • n. a writer of pamphlets conveying a political message.

pan¹ • n. **1** a metal container for cooking food in. **2** a bowl fitted at either end of a pair of scales. **3** Brit. the bowl of a toilet. **4** a hollow in the ground in which water collects. • v. (**pans, panning, panned**) **1** informal criticize harshly. **2** (**pan out**) informal end up or conclude. **3** wash gravel in a shallow bowl to separate out gold.
– ORIGIN Old English.

pan² • v. (**pans, panning, panned**) turn a video or film camera on a horizontal plane to follow a subject or give a panoramic effect.
– ORIGIN short for **PANORAMA**.

pan- • comb. form including everything or everyone: *pan-African*.
– ORIGIN Greek.

panacea /pan-uh-see-uh/ • n. a solution or remedy for all difficulties or diseases.
– ORIGIN Greek *panakeia*.

panache /puh-nash/ • n. impressive confidence of style or manner.
– ORIGIN French, 'plume'.

panama • n. a man's wide-brimmed hat of straw-like material.

– ORIGIN named after the country of *Panama*.

Panamanian /pan-uh-**may**-ni-uhn/ •n. a person from Panama. •adj. relating to Panama.

panatella /pan-uh-**tel**-luh/ •n. a long thin cigar.

– ORIGIN Latin American Spanish *panatela* 'long thin biscuit'.

pancake •n. 1 a thin, flat cake of batter, fried and turned in a pan. 2 theatrical make-up consisting of a flat solid layer of compressed powder.

Pancake Day •n. Shrove Tuesday, when pancakes are traditionally eaten.

panchromatic •adj. (of black-and-white photographic film) sensitive to all visible colours of the spectrum.

pancreas /**pang**-kri-uhss/ •n. (pl. **pancreases**) a large gland behind the stomach which produces digestive enzymes and releases them into the duodenum.

– DERIVATIVES **pancreatic** adj.
– ORIGIN from Greek *pan* 'all' + *kreas* 'flesh'.

panda •n. 1 (also **giant panda**) a large black-and-white bear-like mammal native to bamboo forests in China. 2 (also **red panda**) a raccoon-like Himalayan mammal with thick reddish-brown fur and a bushy tail.

– ORIGIN Nepali.

pandemic /pan-**dem**-ik/ •adj. (of a disease) widespread over a whole country or large part of the world. •n. an outbreak of such a disease.

– ORIGIN from Greek *pan* 'all' + *dēmos* 'people'.

pandemonium /pan-di-**moh**-ni-uhm/ •n. a state of uproar and confusion.

– ORIGIN first meaning 'the place of all demons', in Milton's *Paradise Lost*.

pander •v. (**panders, pandering, pandered**) (**pander to**) indulge someone in an unreasonable desire or bad habit.

– ORIGIN from *Pandare*, a character in Chaucer's *Troilus and Criseyde* who acts as a lovers' go-between.

Pandora's box •n. a process that once begun creates many problems.

– ORIGIN from *Pandora* in Greek mythology, who was sent to earth with a box of evils and let them escape.

p. & p. •abbrev. Brit. postage and packing.

pane •n. a single sheet of glass in a window or door.

– ORIGIN Latin *pannus* 'piece of cloth'.

panegyric /pa-ni-**ji**-rik/ •n. a speech or piece of writing in praise of someone or something.

– ORIGIN Greek *panēgurikos* 'of public assembly'.

panel •n. 1 a section of a door, vehicle, item of clothing, etc. 2 a flat board on which instruments or controls are fixed. 3 a small group of people brought together to investigate or decide on something.

– DERIVATIVES **panelled** (US **paneled**) adj.
– ORIGIN Latin *pannus* 'piece of cloth'.

panel beater •n. Brit. a person whose job is to beat out the bodywork of motor vehicles.

panel game •n. Brit. a broadcast quiz played by a team of people.

panelling (US **paneling**) •n. wooden panels as a decorative wall covering.

panellist (US **panelist**) •n. a member of a panel taking part in a broadcast game or discussion.

pang •n. a sudden sharp pain or painful emotion.

– ORIGIN perh. from **PRONG**.

pangolin /**pang**-guh-lin/ •n. an insect-eating mammal whose body is covered with horny overlapping scales.

– ORIGIN Malay, 'roller'.

panic •n. 1 sudden uncontrollable fear or anxiety. 2 informal frenzied hurry to do something. •v. (**panics, panicking, panicked**) feel sudden uncontrollable fear or anxiety.

– DERIVATIVES **panicky** adj.
– ORIGIN from the Greek god *Pan*, noted for causing terror.

panicle /**pan**-i-k'l/ •n. Bot. a loose branching cluster of flowers.

– ORIGIN Latin *panicula*.

Panjabi •n. (pl. **Panjabis**) var. of **PUNJABI**.

panjandrum /pan-**jan**-druhm/ •n. a self-important person in a position of authority.

– ORIGIN from an invented word in a nonsense verse by Samuel Foote.

pannier •n. a bag or box fitted on either side of the rear wheel of a bicycle or motorcycle, or carried by a donkey or mule.

– ORIGIN Old French *panier*.

panoply /**pan**-uh-pli/ •n. a large and impressive collection or display.

– ORIGIN from Greek *pan* 'all' + *hopla* 'arms'.

panorama •n. 1 a clear view of a wide area. 2 a complete survey of a subject or sequence of events.

– DERIVATIVES **panoramic** adj.
– ORIGIN from Greek *pan* 'all' + *horama* 'view'.

pan pipes •pl. n. a musical instrument made from a row of short pipes fixed together.

– ORIGIN from the Greek god *Pan*.

pansy • n. 1 a plant of the viola family, with brightly coloured flowers. 2 informal, derog. an effeminate or homosexual man.
– ORIGIN French *pensée* 'thought, pansy'.

pant • v. 1 breathe with short, quick breaths. 2 (**pant for**) long for. • n. a short, quick breath.
– ORIGIN Old French *pantaisier* 'be agitated, gasp'.

pantaloons • pl. n. 1 women's baggy trousers gathered at the ankles. 2 hist. men's close-fitting breeches fastened below the calf or at the foot.
– ORIGIN from *Pantalone*, a character in Italian comic theatre represented as a foolish old man wearing pantaloons.

pantechnicon /pan-tek-ni-kuhn/ • n. Brit. a large van for transporting furniture.
– ORIGIN from Greek *pan* 'all' + *tekhnikon* 'piece of art'.

pantheism /pan-thee-i-z'm/ • n. 1 the belief that God is present in all things. 2 the worship or tolerance of many gods.
– DERIVATIVES **pantheist** n. **pantheistic** adj.

pantheon /pan-thi-uhn/ • n. 1 all the gods of a people or religion. 2 an ancient temple dedicated to all the gods. 3 a collection of particularly famous or important people.
– ORIGIN from Greek *pan* 'all' + *theion* 'holy'.

panther • n. 1 a black leopard. 2 N. Amer. a puma or a jaguar.
– ORIGIN Greek *panthēr*.

panties • pl. n. informal knickers.

pantile /pan-tyl/ • n. a curved roof tile.
– ORIGIN from **PAN**[1] + **TILE**.

pantomime • n. Brit. a theatrical entertainment involving music, topical jokes, and slapstick comedy.
– ORIGIN Greek *pantomimos* 'imitator of all'.

pantothenic acid /pan-tuh-then-ik/ • n. a vitamin of the B complex, found in rice, bran, etc., and essential for the oxidation of fats and carbohydrates.
– ORIGIN Greek *pantothen* 'from every side'.

pantry • n. (pl. **pantries**) a small room or cupboard in which food is kept.
– ORIGIN Old French *paneter* 'baker'.

pants • pl. n. 1 Brit. underpants or knickers. 2 esp. N. Amer. trousers.
– ORIGIN short for **PANTALOONS**.

pantyhose • pl. n. N. Amer. women's nylon tights.

pap[1] • n. 1 bland soft or semi-liquid food suitable for babies or invalids. 2 worthless or trivial reading matter or entertainment.
– ORIGIN prob. from Latin *pappare* 'eat'.

pap[2] • n. old use or dialect a woman's breast or nipple.
– ORIGIN prob. Scandinavian.

papa /puh-pah, pop-puh/ • n. N. Amer. or dated a person's father.
– ORIGIN French.

papacy /pay-puh-si/ • n. (pl. **papacies**) the position or period of office of the pope.
– ORIGIN Latin *papa* 'pope'.

papal /pay-p'l/ • adj. relating to the pope or the papacy.

paparazzo /pa-puh-rat-zoh/ • n. (pl. **paparazzi** /pa-puh-rat-zi/) a freelance photographer who pursues celebrities to get photographs of them.
– ORIGIN Italian, the name of a character in Fellini's film *La Dolce Vita*.

papaya /puh-py-uh/ • n. a tropical fruit with orange flesh and small black seeds.
– ORIGIN Spanish and Portuguese.

paper • n. 1 material manufactured in thin sheets from the pulp of wood, used for writing or printing on or as wrapping material. 2 (**papers**) documents. 3 a newspaper. 4 a government report or policy document. 5 an essay or dissertation read at a conference or published in a journal. 6 Brit. a set of exam questions. • v. (**papers, papering, papered**) 1 cover a wall or decorate a room with wallpaper. 2 (**paper something over**) conceal an awkward problem instead of resolving it. • adj. officially recorded but having no real existence or use: *a paper profit*.
– PHRASES **on paper** 1 in writing. 2 in theory rather than in reality.
– DERIVATIVES **papery** adj.
– ORIGIN Old French *papir*.

paperback • n. a book bound in stiff paper or flexible card.

paper boy (or **paper girl**) • n. a boy (or girl) who delivers newspapers to people's homes.

paper clip • n. a piece of bent wire or plastic used for holding several sheets of paper together.

paperknife • n. a blunt knife used for opening envelopes.

paper round • n. a job of regularly delivering newspapers.

paper-thin • adj. very thin or insubstantial.

paper tiger • n. a person or thing that appears threatening but is actually weak.

paperweight • n. a small, heavy object for keeping loose papers in place.

p

paperwork • n. routine work involving written documents.

papier mâché /pa-pi-ay mash-ay/ • n. a mixture of paper and glue that is easily moulded but becomes hard when dry.
– ORIGIN French, 'chewed paper'.

papilla /puh-pil-luh/ • n. (pl. **papillae** /puh-pil-lee/) a small projection on a part of the body or on a plant.
– ORIGIN Latin, 'nipple'.

papilloma /pa-pil-loh-muh/ • n. (pl. **papillomas** or **papillomata** /pa-pil-loh-muh-tuh/) Med. a small wart-like growth.

papist /pay-pist/ derog. • n. a Roman Catholic. • adj. Roman Catholic.

paprika /pap-ri-kuh, puh-pree-kuh/ • n. an orange-red powdered spice made from certain varieties of sweet pepper.
– ORIGIN Hungarian.

Papuan • n. 1 a person from Papua or Papua New Guinea. 2 a group of languages spoken in Papua New Guinea and neighbouring islands. • adj. relating to Papua or its languages.

papyrus /puh-py-ruhss/ • n. (pl. **papyri** /puh-py-ry/ or **papyruses**) a material made in ancient Egypt from the stem of a water plant, used for writing or painting on.
– ORIGIN Greek *papuros*.

par • n. Golf the number of strokes a first-class player should normally require for a particular hole or course.
– PHRASES **above** (or **below** or **under**) **par** above (or below) the usual or expected level. **on a par with** equal to.
– ORIGIN Latin, 'equal'.

para- (also **par-**) • prefix 1 beside; adjacent to: *parallel*. 2 distinct from, but similar to: *paramilitary*.
– ORIGIN Greek *para*.

parable • n. a simple story used to illustrate a moral or spiritual lesson.
– ORIGIN Latin *parabola* 'comparison'.

parabola /puh-rab-uh-luh/ • n. (pl. **parabolas** or **parabolae** /puh-rab-uh-lee/) an open plane curve of the kind formed by the intersection of a cone with a plane parallel to its side.
– ORIGIN Latin.

parabolic /pa-ruh-bol-ik/ • adj. relating to or like a parabola.

paracetamol /pa-ruh-see-tuh-mol, pa-ruh-set-uh-mol/ • n. (pl. **paracetamol** or **paracetamols**) Brit. a drug used to reduce pain and fever.
– ORIGIN from its chemical name.

parachute • n. a cloth canopy which allows a person or heavy object attached to it to descend slowly through the air when dropped from a high position.
• v. (**parachutes**, **parachuting**, **parachuted**) 1 drop by parachute. 2 appoint someone in an emergency or from outside the existing management structure.
– DERIVATIVES **parachutist** n.
– ORIGIN from French *para-* 'protection against' + *chute* 'fall'.

parade • n. 1 a public procession. 2 a formal march or gathering of troops for inspection or display. 3 a series of people or things. 4 a boastful display. 5 Brit. a row of shops. • v. (**parades**, **parading**, **paraded**) 1 walk, march, or display in a parade. 2 display in order to impress people: *he enjoyed being able to parade his knowledge.* 3 (**parade as**) appear falsely to be.
– ORIGIN French, 'a showing'.

parade ground • n. a place where troops gather for parade.

paradigm /pa-ruh-dym/ • n. a typical example, pattern, or model of something.
– DERIVATIVES **paradigmatic** /pa-ruh-dig-mat-ik/ adj.
– ORIGIN Greek *paradeigma*.

paradise • n. 1 (in some religions) heaven. 2 the Garden of Eden. 3 a very pleasant or beautiful place or state.
– ORIGIN Old French *paradis*.

paradox • n. 1 a statement that sounds absurd or seems to contradict itself, but may in fact be true. 2 a person or thing that combines contradictory qualities.
– DERIVATIVES **paradoxical** adj. **paradoxically** adv.
– ORIGIN Greek *paradoxon* 'contrary opinion'.

paraffin • n. 1 (also **paraffin wax**) esp.Brit. a flammable waxy solid obtained from petroleum or shale and used for sealing and waterproofing and in candles. 2 (also **paraffin oil**) Brit. a liquid fuel obtained from petroleum or shale.
– ORIGIN German.

paragliding • n. a sport in which a person glides through the air attached to a wide parachute after jumping from or being hauled to a height.
– DERIVATIVES **paraglider** n.

paragon • n. a person who is a perfect example of a particular quality.
– ORIGIN Italian *paragone* 'touchstone'.

paragraph • n. a distinct section of a piece of writing, beginning on a new line.
– ORIGIN French *paragraphe*.

Paraguayan /pa-ruh-gwy-uhn/ • n. a person from Paraguay. • adj. relating to Paraguay.

parakeet /pa-ruh-keet/ (also **parrakeet**) • n. a small green parrot with a long tail.

– ORIGIN Old French *paroquet*.

parallax /pa-ruhl-laks/ •n. the apparent difference in the position of an object when viewed from different positions.
– ORIGIN Greek *parallaxis* 'a change'.

parallel •adj. **1** (of lines, planes, or surfaces) side by side and having the same distance continuously between them. **2** occurring or existing at the same time or in a similar way: *a parallel universe*. •n. **1** a person or thing that is similar to or can be compared to another. **2** a similarity or comparison. **3** (also **parallel of latitude**) each of the imaginary parallel circles of latitude on the earth's surface. •v. (**parallels, paralleling, paralleled**) **1** run or lie parallel to. **2** be similar or corresponding to.
– PHRASES **in parallel** at the same time.
– ORIGIN Greek *parallēlos*.

 Remember that **parallel** has a double **l** in the middle and a single **l** at the end.

parallel bars •pl. n. a pair of parallel rails used in gymnastics.

parallelogram /pa-ruh-lel-luh-gram/ •n. a plane figure with four straight sides and opposite sides parallel.

Paralympics •pl. n. an international athletic competition for athletes with disabilities.
– DERIVATIVES **Paralympic** adj.
– ORIGIN from *paraplegic* and *Olympics*.

paralyse (esp. US also **paralyze**) •v. (**paralyses, paralysing, paralysed**) **1** cause a person or part of the body to become unable to move. **2** prevent from functioning.

paralysis /puh-ral-i-siss/ •n. (pl. **paralyses** /puh-ral-i-seez/) **1** the loss of the ability to move part or most of the body. **2** inability to act or function.
– ORIGIN Greek *paralusis*.

paralytic •adj. **1** relating to paralysis. **2** Brit. informal very drunk.

paramedic •n. a person who is trained to do medical work but is not a fully qualified doctor.

parameter /puh-ram-i-ter/ •n. **1** something that dictates or limits the way in which something is done: *they set the parameters of the debate.* **2** Math. a quantity which is fixed for the case in question but may vary in other cases.
– ORIGIN from Greek *para-* 'beside' + *metron* 'measure'.

paramilitary •adj. organized on similar lines to a military force. •n. (pl. **paramilitaries**) a member of a paramilitary organization.

paramount •adj. **1** more important than anything else. **2** having supreme power.
– ORIGIN from Old French *par* 'by' + *amont* 'above'.

paramour •n. old use a lover, especially the illicit lover of a married person.
– ORIGIN from Old French *par amour* 'by love'.

paranoia /pa-ruh-noy-uh/ •n. **1** a mental condition in which someone wrongly believes that other people want to harm them or that they are very important. **2** unjustified suspicion and mistrust of other people.
– DERIVATIVES **paranoiac** /pa-ruh-noy-ik/ (also **paranoic** /pa-ruh-noh-ik/) adj. & n.
– ORIGIN Latin.

paranoid •adj. relating to or suffering from paranoia.

paranormal •adj. beyond the scope of normal scientific understanding.

parapet /pa-ruh-pit/ •n. a low protective wall along the edge of a roof, bridge, or balcony.
– ORIGIN French.

paraphernalia /pa-ruh-fer-nay-li-uh/ •n. the equipment needed for a particular activity.
– ORIGIN Latin, 'property owned by a married woman'.

paraphrase •v. (**paraphrases, paraphrasing, paraphrased**) express the meaning of something using different words. •n. a rewording of a passage.

paraplegia /pa-ruh-plee-juh/ •n. paralysis of the legs and lower body.
– DERIVATIVES **paraplegic** adj. & n.
– ORIGIN Greek.

parapsychology •n. the study of things that the mind does that are outside the area of orthodox psychology.

paraquat /pa-ruh-kwot, pa-ruh-kwat/ •n. a poisonous weedkiller.
– ORIGIN from **PARA-** + **QUATERNARY**.

parasailing •n. the sport of gliding through the air attached to a wide parachute while being towed by a motor boat.

parasite •n. **1** an organism which lives in or on another organism and gets its food from it. **2** derog. a person who lives off other people.
– DERIVATIVES **parasitism** n.
– ORIGIN Greek *parasitos* 'person eating at another's table'.

parasitic •adj. **1** living in or on another organism. **2** derog. living off another person.
– DERIVATIVES **parasitical** adj. **parasitically** adv.

p

parasitize /pa-ruh-sy-tyz, pa-ruh-si-tyz/ (or **parasitise**) •v. (**parasitizes**, **parasitizing**, **parasitized**) live in or on something as a parasite.

parasol •n. a light umbrella used to give shade from the sun.
– ORIGIN Italian *parasole*.

paratroops •pl. n. troops equipped to be dropped by parachute from aircraft.
– DERIVATIVES **paratrooper** n.

parboil •v. partly cook something by boiling it.
– ORIGIN Latin *perbullire* 'boil thoroughly'.

parcel •n. 1 an object or objects wrapped in paper in order to be carried or sent by post. 2 a quantity or amount of something: *a parcel of land.* •v. (**parcels**, **parcelling**, **parcelled**; US **parcels**, **parceling**, **parceled**) 1 make something into a parcel by wrapping it. 2 (**parcel something out**) divide something into portions and then share it out.
– ORIGIN Old French *parcelle*.

parch •v. 1 make something dry through strong heat. 2 (as adj. **parched**) informal very thirsty.

parchment •n. 1 a stiff material made from the skin of a sheep or goat, formerly used for writing on. 2 paper treated to resemble parchment.
– ORIGIN Old French *parchemin*.

pardon •n. 1 the action of forgiving someone for a mistake or offence. 2 an official cancellation of the punishment for an offence. •v. 1 forgive a person, mistake, or offence. 2 give an offender an official pardon. •exclam. used to ask a speaker to repeat something because you did not hear or understand it.
– DERIVATIVES **pardonable** adj.
– ORIGIN Latin *perdonare* 'concede'.

pare •v. (**pares**, **paring**, **pared**) 1 trim something by cutting away its outer edges. 2 (**pare something away/down**) gradually reduce something.
– ORIGIN Old French *parer*.

parent •n. 1 a father or mother. 2 an animal or plant from which younger ones are derived. 3 an organization which owns or controls a number of smaller organizations. •v. be or act as a parent to.
– DERIVATIVES **parental** adj. **parenthood** n.
– ORIGIN Latin *parere* 'bring forth'.

parentage •n. the identity and origins of your parents.

parenthesis /puh-ren-thi-siss/ •n. (pl. **parentheses** /puh-ren-thi-seez/) 1 a word or phrase added as an explanation or afterthought, in writing marked off by brackets, dashes, or commas.
2 (**parentheses**) a pair of round brackets ().
– ORIGIN Greek.

parenthetic /pa-ruhn-thet-ik/ •adj. added as an explanation or afterthought.
– DERIVATIVES **parenthetical** adj. **parenthetically** adv.

par excellence /par ek-suh-lonss/ •adj. (after a noun) better or more than all others of the same kind: *a designer par excellence.*
– ORIGIN French, 'by excellence'.

pariah /puh-ry-uh/ •n. an outcast: *they were treated as social pariahs.*
– ORIGIN Tamil, 'hereditary drummers'.

parietal /puh-ry-i-tuhl/ •adj. Anat. relating to the wall of the body or of a body cavity.
– ORIGIN Latin *paries* 'wall'.

parings •pl. n. thin strips pared off from something.

parish •n. 1 (in the Christian Church) a district with its own church and clergy. 2 (also **civil parish**) Brit. the smallest unit of local government in rural areas.
– ORIGIN Old French *paroche*.

parish council •n. the administrative body in a civil parish.

parishioner •n. a person who lives in a particular church parish.

parish register •n. a book recording christenings, marriages, and burials at a parish church.

Parisian /puh-ri-zi-uhn/ •adj. relating to Paris. •n. a person from Paris.

Parisienne /pa-ri-zi-en/ •n. a Parisian girl or woman.

parity /pa-ri-ti/ •n. the state of being equal or equivalent: *the euro's slide to parity with the dollar.*
– ORIGIN Latin *paritas.*

park •n. 1 a large public garden in a town. 2 a large area of woodland and pasture attached to a country house. 3 an area devoted to a specified purpose: *a wildlife park.* 4 an area in which vehicles are parked. •v. stop and leave a vehicle temporarily.
– ORIGIN Old French *parc.*

parka •n. a large windproof hooded jacket.
– ORIGIN Russian.

parking ticket •n. a notice informing a driver of a fine for parking illegally.

Parkinson's disease •n. a progressive disease of the brain and nervous system marked by trembling, muscular rigidity, and slow, imprecise movement.

– ORIGIN named after the English surgeon James *Parkinson*.

parkland (also **parklands**) • n. open land with scattered groups of trees.

parky • adj. Brit. informal chilly.

parlance /par-luhnss/ • n. a way of using words associated with a particular subject: *medical parlance*.
– ORIGIN Old French.

parley /par-li/ • n. (pl. **parleys**) a meeting between opponents or enemies to discuss terms for a truce. • v. (**parleys, parleying, parleyed**) hold a parley.
– ORIGIN perh. from Old French *parlee* 'spoken'.

parliament /par-luh-muhnt/ • n. **1** (**Parliament**) (in the UK) the highest law-making body, consisting of the queen or king, the House of Lords, and the House of Commons. **2** a similar body in other countries.
– ORIGIN Old French *parlement* 'speaking'.

> ☑ Spell **parliament** with **-lia-** in the middle.

parliamentarian • n. a member of a parliament who is experienced in parliamentary procedures.

parliamentary /par-luh-men-tri/ • adj. relating to a parliament.

parliamentary private secretary • n. (in the UK) a Member of Parliament assisting a government minister.

parlour (US **parlor**) • n. **1** dated a sitting room. **2** a shop or business providing particular goods or services: *an ice-cream parlour.* **3** a room or building equipped for milking cows.
– ORIGIN Old French *parlur* 'place for speaking'.

parlous /par-luhss/ • adj. old use dangerously uncertain; precarious.
– ORIGIN from **PERILOUS**.

Parmesan /par-mi-zan/ • n. a hard, dry Italian cheese used chiefly in grated form.
– ORIGIN Italian *Parmigiano* 'of Parma' (an Italian city).

parochial /puh-roh-ki-uhl/ • adj. **1** relating to a parish. **2** having a narrow outlook or range.
– DERIVATIVES **parochialism** n.
– ORIGIN Latin *parochialis*.

parody /pa-ruh-di/ • n. (pl. **parodies**) a piece of writing or music that deliberately copies the style of another, in order to be funny or ironical. • v. (**parodies, parodying, parodied**) produce a parody of.
– DERIVATIVES **parodic** adj. **parodically** adv. **parodist** n.

– ORIGIN Greek *parōidia* 'burlesque poem'.

parole • n. the temporary or permanent release of a prisoner before the end of a sentence, on the condition that they behave well. • v. (**paroles, paroling, paroled**) release a prisoner on the condition that they behave well.
– DERIVATIVES **parolee** n.
– ORIGIN Old French, 'word'.

paroxysm /pa-ruhk-si-z'm/ • n. a sudden attack or outburst: *a paroxysm of weeping.*
– DERIVATIVES **paroxysmal** adj.
– ORIGIN Greek *paroxusmos*.

parquet /par-ki, par-kay/ • n. flooring composed of wooden blocks arranged in a geometric pattern.
– DERIVATIVES **parquetry** n.
– ORIGIN French.

parr • n. (pl. **parr**) a young salmon or trout.

parrakeet • n. var. of **PARAKEET**.

parricide /pa-ri-syd/ • n. **1** the killing of a parent or near relative. **2** a person who commits parricide.
– ORIGIN Latin *parricidium*.

parrot • n. a tropical bird with brightly coloured plumage and a hooked bill, some kinds of which are able to mimic human speech. • v. (**parrots, parroting, parroted**) repeat something without thought or understanding.
– ORIGIN prob. from French dialect *perrot*.

parrot-fashion • adv. Brit. (of something learned or repeated) without thought or understanding.

parry • v. (**parries, parrying, parried**) **1** ward off a weapon or attack. **2** say something in order to avoid answering a question directly. • n. (pl. **parries**) an act of parrying.
– ORIGIN prob. from French *parer*.

parse /parz/ • v. (**parses, parsing, parsed**) analyse a sentence into the parts it is made up of.
– ORIGIN perh. from Old French *pars* 'parts'.

parsec • n. a unit of distance in astronomy, equal to about 3.25 light years.
– ORIGIN from **PARALLAX** and **SECOND²**.

parsimony /par-si-muh-ni/ • n. extreme unwillingness to spend money.
– DERIVATIVES **parsimonious** adj.
– ORIGIN Latin *parsimonia*.

parsley • n. a herb with crinkly or flat leaves, used for seasoning or garnishing food.
– ORIGIN Greek *petroselinon*.

parsnip • n. a long tapering cream-coloured root vegetable.

– ORIGIN Old French *pasnaie*.

parson • n. (in the Church of England) a parish priest.
– ORIGIN Latin *persona* 'person'.

parsonage • n. a church house provided for a parson.

parson's nose • n. informal the piece of fatty flesh at the rump of a cooked fowl.

part • n. **1** a piece or section which is combined with others to make up a whole. **2** some but not all of something. **3** a specified fraction of a whole: *a twentieth part.* **4** a measure allowing comparison between the amounts of different ingredients used in a mixture: *a mix of one part cement to five parts ballast.* **5** a role played by an actor or actress. **6** a person's contribution to a situation. **7** (**parts**) informal a region. • v. **1** move apart or divide to leave a central space. **2** leave someone's company. **3** (**part with**) give up possession of. • adv. partly: *part jazz, part blues.*
– PHRASES **on the part of** used to say someone is responsible for something. **part company** go in different directions. **take the part of** give support to.
– ORIGIN Latin *pars.*

partake • v. (**partakes, partaking, partook**; past part. **partaken**) formal **1** (**partake of**) eat or drink something. **2** (**partake in**) participate in an activity.
– ORIGIN from earlier *partaker* 'person who takes a part'.

parterre /par-**tair**/ • n. a group of flower beds laid out in a formal pattern.
– ORIGIN French.

part exchange • n. Brit. a way of buying something in which you give an article that you own as part of the payment for a more expensive one, paying the balance in money.

parthenogenesis /par-thi-noh-**jen**-i-siss/ • n. Biol. reproduction from an ovum without fertilization.
– ORIGIN from Greek *parthenos* 'virgin' + *genesis* 'creation'.

partial • adj. **1** not complete or whole. **2** favouring one side in a dispute above the other. **3** (**partial to**) having a liking for: *I'm very partial to bacon and eggs.*
– DERIVATIVES **partiality** n. **partially** adv.

participate • v. (**participates, participating, participated**) take part in an activity or event.
– DERIVATIVES **participant** n. **participative** adj. **participator** n. **participatory** adj.
– ORIGIN Latin *participare* 'share in'.

participation • n. the action of taking part in an activity or event.

participle /par-**tiss**-i-p'l/ • n. Grammar a

word formed from a verb (e.g. *going, gone, being, been*) and used as an adjective or noun (as in *burnt toast*) or used to make compound verb forms (*is going, has been*).
– ORIGIN Latin *participium* 'sharing'.

particle • n. **1** a tiny portion of matter. **2** Physics a component of the physical world smaller than an atom, e.g. an electron. **3** Grammar an adverb or preposition that has little meaning, e.g. *in, up, off,* or *over,* used with verbs to make phrasal verbs.
– ORIGIN Latin *particula* 'little part'.

particular • adj. **1** relating to an individual member of a group or class. **2** more than is usual: *particular care.* **3** very careful or concerned about something. • n. a detail.
– PHRASES **in particular** especially.
– ORIGIN Latin *particularis.*

particularity • n. (pl. **particularities**) **1** the quality of being individual. **2** (**particularities**) individual details.

particularize (or **particularise**) • v. (**particularizes, particularizing, particularized**) formal treat something individually or in detail.

particularly • adv. **1** more than is usual; especially. **2** in particular.

particulate /par-**tik**-yuu-luht, par-**tik**-yuu-layt/ • adj. relating to or in the form of minute particles. • n. (**particulates**) matter in the form of minute particles.
– ORIGIN Latin *particula* 'particle'.

parting • n. Brit. a line of scalp revealed by combing the hair away in opposite directions on either side.

parting shot • n. a cutting remark made by someone as they leave.

partisan /par-ti-**zan,** par-ti-**zan**/ • n. **1** a strong supporter of a party or cause. **2** a member of an armed group fighting secretly against an occupying force. • adj. prejudiced.
– ORIGIN French.

partition • n. **1** a light wall or other structure dividing a space into parts. **2** division into parts. • v. **1** divide something into parts. **2** divide a room with a partition.
– ORIGIN Latin.

partitive /**par**-ti-tiv/ • adj. (of a grammatical construction) indicating that only a part of a whole is referred to (e.g. *a slice of bacon, some of the children*).

partly • adv. to some extent; not completely.

partner • n. **1** a person who takes part in a business or other undertaking with another person or a group. **2** either of two people doing something as a pair.

3 either member of a married couple or of an established unmarried couple.
• v. (**partners, partnering, partnered**) be the partner of.
– ORIGIN Old French *parcener*.

partnership • n. **1** the state of being a partner or partners. **2** an association of two or more people as partners.

part of speech • n. a category in which a word is placed in accordance with its grammatical function, e.g. noun, pronoun, adjective, verb.

partook past of PARTAKE.

partridge • n. (pl. **partridge** or **partridges**) a short-tailed game bird with mainly brown plumage.
– ORIGIN Old French *perdriz*.

part song • n. a song with three or more voice parts without musical accompaniment.

part-time • adj. & adv. for only part of the usual working day or week.

parturient /par-tyoor-i-uhnt/ • adj. tech. about to give birth; in labour.

parturition /par-tyuu-ri-sh'n/ • n. tech. the action of giving birth.
– ORIGIN Latin.

party • n. (pl. **parties**) **1** a social gathering of invited guests. **2** an organized political group that puts forward candidates to be elected for government. **3** a group of people taking part in an activity or trip. **4** a person or group forming one side in an agreement or dispute. • v. (**parties, partying, partied**) informal enjoy yourself at a party or dance.
– PHRASES **be party** (or **a party**) **to** be involved in.
– ORIGIN Old French *partie*.

party line • n. a policy or policies officially adopted by a political party.

party politics • pl. n. politics that relate to political parties rather than to the public good.

party-pooper • n. informal a person who spoils other people's fun.

party wall • n. a wall shared by two adjoining buildings or rooms.

parvenu /par-vuh-nyoo/ • n. derog. a person from a poor background who has recently joined a group of wealthy or famous people.
– ORIGIN French, 'arrived'.

pascal /pass-kuhl/ • n. the SI unit of pressure.
– ORIGIN named after the French scientist Blaise *Pascal*.

paschal /pass-kuhl, pahss-kuhl/ • adj. **1** relating to Easter. **2** relating to the Jewish Passover.
– ORIGIN Latin *pascha* 'feast of Passover'.

pas de deux /pah di der/ • n. (pl. **pas de deux**) Ballet a dance for a couple.
– ORIGIN French, 'step of two'.

pasha /rhymes with rasher/ • n. hist. the title of a Turkish officer of high rank.
– ORIGIN Turkish.

pashmina /pash-mee-nuh/ • n. a shawl made from fine-quality goat's wool.
– ORIGIN Persian, 'wool, down'.

paso doble /pa-soh doh-blay/ • n. (pl. **paso dobles**) a fast-paced Latin American ballroom dance.
– ORIGIN Spanish, 'double step'.

pass[1] • v. **1** move or go onward, past, through, or across. **2** change from one state or condition to another. **3** transfer something to someone. **4** kick, hit, or throw the ball to a teammate. **5** (of time) go by. **6** occupy or spend time. **7** be done or said: *not another word passed between them.* **8** come to an end. **9** be successful in an exam, test, or course. **10** declare something to be satisfactory. **11** approve a proposal or verb by voting. **12** express a judgement or opinion.
• n. **1** an act of passing. **2** a success in an exam. **3** an official document allowing the holder to go somewhere or use something. **4** informal a sexual advance. **5** a particular situation: *this is a sad pass.*
– PHRASES **pass away** (of a person) die. **pass off** happen in a specified way. **pass someone/thing off as** present someone or something in a way that gives a false impression. **pass out** become unconscious. **pass something up** refrain from taking up an opportunity.
– DERIVATIVES **passer** n.
– ORIGIN Old French *passer*.

pass[2] • n. a route over or through mountains.
– ORIGIN from PACE[1].

passable • adj. **1** acceptable, but not outstanding. **2** able to be travelled along or on.
– DERIVATIVES **passably** adv.

passage • n. **1** the action of passing. **2** a way through something. **3** a journey by sea or air. **4** the right to pass through somewhere: *a permit for safe passage.* **5** a short section from a book, document, or musical work.

passageway • n. a corridor or other narrow passage between buildings or rooms.

passbook • n. a book issued by a bank or building society to an account holder, recording what has been put into or taken out of the account.

passé /pass-ay/ • adj. no longer fashionable.
– ORIGIN French, 'gone by'.

passenger • n. a person travelling in a

p

vehicle, ship, or aircraft other than the driver, pilot, or crew.
– ORIGIN Old French *passager* 'passing'.

passer-by •n. (pl. **passers-by**) a person who happens to be walking past something or someone.

passerine /pass-uh-ryn, pass-uh-reen/ •adj. referring to birds of a large group having feet adapted for perching and including all songbirds.
– ORIGIN Latin *passer* 'sparrow'.

passim /pass-im/ •adv. (of references) at various places throughout a document.
– ORIGIN Latin, 'everywhere'.

passing •adj. **1** done quickly and casually. **2** (of a similarity) slight. •n. **1** the ending of something. **2** euphem. a person's death.
– PHRASES **in passing** briefly and casually.

passion •n. **1** very strong emotion. **2** intense sexual love. **3** an intense enthusiasm for something. **4** (**the Passion**) Jesus's suffering and death on the cross.
– DERIVATIVES **passionless** adj.
– ORIGIN Latin.

passionate •adj. involving intense emotion, enthusiasm, or sexual love.
– DERIVATIVES **passionately** adv.

passion flower •n. a climbing plant with a flower whose parts are said to suggest objects associated with Jesus's death on the cross.

passion fruit •n. the edible purple fruit of some species of passion flower.

passive •adj. **1** accepting or allowing what happens or what other people do, without resistance. **2** Grammar (of verbs) in which the subject undergoes the action of the verb (e.g. *they were killed* as opposed to the active form *he killed them*). •n. a passive form of a verb.
– DERIVATIVES **passively** adv. **passivity** n.
– ORIGIN Latin *passivus*.

passive resistance •n. non-violent opposition to authority.

passive smoking •n. breathing in smoke from other people's cigarettes, cigars, or pipes.

pass key •n. **1** a key given only to those people who are officially allowed access. **2** a master key.

Passover •n. the major Jewish spring festival, commemorating the liberation of the Israelites from slavery in Egypt.
– ORIGIN from *pass over*, with reference to the exemption of the Israelites from the death of their firstborn (Book of Exodus).

passport •n. **1** an official government document certifying the holder's identity and citizenship and entitling

them to travel abroad. **2** a thing that enables someone to achieve something: *qualifications are a passport to success.*

password •n. a secret word or phrase used to enter a place or use a computer.

past •adj. **1** gone by in time and no longer existing. **2** (of time) that has gone by. **3** Grammar (of a tense) expressing a past action or state. •n. **1** a past period or the events in it. **2** a person's earlier life. **3** Grammar a past tense or form of a verb. •prep. **1** beyond in time or space. **2** in front of or from one side to the other of. **3** beyond the scope or power of. •adv. **1** so as to pass from one side to the other. **2** used to indicate the passage of time.
– ORIGIN from PASS¹.

pasta •n. dough formed into various shapes (e.g. spaghetti, lasagne), cooked as part of a dish or in boiling water.
– ORIGIN Italian, 'paste'.

paste •n. **1** a soft, moist substance. **2** a glue made from water and starch. **3** a hard glassy substance used in making imitation gems. •v. (**pastes, pasting, pasted**) **1** coat or stick something with paste. **2** Computing insert an added section into a document.
– ORIGIN Latin *pasta*.

pasteboard •n. thin board made by pasting together sheets of paper.

pastel •n. **1** a crayon made of powdered pigments bound with gum or resin. **2** a picture drawn with pastels. **3** a pale shade of a colour.
– ORIGIN Italian *pastello*.

paste-up •n. a document prepared for printing by pasting various sections on a backing.

pasteurize /pahss-tyuu-ryz, pahss-chuu-ryz/ (or **pasteurise**) •v. (**pasteurizes, pasteurizing, pasteurized**) make milk safe to drink by heating it to destroy most of the microorganisms in it.
– DERIVATIVES **pasteurization** n.
– ORIGIN named after the French chemist Louis *Pasteur*.

pastiche /pa-steesh/ •n. an artistic work in a style that imitates that of another work, artist, or period.
– ORIGIN Italian *pasticcio*.

pastille /pass-tuhl/ •n. esp. Brit. a small sweet or lozenge.
– ORIGIN Latin *pastillus*.

pastime •n. an activity done regularly for enjoyment.
– ORIGIN from PASS¹ + TIME.

past master •n. a person who is an expert in an activity.

pastor /pah-ster/ •n. a minister in

charge of a Christian church or congregation.

– ORIGIN Latin, 'shepherd'.

pastoral /pahss-tuh-ruhl/
• adj. **1** relating to the farming or grazing of sheep or cattle. **2** (of a creative work) portraying country life. **3** relating to the giving of spiritual guidance by a Christian minister. **4** relating to a teacher's responsibility for the general well-being of pupils or students.

past participle • n. Grammar the form of a verb which is used in forming perfect and passive tenses and sometimes as an adjective, e.g. *looked* in *have you looked?*, *lost* in *lost property*.

pastrami /pass-trah-mi/ • n. highly seasoned smoked beef.

– ORIGIN Yiddish.

pastry • n. (pl. **pastries**) **1** a dough of flour, fat, and water, used as a base or covering in baked dishes such as pies. **2** a cake consisting of sweet pastry with a filling.

– ORIGIN from PASTE.

pasturage • n. land used for grazing cattle or sheep.

pasture • n. land covered with grass, suitable for grazing cattle or sheep.
• v. (**pastures, pasturing, pastured**) put animals to graze in a pasture.

– ORIGIN Latin *pastura* 'grazing'.

pasty¹ /pass-ti/ (also **pastie**) • n. (pl. **pasties**) Brit. a folded pastry case filled with meat and vegetables.

– ORIGIN Old French *pastee*.

pasty² /pay-sti/ • adj. (of a person's skin) unhealthily pale.

pat¹ • v. (**patted, patting**) tap gently with the flat of the hand. • n. **1** an act of patting. **2** a compact mass of a soft substance.

– PHRASES **a pat on the back** an expression of praise or encouragement.

pat² • adj. too quick or easy and not convincing: *a pat answer*.

– PHRASES **have something off** (or **down**) **pat** memorize something perfectly.

– ORIGIN prob. from PAT¹.

patch • n. **1** a piece of material used to mend a hole or strengthen a weak point. **2** a small area differing from its surroundings. **3** a small plot of land: *a cabbage patch*. **4** Brit. informal a brief period of time: *a bad patch*. **5** Brit. informal an area for which someone is responsible or in which they operate. **6** a shield worn over a sightless or injured eye. • v. **1** mend, strengthen, or protect something with a patch. **2** (**patch someone/thing up**) informal treat an injured person or repair something quickly or temporarily. **3** (**patch something up**) informal settle a dispute.

– PHRASES **not a patch on** Brit. informal much less good than.

– ORIGIN perh. from Old French dialect *pieche* 'piece'.

patchwork • n. **1** needlework in which small pieces of cloth in different designs are sewn together to form a larger piece of fabric. **2** a thing composed of many different parts: *a patchwork of educational courses*.

– DERIVATIVES **patchworked** adj.

patchy • adj. **1** existing or happening in small, isolated areas: *patchy fog*. **2** uneven in quality; inconsistent.

– DERIVATIVES **patchily** adv. **patchiness** n.

pate /rhymes with gate/ • n. old use a person's head.

pâté /pa-tay/ • n. a rich savoury paste made from finely minced or mashed meat, fish, or other ingredients.

– ORIGIN French.

pâté de foie gras /pa-tay duh fwah grah/ • n. = FOIE GRAS.

patella /puh-tel-luh/ • n. (pl. **patellae** /puh-tel-lee/) the kneecap.

– ORIGIN Latin, 'small dish'.

patent /pay-t'nt, pa-t'nt/ • n. a government licence giving someone the sole right to make, use, or sell an invention for a set period. • adj. /pay-t'nt/ **1** easily recognizable; obvious: *she smiled with patent insincerity*. **2** made and sold under a patent. • v. obtain a patent for.

– DERIVATIVES **patentable** adj. **patently** /pay-t'nt-li/ adv.

– ORIGIN Latin *patere* 'lie open'.

patent leather • n. glossy varnished leather.

patent medicine • n. a medicine made and sold under a patent and available without prescription.

pater /pay-ter/ • n. Brit. informal, dated father.

– ORIGIN Latin.

paterfamilias /pay-ter-fuh-mi-li-ass/ • n. (pl. **patresfamilias** /pay-treez-fuh-mi-li-ass/) the male head of a family.

– ORIGIN Latin, 'father of the family'.

paternal • adj. **1** relating to or like a father. **2** related through the father.

– DERIVATIVES **paternally** adv.

paternalism • n. the policy of protecting the people you have control over, but also of restricting their freedom or responsibilities.

– DERIVATIVES **paternalist** n. & adj. **paternalistic** adj.

paternity • n. **1** the state of being a father. **2** descent from a father.

paternity suit • n. esp. N. Amer. a court case held to establish the identity of a child's father.

paternoster /pa-ter-noss-ter/ • n. (in the Roman Catholic Church) the Lord's Prayer.
– ORIGIN from Latin *pater noster* 'our father', the first words of the Lord's Prayer.

path • n. **1** a way or track laid down for walking or made by continual treading. **2** the direction in which a person or thing moves. **3** a course of action.
– ORIGIN Old English.

-path • comb. form **1** referring to a person who practises a treatment to cure a disease: *homeopath*. **2** referring to a person who suffers from a disease: *psychopath*.
– ORIGIN from **-PATHY** or from Greek *-pathēs* '-sufferer'.

path-breaking • adj. pioneering; original.

pathetic • adj. **1** arousing pity. **2** informal completely inadequate.
– DERIVATIVES **pathetically** adv.
– ORIGIN Greek *pathētikos* 'sensitive'.

patho- • comb. form relating to disease: *pathology*.
– ORIGIN Greek *pathos* 'suffering'.

pathogen /pa-thuh-juhn/ • n. a microscopic organism that can cause disease.
– DERIVATIVES **pathogenic** adj.

pathological (US **pathologic**) • adj. **1** relating to or caused by a disease. **2** informal beyond your control; compulsive: *a pathological liar*.
– DERIVATIVES **pathologically** adv.

pathology • n. **1** the branch of medicine concerned with the causes and effects of diseases. **2** the typical behaviour of a disease.
– DERIVATIVES **pathologist** n.

pathos /pay-thoss/ • n. a quality that arouses pity or sadness.
– ORIGIN Greek, 'suffering'.

pathway • n. a path or its course.

-pathy • comb. form **1** referring to feelings: *telepathy*. **2** referring to medical treatment: *homeopathy*.
– ORIGIN Greek *patheia* 'feeling'.

patience • n. **1** the ability to accept delay, trouble, or suffering without becoming angry or upset. **2** Brit. a card game for one player.
– ORIGIN Latin *patientia*.

patient • adj. able to accept delay, trouble, or suffering without becoming angry or upset. • n. a person receiving or registered to receive medical treatment.
– DERIVATIVES **patiently** adv.

patina /pa-ti-nuh/ • n. a distinctive surface appearance and texture acquired over time. **2** a soft glow on wooden

furniture produced by age and polishing.
– ORIGIN Latin, 'shallow dish'.

patio • n. (pl. **patios**) a paved area next to a house.
– ORIGIN Spanish.

patio door • n. a large glass sliding door leading to a patio.

patisserie /puh-tiss-uh-ri, puh-tee-suh-ri/ • n. a shop where pastries and cakes are sold.
– ORIGIN French.

patois /pat-wah/ • n. (pl. **patois** /pat-wahz/) the local dialect of a region, especially one with low status in relation to the standard language of the country.
– ORIGIN French, 'rough speech'.

patresfamilias pl. of **PATERFAMILIAS**.

patriarch /pay-tri-ark/ • n. **1** the male head of a family or tribe. **2** a biblical figure regarded as a father of the human race. **3** a powerful or respected older man. **4** a high-ranking bishop in the Roman Catholic Church. **5** the head of an independent Orthodox Church.
– DERIVATIVES **patriarchal** adj.
– ORIGIN Greek *patriarkhēs*.

patriarchy • n. (pl. **patriarchies**) **1** a society in which men hold most or all of the power. **2** a form of social organization in which the father or eldest male is the head of the family.

patrician /puh-tri-sh'n/ • n. an aristocrat. • adj. typical of aristocrats.
– ORIGIN Latin *patricius* 'having a noble father'.

patricide /pa-tri-syd/ • n. **1** the killing of a father by his child. **2** a person who kills their father.
– ORIGIN Latin *patricidium*.

patrimony /pa-tri-muh-ni/ • n. (pl. **patrimonies**) property inherited a person's father or male ancestor.
– ORIGIN Latin *patrimonium*.

patriot /pa-tri-uht, pay-tri-uht/ • n. a person who strongly supports their country and is prepared to defend it.
– DERIVATIVES **patriotic** adj. **patriotically** adv. **patriotism** n.
– ORIGIN Latin *patriota* 'fellow countryman'.

patrol • n. **1** a person or group sent to keep watch over an area. **2** the action of watching over an area. • v. (**patrols**, **patrolling**, **patrolled**) keep watch over an area by regularly walking or travelling around it.
– DERIVATIVES **patroller** n.
– ORIGIN French *patrouiller* 'paddle in mud'.

patron • n. **1** a person who gives financial or other support to a person,

organization, or cause. **2** a regular customer of a restaurant or hotel.
– ORIGIN Latin *patronus* 'protector'.

patronage /pa-truh-nij, pay-truh-nij/ •n. **1** support given by a patron. **2** the giving of help or a job to someone in return for their support. **3** the regular custom attracted by a restaurant or hotel.

patronize (or **patronise**)
•v. (**patronizes, patronizing, patronized**) **1** treat someone in a way that suggests they are inferior. **2** be a regular customer of a restaurant or hotel.

patron saint •n. the protecting or guiding saint of a person or place.

patronymic /pa-truh-**nim**-ik/ •n. a name derived from the name of a father or ancestor, e.g. *O'Brien*.
– ORIGIN Greek *patrōnumikos*.

patter[1] •v. (**patters, pattering, pattered**) **1** make a repeated light tapping sound. **2** run with quick light steps. •n. a repeated light tapping sound.
– ORIGIN from PAT[1].

patter[2] •n. **1** fast continuous talk, such as that used by a comedian. **2** the jargon of a profession or social group.
– ORIGIN from PATERNOSTER (from the fast and mechanical way in which the prayer was often said).

pattern •n. **1** a repeated decorative design. **2** a regular form or order in which a series of things occur: *working patterns*. **3** a model, design, or set of instructions for making something. **4** an example for other people to follow. **5** a sample of cloth or wallpaper.
•v. **1** decorate with a pattern. **2** (**pattern something on/after**) use something as a model for something else.
– ORIGIN from PATRON in the former sense 'something serving as a model'.

patty •n. (pl. **patties**) **1** N. Amer. a small flat cake of minced food, especially meat. **2** a small pie or pasty.
– ORIGIN French *pâté*.

paucity /**paw**-si-ti/ •n. smallness or lack of something: *a paucity of information*.
– ORIGIN Latin *paucus* 'few'.

paunch •n. a stomach that is large or sticks out.
– DERIVATIVES **paunchy** adj.
– ORIGIN Old French *paunche*.

pauper •n. a very poor person.
– ORIGIN Latin, 'poor'.

pause •n. **1** a temporary stop in action or speech. **2** Music a mark (⌢) over a note or rest that is to be lengthened by an unspecified amount. •v. (**pauses, pausing, paused**) stop temporarily.
– ORIGIN Greek *pausis*.

pave •v. (**paves, paving, paved**) cover a piece of ground with flat stones or bricks.
– DERIVATIVES **paving** n.
– ORIGIN Old French *paver*.

pavement •n. **1** Brit. a raised path for pedestrians at the side of a road. **2** N. Amer. the hard surface of a road or street. **3** Geol. a horizontal expanse of bare rock with cracks or joints.
– ORIGIN Latin *pavimentum* 'trodden down floor'.

pavilion •n. **1** Brit. a building at a sports ground used for changing and having drinks and light meals. **2** a decorative shelter in a park or large garden. **3** a marquee used at a show or fair. **4** a temporary display stand at a trade exhibition.
– ORIGIN Old French *pavillon*.

paw •n. an animal's foot that has claws and pads. •v. **1** feel or scrape the ground or another surface with a paw or hoof. **2** informal touch someone in a way that is clumsy or unwanted.
– ORIGIN Old French *poue*.

pawl /pawl/ •n. a pivoted bar or lever whose free end engages with the teeth of a cogwheel or ratchet, allowing it to move or turn in one direction only.
– ORIGIN perh. from German and Dutch *pal*.

pawn[1] •n. **1** a chess piece of the smallest size and value. **2** a person used by other people for their own purposes.
– ORIGIN Old French *poun*.

pawn[2] •v. leave an object with a pawnbroker as security for money lent. •n. the state of being pawned: *everything was in pawn*.
– ORIGIN Old French *pan* 'pledge'.

pawnbroker •n. a person licensed to lend money in exchange for an article left with them, which they can sell if the borrower fails to pay the money back.

pawnshop •n. a pawnbroker's shop.

pawpaw /**paw**-paw/ (also **papaw** /puh-**paw**/) •n. a papaya.
– ORIGIN Spanish and Portuguese *papaya*.

pay •v. (**pays, paying, paid**) **1** give someone money owed to them for work, goods, or as a debt. **2** result in a profit or advantage: *crime doesn't pay*. **3** suffer as a result of an action: *someone's got to pay for all that grief*. **4** give someone attention, respect, or a compliment. **5** visit or call on someone. •n. money paid for work.
– PHRASES **pay someone back** take revenge on someone. **pay off** informal yield good results. **pay someone off** dismiss someone with a final payment. **pay through the nose** informal pay much more than a fair price.

p

– DERIVATIVES **payer** n.
– ORIGIN Old French *payer* 'appease'.

payable • adj. **1** that must be paid. **2** able to be paid.

PAYE • abbrev. (in the UK and South Africa) pay as you earn, a system whereby an employer deducts income tax from an employee's wages to be paid directly to the government.

payee • n. a person to whom money is paid.

paying guest • n. a lodger.

payload • n. **1** passengers and cargo as the part of a vehicle's load for which money is paid. **2** an explosive warhead carried by an aircraft or missile.

paymaster • n. **1** a person who pays another and therefore controls them. **2** an official who pays troops or workers.

payment • n. **1** the action of paying or the process of being paid. **2** an amount paid.

pay-off • n. informal **1** a bribe. **2** the return on investment or on a bet. **3** a final outcome.

payola /pay-oh-luh/ • n. N. Amer. bribery in return for the unofficial promotion of a product in the media.

pay-per-view • n. a television service in which viewers have to pay a fee to watch a particular programme.

payphone • n. a public telephone operated by coins or by a credit or prepaid card.

payroll • n. a list of a company's employees and the amount of money they are to be paid.

Pb • symb. the chemical element lead.
– ORIGIN Latin *plumbum*.

PC • abbrev. **1** personal computer. **2** Brit. police constable. **3** (also **pc**) politically correct; political correctness.

p.c. • abbrev. per cent.

PCB • abbrev. **1** Electron. printed circuit board. **2** Chem. polychlorinated biphenyl, a poisonous compound formed as waste in some industrial processes.

Pd • symb. the chemical element palladium.

PDF • n. Computing **1** a file format for capturing and sending electronic documents in exactly the intended format. **2** a file in this format.
– ORIGIN abbreviation of *Portable Document Format*.

PE • abbrev. physical education.

pea • n. a round green seed within a pod, eaten as a vegetable.
– ORIGIN Old English.

peace • n. **1** freedom from noise or anxiety. **2** freedom from or the ending of war.

– PHRASES **hold your peace** remain silent.
– ORIGIN Old French *pais*.

peaceable • adj. **1** wanting to avoid war. **2** free from conflict; peaceful.
– DERIVATIVES **peaceably** adv.

peaceful • adj. **1** free from noise or anxiety. **2** not involving war or violence. **3** wanting to avoid conflict.
– DERIVATIVES **peacefully** adv. **peacefulness** n.

peacekeeping • n. the use of an international military force to maintain a truce.
– DERIVATIVES **peacekeeper** n.

peace offering • n. a gift given in an attempt to make peace in a conflict.

peacetime • n. a period when a country is not at war.

peach • n. **1** a round fruit with juicy yellow flesh, red and yellow skin, and a stone inside. **2** a pinkish-orange colour. **3** informal an exceptionally good or attractive person or thing.
– DERIVATIVES **peachy** adj.
– ORIGIN Old French *pesche*.

peacock • n. a large male bird with very long tail feathers with eye-like markings that can be fanned out in display.
– ORIGIN Old English.

peahen • n. a large mainly brown bird, the female of the peacock.

peak • n. **1** the pointed top of a mountain. **2** a mountain with a pointed top. **3** Brit. a stiff brim at the front of a cap. **4** the point of highest activity, achievement, or intensity. • v. reach a maximum or the highest point. • adj. maximum.
– ORIGIN prob. from a dialect word meaning 'pointed'.

peaked • adj. (of a cap) having a peak.

peaky • adj. (**peakier**, **peakiest**) Brit. pale from illness or tiredness.
– ORIGIN from former *peak* 'decline in health'.

peal • n. **1** a loud ringing of a bell or bells. **2** a loud repeated or echoing sound of thunder or laughter. **3** a set of bells. • v. ring or resound in a peal.
– ORIGIN from **APPEAL**.

peanut • n. **1** the oval edible seed of a plant native to South America, whose seeds develop in underground pods. **2** (**peanuts**) informal a very small sum of money.

peanut butter • n. a spread made from ground roasted peanuts.

pear • n. a green edible fruit which is narrow at the stalk and widens towards the bottom.
– PHRASES **go pear-shaped** Brit. informal go wrong.
– ORIGIN Old English.

pearl • n. **1** a small, hard, shiny white ball formed within the shell of an oyster and having great value as a gem. **2** a highly valued person or thing.
– ORIGIN Old French *perle*.

pearl barley • n. barley reduced to small round grains by grinding.

pearlescent • adj. having a soft glow resembling that of mother-of-pearl.

pearly • adj. like a pearl in lustre or colour.

Pearly Gates • pl. n. informal the gates of heaven.
– ORIGIN from the Book of Revelation in the Bible.

peasant • n. **1** a poor smallholder or farm labourer of low social status. **2** informal a rude or uneducated person.
– DERIVATIVES **peasantry** n.
– ORIGIN Old French *paisent*.

pea-souper • n. Brit. a very thick yellowish fog.

peat • n. partly decomposed vegetable matter formed in acidic boggy ground, dried for use in gardening and as fuel.
– DERIVATIVES **peaty** adj.
– ORIGIN Latin *peta*.

pebble • n. a small stone made smooth and round by the action of water or sand.
– DERIVATIVES **pebbly** adj.
– ORIGIN Old English.

pebble-dash • n. Brit. mortar with pebbles in it, used as a coating for the outside walls of buildings.

pecan /pee-k'n, pi-kan/ • n. a smooth pinkish-brown nut obtained from a tree of the southern US.
– ORIGIN from an American Indian language.

peccadillo /pek-kuh-dil-loh/ • n. (pl. **peccadilloes** or **peccadillos**) a minor fault.
– ORIGIN Spanish.

peccary /pek-kuh-ri/ • n. (pl. **peccaries**) a piglike mammal found from the south-western US to Paraguay.
– ORIGIN Carib.

peck[1] • v. **1** (of a bird) strike or bite with its beak. **2** kiss lightly and quickly. • n. **1** an act of pecking. **2** a light, quick kiss.

peck[2] • n. a measure of capacity for dry goods, equal to a quarter of a bushel.
– ORIGIN Old French *pek*.

pecker • n. (in phr. **keep your pecker up**) Brit. informal remain cheerful.
– ORIGIN *pecker* prob. in the sense 'beak'.

pecking order • n. a strict order of importance among members of a group.

peckish • adj. informal hungry.

pectin • n. a jelly-like substance present in ripe fruits, used to set jams and jellies.
– ORIGIN Greek *pektos* 'congealed'.

pectoral /pek-tuh-ruhl/ • adj. relating to the breast or chest. • n. a pectoral muscle.
– ORIGIN Latin *pectoralis*.

pectoral muscle • n. each of four large paired muscles which cover the front of the ribcage.

peculiar • adj. **1** strange or odd. **2** (**peculiar to**) belonging only to.
– DERIVATIVES **peculiarly** adv.
– ORIGIN Latin *peculiaris* 'of private property'.

peculiarity • n. (pl. **peculiarities**) **1** an unusual or distinctive feature or habit. **2** the state of being peculiar.

pecuniary /pi-kyoo-ni-uh-ri/ • adj. formal relating to money.
– ORIGIN Latin *pecuniarius*.

pedagogue /ped-uh-gog/ • n. formal a teacher.
– ORIGIN Greek *paidagōgos*, referring to a slave who accompanied a child to school.

pedagogy /ped-uh-go-gi/ • n. the profession or theory of teaching.
– DERIVATIVES **pedagogic** (also **pedagogical**) adj.

pedal /ped-uhl/ • n. **1** each of a pair of foot-operated levers for powering a bicycle or other vehicle. **2** a foot-operated throttle, brake, or clutch control. **3** a foot-operated lever on a piano or organ for sustaining or softening the tone. • v. (**pedals, pedalling, pedalled**; US **pedals, pedaling, pedaled**) work the pedals of a bicycle to move along.
– ORIGIN French *pédale*.

> **USAGE:** Do not confuse the words **pedal** and **peddle. Pedal** is a noun referring to a foot-operated lever, as on a bicycle; as a verb it means 'work the pedals of a bicycle'. **Peddle** is a verb meaning 'sell goods or promote an idea'.

pedalo /ped-uh-loh/ • n. (pl. **pedalos** or **pedaloes**) Brit. a small pedal-operated pleasure boat.

pedal pushers • pl. n. women's calf-length trousers.

pedant /ped-uhnt/ • n. a person who is excessively concerned with minor detail or with displaying specialist knowledge.
– DERIVATIVES **pedantic** adj. **pedantically** adv. **pedantry** n.
– ORIGIN French *pédant*.

peddle • v. (**peddles, peddling, peddled**) **1** travel from house to house to sell goods. **2** sell an illegal drug or stolen item. **3** promote an idea persistently or widely.

p

– ORIGIN from **PEDLAR**.

> **USAGE:** For an explanation of the difference between **pedal** and **peddle**, see the note at **PEDAL**.

peddler • n. var. of **PEDLAR**.

pederasty /ped-uh-rass-ti/ • n. sexual relations between a man and a boy.
– DERIVATIVES **pederast** n.
– ORIGIN Greek *paiderastia*.

pedestal • n. **1** the base or support on which a statue or column is mounted. **2** the supporting column of a washbasin or toilet pan. **3** each of the two supports of a desk or table which has a space for the knees.
– ORIGIN Italian *piedestallo*.

pedestrian • n. a person walking rather than travelling in a vehicle. • adj. dull and boring.
– ORIGIN Latin *pedester* 'going on foot'.

pedestrianize (or **pedestrianise**) • v. (**pedestrianizes, pedestrianizing, pedestrianized**) make a street accessible only to pedestrians.
– DERIVATIVES **pedestrianization** n.

pediatrics • n. US = **PAEDIATRICS**.

pedicure • n. a cosmetic treatment of the feet and toenails.
– ORIGIN French.

pedigree • n. **1** the record of an animal's origins, showing that all the animals from which it is descended are of the same breed. **2** a person's family background or ancestry. **3** the history of a thing.
– ORIGIN from Old French *pé de grue* 'crane's foot', a mark used to represent succession in pedigrees.

pediment • n. the triangular upper part above the entrance to a classical building.
– ORIGIN perh. from **PYRAMID**.

pedlar (esp. US also **peddler**) • n. **1** a travelling trader who sells small goods. **2** a person who sells illegal drugs or stolen goods.
– ORIGIN perh. from dialect *ped* 'pannier'.

pedometer /pi-dom-i-ter/ • n. an instrument for estimating the distance travelled on foot by recording the number of steps taken.
– ORIGIN Latin *pes* 'foot'.

peek • v. **1** look quickly or secretly. **2** stick out slightly so as to be just visible. • n. a quick or secret look.

peel • v. **1** remove the skin from a fruit or vegetable. **2** (of a surface or object) lose parts of its outer layer or covering in small pieces. **3** (**peel something away/off**) remove a thin outer covering.
• n. the outer skin of a fruit or vegetable.
– DERIVATIVES **peelings** pl. n.

– ORIGIN Latin *pilare* 'strip hair from'.

peeler • n. a type of knife for peeling fruit and vegetables.

peen (also **pein**) • n. the rounded or wedge-shaped end of a hammer head opposite the face.
– ORIGIN prob. Scandinavian.

peep[1] • v. **1** look quickly and secretly. **2** (**peep out**) come slowly or partially into view. • n. **1** a quick or secret look. **2** a glimpse of something.

peep[2] • n. a weak or brief high-pitched sound. • v. make a peep.
– PHRASES **not a peep** not the slightest sound or complaint.

peephole • n. a small hole in a door through which callers can be seen.

peeping Tom • n. a person who gains sexual pleasure from secretly watching people undress or engage in sex.
– ORIGIN the name of the tailor said to have watched Lady Godiva ride naked through Coventry.

peep show • n. a form of entertainment in which pictures are viewed through a lens or hole set into a box.

peer[1] • v. (**peers, peering, peered**) look with difficulty or concentration.

peer[2] • n. **1** a member of the nobility in Britain or Ireland. **2** a person who is the same age or has the same status as you.
– ORIGIN Old French.

peerage • n. **1** the title and rank of peer or peeress. **2** (**the peerage**) peers as a whole.

peeress • n. **1** a woman holding the rank of a peer in her own right. **2** the wife or widow of a peer.

peer group • n. a group of people of approximately the same age and status.

peerless • adj. better than all others; unrivalled.

peeved • adj. informal annoyed or irritated.
– ORIGIN from **PEEVISH**.

peevish • adj. irritable.

peewit • n. Brit. a lapwing.

peg • n. **1** a projecting pin or bolt used for hanging things on, securing something in place, or marking a position. **2** a clothes peg. • v. (**pegs, pegging, pegged**) **1** fix, attach, or mark something with a peg or pegs. **2** fix a price or rate at a particular level. **3** (**peg out**) informal die.
– PHRASES **off the peg** Brit. (of clothes) not made to order. **take someone down a peg or two** make someone less arrogant.
– ORIGIN prob. German.

peg leg • n. informal a wooden leg.

pein • n. var. of **PEEN**.

pejorative /pi-jo-ruh-tiv/

• **adj.** expressing contempt or disapproval.
– DERIVATIVES **pejoratively** adv.
– ORIGIN French *péjoratif*.

Pekinese /pee-ki-neez/ • **n.** (pl. **Pekinese**) a small dog with long hair, short legs, and a snub nose.

pelargonium /pe-luh-goh-ni-uhm/ • **n.** a garden plant with red, pink, or white flowers.
– ORIGIN Latin.

pelf • **n.** old use money.
– ORIGIN Old French *pelfre* 'spoils'.

pelican • **n.** a large waterbird with a long bill and a pouch hanging from its throat.
– ORIGIN Greek *pelekan*.

pelican crossing • **n.** (in the UK) a pedestrian crossing with traffic lights operated by pedestrians.

pelisse /pi-leess/ • **n.** hist. a woman's long cloak with armholes or sleeves.
– ORIGIN French.

pellagra /pel-**lag**-ruh, pel-**lay**-gruh/ • **n.** a disease caused by an inadequate diet, in which a person has inflamed skin, diarrhoea, and mental disturbance.
– ORIGIN Italian.

pellet • **n. 1** a small compressed mass of a substance. **2** a piece of small shot or other lightweight bullet.
– ORIGIN Old French *pelote* 'metal ball'.

pell-mell • **adj. & adv.** in a confused or rushed way.
– ORIGIN French *pêle-mêle*.

pellucid /pel-**lyoo**-sid/ • **adj.** literary **1** transparent or semi-transparent; clear. **2** easily understood.
– ORIGIN Latin *pellucidus*.

pelmet • **n.** a narrow border fitted across the top of a window to conceal the curtain fittings.
– ORIGIN prob. from French *palmette* 'small palm leaf'.

pelt[1] • **v. 1** hurl missiles at. **2** (**pelt down**) (of rain) fall very heavily. **3** run very quickly.
– PHRASES (**at**) **full pelt** as fast as possible.

pelt[2] • **n.** the skin of an animal with the fur, wool, or hair still on it.
– ORIGIN Latin *pellis* 'skin'.

pelvic girdle • **n.** (in vertebrates) the enclosing structure formed by the pelvis.

pelvis /pel-viss/ • **n.** (pl. **pelvises** or **pelves** /pel-veez/) the large bony frame at the base of the spine to which the legs are attached.
– DERIVATIVES **pelvic** adj.
– ORIGIN Latin, 'basin'.

Pembs. • **abbrev.** Pembrokeshire.

pen[1] • **n. 1** an instrument for writing or drawing with ink. **2** an electronic device

used to enter commands into a computer. • **v.** (**pens**, **penning**, **penned**) write or compose something.
– ORIGIN Latin *penna* 'feather' (pens were originally made from a quill feather).

pen[2] • **n.** a small enclosure for farm animals. • **v.** (**pens**, **penning**, **penned**) **1** put or keep an animal in a pen. **2** (**pen someone up/in**) confine someone in a restricted space.
– ORIGIN Old English.

penal • **adj. 1** relating to the punishment of offenders under the legal system. **2** very severe: *penal rates of interest.*
– ORIGIN Old French.

penalize (or **penalise**) • **v.** (**penalizes**, **penalizing**, **penalized**) **1** give someone a penalty or punishment. **2** put someone in an unfavourable position.

penalty • **n.** (pl. **penalties**) **1** a punishment for breaking a law, rule, or contract. **2** something unpleasant suffered as a result of an action or circumstance: *feeling cold is one of the penalties of old age.* **3** a penalty kick.

penalty kick • **n.** Football a free shot at the goal awarded to the attacking team after a foul within an area around the goal.

penance • **n. 1** something that you do as punishment for doing wrong. **2** a religious act in which someone confesses their sins to a priest and is given a penance or formal forgiveness.
– ORIGIN Old French.

pence Brit. pl. of **penny** (used for sums of money).

penchant /pon-shon/ • **n.** a strong liking: *a penchant for champagne.*
– ORIGIN French, 'leaning'.

pencil • **n.** an instrument for writing or drawing, consisting of a thin stick of graphite enclosed in a wooden case. • **v.** (**pencils**, **pencilling**, **pencilled**; US **pencils**, **penciling**, **penciled**) **1** write or draw something with a pencil. **2** (**pencil something in**) note something down provisionally.
– ORIGIN Old French *pincel* 'paintbrush'.

pendant • **n. 1** a piece of jewellery that hangs from a necklace chain. **2** a light designed to hang from the ceiling. • **adj.** hanging downwards.
– ORIGIN Old French, 'hanging'.

pendent • **adj.** hanging down.

pending • **adj. 1** awaiting decision or settlement. **2** about to happen. • **prep.** until.
– ORIGIN from **PENDANT**.

pendulous • **adj.** hanging down; drooping.

pendulum • **n.** a weight hung from a fixed point so that it can swing freely,

p

used to regulate the mechanism of a clock.
– ORIGIN Latin, 'thing hanging down'.

peneplain /pee-ni-playn/ • n. a level land surface produced by erosion over a long period.
– ORIGIN Latin *paene* 'almost'.

penetrate • v. (**penetrates, penetrating, penetrated**) **1** force a way into or through: *the shrapnel had penetrated his head.* **2** gain access to an enemy organization or a competitor's market. **3** understand something. **4** (as adj. **penetrating**) (of a sound) clearly heard through or above other sounds. **5** (of a man) insert the penis into the vagina or anus of a sexual partner.
– DERIVATIVES **penetrable** adj. **penetrative** adj. **penetrator** n.
– ORIGIN Latin *penetrare* 'go into'.

penetration • n. **1** the action of penetrating. **2** the extent to which a product is recognized and bought by customers in a particular market: *the company achieved remarkable market penetration.* **3** understanding of complex matters.

penfriend • n. Brit. a person with whom you become friendly by exchanging letters.

penguin • n. a flightless black and white seabird of the southern hemisphere.

penicillin • n. an antibiotic (medicine that destroys bacteria).
– ORIGIN Latin *penicillum* 'paintbrush'.

peninsula • n. a long, narrow piece of land jutting out into a sea or lake.
– DERIVATIVES **peninsular** adj.
– ORIGIN Latin.

USAGE: Do not confuse **peninsula** and **peninsular**. Peninsula is a noun meaning 'a long piece of land jutting out into a sea or lake', whereas **peninsular** is an adjective that means 'relating to a peninsula' (*the peninsular part of Malaysia*).

penis /pee-niss/ • n. (pl. **penises** or **penes** /pee-neez/) the male organ that is used for sex and for urinating.
– DERIVATIVES **penile** adj.
– ORIGIN Latin, 'tail'.

penitent • adj. feeling sorrow and regret for having done wrong. • n. a person who repents or does penance.
– DERIVATIVES **penitence** n. **penitential** adj.
– ORIGIN Latin *paenitere* 'repent'.

penitentiary /pen-i-ten-shuh-ri/ • n. (pl. **penitentiaries**) (in North America) a prison for people convicted of serious crimes.

penknife • n. a small knife with a blade which folds into the handle.

pen name • n. a name used by a writer instead of their real name.

pennant • n. a long, narrow, pointed flag.
– ORIGIN from **PENDANT** and **PENNON**.

penne /pen-nay/ • pl. n. pasta in the form of short wide tubes.
– ORIGIN Italian, 'quills'.

penniless • adj. without money.

pennon • n. = **PENNANT**.
– ORIGIN Old French.

penny • n. (pl. **pennies** (for separate coins); **pence** (for a sum of money)) **1** a British bronze coin worth one hundredth of a pound. **2** a former British coin worth one twelfth of a shilling.
– PHRASES **be two** (or **ten**) **a penny** be plentiful and therefore of little value. **not a penny** no money at all. **the penny dropped** informal someone has finally realized something. **penny wise and pound foolish** economical in small matters but extravagant in large ones.
– ORIGIN Old English.

penny-farthing • n. Brit. an early type of bicycle with a very large front wheel and a small rear wheel.

penny-pinching • adj. unwilling to spend money; miserly.

pennyworth • n. Brit. **1** an amount of something worth a penny. **2** (**your pennyworth**) your contribution to a discussion.

pen pal • n. a penfriend.

pen-pusher • n. informal, derog. a person who works in an office doing routine paperwork.

pension¹ /pen-sh'n/ • n. a regular payment made by the state or a company to retired people and to some widows and disabled people. • v. (**pension someone off**) dismiss someone from employment and pay them a pension.
– DERIVATIVES **pensionable** adj. **pensioner** n.
– ORIGIN Latin, 'payment'.

pension² /pon-syon/ • n. a small hotel in France and other European countries.
– ORIGIN French.

pensive • adj. engaged in deep thought.
– DERIVATIVES **pensively** adv.
– ORIGIN Old French *pensif*.

penta- • comb. form five; having five: *pentagon.*
– ORIGIN Greek *pente*.

pentacle /pen-tuh-k'l/ • n. a pentagram.
– ORIGIN Latin *pentaculum*.

pentagon • n. **1** a plane figure with five straight sides and five angles. **2** (**the Pentagon**) the headquarters of the US Department of Defense.

pentagram • n. a five-pointed star

drawn using a continuous line, used as a mystic and magical symbol.

pentameter /pen-**tam**-i-ter/ • n. a line of verse consisting of five metrical feet.

Pentateuch /**pen**-tuh-tyook/ • n. the first five books of the Old Testament and Hebrew Scriptures.
– ORIGIN Greek.

pentathlon • n. an athletic event consisting of five different activities.
– DERIVATIVES **pentathlete** n.
– ORIGIN Greek.

pentatonic /pen-tuh-**ton**-ik/ • adj. Music consisting of a scale of five notes.

Pentecost /**pen**-ti-kost/ • n. **1** the Christian festival celebrating the coming of the Holy Spirit to the disciples of Jesus, after his Ascension. **2** a Jewish festival that takes place fifty days after the second day of Passover.
– ORIGIN from Greek *pentēkostē hēmera* 'fiftieth day'.

Pentecostal • adj. relating to a Christian movement which emphasizes the gifts of the Holy Spirit, such as 'speaking in tongues' and healing of the sick.
– DERIVATIVES **Pentecostalism** n.

penthouse • n. a flat on the top floor of a tall building.
– ORIGIN Old French *apentis* 'outhouse'.

pent-up • adj. not expressed or released: *pent-up anger.*
– ORIGIN former past part. of PEN².

penultimate • adj. last but one.
– ORIGIN from Latin *paene* 'almost' + *ultimus* 'last'.

penumbra /pi-**num**-bruh/ • n. (pl. **penumbrae** /pi-**num**-bree/ or **penumbras**) the partially shaded outer region of the shadow cast by an object.
– ORIGIN from Latin *paene* 'almost' + *umbra* 'shadow'.

penurious /pi-**nyoor**-i-uhss/ • adj. formal very poor.

penury /**pen**-yuu-ri/ • n. extreme poverty.
– ORIGIN Latin *penuria*.

peon /**pee**-uhn, pay-**on**/ • n. an unskilled Spanish-American worker.
– ORIGIN Portuguese *peão* and Spanish *peón*.

peony /**pee**-uh-ni/ • n. a plant grown for its large pink, white, or red flowers.
– ORIGIN Greek *paiōnia*.

people • pl. n. **1** human beings in general. **2** (**the people**) the ordinary citizens of a country. **3** (pl. **peoples**) the members of a particular nation, community, or ethnic group. **4** (**your people**) dated your relatives. **5** (**your people**) the people who work for you or follow you. • v. (**be peopled**) (of a place) have particular people living in it.

– ORIGIN Old French *poeple*.

> **USAGE:** On the difference between **people** and **persons**, see the note at **PERSON**.

people carrier • n. Brit. a large motor vehicle with three rows of seats.

pep informal • v. (**peps, pepping, pepped**) (**pep someone/thing up**) make someone or something more lively. • n. liveliness or energy.
– DERIVATIVES **peppy** adj.
– ORIGIN from PEPPER.

pepper • n. **1** a hot-tasting powder made from peppercorns, used to flavour food. **2** the fruit of a tropical American plant, of which sweet peppers and chilli peppers are varieties. • v. (**peppers, peppering, peppered**) **1** season something with pepper. **2** (**pepper something with**) scatter something in large amounts over or through something. **3** hit repeatedly with small missiles or gunshot.
– DERIVATIVES **peppery** adj.
– ORIGIN from Sanskrit.

peppercorn • n. the dried berry of a climbing vine, used whole as a spice or ground to make pepper.

peppercorn rent • n. Brit. a very low rent, charged as a sign that payment is necessary.

peppermint • n. **1** a plant of the mint family which produces aromatic leaves and oil, used as a flavouring in food. **2** a sweet flavoured with peppermint oil.

pepperoni /pep-puh-**roh**-ni/ • n. beef and pork sausage seasoned with pepper.
– ORIGIN Italian *peperone* 'chilli'.

pepper spray • n. an aerosol spray containing oils made from cayenne pepper which irritate the eyes, used to disable an attacker.

pep pill • n. informal a pill containing a stimulant drug.

pepsin • n. the chief digestive enzyme in the stomach.
– ORIGIN Greek *pepsis* 'digestion'.

pep talk • n. informal a talk intended to make someone feel more courageous or enthusiastic.

peptic • adj. relating to digestion.
– ORIGIN Greek *peptikos* 'able to digest'.

peptic ulcer • n. an ulcer in the lining of the stomach or small intestine.

peptide • n. a chemical compound consisting of two or more linked amino acids.
– ORIGIN German *Peptid*.

per • prep. **1** for each. **2** by means of. **3** (**as per**) in accordance with.
– ORIGIN Latin.

p

per- • prefix **1** through; all over: *pervade.*
2 completely; very: *perfect.*

peradventure • adv. old use perhaps.
– ORIGIN from Old French *per* (or *par*)
auenture 'by chance'.

perambulate /puh-ram-byuu-layt/
• v. (**perambulates, perambulating,
perambulated**) formal walk or travel from
place to place.
– DERIVATIVES **perambulation** n.
– ORIGIN Latin *perambulare.*

perambulator • n. dated a pram.

per annum • adv. for each year.
– ORIGIN Latin.

percale /per-kayl/ • n. a closely woven
fine cotton fabric.
– ORIGIN French.

per capita /per ka-pi-tuh/ • adv. & adj. for
each person.
– ORIGIN Latin, 'by heads'.

perceive • v. (**perceives, perceiving,
perceived**) **1** become aware of
something through the senses.
2 (**perceive something as**) understand
or interpret something in a particular
way.
– DERIVATIVES **perceivable** adj.
– ORIGIN Old French *perçoivre.*

> ☑ **perceive** follows the usual rule of *i*
> before *e* except after *c*.

per cent (also US **percent**) • adv. by a
specified amount in or for every
hundred. • n. one part in every hundred.

percentage • n. **1** a rate, number, or
amount in each hundred. **2** a proportion
or share, especially a share in profits.

percentile /per-sen-tyl/ • n. Stat. each of
100 equal groups into which a large
group of people can be divided.

perceptible • adj. able to be perceived.
– DERIVATIVES **perceptibly** adv.

perception • n. **1** the ability to see, hear,
or become aware of something through
the senses. **2** a way of understanding or
interpreting something. **3** the ability to
understand the true nature of something; insight.
– ORIGIN Latin.

perceptive • adj. able to understand the
true nature of things.
– DERIVATIVES **perceptively** adv.
perceptiveness n.

perceptual • adj. relating to the ability
to perceive.
– DERIVATIVES **perceptually** adv.

perch¹ • n. **1** a branch, bar, etc. on which a
bird rests or roosts. **2** a high or narrow
seat. • v. **1** sit or rest somewhere. **2** (**be
perched**) (of a building) be above or on
the edge of something.
– ORIGIN Old French *perche.*

perch² • n. (pl. **perch** or **perches**) a
freshwater fish with a spiny fin on its
back.
– ORIGIN Old French *perche.*

perchance • adv. old use by some chance;
perhaps.
– ORIGIN from Old French *par cheance.*

percipient /per-sip-i-uhnt/ • adj. having
insight or understanding.

percolate /per-kuh-layt/
• v. (**percolates, percolating, percolated**)
1 filter through a porous surface or
substance. **2** (of information or ideas)
spread gradually through a group of
people. **3** prepare coffee in a percolator.
– DERIVATIVES **percolation** n.
– ORIGIN Latin *percolare* 'strain through'.

percolator • n. a machine for making
coffee, consisting of a pot in which
boiling water is circulated through a
small chamber that holds the ground
beans.

percussion • n. **1** musical instruments
that are played by being struck or
shaken. **2** the striking of one solid object
with or against another.
– DERIVATIVES **percussionist** n.
– ORIGIN Latin.

perdition /per-di-sh'n/ • n. **1** (in
Christian belief) a state of eternal
damnation into which a sinful person
who has not repented passes after
death. **2** complete and utter ruin.
– ORIGIN Latin.

peregrinations /pe-ri-gri-nay-sh'nz/
• pl. n. old use travel or wandering from
place to place.
– ORIGIN Latin *peregrinari* 'travel abroad'.

peregrine /pe-ri-grin/ • n. a powerful
falcon with a bluish-grey back and wings
and pale underparts.
– ORIGIN Latin, 'pilgrim falcon'.

peremptory /puh-remp-tuh-ri/
• adj. insisting on immediate attention or
obedience: *she dreaded his peremptory
orders.*
– DERIVATIVES **peremptorily** adv.
– ORIGIN Latin *peremptorius* 'deadly'.

perennial • adj. **1** lasting or doing
something for a very long time. **2** (of a
plant) living for several years.
– DERIVATIVES **perennially** adv.
– ORIGIN Latin *perennis* 'lasting the year
through'.

perestroika /pe-ri-stroy-kuh/ • n. the
economic and political reforms
introduced in the former Soviet Union
during the 1980s.
– ORIGIN Russian, 'restructuring'.

perfect • adj. /per-fikt/ **1** having all the
required elements or qualities. **2** free
from any flaw. **3** complete: *it made*

perfect sense. **4** Grammar (of a tense) describing a completed action or a state or habitual action which began in the past (e.g. *they have eaten*). **5** Math. (of a number) equal to the sum of its positive divisors, e.g. the number 6, whose divisors (1, 2, 3) also add up to 6.
• v. /per-**fekt**/ make something perfect or as good as possible.
– DERIVATIVES **perfectible** adj.
– ORIGIN Latin *perfectus* 'completed'.

perfection • n. **1** the state of having all the required elements or qualities. **2** the process of perfecting something.

perfectionism • n. refusal to be satisfied with something unless it is done perfectly.
– DERIVATIVES **perfectionist** n. & adj.

perfectly • adv. **1** in a perfect way. **2** absolutely; completely: *you know perfectly well who it is.*

perfect pitch • n. the ability to recognize the pitch of a note or produce any given note.

perfidious /per-**fid**-i-uhss/ • adj. literary deceitful and disloyal: *a perfidious lover.*

perfidy /per-fi-di/ • n. literary deceit; disloyalty.
– ORIGIN Latin *perfidia*.

perforate /per-fuh-rayt/
• v. (**perforates, perforating, perforated**) pierce and make a hole or holes in something.
– DERIVATIVES **perforation** n. **perforator** n.
– ORIGIN Latin *perforare*.

perforce • adv. formal necessarily; unavoidably.
– ORIGIN from Old French *par force* 'by force'.

perform • v. **1** carry out or complete an action or function. **2** function or do something to a specified standard: *the car performs well at low speeds.* **3** present entertainment to an audience.
– DERIVATIVES **performer** n.
– ORIGIN Old French *parfournir*.

performance • n. **1** the action of performing. **2** an act of performing a play, concert, song, etc. **3** informal a fuss. **4** the capabilities of a machine or product.

performing arts • pl. n. creative activities that are performed in front of an audience, such as drama, music, and dance.

perfume • n. /per-fyoom/ **1** a sweet-smelling liquid used to give a pleasant smell to your body. **2** a pleasant smell.
• v. /per-fyoom/ (**perfumes, perfuming, perfumed**) **1** give a pleasant smell to something. **2** put perfume on or in.
– ORIGIN French *parfum*.

perfumery • n. (pl. **perfumeries**) **1** the making and selling of perfumes. **2** a shop that sells perfumes.
– DERIVATIVES **perfumer** n.

perfunctory /per-fungk-tuh-ri/
• adj. carried out with little effort or thought.
– DERIVATIVES **perfunctorily** adv.
– ORIGIN Latin *perfunctorius* 'careless'.

pergola /per-guh-luh/ • n. an arched structure forming a framework for climbing plants.
– ORIGIN Latin *pergula* 'projecting roof'.

perhaps • adv. **1** expressing uncertainty or possibility. **2** used when making a polite request or suggestion.
– ORIGIN from **PER** + former *hap* 'luck'.

peri- • prefix round; about: *perimeter.*
– ORIGIN Greek *peri.*

perianth /pe-ri-anth/ • n. the outer part of a flower, consisting of the sepals and petals.
– ORIGIN from Greek *peri* 'around' + *anthos* 'flower'.

pericardium /pe-ri-kar-di-uhm/ • n. (pl. **pericardia** /pe-ri-kar-di-uh/) Anat. the membrane enclosing the heart.
– ORIGIN Latin.

pericarp • n. the part of a fruit formed from the wall of the ripened ovary.
– ORIGIN from Greek *peri-* 'around' + *karpos* 'fruit'.

peridot /pe-ri-dot/ • n. a green semi-precious stone.
– ORIGIN French.

perigee /pe-ri-jee/ • n. Astron. the point in the orbit of the moon or a satellite at which it is nearest to the earth.
– ORIGIN from Greek *peri-* 'around' + *gē* 'earth'.

perihelion /pe-ri-hee-li-uhn/ • n. (pl. **perihelia** /pe-ri-hee-li-uh/) the point in a planet's orbit at which it is closest to the sun. Opp. **APHELION**.
– ORIGIN from Greek *peri-* 'around' + *hēlios* 'sun'.

peril • n. a situation of serious or immediate danger.
– ORIGIN Old French.

perilous • adj. full of danger or risk.
– DERIVATIVES **perilously** adv.

perimeter • n. **1** the outermost parts or boundary of an area or object. **2** the continuous line forming the boundary of a closed figure.
– ORIGIN from Greek *peri-* 'around' + *metron* 'measure'.

perinatal /per-i-nay-t'l/ • adj. relating to the time immediately before and after a birth.
– DERIVATIVES **perinatally** adv.

perineum /pe-ri-nee-uhm/ • n. (pl.

p

perinea) Anat. the area between the anus and the genitals.
– DERIVATIVES **perineal** adj.
– ORIGIN Greek *perinaion*.

period •n. **1** a length or portion of time. **2** a major division of geological time, forming part of an era. **3** a lesson in a school. **4** (also **menstrual period**) a monthly flow of blood from the lining of the womb, occurring in women who are not pregnant. **5** N. Amer. a full stop. •adj. belonging to or typical of a past historical time: *period furniture*.
– ORIGIN Greek *periodos* 'course'.

periodic /peer-i-od-ik/ •adj. appearing or occurring at intervals.

periodical •adj. occurring or appearing at intervals. •n. a magazine or newspaper that is published at regular intervals.
– DERIVATIVES **periodically** adv.

periodic table •n. a table of the chemical elements arranged in order of atomic number.

period piece •n. an object or work that is typical of or set in an earlier historical period.

peripatetic /pe-ri-puh-tet-ik/ •adj. travelling from place to place, especially in your work.
– DERIVATIVES **peripatetically** adv.
– ORIGIN Greek *peripatētikos* 'walking up and down'.

peripheral /puh-rif-uh-ruhl/ •adj. **1** relating to or situated on the outer limits of something. **2** of secondary importance. **3** (of a device) able to be attached to and used with a computer, though not a built-in part of it.
– DERIVATIVES **peripherally** adv.

peripheral nervous system •n. the nervous system outside the brain and spinal cord.

periphery /puh-rif-uh-ri/ •n. (pl. **peripheries**) **1** the outer limits or edge of an area or object. **2** the less important part of a subject or group.
– ORIGIN Greek *periphereia* 'circumference'.

periphrasis /puh-rif-ruh-siss/ •n. (pl. **periphrases** /puh-rif-ruh-seez/) the use of an indirect or roundabout way of saying something.
– ORIGIN from Greek *peri-* 'around' + *phrazein* 'declare'.

periscope •n. a tube attached to a set of mirrors or prisms, by which you can see things that are above or behind something else.

perish •v. **1** literary die. **2** literary suffer complete ruin or destruction. **3** rot or decay. **4** (**be perished**) Brit. informal be very cold.
– ORIGIN Latin *perire* 'pass away'.

perishable •adj. (especially of food) likely to rot quickly.

perishing •adj. Brit. informal very cold.

peristalsis /pe-ri-stal-siss/ •n. the contraction and relaxation of the muscles of the intestines, creating movements which push the contents of the intestines forward.
– ORIGIN Greek *peristallein* 'wrap around'.

peritoneum /pe-ri-tuh-nee-uhm/ •n. (pl. **peritoneums** or **peritonea** /pe-ri-tuh-nee-uh/) the membrane lining the cavity of the abdomen and covering the abdominal organs.
– DERIVATIVES **peritoneal** adj.
– ORIGIN Latin.

peritonitis /pe-ri-tuh-ny-tiss/ •n. inflammation of the peritoneum.

periwig •n. hist. a wig.
– ORIGIN French *perruque*.

periwinkle¹ •n. a plant with flat five-petalled flowers.
– ORIGIN Latin *pervinca*.

periwinkle² •n. = **WINKLE**.

perjure •v. (**perjures**, **perjuring**, **perjured**) (**perjure yourself**) tell a lie in a court of law after you have sworn to tell the truth.
– DERIVATIVES **perjurer** n.
– ORIGIN Latin *perjurare* 'swear falsely'.

perjury /per-juh-ri/ •n. the offence of deliberately telling a lie in a court of law after swearing to tell the truth.

perk¹ •v. (**perk up**) become more cheerful or lively.
– ORIGIN perh. from Old French *percher* 'to perch'.

perk² •n. informal a benefit to which an employee is entitled, such as the use of a company car.
– ORIGIN from **PERQUISITE**.

perky •adj. (**perkier**, **perkiest**) cheerful and lively.
– DERIVATIVES **perkily** adv. **perkiness** n.

perm •n. a method of setting the hair in curls and treating it with chemicals so that the style lasts for several months. •v. treat the hair in such a way.

permafrost •n. a thick layer beneath the surface of the soil that remains frozen throughout the year.

permanent •adj. lasting for a long time or forever.
– DERIVATIVES **permanence** n. **permanency** n. **permanently** adv.
– ORIGIN Latin *permanere* 'remain to the end'.

 The ending of **permanent** is **-ent**.

permeable • adj. allowing liquids or gases to pass through.
– DERIVATIVES **permeability** n.

permeate • v. (**permeates, permeating, permeated**) spread throughout.
– DERIVATIVES **permeation** n.
– ORIGIN Latin *permeare* 'pass through'.

Permian /per-mi-uhn/ • adj. Geol. relating to the last period of the Palaeozoic era, about 290 to 245 million years ago, when reptiles increased rapidly in number.
– ORIGIN from *Perm*, a Russian province with deposits from this period.

permissible • adj. allowable.

permission • n. the action of officially allowing someone to do something.

permissive • adj. allowing freedom of behaviour, especially in sexual matters.
– DERIVATIVES **permissiveness** n.

permit • v. /per-mit/ (**permits, permitting, permitted**) 1 officially allow someone to do something. 2 make something possible: *the weather did not permit play.* • n. /per-mit/ an official document giving permission to do something or enter a place.
– ORIGIN Latin *permittere*.

permutation • n. 1 each of several possible ways in which things can be ordered or arranged. 2 Math. the action of changing the arrangement of a set of items.
– ORIGIN Latin.

pernicious /per-nish-uhss/ • adj. having a harmful effect.
– ORIGIN Latin *perniciosus* 'destructive'.

pernickety • adj. Brit. informal fussy.

peroration • n. the concluding part of a speech.
– ORIGIN Latin *perorare* 'speak at length'.

peroxide • n. 1 Chem. a compound containing two oxygen atoms bonded together. 2 hydrogen peroxide, a chemical used as a bleach or disinfectant. • v. (**peroxides, peroxiding, peroxided**) bleach hair with peroxide.

perpendicular /per-puhn-dik-yuu-ler/ • adj. at an angle of 90° to a line, plane, or surface, or to the ground. • n. a perpendicular line.
– ORIGIN Latin *perpendicularis*.

perpetrate /per-pi-trayt/ • v. (**perpetrates, perpetrating, perpetrated**) carry out a bad or illegal action.
– DERIVATIVES **perpetration** n. **perpetrator** n.
– ORIGIN Latin *perpetrare* 'perform'.

perpetual /per-pet-yoo-uhl/ • adj. 1 never ending or changing. 2 so frequent as to seem continual: *their*

perpetual money worries.
– DERIVATIVES **perpetually** adv.
– ORIGIN Latin *perpetualis*.

perpetuate • v. (**perpetuates, perpetuating, perpetuated**) cause something to continue for a long time.
– DERIVATIVES **perpetuation** n.
– ORIGIN Latin *perpetuare*.

perpetuity • n. the state of lasting forever.

perplex • v. puzzle someone.
– ORIGIN Latin *perplexus* 'entangled'.

perplexity • n. (pl. **perplexities**) 1 the state of being puzzled. 2 a puzzling thing.

perquisite /per-kwi-zit/ • n. formal a special right or privilege that comes with your job or position.
– ORIGIN Latin *perquisitum* 'acquisition'.

per se /per say/ • adv. in itself or themselves.
– ORIGIN Latin.

persecute • v. (**persecutes, persecuting, persecuted**) 1 treat someone in a cruel or unfair way over a long period. 2 persistently harass someone.
– DERIVATIVES **persecution** n. **persecutor** n.
– ORIGIN Old French *persecuter*.

persevere • v. (**perseveres, persevering, persevered**) continue in a course of action in spite of difficulty or lack of success.
– DERIVATIVES **perseverance** n.
– ORIGIN Latin *perseverare* 'abide by strictly'.

Persian • n. 1 a person from Persia (now Iran). 2 the language of ancient Persia or modern Iran. 3 a long-haired breed of domestic cat. • adj. relating to Persia or Iran.

persiflage /per-si-flahzh/ • n. formal light teasing or banter.
– ORIGIN French *persifler* 'to banter'.

persimmon /per-sim-muhn/ • n. an edible fruit resembling a large tomato, with very sweet flesh.
– ORIGIN from an American Indian language.

persist • v. 1 continue doing something in spite of difficulty or opposition. 2 continue to exist.
– ORIGIN Latin *persistere* 'continue steadfastly'.

persistent • adj. 1 continuing to do something in spite of difficulty or opposition. 2 continuing or recurring for a long time.
– DERIVATIVES **persistence** n. **persistently** adv.

person • n. (pl. **people** or **persons**) 1 an individual human being. 2 the body of a

human being: *concealed on his person.*
3 Grammar a category used in the classification of pronouns or verb forms according to whether they indicate the speaker (**first person**), the person spoken to (**second person**), or a third party (**third person**).
– PHRASES **in person** actually present.
– ORIGIN Latin *persona* 'mask, character in a play'.

> USAGE: The words **people** and **persons** are not used in exactly the same way. **People** is by far the most common and is used in ordinary writing: *a group of people.* However, **persons** is now found mainly in official or formal writing: *this vehicle is authorized to carry twenty persons.*

-person • comb. form used as a neutral alternative to *-man* in nouns referring to role or status: *salesperson.*

persona /per-**soh**-nuh/ • n. (pl. **personas** or **personae** /per-**soh**-nee/) the aspect of a person's character that is presented to other people: *her public persona.*
– ORIGIN Latin, 'mask, character in a play'.

personable • adj. having a pleasant appearance and character.

personage • n. an important or famous person.
– ORIGIN Old French.

personal • adj. **1** relating or belonging to a particular person. **2** done by a particular person rather than someone else: *a personal appearance.* **3** concerning a person's private life. **4** referring to a person's character or appearance in an offensive way. **5** relating to a person's body.

personal assistant • n. a secretary or administrative assistant working for one particular person.

personal column • n. a section of a newspaper containing private advertisements or messages.

personal computer • n. a computer designed for use by one person.

personal identification number • n. a number you use with your bank card to validate electronic transactions.

personality • n. (pl. **personalities**) **1** the qualities that form a person's character. **2** lively or interesting personal qualities. **3** a celebrity.

personalize (or **personalise**) • v. (**personalizes, personalizing, personalized**) **1** design or produce something to meet someone's individual requirements. **2** make something identifiable as belonging to a particular person. **3** cause an issue or argument to become concerned with personalities or feelings.

– DERIVATIVES **personalization** n.

personally • adv. **1** in person. **2** from your own viewpoint.
– PHRASES **take something personally** interpret a remark as directed against yourself and be upset by it.

personal organizer • n. a loose-leaf notebook incorporating a diary and address book.

personal pronoun • n. each of the pronouns (*I, you, he, she, it, we, they, me, him, her, us,* and *them*) that show person, gender, number, and case.

> USAGE: **I, we, they, he,** and **she** are **subjective** personal pronouns, which means they are used as the subject of the sentence, often coming before the verb (*she lives in Paris*). **Me, us, them, him,** and **her,** on the other hand, are **objective** personal pronouns, which means that they are used as the object of a verb or preposition (*John hates me*). This explains why it is wrong to use *me* in *John and me went to the shops*: the personal pronoun is in subject position, so it must be **I.**
> Where a personal pronoun is used alone, the situation is more difficult. Some people say that statements such as *she's younger than me* are wrong and that the correct form is *she's younger than I.* This is based on the fact that **than** is a conjunction and so the personal pronoun is still in the subject position even though there is no verb (in full it would be *she's younger than I am*). Yet for most people the supposed 'correct' form does not sound natural and it is mainly found in very formal writing; it is usually perfectly acceptable to say *she's younger than me.*

personal stereo • n. a small portable cassette or compact disc player, used with headphones.

persona non grata /per-soh-nuh nohn grah-tuh/ • n. (pl. **personae non gratae** /per-soh-nee nohn grah-tee/) a person who is not welcome somewhere because they have done something unacceptable.
– ORIGIN Latin.

personify /per-**son**-i-fy/ • v. (**personifies, personifying, personified**) **1** represent a quality or an idea in the form of a person. **2** give human characteristics to something non-human.
– DERIVATIVES **personification** n.

personnel /per-suh-**nel**/ • pl. n. the people who work for an organization or the armed forces.
– ORIGIN French, 'personal'.

perspective • n. **1** the art of representing solid objects on a flat

p

surface so as to give the impression of height, width, depth, and relative distance. **2** a particular way of seeing something. **3** understanding of the relative importance of things.
– ORIGIN from Latin *perspectiva ars* 'science of optics'.

perspex • n. trademark a tough transparent plastic used instead of glass.
– ORIGIN Latin *perspicere* 'look through'.

perspicacious /per-spi-**kay**-shuhss/ • adj. quickly gaining insight into and understanding of things.
– DERIVATIVES **perspicacity** n.
– ORIGIN Latin *perspicax* 'seeing clearly'.

perspicuous /per-**spik**-yuu-uhss/ • adj. clearly expressed and easily understood.
– ORIGIN Latin *perspicuus* 'clear'.

perspiration • n. **1** sweat. **2** the process of sweating.

perspire • v. (**perspires, perspiring, perspired**) give out sweat through the pores of the skin.
– ORIGIN Latin *perspirare*.

persuade • v. (**persuades, persuading, persuaded**) use reasoning or argument to make someone do or believe something.
– ORIGIN Latin *persuadere*.

persuasion • n. **1** the action of persuading. **2** a set of beliefs: *writers of all political persuasions.*

persuasive • adj. **1** good at persuading someone to do or believe something. **2** providing sound reasoning or argument.
– DERIVATIVES **persuasively** adv. **persuasiveness** n.

pert • adj. **1** attractively lively or cheeky. **2** (especially of a part of the body) attractively small and well shaped.
– ORIGIN Latin *apertus* 'opened'.

pertain • v. **1** be relevant or appropriate: *matters pertaining to the government.* **2** formal be in existence in a specified place or at a specified time.
– ORIGIN Latin *pertinere* 'extend to'.

pertinacious /per-ti-**nay**-shuhss/ • adj. formal persistent.
– DERIVATIVES **pertinacity** n.
– ORIGIN Latin *pertinax* 'holding fast'.

pertinent • adj. relevant or appropriate.
– DERIVATIVES **pertinence** n. **pertinently** adv.
– ORIGIN Latin *pertinere* 'extend to'.

perturb • v. make someone anxious or unsettled.
– ORIGIN Latin *perturbare*.

perturbation /per-ter-**bay**-sh'n/ • n. **1** anxiety; uneasiness. **2** an alteration in the normal state or path of a system or moving object.

peruse /puh-**rooz**/ • v. (**peruses, perusing, perused**) formal read or examine something thoroughly or carefully.
– DERIVATIVES **perusal** n.
– ORIGIN perh. from PER- + USE.

Peruvian /puh-**roo**-vi-uhn/ • n. a person from Peru. • adj. relating to Peru.

pervade • v. (**pervades, pervading, pervaded**) spread or be present throughout something.
– ORIGIN Latin *pervadere* 'go or come through'.

pervasive • adj. spreading widely through or present everywhere in something.
– DERIVATIVES **pervasively** adv. **pervasiveness** n.

perverse • adj. **1** deliberately choosing to behave in a way that other people find awkward or difficult. **2** contrary to that which is accepted or expected.
– DERIVATIVES **perversely** adv. **perversity** n. (pl. **perversities**).

perversion • n. **1** the action of perverting. **2** abnormal or unacceptable sexual behaviour.

pervert • v. /per-**vert**/ **1** change the form or meaning of something in a way that distorts it. **2** lead someone away from doing what is right, natural, or acceptable. • n. /**per**-vert/ a person whose sexual behaviour is abnormal or unacceptable.
– ORIGIN Latin *pervertere* 'turn about'.

perverted • adj. sexually abnormal or unacceptable.

pervious /per-vi-uhss/ • adj. allowing water to pass through.
– ORIGIN Latin *pervius* 'having a passage through'.

peseta /puh-**say**-tuh/ • n. (until the introduction of the euro in 2002) the basic unit of money of Spain.
– ORIGIN Spanish, 'little weight'.

pesky • adj. informal, esp. N. Amer. annoying.
– ORIGIN perh. from PEST.

peso /**pay**-soh/ • n. (pl. **pesos**) the basic unit of money of several Latin American countries and of the Philippines.
– ORIGIN Spanish, 'weight'.

pessary /**pess**-uh-ri/ • n. (pl. **pessaries**) a small soluble block inserted into the vagina to treat infection or as a contraceptive.
– ORIGIN Latin *pessarium*.

pessimism • n. lack of hope or confidence in the future.
– DERIVATIVES **pessimist** n. **pessimistic** adj.
– ORIGIN Latin *pessimus* 'worst'.

p

pest • n. **1** a destructive animal or insect that attacks crops, food, or livestock. **2** informal an annoying person or thing.
– ORIGIN French *peste* or Latin *pestis* 'plague'.

pester • v. (**pesters, pestering, pestered**) trouble someone with persistent requests or interruptions.
– ORIGIN French *empestrer* 'encumber'.

pesticide • n. a substance for destroying insects or other pests.

pestilence • n. old use a deadly epidemic disease.
– ORIGIN Latin *pestilentia*.

pestilent • adj. deadly.

pestilential • adj. **1** relating to or causing infectious diseases. **2** informal annoying.

pestle /pess-uhl/ • n. a heavy implement with a rounded end, used for crushing and grinding substances in a mortar.
– ORIGIN Latin *pistillum*.

pesto /pess-toh/ • n. a sauce of crushed basil leaves, pine nuts, garlic, Parmesan cheese, and olive oil, served with pasta.
– ORIGIN Italian.

pet[1] • n. **1** an animal or bird kept for companionship or pleasure. **2** a person treated with special favour. • adj. **1** relating to or kept as a pet. **2** favourite or particular: *my pet hate.* • v. (**pets, petting, petted**) **1** stroke or pat an animal. **2** caress someone sexually.

pet[2] • n. a fit of sulking or bad temper.

petal • n. each of the segments forming the outer part of a flower.
– ORIGIN Greek *petalon* 'leaf'.

petard /pi-tard/ • n. (in phr. **be hoist with your own petard**) have problems when your schemes against other people backfire on you.
– ORIGIN French, 'small bomb made of a box filled with powder'.

peter • v. (**peters, petering, petered**) (**peter out**) gradually come to an end.

petersham • n. a corded tape used for stiffening in dresses and hats.
– ORIGIN named after the English army officer Lord *Petersham*.

petiole /pee-ti-ohl/ • n. Bot. the stalk that joins a leaf to a stem.
– ORIGIN Latin *petiolus* 'little foot, stalk'.

petit bourgeois /puh-ti boor-zhwah/ • adj. relating to the lower middle class, especially in being conventional and conservative.
– ORIGIN French, 'little citizen'.

petite • adj. (of a woman) attractively small.
– ORIGIN French, 'small'.

petit four /puh-ti for/ • n. (pl. **petits fours** /puh-ti forz/) a very small fancy cake, biscuit, or sweet.
– ORIGIN French, 'little oven'.

petition • n. **1** an appeal or request, especially a written one signed by many people and presented formally to someone in authority. **2** Law an application to a court for a legal action, writ, etc. • v. make or present a petition to.
– ORIGIN Latin.

petit mal /puh-ti mal/ • n. a mild form of epilepsy with only brief spells of unconsciousness. Compare with **GRAND MAL**.
– ORIGIN French, 'little sickness'.

petit point /puh-ti poynt, puh-ti pwan/ • n. embroidery on canvas, using small diagonal stitches.
– ORIGIN French, 'little stitch'.

pet name • n. a name used to express fondness or familiarity.

petrel /pet-ruhl/ • n. a black and white seabird that flies far from land.
– ORIGIN from St *Peter*, because of the bird's habit of flying low with its legs dangling, and so appearing to walk on the water.

Petri dish /pet-ri, pee-tri/ • n. a shallow transparent dish with a flat lid, used in laboratories.
– ORIGIN named after the German bacteriologist Julius R. *Petri*.

petrify • v. (**petrifies, petrifying, petrified**) **1** paralyse someone with fear. **2** change organic matter into stone by encrusting or replacing its original substance with a mineral deposit.
– DERIVATIVES **petrifaction** n. **petrification** n.
– ORIGIN Latin *petrificare*.

petrochemical • adj. relating to the chemical properties and processing of petroleum and natural gas. • n. a chemical obtained from petroleum and natural gas.
– ORIGIN from **PETROLEUM**.

petrol • n. Brit. a light fuel oil obtained by distilling petroleum and used in internal-combustion engines.

petrol bomb • n. Brit. a simple bomb consisting of a bottle containing petrol and a cloth wick.

petroleum • n. an oil found in layers of rock and refined to produce petrol, paraffin, and diesel oil.
– ORIGIN Latin.

petroleum jelly • n. a semi-transparent substance obtained from petroleum, used as a lubricant or ointment.

petticoat • n. a woman's light under-garment in the form of a skirt or dress.
– ORIGIN from former *petty coat* 'small coat'.

pettifogging • adj. petty; trivial.

– ORIGIN from **PETTY** + former *fogger* 'underhand dealer'.

pettish • adj. childishly sulky.
– DERIVATIVES **pettishly** adv.

petty • adj. (**pettier, pettiest**) **1** of little importance. **2** (of a person's behaviour) small-minded. **3** minor: *a petty official.*
– DERIVATIVES **pettily** adv. **pettiness** n.
– ORIGIN French *petit* 'small'.

petty cash • n. a small amount of money kept in an office for minor payments.

petty officer • n. a rank of non-commissioned officer in the navy.

petulant /pet-yuu-luhnt/ • adj. childishly sulky or bad-tempered.
– DERIVATIVES **petulance** n. **petulantly** adv.
– ORIGIN Latin *petulans* 'impudent'.

petunia /pi-tyoo-ni-uh/ • n. a South American plant with white, purple, or red funnel-shaped flowers.
– ORIGIN from an American Indian word meaning 'tobacco'.

pew • n. **1** (in a church) a long bench with a back. **2** Brit. informal a seat.
– ORIGIN Old French *puye* 'balcony'.

pewter • n. a grey alloy of tin with copper and antimony.
– ORIGIN Old French *peutre*.

pfennig /pfen-nig/ • n. (until the introduction of the euro in 2002) a unit of money of Germany, equal to one hundredth of a mark.
– ORIGIN German.

PG • abbrev. (in the UK) parental guidance, a film classification indicating that some parents may find the film unsuitable for their children.

PGCE • abbrev. (in the UK) Postgraduate Certificate of Education.

pH • n. Chem. a figure expressing how acid or alkaline a substance is (7 is neutral, lower values are more acid and higher values more alkaline).
– ORIGIN from *p* representing German *Potenz* 'power' + *H*, the symbol for hydrogen.

phaeton /fay-tuhn/ • n. hist. a light, open four-wheeled horse-drawn carriage.
– ORIGIN from *Phaethōn* in Greek mythology, who was allowed to drive the chariot of the sun for a day.

phagocyte /fag-uh-syt/ • n. a type of body cell which surrounds and absorbs bacteria and other small particles.
– DERIVATIVES **phagocytic** adj.
– ORIGIN from Greek *phago-* 'eating' + *kutos* 'vessel'.

phalanger /fuh-lan-jer/ • n. a tree-dwelling marsupial native to Australia and New Guinea.
– ORIGIN Greek *phalangion* 'spider's web' (because of its webbed toes).

phalanx /fa-langks/ • n. (pl. **phalanxes**) **1** a group of similar people or things. **2** a body of troops or police officers in close formation.
– ORIGIN Greek.

phallic • adj. relating to or resembling a penis.

phallus /fal-luhss/ • n. (pl. **phalli** /fal-lee/ or **phalluses**) a penis.
– ORIGIN Greek *phallos*.

phantasm /fan-ta-z'm/ • n. literary a thing that exists in the imagination.
– ORIGIN Greek *phantasma*.

phantasmagoria /fan-taz-muh-gor-i-uh/ • n. a sequence of real or imaginary images like that seen in a dream.
– DERIVATIVES **phantasmagoric** adj. **phantasmagorical** adj.
– ORIGIN prob. from French *fantasmagorie*.

phantom • n. **1** a ghost. **2** a thing seen in the imagination. • adj. not really existing.
– ORIGIN Greek *phantasma*.

pharaoh /fair-oh/ • n. a ruler in ancient Egypt.
– DERIVATIVES **pharaonic** /fair-ay-on-ik/ adj.
– ORIGIN Greek *Pharaō*.

> ✓ Remember that **pharaoh** ends with **-aoh**.

Pharisee /fa-ri-see/ • n. a member of an ancient Jewish sect who followed traditional Jewish law very strictly.
– ORIGIN Greek *Pharisaios*.

pharmaceutical /far-muh-syoo-ti-k'l/ • adj. relating to medicinal drugs. • n. a manufactured medicinal drug.
– ORIGIN Greek *pharmakeutikos*.

pharmacist • n. a person qualified to prepare and dispense medicinal drugs.

pharmacology • n. the branch of science concerned with the uses, effects, and action of drugs.
– DERIVATIVES **pharmacological** adj. **pharmacologist** n.
– ORIGIN Greek *pharmakon* 'drug'.

pharmacy • n. (pl. **pharmacies**) **1** a place where medicinal drugs are prepared or sold. **2** the science or practice of preparing and dispensing medicinal drugs.
– ORIGIN Greek *pharmakon* 'drug'.

pharynx /fa-ringks/ • n. (pl. **pharynges** /fa-rin-jeez/) the cavity behind the nose and mouth, connecting them to the oesophagus.
– ORIGIN Greek *pharunx*.

phase • n. **1** a distinct stage in a process of change or development. **2** each of the forms in which the moon or a planet appears, according to the amount that it

is lit up. **3** Physics the stage that a regularly varying quantity (e.g. an alternating electric current) has reached in relation to zero or another chosen value. • v. (**phases, phasing, phased**) **1** carry something out in gradual stages. **2** (**phase something in/out**) gradually introduce or withdraw something.
– ORIGIN French.

PhD • abbrev. Doctor of Philosophy.
– ORIGIN from Latin *philosophiae doctor*.

pheasant • n. a large long-tailed game bird.
– ORIGIN Greek *phasianos* 'bird of Phasis', a river in the Caucasus.

phenol /fee-nol/ • n. Chem. a poisonous white solid obtained from coal tar. Also called CARBOLIC ACID.
– ORIGIN French *phène* 'benzene'.

phenomenal • adj. remarkable or outstanding.
– DERIVATIVES **phenomenally** adv.

phenomenon /fi-nom-i-nuhn/ • n. (pl. **phenomena**) **1** a fact or situation that is seen to exist or happen. **2** a remarkable person or thing.
– ORIGIN Greek *phainomenon* 'thing appearing to view'.

USAGE: The word **phenomenon** comes from Greek, and its plural form is **phenomena**. It is wrong to use **phenomena** as if it were a singular form: say *this is a strange phenomenon*, not *this is a strange phenomena*.

phenotype /fee-noh-typ/ • n. Biol. the observable characteristics of an individual, determined by its genetic make-up and the environment.
– ORIGIN Greek *phainein* 'to show'.

pheromone /fe-ruh-mohn/ • n. a chemical substance released by an animal and causing a response in others of its species.
– ORIGIN from Greek *pherein* 'convey' + HORMONE.

phial /fy-uhl/ • n. a small cylindrical glass bottle.
– ORIGIN Greek *phialē* 'broad flat container'.

philander /fi-lan-der/ • v. (**philanders, philandering, philandered**) (of a man) have casual sexual relationships with women.
– DERIVATIVES **philanderer** n.
– ORIGIN from Greek *philandros* 'fond of men'.

philanthropist • n. a person who donates money to good causes or otherwise helps other people.

philanthropy • n. the practice of donating money or otherwise helping people in need.
– DERIVATIVES **philanthropic** adj.

– ORIGIN Greek *philanthrōpia*.

philately /fi-lat-uh-li/ • n. the collection and study of postage stamps.
– DERIVATIVES **philatelist** n.
– ORIGIN from Greek *philo-* 'loving' + *ateleia* 'exemption from payment'.

-phile • comb. form referring to a person having a liking for a specified thing: *bibliophile*.
– ORIGIN Greek *philos* 'loving'.

philharmonic • adj. (in the names of orchestras) devoted to music.

-philia • comb. form referring to a liking, especially an abnormal liking, for something: *paedophilia*.
– ORIGIN Greek *philia* 'fondness'.

philippic /fi-lip-pik/ • n. a bitter verbal attack.
– ORIGIN Greek *philippikos*, the name given to Demosthenes' speeches against Philip II of Macedon.

Philistine /fil-i-styn/ • n. **1** a member of a people of ancient Palestine who came into conflict with the Israelites. **2** (**philistine**) a person who is uninterested in culture and the arts.
– DERIVATIVES **philistinism** /fil-i-stin-i-z'm/ n.
– ORIGIN Greek *Philistinos*.

philo- • comb. form referring to a liking for a specified thing: *philology*.
– ORIGIN Greek *philos* 'loving'.

philology • n. the study of the structure and historical development of languages.
– DERIVATIVES **philological** adj. **philologist** n.
– ORIGIN Greek *philologia*.

philosopher • n. a person who studies or engages with the fundamental nature of knowledge, reality, and existence.

philosopher's stone • n. (in alchemy) a supposed substance believed to change any metal into gold or silver.

philosophical • adj. **1** relating to the study of philosophy. **2** calm in difficult circumstances.
– DERIVATIVES **philosophically** adv.

philosophize (or **philosophise**) • v. (**philosophizes, philosophizing, philosophized**) talk about serious issues, especially in a boring or pompous way.

philosophy • n. (pl. **philosophies**) **1** the study of the fundamental nature of knowledge, reality, and existence. **2** the theories of a particular philosopher. **3** an attitude that guides a person's behaviour.
– ORIGIN Greek *philosophia* 'love of wisdom'.

philtre /fil-ter/ (US **philter**) • n. a love potion.

– ORIGIN Greek *philtron*.

phlebitis /fli-by-tiss/ • n. Med. inflammation of the walls of a vein.
– ORIGIN Greek *phleps* 'vein'.

phlegm /flem/ • n. **1** thick mucus which forms in the nose and throat, especially when you have a cold. **2** calmness of temperament.
– ORIGIN Greek *phlegma* 'inflammation'.

phlegmatic /fleg-mat-ik/ • adj. calm and unemotional.

phloem /floh-em/ • n. Bot. the tissue in plants which conducts nutrients downwards from the leaves.
– ORIGIN Greek *phloos* 'bark'.

phlox /floks/ • n. a garden plant with clusters of colourful scented flowers.
– ORIGIN Greek, 'flame'.

-phobe • comb. form referring to a person having a fear or dislike of a specified thing: *homophobe*.
– ORIGIN Greek *phobos* 'fear'.

phobia • n. an extreme or irrational fear of something.
– DERIVATIVES **phobic** adj. & n.

-phobia • comb. form extreme or irrational fear or dislike of a specified thing: *arachnophobia*.

phoenix /fee-niks/ • n. (in classical mythology) a bird that burned itself on a funeral pyre and was born again from the ashes.
– ORIGIN Greek *phoinix*.

phone • n. a telephone. • v. (**phones, phoning, phoned**) make a telephone call.

-phone • comb. form referring to an instrument using or connected with sound: *megaphone*.
– ORIGIN Greek *phōnē* 'sound, voice'.

phone book • n. a telephone directory.

phonecard • n. a prepaid card allowing the user to make calls on a public telephone.

phone-in • n. a radio or television programme during which listeners or viewers join in by telephone.

phoneme /foh-neem/ • n. any of the distinct units of sound that distinguish one word from another, e.g. *p, b, d*, and *t* in *pad, pat, bad*, and *bat*.
– ORIGIN Greek *phōnēma* 'sound, speech'.

phonetic • adj. **1** relating to speech sounds. **2** (of a system of spelling) that closely matches the sounds represented. • n. (**phonetics**) the study of speech sounds.
– DERIVATIVES **phonetically** adv.
– ORIGIN Greek *phōnētikos*.

phoney (esp. N. Amer. also **phony**) informal • adj. (**phonier, phoniest**) not genuine. • n. (pl. **phoneys** or **phonies**) a person or thing that is not genuine.
– DERIVATIVES **phoniness** n.

phonic /fon-ik, foh-nik/ • adj. relating to speech sounds.

phono- • comb. form relating to sound: *phonograph*.
– ORIGIN Greek *phōnē* 'sound, voice'.

phonograph • n. Brit. an early form of gramophone.

phonology /fuh-nol-uh-ji/ • n. the system of relationships between the basic speech sounds of a language.

phony • adj. & n. var. of PHONEY.

phosphate /foss-fayt/ • n. Chem. a salt or ester of phosphoric acid.

phosphine /foss-feen/ • n. a foul-smelling gas formed from phosphorus and hydrogen.

phosphor /foss-fer/ • n. a synthetic fluorescent or phosphorescent substance.

phosphorescence • n. light that is given out by a substance without burning or heat.
– DERIVATIVES **phosphorescent** adj.

phosphoric /foss-fo-rik/ • adj. relating to or containing phosphorus.

phosphoric acid • n. Chem. an acid obtained by treating phosphates with sulphuric acid.

phosphorus /foss-fuh-ruhss/ • n. a chemical element in the form of a yellowish wax-like substance which glows in the dark and ignites in the air.
– DERIVATIVES **phosphorous** adj.
– ORIGIN Greek *phōsphoros*.

photo • n. (pl. **photos**) a photograph.

photo- • comb. form **1** relating to light. **2** relating to photography.
– ORIGIN sense 1 from Greek *phōs* 'light'.

photocall • n. Brit. an occasion on which famous people pose for photographers by arrangement.

photocell • n. = PHOTOELECTRIC CELL.

photochemistry • n. the branch of chemistry concerned with the chemical effects of light.
– DERIVATIVES **photochemical** adj.

photocopy • n. (pl. **photocopies**) a photographic copy of a document or picture. • v. (**photocopies, photocopying, photocopied**) make a photocopy of.
– DERIVATIVES **photocopier** n.

photoelectric • adj. involving the emission of electrons from a surface as a result of the action of light.

photoelectric cell • n. a device using a photoelectric effect to generate current.

photo finish • n. a close finish of a race in which the winner is identifiable only from a photograph of competitors crossing the line.

photofit • n. Brit. a picture of a person made up from existing photographs of facial features.

photogenic /foh-tuh-jen-ik/ • adj. **1** looking attractive in photographs. **2** Biol. giving out light.

photograph • n. a picture made with a camera, in which an image is focused on to film and then made visible by chemical treatment. • v. take a photograph of.
– DERIVATIVES **photographer** n. **photographic** adj.

photography • n. the taking and processing of photographs.

photojournalism • n. the taking and publishing of photographs as a means of communicating news.

photometer /foh-tom-i-ter/ • n. an instrument for measuring the strength of light.
– DERIVATIVES **photometric** adj. **photometry** n.

photomontage /foh-toh-mon-tahzh/ • n. a picture consisting of a number of separate photographs placed together or overlapping.

photon /foh-ton/ • n. Physics a particle representing a quantum of light or other electromagnetic radiation.

photo opportunity • n. a photocall.

photosensitive • adj. responding to light.

photostat • n. trademark **1** a machine for making photocopies on special paper. **2** a copy made by a photostat.

photosynthesis • n. the process by which green plants use sunlight to form nutrients from carbon dioxide and water.
– DERIVATIVES **photosynthesize** (or **photosynthesise**) v. **photosynthetic** adj.

phototropism /foh-toh-troh-pi-z'm/ • n. Biol. the moving of a plant or other organism either towards or away from a source of light.

phrasal verb • n. a verb combined with an adverb or preposition to give a new meaning that cannot be worked out from the individual parts, e.g. *give out*.

phrase • n. **1** a small group of words forming a unit within a clause. **2** Music a group of notes forming a distinct unit within a longer passage. • v. (**phrases**, **phrasing**, **phrased**) put something into a particular form of words.
– DERIVATIVES **phrasal** adj.
– ORIGIN Greek *phrasis*.

phrase book • n. a book listing and translating useful expressions in a foreign language.

phraseology /fray-zi-ol-uh-ji/ • n. (pl. **phraseologies**) a particular way in which words are used: *legal phraseology*.

phrasing • n. division of music into phrases.

phrenology /fri-nol-uh-ji/ • n. esp. hist. the study of the shape and size of a person's skull as a supposed indication of their character.
– ORIGIN Greek *phrēn* 'mind'.

phyllo • n. var. of FILO.

phylloquinone /fi-loh-kwi-nohn/ • n. vitamin K₁, a compound found in leafy green vegetables and essential for blood-clotting.
– ORIGIN from Greek *phullon* 'leaf' + QUINONE.

phylum /fy-luhm/ • n. (pl. **phyla** /fy-luh/) a zoological classifying category that ranks above class and below kingdom.
– ORIGIN Greek *phulon* 'race'.

physic • n. old use medicinal drugs or medical treatment.
– ORIGIN Latin *physica*.

physical • adj. **1** relating to the body as opposed to the mind. **2** relating to things that can be seen, heard, or touched. **3** involving bodily contact or activity. **4** relating to physics or the operation of natural forces. • n. a medical examination to find out a person's bodily fitness.
– DERIVATIVES **physicality** n. **physically** adv.

physical chemistry • n. the branch of chemistry concerned with applying the techniques and theories of physics to the study of chemical systems.

physical education • n. instruction in physical exercise and games.

physical geography • n. the branch of geography concerned with natural features.

physical sciences • pl. n. the sciences concerned with the study of inanimate natural objects, including physics, chemistry, and astronomy.

physician • n. a person qualified to practise medicine.

physics • n. **1** the branch of science concerned with the nature and properties of matter and energy. **2** the physical properties and nature of something.
– DERIVATIVES **physicist** n.
– ORIGIN Latin *physica* 'natural things'.

physiognomy /fi-zi-on-uh-mi/ • n. (pl. **physiognomies**) a person's facial features or expression.
– ORIGIN Greek *phusiognōmonia*.

p

physiology •n. 1 the branch of biology concerned with the normal functions of living organisms and their parts. 2 the way in which a living organism or bodily part functions.
– DERIVATIVES **physiological** adj. **physiologist** n.

physiotherapy •n. the treatment of disease or injury by massage and exercise.
– DERIVATIVES **physiotherapist** n.

physique •n. the form, size, and development of a person's body.
– ORIGIN French, 'physical'.

phytochemical •n. any of a group of compounds found in plants that are believed to have beneficial effects.
– ORIGIN Greek *phuton* 'a plant'.

phytoplankton /fy-toh-plangk-tuhn/ •n. Biol. plankton consisting of microscopic plants.
– ORIGIN Greek *phuton* 'a plant'.

pi /py/ •n. the numerical value of the ratio of the circumference of a circle to its diameter (approximately 3.14159).
– ORIGIN from the initial letter of Greek *periphereia* 'circumference'.

pianissimo /pi-uh-niss-i-moh/ •adv. & adj. Music very soft or softly.
– ORIGIN Italian, 'softest'.

piano¹ /pi-an-oh/ •n. (pl. **pianos**) a large musical instrument with a keyboard and metal strings, in which the strings are struck by hammers when the keys are pressed.
– DERIVATIVES **pianist** n.
– ORIGIN from **PIANOFORTE**.

piano² /pi-ah-noh/ •adv. & adj. Music soft or softly.
– ORIGIN Italian.

piano accordion •n. an accordion with a small vertical keyboard like that of a piano.

pianoforte /pi-an-oh-for-tay/ •n. formal = **PIANO**¹.
– ORIGIN from Italian *piano e forte* 'soft and loud'.

pianola /pi-uh-noh-luh/ •n. trademark a piano equipped to be played automatically with a roll of perforated paper which controls the movement of the keys to produce a tune.

piazza /pi-at-zuh/ •n. a public square or marketplace, especially in Italy.
– ORIGIN Italian.

picador /pik-uh-dor/ •n. (in bullfighting) a person on horseback who goads the bull with a lance.
– ORIGIN Spanish.

picaresque /pi-kuh-resk/ •adj. relating to fiction dealing with the adventures of a dishonest but appealing hero.

– ORIGIN Spanish *picaresco*.

piccalilli /pik-kuh-lil-li/ •n. (pl. **piccalillies** or **piccalillis**) a pickle of chopped vegetables, mustard, and hot spices.
– ORIGIN prob. from **PICKLE** and **CHILLI**.

piccaninny /pik-kuh-nin-ni/ (US **pickaninny**) •n. (pl. **piccaninnies**) offens. a small black child.
– ORIGIN Spanish *pequeño* or Portuguese *pequeno* 'little'.

piccolo •n. (pl. **piccolos**) a small flute sounding an octave higher than the ordinary one.
– ORIGIN Italian, 'small flute'.

pick¹ •v. 1 (often **pick something up**) take hold of something and move it. 2 remove a flower or fruit from where it is growing. 3 choose something from a number of alternatives. •n. 1 an act of selecting something. 2 (**the pick of**) informal the best person or thing in a group.
– PHRASES **pick and choose** select only the best from a number of alternatives. **pick at 1** repeatedly pull at something with your fingers. **2** eat something in small amounts. **pick someone's brains** informal obtain information by questioning someone. **pick a fight** provoke an argument or fight. **pick holes in** find fault with. **pick a lock** open a lock with an instrument other than the proper key. **pick on** single someone out for unfair treatment. **pick over** (or **pick through**) sort through a number of items carefully. **pick someone's pockets** steal something from a person's pocket. **pick up** improve or increase. **pick someone up 1** go to collect someone. **2** informal casually strike up a relationship with someone as a sexual approach. **pick something up 1** go to collect something. **2** learn or become aware of something. **3** receive a signal or sound. **pick your way** walk slowly and carefully.
– DERIVATIVES **picker** n.

pick² •n. 1 (also **pickaxe**) a tool consisting of a curved iron bar with pointed ends, fixed at right angles to its handle, used for breaking up hard ground or rock. 2 a plectrum.
– ORIGIN from **PIKE**².

picket •n. 1 a group of people positioned outside a workplace with the aim of persuading other people not to work during a strike. 2 a pointed wooden stake driven into the ground.
•v. (**pickets, picketing, picketed**) act as a picket outside a workplace.
– ORIGIN French *piquet*.

pickings •pl. n. profits or gains.

pickle •n. 1 vegetables or fruit preserved

in vinegar, brine, or mustard, served cold with other food to add flavour. **2 (a pickle)** informal a difficult situation.
• v. (**pickles, pickling, pickled**) **1** preserve food in pickle. **2** (as adj. **pickled**) informal drunk.
– ORIGIN Dutch or German *pekel*.

pick-me-up • n. informal a thing that makes you feel more lively or cheerful.

pickpocket • n. a person who steals from people's pockets.

pickup • n. **1** (also **pickup truck**) a small lorry with low sides. **2** an act of picking up a person or goods.

picky • adj. (**pickier, pickiest**) informal fussy.

picnic • n. a packed meal eaten outdoors, or an occasion when such a meal is eaten. • v. (**picnics, picnicking, picnicked**) have or take part in a picnic.
– PHRASES **be no picnic** informal be difficult or unpleasant.
– DERIVATIVES **picnicker** n.
– ORIGIN French *pique-nique*.

Pict • n. a member of an ancient people inhabiting northern Scotland in Roman times.
– ORIGIN Latin *Picti*.

pictograph (also **pictogram**) • n. **1** a picture representing a word or phrase. **2** a picture representing statistics on a chart, graph, or computer screen.
– ORIGIN Latin *pingere* 'to paint'.

pictorial • adj. relating to or using pictures.
– DERIVATIVES **pictorially** adv.
– ORIGIN Latin *pictorius*.

picture • n. **1** a painting, drawing, or photograph. **2** an image on a television screen. **3** a cinema film. **4** (**the pictures**) the cinema. **5** an impression formed from a description of something. **6** informal a state of being fully informed: *in the picture.* • v. (**pictures, picturing, pictured**) **1** show in a picture. **2** form a mental image of.
– ORIGIN Latin *pictura*.

picture messaging • n. a system that enables digital photos and animated graphics to be sent and received by mobile phone.

picture-postcard • adj. charmingly attractive: *picture-postcard villages.*

picturesque • adj. attractive in a quaint or charming way.

picture window • n. a large window consisting of one pane of glass.

piddling (also **piddly**) • adj. informal ridiculously small or unimportant.
– ORIGIN prob. from PUDDLE.

pidgin • n. a simple form of a language with elements taken from local languages, used for communication between

people not sharing a common language.
– ORIGIN Chinese alteration of English *business*.

pie • n. a baked dish of ingredients encased in or topped with pastry.
– PHRASES **pie in the sky** informal a pleasant idea that is very unlikely to happen.
– ORIGIN prob. the same word as former *pie* 'magpie' (the combination of ingredients being compared to the objects collected by a magpie).

piebald • adj. (of a horse) having irregular patches of two colours.
– ORIGIN from *pie* in *magpie* + *bald* in the former sense 'streaked with white'.

piece • n. **1** a portion separated from the whole. **2** an item used in building something or forming part of a set. **3** a musical or written work. **4** a token used to make moves in a board game. **5** a coin of specified value. • v. (**pieces, piecing, pieced**) (**piece something together**) assemble something from individual parts.
– PHRASES **go to pieces** become so upset that you cannot function normally. **in one piece** unharmed or undamaged.
– ORIGIN Old French.

> ✓ **piece** follows the rule of *i* before *e* except after *c*.

pièce de résistance /pyess duh ray-**ziss**-tonss/ • n. the most important or impressive feature of something.
– ORIGIN French, 'piece (i.e. means) of resistance'.

piecemeal • adj. & adv. done in stages over a period of time.
– ORIGIN from PIECE + an Old English word meaning 'measure'.

piecework • n. work paid for according to the amount produced.

pie chart • n. a diagram in which a circle is divided into sections that each represent a proportion of the whole.

pied /rhymes with ride/ • adj. having two or more different colours.
– ORIGIN first meaning 'black and white like a magpie'.

pied-à-terre /pyay-dah-**tair**/ • n. (pl. **pieds-à-terre** /pyay-dah-**tair**/) a small flat or house for occasional use, that you own in addition to your main home.
– ORIGIN French, 'foot to earth'.

pie-eyed • adj. informal very drunk.

pier • n. **1** a structure that extends into the sea, used as a landing stage for boats or as a place of entertainment. **2** a pillar supporting an arch or bridge.
– ORIGIN Latin *pera*.

pierce • v. (**pierces, piercing, pierced**) **1** make a hole in or through something with a sharp object. **2** force or cut a way through something. **3** (as adj. **piercing**)

very sharp, cold, or high-pitched.
– ORIGIN Old French *percer*.

piety /py-uh-ti/ •n. (pl. **pieties**) **1** the quality of being deeply religious. **2** a conventional belief accepted without thinking: *the accepted pieties of our time*.
– ORIGIN Latin *pietas*.

piffle •n. informal nonsense.

piffling •adj. informal unimportant.

pig •n. **1** a domestic or wild mammal with sparse bristly hair and a flat snout. **2** informal a greedy or dirty person. **3** an oblong mass of iron or lead from a smelting furnace. •v. (**pigs, pigging, pigged**) (often **pig out**) informal gorge yourself with food.
– PHRASES **make a pig's ear of** Brit. informal handle something unskilfully. **a pig in a poke** something that is bought without first being seen.
– DERIVATIVES **piglet** n.
– ORIGIN prob. from an Old English word meaning 'acorn' or 'pig bread'.

pigeon •n. a fat bird with a small head and a cooing voice.
– ORIGIN Old French *pijon* 'young bird'.

pigeonhole •n. **1** each of a set of small compartments where letters or messages may be left for people. **2** a category into which someone or something is placed. •v. (**pigeonholes, pigeonholing, pigeonholed**) place in a particular category.

pigeon-toed •adj. having the toes or feet turned inwards.

piggery •n. (pl. **piggeries**) a farm or enclosure where pigs are kept.

piggish •adj. greedy or dirty.

piggy •adj. like a pig: *little piggy eyes*.

piggyback •n. a ride on someone's back and shoulders.

piggy bank •n. a money box shaped like a pig.

pig-headed •adj. stupidly stubborn.

pig iron •n. crude iron as first obtained from a smelting furnace.

pigment /pig-muhnt/ •n. **1** a natural substance that gives a plant or animal its colour. **2** a substance used for colouring or painting.
– DERIVATIVES **pigmentation** n.
– ORIGIN Latin *pigmentum*.

pigmented •adj. having a natural colour.

pigmy •n. var. of PYGMY.

pigskin •n. leather made from the hide of a pig.

pigsty •n. (pl. **pigsties**) **1** an enclosure for pigs. **2** a very dirty or untidy place.

pigswill •n. kitchen refuse and scraps fed to pigs.

pigtail •n. a plaited length of hair worn

at the back or on each side of the head.

pike¹ •n. (pl. **pike**) a freshwater fish with a long body and sharp teeth.
– ORIGIN from PIKE².

pike² •n. hist. a weapon with a pointed metal head on a long wooden shaft.
– ORIGIN French *pique*.

pike³ •n. a jackknife position in diving or gymnastics.

pikestaff •n. (in phr. **as plain as a pikestaff**) very obvious.
– ORIGIN alteration of *as plain as a packstaff*, the staff being that of a pedlar, on which he rested his pack of wares.

pilaf /pi-laf/ (also **pilau** /pi-low/) •n. a Middle Eastern or Indian dish of spiced rice and often meat and vegetables.
– ORIGIN Turkish.

pilaster /pi-lass-ter/ •n. an architectural feature in the form of a rectangular column incorporated within and projecting slightly from a wall.
– ORIGIN Latin *pilastrum*.

pilchard •n. a small edible fish of the herring family.

pile¹ •n. **1** a heap of things lying one on top of another. **2** informal a large amount. **3** a large imposing building. •v. (**piles, piling, piled**) **1** place things one on top of the other. **2** (**pile up**) form a pile or very large quantity. **3** (**pile something on**) informal exaggerate something for effect. **4** (**pile into/out of**) get into or out of a vehicle in a disorganized way.
– ORIGIN Latin *pila* 'pillar, pier'.

pile² •n. a heavy post driven into the ground to support foundations.
– ORIGIN Old English, 'dart, stake'.

pile³ •n. the soft projecting surface of a carpet or fabric, consisting of the cut ends of many small threads.
– ORIGIN Latin *pilus* 'hair'.

piledriver •n. **1** a machine for driving piles into the ground. **2** Brit. informal a forceful act, blow, or shot.

piles •pl. n. haemorrhoids.
– ORIGIN prob. from Latin *pila* 'ball'.

pile-up •n. a crash involving several vehicles.

pilfer •v. (**pilfers, pilfering, pilfered**) steal things of little value.
– ORIGIN Old French *pelfrer* 'to pillage'.

pilgrim •n. a person who journeys to a holy place for religious reasons.
– ORIGIN Provençal *pelegrin*.

pilgrimage •n. a pilgrim's journey.

pill •n. **1** a small round mass of solid medicine for swallowing whole. **2** (**the Pill**) a contraceptive pill.
– ORIGIN Latin *pilula* 'little ball'.

p

pillage • v. (**pillages, pillaging, pillaged**) (in wartime) rob a place or steal property with violence. • n. the action of pillaging.
– DERIVATIVES **pillager** n.
– ORIGIN Old French.

pillar • n. **1** a tall upright structure used as a support for a building. **2** a person or thing providing reliable support: *he's a pillar of the local community.*
– PHRASES **from pillar to post** from one place to another in an unsatisfactory way.
– DERIVATIVES **pillared** adj.
– ORIGIN Latin *pila* 'pillar'.

pillar box • n. (in the UK) a large red cylindrical public postbox.

pillbox • n. **1** a small round hat. **2** a small round, partly underground, concrete fort.

pillion • n. a seat for a passenger behind a motorcyclist.
– ORIGIN Irish *pillín* 'small cushion'.

pillock • n. Brit. informal a stupid person.
– ORIGIN from former *pillicock* 'penis'.

pillory • n. (pl. **pillories**) a wooden framework with holes for the head and hands, in which offenders were formerly imprisoned and exposed to public abuse. • v. (**pillories, pillorying, pilloried**) attack or ridicule publicly.
– ORIGIN Old French *pilori*.

pillow • n. a cloth bag stuffed with soft material, used to support the head when lying down.
– DERIVATIVES **pillowy** adj.
– ORIGIN Latin *pulvinus* 'cushion'.

pillowcase • n. a removable cloth cover for a pillow.

pillow talk • n. intimate conversation between lovers in bed.

pilot • n. **1** a person who operates the flying controls of an aircraft. **2** a person with local knowledge who is qualified to take charge of a ship entering or leaving a harbour. **3** something done or produced as a test before introducing it more widely. • v. (**pilots, piloting, piloted**) **1** act as a pilot of an aircraft or ship. **2** test a product or scheme before introducing it more widely.
– ORIGIN Latin *pilotus*.

pilot light • n. a small gas burner kept alight permanently to light a larger burner when needed.

pimento /pi-men-toh/ (also **pimiento** /pi-myen-toh/) • n. (pl. **pimentos**) a red sweet pepper.
– ORIGIN Spanish.

pimp • n. a man who controls prostitutes and arranges clients for them, taking a percentage of their earnings in return. • v. act as a pimp.

pimpernel • n. a low-growing plant with bright five-petalled flowers.
– ORIGIN Old French *pimpernelle*.

pimple • n. a small, hard inflamed spot on the skin.
– DERIVATIVES **pimply** adj.
– ORIGIN Old English, 'break out in pustules'.

PIN (also **PIN number**) • abbrev. personal identification number.

pin • n. **1** a thin piece of metal with a sharp point at one end and a round head at the other, used as a fastener. **2** a metal projection from an electric plug or an integrated circuit. **3** a small brooch. **4** Med. a steel rod used to join broken bones while they heal. **5** a metal peg in a hand grenade that prevents it exploding. **6** a skittle. **7** (**pins**) informal legs. • v. (**pins, pinning, pinned**) **1** attach or fasten something with a pin or pins. **2** hold someone firmly so they are unable to move. **3** (**pin someone down**) force someone to be specific. **4** (**pin someone down**) restrict the actions of an enemy by firing at them. **5** (**pin something on**) attribute blame or responsibility to someone.
– ORIGIN Latin *pinna* 'point, edge'.

pina colada /pee-nuh kuh-lah-duh/ • n. a cocktail made with rum, pineapple juice, and coconut.
– ORIGIN Spanish, 'strained pineapple'.

pinafore • n. **1** (also Brit. **pinafore dress**) a collarless, sleeveless dress worn over a blouse or jumper. **2** Brit. a loose sleeveless piece of clothing worn over other clothes to keep them clean.
– ORIGIN from PIN + AFORE.

pinball • n. a game in which small metal balls are shot across a sloping board and score points by striking targets.

pince-nez /panss-nay/ • n. a pair of glasses with a nose clip instead of earpieces.
– ORIGIN French, 'pinches the nose'.

pincer • n. **1** (**pincers**) a tool made of two pieces of metal with blunt inward-curving jaws, used for gripping and pulling things. **2** a front claw of a lobster or similar type of shellfish.
– ORIGIN Old French *pincier* 'to pinch'.

pinch • v. **1** grip flesh tightly between the finger and thumb. **2** (of a shoe) hurt a foot by being too tight. **3** informal steal something. • n. **1** an act of pinching. **2** an amount of an ingredient that can be held between the fingers and thumb.
– PHRASES **at a pinch** if absolutely necessary. **feel the pinch** experience financial hardship.
– ORIGIN Old French *pincier* 'to pinch'.

pincushion • n. a small pad into which

pins are stuck to be stored.

pine¹ •n. (also **pine tree**) an evergreen coniferous tree with clusters of long needle-shaped leaves.
– ORIGIN Latin *pinus*.

pine² •v. (**pines, pining, pined**) **1** become very weak because you miss someone so much. **2** (**pine for**) miss or long for.
– ORIGIN Old English.

pineal gland /py-nee-uhl, pin-i-uhl/ •n. a small gland at the back of the skull within the brain, producing a hormone-like substance in some mammals.
– ORIGIN Latin *pinea* 'pine cone'.

pineapple •n. a large juicy tropical fruit with yellow flesh surrounded by a tough skin.
– ORIGIN from PINE¹ + APPLE.

pine marten •n. a dark brown weasel-like mammal that lives in trees.

pine nut •n. the edible seed of various pine trees.

ping •n. a short high-pitched ringing sound. •v. make a short high-pitched ringing sound.

ping-pong (also US trademark **Ping-Pong**) •n. informal table tennis.

pinhole •n. a very small hole.

pinion¹ /pin-yuhn/ •n. the outer part of a bird's wing including the flight feathers. •v. **1** tie or hold someone by the arms or legs. **2** cut off the pinion of a bird to prevent it from flying.
– ORIGIN Old French *pignon*.

pinion² /pin-yuhn/ •n. a small cogwheel or spindle that engages with a large cogwheel.
– ORIGIN French *pignon*.

pink¹ •adj. **1** of a colour between red and white. **2** relating to homosexuals: *the pink economy.* •n. **1** pink colour or material. **2** (**the pink**) informal the best condition: *in the pink of health.*
– ORIGIN from PINK².

pink² •n. a plant with sweet-smelling pink or white flowers and grey-green leaves.

pink³ •v. cut a zigzag edge on something.
– ORIGIN perh. from German *pinken* 'strike'.

pinking shears •pl. n. large scissors with a serrated blade, used to cut a zigzag edge in cloth.

pinky (also **pinkie**) •n. (pl. **pinkies**) informal the little finger.
– ORIGIN partly from Dutch *pink* 'little finger'.

pin money •n. a small sum of money for spending on small items that are not essential.
– ORIGIN first referring to an allowance to a woman from her husband.

pinna /pin-nuh/ •n. (pl. **pinnae** /pin-

nee/) Anat. the external part of the ear.
– ORIGIN Latin.

pinnace /pin-nis/ •n. esp. hist. a small boat forming part of the equipment of a larger one.
– ORIGIN French *pinace*.

pinnacle •n. **1** the most successful point. **2** a high pointed piece of rock. **3** a small pointed turret on a roof.
– ORIGIN Latin *pinnaculum*.

pinnate /pin-nayt/ •adj. Bot. & Zool. having leaflets or other parts arranged on either side of a stem or axis.
– ORIGIN Latin *pinnatus* 'feathered'.

PIN number •n. see PIN.

pinny •n. (pl. **pinnies**) Brit. informal an apron or pinafore.

pinpoint •v. find the exact position of. •n. a tiny dot. •adj. absolutely precise.

pinprick •n. **1** a prick caused by a pin. **2** a very small dot.

pins and needles •n. a tingling feeling in a limb recovering from numbness.

pinstripe •n. a very narrow pale stripe in dark cloth.
– DERIVATIVES **pinstriped** adj.

pint •n. **1** a unit of liquid or dry capacity equal to one eighth of a gallon, in Britain equal to 0.568 litre. **2** Brit. informal a pint of beer.
– ORIGIN Old French *pinte*.

pintail •n. a duck with a long pointed tail.

pintle •n. a pin or bolt on which a rudder turns.
– ORIGIN Old English, 'penis'.

pint-sized (also **pint-size**) •adj. informal very small.

pin-tuck •n. a very narrow ornamental tuck in a garment.

pin-up •n. a poster featuring a sexually attractive person.

pinwheel •n. esp. N. Amer. a small Catherine wheel firework.

pioneer •n. **1** a person who explores or settles in a new region. **2** a person who develops new ideas or techniques. •v. (**pioneers, pioneering, pioneered**) be a pioneer of a new idea or technique.
– ORIGIN French *pionnier* 'foot soldier'.

pious •adj. **1** deeply religious. **2** pretending to be good or religious so as to impress. **3** (of a hope) sincere but unlikely to be fulfilled.
– DERIVATIVES **piously** adv.
– ORIGIN Latin *pius* 'dutiful'.

pip¹ •n. a small hard seed in a fruit.
– ORIGIN Old French *pepin*.

pip² •n. **1** (**the pips**) Brit. a series of short high-pitched sounds used as a signal on the radio. **2** Brit. a star on the shoulder of an army officer's uniform, showing

p

rank. **3** any of the spots on a playing
card, domino, or dice.

pip³ • v. (in phr. **be pipped at the post**)
Brit. informal be defeated by a small margin
or at the last moment.
– ORIGIN from **PIP¹** or **PIP²**.

pipe • n. **1** a tube used to carry water, gas,
or oil. **2** a device for smoking tobacco,
consisting of a narrow tube that opens
into a small bowl in which the tobacco is
burned. **3** a wind instrument consisting
of a single tube with holes along its
length that are covered by the fingers to
produce different notes. **4** one of the
tubes by which notes are produced in an
organ. **5** (**pipes**) bagpipes. • v. (**pipes**,
piping, **piped**) **1** send water, gas, or oil
through a pipe. **2** transmit music, a
programme, or a signal by wire or cable.
3 play a tune on a pipe. **4** sing or say
something in a high voice. **5** decorate
something with piping.
– PHRASES **pipe down** informal be less noisy.
pipe up say something suddenly.
– ORIGIN Latin *pipare* 'to peep, chirp'.

piped music • n. pre-recorded
background music played through
loudspeakers.

pipe dream • n. a hope or scheme that
will never be realized.
– ORIGIN referring to a dream experienced when smoking an opium pipe.

pipeline • n. a long pipe for carrying oil
or gas over a distance.
– PHRASES **in the pipeline** in the process
of being developed.

pipe organ • n. an organ using pipes
instead of or as well as reeds.

piper • n. a person who plays a pipe or
bagpipes.

pipette /pi-pet/ • n. a thin tube used in a
laboratory for handling small quantities
of liquid, the liquid being drawn into
the tube by suction.
– ORIGIN French, 'little pipe'.

piping • n. **1** lengths of pipe. **2** lines of
icing or cream, used to decorate cakes
and desserts. **3** thin cord covered in
fabric and inserted along a seam or hem
for decoration.
– PHRASES **piping hot** (of food or water)
very hot. [ORIGIN with reference to the
whistling sound made by very hot liquid
or food.]

pipistrelle /pi-pi-strel, pip-i-strel/ • n. a
small insect-eating bat.
– ORIGIN French.

pipit /pi-pit/ • n. a brown songbird of
open country.

pipsqueak • n. informal an unimportant
person.

piquant /pee-kuhnt, pee-kont/
• adj. **1** having a pleasantly sharp or spicy

taste. **2** stimulating to the mind.
– DERIVATIVES **piquancy** n. **piquantly** adv.
– ORIGIN French, 'stinging, pricking'.

pique /peek/ • n. resentment arising
from hurt pride. • v. (**piques, piquing,
piqued**) **1** stimulate interest. **2** (**be
piqued**) feel hurt or resentful.
– ORIGIN French *piquer* 'prick, irritate'.

piqué /pee-kay/ • n. stiff cotton woven in
a ribbed or raised pattern.
– ORIGIN French, 'backstitched'.

piracy • n. **1** the practice of attacking and
robbing ships at sea. **2** the use or
reproduction of a film or recording
without permission and in order to
make a profit.

piranha /pi-rah-nuh/ • n. a freshwater
fish with very sharp teeth.
– ORIGIN Portuguese.

pirate • n. a person who attacks and robs
ships at sea. • adj. **1** (of a film or
recording) that has been reproduced
and used for profit without permission:
pirate videos. **2** (of an organization)
broadcasting radio or television
programmes without official
permission: *a pirate radio station*.
• v. (**pirates, pirating, pirated**)
reproduce a film or recording for profit
without permission.
– ORIGIN Greek *peiratēs*.

pirouette /pi-ruu-et/ • n. (in ballet) an
act of spinning on one foot.
• v. (**pirouettes, pirouetting, pirouetted**)
perform a pirouette.
– ORIGIN French, 'spinning top'.

piscatorial /piss-kuh-tor-i-uhl/
• adj. formal relating to fishing.
– ORIGIN Latin *piscator* 'fisherman'.

Pisces /py-seez/ • n. a constellation (the
Fish or Fishes) and sign of the zodiac,
which the sun enters about 20 February.
– DERIVATIVES **Piscean** /py-see-uhn/ n. &
adj.
– ORIGIN Latin.

piscina /pi-see-nuh/ • n. (pl. **piscinas** or
piscinae /pi-see-nee/) a stone basin near
the altar in some churches, for draining
water used in the Mass.
– ORIGIN Latin, 'fish pond'.

piscine /pi-syn/ • adj. relating to fish.

pistachio /pi-sta-shi-oh/ • n. (pl.
pistachios) the small nut of an Asian
tree, with an edible pale green kernel.
– ORIGIN Greek *pistakion*.

piste /peesst/ • n. a course or run for
skiing.
– ORIGIN French, 'racetrack'.

pistil /piss-til/ • n. Bot. the female organs
of a flower, comprising the stigma, style,
and ovary.
– ORIGIN Latin *pistillum* 'pestle'.

pistol • n. a small gun that is held in one hand.
– ORIGIN French *pistole*.

piston • n. a sliding disc or cylinder fitting closely inside a tube in which it moves up and down as part of an engine or pump.
– ORIGIN Italian *pistone* 'large pestle'.

pit¹ • n. **1** a large hole in the ground. **2** a mine for coal, chalk, etc. **3** a hollow in a surface. **4** a sunken area in a workshop floor allowing access to the underside of a motor vehicle. **5** an area at the side of a track where racing cars are serviced and refuelled. **6** a part of a theatre where an orchestra plays. **7** hist. an enclosure in which animals were made to fight as a form of entertainment. **8** (**the pits**) informal a very bad place or situation.
• v. (**pits, pitting, pitted**) **1** (**pit someone/thing against**) test someone or something in a contest with. **2** make a hollow in the surface of.
– PHRASES **the pit of the stomach** the lower part of the stomach.
– ORIGIN Old English.

pit² esp. N. Amer. • n. the stone of a fruit.
• v. (**pits, pitting, pitted**) remove the stone from a fruit.
– ORIGIN prob. from Dutch.

pit bull terrier • n. a fierce American type of bull terrier.

pitch¹ • n. **1** Brit. an area of ground where outdoor team games are played. **2** the extent to which a sound or tone is high or low. **3** the steepness of a roof. **4** a particular level of intensity: *the crowd were at the right pitch of excitement*. **5** a form of words used to sell or promote something: *a sales pitch*. **6** Brit. a place where a street seller or performer is situated. • v. **1** throw something or fall heavily or roughly. **2** set the voice or a piece of music at a particular pitch. **3** set or aim something at a particular level, target, or audience. **4** set up a tent or camp. **5** (**pitch in**) informal join in enthusiastically with an activity. **6** (**pitch up**) informal arrive. **7** (of a moving ship, aircraft, or vehicle) rock from side to side or from front to back. **8** (as adj. **pitched**) (of a roof) sloping.
– ORIGIN perh. from Old English, 'stigmata'.

pitch² • n. a sticky black substance which hardens on cooling, made from tar or turpentine and used for waterproofing.
– ORIGIN Old English.

pitch-black (also **pitch-dark**)
• adj. completely dark.

pitchblende /pich-blend/ • n. a mineral found in dark pitch-like masses and containing radium.
– ORIGIN German *Pechblende*.

pitched battle • n. a fierce fight involving a large number of people.

pitcher • n. a large jug.
– ORIGIN Old French *pichier* 'pot'.

pitchfork • n. a farm tool with a long handle and two sharp metal prongs, used for lifting hay.
– ORIGIN from former *pickfork*.

piteous • adj. deserving or arousing pity.
– DERIVATIVES **piteously** adv.
– ORIGIN Old French *piteus*.

pitfall • n. a hidden danger or difficulty.

pith • n. **1** spongy white tissue lining the rind of citrus fruits. **2** spongy tissue in the stems and branches of many plants. **3** the most important part of something.
– ORIGIN Old English.

pithead • n. the top of a mineshaft and the area around it.

pith helmet • n. a hat made from the dried pith of a plant, used for protection from the sun.

pithy • adj. **1** (of language or style) concise and expressing a point clearly. **2** (of a fruit or plant) containing much pith.
– DERIVATIVES **pithily** adv. **pithiness** n.

pitiable • adj. **1** deserving or arousing pity. **2** deserving contempt: *a pitiable lack of talent*.

pitiful • adj. **1** deserving or arousing pity. **2** very small or poor.
– DERIVATIVES **pitifully** adv.

pitiless • adj. showing no pity.

piton /pee-ton/ • n. a peg or spike driven into a crack to support a climber or a rope.
– ORIGIN French, 'eye bolt'.

pitta /pit-tuh/ • n. a type of flat bread which can be split open to hold a filling.
– ORIGIN modern Greek, 'cake or pie'.

pittance • n. a very small or inadequate amount of money.
– ORIGIN Old French *pitance* 'pity'.

pitter-patter • n. a sound as of quick light steps or taps. • adv. with this sound.

pituitary gland /pi-tyoo-i-tuh-ri/ • n. a pea-sized gland attached to the base of the brain, which controls growth and development.
– ORIGIN Latin *pituitarius* 'secreting phlegm'.

pity • n. (pl. **pities**) **1** a feeling of sadness and sympathy caused by the sufferings of other people. **2** a cause for regret or disappointment. • v. (**pities, pitying, pitied**) feel pity for.
– ORIGIN Old French *pite* 'compassion'.

pivot • n. **1** the central point, pin, or shaft on which a mechanism turns or is balanced. **2** a person or thing playing a central part in an activity or

p

organization. •v. (**pivots, pivoting, pivoted**) **1** turn or balance on a central point. **2** (**pivot on**) depend on.
– ORIGIN French.

pivotal •adj. **1** of central importance: *a pivotal role*. **2** fixed or turning on a pivot.

pixel •n. any of the tiny areas of light on a display screen which make up an image.
– ORIGIN from *picture element*.

pixelate /pik-suh-layt/ (also **pixellate** or **pixilate**) •v. **1** divide an image into pixels, for display or for storage in a digital format. **2** display a person's image as a small number of large pixels in order to disguise their identity.
– DERIVATIVES **pixelation** n.

pixie (also **pixy**) •n. (pl. **pixies**) an imaginary being portrayed as a tiny man with pointed ears and a pointed hat.

pizza •n. a flat, round base of dough baked with a topping of tomatoes, cheese, and other ingredients.
– ORIGIN Italian, 'pie'.

pizzazz •n. informal liveliness and style.
– ORIGIN prob. invented by Diana Vreeland, fashion editor of *Harper's Bazaar* in the 1930s.

pizzeria /peet-zuh-ree-uh/ •n. a restaurant serving pizzas.
– ORIGIN Italian.

pizzicato /pit-zi-kah-toh/ •adv. & adj. plucking the strings of a musical instrument with your finger.
– ORIGIN Italian, 'pinched'.

pl. •abbrev. **1** (also **Pl.**) place. **2** plural.

placard /pla-kard/ •n. a sign for public display, either fixed to a wall or carried during a demonstration.
– ORIGIN Old French *placquart*.

placate /pluh-kayt/ •v. (**placates, placating, placated**) make someone less angry or hostile.
– DERIVATIVES **placatory** adj.
– ORIGIN Latin *placare*.

place •n. **1** a particular position or area. **2** a portion of space occupied by or set aside for someone or something: *they hurried to their places at the table*. **3** an opportunity to study on a course or be a member of a team. **4** a position in a sequence: *she finished in second place*. **5** the position of a figure in a decimal number. **6** (in place names) a square or short street. •v. (**places, placing, placed**) **1** put in a particular position or situation. **2** find an appropriate place or role for. **3** give a specified position in a sequence to: *the survey placed the company 13th for achievement*. **4** remember where you have seen someone or something. **5** arrange for something to be done: *place a bet*.

– PHRASES **in place of** instead of. **out of place 1** not in the proper position. **2** not suited or in harmony; not fitting in. **put someone in their place** make someone feel less proud or confident. **take place** occur.
– ORIGIN Old French.

placebo /pluh-see-boh/ •n. (pl. **placebos**) a medicine given to a patient to make them feel happier or more confident rather than for any physical effect.
– ORIGIN Latin, 'I shall be acceptable'.

placement •n. **1** the action of putting something in position. **2** Brit. a temporary job undertaken to gain work experience.

placenta /pluh-sen-tuh/ •n. (pl. **placentae** /pluh-sen-tee/ or **placentas**) an organ that is formed in the womb during pregnancy and which supplies blood and nourishment to the fetus through the umbilical cord.
– ORIGIN Latin.

placid •adj. not easily upset or excited.
– DERIVATIVES **placidity** n. **placidly** adv.
– ORIGIN Latin *placidus*.

placing •n. a ranking in a competition.

placket •n. **1** an opening in a garment, covering fastenings or for access to a pocket. **2** a flap of material used to strengthen such an opening.
– ORIGIN from **PLACARD** in a former sense 'garment worn under an open coat'.

plagiarize /play-juh-ryz/ (or **plagiarise**) •v. (**plagiarizes, plagiarizing, plagiarized**) take someone else's work or idea and pretend it is your own.
– DERIVATIVES **plagiarism** n. **plagiarist** n.
– ORIGIN Latin *plagiarius* 'kidnapper'.

plague •n. **1** an infectious disease spread by bacteria and causing fever and delirium. **2** a very large number of destructive insects or animals.
•v. (**plagues, plaguing, plagued**) **1** cause continual trouble to someone. **2** pester someone continually.
– ORIGIN Latin *plaga* 'stroke, wound'.

plaice •n. (pl. **plaice**) an edible brown flatfish with orange spots.
– ORIGIN Old French *plaiz*.

plaid /plad/ •n. fabric woven in a chequered or tartan design.
– ORIGIN Scottish Gaelic, 'blanket'.

plain •adj. **1** simple or ordinary. **2** without a pattern. **3** unmarked: *a plain envelope*. **4** easy to see or understand; clear. **5** (of language) direct. **6** (of a woman or girl) not attractive. **7** sheer; simple: *plain stupidity*. **8** (of a knitting stitch) made by putting the needle through the front of the stitch from left to right. •adv. informal used for emphasis:

that's plain stupid. •n. a large area of flat land with few trees.
– DERIVATIVES **plainly** adv. **plainness** n.
– ORIGIN Latin *planus* 'flat, plain'.

plain chocolate •n. Brit. dark, slightly bitter chocolate without added milk.

plain clothes •pl. n. ordinary clothes rather than uniform.

plain flour •n. Brit. flour that does not contain a raising agent.

plain sailing •n. smooth and easy progress.

plainsong (also **plainchant**)
•n. unaccompanied medieval church music sung by a number of voices together.

plain-spoken •adj. outspoken; blunt.

plaintiff •n. a person who brings a case against someone else in a court of law. Compare with DEFENDANT.
– ORIGIN Old French *plaintif* 'plaintive'.

plaintive •adj. sounding sad and mournful.
– DERIVATIVES **plaintively** adv.
– ORIGIN Old French.

plait •n. Brit. a single length of hair, rope, or other material made up of three or more intertwined strands. •v. form hair, rope, or other material into a plait or plaits.
– ORIGIN Old French *pleit* 'a fold'.

plan •n. 1 a detailed proposal for doing or achieving something. 2 an intention. 3 a scheme for making regular payments towards a pension, insurance policy, etc. 4 a map or diagram. •v. (**plans, planning, planned**) 1 decide on and arrange something in advance. 2 (**plan for**) make preparations for. 3 make a plan of something to be made or built.
– DERIVATIVES **planner** n.
– ORIGIN French.

planar /play-ner/ •adj. Math. relating to or in the form of a plane.

plane¹ •n. 1 a completely flat surface. 2 a level of existence or thought: *the spiritual plane.* •adj. 1 completely flat. 2 relating to two-dimensional surfaces or sizes. •v. (**planes, planing, planed**) 1 (of a bird) soar without moving the wings. 2 (of a boat) skim over the surface of water.
– ORIGIN Latin *planum*.

plane² •n. an aeroplane.

plane³ (also **planer**) •n. a tool used to smooth a wooden surface by cutting shavings from it. •v. (**planes, planing, planed**) smooth a surface with a plane.
– ORIGIN Latin *plana*.

plane⁴ (also **plane tree**) •n. a tall tree with maple-like leaves and a peeling bark.

– ORIGIN Old French.

planet •n. 1 a large round object in space that orbits round a star. 2 (**the planet**) the earth.
– DERIVATIVES **planetary** adj.
– ORIGIN Greek *planētēs*.

planetarium /plan-i-tair-i-uhm/ •n. (pl. **planetariums** or **planetaria** /plan-i-tair-i-uh/) a building in which images of stars, planets, and constellations are projected on to a curved ceiling.
– ORIGIN Latin.

plangent /plan-juhnt/ •adj. literary (of a sound) loud and mournful.
– ORIGIN Latin *plangere* 'to lament'.

plank •n. 1 a long, flat piece of timber, used in flooring. 2 a basic part of a political or other programme: *crime reduction is a central plank of the manifesto.*
– ORIGIN Latin *planca* 'board'.

planking •n. planks used as a building material.

plankton •n. tiny organisms living in the sea or fresh water.
– DERIVATIVES **planktonic** adj.
– ORIGIN Greek *planktos* 'wandering'.

planning •n. 1 the process of making plans for something. 2 the control by local government of building and development in towns and cities.

planning permission •n. Brit. formal permission from local government for building work.

plant •n. 1 a living thing that grows in the ground, having roots with which it absorbs substances and leaves in which it makes nutrients by photosynthesis. 2 a place where an industrial or manufacturing process takes place. 3 machinery used in an industrial or manufacturing process. 4 a person placed in a group as a spy. 5 a thing put among someone's belongings to make them appear guilty of something.
•v. 1 place a seed, bulb, or plant in the ground so that it can grow. 2 place something in a specified position. 3 secretly place a bomb. 4 put something among someone's belongings to make them appear guilty of something. 5 send someone to join a group to act as a spy. 6 fix an idea in someone's mind.
– ORIGIN Latin *planta* 'sprout' and *plantare* 'fix in place'.

plantain¹ /plan-tin, plan-tayn/ •n. a low-growing plant, with a rosette of leaves and green flowers.
– ORIGIN Old French.

plantain² /plan-tin, plan-tayn/ •n. a type of banana eaten as a vegetable.
– ORIGIN Spanish *plá(n)tano*.

plantation •n. 1 a large estate on which

crops such as coffee, sugar, and tobacco are grown. **2** an area in which trees have been planted.

planter •n. **1** a manager or owner of a plantation. **2** a decorative container in which plants are grown.

plaque /plak, plahk/ •n. **1** an inscribed plate or slab fixed to a wall to commemorate a person or event. **2** a sticky deposit on teeth, which encourages the growth of bacteria.
– ORIGIN French.

plasma /plaz-muh/ •n. **1** the colourless fluid part of blood, lymph, or milk, in which cells or fat globules are suspended. **2** Physics a gas of positive ions and free electrons with little or no overall electric charge.
– ORIGIN Greek.

plasma screen •n. a flat display screen which uses an array of cells containing a gas plasma to produce different colours in each cell.

plaster •n. **1** a soft mixture of lime with sand or cement and water for spreading on walls and ceilings to form a smooth hard surface when dried. **2** (also **plaster of Paris**) a hard white substance made by adding water to powdered gypsum, used for setting broken bones and making sculptures and casts. **3** (also **sticking plaster**) Brit. a sticky strip of material for covering cuts and wounds. •v. (**plasters, plastering, plastered**) **1** apply plaster to a wall. **2** coat something thickly with a soft substance. **3** make hair lie flat by applying liquid to it.
– DERIVATIVES **plasterer** n.
– ORIGIN Latin *plastrum*.

plasterboard •n. board made of plaster set between two sheets of paper, used to line interior walls and ceilings.

plastered •adj. informal very drunk.

plastic •n. **1** a chemically produced material that can be moulded into shape while soft and then set into a hard and slightly flexible form. **2** informal credit cards or other plastic cards that can be used as money. •adj. **1** made of plastic. **2** easily shaped. **3** not sincere: *a plastic smile*.
– DERIVATIVES **plastically** adv. **plasticity** n.
– ORIGIN Greek *plastikos*.

plastic bullet •n. a bullet made of PVC or another plastic, used for riot control.

plastic explosive •n. a putty-like explosive capable of being moulded by hand.

plasticine (also **Plasticine**) •n. trademark a soft modelling material.

plasticky •adj. **1** resembling plastic. **2** artificial or of low quality.

plastic surgery •n. surgery performed to repair or reconstruct parts of the body damaged as a result of injury or for cosmetic reasons.

plate •n. **1** a flat dish for holding food. **2** bowls, cups, and other utensils made of gold or silver. **3** a thin, flat piece of metal used to join or strengthen something or forming part of a machine. **4** a small, flat piece of metal with writing on it fixed to a wall or door. **5** a sheet of metal or other material with an image of type or illustrations on it, from which copies are printed. **6** a printed photograph or illustration in a book. **7** a thin, flat structure in a plant or animal body. **8** Geol. each of the several rigid pieces which together make up the earth's surface. •v. (**plates, plating, plated**) cover a metal object with a thin coating of a different metal.
– ORIGIN Old French *plat* 'platter' or *plate* 'sheet of metal'.

plateau /plat-oh/ •n. (pl. **plateaux** /plat-ohz/ or **plateaus**) **1** an area of fairly level high ground. **2** a state of little or no change following a period of activity or progress.
– ORIGIN French.

plate glass •n. thick fine-quality glass used for shop windows and doors.

platelet •n. Physiol. a small disc-shaped cell fragment without a nucleus, found in large numbers in blood and involved in clotting.

platen /plat-uhn/ •n. a cylindrical roller in a typewriter against which the paper is held.
– ORIGIN French *platine* 'flat piece'.

platform •n. **1** a raised level surface on which people or things can stand. **2** a raised structure along the side of a railway track where passengers get on and off trains. **3** a raised structure standing in the sea from which oil or gas wells are drilled. **4** the stated policy of a political party: *seeking election on a platform of low taxes*. **5** an opportunity for the expression or exchange of views. **6** a very thick sole on a shoe.
– ORIGIN French *plateforme* 'ground plan'.

platinum /plat-i-nuhm/ •n. a precious silvery-white metal. •adj. greyish-white or silvery like platinum.
– ORIGIN Spanish *platina*.

platinum blonde •adj. (of hair) very light or silvery blonde.

platinum disc •n. a platinum disc awarded to a recording artist or group for sales above a specified figure.

platitude •n. a remark that has been

used too often to be interesting or thoughtful.
– DERIVATIVES **platitudinous** adj.
– ORIGIN French.

platonic /pluh-ton-ik/ •adj. **1** (of love or friendship) intimate and affectionate but not sexual. **2** (**Platonic**) relating to the ancient Greek philosopher Plato or his ideas.
– DERIVATIVES **platonically** adv.

platoon •n. a subdivision of a company of soldiers.
– ORIGIN French *peloton*.

platter •n. a large flat serving dish.
– ORIGIN Old French *plater*.

platypus /plat-i-puhss/ (also **duck-billed platypus**) •n. (pl. **platypuses**) an egg-laying Australian mammal with a duck-like bill and webbed feet, living partly on land and partly in water.
– ORIGIN Greek *platupous* 'flat-footed'.

plaudits •pl. n. praise.
– ORIGIN Latin *plaudite* 'applaud!'.

plausible •adj. **1** seeming reasonable or probable. **2** skilled at producing persuasive arguments: *a plausible liar.*
– DERIVATIVES **plausibility** n. **plausibly** adv.
– ORIGIN Latin *plaudere* 'applaud'.

play •v. **1** take part in games for enjoyment. **2** take part in a sport or contest. **3** compete against another player or team. **4** take a specified position in a sports team. **5** act the role of a particular character in a play or film. **6** perform a piece of music or perform on a musical instrument. **7** move a piece or display a playing card in your turn in a game. **8** make a CD, tape, or record produce sounds. **9** informal be cooperative: *he needs financial backing, but the banks won't play.* •n. **1** games that are taken part in for enjoyment. **2** the performing of a sporting match: *rain wrecked the second day's play.* **3** a move in a sport or game. **4** the state of being active or effective: *luck came into play.* **5** a piece of writing performed by actors in a theatre or on the television or radio. **6** freedom of movement: *bolts should have half an inch of play.* **7** constantly changing movement: *the play of light across the surface.*
– PHRASES **make great play of** draw attention to something in an exaggerated way. **make a play for** informal attempt to attract or gain. **play about** (or **around**) behave in a casual or irresponsible way. **play along** pretend to cooperate. **play something by ear 1** perform music without having seen a score. **2** (**play it by ear**) informal proceed without having formed a plan. **play something down** disguise the

importance of something. **play for time** use excuses or unnecessary acts to gain time. **play into someone's hands** give someone an advantage without meaning to do so. **play someone off against another** bring one person into conflict with another for your own advantage. **play on** take advantage of someone's weak point. **play up** Brit. informal cause problems. **play with fire** take foolish risks.
– DERIVATIVES **playable** adj.
– ORIGIN Old English, 'to exercise'.

playback •n. the replaying of previously recorded sound or moving images.

playboy •n. a wealthy man who spends his time enjoying himself.

player •n. **1** a person taking part in a sport or game. **2** a person who is influential in a particular area: *a major player in political circles.* **3** a person who plays a musical instrument. **4** a device for playing compact discs, tapes, or records. **5** an actor.

playful •adj. **1** fond of games and amusement. **2** light-hearted.
– DERIVATIVES **playfully** adv. **playfulness** n.

playground •n. an outdoor area provided for children to play in.

playgroup (also **playschool**) •n. Brit. a regular play session for pre-school children, often organized by parents.

playhouse •n. a theatre.

playing card •n. each of a set of rectangular pieces of card with numbers and symbols on one side, used to play various games.

playing field •n. a field used for outdoor team games.

playlist •n. a list of songs or pieces of music chosen to be broadcast on a radio station.

playmate •n. a friend with whom a child plays.

play-off •n. an extra match played to decide the outcome of a contest.

playpen •n. a small portable enclosure in which a baby or small child can play safely.

plaything •n. **1** a toy. **2** a person who is treated as amusing but unimportant.

playtime •n. a period in the school day when children are allowed to go outside and play.

playwright •n. a person who writes plays.

plaza /plah-zuh/ •n. **1** an open public space in a town or city. **2** N. Amer. a shopping centre.
– ORIGIN Spanish, 'place'.

plc (also **PLC**) •abbrev. Brit. public limited company.

p

plea • n. **1** a request made in an urgent and emotional way. **2** a formal statement made by or on behalf of a person charged with an offence in a law court.
– ORIGIN Old French *plait*, *plaid* 'agreement'.

plead • v. (**pleads**, **pleading**, **pleaded** or US & dialect **pled**) **1** make an urgent and emotional request. **2** argue in support of something: *he visited the country to plead his cause*. **3** Law state formally in court whether you are guilty or not guilty of the offence with which you are charged. **4** present something as an excuse for doing or not doing something.
– ORIGIN Old French *plaidier* 'go to law'.

pleading • adj. earnestly appealing: *a pleading look*.
– DERIVATIVES **pleadingly** adv.

pleasant • adj. **1** satisfactory and enjoyable. **2** friendly and likeable.
– DERIVATIVES **pleasantly** adv. **pleasantness** n.
– ORIGIN Old French *plaisant*.

pleasantry • n. (pl. **pleasantries**) **1** an unimportant remark made as part of a polite conversation. **2** a mildly amusing joke.

please • v. (**pleases**, **pleasing**, **pleased**) **1** cause someone to feel happy and satisfied. **2** wish: *do as you please*. **3** (**please yourself**) consider only your own wishes. • adv. used in polite requests or questions, or to accept an offer.
– ORIGIN Old French *plaisir*.

pleased • adj. **1** feeling or showing pleasure and satisfaction. **2** (**pleased to do**) willing or glad to do.

pleasing • adj. giving pleasure or satisfaction.
– DERIVATIVES **pleasingly** adv.

pleasurable • adj. enjoyable.
– DERIVATIVES **pleasurably** adv.

pleasure • n. **1** a feeling of happy satisfaction and enjoyment. **2** an event or activity which you enjoy. **3** a pleasant physical feeling. • adj. intended for enjoyment rather than business: *pleasure boats*. • v. (**pleasures**, **pleasuring**, **pleasured**) give pleasure to.
– PHRASES **at your pleasure** formal as and when you wish.
– ORIGIN Old French *plaisir* 'to please'.

pleat • n. a fold in fabric or a garment, held by stitching the top or side. • v. fold or form fabric into pleats.
– ORIGIN from PLAIT.

pleb • n. informal, derog. a member of the lower social classes.
– ORIGIN from PLEBEIAN.

plebeian /pli-bee-uhn/ • n. **1** a member of the lower social classes. **2** (in ancient Rome) a commoner. • adj. lower-class or unsophisticated.
– ORIGIN Latin *plebs* 'the common people'.

plebiscite /pleb-i-syt/ • n. a vote made by everyone entitled to do so on an important public issue.
– ORIGIN French *plébiscite*.

plectrum • n. (pl. **plectrums** or **plectra**) a thin flat piece of plastic or tortoiseshell used to pluck the strings of a guitar or similar musical instrument.
– ORIGIN Greek *plēktron* 'something with which to strike'.

pled US or dialect past part. of PLEAD.

pledge • n. **1** a solemn promise or undertaking. **2** something valuable given as a guarantee that a debt will be paid or a promise kept. **3** (**the pledge**) a solemn promise not to drink alcohol. **4** a thing given as a token of love, favour, or loyalty. • v. (**pledges**, **pledging**, **pledged**) **1** solemnly promise to do or give something. **2** give something valuable as a guarantee on a loan.
– ORIGIN Old French *plege* 'person acting as surety for another'.

Pleistocene /ply-stuh-seen/ • adj. Geol. relating to the first epoch of the Quaternary period (from 1.64 million to about 10,000 years ago), a time which included the ice ages and the appearance of humans.
– ORIGIN from Greek *pleistos* 'most' + *kainos* 'new'.

plenary /plee-nuh-ri/ • adj. **1** full; complete: *plenary powers*. **2** (of a meeting at a conference or assembly) to be attended by all participants. • n. a plenary meeting.
– ORIGIN Latin *plenus* 'full'.

plenipotentiary /plen-i-puh-ten-shuh-ri/ • n. (pl. **plenipotentiaries**) a person given full power by a government to act on its behalf. • adj. (of power) complete.
– ORIGIN from Latin *plenus* 'full' + *potentia* 'power'.

plenitude • n. formal a large amount of something.
– ORIGIN Old French.

plenteous • adj. literary plentiful.

plentiful • adj. existing in great quantities.
– DERIVATIVES **plentifully** adv.

plenty • pron. a large amount or quantity, or as much as is needed. • n. a situation in which food and other necessities are available in sufficiently large quantities. • adv. informal fully; enough.
– ORIGIN Old French *plente*.

plenum /plee-nuhm/ • n. **1** an assembly of all the members of a group or committee. **2** Physics a space completely

filled with matter, or the whole of space seen in such a way.
– ORIGIN Latin, 'full space'.

pleonasm /plee-oh-na-z'm/ •n. the use of more words than are necessary to express meaning (e.g. *see with your eyes*).
– ORIGIN Greek *pleonasmos*.

plethora /pleth-uh-ruh/ •n. an excessive amount of something: *a plethora of complaints*.
– ORIGIN Latin.

pleura /ploor-uh/ •n. (pl. **pleurae** /ploor-ee/) Anat. each of a pair of membranes lining the thorax and covering the lungs.
– DERIVATIVES **pleural** adj.
– ORIGIN Greek, 'side of the body, rib'.

pleurisy /ploor-i-si/ •n. inflammation of the membranes round the lungs, causing pain during breathing.

plexus •n. (pl. **plexus** or **plexuses**) **1** Anat. a network of nerves or vessels in the body. **2** a complex network or web-like structure.
– ORIGIN Latin, 'plaited formation'.

pliable /ply-uh-b'l/ •adj. **1** easily bent. **2** easily influenced or persuaded.
– DERIVATIVES **pliability** n.
– ORIGIN French.

pliant •adj. pliable.

plié /plee-ay/ •n. Ballet a movement in which a dancer bends the knees and straightens them again, keeping the feet turned out and heels on the ground.
– ORIGIN French, 'bent'.

pliers /ply-erz/ •pl. n. pincers having jaws with flat surfaces, used for gripping small objects or bending wire.
– ORIGIN French *plier* 'to bend'.

plight[1] •n. a dangerous or difficult situation.
– ORIGIN Old French *plit* 'fold'.

plight[2] •v. old use **1** solemnly promise faith or loyalty. **2** (**be plighted to**) be engaged to be married to.
– ORIGIN Old English.

plimsoll (also **plimsole**) •n. Brit. a light rubber-soled canvas sports shoe.
– ORIGIN prob. from the resemblance of the side of the sole to a **PLIMSOLL LINE**.

Plimsoll line •n. a marking on a ship's side showing the limit to which the ship may be legally submerged in the water when loaded with cargo.
– ORIGIN named after the English politician Samuel *Plimsoll*.

plinth •n. a heavy block or slab which supports a statue or forming the base of a column.
– ORIGIN Greek *plinthos* 'tile, brick'.

Pliocene /ply-uh-seen/ •adj. Geol. relating to the last epoch of the Tertiary period (5.2 to 1.64 million years ago), a time when the first hominids appeared.
– ORIGIN from Greek *pleiōn* 'more' + *kainos* 'new'.

PLO •abbrev. Palestine Liberation Organization.

plod •v. (**plods, plodding, plodded**) **1** walk slowly with heavy steps. **2** work slowly and steadily at a dull task. •n. a slow, heavy walk.
– DERIVATIVES **plodder** n.

plonk[1] informal, esp. Brit. •v. set something down heavily or carelessly. •n. a sound like that of something being set down heavily.

plonk[2] •n. Brit. informal cheap wine.
– ORIGIN prob. from *blanc* in French *vin blanc* 'white wine'.

plonker •n. Brit. informal a foolish or incompetent person.
– ORIGIN from **PLONK**[1].

plop •n. a sound like that of a small, solid object dropping into water. •v. (**plops, plopping, plopped**) fall or drop with such a sound.

plosive •adj. referring to a consonant (e.g. *d* and *t*) that is produced by stopping the flow of air coming out of the mouth and then suddenly releasing it.
– ORIGIN from **EXPLOSIVE**.

plot •n. **1** a secret plan to do something illegal or wrong. **2** the main sequence of events in a play, novel, or film. **3** a small piece of ground marked out for building, gardening, etc. •v. (**plots, plotting, plotted**) **1** secretly make plans to carry out something illegal or wrong. **2** invent the plot of a play, novel, or film. **3** mark a route or position on a chart or graph.
– DERIVATIVES **plotter** n.
– ORIGIN Old English; sense 1 is from Old French *complot* 'dense crowd, secret project'.

plough (US **plow**) •n. **1** a large farming implement with one or more blades fixed in a frame, used to turn over and cut furrows in soil. **2** (**the Plough**) Brit. a formation of seven stars in the constellation Ursa Major (the Great Bear). •v. **1** turn up earth with a plough. **2** (**plough through/into**) (of a vehicle) move in a fast or uncontrolled way through or into something. **3** move forward with difficulty or force. **4** (**plough something in**) invest money in a business.
– DERIVATIVES **ploughable** adj. **ploughman** n. (pl. **ploughmen**).
– ORIGIN Old English.

ploughman's lunch •n. Brit. a meal of bread and cheese with pickle and salad.

ploughshare •n. the main cutting blade of a plough.

plover /rhymes with lover/ •n. a wading bird with a short bill.
– ORIGIN Old French.

plow •n. & v. US = PLOUGH.

ploy •n. a cunning act performed to gain an advantage.

pluck •v. 1 take hold of something and quickly remove it from its place. 2 pull out a hair, feather, or similar thing. 3 pull the feathers from a bird's carcass to prepare it for cooking. 4 sound a stringed musical instrument with your finger or a plectrum. •n. courage.
– PHRASES **pluck up courage** summon up enough courage to do something frightening.
– ORIGIN Old English.

plucky •adj. (**pluckier**, **pluckiest**) determined and brave.
– DERIVATIVES **pluckily** adv. **pluckiness** n.

plug •n. 1 a piece of solid material tightly blocking a hole. 2 a device with metal pins that fit into holes in a socket to make an electrical connection. 3 informal an electrical socket. 4 informal a piece of publicity promoting a product or event. 5 a piece of tobacco for chewing. •v. (**plugs**, **plugging**, **plugged**) 1 block a hole. 2 (**plug something in**) connect an appliance to the main electrical supply by means of a socket. 3 (**plug into**) gain access to an information system or area of activity. 4 informal promote a product or event by mentioning it publicly. 5 informal shoot or hit someone. 6 (**plug away**) informal proceed steadily with a task.
– ORIGIN Dutch and German plugge.

plughole •n. Brit. a hole at the lowest point of a bath or sink, through which the water drains away.

plug-in •n. Computing a module or piece of software which can be added to an existing system to give extra features.

plum •n. 1 a soft oval fruit with purple, reddish, or yellow skin, containing a flattish pointed stone. 2 a reddish-purple colour. •adj. informal highly desirable: a plum job.
– ORIGIN Latin prunum.

plumage /ploo-mij/ •n. a bird's feathers.
– ORIGIN Old French.

plumb¹ •v. 1 measure the depth of water. 2 explore or experience something fully: she plumbed the depths of despair. 3 test an upright surface to find out if it is vertical. •n. a heavy object attached to a line for finding the depth of water or whether an upright surface is vertical. •adv. informal exactly: plumb in the centre. •adj. vertical.

– ORIGIN Latin plumbum 'lead'.

plumb² •v. (**plumb something in**) Brit. install a bath, basin, washing machine, etc. and connect it to water and drainage pipes.
– ORIGIN from PLUMBER.

plumber •n. a person who fits and repairs the pipes and fittings of water supply, sanitation, or heating systems.
– ORIGIN Old French plommier 'person working with lead'.

plumbing •n. the system of pipes, tanks, and fittings required for the water supply, heating, and sanitation in a building.

plumb line •n. a line with a heavy weight attached to it, used to find the depth of water or to check that something is vertical.

plume •n. 1 a long, soft feather or set of feathers. 2 a long spreading cloud of smoke or vapour. •v. (**plumes**, **pluming**, **plumed**) 1 (as adj. **plumed**) decorated with feathers. 2 (of smoke or vapour) spread out in a plume.
– ORIGIN Latin pluma 'down'.

plummet •v. (**plummets**, **plummeting**, **plummeted**) 1 fall straight down at high speed. 2 decrease rapidly in value or amount. •n. 1 a steep and rapid fall or drop. 2 a plumb line or weight.
– ORIGIN Old French plommet 'small sounding lead'.

plummy •adj. (**plummier**, **plummiest**) 1 like a plum. 2 Brit. informal (of a person's voice) typical of the English upper classes.

plump¹ •adj. 1 rather fat. 2 full and rounded in shape. •v. (**plump something up**) make something full and rounded.
– DERIVATIVES **plumpness** n.
– ORIGIN Dutch plomp or German plump 'blunt, obtuse'.

plump² •v. 1 set or sit down heavily. 2 (**plump for**) choose one of two or more possibilities.

plum pudding •n. a rich suet pudding containing raisins, currants, and spices.

plumy •adj. resembling or decorated with feathers.

plunder •v. (**plunders**, **plundering**, **plundered**) enter a place by force and steal goods from it. •n. 1 the action of plundering. 2 goods obtained by plundering.
– ORIGIN German plündern 'rob of household goods'.

plunge •v. (**plunges**, **plunging**, **plunged**) 1 fall or move suddenly and uncontrollably. 2 jump or dive quickly and energetically. 3 (**plunge in**) begin a course of action without thought or care. 4 (**be plunged into**) be suddenly

brought into: *the area was plunged into darkness.* **5** push or thrust quickly. • n. an act of plunging.
– PHRASES **take the plunge** informal decide to do something important or difficult after consideration.
– ORIGIN Old French *plungier* 'thrust down'.

plunge pool • n. **1** a small, deep swimming pool. **2** a deep basin at the foot of a waterfall formed by the action of the falling water.

plunger • n. **1** a part of a device that can be pushed down. **2** a rubber cup on a long handle, used to clear blocked pipes by means of suction.

plunk informal • v. play a keyboard or pluck a stringed instrument in a heavy-handed way. • n. a plunking sound.

pluperfect • adj. Grammar (of a tense) referring to an action completed earlier than a past point of time, formed by *had* and the past participle (as in *he had gone by then*).
– ORIGIN from Latin *plus quam perfectum* 'more than perfect'.

plural • adj. **1** more than one in number. **2** Grammar (of a word or form) referring to more than one. • n. Grammar a plural word or form.
– ORIGIN Latin *pluralis*.

pluralism • n. **1** a political system of power-sharing among a number of political parties. **2** the existence or toleration in society of a number of different racial groups or political or religious beliefs. **3** the holding of more than one ecclesiastical position at the same time by one person.
– DERIVATIVES **pluralist** n. & adj. **pluralistic** adj.

plurality • n. (pl. **pluralities**) **1** the state of being plural or more than one. **2** a large number of people or things.

pluralize (or **pluralise**) • v. (**pluralizes**, **pluralizing**, **pluralized**) **1** make something more numerous. **2** give a plural form to a word.

plus • prep. **1** with the addition of. **2** informal together with. • adj. **1** (after a number or amount) at least: *$500,000 plus.* **2** (after a grade) rather better than: *B plus.* **3** (before a number) above zero: *plus 60 degrees centigrade.* **4** having a positive electric charge. • n. **1** (also **plus sign**) the symbol +, indicating addition or a positive value. **2** informal a benefit or advantage. • conj. informal also.
– ORIGIN Latin, 'more'.

plus fours • pl. n. men's baggy trousers that are cut short to fit closely below the knee, formerly worn for hunting and golf.

– ORIGIN so named because the overhang at the knee required an extra four inches of material.

plush • n. a fabric of silk, cotton, or wool, with a long, soft nap. • adj. informal expensively luxurious.
– ORIGIN from former French *pluche*.

Pluto • n. the most remote known planet of the solar system, ninth in order from the sun.

plutocracy /ploo-tok-ruh-si/ • n. (pl. **plutocracies**) **1** government by the wealthy. **2** a society governed by the wealthy.
– ORIGIN from Greek *ploutos* 'wealth' + *kratos* 'strength'.

plutocrat • n. usu. derog. a person who is powerful because they are rich.

plutonium /ploo-toh-ni-uhm/ • n. a radioactive metallic element used as a fuel in nuclear reactors and as an explosive in atomic weapons.
– ORIGIN from PLUTO.

ply[1] • n. (pl. **plies**) **1** a thickness or layer of a material. **2** each of a number of layers or strands of which something is made.
– ORIGIN French *pli* 'a fold'.

ply[2] • v. (**plies**, **plying**, **plied**) **1** work steadily with a tool or at your job. **2** (of a ship or vehicle) travel regularly over a route. **3** (**ply someone with**) keep presenting someone with food, drink, or questions.
– ORIGIN from APPLY.

plywood • n. thin strong board which consists of layers of wood glued together.

PM • abbrev. Prime Minister.

Pm • symb. the chemical element promethium.

p.m. • abbrev. after noon.
– ORIGIN from Latin *post meridiem*.

PMS • abbrev. premenstrual syndrome.

PMT • abbrev. Brit. premenstrual tension.

pneumatic /nyoo-mat-ik/ • adj. containing or operated by air or gas under pressure: *a pneumatic drill.*
– DERIVATIVES **pneumatically** adv.
– ORIGIN Greek *pneumatikos*.

pneumococcus /nyoo-muh-kok-kuhss/ • n. (pl. **pneumococci** /nyoo-muh-kok-ky/) a bacterium associated with pneumonia and some forms of meningitis.

pneumonia /nyoo-moh-ni-uh/ • n. an infection causing inflammation of one or both lungs.
– ORIGIN Greek *pneumōn* 'lung'.

PO • abbrev. **1** postal order. **2** Post Office.

Po • symb. the chemical element polonium.

poach[1] • v. cook something by simmering it in a small amount of liquid.

p

– ORIGIN Old French *pochier*.

poach² • v. **1** catch game or fish illegally in private or protected areas. **2** take or get in an unfair or secret way: *they tried to poach passengers by offering better seats.*
– DERIVATIVES **poacher** n.
– ORIGIN prob. from POKE.

pock • n. a pockmark.
– DERIVATIVES **pocked** adj.
– ORIGIN Old English.

pocket • n. **1** a small bag sewn into or on clothing, used for carrying small articles. **2** a small group or area that is set apart or different from its surroundings: *the city's parks provide pockets of natural beauty.* **3** informal the money you have available: *gifts to suit every pocket.* **4** (in billiards and snooker) an opening at the corner or on the side of a billiard table into which balls are struck. • v. (**pockets, pocketing, pocketed**) **1** put something into your pocket. **2** take something belonging to someone else. **3** earn or win money.
– PHRASES **in someone's pocket** dependent on someone financially and so under their influence. **out of** (or **in**) **pocket** having lost (or gained) money.
– DERIVATIVES **pocketable** adj.
– ORIGIN Old French *pokete* 'little bag'.

pocketbook • n. **1** Brit. a notebook. **2** US a wallet, purse, or handbag.

pocket money • n. Brit. **1** a small sum of money given regularly to a child by their parents. **2** a small amount of money for minor expenses.

pockmark • n. **1** a hollow scar or mark on the skin left by a spot. **2** a mark or hollow area disfiguring a surface.
– DERIVATIVES **pockmarked** adj.

pod¹ • n. a long seed-case of a pea, bean, or similar plant. • v. (**pods, podding, podded**) remove peas or beans from their pods before cooking.

pod² • n. a small herd of whales or similar sea mammals.

podgy • adj. (**podgier, podgiest**) Brit. informal chubby.

podium /poh-di-uhm/ • n. (pl. **podiums** or **podia** /poh-di-uh/) a small platform on which a person stands when conducting an orchestra or giving a speech.
– ORIGIN Greek *podion* 'little foot'.

poem • n. a piece of imaginative writing in verse.
– ORIGIN Greek *poiēma* 'fiction, poem'.

poesy /poh-i-zi/ • n. old use poetry.

poet • n. a person who writes poems.
– DERIVATIVES **poetess** n.

poetic • adj. (also **poetical**) relating to poetry. • n. (**poetics**) the study of

linguistic techniques in poetry and literature.
– DERIVATIVES **poetically** adv.

poetic justice • n. suitable or deserved punishment or reward.

poetic licence • n. freedom to change facts or the normal rules of language for artistic effect.

Poet Laureate • n. (pl. **Poets Laureate**) a poet appointed by the British king or queen, formerly responsible for writing poems for important occasions.

poetry • n. **1** poems as a whole or as a form of literature. **2** a quality of beauty or emotional power: *poetry and fire are balanced in the music.*

po-faced • adj. Brit. serious and disapproving.
– ORIGIN perh. from *po* 'chamber pot'.

pogo stick • n. a toy for bouncing around on, consisting of a pole on a spring with a bar to stand on and a handle at the top.

pogrom /pog-rom/ • n. an organized massacre of an ethnic group, originally that of Jews in Russia or eastern Europe.
– ORIGIN Russian, 'devastation'.

poignant /poy-nyuhnt/ • adj. arousing a sense of sadness or regret.
– DERIVATIVES **poignancy** n.
– ORIGIN Old French, 'pricking'.

poinsettia /poyn-set-ti-uh/ • n. a small shrub with large showy scarlet bracts, which resemble petals.
– ORIGIN named after the American diplomat and botanist Joel R. *Poinsett.*

point • n. **1** the tapered, sharp end of a tool, weapon, or other object. **2** a particular place or moment. **3** an item, detail, or idea. **4** (**the point**) the most important part of what is being discussed. **5** the advantage or purpose of something: *what's the point of it all?* **6** a particular feature or quality: *the building has its good points.* **7** a unit of scoring, value, or measurement. **8** a very small dot or mark. **9** (in geometry) something having position but not magnitude. **10** each of thirty-two directions marked at equal distances round a compass. **11** a narrow piece of land jutting out into the sea. **12** (**points**) Brit. a junction of two railway lines, with a pair of rails that can be moved sideways to allow a train to pass from one line to the other. **13** Brit. an electrical socket. **14** (**points**) a set of electrical contacts in the distributor of a motor vehicle. • v. **1** direct someone's attention in a particular direction by extending your finger. **2** aim something. **3** face in or indicate a particular direction: *a sign pointing left.* **4** (**point something out**) make someone aware of something. **5** (**point to**) indicate that something is likely to happen. **6** fill in the joints of brickwork or masonry with mortar or cement.

– PHRASES **make a point of** make a special effort to do something. **on the point of** on the verge of. **point of view** a particular attitude or opinion.

– ORIGIN Old French *pointe* or *point*.

point-blank •adj. (of a shot or missile) fired from very close to its target. •adv. in a blunt and very direct way: *they refused point-blank to pay the tax.*

point duty •n. Brit. the duties of a police officer stationed at a junction to control traffic.

pointed •adj. **1** having a sharpened or tapered tip or end. **2** (of a remark or look) directed towards a particular person and expressing a clear message.

pointer •n. **1** a long, thin piece of metal on a scale or dial which moves to give a reading. **2** a rod used for pointing to features on a map or chart. **3** a hint or tip. **4** a breed of dog that on scenting game stands rigid looking towards it.

pointillism /ˈpwan-ti-li-z'm/ •n. a way of painting using tiny dots of various pure colours, which become blended in the viewer's eye.

– DERIVATIVES **pointillist** n. & adj.

– ORIGIN French *pointiller* 'mark with dots'.

pointing •n. mortar or cement used to fill the joints of brickwork or masonry.

pointless •adj. having little or no sense or purpose.

– DERIVATIVES **pointlessly** adv. **pointlessness** n.

point-to-point •n. (pl. **point-to-points**) Brit. a cross-country race for horses used in hunting.

poise •n. **1** a graceful way of holding the body. **2** a calm and confident manner. •v. **1** cause something to be balanced or suspended. **2** (as adj. **poised**) calm and confident. **3** (**be poised to do**) be ready to do.

– ORIGIN Old French *pois*.

poison •n. **1** a substance that causes death or injury when swallowed or absorbed by a living organism. **2** a harmful influence: *gossip is a spreading poison.* •v. **1** harm or kill a person or animal with poison. **2** put poison on or in something. **3** have a harmful effect on something.

– DERIVATIVES **poisoner** n.

– ORIGIN Old French, 'magic potion'.

poisoned chalice •n. something offered which seems attractive but which is likely to cause problems to the person receiving it.

poisonous •adj. **1** causing death or injury when swallowed or absorbed by a living organism. **2** very unpleasant or spiteful.

poison pen letter •n. an anonymous letter that is spiteful or abusive.

poke •v. (**pokes, poking, poked**) **1** prod with a finger or a sharp object. **2** (**poke about/around**) look or search around. **3** push or stick out: *she poked her tongue out.* •n. an act of poking.

– PHRASES **poke fun at** make fun of.

poker¹ •n. a metal rod used for prodding and stirring an open fire.

poker² •n. a card game in which the players bet on the value of the hands dealt to them, sometimes using bluff.

– ORIGIN perh. from German *pochen* 'to brag'.

poker face •n. a blank expression that hides your true feelings.

poky (also **pokey**) •adj. (**pokier, pokiest**) (of a room or building) uncomfortably small and cramped.

– ORIGIN from POKE.

polar •adj. **1** relating to the North or South Poles or the regions around them. **2** having an electrical or magnetic field. **3** completely opposite.

polar bear •n. a large white arctic bear.

polarity •n. (pl. **polarities**) **1** the state of having poles or opposites. **2** the direction of a magnetic or electric field.

polarize (or **polarise**) •v. (**polarizes, polarizing, polarized**) **1** divide people into two sharply contrasting groups with different opinions: *the nation's media are polarized in the controversy.* **2** Physics restrict the vibrations of a transverse wave, especially light, to one direction. **3** give magnetic or electric polarity to.

– DERIVATIVES **polarization** n.

Polaroid •n. trademark **1** a material that polarizes the light passing through it, used in sunglasses. **2** a type of camera that produces a finished print rapidly after each exposure.

polder /ˈpohl-der/ •n. (in the Netherlands) a piece of land reclaimed from the sea or a river.

– ORIGIN Dutch.

Pole •n. a person from Poland.

pole¹ •n. a long, thin rounded piece of wood or metal, used as a support. •v. (**poles, poling, poled**) push a boat along with a pole.

– ORIGIN Old English.

pole² •n. **1** either of the two points (**North Pole** or **South Pole**) at opposite ends of the earth's axis. **2** each of the

two opposite points of a magnet at which magnetic forces are strongest. **3** the positive or negative terminal of an electric cell or battery. **4** either of two contrasting opinions.
– PHRASES **be poles apart** have nothing in common.
– ORIGIN Greek *polos* 'axis, sky'.

poleaxe (US also **poleax**) • v. (**poleaxes, poleaxing, poleaxed**) **1** knock down or stun someone with a heavy blow. **2** shock someone greatly. • n. **1** a battleaxe. **2** a butcher's axe used to slaughter animals.
– ORIGIN from POLL + AXE.

polecat • n. **1** a dark brown weasel-like animal with an unpleasant smell. **2** N. Amer. a skunk.
– ORIGIN perh. from Old French *pole* 'chicken' + CAT.

pole dancing • n. erotic dancing which involves swinging around a fixed pole.
– DERIVATIVES **pole dancer** n.

polemic /puh-lem-ik/ • n. **1** a strong verbal or written attack. **2** (also **polemics**) the practice of engaging in fierce discussion. • adj. (also **polemical**) relating to fierce discussion.
– DERIVATIVES **polemicist** n.
– ORIGIN Greek *polemos* 'war'.

polenta /puh-len-tuh/ • n. (in Italian cookery) maize flour or a dough made from this, which is boiled and then fried or baked.
– ORIGIN Latin, 'pearl barley'.

pole position • n. the most favourable position at the start of a motor race.
– ORIGIN from *pole* in horse racing to mean the starting position next to the inside boundary fence.

Pole Star • n. a star located in the part of the sky above the North Pole.

pole vault • n. an athletic event in which competitors attempt to vault over a high bar with the aid of a long pole.

police • n. an official body of people employed by a state to prevent and solve crime and keep public order. • v. (**polices, policing, policed**) **1** keep law and order in an area. **2** ensure that a particular set of rules is obeyed.
– ORIGIN Latin *politia* 'policy'.

policeman (or **policewoman**) • n. (pl. **policemen** or **policewomen**) a member of a police force.

police officer • n. a policeman or policewoman.

police state • n. a state in which police are required by the government to keep secret watch over and control citizens' activities.

police station • n. the building that houses a local police force.

policy[1] • n. (pl. **policies**) a course of action adopted or proposed by an organization or person.
– ORIGIN Greek *politeia* 'citizenship'.

policy[2] • n. (pl. **policies**) a contract of insurance.
– DERIVATIVES **policyholder** n.
– ORIGIN French *police*.

polio • n. = POLIOMYELITIS.

poliomyelitis /poh-li-oh-my-uh-ly-tiss/ • n. an infectious disease that can cause temporary or permanent paralysis.
– ORIGIN from Greek *polios* 'grey' + *muelos* 'marrow'.

Polish /poh-lish/ • n. the language of Poland. • adj. relating to Poland.

polish /po-lish/ • v. **1** make a surface smooth and shiny by rubbing. **2** improve: *he's got to polish up his French.* **3** (**polish something off**) finish something quickly. • n. **1** a substance used to polish something. **2** an act of polishing. **3** shiny appearance produced by polishing. **4** refinement or elegance.
– DERIVATIVES **polisher** n.
– ORIGIN Latin *polire*.

politburo /pol-it-byuu-roh/ • n. (pl. **politburos**) the chief policy-making committee of a communist party, especially that of the former Soviet Union.
– ORIGIN from Russian *politicheskoe byuro* 'political bureau'.

polite • adj. (**politer, politest**) **1** respectful and considerate towards other people; courteous. **2** civilized or well bred: *polite society.*
– DERIVATIVES **politely** adv. **politeness** n.
– ORIGIN Latin *politus* 'polished'.

politic /po-li-tik/ • adj. (of an action) sensible and wise in the circumstances.
– ORIGIN Greek *politikos*.

political • adj. **1** relating to the government or public affairs of a country. **2** related to or interested in politics.
– DERIVATIVES **politically** adv.

political correctness • n. the avoidance of language or behaviour seen as discriminating against or offensive to certain groups of people.

politically correct (or **incorrect**) • adj. showing (or failing to show) political correctness.

political prisoner • n. a person imprisoned for their political beliefs or actions.

political science • n. the study of political activity and behaviour.

politician • n. a person who is involved in politics as a job, either as a holder of or as a candidate for an elected office.

politicize (or **politicise**) • v. (**politicizes,**

politicizing, politicized) **1** cause
someone to become involved in politics.
2 make an issue political.
– DERIVATIVES **politicization** n.

politicking /po-li-ti-king/ • n. esp. derog.
political activity.

politics • n. **1** the activities associated
with governing a country or area, and
with the relations between states. **2** a
particular set of political beliefs.
3 activities concerned with gaining or
using power within an organization or
group: *office politics*.

polity • n. (pl. **polities**) **1** a form of
government. **2** a society as a politically
organized state.
– ORIGIN Greek *politeia* 'citizenship'.

polka /pol-kuh/ • n. a lively dance for
couples.
– ORIGIN Czech *půlka* 'half-step'.

polka dot • n. each of a number of round
dots that are evenly spaced to form a
pattern.

poll /rhymes with pole or doll/ • n. **1** the
process of voting in an election. **2** a
record of the number of votes cast.
• v. **1** record the opinions or votes of a
number of people. **2** (of a candidate in
an election) receive a specified number
of votes.
– ORIGIN perh. from German.

pollack /pol-luhk/ (also **pollock**) • n. (pl.
pollack or **pollacks**) an edible greenish-
brown fish of the cod family.
– ORIGIN perh. from Celtic.

pollard /pol-lerd/ • v. cut the top and
branches off a tree to encourage new
growth.
– ORIGIN from POLL.

pollen • n. a powdery substance
produced by the male part of a flower,
containing the fertilizing agent.
– ORIGIN Latin, 'fine powder'.

pollen count • n. a measure of the
amount of pollen in the air.

pollinate • v. (**pollinates, pollinating,
pollinated**) carry pollen to and fertilize
a flower or plant.
– DERIVATIVES **pollination** n. **pollinator** n.

pollock • n. var. of POLLACK.

pollster /pohl-ster/ • n. a person who
records people's opinions or votes in a
poll.

poll tax • n. a tax paid at the same rate by
every adult.
– ORIGIN from POLL in the former sense
'head'.

pollutant • n. a substance that creates
unpleasant or harmful effects in the air,
soil, or water.

pollute • v. (**pollutes, polluting,
polluted**) make the air, soil, or water

dirty with unpleasant or harmful
substances.
– DERIVATIVES **polluter** n.
– ORIGIN Latin *polluere*.

> ☑ Spell **pollute** and the related word
> **pollution** with a double **l**.

pollution • n. the presence in the air,
soil, or water of a substance with
unpleasant or harmful effects.

polo • n. a game similar to hockey, played
on horseback with a long-handled
mallet.
– ORIGIN from a word in a Tibetan
language meaning 'ball'.

polonaise /pol-uh-nayz/ • n. a slow
stately dance of Polish origin.
– ORIGIN French, 'Polish'.

polo neck • n. Brit. a high, close-fitting
turned-over collar on a sweater.

polonium /puh-loh-ni-uhm/ • n. a rare
radioactive metallic element.
– ORIGIN Latin *Polonia* 'Poland'.

polo shirt • n. a casual short-sleeved
shirt with a collar and two or three
buttons at the neck.

poltergeist /pol-ter-gyst/ • n. a
supernatural being supposedly
responsible for throwing objects about.
– ORIGIN from German *poltern* 'make a
disturbance' + *Geist* 'ghost'.

poltroon /pol-troon/ • n. old use a
complete coward.
– ORIGIN Italian *poltrone*.

poly- • comb. form many; much: *polygon*.
– ORIGIN Greek *polus* 'much', *polloi*
'many'.

polyandry /po-li-an-dri/ • n. the practice
of having more than one husband at the
same time.
– ORIGIN from Greek *anēr* 'male'.

polyanthus /po-li-an-thuhss/ • n. (pl.
polyanthus) a flowering garden plant
that is a hybrid from the wild primrose.
– ORIGIN Greek *anthos* 'flower'.

polychromatic • adj. multicoloured.

polychrome • adj. painted, printed, or
decorated in several colours.
– ORIGIN Greek *khrōma* 'colour'.

polyester • n. a synthetic fibre or resin
used to make fabric for clothes.

polyethylene /po-li-eth-i-leen/ • n. =
POLYTHENE.

polygamy /puh-lig-uh-mi/ • n. the
practice of having more than one wife or
husband at the same time.
– DERIVATIVES **polygamist** n.
polygamous adj.
– ORIGIN Greek *polugamos* 'often
marrying'.

polyglot /po-li-glot/ • adj. knowing or
using several languages.

p

– ORIGIN Greek *poluglōttos* 'many-tongued'.

polygon /po-li-guhn/ • n. a plane figure with three or more straight sides and angles.
– DERIVATIVES **polygonal** /puh-**li**-guh-n'l/ adj.

polygraph • n. a lie detector.

polygyny /puh-**li**-ji-ni/ • n. the practice of having more than one wife at the same time.
– ORIGIN Greek *gunē* 'woman'.

polyhedron /po-li-**hee**-druhn/ • n. (pl. **polyhedra** /po-li-**hee**-druh/ or **polyhedrons**) a solid figure with many plane faces.
– DERIVATIVES **polyhedral** adj.

polymath /po-li-math/ • n. a person with a wide knowledge of many subjects.
– DERIVATIVES **polymathic** adj.
– ORIGIN Greek *polumathēs* 'having learned much'.

polymer /po-li-mer/ • n. Chem. a substance with a molecular structure formed from many identical small molecules bonded together.
– ORIGIN Greek *polumeros* 'having many parts'.

polymerize (or **polymerise**)
• v. (**polymerizes, polymerizing, polymerized**) combine or cause to combine to form a polymer.

polymorphic (also **polymorphous**)
• adj. having several different forms.

Polynesian • n. **1** a person from Polynesia, a large group of Pacific islands including New Zealand and Hawaii. **2** a group of languages spoken in Polynesia. • adj. relating to Polynesia.

polyp /po-lip/ • n. **1** a simple sea creature which remains fixed in the same place, such as coral. **2** Med. a small lump that sticks out from a mucous membrane.
– ORIGIN Greek *polupous*.

polyphonic • adj. (especially of vocal music) in two or more parts, each having a melody of its own.
– ORIGIN Greek *phōnē* 'voice, sound'.

polyphony /puh-**li**-fuh-ni/ • n. the combination in harmony of a number of musical parts, each forming an individual melody.

polysaccharide /po-li-**sak**-kuh-ryd/
• n. a carbohydrate (e.g. starch or cellulose) whose molecules consist of chains of sugar molecules.

polystyrene /po-li-**sty**-reen/ • n. a light synthetic material used especially as packaging.
– ORIGIN from **POLYMER** + **STYRENE**.

polysyllabic • adj. having more than one syllable.

polytechnic • n. (formerly, in Britain) a college offering courses at degree level or below (now called a 'university').

polytheism /po-li-**thee**-i-z'm/ • n. the worship of more than one god.
– DERIVATIVES **polytheistic** adj.
– ORIGIN Greek *polutheos* 'of many gods'.

polythene • n. Brit. a tough, light, flexible plastic, used for packaging.
– ORIGIN from *polyethylene*.

polyunsaturated • adj. (of a fat) having a chemical structure that is thought not to lead to the formation of cholesterol in the blood.
– DERIVATIVES **polyunsaturates** pl. n.

polyurethane /po-li-**yoor**-i-thayn/ • n. a synthetic resin used in paints and varnishes.

polyvinyl acetate • n. a synthetic resin used in paints and adhesives.

Pom • n. = **POMMY**.

pomade /puh-**mayd**, puh-**mahd**/ • n. a scented oil or cream used to make hair glossy and smooth.
– ORIGIN French *pommade*.

pomander /puh-**man**-der, pom-**uhn**-der/ • n. a ball or perforated container of sweet-smelling substances used to perfume a room or cupboard.
– ORIGIN from Latin *pomum de ambra* 'apple of ambergris'.

pomegranate /**pom**-i-gran-it/ • n. a round tropical fruit with a tough orange skin and red flesh containing many seeds.
– ORIGIN from Latin *pomum granatum* 'apple having many seeds'.

pomelo /**pom**-uh-loh/ • n. (pl. **pomelos**) a large citrus fruit similar to a grapefruit.

Pomeranian • n. a small dog of a breed with long silky hair.
– ORIGIN from *Pomerania*, a region of central Europe.

pommel /**pom**-m'l/ • n. **1** the upward curving or projecting front part of a saddle. **2** a rounded knob on the end of the handle of a sword, dagger, or old-fashioned gun.
– ORIGIN Old French *pomel*.

Pommy • n. (pl. **Pommies**) Austral./NZ informal, esp. derog. a British person.

pomp • n. the special clothes, music, and customs that are part of a grand public ceremony.
– ORIGIN Greek *pompē* 'procession'.

pompom (also **pompon**) • n. a small woollen ball attached to a garment for decoration.
– ORIGIN French *pompon* 'tuft, topknot'.

pompous • adj. affectedly solemn,

grand, or self-important.
- DERIVATIVES **pomposity** n. **pompously** adv.

ponce Brit. informal •n. **1** a man who lives off a prostitute's earnings. **2** derog. an effeminate man. •v. (**ponces, poncing, ponced**) (**ponce about/around**) behave in a way that wastes time or looks affected or silly.
- DERIVATIVES **poncey** (also **poncy**) adj.
- ORIGIN perh. from POUNCE.

poncho •n. (pl. **ponchos**) a garment made of a thick piece of woollen cloth with a slit in the middle to go over the head.
- ORIGIN Latin American Spanish.

pond •n. a small area of still water.
- ORIGIN from POUND³.

ponder •v. (**ponders, pondering, pondered**) consider something carefully.
- ORIGIN Latin *ponderare* 'weigh'.

ponderous •adj. **1** slow and clumsy because very heavy. **2** boringly solemn or long-winded: *ponderous newspaper editorials.*
- DERIVATIVES **ponderously** adv.
- ORIGIN Latin *ponderosus.*

pondweed •n. a plant that grows in still or running water.

pong Brit. informal •n. a strong, unpleasant smell. •v. smell strongly and unpleasantly.
- DERIVATIVES **pongy** adj.

poniard /pon-yerd/ •n. hist. a small, thin dagger.
- ORIGIN French *poignard.*

pontiff •n. the Pope.
- ORIGIN Latin *pontifex* 'high priest'.

pontifical /pon-ti-fi-k'l/ •adj. relating to the Pope; papal.

pontificate •v. /pon-ti-fi-kayt/ (**pontificates, pontificating, pontificated**) express your opinions in a pompous and overbearing way.
•n. /pon-ti-fi-kuht/ (also **Pontificate**) (in the Roman Catholic Church) the office of pope or bishop.

pontoon¹ /pon-toon/ •n. Brit. a card game in which players try to obtain cards with a value totalling twenty-one.
- ORIGIN prob. from French *vingt-et-un* 'twenty-one'.

pontoon² /pon-toon/ •n. **1** a flat-bottomed boat or hollow metal cylinder used with others to support a temporary bridge or floating landing stage. **2** a bridge or landing stage supported by pontoons.
- ORIGIN French *ponton.*

pony •n. (pl. **ponies**) a horse of a small breed, especially one below 15 hands.
- ORIGIN prob. from French *poulenet* 'small foal'.

ponytail •n. a hairstyle in which the hair is drawn back and tied at the back of the head.

pony-trekking •n. Brit. the leisure activity of riding across country on a pony or horse.

poo •exclam., n., & v. var. of POOH.

pooch •n. informal a dog.

poodle •n. a breed of dog with a curly coat that is usually clipped.
- ORIGIN German *Pudelhund.*

poof /puuf/ (also **pouf, poofter**) •n. Brit. informal, derog. an effeminate or homosexual man.
- ORIGIN perh. from *puff* in the former sense 'boastful person'.

pooh (also **poo**) informal •exclam. expressing disgust at an unpleasant smell.

pooh-pooh •v. informal dismiss an idea as being silly or impractical.

pool¹ •n. **1** a small area of still water. **2** (also **swimming pool**) an artificial pool for swimming in. **3** a small, shallow patch of liquid lying on a surface.
- ORIGIN Old English.

pool² •n. **1** a supply of vehicles, people, goods, or funds that is shared between a number of people and available for use when needed. **2** (**the pools** or **football pools**) a form of gambling on the results of football matches. **3** a game played on a billiard table using 16 balls. •v. put resources into a common fund to be used by a number of people: *they pooled their wages and bought food.*
- ORIGIN French *poule* 'stake, kitty'.

poolside •n. the area next to a swimming pool.

poop (also **poop deck**) •n. a raised deck at the back of a ship.
- ORIGIN Latin *puppis* 'stern'.

poor •adj. **1** having very little money. **2** of a low standard or quality. **3** (**poor in**) lacking in. **4** deserving pity or sympathy: *he's driven the poor woman away.*
- PHRASES **take a poor view of** regard with disapproval.
- ORIGIN Old French *poure.*

poorhouse •n. Brit. a workhouse.

poorly •adv. in a poor way. •adj. esp. Brit. unwell.

pootle •v. (**pootles, pootling, pootled**) Brit. informal move or travel in a leisurely way.
- ORIGIN from TOOTLE and *poodle* in the same sense.

pop¹ •v. (**pops, popping, popped**) **1** make or cause to make a sudden short explosive sound. **2** go or come quickly or

p

unexpectedly. **3** quickly place something somewhere. **4** (of a person's eyes) open wide and appear to bulge. •n. **1** a sudden short explosive sound. **2** informal, dated a sweet fizzy drink.

pop² •n. (also **pop music**) popular modern commercial music, with a strong melody and beat. •adj. **1** relating to pop music. **2** usu. derog. (of a scientific or academic subject) presented in a way that the general public will understand.

pop³ •n. informal, esp. US father.
– ORIGIN from **PAPA**.

pop art •n. art that uses styles and images from modern popular culture.

popcorn •n. maize kernels which are heated until they burst open and are then eaten as a snack.

pope •n. (often **the Pope**) the Bishop of Rome as head of the Roman Catholic Church.
– ORIGIN Greek *papas* 'bishop, patriarch'.

popery •n. derog. Roman Catholicism.

pop-eyed •adj. informal having bulging or staring eyes.

popgun •n. a child's toy gun which shoots a harmless pellet or cork.

popinjay /pop-in-jay/ •n. dated a vain person who dresses in a showy way.
– ORIGIN Old French *papingay* 'parrot'.

popish •adj. derog. Roman Catholic.

poplar •n. a tall, slender tree with soft wood.
– ORIGIN Latin *populus*.

poplin •n. a cotton fabric with a finely ribbed surface.
– ORIGIN from former French *papeline*.

poppadom /pop-puh-duhm/ •n. (in Indian cookery) a thin circular piece of spiced bread that is fried until crisp.
– ORIGIN Tamil.

popper •n. Brit. informal a press stud.

poppet •n. Brit. informal a pretty or charming child.
– ORIGIN Latin *puppa* 'girl, doll'.

poppy •n. a plant with bright red, pink, or orange flowers and small black seeds.
– ORIGIN Latin *papaver*.

poppycock •n. informal nonsense.
– ORIGIN from Dutch dialect *pap* 'soft' + *kak* 'dung'.

populace /pop-yuu-luhss/ •n. the general public.
– ORIGIN Italian *popolaccio* 'common people'.

popular •adj. **1** liked or admired by many people. **2** intended for or suited to the general public: *the popular press.* **3** (of a belief or attitude) widely held among the general public. **4** (of political activity) carried on by the people as a whole: *a popular revolt.*

– DERIVATIVES **popularly** adv.
– ORIGIN Latin *populus* 'people'.

popularity •n. the state of being liked or supported by many people.

popularize (or **popularise**)
•v. (**popularizes, popularizing, popularized**) **1** make something popular. **2** make something that is scientific or academic understandable or interesting to the general public.
– DERIVATIVES **popularization** n.

populate •v. (**populates, populating, populated**) **1** live in an area and form its population: *the island is populated by 8,000 people.* **2** cause people to settle in a place. **3** add data to a computer database.
– ORIGIN Latin *populare* 'supply with people'.

population •n. **1** all the inhabitants of a place. **2** a particular group within this: *the country's immigrant population.*

populist •adj. wanting or intended to appeal to or represent the interests and views of ordinary people. •n. a populist politician.
– DERIVATIVES **populism** n.

populous •adj. having a large population.

pop-up •n. **1** (of a book or greetings card) containing folded pictures that rise up when opened to form a three-dimensional scene. **2** (of a computer menu or other feature) able to be quickly brought to the screen on top of what is being worked on.

porcelain /por-suh-lin/ •n. **1** a type of fine semi-transparent china. **2** articles made of porcelain.
– ORIGIN Italian *porcellana* 'cowrie shell, china'.

porch •n. a covered shelter over the entrance of a building.
– ORIGIN Old French *porche*.

porcine /por-syn/ •adj. relating to or like a pig or pigs.
– ORIGIN Latin *porcinus*.

porcupine /por-kyuu-pyn/ •n. a large rodent with protective spines on the body and tail.
– ORIGIN from Latin *porcus* 'pig' + *spina* 'thorn'.

pore¹ •n. a tiny opening in the skin or other surface through which gases, liquids, or microscopic particles may pass.
– ORIGIN Greek *poros*.

pore² •v. (**pores, poring, pored**) (**pore over/through**) study or read something with close attention.
– ORIGIN perh. from **PEER¹**.

USAGE: Do not confuse **pore** and **pour**. **Pore** is used with **over** or **through** and means 'study or read closely' (*I spent hours poring over cookery books*), while **pour** means 'flow in a steady stream' (*water poured off the roof*).

---

pork • n. the flesh of a pig used as food.
– ORIGIN Latin *porcus* 'pig'.

porker • n. a young pig raised and fattened for food.

porky informal • adj. fat. • n. (pl. **porkies**) (also **porky pie**) Brit. a lie.

porn (also **porno**) informal
• n. pornography. • adj. pornographic.

pornography • n. pictures, writing, or films that are intended to arouse sexual excitement.
– DERIVATIVES **pornographer** n.
pornographic adj.
– ORIGIN Greek *pornographos* 'writing about prostitutes'.

porous • adj. (of a rock or other material) having tiny spaces through which gases, liquids, or microscopic particles may pass.
– DERIVATIVES **porosity** n.
– ORIGIN Latin *porus* 'pore'.

porphyry /por-fi-ri/ • n. (pl. **porphyries**) a hard, reddish igneous rock containing crystals of feldspar.
– ORIGIN Greek *porphuritēs*.

porpoise /por-puhss, por-poyz/ • n. a small toothed whale with a blunt rounded snout.
– ORIGIN Old French *porpois*.

porridge • n. 1 esp. Brit. a dish consisting of oats or oatmeal heated with water or milk. 2 Brit. informal time spent in prison.
– ORIGIN from **POTTAGE**.

port[1] • n. 1 a town or city with a harbour. 2 a harbour.
– PHRASES **port of call** a place where a ship or person stops on a journey.
– ORIGIN Latin *portus*.

port[2] • n. a strong sweet dark red wine from Portugal.
– ORIGIN from *Oporto*, a port in Portugal from which the wine is shipped.

port[3] • n. the side of a ship or aircraft that is on the left when you are facing forward. Opp. **STARBOARD**.
– ORIGIN prob. originally the side turned towards the port.

port[4] • n. 1 an opening in the side of a ship for boarding or loading. 2 an opening in the body of an aircraft or armoured vehicle through which a gun is fired. 3 a socket in a computer network into which a device is plugged.
– ORIGIN Latin *porta* 'gate'.

portable • adj. able to be easily carried or moved.
– DERIVATIVES **portability** n.

portage /por-tij/ • n. 1 the carrying of a boat or its cargo overland between two waterways. 2 a place at which this is necessary.
– ORIGIN French.

portal • n. 1 a large and impressive doorway or gate. 2 an Internet site providing a directory of links to other sites.
– ORIGIN Latin *porta*.

portcullis • n. a strong, heavy grating that is lowered to block a gateway to a castle.
– ORIGIN from Old French *porte coleice* 'sliding door'.

portend /por-tend/ • v. be a sign or warning that something important or unpleasant is likely to happen.
– ORIGIN Latin *portendere*.

portent /por-tent, por-tuhnt/ • n. a sign or warning that something important or unpleasant is likely to happen.
– ORIGIN Latin *portentum* 'omen, token'.

portentous • adj. 1 being a sign that something important is likely to happen. 2 excessively solemn.

porter[1] • n. 1 a person employed to carry luggage and other loads. 2 a hospital employee who moves equipment or patients around the hospital. 3 dark brown bitter beer.
– ORIGIN Old French *porteour*.

porter[2] • n. Brit. an employee in charge of the entrance of a large building.
– ORIGIN Old French *portier*.

portfolio • n. (pl. **portfolios**) 1 a thin, flat case for carrying drawings, maps, etc. 2 a set of pieces of creative work that demonstrate a person's ability. 3 a range of investments held by a person or organization. 4 the area of responsibility of a government minister.
– ORIGIN Italian *portafogli*.

porthole • n. a small window on the outside of a ship or aircraft.

portico /por-ti-koh/ • n. (pl. **porticoes** or **porticos**) a roof supported by columns at regular intervals, built over the entrance to a building.
– ORIGIN Latin *porticus* 'porch'.

portion • n. 1 a part or a share. 2 an amount of food suitable for or served to one person. • v. divide something into portions.
– ORIGIN Latin.

portly • adj. rather fat.
– ORIGIN Old French *port* 'bearing, gait'.

portmanteau /port-man-toh/ • n. (pl. **portmanteaus** or **portmanteaux** /port-man-tohz/) a large travelling bag that opens into two equal parts.

– ORIGIN French *portemanteau*.

portmanteau word •n. a word made by joining the first part of one word to the end of another, e.g. *brunch* from *breakfast* and *lunch*.

portrait •n. **1** a painting, drawing, or photograph of a person. **2** a written or filmed description.
– DERIVATIVES **portraitist** n.
– ORIGIN Old French *portraire* 'portray'.

portraiture •n. the art of making portraits.

portray •v. **1** show or describe in a work of art or literature. **2** describe in a particular way: *he is portrayed as having relentless energy*.
– DERIVATIVES **portrayal** n.
– ORIGIN Old French *portraire*.

Portuguese /port-yuu-geez, por-chuu-geez/ •n. (pl. **Portuguese**) **1** a person from Portugal. **2** the language of Portugal and Brazil. •adj. relating to Portugal.

Portuguese man-of-war •n. a floating jellyfish-like sea creature with long stinging tentacles.

pose •v. (**poses, posing, posed**) **1** present a problem, danger, or question. **2** sit or stand in a particular position in order to be photographed, painted, or drawn. **3** (**pose as**) pretend to be. **4** behave in a way that is meant to impress people. •n. **1** a position adopted in order to be painted, drawn, or photographed. **2** a way of behaving that is meant to impress or mislead.
– ORIGIN Old French *poser*.

poser •n. **1** a person who behaves in a way that is meant to impress. **2** a puzzling question or problem.

poseur /poh-zer/ •n. a person who poses in order to impress; a poser.
– ORIGIN French.

posh •adj. informal **1** very elegant or luxurious. **2** esp. Brit. upper-class.
– ORIGIN perh. from former slang *posh* 'a dandy'.

posit /poz-it/ •v. (**posits, positing, posited**) put something forward as fact or as a basis for argument.
– ORIGIN Latin, 'placed'.

position •n. **1** a place where someone or something is or should be. **2** a way in which someone or something is placed or arranged: *he raised himself to a sitting position*. **3** a situation. **4** a job. **5** a person's place or importance in relation to other people: *she finished in second position*. **6** a point of view: *the party's position on abortion*. •v. put or arrange in a particular position.
– DERIVATIVES **positional** adj.
– ORIGIN Latin.

positive •adj. **1** showing the presence rather than the absence of particular features: *a positive test result*. **2** expressing agreement, confirmation, or permission. **3** hopeful, favourable, or confident. **4** with no possibility of doubt; certain. **5** (of a quantity) greater than zero. **6** relating to the kind of electric charge opposite to that carried by electrons. **7** (of a photograph) showing light and shade or colours true to the original. **8** (of an adjective or adverb) expressing the basic degree of a quality (e.g. *brave*). Contrasted with COMPARATIVE and SUPERLATIVE. •n. a positive quality.
– DERIVATIVES **positively** adv. **positivity** n.
– ORIGIN Latin *positivus*.

positive discrimination •n. Brit. the policy of providing jobs or other opportunities to people who belong to groups which suffer discrimination.

positivism •n. a system of philosophy that recognizes only things that can be scientifically or logically proved.
– DERIVATIVES **positivist** n. & adj.

positron /poz-i-tron/ •n. Physics a subatomic particle with the same mass as an electron and an equal but positive charge.

posse /poss-i/ •n. **1** N. Amer. hist. a body of men summoned by a sheriff to enforce the law. **2** informal a group of people: *a posse of students*.
– ORIGIN Latin, 'be able, power'.

possess •v. **1** have something as property; own. **2** (also **be possessed of**) have an ability or quality: *he did not possess a sense of humour*. **3** (of a demon or spirit) have complete power over someone. **4** (of an emotion, idea, etc.) dominate someone's mind.
– DERIVATIVES **possessor** n.
– ORIGIN Latin *possidere* 'occupy, hold'.

> ✓ Spell **possess** with a double **s** in the middle as well as a double **s** at the end.

possession •n. **1** the state of owning something. **2** a thing owned. **3** (in sport) temporary control of the ball by a player or team.

possessive •adj. **1** demanding someone gives you their total attention and love. **2** unwilling to share your possessions. **3** Grammar expressing possession (e.g. *theirs, John's*).
– DERIVATIVES **possessively** adv. **possessiveness** n.

possessive determiner •n. Grammar a determiner showing possession (e.g. *my*).

possessive pronoun •n. Grammar a pronoun showing possession (e.g. *mine*).

possibility •n. (pl. **possibilities**) **1** a thing that is possible. **2** the state of being possible. **3** (**possibilities**) general qualities of a promising nature: *the house had possibilities.*

possible •adj. **1** capable of existing, happening, or being done. **2** that may be so, but that is not certain: *the possible cause of the plane crash.*
– ORIGIN Latin *possibilis.*

possibly •adv. **1** perhaps. **2** in accordance with what is possible: *be as noisy as you possibly can.*

possum •n. **1** an Australasian marsupial that lives in trees. **2** N. Amer. informal an opossum.
– ORIGIN from **OPOSSUM**.

post¹ •n. **1** a long, strong, upright piece of timber or metal used as a support or a marker. **2** (**the post**) the starting post or winning post in a race. **3** an Internet posting. •v. **1** display a notice in a public place. **2** announce or publish something. **3** send a message to an Internet bulletin board or newsgroup.
– ORIGIN Latin *postis* 'doorpost'.

post² esp. Brit. •n. **1** the official service or system that delivers letters and parcels. **2** letters and parcels delivered. **3** a single collection or delivery of post. •v. send a letter or parcel via the postal system.
– PHRASES **keep someone posted** keep someone informed of the latest news.
– ORIGIN French *poste* 'station, stand'.

post³ •n. **1** a place where someone is on duty or where an activity is carried out. **2** a job. •v. **1** put a soldier, police officer, etc. in a particular place. **2** send someone to a place to take up a job.
– ORIGIN Italian *posto.*

post- •prefix after: *postgraduate.*
– ORIGIN Latin.

postage •n. **1** the sending of letters and parcels by post. **2** the charge for sending something by post.

postage stamp •n. an adhesive stamp that is stuck on a letter or parcel to show the amount of postage paid.

postal •adj. relating to or sent by post.

postal order •n. Brit. a document that can be bought from the Post Office and sent to someone who exchanges it for money.

postbox •n. a large public box into which letters are posted for collection by the Post Office.

postcard •n. a card for sending a message by post without an envelope.

postcode •n. Brit. a group of letters and

numbers added to a postal address to assist the sorting of mail.

post-coital •adj. occurring or done after sex.

post-date •v. (**post-dates**, **post-dating**, **post-dated**) **1** put a date later than the actual one on a cheque or document. **2** occur at a later date than: *Stonehenge was believed to post-date these structures.*

postdoctoral •adj. (of research) done after the completion of a doctorate.

poster •n. a large printed picture or notice used for decoration or advertisement.

poste restante /pohst ress-tuhnt/ •n. Brit. a department in a post office that keeps letters until they are collected by the person they are addressed to.
– ORIGIN French, 'mail remaining'.

posterior •adj. tech. at or nearer the rear. Opp. **ANTERIOR**. •n. humorous a person's bottom.
– ORIGIN Latin.

posterity •n. all future generations of people.
– ORIGIN Old French *posterite.*

postern /poss-tern/ •n. old use a back or side entrance.
– ORIGIN Old French *posterne.*

postgraduate •adj. relating to study done after completing a first degree. •n. a person engaged in postgraduate study.

post-haste •adv. with great speed.

posthumous /poss-tyuu-muhss/ •adj. happening or appearing after the person involved has died: *he received a posthumous pardon.*
– DERIVATIVES **posthumously** adv.
– ORIGIN Latin *postumus* 'last'.

post-Impressionism •n. a style of art of the late 19th and early 20th centuries in which emphasis was placed on the artist's emotions, as expressed by colour, line, and shape.
– DERIVATIVES **post-Impressionist** n. & adj.

post-industrial •adj. (of an economy or society) no longer relying on heavy industry.

posting¹ •n. esp. Brit. an appointment to a job abroad.

posting² •n. a message sent to an Internet bulletin board or newsgroup.

postman (or **postwoman**) •n. (pl. **postmen** or **postwomen**) Brit. a person who is employed to deliver or collect post.

postmark •n. an official mark stamped on a letter or parcel, giving the date of posting and cancelling the postage stamp. •v. stamp a letter or parcel with a postmark.

p

postmaster (or **postmistress**) • n. a person in charge of a post office.

postmodernism • n. a style and movement in the arts that features a deliberate mixing of different styles and draws attention to artistic traditions.
– DERIVATIVES **postmodern** adj. **postmodernist** n. & adj.

post-mortem • n. 1 an examination of a dead body to find out the cause of death. 2 a detailed discussion of an event made after it has occurred.
– ORIGIN Latin.

post-natal • adj. relating to the period after childbirth.

post office • n. 1 the public department or organization responsible for postal services. 2 a building where postal business is carried on.

post office box • n. a numbered box in a post office where letters are kept until called for.

postpone • v. (**postpones, postponing, postponed**) arrange for something to take place at a time later than was first planned.
– DERIVATIVES **postponement** n.
– ORIGIN Latin *postponere*.

postprandial • adj. formal relating to the period after a meal.
– ORIGIN from Latin *prandium* 'a meal'.

postscript • n. an additional remark at the end of a letter, following the signature.
– ORIGIN Latin *postscriptum* 'thing written under'.

postulant /poss-tyuu-luhnt/ • n. a candidate who wishes to enter a religious order.

postulate /poss-tyuu-layt/ • v. (**postulates, postulating, postulated**) suggest or accept that something is true, as a basis for a theory or discussion.
– DERIVATIVES **postulation** n.
– ORIGIN Latin *postulare* 'ask'.

posture • n. 1 a particular position of the body. 2 the usual way in which a person holds their body: *abdominal exercises aid good posture.* 3 an approach or attitude towards something. • v. (**postures, posturing, postured**) behave in a way that is meant to impress or mislead people.
– DERIVATIVES **postural** adj.
– ORIGIN Latin *positura*.

post-war • adj. occurring or existing after a war.

posy • n. (pl. **posies**) a small bunch of flowers.
– ORIGIN first meaning 'motto or line of verse written inside a ring': from **POESY**.

pot[1] • n. a rounded container used for storage or cooking. • v. (**pots, potting, potted**) 1 plant something in a flowerpot. 2 preserve food in a sealed pot or jar. 3 Billiards & Snooker strike a ball into a pocket. 4 informal hit or kill by shooting.
– PHRASES **go to pot** informal be ruined through neglect. **the pot calling the kettle black** used to suggest that a person is criticizing someone for faults that they have themselves.
– ORIGIN Old English.

pot[2] • n. informal cannabis.
– ORIGIN prob. from Mexican Spanish *potiguaya* 'cannabis leaves'.

potable /poh-tuh-b'l/ • adj. formal (of water) safe to drink.
– ORIGIN French.

potash • n. an alkaline compound of potassium, used in making soap and fertilizers.
– ORIGIN from *pot* + *ash*, because first obtained from a solution made from ashes that was evaporated in a pot.

potassium /puh-tass-i-uhm/ • n. a soft silvery-white reactive metallic element.
– ORIGIN from **POTASH**.

potato • n. (pl. **potatoes**) a starchy plant tuber which is cooked and eaten as a vegetable.
– ORIGIN Spanish *patata* 'sweet potato'.

> ✓ There is no **e** at the end of the singular of **potato**, although you add **-es** to make the plural.

pot belly • n. a large stomach that sticks out.

potboiler • n. informal a book produced purely to make the writer a living by appealing to popular taste.

poteen /po-teen/ • n. (in Ireland) whisky that is made illegally.
– ORIGIN from Irish *fuisce poitín* 'little pot of whisky'.

potent • adj. 1 having great power, influence, or effect: *a potent antibiotic.* 2 (of a man) able to achieve an erection or to reach an orgasm.
– DERIVATIVES **potency** n. (pl. **potencies**).
– ORIGIN Latin, 'being powerful'.

potentate • n. a ruler.
– ORIGIN Latin *potentatus* 'power'.

potential • adj. capable of becoming or developing into something: *a campaign to woo potential customers.* • n. 1 qualities or abilities that may be developed and lead to success: *a young broadcaster with great potential.* 2 (often **potential for/to do**) the possibility of something happening. 3 Physics the difference in voltage between two points in an electric field or circuit.

p

– DERIVATIVES **potentiality** n. **potentially**
adv.
– ORIGIN Latin *potentia* 'power'.

potential energy • n. Physics energy
which a body possesses as a result of its
position or state. Compare with KINETIC
ENERGY.

potentiometer /poh-ten-shi-om-i-ter/
• n. an instrument for measuring or
adjusting an electromotive force.

pothole • n. **1** a deep underground cave
formed by water eroding the rock. **2** a
hole in a road surface.
– DERIVATIVES **potholed** adj.
– ORIGIN from dialect *pot* 'pit'.

potholing • n. exploring potholes as a
sport or pastime.

potion • n. a drink with healing, magical,
or poisonous powers.
– ORIGIN Latin.

pot luck • n. a situation in which you
must take a chance that whatever is
available will be acceptable.

potpourri /poh-poor-i, poh-puh-ree/
• n. (pl. **potpourris**) **1** a mixture of dried
petals and spices placed in a bowl to
perfume a room. **2** a mixture of things.
– ORIGIN French, 'rotten pot'.

potshot • n. a shot aimed unexpectedly
or at random.

pottage • n. old use soup or stew.
– ORIGIN Old French *potage* 'that which is
put into a pot'.

potted • adj. **1** grown or preserved in a
pot. **2** put into a short, understandable
form: *a potted history of Australia.*

potter¹ • v. (**potters, pottering,
pottered**) **1** do minor pleasant tasks in a
relaxed way. **2** move or go in an
unhurried way.

potter² • n. a person who makes pottery.

potter's wheel • n. a flat revolving disc
on which wet clay is shaped into pots.

pottery • n. (pl. **potteries**) **1** articles
made of baked clay. **2** the craft of
making such articles.

potting shed • n. Brit. a shed used for
potting plants and storing garden tools
and supplies.

potty¹ • adj. (**pottier, pottiest**) Brit. informal
1 mad; crazy. **2** very enthusiastic about
someone or something.
– DERIVATIVES **pottiness** n.

potty² • n. (pl. **potties**) a bowl for a young
child to use as a toilet.

pouch • n. **1** a small flexible bag, carried
in a pocket or attached to a belt. **2** a
pocket of skin in an animal's body,
especially that in which animals such as
kangaroos carry their young.
– DERIVATIVES **pouched** adj. **pouchy** adj.
– ORIGIN Old French *poche*.

pouf • n. var. of POOF or POUFFE.

pouffe /poof/ (also **pouf**) • n. a large,
firm cushion used as a seat or stool.
– ORIGIN French.

poulterer • n. Brit. a person who sells
poultry.

poultice /pohl-tiss/ • n. a soft moist mass
traditionally of flour, bran, and herbs,
put on the skin to reduce inflammation.
– ORIGIN Latin *puls* 'pottage, pap'.

poultry /pohl-tri/ • n. chickens, turkeys,
ducks, and geese.
– ORIGIN Old French *pouletrie*.

pounce • v. (**pounces, pouncing,
pounced**) **1** move suddenly so as to seize
or attack. **2** (**pounce on**) take swift
advantage of someone's mistake. • n. an
act of pouncing.

pound¹ • n. **1** a unit of weight equal to
16 oz avoirdupois (0.4536 kg), or 12 oz
troy (0.3732 kg). **2** (also **pound sterling**)
(pl. **pounds sterling**) the basic unit of
money of the UK, equal to 100 pence.
– ORIGIN from Latin *libra pondo*.

pound² • v. **1** hit heavily again and again.
2 walk or run with heavy steps. **3** throb
with a strong regular rhythm. **4** crush or
grind something into a powder or paste.
– ORIGIN Old English.

pound³ • n. a place where stray dogs or
illegally parked vehicles may officially
be taken and kept until claimed.

poundage • n. Brit. **1** a charge made for
every pound in weight of something, or
for every pound sterling in value.
2 weight.

-pounder • comb. form **1** a person or thing
weighing a specified number of pounds:
the shark was a 184-pounder. **2** a gun
designed to fire a shell weighing a
specified number of pounds.

pour • v. **1** flow or cause to flow in a
steady stream. **2** (of rain) fall heavily.
3 prepare and serve a drink. **4** come or
go in large numbers: *letters poured in.*
5 (**pour something out**) express your
feelings freely.
– DERIVATIVES **pourer** n.

> **USAGE:** On the confusion of **pour** with
> **pore**, see the note at PORE².

pout • v. push the lips forward as a sign
of sulking or to look sexually attractive.
• n. a pouting expression.
– DERIVATIVES **pouty** adj.
– ORIGIN perh. from Swedish dialect *puta*
'be inflated'.

poverty • n. **1** the state of being very
poor. **2** the state of being lacking in
quality or amount: *the poverty of her
imagination.*
– ORIGIN Old French *poverte*.

poverty trap • n. Brit. a situation in
which an increase in someone's income

p

results in a loss of state benefits, leaving them no better off.

POW •abbrev. prisoner of war.

powder •n. 1 a mass of fine dry particles. 2 a cosmetic in this form for the face. •v. (**powders, powdering, powdered**) 1 sprinkle or cover a surface or the face with powder. 2 make something into a powder.
– DERIVATIVES **powdery** adj.
– ORIGIN Old French *poudre*.

powder blue •n. a soft, pale blue.

powder keg •n. a situation which is likely suddenly to become dangerous or violent.
– ORIGIN from *powder* in the sense 'gunpowder'.

powder puff •n. a soft pad for putting powder on the face.

powder room •n. euphem. a women's toilet in a public building.

power •n. 1 the ability to do something: *the power of speech.* 2 the ability to influence people or events. 3 the right or authority to do something. 4 political authority or control. 5 a country seen as having international influence and military strength: *a world power.* 6 strength, force, or energy. 7 capacity or performance of an engine or other device. 8 energy that is produced by mechanical, electrical, or other means. 9 Physics the rate of doing work, measured in watts or horse power. 10 Math. the product obtained when a number is multiplied by itself a certain number of times. •v. (**powers, powering, powered**) 1 supply something with mechanical or electrical power. 2 move with speed or force.
– PHRASES **power of attorney** the authority to act for another person in particular legal or financial matters. **the powers that be** the people in authority.
– ORIGIN Old French *poeir*.

powerboat •n. a fast motor boat.
– DERIVATIVES **powerboating** n.

power cut •n. a temporary interruption in an electricity supply.

powerful •adj. 1 having great power. 2 having a strong effect.
– DERIVATIVES **powerfully** adv.

powerhouse •n. a person or thing having great energy or power.

powerless •adj. without the power to take action.

power plant •n. a power station.

power station •n. a building where electrical power is generated.

power steering •n. steering aided by power from the vehicle's engine.

powwow •n. 1 informal a meeting for

discussion. 2 a North American Indian ceremony involving feasting and dancing.
– ORIGIN from a word in a North American Indian language meaning 'magician'.

pox •n. 1 any disease caused by a virus and producing a rash of pus-filled pimples that leave pockmarks on healing. 2 (**the pox**) informal syphilis.
– ORIGIN from *pocks*, plural of POCK.

poxy •adj. Brit. informal of poor quality.

pp •abbrev. 1 (**pp.**) pages. 2 (also **p.p.**) per procurationem (used when signing a letter on someone else's behalf). [ORIGIN Latin, 'through the agency of'.]

PPE •abbrev. philosophy, politics, and economics.

ppm •abbrev. part(s) per million.

PPS •abbrev. 1 post (additional) postscript. 2 Brit. Parliamentary Private Secretary.

PPV •abbrev. pay-per-view.

PR •abbrev. 1 proportional representation. 2 public relations.

Pr •symb. the chemical element praseodymium.

practicable •adj. able to be done successfully.
– DERIVATIVES **practicability** n.

practical •adj. 1 relating to the actual doing or use of something rather than theory: *the candidate should have practical experience of agriculture.* 2 likely to be successful or useful: *practical solutions to common transport problems.* 3 skilled at making or doing things. 4 almost complete; virtual: *it was a practical certainty.* •n. Brit. an exam or lesson in which students have to do or make things.
– DERIVATIVES **practically** adv.
– ORIGIN Greek *praktikos* 'concerned with action'.

practicality •n. (pl. **practicalities**) 1 the state of being practical. 2 (**practicalities**) the real facts or aspects of a situation rather than theories.

practical joke •n. a trick played on someone to make them look silly.

practice •n. 1 the action of doing something rather than the theories about it: *putting policy into practice.* 2 the usual way of doing something. 3 the work, business, or place of work of a doctor, dentist, or lawyer. 4 the doing of something repeatedly to improve your skill: *maths improves with practice.* •v. US = PRACTISE.
– ORIGIN from PRACTISE.

practise (US **practice**) •v. (**practises, practising, practised**; US **practices,**

practicing, practiced) 1 do something repeatedly so as to become skilful. **2** do something regularly as part of your normal behaviour: *irrigation has been practised there for many years.* **3** be working in a particular profession. **4** (as adj. **practised**) expert as a result of much experience. **5** follow the teaching and rules of a particular religion.
– ORIGIN Latin *practicare*.

> **USAGE: Practice** is the correct spelling for the noun in both British and American English: *putting policy into practice.* **Practice** is also the spelling for the verb in American English, but in British English, the verb should be spelled **practise**: *I need to practise my French.*

practitioner • n. a person who practises a particular profession or activity.

pragmatic • adj. dealing with things in a sensible and realistic way.
– DERIVATIVES **pragmatically** adv.
– ORIGIN Greek *pragmatikos* 'relating to fact'.

pragmatism • n. a realistic and sensible attitude or approach to something.
– DERIVATIVES **pragmatist** n.

prairie • n. (in North America) a large open area of grassland.
– ORIGIN French.

prairie dog • n. a type of rodent that lives in burrows in the grasslands of North America.

praise • v. (**praises, praising, praised**) **1** express approval of or admiration for. **2** express thanks to or respect for God or a god. • n. the expression of approval or admiration: *the audience was full of praise for the production.*
– ORIGIN Old French *preisier*.

praiseworthy • adj. deserving praise.
– DERIVATIVES **praiseworthiness** n.

praline /prah-leen, pray-leen/ • n. a smooth substance made from nuts boiled in sugar, used as a filling for chocolates.
– ORIGIN named after Marshal de Plessis-Praslin, the French soldier whose cook invented it.

pram • n. Brit. a four-wheeled vehicle for a baby, pushed by a person on foot.
– ORIGIN from **PERAMBULATOR**.

prance • v. (**prances, prancing, pranced**) **1** walk with exaggerated movements. **2** (of a horse) move with high steps.

prang • v. Brit. informal crash a vehicle.

prank • n. a practical joke or mischievous act.

prankster • n. a person who is fond of playing pranks.

praseodymium /pray-zi-oh-di-mi-uhm/ • n. a silvery-white metallic element.
– ORIGIN German *Praseodym*.

prat • n. Brit. informal a stupid person.

prate • v. (**prates, prating, prated**) talk too much in a silly or boring way.
– ORIGIN Dutch or German *praten*.

pratfall • n. informal a fall on to your bottom.

prattle • v. (**prattles, prattling, prattled**) talk too much in a silly or trivial way. • n. silly or trivial talk.
– ORIGIN German *pratelen*.

prawn • n. an edible shellfish like a large shrimp.

praxis /prak-siss/ • n. practice as opposed to theory.
– ORIGIN Greek, 'doing'.

pray • v. **1** say a prayer. **2** wish or hope strongly for something: *after days of rain, we were praying for sun.* • adv. formal or old use please: *pray continue.*
– ORIGIN Old French *preier*.

prayer • n. **1** a request for help or expression of thanks made to God or a god. **2** (**prayers**) a religious service at which people gather to pray together. **3** an earnest hope or wish.

prayerful • adj. **1** characterized by the use of prayer. **2** liking to pray; devout.

praying mantis • n. see **MANTIS**.

pre- • prefix before: *prearrange.*
– ORIGIN Latin *prae-*.

preach • v. **1** give a religious talk to a group of people. **2** recommend a course of action to someone: *my parents have always preached moderation.* **3** (**preach at**) give moral advice to someone in an annoying or boring way.
– DERIVATIVES **preacher** n.
– ORIGIN Old French *prechier*.

preachy • adj. giving moral advice in a boring or overbearing way.

preamble /pree-am-b'l, pree-am-b'l/ • n. an introduction; an opening statement.
– ORIGIN Latin *praeambulus* 'going before'.

prearrange • v. (**prearranges, prearranging, prearranged**) arrange something beforehand.

prebendary /pre-buhn-duh-ri/ • n. (pl. **prebendaries**) (in the Christian Church) an honorary canon.
– ORIGIN Latin *praebenda* 'pension'.

Precambrian /pree-kam-bri-uhn/ • adj. Geol. relating to the earliest period of the earth's history, ending about 570 million years ago, a time when living organisms first appeared.

precarious • adj. **1** likely to fall or to

p

cause someone to fall: *a precarious pile of books.* **2** uncertain.
– DERIVATIVES **precariously** adv.
– ORIGIN Latin *precarius* 'obtained by begging'.

precast • adj. (of concrete) made into a form that is ready for use in building.

precaution • n. **1** something done in advance to avoid problems or danger. **2** (**precautions**) informal contraception.
– DERIVATIVES **precautionary** adj.
– ORIGIN Latin.

precede • v. (**precedes**, **preceding**, **preceded**) **1** happen before something else in time or order: *a gun battle had preceded the explosions.* **2** go in front of someone.
– ORIGIN Latin *praecedere*.

precedence /press-i-duhnss, pree-si-duhnss/ • n. the state of coming before other people or things in order or importance: *his desire for power took precedence over everything else.*

precedent /press-i-d'nt/ • n. an earlier event, action, or legal case that is taken as an example to be followed in a similar situation.

precentor /pri-sen-ter/ • n. a person who leads the singing or prayers in a religious service.
– ORIGIN Latin *praecinere* 'sing before'.

precept /pree-sept/ • n. a general rule about how to behave or what to think.
– ORIGIN Latin *praeceptum* 'something advised'.

precession • n. **1** the slow movement of the axis of a spinning body around another axis. **2** Astron. the earlier occurrence of equinoxes each year.
– ORIGIN Latin *praecedere* 'go before'.

precinct /pree-singkt/ • n. **1** Brit. an area in a town that is closed to traffic. **2** the area around a place or building, often enclosed by a wall. **3** N. Amer. one of the districts into which a city or town is divided for elections or policing purposes.
– ORIGIN Latin *praecinctum*.

precious • adj. **1** having great value. **2** greatly loved or valued. **3** sophisticated in a way that is artificial and exaggerated.
– PHRASES **precious little** (or **few**) informal very little (or few).
– DERIVATIVES **preciousness** n.
– ORIGIN Latin *pretiosus*.

precious metal • n. a valuable metal such as gold, silver, or platinum.

precious stone • n. a very attractive and valuable piece of mineral, used in jewellery.

precipice • n. a tall and very steep rock face or cliff.

– ORIGIN Latin *praecipitium* 'abrupt descent'.

precipitate • v. /pri-sip-i-tayt/ (**precipitates**, **precipitating**, **precipitated**) **1** make something unpleasant happen suddenly or too soon. **2** cause to move suddenly and with force. **3** Chem. cause a substance to be deposited in solid form from a solution. **4** cause moisture in the atmosphere to condense and fall as rain, sleet, or hail. • adj. /pri-sip-i-tuht/ done or occurring suddenly or without careful thought. • n. /pri-sip-i-tayt, pri-sip-i-tuht/ Chem. a substance precipitated from a solution.
– DERIVATIVES **precipitately** adv. **precipitator** n.
– ORIGIN Latin *praecipitare* 'throw headlong'.

precipitation • n. **1** rain, snow, sleet, or hail. **2** Chem. the action of precipitating a substance from a solution.

precipitous /pri-sip-i-tuhss/ • adj. **1** dangerously high or steep. **2** sudden and considerable: *a precipitous decline in exports.*

precis /pray-si/ (also **précis**) • n. (pl. **precis** /pray-si, pray-seez/) a summary. • v. (**precises** /pray-seez/, **precising** /pray-see-ing/, **precised** /pray-seed/) make a summary of a piece of writing or a discussion.
– ORIGIN French, 'precise'.

precise • adj. **1** expressed very clearly and with sharp detail: *precise directions.* **2** careful about details and accuracy. **3** particular: *at that precise moment the car stopped.*
– DERIVATIVES **precisely** adv.
– ORIGIN Old French *precis.*

precision • n. the state of being precise. • adj. very accurate: *a precision instrument.*

preclude • v. (**precludes**, **precluding**, **precluded**) prevent something from happening or someone from doing something.
– ORIGIN Latin *praecludere* 'shut off'.

precocious /pri-koh-shuhss/ • adj. (of a child) having developed certain abilities or tendencies at an earlier age than usual.
– ORIGIN Latin *praecoquere* 'ripen fully'.

precocity /pri-koss-i-ti/ • n. the state of being precocious.

precognition /pree-kog-ni-sh'n/ • n. knowledge of an event before it happens.

preconceived • adj. (of an idea or opinion) formed before full knowledge or evidence is available.

preconception • n. a preconceived idea or opinion.

precondition • n. something that must exist or happen before other things can happen or be done.

precursor • n. a person or thing that comes before another of the same kind.
– ORIGIN Latin *praecursor*.

pre-date • v. (**pre-dates, pre-dating, pre-dated**) exist or occur at a date earlier than.

predation /pri-**day**-sh'n/ • n. the preying of one animal on others.
– ORIGIN Latin.

predator /**pred**-uh-ter/ • n. **1** an animal that hunts and kills other animals for food. **2** a person who takes advantage of other people.
– ORIGIN Latin *praedator* 'plunderer'.

predatory • adj. **1** (of an animal) killing other animals for food. **2** taking advantage of other people.

predecease • v. (**predeceases, predeceasing, predeceased**) formal die before another person.

predecessor • n. **1** a person who held a job or office before the current holder. **2** a thing that has been followed or replaced by another: *the chapel was built on the site of its predecessor*.
– ORIGIN Latin *praedecessor*.

predestination • n. the Christian belief that everything has been decided or planned in advance by God.

predestine • v. (**predestines, predestining, predestined**) (usu. as adj. **predestined**) (of God or fate) decide in advance that something will happen or that someone will have a particular fate.

predetermine • v. (**predetermines, predetermining, predetermined**) establish or decide something in advance.

predeterminer • n. Grammar a word or phrase that occurs before a determiner, e.g. *both*.

predicament /pri-**dik**-uh-m'nt/ • n. a difficult situation.
– ORIGIN Latin *praedicamentum* 'something declared'.

predicate • n. /**pred**-i-kuht/ Grammar the part of a sentence or clause containing a verb and stating something about the subject (e.g. *went home* in *John went home*). • v. /**pred**-i-kayt/ (**predicates, predicating, predicated**) (**predicate something on**) base something on.
– ORIGIN Latin *praedicare* 'declare'.

predicative /pri-**dik**-uh-tiv/ • adj. Grammar (of an adjective or noun) forming part or the whole of the predicate, as *old* in *the dog is old* (but not in *the old dog*).

predict • v. state that an event will happen in the future.
– DERIVATIVES **predictive** adj. **predictor** n.
– ORIGIN Latin *praedicere*.

predictable • adj. **1** able to be predicted. **2** always behaving or occurring in the way expected and therefore boring.
– DERIVATIVES **predictability** n. **predictably** adv.

prediction • n. **1** a thing predicted; a forecast. **2** the action of predicting.

predilection /pree-di-**lek**-sh'n/ • n. a preference or special liking for something.
– ORIGIN Latin *praediligere* 'prefer'.

predispose • v. (**predisposes, predisposing, predisposed**) make someone likely to be, do, or think something: *certain people are predisposed to become drug abusers*.
– DERIVATIVES **predisposition** n.

predominant • adj. **1** present as the main element: *the bird's predominant colour was white.* **2** having the greatest control or power.
– DERIVATIVES **predominance** n. **predominantly** adv.

predominate • v. (**predominates, predominating, predominated**) **1** be the main part of something. **2** have control or power.

pre-eminent • adj. better than all others; outstanding.
– DERIVATIVES **pre-eminence** n.

pre-empt • v. **1** take action so as to prevent something happening. **2** prevent someone from saying something by speaking first.
– DERIVATIVES **pre-emption** n.
– ORIGIN Latin *praeemere* 'buy in advance'.

pre-emptive • adj. done to prevent someone else from doing something: *a pre-emptive attack.*

preen • v. **1** (of a bird) tidy and clean its feathers with its beak. **2** make yourself look attractive. **3** (**preen yourself**) feel very pleased with yourself.
– ORIGIN prob. from Latin *ungere* 'anoint'.

pre-existing • adj. existing from an earlier time.

prefab • n. informal a prefabricated building.

prefabricated • adj. (of a building) made in sections that can be easily put together on site.

preface /**pref**-uhss/ • n. an introduction to a book, stating its subject or aims. • v. (**prefaces, prefacing, prefaced**) (**preface something with/by**) say or do something to introduce a book, speech, or event.

– DERIVATIVES **prefatory** /pref-uh-tuh-ri/ adj.
– ORIGIN Old French.

prefect • n. **1** Brit. a senior pupil who is appointed to help with discipline in a school. **2** a chief officer, magistrate, or regional governor in certain countries.
– ORIGIN Latin *praeficere* 'put in authority over'.

prefecture • n. (in certain countries) a district under the government of a prefect or governor.

prefer • v. (**prefers**, **preferring**, **preferred**) **1** like someone or something better than another or others. **2** put forward a formal accusation for consideration by a court of law.
– ORIGIN Latin *praeferre* 'carry before'.

preferable • adj. more desirable or suitable.
– DERIVATIVES **preferably** adv.

preference • n. **1** a greater liking for one alternative over another or others. **2** a thing preferred. **3** favour shown to one person over another person or other people: *preference is given to those who make a donation.*

preferential • adj. favouring a particular person or group: *minority businesses were given preferential treatment.*
– DERIVATIVES **preferentially** adv.

preferment • n. formal promotion to a job or position.

prefigure • v. (**prefigures**, **prefiguring**, **prefigured**) be an early sign or version of something: *the violence of this passage prefigures her mature writing.*

prefix • n. **1** a word, letter, or number placed before another. **2** a letter or group of letters placed at the beginning of a word to alter its meaning (e.g. *non-*). • v. **1** add something as a prefix. **2** add a prefix to.

pregnancy • n. (pl. **pregnancies**) the state or period of having a child or young developing in the womb.

pregnant • adj. **1** (of a woman or female animal) having a child or young developing in the womb. **2** full of meaning: *a pregnant pause.*
– ORIGIN Latin *praegnans.*

prehensile /pri-hen-syl/ • adj. (of an animal's limb or tail) capable of grasping things.
– ORIGIN Latin *prehendere* 'to grasp'.

prehistoric • adj. relating to the period before written records.

prehistory • n. **1** the period of time before written records. **2** the early stages of the development of something: *the prehistory of capitalism.*

pre-industrial • adj. before the development of industries on a wide scale.

prejudge • v. (**prejudges**, **prejudging**, **prejudged**) make a judgement about someone or something before having all the necessary information.

prejudice • n. **1** an opinion that is not based on reason or experience: *English prejudice against foreigners.* **2** dislike or unfair behaviour based on such opinions. • v. (**prejudices**, **prejudicing**, **prejudiced**) **1** give rise to prejudice in someone. **2** cause harm to: *delay is likely to prejudice the child's welfare.*
– ORIGIN Latin *praejudicium.*

> ✓ Remember that **prejudice** begins with prej-.

prejudicial • adj. harmful to someone or something.

prelate /prel-uht/ • n. a bishop or other high-ranking Christian priest.
– ORIGIN Latin *praelatus* 'civil dignitary'.

preliminary • adj. happening before or preparing for a main action or event: *preliminary talks.* • n. (pl. **preliminaries**) a preliminary action or event.
– ORIGIN from Latin *prae* 'before' + *limen* 'threshold'.

prelude • n. **1** an action or event acting as an introduction to something more important. **2** a piece of music acting as an introduction to a longer piece.
– ORIGIN Latin *praeludere* 'play beforehand'.

premarital • adj. occurring before marriage.

premature • adj. **1** occurring or done before the proper time: *the sun can cause premature ageing.* **2** (of a baby) born before the normal length of pregnancy is completed.
– DERIVATIVES **prematurely** adv.
– ORIGIN Latin *praematurus* 'very early'.

premeditated • adj. (of an action, especially a crime) planned in advance.
– DERIVATIVES **premeditation** n.

premenstrual • adj. occurring or experienced before menstruation.

premenstrual syndrome • n. a range of symptoms (including emotional tension) experienced by some women before menstruation.

premier • adj. first in importance, order, or position. • n. a Prime Minister or other head of government.
– ORIGIN Old French.

premiere /prem-i-air/ • n. the first performance or showing of a play, film, ballet, or opera. • v. (**premieres**, **premiering**, **premiered**) present the premiere of a play, film, ballet, or opera.

– ORIGIN French *première*.

premiership • n. **1** the office or position of a Prime Minister or other head of government. **2** (**the Premiership**) the top division of professional football in England.

premise /prem-iss/ (Brit. also **premiss**) • n. a statement or idea that forms the basis for a theory, argument, or line of reasoning.

– ORIGIN Old French *premisse*.

premises • pl. n. the building and land occupied by a business.

premium • n. (pl. **premiums**) **1** an amount paid for an insurance policy. **2** an extra sum added to a basic price or other payment. • adj. (of a product) of high quality and more expensive.

– PHRASES **at a premium 1** scarce and in demand. **2** above the usual price.

– ORIGIN Latin *praemium* 'reward'.

Premium Bond • n. (in the UK) a government certificate that pays no interest but is entered in regular draws for cash prizes.

premolar • n. a tooth between the canines and molar teeth.

premonition /prem-uh-ni-sh'n, pree-muh-ni-sh'n/ • n. a strong feeling that something is about to happen.

– DERIVATIVES **premonitory** adj.

– ORIGIN Latin *praemonere* 'forewarn'.

prenatal • adj. N. Amer. before birth.

preoccupation • n. **1** the state of being preoccupied. **2** a matter that fills someone's mind completely.

preoccupy • v. (**preoccupies**, **preoccupying**, **preoccupied**) fill the mind of someone completely: *she was preoccupied with paying the bills.*

preordained • adj. decided or determined beforehand.

prep • n. Brit. informal (especially in a private school) school work done outside lessons.

– ORIGIN from PREPARATION.

prepaid past and past part. of PREPAY.

preparation • n. **1** the action of preparing. **2** something done to prepare for something. **3** a substance that has been prepared for use as a medicine, food, or cosmetic.

preparatory • adj. done in order to prepare for something.

preparatory school • n. **1** Brit. a private school for pupils aged seven to thirteen. **2** N. Amer. a private school that prepares pupils for college or university.

prepare • v. (**prepares**, **preparing**, **prepared**) **1** make something ready for use. **2** make or get ready to do or deal with something: *she took time off to*

prepare for her exams. **3** (**be prepared to do**) be willing to do.

– ORIGIN Latin *praeparare*.

preparedness • n. readiness.

prepay • v. (**prepays**, **prepaying**, **prepaid**) pay for something in advance.

– DERIVATIVES **prepayment** n.

preponderance • n. the state of being greater in number: *the preponderance of women among older people.*

preponderant • adj. greater in number or importance.

– DERIVATIVES **preponderantly** adv.

preponderate • v. (**preponderates**, **preponderating**, **preponderated**) be greater in number or importance.

– ORIGIN Latin *praeponderare* 'weigh more'.

preposition /prep-uh-zi-sh'n/ • n. Grammar a word used with a noun or pronoun to show place, position, time, or method.

– DERIVATIVES **prepositional** adj.

> **USAGE:** A preposition (a word such as *from, to, on, after,* etc.) usually comes before a noun or pronoun and gives information about how, when, or where something has happened (*she arrived after dinner*). Some people believe that a preposition should never come at the end of a sentence, as in *where do you come from?*, and that you should say *from where do you come?* instead. However, this can result in English that sounds very awkward and unnatural, and is not a rule that has to be followed as long as the meaning of what you are saying is clear.
>
> A preposition such as **between** should be followed by an object pronoun such as **me**, **him**, or **us** rather than a subject pronoun such as **I**, **he**, and **we**. It is therefore correct to say *between you and me* and wrong to say *between you and I.*

prepossessing • adj. attractive or appealing in appearance.

preposterous • adj. completely ridiculous or outrageous.

– DERIVATIVES **preposterously** adv.

– ORIGIN Latin *praeposterus* 'reversed, absurd'.

prep school • n. a preparatory school.

prepubescent • adj. relating to the period before puberty.

prepuce /pree-pyooss/ • n. Anat. = FORESKIN.

– ORIGIN French *prépuce*.

prequel • n. a story or film about events which happen before those of an existing work.

– ORIGIN from PRE- + SEQUEL.

Pre-Raphaelite /pree-raf-uh-lyt/ • n. a member of a group of English 19th-century artists who painted in the style of Italian artists from before the time of Raphael. • adj. relating to or typical of the Pre-Raphaelites.

prerequisite /pree-rek-wi-zit/ • n. a thing that must exist or happen before something else can exist or happen: *our solar system is a prerequisite for our existence.* • adj. required before something else can exist or happen.

prerogative /pri-rog-uh-tiv/ • n. a right or privilege belonging to a particular person or group: *owning a car used to be the prerogative of the rich.*
– ORIGIN Latin *praerogativa* 'verdict of the people voting first in the assembly'.

presage /press-ij/ • v. /also pri-sayj/ (**presages, presaging, presaged**) be a sign or warning of: *the clouds above the moor presaged rain.* • n. an omen.
– ORIGIN Latin *praesagire* 'forebode'.

Presbyterian /prez-bi-teer-i-uhn/ • adj. relating to a Protestant Church governed by elders who are all of equal rank. • n. a member of a Presbyterian Church.
– DERIVATIVES **Presbyterianism** n.
– ORIGIN Greek *presbuteros* 'elder'.

presbytery /prez-bi-tuh-ri/ • n. (pl. **presbyteries**) 1 an administrative body in a Presbyterian Church. 2 the house of a Roman Catholic parish priest. 3 the eastern part of a church near the altar.

prescient /press-i-uhnt/ • adj. having knowledge of events before they happen.
– DERIVATIVES **prescience** n.
– ORIGIN Latin *praescire* 'know before-hand'.

prescribe • v. (**prescribes, prescribing, prescribed**) 1 recommend and permit the use of a medicine or treatment. 2 recommend with authority that something should be done.
– ORIGIN Latin *praescribere* 'direct in writing'.

> **USAGE:** Do not confuse **prescribe** and **proscribe**. **Prescribe** means either 'recommend the use of a medicine'(*the doctor prescribed antibiotics*) or 'recommend with authority'. **Proscribe** means 'condemn or forbid' (*gambling was strictly proscribed by the authorities*).

prescription • n. 1 a doctor's written instruction stating that a patient may be issued with a medicine or treatment. 2 the action of prescribing a medicine or treatment. 3 an authoritative recommendation.

prescriptive • adj. stating what should be done; prescribing.

presence • n. 1 the state of being present: *my presence in the flat made her happy.* 2 a person's impressive manner or appearance. 3 a person or thing that seems to be present but is not seen. 4 a group of soldiers or police stationed in a particular place: *the USA would maintain a presence in the region.*
– PHRASES **presence of mind** the ability to remain calm and take quick, sensible action in a difficult situation.

present¹ /pre-z'nt/ • adj. 1 being or occurring in a particular place. 2 existing or occurring now. 3 Grammar (of a tense) expressing an action or state now happening or existing. • n. (**the present**) the period of time now occurring.
– PHRASES **at present** now. **for the present** for now; temporarily.
– ORIGIN Latin *praesens* 'being at hand'.

present² • v. /pri-zent/ 1 give something or introduce someone formally at a ceremony. 2 offer something for consideration or payment. 3 formally introduce someone to someone else. 4 put a show or exhibition before the public. 5 introduce and appear in a television or radio show. 6 be the cause of a problem. 7 give a particular impression to other people: *the EC presented a united front over the crisis.* 8 (**present yourself**) appear at or attend a formal occasion. • n. /pre-z'nt/ a thing given to someone as a gift.
– ORIGIN Latin *praesentare* 'place before'.

presentable • adj. looking clean or smart enough to be seen in public.

presentation • n. the action of presenting something or the way in which it is presented.
– DERIVATIVES **presentational** adj.

presenter • n. Brit. a person who presents a television or radio programme.

presentiment /pri-zen-ti-muhnt/ • n. a feeling that something unpleasant is going to happen.
– ORIGIN from former French *présentiment.*

presently • adv. 1 soon. 2 now.

present participle • n. Grammar the form of a verb, ending in *-ing*, which is used in forming tenses describing continuous action (e.g. *I'm thinking*), as a noun (e.g. *good thinking*), and as an adjective (e.g. *running water*).

preservation • n. the action of keeping something in its original or existing state.

preservative • n. a substance used to prevent food or wood from decaying.

preserve • v. (**preserves, preserving, preserved**) 1 keep something in its original or existing state: *all records of the past were carefully preserved.* 2 keep

something safe from harm. **3** treat food to prevent it from decaying. •n. **1** a type of jam made with fruit boiled with sugar. **2** something seen as reserved for a particular person or group: *jobs that used to be the preserve of men.* **3** esp. N. Amer. a place where game is protected and kept for private hunting.
– DERIVATIVES **preserver** n.
– ORIGIN Latin *praeservare.*

preset •v. (**presets, presetting, preset**) set the controls of an electrical device before using it.

preside •v. (**presides, presiding, presided**) **1** be in charge of a meeting, court, etc. **2** (**preside over**) be in charge of a situation.
– ORIGIN Latin *praesidere.*

presidency •n. (pl. **presidencies**) the job of president or the period of time this is held.

president •n. **1** the elected head of a republic. **2** the head of an organization.
– DERIVATIVES **presidential** adj.

press[1] •v. **1** move into contact with something by using steady force: *the dog pressed against her leg.* **2** push something to operate a device. **3** apply pressure to something to flatten or shape it. **4** move in a particular direction by pushing. **5** (**press on/ahead**) continue in your action. **6** forcefully put forward an opinion or claim. **7** make strong efforts to persuade someone to do something. **8** (of time) be short. **9** (**be pressed for**) have too little of: *I'm really pressed for time.* •n. **1** a device for crushing, flattening, or shaping something. **2** a printing press. **3** (**the press**) newspapers or journalists as a whole. **4** a closely packed mass of people or things.
– ORIGIN Latin *pressare* 'keep pressing'.

press[2] •v. hist. force someone to serve in the army or navy.
– ORIGIN Latin *praestare* 'provide'.

press conference •n. a meeting with journalists in order to make an announcement or answer questions.

press gang •n. hist. a body of men employed to force men to serve in the army or navy. •v. (**press-gang**) force someone into doing something.

pressing •adj. **1** needing urgent action. **2** strongly expressed. •n. an object made by moulding under pressure.

press release •n. an official statement issued to journalists.

press stud •n. Brit. a small fastener with two parts that fit together when pressed.

press-up •n. Brit. an exercise in which a person lies facing the floor and raises

their body by pressing down on their hands.

pressure •n. **1** the steady force brought to bear on an object by something in contact with it. **2** the use of persuasion or threats to make someone do something. **3** a feeling of stress caused by the need to do something: *pressure of work.* **4** the force per unit area applied by a fluid against a surface. •v. (**pressures, pressuring, pressured**) persuade or force someone into doing something.
– ORIGIN Latin *pressura.*

pressure cooker •n. an airtight pot in which food can be cooked quickly under steam pressure.

pressure group •n. a group that tries to influence government policy or public opinion to help a particular cause.

pressurize (or **pressurise**)
•v. (**pressurizes, pressurizing, pressurized**) **1** persuade or force someone into doing something. **2** keep the air pressure in an aircraft cabin the same as it is at ground level.

prestidigitation /press-ti-di-ji-tay-sh'n/ •n. formal magic tricks performed as entertainment.
– ORIGIN French.

prestige /pre-steezh/ •n. respect and admiration resulting from achievements or high quality: *her prestige in Europe was tremendous.*
– ORIGIN French, 'illusion, glamour'.

prestigious /press-ti-juhss/ •adj. having or bringing respect and admiration.

presto •adv. & adj. Music in a quick tempo.
– ORIGIN Italian.

prestressed •adj. (of concrete) strengthened by means of rods or wires inserted under tension before setting.

presumably •adv. as may be supposed; probably.

presume •v. (**presumes, presuming, presumed**) **1** suppose that something is probably true. **2** be bold enough to do something that you should not do: *don't presume to give me orders in my own house.* **3** (**presume on**) take advantage of someone's kindness or friendship.
– ORIGIN Latin *praesumere* 'anticipate'.

presumption •n. **1** an act of presuming something to be true. **2** an idea that is presumed to be true. **3** arrogant or disrespectful behaviour.

presumptuous •adj. behaving with disrespectful boldness.
– DERIVATIVES **presumptuously** adv. **presumptuousness** n.

presuppose •v. (**presupposes, presupposing, presupposed**) **1** depend

on something in order to exist or be true. **2** assume something to be the case.
– DERIVATIVES **presupposition** n.

pretence (US **pretense**) • n. **1** an act or the action of pretending. **2** a claim to have or be something: *he disclaimed any pretence to superiority.*

pretend • v. **1** make it seem that something is the case when in fact it is not. **2** give the appearance of feeling an emotion or having a quality. **3** (**pretend to**) claim to have a particular quality or title.
– ORIGIN Latin *praetendere* 'stretch forth, claim'.

pretender • n. a person who claims a right to a title or position.

pretension • n. **1** (also **pretensions**) a claim to have or be something: *a pub with no pretensions to be a restaurant.* **2** an attempt to impress other people by pretending to be more important or better than you actually are.

pretentious • adj. trying to impress other people by pretending to be more important or better than you actually are.

preternatural /pree-ter-**nach**-uh-ruhl/ • adj. beyond what is normal or natural.
– DERIVATIVES **preternaturally** adv.
– ORIGIN Latin *praeter* 'beyond'.

pretext • n. a false reason used to justify an action.
– ORIGIN Latin *praetextus* 'outward display'.

prettify • v. (**prettifies, prettifying, prettified**) make something look pretty.

pretty • adj. (**prettier, prettiest**) having an attractive or pleasant appearance. • adv. informal to a certain extent; fairly.
– PHRASES **a pretty penny** informal a large sum of money.
– DERIVATIVES **prettily** adv. **prettiness** n.
– ORIGIN Old English, 'cunning, crafty'.

pretzel /**pret**-z'l/ • n. a crisp biscuit in the shape of a knot or stick and flavoured with salt.
– ORIGIN German.

prevail • v. **1** be more powerful than: *it is hard for logic to prevail over emotion.* **2** (**prevail on**) persuade someone to do something. **3** be widespread or current.
– ORIGIN Latin *praevalere*.

prevailing wind • n. a wind from the direction that is most usual at a particular place or time.

prevalent /**prev**-uh-luhnt/ • adj. widespread in a particular area.
– DERIVATIVES **prevalence** n.
– ORIGIN Latin *praevalere* 'prevail'.

prevaricate /pri-**va**-ri-kayt/ • v. (**prevaricates, prevaricating,**

prevaricated) avoid giving a direct answer to a question.
– DERIVATIVES **prevarication** n.
– ORIGIN Latin *praevaricari* 'walk crookedly'.

prevent • v. **1** stop something from happening. **2** stop someone from doing something.
– DERIVATIVES **preventable** adj. **preventer** n. **prevention** n.
– ORIGIN Latin *praevenire* 'precede'.

preventive (also **preventative**) • adj. designed to prevent something from occurring.

preview • n. **1** a viewing or showing of something before it becomes generally available. **2** a review of a forthcoming film, book, or play. • v. give or have a preview of.
– DERIVATIVES **previewer** n.

previous • adj. **1** coming before in time or order: *the events of the previous day.* **2** (**previous to**) before.
– DERIVATIVES **previously** adv.
– ORIGIN Latin *praevius*.

pre-war • adj. occurring or existing before a war.

prey • n. **1** an animal hunted and killed by another animal for food. **2** a person likely to be harmed or deceived by someone or something: *she fell prey to Will's charms.* • v. (**prey on**) **1** hunt and kill an animal for food. **2** take advantage of or cause distress to someone.
– ORIGIN Old French *preie*.

priapic /pry-**ap**-ik/ • adj. relating to men's sexuality.
– ORIGIN Greek *Priapos*, a god of fertility.

price • n. **1** the amount of money for which something is bought or sold. **2** something unwelcome that must be done or given in order to achieve something: *the price of their success was a day spent in discussion.* **3** the odds in betting. • v. (**prices, pricing, priced**) decide the price of something.
– PHRASES **at any price** no matter what is involved. **at a price** at a high cost.
– ORIGIN Old French *pris*.

priceless • adj. **1** very valuable. **2** informal very amusing.

pricey • adj. (**pricier, priciest**) informal expensive.

prick • v. **1** make a small hole in something with a sharp point. **2** cause someone to have a slight prickling feeling: *tears were pricking her eyelids.* • n. a mark, hole, or pain caused by pricking someone or something.
– PHRASES **prick up your ears 1** (of a

horse or dog) make the ears stand erect when alert. **2** (of a person) suddenly begin to pay attention.
– DERIVATIVES **pricker** n.
– ORIGIN Old English.

prickle •n. **1** a small thorn on a plant or a pointed spine on an animal. **2** a tingling feeling on the skin. •v. (**prickles, prickling, prickled**) have a tingling feeling on the skin.
– ORIGIN Old English.

prickly •adj. **1** having small thorns or spines. **2** causing a tingling feeling. **3** easily offended or annoyed.

prickly pear •n. a cactus which produces prickly, pear-shaped fruits.

pride •n. **1** deep pleasure or satisfaction felt if you or people close to you have done something well. **2** a cause or source of this: *the swimming pool is the pride of the village.* **3** self-respect: *he swallowed his pride and asked for help.* **4** an excessively high opinion of yourself. **5** a group of lions. •v. (**prides, priding, prided**) (**pride yourself on**) be especially proud of a quality or skill.
– ORIGIN Old English.

priest •n. **1** a person who is qualified to perform certain religious ceremonies in the Roman Catholic, Orthodox, or Anglican Church. **2** a person who performs ceremonies in a non-Christian religion.
– DERIVATIVES **priesthood** n. **priestly** adj.
– ORIGIN Old English.

priestess •n. a female priest of a non-Christian religion.

prig •n. a person who behaves as if they are morally superior to other people.
– DERIVATIVES **priggish** adj.

prim •adj. very formal and correct and disapproving of anything rude.
– DERIVATIVES **primly** adv.
– ORIGIN prob. from Old French *prin* 'excellent'.

prima ballerina /pree-muh bal-luh-ree-nuh/ •n. the chief female dancer in a ballet or ballet company.
– ORIGIN Italian.

primacy /pry-muh-si/ •n. the fact of being most important.
– ORIGIN Latin *primatia.*

prima donna /pree-muh don-uh/ •n. **1** the chief female singer in an opera or opera company. **2** a very tempera-mental and self-important person.
– ORIGIN Italian, 'first lady'.

primaeval •adj. var. of PRIMEVAL.

prima facie /pry-muh fay-shi-ee/ •adj. & adv. Law accepted as correct until proved otherwise.

– ORIGIN Latin.

primal •adj. relating to early human life; primeval.
– ORIGIN Latin *primalis.*

primary •adj. **1** of chief importance: *the government's primary aim is to reduce unemployment.* **2** earliest in time or order. **3** esp. Brit. relating to education for children between the ages of about five and eleven. •n. (pl. **primaries**) (in the US) a preliminary election to appoint delegates to a party conference or to select candidates for an election.
– DERIVATIVES **primarily** adv.
– ORIGIN Latin *primarius.*

primary care •n. health care provided in the community by doctors and specialist clinics.

primary colour •n. any of a group of colours from which all others can be obtained by mixing.

primate /pry-mayt/ •n. **1** a mammal of an order including monkeys, apes, and humans. **2** (in the Christian Church) an archbishop.
– ORIGIN Latin *primas* 'of the first rank'.

prime¹ •adj. **1** of chief importance. **2** of the highest quality; excellent. **3** (of a number) that can be divided only by itself and one (e.g. 2, 3, 5). •n. **1** a time of greatest vigour or success in a person's life. **2** a prime number.
– ORIGIN Latin *primus* 'first'.

prime² •v. (**primes, priming, primed**) **1** make something, especially a firearm or bomb, ready for use or action. **2** prepare someone for a situation by giving them information. **3** cover a surface with primer.
– ORIGIN prob. from Latin *primus* 'first'.

prime minister •n. the head of a government.

primer¹ •n. a substance painted on a surface as a base coat.

primer² •n. a book for teaching children to read or giving a basic introduction to a subject.
– ORIGIN from Latin *primarius liber* 'primary book'.

prime time •n. the time at which a radio or television audience is expected to be greatest.

primeval /pry-mee-v'l/ (also **primaeval**) •adj. relating to the earliest times in history.
– ORIGIN Latin *primaevus.*

primitive •adj. **1** relating to the earliest times in history or stages in development: *primitive mammals.* **2** referring to a simple form of society that has not yet developed industry or

p

writing. **3** offering a very basic level of comfort. **4** (of behaviour or emotion) not based on reason; instinctive.
– DERIVATIVES **primitively** adv.
– ORIGIN Latin *primitivus* 'first of its kind'.

primogeniture /pry-moh-jen-i-cher/ •n. **1** the state of being the first child born in a family. **2** the system by which the eldest son inherits all his parents' property.
– ORIGIN Latin *primogenitura*.

primordial /pry-mor-di-uhl/ •adj. existing at or from the beginning of time.
– ORIGIN Latin *primordialis* 'first of all'.

primp •v. make small adjustments to your hair, clothes, or make-up.
– ORIGIN from PRIM.

primrose •n. a plant of woods and hedges with pale yellow flowers.
– ORIGIN prob. from Latin *prima rosa* 'first rose'.

primula /prim-yuu-luh/ •n. a plant of a genus that includes primroses and cowslips.
– ORIGIN from Latin *primula veris* 'little first thing'.

Primus /pry-muhss/ •n. trademark a portable cooking stove that burns oil.

prince •n. **1** a son or other close male relative of a king or queen. **2** a male monarch of a small state. **3** (in some European countries) a nobleman.
– ORIGIN Latin *princeps* 'first, chief'.

prince consort •n. the husband of a reigning queen who is himself a prince.

princeling •n. **1** the ruler of a small or unimportant country. **2** a young prince.

princely •adj. **1** relating to or suitable for a prince. **2** (of a sum of money) generous.

Prince of Wales •n. a title granted to the heir apparent to the British throne (usually the eldest son of the king or queen).

princess •n. **1** a daughter or other close female relative of a king or queen. **2** the wife or widow of a prince.

Princess Royal •n. a title that may be given to the eldest daughter of a reigning British king or queen.

principal •adj. most important; main. •n. **1** the most important person in an organization or group. **2** the head of a school or college. **3** a sum of money lent or invested, on which interest is paid. **4** a person for whom someone else acts as a representative.
– DERIVATIVES **principally** adv.
– ORIGIN Latin *principalis* 'first, original'.

USAGE: Do not confuse **principal** and **principle**. Principal is usually an adjective meaning 'main or most important' (*the country's principal cities*), whereas **principle** is a noun that usually means 'a truth or general law used as the basis for something' (*the general principles of law*).

principal boy •n. Brit. a woman who takes the leading male role in a pantomime.

principality •n. (pl. **principalities**) **1** a state ruled by a prince. **2** (**the Principality**) Brit. Wales.

principle •n. **1** a truth or general law that is used as a basis for a theory or system of belief: *a country run on Islamic principles.* **2** (**principles**) rules or beliefs governing the way you behave. **3** a general scientific theorem or natural law: *the principle that gas under pressure heats up.* **4** Chem. an active or characteristic element of a substance.
– PHRASES **in principle** in theory. **on principle** because of your beliefs about what is right and wrong.
– ORIGIN Latin *principium* 'source'.

principled •adj. (of actions or behaviour) based on your beliefs about what is right and wrong.

print •v. **1** produce a book, newspaper, etc. by a mechanical process involving the transfer of words or pictures to paper. **2** produce words or pictures in this way. **3** produce a photographic print from a negative. **4** write words clearly without joining the letters. **5** mark with a coloured design: *a fabric printed with roses.* •n. **1** printed words in a book, newspaper, etc. **2** a mark where something has pressed or touched a surface: *paw prints.* **3** a printed picture or design. **4** a photograph printed on paper from a negative or transparency. **5** a piece of fabric with a coloured design.
– PHRASES **in** (or **out of**) **print** (of a book) available (or no longer available) from the publisher.
– DERIVATIVES **printable** adj.
– ORIGIN Old French *preinte* 'pressed'.

printed circuit •n. an electronic circuit based on thin strips of a conducting material on an insulating board.

printer •n. **1** a person or business involved in printing. **2** a machine for printing.

printing •n. **1** the production of books, newspapers, etc. **2** all the copies of a book printed at one time. **3** handwriting in which the letters are written separately.

printing press •n. a machine for printing from type or plates.

printout • n. a page of printed material from a computer's printer.

prion /pree-on/ • n. a protein particle believed to be the cause of certain brain diseases such as BSE and CJD.
– ORIGIN from *pro(teinaceous) in(fectious particle)*.

prior¹ • adj. **1** coming before in time, order, or importance. **2** (**prior to**) before.
– ORIGIN Latin, 'former, elder'.

prior² • n. (fem. **prioress**) **1** (in an abbey) the person next in rank below an abbot (or abbess). **2** the head of a priory.
– ORIGIN Latin 'former, elder'.

prioritize (or **prioritise**) • v. (**prioritizes, prioritizing, prioritized**) **1** treat something as the most important. **2** decide the order of importance of items or tasks.
– DERIVATIVES **prioritization** n.

priority • n. (pl. **priorities**) **1** the state of being more important: *safety should take priority over any other matter.* **2** a thing seen as more important than other things. **3** Brit. the right to go before other traffic.

priory • n. (pl. **priories**) a monastery or nunnery governed by a prior or prioress.

prise (US **prize**) • v. (**prises, prising, prised**; US **prizes, prizing, prized**) force something open or apart.
– ORIGIN Old French, 'a grasp'.

prism • n. **1** a transparent object with triangular ends, that breaks light up into the colours of the rainbow. **2** a solid geometric figure whose two ends are parallel and of the same size and shape, and whose sides are parallelograms.
– ORIGIN Greek *prisma* 'thing sawn'.

prismatic • adj. **1** relating to or shaped like a prism. **2** (of colours) formed or distributed by a prism.

prison • n. a building where criminals or people awaiting trial are confined.
– ORIGIN Old French *prisun*.

prison camp • n. a camp where prisoners of war or political prisoners are kept.

prisoner • n. **1** a person found guilty of a crime and sent to prison. **2** a person captured and kept confined. **3** a person trapped by a situation: *I was a prisoner of my own fame.*

prisoner of conscience • n. a person imprisoned for their political or religious views.

prisoner of war • n. a person captured and imprisoned by the enemy in war.

prison officer • n. Brit. a guard in a prison.

prissy • adj. too concerned with behaving in a correct and respectable way.

– DERIVATIVES **prissily** adv. **prissiness** n.
– ORIGIN perh. from PRIM and SISSY.

pristine /priss-teen/ • adj. **1** in its original condition: *pristine copies of an early magazine.* **2** clean and fresh as if new.
– DERIVATIVES **pristinely** adv.
– ORIGIN Latin *pristinus* 'former'.

privacy /pri-vuh-si, pry-vuh-si/ • n. a state in which you are not watched or disturbed by other people.

private • adj. **1** for or belonging to a particular person or group only: *his private plane.* **2** (of thoughts or feelings) not to be made known to other people. **3** not sharing thoughts and feelings with other people. **4** (of a service or industry) provided by a person or commercial company rather than the state. **5** working for yourself rather than for the state or an organization. **6** not connected with a person's work or official role: *rumours about his private life.* **7** (of a place) where you will not be disturbed; secluded. • n. (also **private soldier**) a soldier of the lowest rank in the army.
– DERIVATIVES **privately** adv.
– ORIGIN Latin *privatus* 'withdrawn from public life'.

private company • n. Brit. a company whose shares may not be offered to the public for sale.

private detective (also **private investigator**) • n. a detective who is not a police officer and who carries out investigations for private clients.

private enterprise • n. business or industry managed by independent companies rather than the state.

privateer /pry-vuh-teer/ • n. hist. a privately owned armed ship, authorized by a government for use in war.

private eye • n. informal a private detective.

private means • pl. n. Brit. income from investments, property, etc., rather than from employment.

private member • n. (in the UK, Canada, Australia, and New Zealand) a member of a parliament who does not hold a government office.

private parts • pl. n. euphem. a person's genitals.

private school • n. Brit. an independent school financed by the fees paid by pupils.

private secretary • n. **1** a secretary who deals with the personal matters of their employer. **2** a civil servant acting as an assistant to a senior government official.

p

private sector • n. the part of the economy not under direct state control.

privation /pry-vay-sh'n/ • n. a state in which you lack essentials such as food and warmth.
– ORIGIN Latin.

privatize (or **privatise**) • v. (**privatizes, privatizing, privatized**) transfer a business or industry from public to private ownership.
– DERIVATIVES **privatization** n.

privet /pri-vit/ • n. a shrub with small dark green leaves.

privilege • n. 1 a special right or advantage for a particular person or group. 2 an opportunity to do something regarded as a special honour: *she had the privilege of giving the opening lecture.* 3 the rights and advantages of rich and powerful people: *a young man of wealth and privilege.*
– ORIGIN Latin *privilegium* 'law affecting an individual'.

☑ Spell **privilege** with **-lege** at the end.

privileged • adj. 1 having a privilege or privileges. 2 (of information) legally protected from being made public.

privy /pri-vi/ • adj. (**privy to**) sharing in the knowledge of something secret. • n. (pl. **privies**) a toilet in a small shed outside a house.
– ORIGIN Old French *prive* 'private'.

Privy Council • n. a body of advisers appointed by a sovereign or a Governor General.

prize[1] • n. 1 a thing given as a reward to a winner or to mark an outstanding achievement. 2 something of great value that is worth struggling to achieve. • adj. 1 having been or likely to be awarded a prize. 2 outstanding of its kind. • v. (**prizes, prizing, prized**) value highly.
– ORIGIN Old French *preisier* 'praise'.

prize[2] • v. US = PRISE.

prizefight • n. a boxing match for prize money.
– DERIVATIVES **prizefighter** n.

pro[1] • n. (pl. **pros**) informal a professional.

pro[2] • n. (pl. **pros**) (usu. in phr. **pros and cons**) an advantage or argument in favour of something. • prep. & adv. in favour of.
– ORIGIN Latin, 'for, on behalf of'.

pro-[1] • prefix 1 supporting: *pro-choice.* 2 referring to motion forwards, out, or away: *propel.*
– ORIGIN Latin *pro* 'in front of, instead of'.

pro-[2] • prefix before: *proactive.*
– ORIGIN Greek *pro.*

proactive • adj. creating or controlling a situation rather than just responding to it.
– DERIVATIVES **proactively** adv.

probability • n. (pl. **probabilities**) 1 the extent to which something is probable. 2 an event that is likely to happen: *revolution was a strong probability.*

probable • adj. likely to happen or be the case.
– ORIGIN Latin *probabilis.*

probably • adv. almost certainly.

probate • n. the official process of proving that a will is valid.
– ORIGIN Latin *probatum* 'something proved'.

probation • n. 1 the release of an offender from detention or prison on condition that they behave well and report regularly to a supervisor. 2 a period of training and testing a person who has started a new job.
– DERIVATIVES **probationary** adj.

probationer • n. 1 a person serving a probationary period in a job. 2 an offender on probation.

probation officer • n. a person who supervises offenders on probation.

probe • n. 1 an investigation. 2 a blunt-ended surgical instrument for exploring a wound or part of the body. 3 a small measuring or testing device. 4 (also **space probe**) an unmanned exploratory spacecraft. • v. (**probes, probing, probed**) 1 physically explore or examine. 2 investigate a matter closely.
– ORIGIN Latin *proba* 'proof'.

probiotic /proh-by-oh-tik/ • n. a substance which stimulates the growth of beneficial microorganisms, especially the natural bacteria in the intestines.

probity /proh-bi-ti/ • n. honesty and decency.
– ORIGIN Latin *probitas.*

problem • n. something that is difficult to deal with or understand.
– ORIGIN Greek *problēma.*

problematic • adj. presenting a problem.
– DERIVATIVES **problematical** adj.

proboscis /pruh-boss-iss/ • n. (pl. **proboscises** /pruh-boss-eez/ or **proboscises**) 1 the long, flexible nose of a mammal, e.g. an elephant's trunk. 2 an elongated sucking organ or mouthpart of an insect or worm.
– ORIGIN Greek *proboskis* 'means of obtaining food'.

proboscis monkey • n. a monkey native to the forests of Borneo, the male of which has a large dangling nose.

p

procedure • n. **1** an established or official way of doing something. **2** a series of actions done in a certain way.
– DERIVATIVES **procedural** adj.
– ORIGIN French *procédure*.

proceed /pruh-seed/ • v. **1** begin a course of action. **2** go on to do something. **3** (of an action) continue. **4** move forward.
– ORIGIN Latin *procedere*.

proceedings • pl. n. **1** an event or a series of activities. **2** action taken in a court of law to settle a dispute.

proceeds /proh-seedz/ • pl. n. money obtained from an event or activity.

process[1] /proh-seedz/ • n. **1** a series of actions taken towards achieving a particular end. **2** a natural series of changes: *the ageing process.* **3** a summons to appear in a court of law. **4** a natural projection on part of the body or in an organism. • v. **1** perform a series of operations to change or preserve something. **2** operate on electronic data by means of a computer program. **3** deal with something using an established procedure.
– ORIGIN Latin *processus* 'progression'.

process[2] /pruh-sess/ • v. (of a number of people or vehicles) move forward in an orderly way.
– ORIGIN from PROCESSION.

procession • n. **1** a number of people or vehicles moving forward in an orderly way. **2** a large number of people or things coming one after the other.
– ORIGIN Latin.

processor • n. **1** a machine that processes something. **2** a central processing unit in a computer.

pro-choice • adj. supporting the right of a woman to choose to have an abortion.

proclaim • v. **1** announce something officially or publicly. **2** declare someone to be something. **3** show something clearly.
– DERIVATIVES **proclamation** n.
– ORIGIN Latin *proclamare* 'cry out'.

proclivity /pruh-kliv-i-ti/ • n. (pl. **proclivities**) a tendency to do something regularly; an inclination.
– ORIGIN Latin *proclivitas*.

procrastinate /proh-krass-ti-nayt/ • v. (**procrastinates, procrastinating, procrastinated**) delay or postpone action.
– DERIVATIVES **procrastination** n. **procrastinator** n.
– ORIGIN Latin *procrastinare* 'defer till the morning'.

procreate • v. (**procreates, procreating, procreated**) produce young.
– DERIVATIVES **procreation** n. **procreative** adj.

– ORIGIN Latin *procreare* 'generate'.

proctor • n. Brit. an officer in charge of discipline at certain universities.
– ORIGIN Latin *procurator* 'administrator'.

procurator fiscal • n. (pl. **procurators fiscal** or **procurator fiscals**) (in Scotland) a local coroner and public prosecutor.

procure • v. (**procures, procuring, procured**) **1** obtain something. **2** provide a prostitute for someone.
– DERIVATIVES **procurement** n. **procurer** n.
– ORIGIN Latin *procurare* 'manage'.

prod • v. (**prods, prodding, prodded**) **1** poke with a finger or pointed object. **2** stimulate or persuade someone to do something. • n. **1** a poke. **2** a stimulus or reminder. **3** a pointed implement.
– ORIGIN perh. from POKE and dialect *brod* 'to goad, prod'.

prodigal • adj. **1** using money or resources in a wasteful way. **2** lavish. • n. (also **prodigal son**) a person who leaves home and lives a wasteful and extravagant life but returns repentant. [ORIGIN referring to the story in the Gospel of Luke.]
– DERIVATIVES **prodigality** n. **prodigally** adv.
– ORIGIN Latin *prodigalis*.

prodigious /pruh-dij-uhss/ • adj. impressively large.
– DERIVATIVES **prodigiously** adv.
– ORIGIN Latin *prodigiosus*.

prodigy • n. (pl. **prodigies**) **1** a young person with exceptional abilities. **2** an outstanding example of something.
– ORIGIN Latin *prodigium* 'portent'.

produce • v. /pruh-dyooss/ (**produces, producing, produced**) **1** make, manufacture, or create something. **2** cause to happen or exist. **3** show or provide something for inspection or use. **4** administer the financial aspects of a film or broadcast or the staging of a play. **5** supervise the making of a musical recording. • n. /prod-yooss/ things that have been produced or grown: *dairy produce.*
– DERIVATIVES **producer** n. **producible** adj.
– ORIGIN Latin *producere* 'bring forth'.

product • n. **1** an article or substance manufactured for sale. **2** a result: *her suntan was the product of a sunbed.* **3** a substance produced during a natural, chemical, or manufacturing process. **4** Math. a quantity obtained by multiplying quantities together.
– ORIGIN Latin *productum* 'something produced'.

production • n. **1** the action of producing something. **2** the amount

p

of something produced. **3** a film, record, or play regarded as a work that is being or has been made or staged.

production line • n. a sequence of workers and machines in a factory; an assembly line.

productive • adj. **1** producing or able to produce large quantities of goods or crops. **2** achieving or producing a significant amount or result.
– DERIVATIVES **productively** adv.

productivity • n. **1** the state of being able to produce something in large quantities. **2** the efficiency with which things are produced.

profane • adj. **1** not holy or religious: *topics both sacred and profane*. **2** not showing respect for God or holy things. • v. (**profanes, profaning, profaned**) treat something holy with a lack of respect.
– DERIVATIVES **profanation** n.
– ORIGIN Latin *profanus* 'outside the temple'.

profanity • n. (pl. **profanities**) **1** profane behaviour. **2** a swear word.

profess • v. **1** claim that you have a particular quality or feeling. **2** declare your faith in a religion.
– ORIGIN Latin *profiteri* 'declare publicly'.

professed • adj. **1** (of a quality or feeling) claimed openly but often falsely. **2** openly declared.

profession • n. **1** a job or career that needs training and a formal qualification. **2** a body of people engaged in a profession. **3** a claim. **4** a declaration of belief in a religion.

professional • adj. **1** relating or belonging to a profession. **2** engaged in an activity as a paid job rather than as an amateur. **3** appropriate to a professional person; competent or skilful. • n. **1** a person engaged or qualified in a profession. **2** a person who is very skilled in a particular activity.
– DERIVATIVES **professionally** adv.

professionalism • n. the ability or skill expected of a professional.

professor • n. **1** a university academic of the highest rank. **2** N. Amer. a university teacher.
– DERIVATIVES **professorial** adj. **professorship** n.
– ORIGIN Latin.

proffer • v. (**proffers, proffering, proffered**) offer something for someone to accept.
– ORIGIN Old French *proffrir*.

proficient • adj. competent; skilled.
– DERIVATIVES **proficiency** n.
– ORIGIN Latin *proficere* 'to advance'.

profile • n. **1** an outline of a person's face as seen from one side. **2** a short descriptive article about someone. **3** the extent to which a person or organization attracts public notice: *her high profile as an opera star*. • v. (**profiles, profiling, profiled**) **1** write a short article about someone. **2** (**be profiled**) appear in outline.
– PHRASES **keep a low profile** try not to attract attention.
– DERIVATIVES **profiler** n.
– ORIGIN from former Italian *profilo* 'a drawing or border'.

profit • n. **1** a financial gain. **2** advantage; benefit. • v. (**profits, profiting, profited**) benefit, especially financially.
– ORIGIN Latin *profectus* 'progress'.

profitable • adj. **1** (of a business or activity) yielding financial gain. **2** useful: *he'd had a profitable day*.
– DERIVATIVES **profitability** n. **profitably** adv.

profit and loss account • n. an account to which incomes and gains are added and expenses and losses taken away, so as to show the resulting profit or loss.

profiteering • n. the making of a large profit in an unfair way.
– DERIVATIVES **profiteer** n.

profiterole /pruh-fit-uh-rohl/ • n. a small ball of choux pastry filled with cream and covered with chocolate sauce.
– ORIGIN French, 'small profit'.

profit margin • n. the difference between the cost of producing something and the price for which it is sold.

profit-sharing • n. a system in which the people who work for a company receive a direct share of its profits.

profligate /prof-li-guht/ • adj. **1** recklessly extravagant or wasteful. **2** indulging too much in physical pleasures. • n. a profligate person.
– DERIVATIVES **profligacy** n.
– ORIGIN Latin *profligatus* 'dissolute'.

pro forma /proh for-muh/ • adv. & adj. as a matter of form or politeness. • n. a standard document or form.
– ORIGIN Latin.

profound • adj. (**profounder, profoundest**) **1** very great: *profound social change*. **2** showing great knowledge or insight. **3** demanding deep study or thought.
– DERIVATIVES **profoundly** adv. **profundity** n. (pl. **profundities**).
– ORIGIN Latin *profundus* 'deep'.

profuse • adj. done or appearing in large quantities; abundant: *profuse apologies*.
– DERIVATIVES **profusely** adv.

– ORIGIN Latin *profusus* 'lavish'.

profusion /pruh-**fyoo**-zh'n/ •n. an abundance or large quantity.

progenitor /proh-**jen**-i-ter/ •n. 1 an ancestor or parent. 2 the originator of an artistic, political, or intellectual movement.
– ORIGIN Latin.

progeny /**proj**-uh-ni/ •n. offspring.
– ORIGIN Old French *progenie*.

progesterone /pruh-**jess**-tuh-rohn/ •n. a hormone that stimulates the womb to prepare for pregnancy.

progestogen /proh-**jess**-tuh-juhn/ •n. a hormone that maintains pregnancy and prevents further ovulation.

prognosis /prog-**noh**-siss/ •n. (pl. **prognoses** /prog-**noh**-seez/) a forecast, especially of the likely course of an illness.
– ORIGIN Greek.

prognostic /prog-**noss**-tik/ •adj. predicting the likely course of an illness.

prognosticate •v. (**prognosticates, prognosticating, prognosticated**) make a forecast about something.
– DERIVATIVES **prognostication** n. **prognosticator** n.

programmatic •adj. relating to a programme or method.
– DERIVATIVES **programmatically** adv.

programme (US **program**) •n. 1 a planned series of events. 2 a radio or television broadcast. 3 a set of related measures or activities with a long-term aim. 4 a sheet or booklet giving details about a play, concert, or opera. 5 (**program**) a series of software instructions to control the operation of a computer. •v. (**programmes** or **programs, programming, programmed**; US **programs, programing, programed**) 1 (**program**) apply a set of software instructions to control the operation of a computer. 2 cause to behave in a particular way. 3 arrange according to a plan.
– DERIVATIVES **programmable** adj. **programmer** n.
– ORIGIN Greek *programma*.

progress •n. /**proh**-gres/ 1 forward movement towards a destination. 2 development towards a better or more modern state. •v. /pruh-**gres**/ move or develop towards a destination or a more advanced state.
– ORIGIN Latin *progressus* 'an advance'.

progression •n. 1 a gradual movement or development towards a destination or a more advanced state. 2 a number of things coming one after the other.

progressive •adj. 1 happening gradually or in stages. 2 favouring new ideas or social reform. •n. a person who supports social reform.
– DERIVATIVES **progressively** adv.

prohibit •v. (**prohibits, prohibiting, prohibited**) 1 formally forbid something by law or a rule. 2 make something impossible; prevent.
– DERIVATIVES **prohibitory** adj.
– ORIGIN Latin *prohibere* 'keep in check'.

prohibition /proh-hi-**bi**-sh'n, proh-i-**bi**-sh'n/ •n. 1 the action of forbidding or preventing something. 2 an order that forbids something. 3 (**Prohibition**) the prevention by law of the manufacture and sale of alcohol in the US from 1920 to 1933.

prohibitive •adj. 1 forbidding or restricting something. 2 (of a price) excessively high.
– DERIVATIVES **prohibitively** adv.

project •n. /**proj**-jekt/ 1 an enterprise carefully planned to achieve a particular aim. 2 a piece of research work by a student. •v. /pruh-**jekt**/ 1 estimate or forecast something on the basis of present trends. 2 plan something. 3 stick out beyond something else. 4 send forward or outward. 5 cause light, shadow, or an image to fall on a surface. 6 present a particular image to other people.
– ORIGIN Latin *projectum* 'something prominent'.

projectile •n. a missile fired or thrown at a target.

projection •n. 1 a forecast based on present trends. 2 the projecting of an image or sound. 3 a thing that sticks out.
– DERIVATIVES **projectionist** n.

projector •n. a device for projecting slides or film on to a screen.

prolapse /**proh**-laps/ •n. a condition in which a part or organ of the body has slipped from its normal position.
– ORIGIN Latin *prolabi* 'slip forward'.

prolate /**proh**-layt/ •adj. Geom. (of a sphere) lengthened in the direction of a polar diameter.
– ORIGIN Latin *prolatus* 'carried forward'.

prole informal, derog. •n. a member of the working class.
– ORIGIN from **PROLETARIAT**.

proletarian /proh-li-**tair**-i-uhn/ •adj. relating to workers or working-class people. •n. a member of the proletariat.
– ORIGIN Latin *proletarius*.

proletariat •n. workers or working-class people.

pro-life •adj. seeking to ban abortion and euthanasia.
– DERIVATIVES **pro-lifer** n.

proliferate /pruh-lif-uh-rayt/
• v. (**proliferates, proliferating, proliferated**) **1** increase rapidly in number. **2** reproduce rapidly.
– DERIVATIVES **proliferation** n.
– ORIGIN Latin *prolificus*.

prolific • adj. **1** producing much fruit or foliage or many offspring. **2** (of an artist, author, etc.) producing many works.
– DERIVATIVES **prolifically** adv.
– ORIGIN Latin *prolificus*.

prolix /proh-liks, pruh-liks/ • adj. (of speech or writing) long and boring.
– DERIVATIVES **prolixity** n.
– ORIGIN Latin *prolixus* 'poured forth'.

prologue • n. **1** an introductory section or scene in a book, play, or musical work. **2** an event or action leading to another.
– ORIGIN Greek *prologos*.

prolong • v. cause something to last longer.
– DERIVATIVES **prolongation** n.
– ORIGIN Latin *prolongare*.

prolonged • adj. continuing for a long time.

prom • n. informal **1** Brit. = **PROMENADE** (in sense 1). **2** Brit. a promenade concert. **3** N. Amer. a formal dance at a high school or college.

promenade /prom-uh-nahd, prom-uh-nayd/ • n. **1** a paved public walk along a seafront. **2** a leisurely walk, ride, or drive. • v. (**promenades, promenading, promenaded**) go for a leisurely walk, ride, or drive.
– ORIGIN French.

promenade concert • n. Brit. a concert of classical music at which part of the audience stands up rather than sits.

Promethean /pruh-mee-thi-uhn/ • adj. daring or skilful like Prometheus in Greek mythology who stole fire from the gods and gave it to the human race.

promethium /pruh-mee-thi-uhm/ • n. an unstable radioactive metallic chemical element.
– ORIGIN from *Prometheus* (see **PROMETHEAN**).

prominence • n. the state of being prominent.

prominent • adj. **1** important; famous. **2** sticking out: *a man with big, prominent eyes.* **3** particularly noticeable.
– DERIVATIVES **prominently** adv.
– ORIGIN Latin *prominere* 'jut out'.

promiscuous /pruh-miss-kyuu-uhss/ • adj. having many brief sexual relationships.
– DERIVATIVES **promiscuity** n.
– ORIGIN Latin *promiscuus* 'indiscriminate'.

promise • n. **1** an assurance that you will

do something or that something will happen. **2** potential excellence: *he showed great promise as a junior officer.*
• v. (**promises, promising, promised**) **1** make a promise. **2** give good grounds for the expectation that something will happen.
– ORIGIN Latin *promissum*.

Promised Land • n. (**the Promised Land**) (in the Bible) the land of Canaan, promised to Abraham and his descendants in the Book of Genesis.

promising • adj. showing signs of future success.

promissory note • n. a signed document containing a written promise to pay a stated sum.

promo /proh-moh/ • n. (pl. **promos**) informal a promotional film, video, etc.

promontory /prom-uhn-tuh-ri/ • n. (pl. **promontories**) a point of high land jutting out into the sea or a lake.
– ORIGIN Latin *promontorium*.

promote • v. (**promotes, promoting, promoted**) **1** aid the progress of a cause, venture, or aim. **2** publicize a product or celebrity. **3** raise someone to a higher position or rank.
– ORIGIN Latin *promovere* 'move forward'.

promoter • n. **1** the organizer of a sporting event or theatrical production. **2** a supporter of a cause or aim.

promotion • n. **1** activity that supports or encourages something. **2** the publicizing of a product or celebrity. **3** movement to a higher position or rank.
– DERIVATIVES **promotional** adj.

prompt • v. **1** cause something to happen. **2** (**prompt someone to/to do**) cause someone to do something. **3** help or encourage a hesitating speaker. **4** supply a forgotten word or line to an actor. • n. **1** a word or phrase used to prompt an actor. **2** Computing a word or symbol on a screen to show that input is required. • adj. done or acting without delay. • adv. Brit. exactly or punctually: *12 o'clock prompt.*
– DERIVATIVES **promptly** adv.
– ORIGIN Latin *promptus* 'brought to light'.

prompter • n. a person who prompts the actors during a play.

promulgate /prom-uhl-gayt/
• v. (**promulgates, promulgating, promulgated**) **1** make something widely known; promote. **2** officially declare the introduction of a law.
– DERIVATIVES **promulgation** n.
– ORIGIN Latin *promulgare* 'expose to public view'.

prone • adj. **1** (**prone to/to do**) likely to suffer from, do, or experience something unfortunate. **2** lying flat and face downwards.
– ORIGIN Latin *pronus* 'leaning forward'.

prong • n. **1** each of two or more projecting pointed parts on a fork. **2** each of the separate parts of an attack or argument.
– DERIVATIVES **pronged** adj.
– ORIGIN perh. from Low German *prange* 'pinching instrument'.

pronominal /proh-nom-i-n'l/ • adj. relating to pronouns.

pronoun • n. a word used instead of a noun to indicate someone or something already mentioned or known, e.g. *I*, *this*.

pronounce • v. (**pronounces, pronouncing, pronounced**) **1** make the sound of a word or part of a word. **2** declare or announce something. **3** (**pronounce on**) pass judgement or make a decision on.
– DERIVATIVES **pronounceable** adj.
– ORIGIN Latin *pronuntiare*.

pronounced • adj. very noticeable: *a pronounced squint.*

pronouncement • n. a formal public statement.

pronto • adv. informal promptly.
– ORIGIN Spanish.

pronunciation /pruh-nun-si-ay-sh'n/ • n. the way in which a word is pronounced.

☑ Although it is related to *pronounce*, **pronunciation** is spelled **-nun-** in the middle.

proof • n. **1** evidence proving that something is true. **2** the process of proving that something is true. **3** a series of stages in the solving of a mathematical or philosophical problem. **4** a copy of printed material used for making corrections before final printing. **5** a standard used to measure the strength of distilled alcoholic spirits. • adj. (in combination) able to resist: *waterproof.*
– ORIGIN Old French *preove*.

proof positive • n. final or absolute proof of something.

proofread • v. read printed proofs and mark any errors.
– DERIVATIVES **proofreader** n.

prop[1] • n. **1** a pole or beam used as a temporary support. **2** a source of support or assistance. **3** (also **prop forward**) Rugby a forward at either end of the front row of a scrum. • v. (**props, propped, propping**) **1** support with a prop. **2** lean something against something else. **3** (**prop someone/thing**

up) support or help someone or something that would otherwise fail.
– ORIGIN prob. from Dutch *proppe* 'support for vines'.

prop[2] • n. a portable object used on the set of a play or film.
– ORIGIN from **PROPERTY**.

propaganda • n. information that is often biased or misleading, used to promote a political cause or point of view.
– ORIGIN Latin *congregatio de propaganda fide* 'congregation for propagation of the faith'.

☑ Spell **propaganda** with an **a** after the second **p**.

propagandist • n. esp. derog. a person who spreads propaganda.

propagate • v. (**propagates, propagating, propagated**) **1** produce a new plant from a parent plant. **2** promote or spread an idea or knowledge widely.
– DERIVATIVES **propagation** n. **propagator** n.
– ORIGIN Latin *propagare*.

propane /proh-payn/ • n. a flammable gas present in natural gas and used as bottled fuel.

propel • v. (**propels, propelling, propelled**) drive or push forwards.
– ORIGIN Latin *propellere*.

propellant • n. **1** a compressed gas that forces out the contents of an aerosol. **2** a substance used to provide thrust in a rocket engine.

propeller (also **propellor**) • n. a revolving shaft with two or more angled blades, for propelling a ship or aircraft.

propelling pencil • n. a pencil with a thin lead that may be extended as the point is worn away.

propensity • n. (pl. **propensities**) a tendency to behave in a certain way.
– ORIGIN Latin *propensus* 'inclined'.

proper • adj. **1** truly what something is said to be; genuine. **2** (after a noun) according to the precise meaning of the word: *the World Cup proper.* **3** suitable or correct. **4** too concerned to be respectable. **5** (**proper to**) belonging exclusively to.
– ORIGIN Old French *propre*.

proper fraction • n. a fraction that is less than one, with the numerator less than the denominator.

properly • adv. **1** in a suitable or correct way. **2** in the precise sense.

proper noun (also **proper name**) • n. a name for a person, place, or organization, having an initial capital letter. Opp. **COMMON NOUN**.

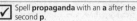

property • n. (pl. **properties**) **1** a thing or things belonging to someone. **2** a building and the land belonging to it. **3** Law the right to the possess, use, or dispose of something. **4** a quality or characteristic: *a perfumed oil with calming properties.*
– ORIGIN Latin *proprietas.*

prophecy /prof-i-si/ • n. (pl. **prophecies**) **1** a prediction about what will happen. **2** the power of prophesying.
– ORIGIN Greek *prophēteia.*

prophesy /prof-i-sy/ • v. (**prophesies, prophesying, prophesied**) predict.

prophet • n. (fem. **prophetess**) **1** (in some religions) a person considered to have been sent by God to teach people about his intentions. **2** a person who predicts the future.
– ORIGIN Greek *prophētēs* 'spokesman'.

prophetic /pruh-fet-ik/
• adj. **1** accurately predicting the future. **2** relating to a prophet or prophecy.
– DERIVATIVES **prophetically** adv.

prophylactic /prof-i-lak-tik/
• adj. intended to prevent disease. • n. a medicine or course of action intended to prevent disease.
– ORIGIN Greek *prophulaktikos.*

propinquity /pruh-ping-kwi-ti/
• n. nearness in time or space.
– ORIGIN Latin *propinquitas.*

propitiate /pruh-pish-i-ayt/
• v. (**propitiates, propitiating, propitiated**) win or regain someone's favour.
– DERIVATIVES **propitiation** n. **propitiatory** adj.
– ORIGIN Latin *propitiare* 'make favourable'.

propitious /pruh-pish-uhss/
• adj. giving or indicating a good chance of success; favourable.

proponent /pruh-poh-nuhnt/ • n. a person who proposes a theory, plan, or project.
– ORIGIN Latin *proponere* 'put forward'.

proportion • n. **1** a part, share, or number considered in relation to a whole. **2** the relationship of one thing to another in terms of size or quantity. **3** the correct relation between things. **4** (**proportions**) dimensions; size.
– PHRASES **sense of proportion** the ability to judge the relative importance of things.
– ORIGIN Latin.

proportional • adj. corresponding in size or amount to something else.
– DERIVATIVES **proportionality** n. **proportionally** adv.

proportional representation • n. a system in which parties in an election gain seats in proportion to the number of votes cast for them.

proportionate • adj. = **PROPORTIONAL.**

proportioned • adj. having parts that relate in size in a particular way to other parts: *a tall, perfectly proportioned woman.*

proposal • n. **1** a plan or suggestion. **2** the action of proposing something. **3** an offer of marriage.

propose • v. (**proposes, proposing, proposed**) **1** put forward an idea or plan for consideration. **2** nominate someone for an official position. **3** make a proposal at a formal meeting. **4** plan or intend something. **5** make an offer of marriage to someone.
– DERIVATIVES **proposer** n.
– ORIGIN Latin *proponere.*

proposition • n. **1** a statement expressing a judgement or opinion. **2** a proposed scheme. **3** a matter to be dealt with: *it's a tough proposition.* • v. informal ask someone to have sex with you.

propound /pruh-pownd/ • v. put forward an idea or theory for consideration.
– ORIGIN Latin *proponere* 'put forward'.

proprietary • adj. **1** relating to an owner or ownership. **2** (of a product) marketed under a registered trade name.
– ORIGIN Latin *proprietarius* 'proprietor'.

proprietary name • n. a name of a product or service registered as a trademark.

proprietor • n. (fem. **proprietress**) **1** the owner of a business. **2** a holder of property.

proprietorial /pruh-pry-uh-tor-i-uhl/
• adj. behaving as if you owned someone or something; possessive.
– DERIVATIVES **proprietorially** adv.

propriety • n. (pl. **proprieties**) **1** correctness of behaviour or morals. **2** the quality of being appropriate. **3** (**proprieties**) the generally accepted rules of behaviour.
– ORIGIN Latin *proprietas* 'property'.

propulsion • n. the action of propelling or driving something forward.
– DERIVATIVES **propulsive** adj.

pro rata /proh rah-tuh, proh ray-tuh/
• adj. proportional. • adv. proportionally.
– ORIGIN Latin, 'according to the rate'.

prosaic /proh-zay-ik/ • adj. **1** (of language) ordinary or unimaginative. **2** dull; mundane: *prosaic day-to-day concerns.*
– DERIVATIVES **prosaically** adv.

proscenium /pruh-see-ni-uhm/ • n. (pl. **prosceniums** or **proscenia** /pruh-see-ni-uh/) **1** the part of a stage in front of

the curtain. **2** (also **proscenium arch**) an arch framing the opening between the stage and the part of the theatre in which the audience sits.
– ORIGIN Greek *proskēnion*.

proscribe • v. (**proscribes, proscribing, proscribed**) **1** officially forbid. **2** criticize or condemn.
– DERIVATIVES **proscription** n.
– ORIGIN Latin *proscribere* 'publish by writing'.

> **USAGE: Proscribe** does not mean the same as **prescribe**: see the note at **PRESCRIBE**.

prose • n. ordinary written or spoken language.
– ORIGIN from Latin *prosa oratio* 'straightforward discourse'.

prosecute • v. (**prosecutes, prosecuting, prosecuted**) **1** take legal proceedings against someone. **2** continue a course of action with the intention of completing it.
– DERIVATIVES **prosecutable** adj.
– ORIGIN Latin *prosequi* 'pursue'.

prosecution • n. **1** the action of taking legal proceedings against someone. **2** (**the prosecution**) the party prosecuting someone in a lawsuit.

prosecutor • n. **1** a person who prosecutes someone. **2** a lawyer who conducts the case against a person accused of a crime.

proselyte /pross-i-lyt/ • n. a person who has been converted from one opinion, religion, or party to another.
– ORIGIN Greek *prosēluthos*.

proselytize /pross-i-li-tyz/ (or **proselytise**) • v. (**proselytizes, proselytizing, proselytized**) convert someone from one religion, opinion, or party to another.
– DERIVATIVES **proselytizer** n.

prosody /pross-uh-di/ • n. **1** the patterns of rhythm and sound used in poetry. **2** the study of these patterns or the rules governing them.
– DERIVATIVES **prosodic** adj.
– ORIGIN Greek *prosōidia* 'song sung to music'.

prospect • n. **1** the possibility of something occurring. **2** a mental picture of a future event. **3** (**prospects**) chances for success. **4** a person who is likely to be successful. **5** a wide view of landscape.
• v. (**prospect for**) search for mineral deposits.
– DERIVATIVES **prospector** n.
– ORIGIN Latin *prospectus* 'view'.

prospective • adj. likely to happen or be in the future.
– DERIVATIVES **prospectively** adv.

prospectus • n. (pl. **prospectuses**) a printed booklet advertising a school or university or giving details of a share offer.
– ORIGIN Latin, 'view, prospect'.

prosper • v. (**prospers, prospering, prospered**) succeed or flourish.
– ORIGIN Latin *prosperare*.

prosperous • adj. rich and successful.
– DERIVATIVES **prosperity** n.

prostate /pross-tayt/ • n. a gland surrounding the neck of the bladder in male mammals that produces a component of semen.
– ORIGIN Greek *prostatēs* 'one that stands before'.

prosthesis /pross-thee-siss/ • n. (pl. **prostheses** /pross-thee-seez/ or **prosthetics** /pross-thet-iks/) an artificial body part.
– DERIVATIVES **prosthetic** /pross-thet-ik/ adj.
– ORIGIN Greek.

prostitute • n. a person who has sex with people for money. • v. (**prostitutes, prostituting, prostituted**) **1** offer someone or yourself as a prostitute. **2** put your abilities to an unworthy use for money.
– DERIVATIVES **prostitution** n.
– ORIGIN Latin *prostituere* 'offer for sale'.

prostrate • adj. /pross-trayt/ **1** lying stretched out on the ground with your face downwards. **2** completely overcome with distress or exhaustion.
• v. /pross-trayt/ (**prostrates, prostrating, prostrated**) **1** (**prostrate yourself**) throw yourself flat on the ground. **2** (**be prostrated**) be completely overcome with stress or exhaustion.
– DERIVATIVES **prostration** n.
– ORIGIN Latin *prosternere*.

protactinium /proh-tak-tin-i-uhm/ • n. a rare radioactive metallic chemical element.

protagonist • n. **1** the leading character in a drama, film, or novel. **2** an important person in a real situation. **3** a person who actively supports a cause or idea.
– ORIGIN Greek *prōtagōnistēs*.

protean /proh-ti-uhn, proh-tee-uhn/ • adj. able to change or adapt.
– ORIGIN from the Greek sea god *Proteus*, who was able to change shape at will.

protect • v. **1** keep safe from harm or injury. **2** (as adj. **protected**) (of a threatened plant or animal species) safeguarded through laws against collecting or hunting.
– ORIGIN Latin *protegere* 'cover in front'.

protection • n. **1** the action of keeping someone or something safe from harm or injury, or the state of being protected.

2 a thing that protects. **3** the payment of money to criminals to prevent them from attacking you or your property.

protectionism •n. the theory or practice of shielding a country's own industries from foreign competition by taxing imports.
– DERIVATIVES **protectionist** n. & adj.

protective •adj. **1** able to or intended to keep someone or something safe from harm or injury. **2** having a strong wish to keep someone safe from harm or injury.
– DERIVATIVES **protectively** adv.

protector •n. **1** a person or thing that keeps someone safe from harm or injury. **2** (**Protector**) hist. a person who ruled a kingdom instead of or on behalf of a king or queen.

protectorate •n. a state that is controlled and protected by another.

protégé /prot-i-zhay, proh-ti-zhay/ •n. (fem. **protégée**) a person who is guided and supported by an older and more experienced person.
– ORIGIN French, 'protected'.

protein •n. any of a group of organic compounds forming part of body tissues and making up an important part of the diet.
– ORIGIN Greek *prōteios* 'primary'.

> ☑ **protein** does not follow the usual rule of *i* before *e* except after *c*.

pro tem /proh tem/ •adv. & adj. for the time being.
– ORIGIN Latin *pro tempore*.

protest •n. /proh-test/ **1** a statement or action expressing disapproval or objection. **2** an organized public demonstration objecting to an official policy. •v. /pruh-test/ **1** express an objection to something that someone has said or done. **2** state something strongly in response to an accusation or criticism: *she protested her innocence.*
– DERIVATIVES **protester** (also **protestor**) n.
– ORIGIN Latin *protestari* 'assert formally'.

Protestant /pro-tiss-tuhnt/ •n. a member or follower of any of the Western Christian Churches that are separate from the Roman Catholic Church. •adj. relating to or belonging to any of the Protestant Churches.
– DERIVATIVES **Protestantism** n.
– ORIGIN from PROTEST.

protestation /prot-i-stay-sh'n/ •n. **1** a firm declaration that something is or is not the case. **2** an objection or protest.

proto- •comb. form **1** original; primitive: *prototype.* **2** first: *protozoan.*
– ORIGIN Greek *prōtos.*

protocol •n. **1** the official system of rules governing affairs of state or diplomatic occasions. **2** the accepted code of behaviour in a particular situation.
– ORIGIN first meaning 'original note of an agreement': from Greek *prōtokollon* 'first page'.

proton /proh-ton/ •n. Physics a subatomic particle with a positive electric charge, occurring in all atomic nuclei.
– ORIGIN Greek, 'first thing'.

protoplasm /proh-tuh-pla-z'm/ •n. Biol. the material comprising the living part of a cell.
– ORIGIN Greek *prōtoplasma.*

prototype •n. a first or earlier form from which other forms are developed or copied.
– DERIVATIVES **prototypical** adj.

protozoan /proh-tuh-zoh-uhn/ •n. a single-celled microscopic animal such as an amoeba.
– ORIGIN from Greek *protos* 'first' + *zōion* 'animal'.

protracted •adj. lasting longer than usual or expected.
– ORIGIN Latin *protrahere* 'prolong'.

protractor •n. an instrument for measuring angles, in the form of a flat semicircle marked with degrees.

protrude •v. (**protrudes, protruding, protruded**) stick out beyond or above a surface.
– ORIGIN Latin *protrudere* 'thrust forward'.

protrusion •n. **1** something that protrudes or sticks out. **2** the action of protruding.

protuberance /pruh-tyoo-buh-ruhnss/ •n. a thing that bulges or sticks out beyond or above a surface.

protuberant •adj. bulging or sticking out.
– ORIGIN Latin *protuberare* 'swell out'.

proud •adj. **1** feeling pride or satisfaction in your own achievements or those of someone close to you. **2** having an excessively high opinion of yourself. **3** having self-respect. **4** (often **proud of**) slightly projecting from a surface.
– PHRASES **do someone proud** informal **1** make someone feel pleased. **2** treat someone very well.
– DERIVATIVES **proudly** adv.
– ORIGIN Old French *prud* 'valiant'.

prove /proov/ •v. (**proves, proving, proved**; past part. **proved** or **proven** /proo-v'n or proh-v'n/) **1** show by evidence or argument that something is true or exists. **2** show or be seen to be: *the*

scheme has proved a great success.
3 (**prove yourself**) show your abilities or courage. **4** (of bread dough) rise through the action of yeast.
– DERIVATIVES **provable** adj.
– ORIGIN Old French *prover*.

> USAGE: **Prove** has two past participles, **proved** and **proven**. You can correctly use either in sentences such as *this hasn't been proved yet* or *this hasn't been proven yet*. However, you should always use **proven** when the word is an adjective coming before the noun: *a proven talent*, not *a proved talent*.

provenance /prov-uh-nuhnss/ • n. **1** the origin or earliest known history of something. **2** a record of ownership of a work of art or an antique.
– ORIGIN French.

Provençal /prov-on-sahl/ • adj. relating to Provence in southern France. • n. **1** a person from Provence. **2** the language of Provence.

provender /prov-in-der/ • n. animal fodder.
– ORIGIN Old French *provendre*.

proverb • n. a short saying stating a general truth or piece of advice.
– ORIGIN Latin *proverbium*.

proverbial • adj. **1** referred to in a proverb or saying. **2** well known.
– DERIVATIVES **proverbially** adv.

provide • v. (**provides**, **providing**, **provided**) **1** make something available for use; supply. **2** (**provide someone with**) equip or supply someone with something. **3** (**provide for**) make enough preparation or arrangements for.
– DERIVATIVES **provider** n.
– ORIGIN Latin *providere* 'attend to'.

provided • conj. on the condition that.

providence • n. the protective care of God or of nature as a spiritual power.

provident • adj. careful in planning for the future.

providential • adj. happening by chance and at a favourable time.
– DERIVATIVES **providentially** adv.

providing • conj. on the condition that.

province • n. **1** a main administrative division of a country or empire. **2** (**the provinces**) the whole of a country outside the capital. **3** (**your province**) your particular area of knowledge, interest, or responsibility.
– ORIGIN Latin *provincia*.

provincial • adj. **1** relating to a province or the provinces. **2** unsophisticated or narrow-minded. • n. a person who lives in the regions outside the capital city of a country.

– DERIVATIVES **provincialism** n. **provinciality** n. **provincially** adv.

provision • n. **1** the action of supplying something. **2** something supplied. **3** (**provision for/against**) arrangements for possible future events or requirements. **4** (**provisions**) supplies of food, drink, or equipment. **5** a condition in a legal document. • v. supply with provisions.

provisional • adj. arranged for the present, possibly to be changed later.
– DERIVATIVES **provisionally** adv.

proviso /pruh-vy-zoh/ • n. (pl. **provisos**) a condition attached to an agreement.
– ORIGIN from Latin *proviso quod* 'it being provided that'.

provocation • n. **1** the causing of a strong reaction in someone. **2** action or speech that arouses a strong reaction.

provocative • adj. **1** deliberately causing annoyance or anger. **2** intended to arouse sexual desire or interest.
– DERIVATIVES **provocatively** adv.

provoke • v. (**provokes**, **provoking**, **provoked**) **1** cause a strong reaction. **2** deliberately make someone feel annoyed or angry. **3** stir someone up to do something.
– ORIGIN Latin *provocare* 'to challenge'.

provost /prov-uhst/ • n. **1** Brit. a person in charge of certain university colleges and public schools. **2** Scottish a mayor.
– ORIGIN Old English.

prow /prow/ • n. the pointed front part of a ship.
– ORIGIN Old French *proue*.

prowess • n. skill or expertise in a particular activity.
– ORIGIN Old French *proesce*.

prowl • v. move about in a stealthy or restless way.
– PHRASES **on the prowl** moving around in a stealthy way.
– DERIVATIVES **prowler** n.

proximate • adj. closest in space, time, or relationship.
– ORIGIN Latin *proximatus* 'drawn near'.

proximity • n. nearness in space, time, or relationship.

proxy • n. (pl. **proxies**) **1** the authority to represent someone else, especially in voting. **2** a person authorized to act on behalf of someone else.
– ORIGIN from former *procuracy* 'the position of a procurator'.

Prozac /proh-zak/ • n. trademark a drug which is taken to treat depression.
– ORIGIN an invented name.

prude • n. a person who is easily shocked by matters relating to sex.
– DERIVATIVES **prudery** n. **prudish** adj.

p

– ORIGIN French *prudefemme* 'good woman and true'.

prudent • adj. acting with or showing care and thought for the future.
– DERIVATIVES **prudence** n. **prudently** adv.
– ORIGIN Latin *prudens*.

prudential • adj. involving or showing care and thought for the future.

prune¹ • n. a dried plum with a black, wrinkled appearance.
– ORIGIN Greek *prounon* 'plum'.

prune² • v. (**prunes, pruning, pruned**) **1** trim a tree or shrub by cutting away dead or unwanted branches or stems. **2** remove unwanted parts from.
– ORIGIN Old French *proignier*.

prurient /proor-i-uhnt/ • adj. having or encouraging an excessive interest in sexual matters.
– DERIVATIVES **prurience** n.
– ORIGIN Latin *prurire* 'itch, be wanton'.

pry¹ • v. (**pries, prying, pried**) enquire too intrusively into a person's private affairs.

pry² • v. (**pries, prying, pried**) esp. N. Amer. = PRISE.
– ORIGIN from PRISE.

PS • abbrev. postscript.

psalm /sahm/ • n. a song or poem in praise of God and contained in the Book of Psalms in the Bible.
– DERIVATIVES **psalmist** n.
– ORIGIN Greek *psalmos* 'song sung to harp music'.

psalter /sawl-ter/ • n. a copy of the Book of Psalms in the Bible.
– ORIGIN Greek *psaltērion* 'stringed instrument'.

psephology /se-fol-uh-ji/ • n. the statistical study of elections and trends in voting.
– DERIVATIVES **psephologist** n.
– ORIGIN Greek *psēphos* 'pebble, vote'.

pseud /syood/ • n. Brit. informal a person who tries to impress other people by pretending to have knowledge or skill.

pseudo /syoo-doh/ • adj. informal not genuine; fake or insincere.

pseudo- • comb. form false; not genuine: *pseudonym*.
– ORIGIN Greek *pseudēs* 'false'.

pseudonym /syoo-duh-nim/ • n. a false name, especially one used by an author.
– ORIGIN from Greek *pseudēs* 'false' + *onoma* 'name'.

pseudonymous /syoo-don-i-muhss/ • adj. writing or written under a false name.

p.s.i. • abbrev. pounds per square inch.

PSNI • abbrev. Police Service of Northern Ireland.

psoriasis /suh-ry-uh-siss/ • n. a skin disease marked by red, itchy, scaly patches.
– ORIGIN Greek.

psych /syk/ • v. **1** (**psych someone up**) informal prepare someone mentally for a difficult task. **2** (**psych someone out**) intimidate an opponent by appearing very confident or aggressive. **3** (as adj. **psyched**) excited and full of anticipation.

psyche /sy-ki/ • n. the human soul, mind, or spirit.
– ORIGIN Greek *psukhē*.

psychedelia /sy-kuh-dee-li-uh/ • n. music or art based on the experiences produced by psychedelic drugs.

psychedelic /sy-kuh-del-ik, sy-kuh-dee-lik/ • adj. **1** (of drugs) producing hallucinations. **2** having bright colours or a swirling pattern.
– ORIGIN from Greek *psyche* 'soul' + *dēlos* 'clear, manifest'.

psychiatrist • n. a doctor specializing in the treatment of mental illness.

psychiatry /sy-ky-uh-tri/ • n. the branch of medicine concerned with mental illness.
– DERIVATIVES **psychiatric** /sy-ki-a-trik/ adj. **psychiatrically** adv.
– ORIGIN from Greek *psukhē* 'soul, mind' + *iatreia* 'healing'.

psychic /sy-kik/ • adj. **1** relating to abilities or events that cannot be explained by natural laws, especially those involving telepathy or clairvoyance. **2** (of a person) appearing to be telepathic or clairvoyant. • n. a person claiming to have psychic powers.
– DERIVATIVES **psychical** adj. **psychically** adv.

psycho • n. (pl. **psychos**) informal a psychopath.

psycho- • comb. form relating to the mind or psychology: *psychotherapy*.
– ORIGIN Greek *psukhē* 'soul, mind'.

psychoanalyse (US **psychoanalyze**) • v. (**psychoanalyses, psychoanalysing, psychoanalysed**; US **psychoanalyzes, psychoanalyzing, psychoanalyzed**) treat someone using psychoanalysis.

psychoanalysis • n. a method of treating mental disorders by investigating the conscious and unconscious elements in the mind.
– DERIVATIVES **psychoanalyst** n. **psychoanalytic** adj.

psychological • adj. **1** relating to the mind. **2** relating to psychology.
– DERIVATIVES **psychologically** adv.

psychological warfare • n. actions intended to reduce an opponent's confidence.

psychology • n. **1** the scientific study of the human mind and its functions. **2** the mental characteristics or attitude of a person.
– DERIVATIVES **psychologist** n.

psychometrics • n. the science of measuring mental abilities and processes.
– DERIVATIVES **psychometric** adj.

psychopath • n. a person having a serious mental illness that causes them to behave violently.
– DERIVATIVES **psychopathic** adj.

psychosis /sy-koh-siss/ • n. (pl. **psychoses** /sy-koh-seez/) a mental disorder in which a person's perception of reality is severely distorted.

psychosomatic /sy-koh-suh-mat-ik/ • adj. **1** (of a physical illness) caused by a mental factor such as stress. **2** relating to the relationship between mind and body.

psychotherapy • n. the treatment of mental disorder by psychological rather than medical means.
– DERIVATIVES **psychotherapeutic** adj. **psychotherapist** n.

psychotic /sy-kot-ik/ • adj. relating to or having a mental disorder in which a person's perception of reality is severely distorted. • n. a person with such an illness.

PT • abbrev. Brit. physical training.

Pt • abbrev. **1** Part. **2** (**pt**) pint. **3** (**Pt.**) Point (on maps). • symb. the chemical element platinum.

PTA • abbrev. parent–teacher association.

ptarmigan /tar-mi-guhn/ • n. a grouse of northern mountains and the Arctic, having grey and black plumage which changes to white in winter.
– ORIGIN Scottish Gaelic.

Pte • abbrev. Brit. Private (in the army).

pterodactyl /te-ruh-dak-til/ • n. a pterosaur of the late Jurassic period, with a long thin head and neck.
– ORIGIN from Greek *pteron* 'wing' + *daktulos* 'finger'.

pterosaur /te-ruh-sor/ • n. a fossil flying reptile of the Jurassic and Cretaceous periods.
– ORIGIN from Greek *pteron* 'wing' + *sauros* 'lizard'.

PTO • abbrev. Brit. please turn over.

Ptolemaic system (also **Ptolemaic theory**) • n. the former theory that the earth is the centre of the universe. Compare with **COPERNICAN SYSTEM**.
– ORIGIN named after the ancient Greek astronomer *Ptolemy*.

Pu • symb. the chemical element plutonium.

pub • n. Brit. a building in which beer and other drinks are served.
– ORIGIN from **PUBLIC HOUSE**.

pub crawl • n. Brit. informal a tour of several pubs, with drinks at each.

puberty • n. the period during which adolescents reach sexual maturity and become able to have children.
– ORIGIN Latin *pubertas*.

pubes /pyoo-beez/ • n. **1** (pl. **pubes**) the lower part of the abdomen at the front of the pelvis, covered with hair from puberty. **2** pl. of **PUBIS**.
– ORIGIN Latin, 'pubic hair, genitals'.

pubescence /pyuu-bess-uhnss/ • n. the time when puberty begins.
– DERIVATIVES **pubescent** adj. & n.
– ORIGIN Latin *pubescere* 'reach puberty'.

pubic • adj. relating to the pubes or pubis.

pubis /pyoo-biss/ • n. (pl. **pubes** /pyoo-beez/) either of a pair of bones forming the two sides of the pelvis.
– ORIGIN from Latin *os pubis* 'bone of the pubes'.

public • adj. **1** relating or available to the people as a whole. **2** involved in the affairs of the community: *a public figure*. **3** intended to be seen or heard by people in general: *a public apology*. **4** provided by the state rather than an independent, commercial company. • n. (**the public**) **1** ordinary people in general. **2** a group of people with a particular interest: *the reading public*.
– DERIVATIVES **publicly** adv.
– ORIGIN Latin *publicus*.

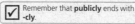
Remember that **publicly** ends with **-cly**.

public address system • n. a system of microphones and loudspeakers used to amplify speech or music.

publican • n. Brit. a person who owns or manages a pub.
– ORIGIN Latin *publicanus*.

publication • n. **1** the action of publishing something. **2** a published book or journal.

public bar • n. Brit. the more plainly furnished bar in a pub.

public company (N. Amer. **public corporation**) • n. a company whose shares are traded freely on a stock exchange.

public enemy • n. a well-known wanted criminal.

public house • n. formal = **PUB**.

publicist • n. a person responsible for publicizing a product or celebrity.

publicity • n. **1** attention given to someone or something by the media. **2** information used for advertising or promotional purposes.

publicize (or **publicise**) • v. (**publicizes, publicizing, publicized**) **1** make something widely known. **2** advertise or promote something.

public limited company • n. (in the UK) a company with shares offered to the public subject to conditions of limited legal responsibility for any company debts.

public relations • pl. n. the business of creating a good public image for an organization or famous person.

public school • n. **1** (in the UK) a private fee-paying secondary school. **2** (chiefly in North America) a school supported by public funds.

public sector • n. the part of an economy that is controlled by the state.

public servant • n. a person who works for the state or for local government.

public transport • n. buses and trains that are available to the public and run on fixed routes.

public utility • n. an organization supplying the community with electricity, gas, water, or sewerage.

publish • v. **1** produce a book, newspaper, journal, or piece of music for public sale. **2** print something in a book, newspaper, or journal so as to make it generally known.
– DERIVATIVES **publishing** n.
– ORIGIN Latin *publicare* 'make public'.

publisher • n. a company or person that publishes books, newspapers, journals, or music.

puce /pyooss/ • n. a dark red or purple-brown colour.
– ORIGIN French, 'flea, flea-colour'.

puck • n. a black disc made of hard rubber, used in ice hockey.

pucker • v. (**puckers, puckering, puckered**) tightly gather into wrinkles or small folds. • n. a wrinkle or small fold.
– ORIGIN prob. from **POCKET**.

puckish • adj. playful; mischievous.

pudding • n. **1** esp. Brit. a cooked dessert. **2** esp. Brit. the dessert course of a meal. **3** a baked or steamed savoury dish made with suet and flour: *steak and kidney pudding.* **4** Brit. the intestines of a pig or sheep stuffed with oatmeal, spices, and meat and boiled.
– ORIGIN prob. from Old French *boudin* 'black pudding'.

pudding basin • n. Brit. a deep round bowl used for cooking steamed puddings.

puddle • n. a small pool of rainwater or other liquid on the ground.
– ORIGIN Old English, 'small ditch'.

pudendum /pyoo-den-duhm/ • n. (pl. **pudenda** /pyoo-den-duh/) the genitals, especially those of a woman.
– ORIGIN from Latin *pudenda membra* 'parts to be ashamed of'.

pudgy • adj. (**pudgier, pudgiest**) informal fat or flabby.

puerile /pyoor-yl/ • adj. childishly silly.
– ORIGIN Latin *puerilis.*

puerility /pyoor-il-i-ti/ • n. (pl. **puerilities**) childish behaviour.

puerperal fever /pyoo-air-puh-ruhl/ • n. fever caused by infection of the womb after childbirth.
– ORIGIN from Latin *puer* 'child, boy' + *parus* 'bearing'.

Puerto Rican /pwair-toh ree-kuhn/ • n. a person from Puerto Rico.
• adj. relating to Puerto Rico.

puff • n. **1** a small amount of air or smoke blown from somewhere. **2** an act of drawing quickly on a pipe, cigarette, or cigar. **3** a light pastry case. **4** Brit. informal breath: *out of puff.* • v. **1** breathe in repeated short gasps. **2** move with short, noisy puffs of air or steam. **3** smoke a pipe, cigarette, or cigar. **4** (**be puffed/puffed out**) be out of breath. **5** (**puff out/up**) swell.
– DERIVATIVES **puffer** n.

puff adder • n. a large African viper which inflates the upper part of its body and hisses loudly when under threat.

puffball • n. a fungus with a large round head which bursts when ripe to release a cloud of spores.

puffery • n. exaggerated praise.

puffin • n. a seabird of the North Atlantic, with a large brightly coloured triangular bill.
– ORIGIN prob. from **PUFF**.

puff pastry • n. light flaky pastry.

puffy • adj. (**puffier, puffiest**) **1** softly rounded: *puffy clouds.* **2** (of a part of the body) swollen and soft.
– DERIVATIVES **puffiness** n.

pug • n. a small dog with a broad flat nose and deeply wrinkled face.
– ORIGIN perh. from German.

pugilist /pyoo-ji-list/ • n. esp. humorous a boxer.
– DERIVATIVES **pugilistic** adj.
– ORIGIN Latin *pugil* 'boxer'.

pugnacious /pug-nay-shuhss/ • adj. eager or quick to argue or fight.
– DERIVATIVES **pugnacity** n.
– ORIGIN Latin *pugnare* 'to fight'.

pug nose • n. a short nose with an upturned tip.

puke informal • v. (**pukes, puking, puked**) vomit. • n. vomit.

pukka /puk-kuh/ • adj. informal **1** genuine. **2** socially acceptable. **3** Brit. excellent.

– ORIGIN Hindi, 'cooked, ripe, substantial'.

pulchritude /pul-kri-tyood/ •n. literary beauty.
– ORIGIN Latin *pulcher* 'beautiful'.

pule /pyool/ •v. (**pules**, **puling**, **puled**) literary cry in a complaining or weak way.

pull •v. 1 apply force to something so as to move it towards yourself. 2 remove something by pulling. 3 move steadily: *the bus pulled away.* 4 move yourself with effort: *she pulled away from him.* 5 strain a muscle or ligament. 6 attract the interest of a potential customer. 7 (**pull at/on**) take deep breaths from a cigarette. 8 informal cancel an event. 9 Brit. informal succeed in attracting someone sexually. 10 informal bring out a weapon for use. •n. 1 an act of pulling. 2 a deep drink of something or a breath of smoke from a cigarette or pipe. 3 a force, influence, or attraction.
– PHRASES **pull back** retreat. **pull someone's leg** deceive someone for a joke. **pull something off** informal succeed in achieving or winning something difficult. **pull out** withdraw. **pull strings** make use of your influence to gain an advantage. **pull yourself together** regain your self-control. **pull your weight** do your fair share of work.
– ORIGIN Old English, 'pluck, snatch'.

pullet •n. a young hen.
– ORIGIN Old French *poulet.*

pulley •n. (pl. **pulleys**) a wheel with a grooved rim around which a rope, chain, or belt passes, used to raise heavy weights.
– ORIGIN Old French *polie.*

pullover •n. a knitted garment put on over the head and covering the top half of the body.

pullulate /pul-yuu-layt/ •v. (**pullulates**, **pullulating**, **pullulated**) 1 reproduce or spread so as to become very widespread. 2 be full of activity.
– ORIGIN Latin *pullulare* 'to sprout'.

pulmonary /pul-muh-nuh-ri/ •adj. relating to the lungs.
– ORIGIN Latin *pulmo* 'lung'.

pulp •n. 1 a soft, wet mass of crushed material. 2 the soft fleshy part of a fruit. 3 a soft, wet mass of fibres made from rags or wood, used in making paper. •v. crush something into a soft, wet mass. •adj. (of writing) popular and badly written: *pulp fiction.*
– DERIVATIVES **pulpy** adj.
– ORIGIN Latin *pulpa.*

pulpit /puul-pit/ •n. a raised platform in a church or chapel from which the preacher gives a sermon.
– ORIGIN Latin *pulpitum* 'platform'.

pulsar /pul-sar/ •n. a type of star that gives off regular rapid pulses of radio waves.
– ORIGIN from *pulsating star.*

pulsate /pul-sayt/ •v. (**pulsates**, **pulsating**, **pulsated**) 1 expand and contract with strong regular movements. 2 produce a regular throbbing feeling or sound.
– DERIVATIVES **pulsation** n.
– ORIGIN Latin *pulsare.*

pulse[1] •n. 1 the regular throbbing of the arteries as blood is sent through them. 2 a single vibration or short burst of sound, electric current, or light. 3 a musical beat or other regular rhythm. •v. (**pulses**, **pulsing**, **pulsed**) pulsate.
– ORIGIN Latin *pulsus* 'beating'.

pulse[2] •n. the edible seeds of some plants of the pea family, such as lentils.
– ORIGIN Latin *puls* 'porridge of meal or pulse'.

pulverize (or **pulverise**) •v. (**pulverizes**, **pulverizing**, **pulverized**) 1 crush something to fine particles. 2 informal utterly defeat.
– DERIVATIVES **pulverizer** n.
– ORIGIN Latin *pulverizare.*

puma •n. a large American wild cat with a tawny or greyish coat.
– ORIGIN from a South American Indian language.

pumice /pum-iss/ •n. a light form of solidified lava, used to remove hard skin.
– ORIGIN Old French *pomis.*

pummel •v. (**pummels**, **pummelling**, **pummelled**; US **pummels**, **pummeling**, **pummeled**) strike repeatedly with the fists.
– ORIGIN from **POMMEL**.

pump[1] •n. a mechanical device using suction or pressure to raise or move liquids, compress gases, or force air into inflatable objects. •v. 1 move by or as if by a pump. 2 fill something with liquid or gas. 3 move vigorously up and down. 4 (**pump something out**) produce something in large quantities or amounts. 5 (as adj. **pumped up**) informal very enthusiastic or excited.
– PHRASES **pump iron** informal exercise with weights.
– ORIGIN Dutch *pomp* 'ship's pump'.

pump[2] •n. Brit. 1 a plimsoll. 2 a light shoe for dancing.

pumpernickel /pum-per-ni-k'l/ •n. dark, heavy German bread made from wholemeal rye.
– ORIGIN German.

pumpkin •n. 1 a large rounded orange-yellow fruit with a thick rind and edible flesh. 2 Brit. = **SQUASH**[2].

p

– ORIGIN from former French *pompon*.

pun •n. a joke that uses the different meanings of a word or the fact that there are words of the same sound and different meanings. •v. (**puns**, **punning**, **punned**) make a pun.

punch¹ •v. **1** hit with the fist. **2** press a button or key on a machine. •n. **1** a blow with the fist. **2** informal effectiveness: *photos give their argument extra punch.*
– ORIGIN from **POUNCE**.

punch² •n. **1** a device or machine for making holes in a material such as paper or metal. **2** a tool or machine for impressing a design on a material. •v. pierce a hole in a material.
– ORIGIN perh. from *puncheon*, in the same sense, or from **PUNCH¹**.

punch³ •n. a drink made from wine or spirits mixed with water, fruit juices, sugar, and spices.
– ORIGIN prob. from a Sanskrit word meaning 'five' (because the drink had five ingredients).

punchbag •n. Brit. a stuffed bag suspended from a rope, used for punching as exercise or training.

punchball •n. Brit. a stuffed ball mounted on a stand, used for punching as exercise or training.

punchbowl •n. **1** a deep bowl for mixing and serving punch. **2** esp. Brit. a deep round hollow in a hilly area.

punch-drunk •adj. confused or numb as a result of being punched many times.

punchline •n. the final part of a joke or story, providing the humour or climax.

punch-up •n. informal, esp. Brit. a brawl.

punchy •adj. (**punchier**, **punchiest**) effective; forceful.

punctilio /pungk-ti-li-oh/ •n. (pl. **punctilios**) a fine or petty point of behaviour or procedure.
– ORIGIN Italian *puntiglio* and Spanish *puntillo* 'small point'.

punctilious /pungk-ti-li-uhss/ •adj. showing great attention to detail or correct behaviour.

punctual •adj. happening at or keeping to the appointed time.
– DERIVATIVES **punctuality** n. **punctually** adv.
– ORIGIN Latin *punctualis*.

punctuate /pungk-chuu-ayt, pungk-tyuu-ayt/ •v. (**punctuates**, **punctuating**, **punctuated**) **1** interrupt at intervals throughout something. **2** put punctuation marks in a piece of writing.
– ORIGIN Latin *punctuare* 'bring to a point'.

punctuation •n. the marks, such as full stop, comma, and brackets, used in writing to separate sentences and to make meaning clear.

puncture •n. a small hole caused by a sharp object. •v. (**punctures**, **puncturing**, **punctured**) make a small hole in something.
– ORIGIN Latin *punctura*.

pundit /pun-dit/ •n. an expert who frequently gives opinions about a subject in public.
– DERIVATIVES **punditry** n.
– ORIGIN Sanskrit, 'learned'.

pungent /pun-juhnt/ •adj. **1** having a sharply strong taste or smell. **2** (of remarks or humour) sharp.
– DERIVATIVES **pungency** n.
– ORIGIN Latin *pungere* 'to prick'.

punish •v. **1** make someone experience something unpleasant for doing something criminal or wrong. **2** treat harshly or unfairly.
– DERIVATIVES **punishable** adj.
– ORIGIN Latin *punire*.

punishment •n. **1** an unpleasant experience imposed on someone as a result of a criminal or wrongful act. **2** the action of punishing. **3** rough treatment.

punitive /pyoo-ni-tiv/ •adj. intended as punishment.

Punjabi /pun-jah-bi, puun-jah-bi/ (also **Panjabi** /pan-jah-bi/) •n. (pl. **Punjabis**) **1** a person from Punjab, a region of NW India and Pakistan. **2** the language of Punjab.

punk •n. **1** (also **punk rock**) a loud, fast form of rock music with aggressive lyrics and behaviour. **2** (also **punk rocker**) an admirer or player of punk music. **3** informal, esp. N. Amer. a worthless person or a criminal. •adj. relating to punk rock.
– ORIGIN perh. from former *punk* 'prostitute' or from **SPUNK**.

punnet •n. Brit. a small light container for fruit.
– ORIGIN perh. from dialect *pun* 'a pound'.

punt¹ /punt/ •n. a long, narrow, flat-bottomed boat that is moved forward with a long pole. •v. travel in a punt.
– ORIGIN Latin *ponto*.

punt² /punt/ Brit. informal •v. bet on or make a risky investment in something. •n. a bet.
– ORIGIN French *ponte* 'player against the bank'.

punt³ /puunt/ •n. the basic unit of money of the Republic of Ireland.
– ORIGIN Irish, 'a pound'.

punter •n. informal **1** esp. Brit. a person who places a bet. **2** Brit. a customer or client.

puny /pyoo-ni/ •adj. (**punier**, **puniest**) **1** small and weak. **2** not very good.
– DERIVATIVES **punily** adv. **puniness** n.

– ORIGIN Old French *puisne* 'junior or inferior person'.

pup •n. **1** a puppy. **2** a young wolf, seal, rat, or other mammal. •v. (**pups, pupping, pupped**) give birth to a pup or pups.
– ORIGIN from **PUPPY**.

pupa /pyoo-puh/ •n. (pl. **pupae** /pyoo-pee/) an insect in the form between larva and adult.
– DERIVATIVES **pupal** adj.
– ORIGIN Latin, 'girl, doll'.

pupate •v. (**pupates, pupating, pupated**) become a pupa.

pupil[1] •n. a person who is being taught by someone.
– ORIGIN Latin *pupillus* 'little boy' and *pupilla* 'little girl'.

pupil[2] •n. the dark circular opening in the centre of the iris of the eye, which alters the amount of light reaching the retina.
– ORIGIN Latin *pupilla* 'little doll' (from the tiny reflected images visible in the eye).

puppet •n. **1** a model of a person or animal which can be moved either by strings or by a hand inside it. **2** a person who is under the control of someone else.
– DERIVATIVES **puppeteer** n. **puppetry** n.
– ORIGIN from **POPPET**.

puppy •n. (pl. **puppies**) a young dog.
– ORIGIN perh. from Old French *poupee* 'doll, toy'.

puppy fat •n. Brit. fat on a child's body which disappears as they grow up.

puppy love •n. strong but short-lived love for someone felt by a young person.

purblind /per-blynd/ •adj. literary **1** partially sighted. **2** lacking awareness or understanding.
– ORIGIN from **PURE** 'utterly' + **BLIND**.

purchase •v. (**purchases, purchasing, purchased**) buy something. •n. **1** the action of buying. **2** a thing bought. **3** firm contact or grip.
– DERIVATIVES **purchaser** n.
– ORIGIN Old French *pourchacier* 'seek to obtain or bring about'.

purdah /per-duh/ •n. the practice in certain Muslim and Hindu societies of screening women from men or strangers.
– ORIGIN Urdu and Persian, 'veil'.

pure •adj. **1** not mixed with any other substance or material. **2** free of impurities. **3** innocent or good. **4** complete; nothing but: *a shout of pure anger.* **5** theoretical rather than practical: *pure mathematics.* **6** (of a sound) perfectly in tune and with a clear tone.
– DERIVATIVES **purely** adv.

– ORIGIN Latin *purus*.

pure-bred •adj. (of an animal) bred from parents of the same breed.

purée /pyoor-ay/ •n. a soft, wet mass of crushed or sieved fruit or vegetables. •v. (**purées, puréeing, puréed**) make a purée of.
– ORIGIN French, 'purified'.

purgation /per-gay-sh'n/ •n. purification.
– ORIGIN Latin.

purgative /per-guh-tiv/ •adj. having a strong laxative effect. •n. a laxative.

purgatory /per-guh-tuh-ri/ •n. (pl. **purgatories**) (in Roman Catholic belief) a place to which the souls of sinners who are making up for their sins go before going to heaven.
– DERIVATIVES **purgatorial** adj.
– ORIGIN Latin *purgatorium*.

purge •v. (**purges, purging, purged**) **1** rid of undesirable things. **2** remove a group of people considered undesirable from an organization. **3** empty your bowels as a result of taking a laxative. •n. an act of purging.
– ORIGIN Latin *purgare* 'purify'.

purify •v. (**purifies, purifying, purified**) make something pure.
– DERIVATIVES **purification** n. **purifier** n.

purist •n. a person who insists on following traditional rules, especially in language or style.
– DERIVATIVES **purism** n. & adj.

puritan •n. **1** (**Puritan**) a member of a group of English Protestants in the 16th and 17th centuries who set out to simplify forms of worship. **2** a person with strong moral beliefs who is critical of the behaviour of other people.
– DERIVATIVES **puritanical** adj.

purity •n. the state of being free from added substances or undesirable influences.

purl •adj. (of a knitting stitch) made by putting the needle through the front of the stitch from right to left.

purler •n. Brit. informal a headlong fall.
– ORIGIN from dialect *purl* 'upset'.

purlieus /per-lyooz/ •pl. n. the area near or surrounding a place.
– ORIGIN prob. from Old French *puralee* 'a walk round to settle boundaries'.

purlin /per-lin/ •n. a horizontal beam that supports the rafters in a roof.
– ORIGIN perh. French.

purloin /per-loyn/ •v. formal steal something.
– ORIGIN Old French *purloigner* 'put away'.

purple •n. a colour between red and blue. •adj. of a colour between red and blue.

p

– DERIVATIVES **purplish** adj. **purply** adj.
– ORIGIN Greek *porphura*, referring to molluscs that yielded a crimson dye.

purple patch • n. Brit. informal a run of success or good luck.

purple prose • n. prose that is too elaborate.

purport • v. /per-**port**/ appear or claim to be someone or be doing something. • n. /**per**-port/ the meaning of something.
– ORIGIN Latin *proportare*.

purpose • n. **1** the reason for which something is done or for which something exists. **2** strong determination. • v. (**purposes, purposing, purposed**) formal have something as your aim.
– PHRASES **on purpose** deliberately.
– ORIGIN Old French *porpos*.

purposeful • adj. having or showing determination.
– DERIVATIVES **purposefully** adv.

purposeless • adj. having no purpose.

purposely • adv. deliberately.

purposive • adj. having a clear purpose.

purr • v. **1** (of a cat) make a low continuous sound expressing contentment. **2** (of a vehicle or engine) move or run smoothly while making a similar sound. • n. a purring sound.

purse • n. **1** esp. Brit. a small pouch for carrying money. **2** N. Amer. a handbag. **3** money for spending. **4** a sum of money given as a prize in a sporting contest. • v. (**purses, pursing, pursed**) form your lips into a tight round shape.
– ORIGIN Latin *bursa*.

purser • n. a ship's officer who keeps the accounts.

pursuance • n. formal the carrying out of a plan or action.

pursuant /per-**syoo**-uhnt/ • adv. (**pursuant to**) formal in accordance with.
– ORIGIN Old French.

pursue • v. (**pursues, pursuing, pursued**) **1** follow someone or something in order to catch or attack them. **2** try to achieve a goal. **3** engage in or continue with an activity. **4** continue to investigate or discuss a subject.
– DERIVATIVES **pursuer** n.
– ORIGIN Old French *pursuer*.

☑ Remember that **pursue** and the related word **pursuit** begin with **pur-**.

pursuit • n. **1** the action of pursuing someone or something. **2** a leisure or sporting activity.

purulent /**pyoor**-uu-luhnt/ • adj. containing or giving out pus.
– ORIGIN Latin *purulentus*.

purvey • v. formal provide or supply food or drink as a business.
– DERIVATIVES **purveyor** n.
– ORIGIN Old French *purveier* 'foresee'.

purview • n. formal the range of the influence or concerns of something: *the case may be within the purview of the legislation.*
– ORIGIN Old French *purveu* 'foreseen'.

pus • n. a thick yellowish or greenish liquid produced in infected tissue.
– ORIGIN Latin.

push • v. **1** apply force to someone or something so as to move them away from yourself. **2** move your body or a part of it into a specified position. **3** move forward by using force. **4** urge someone to greater effort. **5** (**push for**) make persistent demands for something. **6** informal promote the use or acceptance of something. **7** informal sell an illegal drug. • n. **1** an act of pushing. **2** a great effort: *one last push.*
– PHRASES **get** (or **give someone**) **the push** Brit. informal **1** be dismissed (or dismiss someone) from a job. **2** be rejected in (or end) a relationship. **push ahead** carry on with a course of action. **push off** Brit. informal go away. **push in** go in front of people who are already queuing. **push your luck** informal take a risk in the belief that you will continue to be successful.
– DERIVATIVES **pusher** n.
– ORIGIN Old French *pousser*.

pushbike • n. Brit. informal a bicycle.

pushchair • n. Brit. a folding chair on wheels, in which a young child can be pushed along.

pushover • n. informal **1** a person who is easy to influence or defeat. **2** a thing that is easily done.

pushy • adj. (**pushier, pushiest**) too self-assertive or ambitious.
– DERIVATIVES **pushiness** n.

pusillanimous /pyoo-si-**lan**-i-muhss/ • adj. weak or cowardly.
– DERIVATIVES **pusillanimity** /pyoo-si-luh-**nim**-i-ti/ n.
– ORIGIN from Latin *pusillus* 'very small' + *animus* 'mind'.

puss • n. informal a cat.
– ORIGIN prob. from German *pûs* or Dutch *poes*.

pussy • n. (pl. **pussies**) informal a cat.

pussycat • n. informal **1** a cat. **2** a mild-tempered or easy-going person.

pussyfoot • v. (**pussyfoots, pussyfooting, pussyfooted**) act very cautiously.

pussy willow • n. a willow with soft

fluffy catkins that appear before the leaves.

pustule /pus-tyool/ • n. a small blister or pimple containing pus.
– DERIVATIVES **pustular** adj.
– ORIGIN Latin *pustula*.

put • v. (**puts, putting, put**) 1 move something to or place something in a particular position. 2 bring into a particular state: *she tried to put me at ease.* 3 (**put something on/on to**) make a person or thing subject to something: *the decision to put VAT on domestic fuel.* 4 give a value, figure, or limit to. 5 express something in a particular way. 6 (of a ship) go in a particular direction: *the boat put out to sea.* 7 throw a shot or weight as an athletic sport.
– PHRASES **put away** informal 1 consume (food or drink) in large quantities. 2 confine in a prison or psychiatric hospital. **put someone down** informal criticize someone. **put something down** 1 end an uprising or riot by force. 2 kill a sick, old, or injured animal. 3 pay a sum as a deposit. **put someone off** 1 cause someone to feel dislike or lose enthusiasm. 2 distract someone. **put something off** postpone something. **put something on** 1 present or provide a play, service, etc. 2 become heavier by a specified amount. 3 adopt an expression or accent or pretend to be feeling something. **put someone out** inconvenience, upset, or annoy someone. **put someone up** 1 accommodate someone for a short time. 2 propose someone for election or adoption. **put something up** present, provide, or offer something. **put someone up to** informal encourage someone to do something wrong or unwise. **put up with** tolerate.
– ORIGIN Old English.

putative /pyoo-tuh-tiv/ • adj. generally considered to be.
– ORIGIN Latin *putativus*.

put-down • n. informal a humiliating or critical remark.

putrefy /pyoo-tri-fy/ • v. (**putrefies, putrefying, putrefied**) decay or rot and produce a very unpleasant smell.
– DERIVATIVES **putrefaction** n.
– ORIGIN Latin *putrefacere*.

putrescent /pyoo-tress-uhnt/ • adj. becoming putrid; rotting.

putrid • adj. 1 decaying or rotting and producing a very unpleasant smell. 2 informal very unpleasant.
– ORIGIN Latin *putridus*.

putsch /puuch/ • n. a violent attempt to overthrow a government.
– ORIGIN Swiss German, 'thrust, blow'.

putt • v. (**putts, putting, putted**) strike a golf ball gently so that it rolls into or near a hole. • n. a stroke of this kind.
– ORIGIN Scots form of **PUT**.

puttee /put-tee/ • n. a long strip of cloth wound round the leg from ankle to knee for protection and support.
– ORIGIN Hindi, 'band, bandage'.

putter¹ /put-ter/ • n. a golf club used for putting.

putter² /put-ter/ • n. the rapid irregular sound of a small petrol engine. • v. (**putters, puttering, puttered**) move with or make such a sound.

putting green • n. a smooth area of short grass surrounding a hole on a golf course.

putty • n. a paste that is easily pressed into shape and hardens as it sets, used for sealing glass in window frames or filling holes in wood.
– ORIGIN French *potée* 'potful'.

puzzle • v. (**puzzles, puzzling, puzzled**) 1 confuse someone on account of being difficult to understand. 2 (often **puzzle over**) think hard about something that is difficult to understand. • n. 1 a game, toy, or problem designed to test mental skills or knowledge. 2 a person or thing that is difficult to understand.
– DERIVATIVES **puzzlement** n. **puzzler** n.

PVA • abbrev. polyvinyl acetate, a synthetic resin used in paints and glues.

PVC • abbrev. polyvinyl chloride, a synthetic resin used in pipes, flooring, and other products.

pygmy (also **pigmy**) • n. (pl. **pygmies**) 1 (**Pygmy**) a member of a people of very short height living in equatorial Africa. 2 a person who is lacking in a particular respect: *intellectual pygmies.* • adj. very small; dwarf.
– ORIGIN Greek *pugmaios* 'dwarf'.

pyjamas (US **pajamas**) • pl. n. a suit of loose trousers and jacket for sleeping in.
– ORIGIN from the Persian words for 'leg' + 'clothing'.

pylon • n. (also **electricity pylon**) a tall metal structure for carrying electricity cables.
– ORIGIN Greek *pulōn* 'gateway'.

pylorus /py-lor-uhss/ • n. (pl. **pylori** /py-**lor**-l/) the opening from the stomach into the small intestine.
– ORIGIN Greek *pulouros* 'gatekeeper'.

pyramid • n. 1 a very large stone structure with a square or triangular base and sloping sides that meet in a point at the top, especially one built as a royal tomb in ancient Egypt. 2 Geom. a polyhedron of which one face is a polygon and the other faces are triangles with a common vertex.

p

– DERIVATIVES **pyramidal** adj.
– ORIGIN Greek *puramis*.

pyramid selling • n. a system of selling goods in which agency rights are sold to an increasing number of distributors at successively lower levels.

pyre • n. a large heap of wood on which a dead body is ritually burnt.
– ORIGIN Greek *pur* 'fire'.

Pyrex • n. trademark a hard heat-resistant type of glass.

pyridoxine /pi-ri-**dok**-sin, pi-ri-**dok**-seen/ • n. vitamin B$_6$, a compound present chiefly in cereals, liver oils, and yeast.
– ORIGIN from *pyrid(ine)* (a liquid chemical) + *oxy(gen)*.

pyrites /py-ry-**teez**/ (also **iron pyrites** or **pyrite**) • n. a shiny yellow mineral that is a compound of iron and sulphur.
– ORIGIN Greek *puritēs* 'of fire'.

pyro- • comb. form relating to fire: *pyromania*.
– ORIGIN Greek *pur* 'fire'.

pyroclastic /py-ruh-**klass**-tik/ • adj. relating to rock fragments or ash erupted by a volcano, especially as a hot, dense, destructive flow.
– ORIGIN from Greek *klastos* 'broken in pieces'.

pyromania • n. a very strong desire to set fire to things.

– DERIVATIVES **pyromaniac** n.

pyrotechnic /py-ruh-**tek**-nik/ • adj. **1** relating to fireworks. **2** brilliant or spectacular.
– DERIVATIVES **pyrotechnical** adj.

pyrotechnics • pl. n. **1** a firework display. **2** the art of making fireworks or staging firework displays. **3** a spectacular performance or display: *vocal pyrotechnics*.

pyrrhic /**pir**-rik/ • adj. (of a victory) won at too great a cost to have been worthwhile for the person winning.
– ORIGIN named after *Pyrrhus*, an ancient king of Epirus whose victory over the Romans incurred heavy losses.

Pythagoras' theorem • n. the theorem that the square on the hypotenuse of a right-angled triangle is equal in area to the sum of the squares on the other two sides.
– ORIGIN from the name of the ancient Greek mathematician *Pythagoras*.

python • n. a large snake which crushes its prey.
– ORIGIN Greek *Puthōn*, a huge serpent killed by Apollo.

pyx /piks/ • n. (in the Christian Church) the container in which the blessed bread used in the service of Holy Communion is kept.
– ORIGIN Greek *puxis* 'box'.

Qq

Q¹ (also **q**) • n. (pl. **Qs** or **Q's**) the seventeenth letter of the alphabet.

Q² • abbrev. question.

Qatari /ka-**tah**-ri/ • n. a person from Qatar, a country in the Persian Gulf. • adj. relating to Qatar.

QC • abbrev. Law Queen's Counsel.

QED • abbrev. quod erat demonstrandum, used to say that something proves the truth of your claim.
– ORIGIN Latin, 'which was to be demonstrated'.

qt • abbrev. quart(s).

qua /kway, kwah/ • conj. formal in the capacity of.
– ORIGIN Latin.

quack¹ • n. the harsh sound made by a duck. • v. make a quack.

quack² • n. **1** an unqualified person who falsely claims to have medical knowledge. **2** Brit. informal a doctor.
– DERIVATIVES **quackery** n.
– ORIGIN Dutch *quacksalver*.

quad • n. **1** a quadrangle. **2** a quadruplet.

quad bike • n. a motorcycle with four large tyres, for off-road use.

quadrangle • n. **1** a square or rectangular courtyard enclosed by buildings. **2** a four-sided geometrical figure.
– DERIVATIVES **quadrangular** adj.
– ORIGIN from Latin *quadri-* 'four' + *angulus* 'corner, angle'.

quadrant • n. **1** each of four parts of a circle, plane, etc. divided by two lines or planes at right angles. **2** hist. an instrument for measuring altitude in astronomy and navigation.
– ORIGIN Latin *quadrans* 'quarter'.

quadraphonic /kwod-ruh-**fon**-ik/ • adj. (of sound reproduction) transmitted through four channels.

quadrate /kwod-ruht/ • adj. roughly square or rectangular.
– ORIGIN Latin *quadrare* 'make square'.

quadratic /kwod-**rat**-ik/ • adj. Math. involving the second and no higher power of an unknown quantity or variable.

quadrennial /kwod-**ren**-ni-uhl/ • adj. lasting for or recurring every four years.
– ORIGIN from Latin *quadri-* 'four' + *annus* 'year'.

quadri- • comb. form four; having four: *quadriplegia*.
– ORIGIN Latin.

quadriceps /kwod-ri-seps/ • n. (pl. **quadriceps**) a large muscle at the front of the thigh.
– ORIGIN Latin, 'four-headed'.

quadrilateral • n. a four-sided figure. • adj. having four straight sides.

quadrille /kwo-**dril**/ • n. a square dance performed by four couples.
– ORIGIN French.

quadrillion /kwod-**ril**-lyuhn/ • cardinal number a thousand million million.

quadriplegia /kwod-ri-**plee**-juh/ • n. Med. paralysis of all four limbs.
– DERIVATIVES **quadriplegic** adj. & n.

quadruped /kwod-ruu-ped/ • n. an animal which has four feet.
– ORIGIN from Latin *quadru-* 'four' + *pes* 'foot'.

quadruple • adj. **1** consisting of four parts or elements. **2** four times as much or as many. • v. (**quadruples**, **quadrupling**, **quadrupled**) multiply by four.
– ORIGIN Latin *quadruplus*.

quadruplet • n. each of four children born at one birth.

quaff /kwoff/ • v. drink heartily.
– DERIVATIVES **quaffable** adj.

quagmire /kwag-myr, kwog-myr/ • n. **1** a soft boggy area of land that gives way underfoot. **2** a complicated or difficult situation.
– ORIGIN from former *quag* 'a marshy place' + **MIRE**.

quail¹ • n. (pl. **quail** or **quails**) a small short-tailed game bird.
– ORIGIN Old French *quaille*.

quail² • v. feel or show fear or worry.

quaint • adj. attractively unusual or old-fashioned.
– ORIGIN Old French *cointe* 'wise'.

q

quake •v. (**quakes, quaking, quaked**) **1** (of the earth) shake or tremble. **2** shudder with fear. •n. informal an earthquake.
– ORIGIN Old English.

Quaker •n. a member of the Religious Society of Friends, a Christian movement devoted to peaceful principles and rejecting all set forms of worship.
– DERIVATIVES **Quakerism** n.
– ORIGIN from **QUAKE**, perh. referring to the founder's direction to his followers to 'tremble at the Word of the Lord'.

qualification •n. **1** the action of qualifying. **2** a pass of an exam or a successful completion of a course. **3** a quality that makes someone suitable for a job or activity. **4** a statement that restricts the meaning of another statement.

qualify •v. (**qualifies, qualifying, qualified**) **1** meet the necessary standard or conditions to be able to do or receive something. **2** become officially recognized as able to work in a particular profession: *the training needed to qualify as a solicitor.* **3** add restrictions to a statement to limit its meaning. **4** Grammar (of a word or phrase) describe another word in a particular way in order to restrict its meaning (e.g. in *the open door, open* is an adjective which qualifies *door*).
– DERIVATIVES **qualifier** n.
– ORIGIN Latin *qualificare*.

qualitative /kwol-i-tuh-tiv/ •adj. relating to or measured by quality.
– DERIVATIVES **qualitatively** adv.

quality •n. (pl. **qualities**) **1** the standard of how good something is as measured against other similar things. **2** general excellence. **3** a distinctive feature.
– ORIGIN Latin *qualitas*.

quality control •n. a system of maintaining standards in manufactured products by testing a sample to see if it meets the required standard.

qualm /kwahm/ •n. a feeling of doubt or unease.
– ORIGIN perh. from an Old English word meaning 'pain'.

quandary /kwon-duh-ri/ •n. (pl. **quandaries**) a state of uncertainty.
– ORIGIN perh. from Latin *quando* 'when'.

quango /kwang-goh/ •n. (pl. **quangos**) Brit. derog. a semi-public administrative organization that receives financial support from the government, which makes senior appointments to it.
– ORIGIN from the initial letters of *quasi non-governmental organization.*

quanta pl. of **QUANTUM**.

quantify •v. (**quantifies, quantifying, quantified**) express or measure the quantity of.
– DERIVATIVES **quantifiable** adj. **quantification** n. **quantifier** n.

quantitative /kwon-ti-tuh-tiv/ •adj. relating to or measured by quantity.
– DERIVATIVES **quantitatively** adv.

quantity •n. (pl. **quantities**) **1** a certain amount or number. **2** the aspect of something that can be measured in number, amount, size, or weight: *wages depended on quantity of output.* **3** a considerable number or amount.
– ORIGIN Latin *quantitas*.

quantity surveyor •n. Brit. a person who calculates the amount and cost of materials needed for building work.

quantum /kwon-tuhm/ •n. (pl. **quanta**) Physics a distinct quantity of energy corresponding to that involved in the absorption or emission of energy by an atom.
– ORIGIN Latin.

quantum leap •n. a sudden large increase or advance.

quantum mechanics •n. the branch of physics concerned with describing the behaviour of subatomic particles in terms of quanta.

quantum theory •n. a theory of matter and energy based on the idea of quanta.

quarantine •n. a period of isolation for people or animals that have or may have a disease. •v. (**quarantines, quarantining, quarantined**) put a person or animal in quarantine.
– ORIGIN Italian *quarantina* 'forty days'.

quark /kwark/ •n. Physics any of a group of subatomic particles which carry a fractional electric charge and are believed to be building blocks of protons, neutrons, and other particles.
– ORIGIN invented by the American physicist Murray Gell-Mann.

quarrel •n. **1** an angry argument or disagreement. **2** a reason for disagreement. •v. (**quarrels, quarrelling, quarrelled**; US **quarrels, quarreling, quarreled**) **1** have a quarrel. **2** (**quarrel with**) disagree with.
– ORIGIN Latin *querella* 'complaint'.

quarrelsome •adj. likely to quarrel.

quarry[1] •n. (pl. **quarries**) an area of the earth's surface which has been dug open so that stone or other materials can be obtained. •v. (**quarries, quarrying, quarried**) take stone or other materials from a quarry.
– ORIGIN Old French *quarriere*.

quarry[2] •n. (pl. **quarries**) **1** an animal

being hunted. **2** a person or thing being chased or sought.
– ORIGIN Old French *couree* 'parts of a deer given to the hounds'.

quarry tile • n. an unglazed floor tile.
– ORIGIN Old French *quarrel* 'lattice windowpane'.

quart • n. a unit of liquid capacity equal to a quarter of a gallon, equivalent in Britain to approximately 1.13 litres and in the US to approximately 0.94 litre.
– ORIGIN from Latin *quarta pars* 'fourth part'.

quarter • n. **1** each of four equal parts into which something is or can be divided. **2** a period of three months. **3** a quarter-hour. **4** one fourth of a pound weight, equal to 4 ounces avoirdupois. **5** a part of a town or city with a specific character or use: *the business quarter.* **6** a US or Canadian coin worth 25 cents. **7** one fourth of a hundredweight (Brit. 28 lb or US 25 lb). **8** (**quarters**) rooms or lodgings. **9** a person or area regarded as the source of something: *help came from an unexpected quarter.* **10** mercy shown to an opponent: *they gave the enemy no quarter.* • v. (**quarters, quartering, quartered**) **1** divide something into quarters. **2** (**be quartered**) be lodged. **3** hist. cut the body of an executed person into four parts.
– ORIGIN Latin *quartarius*.

quarterback • n. Amer. Football a player stationed behind the centre who directs a team's attacking play.

quarter day • n. Brit. each of four days in the year on which some tenancies begin and end and quarterly payments fall due.

quarterdeck • n. the part of a ship's upper deck near the stern.

quarter-final • n. a match of a knockout competition coming before the semi-final.

quarter-hour (also **quarter of an hour**) • n. a period of fifteen minutes.

quarter-light • n. Brit. a window in the side of a motor vehicle other than a main door window.

quarterly • adj. & adv. produced or occurring once every quarter of a year. • n. (pl. **quarterlies**) a publication produced four times a year.

quartermaster • n. a regimental officer in charge of providing accommodation and supplies.

quarter sessions • pl. n. hist. (in England, Wales, and Northern Ireland) a court of limited powers, held quarterly.

quarterstaff • n. a heavy pole 6–8 feet long, formerly used as a weapon.

quartet • n. **1** a group of four people playing music or singing together. **2** a composition for a quartet. **3** a set of four.
– ORIGIN Italian *quartetto*.

quartile /kwor-tyl/ • n. Stat. each of four equal groups into which a population can be divided.
– ORIGIN Latin *quartilis*.

quarto /kwor-toh/ • n. (pl. **quartos**) a size of page for a book resulting from folding a sheet into four leaves.
– ORIGIN from Latin *in quarto* 'in the fourth'.

quartz • n. a hard mineral consisting of silica, typically occurring as colourless or white hexagonal prisms.
– ORIGIN German *Quarz*.

quartz clock (or **watch**) • n. a clock (or watch) regulated by vibrations of an electrically driven quartz crystal.

quartzite • n. a compact, hard, granular rock consisting mainly of quartz.

quasar /kway-zar/ • n. a kind of galaxy which gives off enormous amounts of energy.
– ORIGIN from *quasi-stellar radio source*.

quash • v. **1** officially reject a legal decision as invalid. **2** suppress or put an end to.
– ORIGIN Old French *quasser* 'annul'.

quasi- /kway-zy/ • comb. form seemingly: *quasi-scientific.*
– ORIGIN Latin, 'as if, almost'.

quaternary /kwuh-ter-nuh-ri/ • adj. **1** fourth in order or rank. **2** (**Quaternary**) Geol. relating to the most recent period in the Cenozoic era, from about 1.64 million years ago to the present.
– ORIGIN Latin *quaternarius*.

quatrain /kwot-rayn/ • n. a verse of four lines, typically with alternate rhymes.
– ORIGIN French.

quatrefoil /kat-ruh-foyl/ • n. an ornamental design of four leaves, resembling a flower or clover leaf.
– ORIGIN from Old French *quatre* 'four' + *foil* 'leaf'.

quattrocento /kwa-troh-chen-toh/ • n. the 15th century as a period of Italian art or architecture.
– ORIGIN Italian, '400' (shortened from *milquattrocento* '1400').

quaver • v. (**quavers, quavering, quavered**) (of a voice) tremble. • n. **1** a tremble in a voice. **2** Brit. a musical note having the value of half a crotchet, shown by a large dot with a hooked stem.
– DERIVATIVES **quavery** adj.
– ORIGIN from dialect *quave* 'quake, tremble'.

q

quay /kee/ • n. a platform alongside or projecting into water for loading and unloading ships.
– ORIGIN Old French *kay*.

quayside • n. a quay and the area around it.

queasy • adj. (**queasier**, **queasiest**) feeling sick.
– DERIVATIVES **queasily** adv. **queasiness** n.
– ORIGIN perh. from Old French *coisier* 'to hurt'.

queen • n. 1 the female ruler of an independent state. 2 (also **queen consort**) a king's wife. 3 the best or most important woman or thing in a field or group. 4 a playing card bearing a picture of a queen, ranking next below a king. 5 the most powerful chess piece, able to move in any direction. 6 a reproductive female in a colony of ants, bees, wasps, or termites. 7 informal a very feminine homosexual man. • v. (**queen it**) (of a woman) act in an unpleasantly superior way.
– DERIVATIVES **queenly** adj.
– ORIGIN Old English.

queen mother • n. the widow of a king and mother of the current king or queen.

Queensberry Rules • pl. n. the standard rules of boxing.
– ORIGIN named after the 9th Marquess of *Queensberry*.

Queen's Counsel • n. a senior barrister appointed on the recommendation of the Lord Chancellor.

Queen's English • n. the English language as correctly written and spoken in Britain.

Queen's evidence • n. Engl. Law evidence for the prosecution given by someone involved in the crime being tried.

Queen's Guide (or **Queen's Scout**) • n. (in the UK) a Guide (or Scout) who has reached the highest rank of proficiency.

Queen's highway • n. Brit. the public road network.

queen-sized (also **queen-size**) • adj. of a larger size than the standard but smaller than king-sized.

queer • adj. 1 strange; odd. 2 informal, derog. (of a man) homosexual. • n. informal, derog. a homosexual man.
– PHRASES **queer someone's pitch** Brit. informal spoil someone's plans or chances of doing something.
– ORIGIN perh. from German *quer* 'oblique, perverse'.

quell • v. 1 put an end to a rebellion or other disorder by force. 2 suppress an unpleasant feeling.
– ORIGIN Old English, 'kill'.

quench • v. 1 satisfy thirst by drinking. 2 put out a fire.
– ORIGIN Old English.

quern /kwern/ • n. a simple hand mill for grinding grain.
– ORIGIN Old English.

querulous /kwe-ruu-luhss, kwe-ryuu-luhss/ • adj. complaining in an irritable way.
– DERIVATIVES **querulously** adv.
– ORIGIN Latin *querulus*.

query • n. (pl. **queries**) a question asking for information or expressing doubt. • v. (**queries**, **querying**, **queried**) ask a query.
– ORIGIN Latin *quaerere* 'ask, seek'.

quest • n. 1 a long or difficult search. 2 (in medieval romance) an expedition by a knight to carry out a specific task. • v. search for something.
– ORIGIN Old French *queste*.

question • n. 1 a sentence worded or expressed so as to obtain information. 2 a doubt or problem. 3 the raising of a doubt or objection: *he obeyed without question*. 4 a matter depending on conditions: *it's only a question of time*. • v. 1 ask questions of someone. 2 express doubt about something.
– PHRASES **in question** 1 being discussed. 2 in doubt. **out of the question** not possible.
– DERIVATIVES **questioner** n.
– ORIGIN Old French.

questionable • adj. 1 open to doubt. 2 likely to be dishonest or morally wrong.

question mark • n. a punctuation mark (?) indicating a question.

questionnaire /kwess-chuh-**nair**/ • n. a set of printed questions written for a survey.
– ORIGIN French.

> ☑ **questionnaire** is spelled with a double **n**.

quetzal /ket-suhl, kwet-suhl/ • n. a long-tailed tropical American bird with iridescent green plumage.
– ORIGIN Aztec, 'bright tail feather'.

queue • n. 1 esp. Brit. a line of people or vehicles waiting their turn for something. 2 Computing a list of data items, commands, etc., stored so as to be retrievable in a definite order. • v. (**queues**, **queuing** or **queueing**, **queued**) esp. Brit. wait in a queue.
– ORIGIN French, 'tail'.

queue-jump • v. Brit. move forward out of turn in a queue.

quibble • n. a slight objection or

criticism. •v. (**quibbles**, **quibbling**, **quibbled**) argue about a trivial matter.
– ORIGIN from former *quib* 'a petty objection'.

quiche /keesh/ •n. a baked flan with a savoury filling thickened with eggs.
– ORIGIN French.

quick •adj. **1** moving fast. **2** lasting or taking a short time: *a quick worker*. **3** with little or no delay. **4** intelligent or alert. •n. (**the quick**) the tender flesh below the growing part of a fingernail or toenail.
– PHRASES **cut someone to the quick** upset someone very much.
– DERIVATIVES **quickly** adv. **quickness** n.
– ORIGIN Old English, 'alive'.

quicken •v. make or become quicker.

quick-fire •adj. **1** fast and unhesitating. **2** (of a gun) firing shots in rapid succession.

quickie informal •n. **1** a rapidly consumed alcoholic drink. **2** a brief act of sex.

quicklime •n. a white caustic alkaline substance consisting of calcium oxide, obtained by heating limestone.

quicksand •n. (also **quicksands**) loose wet sand that sucks in anything resting on it.

quicksilver •n. liquid mercury. •adj. moving or changing rapidly and unpredictably.

quickstep •n. a fast foxtrot dance step.

quick-tempered •adj. easily angered.

quick-witted •adj. able to think or respond quickly.

quid[1] •n. (pl. **quid**) Brit. informal one pound sterling.

quid[2] •n. a lump of chewing tobacco.
– ORIGIN from CUD.

quiddity /kwid-i-ti/ •n. (pl. **quiddities**) the essential nature of a person or thing.
– ORIGIN Latin *quidditas*.

quid pro quo /kwid proh kwoh/ •n. (pl. **quid pro quos**) a favour given in return for something.
– ORIGIN Latin, 'something for something'.

quiescent /kwi-ess-uhnt/ •adj. in a state or period of inactivity.
– DERIVATIVES **quiescence** n.
– ORIGIN Latin *quiescere* 'be still'.

quiet •adj. (**quieter**, **quietest**) **1** making little or no noise. **2** free from activity or excitement. **3** without being disturbed: *a quiet drink*. **4** discreet: *I'll have a quiet word with him*. **5** (of a person) calm and shy. •n. absence of noise or disturbance.
– PHRASES **on the quiet** informal secretly or without drawing attention.
– DERIVATIVES **quietly** adv. **quietness** n.

– ORIGIN Latin *quies* 'rest, quiet'.

> USAGE: Do not confuse **quiet** and **quite**. **Quiet** means 'making little or no noise', as in *he spoke in a quiet voice*, whereas **quite** means 'fairly' or 'completely', as in *it's quite warm* or *I quite agree*.

quieten •v. esp. Brit. make or become quiet and calm.

quietism •n. calm acceptance of things as they are.

quietude •n. a state of calmness and quiet.

quietus /kwy-ee-tuhss/ •n. (pl. **quietuses**) literary death or a cause of death.
– ORIGIN from Latin *quietus est* 'he is quit'.

quiff •n. esp. Brit. a tuft of hair, brushed upwards and backwards from a man's forehead.

quill •n. **1** a main wing or tail feather of a bird. **2** the hollow shaft of a feather. **3** a pen made from a quill feather. **4** a spine of a porcupine or hedgehog.
– ORIGIN prob. from German *quiele*.

quilt •n. **1** a warm bed covering made of padding enclosed between layers of fabric. **2** a bedspread with decorative stitching.
– ORIGIN Old French *cuilte*.

quilted •adj. (of clothes or bedspreads) made of two layers of fabric with padding between them.

quin •n. Brit. informal a quintuplet.

quince •n. the hard, acid, pear-shaped fruit of an Asian tree.
– ORIGIN Old French *cooin*.

quincunx /kwin-kungks/ •n. (pl. **quincunxes**) an arrangement of five objects with four at the corners of a square or rectangle and the fifth at its centre.
– ORIGIN Latin, 'five twelfths'.

quinine /kwi-neen, kwi-neen/ •n. a bitter compound present in cinchona bark, formerly used to treat malaria.
– ORIGIN from a South American Indian word meaning 'bark'.

quinone /kwi-nohn/ •n. Chem. any of a group of organic compounds related to benzene but having two hydrogen atoms replaced by oxygen.
– ORIGIN Spanish *quina* 'cinchona bark'.

quinquennial /kwing-kwen-ni-uhl/ •adj. lasting for or happening every five years.
– ORIGIN from Latin *quinque* 'five' + *annus* 'year'.

quinquereme /kwing-kwi-reem/ •n. an ancient Roman or Greek galley (ship) of

q

a kind believed to have had five oarsman to a bank of oars.
– ORIGIN from Latin *quinque* 'five' + *remus* 'oar'.

quintessence /kwin-**tess**-uhnss/ • n. **1** the perfect or most typical example: *her reply was the quintessence of wit.* **2** a refined essence or extract of a substance.
– ORIGIN from Latin *quinta essentia* 'fifth essence'.

quintessential /kwin-ti-**sen**-sh'l/ • adj. representing the perfect or most typical example.
– DERIVATIVES **quintessentially** adv.

quintet • n. **1** a group of five people playing music or singing together. **2** a composition for a quintet. **3** a set of five.
– ORIGIN Italian *quintetto*.

quintuple /kwin-**tyuu**-p'l, kwin-**tyoo**-p'l/ • adj. **1** consisting of five parts or elements. **2** five times as much or as many.
– ORIGIN Latin *quintuplus*.

quintuplet /kwin-**tyuu**-plit, kwin-**tyoo**-plit/ • n. each of five children born at one birth.

quip • n. a witty remark. • v. (**quips**, **quipping**, **quipped**) make a witty remark.
– ORIGIN perh. from Latin *quippe* 'indeed'.

quire /rhymes with squire/ • n. **1** 25 sheets of paper; one twentieth of a ream. **2** four sheets of paper folded to form eight leaves.
– ORIGIN Old French *quaier*.

quirk • n. **1** a peculiar habit. **2** a strange thing that happens by chance: *a quirk of fate.*

quirky • adj. (**quirkier**, **quirkiest**) having peculiar or unexpected habits or qualities.
– DERIVATIVES **quirkily** adv. **quirkiness** n.

quisling /**kwiz**-ling/ • n. a traitor collaborating with an occupying enemy force.
– ORIGIN from Major Vidkun *Quisling*, who ruled Norway during the Second World War on behalf of the German occupying forces.

quit • v. (**quits**, **quitting**, **quitted** or **quit**) **1** leave a place. **2** resign from a job. **3** informal, esp. N. Amer. stop doing something.
– ORIGIN Old French *quiter*.

quite • adv. **1** to the greatest degree; completely. **2** to a certain extent; moderately. • exclam. expressing agreement.
– ORIGIN from **QUIT**.

> **USAGE:** For an explanation of the difference between **quite** and **quiet**, see the note at **QUIET**.

quits • adj. on equal terms because a debt or score has been settled.
– PHRASES **call it quits** decide to stop doing something.
– ORIGIN perh. from Latin *quietus est* 'he is quit', used as a receipt.

quitter • n. informal a person who gives up easily.

quiver[1] • v. (**quivers**, **quivering**, **quivered**) shake or vibrate with a slight rapid motion. • n. a quivering movement.
– ORIGIN Old English, 'nimble, quick'.

quiver[2] • n. a case for carrying arrows.
– ORIGIN Old French *quiveir*.

quixotic /kwik-**sot**-ik/ • adj. unselfish and idealistic to an impractical extent.
– ORIGIN from Don *Quixote*, hero of a book by the Spanish writer Cervantes.

quiz • n. (pl. **quizzes**) a game or competition involving a set of questions as a test of knowledge. • v. (**quizzes**, **quizzing**, **quizzed**) question someone.

quizzical • adj. showing mild or amused puzzlement.
– DERIVATIVES **quizzically** adv.

quoin /koyn, kwoyn/ • n. **1** an external angle of a wall or building. **2** a cornerstone.
– ORIGIN from **COIN**, in the former senses 'cornerstone' and 'wedge'.

quoit /koyt, kwoyt/ • n. a ring thrown in a game with the aim of it landing over an upright peg.
– ORIGIN prob. French.

quondam /**kwon**-dam/ • adj. formal former.
– ORIGIN Latin, 'formerly'.

quorate /**kwor**-uht/ • adj. Brit. (of a meeting) having a quorum.

quorum /**kwor**-uhm/ • n. (pl. **quorums**) the minimum number of members that must be present at a meeting to make its business valid.
– ORIGIN Latin, 'of whom'.

quota • n. **1** a limited quantity of a product which may be produced, exported, or imported. **2** a share that you are entitled to receive or have to contribute. **3** a fixed number of a group allowed to do something.
– ORIGIN from Latin *quota pars* 'how great a part'.

quotable • adj. suitable for or worth quoting.

quotation • n. **1** a passage or remark repeated by someone other than the person who originally said or wrote it. **2** the action of quoting. **3** a formal statement of the estimated cost of a job.

4 a registration granted to a company enabling their shares to be officially listed and traded on a stock exchange.

quotation mark • n. each of a set of punctuation marks, single (' ') or double (" "), used to mark the beginning and end of a title or quotation.

quote • v. (**quotes, quoting, quoted**) **1** repeat or copy out a passage or remark by another person. **2** (**quote something as**) mention something as an example to support a point: *the figures were quoted as more evidence for the failure of the schools.* **3** give someone an estimated price. **4** give a company a listing on a stock exchange. • n. **1** a quotation. **2** (**quotes**) quotation marks.
– ORIGIN Latin *quotare* 'mark with numbers'.

quoth /*rhymes with* oath/ • v. old use said.
– ORIGIN from former *quethe* 'say'.

quotidian /kwuh-tid-i-uhn/
• adj. **1** daily. **2** ordinary or everyday.
– ORIGIN Latin *quotidianus*.

quotient /kwoh-shuhnt/ • n. **1** Math. a result obtained by dividing one quantity by another. **2** a degree of a quality: *my coolness quotient evaporated on the spot.*
– ORIGIN Latin *quotiens* 'how many times'.

Qur'an /kuh-rahn/ (also **Quran**) • n. = KORAN.

q.v. • abbrev. used to direct a reader to another part of a book for further information.
– ORIGIN from Latin *quod vide* 'which see'.

q

Rr

R¹ (also **r**) • n. (pl. **Rs** or **R's**) the eighteenth letter of the alphabet.
– PHRASES **the three Rs** reading, writing, and arithmetic.

R² • abbrev. **1** rand. **2** Regina or Rex. **3** (**R.**) River.

r • abbrev. **1** radius. **2** right.

RA • abbrev. **1** (in the UK) Royal Academician or Royal Academy. **2** (in the UK) Royal Artillery.

Ra • symb. the chemical element radium.

rabbi /rab-by/ • n. (pl. **rabbis**) a Jewish religious leader or teacher of Jewish law.
– ORIGIN Hebrew, 'my master'.

rabbinic /ruh-bin-ik/ (also **rabbinical**) • adj. relating to rabbis or to Jewish law or teachings.

rabbit • n. **1** a burrowing mammal with long ears and a short tail. **2** the fur of the rabbit. • v. (**rabbits**, **rabbiting**, **rabbited**) **1** (as noun **rabbiting**) hunting for rabbits. **2** Brit. informal chatter. [ORIGIN from *rabbit and pork*, rhyming slang for 'talk'.]
– DERIVATIVES **rabbity** adj.
– ORIGIN prob. from Old French.

rabbit punch • n. a sharp chop with the edge of the hand to the back of the neck.

rabble • n. **1** a disorderly crowd. **2** (**the rabble**) ordinary people seen as common or uncouth.
– ORIGIN perh. from dialect, 'to gabble'.

rabble-rouser • n. a person who stirs up popular opinion for political reasons.

Rabelaisian /rab-uh-lay-zi-uhn/ • adj. like the writings of the French author François Rabelais, especially in being highly imaginative and full of earthy humour.

rabid /rab-id, ray-bid/ • adj. **1** extreme; fanatical: *a rabid anti-Communist.* **2** affected with rabies.
– DERIVATIVES **rabidly** adv.

rabies /ray-beez, ray-biz/ • n. a dangerous disease of dogs and other mammals, caused by a virus that can be transmitted through the saliva to humans, causing madness and convulsions.

– ORIGIN Latin.

RAC • abbrev. (in the UK) Royal Automobile Club.

raccoon /ruh-koon/ (also **racoon**) • n. a greyish-brown American mammal with a black face and striped tail.
– ORIGIN from an American Indian word.

race¹ • n. **1** a competition between runners, horses, or vehicles to see which is fastest over a set course. **2** a situation in which people compete to achieve something: *the race for mayor.* **3** a strong current flowing through a narrow channel. • v. (**races**, **racing**, **raced**) **1** compete in a race. **2** have a race with someone. **3** move or progress rapidly. **4** (of an engine) operate at excessive speed.
– DERIVATIVES **racer** n.
– ORIGIN Old Norse.

race² • n. **1** each of the major divisions of humankind, based on particular physical characteristics. **2** racial origin or the qualities associated with this: *rights based on race.* **3** a group of people sharing the same culture or language: *we Scots were a bloodthirsty race.* **4** a group of people or things with a common feature. **5** a subdivision of a species.
– ORIGIN French.

racecourse • n. a ground or track for horse or dog racing.

racehorse • n. a horse bred and trained for racing.

raceme /ra-seem, ruh-seem/ • n. a flower cluster with the separate flowers along a central stem, the lower flowers developing first. Compare with CYME.
– ORIGIN Latin *racemus* 'bunch of grapes'.

race meeting • n. Brit. a sporting event consisting of a series of horse races held at one course.

race relations • pl. n. relations between members of different races within a country.

racetrack • n. **1** a racecourse. **2** a track for motor racing.

racial • adj. **1** relating to race. **2** relating

to differences or relations between races: *racial discrimination*.
– DERIVATIVES **racially** adv.

racialism • n. racism.
– DERIVATIVES **racialist** n. & adj.

racing • n. a sport that involves competing in races. • adj. **1** moving swiftly. **2** (of a person) following horse racing.

racing car • n. a car built for racing.

racism • n. **1** the belief that each race has certain qualities or abilities, giving rise to the belief that certain races are better than others. **2** discrimination against or hostility towards other races.
– DERIVATIVES **racist** n. & adj.

> ☑ **racism** begins with **rac-** (the only **s** is at the end).

rack[1] • n. **1** a framework for holding or storing things. **2** (**the rack**) hist. a frame on which a person was tortured by being stretched. • v. **1** (also **wrack**) cause great pain to. **2** place in or on a rack. **3** (**rack something up**) accumulate or achieve something.
– PHRASES **rack** (or **wrack**) **your brains** think very hard.
– ORIGIN Dutch *rec* or German *rek*.

> USAGE: The words **rack** and **wrack** are often confused. As a noun, **rack** is always spelled with an **r** (*a magazine rack*). The verb can be spelled **rack** or **wrack**, but only when it means 'cause great pain to' (*he was racked/wracked with guilt*); the meanings 'put in a rack' or 'accumulate or achieve' should always be spelled **rack**.

rack[2] • n. a joint of meat that includes the front ribs.

rack[3] • n. (in phr. **go to rack and ruin**) fall into a bad condition due to neglect.
– ORIGIN Old English, 'vengeance'.

rack-and-pinion • adj. (of a mechanism) using a fixed bar with cogs or teeth that fit into a smaller cog.

racket[1] (also **racquet**) • n. **1** a bat with a stringed round or oval frame, used in tennis, badminton, and squash. **2** (**rackets**) a ball game for two or four people played with rackets in a four-walled court.
– ORIGIN French *raquette*.

racket[2] • n. **1** a loud unpleasant noise. **2** informal a dishonest scheme for obtaining money. • v. (**rackets, racketing, racketed**) make a loud unpleasant noise.
– DERIVATIVES **rackety** adj.

racketeer • n. a person who makes money through dishonest activities.
– DERIVATIVES **racketeering** n.

raconteur /ra-kon-**ter**/ • n. (fem.

raconteuse /ra-kon-**terz**/) a person who tells stories in an interesting way.
– ORIGIN French.

racoon • n. var. of RACCOON.

racquet • n. var. of RACKET[1].

racy • adj. (**racier, raciest**) lively and exciting, especially in a sexual way.
– DERIVATIVES **racily** adv. **raciness** n.

RADA /**rah**-duh/ • abbrev. (in the UK) Royal Academy of Dramatic Art.

radar • n. a system for finding the presence, direction, and speed of aircraft, ships, etc., by sending out pulses of radio waves which are reflected off the object back to the source.
– ORIGIN from *radio detection and ranging*.

radar trap • n. an area of road in which radar is used by the police to detect speeding vehicles.

raddled • adj. showing signs of age or tiredness.
– ORIGIN from RUDDY.

radial • adj. **1** arranged in lines coming out from a central point to the edge of a circle: *radial markings resembling spokes*. **2** (also **radial-ply**) (of a tyre) in which the layers of fabric have their cords running at right angles to the circumference of the tyre.
– DERIVATIVES **radially** adv.
– ORIGIN Latin *radialis*.

radian /**ray**-di-uhn/ • n. an angle of 57.3 degrees, equal to that at the centre of a circle formed by an arc equal in length to the radius.

radiant • adj. **1** shining or glowing brightly. **2** showing great joy, love, or health. **3** (of heat) transmitted by radiation.
– DERIVATIVES **radiance** n. **radiantly** adv.

radiate • v. (**radiates, radiating, radiated**) **1** (with reference to light, heat, or other energy) send out or be sent out in rays or waves. **2** show a strong feeling or quality. **3** spread out from a central point: *rows of cells radiated from a central hall*.
– ORIGIN Latin *radiare*.

radiation • n. **1** energy sent out as electromagnetic waves or subatomic particles. **2** the action of radiating.

radiation sickness • n. illness caused when a person is exposed to X-rays, gamma rays, or other radiation.

radiator • n. **1** a device that radiates heat, consisting of a metal case through which hot water circulates, or one heated by electricity or oil. **2** a cooling device in a vehicle or aircraft engine.

r

radical • adj. **1** relating to the basic nature of something; fundamental: *a radical overhaul of the regulations.* **2** supporting complete political or social reform. **3** departing from tradition; new. **4** Math. relating to the root of a number or quantity. **5** relating to the root or stem base of a plant. • n. **1** a supporter of complete political or social reform. **2** Chem. a group of atoms behaving as a unit in certain compounds.
– DERIVATIVES **radicalism** n. **radically** adv.
– ORIGIN Latin *radix* 'root'.

radical sign • n. Math. the sign √ which indicates the square root of the number following (or a higher root indicated by a raised numeral before the symbol).

radicchio /ra-dee-ki-oh/ • n. (pl. **radicchios**) a variety of chicory with dark red leaves.
– ORIGIN Italian.

radices pl. of RADIX.

radicle /ra-di-k'l/ • n. the part of a plant embryo that develops into the primary root.
– ORIGIN Latin *radicula* 'little root'.

radii pl. of RADIUS.

radio • n. (pl. **radios**) **1** the sending and receiving of electromagnetic waves carrying sound messages. **2** the activity or medium of broadcasting in sound. **3** a device for receiving radio programmes, or for sending and receiving radio messages. • v. (**radioes**, **radioing**, **radioed**) send a message by radio.
– ORIGIN Latin *radius* 'ray'.

radio- • comb. form **1** referring to radio waves or broadcasting: *radiogram.* **2** connected with rays, radiation, or radioactivity: *radiography.*

radioactive • adj. giving out harmful radiation or particles.

radioactivity • n. **1** the sending out of harmful radiation or particles, caused when atomic nuclei break up spontaneously. **2** radioactive particles.

radiocarbon • n. a radioactive isotope of carbon used in carbon dating.

radiogram • n. Brit. dated a combined radio and record player.

radiography • n. the process of taking images by X-rays or other radiation to assist in medical examinations.
– DERIVATIVES **radiographer** n.

radioisotope • n. a radioactive isotope.

radiology • n. the study and use of X-rays and similar radiation in medicine.
– DERIVATIVES **radiological** adj. **radiologist** n.

radiophonic • adj. relating to sound produced electronically.

radio-telephone • n. a telephone using radio transmission.

radio telescope • n. an instrument used to detect radio waves from space.

radiotherapy • n. the treatment of cancer or other disease using X-rays or similar radiation.

radio wave • n. an electromagnetic wave having a frequency in the range 10^4 to 10^{11} or 10^{12} hertz.

radish • n. the crisp, hot-tasting red root of a plant which is eaten raw.
– ORIGIN Latin *radix* 'root'.

radium /ray-di-uhm/ • n. a reactive, radioactive metallic element.
– ORIGIN Latin *radius* 'ray'.

radius /ray-di-uhss/ • n. (pl. **radii** /ray-di-I/ or **radiuses**) **1** a straight line from the centre to the circumference of a circle or sphere. **2** a specified distance from a centre in all directions: *pubs within a two-mile radius.* **3** the thicker and shorter of the two bones in the human forearm.
– ORIGIN Latin, 'spoke, ray'.

radix /ray-diks/ • n. (pl. **radices** /ray-di-seez/) Math. the base of a system of calculation.
– ORIGIN Latin, 'root'.

radon /ray-don/ • n. a rare radioactive gaseous element.
– ORIGIN from RADIUM.

RAF • abbrev. (in the UK) Royal Air Force.

raffia • n. fibre from the leaves of a tropical palm tree, used for making hats, baskets, etc.
– ORIGIN Malagasy (the language of Madagascar).

raffish • adj. slightly disreputable, but in an attractive way.
– ORIGIN from RIFF-RAFF.

raffle • n. a lottery with goods as prizes. • v. (**raffles**, **raffling**, **raffled**) offer something as a prize in a raffle.
– ORIGIN Old French.

raft¹ • n. **1** a flat structure made of pieces of timber fastened together, used as a boat or floating platform. **2** a small inflatable boat.
– ORIGIN Old Norse.

raft² • n. a large amount.
– ORIGIN perh. Scandinavian.

rafter • n. a beam forming part of the internal framework of a roof.
– ORIGIN Old English.

rag¹ • n. **1** a piece of old cloth. **2** (**rags**) old or tattered clothes. **3** informal a low-quality newspaper.
– PHRASES **lose your rag** Brit. informal lose your temper.
– ORIGIN prob. from RAGGED.

rag² • n. Brit. a programme of entertainments organized by students to raise money for charity. •v. (**rags, ragging, ragged**) make fun of someone.

rag³ •n. a piece of ragtime music.

raga /rah-guh/ (also **rag** /rahg/) •n. (in Indian music) a traditional pattern of notes used as a basis for improvising a piece of music.
– ORIGIN Sanskrit, 'colour, musical tone'.

ragamuffin •n. a person in ragged, dirty clothes.
– ORIGIN prob. from RAG¹.

rag-and-bone man •n. Brit. a person who goes from door to door collecting second-hand items to sell.

ragbag •n. a collection of widely different things.

rage •n. violent uncontrollable anger. •v. (**rages, raging, raged**) **1** feel or express violent uncontrollable anger. **2** continue with great force: *the argument raged for days.*
– PHRASES **all the rage** very popular or fashionable for a short time.
– ORIGIN Old French.

ragga /rag-guh/ •n. a style of dance music in which a DJ improvises lyrics over a backing track.
– ORIGIN from RAGAMUFFIN.

ragged /rag-gid/ •adj. **1** (of clothes) old and torn. **2** rough or irregular. **3** not smooth or steady: *he endured our ragged singing.*
– ORIGIN Scandinavian.

raglan •adj. (of a sleeve) continuing in one piece up to the neck of a garment.
– ORIGIN named after Lord *Raglan*, a British commander in the Crimean War.

ragout /ra-goo/ •n. a spicy stew of meat and vegetables.
– ORIGIN French.

ragtag •adj. very varied and lacking organization: *a ragtag force of men.*
– ORIGIN from RAG¹ + TAG¹.

ragtime •n. an early form of jazz music played especially on the piano.
– ORIGIN prob. from the idea of the 'ragged' rhythm.

rag trade •n. informal the clothing or fashion industry.

ragwort •n. a plant with yellow flowers and ragged leaves.

raid •n. **1** a sudden attack on an enemy or a forced entry into a building. **2** a surprise visit by police to arrest suspects or seize illegal goods. •v. make a raid on.
– DERIVATIVES **raider** n.
– ORIGIN Scots, from ROAD.

rail¹ •n. **1** a bar or series of bars fixed on supports or attached to a wall or ceiling, forming part of a fence or used to hang things on. **2** each of the two metal bars laid on the ground to form a railway

track. **3** railways as a means of transport. •v. provide or enclose something with a rail or rails.
– PHRASES **go off the rails** informal begin behaving in an uncontrolled way.
– ORIGIN Old French *reille* 'iron rod'.

rail² •v. (**rail against/at**) complain strongly about.
– ORIGIN French *railler*.

rail³ •n. a waterside bird with grey and brown plumage.
– ORIGIN Old French *raille*.

railcard •n. Brit. a pass entitling the holder to reduced rail fares.

railhead •n. the point at which a railway ends.

railing •n. a fence made of rails.

raillery /rayl-luh-ri/ •n. good-humoured teasing.
– ORIGIN from RAIL².

railroad •n. N. Amer. a railway. •v. informal rush or force someone into doing something.

railway •n. Brit. **1** a track made of rails along which trains run. **2** a system of such tracks with the trains, organization, and staff required to run it.

raiment /ray-muhnt/ •n. old use clothes.
– ORIGIN from ARRAY.

rain •n. **1** the condensed moisture of the atmosphere falling in separate drops. **2** (**rains**) falls of rain. **3** a large quantity of things falling together: *a rain of stones.* •v. **1** (**it rains, it is raining, it rained**) rain falls. **2** (**be rained off**) (of an event) be prevented by rain from continuing or taking place. **3** fall or cause to fall in large quantities.
– ORIGIN Old English.

rainbow •n. an arch of colours in the sky, caused by sunlight shining through water droplets in the atmosphere.

rainbow trout •n. a large trout with reddish sides, native to western North America and introduced elsewhere.

rain check •n. (in phr. **take a rain check**) refuse an offer but imply that you may take it up later.
– ORIGIN referring to a ticket given for later use when an outdoor event is rained off.

raincoat •n. a coat made from waterproofed or water-resistant fabric.

raindrop •n. a single drop of rain.

rainfall •n. the amount of rain falling within an area in a particular time.

rainforest •n. a dense forest found in tropical areas with consistently heavy rainfall.

rainproof •adj. (of an item of clothing) able to keep out the rain.

rainy •adj. (**rainier**, **rainiest**) having a lot of rain.
- PHRASES **a rainy day** a time in the future when money may be needed.

raise •v. (**raises**, **raising**, **raised**) 1 lift or move something upwards or into an upright position. 2 increase the amount, level, or strength of something. 3 cause something to be heard, felt, or considered: *doubts have been raised*. 4 collect or bring together money or people. 5 bring up a child. 6 breed or grow animals or plants. 7 bring a blockade or ban to an end. 8 Brit. informal establish contact with someone by telephone or radio. 9 (**raise something to**) Math. multiply a quantity to a specified power. •n. N. Amer. an increase in salary.
- PHRASES **raise the roof** make a lot of noise, especially by cheering.
- DERIVATIVES **raiser** n.
- ORIGIN Old Norse.

raisin •n. a partially dried grape.
- ORIGIN Old French, 'grape'.

raison d'être /ray-zon de-truh/ •n. (pl. **raisons d'être** /ray-zon de-truh/) the most important reason for someone or something's existence.
- ORIGIN French, 'reason for being'.

Raj /rahj/ •n. (**the Raj**) hist. the period of British rule in India.
- ORIGIN Hindi, 'reign'.

raja /rah-juh/ (also **rajah**) •n. hist. an Indian king or prince.
- ORIGIN Hindi or Sanskrit.

rake[1] •n. a tool consisting of a pole with metal prongs at the end, used for drawing together leaves or cut grass or smoothing soil. •v. (**rakes**, **raking**, **raked**) 1 draw together leaves or grass or smooth soil with a rake. 2 scratch with a sweeping movement. 3 sweep the air with gunfire or a beam of light. 4 (**rake through**) search through. 5 **rake something up/over** revive the memory of something best forgotten.
- PHRASES **rake it in** informal make a lot of money.
- ORIGIN Old English or Old Norse.

rake[2] •n. a fashionable and rich man who lives a disreputable life.
- ORIGIN from former *rakehell* in the same sense.

rake[3] •v. (**rakes**, **raking**, **raked**) set something at a sloping angle. •n. the angle at which something slopes.
- ORIGIN prob. from German *ragen* 'to project'.

rake-off •n. informal a share of the profits from an illegal or underhand deal.

rakish •adj. having a dashing, jaunty, or slightly disreputable appearance.

rally •v. (**rallies**, **rallying**, **rallied**) 1 (with reference to troops) bring or come together again so as to continue fighting. 2 bring or come together in support or for united action: *his family rallied round*. 3 recover in health or strength. 4 (of share, currency, or commodity prices) increase after a fall. •n. (pl. **rallies**) 1 a mass meeting held as a protest or in support of a cause. 2 a long-distance race for motor vehicles over roads or rough country. 3 a quick or strong recovery. 4 (in tennis and other racket sports) a long exchange of strokes between players.
- ORIGIN French *rallier*.

rallying •n. the sport of taking part in a motor rally. •adj. having the effect of calling people to action: *a rallying cry*.

RAM •abbrev. Computing random-access memory.

ram •n. 1 an adult male sheep. 2 a battering ram. 3 a striking or plunging device in a machine. •v. (**rams**, **ramming**, **rammed**) 1 roughly force something into place. 2 hit or be hit with force.
- ORIGIN Old English.

Ramadan /ram-uh-dan/ (also **Ramadhan** /ram-uh-zan/) •n. the ninth month of the Muslim year, during which Muslims fast from dawn to sunset.
- ORIGIN Arabic.

ramble •v. (**rambles**, **rambling**, **rambled**) 1 walk for pleasure in the countryside. 2 talk or write in a confused way and for a long time: *he rambled on about Norman archways*. •n. a walk taken for pleasure in the country-side.
- DERIVATIVES **rambler** n.
- ORIGIN prob. from Dutch *rammelen* 'wander about on heat' (referring to an animal).

rambutan /ram-byoo-tuhn/ •n. the red fruit of a tropical tree, with soft spines and a slightly sour taste.
- ORIGIN Malay.

ramekin /ra-mi-kin/ •n. a small dish for baking and serving an individual portion of food.
- ORIGIN French *ramequin*.

ramifications •pl. n. complex results of an action or event: *any change is bound to have legal ramifications*.

ramify /ra-mi-fy/ •v. (**ramifies**, **ramifying**, **ramified**) form parts that branch out.
- ORIGIN Latin *ramificare*.

ramp •n. 1 a sloping surface joining two different levels. 2 a movable set of steps for entering or leaving an aircraft.
- ORIGIN Old French *ramper* 'creep'.

r

rampage • v. /ram-payj/ (**rampages, rampaging, rampaged**) rush around in a wild and violent way. • n. /ram-payj/ a period of wild and violent behaviour: *thugs went on the rampage through the city.*
– ORIGIN perh. from RAMP and RAGE.

rampant • adj. **1** flourishing or spreading in an uncontrolled way: *rampant inflation.* **2** Heraldry (of an animal) shown standing on its left hind foot with its forefeet in the air: *two lions rampant.*
– ORIGIN Old French, 'crawling'.

rampart • n. a wall built to defend a castle or town, having a broad top with a walkway.
– ORIGIN French *rempart.*

ram raid • n. Brit. a robbery in which a shop window is rammed with a vehicle.

ramrod • n. a rod formerly used to ram down the charge of a firearm.

ramshackle • adj. in a very bad condition.
– ORIGIN from RANSACK.

ran past of RUN.

ranch • n. a large farm in America or Australia, where cattle or other animals are bred. • v. run a ranch.
– DERIVATIVES **rancher** n.
– ORIGIN Spanish *rancho* 'group of people eating together'.

rancid • adj. **1** (of fatty or oily foods) stale and smelling or tasting unpleasant. **2** highly unpleasant.
– DERIVATIVES **rancidity** n.
– ORIGIN Latin *rancidus* 'stinking'.

rancour (US **rancor**) • n. bitter feeling or resentment.
– DERIVATIVES **rancorous** adj.
– ORIGIN Latin *rancor* 'rankness'.

rand /rand/ • n. the basic unit of money of South Africa.
– ORIGIN from *the Rand*, a goldfield district near Johannesburg.

R & B • abbrev. **1** rhythm and blues. **2** a kind of pop music with a vocal style derived from soul.

random • adj. done or happening without a deliberate order, purpose, or choice.
– PHRASES **at random** without thinking or planning in advance.
– DERIVATIVES **randomly** adv. **randomness** n.
– ORIGIN Old French *randon* 'great speed'.

random access • n. the process of storing or finding information on a computer without having to read through items in a particular sequence.

randy • adj. (**randier, randiest**) informal sexually aroused or excited.
– ORIGIN perh. from former Dutch *randen* 'to rant'.

rang past of RING².

range • n. **1** the limits between which something varies: *a population in the range of 250,000 to 1 million.* **2** a set of different things of the same general type: *a wide range of activities.* **3** the distance over which a sound, missile, etc. can travel: *he sat down within range of the rifles.* **4** a line of mountains or hills. **5** a large area of open land for grazing or hunting. **6** an area used as a testing ground for military equipment or for shooting practice. **7** a large cooking stove with several burners or hotplates. • v. (**ranges, ranging, ranged**) **1** vary between particular limits. **2** arrange things in a row or rows or in a particular way. **3** (**be ranged against**) be in opposition to. **4** travel over or cover a wide area.
– ORIGIN Old French, 'row, rank'.

rangefinder • n. an instrument for estimating the distance of an object.

ranger • n. **1** a keeper of a park, forest, or area of countryside. **2** (**Ranger** or **Ranger Guide**) Brit. a senior Guide.

rangy /rayn-ji/ • adj. (of a person) tall and slim with long limbs.

rank¹ • n. **1** a position within the armed forces or an organization. **2** a line or row of people or things. **3** high social position. **4** (**the ranks**) members of the armed forces who are not commissioned officers. **5** (**ranks**) the members of a group: *the ranks of the unemployed.*
• v. **1** give a rank within a system to. **2** hold a specified rank. **3** arrange things in a row or rows.
– PHRASES **break rank** (or **ranks**) fail to support a group to which you belong. **close ranks** unite so as to defend shared interests. **pull rank** use your higher rank to take advantage of someone. **rank and file** the ordinary members of an organization.
– ORIGIN Old French *ranc.*

rank² • adj. **1** having a very unpleasant smell. **2** complete: *a rank amateur.* **3** (of vegetation) growing too thickly.
– ORIGIN Old English, 'proud, sturdy'.

ranking • n. a position on a scale of achievement or importance. • adj. having a specified rank: *high-ranking officers.*

rankle • v. (**rankles, rankling, rankled**) (of a comment or fact) cause continuing annoyance or resentment.
– ORIGIN Old French *rancler* 'fester'.

ransack • v. **1** go hurriedly through a place stealing things and causing damage. **2** search a place thoroughly or destructively.
– ORIGIN Old Norse.

ransom • n. a sum of money demanded

r

or paid for the release of someone who is held captive. •v. obtain the release of someone by paying a ransom.
– PHRASES **hold someone to ransom** force someone to do something by threatening damaging action.
– ORIGIN Old French *ransoun*.

rant •v. speak in a loud and angry way.
– ORIGIN Dutch *ranten* 'talk nonsense'.

rap •v. (**raps, rapping, rapped**) **1** hit a hard surface several times. **2** strike something sharply. **3** informal criticize sharply. **4** say sharply: *he rapped out an order*. •n. **1** a quick, sharp knock or blow. **2** informal a criticism. **3** a type of popular music in which words are spoken rapidly and rhythmically over an instrumental backing. **4** N. Amer. informal a criminal charge: *a murder rap*.
– PHRASES **take the rap** informal be punished or blamed for something.
– DERIVATIVES **rapper** n.
– ORIGIN prob. Scandinavian.

rapacious /ruh-pay-shuhss/ •adj. very greedy.
– ORIGIN Latin *rapere* 'to snatch'.

rapacity /ruh-pa-si-ti/ •n. greed.

rape[1] •v. (**rapes, raping, raped**) **1** (of a man) force someone to have sex with him against their will. **2** spoil or destroy a place. •n. an act of raping someone.
– ORIGIN Latin *rapere* 'seize'.

rape[2] •n. a plant with yellow flowers, grown for its oil-rich seed.
– ORIGIN Latin *rapum, rapa* 'turnip'.

rapid •adj. happening in a short time or at great speed. •pl. n. (**rapids**) a fast-flowing and turbulent stretch of a river.
– DERIVATIVES **rapidity** n. **rapidly** adv.
– ORIGIN Latin *rapidus*.

rapier •n. a thin, light sword.
– ORIGIN French *rapière*.

rapine /ra-pyn, ra-pin/ •n. literary the violent seizure of property.
– ORIGIN Old French.

rapist •n. a man who commits rape.

rapport /rap-por/ •n. a close relationship in which people understand each other and communicate well.
– ORIGIN French.

rapprochement /ra-prosh-mon/ •n. a renewal of friendly relations between two countries or groups.
– ORIGIN French.

rapscallion /rap-skal-li-uhn/ •n. old use a mischievous person.
– ORIGIN perh. from RASCAL.

rapt •adj. completely interested or absorbed in someone or something.
– ORIGIN Latin *raptus* 'seized'.

raptor •n. a bird of prey.
– ORIGIN Latin, 'plunderer'.

rapture •n. **1** intense pleasure or joy.

2 (**raptures**) the expression of intense pleasure or enthusiasm.

rapturous •adj. feeling or expressing intense pleasure or enthusiasm.
– DERIVATIVES **rapturously** adv.

rare[1] •adj. (**rarer, rarest**) **1** not occurring or found very often. **2** unusually good: *a player of rare skill*.
– ORIGIN Latin *rarus*.

rare[2] •adj. (**rarer, rarest**) (of red meat) lightly cooked, so that the inside is still red.
– ORIGIN Old English, 'half-cooked'.

rarebit (also **Welsh rarebit**) •n. a dish of melted cheese on toast.

rarefied /rair-i-fyd/ •adj. **1** (of air) of lower pressure than usual; thin. **2** understood by a limited group of people with particular knowledge.

 Spell **rarefied** with **-ref-** in the middle.

rarely •adv. not often.

raring •adj. informal very eager: *she was raring to go*.
– ORIGIN from ROAR or REAR[2].

rarity •n. (pl. **rarities**) **1** the state of being rare. **2** a thing that is rare.

rascal •n. **1** a mischievous or cheeky person. **2** a dishonest man.
– DERIVATIVES **rascally** adj.
– ORIGIN Old French *rascaille* 'rabble'.

rash[1] •adj. acting or done without considering the possible results.
– DERIVATIVES **rashly** adv.
– ORIGIN Germanic.

rash[2] •n. **1** an area of red spots or patches on a person's skin. **2** an unwelcome series of things happening within a short time: *a rash of strikes*.
– ORIGIN prob. from Old French *rasche* 'sores, scurf'.

rasher •n. a thin slice of bacon.

rasp •n. **1** a coarse file for use on metal, wood, or other hard material. **2** a harsh, grating noise. •v. **1** (of a rough surface or object) scrape something. **2** make a harsh, grating noise.
– ORIGIN Old French *rasper*.

raspberry •n. (pl. **raspberries**) **1** an edible reddish-pink soft fruit. **2** informal a sound made with the tongue and lips, expressing mockery or contempt. [ORIGIN from *raspberry tart*, rhyming slang for 'fart'.]

Rasta /rass-tuh/ •n. informal = RASTAFARIAN.

Rastafarian /rass-tuh-fair-i-uhn, rass-tuh-fah-ri-uhn/ •n. a member of a Jamaican religious movement which believes that Haile Selassie (the former Emperor of Ethiopia) was the Messiah

and that blacks are the chosen people.
– DERIVATIVES **Rastafarianism** n.
– ORIGIN from *Ras Tafari*, the name by which Haile Selassie was known.

rat • n. **1** a rodent resembling a large mouse, considered a serious pest. **2** informal an unpleasant person. • v. (**rats**, **ratting**, **ratted**) (**rat on**) informal **1** inform on someone. **2** break an agreement or promise.
– ORIGIN Old English.

ratable • adj. var. of RATEABLE.

ratafia /ra-tuh-fee-uh/ • n. an almond-flavoured biscuit like a small macaroon.
– ORIGIN French.

ratatouille /ra-tuh-too-i, ra-tuh-twee/ • n. a dish of stewed onions, courgettes, tomatoes, aubergines, and peppers.
– ORIGIN French.

ratbag • n. Brit. informal an unpleasant person.

ratchet • n. a device consisting of a bar or wheel with a set of angled teeth in which a cog, tooth, or pivoted bar fits, allowing movement in one direction only. • v. (**ratchets**, **ratcheting**, **ratcheted**) (**ratchet something up/down**) cause something to rise (or fall) as a step in a process.
– ORIGIN French *rochet*.

rate¹ • n. **1** a measure, quantity, or frequency measured against another: *companies joined the scheme at the rate of ten a month.* **2** the speed with which something moves or happens. **3** a fixed price paid or charged: *a basic rate of pay.* **4** (**rates**) (in the UK) a tax on land and buildings paid to a local authority by a business. • v. (**rates**, **rating**, **rated**) **1** give a standard or value to something according to a particular scale. **2** consider to be of a certain quality or standard: *Atkinson rates him as our top defender.* **3** be worthy of; merit. **4** informal have a high opinion of.
– PHRASES **at any rate** whatever happens or may have happened.
– ORIGIN Latin *rata*.

rate² • v. (**rates**, **rating**, **rated**) old use scold angrily.

rateable (also **ratable**) • adj. able to be rated or estimated.

rateable value • n. (in the UK) a value given to a business property based on its size and location, used to calculate the rates payable by its owner.

rather • adv. **1** (**would rather**) would prefer. **2** to some extent; quite. **3** used to correct something you have said or to be more precise: *I walked, or rather limped, home.* **4** instead of.
– ORIGIN Old English, 'earlier, sooner'.

ratify • v. (**ratifies**, **ratifying**, **ratified**)

give formal consent to.
– DERIVATIVES **ratification** n.
– ORIGIN Latin *ratificare*.

rating • n. **1** a classification or ranking based on quality, standard, or performance. **2** (**ratings**) the estimated audience size of a television or radio programme. **3** Brit. a sailor in the navy who does not hold a commission.

ratio • n. (pl. **ratios**) the relationship between two amounts, showing the number of times one value contains or is contained within the other.
– ORIGIN Latin, 'reckoning'.

ratiocination /ra-ti-oss-i-**nay**-sh'n, ra-shi-oss-i-**nay**-sh'n/ • n. formal thinking in a logical way; reasoning.
– ORIGIN Latin *ratiocinari* 'calculate'.

ration • n. **1** a fixed amount of food, fuel, etc., officially allowed to each person during a shortage. **2** (**rations**) a regular allowance of food supplied to members of the armed forces. • v. limit the supply of food, fuel, etc.
– ORIGIN Latin, 'reckoning, ratio'.

rational • adj. **1** based on reason or logic: *a rational explanation.* **2** able to think sensibly or logically.
– DERIVATIVES **rationality** n. **rationally** adv.

rationale /ra-shuh-**nahl**/ • n. a set of reasons for a course of action or a belief.

rationalism • n. the belief that opinions and actions should be based on reason and knowledge rather than on religious belief or emotions.
– DERIVATIVES **rationalist** n.

rationalize (or **rationalise**) • v. (**rationalizes**, **rationalizing**, **rationalized**) **1** try to find a logical reason for an action or attitude. **2** reorganize a process or system so as to make it more logical. **3** Brit. make a company more efficient by disposing of unwanted staff or equipment.
– DERIVATIVES **rationalization** n.

rat race • n. informal a way of life which is a fiercely competitive struggle for wealth or power.

rattan /ruh-**tan**/ • n. the thin, pliable stems of a tropical climbing palm, used to make furniture.
– ORIGIN Malay.

rattle • v. (**rattles**, **rattling**, **rattled**) **1** make or move with a rapid series of short, sharp sounds. **2** informal make someone nervous or irritated. **3** (**rattle something off**) say or do something quickly and easily. **4** (**rattle on/away**) talk rapidly and at length. • n. **1** a rattling sound. **2** a device or toy that makes a rattling sound.
– ORIGIN Dutch and German *ratelen*.

r

rattlesnake • n. an American viper with horny rings on the tail that produce a rattling sound.

rattletrap • n. informal an old or rickety vehicle.

rattling • adj. informal, dated very: *a rattling good story*.

ratty • adj. (**rattier, rattiest**) 1 resembling a rat. 2 informal in bad condition. 3 Brit. informal irritable.

raucous /raw-kuhss/ • adj. sounding loud and harsh.
– DERIVATIVES **raucously** adv.
– ORIGIN Latin *raucus* 'hoarse'.

raunchy • adj. (**raunchier, raunchiest**) informal sexually exciting or direct.
– DERIVATIVES **raunchiness** n.

ravage • v. (**ravages, ravaging, ravaged**) cause great damage to. • n. (**ravages**) the destruction caused by something.
– ORIGIN French *ravager*.

rave • v. (**raves, raving, raved**) 1 talk angrily or without making sense. 2 speak or write about someone or something with great enthusiasm. • n. a very large event with dancing to loud, fast electronic music.
– ORIGIN prob. from Old French *raver*.

ravel • v. (**ravels, ravelling, ravelled**; US **ravels, raveling, raveled**) (**ravel something out**) untangle something.
– ORIGIN prob. from Dutch *ravelen* 'fray out'.

raven • n. a large black crow. • adj. (of hair) of a glossy black colour.
– ORIGIN Old English.

ravening • adj. (especially of a wild animal) very hungry and searching for food.

ravenous • adj. very hungry.
– DERIVATIVES **ravenously** adv.
– ORIGIN Old French *ravineus*.

raver • n. informal a person who has an exciting or wild social life.

rave review • n. a very enthusiastic review of a play, book, etc.

rave-up • n. Brit. informal a lively party.

ravine /ruh-veen/ • n. a deep, narrow gorge with steep sides.
– ORIGIN French, 'violent rush'.

raving • n. (**ravings**) wild talk that makes no sense. • adj. & adv. informal used for emphasis: *she's not a raving beauty*.

ravioli /rav-i-oh-li/ • pl. n. small pasta cases containing minced meat, cheese, or vegetables.
– ORIGIN Italian.

ravish • v. 1 dated rape someone. 2 (**be ravished**) be filled with great pleasure. 3 (as adj. **ravishing**) very beautiful.
– ORIGIN Old French *ravir*.

raw • adj. 1 (of food) not cooked. 2 (of a material or substance) in its natural state; not processed. 3 new to an activity or job and therefore lacking experience. 4 (of the skin) red and painful from being rubbed or scraped. 5 (of an emotion or quality) strong and undisguised. 6 (of the weather) cold and damp.
– PHRASES **in the raw** informal naked.
– DERIVATIVES **rawness** n.
– ORIGIN Old English.

raw-boned • adj. bony or gaunt.

raw material • n. a basic material from which a product is made.

ray[1] • n. 1 a line of light or other radiation coming from a point. 2 a trace of a good quality: *a ray of hope*.
– ORIGIN Old French *rai*.

ray[2] • n. a broad flat fish with a long thin tail.
– ORIGIN Latin *raia*.

ray[3] (also **re**) • n. Music the second note of a major scale, coming after 'doh' and before 'me'.
– ORIGIN the first syllable of *resonare*, taken from a Latin hymn.

rayon • n. a synthetic fibre or fabric made from viscose.
– ORIGIN invented name.

raze • v. (**razes, razing, razed**) completely destroy a building, town, etc.
– ORIGIN Old French *raser* 'shave closely'.

razor • n. an instrument with a sharp blade, used to shave unwanted hair from the face or body.
– ORIGIN Old French *rasor*.

razor wire • n. metal wire with sharp edges or studded with small sharp blades, used as a barrier.

razzle • n. (in phr. **on the razzle**) Brit. informal out celebrating or enjoying yourself.
– ORIGIN from RAZZLE-DAZZLE.

razzle-dazzle • n. = RAZZMATAZZ.
– ORIGIN from DAZZLE.

razzmatazz (also **razzamatazz**) • n. informal noisy and exciting activity, intended to attract attention.
– ORIGIN prob. from RAZZLE-DAZZLE.

Rb • symb. the chemical element rubidium.

RC • abbrev. 1 Red Cross. 2 Roman Catholic.

Rd • abbrev. Road (used in street names).

RE • abbrev. religious education.

Re • symb. the chemical element rhenium.

re[1] /ree, ray/ • prep. with regard to; about.
– ORIGIN Latin *res* 'thing'.

re[2] • n. var. of RAY[3].

re- • prefix 1 once more; anew: *reactivate*. 2 with return to a previous state: *restore*.
– ORIGIN Latin.

're • abbrev. informal are (usually after the pronouns you, we, and they).

reach • v. **1** stretch out an arm so as to touch or grasp something. **2** be able to touch something with an outstretched arm or leg. **3** arrive at; get as far as: *we reached the bridge in good time.* **4** achieve or come to a particular point or state. **5** make contact with. • n. **1** the distance to which someone can stretch out their arm or arms to touch something: *the ball landed just beyond his reach.* **2** the extent to which someone or something has power, influence, or the ability to do something: *university was out of her reach.* **3** a continuous stretch of river between two bends.
– DERIVATIVES **reachable** adj.
– ORIGIN Old English.

react • v. **1** respond to something in a particular way. **2** interact and undergo a chemical or physical change.

reactant • n. Chem. a substance that takes part in and undergoes change during a reaction.

reaction • n. **1** something done or experienced as a result of an event or situation: *her immediate reaction was one of relief.* **2** (**reactions**) a person's ability to respond to an event. **3** a response by the body to a drug or substance. **4** a way of thinking or behaving that is deliberately different from that of the past. **5** a process in which substances interact causing chemical or physical change.

reactionary • adj. opposing political or social progress or reform. • n. (pl. **reactionaries**) a person holding reactionary views.

reactivate • v. (**reactivates, reactivating, reactivated**) bring something back into action.
– DERIVATIVES **reactivation** n.

reactive • adj. **1** showing a reaction. **2** tending to react chemically.
– DERIVATIVES **reactivity** n.

reactor • n. an apparatus or structure in which nuclear energy is produced in a controlled way.

read /reed/ • v. (**reads, reading, read** /red/) **1** understand the meaning of written or printed words or symbols. **2** speak written or printed words aloud. **3** have a particular wording. **4** discover by reading. **5** interpret in a particular way. **6** (**read something into**) think that something has a meaning that it may not possess. **7** esp. Brit. study a subject at a university. **8** (of a measuring instrument) show a measurement or figure. **9** (of a computer) copy or transfer data. • n. **1** esp. Brit. an act of reading. **2** informal a book that is interesting to read.
– PHRASES **read between the lines** look for or discover a meaning that is not openly stated. **take somethng as read** accept something without the need for discussion. **well read** very knowledgeable as a result of reading widely.
– DERIVATIVES **readable** adj.
– ORIGIN Old English, 'advise'.

reader • n. **1** a person who reads. **2** a book containing extracts of another book or books for teaching purposes. **3** a device that produces on a screen a readable image from a microfiche or microfilm.

readership • n. the readers of a publication as a group.

readily • adv. **1** willingly. **2** easily.

reading • n. **1** an instance of something being read to an audience. **2** a way of interpreting something: *his reading of the situation was justified.* **3** a figure recorded on a measuring instrument. **4** a stage of debate in parliament through which a bill must pass before it can become law.

reading age • n. a child's ability to read, measured by comparing it with the average ability of children of a particular age.

readjust • v. **1** adjust again. **2** adapt to a changed situation.
– DERIVATIVES **readjustment** n.

read-only memory • n. Computing memory read at high speed but not capable of being changed by program instructions.

read-out • n. a visual record or display of the output from a computer or scientific instrument.

read-write • adj. Computing capable of reading existing data and accepting alterations or further input.

ready • adj. (**readier, readiest**) **1** prepared for an activity or situation. **2** made suitable and available for immediate use: *dinner's ready.* **3** easily available or obtained. **4** (**ready to do**) willing or eager to do. **5** quick: *a ready wit.* • n. (**readies** or **the ready**) Brit. informal available money; cash. • v. (**readies,**

r

readying, readied) prepare someone or something for an activity or purpose.
– PHRASES **at the ready** available for immediate use. **make ready** prepare.
– DERIVATIVES **readiness** n.
– ORIGIN Old English.

ready-made • adj. prepared in advance for immediate use.

ready money • n. money in the form of cash that is immediately available.

ready-to-wear • adj. (of clothes) sold through shops rather than made to order for an individual customer.

reagent /ri-ay-juhnt/ • n. a substance that produces a chemical reaction, used in tests and experiments.

real • adj. 1 actually existing or occurring. 2 not artificial; genuine: *the earring was real gold.* 3 worthy of the description; proper: *he's my only real friend.* 4 adjusted for changes in the power of money to buy things: *real incomes had fallen by 30 per cent.* 5 Math. (of a number or quantity) having no imaginary part. • adv. informal, esp. N. Amer. really; very.
– DERIVATIVES **realness** n.
– ORIGIN Latin *realis.*

real ale • n. Brit. beer that is fermented in the cask and served without additional gas pressure.

realign • v. change something to a different position or state.
– DERIVATIVES **realignment** n.

realism • n. 1 the acceptance of, and appropriate response to, a situation as it is. 2 (in art or literature) the presentation of things in a way that is accurate and true to life.
– DERIVATIVES **realist** n. & adj.

realistic • adj. 1 having a sensible and practical idea of what can be achieved. 2 showing things in a way that is accurate and true to life.
– DERIVATIVES **realistically** adv.

reality • n. (pl. **realities**) 1 the state of things as they actually exist: *he refuses to face reality.* 2 a thing that is real. 3 the state of being real. • adj. referring to television programmes based on real people or situations, intended to be entertaining rather than informative: *reality TV.*

realize (or **realise**) • v. (**realizes, realizing, realized**) 1 become fully aware of something as a fact. 2 achieve a wish or plan. 3 be sold for a particular amount. 4 convert property, shares, etc. into money by selling them.
– DERIVATIVES **realizable** adj. **realization** n.

really • adv. 1 in actual fact. 2 very; thoroughly. • exclam. expressing interest, surprise, doubt, or protest.

realm • n. 1 esp. literary a kingdom. 2 a field of activity or interest: *the realm of chemistry.*
– ORIGIN Old French *reaume.*

real property • n. Law property consisting of land or buildings.

real tennis • n. the original form of tennis, played with a solid ball on an enclosed court.

real-time • adj. (of a computer system) in which input data is processed almost immediately.

ream • n. 1 500 sheets of paper. 2 (**reams**) a large quantity.
– ORIGIN Old French *raime.*

reap • v. 1 cut or gather a crop or harvest. 2 receive a reward or benefit as a result of your actions.
– ORIGIN Old English.

reaper • n. 1 a person or machine that harvests a crop. 2 (**the Reaper** or **the Grim Reaper**) death, shown as a cloaked skeleton holding a scythe.

reappear • v. appear again.
– DERIVATIVES **reappearance** n.

reappraisal • n. a new or different assessment of something.

rear¹ • n. 1 the back part of something. 2 (also **rear end**) informal a person's bottom. • adj. at the back.
– PHRASES **bring up the rear** be or come last.
– ORIGIN Old French *rere.*

rear² • v. 1 bring up and care for offspring. 2 breed animals. 3 (of an animal) raise itself upright on its hind legs. 4 (of a building, mountain, etc.) extend to a great height.
– ORIGIN Old English, 'set upright'.

rear admiral • n. a naval rank above commodore and below vice admiral.

rearguard • n. a body of troops protecting the rear of the main force.

rearm • v. provide with or obtain a new supply of weapons.
– DERIVATIVES **rearmament** n.

rearmost • adj. furthest back.

rearrange • v. (**rearranges, rearranging, rearranged**) arrange something again in a different way.
– DERIVATIVES **rearrangement** n.

rearward • adj. directed towards the back. • adv. (also **rearwards**) towards the back.

reason • n. 1 a cause or explanation. 2 good cause to do something: *we have reason to celebrate.* 3 the power to think, understand, and draw conclusions logically. 4 (**your reason**) your sanity. 5 what is right or possible: *I'll answer anything, within reason.* • v. 1 think, understand, and draw conclusions

logically. **2** (**reason with**) persuade someone by logical argument.
- PHRASES **it stands to reason** it is obvious or logical.
- ORIGIN Old French *reisun*.

reasonable •adj. **1** fair and sensible. **2** appropriate in a particular situation: *they had a reasonable time to reply.* **3** fairly good. **4** not too expensive.
- DERIVATIVES **reasonableness** n. **reasonably** adv.

reassemble •v. (**reassembles, reassembling, reassembled**) put something back together.

reassert •v. assert again.

reassess •v. assess again; reconsider.
- DERIVATIVES **reassessment** n.

reassign •v. assign again or differently.
- DERIVATIVES **reassignment** n.

reassure •v. (**reassures, reassuring, reassured**) cause someone to feel less worried or afraid.
- DERIVATIVES **reassurance** n.

rebarbative /ri-bar-buh-tiv/ •adj. formal unattractive and objectionable.
- ORIGIN French *rébarbatif*.

rebate /ree-bayt/ •n. **1** a partial refund to someone who has paid too much for tax, rent, etc. **2** a discount on an amount of money due.
- ORIGIN Old French *rebatre* 'beat back'.

rebel •n. /reb-uhl/ a person who rebels. •v. /ri-bel/ (**rebels, rebelling, rebelled**) **1** fight against or refuse to obey an established government or ruler. **2** resist authority, control, or accepted behaviour.
- ORIGIN Old French *rebelle*.

rebellion •n. **1** an act of rebelling against a government or ruler. **2** opposition to authority or control.

rebellious •adj. rebelling or wanting to rebel.
- DERIVATIVES **rebelliously** adv. **rebelliousness** n.

rebirth •n. **1** a return to life or activity: *a rebirth of faith in the old values.* **2** the process of being born again.

reborn •adj. brought back to life or activity.

rebound •v. /ri-bownd/ **1** bounce back after hitting a hard surface. **2** (**rebound on**) have an unexpected and unpleasant effect on: *his tricks are rebounding on him.* •n. /ree-bownd/ a ball or shot that bounces back.
- PHRASES **on the rebound** while still upset after the ending of a romantic relationship.
- ORIGIN Old French *rebondir*.

rebuff •v. reject in an abrupt or unkind way. •n. an abrupt or unkind rejection.

- ORIGIN from former French *rebuffer*.

rebuild •v. (**rebuilds, rebuilding, rebuilt**) build again.

rebuke •v. (**rebukes, rebuking, rebuked**) criticize or reprimand someone sharply. •n. a sharp criticism.
- ORIGIN Old French *rebuker* 'beat down'.

rebut /ri-but/ •v. (**rebuts, rebutting, rebutted**) claim or prove something to be false.
- ORIGIN Old French *rebuter* 'rebuke'.

rebuttal •n. a claim or proof that something is false.

recalcitrant /ri-kal-si-truhnt/ •adj. unwilling to cooperate; disobedient.
- DERIVATIVES **recalcitrance** n.
- ORIGIN Latin *recalcitrare* 'kick out with the heels'.

recall /ri-kawl/ •v. **1** remember something. **2** make a person remember or think of something. **3** officially order someone to return. **4** (of a manufacturer) request the return of faulty products. •n. /also ree-kawl/ **1** the action of remembering or ability to remember. **2** an act of officially recalling someone or something.

recant /ri-kant/ •v. withdraw a former opinion or belief.
- ORIGIN Latin *recantare* 'revoke'.

recap •v. (**recaps, recapping, recapped**) summarize what has just been said. •n. a summary.

recapitulate /ree-kuh-pit-yuu-layt/ •v. (**recapitulates, recapitulating, recapitulated**) give a summary of what has just been said.
- DERIVATIVES **recapitulation** n.
- ORIGIN Latin *recapitulare* 'go through heading by heading'.

recapture •v. (**recaptures, recapturing, recaptured**) **1** capture a person or animal that has escaped. **2** recover something taken or lost. **3** bring back or experience again a past time, event, or feeling. •n. an act of recapturing.

recast •v. (**recasts, recasting, recast**) **1** cast metal again or differently. **2** present something in a different form.

recce /rek-ki/ •n. Brit. informal an act of reconnaissance.

recede •v. (**recedes, receding, receded**) **1** move back or further away. **2** gradually become weaker or smaller: *her panic receded.* **3** (as adj. **receding**) (of part of the face) sloping backwards.
- ORIGIN Latin *recedere*.

receipt •n. **1** the action of receiving something. **2** a written statement

r

confirming that something has been paid for or received. **3** (**receipts**) an amount of money received over a period by a business.
– ORIGIN Old French *receite*.

receive • v. (**receives**, **receiving**, **received**) **1** be given or paid something. **2** accept or take in something sent or offered. **3** form an idea from an experience. **4** experience or meet with: *the event received wide press coverage.* **5** entertain someone as a guest. **6** admit someone as a member. **7** detect or pick up broadcast signals. **8** (as adj. **received**) widely accepted as true.
– DERIVATIVES **receivable** adj.
– ORIGIN Old French *receivre*.

> ✓ **receive** follows the usual rule of *i* before *e* except after *c*.

received pronunciation • n. the standard form of British English pronunciation, based on educated speech in southern England.

receiver • n. **1** a radio or television apparatus that converts broadcast signals into sound or images. **2** the part of a telephone that converts electrical signals into sounds. **3** (Brit. also **official receiver**) a person appointed to manage the financial affairs of a bankrupt business.

receivership • n. the state of being managed by an official receiver.

recent • adj. having happened or been done only a short time ago.
– DERIVATIVES **recently** adv.
– ORIGIN Latin *recens*.

receptacle /ri-sep-tuh-k'l/ • n. a container.
– ORIGIN Latin *receptaculum*.

reception • n. **1** the action of receiving. **2** the way in which someone or something is received: *an enthusiastic reception.* **3** a formal social occasion held to welcome someone or celebrate an event. **4** esp. Brit. the area in a hotel, office, etc. where visitors are greeted. **5** the quality with which broadcast signals are received.
– ORIGIN Latin.

receptionist • n. a person who greets and deals with clients and visitors to an office, hotel, etc.

receptive • adj. **1** able or willing to receive something. **2** willing to consider new ideas.
– DERIVATIVES **receptivity** n.

receptor /ri-sep-ter/ • n. an organ or cell in the body that responds to a stimulus such as light and transmits a signal to a sensory nerve.

recess /ri-sess, ree-sess/ • n. **1** a small space set back in a wall or set into a surface. **2** (**recesses**) remote or hidden places. **3** a break between sessions of a parliament or law court. • v. set something back into a wall or surface.
– ORIGIN Latin *recessus*.

recession • n. a temporary economic decline during which trade and industrial activity are reduced.
– DERIVATIVES **recessionary** adj.

recessive • adj. (of a gene) appearing in offspring only if a contrary gene is not also inherited. Compare with **DOMINANT**.

recharge • v. (**recharges**, **recharging**, **recharged**) charge a battery or battery-operated device again.
– DERIVATIVES **rechargeable** adj. **recharger** n.

recherché /ruh-shair-shay/ • adj. unusual and not easily understood.
– ORIGIN French, 'carefully sought out'.

recidivist /ri-sid-i-vist/ • n. a person who constantly commits crimes and is not discouraged by being punished.
– DERIVATIVES **recidivism** n.
– ORIGIN French *récidiver* 'fall back'.

recipe • n. **1** a list of ingredients and instructions for preparing a dish. **2** something likely to lead to a particular outcome: *high interest rates are a recipe for disaster.*
– ORIGIN Latin, 'receive!'

recipient /ri-sip-i-uhnt/ • n. a person who receives something.

reciprocal /ri-sip-ruh-k'l/ • adj. **1** given or done in return: *he showed no reciprocal interest in me.* **2** (of an agreement or arrangement) affecting two parties equally. • n. Math. the quantity obtained by dividing the number one by a given quantity.
– DERIVATIVES **reciprocally** adv.

reciprocate • v. (**reciprocates**, **reciprocating**, **reciprocated**) respond to an action or emotion with a similar one.
– ORIGIN Latin *reciprocare* 'move backwards and forwards'.

reciprocity /re-si-pross-i-ti/ • n. a situation in which two parties provide the same help or advantages to each other.

recital • n. **1** the performance of a programme of music by a soloist or small group. **2** a long account of a series of things: *a recital of Adam's failures.*

recitation /re-si-tay-sh'n/ • n. **1** the action of reciting. **2** something that is recited.

recitative /re-si-tuh-teev/ • n. a passage in an opera or oratorio used for conversation or to tell the story, sung in a rhythm like that of ordinary speech.

recite • v. (**recites**, **reciting**, **recited**)

1 repeat a poem or passage aloud from memory in front of an audience. **2** state a set of facts or recount events in order.
– ORIGIN Latin *recitare*.

reckless • adj. without thought or care for the results of an action.
– DERIVATIVES **recklessly** adv. **recklessness** n.
– ORIGIN Old English.

reckon • v. **1** have an opinion about something; think. **2** (**reckon on**) rely on or expect: *they had reckoned on one more day of privacy.* **3** calculate something. **4** (**reckon with** or **without**) take (or fail to take) something into account.
– PHRASES **to be reckoned with** to be treated as important.
– ORIGIN Old English, 'recount, tell'.

reckoning • n. **1** the action of calculating something. **2** a person's opinion. **3** punishment for your actions.
– PHRASES **into** (or **out of**) **the reckoning** among (or not among) those who are likely to be successful.

reclaim • v. **1** recover possession of something. **2** make waste land or land formerly under water usable for growing crops.
– DERIVATIVES **reclamation** n.

recline • v. (**reclines, reclining, reclined**) lean or lie back in a relaxed position.
– DERIVATIVES **recliner** n.
– ORIGIN Latin *reclinare*.

recluse /ri-klooss/ • n. a person who avoids other people and lives alone.
– ORIGIN Old French *reclus* 'shut up'.

reclusive • adj. avoiding the company of other people.

recognition • n. **1** the action of recognizing or the state of being recognized. **2** appreciation or acknowledgement.

recognize (or **recognise**)
• v. (**recognizes, recognizing, recognized**) **1** know someone or something from having come across them before. **2** accept as genuine, legal, or valid: *the qualifications are recognized by the Department of Education.* **3** show official appreciation of.
– DERIVATIVES **recognizable** adj.
– ORIGIN Latin *recognoscere*.

recoil • v. **1** suddenly move back in fear, horror, or disgust. **2** (of a gun) suddenly move backwards as a reaction on firing a bullet or shell. **3** (**recoil on**) have an unpleasant effect on. • n. the action of recoiling.
– ORIGIN Old French *reculer* 'move back'.

recollect /rek-uh-lekt/ • v. remember something.

recollection • n. **1** the action of remembering. **2** a memory.

recommence • v. (**recommences, recommencing, recommenced**) begin again.

recommend • v. **1** put forward as being suitable for a purpose or role. **2** make appealing or desirable: *the house had much to recommend it.*

recommendation • n. **1** a suggestion or proposal as to the best course of action. **2** the action of recommending.

recompense /rek-uhm-penss/
• v. (**recompenses, recompensing, recompensed**) **1** make amends to someone for loss or harm suffered; compensate. **2** pay or reward someone for work. • n. compensation or reward.
– ORIGIN Latin *recompensare*.

reconcile /rek-uhn-syl/ • v. (**reconciles, reconciling, reconciled**) **1** restore friendly relations between people. **2** find a satisfactory way of dealing with things that are opposed to or contradict each other: *an attempt to reconcile freedom with commitment.* **3** (**reconcile someone to**) make someone accept something unwelcome.
– DERIVATIVES **reconcilable** adj.
– ORIGIN Latin *reconciliare*.

reconciliation /rek-uhn-si-li-ay-sh'n/
• n. **1** the end of a disagreement and the return to friendly relations. **2** the action of reconciling opposing ideas or facts.

recondite /rek-uhn-dyt, ri-kon-dyt/
• adj. (of a subject or knowledge) little known.
– ORIGIN Latin *reconditus* 'hidden'.

recondition • v. Brit. bring something back to a good condition; renovate.

reconnaissance /ri-kon-ni-suhnss/
• n. military observation of an area to gain information.
– ORIGIN French.

reconnoitre /rek-uh-noy-ter/ (US **reconnoiter**) • v. (**reconnoitres, reconnoitring, reconnoitred**; US **reconnoiters, reconnoitering, reconnoitered**) make a military observation of an area.
– ORIGIN former French.

reconsider • v. (**reconsiders, reconsidering, reconsidered**) consider something again, with the possibility of changing a decision.
– DERIVATIVES **reconsideration** n.

reconstitute • v. (**reconstitutes, reconstituting, reconstituted**) **1** change the form of an organization. **2** restore dried food to its original state by adding water.
– DERIVATIVES **reconstitution** n.

reconstruct • v. **1** construct again.

r

2 create or act out a past event from evidence.
– DERIVATIVES **reconstruction** n. **reconstructive** adj.

reconvene • v. (**reconvenes, reconvening, reconvened**) meet again after a break.

record • n. /rek-ord/ **1** a permanent account of something that is kept for evidence or information. **2** the previous behaviour or performance of a person or thing: *the team preserved their unbeaten home record.* **3** (also **criminal record**) a list of a person's previous criminal convictions. **4** the best performance or most remarkable event of its kind that has been officially recognized. **5** a thin plastic disc carrying recorded sound in grooves on each surface. • v. /ri-kord/ **1** make a permanent account of something and keep it for evidence or information. **2** convert sound, a broadcast, etc. into permanent form in order to be reproduced later.
– PHRASES **for the record** so that the true facts are recorded. **on** (or **off**) **the record** made (or not made) as an official statement.
– DERIVATIVES **recordable** adj. **recordist** n.
– ORIGIN Latin *recordari* 'remember'.

recorded delivery • n. Brit. a service in which a person receiving an item through the post has to sign a form as a record that it has been delivered.

recorder • n. **1** a device for recording sound, pictures, etc. **2** a person who keeps records. **3** (**Recorder**) (in England and Wales) a barrister appointed to serve as a part-time judge. **4** a simple woodwind instrument with holes along it for the fingers.

recording • n. **1** a piece of music or film that has been recorded. **2** the process of recording something.

record player • n. a device for playing records, with a turntable and a stylus that picks up sound from the groove.

recount[1] /ri-kownt/ • v. tell someone about something.
– ORIGIN Old French *reconter* 'tell again'.

recount[2] • v. /ree-kownt/ count something again. • n. /ree-kownt/ an act of counting something again.

recoup • v. recover an amount of money that has been spent or lost.
– ORIGIN French *recouper* 'cut back'.

recourse • n. **1** a source of help in a difficult situation. **2** (**recourse to**) the use of someone or something as a source of help.
– ORIGIN Latin *recursus*.

recover • v. (**recovers, recovering, recovered**) **1** return to a normal state of health, mind, or strength. **2** find or regain possession or control of: *he recovered his balance.* **3** regain or secure money by legal means or the making of profits.
– DERIVATIVES **recoverable** adj.
– ORIGIN Old French *recoverer*.

re-cover • v. (**re-covers, re-covering, re-covered**) put a new cover on.

recovery • n. (pl. **recoveries**) the action or an act of recovering.

recreate • v. (**recreates, recreating, recreated**) make or do again.

recreation[1] /rek-ri-ay-sh'n/
• n. enjoyable leisure activity.
– DERIVATIVES **recreational** adj.
– ORIGIN Latin.

recreation[2] /ree-kri-ay-sh'n/ • n. the action of making or doing something again.

recreation ground • n. Brit. a piece of public land used for sports and games.

recrimination • n. an accusation in response to one from someone else.
– ORIGIN Latin *recriminari*.

recruit • v. take on someone to serve in the armed forces or to work for an organization. • n. a newly recruited person.
– DERIVATIVES **recruiter** n. **recruitment** n.
– ORIGIN from former French *recrute*.

recta pl. of RECTUM.

rectangle • n. a plane figure with four straight sides and four right angles, and with unequal adjacent sides.
– DERIVATIVES **rectangular** adj.
– ORIGIN Latin *rectangulum.*

rectify • v. (**rectifies, rectifying, rectified**) **1** put right; correct. **2** convert alternating current to direct current.
– DERIVATIVES **rectification** n.
– ORIGIN Latin *rectificare.*

rectilinear /rek-ti-lin-i-er/ • adj. within or moving in a straight line or lines.
– ORIGIN Latin *rectilineus.*

rectitude • n. morally correct behaviour.
– ORIGIN Old French.

recto • n. (pl. **rectos**) a right-hand page of an open book, or the front of a loose document. Contrasted with VERSO.
– ORIGIN Latin, 'on the right'.

rector • n. **1** (in the Church of England) a priest in charge of a parish. **2** (in the Roman Catholic Church) a priest in charge of a church or a religious institution. **3** the head of certain universities, colleges, and schools. **4** (in Scotland) a person elected to represent students on a university's governing body.
– ORIGIN Latin, 'ruler'.

rectory •n. (pl. **rectories**) the house of a rector.

rectum /rek-tuhm/ •n. (pl. **rectums** or **recta** /rek-tuh/) the final section of the large intestine, ending at the anus.
– DERIVATIVES **rectal** adj.
– ORIGIN from Latin *rectum intestinum* 'straight intestine'.

recumbent /ri-kum-buhnt/ •adj. lying down.
– ORIGIN Latin *recumbere*.

recuperate /ri-koo-puh-rayt/
•v. (**recuperates, recuperating, recuperated**) 1 recover from illness or tiredness. 2 regain something lost.
– DERIVATIVES **recuperation** n. **recuperative** adj.
– ORIGIN Latin *recuperare*.

recur •v. (**recurs, recurring, recurred**) happen again or repeatedly.
– DERIVATIVES **recurrence** n.
– ORIGIN Latin *recurrere*.

recurrent •adj. happening often or repeatedly.

recurring decimal •n. a decimal fraction in which a figure or group of figures is repeated indefinitely, as in *0.666 ...*

recusant /rek-yuu-zuhnt/ •n. a person who refuses to obey an authority or a regulation.
– ORIGIN Latin *recusare* 'refuse'.

recycle •v. (**recycles, recycling, recycled**) 1 convert waste into a form in which it can be reused. 2 use something again.
– DERIVATIVES **recyclable** adj. **recycler** n.

red •adj. (**redder, reddest**) 1 of the colour of blood or fire. 2 (of hair or fur) reddish-brown. 3 informal, esp. derog. communist or socialist. •n. 1 red colour or material. 2 informal, esp. derog. a communist or socialist.
– PHRASES **in the red** having spent more than is in your bank account. **see red** informal suddenly become very angry.
– DERIVATIVES **reddish** adj. **redness** n.
– ORIGIN Old English.

red admiral •n. a butterfly having dark wings with red bands and white spots.

red blood cell •n. less technical term for ERYTHROCYTE.

red-blooded •adj. (of a man) full of energy, especially sexual energy.

red-brick •adj. (of a British university) founded in the late 19th or early 20th century and often with buildings of red brick rather than stone, as distinct from the older universities.

red card •n. (in football) a red card shown by the referee to a player being sent off the field.

red carpet •n. a strip of red carpet for

an important visitor to walk along.

redcoat •n. hist. a British soldier.

Red Crescent •n. the equivalent of the Red Cross in Muslim countries.

Red Cross •n. the International Movement of the Red Cross and the Red Crescent, an organization that helps victims of war or natural disaster.

redcurrant •n. a small edible red berry.

redden •v. make or become red.

redecorate •v. (**redecorates, redecorating, redecorated**) decorate again or differently.
– DERIVATIVES **redecoration** n.

redeem •v. 1 make up for the faults or bad aspects of: *a poor debate redeemed by an outstanding speech.* 2 save someone from sin or evil. 3 fulfil a promise. 4 regain possession of something in exchange for payment. 5 exchange a coupon for goods or money. 6 repay a debt.
– DERIVATIVES **redeemable** adj.
– ORIGIN Latin *redimere* 'buy back'.

Redeemer •n. (**the Redeemer**) Jesus.

redemption •n. the action of redeeming or the state of being redeemed.
– DERIVATIVES **redemptive** adj.

redeploy •v. move troops, employees, or resources to a new place or task.
– DERIVATIVES **redeployment** n.

redevelop •v. (**redevelops, redeveloping, redeveloped**) develop again or differently.
– DERIVATIVES **redevelopment** n.

red flag •n. a warning of danger.

red-handed •adj. in or just after the act of doing something wrong.

redhead •n. a person with red hair.

red herring •n. a thing that draws attention away from something important.
– ORIGIN from the use of the scent of a smoked herring in training hounds.

red-hot •adj. 1 so hot as to glow red. 2 very exciting or recent.

redid past of REDO.

Red Indian •n. dated = AMERICAN INDIAN.

redirect •v. direct to a different place or purpose.

rediscover •v. (**rediscovers, rediscovering, rediscovered**) discover something again.
– DERIVATIVES **rediscovery** n.

redistribute •v. (**redistributes, redistributing, redistributed**) distribute again or differently.
– DERIVATIVES **redistribution** n.

red lead •n. a red form of lead oxide used as a pigment.

r

red-letter day •n. an important or memorable day.
– ORIGIN from the practice of highlighting a festival in red on a calendar.

red light •n. a red light instructing moving vehicles to stop.

red-light district •n. an area with many brothels and strip clubs.
– ORIGIN from the use of a red light as the sign of a brothel.

red meat •n. meat that is red when raw, e.g. beef.

redneck •n. informal, derog. a rural working-class white person from the southern US, with conservative views.

redo •v. (**redoes, redoing, redid**; past part. **redone**) do something again or differently.

redolent /red-uh-luhnt/ •adj. (**redolent of/with**) **1** strongly suggestive of: *names redolent of horse racing.* **2** literary strongly smelling of.
– DERIVATIVES **redolence** n.
– ORIGIN Latin *redolere* 'give out a strong smell'.

redouble •v. (**redoubles, redoubling, redoubled**) make or become greater or more intense.

redoubt •n. a temporary or additional fortification.
– ORIGIN French *redoute*.

redoubtable •adj. worthy of respect or fear: *he was a redoubtable debater.*
– ORIGIN Old French *redouter* 'to fear'.

redound /ri-downd/ •v. (**redound to**) formal be to someone's credit.
– ORIGIN Latin *redundare* 'surge'.

red pepper •n. a ripe sweet pepper, red in colour and eaten as a vegetable.

redress •v. /ree-dress/ set right something that is unfair or wrong. •n. /ri-dress/ payment or action to make up for a wrong.
– ORIGIN Old French *redresser*.

redskin •n. dated or offens. an American Indian.

red tape •n. official rules which cause irritation because they take up your time.
– ORIGIN from the red or pink tape used to bind official documents.

reduce •v. (**reduces, reducing, reduced**) **1** make or become less. **2** (**reduce something to**) change something to a different or simpler form. **3** (**reduce someone/thing to**) bring someone or something to a particular state: *she was reduced to stunned silence.* **4** boil a sauce or other liquid so that it becomes thicker. **5** Chem. cause to combine chemically with hydrogen. **6** Chem. cause

to undergo a reaction in which electrons are gained from another substance or molecule. Opp. **OXIDIZE**.
– PHRASES **reduced circumstances** a state in which you have become poor after being more wealthy.
– DERIVATIVES **reducer** n. **reducible** adj.
– ORIGIN Latin *reducere* 'bring back'.

reduction •n. **1** the action of reducing something. **2** the amount by which something is reduced. **3** a smaller copy of a picture or photograph.

reductive •adj. presenting a subject or problem in an oversimplified form.

redundant •adj. **1** no longer needed or useful: *the old skills had become redundant.* **2** Brit. made unemployed because your job is no longer needed.
– DERIVATIVES **redundancy** n. (pl. **redundancies**).
– ORIGIN Latin *redundare* 'surge'.

redwood •n. a giant coniferous tree with reddish wood, found in California and Oregon.

reed •n. **1** a tall plant with a hollow stem, growing in water or on marshy ground. **2** a piece of thin cane or metal which vibrates in a current of air to produce the sound of various musical instruments, as in the mouthpiece of a clarinet or at the base of some organ pipes.
– ORIGIN Old English.

reed organ •n. a keyboard instrument similar to a harmonium, in which air is drawn upwards past metal reeds.

re-educate •v. (**re-educates, re-educating, re-educated**) educate or train someone to behave or think differently.

reedy •adj. **1** (of a sound or voice) high and thin in tone. **2** full of reeds. **3** (of a person) tall and thin.

reef •n. **1** a ridge of jagged rock or coral just above or below the surface of the sea. **2** a vein of gold or other ore. **3** each of several strips across a sail that can be drawn in so as to reduce the area exposed to the wind. •v. take in a reef or the reefs of a sail.
– ORIGIN Old Norse, 'rib'.

reefer •n. informal a cannabis cigarette.
– ORIGIN perh. from Mexican Spanish *grifo* 'smoker of cannabis'.

reefer jacket •n. a thick close-fitting double-breasted jacket.

reef knot •n. esp. Brit. a type of double knot that is very secure.

reek •v. have a very unpleasant smell. •n. a very unpleasant smell.
– ORIGIN Old English, 'give out smoke'.

reel •n. **1** a cylinder on which film, wire,

thread, etc. can be wound. **2** a lively
Scottish or Irish folk dance. • v. **1** (**reel
something in**) bring something towards
you by turning a reel. **2** (**reel something
off**) say something rapidly and with
ease. **3** stagger. **4** feel shocked or
bewildered.
– ORIGIN Old English.

re-elect • v. elect again.
– DERIVATIVES **re-election** n.

re-emerge • v. (**re-emerges,
re-emerging, re-emerged**) emerge
again.
– DERIVATIVES **re-emergence** n.

re-enact • v. act out a past event.
– DERIVATIVES **re-enactment** n.

re-enter • v. (**re-enters, re-entering,
re-entered**) enter again.
– DERIVATIVES **re-entry** n. (pl. **re-entries**).

reeve • n. the chief magistrate of a town
or district in Anglo-Saxon England.
– ORIGIN Old English.

re-examine • v. (**re-examines,
re-examining, re-examined**) examine
again or further.
– DERIVATIVES **re-examination** n.

ref • n. informal (in sports) a referee.

refectory • n. (pl. **refectories**) a room
used for meals in an educational or
religious institution.
– ORIGIN Latin *refectorium*.

refer • v. (**refers, referring, referred**)
1 (**refer to**) write or speak about;
mention. **2** (**refer to**) (of a word or
phrase) describe someone or something.
3 (**refer to**) turn to someone for
information; consult. **4** (**refer someone/
thing to**) pass a person or matter to an
authority or specialist for a decision.
5 fail a candidate in an exam.
– DERIVATIVES **referable** adj.
– ORIGIN Latin *referre* 'carry back'.

referee • n. **1** an official who supervises a
game to ensure that players keep to the
rules. **2** Brit. a person who provides a
reference for someone applying for a
job. **3** a person appointed to assess an
academic work submitted for
publication. • v. (**referees, refereeing,
refereed**) act as a referee of.

reference • n. **1** the action of referring
to something. **2** a mention of a source of
information in a book or article. **3** a
letter from a previous employer giving
information about someone's ability,
used when applying for a new job.
• v. mention or refer to.
– PHRASES **terms of reference** the scope
of an activity or area of knowledge. **with**
(or **in**) **reference to** in relation to.

reference library • n. a library in
which the books are to be consulted in
the building rather than borrowed.

referendum /re-fuh-**ren**-duhm/ • n. (pl.
referendums or **referenda** /re-fuh-**ren**-
duh/) a direct vote by the people of a
country on a single political issue.
– ORIGIN Latin, 'something to be
referred'.

referral • n. the action of referring
someone or something to a specialist or
higher authority.

refill • v. /ree-**fil**/ fill something again.
• n. /**ree**-fil/ an act of filling something
again.
– DERIVATIVES **refillable** adj.

refine • v. (**refines, refining, refined**)
1 remove unwanted substances from.
2 improve something by making minor
changes: *computer applications that have
been refined for years.* **3** (as adj. **refined**)
well educated, elegant, and having good
taste.

refinement • n. **1** the process of
refining. **2** an improvement. **3** the
quality of being well educated, elegant,
and having good taste.

refinery • n. (pl. **refineries**) a factory
where a substance is refined.

refit • v. /ree-**fit**/ (**refits, refitting,
refitted**) replace or repair equipment
and fittings in a ship, building, etc.
• n. /**ree**-fit/ an act of refitting.

reflect • v. **1** throw back heat, light, or
sound from a surface. **2** (of a mirror or
shiny surface) show an image of. **3** show
in a realistic or appropriate way: *schools
should reflect cultural differences.*
4 (**reflect well/badly on**) bring about a
good or bad impression of. **5** (**reflect on**)
think seriously about.
– ORIGIN Latin *reflectere* 'bend back'.

reflecting telescope • n. a telescope
in which a mirror is used to collect and
focus light.

reflection • n. **1** the process of light,
heat, or sound being reflected. **2** an
image formed by reflection. **3** a sign. **4** a
source of shame or blame. **5** serious
thought.

reflective • adj. **1** providing a reflection.
2 thoughtful.
– DERIVATIVES **reflectivity** n.

reflector • n. **1** a piece of glass, plastic,
etc. on the back of a vehicle for
reflecting light. **2** an object or device
which reflects radio waves, sound, or
other waves.

reflex • n. an action done without
conscious thought as a response to
something. • adj. **1** done as a reflex. **2** (of
an angle) more than 180°.
– ORIGIN Latin *reflexus* 'a bending back'.

reflex camera • n. a camera in which

r

the image given by the lens is reflected by an angled mirror to the viewfinder.

reflexive • adj. **1** Grammar (of a pronoun) that refers back to the subject of a clause, e.g. *myself* in the clause *I hurt myself*. **2** Grammar (of a verb or clause) having a reflexive pronoun as its object (e.g. *he washed himself*). **3** done without conscious thought; reflex.
– DERIVATIVES **reflexively** adv.

reflexology • n. a system of massage used to relieve tension and treat illness, based on the theory that there are points on the feet, hands, and head linked to every part of the body.
– DERIVATIVES **reflexologist** n.

refocus • v. (**refocuses, refocusing, refocused** or **refocusses, refocussing, refocussed**) **1** adjust the focus of a lens or your eyes. **2** focus attention on something new or different.

reform • v. **1** make changes in something so as to improve it. **2** make someone improve their behaviour. • n. the making of changes in order to bring about improvements.
– DERIVATIVES **reformer** n.
– ORIGIN Latin *reformare* 'form again'.

re-form • v. form again.

reformation • n. **1** the action of reforming. **2** (**the Reformation**) a 16th-century movement for the reform of the Roman Catholic Church, which ended in the establishment of the Protestant Churches.

reformist • adj. supporting gradual political or social reform. • n. a supporter of such a policy.
– DERIVATIVES **reformism** n.

refract • v. (of water, air, or glass) make a ray of light change direction when it enters at an angle.
– DERIVATIVES **refraction** n.
– ORIGIN Latin *refringere* 'break up'.

refracting telescope • n. a telescope which uses a lens to collect and focus the light.

refractive • adj. (of water, air, or glass) making a ray of light change direction when it enters at an angle.

refractor • n. a lens or other object which makes a ray of light change direction when it enters at an angle.

refractory • adj. **1** stubborn or difficult to control. **2** Med. (of a disease or medical condition) not responding to treatment. **3** tech. heat-resistant.
– ORIGIN Latin *refractarius*.

refrain[1] • v. (**refrain from**) stop yourself from doing something.
– ORIGIN Latin *refrenare*.

refrain[2] • n. the part of a song that is repeated at the end of each verse.
– ORIGIN Latin *refringere* 'break up'.

refresh • v. **1** give new strength or energy to. **2** prompt someone's memory by going over information given previously.

refresher course • n. a course intended to improve or update your skills or knowledge.

refreshing • adj. **1** giving new energy or strength. **2** pleasantly new or different.

refreshment • n. **1** a light snack or drink. **2** the giving of fresh strength or energy.

refrigerate • v. (**refrigerates, refrigerating, refrigerated**) chill food or drink so as to preserve it.
– DERIVATIVES **refrigeration** n.
– ORIGIN Latin *refrigerare*.

refrigerator • n. an appliance or compartment in which food and drink is stored at a low temperature.

refuel • v. (**refuels, refuelling, refuelled**; US **refuels, refueling, refueled**) supply a vehicle with more fuel.

refuge • n. a place or state of safety from danger or trouble: *he took refuge in the French embassy.*
– ORIGIN Latin *refugium*.

refugee • n. a person who has been forced to leave their country because of a war or because they are being persecuted for their beliefs.

refulgent /ri-ful-juhnt/ • adj. literary shining very brightly.
– ORIGIN Latin *refulgere* 'shine out'.

refund • v. /ri-fund/ pay a sum of money back to someone. • n. /ree-fund/ a repayment of a sum of money.
– DERIVATIVES **refundable** adj.
– ORIGIN Latin *refundere* 'pour back'.

refurbish • v. redecorate and improve a building or room.
– DERIVATIVES **refurbishment** n.

refuse[1] /ri-fyooz/ • v. (**refuses, refusing, refused**) **1** state that you are unwilling to do something. **2** state that you are unwilling to give or accept something offered or requested.
– DERIVATIVES **refusal** n.
– ORIGIN Old French *refuser*.

refuse[2] /ref-yooss/ • n. matter thrown away as worthless.
– ORIGIN perh. from Old French *refusé* 'refused'.

refute /ri-fyoot/ • v. (**refutes, refuting, refuted**) prove a statement or person to be wrong.
– DERIVATIVES **refutable** adj. **refutation** n.
– ORIGIN Latin *refutare* 'repel, rebut'.

regain • v. **1** get something back after

losing possession or control of it. **2** get back to a place.

regal • adj. relating to or fit for a monarch, especially in being magnificent or dignified.
– DERIVATIVES **regality** n. **regally** adv.
– ORIGIN Latin *regalis*.

regale • v. (**regales, regaling, regaled**) **1** entertain someone with conversation. **2** supply someone generously with food or drink.
– ORIGIN French *régaler*.

regalia /ri-gay-li-uh/ • n. **1** objects such as the crown and sceptre, symbolizing royalty and used at coronations or other state occasions. **2** the distinctive clothing and objects of an order, rank, or office, worn at formal occasions.
– ORIGIN Latin, 'royal privileges'.

regard • v. **1** think of someone or something in a particular way. **2** look steadily at. • n. **1** concern or care: *she rescued him without regard for herself.* **2** high opinion; respect. **3** a steady look. **4** (**regards**) best wishes.
– PHRASES **as regards** concerning. **with** (or **in**) **regard to** as concerning.
– ORIGIN Old French *regarder* 'to watch'.

regarding • prep. about; concerning.

regardless • adv. **1** (**regardless of**) without concern for. **2** despite what is happening: *they were determined to carry on regardless.*

regatta • n. a sporting event consisting of a series of boat or yacht races.
– ORIGIN Italian, 'a fight or contest'.

regency /ree-juhn-si/ • n. (pl. **regencies**) **1** a period of government by a regent. **2** (**the Regency**) the period when George, Prince of Wales, acted as regent in Britain (1811–20). • adj. (**Regency**) in the neoclassical style of British architecture or furniture popular during the late 18th and early 19th centuries.

regenerate /ri-jen-uh-rayt/ • v. (**regenerates, regenerating, regenerated**) **1** bring new life or strength to. **2** grow new tissue.
– DERIVATIVES **regeneration** n. **regenerative** adj.

regent • n. a person appointed to rule a state because the king or queen is too young or unfit to rule, or is absent. • adj. (after a *noun*) acting as regent: *Prince Regent.*
– ORIGIN Latin, 'ruling'.

reggae /reg-gay/ • n. a style of popular music with a strong beat, originating in Jamaica.
– ORIGIN perh. from Jamaican English *rege-rege* 'quarrel'.

regicide /rej-i-syd/ • n. **1** the killing of a king. **2** a person who kills a king.
– ORIGIN Latin *rex* 'king'.

regime /ray-zheem/ • n. **1** a government, especially one that strictly controls a state. **2** an ordered way of doing something; a system.
– ORIGIN French.

regimen /rej-i-muhn/ • n. a course of medical treatment, diet, or exercise that you follow to improve your health.
– ORIGIN Latin *regere* 'to rule'.

regiment • n. /rej-i-muhnt/ **1** a permanent unit of an army. **2** a large number of people or things. • v. /rej-i-ment/ organize people or things according to a strict system.
– DERIVATIVES **regimental** adj. **regimentation** n.
– ORIGIN Latin *regimentum* 'rule'.

Regina /ri-jy-nuh/ • n. the reigning queen (used following a name or in the titles of lawsuits, e.g. *Regina v. Jones,* the Crown versus Jones).
– ORIGIN Latin.

region • n. **1** an area of a country or the world having particular characteristics: *the equatorial regions.* **2** an administrative district of a city or country. **3** (**the regions**) the parts of a country outside the capital or centre of government. **4** a part of the body.
– PHRASES **in the region of** approximately: *sales in the region of 30 million.*
– DERIVATIVES **regional** adj. **regionally** adv.
– ORIGIN Latin, 'direction, district'.

regionalism • n. loyalty to your own region in cultural and political terms, rather than to central government.
– DERIVATIVES **regionalist** n. & adj.

register • n. **1** an official list or record. **2** a particular part of the range of a person's voice or a musical instrument. **3** the level and style of a piece of writing or speech, varying according to the situation in which it is used. **4** a sliding device controlling a set of organ pipes, or a set of organ pipes controlled by such a device. **5** (in electronic devices) a location in a store of data. • v. (**registers, registering, registered**) **1** enter someone or something in an official list or record. **2** put your name on an official list or record. **3** express an opinion or emotion. **4** become aware of something: *he had not even registered her presence.* **5** (of a measuring instrument) record or show a reading automatically.
– ORIGIN Latin *registrum.*

registered post • n. Brit. a postal service in which the sender can claim compensation if the item sent is damaged, late, or lost.

register office • n. (in the UK) a local government building where civil

r

marriages are performed and births, marriages, and deaths are recorded.

registrar /rej-i-strar, rej-i-**strar**/ • n. **1** an official responsible for keeping official records. **2** the chief administrative officer in a university. **3** Brit. a hospital doctor who is training to be a specialist.

registration • n. **1** the action of registering. **2** (also **registration number**) Brit. the series of letters and figures identifying a motor vehicle and shown on a number plate.

registry • n. (pl. **registries**) a place where official records are kept.

registry office • n. (in non-official use) a register office.

Regius professor /ree-juhss/ • n. (in the UK) the holder of a university professorship founded or appointed by a king or queen.
– ORIGIN Latin *regius* 'royal'.

regress /ri-gress/ • v. return to an earlier or less advanced state.
– DERIVATIVES **regression** n.
– ORIGIN Latin *regredi*.

regressive • adj. **1** returning to an earlier or less advanced state. **2** (of a tax) taking a proportionally greater amount from people on lower incomes.

regret • v. (**regrets, regretting, regretted**) feel or express sorrow or disappointment about something you have done or that you should have done. • n. a feeling of such sorrow or disappointment.
– ORIGIN Old French *regreter* 'lament the dead'.

regretful • adj. feeling or showing regret.

regretfully • adv. **1** in a regretful way. **2** it is regrettable that.

regrettable • adj. giving rise to regret; undesirable.
– DERIVATIVES **regrettably** adv.

regroup • v. form into organized groups again after being attacked or defeated.

regular • adj. **1** following or arranged in a pattern, especially with the same space between one thing and the next: *the association holds regular meetings.* **2** done or happening frequently. **3** doing the same thing often: *regular worshippers.* **4** following or controlled by an accepted standard. **5** usual. **6** Grammar (of a word) following the normal pattern of inflection. **7** belonging to the permanent professional armed forces of a country. **8** (of a geometrical figure) having all sides and all angles equal. **9** informal, dated absolute; complete: *this place is a regular fisherman's paradise.* • n. a regular customer, soldier, etc.
– DERIVATIVES **regularity** n. (pl.

regularities). **regularly** adv.
– ORIGIN Latin *regula* 'rule'.

regularize (or **regularise**)
• v. (**regularizes, regularizing, regularized**) **1** make something regular. **2** make a temporary situation legal or official.

regulate • v. (**regulates, regulating, regulated**) **1** control the rate or speed of a machine or process. **2** control something by means of rules.
– DERIVATIVES **regulator** n.

regulation • n. **1** a rule made by an authority. **2** the action of regulating. • adj. informal conforming to rules or conventions.

regulatory /reg-yuh-luh-tri, reg-yuh-**lay**-tuh-ri/ • adj. acting to regulate something: *a regulatory authority.*

regulo /reg-yuu-loh/ • n. Brit. trademark used before a number to indicate a temperature setting in a gas oven.

regurgitate /ri-ger-ji-tayt/
• v. (**regurgitates, regurgitating, regurgitated**) **1** bring swallowed food up again to the mouth. **2** repeat information without understanding it.
– DERIVATIVES **regurgitation** n.
– ORIGIN Latin *regurgitare*.

rehabilitate • v. (**rehabilitates, rehabilitating, rehabilitated**) **1** prepare someone who has been ill or in prison to resume normal life by training and therapy. **2** restore the reputation of someone previously out of favour.
– DERIVATIVES **rehabilitation** n.
– ORIGIN Latin *rehabilitare*.

rehash • v. reuse old ideas or material with no great change or improvement. • n. a reuse of old ideas or material.

rehearsal • n. **1** a trial performance of a play or other work for later public performance. **2** the action of rehearsing.

rehearse • v. (**rehearses, rehearsing, rehearsed**) **1** practise a play, piece of music, etc. for later public performance. **2** state points that have been made before.
– ORIGIN Old French *rehercier*.

reheat • v. heat again.

rehouse • v. (**rehouses, rehousing, rehoused**) provide someone with new housing.

rehydrate • v. (**rehydrates, rehydrating, rehydrated**) cause something to absorb moisture after dehydration.
– DERIVATIVES **rehydration** n.

reign • v. **1** rule as king or queen. **2** be the dominant quality or aspect: *confusion reigned in the city.* **3** (as adj. **reigning**) currently holding a particular title in sport. • n. **1** the period of rule of a king

r

or queen. **2** the period during which someone or something is best or most important.
– ORIGIN Old French *reignier*.

reimburse /ree-im-berss/
• v. (**reimburses, reimbursing, reimbursed**) repay money to a person who has spent or lost it.
– DERIVATIVES **reimbursement** n.
– ORIGIN Latin *imbursare* 'put in a purse'.

rein • n. **1** a long, narrow strap attached to a horse's bit, used as one of a pair to control the horse. **2** (**reins**) the power to direct and control: *a new chairperson is taking over the reins.* • v. **1** control a horse by pulling on its reins. **2** (**rein someone/thing in/back**) restrain someone or something.
– PHRASES (**a**) **free rein** freedom of action.
– ORIGIN Old French *rene*.

> ☑ The phrase **a free rein**, which comes from the meaning of allowing a horse to move freely without being controlled by reins, is often misinterpreted and wrongly spelled as a *free reign*.

reincarnate /ree-in-kar-nayt/ • v. (**be reincarnated**) be born again in another body.

reincarnation • n. **1** the rebirth of a soul in a new body. **2** a person in whom a soul is believed to have been born again.

reindeer • n. (pl. **reindeer** or **reindeers**) a deer with large branching antlers, found in cold northern regions.
– ORIGIN Old Norse.

reinforce • v. (**reinforces, reinforcing, reinforced**) **1** strengthen or support an object. **2** make a feeling, idea, etc. stronger or more intense. **3** strengthen a military force with additional personnel or equipment.
– ORIGIN French *renforcer*.

reinforced concrete • n. concrete in which metal bars or wire are embedded to strengthen it.

reinforcement • n. **1** the action of strengthening something. **2** (**reinforcements**) extra personnel sent to strengthen an army or similar force.

reinstate • v. (**reinstates, reinstating, reinstated**) restore to a former position or state.
– DERIVATIVES **reinstatement** n.

reinterpret • v. (**reinterprets, reinterpreting, reinterpreted**) interpret something in a new or different light.
– DERIVATIVES **reinterpretation** n.

reintroduce • v. (**reintroduces, reintroducing, reintroduced**) **1** bring something into effect again. **2** put a species of animal or plant back into a

place where it once lived.
– DERIVATIVES **reintroduction** n.

reinvigorate • v. (**reinvigorates, reinvigorating, reinvigorated**) give renewed energy or strength to.

reissue • v. (**reissues, reissuing, reissued**) produce or publish a new supply or different form of a book, record, or other product. • n. a new issue of a product.

reiterate • v. (**reiterates, reiterating, reiterated**) say something again or repeatedly.
– DERIVATIVES **reiteration** n.
– ORIGIN Latin *reiterare* 'go over again'.

reject • v. /ri-jekt/ **1** refuse to accept something faulty or unsatisfactory. **2** refuse to agree to something. **3** fail to show proper affection or care for someone. **4** (of the body) react against a transplanted organ. • n. /ree-jekt/ a rejected person or thing.
– DERIVATIVES **rejection** n.
– ORIGIN Latin *reicere* 'throw back'.

rejig • v. (**rejigs, rejigging, rejigged**) Brit. rearrange something.

rejoice • v. (**rejoices, rejoicing, rejoiced**) feel or show great joy.
– ORIGIN Old French *rejoir*.

rejoin[1] • v. join again.

rejoin[2] • v. say in reply; retort.
– ORIGIN Old French *rejoindre*.

rejoinder • n. a quick or witty reply.

rejuvenate /ri-joo-vuh-nayt/
• v. (**rejuvenates, rejuvenating, rejuvenated**) make someone or something look younger or more lively.
– DERIVATIVES **rejuvenation** n.
– ORIGIN Latin *juvenis* 'young'.

rekindle • v. (**rekindles, rekindling, rekindled**) **1** revive a past feeling, hope, or interest. **2** relight a fire.

relapse • v. /ri-laps/ (**relapses, relapsing, relapsed**) **1** (of a sick or injured person) become ill again after a period of improvement. **2** (**relapse into**) return to a worse state. • n. /ree-laps/ a return to ill health after a temporary improvement.
– ORIGIN Latin *relabi* 'slip back'.

relate • v. (**relates, relating, related**) **1** give an account of something. **2** (**be related**) be connected by blood or marriage. **3** have a connection or link with: *many drowning accidents are related to alcohol use.* **4** (**relate to**) have to do with; concern. **5** (**relate to**) feel sympathy with.
– ORIGIN Latin *referre* 'bring back'.

related • adj. belonging to the same family, group, or type; connected.

relation • n. **1** the way in which two or more people or things are related.

2 (relations) the way in which two or more people or groups feel about and behave towards each other. **3** a relative. **4 (relations)** formal sex or a sexual relationship.
– PHRASES **in relation to** in connection with.

relationship •n. **1** the way in which two or more people or things are connected. **2** the way in which two or more people or groups behave towards each other. **3** a loving and sexual association between two people.

relative /rel-uh-tiv/ •adj. **1** considered in relation or in proportion to something else. **2** existing only in comparison to something else: *months of relative calm ended in April.* **3** Grammar (of a pronoun, determiner, or adverb) referring to an earlier noun, sentence, or clause (e.g. *which* in *a conference in Paris which ended on Friday*). **4** Grammar (of a clause) connected to a main clause by a relative pronoun, determiner, or adverb. •n. a person connected by blood or marriage.
– PHRASES **relative to 1** compared with or in relation to. **2** concerning.

relative atomic mass •n. the ratio of the average mass of one atom of an element to one twelfth of the mass of an atom of carbon-12.

relatively •adv. in comparison or proportion to something else.

relative molecular mass •n. the ratio of the average mass of one molecule of an element or compound to one twelfth of the mass of an atom of carbon-12.

relativism •n. the idea that knowledge, truth, and morality exist in relation to culture, society, or historical context, and are not always the same.
– DERIVATIVES **relativist** n.

relativity •n. **1** the state of being relative to something else. **2** Physics a description of matter, energy, space, and time according to Einstein's theories.

relaunch •v. launch again or in a different form. •n. an instance of relaunching.

relax •v. **1** become less tense, anxious, or rigid. **2** rest from work or engage in a recreational activity. **3** make a rule or restriction less strict.
– ORIGIN Latin *relaxare.*

relaxant •n. a drug that promotes relaxation or reduces tension.

relaxation •n. **1** the state of being free from tension and worry. **2** the action of making something less strict.

relay /ree-lay/ •n. **1** a group of people or animals engaged in a task for a time and then replaced by a similar group. **2** a

race between teams of runners, each team member in turn covering part of the total distance. **3** an electrical device which opens or closes a circuit in response to a current in another circuit. **4** a device to receive, strengthen, and transmit a signal again. •v. /also ri-lay/ **1** receive and pass on information. **2** broadcast by means of a relay.
– ORIGIN Old French *relayer.*

release •v. (**releases, releasing, released**) **1** set someone free from imprisonment. **2** free someone from a duty. **3** allow to move freely. **4** allow information to be generally available. **5** make a film or recording available to the public. •n. **1** the action of setting someone or something free. **2** a film or recording released to the public.
– ORIGIN Old French *relesser.*

relegate •v. (**relegates, relegating, relegated**) place a person or team in a lower rank or position.
– DERIVATIVES **relegation** n.
– ORIGIN Latin *relegare* 'send away'.

relent •v. **1** finally agree to something after refusing it. **2** become less strong or severe.
– ORIGIN from Latin *re-* 'back' + *lentare* 'to bend'.

relentless •adj. **1** never stopping or weakening. **2** harsh or inflexible.
– DERIVATIVES **relentlessly** adv.

relevant •adj. closely connected or appropriate to the current matter.
– DERIVATIVES **relevance** n.
– ORIGIN Latin *relevare* 'raise up'.

reliable •adj. able to be depended on or trusted.
– DERIVATIVES **reliability** n. **reliably** adv.

reliance •n. dependence on or trust in someone or something.
– DERIVATIVES **reliant** adj.

relic •n. **1** an object, custom, or belief surviving from an earlier time. **2** a part of a holy person's body or belongings kept and treated as holy after their death.
– ORIGIN Latin *reliquiae* 'remains'.

relict /rel-ikt/ •n. a thing which has survived from an earlier period.
– ORIGIN Latin *relictus* 'left behind'.

relief •n. **1** a feeling of reassurance and relaxation after anxiety or distress have been removed. **2** a cause of relief. **3** the action of relieving. **4** (also **light relief**) a break in a tense or boring situation. **5** assistance given to people in need or difficulty. **6** a person or group replacing another person or other people who have been on duty. **7** a way of cutting a design into wood, stone, etc. so that parts of it stand out from the surface.

– ORIGIN Latin *relevare* 'raise again'.

relief map • n. a map that shows hills and valleys by shading.

relieve • v. (**relieves, relieving, relieved**) **1** lessen or remove pain, distress, or difficulty. **2** (**be relieved**) stop feeling distressed or anxious. **3** release someone from duty by taking their place. **4** (**relieve someone of**) take a responsibility from someone. **5** bring military support for a place which is under siege. **6** make less boring. **7** (**relieve yourself**) euphem. urinate or defecate.

– DERIVATIVES **reliever** n.

– ORIGIN Old French *relever*.

 relieve follows the usual rule of *i* before e except after c.

religion • n. **1** the belief in and worship of a God or gods. **2** a particular system of faith and worship.

– ORIGIN Latin, 'obligation, reverence'.

religiosity /ri-lij-i-**oss**-i-ti/ • n. the state of being excessively religious.

religious • adj. **1** relating to or believing in a religion. **2** very careful or regular.

– DERIVATIVES **religiously** adv.

relinquish • v. give something up.

– DERIVATIVES **relinquishment** n.

– ORIGIN Latin *relinquere*.

reliquary /**rel**-i-kwuh-ri/ • n. (pl. **reliquaries**) a container for holy relics.

relish • n. **1** great enjoyment. **2** a pleasant feeling of looking forward to something. **3** a highly flavoured sauce or pickle. • v. **1** enjoy something greatly. **2** look forward to something with pleasure.

– ORIGIN Old French *reles* 'remainder'.

relive • v. (**relives, reliving, relived**) live through an experience or feeling again in your imagination.

reload • v. load again.

relocate • v. (**relocates, relocating, relocated**) move to a new place and establish your home or business there.

– DERIVATIVES **relocation** n.

reluctance • n. unwillingness to do something.

reluctant • adj. unwilling and hesitant.

– DERIVATIVES **reluctantly** adv.

– ORIGIN Latin *reluctari* 'struggle against'.

rely • v. (**relies, relying, relied**) (**rely on**) **1** trust or have faith in. **2** be dependent on.

– ORIGIN Old French *relier* 'bind together'.

remade past and past part. of **REMAKE**.

remain • v. **1** stay in the same place or condition. **2** continue to be: *he remained alert.* **3** be left over.

– ORIGIN Latin *remanere*.

remainder • n. **1** a part, number, or amount that is left over. **2** the number which is left over when one quantity does not exactly divide into another.

remains • pl. n. **1** things remaining. **2** historical or archaeological relics. **3** a person's body after death.

remake • v. /ree-**mayk**/ (**remakes, remaking, remade**) make again or differently. • n. /**ree**-mayk/ a film or piece of music that has been filmed or recorded again and re-released.

remand Law • v. place a person charged with a crime on bail or in jail. • n. the state of being remanded.

– ORIGIN Latin *remandare* 'commit again'.

remark • v. **1** say something as a comment. **2** notice something. • n. **1** a comment. **2** the fact of being noticed or commented on.

– ORIGIN French *remarquer* 'note again'.

remarkable • adj. extraordinary or striking.

– DERIVATIVES **remarkably** adv.

rematch • n. a second match or game between two sports teams or players.

remedial • adj. **1** intended as a remedy. **2** provided for children with learning difficulties.

remedy • n. (pl. **remedies**) **1** a medicine or treatment for a disease or injury. **2** a means of dealing with something undesirable. • v. (**remedies, remedying, remedied**) put right an undesirable situation.

– ORIGIN Latin *remedium*.

remember • v. (**remembers, remembering, remembered**) **1** have in or bring to your mind someone or something from the past. **2** keep something necessary in mind: *remember to post the letters.* **3** bring someone to mind by making them a gift or by mentioning them in prayer. **4** (**remember someone to**) pass on greetings from one person to another.

– ORIGIN Latin *rememorari*.

remembrance • n. **1** the action of remembering. **2** a memory. **3** a thing kept or given as a reminder of someone.

Remembrance Sunday (also **Remembrance Day**) • n. (in the UK) the Sunday nearest 11 November, when those who were killed in war are remembered.

remind • v. **1** cause someone to remember to do something. **2** (**remind someone of**) cause someone to think of someone or something because of a resemblance.

reminder • n. **1** a thing that makes

r

someone remember something. **2** a letter sent to remind someone to pay a bill.

reminisce /re-mi-**niss**/ • v. (**reminisces, reminiscing, reminisced**) think or talk contentedly about the past.

reminiscence • n. **1** an account of something that you remember. **2** the enjoyable remembering of past events.
– ORIGIN Latin *reminiscentia*.

reminiscent • adj. **1** (**reminiscent of**) tending to remind you of. **2** with your mind full of memories.

remiss /ri-**miss**/ • adj. lacking care or attention to duty.
– ORIGIN Latin *remittere* 'slacken'.

remission • n. **1** the cancellation of a debt or charge. **2** Brit. the reduction of a prison sentence as a reward for good behaviour. **3** a temporary period during which a serious illness becomes less severe. **4** forgiveness of sins.

remit • v. /ri-**mit**/ (**remits, remitting, remitted**) **1** cancel a debt or punishment. **2** send money in payment. **3** refer a matter for decision to an authority. • n. /**ree**-mit/ esp. Brit. the task officially given to a person or organization.
– ORIGIN Latin *remittere* 'send back'.

remittance • n. **1** a sum of money sent in payment. **2** the action of remitting money.

remix • v. /ree-**miks**/ produce a different version of a musical recording by altering the balance of the separate tracks. • n. /**ree**-miks/ a remixed musical recording.

remnant • n. **1** a small remaining quantity. **2** a piece of cloth left when the greater part has been used or sold.
– ORIGIN Old French *remenant*.

remonstrance • n. a strongly critical protest.

remonstrate /**rem**-uhn-strayt/ • v. (**remonstrates, remonstrating, remonstrated**) make a strongly critical protest.
– DERIVATIVES **remonstration** n.
– ORIGIN Latin *remonstrare* 'demonstrate'.

remorse • n. deep regret or guilt for a wrong that you have done.
– ORIGIN Latin *remorsus*.

remorseful • adj. filled with deep regret or guilt.
– DERIVATIVES **remorsefully** adv.

remorseless • adj. **1** without regret or guilt. **2** (of something unpleasant) relentless.
– DERIVATIVES **remorselessly** adv.

remortgage • v. (**remortgages, remortgaging, remortgaged**) take out another or a different mortgage on a house or flat.

remote • adj. (**remoter, remotest**) **1** far away in space or time. **2** situated far from the main cities or towns: *a remote Welsh valley.* **3** distantly related. **4** having very little connection. **5** (of a chance or possibility) unlikely to occur. **6** unfriendly and distant. **7** (of an electronic device) operating or operated by means of radio or infrared signals. • n. a remote control device.
– DERIVATIVES **remotely** adv. **remoteness** n.
– ORIGIN Latin *remotus* 'removed'.

remote control • n. **1** control of a machine from a distance by means of signals transmitted from a radio or electronic device. **2** a device that controls a machine in this way.
– DERIVATIVES **remote-controlled** adj.

removal • n. **1** the action of taking something off or away from the position occupied. **2** Brit. the transfer of furniture and other contents when moving house.

remove • v. (**removes, removing, removed**) **1** take off or away from the position occupied. **2** abolish or get rid of something. **3** dismiss someone from a post. **4** (**be removed from**) be very different from. **5** (as adj. **removed**) separated by a particular number of steps of descent: *his second cousin once removed.* • n. the extent to which two things are separated: *the chairman was at one remove from what was going on.*
– DERIVATIVES **removable** adj. **remover** n.
– ORIGIN Latin *removere*.

remunerate /ri-**myoo**-nuh-rayt/ • v. (**remunerates, remunerating, remunerated**) pay someone for work done.
– DERIVATIVES **remunerative** adj.
– ORIGIN Latin *remunerari* 'reward'.

remuneration • n. money paid for work.

Renaissance /ri-**nay**-suhnss, ri-**nay**-sonss/ • n. **1** the revival of European art and literature under the influence of classical styles in the 14th–16th centuries. **2** (**renaissance**) a revival of interest in something.
– ORIGIN French, 'rebirth'.

renal /**ree**-n'l/ • adj. tech. relating to the kidneys.
– ORIGIN Latin *renalis*.

rename • v. (**renames, renaming, renamed**) give a new name to.

renascent • adj. becoming active again.
– DERIVATIVES **renascence** n.
– ORIGIN Latin.

rend • v. (**rends, rending, rent**) literary **1** tear something to pieces. **2** cause

someone great distress.
- PHRASES **rend the air** sound piercingly.
- ORIGIN Old English.

render •v. (**renders, rendering, rendered**) **1** provide a service. **2** present something for inspection, consideration, or payment. **3** cause someone to be or become: *she was rendered speechless.* **4** perform a piece of music or drama. **5** melt down fat so as to separate out its impurities. **6** cover a wall with a coat of plaster.
- ORIGIN Old French *rendre.*

rendering •n. **1** a performance of a piece of music or a role in a play. **2** a coat of plaster.

rendezvous /ron-day-voo/ •n. (pl. **rendezvous** /ron-day-voo, ron-day-vooz/) **1** a meeting at an agreed time and place.
•v. (**rendezvouses** /ron-day-vooz/, **rendezvousing** /ron-day-voo-ing/, **rendezvoused** /ron-day-vood/) meet at an agreed time and place.
- ORIGIN French *rendez-vous!* 'present yourselves!'

rendition •n. a performance or version of a dramatic role or a musical work.

renegade /ren-i-gayd/ •n. a person who deserts and betrays an organization, country, or set of principles.
- ORIGIN Spanish *renegado.*

renege /ri-nayg, ri-neeg/ •v. (**reneges, reneging, reneged**) go back on a promise or contract.
- ORIGIN Latin *renegare.*

renegotiate •v. (**renegotiates, renegotiating, renegotiated**) negotiate something again in order to change the original agreed terms.

renew •v. **1** begin again after an interruption. **2** give fresh life or strength to. **3** extend the period of validity of a licence, subscription, or contract. **4** replace something broken or worn out.
- DERIVATIVES **renewal** n.

renewable •adj. **1** capable of being renewed. **2** (of energy or its source) not exhausted when used.

renminbi /ren-min-bi/ •n. (pl. **renminbi**) **1** the system of currency of China. **2** a yuan.
- ORIGIN Chinese.

rennet /ren-nit/ •n. curdled milk from the stomach of a calf, used in curdling milk for cheese.
- ORIGIN prob. from **RUN**.

renounce •v. (**renounces, renouncing, renounced**) **1** formally give up a right or possession. **2** declare that you no longer have a particular belief. **3** abandon a cause, habit, etc.

- ORIGIN Old French *renoncer.*

renovate /ren-uh-vayt/ •v. (**renovates, renovating, renovated**) restore something old to a good state of repair.
- DERIVATIVES **renovation** n. **renovator** n.
- ORIGIN Latin *renovare* 'renew'.

renown •n. the state of being famous and respected.
- DERIVATIVES **renowned** adj.
- ORIGIN Old French *renomer* 'make famous'.

rent¹ •n. a regular payment made to a landlord for the use of property or land.
•v. **1** pay someone for the use of property or land. **2** let someone use something in return for payment.
- ORIGIN Old French *rente.*

rent² •n. a large tear in a piece of fabric.
- ORIGIN from **REND**.

rent³ past and past part. of **REND**.

rental •n. **1** an amount paid as rent. **2** the action of renting. •adj. relating to or available for rent.

renunciation •n. an act of giving up a right or possession.

reoccur •v. (**reoccurs, reoccurring, reoccurred**) occur again or repeatedly.
- DERIVATIVES **reoccurrence** n.

reoffend •v. commit a further offence.
- DERIVATIVES **reoffender** n.

reopen •v. open again.

reorder •v. (**reorders, reordering, reordered**) **1** order again. **2** arrange again. •n. a repeated order for goods.

reorganize (or **reorganise**)
•v. (**reorganizes, reorganizing, reorganized**) change the organization of.
- DERIVATIVES **reorganization** n.

reorient /ree-or-i-ent, ree-o-ri-ent/
•v. **1** change the focus or direction of. **2** (**reorient yourself**) find your bearings again.

rep •n. informal a representative.

repaid past and past part. of **REPAY**.

repair¹ •v. **1** restore something damaged, worn, or faulty to a good condition. **2** set right a breakdown in relations. •n. **1** the action of repairing. **2** a result of repairing. **3** the condition of something: *the cottages were in good repair.*
- DERIVATIVES **repairable** adj. **repairer** n.
- ORIGIN Latin *reparare.*

repair² •v. (**repair to**) formal go to a place.
- ORIGIN Old French *repairer.*

reparable /rep-uh-ruh-b'l/ •adj. able to be repaired or put right.

reparation /rep-uh-ray-sh'n/
•n. **1** something done to make up for a wrong. **2** (**reparations**) compensation for war damage paid by a defeated state.
- ORIGIN Latin.

r

repartee /rep-ar-**tee**/ •n. quick, witty comments or replies.
– ORIGIN French *repartie* 'replied promptly'.

repast /ri-**pahst**/ •n. formal a meal.
– ORIGIN Old French.

repatriate /ree-pat-ri-ayt, ree-**pay**-tri-ayt/ •v. (**repatriates, repatriating, repatriated**) send someone back to their own country.
– DERIVATIVES **repatriation** n.
– ORIGIN Latin *repatriare* 'return to your country'.

repay •v. (**repays, repaying, repaid**) **1** pay back a loan owed to someone. **2** do or give something as a reward for a favour or kindness. **3** Brit. be worth spending time on: *these sites would repay detailed investigation.*
– DERIVATIVES **repayable** adj. **repayment** n.

repayment mortgage •n. Brit. a mortgage in which the borrower repays the money borrowed and interest together in fixed instalments over a fixed period.

repeal •v. officially cancel a law or act of parliament. •n. the action of cancelling a law or act of parliament.
– ORIGIN Old French *repeler.*

repeat •v. **1** say again. **2** do again or more than once. **3** (**repeat itself**) occur again in the same way. **4** esp. Brit. (of food) be tasted again after being swallowed, as a result of indigestion. •n. **1** an instance of repeating. **2** a repeated broadcast of a television or radio programme.
– DERIVATIVES **repeatedly** adj.
– ORIGIN Latin *repetere.*

repel •v. (**repels, repelling, repelled**) **1** drive or force back or away. **2** be disgusting to. **3** (of a magnetic pole or electric field) force away something similarly magnetized or charged. **4** (of a substance) be able to keep something out: *leather uppers to repel moisture.*
– ORIGIN Latin *repellere.*

repellent (also **repellant**) •adj. **1** able to repel a particular thing: *water-repellent nylon.* **2** causing disgust or distaste. •n. **1** a substance that deters insects. **2** a substance used to treat something to make it repel water.

repent •v. feel or express sincere regret or remorse.
– DERIVATIVES **repentance** n. **repentant** adj.
– ORIGIN Old French *repentir.*

repercussions •pl. n. the consequences of an event or action.
– ORIGIN Latin *repercutere* 'push back'.

repertoire /rep-er-twar/ •n. the works known or regularly performed by a performer or company.
– ORIGIN French.

repertory /rep-er-tuh-ri/ •n. (pl. **repertories**) **1** the performance by a company of the plays, operas, or ballets in its repertoire at regular short intervals. **2** = REPERTOIRE.
– ORIGIN Latin *repertorium* 'catalogue, storehouse'.

repetition •n. **1** the action or an instance of repeating. **2** a thing that repeats another.

repetitious •adj. having too much repetition; repetitive.

repetitive •adj. repeated many times or too much.
– DERIVATIVES **repetitively** adv.

repetitive strain injury •n. a condition in which prolonged repetitive action causes pain or weakening in the tendons and muscles involved.

rephrase •v. (**rephrases, rephrasing, rephrased**) express differently.

repine •v. (**repines, repining, repined**) literary be unhappy; fret.

replace •v. (**replaces, replacing, replaced**) **1** take the place of. **2** provide a substitute for. **3** put back in a previous position.
– DERIVATIVES **replaceable** adj.

replacement •n. **1** the action of replacing someone or something. **2** a person or thing that takes the place of another.

replay •v. **1** play back a recording. **2** play a match again. •n. **1** an instance of playing back a recording. **2** a replayed match.

replenish •v. fill up a stock or supply again after some has been used.
– DERIVATIVES **replenishment** n.
– ORIGIN Old French *replenir.*

replete /ri-**pleet**/ •adj. **1** (**replete with**) filled or well-supplied with. **2** very full with food.
– DERIVATIVES **repletion** n.
– ORIGIN Latin *replere* 'fill up'.

replica /**rep**-li-kuh/ •n. an exact copy or model of something.
– ORIGIN Italian.

replicate /**rep**-li-kayt/ •v. (**replicates, replicating, replicated**) make an exact copy of.
– DERIVATIVES **replication** n. **replicator** n.
– ORIGIN Latin *replicare.*

reply •v. (**replies, replying, replied**) **1** say or write something as an answer. **2** respond with a similar action: *they replied to the shelling with a mortar attack.* •n. (pl. **replies**) **1** the action of replying. **2** a spoken or written answer.
– ORIGIN Old French *replier.*

report •v. **1** give a spoken or written

account of something. **2** cover an event or situation as a journalist. **3** (**be reported**) be said or rumoured. **4** make a formal complaint about. **5** present yourself as having arrived or as ready to do something. **6** (**report to**) be responsible to a manager. •n. **1** an account given of a matter after investigation. **2** an account of an event or situation. **3** Brit. a teacher's written assessment of a pupil's progress. **4** a sudden loud noise of an explosion or gunfire.
– ORIGIN Latin *reportare* 'bring back'.

reportage /rep-or-tahzh, ri-por-tij/ •n. the reporting of news by the media.

reported speech •n. a speaker's words reported with the required changes of person and tense (e.g. *he said that he would go*, based on *I will go*). Contrasted with **DIRECT SPEECH**.

reporter •n. a person who reports news for a newspaper or broadcasting company.

repose[1] •n. a state of calm or peace. •v. (**reposes, reposing, reposed**) formal **1** lie down and rest. **2** be placed or kept in a particular place.
– ORIGIN Old French *reposer*.

repose[2] •v. (**reposes, reposing, reposed**) (**repose something in**) place your confidence or trust in.
– ORIGIN from **POSE**.

reposition •v. adjust or alter the position of.

repository /ri-poz-i-tuh-ri/ •n. (pl. **repositories**) **1** a place or container for storage. **2** a person or thing that is full of information or a particular quality.
– ORIGIN Latin *repositorium*.

repossess •v. retake possession of something when a buyer fails to make the required payments.
– DERIVATIVES **repossession** n.

reprehensible •adj. wrong or bad and deserving condemnation.
– ORIGIN Latin *reprehendere* 'to rebuke'.

represent •v. **1** be entitled or appointed to act and speak on behalf of. **2** be a specimen or example of. **3** (**be represented**) be present to a particular degree: *abstraction is well represented in this exhibition.* **4** show or describe something in a particular way. **5** depict something in a work of art. **6** be a symbol of.
– ORIGIN Latin *praesentare*.

representation •n. **1** the action or an instance of representing. **2** an image, model, or other depiction of something. **3** (**representations**) statements made to an authority to pass on an opinion or make a protest.

representational •adj. **1** relating to representation. **2** relating to art which shows the physical appearance of things.

representative •adj. **1** typical of a class or group. **2** containing typical examples of all types: *a representative sample.* **3** (of a law-making assembly) consisting of people chosen to act and speak on behalf of a wider group. •n. **1** a person chosen to act and speak for another person or people. **2** an agent of a firm who visits potential clients to sell its products. **3** an example of a class or group.

repress •v. **1** bring a person or people under control by force. **2** try not to have or show a thought or feeling.
– DERIVATIVES **repressible** adj. **repression** n.
– ORIGIN Latin *reprimere* 'press back'.

repressed •adj. **1** (of a thought or feeling) kept suppressed and unconscious in your mind. **2** having feelings and desires that you do not let yourself show to other people.

repressive •adj. restricting personal freedom.

reprieve •v. (**reprieves, reprieving, reprieved**) **1** cancel the punishment of. **2** abandon or postpone plans to close: *the threatened pits could be reprieved.* •n. **1** the cancellation of a punishment. **2** a short rest from difficulty or danger.
– ORIGIN Old French *reprendre*.

reprimand /rep-ri-mahnd/ •n. a formal statement of disapproval. •v. tell someone formally that they have done something wrong.
– ORIGIN French *réprimande*.

reprint •v. /ree-print/ print again with few or no changes. •n. /ree-print/ an act of reprinting. **2** a copy of a book that has been reprinted.

reprisal /ri-pry-z'l/ •n. a violent or aggressive act done in return for a similar act.
– ORIGIN Old French *reprisaille*.

reprise /ri-preez/ •n. **1** a repeated passage in music. **2** a further performance of something. •v. (**reprises, reprising, reprised**) repeat a piece of music or a performance.
– ORIGIN French, 'taken up again'.

reproach •v. **1** express your disapproval of or disappointment with someone. **2** (**reproach someone with**) accuse someone of: *his wife reproached him with cowardice.* •n. a statement of disapproval or disappointment.
– PHRASES **above** (or **beyond**) **reproach** perfect.
– ORIGIN Old French *reprochier*.

reproachful •adj. expressing disapproval or disappointment.
– DERIVATIVES **reproachfully** adv.

r

reprobate /rep-ruh-bayt/ •n. a person who behaves in an immoral way.
– ORIGIN Latin *reprobare* 'disapprove'.

reproduce •v. (**reproduces, reproducing, reproduced**) 1 produce a copy of. 2 produce something again in a different situation: *the problems are difficult to reproduce in a laboratory.* 3 produce offspring.
– DERIVATIVES **reproducible** adj.

reproduction •n. 1 the action of reproducing. 2 a copy of a work of art. •adj. made to imitate the style of an earlier period or particular craftsman: *reproduction furniture.*
– DERIVATIVES **reproductive** adj.

reproof /ri-proof/ •n. a criticism or reprimand.
– ORIGIN Old French *reprover* 'reprove'.

reprove •v. (**reproves, reproving, reproved**) criticize or reprimand someone.
– ORIGIN Old French *reprover*.

reptile •n. a cold-blooded vertebrate animal, of a class that includes snakes, lizards, crocodiles, turtles, and tortoises.
– DERIVATIVES **reptilian** adj. & n.
– ORIGIN Latin *reptilis* 'crawling'.

republic •n. a state in which power is held by the people and their elected representatives, and which has a president rather than a king or queen.
– ORIGIN Latin *respublica*.

republican •adj. 1 relating to or like a republic. 2 supporting the principles of a republic. 3 (**Republican**) (in the US) supporting the Republican Party. •n. 1 a person in favour of republican government. 2 (**Republican**) (in the US) a member of the Republican Party. 3 (**Republican**) a supporter of a united Ireland.
– DERIVATIVES **republicanism** n.

repudiate /ri-pyoo-di-ayt/ •v. (**repudiates, repudiating, repudiated**) 1 refuse to accept or be associated with. 2 deny the truth or validity of.
– DERIVATIVES **repudiation** n.
– ORIGIN Latin *repudiatus* 'cast off'.

repugnance /ri-pug-nuhnss/ •n. great disgust.
– ORIGIN Latin *repugnare* 'oppose'.

repugnant •adj. disgusting or very unpleasant.

repulse •v. (**repulses, repulsing, repulsed**) 1 drive back an attacking enemy by force. 2 reject or refuse to accept. 3 make someone feel intense dislike or disgust.
– ORIGIN Latin *repellere*.

repulsion •n. 1 a feeling of intense dislike or disgust. 2 Physics a force under the influence of which objects tend to move away from each other.

repulsive •adj. 1 arousing strong distaste or disgust. 2 Physics relating to repulsion between objects.

reputable /rep-yuu-tuh-b'l/ •adj. having a good reputation.

reputation •n. the beliefs or opinions that are generally held about someone or something.

repute •n. 1 the opinion generally held of someone or something. 2 good reputation. •v. 1 (**be reputed**) have a particular reputation. 2 (as adj. **reputed**) generally believed to be so: *the reputed flatness of the country.*
– DERIVATIVES **reputedly** adv.
– ORIGIN Latin *reputare* 'think over'.

request •n. 1 an act of asking politely or formally for something. 2 a thing that is asked for politely or formally. •v. politely or formally ask for something or ask someone to do something.
– ORIGIN Latin *requirere* 'require'.

requiem /rek-wi-uhm, rek-wi-em/ •n. 1 (especially in the Roman Catholic Church) a Mass for the souls of the dead. 2 a musical composition based on such a Mass.
– ORIGIN Latin.

require •v. (**requires, requiring, required**) 1 need something for a purpose. 2 instruct or expect someone to do something. 3 make compulsory: *the minimum required by law.*
– ORIGIN Latin *requirere*.

requirement •n. 1 something that is needed. 2 something that is compulsory.

requisite /rek-wi-zit/ •adj. made necessary by circumstances or regulations. •n. a thing that is necessary for a purpose.
– ORIGIN Latin *requisitus* 'deemed necessary'.

requisition /rek-wi-zi-sh'n/ •n. 1 an official order allowing property or materials to be taken and used. 2 the taking of goods for military or public use. •v. officially take or use property or goods during a war or emergency.

reran past of RERUN.

reredos /reer-doss/ •n. (pl. **reredos**) an ornamental screen at the back of an altar in a church.
– ORIGIN Old French *areredos*.

re-release •v. (**re-releases, re-releasing, re-released**) release a recording or film again. •n. a re-released recording or film.

rerun •v. (**reruns, rerunning, reran**; past

part. **rerun**) show, stage, or perform an event or programme again. •n. a rerun event or programme.

resat past and past part. of RESIT.

reschedule •v. (**reschedules**, **rescheduling**, **rescheduled**) 1 change the time of a planned event. 2 arrange a new scheme of repayments of a debt.

rescind /ri-sind/ •v. cancel a law, order, or agreement.
– ORIGIN Latin *rescindere*.

rescue •v. (**rescues, rescuing, rescued**) save from a dangerous or distressing situation. •n. an act of rescuing or being rescued.
– DERIVATIVES **rescuer** n.
– ORIGIN Old French *rescoure*.

research •n. /ri-serch, ree-serch/ the study of materials and sources in order to establish facts and reach new conclusions. •v. /ri-serch/ carry out research into a subject or for a book, programme, etc.
– DERIVATIVES **researcher** n.
– ORIGIN from former French *recercher*.

research and development •n. (in industry) work directed towards new ideas and improvement of products and processes.

resemblance •n. 1 the fact of looking like or being similar to someone or something. 2 a way in which things look like or are similar to each other.

resemble •v. (**resembles, resembling, resembled**) look like or be similar to: *the fruit resembles a pear.*
– ORIGIN Old French *resembler*.

resent •v. feel bitter or angry about.
– ORIGIN from former French *resentir* 'feel'.

resentful •adj. feeling bitter or indignant about something you think is unfair.
– DERIVATIVES **resentfully** adv.

resentment •n. bitterness or indignation about something you think is unfair.

reservation •n. 1 the action of reserving. 2 an arrangement for something to be reserved. 3 an area of land set aside for occupation by North American Indians or Australian Aboriginals. 4 an expression of doubt about a statement or claim.

reserve •v. (**reserves, reserving, reserved**) 1 keep something for future use. 2 arrange for a seat, ticket, etc. to be kept for the use of a particular person. 3 retain or hold a right or power. •n. 1 a supply of something available for use if required. 2 money kept available by a bank, company, or government. 3 a military force kept to reinforce or

protect other forces, or for use in an emergency. 4 an extra player in a team, serving as a possible substitute. 5 (**the reserves**) the second-choice team. 6 an area of land set aside for wildlife or for a native people. 7 a lack of warmth or openness.
– ORIGIN Latin *reservare* 'keep back'.

reserved •adj. slow to reveal emotion or opinions.

reserve price •n. the price named as the lowest acceptable by the seller for an item sold at auction.

reservist •n. a member of a military reserve force.

reservoir •n. 1 a large lake used as a source of water supply. 2 a container or part of a machine designed to hold fluid. 3 a supply or source of something: *a fine reservoir of comic talent.*
– ORIGIN French.

reset •v. (**resets, resetting, reset**) 1 set something again or differently. 2 set a counter or clock to zero.

resettle •v. (**resettles, resettling, resettled**) settle in a different place.
– DERIVATIVES **resettlement** n.

reshuffle •v. (**reshuffles, reshuffling, reshuffled**) change around the positions of members of a team, especially government ministers. •n. an act of reshuffling.

reside •v. (**resides, residing, resided**) 1 live in a particular place. 2 (of a right or legal power) belong to a person or group. 3 (**reside in**) (of a quality) be present in: *intelligence and judgement reside in old men.*

residence •n. 1 the fact of living somewhere. 2 a person's home. 3 the official house of a government minister or other official.

residency •n. (pl. **residencies**) the fact or period of living in a place or being attached to an institution.

resident •n. 1 a person who lives somewhere on a long-term basis. 2 Brit. a guest in a hotel. •adj. 1 living somewhere on a long-term basis. 2 attached to and working regularly for a particular institution.
– ORIGIN Latin *residere* 'remain'.

residential •adj. 1 suitable for living in. 2 (of a job, course, etc.) requiring someone to live at a particular place.

residual •adj. remaining after the greater part or quantity has gone or been taken away.
– DERIVATIVES **residually** adv.

residue /rez-i-dyoo/ •n. 1 a small amount of something that remains after the main part has gone or been taken.

r

2 a substance that remains after a process such as combustion.
– ORIGIN Latin *residuum*.

residuum /ri-zi-dyoo-uhm/ • n. (pl. **residua** /ri-zi-dyoo-uh/) tech. a chemical residue.
– ORIGIN Latin.

resign • v. **1** voluntarily leave a job. **2** (**be resigned**) accept that something undesirable cannot be avoided.
– ORIGIN Latin *resignare* 'cancel'.

resignation • n. **1** an act of voluntarily leaving a job. **2** a letter stating an intention to leave a job. **3** acceptance of something undesirable but inevitable.

resilient • adj. **1** able to recoil or spring back into shape after bending, stretching, or being compressed. **2** able to recover quickly from difficult conditions.
– DERIVATIVES **resilience** n.
– ORIGIN Latin *resilire* 'leap back'.

resin /rez-in/ • n. **1** a sticky substance produced by some trees. **2** a synthetic polymer used as the basis of plastics, adhesives, or varnishes.
– DERIVATIVES **resinous** adj.
– ORIGIN Latin *resina*.

resist • v. **1** withstand the action or effect of. **2** try to prevent or fight against. **3** refrain from something tempting.
– ORIGIN Latin *resistere*.

resistance • n. **1** the action of resisting. **2** (also **resistance movement**) a secret organization that fights against a political authority. **3** the impeding effect exerted by one thing on another. **4** the ability not to be affected by something. **5** the degree to which a material or device opposes the passage of an electric current.
– DERIVATIVES **resistant** adj.

resistor • n. a device that resists the passage of an electric current.

resit Brit. • v. (**resits, resitting, resat**) take an exam again after failing. • n. an exam held for this purpose.

resolute /rez-uh-loot/ • adj. determined and unwavering.
– DERIVATIVES **resolutely** adv.
– ORIGIN Latin *resolutus* 'loosened, paid'.

resolution • n. **1** a firm decision. **2** a formal expression of opinion or intention by a law-making body. **3** the quality of being determined. **4** the resolving of a problem or dispute. **5** the process of separating something into its individual parts. **6** the degree to which detail is visible in a photograph or on a television screen.

resolve • v. (**resolves, resolving, resolved**) **1** find a solution to a problem. **2** decide firmly on a course of action.

3 (of a law-making body) take a decision by a formal vote. **4** (**resolve something into**) separate something into its individual parts. • n. firm determination.
– DERIVATIVES **resolvable** adj.
– ORIGIN Latin *resolvere*.

resonance • n. **1** the quality of having a deep, clear, ringing sound. **2** the quality of being suggestive of images, memories, or emotions.

resonant • adj. **1** (of sound) deep, clear, and ringing. **2** (of a room, musical instrument, or hollow body) tending to prolong sounds. **3** (**resonant with**) filled with. **4** suggesting images, memories, or emotions.
– ORIGIN Latin *resonare* 'resound'.

resonate • v. (**resonates, resonating, resonated**) make a deep, clear ringing sound.
– DERIVATIVES **resonator** n.

resort • v. (**resort to**) adopt a strategy or course of action so as to resolve a difficult situation. • n. **1** a place visited for holidays or recreation. **2** the action of resorting to something. **3** a strategy or course of action.
– ORIGIN Old French *resortir* 'come or go out again'.

resound /ri-zownd/ • v. **1** fill or be filled with a ringing, booming, or echoing sound. **2** (**resounding**) definite; unmistakable: *a resounding success.*

resource /ri-zorss, ri-sorss/
• n. **1** (**resources**) a stock or supply of materials or assets that can be drawn on when needed. **2** (**resources**) a country's means of supporting itself, as represented by its minerals, land, and other assets. **3** a source of help or information. **4** (**resources**) personal qualities that help you cope with difficult circumstances. • v. (**resources, resourcing, resourced**) provide with resources.
– ORIGIN Old French dialect *resourdre* 'rise again'.

resourceful • adj. able to find quick and clever ways to overcome difficulties.
– DERIVATIVES **resourcefully** adv. **resourcefulness** n.

respect • n. **1** a feeling of admiration for someone because of their qualities or achievements. **2** consideration for the feelings or rights of other people. **3** (**respects**) polite greetings. **4** a particular aspect or point: *the government's record in this respect is a mixed one.* • v. **1** have respect for. **2** avoid harming or interfering with. **3** agree to recognize and observe a law or rule.
– ORIGIN Latin *respectus*.

respectable • adj. **1** regarded by society as being proper, correct, and good.

2 adequate or acceptable; fairly good.
– DERIVATIVES **respectability** n.
respectably adv.

respectful • adj. feeling or showing consideration or admiration for someone.
– DERIVATIVES **respectfully** adv.

respecting • prep. with reference to.

respective • adj. belonging or relating separately to each of two or more people or things: *they chatted about their respective lives.*

respectively • adv. separately and in the order already mentioned.

respell • v. (**respells, respelling, respelled** or esp. Brit. **respelt**) spell a word differently so as to show its pronunciation.

respiration • n. **1** the action of breathing. **2** a single breath. **3** the processes in living organisms involving the production of energy, typically with the intake of oxygen and the release of carbon dioxide.

respirator • n. **1** a device worn over the face to prevent the breathing in of dust, smoke, or other harmful substances. **2** a device that enables someone to breathe when they are unable to do so naturally.

respiratory /ri-spi-ruh-tuh-ri, ress-pi-ruh-tuh-ri/ • adj. relating to breathing.

respiratory tract • n. the passage formed by the mouth, nose, throat, and lungs, through which air passes during breathing.

respire • v. (**respires, respiring, respired**) **1** breathe. **2** (of a plant) carry out respiration.
– ORIGIN Latin *respirare* 'breathe out'.

respite /ress-pyt, ress-pit/ • n. a short period of rest or relief from something difficult or unpleasant.
– ORIGIN Old French *respit.*

respite care • n. temporary care of a sick, elderly, or disabled person, providing relief for the person who usually looks after them.

resplendent /ri-splen-duhnt/ • adj. bright and colourful in an impressive way.
– ORIGIN from Latin *resplendere* 'shine out'.

respond • v. say or do something in reply or as a reaction.
– ORIGIN Latin *respondere.*

respondent • n. **1** Law a person against whom a petition is filed, especially one in an appeal or a divorce case. **2** a person who responds to a questionnaire or an advertisement.

response • n. an answer or reaction.

responsibility • n. (pl. **responsibilities**) **1** the state of being responsible for something or someone. **2** the opportunity or ability to act independently. **3** a thing which you are required to do as part of a job or legal obligation.

responsible • adj. **1** having a duty to do something, or having control over or care for someone. **2** being the cause of something and so able to be blamed or credited for it. **3** capable of being trusted; reliable. **4** (of a job) involving important duties or control over other people. **5** (**responsible to**) having to report to a senior person.
– DERIVATIVES **responsibly** adv.
– ORIGIN Latin *respondere* 'answer'.

responsive • adj. responding readily and with enthusiasm.

rest¹ • v. **1** stop work or movement in order to relax or recover your strength. **2** place or be placed so as to stay in a specified position: *his feet rested on the table.* **3** (**rest on**) depend or be based on. **4** (**rest something in/on**) place trust, hope, or confidence in or on. **5** (**rest with**) (of power, responsibility, etc.) belong to. **6** (of a matter) be left without further action. • n. **1** the state or a period of resting. **2** a motionless state. **3** Music an interval of silence of a specified length. **4** an object that is used to hold or support something.
– ORIGIN Old English.

rest² • n. **1** the remaining part of something. **2** the remaining people or things. • v. remain or be left in a specified condition: *rest assured we will do all we can.*
– ORIGIN Latin *restare* 'remain'.

restart • v. start again. • n. an act of starting again.

restaurant /ress-tuh-ront, ress-tront/ • n. a place where people pay to sit and eat meals that are cooked on the premises.
– ORIGIN French.

restaurateur /ress-tuh-ruh-ter/ • n. a person who owns and manages a restaurant.
– ORIGIN French.

> ✓ Although **restaurateur** is related to *restaurant*, it is not spelled with an *n*.

restful • adj. having a quiet and soothing quality.
– DERIVATIVES **restfully** adv.

rest home • n. an institution where old or frail people live and are cared for.

restitution • n. **1** the restoration of something lost or stolen to its proper owner. **2** payment for injury or loss.

– ORIGIN Latin.

restive • adj. unable to keep still or unwilling to submit to control.
– ORIGIN Old French.

restless • adj. 1 unable to rest or relax as a result of anxiety or boredom. 2 offering no rest: *a restless night*.
– DERIVATIVES **restlessly** adv. **restlessness** n.

restoration • n. 1 the returning of something to a former condition, place, or owner. 2 the repairing or renovating of a building, work of art, etc. 3 the restoring of a previous practice, right, or situation. 4 (**the Restoration**) the re-establishment of Charles II as King of England in 1660, or the period following this.

restorative • adj. having the ability to restore health or strength. • n. a medicine or drink that restores health or strength.

restore • v. (**restores, restoring, restored**) 1 return to a previous condition, place, or owner. 2 repair or renovate a building, work of art, etc. 3 bring back a previous practice, situation, etc.
– DERIVATIVES **restorer** n.
– ORIGIN Latin *restaurare*.

restrain • v. 1 keep someone or something under control or within limits. 2 stop someone moving or acting as they wish.
– ORIGIN Latin *restringere* 'tie back'.

restrained • adj. 1 reserved or unemotional. 2 not richly decorated or brightly coloured.

restraint • n. 1 the action of keeping someone or something under control. 2 a measure or condition that restrains: *the financial restraints of a budget*. 3 a device which limits or prevents freedom of movement. 4 unemotional or controlled behaviour.

restrict • v. 1 put a limit on. 2 stop someone from moving or acting as they wish.
– ORIGIN Latin *restringere* 'tie back'.

restricted • adj. 1 limited in size or amount. 2 Brit. not made public for reasons of national security.

restriction • n. 1 a limiting condition or measure. 2 the limitation or control of someone or something.

restrictive • adj. preventing freedom of action or movement.

restrictive practice • n. Brit. 1 an arrangement by a group of workers to limit output or restrict the entry of new workers in order to protect their jobs. 2 an arrangement that restricts or controls competition between companies.

restroom • n. N. Amer. a toilet in a public building.

restructure • v. (**restructures, restructuring, restructured**) 1 organize differently. 2 convert a debt into another debt that is repayable at a later time.

result • n. 1 a thing that is caused or produced by something else; an outcome. 2 an item of information obtained by experiment or calculation. 3 a final score or mark in a sporting event or exam. 4 a successful outcome: *determination and persistence guarantee results*. • v. 1 happen because of something else. 2 (**result in**) have a specified outcome.
– ORIGIN Latin *resultare* 'spring back'.

resultant • adj. occurring as a result.

resume • v. (**resumes, resuming, resumed**) 1 begin again or continue after an interruption. 2 return to a seat or place.
– ORIGIN Latin *resumere* 'take back'.

résumé /rez-yuu-may/ • n. 1 a summary. 2 N. Amer. a curriculum vitae.
– ORIGIN French, 'resumed'.

resumption • n. the action of beginning something again after an interruption.

resurface • v. (**resurfaces, resurfacing, resurfaced**) 1 put a new coating on a surface. 2 come back up to the surface of deep water. 3 arise again.

resurgent • adj. becoming stronger or more popular again.
– DERIVATIVES **resurgence** n.
– ORIGIN Latin *resurgere* 'rise again'.

resurrect • v. 1 restore someone or something to life. 2 revive a practice or belief.

resurrection • n. 1 the action of resurrecting. 2 (**the Resurrection**) (in Christian belief) the time when Jesus rose from the dead.
– ORIGIN Latin.

resuscitate /ri-suss-i-tayt/ • v. (**resuscitates, resuscitating, resuscitated**) revive someone from unconsciousness.
– DERIVATIVES **resuscitation** n.
– ORIGIN Latin *resuscitare* 'raise again'.

retail • n. the sale of goods to the general public. • v. 1 sell goods to the public. 2 (**retail at/for**) be sold for a specified price.
– DERIVATIVES **retailer** n.
– ORIGIN Old French *retaillier*.

retain • v. 1 continue to have; keep possession of. 2 absorb and continue to hold a substance. 3 keep something in

place. **4** obtain the services of a barrister with a preliminary payment.
– ORIGIN Latin *retinere* 'hold back'.

retainer • n. **1** a thing that holds something in place. **2** a fee paid in advance to a barrister to secure their services. **3** a servant who has worked for a family for a long time.

retake • v. (**retakes, retaking, retook;** past part. **retaken**) **1** take a test or exam again. **2** regain possession of. • n. a test or exam that is retaken.

retaliate /ri-tal-i-ayt/ • v. (**retaliates, retaliating, retaliated**) make an attack in return for a similar attack.
– DERIVATIVES **retaliation** n. **retaliatory** adj.
– ORIGIN Latin *retaliare* 'return in kind'.

retard • v. /ri-tard/ hold back the development or progress of. • n. /ree-tard/ offens. a person who has a mental disability.
– DERIVATIVES **retardation** n.
– ORIGIN Latin *retardare*.

retardant • adj. preventing or inhibiting: *fire-retardant polymers*.

retarded • adj. offens. less developed mentally than is usual for your age.

retch • v. make the sound and movement of vomiting.
– ORIGIN Germanic, 'spittle'.

retention • n. **1** the action of keeping something or holding something in place. **2** failure to remove a substance from the body: *fluid retention*.

retentive • adj. (of a person's memory) able to keep hold of facts and impressions easily.

rethink • v. (**rethinks, rethinking, rethought**) consider a course of action again. • n. an instance of rethinking.

reticent /ret-i-suhnt/ • adj. not revealing your thoughts or feelings readily.
– DERIVATIVES **reticence** n.
– ORIGIN Latin *reticere* 'remain silent'.

reticulated • adj. arranged or marked like a net or network.
– ORIGIN Latin *reticulatus*.

retina /ret-i-nuh/ • n. (pl. **retinas** or **retinae** /ret-i-nee/) a layer at the back of the eyeball containing cells that are sensitive to light and from which impulses are sent to the brain.
– DERIVATIVES **retinal** adj.
– ORIGIN Latin.

retinol /ret-i-nol/ • n. vitamin A.

retinue /ret-i-nyoo/ • n. a group of advisers or assistants accompanying an important person.
– ORIGIN Old French *retenir* 'retain'.

retire • v. (**retires, retiring, retired**) **1** leave your job and stop working, especially because you have reached a particular age. **2** withdraw from a race or match because of injury. **3** leave a place. **4** (of a jury) leave the courtroom to decide the verdict of a trial. **5** go to bed.
– DERIVATIVES **retired** adj. **retiree** n.
– ORIGIN French *retirer* 'draw back'.

retirement • n. **1** the action of retiring. **2** the period of your life after retiring from work.

retiring • adj. avoiding other people; shy.

retook past of **RETAKE**.

retort[1] • v. say something sharp or witty in answer to a remark. • n. a sharp or witty reply.
– ORIGIN Latin *retorquere* 'twist back'.

retort[2] • n. **1** a container or furnace for carrying out a chemical process on a large scale. **2** dated a glass container with a long neck, used in distilling liquids and other chemical operations.
– ORIGIN Latin *retorta*.

retouch • v. improve a painting or photograph by making slight additions or alterations.

retrace • v. (**retraces, retracing, retraced**) **1** go back over the same route that you have just taken. **2** discover and follow a route taken by someone else.

retract • v. **1** withdraw a statement because it is not correct or true. **2** go back on an agreement or promise. **3** draw or be drawn back.
– DERIVATIVES **retractable** adj. **retraction** n. **retractor** n.
– ORIGIN Latin *retrahere* 'draw back'.

retractile /ri-trak-tyl/ • adj. capable of being retracted or drawn back: *retractile claws*.

retrain • v. teach or learn new skills.

retreat • v. **1** (of an army) withdraw from attacking enemy forces. **2** move back from a difficult situation. **3** go to a quiet or secluded place. • n. **1** an act of retreating. **2** a quiet or secluded place. **3** a place where a person goes to be quiet and meditate or pray for a time.
– ORIGIN Latin *retrahere* 'draw back'.

retrench • v. reduce costs or spending in response to economic difficulty.
– DERIVATIVES **retrenchment** n.
– ORIGIN French *retrancher* 'cut out'.

retrial • n. a second or further trial on the same issues and with the same parties.

retribution /ret-ri-byoo-sh'n/ • n. severe punishment in revenge for a wrong or criminal act.
– DERIVATIVES **retributive** /ri-trib-yuu-tiv/ adj.
– ORIGIN Latin.

retrieve • v. (**retrieves, retrieves,**

retrieving) 1 get or bring something back. **2** find or extract information stored in a computer. **3** rescue from a state of difficulty or collapse.
– DERIVATIVES **retrievable** adj. **retrieval** n.
– ORIGIN Old French *retrover* 'find again'.

retriever • n. a dog of a breed used for finding and bringing back game that has been shot.

retro • adj. imitative of a style from the recent past.
– ORIGIN French.

retro- • comb. form **1** back or backwards: *retrogressive*. **2** behind: *retrorocket*.
– ORIGIN Latin *retro*.

retroactive • adj. (especially of a law) taking effect from a date in the past.

retrograde • adj. **1** moving backwards. **2** making a situation worse.
– ORIGIN Latin *retrogradus*.

retrogressive • adj. returning to an earlier and worse state.
– DERIVATIVES **retrogression** n.

retrorocket • n. a small rocket on a spacecraft or missile, fired in the direction of travel to slow it down.

retrospect • n. (in phr. **in retrospect**) when looking back on a past event.

retrospective • adj. **1** looking back on or dealing with past events. **2** (of an exhibition) showing the development of an artist's work over a period of time. • n. a retrospective exhibition.
– DERIVATIVES **retrospectively** adv.

retroussé /ruh-troo-say/ • adj. (of a person's nose) turned up at the tip.
– ORIGIN French, 'tucked up'.

retrovirus /re-troh-vy-ruhss/ • n. any of a group of RNA viruses which insert a DNA copy of their genetic material into the host cell in order to replicate, e.g. HIV.
– DERIVATIVES **retroviral** adj.
– ORIGIN from the initials of *reverse transcriptase* + VIRUS.

retsina /ret-see-nuh/ • n. a Greek white wine flavoured with resin.
– ORIGIN modern Greek.

return • v. **1** come or go back to a place. **2** (**return to**) go back to a particular state or activity. **3** give, send, or put something back. **4** feel, say, or do the same feeling, action, etc. in response: *she returned his kiss.* **5** (of a judge or jury) state a verdict in response to a formal request. **6** yield a profit. **7** elect a person or party to office. • n. **1** an act or the action of returning. **2** a profit from an investment. **3** Brit. a ticket allowing travel to a place and back again. **4** a ticket for an event that has been returned because no longer wanted.
– DERIVATIVES **returnable** adj. **returner** n.

– ORIGIN Old French *returner*.

returnee • n. a person returning to work after a long absence.

reunify • v. (**reunifies, reunifying, reunified**) restore political unity to.
– DERIVATIVES **reunification** n.

reunion • n. **1** the action of bringing or coming together again after a period of separation. **2** a social gathering of people who have not seen each other for some time.

reunite • v. (**reunites, reuniting, reunited**) bring or come together again after a period of separation.

reuse /ree-yooz/ • v. (**reuses, reusing, reused**) use again or more than once.
– DERIVATIVES **reusable** adj.

Rev. • abbrev. Reverend.

rev informal • n. (**revs**) the number of revolutions of an engine per minute. • v. (**revs, revving, revved**) increase the running speed of an engine by pressing the accelerator.

revamp • v. /ree-vamp/ alter something so as to improve its appearance. • n. /ree-vamp/ an improved version.

Revd • abbrev. Brit. Reverend.

reveal • v. **1** make previously unknown or secret information known. **2** cause something hidden to be seen.
– ORIGIN Latin *revelare*.

revealing • adj. **1** giving out interesting information. **2** (of a garment) allowing much of the wearer's body to be seen.

reveille /ri-val-li/ • n. a signal sounded on a bugle or drum to wake up soldiers.
– ORIGIN French *réveillez!* 'wake up!'

revel • v. (**revels, revelling, revelled**; US **revels, reveling, reveled**) **1** enjoy yourself in a lively and noisy way. **2** (**revel in**) gain great pleasure from. • n. (**revels**) lively and noisy celebrations.
– DERIVATIVES **reveller** (US **reveler**) n. **revelry** n. (pl. **revelries**).
– ORIGIN Old French *reveler* 'rise up in rebellion'.

revelation • n. **1** the revealing of something previously unknown. **2** a surprising thing.

revelatory /rev-uh-lay-tuh-ri, rev-uh-luh-tuh-ri/ • adj. revealing something previously unknown.

revenge • n. something harmful done in return for an injury or wrong. • v. (**revenges, revenging, revenged**) **1** (**revenge yourself** or **be revenged**) take revenge for a wrong that has been done to you. **2** take revenge on behalf of someone else or for a wrong.
– ORIGIN Old French *revencher*.

revengeful • adj. eager for revenge.

revenue • n. **1** the income received by an organization. **2** a state's annual income, received from taxes.
– ORIGIN Latin *revenire* 'return'.

reverberate • v. (**reverberates**, **reverberating**, **reverberated**) **1** (of a loud noise) be repeated as an echo. **2** have continuing serious effects.
– DERIVATIVES **reverberation** n.
– ORIGIN Latin *reverberare* 'strike again'.

revere /ri-veer/ • v. (**reveres**, **revering**, **revered**) respect or admire deeply.
– ORIGIN Latin *revereri*.

reverence • n. deep respect.

reverend • adj. a title or form of address to members of the Christian clergy.

reverent • adj. showing deep respect.
– DERIVATIVES **reverential** adj. **reverently** adv.

reverie /rev-uh-ri/ • n. a daydream.
– ORIGIN Old French.

revers /ri-veer/ • n. (pl. **revers** /ri-veerz/) the turned-back edge of a garment revealing the underside.
– ORIGIN French, 'reverse'.

reversal • n. **1** a change to an opposite direction, position, or course of action. **2** a harmful change of fortune.

reverse • v. (**reverses**, **reversing**, **reversed**) **1** move backwards. **2** make something the opposite of what it was. **3** turn the other way round or inside out. **4** cancel a judgement by a lower court or authority. • adj. **1** going in or turned towards the opposite direction. **2** operating or behaving in a way opposite to that which is usual. • n. **1** a complete change of direction or action. **2** (**the reverse**) the opposite. **3** a setback or defeat. **4** the opposite side or face to the observer.
– DERIVATIVES **reversible** adj.
– ORIGIN Latin *revertere* 'turn back'.

reversion • n. a return to a previous state.

revert • v. (**revert to**) return to a previous state.
– ORIGIN Latin *revertere* 'turn back'.

review • n. **1** a formal examination of something so as to make changes if necessary. **2** a critical assessment of a book, play, or other work. **3** a report of an event that has already happened. **4** a ceremonial display and formal inspection of military or naval forces. • v. **1** carry out or write a review of. **2** view or inspect again.
– DERIVATIVES **reviewer** n.
– ORIGIN from former French *reveue*.

revile • v. (**reviles**, **reviling**, **reviled**) criticize in a rude or scornful way.
– ORIGIN Old French *reviler*.

revise • v. (**revises**, **revising**, **revised**) **1** examine and alter a piece of writing. **2** reconsider and change an opinion. **3** Brit. read previous work again in order to prepare for an exam.
– ORIGIN Latin *revisere* 'look at again'.

revision • n. **1** the action of revising something. **2** the study of previous work in preparation for an exam. **3** a revised edition or form of something.

revisionism • n. usu. derog. the reconsideration of accepted theories or principles.
– DERIVATIVES **revisionist** n. & adj.

revitalize (or **revitalise**) • v. (**revitalizes**, **revitalizing**, **revitalized**) give new life and vitality to.
– DERIVATIVES **revitalization** n.

revival • n. **1** an improvement in the condition, strength, or popularity of something. **2** a new production of an old play.

revivalism • n. the promotion of a revival of religious faith.
– DERIVATIVES **revivalist** n. & adj.

revive • v. (**revives**, **reviving**, **revived**) **1** make someone conscious, healthy, or strong again. **2** renew interest in or enthusiasm for something. **3** start doing or using something again.
– ORIGIN Latin *revivere*.

revivify /ree-viv-i-fy/ • v. (**revivifies**, **revivifying**, **revivified**) give new life or strength to.

revoke • v. (**revokes**, **revoking**, **revoked**) officially cancel a decree or decision.
– DERIVATIVES **revocable** adj. **revocation** n.
– ORIGIN Latin *revocare* 'call back'.

revolt • v. **1** rebel against an authority. **2** make someone feel disgust. • n. an act of rebellion.
– ORIGIN French *révolter*.

revolting • adj. very unpleasant; disgusting.

revolution • n. **1** the overthrow of a government or social order by force, in favour of a new system. **2** a great and far-reaching change. **3** motion in orbit or in a circular course around a central point. **4** a single movement around a central point.
– ORIGIN Latin.

revolutionary • adj. **1** involving or causing great change. **2** engaged in or relating to political revolution. • n. (pl. **revolutionaries**) a person who starts or supports a political revolution.

revolutionize (or **revolutionise**) • v. (**revolutionizes**, **revolutionizing**, **revolutionized**) change something completely or fundamentally.

r

revolve • v. (**revolves, revolving, revolved**) **1** move in a circle around a central point. **2** (**revolve about/around**) move in a circular orbit around. **3** (**revolve around**) treat as the most important aspect or element: *her life revolved around her children.*
– ORIGIN Latin *revolvere* 'roll back'.

revolver • n. a pistol with revolving chambers enabling several shots to be fired without reloading.

revue • n. a theatrical show with short sketches, songs, and dances.
– ORIGIN French, 'review'.

revulsion • n. a feeling of disgust and horror.
– ORIGIN Latin.

reward • n. **1** a thing given in recognition of service, effort, or achievement. **2** a fair return for good or bad behaviour.
• v. **1** give a reward to someone to show your appreciation of an action, service, etc. **2** (**be rewarded**) receive what you deserve.
– ORIGIN Old French *reguard* 'regard'.

rewarding • adj. providing satisfaction.

rewind • v. (**rewinds, rewinding, rewound**) wind a film or tape back to the beginning.

rewire • v. (**rewires, rewiring, rewired**) provide a building or room with new electric wiring.

rewrite • v. (**rewrites, rewriting, rewrote**; past part. **rewritten**) write something again in an altered or improved form. • n. an instance of rewriting.

Rf • symb. the chemical element rutherfordium.

RFC • abbrev. Rugby Football Club.

rhapsodize (or **rhapsodise**)
• v. (**rhapsodizes, rhapsodizing, rhapsodized**) express great enthusiasm about someone or something.

rhapsody • n. (pl. **rhapsodies**) **1** an expression of great enthusiasm or joy. **2** an emotional piece of music in one extended movement.
– DERIVATIVES **rhapsodic** adj.
– ORIGIN Greek *rhapsōidia*.

rhea /ree-uh/ • n. a large flightless bird of South American grasslands, resembling a small ostrich with greyish-brown plumage.
– ORIGIN from *Rhea*, the mother of Zeus in Greek mythology.

rhenium /ree-ni-uhm/ • n. a rare silvery-white metallic element.
– ORIGIN Latin *Rhenus* 'Rhine'.

rheology /ri-ol-uh-ji/ • n. the branch of physics concerned with the deformation and flow of matter.
– DERIVATIVES **rheological** adj.
rheologist n.

– ORIGIN Greek *rheos* 'stream'.

rheostat /ree-uh-stat/ • n. an instrument used to control the current in an electrical circuit by varying the amount of resistance in it.
– ORIGIN Greek *rheos* 'stream'.

rhesus factor /ree-suhss/ • n. a substance in red blood cells which can cause disease in a newborn baby whose blood contains the factor while the mother's blood does not.
– ORIGIN from RHESUS MONKEY, in which the substance was first observed.

rhesus monkey /ree-suhss/ • n. a small brown macaque with red skin on the face and rump, native to southern Asia.
– ORIGIN Latin *Rhesus*.

rhetoric /ret-uh-rik/ • n. **1** the art of effective or persuasive speaking or writing. **2** persuasive language that is empty or insincere.
– ORIGIN from Greek *rhētorikē tekhnē* 'art of rhetoric'.

rhetorical /ri-tor-i-k'l/ • adj. **1** relating to rhetoric. **2** intended to persuade or impress. **3** (of a question) asked for effect or to make a statement rather than to obtain an answer.
– DERIVATIVES **rhetorically** adv.

rheumatic /roo-mat-ik/ • adj. relating to or suffering from rheumatism.
– ORIGIN Greek *rheuma* 'stream'.

rheumatic fever • n. an acute fever marked by inflammation and pain in the joints, caused by an infection.

rheumatism • n. any disease marked by inflammation and pain in the joints and muscles.
– ORIGIN Greek *rheumatismos*.

rheumatoid /roo-muh-toyd/
• adj. relating to or resembling rheumatism.

rheumatoid arthritis • n. a disease causing inflammation in the joints.

rheumy /rhymes with gloomy/ • adj. (of the eyes) full of a watery fluid.
– ORIGIN Greek *rheuma* 'stream'.

rhinestone • n. an imitation diamond.
– ORIGIN from French *caillou du Rhin* 'pebble of the Rhine'.

rhino • n. (pl. **rhino** or **rhinos**) informal a rhinoceros.

rhinoceros /ry-noss-uh-ruhss/ • n. (pl. **rhinoceros** or **rhinoceroses**) a large plant-eating mammal with one or two horns on the nose and thick folded skin, found in Africa and South Asia.
– ORIGIN from Greek *rhis* 'nose' + *keras* 'horn'.

rhinoplasty /ry-noh-plass-ti/ • n. (pl. **rhinoplasties**) plastic surgery performed on the nose.

rhizome /ry-zohm/ • n. a horizontal underground plant stem bearing both roots and shoots.
– ORIGIN Greek *rhizōma*.

rhodium /roh-di-uhm/ • n. a hard, dense silvery-white metallic element.
– ORIGIN Greek *rhodon* 'rose'.

rhododendron /roh-duh-den-druhn/ • n. a shrub with large clusters of bright trumpet-shaped flowers.
– ORIGIN from Greek *rhodon* 'rose' + *dendron* 'tree'.

rhomboid /rom-boyd/ • adj. having or resembling the shape of a rhombus. • n. a parallelogram in which adjacent sides are unequal.

rhombus /rom-buhss/ • n. (pl. **rhombuses** or **rhombi** /rom-by/) a quadrilateral whose sides all have the same length.
– ORIGIN Greek *rhombos*.

rhubarb • n. the thick red stems of a plant, which are cooked and eaten as a fruit.
– ORIGIN Latin *rheubarbarum* 'foreign rhubarb'.

rhumba • n. var. of RUMBA.

rhyme • n. 1 a word that has or ends with the same sound as another word. 2 similarity of sound between words or the endings of words. 3 a short poem with rhyming lines. • v. (**rhymes, rhyming, rhymed**) 1 (of a word or line) have or end with the same sound as another word or line. 2 (**rhyme something with**) put a word together with another word that has a similar sound.
– PHRASES **rhyme or reason** logical explanation.
– ORIGIN Old French *rime*.

rhyming slang • n. a type of slang that replaces words with rhyming words, often with the rhyming element omitted (e.g. *butcher's*, short for *butcher's hook*, meaning 'look').

rhyolite /ry-uh-lyt/ • n. a pale, fine-grained volcanic rock similar to granite in composition.
– ORIGIN German *Rhyolit*.

rhythm /ri-*th*uhm/ • n. 1 a strong, regular repeated pattern of music, sound, or movement. 2 a particular pattern of this kind: *a slow waltz rhythm*. 3 the measured flow of words and phrases in verse or prose, as determined by length of and stress on syllables. 4 a regularly recurring sequence of events: *the daily rhythms of the tides*.
– ORIGIN Greek *rhuthmos*.

> ☑ There are two h's in **rhythm**: one after the **r** and one before the **m**.

rhythm and blues • n. popular music of US black origin, arising from a combination of blues and jazz.

rhythmic • adj. 1 having or relating to rhythm. 2 happening regularly.
– DERIVATIVES **rhythmical** adj. **rhythmically** adv.

rhythm section • n. the part of a pop or jazz group supplying the rhythm, in particular the bass and drums.

rib • n. 1 each of a series of thin curved bones attached in pairs to the spine and curving round to protect the chest. 2 a curved structure that supports a vault. 3 a curved strut forming part of the framework of a boat's hull. • v. (**ribs, ribbing, ribbed**) informal tease good-naturedly.
– ORIGIN Old English.

ribald /ri-buhld, ry-bawld/ • adj. humorous in a coarse way.
– ORIGIN Old French *riber* 'be licentious'.

ribaldry • n. coarse humorous talk or behaviour.

riband /ri-buhnd/ • n. old use a ribbon.
– ORIGIN Old French *riban*.

ribbed • adj. having a pattern of raised bands.

ribbon • n. 1 a long, narrow strip of fabric, used for tying something or for decoration. 2 a long, narrow strip. 3 a narrow band of inked material used to produce the characters in some typewriters and computer printers.
– ORIGIN from RIBAND.

ribcage • n. the bony frame formed by the ribs.

riboflavin /ry-boh-flay-vin/ • n. vitamin B_2.
– ORIGIN from *ribose* (a sugar found in DNA) + Latin *flavus* 'yellow'.

ribonucleic acid /ry-boh-nyoo-klay-ik, ry-boh-nyoo-klee-ik/ • n. see RNA.
– ORIGIN from *ribose* (a sugar found in DNA) + NUCLEIC ACID.

rice • n. the grains of a cereal plant which is grown for food on wet land in warm countries.
– ORIGIN Old French *ris*.

ricepaper • n. thin edible paper made from the pith of a shrub, used in oriental painting and in baking biscuits and cakes.

rich • adj. 1 having a great deal of money or property. 2 (of a country) having valuable natural resources or a successful economy. 3 made of or produced with expensive materials or workmanship. 4 plentiful. 5 having something in large amounts: *fruits rich in vitamins*. 6 (of food) containing much fat, sugar, etc.: *rich sauces*. 7 (of a colour, sound, or smell) pleasantly deep and strong. 8 (of soil or land) fertile.

– DERIVATIVES **richness** n.
– ORIGIN Old English.

riches •pl. n. **1** wealth. **2** valuable natural resources.

richly •adv. **1** in a rich way. **2** fully: *a richly deserved holiday.*

Richter scale /rik-ter/ •n. a scale for expressing the strength of an earthquake.
– ORIGIN named after the American geologist Charles F. *Richter.*

rick¹ •n. a stack of hay, corn, or straw.
– ORIGIN Old English.

rick² Brit. •n. a slight sprain or strain in the neck or back. •v. strain the neck or back slightly.
– ORIGIN dialect.

rickets /ri-kits/ •n. a disease of children caused by lack of vitamin D, in which the bones become soft and distorted.
– ORIGIN perh. from Greek *rhakhitis* 'rickets'.

rickety •adj. poorly made and likely to collapse.
– DERIVATIVES **ricketiness** n.

rickshaw •n. a light two-wheeled vehicle pulled by one or more people, used in Asian countries.
– ORIGIN Japanese, 'person-strength-vehicle'.

ricochet •v. (**ricochets** /ri-kuh-shayz/, **ricocheting** /ri-kuh-shay-ing/, **ricocheted** /ri-kuh-shayd/) (of a bullet or fast-moving object) rebound off a surface. •n. /ri-kuh-shay/ **1** a shot or hit that rebounds off a surface. **2** the action of rebounding off a surface.
– ORIGIN French.

ricotta /ri-kot-tuh/ •n. a soft white Italian cheese.
– ORIGIN Italian, 'cooked again'.

rictus /rik-tuhss/ •n. a fixed grimace or grin.
– ORIGIN Latin, 'open mouth'.

rid •v. (**rids**, **ridding**, **rid**) **1** (**rid someone/ thing of**) make someone or something free of an unwanted person or thing. **2** (**be** (or **get**) **rid of**) be freed or relieved of.
– ORIGIN Old Norse.

riddance •n. (in phr. **good riddance**) said to express relief at being rid of someone or something.

ridden past part. of RIDE. •adj. (in combination) full of a particular thing: *guilt-ridden.*

riddle¹ •n. **1** a cleverly worded question that is asked as a game. **2** a puzzling person or thing.
– ORIGIN Old English.

riddle² •v. (**riddles**, **riddling**, **riddled**) **1** make many holes in. **2** fill with something undesirable: *a policy riddled with inadequacies.* •n. a large coarse sieve.
– ORIGIN Old English.

ride •v. (**rides**, **riding**, **rode**; past part. **ridden**) **1** sit on and control the movement of a horse, bicycle, or motorcycle. **2** travel in a vehicle. **3** travel over a route or an area on horseback or on a bicycle or motorcycle: *ride the scenic trail.* **4** be carried or supported by: *surfers rode the waves.* **5** sail or float. **6** (**ride something out**) come safely through something. **7** (**ride on**) depend on. **8** (**ride up**) (of a piece of clothing) gradually move upwards. •n. **1** an act of riding. **2** a roller coaster, roundabout, etc. ridden at a fair or amusement park. **3** a path for horse riding.
– PHRASES **ride high** be successful. **a rough** (or **easy**) **ride** a difficult (or easy) time. **take someone for a ride** informal deceive someone.
– ORIGIN Old English.

rider •n. **1** a person who rides a horse, bicycle, or motorcycle. **2** a condition added to an agreement or document.

ridge •n. **1** a long narrow hilltop or mountain range. **2** a narrow raised band on a surface. **3** Meteorol. a long region of high pressure. **4** the edge formed where the two sloping sides of a roof meet at the top.
– ORIGIN Old English, 'spine, crest'.

ridged •adj. having raised lines on the surface.

ridicule •n. contemptuous mockery. •v. (**ridicules**, **ridiculing**, **ridiculed**) make contemptuous fun of.

ridiculous •adj. very silly or unreasonable; absurd.
– DERIVATIVES **ridiculously** adv.
– ORIGIN Latin *ridiculus* 'laughable'.

riding¹ •n. the sport or activity of riding horses.

riding² •n. (**the East/North/West Riding**) each of three former administrative divisions of Yorkshire.
– ORIGIN Old Norse, 'third part'.

riding crop •n. a short flexible whip with a loop for the hand, used when riding.

Riesling /reez-ling, reess-ling/ •n. a dry white wine made from a variety of grape grown chiefly in Germany and Austria.
– ORIGIN German.

rife •adj. **1** (of something undesirable) widespread. **2** (**rife with**) full of.
– ORIGIN Old English.

riff •n. a short repeated phrase in popular music or jazz.
– ORIGIN from RIFFLE.

riffle •v. (**riffles**, **riffling**, **riffled**) **1** turn over pages quickly and casually. **2** (**riffle**

r

through) search quickly through.
– ORIGIN perh. from **RUFFLE**.

riff-raff • n. people who are considered to be socially unacceptable.
– ORIGIN from Old French *rif et raf* 'one and all'.

rifle¹ • n. a gun with a long spirally grooved barrel to make a bullet spin and thereby increase accuracy over a long distance. • v. (**rifles**, **rifling**, **rifled**) hit or kick a ball hard and straight.
– ORIGIN French *rifler* 'graze, scratch'.

rifle² • v. (**rifles**, **rifling**, **rifled**) search through something hurriedly to find or steal something.
– ORIGIN Old French *rifler* 'plunder'.

rifleman • n. (pl. **riflemen**) a soldier armed with a rifle.

rifle range • n. a place for practising rifle shooting.

rift • n. **1** a crack, split, or break. **2** a serious break in friendly relations.
– ORIGIN Scandinavian.

rift valley • n. a steep-sided valley formed by subsidence of the earth's surface between nearly parallel faults.

rig¹ • v. (**rigs**, **rigging**, **rigged**) **1** provide a boat with sails and rigging. **2** assemble and adjust the equipment of a sailing boat to make it ready for operation. **3** (often **rig something up**) set up a device or structure. **4** (**rig someone out**) provide someone with clothes of a particular type. • n. **1** the arrangement of a boat's sails and rigging. **2** an apparatus for a particular purpose: *a lighting rig*. **3** an oil rig.
– ORIGIN perh. Scandinavian.

rig² • v. (**rigs**, **rigging**, **rigged**) arrange a plan or process in a dishonest way so as to gain an advantage: *the elections had been rigged*.

rigger • n. (in combination) a ship rigged in a particular way: *a square-rigger*.

rigging • n. **1** the system of ropes or chains supporting a ship's masts. **2** the ropes and wires supporting the structure of a hang-glider or parachute.

right • adj. **1** on or towards the side of a person or of a thing which is to the east when the person or thing is facing north. **2** morally good or justified. **3** factually correct. **4** most appropriate: *the right man for the job*. **5** in a satisfactory, sound, or normal condition. **6** relating to a right-wing person or group. **7** Brit. informal complete: *I felt a right idiot*. • adv. **1** on or to the right side. **2** to the furthest extent; completely: *the car spun right off the track*. **3** exactly; directly. **4** correctly or satisfactorily. **5** informal immediately. • n. **1** that which is morally right. **2** an entitlement to have or do

something. **3** (**rights**) the authority to perform, publish, or film a particular work or event. **4** (**the right**) the right-hand side or direction. **5** a right turn. **6** (**the Right**) a right-wing group or political party. • v. **1** restore to a normal or upright position. **2** restore to a normal or correct condition. **3** make up for a wrong.
– PHRASES **by rights** if things were fair or correct. **in your own right** as a result of your own qualifications or efforts. **right away** immediately.
– DERIVATIVES **rightward** adj. & adv.
– ORIGIN Old English.

right angle • n. an angle of 90°, as in a corner of a square.
– PHRASES **at right angles to** forming an angle of 90° with.
– DERIVATIVES **right-angled** adj.

righteous /ry-chuhss/ • adj. morally right or justifiable.
– DERIVATIVES **righteously** adv. **righteousness** n.

rightful • adj. **1** having a legal or moral right to something. **2** correct; fitting.
– DERIVATIVES **rightfully** adv.

right hand • n. **1** the region or direction on the right side. **2** the most important position next to someone. • adj. (**right-hand**) **1** on or towards the right side. **2** done with or using the right hand.

right-hand drive • n. a motor-vehicle steering system with the steering wheel and other controls fitted on the right side.

right-handed • adj. **1** using or done with the right hand. **2** turning to the right.

right-hander • n. a right-handed person.

right-hand man • n. a chief assistant.

rightly • adv. **1** in accordance with what is true or just. **2** with good reason.

right-minded • adj. having views and principles that most people approve of.

right of way • n. **1** the legal right to pass along a specific route through another person's property. **2** a public path through another person's property. **3** the right to go before another vehicle.

right side • n. the side of something intended to be at the top or front.

right wing • n. **1** the conservative or reactionary section of a political party. [ORIGIN see **LEFT WING**.] **2** the right side of a sports team on the field.
– DERIVATIVES **right-winger** n.

rigid • adj. **1** unable to bend or be forced out of shape. **2** not able to be changed or adapted: *rigid rules*.
– DERIVATIVES **rigidity** n. **rigidly** adv.

- ORIGIN Latin *rigidus*.

rigmarole /rig-muh-rohl/ •n. 1 a lengthy and complicated process. 2 a long, rambling story.
- ORIGIN prob. from former *ragman roll*, referring to a legal document recording a list of offences.

rigor mortis /ri-ger mor-tiss/ •n. stiffening of the joints and muscles a few hours after death, lasting from one to four days.
- ORIGIN Latin, 'stiffness of death'.

rigorous •adj. 1 very thorough or accurate. 2 (of a rule or system) strictly applied or followed. 3 harsh or severe: *rigorous military training*.
- DERIVATIVES **rigorously** adv.

> ☑ **rigorous** drops the *u* before the final *r* of **rigour**.

rigour (US **rigor**) •n. 1 the quality of being thorough or severe. 2 (**rigours**) demanding or extreme conditions.
- ORIGIN Latin *rigor* 'stiffness'.

rile •v. (**riles, riling, riled**) informal annoy or irritate.
- ORIGIN from ROIL.

Riley •n. (in phr. **the life of Riley**) informal a luxurious or carefree existence.

rill •n. a small stream.
- ORIGIN prob. German.

rim •n. 1 the upper or outer edge of something circular. 2 a limit or boundary. •v. (**be rimmed**) be provided or marked with a rim.
- ORIGIN Old English, 'a border, coast'.

rime /rym/ •n. tech. & literary hoar frost.
- ORIGIN Old English.

rind •n. the tough outer layer or covering of a fruit, cheese, or piece of bacon.
- ORIGIN Old English.

ring[1] •n. 1 a small circular band of precious metal, worn on a finger. 2 a circular band, object, or mark. 3 an enclosed space in which a sport, performance, or show takes place. 4 a group of people or things arranged in a circle. 5 a group of people working together illegally or secretly: *a drug ring*. •v. 1 surround someone or something. 2 esp. Brit. draw a circle round.
- ORIGIN Old English.

ring[2] •v. (**rings, ringing, rang**; past part. **rung**) 1 make a clear repeated or long-lasting musical or vibrating sound. 2 (**ring with**) echo with such a sound. 3 Brit. call someone by telephone. 4 (**ring off**) Brit. end a telephone call by replacing the receiver. 5 call for attention by sounding a bell. 6 sound (the hour, a peal, etc.) on a bell or bells. 7 (of the ears) be filled with a buzzing or humming sound. 8 (**ring something up**)

record an amount on a cash register. •n. 1 an act of ringing. 2 a clear sound or tone. 3 Brit. informal a telephone call. 4 a quality communicated by something heard: *the tale had a ring of truth*. 2 mark the end (or beginning) of something.
- ORIGIN Old English.

ring binder •n. a binder with ring-shaped clasps that can be opened to pass through holes in paper.

ringdove •n. Brit. a wood pigeon.

ringer •n. 1 a person or device that rings. 2 = DEAD RINGER.

ring-fence •v. Brit. guarantee that funds for a particular purpose will not be spent on anything else. •n. (**ring fence**) a fence completely enclosing a piece of land.

ring finger •n. the finger next to the little finger of the left hand, on which the wedding ring is traditionally worn.

ringing •adj. 1 having a clear repeated or long-lasting musical or vibrating sound. 2 (of a statement) forceful and clear: *a ringing declaration of support*.

ringleader •n. a person who leads other people in crime or causing trouble.

ringlet •n. a corkscrew-shaped curl of hair.
- DERIVATIVES **ringletted** (also **ringleted**) adj.

ringmaster •n. the person directing a circus performance.

ring pull •n. Brit. a ring on a can that is pulled to open it.

ring road •n. Brit. a road encircling a town.

ringside •n. the area beside a boxing ring or circus ring.

ringside seat •n. a very good position from which to observe something.

ringtone •n. a sound made by a mobile phone when an incoming call is received.

ringworm •n. a skin disease occurring in small circular itchy patches, caused by various fungi.

rink •n. 1 (also **ice rink**) an enclosed area of ice for skating, ice hockey, or curling. 2 (also **roller rink**) a smooth enclosed floor for roller skating.
- ORIGIN perh. from Old French *renc* 'rank'.

rinse •v. (**rinses, rinsing, rinsed**) 1 wash something with clean water to remove soap or dirt. 2 remove soap or dirt by washing with clean water. •n. 1 an act of rinsing. 2 an antiseptic liquid for cleansing the mouth. 3 a liquid for conditioning or colouring the hair.
- ORIGIN Old French *rincer*.

riot • n. **1** a violent disturbance caused by an angry crowd. **2** a confused or lavish combination or display: *a riot of colour.* **3** (**a riot**) informal a highly entertaining person or thing. • v. take part in a riot.
– PHRASES **run riot** behave in a violent and uncontrolled way.
– DERIVATIVES **rioter** n.
– ORIGIN Old French *riote* 'debate'.

riotous • adj. **1** involving public disorder. **2** involving wild and uncontrolled behaviour.

RIP • abbrev. rest in peace (used on graves).
– ORIGIN from Latin *requiescat in pace.*

rip¹ • v. (**rips, ripping, ripped**) **1** tear or pull forcibly away. **2** move rapidly: *fire ripped through the house.* **3** (**rip someone off**) informal cheat someone. **4** (**rip something off**) informal steal something. • n. a long tear.
– PHRASES **let rip** informal move or act without restraint.

rip² (also **rip tide**) • n. a stretch of fast-flowing rough water caused by the meeting of currents.
– ORIGIN perh. from **rip¹**.

riparian /ri-**pair**-i-uhn, ry-**pair**-i-uhn/ • adj. relating to or situated on the banks of a river.
– ORIGIN Latin *riparius.*

ripcord • n. a cord that is pulled to open a parachute.

ripe • adj. **1** (of fruit or grain) ready for harvesting and eating. **2** (of a cheese or wine) fully matured. **3** (**ripe for**) having reached a fitting time for. **4** (of a person's age) advanced.
– DERIVATIVES **ripeness** n.
– ORIGIN Old English.

ripen • v. become or make ready for harvesting or eating.

rip-off • n. informal **1** an article that is greatly overpriced. **2** a poor-quality copy.

riposte /ri-**posst**/ • n. a quick clever reply.
– ORIGIN French.

ripping • adj. Brit. informal, dated excellent.

ripple • n. **1** a small wave or series of waves. **2** a sound, feeling, or effect that spreads through a person, group, or place: *a ripple of excitement.* • v. (**ripples, rippling, rippled**) **1** form a series of small waves. **2** (of a sound, feeling, or effect) spread through a person, group, or place.

rip-roaring • adj. full of energy and vigour.

rise • v. (**rises, rising, rose;** past part. **risen**) **1** come or go up. **2** get up from lying, sitting, or kneeling. **3** increase in number, size, strength, or quality. **4** (of land) slope upwards. **5** (of the sun, moon, or stars) appear above the horizon. **6** reach a higher social or professional position. **7** (**rise above**) succeed in not being restricted by: *he struggled to rise above his humble background.* **8** (**rise to**) respond well to a difficult situation. **9** (often **rise up**) rebel. **10** (of a river) have its source in a particular place; begin. • n. **1** an act of rising. **2** an upward slope or hill. **3** Brit. a pay increase.
– ORIGIN Old English.

riser • n. **1** a person who usually gets out of bed at a particular time of the morning: *an early riser.* **2** a vertical section between the treads of a staircase.

risible /ri-zi-b'l/ • adj. causing laughter.
– DERIVATIVES **risibly** adv.
– ORIGIN Latin *risibilis.*

rising • adj. approaching a specified age. • n. a revolt.

rising damp • n. Brit. moisture absorbed from the ground into a wall.

risk • n. **1** a situation that could be dangerous or have a bad outcome. **2** the possibility that something unpleasant will happen. **3** a person or thing causing a risk: *gloss paint can pose a fire risk.* • v. **1** expose to danger or loss. **2** act in such a way that something bad could happen. **3** take a risk by engaging in a particular activity.
– PHRASES **at your own risk** taking responsibility for your own safety or possessions.
– ORIGIN Italian *risco* 'danger'.

risky • adj. (**riskier, riskiest**) involving the possibility of danger or a bad outcome.
– DERIVATIVES **riskily** adv. **riskiness** n.

risotto /ri-**zot**-toh/ • n. (pl. **risottos**) an Italian dish of rice cooked in stock with ingredients such as meat or seafood.
– ORIGIN Italian.

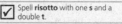 Spell **risotto** with one **s** and a double **t**.

risqué /**riss**-kay, riss-**kay**/ • adj. slightly indecent or rude.
– ORIGIN French.

rissole • n. Brit. a small cake or ball of meat and spices, coated in breadcrumbs and fried.
– ORIGIN French.

rite • n. a religious or other solemn ceremony.
– PHRASES **rite of passage** a ceremony or event that marks an important stage in someone's life.
– ORIGIN Latin *ritus* '(religious) usage'.

ritual • n. **1** a religious or solemn

ceremony involving a series of actions performed according to a set order. **2** a series of actions done regularly and without variation: *her visits became a ritual.* • adj. relating to or done as a ritual.
– DERIVATIVES **ritually** adv.

ritualistic • adj. relating to or done as a ritual.

ritualize (or **ritualise**) • v. (**ritualizes**, **ritualizing**, **ritualized**) make into a ritual by following a pattern of actions or behaviour.
– DERIVATIVES **ritualization** n.

ritzy • adj. (**ritzier**, **ritziest**) informal expensively stylish.
– ORIGIN from *Ritz*, a proprietary name of luxury hotels.

rival • n. **1** a person or thing competing with another for the same thing. **2** a person or thing equal to another in quality: *she has no rivals as a female rock singer.* • v. (**rivals**, **rivalling**, **rivalled**; US **rivals**, **rivaling**, **rivaled**) be equal or comparable to.
– DERIVATIVES **rivalrous** adj.
– ORIGIN Latin *rivalis*.

rivalry • n. (pl **rivalries**) a situation in which two people or groups are competing for the same thing.

riven /ri-vuhn/ • adj. literary torn apart; split.
– ORIGIN Old Norse.

river • n. **1** a large natural flow of water travelling along a channel to the sea, a lake, or another river. **2** a large quantity of a flowing liquid.
– ORIGIN Old French.

riverbank • n. the bank of a river.

riverbed • n. the bed or channel in which a river flows.

rivet /ri-vit/ • n. a short metal pin or bolt for holding together two metal plates. • v. (**rivets**, **riveting**, **riveted**) **1** fasten with a rivet or rivets. **2** (**be riveted**) be completely involved or absorbed.
– ORIGIN Old French.

riviera /ri-vi-air-uh/ • n. a coastal region with a subtropical climate and vegetation, especially that of southern France and northern Italy.
– ORIGIN Italian, 'seashore'.

rivulet /riv-yuu-lit/ • n. a very small stream.
– ORIGIN from former French *riveret* 'small river'.

RM • abbrev. (in the UK) Royal Marines.

RN • abbrev. (in the UK) Royal Navy.

Rn • symb. the chemical element radon.

RNA • n. ribonucleic acid, a substance in living cells which carries instructions from DNA for controlling the synthesis of proteins.

RNLI • abbrev. (in the UK) Royal National Lifeboat Institution.

roach¹ • n. (pl. **roach**) a common freshwater fish of the carp family.
– ORIGIN Old French *roche*.

roach² • n. N. Amer. informal a cockroach.

road • n. **1** a wide way between places, with a hard surface for vehicles to travel on. **2** a way to achieving a particular outcome: *on the road to recovery.*
– ORIGIN Old English, 'journey on horseback'.

roadblock • n. a barrier put across a road by the police or army to stop and examine traffic.

road fund licence • n. Brit. a disc displayed on a vehicle certifying payment of road tax.

road hog • n. informal an inconsiderate motorist.

roadholding • n. the ability of a moving vehicle to remain stable.

roadie • n. informal a person employed by a touring pop or rock group to set up and maintain equipment.

road rage • n. violent anger arising from conflict with the driver of another motor vehicle.

roadshow • n. **1** each of a series of radio or television programmes broadcast from different places. **2** a touring political or promotional campaign.

roadster • n. an open-top car with two seats.

road tax • n. Brit. a tax to be paid on motor vehicles using public roads.

road test • n. **1** a test of the performance of a vehicle on the road. **2** a test of equipment carried out in working conditions.

roadway • n. **1** a road. **2** the part of a road intended for vehicles.

roadworks • pl. n. Brit. repairs to roads or to pipes or cables under them.

roadworthy • adj. (of a vehicle) fit to be driven on roads.
– DERIVATIVES **roadworthiness** n.

roam • v. travel aimlessly over a wide area.

roaming • n. the use of or ability to use a mobile phone on another operator's network, typically while abroad.

roan • adj. (of a horse or cow) having a bay, chestnut, or black coat with hairs of another colour. • n. a roan animal.
– ORIGIN Old French.

roar • n. **1** a long, deep, sound such as that made by a lion, natural force, or engine. **2** a loud, deep sound made by a person as an expression of pain, anger, or great amusement. • v. **1** make a roar. **2** laugh loudly. **3** move, act, or happen very fast.
– ORIGIN Old English.

roaring • adj. informal complete: *a roaring success.*
– PHRASES **do a roaring trade** informal do very good business.

roast • v. **1** cook meat or vegetables in an oven or over a fire. **2** cook coffee beans or nuts in intense heat. **3** become very warm. • adj. (of food) having been baked in a hot oven. • n. a joint of meat that has been roasted.
– ORIGIN Old French *rostir*.

roasting informal • adj. very hot and dry. • n. a severe criticism or reprimand.

rob • v. (**robs, robbing, robbed**) **1** take property unlawfully from a person or place by force or threat of force. **2** deprive someone of something needed or important: *poor health has robbed her of a normal social life.*
– DERIVATIVES **robber** n.
– ORIGIN Old French *rober*.

robbery • n. (pl. **robberies**) the action of robbing a person or place.

robe • n. **1** a loose outer garment reaching to the ankles, worn on formal or ceremonial occasions. **2** a bathrobe or dressing gown. • v. (**robes, robing, robed**) dress someone in a robe.
– ORIGIN Old French, 'garment, booty'.

robin • n. a small songbird of the thrush family, with a red breast and brown back and wings.
– ORIGIN Old French.

robot /roh-bot/ • n. a machine capable of carrying out a complex series of actions automatically.
– ORIGIN Czech *robota* 'forced labour'.

robotic /roh-bot-ik/ • adj. **1** relating to robots. **2** mechanical, stiff, or unemotional. • n. (**robotics**) the branch of technology concerned with the design, construction, and use of robots.
– DERIVATIVES **robotically** adv.

robust • adj. **1** able to withstand heavy use; sturdy or resilient. **2** strong and healthy. **3** determined and forceful: *a robust defence.*
– ORIGIN Latin *robustus* 'firm and hard'.

rock¹ • n. **1** the hard mineral material of the earth's crust. **2** a mass of rock projecting out of the ground or water. **3** a boulder. **4** Geol. any natural material with a particular make-up of minerals. **5** Brit. a kind of hard sweet in the form of a cylindrical stick. **6** informal a diamond or other precious stone.
– PHRASES **on the rocks** informal **1** in difficulties and likely to fail. **2** (of a drink) served undiluted and with ice cubes.
– ORIGIN Latin *rocca*.

rock² • v. **1** move gently to and fro or from side to side. **2** shake something

violently. **3** shock or distress someone greatly. **4** informal dance to or play rock music. • n. **1** (also **rock music**) a form of popular music with a strong beat, played on electric guitars, drums, etc. **2** a rocking movement.
– ORIGIN Old English.

rockabilly • n. a type of popular music combining rock and roll and country music.
– ORIGIN from ROCK AND ROLL and HILLBILLY.

rock and roll (also **rock 'n' roll**) • n. a type of popular dance music originating in the 1950s, having a heavy beat and simple melodies.

rock-bottom • adj. at the lowest possible level.

rock cake • n. esp. Brit. a small currant cake with a hard rough surface.

rock climbing • n. the sport or pastime of climbing rock faces.

rock crystal • n. transparent quartz.

rocker • n. **1** a person who performs or enjoys rock music. **2** a curved piece of wood on the bottom of a rocking chair.
– PHRASES **off your rocker** informal mad.

rockery • n. (pl. **rockeries**) a heaped arrangement of rocks with soil between them, planted with rock plants.

rocket¹ • n. **1** a cylinder-shaped missile or spacecraft propelled by a stream of burning gases. **2** a firework that shoots into the air and then explodes. **3** Brit. informal a severe reprimand. • v. (**rockets, rocketing, rocketed**) move or increase very rapidly and suddenly.
– ORIGIN Italian *rocchetto* 'small spindle (for spinning)'.

rocket² • n. Brit. an edible Mediterranean plant, eaten in salads.
– ORIGIN French *roquette*.

rocketry • n. the branch of science and technology concerned with rockets.

rock garden • n. a rockery.

rocking chair • n. a chair mounted on rockers or springs.

rocking horse • n. a model of a horse mounted on rockers or springs for a child to ride on.

rock plant • n. a plant that grows on or among rocks.

rock pool • n. a pool of water among rocks along a shoreline.

rock salt • n. common salt occurring naturally as a mineral.

rock solid • adj. completely firm or stable.

rocky¹ • adj. (**rockier, rockiest**) **1** made of rock. **2** full of rocks.

rocky² • adj. (**rockier, rockiest**)

1 unsteady or unstable. **2** relating to rock music.

rococo /ruh-koh-koh/ • adj. relating to an elaborately ornate style of European furniture or architecture of the 18th century.
– ORIGIN French.

rod • n. **1** a thin straight bar of wood or metal. **2** a fishing rod. **3** a type of light-sensitive cell in the eye, responsible mainly for black-and-white vision in poor light. Compare with **CONE**.
– ORIGIN Old English.

rode past of **RIDE**.

rodent • n. a mammal of a large group including rats, mice, and squirrels, having strong constantly growing incisors.
– ORIGIN Latin *rodere* 'gnaw'.

rodeo /roh-di-oh, roh-**day**-oh/ • n. (pl. **rodeos**) a contest or entertainment in which cowboys show their skills.
– ORIGIN Spanish.

rodomontade /ro-duh-mon-**tayd**/ • n. literary boastful talk or behaviour.
– ORIGIN Italian *rodomonte* 'boaster'.

roe[1] • n. **1** (also **hard roe**) the mass of eggs contained in the ovaries of a female fish or shellfish, used as food. **2** (**soft roe**) the ripe testes of a male fish, used as food.
– ORIGIN German or Dutch *roge*.

roe[2] (also **roe deer**) • n. (pl. **roe** or **roes**) a small deer with a reddish summer coat that turns greyish in winter.
– ORIGIN Old English.

roebuck • n. a male roe deer.

roentgen /runt-yuhn, rernt-yuhn, ront-yuhn/ • n. a unit of quantity of ionizing radiation.
– ORIGIN named after the German physicist Wilhelm Conrad *Röntgen*.

roger • exclam. your message has been received (used in radio communication).
– ORIGIN from the man's name *Roger*.

rogue • n. **1** a dishonest or immoral man. **2** a mischievous but likeable person. **3** an elephant living apart from the herd.
– ORIGIN prob. from Latin *rogare* 'beg, ask'.

rogues' gallery • n. informal a collection of photographs of known criminals.

roguish • adj. playfully mischievous: *a roguish smile*.

roil /royl/ • v. **1** make a liquid muddy by disturbing the sediment. **2** (of a liquid) move in a turbulent way.
– ORIGIN perh. from Old French *ruiler* 'mix mortar'.

roister /roy-ster/ • v. (**roisters**,

roistering, **roistered**) enjoy yourself or celebrate in a noisy way.
– DERIVATIVES **roisterer** n.
– ORIGIN French *rustre* 'ruffian'.

role • n. **1** an actor's part in a play or film. **2** a person's or thing's function in a particular situation: *religion plays a vital role in society*.
– ORIGIN from former French *roule* 'roll', referring to the roll of paper on which an actor's part was written.

> USAGE: Do not confuse **role** with **roll**. **Role** means 'a part played by an actor', whereas **roll** mainly means 'move by turning over and over' or 'a rolling movement' (*a roll of the dice*).

role model • n. a person who other people look to as an example to be imitated.

role playing (also **role play**) • n. the acting out of a particular role.

roll • v. **1** move by turning over and over. **2** move forward on wheels or with a smooth, wave-like motion. **3** (of a moving ship, aircraft, or vehicle) sway from side to side. **4** (of a machine or device) begin operating. **5** (**roll something up**) turn something flexible over and over on itself to form a cylindrical or round shape. **6** (**roll up**) curl up tightly. **7** flatten something by passing a roller over it or by passing it between rollers. **8** (of a loud, deep sound) reverberate. **9** pronounce an *r* with a trill. • n. **1** a cylinder of flexible material, formed by rolling. **2** a rolling movement. **3** a gymnastic exercise in which the body is rolled into a tucked position and turned in a forward or backward circle. **4** a long, deep, reverberating sound. **5** a very small loaf of bread. **6** an official list or register of names.
– PHRASES **be rolling in it** (or **money**) informal be very rich. **on a roll** informal experiencing a long spell of success or good luck. **roll something out** officially launch a new product. **roll up** informal arrive.
– ORIGIN Old French *roller*.

roll call • n. the reading aloud of a list of names to discover who is present.

roller • n. **1** a rotating cylinder used to move, flatten, or spread something. **2** a small cylinder on which hair is rolled to produce curls. **3** a long swelling wave that appears to roll steadily towards the shore.

Rollerblade • n. trademark a skate with wheels fixed in a single line.
– DERIVATIVES **rollerblader** n. **rollerblading** n.

roller blind •n. a window blind fitted on a roller.

roller coaster •n. a fairground attraction consisting of a light railway track with many tight turns and steep slopes, on which people ride in small open carriages.

roller skate •n. each of a pair of boots having four small wheels and used for gliding across a hard surface.

roller towel •n. a long towel with the ends joined and hung on a roller.

rollicking¹ •adj. cheerfully lively and amusing.
– ORIGIN perh. from ROMP and FROLIC.

rollicking² •n. Brit. informal a severe reprimand.

rolling pin •n. a cylinder for rolling out dough.

rolling stock •n. locomotives, carriages, or other vehicles used on a railway.

rollmop •n. a rolled uncooked pickled herring fillet.
– ORIGIN German *Rollmops*.

roll neck •n. a loosely turned-over collar.

roll-on •adj. (of a deodorant or cosmetic) applied by means of a rotating ball in the neck of the container.

roll-on roll-off •adj. Brit. (of a ferry) in which vehicles are driven directly on at the start of the voyage and driven off at the end of it.

roll-up •n. Brit. informal a hand-rolled cigarette.

roly-poly •adj. informal round and plump. •n. Brit. a pudding made of a sheet of suet pastry covered with jam, formed into a roll, and steamed or baked.
– ORIGIN from ROLL.

ROM •abbrev. Computing read-only memory.

Roman •adj. 1 relating to ancient Rome or its empire or people. 2 relating to modern Rome. 3 referring to the alphabet used for writing Latin, English, and most European languages. 4 (**roman**) (of type) of a plain upright kind used in ordinary print. •n. 1 a person who lives in Rome. 2 (**roman**) roman type.

Roman Catholic •adj. relating to the Roman Catholic Church. •n. a member of this Church.
– DERIVATIVES **Roman Catholicism** n.

Roman Catholic Church •n. the part of the Christian Church which has the Pope as its head.

Romance /roh-manss, roh-manss/ •n. the group of languages descended from Latin, such as French, Spanish, Portuguese, and Italian.
– ORIGIN Latin *Romanicus* 'Roman'.

romance /roh-manss, roh-manss/ •n. 1 a pleasurable feeling of excitement and wonder associated with love. 2 a love affair. 3 a book or film dealing with love in a sentimental or idealized way. 4 a feeling of mystery, excitement, and remoteness from everyday life: *the romance of the past.* 5 a medieval story dealing with adventures of knights. •v. (**romances, romancing, romanced**) try to win the love of someone.
– ORIGIN from ROMANCE.

Roman Empire •n. the empire under Roman rule established in 27 BC and divided into two parts in AD 395.

Romanesque /roh-muh-nesk/ •adj. relating to a style of architecture common in Europe *c.*900–1200, with massive vaulting and round arches.
– ORIGIN French.

Romanian (also **Rumanian**) •n. 1 a person from Romania. 2 the language of Romania. •adj. relating to Romania.

Roman nose •n. a nose with a high bridge.

Roman numeral •n. any of the letters I, V, X, L, C, and D, used as numbers in the ancient Roman system.

romantic •adj. 1 relating to love or romance. 2 showing or regarding life in an unrealistic and idealized way. 3 (**Romantic**) relating to the artistic and literary movement of romanticism. •n. 1 a person with romantic beliefs or attitudes. 2 (**Romantic**) a writer or artist of the Romantic movement.
– DERIVATIVES **romantically** adv.

romanticism •n. a literary and artistic movement which began in the late 18th century and emphasized creative inspiration and individual feeling.

romanticize (or **romanticise**) •v. (**romanticizes, romanticizing, romanticized**) make something seem more attractive and inspiring than it really is.
– DERIVATIVES **romanticization** n.

Romany /roh-muh-ni, ro-muh-ni/ •n. (pl. **Romanies**) 1 the language of the Gypsies. 2 a Gypsy.
– ORIGIN Romany *Rom* 'man, husband'.

Romeo /roh-mi-oh/ •n. (pl. **Romeos**) an attractive, passionate male lover.
– ORIGIN the hero of Shakespeare's *Romeo and Juliet.*

romp •v. 1 play about roughly and energetically. 2 informal achieve something easily: *India romped home with three balls to spare.* •n. a spell of rough and energetic playing about.
– ORIGIN perh. from RAMP.

rompers (also **romper suit**) •pl. n. a

young child's one-piece outer garment.

rondeau •n. (pl. **rondeaux** /ron-doh, ron-dohz/) a poem of ten or thirteen lines with only two rhymes throughout and with the opening words used twice as a refrain.
– ORIGIN French.

rondo /ron-doh/ •n. (pl. **rondos**) a piece of music with a recurring leading theme.
– ORIGIN Italian.

röntgen •n. var. of ROENTGEN.

rood /rood/ •n. a crucifix.
– ORIGIN Old English.

rood screen •n. a screen of wood or stone separating the nave from the chancel of a church.

roof •n. (pl. **roofs**) **1** the upper covering of a building or vehicle. **2** the top inner surface of a covered space: *the roof of the cave fell in.* **3** the upper limit of prices or wages. •v. cover a building with a roof.
– PHRASES **go through the roof** informal (of prices or figures) reach very high levels. **hit** (or **go through**) **the roof** informal suddenly become very angry. **the roof of the mouth** the palate.
– DERIVATIVES **roofer** n.
– ORIGIN Old English.

roofing •n. material for constructing a building's roof.

roof rack •n. a framework for carrying luggage on the roof of a vehicle.

rook[1] •n. a crow with black plumage and a bare face, nesting in colonies in treetops.
– ORIGIN Old English.

rook[2] •n. a chess piece that can move in any direction along a rank or file on which it stands.
– ORIGIN Arabic.

rookery •n. (pl. **rookeries**) a collection of rooks' nests high in a clump of trees.

rookie •n. informal a new recruit or member.
– ORIGIN perh. from RECRUIT.

room /room, ruum/ •n. **1** a part of a building enclosed by walls, floor, and ceiling. **2** (**rooms**) Brit. a set of rooms rented out to lodgers. **3** empty space in which you can do or put things: *there was no room to move.* **4** opportunity or scope: *room for improvement.* •v. N. Amer. share lodgings.
– ORIGIN Old English.

room service •n. the providing of food and drink to hotel guests in their rooms.

roomy •adj. (**roomier, roomiest**) having plenty of space.
– DERIVATIVES **roominess** n.

roost •n. a place where birds or bats regularly settle to rest. •v. (of a bird or

bat) settle or gather for rest.
– ORIGIN Old English.

rooster •n. esp. N. Amer. a male domestic fowl.

root[1] •n. **1** the part of a plant normally below ground, which acts as a support and collects water and nourishment. **2** the part of a bodily structure such as a hair or tooth that is embedded in tissue. **3** the basic cause or origin: *money is the root of all evil.* **4** (**roots**) family, ethnic, or cultural origins. **5** a form from which words have been made by adding prefixes or suffixes or some other change. **6** Math. a number that when multiplied by itself one or more times gives a specified number. •v. **1** cause a plant to establish roots. **2** (**be rooted**) be firmly established. **3** (**be rooted**) stand still through fear or amazement. **4** (**root something out/up**) find and get rid of something.
– PHRASES **put down roots** begin to have a settled life in a place. **take root** become established.
– DERIVATIVES **rootless** adj.
– ORIGIN Old English.

root[2] •v. **1** (of an animal) turn up the ground with its snout in search of food. **2** search through something; rummage. **3** (**root for**) informal support a person or team enthusiastically.
– ORIGIN Old English.

root mean square •n. Math. the square root of the arithmetic mean of the squares of a set of values.

root sign •n. Math. the radical sign.

rootstock •n. **1** a rhizome. **2** a plant on to which another variety is grafted.

root vegetable •n. a vegetable which grows as the root of a plant.

rope •n. **1** a length of thick cord made by twisting together strands of hemp, nylon, etc. **2** a number of objects strung together: *a rope of pearls.* **3** (**the ropes**) the ropes enclosing a boxing or wrestling ring. **4** (**the ropes**) informal the established way of doing something: *I showed her the ropes.* •v. (**ropes, roping, roped**) **1** catch or tie with rope. **2** (**rope someone in/into**) persuade someone to take part in something.
– PHRASES **on the ropes** in a state of near collapse.
– ORIGIN Old English.

ropy (also **ropey**) •adj. (**ropier, ropiest**) Brit. informal poor in quality or health.

Roquefort /rok-for/ •n. trademark a soft blue cheese made from ewes' milk.
– ORIGIN from *Roquefort*-sur-Soulzon, a village in southern France.

rorqual /ror-kwuhl/ •n. a whale of a small group with pleated skin on the

underside, e.g. the blue whale.
– ORIGIN Norwegian *røyrkval* 'fin whale'.

rosary /roh-zuh-ri/ •n. (pl. **rosaries**) **1** (in the Roman Catholic Church) a form of worship in which sets of prayers are repeated. **2** a string of beads for keeping count of prayers said.
– ORIGIN Latin *rosarium* 'rose garden'.

rose¹ •n. **1** a sweet-smelling flower that grows on a prickly bush. **2** a cap with holes in it attached to a shower, the spout of a watering can, or the end of a hose to produce a spray. **3** a warm pink colour.
– PHRASES **rose-coloured spectacles** referring to a viewpoint that is naively optimistic.
– ORIGIN Latin *rosa*.

rose² past of RISE.

rosé /roh-zay/ •n. deep pink wine.
– ORIGIN French, 'pink'.

roseate /roh-zi-uht/ •adj. literary rose-coloured.

rosebud •n. the bud of a rose.

rose hip •n. fuller form of HIP².

rosemary •n. an evergreen shrub with leaves which are used as a herb in cooking.
– ORIGIN from Latin *ros marinus* 'dew of the sea'.

rosette •n. **1** a rose-shaped decoration made of ribbon, worn by supporters of a sports team or political party or awarded as a prize. **2** a design or object resem- bling a rose.
– ORIGIN French, 'little rose'.

rose water •n. scented water made with rose petals.

rose window •n. a circular window in a church with a branching rose-like pattern.

rosewood •n. a close-grained timber of a tropical tree used for making furniture and musical instruments.

Rosh Hashana /rosh huh-shah-nuh/ (also **Rosh Hashanah**) •n. a festival celebrating the Jewish New Year.
– ORIGIN Hebrew, 'head of the year'.

rosin /ro-zin/ •n. a kind of resin, rubbed on the bows of stringed instruments.
– ORIGIN Latin *rosina*.

roster /ross-ter/ •n. **1** a list of people's names and the jobs they have to do at a particular time. **2** a list of sports players available for team selection. •v. (**rosters, rostering, rostered**) put a person's name on a roster.
– ORIGIN Dutch *rooster* 'list'.

rostrum /ross-truhm/ •n. (pl. **rostra** /ross-truh/ or **rostrums**) a platform on which a person stands to make a public

speech, receive a prize, or conduct an orchestra.
– ORIGIN Latin, 'beak'; the word first referred to an orator's platform in ancient Rome, decorated with beak-like projections from captured warships.

rosy •adj. (**rosier, rosiest**) **1** pink. **2** promising; hopeful: *rosy forecasts.*
– DERIVATIVES **rosiness** n.

rot •v. (**rots, rotting, rotted**) decompose; decay. •n. **1** the process or state of decaying. **2** (**the rot**) Brit. a decline in standards: *there's enough talent in the team to stop the rot.* **3** a disease that causes tissue decay in plants. **4** informal, esp. Brit. rubbish: *don't talk rot.*
– ORIGIN Old English.

rota •n. Brit. a list showing when each of a number of people has to do a particular job.
– ORIGIN Latin, 'wheel'.

Rotarian •n. a member of Rotary.

rotary •adj. **1** revolving around a central point. **2** having a rotating part or parts: *a rotary mower.* •n. (**Rotary**) a worldwide charitable society of business and professional people organized into local Rotary clubs.

rotate •v. (**rotates, rotating, rotated**) **1** move in a circle round a central point. **2** (of a job) pass to each member of a group in a regularly recurring order. **3** grow different crops one after the other on the same area of land.
– DERIVATIVES **rotator** n. **rotatory** /roh-tay-tuh-ri/ adj.
– ORIGIN Latin *rotare* 'turn in a circle'.

rotation •n. the action of moving in a circle or doing things in a repeated sequence.
– DERIVATIVES **rotational** adj.

rote •n. the learning of something by regular repetition: *a poem learnt by rote.*

rotisserie /roh-tiss-uh-ri/ •n. a rotating spit for roasting and barbecuing meat.
– ORIGIN French.

rotor •n. **1** the rotating part of a turbine, electric motor, or other device. **2** a hub with a number of blades spreading out from it that is rotated to provide the lift for a helicopter.

rotten •adj. **1** decaying; decomposing. **2** corrupt or immoral. **3** informal very bad. •adv. informal very much: *your mother spoiled you rotten.*
– DERIVATIVES **rottenness** n.
– ORIGIN Old Norse.

rotten borough •n. Brit. (before the Reform Act of 1832) a borough that was able to elect an MP though having very few voters.

rotter •n. informal, dated a cruel or unpleasant person.

Rottweiler /rot-vy-ler, rot-wy-ler/ • n. a large powerful black-and-tan breed of dog.
– ORIGIN from *Rottweil*, a town in SW Germany.

rotund /roh-tund/ • adj. rounded and plump.
– DERIVATIVES **rotundity** n.
– ORIGIN Latin *rotundus*.

rotunda /roh-tun-duh/ • n. a round building or room.
– ORIGIN from Italian *rotonda camera* 'round chamber'.

rouble /roo-b'l/ (also esp. N. Amer. **ruble**) • n. the basic unit of money of Russia and some other former republics of the Soviet Union.
– ORIGIN Russian.

roué /roo-ay/ • n. a man who leads an immoral life.
– ORIGIN French, 'broken on a wheel', referring to the torture thought to be deserved by such a person.

rouge /roozh/ • n. a red powder or cream used for colouring the cheeks.
– ORIGIN French, 'red'.

rough • adj. 1 not smooth or level. 2 not gentle: *rough treatment*. 3 (of weather or the sea) wild and stormy. 4 plain and basic: *rough wooden tables*. 5 harsh in sound or taste. 6 not worked out in every detail: *a rough guess*. 7 informal difficult and unpleasant. • n. 1 a basic version or state: *jot things down in rough first*. 2 esp. Brit. a violent person. 3 (on a golf course) the area of longer grass around the fairway and the green.
• v. 1 (**rough something out**) make a draft or first version of something. 2 (**rough it**) informal live with only very basic necessities. 3 (**rough someone up**) informal beat someone up.
– PHRASES **rough and ready** basic but effective. **rough edges** small flaws in something that is otherwise satisfactory. **rough justice** treatment that is not fair or in accordance with the law. **sleep rough** Brit. sleep outside in uncomfortable conditions.
– DERIVATIVES **roughness** n.
– ORIGIN Old English.

roughage • n. material in cereals, vegetables, and fruit that cannot be digested and which helps food to pass through the gut.

rough and tumble • n. a competitive situation without rules.

roughcast • n. plaster of lime, cement, and gravel, used on outside walls.

rough diamond • n. Brit. a person who is of good character but lacks refinement or education.

roughen • v. make or become rough.

rough-hewn • adj. (of a person) not refined or educated.

roughly • adv. 1 in a rough way. 2 approximately.

roughneck • n. informal 1 a rough, impolite person. 2 an oil-rig worker.

roughshod • adj. (in phr. **ride roughshod over**) fail to consider the wishes or feelings of.

roulade /roo-lahd/ • n. a piece of meat, sponge cake, or other food, spread with a filling and rolled up.
– ORIGIN French.

roulette • n. a gambling game in which a ball is dropped on to a revolving wheel with numbered compartments, the players betting on the number at which the ball comes to rest.
– ORIGIN French, 'small wheel'.

round • adj. 1 shaped like a circle, cylinder, or sphere. 2 having a curved shape. 3 (of a voice or musical tone) rich and smooth. 4 (of a number) expressed in convenient units rather than exactly, for example to the nearest whole number. • n. 1 a circular shape or piece. 2 a route by which a number of people or places are visited in turn: *a newspaper round*. 3 a regular sequence of activities: *the daily round*. 4 each of a sequence of stages in a sports contest. 5 a single division of a boxing or wrestling match. 6 a song for three or more unaccompanied voices or parts, each singing the same theme but starting one after another. 7 the amount of ammunition needed to fire one shot. 8 a set of drinks bought for all the members of a group. 9 Brit. a slice of bread. 10 Brit. the quantity of sandwiches made from two slices of bread. • adv. esp. Brit. 1 so as to move in a circle. 2 so as to cover the whole area surrounding a particular centre. 3 so as to turn and face in the opposite direction. 4 used in describing the position of something: *it's the wrong way round*. 5 so as to surround or give support: *the family rallied round to help her*. 6 so as to reach a new place or position. • prep. esp. Brit. 1 on every side of a central point. 2 so as to encircle. 3 from or on the other side of. 4 so as to cover the whole area of: *she went round the house to check its condition*. • v. 1 pass and go round: *the ship rounded the cape and sailed north*. 2 make a figure less exact but more convenient for calculations: *we'll round the weight up to the nearest kilo*. 3 make or become round in shape.
– PHRASES **round something off 1** smooth the edges of something. 2 complete

something in a suitable or satisfying way: *we rounded off our first day with a beach party.* **round on** make a sudden attack on. **round someone/thing up** collect people or animals together.
– DERIVATIVES **roundness** n.
– ORIGIN Old French.

roundabout • n. Brit. **1** a road junction at which traffic moves in one direction round a central island to reach one of the roads opening on to it. **2** a large revolving device in a playground, for children to ride on. **3** a merry-go-round. • adj. not following a direct route.

rounded • adj. **1** round or curved. **2** complete and balanced: *a rounded human being.*

roundel /rown-d'l/ • n. **1** a small disc. **2** a circular identifying mark painted on military aircraft.
– ORIGIN Old French *rondel.*

rounders • n. a ball game in which players run round a circuit of bases after hitting the ball with a cylindrical wooden bat.

Roundhead • n. hist. a member or supporter of the Parliamentary party in the English Civil War.
– ORIGIN with reference to their short-cropped hair.

roundly • adv. **1** in a firm or thorough way. **2** in a circular shape.

round robin • n. **1** a tournament in which each competitor plays in turn against every other competitor. **2** a petition.

round-table • adj. (of talks or a meeting) at which parties meet on equal terms for discussion.

round trip • n. a journey to a place and back again.

round-up • n. **1** a gathering together of people or things. **2** a summary.

roundworm • n. a parasitic worm with a rounded body, found in the intestines of some mammals.

rouse /rowz/ • v. (**rouses, rousing, roused**) **1** bring or come out of sleep. **2** stir up; arouse: *his evasiveness roused my curiosity.*
– ORIGIN prob. from Old French.

rousing • adj. stirring: *a rousing speech.*

roustabout /rowsst-uh-bowt/ • n. an unskilled or casual labourer.
– ORIGIN perh. from **ROUSE**.

rout¹ /rowt/ • n. **1** a disorderly retreat of defeated troops. **2** a decisive defeat. • v. defeat decisively.
– ORIGIN Old French *rute.*

rout² /rowt/ • v. **1** cut a groove in a surface. **2** rummage; search.
– ORIGIN from **ROOT²**.

route /root/ • n. a way taken in getting

from a starting point to a destination.
• v. (**routes, routeing** or **routing, routed**) send someone or something along a particular course.
– ORIGIN Old French *rute* 'road'.

routine • n. **1** a sequence of actions that is regularly followed. **2** a set sequence in a dance or comedy act. • adj. **1** performed as part of a regular procedure: *a routine inspection.* **2** without variety; dull.
– DERIVATIVES **routinely** adv.
– ORIGIN French.

roux /roo/ • n. (pl. **roux**) a mixture of butter and flour used in making sauces.
– ORIGIN from French *beurre roux* 'browned butter'.

rove • v. (**roves, roving, roved**) **1** travel constantly without a fixed destination. **2** (of eyes) look in all directions.
– DERIVATIVES **rover** n.
– ORIGIN perh. from dialect *rave* 'to stray'.

row¹ /roh/ • n. a number of people or things in a line.
– PHRASES **in a row** informal one after the other.
– ORIGIN Old English.

row² /roh/ • v. **1** propel a boat with oars. **2** row a boat as a sport. • n. a spell of rowing.
– DERIVATIVES **rower** n.
– ORIGIN Old English.

row³ /row/ esp. Brit. • n. **1** an angry quarrel. **2** a loud noise. • v. have a quarrel.

rowan /roh-uhn, row-uhn/ • n. a small tree with white flowers and red berries.
– ORIGIN Scandinavian.

rowdy • adj. (**rowdier, rowdiest**) noisy and disorderly. • n. (pl. **rowdies**) a noisy and disorderly person.
– DERIVATIVES **rowdily** adv. **rowdiness** n. **rowdyism** n.

rowing boat (N. Amer. **rowboat**) • n. a small boat propelled with oars.

rowing machine • n. an exercise machine with oars and a sliding seat.

rowlock /rol-luhk/ • n. Brit. a fitting on the side of a boat for holding an oar.

royal • adj. **1** relating to or having the status of a king or queen. **2** of a quality or size suitable for a king or queen: *a royal fortune.* • n. informal a member of the royal family.
– DERIVATIVES **royally** adv.
– ORIGIN Old French *roial.*

royal blue • n. a deep, vivid blue.

royal icing • n. esp. Brit. hard white icing.

royalist • n. **1** a person who supports the principle of having a king or queen. **2** (**Royalist**) a supporter of the king, Charles I, against Parliament in the English Civil War.
– DERIVATIVES **royalism** n.

royal jelly • n. a substance produced by worker bees and fed by them to larvae which are being raised as potential queen bees.

royalty • n. (pl. **royalties**) **1** people of royal blood or status. **2** the status or power of a king or queen. **3** a sum paid for the use of a patent or to an author or composer for each copy of a work sold or for each time it is performed.

royal warrant • n. a warrant issued by the king or queen indicating that goods or services are supplied to the royal family.

RP • abbrev. received pronunciation.

rpm • abbrev. revolutions per minute.

RSA • abbrev. **1** Republic of South Africa. **2** Royal Society of Arts.

RSJ • abbrev. rolled steel joist.

RSPB • abbrev. (in the UK) Royal Society for the Protection of Birds.

RSPCA • abbrev. (in the UK) Royal Society for the Prevention of Cruelty to Animals.

RSVP • abbrev. répondez s'il vous plaît; please reply (used at the end of invitations).
– ORIGIN French.

Rt Hon. • abbrev. Brit. Right Honourable, a title given to certain government ministers.

Rt Revd (also **Rt Rev.**) • abbrev. Brit. Right Reverend, a title given to a bishop.

Ru • symb. the chemical element ruthenium.

rub • v. (**rubs, rubbing, rubbed**) **1** move back and forth over a surface while pressing against it. **2** apply a substance with a rubbing action. **3** (**rub something down**) dry, smooth, or clean something by rubbing. **4** (**rub something in/into**) work fat into a mixture by breaking and blending it with the fingertips. • n. **1** an act of rubbing. **2** an ointment for rubbing on the skin. **3** (**the rub**) the central difficulty. [ORIGIN from Shakespeare's *Hamlet* (III. i. 65).]
– PHRASES **rub it in** informal firmly draw someone's attention to an embarrassing fact. **rub off** be transferred by contact. **rub something out** esp. Brit. erase pencil marks with a rubber. **rub shoulders** come into contact. **rub someone (up) the wrong way** irritate someone.
– ORIGIN perh. from German *rubben*.

rubato /ruu-bah-toh/ • n. (pl. **rubatos** or **rubati** /ruu-bah-ti/) Music temporary disregard for strict tempo to allow an expressive quickening or slackening.
– ORIGIN Italian, 'robbed'.

rubber¹ • n. **1** a tough elastic substance made from the latex of a tropical tree or

from chemicals. **2** Brit. a piece of rubber used for erasing pencil marks.
– DERIVATIVES **rubbery** adj.

rubber² • n. **1** a series of matches between the same sides in cricket, tennis, etc. **2** a unit of play in the card game bridge.

rubber band • n. a loop of rubber for holding things together.

rubberneck informal • v. turn your head to stare at something as you pass. • n. a person who stares in this way.

rubber plant • n. an evergreen tree of SE Asia with large dark green shiny leaves.

rubber stamp • n. a hand-held device for stamping dates, addresses, etc., on paper. • v. (**rubber-stamp**) approve something automatically without proper consideration.

rubbing • n. an impression of a design on brass or stone, made by placing a sheet of paper over it and rubbing it with chalk or a pencil.

rubbish • n. esp. Brit. **1** waste material. **2** nonsense. • v. Brit. informal criticize and reject something as worthless. • adj. Brit. informal very bad.
– DERIVATIVES **rubbishy** adj.
– ORIGIN Old French *rubbous*.

rubble • n. rough fragments of stone, brick, or concrete.
– ORIGIN perh. from Old French *robe* 'spoils'.

rubella /roo-bel-luh/ • n. a disease transmitted by a virus and with symptoms like mild measles.
– ORIGIN Latin, 'reddish things'.

Rubicon /roo-bi-k'n, roo-bi-kon/ • n. a point of no return.
– ORIGIN a stream marking a boundary between Italy and Gaul; by leading his army across it, Julius Caesar caused a civil war.

rubicund /roo-bi-kuhnd/ • adj. having a reddish complexion.
– ORIGIN Latin *rubicundus*.

rubidium /ruu-bid-i-uhm/ • n. a rare soft silvery reactive metallic element.
– ORIGIN Latin *rubidus* 'red'.

ruble • n. var. of ROUBLE.

rubric /roo-brik/ • n. **1** a heading on a document. **2** a set of instructions or rules. **3** a direction as to how a church service should be conducted.
– ORIGIN first referring to text written in red for emphasis: from Latin *rubrica terra* 'ochre as writing material'.

ruby • n. (pl. **rubies**) **1** a precious stone of a deep red colour. **2** a deep red colour.
– ORIGIN Latin *rubinus*.

ruby wedding • n. Brit. the fortieth

anniversary of a wedding.

RUC • abbrev. hist. Royal Ulster Constabulary.

ruche /roosh/ • n. a frill or pleat of fabric.
– DERIVATIVES **ruched** adj.
– ORIGIN French.

ruck[1] • n. **1** Rugby a loose scrum formed around a player with the ball on the ground. **2** a tightly packed crowd of people.
– ORIGIN prob. Scandinavian.

ruck[2] • v. (**ruck up**) make or form creases or folds.
– ORIGIN Old Norse.

ruck[3] • n. Brit. informal a brawl.
– ORIGIN perh. from **RUCTIONS** or **RUCKUS**.

rucksack /ruk-sak/ • n. a bag with two shoulder straps which allow it to be carried on the back.
– ORIGIN German.

ruckus /ruk-uhss/ • n. a row or commotion.
– ORIGIN perh. from **RUCTIONS** and **RUMPUS**.

ructions • pl. n. Brit. informal angry protests or trouble.
– ORIGIN perh. from **INSURRECTION**.

rudder • n. a hinged upright piece of wood or metal near the back of a boat or an aeroplane, used for steering.
– ORIGIN Old English, 'paddle, oar'.

rudderless • adj. lacking direction; not knowing what to do.

ruddy • adj. (**ruddier, ruddiest**) **1** of a reddish colour. **2** (of a person's face) having a healthy red colour. **3** Brit. informal used as a euphemism for 'bloody'.
– DERIVATIVES **ruddiness** n.
– ORIGIN Old English.

rude • adj. **1** offensively impolite or bad-mannered. **2** referring to sex or the body in an offensive way. **3** very abrupt: *a rude awakening.* **4** esp. Brit. hearty: *rude health.* **5** dated roughly made.
– DERIVATIVES **rudely** adv. **rudeness** n.
– ORIGIN Latin *rudis* 'not wrought'.

rudiment /roo-di-muhnt/
• n. **1** (**rudiments**) the basic facts of a subject. **2** Biol. an undeveloped part or organ.
– ORIGIN Latin *rudimentum.*

rudimentary /roo-di-men-tuh-ri/
• adj. **1** involving only the basic facts or elements: *a rudimentary education.* **2** not highly or fully developed: *a rudimentary stage of evolution.*

rue • v. (**rues, rueing** or **ruing, rued**) bitterly regret a past event or action.
– ORIGIN Old English.

rueful • adj. expressing regret: *a rueful grin.*
– DERIVATIVES **ruefully** adv.

ruff • n. **1** a starched frill worn round the neck. **2** a ring of feathers or hair round the neck of a bird or mammal.
– ORIGIN prob. from **ROUGH**.

ruffian • n. a violent person.
– ORIGIN Old French.

ruffle • v. (**ruffles, ruffling, ruffled**) **1** disturb the smooth surface of. **2** upset or worry: *he had been ruffled by her questions.* **3** (as adj. **ruffled**) gathered into a frill. • n. a gathered frill on a garment.

rufous /roo-fuhss/ • adj. reddish brown in colour.
– ORIGIN Latin *rufus* 'red, reddish'.

rug • n. **1** a small carpet. **2** Brit. a thick woollen blanket.
– ORIGIN prob. Scandinavian.

rugby (also **rugby football**) • n. a team game played with an oval ball that may be kicked, carried, and passed by hand.
– ORIGIN named after *Rugby* School in England.

rugby league • n. a form of rugby played in teams of thirteen.

rugby union • n. a form of rugby played in teams of fifteen.

rugged /rug-gid/ • adj. **1** having a rocky surface. **2** having or requiring toughness and determination. **3** (of a man) having attractively masculine features.
– DERIVATIVES **ruggedly** adv. **ruggedness** n.
– ORIGIN prob. Scandinavian.

rugger • n. Brit. informal rugby.

ruin • n. **1** the destruction or collapse of something. **2** (also **ruins**) a badly damaged or decaying building or the remains of a building. **3** the complete loss of a person's money and property.
• v. **1** completely destroy something. **2** have a very damaging effect on: *the motorway has ruined village life.* **3** make someone very poor or bankrupt.
– ORIGIN Latin *ruina.*

ruination • n. the action of ruining or the state of being ruined.

ruinous • adj. **1** disastrous or destructive. **2** in ruins.

rule • n. **1** a statement of what must be done or not done. **2** control of a country or group: *British rule.* **3** a code of practice and discipline for a religious community. **4** (**the rule**) the normal state of things. **5** a ruler. • v. (**rules, ruling, ruled**) **1** have power over a people or country. **2** have a powerful and restricting influence on: *her whole life was ruled by fear.* **3** state with legal authority that something is the case. **4** informal be very good or the best. **5** make lines on paper.
– PHRASES **as a rule** usually, but not always. **rule of thumb** a fairly accurate guide based on practice rather than

r

theory. **rule something out/in** exclude (or include) something as a possibility.
– ORIGIN Old French *reule*.

ruler • n. **1** a person who rules a people or country. **2** a straight rigid strip of plastic, wood, or metal, marked at regular intervals and used to draw straight lines or measure distances.

ruling • n. a decision or statement made by an authority. • adj. having control: *the ruling party*.

rum[1] • n. an alcoholic spirit made from sugar cane or molasses.
– ORIGIN perh. from former *rumbullion*.

rum[2] • adj. Brit. informal, dated peculiar.

Rumanian • adj. & n. var. of **ROMANIAN**.

rumba /rum-buh/ (also **rhumba**) • n. **1** a rhythmic dance with Spanish and African elements. **2** a ballroom dance based on this.
– ORIGIN Latin American Spanish.

rumble • v. (**rumbles, rumbling, rumbled**) **1** make or move with a continuous deep sound, like thunder. **2** (**rumble on**) (of a dispute) continue in a low-key way. **3** Brit. informal find out the truth about. • n. a continuous deep sound like distant thunder.
– ORIGIN prob. from Dutch *rommelen*.

rumble strip • n. one of a series of raised strips set in a road to warn drivers to slow down.

rumbustious /rum-buss-chuhss, rum-buss-ti-uhss/ • adj. informal, esp. Brit. high-spirited or difficult to control.
– ORIGIN prob. from former *robustious* 'boisterous'.

ruminant • n. a mammal that chews the cud, such as cattle, sheep, or deer.
– ORIGIN Latin *ruminari* 'chew over again'.

ruminate /roo-mi-nayt/ • v. (**ruminates, ruminating, ruminated**) **1** think deeply about something. **2** (of a cow, sheep, etc.) chew the cud.
– DERIVATIVES **rumination** n.

ruminative • adj. thinking deeply about things.

rummage • v. (**rummages, rummaging, rummaged**) search for something in an unmethodical way. • n. an act of rummaging.
– ORIGIN Old French *arrumer* 'stow in a hold'.

rummy • n. a card game in which the players try to form sets and sequences of cards.

rumour (US **rumor**) • n. a story spread among a number of people which is unconfirmed and may be false. • v. (**be rumoured**) be spread as a rumour.
– ORIGIN Latin *rumor* 'noise'.

rump • n. **1** the hind part of the body of a mammal or the lower back of a bird. **2** a part left over from something larger.
– ORIGIN prob. Scandinavian.

rumple • v. (**rumples, rumpling, rumpled**) make something untidy.
– ORIGIN Dutch *rompel* 'wrinkle'.

rumpus • n. (pl. **rumpuses**) a noisy disturbance.

run • v. (**runs, running, ran**; past part. **run**) **1** move fast using your legs. **2** move forcefully or quickly: *the tanker ran aground*. **3** pass: *Helen ran her fingers through her hair*. **4** (of a bus, train, etc.) make a regular journey on a particular route. **5** be in charge of. **6** continue or proceed. **7** function or cause to function. **8** pass into or reach a specified state or level: *inflation is running at 11 per cent*. **9** (**run in**) (of a quality) be common in members of a family. **10** (of a liquid) flow. **11** (of dye or colour) dissolve and spread when wet. **12** stand as a candidate in an election. **13** enter or be entered in a race. **14** publish a story in a newspaper or magazine. **15** transport someone in a car. **16** smuggle goods. • n. **1** an act or spell of running. **2** a journey or route. **3** a course that is regularly used: *a ski run*. **4** a continuous period or sequence: *a run of bad luck*. **5** an enclosed area in which animals or birds may run freely in the open. **6** a rapid series of musical notes. **7** (**the run**) the average type: *she stood out from the general run of women*. **8** (**the run of**) unrestricted use of or access to somewhere. **9** a point scored in cricket or baseball. **10** a ladder in stockings or tights. **11** (**the runs**) informal diarrhoea.
– PHRASES **be run off your feet** be very busy. **on the run** escaping from arrest. **run across** meet or find by chance. **run something by** (or **past**) tell someone about something to find out their opinion. **run down** gradually lose power. **run someone down** knock someone down with a vehicle. **run someone/thing down** criticize someone or something. **run something down** reduce something in size or resources. **run into 1** collide with. **2** meet by chance. **run something off 1** produce a copy on a machine. **2** write or recite something with little effort. **run on** continue without stopping. **run out 1** use up or be used up. **2** become no longer valid. **run someone out** Cricket dismiss a batsman by hitting the bails with the ball while the batsman is still running. **run over** overflow. **run someone over** knock someone down with a vehicle. **run through** (or **over**) go over as a quick rehearsal or reminder. **run someone**

through stab someone so as to kill them. **run something up 1** allow a bill, score, etc. to build up. **2** make something quickly. **run up against** experience a difficulty or problem.
– ORIGIN Old English.

runabout • n. a small car.

runaround • n. (in phr. **give someone the runaround**) informal treat someone badly by giving them misleading information.

runaway • n. a person who has run away from their home or an institution. • adj. **1** (of an animal or vehicle) running out of control. **2** happening quickly or uncontrollably: *runaway success*.

rundown • n. a brief summary. • adj. (**run-down**) **1** in a poor or neglected state. **2** tired and rather unwell.

rune /roon/ • n. **1** a letter of an ancient Germanic alphabet. **2** a symbol with mysterious or magical significance.
– DERIVATIVES **runic** adj.
– ORIGIN Old English, 'secret, mystery'.

rung¹ • n. **1** a horizontal bar on a ladder for a person's foot. **2** a level or rank.
– ORIGIN Old English.

rung² past part. of **RING²**.

run-in • n. **1** Brit. the approach to an action or event. **2** informal a disagreement or fight.

runnel • n. **1** a gutter. **2** a stream.
– ORIGIN from dialect *rindle*.

runner • n. **1** a person or animal that runs. **2** a messenger or agent for a bank, bookmaker, etc. **3** a rod, groove, blade, or roller on which something slides. **4** a shoot of a plant which grows along the ground and can take root at points along its length. **5** a long, narrow rug.
– PHRASES **do a runner** Brit. informal leave hastily to escape something.

runner bean • n. a climbing bean plant with scarlet flowers and long green edible pods.

runner-up • n. (pl. **runners-up**) a competitor or team coming second in a contest.

running • adj. **1** (of water) flowing naturally or supplied through pipes and taps. **2** producing liquid or pus: *a running sore.* **3** continuous or recurring: *a running joke.* **4** (after a noun) in succession: *the third week running.*
– PHRASES **in** (or **out of**) **the running** in (or no longer in) with a chance of success.

running battle • n. a battle which does not occur at a fixed place.

running board • n. a footboard extending along the side of a vehicle.

running commentary • n. a verbal description of events, given as they happen.

running mate • n. esp. N. Amer. an election candidate for the lesser of two linked political positions.

running repairs • pl. n. minor or temporary repairs carried out on machinery while it is in use.

running total • n. a total that is continually adjusted to take account of further items.

runny • adj. (**runnier, runniest**) **1** more liquid in consistency than is usual or expected. **2** (of a person's nose) producing mucus.

run-off • n. a further contest after a clear winner has not emerged in a previous one.

run-of-the-mill • adj. lacking unusual or special aspects; ordinary.

runt • n. the smallest animal in a litter.

run-through • n. **1** a rehearsal. **2** a brief summary.

run-up • n. the period before an important event during which preparations are made.

runway • n. a strip of hard ground where aircraft take off and land.

rupee /roo-pee, ruu-pee/ • n. the basic unit of money of India, Pakistan, and some other countries.
– ORIGIN Sanskrit, 'wrought silver'.

rupture • v. (**ruptures, rupturing, ruptured**) **1** break or burst suddenly. **2** (**be ruptured** or **rupture yourself**) suffer a hernia in the abdomen. **3** disturb good relations. • n. **1** an instance of breaking or bursting. **2** a hernia in the abdomen.
– ORIGIN Latin *ruptura*.

rural • adj. relating to the countryside rather than the town.
– DERIVATIVES **rurality** n. **rurally** adv.
– ORIGIN Latin *ruralis*.

ruse /rooz/ • n. an action intended to deceive or trick someone.
– ORIGIN Old French *ruser* 'use trickery'.

rush¹ • v. **1** move or act with urgent haste. **2** transport something with urgent haste. **3** deal with something too quickly. **4** (of air or a liquid) flow strongly. **5** try to attack or capture a person or place suddenly. • n. **1** a sudden quick movement towards something. **2** a sudden spell of hasty activity: *the pre-Christmas rush.* **3** a sudden strong demand for a product. **4** a sudden strong feeling. **5** informal a sudden thrill experienced after taking certain drugs. **6** (**rushes**) the first prints made of a film after a period of shooting.

r

– ORIGIN Old French *ruser* 'drive back'.

rush² • n. a marsh or waterside plant, some kinds of which are used for matting or baskets.
– ORIGIN Old English.

rush hour • n. a time at the start and end of the working day when traffic is at its heaviest.

rusk • n. esp. Brit. a dry biscuit eaten by babies.
– ORIGIN Spanish or Portuguese *rosca* 'twist, roll of bread'.

russet • adj. reddish brown. • n. **1** a reddish-brown colour. **2** a variety of dessert apple with a slightly rough greenish-brown skin.
– ORIGIN Old French *rousset*.

Russian • n. **1** a person from Russia. **2** the language of Russia. • adj. relating to Russia.

Russian Orthodox Church • n. the national Church of Russia.

Russian roulette • n. a dangerous game of chance in which a person loads a bullet into one chamber of a revolver, spins the cylinder, and then pulls the trigger while pointing the gun at their own head.

rust • n. **1** a reddish-brown flaky coating formed on iron or steel by the effect of moisture, and gradually wearing it away. **2** a disease of plants caused by a fungus, which results in rust-coloured patches. **3** a reddish-brown colour. • v. be affected with rust.
– ORIGIN Old English.

rustic • adj. **1** relating to life in the country. **2** simple and charming in a way seen as typical of the countryside. • n. an unsophisticated country person.
– DERIVATIVES **rusticity** n.
– ORIGIN Latin *rusticus*.

rusticate /russ-ti-kayt/ • v. (**rusticates**, **rusticating**, **rusticated**) **1** Brit. suspend a student from a university as a punishment. **2** (as adj. **rusticated**) (of stonework) shaped in large blocks with sunken joints and a roughened surface.
– ORIGIN Latin *rusticus* 'rustic'.

rustle • v. **1** make or move with a soft

crackling sound. **2** round up and steal cattle, horses, or sheep. **3** (**rustle something up**) informal produce food or a drink quickly. • n. a rustling sound.
– DERIVATIVES **rustler** n.

rustproof • adj. not able to be worn away by rust.

rusty • adj. (**rustier**, **rustiest**) **1** affected by rust. **2** (of knowledge or a skill) weakened by lack of recent practice.
– DERIVATIVES **rustiness** n.

rut¹ • n. **1** a long deep track made by the repeated passing of the wheels of vehicles. **2** a pattern of behaviour that has become dull but is hard to change.
– DERIVATIVES **rutted** adj.
– ORIGIN prob. from Old French *rute* 'road'.

rut² • n. an annual period of sexual activity in some animals, during which the males fight each other for access to the females. • v. (**ruts, rutting, rutted**) engage in such activity.
– ORIGIN Old French.

ruthenium /ruu-thee-ni-uhm/ • n. a hard silvery-white metallic chemical element.
– ORIGIN from *Ruthenia*, a region of central Europe.

rutherfordium /ru-*ther*-for-di-uhm/ • n. a very unstable chemical element made by high-energy atomic collisions.
– ORIGIN named after the New Zealand physicist Ernest *Rutherford*.

ruthless • adj. having no sympathy or pity; hard and selfish.
– DERIVATIVES **ruthlessly** adv. **ruthlessness** n.
– ORIGIN from the old-fashioned word *ruth* 'pity'.

Rwandan /ruu-an-duhn/ (also **Rwandese** /ruu-an-deez/) • n. a person from Rwanda, a country in central Africa. • adj. relating to Rwanda.

rye • n. **1** a cereal plant which grows in poor soils. **2** whisky in which much of the grain used in producing it is rye.
– ORIGIN Old English.

ryegrass • n. a grass used for fodder and lawns.

Ss

S¹ (also **s**) • n. (pl. **Ss** or **S's**) the nineteenth letter of the alphabet.

S² • abbrev. **1** Saint. **2** siemens. **3** small. **4** South or Southern. • symb. the chemical element sulphur.

s • abbrev. second or seconds.

's • contr. informal **1** is. **2** has. **3** us. **4** does.

-'s • suffix **1** showing possession in singular nouns, and also in plural nouns not having a final -s: John's car | the children's teacher. **2** forming the plural of a letter or symbol: 9's.

SA • abbrev. **1** South Africa. **2** South America. **3** South Australia.

sabbath • n. (often **the Sabbath**) a day intended for rest and religious worship, kept by Jews from Friday evening to Saturday evening, and by most Christians on Sunday.
– ORIGIN Hebrew, 'to rest'.

sabbatical /suh-bat-i-k'l/ • n. a period of paid leave granted to a university teacher for study or travel.
– ORIGIN Greek sabbatikos 'of the sabbath'.

saber • n. US = SABRE.

sable /rhymes with table/ • n. **1** a marten with a short tail and dark brown fur, native to Japan and Siberia. **2** the fur of the sable.
– ORIGIN Old French.

sabotage /sab-uh-tahzh/
• v. (**sabotages**, **sabotaging**, **sabotaged**) deliberately destroy or damage. • n. the action of sabotaging.
– ORIGIN French.

saboteur /sab-uh-ter/ • n. a person who sabotages something.
– ORIGIN French.

sabre /say-ber/ (US **saber**) • n. **1** a heavy sword with a curved blade and a single cutting edge. **2** a light fencing sword with a tapering curved blade.
– ORIGIN French.

sabre-rattling • n. the display or threat of military force.

sabretooth (also **sabre-toothed tiger**)
• n. a large extinct member of the cat family with massive curved upper canine teeth.

sac • n. a hollow, flexible structure in the body or a plant, resembling a bag or pouch and containing liquid or air.
– ORIGIN Latin saccus 'sack, bag'.

saccharin /sak-kuh-rin/ • n. a sweet-tasting synthetic substance used as a low-calorie substitute for sugar.
– ORIGIN Greek sakkharon 'sugar'.

saccharine /sak-kuh-rin, sak-kuh-reen/
• adj. too sweet or sentimental.

sacerdotal /sak-er-doh-t'l/ • adj. relating to priests.
– ORIGIN Latin sacerdotalis.

sachet /sa-shay/ • n. Brit. a small sealed bag or packet containing a small quantity of something.
– ORIGIN French, 'little bag'.

sack¹ • n. **1** a large bag made of strong fabric, paper, or plastic, used for storing and carrying goods. **2** (**the sack**) informal dismissal from employment. **3** (**the sack**) informal bed. • v. informal dismiss someone from employment.
– DERIVATIVES **sackable** adj.
– ORIGIN Greek sakkos 'sack, sackcloth'.

sack² • v. forcefully enter, steal from, and destroy a place (used in historical contexts). • n. the sacking of a town or city.
– ORIGIN French sac.

sackcloth • n. a coarse fabric woven from flax or hemp.
– PHRASES **sackcloth and ashes** a sign of remorse or great sadness. [ORIGIN with reference to the wearing of sackcloth and having ashes sprinkled on the head as a sign of penitence (Gospel of Matthew, chapter 11).]

sacking • n. coarse material for making sacks.

sacra pl. of SACRUM.

sacral /say-kruhl, sak-ruhl/ • adj. Anat. relating to the sacrum.

sacrament /sak-ruh-muhnt/ • n. **1** (in the Christian Church) a religious ceremony in which the people taking part are believed to receive the grace of

God. **2** (also **the Blessed Sacrament** or **the Holy Sacrament**) (in Roman Catholic use) bread and wine used in the Eucharist.
– DERIVATIVES **sacramental** adj.
– ORIGIN Latin *sacramentum* 'solemn oath'.

sacred /say-krid/ •adj. **1** connected with a god or goddess and treated as holy. **2** (of writings) relating to the teachings of a religion. **3** religious: *sacred music*.
– ORIGIN Latin *sacrare* 'consecrate'.

sacred cow •n. an idea, custom, or institution that people believe must never be criticized (with reference to the respect of Hindus for the cow as a sacred animal).

sacrifice •n. **1** the killing of an animal or person or the giving up of a possession as an offering to a god or goddess. **2** an animal, person, or object killed or offered in this way. **3** an act of giving up something you value for the sake of something that is more important.
•v. (**sacrifices, sacrificing, sacrificed**) give something as a sacrifice.
– DERIVATIVES **sacrificial** adj.
– ORIGIN Latin *sacrificium*.

sacrilege /sak-ri-lij/ •n. the treating of something sacred or highly valued with great disrespect.
– DERIVATIVES **sacrilegious** adj.
– ORIGIN Latin *sacrilegium*.

> ✓ Spell **sacrilege** with an **i** after the **r**: the ending is **-lege**.

sacristan /sak-ri-stuhn/ •n. a person in charge of a sacristy.

sacristy /sak-ri-sti/ •n. (pl. **sacristies**) a room in a church where a priest prepares for a service, and where things used in worship are kept.
– ORIGIN Latin *sacristia*.

sacrosanct /sak-ruh-sangkt/ •adj. seen as too important or valuable to be changed or questioned.
– ORIGIN Latin *sacrosanctus*.

sacrum /say-kruhm/ •n. (pl. **sacra** /say-kruh/ or **sacrums**) a triangular bone in the lower back between the two hip bones of the pelvis.
– ORIGIN from Latin *os sacrum* 'sacred bone'.

sad •adj. (**sadder, saddest**) **1** feeling sorrow; unhappy. **2** causing sorrow: *a sad story*. **3** informal very inadequate or unfashionable: *his taste in music is sad*.
– DERIVATIVES **sadness** n.
– ORIGIN Old English 'sated, weary'.

sadden •v. make someone unhappy.

saddle •n. **1** a seat with a raised ridge at the front and back, fastened on the back of a horse for riding. **2** a seat on a bicycle

or motorcycle. **3** a low part of a hill or mountain ridge between two higher points. **4** a joint of meat consisting of the two loins. •v. (**saddles, saddling, saddled**) **1** put a saddle on a horse. **2** (**be saddled with**) be burdened with a responsibility or task. **2** in a position of control or responsibility.
– ORIGIN Old English.

saddleback •n. **1** a hill with a ridge along the top that dips in the middle. **2** a pig of a black breed with a white stripe across the back.

saddlebag •n. a bag attached to a saddle.

saddler •n. a person who makes, repairs, or deals in equipment for horses.

saddlery •n. (pl. **saddleries**) **1** saddles and other equipment for horses. **2** a saddler's business or premises.

sadhu /sah-doo/ •n. a Hindu holy man.
– ORIGIN Sanskrit.

sadism /say-di-z'm/ •n. sexual or general pleasure that is gained from hurting or humiliating other people.
– DERIVATIVES **sadist** n. **sadistic** adj. **sadistically** adv.
– ORIGIN named after the French writer the Marquis de *Sade*.

sadly •adv. **1** in a sad way. **2** it is sad that.

sadomasochism /say-doh-mass-uh-ki-z'm/ •n. a sexual practice which is a combination of sadism and masochism.
– DERIVATIVES **sadomasochist** n. **sadomasochistic** adj.

sae •abbrev. Brit. stamped addressed envelope.

safari •n. (pl. **safaris**) an expedition to observe or hunt animals in their natural environment.
– ORIGIN Arabic, 'to travel'.

safari park •n. an area of parkland where wild animals can move freely and may be observed by visitors driving through.

safe •adj. **1** protected from danger or risk. **2** not leading to harm or injury. **3** (of a place) giving security or protection. **4** based on good reasons and not likely to be wrong: *it's a safe bet that they won't sell*. •n. a strong fireproof cabinet with a complex lock, used for storing valuables. **to be on the safe side** so as to be sure of avoiding risks.
– DERIVATIVES **safely** adv.
– ORIGIN Old French *sauf*.

safeguard •n. a measure taken to protect or prevent something.
•v. protect something with a safeguard.

safe house •n. a house in a secret location, used by people in hiding.

safekeeping •n. the keeping of

something in a safe place.

safe seat •n. Brit. a parliamentary seat that is certain to be held by the same party in an election.

safe sex •n. sexual activity in which people protect themselves against sexually transmitted diseases.

safety •n. the condition of being protected from danger, harm, or risk. •adj. designed to prevent injury or damage: *a safety barrier.*

safety belt •n. a belt securing a person to their seat in a vehicle or aircraft.

safety catch •n. a device that prevents a gun being fired or a machine being operated accidentally.

safety match •n. a match that can be lit only by striking it on a specially prepared surface.

safety net •n. 1 a net placed to catch an acrobat in case of a fall. 2 a safeguard against possible hardship.

safety pin •n. a pin with a point that is bent back to the head and is held in a guard when closed.

safety valve •n. a valve that opens automatically to relieve excessive pressure.

saffron •n. an orange-yellow spice used in cooking, made from the dried stigmas of a crocus.
– ORIGIN Arabic.

sag •v. (**sags, sagging, sagged**) 1 sink downwards gradually under weight or pressure. 2 hang down loosely or unevenly. •n. an instance of sagging.
– DERIVATIVES **saggy** adj.
– ORIGIN from German *sacken*, Dutch *zakken* 'subside'.

saga •n. 1 a long traditional story describing heroic adventures. 2 a long, involved account or series of incidents.
– ORIGIN Old Norse, 'narrative'.

sagacious /suh-gay-shuhss/ •adj. having good judgement; wise.
– DERIVATIVES **sagacity** /suh-ga-si-ti/ n.
– ORIGIN Latin *sagax* 'wise'.

sage¹ •n. a Mediterranean plant with greyish-green leaves that are used as a herb in cookery.
– ORIGIN Old French *sauge.*

sage² •n. a very wise man. •adj. wise: *sage remarks.*
– DERIVATIVES **sagely** adv.
– ORIGIN Old French.

Sagittarius /saj-i-tair-i-uhss/ •n. a constellation (the Archer) and sign of the zodiac, which the sun enters about 22 November.
– DERIVATIVES **Sagittarian** n. & adj.
– ORIGIN Latin, 'archer'.

sago /say-goh/ •n. flour or starchy

granules obtained from a palm, often cooked with milk to make a pudding.
– ORIGIN Malay.

sahib /sahb, suh-**heeb**/ •n. (in the Indian subcontinent) a polite form of address for a man.
– ORIGIN Arabic, 'friend, lord'.

said past and past part. of **SAY**.
•adj. referring to someone or something already mentioned: *the said agreement.*

sail •n. 1 a piece of material spread on a mast to catch the wind and propel a boat or ship. 2 a trip in a sailing boat or ship. 3 a flat structure attached to the arm of a windmill to catch the wind. •v. 1 travel in a sailing boat as a sport or pastime. 2 travel in a ship or boat using sails or engine power. 3 begin a voyage. 4 direct or control a boat or ship. 5 move smoothly or confidently. 6 (**sail through**) informal succeed easily at.
– PHRASES **sail close to the wind** behave in a risky way.
– ORIGIN Old English.

sailboard •n. a board with a mast and a sail, used in windsurfing.

sailcloth •n. 1 strong fabric used for making sails. 2 a similar fabric used for making hard-wearing clothes.

sailing boat (or **sailing ship**) •n. Brit. a boat (or ship) with sails.

sailor •n. 1 a person who works as a member of the crew of a ship or boat. 2 a person who sails as a sport or pastime. 3 (**a good/bad sailor**) a person who rarely (or often) becomes seasick.

sailplane •n. a glider designed to be able to fly for a long time.

saint /saynt/, before a name /suhnt/
•n. 1 a holy or good person who Christians believe will go to heaven after death. 2 a person of great goodness who is declared to be a saint by the Church after death. 3 informal a very good or kind person.
– DERIVATIVES **sainthood** n.
– ORIGIN Old French *seint.*

St Bernard •n. a breed of very large dog originally kept to rescue travellers by monks of a hospice on the Great St Bernard, a pass across the Alps.

sainted •adj. dated very good or kind, like a saint.

St Elmo's fire /suhnt el-**mohz**/ •n. a luminous electrical discharge sometimes seen on a ship or aircraft during a storm.
– ORIGIN seen as a sign of protection given by *St Elmo*, the patron saint of sailors.

St George's cross •n. a +-shaped cross, red on a white background.

S

saintly • adj. very holy or good.
– DERIVATIVES **saintliness** n.

saint's day • n. (in the Christian Church) a day on which a saint is particularly honoured.

St Swithin's day • n. 15 July, a Church festival honouring St Swithin and believed to be a day on which, if it rains, it will continue raining for the next forty days.

saith /seth/ archaic 3rd person sing. present of SAY.

saithe /sayth/ • n. an edible North Atlantic fish of the cod family.
– ORIGIN Old Norse.

sake¹ /sayk/ • n. (**for the sake of**) **1** so as to achieve or keep. **2** out of consideration for someone.
– ORIGIN Old English, 'contention'.

sake² /sah-ki, sa-kay/ • n. a Japanese alcoholic drink made from rice.
– ORIGIN Japanese.

salaam /suh-lahm/ • n. a gesture of greeting or respect in Arabic-speaking and Muslim countries, consisting of a low bow with the hand touching the forehead. • v. make a salaam.
– ORIGIN from Arabic, 'peace be upon you'.

salable • adj. var. of SALEABLE.

salacious /suh-lay-shuhss/ • adj. having too much interest in sexual matters.
– ORIGIN Latin *salax*.

salad • n. a cold dish of raw vegetables.
– PHRASES **your salad days** the period when you are young and inexperienced. [ORIGIN from Shakespeare's *Antony and Cleopatra* (I. v. 73).]
– ORIGIN Old French *salade*.

salad cream • n. Brit. a creamy dressing resembling mayonnaise.

salamander /sal-uh-man-der/ • n. **1** an animal with bright markings resembling a newt, that can live in water and on land. **2** a mythical lizard-like creature said to live in fire.
– ORIGIN Greek *salamandra*.

salami /suh-lah-mi/ • n. (pl. **salami** or **salamis**) a type of spicy preserved sausage.
– ORIGIN Italian.

salaried • adj. earning or offering a salary: *a salaried job.*

salary • n. (pl. **salaries**) a fixed regular payment made by an employer to an employee.
– DERIVATIVES **salaried** adj.
– ORIGIN Latin *salarium* 'allowance to buy salt'.

sale • n. **1** the exchange of something for money. **2** (**sales**) the activity or profession of selling. **3** a period in which goods are sold at reduced prices. **4** a public event at which goods are sold or auctioned!
– ORIGIN Old English.

saleable (also **salable**) • adj. good enough to be sold.
– DERIVATIVES **saleability** n.

saleroom • n. Brit. a room in which auctions are held.

salesman (or **saleswoman**) • n. (pl. **salesmen** or **saleswomen**) a person whose job is to sell or promote goods.
– DERIVATIVES **salesmanship** n.

salesperson • n. (pl. **salespeople** or **salespersons**) a salesman or saleswoman.

salient /say-li-uhnt/ • adj. **1** most important: *the salient points of the case.* **2** (of an angle) pointing outwards. • n. a piece of land or a fortified building that juts out to form an angle.
– DERIVATIVES **salience** n.
– ORIGIN Latin *salire* 'to leap'.

saline /say-lyn/ • adj. containing salt.
– DERIVATIVES **salinity** n.
– ORIGIN Latin *sal* 'salt'.

saliva /suh-ly-vuh/ • n. a watery liquid produced by glands in the mouth, helping chewing, swallowing, and digestion.
– DERIVATIVES **salivary** /suh-ly-vuh-ri/ adj.
– ORIGIN Latin.

salivate /sal-i-vayt/ • v. (**salivates**, **salivating**, **salivated**) **1** produce saliva. **2** show great excitement at the prospect of something.
– DERIVATIVES **salivation** n.
– ORIGIN Latin *salivare*.

sallow • adj. (of a person's complexion) yellowish in colour.
– ORIGIN Old English, 'dusky'.

sally • n. (pl. **sallies**) **1** a sudden charge out of a place surrounded by an enemy. **2** a witty or lively reply. • v. (**sallies**, **sallying**, **sallied**) (**sally forth/out**) set out.
– ORIGIN French *saillie*.

salmon /rhymes with gammon/ • n. (pl. **salmon** or **salmons**) a large fish with edible pink flesh, that matures in the sea and moves to freshwater streams to spawn.
– ORIGIN Latin *salmo*.

salmonella /sal-muh-nel-luh/ • n. (pl. **salmonellae** /sal-muh-nel-lee/) a bacterium that occurs mainly in the gut and can cause food poisoning.
– ORIGIN named after the American veterinary surgeon Daniel E. *Salmon*.

salon • n. **1** a place where a hairdresser, beautician, or clothes designer carries out their work. **2** a reception room in a large house. **3** hist. a regular gathering of

writers and artists, held in a fashionable household.
– ORIGIN French.

saloon • n. **1** Brit. a lounge bar in a pub. **2** a large public lounge on a ship. **3** N. Amer. dated a **bar**. **4** Brit. a car with a closed body and separate boot.
– ORIGIN French *salon*.

salopettes /sal-uh-pets/ • pl. n. padded trousers with a high waist and shoulder straps, worn for skiing.
– ORIGIN French *salopette*.

salsa /sal-suh/ • n. **1** a type of Latin American dance music containing elements of jazz and rock. **2** a dance performed to this music. **3** a spicy tomato sauce.
– ORIGIN Spanish, 'sauce'.

salsify /sal-si-fi/ • n. a plant with a long edible root like that of a parsnip.
– ORIGIN French *salsifis*.

salt • n. **1** (also **common salt**) sodium chloride, a white substance in the form of crystals used for flavouring or preserving food. **2** Chem. any compound formed by the reaction of an acid with a base. • adj. containing or treated with salt. • v. **1** season or preserve meat or fish with salt. **2** sprinkle a road or path with salt in order to melt snow or ice. **3** (**salt something away**) informal secretly store something, especially money.
– PHRASES **rub salt into the wound** make a painful experience even more upsetting. **the salt of the earth** a person who is very kind, reliable, or honest. [ORIGIN with reference to the Gospel of Matthew, chapter 5.] **take something with a pinch** (or **grain**) **of salt** be aware that something may be untrue or exaggerated. **worth your salt** good at your job.
– ORIGIN Old English.

salt cellar • n. a container for salt.
– ORIGIN *cellar* is from Old French *salier* 'salt-box'.

saltire /sawl-tyr, sol-tyr/ • n. Heraldry an X-shaped cross.
– ORIGIN Old French *saultoir*.

salt marsh • n. an area of coastal grassland that is regularly flooded by seawater.

salt pan • n. a hollow in the ground in which salt water evaporates to leave a deposit of salt.

saltpetre /sawlt-pee-ter, solt-pee-ter/ (US **saltpeter**) • n. potassium nitrate.
– ORIGIN Latin *salpetra*.

saltwater • adj. relating to or found in the sea.

salty • adj. (**saltier, saltiest**) **1** tasting of or containing salt. **2** (of language or humour) coarse.

– DERIVATIVES **saltiness** n.

salubrious /suh-loo-bri-uhss/ • adj. good for your health: *a salubrious district.*
– ORIGIN Latin *salubris*.

salutary /sal-yuu-tuh-ri/ • adj. (of something unpleasant) producing a good effect because it teaches you something.
– ORIGIN Latin *salutaris*.

salutation • n. a greeting.

salute • n. **1** a gesture of respect or acknowledgement. **2** a raising of a hand to the head, made as a formal military gesture of respect. **3** the shooting of a gun or guns as a formal sign of respect or celebration. • v. (**salutes, saluting, saluted**) **1** make a formal salute to. **2** express admiration and respect for.
– ORIGIN Latin *salutare* 'greet'.

Salvadorean /sal-vuh-dor-i-uhn/ • n. a person from El Salvador, a country in Central America. • adj. relating to El Salvador.

salvage • v. (**salvages, salvaging, salvaged**) **1** rescue a ship or its cargo from loss at sea. **2** save something from being lost or destroyed: *she tried hard to salvage her dignity.* • n. **1** the action of rescuing or saving something. **2** cargo rescued from a wrecked ship.
– DERIVATIVES **salvageable** adj.
– ORIGIN Latin *salvagium*.

salvage yard • n. a place where disused machinery and vehicles are broken up and parts salvaged.

salvation • n. **1** (in Christian belief) the state of being saved from sin, believed to be brought about by faith in Christ. **2** a means of protecting someone from harm or loss: *his only salvation was to outwit the enemy.*
– ORIGIN Latin.

salve • n. **1** an ointment used to soothe or heal the skin. **2** something that reduces guilty feelings: *the idea provided a salve for his guilt.* • v. (**salves, salving, salved**) (**salve your conscience**) do something to make you feel less guilty.
– ORIGIN Old English.

salver • n. a tray.
– ORIGIN French *salve*.

salvia • n. a plant grown for its bright scarlet flowers.
– ORIGIN Latin, 'sage'.

salvo • n. (pl. **salvos** or **salvoes**) **1** a shooting of a number of guns at the same time in a battle. **2** a sudden series of aggressive statements or acts.
– ORIGIN Italian *salva* 'salutation'.

sal volatile /sal vuh-lat-i-li/ • n. a scented solution used as smelling salts.
– ORIGIN Latin, 'volatile salt'.

S

salwar /sul-wah/ (also **shalwar**) •n. a pair of light, loose trousers tapering to a tight fit around the ankles, worn by women from the Indian subcontinent.
– ORIGIN Persian and Urdu.

Samaritan •n. **1** (**good Samaritan**) a kind or helpful person. [ORIGIN with reference to the story of the man from ancient Samaria who helped a man in need whom other people had passed by (Gospel of Luke).] **2** (**the Samaritans**) (in the UK) an organization which counsels those in distress by telephone.

samarium /suh-mair-i-uhm/ •n. a hard silvery-white metallic chemical element.
– ORIGIN named after a Russian official called *Samarsky*.

samba •n. /sam-buh/ a Brazilian dance of African origin. •v. (**sambas, sambaing** /sam-buh-(r)ing/, **sambaed** /sam-buhd/) dance the samba.
– ORIGIN Portuguese.

same •adj. **1** (**the same**) exactly alike. **2** (**this**/**that same**) referring to a person or thing just mentioned. •pron. (**the same**) **1** the same thing as previously mentioned. **2** identical people or things. •adv. in the same way.
– PHRASES **all** (or **just**) **the same** in spite of this.
– DERIVATIVES **sameness** n.
– ORIGIN Old Norse.

samey •adj. Brit. informal lacking in variety.

samizdat /sam-iz-dat/ •n. (in the former Soviet Union) the secret copying and distribution of literature banned by the state.
– ORIGIN Russian, 'self-publishing house'.

samosa /suh-moh-suh/ •n. a triangular fried Indian pastry containing spiced vegetables or meat.
– ORIGIN Persian and Urdu.

samovar /sam-uh-var/ •n. a decorated Russian tea urn.
– ORIGIN Russian, 'self-boiler'.

sampan /sam-pan/ •n. a small boat propelled with an oar at the stern, used in the Far East.
– ORIGIN from Chinese words meaning 'three' and 'board'.

sample •n. **1** a small part or quantity intended to show what the whole is like. **2** a specimen taken for scientific testing. •v. (**samples, sampling, sampled**) **1** take a sample or samples of. **2** get a taste of: *sample some entertaining nights out in Liverpool.* **3** (as noun **sampling**) the process of copying and recording parts of a piece of music in electronic form, to be used in a different piece of music.
– ORIGIN Old French *essample* 'example'.

sampler •n. **1** a piece of embroidery done to demonstrate a person's skill at various stitches. **2** a device for sampling music.

samurai /sam-uh-ry/ •n. (pl. **samurai**) hist. a member of a powerful Japanese military class.
– ORIGIN Japanese.

sanatorium /san-uh-tor-i-uhm/ •n. (pl. **sanatoriums** or **sanatoria** /san-uh-tor-i-uh/) **1** a place for the care of people with a long illness or recovering from illness. **2** Brit. a place in a boarding school for sick children.
– ORIGIN Latin.

sanctify /sangk-ti-fy/ •v. (**sanctifies, sanctifying, sanctified**) **1** make or declare something holy. **2** give religious or official approval to: *love sanctified by the sacrament of marriage.*
– DERIVATIVES **sanctification** n.
– ORIGIN Latin *sanctificare*.

sanctimonious /sangk-ti-moh-ni-uhss/ •adj. making a show of being morally better than other people.
– ORIGIN Latin *sanctimonia* 'sanctity'.

sanction •n. **1** a threatened penalty for disobeying a law or rule. **2** (**sanctions**) measures taken by a state to try to force another state to do something. **3** official permission or approval. •v. give official permission for.
– ORIGIN Latin.

sanctity •n. (pl. **sanctities**) **1** holiness. **2** the state of being very important and worthy of great respect: *the sanctity of human life.*
– ORIGIN Old French *saincite*.

sanctuary •n. (pl. **sanctuaries**) **1** a place of safety. **2** a nature reserve. **3** a place where injured or unwanted animals are cared for. **4** a holy place. **5** the part of the chancel of a church containing the high altar.
– ORIGIN Latin *sanctuarium*.

sanctum /sangk-tuhm/ •n. (pl. **sanctums**) **1** a sacred place. **2** a private place.
– ORIGIN Latin.

sand •n. **1** a substance formed of very fine particles resulting from the erosion of rocks, found on beaches, river beds, the seabed, and deserts. **2** (**sands**) a wide area of sand. •v. **1** smooth a surface with sandpaper or a sander. **2** sprinkle with sand.
– ORIGIN Old English.

sandal •n. a shoe with a partly open upper part or straps attaching the sole to the foot.
– DERIVATIVES **sandalled** (US **sandaled**) adj.
– ORIGIN Greek *sandalon* 'wooden shoe'.

sandalwood •n. the sweet-smelling wood of an Indian or SE Asian tree.

– ORIGIN *sandal* from Latin *sandalum*.

sandbag • n. a bag of sand, used for protection against floods or explosions.
• v. (**sandbags, sandbagging, sandbagged**) protect a building or other structure with sandbags.

sandbank • n. a build-up of sand forming a raised bank in the sea or a river.

sandbar • n. a long, narrow sandbank.

sandblast • v. roughen or clean a surface with a jet of sand driven by compressed air or steam.

sandcastle • n. a model of a castle built out of sand.

sander • n. a power tool used for smoothing a surface.

sandman • n. (**the sandman**) an imaginary man supposed to make children sleep by sprinkling sand in their eyes.

sandpaper • n. paper with sand or another rough substance stuck to it, used for smoothing surfaces.
• v. (**sandpapers, sandpapering, sandpapered**) smooth a surface with sandpaper.

sandpiper • n. a wading bird with a long bill and long legs, found in coastal areas.

sandpit • n. Brit. a shallow box or hollow containing sand, for children to play in.

sandstone • n. rock formed of sand or quartz grains tightly pressed together.

sandstorm • n. a strong wind in a desert carrying clouds of sand.

sandwich • n. 1 two pieces of bread with a filling between them. 2 Brit. a sponge cake of two or more layers with jam or cream between them. • v. 1 (**sandwich something between**) insert something between two people or things.
2 (**sandwich things together**) join two things by putting something between them.
– ORIGIN named after the 4th Earl of *Sandwich*.

sandwich board • n. a pair of advertisement boards connected by straps by which they are hung over a person's shoulders.

sandwich course • n. Brit. a training course with alternate periods of study and work in business or industry.

sandy • adj. (**sandier, sandiest**) 1 covered in or consisting of sand. 2 light yellowish brown.
– DERIVATIVES **sandiness** n.

sane • adj. 1 having a normal mind; not mad. 2 sensible: *sane advice*.
– ORIGIN Latin *sanus* 'healthy'.

sang past of SING.

sangfroid /song-frwah/ • n. the ability

to stay calm in difficult circumstances.
– ORIGIN French, 'cold blood'.

sangria /sang-gree-uh/ • n. a Spanish drink of red wine and lemonade with fruit and spices.
– ORIGIN Spanish, 'bleeding'.

sanguinary /sang-gwi-nuh-ri/ • adj. esp. archaic involving much bloodshed.

sanguine /sang-gwin/ • adj. cheerfully confident about the future.
– ORIGIN Old French, 'blood red'.

Sanhedrin /san-hed-rin, san-hee-drin/ (also **Sanhedrim** /san-hed-rim, san-hee-drim/) • n. the highest court of justice and the supreme council in ancient Jerusalem.
– ORIGIN Hebrew.

sanitarium /san-i-tair-i-uhm/ • n. (pl. **sanitariums** or **sanitaria** /san-i-tair-i-uh/) N. Amer. = SANATORIUM.

sanitary • adj. 1 relating to sanitation.
2 hygienic.
– ORIGIN Latin *sanitas* 'health'.

sanitary towel (N. Amer. **sanitary napkin**) • n. a pad worn by women to absorb menstrual blood.

sanitation • n. arrangements to protect public health, such as the provision of clean drinking water and the disposal of sewage.

sanitize (or **sanitise**) • v. (**sanitizes, sanitizing, sanitized**) 1 make something hygienic. 2 make something unpleasant seem more acceptable.

sanity • n. 1 the condition of being sane.
2 reasonable behaviour.

sank past of SINK.

Sanskrit /san-skrit/ • n. an ancient language of India, still in use as a language of religion and scholarship.
– ORIGIN Sanskrit, 'composed'.

Santa Claus (also informal **Santa**)
• n. Father Christmas.
– ORIGIN Dutch *Sante Klaas* 'St Nicholas'.

sap • n. the liquid that circulates in plants, carrying food to all parts.
• v. (**saps, sapping, sapped**) gradually weaken a person's strength.
– ORIGIN Old English.

sapient /say-pi-uhnt/ • adj. formal wise or intelligent.
– ORIGIN Latin *sapere* 'be wise'.

sapling • n. a young, slender tree.

saponify /suh-pon-i-fy/ • v. (**saponifies, saponifying, saponified**) turn fat or oil into soap by reaction with an alkali.
– ORIGIN Latin *sapo* 'soap'.

sapper • n. a military engineer who lays or finds and defuses mines.
– ORIGIN French *saper* 'dig a trench to approach an enemy position'.

sapphic /saf-fik/ • adj. 1 (**Sapphic**)

relating to the ancient Greek poet Sappho, or her poetry expressing affection for women. **2** formal relating to lesbians.

sapphire /saf-fyr/ •n. **1** a transparent blue precious stone. **2** a bright blue colour.
– ORIGIN Greek *sappheiros*, prob. referring to lapis lazuli.

sappy •adj. (**sappier**, **sappiest**) N. Amer. informal over-sentimental.

saprophyte /sap-ruh-fyt/ •n. Biol. a plant or fungus that lives on decaying matter.
– DERIVATIVES **saprophytic** adj.
– ORIGIN from Greek *sapros* 'putrid' + *phuton* 'plant'.

saraband /sa-ruh-band/ (also **sarabande**) •n. a slow, dignified Spanish dance.
– ORIGIN Spanish and Italian *zarabanda*.

Saracen /sa-ruh-suhn/ •n. an Arab or Muslim at the time of the Crusades.
– ORIGIN Greek *Sarakēnos*.

sarcasm •n. a way of using words which say the opposite of what you mean, in order to upset or mock someone.
– ORIGIN Greek *sarkasmos*.

sarcastic •adj. using words which say the opposite of what you mean, in order to upset or mock someone.
– DERIVATIVES **sarcastically** adv.
– ORIGIN Latin.

sarcoma /sar-koh-muh/ •n. (pl. **sarcomas** or **sarcomata** /sar-koh-muh-tuh/) Med. a cancerous tumour of a kind found chiefly in connective tissue.
– ORIGIN Greek *sarkōma*.

sarcophagus /sar-kof-fuh-guhss/ •n. (pl. **sarcophagi** /sar-kof-fuh-gy/) a stone coffin.
– ORIGIN Latin.

sardine •n. a young pilchard or other small herring-like fish.
– ORIGIN Latin *sardina*.

sardonic /sar-don-ik/ •adj. mocking or cynical: *a sardonic smile*.
– DERIVATIVES **sardonically** adv.
– ORIGIN French *sardonique*.

sardonyx /sar-duh-niks/ •n. onyx (a semi-precious stone) in which white layers alternate with yellow or reddish ones.
– ORIGIN Greek *sardonux*.

sargasso /sar-gass-oh/ •n. a brown seaweed which floats in large masses.
– ORIGIN Portuguese *sargaço*.

sarge •n. informal sergeant.

sari /sah-ri/ (also **saree**) •n. (pl. **saris** or **sarees**) a length of cotton or silk draped around the body, worn by women from the Indian subcontinent.
– ORIGIN Hindi.

sarky •adj. Brit. informal sarcastic.

– DERIVATIVES **sarkily** adv.

sarnie •n. Brit. informal a sandwich.

sarong /suh-rong/ •n. a long piece of cloth wrapped round the body and tucked at the waist or under the armpits.
– ORIGIN Malay, 'sheath'.

SARS (also **Sars**) •abbrev. severe acute respiratory syndrome.

sarsaparilla /sar-suh-puh-ril-luh/ •n. **1** the dried roots of various plants, used as a flavouring. **2** a sweet drink flavoured with this.
– ORIGIN Spanish *zarzaparilla*.

sarsen /sar-suhn/ •n. a sandstone boulder of a kind used at the monument at Stonehenge.
– ORIGIN prob. from **SARACEN**.

sartorial /sah-tor-i-uhl/ •adj. relating to a person's style of dress.
– DERIVATIVES **sartorially** adv.
– ORIGIN Latin *sartor* 'tailor'.

SAS •abbrev. Special Air Service.

sash[1] •n. a long strip of cloth worn over one shoulder or round the waist.
– ORIGIN Arabic 'muslin, turban'.

sash[2] •n. a frame holding the glass in a window.
– ORIGIN from **CHASSIS**.

sashay /sa-shay/ •v. informal walk in a confident way, swinging the hips from side to side.
– ORIGIN French *chassé* 'chased'.

sash window •n. a window with one or two sashes which can be slid up and down to open it.

sassafras /sass-uh-frass/ •n. an extract made from the sweet-smelling leaves or bark of a North American tree, used in medicines and perfumes.
– ORIGIN Spanish *sasafrás*.

Sassenach /sass-uh-nakh, sass-uh-nak/ Scottish & Irish derog. •n. an English person. •adj. English.
– ORIGIN Scottish Gaelic or Irish.

sassy •adj. (**sassier**, **sassiest**) informal confident or cheeky.
– DERIVATIVES **sassiness** n.
– ORIGIN from **SAUCE**.

SAT •abbrev. (in the UK) standard assessment task, a standard test given to schoolchildren to assess their progress.

sat past and past part. of **SIT**.

Satan •n. the Devil.
– ORIGIN Hebrew, 'adversary'.

satanic •adj. relating to Satan.

satanism •n. the worship of Satan.
– DERIVATIVES **satanist** n. & adj.

satchel •n. a shoulder bag with a long strap, used to carry school books.
– ORIGIN Old French *sachel*.

sated •adj. having had as much as you want, or so much that you do not want any more.

– ORIGIN Old English.

sateen /sa-teen/ • n. a cotton fabric with a glossy surface.
– ORIGIN from **SATIN**.

satellite • n. **1** an artificial object placed in orbit round the earth or another planet to collect information or for communication. **2** a natural object that orbits a planet. • adj. (of a country, community, or organization) dependent on or controlled by a larger or more powerful one.
– ORIGIN Latin *satelles* 'attendant'.

> Spell **satellite** with a double **l**.

satellite dish • n. a bowl-shaped aerial which transmits signals to or receives them from a communications satellite.

satellite television • n. television in which the signals are broadcast via satellite.

satiate /say-shi-ayt/ • v. (**satiates, satiating, satiated**) give someone as much or more than they want.
– DERIVATIVES **satiation** n.
– ORIGIN Latin *satiare*.

satiety /suh-ty-i-ti/ • n. the feeling or state of being fully satisfied.

satin • n. a smooth, glossy fabric. • adj. having a smooth, glossy surface or finish.
– DERIVATIVES **satiny** adj.
– ORIGIN Arabic, 'of *Tsinkiang*', a town in China.

satinwood • n. the glossy yellowish wood of a tropical tree, used in making furniture.

satire /sat-yr/ • n. **1** the use of humour, irony, or exaggeration as a form of mockery or criticism. **2** a play or novel using satire.
– DERIVATIVES **satirist** n.
– ORIGIN Latin *satira* 'poetic medley'.

satirical (also **satiric**) • adj. using humour, irony, or exaggeration as a form of mockery or criticism.
– DERIVATIVES **satirically** adv.

satirize /sat-i-ryz/ (or **satirise**) • v. (**satirizes, satirizing, satirized**) mock or criticize by using humour, irony, or exaggeration.

satisfaction • n. **1** the state of being pleased because you have what you want or need. **2** Law the payment of a debt or fulfilment of a duty or claim. **3** something that makes up for an injustice: *the work will stop if they don't get satisfaction.*

satisfactory • adj. acceptable, but not outstanding or perfect.
– DERIVATIVES **satisfactorily** adv.

satisfy • v. (**satisfies, satisfying, satisfied**) **1** please someone by doing or giving them what they want or need. **2** meet a demand, desire, or need.
– ORIGIN Latin *satisfacere* 'to content'.

satrap /sat-rap/ • n. **1** a governor of a province in the ancient Persian empire. **2** a subordinate or local ruler.
– ORIGIN Latin *satrapa*.

satsuma /sat-soo-muh/ • n. a variety of tangerine with a loose skin.
– ORIGIN named after the former Japanese province of *Satsuma*.

saturate /sach-uh-rayt/ • v. (**saturates, saturating, saturated**) **1** soak thoroughly with a liquid. **2** cause a substance to combine with, dissolve, or hold the greatest possible quantity of another substance. **3** supply a market beyond the point at which there is demand for a product.
– ORIGIN Latin *saturare* 'fill, glut'.

saturated • adj. Chem. (of fats) having only single bonds between carbon atoms in their molecules and as a consequence being less easily processed by the body.

saturation • n. the action of saturating or the state of being saturated. • adj. to the fullest extent: *saturation bombing.*

saturation point • n. the stage beyond which no more can be absorbed or accepted.

Saturday • n. the day of the week before Sunday and following Friday.
– ORIGIN from Latin *Saturni dies* 'day of Saturn'.

Saturn • n. a planet of the solar system, sixth in order from the sun and circled by broad flat rings.

saturnine /sat-er-nyn/ • adj. **1** (of a person) serious or gloomy. **2** (of looks) dark and serious.
– ORIGIN Latin *Saturninus* 'of Saturn' (associated with slowness and gloom by astrologers).

satyr /sat-er/ • n. **1** (in Greek mythology) a lustful, drunken woodland god, with a man's head and a horse's ears and tail or (in Roman mythology) with a goat's ears, tail, legs, and horns. **2** a man with strong sexual desires.
– ORIGIN Greek *saturos*.

sauce • n. **1** a liquid substance served with food to add moistness and flavour. **2** informal, esp. Brit. impertinence; cheek.
– ORIGIN Old French.

sauce boat • n. a long, narrow jug for serving sauce.

saucepan • n. a deep cooking pan with a long handle and a lid.

saucer • n. a small shallow dish on which a cup stands.
– ORIGIN Old French *saussier* 'sauce boat'.

s

saucy •adj. (**saucier, sauciest**) informal 1 sexually suggestive in a light-hearted way: *saucy bedroom secrets.* 2 cheeky or impertinent.
– DERIVATIVES **saucily** adv. **sauciness** n.

Saudi /sow-di, saw-di/ •n. (pl. **Saudis**) a person from Saudi Arabia, or a member of its ruling dynasty. •adj. relating to Saudi Arabia or its ruling dynasty.

sauerkraut /sow-er-krowt/ •n. a German dish of chopped pickled cabbage.
– ORIGIN German.

sauna /saw-nuh/ •n. 1 a small room used as a hot-air or steam bath for cleaning and refreshing the body. 2 a session in a sauna.
– ORIGIN Finnish.

saunter •v. (**saunters, sauntering, sauntered**) walk in a slow, relaxed way. •n. a leisurely stroll.

saurian /saw-ri-uhn/ •adj. relating to or like a lizard.
– ORIGIN Greek *sauros* 'lizard'.

sausage •n. 1 a short tube of raw minced meat encased in a skin and grilled or fried before eating. 2 a tube of cooked or preserved spicy meat eaten cold in slices.
– PHRASES **not a sausage** Brit. informal nothing at all.
– ORIGIN Old French *saussiche*.

sausage dog •n. Brit. informal a dachshund.

sausage meat •n. minced meat with spices and cereal, used in sausages or as a stuffing.

sausage roll •n. a piece of sausage meat baked in a roll of pastry.

sauté /soh-tay/ (also **saute**) •adj. fried quickly in a little hot fat. •n. a dish cooked in such a way. •v. (**sautés, sautéing, sautéed** or **sautéd**) fry quickly in a little hot fat.
– ORIGIN French, 'jumped'.

Sauternes /soh-tern/ •n. a sweet white wine from Sauternes in the Bordeaux region of France.

savage •adj. 1 fierce and violent. 2 cruel and vicious: *a savage attack.* 3 uncivilized or primitive. •n. a member of a people seen as primitive and uncivilized. •v. (**savages, savaging, savaged**) 1 attack ferociously. 2 criticize harshly.
– DERIVATIVES **savagely** adv. **savagery** n.
– ORIGIN Old French *sauvage* 'wild'.

savannah (also **savanna**) •n. a grassy plain in tropical regions, with few trees.
– ORIGIN Spanish *sabana.*

savant /sav-uhnt/ •n. a very knowledge-able person.
– ORIGIN French, 'knowing'.

save[1] •v. (**saves, saving, saved**) 1 rescue from harm or danger. 2 store for future use. 3 store data in a computer. 4 avoid the need to use something up: *computers save time.* 5 guard against: *dust jackets save wear and tear on books.* 6 prevent an opponent from scoring a goal or point. 7 (in Christian use) save a soul from being damned. •n. esp. Football an act of preventing a goal.
– PHRASES **save the day** (or **situation**) provide a solution to a problem. **save someone's skin** (or **neck** or **bacon**) rescue someone from difficulty.
– ORIGIN Latin *salvare.*

save[2] •prep. & conj. formal except.
– ORIGIN Latin *salvus* 'safe'.

saveloy /sav-uh-loy/ •n. Brit. a spicy dried pork sausage.
– ORIGIN Italian *cervellata.*

saver •n. 1 a person who regularly saves money through a bank or scheme. 2 something that prevents a resource from being used up: *a space-saver.*

saving •n. 1 a reduction in money, time, or other resource used. 2 (**savings**) money saved. •adj. (in combination) preventing a resource from being wasted: *energy-saving.* •prep. except.

saving grace •n. a good quality which makes up for the faults of someone or something.

saviour (US **savior**) •n. 1 a person who saves someone or something from danger or harm. 2 (**the/our Saviour**) (in Christianity) God or Jesus.
– ORIGIN Old French *sauveour.*

savoir faire /sav-war fair/ •n. the ability to act appropriately in social situations.
– ORIGIN French, 'know how to do'.

savory •n. a plant used as a herb in cookery.
– ORIGIN Latin *satureia.*

savour (US **savor**) •v. 1 fully appreciate the taste of food or drink. 2 enjoy or appreciate something to the full. •n. a characteristic taste or smell.
– ORIGIN Old French.

savoury (US **savory**) •adj. 1 (of food) salty or spicy rather than sweet. 2 morally acceptable or respectable: *the less savoury aspects of the story.* •n. (pl. **savouries**) esp. Brit. a savoury snack.

savoy •n. a cabbage of a variety with wrinkled leaves.
– ORIGIN from *Savoy,* an area of SE France.

savvy informal •n. practical knowledge or understanding. •adj. (**savvier, savviest**) having common sense.
– ORIGIN black and pidgin English imitating Spanish *sabe usted* 'you know'.

saw[1] •n. 1 a hand tool for cutting hard

materials, having a long, thin jagged blade. **2** a power-driven cutting tool with a toothed rotating disc or moving band. • v. (**saws, sawing, sawed**; past part. Brit. **sawn** or N. Amer. **sawed**) **1** cut something with a saw. **2** make rapid movements like those of a saw.
– ORIGIN Old English.

saw² past of SEE¹.

saw³ • n. a proverb or wise saying.
– ORIGIN Old English.

sawdust • n. powdery particles of wood produced by sawing.

sawmill • n. a factory in which logs are sawn by machine.

sawn Brit. past part. of SAW¹.

sawn-off (N. Amer. **sawed-off**) • adj. (of a gun) having had the barrel shortened in order to be easier to handle and to have a wider field of fire.

sawtooth (also **sawtoothed**) • adj. shaped like the jagged projections on the blade of a saw.

sawyer • n. a person who saws timber.

sax • n. informal a saxophone.

saxifrage /saks-i-frayj/ • n. a low-growing plant of rocky or stony ground, with small red, white, or yellow flowers.
– ORIGIN Latin *saxifraga*.

Saxon • n. **1** a member of a Germanic people that conquered and settled in southern England in the 5th–6th centuries. **2** a person from modern Saxony in Germany. • adj. **1** relating to the Saxons who settled in England. **2** relating to modern Saxony.

saxophone /saks-uh-fohn/ • n. a metal wind instrument with a reed.
– DERIVATIVES **saxophonist** /saks-off-uh-nist/ n.
– ORIGIN named after the Belgian instrument-maker Adolphe *Sax*.

say • v. (**says, saying, said**) **1** speak words so as to communicate something. **2** (of a piece of writing or a symbol) convey information or instructions. **3** (of a clock or watch) indicate a time. **4** (**be said**) be claimed or reported. **5** (**say something for**) present a consideration in favour of: *he had nothing to say for himself.* **6** suggest something as an example or theory. • n. an opportunity to state your opinion or to influence events.
– PHRASES **go without saying** be obvious. **say the word** give permission or instructions.
– ORIGIN Old English.

saying • n. a well-known expression containing advice or wisdom.

say-so • n. (usu. **on someone's say-so**) informal the power to decide or allow something.

Sb • symb. the chemical element antimony.
– ORIGIN from Latin *stibium*.

Sc • symb. the chemical element scandium.

scab • n. **1** a crust that forms over a cut or wound as it heals. **2** a skin disease in animals causing itching and hair loss. **3** a plant disease caused by a fungus. **4** informal, derog. a person who refuses to take part in a strike.
– DERIVATIVES **scabby** adj.
– ORIGIN Old Norse.

scabbard /skab-berd/ • n. **1** a cover for the blade of a sword or dagger. **2** a cover for a gun or tool.
– ORIGIN Old French *escalberc*.

scabies /skay-beez/ • n. a skin disease with itching and small raised red spots, caused by a mite.
– ORIGIN Latin.

scabious /skay-bi-uhss/ • n. a plant with blue, pink, or white pincushion-shaped flowers.
– ORIGIN from Latin *scabiosa herba* 'rough, scabby plant'.

scabrous /skay-bruhss, skab-ruhss/ • adj. **1** rough and covered with scabs. **2** indecent or sordid: *scabrous and obscene publications.*
– ORIGIN Latin *scabrosus.*

scaffold • n. **1** a raised wooden platform used formerly for public executions. **2** a structure made using scaffolding.
– ORIGIN Old French *eschaffaut.*

scaffolding • n. a temporary structure made of wooden planks and metal poles, used while building, repairing, or cleaning a building.

scalable (also **scaleable**) • adj. **1** able to be climbed. **2** able to be changed in size or scale.
– DERIVATIVES **scalability** n.

scalar /skay-ler/ Math. & Physics • adj. having only magnitude, not direction. • n. a scalar quantity.
– ORIGIN Latin *scalaris.*

scalawag • n. US = SCALLYWAG.

scald • v. **1** burn with very hot liquid or steam. **2** heat a liquid to near boiling point. **3** dip something briefly in boiling water. • n. a burn caused by hot liquid or steam.
– ORIGIN Latin *excaldare.*

scale¹ • n. **1** each of the small overlapping plates protecting the skin of fish and reptiles. **2** a dry flake of skin. **3** limescale in a kettle, boiler, etc. **4** tartar formed on teeth. • v. (**scales, scaling, scaled**) remove scale or scales from.
– ORIGIN Old French *escale.*

scale² • n. **1** a range of values forming a

system for measuring or grading something: *a pay scale.* **2** a measuring instrument based on such a system. **3** relative size or extent: *he operated on a grand scale.* **4** a ratio of size in a map, model, drawing, or plan. **5** an arrangement of the notes in a system of music in ascending or descending order of pitch. •v. (**scales, scaling, scaled**) **1** climb up or over something high and steep. **2** represent something in measurements in proportion to the size of the original. **3** (**scale something back/ down** or **up**) reduce (or increase) something in size, number, or extent.
– PHRASES **to scale** reduced or enlarged in proportion to something.
– ORIGIN Latin *scala* 'ladder'.

scalene /skay-leen/ •adj. (of a triangle) having sides unequal in length.
– ORIGIN Greek *skalēnos* 'unequal'.

scales •pl. n. an instrument for weighing.
– ORIGIN Old Norse, 'bowl'.

scallion /skal-li-uhn/ •n. N. Amer. a spring onion.
– ORIGIN Old French *scaloun*.

scallop /skol-luhp, skal-luhp/ •n. **1** an edible shellfish with two hinged fan-shaped shells. **2** each of a series of small curves like the edge of a scallop shell, forming a decorative edging. •v. (**scallops, scalloping, scalloped**) decorate something with a series of small curves.
– ORIGIN Old French *escalope*.

scallywag (US also **scalawag**) •n. informal a mischievous person.

scalp •n. **1** the skin covering the top and back of the head. **2** (formerly, among American Indians) the scalp and the hair belonging to it cut away from an enemy's head as a battle trophy. •v. hist. take the scalp of an enemy.
– ORIGIN prob. Scandinavian.

scalpel •n. a knife with a small sharp blade, used by a surgeon.
– ORIGIN Latin *scalpellum* 'small chisel'.

scaly •adj. **1** covered in scales. **2** (of skin) dry and flaking.

scam •n. informal a dishonest scheme.

scamp •n. informal a mischievous person.
– ORIGIN from former *scamp* 'rob on the highway'.

scamper •v. (**scampers, scampering, scampered**) run with quick light steps. •n. an act of running with quick light steps.
– ORIGIN prob. from **SCAMP**.

scampi •pl. n. the tails of large prawns, fried in breadcrumbs.
– ORIGIN Italian.

scan •v. (**scans, scanning, scanned**) **1** look at something quickly in order to

find relevant features or information. **2** move a detector or beam across someone or something. **3** convert a document or picture into digital form for storing or processing on a computer. **4** analyse the metre of a line of verse. **5** (of verse) follow metrical rules. •n. **1** an act of scanning. **2** a medical examination using a scanner. **3** an image obtained by scanning.
– ORIGIN Latin *scandere* 'climb'.

scandal •n. **1** an action or event seen as wrong or unacceptable and causing general outrage. **2** outrage or gossip arising from this.
– ORIGIN Latin *scandalum* 'cause of offence'.

scandalize (or **scandalise**) •v. (**scandalizes, scandalizing, scandalized**) shock a person or group of people by acting in a way which does not conform to accepted or moral behaviour.

scandalous •adj. **1** causing general outrage by being wrong or illegal. **2** (of a state of affairs) shockingly bad.
– DERIVATIVES **scandalously** adv.

Scandinavian •adj. relating to Scandinavia. •n. **1** a person from Scandinavia. **2** the northern branch of the Germanic languages, made up of Danish, Norwegian, Swedish, Icelandic, and Faroese.

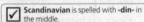 **Scandinavian** is spelled with **-din-** in the middle.

scandium /skan-di-uhm/ •n. a soft silvery-white metallic chemical element.
– ORIGIN Latin.

scanner •n. **1** a machine that examines the body through the use of radiation, ultrasound, etc. **2** a device that scans documents and converts them into digital data.

scansion /skan-sh'n/ •n. **1** the action of scanning a line of verse to determine its rhythm. **2** the rhythm of a line of verse.

scant •adj. hardly any; not enough: *she gave it scant attention.*
– ORIGIN Old Norse, 'short'.

scanty •adj. (**scantier, scantiest**) too little in quantity or amount. •pl. n. (**scanties**) informal women's skimpy knickers.
– DERIVATIVES **scantily** adv.

scapegoat •n. a person who is blamed for the wrongdoings or mistakes of other people. •v. make a scapegoat of someone.
– ORIGIN from former *scape* 'escape' + **GOAT**.

scapula /skap-yuu-luh/ •n. (pl. **scapulae** /skap-yuu-lee/ or **scapulas**) Anat. = **SHOULDER BLADE**.
– ORIGIN Latin.

scapular /skap-yuu-ler/ • adj. Anat. relating to the shoulder or shoulder blade. • n. a short cloak worn by monks, covering the shoulders.

scar¹ • n. **1** a mark left on the skin or within body tissue after the healing of a wound or burn. **2** a lasting effect left after an unpleasant experience. **3** a mark left at the point where a leaf or other part separates from a plant. • v. (**scars, scarring, scarred**) mark or be marked with a scar or scars.
– ORIGIN Greek *eskhara* 'scab'.

scar² • n. a steep high cliff or rock outcrop.
– ORIGIN Old Norse, 'low reef'.

scarab /ska-ruhb/ • n. **1** a large dung beetle, treated as sacred in ancient Egypt. **2** an ancient Egyptian gem in the form of a scarab.
– ORIGIN Greek *skarabeios*.

scarce • adj. **1** (of a resource) available in quantities that are too small to meet the demand for it. **2** rarely found.
– PHRASES **make yourself scarce** informal leave a place.
– DERIVATIVES **scarcity** n.
– ORIGIN Old French *escars*.

scarcely • adv. **1** only just. **2** only a very short time before. **3** used to suggest that something is unlikely: *they could scarcely all be wrong*.

scare • v. (**scares, scaring, scared**) **1** frighten or become frightened. **2** (**scare someone away/off**) drive or keep someone away by fear. • n. **1** a sudden attack of fright. **2** a period of general alarm: *she stopped eating meat because of a health scare*.
– ORIGIN Old Norse.

scarecrow • n. an object made to look like a person, set up to scare birds away from a field where crops are growing.

scarf¹ • n. (pl. **scarves** or **scarfs**) a length or square of fabric worn around the neck or head.
– ORIGIN prob. from Old French *escharpe* 'pilgrim's pouch'.

scarf² • v. join the ends of two pieces of timber or metal by cutting them so that they fit together by overlapping. • n. a joint made by scarfing.
– ORIGIN Old Norse.

scarify /ska-ri-fy/ • v. (**scarifies, scarifying, scarified**) **1** make shallow cuts in the skin. **2** rake out unwanted material from a lawn.
– DERIVATIVES **scarification** n.
– ORIGIN Old French *scarifier*.

scarlatina /skar-luh-tee-nuh/ • n. = SCARLET FEVER.
– ORIGIN Latin.

scarlet • n. a bright red colour.

– ORIGIN Latin *scarlata* 'brightly coloured cloth'.

scarlet fever • n. an infectious disease that particularly affects children, causing fever and a scarlet rash.

scarlet woman • n. esp. humorous a woman known for having many sexual relationships.

scarp • n. a very steep bank or slope.
– ORIGIN Italian *scarpa*.

scarper • v. (**scarpers, scarpering, scarpered**) Brit. informal run away.
– ORIGIN prob. from Italian *scappare* 'to escape'.

scarves pl. of SCARF¹.

scary • adj. (**scarier, scariest**) informal frightening.
– DERIVATIVES **scarily** adv.

scat • v. (**scats, scatting, scatted**) informal go away.
– ORIGIN perh. from SCATTER.

scathing /skay-thing/ • adj. harshly critical.
– ORIGIN Old Norse, 'harm, injure'.

scatological • adj. obsessed with excrement and excretion.
– DERIVATIVES **scatology** n.
– ORIGIN Greek *skōr* 'dung'.

scatter • v. (**scatters, scattering, scattered**) **1** throw a number of things in various random directions. **2** separate and move off in different directions. **3** (**be scattered**) occur or be found at various places.
– ORIGIN prob. from SHATTER.

scatterbrained • adj. disorganized and lacking in concentration.

scatty • adj. Brit. informal absent-minded and disorganized.
– ORIGIN from *scatterbrained*.

scavenge /ska-vinj/ • v. (**scavenges, scavenging, scavenged**) **1** search for and collect anything usable from waste. **2** (of an animal or bird) search for dead animals as food.

scavenger • n. a person or animal that scavenges.
– ORIGIN Old French *escauwer* 'inspect'.

SCE • abbrev. Scottish Certificate of Education.

scenario /si-nah-ri-oh/ • n. (pl. **scenarios**) **1** a possible sequence of future events. **2** a written outline of a film, novel, or stage work.
– ORIGIN Italian.

scene • n. **1** the place where an incident occurs or occurred. **2** a view or landscape as seen by a spectator. **3** an incident: *scenes of violence*. **4** a sequence of continuous action in a play, film, or opera. **5** a public display of emotion or anger. **6** a specified area of activity or

interest: *the literary scene.*
– PHRASES **behind the scenes** out of public view.
– ORIGIN Latin *scena.*

scenery •n. **1** the natural features of a landscape considered in terms of their appearance. **2** the painted background used to represent a place on a stage or film set.

scenic •adj. (of natural scenery) impressive or beautiful.

scent •n. **1** a pleasant smell. **2** perfume. **3** a trail indicated by the smell of an animal. •v. **1** give a pleasant scent to. **2** find or recognize something by using the sense of smell. **3** sense that something is about to happen: *the Premier scented victory.*
– DERIVATIVES **scented** adj.
– ORIGIN Latin *sentire* 'perceive, smell'.

sceptic /skep-tik/ (old use & N. Amer. **skeptic**) •n. a person who questions accepted beliefs or statements.
– DERIVATIVES **scepticism** n.
– ORIGIN Greek *skeptikos.*

sceptical (US **skeptical**) •adj. not easily convinced; having doubts.

sceptre /sep-ter/ (US **scepter**) •n. a staff carried by a king or queen on ceremonial occasions.
– ORIGIN Greek *skēptron.*

Schadenfreude /shah-d'n-froy-duh/ •n. pleasure felt at another person's mistake or misfortune.
– ORIGIN German.

schedule /shed-yool, sked-yool/ •n. **1** a plan for carrying out something, giving lists of intended events and times. **2** a timetable. •v. (**schedules, scheduling, scheduled**) plan for something to happen or for someone to do something.
– DERIVATIVES **scheduler** n.
– ORIGIN Latin *schedula* 'slip of paper'.

scheduled •adj. **1** forming part of a plan or timetable. **2** (of an airline or flight) forming part of a regular service rather than specially chartered.

scheduled caste •n. the official name given in India to the caste considered 'untouchable' in orthodox Hindu scriptures and practice, officially regarded as socially disadvantaged.

schema /skee-muh/ •n. (pl. **schemata** /skee-muh-tuh/ or **schemas**) tech. an outline of a plan or theory.
– ORIGIN Greek *skhēma* 'form, figure'.

schematic •adj. **1** (of a diagram) outlining the main features; simplified. **2** (of thought, ideas, etc.) simplistic and lacking originality.

schematize (or **schematise**) •v. (**schematizes, schematizing, schematized**) arrange or show in outline

or in a simplified form.

scheme •n. **1** a systematic plan for achieving a particular aim. **2** a secret or underhand plan; a plot. **3** an ordered system or pattern: *a classical rhyme scheme.* •v. (**schemes, scheming, schemed**) make secret plans.
– DERIVATIVES **schemer** n.
– ORIGIN Greek *skhēma* 'form'.

scherzo /skair-tsoh/ •n. (pl. **scherzos** or **scherzi** /skair-tsi/) a short lively movement in a symphony or sonata.
– ORIGIN Italian, 'jest'.

schism /si-z'm, ski-z'm/ •n. **1** a deep disagreement between two groups. **2** the formal separation of a Church into two Churches owing to differences in belief.
– ORIGIN Greek *skhisma* 'cleft'.

schismatic •adj. relating to deep disagreement or division.

schist /shist/ •n. a metamorphic rock which consists of layers of different minerals.
– ORIGIN Greek *skhistos* 'split'.

schizoid /skit-soyd/ •adj. having a mental condition similar to schizophrenia.

schizophrenia /skit-suh-free-ni-uh/ •n. a long-term mental disorder whose symptoms include inappropriate actions and feelings and withdrawal from reality into fantasy.
– ORIGIN Latin.

schizophrenic /skits-uh-fren-ik/ •adj. **1** suffering from schizophrenia. **2** informal having contradictory elements. •n. a schizophrenic person.

schmaltz /shmawlts/ •n. informal excessive sentimentality.
– DERIVATIVES **schmaltzy** adj.
– ORIGIN Yiddish.

schmuck /shmuk/ •n. N. Amer. informal a stupid person.
– ORIGIN Yiddish, 'penis'.

schnapps /shnaps/ •n. a strong alcoholic drink resembling gin.
– ORIGIN German *Schnaps* 'dram of liquor'.

schnitzel /shnit-z'l/ •n. a thin slice of veal, coated in breadcrumbs and fried.
– ORIGIN German, 'slice'.

scholar •n. **1** a person who studies a particular subject in detail. **2** a student who holds a scholarship.
– ORIGIN Latin *scholaris.*

scholarly •adj. relating to academic study or dedicated to learning and other academic activities.

scholarship •n. **1** serious academic study. **2** a grant made to support a student's education, awarded on the basis of achievement.

scholastic • adj. relating to schools and education.

scholasticism • n. the system of theology and philosophy taught in medieval universities.

school¹ • n. **1** an institution for educating children. **2** a day's work at school. **3** any institution at which instruction is given in a particular subject. **4** a department of a university. **5** a group of artists, writers, or philosophers sharing similar ideas.
• v. **1** formal or N. Amer. send someone to school; educate. **2** train someone to do something: *his instincts had schooled him to avoid them.*
– PHRASES **school of thought** a particular way of thinking.
– ORIGIN Greek *skholē* 'philosophy'.

school² • n. a large group of fish or sea mammals.
– ORIGIN German or Dutch *schôle*.

schoolchild • n. (pl. **schoolchildren**) a child attending school.

schooling • n. education received at school.

schoolmarm • n. esp. N. Amer. a school-mistress, especially one who is prim and strict.

schoolmaster (or **schoolmistress**) • n. esp. Brit. a teacher in a school.

schoolteacher • n. a person who teaches in a school.

schooner /skoo-ner/ • n. **1** a sailing ship with two or more masts. **2** Brit. a large glass for sherry.
– ORIGIN perh. from dialect *scun* 'skim along'.

schtum /shtuum/ • adj. var. of **SHTUM**.

sciatic /sy-at-ik/ • adj. **1** relating to the hip. **2** affecting the sciatic nerve.
– ORIGIN French *sciatique*.

sciatica • n. pain affecting the back, hip, and outer side of the leg, caused by pressure on the sciatic nerve.

sciatic nerve • n. a major nerve extending from the lower end of the spinal cord down the back of the thigh.

science • n. **1** the systematic study of the structure and behaviour of the physical and natural world through observation and experiment. **2** an organized body of knowledge on any subject.
– ORIGIN Latin *scientia*.

science fiction • n. fiction set in the future and dealing with imagined scientific and technological advances.

science park • n. an area devoted to scientific research or the development of science-based industries.

scientific • adj. **1** relating to or based on science. **2** systematic; methodical.

– DERIVATIVES **scientifically** adv.

scientist • n. a person who has expert knowledge of one or more of the natural or physical sciences.

Scientology • n. trademark a religious system based on the seeking of self-knowledge and spiritual fulfilment through courses of study and training.
– DERIVATIVES **Scientologist** n.
– ORIGIN Latin *scientia* 'knowledge'.

sci-fi • n. informal = **SCIENCE FICTION**.

scimitar /sim-i-ter/ • n. a short sword with a curved blade, used in Eastern countries.
– ORIGIN French *cimeterre* or Italian *scimitarra*.

scintilla /sin-til-luh/ • n. a tiny trace or amount: *not a scintilla of doubt.*
– ORIGIN Latin, 'spark'.

scintillate /sin-ti-layt/ • v. (**scintillates, scintillating, scintillated**) give off flashes of light; sparkle.
– ORIGIN Latin *scintillare* 'to sparkle'.

scintillating • adj. **1** brilliant and exciting. **2** sparkling.

scion /sy-uhn/ • n. **1** a young shoot or twig of a plant that is cut off to create a new plant. **2** a descendant of a notable family.
– ORIGIN Old French *ciun*.

scissors • pl. n. (also **a pair of scissors**) a tool for cutting cloth and paper, consisting of two crossing blades pivoted in the middle. • adj. (**scissor**) (of an action) in which two things move like a pair of scissors: *a scissor kick.*
– ORIGIN Old French *cisoires*.

sclerosis /skluh-**roh**-siss, skleer-**oh**-siss/ • n. Med. **1** abnormal hardening of body tissue. **2** (in full **multiple sclerosis**) a disease involving damage to the sheaths of nerve cells and leading to partial or complete paralysis.
– ORIGIN Greek *sklērōsis*.

scoff¹ • v. speak about something in a scornful way.
– ORIGIN perh. Scandinavian.

scoff² • v. informal eat quickly and greedily.
– ORIGIN Dutch *schoft* 'quarter of a day, meal'.

scold • v. angrily rebuke or criticize.
– ORIGIN prob. from Old Norse, 'person who writes and recites epic poems'.

sconce • n. a candle holder attached to a wall with an ornamental bracket.
– ORIGIN Old French *esconse* 'lantern'.

scone /skon, skohn/ • n. a small plain cake made from flour, fat, and milk.
– ORIGIN perh. from Dutch *schoonbroot* 'fine bread'.

scoop • n. **1** a utensil resembling a spoon, having a short handle and a deep bowl.

2 the bowl-shaped part of a digging machine or dredger. **3** informal a piece of news published or broadcast before other newspapers or broadcast stations know about it. • v. **1** pick something up with a scoop. **2** create a hollow. **3** pick up in a quick, smooth movement.
– ORIGIN German *schöpe* 'waterwheel bucket'.

scoot • v. informal go or leave somewhere quickly.

scooter • n. **1** (also **motor scooter**) a light two-wheeled motorcycle. **2** a child's toy consisting of a footboard mounted on two wheels and a long steering handle, moved by pushing one foot against the ground.

scope • n. **1** the extent of the area or subject matter that something deals with or to which it is relevant: *such questions go beyond the scope of this book.* **2** the opportunity or possibility for doing something.
– ORIGIN Greek *skopos* 'target'.

-scope • comb. form referring to an instrument for observing or examining: *telescope.*
– ORIGIN Greek *skopein* 'look at'.

scorbutic /skor-byoo-tik/ • adj. relating to or affected with scurvy.
– ORIGIN Latin *scorbutus* 'scurvy'.

scorch • v. **1** burn or become burnt on the surface or edges. **2** (as adj. **scorched**) dried out and withered as a result of extreme heat.
– ORIGIN perh. from Old Norse, 'be shrivelled'.

scorcher • n. informal a very hot day.

score • n. **1** the number of points, goals, runs, etc. achieved by a person or side in a game. **2** (pl. **score**) a group or set of twenty. **3** (**scores of**) a large number of. **4** the written music for a composition showing all the vocal and instrumental parts. • v. (**scores, scoring, scored**) **1** gain a point, goal, run, etc. in a game. **2** be worth a number of points. **3** record the score during a game. **4** cut a mark on a surface. **5** (**score something out/ through**) delete part of a piece of writing by drawing a line through it. **6** orchestrate or arrange a piece of music.
– PHRASES **settle a score** take revenge on someone.
– DERIVATIVES **scorer** n.
– ORIGIN Old Norse, 'notch, tally, twenty'.

scoreline • n. Brit. the score in a game or match.

scorn • n. the feeling that someone or something is worthless; contempt. • v. **1** express scorn for. **2** reject in a contemptuous way.

– DERIVATIVES **scornful** adj. **scornfully** adv.
– ORIGIN Old French *escarn*.

Scorpio • n. the eighth sign of the zodiac (the Scorpion), which the sun enters about 23 October.
– DERIVATIVES **Scorpian** n. & adj.
– ORIGIN Latin.

scorpion • n. a creature related to spiders, with pincers and a poisonous sting at the end of its tail.
– ORIGIN Greek *skorpios*.

Scot • n. a person from Scotland.

Scotch • n. (also **Scotch whisky**) whisky made in Scotland. • adj. dated = **SCOTTISH**.
– ORIGIN from **SCOTTISH**.

scotch • v. put an end to.
– ORIGIN perh. related to **SKATE**[1].

Scotch egg • n. Brit. a hard-boiled egg coated in sausage meat, rolled in breadcrumbs, and fried.

scot-free • adv. without suffering any punishment or injury.
– ORIGIN from the former word *scot* 'a tax'.

Scots • adj. = **SCOTTISH**. • n. the form of English used in Scotland.

Scots pine • n. a pine tree grown for timber and other products.

Scottish • adj. relating to Scotland or its people.

Scottish terrier • n. a small rough-haired breed of terrier.

scoundrel • n. a dishonest person.

scour[1] • v. clean by rubbing with something rough or a detergent.
– ORIGIN Old French *escurer*.

scour[2] • v. search a place thoroughly.

scourge /skerj/ • n. **1** a person or thing causing great trouble or suffering: *the scourge of mass unemployment.* **2** hist. a whip used for punishment. • v. (**scourges, scourging, scourged**) **1** cause great suffering to. **2** hist. whip a person or animal with a scourge.
– ORIGIN Old French *escorge*.

Scouse /skowss/ Brit. informal • n. **1** the dialect or accent of people from Liverpool. **2** (also **Scouser**) a person from Liverpool. • adj. relating to Liverpool.
– ORIGIN from *lobscouse*, a stew formerly eaten by sailors.

scout • n. **1** a person sent ahead of a main force to gather information about the enemy. **2** (also **Scout**) a member of the Scout Association, a boys' organization. **3** a person whose job is to find talented performers; a talent scout. **4** an instance

of scouting. •v. **1** make a detailed search to find or discover something. **2** act as a scout.
– ORIGIN Old French *escouter* 'listen'.

scow /skow/ •n. N. Amer. a flat-bottomed sailing dinghy.
– ORIGIN Dutch *schouw* 'ferry boat'.

scowl •n. an angry or bad-tempered expression. •v. frown in an angry or bad-tempered way.
– ORIGIN prob. Scandinavian.

scrabble •v. (**scrabbles, scrabbling, scrabbled**) **1** grope around with your fingers to find or hold on to something. **2** move quickly and awkwardly; scramble.
– ORIGIN Dutch *schrabbelen*.

scrag •v. (**scrags, scragging, scragged**) informal, esp. Brit. handle someone roughly.
– ORIGIN perh. from Scots and northern English *crag* 'neck'.

scraggy •adj. thin and bony.

scram •v. (**scrams, scramming, scrammed**) informal go away quickly.
– ORIGIN prob. from **SCRAMBLE**.

scramble •v. (**scrambles, scrambling, scrambled**) **1** move or make your way quickly and awkwardly, using your hands as well as your feet. **2** make something jumbled and confused. **3** put a broadcast transmission or telephone conversation into a form that can only be understood if received by a decoding device. **4** cook beaten eggs with a little liquid in a pan. **5** (of fighter aircraft) take off immediately in an emergency. **6** informal act in a hurried way: *firms scrambled to win contracts.* •n. **1** an act of moving quickly and awkwardly. **2** Brit. a motorcycle race over rough and hilly ground.

scrambler •n. a device for scrambling a broadcast transmission or telephone conversation.

scrap[1] •n. **1** a small piece or amount of something. **2** (**scraps**) bits of uneaten food left after a meal. **3** waste metal or other material that has been discarded for reprocessing. •v. (**scraps, scrapping, scrapped**) **1** remove something from use. **2** abolish or cancel a plan or law.
– ORIGIN Old Norse.

scrap[2] informal •n. a short fight or quarrel. •v. (**scraps, scrapping, scrapped**) have a short fight or quarrel.
– ORIGIN perh. from **SCRAPE**.

scrapbook •n. a book of blank pages for sticking cuttings, drawings, or pictures in.

scrape •v. (**scrapes, scraping, scraped**) **1** drag or pull a hard or sharp implement across a surface or object to remove dirt or waste matter. **2** rub against a rough or

hard surface. **3** just manage to achieve or pass: *he scrapes a living from a roadside stall.* •n. **1** an act or sound of scraping. **2** an injury or mark caused by scraping. **3** informal an embarrassing or difficult situation.
– ORIGIN Old English, 'scratch with the fingernails'.

scrappy •adj. (**scrappier, scrappiest**) disorganized, untidy, or incomplete.
– DERIVATIVES **scrappiness** n.

scrapyard •n. a place where waste material is collected.

scratch •v. **1** make a long mark or wound on a surface with something sharp. **2** rub a part of your body with your fingernails to relieve itching. **3** (of a bird or mammal) rake the ground with the beak or claws in search of food. **4** cross out writing. **5** withdraw from a competition. **6** cancel or abandon a plan or project. •n. **1** a mark or wound made by scratching. **2** an act of scratching. **3** informal a slight injury. •adj. put together from whatever is available: *a scratch squad.*
– PHRASES **from scratch** from the very beginning. **up to scratch** up to the required standard; satisfactory.

scratch card •n. a card with a section coated in a waxy substance which may be scraped away to reveal whether a prize has been won.

scratchy •adj. (**scratchier, scratchiest**) **1** causing scratching. **2** (of a voice or sound) rough.

scrawl •v. write in a hurried, careless way. •n. hurried, careless handwriting.
– ORIGIN prob. from **CRAWL**.

scrawny •adj. (**scrawnier, scrawniest**) unattractively thin and bony.
– ORIGIN from dialect *scranny*.

scream •v. **1** make a loud, piercing cry or sound expressing great emotion or pain. **2** move very rapidly. •n. **1** a screaming cry or sound. **2** (**a scream**) informal a very funny person or thing.
– ORIGIN perh. Dutch.

scree •n. a mass of small loose stones that form or cover a slope on a mountain.
– ORIGIN prob. from Old Norse, 'landslip'.

screech •n. a loud, harsh cry or sound. •v. make or move with a screech.
– DERIVATIVES **screechy** adj.

screech owl •n. Brit. = **BARN OWL**.

screed •n. **1** a long speech or piece of writing. **2** a layer of material applied to level a floor.
– ORIGIN prob. from **SHRED**.

screen •n. **1** an upright partition used to

divide a room, give shelter, or conceal something. **2** something that provides shelter or concealment. **3** the flat front surface of a television, VDU, or monitor, on which images and data are displayed. **4** a blank surface on which films are projected. **5** (**the screen**) films or television. • v. **1** conceal, protect, or shelter with a screen. **2** show a film or video or broadcast a television programme. **3** protect someone from something dangerous or unpleasant. **4** test someone for the presence or absence of a disease.
– ORIGIN Old French *escren*.

screenplay • n. the script of a film, including acting instructions and scene directions.

screen-print • v. force ink on to a surface through a screen of fine material so as to create a picture or pattern. • n. (**screen print**) a picture or design produced by screen-printing.

screen saver • n. Computing a program which replaces an unchanging screen display with a moving image to prevent damage to the phosphor.

screen test • n. a filmed test to judge whether an actor is suitable for a film role.

screenwriter • n. a person who writes the screenplay for a film.

screw • n. **1** a metal pin with a spiral thread running around it, used to join things together by being turned and pressed in. **2** a cylinder with a spiral ridge running round the outside that can be turned to seal an opening, apply pressure, adjust position, etc. **3** (also **screw propeller**) a ship's or aircraft's propeller. **4** informal, derog. a prison warder. • v. **1** fasten or tighten something with a screw or screws. **2** rotate something so as to attach or remove it by means of a spiral thread. **3** informal cheat or swindle.
– PHRASES **screw someone up** make someone emotionally disturbed. **screw something up 1** crush something into a tight mass. **2** informal make something go wrong.
– ORIGIN Old French *escroue* 'female screw, nut'.

screwball informal, esp. N. Amer. • n. a crazy or eccentric person. • adj. crazy; absurd.

screwdriver • n. a tool with a shaped tip that fits into the head of a screw to turn it.

screwy • adj. informal, esp. N. Amer. rather odd or eccentric.

scribble • v. (**scribbles, scribbling, scribbled**) **1** write or draw carelessly or hurriedly. **2** informal write for a living or as a hobby. • n. a piece of writing or a

picture produced carelessly or hurriedly.
– DERIVATIVES **scribbler** n.
– ORIGIN Latin *scribillare*.

scribe • n. hist. a person who copied out documents.
– DERIVATIVES **scribal** adj.
– ORIGIN Latin *scriba*.

scrim • n. strong, coarse fabric used for heavy-duty lining or upholstery.

scrimmage • n. a confused struggle or fight.
– ORIGIN from SKIRMISH.

scrimp • v. be very careful with money; economize.
– ORIGIN Scots, 'meagre'.

scrip • n. a certificate relating to an issue of additional shares to shareholders in proportion to the shares they already hold.
– ORIGIN short for *subscription receipt*.

script • n. **1** the written text of a play, film, or broadcast. **2** handwriting as distinct from print. **3** Brit. a candidate's written answers in an exam. • v. write a script for.
– ORIGIN Latin *scriptum*.

scriptural • adj. relating to the Bible.

scripture (also **scriptures**) • n. **1** the sacred writings of Christianity contained in the Bible. **2** the sacred writings of another religion.
– ORIGIN Latin *scriptura* 'writings'.

scriptwriter • n. a person who writes a script.
– DERIVATIVES **scriptwriting** n.

scrivener /skriv-uh-ner/ • n. hist. a person who made their living by writing out documents; a clerk.
– ORIGIN Old French *escrivein*.

scrofula /skrof-yuu-luh/ • n. hist. a disease characterized by swollen glands.
– DERIVATIVES **scrofulous** adj.
– ORIGIN Latin *scrofa* 'breeding sow' (said to be subject to the disease).

scroll • n. **1** a roll of parchment or paper for writing or painting on. **2** an ornamental design or carving resembling a partly unrolled scroll. • v. move displayed writing or graphics on a computer screen in order to view different parts of them.
– ORIGIN from former *scrow* 'roll'.

scroll bar • n. a long thin section at the edge of a computer display by which material can be scrolled using a mouse.

Scrooge • n. a person who is mean with money.
– ORIGIN from Ebenezer *Scrooge*, a miser in Charles Dickens's story *A Christmas Carol*.

scrotum /skroh-tuhm/ • n. (pl. **scrota** /skroh-tuh/ or **scrotums**) the pouch of

skin containing the testicles.
- DERIVATIVES **scrotal** adj.
- ORIGIN Latin.

scrounge • v. (**scrounges, scrounging, scrounged**) informal try to get something from other people without having to pay or work for it.
- PHRASES **on the scrounge** trying to get something without working or paying for it.
- DERIVATIVES **scrounger** n.
- ORIGIN from dialect *scrunge* 'steal'.

scrub¹ • v. (**scrubs, scrubbing, scrubbed**) **1** rub hard so as to clean. **2** informal cancel or abandon. • n. an act of scrubbing.
- ORIGIN prob. from German or Dutch *schrobben, schrubben*.

scrub² • n. **1** vegetation consisting mainly of brushwood or stunted trees. **2** land covered with such vegetation.
- DERIVATIVES **scrubby** adj.
- ORIGIN from **SHRUB**.

scrubber • n. **1** a brush for scrubbing. **2** Brit. informal, derog. a woman who has many brief sexual relationships.

scruff¹ • n. the back of a person's or animal's neck.
- ORIGIN from dialect *scuff*.

scruff² • n. Brit. informal a scruffy person.
- ORIGIN from **SCURF**.

scruffy • adj. (**scruffier, scruffiest**) shabby and untidy or dirty.
- DERIVATIVES **scruffiness** n.

scrum • n. **1** Rugby a formation of players in which the forwards of each team push against each other with heads down and the ball is thrown in between them. **2** Brit. informal a disorderly crowd.
- ORIGIN from **SCRUMMAGE**.

scrummage • n. = **SCRUM**.
- ORIGIN from **SCRIMMAGE**.

scrummy • adj. informal delicious.
- ORIGIN from **SCRUMPTIOUS**.

scrump • v. Brit. informal steal fruit from an orchard or garden.
- ORIGIN from dialect, 'withered apple'.

scrumptious • adj. informal very delicious or attractive.

scrumpy • n. Brit. rough strong cider, as made in the west of England.

scrunch • v. **1** make a loud crunching noise. **2** crush or squeeze something into a tight mass. • n. a loud crunching noise.

scruple • n. a feeling of doubt as to whether an action is morally right. • v. (**scruples, scrupling, scrupled**) (**not scruple to do**) not hesitate to do something, even if it may be wrong.
- ORIGIN Latin *scrupus* 'anxiety'.

scrupulous • adj. **1** very careful and

thorough. **2** very concerned to avoid doing wrong.
- DERIVATIVES **scrupulously** adv.

scrutineer • n. Brit. a person who ensures that an election is organized correctly.

scrutinize (or **scrutinise**)
• v. (**scrutinizes, scrutinizing, scrutinized**) examine closely and thoroughly.

scrutiny • n. (pl. **scrutinies**) close and critical examination.
- ORIGIN Latin *scrutinium*.

scuba /skoo-buh/ • n. an aqualung.
- ORIGIN from the initial letters of *self-contained underwater breathing apparatus*.

scuba-diving • n. the sport or pastime of swimming underwater using a scuba.

scud • v. (**scuds, scudding, scudded**) move fast because driven by the wind.

scuff • v. **1** scrape a shoe or other object against something. **2** mark something by scraping it against something. **3** drag your feet when walking. • n. a mark made by scuffing.

scuffle • n. a short, confused fight or struggle. • v. (**scuffles, scuffling, scuffled**) join together in a scuffle.
- ORIGIN prob. Scandinavian.

scull • n. **1** each of a pair of small oars used by a single rower. **2** an oar placed over the back of a boat to propel it with a side to side motion. **3** a light, narrow boat propelled with a scull or a pair of sculls. • v. propel a boat with sculls.
- DERIVATIVES **sculler** n.

scullery • n. (pl. **sculleries**) a small room at the back of a house, used for washing dishes and other dirty household work.
- ORIGIN Old French *escuelerie*.

scullion /skul-li-uhn/ • n. hist. a servant who did the least-skilled kitchen tasks.
- ORIGIN perh. from **SCULLERY**.

sculpt • v. make something by carving stone or wood.

sculptor • n. (fem. **sculptress**) an artist who makes sculptures.

sculpture • n. **1** the art of making three-dimensional figures and shapes by carving stone or wood or casting metal. **2** a work of such a kind. • v. (**sculptures, sculpturing, sculptured**) **1** make something by sculpting. **2** (as adj. **sculptured**) having strong, smooth curves.
- DERIVATIVES **sculptural** adj.
- ORIGIN Latin *sculpere* 'carve'.

scum • n. **1** a layer of dirt or froth on the surface of a liquid. **2** informal a worthless person or group of people.
- DERIVATIVES **scummy** adj.
- ORIGIN German or Dutch *schūm*.

S

scumbag •n. informal an unpleasant person.

scupper[1] •n. a hole in a ship's side to allow water to run away from the deck.
– ORIGIN perh. from Old French *escopir* 'to spit'.

scupper[2] •v. (**scuppers, scuppering, scuppered**) esp. Brit. 1 informal prevent from working or succeeding. 2 sink a ship deliberately.

scurf •n. flakes on the surface of the skin, occurring as dandruff.
– ORIGIN Old English, 'cut to shreds'.

scurrility •n. (pl. **scurrilities**) the quality of being insulting and abusive.

scurrilous /skur-ri-luhss/ •adj. rude and insulting; slanderous.
– ORIGIN Latin *scurrilus*.

scurry •v. (**scurries, scurrying, scurried**) move hurriedly with short quick steps. •n. a situation of hurried and confused movement.
– ORIGIN from HURRY.

scurvy •n. a disease caused by a lack of vitamin C, characterized by bleeding gums and the opening of previously healed wounds.
– ORIGIN from SCURF.

scut •n. the short tail of a hare, rabbit, or deer.

scutter •v. (**scutters, scuttering, scuttered**) esp. Brit. move hurriedly with short steps.
– ORIGIN perh. from SCUTTLE[2].

scuttle[1] •n. a metal container with a lid and a handle, used to store coal for a domestic fire.
– ORIGIN Latin *scutella* 'dish'.

scuttle[2] •v. (**scuttles, scuttling, scuttled**) run with short quick steps.
– ORIGIN prob. from SCUD.

scuttle[3] •v. (**scuttles, scuttling, scuttled**) 1 deliberately cause a scheme to fail. 2 sink your own ship deliberately.
– ORIGIN perh. from Spanish *escotilla* 'hatchway'.

scuzzy •adj. informal dirty and unpleasant.
– ORIGIN prob. from *disgusting*.

scythe •n. a tool used for cutting crops such as grass or corn, with a long curved blade at the end of a long pole. •v. (**scythes, scything, scythed**) 1 cut with a scythe. 2 move through something rapidly and forcefully.
– ORIGIN Old English.

SDLP •abbrev. (in Northern Ireland) Social Democratic and Labour Party.

SE •abbrev. 1 south-east. 2 south-eastern.

Se •symb. the chemical element selenium.

sea •n. 1 the large continuous area of salt water that surrounds the land masses of the earth. 2 a particular area of this. 3 a vast expanse or quantity: *a sea of faces*.
– PHRASES **at sea 1** sailing on the sea. **2** confused; uncertain.
– ORIGIN Old English.

sea anemone •n. a sea creature with a tube-shaped body which bears a ring of stinging tentacles around the mouth.

sea bass •n. a sea fish resembling the freshwater perch.

seabed •n. the ground under the sea.

seabird •n. a bird that lives near the sea.

seaboard •n. a region bordering the sea.

seaborgium /see-borg-i-uhm/ •n. a very unstable chemical element made by high-energy atomic collisions.
– ORIGIN named after the American nuclear chemist Glenn Seaborg.

sea change •n. a great and very noticeable change in a situation.
– ORIGIN from Shakespeare's *The Tempest*.

sea cow •n. a manatee (a mammal that lives in the sea).

sea dog •n. informal an old or experienced sailor.

seafaring •adj. travelling by sea. •n. travel by sea.
– DERIVATIVES **seafarer** n.

seafood •n. shellfish and sea fish as food.

seafront •n. the part of a coastal town next to and facing the sea.

seagoing •adj. 1 (of a ship) suitable for voyages on the sea. 2 relating to sea travel.

seagull •n. a gull.

sea horse •n. a small sea fish with an upright posture and a head and neck suggestive of a horse.

seal[1] •n. 1 a device or substance used to join two things together or to prevent anything from passing between them. 2 a piece of wax with a design stamped into it, attached to a document as a guarantee that it is genuine. 3 a confirmation or guarantee: *the scheme has the government's seal of approval*. •v. 1 fasten or close securely. 2 (**seal something off**) isolate an area by preventing entrance to and exit from it. 3 apply a coating to a surface to prevent fluid passing through it. 4 make something definite; conclude.
– ORIGIN Old French *seel*.

seal[2] •n. a sea mammal with flippers and a streamlined body.
– ORIGIN Old English.

sealant •n. material used to make something airtight or watertight.

sea level •n. the level of the sea's surface, used in calculating the height of geographical features.

sealing wax •n. a mixture of shellac

and rosin with turpentine, used to make seals.

sea lion • n. a large seal of the Pacific Ocean, the male of which has a mane on the neck and shoulders.

seam • n. **1** a line where two pieces of fabric are sewn together. **2** a line where the edges of two pieces of wood or other material touch each other. **3** an underground layer of a mineral such as coal or gold.
– DERIVATIVES **seamed** adj.
– ORIGIN Old English.

seaman • n. (pl. **seamen**) a sailor, especially one below the rank of officer.

sea mile • n. a nautical mile.

seamless • adj. smooth and without seams or obvious joins.
– DERIVATIVES **seamlessly** adv.

seamstress • n. a woman who sews, especially as a job.

seamy • adj. (**seamier**, **seamiest**) immoral and unpleasant; sordid.

seance /say-onss/ • n. a meeting at which people attempt to make contact with the spirits of dead people.
– ORIGIN French.

seaplane • n. an aircraft with floats or skis instead of wheels, designed to land on and take off from water.

seaport • n. a town or city with a harbour for seagoing ships.

sear • v. **1** burn or scorch something with a sudden intense heat. **2** (of pain) be experienced as a sudden burning sensation.
– ORIGIN Old English.

search • v. **1** try to find by looking carefully and thoroughly. **2** examine something thoroughly in order to find something or someone. **3** look for information in a computer network or database by using a search engine. **4** (as adj. **searching**) investigating very deeply: *searching questions.*
• n. an act of searching.
– DERIVATIVES **searchable** adj. **searcher** n.
– ORIGIN Old French *cerchier.*

search engine • n. a computer program that searches for and identifies specified items in a database, used especially for searching the Internet.

searchlight • n. a powerful outdoor electric light with a movable beam.

search party • n. a group of people organized to look for someone or something.

search warrant • n. a legal document authorizing a police officer or other official to enter and search premises.

sea salt • n. salt produced by the evaporation of seawater.

seascape • n. a view or picture of an expanse of sea.

seashell • n. the shell of a marine shellfish.

seashore • n. an area of sandy or rocky land next to the sea.

seasick • adj. suffering from nausea caused by the motion of a ship at sea.
– DERIVATIVES **seasickness** n.

seaside • n. a beach area or holiday resort.

season • n. **1** each of the four divisions of the year (spring, summer, autumn, and winter) marked by particular weather and daylight hours. **2** a period of the year with particular weather, or when a particular activity is done: *the cricket season.* • v. **1** add salt, herbs, or spices to food. **2** make something more interesting. **3** keep wood so as to dry it for use as timber. **4** (as adj. **seasoned**) experienced: *a seasoned traveller.*
– PHRASES **in season 1** (of a fruit or vegetable) plentiful and ready to eat. **2** (of a female mammal) ready to mate.
– ORIGIN Old French *seson.*

seasonable • adj. usual for or appropriate to a particular season.

seasonal • adj. **1** relating to or typical of a particular season of the year. **2** changing according to the season: *seasonal rainfall.*
– DERIVATIVES **seasonally** adv.

seasoning • n. salt, herbs, or spices added to food to improve the flavour.

season ticket • n. a ticket allowing travel within a particular period or admission to a series of events.

seat • n. **1** a thing made or used for sitting on. **2** the part of a chair for sitting on. **3** a sitting place for a passenger in a vehicle or for a member of an audience. **4** a person's buttocks. **5** a place in an elected parliament or council. **6** Brit. a parliamentary constituency. **7** a site or location. **8** Brit. a large country house belonging to an aristocratic family.
• v. **1** arrange for someone to sit somewhere. **2** (**seat yourself** or **be seated**) sit down. **3** (of a place) have enough seats for.
– DERIVATIVES **seating** n.
– ORIGIN Old Norse.

seat belt • n. a belt used to secure someone in the seat of a motor vehicle or aircraft.

sea urchin • n. a sea animal which has a shell covered in spines.

sea wall • n. a wall built to prevent the sea advancing on to an area of land.

seaweed • n. large algae growing in the sea or on rocks at the edge of the sea.

S

seaworthy •adj. (of a boat) in a good enough condition to sail on the sea.
– DERIVATIVES **seaworthiness** n.

sebaceous /si-bay-shuhss/ •adj. tech. producing oil or fat.
– ORIGIN Latin *sebaceus*.

sec¹ •abbrev. secant.

sec² •n. informal a very short time.

secant /see-kuhnt, sek-uhnt/ •n. 1 Math. (in a right-angled triangle) the ratio of the hypotenuse to the shorter side adjacent to an acute angle. 2 Geom. a straight line that cuts a curve in two or more parts.
– ORIGIN Latin *secare* 'to cut'.

secateurs /sek-uh-terz, sek-uh-terz/ •pl. n. Brit. a pair of pruning clippers for use with one hand.
– ORIGIN French, 'cutters'.

secede /si-seed/ •v. (**secedes, seceding, seceded**) withdraw formally from a federation of states or other alliance.
– ORIGIN Latin *secedere* 'withdraw'.

secession /si-sesh-uhn/ •n. the action of withdrawing from a federation or alliance.

secluded •adj. 1 (of a place) sheltered and private. 2 (of a person's life) having little contact with other people.
– ORIGIN Latin *secludere* 'keep away from others'.

seclusion •n. the state of being private and away from other people.

second¹ /sek-uhnd/ •ordinal number 1 that is number two in a sequence; 2nd. 2 lower in position, rank, or importance. 3 (**seconds**) goods of less than perfect quality. 4 (**seconds**) informal a second helping of food at a meal. 5 secondly. 6 a person assisting a contestant in a boxing match or duel. 7 Brit. a place in the second highest grade in an exam for a degree. •v. 1 formally support a nomination or resolution before voting or discussion. 2 express agreement with.
– ORIGIN Latin *secundus*.

second² /sek-uhnd/ •n. 1 the unit of time in the SI system, equal to one sixtieth of a minute. 2 informal a very short time. 3 (also **arc second** or **second of arc**) a measurement of an angle equal to one sixtieth of a minute.
– ORIGIN from Latin *secunda minuta* 'second minute'.

second³ /si-kond/ •v. Brit. temporarily move a worker to another position or role.
– DERIVATIVES **secondment** n.
– ORIGIN from French *en second* 'in the second rank (of officers)'.

secondary •adj. 1 coming after or less important than something primary. 2 relating to education for children from the age of eleven to sixteen or eighteen.
– DERIVATIVES **secondarily** adv.

secondary sexual characteristics •pl. n. physical characteristics developed at puberty which distinguish between the sexes but are not involved in reproduction.

second best •adj. next after the best. •n. a less good alternative.

second class •n. 1 a set of people or things grouped together as the second best. 2 the second-best accommodation in an aircraft, train, or ship. 3 Brit. the second-highest division in the results of the exams for a university degree. •adj. & adv. relating to the second class.

Second Coming •n. (in Christian belief) the expected return of Christ to Earth at the Last Judgement.

second-degree •adj. (of burns) causing blistering but not permanent scars.

second-guess •v. predict someone's actions or thoughts by guesswork.

second-hand •adj. & adv. 1 (of goods) having had a previous owner. 2 learned from other people rather than from your own experience.

secondly •adv. in the second place; second.

second name •n. Brit. a surname.

second nature •n. a habit that has become instinctive.

second person •n. see PERSON (sense 3).

second-rate •adj. of poor quality.

second sight •n. the supposed ability to sense future or distant events.

second string •n. (often in phr. **a second string to one's bow**) an alternative resource or course of action in case another one fails.

second thoughts •pl. n. a change of opinion or decision reached after reconsideration.

second wind •n. fresh energy enabling you to continue with an activity after being tired.

secret •adj. 1 kept from or not known by other people. 2 fond of having or keeping secrets. •n. 1 a thing that other people do not know about. 2 a method of achieving something that is not generally known: *the secret of a happy marriage is compromise*. 3 a thing that is not properly understood: *the secrets of the universe*.
– DERIVATIVES **secrecy** n. **secretly** adv.
– ORIGIN Latin *secretus* 'separate'.

secret agent •n. a spy acting for a country.

secretariat /sek-ri-tair-i-uht/ •n. a governmental administrative office or department.

secretary •n. (pl. **secretaries**) **1** a person employed to type letters, make arrangements, and keep records. **2** a person who carries out these tasks for a society or other organization. **3** the chief assistant of a UK government minister.
– DERIVATIVES **secretarial** adj.
– ORIGIN Latin *secretarius* 'confidential officer'.

> ☑ Spell **secretary** with an **e** after the **r**: the ending is **-ary**.

secretary bird •n. a long-legged African bird of prey, with a crest resembling a quill pen stuck behind the ear.

Secretary General •n. (pl. **Secretaries General**) the chief administrator of some organizations.

Secretary of State •n. **1** (in the UK) the head of a major government department. **2** (in the US) the head of the State Department, responsible for foreign affairs.

secrete[1] /si-kreet/ •v. (**secretes, secreting, secreted**) (of a cell, gland, or organ) produce and discharge a substance.
– DERIVATIVES **secretory** adj.

secrete[2] /si-kreet/ •v. (**secretes, secreting, secreted**) conceal or hide something.
– ORIGIN from SECRET.

secretion •n. **1** a process by which substances are produced and discharged from a cell, gland, or organ. **2** a substance discharged in such a way.
– ORIGIN Latin, 'separation'.

secretive •adj. inclined to hide your feelings and intentions or to withhold information.
– DERIVATIVES **secretively** adv.

secret police •n. a police force working in secret against a government's political opponents.

secret service •n. a government department concerned with spying.

sect •n. a group of people with different religious beliefs from those of a larger group to which they belong.
– ORIGIN Latin *secta* 'following, faction'.

sectarian •adj. relating to a sect or sects.
– DERIVATIVES **sectarianism** n.

section •n. **1** any of the parts into which something is divided or from which it is made up. **2** a distinct group within a larger body of people or things. **3** the shape resulting from cutting a solid by or along a plane. **4** a representation of the internal structure of something as if it has been cut through. •v. divide

something into sections.
– DERIVATIVES **sectional** adj.
– ORIGIN Latin.

sector •n. **1** an area or part that is distinct from others. **2** a distinct part of an economy, society, or field of activity. **3** a part of a circle between two lines drawn from its centre to its circumference.
– ORIGIN Latin, 'cutter'.

secular /sek-yuu-ler/ •adj. **1** not religious or spiritual. **2** (of Christian clergy) not belonging to or living in a monastic or other order.
– DERIVATIVES **secularism** n.
– ORIGIN Latin *saecularis* 'relating to an age or period'.

secure •adj. **1** certain to remain safe. **2** fixed or fastened so as not to give way, become loose, or be lost. **3** feeling free from fear or anxiety. •v. (**secures, securing, secured**) **1** protect against danger or threat. **2** fix or fasten something in a secure way. **3** succeed in obtaining.
– DERIVATIVES **securely** adv.
– ORIGIN Latin *securus*.

security •n. (pl. **securities**) **1** the state of being secure. **2** the safety of a state or organization from terrorism and similar activity. **3** a valuable item given as a guarantee that you will repay a loan. **4** a certificate proving that you own stocks or bonds.

sedan /si-dan/ •n. **1** hist. an enclosed chair carried between two horizontal poles. **2** N. Amer. a car for four or more people.
– ORIGIN perh. from Latin *sella* 'saddle'.

sedate[1] •adj. **1** calm and unhurried. **2** respectable and rather dull.
– DERIVATIVES **sedately** adv.
– ORIGIN Latin *sedare* 'settle'.

sedate[2] •v. (**sedates, sedating, sedated**) give someone a drug to calm them or make them sleep.

sedation •n. the administering of a drug to calm someone or make them sleep.
– ORIGIN Latin.

sedative •adj. making someone calm or sleepy. •n. a drug that makes you calm or sleepy.

sedentary /sed-uhn-tri/ •adj. **1** sitting; seated. **2** tending to sit down a lot; taking little exercise. **3** tending to stay in the same place for much of the time.
– ORIGIN Latin *sedentarius*.

sedge •n. a grass-like plant with triangular stems and small flowers, growing in wet ground.
– ORIGIN Old English.

sediment •n. **1** matter that settles to the bottom of a liquid. **2** Geol. material carried in particles by water or wind and

deposited on land or the seabed.
– DERIVATIVES **sedimentation** n.
– ORIGIN Latin *sedimentum* 'settling'.

sedimentary • adj. (of rock) formed from sediment.

sedition • n. actions or speech urging rebellion against the authority of a state or ruler.
– DERIVATIVES **seditious** adj.
– ORIGIN Latin.

seduce • v. (**seduces, seducing, seduced**) **1** tempt someone into sexual activity. **2** persuade someone to do something unwise.
– DERIVATIVES **seducer** n. **seduction** n. **seductress** n.
– ORIGIN Latin *seducere* 'lead aside'.

seductive • adj. tempting and attractive.
– DERIVATIVES **seductively** adv.

sedulous /sed-yuu-luhss/ • adj. showing dedication and great care.
– DERIVATIVES **sedulously** adv.
– ORIGIN Latin *sedulus* 'zealous'.

sedum /see-duhm/ • n. a plant of a large group having fleshy leaves.
– ORIGIN Latin.

see[1] • v. (**sees, seeing, saw;** past part. **seen**) **1** become aware of someone or something with the eyes. **2** experience or witness. **3** work something out after thinking or from information: *I saw that he was right.* **4** think of someone or something in a particular way. **5** meet someone you know socially or by chance. **6** meet regularly as a boyfriend or girlfriend. **7** consult a specialist or professional. **8** give someone an interview or consultation. **9** guide or lead to a place: *don't bother seeing me out.*
– PHRASES **see someone off** go with a person who is leaving to their point of departure. **see through** realize the true nature of. **see something through** carry on with an undertaking until it is completed. **see to** deal with something or ensure that it is done.
– ORIGIN Old English.

see[2] • n. the district or position of a bishop or archbishop.
– ORIGIN Latin *sedes* 'seat'.

seed • n. **1** a small object produced by a flowering plant that is capable of developing into another such plant. **2** the beginning of a feeling, process, or condition. **3** old use a man's semen. **4** any of the stronger competitors in a sports tournament who have been kept apart from playing each other in the early rounds. • v. **1** sow land with seeds. **2** remove the seeds from. **3** (**be seeded**) be made a seed in a tournament. **2** deteriorate.
– ORIGIN Old English.

seedbed • n. a bed of fine soil in which seeds are grown.

seed leaf • n. a cotyledon.

seedling • n. a young plant raised from seed.

seed money • n. money provided to start up a project.

seedy • adj. (**seedier, seediest**) unpleasant because dirty or immoral.
– DERIVATIVES **seediness** n.

seeing • conj. (**seeing as/that**) because; since.

seek • v. (**seeks, seeking, sought**) **1** try to find or obtain. **2** (**seek someone/thing out**) search for and find someone or something. **3** (**seek to do**) try or want to do. **4** ask for.
– DERIVATIVES **seeker** n.
– ORIGIN Old English.

seem • v. **1** give the impression of being. **2** (**cannot seem to do**) be unable to do, despite having tried.
– ORIGIN Old Norse, 'appropriate'.

seeming • adj. appearing to be real or true; apparent.
– DERIVATIVES **seemingly** adv.

seemly • adj. respectable or in good taste.
– DERIVATIVES **seemliness** n.
– ORIGIN Old Norse, 'fitting'.

seen past part. of SEE[1].

seep • v. (of a liquid) flow or leak slowly through a substance.
– ORIGIN perh. from Old English, 'to soak'.

seepage /see-pij/ • n. the slow escape of a liquid or gas through a material.

seer /rhymes with beer/ • n. a person supposedly able to see visions of the future.

seersucker • n. a fabric with a puckered surface.
– ORIGIN from Persian, 'milk and sugar' (with reference to the stripes of the fabric).

see-saw • n. a long plank balanced on a fixed support, on each end of which children sit and move up and down by pushing the ground with their feet. • v. repeatedly change between two states or positions.
– ORIGIN from SAW[1].

seethe • v. (**seethes, seething, seethed**) **1** be filled with great but unexpressed anger. **2** be crowded with people or things. **3** (of a liquid) boil or churn as if boiling.
– ORIGIN Old English.

see-through • adj. transparent or semi-transparent.

segment • n. /seg-muhnt/ **1** each of the parts into which something is divided.

2 Geom. a part of a circle cut off by a chord, or a part of a sphere cut off by a plane. • v. /seg-**ment**/ divide something into segments.
– DERIVATIVES **segmental** adj. **segmentation** n.
– ORIGIN Latin *segmentum*.

segregate /seg-ri-gayt/ • v. (**segregates**, **segregating**, **segregated**) **1** set people or things apart from the rest or from each other. **2** separate people along racial, sexual, or religious lines.
– ORIGIN Latin *segregare* 'separate from the flock'.

segregation • n. **1** the action of segregating people or things. **2** the enforced separation of different racial groups in a place.

segue /seg-way/ • v. (**segues**, **segueing** or **seguing**) (in music and film) move without interruption from one song or scene to another. • n. an instance of this.
– ORIGIN Italian, 'follows'.

seine /rhymes with rain/ • n. a fishing net which hangs vertically in the water with floats at the top and weights at the bottom.
– ORIGIN Greek *sagēnē*.

seismic /syz-mik/ • adj. **1** relating to earthquakes. **2** very great in size or effect: *seismic pressures affecting American society*.
– DERIVATIVES **seismically** adv.
– ORIGIN Greek *seismos* 'earthquake'.

seismograph /syz-muh-grahf/ • n. an instrument that measures and records details of earthquakes.

seismology /syz-mol-uh-ji/ • n. the branch of science concerned with earthquakes.
– DERIVATIVES **seismologist** n.

seize • v. (**seized**, **seizing**, **seized**) **1** take hold of suddenly and forcibly. **2** take possession of something by force. **3** (of the police or another authority) officially take possession of. **4** take an opportunity eagerly. **5** (**seize on**) take eager advantage of. **6** (often **seize up**) (of a machine or part) become jammed.
– ORIGIN from Latin *ad proprium sacire* 'claim as your own'.

> ☑ **seize** is an exception to the usual rule of *i* before *e* except after *c*.

seizure • n. **1** the action of seizing. **2** a stroke or an epileptic fit.

seldom • adv. not often.
– ORIGIN Old English.

select • v. carefully choose as being the best or most suitable. • adj. **1** carefully chosen as being among the best. **2** used by or made up of wealthy or sophisti-

cated people: *the opera was seen by a select audience*.
– DERIVATIVES **selectable** adj.
– ORIGIN Latin *seligere* 'choose'.

select committee • n. a small parliamentary committee appointed for a special purpose.

selection • n. **1** the action of selecting. **2** a number of selected things. **3** a range of things from which a person can choose something.

selective • adj. **1** relating to selection. **2** tending to choose carefully. **3** (of a process or agent) affecting some things and not others.
– DERIVATIVES **selectively** adv. **selectivity** n.

selector • n. **1** Brit. a person appointed to select a team in a sport. **2** a device for selecting a particular function of a machine.

selenium /si-lee-ni-uhm/ • n. a grey crystalline non-metallic chemical element with semiconducting properties.
– ORIGIN Greek *selēnē* 'moon'.

self • n. (pl. **selves**) **1** a person's essential being that distinguishes them from other people. **2** a person's particular nature or personality: *he was back to his old self*. • pron. (pl. **selves**) yourself.
– ORIGIN Old English.

self- • comb. form relating to, towards, or by yourself or itself: *self-adhesive*.

self-absorbed • adj. obsessed with your own emotions, interests, or situation.
– DERIVATIVES **self-absorption** n.

self-abuse • n. **1** behaviour which causes harm to yourself. **2** dated masturbation.

self-addressed • adj. (of an envelope) addressed to yourself.

self-adhesive • adj. sticking without needing to be moistened.

self-appointed • adj. having taken up a job or title without the approval of other people.

self-assembly • n. the construction of a piece of furniture from materials sold in kit form.

self-assertion • n. confidence in expressing your views.
– DERIVATIVES **self-assertive** adj.

self-assessment • n. **1** assessment of yourself or your performance. **2** Brit. your own calculation of how much tax you owe.

self-assurance • n. confidence in your own abilities or character.
– DERIVATIVES **self-assured** adj.

self-awareness • n. conscious

knowledge of your own character, feelings, etc.
– DERIVATIVES **self-aware** adj.

self-catering • adj. Brit. (of a holiday or accommodation) offering facilities for people to cook their own meals.

self-centred • adj. obsessed with yourself and your life.

self-certification • n. the practice, for the purpose of claiming sick pay, by which an employee rather than a doctor declares in writing that an absence was due to illness.

self-confessed • adj. openly admitting to having certain qualities: *a self-confessed chocoholic.*

self-confidence • n. trust in your abilities, qualities, and judgement.
– DERIVATIVES **self-confident** adj.

self-congratulation • n. excessive pride in your achievements or qualities.
– DERIVATIVES **self-congratulatory** adj.

self-conscious • adj. nervous or awkward because worried about what other people think of you.
– DERIVATIVES **self-consciously** adv.

self-contained • adj. **1** complete in itself. **2** esp. Brit. (of accommodation) having its own kitchen and bathroom and its own private entrance. **3** not depending on or influenced by other people.

self-control • n. the ability to control your emotions or behaviour in difficult situations.
– DERIVATIVES **self-controlled** adj.

self-deception • n. the tendency to deceive yourself into believing that something false is true.

self-defeating • adj. (of an action) preventing rather than achieving a desired result.

self-defence • n. the defence of yourself through physical force.

self-denial • n. the action of not allowing yourself to have or do things that you like.
– DERIVATIVES **self-denying** adj.

self-deprecating • adj. modest about yourself.
– DERIVATIVES **self-deprecation** n.

self-destruct • v. explode or disintegrate automatically.

self-destructive • adj. causing harm to yourself.

self-determination • n. **1** the process by which a country gains independence and runs its own affairs. **2** the right of a person to control their own life.

self-discipline • n. the ability to control your feelings and overcome your weaknesses.

– DERIVATIVES **self-disciplined** adj.

self-doubt • n. lack of confidence in yourself and your abilities.

self-effacing • adj. not wanting to attract attention to yourself.

self-employed • adj. working for yourself as a freelance or the owner of a business rather than for an employer.
– DERIVATIVES **self-employment** n.

self-esteem • n. confidence in your own worth or abilities.

self-evident • adj. not needing to be explained; obvious.

self-explanatory • adj. not needing explanation; clearly understood.

self-expression • n. the expression of your feelings or thoughts, especially in an art form.

self-fertilization (or **self-fertilisation**) • n. the fertilization of plants and some invertebrate animals by their own pollen or sperm.

self-fulfilling • adj. (of prediction) bound to come true because people expect it to and behave in a way that makes it happen.

self-governing • adj. **1** (of a British hospital or school) having opted out of local authority control. **2** (of a country, especially a former colony) administering its own affairs.
– DERIVATIVES **self-government** n.

self-harm • n. deliberate injury to yourself, typically as a sign of a psychological or psychiatric disorder.
• v. commit self-harm.
– DERIVATIVES **self-harmer** n.

self-help • n. reliance on your own efforts and resources to achieve things.

self-image • n. the idea that you have of your appearance, abilities, and personality.

self-importance • n. an exaggerated sense of your own importance.
– DERIVATIVES **self-important** adj.

self-improvement • n. the improvement of your knowledge, status, or character by your own efforts.

self-induced • adj. brought about by yourself.

self-indulgent • adj. allowing yourself to have or do things that you like, especially to an excessive extent.
– DERIVATIVES **self-indulgence** n.

self-inflicted • adj. (of a wound or other harm) caused by yourself.

self-interest • n. your personal interest or advantage.
– DERIVATIVES **self-interested** adj.

selfish • adj. concerned mainly with your own needs or wishes.
– DERIVATIVES **selfishly** adv. **selfishness** n.

selfless • adj. concerned more with the needs and wishes of other people than with your own.

self-made • adj. having become successful or rich by your own efforts: *a self-made billionaire.*

self-opinionated • adj. having too high a regard for your own opinions.

self-perpetuating • adj. (of a thing) able to continue indefinitely without the assistance of anything or anyone else.

self-pity • n. excessive concern with and unhappiness over your own troubles.
– DERIVATIVES **self-pitying** adj.

self-pollination • n. the pollination of a flower by pollen from the same plant.

self-portrait • n. a portrait by an artist of himself or herself.

self-possessed • adj. calm, confident, and in control of your feelings.
– DERIVATIVES **self-possession** n.

self-preservation • n. the protection of yourself from harm or death, regarded as a basic instinct.

self-proclaimed • adj. proclaimed to be such by yourself, without the agreement of other people: *self-proclaimed experts.*

self-raising flour • n. Brit. flour that has baking powder already added.

self-regard • n. **1** consideration for yourself. **2** excessive pride in yourself; vanity.
– DERIVATIVES **self-regarding** adj.

self-regulating • adj. regulating itself without intervention from outside bodies.
– DERIVATIVES **self-regulation** n. **self-regulatory** adj.

self-reliance • n. reliance on your own powers and resources.
– DERIVATIVES **self-reliant** adj.

self-respect • n. pride and confidence in yourself.

self-restraint • n. self-control.

self-righteous • adj. certain that you are totally correct or morally superior.

self-rule • n. government of a state or area by its own people.

self-sacrifice • n. the giving up of your own interests or wishes in order to help other people.
– DERIVATIVES **self-sacrificing** adj.

selfsame • adj. (**the selfsame**) the very same.

self-satisfied • adj. smugly pleased with yourself.
– DERIVATIVES **self-satisfaction** n.

self-seeking • adj. concerned only with your own welfare and interests.

self-service • adj. (of a shop or restaurant) in which customers select goods and pay at a checkout.

self-serving • adj. = SELF-SEEKING.

self-starter • n. an ambitious person who acts on their own initiative.

self-styled • adj. using a description or title that you have given to yourself: *self-styled experts.*

self-sufficient • adj. able to do or produce what you need without outside help.
– DERIVATIVES **self-sufficiency** n.

self-taught • adj. having gained knowledge or skill by reading or experience rather than through formal teaching.

self-worth • n. self-esteem.

sell • v. (**sells**, **selling**, **sold**) **1** hand over something in exchange for money. **2** offer goods or property for sale. **3** (of goods) be bought in specified amounts or for a particular price. **4** (**sell out**) sell all of the stock of something. **5** (**sell up**) sell all of your property or assets. **6** persuade someone that something has particular good qualities. **7** (**sell out**) abandon your principles because it is convenient to do so.
– ORIGIN Old English.

sell-by date • n. a date marked on packaged food giving the date by which it should be sold.

seller • n. **1** a person who sells something. **2** a product that sells in a specified way: *the book became a million-seller.*

selling point • n. a feature of a product for sale that makes it attractive to customers.

sell-off • n. a sale of business assets at a low price, carried out in order to dispose of them rather than as normal trade.

Sellotape • n. Brit. trademark transparent adhesive tape.
– ORIGIN from CELLULOSE + TAPE.

sell-out • n. **1** the selling of the whole stock of something. **2** an event for which all tickets are sold. **3** a sale of a company. **4** a betrayal.

selvedge /sel-vij/ • n. an edge produced on woven fabric during manufacture that prevents it from unravelling.
– ORIGIN from SELF + EDGE.

selves pl. of SELF.

semantic /si-man-tik/ • adj. relating to meaning. • n. (**semantics**) **1** the branch of linguistics concerned with the meaning of words. **2** the meaning of a word, phrase, or piece of writing.
– DERIVATIVES **semantically** adv.
– ORIGIN Greek *sēmantikos* 'significant'.

semaphore • n. a system of sending messages by holding the arms or two

flags in positions that represent letters of the alphabet.
– ORIGIN French *sémaphore*.

semblance • n. the way something looks or seems.
– ORIGIN Old French *sembler* 'seem'.

semen /see-muhn/ • n. the liquid containing spermatozoa that is produced by men and male animals.
– ORIGIN Latin, 'seed'.

semester /si-mess-ter/ • n. a half-year term in a school or university, especially in North America.
– ORIGIN Latin *semestris* 'six-monthly'.

semi • n. (pl. **semis**) informal **1** Brit. a semi-detached house. **2** a semi-final.

semi- • prefix **1** half: *semicircular.* **2** partly: *semi-conscious.*
– ORIGIN Latin.

semi-automatic • adj. (of a firearm) able to load bullets automatically but not fire continuously.

semibreve /sem-i-breev/ • n. Brit. a musical note having the value of four crotchets, shown by a ring with no stem.

semicircle • n. a half of a circle or of its circumference.
– DERIVATIVES **semicircular** adj.

semicolon /sem-i-koh-luhn, sem-i-koh-lon/ • n. a punctuation mark (;) indicating a more noticeable pause than that indicated by a comma.

semiconductor • n. a solid that conducts electricity in certain conditions, but not as well as most metals do.
– DERIVATIVES **semiconducting** adj.

semi-conscious • adj. partially conscious.

semi-detached • adj. Brit. (of a house) joined to another house on one side by a common wall.

semi-final • n. (in sport) a match or round coming immediately before the final.
– DERIVATIVES **semi-finalist** n.

seminal • adj. **1** (of a work, event, or idea) strongly influencing later developments. **2** referring to semen.
– ORIGIN Latin *seminalis*.

seminar /sem-i-nar/ • n. **1** a meeting for discussion or training. **2** a small group of students at university, meeting to discuss topics with a teacher.
– ORIGIN German.

seminary /sem-i-nuh-ri/ • n. (pl. **seminaries**) a training college for priests or rabbis.
– DERIVATIVES **seminarian** /sem-i-nair-i-uhn/ n.
– ORIGIN Latin *seminarium*.

semiotics /sem-i-ot-iks/ • n. the study of signs and symbols.
– DERIVATIVES **semiotic** adj. **semiotician** n.
– ORIGIN Greek *sēmeiotikos* 'of signs'.

semipermeable • adj. (of a membrane) allowing small molecules to pass through it but not large ones.

semi-precious • adj. (of minerals) used as gems but less valuable than precious stones.

semiquaver • n. Brit. a musical note having the value of half a quaver, shown by a large dot with a two-hooked stem.

semi-retired • adj. having retired from employment but continuing to work part-time.

semi-skilled • adj. (of work or a worker) having or needing some, but not full, training.

semi-skimmed • adj. Brit. (of milk) having had some of the cream removed.

Semite /see-myt/ • n. a member of a people speaking a Semitic language, in particular the Jews and Arabs.
– ORIGIN Greek *Sēm* 'Shem', son of Noah in the Bible, from whom these people are traditionally descended.

Semitic /si-mit-ik/ • n. a family of languages that includes Hebrew and Arabic. • adj. relating to Semitic or Semites, especially the Jews and Arabs.

semitone • n. Brit. a musical interval equal to half a tone.

semolina • n. the hard grains left after the milling of flour, used in puddings and in pasta.
– ORIGIN Italian *semolino*.

Semtex • n. a plastic explosive that is easily moulded.
– ORIGIN prob. from *Semtin* (a village in the Czech Republic near the place of production) and **EXPLOSIVE**.

senate • n. **1** the smaller but higher law-making body in the US, US states, France, and other countries. **2** the governing body of a university or college. **3** the state council of the ancient Roman republic and empire.
– ORIGIN Latin *senatus*.

senator • n. a member of a senate.
– DERIVATIVES **senatorial** adj.

send • v. (**sends, sending, sent**) **1** cause something to go or be taken to a destination. **2** move something sharply or quickly. **3** cause to be in a specified state: *the traffic nearly sent me crazy.*
– PHRASES **send someone down** Brit. **1** expel a student from a university. **2** informal sentence someone to imprisonment. **send for 1** order someone to come. **2** order by post. **send someone off** (of a football or rugby

referee) order a player to leave the field and take no further part in the game. **send someone to Coventry** esp. Brit. refuse to speak to someone. **send someone up** informal, esp. Brit. make fun of someone by imitating them.
– DERIVATIVES **sender** n.
– ORIGIN Old English.

send-off •n. a gathering of people to wish good luck to someone who is leaving.

send-up •n. informal an imitation of someone or something, done in order to make fun of them.

Senegalese /sen-i-guh-leez/ •n. (pl. **Senegalese**) a person from Senegal, a country on the coast of West Africa. •adj. relating to Senegal.

senescence /si-ness-uhnss/ •n. the process by which a living thing gradually gets worse with age.
– DERIVATIVES **senescent** adj.
– ORIGIN Latin *senescere* 'grow old'.

seneschal /sen-i-shuhl/ •n. the steward of a noble's or monarch's house in medieval times.
– ORIGIN Latin *seniscalus*.

senile /see-nyl/ •adj. having a loss of mental abilities because of old age.
– DERIVATIVES **senility** n.
– ORIGIN Latin *senilis*.

senior •adj. **1** relating to older people. **2** Brit. relating to schoolchildren above the age of about eleven. **3** US of the final year at a university or high school. **4** (after a name) referring to the elder of two with the same name in a family: *Henry James senior.* **5** high or higher in rank or status. •n. **1** a person who is a specified number of years older than someone else: *she was two years his senior.* **2** (in sport) a competitor of above a certain age or of the highest status. **3** a student at a senior school.
– DERIVATIVES **seniority** n.
– ORIGIN Latin.

senior citizen •n. an elderly person.

senna •n. a laxative made from the dried pods of a tree of warm climates.
– ORIGIN Arabic.

señor /sen-yor/ •n. (in Spanish-speaking countries) a form of address for a man, corresponding to *Mr* or *sir*.
– ORIGIN Spanish.

señora /sen-yor-uh/ •n. (in Spanish-speaking countries) a form of address for a woman, corresponding to *Mrs* or *madam*.

señorita /sen-yuh-ree-tuh/ •n. (in Spanish-speaking countries) a form of address for an unmarried woman, corresponding to *Miss*.

sensation •n. **1** a feeling resulting from something that happens to or comes into contact with the body. **2** the ability to have such feelings. **3** a vague impression: *the eerie sensation that she was being watched.* **4** a widespread reaction of interest and excitement, or a person or thing causing it.

sensational •adj. **1** causing or trying to cause great public interest and excitement. **2** informal very impressive or attractive.
– DERIVATIVES **sensationally** adv.

sensationalism •n. (in the media) the use of exciting or shocking stories or language at the expense of accuracy.
– DERIVATIVES **sensationalist** adj.

sensationalize (or **sensationalise**) •v. (**sensationalizes, sensationalizing, sensationalized**) present information in an exaggerated way, so as to make it seem more interesting or exciting.

sense •n. **1** one of the five faculties of sight, smell, hearing, taste, and touch, by which the body perceives things. **2** a feeling that something is the case. **3** (**sense of**) awareness of or sensitivity to: *a sense of direction.* **4** a sensible and practical attitude. **5** reason or purpose: *there's no sense in standing in the rain.* **6** a meaning of a word or expression.
•v. (**senses, sensing, sensed**) **1** perceive by a sense. **2** be vaguely aware of.
– PHRASES **make sense** be understandable or sensible.
– ORIGIN Latin *sensus* 'faculty of feeling, thought, meaning'.

senseless •adj. **1** unconscious or unable to feel. **2** lacking meaning, purpose, or common sense.

sense organ •n. an organ of the body which responds to external stimuli by sending impulses to the brain.

sensibility •n. (pl. **sensibilities**) **1** the ability to appreciate and respond to emotion or art. **2** (**sensibilities**) the quality of being sensitive to shocking or offensive matters.

sensible •adj. **1** having or showing common sense. **2** practical rather than decorative.
– DERIVATIVES **sensibly** adv.

sensitive •adj. **1** quick to detect or be affected by slight changes. **2** appreciating the feelings of other people. **3** easily offended or upset. **4** needing careful handling because controversial: *sensitive information.*
– DERIVATIVES **sensitively** adv.
– ORIGIN Latin *sensitivus*.

sensitivity •n. (pl. **sensitivities**) **1** the quality of being sensitive. **2** (**sensitivities**) the quality of being likely to be offended or hurt.

S

sensitize (or **sensitise**) • v. (**sensitizes, sensitizing, sensitized**) make sensitive or aware.
– DERIVATIVES **sensitization** n. **sensitizer** n.

sensor • n. a device which detects or measures a physical property.

sensory • adj. relating to sensation or the senses.
– DERIVATIVES **sensorily** adv.

sensual /sen-syuu-uhl, sen-shuu-uhl/ • adj. relating to the senses as a source of pleasure.
– DERIVATIVES **sensuality** n. **sensually** adv.

sensuous /sen-syuu-uhss, sen-shuu-uhss/ • adj. **1** relating to the senses rather than the intellect. **2** physically attractive or pleasing.
– DERIVATIVES **sensuously** adv.
– ORIGIN Latin *sensus* 'sense'.

sent past and past part. of SEND.

sentence • n. **1** a set of words that is complete in itself, conveying a statement, question, exclamation, or command. **2** the punishment given to someone found guilty by a court. • v. (**sentences, sentencing, sentenced**) state in a court that a guilty person is to receive a particular punishment.
– ORIGIN Latin *sententia* 'opinion'.

☑ The ending of **sentence** is spelled **-ence**.

sententious /sen-ten-shuhss/ • adj. tending to make pompous comments on moral issues.
– DERIVATIVES **sententiously** adv.
– ORIGIN Latin *sententia* 'opinion'.

sentient /sen-ti-uhnt, sen-shuhnt/ • adj. able to perceive or feel things.
– DERIVATIVES **sentience** n.
– ORIGIN Latin *sentire* 'to feel'.

sentiment • n. **1** an opinion or feeling. **2** exaggerated feelings of tenderness, sadness, or nostalgia.
– ORIGIN Latin *sentimentum*.

sentimental • adj. having or causing exaggerated feelings of tenderness, sadness, or nostalgia: *sentimental love songs.*
– DERIVATIVES **sentimentality** n. **sentimentally** adv.

sentimentalize (or **sentimentalise**) • v. (**sentimentalizes, sentimentalizing, sentimentalized**) present in a sentimental way.

sentinel /sen-ti-nuhl/ • n. a soldier or guard whose job is to stand and keep watch.
– ORIGIN Italian *sentinella*.

sentry • n. (pl. **sentries**) a soldier stationed to keep guard or to control access to a place.

– ORIGIN perh. from SENTINEL.

sepal /sep-uhl, see-puhl/ • n. each of the leaf-like parts of a flower that surround the petals.
– ORIGIN Greek *skepē* 'covering'.

separable • adj. able to be separated or treated separately.
– DERIVATIVES **separability** n.

separate • adj. /sep-uh-ruht, sep-ruht/ **1** forming a unit by itself. **2** different; distinct. • v. /sep-uh-rayt/ (**separates, separating, separated**) **1** move or come apart. **2** stop living together as a couple. **3** divide into distinct parts. **4** remove something for use or because it is unwanted. **5** form a distinction or boundary between: *six years separated the brothers.* • pl. n. /sep-ruhts/ (**separates**) individual items of clothing designed to be worn together in different combinations.
– DERIVATIVES **separately** adv. **separator** n.
– ORIGIN Latin *separare*.

☑ Spell **separate** with **-par-** in the middle.

separation • n. **1** the action of separating. **2** the state in which a husband and wife remain married but live apart.

separatist • n. a member of a group within a country who want to form an independent state.
– DERIVATIVES **separatism** n.

Sephardi /si-far-di/ • n. (pl. **Sephardim** /si-far-dim/) a Jew of Spanish or Portuguese descent.
– DERIVATIVES **Sephardic** adj.
– ORIGIN Hebrew.

sepia /see-pi-uh/ • n. **1** a reddish-brown colour associated with early photographs. **2** a brown pigment used in art.
– ORIGIN Greek, 'cuttlefish' (the pigment is made from cuttlefish ink).

sepoy /see-poy, si-poy/ • n. hist. an Indian soldier who served the British.
– ORIGIN Urdu and Persian.

seppuku /sep-poo-koo/ • n. = HARA-KIRI.
– ORIGIN Japanese.

sepsis /sep-siss/ • n. the presence in tissues of harmful bacteria, through infection of a wound.
– ORIGIN Greek.

Sept. • abbrev. September.

septa pl. of SEPTUM.

September • n. the ninth month of the year.
– ORIGIN Latin *septem* 'seven' (being originally the seventh month of the Roman year).

septet /sep-tet/ •n. a group of seven people playing music or singing together.
– ORIGIN Latin *septem* 'seven'.

septic /sep-tik/ •adj. (of a wound or a part of the body) infected with bacteria.
– ORIGIN Greek *sēptikos*.

septicaemia /sep-ti-see-mi-uh/ (US **septicemia**) •n. blood poisoning caused by bacteria.

septic tank •n. a underground tank in which sewage decomposes through the action of bacteria before draining away into the ground.

septuagenarian /sep-tyuu-uh-ji-nair-i-uhn/ •n. a person who is between 70 and 79 years old.
– ORIGIN Latin *septuagenarius*.

Septuagint /sep-tyuu-uh-jint/ •n. a Greek version of the Hebrew Bible (or Old Testament).
– ORIGIN Latin *septuaginta* 'seventy' (from the tradition that it was produced by seventy-two translators).

septum /sep-tuhm/ •n. (pl. **septa** /sep-tuh/) a partition separating two cavities in the body, such as that between the nostrils.
– ORIGIN Latin.

septuple /sep-tyuu-p'l, sep-tyoo-p'l/ •adj. consisting of seven parts.
– ORIGIN Latin *septem* 'seven'.

sepulchral /si-pul-kruhl/ •adj. 1 relating to a tomb or burial. 2 gloomy or dismal.
– DERIVATIVES **sepulchrally** adv.

sepulchre /sep-uhl-ker/ (US **sepulcher**) •n. a stone tomb.
– ORIGIN Latin *sepulcrum* 'burial place'.

sequel •n. 1 a book, film, or programme that continues the story of an earlier one. 2 something that takes place after or as a result of an earlier event.
– ORIGIN Latin *sequella*.

sequence •n. 1 a particular order in which related things follow each other. 2 a set of related things that follow each other in a particular order. •v. (**sequences, sequencing, sequenced**) arrange in a sequence.
– DERIVATIVES **sequencer** n.
– ORIGIN Latin *sequentia*.

sequential •adj. following in a logical order or sequence.
– DERIVATIVES **sequentially** adv.

sequester /si-kwess-ter/ •v. (**sequesters, sequestering, sequestered**) 1 isolate or hide away. 2 = SEQUESTRATE.
– ORIGIN Latin *sequestrare* 'commit for safekeeping'.

sequestrate /si-kwess-trayt, see-kwi-strayt/ •v. (**sequestrates, sequestrating, sequestrated**) take legal possession of assets until a debt has been paid.
– DERIVATIVES **sequestration** n. **sequestrator** n.

sequin •n. a small, shiny disc sewn on to clothing for decoration.
– DERIVATIVES **sequinned** (also **sequined**) adj.
– ORIGIN Italian *zecchino*, first referring to a Venetian gold coin.

sequoia /si-kwoy-uh/ •n. a redwood tree.
– ORIGIN named after *Sequoya*, a Cherokee Indian scholar.

sera pl. of SERUM.

seraglio /si-rah-li-oh/ •n. (pl. **seraglios**) 1 the women's apartments in a Muslim house or palace. 2 a harem.
– ORIGIN Italian *serraglio*.

seraph /se-ruhf/ •n. (pl. **seraphim** /se-ruh-fim/ or **seraphs**) a type of angel associated with light and purity.
– DERIVATIVES **seraphic** adj. **seraphically** adv.
– ORIGIN Hebrew.

Serb •n. a person from Serbia.

Serbian •n. 1 the language of the Serbs. 2 a person from Serbia. •adj. relating to Serbia.

serenade •n. a piece of music sung or played outdoors and at night, especially by a man under the window of his lover. •v. (**serenades, serenading, serenaded**) entertain with a serenade.
– ORIGIN Italian *serenata*.

serendipity /se-ruhn-dip-i-ti/ •n. the occurrence of events by chance in a beneficial way.
– DERIVATIVES **serendipitous** adj.
– ORIGIN coined by the English politician Horace Walpole, from *Serendip* (a former name for Sri Lanka).

serene •adj. calm and peaceful.
– DERIVATIVES **serenely** adv. **serenity** n.
– ORIGIN Latin *serenus*.

serf •n. (in the feudal system) an agricultural labourer who was tied to working on a particular estate.
– DERIVATIVES **serfdom** n.
– ORIGIN Latin *servus* 'slave'.

serge /rhymes with urge/ •n. a hard-wearing woollen or worsted fabric.
– ORIGIN Old French *sarge*.

sergeant /sar-juhnt/ •n. 1 a rank of non-commissioned officer in the army or air force above corporal. 2 Brit. a police officer ranking below an inspector.
– ORIGIN Old French *sergent*.

sergeant major •n. a warrant officer in the British army who assists with administrative duties.

S

serial • adj. **1** arranged in or happening in a series. **2** repeatedly committing the same offence: *a serial killer.* • n. a story or play published or broadcast in regular instalments.
– DERIVATIVES **serially** adv.

serialize (or **serialise**) • v. (**serializes, serializing, serialized**) publish or broadcast a story or play in regular instalments.
– DERIVATIVES **serialization** n.

serial number • n. an identification number showing the position of a manufactured item in a series.

series • n. (pl. **series**) **1** a number of similar or related things coming one after another. **2** a sequence of related television or radio programmes.
– ORIGIN Latin, 'row, chain'.

serious • adj. **1** needing careful consideration or action. **2** solemn or thoughtful. **3** sincere and in earnest. **4** dangerous or severe: *serious injury.*
– DERIVATIVES **seriousness** n.
– ORIGIN Latin *serius.*

seriously • adv. in a serious way or to a serious extent.

sermon • n. a talk on a religious or moral subject, especially one given during a church service.
– ORIGIN Latin, 'discourse, talk'.

sermonize (or **sermonise**)
• v. (**sermonizes, sermonizing, sermonized**) give moral advice to someone.

seropositive (or **seronegative**)
• adj. giving a positive (or negative) result in a test of blood serum, especially for the presence of a virus.

serotonin /se-ruh-toh-nin/ • n. a compound present in blood which constricts the blood vessels and brings about the transfer of impulses from one nerve to another.
– ORIGIN from SERUM + TONIC.

serous /see-ruhss/ • adj. relating to or resembling serum.

serpent • n. literary a large snake.
– ORIGIN Latin *serpere* 'to creep'.

serpentine /ser-puhn-tyn/
• adj. winding or twisting.

serrated • adj. having a jagged edge like the teeth of a saw.
– ORIGIN Latin *serratus.*

serration • n. a tooth or point of a serrated edge.

serried • adj. (of rows of people or things) standing close together.
– ORIGIN prob. from French *serré* 'close together'.

serum /seer-uhm/ • n. (pl. **sera** /seer-uh/ or **serums**) the thin liquid which

separates out when blood clots.
– ORIGIN Latin, 'whey'.

servant • n. a person employed to perform domestic duties in a household or for a person.
– ORIGIN Old French.

serve • v. (**serves, serving, served**) **1** perform duties or services for. **2** be employed as a member of the armed forces. **3** spend a period in a job or in prison. **4** present someone with food or drink. **5** attend to a customer in a shop. **6** fulfil a purpose. **7** treat someone in a specified way. **8** (of food or drink) be enough for. **9** (in tennis, badminton, etc.) hit the ball or shuttlecock to begin play for each point of a game. • n. an act of serving in tennis, badminton, etc.
– PHRASES **serve someone right** be someone's deserved punishment.
– ORIGIN Latin *servire.*

server • n. **1** a person or thing that serves. **2** a computer or program which controls or supplies information to a computer network.

servery • n. (pl. **serveries**) Brit. a counter, hatch, or room from which meals are served.

service • n. **1** the action of serving. **2** a period of employment with an organization. **3** help or advice. **4** a formal ceremony of religious worship. **5** a system supplying a public need such as transport, or utilities such as water. **6** a department or organization run by the state: *the probation service.* **7** (**the services**) the armed forces. **8** a set of matching crockery used for serving a meal: *a dinner service.* **9** (in tennis, badminton, etc.) a serve. **10** a regular inspection and maintenance of a vehicle or other machine. • v. (**services, servicing, serviced**) **1** carry out maintenance or repair work on. **2** provide a service or services for. **3** pay interest on a debt.
– PHRASES **in** (or **out of**) **service** available (or not available) for use.
– ORIGIN Latin *servitium* 'slavery'.

serviceable • adj. **1** usable or in working order. **2** useful and hard-wearing rather than attractive.
– DERIVATIVES **serviceability** n.

service area (also **services**) • n. Brit. a roadside area where services are available to motorists.

service charge • n. a charge added to a bill for service in a restaurant.

service industry • n. a business that provides a service for a customer rather than manufacturing things.

serviceman (or **servicewoman**) • n. (pl. **servicemen** or **servicewomen**) a person

S

serving in the armed forces.

service provider •n. a company which provides access to the Internet.

service road •n. a road running parallel to a main road and giving access to houses, shops, or businesses.

service station •n. a garage selling petrol and oil and sometimes offering vehicle maintenance.

serviette •n. Brit. a table napkin.
– ORIGIN Old French.

servile •adj. 1 excessively willing to serve or please other people. 2 relating to a slave or slaves.
– DERIVATIVES **servility** n.
– ORIGIN Latin *servilis*.

serving •n. a quantity of food suitable for or served to one person.

servitor •n. old use a servant or attendant.

servitude /ser-vi-tyood/ •n. the state of being a slave or of being under the complete control of someone more powerful.
– ORIGIN Latin *servitudo*.

servomechanism •n. a powered mechanism producing motion or forces at a higher level of energy than the input level, e.g. in the brakes and steering of large motor vehicles.

sesame /sess-uh-mi/ •n. a tall plant of tropical and subtropical areas, grown for its oil-rich seeds.
– ORIGIN Greek *sēsamon*, *sēsamē*.

session •n. 1 a period devoted to a particular activity: *a training session*. 2 a meeting of a council, court, or law-making body to conduct its business. 3 a period during which council and other meetings are regularly held.
– ORIGIN Latin.

session musician •n. a freelance musician hired to play on recording sessions.

set[1] •v. (**sets**, **setting**, **set**) 1 put, lay, or stand in a specified place or position. 2 bring into a specified state. 3 give someone a task. 4 decide on or fix a time, value, or limit. 5 establish as an example or record. 6 adjust a device as required: *don't set the volume too loud*. 7 prepare a table for a meal. 8 harden into a solid, semi-solid, or fixed state. 9 arrange damp hair into the required style. 10 put a broken or dislocated bone or limb into the correct position for healing. 11 (of the sun or moon) appear to move towards and below the earth's horizon.
– PHRASES **set about** start doing something with determination. **set someone apart** make someone seem superior. **set something aside** 1 temporarily stop using land for growing crops. 2 annul a legal decision.

set forth dated begin a journey. **set something forth** describe something in writing or speech. **set in** (of something unwelcome) begin and seem likely to continue. **set off** begin a journey. **set something off** cause a bomb or alarm to go off. **set on** attack violently. **set out** 1 begin a journey. 2 intend to do something. **set something out** arrange or display something. **set sail** begin a voyage. **set something up** 1 place or erect something in position. 2 establish a business or other organization.
– ORIGIN Old English.

set[2] •n. 1 a number of things or people grouped together. 2 a group of people with shared interests or occupations: *the literary set*. 3 the way in which something is set or positioned: *that cold set of his jaw*. 4 a radio or television receiver. 5 (in tennis and other games) a group of games counting as a unit towards a match. 6 a collection of scenery, stage furniture, etc., used for a scene in a play or film. 7 (in jazz or popular music) a sequence of songs or pieces forming part or all of a live show or recording. 8 Math. a collection of distinct entities satisfying specified conditions and regarded as a unit.
– ORIGIN partly from Old French *sette*, partly from **SET**[1].

set[3] •adj. 1 fixed or arranged in advance. 2 firmly fixed and unchanging. 3 having a fixed wording. 4 ready or likely to do something.

setback •n. a problem that prevents or holds up progress.

set piece •n. 1 a part of a novel, film, etc. that is arranged for maximum effect. 2 Brit. a carefully organized move in a team game.

set play •n. Sport a prearranged manoeuvre carried out from a restart by the team who have the advantage.

set square •n. a right-angled triangular plate for drawing lines, especially at 90°, 45°, 60°, or 30°.

sett •n. the earth or burrow of a badger.
– ORIGIN from **SET**[2].

settee •n. Brit. a long padded seat for more than one person.
– ORIGIN perh. from **SETTLE**[2].

setter •n. a breed of large dog with long hair, trained to stand rigid when scenting game.

setting •n. 1 the way or place in which something is set. 2 a piece of metal in which a precious stone is fixed to form a piece of jewellery. 3 a piece of music composed for particular words. 4 (also **place setting**) a set of crockery and cutlery for one person at a meal.

S

settle[1] • v. (**settles, settling, settled**)
1 reach agreement on a dispute. **2** decide or arrange something finally. **3** make your home in a new place. **4** (often **settle down**) adopt a more steady or secure life. **5** become or make calmer or quieter. **6** sit or place so as to be comfortable or secure. **7** sink or fall slowly downwards. **8** (often **settle in**) begin to feel comfortable in a new situation. **9** pay a debt. **10** (**settle for**) accept something less than satisfactory.
– ORIGIN Old English, 'to seat, place'.

settle[2] • n. a wooden bench with a high back and arms.
– ORIGIN Old English.

settlement • n. **1** the action of settling. **2** an official agreement intended to settle a dispute. **3** a place where people establish a community.

settler • n. a person who settles in an area.

set-to • n. (pl. **set-tos**) informal a fight or argument.

set-up • n. informal **1** the way in which something is organized. **2** an organization or arrangement.

seven • cardinal number one more than six; 7. (Roman numeral: **vii** or **VII**.)
– PHRASES **the seven deadly sins** (in Christian tradition) the sins of pride, covetousness, lust, anger, gluttony, envy, and sloth.
– ORIGIN Old English.

seventeen • cardinal number one more than sixteen; 17. (Roman numeral: **xvii** or **XVII**.)
– DERIVATIVES **seventeenth** ordinal number.

seventh • ordinal number **1** that is number seven in a sequence; 7th. **2** (**a seventh/ one seventh**) each of seven equal parts into which something is divided. **3** a musical interval spanning seven consecutive notes in a scale.

seventy • cardinal number (pl. **seventies**) ten less than eighty; 70. (Roman numeral: **lxx** or **LXX**.)
– DERIVATIVES **seventieth** ordinal number.

sever • v. (**severs, severing, severed**) **1** cut something off or into pieces. **2** put an end to a connection or relationship.
– ORIGIN Old French *severer*.

several • det. & pron. more than two but not many. • adj. separate or respective.
– DERIVATIVES **severally** adv.
– ORIGIN Old French.

severance • n. **1** the ending of a connection or relationship. **2** the state of being separated or cut off.

severance pay • n. money paid to an employee on the early ending of a contract.

severe • adj. **1** (of something bad or difficult) very great. **2** strict or harsh. **3** very plain in style or appearance.
– DERIVATIVES **severely** adv. **severity** n.
– ORIGIN Latin *severus*.

Sèvres /sev-ruh/ • n. a type of elaborately decorated fine porcelain.
– ORIGIN from *Sèvres* in Paris.

sew • v. /soh/ (**sews, sewing, sewed**; past part. **sewn** or **sewed**) **1** join or repair by making stitches with a needle and thread or a sewing machine. **2** (**sew something up**) informal bring something to a favourable conclusion.
– ORIGIN Old English.

sewage /soo-ij/ • n. waste water and excrement carried away in sewers.
– ORIGIN from SEWER.

sewer /soo-er/ • n. an underground pipe for carrying off drainage water and waste matter.
– ORIGIN Old French *seuwiere*.

sewerage • n. **1** the provision of drainage by sewers. **2** US = SEWAGE.

sewing machine • n. a machine with a mechanically driven needle for sewing.

sewn past part. of SEW.

sex • n. **1** either of the two main categories (male and female) into which humans and most other living things are divided on the basis of their reproductive functions. **2** the fact of being male or female. **3** the group of all members of either sex. **4** sexual intercourse. • v. (**sex something up**) informal present something in a more interesting or lively way.
– ORIGIN Latin *sexus*.

sexagenarian /seks-uh-ji-**nair**-i-uhn/ • n. a person between 60 and 69 years old.
– ORIGIN Latin *sexaginta* 'sixty'.

sex appeal • n. the quality of being attractive in a sexual way.

sex chromosome • n. a chromosome concerned in determining the sex of an organism (in mammals the X and Y chromosomes).

sexism • n. prejudice or discrimination on the basis of sex.
– DERIVATIVES **sexist** adj. & n.

sexless • adj. **1** not sexually attractive or active. **2** neither male nor female.

sex life • n. a person's sexual activity and relationships.

sex object • n. a person regarded solely in terms of their sexual attractiveness or availability.

sex symbol • n. a person famous for

their sexual attractiveness.

sextant /**seks**-tuhnt/ • n. an instrument used for measuring the angular distances between objects, used in navigation and surveying.
– ORIGIN from Latin *sextans* 'sixth part'.

sextet • n. **1** a group of six people playing music or singing together. **2** a composition for a sextet. **3** a set of six.
– ORIGIN from Latin *sex* 'six'.

sexton • n. a person who looks after a church and churchyard.
– ORIGIN Old French *segrestein*.

sextuple /**seks**-tyuu-p'l, seks-**tyoo**-p'l/ • adj. **1** made up of six parts. **2** six times as much or as many.
– ORIGIN Latin *sextuplus*.

sextuplet /**seks**-tyuu-plit, seks-**tyoo**-plit/ • n. each of six children born at one birth.

sexual • adj. **1** relating to sex, or to physical attraction or contact between people or animals. **2** relating to the two sexes. **3** (of reproduction) involving the fusion of male and female cells.
– DERIVATIVES **sexualize** (or **sexualise**) v. **sexually** adv.

sexual harassment • n. the making of unwanted sexual advances or remarks to a person, especially at work.

sexual intercourse • n. sexual contact in which a man puts his erect penis into a woman's vagina.

sexuality • n. (pl. **sexualities**) **1** a person's capacity for sexual feelings. **2** a person's sexual preference.

sexual politics • n. relations between the sexes regarded in terms of power.

sexy • adj. (**sexier, sexiest**) **1** sexually attractive or exciting. **2** sexually aroused. **2** informal exciting or interesting.
– DERIVATIVES **sexily** adv. **sexiness** n.

Sg • symb. the chemical element seaborgium.

SGML • abbrev. Computing Standard Generalized Markup Language.

shabby • adj. (**shabbier, shabbiest**) **1** worn out or scruffy. **2** dressed in old or worn clothes. **3** mean and unfair: *a shabby trick*.
– DERIVATIVES **shabbily** adv. **shabbiness** n.
– ORIGIN Germanic.

shack • n. a roughly built hut or cabin. • v. (**shack up with**) informal live with someone as a lover.
– ORIGIN perh. from Mexican.

shackle • n. **1** (**shackles**) a pair of rings connected by a chain, used to fasten a prisoner's wrists or ankles together. **2** (**shackles**) restraints: *the shackles of racism and colonialism*. **3** a metal link

closed by a bolt, used to secure a chain or rope to something. • v. (**shackles, shackling, shackled**) **1** chain with shackles. **2** restrain; limit.
– ORIGIN Old English.

shad • n. (pl. **shad** or **shads**) an edible herring-like sea fish.
– ORIGIN Old English.

shade • n. **1** an area that is dark and cool because it is sheltered from direct sunlight. **2** a form of a colour with regard to how light or dark it is: *various shades of blue*. **3** a variety of something. **4** a slight amount: *I felt a shade anxious*. **5** (**shades**) informal sunglasses. **6** a lampshade. **7** literary a ghost. • v. (**shades, shading, shaded**) **1** screen from direct light. **2** cover or reduce the light of. **3** represent a darker area in a picture with pencil or a block of colour. **4** change gradually: *outrage began to shade into dismay*.
– PHRASES **put someone/thing in the shade** be much better or more impressive than someone or something.
– DERIVATIVES **shader** n.
– ORIGIN Old English.

shading • n. **1** the representation of light and shade on a drawing or map. **2** a very slight variation.

shadow • n. **1** a dark shape or area produced by an object coming between light rays and a surface. **2** partial or complete darkness. **3** sadness or gloom. **4** the slightest trace: *without a shadow of a doubt*. **5** a weak or less good version: *she was a shadow of her former self*. **6** a position of less importance: *he lived in the shadow of his father*. **7** a person who constantly accompanies or secretly follows another. • v. **1** cast a shadow over. **2** accompany or secretly follow someone.
– ORIGIN Old English.

shadow-boxing • n. boxing against an imaginary opponent as a form of training.

shadowy • adj. **1** full of shadows. **2** mysterious or uncertain.

shady • adj. (**shadier, shadiest**) **1** situated in shade. **2** giving shade. **3** informal seeming to be dishonest or illegal.

shaft • n. **1** a long, narrow part forming the handle of a tool or club, the body of a spear or arrow, etc. **2** a ray of light or bolt of lightning. **3** a narrow vertical passage giving access to a mine, accommodating a lift, or providing ventilation. **4** each of a pair of poles between which a horse is harnessed to a vehicle. **5** a cylindrical rotating rod for the transmission of mechanical power in

a machine. •v. informal treat harshly or unfairly.
– ORIGIN Old English.

shag[1] •n. coarse tobacco. •adj. (of pile on a carpet) long and rough.
– ORIGIN Old English.

shag[2] •n. a cormorant (seabird) with greenish-black plumage.
– ORIGIN perh. from SHAG[1].

shaggy •adj. (**shaggier, shaggiest**) 1 (of hair or fur) long, thick, and untidy. 2 having shaggy hair or fur.

shah /rhymes with lah/ •n. hist. a title of the former king of Iran.
– ORIGIN Persian, 'king'.

shake •v. (**shakes, shaking, shook**; past part. **shaken**) 1 move quickly and jerkily up and down or to and fro. 2 tremble with strong emotion. 3 shock or disturb. 4 get rid of or put an end to: *old habits he couldn't shake off.* 5 make a threatening gesture with: *he shook his fist.* •n. 1 an act of shaking. 2 informal a milkshake.
– PHRASES **in two shakes (of a lamb's tail)** informal very quickly. **no great shakes** informal not very good. **shake down** settle down. **shake hands (with someone)** hold someone's right hand in your own when meeting or leaving them, to congratulate them, or as a sign of agreement. **shake someone up** stir someone into action. **shake something up** make major changes to something.
– ORIGIN Old English.

shaker •n. 1 a container for mixing ingredients by shaking. 2 a container with a pierced top from which flour or salt is poured by shaking.

Shakespearean /shayk-**speer**-i-uhn/ (also **Shakespearian**) •adj. relating to the English dramatist William Shakespeare or his works.

shake-up •n. informal a major reorganization.

shako /**shay**-koh, sha-koh/ •n. (pl. **shakos**) a cylindrical military hat with a peak and a plume or pompom.
– ORIGIN from Hungarian *csákó süveg* 'peaked cap'.

shaky •adj. (**shakier, shakiest**) 1 shaking; unsteady. 2 not safe or certain: *a shaky start.*
– DERIVATIVES **shakily** adv. **shakiness** n.

shale •n. soft rock formed from compressed mud or clay, that can be split into thin layers.
– ORIGIN prob. from German *Schale.*

shall •modal verb (3rd sing. present **shall**) 1 used with *I* and *we* to express the future tense. 2 expressing a strong statement, intention, or order. 3 used in questions to make offers or suggestions.
– ORIGIN Old English.

USAGE: The traditional rule is that when forming the future tense, **shall** should be used with **I** and **we** (*I shall be late*), while **will** should be used with **you, he, she, it,** and **they** (*he will not be there*). However, when you want to tell someone what to do or show that you are determined, this rule is reversed: **will** is used with **I** and **we** (*I will not tolerate this*), and **shall** is used with **you, he, she, it,** and **they** (*you shall go to school*). Nowadays, people do not follow these rules so strictly and are more likely to use the shortened forms **I'll, she'll,** etc., especially when speaking.

shallot /shuh-**lot**/ •n. a small vegetable of the onion family.
– ORIGIN French *eschalotte.*

shallow •adj. 1 having a short distance between the top and the bottom; not deep. 2 not thinking or thought out seriously. •n. (**shallows**) a shallow area of water.
– DERIVATIVES **shallowly** adv. **shallowness** n.
– ORIGIN from SHOAL[2].

shalom /shuh-**lom**/ •exclam. said by Jews at meeting or parting.
– ORIGIN Hebrew, 'peace'.

shalt old-fashioned 2nd person sing. of SHALL.

shalwar •n. var. of SALWAR.

sham •n. 1 a thing that is not as good or genuine as it seems to be: *our current free health service is a sham.* 2 a person who pretends to be something they are not. •adj. not genuine; false. •v. (**shams, shamming, shammed**) pretend or pretend to be.
– ORIGIN perh. from SHAME.

shaman /**shay**-muhn, sha-**muhn**/ •n. (pl. **shamans**) (among some peoples) a person believed to be able to contact good and evil spirits.
– DERIVATIVES **shamanic** /shuh-**man**-ik/ adj. **shamanism** n.
– ORIGIN Russian.

shamble •v. (**shambles, shambling, shambled**) walk in a slow, shuffling, awkward way.
– ORIGIN prob. from dialect *shamble* 'ungainly'.

shambles •n. informal a state of complete disorder.
– ORIGIN first meaning 'meat market': from Latin *scamellum* 'little bench'.

shambolic •adj. Brit. informal very disorganized.
– ORIGIN from SHAMBLES.

shame •n. 1 a feeling of embarrassment or distress arising from being aware that you have done something wrong or foolish. 2 loss of respect; dishonour: *the incident brought shame on his family.* 3 a

cause of shame. **4** a cause for regret or disappointment: *it's a shame that he is not better known.* •v. (**shames**, **shaming**, **shamed**) make someone feel ashamed.
– PHRASES **put someone to shame** be much better than someone.
– ORIGIN Old English.

shamefaced •adj. showing shame.

shameful •adj. causing shame.
– DERIVATIVES **shamefully** adv.

shameless •adj. showing no shame.
– DERIVATIVES **shamelessly** adv.
shamelessness n.

shammy •n. (pl. **shammies**) informal a chamois leather.

shampoo •n. **1** a liquid soap for washing the hair. **2** a similar substance for cleaning a carpet, car, etc. **3** an act of washing with shampoo. •v. (**shampoos**, **shampooing**, **shampooed**) wash or clean with shampoo.
– ORIGIN Hindi, 'to press'.

shamrock •n. a clover-like plant with three leaves on each stem, the national emblem of Ireland.
– ORIGIN Irish *seamróg*.

shandy •n. (pl. **shandies**) beer mixed with lemonade or ginger beer.

shanghai /shang-hy/ •v. (**shanghais**, **shanghaiing**, **shanghaied**) informal force or trick someone into doing something.
– ORIGIN first meaning 'force to join a ship's crew': from *Shanghai*, a Chinese seaport.

shank •n. **1** the lower part of a person's leg. **2** the lower part of an animal's foreleg, especially as a cut of meat. **3** the shaft of a tool.
– PHRASES **Shanks's pony** your own legs as a means of transport.
– ORIGIN Old English.

shan't •contr. shall not.

shantung /shan-tung/ •n. a type of soft silk with a coarse surface.
– ORIGIN from *Shantung* in China.

shanty¹ •n. (pl. **shanties**) a small roughly built hut.
– ORIGIN perh. from Canadian French *chantier* 'lumberjack's cabin'.

shanty² •n. (pl. **shanties**) a song in which a solo part alternates with a chorus, sung by sailors when working.
– ORIGIN prob. from French *chantez!* 'sing!'

shanty town •n. a settlement in or near a town where poor people live in shanties.

shape •n. **1** the outward form of someone or something as produced by their outline. **2** a geometric figure such as a rectangle. **3** a piece of material, paper, etc., made or cut in a particular form. **4** the correct or original form of something. **5** organized or well-defined structure or arrangement. **6** a particular condition: *the house was in poor shape.* **7** good physical condition. •v. (**shapes**, **shaping**, **shaped**) **1** give a shape to. **2** have a great influence on: *spiritual teachings shaped by feminism.* **3** (often **shape up**) develop in a particular way. **4** (**shape up**) improve your fitness, behaviour, etc.
– PHRASES **take shape** develop and become more definite or organized.
– DERIVATIVES **shaper** n.
– ORIGIN Old English.

shapeless •adj. lacking a definite or attractive shape.

shapely •adj. (**shapelier**, **shapeliest**) having an attractive shape.
– DERIVATIVES **shapeliness** n.

shard •n. a sharp piece of broken pottery, glass, etc.
– ORIGIN Old English.

share •n. **1** a part of a larger amount which is divided among or contributed by a number of people. **2** any of the equal parts into which a company's wealth is divided, which can be bought by people in return for a proportion of the profits. **3** an amount thought to be normal or acceptable: *the theory has had its share of critics.* •v. (**shares**, **sharing**, **shared**) **1** have or give a share of. **2** have or use jointly with other people: *they shared a flat.* **3** (**share in**) participate in. **4** tell someone about something.
– DERIVATIVES **sharer** n.
– ORIGIN Old English.

shareholder •n. an owner of shares in a company.

sharia /shuh-ree-uh/ •n. Islamic law, based on the teachings of the Koran and the traditions of Muhammad.
– ORIGIN Arabic.

shark¹ •n. a large sea fish with a triangular fin on its back, many kinds of which prey on other animals.

shark² •n. informal a person who dishonestly obtains money from other people.
– ORIGIN perh. from German *Schurke* 'worthless rogue'.

sharkskin •n. a stiff, slightly shiny synthetic fabric.

sharp •adj. **1** having a cutting or piercing edge or point. **2** tapering to a point or edge. **3** sudden and noticeable: *a sharp increase.* **4** clear and definite: *the scene was as sharp in his mind as a film.* **5** (of a feeling) sudden and intense. **6** quick to understand, notice, or respond. **7** quick to take advantage, especially in a dishonest way. **8** (of a food, taste, or

smell) strong and slightly bitter. **9** (of musical sound) strong and true or normal pitch. **10** (of a note or key) higher by a semitone than a specified note or key: *F sharp*. •adv. **1** precisely: *at 7.30 sharp*. **2** suddenly or abruptly. •n. a musical note raised a semitone above natural pitch, shown by the sign ♯.
– DERIVATIVES **sharply** adv. **sharpness** n.
– ORIGIN Old English.

sharpen •v. make or become sharp.
– DERIVATIVES **sharpener** n.

sharpish •adj. fairly sharp. •adv. Brit. informal quickly.

sharp practice •n. dishonest business dealings.

sharpshooter •n. a person skilled in shooting.

sharp-tongued •adj. using harsh or critical language.

sharp-witted •adj. intelligent and shrewd.

shatter •v. (**shatters, shattering, shattered**) **1** break suddenly and violently into pieces. **2** damage or destroy: *the crisis will shatter their confidence*. **3** upset greatly. **4** (as adj. **shattered**) Brit. informal exhausted.

shave •v. (**shaves, shaving, shaved**) **1** remove hair from the face or body by cutting it off close to the skin with a razor. **2** cut a thin slice or slices from something. **3** reduce something by a small amount. **4** pass very close to. •n. an act of shaving.
– ORIGIN Old English.

shaven •adj. shaved.

shaver •n. an electric razor.

shaving •n. a thin strip cut off a surface.

shawl •n. a large piece of fabric worn by women over the shoulders or head or wrapped round a baby.
– ORIGIN Urdu and Persian.

shaykh •n. var. of SHEIKH.

she •pron. (third person sing.) **1** used to refer to a woman, girl, or female animal previously mentioned or easily identified. **2** used to refer to a ship, country, or other thing thought of as female.
– ORIGIN Old English.

sheaf •n. (pl. **sheaves**) **1** a bundle of papers. **2** a bundle of grain stalks tied together after reaping.
– ORIGIN Old English.

shear •v. (**shears, shearing, sheared**; past part. **shorn** or **sheared**) **1** cut the wool off a sheep. **2** cut off something such as hair with scissors or shears. **3** (**be shorn of**) have something taken away from you. **4** break off because of a strain in the structure of something. •n. a strain

produced by pressure in the structure of a substance, so that each layer slides over the next.
– DERIVATIVES **shearer** n.
– ORIGIN Old English.

> USAGE: Do not confuse **shear** and **sheer**. **Shear** means 'cut the wool off a sheep'. As a verb, **sheer** means 'change course quickly' (*the boat sheered off*); **sheer** is also an adjective meaning 'nothing but; absolute' (*sheer hard work*).

shears (also **a pair of shears**) •pl. n. a cutting implement like very large scissors.

sheath /sheeth/ •n. (pl. **sheaths** /sheethz, sheeths/) **1** a cover for the blade of a knife or sword. **2** esp. Brit. a condom. **3** a close-fitting covering. **4** a close-fitting dress.
– ORIGIN Old English.

sheathe /sheeth/ •v. (**sheathes, sheathing, sheathed**) **1** put a knife or sword into a sheath. **2** cover in a close-fitting or protective covering: *her legs were sheathed in black stockings*.

sheath knife •n. a short knife similar to a dagger, carried in a sheath.

sheaves pl. of SHEAF.

shebang /shi-bang/ •n. (in phr. **the whole shebang**) informal the whole thing; everything.

shebeen /shi-been/ •n. a place where alcoholic drink is sold illegally.
– ORIGIN Anglo-Irish *síbín*.

shed¹ •n. **1** a simple building used for storage or to shelter animals. **2** a large building, often with one or more sides open, for storing vehicles or machinery.
– ORIGIN prob. from SHADE.

shed² •v. (**sheds, shedding, shed**) **1** allow leaves, hair, skin, etc. to fall off naturally. **2** get rid of. **3** take off clothes. **4** give off light. **5** Brit. accidentally drop or spill: *a lorry had shed its load*.
– PHRASES **shed tears** cry.
– ORIGIN Old English, 'divide, scatter'.

she'd •contr. she had; she would.

sheen •n. a soft shine on a surface.
– ORIGIN prob. from SHINE.

sheep •n. (pl. **sheep**) a grass-eating mammal with a thick woolly coat, kept in flocks for its wool or meat.
– PHRASES **like sheep** (of people) easily led or influenced.
– ORIGIN Old English.

sheep dip •n. a liquid in which sheep are dipped to clean and disinfect their wool.

sheepdog •n. a breed of dog trained to guard and herd sheep.

sheepish •adj. embarrassed as a result of shame or shyness.

– DERIVATIVES **sheepishly** adv.

sheepshank •n. a knot made in a rope to shorten it temporarily.

sheepskin •n. a sheep's skin with the wool on, made into a garment or rug.

sheer¹ •adj. **1** nothing but; absolute: *sheer hard work.* **2** (of a cliff, wall, etc.) vertical or almost vertical. **3** (of a fabric) very thin. •adv. vertically.
– ORIGIN prob. from SHINE.

> **USAGE:** On the confusion of **sheer** and **shear**, see the note at SHEAR.

sheer² •v. (**sheers, sheering, sheered**) **1** change course quickly. **2** avoid or move away from an unpleasant topic.
– ORIGIN perh. from German *scheren* 'to shear'.

sheet¹ •n. **1** a large rectangular piece of cotton or other fabric, used on a bed to lie on or under. **2** a broad flat piece of metal or glass. **3** a rectangular piece of paper. **4** a wide expanse or moving mass of water, flames, etc.
– ORIGIN Old English.

sheet² •n. a rope attached to the lower corner of a sail, to hold and adjust it.
– ORIGIN Old English, 'lower corner of a sail'.

sheeting •n. material formed into or used as a sheet.

sheet lightning •n. lightning seen as a broad area of light in the sky.

sheet music •n. music published on loose sheets of paper and not bound into a book.

sheikh /shayk, sheek/ (also **shaykh** or **sheik**) •n. **1** the leader of an Arab tribe, family, or village. **2** a leader in a Muslim community or organization.
– ORIGIN Arabic, 'old man, leader'.

sheila •n. Austral./NZ informal a girl or woman.

shekel /rhymes with heckle/ •n. the basic unit of money of modern Israel.
– ORIGIN Hebrew.

shelf •n. (pl. **shelves**) **1** a flat length of wood or other rigid material, fixed horizontally to a wall or forming part of a piece of furniture and used to display or store things. **2** a ledge of rock.
– PHRASES **off the shelf** taken from existing supplies, not made to order. **on the shelf** (of a woman) past an age when she might expect to be married.
– ORIGIN German *schelf*.

shelf life •n. the length of time for which an item remains able to be eaten, used, or sold.

shell •n. **1** the hard protective outer case of an animal such as a shellfish or turtle. **2** the outer covering of an egg, nut kernel, or seed. **3** a metal case filled with explosive, to be fired from a large gun. **4** a hollow case. **5** an outer structure or framework. **6** a light rowing boat for racing. •v. **1** fire explosive shells at. **2** remove the shell or pod from. **3** (**shell something out**) informal pay an amount of money.
– PHRASES **come out of your shell** stop being shy or reserved.
– ORIGIN Old English.

she'll •contr. she shall; she will.

shellac /shuh-lak/ •n. lac resin melted into thin flakes, used for making varnish.
– ORIGIN from SHELL + LAC.

shellfish •n. a water animal that has a shell and that can be eaten, such as a crab or oyster.

shell shock •n. a mental disorder that can affect soldiers who have been in battle for a long time.
– DERIVATIVES **shell-shocked** adj.

shell suit •n. Brit. a casual outfit consisting of a loose top and trousers with a soft lining and a shiny outer layer.

shelter •n. **1** a place giving protection from bad weather or danger. **2** a place providing food and accommodation for homeless people. **3** protection from danger or bad weather: *he waited in the shelter of a rock.* •v. (**shelters, sheltering, sheltered**) **1** provide with shelter. **2** find protection or take cover. **3** (as adj. **sheltered**) protected from the more unpleasant aspects of life.

sheltered housing (also **sheltered accommodation**) •n. Brit. accommodation for elderly or disabled people, staffed by a warden and consisting of private units with some shared facilities.

shelve •v. (**shelves, shelving, shelved**) **1** place an item on a shelf. **2** decide not to continue with a plan for the time being. **3** (of ground) slope downwards.

shelves pl. of SHELF.

shelving •n. shelves.

shenanigans /shi-nan-i-guhnz/ •pl. n. informal **1** secret or dishonest activity. **2** mischievous behaviour.

shepherd •n. a person who looks after sheep. •v. guide or direct: *she shepherded them through the door.*
– DERIVATIVES **shepherdess** n.
– ORIGIN Old English.

shepherd's pie •n. Brit. a dish of minced meat under a layer of mashed potato.

sherbet •n. **1** Brit. a flavoured sweet fizzing powder eaten alone or made into a drink. **2** (in Arab countries) a drink of sweet diluted fruit juices.

S

– ORIGIN Arabic, 'drink'.

 Remember that there is only one **r** in **sherbet**: the ending is -**et**.

sheriff • n. **1** (also **high sheriff**) (in England and Wales) the chief executive officer of the Crown in a county. **2** (in Scotland) a judge. **3** US an elected officer in a county, responsible for keeping the peace.
– ORIGIN Old English.

Sherpa /sher-puh/ • n. (pl. **Sherpa** or **Sherpas**) a member of a Himalayan people living on the borders of Nepal and Tibet.
– ORIGIN Tibetan, 'inhabitant of an Eastern country'.

sherry • n. (pl. **sherries**) a strong wine originally from southern Spain.
– ORIGIN from Spanish *vino de Xeres* 'Xeres wine' (Xeres being the former name of the city of *Jerez de la Frontera*).

she's • contr. she is; she has.

Shetlander • n. a person from the Shetland Islands.

Shetland pony • n. a small breed of pony with a rough coat.

shew • v. old use = SHOW.

Shia /shi-uh/ • n. (pl. **Shia** or **Shias**) **1** one of the two main branches of Islam. **2** a Muslim who follows this branch of Islam.
– ORIGIN Arabic, 'party (of Ali)'.

shiatsu /shi-at-soo/ • n. a Japanese therapy in which pressure is applied with the hands to points on the body.
– ORIGIN Japanese, 'finger pressure'.

shibboleth /shib-buh-leth/ • n. a long-standing belief or principle that many people regard as outdated or no longer important.
– ORIGIN Hebrew, 'ear of corn'; first meaning in English 'a word which a foreigner is unable to pronounce' (according to the Book of Judges, the word was used as a test of nationality because it was difficult to pronounce).

shied past and past part. of SHY².

shield • n. **1** a broad piece of armour held for protection against blows or missiles. **2** a sporting trophy consisting of an engraved metal plate mounted on a piece of wood. **3** a drawing or model of a shield used for displaying a coat of arms. **4** a person or thing that acts as a protective barrier or screen. • v. protect or hide: *the runners were shielded from view by the tunnel.*
– ORIGIN Old English.

shift • v. **1** move or change from one position to another. **2** transfer blame, responsibility, etc. to someone else. **3** Brit. informal move quickly. • n. **1** a slight change in position or direction. **2** a period of time worked by a group of workers who start work as another group finishes. **3** a straight dress without a waist. **4** a key used to switch between two sets of characters or functions on a keyboard. **5** old use a clever or underhand plan.
– PHRASES **shift for yourself** manage without help from other people.
– DERIVATIVES **shifter** n.
– ORIGIN Old English, 'arrange, divide'.

shiftless • adj. lazy and lacking ambition.

shifty • adj. (**shiftier**, **shiftiest**) informal seeming dishonest or untrustworthy.
– DERIVATIVES **shiftily** adv. **shiftiness** n.

Shiite /shee-yt/ • n. a follower of the Shia branch of Islam.

shillelagh /shi-lay-luh, shi-lay-li/ • n. (in Ireland) a wooden cudgel.
– ORIGIN named after the Irish town of *Shillelagh*.

shilling • n. **1** a former British coin worth one twentieth of a pound or twelve pence. **2** the basic unit of money of Kenya, Tanzania, and Uganda.
– ORIGIN Old English.

shilly-shally • v. (**shilly-shallies, shilly-shallying, shilly-shallied**) be unable to make up your mind.
– ORIGIN from *shill I, shall I?*

shim • n. a thin strip of material used in machinery to fill up a space between parts or reduce wear.

shimmer • v. (**shimmers, shimmering, shimmered**) shine with a soft, wavering light. • n. a soft, wavering light or shine.
– DERIVATIVES **shimmery** adj.
– ORIGIN Old English.

shimmy • v. (**shimmies, shimmying, shimmied**) walk or move with a smooth swaying motion.

shin • n. **1** the front of the leg below the knee. **2** a cut of beef from the lower part of a cow's leg. • v. (**shins, shinning, shinned**) (**shin up/down**) climb quickly up or down by gripping with the arms and legs.
– ORIGIN Old English.

shindig • n. informal a large, lively party.
– ORIGIN prob. from SHIN and DIG.

shine • v. (**shines, shining, shone** or **shined**) **1** give out or reflect light. **2** direct a torch or other light somewhere. **3** (of a person's eyes) be bright with an emotion. **4** be very good at something. **5** (past and past part. **shined**) polish something. • n. a quality of brightness.
– PHRASES **take the shine off** make something seem less good. **take a shine to** informal develop a liking for.
– ORIGIN Old English.

shiner • n. informal a black eye.

shingle[1] • n. a mass of small rounded pebbles, especially on a seashore.
– DERIVATIVES **shingly** adj.

shingle[2] • n. **1** a rectangular wooden tile used on walls or roofs. **2** dated a woman's short haircut, tapering from the back of the head to the nape of the neck.
– DERIVATIVES **shingled** adj.
– ORIGIN prob. from Latin *scindula* 'a split piece of wood'.

shingles • n. a disease in which painful blisters form along the path of a nerve or nerves.
– ORIGIN Latin *cingulum* 'girdle'.

Shinto /shin-toh/ • n. a Japanese religion involving the worship of ancestors and nature spirits.
– ORIGIN Chinese, 'way of the gods'.

shinty • n. a Scottish game resembling hockey, played with curved sticks and taller goalposts.

shiny • adj. (**shinier, shiniest**) reflecting light.

ship • n. a large boat for transporting people or goods by sea. • v. (**ships, shipping, shipped**) **1** transport on a ship or by other means. **2** (of a boat) take in water over the side.
– PHRASES **when someone's ship comes in** when a person's fortune is made.
– DERIVATIVES **shipload** n. **shipper** n.
– ORIGIN Old English.

-ship • suffix forming nouns referring to: **1** a quality or condition: *companionship*. **2** status or office: *citizenship*. **3** a skill: *workmanship*. **4** the members of a group: *membership*.
– ORIGIN Old English.

shipboard • adj. used or happening on board a ship.

shipbuilder • n. a person or company that designs and builds ships.
– DERIVATIVES **shipbuilding** n.

shipmate • n. a fellow member of a ship's crew.

shipment • n. **1** the action of transporting goods. **2** an amount of goods shipped.

shipping • n. **1** ships as a whole. **2** the transport of goods.

shipshape • adj. orderly and neat.

shipwreck • n. **1** the sinking or breaking up of a ship at sea. **2** a ship that has sunk or been destroyed at sea. • v. (**be shipwrecked**) suffer a shipwreck.

shipwright • n. a shipbuilder.

shipyard • n. a place where ships are built and repaired.

shire /rhymes with fire/ • n. **1** Brit. a county in England. **2** (**the Shires**) the country areas of the English Midlands regarded as strongholds of traditional country life.
– ORIGIN Old English.

shire horse • n. a heavy powerful breed of horse, used for pulling loads.

shirk • v. avoid work or a duty.
– DERIVATIVES **shirker** n.
– ORIGIN perh. from German *Schurke* 'scoundrel'.

shirred /rhymes with bird/ • adj. (of fabric) gathered by means of threads in parallel rows.

shirt • n. a garment for the upper body, with a collar and sleeves and buttons down the front.
– PHRASES **keep your shirt on** informal stay calm.
– ORIGIN Old English.

shirtsleeves • pl. n. (in phr. **in your shirtsleeves**) wearing a shirt without a jacket over it.

shirtwaister • n. a dress with the bodice shaped like a shirt and a seam at the waist.

shirty • adj. (**shirtier, shirtiest**) Brit. informal bad-tempered or annoyed.

shish kebab /shish ki-bab/ • n. a dish of pieces of meat and vegetables cooked and served on skewers.
– ORIGIN Turkish *şiş kebap*.

shiver[1] • v. (**shivers, shivering, shivered**) shake slightly from fear, cold, or excitement. • n. a trembling movement.
– DERIVATIVES **shivery** adj.
– ORIGIN perh. from Old English, 'jaw'.

shiver[2] • n. a splinter or fragment. • v. (**shivers, shivering, shivered**) break into shivers.
– ORIGIN Germanic, 'to split'.

shoal[1] • n. a large number of fish swimming together. • v. (of fish) form shoals.
– ORIGIN prob. from Dutch *schōle* 'troop'.

shoal[2] • n. **1** an area of shallow water. **2** a submerged sandbank that can be seen at low tide.
– ORIGIN Old English.

shock[1] • n. **1** a sudden upsetting or surprising event or experience. **2** an unpleasant feeling of surprise and distress. **3** a serious medical condition associated with a fall in blood pressure, caused by loss of blood, severe injury, etc. **4** a violent shaking movement caused by an impact, explosion, or earthquake. **5** an electric shock.
• v. **1** make someone feel very surprised and upset. **2** make someone feel outraged or disgusted.
– DERIVATIVES **shockproof** adj.
– ORIGIN French *choc*.

S

shock² •n. an untidy or thick mass of hair.

shock³ •n. a group of twelve sheaves of grain placed upright against each other to allow the grain to dry and ripen.
– ORIGIN perh. from Dutch or German *schok*.

shock absorber •n. a device for absorbing jolts and vibrations on a vehicle.

shocker •n. informal a shocking thing.

shocking •adj. **1** causing shock or disgust. **2** Brit. informal very bad.
– DERIVATIVES **shockingly** adv.

shocking pink •n. a very bright shade of pink.

shock tactics •pl. n. the use of sudden violent or extreme action to shock someone into doing something.

shock therapy (also **shock treatment**) •n. treatment of certain mental illnesses by giving electric shocks to the brain.

shock troops •pl. n. troops trained to carry out sudden attacks.

shock wave •n. a moving wave of very high pressure caused by explosion or by something travelling faster than sound.

shod past and past part. of SHOE.

shoddy •adj. (**shoddier, shoddiest**) **1** badly made or done. **2** dishonest or immoral.
– DERIVATIVES **shoddily** adv. **shoddiness** n.

shoe •n. **1** a covering for the foot with a stiff sole, ending just below the ankle. **2** a horseshoe. **3** a socket on a camera for fitting a flash unit. •v. (**shoes, shoeing, shod**) **1** fit a horse with a shoe or shoes. **2** (**be shod**) be wearing shoes of a particular kind.
– PHRASES **be** (or **put yourself**) **in someone else's shoes** imagine yourself in another person's situation.
– ORIGIN Old English.

shoehorn •n. a curved piece of metal or plastic, used for easing your heel into a shoe. •v. force into a space that is too small.

shoelace •n. a cord or leather strip passed through holes or hooks on opposite sides of a shoe and pulled tight to fasten it.

shoemaker •n. a person who makes footwear as a profession.

shoestring •n. (in phr. **on a shoestring**) informal with only a very small amount of money.

shoe tree •n. a shaped block put into a shoe when it is not being worn to keep it in shape.

shogun /shoh-guhn/ •n. (formerly, in Japan) a hereditary leader of the army.
– ORIGIN Japanese.

shone past and past part. of SHINE.

shoo •exclam. used to drive away an animal or person. •v. (**shoos, shooing, shooed**) drive away by shouting 'shoo'.

shook past of SHAKE.

shoot •v. (**shoots, shooting, shot**) **1** kill or wound a person or animal with a bullet or arrow. **2** fire a gun or other weapon. **3** move suddenly and rapidly. **4** direct a glance, question, or remark at someone. **5** (in sport) kick, hit, or throw the ball in an attempt to score a goal. **6** film or photograph a scene, film, etc. **7** (as adj. **shooting**) (of a pain) sudden and piercing. **8** (of a boat) sweep swiftly down rapids. **9** move a bolt to fasten or unfasten a door. **10** send out buds or shoots. •n. **1** a new part growing from a tree or other plant. **2** an occasion of taking photographs professionally or making a film or video: *a fashion shoot.* **3** an occasion when a group of people hunt and shoot animals or birds for sport.
– PHRASES **shoot your mouth off** informal talk boastfully or too freely. **the whole shooting match** informal everything. **shoot up** informal inject yourself with a narcotic drug.
– ORIGIN Old English.

shooter •n. **1** a person who uses a gun. **2** informal a gun.

shooting gallery •n. a room or fairground booth for shooting at targets.

shooting star •n. a small, rapidly moving meteor that burns up on entering the earth's atmosphere.

shooting stick •n. a walking stick with a handle that unfolds to form a seat and a pointed end which can be stuck in the ground.

shoot-out •n. **1** a gun battle that continues until one side is killed or defeated. **2** Football a tiebreaker decided by each side taking a specified number of penalty kicks.

shop •n. **1** a building or part of a building where goods are sold. **2** a place where things are manufactured or repaired; a workshop. •v. (**shops, shopping, shopped**) **1** go to a shop or shops to buy goods. **2** (**shop around**) look for the best available price or rate for something. **3** Brit. informal inform on someone.
– PHRASES **talk shop** discuss work matters with a colleague when you are not at work.
– DERIVATIVES **shopper** n.
– ORIGIN Old French *eschoppe* 'lean-to booth'.

shopaholic •n. informal a person with an

uncontrollable urge to go shopping.

shop floor • n. Brit. the part of a factory where things are made or assembled by workers.

shopkeeper • n. the owner and manager of a shop.

shoplifting • n. the stealing of goods from a shop by someone pretending to be a customer.
– DERIVATIVES **shoplifter** n.

shopping • n. **1** the buying of goods from shops. **2** goods bought from shops.

shopping centre • n. a group of shops situated together.

shop-soiled • adj. Brit. (of an article) dirty or damaged from being displayed or handled in a shop.

shop steward • n. a person elected by workers in a factory to represent them in dealings with management.

shore¹ • n. **1** the land along the edge of a sea, lake, etc. **2** (**shores**) literary a foreign country: *distant shores*.
– PHRASES **on shore** on land.
– DERIVATIVES **shoreward** adj. & adv. **shorewards** adv.
– ORIGIN Dutch or German *schōre*.

shore² • v. (**shores**, **shoring**, **shored**) (**shore something up**) **1** hold something up with a prop or beam. **2** support or strengthen: *raising interest rates to shore up the dollar*.
– ORIGIN Dutch or German *schore*.

shoreline • n. the line along which a sea, lake, etc. meets the land.

shorn past part. of SHEAR.

short • adj. **1** of a small length in space or time. **2** small in height. **3** smaller than is usual or expected: *a short speech*.
4 (**short of/on**) not having enough of.
5 in scarce supply: *food is short*. **6** rude and abrupt. **7** (of odds in betting) reflecting a high level of probability.
8 (of a vowel) pronounced in a way that takes a shorter time than a long vowel in the same position (e.g. in standard British English the vowel sound in *good*). **9** (of pastry) containing a high proportion of fat to flour and therefore crumbly. • adv. not as far as expected or required: *he pitched the ball short*. • n. Brit. a drink of spirits, served in small measures. • v. have a short circuit.
– PHRASES **be caught short 1** be put at a disadvantage. **2** Brit. informal urgently need to go to the toilet. **for short** as an abbreviation or nickname. **go short** not have enough of something. **in short** to sum up; briefly. **in the short run** (or **term**) in the near future. **make short work of** do, eat, or drink quickly. **short for** an abbreviation or nickname for.

short of 1 less than or not reaching as far as. **2** without doing something; unless something happens. **stop short** stop suddenly.
– DERIVATIVES **shortish** adj. **shortness** n.
– ORIGIN Old English.

shortage • n. a situation in which there is not enough of something needed.

shortbread (also **shortcake**) • n. a rich, crumbly type of biscuit made with butter, flour, and sugar.

short-change • v. **1** cheat someone by giving them less than the correct change. **2** treat someone unfairly by not giving them what they deserve.

short circuit • n. a faulty connection in an electrical circuit in which the current flows along a shorter route than it should do. • v. (**short-circuit**) **1** cause or suffer a short circuit. **2** shorten a process by using a more direct (but often improper) method.

shortcoming • n. a failure to meet a certain standard; a fault or weakness.

shortcrust pastry • n. Brit. crumbly pastry made with flour, fat, and a little water.

short cut • n. **1** a route that is shorter than the usual one. **2** a way of doing something which is quicker than usual.

short division • n. the process of dividing one number by another without writing down the calculations.

shorten • v. make or become shorter.

shortening • n. fat used for making pastry.

shortfall • n. a situation in which there is less of something than is required.

short fuse • n. informal a quick temper.

shorthand • n. a method of writing very quickly by using abbreviations and symbols, used for recording what someone is saying.

short-handed • adj. not having enough or the usual number of staff.

shortlist • n. a list of selected candidates from which a final choice is made.
• v. put on a shortlist.

short-lived • adj. lasting only a short time.

shortly • adv. **1** in a short time; soon.
2 abruptly or sharply.

short-range • adj. **1** able to travel only over short distances. **2** relating to a period of time in the near future.

shorts • pl. n. short trousers that reach to the knees or thighs.

short shrift • n. abrupt and unsympathetic treatment.
– ORIGIN first meaning 'little time

S

allowed for making confession': from **SHRIVE**.

short-sighted • adj. Brit. **1** unable to see things clearly unless they are close to the eyes. **2** not thinking carefully about the consequences of something.
– DERIVATIVES **short-sightedness** n.

short-staffed • adj. without enough or the usual number of staff.

short-tempered • adj. tending to lose your temper quickly.

short wave • n. a radio wave of a wavelength between about 10 and 100 metres (and a frequency of about 3 to 30 megahertz).

shot¹ • n. **1** the firing of a gun, cannon, etc. **2** (in sport) a hit, stroke, or kick of the ball as an attempt to score. **3** informal an attempt. **4** a photograph. **5** a film sequence photographed continuously by one camera. **6** a person with a particular level of ability in shooting: *he was an excellent shot.* **7** (pl. **shot**) a ball of stone or metal fired from a large gun or cannon. **8** (also **lead shot**) tiny lead pellets used in a shotgun. **9** a heavy ball thrown by a shot-putter. **10** the launch of a rocket: *a moon shot.* **11** informal a small drink of spirits. **12** informal an injection of a drug or vaccine.
– PHRASES **like a shot** informal without hesitation. **a shot in the arm** informal a source of encouragement.
– ORIGIN Old English.

shot² past and past part. of **SHOOT**.
• adj. **1** (of coloured cloth) woven with a warp and weft of different colours, giving a contrasting effect when looked at from different angles. **2** interspersed with a different colour: *dark hair shot with silver.*
– PHRASES **get** (or **be**) **shot of** Brit. informal get (or be) rid of. **shot through with** filled with a quality or feature.

shotgun • n. a gun for firing small bullets at short range.

shotgun marriage (also **shotgun wedding**) • n. informal a wedding that has to take place quickly because the bride is pregnant.

shot put • n. an athletic contest in which a very heavy round ball is thrown as far as possible.
– DERIVATIVES **shot-putter** n.

should • modal verb (3rd sing. **should**) **1** used to indicate what is right or ought to be done. **2** used to indicate what is probable. **3** formal used to state what would happen if something else was the case: *if you should change your mind, I'll be at the hotel.* **4** used with *I* and *we* to express a polite request, opinion, or hope.

– ORIGIN past of **SHALL**.

> **USAGE:** As with **shall** and **will**, there are traditional rules as to when to use **should** and when to use **would**. These say that **should** is used with I and **we** (*I said I should be late*), while **would** is used with **you**, **he**, **she**, **it**, and **they** (*you didn't say you would be late*). Nowadays, people do not follow these rules so strictly and are in any case more likely to use the shortened forms **I'd**, **we'd**, etc., especially when speaking, so that the question does not arise.

shoulder • n. **1** the joint between the upper arm or forelimb and the main part of the body. **2** a joint of meat from the upper foreleg and shoulder blade of an animal. **3** a steep sloping side of a mountain. • v. (**shoulders, shouldering, shouldered**) **1** put something heavy over your shoulder or shoulders to carry. **2** take on a responsibility. **3** push aside with your shoulder.
– PHRASES **shoulder arms** hold a rifle against the right side of the body, barrel upwards. **shoulder to shoulder** side by side or acting together.
– ORIGIN Old English.

shoulder bag • n. a bag with a long strap that is hung over the shoulder.

shoulder blade • n. either of the large, flat, triangular bones at the top of the back; the scapula.

shoulder strap • n. **1** a narrow strip of material going over the shoulder from front to back of a garment. **2** a long strap attached to a bag for carrying it over the shoulder.

shouldn't • contr. should not.

shout • v. **1** speak or call out very loudly. **2** (**shout someone down**) prevent someone from speaking or being heard by shouting. • n. **1** a loud cry or call. **2** (**your shout**) Brit. informal your turn to buy a round of drinks.
– PHRASES **in with a shout** Brit. informal having a good chance.
– ORIGIN perh. from **SHOOT**.

shove • v. (**shoves, shoving, shoved**) **1** push roughly. **2** put something somewhere carelessly or roughly. **3** (**shove off**) informal go away. • n. a strong push.
– ORIGIN Old English.

shovel • n. a tool resembling a spade with a broad blade and upturned sides, used for moving earth, snow, etc.
• v. (**shovels, shovelling, shovelled**; US **shovels, shoveling, shoveled**) **1** move earth, snow, etc. with a shovel. **2** (**shovel something down/in**) informal eat food quickly and in large quantities.
– ORIGIN Old English.

show • v. (**shows, showing, showed**; past part. **shown** or **showed**) **1** be or make visible: *wrinkles were starting to show on her face.* **2** offer for inspection or viewing. **3** present an image of: *a postcard showing Mount Etna.* **4** lead or guide. **5** treat in a particular way. **6** be evidence of; prove. **7** make someone understand something by explaining it or doing it yourself. **8** (also **show up**) informal arrive for an appointment. • n. **1** a theatrical performance, especially a musical. **2** a light entertainment programme on television or radio. **3** an event or competition involving the public display of animals, plants, or products. **4** an impressive or pleasing sight. **5** a display of a quality or feeling. **6** an outward display intended to give a false impression: *I made a show of looking bored.* **7** a ridiculous display: *don't make a show of yourself.*
– PHRASES **get the show on the road** informal begin a task, project, or journey. **show your hand** reveal your plans. **show off** try to impress other people by talking about your abilities or possessions. **show something off** display something that is a source of pride. **show of hands** a vote carried out by the raising of hands. **show someone/thing up 1** reveal someone or something to be bad or at fault. **2** informal embarrass or humiliate someone.
– ORIGIN Old English, 'look at, inspect'.

showbiz • n. informal show business.

show business • n. the world of films, television, the theatre, and pop music as a profession or industry.

showcase • n. **1** a glass case used for displaying articles in a shop or museum. **2** an occasion for presenting something favourably. • v. (**showcases, showcasing, showcased**) put on display.

showdown • n. a final meeting or test intended to settle a dispute.

shower /*rhymes with* flower/ • n. **1** a short period of rain or snow. **2** a large number of things that fall or arrive together: *a shower of crumbs.* **3** a piece of equipment that creates a spray of water under which a person stands to wash themselves. **4** an act of washing yourself in a shower. **5** Brit. informal an incompetent group of people. • v. (**showers, showering, showered**) **1** fall or throw in a shower. **2** (**shower someone with**) give a large number of things to someone. **3** wash yourself in a shower.
– ORIGIN Old English.

showery • adj. with frequent showers of rain.

showgirl • n. an actress who sings and dances in a musical or variety show.

show house (also **show home**) • n. Brit. a house on a newly built estate which is furnished and decorated to be shown to possible buyers.

showing • n. **1** a presentation of a cinema film or television programme. **2** a performance of a particular quality: *poor opinion poll showings.*

showjumping • n. the competitive sport of riding horses over a course of obstacles in an arena.
– DERIVATIVES **showjumper** n.

showman • n. (pl. **showmen**) **1** the manager or presenter of a circus, fair, etc. **2** a person who is skilled at entertaining people or getting their attention.
– DERIVATIVES **showmanship** n.

shown past part. of **show**.

show-off • n. informal a person who tries to impress other people by talking about their abilities or possessions.

showpiece • n. an outstanding example of something: *the factory is a showpiece of British industry.*

showplace • n. a place of beauty or interest that attracts many visitors.

showroom • n. a room used to display cars, furniture, or other goods for sale.

show-stopper • n. informal a very impressive performance that receives a great deal of applause.
– DERIVATIVES **show-stopping** adj.

show trial • n. a public trial that is held to influence or satisfy public opinion, rather than to ensure that justice is done.

showy • adj. (**showier, showiest**) very bright or colourful and attracting much attention.
– DERIVATIVES **showily** adv. **showiness** n.

shrank past of **shrink**.

shrapnel /shrap-n'l/ • n. small metal fragments thrown out by an exploding shell or bomb.
– ORIGIN named after General Henry *Shrapnel*, the British inventor.

shred • n. **1** a strip of material that has been torn, cut, or scraped from something. **2** a very small amount: *not a shred of evidence.* • v. (**shreds, shredding, shredded**) tear or cut into shreds.
– DERIVATIVES **shredder** n.
– ORIGIN Old English.

shrew • n. **1** a small mammal resembling a mouse, with a long pointed snout. **2** a bad-tempered woman.
– ORIGIN Old English.

shrewd • adj. having or showing good judgement.

s

- DERIVATIVES **shrewdly** adv. **shrewdness** n.
- ORIGIN from SHREW in the former sense 'evil person or thing'.

shrewish • adj. (of a woman) bad-tempered or nagging.

shriek • v. make a high-pitched piercing cry. • n. a high-pitched piercing cry.

shrike • n. a songbird with a hooked bill, that impales its prey on thorns.

shrill • adj. (of a voice or sound) high-pitched and piercing. • v. make a shrill noise.
- DERIVATIVES **shrillness** n. **shrilly** adv.
- ORIGIN Germanic.

shrimp • n. 1 (pl. **shrimp** or **shrimps**) a small edible shellfish. 2 informal, derog. a small, weak person.
- ORIGIN prob. from German *schrempen* 'to wrinkle'.

shrine • n. 1 a place believed to be holy because it is connected to a holy person or event. 2 a place containing a religious statue or object.
- ORIGIN Old English, 'container for holy relics'.

shrink • v. (**shrinks**, **shrinking**, **shrank**; past part. **shrunk** or (especially as adj.) **shrunken**) 1 become or make smaller. 2 (of clothes) become smaller as a result of being washed in water that is too hot. 3 move back or away in fear or disgust. 4 (**shrink from**) be unwilling to do something. • n. informal a psychiatrist.
- ORIGIN Old English; the noun is from *headshrinker*, an American term for a psychiatrist.

shrinkage • n. the process of shrinking or the amount by which something has shrunk.

shrinking violet • n. informal a very shy person.

shrink-wrap • v. wrap an article in clinging plastic film.

shrive /rhymes with drive/ • v. (**shrives**, **shriving**, **shrove**; past part. **shriven**) old use (of a priest) hear someone's confession, give them a religious duty, and declare them free from sin.
- ORIGIN Old English.

shrivel • v. (**shrivels**, **shrivelling**, **shrivelled**; US **shrivels**, **shriveling**, **shriveled**) wrinkle and shrink through loss of moisture.
- ORIGIN perh. Scandinavian.

shroud • n. 1 a length of cloth in which a dead person is wrapped for burial. 2 a thing that surrounds or hides something. 3 (**shrouds**) a set of ropes supporting the mast of a sailing boat. • v. cover or hide: *the hills were shrouded by mist*.
- ORIGIN Old English, 'garment'.

Shrove Tuesday • n. the day before Ash Wednesday.

shrub • n. a woody plant which is smaller than a tree and divided into separate stems from near the ground.
- DERIVATIVES **shrubby** adj.
- ORIGIN Old English.

shrubbery • n. (pl. **shrubberies**) an area in a garden planted with shrubs.

shrug • v. (**shrugs**, **shrugging**, **shrugged**) 1 raise your shoulders slightly and briefly as a sign that you do not know or care about something. 2 (**shrug something off**) treat something as unimportant. • n. an act of shrugging your shoulders.

shrunk (also **shrunken**) past part. of SHRINK.

shtum /shtuum/ (also **schtum**) • adj. (in phr. **keep shtum**) Brit. informal stay silent.
- ORIGIN Yiddish.

shudder • v. (**shudders**, **shuddering**, **shuddered**) tremble or shake violently, especially from fear or disgust. • n. an act of shuddering.
- ORIGIN Dutch *schūderen*.

shuffle • v. (**shuffles**, **shuffling**, **shuffled**) 1 walk without lifting your feet completely from the ground. 2 move about restlessly while sitting or standing. 3 rearrange a pack of cards by sliding them over each other quickly. 4 rearrange people or things. 5 (**shuffle something off**) avoid a responsibility. • n. an act of shuffling.
- DERIVATIVES **shuffler** n.
- ORIGIN perh. from German *schuffeln*.

shufti /shuuf-ti/ • n. (pl. **shuftis**) Brit. informal a quick look.
- ORIGIN Arabic, 'try to see'.

shun • v. (**shuns**, **shunning**, **shunned**) avoid or reject.
- ORIGIN Old English, 'hate, shrink back'.

shunt • v. 1 push or pull a railway vehicle or vehicles from one set of tracks to another. 2 push or shove. 3 move someone to a less important position.
- ORIGIN perh. from SHUN.

shut • v. (**shuts**, **shutting**, **shut**) 1 move something into position to block an opening. 2 (**shut someone/thing in/out**) keep someone or something in or out by closing a door, gate, etc. 3 prevent access to a place or along a route. 4 (with reference to a shop or other business) stop operating for business. 5 close a book, curtains, etc.
- PHRASES **shut down** stop opening for business, or stop operating. **shut something off** stop something from flowing or working. **shut up** informal stop talking.
- ORIGIN Old English, 'put a bolt in

position to hold fast'.

shutdown •n. an act of closing a factory or of turning off a machine.

shut-eye •n. informal sleep.

shutter •n. 1 each of a pair of hinged panels inside or outside a window that can be closed for security or to keep out the light. 2 a device that opens and closes to expose the film in a camera.
•v. (**shutters, shuttering, shuttered**) close the shutters of a window or building.

shuttle •n. 1 a form of transport that travels regularly between two places. 2 (in weaving) a bobbin for carrying the weft thread across the cloth, between the warp threads. 3 a bobbin carrying the lower thread in a sewing machine.
•v. (**shuttles, shuttling, shuttled**) 1 travel regularly between places. 2 transport in a shuttle.
– ORIGIN Old English, 'dart, missile'.

shuttlecock •n. a light cone-shaped object consisting of a rounded piece of cork or plastic with feathers attached, struck with rackets in badminton.

shy[1] •adj. (**shyer, shyest**) 1 nervous or timid in the company of other people. 2 (**shy of/about**) unwilling or reluctant to do something. 3 (in combination) having a dislike of a particular thing: *camera-shy.* 4 (**shy of**) informal short of. •v. (**shies, shying, shied**) 1 (of a horse) suddenly turn aside in fright. 2 (usu. **shy away from**) avoid something through nervousness or lack of confidence.
– DERIVATIVES **shyly** adv. **shyness** n.
– ORIGIN Old English.

shy[2] •v. (**shies, shying, shied**) throw something at a target.

shyster •n. informal a dishonest person, especially a lawyer.
– ORIGIN perh. from *Scheuster*, the name of a lawyer.

SI •abbrev. Système International, the international system of units of measurement.

Si •symb. the chemical element silicon.

Siamese (also **Siamese cat**) •n. a breed of cat that has short pale fur with a darker face, ears, feet, and tail.
– ORIGIN from *Siam*, the former name for Thailand.

Siamese twins •pl. n. twins whose bodies are joined at birth.

sibilant •adj. literary making a hissing sound. •n. a speech sound made with a hissing effect, e.g. *s, sh.*
– DERIVATIVES **sibilance** n.
– ORIGIN Latin *sibilare* 'hiss'.

sibling •n. a brother or sister.
– ORIGIN Old English, 'relative'.

sibyl •n. (in ancient Greece and Rome) a

woman supposedly able to pass on the messages and prophecies of a god.
– DERIVATIVES **sibylline** adj.
– ORIGIN Greek *Sibulla.*

sic /sik/ •adv. (after a copied or quoted word that appears odd or wrong) written exactly as it stands in the original.
– ORIGIN Latin, 'thus'.

Sicilian •n. a person from Sicily.
•adj. relating to Sicily.

sick •adj. 1 physically or mentally ill. 2 wanting to vomit. 3 (**sick of**) bored by or annoyed about something. 4 informal behaving in an abnormal or cruel way. 5 informal (of humour) dealing with unpleasant subjects in a funny or upsetting way. •n. Brit. informal vomit.
– PHRASES **be sick 1** be ill. **2** Brit. vomit.
– ORIGIN Old English.

sickbay •n. a room or building that is set aside for sick people in a school or on a ship.

sickbed •n. the bed of a person who is ill.

sicken •v. 1 make someone disgusted or appalled. 2 (**be sickening for**) be showing the first symptoms of an illness. 3 (as adj. **sickening**) informal very annoying.
– DERIVATIVES **sickeningly** adv.

sickie •n. Brit. informal a period of sick leave taken when a person is not really ill.

sickle •n. a farming tool for cutting corn, with a semicircular blade.
– ORIGIN Latin *secula.*

sick leave •n. permission to be away from work because of illness.

sickly •adj. (**sicklier, sickliest**) 1 often ill. 2 looking unhealthy. 3 (of flavour, colour, etc.) so bright or sweet as to make you feel sick. 4 too sentimental.

sickness •n. 1 the state of being ill. 2 a particular type of illness or disease. 3 nausea or vomiting.

sicko •n. (pl. **sickos**) informal a perverted person.

side •n. 1 a position to the left or right of an object, place, or central point. 2 either of the two halves into which something can be divided. 3 an upright or sloping surface of something that is not the top, bottom, front, or back. 4 each of the flat surfaces of a solid object, or either of the two surfaces of something flat and thin, e.g. paper. 5 each of the lines forming the boundary of a plane figure. 6 either of the two faces of a record or of the corresponding parts of a cassette tape. 7 a part near the edge of something. 8 a person or group opposing another in a dispute or contest. 9 a sports team. 10 a

S

particular aspect: *he had a disagreeable side.* **11** a person's line of descent as traced through either their father or mother. **12** Brit. informal a television channel. ●adj. additional or less important: *a side dish.* ●v. (**sides, siding, sided**) (**side with/against**) support or oppose one party in a conflict or dispute.
– PHRASES **on the side** informal **1** in addition to your regular job. **2** as a secret additional sexual relationship. **3** (**on the —— side**) rather ——: *he's a little on the large side.* **side by side** close together and facing the same way. **side on** on, from, or towards the side. **take sides** support one person or cause against another.
– DERIVATIVES **sideward** adj. & adv. **sidewards** adv.
– ORIGIN Old English.

sidebar ●n. a short piece of additional information placed alongside a main article in a newspaper or magazine.

sideboard ●n. **1** a flat-topped piece of furniture with cupboards and drawers, used for storing crockery, glasses, etc. **2** (**sideboards**) Brit. sideburns.

sideburns ●pl. n. a strip of hair growing down each side of a man's face in front of his ears.
– ORIGIN reversal of the name of the American General Ambrose *Burnside*, who had sideburns.

sidecar ●n. a small, low vehicle attached to the side of a motorcycle for carrying passengers.

side effect ●n. a secondary, usually bad effect of a drug.

sidekick ●n. informal a person's assistant.

sidelight ●n. Brit. a small additional light on either side of a vehicle's headlights.

sideline ●n. **1** an activity done in addition to a person's main job. **2** either of the two lines along the longer sides of a football field, basketball court, etc. **3** (**the sidelines**) a position of watching a situation rather than being directly involved in it. ●v. (**sidelines, sidelining, sidelined**) **1** prevent a player from playing in a team or game. **2** remove from an influential position.

sidelong ●adj. & adv. to or from one side; sideways.

sidereal /sy-deer-i-uhl/ ●adj. relating to the distant stars or their apparent positions in the sky.
– ORIGIN Latin *sidus* 'star'.

side road ●n. a minor road joining or branching from a main road.

side-saddle ●adv. (of a rider) sitting with both feet on the same side of the horse.

sideshow ●n. **1** a small show or stall at an exhibition, fair, or circus. **2** a minor

incident or issue that takes attention away from the main subject.

side-splitting ●adj. informal very amusing.

sidestep ●v. (**sidesteps, sidestepping, sidestepped**) **1** avoid by stepping sideways. **2** avoid discussing or dealing with a difficult issue.

side street ●n. a minor street.

sideswipe ●n. a critical remark made while discussing another matter.

sidetrack ●v. distract someone from the main thing they are discussing or doing.

sidewalk ●n. N. Amer. a pavement.

sideways ●adv. & adj. **1** to, towards, or from the side. **2** unconventional: *a sideways look at life.*

siding ●n. a short track beside a main railway line, where trains are left.

sidle ●v. (**sidles, sidling, sidled**) walk in a stealthy or timid way.
– ORIGIN from SIDELONG.

siege ●n. **1** a military operation in which enemy forces try to capture a town or building by surrounding it and cutting off its supplies. **2** a similar operation by a police team to force an armed person to surrender.
– PHRASES **lay siege to** begin a siege of.
– ORIGIN Old French *sege* 'a seat'.

☑ **siege** follows the usual rule of *i* before *e* except after *c.*

siemens /see-muhnz/ ●n. Physics the SI unit of conductance.
– ORIGIN named after the German-born British engineer Sir Charles *Siemens*.

sienna ●n. a kind of earth used as a pigment in painting, normally yellowish-brown (**raw sienna**) or deep reddish-brown when roasted (**burnt sienna**).
– ORIGIN from Italian *terra di Sienna* 'earth of *Siena*' (an Italian city).

sierra /si-air-uh/ ●n. (in Spanish-speaking countries or the western US) a long jagged mountain chain.
– ORIGIN Spanish.

Sierra Leonean /si-air-uh li-oh-ni-uhn/ ●n. a person from Sierra Leone, a country in West Africa. ●adj. relating to Sierra Leone.

siesta /si-ess-tuh/ ●n. an afternoon rest or nap, especially in hot countries.
– ORIGIN Spanish.

sieve /siv/ ●n. a utensil consisting of a piece of mesh held in a frame, used for straining solids from liquids or separating coarser from finer particles. ●v. (**sieves, sieving, sieved**) put a substance through a sieve.

– ORIGIN Old English.

 sieve follows the usual rule of *i* before *e* except after *c*.

sift • v. **1** put a substance through a sieve. **2** examine thoroughly to sort out what is important or useful.
– DERIVATIVES **sifter** n.
– ORIGIN Old English.

sigh • v. **1** let out a long, deep, breath expressing sadness, relief, etc. **2** (**sigh for**) literary long for. • n. an act of sighing.
– ORIGIN Old English.

sight • n. **1** the ability to see. **2** the action of seeing: *he hates the sight of blood.* **3** the area or distance within which someone can see or something can be seen. **4** a thing that you see. **5** (**sights**) places of interest to tourists. **6** (**a sight**) informal a person or thing that looks ridiculous or unattractive. **7** (also **sights**) a device that you look through to aim a gun or see with a telescope or similar instrument. • v. **1** manage to see or glimpse. **2** take aim by looking through the sights of a gun.
– PHRASES **at first sight** from the first impression. **catch sight of** glimpse. **in** (or **within**) **sight of** close to being achieved. **lose sight of** fail to consider or be aware of. **on** (or **at**) **sight** as soon as someone or something has been seen. **raise** (or **lower**) **your sights** increase (or lower) your expectations. **set your sights on** hope strongly to achieve. **a sight** —— informal considerably: *she is a sight cleverer than Sarah.* **a sight for sore eyes** informal a person or thing that you are very pleased to see.
– ORIGIN Old English.

USAGE: For an explanation of the difference between **sight** and **site**, see the note at **SITE**.

sighted • adj. **1** having the ability to see; not blind. **2** having a particular kind of sight: *keen-sighted.*

sightless • adj. blind.

sight-read • v. read a musical score and perform it without preparation.

sightseeing • n. the activity of visiting places of interest.
– DERIVATIVES **sightseer** n.

sign • n. **1** an indication that something exists, is happening, or may happen: *I dared not show any sign of weakness.* **2** a signal, gesture, or notice giving information or an instruction. **3** a symbol or word used to represent something in algebra, music, or other subjects. **4** each of the twelve divisions of the zodiac. • v. **1** write your name on a document, letter, etc. to show that you

have written it, or as an indication of agreement. **2** recruit a sports player, musician, etc. by signing a contract. **3** use gestures to give information or instructions.
– PHRASES **sign off** end a letter, broadcast, or other message. **sign on 1** commit yourself to a job. **2** Brit. register as unemployed. **sign someone on** employ someone. **sign up** commit yourself to a job, course of study, etc.
– DERIVATIVES **signer** n.
– ORIGIN Latin *signum* 'mark, token'.

signal[1] • n. **1** a gesture, action, or sound giving information or an instruction. **2** a sign indicating a particular situation. **3** a device that uses lights or a movable arm, used to tell drivers to stop or beware on a road or railway. **4** an electrical impulse or radio wave sent or received. • v. (**signals**, **signalling**, **signalled**; US **signals**, **signaling**, **signaled**) **1** give a signal. **2** indicate by means of a signal.
– DERIVATIVES **signaller** n.
– ORIGIN Latin *signum* 'mark, token'.

signal[2] • adj. noteworthy; striking.
– DERIVATIVES **signally** adv.
– ORIGIN Italian *segnalato* 'distinguished'.

signal box • n. Brit. a building beside a railway track from which signals, points, and other equipment are controlled.

signalman • n. (pl. **signalmen**) a railway worker responsible for operating signals and points.

signatory /sig-nuh-tuh-ri/ • n. (pl. **signatories**) a person, organization, or state that has signed an agreement.
– ORIGIN Latin *signare* 'to sign, mark'.

signature • n. **1** a person's name written in a distinctive way, used in signing a document, letter, etc. **2** the action of signing a document. **3** a distinctive product or quality by which someone or something can be recognized: *the chef produced the pâté that was his signature.*
– ORIGIN Latin *signare* 'to sign'.

signature tune • n. esp. Brit. a special tune used to announce a particular television or radio programme.

signboard • n. a board displaying the name or logo of a business or product.

signet • n. hist. a small seal used to authorize an official document.
– ORIGIN Latin *signetum.*

signet ring • n. a ring with letters or a design set into it.

significance • n. **1** importance. **2** the meaning of something.
– ORIGIN Latin *significantia.*

significant • adj. **1** important or large enough to have an effect or be noticed. **2** having a meaning that is not directly stated: *a significant look.*

– DERIVATIVES **significantly** adv.

significant figure •n. Math. each of the digits of a number that are used to express it to the required degree of accuracy.

signify •v. (**signifies, signifying, signified**) **1** be a sign of; mean. **2** make a feeling or intention known.
– DERIVATIVES **signification** n.
– ORIGIN Latin *significare*.

signing •n. **1** Brit. a person who has recently been recruited to a sports team, record company, etc. **2** a promotional event at which an author signs copies of their book. **3** sign language.

sign language •n. a system of communication used among and with deaf people, consisting of signs made by the hands and face.

signor /see-**nyor**/ •n. a form of address for an Italian-speaking man, corresponding to *Mr* or *sir*.
– ORIGIN Italian.

signora /see-**nyor**-uh/ •n. a form of address for an Italian-speaking married woman, corresponding to *Mrs* or *madam*.
– ORIGIN Italian.

signorina /see-nyuh-**ree**-nuh/ •n. a form of address for an Italian-speaking unmarried woman, corresponding to *Miss*.
– ORIGIN Italian.

signpost •n. a sign on a post, giving the direction and distance to a nearby place. •v. esp. Brit. mark a place or road with a signpost or signposts.

Sikh /seek/ •n. a member of a religion that developed from Hinduism, based on the belief that there is only one God. •adj. relating to Sikhs or Sikhism.
– DERIVATIVES **Sikhism** n.
– ORIGIN Punjabi, 'disciple'.

silage /**sy**-lij/ •n. grass or other green crops that are stored in a silo without being dried, used as animal feed in the winter.
– ORIGIN Spanish *ensilar* 'put into a silo'.

silence •n. **1** complete lack of sound. **2** a situation in which someone is unwilling to speak or discuss something: *he withdrew into sullen silence.* •v. (**silences, silencing, silenced**) **1** prevent someone from speaking. **2** make something silent.
– ORIGIN Latin *silentium*.

silencer •n. a device for reducing the noise made by a gun or (Brit.) an exhaust system.

silent •adj. **1** where there is no sound. **2** not speaking or not spoken aloud: *a silent prayer.* **3** not tending to speak much. **4** (of a film) without a sound-track. **5** (of a letter) written but not pronounced, e.g. *b* in *doubt.*
– DERIVATIVES **silently** adv.

silhouette /si-luu-**et**/ •n. **1** the dark shape and outline of someone or something seen against a lighter background. **2** a picture that shows someone or something as a black shape on a light background. •v. (**silhouettes, silhouetting, silhouetted**) show as a silhouette: *the castle was silhouetted against the sky.*
– ORIGIN named after the French author and politician Étienne de *Silhouette*.

silica /**si**-li-kuh/ •n. a compound of silicon and oxygen that occurs as quartz and is found in sandstone and many other rocks.
– ORIGIN Latin *silex* 'flint'.

silicate /**si**-li-kayt, **si**-li-kuht/ •n. a compound of silica combined with a metal oxide.

silicon /**si**-li-k'n/ •n. a non-metallic chemical element that is a semi-conductor, used in making electronic circuits.
– ORIGIN Latin *silex* 'flint'.

silicon chip •n. a microchip.

silicone /**si**-li-kohn/ •n. a synthetic substance made from silicon, used to make plastics, paints, etc.

silicosis /si-li-**koh**-siss/ •n. a lung disease caused by breathing in dust that contains silica.

silk •n. **1** a fine, soft shiny fibre produced by silkworms, made into thread or fabric. **2** (**silks**) garments made from silk, worn by a jockey. **3** Brit. informal a Queen's Counsel. [ORIGIN because entitled to wear a silk gown.]
– PHRASES **take silk** Brit. become a Queen's Counsel.
– ORIGIN Latin *sericus*.

silken •adj. **1** smooth and shiny like silk. **2** made of silk.

silkworm •n. a caterpillar that spins a silk cocoon from which silk fibre is produced.

silky •adj. (**silkier, silkiest**) **1** smooth and shiny like silk. **2** (of a person's voice) smooth.
– DERIVATIVES **silkily** adv. **silkiness** n.

sill •n. **1** a piece of stone, wood, or metal at the foot of a window or doorway. **2** Geol. a sheet of igneous rock intruded between and parallel with existing strata.
– ORIGIN Old English.

silly •adj. (**sillier, silliest**) **1** lacking in common sense or judgement; foolish. **2** Cricket (of a fielding position) very close to the batsman: *silly mid-on.*
– DERIVATIVES **silliness** n.

– ORIGIN Germanic, 'luck, happiness'.

silo /sy-loh/ • n. (pl. **silos**) **1** a tower on a farm, used to store grain. **2** a pit or airtight structure in which green crops are stored as silage. **3** an underground chamber in which a guided missile is kept ready for firing.
– ORIGIN Spanish.

silt • n. fine sand or clay carried by running water and deposited as a sediment. • v. (**silt up**) fill or block with silt.
– DERIVATIVES **silty** adj.
– ORIGIN prob. Scandinavian.

Silurian /sy-lyoor-i-uhn/ • adj. Geol. relating to the third period of the Palaeozoic era, about 439 to 409 million years ago, a time when the first fish and land plants appeared.
– ORIGIN from *Silures*, the Latin name of a people of ancient Wales.

silver • n. **1** a precious shiny greyish-white metallic element. **2** a shiny grey-white colour. **3** coins made from silver or from a metal that resembles silver. **4** silver dishes, containers, or cutlery. • v. (**silvers, silvering, silvered**) **1** cover or plate with silver. **2** literary give a silvery appearance to: *the moon silvered the turf.*
– PHRASES **be born with a silver spoon in your mouth** be born into a rich upper-class family. **the silver screen** the cinema industry.
– DERIVATIVES **silvery** adj.
– ORIGIN Old English.

silver birch • n. a birch tree with silver-grey bark.

silverfish • n. (pl. **silverfish** or **silverfishes**) a small silvery wingless insect that lives in buildings.

silver jubilee • n. the twenty-fifth anniversary of an important event.

silver medal • n. a medal made of or coloured silver, awarded for second place in a race or competition.

silver plate • n. **1** a thin layer of silver applied as a coating to another metal. **2** plates, dishes, etc. made of or plated with silver.

silverside • n. Brit. the upper side of a round of beef from the outside of the leg.

silversmith • n. a person who makes silver articles.

silver-tongued • adj. persuasive in speaking; eloquent.

silver wedding • n. Brit. the twenty-fifth anniversary of a wedding.

silviculture /sil-vi-kul-cher/ • n. the growing and cultivation of trees.
– DERIVATIVES **silvicultural** adj.
– ORIGIN Latin *silva* 'wood'.

SIM (also **SIM card**) • n. a smart card inside a mobile phone, carrying an identification number unique to the owner, storing personal data, and preventing identification if removed.
– ORIGIN from the initial letters of *subscriber identification module.*

simian /sim-i-uhn/ • adj. relating to or like apes or monkeys. • n. an ape or monkey.
– ORIGIN Latin *simia* 'ape'.

similar • adj. **1** like something but not exactly the same: *the nuts are similar to almonds.* **2** (of geometrical figures) the same in shape but not in size.
– DERIVATIVES **similarity** n. (pl. **similarities**). **similarly** adv.
– ORIGIN Latin *similis* 'like'.

simile /sim-i-li/ • n. a figure of speech in which one thing is compared to another of a different kind, using the words *as* or *like* (e.g. *the family was as solid as a rock*).
– ORIGIN Latin.

similitude /si-mil-i-tyood/ • n. the quality of being similar.

simmer • v. (**simmers, simmering, simmered**) **1** stay or keep just below boiling point. **2** be full of anger or other strong emotion which is only just kept under control. **3** (**simmer down**) become calmer and quieter. • n. a state just below boiling point.
– ORIGIN from dialect *simper* in the same sense.

simony /sy-muh-ni, sim-uh-ni/ • n. esp. hist. the buying or selling of Church privileges such as pardons.
– ORIGIN from *Simon* Magus in the Bible, who offered money to the Apostles.

simper • v. (**simpers, simpering, simpered**) smile in a coy and silly way. • n. a coy and silly smile.

simple • adj. (**simpler, simplest**) **1** easily understood or done. **2** plain and basic: *a simple white blouse.* **3** composed of a single element; not compound. **4** of very low intelligence. **5** of low status; humble. **6** (of interest) payable on the sum loaned only. Compare with **COMPOUND**[1].
– ORIGIN Latin *simplus.*

simple fracture • n. a fracture of a bone only, without breaking of the skin.

simple-minded • adj. not very clever or sensible.

simpleton • n. a foolish or unintelligent person.

simplicity • n. the quality of being simple.

simplify • v. (**simplifies, simplifying, simplified**) make easier to do or understand.

– DERIVATIVES **simplification** n.

simplistic • adj. treating complex issues as more simple than they really are.
– DERIVATIVES **simplistically** adv.

simply • adv. **1** in a simple way. **2** just; merely. **3** absolutely: *the plants are simply wonderful.*

simulacrum /sim-yuu-**lay**-kruhm/ • n. (pl. **simulacra** /sim-yuu-**lay**-kruh/ or **simulacrums**) something that is similar to something else.
– ORIGIN Latin.

simulate • v. (**simulates, simulating, simulated**) **1** imitate the appearance or nature of. **2** use a computer to create conditions that are like those in real life. **3** pretend to feel an emotion.
– DERIVATIVES **simulation** n.
– ORIGIN Latin *simulare* 'copy, represent'.

simulator • n. a machine that imitates the controls and conditions of a real vehicle, process, etc., used for training or testing.

simulcast /sim-uhl-**kahst**/ • n. a broadcast of the same programme on radio and television at the same time.
– ORIGIN from SIMULTANEOUS and BROADCAST.

simultaneous /sim-uhl-**tay**-ni-uhss/ • adj. occurring or done at the same time.
– DERIVATIVES **simultaneity** n. **simultaneously** adv.
– ORIGIN Latin *simul* 'at the same time'.

> ✓ Remember that **simultaneous** ends with **-eous**.

simultaneous equations • pl. n. equations involving two or more unknowns that are to have the same values in each equation.

sin¹ /*rhymes with* tin/ • n. **1** an act that breaks a religious or moral law. **2** an act that causes strong disapproval. • v. (**sins, sinning, sinned**) commit a sin.
– ORIGIN Old English.

sin² /*rhymes with* line/ • abbrev. sine.

sin bin • n. informal (in sport) a place to which offending players can be sent as a penalty during a game.

since • prep. in the period between a time in the past and the present: *what's happened since Monday?* • conj. **1** during or in the time after. **2** because.
• adv. **1** from the time mentioned until the present. **2** ago.
– ORIGIN Old English.

sincere • adj. (**sincerer, sincerest**) not pretending to be or feel anything; genuine and honest.
– DERIVATIVES **sincerely** adv.
– ORIGIN Latin *sincerus* 'clean, pure'.

sincerity • n. the quality of being sincere.

sine /*rhymes with* line/ • n. (in a right-angled triangle) the ratio of the side opposite a particular acute angle to the hypotenuse.
– ORIGIN Latin *sinus* 'curve'.

sinecure /**syn**-i-kyoor, **sin**-i-kyoor/ • n. a job for which the holder is paid but which requires little or no work.
– ORIGIN from Latin *sine cura* 'without care'.

sine die /see-nay **dee**-ay/ • adv. (with reference to proceedings that have been adjourned) with no date set for being restarted.
– ORIGIN Latin, 'without a day'.

sine qua non /si-ni kwah **nohn**/ • n. a thing that is absolutely necessary.
– ORIGIN Latin, 'without which not'.

sinew /**sin**-yoo/ • n. a piece of tough fibrous tissue that joins muscle to bone.
– DERIVATIVES **sinewy** adj.
– ORIGIN Old English.

sinful • adj. **1** wicked or immoral. **2** disgraceful: *a sinful waste.*
– DERIVATIVES **sinfully** adv. **sinfulness** n.

sing • v. (**sings, singing, sang**; past part. **sung**) **1** make musical sounds with the voice in the form of a song or tune. **2** make a whistling sound.
– PHRASES **sing someone's praises** praise someone highly.
– DERIVATIVES **singer** n.
– ORIGIN Old English.

singalong • n. an informal occasion when people sing together in a group.

Singaporean /sing-uh-**por**-i-uhn/ • n. a person from Singapore. • adj. relating to Singapore.

singe • v. (**singes, singeing, singed**) burn the surface of something slightly. • n. a slight burn.
– ORIGIN Old English.

Singhalese /sing-guh-**leez**/ • n. & adj. var. of SINHALESE.

single • adj. **1** one only. **2** designed or suitable for one person. **3** consisting of one part. **4** taken separately from others in a group (used for emphasis): *he wrote down every single word.* **5** not involved in a romantic or sexual relationship. **6** Brit. (of a ticket) valid for an outward journey only. • n. **1** a single person or thing. **2** a short record or CD. **3** (**singles**) a game or competition for individual players. • v. (**singles, singling, singled**) (**single someone/thing out**) choose someone or something from a group for special treatment.
– DERIVATIVES **singly** adv.
– ORIGIN Latin *singulus.*

single-breasted • adj. (of a jacket or coat) fastened by one row of buttons at the centre of the front.

single cream •n. Brit. thin cream with a low fat content.

single currency •n. 1 a currency used by all the members of an economic federation. 2 (also **single European currency**) the currency (the euro) which replaced the national currencies of twelve member states of the European Union in 2002.

single file •n. a line of people or things arranged one behind another.

single-handed •adv. & adj. done without help from other people.
– DERIVATIVES **single-handedly** adv.

single market •n. an association of countries that have few or no restrictions on the movement of goods, money, or people within the group.

single-minded •adj. concentrating on one particular aim.
– DERIVATIVES **single-mindedly** adv. **single-mindedness** n.

single parent •n. a person bringing up a child or children without a partner.

singlet •n. esp. Brit. a vest or similar sleeveless garment.
– ORIGIN from SINGLE.

singleton •n. 1 a single person or thing of its kind. 2 informal a person who is not in a long-term relationship.

sing-song •adj. (of a person's voice) having a repeated rising and falling rhythm. •n. Brit. informal an informal gathering for singing.

singular •adj. 1 Grammar (of a word or form) referring to just one person or thing. 2 very good or great; remarkable. 3 strange or eccentric. •n. Grammar the singular form of a word.
– DERIVATIVES **singularity** n. (pl. **singularities**). **singularly** adv.
– ORIGIN Latin *singularis*.

Sinhalese /sin-huh-leez, sin-uh-leez/ (also **Singhalese** or **Singhalese**) •n. (pl. **Sinhalese** or **Singhalese**) 1 a member of an Indian people forming the majority of the population of Sri Lanka. 2 the language of the Sinhalese. •adj. relating to the Sinhalese.
– ORIGIN Sanskrit, 'Sri Lanka'.

sinister •adj. seeming evil or dangerous.
– DERIVATIVES **sinisterly** adv.
– ORIGIN Latin, 'left'.

sink •v. (**sinks, sinking, sank**; past part. **sunk**) 1 go down below the surface of liquid. 2 (of a ship) go or cause to go to the bottom of the sea. 3 move slowly downwards. 4 gradually decrease in amount or strength. 5 (**sink something into**) force something sharp through a surface. 6 (**sink in**) become fully understood. 7 pass into a particular state: *she sank into sleep.* 8 (**sink

something in/into**) put money or resources into. •n. a fixed basin with a water supply and outflow pipe.
– PHRASES **a sinking feeling** a feeling that something bad has happened or will happen. **sink or swim** fail or succeed by your own efforts.
– ORIGIN Old English.

sinker •n. a weight used to keep a fishing line beneath the water.

sinkhole •n. a hole in the ground caused by water erosion and providing a route for surface water to disappear underground.

sinner •n. a person who sins.

Sino- /sy-noh/ •comb. form Chinese; Chinese and ...: *Sino-American*.
– ORIGIN Latin *Sinae*.

sinology /sy-nol-uh-ji, si-nol-uh-ji/ •n. the study of Chinese language, history, and culture.
– DERIVATIVES **sinologist** n.

sinuous /sin-yuu-uhss/ •adj. 1 having many curves and turns. 2 moving in a graceful, swaying way.
– DERIVATIVES **sinuosity** n. **sinuously** adv.
– ORIGIN Latin *sinuosus*.

sinus /sy-nuhss/ •n. a hollow space within the bones of the face that connects with the inside of the nose.
– ORIGIN Latin, 'a bend'.

sinusitis /si-nuh-sy-tiss/ •n. inflammation of a sinus.

Sioux /soo/ •n. (pl. **Sioux**) a member of a North American Indian people living in the northern Mississippi valley area.

sip •v. (**sips, sipping, sipped**) drink in small mouthfuls. •n. a small mouthful of liquid.
– DERIVATIVES **sipper** n.
– ORIGIN perh. from SUP¹.

siphon (also **syphon**) •n. a tube used to convey liquid upwards from a container and then down to a lower level, using the different fluid pressures at the tube openings to maintain the flow.
•v. 1 draw off or convey liquid with a siphon. 2 (**siphon something off**) take small amounts of money from a source over time.
– ORIGIN Greek, 'pipe'.

sir (also **Sir**) •n. 1 a polite form of address for a man. 2 used as a title before the first name of a knight or baronet.
– ORIGIN from SIRE.

sire /rhymes with fire/ •n. 1 the male parent of an animal. 2 literary a father or other male ancestor. 3 old use a respectful form of address to a king. •v. (**sires, siring, sired**) be the male parent of.
– ORIGIN Old French.

siren •n. 1 a device that makes a long

loud warning sound. **2** Gk Myth. each of a group of creatures who were part woman, part bird, whose singing lured sailors on to rocks. **3** a woman whose sexual attractiveness is regarded as dangerous to men.
– ORIGIN Greek *Seirēn*.

sirloin •n. good-quality beef cut from the loin.
– ORIGIN Old French, 'above the loin'.

sirocco /si-rok-koh/ •n. (pl. **siroccos**) a hot wind blowing from North Africa to southern Europe.
– ORIGIN Arabic, 'east wind'.

sirup •n. US = SYRUP.

SIS •abbrev. (in the UK) Secret Intelligence Service.

sisal /sy-z'l/ •n. fibre made from the leaves of a tropical Mexican plant, used for ropes or matting.
– ORIGIN named after the Mexican port of *Sisal*.

siskin •n. a small yellowish-green finch.
– ORIGIN Dutch *siseken*.

sissy •n. (pl. **sissies**) informal an effeminate or weak person.
– ORIGIN from SISTER.

sister •n. **1** a woman or girl in relation to other children of her parents. **2** a female friend or colleague. **3** a member of a religious order of women. **4** Brit. a senior female nurse. •adj. belonging to the same group or type as something else: *a sister organization.*
– DERIVATIVES **sisterly** adj.
– ORIGIN Old English.

sisterhood •n. **1** the relationship between sisters. **2** closeness and understanding between women. **3** a group of women linked by a shared interest or belief.

sister-in-law •n. (pl. **sisters-in-law**) **1** the sister of a person's wife or husband. **2** the wife of a person's brother or brother-in-law.

Sisyphean /siss-i-**fee**-uhn/ •adj. (of a task) unending.
– ORIGIN from *Sisyphus* in Greek mythology whose punishment was to endlessly roll a large stone to the top of a hill, only for it to roll down again.

sit •v. (**sits**, **sitting**, **sat**) **1** be or put in a position in which your weight is supported by your bottom and your back is upright. **2** be in a particular position or state: *the fridge was sitting in a pool of water.* **3** serve as a member of a council, jury, or other official body. **4** (of a parliament, court of law, or committee) be carrying on its business. **5** Brit. take an exam. **6** (of a table or room) have enough seats for. **7** (**sit for**) pose for an artist or photographer.

– PHRASES **sit in for** temporarily carry out the duties of. **sit something out** not take part in something. **sit tight** informal hold back from taking action. **sit up** go to bed later than usual.
– ORIGIN Old English.

> **USAGE:** It is good English to use the present participle **sitting** rather than the past participle **sat** with the verb 'to be': say *we were sitting there for hours* rather than *we were sat there for hours*.

sitar /si-tar/ •n. a large, long-necked Indian lute.
– ORIGIN Persian.

sitcom •n. informal a situation comedy.

sit-down •adj. (of a protest) in which demonstrators occupy their workplace or sit on the ground in a public place.

site •n. **1** a place where something is or will be located. **2** a place where an event or activity is happening or has happened. **3** a website. •v. (**sites**, **siting**, **sited**) build or locate something in a particular place.
– ORIGIN Latin *situs* 'position'.

> **USAGE:** Do not confuse **site** and **sight**. **Site** means 'a place where something is located or happens' (*the site of a famous temple*), while **sight** means 'the ability to see' (*he lost his sight in an accident*).

Sitka /sit-kuh/ •n. a fast-growing North American spruce tree, grown for its strong lightweight wood.
– ORIGIN from the town of *Sitka* in Alaska.

sitter •n. **1** a person who sits for a portrait. **2** a person who looks after children, pets, or a house while the parents or owners are away.

sitting •n. **1** a period of posing for a portrait. **2** a period of time when a group of people are served a meal. **3** a period of time during which a court of law, committee, or parliament is carrying on its business. •adj. (of an elected representative) currently present or in office.

sitting duck •n. informal a person or thing that is easy to attack.

sitting room •n. esp. Brit. a room for sitting and relaxing in.

sitting tenant •n. Brit. a tenant who is living in rented accommodation.

situate •v. (**situates**, **situating**, **situated**) **1** put in a particular place. **2** (**be situated**) be in a particular situation: *she is now comfortably situated.*
– ORIGIN Latin *situare* 'place'.

situation •n. **1** a set of circumstances existing at a particular time and in a particular place: *the political situation in*

China. **2** the location and surroundings of a place. **3** formal a job.
– DERIVATIVES **situational** adj.

situation comedy • n. a comedy series in which the characters are involved in amusing situations.

sit-up • n. an exercise designed to strengthen the abdominal muscles, in which a person sits up from a horizontal position without using the arms.

six • cardinal number **1** one more than five; 6. (Roman numeral: **vi** or **VI**.) **2** Cricket a hit that reaches the boundary without first bouncing, scoring six runs.
– PHRASES **at sixes and sevens** in a state of confusion. **knock someone for six** Brit. informal surprise someone greatly.
– DERIVATIVES **sixfold** adj. & adv.
– ORIGIN Old English.

six-pack • n. **1** a pack of six cans of beer. **2** informal a set of well-developed stomach muscles.

sixpence • n. Brit. a former coin worth six old pence (2½ p).

six-shooter • n. a revolver with six chambers.

sixteen • cardinal number one more than fifteen; 16. (Roman numeral: **xvi** or **XVI**.)
– DERIVATIVES **sixteenth** ordinal number.

sixth • ordinal number **1** that is number six in a sequence; 6th. **2** (**a sixth/one sixth**) each of six equal parts into which something is divided. **3** a musical interval spanning six consecutive notes in a scale.

sixth-form college • n. Brit. a college for students aged 16–18.

sixth sense • n. a supposed ability to know things by intuition rather than by sight, hearing, etc.

sixty • cardinal number (pl. **sixties**) ten more than fifty; 60. (Roman numeral: **lx** or **LX**.)
– DERIVATIVES **sixtieth** ordinal number.

size¹ • n. **1** the overall measurements or extent of something. **2** each of the series of standard measurements in which articles are made or sold: *the dress was several sizes too big.* • v. (**sizes, sizing, sized**) **1** group things according to size. **2** (**size someone/thing up**) form a judgement of someone or something.
– ORIGIN Old French *sise*.

size² • n. a sticky solution used to glaze paper, stiffen textiles, and prepare plastered walls for decoration. • v. (**sizes, sizing, sized**) treat with size.
– ORIGIN perh. the same as **size**¹.

sizeable (also **sizable**) • adj. fairly large.

sizzle • v. (**sizzles, sizzling, sizzled**) **1** (of food) hiss when being fried. **2** (as adj.

sizzling) informal very hot or exciting.
– DERIVATIVES **sizzler** n.

sjambok /sham-bok/ • n. (in South Africa) a long, stiff whip.
– ORIGIN South African Dutch.

ska /skah/ • n. a style of fast popular music originating in Jamaica.

skate¹ • n. an ice skate or roller skate. • v. (**skates, skating, skated**) **1** move on skates. **2** (**skate over/round/around**) pass over or refer only briefly to a subject or problem.
– PHRASES **get your skates on** Brit. informal hurry up.
– DERIVATIVES **skater** n. **skating** n.
– ORIGIN Dutch *schaats*.

skate² • n. (pl. **skate** or **skates**) an edible sea fish with a flattened diamond-shaped body.
– ORIGIN Old Norse.

skateboard • n. a short narrow board with two small wheels fixed to the bottom of either end, on which a person can ride. • v. ride on a skateboard.
– DERIVATIVES **skateboarder** n.

skedaddle • v. (**skedaddles, skedaddling, skedaddled**) informal leave quickly.

skein /skayn/ • n. a length of thread or yarn, loosely coiled and knotted.
– ORIGIN Old French *escaigne*.

skeletal /skel-i-t'l, skuh-lee-t'l/ • adj. **1** relating to a skeleton. **2** very thin. **3** existing only in outline: *a skeletal plot for a novel.*
– DERIVATIVES **skeletally** adv.

skeleton • n. **1** a framework of bone or cartilage supporting or containing the body of an animal. **2** a supporting framework or structure. **3** a basic outline of a plan, written work, etc. • adj. referring to an essential or minimum number of people: *a skeleton staff.*
– PHRASES **skeleton in the cupboard** a shocking or embarrassing fact that someone wishes to keep secret.
– ORIGIN Greek, 'dried up thing'.

skeleton key • n. a key designed to fit many locks.

skeptic • n. US = SCEPTIC.

sketch • n. **1** a rough drawing or painting. **2** a short humorous scene in a comedy show. **3** a brief written or spoken account. • v. **1** make a sketch of. **2** give a brief account of.
– ORIGIN Italian *schizzo*.

sketchbook (also **sketch pad**) • n. a pad of drawing paper for sketching on.

sketchy • adj. (**sketchier, sketchiest**) not thorough or detailed; rough.

S

– DERIVATIVES **sketchily** adv. **sketchiness** n.

skew • n. a bias towards one particular group or subject: *the paper had a working-class skew.* • v. **1** suddenly change direction or move at an angle. **2** make something biased or distorted.
– ORIGIN Old French *eschiver* 'eschew'.

skewbald • adj. (of a horse) with patches of white and another colour.

skewer • n. a long piece of wood or metal used for holding pieces of food together during cooking. • v. (**skewers**, **skewering**, **skewered**) hold in place or pierce with a skewer or similar sharp implement.

skew-whiff • adv. & adj. Brit. informal not straight; askew.

ski • n. (pl. **skis**) each of a pair of long, narrow pieces of wood, metal, or plastic, attached to boots for travelling over snow. • v. (**skis**, **skiing**, **skied**) travel on skis.
– DERIVATIVES **skiable** adj. **skier** n.
– ORIGIN Norwegian.

skid • v. (**skids**, **skidding**, **skidded**) **1** (of a vehicle) slide sideways in an uncontrolled way. **2** slip; slide. • n. **1** an act of skidding. **2** a runner attached to the underside of an aircraft for use when landing on snow or grass.
– PHRASES **on the skids** informal in a bad state.
– ORIGIN perh. from SKI.

skid row • n. informal, esp. N. Amer. a run-down part of a town where homeless people and alcoholics live.

skiff • n. a light rowing boat, usually for one person.
– ORIGIN Italian *schifo*.

ski jump • n. a steep slope levelling off before a sharp drop to allow a skier to leap through the air.

skilful (US **skillful**) • adj. having or showing skill.
– DERIVATIVES **skilfully** adv. **skilfulness** n.

> ☑ Spell **skilful** with only one **l** in the middle: the spelling **skillful** is American.

ski lift • n. a set of moving seats attached to an overhead cable, used to transport skiers to the top of a run.

skill • n. **1** the ability to do something well. **2** a particular ability.
– ORIGIN Old Norse, 'knowledge'.

skilled • adj. **1** having or showing skill. **2** (of work) requiring special abilities or training.

skillet • n. N. Amer. a frying pan.
– ORIGIN perh. from Old French *escuelete* 'little dish'.

skim • v. (**skims**, **skimming**, **skimmed**)

1 remove a substance from the surface of a liquid. **2** move quickly and lightly over or on a surface or through the air. **3** read through something quickly, noting only the main points. **4** (**skim over**) deal with a subject briefly.
– DERIVATIVES **skimmer** n.
– ORIGIN Old French *escumer*.

skimmed milk (N. Amer. also **skim milk**) • n. milk from which the cream has been removed.

skimp • v. spend less money or use less of something than is really needed in an attempt to economize: *don't skimp on holiday insurance.*

skimpy • adj. (**skimpier**, **skimpiest**) **1** less than is necessary; meagre. **2** (of clothes) short and revealing.

skin • n. **1** the thin layer of tissue forming the outer covering of the body. **2** the skin of a dead animal used for clothing or other items. **3** the peel or outer layer of a fruit or vegetable. **4** an outer layer. • v. (**skins**, **skinning**, **skinned**) **1** remove the skin from. **2** graze a part of the body.
– PHRASES **by the skin of your teeth** only just. **get under someone's skin** informal annoy someone greatly. **have a thick skin** be unaffected by criticism. **it's no skin off my** (or **his** etc.) **nose** informal said to show that you are not upset by something.
– DERIVATIVES **skinless** adj.
– ORIGIN Old English.

skin-deep • adj. not deep or lasting; superficial.

skin-diving • n. the activity of swimming under water without a diving suit, using an aqualung and flippers.
– DERIVATIVES **skin-diver** n.

skinflint • n. informal a very mean person.

skinful • n. Brit. informal enough alcohol to cause drunkenness.

skinhead • n. a young man of a group with close-cropped hair, especially one who is aggressive and racist.

skink • n. a smooth-bodied lizard with short or absent limbs.
– ORIGIN Greek *skinkos*.

skinny • adj. (**skinnier**, **skinniest**) **1** very thin. **2** (of a garment) tight-fitting.
– DERIVATIVES **skinniness** n.

skint • adj. Brit. informal having little or no money.
– ORIGIN from *skinned*, in the same sense.

skintight • adj. (of a garment) very close-fitting.

skip[1] • v. (**skips**, **skipping**, **skipped**) **1** move along lightly, stepping from one foot to the other with a little jump. **2** Brit. jump repeatedly over a rope which is held at both ends and turned over the head and under the feet. **3** omit or move

quickly over part of something being read or watched. **4** fail to attend or deal with: *try not to skip breakfast.* •n. a skipping movement.
– ORIGIN prob. Scandinavian.

skip² •n. Brit. a large open-topped container for holding and carrying away bulky refuse.
– ORIGIN Old Norse, 'basket, bushel'.

ski pants •pl. n. women's stretchy trousers with an elastic strap under each foot.

skipjack (also **skipjack tuna**) •n. a small tuna with dark horizontal stripes.
– ORIGIN from SKIP¹ + JACK.

skipper informal •n. **1** the captain of a ship, boat, or aircraft. **2** the captain of a sports team. •v. (**skippers, skippering, skippered**) be captain of.
– ORIGIN Dutch or German *schipper*.

skirl •n. a shrill sound made by bagpipes. •v. (of bagpipes) make a shrill sound.
– ORIGIN prob. Scandinavian.

skirmish •n. a brief spell of unplanned fighting. •v. take part in a brief unplanned fight.
– DERIVATIVES **skirmisher** n.
– ORIGIN Old French *eskirmir*.

skirt •n. **1** a woman's garment that hangs from the waist and covers part or all of the legs. **2** the part of a coat or dress that hangs below the waist. •v. **1** go round or past the edge of. **2** (also **skirt around**) avoid dealing with.
– ORIGIN Old Norse, 'shirt'.

skirting (also **skirting board**) •n. Brit. a wooden board running along the base of the wall of a room.

skit •n. a short comedy sketch that makes fun of something by imitating it.
– ORIGIN perh. from Old Norse.

skitter •v. (**skitters, skittering, skittered**) move lightly and quickly.

skittish •adj. **1** (of a horse) nervous and inclined to shy. **2** lively or changeable.
– DERIVATIVES **skittishly** adv. **skittishness** n.
– ORIGIN perh. from SKIT.

skittle •n. **1** (**skittles**) a game played with wooden pins set up to be bowled down with a wooden ball. **2** a pin used in the game of skittles.

skive •v. (**skives, skiving, skived**) Brit. informal avoid work or a duty by staying away or leaving early.
– DERIVATIVES **skiver** n.
– ORIGIN perh. from French *esquiver* 'slink away'.

skivvy •n. (pl. **skivvies**) Brit. informal a low-ranking female domestic servant.

skua /skyoo-uh/ •n. a large seabird like a gull.

– ORIGIN Old Norse.

skulduggery (also **skullduggery**) •n. underhand or dishonest behaviour.
– ORIGIN Scots *sculduddery*.

skulk •v. hide or move around in a stealthy way.
– DERIVATIVES **skulker** n.
– ORIGIN Scandinavian.

skull •n. **1** the bony framework that surrounds and protects the brain. **2** informal a person's head or brain.
– PHRASES **skull and crossbones** a picture of a skull with two thigh bones crossed below it, used formerly by pirates and now as a warning symbol.

skullcap •n. a small close-fitting cap without a peak.

skunk •n. a black-and-white striped American mammal able to spray foul-smelling liquid at attackers.
– ORIGIN from an American Indian language.

sky •n. (pl. **skies**) the region of the upper atmosphere seen from the earth. •v. (**skies, skying, skied**) informal hit a ball high into the air.
– PHRASES **the sky is the limit** there is no limit.
– DERIVATIVES **skyward** adj. & adv. **skywards** adv.
– ORIGIN Old Norse, 'cloud'.

sky blue •n. a bright clear blue.

skydiving •n. the sport of jumping from an aircraft and performing acrobatic movements before landing by parachute.
– DERIVATIVES **skydiver** n.

sky-high •adv. & adj. very high.

skylark •n. a lark that sings while in flight. •v. behave in a playful or mischievous way.

skylight •n. a window set in a roof.

skyline •n. an outline of land and buildings seen against the sky.

skyrocket •v. (**skyrockets, skyrocketing, skyrocketed**) informal (of a price or amount) increase very rapidly.

skyscraper •n. a very tall building.

slab •n. **1** a large, thick, flat piece of stone or concrete. **2** a thick slice or piece of cake, bread, etc.

slack¹ •adj. **1** not taut or held tightly; loose. **2** (of business or trade) not busy. **3** careless or lazy. **4** (of a tide) between the ebb and the flow. •n. **1** the part of a rope or line which is not held taut. **2** (**slacks**) casual trousers. •v. **1** (**slack off/up**) become slower or less intense. **2** Brit. informal work slowly.
– DERIVATIVES **slacker** n. **slackly** adv. **slackness** n.
– ORIGIN Old English.

S

slack² • n. coal dust or small pieces of coal.
– ORIGIN prob. German or Dutch.

slacken • v. **1** make or become less active or intense. **2** make or become less tight.

slag • n. **1** stony waste matter that is left when metal has been separated from ore by smelting or refining. **2** Brit. informal, derog. a woman who has many sexual partners. • v. (**slags, slagging, slagged**) (**slag someone off**) Brit. informal criticize someone in a rude way.
– ORIGIN German *slagge*.

slag heap • n. a mound of waste material from a mine or industrial site.

slain past part. of SLAY.

slake • v. (**slakes, slaking, slaked**) satisfy a desire or your thirst.
– ORIGIN Old English, 'become less eager'.

slaked lime • n. calcium hydroxide, a soluble substance produced by combining quicklime with water.

slalom /slah-luhm/ • n. a skiing or canoeing race following a winding course marked out by poles.
– ORIGIN Norwegian, 'sloping track'.

slam • v. (**slams, slamming, slammed**) **1** shut forcefully and loudly. **2** push, put, or hit with great force: *she slammed down the phone.* **3** informal criticize severely. • n. a loud bang caused when a door is slammed.
– ORIGIN prob. Scandinavian.

slammer • n. (**the slammer**) informal prison.

slander • n. the crime of saying something untrue that damages a person's reputation. Compare with LIBEL. • v. (**slanders, slandering, slandered**) make false and damaging statements about someone.
– DERIVATIVES **slanderer** n. **slanderous** adj.
– ORIGIN Old French *esclandre*.

slang • n. very informal words and phrases that are more common in speech than in writing and are used by a particular group of people.
– DERIVATIVES **slangy** adj.

slanging match • n. Brit. a long exchange of insults.

slant • v. **1** slope or lean. **2** present information from a particular point of view. • n. **1** a sloping position. **2** a point of view: *a new slant on science.*
– DERIVATIVES **slantwise** adj. & adv.
– ORIGIN Scandinavian.

slap • v. (**slaps, slapping, slapped**) **1** hit with the palm of the hand or a flat object. **2** hit against something with a slapping sound. **3** (**slap someone down**) informal reprimand someone forcefully. **4** (**slap something on**) put something on

a surface quickly or carelessly. • n. **1** an act of slapping. **2** informal make-up. • adv. (also **slap bang**) informal suddenly and forcefully.
– PHRASES **a slap in the face** an unexpected rejection.

slapdash • adj. done too hurriedly and carelessly.

slapstick • n. comedy based on deliberately clumsy actions and embarrassing events.
– ORIGIN first referring to a device consisting of two pieces of wood joined at one end, used by clowns to make a loud slapping sound.

slap-up • adj. Brit. informal (of a meal) large and extravagant.

slash • v. **1** cut with a violent sweeping movement. **2** informal reduce a price, quantity, or amount greatly. • n. **1** a cut made with a wide, sweeping stroke. **2** a slanting stroke (/) used chiefly between alternatives and in fractions and ratios.
– DERIVATIVES **slasher** n.
– ORIGIN Old French *esclachier* 'break in pieces'.

slat • n. each of a series of thin, narrow pieces of wood or other material, arranged so as to overlap or fit into each other.
– DERIVATIVES **slatted** adj.
– ORIGIN Old French *esclat* 'splinter'.

slate • n. **1** a grey, green, or bluish-purple rock easily split into smooth, flat plates, used as roofing material and formerly for writing on. **2** a list of candidates for election to a post. • v. (**slates, slating, slated**) **1** Brit. informal criticize severely. **2** schedule; plan.
– ORIGIN Old French *esclate* 'splinter'.

slather /sla-ther/ • v. (**slathers, slathering, slathered**) informal spread or smear thickly.

slattern /slat-tern/ • n. dated a dirty, untidy woman.
– DERIVATIVES **slatternly** adj.

slaughter /slaw-ter/ • n. **1** the killing of farm animals for food. **2** the killing of a large number of people in a cruel or violent way. • v. (**slaughters, slaughtering, slaughtered**) **1** kill animals for food. **2** kill people in a cruel or violent way. **3** informal defeat thoroughly.
– DERIVATIVES **slaughterer** n.
– ORIGIN Old Norse, 'butcher's meat'.

slaughterhouse • n. a place where animals are killed for food.

Slav /slahv/ • n. a member of a group of peoples in central and eastern Europe who speak Slavic languages.
– ORIGIN Greek *Sklabos*.

slave • n. **1** hist. a person who was the legal

property of another and was forced to obey them. **2** a person who is strongly influenced or controlled by something: *a slave to fashion.* ●v. (**slaves, slaving, slaved**) work very hard.
– ORIGIN Latin *sclava* 'Slavonic captive'.

slave-driver ●n. informal a person who makes other people work very hard.

slave labour ●n. work that is very demanding and very poorly paid.

slaver¹ /slay-ver/ ●n. hist. a person dealing in or owning slaves.

slaver² /sla-ver, slay-ver/ ●v. (**slavers, slavering, slavered**) let saliva run from the mouth. ●n. saliva running from the mouth.
– ORIGIN prob. from German.

slavery ●n. **1** the state of being a slave. **2** the practice of owning slaves.

slave trade ●n. hist. the buying and selling of people as slaves.

Slavic /slah-vik/ ●n. the group of languages that includes Russian, Polish, and Czech. ●adj. relating to Slavic or the Slavs.

slavish ●adj. following or copying something without trying to be original: *a slavish addiction to fashion.*
– DERIVATIVES **slavishly** adv.

Slavonic /sluh-von-ik/ ●n. & adj. = **Slavic**.

slay ●v. (**slays, slaying, slew;** past part. **slain**) old use or N. Amer. kill in a violent way.
– DERIVATIVES **slayer** n.
– ORIGIN Old English.

sleaze ●n. informal immoral or dishonest behaviour, especially in politics.

sleazy ●adj. (**sleazier, sleaziest**) **1** immoral or dishonest. **2** (of a place) dirty and seedy.
– DERIVATIVES **sleaziness** n.

sled ●n. & v. (**sleds, sledding, sledded**) N. Amer. = **sledge**.
– ORIGIN German *sledde.*

sledge ●n. esp. Brit. **1** a vehicle on runners for travelling over snow or ice, either pushed, pulled, or allowed to slide downhill. **2** a toboggan. ●v. (**sledges, sledging, sledged**) ride on a sledge.
– ORIGIN Dutch *sleedse.*

sledgehammer ●n. a large, heavy hammer.
– ORIGIN Old English.

sleek ●adj. **1** (of hair or fur) smooth and glossy. **2** having a wealthy and smart appearance. **3** elegant and streamlined: *a sleek black car.*
– DERIVATIVES **sleekly** adv.
– ORIGIN from **slick**.

sleep ●n. a state of rest in which the nervous system is inactive, the eyes are closed, the muscles are relaxed, and the mind is unconscious. ●v. (**sleeps, sleeping, slept**) **1** be asleep. **2** (**sleep in**) remain asleep or in bed later than usual. **3** provide a specified number of people with beds or bedrooms. **4** (**sleep with**) have sex or be in a sexual relationship with. **5** (**sleep around**) have many sexual partners.
– PHRASES **put something to sleep** kill an animal painlessly. **sleep on it** informal leave a decision until the next day, so as to have more time to consider it.
– DERIVATIVES **sleepless** adj.
– ORIGIN Old English.

sleeper ●n. **1** Brit. each of the beams on which a railway track rests. **2** Brit. a ring or bar worn in a pierced ear to keep the hole from closing. **3** a sleeping car or a train carrying sleeping cars. **4** a film, book, or play that achieves success after first attracting little attention.

sleeping bag ●n. a warm padded bag to sleep in, especially when camping.

sleeping car ●n. a railway carriage with beds or berths.

sleeping partner ●n. Brit. a partner who puts money into a business but is not involved in running it.

sleeping pill ●n. a tablet used to help a person to sleep.

sleeping policeman ●n. Brit. a hump in the road for slowing down traffic.

sleeping sickness ●n. a tropical disease marked by extreme tiredness.

sleepover ●n. a night spent by children at another person's house.

sleepwalk ●v. walk around while asleep.
– DERIVATIVES **sleepwalker** n.

sleepy ●adj. (**sleepier, sleepiest**) **1** needing or ready for sleep. **2** (of a place) without much activity.
– DERIVATIVES **sleepily** adv. **sleepiness** n.

sleet ●n. rain containing some ice, or snow melting as it falls. ●v. (**it sleets, it is sleeting, it sleeted**) sleet falls.
– DERIVATIVES **sleety** adj.
– ORIGIN Germanic.

sleeve ●n. **1** the part of a piece of clothing that covers the arm. **2** a protective cover for a record. **3** a tube fitting over a rod or smaller tube.
– PHRASES **up your sleeve** kept secret and ready for use when needed.
– DERIVATIVES **sleeved** adj. **sleeveless** adj.
– ORIGIN Old English.

sleigh ●n. a sledge drawn by horses or reindeer.
– ORIGIN Dutch *slee.*

sleight /rhymes with slight/ ●n. (in phr. **sleight of hand**) **1** skilful use of the hands when performing magic tricks. **2** the use of cunning to deceive people.

S

– ORIGIN Old Norse, 'sly'.

slender • adj. (**slenderer**, **slenderest**)
1 gracefully thin. **2** barely enough:
a slender majority.
– DERIVATIVES **slenderness** n.

slept past and past part. of SLEEP.

sleuth /*rhymes with* truth/ • n. informal
a detective.
– DERIVATIVES **sleuthing** n.
– ORIGIN Old Norse, 'track'.

slew¹ • v. turn or slide violently or
uncontrollably.

slew² past of SLAY.

slice • n. **1** a thin, broad piece of food cut
from a larger portion. **2** a portion or
share. **3** a utensil with a broad, flat blade
for lifting foods such as fish. **4** (in
sports) a sliced stroke or shot. • v. (**slices**,
slicing, **sliced**) **1** cut into slices. **2** cut
with a sharp implement. **3** (often **slice
through**) move easily and quickly. **4** (in
sport) hit the ball at a slight angle so
that it spins and curves as it travels.
– DERIVATIVES **slicer** n.
– ORIGIN Old French *esclice* 'splinter'.

slick • adj. **1** done or operating in an
impressively smooth and efficient
way. **2** self-confident but shallow or
insincere. **3** smooth, wet, and slippery or
glossy: *his face was slick with sweat.* • n. **1** a
smooth patch of oil. **2** an application or
amount of a glossy or oily substance.
• v. make hair smooth and glossy with
water, oil, or cream.
– DERIVATIVES **slickly** adv. **slickness** n.
– ORIGIN prob. from Old Norse, 'smooth'.

slide • v. (**slides**, **sliding**, **slid**) **1** move
along a smooth surface while remaining
in contact with it. **2** move smoothly,
quickly, or without being noticed.
2 gradually become lower or worse.
• n. **1** a structure with a smooth sloping
surface for children to slide down. **2** a
smooth stretch of ice for sliding on. **3** an
act of sliding. **4** a rectangular piece of
glass on which an object is placed to be
viewed under a microscope. **5** a small
piece of photographic film held in a
frame and viewed with a projector. **6** Brit.
a hairslide.
– ORIGIN Old English.

slide rule • n. a ruler with a sliding
central strip, marked with logarithmic
scales and used for making calculations.

sliding scale • n. a scale of fees, wages,
etc., that varies according to particular
conditions.

slight • adj. **1** small in degree. **2** not
sturdy and strongly built. **3** rather
superficial: *a slight romantic comedy.*
• v. insult someone by treating them
without proper respect. • n. an insult.
– DERIVATIVES **slightly** adv.

– ORIGIN Old Norse, 'smooth'.

slim • adj. (**slimmer**, **slimmest**)
1 gracefully thin. **2** small in width and
long and narrow in shape. **3** very small:
a slim chance. • v. (**slims**, **slimming**,
slimmed) Brit. make or become thinner.
– DERIVATIVES **slimmer** n.
– ORIGIN German or Dutch.

slime • n. an unpleasantly moist, soft,
and slippery substance.
– ORIGIN Old English.

slimline • adj. **1** slender in design. **2** Brit.
(of food or drink) low in calories.

slimy • adj. (**slimier**, **slimiest**) **1** like or
covered by slime. **2** informal pleasant or
flattering in an insincere way.

sling • n. **1** a flexible loop of fabric used
to support or raise a hanging weight. **2** a
strap or loop used to hurl small missiles.
• v. (**slings**, **slinging**, **slung**) **1** hang or
carry loosely: *he slung the hammock
between two trees.* **2** informal throw
carelessly.
– DERIVATIVES **slinger** n.
– ORIGIN prob. from German.

slingback • n. a shoe held in place by a
strap around the ankle above the heel.

slingshot • n. esp. N. Amer. a hand-held
catapult.

slink • v. (**slinks**, **slinking**, **slunk**) move
quietly in a secretive way.
– ORIGIN Old English, 'crawl, creep'.

slinky • adj. (**slinkier**, **slinkiest**) informal
graceful and curvy.

slip¹ • v. (**slips**, **slipping**, **slipped**) **1** lose
your balance and slide for a short
distance. **2** accidentally slide out of
position or from someone's grasp. **3** fail
to grip a surface. **4** gradually become
worse: *people feel that standards have
slipped.* **5** (usu. **slip up**) make a careless
error. **6** move or place quietly, quickly,
or secretly. **7** get free from: *the balloon
slipped its moorings.* • n. **1** an act of
slipping. **2** a minor or careless mistake.
3 a loose-fitting short petticoat. **4** Cricket a
fielding position close behind and to one
side of the batsman.
– PHRASES **give someone the slip** informal
escape from someone. **let something
slip** reveal something accidentally in
conversation. **slip your mind** forget or
forget to do. **slip of the pen** (or **the
tongue**) a minor mistake in writing (or
speech).
– DERIVATIVES **slippage** n.
– ORIGIN prob. from German *slippen*.

slip² • n. **1** a small piece of paper for
writing on or that gives information. **2** a
cutting taken from a plant for grafting
or planting.
– PHRASES **a slip of a boy/girl/thing** a
small, slim young person.

– ORIGIN prob. from Dutch or German *slippe* 'cut, strip'.

slip³ • n. a creamy mixture of clay and water used for decorating pottery.

slip knot • n. a knot that can be undone by a pull, or that can slide along the rope on which it is tied.

slip-on • adj. (of shoes or clothes) having no fastenings and able to be put on and taken off quickly.

slipped disc • n. an instance of the inner material of a disc between spinal vertebrae protruding through the outer coat, pressing on nearby nerves and causing pain.

slipper • n. a comfortable slip-on shoe that is worn indoors.

slippery • adj. **1** difficult to hold firmly or stand on through being smooth or wet. **2** (of a person) difficult to trust.
– DERIVATIVES **slipperiness** n.

slippery slope • n. a course of action likely to lead to something bad.

slippy • adj. (**slippier, slippiest**) informal slippery.

slip road • n. Brit. a road entering or leaving a motorway or dual carriageway.

slipshod • adj. careless, thoughtless, or disorganized.

slipstream • n. **1** a current of air or water driven back by a revolving propeller or jet engine. **2** the partial vacuum created behind a moving vehicle.

slip-up • n. informal a mistake.

slipway • n. a slope leading into water, used for launching and landing boats and ships or for building and repairing them.

slit • n. a long, narrow cut or opening.
• v. (**slits, slitting, slit**) make a slit in.
– ORIGIN Old English.

slither • v. (**slithers, slithering, slithered**) **1** move smoothly over a surface with a twisting motion. **2** slide unsteadily on a loose or slippery surface.
– DERIVATIVES **slithery** adj.
– ORIGIN from SLIDE.

sliver /*rhymes with* river/ • n. a small, narrow, sharp piece cut or split off a larger piece.
– ORIGIN from dialect *slive* 'cleave'.

Sloane (also **Sloane Ranger**) • n. Brit. informal a fashionable upper-class young woman.
– DERIVATIVES **Sloaney** adj.
– ORIGIN from *Sloane* Square, London + Lone *Ranger*, a fictional cowboy hero.

slob Brit. informal • n. a lazy and untidy person. • v. (**slobs, slobbing, slobbed**) behave in a lazy, untidy way.
– DERIVATIVES **slobbish** adj. **slobby** adj.

– ORIGIN Irish *slab* 'mud'.

slobber • v. (**slobbers, slobbering, slobbered**) **1** have saliva dripping from the mouth. **2** (**slobber over**) show excessive enthusiasm for.
– DERIVATIVES **slobbery** adj.
– ORIGIN prob. from Dutch *slobberen* 'walk through mud'.

sloe /*rhymes with* slow/ • n. the small bluish-black fruit of the blackthorn, with a sharp sour taste.
– ORIGIN Old English.

slog informal • v. (**slogs, slogging, slogged**) **1** work hard over a period of time. **2** move with difficulty or effort. **3** hit forcefully. **4** (**slog it out**) Brit. fight or compete fiercely. • n. a spell of difficult, tiring work or travelling.
– DERIVATIVES **slogger** n.

slogan • n. a short, memorable phrase used in advertising or associated with a political group.
– ORIGIN from Scottish Gaelic *sluagh* 'army' + *gairm* 'shout'.

sloop • n. a type of sailing boat with one mast.
– ORIGIN Dutch *sloep*.

slop • v. (**slops, slopping, slopped**) **1** (of a liquid) spill over the edge of a container. **2** apply something carelessly. **3** (**slop out**) Brit. (in prison) empty the contents of a chamber pot. **4** (**slop about/around**) esp. Brit. relax while dressed in a casual or untidy way. • n. (**slops**) **1** waste liquid. **2** unappetizing semi-liquid food.
– ORIGIN prob. from SLIP³.

slope • n. **1** a surface with one end or side at a higher level than another. **2** a part of the side of a hill or mountain.
• v. (**slopes, sloping, sloped**) **1** slant up or down. **2** Brit. informal move in an aimless way. **3** (**slope off**) informal leave without attracting attention.

sloppy • adj. (**sloppier, sloppiest**) **1** (of a substance) containing too much liquid. **2** careless and disorganized. **3** (of a piece of clothing) casual and loose-fitting. **4** informal too sentimental.
– DERIVATIVES **sloppily** adv. **sloppiness** n.

slosh • v. **1** (of liquid in a container) move around with a splashing sound. **2** move through liquid with a splashing sound. **3** pour liquid clumsily. • n. an act or sound of splashing.
– DERIVATIVES **sloshy** adj.
– ORIGIN from SLUSH.

sloshed • adj. informal drunk.

slot • n. **1** a long, narrow opening into which something may be placed. **2** a place given to someone or something in an arrangement or scheme. • v. (**slots, slotting, slotted**) **1** place or be placed into a slot. **2** (**slot in/into**) fit easily into

S

a new role or situation.
– ORIGIN Old French *esclot*.

sloth /slohth/ •n. **1** laziness. **2** a slow-moving tropical American mammal that hangs upside down from branches.
– DERIVATIVES **slothful** adj.
– ORIGIN Old English.

slot machine •n. a fruit machine or (Brit.) vending machine.

slouch •v. stand, move, or sit in a lazy, drooping way. •n. a lazy, drooping way of standing or sitting.
– PHRASES **be no slouch** informal be good or fast at something.
– DERIVATIVES **slouchy** adj.

slouch hat •n. a hat with a wide flexible brim.

slough[1] /rhymes with plough/ •n. **1** a swamp. **2** a situation without progress or activity.
– ORIGIN Old English.

slough[2] /rhymes with rough/ •v. (of an animal) shed an old skin.
– ORIGIN perh. from German *sluwe* 'peel'.

Slovakian /sluh-vak-i-uhn/ (also **Slovak**) •n. a person from Slovakia. •adj. relating to Slovakia.

Slovene /sloh-veen/ •n. **1** a person from Slovenia. **2** the language of Slovenia.
– DERIVATIVES **Slovenian** n. & adj.

slovenly •adj. **1** untidy and dirty. **2** careless: *slovenly speech*.
– DERIVATIVES **slovenliness** n.
– ORIGIN perh. from Flemish *sloef* 'dirty' or Dutch *slof* 'careless'.

slow •adj. **1** moving or capable of moving only at a low speed. **2** taking a long time. **3** (of a clock or watch) showing a time earlier than the correct time. **4** not quick to understand, think, or learn. **5** with little activity: *sales were slow.* **6** (of an oven) giving off heat gently. •v. (often **slow down/up**) **1** reduce speed. **2** live or work less actively.
– DERIVATIVES **slowly** adv. **slowness** n.
– ORIGIN Old English.

slowcoach •n. Brit. informal a person who acts or moves slowly.

slow cooker •n. a large electric pot used for cooking food very slowly.

slow motion •n. the showing of film or video more slowly than it was made or recorded, so that the action appears much slower than in real life.

slow-worm •n. a small lizard without legs.
– ORIGIN Old English.

slub •n. fabric woven from yarn which contains lumps.

sludge •n. thick, soft, wet mud or waste matter.
– DERIVATIVES **sludgy** adj.

slug[1] •n. **1** a small mollusc like a snail without a shell. **2** informal a small amount of an alcoholic drink. **3** informal, esp. N. Amer. a bullet. •v. (**slugs, slugging, slugged**) gulp a drink, especially alcohol.
– ORIGIN prob. Scandinavian.

slug[2] •v. (**slugs, slugging, slugged**) informal, esp. N. Amer. **1** hit with a hard blow. **2** (**slug it out**) settle a dispute or contest by fighting or competing fiercely.

sluggard •n. a lazy, inactive person.
– ORIGIN from former *slug* 'be lazy'.

sluggish •adj. **1** slow-moving or inactive. **2** not lively or alert.
– DERIVATIVES **sluggishly** adv. **sluggishness** n.

sluice /slooss/ •n. **1** (also **sluice gate**) a sliding device for controlling the flow of water. **2** an artificial channel for carrying off surplus water. **3** an act of rinsing. •v. (**sluices, sluicing, sluiced**) wash or rinse with water.
– ORIGIN Old French *escluse*.

slum •n. **1** a run-down area of a city or town inhabited by very poor people. **2** a house or building unfit to be lived in. •v. (**slums, slumming, slummed**) (**slum it**) informal willingly spend time in uncomfortable conditions or at a lower social level.
– DERIVATIVES **slummy** adj.

slumber literary •v. (**slumbers, slumbering, slumbered**) sleep. •n. a sleep.
– ORIGIN from Scots and northern English *sloom*.

slump •v. **1** sit, lean, or fall heavily and limply. **2** decline greatly or over a long period. •n. a sudden fall in prices or a long period of low economic activity.
– ORIGIN prob. from Norwegian *slumpe* 'to fall'.

slung past and past part. of **SLING**.

slunk past and past part. of **SLINK**.

slur •v. (**slurs, slurring, slurred**) **1** speak in an unclear way. **2** perform a group of musical notes in a smooth, flowing way. •n. **1** an insult or accusation intended to damage someone's reputation. **2** a curved line indicating that musical notes are to be slurred.

slurp •v. eat or drink with a loud sucking sound. •n. a sound of slurping.
– ORIGIN Dutch *slurpen*.

slurry /rhymes with hurry/ •n. a semi-liquid mixture of manure, cement, or coal and water.

slush •n. **1** partially melted snow or ice. **2** informal excessively sentimental talk or writing.
– DERIVATIVES **slushy** adj.

slush fund • n. a reserve of money used for illegal purposes.

slut • n. **1** a woman who has many sexual partners. **2** a woman who is untidy or lazy.
– DERIVATIVES **sluttish** adj. **slutty** adj.

sly • adj. (**slyer**, **slyest**) **1** having a cunning and deceitful nature. **2** (of a remark, glance, or expression) suggesting secret knowledge. **3** done secretly: *a sly sip of water.*
– PHRASES **on the sly** in a secret way.
– DERIVATIVES **slyly** adv. **slyness** n.
– ORIGIN Old Norse, 'cunning'.

Sm • symb. the chemical element samarium.

smack¹ • n. **1** a sharp blow given with the palm of the hand. **2** a loud, sharp sound. **3** a loud kiss. • v. **1** hit with a smack. **2** hit or smash into. **3** part the lips noisily. • adv. **1** in a sudden and violent way. **2** exactly.
– ORIGIN Dutch *smacken*.

smack² • v. (**smack of**) **1** have a flavour or smell of. **2** seem to contain or involve something wrong or unpleasant: *the whole thing smacks of a cover-up.* • n. (**a smack of**) a flavour, smell, or suggestion of.
– ORIGIN Old English.

smack³ • n. Brit. a sailing boat with one mast, used for fishing.
– ORIGIN Dutch *smak*.

smack⁴ • n. informal heroin.
– ORIGIN prob. from Yiddish, 'a sniff'.

smacker • n. informal **1** a loud kiss. **2** Brit. one pound sterling.

small • adj. **1** not large in size, amount, or number. **2** not great in strength, power, or importance. **3** not fully grown; young. **4** (of a business or its owner) operating on a modest scale: *a small farmer.* • n. (**smalls**) Brit. informal underwear. • adv. into small pieces.
– PHRASES **feel** (or **look**) **small** feel (or look) foolish. **small beer** Brit. something unimportant. **the small of the back** the part of a person's back where the spine curves in at the waist. **the small screen** television.
– DERIVATIVES **smallness** n.
– ORIGIN Old English.

small arms • pl. n. portable firearms.

small change • n. **1** coins of low value. **2** something unimportant.

small fry • pl. n. **1** young or small fish. **2** unimportant people or things.

smallholding • n. Brit. a piece of leased agricultural land that is smaller than a farm.
– DERIVATIVES **smallholder** n.

small hours • pl. n. (**the small hours**) the early hours of the morning after midnight.

small intestine • n. the part of the intestine that runs between the stomach and the large intestine.

small-minded • adj. having a narrow outlook.

smallpox • n. a disease spread by a virus, with fever and blisters that leave permanent scars.

small print • n. details printed so that they are not easily noticed in an agreement or contract.

small-scale • adj. of limited size or extent.

small talk • n. polite conversation about unimportant matters.

small-time • adj. informal unimportant.

smarmy • adj. (**smarmier**, **smarmiest**) Brit. informal polite and friendly in an insincere and excessive way.

smart • adj. **1** clean, tidy, and stylish. **2** bright and fresh in appearance: *a smart green van.* **3** (of a place) fashionable and upmarket. **4** quick-witted. **5** esp. N. Amer. clever in a cheeky or sarcastic way. **6** quick: *a smart salute.* • v. **1** give a sharp, stinging pain. **2** feel upset and annoyed.
– PHRASES **look smart** esp. Brit. be quick.
– DERIVATIVES **smartly** adv. **smartness** n.
– ORIGIN Old English.

smart alec (esp. N. Amer. also **smart aleck**) • n. informal a person who is irritating because they behave as if they know everything.

smart card • n. a plastic card on which information is stored in electronic form.

smarten • v. (**smarten up**) make or become smarter.

smartish • adv. informal, esp. Brit. quickly.

smartphone • n. a mobile phone which incorporates a palmtop computer.

smash • v. **1** break violently into pieces. **2** hit or collide forcefully. **3** (in sport) hit the ball hard. **4** completely defeat or destroy. • n. **1** an act or sound of smashing. **2** (also **smash hit**) informal a very successful song, film, or show.

smash-and-grab • adj. Brit. (of a robbery) in which the thief smashes a shop window and seizes goods.

smasher • n. Brit. informal a very attractive or impressive person or thing.

smashing • adj. Brit. informal excellent.

smattering • n. **1** a small amount. **2** a slight knowledge of a language or subject.

smear • v. **1** coat or mark with a greasy or sticky substance. **2** blur or smudge. **3** damage someone's reputation by false accusations. • n. **1** a greasy or sticky mark. **2** a false accusation. **3** a sample

S

thinly spread on a slide for examination under a microscope.
– DERIVATIVES **smeary** adj.
– ORIGIN Old English.

smear test • n. Brit. a test to detect signs of cancer in the neck of the womb.

smell • n. **1** the ability to sense things by means of the organs in the nose. **2** something sensed by the nose; an odour. **3** an act of smelling. • v. (**smells, smelling, smelt** or **smelled**) **1** sense the smell of. **2** sniff at something in order to find out its smell. **3** send out a smell. **4** have a strong or unpleasant smell. **5** detect or sense: *I can smell trouble.*
– PHRASES **smell a rat** informal suspect a trick.

smelling salts • pl. n. (especially in the past) a chemical mixed with perfume, sniffed by someone who feels faint.

smelly • adj. (**smellier, smelliest**) having a strong or unpleasant smell.

smelt[1] • v. extract metal from its ore by a process involving heating and melting.
– DERIVATIVES **smelter** n.
– ORIGIN Dutch or German *smelten.*

smelt[2] past and past part. of **SMELL**.

smelt[3] • n. (pl. **smelt** or **smelts**) a small silvery fish.
– ORIGIN Old English.

smidgen (also **smidgeon** or **smidgin**) • n. informal a tiny amount.
– ORIGIN perh. from Scots *smitch* in the same sense.

smile • v. (**smiles, smiling, smiled**) **1** form the features into a pleased, friendly, or amused expression, with the corners of the mouth turned up. **2** (**smile at/on**) favour: *fortune smiled on him.* • n. an act of smiling.
– ORIGIN perh. Scandinavian.

smiley • adj. informal smiling and cheerful.

smirch /smerch/ • v. **1** make dirty. **2** damage someone's reputation.

smirk • v. smile in a smug or silly way. • n. a smug or silly smile.
– ORIGIN Old English.

smite • v. (**smites, smiting, smote**; past part. **smitten**) **1** (**be smitten**) be affected severely by a disease. **2** (**be smitten**) be strongly attracted to someone or something. **3** literary hit with a hard blow.
– ORIGIN Old English, 'to smear'.

smith • n. **1** a person who works in metal. **2** a blacksmith. • v. treat metal by heating, hammering, and forging it.
– ORIGIN Old English.

smithereens /smi-thuh-reenz/ • pl. n. informal small pieces.
– ORIGIN prob. from Irish *smidirín.*

smithy /smi-thi/ • n. (pl. **smithies**) a blacksmith's workshop.

– ORIGIN Old Norse.

smitten past part. of **SMITE**.

smock • n. **1** a loose dress or blouse with the upper part closely gathered in smocking. **2** a loose overall worn to protect the clothes.
– ORIGIN Old English.

smocking • n. decoration on a garment created by gathering a section of the material into tight pleats and holding them together with a pattern of stitches.

smog • n. fog or haze made worse by smoke or other pollution in the atmosphere.
– DERIVATIVES **smoggy** adj.
– ORIGIN from **SMOKE** and **FOG**.

smoke • n. **1** a visible vapour in the air produced by a burning substance. **2** an act of smoking tobacco. **3** informal a cigarette or cigar. **4** (**the Smoke** or **the Big Smoke**) Brit. a big city. • v. (**smokes, smoking, smoked**) **1** give out smoke. **2** breathe the smoke of a cigarette, pipe, etc. in and out. **3** preserve meat or fish by hanging it in smoke. **4** (**smoke someone/thing out**) drive someone or something out of a place with smoke. **5** (as adj. **smoked**) (of glass) treated so as to darken it.
– PHRASES **go up in smoke** informal (of a plan) come to nothing. **there's no smoke without fire** there is always a reason for a rumour.
– DERIVATIVES **smokable** adj. **smokeless** adj. **smoker** n.
– ORIGIN Old English.

smoke alarm • n. a device that detects and gives a warning of the presence of smoke.

smokeless zone • n. Brit. a district in which it is illegal to create smoke.

smokescreen • n. **1** something intended to disguise someone's real intentions or activities. **2** a cloud of smoke created to conceal military operations.

smokestack • n. a chimney or funnel for discharging smoke from a locomotive, ship, factory, etc.

smoking gun • n. a piece of evidence that proves without doubt that someone is guilty of wrongdoing.

smoking jacket • n. a man's jacket formerly worn while smoking after dinner.

smoky (also **smokey**) • adj. (**smokier, smokiest**) **1** producing or filled with smoke. **2** having the taste or smell of smoked food.
– DERIVATIVES **smokily** adv. **smokiness** n.

smolder • v. US = **SMOULDER**.

smolt /smohlt/ • n. a young salmon or trout after the parr stage, when it migrates to the sea for the first time.

smooch • v. informal **1** kiss and cuddle.
2 Brit. dance slowly in a close embrace.
– DERIVATIVES **smoochy** adj.

smooth • adj. **1** having an even and
regular surface. **2** (of a liquid) without
lumps. **3** (of movement) without jerks.
4 happening without difficulties.
5 charming in a very confident or
flattering way. **6** (of a flavour) not harsh
or bitter. • v. (also **smoothe**) (**smooths** or
smoothes, **smoothing**, **smoothed**)
1 make smooth. **2** (**smooth something
over**) deal successfully with a problem.
– DERIVATIVES **smoothly** adv.
smoothness n.
– ORIGIN Old English.

smoothie • n. **1** a thick, smooth drink of
fresh fruit puréed with milk, yogurt, or
ice cream. **2** informal a charming and
confident man who is often not sincere.

smooth-talking • adj. informal using very
persuasive or flattering language.

smorgasbord /smor-guhz-bord/ • n. a
meal consisting of a range of open
sandwiches and savoury items.
– ORIGIN Swedish.

smote past of SMITE.

smother • v. (**smothers**, **smothering**,
smothered) **1** suffocate someone by
covering the nose and mouth.
2 (**smother someone/thing in/with**)
cover someone or something entirely
with. **3** prevent from happening: *she
smothered a sigh.* **4** make someone feel
overwhelmed by being too protective of
them. **5** put out a fire by covering it.
– ORIGIN Old English.

smoulder (US **smolder**) • v. (**smoulders**,
smouldering, **smouldered**) **1** burn
slowly with smoke but no flame. **2** feel
strong and barely hidden anger, lust, etc.
– ORIGIN Dutch *smeulen*.

SMS • abbrev. Short Message (or
Messaging) Service, a system that
enables mobile phone users to send and
receive text messages.

smudge • v. (**smudges**, **smudging**,
smudged) make or become blurred or
smeared. • n. a smudged mark.
– DERIVATIVES **smudgy** adj.

smug • adj. (**smugger**, **smuggest**) pleased
with yourself in an irritating way.
– DERIVATIVES **smugly** adv. **smugness** n.
– ORIGIN German *smuk* 'pretty'.

smuggle • v. (**smuggles**, **smuggling**,
smuggled) **1** move goods illegally into
or out of a country. **2** take someone or
something somewhere secretly.
– DERIVATIVES **smuggler** n.
– ORIGIN German *smuggelen*.

smut • n. **1** a small flake of soot or dirt.
2 indecent talk, writing, or pictures.
– ORIGIN German *schmutzen*

'make dirty or corrupt'.

smutty • adj. (**smuttier**, **smuttiest**)
1 indecent. **2** dirty or sooty.

Sn • symb. the chemical element tin.
– ORIGIN Latin *stannum* 'tin'.

snack • n. a small quantity of food eaten
between meals or instead of a meal.
• v. eat a snack.
– ORIGIN Dutch.

snaffle • v. (**snaffles**, **snaffling**, **snaffled**)
Brit. informal take something quickly or
secretly for yourself. • n. a simple bit on
a horse's bridle, used with a single set of
reins.
– ORIGIN prob. German or Dutch.

snag • n. **1** an unexpected difficulty. **2** a
sharp or jagged projection. **3** a small
tear. • v. (**snags**, **snagging**, **snagged**)
catch or tear on a sharp projection.
– ORIGIN prob. Scandinavian.

snaggle-toothed • adj. having
irregular or projecting teeth.
– ORIGIN from SNAG.

snail • n. a slow-moving mollusc with a
spiral shell into which it can withdraw
its whole body.
– ORIGIN Old English.

snake • n. a reptile with a long slender
limbless body, many kinds of which
have a poisonous bite. • v. (**snakes**,
snaking, **snaked**) move with the
twisting motion of a snake.
– PHRASES **snake in the grass** a person
who pretends to be someone's friend
but is secretly working against them.
– ORIGIN Old English.

snake charmer • n. an entertainer who
appears to make snakes move by playing
music.

snaky • adj. (**snakier**, **snakiest**) **1** long
and curvy. **2** cold and cunning.

snap • v. (**snaps**, **snapping**, **snapped**)
1 break with a sharp cracking sound.
2 (of an animal) make a sudden bite.
3 open or close with a brisk movement
or sharp sound. **4** (**snap something up**)
quickly buy something that is in short
supply. **5** suddenly lose your self-
control. **6** say something quickly and
irritably. **7** (**snap out of**) informal get out
of a bad mood by a sudden effort. **8** take
a snapshot of. • n. **1** an act or sound of
snapping. **2** a snapshot. **3** Brit. a card game
in which players compete to call 'snap'
as soon as two cards of the same type are
exposed. • adj. done on the spur of the
moment: *a snap decision.*
– ORIGIN prob. from Dutch or German
snappen 'seize'.

snapdragon • n. a plant with brightly
coloured flowers which have a mouth-
like opening.

snapper • n. an edible sea fish noted for
snapping its toothed jaws.

snappish • adj. irritable; snappy.

snappy • adj. (**snappier, snappiest**) informal **1** irritable and sharp. **2** cleverly brief and to the point: *snappy dialogue.* **3** neat and stylish: *a snappy dresser.*
– PHRASES **make it snappy** do it quickly.
– DERIVATIVES **snappily** adv.

snapshot • n. an informal photograph, taken quickly.

snare • n. **1** a trap for catching small animals, consisting of a loop of wire that pulls tight. **2** something likely to lure someone into trouble. **3** (also **snare drum**) a drum with a length of wire stretched across the head to produce a rattling sound. • v. (**snares, snaring, snared**) catch in a snare or trap.
– ORIGIN Old Norse; sense 3 is probably from German or Dutch, 'harp string'.

snarl • v. **1** growl with bared teeth. **2** say something aggressively. • n. an act or sound of snarling.
– DERIVATIVES **snarly** adj.
– ORIGIN Germanic.

snarl-up • n. Brit. informal a traffic jam. • v. (**snarl something up**) entangle or hinder something.
– ORIGIN from SNARE.

snatch • v. **1** grab quickly in a rude or eager way. **2** informal steal or kidnap suddenly. **3** quickly take when the chance presents itself: *he snatched a few hours' sleep.* • n. **1** an act of snatching. **2** a fragment of music or talk.
– ORIGIN perh. from SNACK.

snazzy • adj. (**snazzier, snazziest**) informal smart and stylish.

sneak • v. (**sneaks, sneaking, sneaked** or N. Amer. informal **snuck**) **1** move or take in a secretive way. **2** Brit. informal inform someone in authority of a person's wrongdoings. • n. Brit. informal a telltale. • adj. secret or unofficial: *a sneak preview.*
– ORIGIN perh. from former *snike* 'to creep'.

sneaker • n. esp. N. Amer. a soft shoe worn for sports or casual occasions.

sneaking • adj. (of a feeling) staying in the mind.

sneaky • adj. (**sneakier, sneakiest**) secretive in a sly or guilty way.
– DERIVATIVES **sneakily** adv. **sneakiness** n.

sneer • n. a scornful or mocking smile, remark, or tone of voice. • v. (**sneers, sneering, sneered**) smile or speak in a scornful or mocking way.

sneeze • v. (**sneezes, sneezing, sneezed**) suddenly expel air from the nose and mouth due to irritation of the nostrils. • n. an act of sneezing.
– PHRASES **not to be sneezed at** informal not to be rejected without careful consideration.

– DERIVATIVES **sneezy** adj.
– ORIGIN Old English.

snick • v. cut a small notch in. • n. a small notch or cut.
– ORIGIN prob. from former *snick or snee* 'fight with knives'.

snicker • v. (**snickers, snickering, snickered**) **1** esp. N. Amer. snigger. **2** (of a horse) make a gentle high-pitched neigh. • n. an act or sound of snickering.

snide • adj. disrespectful or mocking in an indirect way.
– DERIVATIVES **snidely** adv.

sniff • v. **1** breath in air audibly through the nose. **2** (**sniff around/round**) informal investigate something secretly. **3** (**sniff something out**) informal discover something by investigation. • n. **1** an act of sniffing. **2** informal a hint. **3** informal a slight chance.
– PHRASES **not to be sniffed at** informal worth having or considering.
– DERIVATIVES **sniffer** n.

sniffer dog • n. a dog trained to find drugs or explosives by smell.

sniffle • v. (**sniffles, sniffling, sniffled**) sniff slightly or repeatedly. • n. **1** an act of sniffling. **2** a slight head cold.
– DERIVATIVES **sniffly** adj.

sniffy • adj. informal scornful.
– DERIVATIVES **sniffily** adv.

snifter • n. Brit.informal a small quantity of an alcoholic drink.

snigger esp. Brit. • v. (**sniggers, sniggering, sniggered**) give a smothered laugh. • n. a smothered laugh.
– ORIGIN from SNICKER.

snip • v. (**snips, snipping, snipped**) cut with scissors using small, quick strokes. • n. **1** an act of snipping. **2** a small piece that has been cut off. **3** Brit. informal a bargain.
– ORIGIN German, 'small piece'.

snipe /*rhymes with* pipe/ • v. (**snipes, sniping, sniped**) (usu. **snipe at**) **1** shoot at someone from a hiding place at long range. **2** criticize in a sly or petty way. • n. (pl. **snipe** or **snipes**) a brown wading bird with a long straight bill.
– ORIGIN prob. Scandinavian.

sniper • n. a hidden gunman who shoots at someone at long range.

snippet • n. a small piece or brief extract.

snitch informal • v. **1** steal something. **2** inform on someone. • n. an informer.

snivel • v. (**snivels, snivelling, snivelled**; US **snivels, sniveling, sniveled**) **1** cry and sniffle. **2** complain in a whining or tearful way.
– ORIGIN Old English, 'mucus'.

snob •n. **1** a person who greatly respects upper-class or rich people and who looks down on people of a lower class. **2** a person who believes that their tastes in a particular area are superior to other people: *a wine snob.*
– DERIVATIVES **snobbery** n. (pl. **snobberies**). **snobby** adj.

snobbish •adj. typical of a snob.
– DERIVATIVES **snobbishly** adv.

snog Brit. informal •v. (**snogs, snogging, snogged**) kiss and cuddle. •n. an act or spell of kissing and cuddling.

snood /snood/ •n. **1** a hairnet worn over the hair at the back of a woman's head. **2** a wide ring of knitted material worn as a hood or scarf.
– ORIGIN Old English.

snook /snook/ •n. (in phr. **cock a snook at**) informal, esp. Brit. openly show contempt or a lack of respect for.

snooker •n. **1** a game played with cues on a billiard table, in which the players use a white cue ball to pocket the other balls in a set order. **2** a position in a game of snooker or pool in which a player cannot make a direct shot at any permitted ball. •v. (**snookers, snookering, snookered**) **1** subject an opponent to a snooker. **2** (**be snookered**) Brit. informal be placed in an impossible position.

snoop informal •v. look around or investigate secretly to find out private information. •n. an act of snooping.
– DERIVATIVES **snooper** n.
– ORIGIN Dutch *snoepen* 'eat on the sly'.

snooty •adj. (**snootier, snootiest**) informal treating people as if they are inferior.
– DERIVATIVES **snootily** adv. **snootiness** n.
– ORIGIN from **SNOUT**.

snooze informal •n. a short, light sleep. •v. (**snoozes, snoozing, snoozed**) have a short, light sleep.
– DERIVATIVES **snoozer** n. **snoozy** adj.

snore •n. a snorting sound in a person's breathing while they are asleep. •v. (**snores, snoring, snored**) make a snorting sound while asleep.
– DERIVATIVES **snorer** n.

snorkel /snor-k'l/ •n. a tube for a swimmer to breathe through while under water. •v. (**snorkels, snorkelling, snorkelled**; US **snorkels, snorkeling, snorkeled**) swim using a snorkel.
– DERIVATIVES **snorkeller** n.
– ORIGIN German *Schnorchel.*

snort •n. **1** an explosive sound made by the sudden forcing of breath through the nose. **2** informal an amount of cocaine that is breathed in through the nose. **3** informal a measure of an alcoholic drink.
•v. **1** make a snort. **2** informal inhale cocaine.
– DERIVATIVES **snorter** n.

snot •n. informal mucus in the nose.
– ORIGIN prob. from Dutch or German.

snotty •adj. (**snottier, snottiest**) informal **1** full of or covered with mucus from the nose. **2** having a superior or arrogant attitude.
– DERIVATIVES **snottiness** n.

snout •n. **1** the projecting nose and mouth of an animal. **2** the projecting front or end of something such as a pistol. **3** Brit. informal a police informer.
– ORIGIN Dutch or German *snūt.*

snow •n. **1** frozen water vapour in the atmosphere that falls in light white flakes. **2** (**snows**) falls of snow. •v. **1** (**it snows, it is snowing, it snowed**) snow falls. **2** (**be snowed in/up**) be unable to leave a place due to heavy snow. **3** (**be snowed under**) be overwhelmed with a large quantity of something.
– ORIGIN Old English.

snowball •n. a ball of packed snow. •v. **1** increase rapidly in size, strength, or importance: *the campaign was snowballing.* **2** throw snowballs at.

snowboard •n. a board resembling a short, broad ski, used for sliding downhill on snow.
– DERIVATIVES **snowboarder** n. **snowboarding** n.

snowbound •adj. **1** prevented from travelling or going out because of snow. **2** (of a place) cut off because of snow.

snowdrift •n. a bank of deep snow heaped up by the wind.

snowdrop •n. a plant which bears drooping white flowers during the late winter.

snowfall •n. **1** a fall of snow. **2** the quantity of snow falling within a particular area in a given time.

snowflake •n. each of the many feathery ice crystals that fall as snow.

snowline •n. the altitude above which some snow remains on the ground throughout the year.

snowman •n. (pl. **snowmen**) a model of a human figure made with compressed snow.

snowmobile •n. a motor vehicle for travelling over snow.

snowplough (US **snowplow**) •n. a device or vehicle for clearing roads of snow.

snowshoe •n. a flat device resembling a tennis racket, which is attached to the sole of a boot and used for walking on snow.

snowstorm •n. a heavy fall of snow accompanied by a high wind.

S

snowy • adj. (**snowier, snowiest**)
1 covered with snow. **2** (of weather or a period of time) having snow falling.
3 pure white.

snowy owl • n. a large northern owl, the male being entirely white.

snub • v. (**snubs, snubbing, snubbed**) ignore or reject scornfully. • n. an act of snubbing. • adj. (of a person's nose) short and turned up at the end.
– ORIGIN Old Norse, 'chide'.

snuck N. Amer. informal past and past part. of SNEAK.

snuff[1] • v. **1** put out a candle. **2** (**snuff something out**) abruptly put an end to something. **3** (**snuff it**) Brit. informal die.

snuff[2] • n. powdered tobacco that is sniffed up the nostril. • v. sniff at.
– ORIGIN prob. from Dutch *snuftabak*; the verb is from Dutch *snuffen* 'to snuffle'.

snuffer • n. a small metal cone on the end of a handle, used to put out a candle.

snuffle • v. (**snuffles, snuffling, snuffled**) **1** breathe noisily through a partially blocked nose. **2** (of an animal) make repeated sniffing sounds. • n. **1** a snuffling sound. **2** (**the snuffles**) informal a cold.
– DERIVATIVES **snuffly** adj.
– ORIGIN prob. from German and Dutch *snuffelen*.

snug • adj. (**snugger, snuggest**) **1** warm and cosy. **2** close-fitting. • n. Brit. a small, cosy bar in a pub or small hotel.
– DERIVATIVES **snugly** adv.
– ORIGIN prob. from German or Dutch.

snuggery • n. (pl. **snuggeries**) a cosy place.

snuggle • v. (**snuggles, snuggling, snuggled**) settle into a warm, comfortable position.
– ORIGIN from SNUG.

so[1] • adv. **1** to such a great extent. **2** extremely; very much. **3** to the same extent; as. **4** referring back to something previously mentioned. **5** similarly: *times have changed and so have I.* **6** in the way described; thus. • conj. **1** therefore. **2** (**so that**) with the result or aim that. **3** and then. **4** in the same way.
– PHRASES **and so on** (or **forth**) and similar things. **or so** approximately. **so long!** informal goodbye. **so much as** even: *without so much as a word.*
– ORIGIN Old English.

so[2] • n. var. of SOH.

soak • v. **1** make or become thoroughly wet by leaving or remaining in liquid. **2** (of a liquid) spread completely throughout. **3** (**soak something up**) absorb a liquid. **4** (**soak something up**) expose yourself to: *soak up the Mediterranean sun.* • n. **1** an act or spell of soaking. **2** informal a heavy drinker.
– ORIGIN Old English.

soaking (also **soaking wet**) • adj. very wet.

so-and-so • n. (pl. **so-and-sos**) informal **1** a person or thing whose name you do not know. **2** a disliked person: *a nosy so-and-so.*

soap • n. **1** a substance used with water for washing and cleaning, made of natural oils or fats combined with an alkali. **2** informal a soap opera. • v. wash with soap.
– ORIGIN Old English.

soapbox • n. **1** a box that someone stands on to make a speech in public. **2** an opportunity for someone to air their views publicly: *I tend to get up on my soapbox about this issue.*

soap opera • n. a television or radio serial dealing with the daily lives of a group of characters.
– ORIGIN so named because such serials were originally sponsored by soap manufacturers.

soapstone • n. a soft rock consisting largely of talc.

soapy • adj. (**soapier, soapiest**) **1** containing or covered with soap. **2** like soap.

soar • v. **1** fly or rise high into the air. **2** maintain height in the air by gliding. **3** increase rapidly above the usual level.
– ORIGIN Old French *essorer*.

sob • v. (**sobs, sobbing, sobbed**) **1** cry with loud gasps. **2** say while sobbing. • n. an act or sound of sobbing.
– ORIGIN perh. Dutch or German.

sober • adj. (**soberer, soberest**) **1** not drunk. **2** serious and sensible. **3** (of a colour) not bright or likely to attract attention. • v. (**sobers, sobering, sobered**) **1** (**sober up**) make or become sober after being drunk. **2** make or become serious.
– DERIVATIVES **soberly** adv.
– ORIGIN Latin *sobrius*.

sobriety /suh-bry-uh-ti/ • n. the state of being sober.

sobriquet /soh-bri-kay/ (also **soubriquet**) • n. a person's nickname.
– ORIGIN French.

sob story • n. informal a story intended to arouse sympathy.

soca /soh-kuh/ • n. calypso music with elements of soul, originally from Trinidad.
– ORIGIN from SOUL and CALYPSO.

so-called • adj. called by the name or term specified.

soccer • n. a form of football played with

a round ball which may not be handled during play except by the goalkeepers, the object being to score goals.
– ORIGIN shortening of *Assoc.* (from **ASSOCIATION FOOTBALL**).

sociable •adj. **1** liking to talk to and spend time with other people. **2** friendly and welcoming: *a very sociable little village.*
– DERIVATIVES **sociability** n. **sociably** adv.
– ORIGIN Latin *sociabilis.*

social •adj. **1** relating to society and its organization. **2** needing the company of other people: *we are social beings as well as individuals.* **3** (of an activity) in which people meet each other for pleasure. **4** (of birds, insects, or mammals) breeding or living in organized communities. •n. an informal social gathering.
– DERIVATIVES **socially** adv.
– ORIGIN Latin *socialis* 'allied'.

social climber •n. derog. a person who is anxious to gain a higher social status.

social contract •n. an unspoken agreement among the members of a society to cooperate for the benefit of all, for example by giving up some individual freedom in return for state protection.

socialism •n. a political and economic theory which holds that a country's land, transport, natural resources, and chief industries should be owned or controlled by the community as a whole.
– DERIVATIVES **socialist** n. & adj.

socialite •n. a person who mixes in fashionable society.

socialize (or **socialise**) •v. (**socializes**, **socializing**, **socialized**) **1** mix socially with other people. **2** make someone behave in a way that is acceptable to society.
– DERIVATIVES **socialization** n.

social science •n. **1** the scientific study of human society and social relationships. **2** a subject within this field, such as economics.

social security •n. (in the UK) money provided by the state for people who are poor or unemployed.

social services •pl. n. services provided by the state for the community, such as education and medical care.

social studies •n. the study of human society.

social work •n. work carried out by people trained to help improve the conditions of people who are poor, old, etc.
– DERIVATIVES **social worker** n.

society •n. (pl. **societies**) **1** people living together in an ordered community. **2** a

community of people living in a country or region, and having shared customs, laws, and organizations. **3** (also **high society**) people who are fashionable, wealthy, and influential. **4** an organization formed for a particular purpose. **5** the situation of being in the company of other people: *she shunned the society of others.*
– DERIVATIVES **societal** adj.
– ORIGIN Latin *societas.*

socio-economic •adj. relating to the interaction of social and economic factors.

sociology •n. the study of the development, structure, and functioning of human society.
– DERIVATIVES **sociological** adj. **sociologist** n.

sociopath /soh-si-oh-path, soh-shi-oh-path/ •n. a person with a mental disorder showing itself in extreme antisocial attitudes and behaviour.

sock •n. **1** a knitted garment for the foot and lower part of the leg. **2** informal a hard blow. •v. informal hit forcefully.
– PHRASES **pull your socks up** informal make an effort to improve. **put a sock in it** Brit. informal stop talking. **sock it to** informal make a strong impression on.
– ORIGIN Greek *sukkhos* 'comic actor's shoe'.

socket •n. **1** a hollow in which something fits or revolves. **2** an electrical device into which a plug or light bulb is fitted.
– ORIGIN Old French *soket* 'small ploughshare'.

Socratic /suh-krat-ik/ •adj. relating to the ancient Greek philosopher Socrates or his ideas.

sod •n. **1** grass-covered ground. **2** a piece of turf.
– ORIGIN Dutch or German *sode.*

soda •n. **1** (also **soda water**) fizzy water. **2** N. Amer. a sweet fizzy drink. **3** a compound of sodium.
– ORIGIN Latin.

soda fountain •n. N. Amer. **1** a device that dispenses soda water or soft drinks. **2** a cafe or counter selling soft drinks, ice cream, etc.

sodden •adj. **1** soaked through. **2** (in combination) having drunk an excessive amount of an alcoholic drink: *whisky-sodden.*
– ORIGIN first meaning 'boiled': from **SEETHE**.

sodium •n. a soft silver-white metallic chemical element of which common salt and soda are compounds.
– ORIGIN from **SODA**.

sodium bicarbonate •n. a soluble

white powder used in fizzy drinks and as a raising agent in baking.

sodium chloride •n. the chemical name for common salt.

sodium hydroxide •n. a strongly alkaline white compound used in industrial processes; caustic soda.

sodomite /sod-uh-myt/ •n. a person who engages in sodomy.

sodomy •n. anal intercourse.
– ORIGIN from the city of *Sodom* in the Bible (Book of Genesis chapter 19).

Sod's Law •n. Brit. = MURPHY'S LAW.

sofa •n. a long padded seat with a back and arms, for two or more people.
– ORIGIN French.

sofa bed •n. a sofa that can be converted into a bed.

soft •adj. 1 easy to mould, cut, compress, or fold. 2 not rough in texture. 3 quiet and gentle: *soft whispers*. 4 (of light or colour) not harsh. 5 not strict or strict enough. 6 informal (of a job or way of life) requiring little effort. 7 informal foolish. 8 (**soft on**) informal have romantic feelings for. 9 (of a drink) not alcoholic. 10 (of a drug) not likely to cause addiction. 11 (of water) free from mineral salts.
– PHRASES **have a soft spot for** be fond of. **a soft** (or **easy**) **touch** informal a person who is easily persuaded.
– DERIVATIVES **softly** adv. **softness** n.
– ORIGIN Old English.

softback •n. = PAPERBACK.

softball •n. a form of baseball played on a smaller field with a larger, softer ball.

soft-boiled •adj. (of an egg) lightly boiled, leaving the yolk soft.

soften •v. 1 make or become soft or softer. 2 (**soften someone up**) make someone more likely to do something.
– DERIVATIVES **softener** n.

soft focus •n. deliberate slight blurring in a photograph or film.

soft fruit •n. Brit. a small fruit without a stone, e.g. a strawberry.

soft furnishings •pl. n. Brit. curtains, chair coverings, and other cloth items used to decorate a room.

soft-hearted •adj. kind and caring.

softie (also **softy**) •n. (pl. **softies**) informal a weak or soft-hearted person.

softly-softly •adj. Brit. cautious and patient.

soft palate •n. the fleshy, flexible part towards the back of the roof of the mouth.

soft-pedal •v. play down the unpleasant aspects of. •n. (**soft pedal**) a pedal on a piano that can be pressed to soften the tone.

soft sell •n. the selling of something in a gently persuasive way.

soft-soap •v. informal use flattery to persuade.

soft target •n. a person or thing that is unprotected or vulnerable.

soft top •n. a car with a roof that can be folded back.

software •n. programs and other operating information used by a computer.

softwood •n. the wood from conifers as opposed to that of broadleaved trees.

softy •n. var. of SOFTIE.

soggy •adj. (**soggier**, **soggiest**) very wet and soft.
– DERIVATIVES **soggily** adv. **sogginess** n.
– ORIGIN from dialect *sog* 'a swamp'.

soh /soh/ (also **so** or **sol**) •n. Music the fifth note of a major scale, coming after 'fah' and before 'lah'.
– ORIGIN the first syllable of *solve*, taken from a Latin hymn.

soi-disant /swah-dee-zon/ •adj. so-called; self-styled: *a soi-disant novelist*.
– ORIGIN French.

soigné /swun-yay/ •adj. (fem. **soignée** /swun-yay/) elegant and well groomed.
– ORIGIN French.

soil[1] •n. 1 the upper layer of earth, in which plants grow. 2 the territory of a particular nation.
– ORIGIN Old French.

soil[2] •v. 1 make dirty. 2 bring discredit to: *the scandal soiled the reputations of all involved.* •n. sewage.
– ORIGIN Old French *soiller*.

soirée /swah-ray/ •n. an evening social gathering for conversation or music.
– ORIGIN French.

sojourn /so-juhn, so-jern/ literary •n. a temporary stay. •v. stay temporarily.
– DERIVATIVES **sojourner** n.
– ORIGIN Old French *sojourner*.

sol •n. var. of SOH.

solace /sol-iss/ •n. comfort in a time of difficulty or sadness. •v. (**solaces**, **solacing**, **solaced**) give comfort to.
– ORIGIN Old French *solas*.

solar /soh-ler/ •adj. relating to the sun or its rays.
– ORIGIN Latin *sol* 'sun'.

solar battery (also **solar cell**) •n. a device that converts the sun's radiation into electricity.

solar eclipse •n. an eclipse in which the sun is hidden by the moon.

solarium /suh-lair-i-uhm/ •n. (pl. **solariums** or **solaria** /suh-lair-i-uh/) 1 a room equipped with sunlamps or sunbeds. 2 a room with large areas of glass to let in sunlight.

– ORIGIN Latin.

solar panel • n. a panel designed to absorb the sun's rays as a source of energy for generating electricity or heating.

solar plexus • n. a network of nerves at the pit of the stomach.

solar power • n. power obtained by harnessing the energy of the sun's rays.

solar system • n. the sun together with the planets, asteroids, comets, etc. in orbit around it.

solar year • n. the time between one spring or autumn equinox and the next, or between one winter or summer solstice and the next (365 days, 5 hours, 48 minutes, and 46 seconds).

sold past and past part. of SELL.

solder /sohl-der/ • n. a soft alloy used for joining metals. • v. (**solders, soldering, soldered**) join with solder.
– ORIGIN Old French *soudure*.

soldering iron • n. an electrical tool for melting and applying solder.

soldier • n. 1 a person who serves in an army. 2 a private in an army. 3 Brit. informal a strip of bread or toast, dipped into a soft-boiled egg. • v. (**soldiers, soldiering, soldiered**) 1 serve as a soldier. 2 (**soldier on**) informal continue doing something in spite of difficulty.
– PHRASES **soldier of fortune** a professional soldier hired to serve in a foreign army.
– DERIVATIVES **soldierly** adj.
– ORIGIN Old French.

soldiery • n. 1 soldiers as a group. 2 military training or knowledge.

sole[1] • n. 1 the underside of a person's foot. 2 the section forming the underside of a piece of footwear.
• v. (**soles, soling, soled**) replace the sole on a shoe.
– ORIGIN Latin *solea* 'sandal, sill'.

sole[2] • n. (pl **sole**) an edible marine flatfish.
– ORIGIN Latin *solea* 'sandal, sill', from its shape.

sole[3] • adj. 1 one and only. 2 belonging or restricted to one person or group.
– DERIVATIVES **solely** adv.
– ORIGIN Latin *sola* 'alone'.

solecism /sol-i-si-z'm/ • n. 1 a grammatical mistake. 2 an instance of bad manners or incorrect behaviour.
– ORIGIN Greek *soloikismos*.

solemn • adj. 1 formal and dignified: *a solemn procession.* 2 not cheerful; serious. 3 deeply sincere: *a solemn oath.*
– DERIVATIVES **solemnly** adv.
– ORIGIN Latin *sollemnis* 'customary'.

solemnity /suh-lem-ni-ti/ • n. (pl.

solemnities) 1 the state of being solemn. 2 (**solemnities**) formal and dignified ceremonies.

solemnize /sol-uhm-nyz/ (or **solemnise**) • v. (**solemnizes, solemnizing, solemnized**) 1 perform a ceremony, especially that of marriage. 2 mark an occasion with a ceremony.

solenoid /sol-uh-noyd, soh-luh-noyd/ • n. a coil of wire which becomes magnetic when an electric current is passed through it.
– ORIGIN Greek *sōlēn* 'channel, pipe'.

solicit • v. (**solicits, soliciting, solicited**) 1 ask for or try to obtain something from someone. 2 (of a prostitute) approach someone and offer sex for money.
– DERIVATIVES **solicitation** n.
– ORIGIN Latin *sollicitare* 'agitate'.

solicitor • n. Brit. a lawyer qualified to deal with property and wills, to advise clients and instruct barristers, and to represent clients in lower courts. Compare with BARRISTER.

solicitous • adj. showing interest or concern about a person's well-being.
– DERIVATIVES **solicitously** adv.

solicitude • n. care or concern.

solid • adj. (**solider, solidest**) 1 firm and stable in shape. 2 strongly built or made. 3 not hollow or having spaces or gaps. 4 consisting of the same substance throughout. 5 (of time) uninterrupted: *two solid hours of entertainment.* 6 able to be relied on: *solid evidence.* 7 Geom. three-dimensional. • n. 1 a solid substance or object. 2 (**solids**) food that is not liquid. 3 a three-dimensional body or shape.
– DERIVATIVES **solidity** n. **solidly** adv.
– ORIGIN Latin *solidus*.

solidarity • n. agreement and support resulting from shared interests, feelings, or opinions.

solidify • v. (**solidifies, solidifying, solidified**) make or become hard or solid.
– DERIVATIVES **solidification** n.

solid-state • adj. (of an electronic device) using solid semiconductors, e.g. transistors, as opposed to valves.

soliloquy /suh-lil-uh-kwi/ • n. (pl. **soliloquies**) a speech in a play in which a character speaks their thoughts aloud when alone.
– ORIGIN Latin *solus* 'alone' + *loqui* 'speak'.

solipsism /sol-ip-siz-uhm/ • n. 1 the view that the self is all that can be known to exist. 2 the quality of being selfish.
– DERIVATIVES **solipsist** n. **solipsistic** adj.

– ORIGIN from Latin *solus* 'alone' + *ipse* 'self'.

solitaire /sol-i-tair, sol-i-**tair**/ • n. 1 Brit. a game for one player played by removing pegs from a board one at a time by moving others over them. 2 N. Amer. the card game patience. 3 a single gem in a piece of jewellery.
– ORIGIN French.

solitary • adj. 1 done or existing alone. 2 (of a place) secluded or isolated. 3 single: *not a solitary shred of evidence.* • n. (pl. **solitaries**) 1 a person living in solitude for personal or religious reasons. 2 informal solitary confinement.
– DERIVATIVES **solitariness** n.
– ORIGIN Latin *solitarius*.

solitary confinement • n. the isolating of a prisoner in a separate cell as a punishment.

solitude • n. the state of being alone.

solo • n. (pl. **solos**) 1 a piece of music or a song or dance for one performer. 2 a flight undertaken by a single pilot. • adj. & adv. for or done by one person. • v. (**soloes, soloing, soloed**) perform a solo.
– ORIGIN Latin *solus* 'alone'.

soloist • n. a musician or singer who performs a solo.

solstice /sol-stiss/ • n. each of the two times in the year, at midsummer and midwinter, when the sun reaches its highest or lowest point in the sky at noon, marked by the longest and shortest days.
– ORIGIN Latin *solstitium*.

soluble • adj. 1 (of a substance) able to be dissolved. 2 (of a problem) able to be solved.
– DERIVATIVES **solubility** n.
– ORIGIN Latin *solubilis*.

solute /sol-yoot/ • n. a substance that is dissolved in another substance.

solution • n. 1 a means of solving a problem. 2 the correct answer to a puzzle. 3 a mixture formed when a substance is dissolved in a liquid. 4 the action of dissolving.
– ORIGIN Latin.

solve • v. (**solves, solving, solved**) find an answer to or way of dealing with a problem or mystery.
– DERIVATIVES **solvable** adj. **solver** n.
– ORIGIN Latin *solvere* 'loosen, unfasten'.

solvency • n. the state of having more money than you owe.

solvent • adj. 1 having more money than you owe. 2 able to dissolve other substances. • n. the liquid in which another substance is dissolved to form a solution.

solvent abuse • n. the deliberate breathing in of the intoxicating fumes of certain solvents, e.g. glue.

Som. • abbrev. Somerset.

Somali /suh-mah-li/ • n. (pl. **Somali** or **Somalis**) 1 a person from Somalia. 2 a member of a mainly Muslim people of Somalia. 3 the language of the Somali. • adj. relating to Somalia.
– DERIVATIVES **Somalian** adj. & n.

somatic /suh-mat-ik/ • adj. relating to the body rather than the mind.
– DERIVATIVES **somatically** adv.
– ORIGIN Greek *sōmatikos*.

sombre (US also **somber**) • adj. 1 dark or dull. 2 very solemn or serious.
– DERIVATIVES **sombrely** adv.
– ORIGIN French.

sombrero /som-brair-oh/ • n. (pl. **sombreros**) a broad-brimmed Mexican hat.
– ORIGIN Spanish.

some • det. 1 an unspecified amount or number of. 2 referring to an unknown or unspecified person or thing. 3 approximately. 4 a considerable amount or number of. 5 a certain small amount or number of: *he liked some music but generally wasn't musical.* 6 expressing admiration: *that was some goal.* • pron. 1 an unspecified number or amount of people or things. 2 a certain small number or amount.
– ORIGIN Old English.

-some • suffix 1 producing: *loathsome.* 2 characterized by being: *wholesome.* 3 apt to: *tiresome.* 4 referring to a group of a specified number: *foursome.*
– ORIGIN Old English.

somebody • pron. someone.

some day (also **someday**) • adv. at some time in the future.

somehow • adv. 1 by one means or another. 2 for an unknown or unspecified reason.

someone • pron. 1 an unknown or unspecified person. 2 an important or famous person.

someplace • adv. & pron. N. Amer. informal somewhere.

somersault • n. a movement in which a person turns head over heels in the air or on the ground and finishes on their feet. • v. perform a somersault.
– ORIGIN Old French *sombresault.*

something • pron. 1 an unspecified or unknown thing. 2 an unspecified or unknown amount or degree. • adv. informal used for emphasis: *my back hurts something terrible.*
– PHRASES **quite** (or **really**) **something** informal something impressive or notable.

something else informal an exceptional person or thing.

sometime •adv. at some unspecified or unknown time. •adj. former: *the sometime editor of the paper.*

sometimes •adv. occasionally.

somewhat •adv. to some extent; rather.

somewhere •adv. **1** in or to an unspecified or unknown place. **2** used to indicate an approximate amount. •pron. some unspecified place.
– PHRASES **get somewhere** informal make progress.

sommelier /so-mel-y-ay/ •n. a waiter who serves wine.
– ORIGIN French, 'butler'.

somnambulism /som-nam-byuu-li-z'm/ •n. formal sleepwalking.
– DERIVATIVES **somnambulist** n.
– ORIGIN Latin *somnus* 'sleep' + *ambulare* 'to walk'.

somnolent /som-nuh-luhnt/ •adj. **1** sleepy. **2** causing sleepiness: *a somnolent summer day.*
– DERIVATIVES **somnolence** n.
– ORIGIN Latin *somnolentus*.

son •n. **1** a boy or man in relation to his parents. **2** a male descendant. **3** (**the Son** or **the Son of Man**) (in Christian belief) Jesus. **4** (also **my son**) a form of address for a boy or younger man.
– ORIGIN Old English.

sonar /soh-nar/ •n. **1** a system for detecting objects under water by giving out sound pulses and measuring their return after being reflected. **2** a device used in this system.
– ORIGIN from *sound navigation and ranging.*

sonata /suh-nah-tuh/ •n. a piece of classical music for a solo instrument, often with a piano accompaniment.
– ORIGIN Italian, 'sounded'.

son et lumière /son ay loo-my-air/ •n. an entertainment held by night at a historic building, telling its history by the use of lighting effects and recorded sound.
– ORIGIN French, 'sound and light'.

song •n. **1** a set of words set to music. **2** singing: *they broke into song.* **3** the musical sounds made by some birds, whales, and insects. **4** literary a poem.
– PHRASES **for a song** informal very cheaply. **on song** Brit. informal performing well. **a song and dance** informal, esp. Brit. a fuss.
– ORIGIN Old English.

songbird •n. a bird with a musical song.

songster •n. (fem. **songstress**) a person who sings.

song thrush •n. a thrush with a song in which phrases are repeated.

songwriter •n. a writer of songs or the music for them.

sonic •adj. relating to or using sound waves.
– DERIVATIVES **sonically** adv.
– ORIGIN Latin *sonus* 'sound'.

sonic boom •n. an explosive noise caused by the shock wave from an object travelling faster than the speed of sound.

son-in-law •n. (pl. **sons-in-law**) the husband of a person's daughter.

sonnet •n. a poem of fourteen lines using a fixed rhyme scheme.
– ORIGIN Italian *sonetto* 'little sound'.

sonny •n. informal an informal form of address to a young boy.

sonogram •n. **1** a graph showing the distribution of energy at different frequencies in a sound. **2** a visual image produced from an ultrasound examination.
– ORIGIN Latin *sonus* 'sound'.

sonography •n. the analysis of sound using an instrument which produces a graph representing its component frequencies.
– DERIVATIVES **sonographic** adj.

sonorous /son-uh-ruhss/ •adj. (of a sound) deep and full.
– DERIVATIVES **sonority** /suh-nor-it-i/ n. **sonorously** adv.
– ORIGIN Latin *sonor* 'sound'.

soon •adv. **1** in or after a short time. **2** early. **3** used to indicate a preference: *I'd just as soon Tim did it.*
– PHRASES **no sooner than** at the very moment that. **sooner or later** eventually.
– DERIVATIVES **soonish** adv.
– ORIGIN Old English.

soot •n. a black powdery substance produced when an organic substance such as coal is burnt.
– ORIGIN Old English.

sooth /rhymes with truth/ •n. old use truth.
– ORIGIN Old English.

soothe •v. (**soothes, soothing, soothed**) **1** gently calm a person or their feelings. **2** make pain or discomfort less intense.
– ORIGIN Old English, 'verify'.

soothsayer •n. a person supposed to be able to foresee the future.

sooty •adj. (**sootier, sootiest**) covered with or coloured like soot.

sop •n. a thing given or done to calm or please someone who is angry or disappointed. •v. (**sops, sopping, sopped**) (**sop something up**) soak up liquid.
– ORIGIN Old English.

s

sophism /soff-i-z'm/ •n. a false argument.
– ORIGIN Greek *sophisma* 'clever device'.

sophist /soff-ist/ •n. a person who uses clever but false arguments.

sophisticate /suh-fiss-ti-kuht/ •n. a person having experience and taste in matters of fashion or culture.

sophisticated •adj. 1 having experience and taste in matters of culture or fashion. 2 (of a machine or system) highly developed and complex.
– DERIVATIVES **sophistication** n.
– ORIGIN Latin *sophisticare* 'tamper with'.

sophistry /soff-iss-tri/ •n. (pl. **sophistries**) 1 the use of clever but false arguments. 2 a false argument.

sophomore /soff-uh-mor/ •n. N. Amer. a second-year university or high-school student.
– DERIVATIVES **sophomoric** adj.
– ORIGIN prob. from **SOPHISM**.

soporific /sop-uh-rif-ik/ •adj. causing drowsiness or sleep.
– ORIGIN Latin *sopor* 'sleep'.

sopping (also **sopping wet**) •adj. wet through.

soppy •adj. (**soppier, soppiest**) Brit. informal 1 sentimental in an excessive or silly way. 2 rather weak and feeble.
– DERIVATIVES **soppily** adv. **soppiness** n.
– ORIGIN from **SOP**.

soprano /suh-prah-noh/ •n. (pl. **sopranos**) the highest singing voice. •adj. (of an instrument) of a high or the highest pitch in its family: *a soprano saxophone*.
– ORIGIN Italian.

sorbet /sor-bay/ •n. a water ice.
– ORIGIN French.

sorcerer •n. (fem. **sorceress**) a person who practises magic.
– DERIVATIVES **sorcery** n.
– ORIGIN Old French *sorcier*.

sordid •adj. 1 dishonest or immoral; arousing moral distaste. 2 very dirty and unpleasant.
– DERIVATIVES **sordidly** adv.
– ORIGIN Latin *sordidus*.

sore •adj. 1 painful or aching. 2 urgent: *we're in sore need of him.* 3 informal, esp. N. Amer. upset and angry. •n. a raw or painful place on the body. •adv. old use very: *sore afraid.*
– PHRASES **sore point** an issue about which someone feels distressed or annoyed. **stand** (or **stick**) **out like a sore thumb** be obviously different.
– DERIVATIVES **soreness** n.
– ORIGIN Old English.

sorely •adv. extremely; greatly.

sorghum /sor-guhm/ •n. a cereal grown in warm regions for grain and animal feed.
– ORIGIN Italian *sorgo*.

sorority /suh-ro-ri-ti/ •n. (pl. **sororities**) N. Amer. a society for female students in a university or college.
– ORIGIN Latin *soror* 'sister'.

sorrel[1] •n. an edible plant with arrow-shaped leaves and a bitter flavour.
– ORIGIN Old French *sorele*.

sorrel[2] •n. 1 a light reddish-brown colour. 2 a horse with a reddish-brown coat.
– ORIGIN Old French *sorel*.

sorrow •n. 1 deep distress caused by loss or disappointment. 2 a cause of sorrow.
– ORIGIN Old English.

sorrowful •adj. 1 feeling or showing sorrow. 2 causing sorrow.
– DERIVATIVES **sorrowfully** adv.

sorry •adj. (**sorrier, sorriest**) 1 feeling sympathy for someone else's misfortune. 2 feeling or expressing regret. 3 in a poor or pitiful state. 4 unpleasant and regrettable: *I kept quiet about the whole sorry business.*
– ORIGIN Old English, 'distressed'.

sort •n. 1 a category of people or things with a common feature or features. 2 informal a person with a specified nature: *he was a friendly sort.* •v. 1 arrange systematically in groups. 2 (often **sort something out**) separate something from a mixed group. 3 (**sort something out**) resolve a problem. 4 (**sort someone out**) informal deal with a troublesome person.
– PHRASES **of a sort** (or **of sorts**) of a rather poor kind. **out of sorts** slightly unwell or unhappy. **sort of** informal to some extent.
– DERIVATIVES **sorter** n.
– ORIGIN Old French *sorte*.

> **USAGE:** The expression *these sort of*, as in *I don't want to answer these sort of questions*, is not grammatical and should be avoided in formal writing. This is because *these* is plural and needs to agree with a plural noun; the correct usage is *these sorts of questions*. See also the note at **KIND**[1].

sorted •adj. Brit. informal 1 organized; arranged. 2 emotionally well balanced.

sortie •n. 1 an attack made by troops from a position of defence. 2 a flight by a single aircraft on a military operation. 3 a short trip.
– ORIGIN French.

SOS •n. 1 an international signal of extreme distress. 2 an urgent appeal for help.
– ORIGIN letters chosen as being easily transmitted and recognized in Morse code.

so-so •adj. neither very good nor very bad.

sot •n. a person who is regularly drunk.
– DERIVATIVES **sottish** adj.
– ORIGIN Latin *sottus* 'foolish person'.

sotto voce /sot-toh voh-chay/ •adv. & adj. in a quiet voice.
– ORIGIN from Italian *sotto* 'under' + *voce* 'voice'.

soubrette /soo-bret/ •n. a pert maidservant or similar minor female role in a comedy.
– ORIGIN from Provençal *soubret* 'coy'.

soubriquet /soo-bri-kay/ •n. var. of SOBRIQUET.

soufflé /soo-flay/ •n. a light, spongy dish made by mixing egg yolks and another ingredient such as cheese or fruit with stiffly beaten egg whites.
– ORIGIN French, 'blown'.

sough /rhymes with how *or* cuff/ •v. literary (of the wind or sea) make a moaning, whistling, or rushing sound.
– ORIGIN Old English.

sought past and past part. of SEEK.
– PHRASES **sought after** in great demand.

souk /sook/ (also **suq**) •n. an Arab market.
– ORIGIN Arabic.

soul •n. 1 the spiritual element of a person, believed to be immortal. 2 a person's inner nature. 3 emotional energy or power; passion: *their performance lacked soul.* 4 a perfect example of a quality: *she's the soul of discretion.* 5 a person: *poor soul.* 6 (also **soul music**) a kind of music using elements of gospel music and rhythm and blues, popularized by black Americans.
– ORIGIN Old English.

soul-destroying •adj. unbearably dull and repetitive.

soulful •adj. expressing deep and often sorrowful feeling: *a soulful glance.*
– DERIVATIVES **soulfully** adv. **soulfulness** n.

soulless •adj. 1 lacking character or interest. 2 lacking human feelings: *soulless dark eyes.*

soulmate •n. a person ideally suited to another.

soul-searching •n. close examination of your emotions and motives.

sound¹ •n. 1 vibrations which travel through air or water and are sensed by the ear. 2 a thing that can be heard. 3 music, speech, and sound effects accompanying a film or broadcast. 4 an impression given by words: *you've had a hard day, by the sound of it.* •v. 1 make a sound. 2 make a sound to show or warn

of something. 3 give a specified impression: *the job sounds great.* 4 (**sound off**) express your opinions forcefully.
– DERIVATIVES **soundless** adj.
– ORIGIN Latin *sonus.*

sound² •adj. 1 in good condition. 2 based on good judgement. 3 financially secure. 4 competent or reliable. 5 (of sleep) deep and unbroken. 6 severe or thorough: *a sound thrashing.* •adv. in a sound way.
– DERIVATIVES **soundly** adv. **soundness** n.
– ORIGIN Old English.

sound³ •v. 1 find out the depth of water in the sea, a lake, or a river using a line, pole, or sound echoes. 2 (**sound someone out**) question someone to find out their opinions.
– DERIVATIVES **sounder** n.
– ORIGIN Old French *sonder.*

sound⁴ •n. a narrow stretch of water forming an inlet or connecting two larger bodies of water.
– ORIGIN Old Norse, 'swimming, strait'.

sound barrier •n. the point at which an aircraft reaches the speed of sound.

sound bite •n. a short memorable extract from a speech or interview.

soundcheck •n. a test of sound equipment before a musical performance or recording.

sound effect •n. a sound other than speech or music made artificially for use in a play, film, etc.

sounding •n. 1 a measurement of the depth of water. 2 (**soundings**) information found out before taking action.

sounding board •n. a person or group with whom new ideas are discussed, in order to find out if they are valid or likely to succeed.

soundproof •adj. preventing sound getting in or out. •v. make soundproof.

sound system •n. a set of equipment for reproducing and amplifying sound.

soundtrack •n. the sound accompaniment to a film.

sound wave •n. a wave of alternate compression and reduction in density by which sound travels through air or water.

soup •n. a savoury liquid dish made by boiling meat, fish, or vegetables in stock or water. •v. (**soup something up**) informal make an engine or other machine more powerful or efficient.
– PHRASES **in the soup** informal in trouble.
– ORIGIN Old French *soupe* 'sop, broth'.

S

soupçon /soop-son/ • n. a very small quantity.
– ORIGIN French.

soup kitchen • n. a place where free food is served to homeless or very poor people.

sour • adj. 1 having a sharp taste like lemon or vinegar. 2 tasting or smelling unpleasantly stale. 3 resentful, bitter, or angry. • v. make or become sour.
– PHRASES **go** (or **turn**) **sour** become less pleasant. **sour grapes** an attitude in which someone pretends to hate something because they cannot have it themselves. [ORIGIN with reference to Aesop's fable *The Fox and the Grapes*.]
– DERIVATIVES **sourly** adv. **sourness** n.
– ORIGIN Old English.

source • n. 1 a place, person, or thing from which something originates. 2 a place where a river or stream begins. 3 a person, book, or document that provides information or evidence. • v. (**sources**, **sourcing**, **sourced**) obtain from a particular source.
– ORIGIN Old French *sourse*.

sour cream • n. cream that has been made sour by adding bacteria.

sourdough • n. bread made from fermenting dough.

sourpuss • n. informal a bad-tempered or sulky person.

souse /sowss/ • v. (**souses**, **sousing**, **soused**) 1 soak in liquid. 2 (as adj. **soused**) pickled or marinaded: *soused herring.*
– ORIGIN Old French *sous* 'pickle'.

soutane /soo-tahn/ • n. a type of long robe worn by Roman Catholic priests.
– ORIGIN Italian *sottana.*

south • n. 1 the direction which is 90° clockwise from east. 2 the southern part of a place. • adj. 1 lying towards or facing the south. 2 (of a wind) blowing from the south. • adv. to or towards the south.
– DERIVATIVES **southbound** adj. & adv.
– ORIGIN Old English.

South African • n. a person from South Africa. • adj. relating to South Africa.

South American • n. a person from South America. • adj. relating to South America.

south-east • n. the direction or region halfway between south and east. • adj. 1 lying towards or facing the south-east. 2 (of a wind) blowing from the south-east. • adv. to or towards the south-east.
– DERIVATIVES **south-eastern** adj.

south-easterly • adj. & adv. in a south-eastward position or direction.

south-eastward • adv. (also south-eastwards) towards the south-east. • adj. in, towards, or facing the south-east.

southerly • adj. & adv. 1 towards or facing the south. 2 (of a wind) blowing from the south.

southern • adj. 1 situated in or facing the south. 2 (usu. **Southern**) coming from or characteristic of the south.
– DERIVATIVES **southernmost** adj.

southerner • n. a person from the south of a region.

Southern Lights • pl. n. the aurora australis.

southpaw • n. a left-handed boxer who leads with the right hand.

south-south-east • n. the direction halfway between south and south-east.

south-south-west • n. the direction halfway between south and south-west.

southward • adj. in a southerly direction. • adv. (also **southwards**) towards the south.

south-west • n. the direction or region halfway between south and west. • adj. 1 lying towards or facing the south-west. 2 (of a wind) blowing from the south-west. • adv. to or towards the south-west.
– DERIVATIVES **south-western** adj.

south-westerly • adj. & adv. in a south-westward position or direction.

south-westward • adv. (also south-westwards) towards the south-west. • adj. in, towards, or facing the south-west.

souvenir /soo-vuh-neer/ • n. a thing that is kept as a reminder of a person, place, or event.
– ORIGIN French.

sou'wester /sow-wess-ter/ • n. a waterproof hat with a broad brim or flap covering the back of the neck.

sovereign • n. 1 a king or queen who is the supreme ruler of a country. 2 a former British gold coin worth one pound sterling. • adj. 1 possessing supreme power. 2 (of a nation) completely independent.
– ORIGIN Old French *soverain.*

> ✓ The ending of **sovereign** is spelled -**eign**.

sovereignty • n. (pl. **sovereignties**) 1 supreme power or authority. 2 a self-governing state.

soviet /soh-vi-uht, sov-i-uht/ • n. 1 (**Soviet**) a citizen of the former Soviet Union. 2 an elected council in the former Soviet Union. • adj. (**Soviet**) relating to the former Soviet Union.
– ORIGIN Russian *sovet* 'council'.

sow[1] /soh/ • v. (**sows, sowing, sowed**; past part. **sown** or **sowed**) **1** plant seed by scattering it on or in the earth. **2** spread something unwelcome: *the new policy has sown confusion and doubt.*
– DERIVATIVES **sower** n.
– ORIGIN Old English.

sow[2] /sow/ • n. an adult female pig.
– ORIGIN Old English.

soya bean • n. an edible bean that is high in protein.
– ORIGIN Malay.

soy sauce (also **soy**) • n. a sauce made with fermented soya beans, used in Chinese and Japanese cooking.
– ORIGIN Chinese.

sozzled • adj. informal very drunk.
– ORIGIN from dialect *sozzle* 'mix sloppily'.

spa • n. **1** a mineral spring considered to have health-giving properties. **2** a place with a mineral spring.
– ORIGIN from *Spa*, a town in Belgium noted for its mineral springs.

space • n. **1** a continuous area or expanse that is free or unoccupied. **2** the dimensions of height, depth, and width within which all things exist and move. **3** (also **outer space**) the physical universe beyond the earth's atmosphere. **4** an interval of time: *forty men died in the space of two days.* **5** the freedom to live and develop as you wish.
• v. (**spaces, spacing, spaced**) **1** position things at a distance from one another. **2** (**be spaced out**) informal be in a state of great happiness or confusion, especially from taking drugs.
– ORIGIN Old French *espace*.

space age • n. (**the space age**) the era that started when the exploration of space became possible. • adj. (**space-age**) having advanced technology: *a space-age control room.*

space capsule • n. a small spacecraft or the part of a larger one that contains the instruments or crew, designed to be returned to earth.

spacecraft • n. (pl. **spacecraft** or **spacecrafts**) a vehicle used for travelling in space.

spaceman • n. (pl. **spacemen**) a male astronaut.

space probe • n. an unmanned exploratory spacecraft.

spaceship • n. a manned spacecraft.

space shuttle • n. a rocket-launched spacecraft, used for journeys between earth and craft orbiting the earth.

space station • n. a large artificial satellite used as a long-term base for manned operations in space.

spacesuit • n. a sealed and pressurized suit designed to allow an astronaut to survive in space.

space–time • n. Physics the concepts of time and three-dimensional space seen as joined in a four-dimensional continuum.

spacious • adj. (of a room or building) having plenty of space.
– DERIVATIVES **spaciousness** n.

spade • n. a tool with a rectangular metal blade and a long handle, used for digging.
– PHRASES **call a spade a spade** speak plainly and frankly.
– ORIGIN Old English.

spades • n. one of the four suits in a pack of playing cards, represented by an upside down black heart with a small stalk.
– PHRASES **in spades** informal in large amounts or to a high degree.
– ORIGIN Italian *spade* 'swords'.

spadework • n. hard or routine work done to prepare for something.

spaghetti /spuh-get-ti/ • pl. n. pasta in long strands.
– ORIGIN Italian, 'little strings'.

spaghetti western • n. informal a western film made in Europe by an Italian director.

spake old use past of SPEAK.

spam • n. **1** trademark a canned meat product made mainly from ham. **2** email which has not been requested, sent to large numbers of Internet users.
• v. (**spams, spamming, spammed**) send email that has not been requested to large numbers of users.
– DERIVATIVES **spammer** n.
– ORIGIN prob. from *spiced ham*: the Internet sense prob. derives from a sketch in the British 'Monty Python' comedy show, in which every item on a cafe's menu includes spam.

span • n. **1** the full extent of something from side to side. **2** the length of time for which something lasts. **3** a wingspan. **4** a part of a bridge between the uprights supporting it. **5** the maximum distance between the tips of the thumb and little finger. • v. (**spans, spanning, spanned**) extend across or over.
– ORIGIN Old English.

spangle • n. **1** a small thin piece of glittering material, used to decorate a garment. **2** a spot of bright colour or light.
– DERIVATIVES **spangled** adj. **spangly** adj.
– ORIGIN Dutch *spange* 'buckle'.

Spaniard /span-yerd/ • n. a person from Spain.

spaniel • n. a breed of dog with a long silky coat and drooping ears.

– ORIGIN Old French *espaigneul* 'Spanish (dog)'.

Spanish • n. the main language of Spain and of much of Central and South America. • adj. relating to Spain or Spanish.

spank • v. slap on the buttocks with the open hand or a flat object. • n. a slap or slaps on the buttocks.

spanking • adj. 1 brisk: *a spanking pace.* 2 informal impressive or pleasing: *a spanking white Rolls Royce.* • n. a series of spanks.

spanner • n. Brit. a tool for gripping and turning a nut or bolt.
– PHRASES **a spanner in the works** a thing that prevents a plan from being carried out successfully.
– ORIGIN German *spannen* 'draw tight'.

spar[1] • n. a thick, strong pole used for a mast or yard on a ship.
– ORIGIN Old French *esparre*.

spar[2] • v. (**spars, sparring, sparred**) 1 make the motions of boxing without landing heavy blows, as a form of training. 2 argue without hostility. • n. a period of sparring.
– ORIGIN Old English, 'strike out'.

spar[3] • n. a crystalline transparent or semi-transparent mineral that is easily split.
– ORIGIN German.

spare • adj. 1 additional to what is needed. 2 not currently in use or occupied. 3 with no excess fat; thin. 4 elegantly simple: *her clothes are spare in style.* • n. an item kept in case another is lost, broken, or worn out. • v. (**spares, sparing, spared**) 1 give something that you have enough of to someone. 2 refrain from killing or harming. 3 protect from something unpleasant.
– PHRASES **go spare** Brit. informal become very angry. **spare no expense** (or **no expense spared**) be prepared to pay any amount. **to spare** left over.
– ORIGIN Old English, 'meagre'.

spare ribs • pl. n. trimmed ribs of pork.
– ORIGIN prob. from German *ribbesper*.

spare tyre • n. 1 an extra tyre carried in a motor vehicle. 2 informal a roll of fat round a person's waist.

sparing • adj. not wasteful; economical.
– DERIVATIVES **sparingly** adv.

spark • n. 1 a small fiery particle produced by burning or caused by friction. 2 a flash of light produced by an electrical discharge. 3 an electrical discharge which ignites the explosive mixture in an internal-combustion engine. 4 a small but concentrated amount: *a tiny spark of anger.* 5 a sense of liveliness and excitement. • v. 1 produce

sparks. 2 ignite a fire. 3 (also **spark something off**) cause: *the announcement sparked off protests.*
– PHRASES **bright spark** a lively person.
– DERIVATIVES **sparky** adj.
– ORIGIN Old English.

sparkle • v. (**sparkles, sparkling, sparkled**) 1 shine brightly with flashes of light. 2 be lively and witty. 3 (as adj. **sparkling**) (of drink) fizzy. • n. 1 a glittering flash of light. 2 liveliness and wit.
– DERIVATIVES **sparkly** adj.

sparkler • n. a hand-held firework that gives out sparks.

spark plug • n. a device for firing the explosive mixture in an internal-combustion engine.

sparrow • n. a small bird with brown and grey plumage.
– ORIGIN Old English.

sparrowhawk • n. a small hawk that preys on small birds.

sparse • adj. thinly scattered.
– DERIVATIVES **sparsely** adv. **sparsity** n.
– ORIGIN Latin *sparsus*.

Spartan • adj. 1 relating to Sparta, a city state in ancient Greece. 2 (**spartan**) not comfortable or luxurious. • n. a citizen of Sparta.

spasm • n. 1 a sudden uncontrollable tightening of a muscle. 2 a sudden brief spell: *a spasm of coughing.*
– ORIGIN Greek *spasmos*.

spasmodic • adj. occurring or done in brief, irregular bursts: *spasmodic fighting.*
– DERIVATIVES **spasmodically** adv.

spastic • adj. 1 relating to or affected by muscle spasm. 2 relating to cerebral palsy. • n. offens. a person with cerebral palsy.
– DERIVATIVES **spasticity** n.
– ORIGIN Greek *spastikos* 'pulling'.

USAGE: You should not use the word **spastic** because many people think it is offensive; say *person with cerebral palsy* instead.

spat[1] past and past part. of SPIT[1].

spat[2] • n. a cloth covering formerly worn by men over the ankles and shoes.
– ORIGIN from *spatterdash*, a long legging formerly worn when riding.

spat[3] • n. informal a petty quarrel.

spate • n. 1 a large number of similar things coming in quick succession. 2 esp. Brit. a sudden flood in a river.

spathe /spayth/ • n. Bot. a large bract (leaf) enclosing the flower cluster of certain plants.
– ORIGIN Greek, 'broad blade'.

spatial /spay-sh'l/ • adj. relating to space.

– DERIVATIVES **spatially** adv.
– ORIGIN Latin *spatium* 'space'.

spatter •v. (**spatters, spattering, spattered**) **1** cover with drops or spots. **2** splash over a surface. •n. a spray or splash.
– ORIGIN from Dutch or German *spatten* 'burst, spout'.

spatula /spat-yuu-luh/ •n. an implement with a broad, flat, blunt blade, used for mixing or spreading.
– ORIGIN Latin.

spatulate /spat-yuu-luht/ •adj. having a broad, rounded end.

spawn •v. **1** (of a fish, frog, etc.) release or deposit eggs. **2** give rise to: *the affair spawned a rash of publications.* •n. the eggs of fish, frogs, etc.
– ORIGIN Old French *espaundre*.

spay •v. sterilize a female animal by removing the ovaries.
– ORIGIN Old French *espeer* 'cut with a sword'.

speak •v. (**speaks, speaking, spoke;** past part. **spoken**) **1** say something. **2** (**speak to**) talk to. **3** communicate in or be able to communicate in a specified language. **4** (**speak up**) speak more loudly. **5** (**speak out/up**) express your opinions frankly and publicly. **6** (**speak for**) express the views or position of. **7** be evidence of: *her behaviour around him spoke strongly of a crush.* **8** (**speak to**) appeal or relate to. **9** make a speech.
– PHRASES **speak in tongues** speak in an unknown language during religious worship, one of the gifts of the Holy Spirit (Acts 2). **speak volumes** convey a great deal without using words.
– ORIGIN Old English.

speakeasy •n. (pl. **speakeasies**) informal (in the US during Prohibition) a secret illegal drinking club.

speaker •n. **1** a person who speaks. **2** a person who speaks a particular language. **3** a person who makes a speech. **4** (**Speaker**) the officer who is in charge of proceedings in a law-making assembly. **5** a loudspeaker.

speaking •adj. **1** used for or involved in speech: *a clear speaking voice.* **2** able to speak a particular language.
– PHRASES **on speaking terms** polite or friendly towards someone.

spear •n. **1** a weapon with a pointed metal tip and a long shaft. **2** a pointed stem of asparagus or broccoli. •v. pierce or strike with a pointed object.
– ORIGIN Old English.

spearhead •n. a person or group leading an attack or movement. •v. lead an attack or movement.

spearmint •n. common garden mint,

used as a herb in cooking.

spec¹ •n. (in phr. **on spec**) informal in the hope of success but without any advance preparation.
– ORIGIN short for *speculation*.

spec² •n. informal a detailed working description.

special •adj. **1** better, greater, or otherwise different from what is usual: *they make a special effort at Christmas.* **2** designed for a particular purpose or occasion. **3** intended for or belonging to a particular person or thing. •n. **1** something designed or organized for a particular occasion or purpose. **2** a dish not on the regular menu but served on a particular day.
– ORIGIN Latin *specialis*.

special constable •n. (in the UK) a person who is trained to act as a police officer on particular occasions.

special effects •pl. n. illusions created for films and television by camerawork, computer graphics, etc.

specialist •n. a person who is highly skilled or knowledgeable in a particular field. •adj. involving detailed knowledge within a field.
– DERIVATIVES **specialism** n.

speciality /spesh-i-al-i-ti/ (N. Amer. & Med. also **specialty**) •n. (pl. **specialities**) **1** a pursuit, area of study, or skill in which someone is an expert. **2** a product for which a person or region is famous. **3** (usu. **specialty**) a branch of medicine or surgery.

specialize (or **specialise**) •v. (**specializes, specializing, specialized**) **1** concentrate on and become expert in a particular skill or area. **2** (**be specialized**) (of an organ or part) be adapted or set apart to serve a special function.
– DERIVATIVES **specialization** n.

specially •adv. **1** for a special purpose. **2** particularly.

special needs •pl. n. particular educational requirements of children with learning difficulties, physical disability, or emotional and behavioural difficulties.

special pleading •n. argument in which the speaker deliberately ignores aspects that are unfavourable to their point of view.

specialty /spesh-uhl-ti/ •n. (pl. **specialties**) N. Amer. & Med. = SPECIALITY.

specie /spee-shee/ •n. money in the form of coins rather than notes.
– ORIGIN Latin *species* 'form, kind'.

species /spee-shiz, spee-sheez, spee-siz/ •n. (pl. **species**) **1** a group of animals or plants consisting of similar individuals capable of breeding with each other. **2** a

kind: *a species of criticism.*
– ORIGIN Latin, 'appearance, form'.

specific /spuh-si-fik/ •adj. **1** clearly defined or identified. **2** precise and clear: *when ordering goods be specific.* **3** (**specific to**) belonging or relating only to. •n. (**specifics**) precise details.
– DERIVATIVES **specifically** adv. **specificity** /spe-si-fis-it-i/ n.
– ORIGIN Latin *specificus.*

specification •n. **1** the action of specifying. **2** (also **specifications**) a detailed description of the design and materials used to make something. **3** a standard of workmanship and materials required in a piece of work.

specify •v. (**specifies**, **specifying**, **specified**) state or identify clearly and definitely.
– DERIVATIVES **specifiable** adj. **specifier** n.

specimen •n. **1** an animal, plant, object, etc. used as an example of its species or type for study or display. **2** a sample for medical testing. **3** a typical example. **4** informal a person or animal of a specific type: *a sorry specimen.*
– ORIGIN Latin, 'pattern, model'.

specious /spee-shuhss/ •adj. **1** seeming reasonable, but actually wrong. **2** misleading in appearance.
– ORIGIN Latin *speciosus* 'fair, plausible'.

speck •n. a tiny spot or particle. •v. mark with small spots.
– ORIGIN Old English.

speckle •n. a small spot or patch of colour. •v. (**speckles**, **speckling**, **speckled**) mark with speckles.
– ORIGIN Dutch *spekkel.*

specs •pl. n. informal a pair of spectacles.

spectacle •n. a visually impressive performance or display.
– PHRASES **make a spectacle of yourself** attract attention by behaving in a ridiculous way in public.
– ORIGIN Latin *spectaculum* 'public show'.

spectacles •pl. n. Brit. a pair of glasses.

spectacular •adj. very impressive, striking, or dramatic. •n. a large and impressive performance or event.
– DERIVATIVES **spectacularly** adv.

spectate •v. (**spectates**, **spectating**, **spectated**) watch an event; be a spectator.

spectator •n. a person who watches at a show, game, or other event.
– ORIGIN Latin.

specter •n. US = SPECTRE.

spectra pl. of SPECTRUM.

spectral[1] •adj. relating to or like a spectre or ghost.
– DERIVATIVES **spectrally** adv.

spectral[2] •adj. relating to spectra or the spectrum.
– DERIVATIVES **spectrally** adv.

spectre (US **specter**) •n. **1** a ghost. **2** a possible unpleasant or dangerous situation: *the spectre of nuclear holocaust.*
– ORIGIN French.

spectrometer /spek-trom-i-ter/ •n. a device for recording and measuring spectra.
– DERIVATIVES **spectrometry** n.

spectroscope •n. a device for producing and recording spectra for examination.

spectroscopy /spek-tross-kuh-pi/ •n. the branch of science concerned with the investigation and measurement of spectra produced when matter interacts with or gives out electromagnetic radiation.

spectrum /spek-truhm/ •n. (pl. **spectra** /spek-truh/) **1** a band of colours produced by separating light into elements with different wavelengths, e.g. in a rainbow. **2** the entire range of wavelengths of light. **3** the components of a sound or other phenomenon arranged according to frequency, energy, etc. **4** a range of beliefs, qualities, etc.: *a wide spectrum of interests.*
– ORIGIN Latin, 'image, apparition'.

speculate /spek-yuu-layt/ •v. (**speculates**, **speculating**, **speculated**) **1** form a theory without firm evidence. **2** invest in stocks, property, or other ventures in the hope of profit but with the risk of loss.
– DERIVATIVES **speculation** n. **speculator** n.
– ORIGIN Latin *speculari* 'observe'.

speculative •adj. **1** based on theory or guesswork rather than knowledge. **2** (of an investment) involving a high risk of loss.
– DERIVATIVES **speculatively** adv.

speculum /spek-yuu-luhm/ •n. (pl. **specula** /spek-yuu-luh/) Med. a metal instrument that is used to make an opening or canal in the body wider to allow inspection.
– ORIGIN Latin, 'mirror'.

sped past and past part. of SPEED.

speech •n. **1** the expression of thoughts and feelings using spoken language. **2** a formal talk delivered to an audience. **3** a sequence of lines written for one character in a play.
– ORIGIN Old English.

speechify •v. (**speechifies**, **speechifying**, **speechified**) deliver a speech in a boring or pompous way.

speechless •adj. unable to speak due to

shock or strong emotion.

speech therapy • n. treatment to help people with speech and language problems.
– DERIVATIVES **speech therapist** n.

speed • n. **1** the rate at which someone or something moves or operates. **2** a fast rate of movement or action. **3** each of the possible gear ratios of a bicycle. **4** the light-gathering power of a camera lens. **5** the sensitivity of photographic film to light. **6** informal an amphetamine drug. • v. (**speeds, speeding, sped** or **speeded**) **1** move more quickly. **2** (**speed up**) move or work more quickly. **3** (of a motorist) travel at a speed greater than the legal limit. **4** old use make prosperous or successful: may God speed you.
– PHRASES **at speed** quickly. **up to speed** fully informed or up to date.
– DERIVATIVES **speeder** n.
– ORIGIN Old English.

speedboat • n. a motor boat designed for high speed.

speed bump (Brit. also **speed hump**) • n. a ridge set in a road to control the speed of vehicles.

speed camera • n. a roadside camera designed to catch speeding vehicles.

speed dating (US trademark **SpeedDating**) • n. an organized activity in which a person has short conversations with a series of people to see if they like each other enough to begin a relationship.

speed dial • n. a function on some telephones which allows numbers to be entered into a memory and dialled with the push of a single button. • v. (**speed-dial**) dial a telephone number by using a speed dial function.

speed limit • n. the maximum speed at which a vehicle may legally travel on a particular stretch of road.

speedometer /spee-**dom**-i-ter/ • n. an instrument on a vehicle's dashboard that indicates its speed.

speedway • n. Brit. a form of motorcycle racing in which the riders race laps around an oval dirt track.

speedwell • n. a small creeping plant with blue or pink flowers.

speedy • adj. (**speedier, speediest**) done, occurring, or moving quickly.
– DERIVATIVES **speedily** adv.

speleology /spee-li-**ol**-uh-ji/ • n. the study or exploration of caves.
– ORIGIN Greek spēlaion 'cave'.

spell¹ • v. (**spells, spelling, spelled** or esp. Brit. **spelt**) **1** write or name the letters that form a word in correct order. **2** (of letters) form a word. **3** lead to: the plans

would spell disaster. **4** (**spell something out**) explain something clearly.
– DERIVATIVES **speller** n.
– ORIGIN Old French espeller.

spell² • n. **1** a form of words thought to have magical power. **2** a state of enchantment caused by a spell.
– ORIGIN Old English, 'narration'.

spell³ • n. a short period of time.

spellbind • v. (**spellbinds, spellbinding, spellbound**) hold the complete attention of: the singer held the audience spellbound.

spellchecker • n. a computer program which checks the spelling of words in a computer document.

spelling • n. the way in which a word is spelled.

spelt past and past part. of SPELL¹.

spend • v. (**spends, spending, spent**) **1** pay out money to buy or hire goods or services. **2** use or use up energy or resources. **3** pass time in a specified way. • n. informal an amount of money paid out.
– PHRASES **spend a penny** Brit. informal, euphem. urinate.
– DERIVATIVES **spender** n.
– ORIGIN Latin expendere 'pay out'.

spendthrift • n. a person who spends money in an extravagant, irresponsible way.

spent past and past part. of SPEND. • adj. used up.

sperm • n. (pl. **sperm** or **sperms**) **1** semen. **2** a spermatozoon.
– ORIGIN Greek sperma 'seed'.

spermatozoon /sper-muh-tuh-**zoh**-on/ • n. (pl. **spermatozoa** /sper-muh-tuh-**zoh**-uh/) the male sex cell of an animal, that fertilizes the egg.
– ORIGIN from Greek sperma 'seed' + zōion 'animal'.

sperm count • n. the number of spermatozoa in a measured amount of semen, used as an indication of a man's fertility.

spermicide • n. a substance that kills sperm, used as a contraceptive.

sperm whale • n. a toothed whale with a massive head, feeding largely on squid.

spew • v. **1** pour out rapidly and in large quantities. **2** informal vomit.
– ORIGIN Old English.

SPF • abbrev. sun protection factor.

sphagnum /**sfag**-nuhm/ • n. a kind of moss that grows on bogs.
– ORIGIN Latin.

sphere • n. **1** a round solid figure in which every point on the surface is at an equal distance from the centre. **2** an area of activity, interest, or expertise: the sphere of foreign affairs.

S

– ORIGIN Greek *sphaira* 'ball'.

spherical • adj. shaped like a sphere.
– DERIVATIVES **spherically** adv.

spheroid /sfeer-oyd/ • n. an object that is roughly the same shape as a sphere.

sphincter /sfingk-ter/ • n. a ring of muscle that surrounds an opening such as the anus, and can be tightened to close it.
– ORIGIN Greek *sphinktēr*.

sphinx • n. an ancient Egyptian stone figure with a lion's body and a human or animal head.
– ORIGIN Greek, first referring to a mythical, winged monster with a woman's head and a lion's body, who set a riddle and killed those who could not solve it.

spic • n. US informal, offens. a Spanish-speaking person from Central or South America or the Caribbean.

spice • n. 1 a strong-tasting vegetable substance used to flavour food. 2 an element providing interest and excitement. • v. (**spices, spicing, spiced**) 1 flavour with spice. 2 (**spice something up**) make something more exciting or interesting.
– ORIGIN Old French *espice*.

spick and span • adj. neat, clean, and well looked after.
– ORIGIN from Old Norse words meaning 'chip' + 'new'.

spicy • adj. (**spicier, spiciest**) 1 strongly flavoured with spice. 2 mildly indecent: *spicy jokes.*
– DERIVATIVES **spicily** adv. **spiciness** n.

spider • n. an eight-legged arachnid (insect-like creature), most kinds of which spin webs in which to capture insects.
– ORIGIN Old English.

spider plant • n. a plant having long narrow leaves with a central yellow stripe.

spidery • adj. long and thin, like a spider's legs: *spidery handwriting.*

spiel /shpeel, speel/ • n. informal an elaborate and insincere speech made to persuade someone to believe or buy something.
– ORIGIN German, 'a game'.

spiffing • adj. Brit. informal, dated excellent.

spigot /spi-guht/ • n. 1 a small peg or plug. 2 US a tap. 3 the plain end of a section of a pipe fitting into the socket of the next one.
– ORIGIN perh. from Provençal *espigou*.

spike¹ • n. 1 a thin, pointed piece of metal or wood. 2 each of several metal points set into the sole of a sports shoe to prevent slipping. • v. (**spikes, spiking,** **spiked**) 1 impale on or pierce with something sharp. 2 form into or cover with sharp points. 3 informal secretly add alcohol or a drug to drink or food. 4 put an end to a plan or undertaking.
– ORIGIN perh. from German or Dutch *spiker.*

spike² • n. Bot. a flower cluster formed of many flower heads attached directly to a long stem.
– ORIGIN Latin *spica* 'ear of corn'.

spikenard /spyk-nahd/ • n. (in the past) a perfumed ointment made from the rhizome (underground stem) of a Himalayan plant.
– ORIGIN from Latin *spica* 'spike' + Greek *nardos* 'spikenard'.

spiky • adj. (**spikier, spikiest**) 1 like a spike or having many spikes. 2 informal easily annoyed.
– DERIVATIVES **spikily** adv. **spikiness** n.

spill¹ • v. (**spills, spilling, spilt** or **spilled**) 1 flow or cause to flow over the edge of a container. 2 move or empty out from a place. • n. 1 an instance of a liquid spilling or the quantity spilt. 2 a fall from a horse or bicycle.
– PHRASES **spill the beans** informal reveal secret information. **spill blood** kill or wound people.
– DERIVATIVES **spillage** n.
– ORIGIN Old English, 'kill, shed blood'.

spill² • n. a thin strip of wood or paper used for lighting a fire.
– ORIGIN Dutch or German.

spilt past and past part. of SPILL¹.

spin • v. (**spins, spinning, spun**) 1 turn round quickly. 2 (of a person's head) have a sensation of dizziness. 3 (of a ball) move through the air with a revolving motion. 4 draw out and twist the fibres of wool, cotton, etc. to convert them into yarn. 5 (of a spider or a silkworm or other insect) produce a web, silk, or cocoon by forcing out a fine thread from a special gland. 6 (**spin something out**) make something last as long as possible. • n. 1 a spinning motion. 2 a fast revolving motion made by an aircraft as it descends rapidly. 3 informal a brief trip in a vehicle for pleasure. 4 a favourable slant given to a news story.
– PHRASES **flat spin** Brit. informal a state of agitation. **spin a yarn** tell a far-fetched story.
– DERIVATIVES **spinner** n.
– ORIGIN Old English.

spina bifida /spy-nuh bi-fi-duh/ • n. a condition present from birth in which part of the spinal cord is exposed through a gap in the backbone, and which can cause paralysis and other problems.

– ORIGIN Latin.

spinach • n. a vegetable with large dark green leaves.
– ORIGIN prob. from Old French *espinache*.

spinal • adj. relating to the spine.

spinal column • n. the spine.

spinal cord • n. the bundle of nerve fibres in the spine that connects all parts of the body to the brain.

spindle • n. 1 a slender rounded rod with tapered ends, used in spinning wool, flax, etc. by hand. 2 a rod acting as an axis that revolves or on which something revolves.
– ORIGIN Old English.

spindly • adj. long or tall and thin.

spin doctor • n. informal a spokesperson for a political party or politician employed to give a favourable interpretation of events to the media.

spindrift • n. 1 spray blown from the crests of waves by the wind. 2 driving snow.
– ORIGIN from former *spoon* 'run before wind or sea' + DRIFT.

spin dryer • n. a machine for drying wet clothes by spinning them in a revolving drum.

spine • n. 1 a series of vertebrae (bones) extending from the skull to the small of the back, enclosing the spinal cord. 2 the part of a book that encloses the inner edges of the pages. 3 a hard pointed projection found on certain plants (e.g. cacti) and animals (e.g. hedgehogs).
– ORIGIN Latin *spina* 'thorn, backbone'.

spine-chiller • n. a story or film that causes terror and excitement.
– DERIVATIVES **spine-chilling** adj.

spineless • adj. 1 (of an animal) having no spine. 2 lacking courage and determination.

spinet /spi-net, spin-it/ • n. a type of small harpsichord.
– ORIGIN Italian *spinetta*.

spine-tingling • adj. informal thrilling or pleasurably frightening.

spinnaker /spin-nuh-ker/ • n. a large three-cornered sail set in front of the mainsail of a racing yacht when the wind is coming from behind.
– ORIGIN prob. from *Sphinx*, the yacht first using such a sail.

spinneret • n. an organ through which the silk, gossamer, or thread of spiders, silkworms, and certain other insects is produced.

spinney • n. (pl. **spinneys**) Brit. a small area of trees and bushes.
– ORIGIN Old French *espinei*.

spinning jenny • n. hist. a machine for spinning with more than one spindle at a time.

spinning wheel • n. a machine for spinning yarn or thread with a spindle driven by a wheel attached to a crank or treadle.

spin-off • n. a product or benefit produced during or after the main activity.

spinster • n. esp. derog. a single woman beyond the usual age for marriage.
– DERIVATIVES **spinsterhood** n.
– ORIGIN first meaning 'woman who spins'.

spiny • adj. (**spinier**, **spiniest**) full of or covered with prickles.

spiracle /spy-ruh-k'l/ • n. Zool. an external opening used for breathing in certain insects, fish, and other animals.
– ORIGIN Latin *spiraculum*.

spiral • adj. winding in a continuous curve around a central point or axis.
• n. 1 a spiral curve, shape, or pattern. 2 a continuous rise or fall of prices, wages, etc., that gradually gets faster.
• v. (**spirals**, **spiralling**, **spiralled**; US **spirals**, **spiraling**, **spiraled**) 1 follow a spiral course. 2 show a continuous and rapid increase or decrease.
– DERIVATIVES **spirally** adv.
– ORIGIN Latin *spiralis*.

spire • n. a tall pointed structure on the top of a church tower.
– ORIGIN Old English, 'tall plant stem'.

spirit • n. 1 the part of a person that consists of their character and feelings rather than their body, often believed to survive after their body is dead. 2 a supernatural being. 3 typical character, quality, or mood: *the spirit of the times.* 4 (**spirits**) a person's mood. 5 courage, energy, and determination. 6 the real meaning of something as opposed to its strict interpretation: *the rule had been broken in spirit if not in letter.* 7 esp. Brit. strong alcoholic drink, such as rum. 8 purified distilled alcohol, such as methylated spirit. • v. (**spirits**, **spiriting**, **spirited**) (**spirit someone/thing away**) take someone or something away rapidly and secretly.
– PHRASES **when the spirit moves someone** when someone feels inclined to do something.
– ORIGIN Latin *spiritus*.

spirited • adj. 1 full of energy, enthusiasm, and determination. 2 having a specified character: *a generous-spirited man.*

spiritless • adj. lacking courage, energy, or determination.

spirit level • n. a sealed glass tube partially filled with a liquid, containing an air bubble whose position reveals whether a surface is perfectly level.

spiritual • adj. **1** relating to the human spirit as opposed to physical things. **2** relating to religion or religious belief. • n. a religious song of a kind associated with black Christians of the southern US.
– DERIVATIVES **spirituality** n. **spiritually** adv.

spiritualism • n. the belief that it is possible to communicate with the spirits of the dead.
– DERIVATIVES **spiritualist** n.

spirituous /spir-it-yoo-uhss/ • adj. old use containing much alcohol.

spirogyra /spy-ruh-jy-ruh/ • n. a type of algae consisting of long green threads.
– ORIGIN from Greek *speira* 'coil' + *guros* 'round'.

spit¹ • v. (**spits**, **spitting**, **spat** or **spit**) **1** force saliva, food, or liquid from the mouth. **2** say in a hostile way. **3** (of a fire or food being cooked) give out small bursts of sparks or hot fat. **4** (**it spits**, **it is spitting**) Brit. light rain falls. • n. **1** saliva. **2** an act of spitting.
– PHRASES **be the spitting image of** (or **be the spit of**) informal look exactly like. **spit and polish** thorough cleaning and polishing. **spit blood** feel or express strong anger. **spit it out** informal say it quickly.
– DERIVATIVES **spitter** n.
– ORIGIN Old English.

spit² • n. **1** a metal rod pushed through meat in order to hold and turn it while it is roasted. **2** a narrow point of land projecting into the sea.
– ORIGIN Old English.

spite • n. a desire to hurt, annoy, or offend. • v. (**spites**, **spiting**, **spited**) deliberately hurt, annoy or offend someone.
– PHRASES **in spite of** without being affected by. **in spite of yourself** although you did not want or expect to do so.
– ORIGIN Old French *despit* 'contempt'.

spiteful • adj. deliberately hurtful.
– DERIVATIVES **spitefully** adv. **spitefulness** n.

spitfire • n. a person with a fierce temper.

spittle • n. saliva.
– ORIGIN from dialect *spattle*.

spittoon /spit-toon/ • n. a container for spitting into.

spiv • n. Brit. informal a flashily dressed man who makes a living by dishonest business dealings.

splash • v. **1** (of a liquid) fall in scattered drops. **2** make wet with scattered drops.

3 move around in water, making it fly about. **4** (**splash down**) (of a spacecraft) land on water. **5** display a story or photograph very noticeably in a newspaper or magazine. **6** (**splash out**) Brit. informal spend money freely. • n. **1** an instance of splashing. **2** a small quantity of liquid splashed on to a surface. **3** a small quantity of liquid added to a drink. **4** a bright patch of colour. **5** informal a noticeable or sensational news story.
– PHRASES **make a splash** informal attract a great deal of attention.
– DERIVATIVES **splashy** adj.

splat • n. informal a sound of something soft and wet or heavy hitting a surface.
– ORIGIN from SPLATTER.

splatter • v. (**splatters**, **splattering**, **splattered**) splash with a sticky or thick liquid. • n. a splash of a sticky or thick liquid.

splay • v. spread out wide apart.
– ORIGIN from DISPLAY.

spleen • n. **1** an organ in the abdomen involved in the production and removal of blood cells and forming part of the immune system. **2** bad temper.
– ORIGIN Greek *splēn*; sense 2 comes from the former belief that bad temper originated in the spleen.

splendid • adj. **1** magnificent; very impressive. **2** informal excellent.
– DERIVATIVES **splendidly** adv.
– ORIGIN Latin *splendidus*.

splendiferous • adj. informal, humorous very good; splendid.

splendour (US **splendor**) • n. magnificent and impressive appearance.

splenetic /spli-net-ik/ • adj. spiteful or bad-tempered.
– ORIGIN Latin *spleneticus*.

splice • v. (**splices**, **splicing**, **spliced**) **1** join a rope or ropes by weaving the strands together at the ends. **2** join pieces of timber, film, or tape at the ends. • n. a place where film, rope, etc. has been spliced together.
– PHRASES **get spliced** Brit. informal get married.
– ORIGIN prob. from Dutch *splissen*.

spliff • n. informal a cannabis cigarette.

splint • n. a strip of rigid material for supporting a broken bone when it has been set.
– ORIGIN Dutch or German *splinte* 'metal plate or pin'.

splinter • n. a small, thin, sharp piece of wood, glass, etc. broken off from a larger piece. • v. (**splinters**, **splintering**, **splintered**) break into splinters.
– DERIVATIVES **splintery** adj.
– ORIGIN Dutch.

splinter group • n. a small organization that has broken away from a larger one.

split • v. (**splits, splitting, split**) 1 break into parts by force. 2 divide into parts or groups. 3 (also **split up**) end a marriage or other relationship. 4 (**be splitting**) informal (of a person's head) be suffering from a bad headache. • n. 1 a tear or crack. 2 an instance of splitting. 3 (**the splits**) (in gymnastics and dance) an act of leaping in the air or sitting down with the legs straight and at right angles to the body.
– PHRASES **split your sides** informal laugh heartily or uncontrollably.
– DERIVATIVES **splitter** n.
– ORIGIN Dutch *splitten* 'break up a ship'.

split end • n. a tip of a person's hair which has split from dryness.

split infinitive • n. a construction consisting of an infinitive with an adverb or other word placed between *to* and the verb.

> **USAGE:** Many people still think that splitting infinitives (putting a word between *to* and the verb) is wrong. They think that you should say *she used secretly to admire him* rather than *she used to secretly admire him*, although this sometimes sounds awkward or gives a different emphasis to what is being said. For this reason, the rule about not splitting infinitives is not followed so strictly today, although it is best not to split them if you are writing.

split-level • adj. 1 (of a room or building) having the floor divided into different levels. 2 (of a cooker) having the oven and hob in separate units.

split pea • n. a pea dried and split in half for cooking.

split screen • n. a cinema, television, or computer screen on which two or more separate images are displayed.

split second • n. a very brief moment of time. • adj. (**split-second**) very rapid or accurate: *split-second timing*.

splodge • n. Brit. a spot or smear.

splosh informal • v. move with a soft splashing sound. • n. a splash.

splotch • n. informal a spot or smear.
– DERIVATIVES **splotchy** adj.
– ORIGIN perh. from SPOT and former *plotch* 'blotch'.

splurge informal • n. a sudden burst of spending money extravagantly. • v. (**splurges, splurging, splurged**) spend money extravagantly.

splutter • v. (**splutters, spluttering, spluttered**) 1 make a series of short explosive spitting or choking sounds. 2 say in a rapid and unclear way. • n. a spluttering sound.

spoil • v. (**spoils, spoiling, spoilt** (esp. Brit.) or **spoiled**) 1 make something less good or enjoyable. 2 (of food) become unfit for eating. 3 harm a child's character by not being strict enough. 4 treat with great or excessive kindness. 5 (**be spoiling for**) be very eager for. • n. (**spoils**) stolen goods.
– ORIGIN Latin *spoliare*.

spoilage • n. the decay of food and other perishable goods.

spoiler • n. 1 a flap on an aircraft wing which can be raised to create drag and so reduce speed. 2 a similar device on a car intended to improve roadholding at high speeds.

spoilsport • n. a person who spoils the pleasure of other people.

spoke¹ • n. 1 each of the bars or rods connecting the centre of a wheel to its rim. 2 each of the metal rods in an umbrella to which the material is attached.
– ORIGIN Old English.

spoke² past of SPEAK.

spoken past part. of SPEAK. • adj. (in combination) speaking in a specified way: *a soft-spoken man*.
– PHRASES **be spoken for** 1 be already claimed. 2 already have a romantic relationship.

spokesman (or **spokeswoman**) • n. (pl. **spokesmen** or **spokeswomen**) a person who makes statements on behalf of a group.

spokesperson • n. (pl. **spokespersons** or **spokespeople**) a spokesman or spokeswoman.

spoliation /spoh-li-ay-shuhn/ • n. 1 the action of destroying or ruining something. 2 the action of plundering.

spondee /spon-dee/ • n. a foot (unit of poetic metre) consisting of two long (or stressed) syllables.
– ORIGIN from Greek *spondeios pous* 'foot of a ritual offering of drink'.

sponge • n. 1 an invertebrate sea creature with a soft porous body. 2 a piece of a light, absorbent substance used for washing, as padding, etc. 3 Brit. a light cake made with eggs, sugar, and flour but little or no fat. • v. (**sponges, sponging** or **spongeing, sponged**) 1 wipe or clean with a wet sponge or cloth. 2 (usu. **sponge off**) informal obtain money or food from other people without giving anything in return.
– ORIGIN Greek *spongos*.

sponge bag • n. Brit. a toilet bag.

sponge pudding • n. Brit. a steamed or baked pudding of fat, flour, and eggs.

sponger • n. informal a person who lives by

obtaining food or money from other people.

spongiform /spun-ji-form/ • adj. tech. having a porous structure or consistency like that of a sponge.

spongy • adj. (**spongier**, **spongiest**) porous, absorbent, or compressible.
– DERIVATIVES **sponginess** n.

sponsor • n. 1 a person or organization that pays for or contributes to the costs of an event in return for advertising. 2 a person who promises to give money to a charity after another person has participated in a fund-raising activity. 3 a person who introduces and supports a proposal for a new law. • v. be a sponsor for.
– DERIVATIVES **sponsorship** n.
– ORIGIN Latin.

 The ending of **sponsor** is spelled **-or**.

spontaneous /spon-tay-ni-uhss/ • adj. 1 done or occurring as a result of an unplanned impulse: *the crowd broke into spontaneous applause.* 2 open, natural, and relaxed. 3 (of a process or event) happening naturally, without being made to do so.
– DERIVATIVES **spontaneity** /spon-tuh-**nay**-i-ti/ n. **spontaneously** adv.
– ORIGIN Latin *spontaneus*.

spoof • n. informal a humorous imitation of something in which its typical features are exaggerated.
– ORIGIN coined by the English comedian Arthur Roberts.

spook informal • n. 1 a ghost. 2 esp. N. Amer. a spy. • v. frighten someone.
– ORIGIN Dutch.

spooky • adj. (**spookier**, **spookiest**) informal sinister or ghostly.
– DERIVATIVES **spookily** adv. **spookiness** n.

spool • n. a cylindrical device on which thread, film, etc. can be wound. • v. wind on to a spool.
– ORIGIN Old French *espole* or German *spôle*.

spoon • n. an implement consisting of a small, shallow bowl on a long handle, used for eating, stirring, and serving food. • v. transfer with a spoon.
– DERIVATIVES **spoonful** n.
– ORIGIN Old English, 'chip of wood'.

spoonbill • n. a tall wading bird having a long bill with a very broad flat tip.

spoonerism • n. a mistake in speech in which the initial sounds or letters of two or more words are accidentally swapped around, as in *you have hissed the mystery lectures*.
– ORIGIN named after the English scholar Revd W. A. *Spooner*.

spoon-feed • v. provide someone with so much help or information that they do not need to think for themselves.

spoor • n. the track or scent of an animal.
– ORIGIN Dutch *spor*.

sporadic /spuh-rad-ik/ • adj. occurring at irregular intervals or only in a few places.
– DERIVATIVES **sporadically** adv.
– ORIGIN Greek *sporadikos*.

spore • n. a tiny reproductive cell produced by plants without vascular systems, fungi, etc.
– ORIGIN Greek *spora* 'sowing, seed'.

sporran /spo-ruhn/ • n. a small pouch worn around the waist so as to hang in front of the kilt as part of men's Scottish Highland dress.
– ORIGIN Scottish Gaelic *sporan*.

sport • n. 1 an activity involving physical effort and skill in which a person or team competes against another or others. 2 informal a person who behaves in a good or specified way when teased or defeated: *be a sport!* 3 pleasure gained from an activity such as hunting. • v. 1 wear a distinctive item. 2 literary play in a lively way.
– ORIGIN from DISPORT.

sporting • adj. 1 connected with or interested in sport. 2 fair and generous towards other people.

sporting chance • n. a reasonable chance of winning or succeeding.

sportive • adj. playful; light-hearted.

sports car • n. a low-built fast car.

sports jacket • n. a man's informal jacket resembling a suit jacket.

sportsman (or **sportswoman**) • n. (pl. **sportsmen** or **sportswomen**) 1 a person who takes part in a sport. 2 a person who behaves in a fair or sporting way.
– DERIVATIVES **sportsmanship** n.

sportswear • n. clothes worn for sport or for casual use.

sporty • adj. (**sportier**, **sportiest**) informal 1 fond of or good at sport. 2 (of clothing) suitable for sport or casual wear. 3 (of a car) compact and with fast acceleration.

spot • n. 1 a small round mark on a surface. 2 a pimple. 3 a particular place, point, or position. • v. (**spots**, **spotting**, **spotted**) 1 notice or recognize someone or something that is difficult to find or that you are searching for. 2 mark with spots. 3 (**it spots**, **it is spotting**) light rain falls.
– PHRASES **on the spot 1** immediately. **2** at the scene of an action or event. **spot on** Brit. informal completely accurate or accurately.

S

– DERIVATIVES **spotted** adj. **spotter** n.
– ORIGIN perh. from Dutch *spotte*.

spot check • n. a test made without warning on a person or thing selected at random. • v. (**spot-check**) make a spot check on.

spotless • adj. absolutely clean or pure.
– DERIVATIVES **spotlessly** adv.

spotlight • n. 1 a lamp projecting a narrow, strong beam of light directly on to a place or person. 2 (**the spotlight**) intense public attention. • v. (**spotlights**, **spotlighting**, **spotlighted** or **spotlit**) light up with a spotlight.

spotty • adj. (**spottier**, **spottiest**) marked with or having spots.

spouse • n. a husband or wife.
– ORIGIN Latin *sponsus*.

spout • n. 1 a projecting tube or lip through or over which liquid can be poured from a container. 2 a stream of liquid flowing out with great force. • v. 1 send out or flow forcibly in a stream. 2 express your views in a lengthy or emphatic way.
– PHRASES **up the spout** Brit. informal useless or ruined.
– ORIGIN from Old Norse, 'to spit'.

sprain • v. wrench the ligaments of a joint so as to cause pain and swelling. • n. the result of wrenching a joint.

sprang past of **SPRING**.

sprat • n. a small edible sea fish of the herring family.
– ORIGIN Old English.

sprawl • v. 1 sit, lie, or fall with the limbs spread out in an awkward way. 2 spread out irregularly over a large area. • n. 1 a sprawling movement. 2 the disorganized expansion of an urban or industrial area into the nearby countryside.
– ORIGIN Old English, 'move the limbs convulsively'.

spray[1] • n. 1 liquid sent through the air in tiny drops. 2 a liquid which can be forced out of an aerosol or other container in a spray. • v. 1 apply liquid in a spray. 2 cover or treat with a spray. 3 (of liquid) be sent through the air in a spray. 4 scatter things over an area.
– DERIVATIVES **sprayer** n.
– ORIGIN from Dutch *spraeyen* 'sprinkle'.

spray[2] • n. 1 a stem or small branch of a tree or plant, bearing flowers and leaves. 2 a bunch of cut flowers arranged in an attractive way.
– ORIGIN Old English.

spray gun • n. a device resembling a gun which is used to spray a liquid such as paint under pressure.

spread • v. (**spreads**, **spreading**, **spread**) 1 open out so as to increase in surface area, width, or length. 2 stretch out limbs, hands, fingers, or wings so that they are far apart. 3 extend over a wide area or a specified period of time. 4 reach or cause to reach more and more people: *panic spread among the crowd.* 5 apply a substance in an even layer. • n. 1 the action of spreading. 2 the extent, width, or area covered by something. 3 the range of something. 4 a soft paste that can be spread on bread. 5 an article or advertisement which covers several pages of a newspaper or magazine. 6 informal a large meal.
– DERIVATIVES **spreadable** adj. **spreader** n.
– ORIGIN Old English.

spreadeagle • v. (**be spreadeagled**) be stretched out with the arms and legs extended.

spreadsheet • n. a computer program in which figures arranged in a grid can be manipulated and used in calculations.

spree • n. a spell of unrestrained activity: *a shopping spree.*

sprig • n. a small stem bearing leaves or flowers, taken from a bush or plant.
– ORIGIN German *sprick*.

sprightly • adj. (**sprightlier**, **sprightliest**) (especially of an old person) lively; energetic.
– DERIVATIVES **sprightliness** n.
– ORIGIN from **SPRITE**.

spring • v. (**springs**, **springing**, **sprang** or N. Amer. **sprung**; past part. **sprung**) 1 move suddenly or quickly upwards or forwards. 2 move or do suddenly: *the drawer sprang open.* 3 (**spring from**) come or appear from. 4 (**spring up**) suddenly develop or appear. 5 (as adj. **sprung**) (of a vehicle or item of furniture) having springs. • n. 1 the season after winter and before summer. 2 a spiral metal coil that can be pressed or pulled but returns to its former shape when released. 3 a sudden jump upwards or forwards. 4 a place where water wells up from an underground source. 5 elastic quality.
– PHRASES **spring a leak** (of a boat or container) develop a leak.
– ORIGIN Old English.

spring balance • n. a balance that measures weight by the tension of a spring.

springboard • n. 1 a flexible board from which a diver or gymnast may jump in order to push off more powerfully. 2 a thing providing driving force to an action or enterprise.

springbok • n. a southern African gazelle that leaps when disturbed.
– ORIGIN Afrikaans.

S

spring chicken • n. informal a young person: *I'm no spring chicken.*

spring clean • n. Brit. a thorough cleaning of a house or room. • v. (**spring-clean**) clean thoroughly.

springer (also **springer spaniel**) • n. a small spaniel of a breed originally used to drive game birds out of cover.

spring greens • pl. n. the leaves of young cabbage plants of a variety that does not develop a heart.

spring-loaded • adj. containing a compressed or stretched spring pressing one part against another.

spring onion • n. Brit. a small onion with a long green stem, eaten in salads.

spring roll • n. a Chinese snack consisting of a pancake filled with vegetables and sometimes meat, rolled into a cylinder and fried.

spring tide • n. a tide just after a new or full moon, when there is the greatest difference between high and low water.

springy • adj. (**springier, springiest**) springing back quickly when squeezed or stretched.
– DERIVATIVES **springily** adv. **springiness** n.

sprinkle • v. (**sprinkles, sprinkling, sprinkled**) **1** scatter or pour small drops or particles over an object or surface. **2** distribute something randomly throughout something else. • n. a small amount that is sprinkled.
– ORIGIN perh. from Dutch *sprenkelen.*

sprinkler • n. **1** a device for watering lawns. **2** an automatic fire extinguisher installed in a ceiling.

sprinkling • n. a small, thinly distributed amount.

sprint • v. run at full speed over a short distance. • n. **1** an act of sprinting. **2** a short, fast race.
– DERIVATIVES **sprinter** n.
– ORIGIN from Swedish *spritta.*

sprit • n. Sailing a small pole reaching diagonally from a mast to the upper outer corner of a sail.
– ORIGIN Old English, 'punting pole'.

sprite • n. an elf or fairy.
– ORIGIN a shortening of **spirit.**

spritz • v. spray liquid in quick short bursts at or on to.
– ORIGIN German *spritzen* 'to squirt'.

spritzer • n. a mixture of wine and soda water.
– ORIGIN German, 'a splash'.

sprocket • n. each of several projections on the rim of a wheel that engage with the links of a chain or with holes in film, tape, or paper.

sprout • v. **1** produce plant shoots or

grow hair. **2** appear or develop in large numbers: *multiplexes are sprouting up around the country.* • n. **1** a shoot of a plant. **2** a Brussels sprout.
– ORIGIN Germanic.

spruce¹ • adj. neat and smart.
• v. (**spruces, sprucing, spruced**) (**spruce someone/thing up**) make someone or something smarter.
– ORIGIN perh. from **spruce**² in the former sense 'Prussian'.

spruce² • n. a coniferous tree with a conical shape and hanging cones.
– ORIGIN from former *Pruce* 'Prussia'.

sprung past part. and N. Amer. past of **spring.**

spry • adj. (of an old person) lively.

spud • n. informal a potato.

spume /spyoom/ • n. literary froth or foam that is found on waves.
– ORIGIN Latin *spuma.*

spun past and past part. of **spin.**

spunk • n. informal courage and determination.
– DERIVATIVES **spunky** adj. (**spunkier, spunkiest**).
– ORIGIN perh. from **spark** and former *funk* 'spark'.

spur • n. **1** a device with a small spike or a spiked wheel, worn on a rider's heel for urging a horse forward. **2** an encouragement: *wars act as a spur to invention.* **3** a projection from a mountain. **4** a short branch road or railway line. **5** Bot. a slender projection from the base of a flower. • v. (**spurs, spurring, spurred**) **1** urge a horse forward with spurs. **2** encourage someone.
– PHRASES **on the spur of the moment** on an impulse; without thinking.
– ORIGIN Old English.

spurge • n. a plant or shrub with milky latex and small greenish flowers.
– ORIGIN Old French *espurge.*

spurious /rhymes with curious/ • adj. **1** false or fake. **2** (of reasoning) apparently but not actually correct.
– ORIGIN Latin *spurius* 'false'.

spurn • v. reject with contempt.
– ORIGIN Old English.

spurt • v. **1** gush out in a sudden stream. **2** move with a sudden burst of speed. • n. **1** a sudden gushing stream. **2** a sudden burst of activity or speed.

sputter • v. (**sputters, sputtering, sputtered**) **1** make a series of soft explosive sounds. **2** say in a rapid and unclear way; splutter.
– ORIGIN Dutch *sputteren.*

sputum • n. a mixture of saliva and

mucus coughed up from the throat or lungs.
– ORIGIN Latin.

spy •n. (pl. **spies**) **1** a person employed to collect and report secret information on an enemy or competitor. **2** a device that observes people secretly. •v. (**spies**, **spying**, **spied**) **1** be a spy. **2** (**spy on**) watch secretly. **3** see or notice: *he could spy a figure in the distance.*
– ORIGIN Old French *espier* 'espy'.

spyglass •n. a small telescope.

sq. •abbrev. square.

squab /skwob/ •n. a young pigeon that is yet to leave the nest.

squabble •n. a noisy quarrel about an unimportant matter. •v. (**squabbles**, **squabbling**, **squabbled**) quarrel about an unimportant matter.

squad •n. **1** a small number of soldiers assembled for drill or working together. **2** a group of sports players from which a team is chosen. **3** a division of a police force dealing with a particular type of crime.
– ORIGIN Italian *squadra* 'square'.

squad car •n. a police patrol car.

squaddie •n. (pl. **squaddies**) Brit. informal a private soldier.

squadron •n. **1** an operational unit in an air force. **2** a main division of an armoured or cavalry regiment. **3** a group of warships on a particular duty.
– ORIGIN Italian *squadrone* 'soldiers in a square formation'.

squalid •adj. **1** very dirty and unpleasant. **2** highly immoral or dishonest: *a squalid attempt to buy votes.*
– ORIGIN Latin *squalidus.*

squall •n. a sudden violent gust of wind or a localized storm. •v. (of a baby) cry noisily and continuously.
– DERIVATIVES **squally** adj.
– ORIGIN prob. from SQUEAL.

squalor /rhymes with collar/ •n. the state of being dirty and unpleasant.

squander •v. (**squanders**, **squandering**, **squandered**) waste money, time, etc. in a reckless or foolish way.

square •n. **1** a plane figure with four equal straight sides and four right angles. **2** an open four-sided area surrounded by buildings. **3** the product of a number multiplied by itself. **4** an area within a military barracks or camp used for drill. **5** an L-shaped or T-shaped instrument used for obtaining or testing right angles. **6** informal an old-fashioned or boring person. •adj. **1** having the shape of a square. **2** having or forming a right angle. **3** (of a unit of measurement) equal to the area of a square

whose side is of the unit specified. **4** (after a noun) referring to the length of each side of a square shape or object: *the room was ten metres square.* **5** at right angles. **6** level or parallel. **7** broad and solid in shape. **8** informal old-fashioned or boringly conventional. •adv. directly; straight. •v. (**squares**, **squaring**, **squared**) **1** make square or rectangular. **2** (as adj. **squared**) marked out in squares. **3** multiply a number by itself. **4** (**square with**) agree or be consistent with: *do those claims square with the facts?* **5** settle a bill or debt. **6** make the score of a match or game even. **7** bring the shoulders into a position in which they appear square and broad.
– PHRASES **back to square one** informal back to where you started. **2** do something considered to be impossible. **a square deal** see DEAL¹. **a square peg in a round hole** see PEG. **square up** take up the position of a person about to fight.
– DERIVATIVES **squarish** adj.
– ORIGIN Old French *esquare.*

square-bashing •n. Brit. informal military drill performed repeatedly on a barrack square.

square dance •n. a country dance that starts with four couples facing one another in a square.

squarely •adv. in a straightforward way; directly.

square meal •n. a large and balanced meal.

square measure •n. a unit of measurement relating to area.

square number •n. the product of a number multiplied by itself, e.g. 1, 4, 9.

square-rigged •adj. (of a sailing ship) having the main sails at right angles to the length of the ship.

square root •n. a number which produces a specified quantity when multiplied by itself.

squash¹ •v. **1** crush or squeeze something so that it becomes flat, soft, or out of shape. **2** force into a restricted space. **3** put an end to: *the revolt was squashed.* •n. **1** a state of being squashed. **2** Brit. a concentrated liquid made from fruit juice and sugar, diluted to make a drink. **3** (also **squash rackets**) a game in which two players use rackets to hit a small rubber ball against the walls of a closed court.
– DERIVATIVES **squashy** adj.
– ORIGIN from QUASH.

squash² •n. (pl. **squash** or **squashes**) a gourd with flesh that can be cooked and eaten as a vegetable.

S

– ORIGIN from a North American Indian language.

squat • v. (**squats, squatting, squatted**) **1** crouch or sit with the knees bent and the heels close to the bottom or thighs. **2** unlawfully occupy an uninhabited building or area of land. • adj. (**squatter, squattest**) short or low and wide. • n. **1** a squatting position. **2** a building occupied unlawfully.
– DERIVATIVES **squatter** n.
– ORIGIN Old French *esquatir* 'flatten'.

squat thrust • n. an exercise in which the legs are thrust backwards to their full extent from a squatting position with the hands on the floor.

squaw /skwaw/ • n. offens. an American Indian woman or wife.
– ORIGIN from a North American Indian language.

squawk • v. **1** (of a bird) make a loud, harsh noise. **2** say something in a loud, ugly tone. • n. an act of squawking.

squeak • n. **1** a short, high-pitched sound or cry. **2** a single remark or sound: *I didn't hear a squeak from him.* • v. **1** make a squeak. **2** say something in a high-pitched tone. **3** informal only just manage to achieve something.
– PHRASES **a narrow squeak** Brit. informal something that is only just achieved.
– DERIVATIVES **squeaker** n. **squeaky** adj. (**squeakier, squeakiest**).

squeaky clean • adj. informal **1** completely clean. **2** morally correct; very good.

squeal • n. a long, high-pitched cry or noise. • v. **1** make a squeal. **2** say something in a high-pitched tone. **3** (often **squeal on**) informal inform on someone.
– DERIVATIVES **squealer** n.

squeamish • adj. **1** easily disgusted or made to feel sick. **2** having very strong moral views.
– DERIVATIVES **squeamishly** adv. **squeamishness** n.
– ORIGIN Old French *escoymos*.

squeegee /skwee-jee/ • n. a scraping tool with a rubber-edged blade, used for cleaning windows.
– ORIGIN from SQUEEZE.

squeeze • v. (**squeezes, squeezing, squeezed**) **1** firmly press from opposite or all sides. **2** extract liquid or a soft substance from something by squeezing. **3** (**squeeze in/into/through**) manage to get into or through a restricted space. **4** (**squeeze someone/thing in**) manage to find time for someone or something. • n. **1** an act of squeezing or the state of being squeezed. **2** a hug. **3** a small amount of liquid produced by squeezing. **4** a strong financial demand or pressure: *a squeeze on profits.*
– PHRASES **put the squeeze on** informal pressurize someone into doing something.
– DERIVATIVES **squeezable** adj. **squeezer** n. **squeezy** adj.

squelch • v. make a soft sucking sound such as that made by treading in thick mud. • n. a squelching sound.
– DERIVATIVES **squelchy** adj.

squib • n. a small firework that hisses before exploding.

squid • n. (pl. **squid** or **squids**) a mollusc that lives in the sea, with a long body, eight arms, and two long tentacles.

squidgy • adj. (**squidgier, squidgiest**) informal, esp. Brit. soft and moist.

squiffy • adj. Brit. informal slightly drunk.

squiggle • n. a short line that curls and loops irregularly.
– DERIVATIVES **squiggly** adj.
– ORIGIN perh. from SQUIRM and WIGGLE or WRIGGLE.

squillion • cardinal number informal an indefinite very large number.
– ORIGIN humorous formation on the pattern of *billion*.

squint • v. **1** look at someone or something with partly closed eyes. **2** partly close the eyes. **3** have a squint affecting one eye. • n. **1** a permanent condition in which one eye does not look in the same direction as the other. **2** informal a quick or casual look.
– ORIGIN perh. from Dutch *schuinte* 'slant'.

squire • n. **1** a country gentleman. **2** Brit. informal used as a friendly form of address by one man to another. **3** hist. a young nobleman acting as an attendant to a knight before becoming a knight himself.
– ORIGIN Old French *esquier* 'esquire'.

squirm • v. **1** wriggle or twist the body from side to side. **2** be embarrassed or ashamed. • n. a wriggling movement.
– ORIGIN prob. from WORM.

squirrel • n. a rodent with a bushy tail that lives in trees. • v. (**squirrels, squirrelling, squirrelled**; US also **squirrels, squirreling, squirreled**) (**squirrel something away**) hide money or valuables in a safe place.
– ORIGIN Old French *esquireul*.

squirt • v. **1** force out liquid in a thin jet from a small opening. **2** wet with a jet of liquid. • n. **1** a thin jet of liquid. **2** informal a weak or insignificant person.

squish • v. **1** make a soft squelching sound. **2** informal squash something. • n. a soft squelching sound.
– DERIVATIVES **squishy** adj.

Sr •symb. the chemical element strontium.

Sri Lankan /sri lang-kuhn, shri lang-kuhn/ •n. a person from Sri Lanka.
•adj. relating to Sri Lanka.

SS¹ •abbrev. **1** Saints. **2** steamship.

SS² •n. the Nazi special police force.
– ORIGIN short for German *Schutzstaffel* 'defence squadron'.

St •abbrev. **1** Saint. **2** (usu. **St.**) Street.

st •abbrev. stone (in weight).

stab •v. (**stabs**, **stabbing**, **stabbed**) **1** thrust a knife or other pointed weapon into. **2** thrust a pointed object at. **3** (of a pain) cause a sudden sharp feeling.
•n. **1** an act of stabbing. **2** a sudden sharp feeling or pain. **3** (**a stab at**) informal an attempt to do.

stability •n. the state of being stable.

stabilize (or **stabilise**) •v. (**stabilizes**, **stabilizing**, **stabilized**) make or become stable.
– DERIVATIVES **stabilization** n.

stabilizer (or **stabiliser**)
•n. **1** (**stabilizers**) Brit. a pair of small supporting wheels fitted on a child's bicycle. **2** a device used to stabilize a ship or aircraft. **3** a substance which prevents the breakdown of emulsions in food or paint.

stable¹ •adj. (**stabler**, **stablest**) **1** not likely to give way or overturn; firmly fixed. **2** not worsening in health after an injury or operation. **3** not easily upset or disturbed; sane and sensible. **4** not likely to change or fail. **5** not liable to undergo chemical decomposition or radioactive decay.
– DERIVATIVES **stably** adv.
– ORIGIN Latin *stabilis*.

stable² •n. **1** a building for housing horses. **2** a place where racehorses are kept and trained. •v. (**stables**, **stabling**, **stabled**) put or keep a horse in a stable.
– ORIGIN Old French *estable* 'stable, pigsty'.

stablemate •n. a horse from the same stable as another.

stabling •n. accommodation for horses.

staccato /stuh-kah-toh/ •adv. & adj. Music with each sound or note sharply separated from the others. •n. (pl. **staccatos**) **1** Music a staccato passage or performance. **2** a series of short, detached sounds or words.
– ORIGIN Italian, 'detached'.

stack •n. **1** a neat pile of objects. **2** a rectangular or cylindrical pile of hay, straw, etc. **3** informal a large quantity. **4** a chimney. •v. **1** arrange in a stack. **2** fill or cover with stacks of things. **3** cause aircraft to fly at different altitudes while waiting to land. **4** arrange a pack of cards dishonestly. **5** (**be stacked against/in favour of**) (of a situation) be very likely to produce an unfavourable or favourable outcome for.
– DERIVATIVES **stackable** adj. **stacker** n.
– ORIGIN Old Norse, 'haystack'.

stadium /stay-di-uhm/ •n. (pl. **stadiums** or **stadia** /stay-di-uh/) an athletic or sports ground with rows of seats for spectators.
– ORIGIN Greek *stadion* 'racing track'.

staff •n. **1** the employees of an organization. **2** a group of army officers assisting a commanding officer. **3** a long stick used as a support or weapon. **4** a rod or sceptre held as a sign of office or authority. **5** Music a stave. •v. provide an organization with staff.
– ORIGIN Old English.

staff nurse •n. Brit. an experienced hospital nurse less senior than a sister.

staffroom •n. esp. Brit. a common room for teachers in a school or college.

Staffs. •abbrev. Staffordshire.

stag •n. a fully adult male deer.
– ORIGIN Old Norse, 'male bird'.

stag beetle •n. a large dark beetle, the male of which has large jaws resembling antlers.

stage •n. **1** a point, period, or step in a process. **2** a raised floor or platform on which actors, entertainers, or speakers perform. **3** (**the stage**) the acting profession. **4** a part of a journey. **5** each of two or more sections of a rocket or spacecraft that are discarded in turn when their fuel is exhausted.
•v. (**stages**, **staging**, **staged**) **1** present a performance of a play or other show. **2** organize a public event. **3** cause something notable to happen: *she's going to stage a comeback.*
– ORIGIN Old French *estage* 'dwelling'.

stagecoach •n. a closed horse-drawn vehicle formerly used to carry passengers along a regular route.

stage direction •n. an instruction in a play script indicating the position or tone of an actor, or specifying sound effects, lighting, etc.

stage door •n. an actors' entrance from the street to the backstage area of a theatre.

stage fright •n. nervousness before or during a performance.

stagehand •n. a person dealing with scenery or props during a play.

stage-manage •v. arrange and control something carefully to create a particular effect.

stage manager •n. the person

S

responsible for lighting and other technical arrangements for a stage play.

stage name • n. a name taken for professional purposes by an actor.

stage-struck • adj. having a passionate wish to become an actor.

stage whisper • n. a loud whisper by an actor on stage, intended to be heard by the audience.

stagey • adj. var. of STAGY.

stagger • v. (**staggers, staggering, staggered**) **1** walk or move unsteadily, as if about to fall. **2** astonish someone greatly. **3** spread payments, events, etc. over a period of time. **4** arrange objects or parts so that they are not in line. • n. an act of staggering.
– ORIGIN Old Norse.

staging • n. **1** a way of staging a play. **2** a temporary platform for working on.

staging post • n. a place at which people or vehicles regularly stop during a journey.

stagnant • adj. **1** (of water or air) not moving and often having an unpleasant smell. **2** showing little activity.
– ORIGIN Latin *stagnare* 'form a pool of standing water'.

stagnate • v. (**stagnates, stagnating, stagnated**) become stagnant or inactive.
– DERIVATIVES **stagnation** n.

stag night • n. an all-male celebration, especially one held for a man about to be married.

stagy (also **stagey**) • adj. excessively theatrical or exaggerated.
– DERIVATIVES **stagily** adv. **staginess** n.

staid • adj. respectable, unadventurous, and rather dull.
– ORIGIN from STAY¹.

stain • v. **1** mark or discolour with something that is not easily removed. **2** damage someone's reputation. **3** colour with a dye or chemical. • n. **1** a discoloured patch or dirty mark that is difficult to move. **2** a thing that damages a person's reputation. **3** a dye or chemical used to colour materials.
– ORIGIN Old French *desteindre*.

stained glass • n. coloured glass used to form pictures or designs, used for church windows.

stainless steel • n. a form of steel containing chromium, resistant to tarnishing and rust.

stair • n. **1** each of a set of fixed steps. **2** (**stairs**) a set of fixed steps leading from one floor of a building to another.
– ORIGIN Germanic, 'climb'.

staircase (also **stairway**) • n. a set of stairs and its surrounding structure.

stairwell • n. a shaft in which a staircase is built.

stake¹ • n. **1** a strong post with a point at one end, driven into the ground to support a tree, form part of a fence, etc. **2** (**the stake**) hist. a wooden post to which a person was tied before being burned alive. • v. (**stakes, staking, staked**) **1** support a plant with a stake. **2** (often **stake something out**) state your position or assert your rights forcefully. **3** (**stake someone/thing out**) informal keep a place or person under secret observation.
– ORIGIN Old English.

stake² • n. **1** a sum of money gambled. **2** a share or interest in a business or situation. **3** (**stakes**) prize money. **4** (**stakes**) a competitive situation: *we'll keep you one step ahead in the fashion stakes.* • v. (**stakes, staking, staked**) gamble money or something of value.
– PHRASES **at stake 1** at risk. **2** in question.
– ORIGIN perh. from STAKE¹.

stakeholder • n. a person with an interest or concern in a business, project, etc.
– DERIVATIVES **stakeholding** n. & adj.

stake-out • n. informal a period of secret observation.

stalactite /sta-luhk-tyt/ • n. a tapering structure hanging from the roof of a cave, formed of calcium salts deposited by dripping water.
– ORIGIN Greek *stalaktos* 'dripping'.

stalagmite /sta-luhg-myt/ • n. a tapering column rising from the floor of a cave, formed of calcium salts deposited by dripping water.
– ORIGIN Greek *stalagma* 'a drop'.

stale • adj. (**staler, stalest**) **1** (of food) no longer fresh or pleasant to eat. **2** no longer new and interesting. **3** no longer interested or enthusiastic.
– DERIVATIVES **staleness** n.
– ORIGIN prob. from Old French *estaler* 'to halt'.

stalemate • n. **1** Chess a position counting as a draw, in which a player is not in check but can only move into check. **2** a situation in which further progress by opposing sides seems impossible.

Stalinism • n. the policies adopted by the Soviet Communist Party leader and head of state Joseph Stalin, based on dictatorial state control and the pursuit of communism.
– DERIVATIVES **Stalinist** n. & adj.

stalk¹ • n. **1** the main stem of a plant. **2** the attachment or support of a leaf,

flower, or fruit. **3** a slender support or stem of an object.
– ORIGIN prob. from an Old English word meaning 'rung of a ladder'.

stalk² • v. **1** follow stealthily. **2** harass someone with unwanted and obsessive attention. **3** walk in a proud, stiff, or angry way.
– DERIVATIVES **stalker** n.
– ORIGIN Old English.

stalking horse • n. a person or thing that is used to disguise a person's real intentions.

stall • n. **1** a stand, booth, or compartment where goods are sold in a market. **2** an individual compartment for an animal in a stable or cowshed. **3** a stable or cowshed. **4** (also **starting stall**) a compartment in which a horse is held before the start of a race. **5** a compartment for one person in a set of toilets or shower cubicles. **6** (**stalls**) Brit. the ground-floor seats in a theatre. **7** a seat in the choir or chancel of a church.
• v. **1** (of a motor vehicle or its engine) stop running. **2** stop making progress. **3** delay by putting something off until later: *she was stalling for time.* **4** (of an aircraft) be moving too slowly to allow it to be controlled effectively.
– ORIGIN Old English.

stallholder • n. Brit. a person in charge of a market stall.

stallion • n. an adult male horse that has not been castrated.
– ORIGIN Old French *estalon*.

stalwart /stawl-wert, stol-wert/ • adj. **1** loyal, reliable, and hard-working. **2** dated strongly built and sturdy. • n. a loyal and reliable supporter or member of an organization.
– ORIGIN Scots.

stamen /stay-muhn/ • n. the male fertilizing organ of a flower.
– ORIGIN Latin, 'thread'.

stamina • n. the ability to keep up physical or mental effort over a long period.
– ORIGIN Latin, plural of **STAMEN** in the sense 'threads spun by the Fates'.

stammer • v. (**stammers, stammering, stammered**) speak or say with difficulty, repeating the first letters of words and often pausing. • n. a tendency to stammer.
– DERIVATIVES **stammerer** n.
– ORIGIN Old English.

stamp • v. **1** bring your foot down heavily on the ground or an object. **2** walk with heavy, forceful steps. **3** (**stamp something out**) put an end to by taking decisive action: *measures to stamp out BSE.* **4** press against something

with a device that leaves a mark or pattern. **5** (**stamp something on**) fix something in the mind: *the date was stamped on his memory.* • n. **1** a small piece of paper stuck to a letter or parcel to show that postage has been paid. **2** an instrument for stamping a pattern or mark. **3** a mark or pattern made by a stamp. **4** a distinctive impression or quality. **5** a particular class or type: *men of his own stamp.* **6** an act of stamping the foot.
– DERIVATIVES **stamper** n.
– ORIGIN Germanic.

stamp duty • n. a duty which must be paid for the legal recognition of certain documents.

stampede • n. **1** a sudden panicked rush of a number of horses, cattle, etc. **2** a sudden rapid movement or reaction of a large group of people due to interest or panic. • v. (**stampedes, stampeding, stampeded**) take part in or cause a stampede.
– ORIGIN Spanish *estampida* 'crash'.

stamping ground • n. a place that a person regularly visits or spends time at.

stance /stahnss, stanss/ • n. **1** the way in which someone stands. **2** an attitude towards something; a standpoint.
– ORIGIN French.

stanch /stawnch/ • v. US = **STAUNCH²**.

stanchion /stan-shuhn/ • n. an upright bar, post, or frame forming a support or barrier.
– ORIGIN Old French *stanchon*.

stand • v. (**stands, standing, stood**) **1** be in or rise to an upright position, supported by the feet. **2** place or be situated in a particular position. **3** move somewhere while standing: *stand aside.* **4** remain stationary or unchanged. **5** be in a specified state or condition. **6** adopt a particular attitude towards an issue. **7** be likely to do something: *investors stood to lose heavily.* **8** tolerate or like: *I can't stand it.* **9** Brit. be a candidate in an election. • n. **1** an attitude towards a particular issue. **2** a determined effort to hold your ground or resist something. **3** a stopping of movement or progress. **4** a large structure for spectators to sit or stand in at different levels. **5** a raised platform for a band, orchestra, or speaker. **6** a rack, base, or item of furniture for holding or displaying something. **7** a stall from which goods are sold or displayed. **8** (**the stand**) a witness box in a law court.
– PHRASES **stand by 1** watch without becoming involved. **2** support someone or abide by a promise. **3** be ready to take action if needed. **stand down** (also

S

stand aside) resign from or leave a job. **stand for 1** be an abbreviation of or symbol for. **2** put up with; tolerate. **stand in** act as a deputy for someone. **stand out 1** stick out or be easily noticeable. **2** be clearly better. **stand trial** be tried in a court of law. **stand someone up** informal fail to keep a date with someone. **stand up for** speak or act in support of. **stand up to 1** resist someone in a spirited way. **2** resist the harmful effects of something.

– ORIGIN Old English.

USAGE: It is good English to use the present participle **standing** rather than the past participle **stood** with the verb 'to be': say *we were standing there for hours* rather than *we were stood there for hours*.

stand-alone • adj. (of computer hardware or software) able to operate independently of other hardware or software.

standard • n. **1** a level of quality or achievement. **2** a required or accepted level of quality or achievement. **3** something used as a measure in order to make comparisons. **4** (**standards**) principles of good behaviour. **5** a military or ceremonial flag. • adj. **1** used or accepted as normal or average. **2** (of a size, measure, etc.) regularly used or produced. **3** (of a work, writer, etc.) viewed as having authority and so widely read.

– ORIGIN Old French *estendart*.

standard-bearer • n. **1** a leading figure in a cause or movement. **2** a soldier carrying the flag of a unit, regiment, or army.

Standard Grade • n. (in Scotland) an exam equivalent to the GCSE.

standardize (or **standardise**) • v. (**standardizes, standardizing, standardized**) make something meet or follow a standard.

– DERIVATIVES **standardization** n.

standard lamp • n. a lamp with a tall stem whose base stands on the floor.

standard of living • n. the amount of money and level of comfort available to a person or community.

standby • n. (pl. **standbys**) **1** readiness for duty or immediate action. **2** a person or thing ready to be used in an emergency. • adj. (of tickets for a journey or performance) sold only at the last minute if still available.

stand-in • n. a person who stands in or deputizes for another.

standing • n. **1** the position, status, or reputation of someone or something. **2** the length of time that something has existed: *a problem of long standing.* • adj. **1** remaining in force or use; permanent. **2** (of a jump or start of a race) performed from rest or an upright position.

standing joke • n. something regularly causing amusement.

standing order • n. Brit. **1** an instruction to a bank to make regular fixed payments to someone. **2** an order placed on a regular basis with a retailer.

standing ovation • n. a long period of applause during which the audience rise to their feet.

stand-off • n. a deadlock between two equally matched opponents.

stand-off half • n. Rugby a halfback who forms a link between the scrum half and the three-quarters.

stand-offish • adj. informal unfriendly and cold.

standpipe • n. a vertical pipe extending from a water supply, connecting a temporary tap to the mains.

standpoint • n. an attitude towards a particular issue.

standstill • n. a situation without movement or activity.

stand-up • adj. (of comedy or a comedian) performed or performing by telling jokes to an audience.

stank past of STINK.

stanza /stan-zuh/ • n. a group of lines forming the basic unit in a poem; a verse.

– ORIGIN Italian, 'standing place, stanza'.

staphylococcus /staf-fi-luh-kok-kuhss/ • n. (pl. **staphylococci** /staf-fi-luh-kok-ky/) a bacterium of a group including many kinds that cause pus to be formed.

– ORIGIN from Greek *staphulē* 'bunch of grapes' + *kokkos* 'berry'.

staple¹ • n. **1** a small piece of wire used to fasten papers together. **2** a small U-shaped metal bar that is driven into wood to hold things in place. • v. (**staples, stapling, stapled**) secure with a staple or staples.

– DERIVATIVES **stapler** n.

– ORIGIN Old English, 'pillar'.

staple² • n. **1** a main item of trade or production. **2** a main or important element of something. • adj. main or important: *a staple food.*

– ORIGIN German or Dutch *stapel* 'pillar, emporium'.

star • n. **1** a huge mass of burning gas which is visible as a glowing point in the night sky. **2** a shape with five or six points representing a star, often used to indicate a category of excellence. **3** a

famous or talented entertainer or sports player. **4** an outstanding person or thing. • v. (**stars, starring, starred**) **1** (of a film, play, etc.) have someone as a leading performer. **2** (of a performer) have a leading role in a film, play, etc.
– ORIGIN Old English.

star anise • n. a small star-shaped fruit with an aniseed flavour, used in Asian cookery.

starboard /star-bord, star-berd/ • n. the side of a ship or aircraft on the right when a person is facing forward. Opp. **PORT³**.
– ORIGIN Old English, 'rudder side'.

starch • n. **1** a carbohydrate which is obtained from cereals and potatoes and is an important part of the human diet. **2** powder or spray made from starch, used to stiffen fabric. • v. stiffen fabric with starch.
– ORIGIN Old English, 'stiffened'.

starchy • adj. **1** (of food) containing a great deal of starch. **2** informal (of a person) stiff and formal.
– DERIVATIVES **starchily** adv. **starchiness** n.

star-crossed • adj. literary (of love or lovers) fated to be unlucky.

stardom • n. the state of being a famous entertainer or sports player.

stare • v. (**stares, staring, stared**) look at someone or something with great concentration and the eyes wide open. • n. an act of staring.
– ORIGIN Old English.

starfish • n. (pl. **starfish** or **starfishes**) a sea creature having a flattened body with five or more arms extending from a central point.

starfruit • n. = **CARAMBOLA**.

stargazer • n. informal an astronomer or astrologer.

stark • adj. **1** severe or bare in appearance. **2** unpleasantly or sharply clear. **3** complete; sheer: *stark terror.*
– PHRASES **stark naked** completely naked.
– DERIVATIVES **starkly** adv. **starkness** n.
– ORIGIN Old English.

starkers • adj. Brit. informal completely naked.

starlet • n. informal a promising young actress or performer.

starlight • n. light coming from the stars.
– DERIVATIVES **starlit** adj.

starling • n. a songbird with dark shiny plumage.
– ORIGIN Old English.

Star of David • n. a six-pointed shape made up of two equilateral triangles, used as a Jewish and Israeli symbol.

starry • adj. (**starrier, starriest**) **1** full of

or lit by stars. **2** informal relating to stars in entertainment.

starry-eyed • adj. full of hopes or emotion in a way that is not realistic.

Stars and Stripes • pl. n. the national flag of the US.

starship • n. (in science fiction) a large spaceship for travel between stars.

star sign • n. a sign of the zodiac.

star-struck • adj. fascinated by famous actors and actresses.

star-studded • adj. informal featuring a number of famous people.

start • v. **1** begin to do, be, or happen. **2** make something happen or operate. **3** begin to operate. **4** begin to move or travel. **5** jump or jerk from surprise. • n. **1** the point at which something begins. **2** an act of beginning. **3** an amount of time or distance given to a competitor as an advantage at the beginning of a race. **4** a sudden movement of surprise.
– PHRASES **for a start** in the first place. **start out** (or **up**) begin a project or business. **to start with** as the first thing to be taken into account.
– ORIGIN Old English, 'to caper, leap'.

starter • n. **1** a person or thing that starts. **2** esp. Brit. the first course of a meal. **3** an automatic device for starting a machine.

starting block • n. a block for bracing the feet of a runner at the start of a race.

starting price • n. the final odds at the start of a horse race.

startle • v. (**startles, startling, startled**) make someone feel sudden shock or alarm.
– DERIVATIVES **startled** adj.
– ORIGIN Old English, 'kick, struggle'.

startling • adj. very surprising, astonishing, or remarkable.
– DERIVATIVES **startlingly** adv.

starve • v. (**starves, starving, starved**) **1** suffer or die from hunger. **2** make someone suffer or die by preventing them from eating. **3** (**be starving** or **starved**) informal feel very hungry. **4** (**be starved of**) be deprived of.
– DERIVATIVES **starvation** n.
– ORIGIN Old English, 'to die'.

stash informal • v. store safely in a secret place. • n. a secret store of something.

stasis /stay-sis/ • n. formal or tech. a period or state when there is no change or development.
– ORIGIN Greek, 'standing, stoppage'.

state • n. **1** the condition of someone or something at a particular time. **2** a nation or territory considered as an organized political unit under one

S

government. **3** an area forming part of a federal republic. **4 (the States)** the United States of America. **5** the government of a country. **6** ceremony associated with monarchy or government: *he was buried in state*. **7 (a state)** informal an agitated, untidy, or dirty condition. •v. **(states, stating, stated)** express definitely in speech or writing.
– PHRASES **state-of-the-art** using the newest ideas and most up-to-date features. **the state of play** Brit. **1** the score at a particular time in a cricket or football match. **2** the current situation.
– DERIVATIVES **statehood** n.
– ORIGIN partly from ESTATE, partly from Latin *status* 'standing'.

stateless •adj. not recognized as a citizen of any country.

stately •adj. **(statelier, stateliest)** dignified, grand, or impressive.
– DERIVATIVES **stateliness** n.

stately home •n. Brit. a large and impressive house occupied or formerly occupied by an aristocratic family.

statement •n. **1** a clear expression of something in speech or writing. **2** a formal account of facts or events given to the police or in court. **3** a document setting out what has been paid into and out of a bank account.

stateroom •n. **1** a private room on a ship. **2** a large room in a palace or public building, for use on formal occasions.

state school •n. Brit. a school funded and controlled by the state.

stateside •adj. & adv. informal relating to or towards the US.

statesman (or **stateswoman**) •n. (pl. **statesmen** or **stateswomen**) an experienced and respected political leader or figure.

static /stat-tik/ •adj. **1** not moving, changing, or active. **2** Physics relating to bodies at rest or forces in equilibrium. Often contrasted with DYNAMIC. **3** (of an electric charge) acquired by objects that cannot conduct a current. •n. **1** static electricity. **2** crackling on a telephone, radio, etc.
– DERIVATIVES **statically** adv.
– ORIGIN Greek *statikos* 'causing to stand'.

static electricity •n. a stationary electric charge produced by friction, causing sparks or crackling or the attraction of dust or hair.

station •n. **1** a place where passenger trains stop on a railway line. **2** a place where a specified activity or service is based: *a radar station*. **3** a broadcasting company. **4** the place where someone or something stands or is placed. **5** a person's social rank or position. **6** Austral./

NZ a large sheep or cattle farm. •v. put someone in a specified position.
– ORIGIN Latin.

stationary •adj. not moving or changing.

USAGE: Do not confuse **stationary** and **stationery**. **Stationary** means 'not moving or changing' (*the lorry crashed into a stationary car*), while **stationery** means 'paper and other writing materials'.

stationer •n. a person who sells stationery.
– ORIGIN Latin *stationarius* 'tradesman at a fixed location'.

stationery •n. paper and other materials needed for writing.

stationmaster •n. a person in charge of a railway station.

station wagon •n. N. Amer. & Austral./NZ an estate car.

statistic •n. a fact or piece of data obtained from a study of a large quantity of numerical information.
– ORIGIN German *Statistik*.

statistical •adj. relating to statistics.
– DERIVATIVES **statistically** adv.

statistics •n. the collection and analysis of large quantities of information in the form of numbers.
– DERIVATIVES **statistician** n.

statuary /stat-yoo-ri/ •n. statues as a whole.

statue •n. a carved or cast figure of a person or animal.
– ORIGIN Latin *statua*.

statuesque /sta-tyuu-esk, sta-chuu-esk/ •adj. (of a woman) tall, graceful, and dignified.

statuette •n. a small statue.

stature •n. **1** a person's natural height when standing. **2** a person's reputation or importance.
– ORIGIN Latin *statura*.

status •n. **1** a person's social or professional position in relation to other people. **2** high rank or social standing. **3** the situation at a particular time. **4** the official classification given to someone or something.
– ORIGIN Latin, 'standing'.

status quo /stay-tuhss kwoh/ •n. the existing situation.
– ORIGIN Latin, 'the state in which'.

status symbol •n. a possession intended to show a person's wealth or high status.

statute •n. **1** a written law. **2** a rule of an organization.
– ORIGIN Latin *statutum* 'thing set up'.

statute book •n. **(the statute book)** the whole of a nation's laws.

statute law • n. all the written laws of a parliament, country, etc., as a group.

statutory • adj. **1** required or permitted by law. **2** done or happening regularly and so expected.
– DERIVATIVES **statutorily** adv.

staunch[1] /stawnch/ • adj. very loyal and committed.
– DERIVATIVES **staunchly** adv.
– ORIGIN Old French *estanche* 'watertight'.

staunch[2] /stawnch, stahnch/ (US **stanch**) • v. stop or slow down a flow of something, especially blood.
– ORIGIN Old French *estanchier*.

stave • n. **1** any of the lengths of wood fixed side by side to make a barrel, bucket, etc. **2** a strong post or pole. **3** (also **staff**) Music a set of five parallel lines on or between which a note is written to indicate its pitch.
• v. **1** (**staves, staving, staved** or **stove**) (**stave something in**) break something by forcing it inwards. **2** (past and past part. **staved**) (**stave something off**) stop or delay something bad.
– ORIGIN from *staves*, former plural of STAFF.

stay[1] • v. **1** remain in the same place. **2** remain in a specified state or position: *inflation will stay down*. **3** live somewhere temporarily as a visitor or guest. **4** stop, delay, or prevent. • n. **1** a period of staying somewhere. **2** a suspension or postponement of the proceedings of a law court: *a stay of execution*. **3** (**stays**) hist. a corset made of two pieces laced together and stiffened by strips of whalebone.
– PHRASES **stay on** continue to work or be somewhere after other people have left. **stay put** remain somewhere without moving.
– DERIVATIVES **stayer** n.
– ORIGIN Old French *ester*.

stay[2] • n. a large rope, wire, or cable used to support or brace something such as a ship's mast.
– ORIGIN Old English.

staying power • n. informal endurance or stamina.

STD • abbrev. **1** sexually transmitted disease. **2** Brit. subscriber trunk dialling.

stead • n. (in phr. **in someone's/ something's stead**) instead of someone or something: *she was appointed in his stead.*
– PHRASES **stand someone in good stead** be useful to someone in the future.
– ORIGIN Old English.

steadfast • adj. not changing in your attitudes or aims.
– DERIVATIVES **steadfastly** adv. **steadfastness** n.

– ORIGIN Old English, 'standing firm'.

steady • adj. (**steadier, steadiest**) **1** firmly fixed, supported, or balanced. **2** not faltering or wavering. **3** sensible and reliable. **4** regular, even, and continuous in development, frequency, or strength. • v. (**steadies, steadying, steadied**) make or become steady.
– PHRASES **go steady** informal have a regular romantic or sexual relationship with someone.
– DERIVATIVES **steadily** adv. **steadiness** n.

steak • n. **1** high-quality beef from the hindquarters of the animal, cut into thick slices for grilling or frying. **2** a thick slice of other meat or fish. **3** poorer-quality beef for stewing.
– ORIGIN Old Norse.

steal • v. (**steals, stealing, stole**; past part. **stolen**) **1** take something without permission and without intending to return it. **2** move quietly or secretively. • n. informal a bargain.
– PHRASES **steal a look** (or **glance**) take a quick and secret look at someone or something. **steal the show** attract the most attention and praise.
– DERIVATIVES **stealer** n.
– ORIGIN Old English.

stealth • n. cautious and secretive action or movement.
– ORIGIN prob. from STEAL.

stealth tax • n. a tax charged in such a way that it is not noticed as a tax.

stealthy • adj. (**stealthier, stealthiest**) cautious and secretive.
– DERIVATIVES **stealthily** adv. **stealthiness** n.

steam • n. **1** the hot vapour into which water is converted when heated, which condenses in the air into a mist of tiny water droplets. **2** power produced from steam under pressure. **3** energy or force of movement: *the dispute gathered steam.* • v. **1** give off or produce steam. **2** (**steam up**) mist over with steam. **3** cook food by heating it in steam from boiling water. **4** clean or treat with steam. **5** (of a ship or train) travel under steam power. **6** informal move quickly or forcefully.
– PHRASES **let off steam** informal get rid of suppressed energy or strong emotion.
– ORIGIN Old English.

steamboat • n. a boat propelled by a steam engine.

steam engine • n. **1** an engine that uses the expansion or rapid condensation of steam to generate power. **2** a steam locomotive.

steamer • n. **1** a ship or boat powered by steam. **2** a type of saucepan in which food can be steamed.

S

steam iron • n. an electric iron that gives off steam from holes in its flat surface.

steamroller • n. a heavy, slow-moving vehicle with a roller, used to flatten the surfaces of roads during construction. • v. (**steamrollers, steamrollering, steamrollered**) **1** force someone into doing something. **2** forcibly pass a law.

steamship • n. a ship that is propelled by a steam engine.

steamy • adj. (**steamier, steamiest**) **1** producing or filled with steam. **2** hot and humid. **3** informal involving passionate sexual activity.

steed • n. old use a horse.
– ORIGIN Old English.

steel • n. **1** a hard, strong metal that is an alloy of iron with carbon, used as a structural material and in manufacturing. **2** strength and determination: *nerves of steel.* • v. mentally prepare yourself for something difficult.
– ORIGIN Old English.

steel band • n. a band that plays music on drums made from empty oil containers.

steel wool • n. fine strands of steel matted together into a mass, used to clean or smooth things.

steelworks • n. a factory where steel is produced.

steely • adj. (**steelier, steeliest**) **1** like steel in colour, brightness, or strength. **2** coldly determined.
– DERIVATIVES **steeliness** n.

steep¹ • adj. **1** rising or falling sharply. **2** (of a rise or fall in an amount) very large or rapid. **3** informal (of a price or demand) excessive.
– DERIVATIVES **steeply** adv. **steepness** n.
– ORIGIN Old English, 'extending to a great height'.

steep² • v. **1** soak in water or other liquid. **2** (**be steeped in**) have a great deal of a particular quality: *a city steeped in history.*
– ORIGIN Germanic.

steepen • v. become or make steeper.

steeple • n. a church tower and spire. • v. place the fingers or hands together so that they form an upward-pointing V-shape.
– ORIGIN Old English.

steeplechase • n. **1** a horse race run on a racecourse with ditches and hedges as jumps. **2** a running race in which runners must clear hurdles and water jumps.
– DERIVATIVES **steeplechaser** n. **steeplechasing** n.
– ORIGIN because the race was originally

run across country, with a steeple marking the finishing point.

steeplejack • n. a person who climbs tall structures such as chimneys and steeples in order to repair them.

steer¹ • v. **1** guide or control the movement of a vehicle, ship, or aircraft. **2** direct or guide: *I always steer the conversation back to work.*
– PHRASES **steer clear of** take care to avoid.
– DERIVATIVES **steerable** adj. **steerer** n.
– ORIGIN Old English.

steer² • n. a bullock.
– ORIGIN Old English.

steerage • n. hist. the cheapest accommodation in a ship.

steering • n. the mechanism in a vehicle, ship, or aircraft which allows it to be steered.

steering column • n. a shaft that connects the steering wheel of a vehicle to the rest of the steering mechanism.

steering committee (also **steering group**) • n. a committee that decides on the priorities or order of business of an organization.

steering wheel • n. a wheel that a driver turns in order to steer a vehicle.

steersman • n. (pl. **steersmen**) a person who steers a boat or ship.

stein /styn/ • n. a large earthenware beer mug.
– ORIGIN German, 'stone'.

stellar /stel-ler/ • adj. **1** relating to a star or stars. **2** informal excellent; outstanding.
– ORIGIN Latin *stellaris.*

stem¹ • n. **1** the main long thin part of a plant or shrub. **2** the stalk supporting a fruit, flower, or leaf. **3** a long, thin supporting part, such as that of a wine glass or tobacco pipe. **4** a vertical stroke in a letter or musical note. **5** Grammar the root or main part of a word, to which other elements are added. • v. (**stems, stemming, stemmed**) (**stem from**) be caused by or come from.
– ORIGIN Old English.

stem² • v. (**stems, stemming, stemmed**) stop or slow down the flow or progress of something.
– ORIGIN Old Norse.

stench • n. a strong and very unpleasant smell.
– ORIGIN Old English.

stencil • n. a thin sheet of card, plastic, or metal with a pattern or letters cut out of it, used to produce a design on the surface below by applying ink or paint through the holes. • v. (**stencils, stencilling, stencilled;** US **stencils,**

stenciled, **stenciling**) decorate with a stencil.
– ORIGIN Old French *estanceler* 'decorate brightly'.

stenographer /sti-nog-ruh-fer/ •n. N. Amer. a shorthand typist.
– ORIGIN Greek *stenos* 'narrow'.

stentorian /sten-tor-i-uhn/ •adj. (of a person's voice) loud and powerful.
– ORIGIN from *Stentor*, a herald in the Trojan War.

step •n. **1** an act of lifting and putting down the foot or feet in walking. **2** the distance covered by a step. **3** a flat surface on which to place the foot when moving from one level to another. **4** a position or grade in a scale or ranking. **5** a measure or action taken to achieve something: *a major step forward*. **6** (**steps** or **a pair of steps**) Brit. a stepladder.
•v. (**steps**, **stepping**, **stepped**) lift and put down the foot or feet.
– PHRASES **in** (or **out of**) **step 1** walking, marching, or dancing in the same (or a different) rhythm and pace as other people. **2** in accordance (or not in accordance) with what other people are doing or thinking. **step down** withdraw or resign from a job. **step in** become involved in a difficult situation. **step out of line** behave inappropriately or disobediently. **step something up** increase the amount, speed, or strength of something.
– ORIGIN Old English.

step- •comb. form referring to a relationship resulting from a remarriage: *stepmother*.
– ORIGIN Old English.

step aerobics •pl. n. a type of aerobics that involves stepping up on to and down from a block.

stepbrother •n. a son of a person's stepmother or stepfather.

stepchild •n. (pl. **stepchildren**) a child of a person's husband or wife by a previous marriage.

stepdaughter •n. a daughter of a person's husband or wife by a previous marriage.

stepfather •n. a man who is married to a person's mother after their parents are divorced or their father dies.

stephanotis /stef-fuh-noh-tiss/ •n. a climbing plant with waxy white flowers.
– ORIGIN Greek, 'fit for a wreath'.

stepladder •n. a short folding ladder with flat steps and a small platform.

stepmother •n. a woman who is married to a person's father after their parents are divorced or their mother dies.

steppe /step/ •n. a large area of flat grassland without trees in SE Europe or Siberia.
– ORIGIN Russian *step'*.

stepping stone •n. **1** a raised stone on which to step when crossing a stream. **2** something that helps a person to progress towards a goal.

stepsister •n. a daughter of a person's stepmother or stepfather.

stepson •n. a son of a person's husband or wife by a previous marriage.

-ster •suffix **1** referring to a person engaged in or associated with a particular activity: *gangster*. **2** referring to a person having a particular quality: *youngster*.
– ORIGIN Old English.

stereo /ste-ri-oh/ •n. (pl. **stereos**) **1** stereophonic sound. **2** a stereophonic CD player, record player, etc.
•adj. stereophonic.

stereophonic •adj. (of sound reproduction) using two or more channels so that the sound seems to come from more than one source.
– ORIGIN Greek *stereos* 'solid'.

stereoscopic •adj. **1** able to see objects as three-dimensional forms. **2** (of a photograph) taken with a special device to give a three-dimensional impression of something.

stereotype •n. an oversimplified idea of the typical characteristics of a person or thing. •v. (**stereotypes**, **stereotyping**, **stereotyped**) represent in an over-simplified way.

stereotypical •adj. relating to a stereotype.
– DERIVATIVES **stereotypically** adv.

sterile •adj. **1** not able to produce children, young, crops, or fruit. **2** free from bacteria or other living microorganisms. **3** not imaginative, creative, or exciting.
– DERIVATIVES **sterilely** adv. **sterility** n.
– ORIGIN Latin *sterilis*.

sterilize (or **sterilise**) •v. (**sterilizes**, **sterilizing**, **sterilized**) **1** make free from bacteria. **2** make a person or animal unable to produce offspring by removing or blocking the sex organs.
– DERIVATIVES **sterilization** n.

sterling •n. British money.
•adj. excellent: *she does sterling work*.
– ORIGIN prob. from Old English *steorra* 'star' (because some Norman pennies bore a small star).

sterling silver •n. silver of at least 92¼ per cent purity.

stern¹ •adj. **1** serious, disapproving, or strict. **2** severe or difficult: *a stern test of technique*.

S

– DERIVATIVES **sternly** adv. **sternness** n.
– ORIGIN Old English.

stern² • n. the rear of a ship or boat.
– ORIGIN prob. from Old Norse, 'steering'.

sternum /ster-nuhm/ • n. (pl. **sternums** or **sterna** /ster-nuh/) the breastbone.
– ORIGIN Greek *sternon* 'chest'.

steroid /ste-royd, steer-oyd/ • n. **1** any of a class of organic compounds that includes certain hormones and vitamins. **2** an anabolic steroid.
– ORIGIN from **STEROL**.

sterol /steer-ol, ste-rol/ • n. Biochem. any of a group of natural unsaturated steroid alcohols, such as cholesterol.
– ORIGIN from the ending of words such as **CHOLESTEROL**.

stertorous /ster-tuh-ruhss/ • adj. (of breathing) noisy and laboured.
– ORIGIN Latin *stertere* 'to snore'.

stethoscope /steth-uh-skohp/ • n. a medical instrument for listening to the action of someone's heart or breathing, having a disc that is placed against the chest and two tubes connected to earpieces.
– ORIGIN from Greek *stēthos* 'breast' + *skopein* 'look at'.

Stetson /stet-suhn/ • n. (trademark in the US) a hat with a high crown and a very wide brim, traditionally worn by cowboys.
– ORIGIN named after the American hat manufacturer John B. *Stetson*.

stevedore /stee-vuh-dor/ • n. a person employed at a dock to load and unload ships.
– ORIGIN Spanish *estivador*.

stew • n. **1** a dish of meat and vegetables cooked slowly in liquid in a closed dish. **2** informal a state of anxiety or agitation. • v. **1** cook slowly in liquid in a closed dish. **2** Brit. (of tea) become strong and bitter with prolonged brewing. **3** informal be in a stuffy atmosphere. **4** informal be agitated or anxious.
– ORIGIN Old French *estuve*.

steward • n. **1** a person who looks after the passengers on a ship or aircraft. **2** a person responsible for supplies of food to a college, club, etc. **3** an official who supervises arrangements at a large public event. **4** a person employed to manage a large house or estate.
– DERIVATIVES **stewardship** n.
– ORIGIN Old English.

stewardess • n. a woman who looks after the passengers on a ship or aircraft.

stick¹ • n. **1** a thin piece of wood that has fallen or been cut off a tree. **2** a piece of trimmed wood used for support in walking or as a weapon. **3** (in hockey, polo, etc.) a long, thin implement used to hit or direct the ball or puck. **4** a long, thin object: *a stick of dynamite*. **5** Brit. informal severe criticism. **6** Brit. informal remote country areas. **7** (**the sticks**)
– ORIGIN Old English.

stick² • v. (**sticks, sticking, stuck**) **1** push something pointed into or through something. **2** (**stick in/into/through**) be fixed with its point embedded in something. **3** protrude or extend in a particular direction: *his front teeth stick out*. **4** informal put somewhere in a quick or careless way. **5** cling or fasten very tightly to something; adhere. **6** (**be stuck**) be fixed in a particular position or unable to move. **7** (**be stuck**) be unable to continue with a task or solve something.
– PHRASES **be stuck with** informal be unable to get rid of or escape from. **get stuck in** (**or into**) Brit. informal start doing something with determination. **stick it out** informal put up with or carry on with something difficult. **stick out** be very noticeable. **stick to** continue doing or using. **stick up for** support or defend a person.
– ORIGIN Old English.

sticker • n. a sticky label or notice.

stick insect • n. a long, thin insect that resembles a twig.

stick-in-the-mud • n. informal a person who resists change.

stickleback • n. a small freshwater or coastal fish with sharp spines along its back.
– ORIGIN from Old English words meaning 'thorn' + 'back'.

stickler • n. a person who insists on a certain quality or type of behaviour.
– ORIGIN Old English, 'set in order'.

stick-up • n. informal a robbery in which a gun is used to threaten people.

sticky • adj. (**stickier, stickiest**) **1** tending or designed to stick. **2** like glue in texture. **3** (of the weather) hot and humid. **4** difficult or awkward. • n. (pl. **stickies**) a piece of paper with an adhesive strip on one side, used for leaving notes.
– DERIVATIVES **stickily** adv. **stickiness** n.

stiff • adj. **1** not easily bent. **2** difficult to turn or operate. **3** unable to move easily and without pain. **4** not relaxed or friendly. **5** severe or strong: *stiff fines*. • n. informal a dead body.
– PHRASES **stiff upper lip** the tendency to endure difficulty without complaining or showing your feelings.
– DERIVATIVES **stiffly** adv. **stiffness** n.
– ORIGIN Old English.

stiffen • v. **1** make or become stiff. **2** make or become stronger.

– DERIVATIVES **stiffener** n.

stiff-necked •adj. proud and stubborn.

stifle •v. (**stifles, stifling, stifled**)
1 prevent someone from breathing freely; suffocate. **2** restrain or prevent a reaction or activity.
– ORIGIN perh. from Old French *estouffer*.

stifling •adj. unpleasantly hot and stuffy.

stigma /stig-muh/ •n. (pl. **stigmas** or in sense 2 **stigmata** /stig-mah-tuh, stig-muh-tuh/) **1** a mark or sign of disgrace. **2** (**stigmata**) (in Christian tradition) marks on a person's body corresponding to those left on Christ's body by the Crucifixion. **3** the part of a plant's pistil that receives the pollen during pollination.
– ORIGIN Greek, 'mark made by a pointed instrument'.

stigmatize (or **stigmatise**)
•v. (**stigmatizes, stigmatizing, stigmatized**) regard or treat as worthy of disgrace or disapproval.
– DERIVATIVES **stigmatization** n.

stile •n. an arrangement of steps set into a fence or wall that allows people to climb over.
– ORIGIN Old English.

stiletto •n. (pl. **stilettos**) **1** esp. Brit. a thin, high heel on a woman's shoe. **2** a short dagger with a tapering blade.
– ORIGIN Italian, 'little dagger'.

☑ Spell **stiletto** with one **l** and a double **t**.

still[1] •adj. **1** not moving. **2** Brit. (of a drink) not fizzy. •n. **1** a state of deep and quiet calm. **2** a photograph or a single shot from a cinema film. •adv. **1** even now or at a particular time. **2** nevertheless. **3** even: *better still*. •v. make or become still.
– DERIVATIVES **stillness** n.
– ORIGIN Old English.

still[2] •n. a device for distilling alcoholic drinks such as whisky.
– ORIGIN from DISTIL.

stillbirth •n. the birth of an infant that has died in the womb.

stillborn •adj. (of an infant) born dead.

still life •n. a painting or drawing of an arrangement of objects such as flowers or fruit.

stilt •n. **1** either of a pair of upright poles with supports for the feet, enabling the user to walk above the ground. **2** each of a set of posts supporting a building.
– ORIGIN Germanic.

stilted •adj. (of speech or writing) stiff and unnatural.

Stilton •n. trademark a kind of strong, rich blue cheese.

– ORIGIN because it was formerly sold at *Stilton* in Cambridgeshire.

stimulant •n. **1** a substance that raises levels of activity in the body. **2** something that increases activity, interest, or enthusiasm.

stimulate •v. (**stimulates, stimulating, stimulated**) **1** raise levels of physiological or nervous activity in the body. **2** make more active, interested, or enthusiastic.
– DERIVATIVES **stimulation** n. **stimulator** n. **stimulatory** adj.
– ORIGIN Latin *stimulare* 'urge, goad'.

stimulus /stim-yuu-luhss/ •n. (pl. **stimuli** /stim-yuu-ly, stim-yuu-lee/) something that causes a reaction or that promotes activity, interest, etc.
– ORIGIN Latin, 'goad, spur, incentive'.

sting •n. **1** a sharp-pointed organ of an insect, capable of making a wound by injecting poison. **2** any of a number of tiny hairs on some plants, causing inflammation if touched. **3** a wound from a sting. **4** a sharp tingling feeling or hurtful effect. •v. (**stings, stinging, stung**) **1** wound with a sting. **2** produce a stinging feeling. **3** hurt or upset someone. **4** (**sting someone into**) provoke someone to do something.
– DERIVATIVES **stinger** n.
– ORIGIN Old English.

stinging nettle •n. a nettle covered in stinging hairs.

stingray •n. a ray (fish) with a long poisonous spine at the base of the tail.

stingy /stin-ji/ •adj. (**stingier, stingiest**) informal not generous; mean.
– DERIVATIVES **stingily** adv. **stinginess** n.
– ORIGIN perh. from STING.

stink •v. (**stinks, stinking, stank** or **stunk**; past part. **stunk**) **1** have a strong unpleasant smell. **2** informal be very bad or unpleasant. •n. **1** a strong, unpleasant smell. **2** informal a row or fuss.
– ORIGIN Old English.

stinker •n. informal a very unpleasant person or thing.

stinking •adj. **1** smelling very unpleasant. **2** informal very bad or unpleasant. •adv. informal very: *stinking rich*.

stinky •adj. (**stinkier, stinkiest**) informal having a strong unpleasant smell.

stint •v. (**stint on**) be very economical or mean about spending or providing something: *he doesn't stint on wining and dining*. •n. a period of work.
– ORIGIN Old English, 'make blunt'.

stipend /sty-pend/ •n. a fixed regular sum paid as a salary to a priest, teacher, or public official.

S

– ORIGIN Latin *stipendium*.

stipendiary /sty-pen-di-uh-ri/
• adj. receiving a stipend; working for
pay.

stipple • v. (**stipples, stippling, stippled**)
1 mark a surface with many small dots.
2 produce a decorative effect on paint or
other material by roughening the
surface when wet.
– ORIGIN Dutch *stippelen* 'to prick'.

stipulate /stip-yuu-layt/ • v. (**stipulates,
stipulating, stipulated**) demand or
specify a requirement as part of an
agreement.
– DERIVATIVES **stipulation** n.
– ORIGIN Latin *stipulari*.

stir[1] • v. (**stirs, stirring, stirred**) **1** move an
implement round and round in a liquid
or soft substance to mix it. **2** move
slightly or begin to be active. **3** wake or
get out of bed. **4** (also **stir something
up**) arouse a strong feeling in someone.
5 Brit. informal deliberately cause trouble
by spreading rumours. • n. **1** an act of
stirring. **2** a disturbance or commotion.
– DERIVATIVES **stirrer** n.
– ORIGIN Old English.

stir[2] • n. informal prison.
– ORIGIN perh. from Romany *sturbin* 'jail'.

stir-crazy • adj. informal mentally
disturbed as a result of being
imprisoned.

stir-fry • v. fry food quickly over a high
heat while stirring it briskly.

stirring • adj. causing great excitement
or strong emotion. • n. a first sign of
activity, movement, or emotion.

stirrup • n. each of a pair of loops
attached at either side of a horse's
saddle to support the rider's foot.
– ORIGIN Old English.

stirrup pump • n. a hand-operated
water pump with a footrest resembling
a stirrup.

stitch • n. **1** a loop of thread or yarn made
by a single pass of the needle in sewing,
knitting, or crochet. **2** a method of
sewing, knitting, or crochet that
produces a particular pattern. **3** informal
the smallest item of clothing: *swimming
with not a stitch on.* **4** a sudden sharp pain
in the side of the body, caused by hard
exercise. • v. make or mend with stitches.
– PHRASES **in stitches** informal laughing
uncontrollably. **stitch someone up** Brit.
informal make someone appear guilty of
something they did not do.
– DERIVATIVES **stitcher** n. **stitching** n.
– ORIGIN Old English.

stoat • n. a small brown mammal of the
weasel family.

stock • n. **1** a supply of goods or materials
available for sale or use. **2** farm animals

bred and kept for their meat or milk.
3 the capital raised by a company
through the selling of shares. **4** (**stocks**)
shares in a company. **5** (in the UK)
securities issued by the government in
fixed units with a fixed rate of interest.
6 water in which bones, meat, fish, or
vegetables have been slowly simmered.
7 a person's ancestry. **8** a breed, variety,
or population of an animal or plant.
9 the trunk or stem of a tree or shrub.
10 the part of a rifle or other gun which
is held against the shoulder when firing
it. **11** a plant with sweet-smelling white,
pink, or lilac flowers. **12** (**the stocks**) hist.
a wooden structure with holes for a
person's feet and hands, in which
criminals were locked as a public
punishment. • adj. **1** (of a product)
usually kept in stock; regularly
available. **2** constantly recurring or
conventional: *stock characters.* • v. **1** have
or keep a stock of. **2** provide or fill with a
stock of something. **3** (**stock up**) collect
stocks of something.
– PHRASES **take stock** assess a situation.
– ORIGIN Old English, 'trunk, post'.

stockade • n. a barrier or enclosure
formed from upright wooden posts.
– ORIGIN from former French *estocade*.

stockbreeder • n. a farmer who breeds
livestock.

stockbroker • n. a person who buys and
sells stocks and shares on behalf of
clients.
– DERIVATIVES **stockbroking** n.

stock car • n. an ordinary car that has
been strengthened for use in a type of
race in which cars collide with each
other.

stock cube • n. a cube of dried meat,
vegetable, or fish stock for use in
cooking.

stock exchange • n. a market in which
stocks and shares are bought and sold.

stocking • n. **1** either of a pair of
women's close-fitting nylon garments
covering the foot and leg. **2** US or old use
a long sock worn by men.
– DERIVATIVES **stockinged** adj.
– ORIGIN from *stock* in the dialect sense
'stocking'.

stocking stitch • n. a knitting stitch
consisting of alternate rows of plain and
purl stitch.

stock-in-trade • n. the typical subject
or commodity a person or company uses
or deals in.

stockist • n. Brit. a retailer that sells a
particular type of goods.

stockman • n. (pl. **stockmen**) a person
who looks after livestock.

stock market • n. a stock exchange.

stockpile • n. a large stock of goods or materials that has been gathered together. • v. (**stockpiles, stockpiling, stockpiled**) gather together a large stock of things.

stockpot • n. a pot in which stock is made by long, slow cooking.

stock-still • adv. completely still.

stocktaking • n. the action of recording the amount of stock held by a business.

stocky • adj. (**stockier, stockiest**) (of a person) short and sturdy.

stodge • n. Brit. informal food that is heavy and filling.
– ORIGIN prob. from STUFF and *podge* 'fat'.

stodgy • adj. (**stodgier, stodgiest**) Brit. **1** (of food) heavy and filling. **2** rather serious and dull: *stodgy English teachers*.
– DERIVATIVES **stodgily** adv. **stodginess** n.

stoep /stoop/ • n. S. Afr. a veranda in front of a house.
– ORIGIN Afrikaans.

stoic /stoh-ik/ • n. a person who can endure pain and hardship without showing their feelings. • adj. stoical.
– DERIVATIVES **stoicism** n.
– ORIGIN Greek *stōïkos*.

stoical • adj. enduring pain and hardship without showing your feelings.
– DERIVATIVES **stoically** adv.

stoke • v. (**stokes, stoking, stoked**) **1** add coal to a fire, furnace, etc. **2** encourage a strong emotion. **3** (**stoke up**) informal eat a large quantity of food for energy.

stoker • n. a person who tends the furnace on a steamship or steam train.
– ORIGIN Dutch.

stole¹ • n. a woman's long scarf or shawl, worn loosely over the shoulders.
– ORIGIN Greek, 'clothing'.

stole² past of STEAL.

stolen past part. of STEAL.

stolid • adj. calm, dependable, and showing little emotion.
– DERIVATIVES **stolidity** n. **stolidly** adv.
– ORIGIN Latin *stolidus*.

stoma /stoh-muh/ • n. (pl. **stomas** or **stomata** /stoh-muh-tuh/) tech. **1** a tiny pore in a leaf or stem of a plant, allowing movement of gases in and out. **2** a small mouth-like opening in some invertebrate animals.
– ORIGIN Greek, 'mouth'.

stomach • n. **1** the organ of the body in which the first part of digestion occurs. **2** the belly. **3** an appetite or desire for something: *they had no stomach for a fight*. • v. **1** consume food or drink without feeling sick. **2** accept an unpleasant person or thing.
– ORIGIN Greek *stomakhos* 'gullet'.

stomach pump • n. a syringe attached to a long tube, used for removing the contents of a person's stomach.

stomata pl. of STOMA.

stomp • v. tread heavily and noisily.
– ORIGIN from STAMP.

stone • n. **1** the hard non-metallic mineral material which rock is made of. **2** a small piece of stone on the ground. **3** a piece of stone shaped as a memorial or to mark out a boundary. **4** a gem. **5** a hard seed in certain fruits. **6** (pl. **stone**) Brit. a unit of weight equal to 14 lb (6.35 kg). • v. (**stones, stoning, stoned**) **1** throw stones at. **2** remove the stone from a fruit. • adv. completely: *stone cold*.
– PHRASES **leave no stone unturned** try everything possible in order to achieve something. **a stone's throw** a short distance.
– ORIGIN Old English.

Stone Age • n. a period that came before the Bronze Age, when weapons and tools were made of stone.

stonechat • n. a small bird with a call resembling two stones being knocked together.

stone circle • n. a prehistoric monument consisting of stones arranged in a circle.

stoned • adj. informal strongly affected by drugs or alcohol.

stoneground • adj. (of flour) ground with millstones.

stonemason • n. a person who prepares and builds with stone.

stonewall • v. delay or block a person or process by refusing to answer questions or by giving evasive replies.

stoneware • n. a type of hard and impermeable pottery.

stonewashed • adj. (of a garment or fabric) washed with small stones to produce a worn or faded appearance.

stonework • n. the parts of a building that are made of stone.

stony • adj. (**stonier, stoniest**) **1** full of stones. **2** made of or resembling stone. **3** cold and unfeeling.
– DERIVATIVES **stonily** adv.

stood past and past part. of STAND.

stooge • n. **1** derog. a less important person used by another to do routine or unpleasant work. **2** a performer whose act involves being the butt of a comedian's jokes.

stool • n. **1** a seat without a back or arms. **2** Med. a piece of faeces.
– PHRASES **fall between two stools** Brit. fail to be either of two satisfactory alternatives.
– ORIGIN Old English.

S

stool pigeon •n. informal a police informer.
– ORIGIN from the former use of a pigeon fixed to a stool as a decoy.

stoop •v. 1 bend the head or body forwards and downwards. 2 have the head and shoulders permanently bent forwards. 3 lower your standards to do something morally wrong: *he wouldn't stoop to thieving.* •n. a stooping posture.
– ORIGIN Old English.

stop •v. (**stops, stopping, stopped**) 1 come or bring to an end. 2 prevent from happening or from doing something. 3 no longer move or operate. 4 (of a bus or train) call at a place to pick up or set down passengers. 5 Brit. informal stay somewhere for a short time. 6 block or close up a hole or leak. 7 refuse to supply as usual; withhold. 8 instruct a bank to withhold payment on a cheque. •n. 1 an act of stopping. 2 a place where a bus or train regularly stops. 3 an object or part of a mechanism which prevents movement. 4 a set of organ pipes of a particular tone and range of pitch.
– PHRASES **pull out all the stops** make a very great effort to achieve something. [ORIGIN with reference to the stops of an organ.]
– ORIGIN Old English.

stopcock •n. an externally operated valve regulating the flow of a liquid or gas through a pipe.

stopgap •n. a temporary solution or substitute.

stoppage •n. 1 an instance of stopping. 2 an instance of industrial action. 3 a blockage. 4 (**stoppages**) Brit. deductions from wages by an employer for tax, National Insurance, etc.

stoppage time •n. = INJURY TIME.

stopper •n. a plug for sealing a hole. •v. (**stoppers, stoppering, stoppered**) seal with a stopper.

stop press •n. Brit. late news added to a newspaper either just before or during printing.

stopwatch •n. a special watch with buttons that start and stop the display, used to time races.

storage •n. 1 the action of storing. 2 space available for storing.

storage heater •n. Brit. an electric heater that stores up heat during the night and releases it during the day.

store •n. 1 an amount or supply kept for use as needed. 2 (**stores**) equipment and food kept for use by an army, navy, or other institution. 3 a place where things are kept for future use or sale. 4 Brit. a large shop selling different types of goods. 5 N. Amer. a shop. •v. (**stores,**

storing, stored) 1 keep for future use. 2 enter information in the memory of a computer.
– PHRASES **in store** about to happen. **set store by** consider to be of a particular level of importance.
– ORIGIN Old French *estore*.

storehouse •n. a building used for storing goods.

storey (N. Amer. also **story**) •n. (pl. **storeys** or **stories**) a floor or level of a building.
– ORIGIN Latin *historia* 'history'.

> USAGE: Do not confuse **storey** with **story**. Storey means 'a floor of a building' (*a three-storey house*), while **story** means 'an account told for entertainment' (*an adventure story*). In American English, the spelling **story** is used for both senses.

stork •n. a tall long-legged bird with a long heavy bill and white and black plumage.
– ORIGIN Old English.

storm •n. 1 a violent disturbance of the atmosphere with strong winds and rain, thunder, lightning, or snow. 2 an uproar or controversy: *the book caused a storm in America.* •v. 1 move angrily or forcefully. 2 (of troops) suddenly attack and capture a place. 3 shout angrily.
– PHRASES **a storm in a teacup** Brit. great anger or excitement about a trivial matter. **take something by storm** 1 capture a place by a sudden attack. 2 have great and rapid success in a place.
– ORIGIN Old English.

storm cloud •n. a heavy, dark rain cloud.

storm drain •n. a drain built to carry away excess water in times of heavy rain.

storm petrel •n. a small petrel (bird) with blackish plumage.

storm trooper •n. a member of a Nazi military force.

stormy •adj. (**stormier, stormiest**) 1 affected by a storm. 2 full of angry or violent outbursts of feeling.

story¹ •n. (pl. **stories**) 1 an account of imaginary or real people and events told for entertainment. 2 an item of news. 3 informal a lie.
– ORIGIN Old French *estorie*.

> USAGE: For an explanation of the difference between **story** and **storey**, see the note at STOREY.

story² •n. N. Amer. = STOREY.

storybook •n. a book containing a story or stories for children. •adj. perfect, as things typically are in children's stories: *a storybook romance.*

storyline • n. the plot of a novel, play, film, etc.

stoup /stoop/ • n. a basin for holy water in a church.
– ORIGIN Old Norse.

stout • adj. **1** rather fat or heavily built. **2** (of an object) sturdy and thick. **3** brave and determined: *he put up a stout defence.* • n. a kind of strong, dark beer brewed with roasted malt or barley.
– DERIVATIVES **stoutly** adv.
– ORIGIN Old French.

stove[1] • n. an apparatus for cooking or heating that operates by burning fuel or using electricity.
– ORIGIN Dutch or German.

stove[2] past and past part. of **STAVE**.

stow • v. **1** pack or store an object tidily. **2** (**stow away**) hide on a ship, aircraft, etc. so as to travel secretly or without paying.
– DERIVATIVES **stowage** n.
– ORIGIN from **BESTOW**.

stowaway • n. a person who stows away.

strabismus /struh-biz-muhss/ • n. the condition of having a squint.
– ORIGIN Greek *strabismos*.

straddle • v. (**straddles, straddling, straddled**) **1** sit or stand with one leg on either side of. **2** extend across both sides of.
– ORIGIN from dialect *striddling* 'astride'.

strafe /strahf, strayf/ • v. (**strafes, strafing, strafed**) attack with machine-gun fire or bombs from low-flying aircraft.
– ORIGIN from the German First World War catchphrase *Gott strafe England* 'may God punish England'.

straggle • v. (**straggles, straggling, straggled**) **1** trail slowly behind the person or people in front. **2** grow or spread out in an untidy way.
– DERIVATIVES **straggler** n. **straggly** adj.
– ORIGIN perh. from dialect *strake* 'go'.

straight • adj. **1** extending in one direction only; without a curve or bend. **2** properly positioned so as to be level, upright, or symmetrical. **3** in proper order or condition. **4** honest and direct. **5** (of thinking) clear and logical. **6** in continuous succession: *his fourth straight win.* **7** (of an alcoholic drink) undiluted. **8** (of drama) serious. **9** informal conventional or respectable. **10** informal heterosexual. • adv. **1** in a straight line or in a straight way. **2** without delay. • n. the straight part of something.
– PHRASES **straight away** immediately.
– DERIVATIVES **straightness** n.
– ORIGIN from **STRETCH**.

straight angle • n. Math. an angle of 180°.

straighten • v. **1** make or become straight. **2** stand or sit erect after bending.

straight-faced • adj. having a blank or serious facial expression.
– DERIVATIVES **straight face** n.

straightforward • adj. **1** easy to do or understand. **2** honest and open.
– DERIVATIVES **straightforwardly** adv.

straightjacket • n. var. of **STRAITJACKET**.

straight-laced • adj. var. of **STRAIT-LACED**.

straight man • n. a person in a show whose role is to provide a comedian with opportunities to make jokes.

strain[1] • v. **1** force yourself or a part of your body to make an unusually great effort. **2** injure a muscle, limb, or organ by making it work too hard. **3** make great or excessive demands on. **4** pull or push forcibly at something. **5** pour a mainly liquid substance through a sieve to separate out any solid matter. • n. **1** force tending to strain something to an extreme degree. **2** an injury caused by straining a muscle, limb, etc. **3** a severe demand on strength or resources. **4** a state of tension or exhaustion caused by severe demands on a person's strength or resources. **5** the sound of a piece of music as it is played.
– ORIGIN Old French *estreindre*.

strain[2] • n. **1** a distinct breed or variety of an animal, plant, or other organism. **2** a tendency in a person's character.
– ORIGIN Old English, 'acquisition, gain'.

strained • adj. **1** not relaxed or comfortable. **2** produced by deliberate effort; not graceful or spontaneous.

strainer • n. a device for straining liquids, having holes punched in it or made of wire mesh.

strait • n. **1** (also **straits**) a narrow passage of water connecting two seas or other large areas of water. **2** (**straits**) a situation of trouble or difficulty: *the economy is in dire straits.*
– ORIGIN Old French *estreit* 'narrow'.

straitened • adj. without enough money; poor: *straitened circumstances.*

straitjacket (also **straightjacket**) • n. **1** a strong garment with long sleeves which can be tied together to confine the arms of a violent prisoner or mental patient. **2** something which severely restricts freedom of action or development.

strait-laced (also **straight-laced**) • adj. having very strict moral attitudes.

strand[1] • v. **1** drive or leave aground on a shore. **2** leave without the means to move from a place: *the lorries are stranded*

S

in France. •**n.** literary a beach or shore.
– ORIGIN Old English.

strand² •**n. 1** a single thin length of thread, wire, etc. **2** a single hair or thin lock of hair. **3** an element that forms part of a complex whole.

strange •**adj. 1** unusual or surprising. **2** not previously visited, seen, or encountered: *she found herself in bed in a strange place.*
– DERIVATIVES **strangely** adv. **strangeness** n.
– ORIGIN Old French *estrange.*

stranger •**n. 1** a person you do not know. **2** a person who does not know, or is not known in, a particular place.

strangle •**v. (strangles, strangling, strangled) 1** kill or injure someone by squeezing their neck. **2** prevent from growing or developing.
– DERIVATIVES **strangler** n.
– ORIGIN Old French *estrangler.*

stranglehold •**n. 1** a grip around a person's neck that deprives them of oxygen and so can kill them. **2** complete or overwhelming control.

strangulation •**n.** the action of strangling someone, or the state of being strangled.

strap •**n. 1** a strip of flexible material used for fastening, securing, carrying, or holding on to. **2 (the strap)** punishment by beating with a leather strap.
•**v. (straps, strapping, strapped) 1** fasten or secure with a strap. **2** Brit. wrap adhesive plaster round an injured part of the body.
– DERIVATIVES **strapless** adj. **strappy** adj.
– ORIGIN dialect form of STROP¹.

strapping •**adj.** (of a person) big and strong.

strata pl. of STRATUM.

stratagem /stra-tuh-juhm/ •**n.** a plan or scheme intended to outwit an opponent.
– ORIGIN Greek *stratēgēma.*

strategic /struh-tee-jik/ •**adj. 1** forming part of a long-term plan to achieve a particular purpose. **2** relating to the gaining of long-term military advantage. **3** (of weapons) intended to be fired at industrial areas and communication centres in enemy territory rather than used in a battle. Often contrasted with TACTICAL.
– DERIVATIVES **strategically** adv.

strategy /stra-ti-ji/ •**n. (pl. strategies) 1** a plan designed to achieve a particular long-term aim. **2** the art of planning and directing military activity in a war or battle. Often contrasted with **tactics** (see TACTIC).
– DERIVATIVES **strategist** n.
– ORIGIN Greek *stratēgia* 'generalship'.

stratify /stra-ti-fy/ •**v. (stratifies, stratifying, stratified)** (usu. as adj. **stratified) 1** form or arrange into strata. **2** arrange or classify.
– DERIVATIVES **stratification** n.

stratosphere /stra-tuh-sfeer/ •**n. 1** the layer of the earth's atmosphere above the troposphere and below the mesosphere. **2** informal the very highest levels of something.
– DERIVATIVES **stratospheric** /stra-tuhss-fe-rik/ adj.

stratum /strah-tuhm/ •**n. (pl. strata** /strah-tuh/) **1** a layer or a series of layers of rock. **2** a thin layer within any structure. **3** a level or class of society.
– ORIGIN Latin, 'something laid down'.

stratus /strah-tuhss, stray-tuhss/ •**n.** cloud forming a continuous horizontal grey sheet.
– ORIGIN Latin, 'strewn'.

straw •**n. 1** dried stalks of grain, used as fodder or bedding for animals and for thatching, packing, etc. **2** a single dried stalk of grain. **3** a thin hollow tube of paper or plastic for sucking drink from a container. **4** a pale yellow colour.
– PHRASES **clutch at straws** turn in desperation to something which is unlikely to be helpful. **draw the short straw** be chosen to do something unpleasant. **the last** (or **final) straw** a further difficulty that comes after a series of difficulties and makes a situation unbearable.
– ORIGIN Old English.

strawberry •**n. (pl. strawberries)** a sweet red fruit with many seeds on the surface.

strawberry blonde •**adj.** (of hair) light reddish-blonde in colour.

straw poll •**n.** an unofficial test of opinion.

stray •**v. 1** move away aimlessly from a group or from the right course or place. **2** (of the eyes or a hand) move idly in a particular direction. •**adj. 1** not in the right place; separated from a group. **2** (of a domestic animal) having no home or having wandered away from home. •**n.** a stray person or thing.
– ORIGIN Old French *estrayer.*

streak •**n. 1** a long, thin mark. **2** an element of a particular kind in someone's character: *a ruthless streak.* **3** a series of successes or failures: *a winning streak.* •**v. 1** mark with streaks. **2** move very fast. **3** informal run naked in a public place to shock or amuse people.
– DERIVATIVES **streaker** n.
– ORIGIN Old English.

streaky •**adj. (streakier, streakiest) 1** having streaks. **2** Brit. (of bacon) from

the belly of a pig, so having alternate strips of fat and lean meat.
– DERIVATIVES **streakiness** n.

stream • n. **1** a small, narrow river. **2** a continuous flow of liquid, air, gas, people, etc. **3** Brit. a group in which schoolchildren of the same age and ability are taught. • v. **1** run or move in a continuous flow. **2** (usu. **be streaming**) run with tears, sweat, or other liquid. **3** float out in the wind. **4** Brit. put schoolchildren in streams.
– PHRASES **on stream** in or into operation or existence.
– ORIGIN Old English.

streamer • n. a long, narrow strip of material used as a decoration or flag.

streaming • adj. (of a cold) accompanied by running of the nose and eyes.

streamline • v. (**streamlines, streamlining, streamlined**) **1** (**be streamlined**) have a shape that presents very little resistance to a flow of air or water, increasing speed and ease of movement. **2** make an organization or system more efficient by using faster or simpler working methods.

street • n. a public road in a city, town, or village. • adj. **1** relating to fashionable young people living in cities and towns: *street style*. **2** homeless: *street children*.
– PHRASES **on the streets 1** homeless. **2** working as a prostitute.
– ORIGIN from Latin *strāta via* 'paved way'.

streetcar • n. N. Amer. a tram.

street value • n. the price for which something that is illegal or has been illegally obtained, especially drugs, can be sold.

streetwalker • n. a prostitute who seeks clients in the street.

streetwise • adj. informal having the skills and knowledge necessary for dealing with the difficulties and dangers of life in a large city.

strength /strength, strengkth/ • n. **1** the quality of being strong. **2** a good or useful quality. **3** the number of people making up a group. **4** the number of people that makes a group complete: *100 staff below strength*.
– PHRASES **go from strength to strength** progress with increasing success. **on the strength of** on the basis of.
– ORIGIN Old English.

✓ Remember that **strength** is spelled with a **g** before the **-th**.

strengthen • v. make or become stronger.

strenuous /stren-yuu-uhss/ • adj. requiring or using great exertion.

– DERIVATIVES **strenuously** adv.
– ORIGIN Latin *strenuus* 'brisk'.

streptococcus /strep-tuh-**kok**-kuhss/ • n. (pl. **streptococci** /strep-tuh-**kok**-ky/) a bacterium of a large genus including some which can cause various serious infections.
– DERIVATIVES **streptococcal** adj.
– ORIGIN Greek *streptos* 'twisted'.

streptomycin /strep-toh-**my**-sin/ • n. an antibiotic used against tuberculosis.
– ORIGIN from Greek *streptos* 'twisted' + *mukēs* 'fungus'.

stress • n. **1** pressure or tension exerted on an object. **2** a state of mental or emotional strain. **3** particular emphasis. **4** emphasis given to a syllable or word in speech. • v. **1** emphasize a point, statement, etc. when speaking or writing. **2** give emphasis to a syllable or word when pronouncing it. **3** subject to pressure, tension, or strain.
– ORIGIN from DISTRESS, or partly from Old French *estresse* 'narrowness'.

stressful • adj. causing mental or emotional stress.

stretch • v. **1** (of something soft or elastic) be able to be made longer or wider without tearing or breaking. **2** pull something tightly from one point to another. **3** extend your body or a part of your body to its full length. **4** extend over an area or period of time. **5** (of finances or resources) be enough for a particular purpose. **6** make demands on. • n. **1** an act of stretching. **2** the fact of being stretched. **3** the capacity to stretch or be stretched; elasticity. **4** a continuous expanse or period: *a treacherous stretch of road*.
– PHRASES **at full stretch** using the maximum amount of your resources or energy. **stretch your legs** go for a short walk.
– DERIVATIVES **stretchy** adj. (**stretchier, stretchiest**).
– ORIGIN Old English.

stretcher • n. a framework of two poles with a long piece of canvas slung between them, used for carrying sick, injured, or dead people. • v. (**stretchers, stretchering, stretchered**) carry on a stretcher.

strew • v. (**strews, strewing, strewed**; past part. **strewn** or **strewed**) **1** scatter untidily over a surface or area. **2** (**be strewn with**) be covered with untidily scattered things.
– ORIGIN Old English.

stria /stry-uh/ • n. (pl. **striae** /stry-ee/) tech. a line, ridge, or groove.
– ORIGIN Latin, 'furrow'.

striated /stry-ayt-id/ • adj. **1** marked with a series of ridges or grooves.

2 striped or streaked.
– DERIVATIVES **striation** n.

stricken North American or old-fashioned past part. of **STRIKE**.
•adj. **1** seriously affected by something unpleasant. **2** (of a face or look) showing great distress.

strict •adj. **1** demanding that rules about behaviour are obeyed. **2** (of a rule) requiring complete obedience. **3** following rules or beliefs exactly: *a strict vegetarian.* **4** exact and clearly defined.
– DERIVATIVES **strictly** adv. **strictness** n.
– ORIGIN Latin *strictus* 'tightened'.

stricture /strik-cher/ •n. **1** a rule restricting behaviour or action. **2** a sternly critical remark.

stride •v. (**strides, striding, strode**) walk with long, decisive steps. •n. **1** a long, decisive step. **2** the length of a step in running or walking. **3** a step made towards an aim. **4** (**your stride**) a good or regular rate of progress.
– PHRASES **take something in your stride** deal calmly with something difficult.
– ORIGIN Old English.

strident •adj. **1** loud and harsh. **2** presenting a point of view in a way that is too forceful.
– DERIVATIVES **stridency** n. **stridently** adv.
– ORIGIN Latin *stridere* 'creak'.

strife •n. angry or bitter disagreement.
– ORIGIN Old French *estrif*.

strike •v. (**strikes, striking, struck**) **1** deliver a blow to. **2** come into forcible contact with. **3** (in sport) hit or kick a ball. **4** light a match by rubbing it against a rough surface. **5** (of a disaster, disease, etc.) occur suddenly and have harmful effects on: *an earthquake struck the island.* **6** attack suddenly. **7** (**strike something into**) cause a strong emotion in: *his name struck terror into their hearts.* **8** cause to become suddenly: *he was struck dumb.* **9** suddenly come into the mind of: *a thought struck her.* **10** (of employees) refuse to work as a form of organized protest. **11** discover unexpectedly. **12** (**strike someone off**) officially remove someone from membership of a professional group. **13** (**strike out**) start out on a new or independent course. **14** reach an agreement or compromise. **15** (of a clock) show the time by sounding a chime or stroke. •n. **1** an act of striking by employees. **2** a refusal to do something as an organized protest: *a rent strike.* **3** a sudden attack. **4** (in sport) an act of striking a ball.
– PHRASES **strike up** begin to play a piece of music. **strike something up** begin a friendship or conversation with someone.
– ORIGIN Old English, 'go, flow'.

striker •n. **1** an employee who is on strike. **2** (chiefly in football) a forward or attacker.

striking •adj. **1** very noticeable. **2** very good-looking or beautiful.
– DERIVATIVES **strikingly** adv.

string •n. **1** material consisting of threads twisted together to form a thin length. **2** a piece of such material. **3** a length of catgut or wire on a musical instrument, producing a note by vibration. **4** (**strings**) the stringed instruments in an orchestra. **5** a piece of catgut, nylon, etc., interwoven with others to form the head of a sports racket. **6** a set of things tied or threaded together on a thin cord. **7** a sequence of similar items or events: *a string of blockbusters.* •v. (**strings, stringing, strung**) **1** thread things on a string. **2** (**be strung** or **be strung out**) be arranged in a long line. **3** fit a string or strings to a musical instrument, a racket, or a bow.
– PHRASES **no strings attached** informal there are no special conditions or restrictions. **string someone up** kill someone by hanging them.
– DERIVATIVES **stringed** adj.
– ORIGIN Old English.

string bean •n. any of various beans eaten in their pods.

stringent /strin-juhnt/ •adj. (of regulations or requirements) strict and precise; requiring complete obedience.
– DERIVATIVES **stringency** n.
– ORIGIN Latin *stringere* 'draw tight'.

string quartet •n. a chamber music group made up of first and second violins, viola, and cello.

stringy •adj. (**stringier, stringiest**) **1** resembling string. **2** (of food) tough and fibrous.

strip¹ •v. (**strips, stripping, stripped**) **1** remove all coverings or clothes from. **2** take off your clothes. **3** leave a room, vehicle, etc. bare of accessories or fittings. **4** remove paint or varnish from a surface. **5** (**strip someone of**) deprive someone of rank, power, or property. •n. **1** an act of undressing. **2** Brit. the identifying outfit worn by the members of a sports team while playing.
– ORIGIN Germanic.

strip² •n. **1** a long, narrow piece of cloth, paper, etc. **2** a long, narrow area of land.
– ORIGIN German *strippe* 'strap, thong'.

stripe •n. **1** a long narrow band or strip of a different colour or texture from its surroundings. **2** a V-shaped stripe sewn

on to a uniform to show military rank.
• v. (**stripes**, **striping**, **striped**) mark with stripes.
– DERIVATIVES **striped** adj. **stripy** (also **stripey**) adj.
– ORIGIN perh. from Dutch or German.

strip light • n. Brit. a fluorescent lamp in the shape of a tube.

stripling • n. old use a young man.
– ORIGIN prob. from STRIP² (from the idea of 'narrowness', i.e. slimness).

stripper • n. **1** a device or substance for stripping paint or varnish off a surface. **2** a striptease performer.

strip-search • v. search someone for concealed drugs, weapons, or other items, by stripping off their clothes.

striptease • n. a form of entertainment in which a performer gradually undresses to music in a sexually exciting way.

strive • v. (**strives**, **striving**, **strove** or **strived**; past part. **striven** or **strived**) **1** make great efforts. **2** (**strive against**) fight vigorously against.
– ORIGIN Old French *estriver*.

strobe • n. a stroboscope. • v. (**strobes**, **strobing**, **strobed**) flash at rapid intervals.

stroboscope /stroh-buh-skohp/ • n. an instrument which shines a bright light at rapid intervals so that a moving person or object appears stationary.
– DERIVATIVES **stroboscopic** adj.
– ORIGIN Greek *strobos* 'whirling'.

strode past of STRIDE.

stroke • n. **1** an act of hitting. **2** Golf an act of hitting the ball with a club, as a unit of scoring. **3** a sound made by a striking clock. **4** an act of stroking with the hand. **5** a mark made by drawing a pen, pencil, or paintbrush once across paper or canvas. **6** a line forming part of a written or printed character. **7** a short diagonal line separating characters or figures. **8** one of a series of repeated movements. **9** a style of swimming. **10** the action of moving the oar in rowing. **11** a sudden disabling attack or loss of consciousness caused by an interruption in the flow of blood to the brain. • v. (**strokes**, **stroking**, **stroked**) gently move your hand over.
– PHRASES **at a stroke** by a single action which has immediate effect. **stroke of luck** a fortunate and unexpected occurrence.
– ORIGIN Old English.

stroll • v. walk in a leisurely way. • n. a short, leisurely walk.
– ORIGIN prob. from German *strollen*.

strong • adj. (**stronger**, **strongest**) **1** physically powerful. **2** done with or exerting great force. **3** able to withstand great force or pressure. **4** secure, stable, or firmly established. **5** great in power, influence, or ability: *a strong leader*. **6** (of something seen, heard, or smelt) very intense: *a strong smell*. **7** (of language) forceful and using swear words. **8** full-flavoured. **9** (of a solution or drink) containing a large proportion of a substance. **10** used after a number to indicate the size of a group: *a crowd several thousands strong*. **11** (of verbs) forming the past tense and past participle by a change of vowel within the stem rather than by addition of a suffix (e.g. *swim*, *swam*, *swum*).
– PHRASES **going strong** informal continuing to be healthy, vigorous, or successful. **your strong point** something you are very good at.
– DERIVATIVES **strongly** adv.
– ORIGIN Old English.

strong-arm • adj. using force or violence.

strongbox • n. a small lockable metal box in which valuables may be kept.

stronghold • n. **1** a place of strong support for a cause or political party. **2** a place that has been strengthened against attack.

strongroom • n. a room, typically one in a bank, designed to protect valuable items against fire and theft.

strontium /stron-ti-uhm/ • n. a soft silver-white metallic chemical element.
– ORIGIN from *Strontian* in Scotland.

strop¹ • n. a strip of leather used for sharpening razors.
– ORIGIN prob. from Latin *stroppus* 'thong'.

strop² • n. Brit. informal a temper.

stroppy • adj. (**stroppier**, **stroppiest**) Brit. informal bad-tempered.
– ORIGIN perh. from OBSTREPEROUS.

strove past of STRIVE.

struck past and past part. of STRIKE.

structural • adj. relating to or forming part of a structure.
– DERIVATIVES **structurally** adv.

structuralism • n. a theory that pieces of writing, languages, and social systems should be seen as a structure whose various parts have meaning only when considered in relation to each other.
– DERIVATIVES **structuralist** n. & adj.

structure • n. **1** the arrangement of and relations between the parts of something complex. **2** a building or other object constructed from several parts. **3** the quality of being well organized. • v. (**structures**, **structuring**, **structured**) arrange according to a system or plan.

– ORIGIN Latin *structura*.

strudel /stroo-duhl/ • n. a dessert of thin pastry rolled up round a fruit filling and baked.
– ORIGIN German, 'whirlpool'.

struggle • v. (**struggles, struggling, struggled**) **1** make great efforts to get free. **2** try hard under difficult circumstances to do something. **3** make your way with difficulty. • n. **1** an act of struggling. **2** a very difficult task.

strum • v. (**strums, strumming, strummed**) play a guitar or similar instrument by sweeping the thumb or a plectrum up or down the strings.

strumpet • n. old use a woman who has many sexual partners.

strung past and past part. of **STRING**.

strut • n. **1** a bar used to support or strengthen a structure. **2** a proud, confident walk. • v. (**struts, strutting, strutted**) walk in a proud, confident way, with your back straight and head up.
– ORIGIN Old English, 'stick out stiffly'.

strychnine /strik-neen/ • n. a bitter and highly poisonous substance obtained from the fruit of an Asian tree.
– ORIGIN Greek *strukhnos*, referring to a kind of nightshade.

Stuart (also **Stewart**) • adj. relating to the royal family ruling Scotland 1371–1714 and Britain 1603–1714 (interrupted by the Commonwealth 1649–60).

stub • n. **1** the remaining part of a pencil, cigarette, or similar-shaped object after use. **2** a shortened or unusually short thing. **3** the counterfoil of a cheque, ticket, or other document. • v. (**stubs, stubbing, stubbed**) **1** accidentally strike your toe against something. **2** (often **stub something out**) put a cigarette out by pressing the lighted end against something.
– ORIGIN Old English, 'stump of a tree'.

stubble • n. **1** the cut stalks of cereal plants left in the ground after harvesting. **2** short, stiff hairs growing on a man's face when he has not shaved for a while.
– DERIVATIVES **stubbly** adj.
– ORIGIN Old French *stuble*.

stubborn • adj. **1** determined not to change your attitude or position. **2** difficult to move, remove, or cure: *a stubborn stain*.
– DERIVATIVES **stubbornly** adv. **stubbornness** n.

stubby • adj. (**stubbier, stubbiest**) short and thick.

stucco • n. fine plaster used for coating wall surfaces or moulding into architectural decorations.
– DERIVATIVES **stuccoed** adj.
– ORIGIN Italian.

stuck past and past part. of **STICK**[2].

stuck-up • adj. informal unfriendly towards other people because you believe that you are superior to them.

stud[1] • n. **1** a piece of metal with a large head, that pierces and projects from a surface. **2** Brit. a small projection fixed to the base of a shoe or boot to provide better grip. **3** a small piece of jewellery which is pushed through a pierced ear or nostril. **4** a device for fastening a collar to a shirt, consisting of two buttons joined with a bar. • v. (**studs, studding, studded**) **1** decorate with studs or similar small objects. **2** strew or scatter: *the sky was studded with stars*.
– ORIGIN Old English, 'post'.

stud[2] • n. **1** an establishment where horses are kept for breeding. **2** (also **stud horse**) a stallion. **3** informal a man who has many sexual partners or is considered sexually desirable.
– ORIGIN Old English.

student • n. **1** a person studying at a university or college. **2** a school pupil. **3** a person who takes a particular interest in a subject. • adj. referring to someone who is studying to enter a profession: *a student nurse*.
– ORIGIN Latin *studere* 'apply yourself to'.

studio • n. (pl. **studios**) **1** a room where an artist works or where dancers practise. **2** a room from which television or radio programmes are broadcast, or in which they are recorded. **3** a place where film or sound recordings are made.
– ORIGIN Italian.

studio flat • n. Brit. a flat containing one main room.

studious • adj. **1** spending a lot of time studying or reading. **2** done deliberately or with great care.
– DERIVATIVES **studiously** adv.

study • n. (pl. **studies**) **1** the reading of books or examination of other materials to gain knowledge. **2** a detailed investigation into a subject or situation. **3** a room for reading, writing, or academic work. **4** a piece of work done for practice or as an experiment.
• v. (**studies, studying, studied**) **1** make a study of; learn about. **2** apply yourself to study. **3** look at closely in order to observe or read. **4** (as adj. **studied**) done with deliberate and careful effort: *studied politeness*.
– ORIGIN Latin *studium* 'zeal'.

stuff • n. **1** matter, material, articles, or activities of a particular or unspecified kind. **2** basic characteristics: *Helen was*

made of sterner stuff. **3** (**your stuff**) informal the things you are knowledgeable about or experienced in: *he knows his stuff*. • v. **1** fill tightly with something. **2** force tightly or hastily into a container or space. **3** fill out the skin of a dead animal or bird with material to restore its original shape and appearance. **4** fill the inside of an item of food with another type of food.
– ORIGIN Old French *estoffe* 'material'.

stuffed shirt • n. informal an old-fashioned, pompous person.

stuffing • n. **1** a mixture used to stuff poultry or meat before cooking. **2** padding used to stuff cushions, furniture, or soft toys.

stuffy • adj. (**stuffier, stuffiest**) **1** lacking fresh air or ventilation. **2** conventional and narrow-minded. **3** (of a person's nose) blocked up.
– DERIVATIVES **stuffiness** n.

stultify /stul-ti-fy/ • v. (**stultifies, stultifying, stultified**) (usu. as adj. **stultifying**) make someone feel bored or drained of energy.
– DERIVATIVES **stultification** n. **stultifyingly** adv.
– ORIGIN Latin *stultificare*.

stumble • v. (**stumbles, stumbling, stumbled**) **1** trip and lose your balance. **2** walk unsteadily. **3** make a mistake in speaking. **4** (**stumble across/on/upon**) find by chance. • n. an act of stumbling.
– ORIGIN Old Norse.

stumbling block • n. an obstacle.

stump • n. **1** the part of a tree trunk that sticks up from the ground after the rest has fallen or been cut down. **2** a remaining piece of something. **3** Cricket each of the three upright pieces of wood which form a wicket. • v. **1** informal baffle someone. **2** Cricket dismiss a batsman by dislodging the bails with the ball while the batsman is out of the crease but not running. **3** (**stump something up**) Brit. informal pay a sum or money.
– ORIGIN German *stumpe* or Dutch *stomp*.

stumpy • adj. short and thick; squat.

stun • v. (**stuns, stunning, stunned**) **1** knock unconscious or into a semi-conscious state. **2** astonish and shock someone so that they are temporarily unable to react.
– ORIGIN Old French *estoner* 'astonish'.

stung past and past part. of STING.

stunk past and past part. of STINK.

stunner • n. informal a strikingly beautiful or impressive person or thing.

stunning • adj. very impressive or attractive.
– DERIVATIVES **stunningly** adv.

stunt[1] • v. slow down the growth or development of.
– ORIGIN Germanic.

stunt[2] • n. **1** an action displaying spectacular skill and daring. **2** something unusual done to attract attention: *a publicity stunt*.

stuntman (or **stuntwoman**) • n. (pl. **stuntmen** or **stuntwomen**) a person taking an actor's place in performing dangerous stunts.

stupefy /styoo-pi-fy/ • v. (**stupefies, stupefying, stupefied**) **1** make someone unable to think properly. **2** astonish and shock.
– DERIVATIVES **stupefaction** n.
– ORIGIN Latin *stupefacere*.

stupendous /styoo-pen-duhss/ • adj. very impressive.
– ORIGIN Latin *stupendus* 'to be wondered at'.

stupid • adj. (**stupider, stupidest**) **1** lacking intelligence or common sense. **2** informal used to express exasperation or annoyance: *your stupid paintings*! **3** dazed and unable to think clearly.
– DERIVATIVES **stupidity** n. **stupidly** adv.
– ORIGIN Latin *stupidus*.

stupor /styoo-per/ • n. a state of being dazed or nearly unconscious.
– ORIGIN Latin.

sturdy • adj. (**sturdier, sturdiest**) **1** strongly and solidly built or made. **2** confident and determined.
– DERIVATIVES **sturdily** adv. **sturdiness** n.
– ORIGIN Old French *esturdi* 'dazed'.

sturgeon /ster-juhn/ • n. a very large fish with bony plates on the body, from whose roe caviar is made.
– ORIGIN Old French.

stutter • v. (**stutters, stuttering, stuttered**) **1** have difficulty speaking as a result of the involuntary repetition of the first sounds of a word. **2** (of a machine or gun) produce a series of short, sharp sounds. • n. a tendency to stutter while speaking.
– DERIVATIVES **stutterer** n.
– ORIGIN Germanic.

sty[1] • n. (pl. **sties**) a pigsty.
– ORIGIN Old English.

sty[2] (also **stye**) • n. (pl. **sties** or **styes**) an inflamed swelling on the edge of an eyelid.
– ORIGIN from a Old English word meaning 'riser' + EYE.

Stygian /sti-ji-uhn/ • adj. literary very dark.
– ORIGIN from the *Styx*, an underworld river in Greek mythology.

style • n. **1** a way of doing something. **2** a distinctive appearance, design, or arrangement. **3** a way of painting, writing, etc., characteristic of a

particular period, person, etc. **4** elegance and sophistication. **5** a narrow extension of a plant's ovary, bearing the stigma.
• v. (**styles, styling, styled**) **1** design, make, or arrange in a particular form. **2** give a particular name, description, or title to.
– ORIGIN Latin *stilus* 'stylus, style'.

styli pl. of STYLUS.

stylish • adj. **1** having or displaying a good sense of style. **2** fashionably elegant.
– DERIVATIVES **stylishly** adv. **stylishness** n.

stylist • n. a person who designs fashionable clothes or cuts hair.

stylistic • adj. relating to style.
– DERIVATIVES **stylistically** adv.

stylized (or **stylised**) • adj. represented in a non-realistic style.

stylus /sty-luhss/ • n. (pl. **styli** /sty-ly/) **1** a hard point following a groove in a gramophone record and transmitting the recorded sound for reproduction. **2** a pointed implement used for scratching or tracing letters or engraving. **3** a pen-like device used to input handwriting directly into a computer.
– ORIGIN Latin *stilus*.

stymie /sty-mi/ • v. (**stymies, stymying** or **stymieing, stymied**) informal prevent or slow down the progress of.
– ORIGIN a golfing term.

styptic /stip-tik/ • adj. able to make bleeding stop.
– ORIGIN Greek *stuptikos*.

styrene /sty-reen/ • n. Chem. an unsaturated liquid hydrocarbon obtained from petroleum and used to make plastics.
– ORIGIN from *styrax*, a resin obtained from a tree.

styrofoam • n. (trademark in the US) a kind of polystyrene, used for making food containers.
– ORIGIN from POLYSTYRENE + FOAM.

suave /swahv/ • adj. (**suaver, suavest**) (of a man) charming, confident, and elegant.
– DERIVATIVES **suavely** adv. **suavity** n.
– ORIGIN Latin *suavis* 'agreeable'.

sub informal • n. **1** a submarine. **2** a substitute. **3** Brit. a subscription.
• v. (**subs, subbing, subbed**) act as a substitute.

sub- • prefix **1** under: *submarine*. **2** lower in rank or importance: *subaltern*. **3** below; less than: *sub-zero*. **4** secondary or subsequent: *subdivision*.
– ORIGIN Latin *sub* 'under, close to'.

subaltern /sub-uhl-tern/ • n. an officer in the British army below the rank of captain.

– ORIGIN from Latin *sub-* 'next below' + *alternus* 'every other'.

sub-aqua • adj. relating to swimming or exploring under water, especially with an aqualung.

subatomic • adj. smaller than or occurring within an atom.

subcategory • n. (pl. **subcategories**) a secondary or less important category.

subcommittee • n. a committee consisting of some members of a larger committee, formed in order to study a subject in more detail.

subconscious • adj. relating to the part of the mind of which you are not fully aware but which influences your actions and feelings. • n. (**your/the subconscious**) this part of the mind.
– DERIVATIVES **subconsciously** adv.

subcontinent • n. a large part of a continent considered as a particular area, such as North America.

subcontract /sub-kuhn-trakt/
• v. employ a firm or person outside your company to do work as part of a larger project.

subcontractor • n. a firm or person that carries out work for a company as part of a larger project.

subculture • n. a distinct group within a society or class, having beliefs or interests that are different from those of the larger group.

subcutaneous • adj. situated or applied under the skin.

subdivide • v. (**subdivides, subdividing, subdivided**) divide something into smaller parts.
– DERIVATIVES **subdivision** n.

subdue • v. (**subdues, subduing, subdued**) **1** overcome, quieten, or bring under control. **2** bring a country under control by force.
– ORIGIN Latin *subducere* 'draw from below'.

subdued • adj. **1** quiet and rather thoughtful or depressed. **2** (of colour or lighting) soft; muted.

subedit • v. (**subedits, subediting, subedited**) Brit. check and correct the written part of a newspaper, magazine, etc. before printing.
– DERIVATIVES **subeditor** n.

subgroup • n. a small group that is part of a larger group.

subheading • n. a heading given to a section within a larger piece of writing.

subhuman • adj. not behaving like a human being or not fit for human beings.

subject • n. /sub-jikt, sub-jekt/ **1** a person or thing that is being discussed,

studied, or dealt with. **2** a branch of knowledge studied or taught. **3** Grammar the word or words in a sentence that name who or what performs the action of the verb. **4** a member of a country or state that is ruled by a king or queen.
• adj. /sub-jikt, sub-jekt/ (**subject to**) **1** likely or able to be affected by something bad. **2** dependent on something in order to happen. **3** under the control or authority of. • adv. /sub-jikt, sub-jekt/ (**subject to**) if certain conditions are fulfilled. • v. /suhb-jekt/ (**subject someone/thing to**) **1** make someone or something undergo an unpleasant experience. **2** bring a person or country under your control or authority.
– DERIVATIVES **subjection** n.
– ORIGIN Latin *subicere* 'bring under'.

subjective • adj. **1** based on or influenced by personal opinions. **2** Grammar relating to a case of nouns and pronouns used for the subject of a sentence.
– DERIVATIVES **subjectively** adv. **subjectivity** n.

subject matter • n. the ideas, information, or theme of a book, work of art, speech, etc.

sub judice /sub joo-di-si/ • adj. being considered by a court of law and therefore forbidden to be publicly discussed elsewhere.
– ORIGIN Latin, 'under a judge'.

subjugate /sub-juu-gayt/
• v. (**subjugates, subjugating, subjugated**) conquer and bring under control.
– DERIVATIVES **subjugation** n.
– ORIGIN Latin *subjugare* 'bring under a yoke'.

subjunctive /suhb-jungk-tiv/
• adj. Grammar (of a form of a verb) expressing what is imagined or wished or possible.
– ORIGIN Latin *subjunctivus*.

> **USAGE:** The **subjunctive** form of a verb is used to express what is imagined, wished, or possible. It is usually the same as the ordinary (**indicative**) form of the verb except in the third person singular (*he, she,* or *it*), where the normal **-s** ending is omitted. For example, you should say *face* rather than *faces* in the sentence *the report recommends that he face the tribunal*. The subjunctive is also different from the indicative when using the verb 'to be'; for example, you should say *I were* rather than *I was* in the sentence *I wouldn't try it if I were you*.

sublet /sub-let/ • v. (**sublets, subletting, sublet**) let a property or a part of a property that you are already renting yourself to someone else.

sublimate /sub-li-mayt/
• v. (**sublimates, sublimating, sublimated**) **1** transform into a purer or idealized form. **2** Chem. = SUBLIME.
– DERIVATIVES **sublimation** n.
– ORIGIN Latin *sublimare* 'raise up'.

sublime • adj. (**sublimer, sublimest**) **1** of very high quality and causing great admiration. **2** extreme: *the sublime confidence of youth.* • v. Chem. (**sublimes, subliming, sublimed**) (of a solid substance) change directly into vapour when heated, forming a solid deposit again on cooling.
– DERIVATIVES **sublimely** adv.
– ORIGIN Latin *sublimis*.

subliminal /suhb-lim-i-n'l/ • adj. (of a stimulus or mental process) affecting someone's mind without their being aware of it.
– DERIVATIVES **subliminally** adv.
– ORIGIN from SUB- + Latin *limen* 'threshold'.

sub-machine gun • n. a hand-held lightweight machine gun.

submarine • n. a streamlined warship designed to operate under the sea for long periods. • adj. existing or done under the surface of the sea.
– DERIVATIVES **submariner** /suhb-ma-ri-ner/ n.

submerge • v. (**submerges, submerging, submerged**) **1** push or hold under water. **2** go below the surface of water. **3** completely cover or hide.
– ORIGIN Latin *submergere*.

submerse • v. (**submerses, submersing, submersed**) tech. submerge.
– DERIVATIVES **submersion** n.

submersible • adj. designed to operate under water. • n. a small boat or craft that is submersible.

submicroscopic • adj. too small to be seen by an ordinary microscope.

submission • n. **1** the action of submitting something. **2** a proposal or application submitted for consideration.

submissive • adj. very obedient or passive.

submit • v. (**submits, submitting, submitted**) **1** accept or give in to the authority, control, or greater strength of. **2** present a proposal or application for consideration or judgement.
– ORIGIN Latin *submittere*.

subnormal • adj. not meeting standards or reaching a level regarded as normal.

subordinate • adj. /suh-bor-di-nuht/ **1** lower in rank or position. **2** less

S

important. •n. /suh-**bor**-di-nuht/ a person under the authority of another. •v. /suh-**bor**-di-nayt/ (**subordinates, subordinating, subordinated**) treat as less important.
– DERIVATIVES **subordination** n.
– ORIGIN Latin *subordinatus* 'placed in an inferior rank'.

subordinate clause •n. a clause that forms part of and is dependent on a main clause (e.g. *when it rang* in *she answered the phone when it rang*).

suborn /suh-**born**/ •v. pay or persuade someone to commit an unlawful act such as perjury.
– ORIGIN Latin *subornare* 'incite secretly'.

subplot •n. a plot in a play, novel, etc. that is secondary to the main plot.

subpoena /suhb-**pee**-nuh/ •n. a written order instructing someone to attend a court of law. •v. (**subpoenas, subpoenaing, subpoenaed** or **subpoena'd**) summon with a subpoena.
– ORIGIN from Latin *sub poena* 'under penalty'.

subroutine •n. Computing a set of instructions designed to perform a frequently used operation within a program.

sub-Saharan •adj. from or forming part of the African regions south of the Sahara Desert.

subscribe •v. (**subscribes, subscribing, subscribed**) 1 (often **subscribe to**) arrange to receive something regularly by paying in advance. 2 (**subscribe to**) contribute a sum of money to a project or cause on a regular basis. 3 apply to take part in: *the course is fully subscribed.* 4 (**subscribe to**) express agreement with an idea or proposal.
– DERIVATIVES **subscriber** n.
– ORIGIN Latin *subscribere* 'write below'.

subscript •adj. (of a letter, figure, or symbol) written or printed below the line.

subscription •n. 1 the action of subscribing. 2 a payment to subscribe to something.

subsection •n. a division of a section.

subsense •n. a related but less important sense of a word defined in a dictionary.

subsequent •adj. coming after something in time.
– DERIVATIVES **subsequently** adv.
– ORIGIN Latin *subsequi* 'follow after'.

subservient •adj. 1 too willing to obey other people. 2 less important.
– DERIVATIVES **subservience** n.

subset •n. 1 a part of a larger group of related things. 2 Math. a set of which all

the elements are contained in another set.

subside •v. (**subsides, subsiding, subsided**) 1 become less strong, violent, or severe. 2 (of water) go down to a lower or the normal level. 3 (of a building) sink lower into the ground. 4 (of the ground) cave in; sink. 5 (**subside into**) give way to a strong feeling.
– ORIGIN Latin *subsidere*.

subsidence /suhb-sy-duhnss, sub-si-duhnss/ •n. the gradual caving in or sinking of an area of land.

subsidiary •adj. 1 related but less important. 2 (of a company) controlled by another company. •n. (pl. **subsidiaries**) a subsidiary company.
– ORIGIN Latin *subsidiarius*.

subsidize (or **subsidise**) •v. (**subsidizes, subsidizing, subsidized**) 1 support an organization or activity financially. 2 pay part of the cost of producing something to reduce its price.
– DERIVATIVES **subsidization** n.

subsidy •n. (pl. **subsidies**) 1 a sum of money given to an industry or business from public funds to help keep the price of a product or service low. 2 a sum of money granted to support an under-taking that is in the public interest.
– ORIGIN Latin *subsidium* 'assistance'.

subsist •v. manage to stay alive, especially with limited resources.
– ORIGIN Latin *subsistere* 'stand firm'.

subsistence •n. the action or fact of subsisting. •adj. (of production) at a level which is enough only for your own use, without anything left over for trade: *subsistence agriculture.*

subsistence level (also **subsistence wage**) •n. a standard of living (or wage) that provides only the basic necessities of life.

subsoil •n. the soil lying immediately under the surface soil.

subsonic •adj. relating to or flying at a speed or speeds less than that of sound.

substance •n. 1 a type of solid, liquid, or gas that has particular qualities. 2 the physical matter of which a person or thing consists. 3 the quality of being based on facts or truth: *the claim has no substance.* 4 the quality of being important: *a man of substance.* 5 the most important or essential part or meaning. 6 the subject matter of a piece of writing or work of art. 7 an intoxicating or narcotic drug, especially an illegal one.
– PHRASES **in substance** essentially.
– ORIGIN Latin *substantia* 'being'.

substandard • adj. below the usual or required standard.

substantial • adj. **1** of great importance, size, or value. **2** strongly built or made.

substantially • adv. **1** considerably. **2** for the most part; mainly: *things will remain substantially the same.*

substantiate /suhb-stan-shi-ayt/ • v. (**substantiates, substantiating, substantiated**) provide evidence to prove that something is true.
– ORIGIN Latin *substantiare* 'give substance'.

substantive /sub-stuhn-tiv, suhb-stan-tiv/ • adj. important or meaningful.
– DERIVATIVES **substantively** adv.

substation • n. a set of equipment reducing the high voltage of electrical power transmission to that suitable for supply to consumers.

substitute • n. **1** a person or thing acting or used in place of another. **2** a sports player who is allowed to replace another after a match has begun. • v. (**substitutes, substituting, substituted**) take the place of; use instead of: *frozen peas can be substituted for fresh.*
– DERIVATIVES **substitution** n.
– ORIGIN Latin *substituere*.

substratum • n. (pl. **substrata**) a layer of rock or soil beneath the surface of the ground.

subsume • v. (**subsumes, subsuming, subsumed**) include or absorb in something else.
– ORIGIN Latin *subsumere*.

subtenant • n. a person who rents property from a tenant.

subtend • v. Geom. (of a line, arc, etc.) form an angle at a particular point when straight lines from its extremities meet.
– ORIGIN Latin *subtendere*.

subterfuge /sub-ter-fyooj/ • n. secret or dishonest actions used in order to achieve an aim.
– ORIGIN Latin *subterfugere* 'escape secretly'.

subterranean /sub-tuh-ray-ni-uhn/ • adj. existing or happening under the earth's surface.
– DERIVATIVES **subterraneous** adj.
– ORIGIN Latin *subterraneus*.

subtext • n. an underlying theme in a speech or piece of writing.

subtitle • n. **1** (**subtitles**) captions displayed at the bottom of a cinema or television screen that translate the dialogue. **2** a secondary title of a published work. • v. (**subtitles, subtitling, subtitled**) provide with a subtitle or subtitles.

subtle /suh-t'l/ • adj. (**subtler, subtlest**) **1** so delicate or precise as to be difficult to analyse or describe. **2** good at noticing and understanding things. **3** done in a clever but understated way: *subtle lighting.* **4** using clever and indirect methods to achieve something.
– DERIVATIVES **subtlety** n. (pl. **subtleties**). **subtly** adv.
– ORIGIN Latin *subtilis*.

> ✓ Remember that **subtle** has a silent **b** before the **t**.

subtotal • n. the total of one set within a larger group of figures to be added.

subtract • v. take away a number or amount from another to calculate the difference.
– DERIVATIVES **subtraction** n. **subtractive** adj.
– ORIGIN Latin *subtrahere* 'draw away'.

subtropical • adj. relating to the regions near or next to the tropics.

suburb • n. an outlying residential district of a city.
– ORIGIN from Latin *sub-* 'near to' + *urbs* 'city'.

suburban • adj. **1** relating to or like a suburb. **2** boringly conventional.

suburbanite • n. a person who lives in a suburb.

suburbia • n. suburbs and the way of life of their inhabitants.

subversive • adj. trying to damage or weaken the power of an established system or institution. • n. a subversive person.
– DERIVATIVES **subversively** adv.

subvert • v. damage or weaken the power of an established system or institution.
– DERIVATIVES **subversion** n.
– ORIGIN Latin *subvertere*.

subway • n. **1** Brit. a passage under a road for use by pedestrians. **2** N. Amer. an underground railway.

sub-zero • adj. (of temperature) below freezing.

succeed • v. **1** achieve an aim or purpose. **2** gain fame, wealth, or social status. **3** take over a job, role, or title, from someone else. **4** become the new rightful holder of a position, title, etc.: *James I succeeded to the throne in 1603.* **5** come after and take the place of.
– ORIGIN Latin *succedere* 'come close after'.

success • n. **1** the accomplishment of an aim or purpose. **2** the gaining of fame, wealth, or social status. **3** a person or thing that achieves success.

– ORIGIN Latin *successus*.

 Spell **success** and **successful** with a double **c** and a double **s**.

successful • adj. **1** having achieved an aim or purpose. **2** having achieved fame, wealth, or social status.
– DERIVATIVES **successfully** adv.

succession • n. **1** a number of people or things following one after the other. **2** the action or right of inheriting a position, title, etc.
– PHRASES **in quick succession** following one another at short intervals. **in succession** following one after the other without interruption.

successive • adj. following one another or following others.
– DERIVATIVES **successively** adv.

successor • n. a person or thing that succeeds another.

succinct /suhk-singkt/ • adj. briefly and clearly expressed.
– DERIVATIVES **succinctly** adv.
– ORIGIN Latin *succingere* 'tuck up'.

succour /suk-ker/ (US **succor**) • n. help and support in times of hardship and distress. • v. give help to.
– ORIGIN Latin *succursus*.

succubus /suk-kyuu-buhss/ • n. (pl. **succubi** /suk-kyuu-by/) a female demon believed to have sex with sleeping men.
– ORIGIN Latin, 'prostitute'.

succulent • adj. **1** (of food) tender, juicy, and tasty. **2** (of a plant) having thick fleshy leaves or stems adapted to storing water. • n. a succulent plant.
– DERIVATIVES **succulence** n.
– ORIGIN Latin *succulentus*.

succumb • v. **1** give in to pressure, temptation, etc. **2** die from the effect of a disease or injury.
– ORIGIN Latin *succumbere*.

such • det., predet., & pron. **1** of the type previously mentioned. **2** (**such —— as/that**) of the type about to be mentioned. **3** to so high a degree; so great: *autumn's such a beautiful season.*
– PHRASES **as such** in the exact sense of the word. **such as 1** for example. **2** of a kind that; like.
– ORIGIN Old English.

suchlike • pron. things of the type mentioned: *old chairs, tables, and suchlike.* • det. of the type mentioned.

suck • v. **1** draw something into the mouth by tightening the lip muscles and breathing in. **2** hold something in the mouth and draw at it by tightening the lip and cheek muscles. **3** pull forcefully in a particular direction: *he was sucked under the surface of the river.* **4** (**suck someone in/into**) involve someone in a

situation or activity, especially against their will. **5** (**suck up to**) informal try to please someone in authority in order to gain advantage for yourself. **6** N. Amer. informal be very bad or unpleasant. • n. an act of sucking.
– ORIGIN Old English.

sucker • n. **1** a rubber cup that sticks to a surface by suction. **2** an organ that allows an animal to cling to a surface by suction. **3** informal a person who is easily fooled. **4** (**a sucker for**) informal a person who is especially influenced by or fond of a particular thing: *I was a sucker for flattery.* **5** a shoot springing from the base of a tree or other plant.

suckle • v. (**suckles, suckling, suckled**) (with reference to a baby or young animal) feed from the breast or teat.

suckling • n. a young child or animal that is still feeding on its mother's milk.

sucrose /soo-krohz/ • n. a compound which is the chief component of cane or beet sugar.
– ORIGIN French *sucre* 'sugar'.

suction • n. the process of removing air or liquid from a space or container, creating a partial vacuum that causes something else to be sucked in or surfaces to stick together.
– ORIGIN Latin.

Sudanese /soo-duh-neez/ • n. a person from the Sudan in north-east Africa. • adj. relating to the Sudan.

sudden • adj. occurring or done quickly and unexpectedly.
– DERIVATIVES **suddenly** adv. **suddenness** n.
– ORIGIN Old French *sudein*.

sudden death • n. a means of deciding the winner in a tied match, in which play continues and the winner is the first side or player to score.

sudden infant death syndrome • n. tech. = COT DEATH.

suds • pl. n. froth made from soap and water.
– ORIGIN prob. from SEETHE.

sue • v. (**sues, suing, sued**) **1** take legal action against a person or institution. **2** (**sue for**) formal appeal formally to a person for: *they sued for peace.*
– ORIGIN Old French *suer*.

suede • n. leather with the flesh side rubbed to make a velvety nap.
– ORIGIN from French *gants de Suède* 'gloves of Sweden'.

suet • n. the hard white fat on the kidneys of cattle, sheep, and other animals, used in making puddings, pastry, etc.
– ORIGIN Old French.

suffer •v. (**suffers, suffering, suffered**) **1** experience something bad or unpleasant. **2** (**suffer from**) be affected by an illness or condition. **3** become or appear worse in quality: *his relationship with Anne did suffer.* **4** old use tolerate.
– DERIVATIVES **sufferer** n.
– ORIGIN Latin *sufferre.*

sufferance •n. lack of objection rather than actual approval; toleration.

suffice /suh-fyss/ •v. (**suffices, sufficing, sufficed**) **1** be enough or adequate. **2** meet the needs of.
– ORIGIN Latin *sufficere.*

sufficiency •n. (pl. **sufficiencies**) **1** the quality of being enough or adequate. **2** an adequate amount.

sufficient •adj. & adv. enough; adequate.
– DERIVATIVES **sufficiently** adv.

suffix /suf-fiks/ •n. a letter or group of letters added at the end of a word to form another word (e.g. *-ation*).

suffocate •v. (**suffocates, suffocating, suffocated**) **1** die or cause to die from lack of air or inability to breathe. **2** feel trapped.
– DERIVATIVES **suffocation** n.
– ORIGIN Latin *suffocare* 'stifle'.

suffrage /suf-frij/ •n. the right to vote in political elections.
– ORIGIN Latin *suffragium.*

suffragette /suf-fruh-jet/ •n. hist. a woman who campaigned for women to be given the right to vote in political elections.

suffuse /suh-fyooz/ •v. (**suffuses, suffusing, suffused**) gradually spread through or over.
– DERIVATIVES **suffusion** n.
– ORIGIN Latin *suffundere* 'pour into'.

Sufi /soo-fi/ •n. (pl. **Sufis**) a member of a Muslim group leading a very religious, strict, and simple life.
– DERIVATIVES **Sufism** n.
– ORIGIN Arabic.

sugar •n. **1** a sweet crystalline substance obtained from sugar cane and sugar beet. **2** any of the class of soluble crystalline sweet-tasting carbohydrates found in plant and animal tissue, including sucrose and glucose.
•v. **1** sweeten, sprinkle, or coat with sugar. **2** make more pleasant.
– ORIGIN Old French *sukere.*

sugar beet •n. a type of beet (plant) from which sugar is extracted.

sugar cane •n. a tropical grass with tall thick stems from which sugar is extracted.

sugar daddy •n. informal a rich older man who gives presents and money to a much younger woman.

sugar snap •n. a type of mangetout pea with thick pods.

sugar soap •n. Brit. an alkaline preparation containing washing soda and soap, used for cleaning or removing paint.

sugary •adj. **1** coated in or containing much sugar. **2** too sentimental.

suggest •v. **1** put forward an idea or plan for consideration. **2** make someone think that something exists or is the case. **3** say or express indirectly. **4** (**suggest itself**) (of an idea) come into a person's mind.
– ORIGIN Latin *suggerere.*

suggestible •adj. quick to accept other people's ideas or suggestions; easily influenced.

suggestion •n. **1** an idea or plan put forward for consideration. **2** something that suggests or indicates a certain fact or situation. **3** a slight trace or indication: *a suggestion of a smile.*

suggestive •adj. **1** making someone think of something. **2** (of a remark, joke, etc.) making someone think about sex.
– DERIVATIVES **suggestively** adv.

suicide •n. **1** the action of killing yourself deliberately. **2** a person who commits suicide. **3** a course of action which is likely to be very damaging to your career, position in society, etc.
•adj. referring to a military operation carried out by people who do not expect to survive it: *a suicide bomber.*
– DERIVATIVES **suicidal** adj. **suicidally** adv.
– ORIGIN from Latin *sui* 'of yourself' + *caedere* 'kill'.

suit /*rhymes with* boot/ •n. **1** a set of clothes made of the same fabric, consisting of a jacket and trousers or a skirt. **2** a set of clothes for a particular activity. **3** any of the sets into which a pack of playing cards is divided (spades, hearts, diamonds, and clubs). **4** a lawsuit. **5** the process of trying to win a woman's affection with a view to marriage. •v. **1** be convenient for or acceptable to. **2** (of clothes, colours, etc.) be right for someone's features or figure. **3** (**suit yourself**) do exactly what you want.
– ORIGIN Old French *siwte.*

suitable •adj. right or appropriate for a particular person, purpose, or situation.
– DERIVATIVES **suitability** n. **suitably** adv.

suitcase •n. a case with a handle and a hinged lid, used for carrying clothes and other personal possessions.

suite /sweet/ •n. **1** a set of rooms for one person's or family's use. **2** a set of furniture of the same design. **3** (in music) a set of instrumental

S

compositions to be played one after the other. **4** a set of pieces from an opera or musical arranged as one instrumental work.
– ORIGIN French.

suitor /soo-ter/ •n. a man who wants to marry a particular woman.

sulfur etc. •n. US = SULPHUR etc.

sulk •v. be silent, miserable, and bad-tempered as a result of annoyance or disappointment. •n. a period of sulking.

sulky •adj. (**sulkier, sulkiest**) miserable, bad-tempered, and resentful.
– DERIVATIVES **sulkily** adv.
– ORIGIN perh. from former *sulke* 'hard to dispose of'.

sullen •adj. bad-tempered and sulky.
– DERIVATIVES **sullenly** adv.
– ORIGIN Old French *sulein*.

sully •v. (**sullies, sullying, sullied**) literary spoil the purity or cleanliness of.
– ORIGIN perh. from French *souiller* 'to soil'.

sulphate (US **sulfate**) •n. Chem. a salt or ester of sulphuric acid.

sulphide /sul-fyd/ (US **sulfide**) •n. Chem. a compound of sulphur with another element or group.

sulphur (US & Chem. **sulfur**) •n. a non-metallic chemical element which easily catches fire, typically found in the form of yellow crystals.
– ORIGIN Latin *sulfur, sulphur*.

sulphur dioxide •n. a colourless poisonous gas formed by burning sulphur.

sulphuric /sul-fyoor-ik/ (US **sulfuric**) •adj. containing sulphur or sulphuric acid.

sulphuric acid •n. a strong corrosive acid.

sulphurous (US **sulfurous**) •adj. containing or obtained from sulphur.

sultan •n. a Muslim ruler.
– DERIVATIVES **sultanate** n.
– ORIGIN Arabic, 'power, ruler'.

sultana •n. **1** Brit. a seedless raisin. **2** a wife of a sultan.
– ORIGIN Italian.

sultry •adj. (**sultrier, sultriest**) **1** (of the weather) hot and humid. **2** suggesting sexual passion.
– ORIGIN from former *sulter* 'swelter'.

sum •n. **1** a particular amount of money. **2** (also **sum total**) the total amount resulting from the addition of two or more numbers or amounts. **3** a calculation in arithmetic. •v. (**sums, summing, summed**) **1** (**sum someone/ thing up**) concisely describe the nature or character of: *selfish—that summed her*

up. **2** (**sum something up** or **sum up**) summarize something briefly.
– ORIGIN Latin *summa* 'main part'.

summarize (or **summarise**)
•v. (**summarizes, summarizing, summarized**) give a brief statement of the main points of something.

summary •n. (pl. **summaries**) a brief statement of the main points of something. •adj. **1** not including unnecessary details. **2** (of a legal process or judgement) done or made immediately and without following the normal legal procedures.
– DERIVATIVES **summarily** adv.
– ORIGIN Latin *summarius*.

> **USAGE:** Do not confuse **summary** and **summery**. A **summary** is a brief statement of the main points of something (*a summary of today's news*), whereas **summery** is an adjective meaning 'typical of or suitable for summer' (*summery weather*).

summation /sum-may-sh'n/ •n. **1** the process of adding things together. **2** the action of summing something up. **3** a summary.

summer •n. the season after spring and before autumn.
– DERIVATIVES **summery** adj.
– ORIGIN Old English.

summer house •n. a small building in a garden, used for relaxing in during fine weather.

summer school •n. a course of lectures held during school and university summer vacations.

summer time •n. Brit. time as advanced one hour ahead of standard time so that it is light for an extra hour in the evening.

summing-up •n. **1** a summary. **2** a judge's review of the evidence at the end of a case heard in a court of law.

summit •n. **1** the highest point of a hill or mountain. **2** the highest possible level of achievement. **3** a meeting between heads of government.
– ORIGIN Old French *somete*.

summon •v. **1** instruct someone to be present. **2** urgently ask for help. **3** call people to attend a meeting. **4** make an effort to produce a quality or reaction from within yourself: *she managed to summon up a smile*.
– ORIGIN Latin *summonere* 'give a hint'.

summons •n. (pl. **summonses**) **1** an order to appear in a law court. **2** an act of summoning.

sumo /soo-moh/ •n. Japanese wrestling in which a wrestler must not go outside a circle or touch the ground with any

part of his body except the soles of his feet.
– ORIGIN Japanese.

sump • n. the base of an internal-combustion engine, which serves as a reservoir of oil for the lubrication system.
– ORIGIN Dutch or German *sump* 'marsh'.

sumptuous • adj. splendid and expensive-looking.
– DERIVATIVES **sumptuously** adv.
– ORIGIN Latin *sumptuosus*.

sum total • n. = SUM (in sense 2).

sun • n. **1** (also **Sun**) the star round which the earth orbits. **2** any similar star. **3** the light or warmth received from the sun.
• v. (**suns, sunning, sunned**) (**sun yourself**) sit or lie in the sun.
– PHRASES **under the sun** in existence.
– ORIGIN Old English.

sun-baked • adj. exposed to the heat of the sun.

sunbathe • v. (**sunbathes, sunbathing, sunbathed**) sit or lie in the sun to get a suntan.
– DERIVATIVES **sunbather** n.

sunbeam • n. a ray of sunlight.

sunbed • n. Brit. **1** a long chair for lying on while sunbathing. **2** an apparatus for getting an artificial tan, consisting of two banks of sunlamps between which you lie or stand.

sunblock • n. a cream or lotion for protecting the skin from sunburn.

sunburn • n. inflammation of the skin caused by too much exposure to the ultraviolet rays of the sun.
– DERIVATIVES **sunburned** (or **sunburnt**) adj.

suncream • n. a cream used for protecting the skin from sunburn.

sundae • n. a dish of ice cream with added fruit, nuts, and syrup.
– ORIGIN perh. from **SUNDAY**, either because the dish was made with ice cream left over from Sunday, or because it was sold only on Sundays.

Sunday • n. the day of the week before Monday and following Saturday, observed by Christians as a day of religious worship.
– ORIGIN Old English, 'day of the sun'.

Sunday best • n. a person's best clothes.

Sunday school • n. a class held on Sundays to teach children about Christianity or Judaism.

sunder • v. (**sunders, sundering, sundered**) literary split apart.
– ORIGIN Old English.

sundial • n. an instrument showing the time by the shadow cast by a pointer.

sundown • n. sunset.

sundress • n. a light, loose sleeveless dress.

sun-dried • adj. dried in the sun, as opposed to by artificial heat.

sundry • adj. of various kinds.
• n. (**sundries**) various items not important enough be mentioned individually.
– ORIGIN Old English, 'distinct, separate'.

sunflower • n. a tall plant with very large golden flowers, grown for its edible seeds which produce oil.

sung past part. of SING.

sunglasses • pl. n. glasses tinted to protect the eyes from sunlight.

sunk past part. of SINK.

sunken • adj. **1** having sunk. **2** at a lower level than the surrounding area.
– ORIGIN former past part. of SINK.

sun-kissed • adj. made warm or brown by the sun.

sunlamp • n. a lamp giving off ultraviolet rays, used to produce an artificial suntan.

sunlight • n. light from the sun.
– DERIVATIVES **sunlit** adj.

Sunni /suu-ni, sun-ni/ • n. (pl. **Sunni** or **Sunnis**) **1** one of the two main branches of Islam. **2** a Muslim who follows the Sunni branch of Islam.
– ORIGIN Arabic, 'custom, standard rule'.

sunny • adj. (**sunnier, sunniest**) **1** bright with or receiving much sunlight. **2** cheerful: *a sunny smile.*

sunrise • n. **1** the time in the morning when the sun rises. **2** the colours and light visible in the sky at sunrise.

sunroof • n. a panel in the roof of a car that can be opened for extra ventilation.

sunscreen • n. a cream or lotion rubbed on to the skin to protect it from the sun.

sunset • n. **1** the time in the evening when the sun sets. **2** the colours and light visible in the sky at sunset.

sunshade • n. a parasol or awning giving protection from the sun.

sunshine • n. sunlight unbroken by cloud.
– DERIVATIVES **sunshiny** adj.

sunspot • n. a temporary darker and cooler patch on the sun's surface.

sunstroke • n. heatstroke caused by staying out too long in hot sunlight.

suntan • n. a golden-brown colouring of the skin caused by spending time in the sun.
– DERIVATIVES **suntanned** adj.

sunup • n. esp. N. Amer. sunrise.

sup[1] • v. (**sups, supping, supped**) dated or N. English take drink or liquid food by sips or spoonfuls. • n. a sip.
– ORIGIN Old English.

s

sup² • v. (**sups**, **supping**, **supped**) dated eat supper.
– ORIGIN Old French *super*.

super • adj. informal excellent.

super- • comb. form **1** above; over; beyond: *superstructure.* **2** to a great or extreme degree: *supercool.* **3** extra large of its kind: *superpower.*
– ORIGIN Latin *super.*

superannuate • v. (**superannuates**, **superannuating**, **superannuated**) **1** cause someone to retire with a pension. **2** (as adj. **superannuated**) too old or outdated to be effective or useful.
– ORIGIN from Latin *super-* 'over' + *annus* 'year'.

superannuation • n. regular payment made into a fund by an employee towards a future pension.

superb • adj. **1** very good; excellent. **2** magnificent or impressive.
– DERIVATIVES **superbly** adv.
– ORIGIN Latin *superbus.*

superbug • n. informal a bacterium or insect which has developed resistance to antibiotics or pesticides.

supercharge • v. (**supercharges**, **supercharging**, **supercharged**) (usu. as adj. **supercharged**) **1** provide an engine with a supercharger. **2** give extra power or intensity to: *a supercharged collection of dance tracks.*

supercharger • n. a device that increases the efficiency of an internal-combustion engine by raising the pressure of the fuel and air supplied to it.

supercilious • adj. behaving in a way that shows you think you are better than other people.
– ORIGIN Latin *superciliosus* 'haughty'.

supercomputer • n. a particularly powerful mainframe computer.

superconductivity • n. Physics the property of zero electrical resistance in some substances at very low temperatures.
– DERIVATIVES **superconducting** adj. **superconductor** n.

supercool • v. Chem. cool a liquid below its freezing point without solidification or crystallization.

superego • n. (pl. **superegos**) the part of the mind that acts as a conscience, reflecting social standards that have been learned. Compare with EGO and ID.

superficial • adj. **1** existing or happening at or on the surface. **2** appearing to be real or true until examined more closely: *the resemblance is superficial.* **3** not thorough: *a superficial reading of the document.* **4** lacking the ability to think deeply about things.
– DERIVATIVES **superficiality** n. (pl. **superficialities**). **superficially** adv.
– ORIGIN Latin *superficialis.*

superfluity /soo-per-floo-it-i/ • n. (pl. **superfluities**) **1** an unnecessarily or excessively large amount or number of something. **2** an unnecessary thing.

superfluous /soo-per-floo-uhss/ • adj. unnecessary because more than is needed: *avoid asking for superfluous information.*
– ORIGIN Latin *superfluus.*

superglue • n. a very strong quick-setting glue.

supergrass • n. Brit. informal a police informer who gives information about the criminal activities of a large number of people.

superhero • n. (pl. **superheroes**) a fictional hero with superhuman powers.

superhuman • adj. having or showing exceptional ability or powers.

superimpose • v. (**superimposes**, **superimposing**, **superimposed**) place or lay one thing over another.
– DERIVATIVES **superimposition** n.

superintend • v. manage an activity or organization.
– ORIGIN Latin *superintendere.*

superintendent • n. **1** a person who manages an organization or activity. **2** (in the UK) a police officer ranking above chief inspector.

superior • adj. **1** higher in status, quality, or power. **2** high in quality. **3** thinking that you are better than other people; conceited. • n. a person of higher rank.
– ORIGIN Latin, 'higher'.

superiority • n. the state of being superior.

superlative /soo-per-luh-tiv/ • adj. **1** of the highest quality or degree. **2** Grammar (of an adjective or adverb) expressing the highest degree of a quality (e.g. *bravest*). Contrasted with POSITIVE and COMPARATIVE. • n. an exaggerated expression of praise.
– DERIVATIVES **superlatively** adv.
– ORIGIN Latin *superlativus.*

superman (or **superwoman**) • n. (pl. **supermen** or **superwomen**) informal an exceptionally strong or intelligent person.

supermarket • n. a large self-service shop selling foods and household goods.

supermodel • n. a very successful and famous fashion model.

supernatural • adj. caused by a force that cannot be explained by science or the laws of nature. • n. (**the**

supernatural) supernatural events.
– DERIVATIVES **supernaturally** adv.

supernova /soo-per-**noh**-vuh/ • n. (pl.
supernovae /soo-per-**noh**-vee/ or
supernovas) a star that undergoes a
catastrophic explosion, becoming
suddenly very much brighter.

supernumerary /soo-per-**nyoo**-muh-
ruh-ri/ • adj. **1** more than is normally
needed; extra. **2** not belonging to a
regular staff but employed for extra
work. • n. (pl. **supernumeraries**) an extra
person or thing.
– ORIGIN Latin *supernumerarius* 'soldier
added to a legion after it is complete'.

superpower • n. a very powerful and
influential country.

superscript • adj. (of a letter, figure, or
symbol) written or printed above the
line.

supersede /soo-per-**seed**/
• v. (**supersedes, superseding,
superseded**) take the place of someone
or something previously in authority or
use.
– ORIGIN Latin *supersedere* 'be superior
to'.

> The ending of **supersede** is spelled
> **-sede**.

supersonic • adj. relating to a speed
greater than that of sound.
– DERIVATIVES **supersonically** adv.

superstar • n. a very famous and
successful performer or sports player.

superstate • n. a large and powerful
state formed from a union of several
nations.

superstition • n. **1** irrational belief in
supernatural events. **2** a belief that
supernatural influences can bring good
or bad luck.
– ORIGIN Latin.

superstitious • adj. believing in the
supernatural and its influence to bring
good or bad luck.
– DERIVATIVES **superstitiously** adv.

superstore • n. a very large out-of-town
supermarket.

superstructure • n. **1** a structure built
on top of something else. **2** the part of a
building above its foundations. **3** the
parts of a ship, other than masts and
rigging, above its hull and main deck.

supertanker • n. a very large oil tanker.

supervene /soo-per-**veen**/
• v. (**supervenes, supervening,
supervened**) happen so as to interrupt
or change an existing situation.
– ORIGIN Latin *supervenire* 'come in
addition'.

supervise • v. watch and direct the

performance of a task or the work of a
person.
– DERIVATIVES **supervision** n. **supervisor**
n. **supervisory** adj.
– ORIGIN Latin *supervidere* 'survey,
supervise'.

supine /soo-**pyn**/ • adj. **1** lying face
upwards. **2** failing to act as a result of
laziness or weakness.
– DERIVATIVES **supinely** adv.
– ORIGIN Latin *supinus* 'bent backwards'.

supper • n. a light or informal evening
meal.
– ORIGIN Old French *super* 'to sup'.

supplant • v. take the place of: *another
technology might supplant the CD.*
– ORIGIN Latin *supplantare* 'trip up'.

supple • adj. (**suppler, supplest**) bending
and moving easily; flexible.
– DERIVATIVES **suppleness** n.
– ORIGIN Latin *supplex* 'submissive'.

supplement • n. **1** a thing added to
something else to improve or complete
it. **2** a separate section added to a
newspaper or magazine. **3** an additional
charge payable for an extra service or
facility. • v. add an extra element or
amount to.
– DERIVATIVES **supplemental** adj.
supplementation n.
– ORIGIN Latin *supplementum*.

supplementary • adj. completing or
improving something.

suppliant /sup-pli-uhnt/ • n. a person
who makes a humble request.

supplicate /sup-pli-kayt/
• v. (**supplicates, supplicating,
supplicated**) humbly ask or beg for
something.
– DERIVATIVES **supplicant** n.
supplication n.
– ORIGIN Latin *supplicare* 'implore'.

supply • v. (**supplies, supplying,
supplied**) make something needed or
wanted available to someone; provide.
• n. (pl. **supplies**) **1** a stock or amount of
something supplied or available. **2** the
action of supplying. **3** (**supplies**)
provisions and equipment necessary for
an army or expedition.
– PHRASES **supply and demand** the
amount of goods or services available
and the desire of buyers for them,
considered as factors deciding the price.
– DERIVATIVES **supplier** n.
– ORIGIN Latin *supplere* 'fill up'.

support • v. **1** bear all or part of the
weight of. **2** give help, encouragement,
or approval to. **3** be actively interested
in a sports team. **4** provide with a home
and the necessities of life. **5** provide
enough food and water for life to exist.
6 confirm or back up: *the studies support*

our findings. • n. **1** a person or thing that supports. **2** the action of supporting. **3** help, encouragement, or approval.
– ORIGIN Latin *supportare*.

supporter • n. a person who supports a sports team, political party, etc.

supportive • adj. providing encouragement or emotional help.

suppose • v. (**supposes, supposing, supposed**) **1** think that something is true or likely, but lack proof. **2** (of a theory or argument) require that something is the case as a necessary condition. **3** (**be supposed to do**) be required or expected to do.
– ORIGIN Latin *supponere*.

supposedly • adv. according to what is generally believed.

supposition • n. a belief held without proof or certain knowledge.

suppository • n. (pl. **suppositories**) a small piece of a medical substance that dissolves when placed in the rectum or vagina.
– ORIGIN Latin *suppositorium* 'thing placed underneath'.

suppress • v. **1** forcibly put an end to. **2** prevent from acting or developing. **3** prevent from being stated or published.
– DERIVATIVES **suppression** n. **suppressive** adj. **suppressor** n.
– ORIGIN Latin *supprimere* 'press down'.

 Spell **suppress** with a double **p**.

suppressant • n. a drug which prevents a bodily function from working.

suppurate /sup-pyuh-rayt/ • v. (**suppurates, suppurating, suppurated**) form or give off pus.
– DERIVATIVES **suppuration** n.
– ORIGIN from Latin *sub-* 'below' + *pus* 'pus'.

supranational • adj. having power or influence that goes beyond national boundaries or governments.
– ORIGIN from Latin *supra* 'above, beyond'.

supremacist • n. a person who believes that a particular group, especially a racial group, is superior to all others.
– DERIVATIVES **supremacism** n.

supremacy /soo-prem-uh-si/ • n. the state of being superior to all others in authority, power, or status.

supreme • adj. **1** highest in authority, rank, or importance. **2** very great or greatest.
– DERIVATIVES **supremely** adv.
– ORIGIN Latin *supremus* 'highest'.

supreme court • n. the highest law court in a country or state.

supremo /soo-pree-moh/ • n. (pl. **supremos**) Brit. informal a person in charge of an organization or with great skill in a particular area.
– ORIGIN Spanish, 'supreme'.

suq • n. var. of SOUK.

sur- • prefix = SUPER-.
– ORIGIN French.

surcharge • n. an extra charge or payment. • v. (**surcharges, surcharging, surcharged**) make someone pay an extra charge.

surd /rhymes with curd/ • n. Math. a number which cannot be expressed as a ratio of two whole numbers.
– ORIGIN Latin *surdus* 'deaf, mute'.

sure • adj. **1** completely confident that you are right. **2** (**sure of/to do something**) certain to receive, get, or do. **3** undoubtedly true. **4** steady and confident.
– PHRASES **be sure to do** do not fail to do. **make sure** confirm or ensure.
– DERIVATIVES **sureness** n.
– ORIGIN Old French *sur*.

sure-fire • adj. informal certain to succeed.

sure-footed • adj. **1** unlikely to stumble or slip. **2** confident and competent.

surely • adv. **1** it must be true that. **2** certainly. **3** in a confident way.

surety /shoor-i-ti/ • n. (pl. **sureties**) **1** a person who accepts responsibility if another person fails to pay a debt, appear in court, etc. **2** money given as a guarantee that someone will do something.

surf • n. waves that break and form foam on a seashore or reef. • v. **1** stand or lie on a surfboard and ride on the crest of a wave towards the shore. **2** move from site to site on the Internet.
– DERIVATIVES **surfer** n. **surfing** n.

surface • n. **1** the outside part or uppermost layer of something. **2** the upper limit of a body of liquid. **3** outward appearance as distinct from less obvious aspects. • adj. **1** relating to or occurring on the surface. **2** outward or superficial: *surface politeness.* • v. (**surfaces, surfacing, surfaced**) **1** rise or come up to the surface. **2** become apparent. **3** provide with a particular surface.
– ORIGIN French.

surface tension • n. the tension of the surface film of a liquid, which tends to minimize surface area.

surfboard • n. a long, narrow board used in surfing.

surfeit • n. an excessive amount of something.
– ORIGIN Old French.

surge •n. **1** a sudden powerful forward or upward movement. **2** a sudden large temporary increase. **3** a powerful rush of an emotion. •v. (**surges, surging, surged**) **1** move suddenly and powerfully forward or upward. **2** increase suddenly and powerfully.
– ORIGIN Latin *surgere* 'to rise'.

surgeon •n. **1** a medical practitioner qualified to practise surgery. **2** a doctor in the navy.
– ORIGIN Old French *serurgien*.

surgery •n. (pl. **surgeries**) **1** the medical treatment of injuries or disorders by cutting open the body and removing or repairing parts. **2** Brit. a place where a doctor or nurse treats or advises patients. **3** Brit. an occasion on which an MP, lawyer, or other professional person gives advice.

surgical •adj. **1** relating to or used in surgery. **2** worn to correct or relieve an injury, illness, or deformity: *surgical stockings*. **3** done with great precision: *surgical bombing*.
– DERIVATIVES **surgically** adv.

surgical spirit •n. Brit. methylated spirit used for cleaning the skin before injections or surgery.

surly •adj. (**surlier, surliest**) bad-tempered and unfriendly.
– DERIVATIVES **surlily** adv. **surliness** n.
– ORIGIN from former *sirly* 'haughty' (from SIR).

surmise /ser-myz/ •v. (**surmises, surmising, surmised**) believe something to be so without having evidence. •n. a guess.
– ORIGIN Old French, 'accused'.

surmount •v. **1** overcome a difficulty. **2** stand or be placed on top of.

surname •n. an inherited name shared by all members of a family.

surpass •v. **1** be greater or better than. **2** (as adj. **surpassing**) old use outstanding.

surplice /ser-pliss/ •n. a loose white garment worn over a cassock by Christian clergy and members of church choirs.
– ORIGIN Old French *sourpelis*.

surplus •n. **1** an amount left over when requirements have been met. **2** the amount by which the amount of money received is greater than the amount of money spent over a specific period. •adj. more than what is needed or used.
– ORIGIN from Latin *super-* 'in addition' + *plus* 'more'.

surprise •n. **1** a feeling of mild astonishment or shock caused by something unexpected. **2** an unexpected or astonishing thing. •v. (**surprises, surprising, surprised**) **1** make someone feel surprise. **2** capture, attack, or discover suddenly and unexpectedly.
– ORIGIN Old French.

☑ Remember that **surprise** has two **r**'s, one before and one after the **p**.

surreal •adj. very strange, like a dream.
– DERIVATIVES **surreally** adv.

surrealism •n. a 20th-century movement in art and literature in which unrelated images are combined in a strange or irrational way.
– DERIVATIVES **surrealist** n. & adj. **surrealistic** adj.

surrender •v. (**surrenders, surrendering, surrendered**) **1** give in to an opponent and submit to their authority. **2** give up a person, right, or possession on demand. **3** (**surrender to**) abandon yourself completely to a powerful emotion or influence. •n. an act of surrendering.
– ORIGIN Old French *surrendre*.

surreptitious /sur-ruhp-ti-shuhss/ •adj. done secretly.
– DERIVATIVES **surreptitiously** adv.
– ORIGIN Latin *surreptitius* 'obtained secretly'.

surrogate /sur-ruh-guht/ •n. **1** a person who stands in for another in a role or office. **2** (in the Christian Church) a bishop's deputy who grants marriage licences.
– DERIVATIVES **surrogacy** n.
– ORIGIN Latin *surrogare* 'elect as a substitute'.

surrogate mother •n. a woman who bears a child on behalf of another woman.

surround •v. **1** be all round; encircle. **2** be associated with: *the incident was surrounded by controversy*. •n. a border or edging.
– ORIGIN Latin *superundare* 'overflow'.

surroundings •pl. n. the conditions or area around a person or thing: *a school in rural surroundings*.

surtax •n. an extra tax on something already taxed.

surtitle •n. a caption projected on a screen above the stage in an opera, translating the words being sung.

surveillance /ser-vay-luhnss/ •n. close observation of a suspected spy or criminal.
– ORIGIN French.

survey •v. /ser-vay/ (**surveys, surveying, surveyed**) **1** look carefully and thoroughly at. **2** examine and record the features of an area of land to produce a map or description. **3** Brit. examine and report on the condition of a building. **4** question a group of people to

investigate their opinions. •n. /ser-vay/ **1** a general view, examination, or description. **2** an investigation of the opinions or experience of a group of people, based on a series of questions. **3** an act of surveying. **4** a map or report obtained by surveying.
– ORIGIN Old French *surveier*.

surveyor •n. a person who surveys land, buildings, etc. as a profession.

survival •n. **1** the state of surviving. **2** an object or practice that has survived from an earlier time.

survivalist •n. a person who practises outdoor survival skills as a sport or hobby.
– DERIVATIVES **survivalism** n.

survive •v. (**survives, surviving, survived**) **1** continue to live or exist. **2** continue to live in spite of an accident or ordeal. **3** remain alive after the death of: *he was survived by his wife.*
– DERIVATIVES **survivable** adj. **survivor** n.
– ORIGIN Old French *sourvivre*.

susceptibility •n. (pl. **susceptibilities**) **1** the state of being harmed or influenced. **2** (**susceptibilities**) a person's sensitive feelings.

susceptible /suh-sep-ti-b'l/ •adj. **1** (often **susceptible to**) likely to be influenced or harmed by a particular thing. **2** easily influenced by emotions.
– ORIGIN Latin *susceptibilis*.

sushi /soo-shi/ •n. a Japanese dish consisting of small balls or rolls of cold rice with vegetables, egg, or raw seafood.
– ORIGIN Japanese.

suspect •v. /suh-spekt/ **1** believe to be likely or possible. **2** believe that someone is guilty of a crime or offence, without definite proof. **3** doubt that something is genuine or true. •n. /susspekt/ a person suspected of a crime or offence. •adj. /suss-pekt/ possibly dangerous or false: *a suspect package.*
– ORIGIN Latin *suspicere* 'mistrust'.

suspend •v. **1** stop something temporarily. **2** temporarily bar someone from a job or from attending school, as a punishment or during investigation. **3** postpone or delay an action, event, or judgement. **4** (as adj. **suspended**) Law (of a sentence) not enforced as long as no further offence is committed within a specified period. **5** hang from something.
– ORIGIN Latin *suspendere*.

suspended animation •n. a state in which most of the functions of an animal or plant stop for a time, without death.

suspender •n. **1** Brit. an elastic strap attached to a belt or garter, fastened to the top of a stocking to hold it up. **2** (**suspenders**) N. Amer. braces for holding up trousers.

suspender belt •n. Brit. a woman's undergarment made up of a decorative belt and suspenders.

suspense •n. a state of excited or anxious uncertainty about what may happen.
– DERIVATIVES **suspenseful** adj.
– ORIGIN Old French *suspens* 'abeyance'.

suspension •n. **1** the action of suspending something or the state of being suspended. **2** the temporary barring of someone from a job or from school, especially as a punishment. **3** the system of springs and shock absorbers which supports a vehicle on its wheels. **4** a mixture in which particles are dispersed throughout a fluid.

suspension bridge •n. a bridge in which the deck is suspended from cables running between towers.

suspicion •n. **1** a feeling that something is possible or that someone has done something wrong. **2** distrust of someone or something. **3** a very slight trace: *a suspicion of a smile.*
– ORIGIN Old French *suspeciun*.

suspicious •adj. **1** having a feeling that someone has done something wrong. **2** seeming to be dishonest or dangerous: *a suspicious package.* **3** (also **suspicious of**) not able to trust someone or something.
– DERIVATIVES **suspiciously** adv.

suss •v. (**susses, sussing, sussed**) (often **suss someone/thing out**) Brit. informal realize or understand the true nature of.
– ORIGIN from **SUSPECT**.

sustain •v. **1** support someone physically or mentally. **2** keep something going over time or continuously. **3** suffer something unpleasant. **4** decide that a claim is valid. **5** bear the weight of an object.
– ORIGIN Latin *sustinere*.

sustainable •adj. **1** able to be continued or sustained. **2** (of industry, development, or agriculture) avoiding using up natural resources.
– DERIVATIVES **sustainability** n. **sustainably** adv.

sustenance •n. **1** food and drink as needed to keep someone alive. **2** the process of making something continue.

suture /soo-cher/ •n. **1** a stitch or stitches holding together the edges of a wound or surgical cut. **2** a thread used for stitching a wound or cut.
•v. (**sutures, suturing, sutured**) stitch up a wound or cut.

– ORIGIN Latin *sutura*.

suzerainty /soo-zuh-rayn-ty/ • n. the right of one country to rule over another country that has its own ruler but is not fully independent.
– DERIVATIVES **suzerain** n.
– ORIGIN French.

svelte • adj. slender and elegant.
– ORIGIN Italian *svelto*.

Svengali /sven-gah-li/ • n. a person who exercises a controlling influence on another.
– ORIGIN from *Svengali*, a character in George du Maurier's novel *Trilby*.

SW • abbrev. **1** south-west. **2** south-western.

swab • n. **1** a pad used for cleaning wounds or taking a sample from the body for testing. **2** a sample taken with a swab. • v. (**swabs, swabbing, swabbed**) **1** clean with an absorbent pad. **2** wash a floor or ship's deck with a mop or cloth.
– ORIGIN Dutch *zwabber* 'sailor who cleans a ship's deck'.

swaddle • v. (**swaddles, swaddling, swaddled**) wrap in clothes or cloth.
– ORIGIN from SWATHE².

swaddling clothes • pl. n. strips of cloth formerly wrapped round a newborn baby to calm it.

swag • n. **1** an ornamental garland of flowers, fruit, or greenery. **2** a curtain fastened to hang in a drooping curve. **3** informal money or goods taken by a thief or burglar.
– ORIGIN prob. from Scandinavian.

swagger • v. (**swaggers, swaggering, swaggered**) walk or behave in a very confident or arrogant way. • n. a swaggering walk.
– ORIGIN prob. from SWAG.

Swahili /swuh-hee-li, swah-hee-li/ • n. a Bantu language widely spoken in East Africa.
– ORIGIN Arabic, 'coasts'.

swain • n. **1** literary a young male lover. **2** old use a country youth.
– ORIGIN Old Norse, 'lad'.

swallow¹ • v. **1** pass food, drink, or saliva down the throat. **2** take in or cover completely: *the dark mist swallowed her up.* **3** completely use up money or resources. **4** believe something unlikely without question. **5** put up with unfair treatment. **6** resist expressing a feeling or words. • n. an act of swallowing.
– ORIGIN Old English.

swallow² • n. a swift-flying songbird with a forked tail.
– ORIGIN Old English.

swallow dive • n. Brit. a dive performed with the arms outspread until close to the water.

swallowtail • n. a large brightly coloured butterfly with tail-like projections on the hind wings.

swam past of SWIM.

swami /swah-mi/ • n. (pl. **swamis**) a male Hindu religious teacher.
– ORIGIN Hindi, 'master, prince'.

swamp • n. a bog or marsh. • v. **1** flood with water. **2** overwhelm with too much of something: *the country was swamped with goods from abroad.*
– DERIVATIVES **swampy** adj.
– ORIGIN prob. from a Germanic word meaning 'sponge' or 'fungus'.

swan • n. a large white waterbird with a long flexible neck and webbed feet. • v. (**swans, swanning, swanned**) Brit. informal go around enjoying yourself in a way that makes other people jealous or annoyed.
– ORIGIN Old English.

swank informal • v. show off your wealth, knowledge, or achievements. • n. behaviour or talk intended to impress other people.

swanky • adj. (**swankier, swankiest**) informal **1** stylishly luxurious and expensive. **2** inclined to show off.

swansong • n. the final performance or activity of a person's career.
– ORIGIN suggested by German *Schwanengesang*, referring to a mythical song sung by a dying swan.

swap (also **swop**) • v. (**swaps, swapping, swapped**) exchange or substitute one thing for another. • n. an act of exchanging one thing for another.

sward /sword/ • n. literary an expanse of short grass.
– ORIGIN Old English, 'skin'.

swarf /swahf/ • n. fine chips or filings produced by machining.
– ORIGIN Old English or Old Norse.

swarm • n. **1** a large group of insects flying closely together. **2** a large number of honeybees that leave a hive with a queen in order to establish a new colony. **3** a large group of people or things. • v. **1** move in or form a swarm. **2** (**swarm with**) be crowded or overrun with. **3** (**swarm up**) climb rapidly by gripping something with the hands and feet.
– ORIGIN Old English.

swarthy • adj. (**swarthier, swarthiest**) having a dark skin.
– ORIGIN Old English.

swashbuckling • adj. having daring and romantic adventures.
– DERIVATIVES **swashbuckler** n.

swastika /swoss-ti-kuh/ • n. an ancient symbol in the form of an equal-armed cross with each arm bent at a right

angle, used (in clockwise form) as the emblem of the German Nazi party.
– ORIGIN Sanskrit, 'well-being'.

swat /rhymes with hot/ • v. (**swats, swatting, swatted**) hit or crush with a sharp blow from a flat object.
– ORIGIN northern English and US form of **SQUAT**.

swatch • n. **1** a piece of fabric used as a sample. **2** a number of fabric samples bound together.

swathe¹ /swayth/ (N. Amer. also **swath** /swawth/) • n. (pl. **swathes** or **swaths** /swaythz, swawths/) **1** a row or line of grass, corn, etc. as it falls when cut down. **2** a broad strip or area: *vast swathes of countryside.*
– ORIGIN Old English, 'track, trace'.

swathe² /swayth/ • v. (**swathes, swathing, swathed**) wrap in several layers of fabric.
– ORIGIN Old English.

sway • v. **1** move slowly and rhythmically backwards and forwards or from side to side. **2** make someone change their opinion: *he's easily swayed.* • n. **1** a swaying movement. **2** power, influence, or control: *different kings held sway in different regions.*
– ORIGIN perh. from German *swājen* 'be blown to and fro' or Dutch *zwaaien* 'swing'.

swear • v. (**swears, swearing, swore**; past part. **sworn**) **1** promise solemnly or on oath. **2** make someone promise to do something: *I am sworn to secrecy.* **3** use offensive or obscene language.
– PHRASES **swear by** informal have great confidence in. **swear someone in** admit someone to a post or job by directing them to take a formal oath. **swear off** informal promise to stop doing or give up.
– ORIGIN Old English.

swear word • n. an offensive or obscene word.

sweat • n. moisture given out through the pores of the skin, especially in reaction to heat, effort, or anxiety. • v. (**sweats, sweating, sweated** or N. Amer. **sweat**) **1** give off sweat. **2** make a great deal of effort: *I've sweated over this for six months.* **3** be very anxious. **4** (of a substance) give off moisture. **5** cook chopped vegetables slowly with a small amount of fat.
– PHRASES **break sweat** informal make a great physical effort. **no sweat** informal no problem.
– ORIGIN Old English.

sweatband • n. a band of absorbent material worn to soak up sweat.

sweater • n. a pullover with long sleeves.

sweatpants • pl. n. loose, warm trousers with an elasticated or drawstring waist.

sweatshirt • n. a loose knitted cotton sweater.

sweatshop • n. a factory or workshop employing workers for long hours in poor conditions.

sweaty • adj. (**sweatier, sweatiest**) soaked in or causing sweat.
– DERIVATIVES **sweatily** adv.

swede • n. **1** (**Swede**) a person from Sweden. **2** Brit. a round yellow root vegetable.

Swedish • n. the Scandinavian language of Sweden. • adj. relating to Sweden.

sweep • v. (**sweeps, sweeping, swept**) **1** clean an area by brushing away dirt or litter. **2** move forcefully or quickly. **3** (**sweep something away/aside**) remove or abolish something quickly and suddenly. **4** search an area. **5** affect swiftly and widely: *violence swept the country.* • n. **1** an act of sweeping. **2** a long, swift curving movement. **3** a long curved stretch of road, river, etc. **4** the range of something. **5** (also **chimney sweep**) a person whose job is cleaning out the soot from chimneys.
– PHRASES **sweep the board** win every event or prize in a contest.
– ORIGIN Old English.

sweeper • n. **1** a person or device that cleans by sweeping. **2** Football a player stationed behind the other defenders, free to defend at any point across the field.

sweeping • adj. **1** extending or performed in a long, continuous curve. **2** wide in range or effect. **3** (of a statement) too general. • n. (**sweepings**) dirt or refuse collected by sweeping.

sweepstake (also **sweepstakes**) • n. a form of gambling in which the winner receives all the money bet by the other participants.

sweet • adj. **1** having the pleasant taste of sugar or honey. **2** having a pleasant smell. **3** (of air, water, etc.) fresh and pure. **4** kind and thoughtful. **5** pleasant or satisfying. **6** charming and endearing: *a sweet little cat.* • n. Brit. **1** a small piece of confectionery made with sugar. **2** a sweet dish forming a course of a meal.
– DERIVATIVES **sweetly** adv.
– ORIGIN Old English.

sweet-and-sour • adj. cooked with sugar and either vinegar or lemon.

sweetbread • n. the thymus gland or pancreas of an animal, used for food.

sweetcorn • n. a variety of maize with sweet kernels that are eaten as a vegetable.

S

sweeten • v. **1** make or become sweet or sweeter. **2** make more pleasant or acceptable.

sweetener • n. **1** a substance used to sweeten food or drink. **2** informal a bribe.

sweetheart • n. a person who is in love with someone.

sweetie • n. informal **1** Brit. a sweet. **2** used as a term of affection.

sweetmeat • n. old use a sweet or item of sweet food.

sweetness • n. the quality of being sweet.
– PHRASES **sweetness and light** pleasantness or harmony.

sweet pea • n. a climbing plant of the pea family with colourful sweet-smelling flowers.

sweet pepper • n. a large variety of pepper with a mild or sweet flavour.

sweet potato • n. the edible tuber of a tropical climbing plant, with pinkish-orange flesh.

sweet-talk • v. informal use charm or flattery to persuade someone to do something.

sweet tooth • n. a great liking for sweet foods.

sweet william • n. a sweet-smelling plant with clusters of vivid red, pink, or white flowers.

swell • v. (**swells, swelling, swelled**, past part. **swollen** or **swelled**) **1** become larger or rounder in size. **2** increase in strength, amount, or volume. • n. **1** a full or gently rounded form. **2** a gradual increase in sound, amount, or strength. **3** a slow, regular movement of the sea in rolling waves that do not break. • adj. N. Amer. informal, dated excellent.
– ORIGIN Old English.

swelling • n. a place on the body that has swollen as a result of illness or an injury.

swelter • v. (**swelters, sweltering, sweltered**) be uncomfortably hot.
– ORIGIN Germanic.

swept past and past part. of SWEEP.

swerve • v. (**swerves, swerving, swerved**) abruptly go off from a straight course. • n. an abrupt change of course.
– ORIGIN Old English, 'leave, turn aside'.

swift • adj. **1** happening quickly or promptly. **2** moving or capable of moving at high speed. • n. a fast-flying bird with long, slender wings.
– DERIVATIVES **swiftly** adv. **swiftness** n.
– ORIGIN Old English.

swig informal • v. (**swigs, swigging, swigged**) drink quickly. • n. a swift drink.

swill • v. Brit. **1** rinse out with large amounts of water. **2** (of liquid) swirl round in a container or cavity. • n. waste food mixed with water for feeding to pigs.
– ORIGIN Old English.

swim • v. (**swims, swimming, swam**; past part. **swum**) **1** propel yourself through water by moving the arms and legs. **2** be immersed in or covered with liquid. **3** experience a dizzily confusing feeling. • n. a period of swimming.
– PHRASES **in the swim** involved in current events.
– DERIVATIVES **swimmer** n.
– ORIGIN Old English.

swimming costume • n. Brit. a woman's one-piece swimsuit.

swimmingly • adv. informal smoothly and satisfactorily.

swimming pool • n. an artificial pool for swimming in.

swimming trunks • pl. n. shorts worn by men for swimming.

swimsuit • n. a woman's one-piece swimming costume.

swimwear • n. clothing worn for swimming.

swindle • v. (**swindles, swindling, swindled**) use deception to obtain money or possessions from someone. • n. a scheme designed to obtain money dishonestly.
– DERIVATIVES **swindler** n.
– ORIGIN German *schwindeln* 'tell lies'.

swine • n. **1** (pl. **swine**) esp. formal or N. Amer. a pig. **2** (pl. **swine** or **swines**) informal an unpleasant person.
– DERIVATIVES **swinish** adj.
– ORIGIN Old English.

swing • v. (**swings, swinging, swung**) **1** move back and forth or from side to side while hanging. **2** move by grasping a support and leaping. **3** move in a smooth, curving line. **4** (**swing at**) attempt to hit someone. **5** change from one opinion, mood, or situation to another. **6** have a decisive influence on a vote or decision. **7** informal succeed in bringing about: *we might be able to swing something.* • n. **1** a seat hanging from ropes or chains, on which someone can sit and swing. **2** an act of swinging. **3** a clear change in public opinion. **4** a style of jazz or dance music with an easy flowing rhythm.
– PHRASES **get into the swing of things** Brit. informal become used to an activity. **in full swing** at the height of activity.
– DERIVATIVES **swinger** n. **swingy** adj.
– ORIGIN Old English, 'to beat, whip'.

swingboat • n. esp. Brit. a boat-shaped swing seating several people, found at fairs.

swing door • n. a door that can be

opened in either direction and swings back when released.

swingeing /swin-jing/ •adj. Brit. severe or otherwise extreme: *swingeing cuts in expenditure.*
– ORIGIN Old English, 'shatter'.

swinging •adj. informal lively, exciting, and fashionable.

swipe informal •v. (**swipes, swiping, swiped**) **1** hit or try to hit with a swinging blow. **2** steal something. **3** pass a swipe card through an electronic reader. •n. **1** a sweeping blow. **2** a verbal attack.
– ORIGIN perh. from SWEEP.

swipe card •n. a plastic card carrying coded information which is read when the card is slid through an electronic device.

swirl •v. move in a twisting or spiralling pattern. •n. a swirling movement or pattern.
– DERIVATIVES **swirly** adj.
– ORIGIN perh. German or Dutch.

swish •v. move with a soft rushing sound. •n. a soft rushing sound or movement. •adj. Brit. informal impressively smart.

Swiss •adj. relating to Switzerland or its people. •n. (pl. **Swiss**) a person from Switzerland.

Swiss roll •n. Brit. a flat rectangular sponge cake spread with jam or cream and rolled up.

switch •n. **1** a device for making and breaking an electrical connection. **2** a change from one thing to another. **3** a flexible shoot cut from a tree. •v. **1** change in position, direction, or focus. **2** exchange one thing for another. **3** (**switch something off/on**) turn an electrical connection off or on. **4** (**switch off**) informal stop paying attention.
– DERIVATIVES **switcher** n.
– ORIGIN prob. from German.

switchback •n. **1** Brit. a road with alternate sharp ascents and descents. **2** a roller coaster.

switchblade •n. N. Amer. a flick knife.

switchboard •n. a device for routing telephone calls within an organization.

switched-on •adj. Brit. informal aware of what is going on or what is up to date.

swivel •v. (**swivels, swivelling, swivelled**; US **swivels, swiveling, swiveled**) turn round, or around a central point. •n. a connecting device between two parts enabling one to revolve without turning the other.
– ORIGIN Old English, 'move, sweep'.

swizz •n. Brit. informal a disappointment or minor swindle.
– ORIGIN prob. from SWINDLE.

swizzle stick •n. a stick used for frothing up or taking the fizz out of drinks.

swollen past part. of SWELL.

swoon literary •v. faint from extreme emotion. •n. an instance of fainting.
– ORIGIN Old English, 'overcome'.

swoop •v. **1** move rapidly downwards through the air. **2** carry out a sudden raid. •n. an act of swooping.
– PHRASES **at** (or **in**) **one fell swoop** see FELL⁴.
– ORIGIN perh. from SWEEP.

swop •v. & n. var. of SWAP.

sword •n. **1** a weapon with a long metal blade and a handle, used for thrusting or striking. **2** (**the sword**) literary military power; violence.
– PHRASES **put someone to the sword** kill someone in war.
– ORIGIN Old English.

swordfish •n. (pl. **swordfish** or **swordfishes**) a large sea fish with a sword-like snout.

swordplay •n. fencing with swords or foils.

swordsman •n. (pl. **swordsmen**) a man who fights with a sword.

swore past of SWEAR.

sworn past part. of SWEAR. •adj. **1** given under oath. **2** determined to remain the specified thing: *sworn enemies.*

swot Brit. informal •v. (**swots, swotting, swotted**) (also **swot up**) study hard. •n. derog. a person who spends a lot of time studying.
– DERIVATIVES **swotty** adj.
– ORIGIN from SWEAT.

swum past part. of SWIM.

swung past and past part. of SWING.

sybarite /si-buh-ryt/ •n. a person who is very fond of luxury and pleasure.
– DERIVATIVES **sybaritic** adj.
– ORIGIN first referring to a person from *Sybaris,* an ancient Greek city in Italy.

sycamore •n. **1** a European tree of the maple family. **2** N. Amer. a plane tree.
– ORIGIN Greek *sukomoros.*

sycophant /si-kuh-fant/ •n. a person who flatters someone important to try to gain favour with them.
– DERIVATIVES **sycophancy** n. **sycophantic** adj.
– ORIGIN Greek *sukophantēs* 'informer'.

syllabic /si-lab-ik/ •adj. relating to or based on syllables.

syllable /si-luh-b'l/ •n. a unit of pronunciation having one vowel sound and forming all or part of a word (e.g. *butter* has two syllables).
– ORIGIN Greek *sullabē.*

syllabub /sil-uh-bub/ •n. a whipped cream dessert, typically flavoured with white wine or sherry.

syllabus /sil-uh-buhss/ •n. (pl. **syllabuses** or **syllabi** /sil-luh-by/) the subjects in a course of study or teaching.
– ORIGIN Latin.

syllogism /si-luh-ji-z'm/ •n. a form of reasoning in which a conclusion is drawn from two propositions (e.g. *all dogs are animals; all animals have four legs; therefore all dogs have four legs*).
– ORIGIN Greek *sullogismos*.

sylph /silf/ •n. 1 an imaginary spirit of the air. 2 a slender woman or girl.
– ORIGIN Latin *sylphes* (plural).

sylvan •adj. literary relating to woods; wooded: *a sylvan setting*.
– ORIGIN Latin *silva* 'a wood'.

symbiosis /sim-by-oh-siss/ •n. (pl. **symbioses** /sim-by-oh-seez/) Biol. a situation in which two different organisms live with and are dependent on each other, to the advantage of both.
– DERIVATIVES **symbiotic** /sim-by-ot-ik/ adj.
– ORIGIN Greek *sumbiôsis*.

symbol •n. 1 a thing or person that represents something else: *the limousine was a symbol of his wealth*. 2 a sign, letter, or mark that has a fixed meaning, especially in music, science, or mathematics.
– ORIGIN Greek *sumbolon* 'mark, token'.

symbolic •adj. 1 acting as a symbol. 2 involving the use of symbols or symbolism.
– DERIVATIVES **symbolically** adv.

symbolism •n. the use of symbols to represent ideas or qualities.
– DERIVATIVES **symbolist** n. & adj.

symbolize (or **symbolise**)
•v. (**symbolizes, symbolizing, symbolized**) 1 be a symbol of. 2 represent by means of symbols.

symmetrical •adj. made up of exactly similar parts facing each other or around an axis; showing symmetry.
– DERIVATIVES **symmetric** adj. **symmetrically** adv.

symmetry /sim-mi-tri/ •n. (pl. **symmetries**) 1 the quality of being made up of exactly similar parts facing each other or around an axis. 2 the quality of being the same or very similar.
– ORIGIN Latin *symmetria*.

☑ Remember that **symmetry** has a double **m** in the middle.

sympathetic •adj. 1 showing kindness or understanding. 2 showing approval of an idea or action. 3 pleasing or likeable.

4 referring to the part of the nervous system supplying the internal organs, blood vessels, and glands.
– DERIVATIVES **sympathetically** adv.

sympathize (or **sympathise**)
•v. (**sympathizes, sympathizing, sympathized**) 1 feel or express sympathy. 2 support an opinion or political movement.
– DERIVATIVES **sympathizer** n.

sympathy •n. (pl. **sympathies**) 1 the feeling of being sorry for someone. 2 understanding between people. 3 support for or approval of something.
– PHRASES **in sympathy** in keeping; in harmony.
– ORIGIN Greek *sumpatheia*.

symphonic •adj. relating to or having the form of a symphony.

symphony •n. (pl. **symphonies**) a musical composition for a full orchestra, typically in four movements.
– ORIGIN Greek *sumphônia*.

symphony orchestra •n. a large classical orchestra, including string, woodwind, brass, and percussion instruments.

symposium /sim-poh-zi-uhm/ •n. (pl. **symposia** /sim-poh-zi-uh/ or **symposiums**) a conference to discuss a particular academic subject.
– ORIGIN Greek *sumposion*.

symptom •n. 1 a change in the body or mind which is the sign of a disease. 2 a sign of an undesirable situation.
– ORIGIN Greek *sumptôma*.

symptomatic •adj. acting as a symptom or sign of something.
– DERIVATIVES **symptomatically** adv.

syn- (also **sym-** before *b*, *m*, and *p*; **syl-** before *l*) •prefix united: *syndrome*.
– ORIGIN Greek *sun* 'with'.

synagogue /sin-uh-gog/ •n. a building where Jewish people meet for religious worship and instruction.
– ORIGIN Greek *sunagôgê* 'meeting'.

synapse /sy-naps, si-naps/ •n. a gap between two nerve cells, across which impulses are conducted.
– DERIVATIVES **synaptic** adj.
– ORIGIN Greek *sunapsis*.

sync (also **synch**) •n. informal synchronization.
– PHRASES **in** (or **out of**) **sync** working well (or badly) together.

synchromesh •n. a system of gear changing in which the gearwheels are made to revolve at the same speed during engagement.

synchronicity /sing-kruh-nis-it-i/ •n. the occurrence of events at the same time, which appear to be related but have no obvious connection.

S

synchronize (or **synchronise**)
• v. (**synchronizes, synchronizing, synchronized**) cause to happen or operate at the same time or rate.
– DERIVATIVES **synchronization** n. **synchronizer** n.

synchronous /sing-kruh-nuhss/
• adj. existing or occurring at the same time.
– DERIVATIVES **synchronously** adv.
– ORIGIN Greek *sunkhronos*.

synchrony /sing-kruh-ni/ • n. the state of operating or developing at the same rate as something else.

syncline /sing-klyn/ • n. a ridge or fold of rock in which the strata slope upwards from the axis.
– ORIGIN from Greek *klinein* 'to lean'.

syncopated /sing-kuh-payt-id/ • adj. (of music or a rhythm) having the beats or accents altered so that strong beats become weak and vice versa.
– DERIVATIVES **syncopation** n.
– ORIGIN from Greek *sunkopē* 'a cutting off'.

syncretism /sing-kri-ti-z'm/ • n. the combining of different religions, cultures, or ways of thinking.
– DERIVATIVES **syncretic** adj.
– ORIGIN Greek *sunkrētizein* 'unite against a third party'.

syndicate • n. /sin-di-kuht/ a group of people or organizations that combine to promote a common interest. • v. /sin-di-kayt/ (**syndicates, syndicating, syndicated**) 1 control or manage by a syndicate. 2 sell an article or photograph to be published in several different newspapers.
– DERIVATIVES **syndication** n.

syndrome • n. 1 a group of medical symptoms which consistently occur together. 2 a set of opinions or behaviour that is typical of a particular group of people.
– ORIGIN Greek *sundromē*.

synecdoche /si-nek-duh-ki/ • n. a figure of speech in which a part is made to represent the whole or vice versa, as in *England lost by six wickets* (meaning 'the English cricket team').
– ORIGIN Greek *sunekdokhē*.

synergy /sin-er-ji/ (also **synergism**)
• n. cooperation of two or more people or things to produce a combined effect greater than the sum of their separate effects.
– ORIGIN Greek *sunergos* 'working together'.

synod /si-nod/ • n. an official meeting of the ministers and other members of a Christian Church.
– ORIGIN Greek *sunodos* 'meeting'.

synonym /sin-uh-nim/ • n. a word or phrase that means the same as another word or phrase in the same language.
– ORIGIN Greek *sunōnumon*.

synonymous /si-non-i-muhss/
• adj. 1 (of a word or phrase) having the same meaning as another word or phrase in the same language. 2 closely associated with something: *his name was synonymous with victory.*
– DERIVATIVES **synonymously** adv.

synopsis /si-nop-siss/ • n. (pl. **synopses** /si-nop-seez/) a brief summary or outline.
– ORIGIN Greek.

synoptic • adj. 1 relating to a synopsis. 2 (**Synoptic**) referring to the Gospels of Matthew, Mark, and Luke, which describe events from a similar point of view.

synovial /sy-noh-vi-uhl/ • adj. relating to a type of joint in the body that is enclosed in a flexible membrane which contains a lubricating fluid.
– ORIGIN Latin *synovia*.

syntax • n. 1 the arrangement of words and phrases to create sentences. 2 a set of rules for the formation of sentences.
– DERIVATIVES **syntactic** adj. **syntactical** adj.
– ORIGIN Greek *suntaxis*.

synthesis /sin-thuh-siss/ • n. (pl. **syntheses** /sin-thuh-seez/) 1 the combination of parts to form a connected whole. 2 the production of chemical compounds by reaction from simpler materials.
– ORIGIN Greek *sunthesis*.

synthesize /sin-thuh-syz/ (or **synthesise**) • v. (**synthesizes, synthesizing, synthesized**) 1 make by chemical synthesis. 2 combine parts into an organized whole. 3 produce sound with a synthesizer.

synthesizer (or **synthesiser**) • n. an electronic musical instrument that produces sounds by generating and combining signals of different frequencies.

synthetic /sin-thet-ik/ • adj. 1 made by chemical synthesis, especially to imitate a natural product: *synthetic rubber.* 2 not genuine; insincere. • n. a synthetic material.
– DERIVATIVES **synthetically** adv.

syphilis /si-fi-liss/ • n. a serious sexually transmitted disease spread by bacteria.
– DERIVATIVES **syphilitic** adj. & n.
– ORIGIN Latin.

syphon • n. & v. var. of SIPHON.

Syrian • n. a person from Syria.
• adj. relating to Syria.

syringe /si-rinj/ • n. a tube with a nozzle

and piston for sucking in and forcing out liquid in a thin stream, often one fitted with a hollow needle for injecting drugs or withdrawing bodily fluids.
• v. (**syringes, syringing, syringed**) spray liquid into or over something with a syringe.
– ORIGIN Latin *syringa*.

syrup (US also **sirup**) • n. **1** a thick sweet liquid made by dissolving sugar in boiling water. **2** a thick sweet liquid containing medicine or used as a drink: *cough syrup*.
– ORIGIN Arabic, 'beverage'.

syrupy (US also **sirupy**) • adj. **1** thick or sweet, like syrup. **2** excessively sentimental.

system • n. **1** a set of things working together as a mechanism or network. **2** a person's body. **3** Computing a group of related hardware units or programs or both. **4** an organized scheme or method. **5** the state of being well organized.

6 (**the system**) the laws and rules that control society.
– ORIGIN Greek *sustēma*.

systematic • adj. done or acting according to a system; methodical.
– DERIVATIVES **systematically** adv.

systematize (or **systematise**)
• v. (**systematizes, systematizing, systematized**) arrange things according to an organized system.
– DERIVATIVES **systematization** n.

systemic /si-stem-ik, si-steem-ik/
• adj. relating to a system as a whole.

systems analyst • n. a person who studies a complex process or operation in order to improve its efficiency.

systole /siss-tuh-li/ • n. the phase of the heartbeat when the heart muscle contracts and pumps blood into the arteries.
– DERIVATIVES **systolic** /si-stol-lik/ adj.
– ORIGIN Greek *sustolē*.

Tt

T (also **t**) • n. (pl. **Ts** or **T's**) the twentieth letter of the alphabet.
– PHRASES **to a T** informal to perfection.

t • abbrev. ton(s).

TA • abbrev. (in the UK) Territorial Army.

Ta • symb. the chemical element tantalum.

ta • exclam. Brit. informal thank you.

tab¹ • n. **1** a small flap or strip of material attached to something. **2** informal, esp. N. Amer. a restaurant bill. **3** N. Amer. a ring pull.
– PHRASES **keep tabs on** informal monitor the activities of. **pick up the tab** informal pay for something.
– ORIGIN perh. from TAG¹.

tab² • n. = TABULATOR. • v. (**tabs**, **tabbing**, **tabbed**) = TABULATE.

tab³ • n. informal a tablet containing an illicit drug.

tabard /tab-erd, tab-ard/ • n. a sleeveless jacket consisting only of front and back pieces with a hole for the head.
– ORIGIN Old French tabart.

tabby • n. (pl. **tabbies**) a grey or brownish cat with dark stripes.
– ORIGIN French tabis 'striped silk taffeta'.

tabernacle /tab-er-na-k'l/ • n. **1** (in the Bible) a tent used by the Israelites to house the Ark of the Covenant during the Exodus. **2** a Mormon or Nonconformist place of worship.
– ORIGIN Latin tabernaculum 'tent'.

tabla /tab-luh, tub-luh/ • n. a pair of small hand drums fixed together, used in Indian music.
– ORIGIN Arabic, 'drum'.

table • n. **1** a piece of furniture with a flat top supported by legs, for eating, writing, or working at. **2** a set of facts or figures displayed in rows or columns. **3** (**tables**) multiplication tables. • v. (**tables**, **tabling**, **tabled**) Brit. formally present something for discussion at a meeting.
– PHRASES **on the table** available for discussion. **turn the tables** reverse a situation to your own advantage.

– ORIGIN Latin tabula 'tablet, list'.

tableau /tab-loh/ • n. (pl. **tableaux** or **tableaus** /tab-lohz/) a group of models or motionless figures representing a scene.
– ORIGIN French, 'picture'.

tablecloth • n. a cloth spread over a table.

table d'hôte /tah-bluh doht/ • n. a restaurant menu or meal offered at a fixed price and with limited choices.
– ORIGIN French, 'host's table'.

tableland • n. a broad, high, level region; a plateau.

table manners • pl. n. behaviour that is considered polite while eating at a table.

tablespoon • n. **1** a large spoon for serving food. **2** the amount held by a tablespoon, in the UK considered to be 15 millilitres.
– DERIVATIVES **tablespoonful** n.

tablet • n. **1** a slab of stone, clay, or wood on which an inscription is written. **2** esp. Brit. a pill.
– ORIGIN Old French tablete.

table tennis • n. a game played with small bats and a small, hollow ball hit across a table divided by a net.

tableware • n. crockery, cutlery, and glassware used for serving and eating meals.

table wine • n. wine of moderate quality considered suitable for drinking with a meal.

tabloid • n. a newspaper having pages half the size of those of a broadsheet, written in a popular style.
– DERIVATIVES **tabloidization** (or **tabloidisation**) n.
– ORIGIN first referring to a tablet of medicine; the current sense reflects the idea of information being presented in a form that is easily digested.

taboo • n. (pl. **taboos**) a social or religious custom placing a ban or restriction on a particular thing or person. • adj. banned or restricted by social custom: *sex was a taboo subject*.

– ORIGIN Tongan, 'forbidden'.

tabular /tab-yuu-ler/ •adj. (of data) made up of or presented in columns or tables.
– ORIGIN Latin *tabularis*.

tabulate /tab-yuu-layt/ •v. (**tabulates, tabulating, tabulated**) arrange data in the form of columns or tables.
– DERIVATIVES **tabulation** n.

tabulator •n. a facility in a word-processing program, or a device on a typewriter, for advancing to set positions in order to produce columns or tables.

tachograph /tak-uh-grahf/ •n. a tachometer used in commercial road vehicles to provide a record of vehicle speed over a period.
– ORIGIN Greek *takhos* 'speed'.

tachometer /ta-kom-i-ter/ •n. an instrument which measures the working speed of an engine.

tachycardia /ta-ki-kar-di-uh/ •n. an abnormally rapid heart rate.
– ORIGIN from Greek *takhus* 'swift' + *kardia* 'heart'.

tacit /ta-sit/ •adj. understood or meant without being stated: *tacit agreement.*
– DERIVATIVES **tacitly** adv.
– ORIGIN Latin *tacitus* 'silent'.

taciturn /ta-si-tern/ •adj. saying little.
– DERIVATIVES **taciturnity** n.
– ORIGIN Latin *taciturnus*.

tack[1] •n. 1 a small broad-headed nail. 2 N. Amer. a drawing pin. 3 a long stitch used to fasten fabrics together temporarily. 4 a course of action. 5 Sailing an act of tacking. •v. 1 fasten or fix with tacks. 2 (**tack something on**) add something to something already existing. 3 change the direction of a sailing boat so that the wind blows into the sails from the opposite side.
– ORIGIN prob. from Old French *tache* 'clasp, large nail'.

tack[2] •n. equipment used in horse riding.
– ORIGIN from **TACKLE**.

tack[3] •n. informal cheap, shoddy, or tasteless material.
– ORIGIN from **TACKY**[2].

tackle •n. 1 the equipment needed for a task or sport. 2 a mechanism consisting of ropes, pulley blocks, and hooks for lifting heavy objects. 3 (in sport) an act of tackling an opponent. •v. (**tackles, tackling, tackled**) 1 make an effort to deal with a difficult task. 2 begin to talk to someone about a difficult issue. 3 (in football, hockey, rugby, etc.) try to take the ball from or prevent the movement of an opponent.
– DERIVATIVES **tackler** n.
– ORIGIN prob. from German *takel*.

tacky[1] •adj. (**tackier, tackiest**) (of glue, paint, etc.) slightly sticky because not fully dry.

tacky[2] •adj. (**tackier, tackiest**) informal showing poor taste and quality.
– DERIVATIVES **tackiness** n.

taco /ta-koh, tah-koh/ •n. (pl. **tacos**) (in Mexican cookery) a folded tortilla filled with spicy meat or beans.
– ORIGIN Spanish, 'plug, wad'.

tact •n. sensitivity and skill in dealing with other people or with difficult issues.
– ORIGIN Latin *tactus* 'touch, sense of touch'.

tactful •adj. having or showing tact.
– DERIVATIVES **tactfully** adv.

tactic •n. 1 an action or plan that is intended to achieve something. 2 (**tactics**) the art of directing and organizing the movement of armed forces and equipment during a war. Often contrasted with **STRATEGY**.
– DERIVATIVES **tactician** n.
– ORIGIN from Greek *taktikē tekhnē* 'art of tactics'.

tactical •adj. 1 done or planned to achieve a particular end. 2 (of weapons) for use in direct support of military or naval operations. Often contrasted with **STRATEGIC**. 3 Brit. (of voting) aimed at preventing the strongest candidate from winning by supporting the next strongest, regardless of your true political preference.
– DERIVATIVES **tactically** adv.

tactile •adj. 1 relating to the sense of touch. 2 liking to touch other people in a friendly way.
– ORIGIN Latin *tactilis*.

tactless •adj. showing a lack of tact; thoughtless and insensitive.
– DERIVATIVES **tactlessly** adv. **tactlessness** n.

tad informal •adv. (**a tad**) to a small extent. •n. a small amount.
– ORIGIN perh. from **TADPOLE**.

tadpole •n. the larva of a frog or toad, at the stage when it lives in water and has gills and a tail.
– ORIGIN from an Old English word meaning 'toad' + **POLL**.

tae kwon do /ty kwon doh/ •n. a modern Korean martial art similar to karate.
– ORIGIN Korean, 'art of hand and foot fighting'.

taffeta /taf-fi-tuh/ •n. a fine shiny silk or similar synthetic fabric.
– ORIGIN Latin.

taffrail •n. a rail round a ship's stern.

– ORIGIN Dutch *tafereel*.

Taffy (also **Taff**) • n. (pl. **Taffies**) Brit. informal, usu. offens. a Welshman.
– ORIGIN representing a supposed Welsh pronunciation of the man's name *Davy* or *David* (Welsh *Dafydd*).

tag[1] • n. **1** a label identifying something or giving information about it. **2** an electronic device attached to someone to monitor their movements. **3** a nickname or description by which someone or something is widely known. **4** a nickname or other identifying mark written as the signature of a graffiti artist. **5** a frequently repeated quotation or phrase. **6** a metal or plastic point at the end of a shoelace. • v. (**tags, tagging, tagged**) **1** attach a tag to. **2** (**tag something on/to**) add something to the end of something else as an after-thought. **3** (**tag along/on**) accompany someone without being invited. **4** (of a graffiti artist) write a tag or nickname on a surface.

tag[2] • n. a children's game in which one player chases the rest, and anyone who is caught then becomes the person doing the chasing.
– ORIGIN perh. from TIG.

tagliatelle /tal-yuh-tel-li/ • pl. n. pasta in narrow ribbons.
– ORIGIN Italian.

tag wrestling • n. a form of wrestling involving pairs of wrestlers who fight as a team, each taking turns in the ring.

tahini /tah-hee-ni/ • n. a Middle Eastern paste or spread made from ground sesame seeds.
– ORIGIN modern Greek *takhini*.

Tahitian /tah-hee-shuhn/ • n. **1** a person from Tahiti. **2** the language of Tahiti. • adj. relating to Tahiti.

t'ai chi /ty chee/ (also **t'ai chi ch'uan** /ty chee chwahn/) • n. a Chinese martial art and system of exercises, consisting of sequences of very slow controlled movements.
– ORIGIN Chinese, 'great ultimate boxing'.

taiga /ty-guh/ • n. swampy coniferous forest of high northern latitudes, especially that between the tundra and steppes of Siberia.
– ORIGIN Mongolian.

tail • n. **1** the part at the rear of an animal that sticks out from the rest of the body. **2** something resembling an animal's tail in shape or position. **3** the rear part of an aircraft, with the tailplane and rudder. **4** the final, more distant, or weaker part: *the tail of a hurricane.* **5** (**tails**) the side of a coin without the image of a head on it. **6** (**tails**) informal a tailcoat. **7** informal a person secretly following another to

observe their movements. • v. **1** informal secretly follow and observe. **2** (**tail off/away**) gradually become smaller or weaker. **3** (**tail back**) Brit. (of traffic) become congested and form a long stationary queue.
– PHRASES **on someone's tail** informal following someone closely. **with your tail between your legs** informal dejected or humiliated.
– DERIVATIVES **tailless** adj.
– ORIGIN Old English.

tailback • n. Brit. a long queue of traffic extending back from a busy junction or other obstruction.

tailcoat • n. Brit. a man's formal coat, with a long skirt divided at the back into tails and cut away in front.

tail end • n. the last part of something.

tail fin • n. **1** a fin at the rear of a fish's body. **2** a projecting vertical surface on the tail of an aircraft, providing stability.

tailgate • n. **1** a hinged flap at the back of a lorry. **2** the door at the back of an estate or hatchback car.

tailor • n. a person who makes men's clothing for individual customers. • v. **1** make clothes to fit individual customers. **2** make or adapt for a particular purpose or person.
– ORIGIN Old French *taillour* 'cutter'.

tailored • adj. (of clothes) smart, fitted, and well cut.

tailoring • n. **1** the activity or occupation of a tailor. **2** the style or cut of a garment or garments.

tailor-made • adj. made or adapted for a particular purpose or person.

tailpiece • n. a part added to the end of a piece of writing.

tailplane • n. Brit. a small wing at the tail of an aircraft.

tailspin • n. a fast revolving motion made by a rapidly descending aircraft.

tailwind • n. a wind blowing from behind a vehicle or aircraft.

taint • v. **1** contaminate or pollute. **2** affect with an undesirable quality: *his reputation was tainted by scandal.* • n. a trace of an undesirable quality or substance.
– ORIGIN Old French *teint* 'tinged'.

Taiwanese /ty-wuh-neez/ • n. (pl. **Taiwanese**) a person from Taiwan. • adj. relating to Taiwan.

take • v. (**takes, taking, took**; past part. **taken**) **1** reach for and hold. **2** occupy a place or position. **3** gain possession of by force. **4** carry or bring with you. **5** remove from a place. **6** subtract.

7 consume as food, drink, medicine, or drugs. **8** bring into a particular state: *the invasion took Europe to the brink of war.* **9** experience or be affected by: *the lad took a savage beating.* **10** use as a route or a means of transport. **11** accept or receive. **12** require or use up. **13** hold: *the hotel takes just 20 guests.* **14** act on an opportunity. **15** see or deal with in a particular way: *he took it as an insult.* **16** tolerate: *I can't take it any more.* **17** undertake or perform an action or task. **18** study a subject. **19** do an exam or test. **20** make a photograph with a camera. • n. **1** a sequence of sound or part of a film photographed or recorded continuously. **2** a particular version of or approach to something: *his whimsical take on life.* **3** an amount gained from one source or in one session.
– PHRASES **take after** resemble a parent or ancestor. **take something as read** Brit. assume something. **take something back** withdraw a statement. **take someone in** cheat or deceive someone. **take something in 1** make a garment tighter by altering its seams. **2** encompass or understand something. **take someone/thing in hand 1** undertake to control or reform someone. **2** start dealing with a task. **take it out of** exhaust someone. **take off 1** become airborne. **2** leave hastily. **take someone/thing off 1** remove clothing. **2** informal mimic someone. **take someone/thing on 1** engage someone as an employee. **2** undertake a task. **3** begin to have a particular meaning or quality. **take something out on** relieve your frustration or anger by treating someone badly. **take over** assume control of or responsibility for something. **take your time** not hurry. **take to 1** get into the habit of. **2** start to like or develop an ability for. **3** go to a place to escape danger. **take something up 1** become interested in a pursuit. **2** occupy time, space, or attention. **3** pursue a matter further. **take someone up on** accept an offer or challenge from someone. **take up with** begin to associate with.
– DERIVATIVES **taker** n.
– ORIGIN Old Norse.

takeaway • n. Brit. **1** a restaurant or shop selling cooked food to be eaten elsewhere. **2** a meal of such food.

take-home pay • n. an employee's wages or salary after the tax and insurance have been taken out.

take-off • n. **1** the action of becoming airborne. **2** informal an act of mimicking someone or something.

takeout • n. N. Amer. a takeaway.

takeover • n. an act of taking control of something such as a company from someone else.

taking • n. (**takings**) the amount of money earned by a business from the sale of goods or services.
– PHRASES **for the taking** available to take advantage of.

talc • n. **1** talcum powder. **2** a soft mineral that is a form of magnesium silicate.

talcum powder • n. the mineral talc in powdered form used on the skin to make it feel smooth and dry.
– ORIGIN Latin.

tale • n. **1** a story. **2** a lie.
– ORIGIN Old English.

talent • n. **1** natural ability or skill. **2** people possessing natural ability or skill. **3** Brit. informal people seen in terms of their sexual attractiveness. **4** an ancient weight and unit of currency.
– DERIVATIVES **talented** adj. **talentless** adj.
– ORIGIN Greek *talanton* 'weight, sum of money': sense 1 comes from the parable of the talents (Gospel of Matthew, chapter 25).

talent scout • n. a person whose job is searching for talented performers.

talisman /tal-iz-muhn/ • n. (pl. **talismans**) an object thought to have magic powers and to bring good luck.
– DERIVATIVES **talismanic** /tal-iz-**man**-ik/ adj.
– ORIGIN Arabic.

talk • v. **1** speak in order to give information or express ideas or feelings. **2** be able to speak. **3** (**talk something over/through**) discuss something thoroughly. **4** (**talk back**) reply in a defiant or cheeky way. **5** (**talk down to**) speak to someone in a way that suggests you feel superior to them. **6** (**talk someone round**) persuade someone to accept or agree to something. **7** (**talk someone into/out of**) convince someone to do or not to do something. **8** reveal secret information.
• n. **1** conversation. **2** a speech or lecture. **3** (**talks**) formal discussions. **4** rumour or gossip.
– DERIVATIVES **talker** n.
– ORIGIN from TALE or TELL.

talkative • adj. fond of talking.

talking point • n. a topic that causes discussion or argument.

talking-to • n. informal a sharp reprimand.

talk show • n. a chat show.

tall • adj. **1** of great or more than average height. **2** measuring a specified distance from top to bottom.
– PHRASES **a tall order** an unreasonable or difficult demand. **tall story** (or **tale**) an account of something that is difficult to

believe and seems unlikely to be true.
– DERIVATIVES **tallish** adj. **tallness** n.
– ORIGIN prob. from Old English, 'swift, prompt'.

tallboy •n. Brit. a tall chest of drawers in two sections, one standing on the other.

tallow /tal-loh/ •n. a hard substance made from animal fat, used (especially in the past) in making candles and soap.
– ORIGIN perh. from German.

tall ship •n. a sailing ship with a high mast or masts.

tally •n. (pl. **tallies**) 1 a current score or amount. 2 a record of a score or amount. 3 (also **tally stick**) hist. a piece of wood marked with notches as a record of the items in an account. •v. (**tallies, tallying, tallied**) 1 agree or correspond. 2 calculate the total number of.
– ORIGIN Old French *tallie*.

tally-ho •exclam. a huntsman's cry to the hounds on sighting a fox.
– ORIGIN prob. from French *taïaut*.

Talmud /tal-muud/ •n. a collection of ancient writings on Jewish civil and ceremonial law and legend.
– DERIVATIVES **Talmudic** adj.
– ORIGIN Hebrew, 'instruction'.

talon •n. a claw of a bird of prey.
– ORIGIN Old French, 'heel'.

talus /tay-luhss/ •n. (pl. **tali** /tay-ly/) the bone in the ankle that forms a movable joint with the shin bone.
– ORIGIN Latin, 'ankle, heel'.

tamarind /tam-uh-rind/ •n. sticky brown pulp obtained from the pod of a tropical African tree, used in Asian cookery.
– ORIGIN Arabic, 'Indian date'.

tamarisk /tam-uh-risk/ •n. a shrub or small tree with tiny scale-like leaves on slender branches.
– ORIGIN Latin *tamariscus*.

tambour /tam-boor/ •n. hist. a small drum.
– ORIGIN French, 'drum'.

tambourine /tam-buh-reen/ •n. a percussion instrument like a shallow drum with metal discs around the edge, played by being shaken or hit with the hand.
– ORIGIN French *tambourin* 'small tambour'.

tame •adj. 1 (of an animal) not dangerous or frightened of people. 2 not exciting, adventurous, or controversial. 3 informal (of a person) willing to cooperate. •v. (**tames, taming, tamed**) 1 make an animal tame. 2 make less powerful and easier to control.
– DERIVATIVES **tamely** adv. **tamer** n.
– ORIGIN Old English.

Tamil •n. 1 a member of a people living in parts of South India and Sri Lanka. 2 the language of the Tamils.

tam-o'-shanter /tam-uh-shan-ter/ •n. a round Scottish cap with a bobble in the centre.
– ORIGIN named after the hero of Robert Burns's poem *Tam o' Shanter*.

tamp •v. firmly ram or pack a substance down or into something.
– ORIGIN prob. from French *tampon* 'tampon, plug'.

tamper •v. (**tampers, tampering, tampered**) (**tamper with**) interfere with something without permission or so as to cause damage.
– ORIGIN from TEMPER.

tampon •n. a plug of soft material put into the vagina to absorb blood during a woman's period.
– ORIGIN French.

tan¹ •n. 1 a yellowish-brown colour. 2 a golden-brown shade of skin developed by pale-skinned people after being in the sun. •v. (**tans, tanning, tanned**) 1 become golden-brown from being in the sun. 2 convert animal skin into leather.
– ORIGIN Old English.

tan² •abbrev. tangent.

tandem •n. a bicycle with seats and pedals for two riders, one behind the other.
– PHRASES **in tandem** 1 alongside each other. 2 one behind another.
– ORIGIN Latin, 'at length'.

tandoor /tan-door, tan-door/ •n. a clay oven of a type used originally in northern India and Pakistan.
– ORIGIN Arabic.

tandoori /tan-door-i/ •adj. (of Indian food) cooked in a tandoor.

tang •n. 1 a strong taste, flavour, or smell. 2 the projection on the blade of a tool by which the blade is held firmly in the handle.
– ORIGIN Old Norse.

tangent /tan-juhnt/ •n. 1 a straight line or plane that touches a curve or curved surface at a point, but if extended does not cross it at that point. 2 Math. the ratio of the sides (other than the hypotenuse) opposite and adjacent to an angle in a right-angled triangle. 3 a completely different line of thought or action: *her mind went off at a tangent*.
– ORIGIN Latin *tangere* 'to touch'.

tangential /tan-jen-sh'l/ •adj. 1 relating to or along a tangent. 2 only slightly connected or relevant.
– DERIVATIVES **tangentially** adv.

tangerine •n. 1 a small citrus fruit with a loose skin. 2 a deep orange-red colour.

– ORIGIN from *Tanger*, the former name of *Tangier* in Morocco.

tangible /tan-ji-b'l/ • adj. **1** able to be perceived by touch. **2** definite or real: *we need tangible results.*
– DERIVATIVES **tangibility** n. **tangibly** adv.
– ORIGIN Latin *tangibilis.*

tangle • v. (**tangles, tangling, tangled**) **1** twist strands into a knotted mass. **2** (**tangle with**) informal become involved in a conflict with. • n. **1** a knotted mass of something twisted together. **2** a muddle.
– ORIGIN prob. Scandinavian.

tango • n. (pl. **tangos**) a Latin American ballroom dance with a strong rhythm and abrupt pauses. • v. (**tangoes, tangoing, tangoed**) dance the tango.
– ORIGIN Latin American Spanish.

tangy • adj. (**tangier, tangiest**) having a strong, sharp flavour or smell.
– DERIVATIVES **tanginess** n.

tank • n. **1** a large container or storage chamber for liquid or gas. **2** the container holding the fuel supply in a motor vehicle. **3** a container with clear sides in which to keep fish. **4** a heavy armoured fighting vehicle carrying guns and moving on a continuous metal track.
– DERIVATIVES **tankful** n.
– ORIGIN perh. from a word in an Indian language meaning 'underground cistern'.

tankard • n. a tall beer mug with a handle and sometimes a hinged lid.
– ORIGIN perh. from Dutch *tanckaert.*

tank engine • n. a steam locomotive carrying fuel and water holders in its own frame, not in a separate wagon.

tanker • n. a ship, road vehicle, or aircraft for carrying liquids in bulk.

tankini /tan-kee-ni/ • n. a women's two-piece swimsuit combining a top half like a tank top with a bikini bottom.

tank top • n. a sleeveless top worn over a shirt or blouse.

tannery • n. (pl. **tanneries**) a place where animal hides are tanned.

tannic acid • n. = TANNIN.

tannin • n. a bitter-tasting substance present in the bark of some trees, and in tea and grapes.
– DERIVATIVES **tannic** adj.
– ORIGIN French *tanin.*

tannoy • n. Brit. trademark a type of public address system.
– ORIGIN from *tantalum alloy*, a substance used in the system.

tantalize (or **tantalise**) • v. (**tantalizes, tantalizing, tantalized**) tease someone by showing or promising them something that they cannot have.

– ORIGIN from *Tantalus* in Greek mythology, who was punished by being provided with fruit and water which moved away when he reached for them.

tantalum /tan-tuh-luhm/ • n. a hard silver-grey metallic chemical element.
– ORIGIN from *Tantalus* (see TANTALIZE).

tantamount • adj. (**tantamount to**) equivalent in seriousness to.
– ORIGIN from Italian *tanto montare* 'amount to as much'.

tantra /tan-truh/ • n. a Hindu or Buddhist piece of writing dealing with mystical or magical practices.
– DERIVATIVES **tantric** adj.
– ORIGIN Sanskrit, 'loom, doctrine'.

tantrum • n. an uncontrolled outburst of anger and frustration.

Tanzanian /tan-zuh-nee-uhn/ • n. a person from Tanzania, a country in East Africa. • adj. relating to Tanzania.

Taoiseach /tee-shuhkh/ • n. the Prime Minister of the Irish Republic.
– ORIGIN Irish, 'chief, leader'.

Taoism /tow-i-z'm/ • n. a Chinese philosophy based on the belief that everything in the universe is connected and that a person should try to balance the opposing principles of yin and yang to reach a calm acceptance of life.
– DERIVATIVES **Taoist** n. & adj.
– ORIGIN Chinese, 'the right way'.

tap[1] • n. **1** a device by which a flow of liquid or gas from a pipe or container can be controlled. **2** a device connected to a telephone for listening secretly to conversations. • v. (**taps, tapping, tapped**) **1** draw liquid through the tap or spout of a cask, barrel, etc. **2** draw sap from a tree by cutting into it. **3** take some of a supply. **4** connect a device to a telephone so as to listen to conversations secretly.
– PHRASES **on tap** informal freely available whenever needed.
– ORIGIN Old English, 'stopper for a cask'.

tap[2] • v. (**taps, tapping, tapped**) **1** strike with a quick light blow or blows. **2** strike lightly and repeatedly against something else. • n. **1** a quick light blow. **2** a piece of metal attached to the toe and heel of a tap dancer's shoe.
– ORIGIN Old French *taper.*

tapas /tap-uhss/ • pl. n. small Spanish savoury dishes served with drinks at a bar.
– ORIGIN Spanish, 'lid' (because the dishes were served on a dish balanced on the glass of a drink).

tap dance • n. a dance performed wearing shoes fitted with metal taps, characterized by rhythmical tapping of the toes and heels.

– DERIVATIVES **tap dancer** n. **tap-dancing** n.

tape • n. **1** light, flexible material in a narrow strip, used to hold, fasten, or mark off something. **2** (also **adhesive tape**) a strip of paper or plastic coated with a sticky substance, used to stick things together. **3** a kind of tape with magnetic properties, used for recording sound, pictures, or computer data. **4** a cassette or reel containing magnetic tape. • v. (**tapes, taping, taped**) **1** record sound or pictures on magnetic tape. **2** fasten, attach, or mark off with tape.
– ORIGIN Old English.

tape measure • n. a strip of tape marked for measuring the length of something.

taper • v. (**tapers, tapering, tapered**) **1** reduce in thickness towards one end. **2** (**taper off**) gradually lessen. • n. a slender candle.
– ORIGIN Old English.

tape recorder • n. a device for recording sounds on magnetic tape and then reproducing them.
– DERIVATIVES **tape recording** n.

tapestry • n. (pl. **tapestries**) a piece of thick fabric with designs woven or embroidered on it.
– ORIGIN Old French *tapisserie*.

tapeworm • n. a flatworm with a long ribbon-like body, the adult of which lives as a parasite in the intestines.

tapioca /ta-pi-oh-kuh/ • n. a starchy substance in the form of hard white grains, obtained from cassava and used for making puddings and other dishes.
– ORIGIN Tupi-Guarani (an American Indian language), 'squeezed-out dregs'.

tapir /tay-peer/ • n. an animal like a pig with a long flexible snout, found in tropical America and Malaysia.
– ORIGIN Tupi (an American Indian language).

tappet • n. a moving part in a machine which transmits motion in a straight line between a cam and another part.
– ORIGIN from TAP².

taproom • n. a room in a pub in which beer is served from barrels.

taproot • n. a tapering root growing straight downwards and forming the centre from which other roots spring.

tar¹ • n. **1** a dark, thick flammable liquid distilled from wood or coal, used in road-making and for preserving timber. **2** a similar substance formed by burning tobacco. • v. (**tars, tarring, tarred**) cover with tar.
– PHRASES **tar and feather** smear someone with tar and then cover them with feathers as a punishment. **tar**

people with the same brush consider certain people to have the same faults.
– ORIGIN Old English.

tar² • n. informal, dated a sailor.
– ORIGIN perh. short for TARPAULIN, formerly used as a nickname for a sailor.

taramasalata /ta-ruh-muh-suh-lah-tuh/ • n. a Greek dip made from the roe of cod or other fish.
– ORIGIN from modern Greek *taramas* 'roe' + *salata* 'salad'.

tarantula /tuh-ran-tyuu-luh/ • n. **1** a very large hairy spider found chiefly in tropical and subtropical America. **2** a large black spider of southern Europe.
– ORIGIN Italian *tarantola*.

tardy • adj. (**tardier, tardiest**) **1** late. **2** slow to act or respond.
– DERIVATIVES **tardily** adv. **tardiness** n.
– ORIGIN Latin *tardus*.

tare¹ /tair/ • n. **1** a vetch (plant). **2** (in the Bible) a type of weed.

tare² /tair/ • n. the weight of a vehicle without its fuel or load.
– ORIGIN French, 'deficiency'.

target • n. **1** a person, object, or place selected as the aim of an attack. **2** a board marked with a series of circles sharing the same centre, aimed at in archery or shooting. **3** a result which you aim to achieve: *a sales target*.
• v. (**targets, targeting, targeted**) **1** select as an object of attention or attack. **2** aim or direct.
– PHRASES **on** (or **off**) **target** succeeding (or not succeeding) in hitting or achieving the thing aimed at.
– ORIGIN Old English, 'round shield'.

tariff • n. **1** a tax to be paid on a particular class of imports or exports. **2** a list of the fixed prices in a business such as a hotel or restaurant.
– ORIGIN Italian *tariffa*.

> ✓ Spell **tariff** with one **r** and a double **f**.

tarmac • n. **1** (trademark in the UK) material used for surfacing roads or other outdoor areas, consisting of broken stone mixed with tar. **2** (**the tarmac**) a runway or other area surfaced with tarmac. • v. (**tarmacs, tarmacking, tarmacked**) surface an area with tarmac.
– ORIGIN from TAR¹ + MACADAM.

tarn • n. a small mountain lake.
– ORIGIN Old Norse.

tarnish • v. **1** cause metal to lose its shine by exposure to air or damp. **2** damage or spoil: *the company's reputation was tarnished.* • n. a film or stain formed on an exposed surface of a mineral or metal.
– ORIGIN French *ternir*.

tarot /ta-roh/ • n. a set of special playing

cards used for fortune telling.
– ORIGIN French.

tarpaulin /tar-por-lin/ •n. **1** heavy waterproof cloth. **2** a sheet of this used as a covering.
– ORIGIN prob. from TAR¹ + PALL¹.

tarragon /ta-ruh-guhn/ •n. a herb with narrow sweet-smelling leaves, used in cooking.
– ORIGIN Latin *tragonia* and *tarchon*.

tarry¹ /rhymes with starry/ •adj. relating to or covered with tar.

tarry² /rhymes with marry/ •v. (**tarries**, **tarrying**, **tarried**) literary stay longer than intended.

tarsal /tar-s'l/ •adj. relating to the tarsus. •n. a bone of the tarsus.

tarsier /tah-si-er/ •n. a small tree-dwelling primate with very large eyes, native to the islands of SE Asia.
– ORIGIN French.

tarsus /tar-suhss/ •n. (pl. **tarsi** /tar-sy/) the group of small bones in the ankle and upper foot.
– ORIGIN Greek *tarsos* 'flat of the foot, the eyelid'.

tart¹ •n. an open pastry case containing a sweet or savoury filling.
– DERIVATIVES **tartlet** n.
– ORIGIN Old French *tarte*.

tart² informal •n. **1** derog. a woman who has many sexual partners. **2** a prostitute. •v. **1** (**tart yourself up**) Brit. make yourself look attractive with clothes or make-up. **2** (**tart something up**) improve something's appearance.
– DERIVATIVES **tarty** adj.
– ORIGIN prob. from SWEETHEART.

tart³ •adj. **1** sharp or acid in taste. **2** (of a remark or tone of voice) sharp or hurtful.
– DERIVATIVES **tartly** adv. **tartness** n.
– ORIGIN Old English, 'harsh, severe'.

tartan •n. **1** a pattern of coloured checks and intersecting lines. **2** woollen cloth with a tartan pattern.
– ORIGIN perh. from Old French *tertaine*, referring to a kind of cloth.

Tartar /tar-ter/ •n. **1** hist. a member of a group of central Asian peoples who conquered much of Asia and eastern Europe in the early 13th century. **2** (**tartar**) a person who is fierce or difficult to deal with.
– ORIGIN from *Tatar*, the name of a tribe formerly living in parts of Russia and Ukraine.

tartar /tar-ter/ •n. **1** a hard deposit that forms on the teeth and contributes to their decay. **2** a deposit formed during the fermentation of wine.
– PHRASES **cream of tartar** an acidic compound produced during the fermentation of wine, used chiefly in baking powder.
– ORIGIN Greek *tartaron*.

tartare /tah-tah/ •adj. (of fish or meat) served raw, seasoned, and shaped into small patties: *steak tartare*.
– ORIGIN French, 'Tartar'.

tartare sauce /tah-tuh/ (also **tartar sauce**) •n. a cold sauce consisting of mayonnaise mixed with chopped onions, gherkins, and capers.

tartaric acid •n. an organic acid found in unripe grapes and used in baking powders and as a food additive.
– ORIGIN from TARTAR.

tartrazine /tah-truh-zeen/ •n. a bright yellow synthetic dye made from tartaric acid and used to colour food, drugs, and cosmetics.

task •n. a piece of work to be done. •v. (**task someone with**) give someone a task.
– PHRASES **take someone to task** rebuke or criticize someone.
– ORIGIN Old French *tasche*.

task force •n. **1** an armed force organized for a special operation. **2** a group of people specially organized for a task.

taskmaster •n. a person who imposes a demanding workload on someone.

Tasmanian devil •n. a heavily built aggressive marsupial with a large head, powerful jaws, and mainly black fur, found only in the Australian state of Tasmania.

tassel •n. **1** a tuft of hanging threads, knotted together at one end and used for decoration. **2** the tufted head of some plants.
– DERIVATIVES **tasselled** (US **tasseled**) adj.
– ORIGIN Old French, 'clasp'.

taste •n. **1** the way a particular substance is perceived when it comes into contact with the mouth. **2** the sense by which taste is perceived. **3** a small amount of food or drink taken as a sample. **4** a brief experience of something. **5** a liking for something. **6** the ability to pick out what is of good quality or appropriate: *I liked his taste in clothes*. •v. (**tastes, tasting, tasted**) **1** perceive the flavour of. **2** have a particular flavour. **3** test the flavour of something by eating or drinking a small amount of it. **4** have a brief experience of.
– PHRASES **to taste** according to your personal liking.
– ORIGIN Old French *taster* 'try, taste'.

taste bud •n. any of the clusters of nerve endings on the tongue and in the lining of the mouth which provide the sense of taste.

tasteful • adj. showing good judgement as to quality, appearance, or appropriate behaviour: *a tasteful lounge bar.*
– DERIVATIVES **tastefully** adv.

tasteless • adj. **1** lacking flavour. **2** not showing good judgement as to quality, appearance, or appropriate behaviour.
– DERIVATIVES **tastelessly** adv.

taster • n. **1** a person who tests food or drink by tasting it. **2** Brit. a sample of something.

tasty • adj. (**tastier, tastiest**) **1** (of food) having a pleasant flavour. **2** Brit. informal attractive; appealing.

tat • n. Brit. informal tasteless or badly made articles.
– ORIGIN prob. from TATTY.

tattered • adj. **1** old and torn. **2** ruined; in tatters.

tatters • pl. n. irregularly torn pieces of cloth, paper, etc.
– PHRASES **in tatters** destroyed; ruined.
– ORIGIN Old Norse, 'rags'.

tatting • n. **1** a kind of knotted lace made by hand with a small shuttle. **2** the process of making this lace.

tattle • n. gossip. • v. (**tattles, tattling, tattled**) engage in gossip.
– ORIGIN Flemish *tatelen, tateren.*

tattoo¹ • n. (pl. **tattoos**) **1** Brit. a military display consisting of music, marching, and exercises. **2** a rhythmic tapping or drumming. **3** an evening drum or bugle signal calling soldiers back to their quarters.
– ORIGIN Dutch *taptoe!* 'close the tap of the cask!'

tattoo² • n. (pl. **tattoos**) a permanent design made on the skin by making small holes in it with a needle and filling them with coloured ink. • v. (**tattoos, tattooing, tattooed**) mark a person's skin in this way.
– DERIVATIVES **tattooist** n.
– ORIGIN from a language of Polynesia.

tatty • adj. (**tattier, tattiest**) informal worn and shabby.
– ORIGIN Old English, 'rag'.

taught past and past part. of TEACH.

taunt • n. a remark made in order to anger, upset, or provoke someone. • v. provoke or upset with taunts.
– ORIGIN from French *tant pour tant* 'tit for tat'.

taupe /rhymes with rope/ • n. a grey colour with a brown tinge.
– ORIGIN French, 'mole, moleskin'.

Taurus /taw-ruhss/ • n. a constellation (the Bull) and sign of the zodiac, which the sun enters about 21 April.
– DERIVATIVES **Taurean** /taw-ree-uhn/ n. & adj.
– ORIGIN Latin.

taut • adj. **1** stretched or pulled tight. **2** (of muscles or nerves) tense.
– DERIVATIVES **tauten** v. **tautly** adv.
– ORIGIN perh. from TOUGH.

tautology /taw-tol-uh-ji/ • n. (pl. **tautologies**) the saying or writing of the same thing over again in different words, seen as a fault of style (e.g. *they arrived one after the other in succession*).
– DERIVATIVES **tautological** adj. **tautologous** adj.
– ORIGIN from Greek *tauto-* 'same' + *logos* 'word'.

tavern • n. old use or N. Amer. an inn or pub.
– ORIGIN Old French *taverne.*

taverna /tuh-ver-nuh/ • n. a small Greek restaurant.
– ORIGIN modern Greek.

tawdry • adj. (**tawdrier, tawdriest**) **1** showy but cheap and of poor quality. **2** sleazy or unpleasant.
– DERIVATIVES **tawdriness** n.
– ORIGIN short for *tawdry lace*, from *St Audrey's lace*, a fine silk lace or ribbon.

tawny • adj. (**tawnier, tawniest**) of an orange-brown or yellowish-brown colour.
– ORIGIN Old French *tane.*

tawny owl • n. a common owl with either reddish-brown or grey plumage, and a quavering hoot.

tax • n. money that must be paid to the state, charged as a proportion of personal income and business profits or added to the cost of some goods and services. • v. **1** impose a tax on. **2** pay tax on a vehicle. **3** make heavy demands on: *the ordeal would severely tax her strength.* **4** accuse someone of doing something wrong.
– DERIVATIVES **taxable** adj.
– ORIGIN Latin *taxare* 'to censure, charge'.

taxation • n. **1** the imposing of tax. **2** money paid as tax.

tax avoidance • n. the arrangement of your financial affairs so as to pay only the minimum of tax that is legally required.

tax break • n. informal a tax reduction or advantage allowed by the government.

tax-deductible • adj. allowed to be deducted from income before the amount of tax to be paid is calculated.

tax disc • n. Brit. a circular label displayed on the windscreen of a vehicle, showing that road tax has been paid.

tax evasion • n. the illegal non-payment or underpayment of tax.

tax exile • n. a wealthy person who chooses to live in a country with low taxes.

tax haven • n. a country or independent area where taxes are low.

taxi • n. (pl. **taxis**) a motor vehicle licensed to transport passengers to the place of their choice in return for payment of a fare. • v. (**taxies, taxiing, taxied**) (of an aircraft) move slowly along the ground before take-off or after landing.
– ORIGIN short for *taxicab* or *taximeter cab*.

taxicab • n. a taxi.

taxidermy /tak-si-der-mi/ • n. the art of preparing, stuffing, and mounting the skins of dead animals so that they look like living ones.
– DERIVATIVES **taxidermist** n.
– ORIGIN from Greek *taxis* 'arrangement' + *derma* 'skin'.

taximeter • n. a device used in taxis that automatically records the distance travelled and the fare to be paid.
– ORIGIN French *taximètre*.

taxing • adj. physically or mentally demanding.

taxi rank (N. Amer. **taxi stand**) • n. a place where taxis park while waiting to be hired.

taxman • n. (pl. **taxmen**) informal an inspector or collector of taxes.

taxonomy /taks-on-uh-mi/ • n. 1 the branch of science concerned with classification. 2 a system of classifying things.
– DERIVATIVES **taxonomic** adj. **taxonomist** n.
– ORIGIN from Greek *taxis* 'arrangement' + *-nomia* 'distribution'.

taxpayer • n. a person who pays taxes.

tax return • n. a form on which a taxpayer makes a statement of their income and personal circumstances, used to assess how much tax that person should pay.

tax year • n. a year as reckoned for the purposes of taxation (in Britain from 6 April).

TB • abbrev. tubercle bacillus; tuberculosis.

Tb • symb. the chemical element terbium.

TBA • abbrev. to be arranged (or announced).

TBC • abbrev. to be confirmed.

T-bone • n. a large piece of loin steak containing a T-shaped bone.

tbsp (also **tbs**) (pl. **tbsp** or **tbsps**) • abbrev. tablespoonful.

Tc • symb. the chemical element technetium.

Te • symb. the chemical element tellurium.

te (N. Amer. **ti**) • n. Music the seventh note of a major scale, coming after 'lah'.
– ORIGIN alteration of former *si*, adopted

to avoid having two notes (*soh* and *si*) beginning with the same letter.

tea • n. 1 a hot drink made by soaking the dried leaves of an evergreen Asian shrub (the tea plant) in boiling water. 2 the dried leaves used to make tea. 3 a drink made from the leaves, fruits, or flowers of other plants. 4 Brit. a light afternoon meal consisting of sandwiches, cakes, etc., with tea to drink. 5 Brit. a cooked evening meal.
– ORIGIN Chinese.

tea bag • n. a small sachet containing tea leaves, on to which boiling water is poured to make tea.

tea break • n. Brit. a short rest period during the working day.

teacake • n. Brit. a light sweet bun containing dried fruit.

teach • v. (**teaches, teaching, taught**) 1 give information about a particular subject to a class or pupil. 2 show someone how to do something. 3 make someone realize, understand, or be less likely to do something: *the experience taught me the real value of money.*
– DERIVATIVES **teaching** n.
– ORIGIN Old English, 'show'.

teacher • n. a person who teaches in a school.

tea chest • n. a light metal-lined wooden box in which tea is transported.

tea cloth • n. a tea towel.

tea cosy • n. a thick or padded cover placed over a teapot to keep the tea hot.

teacup • n. a cup from which tea is drunk.

tea dance • n. a social occasion which consists of afternoon tea and dancing.

teak • n. hard wood used in shipbuilding and for making furniture, obtained from a tree native to India and SE Asia.
– ORIGIN Portuguese *teca*.

teal • n. (pl. **teal** or **teals**) 1 a small freshwater duck. 2 (also **teal blue**) a dark greenish-blue colour.

team • n. 1 a group of players forming one side in a competitive game or sport. 2 two or more people working together. 3 two or more horses harnessed together to pull a vehicle. • v. 1 (**team up**) come together as a team to achieve a shared goal. 2 (**team something with**) match something with: *a pinstripe suit teamed with a white shirt.*
– ORIGIN Old English.

teammate • n. a fellow member of a team.

team player • n. a person who plays or works well as a member of a team.

team spirit • n. trust and cooperation among the members of a team.

teamwork •n. organized effort as a group.

teapot •n. a pot with a handle, spout, and lid, in which tea is prepared.

tear¹ /rhymes with rare/ •v. (**tears, tearing, tore**; past part. **torn**) **1** rip a hole or split in. **2** (usu. **tear something up**) pull something apart or to pieces. **3** damage a muscle or ligament by overstretching it. **4** (usu. **tear something down**) demolish or destroy something. **5** (**tear something apart**) destroy good relations between people. **6** (**be torn**) be unsure of which of two options or parties to choose or support. **7** informal move very quickly. **8** (**tear into**) attack verbally. •n. a hole or split caused by tearing.
– ORIGIN Old English.

tear² /rhymes with rear/ •n. a drop of clear salty liquid produced by glands in a person's eye when they are crying or when the eye is irritated.
– PHRASES **in tears** crying.
– DERIVATIVES **teary** adj.
– ORIGIN Old English.

tearaway •n. Brit. a person who behaves in a wild or reckless way.

teardrop •n. a single tear. •adj. shaped like a tear.

tear duct •n. a passage through which tears pass from the glands which produce them to the eye or from the eye to the nose.

tearful •adj. **1** crying or about to cry. **2** causing tears: a tearful farewell.
– DERIVATIVES **tearfully** adv.

tear gas •n. gas that causes severe irritation to the eyes, used in warfare and riot control.

tear-jerker •n. informal a very sad story, film, or song.

tea room •n. a small restaurant or cafe where tea and other light refreshments are served.

tea rose •n. a garden rose having flowers that are pale yellow tinged with pink, and a delicate scent like that of tea.

tease •v. (**teases, teasing, teased**) **1** playfully make fun of or attempt to provoke. **2** tempt sexually. **3** (**tease something out**) find out something by searching through a mass of information. **4** gently pull tangled wool, hair, etc. into separate strands. •n. informal a person who teases.
– ORIGIN Old English.

teasel (also **teazle**) •n. a tall prickly plant with spiny purple flower heads.
– ORIGIN Old English.

teaser •n. informal a tricky question or problem.

tea set •n. a set of crockery for serving tea.

teaspoon •n. **1** a small spoon used for adding sugar to and stirring hot drinks. **2** the amount held by a teaspoon, in the UK considered to be 5 millilitres.
– DERIVATIVES **teaspoonful** n.

teat •n. **1** one of the parts of a female animal's body from which milk is sucked by the young; a nipple. **2** Brit. a plastic nipple-shaped device by which a baby or young animal can suck milk from a bottle.
– ORIGIN Old French tete.

tea towel •n. esp. Brit. a cloth for drying washed crockery, cutlery, and glasses.

tea tree •n. an Australasian flowering shrub or small tree which yields an oil valued for its antiseptic qualities.

teazle •n. var. of TEASEL.

technetium /tek-nee-shi-uhm/ •n. an unstable radioactive metallic element made by high-energy collisions.
– ORIGIN Greek tekhnētos 'artificial'.

technical •adj. **1** relating to the practical skills of a particular subject, art, or craft. **2** relating to the practical use of machinery and methods in science and industry. **3** requiring specialized knowledge in order to be understood. **4** according to the law or rules when applied strictly: a technical violation of the treaty.
– DERIVATIVES **technically** adv.
– ORIGIN Greek tekhnē 'art'.

technical college •n. a college of further education providing courses in applied sciences and other practical subjects.

technicality •n. (pl. **technicalities**) **1** a small formal detail in a set of rules. **2** (**technicalities**) details of theory or practice in a particular field. **3** the use of technical terms or methods.

technical knockout •n. Boxing the ending of a fight by the referee because a contestant is unable to continue, the opponent being declared the winner.

technician •n. **1** a person employed to look after technical equipment or do practical work in a laboratory. **2** a person skilled in the technique of an art, science, craft, or sport.

Technicolor •n. **1** trademark a process of producing cinema films in colour. **2** (**technicolor** or Brit. also **technicolour**) informal vivid colour.

technique •n. **1** a particular way of doing something, especially something requiring special skills. **2** a person's

level of practical skill.
– ORIGIN French.

techno • n. a style of fast electronic dance music, with a strong beat and few or no vocals.
– ORIGIN short for technological (see **TECHNOLOGY**).

technocracy /tek-nok-ruh-si/ • n. (pl. **technocracies**) a social or political system in which scientific or technical experts hold a great deal of power.
– DERIVATIVES **technocrat** n.

technology • n. (pl. **technologies**) 1 the application of scientific knowledge for practical purposes. 2 machinery and equipment developed from such scientific knowledge. 3 the branch of knowledge concerned with applied sciences.
– DERIVATIVES **technological** adj. **technologically** adv. **technologist** n.
– ORIGIN Greek *tekhnologia* 'systematic treatment'.

technophobe • n. a person who dislikes or fears new technology.
– DERIVATIVES **technophobia** n. **technophobic** adj.

tectonic /tek-ton-ik/ Geol. • adj. relating to the structure of the earth's crust and the large-scale processes which take place within it. • n. (**tectonics**) large-scale processes affecting the structure of the earth's crust.
– ORIGIN Greek *tektonikos*.

teddy • n. (pl. **teddies**) 1 (also **teddy bear**) a soft toy bear. 2 a woman's all-in-one undergarment.
– ORIGIN from *Teddy*, informal form of the man's name *Theodore*, with reference to the US President *Theodore* Roosevelt, an enthusiastic bear hunter.

Teddy boy • n. (in Britain during the 1950s) a young man of a group who wore clothes based on Edwardian fashion, had their hair slicked up in a quiff, and liked rock-and-roll music.
– ORIGIN from *Teddy*, informal form of the man's name *Edward*.

tedious • adj. too long, slow, or dull.
– DERIVATIVES **tediously** adv.
– ORIGIN Latin *taedium* 'tedium'.

tedium • n. the state of being tedious.

tee • n. 1 a cleared space on a golf course, from which the ball is struck at the beginning of play for each hole. 2 a small peg placed in the ground to support a golf ball before it is struck from a tee. • v. (**tees, teeing, teed**) Golf 1 (**tee up**) place the ball on a tee ready to make the first stroke of the round or hole. 2 (**tee off**) begin a round or hole by playing the ball from a tee.

teem¹ • v. (**teem with**) be full of or swarming with.
– ORIGIN Old English, 'give birth to'.

teem² • v. (of rain) fall heavily.
– ORIGIN Old Norse, 'to empty'.

teen informal • adj. relating to teenagers. • n. a teenager.

-teen • suffix forming the names of numerals from 13 to 19.
– ORIGIN Old English.

teenage • adj. relating to a teenager or teenagers.
– DERIVATIVES **teenaged** adj.

teenager • n. a person aged between 13 and 19 years.

teens • pl. n. the years of a person's age from 13 to 19.

teensy • adj. (**teensier, teensiest**) informal very tiny.
– ORIGIN prob. from **TEENY**.

teeny • adj. (**teenier, teeniest**) informal tiny.
– ORIGIN from **TINY**.

teeny-bopper • n. informal a young teenager who follows the latest fashions in clothes and pop music.

teeny-weeny (also **teensy-weensy**) • adj. informal very tiny.

teepee • n. var. of TEPEE.

tee shirt • n. var. of T-SHIRT.

teeter • v. (**teeters, teetering, teetered**) 1 move or balance unsteadily. 2 be unable to decide between different options.
– ORIGIN Old Norse, 'shake, shiver'.

teeth pl. of TOOTH.

teethe • v. (**teethes, teething, teethed**) (of a baby) develop its first teeth.

teething troubles (also **teething problems**) • pl. n. short-term problems that occur in the early stages of a new project.

teetotal • adj. choosing never to drink alcohol.
– DERIVATIVES **teetotalism** n. **teetotaller** n.
– ORIGIN from **TOTAL** (referring to total abstinence from all alcohol).

TEFL /tef-uhl/ • abbrev. teaching of English as a foreign language.

Teflon /tef-lon/ • n. trademark a tough synthetic substance used to make seals and to coat non-stick cooking utensils.

tele- /tel-i/ • comb. form 1 to or at a distance: *telecommunications*. 2 relating to television: *telethon*. 3 done by means of the telephone: *telesales*.
– ORIGIN Greek, 'far off'. Senses 2 and 3 are abbreviations.

telecast • n. a television broadcast. • v. transmit by television.

telecommunications • pl. n. the

t

technology concerned with long-distance communication by means of cable, telephone, broadcasting, satellite, etc.

telecoms (also **telecomms**)
• n. telecommunications.

telegenic /te-li-jen-ik/ • adj. having an appearance or manner that is attractive on television.

telegram • n. a message sent by telegraph and delivered in written or printed form, now used in the UK only for international messages.

telegraph • n. a system or device for transmitting messages from a distance along a wire, especially one creating signals by making and breaking an electrical connection. • v. 1 dated send a message by telegraph. 2 convey a message, especially by body language.
– DERIVATIVES **telegraphy** n.

telegraphic • adj. relating to telegraphs or telegrams.

telegraph pole • n. a tall pole used to carry telegraph or telephone wires above the ground.

telekinesis /te-li-ki-nee-siss/ • n. the supposed ability to move objects at a distance by mental power or other non-physical means.
– DERIVATIVES **telekinetic** adj.
– ORIGIN Greek *kinēsis* 'motion'.

telemarketing • n. the marketing of goods or services by telephone calls to potential customers.

teleology /tel-i-ol-uh-ji, tee-li-ol-uh-ji/ • n. the philosophical theory that all things in nature have a purpose and happen because of that.
– DERIVATIVES **teleological** adj.
– ORIGIN from Greek *telos* 'end' + *logos* 'reason'.

telepathy • n. the supposed communication of thoughts or ideas by means other than the known senses.
– DERIVATIVES **telepathic** adj.

telephone • n. 1 a system for transmitting voices over a distance using wire or radio, by converting sound vibrations to electrical signals. 2 an instrument used as part of such a system, having a handset with a transmitting microphone and a set of numbered buttons by which a connection can be made to another such instrument. • v. (**telephones, telephoning, telephoned**) contact by telephone.
– DERIVATIVES **telephonic** adj. **telephonically** adv.

telephone box • n. Brit. a public booth or enclosure housing a payphone.

telephone directory • n. a book listing the names, addresses, and telephone numbers of the people in a particular area.

telephone exchange • n. a set of equipment that connects telephone lines during a call.

telephone number • n. a number given to a particular telephone and used in making connections to it.

telephonist • n. Brit. an operator of a telephone switchboard.

telephony /ti-lef-fuh-ni/ • n. the working or use of telephones.

telephoto lens • n. a lens that produces a magnified image of a distant object.

teleprinter • n. Brit. a device for transmitting telegraph messages as they are keyed, and for printing messages received.

telesales • pl. n. esp. Brit. the selling of goods or services over the telephone.

telescope • n. an instrument designed to make distant objects appear nearer, containing an arrangement of lenses, or of curved mirrors and lenses, by which rays of light are collected and focused and the resulting image magnified.
• v. (**telescopes, telescoping, telescoped**) 1 (of an object made up of several tubes fitting into each other) slide into itself so as to become smaller. 2 condense or combine so as to occupy less space or time: *at sea the years are telescoped into hours.*
– DERIVATIVES **telescopic** adj.

teletext • n. a news and information service transmitted to televisions with appropriate receivers.

telethon • n. a long television programme broadcast to raise money for a charity.
– ORIGIN from **TELE-** + *marathon*.

televangelist • n. esp. N. Amer. an evangelical preacher who appears regularly on television.

televise • v. (**televises, televising, televised**) broadcast on television.

television • n. 1 a system for converting visual images with sound into electrical signals, transmitting them, and displaying them electronically on a screen. 2 (also **television set**) a device with a screen for receiving television signals. 3 the process or business of broadcasting programmes on television.
– DERIVATIVES **televisual** adj.

telex • n. 1 an international system in which printed messages are transmitted and received by teleprinters. 2 a device used for this. 3 a message sent by this system. • v. send a message to someone by telex.

– ORIGIN from **TELEPRINTER** and **EXCHANGE**.

tell • v. (**tells, telling, told**)
1 communicate information to someone.
2 instruct someone to do something.
3 express in words: *he tried to make them laugh by telling jokes.* **4** (**tell on**) informal inform on. **5** (**tell someone off**) informal reprimand someone. **6** establish or determine that something is the case: *you can tell they're in love.* **7** be able to recognize a difference. **8** (of an experience) have a noticeable effect on someone.
– PHRASES **tell tales** gossip about another person's secrets or wrongdoings. **tell the time** be able to find out the time from reading the face of a clock or watch.
– ORIGIN Old English, 'relate, count'.

teller • n. **1** esp. N. Amer. a person who deals with customers' transactions in a bank. **2** a person appointed to count votes. **3** a person who tells something.

telling • adj. having a striking or revealing effect.
– DERIVATIVES **tellingly** adv.

telling-off • n. (pl. **tellings-off**) Brit. informal a reprimand.

telltale • adj. revealing something: *the telltale signs of a woman in love.* • n. Brit. a person who reports things that other people have done wrong or reveals their secrets.

tellurium /tel-lyoor-i-uhm/ • n. a silvery-white crystalline non-metallic element with semiconducting properties.
– ORIGIN Latin *tellus* 'earth'.

telly • n. (pl. **tellies**) Brit. informal = **TELEVISION**.

temerity /ti-me-ri-ti/ • n. very confident or bold behaviour, likely to be considered rude or disrespectful by other people.
– ORIGIN Latin *temeritas*.

temp informal • n. an employee who is employed on a temporary basis. • v. work as a temp.

temper • n. **1** a person's state of mind: *she regained her good temper.* **2** a tendency to become angry easily. **3** an angry state of mind. **4** the degree of hardness of a metal. • v. (**tempers, tempering, tempered**) **1** harden a metal by reheating and then cooling it. **2** make something less extreme by adding something that balances or modifies it: *their idealism is tempered with realism.*
– PHRASES **keep** (or **lose**) **your temper** manage (or fail to manage) to control your anger.
– ORIGIN Latin *temperare* 'mingle'.

tempera /tem-puh-ruh/ • n. a method of

painting with powdered colours mixed with egg yolk.
– ORIGIN from Italian *pingere a tempera* 'paint in distemper'.

temperament • n. a person's nature in terms of the effect it has on their behaviour.
– ORIGIN Latin *temperamentum* 'correct mixture'.

temperamental • adj. **1** relating to or caused by temperament. **2** tending to change mood in an unreasonable way.
– DERIVATIVES **temperamentally** adv.

temperance • n. complete avoidance of drinking alcohol.
– ORIGIN Old French *temperaunce*.

temperate • adj. **1** (of a region or climate) having mild temperatures. **2** showing self-control.
– ORIGIN Latin *temperatus*.

temperature • n. **1** the degree of heat present in a place, substance, or object. **2** a body temperature above the normal. **3** the degree of excitement or tension in a situation: *the temperature of the debate lowered.*
– ORIGIN Latin *temperatura* 'the state of being mixed'.

 Spell **temperature** with **-era-** in the middle.

tempest • n. a violent windy storm.
– ORIGIN Latin *tempestas* 'weather, storm'.

tempestuous /tem-pess-tyoo-uhss/ • adj. **1** very stormy. **2** full of strong and changeable emotion: *a tempestuous relationship.*

tempi pl. of **TEMPO**.

template /tem-playt/ • n. **1** a shaped piece of rigid material used as a pattern for cutting out, shaping, or drilling. **2** something serving as a model for other people to copy.
– ORIGIN prob. from *temple* 'device in a loom for keeping the cloth stretched'.

temple[1] • n. **1** a building used for the worship of a god or gods. **2** (**the Temple**) either of two ancient religious buildings of the Jews in Jerusalem.
– ORIGIN Latin *templum* 'open or consecrated space'.

temple[2] • n. the flat part either side of the head between the forehead and the ear.
– ORIGIN Old French.

tempo /tem-poh/ • n. (pl. **tempos** or **tempi** /tem-pi/) **1** the speed at which a passage of music is played. **2** the pace of an activity or process.
– ORIGIN Italian.

temporal[1] /tem-puh-ruhl/
• adj. **1** relating to time. **2** relating to the

physical world rather than to spiritual matters.
– DERIVATIVES **temporally** adv.
– ORIGIN Latin *temporalis*.

temporal² /tem-puh-ruhl/ • adj. relating to or situated in the temples of the head.

temporary • adj. lasting for only a short time.
– DERIVATIVES **temporarily** adv.
– ORIGIN Latin *temporarius*.

temporize (or **temporise**)
• v. (**temporizes, temporizing, temporized**) delay making a decision so as to gain time.
– ORIGIN French *temporiser* 'bide your time'.

tempt • v. 1 try to persuade someone to do something which is appealing but wrong or unwise. 2 (**be tempted to do**) have an urge or inclination to do: *I was tempted to look at my watch.* 3 entice or attract: *programmes designed to tempt young people into engineering.*
– PHRASES **tempt fate** (or **providence**) do something risky or dangerous.
– DERIVATIVES **tempter** n. **tempting** adj.
– ORIGIN Latin *temptare* 'handle, test'.

temptation • n. 1 the action of tempting or the state of being tempted. 2 a tempting thing.

temptress • n. a sexually attractive woman who sets out to make a man desire her.

ten • cardinal number one more than nine; 10. (Roman numeral: **x** or **X**.)
– PHRASES **ten out of ten** referring to an excellent performance. **ten to one** very probably.
– DERIVATIVES **tenfold** adj. & adv.
– ORIGIN Old English.

tenable • adj. 1 able to be defended against attack or objection. 2 (of a post, grant, etc.) able to be held or used for a particular period: *a scholarship tenable for three years.*
– ORIGIN French.

tenacious /ti-nay-shuhss/ • adj. 1 firmly holding on to something. 2 continuing to exist or do something for longer than might be expected: *a tenacious belief.*
– DERIVATIVES **tenaciously** adv. **tenacity** /ti-**nass**-i-ti/ n.
– ORIGIN Latin *tenere* 'to hold'.

tenancy • n. (pl. **tenancies**) possession of land or property as a tenant.

tenant • n. 1 a person who rents land or property from a landlord. 2 Law a person privately owning land or property.
• v. occupy property as a tenant.
– ORIGIN Old French, 'holding'.

tenant farmer • n. a person who farms rented land.

tench • n. (pl. **tench**) a freshwater fish of the carp family.
– ORIGIN Old French *tenche*.

Ten Commandments • pl. n. (in the Bible) the rules of conduct given by God to Moses on Mount Sinai.

tend¹ • v. 1 frequently behave in a particular way or have a certain characteristic. 2 go or move in a particular direction.
– ORIGIN Latin *tendere* 'stretch, tend'.

tend² • v. care for or look after.
– ORIGIN from **ATTEND**.

tendency • n. (pl. **tendencies**) 1 an inclination to behave in a particular way. 2 a group within a larger political party or movement.

☑ Remember that **tendency** ends with -**ency**.

tendentious /ten-den-shuhss/ • adj. expressing a strong opinion, especially a controversial one.
– ORIGIN German *tendenziös*.

tender¹ • adj. (**tenderer, tenderest**) 1 gentle and kind. 2 (of food) easy to cut or chew. 3 (of a part of the body) painful to the touch. 4 young and vulnerable. 5 easily damaged.
– DERIVATIVES **tenderly** adv. **tenderness** n.
– ORIGIN Old French *tendre*.

tender² • v. (**tenders, tendering, tendered**) 1 offer or present formally. 2 make a formal written offer to carry out work, supply goods, etc. for a stated fixed price. 3 offer money as payment.
• n. a tendered offer.
– ORIGIN Latin *tendere* 'stretch, hold out'.

tender³ • n. 1 a vehicle used by a fire service for carrying equipment. 2 a wagon attached to a steam locomotive to carry fuel and water. 3 a boat used to ferry people and supplies to and from a ship.
– ORIGIN from **TEND²** or **ATTEND**.

tender-hearted • adj. having a kind, gentle, or sentimental nature.

tenderize (or **tenderise**)
• v. (**tenderizes, tenderizing, tenderized**) make meat more tender by beating or slow cooking.

tenderloin • n. the tenderest part of a loin of beef, pork, etc., taken from under the short ribs in the hindquarters.

tendinitis /ten-di-ny-tiss/ (also **tendonitis** /ten-duh-ny-tiss/)
• n. inflammation of a tendon.

tendon /ten-duhn/ • n. a strong band or cord of tissue attaching a muscle to a bone.
– ORIGIN Greek *tenōn* 'sinew'.

tendril • n. 1 a thread-like part of a climbing plant, which stretches out and

twines round any suitable support. **2** a slender ringlet of hair.
– ORIGIN prob. from Old French *tendron* 'young shoot'.

tenebrous /ten-i-bruhss/ •adj. literary dark; shadowy.
– ORIGIN Latin *tenebrosus*.

tenement /ten-uh-muhnt/ •n. a large house divided into several separate flats.
– ORIGIN Latin *tenementum*.

tenet /ten-it/ •n. a central principle or belief.
– ORIGIN Latin, 'he holds'.

ten-gallon hat •n. a large, broad-brimmed hat, traditionally worn by cowboys.

tenner •n. Brit. informal a ten-pound note.

tennis •n. a game for two or four players, who use rackets to strike a ball over a net stretched across a grass or clay court.
– ORIGIN prob. from Old French *tenez* 'take, receive' (called by the server in the game of real tennis).

tennis elbow •n. inflammation of the tendons of the elbow caused by overuse of the forearm muscles.

tenon /ten-uhn/ •n. a projecting piece of wood made to be inserted into a mortise in another piece of wood.
– ORIGIN French.

tenor¹ •n. a singing voice between baritone and alto or countertenor, the highest of the ordinary adult male range. •adj. referring to an instrument of the second or third lowest pitch in its family: *a tenor sax.*
– ORIGIN Latin *tenere* 'to hold' (because the tenor part 'held' the melody).

tenor² •n. the general meaning or nature of something: *the even tenor of her marriage.*
– ORIGIN Latin, 'course'.

tenpin •n. a skittle used in tenpin bowling.

tenpin bowling •n. a game in which ten skittles are set up at the end of a track and bowled down with hard balls.

tense¹ •adj. **1** stretched tight or rigid. **2** feeling, causing, or showing anxiety and nervousness. •v. (**tenses, tensing, tensed**) make or become tense.
– DERIVATIVES **tensely** adv. **tenseness** n.
– ORIGIN Latin *tensus.*

tense² •n. Grammar a set of forms of a verb that indicate the time or completeness of the action expressed by the verb.
– ORIGIN Latin *tempus* 'time'.

tensile /ten-syl/ •adj. **1** relating to tension. **2** capable of being drawn out or stretched.

tensile strength •n. the resistance of a material to breaking under tension.

tension •n. **1** the state of being stretched tight. **2** mental or emotional strain. **3** a situation in which there is strain because of differing views or aims: *months of tension between the military and the government.* **4** the degree of stitch tightness in knitting and machine sewing. **5** voltage of a particular magnitude: *high tension.*
– DERIVATIVES **tensional** adj.

tent •n. a portable shelter made of cloth, supported by one or more poles and stretched tight by cords attached to pegs driven into the ground.
– ORIGIN Old French *tente.*

tentacle •n. a long thin flexible part extending from the body of an animal, used for feeling or holding things, or for moving about.
– DERIVATIVES **tentacled** adj.
– ORIGIN Latin *tentaculum.*

tentative •adj. **1** done without confidence; hesitant: *a few tentative steps.* **2** not certain or fixed: *a tentative conclusion.*
– DERIVATIVES **tentatively** adv. **tentativeness** n.
– ORIGIN Latin *tentativus.*

tenterhook •n. (in phr. **on tenterhooks**) in a state of nervous suspense.
– ORIGIN first meaning a hook used to fasten cloth on a *tenter*, a framework on which fabric was held during manufacture.

tenth •ordinal number **1** that is number ten in a sequence; 10th. **2** (**a tenth/one tenth**) each of ten equal parts into which something is divided. **3** a musical interval spanning an octave and a third in a scale.

tenuous •adj. **1** very slight or weak: *a tenuous distinction.* **2** very slender or fine.
– DERIVATIVES **tenuously** adv.
– ORIGIN Latin *tenuis* 'thin'.

tenure /ten-yer/ •n. **1** the conditions under which land or buildings are held or occupied. **2** the holding of a job. **3** guaranteed permanent employment after a probationary period.
– ORIGIN Old French.

tenured •adj. having a permanent post.

tepee /tee-pee/ (also **teepee** or **tipi**) •n. a cone-shaped tent made of skins or cloth on a frame of poles, used by American Indians.
– ORIGIN Sioux, 'dwelling'.

tepid •adj. **1** lukewarm. **2** not enthusiastic: *a tepid response.*
– ORIGIN Latin *tepidus.*

tequila /ti-kee-luh/ •n. a Mexican

t

alcoholic spirit made from a plant.
– ORIGIN named after the town of *Tequila*
in Mexico.

terabyte •n. a unit of information
stored in a computer, equal to one
million million (10^{12}) or (strictly) 2^{40}
bytes.
– ORIGIN Greek *teras* 'monster'.

terbium /ter-bi-uhm/ •n. a silvery-white
metallic chemical element.
– ORIGIN from *Ytterby*, a Swedish quarry
where it was first found.

tercentenary •n. (pl. **tercentenaries**) a
three-hundredth anniversary.
– ORIGIN Latin *ter* 'thrice'.

tergiversation /ter-ji-vuh-say-sh'n/
•n. the use of language that is evasive or
has more than one possible meaning.
– ORIGIN Latin *tergiversari* 'turn your
back'.

term •n. 1 a word or phrase used to
describe a thing or to express an idea.
2 (**terms**) language used on a particular
occasion: *a protest in the strongest possible
terms.* 3 (**terms**) requirements or
conditions laid down or agreed.
4 (**terms**) relations between people:
we're on good terms. 5 a period for which
something lasts or is intended to last.
6 each of the periods in the year during
which teaching is given in a school or
college or during which a law court
holds sessions. 7 (also **full term**) the
completion of a normal length of
pregnancy. 8 Math. each of the quantities
in a ratio, series, or mathematical
expression. •v. call by a particular term.
– PHRASES **come to terms with** become
able to accept or deal with. **terms of
reference** Brit. the scope of an inquiry or
discussion.
– DERIVATIVES **termly** adj. & adv.
– ORIGIN Latin *terminus* 'end, limit'.

termagant /ter-muh-guhnt/ •n. a bad-
tempered or overbearing woman.
– ORIGIN Italian *Trivagante* 'thrice-
wandering', referring to a violent
imaginary god or goddess in medieval
morality plays.

terminable •adj. 1 able to be terminated. 2 coming to an end after a certain
time.

terminal •adj. 1 relating to or situated
at the end. 2 (of a disease) predicted to
lead to a person's death. •n. 1 the station
at the end of a railway or bus route. 2 a
departure and arrival building for
passengers at an airport. 3 a point of
connection for closing an electric
circuit. 4 a keyboard and screen
connected to a central computer system.
– DERIVATIVES **terminally** adv.
– ORIGIN Latin *terminalis*.

terminal velocity •n. Physics the
constant speed that a freely falling
object reaches when the resistance of
the medium through which it is falling
prevents it from moving any faster.

terminate •v. (**terminates, terminating,
terminated**) 1 bring to an end.
2 (**terminate in**) have an end at or in.
3 (of a train or bus service) end its
journey. 4 end a pregnancy at an early
stage by a medical procedure.
– DERIVATIVES **termination** n.
terminator n.

terminology •n. (pl. **terminologies**) the
set of terms used in a subject of study,
profession, etc.
– DERIVATIVES **terminological** adj.

terminus •n. (pl. **termini** /ter-mi-ny/ or
terminuses) a railway or bus terminal.
– ORIGIN Latin, 'end, limit'.

termite /ter-myt/ •n. a small, soft-
bodied insect which feeds on wood and
lives in colonies in large nests of earth.
– ORIGIN Latin *termes* 'woodworm'.

tern /rhymes with fern/ •n. a white
seabird with long pointed wings and a
forked tail.
– ORIGIN Scandinavian.

ternary /ter-nuh-ri/ •adj. 1 composed of
three parts. 2 Math. using three as a base.
– ORIGIN Latin *ternarius*.

terpsichorean /terp-si-kuh-ree-uhn/
•adj. formal relating to dancing.
– ORIGIN from *Terpsichore*, the ancient
Greek and Roman Muse of dance.

terrace •n. 1 each of a series of flat areas
on a slope, used for growing plants and
crops. 2 a patio. 3 Brit. a row of houses in
the same style built in one block. 4 Brit. a
flight of wide, shallow steps providing
standing room for spectators in a
stadium. •v. (**terraces, terracing,
terraced**) make sloping land into
terraces.
– DERIVATIVES **terracing** n.
– ORIGIN Old French, 'rubble, platform'.

terraced •adj. Brit. (of a house) forming
part of a terrace.

terracotta /te-ruh-kot-tuh/
•n. 1 brownish-red earthenware that has
not been glazed, used as a decorative
building material and in modelling. 2 a
strong brownish-red colour.
– ORIGIN from Italian *terra cotta* 'baked
earth'.

terra firma /te-ruh fer-muh/ •n. dry
land; the ground.
– ORIGIN Latin, 'firm land'.

terrain /te-rayn/ •n. a stretch of land
seen in terms of its physical features:
rough terrain.
– ORIGIN French.

terra incognita /te-ruh in-kog-ni-tuh/

• n. unknown territory.
– ORIGIN Latin, 'unknown land'.

terrapin • n. a small freshwater turtle.
– ORIGIN from an American Indian language.

terrarium /ter-rair-i-uhm/ • n. (pl. **terrariums** or **terraria** /ter-rair-i-uh/) **1** a glass-fronted case for keeping small reptiles, amphibians, etc. **2** a sealed transparent container in which plants are grown.
– ORIGIN Latin *terra* 'earth'.

terrazzo /te-rat-zoh/ • n. flooring material consisting of chips of marble or granite set in concrete and polished smooth.
– ORIGIN Italian, 'terrace'.

terrestrial /tuh-ress-tri-uhl/ • adj. **1** relating to the earth or dry land. **2** (of an animal or plant) living on or in the ground. **3** (of television broadcasting) using ground-based equipment rather than a satellite.
– ORIGIN Latin *terrestris*.

terrible • adj. **1** very bad, serious, or unpleasant. **2** unhappy, guilty, or unwell: *I felt terrible about forgetting her name*. **3** causing terror.
– ORIGIN Latin *terribilis*.

terribly • adv. **1** extremely. **2** very badly.

terrier • n. a small breed of dog originally used to hunt animals that live underground.
– ORIGIN from Old French *chien terrier* 'earth dog'.

terrific • adj. **1** of great size, amount, or strength. **2** informal excellent.
– DERIVATIVES **terrifically** adv.
– ORIGIN Latin *terrificus*.

terrify • v. (**terrifies, terrifying, terrified**) make someone feel terror.

terrine /tuh-reen/ • n. a mixture of chopped meat, fish, or vegetables that is pressed into a container and served cold.
– ORIGIN French, 'large earthenware pot'.

territorial • adj. **1** relating to an area of land or sea that is owned by a particular country. **2** (of an animal) having and defending a territory. • n. (**Territorial**) (in the UK) a member of the Territorial Army.
– DERIVATIVES **territoriality** n. **territorially** adv.

Territorial Army • n. (in the UK) a military reserve force of people who volunteer to train as soldiers in their spare time.

territorial waters • pl. n. the waters under the control of a state, especially those within a stated distance from its coast.

territory • n. (pl. **territories**) **1** an area

under the control of a ruler or state. **2** (**Territory**) an organized division of a country not having the full rights of a state. **3** an area defended by an animal against others of the same sex or species. **4** an area in which a person has special rights, responsibilities, or knowledge.
– ORIGIN Latin *territorium*.

terror • n. **1** extreme fear. **2** a cause of terror. **3** the use of terror to intimidate people: *weapons of terror*. **4** informal a person that causes trouble or annoyance.
– ORIGIN Latin.

terrorism • n. the unofficial or unauthorized use of violence and intimidation in the attempt to achieve political aims.
– DERIVATIVES **terrorist** n. & adj.

terrorize (or **terrorise**) • v. (**terrorizes, terrorizing, terrorized**) threaten and frighten someone over a period of time.

terry • n. fabric with raised loops of thread on both sides.

terse • adj. (**terser, tersest**) using few words; abrupt.
– DERIVATIVES **tersely** adv. **terseness** n.
– ORIGIN Latin *tersus* 'wiped, polished'.

tertiary /ter-shuh-ri/ • adj. **1** third in order or level. **2** Brit. (of education) at a level beyond that provided by schools. **3** (of medical treatment) provided at a specialist institution. **4** (**Tertiary**) Geol. relating to the first period of the Cenozoic era, about 65 to 1.64 million years ago.
– ORIGIN Latin *tertiarius*.

terylene • n. Brit. trademark a polyester fibre used to make clothing, bed linen, etc.

TESL • abbrev. teaching of English as a second language.

tesla /tess-luh, tez-luh/ • n. Physics the SI unit of magnetic flux density.
– ORIGIN named after the American electrical engineer Nikola *Tesla*.

TESOL /tee-sol/ • abbrev. teaching of English to speakers of other languages.

tessellated /tess-uh-lay-tid/ • adj. (of a floor) decorated with mosaics.
– DERIVATIVES **tessellation** n.
– ORIGIN Latin *tessellare* 'decorate with mosaics'.

tessera /tess-uh-ruh/ • n. (pl. **tesserae** /tess-uh-ree, **tess**-uh-ray/) a small tile or block of stone used in a mosaic.
– ORIGIN Greek.

tessitura /tess-i-tyoor-uh/ • n. Music the range within which most notes of a vocal part fall.
– ORIGIN Italian, 'texture'.

test[1] • n. **1** a procedure intended to

establish the quality, performance, or reliability of something. **2** a short examination of skill or knowledge. **3** a means of testing something. **4** a difficult situation that reveals the strength or quality of someone or something. **5** an examination of part of the body or a body fluid for medical purposes. **6** Chem. a procedure for identifying a substance or revealing whether it is present. **7** (**Test**) a Test match. • v. **1** subject to a test. **2** touch or taste before proceeding further. **3** severely try someone's endurance or patience.
– PHRASES **test the water** find out feelings or opinions before proceeding further.
– ORIGIN Latin *testum* 'earthen pot'.

test² • n. the shell or tough outer covering of some invertebrates and protozoans.
– ORIGIN Latin *testa* 'tile, jug, shell'.

testa /tess-tuh/ • n. (pl. **testae** /tess-tee/) the protective outer covering of a seed.
– ORIGIN Latin, 'tile, shell'.

testament • n. **1** a person's will. **2** evidence or proof of a fact, event, or quality: *the show's success is a testament to her talent.*
– ORIGIN Latin *testamentum* 'a will'.

testamentary • adj. relating to a will.

testate /tess-tayt/ • adj. having made a valid will before dying.
– ORIGIN Latin *testatus* 'testified'.

testator /tess-tay-ter/ • n. (fem. **testatrix** /tess-tay-triks/) a person who has made a will or given a legacy.
– ORIGIN Latin.

test card • n. Brit. a still television picture transmitted outside normal programme hours to help judge the quality of the image.

test case • n. Law a case setting an example for future cases.

test-drive • v. drive a motor vehicle to judge its performance and quality.

tester • n. **1** a person or device that tests something. **2** a sample of a product allowing customers to try it before buying.

testicle • n. either of the two oval organs that produce sperm in male mammals, enclosed in the scrotum behind the penis.
– DERIVATIVES **testicular** adj.
– ORIGIN Latin *testiculus*.

testify • v. (**testifies**, **testifying**, **testified**) **1** give evidence as a witness in a law court. **2** (**testify to**) be evidence or proof of: *luxurious villas testify to the wealth here.*
– ORIGIN Latin *testificari*.

testimonial /tess-ti-moh-ni-uhl/ • n. **1** a

formal statement of a person's good character and qualifications. **2** a public tribute to someone and their achievements.

testimony • n. (pl. **testimonies**) **1** a formal statement, especially one given in a court of law. **2** (**testimony to**) evidence or proof of something.
– ORIGIN Latin *testimonium*.

testis /tess-tiss/ • n. (pl. **testes** /tess-teez/) an organ which produces sperm.
– ORIGIN Latin, 'witness'.

Test match • n. an international cricket or rugby match played between teams representing two different countries.

testosterone /tess-toss-tuh-rohn/ • n. a steroid hormone that stimulates the development of male secondary sexual characteristics.
– ORIGIN from TESTIS.

test pilot • n. a pilot who flies new or modified aircraft to test their performance.

test tube • n. a thin glass tube closed at one end, used to hold material for laboratory testing or experiments.

test-tube baby • n. informal a baby conceived by in vitro fertilization.

testy • adj. (**testier**, **testiest**) easily irritated.
– DERIVATIVES **testily** adv. **testiness** n.
– ORIGIN first meaning 'headstrong': from Old French *teste* 'head'.

tetanus /tet-uh-nuhss/ • n. a disease causing the muscles to stiffen and go into spasms, spread by bacteria.
– ORIGIN Latin.

tetchy • adj. (**tetchier**, **tetchiest**) bad-tempered and irritable.
– DERIVATIVES **tetchily** adv. **tetchiness** n.
– ORIGIN prob. from Old French *teche* 'blotch, fault'.

tête-à-tête /tayt-ah-tayt/ • n. (pl. **tête-à-tête** or **tête-à-têtes** /tayt-ah-tayt/) a private conversation between two people.
– ORIGIN French, 'head-to-head'.

tether • v. (**tethers**, **tethering**, **tethered**) tie an animal with a rope or chain so as to restrict its movement. • n. a rope or chain used to tether an animal.
– ORIGIN Old Norse.

tetra- (also **tetr-** before a vowel) • comb. form four; having four: *tetrahedron.*
– ORIGIN Greek *tettares* 'four'.

tetrahedron /tet-ruh-hee-druhn/ • n. (pl. **tetrahedra** /tet-ruh-hee-druh/ or **tetrahedrons**) a solid with four plane triangular faces.

tetralogy /ti-tral-uh-ji/ • n. (pl. **tetralogies**) a group of four related books, plays, operas, etc.

tetrameter /ti-tram-i-ter/ •n. a line of verse made up of four metrical feet.

tetrapod /te-truh-pod/ •n. an animal of a group which includes all vertebrates apart from fish.
– ORIGIN Greek *tetrapous* 'four-footed'.

Teuton /tyoo-tuhn/ •n. a member of an ancient Germanic people who lived in Jutland.
– ORIGIN Latin *Teutones* (plural).

Teutonic /tyoo-ton-ik/ •adj. 1 relating to the Teutons. 2 informal, usu. derog. displaying qualities thought to belong to Germans.

text •n. 1 a book or other written or printed work. 2 the main part of a written work as distinct from appendices, illustrations, etc. 3 written or printed words or computer data. 4 a written work chosen as a subject of study. 5 a passage from the Bible as the subject of a sermon. 6 a text message.
•v. send a text message to.
– DERIVATIVES **texter** n. **texting** n.
– ORIGIN Latin *textus* 'tissue, literary style'.

textbook •n. a book used as a standard work for the study of a subject.
•adj. done in exactly the recommended way: *a textbook example of damage control.*

textile •n. a type of cloth or woven fabric. •adj. relating to fabric or weaving.
– ORIGIN Latin *textilis*.

text message •n. an electronic message sent and received via mobile phone.
– DERIVATIVES **text messaging** n.

textual •adj. relating to a text or texts.
– DERIVATIVES **textually** adv.

texture •n. the feel, appearance, or consistency of a surface, substance, or fabric. •v. (**textures**, **texturing**, **textured**) give a rough or raised texture to.
– DERIVATIVES **textural** adj.
– ORIGIN Latin *textura* 'weaving'.

TGV •n. a French high-speed passenger train.
– ORIGIN abbreviation of French *train à grande vitesse*.

Th •symb. the chemical element thorium.

Thai /ty/ •n. (pl. **Thai** or **Thais**) 1 a person from Thailand. 2 the official language of Thailand.
– ORIGIN Thai, 'free'.

thalidomide /thuh-lid-uh-myd/ •n. a drug formerly used as a sedative, but found to cause malformation of the

fetus when taken in early pregnancy.

thallium /thal-li-uhm/ •n. a soft silvery-white metallic chemical element whose compounds are very poisonous.
– ORIGIN Greek *thallos* 'green shoot'.

than •conj. & prep. 1 used to introduce the second part of a comparison. 2 used to introduce an exception or contrast. 3 used in expressions indicating one thing happening immediately after another.
– ORIGIN Old English.

> **USAGE:** For an explanation of whether to use **I** and **we** or **me** and **us** after **than**, see the note at **PERSONAL PRONOUN**.

thane /thayn/ •n. 1 (in Anglo-Saxon England) a nobleman granted land by the king or a higher-ranking nobleman. 2 (in medieval Scotland) a nobleman who held land from a Scottish king.
– ORIGIN Old English, 'servant, soldier'.

thank •v. 1 express gratitude to. 2 ironic blame or hold responsible: *you have only yourself to thank.*
– PHRASES **thank you** a polite expression of gratitude.
– ORIGIN Old English.

thankful •adj. 1 pleased and relieved. 2 expressing gratitude.
– DERIVATIVES **thankfulness** n.

thankfully •adv. 1 in a thankful way. 2 fortunately.

thankless •adj. 1 (of a job or task) unpleasant and unlikely to be appreciated by other people. 2 not showing or feeling gratitude.

thanks •pl. n. 1 an expression of gratitude. 2 thank you.
– PHRASES **no thanks to** despite the unhelpfulness of. **thanks to** due to.
– ORIGIN Old English.

thanksgiving •n. 1 the expression of gratitude to God. 2 (**Thanksgiving**) (in North America) a national holiday commemorating a harvest festival celebrated by the Pilgrim Fathers, held in the US on the fourth Thursday in November and in Canada on the second Monday in October.

that •pron. & det. 1 (pl. **those**) used to refer to a person or thing seen or heard by the speaker or already mentioned or known. 2 (pl. **those**) referring to the more distant of two things near to the speaker. 3 (as pronoun) (pl. **that**) used instead of which, who, when, etc. to introduce a clause that defines or identifies something: *the woman that owns the place.* •adv. 1 to such a degree; so. 2 informal very: *he wasn't that far away.*
•conj. introducing a statement or

suggestion: *she said that she'd be late.*
– ORIGIN Old English.

> **USAGE:** When is it right to use **that** and when should you use **which**? The general rule is that, when introducing clauses that define or identify something, it is acceptable to use **that** or **which**: *a book which aims to simplify scientific language* or *a book that aims to simplify scientific language.* You should use **which**, but never **that**, to introduce a clause giving additional information: *the book, which costs £15, has sold over a million copies,* not *the book, that costs £15, has sold over a million copies.*

thatch • n. **1** a roof covering of straw, reeds, or similar material. **2** informal a person's hair. • v. cover with thatch.
– DERIVATIVES **thatcher** n.
– ORIGIN Old English, 'cover'.

thaw • v. **1** become or make liquid or soft after being frozen. **2** (**it thaws, it is thawing, it thawed**) the weather becomes warmer and causes snow and ice to melt. **3** make or become friendlier. • n. **1** a period of warmer weather that thaws ice and snow. **2** an increase in friendliness.
– ORIGIN Old English.

the • det. **1** used to refer to one or more people or things already mentioned or easily understood; the definite article. **2** used to refer to someone or something that is the only one of its kind: *the sun.* **3** used to refer to something in a general rather than specific way: *the computer has changed our way of life.*
– ORIGIN Old English.

theatre (US **theater**) • n. **1** a building in which plays and other dramatic performances are given. **2** the writing and production of plays. **3** the dramatic quality of a play: *this is intense, moving theatre.* **4** (also **lecture theatre**) a room for lectures with seats in tiers. **5** Brit. an operating theatre. **6** the area in which something happens: *a new theatre of war has opened up.*
– ORIGIN Greek *theatron.*

theatrical • adj. **1** relating to acting, actors, or the theatre. **2** exaggerated and too dramatic. • pl. n. (**theatricals**) theatrical performances or behaviour.
– DERIVATIVES **theatricality** n. **theatrically** adv.

theatrics /thi-a-triks/ • pl. n. theatricals.

thee • pron. old use or dialect you (as the singular object of a verb or preposition).
– ORIGIN Old English.

theft • n. the action or crime of stealing.
– ORIGIN Old English.

their • possess. det. **1** belonging to or associated with the people or things previously mentioned or easily identified. **2** belonging to or associated with a person whose sex is not specified (used in place of either 'his' or 'his or her'). **3** (**Their**) used in titles.
– ORIGIN Old Norse.

> **USAGE:** Do not confuse **their**, **there**, and **they're**. **Their** means 'belonging to them' (as in *I went round to their house*), while **there** means 'in, at, or to that place' (as in *it will take an hour to get there*), and **they're** is short for 'they are' (as in *they're going to be late*).
> For an explanation of the use of **their** in the singular to mean 'his or her', see the note at **THEY**.

theirs • possess. pron. used to refer to something belonging to or associated with two or more people or things previously mentioned.

> ✓ No apostrophe: **theirs** not *their's.*

theism /thee-i-z'm/ • n. belief in the existence of a god or gods, specifically of a creator who intervenes in the universe. Compare with **DEISM**.
– DERIVATIVES **theist** n. **theistic** adj.
– ORIGIN Greek *theos* 'god'.

them • pron. (third person pl.) **1** used as the object of a verb or preposition to refer to two or more people or things previously mentioned or easily identified. **2** referring to a person whose sex is not specified (used in place of either 'him' or 'him or her').
– ORIGIN Old Norse.

> **USAGE:** For an explanation of the use of **them** in the singular to mean 'his or her', see the note at **THEY**.

thematic • adj. arranged according to subject or connected with a subject.
– DERIVATIVES **thematically** adv.

theme • n. **1** a subject of a talk, piece of writing, etc. **2** a prominent or frequently recurring melody or group of notes in a musical composition. **3** an idea that is often repeated in a work of art or literature. **4** (also **theme tune** or **music**) a piece of music played at the beginning and end of a film or programme. • adj. (of a restaurant or pub) designed in the style of a particular country, historical period, etc.
– ORIGIN Greek *thema* 'proposition'.

theme park • n. a large amusement park based around a particular idea.

themself • pron. (third person sing.) informal used instead of 'himself' or 'herself' to refer to a person whose sex is not specified.

themselves • pron. (third person pl.) **1** used as the object of a verb or preposition to refer to a group of people or things previously mentioned as the subject of the clause. **2** they or them personally. **3** used instead of 'himself' or 'herself' to refer to a person of unspecified sex.

then • adv. **1** at that time. **2** after that. **3** also. **4** therefore.
– PHRASES **but then (again)** on the other hand. **then and there** immediately.
– ORIGIN Old English.

thence (also **from thence**) • adv. formal **1** from a place or source previously mentioned. **2** as a consequence.

thenceforth (also **thenceforward**) • adv. old use or formal from that time, place, or point onward.

theocracy /thi-ok-ruh-si/ • n. (pl. **theocracies**) a system of government in which priests rule in the name of God or a god.
– DERIVATIVES **theocratic** adj.
– ORIGIN Greek *theos* 'god'.

theodolite /thi-od-uh-lyt/ • n. an instrument with a rotating telescope used in surveying for measuring horizontal and vertical angles.
– ORIGIN Latin *theodelitus*.

theologian /thi-uh-loh-juhn/ • n. a person who is an expert in or is studying theology.

theology • n. (pl. **theologies**) **1** the study of God and religious belief. **2** a system of religious beliefs and theory: *Christian theology.*
– DERIVATIVES **theological** adj. **theologically** adv. **theologist** n.

theorem /theer-uhm/ • n. **1** Physics & Math. a general proposition or rule that can be proved by reasoning. **2** Math. a rule expressed by symbols or formulae.
– ORIGIN Greek *theōrēma* 'proposition'.

theoretical (also **theoretic**) • adj. **1** concerned with the theory of a subject rather than its practical application. **2** based on theory rather than experience or practice: *British players have a theoretical advantage.*
– DERIVATIVES **theoretically** adv.

theoretician /theer-uh-ti-sh'hn/ • n. a

person who develops or studies the theory of a subject.

theorist • n. a theoretician.

theorize (or **theorise**) • v. (**theorizes**, **theorizing**, **theorized**) form a theory or theories about something.

theory • n. (pl. **theories**) **1** an idea or set of ideas that is intended to explain something. **2** a set of principles on which an activity is based: *a theory of education.*
– PHRASES **in theory** in an ideal situation, but probably not in reality.
– ORIGIN Greek *theōria* 'speculation'.

theosophy /thi-oss-uh-fi/ • n. a philosophy which believes that a knowledge of God may be achieved through such things as intuition, meditation, and prayer.
– DERIVATIVES **theosophical** adj.
– ORIGIN Greek *theosophos* 'wise concerning God'.

therapeutic /the-ruh-pyoo-tik/ • adj. **1** relating to the healing of disease. **2** having a good effect on the body or mind.
– DERIVATIVES **therapeutically** adv.

therapy • n. (pl. **therapies**) **1** treatment intended to relieve or heal a physical disorder or illness. **2** the treatment of mental or emotional problems using psychological methods.
– DERIVATIVES **therapist** n.
– ORIGIN Greek *therapeia* 'healing'.

there • adv. **1** in, at, or to that place or position. **2** on that issue. **3** used in attracting attention to someone or something. **4** (**there is/are**) used to indicate the fact or existence of something. • exclam. used to comfort someone.
– PHRASES **here and there** in various places. **there and then** immediately.
– ORIGIN Old English.

thereabouts (also **thereabout**) • adv. near that place, time, or figure.

thereafter • adv. formal after that time.

thereat • adv. old use or formal at that place.

thereby • adv. by that means; as a result of that.

therefore • adv. for that reason.

therein • adv. formal in that place, document, or respect.

thereof • adv. formal of the thing just mentioned.

thereon • adv. formal on or following from the thing just mentioned.

there's • contr. **1** there is. **2** there has.

thereto • adv. formal to that or that place.

thereupon • adv. formal immediately or shortly after that.

therewith • adv. old use or formal **1** with or in the thing mentioned. **2** soon or immediately after that.

thermal • adj. **1** relating to heat. **2** (of a garment) made of a fabric that provides good insulation to keep the body warm. • n. **1** an upward current of warm air, used by birds, gliders, and balloonists to gain height. **2** (**thermals**) thermal underwear.
– DERIVATIVES **thermally** adv.
– ORIGIN Greek *thermē* 'heat'.

thermal spring • n. a spring of naturally hot water.

thermionic /ther-mi-on-ik/ • adj. relating to the emission of electrons from substances heated to very high temperatures.

thermocouple • n. a device for measuring or sensing a temperature difference, consisting of two wires of different metals connected at two points, between which a voltage is developed in proportion to any temperature difference.

thermodynamics • n. the branch of science concerned with the relations between heat and other forms of energy involved in physical and chemical processes.
– DERIVATIVES **thermodynamic** adj. **thermodynamically** adv.

thermoelectric • adj. producing electricity by a difference of temperatures.

thermometer • n. an instrument for measuring temperature, typically consisting of a glass tube marked with a temperature scale and containing mercury or alcohol which expands when heated.

thermonuclear • adj. relating to or using nuclear fusion reactions that occur at very high temperatures.

thermoplastic • adj. (of a substance) becoming plastic when heated.

thermoregulation • n. Physiol. the control of body temperature.

Thermos • n. trademark a vacuum flask.
– ORIGIN Greek, 'hot'.

thermosetting • adj. (of a substance) setting permanently when heated.

thermosphere • n. the upper region of the atmosphere above the mesosphere.

thermostat /ther-muh-stat/ • n. a device that automatically controls temperature or activates a device at a set temperature.

– DERIVATIVES **thermostatic** adj. **thermostatically** adv.

thesaurus /thi-saw-ruhss/ • n. (pl. **thesauri** /thi-saw-ry/ or **thesauruses**) a book containing lists of words which have the same, similar, or a related meaning.
– ORIGIN Greek *thēsauros* 'storehouse, treasure'.

these pl. of THIS.

thesis /thee-siss/ • n. (pl. **theses** /thee-seez/) **1** a statement or theory put forward to be supported or proved. **2** a long piece of written work involving personal research, written as part of a university degree.
– ORIGIN Greek, 'placing, a proposition'.

thespian /thess-pi-uhn/ • adj. relating to drama and the theatre. • n. an actor or actress.
– ORIGIN from the ancient Greek dramatic poet *Thespis*.

they • pron. (third person pl.) **1** used to refer to two or more people or things previously mentioned or easily identified. **2** people in general. **3** used to refer to a person whose sex is not specified (in place of either 'he' or 'he or she').
– ORIGIN Old Norse.

> **USAGE:** Many people now think that the traditional use of **he** to refer to a person of either sex is old-fashioned and sexist; the alternative, **he or she**, is rather clumsy. For this reason, **they** (with its counterparts **them** or **their**) have become acceptable instead, as in *anyone can join if they are a resident* and *each to their own.*

they'd • contr. **1** they had. **2** they would.

they'll • contr. **1** they shall. **2** they will.

they're • contr. they are.

> **USAGE:** For an explanation of the difference between **they're**, **their**, and **there**, see the note at THEIR.

they've • contr. they have.

thiamine /thy-uh-meen/ (also **thiamin** /thy-uh-min/) • n. vitamin B$_1$, a compound found in unrefined cereals, beans, and liver.
– ORIGIN Greek *theion* 'sulphur'.

thick • adj. **1** with opposite sides or surfaces relatively far apart. **2** (of a garment or fabric) made of heavy material. **3** made up of a large number of things or people close together: *thick forest.* **4** (**thick with**) densely filled or covered with. **5** (of the air or atmosphere) heavy, dense, or difficult to see through. **6** (of a liquid or a semi-liquid substance) relatively firm in consistency. **7** informal stupid. **8** (of a voice)

hoarse or husky. **9** (of an accent) very marked and difficult to understand. **10** informal having a very close, friendly relationship. •n. (**the thick**) the middle or the busiest part: *in the thick of battle.*
– PHRASES **thick and fast** rapidly and in great numbers. (**as**) **thick as thieves** informal very close or friendly. **through thick and thin** under all circumstances, no matter how difficult.
– DERIVATIVES **thickly** adv.
– ORIGIN Old English.

thicken •v. make or become thick or thicker.
– PHRASES **the plot thickens** the situation is becoming more complicated and puzzling.
– DERIVATIVES **thickener** n.

thickening •n. **1** a thicker area or part. **2** a substance added to a liquid to make it thicker.

thicket •n. a dense group of bushes or trees.
– ORIGIN Old English.

thickness •n. **1** the distance through an object, as distinct from width or height. **2** the state or quality of being thick. **3** a layer of material. **4** a thicker part of something: *beams set into the thickness of the wall.*

thickset •adj. heavily or solidly built.

thief •n. (pl. **thieves**) a person who steals another person's property.
– ORIGIN Old English.

> ☑ **thief** follows the usual rule of *i* before *e* except after *c*.

thieve •v. (**thieves**, **thieving**, **thieved**) steal things.
– DERIVATIVES **thievery** n.

thigh •n. the part of the leg between the hip and the knee.
– ORIGIN Old English.

thimble •n. a small metal or plastic cap worn to protect the finger and push the needle in sewing.
– ORIGIN Old English.

thimbleful •n. a small quantity of something.

thin •adj. (**thinner**, **thinnest**) **1** having opposite surfaces or sides close together. **2** (of a garment or fabric) made of light material. **3** having little flesh or fat on the body. **4** having few parts or members in relation to the area covered or filled: *a thin crowd.* **5** not dense or heavy. **6** containing much liquid and not much solid substance. **7** (of a sound) faint and high-pitched. **8** weak and inadequate: *the evidence is rather thin.* •v. (**thins**, **thinning**, **thinned**) **1** make or become less thick. **2** (often **thin something out**) remove some

plants from an area to allow the others more room to grow.
– PHRASES **into thin air** so as to become invisible or non-existent.
– DERIVATIVES **thinly** adv. **thinness** n.
– ORIGIN Old English.

thine •possess. pron. & possess. det. old use your or yours.
– ORIGIN Old English.

thing •n. **1** an inanimate object. **2** an unspecified object, action, activity, etc. **3** (**things**) personal belongings or clothing. **4** (**things**) unspecified matters: *how are things?* **5** (**the thing**) informal what is needed, acceptable, or fashionable. **6** (**your thing**) informal your special interest.
– ORIGIN Old English.

thingamajig /thing-uh-muh-jig/ •n. = THINGUMMY.

thingummy /thing-uh-mi/ •n. (pl. **thingummies**) informal a person or thing whose name you have forgotten, do not know, or do not want to mention.

thingy •n. (pl. **thingies**) = THINGUMMY.

think •v. (**thinks**, **thinking**, **thought**) **1** have a particular opinion, belief, or idea about someone or something. **2** direct your mind towards someone or something. **3** (**think of/about**) take into account or consideration. **4** (**think of/about**) consider the possibility or advantages of: *he was thinking of going to America.* **5** (**think of**) call something to mind. •n. an act of thinking.
– PHRASES **think better of** decide not to do something after reconsidering it. **think nothing** (or **little**) **of** consider an activity other people see as odd, wrong, or difficult to be easy or normal. **think something over** consider something carefully. **think twice** consider a course of action carefully before going ahead with it. **think something up** informal invent something.
– DERIVATIVES **thinker** n.
– ORIGIN Old English.

thinking •n. a person's ideas or opinions. •adj. intelligent: *MacLean is the thinking man's player.*
– PHRASES **put on your thinking cap** informal think hard about a problem.

think tank •n. a group of experts providing advice and ideas on particular political or economic problems.

thinner •n. a solvent used to thin paint or other solutions.

third •ordinal number **1** that is number three in a sequence; 3rd. **2** (**a third/one third**) each of three equal parts into which something is divided. **3** a musical interval spanning three consecutive notes in a scale. **4** Brit. a place in the third

grade in the exams for a university degree.
– DERIVATIVES **thirdly** adv.
– ORIGIN Old English.

third class • n. **1** a set of people or things grouped together as the third best. **2** Brit. the third-highest division in the results of the exams for a university degree. **3** hist. the cheapest and least comfortable accommodation in a train or ship. • adj. & adv. relating to the third class.

third-degree • adj. (of burns) being of the most severe kind, affecting tissue below the skin. • n. (**the third degree**) long and harsh questioning to obtain information or a confession.

third party • n. a person or group besides the two main ones involved in a situation or dispute. • adj. Brit. (of insurance) covering damage or injury suffered by someone other than the person who is insured.

third person • n. **1** a third party. **2** see **PERSON** (sense 3).

third-rate • adj. of very poor quality.

Third Reich /rykh, ryk/ • n. the Nazi regime in Germany, 1933–45.
– ORIGIN German *Reich* 'empire'.

third way • n. a political agenda which is moderate and based on general agreement rather than left- or right-wing.

Third World • n. the developing countries of Asia, Africa, and Latin America.
– ORIGIN first used to distinguish the developing countries from the capitalist and Communist blocs.

thirst • n. **1** a feeling of needing or wanting to drink. **2** the state of not having enough water to stay alive. **3** (**thirst for**) a strong desire for. • v. **1** (**thirst for/after**) have a strong desire for. **2** old use feel a need to drink.
– ORIGIN Old English.

thirsty • adj. (**thirstier, thirstiest**) **1** feeling or causing thirst: *modelling is thirsty work.* **2** (of an engine or plant) consuming a lot of fuel or water. **3** (**thirsty for**) having or showing a strong desire for.
– DERIVATIVES **thirstily** adv. **thirstiness** n.

thirteen • cardinal number one more than twelve; 13. (Roman numeral: **xiii** or **XIII**.)
– DERIVATIVES **thirteenth** ordinal number.
– ORIGIN Old English.

thirty • cardinal number (pl. **thirties**) ten less than forty; 30. (Roman numeral: **xxx** or **XXX**.)
– DERIVATIVES **thirtieth** ordinal number.
– ORIGIN Old English.

this • pron. & det. (pl. **these**) **1** used to identify a specific person or thing close

at hand, just mentioned, or being indicated or experienced. **2** referring to the nearer of two things close to the speaker. **3** (as determiner) used with periods of time related to the present: *how are you this morning?* • adv. to the degree or extent indicated.
– ORIGIN Old English.

thistle • n. a plant with a prickly stem and leaves and rounded heads of purple flowers.
– ORIGIN Old English.

thistledown • n. the light fluffy down of thistle seeds, which enable them to be blown about in the wind.

thither • adv. old use or literary to or towards that place.
– ORIGIN Old English.

tho' (also **tho**) • conj. & adv. informal spelling of **THOUGH**.

thole /thohl/ (also **thole pin**) • n. a pin fitted to the gunwale of a rowing boat, on which an oar turns.
– ORIGIN Old English.

thong • n. **1** a narrow strip of leather or other material, used as a fastening or as the lash of a whip. **2** a pair of knickers or skimpy bathing garment like a G-string.
– ORIGIN Old English.

thorax /thor-aks/ • n. (pl. **thoraces** /thor-uh-seez/ or **thoraxes**) **1** the part of the body between the neck and the abdomen. **2** the middle section of the body of an insect, bearing the legs and wings.
– DERIVATIVES **thoracic** adj.
– ORIGIN Greek.

thorium /thor-i-uhm/ • n. a white radioactive metallic chemical element.
– ORIGIN named after *Thor*, the Scandinavian god of thunder.

thorn • n. **1** a stiff, sharp-pointed woody projection on a plant. **2** a thorny bush, shrub, or tree.
– PHRASES **a thorn in someone's side** (or **flesh**) a source of continual annoyance or trouble.
– ORIGIN Old English.

thorny • adj. (**thornier, thorniest**) **1** having many thorns or thorn bushes. **2** causing trouble or difficulty.

thorough • adj. **1** complete with regard to every detail. **2** performed with or showing great care and completeness. **3** absolute; utter: *he is a thorough nuisance.*
– DERIVATIVES **thoroughly** adv. **thoroughness** n.
– ORIGIN Old English, 'through'.

thoroughbred • adj. (of an animal, especially a horse) of pure breed. • n. a thoroughbred animal.

thoroughfare • n. a road or path

forming a route between two places.

thoroughgoing •adj. **1** involving or dealing with every detail or aspect. **2** complete; absolute.

those pl. of THAT.

thou[1] •pron. old use or dialect you (as the singular subject of a verb).
– ORIGIN Old English.

thou[2] •n. (pl. **thou** or **thous**) **1** informal a thousand. **2** one thousandth of an inch.

though •conj. **1** despite the fact that; although. **2** however; but. •adv. however: *he was able to write, though.*
– ORIGIN Old English.

thought[1] •n. **1** an idea or opinion produced by thinking, or that occurs suddenly in the mind. **2** the process of thinking. **3** (**your thoughts**) your mind. **4** careful consideration: *I haven't given it much thought.* **5** (**thought of**) an intention, hope, or idea of: *they had no thought of surrender.* **6** the forming of opinions or the opinions so formed: *traditions of Western thought.*
– ORIGIN Old English.

thought[2] past and past part. of THINK.

thoughtful •adj. **1** deep in thought. **2** showing careful consideration. **3** showing consideration for other people.
– DERIVATIVES **thoughtfully** adv. **thoughtfulness** n.

thoughtless •adj. **1** not showing consideration for other people. **2** without considering the consequences of something.
– DERIVATIVES **thoughtlessly** adv. **thoughtlessness** n.

thousand •cardinal number **1** (**a/one thousand**) the number equivalent to the product of a hundred and ten; 1,000. (Roman numeral: **m** or **M**.) **2** (**thousands**) informal an unspecified large number.
– DERIVATIVES **thousandth** ordinal number.
– ORIGIN Old English.

thrall /thrawl/ •n. the state of being in another's power: *she was in thrall to her husband.*
– ORIGIN Old Norse, 'slave'.

thrash •v. **1** beat someone or something repeatedly and violently with a stick or whip. **2** move in a violent or uncontrolled way. **3** informal defeat heavily. **4** (**thrash something out**) discuss an issue frankly and thoroughly so as to reach a decision.
– ORIGIN Old English.

thread •n. **1** a thin strand of cotton, nylon, or other fibres used in sewing or weaving. **2** a long thin line or piece of something. **3** (also **screw thread**) a spiral ridge on the outside of a screw or

bolt or on the inside of a cylindrical hole, to allow two parts to be screwed together. **4** a theme running through a situation or piece of writing. •v. **1** pass a thread through. **2** move or weave in and out of obstacles. **3** (as adj. **threaded**) (of a hole, screw, etc.) having a screw thread.
– ORIGIN Old English.

threadbare •adj. thin and tattered with age.

threadworm •n. a thin, thread-like worm, living as a parasite.

threat •n. **1** a stated intention to harm someone, especially if they do not do what you want. **2** a person or thing likely to cause harm or danger. **3** the possibility of trouble or danger.
– ORIGIN Old English, 'oppression'.

threaten •v. **1** state your intention to harm someone or to cause trouble if you do not get what you want. **2** put at risk: *a broken finger threatened his career.* **3** seem likely to produce an unwelcome result.

three •cardinal number one more than two; 3. (Roman numeral: **iii** or **III**.)
– DERIVATIVES **threefold** adj. & adv.
– ORIGIN Old English.

three-dimensional •adj. having or appearing to have length, breadth, and depth.

3G •adj. (of telephone technology) third-generation.

three-legged race •n. a race run by pairs of people, one member of each pair having their left leg tied to the right leg of the other.

three-line whip •n. (in the UK) a written notice, underlined three times to stress its urgency, requiring members of a political party to attend a vote in parliament.

threepence /threp-uhnss, thrup-uhnss/ •n. Brit. the sum of three pence before decimalization (1971).

threepenny bit /thri-puh-ni, thru-puh-ni/ •n. Brit. hist. a coin worth three old pence (1¼ p).

three-piece •adj. **1** (of a set of furniture) consisting of a sofa and two armchairs. **2** (of a set of clothes) consisting of trousers or a skirt with a waistcoat and jacket.

three-point turn •n. a method of turning a vehicle round in a narrow space by moving forwards, backwards, and forwards again in a sequence of arcs.

three-quarter •n. Rugby each of four players in a team positioned across the field behind the halfbacks.

threescore •cardinal number literary sixty.

threesome •n. a group of three people.

threnody /thren-uh-di/ •n. (pl. **threnodies**) a song, piece of music, or poem expressing grief or regret.
– ORIGIN Greek *thrēnōidia*.

thresh •v. separate grains of corn from the rest of the plant.
– DERIVATIVES **thresher** n.
– ORIGIN Old English.

threshold /thresh-ohld, thresh-hohld/ •n. 1 a strip of wood or stone forming the bottom of a doorway. 2 a level or point at which something is about to begin: *she was on the threshold of a dazzling career*.
– ORIGIN Old English.

> ☑ Spell **threshold** with only one **h** in the middle.

threw past of THROW.

thrice /thryss/ •adv. old use or literary 1 three times. 2 very: *I was thrice blessed*.
– ORIGIN Old English.

thrift •n. 1 carefulness and economy in the use of money and other resources so as to avoid waste. 2 a plant with low-growing tufts of slender leaves and rounded pink flower heads, found on sea cliffs and mountains.
– ORIGIN Old Norse, 'grasp'.

thriftless •adj. spending money in an extravagant and wasteful way.

thrifty •adj. (**thriftier, thriftiest**) careful and economical with money.

thrill •n. 1 a sudden feeling of excitement and pleasure. 2 an exciting or pleasurable experience. 3 a wave of emotion or sensation: *a thrill of excitement ran through her*. •v. 1 give someone a sudden feeling of excitement and pleasure. 2 (**thrill to**) experience something exciting.
– DERIVATIVES **thrilling** adj.
– ORIGIN from dialect *thirl* 'pierce, bore'.

thriller •n. a novel, play, or film with an exciting plot, typically involving crime or spying.

thrips /thrips/ (also **thrip**) •n. (pl. **thrips**) a tiny black insect which sucks plant sap, noted for swarming on warm still summer days.
– ORIGIN Greek, 'woodworm'.

thrive •v. (**thrives, thriving, thrived** or **throve**; past part. **thrived** or **thriven**) 1 grow or develop well or vigorously. 2 prosper; flourish.
– ORIGIN Old Norse, 'grasp'.

thro' •prep., adv., & adj. literary or informal = THROUGH.

throat •n. 1 the passage which leads from the back of the mouth, through which food passes to the oesophagus and air passes to the lungs. 2 the front part of the neck.

– PHRASES **be at each other's throats** be arguing or fighting. **force something down someone's throat** force something on a person's attention. **stick in your throat** be unwelcome or hard to accept.
– ORIGIN Old English.

throaty •adj. (**throatier, throatiest**) (of a voice or other sound) deep and husky.
– DERIVATIVES **throatily** adv.

throb •v. (**throbs, throbbing, throbbed**) 1 beat or sound with a strong, regular rhythm. 2 feel pain in a series of pulsations. •n. a strong, regular beat or sound.

throes /throhz/ •pl. n. severe or violent pain and struggle.
– PHRASES **in the throes of** in the middle of doing or dealing with something difficult or traumatic.
– ORIGIN perh. from Old English, 'calamity'.

thrombosis /throm-boh-siss/ •n. (pl. **thromboses** /throm-boh-seez/) the formation of a blood clot in a blood vessel or the heart.
– ORIGIN Greek, 'curdling'.

throne •n. 1 a chair for a king, queen, or bishop, used during ceremonies. 2 (**the throne**) the power or rank of a king or queen.
– ORIGIN Greek *thronos* 'elevated seat'.

throng •n. a large, densely packed crowd. •v. gather somewhere in large numbers.
– ORIGIN Old English.

throttle •n. a device controlling the flow of fuel or power to an engine. •v. (**throttles, throttling, throttled**) 1 attack or kill by choking or strangling. 2 control an engine or vehicle with a throttle.
– ORIGIN perh. from THROAT.

through •prep. & adv. 1 moving in one side and out of the other side of an opening or place. 2 (prep.) expressing the location of something beyond an opening or an obstacle: *the approach to the church is through a gate*. 3 continuing in time towards: *she struggled through until pay day*. 4 from beginning to end: *we sat through some boring speeches*. 5 by means of. 6 (adv.) so as to be connected by telephone. •adj. 1 (of public transport or a ticket) continuing or valid to the final destination. 2 (of traffic, roads, etc.) passing straight through a place. 3 having successfully passed to the next stage of a competition. 4 informal having finished an activity, relationship, etc.
– ORIGIN Old English.

throughout •prep. & adv. all the way through.

throughput • n. the amount of material or items passing through a system or process.

throve past of THRIVE.

throw • v. (**throws, throwing, threw;** past part. **thrown**) **1** send something from your hand through the air by a rapid movement of the arm and hand. **2** move or place hurriedly or roughly. **3** direct or cast light, an expression, etc. in a particular direction. **4** send suddenly into a particular state: *the country was thrown into chaos.* **5** confuse or put off. **6** have a tantrum. **7** hold a party. **8** make a clay pot, dish, etc. on a potter's wheel. • n. **1** an act of throwing. **2** a light cover for furniture. **3** (**a throw**) informal a single turn, round, or item.
– PHRASES **throw something away 1** get rid of something useless or unwanted. **2** fail to make use of an opportunity. **2** withdraw; give up. **throw in 1** include (something extra) with something that is being sold or offered. **2** make (a remark) casually as an interjection in a conversation. **2** admit defeat. **throw oneself into** start to do with enthusiasm and vigour. **throw open** make generally accessible. **throw someone/thing out 1** force someone to leave. **2** get rid of something useless or unwanted. **throw up** informal vomit.
– ORIGIN Old English, 'to twist, turn'.

throwaway • adj. **1** intended to be thrown away after being used once or a few times. **2** (of a remark) said casually or without careful thought.

throwback • n. a person or thing that resembles someone or something that existed in the past.

throw-in • n. Football & Rugby the act of throwing the ball from the sideline to restart the game after the ball has gone out of play.

thru • prep., adv., & adj. informal = THROUGH.

thrum • v. (**thrums, thrumming, thrummed**) make a continuous rhythmic humming sound. • n. a continuous rhythmic humming sound.

thrush¹ • n. a songbird with a brown back and spotted breast.
– ORIGIN Old English.

thrush² • n. infection of the mouth and throat or the genitals by a yeast-like fungus.

thrust • v. (**thrusts, thrusting, thrust**) **1** push suddenly or violently. **2** make your way forcibly. **3** (**thrust something on**) force someone to accept or deal with something. • n. **1** a sudden or violent lunge or attack. **2** the main point of an argument. **3** the force produced by an engine to propel a jet or rocket.

– ORIGIN Old Norse.

thrusting • adj. aggressively ambitious.

thud • n. a dull, heavy sound. • v. (**thuds, thudding, thudded**) move, fall, or strike something with a thud.
– ORIGIN prob. from Old English, 'to thrust, push'.

thug • n. a violent and aggressive man.
– DERIVATIVES **thuggery** n. **thuggish** adj.
– ORIGIN Hindi, 'swindler, thief'.

thulium /thyoo-li-uhm/ • n. a soft silvery-white metallic chemical element.
– ORIGIN from *Thule*, a country said in ancient times to be the northernmost part of the world.

thumb • n. the short, thick first digit of the hand. • v. **1** press with the thumb. **2** turn over pages with the thumb. **3** (as adj. **thumbed**) (of a book's pages) worn or dirty from repeated handling. **4** ask for a free ride in a passing vehicle by signalling with the thumb.
– PHRASES **thumbs up** (or **down**) informal an indication of satisfaction or approval (or of rejection or failure). **under someone's thumb** completely under someone's control.
– ORIGIN Old English.

thumb index • n. a set of lettered notches cut down the side of a book to make it easier to find the section wanted.

thumbnail • n. the nail of the thumb. • adj. brief or concise: *a thumbnail sketch.*

thumbscrew • n. an instrument of torture that crushes the thumbs.

thumbtack • n. N. Amer. a drawing pin.

thump • v. **1** hit heavily with the fist or a blunt object. **2** put down forcefully or noisily. **3** (of a person's heart or pulse) beat strongly. • n. a heavy dull blow or noise.

thumping • adj. **1** pounding; throbbing. **2** Brit. informal impressively large: *a thumping 64 per cent majority.*

thunder • n. **1** a loud rumbling or crashing noise heard after a lightning flash due to the expansion of rapidly heated air. **2** a loud deep resounding noise. • v. **1** (**it thunders, it is thundering, it thundered**) thunder sounds. **2** make a loud deep resounding noise. **3** speak loudly and angrily.
– DERIVATIVES **thundery** adj.
– ORIGIN Old English.

thunderbolt • n. a flash of lightning with a crash of thunder at the same time.

thunderclap • n. a crash of thunder.

thundercloud • n. a cloud with a towering or spreading top, charged with electricity and producing thunder and lightning.

thunderous • adj. **1** very loud. **2** (of a person's expression) very angry or threatening.

thunderstorm • n. a storm with thunder and lightning.

thunderstruck • adj. very surprised or shocked.

thurible /thyoor-ib-uhl/ • n. a container in which incense is burnt; a censer.
– ORIGIN Latin *thuribulum*.

Thursday • n. the day of the week before Friday and following Wednesday.
– ORIGIN Old English, 'day of thunder' (named after the Germanic thunder god *Thor*).

thus • adv. formal **1** as a result of this; therefore. **2** in this way. **3** to this point; so.
– ORIGIN Old English.

thwack • v. hit with a sharp blow. • n. a sharp blow.

thwart /thwort/ • v. prevent someone from accomplishing something.
– ORIGIN Old Norse, 'transverse'.

thy (also **thine** before a vowel) • possess. det. old use or dialect your.
– ORIGIN Old English.

thyme /rhymes with time/ • n. a sweet-smelling plant of the mint family, used as a herb in cooking.
– ORIGIN Greek *thumon*.

thymus /thy-muhss/ • n. (pl. **thymi** /thy-my/) a gland in the neck which produces white blood cells for the immune system.
– ORIGIN Greek *thumos*.

thyroid /thy-royd/ • n. (also **thyroid gland**) a large gland in the neck which produces hormones regulating growth and development.
– ORIGIN from Greek *khondros thureoeidēs* 'shield-shaped cartilage'.

thyself • pron. (second person sing.) old use or dialect yourself.

Ti • symb. the chemical element titanium.

ti • n. N. Amer. = TE.

tiara • n. a semicircular jewelled ornamental band worn on the front of a woman's hair.
– ORIGIN Greek.

Tibetan • n. **1** a person from Tibet. **2** the language of Tibet. • adj. relating to Tibet.

tibia /ti-bi-uh/ • n. (pl. **tibiae** /ti-bi-ee/ or **tibias**) the inner of the two bones between the knee and the ankle, parallel with the fibula.
– ORIGIN Latin, 'shin bone'.

tic • n. a recurring spasm in the muscles of the face.
– ORIGIN Italian *ticchio*.

tick¹ • n. **1** Brit. a mark (✓) used to show

that something is correct or has been chosen or checked. **2** a regular short, sharp sound. **3** Brit. informal a moment. • v. **1** esp. Brit. mark with a tick. **2** make regular ticking sounds. **3** (**tick away/by/past**) (of time) keep passing. **4** (**tick over**) (of an engine) run slowly while the vehicle is not moving. **5** (**tick over**) work or operate slowly or at a minimum level. **6** (**tick someone off**) Brit. informal reprimand someone.
– ORIGIN prob. Germanic.

tick² • n. a tiny creature related to the spiders, which attaches itself to the skin and sucks blood.
– ORIGIN Old English.

tick³ • n. (in phr. **on tick**) on credit.
– ORIGIN prob. from the phrase *on the ticket*, referring to a promise to pay.

ticker • n. informal a person's heart.

ticker tape • n. a continuous paper strip on which information is printed by a machine.

ticket • n. **1** a piece of paper or card giving the holder the right to be admitted to a place or event or to travel on public transport. **2** an official notice of a parking or driving offence. **3** a label attached to an item in a shop, giving its price, size, etc. • v. (**tickets, ticketing, ticketed**) issue with a ticket.
– ORIGIN Old French *estiquet*.

ticking • n. a hard-wearing material used to cover mattresses.
– ORIGIN prob. from Greek *thēkē* 'case'.

tickle • v. (**tickles, tickling, tickled**) **1** lightly touch in a way that causes itching or twitching and often laughter. **2** be appealing or amusing to. • n. an act of tickling, or the sensation of being tickled.
– DERIVATIVES **tickly** adj.
– ORIGIN perh. from TICK¹, or from Scots and dialect *kittle* 'to tickle'.

ticklish • adj. **1** sensitive to being tickled. **2** (of a situation or problem) requiring careful handling; tricky.

tidal • adj. relating to or affected by tides.
– DERIVATIVES **tidally** adv.

tidal wave • n. an exceptionally large ocean wave, caused by an earthquake, storm, etc.

tidbit • n. US = TITBIT.

tiddler • n. Brit. informal **1** a small fish. **2** a young or unusually small person or thing.
– ORIGIN perh. from TIDDLY² or *tittlebat*, a child's word for *stickleback*.

tiddly¹ • adj. (**tiddlier, tiddliest**) informal, esp. Brit. slightly drunk.
– ORIGIN perh. from former slang

tiddlywink, referring to an unlicensed pub.

tiddly² •adj. (**tiddlier**, **tiddliest**) Brit. informal little; tiny.

tiddlywinks •n. a game in which small plastic counters are flicked into a central container, using a larger counter.

tide •n. **1** the alternate rising and falling of the sea due to the attraction of the moon and sun. **2** a powerful surge of feeling or trend of events: *the tide of racism sweeping Europe.* •v. (**tides**, **tiding**, **tided**) (**tide someone over**) help someone through a difficult period.
– ORIGIN Old English, 'time, period, era'.

tideline •n. a line made by the sea on a beach at the highest point of a tide.

tidemark •n. Brit. informal a dirty mark left around the inside of a bath at the level reached by the water.

tidewater •n. water brought or affected by tides.

tidings •pl. n. literary news; information.
– ORIGIN Old English.

tidy •adj. (**tidier**, **tidiest**) **1** arranged neatly and in order. **2** liking to keep yourself and your possessions neat and in order. **3** informal (of a sum of money) considerable. •n. (pl. **tidies**) **1** (also **tidy-up**) Brit. an act of tidying. **2** a container for holding small objects. •v. (**tidies**, **tidying**, **tidied**) **1** (often **tidy someone/thing up**) make someone or something tidy. **2** (**tidy something away**) put something away for the sake of tidiness.
– DERIVATIVES **tidily** adv. **tidiness** n.
– ORIGIN first meaning 'timely': from TIDE.

tie •v. (**ties**, **tying**, **tied**) **1** attach or fasten with string, cord, etc. **2** form into a knot or bow. **3** restrict to a particular situation or place. **4** connect; link. **5** achieve the same score or ranking as another competitor. •n. (pl. **ties**) **1** a thing that ties. **2** a strip of material worn beneath a collar, tied in a knot at the front. **3** a result in a game or match in which two or more competitors are equal. **4** Brit. a sports match in which the winners proceed to the next round of the competition. **5** Music a curved line above or below two notes of the same pitch indicating that they are to be played as one note. **6** a rod or beam holding parts of a structure together.
– PHRASES **tie in** fit or be in harmony. **tie someone up 1** restrict someone's movement by binding their limbs. **2** informal occupy someone so that they have no time for any other activity. **tie something up** settle something in a satisfactory way.
– ORIGIN Old English.

tiebreaker (also **tiebreak**) •n. a means

of deciding a winner from competitors who are equal at the end of a game or match.

tied •adj. Brit. **1** (of accommodation) rented by someone on condition that they work for the owner. **2** (of a pub) owned and controlled by a brewery.

tie-dye •v. produce patterns on fabric by tying knots in it before it is dyed.

tie-in •n. **1** a connection or association. **2** a product produced to take commercial advantage of a related film, book, etc.

tiepin •n. an ornamental pin for holding a tie in place.

tier •n. one of a series of rows or levels placed one above and behind the other.
– DERIVATIVES **tiered** adj.
– ORIGIN French *tire* 'sequence, order'.

tie-up •n. a link or connection.

tiff •n. informal a trivial quarrel.
– ORIGIN prob. dialect.

tiffin •n. dated or Indian a snack or light meal.

tig •n. Brit. = TAG².
– ORIGIN perh. from TICK¹.

tiger •n. a large member of the cat family, with a yellow-brown coat striped with black, native to the forests of Asia.
– ORIGIN Greek *tigris*.

tiger lily •n. a tall Asian lily which has orange flowers spotted with black or purple.

tiger moth •n. a moth with boldly spotted and streaked wings.

tiger prawn (also **tiger shrimp**) •n. a large edible prawn marked with dark bands.

tight •adj. **1** fixed, closed, or fastened firmly. **2** (of clothes) close-fitting. **3** well sealed against something such as water or air. **4** (of a rope, fabric, or surface) stretched so as to leave no slack. **5** (of an area or space) allowing little room for movement. **6** (of people or things) closely packed together. **7** (of a form of control) strict: *security was tight.* **8** (of money or time) limited. **9** Brit. informal mean; ungenerous. •adv. very firmly, closely, or tensely.
– DERIVATIVES **tightly** adv. **tightness** n.
– ORIGIN prob. from Germanic.

tighten •v. make or become tight or tighter.

tight-fisted •adj. informal not willing to spend or give much money.

tight-knit (also **tightly knit**) •adj. (of a group of people) closely linked by strong relationships and common interests.

tight-lipped •adj. unwilling to give away information or express emotion.

t

tightrope •n. a rope or wire stretched high above the ground, on which acrobats balance.

tights •pl. n. a close-fitting garment made of stretchy material, covering the hips, legs, and feet.

tigress •n. a female tiger.

tikka /tik-uh, tee-kuh/ •n. an Indian dish of pieces of meat or vegetables marinated in a spice mixture.
– ORIGIN Punjabi.

tilde /til-duh/ •n. an accent (˜) placed over Spanish *n* or Portuguese *a* or *o* to change the way they are pronounced.
– ORIGIN Spanish.

tile •n. a thin square or rectangular piece of baked clay, concrete, cork, etc., used for covering roofs, floors, or walls.
•v. (**tiles, tiling, tiled**) cover with tiles.
– PHRASES **on the tiles** informal, esp. Brit. having a lively night out.
– DERIVATIVES **tiler** n.
– ORIGIN Latin *tegula*.

tiling •n. a surface covered by tiles.

till¹ •prep. & conj. less formal way of saying UNTIL.
– ORIGIN Old English (not a shortened form of *until*).

> **USAGE:** Although **till** and **until** have the same meaning, **till** is felt to be more informal and is used more often in speech than in writing. It is also more usual to use **until** at the beginning of a sentence.

till² •n. a cash register or drawer for money in a shop, bank, or restaurant.

till³ •v. prepare land for growing crops.
– ORIGIN Old English, 'strive for'.

tiller •n. a horizontal bar fitted to the head of a boat's rudder post and used for steering.
– ORIGIN Old French *telier* 'weaver's beam, stock of a crossbow'.

tilt •v. **1** move into a sloping position. **2** change in attitude or tendency: *the balance of power tilted towards the workers.* **3** (**tilt at**) hist. (in jousting) thrust at someone with a lance. •n. **1** a tilting position or movement. **2** (**tilt at**) an attempt at winning something. **3** a bias or tendency. **4** hist. a joust.
– PHRASES (**at**) **full tilt** with maximum speed or force.
– ORIGIN perh. from Old English, 'unsteady'.

tilth •n. the condition of soil that has been prepared for crops.
– ORIGIN Old English.

timber •n. **1** wood prepared for use in building and carpentry. **2** a wooden beam used in building.
– DERIVATIVES **timbered** adj.
– ORIGIN Old English, 'a building'.

timbre /tam-ber/ •n. **1** the quality of a musical sound or voice as distinct from its pitch and strength. **2** distinctive quality or character.
– ORIGIN French.

time •n. **1** the unlimited continued progress of existence and events in the past, present, and future. **2** (also **times**) a point or period of time: *Victorian times.* **3** a point of time as measured in hours and minutes past midnight or noon: *the time is 9.30.* **4** the right or agreed moment to do something: *the departure time.* **5** (**a time**) an indefinite period. **6** the length of time taken to complete an activity. **7** time as available or used: *a waste of time.* **8** an instance of something happening or being done: *this is the first time I have got into debt.* **9** (**times**) (following a number) expressing multiplication. **10** the rhythmic pattern or tempo of a piece of music. **11** the normal rate of pay for time spent working. **12** Brit. the moment at which the opening hours of a pub end. **13** informal a prison sentence. •v. (**times, timing, timed**) **1** arrange a time for. **2** do at a particular time. **3** measure the time taken by. **4** (**time something out**) (of a computer or a program) cancel an operation automatically because a set interval of time has passed.
– PHRASES **behind the times** not aware of or using the latest ideas or techniques. **for the time being** until some other arrangement is made. **in time 1** not late. **2** eventually. **on time** punctual; punctually. **time will tell** the truth about something will be established in the future.
– ORIGIN Old English.

time-and-motion study •n. a study of the efficiency of a company's working methods.

time bomb •n. a bomb designed to explode at a set time.

time capsule •n. a container holding objects typical of the present time that is buried for discovery in the future.

time frame •n. a specified period of time.

time-honoured •adj. (of a custom or tradition) respected or valued because it has existed for a long time.

timekeeper •n. **1** a person who records the amount of time taken by a process or activity. **2** a person regarded in terms of how punctual they are.
– DERIVATIVES **timekeeping** n.

time-lapse •adj. (of a photographic technique) taking a sequence of frames at set intervals to record changes that take place slowly over time.

timeless • adj. not affected by the passage of time or changes in fashion.
– DERIVATIVES **timelessly** adv. **timelessness** n.

timely • adj. done or occurring at a good or appropriate time.
– DERIVATIVES **timeliness** n.

time off • n. time spent away from your usual work or studies.

timepiece • n. an instrument for measuring time; a clock or watch.

timer • n. **1** a device that stops or starts a machine at a preset time. **2** a device that records the amount of time taken by something.

timescale • n. the time allowed for or taken by a process or series of events.

time-server • n. a person who makes very little effort at work because they are waiting to leave or retire.

timeshare • n. an arrangement in which joint owners use a property as a holiday home at different specified times.

time sheet • n. a piece of paper for recording the number of hours worked.

time signature • n. a sign in the form of two numbers at the start of a piece of music showing the number of beats in a bar.

timetable • n. a list or plan of times at which events are scheduled to take place. • v. (**timetables, timetabling, timetabled**) schedule to take place at a particular time.

time trial • n. (in various sports) a test of a competitor's individual speed over a set distance.

timid • adj. (**timider, timidest**) not brave or confident.
– DERIVATIVES **timidity** n. **timidly** adv.
– ORIGIN Latin *timidus*.

timing • n. **1** the choice, judgement, or control of when something should be done. **2** a particular time when something happens.

timorous /tim-uh-ruhss/ • adj. nervous or lacking in confidence.
– DERIVATIVES **timorously** adv. **timorousness** n.
– ORIGIN Latin *timorosus*.

timpani /tim-puh-ni/ (also **tympani**) • pl. n. kettledrums.
– ORIGIN Italian.

tin • n. **1** a silvery-white metallic chemical element. **2** an airtight container with a lid, made of tinplate or aluminium. **3** Brit. a sealed tinplate or aluminium container for preserving food; a can. **4** an open metal container for baking food. • v. (**tins, tinning, tinned**) **1** cover with a thin layer of tin. **2** (as adj. **tinned**) Brit. preserved in a tin.

– ORIGIN Old English.

tincture /tingk-cher/ • n. **1** a medicine made by dissolving a drug in alcohol. **2** a slight trace.
– ORIGIN Latin *tinctura* 'dyeing'.

tinder • n. dry material which burns easily, used for lighting a fire.
– ORIGIN Old English.

tinderbox • n. hist. a box containing tinder, flint, a steel, and other items for lighting fires.

tine /rhymes with line/ • n. a prong or sharp point, especially of a fork.
– DERIVATIVES **tined** adj.
– ORIGIN Old English.

tinfoil • n. metal foil used for covering or wrapping food.

ting • n. a sharp, clear ringing sound. • v. make a sharp, clear ringing sound.

tinge • v. (**tinges, tinging** or **tingeing, tinged**) **1** colour something slightly. **2** give a small amount of a quality to: *a visit tinged with sadness.* • n. a slight trace of a colour or quality.
– ORIGIN Latin *tingere* 'to dip or colour'.

tingle • v. (**tingles, tingling, tingled**) experience a slight prickling or stinging feeling. • n. a slight prickling or stinging feeling.
– DERIVATIVES **tingly** adj.
– ORIGIN perh. from TINKLE.

tinker • n. **1** a travelling mender of pots, kettles, etc. **2** an act of tinkering with something. • v. (**tinkers, tinkering, tinkered**) (**tinker with**) try to repair or improve something by making many small changes.

tinkle • v. (**tinkles, tinkling, tinkled**) make a light, clear ringing sound. • n. a light, clear ringing sound.
– DERIVATIVES **tinkly** adj.

tinnitus /tin-ni-tuhss, ti-ny-tuhss/ • n. Med. ringing or buzzing in the ears.
– ORIGIN Latin.

tinny • adj. **1** having a thin, metallic sound. **2** made of thin or poor-quality metal.

tinplate • n. sheet steel or iron coated with tin.

tinpot • adj. informal not significant or effective: *a tinpot dictator.*

tinsel • n. thin strips of shiny metal foil attached to a length of thread, used for decoration.
– DERIVATIVES **tinselly** adj.
– ORIGIN Old French *estincele* 'spark'.

Tinseltown • n. the glamorous but artificial world of Hollywood and its film industry.

tinsmith • n. a person who makes or repairs articles made of tin or tinplate.

tint • n. **1** a shade of a colour. **2** a dye for

colouring the hair. • v. **1** colour something slightly. **2** dye the hair.
– ORIGIN Latin *tinctus* 'dyeing'.

tintinnabulation /tin-tin-nab-yuu-**lay**-sh'n/ • n. a ringing or tinkling sound.
– ORIGIN Latin *tintinnabulum* 'tinkling bell'.

tin whistle • n. a metal musical instrument like a small flute.

tiny • adj. (**tinier**, **tiniest**) very small.
– DERIVATIVES **tinily** adv. **tininess** n.

tip[1] • n. **1** the pointed or rounded end of something thin or tapering. **2** a small part fitted to the end of an object. • v. (**tips**, **tipping**, **tipped**) (usu. as adj. **tipped**) attach to or cover the tip of.
– PHRASES **on the tip of your tongue** almost but not quite spoken or coming to mind.
– ORIGIN Old Norse.

tip[2] • v. (**tips**, **tipping**, **tipped**) **1** overbalance so as to fall or turn over. **2** be or put in a sloping position. **3** empty out the contents of a container by holding it at an angle. • n. **1** Brit. a place where rubbish is left. **2** informal a dirty or untidy place.
– ORIGIN perh. Scandinavian.

tip[3] • n. **1** a small extra sum of money given to someone for good service. **2** a piece of practical advice. **3** a prediction about the likely winner of a race or contest. • v. (**tips**, **tipping**, **tipped**) **1** give a tip to. **2** Brit. predict that someone is likely to win or achieve something. **3** (**tip someone off**) informal give someone secret information.
– ORIGIN prob. from TIP[1].

tipi • n. var. of TEPEE.

tip-off • n. informal a piece of secret information.

tippet • n. a long piece of fur worn around the neck, or the neck and shoulders, by women.
– ORIGIN prob. from TIP[1].

tipple • v. (**tipples**, **tippling**, **tippled**) drink alcohol regularly. • n. informal an alcoholic drink.
– DERIVATIVES **tippler** n.

tipstaff • n. a sheriff's officer; a bailiff.
– ORIGIN from *tipped staff*, a bailiff's metal-tipped staff.

tipster • n. a person who gives tips as to the likely winner of a race or contest.

tipsy • adj. (**tipsier**, **tipsiest**) slightly drunk.
– DERIVATIVES **tipsily** adv. **tipsiness** n.
– ORIGIN from TIP[2].

tiptoe • v. (**tiptoes**, **tiptoeing**, **tiptoed**) walk quietly and carefully with the heels raised.

– PHRASES **on tiptoe** (or **tiptoes**) with the heels raised.

tip-top • adj. of the very best quality.

tirade /ty-**rayd**, ti-**rayd**/ • n. a long angry speech.
– ORIGIN French.

tiramisu /tir-uh-mi-**soo**/ • n. an Italian dessert consisting of sponge cake soaked in coffee and brandy, with powdered chocolate and mascarpone cheese.
– ORIGIN from Italian *tira mi sù* 'pick me up'.

tire[1] • v. (**tires**, **tiring**, **tired**) **1** make or become in need of rest or sleep. **2** make someone feel impatient or bored. **3** (**tire of**) become impatient or bored with.
– ORIGIN Old English.

tire[2] • n. US = TYRE.

tired • adj. **1** in need of sleep or rest. **2** (**tired of**) bored with. **3** (of a statement or idea) uninteresting because too familiar.
– DERIVATIVES **tiredly** adv. **tiredness** n.

tireless • adj. having or showing great effort or energy.
– DERIVATIVES **tirelessly** adv.

tiresome • adj. making you feel bored or impatient.
– DERIVATIVES **tiresomely** adv.

'tis • contr. literary it is.

tisane /ti-**zan**/ • n. a herb tea.
– ORIGIN French.

tissue /ti-**shoo**/ • n. **1** any of the distinct types of material of which animals or plants are made, consisting of specialized cells. **2** a paper handkerchief.
– PHRASES **a tissue of lies** a story that is full of lies.
– DERIVATIVES **tissuey** adj.
– ORIGIN Old French *tissu* 'woven'.

tissue paper • n. very thin, soft paper.

tit[1] • n. a small insect-eating songbird; a titmouse.
– ORIGIN prob. Scandinavian.

tit[2] • n. (in phr. **tit for tat**) a situation in which a person insults or hurts someone to retaliate for something they have done.
– ORIGIN from former *tip for tap*, from TIP[2].

Titan /**ty**-tuhn/ • n. **1** any of a family of giant gods in Greek mythology. **2** (**titan**) a person who is very strong, clever, or important.

titanic • adj. very strong, large, or powerful.

titanium /ti-**tay**-ni-uhm, ty-**tay**-ni-uhm/ • n. a silver-grey metal used in strong, corrosion-resistant alloys.
– ORIGIN from TITAN.

titbit (US **tidbit**) • n. **1** a small piece of

tasty food. **2** a small item of very interesting information.
– ORIGIN from dialect *tid* 'tender' + BIT¹.

titch • n. Brit. informal a small person.
– DERIVATIVES **titchy** adj.
– ORIGIN from *Little Tich*, stage name of Harry Relph, an English music-hall comedian.

tithe /tyth/ • n. one tenth of what people produced or earned in a year, formerly taken as a tax to support the Church.
– ORIGIN Old English, 'tenth'.

titillate /ti-til-layt/ • v. (**titillates, titillating, titillated**) interest or excite someone, especially in a sexual way.
– DERIVATIVES **titillation** n.
– ORIGIN Latin *titillare* 'tickle'.

> **USAGE:** Do not confuse **titillate** with **titivate**. **Titillate** means 'interest or excite someone, especially sexually', whereas **titivate** means 'make smarter or more attractive'.

titivate /ti-ti-vayt/ • v. (**titivates, titivating, titivated**) informal make smarter or more attractive.
– DERIVATIVES **titivation** n.
– ORIGIN perh. from TIDY.

title • n. **1** the name of a book, musical composition, or other work. **2** a name that describes someone's position or job. **3** a word, such as *Dr*, *Mrs*, or *Lord*, used before or instead of someone's name to indicate their rank or profession. **4** the position of being the champion of a major sports competition. **5** a caption or credit in a film or broadcast. **6** the legal right to own something, especially land or property. • v. (**titles, titling, titled**) give a title to.
– ORIGIN Latin *titulus*.

titled • adj. having a title indicating nobility or rank.

title deed • n. a legal document giving evidence of a person's right to own a property.

title role • n. the role in a play or film from which the work's title is taken.

titmouse • n. (pl. **titmice**) = TIT¹.
– ORIGIN from TIT¹ + the former word *mose* 'titmouse'.

titrate /ty-trayt/ • v. (**titrates, titrating, titrated**) Chem. calculate the amount of a substance in a solution by measuring the volume of a standard reagent required to react with it.
– DERIVATIVES **titration** n.
– ORIGIN French *titre* 'fineness of alloyed gold or silver'.

titter • n. a short, quiet laugh. • v. (**titters, tittering, tittered**) laugh quietly.

tittle • n. a tiny amount.
– ORIGIN Latin *titulus* 'title'.

tittle-tattle • n. gossip. • v. engage in gossip.
– ORIGIN from TATTLE.

titular /tit-yuu-ler/ • adj. **1** relating to a title. **2** holding a formal position or title without any real authority.
– DERIVATIVES **titularly** adv.

tizzy (also **tizz**) • n. (pl. **tizzies** or **tizzes**) informal a state of nervous excitement or worry.

T-junction • n. Brit. a road junction at which one road joins another at right angles without crossing it.

Tl • symb. the chemical element thallium.

TLC • abbrev. informal tender loving care.

Tm • symb. the chemical element thulium.

TNT • abbrev. trinitrotoluene, a high explosive.

to • prep. **1** in the direction of. **2** situated in the direction mentioned from: *there are mountains to the north.* **3** so as to reach a particular state. **4** identifying the person or thing affected by an action: *you were unkind to her.* **5** indicating that people or things are related, linked, or attached. **6** esp. Brit. (in telling the time) before the hour specified. **7** indicating a rate of return: *ten miles to the gallon.* **8** introducing the second part of a comparison: *the club's nothing to what it once was.* • infinitive marker used with the base form of a verb to indicate that the verb is in the infinitive. • adv. so as to be closed or nearly closed.
– PHRASES **to and fro** in a constant movement backwards and forwards or from side to side.
– ORIGIN Old English.

> **USAGE:** Do not confuse **to** with **too** or **two**. **To** mainly means 'in the direction of' (*the next train to London*), while **too** means 'excessively' (*she was driving too fast*) or 'in addition'. **Two** is a number meaning 'one less than three' (*we met two years ago*).

toad • n. a tailless amphibian with a short stout body and short legs.
– ORIGIN Old English.

toadflax • n. a plant with yellow or purple flowers that resemble those of the snapdragon.

toad-in-the-hole • n. Brit. a dish consisting of sausages baked in batter.

toadstool • n. a fungus, typically in the form of a rounded cap on a stalk.

toady • n. (pl. **toadies**) a person who behaves in an excessively respectful way towards someone in order to gain their favour. • v. (**toadies, toadying, toadied**) act in an excessively respectful way to gain someone's favour.

– ORIGIN prob. from *toad-eater*, a charlatan's assistant who ate toads (regarded as poisonous) to demonstrate the power of the charlatan's remedy.

toast • n. **1** sliced bread that has been browned by putting it close to a source of heat, such as a grill or fire. **2** an act of raising glasses at a gathering and drinking together in honour of a person or thing. **3** a person who is respected or admired: *he was the toast of Oxford.* • v. **1** brown bread under a grill or near another source of heat. **2** drink a toast to.
– ORIGIN Old French *toster* 'roast'; sense 2 came from the idea that the name of the lady whose health was being drunk flavoured the drink like the pieces of spiced toast formerly placed in wine.

toaster • n. an electrical device for making toast.

toasting fork • n. a long-handled fork for making toast in front of a fire.

toastmaster (or **toastmistress**) • n. an official responsible for proposing toasts and making other announcements at a large social event.

tobacco • n. (pl. **tobaccos**) the dried nicotine-rich leaves of an American plant, used for smoking or chewing.
– ORIGIN Spanish *tabaco*.

tobacconist • n. esp. Brit. a shopkeeper who sells cigarettes and tobacco.

toboggan • n. a light, narrow vehicle on runners, used for sliding downhill over snow or ice.
– DERIVATIVES **tobogganist** n.
– ORIGIN from a North American Indian language.

toby jug • n. a beer jug or mug in the form of a seated old man wearing a three-cornered hat.
– ORIGIN prob. from a poem about *Toby Philpot*, a soldier who liked to drink.

toccata /tuh-kah-tuh/ • n. a musical composition for a keyboard instrument designed to show the performer's touch and technique.
– ORIGIN Italian, 'touched'.

tocopherol /to-kof-fuh-rol/ • n. vitamin E.
– ORIGIN from Greek *tokos* 'offspring' + *pherein* 'to bear'.

tocsin /tok-sin/ • n. old use an alarm bell or signal.
– ORIGIN Provençal *tocasenh*.

tod • n. (in phr. **on your tod**) Brit. informal on your own.
– ORIGIN from rhyming slang *Tod Sloan*, an American jockey.

today • adv. **1** on or during this present day. **2** at the present period of time.

• n. **1** this present day. **2** the present period of time.
– ORIGIN Old English, 'on this day'.

toddle • v. (**toddles, toddling, toddled**) **1** (of a young child) move with short unsteady steps while learning to walk. **2** informal go somewhere in a casual or leisurely way. • n. an act of toddling.

toddler • n. a young child who is just beginning to walk.

toddy • n. (pl. **toddies**) a drink made of spirits with hot water and sugar.
– ORIGIN Sanskrit, 'palmyra' (referring to a palm tree with a naturally alcoholic sap).

to-do • n. informal a commotion or fuss.
– ORIGIN from *much to do* 'much needing to be done'.

toe • n. **1** any of the five digits at the end of the foot. **2** the lower end or tip of something. • v. (**toes, toeing, toed**) push or touch with the toes.
– PHRASES **on your toes** ready and alert. **toe the line** obey authority.
– ORIGIN Old English.

> ☑ The correct spelling is **toe the line** (not *tow*).

toecap • n. a piece of steel or leather on the front part of a boot or shoe.

toehold • n. a small foothold.

toenail • n. a nail on the upper surface of the tip of each toe.

toerag • n. Brit. informal an unpleasant or disliked person.
– ORIGIN first referring to a rag wrapped round the foot as a sock, such as might be worn by a homeless person.

toff • n. Brit. informal, derog. a rich upper-class person.
– ORIGIN perh. from **TUFT**, referring to a gold cap tassel worn by titled under-graduates at Oxford and Cambridge.

toffee • n. a kind of firm sweet which softens when sucked or chewed, made by boiling together sugar and butter.

toffee apple • n. Brit. an apple coated with a layer of toffee and fixed on a stick.

toffee-nosed • adj. Brit. informal snobbish.

tofu /toh-foo/ • n. a soft white substance made from mashed soya beans, used in Asian and vegetarian cookery.
– ORIGIN Chinese, 'rotten beans'.

tog[1] informal • n. (**togs**) clothes. • v. (**be togged up/out**) be fully dressed for a particular occasion or activity.
– ORIGIN prob. from former criminals' slang *togeman* 'light cloak'.

tog[2] • n. Brit. a unit for measuring the

insulating properties of clothes and quilts.
– ORIGIN from **TOG**¹, on the pattern of an earlier unit called the *clo* (first part of *clothes*).

toga /toh-guh/ • n. a loose outer garment made of a single piece of cloth, worn by the citizens of ancient Rome.
– ORIGIN Latin.

together • adv. **1** with or near to another person or people. **2** so as to touch, combine, or be united. **3** regarded as a whole. **4** (of two people) married or in a sexual relationship. **5** at the same time. **6** without interruption. • adj. informal sensible, calm, or well organized.
– PHRASES **together with** as well as.
– DERIVATIVES **togetherness** n.
– ORIGIN Old English.

toggle • n. a narrow piece of wood or plastic attached to a coat or jacket, pushed through a loop to act as a fastener.

toggle switch • n. an electric switch operated by means of a projecting lever that is moved up and down.

Togolese /toh-guh-leez/ • n. (pl. **Togolese**) a person from Togo, a country in West Africa. • adj. relating to Togo.

toil • v. **1** work very hard. **2** move somewhere slowly and with difficulty. • n. exhausting work.
– DERIVATIVES **toiler** n.
– ORIGIN Old French *toiler* 'strive'.

toilet • n. **1** a large bowl for urinating or defecating into. **2** dated the process of washing yourself, dressing, and attending to your appearance.
– ORIGIN first referring to a cloth cover for a dressing table: from French *toilette* 'cloth'.

toilet bag • n. Brit. a waterproof bag for holding toothpaste, soap, etc. when travelling.

toiletries • pl. n. articles used in washing and taking care of the body, such as soap and shampoo.

toilette /twah-let/ • n. = TOILET (in sense 2).
– ORIGIN French (see TOILET).

toilet-train • v. teach a young child to use the toilet.

toilet water • n. a diluted form of perfume.

toilsome • adj. old use involving hard work or effort.

token • n. **1** a thing that represents a fact, quality, or feeling. **2** a voucher that can be exchanged for goods or services. **3** a metal or plastic disc used to operate a machine. • adj. done just for the sake of

appearances: *cases like this often bring token fines.*
– ORIGIN Old English.

tokenism • n. the practice of doing something in a superficial way, so as to be seen to be obeying the law or satisfying a particular group of people.
– DERIVATIVES **tokenistic** adj.

told past and past part. of TELL.

tolerable • adj. **1** able to be tolerated or endured. **2** fairly good.
– DERIVATIVES **tolerably** adv.

tolerance • n. **1** the ability to accept things you dislike or disagree with. **2** the ability to endure specified conditions or treatment. **3** an allowable amount of variation of a measurement.

tolerant • adj. **1** able to accept things you dislike or disagree with. **2** able to endure specified conditions or treatment: *rye is tolerant of drought*.
– DERIVATIVES **tolerantly** adv.

tolerate • v. (**tolerates, tolerating, tolerated**) **1** allow something that you dislike or disagree with to happen or continue. **2** patiently accept something unpleasant. **3** be able to be exposed to a drug, toxin, etc. without a bad reaction.
– DERIVATIVES **toleration** n.
– ORIGIN Latin *tolerare* 'endure'.

toll¹ /tohl/ • n. **1** a charge payable to use some roads or bridges. **2** the number of deaths or casualties arising from an accident, war, etc. **3** the cost or damage resulting from something.
– ORIGIN Greek *telōnion* 'toll house'.

toll² /tohl/ • v. **1** (of a bell) sound with slow, even strokes. **2** (of a bell) announce the time, a service, or a person's death. • n. a single ring of a bell.
– ORIGIN prob. from dialect *toll* 'drag, pull'.

tollbooth • n. a roadside kiosk where tolls are paid.

toll gate • n. a barrier across a road where a toll must be paid to go through.

tom • n. the male of various animals, especially a domestic cat.
– ORIGIN from the man's name *Thomas*.

tomahawk /tom-uh-hawk/ • n. a light axe formerly used by American Indians.
– ORIGIN from a North American Indian language.

tomato • n. (pl. **tomatoes**) a glossy red fruit, eaten as a vegetable or in salads.
– ORIGIN from a Central American Indian language.

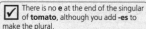 There is no **e** at the end of the singular of **tomato**, although you add **-es** to make the plural.

tomb • n. **1** a burial place consisting of a stone structure above ground or a large

underground vault. **2** a monument to a dead person, built over their burial place. **3** (**the tomb**) literary death.
– ORIGIN Greek *tumbos*.

tombola /tom-boh-luh/ •n. Brit. a game in which tickets are drawn from a revolving drum to win prizes.
– ORIGIN Italian.

tomboy •n. a girl who enjoys rough, noisy activities traditionally associated with boys.
– DERIVATIVES **tomboyish** adj.

tombstone •n. a flat inscribed stone standing or laid over a grave.

tomcat •n. a male domestic cat.

Tom, Dick, and Harry •n. ordinary people in general.

tome •n. humorous a large, serious book.
– ORIGIN Greek *tomos* 'roll of papyrus, volume'.

tomfoolery •n. silly behaviour.

Tommy •n. (pl. **Tommies**) informal a British private soldier.
– ORIGIN from a use of the name *Thomas Atkins* in examples of completed forms in the British army.

tomography /tuh-mog-ruh-fi/ •n. a technique for displaying a cross section through a human body or other solid object using X-rays or ultrasound.
– DERIVATIVES **tomographic** adj.
– ORIGIN Greek *tomos* 'slice'.

tomorrow •adv. **1** on the day after today. **2** in the near future. •n. **1** the day after today. **2** the near future.

> ☑ Remember that **tomorrow** has one **m** and a double **r**.

tomtit •n. a small tit or similar bird.

tom-tom •n. a drum beaten with the hands.
– ORIGIN Hindi.

ton /tun/ •n. **1** (also **long ton**) a unit of weight equal to 2,240 lb avoirdupois (1016.05 kg). **2** (also **short ton**) esp. N. Amer. a unit of weight equal to 2,000 lb avoirdupois (907.19 kg). **3** a metric ton. **4** (also **displacement ton**) a unit of measurement of a ship's weight equal to 2,240 lb or 35 cu. ft (0.99 cubic metres). **5** (also **tons**) informal a large number or amount. **6** Brit. informal a speed of hundred miles an hour. •adv. (**tons**) Brit. informal much; a great deal.
– ORIGIN from **TUN**.

tonal /toh-n'l/ •adj. **1** relating to tone. **2** (of music) written using traditional keys and harmony.
– DERIVATIVES **tonally** adv.

tonality •n. (pl. **tonalities**) the character of a piece of music as determined by the key in which it is played.

tone •n. **1** a musical sound with reference to its pitch, quality, and strength. **2** the sound of a person's voice, expressing a feeling or mood. **3** general character: *trust her to lower the tone of the conversation.* **4** a basic interval in classical Western music, equal to two semitones. **5** a particular brightness, deepness, or shade in a colour. **6** the normal level of firmness in a resting muscle. •v. (**tones, toning, toned**) **1** (often **tone something up**) make the body or a muscle stronger or firmer. **2** (**tone something down**) make something less harsh, extreme, or intense.
– ORIGIN Greek *tonos* 'tension, tone'.

tone-deaf •adj. unable to notice differences of musical pitch accurately.

tone poem •n. a piece of orchestral music describing a subject taken from mythology, literature, history, etc.

toner •n. **1** a liquid applied to the skin to reduce oiliness and improve its condition. **2** a powder used in photocopiers.

Tongan /tong-uhn, tong-guhn/ •n. **1** a person from Tonga, an island group in the South Pacific. **2** the language spoken in Tonga. •adj. relating to Tonga.

tongs •pl. n. a tool with two movable arms that are joined at one end, used for picking up and holding things.
– ORIGIN Old English.

tongue •n. **1** the fleshy organ in the mouth, used for tasting, licking, swallowing, and (in humans) producing speech. **2** the tongue of an ox or lamb as food. **3** a person's way of speaking: *she has a sharp tongue.* **4** a language. **5** a strip of leather or fabric under the laces in a shoe. **6** the clapper of a bell.
•v. (**tongues, tonguing, tongued**) **1** sound a note distinctly on a wind instrument by interrupting the air flow with the tongue. **2** lick with the tongue.
– PHRASES **the gift of tongues** the power of speaking in unknown languages, believed to be one of the gifts of the Holy Spirit. **hold your tongue** informal remain silent. **lose your tongue** be unable to express yourself after a shock. (**with**) **tongue in cheek** not seriously meaning what you are saying.
– ORIGIN Old English.

tongue and groove •n. wooden boards which are placed next to each other and joined by means of interlocking ridges and grooves down their sides.

tongue-lashing •n. a severe scolding.

tongue-tied •adj. too shy or

embarrassed to speak.

tongue-twister • n. a sequence of words that are difficult to pronounce quickly.

tonic • n. 1 a drink taken as a medicine, to give a feeling of energy or well-being. 2 something that makes someone feel happier or healthier. 3 (also **tonic water**) a fizzy soft drink with a bitter flavour, used as a mixer with gin or other spirits.
– ORIGIN Greek *tonikos* 'for stretching'.

tonic sol-fa • n. a system of associating each note of a musical scale with a particular syllable (usually doh, ray, me, fah, soh, la, te), used to teach singing.

tonight • adv. on the evening or night of the present day. • n. the evening or night of the present day.

tonnage • n. 1 weight in tons. 2 the size or carrying capacity of a ship measured in tons.

tonne /tun/ • n. = METRIC TON.
– ORIGIN French.

tonsil • n. either of two small masses of tissue in the throat, one on each side of the root of the tongue.
– ORIGIN Latin *tonsillae* (plural).

tonsillectomy /ton-sil-**lek**-tuh-mi/ • n. (pl. **tonsillectomies**) a surgical operation to remove the tonsils.

tonsillitis • n. inflammation of the tonsils.

tonsorial /ton-**sor**-i-uhl/ • adj. esp. humorous relating to hairdressing.
– ORIGIN Latin *tonsor* 'barber'.

tonsure /ton-syer, ton-sher/ • n. a circular area on a monk's or priest's head where the hair is shaved off.
– ORIGIN Latin *tonsura*.

too • adv. 1 to a higher degree than is desirable, allowed, or possible; excessively. 2 in addition; also. 3 informal very: *you're too kind*.
– ORIGIN Old English.

> USAGE: On the difference between **too**, **to**, and **two**, see the note at **TO**.

took past of TAKE.

tool • n. 1 an implement or device used to carry out a particular function. 2 a thing used to help perform a job. 3 a person used by another. • v. 1 impress a design on leather with a heated tool. 2 equip with tools for industrial production.
– ORIGIN Old English.

toolbar • n. Computing a strip of icons used to perform certain functions.

toolmaker • n. a person who makes and repairs tools for use in a manufacturing process.

toot • n. a short, sharp sound made by a

horn, trumpet, or similar instrument.
• v. make a toot.
– ORIGIN perh. from German *tüten*.

tooth • n. (pl. **teeth**) 1 each of a set of hard enamel-coated structures in the jaws, used for biting and chewing. 2 a cog on a gearwheel or a point on a saw or comb. 3 (**teeth**) power or effectiveness: *the law would be fine if it had teeth.*
– PHRASES **fight tooth and nail** fight very fiercely. **in the teeth of 1** directly against the wind. **2** in spite of opposition.
– DERIVATIVES **toothed** adj.
– ORIGIN Old English.

toothache • n. pain in a tooth or teeth.

toothbrush • n. a small brush with a long handle, used for cleaning the teeth.

toothed whale • n. any of the large group of whales with teeth, including killer whales and dolphins.

tooth fairy • n. a fairy said to take children's milk teeth after they fall out and leave a coin under their pillow.

toothless • adj. 1 having no teeth. 2 lacking power or effectiveness.

toothpaste • n. a paste used for cleaning the teeth.

toothpick • n. a thin, pointed piece of wood or plastic used for removing bits of food stuck between the teeth.

toothsome • adj. 1 (of food) temptingly tasty. 2 informal attractive.

toothy • adj. (**toothier**, **toothiest**) having or showing large noticeable teeth: *he gave a toothy grin.*
– DERIVATIVES **toothily** adv.

tootle • v. (**tootles**, **tootling**, **tootled**) make a series of sounds on a horn, trumpet, etc.
– ORIGIN from TOOT.

tootsie /tuut-si/ (also **tootsy**) • n. (pl. **tootsies**) informal 1 a person's foot. 2 a young woman.
– ORIGIN from FOOT.

top¹ • n. 1 the highest or uppermost point, part, or surface. 2 a thing placed on, fitted to, or covering the upper part of something. 3 (**the top**) the highest or most important rank, level, or position. 4 the utmost degree: *she shouted at the top of her voice.* 5 esp. Brit. the end that is furthest away: *the bus stop at the top of the road.* 6 an item of clothing covering the upper part of the body. • adj. highest in position, rank, or degree: *the top floor.* • v. (**tops**, **topping**, **topped**) 1 be more, better, or taller than. 2 be at the highest place or rank in. 3 reach the top of a hill or rise. 4 provide with a top or topping. 5 Brit. informal kill someone.
– PHRASES **on top** in addition. **on top of 1** so as to cover. **2** very near to. **3** in

control of. **4** in addition to. **on top of the world** informal very happy. **over the top** informal, esp. Brit. excessive or exaggerated. **top off** finish (something) in a memorable way. **2** reach an upper limit. **top something up** esp. Brit. **1** add to a number or amount to bring it up to a certain level. **2** fill up a partly full container.
– DERIVATIVES **topmost** adj.
– ORIGIN Old English.

top² • n. a toy with a rounded top and pointed base, that can be set to spin.
– ORIGIN Old English.

topaz • n. a colourless, yellow, or pale blue precious stone.
– ORIGIN Greek *topazos*.

topcoat • n. **1** an overcoat. **2** an outer coat of paint.

top dog • n. informal a person who is successful or dominant in their field.

top-drawer • adj. informal of the highest quality or social class.

tope • v. (**topes, toping, toped**) literary frequently drink too much alcohol.
– DERIVATIVES **toper** n.
– ORIGIN perh. from former *top* 'overbalance'.

top flight • n. the highest rank or level.

topgallant /top-gal-luhnt, tuh-gal-luhnt/ • n. **1** the section of a square-rigged sailing ship's mast immediately above the topmast. **2** a sail set on a topgallant mast.

top hat • n. a man's formal black hat with a high cylindrical crown.

top-heavy • adj. **1** too heavy at the top and likely to be unstable. **2** (of an organization) having too large a number of senior executives.

topiary /toh-pi-uh-ri/ • n. (pl. **topiaries**) **1** the art of clipping shrubs into decorative shapes. **2** shrubs clipped into decorative shapes.
– ORIGIN Latin *topiarius* 'ornamental gardener'.

topic • n. a subject of a written work, speech, or conversation.
– ORIGIN from Greek *ta topika*, 'matters concerning commonplaces'.

topical • adj. **1** relating to or dealing with current affairs. **2** relating to a particular subject.
– DERIVATIVES **topicality** n. **topically** adv.

topknot • n. **1** a knot of hair arranged on the top of the head. **2** a tuft or crest of hair or feathers on the head of an animal or bird.

topless • adj. having the breasts uncovered.

topmast /top-mahst, top-muhst/ • n. the second section of a square-rigged sailing ship's mast, immediately above the lower mast.

top-notch • adj. informal of the highest quality.

topography /tuh-pog-ruh-fi/ • n. **1** the arrangement of the physical features of an area. **2** a representation of the physical features of an area on a map.
– DERIVATIVES **topographic** adj. **topographical** adj.
– ORIGIN Greek *topos* 'place'.

topology /tuh-pol-uh-ji/ • n. the study of geometrical properties and spatial relations which remain unaffected by certain changes in shape or size of figures.
– DERIVATIVES **topological** adj.

topper • n. informal a top hat.

topping • n. a layer of food poured or spread over another food.

topple • v. (**topples, toppling, toppled**) **1** overbalance and fall down. **2** remove a government or leader from power.
– ORIGIN from **top¹**.

topsail /top-sayl, top-s'l/ • n. **1** a sail on a ship's topmast. **2** a sail set lengthwise, above the gaff.

top secret • adj. highly secret.

topside • n. Brit. the outer side of a round of beef.

topsoil • n. the top layer of soil.

topspin • n. a fast forward spin given to a moving ball, resulting in a curved path or a strong forward motion on rebounding.

topsy-turvy • adj. & adv. **1** upside down. **2** in a state of confusion.
– ORIGIN prob. from **top¹** and former *terve* 'overturn'.

top-up • n. Brit. an additional amount or portion that restores something to a former level.

toque /tohk/ • n. **1** a woman's small hat, typically having a narrow, closely turned-up brim. **2** a tall white hat worn by chefs.
– ORIGIN French.

tor • n. a steep hill or rocky peak.
– ORIGIN perh. Celtic.

Torah /tor-uh, tor-ah/ • n. (in Judaism) the law of God as revealed to Moses and recorded in the Pentateuch.
– ORIGIN Hebrew, 'instruction, law'.

torch • n. **1** Brit. a portable battery-powered electric lamp. **2** esp. hist. a piece of wood or cloth soaked in tallow and ignited. • v. informal set fire to.
– PHRASES **carry a torch for** be in love with someone who is not in love with you.
– ORIGIN Latin *torqua, torques* 'necklace'.

tore past of **tear¹**.

toreador /to-ri-uh-dor/ •n. a bullfighter, especially one on horseback.
– ORIGIN Spanish.

torment •n. /tor-ment/ **1** great suffering. **2** a cause of suffering.
•v. /tor-ment/ **1** make someone suffer greatly. **2** annoy or tease unkindly.
– DERIVATIVES **tormentor** n.
– ORIGIN Latin *tormentum* 'instrument of torture'.

torn past part. of TEAR¹.

tornado /tor-nay-doh/ •n. (pl. **tornadoes** or **tornados**) a violently rotating wind storm having the appearance of a funnel-shaped cloud.
– ORIGIN perh. from Spanish *tronada* 'thunderstorm'.

torpedo •n. (pl. **torpedoes**) a long narrow underwater missile fired from a ship, submarine, or an aircraft.
•v. (**torpedoes, torpedoing, torpedoed**) **1** attack with a torpedo or torpedoes. **2** ruin a plan or project.
– ORIGIN first meaning an electric ray (fish): from Latin, 'numbness'.

torpid •adj. inactive and lacking energy.
– DERIVATIVES **torpidity** n. **torpidly** adv.
– ORIGIN Latin *torpidus*.

torpor /tor-per/ •n. the state of being inactive and lacking in energy.
– ORIGIN Latin.

torque /tork/ •n. a force that tends to cause rotation.
– ORIGIN Latin *torquere* 'to twist'.

torrent •n. **1** a strong and fast-moving stream of water or other liquid. **2** an overwhelming outpouring: *a torrent of abuse.*
– ORIGIN French.

torrential •adj. (of rain) falling rapidly and heavily.

torrid •adj. **1** very hot and dry. **2** full of sexual passion. **3** Brit. full of difficulty.
– ORIGIN Latin *torridus*.

torsion /tor-sh'n/ •n. the action of twisting or the state of being twisted.
– DERIVATIVES **torsional** adj.
– ORIGIN Latin.

torso •n. (pl. **torsos**) the trunk of the human body.
– ORIGIN Italian, 'stalk, stump'.

tort •n. Law a wrongful act or a violation of a right (other than under contract) leading to legal liability.
– ORIGIN Latin *tortum* 'wrong, injustice'.

torte /tor-tuh, tort/ •n. (pl. **torten** /tor-tuhn/ or **tortes**) a sweet cake or tart.
– ORIGIN German.

tortellini /tor-tuhl-lee-ni/ •pl. n. stuffed pasta parcels rolled and formed into small rings.
– ORIGIN Italian.

tortilla /tor-tee-yuh/ •n. **1** (in Mexican cookery) a thin, flat maize pancake. **2** (in Spanish cookery) an omelette.
– ORIGIN Spanish, 'little cake'.

tortoise /tor-tuhss/ •n. a slow-moving land reptile with a rounded shell into which it can draw its head and legs.
– ORIGIN Latin *tortuca*.

tortoiseshell •n. **1** the semi-transparent mottled yellow and brown shell of certain turtles, used to make jewellery or ornaments. **2** a domestic cat with markings resembling tortoiseshell. **3** a butterfly with mottled orange, yellow, and black markings.

tortuous /tor-chuu-uhss, tor-tyuu-uhss/ •adj. **1** full of twists and turns. **2** excessively lengthy and complex.
– DERIVATIVES **tortuosity** n. **tortuously** adv.
– ORIGIN Latin *tortuosus*.

torture •n. **1** the action of causing severe pain to someone as a punishment or to make them do something. **2** great suffering or anxiety.
•v. (**tortures, torturing, tortured**) cause to suffer severe pain.
– DERIVATIVES **torturer** n.
– ORIGIN Latin *tortura* 'torment'.

torturous •adj. involving or causing pain or suffering.

Tory •n. (pl. **Tories**) a member or supporter of the British Conservative Party.
– DERIVATIVES **Toryism** n.
– ORIGIN first referring to Irish peasants dispossessed by English settlers and living as robbers: prob. from Irish *toraidhe* 'outlaw'.

tosh •n. Brit. informal nonsense.

toss •v. **1** throw lightly or casually. **2** move from side to side or back and forth. **3** jerk the head or hair sharply backwards. **4** throw a coin into the air so as to make a decision, based on which side of the coin faces uppermost when it lands. **5** shake or turn food in a liquid to coat it lightly. •n. an act of tossing.
– PHRASES **not give** (or **care**) **a toss** Brit. informal not care at all. **toss something off** produce something rapidly or without thought or effort.

toss-up •n. informal **1** the tossing of a coin to make a decision. **2** a situation in which any of two or more outcomes is equally possible.

tot¹ •n. **1** a very young child. **2** esp. Brit. a small drink of spirits.

tot² •v. (**tots, totting, totted**) (**tot something up**) esp. Brit. **1** add up numbers or amounts. **2** collect something over time.

t

– ORIGIN from **TOTAL** or Latin *totum* 'the whole'.

total • adj. **1** comprising the whole number or amount. **2** complete: *a total stranger*. • n. a total number or amount. • v. (**totals**, **totalling**, **totalled**; US **totals**, **totaling**, **totaled**) **1** amount to a total number. **2** find the total of.
– DERIVATIVES **totally** adv.
– ORIGIN Latin *totalis*.

total eclipse • n. an eclipse in which the whole of the disc of the sun or moon is covered.

totalitarian /toh-tal-i-**tair**-i-uhn/ • adj. (of a system of government) consisting of only one leader or party and having complete power and control. • n. a person in favour of a totalitarian government.
– DERIVATIVES **totalitarianism** n.

totality • n. **1** the whole of something. **2** Astron. the time during which the sun or moon is totally covered during an eclipse.

totalizator (or **totalisator**) • n. **1** a device showing the number and amount of bets staked on a race. **2** = **TOTE¹**.

tote¹ • n. (**the tote**) informal a system of betting based on the use of the totalizator, in which winnings are calculated according to the amount staked rather than odds offered.

tote² • v. (**totes**, **toting**, **toted**) informal carry something.
– ORIGIN prob. dialect.

tote bag • n. a large bag for carrying a number of items.

totem /**toh**-tuhm/ • n. a natural object or animal believed by a particular society to have spiritual meaning and adopted by it as an emblem.
– DERIVATIVES **totemic** /toh-**tem**-ik/ adj.
– ORIGIN from a North American Indian language.

totem pole • n. a pole on which totems are hung or on which the images of totems are carved.

totter • v. (**totters**, **tottering**, **tottered**) **1** move in an unsteady way. **2** shake or rock as if about to collapse. **3** be insecure or about to fail. • n. an unsteady walk.
– DERIVATIVES **tottery** adj.
– ORIGIN Dutch *touteren* 'to swing'.

totty • n. Brit. informal girls or women regarded as sexually desirable.
– ORIGIN from **TOT¹**.

toucan /**too**-kuhn/ • n. a tropical American bird with a massive bill and brightly coloured plumage.
– ORIGIN from a South American Indian language.

touch • v. **1** come into or be in physical contact with. **2** bring the hand or another part of the body into contact with. **3** have an effect on. **4** harm or interfere with. **5** use or consume: *I haven't touched a cent of the money.* **6** (**be touched**) feel moved with gratitude or sympathy. • n. **1** an act or way of touching. **2** the ability to be aware of something through physical contact, especially with the fingers. **3** a small amount. **4** a distinctive detail or feature. **5** a distinctive or skilful way of dealing with something: *a sure political touch.*
– PHRASES **in touch 1** in or into communication. **2** possessing up-to-date knowledge. **lose touch** no longer be in communication. **out of touch** lacking awareness or up-to-date knowledge. **touch down** (of an aircraft or spacecraft) land. **touch on** deal briefly with a subject. **touch something up** make small improvements to something.
– DERIVATIVES **touchable** adj.
– ORIGIN Old French *tochier*.

touch-and-go • adj. (of an outcome) possible but very uncertain.

touchdown • n. **1** the moment at which an aircraft touches down. Rugby & Amer. Football an act of scoring by touching the ball down behind the opponents' goal line.

touché /too-**shay**/ • exclam. **1** used to acknowledge a good point made at your expense. **2** (in fencing) used to acknowledge a hit by an opponent.
– ORIGIN French, 'touched'.

touching • adj. arousing gratitude or sympathy; moving. • prep. concerning.

touchline • n. Rugby & Football the boundary line on each side of the field.

touchpaper • n. a strip of paper treated with saltpetre, for setting light to fireworks or gunpowder.

touch screen • n. a display device which allows the user to interact with a computer by touching areas on the screen.

touchstone • n. **1** a standard by which something is judged. **2** a piece of stone formerly used for testing alloys of gold by observing the colour of the mark which they made on it.

touch-tone • adj. (of a telephone) generating tones to dial rather than pulses.

touch-type • v. type using all of the fingers and without looking at the keys.

touchy • adj. (**touchier**, **touchiest**) **1** quick to take offence. **2** (of a situation or issue) requiring careful handling.
– DERIVATIVES **touchiness** n.

– ORIGIN perh. from **TETCHY**, influenced by **TOUCH**.

touchy-feely • adj. informal, usu. derog. openly expressing affection or other emotions.

tough • adj. **1** strong enough to withstand wear and tear. **2** able to endure difficulty or pain. **3** strict: *tough anti-smoking laws.* **4** involving difficulty or problems. **5** (of a person) rough or violent. • n. informal a rough and violent man.
– DERIVATIVES **toughness** n.
– ORIGIN Old English.

toughen • v. make or become tough.

toupee /too-pay/ • n. a small wig or hairpiece worn to cover a bald spot.
– ORIGIN French.

tour • n. **1** a journey for pleasure in which several different places are visited. **2** a short trip to view or inspect something. **3** a series of performances or sports matches in several different places. • v. make a tour of.
– ORIGIN Old French, 'turn'.

tour de force /toor duh **forss**/ • n. (pl. **tours de force** /toor duh **forss**/) a performance or achievement accomplished with great skill.
– ORIGIN French, 'feat of strength'.

tourer • n. a car, caravan, or bicycle designed for touring.

tourism • n. the business of organizing and operating holidays and visits to places of interest.

tourist • n. **1** a person who travels for pleasure. **2** Brit. a member of a touring sports team.

tourist class • n. the cheapest accommodation or seating in a ship, aircraft, or hotel.

touristy • adj. informal, usu. derog. appealing to or visited by many tourists.

tourmaline /toor-muh-lin, toor-muh-leen/ • n. a brittle grey or black mineral used as a gemstone and in electrical devices.
– ORIGIN Sinhalese, 'carnelian'.

tournament • n. **1** a series of contests between a number of competitors. **2** a medieval sporting event in which knights jousted with blunted weapons for a prize.
– ORIGIN Old French *torneiement.*

tourney /toor-ni, ter-ni/ • n. (pl. **tourneys**) a medieval joust.
– ORIGIN Old French *tornei.*

tourniquet /toor-ni-kay, tor-ni-kay/ • n. a cord or tight bandage which is tied around a limb to stop the flow of blood through an artery.
– ORIGIN French.

tour operator • n. a travel agent specializing in package holidays.

tousle /tow-z'l/ • v. (**tousles, tousling, tousled**) make a person's hair untidy.
– ORIGIN Germanic.

tout /towt/ • v. **1** attempt to sell something. **2** try to persuade people that someone or something is of value. **3** Brit. resell a ticket for a popular event at a price higher than the official one. • n. (also **ticket tout**) Brit. a person who buys up tickets for an event to resell them at a profit.
– ORIGIN Germanic.

tow[1] • v. use a vehicle or boat to pull another vehicle or boat along. • n. an act of towing.
– PHRASES **in tow 1** (also **on tow**) being towed. **2** accompanying or following someone.
– ORIGIN Old English.

 The correct spelling is **toe the line** (not *tow*).

tow[2] • n. short coarse fibres of flax or hemp, used for making yarn.
– ORIGIN Old English.

towards (esp. N. Amer. also **toward**) • prep. **1** in the direction of. **2** getting nearer to a time or aim. **3** in relation to. **4** contributing to the cost of.
– ORIGIN Old English.

towel • n. a piece of absorbent cloth or paper used for drying. • v. (**towels, towelling, towelled;** US **towels, toweling, toweled**) dry with a towel.
– ORIGIN Old French *toaille.*

towelling (US **toweling**) • n. absorbent cloth used for towels and bathrobes.

tower • n. **1** a tall, narrow building or part of a building. **2** a tall structure that houses machinery, operators, etc. **3** a tall structure used as a container or for storage. • v. (**towers, towering, towered**) rise to or reach a great height.
– ORIGIN Old English.

tower block • n. Brit. a tall modern building containing many floors of offices or flats.

towering • adj. **1** very tall. **2** very great or important: *a towering rage.*

town • n. **1** a settlement larger than a village and generally smaller than a city. **2** the central part of a town or city, with its business or shopping area. **3** densely populated areas, as contrasted with the country or suburbs.
– PHRASES **go to town** informal do something thoroughly and enthusiastically. **on the town** informal enjoying the nightlife of a city or town.
– ORIGIN Old English, 'homestead, village'.

t

town clerk • n. (in the UK, until 1974) the secretary and legal adviser of a town corporation.

town council • n. (especially in the UK) a town's elected governing body.
– DERIVATIVES **town councillor** n.

town crier • n. hist. a person employed to make public announcements in the streets.

town hall • n. a building housing local government offices.

town house • n. 1 a tall, narrow terrace house, generally having three or more floors. 2 a house in a town or city owned by someone who has another property in the country.

townie • n. informal a person who lives in a town.

town planning • n. the planning and control of the construction, growth, and development of a town or other urban area.
– DERIVATIVES **town planner** n.

township • n. (in South Africa) a suburb or city where mainly black people live, formerly selected for black occupation by apartheid laws.
– ORIGIN Old English.

townspeople (also **townsfolk**) • pl. n. the people living in a town or city.

towpath • n. a path beside a river or canal, originally used as a path for horses towing barges.

tow rope • n. a rope or cable used in towing.

toxaemia /tok-see-mi-uh/ (US **toxemia**) • n. 1 blood poisoning by toxins from a local bacterial infection. 2 a condition in pregnancy characterized especially by high blood pressure.
– ORIGIN from Latin *toxicum* 'poison'.

toxic • adj. 1 poisonous. 2 relating to or caused by poison.
– DERIVATIVES **toxicity** n.
– ORIGIN Latin *toxicum* 'poison'.

toxicology /toks-i-kol-uh-ji/ • n. the branch of science concerned with the nature and effects of poisons.
– DERIVATIVES **toxicological** adj. **toxicologist** n.

toxin • n. a poison produced by a microorganism or other organism, to which the body reacts by producing antibodies.

toy • n. 1 an object for a child to play with. 2 a gadget or machine that provides amusement for an adult. • v. (**toy with**) 1 consider an idea casually. 2 move or touch something absent-mindedly or nervously. 3 eat or drink in an unenthusiastic way. • adj. (of a breed of dog) much smaller than is normal for the breed.

toy boy • n. Brit. informal a male lover who is much younger than his partner.

trace[1] • v. (**traces, tracing, traced**) 1 find by careful investigation. 2 find or describe the origin or development of. 3 follow the course or position of something with the eye, mind, or finger. 4 copy a drawing or map by drawing over its lines on a piece of transparent paper placed on top of it. 5 draw a pattern or outline. • n. 1 a mark or other sign that something has existed or passed by. 2 a very small amount. 3 a barely noticeable indication: *a trace of a smile*. 4 a line or pattern on paper or a screen, showing something that a machine is recording.
– DERIVATIVES **traceable** adj.
– ORIGIN Old French *tracier*.

trace[2] • n. each of the two side straps, chains, or ropes by which a horse is attached to a vehicle that it is pulling.
– ORIGIN Old French *trais*.

trace element • n. a chemical element present or required only in tiny amounts.

tracer • n. a bullet or shell whose course is made visible by a trail of flames or smoke, used to assist in aiming.

tracery • n. (pl. **traceries**) 1 a decorative design of holes and outlines in stone, especially in a window. 2 a delicate branching pattern.

trachea /truh-kee-uh/ • n. (pl. **tracheae** /truh-kee-ee/ or **tracheas**) the tube carrying air between the larynx and the lungs; the windpipe.
– DERIVATIVES **tracheal** /tray-ki-uhl/ adj.
– ORIGIN from Greek *trakheia artēria* 'rough artery'.

tracheotomy /tra-ki-ot-uh-mi/ (also **tracheostomy** /tra-ki-oss-tuh-mi/) • n. (pl. **tracheotomies**) a surgical cut in the windpipe, made to enable someone to breathe when the windpipe is blocked.

tracing • n. 1 a copy of a drawing or map made by tracing. 2 a faint or delicate mark or pattern.

track • n. 1 a rough path or small road. 2 a prepared course or circuit for racing. 3 a mark or line of marks left by a person, animal, or vehicle in passing. 4 a continuous line of rails on a railway. 5 a section of a record, compact disc, or cassette tape containing one song or piece of music. 6 a strip or rail along which something such as a curtain may be moved. 7 a jointed metal band around the wheels of a heavy vehicle.
• v. 1 follow the trail or movements of. 2 (**track someone/thing down**) find

someone or something after a thorough search. **3** follow a particular course. **4** (of a film or television camera) move along with the subject being filmed.

– PHRASES **keep** (or **lose**) **track of** keep (or fail to keep) fully aware of or informed about. **on the right** (or **wrong**) **track** following a course likely to result in success (or failure).

– DERIVATIVES **tracker** n.

– ORIGIN Old French *trac*.

trackball • n. a small ball set in a holder that can be rotated by hand to move a cursor on a computer screen.

track events • pl. n. athletic events that take place on a running track.

tracking • n. Electron. the maintenance of a constant difference in frequency between connected circuits or parts.

track record • n. the past achievements or performance of a person, organization, or product.

tracksuit • n. an outfit consisting of a sweatshirt and loose trousers.

tract[1] • n. **1** a large area of land. **2** a major passage in the body: *the digestive tract.*

– ORIGIN Latin *tractus* 'drawing'.

tract[2] • n. a pamphlet containing a short piece of religious or political writing.

– ORIGIN prob. from Latin *tractatus* 'treatise'.

tractable • adj. **1** easy to control or influence. **2** (of a problem) easy to deal with.

– DERIVATIVES **tractability** n.

– ORIGIN Latin *tractabilis.*

traction • n. **1** the action of pulling something along a surface. **2** the power used for pulling. **3** a way of treating a fractured bone by gradually pulling it back into position. **4** the grip of a tyre on a road or a wheel on a rail.

– ORIGIN Latin.

traction engine • n. a steam- or diesel-powered road vehicle used for pulling very heavy loads.

tractor • n. a powerful motor vehicle with large rear wheels, used for pulling farm machinery.

– ORIGIN Latin.

trad • adj. informal (especially of music) traditional.

trade • n. **1** the buying and selling of goods and services. **2** a particular area of commercial activity: *the tourist trade.* **3** a job requiring manual skills and special training: *a carpenter by trade.* **4** (**the trade**) the people engaged in a particular area of business. • v. (**trades, trading, traded**) **1** buy and sell goods and services. **2** buy or sell a particular item. **3** exchange something for something else. **4** (**trade something in**)

exchange a used article as part of a payment for another. **5** (**trade on**) take advantage of. **6** (**trade something off**) exchange something of value as part of a compromise.

– DERIVATIVES **tradable** (or **tradeable**) adj. **trader** n.

– ORIGIN German, 'track'.

trademark • n. **1** a symbol, word, or words chosen to represent a company or product. **2** a distinctive characteristic.

trade name • n. **1** a name that has the status of a trademark. **2** a name by which something is known in a particular trade or profession.

trade-off • n. a balance achieved between two desirable but conflicting things; a compromise.

tradescantia /trad-i-skan-ti-uh/ • n. an American plant with triangular three-petalled flowers.

– ORIGIN named after the English botanist John *Tradescant.*

tradesman • n. (pl. **tradesmen**) **1** a person who owns a small shop. **2** a person engaged in a skilled trade.

trade surplus • n. the amount by which the value of a country's exports is more than the cost of its imports.

trade union (Brit. also **trades union**) • n. an organized association of workers formed to work for their rights and interests.

– DERIVATIVES **trade unionist** (also **trades unionist**) n.

trade wind • n. a wind blowing steadily towards the equator from the north-east in the northern hemisphere or from the south-east in the southern hemisphere.

– ORIGIN from former *blow trade* 'blow steadily'.

trading estate • n. Brit. a specially designed industrial and commercial area.

trading post • n. a store or small settlement established for trading in a remote place.

tradition • n. **1** the passing on of customs or beliefs from generation to generation. **2** a long-established custom or belief passed on from generation to generation. **3** a method or style established by an artist, writer, or movement, and followed by other people.

– ORIGIN Latin.

traditional • adj. relating to or following tradition: *traditional music.*

– DERIVATIVES **traditionally** adv.

traditionalism • n. the belief that traditions should be followed and change should be limited.

– DERIVATIVES **traditionalist** n. & adj.

t

traduce /truh-dyooss/ • v. (**traduces, traducing, traduced**) say unpleasant or untrue things about someone.
– ORIGIN Latin *traducere* 'expose to ridicule'.

traffic • n. **1** vehicles moving on public roads. **2** the movement of ships or aircraft. **3** the transport of goods or passengers as a business. **4** the messages or signals sent through a communications system. **5** the action of trading in something illegal. • v. (**traffics, trafficking, trafficked**) deal or trade in something illegal.
– DERIVATIVES **trafficker** n.
– ORIGIN French *traffique*.

traffic calming • n. the deliberate slowing of traffic in residential areas, by building road humps or other obstructions.

traffic island • n. a raised area in the middle of a road which provides a safe place for pedestrians to stand.

traffic jam • n. a line or lines of traffic at or almost at a standstill.

traffic lights • pl. n. a set of automatic coloured lights for controlling traffic.

traffic warden • n. Brit. an official who locates and reports on vehicles breaking parking regulations.

tragedian /truh-jee-di-uhn/ • n. **1** (fem. **tragedienne** /truh-jee-di-en/) an actor or actress who plays tragic roles. **2** a writer of tragedies.

tragedy • n. (pl. **tragedies**) **1** an event causing great sadness or suffering. **2** a serious play with an unhappy ending.
– ORIGIN Greek *tragōidia*.

tragic • adj. **1** very sad or upsetting. **2** relating to tragedy in a literary work.
– DERIVATIVES **tragically** adv.

tragicomedy • n. (pl. **tragicomedies**) a play or novel containing elements of both comedy and tragedy.
– DERIVATIVES **tragicomic** adj.

trail • n. **1** a mark or a series of signs left by someone or something in passing. **2** a track or scent used in following someone or hunting an animal. **3** a beaten path through rough country. **4** a route planned or followed by a purpose: *the tourist trail.* **5** a long thin part stretching behind or hanging down from something: *trails of ivy.* • v. **1** draw or be drawn along behind. **2** follow the trail of. **3** walk or move slowly or wearily. **4** (**trail away/off**) (of the voice or a speaker) fade gradually before stopping. **5** be losing to an opponent in a contest. **6** (of a plant) grow along the ground or so as to hang down.
– ORIGIN Old French *traillier* 'to tow' or German *treilen* 'haul a boat'.

trailblazer • n. **1** a person who is the first to do something new. **2** a person who makes a new track through wild country.
– DERIVATIVES **trailblazing** n. & adj.

trailer • n. **1** an unpowered vehicle pulled by another. **2** the rear section of an articulated lorry. **3** an extract from a film or programme used to advertise it. **4** N. Amer. a caravan.

trailer truck • n. US an articulated lorry.

train • v. **1** teach a skill or type of behaviour to a person or animal. **2** be taught a skill or type of behaviour. **3** make or become physically fit through a course of exercise and diet. **4** (**train something on**) point something at. **5** make a plant grow in a particular direction. • n. **1** a series of railway carriages or wagons moved by a locomotive. **2** a number of vehicles or pack animals moving in a line. **3** a series of connected events or thoughts. **4** a long piece of trailing material attached to the back of a formal dress or robe.
– PHRASES **in train** in progress.
– DERIVATIVES **training** n.
– ORIGIN Old French *trahiner*.

trainee • n. a person being trained for a particular job or profession.

trainer • n. **1** a person who trains people or animals. **2** Brit. a soft shoe for sports or casual wear.

training college • n. (in the UK) a college where future teachers are trained.

trainspotter • n. Brit. **1** a person who collects locomotive numbers as a hobby. **2** a person who is obsessively interested in every detail of a hobby or subject.
– DERIVATIVES **trainspotting** n.

traipse • v. (**traipses, traipsing, traipsed**) walk or move wearily or reluctantly. • n. a boring or tiring walk.

trait /trayt, tray/ • n. **1** a distinguishing quality or characteristic. **2** a characteristic that is determined by a gene.
– ORIGIN French.

traitor • n. a person who betrays their country or a cause.
– DERIVATIVES **traitorous** adj.
– ORIGIN Old French *traitour*.

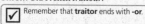 Remember that **traitor** ends with **-or**.

trajectory /truh-jek-tuh-ri/ • n. (pl. **trajectories**) the path followed by a moving object.
– ORIGIN Latin *trajectoria*.

tram (also **tramcar**) • n. Brit. a passenger vehicle powered by electricity and running on rails laid in a road.

– ORIGIN German and Dutch *trame* 'beam, barrow shaft'.

tramlines • pl. n. **1** rails for a tram. **2** informal a pair of parallel lines at the sides of a tennis court or at the sides or back of a badminton court.

trammel • n. (**trammels**) literary restrictions on someone's freedom of action. • v. (**trammels**, **trammelling**, **trammelled**; US **trammels**, **trammeling**, **trammeled**) restrict the freedom of.
– ORIGIN Old French *tramail*.

tramp • v. **1** walk heavily or noisily. **2** walk wearily over a long distance. • n. **1** a homeless person who travels around and lives by begging or doing casual work. **2** the sound of heavy steps. **3** a long walk. **4** a cargo ship running between many different ports rather than sailing a fixed route. **5** N. Amer. informal a woman who has many sexual partners.
– DERIVATIVES **tramper** n. **trampy** adj.
– ORIGIN prob. German.

trample • v. (**tramples**, **trampling**, **trampled**) **1** tread on and crush. **2** (**trample on/over**) treat with contempt.
– ORIGIN from **TRAMP**.

trampoline • n. a strong fabric sheet connected by springs to a frame, used as a springboard and landing area in doing acrobatic or gymnastic exercises.
– DERIVATIVES **trampolining** n.
– ORIGIN Italian *trampolino*.

tramway • n. Brit. **1** a set of rails for a tram. **2** a tram system.

trance • n. **1** a half-conscious state in which someone does not respond to things that happen to them. **2** a state of not paying attention. **3** (also **trance music**) a type of electronic dance music with hypnotic rhythms.
– ORIGIN Old French *transir* 'depart, fall into a trance'.

tranche /rhymes with branch/ • n. any of the parts into which an amount of money or a number of shares in a company is divided.
– ORIGIN Old French, 'slice'.

tranquil • adj. free from disturbance; calm.
– DERIVATIVES **tranquillity** (also **tranquility**) n. **tranquilly** adv.
– ORIGIN Latin *tranquillus*.

tranquillize (or **tranquillise**; US **tranquilize**) • v. (**tranquillizes**, **tranquillizing**, **tranquillized**) give a calming or sedative drug to.

tranquillizer (or **tranquilliser**; US **tranquilizer**) • n. a medicinal drug taken to reduce tension or anxiety.

trans- • prefix **1** across; beyond: *transcontinental.* **2** on or to the other side of: *transatlantic.* **3** into another state or place: *translate.*
– ORIGIN from Latin *trans* 'across'.

transact • v. conduct or carry out business.

transaction • n. **1** an instance of buying or selling. **2** the action of conducting business.
– ORIGIN Latin.

transatlantic • adj. **1** crossing the Atlantic. **2** concerning countries on both sides of the Atlantic, especially Britain and the US. **3** relating to or situated on the other side of the Atlantic.

transceiver • n. a combined radio transmitter and receiver.

transcend • v. **1** be or go beyond the range or limits of. **2** be better than.
– ORIGIN Latin *transcendere*.

transcendent • adj. **1** going beyond normal or physical human experience. **2** (of God) existing apart from and not limited by the material universe.
– DERIVATIVES **transcendence** n.

transcendental • adj. going beyond human knowledge and into a spiritual area.
– DERIVATIVES **transcendentally** adv.

Transcendental Meditation • n. (trademark in the US) a technique for relaxation and promoting harmony by meditation and repetition of a mantra.

transcontinental • adj. crossing or extending across a continent or continents.

transcribe • v. (**transcribes**, **transcribing**, **transcribed**) **1** put thoughts, speech, or data into written or printed form. **2** make a copy of something in another alphabet or language. **3** arrange a piece of music for a different instrument or voice.
– DERIVATIVES **transcriber** n.
– ORIGIN Latin *transcribere*.

transcript • n. a written or printed version of material that was originally spoken or presented in another form.
– ORIGIN Latin *transcriptum*.

transcription • n. **1** a transcript. **2** the action of transcribing. **3** a piece of music transcribed for a different instrument or voice.

transducer • n. a device that converts variations in a physical quantity (such as pressure or brightness) into an electrical signal, or vice versa.
– DERIVATIVES **transduction** n.
– ORIGIN Latin *transducere* 'lead across'.

transect • v. tech. cut across or make a transverse section in.

– DERIVATIVES **transection** n.
– ORIGIN from **TRANS-** + Latin *secare* 'divide by cutting'.

transept /tran-sept, trahn-sept/ •n. (in a cross-shaped church) either of the two parts extending at right angles from the nave.
– ORIGIN Latin *transeptum*.

transexual •n. var. of **TRANSSEXUAL**.

transfer •v. (**transfers, transferring, transferred**) **1** move someone or something from one place to another. **2** move to another department, job, team, etc. **3** change to another place, route, or means of transport during a journey. **4** pass property or a right or responsibility to another person.
•n. **1** an act or the action of transferring. **2** Brit. a small coloured picture or design on paper, which can be transferred to another surface by being pressed or heated.
– DERIVATIVES **transferable** adj. **transferee** n. **transferor** n. **transferral** n.
– ORIGIN Latin *transferre*.

transference •n. the action of transferring something from one place to another.

transfigure •v. (**be transfigured**) be transformed into something more beautiful or spiritual.
– DERIVATIVES **transfiguration** n.
– ORIGIN Latin *transfigurare*.

transfix •v. **1** make motionless with horror, wonder, or astonishment. **2** pierce with a sharp object.
– ORIGIN Latin *transfigere*.

transform •v. **1** change or be changed in appearance, form, or nature. **2** change the voltage of an electric current.

transformation •n. a marked change in nature, form, or appearance.
– DERIVATIVES **transformational** adj.

transformer •n. a device for changing the voltage of an alternating electric current.

transfusion •n. a medical process in which blood is transferred from one person to another.
– ORIGIN Latin *transfundere* 'pour from one container to another'.

transgenic /tranz-jen-ik/ •adj. containing genetic material into which DNA from a different organism has been artificially added.

transgress •v. go beyond the limits of what is morally, socially, or legally acceptable.
– DERIVATIVES **transgression** n. **transgressive** adj. **transgressor** n.
– ORIGIN Latin *transgredi* 'step across'.

transient /tran-zi-uhnt, trahn-zi-uhnt/ •adj. **1** lasting only for a short time. **2** staying or working in a place for a short time only. •n. a person who stays or works in a place for a short time.
– DERIVATIVES **transience** n. **transiently** adv.
– ORIGIN Latin *transire* 'go across'.

transistor •n. **1** a semiconductor device with three connections, able to amplify or rectify an electric current. **2** (also **transistor radio**) a portable radio using circuits containing transistors.
– ORIGIN from **TRANSFER** + **RESISTOR**.

transit •n. **1** the carrying of people or things from one place to another. **2** an act of passing through or across a place.
– ORIGIN Latin *transitus*.

transition •n. the process or a period of changing from one state or condition to another.
– DERIVATIVES **transitional** adj.

transition metal •n. any of the set of metallic chemical elements occupying the central block in the periodic table, e.g. iron, manganese, chromium, and copper.

transitive /tran-zi-tiv/ •adj. Grammar (of a verb) able to take a direct object, e.g. *saw* in *he saw the donkey*. Opp. **INTRANSITIVE**.
– DERIVATIVES **transitivity** n.
– ORIGIN Latin *transitivus*.

transitory /tran-zi-tuh-ri/ •adj. lasting for a short time.
– DERIVATIVES **transitoriness** n.
– ORIGIN Latin *transitorius*.

translate •v. (**translates, translating, translated**) **1** express the sense of words or writing in another language. **2** be expressed or able to be expressed in another language. **3** (**translate into**) convert or be converted into another form or medium.
– DERIVATIVES **translatable** adj.
– ORIGIN Latin *translatus* 'carried across'.

translation •n. **1** the action of translating. **2** a word or written work that is translated.

translator •n. a person who translates from one language into another.

transliterate •v. (**transliterates, transliterating, transliterated**) write a letter or word using the corresponding letters of a different alphabet or language.
– DERIVATIVES **transliteration** n.
– ORIGIN from **TRANS-** + Latin *littera* 'letter'.

translucent /tranz-loo-suhnt/ •adj. allowing light to pass through partially; semi-transparent.
– DERIVATIVES **translucence** (also **translucency**) n.

– ORIGIN Latin *translucere* 'shine through'.

transmigration • n. (in some beliefs) the passing of a person's soul after their death into another body.

transmission • n. **1** the passing of something from one person or place to another. **2** a programme or signal that is transmitted. **3** the mechanism by which power is transmitted from an engine to the axle in a vehicle.

transmit • v. (**transmits, transmitting, transmitted**) **1** pass something from one place or person to another. **2** broadcast or send out an electrical signal or a radio or television programme. **3** allow heat, light, or other energy to pass through a medium.
– DERIVATIVES **transmissible** adj. **transmittal** n.
– ORIGIN Latin *transmittere*.

transmitter • n. a device used to produce and transmit electromagnetic waves carrying messages or signals, especially those of radio or television.

transmogrify /tranz-mog-ri-fy/ • v. (**transmogrifies, transmogrifying, transmogrified**) humorous change into something completely different.
– DERIVATIVES **transmogrification** n.

transmute /tranz-myoot/ • v. (**transmutes, transmuting, transmuted**) change in form, nature, or substance.
– DERIVATIVES **transmutation** n.
– ORIGIN Latin *transmutare*.

transnational • adj. extending or operating across national boundaries.

transom /tran-suhm/ • n. **1** the flat surface forming the stern of a boat. **2** a strengthening crossbar above a door or window.
– ORIGIN Old French *traversin*.

transparency • n. (pl. **transparencies**) **1** the condition of being transparent. **2** a positive transparent photograph printed on plastic or glass, and viewed using a slide projector.

transparent /tranz-pa-ruhnt, tranz-pair-uhnt/ • adj. **1** allowing light to pass through so that objects behind can be distinctly seen. **2** obvious or evident.
– DERIVATIVES **transparently** adv.
– ORIGIN Latin *transparere* 'shine through'.

transpire • v. (**transpires, transpiring, transpired**) **1** come to be known or prove to be true. **2** take place; happen. **3** (of a plant or leaf) give off water vapour through the stomata (tiny pores in the surface).
– DERIVATIVES **transpiration** n.
– ORIGIN Latin *transpirare*.

USAGE: The standard sense of **transpire** is 'come to be known' (*it transpired that he had bought a house*). From this, a newer sense developed, meaning 'happen' (*I'm going to find out what transpired*). This sense is sometimes criticized for being an unnecessarily long word used where **occur** or **happen** would do just as well.

transplant • v. /tranz-plahnt/ **1** transfer to another place or situation. **2** take living tissue or an organ and put it in another part of the body or in another body. • n. /tranz-plahnt/ **1** an operation in which an organ or tissue is transplanted. **2** a person or thing that has been transplanted.
– DERIVATIVES **transplantation** n.
– ORIGIN Latin *transplantare*.

transponder • n. a device for receiving a radio signal and automatically transmitting a different signal.
– ORIGIN from TRANSMIT and RESPOND.

transport • v. /tran-sport/ **1** carry people or goods from one place to another by means of a vehicle, aircraft, or ship. **2** (**be transported**) be overwhelmed with a strong emotion. **3** hist. send a convict to a distant country as a punishment. • n. /tran-sport/ **1** a system or means of transporting people or goods. **2** the transporting of people or goods. **3** a large vehicle, ship, or aircraft for carrying troops or stores. **4** (**transports**) overwhelmingly strong emotions.
– DERIVATIVES **transportability** n. **transportable** adj. **transportation** n.
– ORIGIN Latin *transportare* 'carry across'.

transport cafe • n. Brit. a roadside cafe for drivers of haulage vehicles.

transporter • n. a large vehicle used to carry heavy objects.

transpose • v. (**transposes, transposing, transposed**) **1** make two or more things change places with each other. **2** move to a different place or situation. **3** write or play music in a different key from the original.
– DERIVATIVES **transposable** adj. **transposition** n.
– ORIGIN Old French *transposer*.

transsexual (also **transexual**) • n. a person born with the physical characteristics of one sex who emotionally and psychologically feels that they belong to the opposite sex.

trans-ship • v. transfer cargo from one ship or other form of transport to another.
– DERIVATIVES **trans-shipment** n.

transubstantiation • n. (in Christian belief) the doctrine that when the bread

and wine of the Eucharist have been consecrated they become the body and blood of Jesus.
– ORIGIN Latin *transubstantiare* 'change in substance'.

transuranic /tranz-yuu-**ran**-ik/ • adj. (of a chemical element) having a higher atomic number than uranium (92).

transverse • adj. placed or extending across something.
– DERIVATIVES **transversely** adv.
– ORIGIN Latin *transvertere* 'turn across'.

transvestite • n. a person, especially a man, who gains pleasure from dressing in clothes usually worn by the opposite sex.
– DERIVATIVES **transvestism** n.
– ORIGIN German *Transvestit*.

trap • n. 1 a device, pit, or enclosure designed to catch and hold animals. 2 an unpleasant situation from which it is difficult to escape. 3 a trick causing someone to do something that they do not intend or that will affect them badly. 4 a container or device used to collect a specified thing. 5 a light, two-wheeled carriage pulled by a horse or pony. 6 the compartment from which a greyhound is released at the start of a race. 7 a curve in the waste pipe from a bath, basin, or toilet that is always full of liquid to prevent the upward passage of gases. 8 a device for hurling a clay pigeon into the air. 9 informal a person's mouth. • v. (**traps, trapping, trapped**) 1 catch or hold in a trap. 2 trick into doing something.
– ORIGIN Old English.

trapdoor • n. a hinged or removable panel in a floor, ceiling, or roof.

trapeze (also **flying trapeze**) • n. a horizontal bar hanging by two ropes high above the ground, used by acrobats in a circus.
– ORIGIN French.

trapezium /truh-**pee**-zi-uhm/ • n. (pl. **trapezia** /truh-**pee**-zi-uh/ or **trapeziums**) Geom. 1 Brit. a quadrilateral with one pair of sides parallel. 2 N. Amer. a quadrilateral with no sides parallel.
– ORIGIN Latin.

trapezoid /truh-**pee**-zoyd, tra-pi-**zoyd**/ • n. Geom. 1 Brit. a quadrilateral with no sides parallel. 2 N. Amer. a quadrilateral with one pair of sides parallel.

trapper • n. a person who traps wild animals.

trappings • pl. n. 1 the signs or objects associated with a particular situation or role: *the trappings of success.* 2 a horse's ornamental harness.
– ORIGIN Old French *drap* 'drape'.

Trappist • n. a monk belonging to a branch of the Cistercian order of monks who speak only in certain situations.
– ORIGIN French *trappiste*.

trash • n. 1 N. Amer. waste material. 2 poor-quality writing, art, etc. 3 N. Amer. a person or people of very low social status. • v. informal, esp. N. Amer. wreck or destroy something.
– DERIVATIVES **trashy** adj. (**trashier, trashiest**).

trash can • n. N. Amer. a dustbin.

trattoria /trat-tuh-**ree**-uh/ • n. an Italian restaurant.
– ORIGIN Italian.

trauma /**traw**-muh, **trow**-muh/ • n. (pl. **traumas**) 1 a deeply distressing experience. 2 Med. physical injury. 3 emotional shock following a stressful event.
– DERIVATIVES **traumatic** adj. **traumatically** adv.
– ORIGIN Greek, 'wound'.

traumatize (or **traumatise**) • v. (**traumatizes, traumatizing, traumatized**) cause someone to experience lasting shock as a result of a disturbing experience or physical injury.

travail /**tra**-vayl/ (also **travails**) • n. old use painful or laborious effort.
– ORIGIN Old French.

travel • v. (**travels, travelling, travelled;** US also **travels, traveling, traveled**) 1 go on from one place to another, especially over a long distance. 2 go along a road or through a region. 3 move at a particular speed, in a particular direction, or over a particular distance: *light travels faster than sound.* • n. 1 the action of travelling. 2 (**travels**) journeys, especially abroad. • adj. (of a device) small enough to be packed for use when travelling: *a travel iron.*
– ORIGIN from TRAVAIL.

travel agency • n. an agency that makes the necessary arrangements for travellers.
– DERIVATIVES **travel agent** n.

travelled • adj. 1 having travelled to many places. 2 used by people travelling: *a well-travelled route.*

traveller (US also **traveler**) • n. 1 a person who is travelling or who often travels. 2 (usu. **Traveller**) Brit. a Gypsy.

traveller's cheque • n. a cheque for a fixed amount that may be exchanged for cash or used to pay for things abroad.

travelling salesman • n. a representative of a firm who visits businesses to show samples and gain orders.

travelogue • n. a film, book, or illustrated talk about a person's travels.

travel-sick • adj. feeling sick when travelling in a vehicle, boat, or aircraft.
– DERIVATIVES **travel-sickness** n.

traverse /tra-verss, truh-verss/
• v. (**traverses, traversing, traversed**) travel or extend across or through something.
– DERIVATIVES **traversable** adj. **traversal** n.
– ORIGIN Latin *traversare*.

travesty /tra-vi-sti/ • n. (pl. **travesties**) an absurd or distorted representation of something: *the trial was a travesty of justice.* • v. (**travesties, travestying, travestied**) represent in an absurd or distorted way.
– ORIGIN French *travestir* 'to disguise'.

trawl • v. **1** catch fish with a trawl net or seine. **2** search thoroughly. • n. **1** an act of trawling. **2** (also **trawl net**) a large wide-mouthed fishing net dragged by a boat along the bottom of the sea or a lake.
– ORIGIN prob. from Dutch *traghelen* 'to drag'.

trawler • n. a fishing boat used for trawling.

tray • n. a flat container with a raised rim, used for carrying things.
– ORIGIN Old English.

treacherous • adj. **1** not loyal or able to be trusted. **2** having hidden or unpredictable dangers: *treacherous currents.*
– DERIVATIVES **treacherously** adv.
– ORIGIN Old French *trecherous.*

✓ Spell **treacherous** and **treachery** with **trea-** at the beginning.

treachery • n. behaviour that involves betraying a person's trust in you.

treacle • n. Brit. **1** molasses. **2** golden syrup.
– ORIGIN Greek *thēriakē* 'antidote against venom'.

treacly • adj. **1** resembling treacle; thick or sticky. **2** excessively sentimental: *treacly film music.*

tread • v. (**treads, treading, trod**; past part. **trodden** or **trod**) **1** walk in a specified way. **2** press down or crush with the feet. **3** walk on or along. • n. **1** a way or the sound of walking. **2** the top surface of a step or stair. **3** the part of a vehicle tyre that grips the road. **4** the part of the sole of a shoe that rests on the ground.
– PHRASES **tread water** stay in an upright position in deep water by moving the feet with a walking movement.
– ORIGIN Old English.

treadle • n. a lever worked by the foot to operate a machine.
– ORIGIN Old English, 'stair, step'.

treadmill • n. **1** a large wheel turned by the weight of people or animals treading on steps fitted into it, formerly used to drive machinery. **2** a device used for exercise, consisting of a continuous moving belt on which to walk or run. **3** a job or situation that is tiring or boring.

treason (also **high treason**) • n. the crime of betraying your country.
– DERIVATIVES **treasonable** adj. **treasonous** adj.
– ORIGIN Old French *treisoun.*

treasure • n. **1** a quantity of precious metals, gems, or other valuable objects. **2** a very valuable object. **3** informal a much loved or highly valued person.
• v. (**treasures, treasuring, treasured**) **1** look after a valuable or valued item carefully. **2** value highly.
– ORIGIN Old French *tresor.*

treasure hunt • n. a game in which players search for hidden objects by following a trail of clues.

treasurer • n. a person appointed to manage the finances of a society, company, etc.

treasure trove • n. **1** a store of valuable or pleasant things. **2** Engl. Law (abolished in 1996) valuables of unknown ownership that are found hidden and declared the property of the Crown.
– ORIGIN from Old French *tresor trové* 'found treasure'.

treasury • n. (pl. **treasuries**) **1** the funds or revenue of a state, institution, or society. **2** (**Treasury**) (in some countries) the government department responsible for the overall management of the economy.

treat • v. **1** behave towards or deal with someone or something in a particular way. **2** give medical care or attention to. **3** apply a process or a substance to. **4** present or discuss a subject. **5** (**treat someone to**) pay for someone's food, drink, or entertainment. **6** (**treat yourself**) do or have something very enjoyable. • n. **1** a surprise gift, event, etc. that gives great pleasure. **2** (**your treat**) an act of paying for someone's food, drink, or entertainment.
– DERIVATIVES **treatable** adj.
– ORIGIN Old French *traitier.*

treatise /tree-tiss, tree-tiz/ • n. a written work dealing formally and systematically with a subject.
– ORIGIN Old French *tretis.*

treatment • n. **1** a way of behaving towards someone or dealing with something. **2** medical care for an illness or injury. **3** the use of a substance or process to preserve or give particular properties to something: *treatment of* *hazardous waste.* **4** the presentation or discussion of a subject.

treaty •n. (pl. **treaties**) a formal agreement between states.
– ORIGIN Old French *traite.*

treble¹ •adj. **1** consisting of three parts. **2** multiplied or occurring three times. •pron. an amount which is three times as large as usual. •v. (**trebles, trebling, trebled**) make or become three times as large or as many.
– ORIGIN Latin *triplus* 'triple'.

treble² •n. **1** a high-pitched voice, especially a boy's singing voice. **2** the high-frequency output of a radio or audio system.
– ORIGIN from **TREBLE¹**.

treble clef •n. Music a clef placing G above middle C on the second-lowest line of the stave.

tree •n. a woody perennial plant consisting of a trunk and branches, that can grow to a considerable height.
– DERIVATIVES **treeless** adj.
– ORIGIN Old English.

tree diagram •n. a diagram with a structure of branching connecting lines.

tree fern •n. a large palm-like fern with a stem that resembles a tree trunk.

tree house •n. a structure built in a tree for children to play in.

treeline •n. the height on a mountain above which trees are unable to grow.

tree ring •n. each of a number of rings in the cross section of a tree trunk, representing a single year's growth.

tree surgeon •n. a person who treats old or damaged trees in order to preserve them.

trefoil /tre-foyl, tree-foyl/ •n. **1** a small plant with yellow flowers and clover-like leaves. **2** ornamental stonework in the form of three rounded lobes like a clover leaf.
– ORIGIN Latin *trifolium.*

trek •n. a long difficult journey, especially one made on foot. •v. (**treks, trekking, trekked**) go on a trek.
– DERIVATIVES **trekker** n.
– ORIGIN South African Dutch *trekken* 'to pull, travel'.

trellis •n. a framework of bars used as a support for climbing plants.
– ORIGIN Old French *trelis.*

tremble •v. (**trembles, trembling, trembled**) **1** shake uncontrollably through fear, excitement, or weakness. **2** be in a state of great worry or fear. **3** (of a thing) shake slightly. •n. a trembling feeling, movement, or sound.
– DERIVATIVES **trembly** adj. (informal).
– ORIGIN Old French *trembler.*

trembler •n. Brit. an automatic vibrator for making and breaking an electric circuit.

tremendous •adj. **1** very great in amount, scale, or intensity. **2** informal very good or impressive.
– DERIVATIVES **tremendously** adv.
– ORIGIN Latin *tremendus.*

tremolo •n. (pl. **tremolos**) a wavering effect in singing or created when playing some musical instruments.
– ORIGIN Italian.

tremor •n. **1** a quivering movement that cannot be controlled. **2** (also **earth tremor**) a slight earthquake. **3** a sudden feeling of fear or excitement.
– ORIGIN Latin.

tremulous •adj. **1** shaking or quivering slightly. **2** nervous; timid.
– DERIVATIVES **tremulously** adv. **tremulousness** n.
– ORIGIN Latin *tremulus.*

trench •n. **1** a long, narrow ditch. **2** a long ditch dug by troops to provide shelter from enemy fire. **3** (also **ocean trench**) a long, deep depression in the ocean bed.
– ORIGIN Old French *trenche.*

trenchant /tren-chuhnt/ •adj. (of speech or writing) expressed strongly and clearly.
– DERIVATIVES **trenchantly** adv.
– ORIGIN Old French, 'cutting'.

trench coat •n. a belted double-breasted raincoat.

trencher •n. hist. a wooden plate or platter.
– ORIGIN Old French *trenchour.*

trencherman •n. (pl. **trenchermen**) humorous a person who eats heartily.

trench warfare •n. warfare in which opposing troops fight from trenches facing each other.

trend •n. **1** a general direction in which something is developing or changing: *an upward trend in sales.* **2** a fashion.
– ORIGIN Old English, 'revolve, rotate'.

trendsetter •n. a person who leads the way in fashion or ideas.
– DERIVATIVES **trendsetting** adj.

trendy informal •adj. (**trendier, trendiest**) very fashionable or up to date.
– DERIVATIVES **trendily** adv. **trendiness** n.

trepidation •n. a feeling of fear or nervousness about something that may happen.
– ORIGIN Latin.

trepidatious /tre-pi-**day**-shuss/ •adj. informal apprehensive or nervous.

trespass •v. **1** enter someone's land or property without their permission. **2** (**trespass on**) take advantage of

someone's time, good nature, etc. **3** (**trespass against**) old use do wrong or harm to. •n. **1** Law entry to a person's land or property without their permission. **2** old use a sin or other bad act.
– DERIVATIVES **trespasser** n.
– ORIGIN Old French *trespasser* 'pass over, trespass'.

tress •n. a long lock of a woman's hair.
– ORIGIN Old French *tresse*.

trestle •n. a framework made of a horizontal beam supported by two pairs of sloping legs, used in pairs to support a flat surface such as a table top.
– ORIGIN Old French *trestel*.

trestle table •n. a table consisting of a board or boards laid on trestles.

trews /trooz/ •pl. n. esp. Brit. trousers.
– ORIGIN Irish or Scottish Gaelic.

tri- /try/ •comb. form three; having three: *triathlon*.
– ORIGIN Latin *tres*, Greek *treis* 'three'.

triable /try-uh-b'l/ •adj. (of an offence or case) liable to trial in a court of law.

triad /try-ad/ •n. **1** a group of three related people or things. **2** (also **Triad**) a Chinese secret society involved in organized crime.
– DERIVATIVES **triadic** adj.
– ORIGIN Greek *trias*.

triage /tree-ahzh, try-ij/ •n. (in a hospital or in war) the assessment of the seriousness of wounds or illnesses to decide the order in which a large number of patients should be treated. •v. (**triages, triaging, triaged**) decide the order of treatment of patients.
– ORIGIN French.

trial •n. **1** a formal examination of evidence in a court of law to decide if a person is guilty of a crime. **2** a test of performance, qualities, or suitability. **3** (**trials**) an event in which horses or dogs compete or perform. **4** a test of a person's endurance or patience. •v. (**trials, trialling, trialled**; US **trials, trialing, trialed**) test something to assess its suitability or performance.
– PHRASES **on trial 1** being tried in a court of law. **2** undergoing tests. **trial and error** the process of experimenting with various methods until you find the most successful.
– ORIGIN Latin *triallum*.

trialist (Brit. also **triallist**) •n. a person who participates in a sports trial.

trial run •n. a preliminary test of a new system or product.

triangle •n. **1** a plane figure with three straight sides and three angles. **2** a musical instrument consisting of a steel rod bent into a triangle, played by

hitting it with a rod. **3** an emotional relationship involving a couple and a third person with whom one of them is involved.
– ORIGIN Latin *triangulum*.

triangular •adj. **1** shaped like a triangle. **2** involving three people or groups.

triangulate /try-ang-gyuu-layt/ •v. (**triangulates, triangulating, triangulated**) (in surveying) divide an area into triangles in order to determine the distances and relative positions of points.
– DERIVATIVES **triangulation** n.

Triassic /try-ass-ik/ •adj. Geol. referring to the earliest period of the Mesozoic era (about 245 to 208 million years ago), a time when the first dinosaurs, ammonites, and primitive mammals appeared.
– ORIGIN Latin *trias* 'set of three', because the strata are divisible into three groups.

triathlon /try-ath-lon/ •n. an athletic contest involving three different events, typically swimming, cycling, and long-distance running.
– DERIVATIVES **triathlete** n.
– ORIGIN from TRI-, on the pattern of *decathlon*.

tribal •adj. relating to a tribe or tribes.
– DERIVATIVES **tribally** adv.

tribalism •n. behaviour and attitudes that are based on a person's loyalty to a tribe or other social group.

tribe •n. **1** a social group in a traditional society consisting of linked families or communities sharing customs and beliefs. **2** a category in scientific classification that ranks above genus and below family. **3** (**tribes**) informal large numbers of people.
– ORIGIN Latin *tribus*.

USAGE: The word **tribe** can cause offence when used to refer to a community living within a traditional society today, and it is better in such cases to use alternative terms such as **community** or **people**. However, when talking about such communities in the past, it is perfectly acceptable to say **tribe**: *the area was inhabited by Slavic tribes.*

tribesman (or **tribeswoman**) •n. (pl. **tribesmen** or **tribeswomen**) a member of a tribe in a traditional society.

tribulation /trib-yuu-lay-sh'n/ •n. a cause or state of difficulty or suffering.
– ORIGIN Latin.

tribunal /try-byoo-nuhl, tri-byoo-nuhl/ •n. **1** Brit. a group of people established to settle certain types of dispute. **2** a court of justice.
– ORIGIN Latin, 'raised platform provided for a magistrate's seat'.

t

tribune •n. (in ancient Rome) an official chosen by the ordinary people to protect their interests.
– ORIGIN Latin *tribunus* 'head of a tribe'.

tributary /trib-yuu-tuh-ri/ •n. (pl. **tributaries**) **1** a river or stream flowing into a larger river or lake. **2** hist. a person or state that pays money to another more powerful state or ruler.
– ORIGIN Latin *tributarius*.

tribute •n. **1** an act, statement, or gift that is intended to show gratitude, respect, or admiration. **2** something that indicates the worth of something else: *his victory was a tribute to his persistence*. **3** hist. payment made regularly by a state to a more powerful one.
– ORIGIN Latin *tributum*.

trice /rhymes with nice/ •n. (in phr. **in a trice**) in a moment.
– ORIGIN first meaning 'a tug': from Dutch *trisen* 'pull sharply'.

triceps /try-seps/ •n. (pl. **triceps**) the large muscle at the back of the upper arm.
– ORIGIN Latin, 'three-headed'.

trichology /tri-kol-uh-ji/ •n. the branch of medicine concerned with the hair and scalp.
– DERIVATIVES **trichologist** n.
– ORIGIN Greek *thrix* 'hair'.

trick •n. **1** an act or scheme intended to deceive or outwit someone. **2** a skilful act performed for entertainment. **3** an illusion: *a trick of the light*. **4** a habit or mannerism. **5** (in bridge, whist, etc.) a sequence of cards forming a single round of play. •adj. intended to trick: *a trick question*. •v. **1** cunningly deceive or outwit someone. **2** (**trick someone into/out of**) deceive someone into doing or parting with something.
– PHRASES **do the trick** informal achieve the required result. **trick or treat** a children's custom of calling at houses at Halloween with the threat of pranks if they are not given a small gift.
– DERIVATIVES **trickery** n.
– ORIGIN Old French *triche*.

trickle •v. (**trickles, trickling, trickled**) **1** (of a liquid) flow in a small stream. **2** come or go slowly or gradually: *details began to trickle out*. •n. **1** a small flow of liquid. **2** a small number of people or things moving slowly.

trickster •n. a person who cheats or deceives people.

tricksy •adj. **1** clever in an inventive way. **2** playful or mischievous.

tricky •adj. (**trickier, trickiest**) **1** needing care and skill because difficult or awkward. **2** deceitful or crafty.
– DERIVATIVES **trickily** adv. **trickiness** n.

tricolour /tri-kuh-ler/ (US **tricolor**) •n. a flag with three bands of different colours, especially the French national flag.

tricorne /try-korn/ (also **tricorn**) •n. a hat with a brim turned up on three sides.
– ORIGIN Latin *tricornis*.

tricuspid /try-kus-pid/ •n. a tooth with three cusps or points.
– ORIGIN from Latin *tri-* 'three' + *cuspis* 'sharp point'.

tricycle •n. a vehicle similar to a bicycle, but having three wheels, two at the back and one at the front.

trident •n. a three-pronged spear.
– ORIGIN Latin.

tried past and past part. of **TRY**.

triennial /try-en-ni-uhl/ •adj. lasting for or recurring every three years.

trier •n. a person who always makes an effort, however unsuccessful they may be.

trifle •n. **1** a thing of little value or importance. **2** a small amount. **3** Brit. a cold dessert of sponge cake and fruit covered with layers of custard, jelly, and cream. •v. (**trifles, trifling, trifled**) (**trifle with**) treat without seriousness or respect.
– DERIVATIVES **trifler** n.
– ORIGIN Old French *truffler* 'mock'.

trifling •adj. unimportant or trivial.

trigger •n. **1** a device that releases a spring or catch and so sets off a gun or mechanism. **2** an event that causes something to happen. •v. (**triggers, triggering, triggered**) **1** cause a device to function. **2** cause to happen.
– ORIGIN Dutch *trekker*.

trigger-happy •adj. excessively ready and quick to respond by shooting someone.

trigonometry /tri-guh-nom-i-tri/ •n. the branch of mathematics concerned with the relationships between the sides and angles of triangles and with the functions of angles.
– DERIVATIVES **trigonometric** adj.
– ORIGIN Greek *trigōnos* 'three-cornered'.

trike •n. informal a tricycle.

trilateral •adj. **1** shared by or involving three parties: *trilateral talks*. **2** Geom. on or with three sides.

trilby •n. (pl. **trilbies**) esp. Brit. a soft felt hat with a narrow brim and indented crown.
– ORIGIN from the heroine of George du Maurier's novel *Trilby*, in the stage version of which such a hat was worn.

trilingual • adj. **1** speaking three languages fluently. **2** written or carried out in three languages.

trill • n. a quavering or warbling sound. • v. make a quavering or warbling sound.
– ORIGIN Italian *trillo*.

trillion • cardinal number (pl. **trillions** or (with numeral or quantifying word) **trillion**) **1** a million million $(1,000,000,000,000$ or $10^{12})$. **2** Brit. dated a million million million $(1,000,000,000,000,000,000$ or $10^{18})$. **3** (**trillions**) informal a very large number or amount.
– DERIVATIVES **trillionth** ordinal number.

trilobite /try-loh-byt/ • n. a fossil marine arthropod (invertebrate creature) with a rear part divided into three segments.
– ORIGIN from Greek *tri-* 'three' + *lobos* 'lobe'.

trilogy • n. (pl. **trilogies**) a group of three related novels, plays, or films.

trim • v. (**trims**, **trimming**, **trimmed**) **1** cut away unwanted parts from something: *trim the fat off the meat.* **2** reduce the size, amount, or number of. **3** decorate something along its edges. **4** adjust a sail to take advantage of the wind. • n. **1** decoration along the edges of something. **2** the upholstery or interior lining of a car. **3** an act of trimming. **4** good condition or order.
• adj. (**trimmer**, **trimmest**) **1** neat and smart. **2** slim and fit.
– PHRASES **in trim** slim and fit.
– DERIVATIVES **trimmer** n.
– ORIGIN Old English, 'arrange'.

trimaran /try-muh-ran/ • n. a yacht with three hulls side by side.
– ORIGIN from TRI- + CATAMARAN.

trimester /try-mess-ter/ • n. **1** a period of three months, as a division of the duration of pregnancy. **2** N. Amer. each of the three terms in an academic year.
– ORIGIN Latin *trimestris*.

trimming • n. **1** (**trimmings**) small pieces trimmed off. **2** decoration for clothing or furniture. **3** (**the trimmings**) the traditional accompaniments to something: *roast turkey with all the trimmings.*

Trinitarian /tri-ni-tair-i-uhn/ • adj. relating to the Christian doctrine of the Trinity. • n. a Christian who believes in the doctrine of the Trinity.
– DERIVATIVES **Trinitarianism** n.

trinity • n. (pl. **trinities**) **1** (**the Trinity** or **the Holy Trinity**) (in Christian belief) the three persons (Father, Son, and Holy Spirit) that together make up God. **2** a group of three people or things.
– ORIGIN Latin *trinitas*.

trinket • n. a small ornament or item of jewellery that is of little value.

trio • n. (pl. **trios**) **1** a set or group of three. **2** a group of three musicians.
– ORIGIN Italian.

triode /try-ohd/ • n. a semiconductor device with three connections, typically allowing the flow of current in one direction only.
– ORIGIN from TRI- + ELECTRODE.

trip • v. (**trips**, **tripping**, **tripped**) **1** catch the foot on something and stumble or fall. **2** (**trip up**) make a mistake. **3** walk, run, or dance with quick light steps. **4** (of words) flow lightly and easily. **5** activate a mechanism. **6** (of part of an electric circuit) disconnect automatically as a safety measure. **7** informal experience hallucinations as a result of taking a drug such as LSD. • n. **1** a journey or excursion. **2** an instance of tripping or falling. **3** informal a period of hallucinations caused by taking a drug. **4** informal a self-indulgent attitude or activity: *a power trip.* **5** a device that trips a mechanism or circuit.
– PHRASES **trip the light fantastic** humorous dance. [ORIGIN from 'Trip it as you go On the light fantastic toe' (Milton's *L'Allegro*).]
– ORIGIN Dutch *trippen* 'to skip, hop'.

tripartite /try-par-tyt/ • adj. **1** consisting of three parts. **2** shared by or involving three parties.

tripe • n. **1** the stomach of a cow or sheep used as food. **2** informal nonsense; rubbish.
– ORIGIN Old French, 'entrails of an animal'.

triple • adj. **1** consisting of or involving three things or people. **2** having three times the usual size, quality, or strength. • predet. three times as much or as many. • n. a thing that is three times as large as usual or is made up of three parts. • v. (**triples**, **tripling**, **tripled**) make or become three times as much or as many.
– DERIVATIVES **triply** adv.
– ORIGIN Old French.

triple jump • n. an athletic event in which competitors attempt to jump as far as possible by performing a hop, a step, and a jump from a running start.

triplet • n. **1** each of three children or animals born at the same birth. **2** a group of three equal musical notes to be performed in the time of two or four. **3** a set of three rhyming lines of verse.

triple time • n. musical time with three beats to the bar.

triplicate • adj. /trip-li-kuht/ existing in three copies or examples. • v. /trip-li-kayt/ (**triplicates**, **triplicating**,

triplicated) 1 make three copies of. **2** multiply by three.
– DERIVATIVES **triplicity** /tri-**pliss**-i-ti/ n.
– ORIGIN Latin *triplicare* 'make three'.

tripod /**try**-pod/ •n. a three-legged stand for supporting a camera or other device.
– ORIGIN Greek.

tripos /**try**-poss/ •n. the final honours exam for a BA degree at Cambridge University.
– ORIGIN Latin *tripus* 'tripod', with reference to the stool on which a graduate sat to deliver a satirical speech at the degree ceremony.

tripper •n. Brit. informal a person who goes on a pleasure trip.

triptych /**trip**-tik/ •n. **1** a picture or carving on three panels, hinged together vertically and used as an altarpiece. **2** a set of three related artistic works.

tripwire •n. a wire that is stretched close to the ground and sets off a trap, explosion, or alarm when disturbed.

trireme /**try**-reem/ •n. an ancient Greek or Roman warship with three banks of oars.
– ORIGIN Latin *triremis*.

trisect /**try**-sekt/ •v. divide into three parts.
– ORIGIN from **TRI-** + Latin *secare* 'cut'.

trite •adj. (of a remark or idea) unoriginal and dull because of overuse.
– ORIGIN Latin *tritus* 'rubbed'.

triumph •n. **1** a great victory or achievement. **2** the state of being victorious or successful. **3** joy or satisfaction resulting from a success or victory. **4** a highly successful example: *their marriage was a triumph of togetherness.* •v. achieve victory or success.
– DERIVATIVES **triumphal** adj.
– ORIGIN Latin *triumphus.*

triumphalism •n. excessive rejoicing over your own success or achievements.
– DERIVATIVES **triumphalist** adj. & n.

triumphant •adj. **1** having won a battle or contest. **2** joyful after a victory or achievement.
– DERIVATIVES **triumphantly** adv.

triumvirate /**try**-um-vi-ruht/ •n. **1** a group of three powerful or important people or things. **2** (in ancient Rome) a group of three men holding power.
– ORIGIN from Latin *trium virorum* 'of three men'.

trivet •n. **1** a metal stand on which hot dishes are placed. **2** an iron tripod placed over a fire for a cooking pot or kettle to stand on.
– ORIGIN prob. from Latin *tripes* 'three-legged'.

trivia /**tri**-vi-uh/ •pl. n. unimportant details or pieces of information.
– ORIGIN Latin.

trivial •adj. not very important or serious.
– DERIVATIVES **triviality** n. (pl. **trivialities**). **trivially** adv.
– ORIGIN first meaning 'belonging to the trivium' (an introductory course at a medieval university involving the study of grammar, rhetoric, and logic): from Latin *trivium*, literally 'place where three roads meet'.

trivialize (or **trivialise**) •v. (**trivializes**, **trivializing**, **trivialized**) make something seem less important or complex than it really is.
– DERIVATIVES **trivialization** n.

trochee /**troh**-kee/ •n. a foot (unit of poetic metre) consisting of one long or stressed syllable followed by one short or unstressed syllable.
– DERIVATIVES **trochaic** adj.
– ORIGIN from Greek *trokhaios pous* 'running foot'.

trod past and past part. of TREAD.

trodden past part. of TREAD.

troglodyte /**trog**-luh-dyt/ •n. a person who lives in a cave.
– DERIVATIVES **troglodytic** adj.
– ORIGIN Greek *trōglodutēs.*

troika /**troy**-kuh/ •n. **1** a Russian vehicle pulled by a team of three horses side by side. **2** a group of three people working together.
– ORIGIN Russian.

Trojan /**troh**-juhn/ •n. an inhabitant of ancient Troy in Asia Minor. •adj. relating to ancient Troy.
– PHRASES **work like a Trojan** work very hard.

Trojan Horse •n. something intended to weaken or defeat an enemy secretly.
– ORIGIN from the hollow wooden statue of a horse in which the ancient Greeks are said to have hidden themselves in order to enter Troy.

troll[1] /rhymes with doll or dole/ •n. (in folklore) an ugly giant or dwarf that lives in a cave.
– ORIGIN Old Norse and Swedish, 'witch'.

troll[2] /rhymes with dole or doll/ •v. fish by trailing a baited line along behind a boat.
– DERIVATIVES **troller** n.

trolley •n. (pl. **trolleys**) **1** Brit. a large metal basket on wheels, for transporting heavy or bulky items such as shopping. **2** a small table on wheels used to convey food and drink. **3** (also **trolley wheel**) a wheel attached to a pole, used for collecting current from an overhead electric wire to drive a tram.

– PHRASES **off your trolley** informal mad.
– ORIGIN perh. from TROLL².

trolleybus •n. Brit. a bus powered by electricity obtained from overhead wires by means of a trolley wheel.

trollop •n. dated or humorous a woman who has many sexual partners.
– ORIGIN perh. from former *trull* 'prostitute'.

trombone •n. a large brass wind instrument with a sliding tube which is moved to produce different notes.
– DERIVATIVES **trombonist** n.
– ORIGIN French or Italian.

trompe l'œil /tromp loy/ •n. (pl. **trompe l'œils** /tromp loy/) a method of painting that creates the illusion of a three-dimensional object or space.
– ORIGIN French, 'deceives the eye'.

troop •n. **1** (**troops**) soldiers or armed forces. **2** a unit of an armoured or cavalry division. **3** a group of people or animals of a particular kind: *a troop of musicians.* •v. come or go as a group.
– PHRASES **troop the colour** Brit. perform the ceremony of parading a regiment's flag along ranks of soldiers.
– ORIGIN French *troupe*.

troop carrier •n. a large aircraft or armoured vehicle designed for transporting troops.

trooper •n. **1** a private soldier in a cavalry or armoured unit. **2** US a state police officer. **3** esp. US a mounted police officer.

trope /rhymes with rope/ •n. a figurative or metaphorical use of a word or expression.
– ORIGIN Greek *tropos* 'turn, trope'.

trophy •n. (pl. **trophies**) **1** a cup or other decorative object awarded as a prize. **2** a souvenir of an achievement, e.g. a head of an animal killed when hunting.
– ORIGIN French *trophée*.

tropic •n. **1** the line of latitude 23°26′ north (**tropic of Cancer**) or south (**tropic of Capricorn**) of the equator. **2** (**the tropics**) the region between the tropics of Cancer and Capricorn.
– ORIGIN Greek *tropikos*.

tropical •adj. **1** relating to the tropics. **2** very hot and humid.
– DERIVATIVES **tropically** adv.

tropical storm (also **tropical cyclone**) •n. a localized, very intense low-pressure wind system with winds of hurricane force, forming over tropical oceans.

tropism /troh-pi-z'm, trop-i-z'm/ •n. Biol. the turning of all or part of an organism in a particular direction in response to an external stimulus.
– ORIGIN Greek *tropos* 'turning'.

troposphere /tro-puh-sfeer, troh-puh-sfeer/ •n. the lowest region of the atmosphere, extending from the earth's surface to a height of about 6–10 km (the lower boundary of the stratosphere).
– ORIGIN Greek *tropos* 'turning'.

trot •v. (**trots, trotting, trotted**) **1** (of a horse) move at a pace faster than a walk. **2** (of a person) run at a moderate pace with short steps. **3** (**trot something out**) informal produce an account that has been produced many times before. •n. **1** a trotting pace. **2** an act of trotting. **3** (**the trots**) informal diarrhoea.
– PHRASES **on the trot** Brit. informal one after another.
– ORIGIN Latin *trottare*.

troth /trohth, troth/ •n. (in phr. **pledge** (or **plight**) **your troth**) make a solemn promise to marry someone.
– ORIGIN from TRUTH.

Trotskyism •n. the political or economic principles of the Russian revolutionary Leon Trotsky, especially the theory that socialism should be established throughout the world by continuing revolution.
– DERIVATIVES **Trotskyist** n. & adj. **Trotskyite** n. & adj. (derog.).

trotter •n. a pig's foot.

troubadour /troo-buh-dor/ •n. (in medieval France) a travelling poet who composed and sang in the Provençal language.
– ORIGIN French.

trouble •n. **1** difficulty or problems. **2** effort made to do something. **3** a cause of worry or inconvenience. **4** a situation in which a person is likely to be punished or blamed: *he's been in trouble with the police.* **5** public disorder or unrest. •v. (**troubles, troubling, troubled**) **1** cause distress or inconvenience to. **2** (as adj. **troubled**) experiencing problems or anxiety. **3** (**trouble about/over/with**) be anxious about. **4** (**trouble to do**) make the effort to do.
– ORIGIN Old French *truble*.

troublemaker •n. a person who regularly causes trouble.

troubleshooter •n. a person who investigates and solves problems in an organization.
– DERIVATIVES **troubleshooting** n.

troublesome •adj. causing difficulty or annoyance.

trouble spot •n. a place where difficulties or conflict regularly occur.

troublous •adj. old use full of troubles: *troublous times.*

trough •n. **1** a long, narrow open

container for animals to eat or drink out of. **2** a channel used to convey water. **3** Meteorol. a long region of low pressure. **4** a point of low activity or achievement.
– ORIGIN Old English.

trounce • v. (**trounces, trouncing, trounced**) defeat heavily in a contest.

troupe • n. a group of entertainers who tour to different venues.
– ORIGIN French.

trouper • n. **1** an entertainer with long experience. **2** a reliable and uncomplaining person.

trouser • v. (**trousers, trousering, trousered**) Brit. informal receive or take something for yourself.

trousers • pl. n. an outer garment covering the body from the waist to the ankles, with a separate part for each leg.
– PHRASES **wear the trousers** informal be the dominant partner in a relationship.
– ORIGIN Irish and Scottish Gaelic.

trousseau /troo-soh/ • n. (pl. **trousseaux** or **trousseaus** /troo-sohz/) the clothes, linen, and other belongings collected by a bride for her marriage.
– ORIGIN French, 'small bundle'.

trout • n. (pl. **trout** or **trouts**) an edible fish of the salmon family, found chiefly in fresh water.
– ORIGIN Old English.

trove • n. a store of valuable or delightful things.
– ORIGIN from **TREASURE TROVE**.

trowel • n. **1** a small hand-held tool with a curved scoop for lifting plants or earth. **2** a small tool with a flat, pointed blade, used to apply and spread mortar or plaster.
– ORIGIN Latin *truella*.

troy (also **troy weight**) • n. a system of weights used for precious metals and gems, with a pound of 12 ounces or 5,760 grains. Compare with **AVOIRDUPOIS**.
– ORIGIN from a weight used at the fair of *Troyes* in France.

truant • n. a pupil who stays away from school without permission or explan-ation. • adj. wandering; straying: *her truant husband*. • v. (also esp. Brit. **play truant**) (of a pupil) stay away from school without permission or explan-ation.
– DERIVATIVES **truancy** n.
– ORIGIN first referring to a beggar: from Old French.

truce • n. an agreement between enemies to stop fighting for a certain time.
– ORIGIN Old English, 'belief, trust'.

truck¹ • n. **1** a large road vehicle, used for carrying goods or troops. **2** Brit. an open railway vehicle for carrying goods.
– ORIGIN perh. from former *truckle* 'wheel, pulley'.

truck² • n. (in phr. **have no truck with**) refuse to deal or be associated with.
– ORIGIN prob. from Old French.

trucker • n. a long-distance lorry driver.

truculent /truk-yuu-luhnt/ • adj. quick to argue or fight.
– DERIVATIVES **truculence** n. **truculently** adv.
– ORIGIN Latin *truculentus*.

trudge • v. (**trudges, trudging, trudged**) walk slowly and with heavy steps. • n. a long and tiring walk.

true • adj. (**truer, truest**) **1** in accordance with fact or reality. **2** rightly so called: *true love*. **3** real or actual: *my true intentions*. **4** accurate and exact. **5** upright or level. **6** loyal or faithful. **7** (**true to**) in keeping with a standard or expectation.
– PHRASES **come true** actually happen or become the case. **out of true** not in the correct or exact shape or alignment.
– DERIVATIVES **trueness** n.
– ORIGIN Old English, 'steadfast, loyal'.

true north • n. north according to the earth's axis, not magnetic north.

truffle • n. **1** an underground fungus that resembles a rough-skinned potato, eaten as a delicacy. **2** a soft chocolate sweet.
– ORIGIN a former French word.

trug • n. Brit. a shallow oblong wooden basket, used for carrying garden flowers, fruit, and vegetables.
– ORIGIN perh. a dialect form of **TROUGH**.

truism • n. a statement that is obviously true and says nothing new or interesting.

truly • adv. **1** in a truthful way. **2** genuinely or properly. **3** really.
– PHRASES **yours truly 1** used as a formula for ending a letter. **2** humorous used to refer to yourself.

 There is no **e** in **truly**.

trump • n. **1** (in bridge, whist, etc.) a playing card of the suit chosen to rank above the others, which can win a trick where a card of a different suit has been led. **2** (also **trump card**) a valuable resource that may be used as a surprise to gain an advantage. • v. **1** play a trump on a card of another suit. **2** beat by saying or doing something better. **3** (**trump something up**) invent a false accusation or excuse.
– PHRASES **come** (or **turn**) **up trumps** informal, esp. Brit. **1** have a better outcome than expected. **2** be especially generous or helpful.

– ORIGIN from TRIUMPH.

trumpery • n. (pl. **trumperies**) old use articles that are superficially attractive but have little real worth.
– ORIGIN Old French *tromperie*.

trumpet • n. 1 a brass musical instrument with a flared end. 2 something shaped like a trumpet, such as a flower head. 3 the loud cry of an elephant.
• v. (**trumpets, trumpeting, trumpeted**) 1 play a trumpet. 2 (of an elephant) make its typical loud cry. 3 proclaim widely or loudly.
– PHRASES **blow your own trumpet** esp. Brit. talk boastfully about your achievements.
– DERIVATIVES **trumpeter** n.
– ORIGIN Old French *trompette*.

truncate /trung-kayt/ • v. (**truncates, truncating, truncated**) shorten by cutting off the top or the end.
– DERIVATIVES **truncation** n.
– ORIGIN Latin *truncare* 'maim'.

truncheon /trun-chuhn/ • n. esp. Brit. a short thick stick carried as a weapon by a police officer.
– ORIGIN Old French *tronchon* 'stump'.

trundle • v. (**trundles, trundling, trundled**) move or roll slowly and unevenly.
– ORIGIN from dialect *trendle* 'revolve'.

trunk • n. 1 the main woody stem of a tree. 2 a person's or animal's body apart from the limbs and head. 3 the long nose of an elephant. 4 a large box with a hinged lid for storing or transporting clothes and other articles. 5 N. Amer. the boot of a car. • adj. relating to the main routes of a transport or communication network: *a trunk road*.
– ORIGIN Latin *truncus*.

trunk call • n. Brit. dated a long-distance telephone call made within a country.

trunks • pl. n. men's shorts worn for swimming or boxing.

truss • n. 1 a framework of rafters, posts, and bars which supports a roof, bridge, or other structure. 2 a padded belt worn to support a hernia. 3 a compact cluster of flowers or fruit growing on one stalk.
• v. 1 bind or tie up tightly. 2 tie up the wings and legs of a bird before cooking. 3 support with a truss or trusses.
– ORIGIN Old French *trusser* 'bind in'.

trust • n. 1 firm belief in the reliability, truth, or ability of someone or something. 2 acceptance of the truth of a statement without proof. 3 the state of being responsible for someone or something. 4 an arrangement whereby a person (a trustee) holds property as its nominal owner for the benefit of another person or people. 5 an

organization managed by trustees.
• v. 1 have trust in. 2 (**trust someone with**) have the confidence to allow someone to have, use, or look after. 3 (**trust someone/thing to**) give someone or something to another person for safekeeping. 4 (**trust to**) rely on luck, fate, etc. 5 hope: *I trust that you have enjoyed this book.*
– DERIVATIVES **trusted** adj.
– ORIGIN Old Norse, 'strong'.

trustee • n. a person given legal powers to hold and manage property for the benefit of another person or people.
– DERIVATIVES **trusteeship** n.

trustful • adj. having total trust in someone.
– DERIVATIVES **trustfully** adv.

trust fund • n. a fund consisting of money or property that is held and managed for another person by a trust.

trusting • adj. tending to trust other people; not suspicious.
– DERIVATIVES **trustingly** adv.

trustworthy • adj. honest, truthful, and reliable.
– DERIVATIVES **trustworthiness** n.

trusty • adj. (**trustier, trustiest**) old use or humorous reliable or faithful.

truth /trooth/ • n. (pl. **truths** /troothz, trooths/) 1 the state of being true. 2 (also **the truth**) that which is true; true facts. 3 a fact or belief that is accepted as true.
– ORIGIN Old English.

truthful • adj. 1 telling or expressing the truth. 2 lifelike.
– DERIVATIVES **truthfully** adv. **truthfulness** n.

try • v. (**tries, trying, tried**) 1 make an attempt to do something. 2 (also **try something out**) test something new or different to see if it is suitable, effective, or pleasant. 3 attempt to open a door. 4 (**try something on**) put on an item of clothing to see if it fits or suits you. 5 make severe demands on: *you are trying my patience.* 6 put someone on trial. 7 investigate and decide a case in a formal trial. • n. (pl. **tries**) 1 an attempt. 2 an act of testing something new or different. 3 Rugby an act of touching the ball down behind the opposing goal line, scoring points and entitling the scoring side to a kick at goal.
– PHRASES **tried and tested** (or **true**) having proved effective or reliable before. **try your hand at** attempt to do something for the first time. **try it on** Brit. informal 1 attempt to seduce someone. 2 deliberately test someone's patience.
– ORIGIN Old French *trier* 'sift'.

t

trying •adj. difficult or annoying.

tryst /trist/ •n. literary a private, romantic meeting between lovers.
– ORIGIN Latin *trista* 'an appointed place in hunting'.

tsar /zar, tsar/ (also **czar** or **tzar**) •n. an emperor of Russia before 1917.
– DERIVATIVES **tsarist** n. & adj.
– ORIGIN Russian.

tsarina /zah-ree-nuh, tsah-ree-nuh/ (also **czarina** or **tzarina**) •n. an empress of Russia before 1917.

tsetse /tet-si, tset-si/ (also **tsetse fly**) •n. an African bloodsucking fly which transmits sleeping sickness and other diseases.
– ORIGIN from a southern African language.

T-shirt (also **tee shirt**) •n. a short-sleeved casual top, having the shape of a T when spread out flat.

tsp •abbrev. (pl. **tsp** or **tsps**) teaspoonful.

T-square •n. a T-shaped instrument for drawing or testing right angles.

tsunami /tsoo-nah-mi/ •n. (pl. **tsunami** or **tsunamis**) a tidal wave caused by an earthquake or other disturbance.
– ORIGIN Japanese, 'harbour wave'.

tub •n. **1** a low, wide, open container with a flat bottom. **2** a small plastic or cardboard container for food. **3** informal a bath. **4** informal a short, broad boat that is awkward to manoeuvre.
– DERIVATIVES **tubful** n.
– ORIGIN prob. German or Dutch.

tuba •n. a large low-pitched brass wind instrument.
– ORIGIN Latin, 'trumpet'.

tubby •adj. (**tubbier, tubbiest**) informal (of a person) short and rather fat.
– DERIVATIVES **tubbiness** n.

tube •n. **1** a long, hollow cylinder for conveying or holding something. **2** a flexible metal or plastic container sealed at one end and having a cap at the other: *a toothpaste tube.* **3** a hollow cylindrical organ or structure in an animal or plant. **4** (**the Tube**) Brit. trademark the underground railway system in London.
– ORIGIN Latin *tubus*.

tuber •n. **1** a thickened underground part of a stem or rhizome, e.g. that of the potato, bearing buds from which new plants grow. **2** a thickened fleshy root, e.g. of the dahlia.
– ORIGIN Latin, 'hump, swelling'.

tubercle /tyoo-ber-k'l/ •n. **1** a small lump on a bone or on the surface of an

animal or plant. **2** a small rounded swelling in the lungs or other tissues, characteristic of tuberculosis.
– ORIGIN Latin *tuberculum* 'small lump or swelling'.

tubercle bacillus •n. the bacterium that causes tuberculosis.

tubercular /tyuu-ber-kyuu-ler/ •adj. **1** relating to or affected with tuberculosis. **2** having or covered with tubercles.

tuberculosis /tyuu-ber-kyuu-loh-siss/ •n. an infectious disease transmitted by a bacterium, in which tubercles (small swellings) appear in the tissues, especially the lungs.

tuberculous /tyuu-ber-kyuu-luhss/ •adj. = TUBERCULAR.

tuberose /tyoo-buh-rohz/ •n. a Mexican plant with heavily scented white waxy flowers and a bulb-like base.

tuberous /tyoo-buh-ruhss/ •adj. (of a plant) having or forming a tuber or tubers.

tubing •n. a length or lengths of material in the form of tubes.

tub-thumping •n. informal the expression of opinions in a loud and aggressive way.

tubular •adj. **1** long, round, and hollow like a tube. **2** made from a tube or tubes.

tubular bells •pl. n. an orchestral instrument consisting of a row of hanging metal tubes struck with a mallet.

tubule /tyoo-byool/ •n. a tiny tube.
– ORIGIN Latin *tubulus*.

TUC •abbrev. (in the UK) Trades Union Congress.

tuck •v. **1** push, fold, or turn under or between two surfaces. **2** (**tuck someone in/up**) settle someone in bed by pulling the edges of the bedclothes firmly under the mattress. **3** (often **tuck something away**) put or keep something in a safe or secret place. **4** (**tuck in/into**) informal eat food heartily. **5** make a flattened, stitched fold in a garment or material. •n. **1** a flattened, stitched fold in a garment or material. **2** Brit. informal food eaten by children at school as a snack.
– ORIGIN Old English, 'punish, ill-treat'.

tucker •n. Austral./NZ informal food.

-tude •suffix forming abstract nouns such as *solitude*.
– ORIGIN Latin *-tudo*.

Tudor •adj. relating to the English royal dynasty which held the throne from 1485 to 1603.

Tuesday •n. the day of the week before Wednesday and following Monday.

– ORIGIN named after the Germanic god *Tīw*.

tufa /tyoo-fuh/ • n. **1** a rock composed of calcium carbonate and formed as a deposit from mineral springs. **2** = TUFF.
– ORIGIN Italian.

tuff /*rhymes with* tough/ • n. rock formed from volcanic ash.
– ORIGIN Latin *tofus*.

tuffet • n. **1** a tuft or clump. **2** a footstool or low seat.
– ORIGIN from TUFT.

tuft • n. a bunch of threads, grass, or hair, held or growing together at the base.
– DERIVATIVES **tufted** adj. **tufty** adj.
– ORIGIN prob. from Old French *tofe*.

tug • v. (**tugs**, **tugging**, **tugged**) pull hard or suddenly. • n. **1** a hard or sudden pull. **2** (also **tugboat**) a small, powerful boat for towing larger boats and ships.
– ORIGIN from TOW¹.

tug of war • n. a contest in which two teams pull at opposite ends of a rope until one drags the other over a central line.

tuition • n. teaching or instruction.
– ORIGIN Latin.

tulip • n. a spring-flowering plant with boldly coloured cup-shaped flowers.
– ORIGIN French *tulipe*.

tulle /tyool/ • n. a soft, fine net material, used for making veils and dresses.
– ORIGIN from *Tulle*, a town in SW France.

tumble • v. (**tumbles**, **tumbling**, **tumbled**) **1** fall suddenly, clumsily, or headlong. **2** move in an uncontrolled way: *they tumbled from the vehicle*. **3** decrease rapidly in amount or value. **4** (**tumble to**) informal suddenly realize. • n. **1** a sudden or clumsy fall. **2** an untidy or confused arrangement or state: *a tumble of untamed curls*. **3** an acrobatic feat such as a cartwheel.
– ORIGIN German *tummelen*.

tumbledown • adj. (of a building) falling or fallen into ruin.

tumble dryer • n. Brit. a machine that dries washed clothes by spinning them in hot air inside a rotating drum.

tumbler • n. **1** a drinking glass with straight sides and no handle or stem. [ORIGIN formerly having a rounded bottom so that it could not be put down until emptied.] **2** an acrobat. **3** a part of a lock that holds the bolt until lifted by a key.

tumbleweed • n. N. Amer. & Austral./NZ a plant of dry regions which breaks off near the ground in late summer, forming light masses blown about by the wind.

tumbril /tum-bril/ (also **tumbrel**) • n. hist. an open cart that tilted backwards to empty out its load, used to take prisoners to the guillotine during the French Revolution.
– ORIGIN Old French *tomberel*.

tumescent /tyuu-mess-uhnt/ • adj. swollen or becoming swollen.
– DERIVATIVES **tumescence** n.

tumid /tyoo-mid/ • adj. (of a part of the body) swollen.
– ORIGIN Latin *tumidus*.

tummy • n. (pl. **tummies**) informal a person's stomach or abdomen.
– ORIGIN a child's pronunciation of STOMACH.

tummy button • n. informal a person's navel.

tumour (US **tumor**) • n. a swelling of a part of the body caused by an abnormal growth of tissue.
– ORIGIN Latin *tumor*.

tumult • n. **1** a loud, confused noise, as caused by a mass of people. **2** confusion or disorder.
– ORIGIN Latin *tumultus*.

tumultuous /tyuu-mul-tyuu-uhss/ • adj. **1** very loud or uproarious. **2** excited, confused, or disorderly.

tumulus /tyoo-myuu-luhss/ • n. (pl. **tumuli** /tyoo-myuu-ly/) an ancient burial mound.
– ORIGIN Latin.

tun • n. a large beer or wine cask.
– ORIGIN Latin *tunna*.

tuna • n. (pl. **tuna** or **tunas**) a large edible fish of warm seas.
– ORIGIN Spanish *atún*.

tundra /tun-druh/ • n. a vast, flat, treeless Arctic region of Europe, Asia, and North America in which the subsoil is permanently frozen.
– ORIGIN Lappish (the language of Lapland).

tune • n. a sequence of notes that form a piece of music; a melody. • v. (**tunes**, **tuning**, **tuned**) **1** (also **tune up**) adjust a musical instrument to the correct pitch. **2** adjust a radio or television to a particular frequency. **3** adjust an engine or balance mechanical parts so that they run smoothly and efficiently. **4** adjust or adapt to a purpose or situation: *the animals are finely tuned to life in the desert*.
– PHRASES **in** (or **out of**) **tune** in (or not in) the correct musical pitch. **to the tune of** informal amounting to or involving a particular sum of money.
– DERIVATIVES **tunable** (also **tuneable**) adj.
– ORIGIN from TONE.

tuneful • adj. having a pleasing tune.
– DERIVATIVES **tunefully** adv.

t

tuneless • adj. not having a pleasing tune.
– DERIVATIVES **tunelessly** adv.

tuner • n. **1** a person who tunes musical instruments, especially pianos. **2** a part of a stereo system that receives radio signals.

tungsten /tung-stuhn/ • n. a hard grey metallic element with a very high melting point, used to make electric light filaments.
– ORIGIN Swedish.

tunic • n. **1** a loose sleeveless garment reaching to the thigh or knees. **2** a close-fitting short coat worn as part of a uniform.
– ORIGIN Latin *tunica*.

tuning fork • n. a two-pronged steel device used for tuning musical instruments, which vibrates when hit against a surface to give a note of specific pitch.

Tunisian /tyoo-ni-zi-uhn/ • n. a person from Tunisia. • adj. relating to Tunisia.

tunnel • n. a passage built underground for a road or railway, or dug by a burrowing animal. • v. (**tunnels, tunnelling, tunnelled**; US **tunnels, tunneling, tunneled**) dig or force a passage underground or through something.
– ORIGIN Old French *tonel* 'small cask'.

tunnel vision • n. **1** a condition in which things cannot be seen properly if they are not straight ahead. **2** informal the tendency to focus only on a single or limited aspect of a subject or situation.

tunny • n. (pl. **tunny** or **tunnies**) a tuna.
– ORIGIN Greek *thunnos*.

tup esp. Brit. • n. a ram. • v. (**tups, tupping, tupped**) (of a ram) mate with a ewe.

tuppence • n. Brit. = TWOPENCE.

tuppenny • adj. Brit. = TWOPENNY.

turban • n. a long length of material wound round the head, worn by Muslim and Sikh men.
– DERIVATIVES **turbaned** (also **turbanned**) adj.
– ORIGIN Persian.

turbid /ter-bid/ • adj. (of a liquid) cloudy or muddy; not clear.
– DERIVATIVES **turbidity** n.
– ORIGIN Latin *turbidus*.

turbine /ter-byn, ter-bin/ • n. a machine for producing power in which a wheel or rotor is made to revolve by a fast-moving flow of water, steam, gas, or air.
– ORIGIN Latin *turbo* 'spinning top, whirl'.

turbo /ter-boh/ • n. (pl. **turbos**) = TURBOCHARGER.

turbocharger • n. a supercharger driven by a turbine powered by the engine's exhaust gases.
– DERIVATIVES **turbocharged** adj.

turbofan • n. a jet engine in which a turbine-driven fan provides additional thrust.

turbojet • n. a jet engine in which the exhaust gases also operate a turbine-driven device for compressing the air drawn into the engine.

turboprop • n. a jet engine in which a turbine is used to drive a propeller.

turbot • n. (pl. **turbot** or **turbots**) an edible flatfish which has large bony swellings on the body.
– ORIGIN Scandinavian.

turbulence • n. **1** violent or unsteady movement of air or water, or of some other fluid. **2** conflict or confusion: *political turbulence.*

turbulent /ter-byuu-luhnt/ • adj. **1** involving much conflict, disorder, or confusion. **2** (of air or water) moving unsteadily or violently.
– DERIVATIVES **turbulently** adv.
– ORIGIN Latin *turbulentus* 'full of commotion'.

tureen /tyuu-reen, tuh-reen/ • n. a deep covered dish from which soup is served.
– ORIGIN French *terrine* 'large earthenware pot'.

turf • n. (pl. **turfs** or **turves**) **1** grass and the surface layer of earth held together by its roots. **2** a piece of turf cut from the ground. **3** (**the turf**) horse racing or racecourses generally. **4** (**someone's turf**) informal a place or area in which someone has special rights, knowledge, or responsibility. • v. **1** (**turf someone off/out**) informal, esp. Brit. force someone to leave a place. **2** cover an area of ground with turf.
– ORIGIN Old English.

turf accountant • n. Brit. formal a bookmaker.

turgid /ter-jid/ • adj. **1** swollen or full: *a turgid river.* **2** (of language or style) pompous and boring.
– DERIVATIVES **turgidity** n.
– ORIGIN Latin *turgidus*.

Turk • n. a person from Turkey.

turkey • n. (pl. **turkeys**) **1** a large game bird native to North America, which is bred for food. **2** informal something that is very unsuccessful or of very poor quality.
– PHRASES **talk turkey** N. Amer. informal talk frankly and openly.
– ORIGIN short for TURKEYCOCK, first referring to the guineafowl (which was imported through Turkey), and then wrongly to the American bird.

turkeycock • n. a male turkey.

Turkic /ter-kik/ •adj. referring to a large group of Asian languages, including Turkish and Azerbaijani.

Turkish •n. the language of Turkey. •adj. relating to Turkey or its language.

Turkish bath •n. **1** a cleansing treatment that involves sitting in a room filled with very hot air or steam, followed by washing and massage. **2** a building or room where such a treatment is available.

Turkish delight •n. a sweet consisting of flavoured gelatin coated in icing sugar.

turmeric /ter-muh-rik/ •n. a bright yellow powder obtained from a plant of the ginger family, used as a spice in Asian cookery.
– ORIGIN perh. from French *terre mérite* 'deserving earth'.

turmoil •n. a state of great disturbance, confusion, or uncertainty.

turn •v. **1** move around a central point. **2** move so as to face or go in a different direction. **3** make or become: *Emma turned pale.* **4** shape something on a lathe. **5** (of the tide) change from coming in to going out or vice versa. **6** twist or sprain an ankle. •n. **1** an act of turning. **2** a bend in a road, river, etc. **3** a place where a road meets or branches off another. **4** the time when a member of a group must or is allowed to do something: *it was his turn to speak.* **5** a time when one period of time ends and another begins: *the turn of the century.* **6** a change in circumstances: *the latest turn of events.* **7** a short walk or ride. **8** a brief feeling of illness: *a funny turn.* **9** a short performance: *a comic turn.* **10** one round in a coil of rope or other material.
– PHRASES **at every turn** on every occasion. **be turned out** be dressed in a particular way. **do someone a good turn** do something that is helpful for someone. **in turn** one after the other. **out of turn** at a time when it is inappropriate or not your turn. **take turns** (or Brit. **take it in turns**) (of two or more people) do something alternately or one after the other. **to a turn** to exactly the right degree. **turn someone away** refuse to allow someone to enter a place. **turn someone/thing down 1** reject something offered or proposed by someone. **2** reduce the volume or strength of sound, heat, etc. produced by a device by adjusting its controls. **turn in** informal go to bed in the evening. **turn someone/thing in** hand someone or something over to the authorities. **turn someone off** informal make someone feel bored or disgusted. **turn something off/**
on stop or start the operation of something by means of a tap, switch, or button. **turn of mind** a particular way of thinking. **turn on** suddenly attack. **turn someone on** informal excite someone sexually. **turn something out 1** switch off an electric light. **2** produce something. **3** empty your pockets. **turn out 1** prove to be the case. **2** be present at an event. **turn over** (of an engine) start or continue to run properly. **turn someone over** hand someone over to the care or custody of a person in authority. **turn tail** informal turn round and run away. **turn to 1** start doing or becoming involved with. **2** go to for help or information. **turn up 1** be found, especially by chance. **2** put in an appearance. **turn something up 1** increase the volume or strength of sound, heat, etc. produced by a device by adjusting its controls. **2** reveal or discover something.
– ORIGIN Latin *tornare*.

turnaround (also **turnround**) •n. **1** a sudden or unexpected change. **2** the process of completing a task, or the time needed to do this.

turncoat •n. a person who deserts one party or cause in order to join an opposing one.

turning •n. **1** a place where a road branches off another. **2** the action of using a lathe.

turning point •n. a time when a decisive change happens, especially one with good results.

turnip •n. a round root vegetable with white or cream flesh.
– ORIGIN from an unknown first element + Latin *napus* 'turnip'.

turnkey •n. (pl. **turnkeys**) old use a jailer.

turn-off •n. **1** a junction at which a road branches off. **2** informal a person or thing that makes someone feel bored or disgusted.

turn-on •n. informal a person or thing that makes someone feel sexually excited.

turnout •n. the number of people attending or taking part in an event.

turnover •n. **1** the amount of money taken by a business in a particular period. **2** the rate at which employees leave a workforce and are replaced. **3** the rate at which goods are sold and replaced in a shop. **4** a small pie made by folding a piece of pastry over on itself to enclose a filling.

turnpike •n. **1** hist. a toll gate. **2** hist. a road on which a toll was collected. **3** US a motorway on which a toll is charged.
– ORIGIN first meaning a spiked barrier

fixed across a road as a defence: from PIKE².

turnround • n. var. of TURNAROUND.

turnstile • n. a mechanical gate with revolving horizontal arms that allow only one person at a time to pass through.

turntable • n. a circular revolving platform or support, e.g. for the record in a record player.

turn-up • n. Brit. **1** the end of a trouser leg folded upwards on the outside. **2** informal an unusual or unexpected event.

turpentine /ter-puhn-tyn/ • n. **1** a substance produced by certain trees, distilled to make oil of turpentine. **2** (also **oil of turpentine**) a strong-smelling oil distilled from this substance, used in mixing and thinning paints and varnishes and for cleaning paintbrushes.
– ORIGIN Old French *terebentine*.

turpitude /ter-pi-tyood/ • n. formal wickedness.
– ORIGIN Latin *turpitudo*.

turps • n. informal turpentine.

turquoise /ter-kwoyz, ter-kwahz/ • n. **1** a greenish-blue or sky-blue semi-precious stone. **2** a greenish-blue colour.
– ORIGIN Old French *turqueise* 'Turkish stone'.

turret • n. **1** a small tower at the corner of a building or wall. **2** an armoured tower, usually one that revolves, for a gun and gunners in a ship, aircraft, fort, or tank.
– DERIVATIVES **turreted** adj.
– ORIGIN Old French *tourete* 'small tower'.

turtle • n. a sea or freshwater reptile with a bony or leathery shell and flippers or webbed toes.
– PHRASES **turn turtle** (of a boat) turn upside down.
– ORIGIN prob. from French *tortue* 'tortoise'.

turtle dove • n. a small dove with a soft purring call.
– ORIGIN Latin *turtur*.

turtleneck • n. **1** Brit. a high, round, close-fitting neck on a knitted garment. **2** N. Amer. = POLO NECK.

turves pl. of TURF.

Tuscan /tuss-kuhn/ • adj. relating to Tuscany in central Italy.

tusk • n. a long pointed tooth which protrudes from a closed mouth, as one of a pair in the elephant, walrus, or wild boar.
– DERIVATIVES **tusked** adj.
– ORIGIN Old English.

tussle • n. a vigorous struggle or scuffle.
• v. (**tussles**, **tussling**, **tussled**) engage in a tussle.

– ORIGIN perh. from dialect *touse* 'handle roughly'.

tussock /tus-suhk/ • n. a dense clump or tuft of grass.
– DERIVATIVES **tussocky** adj.
– ORIGIN perh. from dialect *tusk* 'tuft'.

tutee /tyoo-tee/ • n. a student or pupil of a tutor.

tutelage /tyoo-ti-lij/ • n. **1** protection of or authority over someone or something. **2** instruction; tuition.
– ORIGIN Latin *tutela* 'keeping'.

tutelary /tyoo-ti-luh-ri/ • adj. serving as a protector, guardian, or patron.

tutor • n. **1** a private teacher who teaches a single pupil or a very small group. **2** esp. Brit. a university or college teacher responsible for the teaching and supervision of students assigned to them. **3** Brit. a book of instruction in a particular subject. • v. act as a tutor to.
– ORIGIN Latin.

tutorial • n. **1** a period of tuition given by a university or college tutor. **2** a book or computer program giving information about a subject or explaining how something is done.
• adj. relating to a tutor or the work of a tutor.

tutti /tuut-ti/ • adv. & adj. Music with all voices or instruments together.
– ORIGIN Italian.

tutti-frutti /toot-ti-froot-ti/ • n. (pl. **tutti-fruttis**) a type of ice cream containing mixed fruits.
– ORIGIN Italian, 'all fruits'.

tutu /too-too/ • n. a female ballet dancer's costume consisting of a bodice and a very short, stiff attached skirt made of many layers of fabric and sticking out from the waist.
– ORIGIN French.

tux • n. informal, esp. N. Amer. a tuxedo.

tuxedo /tuk-see-doh/ • n. (pl. **tuxedos** or **tuxedoes**) esp. N. Amer. **1** a man's dinner jacket. **2** a formal evening suit including such a jacket.
– DERIVATIVES **tuxedoed** adj.
– ORIGIN from *Tuxedo* Park, the site of a country club in New York.

TV • abbrev. television.

twaddle • n. informal trivial or silly speech or writing.

twain • cardinal number old use = TWO.
– ORIGIN Old English.

twang • n. **1** a strong ringing sound such as that made by the plucked string of a musical instrument. **2** a distinctive nasal way of speaking. • v. make a twang.
– DERIVATIVES **twangy** adj.

'twas • contr. old use or literary it was.

tweak • v. **1** twist or pull with a small but

sharp movement. **2** informal improve by making fine adjustments. • n. an act of tweaking.
– ORIGIN prob. from dialect *twick* 'pull sharply'.

twee • adj. Brit. too quaint or sentimental.
– ORIGIN from a child's pronunciation of SWEET.

tweed • n. **1** a rough woollen cloth flecked with mixed colours. **2** (**tweeds**) clothes made of tweed.
– DERIVATIVES **tweedy** adj.
– ORIGIN from a Scots form of TWILL.

tweet • n. the chirp of a small or young bird. • v. make a chirping noise.

tweeter • n. a loudspeaker designed to reproduce high frequencies.

tweeze • v. (**tweezes, tweezing, tweezed**) pluck or pull with tweezers.

tweezers • pl. n. (also **pair of tweezers**) a small instrument like a pair of pincers for plucking out hairs and picking up small objects.
– ORIGIN from former *tweeze* 'case of surgical instruments'.

twelfth /twelfth/ • ordinal number **1** that is number twelve in a sequence; 12th. **2** (**a twelfth/one twelfth**) each of twelve equal parts into which something is divided. **3** a musical interval spanning an octave and a fifth in a scale.

> ☑ Spell **twelfth** with an **f** after the **l**.

Twelfth Night • n. **1** 6 January, the feast of the Epiphany. **2** the evening of 5 January, formerly the twelfth and last day of Christmas festivities.

twelve • cardinal number two more than ten; 12. (Roman numeral: **xii** or **XII**.)
– ORIGIN Old English.

twelvemonth • n. old use a year.

twenty • cardinal number (pl. **twenties**) ten less than thirty; 20. (Roman numeral: **xx** or **XX**.)
– DERIVATIVES **twentieth** ordinal number.
– ORIGIN Old English.

24-7 (also **24/7**) • adv. informal twenty-four hours a day, seven days a week; all the time.

twenty-twenty vision (also **20/20 vision**) • n. normal vision.

'twere • contr. old use or literary it were.

twerp • n. informal a silly person.

twice • adv. **1** two times. **2** double in degree or quantity.
– ORIGIN Old English.

twiddle • v. (**twiddles, twiddling, twiddled**) play or fiddle with something in an aimless or nervous way. • n. an act of twiddling.

– PHRASES **twiddle your thumbs** have nothing to do.
– DERIVATIVES **twiddly** adj.

twig¹ • n. a slender woody shoot growing from a branch or stem of a tree or shrub.
– DERIVATIVES **twiggy** adj.
– ORIGIN Old English.

twig² • v. (**twigs, twigging, twigged**) Brit. informal come to understand or realize something.

twilight • n. **1** the soft glowing light from the sky when the sun is below the horizon. **2** a period or state of gradual decline: *the twilight of his career.*
– ORIGIN from Old English, 'two' + LIGHT¹.

twilight zone • n. a situation or area of thought which is not clearly defined.

twilit • adj. dimly lit by twilight.

twill • n. a fabric woven so as to have a surface of parallel diagonal ridges.
– DERIVATIVES **twilled** adj.
– ORIGIN Old English, 'two'.

twin • n. **1** one of two children or animals born at the same birth. **2** a thing that is exactly like another. • adj. **1** forming or being one of a pair of twins or matching things. **2** (of a bedroom) containing two single beds. • v. (**twins, twinning, twinned**) **1** link or combine as a pair. **2** Brit. link a town with another in a different country, for the purposes of cultural exchange.
– ORIGIN Old English.

twine • n. strong string consisting of strands of hemp or cotton twisted together. • v. (**twines, twining, twined**) wind round something.
– ORIGIN Old English, 'thread, linen'.

twinge • n. **1** a sudden sharp pain. **2** a brief, sharp pang of emotion.
– ORIGIN Old English, 'pinch, wring'.

twinkle • v. (**twinkles, twinkling, twinkled**) **1** (of a star or light) shine with a gleam that changes constantly from bright to faint. **2** (of a person's eyes) sparkle with amusement or liveliness. • n. a twinkling sparkle or gleam.
– PHRASES **in a twinkling of an eye** in an instant.
– DERIVATIVES **twinkly** adj.
– ORIGIN Old English.

twinkle-toed • adj. informal nimble and quick on your feet.

twinset • n. esp. Brit. a woman's matching cardigan and jumper.

twirl • v. spin quickly and lightly round. • n. **1** an act of twirling. **2** a spiral shape.
– DERIVATIVES **twirly** adj.
– ORIGIN prob. from former *trill* 'twiddle, spin'.

t

twist • v. 1 bend, curl, or distort. 2 turn or bend round or into a different direction. 3 force out of the natural position: *she twisted her ankle.* 4 take or have a winding course. 5 deliberately change the meaning of something. 6 (as adj. **twisted**) strange or abnormal in an unpleasant way; perverted. • n. 1 an act of twisting. 2 a thing with a spiral shape. 3 a new or unexpected development or way of treating something: *the plot includes a clever twist.* 4 (**the twist**) a dance with a twisting movement of the body, popular in the 1960s.
– PHRASES **round the twist** Brit. informal crazy. **twist someone's arm** informal forcefully persuade someone to do something that they are reluctant to do.
– DERIVATIVES **twisty** adj.
– ORIGIN Old English.

twister • n. 1 Brit. informal a swindler or dishonest person. 2 N. Amer. a tornado.

twit[1] • n. informal, esp. Brit. a silly person.
– ORIGIN perh. from TWIT[2].

twit[2] • v. (**twits, twitting, twitted**) informal tease good-humouredly.
– ORIGIN Old English, 'reproach with'.

twitch • v. make a short jerking movement. • n. 1 a twitching movement. 2 a pang: *he felt a twitch of annoyance.*
– ORIGIN Germanic.

twitcher • n. Brit. informal a birdwatcher intent on spotting rare birds.

twitchy • adj. (**twitchier, twitchiest**) informal nervous.

twitter • v. (**twitters, twittering, twittered**) 1 (of a bird) make a series of short high sounds. 2 talk rapidly in a nervous or silly way. • n. 1 a twittering sound. 2 informal an agitated or excited state.

'twixt • contr. betwixt.

two • cardinal number one less than three; 2. (Roman numeral: **ii** or **II**.)
– PHRASES **put two and two together** draw an obvious conclusion from the evidence available. **two by two** side by side in pairs.
– DERIVATIVES **twofold** adj. & adv.
– ORIGIN Old English.

> USAGE: For an explanation of the difference between **two**, **to**, and **too**, see the note at TO.

two-bit • adj. N. Amer. informal insignificant, cheap, or worthless.

two-dimensional • adj. having or appearing to have length and breadth but no depth.

two-faced • adj. insincere and deceitful.

twopence /tup-puhnss/ (also **tuppence**) • n. Brit. 1 the sum of two pence before decimalization (1971).

2 informal anything at all: *he didn't care twopence.*

twopenn'orth /too-pen-nuhth/ • n. an amount that is worth or costs twopence.
– PHRASES **add** (or **put in**) **your twopenn'orth** informal give your opinion.

twopenny /tup-puh-ni/ (also **tuppeny**) • adj. Brit. costing two pence before decimalization (1971).

twopenny-halfpenny • adj. Brit. informal insignificant or worthless.

two-piece • adj. consisting of two matching items.

twosome • n. a set of two people or things.

two-step • n. a dance with long sliding steps in march or polka time.

two-time • v. informal be unfaithful to a lover or a husband or wife.

two-way • adj. 1 involving movement or communication in opposite directions. 2 (of a switch) permitting a current to be switched on or off from either of two points.
– PHRASES **two-way street** a shared obligation: *trust is a two-way street.*

two-way mirror • n. a panel of glass that can be seen through from one side and is a mirror on the other.

tycoon • n. a wealthy, powerful person in business or industry.
– ORIGIN Japanese, 'great lord'.

tying pres. part. of TIE.

tyke • n. informal a mischievous child.
– ORIGIN Old Norse, 'bitch'.

tympani • pl. n. var. of TIMPANI.

tympanum /tim-puh-nuhm/ • n. (pl. **tympanums** or **tympana** /tim-puh-nuh/) the eardrum.
– ORIGIN Greek *tumpanon* 'drum'.

Tynwald /tin-wuhld/ • n. the parliament of the Isle of Man.
– ORIGIN Old Norse, 'place of assembly'.

type • n. 1 a category of people or things that share particular qualities or features: *a new type of battery.* 2 informal a person of a particular nature: *a sporty type.* 3 printed characters or letters. • v. (**types, typing, typed**) write using a typewriter or computer.
– DERIVATIVES **typing** n.
– ORIGIN Greek *tupos* 'impression, type'.

typecast • v. (**be typecast**) (of an actor) be repeatedly cast in the same type of role because their appearance is appropriate or they are known for such roles.

typeface • n. a particular design of printed characters or letters.

typescript • n. a typed copy of a written work.

typeset • v. (**typesets, typesetting,**

typeset) arrange or generate the data or type for text to be printed.
– DERIVATIVES **typesetter** n. **typesetting** n.

typewriter •n. an electric, electronic, or manual machine with keys for producing characters similar to printed ones.
– DERIVATIVES **typewriting** n. **typewritten** adj.

typhoid (also **typhoid fever**) •n. an infectious fever caused by bacteria, resulting in red spots on the chest and abdomen and severe irritation of the intestines.
– ORIGIN from TYPHUS.

typhoon /ty-foon/ •n. a tropical storm with very high winds, occurring in the region of the Indian Ocean or the western Pacific Ocean.
– ORIGIN partly from Arabic, partly from a Chinese dialect word meaning 'big wind'.

typhus /ty-fuhss/ •n. an infectious disease caused by bacteria, resulting in a purple rash, headaches, fever, and usually delirium.
– ORIGIN Greek *tuphos* 'smoke, stupor'.

typical •adj. **1** having the distinctive qualities of a particular type of person or thing: *a typical example of a small American town.* **2** characteristic of a particular person or thing.
– DERIVATIVES **typically** adv.

typify •v. (**typifies**, **typifying**, **typified**) be typical of.

typist •n. a person skilled in typing and employed for this purpose.

typo /ty-poh/ •n. (pl. **typos**) informal a

small mistake in typed or printed writing.

typography /ty-pog-ruh-fi/ •n. **1** the art or process of preparing material for printing, especially of designing how printed text will appear. **2** the style and appearance of printed text.
– DERIVATIVES **typographer** n. **typographic** adj. **typographical** adj.

tyrannical •adj. using power over other people in a cruel and unfair way.
– DERIVATIVES **tyrannically** adv.

tyrannize /ti-ruh-nyz/ (or **tyrannise**) •v. (**tyrannizes**, **tyrannizing**, **tyrannized**) rule or dominate in a cruel or oppressive way.

tyrannosaurus rex /ti-ran-nuh-sor-uhss recks/ •n. a very large meat-eating dinosaur with powerful jaws and small claw-like front legs.
– ORIGIN from Greek *turannos* 'tyrant' + *sauros* 'lizard'.

tyranny •n. (pl. **tyrannies**) cruel and oppressive government or rule.
– DERIVATIVES **tyrannous** adj.

tyrant •n. **1** a cruel and oppressive ruler. **2** a person who uses their power in a cruel or unfair way.
– ORIGIN Greek *turannos*.

tyre (US **tire**) •n. a rubber covering that is inflated or that surrounds an inflated inner tube, that fits around a wheel to form a soft contact with the road.
– ORIGIN prob. from ATTIRE.

tyro /ty-roh/ •n. (pl. **tyros**) a beginner or novice.
– ORIGIN Latin, 'recruit'.

tzar •n. var. of TSAR.

tzarina •n. var. of TSARINA.

Uu

U¹ (also **u**) •n. (pl. **Us** or **U's**) the twenty-first letter of the alphabet.

U² •abbrev. **1** (in names of sports clubs) United. **2** Brit. universal (referring to films classified as suitable for everyone to see). •symb. the chemical element uranium.

U-bend •n. a section of a waste pipe shaped like a U.

uber- /oo-ber/ (also **über-**) •prefix referring to an outstanding or supreme example of a person or thing: *an uberbabe.*
– ORIGIN German *über* 'over'.

ubiquitous /yoo-bi-kwi-tuhss/ •adj. present, appearing, or found everywhere.
– DERIVATIVES **ubiquitously** adv. **ubiquity** n.
– ORIGIN Latin *ubique* 'everywhere'.

U-boat •n. a German submarine of the First or Second World War.
– ORIGIN German *U-Boot*, short for *Unterseeboot* 'undersea boat'.

UCAS /yoo-kass/ •abbrev. (in the UK) Universities and Colleges Admissions Service.

UDA •abbrev. Ulster Defence Association.

udder •n. the milk-producing gland of female cattle, sheep, goats, horses, etc., hanging near the hind legs as a bag-like organ with two or more teats.
– ORIGIN Old English.

UDR •abbrev. Ulster Defence Regiment.

UEFA /yoo-ee-fuh, yoo-ay-fuh/ •abbrev. Union of European Football Associations.

UFO •n. (pl. **UFOs**) a mysterious object seen in the sky for which it is claimed no scientific explanation can be found, believed by some to be a vehicle carrying beings from outer space.
– ORIGIN short for *unidentified flying object*.

Ugandan /yoo-gan-duhn/ •n. a person from Uganda. •adj. relating to Uganda.

Ugli fruit /ug-li/ •n. (pl. **Ugli fruit**) trademark a mottled green and yellow citrus fruit which is a cross between a grapefruit and a tangerine.
– ORIGIN from UGLY.

ugly •adj. (**uglier, ugliest**) **1** unpleasant or unattractive in appearance. **2** hostile or threatening: *the mood in the room turned ugly.*
– DERIVATIVES **ugliness** n.
– ORIGIN Old Norse, 'to be dreaded'.

ugly duckling •n. a person who unexpectedly turns out to be beautiful or talented.
– ORIGIN from one of Hans Christian Andersen's fairy tales, in which the 'ugly duckling' becomes a swan.

UHF •abbrev. ultra-high frequency.

UHT •abbrev. Brit. ultra heat treated (a process used to extend the shelf life of milk).

UK •abbrev. United Kingdom.

Ukrainian /yoo-kray-ni-uhn/ •n. **1** a person from Ukraine. **2** the language of Ukraine. •adj. relating to Ukraine.

ukulele /yoo-kuh-lay-li/ •n. a small four-stringed guitar of Hawaiian origin.
– ORIGIN Hawaiian, 'jumping flea'.

ulcer •n. an open sore on the body or on an internal organ.
– DERIVATIVES **ulcerous** adj.
– ORIGIN Latin *ulcus*.

ulcerate •v. (**ulcerates, ulcerating, ulcerated**) develop into or become affected by an ulcer.
– DERIVATIVES **ulceration** n.

-ule •suffix forming nouns conveying smallness: *capsule.*
– ORIGIN Latin *-ulus, -ula, -ulum.*

ullage /ul-lij/ •n. **1** the amount by which a container falls short of being full. **2** loss of liquid by evaporation or leakage.
– ORIGIN Old French *euillier* 'fill up'.

ulna /ul-nuh/ •n. (pl. **ulnae** /ul-nee/ or **ulnas**) the thinner and longer of the two bones in the human forearm.
– DERIVATIVES **ulnar** adj.
– ORIGIN Latin.

ulster •n. a long, loose overcoat made of rough cloth, worn by men.

– ORIGIN from *Ulster* in Ireland, where it was originally sold.

Ulsterman (or **Ulsterwoman**) • n. (pl. **Ulstermen** or **Ulsterwomen**) a person from Northern Ireland or Ulster.

ulterior • adj. other than what is obvious or has been admitted: *she had some ulterior motive in coming.*
– ORIGIN Latin, 'further, more distant'.

ultimate • adj. **1** being or happening at the end of a process; final. **2** being the best or most extreme example of its kind: *the ride gained the ultimate accolade of three stars.* **3** basic or fundamental: *atoms are the ultimate constituents of anything that exists.* • n. (**the ultimate**) the best of its kind that is imaginable: *the ultimate in decorative luxury.*
– DERIVATIVES **ultimately** adv.
– ORIGIN Latin *ultimatus.*

ultimatum /ul-ti-may-tuhm/ • n. (pl. **ultimatums** or **ultimata** /ul-ti-may-tuh/) a final warning that action will be taken against you if you do not agree to another party's demands.
– ORIGIN Latin, 'thing that has come to an end'.

ultra informal • adv. very: *ultra modern furniture.*

ultra- • prefix **1** beyond; on the other side of: *ultramarine.* **2** extreme; extremely: *ultramicroscopic.*
– ORIGIN Latin *ultra.*

ultra-high frequency • n. a radio frequency in the range 300 to 3,000 megahertz.

ultramarine • n. a brilliant deep blue pigment and colour.
– ORIGIN Latin *ultramarinus* 'beyond the sea' (because the pigment was obtained from lapis lazuli, which was imported).

ultrasonic • adj. involving sound waves with a frequency above the upper limit of human hearing. • n. (**ultrasonics**) **1** the science and application of ultrasonic waves. **2** ultrasound.
– DERIVATIVES **ultrasonically** adv.

ultrasound • n. sound or other vibrations having an ultrasonic frequency, used in medical scans.

ultraviolet • n. electromagnetic radiation having a wavelength just shorter than that of violet light but longer than that of X-rays.
• adj. referring to such radiation.

ululate /yoo-lyuu-layt, ul-yuu-layt/
• v. (**ululates, ululating, ululated**) howl or wail.
– DERIVATIVES **ululation** n.
– ORIGIN Latin *ululare.*

umbel /um-buhl/ • n. a flower cluster in which stalks spring from a common centre and form a flat or curved surface.

– ORIGIN Latin *umbella* 'sunshade'.

umber /rhymes with number/ • n. a natural pigment, normally dark yellowish-brown in colour (**raw umber**) or dark brown when roasted (**burnt umber**).
– ORIGIN from French *terre d'ombre,* 'earth of shadow'.

umbilical /um-bil-i-k'l, um-bi-ly-k'l/
• adj. relating to the navel or the umbilical cord.
– DERIVATIVES **umbilically** adv.

umbilical cord • n. a flexible cord-like structure containing blood vessels, attaching a fetus to the placenta while it is in the womb.

umbilicus /um-bil-li-kuhss, um-bi-ly-kuhss/ • n. (pl. **umbilici** /um-bil-li-sy, um-bi-ly-sy/ or **umbilicuses**) the navel.
– ORIGIN Latin.

umbra /um-bruh/ • n. (pl. **umbras** or **umbrae** /um-bree/) the dark central part of the shadow cast by the earth or the moon in an eclipse.
– ORIGIN Latin, 'shade'.

umbrage /um-brij/ • n. (in phr. **take umbrage**) take offence or become annoyed.
– ORIGIN first meaning 'shade, ground for suspicion': from Latin *umbra.*

umbrella • n. a device consisting of a circular fabric canopy on a folding metal frame supported by a central rod, used as protection against rain.
• adj. including or containing many different parts: *an umbrella organization.*
– ORIGIN Italian *ombrella.*

umlaut /uum-lowt/ • n. a mark (¨) used over a vowel in some languages to indicate how it should be pronounced.
– ORIGIN German.

umpire • n. (in certain sports) an official who supervises a game to ensure that players keep to the rules and who settles disputes arising from the play.
• v. (**umpires, umpiring, umpired**) act as an umpire.
– ORIGIN Old French *nonper* 'not equal'.

umpteen • cardinal number informal very many.
– DERIVATIVES **umpteenth** ordinal number.

UN • abbrev. United Nations.

un-¹ • prefix **1** (added to adjectives, participles, and their derivatives) not: *unacademic.* **2** (added to nouns) a lack of: *untruth.*
– ORIGIN Old English.

> **USAGE:** For an explanation of the difference between the prefixes **un-** and **non-**, see the note at **NON-**.

un-² • prefix added to verbs: **1** referring to the reversal or cancellation of an action

or state: *unsettle.* **2** referring to deprivation, separation, or change to a lesser state: *unmask.*
– ORIGIN Old English.

unabashed • adj. not embarrassed or ashamed.

unabated • adj. without any reduction in intensity or strength.

unable • adj. not having the skill, means, strength, or opportunity to do something.

unabridged • adj. (of a novel, play, speech, etc.) not cut or shortened.

unacceptable • adj. not satisfactory or allowable.
– DERIVATIVES **unacceptability** n. **unacceptably** adv.

unaccompanied • adj. **1** having no companion or escort. **2** without instrumental accompaniment. **3** without something specified occurring at the same time.

unaccountable • adj. **1** unable to be explained. **2** not responsible for or required to explain the outcome of something.
– DERIVATIVES **unaccountably** adv.

unaccounted • adj. (**unaccounted for**) not taken into consideration or explained.

unaccustomed • adj. **1** not usual or customary. **2** (**unaccustomed to**) not familiar with or used to.

unacknowledged • adj. **1** existing or having taken place but not accepted or admitted to. **2** (of a person or their work) deserving recognition but not receiving it.

unacquainted • adj. **1** (**unacquainted with**) having no experience of or familiarity with. **2** not having met before.

unadorned • adj. not decorated; plain.

unadulterated • adj. **1** not mixed with any different or inferior substances. **2** complete; total: *pure, unadulterated jealousy.*

unadventurous • adj. not offering, involving, or eager for new or exciting things.

unadvisedly • adv. in an unwise or rash way.

unaffected • adj. **1** feeling or showing no effects. **2** (of a person) sincere and genuine.

unaffiliated • adj. not officially attached to or connected with an organization.

unaffordable • adj. too expensive to be afforded by the average person.

unafraid • adj. feeling no fear.

unaided • adj. without any help.

unalike • adj. differing from each other.

unalloyed • adj. **1** (of metal) not alloyed. **2** complete; total: *unalloyed delight.*

unaltered • adj. remaining the same.

unambiguous • adj. not open to more than one interpretation; clear in meaning.
– DERIVATIVES **unambiguously** adv.

unambitious • adj. **1** not motivated by a strong desire to succeed. **2** (of a plan or piece of work) not involving anything new, exciting, or demanding.

un-American • adj. **1** not American in nature. **2** US against the interests of the US and therefore treasonable.

unanimous /yoo-nan-i-muhss/ • adj. **1** fully in agreement. **2** (of an opinion, decision, or vote) held or carried by everyone involved.
– DERIVATIVES **unanimity** /yoo-nuh-nim-i-ti/ n. **unanimously** adv.
– ORIGIN Latin *unanimus.*

unannounced • adj. without warning or notice: *he arrived unannounced.*

unanswerable • adj. **1** unable to be answered. **2** unable to be proved wrong.

unanswered • adj. not answered.

unapologetic • adj. not sorry for your actions.
– DERIVATIVES **unapologetically** adv.

unappealing • adj. not inviting or attractive.

unappetizing (or **unappetising**) • adj. not inviting or attractive.

unappreciated • adj. not fully understood, recognized, or valued.

unappreciative • adj. not fully understanding or recognizing something.

unapproachable • adj. not welcoming or friendly.

unarguable • adj. not able to be disagreed with.
– DERIVATIVES **unarguably** adv.

unarmed • adj. not equipped with or carrying weapons.

unashamed • adj. feeling or showing no guilt or embarrassment.
– DERIVATIVES **unashamedly** adv.

unasked • adj. **1** (of a question) not asked. **2** without being asked or invited.

unassailable • adj. unable to be attacked, questioned, or defeated.

unassisted • adj. not helped by anyone or anything.

unassuming • adj. not wanting to draw attention to yourself or your abilities.

unattached • adj. without a husband or wife or established lover.

unattainable • adj. not able to be reached or achieved.

unattended • adj. without the owner or a responsible person present; not being watched or looked after.

unattractive • adj. not pleasing, appealing, or inviting.
– DERIVATIVES **unattractively** adv. **unattractiveness** n.

unattributed • adj. (of a quotation, story, or work of art) of unknown or unpublished origin.
– DERIVATIVES **unattributable** adj.

unauthorized (or **unauthorised**) • adj. not having official permission or approval.

unavailable • adj. **1** not able to be used or obtained. **2** (of a person) not free to do something.
– DERIVATIVES **unavailability** n.

unavailing • adj. achieving little or nothing.

unavoidable • adj. not able to be avoided or prevented.
– DERIVATIVES **unavoidably** adv.

unaware • adj. having no knowledge of a situation or fact. • adv. (**unawares**) so as to surprise someone; unexpectedly.

unbalanced • adj. **1** emotionally or mentally disturbed. **2** not giving equal coverage or treatment to all aspects of something.

unbearable • adj. not able to be endured.
– DERIVATIVES **unbearably** adv.

unbeatable • adj. not able to be bettered or beaten.

unbeaten • adj. not defeated or bettered.

unbecoming • adj. **1** not flattering: *an unbecoming red dress.* **2** (of behaviour) improper or inappropriate.

unbeknown (also **unbeknownst**) • adj. (**unbeknown to**) without the knowledge of.

unbelievable • adj. **1** unlikely to be true. **2** extraordinary.
– DERIVATIVES **unbelievably** adv.

unbeliever • n. a person without religious belief.

unbend • v. (**unbends, unbending, unbent**) **1** straighten. **2** become less formal or strict.

unbending • adj. unwilling to change your mind; inflexible.

unbiased (also **unbiassed**) • adj. showing no prejudice.

unbidden • adj. without having been invited.

unblemished • adj. not damaged or marked in any way.

unblock • v. remove an obstruction from.

unblushing • adj. not feeling or showing embarrassment or shame.

– DERIVATIVES **unblushingly** adv.

unborn • adj. (of a baby) not yet born.

unbound • adj. not bound or tied up.

unbounded • adj. having no limits.

unbowed • adj. not having been defeated.

unbreakable • adj. not able to be broken.

unbridgeable • adj. (of a gap or difference between two people) not able to be closed or made less significant.

unbridled • adj. uncontrolled: *unbridled lust.*

unbroken • adj. **1** not broken or interrupted. **2** (of a record in sport) not beaten. **3** (of a horse) not broken in.

unbuckle • v. (**unbuckles, unbuckling, unbuckled**) unfasten the buckle of.

unburden • v. (**unburden yourself**) confide in someone about a worry or problem.

unbutton • v. unfasten the buttons of.

uncalled • adj. (**uncalled for**) undesirable and unnecessary.

uncanny • adj. strange or mysterious.
– DERIVATIVES **uncannily** adv.

uncared • adj. (**uncared for**) not looked after properly.

uncaring • adj. not sympathetic to or concerned for other people.

unceasing • adj. not stopping; continuous.
– DERIVATIVES **unceasingly** adv.

unceremonious • adj. rude or abrupt.
– DERIVATIVES **unceremoniously** adv.

uncertain • adj. **1** not known, reliable, or definite. **2** not completely confident or sure.
– PHRASES **in no uncertain terms** clearly and forcefully.
– DERIVATIVES **uncertainly** adv.

uncertainty • n. (pl. **uncertainties**) **1** the state of being uncertain. **2** something that is uncertain or makes you feel uncertain.

unchallengeable • adj. not able to be questioned or opposed.

unchallenged • adj. not questioned or opposed.

unchangeable • adj. not liable to change or able to be altered.

unchanged • adj. not changed; unaltered.

unchanging • adj. remaining the same.

uncharacteristic • adj. not typical of a particular person or thing.
– DERIVATIVES **uncharacteristically** adv.

uncharitable • adj. unkind or unsympathetic to other people.
– DERIVATIVES **uncharitably** adv.

uncharted • adj. (of an area of land or sea) not mapped or surveyed.

u

unchecked • adj. (of something undesirable) not controlled or restrained.

unchristian • adj. **1** not in line with the teachings of Christianity. **2** unkind or unfair.

uncivil • adj. not polite.

uncivilized (or **uncivilised**) • adj. **1** (of a place or people) not having developed a modern culture or way of life. **2** not behaving in accordance with accepted moral standards.

unclaimed • adj. not having been claimed.

unclasp • v. unfasten a clasp or similar device.

unclassified • adj. not classified.

uncle • n. the brother of a person's father or mother or the husband of a person's aunt.
– ORIGIN Latin *avunculus* 'maternal uncle'.

unclean • adj. **1** not clean; dirty. **2** morally wrong. **3** (of food) considered impure and forbidden by a particular religion.

uncleanliness • n. the state of being dirty.

unclear • adj. not easy to see, hear, or understand.

unclench • v. release a clenched part of the body.

Uncle Sam • n. the United States or its government, often shown as a man with a tall hat and white beard.

unclog • v. (**unclogs**, **unclogging**, **unclogged**) remove a blockage from.

unclothed • adj. naked.

unclouded • adj. **1** (of the sky) not dark or overcast. **2** not spoiled by anything: *unclouded happiness.*

uncluttered • adj. not cluttered by too many objects or unnecessary items.

uncoil • v. straighten from a coiled position.

uncoloured (US **uncolored**) • adj. **1** having no colour. **2** not influenced: *her views were uncoloured by her husband's.*

uncomfortable • adj. **1** not physically comfortable. **2** uneasy or awkward.
– DERIVATIVES **uncomfortably** adv.

uncommercial • adj. not making or intended to make a profit.

uncommon • adj. **1** out of the ordinary; unusual. **2** remarkably great.
– DERIVATIVES **uncommonly** adv.

uncommunicative • adj. unwilling to talk or give out information.

uncompetitive • adj. not cheaper or better than others and therefore not able to compete commercially.

uncomplaining • adj. not complaining.
– DERIVATIVES **uncomplainingly** adv.

uncomplicated • adj. simple or straightforward.

uncomplimentary • adj. rude or insulting.

☑ Spell **uncomplimentary** with **-li-** in the middle.

uncomprehending • adj. unable to understand something.
– DERIVATIVES **uncomprehendingly** adv.

uncompromising • adj. **1** unwilling to change your mind or behaviour. **2** harsh or relentless.
– DERIVATIVES **uncompromisingly** adv.

unconcealed • adj. not concealed; obvious.

unconcern • n. a lack of worry or interest.

unconcerned • adj. not concerned or interested.

unconditional • adj. not subject to any conditions.
– DERIVATIVES **unconditionally** adv.

unconfined • adj. **1** not confined to a limited space. **2** (of joy or excitement) very great.

unconfirmed • adj. not yet proved to be true.

uncongenial • adj. **1** not friendly or pleasant to be with. **2** not suitable: *the atmosphere was uncongenial to good conversation.*

unconnected • adj. **1** not joined together or to something else. **2** not associated or linked in a sequence.

unconscionable /un-kon-shuh-nuh-b'l/ • adj. not right or reasonable.
– DERIVATIVES **unconscionably** adv.
– ORIGIN from former *consciable* 'conscientious'.

unconscious • adj. **1** not awake and aware of and responding to your surroundings. **2** done or existing without realizing. **3** (**unconscious of**) unaware of. • n. (**the unconscious**) the part of the mind which cannot be accessed by the conscious mind but which affects behaviour and emotions.
– DERIVATIVES **unconsciously** adv. **unconsciousness** n.

unconstitutional • adj. not in accordance with the constitution of a country or the rules of an organization.
– DERIVATIVES **unconstitutionally** adv.

unconstrained • adj. not restricted or limited.

uncontaminated • adj. not contaminated.

uncontested • adj. not contested or challenged.

u

uncontrollable • adj. not controllable.
– DERIVATIVES **uncontrollably** adv.

uncontrolled • adj. not controlled.

uncontroversial • adj. not controversial.
– DERIVATIVES **uncontroversially** adv.

unconventional • adj. not following what is generally done or believed.
– DERIVATIVES **unconventionality** n. **unconventionally** adv.

unconvinced • adj. not certain that something is true or can be relied on.

unconvincing • adj. failing to convince or impress.
– DERIVATIVES **unconvincingly** adv.

uncooked • adj. not cooked; raw.

uncool • adj. informal not fashionable or impressive.

uncooperative • adj. unwilling to help other people or do what they ask.

uncoordinated • adj. **1** badly organized. **2** clumsy.

uncorroborated • adj. not supported or confirmed by evidence.

uncountable • adj. too many to be counted.

uncouth • adj. lacking good manners.
– ORIGIN Old English, 'unknown'.

uncover • v. (**uncovers, uncovering, uncovered**) **1** remove a cover or covering from. **2** discover something previously secret or unknown.

uncovered • adj. not covered.

uncritical • adj. not willing to criticize or judge something.
– DERIVATIVES **uncritically** adv.

uncross • v. move something back from a crossed position.

uncrowned • adj. not formally crowned as a king or queen.

unction /ungk-sh'n/ • n. **1** formal the smearing of someone with oil or ointment as a religious ceremony. **2** excessive politeness or flattery.
– ORIGIN Latin.

unctuous /ungk-tyuu-uhss/ • adj. excessively flattering or friendly.
– DERIVATIVES **unctuously** adv.

uncultivated • adj. **1** (of land) not used for growing crops. **2** not highly educated.

uncultured • adj. not having good taste, manners, or education.

uncut • adj. not cut.

undamaged • adj. not damaged.

undated • adj. not provided or marked with a date.

undaunted • adj. not discouraged by difficulty, danger, or disappointment.

undeceive • v. (**undeceives, undeceiving, undeceived**) tell someone that an idea or belief is mistaken.

undecided • adj. **1** (of a person) not having made a decision. **2** not settled or resolved.

undefeated • adj. not defeated.

undefined • adj. not clear or defined.
– DERIVATIVES **undefinable** adj.

undemanding • adj. not demanding.

undemocratic • adj. not according to the principles of democracy.
– DERIVATIVES **undemocratically** adv.

undemonstrative • adj. not tending to express feelings openly.

undeniable • adj. unable to be denied or questioned.
– DERIVATIVES **undeniably** adv.

under • prep. **1** extending or directly below. **2** at a lower level, layer, or grade than. **3** expressing control by another person: *I was under his spell.* **4** according to the rules of. **5** used to express grouping or classification. **6** undergoing a process: *the hotel is still under construction.* • adv. extending or directly below something.
– PHRASES **under way 1** having started and making progress. **2** (of a boat) moving through the water.
– ORIGIN Old English.

under- • prefix **1** below; beneath: *undercover.* **2** lower in status: *undersecretary.* **3** insufficiently; incompletely: *undernourished.*

underachieve • v. (**underachieves, underachieving, underachieved**) do less well than is expected.
– DERIVATIVES **underachievement** n. **underachiever** n.

underage • adj. too young to take part legally in a particular activity.

underarm • adj. & adv. (of a throw or stroke in sport) made with the arm or hand below shoulder level. • n. a person's armpit.

underbelly • n. (pl. **underbellies**) **1** the soft underside of an animal. **2** a hidden unpleasant or criminal part of society.

undercarriage • n. **1** a wheeled structure beneath an aircraft which supports the aircraft on the ground. **2** the supporting frame under the body of a vehicle.

undercharge • v. (**undercharges, undercharging, undercharged**) charge someone a price or amount that is too low.

underclass • n. the lowest social class in a country or community, consisting of the poor and unemployed.

underclothes • pl. n. clothes worn under others next to the skin.
– DERIVATIVES **underclothing** n.

u

undercoat • n. a layer of paint applied after the primer and before the topcoat.

undercover • adj. & adv. involving secret work for investigation or spying.

undercurrent • n. **1** a current of water below the surface and moving in a different direction from any surface current. **2** an underlying feeling or influence.

undercut • v. (**undercuts, undercutting, undercut**) **1** offer goods or services at a lower price than a competitor. **2** cut or wear away the part under. **3** weaken; undermine: *the chairman's authority was being undercut.*

underdeveloped • adj. **1** not fully developed. **2** (of a country or region) not advanced economically.

underdog • n. a competitor thought to have little chance of winning a fight or contest.

underdone • adj. (of food) not cooked enough.

underdress • v. (**be underdressed**) be dressed too plainly or informally for a particular occasion.

underemployed • adj. not having enough work.
– DERIVATIVES **underemployment** n.

underestimate • v. (**underestimates, underestimating, underestimated**) **1** estimate something to be smaller or less important than it really is. **2** think of someone as less capable than they really are. • n. an estimate that is too low.
– DERIVATIVES **underestimation** n.

underfed • adj. not fed or nourished enough.

underfelt • n. Brit. felt laid under a carpet for protection or support.

underfoot • adv. **1** under the feet; on the ground. **2** constantly present and in your way.

underfund • v. fail to provide with enough funding.
– DERIVATIVES **underfunding** n.

undergarment • n. an article of underclothing.

undergo • v. (**undergoes, undergoing, underwent**; past part. **undergone**) experience something unpleasant or difficult.
– ORIGIN Old English, 'undermine'.

undergraduate • n. a student at a university who has not yet taken a first degree.

underground • adj. & adv. **1** beneath the surface of the ground. **2** in secrecy or hiding. • n. **1** Brit. an underground railway. **2** a secret group or movement working against an existing government.

undergrowth • n. a dense growth of shrubs and other plants.

underhand • adj. acting or done in a secret or dishonest way.

underlay¹ • n. material laid under a carpet for protection or support.
• v. (**underlays, underlaying, underlaid**) place something under something else to support or raise it.

underlay² past tense of UNDERLIE.

underlie • v. (**underlies, underlying, underlay**; past part. **underlain**) lie or be situated under.
– DERIVATIVES **underlying** adj.

underline • v. (**underlines, underlining, underlined**) **1** draw a line under a word or phrase for emphasis. **2** emphasize something.

underling • n. esp. derog. a person of lower status.

underlying pres. part. of UNDERLIE.

underman • v. (**undermans, undermanning, undermanned**) fail to provide with enough workers.

undermine • v. (**undermines, undermining, undermined**) **1** damage or weaken: *this could undermine years of hard work.* **2** wear away the base of a rock formation. **3** dig beneath a building so as to make it collapse.

underneath • prep. & adv. **1** situated directly below. **2** so as to be hidden by. • n. the part or side facing towards the ground.
– ORIGIN Old English.

undernourished • adj. not having enough food or the right type of food for good health.
– DERIVATIVES **undernourishment** n.

underpaid past and past part. of UNDERPAY.

underpants • pl. n. an undergarment covering the lower part of the body and having two holes for the legs.

underpart • n. a lower part or portion.

underpass • n. a road or tunnel passing under another road or a railway.

underpay • v. (**underpays, underpaying, underpaid**) pay too little to someone or for something.

underperform • v. perform less well than expected.
– DERIVATIVES **underperformance** n.

underpin • v. (**underpins, underpinning, underpinned**) **1** support a structure from below by laying a solid foundation or replacing weak materials with stronger ones. **2** support or form the basis for an argument, claim, etc.

underplay • v. try to make something seem less important than it really is.

underprivileged • adj. not enjoying

the same rights or standard of living as the majority of the population.

underrate • v. (**underrates, underrating, underrated**) fail to recognize the real extent, value, or importance of.

☑ Remember that **underrate** is spelled with a double **r** in the middle.

underscore • v. (**underscores, underscoring, underscored**) = UNDERLINE.

undersea • adj. relating to or situated below the sea or the surface of the sea.

undersecretary • n. (pl. **undersecretaries**) (in the UK) a junior minister or senior civil servant.

undersell • v. (**undersells, underselling, undersold**) sell something at a lower price than a competitor.

undershirt • n. N. Amer. an undergarment worn under a shirt; a vest.

undershoot • v. (**undershoots, undershooting, undershot**) fall short of a point or target.

underside • n. the bottom or lower side or surface of something.

undersigned • n. (**the undersigned**) formal the person or people who have signed the document in question.

undersized (also **undersize**) • adj. smaller than the usual size.

underskirt • n. a petticoat.

undersold past and past part. of UNDERSELL.

underspend • v. (**underspends, underspending, underspent**) spend too little or less than has been planned.

understaffed • adj. (of an organization) having too few members of staff to operate effectively.

understand • v. (**understands, understanding, understood**) **1** know or realize the intended meaning of words or a speaker. **2** be aware of the importance or cause of. **3** know how someone feels or why they behave in a particular way. **4** believe to be the case from information received: *I understand you're at university.* **5** mentally supply a word that is not actually given in a sentence.

understandable • adj. **1** able to be understood. **2** to be expected; normal or reasonable.
– DERIVATIVES **understandably** adv.

understanding • n. **1** the ability to understand something. **2** a person's intellect. **3** a person's judgement of a situation. **4** sympathetic awareness or tolerance. **5** an informal or unspoken agreement. • adj. sympathetically aware of other people's feelings.

– DERIVATIVES **understandingly** adv.

understate • v. (**understates, understating, understated**) describe or represent something as being smaller or less important than it really is.
– DERIVATIVES **understatement** n.

understated • adj. presented or expressed in a subtle and effective way.

understood past and past part. of UNDERSTAND.

understudy • n. (pl. **understudies**) an actor who learns another's role in order to be able to act in their absence. • v. (**understudies, understudying, understudied**) be an understudy for.

undertake • v. (**undertake, undertaking, undertook**; past part. **undertaken**) **1** make yourself responsible for and begin an activity. **2** formally guarantee or promise to do.

undertaker • n. a person whose business is preparing dead bodies for burial or cremation and making arrangements for funerals.

undertaking • n. **1** a formal promise to do something. **2** a task that is taken on. **3** the management of funerals as a profession.

undertone • n. **1** a subdued or muted tone of sound or colour. **2** an underlying quality or feeling.

undertow • n. = UNDERCURRENT.

underuse • v. /un-der-yooz/ (**underuses, underusing, underused**) fail to use something enough. • n. /un-der-yooss/ insufficient use of something.

underutilize (or **underutilise**) • v. (**underutilizes, underutilizing, underutilized**) = UNDERUSE.

undervalue • v. (**undervalues, undervaluing, undervalued**) **1** fail to appreciate. **2** underestimate how much something is worth.

underwater • adj. & adv. situated or occurring beneath the surface of the water.

underway • adj. var. of under way (see UNDER).

USAGE: The spelling **underway** is best avoided in formal writing: use **under way** instead.

underwear • n. clothing worn under other clothes next to the skin.

underweight • adj. below a weight considered normal or desirable.

underwent past of UNDERGO.

underwhelm • v. humorous fail to impress or make a good impact on.
– ORIGIN from OVERWHELM.

underwired • adj. (of a bra) having a

u

semicircular wire support stitched under each cup.

underworld • n. **1** the world of criminals or of organized crime. **2** (in myths and legends) the home of the dead, imagined as being under the earth.

underwrite • v. (**underwrites, underwriting, underwrote**; past part. **underwritten**) **1** sign and accept legal responsibility for an insurance policy. **2** finance or otherwise support or guarantee something.
– DERIVATIVES **underwriter** n.

undeserved • adj. not deserved or earned.
– DERIVATIVES **undeservedly** adv.

undeserving • adj. not deserving or worthy of something good.

undesirable • adj. harmful, offensive, or unpleasant. • n. an unpleasant or offensive person.
– DERIVATIVES **undesirability** n. **undesirably** adv.

undesired • adj. not wanted or desired.

undetectable • adj. not able to be detected.

undetected • adj. not detected or discovered.

undetermined • adj. not firmly decided or settled.

undeterred • adj. persevering despite setbacks.

☑ Spell **undeterred** with one **t** and a double **r**.

undeveloped • adj. not having developed or been developed.

undeviating • adj. constant and steady.

undid past of UNDO.

undies • pl. n. informal articles of underwear.

undifferentiated • adj. not different or recognized as different.

undigested • adj. **1** (of food) not digested. **2** (of information) not having been properly understood or absorbed.

undignified • adj. appearing foolish.

undiluted • adj. **1** (of a liquid) not diluted. **2** not moderated or weakened in any way: *pure, undiluted happiness.*

undiminished • adj. not reduced or lessened.

undiplomatic • adj. insensitive and tactless.

undisciplined • adj. uncontrolled in behaviour or manner.

undisclosed • adj. not revealed or made known.

undiscovered • adj. not discovered.

undiscriminating • adj. lacking good judgement or taste.

undisguised • adj. (of a feeling) not disguised or concealed.

undismayed • adj. not dismayed or discouraged by a setback.

undisputed • adj. not disputed or called in question.

undistinguished • adj. not very good or impressive.

undisturbed • adj. not disturbed.

undivided • adj. **1** not divided, separated, or broken into parts. **2** devoted completely to one object: *you have my undivided attention.*

undo • v. (**undoes, undoing, undid**; past part. **undone**) **1** unfasten or loosen. **2** cancel or reverse the effects of a previous action. **3** formal cause the downfall of: *Iago's hatred of women undoes him.*

undocumented • adj. not recorded in or proved by documents.

undoing • n. a person's ruin or downfall.

undone • adj. **1** not tied or fastened. **2** not done or finished. **3** old use or humorous ruined by a disastrous setback.

undoubted • adj. not questioned or doubted by anyone.
– DERIVATIVES **undoubtedly** adv.

undreamed /un-dreemd, un-dremt/ (Brit. also **undreamt** /un-dremt/) • adj. (**undreamed of**) not previously thought to be possible.

undress • v. **1** (also **get undressed**) take off your clothes. **2** take the clothes off someone else. • n. the state of being naked or only partially clothed.

undressed • adj. **1** wearing no clothes. **2** not treated, processed, or prepared for use. **3** (of food) not having a dressing.

undrinkable • adj. not fit to be drunk because of impurity or poor quality.

undue • adj. more than is reasonable or necessary; excessive.
– DERIVATIVES **unduly** adv.

undulate /un-dyuu-layt/ • v. (**undulates, undulating, undulated**) **1** move with a smooth wave-like motion. **2** have a wavy form or outline.
– DERIVATIVES **undulation** n.
– ORIGIN Latin *undulatus.*

undyed • adj. (of fabric) not dyed; of its natural colour.

undying • adj. lasting forever.

unearned • adj. not earned or deserved.

unearned income • n. income from private means (such as investments) rather than from work.

unearth • v. **1** find in the ground by digging. **2** discover by investigation or searching.

unearthly • adj. **1** unnatural or mysterious. **2** informal unreasonably early or inconvenient: *an unearthly hour.*

unease • n. anxiety or discontent.

uneasy • adj. (**uneasier, uneasiest**)
1 anxious or uncomfortable. **2** liable to change; not settled: *an uneasy truce.*
– DERIVATIVES **uneasily** adv. **uneasiness** n.

uneatable • adj. not fit to be eaten.

uneaten • adj. not eaten.

uneconomic • adj. not profitable or making efficient use of resources.

uneconomical • adj. wasteful of money or other resources.

unedifying • adj. distasteful or unpleasant.

uneducated • adj. poorly educated.

unelectable • adj. very likely to be defeated at an election.

unelected • adj. (of an official) not elected.

unembarrassed • adj. not feeling or showing embarrassment.

unemotional • adj. not having or showing strong feelings.
– DERIVATIVES **unemotionally** adv.

unemployable • adj. not able to get paid employment because of a lack of skills or qualifications.

unemployed • adj. **1** without a paid job but available to work. **2** (of a thing) not in use.

unemployment • n. **1** the state of being unemployed. **2** the number or proportion of unemployed people.

unemployment benefit • n. payment made by the state or a trade union to an unemployed person.

unencumbered • adj. not having any burden or obstacle to progress.

unending • adj. seeming to last or continue for ever.

unendurable • adj. not able to be tolerated or endured.

unenlightened • adj. not reasonable and tolerant in outlook.

unenterprising • adj. lacking initiative or resourcefulness.

unenthusiastic • adj. not having or showing enthusiasm.
– DERIVATIVES **unenthusiastically** adv.

unenviable • adj. difficult, undesirable, or unpleasant.

unequal • adj. **1** not equal in quantity, size, or value. **2** not fair or evenly balanced. **3** (**unequal to**) not having the ability or resources to meet a challenge.
– DERIVATIVES **unequally** adv.

unequalled (US **unequaled**) • adj. better or greater than all others.

unequivocal /un-i-kwiv-uh-k'l/ • adj. leaving no doubt; clear in meaning: *an unequivocal answer.*

– DERIVATIVES **unequivocally** adv.

unerring • adj. always right or accurate.
– DERIVATIVES **unerringly** adv.

UNESCO /yoo-ness-koh/ • abbrev. United Nations Educational, Scientific, and Cultural Organization.

unethical • adj. not morally correct.
– DERIVATIVES **unethically** adv.

uneven • adj. **1** not level or smooth. **2** not regular, consistent, or equal.
– DERIVATIVES **unevenly** adv. **unevenness** n.

uneventful • adj. not marked by interesting or exciting events.
– DERIVATIVES **uneventfully** adv.

unexceptionable • adj. not able to be objected to, but not particularly new or exciting.

unexceptional • adj. not out of the ordinary; usual.
– DERIVATIVES **unexceptionally** adv.

unexciting • adj. not exciting; dull.

unexpected • adj. not expected or thought likely to happen.
– DERIVATIVES **unexpectedly** adv. **unexpectedness** n.

unexplained • adj. not made clear or accounted for.
– DERIVATIVES **unexplainable** adj.

unexplored • adj. not explored, investigated, or evaluated.

unexposed • adj. **1** not exposed. **2** (**unexposed to**) not introduced to or knowing about.

unexpressed • adj. (of a thought or feeling) not communicated or made known.

unexpurgated • adj. (of a written work) complete and containing all the original material.

unfailing • adj. **1** without error. **2** reliable or constant.
– DERIVATIVES **unfailingly** adv.

unfair • adj. not based on or showing fairness.
– DERIVATIVES **unfairly** adv. **unfairness** n.

unfaithful • adj. **1** not faithful; disloyal. **2** having sex with a person other than your husband, wife, or established lover.

unfamiliar • adj. **1** not known or recognized. **2** (**unfamiliar with**) not having knowledge or experience of.
– DERIVATIVES **unfamiliarity** n.

unfashionable • adj. not fashionable or popular.
– DERIVATIVES **unfashionably** adv.

unfasten • v. open the fastening of.

unfathomable • adj. **1** too strange or difficult to be understood. **2** impossible to measure the depth or extent of.
– DERIVATIVES **unfathomably** adv.

unfavourable (US **unfavorable**)

u

• adj. 1 expressing lack of approval.
2 unlikely to lead to success:
unfavourable circumstances.
– DERIVATIVES **unfavourably** adv.

unfazed • adj. informal not surprised or worried by something unexpected.

unfeasible • adj. inconvenient or impractical.
– DERIVATIVES **unfeasibly** adv.

unfeeling • adj. unsympathetic, harsh, or cruel.

unfeigned • adj. genuine; sincere.

unfertilized (or **unfertilised**) • adj. not fertilized.

unfettered • adj. unrestrained or uninhibited.

unfilled • adj. vacant or empty.

unfinished • adj. not finished.

unfit • adj. 1 unsuitable or inadequate for something. 2 not in good physical condition.

unfitted • adj. unfit for something.

unfitting • adj. unsuitable or unbecoming.

unfixed • adj. 1 unfastened; loose.
2 uncertain or variable.

unflagging • adj. tireless or persistent.

unflappable • adj. informal calm in a crisis.

unflattering • adj. not flattering.
– DERIVATIVES **unflatteringly** adv.

unflinching • adj. not afraid or hesitant.
– DERIVATIVES **unflinchingly** adv.

unfocused (also **unfocussed**)
• adj. 1 not focused; out of focus.
2 without a specific aim or direction.

unfold • v. 1 open or spread out from a folded position. 2 reveal or be revealed.

unforced • adj. produced naturally and without effort.

unforeseen • adj. not anticipated or predicted.
– DERIVATIVES **unforeseeable** adj.

> ✓ Remember that **unforeseen** is spelled with an **e** after the **r**.

unforgettable • adj. highly memorable.
– DERIVATIVES **unforgettably** adv.

unforgivable • adj. so bad as to be unable to be forgiven or excused.
– DERIVATIVES **unforgivably** adv.

unforgiven • adj. not forgiven.

unforgiving • adj. 1 not willing to forgive or excuse faults. 2 (of conditions) harsh; hostile.

unformed • adj. 1 without a definite form. 2 not fully developed.

unforthcoming • adj. 1 not willing to give out information. 2 not available when needed.

unfortunate • adj. 1 having or marked by bad luck; unlucky. 2 regrettable or inappropriate. • n. a person who suffers bad fortune.
– DERIVATIVES **unfortunately** adv.

unfounded • adj. having no basis in fact:
unfounded rumours.

unfreeze • v. (**unfreezes**, **unfreezing**, **unfroze**; past part. **unfrozen**) 1 thaw something frozen. 2 remove restrictions on the use of an asset.

unfriendly • adj. (**unfriendlier**, **unfriendliest**) not friendly.
– DERIVATIVES **unfriendliness** n.

unfroze past of UNFREEZE.

unfrozen past part. of UNFREEZE.

unfulfilled • adj. not fulfilled.
– DERIVATIVES **unfulfilling** adj.

unfunny • adj. (of something meant to be funny) not amusing.

unfurl • v. spread out something that is rolled or folded.

unfurnished • adj. without furniture.

ungainly • adj. clumsy; awkward.
– DERIVATIVES **ungainliness** n.
– ORIGIN from former *gainly* 'graceful', from Old Norse.

ungenerous • adj. not generous; mean.

ungentlemanly • adj. (of a man's behaviour) not well-mannered or pleasant.

ungodly • adj. 1 disrespectful to God; wicked. 2 informal inconveniently early or late: *calls at ungodly hours*.
– DERIVATIVES **ungodliness** n.

ungovernable • adj. impossible to control or govern.

ungraceful • adj. lacking in grace; clumsy.
– DERIVATIVES **ungracefully** adv.

ungracious • adj. not polite, kind, or pleasant.
– DERIVATIVES **ungraciously** adv.

ungrammatical • adj. not following grammatical rules.
– DERIVATIVES **ungrammatically** adv.

ungrateful • adj. not feeling or showing gratitude.
– DERIVATIVES **ungratefully** adv.
ungratefulness n.

unguarded • adj. 1 without protection or a guard. 2 not well considered; careless: *an unguarded remark*.

unguent /ung-gwuhnt/ • n. a soft greasy or thick substance used as ointment or for lubrication.
– ORIGIN Latin *unguentum*.

ungulate /ung-gyuu-luht, ung-gyuu-layt/ • n. Zool. a mammal with hoofs.
– ORIGIN Latin *ungulatus*.

unhand • v. old use release from your grasp.

unhappy • adj. (**unhappier**, **unhappiest**)

1 not happy. **2** not lucky; unfortunate.
- DERIVATIVES **unhappily** adv.
unhappiness n.

unharmed • adj. not harmed.

unhealthy • adj. (**unhealthier**, **unhealthiest**) **1** in poor health. **2** not good for the health.
- DERIVATIVES **unhealthily** adv.
unhealthiness n.

unheard • adj. **1** not heard or listened to. **2** (**unheard of**) previously unknown.

unheeded • adj. heard or noticed but ignored.

unheeding • adj. not paying attention.

unhelpful • adj. not helpful.
- DERIVATIVES **unhelpfully** adv.

unheralded • adj. not previously announced; without warning.

unhesitating • adj. without doubt or hesitation.
- DERIVATIVES **unhesitatingly** adv.

unhinge • v. (**unhinges**, **unhinging**, **unhinged**) make someone mentally unbalanced.

unhistorical • adj. not in accordance with history or historical study.

unholy • adj. **1** wicked or sinful. **2** (of an alliance) likely to be harmful. **3** informal dreadful: *an unholy row*.

unhoped • adj. (**unhoped for**) beyond your hopes or expectations.

unhorse • v. (**unhorses**, **unhorsing**, **unhorsed**) drag or cause to fall from a horse.

unhurried • adj. moving or acting without urgency.
- DERIVATIVES **unhurriedly** adv.

unhurt • adj. not hurt or harmed.

unhygienic • adj. not hygienic.

uni • n. (pl. **unis**) informal university.

uni- • comb. form one; having or made up of one: *unicycle*.
- ORIGIN Latin *unus*.

unicameral /yoo-ni-kam-uh-ruhl/ • adj. (of a law-making body) having a single chamber.
- ORIGIN Latin *camera* 'chamber'.

UNICEF /yoo-ni-sef/ • abbrev. United Nations Children's (originally International Children's Emergency) Fund.

unicellular • adj. Biol. consisting of a single cell.

unicorn • n. a mythical animal represented as a horse with a single horn projecting from its forehead.
- ORIGIN Latin *unicornis*.

unicycle • n. a cycle with a single wheel.
- DERIVATIVES **unicyclist** n.

unidentifiable • adj. unable to be identified.

unidentified • adj. not recognized or identified.

unification • n. the process of being unified.

uniform • adj. not varying; the same in all cases and at all times. • n. the distinctive clothing worn by members of the same organization or school.
- DERIVATIVES **uniformed** adj. **uniformity** n. **uniformly** adv.
- ORIGIN Latin *uniformis*.

unify /yoo-ni-fy/ • v. (**unifies**, **unifying**, **unified**) make or become united or uniform.
- DERIVATIVES **unifier** n.
- ORIGIN Latin *unificare*.

unilateral • adj. performed by or affecting only one person, group, etc.
- DERIVATIVES **unilaterally** adv.

unimaginable • adj. impossible to imagine or understand.
- DERIVATIVES **unimaginably** adv.

unimaginative • adj. not using or showing imagination; dull.
- DERIVATIVES **unimaginatively** adv.

unimpaired • adj. not weakened or damaged.

unimpeachable • adj. beyond doubt or criticism: *an unimpeachable witness*.
- DERIVATIVES **unimpeachably** adv.

unimpeded • adj. not obstructed or hindered.

unimportant • adj. lacking in importance.
- DERIVATIVES **unimportance** n.

unimpressed • adj. not impressed.

unimpressive • adj. not impressive.

uninformed • adj. lacking awareness or understanding of the facts.

uninhabitable • adj. not suitable for living in.

uninhabited • adj. without inhabitants.

uninhibited • adj. expressing yourself or acting freely.
- DERIVATIVES **uninhibitedly** adv.

uninitiated • adj. without the necessary special knowledge or experience.

uninjured • adj. not harmed or damaged.

uninspired • adj. **1** not original or imaginative; dull. **2** not excited.

uninspiring • adj. not exciting or interesting.

unintelligent • adj. lacking intelligence.

unintelligible • adj. impossible to understand.
- DERIVATIVES **unintelligibility** n. **unintelligibly** adv.

unintended • adj. not planned or meant.

unintentional • adj. not done on purpose.

u

– DERIVATIVES **unintentionally** adv.

uninterested • adj. not interested or concerned.

> **USAGE:** For an explanation of the difference between **uninterested** and **disinterested**, see the note at **DISINTERESTED**.

uninteresting • adj. not interesting.

uninterrupted • adj. **1** continuous. **2** not obstructed: *a location with uninterrupted views.*

uninvited • adj. arriving or acting without invitation.

uninviting • adj. not attractive; unpleasant.

uninvolved • adj. not involved.

union • n. **1** the action of uniting or the fact of being united: *he supported closer economic union with Europe.* **2** a state of harmony or agreement. **3** a marriage. **4** a society or association formed by people with a common interest or purpose, especially a trade union. **5** (also **Union**) a political unit consisting of a number of states or provinces with the same central government.
– ORIGIN Latin, 'unity'.

unionist • n. **1** a member of a trade union. **2** (**Unionist**) a person in favour of the union of Northern Ireland with Great Britain.
– DERIVATIVES **unionism** n.

unionize (or **unionise**) • v. (**unionizes, unionizing, unionized**) join or cause to join a trade union.
– DERIVATIVES **unionization** n.

Union Jack (also **Union flag**) • n. the national flag of the United Kingdom.

unipolar • adj. having or relating to a single pole.

unique • adj. **1** being the only one of its kind. **2** (**unique to**) belonging or connected to one particular person, group, or place. **3** very special or unusual.
– DERIVATIVES **uniquely** adv. **uniqueness** n.
– ORIGIN French.

unisex • adj. designed to be suitable for both sexes.

unison • n. **1** the fact of two or more things being said or happening at the same time. **2** a coincidence in pitch of musical sounds or notes.
– ORIGIN Latin *unisonus.*

unit • n. **1** an individual thing, group, or person that is complete in itself but that can also form part of something larger. **2** a device, part, or item of furniture with a specified function: *a sink unit.* **3** a self-contained section of a building or group of buildings. **4** a subdivision of a

larger military grouping. **5** a fixed quantity that is used as a standard measurement. **6** one as a number or quantity.
– ORIGIN Latin *unus.*

Unitarian /yoo-ni-tair-i-uhn/ • n. a member of a Christian Church that believes in the unity of God and rejects the idea of the Trinity.
– DERIVATIVES **Unitarianism** n.
– ORIGIN Latin *unitarius.*

unitary • adj. **1** single; uniform. **2** relating to a unit or units.

unitary authority (also **unitary council**) • n. (chiefly in the UK) a division of local government established in place of a two-tier system of local councils.

unite • v. (**unites, uniting, united**) come or bring together for a common purpose or to form a whole.
– DERIVATIVES **united** adj.
– ORIGIN Latin *unire* 'join together'.

unit trust • n. Brit. a company that invests money in a range of businesses on behalf of individual people, who can buy small units of investment.

unity • n. (pl. **unities**) **1** the state of being united or forming a whole. **2** a thing forming a complex whole. **3** Math. the number one.

universal • adj. **1** involving or done by all people or things in the world or in a particular group. **2** true or applicable in all cases.
– DERIVATIVES **universality** n. **universally** adv.

universalize (or **universalise**) • v. (**universalizes, universalizing, universalized**) make universal or available to all.
– DERIVATIVES **universalization** n.

universal joint • n. a joint which can transmit rotary power by a shaft at any selected angle.

universal suffrage • n. the right of all adults (with minor exceptions) to vote in political elections.

universe • n. all existing matter and space considered as a whole.
– ORIGIN Latin *universus* 'combined into one, whole'.

university • n. (pl. **universities**) a high-level educational institution in which students study for degrees and academic research is done.
– ORIGIN Latin *universitas* 'the whole'.

unjust • adj. not fair.
– DERIVATIVES **unjustly** adv.

unjustifiable • adj. impossible to justify.
– DERIVATIVES **unjustifiably** adv.

unjustified • adj. not justified.

unkempt • adj. having an untidy appearance.
– ORIGIN from Old English, 'combed'.

unkind • adj. not caring or kind; rather cruel.
– DERIVATIVES **unkindly** adv. **unkindness** n.

unknowable • adj. not able to be known.
– DERIVATIVES **unknowability** n.

unknowing • adj. not knowing or aware.
– DERIVATIVES **unknowingly** adv.

unknown • adj. not known or familiar. • n. an unknown person or thing.
– PHRASES **unknown to someone** without someone being aware of something.

unknown quantity • n. a person or thing whose ability or value is not yet known.

Unknown Soldier • n. an unidentified member of a country's armed forces killed in war, buried in a national memorial to represent all those killed but unidentified.

unlabelled (US **unlabeled**) • adj. without a label.

unlace • v. (**unlaces, unlacing, unlaced**) undo the laces of.

unladen • adj. not carrying a load.

unladylike • adj. not appropriate for or typical of a well-bred woman.

unlamented • adj. not mourned or regretted.

unlatch • v. unfasten the latch of.

unlawful • adj. not obeying or allowed by law or rules.
– DERIVATIVES **unlawfully** adv.

unleaded • adj. (of petrol) without added lead.

unlearn • v. (**unlearns, unlearning, unlearned** or **unlearnt**) try to forget something that has been learned.

unlearned[1] /un-ler-nid/ • adj. not well educated.

unlearned[2] /un-lernd/ (also **unlearnt** /un-lernt/) • adj. not having been learned.

unleash • v. set free.

unleavened • adj. (of bread) made without yeast or other raising agent.

unless • conj. except when; if not.
– ORIGIN from ON or IN + LESS.

unlettered • adj. poorly educated or unable to read and write.

unlicensed • adj. not having a licence for the sale of alcoholic drinks.

unlike • prep. 1 different from; not like. 2 in contrast to: *unlike Tim, she was not superstitious.* 3 uncharacteristic of. • adj. different from each other.

> **USAGE:** It is not good English to use **unlike** as a conjunction (a word connecting words or clauses of a sentence together), as in *she was behaving unlike she'd ever behaved before.* You should use **as** with a negative instead: *she was behaving as she'd never behaved before.*

unlikely • adj. (**unlikelier, unlikeliest**) not likely to happen, be done, or be true.
– DERIVATIVES **unlikelihood** n.

unlimited • adj. not limited; infinite.

unlined[1] • adj. not marked with lines or wrinkles.

unlined[2] • adj. without a lining.

unlisted • adj. not included in a list of stock exchange prices or telephone numbers.

unlit • adj. 1 not provided with lighting. 2 not having been lit.

unlived • adj. (**unlived in**) not appearing to be inhabited.

unload • v. 1 remove goods from a vehicle, ship, etc. 2 informal get rid of.

unlock • v. unfasten the lock of a door, container, etc. using a key.

unlooked • adj. (**unlooked for**) unexpected.

unloose • v. (**unlooses, unloosing, unloosed**) undo or release.

unloosen • v. = UNLOOSE.

unloved • adj. loved by no one.

unlovely • adj. not attractive; ugly.

unlucky • adj. (**unluckier, unluckiest**) having, bringing, or resulting from bad luck.
– DERIVATIVES **unluckily** adv.

unmade • adj. 1 (of a bed) not arranged tidily. 2 Brit. (of a road) without a hard, smooth surface.

unman • v. (**unmans, unmanning, unmanned**) literary deprive of manly qualities such as self-control or courage.

unmanageable • adj. difficult or impossible to manage or control.
– DERIVATIVES **unmanageably** adv.

unmanned • adj. not having or needing a crew or staff.

unmannerly • adj. not well mannered.

unmarked • adj. 1 not marked. 2 not noticed.

unmarried • adj. not married.

unmask • v. reveal the true character of.

unmatched • adj. not matched or equalled.

unmentionable • adj. too embarrassing or offensive to be spoken about.

unmerciful • adj. showing no mercy.
– DERIVATIVES **unmercifully** adv.

unmerited • adj. not deserved.

unmetalled • adj. Brit. (of a road) not having a hard surface.

u

unmindful • adj. (**unmindful of**) not conscious or aware of.

unmissable • adj. that should not or cannot be missed.

unmistakable (also **unmistakeable**) • adj. not able to be mistaken for anything else.

– DERIVATIVES **unmistakably** adv.

unmitigated • adj. absolute: *an unmitigated disaster.*

unmotivated • adj. **1** not motivated or enthusiastic. **2** without apparent motive: *an unmotivated attack.*

unmoved • adj. **1** not affected by emotion or excitement. **2** not changed in purpose or position.

unmoving • adj. not moving; still.

unmusical • adj. **1** not pleasing to the ear. **2** (of a person) unable to play or enjoy music.

unnameable • adj. unmentionable.

unnamed • adj. not named.

unnatural • adj. **1** different from what is found in nature. **2** different from what is normal or expected.

– DERIVATIVES **unnaturally** adv.

unnavigable • adj. not able to be sailed on by ships or boats.

unnecessary • adj. not necessary, or more than is necessary.

– DERIVATIVES **unnecessarily** adv.

> ☑ Spell **unnecessary** with a double **n**, a single **c**, and a double **s**.

unnerve • v. (**unnerves, unnerving, unnerved**) make someone feel nervous or frightened.

– DERIVATIVES **unnerving** adj.

unnoticeable • adj. not easily seen or noticed.

unnoticed • adj. not noticed.

unnumbered • adj. **1** not given a number. **2** not counted, or not able to be counted.

unobserved • adj. not seen.

unobstructed • adj. not obstructed.

unobtainable • adj. not able to be obtained.

unobtrusive • adj. not conspicuous or attracting attention.

– DERIVATIVES **unobtrusively** adv.

unoccupied • adj. not occupied.

unofficial • adj. not officially authorized or confirmed.

– DERIVATIVES **unofficially** adv.

unopened • adj. not opened.

unopposed • adj. not opposed; unchallenged.

unorganized (or **unorganised**) • adj. not organized.

unoriginal • adj. lacking originality.

– DERIVATIVES **unoriginality** n. **unoriginally** adv.

unorthodox • adj. different from what is usual, traditional, or accepted.

– DERIVATIVES **unorthodoxy** n.

unostentatious • adj. not ostentatious; simple.

unpack • v. remove the contents of a suitcase, bag, or package.

unpaid • adj. **1** (of a debt) not yet paid. **2** (of work or leave) done or taken without payment. **3** not receiving payment for work done.

unpalatable • adj. **1** not pleasant to taste. **2** difficult to accept.

unparalleled • adj. having no equal; exceptional.

unpardonable • adj. (of a fault or offence) unforgivable.

– DERIVATIVES **unpardonably** adv.

unparliamentary • adj. (of language) against the rules of behaviour of a parliament.

unpasteurized (or **unpasteurised**) • adj. not pasteurized.

unpatriotic • adj. not patriotic.

unpaved • adj. lacking a metalled or paved surface.

unperson • n. (pl. **unpersons**) a person whose name or existence is officially denied or ignored.

unperturbed • adj. not concerned or worried.

unpick • v. **1** undo the stitches from a piece of sewing. **2** carefully analyse the different elements of.

unpin • v. (**unpins, unpinning, unpinned**) unfasten or detach by removing a pin or pins.

unpitying • adj. not feeling or showing pity.

unplanned • adj. not planned.

unplayable • adj. **1** not able to be played or played on: *the pitch was unplayable.* **2** (of music) too difficult to perform.

unpleasant • adj. **1** not pleasant. **2** not friendly or kind.

– DERIVATIVES **unpleasantly** adv.

unpleasantness • n. **1** the state of being unpleasant. **2** bad feeling or quarrelling between people.

unplug • v. (**unplugs, unplugging, unplugged**) **1** disconnect an electrical device by removing its plug from a socket. **2** remove a blockage from. **3** (adj. **unplugged**) trademark (of pop or rock music) performed or recorded with acoustic rather than electrically amplified instruments.

unplumbed • adj. **1** not provided with

plumbing. **2** not fully explored or understood.
– DERIVATIVES **unplumbable** adj.

unpolished • adj. **1** not having a polished surface. **2** (of a performance or piece of work) not having been refined or perfected.

unpopular • adj. not liked or popular.
– DERIVATIVES **unpopularity** n.

unpopulated • adj. without inhabitants.

unpractised (US **unpracticed**) • adj. not trained or experienced.

unprecedented • adj. never done or known before.
– DERIVATIVES **unprecedentedly** adv.

unpredictable • adj. **1** not able to be predicted. **2** changeable or unreliable.
– DERIVATIVES **unpredictability** n. **unpredictably** adv.

unprejudiced • adj. without prejudice; unbiased.

unpremeditated • adj. not planned beforehand.

unprepared • adj. **1** not ready or able to deal with something. **2** not made ready for use.

unprepossessing • adj. not attractive or impressive.

unpretentious • adj. not pretentious; modest or unassuming.

unprincipled • adj. not acting in accordance with moral principles.

unprintable • adj. (of words, comments, or thoughts) too offensive to be published.

unproblematic • adj. not presenting a problem or difficulty.
– DERIVATIVES **unproblematically** adv.

unproductive • adj. **1** not producing or able to produce large amounts of goods, crops, etc. **2** not achieving much; not very useful.

unprofessional • adj. not in accordance with professional standards or behaviour.
– DERIVATIVES **unprofessionally** adv.

unprofitable • adj. **1** not making a profit. **2** not helpful or useful.

unpromising • adj. not giving hope of future success or good results.

unprompted • adj. without being prompted.

unpronounceable • adj. too difficult to pronounce.

unprotected • adj. **1** not protected or kept safe from harm. **2** (of sex) performed without using a condom.

unproven /un-proo-vuhn, un-proh-vuhn/ (also **unproved**) • adj. **1** not shown by evidence or argument as true. **2** not tried and tested.

unprovoked • adj. (of an attack, crime, etc.) not directly provoked.

unpublished • adj. **1** (of a work) not published. **2** (of an author) having no writings published.

unpunished • adj. (of an offence or offender) not receiving any punishment or penalty.

unputdownable • adj. informal (of a book) so absorbing that you cannot stop reading it.

unqualified • adj. **1** not having the necessary qualifications or requirements. **2** complete: *an unqualified success.*

unquantifiable • adj. impossible to express or measure.

unquenchable • adj. not able to be quenched or satisfied.

unquestionable • adj. not able to be denied or doubted.
– DERIVATIVES **unquestionably** adv.

unquestioned • adj. **1** not denied or doubted. **2** accepted without question.

unquiet • adj. **1** unable to be still; restless. **2** anxious.

unravel • v. (**unravels**, **unravelling**, **unravelled**; US **unravels**, **unraveling**, **unraveled**) **1** undo twisted, knitted, or woven threads. **2** become undone. **3** solve a mystery or puzzle. **4** begin to fail or collapse: *the peace process began to unravel.*

unreachable • adj. unable to be reached or contacted.

unreactive • adj. having little tendency to react chemically.

unread • adj. not having been read.

unreadable • adj. **1** not clear enough to read. **2** too dull or difficult to be worth reading.

unready • adj. not ready or prepared.

unreal • adj. **1** strange and not seeming real. **2** not related to reality; unrealistic.
– DERIVATIVES **unreality** n.

unrealistic • adj. **1** not showing things in a realistic way. **2** not having a sensible understanding of what can be achieved.
– DERIVATIVES **unrealistically** adv.

unrealized (or **unrealised**) • adj. **1** achieved or created. **2** not converted into money: *unrealized property assets.*

unreason • n. lack of reasonable thought.

unreasonable • adj. **1** not based on good sense. **2** beyond the limits of what is acceptable or achievable.
– DERIVATIVES **unreasonableness** n. **unreasonably** adv.

unreasoning • adj. not guided by or based on reason.

unrecognizable (or **unrecognisable**)

• adj. not able to be recognized.
– DERIVATIVES **unrecognizably** adv.

unrecognized (or **unrecognised**)
• adj. **1** not identified from previous encounters or knowledge. **2** not accepted as valid.

unreconstructed • adj. not converted to the current political theory or movement.

unrecorded • adj. not recorded.

unrefined • adj. **1** not processed to remove impurities. **2** not elegant or cultured.

unregenerate /un-ri-jen-uh-ruht/
• adj. not reforming; stubbornly wrong or bad.

unregistered • adj. not officially recognized and recorded.

unregulated • adj. not controlled by regulations or laws.

unrehearsed • adj. not rehearsed.

unrelated • adj. not related.

unreleased • adj. (especially of a film or recording) not released.

unrelenting • adj. **1** not stopping or becoming less severe. **2** not giving in to other people's requests.
– DERIVATIVES **unrelentingly** adv.

unreliable • adj. not able to be relied on.
– DERIVATIVES **unreliability** n. **unreliably** adv.

unrelieved • adj. lacking variation or change; boring.

unremarkable • adj. not particularly interesting or surprising.

unremarked • adj. not noticed or remarked on.

unremitting • adj. never relaxing or slackening.
– DERIVATIVES **unremittingly** adv.

unremunerative • adj. bringing little or no profit or income.

unrepeatable • adj. **1** not able to be repeated. **2** too offensive or shocking to be said again.

unrepentant • adj. showing no regret for your wrongdoings.
– DERIVATIVES **unrepentantly** adv.

unrepresentative • adj. not typical of a class, group, or body of opinion.

unrequited • adj. (of love) not returned.
– ORIGIN from *requite* 'make a suitable return for'.

unreserved • adj. **1** without doubts or reservations; complete. **2** honest and open. **3** not set apart or booked in advance.
– DERIVATIVES **unreservedly** adv.

unresolved • adj. (of a problem, dispute, etc.) not resolved.

unresponsive • adj. not responsive.

unrest • n. **1** a state of rebellious discontent in a group of people. **2** a state of uneasiness.

unrestrained • adj. not restrained or restricted.
– DERIVATIVES **unrestrainedly** adv.

unrestricted • adj. not limited or restricted.

unrewarding • adj. not rewarding or satisfying.

unripe • adj. not ripe.

unrivalled (US **unrivaled**) • adj. greater or better than all others.

unroll • v. open out something that is rolled up.

unromantic • adj. not romantic.

unruffled • adj. (of a person) calm and unconcerned.

unruly • adj. (**unrulier**, **unruliest**) disorderly and disruptive.
– DERIVATIVES **unruliness** n.
– ORIGIN from former *ruly* 'orderly', from **RULE**.

unsafe • adj. **1** not safe; dangerous. **2** Law (of a verdict or conviction) not based on trustworthy evidence and likely to be unjust. **3** (of sexual activity) in which people do not take precautions to protect themselves against sexually transmitted diseases such as Aids.

unsaid past and past part. of **UNSAY**.
• adj. not said.

unsaleable (also **unsalable**) • adj. not able to be sold.

unsalted • adj. not salted.

unsanitary • adj. not hygienic.

unsatisfactory • adj. not good enough.
– DERIVATIVES **unsatisfactorily** adv.

unsatisfied • adj. not satisfied.

unsatisfying • adj. not satisfying.

unsaturated • adj. Chem. (of fats) having double and triple bonds between carbon atoms in their molecules and as a consequence being more easily processed by the body.

unsavoury (US **unsavory**)
• adj. **1** unpleasant to taste, smell, or look at. **2** not morally respectable: *an unsavoury reputation.*

unsay • v. (**unsays**, **unsaying**, **unsaid**) withdraw a statement.

unscarred • adj. not scarred or damaged.

unscathed • adj. without suffering any injury, damage, or harm.

unscented • adj. not scented.

unscheduled • adj. not scheduled.

unschooled • adj. **1** lacking schooling or training. **2** natural and spontaneous.

unscientific • adj. not in accordance with scientific principles or methods.
– DERIVATIVES **unscientifically** adv.

u

unscrew • v. unfasten by twisting.

unscripted • adj. said without a prepared script; unplanned.

unscrupulous • adj. without moral principles; dishonest or unfair.
– DERIVATIVES **unscrupulously** adv.

unsealed • adj. not sealed.

unseasonable • adj. (of weather) unusual for the time of year.
– DERIVATIVES **unseasonably** adv.

unseasonal • adj. unusual or inappropriate for the time of year.

unseasoned • adj. **1** (of food) not flavoured with salt, pepper, or other spices. **2** (of timber) not treated or matured.

unseat • v. **1** cause to fall from a saddle or seat. **2** remove from a position of power.

unsecured • adj. (of a loan) made without an asset given as security.

unseeded • adj. (of a competitor in a sports tournament) not seeded.

unseeing • adj. with your eyes open but without noticing or seeing anything.

unseemly • adj. (of behaviour or actions) not proper or appropriate.
– DERIVATIVES **unseemliness** n.

unseen • adj. **1** not seen or noticed. **2** esp. Brit. (of a passage for translation in an exam) not previously read or prepared.

unselfconscious • adj. not shy or embarrassed.
– DERIVATIVES **unselfconsciously** adv.

unselfish • adj. not selfish.
– DERIVATIVES **unselfishly** adv.

unsentimental • adj. not showing or influenced by sentimental feelings.

unserviceable • adj. not in working order; unfit for use.

unsettle • v. (**unsettles, unsettling, unsettled**) make anxious; disturb.
– DERIVATIVES **unsettling** adj.

unsettled • adj. **1** changeable or likely to change: *unsettled weather*. **2** agitated; uneasy. **3** not yet resolved.

unshackle • v. (**unshackles, unshackling, unshackled**) release from restraints; set free.

unshakeable (also **unshakable**)
• adj. (of a belief, feeling, etc.) firm and unable to be changed or disputed.

unshaken • adj. strong and unwavering.

unshaven • adj. not having shaved or been shaved.

unsheathe • v. (**unsheathes, unsheathing, unsheathed**) pull a knife or similar weapon out of a sheath.

unshockable • adj. impossible to shock.

unsightly • adj. unpleasant to look at; ugly.

– DERIVATIVES **unsightliness** n.

unsigned • adj. not identified or authorized by a person's signature.

unsinkable • adj. unable to be sunk.

unskilful (US **unskillful**) • adj. not having or showing skill.
– DERIVATIVES **unskilfully** adv.

> ☑ Spell **unskilful** with only one **l** in the middle: the spelling **unskillful** is American.

unskilled • adj. not having or needing special skill or training.

unsmiling • adj. not smiling; serious or unfriendly.

unsociable • adj. **1** not enjoying the company of other people. **2** not likely to produce friendly relationships between people: *watching TV is an unsociable activity*.

unsocial • adj. **1** Brit. (of hours of work) falling outside the normal working day and so socially inconvenient. **2** anti-social.

unsold • adj. (of an item) not sold.

unsolicited • adj. not asked for.

unsolved • adj. not solved.

unsophisticated • adj. **1** lacking experience of cultured society. **2** not complicated or highly developed; basic.

unsound • adj. **1** not safe or strong; in poor condition. **2** not based on reliable evidence or reasoning.

unsparing • adj. merciless; severe.

unspeakable • adj. **1** not able to be expressed in words. **2** too bad or horrific to express in words.
– DERIVATIVES **unspeakably** adv.

unspecific • adj. not specific; vague.

unspecified • adj. not stated clearly.

unspectacular • adj. not spectacular; unremarkable.

unspoilt (also **unspoiled**) • adj. (of a place) largely unaffected by building or development.

unspoken • adj. understood without being expressed in speech: *an unspoken rule*.

unsporting • adj. not fair or generous.

unsportsmanlike • adj. not behaving according to the spirit of fair play in a particular sport.

unsprung • adj. not provided with springs.

unstable • adj. (**unstabler, unstablest**) **1** likely to change or collapse. **2** prone to mental health problems or sudden changes of mood.

unstated • adj. not stated.

unsteady • adj. (**unsteadier,**

u

unsteadiest) **1** liable to fall or shake; not firm. **2** not uniform or regular.
– DERIVATIVES **unsteadily** adv. **unsteadiness** n.

unstick • v. (**unsticks, unsticking, unstuck**) separate a thing stuck to another.

unstinting • adj. given or giving freely.

unstoppable • adj. impossible to stop or prevent.
– DERIVATIVES **unstoppably** adv.

unstressed • adj. (of a syllable) not pronounced with stress.

unstructured • adj. without formal organization or structure.

unstuck past and past part. of UNSTICK.
– PHRASES **come unstuck** informal fail.

unstudied • adj. natural and unaffected.

unsubstantial • adj. having little or no solidity or reality.

unsubstantiated • adj. not supported or proven by evidence.

unsubtle • adj. obvious; clumsy.

unsuccessful • adj. not successful.
– DERIVATIVES **unsuccessfully** adv.

unsuitable • adj. not right or suitable for a particular purpose or occasion.
– DERIVATIVES **unsuitability** n. **unsuitably** adv.

unsuited • adj. not right or appropriate.

unsullied • adj. not spoiled.

unsung • adj. not celebrated or praised: *unsung heroes.*

unsupervised • adj. not done or acting under supervision.

unsupported • adj. **1** not supported. **2** not proved to be true by evidence.

unsure • adj. **1** lacking confidence. **2** not fixed or certain.

unsurfaced • adj. (of a road or path) not provided with a hard upper layer.

unsurpassed • adj. better or greater than any other.

unsurprising • adj. expected and so not causing surprise.
– DERIVATIVES **unsurprisingly** adv.

unsuspected • adj. **1** not known or thought to exist. **2** not regarded with suspicion.

unsuspecting • adj. not aware of the presence of danger; feeling no suspicion.

unsustainable • adj. **1** not able to be maintained at the current level. **2** upsetting the ecological balance by using up natural resources.

unswayed • adj. not influenced or affected.

unsweetened • adj. (of food or drink) without added sugar or sweetener.

unswerving • adj. not changing or becoming weaker.
– DERIVATIVES **unswervingly** adv.

unsymmetrical • adj. not symmetrical.

unsympathetic • adj. **1** not sympathetic. **2** not supporting an idea or action. **3** not likeable: *an unsympathetic character.*
– DERIVATIVES **unsympathetically** adv.

unsystematic • adj. not done or acting according to a fixed plan.
– DERIVATIVES **unsystematically** adv.

untainted • adj. not tainted.

untamed • adj. not tamed or controlled.
– DERIVATIVES **untameable** (also **untamable**) adj.

untangle • v. (**untangles, untangling, untangled**) **1** free from tangles. **2** free from complications or confusion.

untapped • adj. (of a resource) available but not yet exploited or used.

untarnished • adj. **1** (of metal) not tarnished. **2** not spoiled.

untasted • adj. (of food or drink) not sampled.

untaught • adj. **1** not having been taught or educated. **2** natural or spontaneous.

untenable • adj. not able to be defended against criticism or attack.

untended • adj. not cared for or looked after.

untested • adj. not subjected to testing; unproven.

unthinkable • adj. too unlikely or unpleasant to be considered a possibility.
– DERIVATIVES **unthinkably** adv.

unthinking • adj. without proper consideration.
– DERIVATIVES **unthinkingly** adv.

unthreatening • adj. not threatening.

untidy • adj. (**untidier, untidiest**) **1** not arranged tidily. **2** not inclined to be neat.
– DERIVATIVES **untidily** adv. **untidiness** n.

untie • v. (**unties, untying, untied**) undo or unfasten something tied.

until • prep. & conj. up to the point in time or the event mentioned.
– ORIGIN from Old Norse *und* 'as far as' + TILL[1].

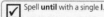 Spell **until** with a single **l**.

untimely • adj. **1** happening or done at an unsuitable time. **2** (of a death or end) happening too soon or sooner than normal.
– DERIVATIVES **untimeliness** n.

untiring • adj. continuing at the same rate without loss of energy.

untitled • adj. **1** (of a book or other work) having no title. **2** not having a title indicating high rank.

unto • prep. **1** old use = **TO**. **2** old use = **UNTIL**.
– ORIGIN from **UNTIL**.

untold • adj. **1** too much or too many to be counted. **2** not narrated or recounted.

untouchable • adj. **1** not able to be touched or affected. **2** unable to be rivalled. • n. offens. a member of the lowest caste in Hindu society.
– DERIVATIVES **untouchability** n.

USAGE: The use of the term **untouchable** to refer to a member of the lowest Hindu social class is now illegal in India and Pakistan. The official term today is **scheduled caste**.

untouched • adj. **1** not handled, used, or tasted. **2** not affected, changed, or damaged in any way.

untoward • adj. unexpected and unwelcome.

untraceable • adj. unable to be found or traced.

untrained • adj. not having been trained in a particular skill.

untrammelled (US also **untrammeled**) • adj. not restricted or hampered.

untranslatable • adj. not able to be translated.

untreatable • adj. for whom or which no medical care is available or possible.

untreated • adj. **1** not given medical care. **2** not treated by the use of a chemical, physical, or biological agent.

untried • adj. not yet tested; without experience.

untrodden • adj. not having been walked on.

untroubled • adj. not troubled.

untrue • adj. **1** false. **2** not faithful or loyal.

untrustworthy • adj. unable to be trusted.

untruth • n. (pl. **untruths**) **1** a lie. **2** the quality of being false.

untruthful • adj. not truthful.
– DERIVATIVES **untruthfully** adv.

untutored • adj. not formally taught or trained.

untying pres. part. of **UNTIE**.

untypical • adj. uncharacteristic or unusual.
– DERIVATIVES **untypically** adv.

unusable • adj. not fit to be used.

unused • adj. **1** not used. **2** (**unused to**) not accustomed to.

unusual • adj. **1** not often done or occurring. **2** remarkable or interesting because different.
– DERIVATIVES **unusually** adv.

unutterable • adj. too great or awful to describe.
– DERIVATIVES **unutterably** adv.

unuttered • adj. not spoken or expressed.

unvaried • adj. not varied.

unvarnished • adj. **1** not varnished. **2** plain and straightforward: *the unvarnished truth*.

unvarying • adj. not varying.
– DERIVATIVES **unvaryingly** adv.

unveil • v. **1** remove a veil or covering from. **2** show or announce publicly for the first time.

unverifiable • adj. unable to be verified.

unverified • adj. not verified.

unversed • adj. (**unversed in**) not experienced or skilled in.

unvoiced • adj. **1** not expressed in words. **2** (of a speech sound) produced without vibration of the vocal cords.

unwaged • adj. Brit. **1** unemployed or doing unpaid work. **2** (of work) unpaid.

unwanted • adj. not wanted.

unwarrantable • adj. unjustifiable.
– DERIVATIVES **unwarrantably** adv.

unwarranted • adj. not warranted.

unwary • adj. not cautious.

unwashed • adj. not washed.
– PHRASES **the (great) unwashed** derog. ordinary people; the masses.

unwatchable • adj. too disturbing or boring to watch.

unwatched • adj. not watched.

unwavering • adj. not wavering; steady or resolute.
– DERIVATIVES **unwaveringly** adv.

unweaned • adj. not weaned.

unwearying • adj. never tiring or slackening.

unwed • adj. not married.

unwelcome • adj. not welcome.

unwelcoming • adj. unfriendly or inhospitable.

unwell • adj. ill.

unwholesome • adj. not wholesome.

unwieldy • adj. hard to move or manage because of its size, shape, or weight.
– ORIGIN from **WIELD**.

 unwieldy follows the usual rule of *i* before *e* except after *c*.

unwilling • adj. not willing.
– DERIVATIVES **unwillingly** adv. **unwillingness** n.

unwind • v. (**unwinds, unwinding, unwound**) **1** undo after winding. **2** relax after a period of work or tension.

unwise • adj. foolish.
– DERIVATIVES **unwisely** adv.

unwitting • adj. **1** not aware of the full

u

facts. **2** unintentional.
– ORIGIN Old English, 'not knowing'.

unwonted /un-**wohn**-tid/ • adj. not usual or expected.

unworkable • adj. impractical.

unworldly • adj. **1** having little awareness of the realities of life. **2** not seeming to belong to this world.
– DERIVATIVES **unworldliness** n.

unworried • adj. not worried.

unworthy • adj. (**unworthier, unworthiest**) not deserving attention, effort, or respect.
– DERIVATIVES **unworthiness** n.

unwound past and past part. of UNWIND.

unwrap • v. (**unwraps, unwrapping, unwrapped**) remove the wrapping from.

unwritten • adj. not written.

unyielding • adj. not yielding.

unzip • v. (**unzips, unzipping, unzipped**) **1** unfasten the zip of. **2** Computing expand a compressed file.

up • adv. **1** towards a higher place or position. **2** to the place where someone is: *he crept up behind her.* **3** at or to a higher level or value. **4** into the desired or a proper condition: *the government set up an inquiry.* **5** out of bed. **6** in a publicly visible place: *sticking up posters.* **7** (of the sun) visible in the sky. **8** towards the north. **9** Brit. towards or in the capital or a major city. **10** into a happy mood.
• prep. **1** from a lower to a higher point of. **2** from one end of a street or other area to another. • adj. **1** directed or moving towards a higher place or position. **2** at an end. **3** (of the road) being repaired. **4** cheerful. **5** (of a computer system) working properly.
• v. (**ups, upping, upped**) increase a level or amount.
– PHRASES **something is up** informal something unusual is happening. **up against** close to or touching. **up and down** in various places throughout. **up before** appearing for a hearing in the presence of a judge, magistrate, etc. **up for 1** available for. **2** being considered for. **3** (often **up for it**) informal ready to take part in something. **up to 1** as far as. **2** (also **up until**) until. **what's up?** informal **1** what is going on? **2** what is the matter?
– ORIGIN Old English.

up- • prefix **1** (added to verbs and their derivatives) upwards: *upturned.* **2** (added to verbs and their derivatives) to a more recent time: *update.* **3** (added to nouns) referring to motion up: *uphill.* **4** (added to nouns) higher: *upland.*

up-and-coming • adj. likely to become successful.

upbeat • adj. positive and cheerful or

enthusiastic. • n. (in music) an unstressed beat coming before a stressed beat.

upbraid • v. scold or criticize.
– ORIGIN Old English, 'allege as a basis for censure'.

upbringing • n. the way in which a person is taught and looked after as a child.

upcoming • adj. forthcoming.

upcountry • adv. & adj. inland.

update • v. /up-**dayt**/ (**updates, updating, updated**) **1** make more modern. **2** give the latest information to. • n. /**up**-dayt/ an act of updating or an updated version.

upend • v. set or turn something on its end or upside down.

upfield • adv. (in sport) in or to a position nearer to the opponents' end of a field.

upfront informal • adv. (usu. **up front**) **1** at the front; in front. **2** (of a payment) in advance. • adj. **1** not trying to hide your thoughts or intentions; honest and frank. **2** (of a payment) made in advance.

upgrade • v. (**upgrades, upgrading, upgraded**) raise to a higher standard or rank. • n. an act of upgrading, or an upgraded version.
– DERIVATIVES **upgradeable** (also **upgradable**) adj.

upheaval • n. a violent or sudden change or disruption.

uphill • adv. towards the top of a slope. • adj. **1** sloping upwards. **2** difficult: *an uphill struggle.*

uphold • v. (**upholds, upholding, upheld**) **1** confirm or support. **2** maintain a custom or practice.

upholster /up-**hohl**-ster, up-**hol**-ster/ • v. (**upholsters, upholstering, upholstered**) provide an armchair, sofa, etc. with a soft, padded covering.
– DERIVATIVES **upholsterer** n.
– ORIGIN from UPHOLD in the former sense 'keep in repair'.

upholstery • n. **1** the soft, padded covering on an armchair, sofa, etc. **2** the art or practice of upholstering furniture.

upkeep • n. **1** the process of keeping something in good condition. **2** the cost of this or of supporting a person.

upland • n. (also **uplands**) an area of high or hilly land.

uplift • v. **1** raise. **2** (**be uplifted**) (of an island, mountain, etc.) be created by an upward movement of the earth's surface. **3** make more hopeful or happy. • n. **1** an act of uplifting. **2** support from a garment for a woman's bust. **3** a feeling of fresh hope or happiness.

uplighter • n. a lamp designed to throw light upwards.

upmarket • adj. & adv. esp. Brit. expensive and of high quality.

upon • prep. formal = ON.

upper • adj. **1** situated above another part. **2** higher in position or status. **3** situated on higher ground. • n. **1** the part of a boot or shoe above the sole. **2** informal a stimulating drug.

– PHRASES **have the upper hand** have an advantage or control. **the upper crust** informal the upper classes.

upper case • n. capital letters.

upper class • n. the social group with the highest status. • adj. relating to the upper class.

uppercut • n. a punch delivered with an upwards motion and the arm bent.

upper house (also **upper chamber**) • n. the higher house in a parliament with two chambers.

uppermost • adj. highest in place, rank, or importance. • adv. at or to the uppermost position.

upper school • n. (in the UK) a secondary school for children aged from about fourteen upwards.

uppish • adj. informal self-assertive and arrogant.

uppity • adj. informal self-important.

– ORIGIN from UP.

upright • adj. **1** vertical; erect. **2** greater in height than breadth. **3** strictly honest or respectable. **4** (of a piano) having vertical strings. • adv. in or into an upright position. • n. a vertical post, structure, or line.

uprising • n. a rebellion.

upriver • adv. & adj. towards or situated at a point nearer the source of a river.

uproar • n. **1** a loud and emotional noise or disturbance. **2** a public expression of outrage.

– ORIGIN Dutch *uproer*.

uproarious • adj. **1** very noisy and lively. **2** very funny.

– DERIVATIVES **uproariously** adv.

uproot • v. **1** pull a plant, tree, etc. out of the ground. **2** move someone from their home or usual surroundings.

upscale • adj. & adv. N. Amer. upmarket.

upset • v. /up-set/ (**upsets**, **upsetting**, **upset**) **1** make unhappy, disappointed, or worried. **2** knock over. **3** disrupt or disturb. • n. /up-set/ **1** an unexpected result or situation. **2** a state of being upset. **3** a disturbance of a person's digestive system. • adj. **1** /up-set/ unhappy, disappointed, or worried. **2** /up-set/ (of a person's stomach) having disturbed digestion.

– DERIVATIVES **upsetting** adj.

upshot • n. the eventual outcome or conclusion.

upside • n. the positive aspect of something.

upside down • adv. & adj. **1** with the upper part where the lower part should be. **2** in or into total disorder.

– ORIGIN from *up so down*, perh. meaning 'up as if down'.

upstage • adv. & adj. at or towards the back of a stage. • v. (**upstages**, **upstaging**, **upstaged**) draw attention away from someone else and towards yourself.

upstairs • adv. on or to an upper floor. • adj. situated on an upper floor. • n. an upper floor.

upstanding • adj. honest and respectable.

upstart • n. derog. a person who has suddenly become important and behaves arrogantly.

upstate • adj. & adv. US in or to a part of a state remote from its large cities.

upstream • adv. & adj. situated or moving in the direction opposite to that in which a stream or river flows.

upstroke • n. an upwards stroke.

upsurge • n. an increase.

upswing • n. an upward trend.

uptake • n. the action of taking up or making use of something.

– PHRASES **be quick** (or **slow**) **on the uptake** informal be quick (or slow) to understand something.

uptempo • adj. & adv. Music played with a fast or increased tempo.

upthrust • n. **1** Physics the upward force that a fluid exerts on a body floating in it. **2** Geol. the upward movement of part of the earth's surface.

uptight • adj. informal **1** nervously tense or angry. **2** unable to express your feelings and desires.

up to date • adj. using or aware of the latest developments and trends.

uptown • adj. & adv. esp. N. Amer. in or into the residential area of a town or city.

upturn • n. an improvement or upward trend.

upturned • adj. turned upwards or upside down.

upward • adv. (also **upwards**) towards a higher level. • adj. moving or leading towards a higher level.

– PHRASES **upwards of** more than.

– DERIVATIVES **upwardly** adv.

upwind • adv. & adj. into the wind.

uranium /yuu-ray-ni-uhm/ • n. a radioactive metallic chemical element used as a fuel in nuclear reactors.

u

– ORIGIN from **Uranus**.

Uranus /yoo-ray-nuhss, yoo-ruh-nuhss/ • n. a planet of the solar system, seventh in order from the sun.

urban • adj. relating to a town or city.
– ORIGIN Latin *urbanus*.

urbane /er-bayn/ • adj. (of a man) confident, polite, and at ease in social situations.
– ORIGIN first meaning 'urban': from Latin *urbanus*.

urbanite • n. informal a town or city dweller.

urbanity • n. an urbane quality or manner.

urbanize (or **urbanise**) • v. (**urbanizes, urbanizing, urbanized**) **1** build towns and cities in a country area. **2** make someone accustomed to living in a town or city rather than a country area.
– DERIVATIVES **urbanization** n.

urban myth (also N. Amer. **urban legend**) • n. an entertaining story or piece of information of uncertain origin that is circulated as though it were true.

urchin • n. a poor child dressed in ragged clothes.
– ORIGIN Old French *herichon* 'hedgehog'.

Urdu /oor-doo, er-doo/ • n. a language closely related to Hindi, the official language of Pakistan and widely used in India.
– ORIGIN Persian, 'language of the camp'.

-ure • suffix forming nouns: **1** referring to an action, process, or result: *closure.* **2** referring to an office or function: *judicature.* **3** referring to a group of people: *legislature.*
– ORIGIN Latin *-ura.*

urea /yuu-ree-uh/ • n. a colourless compound found in urine.
– ORIGIN Latin.

ureter /yuu-ree-ter/ • n. the duct by which urine passes from the kidney to the bladder.
– ORIGIN Greek *ourētēr.*

urethra /yuu-ree-thruh/ • n. the duct by which urine passes out of the body, and which in males also carries semen.
– DERIVATIVES **urethral** adj.
– ORIGIN Greek *ourēthra.*

urge • v. (**urges, urging, urged**) **1** encourage or earnestly ask someone to do something. **2** strongly recommend. • n. a strong desire or impulse.
– ORIGIN Latin *urgere* 'press, drive'.

urgent • adj. **1** requiring immediate action or attention. **2** earnest and insistent.
– DERIVATIVES **urgency** n. **urgently** adv.

urinal /yuu-ry-nuhl, yoor-i-nuhl/ • n. a container attached to the wall in a public toilet, into which men urinate.

urinary • adj. **1** relating to urine. **2** referring to the organs, structures, and ducts in which urine is produced and passed out of the body.

urinate • v. (**urinates, urinating, urinated**) pass urine out of the body.
– DERIVATIVES **urination** n.
– ORIGIN Latin *urinare.*

urine /yoo-rin, yoo-ryn/ • n. a yellowish fluid stored in the bladder and discharged through the urethra, made up of water and waste substances removed from the blood by the kidneys.
– ORIGIN Latin *urina.*

URL • abbrev. uniform (or universal) resource locator, the address of a World Wide Web page.

urn • n. **1** a tall vase with a stem and base, especially one for storing a cremated person's ashes. **2** a large metal container with a tap, in which tea or coffee is made and kept hot.
– ORIGIN Latin *urna.*

urology /yuu-rol-uh-ji/ • n. the branch of medicine concerned with the urinary system.
– DERIVATIVES **urological** adj. **urologist** n.

ursine /er-syn/ • adj. relating to bears.
– ORIGIN Latin *ursinus.*

Uruguayan /yoor-uh-gwy-uhn/ • n. a person from Uruguay. • adj. relating to Uruguay.

US • abbrev. United States.

us • pron. (first person pl.) **1** used by a speaker to refer to himself or herself and another person or people as the object of a verb or preposition. **2** used after the verb 'to be' and after 'than' or 'as'.
– ORIGIN Old English.

> **USAGE:** For an explanation of whether to use **us** or **we** following **than**, see the note at **PERSONAL PRONOUN**.

USA • abbrev. United States of America.

usable (also **useable**) • adj. able to be used.
– DERIVATIVES **usability** n.

usage • n. **1** the action of using something or the fact of being used: *a survey of water usage.* **2** the way in which words are used in a language.

> **usage** only has one **e**, at the end.

USB • abbrev. universal serial bus, a connector which enables any of a variety of devices to be plugged into a computer.

use • v. /yooz/ (**uses, using, used**) **1** do something with a device or object, or adopt a method, as a means of achieving a purpose: *the table can also be used as a desk.* **2** take or consume an amount of

something from a limited supply. **3** (**use something up**) consume the whole of something. **4** treat in a particular way. **5** exploit unfairly. **6** /yoosst/ (**used to**) did repeatedly or existed in the past. **7** /yoosst/ (**be/get used to**) be or become familiar with through experience.
• n. /yooss/ **1** the action of using something or the state of being used. **2** the ability or power to exercise something: *he lost the use of his legs.* **3** a purpose for something or a way in which something can be used: *the herb has various uses in cookery.* **4** value: *what's the use of crying?*
– PHRASES **make use of** use.
– ORIGIN Old French *user*.

useable • adj. var. of USABLE.

used • adj. **1** having already been used. **2** second-hand.

useful • adj. **1** able to be used for a practical purpose or in several ways. **2** Brit. informal skilful.
– DERIVATIVES **usefully** adv. **usefulness** n.

useless • adj. **1** serving no purpose. **2** informal having little ability or skill.
– DERIVATIVES **uselessly** adv. **uselessness** n.

user • n. a person who uses or operates something.

user-friendly • adj. easy to use or understand.

usher • n. **1** a person who shows people to their seats in a theatre or cinema or in church. **2** an official in a law court who swears in jurors and witnesses and generally keeps order. • v. (**ushers, ushering, ushered**) **1** show or guide someone somewhere. **2** (**usher something in**) cause or mark the start of something new.
– ORIGIN Old French *usser* 'doorkeeper'.

usherette • n. a woman who shows people to their seats in a cinema or theatre.

USSR • abbrev. hist. Union of Soviet Socialist Republics.

usual • adj. happening or done most of the time or in most cases. • n. (**the usual**) informal the drink someone regularly prefers.
– DERIVATIVES **usually** adv.
– ORIGIN Latin *usualis*.

usurious /yoo-zhoor-i-uhss, yoo-zyoor-i-uhss/ • adj. relating to usury.

usurp /yuu-zerp/ • v. take over someone's position or power illegally or by force.
– DERIVATIVES **usurpation** n. **usurper** n.
– ORIGIN Latin *usurpare* 'seize for use'.

usury /yoo-zhuh-ri/ • n. the practice of lending money at unreasonably high rates of interest.

– DERIVATIVES **usurer** n.
– ORIGIN Latin *usura*.

utensil • n. a tool or container, especially for household use.
– ORIGIN Latin *utensilis* 'usable'.

uterine /yoo-tuh-ryn/ • adj. relating to the womb (uterus).

uterus /yoo-tuh-ruhss/ • n. (pl. **uteri** /yoo-tuh-ry/) the womb.
– ORIGIN Latin.

utilitarian /yuu-ti-li-tair-i-uhn/ • adj. **1** useful or practical rather than attractive. **2** relating to utilitarianism.

utilitarianism • n. the belief that the right course of action is the one that will lead to the greatest happiness of the greatest number of people.

utility • n. (pl. **utilities**) **1** the state of being useful or profitable. **2** an organization supplying electricity, gas, water, or sewerage to the public.
• adj. having several functions or uses.
– ORIGIN Latin *utilitas*.

utility room • n. a room where a washing machine and other domestic equipment are kept.

utility vehicle • n. a lorry with low sides, used for small loads.

utilize (or **utilise**) • v. (**utilizes, utilizing, utilized**) make practical and effective use of.
– DERIVATIVES **utilization** n.
– ORIGIN French *utiliser*.

utmost • adj. most extreme; greatest.
• n. (**the utmost**) the greatest or most extreme extent or amount.
– ORIGIN Old English, 'outermost'.

Utopia /yoo-toh-pi-uh/ • n. an imagined place or society where everything is perfect.
– ORIGIN the title of a book by Sir Thomas More, from Greek *ou* 'not' + *topos* 'place'.

utopian • adj. relating to or aiming for a situation in which everything is perfect.
• n. an idealistic reformer.
– DERIVATIVES **utopianism** n.

utter[1] • adj. complete; absolute.
– DERIVATIVES **utterly** adv.
– ORIGIN Old English, 'outer'.

utter[2] • v. (**utters, uttering, uttered**) make a sound, or say something.
– ORIGIN Dutch *úteren* 'speak, make known'.

utterance • n. **1** a word, statement, or sound uttered. **2** the action of uttering something.

uttermost • adj. & n. utmost.

U-turn • n. **1** the turning of a vehicle in a U-shaped course so as to face the opposite way. **2** a reversal of policy.

UV • abbrev. ultraviolet.

u

uvula /yoo-vyuu-luh/ •n. (pl. **uvulae** /yoo-vyuu-lee/) a fleshy part of the soft palate which hangs above the throat.
– ORIGIN Latin, 'little grape'.

uxorious /uk-sor-i-uhss/ •adj. (of a man) very fond of his wife.
– ORIGIN Latin *uxoriosus*.

Uzi /oo-zi/ •n. a type of sub-machine gun.
– ORIGIN from the name of *Uziel* Gal, the Israeli army officer who designed it.

Vv

V¹ (also **v**) •n. (pl. **Vs** or **V's**) **1** the twenty-second letter of the alphabet. **2** the Roman numeral for five.

V² •abbrev. volt(s). •symb. the chemical element vanadium.

v (also **v.**) •abbrev. **1** Grammar verb. **2** versus. **3** very.

vacancy •n. (pl. **vacancies**) **1** an unoccupied position or job. **2** an available room in a hotel, guest house, etc. **3** empty space.

vacant •adj. **1** empty. **2** (of a position) not filled. **3** showing no intelligence or interest.
– DERIVATIVES **vacantly** adv.

vacate /vay-kayt, vuh-kayt/ •v. (**vacates**, **vacating**, **vacated**) **1** go out of a place, leaving it empty. **2** give up a position or job.
– ORIGIN Latin *vacare* 'leave empty'.

vacation •n. **1** a holiday period between terms in universities and law courts. **2** N. Amer. a holiday. **3** the action of vacating a place. •v. N. Amer. take a holiday.
– DERIVATIVES **vacationer** n.

vaccinate /vak-si-nayt/ •v. (**vaccinates**, **vaccinating**, **vaccinated**) treat with a vaccine to produce immunity against a disease.
– DERIVATIVES **vaccination** n.

> ☑ Remember that **vaccinate**, **vaccination**, and **vaccine** are spelled with a double **c**.

vaccine /vak-seen/ •n. a substance injected into the body to cause it to produce antibodies and so provide immunity against a disease.
– ORIGIN Latin *vaccinus*.

vacillate /va-si-layt/ •v. (**vacillates**, **vacillating**, **vacillated**) keep changing your mind about something.
– DERIVATIVES **vacillation** n.
– ORIGIN Latin *vacillare* 'sway'.

vacuole /vak-yuu-ohl/ •n. Biol. a space inside a cell, enclosed by a membrane and containing fluid.
– ORIGIN Latin *vacuus* 'empty'.

vacuous /vak-yuu-uhss/ •adj. showing a lack of thought or intelligence.
– DERIVATIVES **vacuity** /vuh-kyoo-i-ti/ n.
– ORIGIN Latin *vacuus* 'empty'.

vacuum /vak-yuu-uhm, vak-yuum/ •n. (pl. **vacuums** or **vacua** /vak-yuu-uh/) **1** a space that is completely empty of all matter. **2** a space or container from which the air has been completely or partly removed. **3** a gap left by the loss of someone or something important. **4** (pl. **vacuums**) a vacuum cleaner. •v. clean with a vacuum cleaner.
– ORIGIN Latin.

vacuum cleaner •n. an electrical device that collects dust by means of suction.

vacuum flask •n. esp. Brit. a container that keeps a substance hot or cold by means of a double wall enclosing a vacuum.

vacuum-pack •v. seal a product in a pack or wrapping with the air removed.

vacuum tube •n. a sealed glass tube containing a near vacuum which allows the free passage of electric current.

vade mecum /vah-di may-kuhm, vay-di mee-kuhm/ •n. a handbook or guide kept constantly at hand.
– ORIGIN Latin, 'go with me'.

vagabond /vag-uh-bond/ •n. **1** a person who has no settled home or job; a vagrant. **2** old use a rogue.
– ORIGIN Latin *vagabundus*.

vagary /vay-guh-ri/ •n. (pl. **vagaries**) an unexpected and mysterious change.
– ORIGIN Latin *vagari* 'wander'.

vagina /vuh-jy-nuh/ •n. (pl. **vaginas**) the muscular tube leading from the external genitals to the cervix in women and most female mammals.
– DERIVATIVES **vaginal** adj.
– ORIGIN Latin, 'sheath, scabbard'.

vagrant /vay-gruhnt/ •n. a person who has no settled home or job. •adj. living as a vagrant.
– DERIVATIVES **vagrancy** n.
– ORIGIN Old French *vagarant* 'wandering about'.

vague •adj. **1** not certain or definite. **2** thinking or expressing yourself in a

v

way that is not clear or detailed.
- DERIVATIVES **vaguely** adv. **vagueness** n.
- ORIGIN Latin *vagus* 'wandering, uncertain'.

vain • adj. **1** having too high an opinion of yourself. **2** useless or meaningless: *a vain boast.*
- PHRASES **in vain** without success. **take someone's name in vain** use someone's name in a way that shows a lack of respect.
- DERIVATIVES **vainly** adv.
- ORIGIN Latin *vanus* 'empty'.

vainglory • n. literary too much pride in yourself or your achievements.
- DERIVATIVES **vainglorious** adj.

valance /va-luhnss/ • n. a length of fabric attached to the base of a bed beneath the mattress to cover the space below.
- ORIGIN perh. from Old French *avaler* 'descend'.

vale • n. literary a valley.
- ORIGIN Latin *vallis*.

valediction /va-li-dik-sh'n/ • n. **1** the action of saying farewell. **2** a farewell speech.
- ORIGIN from Latin *vale* 'goodbye' + *dicere* 'to say'.

valedictory /va-li-dik-tuh-ri/ • adj. serving as a farewell.

valency /vay-luhn-si/ (or **valence** /vay-luhnss/) • n. (pl. **valencies**) the combining power of a chemical element, as measured by the number of hydrogen atoms it can displace or combine with.
- ORIGIN Latin *valentia* 'power'.

valentine • n. **1** a card sent on St Valentine's Day (14 February) to a person you love or are attracted to. **2** a person to whom you send such a card.

valerian /vuh-leer-i-uhn/ • n. **1** a plant with clusters of small pink, red, or white flowers. **2** a sedative drug obtained from a valerian root.
- ORIGIN Latin *valeriana*.

valet /va-lay, va-lit/ • n. **1** a man's male attendant, responsible for looking after his clothes and other personal needs. **2** N. Amer. a person employed to clean or park cars. • v. (**valets, valeting, valeted**) **1** act as a valet to. **2** clean a car as a professional service.
- ORIGIN French.

valetudinarian /va-li-tyoo-di-nair-i-uhn/ • n. a person who is in poor health or who worries too much about their health.
- ORIGIN Latin *valetudinarius* 'in ill health'.

valiant • adj. showing courage or determination.
- DERIVATIVES **valiantly** adv.

- ORIGIN Old French *vailant*.

valid • adj. **1** (of a reason, argument, etc.) sound or logical. **2** legally binding or officially acceptable.
- DERIVATIVES **validity** n. **validly** adv.
- ORIGIN Latin *validus* 'strong'.

validate • v. (**validates, validating, validated**) **1** check or prove the validity of. **2** make or declare legally valid.
- DERIVATIVES **validation** n.

valise /vuh-leez/ • n. a small travelling bag or suitcase.
- ORIGIN French.

Valium /va-li-uhm/ • n. trademark a tranquillizing drug used to relieve anxiety.

valley • n. (pl. **valleys**) a low area between hills or mountains.
- ORIGIN Latin *vallis*.

valorize /va-luh-ryz/ (or **valorise**) • v. (**valorizes, valorizing, valorized**) give value or validity to.
- DERIVATIVES **valorization** n.
- ORIGIN French *valorisation*.

valour (US **valor**) • n. great courage in the face of danger.
- DERIVATIVES **valorous** adj.
- ORIGIN Latin *valor*.

valuable • adj. **1** worth a great deal of money. **2** very useful or important. • n. (**valuables**) valuable items.
- DERIVATIVES **valuably** adv.

valuation • n. an estimate of how much something is worth.

value • n. **1** the importance or usefulness of something. **2** the amount of money that something is worth. **3** (**values**) standards of behaviour. **4** Math. the amount represented by a letter, symbol, or number. **5** the relative length of the sound represented by a musical note. • v. (**values, valuing, valued**) **1** estimate the value of. **2** consider to be important or useful.
- DERIVATIVES **valueless** adj. **valuer** n.
- ORIGIN Old French.

value added tax • n. a tax on the amount by which goods rise in value at each stage of production.

valve • n. **1** a device for controlling the flow of a liquid or gas through a pipe or duct. **2** a cylindrical mechanism used to vary the length of the tube in a brass musical instrument. **3** a structure in the heart or in a blood vessel that allows blood to flow in one direction only. **4** each of the two parts of the hinged shell of a bivalve mollusc such as an oyster or mussel.
- ORIGIN Latin *valva* 'leaf of a folding or double door'.

valvular • adj. relating to or having a valve or valves.

vamoose /vuh-mooss/ • v. (**vamooses, vamoosing, vamoosed**) informal leave hurriedly.
– ORIGIN Spanish *vamos* 'let us go'.

vamp¹ • n. the upper front part of a boot or shoe. • v. (**vamp something up**) informal improve something by adding something more interesting.
– ORIGIN first referring to the foot of a stocking: from Old French *avant* 'before' + *pie* 'foot'.

vamp² • n. informal a woman who uses her sexual attractiveness to control men.
– DERIVATIVES **vampish** adj.
– ORIGIN short for VAMPIRE.

vampire /vam-pyr/ • n. **1** (in folklore) a dead person supposed to leave their grave at night to drink the blood of living people. **2** (also **vampire bat**) a small bat that feeds on blood by piercing the skin with its teeth, found mainly in tropical America.
– DERIVATIVES **vampiric** /vam-pi-rik/ adj. **vampirism** n.
– ORIGIN Hungarian *vampir*.

van¹ • n. **1** a motor vehicle used for moving goods or people. **2** Brit. a railway carriage used for luggage, mail, etc.
– ORIGIN shortening of CARAVAN.

van² • n. (**the van**) the leading part of an advancing group.
– ORIGIN short for VANGUARD.

vanadium /vuh-nay-di-uhm/ • n. a hard grey metallic chemical element, used to make alloy steels.
– ORIGIN from an Old Norse name of the Scandinavian goddess Freyja.

vandal • n. a person who deliberately destroys or damages property.
– DERIVATIVES **vandalism** n.
– ORIGIN Latin *Vandalus*, referring to a Germanic people that plundered parts of Europe in the 4th and 5th centuries.

vandalize (or **vandalise**) • v. (**vandalizes, vandalizing, vandalized**) deliberately destroy or damage property.

vane • n. **1** a broad blade attached to a rotating axis or wheel which is moved by wind or water, forming part of a windmill, propeller, or turbine. **2** a weathervane.
– ORIGIN Germanic.

vanguard • n. **1** the leading part of an advancing army. **2** a group of people leading the way in new developments or ideas.
– ORIGIN Old French *avantgarde*.

vanilla • n. a substance obtained from the pods of a tropical orchid or produced artificially, used as a flavouring.
– ORIGIN Spanish *vainilla* 'pod'.

vanish • v. **1** disappear suddenly and completely. **2** gradually stop existing.
– ORIGIN Old French *esvanir*.

vanishing point • n. the point in the distance at which receding parallel lines appear to meet.

vanity • n. (pl. **vanities**) **1** too much pride in your own appearance or achievements. **2** the quality of being pointless or futile: *the vanity of human wishes*.
– ORIGIN Latin *vanitas*.

vanity case • n. a small case fitted with a mirror and compartments for make-up.

vanity unit • n. a unit made up of a washbasin set into a flat top with cupboards beneath.

vanquish /vang-kwish/ • v. literary defeat thoroughly.
– ORIGIN Old French *vainquir*.

vantage /vahn-tij/ (also **vantage point**) • n. a place or position giving a good view.
– ORIGIN Old French *avantage* 'advantage'.

vapid /vap-id/ • adj. lacking interest, intelligence, or originality.
– DERIVATIVES **vapidity** n.
– ORIGIN Latin *vapidus*.

vaporize (or **vaporise**) • v. (**vaporizes, vaporizing, vaporized**) convert a substance into vapour.
– DERIVATIVES **vaporization** n.

vaporizer (or **vaporiser**) • n. a device that is used to breathe in medicine in the form of a vapour.

vapour (US **vapor**) • n. **1** moisture or another substance that is diffused or suspended in the air. **2** Physics a gaseous substance that can be made into liquid by pressure alone.
– DERIVATIVES **vaporous** adj.
– ORIGIN Latin *vapor* 'steam, heat'.

vapour trail • n. a trail of condensed water from an aircraft or rocket at high altitude, seen as a white streak against the sky.

variable • adj. **1** often changing or likely to change; not consistent: *the photos are of variable quality*. **2** able to be changed. **3** Math. (of a quantity) able to take on different numerical values. • n. a variable situation, feature, or quantity.
– DERIVATIVES **variability** n. **variably** adv.

variance • n. the amount by which something changes or is different from something else.
– PHRASES **at variance** (**with**) disagreeing with or opposing.

variant • n. a form or version that varies

V

from other forms of the same thing.

variation • n. **1** a change or slight difference in condition, amount, or level. **2** a different or distinct form or version. **3** a new but still recognizable version of a musical theme.
– DERIVATIVES **variational** adj.

varicoloured /vair-i-kul-erd/ (US **varicolored**) • adj. consisting of several different colours.

varicose /va-ri-kohss, va-ri-kuhss/ • adj. (of a vein) swollen, twisted, and lengthened, as a result of poor circulation.
– ORIGIN Latin *varicosus*.

varied • adj. involving a number of different types or elements: *a long and varied career.*

variegated /vair-i-gay-tid/ • adj. having irregular patches or streaks of a different colour or colours.
– DERIVATIVES **variegation** /vair-i-gay-sh'n/ n.
– ORIGIN Latin *variegare* 'make varied'.

variety • n. (pl. **varieties**) **1** the quality of being different or varied. **2** (**a variety of**) a number of things of the same general type that are distinct in character. **3** a thing which differs in some way from others of the same general class: *fifty varieties of pasta.* **4** a form of entertainment made up of a series of different acts, such as singing, dancing, and comedy. **5** a subdivision of a species.
– ORIGIN Latin *varietas*.

various • adj. different from one another; of different kinds or sorts. • det. & pron. more than one; individual and separate.
– DERIVATIVES **variously** adv.
– ORIGIN Latin *varius* 'changing, diverse'.

varlet /var-lit/ • n. **1** old use a rogue or rascal. **2** hist. a male servant.
– ORIGIN Old French, from *valet* (see VALET).

varnish • n. **1** resin dissolved in a liquid, applied to wood or metal to give a hard, clear, shiny surface when dry. **2** nail varnish. • v. apply varnish to.
– ORIGIN Old French *vernis*.

varsity • n. (pl. **varsities**) **1** Brit. dated or S. Afr. university. **2** N. Amer. a sports team representing a university or college.
– ORIGIN shortening of UNIVERSITY.

vary • v. (**varies, varying, varied**) **1** differ in size, degree, or nature from something else of the same general class: *the houses vary in price.* **2** change from one form or state to another. **3** alter something to make it less uniform.
– ORIGIN Latin *variare*.

vascular /vass-kyuu-ler/ • adj. referring

to the system of vessels for carrying blood or (in plants) sap, water, and nutrients.
– ORIGIN Latin *vascularis*.

vas deferens /vass def-uh-renz/ • n. (pl. **vasa deferentia** /vay-suh def-uh-ren-shuh/) either of the ducts which convey sperm from the testicles to the urethra.
– ORIGIN from Latin *vas* 'vessel, duct' + *deferens* 'carrying away'.

vase • n. a decorative container used as an ornament or for displaying cut flowers.
– ORIGIN French.

vasectomy /vuh-sek-tuh-mi/ • n. (pl. **vasectomies**) the surgical cutting and sealing of part of each vas deferens as a means of sterilization.

Vaseline /vass-uh-leen/ • n. trademark a type of petroleum jelly used as an ointment and lubricant.
– ORIGIN from German *Wasser* 'water' + Greek *elaion* 'oil'.

vassal /vass-uhl/ • n. **1** (in the feudal system) a man who promised to fight for a monarch or lord in return for holding a piece of land. **2** a country that is controlled by or dependent on another.
– ORIGIN Latin *vassallus* 'retainer'.

vast • adj. of very great extent or quantity; huge.
– DERIVATIVES **vastly** adv. **vastness** n.
– ORIGIN Latin *vastus* 'void, immense'.

VAT • abbrev. value added tax.

vat • n. a large tank or tub used to hold liquid.
– ORIGIN Germanic.

Vatican • n. the official residence of the Pope in Rome.

vaudeville /vaw-duh-vil, voh-duh-vil/ • n. a type of entertainment featuring a mixture of musical and comedy acts.
– DERIVATIVES **vaudevillian** adj. & n.
– ORIGIN French.

vault[1] • n. **1** a roof in the form of an arch or a series of arches. **2** a large room used for storage, especially in a bank. **3** a chamber beneath a church or in a graveyard, used for burials.
– DERIVATIVES **vaulted** adj.
– ORIGIN Old French *voute*.

vault[2] • v. jump over something in a single movement, using your hands or a pole to push yourself. • n. an act of vaulting.
– DERIVATIVES **vaulter** n.
– ORIGIN Old French *volter* 'turn a horse'.

vaulting • n. the arrangement of vaults in a roof or ceiling.

vaulting horse • n. a padded wooden

block used for vaulting over by gymnasts and athletes.

vaunted /rhymes with haunted/
• adj. much praised or boasted about.
– ORIGIN Latin vantare.

VC • abbrev. Victoria Cross.

VCR • abbrev. video cassette recorder.

VD • abbrev. venereal disease.

VDU • abbrev. Brit. visual display unit.

veal • n. meat from a young calf.
– ORIGIN Old French veel.

vector /vek-ter/ • n. **1** Math. & Physics a quantity having direction as well as magnitude, especially as determining the position of one point in space relative to another. **2** the carrier of a disease or infection.
– DERIVATIVES **vectorial** adj.
– ORIGIN Latin, 'carrier'.

Veda /vay-duh, vee-duh/ • n. the most ancient Hindu scriptures.
– ORIGIN Sanskrit, 'sacred knowledge'.

VE day • n. the day (8 May) marking the Allied victory in Europe in 1945.
– ORIGIN short for Victory in Europe.

veer • v. (**veers, veering, veered**) **1** change direction suddenly. **2** (of the wind) change direction clockwise around the points of the compass. • n. a sudden change of direction.
– ORIGIN French virer.

veg¹ /vej/ • n. (pl. **veg**) Brit. informal vegetables, or a vegetable.

veg² /vej/ • v. (**vegges, vegging, vegged**) (**veg out**) informal relax completely.
– ORIGIN from **VEGETATE**.

vegan /vee-guhn/ • n. a person who does not eat or use any animal products.
– DERIVATIVES **veganism** n.
– ORIGIN from **VEGETARIAN**.

vegetable /vej-tuh-b'l, vej-i-tuh-b'l/
• n. **1** a plant used as food. **2** informal, offens. a person who is incapable of normal mental or physical activity as a result of brain damage.
– ORIGIN Latin vegetabilis 'animating'.

✓ **vegetable** is spelled with an **e** after the **g**, as well as one before it.

vegetable oil • n. an oil obtained from plants, e.g. olive oil or sunflower oil.

vegetal /vej-i-tuhl/ • adj. formal relating to plants.
– ORIGIN Latin vegetalis.

vegetarian • n. a person who does not eat meat or fish. • adj. eating or including no meat or fish.
– DERIVATIVES **vegetarianism** n.

vegetate • v. (**vegetates, vegetating, vegetated**) spend time in a dull and inactive way that involves little mental stimulation.

– ORIGIN Latin vegetare 'enliven'.

vegetation • n. plants in general.

vegetative /vej-i-tuh-tiv/
• adj. **1** relating to vegetation or the growth of plants. **2** relating to reproduction or breeding by asexual means. **3** (of a person) alive but in a coma and showing no sign of brain activity.

veggie burger • n. a savoury cake resembling a hamburger but made with vegetables or soya instead of meat.

vehement /vee-uh-muhnt/
• adj. showing strong feeling.
– DERIVATIVES **vehemence** n. **vehemently** adv.
– ORIGIN Latin, 'impetuous, violent'.

vehicle /vee-i-k'l/ • n. **1** a thing used for transporting people or goods on land, such as a car or lorry. **2** a means of expressing something: she used paint as a vehicle for her ideas. **3** a film, programme, song, etc., intended to display the leading performer to the best advantage.
– DERIVATIVES **vehicular** /vi-hik-yuu-ler/ adj.
– ORIGIN Latin vehiculum.

veil • n. **1** a piece of fine material worn to protect or hide the face. **2** a piece of fabric forming part of a nun's headdress, resting on the head and shoulders. **3** a thing that hides or disguises. • v. **1** cover with a veil. **2** (as adj. **veiled**) partially hidden or disguised.
– ORIGIN Latin velum 'sail, veil'.

vein • n. **1** any of the tubes forming part of the circulation system by which blood is carried from all parts of the body towards the heart. **2** (in general use) a blood vessel. **3** a very thin rib running through a leaf. **4** (in insects) a hollow rib forming part of the supporting framework of a wing. **5** a streak of a different colour in wood, marble, cheese, etc. **6** a fracture in rock containing a deposit of minerals or ore. **7** a source of a quality: a rich vein of humour.
– DERIVATIVES **veined** adj.
– ORIGIN Old French veine.

Velcro • n. trademark a fastener made up of two strips of fabric which stick together when pressed.
– ORIGIN from French velours croché 'hooked velvet'.

veld /velt/ (also **veldt**) • n. open, uncultivated country or grassland in southern Africa.
– ORIGIN Afrikaans, 'field'.

vellum /vel-luhm/ • n. fine parchment made from animal skin.
– ORIGIN Old French velin.

V

velociraptor /vi-los-si-rap-ter/ • n. a small meat-eating dinosaur with a large slashing claw on each foot.
– ORIGIN Latin.

velocity /vi-loss-i-ti/ • n. (pl. **velocities**) 1 the speed of something in a given direction. 2 (in general use) speed.
– ORIGIN Latin *velocitas*.

velodrome /vel-uh-drohm/ • n. a cycle-racing track with steeply banked curves.
– ORIGIN French.

velour /vuh-loor/ • n. a plush woven fabric resembling velvet.
– ORIGIN French *velours* 'velvet'.

velvet • n. a fabric of silk, cotton, or nylon with a thick short pile on one side.
– DERIVATIVES **velvety** adj.
– ORIGIN Old French *veluotte*.

velveteen • n. a cotton fabric with a pile resembling velvet.

venal /vee-n'l/ • adj. open to bribery.
– DERIVATIVES **venality** n.
– ORIGIN Latin *venum* 'thing for sale'.

vend • v. offer small items for sale.
– ORIGIN Latin *vendere* 'sell'.

vendetta /ven-det-tuh/ • n. 1 a prolonged feud between families in which people are murdered in return for previous murders. 2 a prolonged bitter quarrel with someone.
– ORIGIN Italian.

vending machine • n. a machine that dispenses small articles when a coin or token is inserted.

vendor (US also **vender**) • n. 1 a person or company offering something for sale. 2 Law a person who is selling a property.

veneer /vi-neer/ • n. 1 a thin decorative covering of fine wood applied to a cheaper wood or other material. 2 an attractive appearance that disguises someone or something's true nature or feelings.
– DERIVATIVES **veneered** adj.
– ORIGIN German *furnieren*.

venerable • adj. 1 greatly respected because of age, wisdom, or character. 2 (in the Anglican Church) a title given to an archdeacon.

venerate /ven-uh-rayt/ • v. (**venerates**, **venerating**, **venerated**) regard with great respect.
– DERIVATIVES **veneration** n.
– ORIGIN Latin *venerari* 'revere'.

venereal /vi-neer-i-uhl/ • adj. 1 relating to venereal disease. 2 formal relating to sexual intercourse or sexual desire.
– ORIGIN Latin *venereus*.

venereal disease • n. a disease caught by having sex with a person who is already infected.

Venetian /vi-nee-sh'n/ • adj. relating to Venice. • n. a person from Venice.

venetian blind • n. a window blind consisting of horizontal slats which can be turned to control the amount of light that passes through.

Venezuelan /ve-ni-zway-luhn/ • n. a person from Venezuela. • adj. relating to Venezuela.

vengeance /ven-juhnss/ • n. the action of punishing or harming someone in return for what they have done to you or someone close to you.
– PHRASES **with a vengeance** with great intensity.
– ORIGIN Old French.

> ☑ **vengeance** is spelled with an **e** after the **g**.

vengeful • adj. wanting to punish or harm someone in return for something they have done.
– DERIVATIVES **vengefully** adv. **vengefulness** n.

venial /vee-ni-uhl/ • adj. 1 (in Christian belief) referring to a sin that will not deprive the soul of divine grace. Often contrasted with MORTAL. 2 (of a fault or offence) slight and pardonable.
– ORIGIN Latin *venialis*.

venison /ven-i-s'n/ • n. meat from a deer.
– ORIGIN Old French *venesoun*.

Venn diagram • n. a diagram representing mathematical sets as circles, common elements of the sets being represented by overlapping sections of the circles.
– ORIGIN named after the English logician John Venn.

venom • n. 1 poisonous fluid produced by animals such as snakes and scorpions and injected by biting or stinging. 2 extreme hatred or bitterness.
– ORIGIN Old French *venim*.

venomous • adj. 1 producing venom. 2 full of hatred or bitterness.
– DERIVATIVES **venomously** adv.

venous /vee-nuhss/ • adj. relating to a vein or the veins.

vent¹ • n. an opening that allows air, gas, or liquid to pass out of or into a confined space. • v. 1 express a strong emotion freely. 2 allow air, gas, or liquid to pass through an outlet.
– ORIGIN French *vent* 'wind' or *éventer* 'expose to air'.

vent² • n. a slit in a garment.
– ORIGIN Old French *fente* 'slit'.

ventilate • v. (**ventilates**, **ventilating**, **ventilated**) 1 cause air to enter and circulate freely in a room or building. 2 discuss an opinion or issue in public.
– DERIVATIVES **ventilation** n.
– ORIGIN Latin *ventilare* 'blow'.

ventilator • n. **1** a machine or opening for ventilating a room or building. **2** a machine that pumps air in and out of a person's lungs to help them to breathe.

ventral • adj. tech. relating to the underside or abdomen. Compare with DORSAL.
– DERIVATIVES **ventrally** adv.
– ORIGIN Latin *venter* 'belly'.

ventricle /ven-tri-k'l/ • n. each of the two larger and lower cavities of the heart.
– DERIVATIVES **ventricular** /ven-**trik**-yuu-ler/ adj.
– ORIGIN Latin *ventriculus*.

ventriloquist /ven-**tril**-uh-kwist/ • n. an entertainer who makes their voice seem to come from a dummy of a person or animal.
– DERIVATIVES **ventriloquism** n.
– ORIGIN from Latin *venter* 'belly' + *loqui* 'speak'.

venture • n. **1** a risky or daring journey or undertaking. **2** a business enterprise involving considerable risk.
• v. (**ventures, venturing, ventured**) **1** dare to do something dangerous or risky. **2** dare to say something bold.
– DERIVATIVES **venturer** n.
– ORIGIN shortening of ADVENTURE.

venture capital • n. capital invested in a project in which there is a large element of risk.

venturesome • adj. willing to do something difficult or risky.

venue /ven-yoo/ • n. the place where an event or meeting is held.
– ORIGIN Old French, 'a coming'.

Venus • n. a planet of the solar system, second in order from the sun and the brightest object in the sky after the sun and moon.

Venus flytrap • n. a plant with hinged leaves that spring shut on and digest insects which land on them.

veracious /vuh-**ray**-shuhss/ • adj. formal speaking or representing the truth.
– ORIGIN Latin *verus* 'true'.

veracity /vuh-**rass**-i-ti/ • n. the quality of being true or accurate.

veranda /vuh-**ran**-duh/ (also **verandah**) • n. a roofed structure with an open front along the outside of a house, level with the ground floor.
– ORIGIN Portuguese *varanda* 'railing'.

verb • n. a word used to describe an action, state, or occurrence, such as *hear*, *become*, or *happen*.
– ORIGIN Latin *verbum* 'word, verb'.

verbal • adj. **1** relating to or in the form of words. **2** spoken rather than written. **3** relating to a verb.

– DERIVATIVES **verbally** adv.

verbalize (or **verbalise**) • v. (**verbalizes, verbalizing, verbalized**) express in words.
– DERIVATIVES **verbalization** n.

verbal noun • n. a noun formed as an inflection of a verb, such as *smoking* in *smoking is forbidden*.

verbatim /ver-**bay**-tim/ • adv. & adj. in exactly the same words as were used originally; word for word.
– ORIGIN Latin.

verbena /ver-**bee**-nuh/ • n. an ornamental plant with bright showy flowers.
– ORIGIN Latin, 'sacred bough'.

verbiage /ver-bi-ij/ • n. excessively long or technical speech or writing.
– ORIGIN French.

verbose /ver-**bohss**/ • adj. using more words than are needed.
– DERIVATIVES **verbosity** /ver-**boss**-i-ti/ n.
– ORIGIN Latin *verbosus*.

verdant /ver-duhnt/ • adj. green with grass or other lush vegetation.
– ORIGIN perh. from Old French *verdeant*.

verdict • n. **1** a formal decision made by a jury in a court of law as to whether a person is innocent or guilty. **2** an opinion or judgement made after testing or trying something.
– ORIGIN Old French *verdit*.

verdigris /ver-di-gree, ver-di-greess/ • n. a bright bluish-green substance formed on copper or brass by oxidation.
– ORIGIN from Old French *vert de Grece* 'green of Greece'.

verdure /ver-dyer/ • n. lush green vegetation.
– ORIGIN Old French *verd* 'green'.

verge • n. **1** an edge or border. **2** Brit. a grass edging by the side of a road or path. **3** a limit beyond which something will happen: *she was on the verge of tears.*
• v. (**verges, verging, verged**) (**verge on**) be very close or similar to.
– ORIGIN Old French.

verger • n. an official in a church who acts as a caretaker and attendant.
– ORIGIN Old French.

verify /**ve**-ri-fy/ • v. (**verifies, verifying, verified**) make sure or show that something is true, accurate, or justified.
– DERIVATIVES **verifiable** adj. **verification** n.
– ORIGIN Latin *verificare*.

verily • adv. old use truly; certainly.
– ORIGIN from French.

verisimilitude /ve-ri-si-**mil**-i-tyood/ • n. the appearance of being true or real.
– ORIGIN Latin *verisimilitudo*.

veritable • adj. rightly so called (used

verity •n. (pl. **verities**) **1** a true principle or belief. **2** truth.
– ORIGIN Latin *veritas*.

vermicelli /ver-mi-**chel**-li, ver-mi-**sel**-li/ •pl. n. **1** pasta made in long thin threads. **2** Brit. shreds of chocolate used to decorate cakes.
– ORIGIN Italian, 'little worms'.

vermiform •adj. tech. resembling or having the form of a worm.

vermilion /ver-**mil**-yuhn/ •n. a brilliant red pigment or colour.
– ORIGIN Old French *vermeillon*.

vermin •n. **1** wild mammals and birds which harm crops, farm animals, or game, or which carry disease. **2** worms or insects that live on the bodies of animals or people. **3** people who are very unpleasant or dangerous to society.
– DERIVATIVES **verminous** adj.
– ORIGIN Old French.

vermouth /ver-**muhth**, ver-**mooth**/ •n. a red or white wine flavoured with herbs.
– ORIGIN French *vermout*.

vernacular /ver-**nak**-yuu-ler/ •n. the language or dialect spoken by the ordinary people of a country or region.
– ORIGIN Latin *vernaculus* 'native'.

vernal /**ver**-n'l/ •adj. relating to the season of spring.
– ORIGIN Latin *vernalis*.

vernier /**ver**-ni-er/ •n. a small movable graduated scale for indicating fractions of the main scale on a measuring device.
– ORIGIN named after the French mathematician Pierre *Vernier*.

verruca /vuh-**roo**-kuh/ •n. (pl. **verrucae** /vuh-**roo**-kee/ or **verrucas**) a contagious wart on the sole of the foot.
– ORIGIN Latin.

versatile •adj. able to adapt or be adapted to many different functions or activities.
– DERIVATIVES **versatility** n.
– ORIGIN Latin *versatilis*.

verse •n. **1** writing arranged with a regular rhythm, and often having a rhyme. **2** a group of lines that form a unit in a poem or song. **3** each of the short numbered divisions of a chapter in the Bible or other scripture.
– ORIGIN Latin *versus* 'furrow, line of writing'.

versed •adj. (**versed in**) experienced or skilled in; knowledgeable about.
– ORIGIN Latin *versatus*.

versify •v. (**versifies**, **versifying**, **versified**) write verse or turn a piece of writing into verse.

– DERIVATIVES **versification** n.

version •n. **1** a form of something that differs in some way from other forms of the same type of thing: *the car comes in two-door and four-door versions.* **2** an account of something told from a particular person's point of view.
– ORIGIN Latin.

verso /**ver**-soh/ •n. (pl. **versos**) a left-hand page of an open book, or the back of a loose document. Contrasted with RECTO.
– ORIGIN from Latin *verso folio* 'on the turned leaf'.

versus •prep. **1** against. **2** as opposed to.
– ORIGIN Latin, 'towards'.

vertebra /**ver**-ti-bruh/ •n. (pl. **vertebrae** /**ver**-ti-bray, **ver**-ti-bree/) each of the series of small bones forming the backbone.
– DERIVATIVES **vertebral** adj.
– ORIGIN Latin.

vertebrate /**ver**-ti-bruht/ •n. an animal having a backbone, including mammals, birds, reptiles, amphibians, and fish.

vertex /**ver**-teks/ •n. (pl. **vertices** /**ver**-ti-seez/ or **vertexes**) **1** the highest point. **2** each angular point of a polygon, triangle, or other geometrical figure. **3** a meeting point of two lines that form an angle.
– ORIGIN Latin, 'whirlpool, vertex'.

vertical •adj. at a right angle to a horizontal line or surface; having the top directly above the bottom. •n. **1** (**the vertical**) a vertical line or surface. **2** an upright structure.
– DERIVATIVES **verticality** n. **vertically** adv.
– ORIGIN Latin *verticalis*.

vertiginous /ver-**tij**-i-nuhss/ •adj. very high or steep and causing giddiness.
– DERIVATIVES **vertiginously** adv.

vertigo /**ver**-ti-goh/ •n. a feeling of giddiness caused by looking down from a great height.
– ORIGIN Latin, 'whirling'.

vervain /**ver**-vayn/ •n. a plant with small blue, white, or purple flowers, used in herbal medicine.
– ORIGIN Old French *verveine*.

verve •n. vigour, spirit, and style.
– ORIGIN French.

very •adv. in a high degree. •adj. **1** actual; precise. **2** emphasizing an extreme point in time or space: *the very beginning.* **3** mere: *the very thought of drink made him feel sick.*
– ORIGIN Latin *verus* 'true'.

Very Reverend •adj. a title given to a dean in the Anglican Church.

vesicle /**ves**-si-k'l, **vee**-si-k'l/ •n. **1** a small fluid-filled sac or cyst in an animal

V

or plant. **2** a blister full of clear fluid.
– ORIGIN Latin *vesicula* 'small bladder'.

vespers • n. a service of evening prayer.
– ORIGIN Latin *vesperas* 'evensong'.

vessel • n. **1** a ship or large boat. **2** a tube
or duct carrying a fluid within the body,
or within a plant. **3** a bowl, cup, or other
container for liquids.
– ORIGIN Old French *vessele*.

vest • n. **1** Brit. a sleeveless undergarment
worn on the upper part of the body. **2** a
sleeveless garment worn for a particular
purpose: *a bulletproof vest*. **3** N. Amer. &
Austral. a waistcoat or sleeveless jacket.
• v. **1** (**vest something in**) give power,
property, etc. to someone. **2** (usu. **be
vested with**) give someone the legal
right to power, property, etc.
– ORIGIN Latin *vestis* 'garment'.

Vestal Virgin • n. (in ancient Rome) a
virgin dedicated to the goddess Vesta
and vowed to chastity.

vested interest • n. a personal reason
for wanting something to happen.

vestibule /vess-ti-byool/ • n. a room or
hall just inside the outer door of a
building.
– ORIGIN Latin *vestibulum* 'entrance
court'.

vestige /vess-tij/ • n. **1** a remaining trace
of something that once existed: *the last
vestiges of colonialism*. **2** the smallest
amount.
– ORIGIN Latin *vestigium* 'footprint'.

vestigial /ve-sti-ji-uhl, ve-sti-juhl/
• adj. forming a very small remaining
part.

vestment • n. a robe worn by the clergy
or members of a choir during church
services.
– ORIGIN Latin *vestimentum*.

vestry • n. (pl. **vestries**) a room in a
church, used as an office and for
changing into ceremonial robes.
– ORIGIN Latin *vestiarium*.

vet[1] • n. esp. Brit. a veterinary surgeon.
• v. (**vets, vetting, vetted**) **1** check or
examine very carefully. **2** Brit. investigate
a person's background before employing
them.

vet[2] • n. N. Amer. informal a veteran.

vetch • n. a plant with purple, pink, or
yellow flowers, grown for silage or
fodder.
– ORIGIN Old French *veche*.

veteran • n. **1** a person who has had
many years of experience in a particular
field. **2** a person who used to serve in the
armed forces.
– ORIGIN Latin *veteranus*.

veteran car • n. Brit. an old car,
specifically one made before 1919.

veterinarian • n. N. Amer. = VETERINARY
SURGEON.

veterinary /vet-uhn-ri, vet-ri-nuh-ri/
• adj. relating to the treatment of
diseases and injuries in animals.
– ORIGIN Latin *veterinarius*.

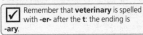
> ✓ Remember that **veterinary** is spelled
> with **-er-** after the **t**: the ending is
> **-ary**.

veterinary surgeon • n. Brit. a person
qualified to treat diseased or injured
animals.

veto /vee-toh/ • n. (pl. **vetoes**) **1** a right to
reject a decision or proposal made by a
law-making body. **2** any refusal to allow
something. • v. (**vetoes, vetoing,
vetoed**) **1** use a veto against. **2** refuse to
allow.
– ORIGIN Latin, 'I forbid'.

vex • v. make annoyed or worried.
– DERIVATIVES **vexation** n.
– ORIGIN Latin *vexare* 'shake'.

vexatious • adj. causing annoyance or
worry.

vexed • adj. **1** (of an issue) difficult to
resolve and causing much debate: *the
vexed question of Europe*. **2** annoyed or
worried.

VHF • abbrev. very high frequency.

VHS • abbrev. trademark video home system
(as used by domestic video recorders).

via /vy-uh, vee-uh/ • prep. **1** travelling
through a place on the way to a
destination. **2** by way of; through. **3** by
means of.
– ORIGIN Latin, 'way, road'.

viable /vy-uh-b'l/ • adj. **1** capable of
working successfully; feasible. **2** (of a
plant, animal, or cell) capable of
surviving or living successfully.
– DERIVATIVES **viability** n.
– ORIGIN French.

viaduct • n. a long bridge-like structure
carrying a road or railway across a valley
or other low ground.
– ORIGIN from Latin *via* 'way' + *ducere* 'to
lead'.

Viagra /vy-ag-ruh/ • n. trademark a
synthetic compound used to help a man
achieve an erection.
– ORIGIN prob. from *virility* and the name
Niagara.

vial /vy-uhl/ • n. a small container used
for holding liquid medicines.
– ORIGIN from PHIAL.

viands /vy-uhndz/ • pl. n. old use food.
– ORIGIN Old French *viande*.

viaticum /vy-at-i-kuhm/ • n. (pl. **viatica**
/vy-at-i-kuh/) the Eucharist as given to a
person who is dying or in danger of
death.
– ORIGIN Latin.

v

vibe (also **vibes**) • n. informal the atmosphere produced by a place or a mood passing between people.

vibrant • adj. **1** full of energy and enthusiasm. **2** (of sound) strong or resonant. **3** (of colour) bright.
– DERIVATIVES **vibrancy** n. **vibrantly** adv.
– ORIGIN Latin *vibrare* 'vibrate'.

vibraphone /vy-bruh-fohn/ • n. an electrical musical instrument with tuned metal bars that give a vibrato effect.

vibrate • v. (**vibrates, vibrating, vibrated**) **1** move with small movements rapidly to and fro. **2** (of a sound) resonate.
– DERIVATIVES **vibratory** adj.
– ORIGIN Latin *vibrare*.

vibration • n. an instance or the state of vibrating.
– DERIVATIVES **vibrational** adj.

vibrato /vi-brah-toh/ • n. a rapid, slight variation in pitch in singing or playing some musical instruments.
– ORIGIN Italian.

vibrator • n. a vibrating device used for massage or sexual stimulation.

viburnum /vy-ber-nuhm/ • n. (pl. **viburnums**) a shrub or small tree with clusters of small white flowers.
– ORIGIN Latin, 'wayfaring tree'.

vicar • n. (in the Church of England) a priest in charge of a parish.
– ORIGIN Old French *vicaire*.

vicarage • n. the house of a vicar.

vicarious /vi-kair-i-uhss, vy-kair-i-uhss/ • adj. experienced in the imagination after watching or reading about another person's actions or feelings: *vicarious excitement.*
– DERIVATIVES **vicariously** adv.
– ORIGIN Latin *vicarius* 'substitute'.

vice¹ • n. **1** immoral or wicked behaviour. **2** criminal activities involving prostitution, pornography, or drugs. **3** an immoral or bad quality in a person's character. **4** a bad habit.
– ORIGIN Old French.

vice² (US **vise**) • n. a metal tool with movable jaws which are used to hold an object firmly in place while work is done on it.
– ORIGIN Old French *vis*.

vice- • comb. form next in rank to and able to deputize for: *vice-president.*
– ORIGIN Latin *vice* 'in place of'.

vice admiral • n. a high rank of naval officer, above rear admiral and below admiral.

vice chancellor • n. a deputy chancellor of a British university who is in charge of its administration.

vice-president • n. an official or executive serving as a deputy to a president.

viceregal • adj. relating to a viceroy.

viceroy • n. a person sent by a king or queen to govern a colony.
– ORIGIN former French.

vice versa /vyss ver-suh, vy-suh ver-suh/ • adv. reversing the order of the items just mentioned.
– ORIGIN Latin, 'in-turned position'.

vicinity • n. (pl. **vicinities**) the area near or surrounding a place.
– ORIGIN Latin *vicinitas*.

vicious • adj. **1** cruel or violent. **2** (of an animal) wild and dangerous.
– DERIVATIVES **viciously** adv. **viciousness** n.
– ORIGIN Latin *vitiosus*.

> ✓ The beginning of **vicious** is spelled **vici-** (no s).

vicious circle • n. a situation in which one problem leads to another, which then makes the first one worse.

vicissitudes /vi-siss-i-tyoodz/ • pl. n. changes of circumstances or fortune.
– ORIGIN Latin *vicissitudo.*

victim • n. **1** a person harmed or killed as a result of a crime or accident. **2** a person who has been tricked: *the victim of a hoax.*
– PHRASES **fall victim to** be hurt, killed, or destroyed by.
– DERIVATIVES **victimhood** n.
– ORIGIN Latin *victima.*

victimize (or **victimise**) • v. (**victimizes, victimizing, victimized**) single someone out for cruel or unfair treatment.
– DERIVATIVES **victimization** n. **victimizer** n.

victor • n. a person who defeats an opponent in a battle, game, or competition.
– ORIGIN Latin.

Victorian • adj. relating to the reign of Queen Victoria (1837–1901), or to the attitudes associated with that period.

Victoriana • pl. n. articles from the Victorian period.

Victoria plum • n. Brit. a large red dessert plum.

victorious • adj. having won a victory.
– DERIVATIVES **victoriously** adv.

victory • n. (pl. **victories**) an act of defeating an opponent in a battle, game, or competition.
– ORIGIN Latin *victoria.*

victual /vi-t'l/ dated • n. (**victuals**) food or provisions. • v. (**victuals, victualling, victualled**; US **victuals, victualing, victualed**) provide with food or other stores.
– ORIGIN Latin *victualis.*

victualler /vi-t'l-er/ •n. Brit. a person who is licensed to sell alcoholic drinks.

vicuña /vi-koo-nyuh, vy-kyoo-nuh/ •n. 1 a wild relative of the llama, having fine silky wool. 2 cloth made from the wool of the vicuña.
– ORIGIN from a South American Indian language.

video •n. (pl. **videos**) 1 a system of recording and reproducing moving images using magnetic tape. 2 a film or other recording on magnetic tape. 3 a cassette of videotape. 4 Brit. a video recorder. •v. (**videoes, videoing, videoed**) film or make a video recording of.
– ORIGIN Latin *videre* 'to see'.

videoconference •n. an arrangement in which television sets linked to telephone lines are used to allow a group of people to talk to and see each other.
– DERIVATIVES **videoconferencing** n.

videodisc •n. a CD-ROM or other disc used to store images.

video game •n. a computer game played on a VDU screen.

videophone •n. a telephone device transmitting and receiving a visual image as well as sound.

video recorder •n. a machine linked to a television set, used for recording programmes and playing videotapes.

videotape •n. 1 magnetic tape for recording and reproducing images and sound. 2 a cassette on which this magnetic tape is held. •v. (**videotapes, videotaping, videotaped**) record on videotape.

vie •v. (**vies, vying, vied**) compete eagerly with other people in order to do or achieve something.
– ORIGIN prob. from the former word *envy*, from Latin *invitare* 'challenge'.

Viennese /vee-uh-neez/ •n. (pl. **Viennese**) a person from Vienna. •adj. relating to Vienna.

Vietnamese •n. (pl. **Vietnamese**) 1 a person from Vietnam. 2 the language of Vietnam. •adj. relating to Vietnam.

view •n. 1 the ability to see something or to be seen from a particular position: *the mountains came into view.* 2 something seen from a particular position, especially beautiful scenery. 3 an attitude or opinion. •v. 1 look at or inspect. 2 regard in a particular way: *she views beggars as potential thieves.* 3 inspect a house or other property with the intention of buying or renting it. 4 watch something on television.
– PHRASES **in view** able to be seen; visible. **in view of** because or as a result of. **with**

a view to with the aim or intention of.
– DERIVATIVES **viewable** adj.
– ORIGIN Old French *vieue*.

viewer •n. 1 a person who views something. 2 a device for looking at film transparencies or similar photographic images.

viewership •n. the audience for a particular television programme or channel.

viewfinder •n. a device on a camera that the user looks through to see what will appear in the photograph.

viewpoint •n. 1 a position giving a good view. 2 an opinion or point of view.

viewscreen •n. the screen on a television, computer, or similar device on which images and information are displayed.

vigil /vi-jil/ •n. a period of staying awake during the night to keep watch or pray.
– ORIGIN Latin, 'awake'.

vigilant •adj. keeping careful watch for possible danger or difficulties.
– DERIVATIVES **vigilance** n. **vigilantly** adv.
– ORIGIN Latin *vigilare* 'keep awake'.

vigilante /vi-ji-lan-ti/ •n. a member of a group of people who take it on themselves to prevent crime or punish offenders without legal authority.
– DERIVATIVES **vigilantism** n.
– ORIGIN Spanish, 'vigilant'.

vignette /vee-nyet, vi-nyet/ •n. 1 a brief, vivid description or episode. 2 a small illustration or portrait photograph which fades into its background without a definite border.
– ORIGIN French.

vigorous •adj. 1 strong, healthy, and full of energy. 2 involving physical strength, effort, or energy.
– DERIVATIVES **vigorously** adv. **vigorousness** n.

> ✓ **vigorous** drops the *u* before the *r* of **vigour**.

vigour (US **vigor**) •n. 1 physical strength and good health. 2 effort, energy, and enthusiasm.
– ORIGIN Latin *vigor*.

Viking •n. a member of the Scandinavian seafaring people who settled in parts of Britain and elsewhere in NW Europe between the 8th and 11th centuries.
– ORIGIN Old Norse.

vile •adj. 1 very unpleasant. 2 wicked; morally bad.
– DERIVATIVES **vilely** adv. **vileness** n.
– ORIGIN Latin *vilis* 'cheap, base'.

vilify /vil-i-fy/ •v. (**vilifies, vilifying, vilified**) speak or write about someone in a very abusive way.
– DERIVATIVES **vilification** n.

– ORIGIN Latin *vilificare*.

villa •n. **1** Brit. a rented holiday home abroad. **2** (especially in continental Europe) a large country house in its own grounds. **3** a large country house of Roman times.
– ORIGIN Latin.

village •n. **1** a community in a country area that is smaller than a town. **2** a self-contained district within a town or city.
– DERIVATIVES **villager** n. **villagey** adj.
– ORIGIN Old French.

villain •n. **1** a wicked person. **2** a bad character in a novel or play whose evil actions are important to the plot.
– DERIVATIVES **villainous** adj. **villainy** n. (pl. **villainies**).
– ORIGIN first meaning 'an unsophisti-cated country person': from Old French *vilein*.

villein /vil-luhn, vil-layn/ •n. (in medieval England) a poor man who had to work for a lord in return for a small piece of land on which to grow food.
– ORIGIN from **VILLAIN**.

villus /vil-luhss/ •n. (pl. **villi** /vil-ly/) any of many tiny finger-like growths of tissue on some membranes of the body, especially the small intestine.
– ORIGIN Latin, 'shaggy hair'.

vim •n. informal energy; enthusiasm.
– ORIGIN perh. from Latin *vis* 'energy'.

vinaigrette /vi-ni-gret, vi-nay-gret/ •n. a salad dressing of oil, wine vinegar, and seasoning.
– ORIGIN French.

vindaloo /vin-duh-loo/ •n. (pl. **vindaloos**) a very hot Indian curry.
– ORIGIN prob. from Portuguese *vin d'alho* 'wine and garlic sauce'.

vindicate /vin-di-kayt/ •v. (**vindicates, vindicating, vindicated**) **1** clear some-one of blame or suspicion. **2** show to be right or justified.
– DERIVATIVES **vindication** n.
– ORIGIN Latin *vindicare* 'claim, avenge'.

vindictive •adj. having a strong or spiteful desire for revenge.
– DERIVATIVES **vindictively** adv. **vindictiveness** n.
– ORIGIN Latin *vindicta* 'vengeance'.

vine •n. **1** a climbing plant, especially one that produces grapes. **2** the stem of a climbing plant.
– ORIGIN Latin *vinea* 'vineyard, vine'.

vinegar •n. a sour liquid made from wine, beer, or cider, used as a seasoning or for pickling.
– DERIVATIVES **vinegary** adj.
– ORIGIN from Old French *vyn egre* 'sour wine'.

vineyard /vin-yard/ •n. a plantation of grapevines, producing grapes used in winemaking.

vinification /vin-i-fi-kay-sh'n/ •n. the conversion of grape juice or other vegetable extract into wine by fermentation.

vino •n. (pl. **vinos**) informal, esp. Brit. wine, especially that which is cheap.
– ORIGIN Spanish and Italian, 'wine'.

vinous /vy-nuhss/ •adj. relating to or resembling wine.

vintage •n. **1** the year or place in which wine was produced. **2** a wine of high quality made from the crop of a single specified district in a good year. **3** the harvesting of grapes for winemaking. **4** the wine of a particular season. **5** the time that something was produced.
•adj. **1** referring to high-quality wine. **2** (of something from the past) of high quality: *a vintage film*.
– ORIGIN Old French *vendange*.

vintage car •n. Brit. an old car, specific-ally one made between 1919 and 1930.

vintner /vint-ner/ •n. a wine merchant.
– ORIGIN Old French *vinetier*.

vinyl /vy-n'l/ •n. a type of strong plastic, used in making floor coverings, paint, and gramophone records.
– ORIGIN Latin *vinum* 'wine'.

viol /vy-uhl/ •n. a musical instrument of the Renaissance and baroque periods, resembling a violin but with six strings.
– ORIGIN Provençal *viola*.

viola¹ /vi-oh-luh/ •n. an instrument of the violin family, larger than the violin and tuned a fifth lower.
– ORIGIN Italian and Spanish.

viola² /vy-uh-luh/ •n. a plant of a group that includes pansies and violets.
– ORIGIN Latin, 'violet'.

violate •v. (**violates, violating, violated**) **1** break a rule or formal agreement. **2** treat with disrespect. **3** esp. literary rape someone.
– DERIVATIVES **violation** n. **violator** n.
– ORIGIN Latin *violare* 'treat violently'.

violence •n. **1** behaviour involving physical force intended to hurt, damage, or kill. **2** the power of a destructive natural force. **2** strength of emotion.

violent •adj. **1** using or involving violence. **2** very forceful or powerful: *violent dislike*.
– DERIVATIVES **violently** adv.
– ORIGIN Latin, 'vehement, violent'.

violet •n. **1** a small plant with purple, blue, or white five-petalled flowers. **2** a bluish-purple colour.
– ORIGIN Old French *violette*.

violin •n. a musical instrument having

four strings, played with a bow.
– DERIVATIVES **violinist** n.
– ORIGIN Italian *violino* 'small viola'.

violist /vi-**oh**-list/ • n. a viola player.

violoncello /vy-uh-luhn-**chel**-loh/
• n. formal = CELLO.
– ORIGIN Italian.

VIP • n. a very important person.

viper • n. a poisonous snake with large
fangs and a patterned body.
– ORIGIN Latin *vipera*.

virago /vi-**rah**-goh/ • n. (pl. **viragos** or
viragoes) a domineering, violent, or
bad-tempered woman.
– ORIGIN Latin, 'heroic woman, female
warrior'.

viral • adj. relating to or caused by a virus
or viruses.
– DERIVATIVES **virally** adv.

virgin • n. 1 a person who has never had
sexual intercourse. 2 (**the Virgin**) the
Virgin Mary. 3 a person who is
inexperienced in a particular activity: *a
political virgin.* • adj. 1 having had no
sexual experience. 2 not yet used or
exploited: *virgin forest.* 3 (of olive oil)
made from the first pressing of olives.
– DERIVATIVES **virginal** adj.
– ORIGIN Latin *virgo*.

Virgin Birth • n. the Christian doctrine
of Jesus's birth from a mother, Mary,
who was a virgin.

Virginia creeper • n. a North American
climbing plant, grown for its red
autumn foliage.

virginity • n. the state of never having
had sexual intercourse.

Virgo • n. a constellation (the Virgin) and
sign of the zodiac, which the sun enters
about 23 August.
– DERIVATIVES **Virgoan** n. & adj.
– ORIGIN Latin.

viridian /vi-**rid**-i-uhn/ • n. a bluish-green
pigment or colour.
– ORIGIN Latin *viridis* 'green'.

virile • adj. (of a man) strong, energetic,
and having a strong sex drive.
– DERIVATIVES **virility** n.
– ORIGIN Latin *virilis*.

virology /vy-**rol**-uh-ji/ • n. the branch of
science concerned with the study of
viruses.
– DERIVATIVES **virological** adj. **virologist** n.

virtual • adj. 1 almost or nearly the thing
described, but not completely: *the virtual
absence of border controls.* 2 not existing
in reality but made by computer
software to appear to do so.
– DERIVATIVES **virtuality** n. **virtually** adv.
– ORIGIN Latin *virtualis*.

virtual reality • n. a system in which
images that look like real, three-

dimensional objects are created by
computer.

virtue /**ver**-tyoo/ • n. 1 behaviour
showing high moral standards. 2 a good
or desirable personal quality. 3 old use
virginity or chastity.
– PHRASES **by virtue of** as a result of.
– ORIGIN Latin *virtus* 'valour, merit'.

virtuoso /ver-tyoo-**oh**-soh/ • n. (pl.
virtuosi /ver-tyoo-**oh**-si/ or **virtuosos**) a
person highly skilled in music or
another art.
– DERIVATIVES **virtuosic** adj. **virtuosity** n.
– ORIGIN Italian, 'learned, skilful'.

virtuous • adj. 1 having high moral
standards. 2 old use chaste.
– DERIVATIVES **virtuously** adv.

virulent /vi-**ruu**-luhnt, vir-**yuu**-luhnt/
• adj. 1 (of a disease or poison) having a
very harmful effect. 2 (of a virus)
spreading very quickly. 3 bitterly
hostile: *a virulent attack.*
– DERIVATIVES **virulence** n. **virulently** adv.
– ORIGIN Latin *virulentus* 'poisonous'.

virus /**vy**-ruhss/ • n. 1 a submicroscopic
particle, typically consisting of nucleic
acid coated in protein, which can cause
infection or disease and can only
multiply within the cells of a host
organism. 2 an infection or disease
caused by a virus. 3 (also **computer
virus**) a piece of code introduced
secretly into a computer system in order
to damage or destroy data.
– ORIGIN Latin, 'slimy liquid, poison'.

visa /**vee**-zuh/ • n. a note on a passport
indicating that the holder is allowed to
enter, leave, or stay for a specified time
in a country.
– ORIGIN Latin.

visage /**vi**-zij/ • n. literary a person's facial
features or expression.
– ORIGIN Old French.

vis-à-vis /veez-ah-**vee**/ • prep. in
relation to.
– ORIGIN French, 'face to face'.

viscera /**viss**-uh-ruh/ • pl. n. the internal
organs of the body, especially those in
the abdomen.
– ORIGIN Latin.

visceral • adj. 1 relating to the body's
internal organs. 2 relating to deep
inward feelings rather than to the
intellect.
– DERIVATIVES **viscerally** adv.

viscid /**viss**-id/ • adj. having a sticky
consistency.
– ORIGIN Latin *viscidus*.

viscose /**viss**-kohz, **viss**-kohss/ • n. rayon
fabric made from treating cellulose with
certain chemicals.
– ORIGIN Latin *viscus* 'birdlime'.

viscosity /viss-**koss**-i-ti/ • n. (pl.

V

viscosities) the state of being thick, sticky, and semi-fluid in consistency.

viscount /vy-kownt/ • n. a British nobleman ranking above a baron and below an earl.
– ORIGIN Latin *vicecomes*.

viscountess /vy-kown-tiss/ • n. the wife or widow of a viscount, or a woman holding the rank of viscount in her own right.

viscous /viss-kuhss/ • adj. having a thick, sticky consistency between solid and liquid.
– ORIGIN Latin *viscosus*.

vise • n. US = VICE².

visibility • n. 1 the state of being able to see or be seen. 2 the distance that a person can see, depending on light and weather conditions.

visible • adj. able to be seen or noticed.
– DERIVATIVES **visibly** adv.
– ORIGIN Latin *visibilis*.

vision • n. 1 the ability to see. 2 the ability to think about the future with imagination or wisdom. 3 an experience of seeing something in the mind, or in a dream or trance. 4 the images seen on a television screen. 5 a person or sight of great beauty.
– ORIGIN Latin.

visionary • adj. 1 thinking about the future with imagination or wisdom. 2 relating to supernatural or dreamlike visions. • n. (pl. **visionaries**) a person with imaginative and original ideas about the future.

visit • v. (**visits, visiting, visited**) 1 go to see and spend time with someone. 2 go to see and spend time in a place. 3 access and view a website or web page. 4 literary cause something harmful or unpleasant to affect someone: *they were visited with an epidemic.* • n. 1 an act of visiting. 2 a temporary stay at a place.
– ORIGIN Latin *visitare*.

visitant • n. 1 literary a ghost. 2 old use a visitor.

visitation • n. 1 an official or formal visit. 2 the appearance of a god or goddess, or other supernatural being. 3 a disaster or difficulty seen as a punishment from God: *a visitation of the plague.* 4 (**the Visitation**) the visit of the Virgin Mary to Elizabeth related in the Gospel of Luke, chapter 1.

visitor • n. 1 a person visiting a person or place. 2 a bird present in a particular area for only part of the year.

visor /vy-zer/ (also **vizor**) • n. 1 a movable part of a helmet that can be pulled down to cover the face. 2 a screen for protecting the eyes from unwanted

light. 3 N. Amer. a peak at the front of a cap.
– ORIGIN Old French *viser*.

vista • n. a pleasing view.
– ORIGIN Italian, 'view'.

visual • adj. relating to seeing or sight. • n. a picture, piece of film, or display used to illustrate or accompany something.
– DERIVATIVES **visually** adv.
– ORIGIN Latin *visualis*.

visual display unit • n. Brit. a device for displaying information from a computer on a screen.

visualize (or **visualise**) • v. (**visualizes, visualizing, visualized**) form an image of something in the mind.
– DERIVATIVES **visualization** n. **visualizer** n.

vital • adj. 1 absolutely necessary. 2 essential for life: *the vital organs.* 3 full of energy. • n. (**vitals**) the body's important internal organs.
– DERIVATIVES **vitally** adv.
– ORIGIN Latin *vitalis*.

vitality • n. the state of being strong and active.

vitalize (or **vitalise**) • v. (**vitalizes, vitalizing, vitalized**) give strength and energy to.

vital signs • pl. n. measurements, specifically pulse rate, temperature, rate of breathing, and blood pressure, that indicate the state of a patient's essential body functions.

vital statistics • pl. n. informal the measurements of a woman's bust, waist, and hips.

vitamin /vi-tuh-min, vy-tuh-min/ • n. any of a group of organic compounds which are present in many foods and are essential for normal nutrition.
– ORIGIN from Latin *vita* 'life' + *amine*, because vitamins were originally thought to contain an amino acid.

vitamin A • n. retinol, a compound which is essential for growth and vision in dim light and is found in vegetables, egg yolk, and fish liver oil.

vitamin B • n. any of a group of substances essential for the working of certain enzymes in the body.

vitamin C • n. ascorbic acid, a compound found in citrus fruits and green vegetables, essential in maintaining healthy connective tissue.

vitamin D • n. any of a group of compounds found in liver and fish oils, essential for the absorption of calcium.

vitamin E • n. tocopherol, a compound found in wheatgerm oil, egg yolk, and leafy vegetables and important in stabilizing cell membranes.

vitamin K •n. any of a group of compounds found mainly in green leaves and essential for the blood-clotting process.

vitiate /vi-shi-ayt/ •v. (**vitiates, vitiating, vitiated**) formal make something less good or effective.
– ORIGIN Latin *vitiare* 'impair'.

viticulture /vi-ti-kul-cher/ •n. **1** the cultivation of grapevines. **2** the study of grape cultivation.
– DERIVATIVES **viticultural** adj. **viticulturist** n.
– ORIGIN from Latin *vitis* 'vine'.

vitreous /vi-tri-uhss/ •adj. resembling or containing glass.
– ORIGIN Latin *vitreus*.

vitreous humour •n. the transparent jelly-like tissue filling the eyeball behind the lens.

vitrify /vi-tri-fy/ •v. (**vitrifies, vitrifying, vitrified**) convert into glass or a glass-like substance by exposure to heat.
– DERIVATIVES **vitrification** n.
– ORIGIN Latin *vitrum* 'glass'.

vitriol /vi-tri-uhl/ •n. **1** extreme bitterness or malice. **2** old use sulphuric acid.
– DERIVATIVES **vitriolic** adj.
– ORIGIN Latin *vitriolum*.

vituperation /vi-tyoo-puh-ray-sh'n/ •n. bitter and abusive language.
– DERIVATIVES **vituperative** adj.
– ORIGIN Latin.

viva[1] /vee-vuh/ •exclam. long live! (used to express praise or support).
– ORIGIN Italian.

viva[2] /vy-vuh/ (also **viva voce** /vy-vuh voh-chi/) •n. Brit. an oral exam for an academic qualification.
– ORIGIN Latin *viva voce* 'with the living voice'.

vivace /vi-vah-chay/ •adv. & adj. Music in a lively and brisk way.
– ORIGIN Italian.

vivacious /vi-vay-shuhss, vy-vay-shuhss/ •adj. attractively lively.
– DERIVATIVES **vivaciously** adv. **vivacity** /vi-vas-it-i/ n.
– ORIGIN Latin *vivax* 'lively, vigorous'.

vivarium /vi-vair-i-uhm, vy-vair-i-uhm/ •n. (pl. **vivaria** /vi-vair-i-uh, vy-vair-i-uh/) a place for keeping animals in conditions similar to their natural environment for study or as pets.
– ORIGIN Latin, 'warren, fish pond'.

vivid •adj. **1** producing powerful feelings or strong, clear images in the mind: *a vivid description.* **2** (of a colour) very deep or bright.
– DERIVATIVES **vividly** adv. **vividness** n.

– ORIGIN Latin *vividus* 'lively, vigorous'.

vivify /vi-vi-fy/ •v. (**vivifies, vivifying, vivified**) make more lively or interesting.
– ORIGIN Latin *vivificare*.

viviparous /vi-vip-uh-ruhss/ •adj. (of an animal) giving birth to live young which have developed inside the body of the parent. Compare with **OVIPAROUS**.
– ORIGIN Latin *viviparus*.

vivisection •n. the practice of operating on live animals for scientific research (used by people opposed to such work).
– ORIGIN Latin *vivus* 'living'.

vixen •n. **1** a female fox. **2** a spirited or quarrelsome woman.
– ORIGIN perh. from Old English, 'of a fox'.

Viyella /vy-el-luh/ •n. trademark a fabric made from a mixture of cotton and wool.
– ORIGIN from *Via Gellia*, a valley in Derbyshire.

viz. •adv. namely; in other words.
– ORIGIN short for Latin *videlicet*.

vizier /vi-zeer/ •n. hist. an important official in some Muslim countries.
– ORIGIN Arabic.

vizor •n. var. of **VISOR**.

VLF •abbrev. very low frequency (referring to radio waves of frequency 3–30 kilohertz and wavelength 10–100 kilometres).

V-neck •n. a neckline that has straight sides meeting at a point to form a V shape.
– DERIVATIVES **V-necked** adj.

vocabulary •n. (pl. **vocabularies**) **1** all the words used in a particular language or activity. **2** all the words known to an individual person. **3** a list of words and their meanings, accompanying a piece of specialist or foreign writing.
– ORIGIN Latin *vocabularius*.

> ☑ The ending of **vocabulary** is **-ary**.

vocal •adj. **1** relating to the human voice. **2** expressing opinions or feelings freely or loudly. **3** (of music) consisting of or including singing. •n. (also **vocals**) a part of a piece of music that is sung.
– DERIVATIVES **vocally** adv.
– ORIGIN Latin *vocalis*.

vocal cords •pl. n. the folds of the lining of the larynx that vibrate in the airstream to produce the voice.

vocalist •n. a singer.

vocalize /voh-kuh-lyz/ (or **vocalise**) •v. (**vocalizes, vocalizing, vocalized**) **1** produce a sound or word. **2** express something with words. **3** sing with

several notes to one vowel.
– DERIVATIVES **vocalization** n.

vocation • n. **1** a strong feeling that you ought to pursue a particular career or occupation. **2** a person's career or occupation.
– ORIGIN Latin.

vocational • adj. relating to a particular occupation and its skills or knowledge.
– DERIVATIVES **vocationally** adv.

vocative /vok-uh-tiv/ • n. Grammar the case used in addressing a person or thing.
– ORIGIN Latin *vocativus*.

vociferous /vuh-sif-uh-ruhss/ • adj. expressing opinions in a loud and forceful way: *he was a vociferous opponent of the takeover.*
– DERIVATIVES **vociferously** adv.
– ORIGIN Latin *vociferari* 'exclaim'.

vodka • n. a clear Russian alcoholic spirit made from rye, wheat, or potatoes.
– ORIGIN Russian, 'little water'.

vogue • n. the fashion or style current at a particular time.
– DERIVATIVES **voguish** adj.
– ORIGIN French.

voice • n. **1** the sound produced in a person's larynx and uttered through the mouth, as speech or song. **2** the ability to speak or sing. **3** the range of pitch or type of tone with which a person sings, e.g. soprano. **4** a vocal part in a musical composition. **5** an opinion or the right to express an opinion. **6** Grammar a form of a verb showing the relation of the subject to the action. • v. (**voices, voicing, voiced**) **1** express in words. **2** (as adj. **voiced**) (of a speech sound) produced with vibration of the vocal cords.
– ORIGIN Old French *vois*.

voice box • n. the larynx.

voiceless • adj. (of a speech sound) produced without vibration of the vocal cords.

voicemail • n. a centralized electronic system which can store messages from telephone callers.

voice-over • n. a piece of speech giving information in a film or broadcast that is spoken by a person who is not seen on the screen.

void • adj. **1** not valid or legally binding. **2** completely empty. **3** (**void of**) free from; lacking. • n. a completely empty space. • v. **1** discharge or drain away water, gases, or waste matter. **2** esp. N. Amer. declare to be no longer valid.
– ORIGIN Old French *vuide*.

voila /vwa-lah/ • exclam. there it is; there you are.
– ORIGIN French *voilà*.

voile /voyl, vwahl/ • n. a thin, semi-transparent fabric.
– ORIGIN French, 'veil'.

VOIP • abbrev. voice over Internet protocol, a technology for making telephone calls over the Internet in which speech sounds are converted into binary data.

volatile /vol-uh-tyl/ • adj. **1** liable to change rapidly and unpredictably: *volatile currency markets.* **2** (of a substance) easily evaporated at normal temperatures. • n. a substance that is easily evaporated at normal temperatures.
– DERIVATIVES **volatility** n.
– ORIGIN Latin *volare* 'to fly'.

vol-au-vent /vol-oh-von/ • n. a small round case of puff pastry filled with a savoury mixture.
– ORIGIN French, 'flight in the wind'.

volcanic • adj. relating to or produced by a volcano or volcanoes.
– DERIVATIVES **volcanically** adv.

volcanism (also **vulcanism**) • n. volcanic activity or phenomena.

volcano • n. (pl. **volcanoes** or **volcanos**) a mountain that has a crater or opening through which lava, rock, hot vapour, and gas are or have been forced from the earth's crust.
– ORIGIN Latin *Volcanus* 'Vulcan', the Roman god of fire.

vole • n. a small mouse-like rodent with a rounded muzzle.
– ORIGIN Norwegian *vollmus* 'field mouse'.

volition /vuh-li-sh'n/ • n. a person's power to choose freely and make their own decisions.
– DERIVATIVES **volitional** adj.
– ORIGIN Latin.

volley • n. (pl. **volleys**) **1** a number of bullets, arrows, or other missiles fired at one time. **2** a series of questions, insults, etc. directed rapidly at someone. **3** (in sport) a hit of the ball made before it touches the ground. • v. (**volleys, volleying, volleyed**) hit the ball before it touches the ground.
– DERIVATIVES **volleyer** n.
– ORIGIN French *volée*.

volleyball • n. a team game in which a ball is hit by hand over a net and points are scored if the ball touches the ground on the opponent's side of the court.

volt • n. the SI unit of electromotive force, the difference of potential that would carry one ampere of current against a resistance of one ohm.
– ORIGIN named after the Italian physicist Alessandro *Volta*.

voltage • n. an electromotive force or

potential difference expressed in volts.

voltaic /vol-**tay**-ik/ •adj. referring to electricity produced by chemical action in a primary battery.

volte-face /volt-**fass**/ •n. an abrupt and complete reversal of attitude or policy.
– ORIGIN French.

voltmeter •n. an instrument for measuring electric potential in volts.

voluble /vol-yuu-b'l/ •adj. speaking easily and at length.
– DERIVATIVES **volubility** n. **volubly** adv.
– ORIGIN Latin *volvere* 'to roll'.

volume •n. **1** the amount of space occupied by a substance or object or enclosed within a container. **2** the amount of something: *the growing volume of traffic.* **3** degree of loudness. **4** a book, especially one forming part of a larger work or series. **5** fullness of the hair.
– ORIGIN first referring to a roll of parchment with writing on: from Latin *volumen* 'a roll'.

volumetric /vol-yuu-**met**-rik/ •adj. relating to the measurement of volume.
– DERIVATIVES **volumetrically** adv.

voluminous /vuh-**loo**-mi-nuhss/ •adj. **1** (of clothing) loose and full. **2** (of writing) very lengthy.
– DERIVATIVES **voluminously** adv.
– ORIGIN from Latin *voluminosus* 'having many coils' or *volumen* 'a roll'.

volumize (or **volumise**) •v. (**volumizes**, **volumizing**, **volumized**) give volume or body to hair.

voluntary •adj. **1** done or acting of your own free will. **2** working or done without payment. **3** under the conscious control of the brain. •n. (pl. **voluntaries**) an organ solo played before, during, or after a church service.
– DERIVATIVES **voluntarily** adv.
– ORIGIN Latin *voluntarius*.

volunteer •n. **1** a person who freely offers to do something. **2** a person who works for an organization without being paid. **3** a person who freely joins the armed forces. •v. (**volunteers**, **volunteering**, **volunteered**) **1** freely offer to do something. **2** say or suggest something without being asked.
– ORIGIN French *volontaire* 'voluntary'.

voluptuary /vuh-**lup**-tyuu-uh-ri, vuh-**lup**-chuu-uh-ri/ •n. (pl. **voluptuaries**) a person who enjoys sensual or sexual pleasure very much.
– ORIGIN Latin *voluptuarius*.

voluptuous /vuh-**lup**-tyuu-uhss, vuh-**lup**-chuu-uhss/ •adj. **1** (of a woman) having a full, sexually attractive body. **2** giving sensual pleasure.
– DERIVATIVES **voluptuously** adv. **voluptuousness** n.
– ORIGIN Latin *voluptuosus*.

vomit •v. (**vomits**, **vomiting**, **vomited**) **1** bring up food and other matter from the stomach through the mouth. **2** send out something in an uncontrolled stream. •n. food and other matter vomited from the stomach.
– ORIGIN Latin *vomere* 'to vomit'.

voodoo •n. a religious cult of African origin practised chiefly in the Caribbean, involving sorcery, possession by spirits, and elements of Roman Catholic ritual.
– ORIGIN from an African language.

voracious /vuh-**ray**-shuhss/ •adj. **1** wanting or eating great quantities of food. **2** doing something eagerly and enthusiastically: *his voracious reading of literature.*
– DERIVATIVES **voraciously** adv. **voracity** /vuh-**ras**-it-i/ n.
– ORIGIN Latin *vorax*.

-vorous /vuh-ruhss/ •comb. form feeding on a specified food: *carnivorous.*
– DERIVATIVES **-vore** comb. form.
– ORIGIN Latin *vorare* 'devour'.

vortex /**vor**-teks/ •n. (pl. **vortexes** or **vortices** /**vor**-ti-seez/) a whirling mass of water or air.
– ORIGIN Latin, 'eddy'.

votary /**voh**-tuh-ri/ •n. (pl. **votaries**) **1** a person who has taken vows to dedicate their life to God or religious service. **2** a devoted follower or supporter: *a votary of the arts.*
– ORIGIN Latin *vovere* 'vow'.

vote •n. **1** a formal indication of a choice between two or more candidates or courses of action. **2** (**the vote**) the right to participate in an election. **3** (**the vote**) a particular group of voters or the votes cast by them: *the green vote.* •v. (**votes**, **voting**, **voted**) give or register a vote.
– PHRASES **vote of** (**no**) **confidence** a vote showing that a majority continues to support (or no longer supports) the policy of a leader or governing body.
– DERIVATIVES **voter** n.
– ORIGIN Latin *votum* 'a vow, wish'.

votive •adj. offered to a god as a sign of gratitude.
– ORIGIN Latin *votivus*.

vouch •v. (**vouch for**) **1** confirm that something is true or accurate. **2** say that someone is who they claim to be or that they are reliable or honest.
– ORIGIN Old French *voucher* 'summon'.

voucher •n. a piece of paper that entitles the holder to a discount, or that may be exchanged for goods or services.

vouchsafe • v. (**vouchsafes, vouchsafing, vouchsafed**) give or say in a gracious or superior way.
– ORIGIN first as *vouch* something *safe* on someone, i.e. 'guarantee that something is granted to someone'.

vow • n. a solemn promise. • v. solemnly promise to do something.
– ORIGIN Old French *vou*.

vowel • n. **1** a speech sound in which the mouth is open and the tongue is not touching the top of the mouth, the teeth, or the lips. **2** a letter representing a vowel, such as *a, e, i, o, u.*
– ORIGIN Old French *vouel*.

vox pop • n. Brit. informal popular opinion as represented by informal comments from members of the public.
– ORIGIN short for Latin *vox populi* 'the people's voice'.

voyage • n. a long journey by sea or in space. • v. (**voyages, voyaging, voyaged**) go on a voyage.
– DERIVATIVES **voyager** n.
– ORIGIN Old French *voiage*.

voyeur /vwa-yer, voy-er/ • n. **1** a person who gains sexual pleasure from watching other people when they are naked or taking part in sexual activity. **2** a person who enjoys seeing the pain or distress of other people.
– DERIVATIVES **voyeurism** n. **voyeuristic** adj. **voyeuristically** adv.
– ORIGIN French.

vs • abbrev. versus.

V-sign • n. Brit. a rude gesture made by holding up the hand with the back facing outwards and making a V shape with the first two fingers.

VSO • abbrev. Voluntary Service Overseas.

vulcanism • n. var. of VOLCANISM.

vulcanite /vul-kuh-nyt/ • n. hard black vulcanized rubber.
– ORIGIN from *Vulcan*, the Roman god of fire.

vulcanize (or **vulcanise**) • v. (**vulcanizes, vulcanizing, vulcanized**) harden rubber by treating it with sulphur at a high temperature.
– DERIVATIVES **vulcanization** n.

vulgar • adj. **1** lacking sophistication or good taste. **2** referring to sex or bodily functions in a rude way. **3** dated relating to ordinary people.
– DERIVATIVES **vulgarity** n. (pl. **vulgarities**). **vulgarly** adv.
– ORIGIN Latin *vulgaris*.

vulgar fraction • n. Brit. a fraction shown by numerator and denominator (numbers above and below the line), not decimally.

vulgarian /vul-gair-i-uhn/ • n. a person who lacks good taste and sophistication.

vulgarism • n. a word or expression that refers to sex or bodily functions in a rude way.

vulgarize (or **vulgarise**) • v. (**vulgarizes, vulgarizing, vulgarized**) spoil something by making it ordinary or less refined.
– DERIVATIVES **vulgarization** n.

Vulgate /vul-gayt/ • n. the main Latin version of the Bible, prepared in the 4th century and later revised and adopted as the official version for the Roman Catholic Church.
– ORIGIN from Latin *vulgata editio* 'edition prepared for the public'.

vulnerable /vul-nuh-ruh-b'l/ • adj. exposed to being attacked or harmed.
– DERIVATIVES **vulnerability** n. (pl. **vulnerabilities**). **vulnerably** adv.
– ORIGIN Latin *vulnerabilis*.

> ✓ Remember that **vulnerable** is spelled with an **l** before the **n**.

vulpine /vul-pyn/ • adj. relating to or resembling a fox or foxes.
– ORIGIN Latin *vulpinus*.

vulture /vul-cher/ • n. **1** a large bird of prey without feathers on the head and neck, that feeds on dead animals. **2** a person who tries to benefit from the difficulties of other people.
– ORIGIN Latin *vulturius*.

vulva /vul-vuh/ • n. the female external genitals.
– ORIGIN Latin, 'womb'.

vying pres. part. of VIE.

Ww

W¹ (also **w**) • n. (pl. **Ws** or **W's**) the twenty-third letter of the alphabet.

W² • abbrev. **1** watt(s). **2** West or Western. • symb. the chemical element tungsten. [ORIGIN Latin *wolframium*.]

w • abbrev. with.

wacko (also **whacko**) informal, esp. N. Amer. • adj. mad; insane. • n. (pl. **wackos** or **wackoes**) a mad person.

wacky (also **whacky**) • adj. (**wackier**, **wackiest**) informal funny or amusing in a slightly odd way.
– DERIVATIVES **wackily** adv. **wackiness** n.
– ORIGIN from **WHACK**.

wad /wod/ • n. **1** a lump or bundle of a soft material, used for padding, stuffing, or wiping. **2** a bundle of paper or banknotes. • v. (**wads**, **wadding**, **wadded**) **1** compress a soft material into a wad. **2** line or fill with soft material.
– DERIVATIVES **wadding** n.
– ORIGIN perh. from Dutch *watten* or French *ouate* 'padding'.

waddle • v. (**waddles**, **waddling**, **waddled**) walk with short steps and a clumsy swaying motion. • n. a waddling way of walking.
– ORIGIN perh. from **WADE**.

wade • v. (**wades**, **wading**, **waded**) **1** walk through water or mud. **2** (**wade through**) read through a long piece of writing with effort. **3** (**wade in/into**) informal attack or intervene in a forceful way.
– ORIGIN Old English, 'move onward'.

wader • n. **1** a long-legged bird that feeds in shallow water. **2** (**waders**) high waterproof boots, used by anglers.

wadi /wah-di, wod-i/ • n. (pl. **wadis**) (in Arabic-speaking countries) a valley, ravine, or channel that is dry except in the rainy season.
– ORIGIN Arabic.

wafer • n. **1** a very thin, light, crisp sweet biscuit. **2** a thin disc of unleavened bread used in the service of Holy Communion. **3** a very thin slice of a semiconductor crystal used in solid-state electric circuits.
– ORIGIN Old French *gaufre* 'honeycomb'.

wafer-thin • adj. very thin or thinly.

waffle¹ Brit. informal • v. (**waffles**, **waffling**, **waffled**) speak or write at length in a vague or trivial way. • n. lengthy but vague or trivial talk or writing.
– DERIVATIVES **waffler** n. **waffly** adj.
– ORIGIN from dialect *waff* 'yelp'.

waffle² • n. a small crisp batter cake, eaten hot with butter or syrup.
– ORIGIN Dutch *wafel*.

waft /woft/ • v. **1** move easily or gently through the air. **2** move along with a gliding motion: • n. **1** a scent carried in the air. **2** a gentle movement of air.
– ORIGIN German or Dutch *wachten* 'to guard'.

wag¹ • v. (**wags**, **wagging**, **wagged**) move rapidly to and fro. • n. a wagging movement.
– ORIGIN Old English, 'to sway'.

wag² • n. informal a person who likes making jokes.
– ORIGIN prob. from former *waghalter* 'person likely to be hanged'.

wage • n. (also **wages**) **1** a fixed regular payment for work. **2** the result or effect of doing something wrong: *disasters are the wages of sin.* • v. (**wages**, **waging**, **wages**) carry on a war or campaign.
– ORIGIN Old French.

wager • n. & v. = BET.
– ORIGIN Old French, 'to wage'.

waggish • adj. informal humorous in a playful way.

waggle • v. (**waggles**, **waggling**, **waggled**) move with short quick movements from side to side or up and down. • n. an act of waggling.
– DERIVATIVES **waggler** n. **waggly** adj.
– ORIGIN from **WAG¹**.

wagon (Brit. also **waggon**) • n. **1** a vehicle, especially a horse-drawn one, for transporting goods. **2** Brit. a railway vehicle for carrying goods in bulk.
– PHRASES **on** (or **off**) **the wagon** informal drinking (or not drinking) any alcohol.
– DERIVATIVES **wagoner** n.
– ORIGIN Dutch *wagen*.

w

wagtail • n. a slender songbird with a long tail that wags up and down.

waif • n. 1 a homeless and helpless person, especially a child. 2 a person who appears thin or pale.
– DERIVATIVES **waiflike** adj.
– ORIGIN first referring to an unclaimed piece of property: from Old French *gaif*.

wail • n. 1 a long high-pitched cry of pain, grief, or anger. 2 a long high-pitched sound. • v. make a long high-pitched cry or sound.
– DERIVATIVES **wailer** n.
– ORIGIN Old Norse.

wain • n. old use a wagon or cart.
– ORIGIN Old English.

wainscot /wayn-skot, wayn-skuht/ (also **wainscoting** or **wainscotting**) • n. an area of wooden panelling on the lower part of the walls of a room.
– ORIGIN German *wagenschot*.

waist • n. 1 the part of the body below the ribs and above the hips. 2 a narrow part in the middle of something such as a violin.
– ORIGIN prob. from Old English.

waistband • n. a strip of cloth forming the waist of a skirt or a pair of trousers.

waistcoat /wayst-koht, wess-kit/ • n. Brit. a close-fitting waist-length item of clothing with buttons down the front and no sleeves or collar.

waistline • n. the measurement around a person's body at the waist.

wait • v. 1 stay where you are or delay action until a particular time or event. 2 be delayed or postponed. 3 (**wait on**) act as an attendant to. 4 serve food and drink to people at a meal or in a restaurant. • n. a period of waiting.
– PHRASES **in wait** watching for someone and preparing to attack them.
– ORIGIN Old French *waitier*.

waiter (or **waitress**) • n. a person whose job is to serve customers at their tables in a restaurant.

waiting list • n. a list of people waiting for something that is not immediately available, such as housing.

waive • v. (**waives, waiving, waived**) choose not to insist on or demand a right or claim.
– ORIGIN Old French *gaiver* 'allow to become a waif, abandon'.

waiver • n. 1 an act of not insisting on a right or claim. 2 a document recording this.

wake[1] • v. (**wakes, waking, woke**; past part. **woken**) 1 (often **wake up**) stop or cause to stop sleeping. 2 bring to life; stir: *his voice wakes desire.* 3 (**wake up to**) become alert to or aware of. • n. a

watch held beside the body of someone who has died. 2 a party held after a funeral.
– ORIGIN Old English.

wake[2] • n. a trail of disturbed water or air left by the passage of a ship or aircraft.
– PHRASES **in the wake of** following as a result of.
– ORIGIN prob. from Old Norse, 'hole or opening in ice'.

wakeful • adj. 1 unable or not needing to sleep. 2 alert and aware of possible dangers.
– DERIVATIVES **wakefulness** n.

waken • v. wake from sleep.
– ORIGIN Old English, 'be aroused'.

walk • v. 1 move at a fairly slow pace using the legs. 2 travel over a route or area on foot. 3 accompany someone on foot. 4 take a dog out for exercise. • n. 1 a journey on foot. 2 an unhurried rate of movement on foot. 3 a person's way of walking. 4 a path for walking.
– PHRASES **walk off with** (or **away with**) informal 1 steal something. 2 win something. **walk of life** the position within society that someone holds. **walk over** informal 1 treat someone unfairly or thoughtlessly. 2 defeat someone easily.
– DERIVATIVES **walker** n.
– ORIGIN Old English, 'roll, wander'.

walkabout • n. 1 esp. Brit. an informal stroll among a crowd conducted by an important visitor. 2 a journey (originally on foot) undertaken by an Australian Aboriginal in order to live in the traditional way.

walkie-talkie • n. a portable two-way radio.

walk-in • adj. (of a storage area) large enough to walk into.

walking stick • n. a stick with a curved handle used for support when walking.

Walkman • n. (pl. **Walkmans** or **Walkmen**) trademark a type of personal stereo.

walk-on • adj. (of a part in a play or film) small and not involving any speaking.

walkout • n. a sudden angry departure as a protest or strike.

walkover • n. an easy victory.

walkway • n. a raised passageway in a building, or a wide path outdoors.

wall • n. 1 a continuous upright structure forming a side of a building or room, or enclosing or dividing an area of land. 2 a barrier: *a wall of silence.* 3 Football a line of defenders forming a barrier against a free kick taken near the penalty area. 4 the outer layer or lining of a body

organ or cavity. • v. enclose or block by building a wall.
– PHRASES **drive someone** (or **go**) **up the wall** informal make someone (or become) very irritated. **go to the wall** informal (of a business) fail. **wall-to-wall 1** (of a carpet) fitted to cover an entire floor. **2** informal very numerous or plentiful.
– DERIVATIVES **walling** n.
– ORIGIN Latin *vallum* 'rampart'.

wallaby • n. (pl. **wallabies**) an Australian marsupial resembling a small kangaroo.
– ORIGIN Dharuk (an Aboriginal language).

wallah /wol-luh/ • n. Ind. or informal a person of a specified kind or having a specified role: *an office wallah*.
– ORIGIN from Hindi, 'doer, fellow'.

wall bars • pl. n. Brit. parallel horizontal bars attached to the wall of a gymnasium, on which exercises are performed.

wallet • n. a pocket-sized, flat, folding holder for money and plastic cards.
– ORIGIN prob. from Germanic.

wall-eyed • adj. having an eye or eyes that squint outwards.
– ORIGIN Old Norse.

wallflower • n. **1** a plant with sweet-smelling flowers that bloom in early spring. **2** informal a girl who does not have a man to dance with at a dance or party.

Walloon /wol-loon/ • n. **1** a member of a people who speak a French dialect and live in southern and eastern Belgium and neighbouring parts of France. **2** the French dialect spoken by the Walloons.
– ORIGIN French *Wallon*.

wallop informal • v. (**wallops, walloping, walloped**) **1** hit very hard. **2** heavily defeat an opponent. • n. a heavy blow.
– ORIGIN Old French *waloper* 'to gallop'.

wallow • v. **1** roll about or lie in mud or water. **2** (of a boat or aircraft) roll from side to side. **3** (**wallow in**) indulge without restraint in something enjoyable. • n. **1** an act of wallowing. **2** an area of mud or shallow water where mammals go to wallow.
– ORIGIN Old English.

wallpaper • n. **1** paper pasted in strips over the walls of a room to provide a decorative surface. **2** an optional background pattern or picture on a computer or mobile phone screen.
• v. (**wallpapers, wallpapering, wallpapered**) apply wallpaper to a wall or room.

wally • n. (pl. **wallies**) Brit. informal a silly or incompetent person.
– ORIGIN perh. a shortened form of the man's name *Walter*.

walnut • n. **1** an edible wrinkled nut with a hard round shell. **2** the tree which produces walnuts, with valuable ornamental wood.
– ORIGIN Old English.

walrus • n. a large sea mammal with two large downward-pointing tusks, found in the Arctic Ocean.
– ORIGIN prob. Dutch.

waltz /wawlts, wolts/ • n. a ballroom dance in triple time performed by a couple, who turn round and round as they progress around the dance floor.
• v. **1** dance a waltz. **2** move or behave in a casual or inconsiderate way: *she waltzed in and took all the credit.*
– ORIGIN German *Walzer*.

waltzer • n. a fairground ride in which cars spin round as they are carried round a track that moves up and down.

wan /won/ • adj. **1** (of a person) pale and appearing ill or exhausted. **2** (of light) pale. **3** (of a smile) weak or strained.
– DERIVATIVES **wanly** adv.
– ORIGIN Old English, 'dark'.

wand • n. **1** a rod used in casting magic spells or performing tricks. **2** a rod held as a symbol of office. **3** a hand-held electronic device passed over a bar code to read the data.
– ORIGIN Old Norse.

wander • v. (**wanders, wandering, wandered**) **1** walk or move in a leisurely, casual, or aimless way. **2** move slowly away from a fixed point or place: *please don't wander off again.* • n. an act or spell of wandering.
– DERIVATIVES **wanderer** n.
– ORIGIN Old English.

wanderlust • n. a strong desire to travel.
– ORIGIN German.

wane • v. (**wanes, waning, waned**) **1** (of the moon) appear to become smaller each day through having a decreasing area of its surface illuminated. **2** (of a state or feeling) become weaker.
– PHRASES **on the wane** becoming weaker.
– ORIGIN Old English, 'lessen'.

wangle • v. (**wangles, wangling, wangled**) informal obtain something desired by trickery or persuasion.

wannabe /won-nuh-bee/ • n. informal, derog. a person who tries to be like someone famous.

want • v. **1** feel a need or desire to have or do. **2** (**be wanted**) (of a suspected criminal) be sought by the police. **3** informal ought or need to do something: *you don't want to believe all you hear.* **4** (often **want for**) literary lack something desirable or essential. **5** desire someone

sexually. **6** informal, esp. Brit. (of a thing) need something to be done: *the wheel wants greasing.* • n. **1** lack or shortage. **2** the state of being poor; poverty. **3** a desire.
– ORIGIN Old Norse, 'be lacking'.

wanting • adj. **1** lacking in something required or desired. **2** not good enough: *workers who are found wanting face dismissal.*

wanton /won-t'n/ • adj. **1** (of a cruel or violent action) deliberate and unprovoked. **2** having many sexual partners.
– DERIVATIVES **wantonly** adv. **wantonness** n.
– ORIGIN from former *wan-* 'badly' + Old English *togen* 'trained'.

WAP • abbrev. Wireless Application Protocol, a means of enabling a mobile phone to browse the Internet and display data.

wapiti /wop-i-ti/ • n. (pl. **wapitis**) a large North American red deer.
– ORIGIN Shawnee (an American Indian language), 'white rump'.

War. • abbrev. Warwickshire.

war • n. **1** a state of armed conflict between different nations, states, or groups. **2** a prolonged contest between rivals or campaign against something undesirable: *a war on drugs.* • v. (**wars, warring, warred**) engage in a war.
– PHRASES **be on the warpath** be very angry with someone.
– ORIGIN Old French *guerre*.

warble • v. (**warbles, warbling, warbled**) **1** (of a bird) sing with constantly changing notes. **2** (of a person) sing in a trilling or quavering voice. • n. a warbling sound.
– ORIGIN Old French *werbler*.

warbler • n. a small songbird with a warbling song, typically living in trees and bushes.

war chest • n. a reserve of funds used for fighting a war.

war crime • n. an act carried out during a war that violates accepted international rules of war.

ward • n. **1** a room or division in a hospital for one or more patients. **2** a division of a city or borough that is represented by a councillor or councillors. **3** a young person under the care and control of a guardian appointed by their parents or a court. **4** any of the ridges or bars in a lock which prevent the turning of any key without corresponding grooves. • v. (**ward someone/thing off**) prevent someone or something from harming or affecting you.

– ORIGIN Old English, 'keep safe, guard'.

-ward (also **-wards**) • suffix **1** (usu. **-wards**) (forming adverbs) towards the specified place or direction: *homewards.* **2** (usu. **-ward**) (forming adjectives) turned or tending towards: *upward.*
– ORIGIN Old English.

warden • n. **1** a person responsible for supervising a particular place or procedure. **2** Brit. the head of certain schools, colleges, or other institutions. **3** esp. N. Amer. a prison governor.
– ORIGIN Old French *wardein, guarden* 'guardian'.

warder • n. (fem. **wardress**) esp. Brit. a prison guard.
– ORIGIN Old French *warder* 'to guard'.

wardrobe • n. **1** a large, tall cupboard for hanging clothes in. **2** a person's entire collection of clothes. **3** the costume department or costumes of a theatre or film company.
– ORIGIN Old French *warderobe, garderobe* 'private chamber'.

wardroom • n. a room on a warship where commissioned officers eat.

-wards • suffix var. of **-WARD**.

ware • n. **1** pottery of a specified type: *porcelain ware.* **2** manufactured articles of a specified type. **3** (**wares**) articles offered for sale.
– ORIGIN Old English, 'commodities'.

warehouse • n. **1** a large building where raw materials or manufactured goods are stored. **2** a large wholesale or retail store.

warfare • n. the activities involved in fighting a war.

war game • n. **1** a military exercise carried out to test or improve tactics. **2** a mock military conflict carried out as a game or sport.

warhead • n. the explosive head of a missile, torpedo, or similar weapon.

warhorse • n. informal a person such as a soldier or politician who has fought many campaigns or contests.

warlike • adj. **1** tending to wage war; hostile: *a warlike clan.* **2** relating to or prepared for war.

warlock • n. a man who practises witchcraft.
– ORIGIN Old English, 'traitor, monster', also 'the Devil'.

warlord • n. a military commander, especially one controlling a region.

warm • adj. **1** at a fairly high temperature. **2** (of clothes or coverings) made of a material that helps the body to retain heat. **3** enthusiastic, affectionate, or kind: *a warm welcome.* **4** (of a colour) containing red, yellow, or

orange tones. **5** (of a scent or trail) fresh and easy to follow. **6** close to finding or guessing something. •v. **1** make or become warm. **2** (**warm to/towards**) become more interested in or enthusiastic about. •n. (**the warm**) a warm place or area.
– PHRASES **warm up 1** prepare for exercise by doing gentle stretches and exercises. **2** (of an engine or electrical device) reach a temperature high enough to operate efficiently. **warm something up** entertain an audience to make them more enthusiastic before the arrival of the main act.
– DERIVATIVES **warmer** n. **warmly** adv. **warmness** n.
– ORIGIN Old English.

warm-blooded •adj. **1** (of animals, chiefly mammals and birds) maintaining a constant body temperature by their body's chemical processes. **2** passionate.

warm-hearted •adj. sympathetic and kind.

warmonger /wor-mung-ger/ •n. a person who tries to bring about war.

warmth •n. **1** the quality, state, or feeling of being warm. **2** enthusiasm, affection, or kindness: *she smiled with real warmth.* **3** strength of emotion.

warn •v. **1** inform someone of a possible danger or problem. **2** advise someone not to do something wrong or foolish. **3** (**warn someone off**) order someone to keep away or to refrain from doing something.
– ORIGIN Old English.

warning •n. **1** a statement or event that indicates a possible danger or problem. **2** advice against wrong or foolish actions. **3** advance notice of something.

warp •v. **1** bend or twist out of shape as a result of heat or damp. **2** make abnormal or strange: *his hatred has warped his judgement.* •n. **1** a distortion or twist in shape. **2** (in weaving) the lengthwise threads on a loom over and under which the weft threads are passed to make cloth.
– ORIGIN Old English.

warpaint •n. **1** paint traditionally used in some societies to decorate the face and body before battle. **2** informal elaborate or excessive make-up.

warplane •n. an aircraft designed and equipped to engage in air combat or to drop bombs.

warrant •n. **1** an official authorization giving the police or another body the power to make an arrest, search somewhere, etc. **2** a document entitling the holder to receive goods, money, or services. **3** justification or authority: *there is no warrant for this assumption.*

•v. **1** make necessary or justify a course of action. **2** officially state or guarantee.
– ORIGIN first meaning 'protector', 'protect from danger': from Old French *guarant*, *guarantir*.

warrant officer •n. a rank of officer in the army, RAF, or US navy, below the commissioned officers and above the non-commissioned officers.

warranty •n. (pl. **warranties**) **1** a written guarantee promising to repair or replace an article if necessary within a specified period. **2** a guarantee made by a person insured that certain statements are true or that certain conditions shall be fulfilled, the breach of which will make the policy invalid.

warren •n. **1** a network of interconnecting rabbit burrows. **2** a complex network of paths or passages.
– ORIGIN Old French *garenne* 'game park'.

warrior •n. a brave or experienced soldier or fighter.
– ORIGIN Old French *werreior*, *guerreior*.

warship •n. a ship equipped with weapons and designed to take part in warfare at sea.

wart •n. **1** a small, hard growth on the skin, caused by a virus. **2** any rounded growth on the skin of an animal or the surface of a plant.
– PHRASES **warts and all** informal including faults or unattractive qualities.
– DERIVATIVES **warty** adj.
– ORIGIN Old English.

warthog •n. an African wild pig with a large head, warty lumps on the face, and curved tusks.

wartime •n. a period during which a war is taking place.

wary •adj. (**warier**, **wariest**) (often **wary of**) cautious about possible dangers or problems.
– DERIVATIVES **warily** adv. **wariness** n.
– ORIGIN Old English, 'be on your guard'.

was 1st and 3rd person sing. past of **BE**.

wash •v. **1** clean with water and, typically, soap or detergent. **2** (of flowing water) carry or move in a particular direction. **3** be carried by flowing water. **4** (**wash over**) occur all around without greatly affecting someone. **5** informal seem convincing or genuine: *excuses just don't wash with us.* •n. **1** an act of washing. **2** a quantity of clothes needing to be or just having been washed. **3** the water or air disturbed by a moving boat or aircraft. **4** a medicinal or cleansing liquid: *antiseptic skin wash.* **5** a thin coating of paint or metal. **6** silt or gravel carried by water and deposited as sediment.
– PHRASES **be washed out** be postponed

W

or cancelled because of rain. **come out in the wash** informal be resolved eventually. **wash your hands of** take no further responsibility for. [ORIGIN with reference to Pontius Pilate washing his hands after the condemnation of Christ (Gospel of Matthew, chapter 27).] **wash up** esp. Brit. wash crockery and cutlery after use.
– DERIVATIVES **washable** adj.
– ORIGIN Old English.

washbasin • n. a basin for washing the hands and face.

washboard • n. **1** a ridged or corrugated board against which clothes are scrubbed during washing. **2** a similar board played as a percussion instrument by scraping. • adj. (of a person's stomach) lean and with well-defined muscles.

washed out • adj. **1** faded by repeated washing. **2** pale and tired.

washed-up • adj. informal no longer effective or successful.

washer • n. **1** a person or device that washes. **2** a small flat ring fixed between a nut and bolt to spread the pressure or between two joining surfaces to prevent leakage.

washerwoman • n. (pl. **washerwomen**) a woman whose occupation is washing clothes.

washing • n. a quantity of clothes, bedlinen, etc. that is to be washed or has just been washed.

washing machine • n. a machine for washing clothes, bedlinen, etc.

washing powder • n. Brit. powdered detergent for washing laundry.

washing soda • n. sodium carbonate, used dissolved in water for washing and cleaning.

washing-up • n. Brit. crockery, cutlery, and other kitchen utensils that are to be washed.

washout • n. informal a disappointing failure.

washroom • n. N. Amer. a room with washing and toilet facilities.

washstand • n. esp. hist. a piece of furniture designed to hold a jug, bowl, or basin for washing the hands and face.

wasn't • contr. was not.

Wasp (also **WASP**) • n. N. Amer. an upper- or middle-class American white Protestant, thought to be a member of the most powerful social group.
– ORIGIN from *white Anglo-Saxon Protestant*.

wasp • n. a stinging winged insect which nests in complex colonies and has a black- and yellow-striped body.
– ORIGIN Old English.

waspish • adj. sharply irritable.
– DERIVATIVES **waspishly** adv.

wasp-waisted • adj. having a very narrow waist.

wassail /wos-sayl, wos-s'l/ old use • n. **1** spiced ale or mulled wine drunk during celebrations for Twelfth Night and Christmas Eve. **2** lively festivities involving the drinking of much alcohol. • v. **1** celebrate with much alcohol. **2** go carol-singing at Christmas.
– ORIGIN Old Norse, 'be in good health!'

wastage • n. **1** the action of wasting something. **2** an amount wasted. **3** (also **natural wastage**) Brit. the reduction in the size of a workforce through people willingly resigning or retiring rather than being made redundant.

waste • v. (**wastes**, **wasting**, **wasted**) **1** use more of something than is necessary or useful. **2** fail to make good use of: *we're wasted in this job.* **3** (**be wasted on**) not be appreciated by. **4** (often **waste away**) gradually become weaker and thinner. **5** N. Amer. informal kill someone. **6** (as adj. **wasted**) informal under the influence of alcohol or illegal drugs. • adj. **1** discarded as no longer useful or required. **2** (of an area of land) not used, cultivated, or built on. • n. **1** an instance of wasting something. **2** material that is not wanted or cannot be used. **3** a large area of barren, uninhabited land.
– PHRASES **go to waste** be wasted. **lay waste (to)** completely destroy.
– ORIGIN Old French.

USAGE: Do not confuse **waste** with **waist**. Waste means 'use more of something than is necessary or useful' (*we can't afford to waste electricity*), whereas **waist** means 'the part of a person's body between the ribs and the hips' (*he put his arm around her waist*).

waste-disposal unit • n. Brit. an electric device fitted to the waste pipe of a kitchen sink for grinding up food waste.

wasteful • adj. using or using up something carelessly or extravagantly.
– DERIVATIVES **wastefully** adv. **wastefulness** n.

wasteland • n. a barren or empty area of land.

waster • n. **1** a wasteful person or thing. **2** informal a person who does little or nothing of value.

wastrel /way-struhl/ • n. literary a wasteful or worthless person.

watch • v. **1** look at with attention or interest. **2** keep under careful observation. **3** treat with caution or control: *watch what you say!* **4** (**watch**

for) look out for. **5** (**watch out**) be careful. •n. **1** a small timepiece usually worn on a strap on the wrist. **2** an instance of watching. **3** a period of keeping watch during the night. **4** a fixed period of duty on a ship, usually lasting four hours. **5** a shift worked by firefighters or police officers.
– PHRASES **keep watch** keep alert for danger or trouble. **watch your back** protect yourself against unexpected danger.
– DERIVATIVES **watcher** n.
– ORIGIN Old English.

watchable • adj. (of a film or television programme) fairly enjoyable to watch.

watchdog • n. **1** a dog kept to guard private property. **2** a person or group that monitors the practices of companies providing a particular service.

watchful • adj. alert to possible difficulty or danger.
– DERIVATIVES **watchfully** adv. **watchfulness** n.

watching brief • n. **1** an interest in a proceeding in which you are not directly involved. **2** Law, Brit. instructions held by a barrister to follow a case on behalf of a client who is not directly involved.

watchman • n. (pl. **watchmen**) a man employed to look after an empty building.

watchtower • n. a tower built to create a high observation point.

watchword • n. a word or phrase expressing the central aim or belief of a person or group.

water • n. **1** the liquid which forms the seas, lakes, rivers, and rain and is the basis of the fluids of living things. **2** (**waters**) an area of sea under the legal authority of a particular country. **3** (**waters**) the fluid surrounding a fetus in the womb, especially as passed from a woman's body shortly before she gives birth. **4** (**the waters**) the water of a mineral spring used for medicinal purposes. • v. (**waters, watering, watered**) **1** pour water over a plant or an area of ground. **2** give a drink of water to an animal. **3** (of the eyes or mouth) produce tears or saliva. **4** dilute with water. **5** (**water something down**) make something less forceful or controversial by changing or leaving out things. **6** (of a river) flow through an area.
– PHRASES **hold water** (of a theory) seem valid or reasonable. **under water** submerged; flooded. **water on the brain** informal hydrocephalus. **water under the**

bridge past events that are over and done with.
– DERIVATIVES **waterless** adj.
– ORIGIN Old English.

water-based • adj. (of a substance or solution) using or having water as a main ingredient.

waterbed • n. a bed with a water-filled rubber or plastic mattress.

water biscuit • n. a thin, crisp unsweetened biscuit made from flour and water.

water buffalo • n. a large black Asian buffalo with heavy swept-back horns, used for carrying heavy loads.

water cannon • n. a device that sends out a powerful jet of water, used to disperse a crowd.

water chestnut • n. the crisp, white-fleshed tuber of a tropical plant, used in oriental cookery.

water closet • n. dated a flush toilet.

watercolour (US **watercolor**) • n. **1** artists' paint that is thinned with water rather than oil. **2** a picture painted with watercolours. **3** the art of painting with watercolours.
– DERIVATIVES **watercolourist** n.

watercourse • n. a brook, stream, or artificially constructed water channel.

watercress • n. a cress which grows in running water and whose strong-tasting leaves are used in salad.

water diviner • n. Brit. a person who searches for underground water by using a divining rod.

waterfall • n. a stream of water falling from a height, formed when a river or stream flows over a precipice or steep slope.

water feature • n. a pond or fountain in a garden.

waterfowl • pl. n. ducks, geese, or other large birds living in water.

waterfront • n. a part of a town or city alongside a body of water.

waterhole • n. a hollow in which water collects, typically one at which animals drink.

water ice • n. a frozen dessert consisting of fruit juice or purée in a sugar syrup.

watering can • n. a portable water container with a long spout and a removable cap with tiny holes in it, used for watering plants.

watering hole • n. **1** a waterhole from which animals regularly drink. **2** informal a pub or bar.

watering place • n. **1** a watering hole. **2** a spa or seaside resort.

water level • n. the height reached by a body of water.

w

water lily • n. a plant that grows in water, with large round floating leaves and large cup-shaped flowers.

waterline • n. 1 the level normally reached by the water on the side of a ship. 2 a line on a shore, riverbank, etc. marking the level reached by the sea or a river.

waterlogged • adj. saturated with or full of water.
– ORIGIN from former *waterlog* 'make a ship unmanageable by flooding'.

water main • n. the main pipe in a water supply system.

watermark • n. a faint design made in some paper that can be seen when held against the light, identifying the maker.

water meadow • n. a meadow that is periodically flooded by a stream or river.

watermelon • n. a large melon-like fruit with smooth green skin, red pulp, and watery juice.

watermill • n. a mill worked by a waterwheel.

water pistol • n. a toy pistol that shoots a jet of water.

water polo • n. a seven-a-side game played by swimmers in a pool, with a ball like a football that the players try to throw into their opponents' net.

waterproof • adj. unable to be penetrated by water. • n. Brit. a waterproof garment. • v. make waterproof.

water rat • n. 1 a large rat-like rodent living both on land and in water. 2 Brit. a water vole.

water-resistant • adj. partially able to resist the penetration of water.

watershed • n. 1 an area of land that separates waters flowing to different rivers, basins, or seas. 2 a turning point in a situation. 3 Brit. the time after which programmes that are unsuitable for children are broadcast on television.
– ORIGIN from **WATER** + *shed* in the sense 'ridge of high ground'.

waterside • n. the area next to a sea, lake, or river.

waterski • n. (pl. **waterskis**) each of a pair of skis enabling the wearer to skim the surface of the water when towed by a motor boat. • v. (**waterskis, waterskiing, waterskied**) travel on waterskis.
– DERIVATIVES **waterskier** n.

waterspout • n. a funnel-shaped column of water and spray formed by a whirlwind occurring over the sea.

water table • n. the level below which the ground is saturated with water.

watertight • adj. 1 closely sealed, fastened, or fitted so as to prevent water

passing through. 2 (of an argument or account) unable to be called into question.

water tower • n. a tower that supports a water tank at a height to create enough pressure to distribute the water through a system of pipes.

water vole • n. a large vole living both on land and in water, which digs burrows in the banks of rivers.

waterway • n. a river, canal, or other route for travel by water.

waterwheel • n. a large wheel driven by flowing water, used to work machinery or to raise water to a higher level.

water wings • pl. n. inflated floats fixed to the arms of someone learning to swim to help them stay afloat.

waterworks • pl. n. an establishment for managing a water supply.
– PHRASES **turn on the waterworks** informal start crying.

watery • adj. 1 consisting of, containing, or like water. 2 (of food or drink) thin or tasteless as a result of containing too much water. 3 weak or pale: *watery sunlight.*

watt • n. the SI unit of power, equivalent to one joule per second and corresponding to the rate of energy in an electric circuit where the potential difference is one volt and the current one ampere.
– ORIGIN named after the Scottish engineer James *Watt*.

wattage • n. an amount of electrical power expressed in watts.

wattle¹ /wot-t'l/ • n. a material for making fences, walls, etc., consisting of rods interlaced with twigs or branches.
– ORIGIN Old English.

wattle² /wot-t'l/ • n. a fleshy lobe hanging from the head or neck of the turkey and some other birds.

wattle and daub • n. a material formerly used in building walls, consisting of wattle covered with mud or clay.

wave • v. (**waves, waving, waved**) 1 move your hand to and fro in greeting or as a signal. 2 move something held in your hand to and fro. 3 move to and fro with a swaying motion while remaining fixed to one point. 4 style hair so that it curls slightly. • n. 1 a ridge of water moving along the surface of the sea or arching and breaking on the shore. 2 a sudden occurrence of or increase in a phenomenon or emotion: *a wave of panic swept over her.* 3 a gesture made by waving your hand. 4 a slightly curling lock of hair. 5 Physics a periodic

disturbance of the particles of a substance without overall movement of the particles, as in the transmission of sound, light, heat, etc.
– PHRASES **make waves** informal **1** create a significant impression. **2** cause trouble.
– ORIGIN Old English.

waveband • n. a range of wavelengths between two given limits, used in radio transmission.

waveform • n. Physics a curve showing the shape of a wave at a given time.

wavelength • n. **1** Physics the distance between successive crests of a wave of sound, light, radio waves, etc. **2** one person's way of thinking when communicated to another person: *we weren't on the same wavelength.*

wavelet • n. a small wave.

waver • v. (**wavers, wavering, wavered**) **1** move quiveringly; flicker. **2** begin to weaken; falter. **3** be indecisive.
– ORIGIN Old Norse, 'flicker'.

wavy • adj. (**wavier, waviest**) having or consisting of a series of wave-like curves.
– DERIVATIVES **waviness** n.

wax¹ • n. **1** a substance produced by bees to make honeycombs; beeswax. **2** a soft solid oily substance that melts easily, used for making candles or polishes.
• v. **1** polish or treat with wax. **2** remove hair from a part of the body by applying melted wax and then peeling it off together with the hairs.
– ORIGIN Old English.

wax² • v. **1** (of the moon) gradually have a larger part of its visible surface lit up, so that it appears to increase in size. **2** literary become larger or stronger. **3** speak or write in a particular way: *they waxed lyrical about the old days.*
– ORIGIN Old English.

waxen • adj. **1** having a smooth, pale, semi-transparent surface like that of wax. **2** old use or literary made of wax.

waxwing • n. a crested songbird, mainly pinkish-brown and with bright red tips to some wing feathers.

waxwork • n. **1** a lifelike dummy modelled in wax. **2** (**waxworks**) an exhibition of waxworks.

waxy • adj. (**waxier, waxiest**) like wax in consistency or appearance.
– DERIVATIVES **waxiness** n.

way • n. **1** a method, style, or manner of doing something. **2** the typical manner in which someone behaves or in which something happens. **3** a road, track, path, or street. **4** a route or means taken in order to reach, enter, or leave a place. **5** the route along which someone or something is travelling or would travel

if unobstructed: *he blocked her way.* **6** a specified direction. **7** the distance in space or time between two points: *September was a long way off.* **8** informal a particular area: *they live over Maidenhead way.* **9** a particular aspect: *I've changed in every way.* **10** a particular condition or state: *the family was in a poor way.* **11** (**ways**) parts into which something divides or is divided. **12** forward motion of a ship or boat through water.
• adv. informal at or to a considerable distance or extent.
– PHRASES **by the way** incidentally. **by way of 1** via. **2** as a form of. **3** by means of. **come your way** happen or become available to you. **get** (or **have**) **your** (**own**) **way** get or do what you want in spite of opposition. **give way 1** yield. **2** collapse or break under pressure. **3** Brit. allow someone or something else to be or go first. **4** (**give way to**) be replaced or superseded by. **go your way** (of events, circumstances, etc.) be favourable to you. **have a way with** have a particular talent for dealing with or ability in. **have your way with** humorous have sex with. **lead the way** go first along a route or be the first to do something. **one way and another** (or **one way or the other**) **1** taking most considerations into account. **2** by some means. **on the** (or **your** or **its**) **way** about to arrive or happen. **on the** (or **your** or **its**) **way out** informal going out of fashion or favour. **the other way round** (or **around**; Brit. also **about**) **1** in the opposite position or direction. **2** the opposite of what is expected or supposed. **out of the way 1** (of a place) remote. **2** dealt with or finished. **3** no longer an obstacle to someone's plans. **4** unusual or exceptional. **ways and means** the methods and resources for achieving something.
– ORIGIN Old English.

waybill • n. a list of passengers or goods being carried on a vehicle.

wayfarer • n. literary a person who travels on foot.
– DERIVATIVES **wayfaring** n. & adj.

waylay • v. (**waylays, waylaying, waylaid**) **1** intercept someone in order to attack them. **2** stop someone and keep them in conversation.

waymark • n. (also **waymarker**) a sign forming one of a series used to mark out a footpath or similar route.

way-out • adj. informal very unconventional or experimental.

-ways • suffix forming adjectives and adverbs of direction or manner: *lengthways.*

w

wayside • n. the edge of a road.
– PHRASES **fall by the wayside** fail to continue with an undertaking. [ORIGIN with biblical reference to the Gospel of Luke, chapter 8.]

way station • n. N. Amer. a stopping place on a journey.

wayward • adj. difficult to control because of unpredictable or wilful behaviour.
– DERIVATIVES **waywardness** n.
– ORIGIN shortening of former *awayward* 'turned away'.

wazzock /waz-zuhk/ • n. Brit. informal a stupid or annoying person.

Wb • abbrev. weber(s).

WBA • abbrev. World Boxing Association.

WBC • abbrev. World Boxing Council.

WC • abbrev. Brit. water closet.

we • pron. (first person pl.) **1** used by a speaker to refer to himself or herself and one or more other people considered together. **2** people in general. **3** used in formal contexts for or by a royal person, or by a writer, to refer to himself or herself. **4** you (used in a superior way): *how are we today?*
– ORIGIN Old English.

USAGE: For an explanation of whether to use **we** or **us** following *than*, see the note at **PERSONAL PRONOUN**.

weak • adj. **1** lacking physical strength and energy. **2** likely to break or give way under pressure. **3** not secure, stable, or firmly established. **4** lacking power, influence, or ability. **5** lacking intensity: *a weak light from a single street lamp.* **6** (of a liquid or solution) heavily diluted. **7** not convincing or forceful. **8** (of verbs) forming the past tense and past participle by addition of a suffix (in English, typically -*ed*).
– PHRASES **the weaker sex** dated women seen as a group.
– ORIGIN Old English.

weaken • v. make or become weak.

weak-kneed • adj. lacking determination or courage.

weakling • n. a weak person or animal.

weakly • adv. in a weak way.
• adj. (**weaklier**, **weakliest**) weak or sickly.

weakness • n. **1** the state of being weak. **2** a disadvantage or fault. **3** a person or thing that you cannot resist or you like too much. **4** (**weakness for**) a self-indulgent liking for something.

weal¹ /rhymes with feel/ (also esp. Med. **wheal**) • n. a red, swollen mark left on flesh by a blow or pressure.
– ORIGIN variant of *wale*, meaning 'a ridge on woven fabric'.

weal² /rhymes with feel/ • n. formal that which is best for someone or something: *guardians of the public weal.*
– ORIGIN Old English, 'wealth, well-being'.

wealth • n. **1** a large amount of money, property, or possessions. **2** the state of being rich. **3** a large amount of something desirable.
– ORIGIN from WELL¹ or WEAL².

wealthy • adj. (**wealthier**, **wealthiest**) rich.

wean¹ • v. **1** make a young mammal used to food other than its mother's milk. **2** (often **wean someone off**) make someone give up a habit or addiction. **3** (**be weaned on**) be strongly influenced by something from an early age.
– ORIGIN Old English.

wean² • n. Scottish & N. English a young child.
– ORIGIN from *wee ane* 'little one'.

weapon • n. **1** a thing designed or used to cause physical harm or damage. **2** a means of gaining an advantage or defending yourself.
– DERIVATIVES **weaponry** n.
– ORIGIN Old English.

weapon of mass destruction • n. a nuclear, biological, or chemical weapon able to cause widespread destruction and loss of life.

wear • v. (**wears**, **wearing**, **wore**; past part. **worn**) **1** have on your body as clothing, decoration, or protection. **2** display a particular facial expression. **3** damage or destroy by friction or continued use. **4** withstand continued use to a particular degree: *the fabric wears well wash after wash.* **5** (**wear off**) lose effectiveness or strength. **6** (**wear someone down**) overcome someone by persistence. **7** (**wear someone out**) exhaust someone. **8** (as adj. **wearing**) mentally or physically tiring. **9** (**wear on**) (of time) pass in a slow or boring way. • n. **1** clothing suitable for a particular purpose or of a particular type. **2** damage caused by continuous use. **3** the capacity for withstanding such damage.
– PHRASES **wear thin** be gradually used up.
– DERIVATIVES **wearable** adj. **wearer** n.
– ORIGIN Old English.

wearisome • adj. making you feel tired or bored.

weary • adj. (**wearier**, **weariest**) **1** tired. **2** causing tiredness. **3** (often **weary of**) reluctant to experience any more of.
• v. (**wearies**, **wearying**, **wearied**) **1** make weary. **2** (**weary of**) grow tired of.

– DERIVATIVES **wearily** adv. **weariness** n.
– ORIGIN Old English.

weasel • n. **1** a small slender meat-eating mammal related to the stoat, with reddish-brown fur. **2** informal a deceitful or treacherous person.
– DERIVATIVES **weaselly** adj.
– ORIGIN Old English.

weather • n. the state of the atmosphere at a place and time in terms of temperature, wind, rain, etc. • adj. referring to the side from which the wind is blowing. Contrasted with LEE. • v. (**weathers, weathering, weathered**) **1** wear away or change in form or appearance by being exposed to the weather for a long time. **2** come through a difficult or dangerous situation safely.
– PHRASES **keep a weather eye on** be watchful for developments. **make heavy weather of** informal have unnecessary difficulty in dealing with a task or problem. **under the weather** informal slightly unwell or depressed.
– ORIGIN Old English.

weather-beaten • adj. damaged, worn, or tanned through being exposed to the weather.

weatherboard esp. Brit. • n. **1** a sloping board attached to the bottom of an outside door to keep out the rain. **2** each of a series of horizontal boards nailed to outside walls with edges overlapping to keep out the rain.

weathercock • n. a weathervane in the form of a cockerel.

weatherman (or **weatherwoman**) • n. (pl. **weathermen** or **weatherwomen**) a person who broadcasts a description and forecast of weather conditions.

weather station • n. an observation post where weather and atmospheric conditions are observed and recorded.

weathervane • n. a revolving pointer that shows the direction of the wind.

weave¹ • v. (**weaves, weaving, wove**; past part. **woven** or **wove**) **1** make fabric by interlacing long threads passing in one direction with others at a right angle to them. **2** make basketwork or a wreath by interlacing rods or flowers. **3** (**weave something into**) make facts, events, or other elements into a story. • n. a particular way in which fabric is woven: *cloth of a very fine weave.*
– ORIGIN Old English.

weave² • v. (**weaves, weaving, weaved**) move from side to side to get around obstructions.
– ORIGIN prob. from Old Norse, 'to wave, brandish'.

weaver • n. **1** a person who weaves

fabric. **2** (also **weaver bird**) a songbird of tropical Africa and Asia, which builds elaborate nests.

web • n. **1** a network of fine threads made by a spider to catch its prey. **2** a complex system of interconnected elements: *a web of lies.* **3** (**the Web**) the World Wide Web. **4** a membrane between the toes of a swimming bird or other animal living in water.
– ORIGIN Old English.

webbed • adj. (of an animal's feet) having the toes connected by a web.

webbing • n. strong, closely woven fabric used chiefly for making straps and belts and for supporting the seats of upholstered chairs.

webcam • n. (trademark in the US) a video camera connected to a computer, so that its images may be seen by Internet users.

webcast • n. a live video broadcast of an event transmitted across the Internet.

weber /vay-ber/ • n. the SI unit of magnetic flux, sufficient to cause an electromotive force of one volt in a circuit of one turn when generated and removed in one second.
– ORIGIN named after the German physicist Wilhelm Eduard *Weber*.

web-footed • adj. having webbed feet.

weblog • n. a personal website on which someone regularly records their opinions or experiences and creates links to other sites.

webmaster • n. a person who is responsible for a particular server on the Internet.

web page • n. a hypertext document which can be accessed via the Internet.

website • n. a location connected to the Internet that maintains one or more web pages.

wed • v. (**weds, wedding, wedded** or **wed**) **1** formal or literary marry. **2** formal or literary give or join in marriage. **3** (as adj. **wedded**) relating to marriage: *wedded bliss.* **4** combine two desirable factors or qualities. **5** (**be wedded to**) be entirely devoted to a particular activity or belief.
– ORIGIN Old English.

we'd • contr. **1** we had. **2** we should or we would.

wedding • n. a marriage ceremony.

wedding breakfast • n. Brit. a celebratory meal eaten just after a wedding (at any time of day) by the couple and their guests.

wedding march • n. a piece of march music played at the entrance of the bride or the exit of the couple at a wedding.

w

wedding ring •n. a ring worn by a married person, given to them by their husband or wife at their wedding.

wedge •n. **1** a piece of wood, metal, etc. with a thick end that tapers to a thin edge, that is driven between two objects or parts of an object to secure or separate them. **2** a wedge-shaped thing or piece. **3** a golf club with a low, angled face for hitting the ball as high as possible into the air. **4** a shoe with a fairly high heel forming a solid block with the sole. •v. (**wedges, wedging, wedged**) **1** fix in position using a wedge. **2** force into a narrow space.
– PHRASES **drive a wedge between** cause a disagreement or hostility between. **the thin end of the wedge** informal an action unimportant in itself but which is likely to lead to more serious developments.
– ORIGIN Old English.

Wedgwood /wej-wuud/ •n. trademark a type of pottery made by the English potter Josiah Wedgwood and his successors.

wedlock •n. formal the state of being married.
– PHRASES **born in** (or **out of**) **wedlock** born of married (or unmarried) parents.
– ORIGIN Old English, 'marriage vow'.

Wednesday •n. the day of the week before Thursday and following Tuesday.
– ORIGIN Old English, named after the Germanic god *Odin*.

> ✓ Remember that **Wednesday** is spelled with a **d** before the **n**.

wee •adj. (**weer, weest**) esp. Sc. little.
– ORIGIN Old English.

weed •n. **1** a wild plant growing where it is not wanted and in competition with plants which have been deliberately grown. **2** informal cannabis. **3** (**the weed**) informal tobacco. **4** Brit. informal a weak or skinny person. •v. **1** remove weeds from. **2** (**weed someone/thing out**) remove unwanted items or members from a group.
– ORIGIN Old English.

weedkiller •n. a substance used to destroy weeds.

weedy •adj. (**weedier, weediest**) **1** containing or covered with many weeds. **2** Brit. informal thin and weak.

week •n. **1** a period of seven days. **2** the period of seven days generally reckoned from and to midnight on Saturday night. **3** Brit. (preceded by a specified day) a week after that day. **4** the five days from Monday to Friday, or the time spent working during this period.
– ORIGIN Old English.

weekday •n. a day of the week other than Sunday or Saturday.

weekend •n. Saturday and Sunday.
•v. informal spend a weekend somewhere.

weekender •n. a person who spends weekends away from their main home.

weekly •adj. **1** done, produced, or happening once a week. **2** calculated in terms of a week: *weekly income.*
•adv. once a week. •n. (pl. **weeklies**) a newspaper or other publication issued every week.

weeny •adj. (**weenier, weeniest**) informal tiny.
– ORIGIN from **WEE**.

weep •v. (**weeps, weeping, wept**) **1** shed tears. **2** discharge liquid: *the sores began to weep.* **3** (as adj. **weeping**) used in names of trees and shrubs with drooping branches, e.g. **weeping willow**. •n. a period of shedding tears.
– ORIGIN Old English.

weepie (also **weepy**) •n. (pl. **weepies**) informal a sentimental or emotional film, novel, or song.

weepy •adj. (**weepier, weepiest**) informal **1** tearful. **2** sentimental.
– DERIVATIVES **weepily** adv. **weepiness** n.

weevil /wee-v'l/ •n. a small beetle with a long snout, several kinds of which feed on crops or stored foodstuffs.
– ORIGIN Old English.

weft •n. (in weaving) the crosswise threads that are passed over and under the warp threads on a loom to make cloth.
– ORIGIN Old English.

weigh •v. **1** find out how heavy someone or something is. **2** have a specified weight. **3** (**weigh something out**) measure and take out a portion of a particular weight. **4** (**weigh someone down**) be heavy and troublesome to someone. **5** (**weigh on**) be depressing or worrying to: *his unhappiness weighed on my mind.* **6** (**weigh in**) (of a boxer or jockey) be officially weighed before or after a contest. **7** (often **weigh something up**) assess the nature or importance of something. **8** (often **weigh against**) influence a decision or action: *the evidence weighed heavily against him.* **9** (**weigh in**) informal make a forceful contribution to a competition or argument. **10** (**weigh on**) join in or attack forcefully or enthusiastically.
– PHRASES **weigh anchor** (of a boat) take up the anchor when ready to sail.
– ORIGIN Old English.

weighbridge •n. a machine for weighing vehicles, set into the ground to be driven on to.

weigh-in •n. an official weighing, e.g. of boxers before a fight.

weight •n. **1** the heaviness of a person

or thing. **2** Physics the force exerted on the mass of a body by a gravitational field. **3** the quality of being heavy. **4** a unit or system of units used for expressing how much something weighs. **5** a piece of metal known to weigh a definite amount and used on scales to determine how heavy something is. **6** a heavy object. **7** (**weights**) heavy blocks or discs used in weightlifting or weight training. **8** ability to influence decisions or actions: *their recommendation will carry great weight.* **9** the importance attached to something. **10** a feeling of pressure or worry: *a weight on your mind.* •v. **1** make heavier or keep in place with a weight. **2** attach importance or value to. **3** (**be weighted**) be planned or arranged so as to give one party an advantage.
– PHRASES **be worth your/its weight in gold** be very useful or helpful. **throw your weight about** (or **around**) informal assert yourself in an unpleasant way.
– ORIGIN Old English.

weighting •n. **1** adjustment made to take account of special circumstances. **2** Brit. additional wages or salary paid to allow for a higher cost of living in a particular area.

weightless •adj. (of a body) not apparently acted on by gravity.
– DERIVATIVES **weightlessness** n.

weightlifting •n. the sport or activity of lifting barbells or other heavy weights.
– DERIVATIVES **weightlifter** n.

weight training •n. physical training that involves lifting weights.

weighty •adj. (**weightier**, **weightiest**) **1** heavy. **2** very serious and important. **3** very influential.

weir /rhymes with here/ •n. **1** a low dam built across a river to raise the level of water upstream or control its flow. **2** an enclosure of stakes set in a stream as a trap for fish.
– ORIGIN Old English.

weird •adj. **1** strange in a frightening way. **2** informal very strange.
– DERIVATIVES **weirdly** adv. **weirdness** n.
– ORIGIN Old English, 'destiny, fate'.

☑ **weird** is an exception to the usual rule of *i* before *e* except after *c*.

weirdo •n. (pl. **weirdos**) informal a strange or eccentric person.

welch /welch/ •v. var. of WELSH.

welcome •n. **1** an instance or way of greeting someone. **2** a pleased or approving reaction. •exclam. used to greet someone in a friendly way.
•v. (**welcomes**, **welcoming**, **welcomed**) **1** greet someone who is arriving in a

polite or friendly way. **2** be glad to receive or hear of. •adj. **1** (of a guest or new arrival) gladly received. **2** very pleasing because much needed or desired: *welcome news for the government.* **3** allowed or invited to do a particular thing.
– ORIGIN Old English, 'a person whose coming is pleasing'.

weld •v. **1** join metal parts together by heating the surfaces to the point of melting and pressing or hammering them together. **2** make an article in this way. **3** make two things combine into a whole. •n. a welded joint.
– DERIVATIVES **welder** n.
– ORIGIN from WELL² in the former sense 'melt or weld heated metal'.

welfare •n. **1** the health, happiness, and fortunes of a person or group. **2** organized practical or financial help provided to help people in need.
– ORIGIN from WELL¹ + FARE.

welfare state •n. a system under which the state undertakes to protect the health and well-being of its citizens by means of grants, pensions, and other benefits.

well¹ •adv. (**better**, **best**) **1** in a good way. **2** in prosperity or comfort: *they lived well.* **3** in a favourable or approving way. **4** thoroughly: *add the lemon juice and mix well.* **5** to a great extent or degree: *everything was planned well in advance.* **6** Brit. informal very; extremely: *he was well out of order.* **7** very probably; in all likelihood: *she could well afford to pay for it herself.* **8** without difficulty: *she could well afford to pay for it herself.* **9** with good reason. **10** old use luckily; at a good time: *hail fellow, well met.*
•adj. (**better**, **best**) **1** in good health. **2** in a satisfactory state or position. **3** sensible; advisable. •exclam. used to express surprise, anger, resignation, etc., or when pausing in speech.
– PHRASES **as well** (or **just as well**) **1** with equal reason or an equally good result. **2** sensible, appropriate, or desirable. **leave** (or **let**) **well alone** avoid interfering with or trying to improve something. **well and truly** completely.
– ORIGIN Old English.

USAGE: The adverb **well** is often used with a past participle (such as *known*) to form compound adjectives: **well known**, **well dressed**, and so on. Such adjectives should be written without a hyphen when they are used alone after a verb (*she is well known as a writer*) but with a hyphen when they come before a noun (*a well-known writer*).

well² •n. **1** a shaft sunk into the ground to obtain water, oil, or gas. **2** a hollow

w

made to hold liquid. **3** a plentiful source or supply. **4** an enclosed space in the middle of a building, giving room for stairs or a lift or allowing in light or air. • v. (often **well up**) **1** (of a liquid) rise up to the surface and spill or be about to spill. **2** (of an emotion) arise and become stronger.
– ORIGIN Old English.

we'll • contr. we shall; we will.

well advised • adj. sensible; wise.

well appointed • adj. (of a building or room) having a high standard of equipment or furnishing.

well balanced • adj. mentally and emotionally stable.

well-being • n. the state of being comfortable, healthy, or happy.

well bred • adj. polite and well brought up.

well built • adj. (of a person) strong and sturdy.

well disposed • adj. having a positive, sympathetic, or friendly attitude.

well done • adj. **1** carried out in a successful or satisfactory way. **2** (of food) thoroughly cooked. • exclam. used to express congratulation or approval.

well endowed • adj. having plentiful supplies of a resource.

well founded • adj. based on good evidence or reasons.

well heeled • adj. informal wealthy.

wellie • n. var. of WELLY.

wellington (also **wellington boot**) • n. Brit. a knee-length waterproof rubber or plastic boot.
– ORIGIN named after the British soldier and Prime Minister the 1st Duke of *Wellington*.

well known • adj. known widely or thoroughly.

well meaning (also **well meant**) • adj. having good intentions but not necessarily the desired effect.

well-nigh • adv. esp. literary almost.

well off • adj. **1** wealthy. **2** in a good situation or circumstances.

well preserved • adj. (of an old person) showing little sign of ageing.

well rounded • adj. **1** having a pleasing curved shape. **2** (of a person) plump. **3** having a personality that is fully developed in all aspects.

well spoken • adj. speaking in an educated and refined way.

wellspring • n. literary **1** a plentiful source of something: *a wellspring of creativity.* **2** the place where a spring comes out of the ground.

well-to-do • adj. wealthy; prosperous.

well travelled • adj. **1** (of a person) having travelled widely. **2** (of a route) much followed by travellers.

well trodden • adj. much followed by travellers.

well turned • adj. **1** (of a phrase or compliment) elegantly expressed. **2** (of a woman's ankle or leg) attractively shaped.

well-wisher • n. a person who desires happiness or success for someone else, or who expresses such a desire.

well worn • adj. **1** showing signs of extensive use or wear. **2** (of a phrase or idea) used or repeated so often that it no longer has interest or significance.

welly (also **wellie**) • n. (pl. **wellies**) Brit. informal **1** = WELLINGTON. **2** power or vigour.

Welsh • n. the language of Wales. • adj. relating to Wales.
– DERIVATIVES **Welshman** n. (pl. **Welshmen**). **Welshness** n. **Welshwoman** n. (pl. **Welshwomen**).

welsh (also **welch**) • v. (**welsh on**) fail to repay a debt or fulfil an obligation.

Welsh rarebit (also **Welsh rabbit**) • n. = RAREBIT.

welt • n. **1** a leather rim round the edge of the upper of a shoe, to which the sole is attached. **2** a ribbed, reinforced, or decorative border in a garment. **3** a weal.

welter • n. a large number of disordered items.
– ORIGIN Dutch or German *welteren* 'writhe, wallow'.

welterweight • n. a weight in boxing and other sports intermediate between lightweight and middleweight.

wen • n. a boil or other swelling or growth on the skin.
– ORIGIN Old English.

wench /wench/ • n. old use or humorous a girl or young woman.
– ORIGIN from former *wenchel* 'child, servant, prostitute'.

wend • v. (**wend your way**) go slowly or by an indirect route.
– ORIGIN Old English, 'to turn, depart'.

Wendy house • n. Brit. a toy house large enough for children to play in.
– ORIGIN named after the house built around *Wendy* in J. M. Barrie's play *Peter Pan*.

went past of GO.

wept past and past part. of WEEP.

were 2nd person sing. past, pl. past, and past subjunctive of BE.

we're • contr. we are.

weren't • contr. were not.

werewolf /wair-wuulf, weer-wuulf/ • n. (pl. **werewolves**) (in folklore) a person who periodically changes into a wolf, typically when there is a full moon.

– ORIGIN Old English.

Wesleyan • adj. relating to the teachings of the English preacher John Wesley or the main branch of the Methodist Church which he founded. • n. a follower of Wesley or of the main Methodist tradition.

west • n. 1 the direction in which the sun sets at the equinoxes. 2 the western part of a place. 3 (**the West**) Europe and North America seen in contrast to other civilizations. 4 (**the West**) hist. the non-Communist states of Europe and North America. • adj. 1 lying towards or facing the west. 2 (of a wind) blowing from the west. • adv. to or towards the west.

– DERIVATIVES **westbound** adj. & adv.

– ORIGIN Old English.

westerly • adj. & adv. 1 towards or facing the west. 2 (of a wind) blowing from the west.

western • adj. 1 situated in or facing the west. 2 (usu. **Western**) coming from or typical of the west, in particular Europe and North America. • n. a film or novel about cowboys in western North America.

– DERIVATIVES **westernmost** adj.

Western Church • n. the part of the Christian Church originating in the Western Roman Empire, including the Roman Catholic, Anglican, Lutheran, and Reformed Churches.

westerner • n. a person from the west of a region.

westernize (or **westernise**) • v. (**westernizes, westernizing, westernized**) bring a country, system, etc. under the influence of the cultural, economic, or political systems of Europe and North America.

– DERIVATIVES **westernization** n.

West Indian • n. a person from the West Indies, or a person of West Indian descent. • adj. relating to the West Indies.

west-north-west • n. the direction halfway between west and north-west.

west-south-west • n. the direction halfway between west and south-west.

westward • adj. towards the west. • adv. (also **westwards**) in a westerly direction.

wet • adj. (**wetter, wettest**) 1 covered or saturated with liquid. 2 (of the weather) rainy. 3 involving the use of water or liquid. 4 (of paint, ink, etc.) not yet having dried or hardened. 5 Brit. informal lacking forcefulness or strength of character. • v. (**wets, wetting, wet** or

wetted) 1 cover or touch with liquid. 2 urinate in or on. 3 (**wet yourself**) urinate without meaning to. • n. 1 liquid that makes something damp. 2 (**the wet**) rainy weather. 3 Brit. informal a feeble person.

– PHRASES **wet behind the ears** informal lacking experience. **wet your whistle** informal have a drink.

– DERIVATIVES **wetly** adv. **wetness** n.

– ORIGIN Old English.

wet blanket • n. informal a person who spoils other people's enjoyment with their disapproving or unenthusiastic attitude.

wet dream • n. an erotic dream that causes involuntary ejaculation of semen.

wether /rhymes with weather/ • n. a castrated ram.

– ORIGIN Old English.

wetland • n. (also **wetlands**) swampy or marshy land.

wet nurse • n. esp. hist. a woman employed to breastfeed another woman's child.

wet rot • n. a brown fungus causing decay in moist timber.

wetsuit • n. a close-fitting rubber garment covering the entire body, worn for warmth in water sports or diving.

we've • contr. we have.

whack informal • v. 1 strike forcefully with a sharp blow. 2 defeat heavily. 3 place or insert roughly or carelessly. • n. 1 a sharp blow. 2 a try or attempt. 3 Brit. a specified share of or contribution to something: *he paid a fair whack of the bill.*

– PHRASES **top** (or **full**) **whack** esp. Brit. the maximum price or rate.

whacked (also **whacked out**) • adj. Brit. informal completely exhausted.

whacking • adj. Brit. informal very large.

whacko • adj. & n. (pl. **whackos**) var. of **WACKO**.

whacky • adj. var. of **WACKY**.

whale • n. (pl. **whale** or **whales**) a very large sea mammal with a horizontal tail fin and a blowhole on top of the head for breathing.

– PHRASES **have a whale of a time** informal enjoy yourself very much.

– ORIGIN Old English.

whalebone • n. a hard substance which grows in a series of thin parallel plates in the upper jaw of some whales and is used by them to strain plankton from the seawater.

whaler • n. 1 a ship used for hunting whales. 2 a sailor whose job is to hunt whales.

whaling • n. the practice or industry of

w

hunting and killing whales for their oil, meat, or whalebone.

wham • informal • exclam. used to express the sound of a hard impact or the idea of a sudden and dramatic event. • v. (**whams, whamming, whammed**) strike something forcefully.

whammy • n. (pl. **whammies**) informal an event with a powerful and unpleasant effect; a blow.

whap • v. (**whaps, whapping, whapped**) v. & n. esp. N. Amer. var. of **whop**.

wharf /worf/ • n. (pl. **wharves** or **wharfs**) a level quayside area to which a ship may be moored to load and unload.
– ORIGIN Old English.

what • pron. & det. **1** asking for information about something. **2** (as pronoun) asking for repetition of something not heard or confirmation of something not understood. **3** (as pronoun) the thing or things that. **4** no matter what; whatever. **5** used to emphasize something surprising or remarkable. • adv. **1** to what extent? **2** informal, dated used for emphasis or to invite agreement.
– PHRASES **what for?** informal for what reason? **what's what** informal what is useful or important. **what with** because of.
– ORIGIN Old English.

whatever • pron. & det. everything or anything that; no matter what. • pron. used for emphasis instead of 'what' in questions. • adv. **1** at all; of any kind. **2** informal no matter what happens.

whatnot • n. informal an unidentified or unspecified item or items similar to the ones mentioned.

whatsit • n. informal a person or thing whose name you cannot remember, do not know, or do not want to specify.

whatsoever • adv. at all. • det. & pron. old use whatever.

wheal • n. var. of **weal**¹.

wheat • n. a cereal widely grown in temperate countries, the grain of which is ground to make flour.
– ORIGIN Old English.

wheatear • n. a songbird with black and grey, buff, or white plumage and a white rump.
– ORIGIN prob. from **white** + **arse**.

wheaten • adj. made of wheat.

wheatgerm • n. a nutritious foodstuff consisting of the centre parts of grains of wheat.

wheatmeal • n. flour made from wheat from which some of the bran has been removed.

wheedle • v. (**wheedles, wheedling, wheedled**) use flattery or terms of affection to persuade someone to do something.
– ORIGIN perh. from German *wedeln* 'cringe, fawn'.

wheel • n. **1** a circular object that revolves on an axle, fixed below a vehicle to enable it to move along or forming part of a machine. **2** something resembling a wheel or having a wheel as its essential part. **3** (**the wheel**) a steering wheel. **4** (**wheels**) informal a car. **5** a turn or rotation. • v. **1** push or pull something with wheels. **2** carry or convey on something with wheels. **3** fly or turn in a wide circle or curve. **4** turn round quickly to face another way. **5** (**wheel something on/out**) informal resort to something that has been frequently seen or heard before.
– PHRASES **wheel and deal** take part in commercial or political scheming.
– ORIGIN Old English.

wheelbarrow • n. a small cart with a single wheel at the front and two supporting legs and two handles at the rear, used for carrying loads in building or gardening.

wheelbase • n. the distance between the front and rear axles of a vehicle.

wheelchair • n. a chair on wheels for an invalid or disabled person.

wheel clamp • n. Brit. a device placed around the wheel of an illegally parked car to prevent it from being driven away.

wheeler • n. (in combination) a vehicle having a specified number of wheels: *a three-wheeler*.

wheeler-dealer (also **wheeler and dealer**) • n. a person who takes part in commercial or political scheming.

wheelhouse • n. a shelter for the person at the wheel of a boat or ship.

wheelie • n. informal a manoeuvre in which a bicycle or motorcycle is ridden for a short distance with the front wheel raised off the ground.

wheelie bin (also **wheely bin**) • n. Brit. informal a large rubbish bin on wheels.

wheelspin • n. the rotation of a vehicle's wheels without movement of the vehicle forwards or backwards.

wheelwright • n. esp. hist. a person who makes or repairs wooden wheels.

wheeze • v. (**wheezes, wheezing, wheezed**) **1** breathe with a whistling or rattling sound in the chest, as a result of a blockage in the air passages. **2** (of a device) make an irregular rattling or spluttering sound. • n. **1** a sound of a person wheezing. **2** Brit. informal a clever or amusing scheme or trick.
– DERIVATIVES **wheezily** adv. **wheeziness** n. **wheezy** adj.

– ORIGIN prob. from Old Norse, 'to hiss'.

whelk • n. a shellfish with a heavy pointed spiral shell, some kinds of which are eaten as food.
– ORIGIN Old English.

whelp • n. esp. old use **1** a puppy. **2** derog. a boy or young man. • v. give birth to a puppy.
– ORIGIN Old English.

when • adv. **1** at what time? **2** how soon? **3** in what circumstances? **4** at which time or in which situation. • conj. **1** at or during the time that. **2** at any time that; whenever. **3** after which; and just then. **4** in view of the fact that: *why buy when you can borrow?* **5** although; whereas.
– ORIGIN Old English.

whence (also **from whence**) • adv. formal or old use **1** from what place or source? **2** from which; from where. **3** to the place from which. **4** as a consequence of which.

whenever • conj. **1** at whatever time; on whatever occasion. **2** every time that. • adv. used for emphasis instead of 'when' in questions.

whensoever • conj. & adv. formal word for WHENEVER.

where • adv. **1** in or to what place or position? **2** in what direction or respect? **3** at, in, or to which. **4** the place or situation in which. **5** in or to a place or situation in which.
– ORIGIN Old English.

whereabouts • adv. where or approximately where? • n. the place where someone or something is.

whereas • conj. **1** in contrast or comparison with the fact that. **2** taking into consideration the fact that.

> ☑ **whereas** has an **e** before the **a**.

whereat • adv. & conj. old use or formal at which.

whereby • adv. by which.

wherefore old use • adv. for what reason? • adv. & conj. as a result of which.

wherein • adv. formal **1** in which. **2** in what place or respect?

whereof • adv. formal of what or which.

wheresoever • adv. & conj. formal word for WHEREVER.

whereupon • conj. immediately after which.

wherever • adv. **1** in or to whatever place. **2** used for emphasis instead of 'where' in questions. • conj. in every case when.

wherewithal • n. the money or other resources needed for a particular purpose.

wherry /*rhymes with* sherry/ • n. (pl. **wherries**) **1** a light rowing boat used chiefly for carrying passengers. **2** Brit. a large light barge.

whet /wet/ • v. (**whets, whetting, whetted**) **1** sharpen the blade of a tool or weapon. **2** arouse or stimulate someone's desire, interest, or appetite.
– ORIGIN Old English.

whether • conj. **1** expressing a doubt or choice between alternatives. **2** expressing an enquiry or investigation. **3** indicating that a statement applies whichever of the alternatives mentioned is the case.
– ORIGIN Old English.

> **USAGE:** For an explanation on whether to use **whether** or **if**, see the note at **IF**.

whetstone • n. a fine-grained stone used for sharpening cutting tools.

whey /way/ • n. the watery part of milk that remains after curds have formed.
– ORIGIN Old English.

which • pron. & det. **1** asking for information specifying one or more people or things from a definite set. **2** used to refer to something previously mentioned when introducing a clause giving further information.
– ORIGIN Old English.

> **USAGE:** On the difference between **which** and **that**, see the note at **THAT**.

whichever • det. & pron. **1** any which; that or those which. **2** regardless of which.

whiff • n. **1** a smell that is smelt only briefly or faintly. **2** Brit. informal an unpleasant smell. **3** a trace or hint of something bad or exciting: *a whiff of scandal.* **4** a puff or breath of air or smoke.

whiffy • adj. (**whiffier, whiffiest**) Brit. informal having an unpleasant smell.

Whig • n. hist. a member of a British political party that was succeeded in the 19th century by the Liberal Party.
– ORIGIN prob. a shortening of Scots *whiggamore*, the nickname of 17th-century Scottish rebels.

while • n. **1** (**a while**) a period of time. **2** (**a while**) for some time. **3** (**the while**) at the same time; meanwhile. • conj. **1** at the same time as. **2** whereas (indicating a contrast). **3** although. • adv. during which. • v. (**whiles, whiling, whiled**) (**while something away**) pass time in a leisurely way.
– PHRASES **worth while** (or **worth your while**) worth the time or effort spent.
– ORIGIN Old English.

whilst • conj. & adv. esp. Brit. while.

W

whim • n. a sudden desire or change of mind.

whimper • v. (**whimpers, whimpering, whimpered**) make a series of low, feeble sounds expressing fear, pain, or discontent. • n. a whimpering sound.

whimsical • adj. 1 playfully old-fashioned or fanciful. 2 showing sudden changes of behaviour.
– DERIVATIVES **whimsicality** n. **whimsically** adv.

whimsy (also **whimsey**) • n. (pl. **whimsies** or **whimseys**) 1 playfully old-fashioned or fanciful behaviour or humour. 2 a fanciful or odd thing. 3 a whim.
– ORIGIN prob. from former *whim-wham* 'trinket, whim'.

whin • n. esp. N. English gorse.
– ORIGIN prob. Scandinavian.

whinchat /win-chat/ • n. a small songbird with a brown back and orange-buff throat and neck.

whine • n. 1 a long, high-pitched complaining cry. 2 a long, high-pitched unpleasant sound. • v. (**whines, whining, whined**) 1 give or make a whine. 2 complain in a sulky way.
– DERIVATIVES **whiny** (also **whiney**) adj.
– ORIGIN Old English, 'whistle through the air'.

whinge Brit. informal • v. (**whinges, whingeing, whinged**) complain persistently and irritably. • n. an act of whingeing.
– DERIVATIVES **whinger** n.
– ORIGIN Old English.

whinny • n. (pl. **whinnies**) a gentle, high-pitched neigh. • v. (**whinnies, whinnying, whinnied**) (of a horse) make a gentle, high-pitched neigh.

whip • n. 1 a length of leather or cord fastened to a handle, used for beating a person or urging on an animal. 2 an official of a political party appointed to maintain parliamentary discipline among its members. 3 Brit. a written notice from such an official requesting that members of the party attend to vote in a debate. 4 a dessert made from cream or eggs beaten into a light fluffy mass. • v. (**whips, whipping, whipped**) 1 beat a person or animal with a whip. 2 (of a flexible object or rain or wind) strike or beat violently. 3 move or take something out fast or suddenly. 4 beat cream, eggs, etc. into a froth. 5 Brit. informal steal something.
– PHRASES **whip someone/thing up** 1 make or prepare something very quickly. 2 stimulate a particular feeling in someone. 3 deliberately excite or provoke someone.

– ORIGIN prob. from German and Dutch *wippen* 'swing, leap, dance'.

whipcord • n. 1 thin, tough, tightly twisted cord used for making the flexible end part of whips. 2 a closely woven ribbed fabric.

whiplash • n. 1 the lashing action of a whip. 2 the flexible part of a whip. 3 injury caused by a severe jerk to the head.

whippersnapper • n. informal a young and inexperienced but overconfident person.
– ORIGIN perh. representing *whipsnapper*, expressing noise and unimportance.

whippet • n. a small slender dog, bred for racing.
– ORIGIN partly from former *whippet* 'move briskly'.

whipping boy • n. a person who is blamed or punished for other people's faults or mistakes.
– ORIGIN first referring to a boy educated with a young prince and punished instead of him.

whippoorwill /wip-per-wil/ • n. a American nightjar with a distinctive call.

whippy • adj. flexible; springy.

whip-round • n. Brit. informal a collection of contributions of money for a particular purpose.

whipsaw • n. a saw with a narrow blade and a handle at both ends.

whirl • v. 1 move rapidly round and round. 2 (of the head or mind) seem to spin round. • n. 1 a rapid movement round and round. 2 frantic activity: *the mad social whirl.* 3 a sweet or biscuit with a spiral shape.
– PHRASES **give something a whirl** informal give something a try. **in a whirl** in a state of confusion.
– ORIGIN prob. from Old Norse.

whirligig • n. 1 a toy that spins round, e.g. a top or windmill. 2 a roundabout at a fair.
– ORIGIN from WHIRL + former *gig* 'toy for whipping'.

whirlpool • n. 1 a current of water whirling in a circle, often drawing floating objects towards its centre. 2 (also **whirlpool bath**) a heated pool in which hot bubbling water is continuously circulated.

whirlwind • n. 1 a column of air moving rapidly round and round in a funnel shape. 2 a situation in which many things happen very quickly: *a whirlwind of activities.* • adj. happening very quickly or suddenly: *a whirlwind romance.*

whirr (also **whir**) • v. (**whirs** or **whirrs**,

whirring, whirred) (of something rapidly rotating or moving to and fro) make a low, continuous, regular sound. •n. a whirring sound.
– ORIGIN prob. Scandinavian.

whisk •v. **1** move or take suddenly, quickly, and lightly. **2** beat a substance with a light, rapid movement. •n. **1** a utensil for whisking eggs or cream. **2** a bunch of grass, twigs, or bristles for flicking away dust or flies. **3** a brief, rapid action or movement.
– ORIGIN Scandinavian.

whisker •n. **1** a long hair or bristle growing from the face or snout of an animal. **2** (**whiskers**) the hair growing on a man's face. **3** (**a whisker**) informal a very small amount.
– DERIVATIVES **whiskery** adj.
– ORIGIN from **whisk**.

whisky (also Irish & US **whiskey**) •n. (pl. **whiskies**) a spirit distilled from malted grain, especially barley or rye.
– ORIGIN from Irish and Scottish Gaelic *uisge beatha* 'water of life'.

whisper •v. (**whispers, whispering, whispered**) **1** speak very softly. **2** literary rustle or murmur softly. •n. **1** something whispered, or a whispering tone of voice. **2** literary a soft rustling or murmuring sound. **3** a rumour or piece of gossip. **4** a slight trace.
– DERIVATIVES **whisperer** n. **whispery** adj.
– ORIGIN Old English.

whist /wist/ •n. a card game in which points are scored according to the number of tricks won.
– ORIGIN earlier as *whisk*: perh. from **whisk** (with reference to whisking away the tricks).

whistle •n. **1** a clear, high-pitched sound made by forcing breath through pursed lips, or between the teeth. **2** any similar high-pitched sound. **3** an instrument used to produce a whistling sound. •v. (**whistles, whistling, whistled**) **1** give out a whistle. **2** produce a tune in such a way. **3** move rapidly through the air or a narrow opening with a whistling sound. **4** blow a whistle. **5** (**whistle for**) wish for or expect something which will not happen.
– PHRASES **blow the whistle on** informal bring a secret activity to an end by informing on the person responsible. (**as**) **clean as a whistle** very clean.
– DERIVATIVES **whistler** n.
– ORIGIN Old English.

whistle-blower •n. informal a person who informs on someone engaged in a secret or illegal activity.

whistle-stop •adj. very fast and with only brief pauses.

whit /wit/ •n. a very small part or amount.
– PHRASES **not a whit** not at all.
– ORIGIN prob. from an Old English word meaning 'thing, creature, small amount'.

white •adj. **1** having the colour of milk or fresh snow. **2** very pale. **3** relating to a human group having light-coloured skin. **4** Brit. (of coffee or tea) served with milk or cream. **5** (of food such as bread or rice) light in colour through having been refined. **6** (of wine) made from white grapes, or dark grapes with the skins removed, and having a yellowish colour. **7** innocent and pure. •n. **1** white colour. **2** (also **whites**) white clothes or material. **3** the visible pale part of the eyeball around the iris. **4** the outer part which surrounds the yolk of an egg; the albumen. **5** a member of a light-skinned people.
– DERIVATIVES **whitely** adv. **whiteness** n. **whitish** adj.
– ORIGIN Old English.

white ant •n. = TERMITE.

whitebait •n. the small silvery-white young of herrings, sprats, and similar sea fish as food.

white belt •n. a white belt worn by a beginner in judo or karate.

white blood cell •n. less technical term for LEUCOCYTE.

whiteboard •n. a wipeable board with a white surface used for teaching or presentations.

white-collar •adj. relating to the work done or people who work in an office or other professional environment.

white elephant •n. a possession that is useless or troublesome.
– ORIGIN from the story that the kings of Siam (now Thailand) gave such animals to courtiers they disliked, in order to ruin them financially by the great cost of looking after the animals.

white feather •n. a white feather given to someone as a sign that they are considered a coward.
– ORIGIN with reference to a white feather in the tail of a game bird, being a mark of bad breeding.

whitefish •n. (pl. **whitefish** or **whitefishes**) a mainly freshwater fish of the salmon family, widely used as food.

white flag •n. a white flag or cloth used as a symbol of surrender, truce, or a wish to negotiate.

whitefly •n. (pl. **whitefly** or **whiteflies**) a minute winged bug covered with powdery white wax, damaging plants by feeding on sap and coating them with honeydew.

white gold •n. a silver-coloured alloy of

gold with another metal.

whitehead •n. informal a pale or white-topped pimple on the skin.

white heat •n. the temperature or state of something that is so hot that it gives out white light.

white hope (also **great white hope**) •n. a person expected to bring much success to a team or organization.
– ORIGIN first referring to a white boxer believed capable of beating the first black world heavyweight champion.

white-hot •adj. so hot as to glow white.

white-knuckle •adj. causing fear or nervous excitement.
– ORIGIN with reference to the effect caused by gripping tightly to steady yourself on a fairground ride.

white lie •n. a harmless lie told to avoid hurting someone's feelings.

white light •n. apparently colourless light containing all the wavelengths of the visible spectrum at equal intensity (such as ordinary daylight).

white magic •n. magic used only for good purposes.

white meat •n. pale meat such as chicken or turkey.

whiten •v. make or become white.
– DERIVATIVES **whitener** n.

white noise •n. noise containing many frequencies with equal intensities.

white-out •n. a dense blizzard.

White Paper •n. (in the UK) a government report giving information about or proposals concerning a particular issue.

white sauce •n. a sauce consisting of flour blended and cooked with butter and milk or stock.

white spirit •n. Brit. a colourless liquid distilled from petroleum, used as a paint thinner and solvent.

white tie •n. 1 a white bow tie worn by men as part of full evening dress. 2 full evening dress.

white trash •n. N. Amer. derog. poor white people.

whitewash •n. 1 a solution of lime or chalk and water, used for painting walls white. 2 a deliberate concealment of someone's mistakes or faults. 3 informal a victory by the same side in every game of a series. •v. 1 paint with whitewash. 2 conceal mistakes or faults.

white water •n. a fast shallow stretch of water in a river.

white witch •n. a person who uses witchcraft to help other people.

whither old use or literary •adv. 1 to what place or state? 2 what is the likely future of? 3 to which (with reference to a

place). 4 to whatever place.
– ORIGIN Old English.

whiting¹ •n. (pl. **whiting**) a slender-bodied sea fish with white edible flesh.
– ORIGIN Dutch *wijting*.

whiting² •n. ground chalk used for purposes such as whitewashing and cleaning metal plate.

Whitsun /wit-suhn/ •n. Whitsuntide.

Whit Sunday •n. the seventh Sunday after Easter, a Christian festival commemorating the descent of the Holy Spirit at Pentecost (Acts, chapter 2).
– ORIGIN Old English, 'white Sunday'.

Whitsuntide /wit-suhn-tyd/ •n. the weekend or week including Whit Sunday.

whittle •v. (**whittles, whittling, whittled**) 1 carve wood by repeatedly cutting small slices from it. 2 make an object by whittling wood. 3 (**whittle something away/down**) gradually reduce something.
– ORIGIN from dialect *whittle* 'knife'.

whizz (also esp. N. Amer. **whiz**) •v. (**whizzes, whizzing, whizzed**) 1 move quickly through the air with a whistling sound. 2 move or go fast. 3 (**whizz through**) do or deal with quickly. •n. 1 a whizzing sound. 2 informal a fast movement or brief journey. 3 (also **wiz**) informal a person who is very clever at something. [ORIGIN influenced by **wizard**.]
– DERIVATIVES **whizzy** adj.

whizz-kid (also **whiz-kid**) •n. informal a young person who is very successful or highly skilled.

WHO •abbrev. World Health Organization.

who •pron. 1 what or which person or people? 2 introducing a clause giving further information about a person or people previously mentioned.
– ORIGIN Old English.

> **USAGE:** When writing, **who** should be used as the subject of a verb (*who decided this?*) and **whom** should be used as the object of a verb or preposition (*whom do you think we should support?*). When speaking, however, most people think it is acceptable to use **who** instead of **whom**, as in *who do you think we should support?*

whoa /woh/ •exclam. used as a command to a horse to stop or slow down.

who'd •contr. 1 who had. 2 who would.

whodunnit (US **whodunit**) •n. informal a story or play about a murder in which the identity of the murderer is not revealed until the end.

whoever •pron. 1 the person or people who; any person who. 2 regardless of who. **3** used for emphasis instead of 'who' in questions.

whole •adj. **1** complete; entire. **2** used to emphasize a large extent or number: *a whole range of issues.* **3** in one piece. •n. **1** a thing that is complete in itself. **2** (**the whole**) all of something. •adv. informal entirely; wholly: *a whole new meaning.*
– PHRASES **as a whole** as a single unit; overall. **on the whole** taking everything into account; in general. **the whole nine yards** informal, esp. N. Amer. everything possible or available.
– DERIVATIVES **wholeness** n.
– ORIGIN Old English.

wholefood •n. (also **wholefoods**) Brit. food that has been processed as little as possible and is free from additives.

wholehearted •adj. completely sincere and committed.
– DERIVATIVES **wholeheartedly** adv.

wholemeal •adj. Brit. referring to flour or bread made from wholewheat, including the husk.

whole number •n. a number without fractions; an integer.

wholesale •n. the selling of goods in large quantities to be sold to the public by others. •adv. **1** being sold in such a way. **2** as a whole and in an indiscriminate way. •adj. done on a large scale. •v. (**wholesales**, **wholesaling**, **wholesaled**) sell goods wholesale.
– DERIVATIVES **wholesaler** n.

wholesome •adj. **1** good for health and physical well-being. **2** morally good or beneficial.

wholewheat •n. whole grains of wheat including the husk.

wholly /hohl-li, hoh-li/ •adv. entirely; fully.

whom •pron. used instead of 'who' as the object of a verb or preposition.

whomever •pron. formal used instead of 'whoever' as the object of a verb or preposition.

whomp /womp/ N. Amer. informal •v. strike heavily. •n. a thump.

whomsoever •relative pronoun formal used instead of 'whosoever' as the object of a verb or preposition.

whoop /woop/ •n. a loud cry of joy or excitement. •v. give or make a whoop.

whoopee •exclam. /wuu-pee/ informal expressing wild excitement or joy.
– PHRASES **make whoopee** celebrate wildly.

whooping cough /hoo-ping/ •n. a contagious disease chiefly affecting children, caused by bacteria and characterized by coughs followed by a rasping indrawn breath.

whoops •exclam. informal expressing mild dismay.

whoosh /wuush, woosh/ (also **woosh**) •v. move quickly or suddenly and with a rushing sound. •n. a sudden movement with a rushing sound.

whop /wop/ (esp. N. Amer. also **whap**) informal •v. (**whops**, **whopping**, **whopped**) hit hard. •n. a heavy blow or its sound.
– ORIGIN from dialect *wap* 'strike'.

whopper •n. informal **1** a very large thing. **2** a complete or blatant lie.

whopping •adj. informal very large.

whore /rhymes with door/ •n. **1** a prostitute. **2** derog. a woman who has many sexual partners.
– ORIGIN Old English.

whorehouse •n. informal a brothel.

whorl /worl, werl/ •n. **1** each of the turns in the spiral shell of a mollusc. **2** a coil of leaves, flowers, or branches encircling a stem. **3** a complete circle in a fingerprint.
– ORIGIN prob. from **WHIRL**.

who's •contr. **1** who is. **2** who has.

> **USAGE:** Do not confuse **who's** with **whose**. **Who's** is short for either **who is** or **who has**, as in *he has a son who's a doctor* or *who's done the reading?*, whereas **whose** means 'belonging to or associated with which person' or 'of whom or which', as in *whose coat is this?* or *he's a man whose opinion I respect.*

whose •possess. det. & pron. **1** belonging to or associated with which person. **2** (as possess. det.) of whom or which.
– ORIGIN Old English.

whosever •relative pronoun & det. belonging to or associated with whichever person; whoever's.

whosoever •pron. formal term for **WHOEVER**.

why •adv. **1** for what reason or purpose? **2** on account of which; the reason that: *that's why they are still friends.* •exclam. expressing surprise or annoyance, or used for emphasis. •n. (pl. **whys**) a reason or explanation.
– ORIGIN Old English.

WI •abbrev. **1** West Indies. **2** Brit. Women's Institute.

Wicca /wik-kuh/ •n. the religious cult of modern witchcraft.
– DERIVATIVES **Wiccan** adj. & n.
– ORIGIN Old English, 'witch'.

wick •n. a length of thread up which liquid fuel is drawn to the flame in a candle, lamp, or lighter.
– PHRASES **get on someone's wick** Brit. informal annoy someone.

w

– ORIGIN Old English.

wicked •adj. (**wickeder**, **wickedest**) **1** evil or morally wrong. **2** playfully mischievous. **3** informal excellent; very good.
– DERIVATIVES **wickedly** adv. **wickedness** n.
– ORIGIN prob. from **WICCA**.

wicker •n. twigs plaited or woven to make items such as furniture and baskets.
– DERIVATIVES **wickerwork** n.
– ORIGIN Scandinavian.

wicket •n. **1** Cricket each of the sets of three stumps with two bails across the top at either end of the pitch, defended by a batsman. **2** a small door or gate.
– ORIGIN Old French *wiket*.

wicketkeeper •n. Cricket a fielder positioned close behind a batsman's wicket.

wide •adj. (**wider**, **widest**) **1** of great or more than average width. **2** extending a specified distance from side to side. **3** open to the full extent. **4** including a great variety of people or things. **5** spread among a large number or over a large area. **6** (in combination) extending over the whole of: *industry-wide*. **7** at a distance from a point or target. •adv. **1** to the full extent. **2** far from a point or target. **3** (especially in football) at or near the side of the field.
– PHRASES **wide awake** fully awake. **wide of the mark** not accurate.
– DERIVATIVES **widely** adv.
– ORIGIN Old English.

wide-angle •adj. (of a camera lens) covering a wider view than a standard lens.

wide boy •n. Brit. informal a man involved in petty criminal activities.

wide-eyed •adj. **1** having the eyes wide open in amazement. **2** inexperienced; innocent.

widen •v. make or become wider.

widescreen •n. a cinema or television screen presenting a wide field of vision in relation to height.

widespread •adj. spread among a large number or over a large area.

widgeon •n. var. of **WIGEON**.

widget /wi-jit/ •n. informal a small gadget or mechanical device.
– ORIGIN perh. from **GADGET**.

widow •n. **1** a woman whose husband has died and who has not married again. **2** humorous a woman whose husband is often away taking part in a specified activity: *a golf widow*. •v. (**be widowed**) become a widow or widower.
– ORIGIN Old English.

widower •n. a man whose wife has died and who has not married again.

widowhood •n. the state or period of being a widow or widower.

widow's peak •n. a V-shaped growth of hair towards the centre of the forehead.

widow's weeds •pl. n. black clothes worn by a widow in mourning.
– ORIGIN *weeds* is used in the former sense 'clothes' and is from Old English.

width /with, width/ •n. **1** the measurement or extent of something from side to side. **2** a piece of something at its full extent from side to side. **3** wide range or extent: *the width of his interests*.

widthways (also **widthwise**) •adv. in a direction parallel with a thing's width.

wield •v. **1** hold and use a weapon or tool. **2** have and be able to use power or influence.
– DERIVATIVES **wielder** n.
– ORIGIN Old English, 'govern, subdue, direct'.

> ☑ **wield** follows the usual rule of *i* before *e* except after *c*.

wife •n. (pl. **wives**) a married woman in relation to her husband.
– DERIVATIVES **wifely** adj.
– ORIGIN Old English, 'woman'.

wig •n. a covering for the head made of real or artificial hair.
– ORIGIN shortening of *periwig* (a man's wig worn in the past), from French *perruque*.

wigeon /rhymes with pigeon/ (also **widgeon**) •n. a duck with mainly reddish-brown and grey plumage.
– ORIGIN perh. suggested by **PIGEON**.

wiggle •v. (**wiggles**, **wiggling**, **wiggled**) move with short movements up and down or from side to side. •n. a wiggling movement.
– DERIVATIVES **wiggler** n. **wiggly** adj.
– ORIGIN German and Dutch *wiggelen*.

wigwam •n. a dome-shaped or conical home made by fastening skins or other material over a framework of poles (as used formerly by some North American Indian peoples).
– ORIGIN from a word meaning 'their house' in a North American Indian language.

wild •adj. **1** (of animals or plants) living or growing in the natural environment. **2** (of scenery or a region) not inhabited or changed by people. **3** lacking discipline or control. **4** not civilized; primitive. **5** not based on reason or evidence: *a wild guess*. **6** (of looks, appearance, etc.) showing strong

emotion. **7** informal very enthusiastic or excited. **8** informal very angry. • n. **1** (**the wild**) a natural state. **2** (also **the wilds**) a remote area with no or few inhabitants.
– DERIVATIVES **wildly** adv. **wildness** n.
– ORIGIN Old English.

wild card • n. **1** a playing card that can have any value, suit, colour, or other property in a game according to the choice of the player holding it. **2** a person or thing whose qualities are uncertain. **3** Computing a character that will match any character or sequence of characters in a search.

wildcat • n. a small Eurasian and African cat, typically grey with black markings and a bushy tail. • adj. (of a strike) sudden and unofficial.

wild duck • n. a mallard.

wildebeest /wil-duh-beest, vil-duh-beest/ • n. (pl. **wildebeest** or **wildebeests**) = GNU.
– ORIGIN Afrikaans, 'wild beast'.

wilderness • n. **1** a wild region that is very difficult to live in. **2** a state of being out of political favour or office.
– ORIGIN Old English, 'land inhabited only by wild animals'.

wildfire • n. (in phr. **spread like wildfire**) spread very quickly.
– ORIGIN first meaning 'a highly flammable liquid used in warfare'.

wildfowl • pl. n. birds that are hunted as game.

wild goose chase • n. a hopeless search for something that is impossible to find.

wildlife • n. the native animals of a region.

wild rice • n. a tall American grass with edible grains, related to rice.

wiles • pl. n. cunning methods used by someone to get what they want.
– ORIGIN perh. from Old Norse, 'craft'.

wilful (US also **willful**) • adj. **1** (of a bad act) deliberate. **2** stubborn and determined.
– DERIVATIVES **wilfully** adv. **wilfulness** n.

☑ Spell **wilful** with only one **l** in the middle: the spelling **willful** is American.

will[1] • modal verb (3rd sing. present **will**; past **would**) **1** expressing the future tense. **2** expressing a strong intention about the future. **3** expressing events that are certain to occur: *accidents will happen.* **4** expressing a request: *will you stop here, please?* **5** expressing desire, consent, or willingness: *will you have a cognac?* **6** expressing facts about ability or capacity: *it will float on water.*
– ORIGIN Old English.

USAGE: For an explanation of the difference between **will** and **shall**, see the note at **SHALL**.

will[2] • n. **1** a person's power to decide on something and take action. **2** (also **willpower**) a person's ability to control their actions and thoughts. **3** a desire or intention: *the will to live.* **4** a legal document containing a person's instructions about what should be done with their money and property after their death. • v. **1** intend or desire something to happen. **2** bring about by the use of mental powers. **3** leave something to someone in a will.
– PHRASES **at will** at whatever time or in whatever way you wish.
– ORIGIN Old English.

willies • pl. n. (**the willies**) informal a feeling of nervousness or uneasiness.

willing • adj. **1** ready, eager, or prepared to do something. **2** given or done readily.
– DERIVATIVES **willingly** adv. **willingness** n.

will-o'-the-wisp • n. **1** a person or thing that is difficult or impossible to reach or catch. **2** a dim, flickering light seen hovering at night over marshy ground, thought to be caused by natural gases burning.
– ORIGIN first as *Will with the wisp*, the sense of *wisp* being 'handful of lighted hay'.

willow • n. a tree or shrub which typically grows near water, has narrow leaves, and bears catkins.
– ORIGIN Old English.

willowherb • n. a plant with long narrow leaves and pink or pale purple flowers.

willow pattern • n. a design in pottery featuring a Chinese scene depicted in blue on white, typically including people on a bridge, a willow tree, and birds.

willowy • adj. **1** (of a person) tall and slim. **2** bordered, shaded, or covered by willows.

willy-nilly • adv. **1** whether you like it or not. **2** without direction or planning.
– ORIGIN later spelling of *will I, nill I* 'I am willing, I am unwilling'.

wilt[1] • v. **1** (of a plant) become limp through loss of water or heat or disease; droop. **2** feel weak and tired.
– ORIGIN perh. from dialect *welk* 'lose freshness', from German.

wilt[2] old-fashioned 2nd person sing. of **WILL**[1].

Wilts. • abbrev. Wiltshire.

wily /rhymes with highly/ • adj. (**wilier**,

wiliest) clever in a cunning or crafty way.
- DERIVATIVES **wiliness** n.

wimp informal • n. a timid or weak person. • v. (**wimp out**) fail to do something as a result of fear or lack of confidence.
- DERIVATIVES **wimpish** adj. **wimpy** adj.
- ORIGIN perh. from WHIMPER.

wimple • n. a cloth headdress covering the head, neck, and sides of the face, formerly worn by women and still by some nuns.
- ORIGIN Old English.

win • v. (**wins, winning, won**) **1** be the most successful in a contest or conflict. **2** gain as a result of success in a contest, conflict, or bet: *you could win a trip to Australia.* **3** gain someone's attention, support, or love. **4** (**win someone over**) gain someone's support or favour. **5** (**win out/through**) manage to succeed or achieve something by effort. • n. a victory in a game or contest.
- DERIVATIVES **winnable** adj.
- ORIGIN Old English, 'strive, contend', also 'subdue and take possession of, gain'.

wince • v. (**winces, wincing, winced**) give a slight unintentional grimace or flinch due to pain or distress. • n. an instance of wincing.
- ORIGIN Old French *guenchir* 'turn aside'.

winceyette /win-si-et/ • n. Brit. a lightweight brushed cotton fabric, used especially for nightclothes.
- ORIGIN from *wincey*, a lightweight wool and cotton fabric.

winch • n. a hauling or lifting device consisting of a rope or chain winding around a horizontal rotating drum, turned by a crank or motor. • v. hoist or haul with a winch.
- ORIGIN Old English, 'reel, pulley'.

wind[1] /wind/ • n. **1** a natural movement of the air. **2** breath as needed in physical effort, speech, or playing an instrument. **3** Brit. air swallowed while eating or gas generated in the stomach and intestines by digestion. **4** meaningless talk. **5** wind or woodwind instruments forming a band or section of an orchestra.
• v. **1** make someone unable to breathe easily because of physical effort or a blow to the stomach. **2** Brit. make a baby bring up wind after feeding by patting its back.
- PHRASES **get wind of** informal hear a rumour of. **put the wind up** Brit. informal alarm or frighten someone.
- DERIVATIVES **windless** adj.
- ORIGIN Old English.

wind[2] /wynd/ • v. (**winds, winding, wound** /wownd/) **1** move in or take a

twisting or spiral course. **2** pass something around a thing or person so as to encircle or enfold them. **3** (of something long) twist or be twisted around itself or a core. **4** make a clockwork device work by turning a key or handle. **5** turn a key or handle several times. **6** move an audio tape, videotape, or a film backwards or forwards. • n. a single turn made when winding a key or handle.
- PHRASES **wind down 1** (of a clockwork mechanism) gradually lose power. **2** (also **wind something down**) draw or bring something gradually to a close. **3** informal relax after stress or excitement. **wind up** informal end up in a specified state, situation, or place. **wind someone up** Brit. informal tease or irritate someone. **wind something up** bring something to an end.
- DERIVATIVES **winder** n.
- ORIGIN Old English, 'go rapidly', 'twine'.

windbag • n. informal a person who talks a great deal but says little of any value.

windbreak • n. a screen, wall, or row of trees that provides shelter from the wind.

windcheater • n. Brit. a wind-resistant jacket with a close-fitting neck, waistband, and cuffs.

wind chill • n. the cooling effect of wind on a surface.

wind chimes • pl. n. pieces of glass, metal rods, or similar items, hung near a door or window so as to chime in the draught.

windfall • n. **1** a piece of unexpected good luck. **2** an apple or other fruit blown from a tree by the wind.

wind farm • n. an area containing a group of energy-producing windmills or wind turbines.

winding /*rhymes with* finding/ • adj. having a twisting or spiral course. • n. **1** a twisting movement or course. **2** a thing that winds or is wound round something.

winding sheet • n. a sheet in which a corpse is wrapped for burial; a shroud.

wind instrument • n. **1** a musical instrument in which sound is produced by the vibration of air, typically by the player blowing into the instrument. **2** a woodwind instrument as distinct from a brass instrument.

windjammer • n. hist. a merchant sailing ship.

windlass • n. a winch, especially one on a ship or in a harbour.
- ORIGIN prob. from Old Norse, 'winding pole'.

windmill • n. a building with sails or

vanes that turn in the wind and produce power to grind corn, generate electricity, or draw water.

window • n. **1** an opening in a wall of a building or vehicle, fitted with glass to let in light and allow people to see out. **2** an opening through which customers are served in a bank, ticket office, etc. **3** a framed area on a computer screen for viewing information. **4** a transparent panel in an envelope to show an address. **5** an opportunity for action.
– DERIVATIVES **windowless** adj.
– ORIGIN Old Norse.

window box • n. a long narrow box in which flowers are grown on an outside window sill.

window dressing • n. **1** the arrangement of a display in a shop window. **2** the presentation of something in a superficially attractive way to give a good impression.

window frame • n. a frame holding the glass of a window.

window ledge • n. a window sill.

windowpane • n. a pane of glass in a window.

window seat • n. **1** a seat below a window, especially one in a bay or alcove. **2** a seat next to a window in an aircraft or train.

window-shop • v. look at the goods displayed in shop windows, especially without intending to buy.
– DERIVATIVES **window-shopper** n.

windowsill • n. a ledge or sill forming the bottom part of a window.

windpipe • n. the air passage from the throat to the lungs; the trachea.

windproof • adj. (of an item of clothing or fabric) giving protection from the wind.

windscreen • n. Brit. a glass screen at the front of a motor vehicle.

windscreen wiper • n. Brit. a device consisting of a rubber blade on a moving arm, for keeping a windscreen clear of rain.

windshield • n. N. Amer. a windscreen.

windsock • n. a light, flexible cylinder or cone mounted on a mast to show the direction and strength of the wind.

windsurfing • n. the sport of riding on a sailboard on water.
– DERIVATIVES **windsurf** v. **windsurfer** n.

windswept • adj. **1** exposed to strong winds. **2** (of a person's hair or appearance) untidy after being in the wind.

wind tunnel • n. a tunnel-like structure for producing an airstream, in order to investigate flow or the effect of wind on an aircraft or object.

wind-up • n. Brit. informal an attempt to tease or irritate someone.

windward • adj. & adv. facing the wind or on the side facing the wind. Contrasted with LEEWARD. • n. the side from which the wind is blowing.

windy¹ /win-di/ • adj. (**windier**, **windiest**) marked by or exposed to strong winds.
– DERIVATIVES **windily** adv. **windiness** n.

windy² /wyn-di/ • adj. following a winding course.

wine • n. **1** an alcoholic drink made from fermented grape juice. **2** a fermented alcoholic drink made from other fruits or plants.
– DERIVATIVES **winey** (also **winy**) adj.
– ORIGIN Old English.

wine bar • n. a bar or small restaurant that specializes in serving wine.

wine cellar • n. **1** a cellar for storing wine. **2** a stock of wine.

wine glass • n. a glass with a stem and foot, used for drinking wine.

wine list • n. a list of the wines available in a restaurant.

winemaker • n. a producer of wine.
– DERIVATIVES **winemaking** n.

winery • n. (pl. **wineries**) a place where wine is made.

wing • n. **1** a modified forelimb or other part enabling a bird, bat, or insect to fly. **2** a rigid horizontal structure projecting from both sides of an aircraft and supporting it in the air. **3** a part of a large building. **4** a group within an organization such as a political party having particular views or a particular function. **5** (**the wings**) the sides of a theatre stage out of view of the audience. **6** the part of a football, rugby, or hockey field close to the sidelines. **7** an attacking player positioned near the sidelines. **8** Brit. a raised part of the body of a vehicle above the wheel.
• v. **1** fly or move quickly as if flying. **2** shoot a person or bird so as to wound in the arm or wing. **3** (**wing it**) informal speak or act without preparation.
– PHRASES **in the wings** ready for use or action at the appropriate time. **on the wing** (of a bird or insect) in flight. **take wing** fly away. **under your wing** in or into your protective care.
– DERIVATIVES **winged** adj. **wingless** adj.
– ORIGIN Old Norse.

wingbeat (also **wingstroke**) • n. one complete set of motions of a wing in flying.

wing chair • n. an armchair with side

W

pieces projecting forwards from a high back.

wing collar • n. a high stiff shirt collar with turned-down corners.

winger • n. **1** an attacking player on the wing in football, hockey, etc. **2** (in combination) a member of a specified political wing: *a Tory right-winger.*

wing mirror • n. a rear-view mirror projecting from the side of a vehicle.

wing nut • n. a nut with a pair of projections for the fingers to turn it on a screw.

wingspan • n. the full extent from tip to tip of the wings of an aircraft, bird, etc.

wink • v. **1** close and open one eye quickly as a signal of affection or greeting or to convey a message. **2** shine or flash on and off. • n. an act of winking.
– PHRASES **in the wink of an eye** (or **in a wink**) very quickly. **not sleep a wink** (or **not get a wink of sleep**) not sleep at all.
– ORIGIN Old English.

winkle • n. a small edible shellfish with a spiral shell. • v. (**winkles, winkling, winkled**) (**winkle something out**) esp. Brit. take out or obtain something with difficulty.
– ORIGIN shortening of PERIWINKLE².

winkle-picker • n. Brit. informal a shoe with a long pointed toe, popular in the 1950s.

winner • n. **1** a person or thing that wins. **2** informal a successful or highly promising thing.

winning • adj. **1** gaining, resulting in, or relating to victory. **2** attractive or charming. • n. (**winnings**) money won, especially by gambling.
– DERIVATIVES **winningly** adv.

winning post • n. a post marking the end of a race.

winnow • v. **1** blow air through grain in order to remove the chaff. **2** remove people or things from a group until only the best ones are left: *we had to winnow out the losers.*
– ORIGIN Old English.

wino • n. (pl. **winos**) informal a homeless person who drinks excessive amounts of alcohol.

winsome • adj. attractive or appealing.
– DERIVATIVES **winsomely** adv. **winsomeness** n.
– ORIGIN Old English, 'joy'.

winter • n. the coldest season of the year, after autumn and before spring. • v. (**winters, wintering, wintered**) spend the winter in a particular place. • adj. (of crops) sown in autumn for harvesting the following year.
– ORIGIN Old English.

wintergreen • n. **1** an American shrub whose leaves produce oil. **2** (also **oil of wintergreen**) a pungent oil obtained from wintergreen or from birch bark, used as a medicine or flavouring.

Winter Olympics • pl. n. an international contest of winter sports held every four years at a two-year interval from the Olympic Games.

winter sports • pl. n. sports performed on snow or ice.

wintertime • n. the season or period of winter.

wintry • adj. (**wintrier, wintriest**) typical of winter; very cold or bleak.

> ✓ Although **wintry** is related to *winter,* it ends with **-try.**

wipe • v. (**wipes, wiping, wiped**) **1** clean or dry something by rubbing with a cloth or the hand. **2** remove dirt or moisture by wiping. **3** (usu. **wipe something up**) remove or eliminate something. **4** (**wipe someone out**) kill a large number of people. **5** erase data from a tape, computer, etc. • n. **1** an act of wiping. **2** an absorbent disposable cleaning cloth.
– DERIVATIVES **wipeable** adj. **wiper** n.
– ORIGIN Old English.

wire • n. **1** metal drawn out into a thin flexible strand or rod. **2** a length or quantity of wire used for fencing, to carry an electric current, etc. **3** a concealed electronic listening device. **4** informal, esp N. Amer. a telegram. • v. (**wires, wiring, wired**) **1** install electric circuits or wires in something. **2** provide, fasten, or reinforce with wire. **3** informal, esp. N. Amer. send a telegram to.
– PHRASES **down to the wire** informal until the very last minute.
– ORIGIN Old English.

wire brush • n. a brush with tough wire bristles for cleaning hard surfaces.

wired • adj. informal **1** making use of computers and information technology to transfer or receive information. **2** nervous or on edge.

wireless • n. dated, esp. Brit. **1** a radio receiving set. **2** broadcasting using radio signals. • adj. lacking or not needing wires.

wiretapping • n. the practice of tapping a telephone line to monitor conversations secretly.

wire wool • n. Brit. = STEEL WOOL.

wireworm • n. the worm-like larva of a kind of beetle, which feeds on roots and can cause damage to crops.

wiring • n. a system of wires providing electric circuits for a device or building.

wiry • adj. (**wirier, wiriest**) **1** resembling

wire in form and texture. **2** lean, tough, and sinewy.

wisdom • n. **1** the quality of having experience, knowledge, and good judgement. **2** the body of knowledge and experience that develops within a society or period: *oriental wisdom.*

wisdom tooth • n. each of the four molars at the back of the mouth which usually appear at about the age of twenty.

wise¹ • adj. **1** having or showing experience, knowledge, and good judgement. **2** (**wise to**) informal aware of.
• v. (**wises, wising, wised**) (**wise up**) informal become alert or aware.
– DERIVATIVES **wisely** adv.
– ORIGIN Old English.

wise² • n. old use the way or extent of something.
– ORIGIN Old English.

-wise • suffix **1** forming adjectives and adverbs of manner or respect: *clockwise.* **2** informal concerning: *security-wise.*

wiseacre /wyz-ay-ker/ • n. a person who pretends to be wise or knowledgeable.
– ORIGIN Dutch *wijsseggher* 'soothsayer'.

wisecrack informal • n. a witty remark or joke. • v. make a wisecrack.
– DERIVATIVES **wisecracker** n.

wise guy • n. informal, esp. N. Amer. a person who makes sarcastic or cheeky remarks to demonstrate their cleverness.

wish • v. **1** desire something that cannot or probably will not happen. **2** want to do something. **3** want someone to do something or something to be done. **4** express a hope that someone has happiness or success. **5** (**wish someone/ thing on**) hope that someone has to deal with someone or something unpleasant.
• n. **1** a desire or hope. **2** (**wishes**) an expression of a hope for someone's happiness, success, or welfare. **3** a thing wished for.
– ORIGIN Old English.

wishbone • n. a forked bone between the neck and breast of a bird.

wishful • adj. **1** having or expressing a wish for something to happen. **2** based on impractical wishes rather than facts: *wishful thinking.*
– DERIVATIVES **wishfully** adv.

wish-fulfilment • n. the satisfying of wishes in dreams or fantasies.

wishing well • n. a well into which you drop a coin and make a wish.

wishy-washy • adj. not firm or forceful; feeble: *wishy-washy liberalism.*

wisp • n. a small thin bunch, strand, or amount of something.
– DERIVATIVES **wispy** adj.

wisteria /wi-steer-i-uh/ (also **wistaria** /wi-stair-i-uh/) • n. a climbing shrub with hanging clusters of pale bluish-lilac flowers.
– ORIGIN named after the American anatomist Caspar *Wistar* (or *Wister*).

wistful • adj. having or showing a feeling of vague or regretful longing.
– DERIVATIVES **wistfully** adv. **wistfulness** n.
– ORIGIN prob. from former *wistly* 'intently', influenced by **WISHFUL**.

wit • n. **1** (also **wits**) the capacity for inventive thought and quick under-standing; keen intelligence. **2** a nat-ural talent for using words and ideas in a quick, clever, and amusing way. **3** a witty person.
– PHRASES **be at your wits' end** be so worried that you do not know what to do.
– ORIGIN Old English.

witch • n. **1** a woman thought to have evil magic powers. **2** a person who follows or practises modern witchcraft. **3** informal an ugly or disliked old woman.
– DERIVATIVES **witchy** adj.
– ORIGIN Old English.

witchcraft • n. the practice of magic, especially the use of spells and the calling up of evil spirits. See also **WICCA**.

witch doctor • n. (among tribal peoples) a person believed to have magic powers of healing, seeing the future, etc.

witchery • n. the practice of magic.

witchetty grub /wit-chi-ti/ • n. a large whitish wood-eating larva of a beetle or moth, eaten as food by some Australian Aboriginals.
– ORIGIN from words in an Aboriginal language meaning 'hooked stick for extracting grubs' + 'grub'.

witch hazel • n. a lotion made from the bark and leaves of a shrub, used for treating injuries on the skin.
– ORIGIN *wych*, used in names of trees with flexible branches, is from Old English.

witch-hunt • n. a campaign directed against a person or people whose views are seen as unacceptable or a threat to society.

witching hour • n. midnight, regarded as the time when witches are supposed to be active.
– ORIGIN with reference to *the witching time of night* from Shakespeare's *Hamlet* (III. ii. 377).

with • prep. **1** accompanied by. **2** in the same direction as. **3** possessing; having. **4** indicating the instrument used to perform an action or the material used for a purpose: *cut the fish with a knife.* **5** in opposition to or competition with.

w

6 indicating the way or attitude in which a person does something. **7** indicating responsibility: *leave it with me.* **8** in relation to. **9** affected by. **10** employed by. **11** using the services of. **12** indicating separation or removal from something.

– PHRASES **with it** informal **1** up to date or fashionable. **2** alert and able to understand things quickly.

– ORIGIN Old English.

withal /wi-*thawl*/ old use •adv. in addition.

withdraw •v. (**withdraws**, **withdrawing**, **withdrew**; past part. **withdrawn**) **1** remove or take away something. **2** leave or cause to leave a place. **3** stop taking part in an activity or being a member of a team or organization. **4** take back something said. **5** take money out of an account. **6** go away to another place to be quiet or private. **7** stop taking an addictive drug.

withdrawal •n. **1** the action or an act of withdrawing. **2** the process of giving up an addictive drug.

> ☑ Remember that **withdrawal** ends with **-wal**.

withdrawn past part. of **WITHDRAW**. •adj. very shy or reserved.

wither •v. (**withers**, **withering**, **withered**) **1** (of a plant) become dry and shrivelled. **2** become shrunken or wrinkled from age or disease. **3** become weaker; decline. **4** (as adj. **withering**) scornful: *a withering look.*

– ORIGIN prob. a variant of **WEATHER**.

withers •pl. n. the highest part of a horse's back, lying at the base of the neck above the shoulders.

– ORIGIN prob. from former *widersome*.

withhold •v. (**withholds**, **withholding**, **withheld**) **1** refuse to give something due to or wanted by another person. **2** suppress or hold back an emotion or reaction.

> ☑ **withhold** is spelled with a double **h**.

within •prep. **1** inside. **2** inside the range or bounds of. **3** occurring inside a particular period of time. **4** not further off than (used with distances). •adv. **1** inside. **2** internally or inwardly.

without •prep. **1** not accompanied by or having the use of. **2** in which the action mentioned does not happen. •adv. old use outside.

withstand •v. (**withstands**, **withstanding**, **withstood**) **1** remain undamaged or unaffected by. **2** offer strong resistance to.

withy /wi-*thi*/ •n. (pl. **withies**) a tough flexible willow branch, used for making baskets or tying things.

– ORIGIN Old English.

witless •adj. foolish; stupid.

witness •n. **1** a person who sees an event take place. **2** a person giving sworn evidence to a court of law or the police. **3** a person who is present at the signing of a document and signs it themselves to confirm this. •v. **1** be a witness to. **2** be the place or period in which an event takes place: *the 1960s witnessed a drop in churchgoing.*

– ORIGIN Old English.

witness box (N. Amer. **witness stand**) •n. the place in a court of law from where a witness gives evidence.

witter •v. (**witters**, **wittering**, **wittered**) (usu. **witter on**) Brit. informal speak at length about trivial things.

witticism •n. a witty remark.

witting •adj. aware of what you are doing.

– DERIVATIVES **wittingly** adv.

– ORIGIN Old English, 'to know'.

witty •adj. (**wittier**, **wittiest**) showing or having the ability to say clever and amusing things.

– DERIVATIVES **wittily** adv. **wittiness** n.

wives pl. of **WIFE**.

wiz •n. var. of **WHIZZ** (in sense 3).

wizard •n. **1** a man who has magical powers. **2** a person who is very skilled in a particular area. **3** a computer software tool that automatically guides a user through a process. •adj. Brit. informal, dated excellent.

– DERIVATIVES **wizardly** adj.

– ORIGIN first meaning 'philosopher, wise man': from **WISE**[1].

wizardry •n. **1** the art or practice of magic. **2** great skill in a particular area.

wizened /wi-*zuhnd*/ •adj. shrivelled or wrinkled with age.

– ORIGIN from former *wizen* 'shrivel', from Old English.

WMD •abbrev. weapon (or weapons) of mass destruction.

woad /rhymes with road/ •n. a plant whose leaves were formerly used to make blue dye.

– ORIGIN Old English.

wobble •v. (**wobbles**, **wobbling**, **wobbled**) **1** move unsteadily from side to side. **2** (of the voice) tremble. •n. a wobbling movement or sound.

– ORIGIN Germanic.

wobbler •n. **1** a person or thing that wobbles. **2** = **WOBBLY**.

wobbly •adj. (**wobblier**, **wobbliest**) **1** tending to wobble. **2** weak and

unsteady from illness, tiredness, or anxiety. •n. Brit. informal a fit of temper or panic.
– DERIVATIVES **wobbliness** n.

wodge •n. Brit. informal a large piece or amount.
– ORIGIN from WEDGE.

woe •n. literary **1** great sorrow or distress. **2** (**woes**) troubles or problems.
– PHRASES **woe betide someone** a person will be in trouble if they do a specified thing.
– ORIGIN Old English.

woebegone /woh-bi-gon/ •adj. looking sad or miserable.
– ORIGIN from WOE + former *begone* 'surrounded'.

woeful •adj. **1** very sad or miserable. **2** very bad.
– DERIVATIVES **woefully** adv.

wog •n. Brit. informal, offens. a person who is not white.

woggle •n. a loop or ring through which the ends of a Scout's neckerchief are threaded.

wok •n. a bowl-shaped frying pan used in Chinese cookery.
– ORIGIN Chinese.

woke past of WAKE¹.

woken past part. of WAKE¹.

wold /rhymes with cold/ •n. (especially in British place names) a piece of high, open, uncultivated land.
– ORIGIN Old English.

wolf •n. (pl. **wolves**) a wild animal of the dog family, that lives and hunts in packs. •v. (**wolfs**, **wolfing**, **wolfed**) (usu. **wolf something down**) eat food quickly and greedily.
– PHRASES **cry wolf** raise repeated false alarms, so that when you really need help you are ignored. [ORIGIN with reference to the fable of the shepherd boy who tricked people with false cries of 'Wolf!'] **keep the wolf from the door** have enough money to be able to buy food.
– DERIVATIVES **wolfish** adj.
– ORIGIN Old English.

wolfhound •n. a dog of a large breed originally used to hunt wolves.

wolfram /wuul-fruhm/ •n. tungsten or its ore.
– ORIGIN German.

wolf whistle •n. a whistle with a rising and falling pitch, used to express sexual attraction or admiration. •v. (**wolf-whistle**) whistle at someone to express sexual attraction.

wolverine /wuul-vuh-reen/ •n. a heavily built mammal with a long brown coat and a bushy tail, native to

northern tundra and forests.
– ORIGIN from *wolv-*, plural stem of WOLF.

wolves pl. of WOLF.

woman •n. (pl. **women**) **1** an adult human female. **2** a female worker or employee. **3** a wife or lover.
– DERIVATIVES **womanliness** n. **womanly** adj.
– ORIGIN from the Old English words for WIFE and MAN.

womanhood •n. **1** the state or period of being a woman. **2** women as a group. **3** the qualities associated with women, such as femininity.

womanish •adj. derog. suitable for or typical of a woman.

womanize (or **womanise**) •v. (**womanizes**, **womanizing**, **womanized**) (of a man) have many casual sexual relationships with women.
– DERIVATIVES **womanizer** n.

womankind •n. women as a group.

womb •n. the organ in the body of a woman or female mammal in which offspring develop before birth.
– ORIGIN Old English.

wombat /wom-bat/ •n. a burrowing Australian marsupial (mammal) which resembles a small bear with short legs.
– ORIGIN from an extinct Aboriginal language.

women pl. of WOMAN.

womenfolk •pl. n. the women of a family or community considered as a group.

women's liberation (also informal **women's lib**) •n. a movement supporting the freedom of women to have the same rights, status, and treatment as men (now usually replaced by the term *feminism*).

won past and past part. of WIN.

wonder •n. **1** a feeling of amazement and admiration caused by something beautiful, unexpected, or unfamiliar. **2** a cause of wonder. •v. (**wonders**, **wondering**, **wondered**) **1** desire to know something. **2** feel doubt. **3** feel amazement and admiration. •adj. having remarkable qualities or abilities: *a wonder drug.*
– PHRASES **no wonder** it is not surprising.
– ORIGIN Old English.

wonderful •adj. very good, pleasant, or remarkable.
– DERIVATIVES **wonderfully** adv. **wonderfulness** n.

wonderland •n. a place full of wonderful things.

wonderment •n. a state of awed admiration or respect.

W

wondrous • adj. literary causing amazement and admiration.
– DERIVATIVES **wondrously** adv.

wonky • adj. (**wonkier, wonkiest**) informal **1** not straight; crooked. **2** unsteady or faulty.
– DERIVATIVES **wonkily** adv. **wonkiness** n.

wont /wohnt/ • n. (**your wont**) formal your normal behaviour. • adj. literary in the habit of doing something; accustomed.
– ORIGIN Old English.

won't • contr. will not.

wonted /wohn-tid/ • adj. literary usual.

WOO • v. (**woos, wooing, wooed**) **1** try to gain a woman's love. **2** try to gain a person's support or custom.
– DERIVATIVES **wooer** n.
– ORIGIN Old English.

wood • n. **1** the hard fibrous material forming the trunk and branches of a tree or shrub, used for fuel or timber. **2** (also **woods**) a small forest. **3** (**the wood**) wooden barrels used for storing alcoholic drinks. **4** a golf club with a wooden or other head that is relatively broad from face to back. **5** = BOWL².
– PHRASES **be unable to see the wood for the trees** fail to grasp the main issue because of over-attention to details. **out of the woods** out of difficulty. **touch wood** touch something wooden to ward off bad luck.
– ORIGIN Old English.

woodbine • n. Brit. the common honeysuckle.

woodchip • n. esp. Brit. wallpaper with small chips of wood embedded in it to give a grainy surface texture.

woodchuck • n. a North American marmot (rodent) with a heavy body and short legs.
– ORIGIN from an American Indian name (by association with WOOD).

woodcock • n. (pl. **woodcock**) a long-billed woodland bird of the sandpiper family, with brown plumage.

woodcut • n. a print of a type made from a design cut in relief in a block of wood.

woodcutter • n. a person who cuts down trees for wood.

wooded • adj. (of land) covered with woods.

wooden • adj. **1** made of or resembling wood. **2** stiff and awkward in speech or behaviour.
– DERIVATIVES **woodenly** adv. **woodenness** n.

wooden spoon • n. Brit. the last place in a race or competition.
– ORIGIN from the former practice of giving a spoon to the candidate coming last in the Cambridge mathematical tripos (exam).

woodland • n. (also **woodlands**) land covered with trees.

woodlouse • n. (pl. **woodlice**) a small insect-like creature with a grey segmented body which it is able to roll into a ball.

woodpecker • n. a bird with a strong bill and a stiff tail, typically pecking at tree trunks to find insects.

wood pigeon • n. a common large pigeon, mainly grey with white patches forming a ring round its neck.

wood pulp • n. wood fibre reduced chemically or mechanically to pulp and used in the manufacture of paper.

woodruff (also **sweet woodruff**) • n. a white-flowered plant with sweet-scented leaves used to flavour drinks and in perfumery.
– ORIGIN Old English.

woodsman • n. (pl. **woodsmen**) a forester, hunter, or woodcutter.

woodturning • n. the activity of shaping wood with a lathe.
– DERIVATIVES **woodturner** n.

woodwind • n. wind instruments other than brass instruments forming a section of an orchestra.

woodwork • n. **1** the wooden parts of a room, building, or other structure. **2** Brit. the activity or skill of making things from wood.
– PHRASES **come out of the woodwork** (of an undesirable person or thing) suddenly appear.
– DERIVATIVES **woodworker** n. **woodworking** n.

woodworm • n. **1** the wood-boring larva of a kind of small brown beetle. **2** the damaged condition of wood resulting from infestation with woodworm.

woody • adj. (**woodier, woodiest**) **1** covered with trees. **2** made of or resembling wood.
– DERIVATIVES **woodiness** n.

woof¹ /woof/ • n. the barking sound made by a dog. • v. (of a dog) bark.

woof² /woof/ • n. = WEFT.
– ORIGIN Old English.

woofer /woo-fer, wuu-fer/ • n. a loud-speaker designed to reproduce low frequencies.

wool • n. **1** the fine soft hair forming the coat of a sheep, goat, or similar animal. **2** a metal or mineral made into a mass of fine fibres.
– PHRASES **pull the wool over someone's eyes** deceive someone.
– ORIGIN Old English.

wool-gathering •n. aimless thought or daydreaming.

woollen (US **woolen**) •adj. **1** made of wool. **2** relating to the production of wool. •n. (**woollens**) woollen garments.

woolly •adj. (**woollier, woolliest**) **1** made of wool. **2** (of an animal or plant) covered with wool or hair resembling wool. **3** resembling wool. **4** confused or unclear: *woolly thinking.* •n. (pl. **woollies**) informal, esp. Brit. a woollen jumper or cardigan.

– DERIVATIVES **woolliness** n.

Woolsack •n. (in the UK) the Lord Chancellor's wool-stuffed seat in the House of Lords.

woosh •v. & n. var. of WHOOSH.

woozy •adj. (**woozier, wooziest**) informal unsteady, dizzy, or dazed.

– DERIVATIVES **woozily** adv. **wooziness** n.

wop •n. informal, offens. an Italian or other southern European.

– ORIGIN perh. from Italian *guappo* 'bold, showy'.

Worcester sauce (also **Worcestershire sauce**) •n. a tangy sauce containing soy sauce and vinegar.

Worcs. •abbrev. Worcestershire.

word •n. **1** a single unit of language which has meaning and is used with others to form sentences. **2** a remark or statement. **3** (**a word**) even the smallest amount of something spoken or written: *don't believe a word.* **4** (**words**) angry talk. **5** (**the word**) a command, slogan, or signal. **6** (**your word**) a person's version of the truth. **7** (**your word**) a promise. **8** information or news. •v. express in particular words.

– PHRASES **have a word** speak briefly to someone. **in so many words** precisely in the way mentioned. **in a word** briefly. **take someone's word** (**for it**) believe what someone says or writes without checking for yourself. **word of mouth** speaking as a means of conveying information.

– DERIVATIVES **wordless** adj.

– ORIGIN Old English.

wording •n. the way in which something is expressed in words.

word-perfect •adj. (of an actor or speaker) knowing a part or speech by heart.

wordplay •n. the witty exploitation of the meanings of words.

word processor •n. a computer or program for creating, editing, storing, and printing a piece of writing.

wordsmith •n. a skilled user of words.

wordy •adj. using or expressed in too many words.

– DERIVATIVES **wordiness** n.

wore past of WEAR.

work •n. **1** activity involving mental or physical effort done in order to achieve a result. **2** the activity or job that a person does to earn money. **3** a task or tasks to be done. **4** a thing or things done or made. **5** (**works**) esp. Brit. a place where industrial or manufacturing processes are carried out. **6** (**works**) esp. Brit. activities involving construction or repair. **7** (**works**) the mechanism of a machine. **8** a defensive military structure. •v. (**works, working, worked** or old use **wrought**) **1** do work as a job. **2** make someone do work. **3** (of a machine or system) function properly. **4** operate a machine. **5** have the desired result: *her plan worked admirably.* **6** bring a material or mixture to a desired shape or consistency. **7** produce an article or design using a specified material or sewing stitch. **8** cultivate land or extract materials from a mine or quarry. **9** move gradually or with difficulty into another position.

– PHRASES **get worked up** become excited, angry, or stressed. **have your work cut out** be faced with a hard or lengthy task. **work out 1** develop in a good or specified way. **2** engage in vigorous physical exercise. **work someone out** understand someone's character. **work something out 1** solve a sum or calculate an amount. **2** plan something in detail. **work someone over** informal beat someone up. **work your passage** pay for your journey on a ship with work instead of money. **work to rule** esp. Brit. follow official working rules and hours exactly in order to reduce output and efficiency, as a form of industrial action. **work up to** proceed gradually towards something more advanced.

– ORIGIN Old English.

workable •adj. **1** able to be shaped, dug, etc. **2** capable of producing the desired result.

workaday •adj. not special; ordinary.

workaholic •n. informal a person who works very hard and finds it difficult to stop working.

workbench •n. a bench at which carpentry or other mechanical or practical work is done.

worker •n. **1** a person who works. **2** a person who achieves a specified thing: *a miracle-worker.* **3** a neuter or undeveloped female bee, wasp, ant, etc., large numbers of which perform the basic work of a colony.

work experience •n. Brit. short-term experience of employment, arranged for

W

older pupils by schools.

workforce • n. the people engaged in or available for work in a particular area, firm, or industry.

workhorse • n. a person or machine that works hard and reliably over a long period.

workhouse • n. hist. (in the UK) a public institution in which poor people received food and lodging in return for work.

working • adj. **1** having a job; in paid employment. **2** doing manual work. **3** functioning or able to function. **4** used as the basis for work or discussion and likely to be changed later: *a working title.* • n. **1** the parts of a mine or quarry from which minerals are being extracted. **2** (**workings**) the way in which a machine, organization, or system operates. **3** (**workings**) a record of the calculations made in solving a mathematical problem.

working capital • n. the capital of a business which is used in its day-to-day trading operations.

working class • n. the social group made up largely of people who do manual or industrial work. • adj. relating to the working class.

working party (also **working group**) • n. Brit. a group appointed to study and report on a particular question and make recommendations.

workload • n. the amount of work to be done by someone or something.

workman • n. (pl. **workmen**) a man employed to do manual work.

workmanlike • adj. showing efficient skill.

workmanship • n. the degree of skill with which a product is made or a job done.

workmate • n. esp. Brit. a person with whom you work.

work of art • n. a creative product with strong imaginative or artistic appeal.

workout • n. a session of physical exercise.

work permit • n. an official document giving a foreigner permission to take a job in a country.

workpiece • n. an object being worked on with a tool or machine.

worksheet • n. **1** a paper listing questions or tasks for students. **2** a paper recording work done or in progress.

workshop • n. **1** a room or building in which things are made or repaired. **2** a meeting for discussion and activity on a particular subject or project.

work-shy • adj. unwilling to work.

workspace • n. **1** an area rented or sold for commercial purposes. **2** Computing a memory storage facility for temporary use.

workstation • n. a desktop computer terminal, typically one that is part of a network.

worktop • n. Brit. a flat surface for working on.

world • n. **1** (**the world**) the earth with all its countries and peoples. **2** a region or group of countries: *the English-speaking world.* **3** all that belongs to a particular period or area of activity: *the theatre world.* **4** (**your world**) your life and activities. **5** (**the world**) secular or material matters as opposed to spiritual or religious ones. **6** a planet. **7** (**a/the world**) a very large amount of: *that makes a world of difference.*
– PHRASES **the best of both** (or **all possible**) **worlds** the benefits of widely differing situations, enjoyed at the same time. **out of this world** informal very enjoyable or impressive.
– ORIGIN Old English.

world-beater • n. a person or thing that is better than all others in its field.
– DERIVATIVES **world-beating** adj.

world-class • adj. of or among the best in the world.

World Cup • n. a competition between teams from many countries in a sport.

world English • n. the English language including all of its regional varieties around the world.

worldly • adj. (**worldlier**, **worldliest**) **1** relating to material things rather than spiritual ones. **2** experienced and sophisticated.
– DERIVATIVES **worldliness** n.

worldly-wise • adj. having enough experience not to be easily shocked or cheated.

world music • n. traditional music from the developing world, sometimes incorporating elements of Western popular music.

world order • n. a system established internationally for preserving global political stability.

world power • n. a country that has great influence in international affairs.

world-ranking • adj. among the best in the world.

world war • n. a war involving many large nations in different parts of the world, especially the wars of 1914–18 and 1939–45.

world-weary • adj. bored with or cynical about life.

worldwide • adj. extending or applicable throughout the world. • adv. throughout the world.

World Wide Web • n. an extensive information system on the Internet providing facilities for documents to be connected to other documents by hypertext links.

worm • n. **1** an earthworm or other creeping or burrowing invertebrate animal with a long, thin, soft body and no limbs. **2** (**worms**) parasites that live in the intestines. **3** a maggot regarded as eating dead bodies buried in the ground: *food for worms.* **4** informal a weak or disliked person. • v. **1** (**worm your way**) move by crawling or wriggling. **2** (**worm your way into**) gradually move into a situation in order to gain advantage. **3** (**worm something out of**) obtain information from someone by continual questions.
– ORIGIN Old English.

worm cast • n. a coiled mass of soil, mud, or sand thrown up at the surface by a burrowing worm.

wormhole • n. a hole made by a burrowing insect larva or worm in wood, fruit, etc.

wormwood • n. a woody shrub with a bitter taste, used as an ingredient of vermouth and in medicine.
– ORIGIN Old English.

wormy • adj. (**wormier, wormiest**) worm-eaten or full of worms.

worn past part. of WEAR. • adj. **1** damaged by wear. **2** very tired.

worn out • adj. **1** exhausted. **2** so damaged by wear as to be no longer usable.

worried • adj. feeling, showing, or expressing anxiety.
– DERIVATIVES **worriedly** adv.

worrisome • adj. causing anxiety or concern.

worry • v. (**worries, worrying, worried**) **1** feel or cause to feel troubled over actual or possible difficulties. **2** annoy or disturb someone. **3** (of a dog) tear at or pull about with the teeth. **4** (of a dog) chase and attack livestock. • n. (pl. **worries**) **1** the state of being troubled over actual or possible difficulties. **2** a source of anxiety.
– DERIVATIVES **worrier** n.
– ORIGIN Old English, 'strangle'.

worry beads • pl. n. a string of beads that a person fingers so as to stay relaxed and calm.

worse • adj. **1** less good, satisfactory, or pleasing. **2** more serious or severe. **3** more ill or unhappy. • adv. **1** less well. **2** more seriously or severely. • n. a worse event or situation.

– PHRASES **worse off** less fortunate or wealthy.
– ORIGIN Old English.

worsen • v. make or become worse.

worship • n. **1** the practice of showing deep respect for and praying to God or a god or goddess. **2** religious rites and ceremonies. **3** great admiration or respect for someone. **4** (**His/Your Worship**) esp. Brit. a title of respect for a magistrate or mayor. • v. (**worships, worshipping, worshipped**; US also **worships, worshiping, worshiped**) **1** offer praise and prayers to God or a god or goddess. **2** feel great admiration or respect for.
– DERIVATIVES **worshipper** n.
– ORIGIN Old English, 'worthiness, acknowledgement of worth'.

worshipful • adj. **1** feeling or showing great respect and admiration. **2** (**Worshipful**) Brit. a title given to Justices of the Peace.

worst • adj. most bad, severe, or serious. • adv. **1** most severely or seriously. **2** least well. • n. the worst part, event, or situation. • v. get the better of; defeat.
– PHRASES **do your worst** do as much damage as you can.
– ORIGIN Old English.

worsted /wuus-tid/ • n. smooth and close-textured woollen fabric made from a fine yarn.
– ORIGIN from *Worstead*, a parish in Norfolk, England.

worth • adj. **1** equivalent in value to the sum or item specified. **2** deserving to be treated or regarded in the way specified: *the museums are worth a visit.* **3** having income or property amounting to a specified sum. • n. **1** the value or merit of someone or something. **2** an amount of a commodity equivalent to a specified sum of money: *hundreds of pounds worth of clothes.*
– PHRASES **for all you are worth** informal as energetically or enthusiastically as you can.
– ORIGIN Old English.

worthless • adj. **1** having no real value or use. **2** having no good qualities.
– DERIVATIVES **worthlessness** n.

worthwhile • adj. worth the time, money, or effort spent.

worthy • adj. (**worthier, worthiest**) **1** deserving effort, attention, or respect. **2** deserving or good enough: *issues worthy of further consideration.* **3** well intentioned but rather dull or unimaginative. • n. (pl. **worthies**) usu. humorous a person important in a particular sphere: *local worthies.*

w

– DERIVATIVES **worthily** adv. **worthiness** n.

-worthy • comb. form **1** deserving of a specified thing: *newsworthy.* **2** suitable for a specified thing: *roadworthy.*

would • modal verb (3rd sing. present **would**) **1** past of **WILL**[1], in various senses. **2** (expressing the conditional mood) indicating the result of an imagined event. **3** expressing a desire or inclination. **4** expressing a polite request. **5** expressing an opinion or assumption: *I would have to agree.* **6** literary expressing a wish or regret: *would that he had lived to finish it.*

> USAGE: For an explanation of the difference between **would** and **should**, see the note at **SHOULD**.

would-be • adj. usu. derog. desiring or hoping to be a specified type of person: *a would-be actress.*

wouldn't • contr. would not.

wouldst old-fashioned 2nd person sing. of **WOULD**.

wound[1] /woond/ • n. **1** a bodily injury caused by a cut, blow, or other impact. **2** something that hurts a person's feelings. • v. **1** inflict a wound on. **2** hurt someone's feelings.
– ORIGIN Old English.

wound[2] past and past part. of **WIND**[2].

wove past of **WEAVE**[1].

woven past part. of **WEAVE**[1].

wow informal • exclam. expressing astonishment or admiration. • n. a sensational success. • v. impress and excite greatly.

WP • abbrev. word processing or word processor.

WPC • abbrev. (in the UK) woman police constable.

wpm • abbrev. words per minute (used after a number to indicate typing speed).

wrack[1] • v. var. of **RACK**[1].

> USAGE: For an explanation of the difference between **wrack** and **rack**, see the note at **RACK**[1].

wrack[2] • n. a coarse brown seaweed which grows on the shoreline.
– ORIGIN prob. from Dutch *wrak* 'shipwreck'.

wraith /rayth/ • n. a ghost or ghostly image of someone, especially one seen shortly before or after their death.

wrangle • n. a long and complicated dispute or argument. • v. (**wrangles, wrangling, wrangled**) engage in a wrangle.
– DERIVATIVES **wrangler** n.

– ORIGIN perh. from German *wrangen* 'to struggle'.

wrap • v. (**wraps, wrapping, wrapped**) **1** cover or enclose in paper or soft material. **2** encircle or wind round: *he wrapped an arm around her waist.* **3** (in word processing) cause a word or words to be carried over to a new line automatically. **4** informal finish filming or recording. • n. **1** a loose outer garment or piece of material. **2** paper or material used for wrapping.
– PHRASES **be wrapped up in** be so involved in something that you do not notice anyone else. **under wraps** kept secret. **wrap up** (also **wrap someone up**) put on or dress someone in warm clothes. **wrap something up** complete a meeting or deal.
– DERIVATIVES **wrapping** n.

wrapper • n. a piece of paper or other material used for wrapping something.

wrasse /rass/ • n. (pl. **wrasse** or **wrasses**) a brightly coloured sea fish with thick lips and strong teeth.
– ORIGIN Cornish *wrah.*

wrath /roth, rawth/ • n. extreme anger.
– ORIGIN Old English.

wrathful • adj. literary full of or showing great anger.
– DERIVATIVES **wrathfully** adv.

wreak • v. **1** cause a great amount of damage or harm. **2** take revenge on someone.
– ORIGIN Old English, 'drive (out), avenge'.

wreath /reeth/ • n. (pl. **wreaths** /reeths, reethz/) **1** an arrangement of flowers or leaves fastened in a ring and used for decoration or for placing on a grave. **2** a curl or ring of smoke or cloud.
– ORIGIN Old English.

wreathe /reeth/ • v. (**wreathes, wreathing, wreathed**) **1** surround or encircle: *he sat wreathed in smoke.* **2** entwine round or over something.
– ORIGIN from **WRITHE**.

wreck • n. **1** the destruction of a ship at sea. **2** a ship destroyed at sea. **3** a building, vehicle, etc. that has been destroyed or badly damaged. **4** a person in a very bad physical or mental state. • v. **1** destroy a ship by sinking or breaking up. **2** destroy or badly damage a structure or vehicle. **3** spoil something completely.
– DERIVATIVES **wrecker** n.
– ORIGIN Old French *wrec.*

wreckage • n. the remains of something that has been badly damaged or destroyed.

wrecked • adj. informal **1** exhausted. **2** Brit. very drunk.

Wren •n. (in the UK) a member of the former Women's Royal Naval Service.
– ORIGIN from the abbreviation *WRNS*.

wren •n. a very small songbird with a cocked tail.
– ORIGIN Old English.

wrench •v. 1 pull or twist suddenly and violently. 2 twist and injure a part of the body. •n. 1 a sudden violent twist or pull. 2 a feeling of sadness or distress on leaving a person or place. 3 an adjustable tool like a spanner, used for gripping and turning nuts or bolts.
– ORIGIN Old English.

wrest /rest/ •v. 1 forcibly pull something from a person's grasp. 2 take power or control from someone after a struggle.
– ORIGIN Old English.

wrestle •v. (**wrestles, wrestling, wrestled**) 1 take part in a fight or contest that involves close grappling with an opponent. 2 struggle with a difficulty or problem. 3 move an object with difficulty. •n. 1 a wrestling bout or contest. 2 a hard struggle.
– DERIVATIVES **wrestler** n. **wrestling** n.

wretch •n. 1 a person who you feel sympathy for. 2 informal a disliked or unpleasant person.
– ORIGIN Old English.

wretched •adj. (**wretcheder, wretchedest**) 1 in a very unhappy or unfortunate state. 2 very bad or unpleasant. 3 used to express anger or annoyance: *she disliked the wretched man intensely.*
– DERIVATIVES **wretchedly** adv.

wriggle •v. (**wriggles, wriggling, wriggled**) 1 twist and turn with quick short movements. 2 (**wriggle out of**) avoid doing something that you should do. •n. a wriggling movement.
– DERIVATIVES **wriggler** n. **wriggly** adj.
– ORIGIN German *wriggelen.*

wright •n. old use (except in combination) a maker or builder: *playwright.*
– ORIGIN Old English.

wring •v. (**wrings, wringing, wrung**) 1 squeeze and twist something to force liquid from it. 2 twist and break an animal's neck. 3 squeeze someone's hand tightly. 4 (**wring something from/ out of**) obtain something with difficulty.
– DERIVATIVES **wringer** n.
– ORIGIN Old English.

wringing •adj. very wet.

wrinkle •n. a slight line or fold, especially in fabric or on the skin of the face. •v. (**wrinkles, wrinkling, wrinkled**) make or become wrinkled.
– ORIGIN perh. from Old English, 'sinuous'.

wrinkly •adj. (**wrinklier, wrinkliest**) full of wrinkles. •n. (pl. **wrinklies**) Brit. informal, derog. an old person.

wrist •n. the joint connecting the hand with the forearm.
– ORIGIN Old English.

wristband •n. a band worn round the wrist.

wristwatch •n. a watch worn on a strap round the wrist.

writ[1] •n. an official document from a court of law or other legal authority, ordering a person to do or not to do something.
– ORIGIN Old English.

writ[2] •v. old-fashioned past part. of **WRITE**.
– PHRASES **writ large** in an obvious or exaggerated form.

write •v. (**writes, writing, wrote**; past part. **written**) 1 mark letters, words, or other symbols on a surface, with a pen, pencil, or similar implement. 2 compose and send a letter to someone. 3 compose a book or other written work. 4 compose a musical work. 5 fill out a cheque or form.
– PHRASES **write something off** 1 (**write someone/thing off**) dismiss someone or something as insignificant. 2 cancel an outstanding debt. 3 Brit. damage a vehicle so badly that it cannot be repaired.
– DERIVATIVES **writable** adj.
– ORIGIN Old English.

write-off •n. Brit. a vehicle that is too badly damaged to be repaired.

writer •n. a person who has written a particular work, or who writes books or articles as an occupation.
– PHRASES **writer's block** the condition of being unable to think of what to write. **writer's cramp** pain or stiffness in the hand caused by excessive writing.

writerly •adj. 1 relating to a professional author. 2 deliberately literary in style.

write-up •n. a newspaper review of a recent event, performance, etc.

writhe /ryth/ •v. (**writhes, writhing, writhed**) twist or squirm in pain, distress, or other strong emotion.
– ORIGIN Old English, 'make into coils, plait'.

writing •n. 1 the activity or skill of writing. 2 written work. 3 (**writings**) a group of written works by a particular author or on a particular subject. 4 a sequence of letters or symbols forming words.
– PHRASES **the writing is on the wall** there are clear signs that something unpleasant is going to happen. [ORIGIN with reference to Belshazzar's feast in

w

the Bible (Book of Daniel, chapter 5), at which mysterious writing appeared on the wall foretelling Belshazzar's overthrow.]

written past part. of WRITE.

wrong •adj. **1** not correct or true; mistaken or in error. **2** unjust, dishonest, or immoral. **3** in a bad or abnormal condition: *something is wrong with the pump.* •adv. **1** in a mistaken or undesirable way or direction. **2** with an incorrect result. •n. an unjust, dishonest, or immoral action. •v. **1** act unjustly towards someone. **2** mistakenly think that someone has bad motives.
– PHRASES **get hold of the wrong end of the stick** misunderstand something. **in the wrong** responsible for a mistake or offence. **on the wrong side of 1** out of favour with. **2** somewhat more than a specified age.
– DERIVATIVES **wrongly** adv. **wrongness** n.
– ORIGIN Old Norse, 'awry, unjust'.

wrongdoing •n. illegal or dishonest behaviour.
– DERIVATIVES **wrongdoer** n.

wrong-foot •v. Brit. **1** (in a game) play so as to catch an opponent off balance. **2** place someone in a difficult situation by saying or doing something that is unexpected.

wrongful •adj. not fair, just, or legal.
– DERIVATIVES **wrongfully** adv.

wrong-headed •adj. having or showing bad judgement.

wrote past tense of WRITE.

wroth /rohth, roth/ •adj. old use angry.
– ORIGIN Old English.

wrought /rhymes with bought/

•adj. **1** (of metals) beaten out or shaped by hammering. **2** (in combination) made in the specified way: *well-wrought.*
– ORIGIN old-fashioned past and past participle of WORK.

wrought iron •n. a tough form of iron suitable for forging or rolling rather than casting.

wrung past and past part. of WRING.

wry /ry/ •adj. (**wryer**, **wryest** or **wrier**, **wriest**) **1** using or expressing dry, mocking humour: *a wry smile.* **2** (of a person's face) twisted into an expression of disgust, disappointment, or annoyance. **3** bending or twisted to one side.
– DERIVATIVES **wryly** adv.
– ORIGIN Old English, 'tend, incline'.

wryneck •n. a bird of the woodpecker family, with brown plumage and a habit of twisting its head backwards.

WSW •abbrev. west-south-west.

WTO •abbrev. World Trade Organization.

wunderkind /vuun-der-kind/ •n. (pl. **wunderkinds** or **wunderkinder** /vuun-der-kin-der/) a person who is very successful at a young age.
– ORIGIN German.

Wurlitzer /wer-lit-ser/ •n. trademark a large pipe organ or electric organ.
– ORIGIN named after the American instrument-maker Rudolf *Wurlitzer.*

wuss /rhymes with puss/ •n. informal a feeble person.

WWI •abbrev. World War I.

WWII •abbrev. World War II.

WWF •abbrev. **1** World Wide Fund for Nature. **2** World Wrestling Federation.

WWW •abbrev. World Wide Web.

w

Xx

X¹ (also **x**) •n. (pl. **Xs** or **X's**) **1** the twenty-fourth letter of the alphabet. **2** referring to an unknown or unspecified person or thing. **3** (usu. **x**) the first unknown quantity in an algebraic expression. **4** referring to the main or horizontal axis in a system of coordinates. **5** a cross-shaped written symbol, used to indicate an incorrect answer or to symbolize a kiss. **6** the Roman numeral for ten.

X² •symb. (formerly in the UK and US) a classification of films as suitable for adults only.

X chromosome •n. (in humans and other mammals) a sex chromosome, two of which are normally present in female cells (known as XX) and only one in male cells (known as XY). Compare with **Y CHROMOSOME**.

Xe •symb. the chemical element xenon.

xenon /zen-on, zee-non/ •n. an inert gaseous chemical element, present in trace amounts in the air and used in some kinds of electric light.
– ORIGIN Greek *xenos* 'strange'.

xenophobia /zen-uh-foh-bi-uh/ •n. strong dislike or fear of people from other countries.
– DERIVATIVES **xenophobe** n. **xenophobic** adj.
– ORIGIN Greek *xenos* 'stranger'.

xerography /zeer-og-ruh-fi/ •n. a dry copying process in which powder sticks to parts of a surface remaining electrically charged after being exposed to light from an image of the document to be copied.
– DERIVATIVES **xerographic** adj.
– ORIGIN Greek *xēros* 'dry'.

Xerox /zeer-oks, ze-roks/ •n. trademark **1** a xerographic copying process. **2** a copy made using such a process. •v. (**xerox**) copy a document using xerography.
– ORIGIN from **XEROGRAPHY**.

Xmas /kriss-muhss, eks-muhss/ •n. informal Christmas.
– ORIGIN *X* representing the initial Greek character of Greek *Khristos* 'Christ'.

XML •abbrev. Extensible Markup Language.

X-rated •adj. **1** pornographic or indecent. **2** (formerly) referring to a film given an X classification.

X-ray •n. **1** an electromagnetic wave of very short wavelength, able to pass through many solids and so make it possible to see into or through them. **2** an image of the internal structure of an object produced by passing X-rays through it. •v. photograph or examine with X-rays.
– ORIGIN from *X*- (because, when first discovered, the nature of the rays was unknown).

xylem /zy-luhm/ •n. the tissue in plants which carries water and nutrients upwards from the root and also helps to form the woody part of the stem.
– ORIGIN Greek *xulon* 'wood'.

xylophone /zy-luh-fohn/ •n. a musical instrument played by striking a row of wooden bars with small hammers.
– ORIGIN Greek *xulon* 'wood'.

x

Yy

Y¹ (also **y**) •n. (pl. **Ys** or **Y's**) **1** the twenty-fifth letter of the alphabet. **2** referring to an unknown or unspecified person or thing. **3** (usu. **y**) the second unknown quantity in an algebraic expression. **4** referring to the secondary or vertical axis in a system of coordinates.

Y² •symb. the chemical element yttrium.

y •abbrev. year(s).

-y¹ •suffix forming adjectives: **1** full of; having the quality of: *messy*. **2** inclined to; apt to: *sticky*.
– ORIGIN Old English.

-y² •suffix forming nouns: **1** referring to a state or quality: *jealousy*. **2** referring to an action or its result: *victory*.
– ORIGIN from Latin *-ia, -ium* or Greek *-eia, -ia*.

-y³ (also **-ey** or **-ie**) •suffix forming diminutive nouns, affectionate names, etc.: *granny*.
– ORIGIN Scots.

Y2K •abbrev. year 2000 (with reference to the millennium bug).

yacht /yot/ •n. **1** a medium-sized sailing boat equipped for cruising or racing. **2** a powered boat equipped for cruising.
– DERIVATIVES **yachting** n. **yachtsman** n. (pl. **yachtsmen**). **yachtswoman** n. (pl. **yachtswomen**).
– ORIGIN Dutch *jaghte*.

> ✓ Remember that the ending of **yacht** is spelled **-acht**.

yack •n. & v. var. of YAK².

yahoo /yah-hoo, yuh-hoo/ •n. informal a rude, coarse, or violent person.
– ORIGIN the name of an imaginary people in Jonathan Swift's *Gulliver's Travels*.

Yahweh /yah-way/ •n. a form of the Hebrew name of God used in the Bible.
– ORIGIN Hebrew.

yak¹ •n. a large ox with shaggy hair and large horns, used in Tibet for carrying loads and for its milk, meat, and hide.
– ORIGIN Tibetan.

yak² (also **yack**) informal •v. (**yaks, yakking, yakked**) talk at length about unimportant or boring subjects. •n. a

trivial or lengthy conversation.

Yale •n. trademark a type of lock with a latch bolt and a flat key with a serrated edge.
– ORIGIN named after the American locksmith Linus *Yale* Jr.

yam •n. **1** the starchy tuber of a tropical climbing plant, eaten as a vegetable. **2** N. Amer. a sweet potato.
– ORIGIN Portuguese *inhame* or former Spanish *iñame*.

yammer informal •v. (**yammers, yammering, yammered**) talk loudly and without pausing. •n. loud and continuous noise.
– ORIGIN Old English, 'to lament'.

yang •n. (in Chinese philosophy) the active male principle of the universe. Contrasted with YIN.
– ORIGIN Chinese, 'male genitals, sun'.

Yank •n. informal, usu. derog. an American.

yank informal •v. pull quickly and hard. •n. a sudden hard pull.

Yankee •n. informal **1** usu. derog. an American. **2** US a person from New England or one of the northern states. **3** hist. a Federal soldier in the US Civil War.
– ORIGIN perh. from Dutch *Jan* 'John'.

yap •v. (**yaps, yapping, yapped**) **1** give a sharp, shrill bark. **2** informal talk at length in an irritating way. •n. a sharp, shrill bark.
– DERIVATIVES **yappy** adj.

yard¹ •n. **1** a unit of length equal to 3 feet (0.9144 metre). **2** a square or cubic yard, especially of sand or other building materials. **3** a long piece of wood slung across a ship's mast for a sail to hang from.
– ORIGIN Old English.

yard² •n. **1** esp. Brit. a piece of enclosed ground next to a building. **2** an area of land used for a particular purpose or business: *a builder's yard*. **3** N. Amer. the garden of a house.
– ORIGIN Old English, 'home, region'.

yardage •n. a distance or length measured in yards.

yardarm • n. either end of a ship's yard supporting a sail.

Yardie • n. informal **1** (among Jamaicans) a fellow Jamaican. **2** (in the UK) a member of a Jamaican or West Indian gang of criminals.
– ORIGIN Jamaican English *yard* 'house, home'.

yardstick • n. **1** a standard used for judging how good or successful something is. **2** a measuring rod a yard long.

yarmulke /yar-muul-kuh/ (also **yarmulka**) • n. a skullcap worn in public by Orthodox Jewish men or during prayer by other Jewish men.
– ORIGIN Yiddish.

yarn • n. **1** spun thread used for knitting, weaving, or sewing. **2** informal a long or rambling story.
– ORIGIN Old English.

yarrow • n. a plant with feathery leaves and heads of small white or pale pink flowers, used in herbal medicine.
– ORIGIN Old English.

yashmak /yash-mak/ • n. a veil concealing all of the face except the eyes, worn by some Muslim women in public.
– ORIGIN Turkish.

yaw • v. (of a moving ship or aircraft) turn to one side or from side to side. • n. yawing movement of a ship or aircraft.

yawl • n. a kind of sailing boat with two masts.
– ORIGIN German *jolle* or Dutch *jol*.

yawn • v. **1** open the mouth wide and breathe in deeply due to tiredness or boredom. **2** (as adj. **yawning**) wide open: *a yawning chasm.* • n. **1** an act of yawning. **2** informal a boring event.
– ORIGIN Old English.

yawp • n. a harsh or hoarse cry or yelp. • v. shout or exclaim hoarsely.

yaws • n. a contagious tropical disease caused by a bacterium that enters cuts on the skin and may cause deep ulcers.
– ORIGIN prob. from Carib.

Yb • symb. the chemical element ytterbium.

Y chromosome • n. (in humans and other mammals) a sex chromosome which is normally present only in male cells, which are known as XY. Compare with **X** CHROMOSOME.

yd • abbrev. yard (measure).

ye¹ • pron. (second person pl.) pl. of **THOU**¹.
– ORIGIN Old English.

ye² • det. old use = **THE**.
– ORIGIN from a misunderstanding of the Old English letter þ (now written *th*),

which could be written as y, so that *the* could be written *ye*.

yea • adv. old use or formal yes.
– ORIGIN Old English.

yeah (also **yeh**) • exclam. & n. informal = **YES**.

year • n. **1** the time taken by the earth to make one complete orbit around the sun. **2** (also **calendar year**) the period of 365 days (or 366 days in leap years) starting from the first of January. **3** a period of the same length as this starting at a different point. **4** a similar period used for reckoning time according to other calendars. **5** (**your years**) your age or time of life. **6** (**years**) informal a very long time. **7** a set of students of similar ages who enter and leave a school or college at the same time.
– PHRASES **year in, year out** continuously or repeatedly over a period of years.
– ORIGIN Old English.

yearbook • n. an annual publication giving details of events of the previous year, especially those connected with a particular area of activity.

yearling • n. an animal of a year old, or in its second year.

yearly • adj. & adv. happening or produced once a year or every year.

yearn /yern/ • v. have a strong feeling of loss and longing for something.
– DERIVATIVES **yearning** n. & adj.
– ORIGIN Old English.

year-on-year • adj. (of figures, prices, etc.) as compared with the corresponding ones from a year earlier.

year-round • adj. happening or continuing throughout the year.

yeast • n. **1** a microscopic single-celled fungus capable of converting sugar into alcohol and carbon dioxide. **2** a greyish-yellow substance formed from this, used to make bread dough rise and to ferment beer.
– DERIVATIVES **yeasty** adj.
– ORIGIN Old English.

yell • n. a loud, sharp cry. • v. shout loudly.
– ORIGIN Old English.

yellow • adj. **1** of the colour of egg yolks or ripe lemons. **2** informal cowardly. • n. yellow colour. • v. (of paper, fabric, etc.) become slightly yellow with age.
– DERIVATIVES **yellowish** adj.
– ORIGIN Old English.

yellow-belly • n. informal a coward.

yellow card • n. (in football) a yellow card shown by the referee to a player being cautioned.

yellow fever • n. a tropical disease caused by a virus transmitted by mosquitoes, causing fever and jaundice and often death.

y

yellowhammer • n. a bunting (songbird), the male of which has a yellow head, neck, and breast.
– ORIGIN -*hammer* is perh. from Old English *amore* (a kind of bird).

Yellow Pages • pl. n. (trademark in the UK) a telephone directory printed on yellow paper and listing businesses and other organizations according to the goods or services they offer.

yelp • n. a short sharp cry. • v. make a yelp or yelps.
– ORIGIN Old English, 'to boast'.

Yemeni /yem-uh-ni/ • n. a person from Yemen. • adj. relating to Yemen.

yen[1] • n. (pl. **yen**) the basic unit of money of Japan.
– ORIGIN Japanese, 'round'.

yen[2] • n. informal a strong desire to have or do something.
– ORIGIN Chinese.

yeoman /yoh-muhn/ • n. (pl. **yeomen**) hist. 1 a man owning a house and a small area of farming land. 2 a servant in a royal or noble household.
– ORIGIN prob. from **YOUNG** + **MAN**.

Yeoman of the Guard • n. a member of the British king or queen's bodyguard (now having only ceremonial duties).

yeomanry • n. hist. yeomen as a group.

Yeoman Warder • n. a warder at the Tower of London.

yes • exclam. 1 used to give a response in favour of something. 2 used to reply to someone who is asking you something or trying to attract your attention. 3 used to express delight. • n. (pl. **yeses** or **yesses**) an answer or vote in favour of something.
– ORIGIN Old English.

yes-man • n. informal a person who always agrees with people in authority.

yesterday • adv. on the day before today. • n. 1 the day before today. 2 the recent past.
– ORIGIN Old English.

yesteryear • n. literary last year or the recent past.

yet • adv. 1 up until now or then. 2 as soon as this: *wait, don't go yet.* 3 from now into the future for a specified length of time. 4 referring to something that will or may happen in the future. 5 still; even: *snow, snow, and yet more snow.* 6 in spite of that. • conj. but at the same time.
– ORIGIN Old English.

yeti /yet-i/ • n. a large hairy manlike creature said to live in the highest part of the Himalayas.
– ORIGIN Tibetan, 'little manlike animal'.

yew • n. an evergreen coniferous tree

with poisonous red fruit and springy wood.
– ORIGIN Old English.

Y-fronts • pl. n. Brit. trademark men's or boys' underpants with a seam at the front in the shape of an upside-down Y.

YHA • abbrev. (in the UK) Youth Hostels Association.

Yid • n. informal, offens. a Jew.

Yiddish /yid-dish/ • n. a language used by Jews from central and eastern Europe, originally a German dialect with words from Hebrew and several modern languages. • adj. relating to Yiddish.
– ORIGIN from Yiddish *yidish daytsh* 'Jewish German'.

yield • v. 1 produce or provide a natural or industrial product. 2 produce a result or gain. 3 give way to demands or pressure. 4 give up possession of. 5 (of a mass or structure) give way under force or pressure. • n. an amount or result yielded.
– ORIGIN Old English, 'pay, repay'.

> ✓ **yield** follows the usual rule of *i* before *e* except after *c*.

yin • n. (in Chinese philosophy) the passive female principle of the universe. Contrasted with **YANG**.
– ORIGIN Chinese, 'feminine, moon'.

yippee • exclam. expressing wild excitement or delight.

ylang-ylang /ee-lang-ee-lang/ • n. a sweet-scented oil obtained from the flowers of a tropical tree, used in perfumes and in aromatherapy.
– ORIGIN Tagalog (a language of the Philippines).

YMCA • abbrev. Young Men's Christian Association.

yob • n. Brit. informal a rude and aggressive young man.
– DERIVATIVES **yobbery** n. **yobbish** adj.
– ORIGIN from **BOY** (spelled backwards).

yobbo • n. (pl. **yobbos** or **yobboes**) Brit. informal a yob.

yodel /yoh-d'l/ • v. (**yodels, yodelling, yodelled**; US **yodels, yodeling, yodeled**) sing or call in a style that alternates rapidly between a normal voice and a very high voice. • n. a song or call of this type.
– DERIVATIVES **yodeller** n.
– ORIGIN German *jodeln*.

yoga • n. a Hindu spiritual discipline, a part of which, including breathing exercises and the holding of specific body positions, is widely practised for health and relaxation.
– DERIVATIVES **yogic** adj.
– ORIGIN Sanskrit, 'union'.

yogi • n. (pl. **yogis**) a person who is skilled in yoga.
– ORIGIN Sanskrit.

yogurt /yog-ert, yoh-gert/ (also **yoghurt** or **yoghourt**) • n. a thick liquid food prepared from milk with bacteria added.
– ORIGIN Turkish.

yoke • n. **1** a piece of wood fastened over the necks of two animals and attached to a plough or cart in order for them to pull it. **2** (pl. **yoke** or **yokes**) a pair of yoked animals. **3** a frame fitting over the neck and shoulders of a person, used for carrying buckets or baskets. **4** something that restricts freedom or is a burden: *the yoke of imperialism.* **5** a part of an item of clothing that fits over the shoulders and to which the main part of the garment is attached. • v. (**yokes**, **yoking**, **yoked**) **1** join together or attach with a yoke. **2** bring people or things into a close relationship: *we are yoked to the fates of others.*
– ORIGIN Old English.

yokel /yoh-k'l/ • n. an unsophisticated country person.
– ORIGIN perh. from dialect *yokel* 'green woodpecker'.

yolk /rhymes with poke/ • n. the yellow inner part of a bird's egg, which is rich in protein and fat and nourishes the developing embryo.
– ORIGIN Old English.

Yom Kippur /yom kip-**poor**, yom kip-per/ • n. the most solemn religious fast of the Jewish year, the last of the ten days of penitence that begin with Rosh Hashana (the Jewish New Year).
– ORIGIN Hebrew, 'day of atonement'.

yon literary or dialect • det. & adv. yonder; that. • pron. that person or thing over there.
– ORIGIN Old English.

yonder old use or dialect • adv. over there. • det. that or those (referring to something situated at a distance).

yonks • pl. n. Brit. informal a very long time.
– ORIGIN perh. from **donkey's years** (see DONKEY).

yore • n. (in phr. **of yore**) literary of former times or long ago.
– ORIGIN Old English.

Yorkist • n. a follower of the House of York in the Wars of the Roses. • adj. relating to the House of York.

Yorks. • abbrev. Yorkshire.

Yorkshire pudding • n. a baked batter pudding typically eaten with roast beef.

Yorkshire terrier • n. a small long-haired grey and brown breed of terrier.

you • pron. (second person sing. or pl.) **1** used to refer to the person or people that the speaker is addressing. **2** used to refer to

the person being addressed together with other people of the same sort: *you Americans.* **3** used to refer to any person in general.
– ORIGIN Old English.

you'd • contr. **1** you had. **2** you would.

you'll • contr. you will; you shall.

young • adj. (**younger**, **youngest**) **1** having lived or existed for only a short time. **2** relating to or characteristic of young people. • pl. n. young children or animals; offspring.
– DERIVATIVES **youngish** adj.
– ORIGIN Old English.

young offender • n. Law (in the UK) a criminal from 14 to 17 years of age.

youngster • n. a young person.

your • possess. det. **1** belonging to or associated with the person or people that the speaker is addressing. **2** belonging to or associated with any person in general. **3** (**Your**) used when addressing the holder of certain titles.
– ORIGIN Old English.

> **USAGE:** Do not confuse the possessive **your** meaning 'belonging to you' (as in *let me talk to your daughter*) with the form **you're**, which is short for **you are** (as in *you're a good cook*).

you're • contr. you are.

yours • possess. pron. used to refer to something belonging to or associated with the person or people that the speaker is addressing.

> ☑ No apostrophe: **yours** not *your's*.

yourself • pron. (second person sing.) (pl. **yourselves**) **1** used as the object of a verb or preposition when this is the same as the subject of the clause and the subject is the person or people being addressed. **2** you personally.

youth • n. (pl. **youths**) **1** the period of life between childhood and adult age. **2** the qualities of energy, freshness, immaturity, etc. associated with being young. **3** young people. **4** a young man.
– ORIGIN Old English.

youth club (also **youth centre**) • n. a place or organization providing leisure activities for young people.

youthful • adj. **1** young or seeming young. **2** characteristic of young people.
– DERIVATIVES **youthfully** adv. **youthfulness** n.

youth hostel • n. a place providing cheap accommodation, aimed mainly at young people on holiday.

you've • contr. you have.

yowl /rhymes with fowl/ • n. a loud

y

wailing cry of pain or distress. • v. make such a cry.

yo-yo • n. (pl. **yo-yos**) (trademark in the UK) a toy consisting of a pair of joined discs with a deep groove between them in which string is attached and wound, which can be spun down and up by its weight as the string unwinds and rewinds. • v. (**yo-yoes**, **yo-yoing**, **yo-yoed**) move up and down repeatedly.
– ORIGIN prob. from a language of the Philippines.

YTS • abbrev. Youth Training Scheme.

ytterbium /it-ter-bi-uhm/ • n. a silvery-white metallic chemical element.
– ORIGIN from *Ytterby* in Sweden.

yttrium /it-tri-uhm/ • n. a greyish-white metallic chemical element.
– ORIGIN from *Ytterby* (see **YTTERBIUM**).

yuan /yuu-ahn/ • n. (pl. **yuan**) the basic unit of money of China.
– ORIGIN Chinese, 'round'.

yucca /yuk-kuh/ • n. a plant with sword-like leaves, native to warm regions of the US and Mexico.

– ORIGIN Carib.

yuck (also **yuk**) • exclam. informal used to express disgust.
– DERIVATIVES **yucky** (also **yukky**) adj.

Yugoslav /yoo-guh-slahv/ • n. a person from any of the states of the former Yugoslavia.
– DERIVATIVES **Yugoslavian** n. & adj.

Yule (also **Yuletide**) • n. old use Christmas.
– ORIGIN Old English or Old Norse.

yule log • n. **1** a large log traditionally burnt in the hearth on Christmas Eve. **2** a log-shaped chocolate cake eaten at Christmas.

yummy • adj. (**yummier**, **yummiest**) informal very good to eat; delicious.

yuppie (also **yuppy**) • n. (pl. **yuppies**) informal derog. a well-paid young middle-class professional person working in a city.
– ORIGIN from the initial letters of *young urban professional*.

YWCA • abbrev. Young Women's Christian Association.

y

Zz

Z /zed, US zee/ (also **z**) • n. (pl. **Zs** or **Z's**)
1 the twenty-sixth letter of the alphabet.
2 (usu. **z**) the third unknown quantity in an algebraic expression. **3** used in repeated form to represent buzzing or snoring.

zabaglione /za-ba-lyoh-ni/ • n. an Italian dessert made of whipped egg yolks, sugar, and wine.
– ORIGIN Italian.

Zairean /zy-eer-i-uhn/ (also **Zairian**) • n. a person from the Democratic Republic of Congo (known as Zaire from 1971–97). • adj. relating to Zaire.

Zambian /zam-bi-uhn/ • n. a person from Zambia. • adj. relating to Zambia.

zany • adj. (**zanier, zaniest**) amusingly unconventional and individual.
– DERIVATIVES **zanily** adv. **zaniness** n.
– ORIGIN Italian *zani* or *zanni*, a form of *Gianni, Giovanni* 'John', a clown in traditional Italian comedy.

zap • v. (**zaps, zapping, zapped**) informal
1 destroy someone or something.
2 move or propel suddenly and rapidly.
3 use a remote control to change television channels, operate a video recorder, etc.

zeal /zeel/ • n. great energy or enthusiasm for a cause or aim.
– ORIGIN Greek *zēlos*.

zealot /zel-uht/ • n. a person who follows a religion, cause, or policy very strictly or enthusiastically.
– DERIVATIVES **zealotry** n.

zealous /zel-uhss/ • adj. having or showing great energy or enthusiasm for a cause or aim.
– DERIVATIVES **zealously** adv. **zealousness** n.

zebra /zeb-ruh, zee-bruh/ • n. an African wild horse with black and white stripes and an erect mane.
– ORIGIN Italian, Spanish, or Portuguese, first meaning 'wild ass'.

zebra crossing • n. Brit. a pedestrian street crossing marked with broad white stripes.

zebu /zee-boo/ • n. a breed of domestic-

ated ox with a humped back.
– ORIGIN French.

zeitgeist /zyt-gysst/ • n. the characteristic spirit or mood of a particular period of history.
– ORIGIN German.

Zen • n. a type of Buddhism emphasizing the value of meditation and intuition.
– ORIGIN Japanese, 'meditation'.

zenith /zen-ith/ • n. **1** the time at which someone or something is most powerful or successful. **2** the point in the sky directly overhead. **3** the highest point in the sky reached by the sun or moon.
– ORIGIN Arabic, 'path over the head'.

zephyr /zef-fer/ • n. literary a soft, gentle breeze.
– ORIGIN Greek *zephuros* 'god of the west wind, west wind'.

Zeppelin /zep-puh-lin/ • n. hist. a large German airship of the early 20th century.
– ORIGIN named after Ferdinand, Count von *Zeppelin*, German airship pioneer.

zero /rhymes with hero/ • cardinal number (pl. **zeros**) **1** the figure 0; nought.
2 a point on a scale or instrument from which a positive or negative quantity is reckoned. **3** a temperature of 0°C (32°F), marking the freezing point of water.
4 the lowest possible amount or level.
• v. (**zeroes, zeroing, zeroed**) **1** adjust an instrument to zero. **2** set the sights of a gun for firing. **3** (**zero in on**) take aim at or focus attention on.
– ORIGIN Arabic, 'cipher'.

zero hour • n. the time at which a military or other operation is set to begin.

zero tolerance • n. strict enforcement of the law regarding any form of antisocial behaviour.

zest • n. **1** great enthusiasm and energy.
2 the quality of being exciting or interesting. **3** the outer coloured part of the peel of an orange, lemon, or lime, used as flavouring.
– DERIVATIVES **zestful** adj. **zesty** adj.
– ORIGIN French *zeste*.

z

ziggurat /zig-guh-rat/ • n. (in ancient Mesopotamia) a tiered structure in the shape of a pyramid, often with a temple on the top.
– ORIGIN from an ancient Semitic language.

zigzag • n. a line or course having sharp alternate right and left turns. • adj. & adv. veering to right and left alternately.
• v. (**zigzags, zigzagging, zigzagged**) take a zigzag course.
– ORIGIN German *Zickzack*.

zilch /zilch/ • pron. informal nothing.
– ORIGIN perh. from a Mr *Zilch*, a character in a magazine.

zillion • cardinal number informal a very large number of people or things.
– DERIVATIVES **zillionth** ordinal number.
– ORIGIN from *Z* + **MILLION**.

Zimbabwean /zim-bahb-wi-uhn, zim-**bab**-wi-uhn/ • n. a person from Zimbabwe. • adj. relating to Zimbabwe.

Zimmer /zim-mer/ (also **Zimmer frame**) • n. trademark a kind of walking frame.
– ORIGIN from *Zimmer* Orthopaedic Limited, the name of the manufacturer.

zinc /zingk/ • n. a silvery-white metallic chemical element which is used in making brass and for coating iron and steel as a protection against corrosion.
– ORIGIN German *Zink*.

zing informal • n. energy or excitement.
• v. move swiftly.
– DERIVATIVES **zingy** adj.

zinnia /zin-ni-uh/ • n. a plant of the daisy family with bright showy flowers.
– ORIGIN named after the German physician and botanist Johann G. *Zinn*.

Zion /zy-uhn/ (also **Sion** /sy-uhn/) • n. 1 the Jewish people or religion. 2 (in Christian thought) the heavenly city or kingdom of heaven.
– ORIGIN Hebrew, the name of the hill of Jerusalem on which the city of David was built.

Zionism /zy-uh-ni-z'm/ • n. a movement for the development and protection of a Jewish nation in Israel.
– DERIVATIVES **Zionist** n. & adj.

zip • n. 1 esp. Brit. a fastener consisting of two flexible strips of metal or plastic with interlocking projections that are closed or opened by pulling a slide along them. 2 informal energy; liveliness.
• v. (**zips, zipping, zipped**) 1 fasten something with a zip. 2 informal move at high speed. 3 Computing compress a file so that it takes up less space.

zip code (also **ZIP code**) • n. US a post-code.
– ORIGIN from the initial letters of *zone improvement plan*.

zipper esp. N. Amer. • n. a zip fastener.

• v. (**zippers, zippering, zippered**) fasten with a zipper.

zippy • adj. (**zippier, zippiest**) informal 1 bright, fresh, or lively. 2 speedy.

zip-up • adj. esp. Brit. fastened with a zip.

zircon /zer-kuhn/ • n. a mineral that is brown or semi-transparent, used as a gem and in industry.
– ORIGIN German *Zirkon*.

zirconium /zer-koh-ni-uhm/ • n. a hard silver-grey metallic chemical element.

zit • n. informal a spot on the skin.

zither /zi-ther/ • n. a musical instrument with numerous strings stretched across a flat box, placed horizontally and played with the fingers and a plectrum.
– ORIGIN German.

zloty /zlo-ti/ • n. (pl. same, **zlotys**, or **zloties**) the basic unit of money of Poland.
– ORIGIN Polish, 'golden'.

Zn • symb. the chemical element zinc.

zodiac /zoh-di-ak/ • n. an area of the sky in which the sun, moon, and planets appear to lie, divided by astrologers into twelve equal divisions or signs.
– DERIVATIVES **zodiacal** /zuh-dy-uh-k'l/ adj.
– ORIGIN Greek *zōidiakos*.

zombie • n. 1 a corpse supposedly brought back to life by witchcraft. 2 informal a lifeless or completely unresponsive person.
– ORIGIN West African.

zombify • v. (**zombifies, zombifying, zombified**) informal deprive someone of energy or vitality.

zone • n. 1 an area that has particular characteristics or a particular use. 2 (also **time zone**) an area where a common standard time is used.
• v. (**zones, zoning, zoned**) divide into zones.
– DERIVATIVES **zonal** adj.
– ORIGIN Greek, 'girdle'.

zonk • v. informal 1 (**zonk out**) fall suddenly and heavily asleep. 2 (as adj. **zonked**) under the influence of drugs or alcohol.

zoo • n. 1 a place which keeps wild animals for study, conservation, or display to the public. 2 informal a confused or chaotic situation.
– ORIGIN short for *zoological garden*.

zookeeper • n. a person employed to look after the animals in a zoo.

zoology /zoo-ol-uh-ji/ • n. 1 the scientific study of animals. 2 the animal life of a particular area or time.
– DERIVATIVES **zoological** adj. **zoologist** n.
– ORIGIN Greek *zōion* 'animal'.

zoom • v. 1 move or travel very quickly.

2 (of a camera) change smoothly from a long shot to a close-up or vice versa.

zoom lens • n. a lens allowing a camera to zoom by varying the distance between the centre of the lens and its focus.

Zoroastrianism /zo-roh-ass-tri-uh-ni-z'm/ • n. a religion of ancient Persia based on the worship of a single god, founded by the prophet Zoroaster (also called Zarathustra) in the 6th century BC.

– DERIVATIVES **Zoroastrian** adj. & n.

Zr • symb. the chemical element zirconium.

zucchini /zuu-kee-ni/ • n. (pl. **zucchini** or **zucchinis**) N. Amer. a courgette.
– ORIGIN Italian, 'little gourds'.

Zulu /zoo-loo/ • n. **1** a member of a South African people. **2** the language of the Zulus.

zygote /zy-goht/ • n. Biol. a cell resulting from the joining of two gametes.
– ORIGIN Greek *zugōtos* 'yoked'.